1974 BRITANNICA BOOK OF THE YEAR

ENCYCLOPÆDIA BRITANNICA, INC.

HELEN HEMINGWAY BENTON, Publisher

Chicago, Toronto, London, Geneva, Sydney, Tokyo, Manila, Johannesburg, Seoul

Library of Congress Catalog Card Number: 38–12082
International Standard Book Number: 0–85229–294–5

BRITANNICA BOOK OF THE YEAR

(*Trademark Reg. U.S. Pat. Off.*)
Printed in U.S.A.

THE UNIVERSITY OF CHICAGO

The Britannica Book of the Year is published with the editorial advice of the faculties of the University of Chicago

In Memoriam

WILLIAM BENTON (1900–1973)

Publisher of *Encyclopædia Britannica* (1943–1973)

Born in Minneapolis, Minn., and brought up there and in Montana, William Benton was destined by character and circumstance to carve out one of the great 20th-century careers in communications. In his early years an advertising man, he sold his interest in Benton and Bowles to enter the field of education, joining his friend Robert M. Hutchins at the University of Chicago. In 1941, as vice-president of the university, he dedicated himself to the task of acquiring *Encyclopædia Britannica* for it. The university accepted the gift in 1943, committing to him the management and common stock control. His third career was in politics. As assistant secretary of state under President Harry S. Truman, as U.S. senator from Connecticut, and as U.S. representative to the Executive Board of UNESCO, he furthered freedom and the cause of education throughout the world. At his death in New York City on March 18, 1973, the great encyclopaedia to which he had dedicated his life was the reference standard of the English-speaking nations. His name will live on as a symbol of light and liberty.

The Publisher's Message

Looking back over 1973, I find it difficult to believe that so many different, strange, and unexpected things happened in so short a span of time. A former U.S. president, the most famous artist of the century, a great cellist, a poet of peace, and numerous other musicians, poets, artists, and statesmen died during the year, leaving us their gifts. Governments fell and others came into being; one war ended and another began. The direst predictions of some of our prophets came closer to fulfillment, as crises of energy, inflation, and ecology drew closer.

Yet through it all the daily progress of ordinary human events continued. This book is about the crises, but it is also about that daily progress. It deals with a constitutional crisis in the United States as well as with the sustained, if slow and quiet, movement of its citizens toward greater realization of their rights and opportunities. It is about international relations that, while verging on war, also inched toward détente. And it is also about all of us—farmers, labour union members, white collar workers, refugees—who somehow left our mark on 1973.

To encompass the extraordinary variety of events during 1973, the editors have selected four feature articles and an array of special reports—18 to be exact—to complement the annual reference reports. The feature section focuses on important world developments during the year: changes in the balance of power and in relations among nations; ominous world monetary developments; and the emergence of Japan as a great economic power. These extended articles are contributed by persons who are eminent in their respective fields. Taken together they demonstrate that we have indeed become one world, and that we can no longer safely pretend that one nation can profit or advance at the expense of another.

Special reports appear throughout the book, in association with the articles to which they most directly relate. This year's reports range from historian Basil Davidson's observations on the continuing conflict along the Zambezi River in southern Africa to psychiatrist Thomas Szasz's analysis of our treatment of mental patients. They include reports from Australia, Canada, and Northern Ireland on issues of current concern to the citizens of those countries, as well as analyses of social services, education, and housing programs on both sides of the Atlantic. Among this year's special reports is an article on the progress of the U.S. women's movement that marks the debut of a new Yearbook section. And, inevitably, the special reports include two articles on aspects of the U.S. Watergate scandals: the first an analysis of the constitutional implications of the crisis by historian Henry Steele Commager, the second a brief look at its effects on one segment of President Nixon's Silent Majority.

We present this book to you with pride in its contents and faith in our common future. It was quite a year. Without a doubt, the ups and downs of 1973 should remind us that we have not yet learned to live with one another or with nature. But some of the lessons learned from 1973 were important to learn, and I would like to think that they will carry forward into 1974—and beyond.

Helen H. Benton

Contents

THE ROAD TO A NEW JAPAN

by Kakuei Tanaka

Kakuei Tanaka was elected prime minister of Japan on July 5, 1972, after 25 years as a member of the Diet. Long a leader in the movement to redirect national priorities, he published in 1972 Nihon Retto (Building a New Japan), *a book that swept the nation. The following article reflects the continuing development of his goals for Japan. Although its preparation, in September 1973, preceded the energy crisis, which may have the effect of postponing his plans, the article stands as a definitive statement of the prime minister's long-range objectives.*

From our bitter experience in World War II 30 years ago, we Japanese have learned in our heart the limitations of power. Since then, we have adopted a "peace constitution" without precedent in world history. We have renounced force as a means of settling international disputes and have resolved to abandon any recourse to nuclear weapons. We have come to live as a nation devoted to peace.

Over the years there have been repeated regional conflicts, but fundamentally the cold war animosity between East and West which shaped the postwar era has now been broken. Mankind has been wise enough to see the barrenness of solutions imposed by force. The grave issues facing the world today—the advancing global menace of pollution, the depletion of the world's natural and energy resources, impending food shortages, inflation, and the "North-South" problem of growing disparity between the developed and developing countries—these are matters that cannot be solved by naked force.

In a sense, Japan itself can be said to contain, in concentrated and accentuated form, many of the contradictions now facing human society. This country's "miraculous" postwar economic growth enabled us to build a sophisticated industrial state on a very small land base and in a very short time. Yet Japan today faces urban problems, pollution, the generation gap, educational disorder, and other difficulties common to all advanced nations. At the same time we must cope with inadequate housing, shortages of capital, insufficient provisions for social security, and other problems usually associated with a developing country. To carry the analogy further, the various disparities between urban and rural areas in Japan may be said to constitute a domestic North-South problem within a single country.

Japan's rapid economic growth has given it the potential to conquer these internal problems. The Japanese archipelago is favoured by the richness of nature and its graceful changes. In the century since the Meiji Restoration, the Japanese people have absorbed the sophisticated industrial civilization developed by the West and made it their own. At the same time, they have preserved the delicate and sensitive cultural traditions handed down by their ancestors. There are now more than 100 million Japanese, cheerful, hardworking people with deep sensibilities. They should set out to create a new kind of civilized society dedicated to the restoration of human values.

If one were to characterize the course we are setting, it would be with the words "peace" and "welfare." In the outside world, we should maintain steadfastly the same peaceful way of life that Japan as a nation has pursued consistently throughout the quarter century since the war. At home, Japan must strive to reconstitute a nation of local communities in which nature, culture, and industry can be harmoniously blended and where people can work, live, and enjoy themselves in peace. We do not stress welfare merely as a device for putting people's minds temporarily at ease. Rather, the whole idea of welfare must be considered within a historical perspective of long-ranging plans supported by the diligence that has been a part of man since earliest times. The success of this undertaking would put Japan in the forefront of those who are building a new human society for the 21st century.

Toward True Affluence. Defeated in World War II in 1945, Japan struggled to its feet in the midst of an endless sea of ruins. Forty-four percent of its territory was lost. The four islands remaining overflowed with hordes of unemployed, as soldiers and civilians were repatriated from overseas. Industrial output fell to a mere one-sixth of its prewar (1935–37) level. Even today, I cannot forget the picture of men struggling with plans for the nation's economic recovery while fighting to eke out their own bare subsistence, clothes tattered and stomachs empty.

It took fully ten years before the people's standard of living could be raised to prewar levels. The 1965 Economic White Paper used the phrase "It is no longer postwar" to point out that the Japanese economy had finished its recovery period and was entering a new era of development. It was at this time that the curtain went up on Japan's era of rapid economic growth. Such industries as petroleum refining, petrochemicals, iron and steel, automobiles, and electrical home appliances emerged one after the other in a remarkable growth of heavy industry. In an expanding cycle, investment attracted still more investment. Chronic unemployment was eliminated, and the labour market became tight. Wage and salary incomes went up steadily, while a boom market developed in television sets and automobiles.

In 1964 the Olympic Games were held in Tokyo. In the same year Japan received art. 8 status as a member of the International Monetary Fund and joined the Organization for Economic Cooperation and Development, a body dedicated to the principle of liberalizing capital transactions.

Holding to an open economic system itself, Japan put to sea in the rough waters of international economic competition. Industry became better able to compete internationally, and our balance of international payments went into the black in 1968, thus removing balance of payments difficulties as a ceiling on growth. Japan's rate of real economic growth from 1955 to 1970 averaged 10.4% per annum. During this period the scale of the national economy (as measured by its gross national product) increased almost four and a half times to become the second largest in the free world, surpassed only by that of the United States. This transformation was realized thanks to our people's diligence, their outstanding adaptability, and a vigorous entrepreneurial spirit. Add to this the facts of an abundant and well-educated labour force, a high savings rate, and the rapid technological progress made possible by the ambitious introduction of overseas techniques.

Today, however, circumstances both within and outside Japan have changed drastically. As we move toward a postindustrial society—*i.e.*, the information-oriented society—people are seeking a different form of affluence. The very context of the term affluence is shifting, from the affluence of industry to the affluence of the individual, from affluence in the economic "flow" of things to affluence in the economic "stock," and from the idea of simple economic or materialistic well-being to a well-being expressed by personal fulfillment and the enjoyment of leisure time.

In the age of "production-first," we had one widely accepted set of values: if the individual devoted himself totally to doing his best at his particular job, the whole enterprise would prosper, the national wealth would increase, and his own standard of living and social position would be improved in the bargain. Today, however, people are judging both their natural environment and their work environment by new standards. They are now seeking self-fulfillment not only in their work but also through active participation in cultural activities, sports, and various other aspects of social life.

In order to meet these changing conditions, a drastic reorientation is called for. The basic focus of the government's policy must be shifted, away from the emphasis on expanded production and exports to a new emphasis on better living. A congenial workplace, an emotionally rewarding life, and diverse opportunities for recreation should be the prime goals of our domestic policy. We should also guarantee that the workingman will be able to enjoy his old age in comfort and that full medical care will be provided to those unfortunately stricken by illness.

Yet a society that provides for the welfare of its people must also be a society that respects people, a society in which each individual through his own free choice is able to develop his own potential fully. We do not mean to form an egocentric and fragmented society. Rights are always accompanied by duties, choices by responsibilities. A truly civilized society recognizes the dignity of man and is based on freedom and democracy.

Getting down to specifics, we cannot begin to discuss the problems facing today's society without speaking of the ways in which the nation's land is utilized.

Modern industry, seeking the advantages of concentration, gathers in the major metropolises. Seeking higher wages and easier living, people flood into those same urban centres in its wake. Concentration begets further concentration, and competition generates the energy for economic development. As the recent economic history of so many nations shows, economic development is brought about by population shifts from primary to secondary and then tertiary industries, namely, by the movement of industry and population from rural into

"The Japanese people . . . have preserved the delicate and sensitive cultural traditions handed down by their ancestors."

JOHN LAUNOIS—BLACK STAR

urban areas. Japan is no exception to this general pattern. The national census shows that our country's urban population has expanded by some 40 million people in 20 years.

This concentration of industry and population has been conspicuous along the Pacific Coast belt, particularly in the three great urban centres of Tokyo, Osaka, and Nagoya. The population in these three metropolitan areas increased by 10,620,000 from 1960 to 1970 to reach 45,580,000 (or 43.9% of the nation's total). Japan has a total area of about 370,000 sq.km. (143,000 sq.mi.), slightly less than the single state of California in the United States. And on a mere 1% of this land the population has increased by an amount greater than the total population of Sweden.

As a result, the urban areas are ailing, exhausted, frustrated, and overcrowded melting pots. Pollution, land scarcities, housing shortages, waste-disposal problems, water shortages, rising prices, and similar problems are becoming ever more serious. On the other hand, the rural population has grown older as young people have moved out. The farming areas are losing the energy vital to growth.

Taking 1968, the centennial of the Meiji Restoration, as a turning point, I believe the advantages of urbanization have today become clear disadvantages. It is imperative that we redirect this torrential flow of urban concentration and spread our people's energies throughout the entire Japanese archipelago. We must solve the problems of overcongestion and underpopulation simultaneously, by making both the great cities and the country areas fit once more for decent human living.

Japan has one of the world's largest merchant fleets and leads the nations of the world in shipbuilding.

GEORG GERSTER—RAPHO GUILLUMETTE

Sharing Prosperity with the World. As the crew aboard this "spaceship earth," the human race must share an awareness of the problems of its own survival. Sprawling global pollution, diminishing energy resources, and other grave problems cannot be solved with a selfish me-first attitude.

Fortunately, international politics in the quarter century since the end of World War II has moved from an era of military confrontation to one of dialogue. Within this context, Japan has become a major economic power. But Japan should not merely be a beneficiary of peace. We also have a duty to participate actively in creating a new peace and building a new economic order. Two things are important here. First, we must maintain the kind of general good fellowship among nations in which frank discussions can always take place. Second, we must be sufficiently flexible in handling our own internal affairs so that we can make the changes dictated by international circumstances.

Poor in resources below the ground, yet housing a population of more than 100 million on its very limited land, Japan has had to form a trade pattern of importing raw materials and energy from all corners of the world, processing them to give them added value, and then exporting them abroad as finished products. An economy such as this can develop only within an international environment of economic freedom. Accordingly, Japan has been foremost among those calling for a new round of multilateral negotiations looking toward sweeping liberalization and expansion in world trade. We feel we must discard the past attitude of concentrating on the benefits of the *existing* international economic order. Instead, we must participate actively in averting protectionism, in securing opportunities for the less developed nations to "take off" economically, and in otherwise creating a new and more sophisticated international economic order.

At the same time, it is important that we have a clear understanding and appreciation of other people's histories and cultures, if we are to transcend differences of language and tradition. As we promote international economic harmony, we should also encourage greater exchanges in academic, cultural, athletic, and other fields. Through such interactions, we can forge bonds of mutual trust and friendship that no amount of money can buy.

The solution of the North-South problem is an especially critical issue. True, the developing nations of the "South" achieved an average growth rate of 5.5% during the 1960s, surpassing the average 4.8% growth of the advanced "Northern" nations. But their populations experienced such an explosive increase during this same period that the gap between North and South in per capita income actually widened. At the same time, as the industrial growth of some developing countries has surpassed the lagging economies of others, we see developing a new "North-South problem within the

South." This situation has been aggravated still further during 1973 by irregular turns of the weather, which created grave food shortages and even famine conditions in some nations.

Our country has extended economic cooperation to the developing nations in the amount of $2,730,000,000 (0.93% of GNP) during 1972. Of this, $610 million (0.21% of GNP) was official development assistance. By 1980 this economic cooperation must be expanded to more than $7.5 billion, and it is evident that this aid should be extended to all the nations of Asia, Africa, and Latin America that have relations with Japan. In the case of the Middle Eastern nations, whose oil resources have made them prosperous, this aid should include know-how assistance for processing their resources, desalinating their seawater, and making their deserts bloom.

Our offer of assistance to the developing nations is in frank repentance for a past tendency to seek profits for ourselves alone. So it is imperative that Japan faithfully develop formulas that truly serve the needs of these nations, remembering that the road to industrialization and modernity on which many of these nations are setting out is the same path taken by Japan in the hundred years since the Meiji Restoration.

The time is past when a small number of advanced nations can settle the problems of the international economy among themselves. Japan must heed the demand of the developing nations that the international division of labour be reorganized fairly and reasonably. We must carry out internal reforms to the same purpose. Beginning with the countries of the South, Japan must move to form an economic society open to the developing nations and to the world at large.

Industrial Adjustment from a New Perspective. If we are to share our prosperity with the rest of the world and create a truly vital welfare society, we must carry out a drastic industrial adjustment. Heavy industry played a historic role as the central driving force for the entire economy during our era of rapid growth. It also caused excessive consumption of our resources and increasingly serious pollution problems, while intensifying friction with other nations over our foreign trade. In the future, we must not select industries merely for purposes of economic growth. We must also ask ourselves: Do they cause pollution and destroy environment? At the same time: Do they offer work in which people can take pride and which they enjoy doing?

Our country does not need to have every type of industry within its own borders. Rather we should defer to other nations in the case of industries that are more properly theirs and adjust our own industries in such a way as to accommodate the industrialization of the developing countries, as well as to further the horizontal division of labour among the advanced nations.

In order to come to terms with those developing countries that are trying to industrialize themselves, we should arrange to have raw materials receive their primary or secondary processing in the country of origin or at some midway point, insofar as this is possible. Japan can then import these semiprocessed materials. With this in mind, the Japanese industrial establishment must shift its emphasis from heavy industry to the knowledge-intensive industries that capitalize on know-how and creativity. For the added value they create, they consume relatively small quantities of raw materials and energy and generate less pollution.

This knowledge-intensification of the industrial structure offers many possibilities—the development of new products, further sophistication of existing products, and systemization of conventional industrial processes. Already some industry groups suited to the new age have emerged. Examples include the research-intensive industries (computers, aircraft, electric automobiles, industrial robots, underwater exploration); sophisticated assembly industries (communications equipment, business machines, pollution-prevention equipment, educational equipment, prefabricated housing); fashion industries (quality clothing, furniture, household utensils); and the industries that create and provide knowledge or information itself (data-processing services, video industries, systems engineering).

In contrast to resource-dependent heavy industries that constantly pursue quantitative expansion, these knowledge-intensive industries hold great potential for smaller firms, for here the key growth factor is the quality of the people responsible for intellectual activities. Of course, the role of heavy industries is still important. We must not forget to distribute these appropriately throughout the Japanese archipelago, keeping in mind the establishment of an international division of labour.

Step by step with the knowledge-intensification of the industrial sector, it is also necessary to define long-term development policies for the agricultural sector. Farming, fishing, and forestry, as well as the towns and villages supported by these primary industries, have vital roles to play in building a welfare society. They ensure a stable supply of food, without which people's very lives would be jeopardized. They also provide a good life in the midst of the green countryside. Finally, they play a role in protecting and managing Japan's natural beauty.

The worldwide food shortage in 1973 once again demonstrated that when a nation relies overmuch on getting its food from foreign sources, there is no guarantee that it will always be provided with a stable supply. The immediate, obvious cause of this year's tight supply and demand situation was the coincidence of massive Soviet and Chinese grain purchases and poor harvests throughout the world. But this was not solely a "coincidence." The supply of feed grains cannot keep up with the steady increase in the demand for livestock. Though there may be years in which the demand can be met easily, it is possible that foodstuffs will be in constant undersupply from now on.

Japan is 100% self-sufficient in rice, its staple food. Yet this country is only 42% self-sufficient vis-à-vis its total grain demand, if feed grains are included. This rate is the lowest among the industrial nations. Given the fluctuations in the international food market, Japan must maintain its 100% self-sufficiency in rice and must also strive to establish significant domestic production of wheat, soybeans, and pasture grasses. Still, it will be impossible to attain 100% self-sufficiency immediately. Japan will have to continue diversifying its import sources while simultaneously promoting "develop-and-import" projects to meet its needs.

According to the 1972 White Paper on Agriculture, farm income levels were only 54% of the average daily wage in manufacturing industry (*i.e.*, for full-time employees in establishments with more than five employees). Thus people engaged in farming are forced to find additional jobs or to leave their farming communities in search of outside income.

In 1972 there were 6,820,000 persons employed in farming. This is only 13.3% of the total employed population! From before World War II until 1953, Japan's agricultural work force stood at about 15 million. Every year, about 400,000 new school graduates remained on the farm to carry on the family work. Yet 20 years later, in 1972, the number of new school graduates going into farming had dropped to a mere 22,000, one-twentieth of the old figure. The agricultural work force has been more than halved. Considered by age grouping, the farm labour force has become top-heavy; it lacks the energy of youth.

In order to cope with this situation and maintain a stable supply of basic foodstuffs, we must promote more efficient and higher-profit agriculture through mechanization, modernization, better organization, and consolidation into larger farm units, all the while selecting crops that suit the climatic and soil characteristics and the farm infrastructure of each region. In so doing, it would be well to expand the average farm size to about 20 ha. per full-time farm family. This would inevitably involve the use of cooperatives, subcontracting, or salaried farming. At present, the strong attachment to an ownership pattern of widely scattered, minuscule plots makes it difficult for any one farmer to expand the scale of his operations on his own.

To enlarge the operational scale of farms, a nationwide land-utilization plan must be formulated; permanent farmlands must be selected and designated by farmland-use unions formed by the farmers themselves. Financial assistance must be provided so that farmers on these lands can make concentrated improvements in their infrastructure. At the same time, while respecting the vested rights of landed farmers, the present Agricultural Land Law must be reexamined and agrarian land policies adopted in coordination with national land-use plans. We must put more farmland back in circulation.

The role of forested areas in protecting Japan's foliage and water resources cannot be overemphasized. It is only after thorough forest- and water-conservation measures have been taken that industrial development is possible and the formation of regional societies, urban and rural, can be safely advanced. Most of today's forests were planted and cultivated by our ancestors. We must preserve these forests handed down to us over the ages and must expand them to provide a more bountiful heritage for future generations. If need be, I would examine some effective means of investing government funds to this end.

Fishing provides those seafoods that are such an indispensable part of the Japanese diet. It is imperative that water pollution be prevented in order to further safe fishing. While it is obvious that strict regulations will be needed to keep our rivers and oceans from being further polluted by industrial or other effluents, efforts must also be made to clean up those already polluted bays and shores of the Japanese archipelago.

The progressive reorganization of industrial activity will make industry more knowledge-intensive and agriculture more efficient. Inevitably, in the process, the flow of goods and technologies will take on a more international flavour. There will be increasing overseas processing of raw materials, importation of labour-intensive products, and develop-and-import arrangements for agricultural products. We must think of these issues not in terms of Japan's interests alone but rather with a view toward sharing our prosperity. We should consider moving our technology overseas, while helping to build a social infrastructure that will permit this transplanted technology to take root, put out branches, and bear fruit in the partner nations, in keeping with their respective stages of development and their economic, social, and cultural backgrounds.

Only by this kind of cumulative effort can we put a restructured Japanese industry on the right track, operating within the context of a stable, international order. We must be extremely careful that any move of Japanese industries overseas is not interpreted as exporting pollution, and that develop-and-import schemes are not seen as depriving the host country of the productive potential of its land. This concern should be both our pride and our guiding principle.

While we change our industrial structure to fit a global perspective, I should also like to stress the corollary importance of industrial relocation within Japan. If the Japanese economy continues to grow at an annual rate of 10% from its 1970 GNP of 73 trillion yen, our GNP will reach 304 trillion yen (in 1970 prices) by 1985. If the average growth is 8.5% per annum this will be 248 trillion yen, while an annual average of 7.5% will result in a GNP of 216 trillion yen. Even if the rate of economic growth is held to 5% per annum—a rate that could virtually create a depression—the 1985 GNP would still be as high as 152 trillion yen. With the economy growing to such massive proportions, it will be difficult to develop it properly unless its geographic imbalances are rectified.

Accordingly, Japan must halt the further concentration of industry in its already overindustrialized Pacific coastal region. We must redirect this flow from the crowded cities to outlying areas. Some of the goals here are to reduce the value of industrial shipments from the Pacific coastal belt from their present 73% of the national total to 50% by 1985, and to halve the expense of industrial sites in and around Tokyo, Osaka, and Nagoya. The necessary legal, fiscal, and tax measures have already been readied. The Industrial Relocation and Coal Mining Area Development Public Corporation (soon to be reorganized as the Comprehensive National Land Development Public Corporation) has already begun its operations as the implementing agency.

The regional dispersion of industry may be divided into two main currents. The mainstream involves the development of inland-type industries in outlying cities and agricultural communities. Most of these inland industries are knowledge-intensive. Because they consume relatively less raw material and generate little environmental pollution or disruption, they can be organized into industrial parks, located in outlying cities and rural areas, with appropriate attention paid to cooperation and harmony with the local community.

Parallel to this plan is the second current: the regional dispersion of the basic-resource industries on the coast. While an increasing number of plants will locate overseas, as already mentioned, it is hoped that those that remain will build large-scale and pollution-free industrial sites well away from the three major metropolitan areas. Such sites should be a considerable distance apart. There should be spacious greenbelts, parks, streams, recreational lakes, and playgrounds in and around the industrial parks. One could envision cattle grazing in some of these buffer zones or greenbelts, creating a new concept of the industrial park as a place where nature and modern technology coexist in harmony.

In considering the regional dispersion of industry, I should like to stress that it is precisely in those snowy, single-crop areas that constitute fully half the Japanese land area that industrialization should be promoted. All the advanced industrial nations are at least as far north as Japan, and in all of them heavy industry has concentrated in the northern part of the country while the south has been traditionally agricultural. Only Japan has flown in the face of this pattern. Here, too, it is necessary to change our traditional practices.

The relocation of industry and the reform of the agricultural structure are one and the same problem. Introducing industry into outlying cities and agricultural villages will provide new employment opportunities for the people there. Thus stimulated, commerce and service will develop, yielding still more job opportunities and greater employment diversification. The agricultural work force will inevitably shrink as farming increases in scale and becomes more efficient. Yet the people thus displaced will be able to find work within commuting distance from their homes. This should resolve the tragedy of the seasonal workers, the men who have to leave home to find nonfarming work during the off-season. It will also halt the exodus from rural Japan. It is only when those employed in agriculture and those who leave the farm are able to enjoy life together in the same local community that our task of industrial adjustment, in its broader perspective, will have been completed.

Toward a More Appealing Life. Tokyo, Osaka, Nagoya, and other cities have become monsters of overcrowding. We must take immediate steps to free the people of these metropolitan areas from pollution, traffic congestion, water scarcities, abnormally high land prices, housing shortages, and the other ills that afflict them. It is impossible, however, to resolve the basic problem simply by rebuilding the cities. This would be treating symptoms. Urban renewal by itself would only attract more people to the metropolitan areas.

The population of the Tokyo megalopolis (Tokyo and the seven neighbouring prefectures) was 30,260,000 in 1970, an increase of 3,290,000 over 1965. If the area's population continues to grow at this pace, it is bound to reach the 40-million mark by 1985. It is now difficult to secure adequate amounts of water and electrical power in the area. In the most crowded part of the megalopolis

"The Japanese land is richly blessed by nature." Here, in southern Japan, the land is used for terraced farming.

BURT GLINN—MAGNUM

PAOLO KOCH—RAPHO GUILLUMETTE

Sophisticated equipment helps the staff of Tokyo's Metropolitan Police Traffic Information and Control Centre monitor the city's congested traffic.

(Tokyo and the three adjacent prefectures), it is physically impossible to provide the housing, educational facilities, transit systems, waste-disposal plants, and other services necessary to support such a huge population. Even the supply of fresh food for the table becomes uncertain.

If this reckless expansion is to be stopped, the relocation of industry must be supplemented by vigorous efforts to disperse government administrative functions. In conjunction with this, we should pour our efforts into strengthening the bases of provincial life by building and improving what one might call the basic inventory of our social capital. In this way, it should be possible to strengthen the integrity of regional functions and to develop regional cities with their own fresh and fully individual charm. We must work to delineate functions and share burdens between the major metropolises and the local cities, among local cities themselves, and between these cities and the farm villages. Only when such a balanced regional structure is achieved can we put any workable urban renovation into effect.

The balanced development of our land must be supported with outstanding transportation and communications networks. Thus, some 7,000 km. (4,350 mi.) of superexpressway trunk railways and 10,000 km. (6,200 mi.) of expressways are to be built by 1985, putting every point in the Japanese archipelago within one day's journey of any other point. In addition to Japan's present 200-kph (125-mph) superexpressway railways, I would also like to perfect linear-motor-powered superexpress lines capable of speeds up to 500 kph (310 mph). Work has already begun on linking the main islands with the three bridge routes between Shikoku and Honshu and on the Seikan Tunnel between Honshu and Hokkaido. At the same time, improvement and expansion of the industrial ports, distribution centres, and airports become more important as population and industry are dispersed. A comprehensive transportation system for goods and people must be established as soon as possible, including the prompt construction of nationwide pipeline facilities.

As our postindustrial society brings increased computerization, we should restructure the entire communications system. In addition to the existing telephone lines, a million or more data-transmission circuits must be created through the use of broader regional exchanges. In restructuring our data-transmission facilities, it is important to give priority to those isolated areas that have hitherto been neglected. Plans should also be developed for new social-information systems combining cable television and data-transmission facilities for education, medical care, distribution, pollution-prevention, traffic control, and other needs.

The attraction of Tokyo and other huge cities lies in the concentration of information, the freedom of options, convenience, and stimulation available in them. Yet this very attractiveness has given rise to the disadvantages of urban life. The basic urban problem is that of rectifying these disadvantages without turning urban life into a minus quantity.

The basic strategy in urban renovation should be to make facilities more compact. Instead of our present horizontal cities with their small buildings sprawling over wide areas, we should build high-rise, vertical cities.

Only in this way will it be possible to utilize the land fully and to generate the necessary space for widening roads, rebuilding homes, and implementing other aspects of urban renewal. This will also yield the space for a wide variety of facilities designed to help improve the conditions of human life, such as parks, plazas, athletic grounds, and bicycling paths. Whether by restoring the community spirit through community sports or by fostering a sense of togetherness in shady parks made for quiet conversation, we must alleviate the sense of isolation so common to our big cities.

The verticalization of our cities, however, does not mean building high-rise structures everywhere. Rather, it would be better to punctuate the city's landscape by distributing high-rise sections and low-rise sections appropriately throughout the city. New financial arrangements for facilitating redevelopment should be devised. Disaster-prevention facilities to protect the lives of our people in case of fire or earthquake must also receive immediate attention.

Among the many urban problems crying out for solution is that of city traffic. As of February 1972 there were as many as 21 million motor vehicles in Japan, and the number is expected to exceed 40 million by 1985. The traffic congestion and automobile-generated pollution in our major cities will get far worse unless something is done. We should make the widest possible use of public mass-transit facilities, as well as improving them through the use of new systems and data-processing technologies. Measures restricting automobile traffic within the over-crowded downtown areas must also receive serious study.

The many outlying cities dotting Japan, blessed as they are with unspoiled nature and a rich cultural tradition, may be ideally suited to the creation of fresh and attractive sites for both residential and recreational use. This must not mean a drab uniformity in which each provincial city seeks to become a miniature Tokyo. Rather, we should build cities of character.

The methods to be used in building up provincial cities can be divided into three categories. The first involves strengthening the administrative functions of cities that will serve as the centres of regional projects. All of these cities have the common problem of building new urban areas in line with regional plans and renovating existing urban areas so as to provide general hospitals, universities, and other educational, medical, cultural, and amusement facilities. Fashion-related industries, research-and-development-intensive industries, information industries, and service industries may be brought into these cities to stimulate their development.

The second category involves the improvement of cities that already play a major role as regional economic, social, and cultural centres and have accumulated many urban functions. In addition to improving their educational, medical, cultural, and recreational facilities and expanding their service functions for the surrounding areas, it will be necessary to build industrial parks on their outskirts and to bring in knowledge-intensive industries. Universities must also be included. Positive efforts should be made to avoid simply enriching existing downtown areas. Thus we should build new urban areas around universities and industrial parks a short distance from present centres.

The third category involves moving industry and academia from the five largest cities to areas that have virtually no urban functions at present. We can make these into the nuclei of new cities.

In promoting provincial urban improvement along such lines, plans must be drawn up so that economic, social, and other benefits accrue to the broader region, including farm villages. If we think of these new cities as flowers blossoming on the land, it is only just that the surrounding areas enjoy their beautiful colours and fragrances.

It is anticipated that the population of provincial cities will grow by approximately 15 million by 1985. I would like to absorb most of this expansion in new towns, including those planned to be built on the outskirts of existing urban centres and those to be developed where no real cities now exist. In such new towns we should be able to apply the latest in technology to assure pollution-free work places, comfortable and pleasant homes, and public recreational areas full of sunshine and greenery.

I should like to stress that the dispersion of universities to outlying areas is an important strategic device, both for solving urban overcrowding and for fostering provincial cities. At present Japan has approximately 950 institutions of higher education with a total student body of some 1,840,000. As many as 61% of these students are in metropolitan Tokyo and other major cities. The improvement of regional institutions of higher learning should be an essential aspect of any plan for building a new Japan.

The most important concept of all is that local communities actively participate in development; they must be not merely beneficiaries. We must not force this national land development upon unwilling or dissenting communities without regard for their wishes. The role of the state is to clarify the perspective for the future from a national point of view and then to suggest the role of each locality within this larger framework. The different localities must then decide on their own plans and make their own policy choices based on this information. In the process, there should be continuing dialogue and frank exchanges of opinion between the national government and the local governmental bodies. At the same time, local governmental bodies must incorporate the wishes and opinions of local residents and seek their understanding and cooperation.

The Harmony of Nature and the Works of Man. The Japanese land is richly blessed by nature. Yet we must not allow ourselves to take nature for granted.

The study of ecology has clearly shown how nature maintains its vital balance through fragile chains of events. When we set out to reorganize the nation's land for better productivity, better living, and better leisure, it is absolutely essential that we make every effort to prevent these human activities from causing irrevocable damage to nature's cycles. Should we neglect such considerations, nature will surely retaliate and make us pay a heavy price in pollution and environmental disruption.

In considering the development of industry and living space, we must think of nature and human activity as part of one all-embracing system. We should always make thorough predevelopment surveys, keeping in mind that the scope of development should remain within the limits of nature's ability to accommodate it. For example, we should hold down effluent emission and pollution to conform with nature's cleansing capacity.

If we do this, the approach to developing pollution-prevention technologies will probably change. Research and development will be encouraged on closed systems that discharge no pollutants but instead recover and recycle them within the production process. This is a new, wide-open frontier for Japan's technological development.

In talking about the relationship between man and nature, I especially want to emphasize the conservation and rejuvenation of our green areas. Even children know the role that green areas play in maintaining the atmospheric cycle. What is more, as surely as water is central to human life, these small patches of green are absolutely essential to man's peace of mind. I would like to provide ample space and rich greenbelts near factories as well as in towns and villages. The little grove of trees around the village shrine has long been a place of spiritual repose for the Japanese people. Similarly, our development should strike a new balance between nature and man's works.

We cannot think of reconstructing the nation's land use without attacking the problem of the land itself. There is a strong popular mood that seeks to reconcile land ownership, which has sometimes been stressed as an absolute right, with the public welfare. The general public would react favourably to placing some limits on land ownership. The concentration of people and industry in the major urban areas has brought chaos to land-use patterns there. Land prices have been driven to abnormal heights resulting in serious housing problems. In and around our cities, the average man's dream of owning a home of his own has all but faded. This problem has been compounded, unfortunately, by a rash of land speculation, not only in the big cities but throughout the nation.

The Tokaido Express hurtles between Tokyo and Osaka at a speed of 125 miles per hour.

JOHN LAUNOIS—BLACK STAR

In the long run, the project to remodel Japan will no doubt contribute to solving the land problem by tending to equalize demand everywhere, but it has short-term dangers. To overcome them, we must develop land policies giving the maximum priority possible under the constitution to the public welfare. This is why legislation was proposed to create a new Comprehensive Land Developments Law.

The basis for land policy is to set up a comprehensive land-utilization plan embracing the entire nation. It must accurately reflect the aspirations of the local people. It must focus on striking an overall balance between land use and conservation, on facilitating the creation of broader regional economic spheres, and on alloting different functions to the various regions in a way that makes sense nationally. This plan must be more than a mere exercise in colouring maps. It must have the force of law behind it. Again, so that land transactions will not be subject to the whims and caprices of landholders, it will be necessary to provide some public checks on the transfer of titles to the land. To do this, the government should not only widen its system of publicly posting land prices and establishing clear criteria for them, it should also give national and local governments, as well as public corporations, priority-acquisition rights to land for public uses. The tax system must also be utilized to keep vast profits from being made on land trading and speculation.

Water, along with land, is a national resource indispensable to life. Traditionally Japan has had abundant rainfall and has been blessed with rich water resources. Looking at the average rainfall per capita, however, Japan has only one-fifth as much water as the United States or the Soviet Union. Moreover, many of Japan's rivers are fast-flowing and the rainfall is concentrated in the rainy and typhoon seasons.

"The Japanese," it has been said, "have come to think that water and security can be had for nothing." Even now, we speak of a spendthrift as one whose money "flows like water." Yet this common notion must now be revised. As rapid economic growth and an increasingly sophisticated way of life have given rise to greatly expanded demand, the water situation has come to approach crisis proportions. Already, it has become standard for the water supply to be restricted around Tokyo and Osaka in summer. This situation, too, impels us to make haste in restructuring our land uses.

It will be difficult, however, to surmount the crisis simply by dispersing demand. We must make every effort to promote the in-plant recycling and reuse of industrial water. Thought should be given to legislation on guidance and assistance for rationalizing water uses. It is also important that new artificial sources of water be created. While the Ministry of International Trade and Industry is supporting research and development on ways of processing sewage and industrial effluents for reuse, we should also expend some effort on the recycling of household and commercial utility water. Attention must also be devoted to the desalinization of seawater.

Japan's land has always been poor in natural resources, yet it is no exaggeration to say that this weakness contributed to Japan's growth and development after World War II. Generally, there was a worldwide sufficiency in the supply of raw materials. Japan, building or improving industrial and distribution ports to take best advantage of its coastline, was able to import materials from whatever overseas sources it chose. There was no need to rely upon domestic sources. As tankers and ore carriers became bigger and faster, this tendency was strengthened.

This situation is now changing rapidly. Moreover, it has been widely pointed out that the consumption of large quantities of cheap raw materials places an excessive burden on the natural environment and aggravates the problems of pollution. In line with its basic policy of pursuing peace and welfare, Japan must escape this trap of energy overexploitation as quickly as possible.

The basic tone of policy must be to promote multifaceted resources development and procurement, fully respecting the spirit of international cooperation. In line with this, we must make special efforts to save energy and resources in our own domestic land use. The knowledge-intensification of the industrial structure, mentioned earlier, is also a step in this direction. In addition, policies should be developed for saving resources and energy and for multiple recycling within the production process. Especially in the field of recycling and reuse, systematic research and development should be encouraged.

Possible new sources of clean energy also require study. In addition to atomic power, for which research and development have already begun, I would like to have Japan start work on other revolutionary new technologies for the 21st century, such as solar energy, tidal energy, geothermal energy, coal gasification, and hydrogen energy. Here, too, is a frontier in our battle to make Japan once more a land of bright sunshine and blue skies.

Revolutionizing Economic and Social Management. Until now, the management of the Japanese economy has aimed at catching up with the advanced nations. Government policies have focused on maintaining and expanding economic growth. Businesses have come to see their main objective as enlarging their scale of operations. As a result, the Japanese economy has become one of the strongest in the world. Now, however, there are strong demands that we apply the proceeds of our growth—not to mention the economic strength accruing from it—to enhance the public welfare and to advance international cooperation.

The first steps to take are financial. Public financing will play a major role here. It is fundamental that we move in the direction of economic management with sound financial leadership. In doing so, our fiscal managers should cease attempting to balance each year's budget and instead emphasize fiscal balance over a longer period. This means the development of aggressive financial policies that envisage defraying our expenses not merely in this generation but also in future generations. Although the idea of not wanting to leave any debts to posterity may at first seem praiseworthy, it is not so kind as it seems. If we pass along our so-called social capital in its present inadequate state, the succeeding generations will be inheriting the worst kind of problems.

By the same token, if the fruits of growth are to contribute to a higher standard of living for all people, we must expand still further the allocation of resources to the public sector, all the while taking care to avoid inflation. To get maximum effect with limited resources, we should direct our efforts toward development works that will effectively utilize the land, such as trunk transportation and communications networks, the improvement of our life and leisure, and other projects directly linked to a better life for the people. In this, it should be made clear that the pump-priming and strategic investment of government funds is desirable and that belated investment in proven approaches only serves to increase the burden on the public coffers.

The question of expanding social security guarantees poses important problems for government policy. We must promptly formulate long-term plans while, at the same time, allocating expanded funding and making real improvements in the system now. I envision three kinds of social security guarantees for the future: (1) all the aged

The modern high-rise building has become commonplace in Tokyo, which has been largely rebuilt since World War II.

H. W. SILVESTER—RAPHO GUILLUMETTE

are entitled to receive pensions; (2) the popular demand for health care will be met with high-quality preventive medicine, therapy, and rehabilitation; and (3) we will make an adequate response to the general public demand for greater social welfare facilities.

At the same time, we must make every effort to secure the best possible educational environment. Nor can we forget positive policies for increasing the wealth of the workingman to reward him for his prodigious efforts as the driving force behind our economic development. Although working people—and this means most of the Japanese population—have had their incomes improved to some extent by higher wage levels, they are still conspicuously poor in terms of such assets as capital savings or home ownership. As one link in the overall policy of building a new Japan, I would like to prepare residential land for five million dwellings throughout the country and to provide five million high-rise apartments in the major suburban areas by 1985.

Japan is currently beset by skyrocketing prices, attributable to the rising prices of international commodities resulting from global inflation, as well as to our boom in domestic demand. This global inflation overruns our shores like an incoming tide. To stem it, it is necessary to strengthen international anti-inflationary cooperation. At home we must continue the vigorous enforcement of price control policies and check absolutely the spread of any inflationary mood.

Along with the flexible management of public finances from the long-term perspective, we must also actively introduce new policy techniques. It is essential to use taxation as a tool for implementing policy; namely, by means of prohibitive taxes and incentive taxes. West Germany's use of its tax system to regulate the establishment of a comprehensive transport system is well known. If overloaded trucks travel the roads, the highways will be damaged. It is necessary to shift this excess haulage to railways or, if railways prove unable to handle it all, then to waterway shipping. Accordingly, West Germany has levied taxes of more than DM. 16,700 (about 1.6 million yen) on a six-ton truck—clearly a prohibitive tax. At the same time, it is an incentive tax impelling shippers to use the railways and waterways for hauling heavy loads. Such thinking should also be fully utilized in the task of building a new Japan, whether it be for verticalizing our cities or dispersing our industrial concentrations.

It is imperative that the government not take the sole initiative in these works. We must also devise tax incentives, interest supplementation, and other such means to effectively control and use that private capital, know-how, and vitality that have been accumulated during the country's growth and development. Cooperation between the public and private sectors should be flexible, with appropriate systems and assistance for delegating work to private industry in a unique meshing of the public interest with the profit motive. Sometimes it may be necessary to ensure the public character of a project or obtain private capital for large investment projects that yield no return for long periods. In such cases I would hope we might prudently foster such new formulas as the third-sector idea, in which an organization like the Comprehensive National Land Development Public Corporation will lay the foundations of the project and then, in accordance with strict guidelines, turn the construction and improvement over to private enterprise.

It is fundamental to a free economic system that private enterprise be able to give full rein to its spontaneous creativity and vigorous entrepreneurial spirit. Nevertheless, the bases of economic and social management have changed. The demands that private industry be subject to the rules of society have grown louder, whether in the areas of international trust, conserving nature and raw materials in a disciplined way, harmonizing with the local community, or respecting the sovereignty of the consumer. If industry is to respond, it must strengthen its capacity for responsible action on its own initiative. The establishment and observation of new rules is not an area that should await piecemeal intervention by governments. It is imperative that common criteria be clarified and backed by a broad consensus at all levels within the international and domestic economic communities. Such criteria are already being established for overseas investment and trading-company activities. This correct balance between freedom and regulation should be basic to the new economic society of the future.

* * *

During the quarter century since World War II, we have built the first highly industrialized nation in Asia. We are now prepared to cope with the task of creating a new Japan dedicated to peace and welfare. We seek to make Japan, our motherland, a more beautiful, more hospitable, and more spiritually enriching place to live. We also seek to build bonds of friendship with all people.

In 1947 I won my seat in the House of Representatives in the first general election conducted under the new constitution. Beginning with the Comprehensive National Land Development Law of 1950, I have taken the initiative in urging legislation that has resulted in revising the Road Law, introducing the toll road system, establishing the gasoline tax, and enacting the Water Resources Development Promotion Law. In 1968 I wrote the General Principles of Urban Policy. In 1972 I published *Nihon Retto* (English title *Building a New Japan: A Plan for Remodeling the Japanese Archipelago*). Since then, the Honshu-Shikoku Bridge Authority has been created, the Nationwide Shinkansen (superexpress railways) Extension Law has been enacted, the automobile weight tax has been put into force, and the Industrial Relocation Promotion Law has been passed. This series of important policy measures that make up the backbone of the remodeling of the Japanese archipelago is indeed the realization, step by step, of the philosophy contained in my plan.

The road to remodeling Japan is steep and rocky, but unless we accept this challenging task now, Japan will sooner or later come to an impasse. But youth always pulls in new directions that usher in a new age. This is their privilege. I only hope that the young people, upon whose shoulders the future of Japan will rest, will find a rewarding challenge in striving to obtain the ideal, dedicating themselves to mankind, and thus marking their place in history.

INFLATION: A WORLDWIDE DISASTER

by Irving S. Friedman

The world is confronted by a persistent global inflation, and there are strong expectations that it will continue for years to come. This poses a grave threat to all countries, irrespective of size, wealth, political structure, or social ideology. Today's inflation is rooted in the attitudes and experiences of the Great Depression of the 1930s and World War II, and in a number of mutually reinforcing trends that emerged in the aftermath of the war. Because it is fundamentally different from past inflations, and because it varies from country to country in many important respects, a successful attack on it requires new approaches adapted to the conditions and dynamics of each country, coupled with practical day-to-day international collaboration.

The Great Depression gave rise to the firm conviction that such a disaster must not be allowed to happen again. The despair and political turmoil created by years of high unemployment and economic stagnation had wrecked a decade of effort to reestablish a functioning world economy and create a stable international order. Despite the widespread pacifism of the post-World War I period, the breakdown of the world economy had brought political unrest and conflicts, culminating in the rise of Nazism and the horrors of World War II. No one could ever again make the mistake of believing that the achievement of world peace could be separated from the achievement of world prosperity.

The failure to overcome massive unemployment in the 1930s was a failure to understand the causes of economic stagnation, combined with a reluctance to adopt the policies of those who did. Rather belatedly, John Maynard Keynes and others had explained the causes and pointed to the remedies, but even where governments tried their approach, they did so halfheartedly and ineffectively. Ironically, the experience of World War II was more convincing than all the peacetime expositions, because it demonstrated that full employment and economic growth could be commanded into existence by governments. In the postwar world, the New Economics became orthodox and conventional and was soon adopted as the foundation for the fiscal policies of many governments. Avoidance of prolonged, large-scale unemployment became the firmest tenet in economic theology and practice. For many countries, the definition of what constituted an acceptable rate of unemployment, even during recessions, was lower than the actual rates experienced in periods of prosperity before World War II.

Closely related to the commitment to full employment and economic growth, but distinct from it, was the governmental commitment to welfare. The English statesman Disraeli, among others, had deplored the fact that even the extraordinary increases in national output and wealth stemming from industrialization had not eliminated widespread poverty. Indeed, a new and growing class of urban poor lived deplorable and excruciatingly insecure existences. Even before World War I, a few countries—Australia, for example, and Germany under Bismarck—had taken steps to ameliorate the worst aspects of poverty. Until World War II, however, the dominant philosophy was that it was not the responsibility of government to eliminate these social ills or ameliorate their effects; only the most destitute of widows and orphans were to be public responsibilities.

World War II saw a dramatic change in attitude. Governments had proved their miraculous powers. The horrors of war had strengthened the feeling that all human beings are precious. These views came together in an insistence that governments undertake to provide basic needs, to eliminate dire poverty and insecurity. What ethical and religious leaders had urged for millennia was to be accomplished, not in some distant future, but now.

Government budgets reflected these new responsibilities. Like full employment, these social aims became common to political groups of all persuasions. Some went further than others, but they all acted much more alike than they sounded on the hustings. Indeed, as the years passed, new areas of social responsibility were added: higher education, housing, medical care, recreation, day care for children, retirement income, even guaranteed minimum annual incomes—the process still goes on. Poverty and insecurity are still the lot of many. Nevertheless, vast numbers of people have been lifted from subhuman to human conditions, and nowhere is the responsibility of government in this regard seriously contested.

For many, full employment and economic growth meant rising incomes and expectations of even greater rises in the future. Nor—given the governmental acceptance of responsibility for the well-being of all—were such expectations limited to the relatively prosperous. They also dominated the attitudes of the poor. Further, for those earning good incomes, consumption no longer had to be limited in order to save for the education of children, prolonged unemployment, retirement, and medical care.

Irving S. Friedman, professor in residence at the World Bank, was formerly the economic adviser to its president and a director of the International Monetary Fund. He is author of several books, including Inflation: A World-Wide Disaster, *published by Houghton Mifflin in 1973.*

Simultaneously, as wartime technological innovations were applied to the civilian sector, the content of these expectations was vastly altered by a greatly improved range of goods. TV, transistor radios, jet airplanes, satellite communications, new fibres, new construction techniques and styles for housing, commercial buildings, and factories all whetted the appetite. Servicing of these technological wonders became a major need. Mass advertising, made global and simultaneous by the new methods of communication, educated consumers and producers as to what they should wish to consume and produce. New financing arrangements made everyone a potential buyer of products well beyond his current income. Consumption gave way to consumerism, and standards of living were related not to current income but to expectations of rising incomes coupled with easy access to credit.

These forces alone were enough to explain why the worldwide demand for goods and services after World War II outdistanced anything known before, chronically exceeding productive capacity despite the unprecedented growth of the world economy by over 5% per year. But other major factors were also operative. One was the population explosion. World population, which amounted to about 2,295,000,000 in 1940, had increased by almost 200 million by 1950 despite the massive slaughter in World War II. In the 1950s it rose by 500 million—more than the total population of Europe. Nearly 650 million were added in the 1960s, and by 1973 the world was inhabited by well over 3,850,000,000 people—1,370,000,000 more than in 1950. And all these people were demanding more goods and services. Thus, while the world population rose by 46% between 1950 and 1970, the "economic" population rose much more, particularly if changes in age composition (many more young and more old) are taken into account.

At least two other forces need to be mentioned: the nation-state explosion and the cold-hot war.

The postwar period saw the breakup of the colonial system. World War II had greatly strengthened nationalistic feelings, and the European powers, weakened by war, found their empires were no longer viable. In 1945 the United Nations had 51 members; by September 1973 it had grown to 135, largely through the admission of new nations carved from former colonial territories. Furthermore, countries such as China and the Latin-American nations, which were nominally sovereign before the war, began to assume a more independent stance. Irrespective of their economic viability, and burdened in many cases by an overwhelming assortment of social and political problems, the new nations nevertheless took on not only such traditional responsibilities and trappings of independence as police forces, armies, elementary schools, and government buildings, but also such new ones as steel mills, universities, and commitments to improved material well-being for all. An independent state is a much greater source of demand for the world's goods and services than the same territory was as a colony. At the same time, independence does not radically improve productive capacity, at least not for many years.

The cold war meant the continuation of military expenditures at wartime levels. At times it became the cold-hot war, making even greater demands on available resources. Unlike World War II, the new military-political situation was not accompanied by public willingness to accept reduced consumption and increased taxes. The cold-hot war, however, is too often seen as *the* cause of widespread inflation, particularly in the United States. It was not the primary cause of either postwar prosperity or postwar inflation. Other forces would probably have made for persistent worldwide inflation, even if international tensions had been greatly reduced. But the burdens of wars and armament were piled on top of already excessive demand pressures. They helped to accelerate an inflation that already had great momentum.

Finally, more recent developments have further widened the disparity between world demand and world capacity to produce. Among the leading examples are the

Inflation has affected individuals all over the world. In Paris young people without jobs search the advertisement pages of a newspaper outside the publisher's office. In London a businessman stops to scan a paper for news of the government's latest economic measures.

LEFT, PHELPS—RAPHO GUILLUMETTE; RIGHT, CENTRAL PRESS/PICTORIAL PARADE huge increases in the demand for natural fuels for energy, particularly oil; the need for other industrial raw materials such as copper, tin, and rubber; the greatly heightened demand for foodstuffs; the increasingly obvious need for environmental protective devices; and the worldwide trend toward urbanization, with its concomitant demand for resources to restructure cities and their related educational, police, transportation, sanitation, lighting, and medical services systems.

Meanwhile, labour-management relations were undergoing a dramatic change. The extensive, prolonged, and often violent industrial strife that had marked the 1920s and 1930s became the exception in most industrial countries. Given the strong demand for labour and frequent critical labour shortages, plus an environment of rising prices that readily absorbed rising wage costs, the conditions that had led to the industrial disputes of earlier years no longer obtained. Trade unions became larger and more powerful politically as well as industrially, so that political parties and governments often depended on them for survival. Management, at times, expressed concern over the power of the unions or over rising wage costs, but it did so rather quietly, since a mutually satisfactory peace could be made with labour and profits could be defended by passing on the increased costs to the consumer. Steadily rising wages strengthened the expectations of future wage rises; they strengthened, reinforced, and interacted with the expectations of rising prices. It became impossible to say either that wage increases pushed up prices or that demand pulled up prices. They were part and parcel of the same phenomenon.

Closely related was the further strengthening of monopolistic practices in modern industry. Giant firms combined to form giant conglomerates. Prices were greatly influenced by the management decisions of a few firms that dominated some industries rather than being decided under competitive market conditions. This situation had been evolving for decades before World War II, but the process accelerated. In many countries, it was encouraged by governments; in a few countries, like the United States, antimonopoly laws existed but had limited effects. The "administered" prices set by giant firms were designed to make the most money for the firms over time. Prices could be lowered to drive out competitors or raised to increase profits if there was no fear of competition. In the main, large firms tend to favour price stability, since this facilitates management of the entire productive and sales process. In an environment of generally rising prices, "administered" prices will also go up like any others, although they may rise jerkily, in steps, rather than smoothly. At the same time, the incentives to improve products and service are greatly weakened.

Monopolistic practices by themselves would not have resulted in persistent inflation. In fact, it is likely that the persistent inflation has been more important in promoting monopolies than monopolistic practices have been in promoting persistent inflation. The larger and more diversified firm is better able to survive the difficulties created by persistent inflation than the smaller firm. The customer is the greatest threat to monopoly, and during inflation the customer is in a greatly weakened position.

A New Kind of Inflation. Modern inflation is persistent and worldwide, unlike its predecessors which, arising from very different causes and existing under very different conditions, were temporary and usually confined to a few countries at any one time. Everywhere people and their governments now expect that inflation will continue, even if business conditions turn downward. This conviction derives from three decades of experience.

Persistent inflation has been worldwide since 1940. By a process of self-mesmerization, many in the developed countries—including those who should have known better—convinced themselves that low rates of inflation were tolerable if not desirable, at worst a small price to pay for avoiding prolonged unemployment. It was erroneously believed that very high rates of inflation were a disease of the poorer nations, particularly those south of the Panama Canal. It was also erroneously believed that in any case, the richer industrial countries could rid themselves of these low rates of inflation by accepting somewhat higher rates of unemployment.

These continuing low rates of inflation in the industrial countries were the seeds that gave birth to expectations of persistent inflation. They reflected the continuing disparity between world demand and world supply. They did not reflect cyclical conditions but, rather, a fundamental imbalance for which there was no automatic corrective mechanism. Indeed, the persistent inflation not only failed to stimulate output sufficient to meet demand, but even exacerbated the imbalance by discouraging investment in the production of needed consumption goods and housing. The toleration of low rates of inflation until expectations of persistent inflation had become commonplace everywhere was the fatal error in the thinking and policies of governments in the years following World War II.

Now inflation rates are high in the industrial countries, and it is evident that even the richest of them all—the United States—can experience price inflation at annual rates of 10, 20, 30, or 40% or more. Now it becomes obvious that the myopic view of serious inflation as a problem largely confined to the less developed countries is wrong. The industrial countries, however, have still not accepted the idea that their inflation is novel, persistent, and truly international. It is not merely a repetition of past temporary experiences in a more virulent form. It is international not only in the sense that it is being experienced simultaneously by many countries, but also in a more profound sense: it is international in its causes and effects and is incapable of separate national solutions.

During the Depression "beggar thy neighbour" policies were adopted. Imports were reduced and exports were pushed in an effort to stimulate both domestic business and employment. In the 1970s countries are again becoming more nationalistic as they try to deal with their domestic inflations. Their policies, if successful, could help control their inflations, but only at the expense of worsening inflation in other countries. But these defensive measures will not work for long, because the aggravated inflation abroad will come right back again through import prices, exports, and movements of funds. Countries are now caught on the horns of a painful dilemma. A balance of payments deficit helps the domestic economy because it means more goods are being added to the economy than are being exported, but the deficit weakens national and international confidence in the country's money and economic management. A balance of payments surplus strengthens this confidence but it worsens the inflationary situation because it means more is being exported than is being imported, thus reducing the amount of goods available in an economy already suffering from a scarcity of goods relative to demand. "Inflate thy neighbour" is as futile a policy in the 1970s as "beggar thy neighbour" was in the 1930s.

It is becoming fashionable to say that inflation is inevitable and is here to stay. The author's own conviction is that the present inflation is persistent and that strong, stubborn expectations of continuing inflation are universal, but the inflation will end. The only question is how. Inflation can be brought to an end in a chaotic, destructive manner or in an orderly, constructive manner. Great damage has been done to societies and their economies, but the choice still exists.

Stubbornness in Error. Given the enormity and universality of postwar needs and demands, it is not surprising that inflationary forces persisted and grew more intractable. What is disappointing is that economists, concerned private leaders of business, finance, and labour, and politicians and policymakers failed so completely to diagnose the problem correctly and thus failed to advocate effective remedies. While the now traditional Keynesian framework was being accepted, and even political "conservatives" in the United States, Britain, West Germany, and elsewhere acquiesced in the new leadership role of government and its expanded responsibilities, the implications of the new domestic and global conditions were not appreciated.

The New Economics, like classical economics, remains a highly useful device for understanding current economic phenomena, but it does not go far enough in providing an adequate diagnosis. Too often its practitioners start with the erroneous assumption that the world economy is essentially the same as it was before World War II, although the scale is bigger and there are a few new wrinkles. They fail to see that, in the meantime, we have had earthquakes that have dramatically raised new mountain ranges, created new valleys, and obliterated familiar landmarks.

Modern societies are fundamentally different from prewar societies. They are deeply concerned not only with the general level of demand but also with the structure and distribution of consumption. Because economists have not understood this, they have failed to see that modern inflation is a different phenomenon. They continue to discuss inflation in traditional terms, giving these terms a time-honoured but erroneous context. It is possible to use traditional terms to describe new phenomena—doctors still talk of "headaches"—but then the context of the words must conform to new conditions. Thus we speak of "persistent inflation" and expectations of persistent inflation, instead of merely "inflation." This has the advantage of familiarity—people know that "inflation" means rising prices, costs, and wages—while at the same time, the use of the word "persistent" indicates novelty.

Persistent inflation means continuing price, cost, and wage increases and much more. It means steadily rising wholesale and consumer price indices, climbing money wages, higher public utility rates, higher interest rates for loans, and increased money supply, more bank credit, and ever higher levels of government expenditures and receipts, including taxation. The fact that these trends continue for years despite changes in business conditions is an essential clue to the evolution of persistent inflation. The critical element, however, is the presence of expectations of continuing inflation. When consumers, producers, traders, bankers, artists, scientists, gamblers, governments—in short, everyone—expect these rising trends are here to stay, then social and political as well as economic behaviour changes radically.

The old descriptions of incentives and responses are no longer apt because the expectation of continuing inflation cuts across all human behaviour. In any one day's activities, everyone can find for himself scores of cases in which he would have acted differently—professionally, socially, or otherwise—if he had expected future prices and wages to decline.

Thus, persistent inflation has many manifestations that "temporary" inflation does not. The lower-income family seeks housing and finds that low-income housing is disappearing. The pensioner and his wife who retired ten years ago on a seemingly adequate pension now qualify for the relief rolls. The poor black family discovers that ham hocks are costly and hard to find. Pollution becomes intolerable in Los Angeles and Tokyo as city finances flounder in the maze of problems caused by inflation. Garbage piles up in New York City as sanitation workers try to defend their meagre living standards, even at the expense of great hardship to the city's residents. Products decrease in size and worsen in quality, and service deteriorates.

There is more. The sailing enthusiast considers giving up sailing because of congestion, greatly increased marina fees, and water pollution. The young couple is already swamped and chronically worried by consumer debt because their furnishings, purchased on credit, are expensive relative to their income. A college graduate finds he can earn more as a taxi driver than in a job that will utilize his education—if he can find such a job at all. The homeowner cannot afford to paint his house, even though this accelerates deterioration and means more expensive repairs later. The apartment dweller sees his rent rise while services in his building worsen sharply. The worker finds his bus service becoming less frequent and more crowded and less dependable (even leaving aside the increase in fares).

The small store owner has great difficulty deciding how much merchandise he can afford to stock in the face of uncertainty as to operating costs, including the availability and costs of credit, rent, labour, and utilities, coupled with uncertainty as to what the market will tolerate in the way of higher prices. The large firm faces bottlenecks and shortages in many areas of production and distribution. The banker is eager to accommodate customers, but is reluctant to lock himself into firm commitments on the amount, interest rate, and maturity of loans when he cannot foresee what will happen to deposits, reserve requirements, or the prime rate. Substantial firms with experienced management are unable to cope with this peculiar prosperity and are glad to be absorbed by a conglomerate—which is unable to provide the same leadership, initiative, skills, and dedication. The investor views all these uncertainties, wonders where it will all end, and decides he is well advised to buy diamonds, gold, or real estate or keep funds abroad instead of buying equities or bonds that would finance increases in productive capacity at home.

The schoolteacher moonlights as a clerk in a local store or goes on strike because schoolteachers are not paid enough to support their families in a manner commensurate with their standing in the community. Government officials become increasingly corrupt as their salaries become increasingly inadequate. The voter becomes deeply disillusioned with his government as he sees political leaders gain office on the basis of promises they cannot fulfill, even though the promises seem quite reasonable when considered separately—lower taxes, more schools, better transportation, more jobs, cheaper power, protection of the environment, less crime, and an end to inflation.

Heads of families are puzzled when children readily accept ways of life at odds with their upbringing. In India the traditional family system breaks down because parents cannot support young people or help them improve their education. Young mothers work and feel guilty because they are not at home with their infants. Clergymen wonder why their congregations seem so materialistic and selfish, despite the strong strain of ethical concern in modern thinking. The United States government limits food exports at the very time when it is trying to strengthen the international position of the dollar. Major sections of society believe that price and wage controls will not work (in part because they require widespread public support) and that the control period will be followed by more price and wage increases.

The list could be expanded almost indefinitely. The social and political manifestations of persistent inflation vary markedly from country to country and from community to community, but they add up to widespread discontent, concern, frustration, and alienation—a deepening sense that one is running faster and faster only to find that one is going backward. Modern societies have shown remarkable resiliency—disrupted by major wars, internal violence, and economic disaster, they have survived and progressed. At the same time, they are highly vulnerable because of the intricate interlinking of their many activities. A break in any link—transportation, policing, water supply, fuels, communications, education, sanitation, health services, food production and distribution—can disrupt the entire society. Repeated disruptions increase popular anger, discontent, and alienation. Social and political explosions result. The cause may be perceived as some current event; what has been hidden is the steady undermining of the foundations.

It is for such reasons that the author, in his book *Inflation: A World-Wide Disaster,* has stressed the grave social and political effects of modern inflation. Only when these effects are sufficiently appreciated will the public be prepared for a serious and sustained attack on the problem.

Attempts to deal with modern inflation have nearly always failed because it was assumed that individuals, firms, and governments would behave as they would have under conditions of "temporary" inflation. For example, in different times raising interest rates on loans to very high levels would have curtailed the demand for loans drastically and might well have initiated a stock market collapse and a major depression. Under existing conditions, such a move may actually increase the demand for loans, possibly after an initial shock period of accommodation to the new situation. Individuals may be convinced from past experience that even unprecedentedly high interest rate levels will be followed by still higher levels, so that it is best to borrow immediately. Higher interest rates are themselves seen as a sign of the strength of inflation. The increased cost of borrowing can be passed on to the final purchaser of a product or service or, if necessary, it can be financed by borrowing more. Further, the increased interest costs are tax deductible—an important consideration as rising money incomes move more and more people into higher income tax brackets, even though their jobs and real income (*i.e.,* the purchasing power of their money incomes) remain unchanged.

Similarly, higher taxes may not have the expected effect of reducing consumption and investment demand. The consumer simply uses his savings. Savings become less attractive as inflation persists; better to use savings that are declining in purchasing power than to forego desired consumption or investment, since the desired goods and services will only cost more in subsequent months and years. Another time-honoured "anti-inflationary" measure is to keep wages down, but who expects that wages will continue to be held down long enough to end inflation? Therefore, wage limitations are seen as temporary, and the wage earner maintains consumption by using consumer credit, savings, and other methods.

What is needed is to end expectations of persistent inflation. Given the failure to understand this, necessary remedies have been neglected. Those remedies will be unavoidably painful, but not as painful as they will become if the inflationary process is allowed to go on—and not nearly as painful as the end result of that process: erosion of the fabric of existing organized societies.

The U.S. Case. While persistent worldwide inflation is evident in every country, the U.S., by virtue of its size and extraordinary international presence, is of preeminent importance. By itself it accounts for about one-third of world output. Throughout the 1950s and most of the 1960s, Americans tended to feel that, except for the effects of the Korean War and, later, the war in Vietnam, serious inflation was a problem of other countries, particularly those in Latin America. This attitude prevailed despite the fact that prices in the U.S. rose year after year, through both prosperity and recession. The low annual rates of inflation in the U.S.—about 2 to 3%—lulled the public, the academic community, and officialdom into complacency. The presence of higher inflation—rates 3 to 5% a year—in most European countries helped foster that complacency, since the higher prices abroad helped the U.S. to maintain a favourable international trade balance throughout the 1950s and 1960s.

By the end of the 1960s, however, the expansionary pressures of consumerism, defense needs (accelerated by the Vietnam war), and continuing government social programs combined to accelerate the pace of price increases. In 1969 Pres. Richard Nixon moved to cool the economy through the use of classic measures—federal budget restraint and a tight Federal Reserve monetary policy. Economic activity slowed down at an unexpectedly rapid rate, unemployment rose to 6%, and the administration found itself in the midst of a mild recession. At the same time, despite the recession, prices still tended to rise. This state of affairs was admittedly puzzling to many, though it is readily explained in terms of persistent inflation and the accompanying inflationary psychology.

Like his predecessors, President Nixon found that his ability to change the inherited pattern of government expenditure was severely limited. It was supported not only by vested interests desiring to continue the status quo but also by a wide public consensus on the responsibilities of government. Nevertheless, emphasis was and still is being placed on fiscal economies—as though reductions in government expenditures sufficient to dampen significantly or eliminate inflationary pressures were possible. Viewed realistically, such reductions appear to be outside the realm of practical politics, irrespective of their desirability. In 1970 U.S. economic managers were not armed (or at least acted as though they were not armed) with the crucial insight as to the true nature of modern inflation. Consequently, the continued rise in prices during and beyond 1970 began to take on alarming dimensions.

By mid-1971 the rapid and continued increase in U.S. prices had taken a heavy toll on the competitiveness of U.S. goods in relation to those of Europe and Japan. In the summer of that year, the U.S. announced a shocking piece of economic news: the existence of a U.S. international trade deficit, the first in a generation. This startling revelation, however, only began to jog the perceptions of the U.S. public and of officials who remained wedded to the idea that inflation was a temporary condition that could be restrained by traditional economic policies. Even then, very few related the trade deficit to the burgeoning rate of persistent inflation.

Observers abroad, while also slow to perceive the crucial role of persistent inflation in the U.S. trade turnabout, were equally alarmed by the figures. The U.S. trade deficit bolstered the fears of foreign businessmen and government officials (whose countries held tens of billions of U.S. dollars) that the U.S. dollar, the mainstay of the international monetary system, had become a seriously weakened currency. These fears had been growing for some time, as the outflow of U.S. dollars to Europe and Japan had increased to the point where foreign dollar holdings exceeded, by tens of billions of dollars, the supply of U.S. gold that supported the value of those dollars. Not surprisingly, foreign holders of dollars rushed to trade them in for the currencies of other countries (notably of Japan and West Germany) whose national economies and international trade positions seemed more reassuring.

At the same time, persistent inflation in those countries, combined with worldwide scarcities, cast doubt on the attractiveness of financial assets as longer-term havens for money savings. Simultaneously with a flight from the dollar, there was a flight from all currencies into physical assets like gold, real estate, commodities, and favoured productive enterprises. The ensuing mad scramble in international currency markets resulted in repeated runs on the U.S. dollar and chaos for the international monetary system.

Amid these conditions, the United States acted in a dramatic and totally unexpected way. Despite his strong personal antagonism to wage and price controls, President Nixon surprised the world on Aug. 15, 1971, by announcing a devaluation of the dollar in terms of gold, a suspension of the convertibility of the dollar into gold, and a comprehensive wage-price freeze with the creation of a Cost of Living Council to enforce the freeze. This action dealt a crippling—if not a death—blow to the international monetary system that had been in existence since the Bretton Woods, N.H., conference of 1944. It unilaterally severed the connection between the dollar and gold, the tie around which the value of every currency in the world had been defined. Thenceforth, the international monetary system was in flux, awaiting international agreement as to the new roles of the dollar, gold, and their substitutes.

The U.S. public got its first experience with peacetime regulation of the economy. Through four successive phases of controls, the administration, Congress, and the public began to sense—but failed to grasp—the dominant influence of inflationary expectations, chronic excess demand, widespread production bottlenecks and scarcities, and the resultant persistent inflation. When Phases One and Two "succeeded" in restraining inflation to an annual rate of 3.4%, the administration, pressured by both business and labour, felt it could relax the controls program. But no sooner had controls been relaxed (in January 1973) than prices began to soar. By mid-1973 inflation held first place among national issues of greatest concern to the public, surpassing even the Watergate scandals. Wholesale prices of all goods, not just agricultural goods, rose to an annual rate of over 20%, an incredible figure to the many who had believed the U.S. economy was immune to high rates of inflation.

The administration weaved unhappily among policy alternatives. Its course was made all the more uncertain in that it disliked wage-price controls and said so publicly. Phase Four of the controls program, if "successful," would only reduce the annual rate of price increase. Meanwhile, this relatively rigid set of rules was accompanied by a tight money policy that pushed interest rates to all-time highs. Reducing the rate of inflation is desirable, of course, but it does not get at the roots of persistent inflation. It does not end expectations of continued price rises in the future. Until this is done, rates of inflation will be reduced only to rise again.

The aim of any anti-inflationary program must be a zero rate of inflation, not a "low" rate of inflation. Low rates may be acceptable targets during periods of temporary inflation, when expectations are that the low rates will be followed by a zero rate or even by declining prices. Nowhere, however, does this situation prevail today. The path from high rates to a zero rate may well pass through lower rates for some time, but the problem of modern inflation will be tackled only if it is clear throughout that the target is zero, that the policies are designed to achieve this target, that the mechanism is suitable, that the economic managers are determined, and that the necessary political support exists.

An alternative is the establishment of much more comprehensive governmental controls over all aspects of economic behaviour. For this to even seem successful it must be accompanied either by widespread public support or by acquiescence achieved through drastic coercion. These preconditions are not present in the United States—or in most countries. Even if they were, the persistent inflation would remain as long as the imbalance between demand and supply existed. The price and wage effects of inflation might conceivably be suppressed, but the inflation would then be manifested in black markets, shoddier goods, a much narrower range of goods, rapid deterioration as servicing became more inefficient or unavailable, disappearance of less expensive goods, increased moonlighting, industrial strife, and more crime. At best, a tightly controlled society is a huge price to pay for ending inflation. In any case, it is not an effective way.

As 1973 ended, President Nixon continued to advocate paring federal expenditures, and there was increased talk of tax increases—signs that the seriousness of the inflation was recognized and that politically courageous steps were being contemplated. The danger remained, however, that as long as the anatomy of the phenomenon was not adequately understood, the remedies might well prove ineffective and might even worsen the disease.

The European and Japanese Experience. The phenomenon of persistent inflation is no more appreciated in Europe than in the U.S. In their attempts to cope with the same entrenched and growing inflationary pressures, every European country, over the last several years, has introduced some form of wage and price controls, as well as restrictive monetary and fiscal policies. In almost all cases, the failure actually to eliminate inflation has left them wide open to rapid acceleration of their inflation rates from low to alarmingly high. In November 1972 the Council of Ministers of the European Economic Community met to consider a common attack on inflation. Not surprisingly, in view of the conventional wisdom, the council established, as a goal, a 4% rate of annual increase in the member states' consumer price indices for 1973. Elimination of inflation was seemingly not considered.

Despite the widespread introduction (and, in some cases, reintroduction) of controls and restrictive monetary and fiscal policies, steeply rising prices continue to plague the European countries. By June 1973 inflation in Europe was running at twice the 4% target. Italy's annual inflation rate by midyear was 11.5%; France had the region's lowest rate, 7.4%. The Japanese experience was similar. As of mid-1973 inflation was at an annual rate of 11.1%. The Japanese were also attempting to restrain the national inflation through a series of fiscal, monetary, and tariff programs.

The Less Developed Countries. In the less developed countries, inflation continues to be a problem of the first magnitude. It threatens all efforts to create more productive and equitable societies. Its social and political effects are seen daily in repeated governmental crises. In many respects, less developed countries are more resilient than industrialized societies because they are not as highly integrated. On the other hand, their widespread poverty leaves very little margin before the effects of inflation become explosive.

In Latin America, Chile, Uruguay, and Argentina have recently experienced the world's highest inflation rates: over 60% in each country. During the year Chile underwent a military takeover as the socioeconomic situation under the Allende government became intolerable. Taken as a whole, the less developed world is experiencing an inflation rate on the order of 15%. Rates of about 10% or more are common, existing, for example, in Indonesia, Pakistan, and the Philippines. In India continuing inflation even during industrial recession and cutbacks in foreign aid have forced planners to reduce drastically the physical development targets of the five-year plan scheduled to begin in 1974.

A Program for Zero Inflation. Policymakers and the public alike must appreciate that we are in the midst of an unprecedented century of inflation. Inflation is now a persistent—not a temporary—phenomenon. Equally important is the realization that persistent inflation is worldwide in scale, common to all regions of the globe and to all stages of development. Campaigns to restrain inflation are also common to most countries, including every Western European state, Japan, and the U.S. In every case, these campaigns consist of traditional fiscal and monetary policies in combination with wage and price controls. In every case, the aim is to restrain price increases to some acceptable level, and, in almost every case, anti-inflation programs have failed to achieve that aim. Nowhere has the elimination of persistent inflation without severe recession or depression been posited as a viable goal.

These conditions suggest the prevalence of erroneous conceptions of the world economy. It must be realized that, under current supply and demand conditions, a seemingly low rate of inflation can easily accelerate to an uncontrollable pace, even when relatively restrictive price, wage, fiscal, and monetary policies are applied. There is an ever present likelihood that, at some point in this acceleration, social and economic objectives will be sacrificed. Persistent inflation is an unrelenting enemy of full employment, improved general well-being, and the elimination of poverty and chronic insecurity. Any modern nation eager to pursue these objectives must, therefore, make zero inflation its goal.

This is a hard decision. It must be taken with keen awareness of its broad implications and in response to a widespread conviction that the societal effects of continuing inflation are intolerable. The process can be greatly facilitated by a clarification of what each citizen wants for his country—its social priorities, its economic institutions and practices, its political processes. Equally important, the basic operating assumptions for the management of the economy need to be made explicit and largely agreed upon.

Goals could include high levels of employment, avoidance of prolonged and severe unemployment, steady progress in eliminating poverty, increasing opportunities for all groups, improved quality of life, sharing by all in material improvements, and expansion in the international exchange of goods and services. Certain questions will need to be answered in advance; for example, the role of government in dealing in social and economic management, the acceptability of attempts to influence the pattern of consumption through fiscal and credit devices, the acceptability and feasibility of long-term reliance on government directives and controls, the desirability of increasing savings and investment, and the possibilities of strengthening mechanisms for broad participation in the public debate on these subjects.

The precise content of the program to end inflation will be grist in the mill of politics for years to come.

We cannot be certain in advance that any set of policies will succeed. Therefore, any program will need to be flexible. But there should be no doubt about one key aspect—that the program will continue until persistent inflation is ended and expectations that persistent inflation will continue are eliminated. An apt analogy is to the national determination to win a popularly supported war. No one is sure how to do it, but the national purpose is not obscured by this uncertainty, nor is the ability to act paralyzed by differences over strategy and tactics.

Regardless of details, however, the national anti-inflation effort must start from the premise that it is attacking root causes. What is needed is a carefully selective attack on the scarcities and bottlenecks that exist in the supply of needed goods and services and, simultaneously, a carefully selective effort to change the pattern of consumption. Traditional fiscal, monetary, and wage-price controls will be useful tools, but only if they are used in combination with others and only if they mesh with actions being taken in other countries.

Tax legislation, interest rates, and credit policies must be used to achieve desired changes in consumption. It is not enough to aim at "reducing" or "increasing" consumption; the composition of consumption must be changed as well. Luxury taxes for certain products may need to be much higher. Investment incentives for producing such goods might be nil, while investment tax incentives for producing widely used goods might be made more attractive. Credit mechanisms can be used in a similar way. Savings must be encouraged; for example, interest earned on savings deposits or earned income that is saved could be made nontaxable. With changes in consumption will come changes in investment and output, and increased production of needed commodities will provide the underpinning for the elimination of inflationary expectations.

Thus, imaginative tax and credit policies can be used to discourage certain types of consumption, to economize on the use of industrial raw materials, to encourage savings, and to encourage patterns of production that will strengthen the national zero-inflation program. The national anti-inflation program should also provide mechanisms for the allocation of national resources among leading national priorities, including urban renewal, medical care and research, housing, more equitable income, defense, education, and transportation. Decisions about these priorities must take place at the grass-roots level.

Given the international scope of persistent inflation, any national program must include provisions for international cooperation in dealing with international supply and demand for food, energy, and other resources. If the international aspects of the problem are ignored, the national program may well be defeated by the effects of inflation abroad.

Once the desirability of such a program has been widely accepted in a number of countries, the national anti-inflation campaign can proceed with its substantive efforts. Initially, the government must acquire information about the economy that will enable policymakers and the public to understand the inflationary psychology and demand conditions that are the root causes of persistent inflation. An effort must be made to balance demand and supply, but with much more attention to the composition of demand and the structure of supply than has been given in the past. It is vitally important that scarce resources be channeled into areas that will increase productive capacity, for this latter achievement lies at the heart of a comprehensive anti-inflation program. Only through increased productive capacity can the desired social welfare and other goals be met. To this end, rampant consumerism must be transformed into reasonable consumption, and private investment must help in the transformation.

The international dimension of the problem can be attacked by giving new responsibilities and support to such existing institutions as the International Monetary Fund, the World Bank Group, the Food and Agriculture Organization, the new UN Environment Program, and the various regional development banks. These institutions can take an overview of national conditions and policies and help to bring about the needed equilibrium between world supply and world demand.

Fortunately, the elimination of persistent inflation is consistent with the achievement of other aims of modern societies, from the restructuring of cities to the elimination of pollution. The existence of persistent inflation reflects the fact that a wide range of problems are not being handled properly. Conversely, as long as persistent inflation continues, the world's other major social, political—and economic—problems cannot be solved.

For those who fear that the effort to end persistent inflation implies an excessive degree of government intervention, it should be borne in mind that persistent inflation itself makes government intervention inevitable. Only when persistent inflation is ended will it be possible to make a true choice between a type of society in which government intervention is kept to a minimum and a society that tolerates a high degree of government intervention. Persistent inflation is destroying our political choices, just as it is destroying our economic and social choices.

PROSPECTS FOR EUROPEAN SECURITY

by Christoph Bertram

Ten years ago, European security would have been a straightforward issue within a clearly defined international system: it would have been synonymous with the military security of Western Europe. Its problems would have been, above all, to maintain and strengthen the Atlantic alliance, to provide means of defense deemed adequate to deter a Soviet attack, and to promote harmony and political accommodation both among the states of Western Europe and between them and the United States. Today, the subject has become more ambiguous. It still includes the traditional ingredients of Western European security and defense, but deterrence is no longer the only yardstick for their adequacy, the threat has become less definable, and accommodation is sought not only between allies but between East and West as well.

The international system as we have known it since the end of World War II is in a state of flux, while the contours of a new system have not yet become clearly visible. We are living in an era of political maneuver, to use Marshall Shulman's term, where not only the superpowers of East and West are jockeying for new positions but where states and societies within the West are working out new relationships.

Old Problems in a New Setting. This is not to say that the problem is new or that the instruments of security set up in Western Europe during the past 25 years are out of date. Security for Western Europe then and now means military security against the Soviet Union and political security to define and implement the legitimate interests of states and societies. But today many of the elements that provided the unquestioned basis for Western European security policies are in a state of uncertainty. The task would be more manageable if the future of U.S. policy toward Western Europe were clear, if Soviet aims were less ambiguous, if the extent of Soviet-U.S. entente were defined, if the ability of Western Europe to jointly organize political cohesion and military resources were predictable. Even then the problem would not be easy; as it is, it must be tackled against a moving background.

Perhaps the best example of the new complexity is provided by the negotiations between NATO and the Warsaw Pact on the mutual reduction of military forces, which, after an exploratory meeting in the first half of 1973, started in earnest on October 30 in Vienna. On the surface, these negotiations aim at reducing the military burden and maintaining the military balance at lower cost for both sides. But they raise much more fundamental questions. How will a reduction of forces affect the U.S. security commitment to Europe? Will East-West negotiations in Europe amount to more than a Soviet-U.S. deal, confirming and broadening the trend toward superpower bilateralism? Will the Western alliance stand the strain of joint protracted negotiations with the East? Will the negotiations for the reduction of military forces restrict the ability of the alliance to restructure its military effort and streamline its armed forces to best advantage? Will they make Western European political and defense integration more difficult by creating a special zone of inspected force reductions in the centre of Europe? Will they serve to limit the Soviet ability to interfere militarily within and outside the Warsaw Pact area?

Rather than displaying premature hopes and making concessions to an uncertain future, East-West diplomacy in the era of political maneuver will at first be subject to fairly conservative guidelines: caution, limited cooperation, and delimitation.

Caution dictates that the existing structures of European security, NATO and the Warsaw Pact and their organizations, be maintained. This is apparent in both parts of Europe. In the East, the Soviet Union and some of its allies proclaim the further consolidation of the "community of socialist states" as their primary aim in Europe. In the West, the preference of European governments would probably be to improve alliance coordination and procedures, but uncertainty over the future of the U.S. commitment has made them more responsive to the idea of strengthening the European caucus within the alliance and of exploring the possibilities of closer Western European defense cooperation.

Limited cooperation is the result of two opposing considerations. The first is that cooperation among European states across the dividing line is recognized as more natural than confrontation. For the Soviet Union and the Eastern European countries, economic and technological cooperation with the West has, indeed, been one of the major motives for détente. The second consideration is that cooperation should not lead to interdependence. While each side may want to use cooperation to influence the other, neither wants to be irrevocably tied down.

Delimitation is a term originally coined by East Germany after the Basic Treaty on relations between the two German states had been negotiated in late 1972. *Abgrenzung,* as interpreted by East Germany, means that arrangements between states with different social systems must not lead to a blurring of differences or to destabilizing interpenetration. The monolithic regimes in the

---

Christoph Bertram is assistant director of the International Institute for Strategic Studies, London, and editor of the Institute's journal Survival. *In 1972 he published* Mutual Force Reductions in Europe: The Political Aspects.

East view with apprehension the effects that uncontrolled contact with the pluralistic West might have on their own citizens; while aware that cooperation between East and West is impossible without greater contact, they would like to preempt the dangers this might portend by ideological vigilance and domestic consolidation. But delimitation, while an Eastern term, is to some extent also a Western concern. The pluralistic societies of Western Europe are not worried about human contacts or ideological struggles. Rather, delimitation is endorsed by the West as a barrier against Soviet influence over Western affairs. Détente, multilateral East-West conferences, negotiations on troop reductions, all-European institutions, and Soviet-U.S. arrangements are feared by many in Western Europe because they might offer a skillful Soviet diplomacy the chance to sow seeds of disunity and exploit Western differences.

Détente and the Superpowers. Détente is not a new phenomenon, least of all in Europe. It has been the subject of international conferences and summit meetings since the mid-1950s. The new factor in the 1970s is that détente has become operational policy. This is due, above all, to two more or less simultaneous developments. The first has been West Germany's *Ostpolitik.* In 1969 the new government in Bonn set out to come to terms with the division of Germany, first by recognizing the existing border in Europe in treaties with the Soviet Union and Poland, then by negotiating a settlement, if not a solution of the German problem, with the other German state. More important was the second development: détente between the Soviet Union and the United States. Its main cause was not the European situation, and it would have taken shape even without West Germany's *Ostpolitik.* But it could not and cannot fail to influence European policies and European security.

Superpower bilateralism has long been a major aim of Soviet foreign policy. For many years inferior in strategic power and owing its superpower status to its European stronghold rather than to worldwide influence, the Soviet Union saw parity with the United States as an obvious objective and superpower bilateralism as its obvious expression. There has also been the growing Soviet concern over China. Bilateralism and cooperation with the United States promises a number of dividends: access to the world's most advanced economy and technology, respect for Soviet interests in exchange for respect for U.S. interests, and joint crisis control. Finally, détente may be the only way for the Soviet Union to maintain parity; if past experience is anything to go by, uncontrolled rivalry in the field of strategic weapons could lead to major new U.S. efforts and possibly to U.S. superiority.

For the United States, the reasons for the new relationship are more complex. In his 1973 foreign policy report, Pres. Richard Nixon presented the major considerations. Superpower détente was possible for two seemingly contradictory reasons: because the Soviet Union had become weaker politically and stronger strategically. "The more equal strategic balance" made it possible for the Soviet Union to enter into negotiations and agreements on strategic arms control. At the same time, "divisions within the Communist world" and "the economic revival of Western Europe and Japan" would reduce Soviet abilities to exploit the rapprochement with the United States to divide the Western alliance systems.

This view explains the timing of U.S. *Ostpolitik* and also hints at one of its major substantive incentives: the desire to stabilize the strategic competition. The recognition that an uncontrolled rivalry in the field of strategic weapons would be not only costly but also—and this is more important—potentially destabilizing led naturally to the conviction that a common effort toward stabilization by the strategic superpowers was required. It was, therefore, only logical that the most visible efforts toward negotiation and agreement between the Soviet Union and the United States have been made in the field of limiting strategic weaponry.

From the start, however, neither superpower regarded détente as limited to the military strategic relationship. Increasingly, arrangements in the arms-control field have become expressions of, and vehicles for, the overall political evolution between the Soviet Union and the United States.

The architects of U.S. *Ostpolitik,* Nixon and Henry Kissinger, remain convinced that fundamental differences persist between the United States and the Soviet Union. They are suspicious of long-term Soviet motives and ambitions. Because of this, and contrary to the fears expressed in the past by some of America's allies, U.S. *Ostpolitik* does not aspire to a superpower condominium; this would require a solid basis of mutual trust in the compatibility of Soviet-U.S. interests and in the sincerity of Soviet leaders. Rather, it aims to restrain Soviet power and to create Soviet respect for the interests the United States regards as vital. To achieve this, the United States seeks to create, through cooperation, vested Soviet interests in maintaining good relations, and through firmness, including military efforts, Soviet respect for American objectives.

The Middle East crisis of October 1973 has provided the latest and, perhaps, the most telling demonstration of this relationship. From the start, both sides were in constant contact, and even the fact that each side was supplying arms in considerable quantity to its client states in the area did not disrupt the ongoing consultations between Moscow and Washington. The swiftness with which the joint Soviet-U.S. cease-fire proposal was negotiated during Secretary Kissinger's trip to Moscow on October 20 underlines the degree of prior close liaison and preparation.

At the same time, along with the conciliatory gestures, each side was signaling to the other its determination not to be outmaneuvered. Both sides were increasing their naval presence in the Mediterranean. When developments on the ground between Israel and Egypt seemed to prompt a Soviet decision to send forces to the Suez Canal to police the cease-fire, the United States brought part of its forces, including strategic forces, to a state of alert. The demonstration had its effect. Its magnitude might have been influenced by fear that the Soviet Union wanted to exploit the U.S. crisis of leadership; an excess of firmness was seen as the best way to demonstrate not only U.S. interests but also the resolve of a president weakened by the Watergate crisis. However, it is worth bearing in mind that the real surprise was not the demonstration of force by both sides, but their simultaneous desire to accommodate each other's vital interests regardless of it. It is also worth bearing in mind that for neither superpower is détente the result of affection and trust but of the recognition that the two will have to live together.

The past years have helped to clarify some of the ambiguities of détente. The first clarification has been that détente is not confined to some parts of the superpower relationship but applies across the board. A regional event affects the total relationship.

The second clarification is that stability is in the interest of both superpowers, in both the strategic and the general political field. This is particularly visible in Europe. To all intents and purposes, the United States has recognized the political status quo in Eastern Europe and, with it, Soviet security interests there. In return, the Soviet Union has recognized the legitimacy of the U.S. military presence in Europe, through the four-power agreement on Berlin of September 1971 and through Soviet willingness to accept the United States as a full member of the Conference on Security and Cooperation in Europe.

The third major clarification is that contact and general goodwill are more important than concrete agreements. For the Soviets this is nothing new; to be accepted as an equal in the dialogue with the other superpower is, for the Soviet Union, perhaps, the most significant achievement of strategic efforts and of détente. The U.S. side, however, has always stressed that Soviet-U.S. differences "could not be hidden merely by expressions of goodwill; they could only be resolved by precise solutions of major issues" (*U.S. Foreign Policy for the 1970s,* May 3, 1973). Any "precise solution of major issues," however, produces its own dynamics and its significance resides in its symbolic value for the Soviet-U.S. relationship as a whole.

A Model for Europe? The "era of political maneuver" and the practice of Soviet-U.S. détente have highlighted the differences, rather than confirmed the similarities, between a European and a superpower concept of détente.

Détente with the Soviet Union is, for the Western Europeans, accompanied by military inferiority. If they want to influence Soviet policy, they can scarcely hope to do so by military power—unlike their U.S. ally.

The fact that Western European states are regional powers and concerned with Soviet restraint mainly in Europe and the immediate vicinity facilitates their task because it reduces the areas of friction. But it complicates their task in two respects: Europe is the area of primary Soviet interest, so there is little room for Soviet concessions there; and the regional interests of Western Europe deprive governments of the ability to trade off good Western European behaviour elsewhere against good Soviet behaviour in Europe, as the United States would be able to do. What is more, Western European interests in détente are less compatible with Soviet views than U.S. interests are. Stability without change in Europe is the motto of the superpowers. For Western Europe, having to live with the Soviet superpower and bordering on the Soviet sphere of control, stability is important not

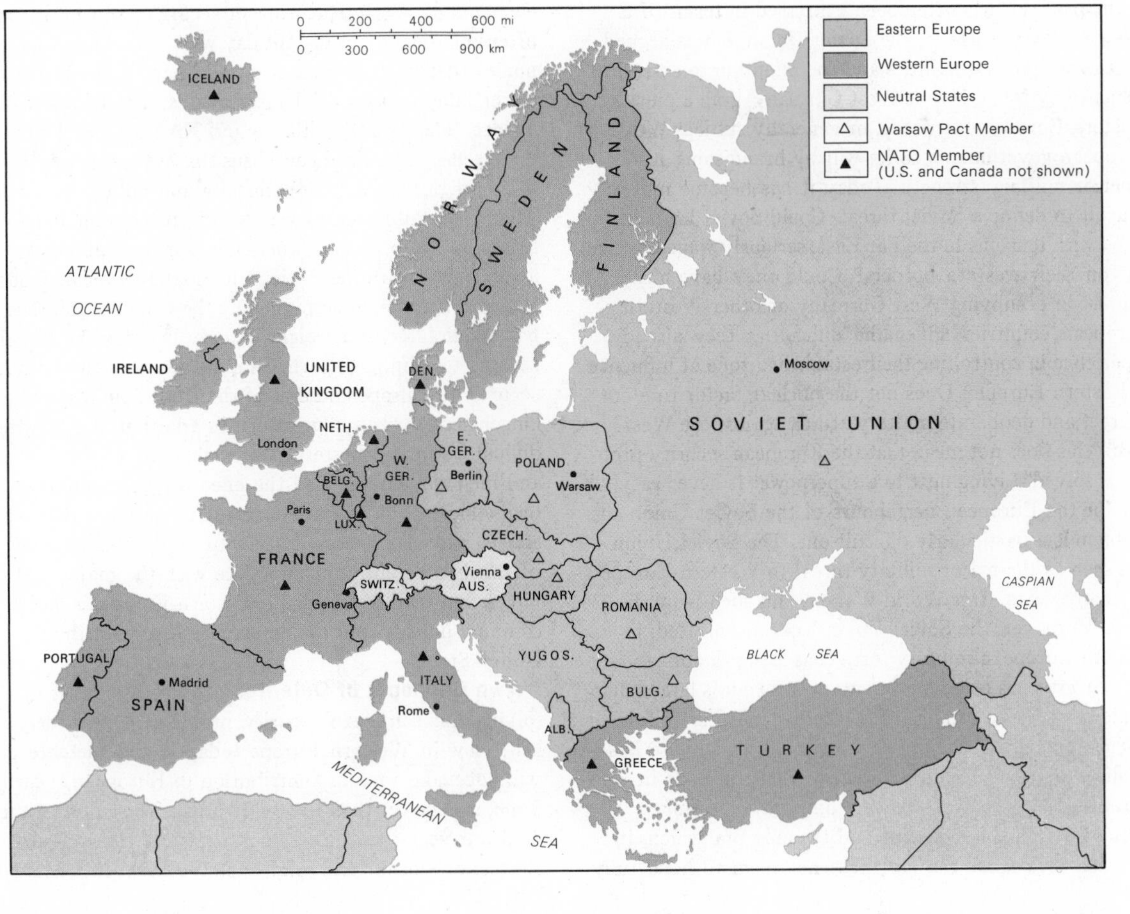

just for its own sake but because it will permit gradual change toward a more secure Europe.

Neither the United States nor the Soviet Union has any desire to see their relationship complicated by events in Europe. In the past, the Soviet Union has displayed a clear desire to separate European from superpower détente, and this will become even more marked if contact with European states and societies and the emotional appeal of Europe should produce strains within its power sphere in Eastern Europe. The United States, for its part, has no wish to have its *Ostpolitik* rendered more difficult by its European allies. As the most powerful state in the West, the United States feels it is much better suited than the middle and small states of Western Europe to extract maximum concessions and maximum restraints from the Soviet Union. It also sees itself as acting for the West as a whole and entitled to the support of its allies.

This is a true alliance dilemma, demonstrated again during the Middle East crisis. Unlike the Soviet Union, the United States cannot command its allies but must convince them. Unlike the Soviet satellites, Western European governments can choose whether to endorse or to disapprove U.S. policy. The United States will rightly argue that there are specific concerns and procedures in superpower détente; the Europeans will rightly point out that there are equally specific concerns and procedures in European détente. Unless both views can be accommodated, détente could prove disruptive to the Atlantic relationship and, with it, to European security.

The Problem of European Security. The European security problem is how to live with the Soviet superpower. In the past this has often been expressed in terms of a defined "Soviet threat"; the Soviet Union, it was argued, has the military capabilities and the intention to extend its influence by force, invade West Germany, grab a piece of Western European territory, or generally subject Western European governments to its will by brandishing its superior military strength. Today it has become more difficult to define a Soviet threat. Could Soviet leaders, faced with tensions in the Far East, seriously want to wage war on their western borders? Could they have any interest in occupying West Germany or other Western European countries, given the difficulties they already experience in controlling their established zone of influence in Eastern Europe? Does not the nuclear factor rule out a direct and deliberate military attack against the West?

But this does not mean that the European security problem is solved. Living next to a superpower is never easy, and for the European neighbours of the Soviet Union the problem is a particularly difficult one. The Soviet Union was seen as the major military threat to Western Europe for many years after World War II, and such fears die hard. Moreover, the Soviet Union has concentrated, in Eastern Europe, a military force that raises doubts about the peacefulness of Soviet intentions, since it is larger than would seem to be required for internal policing or for defense against NATO forces. The Soviet Union also has a tradition of using military force for political ends in Europe—1953, 1956, 1968—the only power to take military action since the war and the only one which, in the case of Yugoslavia, still does not seem to have fully recognized the status quo. Finally, the Soviet system is closed; the secrecy of its regime would make it difficult to trust the Soviet superpower, even if its traditions in Europe were unambiguously peaceful.

In addition, the nature of Soviet control over Eastern Europe raises a specific security concern. The very rigidity of this control, while in general succeeding in imposing bloc discipline, has increased the explosive effect of the few crises that have erupted in Eastern Europe. The use of Soviet military force there has demonstrated the absence of more peaceful means of crisis control. Although the Soviet Union has prevented these crises from getting out of hand so far, there is no guarantee that this will remain true in the future.

The power and practice of the Soviet Union constitute the security problem for Western European governments. How can they meet it?

In the past, they have sought to deter an expansion of Soviet military power and an increase of Soviet political influence by jointly organizing defense, together with the United States, in the Atlantic alliance and by some coordination of their policies toward the East. This has been highly successful. At the least, the alliance's effect on European security has been twofold: it has provided Western European governments with the confidence they needed to stand firm in the face of Soviet military power, and, by linking the European region to the United States and its nuclear deterrent, it has diminished the usefulness of military force in the pursuit of Soviet objectives outside the Eastern sphere.

Thus, defense and deterrence will remain essential elements of Western European security, and until that often-mentioned but distant day when a credible European nuclear deterrent has materialized, there is no alternative to the alliance with the United States. The details will change. The Atlantic alliance and NATO as we know them reflect a political consensus that was established when Western Europe was economically and politically weak, when the United States was willing to commit itself firmly to Europe, and when the prospect of some arrangement with the Soviet Union seemed bleak. Today Western Europe, underpinned by the Common Market, has acquired greater weight, if only because the U.S. is seeking to relinquish part of its burden, and the military security of Europe and that of the United States are no longer necessarily synonymous. In addition, the growing difficulties for all Western governments in procuring money and men for defense and the effect of new military technologies will produce changes in national defense efforts and in the organization of NATO. But none of this is inherently incompatible with the major principles that form the basis of Western European security: common defense and the deterrence link with the United States.

Two Concepts of Détente. Can détente assist in solving the European security problem? One widely held view in Western Europe today is that détente will not make a major contribution to European security. True, it is better than the political confrontation of the cold war years. It can help do away with unnecessary sources of tension, and joint East-West institutions might serve as a means of joint crisis management. But little is expected beyond this since Soviet policy will not be changed from the outside but only by slow internal evolution. According to this view, the best policy for Western Europe is to give priority to Western European integration and alliance cohesion.

The other concept of European détente is more ambitious, more dynamic, and also more risky. It regards détente as a means of controlled change—change in East-West relations, but also change within the Soviet and Eastern European systems. It argues that the European security problem cannot be neatly separated into Soviet policy toward Western Europe and Soviet policy within Eastern Europe. Rigid Soviet control in the East can produce crises that affect Western Europe, and Soviet worries about the cohesion of the Eastern bloc could lead to a more aggressive Soviet policy toward the rest of Europe. This concept also implies greater awareness of the risks of détente to the Eastern regimes and more confidence that the risks of détente for the West can be dealt with adequately.

How should change be encouraged? Soviet and Eastern European regimes are not monolithic blocs but power coalitions. The Western aim should be to strengthen the position of those who are more interested in economic and other contacts with the West, who are less worried than the orthodox ideologists by diversity within Eastern Europe, who are more aware of the need for changes within the Soviet economic and political structure and more confident that these changes can be implemented without weakening the political system. The aim is not to undermine Soviet power but to change its quality, not to woo Soviet satellites away from their *contrôleur* and protector but to turn them into Soviet allies in an alliance based on loyalty and self-interest rather than coercion. Cooperation and contact may lead over time to a more flexible Soviet policy in Eastern Europe and to an understanding of the security interests and needs of Western Europe.

How should change be controlled? Only if détente avoids new crises and insecurities can the learning process have the desired effect of improving European security. Left to itself, détente might not only undermine cohesion in the West and produce, among Western societies, an illusion of peace. It can also endanger the power basis in Eastern Europe—by prompting a competition for Western goods, technologies, and credits and, more important, by exposing the closed and rigid Communist societies and economic structures to contact with Western pluralistic concepts and techniques. Change, therefore, must be carefully prescribed if stability—and security—are not to suffer.

These considerations give particular significance to multilateral East-West institutions and negotiations such as the Conference on Security and Cooperation in Europe. Such negotiations increase, at least formally, the margin of maneuver for Eastern European states, since they are based on the assumption that all states are sovereign and independent; at the same time, they encourage the coordination of policies within each alliance. Thus the Soviet Union need not fear a loss of control in Eastern Europe and may even gradually recognize that the cohesion of its bloc will not break down if a greater degree of autonomy is granted to the members. Multilateral institutions in Europe provide a constant framework for dialogue and crisis control. They can both further détente and channel it.

To implement the dynamic concept of détente, a general agreement on principles of relations and rules of behaviour—ranging from the nonuse of force to respect for human rights—is highly desirable. But resolutions on principles will be largely meaningless unless complemented by joint multilateral institutions; only then can they grow, as part of an organized process of dialogue and cooperation, into respected rules. The dynamic concept sees European détente as an institutionalized process in which institutions and agreed principles create a habit of respect for the legitimate security interests of each side.

This concept is, however, both risky and uncertain. Will a protracted process of multilateral diplomatic dialogue and joint East-West institutions increase Soviet influence over Western European and Atlantic matters and weaken Western European integration? Perhaps, but this will depend on the Western Europeans themselves and the degree to which they allow themselves to be influenced and deflected from the route of integration and alliance solidarity. Will it produce strains between Western Europe and the United States and speed up the reduction of U.S. forces in Europe? Possibly, but if the past few years are any guide, U.S. forces will be reduced because the Americans pull, not because the Soviets push. Will protracted negotiations lay bare the lack of unity in the West while demonstrating bloc discipline in the East? Maybe, but this will depend on the ability of the Western states to work out a common position regarding détente—which would be necessary regardless of the type of negotiation procedure chosen; in point of fact, political coordination of the nine Common Market countries during the various phases of the European security conference has worked remarkably well. Will protracted and institutionalized negotiations create the illusion of peace in Western societies? Perhaps, but pious resolutions passed by an all-European summit meeting and never followed up are even more likely to have this effect.

At first glance, a kind of dynamic approach to détente negotiations also seems to be favoured by most Eastern European states and, after initial reluctance, by the Soviet Union. They attach considerable importance to all-European resolutions, in an obvious desire to achieve an unambiguous and formal confirmation of the territorial and the political status quo in Europe. But they have also been the first to advocate a series of security conferences and to favour some joint consultative institution to provide continuity between the various East-West meetings. There seem to be three major reasons behind this attitude. First, there is the fear on the part of the Eastern European states that they might be left out of serious East-West negotiations and agreements unless a multilateral framework for European détente is assured. Second, there is the hope that an established framework of East-West dialogue might make certain degrees of Western European integration, particularly a European nuclear force, more difficult to attain. Third, a series of East-West conferences might serve to channel détente and avoid the risks of uncontrolled contact and the competition of bilateral diplomacy.

If the East favours a series of conferences and joint institutions, the West need not necessarily oppose them. The view that the advantage of one side is the disadvantage of the other has never been a satisfactory guideline, since the assumed adversary may be wrong or the interests of both sides may be compatible. The fact that the Eastern position leans toward the dynamic approach to détente in Europe does not rule out this approach for the West. There is no proof that it will actually promote security in Europe; it offers no more than a chance. If the chance is not to be missed, it must be tested. This test will come, above all, in two areas: can détente curb the use of military power? Can cooperation produce the desired change?

European Détente and Military Power. There is no doubt that the Soviet Union is the dominant military power in Europe and that there the forces of the Warsaw Pact enjoy military superiority over the forces of NATO. If détente in Europe is to be more than atmosphere and trade, it will have to curb Soviet military superiority in the region. As long as the Western Europeans feel exposed to Soviet military power, they will not be able to trust fully Soviet declarations of peaceful intentions.

There are no easy solutions. First, there can be no global balance between the Soviet Union and Western Europe. The Soviet Union is a global power, Western Europe is not. The Soviets cannot be expected to give up one of the major attributes of their superpower status just to disperse European fears.

Second, it is difficult even to conceive of a regional balance in Europe with both sides holding equivalent forces. The Soviet Union would retain its ability to reinforce its troops in Europe; its geographic advantages cannot be negotiated away. A symmetrical ceiling on forces in Europe would also imply symmetrical military purposes, but Soviet forces, unlike the forces of NATO, have a double function: to defend against the West and to underpin Soviet control in the East. Finally, defense efforts in East and West are subject to different pressures; *e.g.*, the financial constraints and manpower shortages in the West have no equivalent.

Third, a reduction of forces on both sides, as is currently being negotiated between NATO and Warsaw Pact countries in Vienna, is not the most promising way to deal with the problem. Military forces are sources of both trust and distrust. NATO forces provide confidence for Western Europeans; Soviet forces give assurance to the Soviets. If mutual reductions in Europe should erode this confidence, they will scarcely serve détente. This is not to say that all reductions should be avoided or that negotiations on equal force ceilings in Eastern and Western Europe should be ruled out. After all, a sizable reduction of Soviet forces in Eastern Europe—and, even more so, an agreement to equalize NATO and Warsaw Pact forces—would be better than the present state of imbalance. The point here is that they will not in themselves remove Western European anxieties. Trust will come only when each side understands the other's security needs and is convinced that these are compatible with its own. In Europe this will require first of all a mutual understanding of the relationship between military power and political détente.

The Western view is that détente must lead to a gradual elimination of military forces as political factors in Europe. The Soviet view is different: détente is seen as the result of efforts made by the Soviet Union and its allies to acquire greater military, economic, and political power; only this, it is argued, has induced capitalist countries to accept peaceful coexistence. Increasing the number of Soviet forces in Eastern Europe in time of peace is, from this point of view, not a contradiction to détente. The Soviet refusal, in the Vienna talks, to discuss measures that would restrict the use of military force is not regarded as incompatible with Soviet advocacy, in the Conference on Security and Cooperation in Europe, of a declaration on the nonuse of force.

This Soviet view may not rule out force reduction agreements of some sort, since they may be entered into for reasons unrelated to European détente. But it will deprive such agreements of the trust-creating effect they could otherwise have. It could turn out to be not only contradictory to Western concepts but also counterproductive to one major Eastern aim: preventing the formation of a European nuclear force. Western Europe, caught between the Soviet Union, which holds that its superior military strength is a postulate of détente, and the United States, which argues that détente allows it to reduce forces in Europe, may regard nuclear weapons as the best way to safeguard the security détente would have denied it.

Cooperation and Change. The issue that has highlighted the problem more than any other is that of cultural exchange and the free movement of people, information, and ideas between East and West. It is here that the differences between the Western and Eastern systems are most visible and that change might be most unsettling.

The different emphases that East and West give to the free movement of people, ideas, and information stem from their different concepts of détente. For the East, the improvement of relations between states is sufficient; for the West, the improvement of individual liberties is desirable. Eastern governments, in turn, see the Western delegations' insistence, at the Geneva security conference negotiations, that this promise be included in the conference agreements as an attempt to interfere in the internal affairs of the socialist countries.

The differences are not necessarily irreconcilable. Soviet and Eastern European leaders realize that change and interference are inevitable if their countries are to cooperate on a large scale with Western industries, apply Western technologies, and learn Western methods. They do, however, want to keep these changes to a minimum and to control them as much as possible. In turn, most politicians in the West realize that détente would be made more difficult if the principle of freer movement were to be advanced more rapidly than Soviet and Eastern leaders think their systems can tolerate.

While it would be wrong to overlook the problems that greater contact with Western ideas and methods can pose for the Soviet Union, it would equally be wrong to be hypnotized by them. There is no absolute barrier against change. In Eastern Europe internal policies and practices differ from country to country in spite of Soviet control. The Soviet dissenters Andrey D. Sakharov and Aleksandr I. Solzhenitsyn were able to speak out, in 1973, if only in the Western press, after a major press campaign had started against them. The emigration restrictions on Soviet Jews were further lifted, and a law that had imposed a special tax on emigrants was no longer applied. Change, after all, is occurring.

To what extent can the West use the Soviet desire for détente to bring about changes in Soviet policy, and at what point do such attempts become counterproductive? The large-scale emigration of Soviet Jews would scarcely have been possible if the Soviet government had not felt under pressure from Western public opinion and realized that this might make it difficult to reach agreement with Western governments. Similarly, the fate of Sakharov and Solzhenitsyn would probably have been very different if the Western press had not called attention to their predicament. Perhaps one of the lessons of recent months has been that governments are in the least favourable position to press for domestic change in the Soviet system. A governmental demarche on behalf of Sakharov would have been seen—and rightly—as an attempt to interfere in Soviet internal affairs. The situation is different when public or parliamentary opinion takes up such issues. The Soviet Union can then claim that it is not bowing to foreign pressure but is exerting pressure of its own in order to strengthen the position of a détente-minded government. But this is a delicate operation for which Western public opinion is not necessarily well suited. No more must be demanded of the Soviet leadership than it can provide without losing too much face internally, and the credibility of Western governments to enter agreements with the East must not be undermined.

Can Western cooperation in one field be traded off against Eastern cooperation in another? Western European economic superiority, say, against Soviet military superiority? Détente is, after all, the result of many considerations, not the least of them economic, and this kind of bargain would seem natural enough at first glance. But the obstacles are formidable. There is the difference of view in East and West on how détente should affect military forces; there is the Soviet reluctance to admit military superiority and economic inferiority, as well as the fear that across-the-board bargaining would interfere much more in the internal affairs of the socialist states than would be the case if economic, military, and cultural matters were looked at in isolation. As with many other aspects of détente, this may change over time. If the Soviet Union should one day decide that its military superiority in Europe was no longer politically useful, it might be quick to turn force reductions into economic bargaining counters.

An Uncertain Outlook. The year 1973 was one of ambiguities in East-West relations. On the one hand, formal negotiations on force reductions and European security and cooperation were started; détente ceased to be a matter of atmospherics and expectations and became a matter of tough professional and protracted negotiations, losing some of its former glitter in the process. On the other hand, the year demonstrated the growing pains of détente. There were disputes over the interpretation of the four-power Berlin agreement. Concern over internal repression in the Soviet Union increased as détente made the border between East and West more transparent. Soviet and Eastern European expectations of the economic dividends of détente were disappointed. In the Middle East crisis, the two superpowers showed that, for them, détente and demonstrations of force are not incompatible but complementary. In the West, the need to work out a new Atlantic structure and to develop the political organization of Western Europe has made détente a secondary concern for most Western European countries. The starting positions on both sides of the Atlantic are clear enough. The U.S. wants its European allies to shoulder a greater part of the defense effort in the alliance, to reassess military structures and doctrine in NATO, to accept a reduction of U.S. forces in Europe without reducing their own, and to accommodate U.S. trade and monetary interests. The Western Europeans, while resigning themselves to some reduction of U.S. forces and being prepared, in various degrees, to shoulder part of the burden and to seek arrangements in the trade and monetary field that take U.S. interests into account, desire in turn a reaffirmation of the U.S. commitment to Europe and U.S. readiness to consult and coordinate with them as serious partners. But while the aims are clear, the implementation is far from easy. Is the present U.S. administration, even if its wishes are granted, capable of making long-term commitments, in the light of the uncertain political scene in the United States? Are the Western Europeans sufficiently willing to compromise for the sake of European unity? And will the necessary political leadership be forthcoming, or will it be niggled away by short-sighted nationalism and tactical concerns?

Where does this leave détente? Not surprisingly, the question that détente was supposed to render obsolete is again being asked in the West (and, presumably, in the East): Who needs détente more—they or we? In the West there is a tendency to concentrate on Eastern economic weaknesses and on Western economic strengths, and to deduce that the East needs cooperation more. In the East disappointment over the meagre dividends in trade and credits that détente has so far produced may have strengthened the ranks of those who believe that the political price of détente might be too high.

If this attitude should become dominant, the chance that détente offers for European security will be lost. Western Europe will find itself in a worse position if both East and West, rather than seeking to enlarge the area of compatible interests, play off their different superiorities against each other. The Soviet Union, having fewer cards to play, will pursue further a policy of military strength in Europe and of superpower arrangements with the United States. The process of learning and mutual accommodation will have ended before it really started.

It is important to keep this process alive.

THE THIRD WORLD BIDS FOR POWER

by Colin Legum

Third world politics changed dramatically in 1973, especially with the successful deployment of oil as a weapon of politics by the Arab oil-producing nations; this raised questions about both the future role of oil in a time of growing world concern over the energy crisis and the possible political use to which other strategic primary commodities and minerals might be put by the less developed countries. The alignment of virtually all the nations of the third world in support of the Arab cause against Israel marked a further step in the gradual evolution of "third force" alliances in world affairs over issues held to be of direct concern, such as Indochina and the white-dominated regimes in Africa.

The agreement to end international involvement in Vietnam contributed substantially to raising morale in the third world, since its leaders saw in U.S. withdrawal a vindication of their own presuppositions that economic and military power were insufficient to defeat the independent spirit of small nations that believed themselves to be the victims of aggression. However, the third world was deeply ambivalent over the other major international development of 1973: the ripening détente between the West (especially the U.S.) and the Soviet Union on the one side, and China on the other. While they welcomed the possibility of a more relaxed international climate, they were suspiciously anxious about the implications for their own interests in a world dominated by collaborating superpowers.

Origins and Growth. The attitudes of the third world and its relations with the major powers can be best understood in the context of the forces that gave birth to this movement. The third world consists mainly of states that for long periods up to World War II were under foreign (mostly Western) domination. Although most of the Latin-American nations had gained their political independence in the first half of the 19th century, they were slow to identify themselves with the alliance of former colonial countries; this movement received its main impetus only after the liberation of the Afro-Asian peoples, who at their gathering in Bandung (Indonesia) in 1955 first expressed the idea of a third world determined to disengage itself from the cold war politics of the major powers. While the "Bandung spirit" still survives, the original idea of an Afro-Asian group gave way in the 1960s to the larger concept of nonaligned nations, including some European countries (notably Yugoslavia) and a number of Latin-American and Caribbean states. Nonalignment was informally institutionalized at a conference held in Belgrade, Yugos., in 1961, where 24 nations came together. Their numbers had increased to 47 at the second conference, held in Cairo in 1964, to 54 at the third conference in Lusaka (Zambia) in 1970, and to 76 at the 1973 conference held in Algiers.

The conference of nonaligned nations is only one of a number of groupings and organizations through which the third world seeks to mobilize its diverse forces to act as pressure groups within the international system. The best organized of the regional groups is the Organization of African Unity (OAU), to which all independent African states (barring only South Africa) belong. The Arab League, after playing a militant but divisive role under the late Gamal Abd-an-Nasser's leadership, has declined in influence; while the competing pan-Islamic federations operate sporadically rather than consistently. All the less developed countries work together through the so-called Committee of 77 (by 1973 composed of more than 100 members), which serves as a caucus within the UN Conference on Trade and Development (UNCTAD), the International Development Association (IDA), and the International Monetary Fund (IMF)—the three major arenas of economic confrontation between developed and less developed countries. The Committee of 77 is strongly reinforced by three regional UN organizations, the Economic Commission for Africa (ECA), the Economic Commission for Latin America (ECLA), and the Economic Commission for Asia and the Far East (ECAFE). In addition, there are functional groupings such as the International Committee of Copper Exporting Countries (CIPAC) and the Organization of Petroleum Exporting Countries (OPEC) with its Arab

---

Colin Legum is associate editor and Commonwealth correspondent of the London Observer. *He has written and edited numerous books on African political affairs and attended the Conference of Nonaligned Nations held in Algiers, September 1973.*

HENRI BUREAU—SYGMA

At the fourth conference of nonaligned nations held in Algiers in September 1973: left, Houari Boumediénne of Algeria addressing the assembly; top, Yasir Arafat of the Palestine Liberation Organization; bottom left, Fidel Castro of Cuba; bottom right, Indira Gandhi of India.

subgroup (OAPEC), which framed and operated the 1973 oil boycott.

The various strands of this network of third world organizations are brought together in the Afro-Asian–Latin-American–Caribbean Group at UN headquarters, which serves as a forum to coordinate policies and determine strategy. The third world insists on treating the UN as the centre of the world political scene and sees the world body as its only effective international platform; without it the third world nations would find it difficult to fulfill a collective role in international decision-making. Support for the UN Charter is one of the fundamental points of unity within the third world.

This tricontinental grouping is frequently described as the "Afro-Asian bloc," but this is a fundamental error. The politics of the third world are much too fluid and diffuse to be regarded as a "bloc"; they lack the essential disciplining power of the major world "blocs" that they would need to be classified as more than a loose grouping of nations that can form ad hoc coalitions of pressure groups to cooperate over specific issues, mainly those touching their relations with the big powers, colonialism, and economic development; there are many issues over which the third world remains deeply divided. No single dominant force within the third world is able to whip all its constituent parts into loyal obedience to a particular policy.

The fundamental ideas that have contributed to the growth of the concept of the third world grew out of the struggle over the redistribution of world power, which has been at the nub of international politics since the Yalta Conference of 1945: on one hand, the anxious search for an equilibrium between the U.S. and the Soviet Union, and later China; and, on the other, the dissolution of the old colonial empires and the consequent attempts by the new nations to form an international system lying outside the rival spheres of the great powers. The Soviet Union, the U.S., and China have all tried in their various ways to use the struggles of the colonial peoples in maneuvers against one another; after 1947, however, the newly independent states began to use their growing numbers and strength in an effort to disengage themselves from the struggles of the great powers and to become the agents of their own destiny.

This active disengagement—described variously as "positive neutrality," "noncommitment," and nonalignment—gave rise to the beginning of a third world with its own ideas of international society and its own set of loyalties. The principal rooted objections are against membership in any of the military alliance systems (NATO, SEATO, and the Warsaw Pact); against foreign military bases on their soil; and against economic dependency relationships with any of the major economic systems. They refuse to be bullied by their old colonial masters, and they refuse to be dictated to by new masters. They refuse to be taken for granted, and they refuse to be bribed by economic aid with strings attached. They are too newly freed from foreign control to be willing to accept its reestablishment in any form. These basic elements constitute the emotions and ideas of the third world, and they provide the kind of perspective required to consider the many important events witnessed in 1973 in the attempts to secure a redistribution of world power.

The Algiers Conference. The fourth summit meeting of nonaligned nations was dominated by five major issues: the Middle East crisis; the economic relations between the developed and less developed countries; the détente among the major world powers; the struggles of the "liberation movements" in southern Africa and the Portuguese territories; and the desire to create nuclear-free peace zones in the Indian Ocean and the Mediterranean. Attempts to "purify" the nonaligned movement by adopting more rigid qualifications for membership were strongly resisted by Yugoslavia's Marshal Tito and others; the broad consensus was in favour of widening the area of membership by inviting more countries from Europe and Latin America. Venezuela, Colombia, Brazil, Bolivia, Ecuador, Panama, Mexico, Uruguay, and Barbados decided on observer status, along with Austria, Sweden, and Finland; Australia and New Zealand did not accept invitations to attend as observers.

The hostile attitude of the Soviet Union toward certain tendencies in the nonaligned nations—especially the growing habit of regarding the Soviet bloc and the Western bloc as equally unacceptable—produced strongly adverse reactions, while China's unqualified approval of this tendency won general sympathy.

The site of the conference, an Arab capital, ensured that the Middle East crisis would dominate the political debate; but the summit also gave strong support to the "liberation movements" in South Africa, Rhodesia, South West Africa, and the Portuguese territories. Support was promised for a new challenge against Portugal by backing a move to declare Guinea-Bissau (Portuguese Guinea) as an independent republic; when this step was taken in late September, more than 70 nonaligned nations, as well as the Soviet bloc and China, recognized the new state. They supported a resolution welcoming its new status which was introduced at the UN General Assembly in November. In this way collective nonaligned support was mobilized to exert maximum pressure against Portugal and its allies.

Middle East Crisis. The Algiers summit presaged a new Arab confrontation with Israel. A resolution sharply condemnatory of the Jewish state was adopted, and private assurances were sought that unless Israel agreed to withdraw from all the occupied Arab territories, third world countries should break diplomatic relations with it in an effort to isolate Israel within the world community. For the first time in some years all the Arab countries came together at Algiers. Saudi Arabia, whose King Faisal played a key role in using oil as a political weapon against Israel's supporters, was represented for the first time at a meeting of nonaligned leaders; previously it had been regarded as pro-U.S.

The architect of the idea of using oil as a political weapon was Nadim Pachachi of Iraq, the former secretary-general of OPEC. Shortly before the Algiers meeting, Pres. Anwar as-Sadat of Egypt had visited a number of Arab capitals to win support for the use of this weapon at the appropriate time. Thus, for the first time, the third world used its economic resources to exert greater leverage in support of one of its causes.

Although most of the third world countries readily supported the Moscow agreement between the U.S. and the Soviet Union to bring about a cease-fire in the Arab-Israeli war of October 1973, they were deeply unhappy about the peremptory manner in which the two superpowers had introduced their proposals to the Security Council, demanding a vote without discussion. The nonaligned nations were, however, able to play an effective role in saving the cease-fire when on October 25 relations between Moscow and Washington became strained. Eight members of the nonaligned group at the UN (Guinea, India, Indonesia, Kenya, Panama, Peru, Sudan, and Yugoslavia) quickly produced Resolution 340, which provided the framework for an international peace-keeping force to be sent to the Middle East.

International Economic Relations. The third world continues to feel itself deeply discriminated against by all the richer nations because of the way in which they are still able to control the terms of world trade and the fixing of prices for primary commodities. This concern was greatly increased by the consequences to themselves of currency devaluations by the major nations, which greatly added to the cost of their imports from the industrialized countries without compensating increases in the prices of their own primary commodity exports, except for oil, cocoa, and copper. They continue to feel that the policies adopted through UNCTAD do not measure up to their needs, and they were deeply disappointed by the failure to get agreement for their proposals at the meeting of the International Monetary Fund held in Nairobi, Kenya, in 1973.

One significant reaction to their lack of bargaining power in fixing world prices for minerals and primary commodities has been the growing support for either outright nationalization of major economic resources (as has begun to occur in the oil industry in the Middle East); or for unilateral fixing of oil prices at much higher figures than before; or for the now almost universal insistence on partnership arrangements between foreign investors and governments in key industries. Thus, the third world countries increasingly are establishing national control over their major economic resources. With this development so widespread it is no longer so easy for the stronger powers to apply economic pressures against individual countries that resort to such measures; thus, through the collective strength of the weaker nations, it is becoming possible in certain cases to begin the process of changing the balance of power between the richer and poorer nations. But while such measures are feasible in the case of oil, copper, and a few of the strategic minerals in short world supply, it is difficult, as yet, to see how this method could be adapted to apply to primary commodities that are more plentiful.

Conclusion. Although the third world still remains conceptual rather than actual, the attempts over the last decade to institutionalize relations within it through political and functional organizations have begun to give it a clearer reality. And although there are strong differences of policy, and even competing interests, among the constituent elements of the third world, it is now possible to detect the growth of an authentic and effective international lobby which seeks to play a role independent of any of the major powers.

1973 Chronology of major events

JANUARY

1

Treaty of Accession, by which the U.K., Ireland, and Denmark formally became part of the EEC, went into effect.

Maltese Prime Minister Dom Mintoff refused Britain's first quarterly rent payment for use of the naval base facilities on Malta; Britain had previously rejected Mintoff's demand for higher payments to compensate for loss of value of the pound.

3

Egyptian government closed all institutions of higher education as month-long student disturbances at Cairo University continued.

First session of the 93rd U.S. Congress convened in Washington, D.C.; House Democrats elected Rep. Thomas P. O'Neill, Jr. (Mass.), as majority leader to replace Hale Boggs (La.), whose light plane had disappeared over Alaska in 1972.

Philippine Pres. Ferdinand Marcos offered "selective amnesty" to Muslim rebels on Mindanao and ordered a temporary halt to military operations against them.

4

Speech from the throne, read at the opening of the 29th Canadian Parliament in Ottawa, included calls for the creation of more jobs, social security reform, and tax relief; the New Democratic Party indicated it would support the minority Liberal government of Prime Minister Pierre Elliott Trudeau for the time being.

5

U.S. Pres. Richard M. Nixon announced a reorganization of the executive branch, putting into effect as much of his 1971 plan as was possible without congressional approval.

6

François-Xavier Ortoli, French economist, took over as president of the EEC Commission, replacing retiring Sicco Mansholt.

Hanoi radio reported that North Vietnamese Premier Pham Van Dong had ordered a national emergency in order to cope with the effects of the heavy U.S. bombing of December 1972.

8

U.S. presidential adviser Henry Kissinger and North Vietnamese negotiator Le Duc Tho resumed their secret talks on a Vietnamese cease-fire in Paris.

Fierce fighting between Israeli and Syrian forces was reported along the Golan Heights.

9

Australian Maritime Union ended its boycott of U.S. ships, called two weeks earlier to protest U.S. bombing of North Vietnam.

Rhodesia closed its border with Zambia, following the killing of two South African policemen by a land mine near Victoria Falls the preceding day.

10

Egyptian Pres. Anwar as-Sadat and Libyan leader Muammar al-Qaddafi completed talks in Tripoli, Libya, on the projected unification of their two countries and on Middle East tensions.

Thai Prime Minister Thanom Kittikachorn announced that the U.S. would keep its bases in Thailand after a Vietnam cease-fire.

11

Pres. Nixon announced Phase Three of his economic stabilization program, replacing most mandatory wage and price controls with "voluntary cooperation."

Major reorganization of the U.S. Army's domestic command structure was announced.

12

French Pres. Georges Pompidou ended two days of talks with U.S.S.R. Communist Party General Secy. Leonid I. Brezhnev at a country estate near Minsk, U.S.S.R.

14

Miami Dolphins won the National Football League championship by defeating the Washington Redskins 14–7.

15

Pres. Nixon ordered all offensive military operations against North Vietnam halted, citing progress in the peace talks.

Israeli Prime Minister Golda Meir and the Roman Catholic pontiff, Pope Paul VI, held an unprecedented meeting at the Vatican.

Greek government announced that it was relinquishing direct U.S. military aid, but would continue to buy U.S. military equipment.

Preliminary meetings for the proposed European security conference resumed at Helsinki, Fin.

16

Lunokhod 2, unmanned Soviet lunar vehicle, landed on the moon.

17

Philippine Pres. Marcos proclaimed a new constitution under which he would rule indefinitely, and permanently extended the martial law he had reinstated on January 7, when he had also postponed the constitutional plebiscite scheduled for January 15.

U.K. Prime Minister Edward Heath, in a nationally televised press conference, outlined Stage Two of his anti-inflation program.

Indian Food Minister Fakhruddin Ali Ahmed announced that India was purchasing at least two million tons of food grains to help relieve the worst drought in a decade.

Pres. Nixon authorized unlimited importation of home heating oil and diesel fuel oil through April 30 and relaxation of restrictions on the importation of crude oil as increasingly critical shortages were reported in the U.S.

18

Joint statement said that U.S. adviser Kissinger and North Vietnamese negotiator Tho would meet again January 23 "for the purpose of completing the text of an agreement"; heavy fighting flared near Saigon and on South Vietnam's northern front as both sides sought as much territory as possible before a cease-fire.

Finnish Parliament passed a special law extending the term of Pres. Urho Kaleva Kekkonen, due to expire March 1, 1974, for four more years without a new election.

20

Pres. Nixon and Vice-Pres. Spiro T. Agnew were sworn in for their second terms at inauguration ceremonies in Washington.

Published texts of Soviet legislative acts revealed that the controversial educational exit tax had been officially adopted by the Soviet government.

Amilcar Cabral, leader of the African Party for the Independence of Guinea and Cape Verde, was assassinated in front of his house in Conakry, Guinea.

22

Former U.S. Pres. Lyndon B. Johnson died following an apparent heart attack at the LBJ ranch in Johnson City, Tex.

U.S. Supreme Court, in a ruling based on the constitutional right of privacy, ruled that states may not prevent a woman from obtaining an abortion during the first six months of pregnancy.

West German Chancellor Willy Brandt and French Pres. Pompidou began their semiannual talks in Paris with ceremonies marking the tenth anniversary of the Franco-West German friendship treaty.

Australian Prime Minister Gough Whitlam and New Zealand Prime Minister Norman Kirk concluded two days of talks in Wellington, N.Z.

Chilean Pres. Salvador Allende Gossens placed the armed forces in charge of distributing essential products.

23

Pres. Nixon announced that presidential adviser Kissinger and North Vietnamese negotiator Tho had initialed an agreement earlier that day in Paris to end the Vietnam war; a simultaneous announcement was made in Hanoi.

Swiss National Bank announced temporary suspension of its intervention in exchange markets, permitting the Swiss franc to float freely; the previous day the Italian government had set up a two-tier foreign exchange system in an effort to stop speculation against the lira.

Eldfell volcano on Heimaey Island, Iceland, dormant for thousands of years, erupted, forcing evacuation of the town of Vestmannaeyjar.

24

U.S. Ambassador to Haiti Clinton Knox, held prisoner for nearly 20 hours by three armed Haitians, was freed after the Haitian government agreed to the release of 12 Haitian prisoners, payment of a $70,000 ransom, and the granting of safe conduct to Mexico.

Australian Atty. Gen. Lionel Murphy, ending ten days of talks in London, said he hoped that all constitutional and legal ties between Australia and the U.K. would be ended "within a year."

U.S. Secy. of State William Rogers and North Vietnamese Foreign Minister Nguyen Duy Trinh sign cease-fire agreement in Paris . . . January 27

A.F.P./PICTORIAL PARADE

A.F.P./PICTORIAL PARADE

26

Edmond Leburton was sworn in as Belgian prime minister at the head of a three-party coalition government, ending a two-month government crisis.

27

Vietnam peace agreement was formally signed in Paris by representatives of North and South Vietnam, the U.S., and the Viet Cong; the U.S. and North Vietnam began exchanging lists of prisoners.

28

Arab Joint Defense Council announced its decision to place Jordan's armed forces under the command of Egyptian War Minister Ahmed Ismail, who was reported a week earlier to have been given command of the Egyptian, Syrian, and Libyan forces.

29

Pres. Nixon submitted to Congress a $268.7 billion budget for fiscal 1974 calling for drastic cuts in or the elimination of more than 100 antipoverty and aid-to-education programs.

Test truce ordered by Pres. Lon Nol went into effect in Cambodia.

30

Pres. Nixon's Economic Report to Congress and its accompanying annual report of the Council of Economic Advisers predicted a strongly expanding U.S. economy in 1973; the administration's proposals for reform of the international monetary system were attached to the report.

Two former officials of Pres. Nixon's reelection campaign committee, G. Gordon Liddy and James W. McCord, Jr., were found guilty of attempting to spy on Democratic National Committee headquarters in the Watergate building complex, Washington, D.C.; five other defendants had pleaded guilty.

U.S. Vice-Pres. Agnew held talks with South Vietnamese Pres. Nguyen Van Thieu in Saigon on the first stop of an extensive Asian tour.

31

Military commissions set up to monitor the Vietnam cease-fire had their first official meeting in Saigon following several days of delays because of procedural disputes.

Representatives of the Laotian government and the Pathet Lao began secret peace negotiations in Vientiane.

Pres. Nixon announced at an impromptu news conference that presidential adviser Kissinger would go to Hanoi to discuss implementation of the Vietnam cease-fire and postwar aid arrangements and defended his "absolutely clear" constitutional right to impound funds appropriated by Congress.

Preliminary talks between NATO and Warsaw Pact powers, looking toward a conference on mutual and balanced force reductions in Central Europe, opened in Vienna.

FEBRUARY

2

U.K. Prime Minister Heath ended two days of talks with Pres. Nixon in Washington and at Camp David, Md.

Philippine Pres. Marcos offered amnesty to Communists and other "subversives," but not to their leaders.

Pope Paul VI nominated 30 new cardinals, bringing membership of the College of Cardinals to 145.

Pres. Nixon sent Congress the first of a series of state of the union messages reiterating his intention to "draw the line" on spending.

4

Israel announced it was building a fleet of high-speed, long-range-missile "Flash" boats, intended to more than triple its striking force.

Zambian Pres. Kenneth Kaunda said Zambia would keep its border with Rhodesia closed, despite a Rhodesian announcement it would be reopened, and would continue with arrangements made after the border closing to ship its copper exports over other routes.

5

International truce observers began taking up positions in the South Vietnamese countryside as cease-fire violations continued.

One of the first U.S. prisoners of war to return from Vietnam . . . February 12

ALLEN—GAMMA

Dominican government ordered the arrest of several opposition leaders, including former Pres. Juan Bosch, closed schools and radio stations in Santo Domingo, and sent troops to pursue a small band of guerrillas reported to have landed on the southern coast the previous day.

6

Argentine government barred former dictator Juan Perón from returning to Argentina before the general elections in March and began taking legal steps to dissolve the Peronista coalition.

Jordanian King Hussein I received assurances of continued U.S. military and economic assistance during talks in Washington with Pres. Nixon.

7

General strike by Northern Ireland Protestants paralyzed Belfast; the strike protested the internment of two Protestants in connection with a grenade attack on a bus during a fresh wave of violence in recent days, the first application to Protestants of antiterrorist orders previously used only against the Irish Republican Army (IRA).

U.S. Senate voted, 77–0, to establish the Select Committee to Investigate the 1972 Presidential Campaign Activities to conduct a probe of the Watergate affair.

8

One-day strike on the Penn Central Railroad ended when the U.S. Congress passed and sent to the president special legislation forbidding the railroad from reducing train crews for 90 days.

Archbishop Makarios III was proclaimed president of Cyprus for a third five-year term when no other candidates registered for the election.

11

Egyptian Prime Minister Aziz Sidky announced that his government would adopt a "war budget."

Gen. Alfredo Stroessner was elected to a fifth consecutive term as president of Paraguay.

12

First group of U.S. prisoners of war to be freed by North Vietnam was flown from Hanoi to Clark Air Force Base in the Philippines.

Week-long rebellion by the Uruguayan military ended with an agreement whereby Pres. Juan María Bordaberry remained in office but the military took effective control of the government.

U.S. Treasury Secy. George P. Shultz announced a 10% devaluation of the dollar, raising the price of gold from $38 to $42.22 per ounce.

13

Japan permitted the yen to float; Italy announced that the "commercial lira" would be floated to achieve a moderate devaluation.

14

Communiqué growing out of talks in Hanoi between U.S. presidential adviser Kissinger and North Vietnamese Premier Dong announced agreement to create a Joint Economic Commission to channel U.S. reconstruction aid to the North.

British gasworkers struck or began working to rule in support of a pay claim in excess of anti-inflation ceilings; Prime Minister Heath said he would make no exceptions to his anti-inflation policy.

15

Pres. Nixon, in a message on environment and natural resources, asked Congress for legislation phasing out crop allotments and direct farm subsidies, and also called for federal safety standards for drinking water.

U.S. and Cuba signed a five-year agreement designed to curb airline hijacking; Canada and Cuba signed a similar document.

New Zealand government, following Australia's lead, confirmed that it planned to continue participation in the five-power Singapore-Malaysia defense arrangement (ANZUK), despite pre-election pledges to the contrary.

16

Athens University students and police clashed in downtown Athens in a widening conflict between the Greek government and students.

Maltese government accepted the British government's regular quarterly payment for use of the island's naval facilities; five other NATO nations increased their payments to compensate for devaluation of the pound.

Former Col. Francisco Caamaño Deñó, leader of the constitutionalist forces in the Dominican Republic during the 1965 disturbances, was reportedly killed in the mountains, where he had been leading the invading guerrilla force.

17

L. Patrick Gray III, acting director of the FBI since the death of J. Edgar Hoover in 1972, was nominated by Pres. Nixon to be permanent director.

Joint Military Commission in Vietnam issued an urgent appeal that South Vietnamese and Communist forces end their fighting.

18

West German government announced a series of tax increases and a sharply trimmed budget in measures aimed at curbing inflation.

New York Times published an article suggesting that a Euphronius vase that had been purchased by New York's Metropolitan Museum of Art for $1 million had been smuggled out of Italy.

19

U.S. Circuit Court Judge Otto Kerner was found guilty of 17 charges in connection with the purchase and sale of racetrack stock when he was governor of Illinois.

RICHARD ERBOES—GAMMA

Oglala Sioux Indians occupy Wounded Knee, S.D. . . . February 27

Canadian Finance Minister John Turner presented an $18.9 billion fiscal 1974 budget, including income tax cuts and pension increases, to the House of Commons.

21

Israeli fighter planes shot down a Libyan commercial jet with 113 persons aboard that had become lost over Israeli-held territory while attempting to land at Cairo airport.

Laotian government of Premier Prince Souvanna Phouma and the Pathet Lao signed a peace agreement in Vientiane.

22

Remains of French Marshal Philippe Pétain, stolen by right-wing extremists from his grave on the Ile d'Yeu, were reburied there after having been found in a Paris suburb.

Joint communiqué issued following U.S. presidential adviser Kissinger's five-day visit to Peking included an announcement that the U.S. and China would set up liaison offices in each other's capital.

23

Six European central banks intervened to support the dollar as the price of gold on the London market reached $95 an ounce.

Pres. Nixon met with Hafez Ismail, national security adviser to Egyptian Pres. Sadat, in Washington.

Foreign ministers of the South Vietnamese government and the Viet Cong met alone in Paris for the first time and agreed to open political talks in March.

26

Three lawsuits were filed in U.S. district courts seeking to prevent further dismantling of the Office of Economic Opportunity (OEO) by charging that recent cutbacks and changes there violated the separation of powers doctrine of the Constitution.

Rhodesia suspended postal service with Zambia as part of a protest of the arrest of a train engineer by Zambian troops at the Victoria Falls border bridge the day before.

27

North Vietnam said there would be no further release of U.S. prisoners until conditions of the cease-fire were implemented; in response, Pres. Nixon ordered Secy. of State William P. Rogers not to return to the International Conference on Vietnam, convened in Paris the previous day, until release arrangements were complete; minesweeping of Haiphong Harbour and withdrawal of U.S. troops from Vietnam stopped.

Harry Sears, former head of Pres. Nixon's reelection drive in New Jersey, testified in federal court that Robert L. Vesco, a financier charged with securities fraud, had made a secret $200,000 contribution to Nixon's reelection campaign on April 10, 1972, three days after the new political contributions disclosure law went into effect.

First full-scale strike by U.K. civil servants opened a series of strikes opposing the government's anti-inflation program.

Wounded Knee, on the Oglala Sioux reservation in South Dakota, was occupied by members of the American Indian Movement, who demanded an investigation of federal treatment of Indians.

Australian Gov.-Gen. Paul Hasluck, opening the 28th Australian Parliament, outlined a comprehensive legislative program designed to implement the Labour Party's campaign promises.

28

U.S. Secy. of State Rogers received assurances in Paris from North Vietnamese Foreign Minister Nguyen Duy Trinh that discussions on the release of prisoners would resume in Saigon.

Fianna Fail Party of Irish Prime Minister John Lynch lost Irish general elections to a coalition of the Labour and Fine Gael parties led by Liam Cosgrave.

MARCH

1

Pres. Nixon sent Congress a "human resources" message in which he announced that he had abandoned his guaranteed annual income plan for the present; he also defended his budget cuts in social service spending.

Reports of civil war between the Hutu and Tutsi tribes in Rwanda were published.

Israeli Prime Minister Meir, on a ten-day U.S. visit, met in Washington with Pres. Nixon.

2

Representatives of 80 countries agreed in Washington to a treaty outlawing trade in 375 endangered wildlife species.

Foreign exchange markets were closed in London, Brussels, Frankfurt, Amsterdam, Vienna, and Tokyo in the face of a new international monetary crisis.

Agreement guaranteeing the Vietnam settlement was signed by the 12 nations attending the Paris conference.

4

Black September terrorists surrendered to Sudanese authorities after having occupied the Saudi Arabian embassy in Khartoum for almost three days, during which they had killed the U.S. ambassador and chargé d'affaires and the Belgian chargé and held three other persons hostage.

Opposition coalition retained its control of both houses of Congress in Chilean elections but fell far short of the two-thirds majority needed to veto government legislation or impeach Pres. Allende.

6

U.K. Chancellor of the Exchequer Anthony Barber presented to Parliament a "broadly neutral" budget designed to maintain a 5% economic growth rate without inducing further inflation.

7

Awami League of Prime Minister Mujibur Rahman won 292 of 300 National Assembly seats in Bangladesh's first national elections.

South Vietnam and the Viet Cong reached agreement on a second phase of prisoner exchange, ending a two-day impasse during which the Communists had boycotted the Joint Military Commission.

8

Referendum in Northern Ireland overwhelmingly favoured maintaining ties with the U.K., but most Catholics boycotted the polls.

Three Cypriot bishops, supporters of opposition leader Gen. Georgios Grivas, ordered the defrocking of Archbishop Makarios for refusing to resign as president of Cyprus.

9

White House warned that Pres. Nixon would veto some 15 funding bills if Congress passed them or would impound funds if the vetos were overridden.

10

Bermuda Gov. Sir Richard Sharples and his aide-de-camp were assassinated outside the governor's residence in Hamilton.

11

Gaullists won an absolute majority in the National Assembly in the second round of French parliamentary elections, a marked contrast to the first round a week earlier in which leftists had made heavy gains.

Peronista presidential candidate Héctor J. Cámpora won 49% of the vote in the first Argentine elections since 1965.

12

Second phase of the U.S.-U.S.S.R. strategic arms limitation talks (SALT II) resumed in Geneva, having been in recess since December 1972.

China released John T. Downey, a U.S. Central Intelligence Agency (CIA) agent held prisoner since his plane was shot down over China in 1952.

Malaysia announced its withdrawal from the Asian and Pacific Council on the ground that the organization "has done nothing."

EEC agricultural ministers agreed on a program to phase out Britain's farm subsidy payments over a five-year period.

13

Negotiators for major U.S. railroads and rail unions reached tentative agreement on an 18-month contract.

Syrian voters approved the country's first permanent constitution since 1961 in a two-day referendum; Sunni Muslims in central Syria, who had demonstrated against the document's failure to declare Islam the state religion, boycotted the election.

14

U.S. announced a partial lifting of the arms embargo imposed against India and Pakistan during the December 1971 war.

15

Pres. Nixon, at an unscheduled press conference, said he had expressed "concern" to Hanoi over the continuing movement of military equipment into South Vietnam and repeated his opposition to price controls on raw agricultural products.

17

Cambodian Air Force pilot flying a stolen plane bombed the presidential palace in Phnom Penh, killing 43 and wounding 50; Pres. Lon Nol, who escaped unhurt, declared a state of emergency and suspended civil liberties.

19

Foreign exchange markets reopened, following a 17-day shutdown, under the terms of a loosely formulated settlement of the international monetary crisis; the currencies of six EEC nations were floated jointly against the dollar and the West German mark was revalued 3% against the other five currencies.

Nixon administration released details of its proposed Better Schools Act, which would replace 32 programs of federal aid with revenue sharing.

Representatives of the South Vietnamese government and the Viet Cong began full-scale political talks in Paris.

20

U.K. White Paper on Northern Ireland proposed formation of an 80-member assembly chosen by a system of proportional representation that would give Catholics a greater voice in government.

Kuwait closed its border with Iraq following a border clash between Kuwaiti and Iraqi troops.

Shah of Iran Mohammed Reza Pahlavi announced nationalization of the foreign-operated oil industry, in effect nullifying a contract with the oil companies that was to expire in 1979.

Formation of a coalition government in San Marino ended the country's most serious political crisis in 15 years; the Cabinet had resigned January 22 over economic reform plans.

French air traffic controllers returned to work after a month-long strike during which many foreign airlines suspended service over France.

21

U.S. Supreme Court upheld the constitutionality of financing of public schools by states through local property taxes, reversing a lower court decision.

Libyan fighter planes attacked an unarmed U.S. Air Force C-130 transport plane over the eastern Mediterranean.

U.S. vetoed a UN Security Council resolution urging the U.S. and Panama to reach an equitable resolution on the future of the Panama Canal on the final day of a five-day council meeting on Latin-American problems held in Panama City.

22

Pres. Nixon submitted to Congress a proposed complete revamping of the U.S. criminal code that would make the death penalty mandatory for certain crimes and abolish insanity as a defense except in extreme cases.

Dow Jones industrial average closed at 925.20, its lowest point in ten months, after falling 24 points in two days.

Pres. Nixon, in an annual report to Congress of the President's Council on International Economic Policy, indicated he would ask for complete discretionary power to adjust tariffs.

Indonesian People's Consultative Congress reelected Suharto to a second five-year term as president.

23

Convicted Watergate conspirator McCord was reported to have told the Watergate committee that he had at least hearsay evidence that some White House officials had prior knowledge of the break-in and that perjury had been committed during the Watergate trial.

Pres. Nixon, in the face of threatened gasoline shortages, removed the volume restriction on oil imports into the U.S.

26

U.S. banks put through a general increase in the prime interest rate from $6\frac{1}{4}$ to $6\frac{1}{2}$%, ending a week-long dispute between the U.S. administration and banks that had attempted to raise the rate to $6\frac{3}{4}$%.

Black September terrorists occupy Saudi Arabian embassy at Khartoum . . . March 4

HENRI BUREAU—GAMMA

White House announced the Joint Military Commission in Saigon had agreed to complete by March 29 both prisoner returns, including those U.S. prisoners held in Laos, and the withdrawal of remaining U.S. troops.

Philippine government reported that its forces had killed some 200 of a force of Muslim rebels that had seized a Mindanao town four days before.

27

White House said the U.S. would continue bombing raids in Cambodia until Communist forces stopped offensive operations and agreed to a cease-fire.

Canadian External Affairs Minister Mitchell Sharp warned that Canada would withdraw from the International Commission of Control and Supervision in Vietnam unless prospects for peace improved.

28

Egyptian Pres. Sadat proclaimed himself military governor-general of Egypt with power to declare martial law; two days earlier he had taken over the additional duties of prime minister from Aziz Sidky, who had resigned under pressure.

29

Last U.S. prisoners of war held by Communist forces in Vietnam were released and the last U.S. troops withdrawn from South Vietnam, a day later than called for in the cease-fire agreement; former POWs began releasing stories in the U.S. of the physical and mental torture inflicted on them during their captivity.

United Steelworkers of America approved an agreement with major U.S. steel manufacturers, to last through July 1977, that included a no-strike clause and provisions for arbitration of disputes.

Italian Justice Minister Guido Gonella conceded in the Chamber of Deputies that police had purchased 109 electronic surveillance devices but denied that they had been used for anything but legally authorized wiretaps; widespread rumours suggested that private and government spy rings had bugged telephones of political figures, including Pres. Giovanni Leone, business executives, newspapers, and foreign governments.

APRIL

2

U.S. Court of Appeals in St. Louis, Mo., ruled that Pres. Nixon's impounding of highway funds appropriated by Congress was illegal.

Soviet government announced a major industrial reorganization consolidating plants into large "production associations."

International Telephone and Telegraph (ITT) chairman Harold Geneen told a U.S. Senate subcommittee that he would accept as true the testimony of a CIA official who had charged that Geneen had offered the CIA money to help prevent the election of Chilean Pres. Allende.

Stage Two of U.K. Prime Minister Heath's anti-inflation program went into effect.

3

U.S. Senate failed to override Pres. Nixon's March 27 veto of a $2.6 billion vocational rehabilitation bill, the first of 15 bills the president had said he would veto.

Spanish police fired into 1,500 demonstrating construction workers in a Barcelona suburb; one worker was killed.

4

Cambodian government declared a "state of national danger" as Khmer Rouge troops closed part of Highway 5, the last remaining supply route to Phnom Penh.

5

French Pres. Pompidou approved 21 ministers of a new Cabinet of reappointed Premier Pierre Messmer; Michel Jobert became foreign minister, replacing Maurice Schumann, who had failed to win reelection, and Robert Galley replaced Michel Debré, who had resigned as defense minister following a massive student demonstration on April 2 against his new draft rules.

Pres. Nixon withdrew the nomination of L. Patrick Gray as FBI director, following severe criticism in the Senate Judiciary Committee nomination hearings of his having given FBI reports on the Watergate break-in to presidential counsel John W. Dean III.

U.S. Labor Department announced that the wholesale price index rose at the annual rate of 21.5% in the first three months of 1973, the highest such increase since the Korean War.

American Indian Movement leaders and representatives of the U.S. government agreed to a cease-fire in the 37-day siege of Wounded Knee, S.D.

6

Athens University senate resigned after the Greek government prevented it from carrying out part of an offer accepted by the students in ending their eight-week strike on March 26.

Sen. Fahri Koruturk was elected president of Turkey by Parliament on the 15th ballot, breaking a 24-day deadlock.

Sweden became the first Western nation to recognize North Korea.

7

Week-long meat boycott organized by U.S. consumer groups ended with no significant decline in prices, despite widespread participation.

Helicopter carrying international observers of the Vietnam cease-fire was shot down by a Viet Cong missile, killing all nine persons aboard.

8

Pablo Picasso died at his home at Mougins, France, at the age of 91.

India took over administrative control of Sikkim at the request

DANIEL LE BOURNOT—GAMMA

Palestinian mourners honour victims of Israeli raid into Lebanon . . . April 10

of Chogyal Palden Thondup Namgyal after two weeks of demonstrations triggered by opposition claims that the chogyal had rigged State Council elections.

9

Arab guerrillas attacked the residence of the Israeli ambassador to Cyprus and unsuccessfully tried to hijack an Israeli airliner at Nicosia airport.

Danish workers and employers accepted a two-year wage agreement prepared by a state mediator, ending the country's worst labour crisis since the 1930s.

10

Israeli strike force, in a night-time raid, attacked buildings used by Palestinians in Beirut and Saida, Lebanon, killing three prominent Palestinian leaders; Lebanese Prime Minister Saeb Salam submitted his resignation.

Pakistani National Assembly approved the country's new democratic constitution.

Ephraim Katchalski was elected by the Knesset to replace Zalman Shazar, whose term as president of Israel was to expire May 25; Katchalski said he would hebraize his name to Katzir.

11

U.S. Environmental Protection Agency granted the automobile industry a one-year delay in meeting 1975 emission-control standards.

U.S. District Court Judge William Jones ordered OEO Director Howard Phillips to cease efforts to dismantle the agency, calling them "in excess of statutory authority."

12

U.S. presidential adviser Gen. Alexander Haig, Jr., reported to Pres. Nixon on his three-day trip to assess truce violations in South Vietnam and military situations in Cambodia and Laos.

Swaziland King Sobhuza II set aside the constitution and took over personal control of the country.

13

Japanese government adopted a program to curb inflation.

U.K. Labour Party won control of the Greater London Council and of six new metropolitan county councils in local elections.

14

U.S.-owned oil installation near Saida, Lebanon, was blown up by the previously unknown Lebanese Revolutionary Guard.

South Vietnamese Pres. Thieu returned to Saigon from a two-week tour of the U.S., Western Europe, and Asia.

15

Libyan leader Qaddafi announced a five-point reform program that included the purging of political deviationists and implementation of Islamic thought.

Peronista candidates won nearly all Senate seats and provincial governorships at stake in the second round of Argentine national elections.

16

U.S. Defense Department informed Congress that it planned to close or cut back 274 military installations.

U.S. planes resumed bombing of North Vietnamese positions in Laos after reports that a town on the Plaine des Jarres had been overrun.

17

Pres. Nixon announced that "major developments" had resulted from a new inquiry he had initiated into the Watergate case, and that White House aides would be permitted to testify before the Senate investigating committee under certain conditions; presidential Press Secy. Ronald L. Ziegler said previous statements denying White House involvement in Watergate were now "inoperative."

Indian occupying Wounded Knee was severely wounded in renewed shooting between the Indians and U.S. marshals and FBI agents.

Philippine Armed Forces chief, Gen. Romeo C. Espino, announced that amnesty for Muslim rebels in southwestern Mindanao had been canceled and that a new military offensive against them was planned.

19

U.S. announced that mine-clearing operations in North Vietnam and U.S.-North Vietnamese talks on economic assistance had been halted in response to North Vietnamese violations of the cease-fire agreement.

West German Chancellor Brandt and Yugoslav Pres. Tito agreed to settle Yugoslavia's outstanding war claims against Germany by means of long-term economic cooperation.

U.S. Atty. Gen. Richard Kleindienst removed himself from the Watergate investigation because many of his friends and associates were involved; this action followed reports that Jeb Stuart Magruder, an official of the Committee for the Re-election of the President (CRP), had accused former Atty. Gen. John Mitchell and presidential counsel Dean of planning the Watergate bugging; Dean issued a statement that he would not "become a scapegoat" in the case.

20

Former U.S. Atty. Gen. Mitchell testified before the federal grand jury investigating Watergate and later met with reporters, telling them that he had "heard discussions" of the bugging plans but had not approved them.

Pakistani Pres. Zulfikar Ali Bhutto rejected conditions of a proposal by India and Bangladesh that would have permitted a three-way exchange of prisoners taken in the 1971 war.

Amin Hafez became prime minister of Lebanon.

22

Israel protested to France the alleged transfer to Egypt of Mirage jets sold by France to Libya.

23

U.S. presidential adviser Kissinger, in an address before the annual meeting of the Associated Press, proposed a new "Atlantic Charter" involving major changes in economic, military, and diplomatic ties between the U.S., Canada, Western Europe, and Japan.

U.S.S.R. Communist Party General Secy. Brezhnev told a group of U.S. senators visiting Moscow that his country looked forward to expanded trade with the U.S., and that the education tax on emigrants from the U.S.S.R. had been suspended.

24

Cambodian Pres. Lon Nol replaced his Cabinet, which had resigned April 17, with a four-man High Political Council that included opposition leaders Sisowath Sirik Matak, In Tam, and Cheng Heng.

25

Australian Prime Minister Whitlam ended a six-day visit to Great Britain during which he discussed possible changes in the legal ties between the two countries.

26

Mexican Pres. Luis Echeverría Álvarez ended a month-long "mission of peace" to Canada, the U.K., Belgium, France, the U.S.S.R., and China, during which he received assurances from China and France that they would sign the treaty barring nuclear arms from Latin America.

27

L. Patrick Gray resigned as acting FBI director, following reports that he had burned, at the urging of White House counsel Dean and presidential adviser John D. Ehrlichman, sensitive files taken from the safe of convicted Watergate conspirator E. Howard Hunt, Jr.; William Ruckelshaus, administrator of the Environmental Protection Agency, was named temporary FBI head.

Central Committee of the Soviet Communist Party approved a major series of personnel changes in the Politburo.

U.S. Senate Foreign Relations subcommittee released Defense Department information indicating that the pattern of U.S. bombing in Cambodia had shifted from attacks on North Vietnamese communications lines to support for Cambodian troops against rebel forces.

28

U.S.S.R. announced the "completion" of the flight program of Salyut 2, the orbital workshop launched April 3; Western tracking stations had indicated the craft was damaged on April 14.

Japanese government and labour leaders reached a compromise agreement ending the worst labour crisis in Japan's history.

30

U.S. Atty. Gen. Kleindienst, presidential aides Ehrlichman and H. R. Haldeman, and White House counsel Dean resigned as a result of the Watergate affair; Defense Secy. Elliot Richardson was named to replace Kleindienst; Pres. Nixon, in a nationwide television address, accepted "responsibility" for the affair but said he was not personally involved.

Former White House aide Charles Colson reportedly admitted that among the White House papers destroyed by L. Patrick Gray was a cable forged by Watergate conspirator Hunt to implicate Pres. John Kennedy in the 1963 assassination of South Vietnamese Pres. Ngo Dinh Diem.

Pres. Nixon signed a compromise bill extending his power to impose wage and price controls until April 30, 1974.

MAY

1

May Day work stoppage, called by the U.K.'s Trades Union Congress and the Labour Party to protest the government's economic programs, involved some 1.6 million workers; TUC had announced "reluctant acquiescence" to the Stage Two guidelines on April 25.

EEC agricultural ministers reached a compromise agreement on guaranteed minimum prices to be paid to farmers during 1973–74.

2

Communiqué issued following two days of talks between Pres. Nixon and West German Chancellor Brandt in Washington called for "a comprehensive Atlantic partnership among equals."

3

Mississippi River and its tributaries rose to new record levels following heavy rains; damage resulting from some two months of flooding was estimated at $322 million.

4

Gen. Haig was appointed presidential assistant on an "interim" basis, assuming most of the duties of H. R. Haldeman.

Finnish Foreign Trade Minister Jussi Linnamo resigned because of his involvement in a scandal resulting from the news leak of a secret document concerning discussions between Pres. Kekkonen and Soviet Communist Party General Secy. Brezhnev in 1972.

7

Rightist demonstrators paraded through Madrid demanding that the Spanish Cabinet resign and more power be given to the Army and police, in a demonstration triggered by the fatal stabbing of a policeman during a Communist Party parade on May Day.

Israel marked the 25th anniversary of its independence with a military parade in Jerusalem.

U.S. consul general in Guadalajara, Mex., Terrance G. Leonhardy, who had been kidnapped by left-wing guerrillas May 4, was released unharmed after the Mexican government agreed to demands, including the safe conduct to Cuba of 30 "political prisoners."

8

Siege of Wounded Knee ended after 70 days as occupying Indians surrendered under terms of a new cease-fire worked out on May 5.

Chogyal of Sikkim signed an agreement providing for more democratic government.

Flooding of Mississippi valley in Missouri continues, due to heavy rains . . . May 3

WIDE WORLD

9

U.S. presidential adviser Kissinger left the U.S.S.R. for London following four days of talks with Soviet officials.

Rainer Barzel resigned as parliamentary leader of the West German Christian Democratic Union when the party rejected his stand favouring UN membership for East and West Germany.

10

Pres. Nixon announced a major government reorganization, including the appointment of former CIA director James Schlesinger as defense secretary, William Colby as CIA director, and former Treasury Secy. John Connally, who had joined the Republican Party on May 2, as special adviser to the president; the "supercabinet" system adopted in January was abandoned.

Former U.S. Atty. Gen. Mitchell and former Commerce Secy. Maurice Stans were indicted in New York along with Harry Sears and Robert Vesco on charges growing out of Vesco's secret contribution to the Nixon campaign.

11

West German Bundestag ratified the treaty establishing formal relations between East and West Germany.

Mistrial was declared in the Pentagon papers case and all charges were dropped against the defendants, Daniel Ellsberg and Anthony Russo, because of government misconduct.

Netherlands Labour Party leader Joop den Uyl was sworn in as prime minister at the head of a five-party centre-left government, ending a 164-day government crisis, the longest in The Netherlands' history.

12

UN Food and Agriculture Organization reported that famine, resulting from a five-year drought, threatened about ten million people south of the Sahara Desert.

14

Skylab, first U.S. orbiting space station, was damaged shortly after launch from Cape Kennedy, Fla.

U.S. Sen. Stuart Symington (Dem., Mo.) reported that, according to testimony before the Senate Armed Services Committee, the administration had attempted to involve the CIA in the Watergate affair.

NATO and Warsaw Pact representatives opened formal preparatory talks in Vienna on mutual force reductions in Europe.

EEC and Norway signed a free trade agreement bringing Norway into line with other EFTA members that had not joined the EEC.

17

Lebanese government and Palestinian guerrillas announced an agreement ending fighting that had broken out following the kidnapping of two Lebanese officers by guerrillas on May 1.

U.S. Senate select committee investigating the Watergate affair opened public hearings in Washington.

IRA guerrillas bombed Aldergrove airport outside Belfast, N.Ire., in what a U.K. spokesman described as a new offensive to disrupt upcoming elections.

18

Watergate conspirator McCord testified before the Senate select committee that a former White House aide, John Caulfield, had offered him executive clemency in return for his silence.

Archibald Cox, former U.S. solicitor general, was named by Elliot Richardson, nominee for U.S. attorney general, as special Watergate prosecutor.

19

Argentine government ended a state of emergency that had been in effect throughout most of the country since May 1, when the military had taken power in a crisis triggered by the assassination April 30 of retired Rear Adm. Hermes Quijada by leftists.

Soviet-West German agreements on economic, industrial, and technical cooperation were signed by West German Chancellor Brandt and Soviet Communist Party General Secy. Brezhnev during Brezhnev's four-day visit to Bonn, the first such trip to West Germany by a Soviet leader.

Australia and China announced agreement on a trade pact including most-favoured-nation treatment.

20

Swiss voters, in a national referendum, repealed two anti-Catholic articles that had been in the constitution since 1874.

21

U.K. Chancellor of the Exchequer Barber announced drastic cuts in government spending in an effort to curb overheating in the economy.

U.S. Supreme Court upheld an appellate court ruling that the proposed merger of predominantly black Richmond, Va., schools with predominantly white suburban school districts was unconstitutional.

22

South African government introduced in Parliament a bill giving blacks a limited right to strike.

Pres. Nixon released a statement on the Watergate affair in which he admitted limiting the investigation into the matter because of "national security" but said his aides had exceeded his instructions in attempting a cover-up.

23

U.S. presidential adviser Kissinger and North Vietnamese negotiator Tho ended a week of discussions in Paris regarding plans for implementation of the Vietnam cease-fire; Kissinger reported that the discussions would resume in two weeks.

COURTESY, NASA

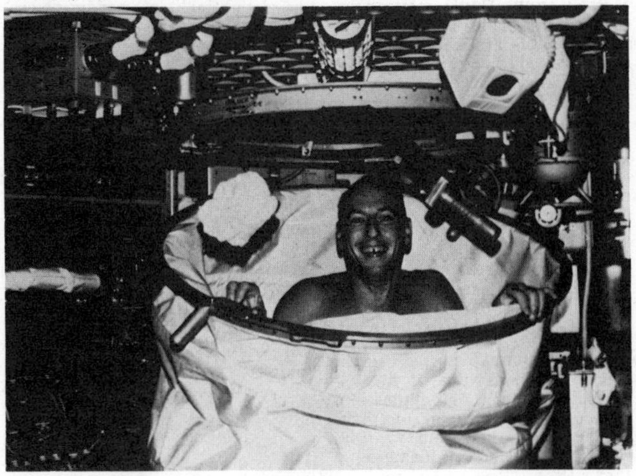

U.S. astronaut Charles Conrad demonstrates Skylab shower facilities . . . May 26

U.S. House of Representatives upheld a presidential veto of a bill that would have required Senate confirmation of the director and deputy director of the Office of Management and Budget.

U.S. agreed to grant commonwealth status to the Mariana Islands under a preliminary pact announced in Agana, Guam.

Australia and Papua New Guinea agreed on a timetable leading toward internal self-government for Papua New Guinea on Dec. 1, 1973, and independence in 1975.

24

New York Times published details of a 1970 White House plan for massive domestic espionage that was allegedly abandoned because of opposition from then FBI Director Hoover; secret White House intelligence unit was established instead.

Lord Jellicoe resigned as Britain's lord privy seal after his name had been linked with a ring of prostitutes; Lord Lambton, who had resigned May 22 as aviation secretary for similar reasons, was issued summonses alleging possession of cannabis and amphetamines.

Greek Defense Ministry announced it had broken up a planned coup by active and retired navy officers.

U.S. Commerce Department reported that during April the U.S. had had its first trade surplus since September 1971.

25

U.S. and Switzerland signed a treaty designed to help the U.S. trace funds hidden in Swiss banks by organized crime figures.

Police rebellion in Uttar Pradesh, India, that had grown out of labour disputes and had resulted in at least 40 deaths in four days of fighting, ended with the surrender of the last armoury held by mutineers to Indian Army troops.

26

Icelandic gunboat shelled a British trawler fishing within Iceland's extended 50-mi. fishing limits; a week previously Britain had sent navy warships to protect the fishing vessels.

U.S. astronauts Charles Conrad, Jr., Joseph Kerwin, and Paul Weitz, sent into orbit from Cape Kennedy the previous day, repaired damages to Skylab that permitted their extended stay in space.

National Progressive slate of the Baath, Communist, and Socialist parties won a 70% majority in Syria's first parliamentary elections in more than ten years.

28

Ugandan Pres. Amin and Tanzanian Pres. Julius Nyerere, attending the tenth anniversary summit conference of the Organization of African Unity in Addis Ababa, Eth., signed an agreement, mediated by Emperor Haile Selassie I, designed to end their year-long dispute.

U.S. Secy. of State Rogers completed a tour of eight Latin-American countries; students had rioted in several cities in protest against his visit.

Bolivian Pres. Hugo Banzer Suárez assumed temporary command of the armed forces in an apparent attempt to weather a crisis resulting from the murder of former Col. Andres Selich, who had been accused of participating in a right-wing plot to overthrow the government.

29

Canadian government announced that it intended to withdraw from the International Commission of Control and Supervision in Vietnam within 60 days because the observers were not being permitted to do their jobs properly.

Sadanori Yamanaka was named Japanese defense minister, succeeding Keikichi Masuhara, who resigned after being accused of using the emperor's prestige to increase defense spending; Liberal Democrat Shigesaburo Maeo was named speaker of the House of Representatives, replacing Umekichi Nakamura, whose resignation the previous day had ended an opposition boycott of the House that had begun May 11 to protest proposed election law changes.

U.S. Air Force Col. Theodore Guy, who had been a prisoner in North Vietnam for four years, filed formal charges of misconduct against eight other former POWs.

30

Czechoslovakia and West Germany agreed on terms of a treaty to normalize their relations.

Erskine Childers, candidate of Fianna Fail and a Protestant, was elected president of Ireland to succeed Eamon de Valera.

Unionist Party won 210 of 526 seats on local councils in Northern Ireland elections; Social Democratic and Labour Party, the largest Catholic group, gained 82 seats.

31

U.S. Senate voted, 63–19, to cut off all funds for combat activities in Laos and Cambodia; a milder measure had previously been passed by the House.

JUNE

1

Greek Cabinet abolished the Greek monarchy, naming Prime Minister Georgios Papadopoulos as provisional president.

Pres. Nixon and French Pres. Pompidou ended two days of talks in Reykjavik, Iceland, without producing any concrete agreements.

British Honduras officially changed its name to Belize.

6

UN Security Council opened a general debate on the Middle East; Egypt renewed demands that Israel withdraw from captured Arab territories.

Pres. Nixon announced the appointment of presidential adviser Haig as permanent White House chief of staff, replacing Haldeman; of former Defense Secy. Melvin R. Laird as chief domestic adviser, replacing Ehrlichman; and of White House Press Secy. Ziegler as presidential assistant, replacing Communications Director Herbert Klein, whose resignation had been announced the preceding day.

West German Pres. Gustav Heinemann completed ratification proceedings by signing the treaty normalizing relations between East and West Germany.

U.S. Treasury Secy. Shultz delivered to a monetary conference in Paris the U.S. rejection of European pleas that the U.S. intervene to support the dollar, which rallied on world markets after having fallen to new lows earlier in the week.

Swedish Riksdag gave preliminary approval to new constitutional measures that would eliminate most of the powers of the monarch after the death of Gustaf VI Adolf and lower the voting age to 18.

7

U.S. Labor Department announced that the wholesale price index rose 2%, seasonally adjusted, in May, the highest peacetime rate since World War II.

West German Chancellor Brandt began a five-day official visit to Israel.

UN Food and Agriculture Organization warned of possible famine, listing 28 nations in wide areas of Latin America, Asia, Africa, and the Middle East stricken by the worst prolonged droughts in 25 years.

Icelandic government claimed that "unlawful" behaviour on the part of a British warship had caused it to collide with an Icelandic Coast Guard vessel in disputed waters; the British government said the warship had been rammed deliberately.

8

Generalissimo Francisco Franco Bahamonde resigned as premier of Spain, appointing Adm. Luis Carrero Blanco to succeed him, but retained the title of chief of state.

9

Secretariat won the Belmont Stakes in record time to become the first horse to win Thoroughbred racing's Triple Crown since 1948.

11

Libya nationalized a U.S. oil firm, making it clear that the action was in retaliation for U.S. pro-Israeli policy.

12

Italian Premier Giulio Andreotti and his coalition Cabinet resigned; two weeks earlier the Republican Party had withdrawn from the coalition.

13

Agreement aimed at strengthening the Vietnamese cease-fire was signed in Paris by representatives of the U.S., North and South Vietnam, and the Viet Cong.

Pres. Nixon imposed a freeze on all prices for as long as 60 days, excluding only raw agricultural products and rents.

14

U.S.S.R. Communist Party General Secy. Brezhnev held an unprecedented meeting with 11 U.S. newsmen in his Kremlin offices.

Japanese Finance Ministry announced that Japan's balance of payments had shown a record deficit for the third straight month; the Ministry of International Trade announced the dropping of self-imposed quotas on export sales.

Lebanese Prime Minister Hafez resigned; two days earlier Hafez had been forced to postpone a vote of confidence in his new government when two Cabinet members resigned to support Sunni Muslim demands for a stronger government.

U.S. bombers struck Khmer Rouge troop concentrations in Cambodia for the 100th straight day; in South Vietnam the government military command and the Viet Cong, in compliance with the new Paris agreement, ordered troops to stop shooting.

ALAIN NOGUES—SYGMA

Emergency food supplies are distributed in drought-ravaged Upper Volta . . . June 7

15

NATO foreign ministers, meeting in Copenhagen, agreed to review their countries' political, economic, and military relationships in light of vast changes in the international situation.

18

Brazilian Pres. Emílio Garrastazú Médici announced that he would be succeeded in 1974 by retired Gen. Ernesto Geisel.

Dow Jones industrial average dropped 13.47 points to close at 875.08, its lowest closing since Dec. 17, 1971.

19

U.S.S.R. Communist Party General Secy. Brezhnev, in the U.S. on a state visit, and Pres. Nixon signed Soviet-U.S. executive agreements on transportation, oceanography, agricultural research, and cultural exchange.

20

Plane carrying former dictator Perón to Argentina from exile in Spain was forced to land at a military airfield when rioting broke out among rival Peronist groups waiting at the Buenos Aires airport for his arrival.

Chilean Senate censured and dismissed two Cabinet ministers for their alleged involvement in the 63-day-old El Teniente copper mine strike; the Communist-led Central Labour Federation called a 24-hour strike to support the government's handling of the strike while physicians, teachers, students, and professional workers joined walkouts supporting the miners.

Czechoslovak and West German foreign ministers initialed a treaty declaring the 1938 Munich agreement void, thus opening the way for resumption of diplomatic relations between the two countries.

21

Pres. Nixon and U.S.S.R. Communist Party General Secy. Brezhnev signed a declaration of principles in which they agreed to speed up SALT negotiations and to complete a new arms limitation agreement by the end of 1974.

U.S. Supreme Court handed down new and stricter guidelines for defining obscenity and ruled that local authorities could apply local community standards to suspect material; the court also stated, in a decision involving the Denver, Colo., school board, that segregation would be treated the same in Northern and Southern schools.

22

Pres. Nixon and U.S.S.R. Communist Party General Secy. Brezhnev signed an agreement aimed at avoiding confrontations that could lead to nuclear war.

Three Skylab astronauts returned safely to earth after spending a record 28 days in space during which they made two major repairs to the orbiting vehicle.

French Pres. Pompidou and West German Chancellor Brandt ended their semiannual meeting without reaching agreement on the proposed summit meeting between leaders of the EEC nations and Pres. Nixon.

23

Australian Prime Minister Whitlam announced Australia would join New Zealand in a joint naval demonstration protesting planned French nuclear tests in the Pacific.

South Korean Pres. Park Chung Hee announced that he would drop his opposition to the entry of both North and South Korea into the UN; North Korea later rejected the proposal.

24

Indian Prime Minister Indira Gandhi ended an eight-day official visit to Canada.

25

Joint communiqué issued by Pres. Nixon and U.S.S.R. Communist Party General Secy. Brezhnev at the end of Brezhnev's U.S. visit announced that talks on mutual troop reduction in Europe would begin Oct. 30, 1973, in Vienna.

Former White House counsel Dean began his testimony before the Senate Watergate committee by reading a 245-page statement implicating Pres. Nixon and his top aides in the Watergate affair and its cover-up.

U.S. Supreme Court declared unconstitutional New York, Pennsylvania, South Carolina, and Mississippi state laws permitting state aid to parochial schools.

26

U.S.S.R. Communist Party General Secy. Brezhnev began two days of talks with French Pres. Pompidou in Paris.

Acting OEO Director Phillips resigned in compliance with a district court ruling that he was serving illegally; Pres. Nixon appointed Alvin J. Arnett as his replacement.

Argentine police reported that the country's latest wave of kidnappings had claimed ten victims in a 24-hour period, bringing to 14 the number being held and to more than 70 the number kidnapped so far in 1973.

EEC foreign ministers, meeting in Luxembourg, agreed on a joint stand for the forthcoming meetings of the General Agreement on Tariffs and Trade (GATT).

27

Uruguayan Pres. Bordaberry dissolved Congress and created a Council of State, ending 40 years of constitutional government; the National Labour Confederation called an indefinite general strike.

U.S. government imposed an immediate embargo on the export of soybeans, cottonseed, and their oil and meal by-products in an effort to forestall a national shortage.

China exploded its 15th nuclear device in the atmosphere at its Lop Nor test site.

28

NATO and Warsaw Pact nations concluded five months of preparatory talks by agreeing in Vienna to open formal talks on mutual force reductions on October 30 but without agreeing on an agenda.

Canadian government issued a report stating that Canadian energy supplies would be adequate for the foreseeable future providing that Canada was not expected to use them to solve the U.S. energy crisis.

Northern Ireland voters gave a majority of seats in a proposed legislative assembly to parties supporting the British government's plan for sharing of power between Catholics and Protestants.

29

Attempted military coup in Chile was crushed by troops loyal to Pres. Allende.

West Germany revalued the mark by 5.5% against currencies participating in the EEC float.

30

Khmer Rouge troops launched a strong offensive near the Cambodian provincial capital of Kompong Speu as heavy fighting also continued in a number of places around Phnom Penh.

U.S. Congress gave final approval to a compromise with Pres. Nixon that would end U.S. bombing in Cambodia by August 15 unless Congress approved an extension; congressional leaders had threatened to attach an amendment providing for an immediate cutoff to all supplemental funding bills for government agencies.

JULY

1

Partido Revolucionario Institucional retained firm control of most national, state, and local offices in Mexican general elections.

Iraqi government announced that it had crushed a coup attempt led by Col. Nazem Kazzar, the chief of internal security; the defense minister was killed and the interior minister wounded during the attempt.

2

U.S. government imposed new controls on the export of iron and steel scrap and announced the resumption of soybean exporting on a reduced basis.

Strike at Chile's El Teniente copper mine ended after 75 days.

3

Conference on Security and Co-operation in Europe opened in Helsinki, Fin., with the foreign ministers of 35 nations in attendance.

U.S. Army and Navy announced that charges against seven former U.S. prisoners of war brought by Col. Guy were being dropped; an eighth POW charged by Guy had committed suicide on June 27.

5

Rwanda government was overturned in a bloodless coup led by the defense minister, Maj. Gen. Juvénal Habyalimana.

6

Chinese representative to the U.S., Huang Chen, and Pres. Nixon conferred at San Clemente, Calif.

American Airlines chairman George A. Spater announced that his company had been pressured into contributing an illegal corporate gift to the 1972 Nixon campaign.

7

First phase of the European security conference ended in Helsinki with an agreement to resume negotiations in Geneva on September 18.

8

Mariano Rumor, heading a centre-left coalition, was sworn in as premier of Italy.

New Lebanese Cabinet was formed, headed by Prime Minister Takieddin as-Solh, following 17 days of consultations and party maneuvers.

9

Uganda Pres. Idi Amin permitted the release of 112 U.S. Peace Corps volunteers who had been detained at Entebbe for over two days while he determined whether or not they were "mercenaries."

U.S. Secy. of State Rogers and Czechoslovak Foreign Minister Bohuslav Chnoupek signed a consular agreement between their two countries in Prague.

Two weeks of meetings in Cairo between Libyan leader Qaddafi and Egyptian Pres. Sadat ended without agreement on the complete merger of the two countries.

Clarence M. Kelley, former Kansas City, Mo., police chief, was sworn in as director of the FBI.

10

Bahamas became independent of Great Britain.

The Times (London) published an article by a Roman Catholic priest, Adrian Hastings, in which he said he had learned from Spanish missionaries that Portuguese forces had massacred at least 400 persons in a Mozambique village on Dec. 16, 1972.

Pakistani National Assembly voted to give Pres. Bhutto authority to recognize Bangladesh when it was "in the best national interest of Pakistan to do so."

12

Former U.S. Atty. Gen. Mitchell ended three days of testimony before the Senate Watergate committee during which he denied he had authorized the Watergate break-in and said he had tried to shield Nixon from knowledge of various "White House horrors."

13

Argentine Pres. Cámpora resigned, clearing the way for former dictator Perón to obtain the presidency in new elections.

14

Synod of the Orthodox Church deposed three Cypriot bishops who had previously proclaimed the deposition of the president of Cyprus, Archbishop Makarios.

15

Two Canadian officials of the International Commission of Control and Supervision in Vietnam were freed after being held for 17 days by the Viet Cong.

16

Former presidential aide Alexander P. Butterfield revealed to the Senate Watergate committee that Pres. Nixon's conversations and telephone calls in the White House and the Executive Office Building had been tape recorded without the knowledge of the other participants.

Portuguese Premier Marcello Caetano began a state visit to Britain despite protests stemming from reports of massacres by government troops in Portuguese Africa.

Guyanan Prime Minister Forbes Burnham's People's National Congress won a two-thirds majority in parliamentary elections.

U.S. Defense Department admitted that the U.S. had carried out thousands of bombing raids in Cambodia prior to the U.S. incursion into Cambodia in May 1970 and that records had been falsified to keep the raids secret.

17

Afghanistan King Mohammad Zahir Shah was deposed after a 40-year reign in a coup led by his brother-in-law, Lieut. Gen. Mohammad Daud Khan, a former prime minister; the king was undergoing medical treatment in Italy at the time.

Jordan severed diplomatic relations with Tunisia in response to Tunisian Pres. Habib Bourguiba's earlier statement calling for King Hussein's resignation and the creation of a Palestinian state on the East and West banks of the Jordan River.

Cambodian government ordered conscription of men between 18 and 35 as Khmer Rouge forces intensified their threat to Phnom Penh despite continued massive U.S. bombing.

18

Pres. Nixon announced his Phase Four economic program, based on a mixture of voluntary and mandatory controls on prices, wages, and profits, which would begin August 12; price restrictions were lifted on all foods except beef, which would remain frozen until September 12.

U.S. Treasury Secy. Shultz and Arthur Burns, chairman of the Federal Reserve Board, issued a joint statement revealing that the board had been intervening in foreign exchange markets in order to support the dollar since July 10; despite these efforts, the market value of the dollar had fallen July 12 after a three-day rally that had been spurred by the belief that central banks were intervening in currency markets.

19

British government announced it planned to adopt a new system of tax credits that would include a form of negative income tax.

21

France began a round of nuclear tests at Mururoa Atoll in the South Pacific, despite international protests, an interim injunction by the International Court of Justice, and the stationing of a New Zealand Navy ship with the immigration minister aboard 12 mi. off the atoll.

Caravan of some 30,000 Libyans journeying to Cairo to urge immediate merger of Libya and Egypt was ordered to return to Libya by Libyan leader Qaddafi in response to demands by Egyptian Pres. Sadat.

23

Libyan leader Qaddafi withdrew his resignation as chairman of the Revolutionary Command Council, submitted July 11 in what Qaddafi had described as an effort to clear the way for merger between Libya and Egypt.

24

Japan Air Lines jet, hijacked out of Amsterdam July 20 by pro-Palestinian guerrillas and flown initially to Dubai, was blown up at Benghazi, Libya, shortly after the passengers and crew had been evacuated.

Shah of Iran arrived in the U.S. for a state visit.

25

U.S. District Court Justice Orrin Judd ruled in New York that the U.S. bombing in Cambodia was unlawful and should be halted; he granted a 48-hour stay to permit appeals.

26

Nonoperating employees began a series of rotating strikes against the Canadian National Railways.

Chilean truckers began a nationwide strike.

Pres. Nixon formally defied subpoenas issued by the Senate Watergate committee and Special Prosecutor Cox that had ordered him to release tapes of his White House conversations.

EEC Council of Ministers and representatives of 40 African, Caribbean, and Pacific nations ended a two-day meeting in Brussels at which they agreed to begin serious negotiations on their future relations on October 17.

27

Capt. Arturo Araya, Chilean Pres. Allende's naval aide-de-camp, was assassinated at his home in Santiago.

Bank of England raised the bank loan rate to a record high of 11.5% and West Germany eased its tight money policy in moves aimed at halting the sliding of the dollar and the pound on world currency markets.

28

U.S. astronauts Alan Bean, Owen Garriott, and Jack Lousma were launched into space for a planned 59-day mission in Skylab.

Philippine voters concluded a two-day plebiscite approving the retention of Pres. Marcos in office after 1973.

29

Agreement between the Laotian government and the Pathet Lao, setting broad outlines for a political and military settlement of the Laotian conflict, was reported.

30

New Greek constitution was approved by more than 78% of the voters in a nationwide referendum.

Former presidential aide Haldeman told the Senate Watergate committee that Pres. Nixon had allowed him to listen to some of the White House tapes and that they did not incriminate the president; earlier John Ehrlichman had ended four and a half days of testimony before the committee.

Gen. Earle G. Wheeler, former chairman of the U.S. Joint Chiefs of Staff, told the Senate Armed Services Committee that Pres. Nixon had personally ordered that the bombing of Cambodia in late 1969 and early 1970 be kept secret.

Japan Air Lines jet destroyed by pro-Palestinian guerrillas at Benghazi, Libya . . . July 24

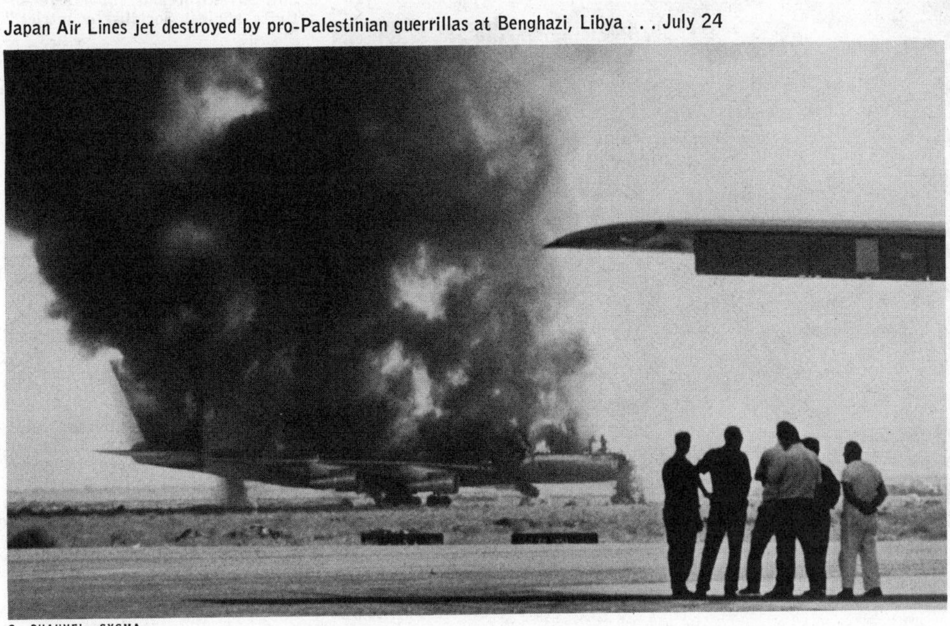

G. CHAUVEL—SYGMA

Australian Prime Minister Whitlam met with Pres. Nixon at the White House.

31

First session of the new Northern Ireland legislature in Belfast was disrupted by militant Protestants.

Canada formally ended its participation in the Vietnam peacekeeping operation; U.S. officials announced that its place would be taken by Iran.

AUGUST

1

Communiqué issued after two days of meetings in Washington between Pres. Nixon and Japanese Prime Minister Tanaka included announcement of a planned exchange of visits between Nixon and Emperor Hirohito.

U.S. Department of Agriculture (USDA) announced that cattle slaughter had fallen about 20% from the previous week as ranchers withheld beef cattle from the market because of the government freeze on beef prices.

2

Cambodian government established roadblocks half a mile from Phnom Penh in an effort to counter a new Khmer Rouge offensive.

3

Pres. Nixon warned in a letter to congressional leaders that the scheduled bombing halt in Cambodia could have "dangerous potential consequences"; in another congressional message Nixon outlined a proposed major restructuring of the U.S. banking system.

Public transportation in Santiago, Chile, was brought to a virtual halt by strikes.

4

U.S. Supreme Court Justice William O. Douglas upheld the July 25 injunction ordering an immediate end to U.S. bombing in Cambodia; hours later Justice Thurgood Marshall, supported by the seven other justices, overturned Douglas' ruling.

South Vietnamese government troops repulsed a Communist attack near Kon Tum as fighting intensified in Vietnam.

5

Two Arab terrorists surrendered to Greek police after killing three persons, wounding 55, and holding 35 hostage in an attack at Athens airport on passengers waiting to board a flight for New York; the terrorists had believed the flight was bound for Tel Aviv.

6

U.S. B-52, on a raid in support of Cambodian government troops, mistakenly bombed the friendly village of Neak Luong 38 mi. S of Phnom Penh, killing 137 persons and wounding more than 250.

Nixon administration released an estimate indicating that about $10 million had been spent for security at homes used frequently by Pres. Nixon and his family; previous accountings of these expenses had been much lower.

U.K. Defense Ministry admitted that it had encouraged Kenneth Littlejohn to infiltrate the IRA, but denied he had been authorized to commit criminal acts; Littlejohn and his brother Keith had been sentenced to prison in Ireland August 3 for robbing a Dublin bank in 1972.

EEC Commission announced it had banned all exports of hard wheat from the Community effective August 4 to protect European supplies in face of the worldwide wheat shortage.

7

U.S. Vice-Pres. Agnew was reported to be under federal investigation for possible violations of the criminal law; allegations involved kickbacks from construction companies while Agnew was executive of Baltimore (Md.) County.

Senate Watergate committee recessed until September after hearing 33 witnesses and compiling more than 7,500 pages of testimony.

Soviet geneticist Zhores Medvedev, working in London since January, was deprived of his Soviet citizenship and told not to return to the U.S.S.R.

9

Mars 7, the fourth in a series of launchings of Mars probes begun July 21, was launched by the U.S.S.R.

French Economy and Finance Minister Valéry Giscard d'Estaing announced plans to liberalize the exchange regulations introduced in November 1968 to avoid devaluation of the franc.

10

Pres. Nixon signed a farm bill designed to encourage increased production by means of a new method of subsidizing main crops.

Communiqué issued at the close of the meeting of Commonwealth heads of government in Ottawa included support for majority rule in Rhodesia.

U.S. presidential adviser Laird denied that he had approved falsified reporting to conceal U.S. bombing in Cambodia when he was defense secretary, although he had authorized a "separate reporting system"; the previous day the Pentagon had released a classified memo indicating that Laird had given such approval.

11

Spokesman for the Palestine Liberation Organization said that Palestinian guerrilla leader George Habash and his deputy, Salah Salah, had, at the last minute, changed their plans to be aboard a Middle East Airlines jetliner intercepted by Israeli jets the previous day while en route from Beirut, Lebanon, to Baghdad, Iraq.

13

Pres. Nixon signed a highway funding bill that would permit the use of Federal Highway Trust Fund money for mass transit.

South Korean opposition leader Kim Dae Jung was freed outside his Seoul home five days after his abduction from a Tokyo hotel.

14

New Pakistani constitution went into effect; Chaudhri Fazal Elahi was sworn in as president and Zulfikar Ali Bhutto as prime minister.

Dollar climbed to a six-week high and gold fell to a three-month low on the London market, in a reversal of recent trends attributed to record-high interest rates in the U.S. and U.K.

Two teen-agers were indicted after confessing to having taken part in the torture and killing of 27 boys in the Houston, Tex., area; one of the young men admitted killing the leader of the murder ring, a 33-year-old homosexual.

Sixteen districts in the Punjab, Pakistan, were declared disaster areas as a result of extensive flooding of the Indus River.

15

Pres. Nixon, in a nationally televised address, again accepted responsibility for Watergate but denied any personal involvement in the affair; he urged the nation to leave the case to the courts and turn its attention to "matters of far greater importance."

U.S. combat participation in Cambodia ended, although supply and reconnaissance activities were to be continued; Pres. Nixon accused Congress of undermining "the prospects for world peace" by forcing the halt.

U.S.S.R. Communist Party General Secy. Brezhnev, in a televised speech made at a rally in Alma Ata, Kazakhstan, accused China of pursuing a policy "based on rabid anti-Sovietism and subversive activity against Socialist countries."

17

U.S. Defense Secy. Schlesinger announced that the U.S.S.R. had successfully tested multiple independently targeted reentry vehicles (MIRVs), thus apparently drawing abreast of the U.S. in missile technology.

U.S. Commerce Department reported that corporate profits in the second quarter of 1973 were 37% above the 1972 level and that the federal budget showed a surplus of $100 million for the second quarter of 1973, compared with deficits in the first quarter and for 1972.

Syria reopened its border with Lebanon, closed May 8 during heavy fighting between Lebanese troops and Palestinian guerrillas.

19

Georgios Papadopoulos was sworn in for an eight-year term as the first president of Greece; ves-

The St. Louis National Stockyards stands empty as farmers withhold beef cattle . . . August 1

UPI COMPIX

tiges of martial law in effect since 1967 were lifted and amnesty was granted to some political prisoners.

20

Bolivian Interior Minister Col. Walter Castro Avendano announced the government had crushed a planned right-wing coup led by former Health Minister Carlos Valverde Barbery.

Laotian troops loyal to Premier Souvanna Phouma crushed an attempted right-wing military coup; the coup leader, exiled Brig. Gen. Thao Ma, died after his plane crashed at Vientiane airport.

Pres. Nixon, speaking before the national convention of Veterans of Foreign Wars in New Orleans, La., defended the secret bombing of Cambodia in 1969; a scheduled motorcade was canceled when the Secret Service announced that it had uncovered a "possible conspiracy" to assassinate the president.

Five-day lull in fighting ended in Cambodia as Khmer Rouge forces attacked Cambodian government troops at two provincial capitals.

21

Exiled Cambodian chief of state Prince Norodom Sihanouk, at a news conference in Peking, denied Pres. Nixon's claim made in his New Orleans speech the previous day that he had approved the secret U.S. bombing of Cambodia in 1969.

22

Pres. Nixon, at his first press conference in five months, announced that William Rogers had resigned as U.S. secretary of state and that presidential aide Kissinger had been named to replace him.

24

Scotland Yard officially blamed the Provisional wing of the IRA for the series of letter and fire bombs that had disrupted London since August 18.

Japanese Cabinet decided to postpone an economic conference with South Korea, planned for September 7–8, because of tensions between the two countries growing out of the kidnapping of South Korean opposition leader Kim.

27

Soviet economist Viktor Krasin and historian Pyotr Yakir confessed at their trial in Moscow that they had taken part in various subversive activities aimed at slandering the Soviet Union.

28

India and Pakistan signed an agreement in New Delhi providing for settlement of the problems remaining from the 1971 war.

Chilean Pres. Allende appointed a new Cabinet, his 22nd in nearly three years, the day after the resignation of the last of the armed forces commanders appointed to the previous Cabinet on August 9; shopkeepers went on strike, joining professionals, doctors, and farm workers supporting striking transport workers.

Stockholm police stormed a bank vault and captured a gunman and his companion who had held four persons hostage in the vault since August 23.

Tenth congress of the Chinese Communist Party ended after adopting a new party constitution, formally expelling the late defense minister Lin Piao, and confirming the leadership of Chairman Mao Tse-tung.

Zambian Pres. Kaunda named Mainza Chona as the country's first prime minister under a new constitution signed by Kaunda on August 25.

29

Seven persons were reported to have died in an outbreak of cholera in Naples, Italy.

Egyptian Pres. Sadat and Libyan leader Qaddafi signed an agreement proclaiming a "unified Arab state"; the merger was to take place in a series of steps, beginning with the formation of a constituent assembly on September 1.

U.K. Prime Minister Heath ended a two-day visit to Northern Ireland during which he held talks with Protestant and Catholic leaders.

Soviet press began a campaign denouncing the views of dissident atomic physicist Andrey D. Sakharov, who had warned August 21 that the West should beware of détente on Soviet terms.

30

USDA announced that average U.S. farm prices had risen 20% between July 15 and August 15 and were 62% above the 1972 level.

Striking railroad employees stormed the Canadian Parliament building in Ottawa to protest a proposed bill designed to end the nationwide rail strike, which had begun August 24.

White House said Pres. Nixon would appeal Judge John J. Sirica's order of the day before that Nixon produce tapes of his White House conversations for Sirica's private inspection, in a ruling on a petition by Special Prosecutor Cox.

SEPTEMBER

1

Libya announced the nationalization of 51% of foreign oil companies operating in the country.

2

Canadian railroads resumed operations the day after Parliament approved a bill ordering striking employees back to work.

4

Secret indictments on charges arising from the 1971 break-in of the office of Daniel Ellsberg's former psychiatrist were returned by a Los Angeles County grand jury against four former Nixon administration officials.

5

Fourth conference of nonaligned nations opened in Algiers.

7

Five Palestinian guerrillas belonging to a formerly unknown organization landed in Kuwait with hostages captured when they broke into the Saudi Arabian embassy in Paris.

9

Sudanese Pres. Gaafar Nimeiry ended a four-day state of siege imposed as a result of student and worker unrest.

Australian Prime Minister Whitlam announced a 5% revaluation of the Australian dollar.

10

Pres. Nixon sent Congress a second state of the union message in which he urged passage of the more than 50 bills proposed by the administration.

Bombs exploded at two London railroad stations injuring 13 persons in the third week of fire and letter bombings in Britain; these bombings coincided with the opening of the trial of ten persons accused of earlier bombings.

Centrist coalition government of Norwegian Prime Minister Lars Korvald failed to win enough seats in the Storting in Norwegian general elections to maintain it in office.

11

Leftist government of Chilean Pres. Allende was overthrown by a military coup; Allende was reported to have committed suicide.

Icelandic Cabinet threatened to break diplomatic ties with Britain if British ships "continued ramming" Icelandic vessels.

French Pres. Pompidou arrived in China for an official visit.

12

Eleven black miners were killed by South African police at the Western Deep Levels gold mine in Carletonville during a riot over wages.

Cambodian government reported it had won the battle for Kompong Cham.

Egypt resumed diplomatic relations with Jordan, broken in 1972 after Jordanian King Hussein proposed a federation of Jordan and the Israeli-occupied West Bank territories.

GATT ministerial conference, meeting in Tokyo, reached preliminary agreement on a "basic approach" to the formal GATT negotiations, scheduled to begin in October in Geneva.

13

Syrian and Israeli jets clashed in an air battle over the Mediterranean; Israel claimed to have downed 13 Syrian planes while the Syrians said Israel had lost 5.

Chilean military junta named the Army chief, Gen. Augusto Pinochet Ugarte, as the country's president and swore in a Cabinet consisting of ten military officers, three national police officers, and two civilians.

U.S. Court of Appeals for the District of Columbia urged an out-of-court settlement of the White House tapes dispute.

14

Representatives of the Laotian government and the Pathet Lao signed an agreement to set up a coalition government.

15

King Gustaf VI Adolf of Sweden died at the age of 90 and was succeeded by his grandson Carl XVI Gustaf.

East and West Germany and the Bahamas were accepted as members of the UN at the opening session of the 28th General Assembly; Leopoldo Benites of Ecuador was elected assembly president.

Second stage of the Conference on Security and Cooperation in Europe opened in Geneva.

Cambodian high command announced that government troops had reopened Route 4, the main road between Phnom Penh and the port of Kompong Som.

Chilean soldiers fire on presidential palace during military coup . . . September 11

S. JULIENNE—SYGMA

WIDE WORLD

Juan Perón and his wife Isabel greet supporters during Argentine campaign . . . September 23

16

Swedish general elections resulted in a tie in the Riksdag between the governing Social Democrats and the nonsocialists.

UNICEF reported that at least 50,000 persons had died in a drought-induced famine in Welo and Tigre provinces of Ethiopia.

17

United Automobile Workers and the Chrysler Corp. reached a tentative agreement on a new three-year contract, ending a strike that had begun at midnight September 14.

Prime Minister Heath and Irish Prime Minister Cosgrave met outside Dublin, during the first official visit of a U.K. prime minister to the Irish Republic, without reaching agreement on the timetable for establishing the proposed Council of Ireland.

The Netherlands revalued the guilder upward by 5% as part of an anti-inflation program.

18

Jordanian King Hussein declared amnesty for some 1,500 political prisoners, including Palestinian guerrilla leader Abu Daoud, in a move to further Arab reconciliation.

19

India and Pakistan began an exchange of the more than 250,000 persons isolated by the 1971 war.

EEC delivered to the U.S. a proposal for a joint declaration of principles in which both the U.S. and the EEC would promise to "intensify cooperation on the basis of equality."

Pakistani Prime Minister Bhutto ended two days of conferences with Pres. Nixon in Washington, D.C., but failed to have the ban on arms sales to Pakistan lifted.

20

Special Prosecutor Cox and Pres. Nixon's lawyers told the U.S. Court of Appeals that they had failed to reach an out-of-court settlement regarding the White House tapes.

Billie Jean King defeated Bobby Riggs, 6–4, 6–3, 6–3, in a $100,000 tennis match in Houston, Tex., billed as the battle of the sexes.

21

U.S. Labor Department reported that the consumer price index rose 1.9% seasonally adjusted during August, or 22.8% at a seasonally adjusted annual rate; this steepest monthly rise in 26 years reflected the removal of federal price ceilings on food in July.

23

Japanese Diet passed two measures to boost the size and scope of the Self-Defense Forces, despite a September 7 district court ruling that such forces were unconstitutional.

Juan Perón and his wife Isabel were elected president and vice-president of Argentina; they received 61.8% of the 12 million votes cast.

24

Annual meeting of the International Monetary Fund opened in Nairobi, Kenya; two days earlier the IMF had announced that agreement on currency exchange rates and related international monetary problems would be delayed for at least a year.

25

Skylab 2 astronauts returned to earth after 59½ days in orbit.

Soviet Foreign Minister Andrey Gromyko, addressing the UN General Assembly, repeated an earlier suggestion that all five permanent members of the Security Council reduce their military budgets by 10%.

SALT II resumed in Geneva.

26

U.S. House Speaker Carl Albert (Dem., Okla.) refused to act on Vice-Pres. Agnew's request of the previous day, that the House investigate charges against him on the ground that it was the only proper forum for a case involving an incumbent vice-president.

U.S. Senate approved an amendment calling for a 40% reduction in U.S. overseas military forces and then, after intensive administration lobbying, reversed itself on a later vote.

27

U.S.S.R. announced that it had ratified two UN covenants on human rights.

28

Lawyers for Vice-Pres. Agnew brought suit in federal district court in Baltimore asking that the grand jury investigation of Agnew, begun the day before, be halted.

29

Two Soviet cosmonauts returned to earth after a two-day orbital flight in Soyuz 12, the first manned Soviet space flight since June 1971.

Austrian government, in return for the release of three Soviet Jews and an Austrian customs official seized by Palestinian guerrillas on a Moscow–Vienna train, announced that it would no longer permit group transit through Austria of Soviet Jews emigrating to Israel and would close the Schönau Castle transit facility.

OCTOBER

3

East German Parliament elected Premier Willi Stoph chief of state and Horst Sindermann premier, in changes necessitated by the death of Walter Ulbricht on August 1.

5

Catholic and Protestant leaders in Northern Ireland met formally for the first time in two years for talks on a new coalition government.

Finland signed an industrial free trade pact with the EEC.

6

Egyptian and Syrian forces attacked Israeli-held territory on the east bank of the Suez Canal and in the Golan Heights; major fighting was reported on both fronts.

8

Egypt claimed control of the entire eastern bank of the Suez Canal; Syria said its forces had retaken a large part of the Golan Heights.

Civilian Cabinet headed by Spyros Markezinis, who had been named prime minister on October 1, was installed in Greece.

U.K. Prime Minister Heath announced rules for Stage Three of an anti-inflation program, easing controls on wages and tightening controls on prices and profits.

10

U.S. Vice-Pres. Agnew resigned and pleaded no contest to one count of income tax evasion; the Justice Department dropped all pending charges against him and he was fined $10,000 and placed on three years' probation.

Japanese Prime Minister Tanaka, on the last day of a 16-day tour of four nations, ended talks with Soviet officials in Moscow without gaining assurances of a formal peace treaty with the U.S.S.R.

11

Israeli tank force broke through Syrian defenses on the Golan Heights and pushed past the 1967 cease-fire line toward Damascus.

12

Pres. Nixon announced he would nominate House Republican leader Gerald Ford of Michigan as the next U.S. vice-president.

U.S. Circuit Court of Appeals for the District of Columbia ordered that Pres. Nixon turn over the disputed White House tapes to Judge Sirica.

13

Canadian Prime Minister Trudeau and Chinese Premier Chou signed a three-year trade agreement during a state visit by Trudeau to Peking; an agreement by which China would buy 224,000,000 bu. of Canadian wheat over three years had been announced October 5.

14

Egyptian forces staged an all-day offensive along the 100-mi. Sinai front following a three-day lull in which large amounts of men and equipment had been moved across the Suez Canal.

Thai King Bhumibol Adulyadej named Sanya Thammasak prime minister after the military government of Thanom Kittikachorn resigned following a week of student riots.

Republican People's Party led but failed to win a parliamentary majority in Turkish elections.

15

Israeli task force crossed to the west bank of the Suez Canal and was reportedly attacking Egyptian missile sites and other targets.

U.S. State Department confirmed that an airlift of arms to Israel was under way to balance the "massive" shipments to Egypt and Syria that it said were being made by the U.S.S.R.

16

Nobel Peace Prize was awarded to U.S. Secy. of State Kissinger and North Vietnamese negotiator Tho for their negotiations leading to the end of U.S. involvement in Vietnam.

U.K. Prime Minister Heath and Icelandic Prime Minister Olafur Johannesson, after two days of talks in London, agreed on an interim settlement of their fishing dispute; the U.K. had agreed October 2 to withdraw its warships and tugboats from the 50-mi. zone around Iceland in response to a September 27 ultimatum in which Iceland threatened to break relations.

Labour Party leader Trygve Bratteli was sworn in as prime minister of Norway replacing Lars Korvald, who had resigned October 12.

17

Organization of Arab Petroleum Exporting Countries (OAPEC), meeting in Kuwait, agreed on a coordinated program of cutting the flow of oil by 5% each month in order to force the U.S. to change its Middle East policy; the day before the six largest Persian Gulf oil-producing nations announced a 17% rise in the price of their crude oil and a 70% rise in oil company taxes.

19

First National City Bank of New York lowered its prime rate to 9.75% a little more than a month after setting it at a record 10%; it was the first significant decline in the rate in nearly two years.

Lebanese police and army units stormed the Beirut branch of the Bank of America and captured Arab guerrillas threatening to blow it up; one hostage and two guerrillas were killed.

U.S. Labor Department announced that the consumer price index had risen only 0.3% in September, although it was still 7.4% higher than a year before.

Pres. Nixon announced a compromise plan whereby summaries of the White House tapes would be made available to the federal court and the Senate Watergate committee and the tapes themselves would be verified by Sen. John Stennis (Dem., Miss.); as part of the compromise the special prosecutor was to stop trying to obtain presidential tapes or papers through the courts.

20

Israeli forces pushed out in three directions from their bridgehead on the west bank of the Suez Canal; an Israeli spokesman said the road from Ismailia to Suez city had been cut.

Special Prosecutor Cox, in a news conference, refused to stop his efforts to get presidential tapes and papers; Atty. Gen. Richardson resigned rather than obey Pres. Nixon's order to fire Cox and disband his task force; Deputy Atty. Gen. Ruckelshaus also refused and was himself fired; Cox was finally fired by Solicitor General Robert Bork, who was then named acting attorney general.

Sydney (Austr.) Opera House was officially opened by Queen Elizabeth II after 14 years of difficulty-plagued construction.

Viet Cong made public orders to its forces indicating that it planned increased fighting in South Vietnam.

21

Kuwait, Bahrain, Qatar, and Dubai announced a boycott of oil shipments to the U.S., making the Arab oil embargo complete; Saudi Arabia had announced it was cutting off U.S.-bound oil the day before and Libya had done so on October 19.

Oakland Athletics won their second consecutive World Series, defeating the New York Mets 5–2 in the seventh game.

22

UN Security Council adopted a Middle East cease-fire proposal formulated by U.S. Secy. of State Kissinger and Soviet party leader Brezhnev during talks in Moscow on October 20–21.

23

Israeli and Egyptian forces continued full-scale war on the Suez front despite the UN cease-fire; Israeli forces were reported to have surrounded and cut off the Egyptian 3rd Army.

Ethiopia became the ninth African nation to break diplomatic relations with Israel since the outbreak of fighting.

Pres. Nixon, amid mounting public criticism of his firing of Cox and Ruckelshaus and the resignation of Richardson, agreed to turn the nine disputed White House tapes over to Judge Sirica.

Four Canadian paper mills resumed production following union ratification of new wage pacts; strikes causing severe newsprint shortages in the U.S. continued at several other mills.

North Vietnamese negotiator Tho announced that he would not accept the Nobel Peace Prize because "peace has not yet really been established in South Vietnam."

Former special prosecutor Cox was reported to have obtained a letter to Pres. Nixon from a dairy cooperative representative suggesting that higher import quotas on dairy products had been imposed in exchange for a large contribution by the dairy industry to the Nixon campaign fund.

24

Syria accepted the UN cease-fire and fighting on the Syrian front virtually ceased.

Pres. Nixon vetoed a war powers bill that would have limited the president's ability to wage undeclared war without consulting Congress.

25

Israeli Defense Minister Moshe Dayan offered to resign following criticism of Israel's war preparedness; Prime Minister Meir rejected the offer.

"Precautionary alert" of all U.S. forces was ordered in response to possible Soviet efforts to place troops in the Middle East; the crisis eased when the U.S.S.R. joined in approving a UN Security Council resolution establishing a peacekeeping force in the Middle East but barring the major powers from the force; the resolution also repeated earlier calls for a cease-fire.

26

Widespread violence in Northern Ireland included at least 17 bomb explosions and more than 50 bomb scares.

Pres. Nixon held a news conference in which he gave his version of the alert call and recent Watergate developments and displayed marked displeasure with "vicious" media reporting.

U.S. criticized strongly "a number" of its NATO allies for separating themselves publicly from U.S. policies and actions in the Middle East.

ALEX OZOLINS—AUSTRALIAN INFORMATION SERVICE

Fireworks light up the Sydney Opera House during opening festivities . . . October 20

28

Israel agreed to allow the resupplying of the Egyptian 3rd Army following the first direct meeting, in the Sinai, of high Egyptian and Israeli representatives since 1956.

UN report said drought had resulted in 50,000–100,000 deaths in Ethiopia.

Portuguese general elections gave all 150 National Assembly seats to the ruling National Popular Action Party; the opposition Democratic Party had withdrawn from the elections by October 25, charging police harassment and calling the vote a fraud.

29

White House urged Congress to lay aside the administration's request for power to liberalize trade with the U.S.S.R. as being "inappropriate" while Middle East negotiations were under way.

Liberal Party won a landslide victory in Quebec provincial elections.

New York Times reported that former Deputy Atty. Gen. Kleindienst had told former special prosecutor Cox that Pres. Nixon had intervened in a Justice Department antitrust case against ITT; the White House denounced the leaking of "confidential" information but did not deny its substance.

30

White House announced that Pres. Nixon would meet in upcoming days with acting Egyptian Foreign Minister Ismail Fahmy and Israeli Prime Minister Meir as part of an intensified effort to clear the way for Egyptian-Israeli negotiations.

The Netherlands imposed a ban on Sunday pleasure driving and called on other EEC members to abide by rules for the free movement of oil within the Community; Libya became the seventh Arab country to suspend oil deliveries to The Netherlands.

Australian Prime Minister Whitlam and Japanese Prime Minister Tanaka agreed at talks in Tokyo to begin immediate negotiations on a treaty to formalize, stabilize, and broaden relations.

Negotiations on mutual troop reductions in Central Europe opened between the Warsaw Pact and NATO nations in Vienna.

31

Judge Sirica announced that White House lawyers had informed him that two of the nine subpoenaed tapes had never been made.

U.S. military alert was ended when the last 350,000 troops were returned to normal status; the Defense Department reported that Soviet troop alerts in the U.S.S.R. and Eastern Europe appeared to have ended.

NOVEMBER

1

Pres. Nixon announced he was nominating Sen. William B. Saxbe (Rep., O.) as his fourth attorney general; Leon Jaworski was appointed special Watergate prosecutor.

2

Syrian Deputy Foreign Minister M. Z. Ismail met in Washington with Secy. of State Kissinger to discuss Middle East cease-fire problems in the first significant diplomatic contact between the two countries in a year.

4

Joint communiqué issued at the end of a four-day visit to China by Australian Prime Minister Whitlam disclosed a three-year wheat-sales agreement and Chinese backing for an expanded Australian role in Asia.

Fierce fighting between North Vietnamese and South Vietnamese forces was reported near the Cambodian border.

5

East Germany announced it would double the compulsory minimum currency exchange required of Westerners visiting East Germany.

OAPEC announced, following a two-day meeting in Kuwait, that each of the countries would reduce oil production to 75% of its September output, with an additional 5% drop planned for December.

U.S. Secy. of State Kissinger arrived in Rabat, Morocco, at the start of a Middle East peace mission.

6

EEC foreign ministers adopted a joint resolution at the end of a two-day meeting in Brussels calling on Israel and Egypt to return to the cease-fire lines of October 22 and on Israel to end the territorial occupation maintained since 1967.

State and local elections in the U.S. saw Democrat Brendan T. Byrne elected governor of New Jersey and Republican Mills E. Godwin winning narrowly in Virginia; Abraham D. Beame overwhelmed three other candidates in the New York City mayoralty race; Detroit, Raleigh, N.C., Dayton, O., and Grand Rapids, Mich., elected black mayors.

7

U.S. Congress overrode Pres. Nixon's veto of a bill limiting presidential powers to wage war without congressional approval.

U.S. and Egypt announced they would resume diplomatic relations, ended six years before, following a meeting between Secy. of State Kissinger and Pres. Sadat in Cairo.

Pres. Nixon asked Congress for far-reaching and various powers to deal with the oil shortage; in a television address asking the people to cooperate in coping with oil shortages, Nixon departed from his prepared text to declare that he would not resign.

8

U.S. State Department announced it was closing the embassy in Uganda and withdrawing the chargé d'affaires; Uganda Pres. Idi Amin had ordered the U.S. Marine security guards at the embassy out of the country on October 29, charging them with subversive activities.

Danish Parliament was dissolved and elections were scheduled for December 4, following a split in the government over tax proposals.

9

Pres. Nixon began a series of meetings with Republican members of Congress to counteract serious declines in public confidence in his leadership.

11

Egypt and Israel signed a U.S.-sponsored, six-point cease-fire agreement and immediately began direct discussions on how to implement it.

13

West German Chancellor Brandt outlined to the European Parliament a six-point plan to accelerate EEC political, economic, and social unification.

U.K. and Iceland announced an interim agreement formally ending the fishing dispute between the two countries.

U.K. Home Secy. Robert Carr announced a state of emergency giving the U.K. government broad powers to regulate fuel distribution and take over public and private transport as labour disputes continued in the coal and electric power industries; the worst monthly trade deficit in British history was reported and the Bank of England and the government adopted restrictive monetary policies.

U.S. Federal Reserve Board Chairman Burns announced that the U.S. and six European countries had terminated the two-tier gold agreement of March 1968 at a meeting of central bank officials in Basel, Switz.

14

Joint communiqué ending Secy. of State Kissinger's visit to China said that China and the U.S. had agreed to continue efforts to promote normalization of relations.

Israeli and Egyptian negotiators ended a three-day impasse over implementation of their cease-fire pact by agreeing to an immediate exchange of prisoners.

Princess Anne of Britain and Capt. Mark Phillips were married in Westminster Abbey.

15

U.S. Commerce Department announced that the balance of payments surplus for the third quarter of 1973 was $2,150,000,000, the largest on record.

16

Pres. Nixon signed a bill authorizing construction of a trans-Alaska oil pipeline.

Japanese government announced emergency rationing of oil and electric power for industry and appealed for voluntary conservation of fuel at home.

Skylab 3 crew was launched from Kennedy Space Center for a planned record 84-day mission following a 6-day delay caused by problems with the Saturn 1-B rocket.

17

Greek Pres. Papadopoulos imposed martial law in an attempt to quell two weeks of demonstrations demanding his resignation; police broke up a student sit-in begun November 14 at the Athens Polytechnic Institute.

U.K. Prime Minister Heath and French Pres. Pompidou concluded two days of talks in Chequers and signed a treaty to open the way for construction of a tunnel under the English Channel.

18

OAPEC announced that petroleum supplies would not be cut back any further to most European countries; embargoes against The Netherlands and the U.S. would continue.

Israeli Cabinet ordered a judicial inquiry into the nation's failures and shortcomings in the October war; a military probe had been ordered November 11.

19

Lone pilot bombed the presidential palace in Phnom Penh, Cambodia, killing three persons; Pres. Lon Nol escaped uninjured.

U.S. Supreme Court agreed to review a federal district court plan ordering the integration of the predominantly black Detroit school system with heavily white suburban school systems, using extensive busing.

21

Northern Ireland political leaders agreed on a compromise plan for creating an 11-member executive that would share the government between Protestants and Catholics.

U.K. coal miners rejected a government offer to settle their pay dispute and continued a week-old ban on overtime work that had cut coal production 20%.

Judge Sirica ordered that the existing subpoenaed White House tapes be turned over to him by November 26 to ensure their safety, following disclosure of an 18-minute gap in one of them.

22

Saudi Arabian Oil Minister Ahmad Zaki al-Yamani threatened to cut oil production by 80% if the U.S., Europe, or Japan tried countermeasures and threatened to blow up oil fields if the U.S. took military action.

Japan called on Israel to withdraw from Arab lands captured in 1967, saying it might "reconsider" its relations with Israel.

25

Greek Pres. Papadopoulos was ousted in a bloodless coup and replaced by Lieut. Gen. Phaidon Gizikis.

Israel agreed "in principle" to a U.S. proposal for peace talks with Egypt, Syria, and Jordan to begin on December 18.

Pres. Nixon announced a series of measures designed to offset an expected 10–17% fuel shortage.

26

Canadian House of Commons passed by acclamation a bill that would put strict controls on a broad range of foreign investments in Canada.

27

French Pres. Pompidou and West German Chancellor Brandt ended two days of talks in Paris on the oil crisis, European defense, and other EEC issues.

Panamanian officials and U.S. Ambassador at Large Ellsworth Bunker resumed talks in Panama City, deadlocked since March 1972, on a new treaty for the Panama Canal and Zone.

Rose Mary Woods, Pres. Nixon's personal secretary, testified in Judge Sirica's court that she had accidentally erased 5 minutes of one of the subpoenaed tapes but could not account for the rest of the 18-minute gap.

Senate Watergate committee suspended hearings on campaign financing to give staff more time to complete several investigations.

28

Summit meeting of 15 Arab nations ended after three days in Staoueli, Alg., with the announcement of an embargo on oil exports to Portugal, Rhodesia, and South Africa and by endorsing "political efforts" toward a Middle East peace; the previous day the group had exempted Japan and the Philippines from the scheduled 5% export cut for December.

29

Israeli and Egyptian military talks broke down over the disengagement of forces along the Suez Canal.

Saudi Arabian Oil Minister Yamani described the U.K., France, and Spain as "friendly" and said they would be exempted from the scheduled January 5% oil cutback.

U.S.S.R. and India signed a 15-year cooperation agreement in New Delhi during a visit by Soviet party leader Brezhnev.

DECEMBER

1

David Ben-Gurion, first prime minister of Israel, died in Tel Aviv.

Libya closed its embassy in Cairo apparently in protest to Egypt's conduct of the war with Israel.

2

William Whitelaw was named employment secretary and was replaced as Northern Ireland secretary by Francis Pym, as part of a U.K. Cabinet reshuffle.

3

Viet Cong rocket destroyed an estimated 30–45% of South Vietnam's civilian oil reserves at a depot southeast of Saigon.

U.S. Senate approved and Pres. Nixon signed a bill extending the federal debt limit, which had expired November 30, leaving the government without funds; earlier the Senate had voted to drop an amendment to the bill calling for campaign financing from public funds, after failing to end a filibuster.

Pioneer 10, U.S. unmanned spacecraft, reached its closest approach to Jupiter, 21 months after its launch.

4

U.S. truck drivers began blocking key highways to protest the effects that rising fuel costs and lower speed limits would have on their incomes.

Pres. Nixon announced the appointment of William E. Simon as head of a new Federal Energy Office; John A. Love had resigned the previous day as the administration's chief energy adviser.

5

Zambian Pres. Kaunda was reelected unopposed to a third term.

Romanian Pres. Nicolae Ceausescu, on a two-day state visit to the U.S., joined Pres. Nixon in signing a statement of principle pledging "continued development of friendly relations."

Danish Prime Minister Anker Jørgensen resigned the day following the defeat of his Social Democratic Party in general elections.

U.S. Senate completed congressional action on the first regular foreign aid authorization in two years, one of $2.4 billion.

French Finance Minister Giscard d'Estaing announced sweeping measures to control inflation; a general strike to protest government economic policies was scheduled for the following day.

6

Gerald R. Ford took office as 40th vice-president of the U.S., one hour after the House completed congressional action on his nomination.

8

Pres. Nixon made public information about his personal finances, including his income tax returns, to "remove doubts" raised in persistent reports that he had profited improperly from office.

9

Council of Ireland to deal with mutual problems of the Republic of Ireland and Northern Ireland was established by an agreement reached at a conference between U.K. Prime Minister Heath and Irish and Northern Ireland leaders at Sunningdale, Eng.

Arab oil ministers meeting in Kuwait ordered an additional 5% cutback in oil production to begin January 1.

Democratic Action Party of opposition presidential candidate Carlos Andrés Pérez swept Venezuelan general elections.

10

NATO foreign ministers opened a two-day meeting in Brussels; U.S. Secy. of State Kissinger and French Foreign Minister Jobert clashed over whether the improvement in U.S.-Soviet relations jeopardized the security of Western Europe.

11

Czechoslovakia and West Germany signed a treaty establishing diplomatic relations and voiding the 1938 Munich pact; an exchange of notes called for further talks to resolve difficulties over representation of West Berlin institutions.

13

U.K. Prime Minister Heath announced the imposition of a three-day workweek in most industries, effective Jan. 1, 1974, in response to sweeping disruptions in energy supplies.

U.S. Energy Office Director Simon announced new energy-saving measures calling for voluntary compliance; truck drivers started a two-day protest on the effects of the fuel shortage.

15

EEC heads of state ended a two-day summit conference in Copenhagen at which they had issued a declaration on "European identity," agreed to develop a common energy policy, and reaffirmed their November 6 statement calling for Israel to withdraw from Arab lands, despite the appearance of four Arab foreign ministers seeking stronger anti-Israeli action.

J. Paul Getty III, grandson of a U.S. oil magnate, was found in southern Italy over five months after his disappearance and following payment of a reported $2.8 million ransom.

16

Thai King Bhumibol Adulyadej dissolved the National Assembly, in a move toward the establishment of a new constitution.

17

U.S. Secy. of State Kissinger concluded five days of talks in seven Middle East capitals discussing questions involving the opening of a Middle East peace conference.

Arab guerrillas killed 31 persons at Rome airport and hijacked a West German airliner to Athens where they demanded the release of Palestinian terrorists being held there.

18

Senate Watergate committee voted unanimously to subpoena hundreds of White House documents related to the Watergate break-in and campaign financing.

EEC foreign ministers ended a two-day conference in Brussels without agreeing on implementation of the directives of the EEC summit meeting.

19

Pres. Nixon signed a Health, Education, and Welfare and Labor Department appropriations bill and released $1.1 billion in impounded education and health funds.

U.S. Commerce Department reported that the U.S. basic balance of payments for the third quarter of 1973 showed a $2,540,000,000 surplus, in contrast to a $2,650,000,000 deficit for the same period of 1972.

20

French Pres. Pompidou, in a television address, reaffirmed his confidence in Premier Messmer, whose ouster was being demanded in press and political circles.

Spanish Premier Carrero was assassinated by an explosion as his car was being driven away from a Madrid church.

U.S. Congress passed a $73.7 billion defense appropriation for fiscal 1974 and compromise manpower legislation.

21

First peace conference between Israel and Arab countries opened in Geneva.

U.S. Congress gave final approval to legislation increasing Social Security benefits by 11% in two stages and cleared a bill reorganizing the northeast railroad system.

Judge Sirica released to Special Prosecutor Jaworski those portions of the subpoenaed tapes and documents that he had ruled were related to the Watergate affair.

22

First session of the 93rd U.S. Congress adjourned after abandoning efforts to pass major emergency energy legislation.

Pope Paul VI met with African leaders to discuss Vatican proposals to make Jerusalem an international city.

Japanese Cabinet adopted a series of radical measures to cope with the economic crisis, including a declaration of a state of emergency, the ordering of a 20% reduction in the use of oil and electricity in major industries beginning January 1, and approval of an "austerity" budget for 1974.

25

OAPEC announced in a surprise move that the flow of oil to most countries would be increased, while embargoes against the U.S. and The Netherlands would continue.

26

Japanese Cabinet delayed oil and electricity cutbacks in view of the OAPEC announcement; in an effort to protect its balance of payments the government tightened regulations on business investments abroad.

Soyuz 13, Soviet manned spacecraft, ended an eight-day earth orbiting flight that was reported to be a test of the craft to be used in a joint U.S.-Soviet mission in 1975.

27

U.S. Justice Department filed a civil antitrust suit against Mid-America Dairymen Inc., a milk marketing cooperative that had contributed heavily to the 1972 Nixon presidential campaign; similar suits were pending against two other milk groups.

28

U.K. electrical engineers accepted a government pay offer and agreed to end their eight-week ban on overtime and emergency work; a similar action by coal miners continued.

Comet Kohoutek made its closest approach to the sun, having failed to appear as spectacular as had been predicted.

South Korean Pres. Park announced new restrictions on press freedom despite month-long demonstrations demanding a return to democratic rule.

29

Spanish Chief of State Franco named Interior Minister Carlos Arias Navarro premier.

Turkish Pres. Koruturk asked acting Prime Minister Naim Talu to form a coalition Cabinet to govern until new general elections could be held in 1974; several efforts to form a government had failed since the October 14 general elections.

31

Libya, Nigeria, Bolivia, and Indonesia announced 60–80% increases in the prices of their crude oil, following a pattern set by the Persian Gulf states on December 23 at a meeting in Teheran, Iran; Venezuela had announced a comparable increase December 28.

Labour Party of Israeli Prime Minister Meir lost some seats but retained control of the Knesset in Israeli general elections.

Dow-Jones industrial average closed at 850.86, 169.16 points below the 1972 closing figure, after having fallen gradually from a record high in January and staging a strong recovery in October; gold prices in London reached their highest level in four months; the U.S. dollar had reached its highest level since February on December 28.

Gerald R. Ford (centre) is sworn in as U.S. vice-president in Capitol ceremony . . . December 6

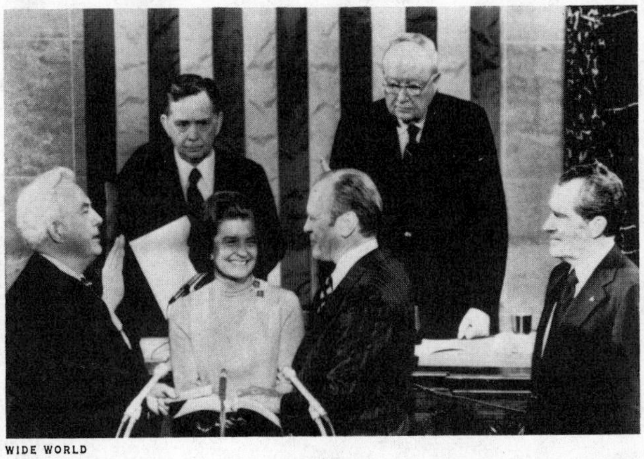

WIDE WORLD

1973

Advertising

The population explosion, diminishing natural resources, the environment, pollution—once the preserve of cranks and lone campaigners, these subjects had become respectable by the late '60s, an increasing preoccupation of the early '70s, and real anxieties in 1973. This became apparent when a fuel shortage first hit the U.S. in May, long before the Middle East war and the Arab oil boycott later in the year. Among other raw materials in short supply was newsprint.

Though these events did not detract from the prosperity that the advertising business as a whole enjoyed in 1973, they were omens. The advertising of petroleum was cut drastically, and some U.S. companies with media contracts shifted their ground and advised their customers to "go easy on the gas pedal." The shortage of newsprint was felt around the world; in countries like India, reluctant to part with foreign exchange to meet the higher cost, editorial and advertising pages were cut. In Europe the waiting list for space in major print media grew longer, a situation aggravated by an acute shortage of television time that in some instances necessitated advance payment and up to a year's prebooking.

The availability of television time was determined by the need to maintain a balance between program material and advertising, and was a matter of government policy in many countries. However, the shortage of print media could result in greater pressure for a relaxation of the rules, particularly in countries like West Germany, where the ratio of advertising was low (20 minutes before 8 P.M.), and Italy, where the advertiser was obliged to contain his advertising message within a package of entertainment material that he provided.

Despite these gloomy observations, indications were that the final figures for 1973 would show it had been a boom year for the advertising business. In Britain 1972 had been a year of recovery, with advertising expenditure reaching a record £708 million. This represented a true increase of some 11% over 1971, the first significant increase in real terms for many years. All media did well. Of total advertising expenditure, 26.5% went to regional newspapers, 24.9% to television, and 18.4% to the national press. The trade and technical press accounted for 8.6% and magazines and periodicals for 8.5%.

Figures from other countries indicated similar growth. In West Germany, media advertising in 1972 was 11% above 1971, with magazines holding the major share of expenditure at 40.95%; newspapers accounted for 30.98%, television for 16.35% (reflecting the restricted buying situation), trade publications for 6.50%, and radio for 5.22%. Total expenditure through agencies was estimated at DM. 4,310,000,000. In France the 1972 increase was 6%, with a 7% growth forecast for 1973. Media shares in 1972 were press 68%, television 13%, outdoor 11%, radio 7%, and cinema 1%; it was expected that 1973 would show a 2% growth in television at the expense of the press. Other countries experiencing increases in 1972 included Belgium 11%, Sweden 5%, Denmark 8.06%, Japan 11.6%, Mexico 10%, and South Africa 15%. The 1973 forecast for Brazil was a phenomenal 25%.

According to an *Advertising Age* survey of major media organizations, national advertising volume in major media in the U.S. in 1973 was expected to be 5% above the 1972 total of $10.6 billion. Projected national ad volume in newspapers was $1.1 billion, the same as in 1972, but national and local volume combined were forecast at $7,480,000,000 to $7.5 billion, compared with $7 billion a year earlier. Twelve percent gains were predicted both for total network, spot, and local TV ad revenues (to $4,560,000,000) and for network TV (to $2,020,000,000). Magazine advertising was expected to rise to $1,310,000,000 from $1,290,000,000. Ad volume projections of $930 million for business publications represented an anticipated gain of 5.4%. Network radio expected a $1 million gain, to $60 million. Outdoor advertising's projected $340,095,000 total was 5% ahead of 1972, and direct mail was expected to rise 5% over the 1972 figure of $2.4 billion to $2.5 billion.

While advertisers, media, and agencies were busy about their business, bureaucrats around the world were seeking ways to meet, and in some cases encourage, the pressures of consumerism. Focal points for much of this activity were the European Commission in Brussels and the Council of Europe in Strasbourg. Late in 1972 the Commission discussed the "harmonization of legislation on unfair competition" within the EEC countries, part of which concerned misleading advertising, including denigration and comparative advertising, premiums, and promotions. The subject was of vital importance to the advertising industry, which presented its views to the Commission through a formal memorandum from the European Association of Advertising Agencies. The opinion was expressed that advertising interests were not opposed in principle to the harmonization of such laws but were greatly concerned over matters of definition and execution and many points of detail.

Another matter in the political arena was a proposal before the consultative assembly of the Council of Europe to reduce consumption of products containing tobacco and alcohol and to prohibit advertising for these products. Again the European Association of Advertising Agencies was active in bringing together interested parties to ensure that opposition views were represented. In consequence, the assembly's final recommendation to the Committee of Ministers took a much milder line than had been feared.

In Norway legislation banning all advertising of alcoholic drinks and tobacco was held in abeyance because of trade agreements with foreign suppliers. Mexico City removed all outdoor posters, billboards, and neon signs along the main highway circling the city. Belgium placed statutory restrictions on the advertising of medicines.

Late in the year the U.S. Federal Trade Commission (FTC) virtually dismissed two major ad cases, against Wonder bread (ITT Continental) and Hi-C drink (Coca-Cola Co.). By so doing, the FTC, now under the leadership of Chairman Lewis Engman, appeared to be backing off from some of the positions introduced during the tenure of Engman's predecessor, Miles Kirkpatrick. These included ordering corrective advertising, requiring affirmative disclosures in TV ads, and maintaining that advertisers had an obligation to be "fair" to children, though in August Engman urged the industry to develop a code for children's advertising. A limited cease and desist order was issued prohibiting ITT Continental and its agency, Ted Bates & Co., from making nutritional claims ("rich in vitamins," "enriched") for any food without stating the brand, product, or product category with which the comparison was being made. The

Aden:
see Yemen, People's Democratic Republic of

HEALTH EDUCATION COUNCIL

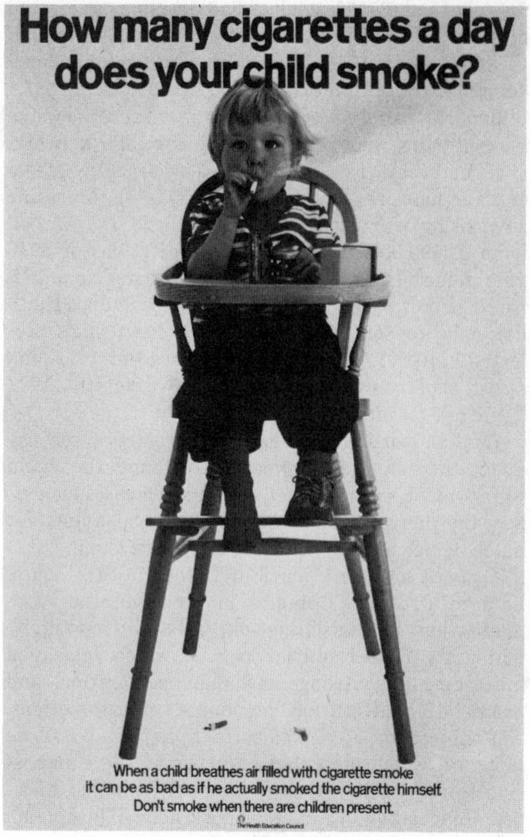

How many cigarettes a day does your child smoke?
When a child breathes air filled with cigarette smoke it can be as bad as if he actually smoked the cigarette himself.
Don't smoke when there are children present.

One of a series in the British Health Education Council's 1973 smoking and health campaign, this poster urges adults to consider the hazards not only of smoking, but of secondary smoking—taking in the smoke created by another's cigarette.

Hi-C case was dismissed when the FTC decided that its own staff had read unwarranted comparisons with orange juice into certain Hi-C ads.

The industry got support from an unexpected quarter when John W. Pettit of the Federal Communications Commission told an Association of National Advertisers seminar that he felt the ban on broadcast cigarette advertising was an "unmitigated disaster" and "deserves a decent burial." Meanwhile, however, Pres. Richard Nixon in the fall signed into law a congressional ban on broadcast advertising for little cigars.

The National Advertising Review Board, the industry's two-year-old self-regulating group, decided a number of cases. In one involving Bristol-Myers' claim that Ultra Ban 5000 "can keep you drier than any leading anti-perspirant spray," the NARB decided that in instances where advertisers considered supporting data to be confidential trade secrets, they would not be required to disclose them. The NARB also upheld a claim by J. B. Williams Co., marketer of Sominex, that ads for Nytol sleeping aid, made by the Block Drug Co., were misleading because they used selected portions of a medical study out of context. An NARB panel unanimously ruled that a Volkswagen of America print ad was misleading because of certain omissions in comparing VW's warranty with those of competitors.

The body dismissed a complaint against American Oil Co. TV commercials starring singer Johnny Cash after finding that survey data substantiated the challenged claim that "more new car buyers switch to the gasoline at American than any other brand." It also held that his appearance did not constitute a testimonial, since he appeared as a presenter, not an endorser. Also dismissed was a complaint against the STP Corp., after test data were found to support the claim that Double-Power gasoline additive "keeps an automobile clean and in tune." A negotiated settlement involved Ralston Purina Co. print ads for Chuck Wagon dog food. Because a photograph depicted chunks of dog food made from soybeans instead of meat, the company agreed to drop the possibly misleading words "tender, juicy chunks." NARB's first chairman, Charles W. Yost, resigned and was succeeded by Edwin D. Etherington, a businessman, educator, and lawyer.

Sexual permissiveness in advertising continued to be a subject of controversy. Advertisers claimed that they did not lead in these matters but followed the editorial climate already established by the media. Differing standards were highlighted by the affair of the Rizzoli awards, an annual presentation for "the most effective press campaigns in Europe," sponsored by a major Italian publishing group and judged by a panel assembled from all parts of the continent. When it became clear that a graphic and provocative advertisement on venereal disease by a Swedish contraceptive manufacturer was amassing a large number of votes, the rules had to be changed. As *Adweek* put it: "How could a group of pious women's magazines in Italy be seen to give a big prize to a gleefully dirty picture for a forbidden product!"

Among media developments of particular interest to advertisers, commercial radio finally became a reality in Britain when London Broadcasting went on the air at 6 A.M. October 8. Capital Radio followed later the same month, and Radio Clyde, Radio Birmingham, and Radio Manchester were scheduled to follow in 1974. A new and unlikely advertising medium appeared with the youth craze for displaying well-known trademarks on clothing, notably the seat of the pants. Advertisers were quick to cooperate with manufacturers of pants and T-shirts, thereby enjoying the benefit of walking billboards free of space costs.

Advertising Age listed the top ten agencies in the world in 1972 as J. Walter Thompson Co., with billings of $772 million; Dentsu Advertising Ltd., $684 million; McCann-Erickson (part of Interpublic Group), $636 million; Young & Rubicam, $563 million; Leo Burnett Co., $471 million; Ted Bates & Co., $457 million; SSC&B-Lintas International, $409 million; Ogilvy & Mather International, $406 million; Batten, Barton, Durstine & Osborn, $370 million; and Doyle Dane Bernbach, $232 million.

After a year of indecision, Batten, Barton, Durstine & Osborn went public during the year. At the same time, Clinton E. Frank, Inc., returned to privately held status after indicating disappointment at the market reception of its stock, first offered in 1971. At that time, the stock sold for $15.50; the agency's buyback price was $10.75. Doyle Dane Bernbach completed a repurchase program begun earlier in the year, buying 8%, or 149,300 shares, of its outstanding stock on the open market. Burton Sohigian Inc. went public with a limited offering of 38% of its stock.

Lando Inc. of Pittsburgh, Pa., and Bishopric & Fielden of Miami, Fla., merged to form the $24 million Lando-Bishopric agency. Young & Rubicam acquired Sudler & Hennessey, largest U.S. agency in the medical advertising field, and Wunderman, Ricotta & Kline, the country's biggest agency in the area of direct response marketing. Winius-Brandon Co., St. Louis, Mo., was merged into Batz-Hodgson-Neuwoehner, forming a combined $18 million operation. In Europe, Publicis Conseil, second largest agency in France, acquired Dr. Rudolf Farner Advertising Agency Group, making Publicis the largest European-owned agency on the continent. In 1972 Publicis billed $82 million and the Farner group, $41,470,000.

The first East-West agreement was concluded when Marsteller, an agency concerned mostly with industrial advertising, signed an agreement with Vneshtorgreklama of Moscow, the Soviet state agency, to help U.S. firms market their products in the Soviet Union. Marsteller also concluded a merger with a Japanese agency, Fuji Ad. Systems Co., and set up Marsteller-Fuji, a fifty–fifty partnership. Also in Japan, Daiko and Hakuhodo were talking of merger in order to offer more competition to Dentsu. The combined billings of the two agencies, amounting to $341 million, would be about half of Dentsu's total. Dentsu had full-service offices in New York, Los Angeles, and Hong Kong, but these represented only 3% of its billings. Further overseas expansion was forecast.

Grant Advertising International sold its Australian interests, with billings of some $3 million, to a local agency, Insight Pty. In Africa, Grant was negotiating to sell its business in Rhodesia, Kenya, Zambia, and South Africa to Interpublic for a reputed $1 million. Batten, Barton, Durstine & Osborn opened in São Paulo, Braz., and acquired a 71.5% interest in the biggest West German-owned agency, Team. In Australia, despite local hostility to the growing U.S. influence, BBDO obtained a 35% interest in Clemenger Australia, with billings of $18 million. Grey Advertising was another major U.S. agency to acquire an interest in Australia with the purchase of Claude Mooney Limited. Ogilvy & Mather acquired the largest Scandinavian agency, Svenska Telegrambyrån, with offices in Sweden, Denmark, Norway, and Finland and a 50% share in a Danish agency.

Some 652 U.S. advertising agencies billed a record $11.3 billion in 1972, $800 million more than 624 agencies billed in 1971. Although indications were that agency payrolls were still being cut, the paring process had slowed to the point where only 675 people were let go in the 66 agencies billing over $25 million; in 1971 those agencies had lopped payrolls by 2,660 people. Among agencies in the $10 million–$25 million category, only 50 people were dismissed in 1972, compared with 303 the year before.

A total of 213 major accounts (billing $350,000 and over) changed agencies in 1972, redistributing a total of $455,295,000 in billings. The largest single move was the switch of the $23 million American Motors account from Wells, Rich, Greene to Cunningham & Walsh (passenger cars), Hoefer, Dieterich & Brown (international advertising), and Mace Advertising (dealer advertising, shared with Cunningham and Walsh). In the first half of 1973, a total of $226,350,000 in billings from 112 major advertisers changed hands. The biggest move of the period was Liggett & Myers' reassignment of $15 million in cigarette billings from J. Walter Thompson Co. to Cunningham & Walsh and Norman, Craig & Kummel.

Advertising outlays by the 100 leading national advertisers in the U.S. rose 7.5% in 1972, from $4.9 billion to $5,270,000,000. It was the biggest increase for the leaders in 13 years (since a 9% rise in 1959). In the top 100 for the first time was the U.S. government, ranked as the 22nd largest advertiser, with outlays of $65,828,000, up one-third over 1971. Most of the increase went for armed services recruiting in connection with abolition of the draft, but a wide range of public service messages were sponsored by various federal agencies, among them the Postal Service.

WALTER ZURLINDEN—LIAISON

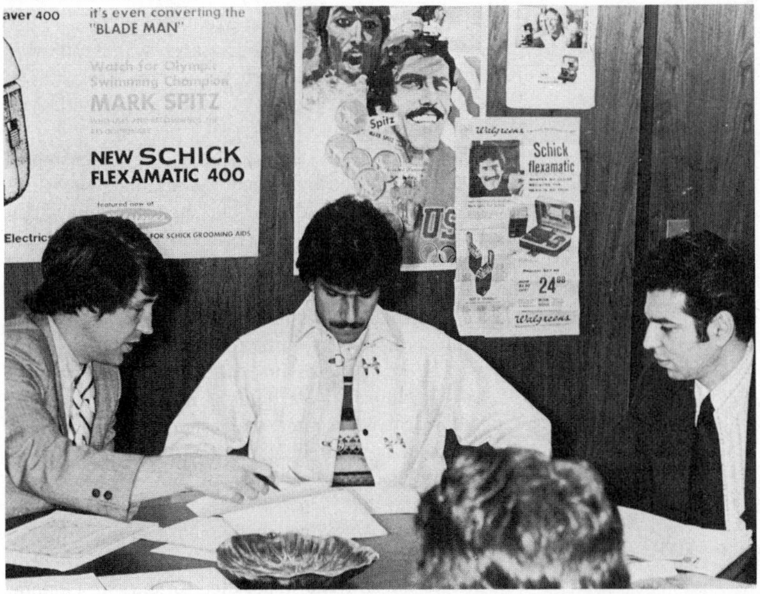

1972 Olympic swimming champion Mark Spitz (centre) in a different role. In 1973 he signed a lucrative agreement with Schick, a shaving products company, and promoted their items in several media campaigns.

The leading U.S. advertisers, according to figures compiled by *Advertising Age,* were Procter & Gamble, with an expenditure of $275 million, and Sears, Roebuck and Co., which spent $215 million. Others in the top ten were General Foods, $170 million; General Motors, $146 million; Warner-Lambert, $134 million; Ford Motor Co., $132 million; American Home Products Corp., $116 million; Bristol-Myers, $115 million; Colgate-Palmolive, $105 million; and Chrysler Corp., $95 million.

The top ten advertisers in Britain in 1972 were Co-op (local stores), £2,090,000; C & A Modes, £2,023,000; Guinness, £1,993,000; Brentford Nylons, £1,636,000; Weetabix, £1,516,000; Milk Marketing Board, £1,416,000; Ariel washing powder, £1,364,000; Blue Band margarine, £1,338,000; Oxo, £1,284,000; and Persil, £1,281,000. Of these, the Co-op spent the most in the press (£1,837,000) and Guinness the most in television (£1,657,000). In 1972, 22 of Britain's advertisers spent over £1 million.

Colgate-Palmolive was the leading advertiser in France, with $21,340,000, followed by Lever, $10,224,000; Henkel, $8 million; and Procter & Gamble, $7,560,000. In West Germany publishing spent the most among product groups, with a total expenditure of $74 million; next in line were skin and grooming products, automobiles, alcoholic beverages, pharmaceuticals, cigarettes, and detergents.

(GEOFFREY DEMPSEY; JARLATH JOHN GRAHAM)

See also Consumer Affairs; Industrial Review; Merchandising; Publishing; Telecommunications; Television and Radio.

Afghanistan

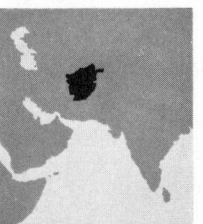

A republic in central Asia, Afghanistan is bordered by the U.S.S.R., China, Pakistan, and Iran. Area: 251,823 sq.mi. (652,221 sq.km.). Pop. (1972 est.): 17,882,326, including (1963 est.) Pashtoon 59%; Tadzhik 29%; Uzbek 5%; Hazara 3%. Cap. and largest city: Kabul (pop., 1972 est., 329,227). Language: Dari Persian and Pashto. Religion: Muslim. King until July 17, 1973, Mohammad Zahir Shah; prime ministers, Mohammad Musa Shafiq and, after July 17, Lieut. Gen. Sardar Mohammad Daud Khan; president after July 17, Mohammad Daud Khan.

The 40-year reign of King Mohammad Zahir Shah came to an end in 1973. The monarch was deposed in July in a coup led by his brother-in-law, Mohammad Daud Khan (*see* Biography), who proclaimed a republic with himself as head.

Afghanistan's internal situation at the beginning of 1973 was dominated by difficulties arising from three successive seasons of drought in the central and northern areas of the country. In Ghor Province, the shortage was particularly bad; famine was widespread and there were many deaths from starvation. The Cabinet headed by Abdul Zahir had come under severe criticism for its alleged failure to cope with the emergency; and after a massive vote of no confidence in the Lower House of Parliament in December 1972, King Zahir Shah accepted the resignation of the government and appointed Mohammad Shafiq to form a new administration which took office later in the month. Shafiq had been prominent in shaping the constitution of 1964, which banned members of the royal family from public office, and had thereby brought to an end the quasi-dictatorship of General Daud, the king's cousin and brother-in-law, who had virtually ruled Afghanistan from 1953 to 1963. The new prime minister set to work to deal with the economic crisis, mobilizing young officials, students, and army officers into a relief corps to distribute the foreign aid that poured into the country from the U.S. and from international agencies. Even so, it was estimated that approximately 80,000 people had died of starvation before supplies could reach them.

Although massive Soviet and U.S. aid programs, supplemented by less ambitious efforts sponsored by China, Britain, France, India, and other countries, had done much to improve roads, power supplies, irrigation, and other essential elements of an economic substructure on which future progress could be based, the gap that divided Kabul from the outlying and backward areas showed little signs of closing. In those parts of the country the authority of the central government remained minimal, and small notice was taken of the men selected for Parliament. Thus, the capital tended to be a world of its own, where governments changed, where unrest was chronic, and where the country found almost its only link with the outside world.

That such a situation was inherently unstable was shown in July when King Zahir Shah, whose personality had for many years ensured an element of continuity, absented himself in Europe for medical treatment. While he was out of the country, Daud, who had long resented his exclusion from power, took advantage of some discontent over promotions in the armed forces, along with student unrest and resentment among the educated classes against unemployment, to depose the king by a military coup and proclaim a republic with himself as president. He announced his adherence to Afghanistan's traditional policy of nonalignment, but was an acknowledged friend of the Soviet Union and a firm supporter of secessionist movements in the Pashto-speaking areas of Pakistan, the North-West Frontier Province and Baluchistan—an outlook that seemed likely to revive the friction with Pakistan that had marked his earlier period of power.

Radio Kabul in September announced the discovery of an allegedly Pakistan-backed plot to overthrow the new regime. A large number of army officers were arrested including former prime minister Mohammad Hashim Maiwandwal, who was later reported to have hanged himself while awaiting trial.

(L. F. RUSHBROOK WILLIAMS)

AFGHANISTAN

Education. (1970–71) Primary, pupils 540,687, teachers 13,117; secondary, pupils 107,609, teachers 4,248; vocational, pupils 7,646, teachers 773; teacher training, students 6,444, teachers 845; higher, students 7,397, teaching staff (1969–70) 881.

Finance. Monetary unit: afghani, with (Sept. 17, 1973) an official rate of 45 afghanis to U.S. $1 (free rate of 108.50 afghanis = £1 sterling) and a free rate of 62.25 afghanis to U.S. $1 (150 afghanis = £1 sterling). Gold, SDRs, and foreign exchange, central bank: (June 1973) U.S. $53,720,000; (June 1972) U.S. $51.7 million. Budget (1970–71 est.): revenue 6,269,000,000 afghanis; expenditure 8,175,000,000 afghanis. Money supply: (May 1973) 9,454,000,000 afghanis; (May 1972) 7,899,000,000 afghanis.

Foreign Trade. (1970–71) Imports 6,258,000,000 afghanis; exports 7,110,000,000 afghanis. Import sources (1970): U.S.S.R. 27%; Japan 18%; India 14%; U.S. 8%; West Germany 7%; Pakistan 6%; Iran 5%. Export destinations (1970): U.S.S.R. 30%; Pakistan 19%; West Germany 13%; U.K. 13%; India 9%. Main exports: fruits and nuts 34%; natural gas 17%; karakul (Persian lamb) skins 12%; cotton 10%; wool 8%.

Transport and Communications. Roads (1970) *c.* 6,700 km. (including *c.* 2,000 km. with asphalt). Motor vehicles in use (1969): passenger 30,800; commercial (including buses) 18,200. Air traffic (1971): 171 million passenger-km.; freight 2,166,000 net ton-km. Telephones (Jan. 1971) 21,000. Radio receivers (Dec. 1968) 248,000.

Agriculture. Production (in 000; metric tons; 1972; 1971 in parentheses): corn *c.* 680 (*c.* 700); wheat *c.* 2,000 (1,915); rice (1971) 350, (1970) 366; barley *c.* 320 (355); cotton, lint *c.* 29 (*c.* 27); wool (1971) *c.* 17, (1970) 16. Livestock (in 000; 1971–72): cattle *c.* 3,750; sheep (1970–71) *c.* 22,900 (including *c.* 6,800 karakul); horses *c.* 400; asses *c.* 1,300; goats (1970–71) *c.* 3,300; camels (1970–71) *c.* 300.

Industry. Production (in 000; metric tons; 1971–72): salt 36; cotton yarn 6; cotton fabrics (m.) 62,000; coal (1969–70) 136; electricity (kw-hr.; 1970–71) 326,000; cement (1969–70) 180.

Aerospace Industry: *see* Astronautics; Defense; Industrial Review; Transportation

African Affairs

The worst drought of the 20th century brought disaster to seven countries of Africa and added to the continent's economic difficulties in 1973. While world increases in commodity prices helped the leading exporting nations, the continuing world monetary crisis seriously affected most countries. The wars in the Portuguese territories—especially in Mozambique and Guinea—increased in violence; tensions built up along the Zambezi River frontier dividing white-ruled from black-ruled Africa and there were fears of new hostilities in the Horn of Africa (Ethiopia, Somalia, and the French Territory of the Afars and Issas). With only one military coup during the year, in Rwanda, and a palace coup by King Sobhuza II of Swaziland, there was some evidence of less internal political instability than in previous years. An important development was the almost universal African support given to the Arab cause in the Middle East conflict, with the consequent breaking of diplomatic relations with Israel.

The Drought. An extended drought devastated the lives of an estimated seven million people in Ethiopia and in six states fringing the Sahara Desert—Mali, Mauritania, Senegal, Chad, Niger, and Upper Volta. A permanent interstate committee and a special fund, established at a summit meeting of the six states, set a target of $1.5 billion to be spent combating drought conditions and stemming the desert, which was advancing southward.

Wars and Coups. At the northeastern end of the continent, in the Horn of Africa, the long-standing dispute between Ethiopia and Somalia deteriórated to the point where open hostilities were feared. The Organization of African Unity (OAU) appointed a mediation committee to reduce the tensions.

The year's only military coup occurred in Rwanda. The bloodless coup seemed to stem from dissension among rival factions of the ruling Hutu tribe. Hutus from the southern region of the country had dominated government positions, while northern Hutus who were dominant in the Army wanted a greater share in ruling Rwanda. The palace coup in Swaziland by King Sobhuza II in April brought no fundamental changes to the country although it swept aside the constitution of independence.

Portugal during the year committed additional manpower and money to fighting the three wars in Angola, Mozambique, and Portuguese Guinea, where it had been engaged for 12 years in defending its traditional policies against the challenge of guerrilla-type liberation movements. The policies of Premier Marcello Caetano toward Portugal's African territories became a divisive issue within Portugal itself in the general election of October 1973 and strained its international relations. Allegations of atrocities by Portuguese troops in Mozambique caused special concern in Britain in the year of the 600th anniversary celebrations of the Anglo-Portuguese treaty. The main focus of the allegations was a massacre reported by missionaries of the Burgos Fathers order that had allegedly occurred in the Mozambique village of Wiriyamu. Although Caetano paid a state visit to London, Britain later subscribed to a communiqué at the Commonwealth heads of government conference in Ottawa calling on Portugal's friends to press for negotiated independence of the Portuguese colonies. Reforms introduced by Portugal to confer a measure of autonomy on the territories within the framework of a unified Portuguese state failed to produce a respite from diplomatic or military pressures. Portugal in 1973 devoted 41% of its total government expenditure to keeping 120,000 black and white troops in the field.

Divisions among the three guerrilla movements fighting in Angola gave the Portuguese some respite there, but the situation became less favourable in the other two territories. The assassination on January 20 of Amilcar Cabral (*see* OBITUARIES), the 48-year-old leader of the African Party for the Independence of Guinea and Cape Verde (PAIGC), did not produce a significant change in Portuguese Guinea. An assembly elected in the "liberated areas" proclaimed the independence of Guinea-Bissau on September 24. It gained diplomatic recognition from more than 70 countries, including most African states, the nonaligned nations, the Soviet bloc, and China. Increasingly sophisticated weapons, supplied mainly by the U.S.S.R., were in use in Guinea and in Mozambique, where the Front for the Liberation of Mozambique (Frelimo) increased its threat to the strategically sensitive Tete Province abutting on Rhodesia and opened up a new front in the Manica e Sofala region.

Frelimo's successes along the Rhodesian frontier also opened the way for a tougher guerrilla challenge by one of the Rhodesian liberation movements, the Zimbabwe African National Union, to the regime of Ian Smith in Rhodesia. Another guerrilla movement, the South West African People's Organization (SWAPO), increased its attacks through the Caprivi Strip against South West Africa (Namibia). (*See* Special Report.)

Southern Africa. These growing guerrilla threats to the white-ruled states had several consequences. On January 9 the Rhodesian regime closed the frontier with Zambia on the Zambezi River. This action, criticized by Rhodesia's Portuguese and South African allies, heightened tensions along this dangerous frontier. Although Ian Smith later decided to reopen the frontier, Zambia ordered it to remain closed. Consequently, the already strained relations between Zambia's Pres. Kenneth Kaunda (*see* BIOGRAPHY) and his white-ruled neighbours deteriorated. The UN Security Council appealed on March 10 for international support to help Zambia sustain its economy while alternative trade routes were being opened up. South Africa's prime minister, B. J. Vorster, widened his previous commitment to Rhodesia by offering to send troops to help fight guerrillas wherever his help was

continued on page 59

CAMERA PRESS/PICTORIAL PARADE

African workers, supervised by Chinese engineers, lay down a section of the Tanzam railway. Construction of the railway, linking the Zambian copper mines with the harbour at Dar es Salaam, Tanzania, was being financed with an interest-free loan from the People's Republic of China.

CONFRONTATION ALONG THE ZAMBEZI

By Basil Davidson

Always latent in the long process of European withdrawal from political control of colonies in Africa, the subcontinental conflict in southern Africa became for the first time a major issue of world concern in 1973. Crystallized along the middle course of the west–east flowing Zambezi, a river increasingly seen since 1964 as the frontier of confrontation between regimes of black majority rule to the north and those of white supremacy to the south, this conflict had already spread far beyond the region of the Zambezi itself. All the vast areas of the southerly half of Africa were evidently now involved.

Many developments over many years had made their contribution to a rising tide of subcontinental violence. Observers had watched the drama as it intensified with the clash between white repression and black resistance. The area had received rather little attention in the clamour of the times, but events during 1973 struck the note of coming emergency in an altogether new tone. Elsewhere, the war in Vietnam was nearing its end—though soon to be followed by a new war in the Middle East. Was it possible that another such disaster could now engulf the countries of southern Africa?

The question had been put, but had seemed alarmist. By 1973 it appeared less so. The various strands of tension, whether in one of these countries or another, were perceived to have drawn into a single knot. There was no longer, it now transpired, a series of separate territorial "questions," Portuguese or Rhodesian, South African or Namibian, generally regarded previously as more or less unrelated and capable of separate resolution. What now thrust itself upon the scene was an overriding "question" far more full of menace: the doubtful future of southern Africa regarded as a whole.

Crucial developments began early in 1973. On January 24 the Zambian representative at the United Nations asked for an urgent meeting of the Security Council to consider serious acts of aggression committed against his country by the illegal regime in Rhodesia. This followed Rhodesia's closing of its border with Zambia on January 9 in protest against alleged guerrilla incursions from the north (blamed for the killing by a land mine on January 8 of two South African policemen working with the Rhodesian security forces), and the laying of mines, presumed to be Rhodesian, on the Zambian side. In a series of incidents these mines killed several Zambians and wounded others.

The Security Council met on January 29 and heard the Zambian representative declare that the Rhodesian government, in closing the border and thus cutting Zambia's rail communications through Rhodesia, had opened economic warfare on his country; he asked for financial aid to help Zambia meet this problem. The Security Council duly passed two resolutions, the more important of which condemned "all the acts of provocation and harassment . . . against the Republic of Zambia by the illegal régime in collusion with . . . South Africa"; demanded "the immediate and total withdrawal of South African military and armed forces from . . . Rhodesia"; and decided to send a special mission to investigate.

Strong though it was, this resolution was passed by 13 votes without opposition, and with only Britain and the U.S. abstaining. Only a year earlier it would probably have received several outright rejections. The Security Council's special mission, which visited Zambia on February 12–16, recommended aid, and UN Secretary-General Kurt Waldheim deployed two representatives to prepare detailed proposals. Very clearly by this time, these proposals seemed likely to serve as a pattern for others of a far wider nature. Nothing short of majority rule, warned Pres. Kenneth Kaunda of Zambia, could now stop the escalation toward catastrophe in southern Africa. The Security Council manifestly thought so too.

Basic Factors. In examining the background to the current situation some key dates may usefully be isolated. Just ten years earlier, in February 1963, the British protectorate of Nyasaland was granted what Britain called "responsible self-government," in fact a preliminary to the independence of this country, which became Malawi in July 1964. More telling in the wider picture, the British decision effectively ended the white-dominated Federation of Rhodesia and Nyasaland, formed as a result of settler pressure in 1953. This opened the way for the independence of Northern Rhodesia, which became Zambia in October 1964. Another "front line" territory had meanwhile gone the same way in December 1961 with the independence of Tanganyika, afterward joined with Zanzibar as Tanzania. Similarly relevant in this context, the Belgian Congo had become independent in June 1960.

This process had many consequences. For one important thing, it gave fresh hope to banned nationalist movements south of the Zambezi, as well as in the great "flank guards" of the white supremacist system, the Portuguese colonies of Angola and Mozambique; it also gave those movements bases from which they could mount operations, political or military, in their own countries. The nationalist parties of the north might harbour hesitations about supporting their brothers in lands not yet free, and their leaders were divided on the subject. Although he minimally shifted his stance on this in mid-1973, Pres. H. Kamuzu Banda of Malawi refused all support and drew close to his white neighbours; farther away, in the former Belgian Congo, now Zaire, Pres. Mobutu Sese Seko has done in practice much the same. Yet the leaders of the two states that have mattered most in this context, Presidents Kaunda of Zambia and Julius Nyerere of Tanzania, at once made clear that aid to other nationalists, especially in countries of the supremacist system, was for them a natural right and duty as a contribution toward those necessary political and social advances that alone could bring peace to the subcontinent.

Southward, the rulers of South Africa watched all this with a calculating patience, intent on finding where their influence could enter. But their calculations were now upset, and rudely, from an unexpected quarter. This was Rhodesia. Although formally subject to the British crown, Southern Rhodesia's white minority had since 1923 enjoyed full internal self-rule with little interference from London, and had used this to install a racist system differing in no essentials from that of South Africa. By 1965 whites numbered fewer than 250,000 in an African population past the four-million mark. At that time, they demanded constitutional independence of Britain on the basis of the existing supremacist system, but found themselves refused. During November 1965 the great majority of these settlers accordingly backed the extremist course of declaring unilateral independence. This coup d'etat was rejected by the British, who forthwith applied economic sanctions, soon widened by UN support. These sanctions proved quite inadequate to overthrow the illegal regime thanks to the aid it received from South Africa and Portugal, and from a host of profiteering sanctions-breakers

---

Basil Davidson is an author and historian. His recent works include The African Past; The Africans: An Entry to Cultural History; *and* In the Eye of the Storm: Angola's People.

throughout the world. But sanctions were maintained, and, to that extent, they greatly added to the isolation of the "white bastion" south of the Zambezi.

This far-ranging radicalization of the situation in Rhodesia was deeply if privately deplored by the men in Pretoria, South Africa's capital. Their calculations had in the mid-1960s led them to embark upon an "outward looking" policy aimed at winning an economic and then political dominance for South Africa among the newly independent black states. This plan flowed partly from a belief that a highly capitalized South African economy could fashion a southern and central African "common market" or "co-prosperity sphere" under Pretoria's control, and partly from the logic of apartheid. Inside South Africa, apartheid was in the process of reorganizing the old native reserves or homelands into an "orbit" of subordinate black "states" known familiarly as Bantustans. The three British High Commission Territories within or along the frontiers of South Africa were soon to become independent, Basutoland (Lesotho) and Bechuanaland (Botswana) in 1966 and Swaziland in 1968, and these were to form, as they since have, a second "orbit" of compliant black polities revolving round the sun of Pretoria. More ambitiously, it was hoped that a third and outer "orbit" could be formed to the north. The Malawi of President Banda (like the Malagasy of the then Pres. Philibert Tsiranana) duly complied. and there were hopes of drawing in Zambia and even distant Zaire, two countries of great mineral wealth. Finally, South African investment in mineral research and extraction, and in hydroelectric projects, whether on the Cunene or Zambezi (Cabora Bassa), was steadily increased in Angola and Mozambique.

The whole "grand design" seemed promising, and it is no doubt ironic that it was the white Rhodesians, more than anyone else, who overturned it. Although outwardly supported by the South African government, whose electorate would have tolerated nothing else, the illegal regime of Ian Smith in Rhodesia in fact raised a formidable barrier to any northward extension of South African influence, and the "common market" plan steadily faded after 1966. Other factors also developed to frustrate South African ambitions. Western criticism of apartheid and its consequences was much reinforced by liberal and Christian opinion. South Africa's cultural isolation deepened as actors and other artists refused to visit the country, and white South African sportsmen found themselves increasingly barred from competing abroad. If divided on many other issues, the Organization of African Unity was largely solid on this one. UN denunciation sharpened.

Such was the trend of the early 1970s. Supremely confident of Western backing and well used to the jagged strains of apartheid, most South African whites seemed barely aware of any impending troubles. Behind the scenes, however, their leaders were less happy. For the 1960s had brought another development in the north, the use of guerrilla warfare in the service of an awakened and even radical African struggle to be free. And this warfare, implied forerunner of what might also come to happen farther south, had not failed.

The Guerrilla Effort. Measured militarily, the wars of armed resistance launched against Portuguese colonial rule by nationalists of Angola, Mozambique, and Guinea-Bissau have already achieved remarkable gains. Though experiencing many shifts of fortune, the fighting movements of these countries have grown continuously in strength since the early 1960s. In certain respects they are perhaps the most successful guerrilla efforts of modern history. By 1973 the Portuguese regime had fielded armies in Africa totaling about 150,000 men, much the largest ever raised in Portugal, and representing a probable maximum possible metropolitan conscription on the basis of four years' military service for all able men between the ages of 18 and 45. By per capita comparison of populations, these troops comprise a force some seven times greater than the largest U.S. army engaged in Southeast Asia. Yet there was no sign in 1973 that

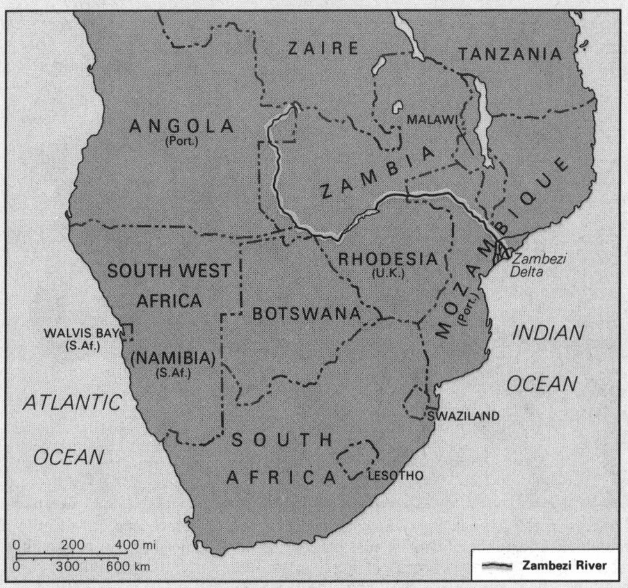

they were within sight of containing their nationalist opponents, much less of crushing them.

Indeed, the trend appeared to be against Portugal. In Guinea-Bissau, for example, nationalist units began shooting down Portuguese jet bombers and other warplanes in March 1973 with what were evidently "homing" ground-to-air missiles; this deployment of new weaponry could be expected, on past form, to appear in Angola and Mozambique as well, thus robbing the Portuguese of their unchallenged air superiority. Though operations in Angola were making little progress, largely through the continued refusal of the Zaire government to afford guerrillas access to Angola by way of Zaire's long common frontier, this was far from true in Mozambique. There the nationalists had improved their penetration of the strategically crucial Tete district lying between Malawi and Rhodesia, and crossed south over the Zambezi in 1972, while continuing to maintain their hold on the northern districts of Cabo Delgado and Niassa. By mid-1973 they were reported by both sides to be astride the Pungwe River, and therefore adjacent to Rhodesia's lines of communication with the Indian Ocean.

Measured politically, the nationalist movements have likewise shown themselves resourcefully original. While owing much to aid in military material from Communist states, they are movements of an indigenous and undoubtedly independent nature, vowed to social and political change within the frameworks and conditions of their own countries. Their basic policies aim at building new social structures and institutions in place of the imposed patterns of Portuguese autocracy and such traditional patterns as have survived the colonial period.

They are thus modernizing and nonracist movements that reject the mere reform of existing institutions and see current Portuguese gestures toward reform as illusory or, at best, a mere tinkering with the problems of indigenous development. By 1973 they had given ample evidence of their intentions by the use they were making of areas liberated from Portuguese control. There, as many visitors have reported, they are laying the foundations of new systems of self-rule based on elective village committees and the promotion of modern education and social services. In 1972 the nationalists of Guinea-Bissau set another precedent for Angola and Mozambique by holding a general election throughout their liberated areas for a national assembly. In September 1973 this assembly proclaimed the country's independence, even while the capital and some part of its territory were still in Portuguese hands. Sixty-six nations immediately recognized the new nation.

This emphasis on political change by work at the grass roots, aiming at social and cultural unity within a new national con-

A.F.P. / PICTORIAL PARADE

Members of the African Party for the Independence of Guinea and Cape Verde proclaim the Republic of Guinea-Bissau, Sept. 24, 1973. Formed by an assembly elected in the "liberated areas" of Portuguese Guinea, the new nationalist government was recognized by China, the U.S.S.R., and many other nations.

sciousness, was an evidently vital reason for the nationalists' military success. Not surprisingly, it began to have its influence elsewhere. A new guerrilla resistance launched inside Rhodesia during 1973 appeared to have sprung from the same policies. By midyear the Rhodesian authorities were admitting that significant parts of the northeastern areas had passed out of their sure control. Emergencies were proclaimed, and reservists called up. There was the prospect of a long struggle with a nationalist movement that had much matured from its earlier reverses. Even among Rhodesia's orthodox white settlers, voices were being heard to say that if majority rule was not conceded, as things were going now it would eventually be taken.

The South African Dilemma. From the foregoing it is clear that the overall balance in southern Africa has changed considerably. The Portuguese may well persevere with their enormous effort, but there is nothing to indicate that they can restore their colonial control of 1960. In the end, failing this, they must either make an attempt at settlement on whatever terms they can get, or else withdraw. The illegal Rhodesian regime can go on defying economic sanctions and political isolation from the world at large, yet it can do this only at the price of growing violence and counterviolence, and a corresponding financial and military drain on its indispensable ally, South Africa. Throughout these regions, the cause of black equality is on the ascendant. But what of South Africa, the "giant in the south," where all keys to the future of this subcontinent must ultimately lie?

Outwardly, the apartheid system appears impregnably strong, and in many ways undoubtedly is so. It commands an advanced industrial economy that has already achieved an impressive degree of independence within the wider system of the West. Its energies are constantly fueled by new inflows of investment from the U.S., Britain, France, West Germany, Japan, and other countries. Its armed forces are admittedly small, but they are highly trained and equipped with an abundance of the most sophisticated weapons, perhaps now including nuclear missiles. Its political and cultural isolation may have deepened, but its vital links with the most advanced countries of the West are in no way weakened, and these links are military (or at least naval) as well as economic.

Yet this is a strength that becomes increasingly hard to employ in the Africa that now lies beyond the South African frontiers. There are two chief reasons for this difficulty. The first, and in the long run perhaps the more influential, is that the new and rising tensions caused by white revolt in Rhodesia, allied to colonial intransigence in Angola and Mozambique, have tended steadily to lessen Central African reliance upon South African markets and production. That reliance may still be considerable, but it is not growing and may dwindle further.

South Africa's second difficulty in deploying its strength lies in a critical shortage of white manpower for military purposes. It is one thing to station a few thousand all-white troops in Rhodesia, and a few thousand more in Mozambique or Angola (and even so the South African government has departed from tradition by arming a few Coloured volunteers for service under white officers in the Caprivi Strip of Namibia). Should, however, the Portuguese continue to fail in containing nationalist advances, it would be quite another thing for South Africa to mount and maintain over a long period the large expeditionary forces that would be required by any attempt to succeed where the Portuguese fail. The South African white population is only half the size of Portugal's. Even if this white minority could be placed on a total and prolonged war footing it could scarcely supply such forces, and it must remain very much an open question whether the regime would be willing and able to raise large levies of black as well as Coloured troops ready to serve its cause, as the Portuguese have done.

Yet it will become increasingly hard for Pretoria simply to stand by and watch the gradual disintegration of supremacist structures outside the boundaries of its "fortress." For this would mean accepting the eventual prospect of nationalist movements and ultimately governments, along these boundaries, of a kind quite opposed to any fake independence within their own countries, and as much disposed to help their brethren inside the "fortress" as other Africans have helped them. The dilemma for South Africa and its friends abroad is likely to be tough, and there is no doubt that they know this.

Much will, of course, depend upon how far Pretoria can expect further support from its friends abroad in one or another type of intervention, whether direct or indirect; and, vice versa, on how far such intervention may be challenged by the Africans' friends abroad. The chances of a major world "confrontation along the Zambezi" are clearly present. But aside from these considerations, there appear to be two or possibly three options for Pretoria. One is to continue as at present, giving the Rhodesians and Portuguese just enough men and money to keep up their repressive effort in the hope that this will after all suffice. Parallel with this, the already adopted practice of armed incursions, bombings, and politically subversive adventures or assassinations in Zambia or Tanzania can be increased. Informed Central African opinion expects that it will be, whether by the Portuguese or Rhodesians or even South Africans, believing that these allies can in any case count on covert protection from the West and a UN Security Council consequently robbed of teeth.

If all such operations prove insufficient, there is a variant, if hazardous, form of this first option. This would consist of launching major air and ground strikes against Zambia and perhaps Tanzania, while sending large forces into Angola and Mozambique, with the dual aim of destroying support for the liberation movements and holding at least the southern and perhaps central areas of Angola and Mozambique, where South African interests are much involved. This, too, is what a number of leading Africans have begun to think may yet come to pass, for they judge again, rightly or not, that even so desperate a widening of the conflict would be somehow "covered" by South Africa's friends abroad. The objections to adopting it are enormous from Pretoria's standpoint, whether because of the internal strains it would impose or because of the open challenge it would present to the rest of the world. Yet the possibility of some such savage dénouement, already hinted at in threats by Pretoria spokesmen, cannot be dismissed.

A third option for South Africa would be to accept the changing balance in the subcontinent, come to terms with the liberation movements, abandon the illegal regime in Rhodesia, and admit at least a large relaxation of apartheid at home. As there was no evidence in 1973 that any serious thought was being given to such a course, the current upheavals in southern Africa might well be the prelude to far greater ones.

continued from page 55

requested. South Africa's army chief, Lieut. Gen. Magnus Malan, said in September that the republic found itself in "a state of war of low intensity and high intensity." In September, too, the Chinese-built Tanzam railway line reached the Zambia frontier with Tanzania; this held out the promise that by 1974 Zambia would have access to the sea through Tanzania to the port of Dar es Salaam.

A general strike among black workers in South Africa began in South West Africa (Namibia) at the end of 1972 and continued into January 1973. This unexpected display of militancy served to sharpen the focus of international attention on this disputed territory and led to renewed offers by Vorster to negotiate its future with the UN secretary-general; it also increased internal opposition to South Africa's official policies of creating separate homelands, especially in Ovamboland, which bordered on Angola and lay close to Zambia. A state of emergency was declared. The elections for the first territorial authority assembly for the Ovambos' homeland were heavily boycotted.

South Africa's relations with its three small neighbours—Lesotho, Botswana, and Swaziland—continued to worsen during the year. Lesotho's prime minister, Chief Leabua Jonathan, who had ended the state of emergency proclaimed in his own kingdom in 1970 in order to begin talks about a new constitution, continued the attacks he had started two years earlier on South Africa over what he termed its inflexible attitude on apartheid; this attitude, he warned, would plunge the whole area into violent bloodshed. Nothing came of proposed talks between himself and Vorster during the year. When Chief Jonathan called for UN observers to be present at the inquiry into the shooting of black miners at the Western Deep Levels mine in September, Vorster warned him not to test the republic too far. Relations with Botswana's president, Sir Seretse Khama, also remained uneasy. Sir Seretse had previously offended the republic by his outspoken criticisms of its apartheid policies. When Sir Seretse signed a joint communiqué with Tanzania's Pres. Julius Nyerere in September, in which mention was made of the role of liberation movements, Vorster demanded an explanation from the Botswanan leader. Although there was no open rift with Swaziland, its leaders joined with Botswana and Lesotho in calling for talks with South Africa (all were members of the Southern African Customs Union) to discuss what they claimed were unilateral decisions taken by South Africa on devaluation, currency, and trade policies, decisions that adversely affected their own countries.

By the end of the year no significant changes of power had occurred in southern Africa. However, concern about the growing effectiveness of the guerrilla movements, especially in Mozambique, had heightened the sense of insecurity in an already tense part of the continent.

The Organization of African Unity. This pan-African alliance of all independent states in the continent (except for South Africa) celebrated its tenth anniversary in Addis Ababa, Eth., in May. The occasion was not marked by the tensions of previous summit meetings despite ominous threats of conflict between Ethiopia and Somalia and an initiative by Libya's leader Muammar al-Qaddafi (*see* BIOGRAPHY) calling for a boycott of Ethiopia unless it either broke its ties with Israel or changed the place of the meeting from Addis Ababa to Cairo. There was little support for his attitude (although Ethiopia did in fact break diplomatic relations with Israel later in the year).

Nigeria's prestigious Gen. Yakubu Gowon (*see* BIOGRAPHY) was elected chairman of the OAU. The organization adopted two declarations of policy. A political declaration reaffirmed support for the movements struggling to achieve majority rule in the southern African and Portuguese territories, and promised increased support through the OAU's African Liberation Committee (ALC). The economic declaration defined the continent's goal to increase its economic independence from external powers by, for example, greater intra-African cooperation and by working toward a more favourable international trade and monetary system. During the summit a dramatic reconciliation occurred between Uganda's Gen. Idi Amin and Tanzania's President Nyerere, whose two countries had come to the brink of conflict in 1972. The OAU also decided to give full support to the continent's international aspiration of noninvolvement with either of the world's major military blocs by supporting the conference of nonaligned nations, which held a summit meeting in Algiers in September.

Intra-African Relations. The process of fission and fusion continued to characterize relations between a number of African states. While relations between Ethiopia-Somalia worsened during the year, those between Tanzania-Uganda, Chad-Libya, and Ethiopia-Sudan improved. The feud between Libya's leader Qaddafi and Morocco's King Hassan continued bitterly, but mainly at the level of radio warfare. Other relations within North Africa showed visible signs of improvement, largely the result of the increasingly influential role of Algeria's Pres. Houari Boumédienne. Tunisia's Pres. Habib Bourguiba advocated a new approach to unity in the region by seeking the unification of Tunisia, Algeria, Mauritania, and Libya into a single Arab state. Relations between Egypt and Libya deteriorated over the latter's impatient attempts to move quickly toward unity between the two countries and Syria within the framework of the Federation of Arab Republics agreed upon in 1972. This possibility seemed to have receded because of Qaddafi's impetuous demands on Egypt's Pres. Anwar as-Sadat (*see* BIOGRAPHY) and his decision not to commit Libya fully in the October war against Israel.

In West Africa, relations between Guinea and the Ivory Coast entered a new period of strain following allegations by the former's Pres. Sékou Touré that Ivory Coast Pres. Félix Houphouët-Boigny was supporting opponents of his regime. General Gowon maintained Nigeria's new role as a leader among African states by extensive visits throughout the continent; one of his primary aims was to bridge the political and economic "frontiers" that still kept parts of French-speaking Africa separate from those nations speaking English.

Zaire's Pres. Mobutu Sese Seko played a similar role in equatorial and central Africa. His own relations with his neighbour, the Congo, remained friendly; and he intervened on a number of occasions to mediate between Rwanda-Burundi, Tanzania-Uganda, and Tanzania-Burundi. His most significant role was in developing a new détente between Zaire, Tanzania, and Zambia, whose three leaders began meeting at regular intervals.

It was, however, in the field of economic relations that intra-African relations expanded most steadily. More than 100 intra-African organizations for functional cooperation operated regularly, largely under the umbrella of the UN Economic Commission for Africa (ECA).

External Relations. Five major issues continued to delineate the continent's relations with the outside world. The overriding factor remained the desire among a growing number of African countries to adopt more clearly consistent policies on nonalignment in their dealings with the major powers. Flowing directly from this was their concern to achieve a different kind of relationship with both the Western and Communist countries over trade and financial relations, with both systems coming in for heavy criticism. There was much greater concern about the role of Western multinational corporations in the continent's economy.

Future relations between Africa and Europe were foreshadowed by two parallel developments: the negotiations begun over future African ties with the European Economic Community (*see* below), and the loosening of the old bonds between French-speaking African countries and France. This latter development was particularly significant. It began in 1972 when serious internal crises emerged in the Common Organization of Africa, Malagasy, and Mauritius (OCAM), resulting in the withdrawal of Mauritania, Zaire, and the Congo. This development continued in 1973 when Malagasy, Cameroon, and Chad also withdrew, leaving only 10 of the original 16 members. Most of the retiring members charged OCAM with perpetuating links with France, an allegation hotly denied by the rest of the members. This changing relationship with France was also evident in the case of membership in the franc zone, from which Mauritania and Malagasy withdrew. A new group, the West African Economic Community (CEAO), was formed by the Ivory Coast, Senegal, Mauritania, Mali, Niger, and Upper Volta, to replace the largely ineffective Central African Customs and Economic Union (UDEAC) of the French-speaking West African states.

The other two issues that seriously affected foreign relations were the situation in the Middle East and

KEYSTONE

Workers at the port of Dakar, Senegal, shovel grain into sacks for distribution. Thousands of tons of grain, contributed as part of an international effort to relieve famine in drought-stricken West Africa, were stockpiled at Dakar harbour during 1973.

Western policies toward South Africa and Portugal. The Arab stand on the Middle East, which had achieved significant support in 1972 when a number of countries broke diplomatic relations with Israel, continued in 1973. Up to the end of the year, 27 African states (including some with marked sympathy for Israel) had severed diplomatic relations with Israel, more than half of them during the October war. These included Kenya and Ethiopia, whose leaders, Pres. Jomo Kenyatta and Emperor Haile Selassie, were regarded as founding fathers of African nationalism. For Israel these diplomatic reverses were a bitter outcome of painstaking efforts over many years to gain the friendship of Africa through its technical assistance programs, helping African farmers to irrigate desert lands south of the Sahara and to plant new soil-holding crops; Israel had sent its skilled manpower—physicians, nurses, teachers, agronomists, engineers, architects, scientists, and construction teams—to Africa in return for a degree of support at the UN for its stand on direct negotiations with the Arabs.

The African commitment to its own "unfinished revolution," aimed at completing the decolonization process by removing "the last vestige of white minority rule," continued to dominate political attitudes. In pursuit of this objective, the great majority of African states continued to adopt a common stand in applying pressures on the major Western countries through the UN, the Commonwealth of Nations, and other international organizations. A significant shift of opinion more critical of France over its arms and other policies toward South Africa was noticeable, while the United States came under attack especially over the consequences of the U.S. Senate's decision to breach the UN sanctions program against Rhodesia by allowing the importation of chrome and other strategically important minerals.

Economy. Africa's population continued to grow by about 2.7% per year with a real growth of income of less than 1% as against a target of 3.5%. The continuing crisis in international finance, and especially the devaluation of some of the major world currencies, directly affected the costs of African imports. The increases in these costs for most countries were not offset by the general rise in commodity prices, especially for cocoa and copper. The continent's economic strategy was discussed at a number of major conferences, such as those of the ECA and the OAU and the nonaligned nations summit at Algiers. As a result of these discussions a continental strategy of economic development emerged. This found its clearest expression in the African Declaration on Cooperation, Development, and Economic Independence adopted at Abidjan, Ivory Coast, in May; this was subsequently substantially incorporated into the OAU's economic declaration.

Considerable time was spent in discussing Africa's future relations with the EEC, especially in the light of Britain's entry into the Community, which was made conditional on the right of 20 Commonwealth members to acquire rights of associate membership similar to those previously granted to the 19 mainly French-speaking African states that were signatories to the Yaoundé Convention. Nigeria at first refused to consider any terms for "association," a term that it held implied an inferior status. But when it seemed as if this attitude might divide the African nations, Nigeria agreed to participate in negotiations provided that all African countries were included. The EEC agreed to include countries previously excluded—Ethiopia, Liberia, Sudan, and Guinea.

The greater part of the year was taken up in trying to find agreement among the Africans themselves about the terms they required of the EEC. Finally, at a meeting of African ministers of trade and development held in Abidjan in May, agreement was reached on the general principles to coordinate and harmonize the attitudes of the nations in all negotiations so as to safeguard their interests against decisions prejudicial to African economies or inter-African cooperation; and to ensure that "in agreements with developed market-economy countries, the provision of aid was not conditioned by a particular form of relationship." Although agreement was reached on general principles, it proved harder to win similar agreements on the details of a form of relationship with the EEC, especially over such contentious questions as rights of reciprocity for Europe in African markets. It was not until August that the African nations were in sufficient agreement among themselves to begin their negotiations with the EEC in Brussels.

Communications. The Trans-African Highway, which was to link the Indian Ocean coast and the Atlantic coast of the continent, continued to progress. There was also a decision that this highway should be linked with a northern highway across the Sahara, from El Goléa to In-Salah, to bring Algeria, Mauritania, Mali, and Niger into the new system of international road links. The OAU also decided to establish an investment fund to create a pan-African telecommunications network.

The completion of the railway link between Tanzania and Zambia, expected in 1974, would provide a complete railway network system linking the southern, central, and eastern African countries from Dar es Salaam, on the Indian Ocean to Lobito, Angola, on the Atlantic coast. It would also provide an outlet to Cape Town through the Rhodesian and South African railway system. (COLIN LEGUM)

See also Dependent States; Refugees; articles on the various political units.

ENCYCLOPÆDIA BRITANNICA FILMS. *Africa: Living in Two Worlds* (1970); *Boy of Botswana* (1970); *City Boy of the Ivory Coast* (1970); *A Family of Liberia* (1970); *Two Boys of Ethiopia* (1970); *Youth Builds a Nation in Tanzania* (1970); *Silent Safari* (1972); *Elephant* (1973); *Giraffe* (1973); *Lion* (1973); *Zebra* (1973); *Cheetah* (1973).

Agriculture and Fisheries

For the world's farmers, 1973 was extraordinary in many ways.

New production records were set for important crops and in some portions of the livestock sector of the world's agricultural economy. This was accomplished despite severe drought and flood damage in some areas and some civil disturbance.

Prices of agricultural raw materials and foodstuffs rose to unprecedented levels, with the increase amounting to at least 10% overall. Among the contributing factors were a wild scramble among nations attempting to assure themselves of minimum basic food reserves as the extent of the 1972 Soviet crop failure became known, and the instability of the world monetary situation.

There was a dawning realization of a potentially very precarious situation, as reserves of basic foodstuffs were drawn down to critical levels following the poor crops of 1972. Addeke H. Boerma, director general of the UN Food and Agriculture Organization, termed the situation intolerable. Production was at peak levels, yet reserves of important staples were dwindling and a single season's bad weather could produce a food crisis. Reiterating an earlier proposal for a coordinated stockpiling policy by major producing countries, Boerma called on the five main producer countries to consider increasing grain exports and reducing the use of wheat as an animal feedstuff, and to discuss ways of sharing available supplies according to some internationally accepted criteria.

WORLD FOOD SUPPLIES

Food supplies in 1972–73 were reduced to critically low levels, unmatched in any year since the end of World War II. Droughts and other reverses in one or more important producing regions are commonplace, but in 1972–73 they were unusually numerous and severe. Grain harvests declined more than 3% from a year earlier, producing a combined shortfall of some 39 million metric tons of wheat, rice, and feed grains. The effect was serious, primarily because of the distribution of production and the occurrence of large shortfalls in certain important areas. The situation was further exacerbated by disruptions in the patterns of trade, and prices rose sharply.

The FAO estimated that total food production in 1972 had declined to an index of 125 (1961–65 = 100) from 126 a year earlier, while population rose from an index of 117 to 119. The resulting overall reduction of 3% in per capita food production was unevenly divided; it amounted to 2% in the developed market economies, while a 4% reduction in less developed regions reduced food availability to the level prevailing in 1961–65. Throughout most of 1973 uncertainty about the adequacy of food supplies spurred demand and exerted heavy pressure on prices of wheat, feed grains, oilseed crops, and meat. In many instances, governments restrained the export of some food commodities in order to maintain domestic supplies. In the U.S., the sale of record quantities of grains—particularly to the U.S.S.R.—was scrutinized by Congress.

Generally speaking, the official U.S. view was that the 1972–73 crisis was the result of cyclical and weather-induced shortfalls, and that production trends throughout the world indicated an ability to produce sufficient supplies, at least through the next few decades. Even so, without an eventual reduction in the rate of growth of world population there could be no long-run solution to the world food problem. A special meeting of the principal wheat-exporting countries was called in Rome in September to assess the current situation with respect to wheat, stocks of

Table I. Indexes of Food and Agricultural Production
Average 1961–65=100

Region	Total agricultural production			Per capita food production		
	1972*	1971	1968–70	1972*	1971	1968–70
Western Europe	120	121	115	113	114	110
North America	117	118	110	109	113	106
Oceania	121	124	121	107	111	111
Far East (excluding China and Japan)	121	125	118	97	102	102
Near East (excluding Israel)	136	127	122	106	101	104
Africa (excluding South Africa)	125	124	116	101	102	101
Eastern Europe and the U.S.S.R.	132	132	125	121	122	119
Other developed countries (Japan, South Africa, and Israel)	126	121	122	113	111	114
All above regions† (world)	124	124	118	105	108	106

*Preliminary.
†Excluding China.
Source: Food and Agriculture Organization of the United Nations, *The State of Food and Agriculture 1973*.

which had been reported at a 20-year low. At the meeting, an FAO prediction, based on an estimate by the International Wheat Council that 1973–74 wheat supplies would fall short of requirements by some 9 million metric tons, was modified on the basis of new information. Export availabilities were placed in the range of 59 million–62 million metric tons, against import requirements on the order of 62 million–65 million tons, and there were some indications that a good Soviet crop might ease the situation further. The U.S. assured the meeting that its wheat stocks, though shrinking, would be sufficient to meet world demands in 1973–74.

Consumption, Expenditures, and Prices. Smaller supplies and higher prices reduced per capita food consumption in 1972–73. Some improvement in the supply situation was anticipated in 1973 as prospects for better crops were reported, but with stocks drawn down to low levels, it was clear that supplies would depend heavily on the outcome of 1973 harvests. Food prices everywhere continued to rise throughout 1973, as inflationary pressures were reinforced by shortages. (*See* Table II.)

Per capita consumption of all foods in the U.S. was expected to decline about 1% in 1973—the first decline since 1965. Consumption of livestock products was 2% less than a year earlier, and this was expected to offset a 1% increase in the combined use of fruits, vegetables, and cereals. Consumption of red meat was about 9 lb. less per person than the 189 lb. consumed in 1972, and both beef and pork were affected. Per capita use of fishery products was expected to show a slight increase from the 12.2-lb. average reported for 1972. Consumption of chicken was declining, and per capita egg consumption was at its lowest level since the mid-1930s. In the dairy product category, cheese consumption rose 5% while consumption of fluid milk and cream appeared to be unchanged. Per capita consumption of cereal grains and sugar was also expected to remain about the same.

As of the second quarter of 1973, U.S. consumers were paying about 9% more for food than in 1972. Total food expenditures in 1972 were estimated at $125 billion, compared with $117.5 billion in 1971, and

Table II. Recent Food Price Index Changes in Selected Countries, 1973

Country and month		Index 1963=100	Percentage change from: Previous month	Three months	One year
United States	May	151.2	+1.00	+5.15	+12.75
	June	153.3	+1.39	+3.93	+13.64
	July	154.5	+.78	+3.21	+13.44
Canada	May	149.8	+.81	+3.81	+14.61
	June	152.7	+1.94	+5.46	+16.74
Japan	May	187.3	+1.52	+7.27	+12.29
	June	184.9	−1.28	+1.93	+12.15
	July	186.1	+.65	+.87	+12.92
United Kingdom	May	184.5	+1.77	+5.25	+16.26
	June	185.5	+.54	+3.86	+14.86
	July	185.5	+0	+2.32	+14.86
Denmark	May	204	+1.49	+4.08	+17.24
	June	207	+1.47	+5.08	+15.64
	July	211	+1.93	+4.98	+17.88
Germany	May	136.6	+1.04	+3.17	+10.16
	June	137.8	+.88	+3.38	+9.71
Italy	May	152.5	+1.46	+4.67	+13.47
	June	153.7	+.79	+5.06	+13.35
	July	154.5	+.52	+2.86	+13.27
Belgium	May	169.7	+8.30	+10.19	+18.26
	June	170.6	+.53	+10.21	+17.41
	July	169.7	+.53	+8.30	+15.13
France*	May	122.7	+.57	+2.25	+8.68
	June	124.3	+1.30	+2.90	+9.04
	July	125.2	+.72	+2.62	+9.25

*Index, 1970=100. National statistical series for selected countries.
Source: U.S. Department of Agriculture, Foreign Agricultural Service, *Foreign Agriculture* (Oct. 8, 1973).

second quarter 1973 food expenditures were running at a seasonally adjusted annual rate of $135.8 billion, including $106.2 billion for food used at home. According to the U.S. Department of Agriculture (USDA), food accounted for 15.6% of disposable personal income, compared with 15.7% a year earlier. The Organization for Economic Cooperation and Development reported that in 1971 food expenditures as a percentage of disposable income amounted to 20.6% in Canada, 16.7% in the U.S., 26.6% in Japan, 24.2% in West Germany, and 18.9% in The Netherlands.

Food prices in the U.S. rose throughout 1972–73. Price controls on processed foods were retained under Phase Three of the administration's economic program, announced early in the year, but raw agricultural products were not subject to controls, and meat prices, especially, rose steeply throughout the winter. By March several consumer groups were planning a one-week boycott of beef, pork, and lamb. The administration had consistently rejected the idea of controlling such products on the grounds that it would breed market distortion and cause shortages. As plans for the boycott proceeded, however, Pres. Richard Nixon, in what appeared to be a sudden reversal of policy, announced a price freeze on beef, pork, and lamb at the retail level. The results of the boycott were uncertain. Meat sales in some areas were reported to be off as much as 80%, but the action was generally considered insufficient to bring about a general decline in prices. At the end of June, the government reported that food prices during the first half of the year had risen at an annual rate of 25%.

On July 18 President Nixon announced another major change in the administration's management of the economy. Phase Four ended the freeze on most retail food prices but continued the freeze on beef until September 12, presumably to spread out the price bulge that was expected to occur when controls ended. The delay in ending beef controls was bitterly criticized by livestock producers and packers; supplies were withheld, several packers were forced to shut down, and in some areas beef disappeared from meat counters. An attempt by Congress to legislate an end to the freeze failed, but controls were lifted a few days early, on September 9.

Meanwhile, on September 5, the USDA raised the milk price floor by nearly 13%. The action revived criticism of a controversial increase of 27 cents per hundredweight granted by the government in March 1971. Consumer groups charged that the dairy industry had influenced the action by heavy contributions to the Nixon campaign treasury, although the president denied any connection.

Although it was difficult to isolate a single cause for the food price spiral, a midyear report by the General Accounting Office indicated that heavy sales of wheat and feed grains to the U.S.S.R. were largely responsible. Many observers implicated other forces, including inflation, heavy export demand for U.S. food and feed grains by Europe and Japan, devaluation of the dollar, and perhaps speculation. Consumers were slow to return to beef when supplies reappeared, and this, together with the arrival of plentiful harvest produce on the market, kept retail food prices lower than had been predicted during the autumn months. Most experts felt that this was a temporary phenomenon, however, and at year's end food prices began to rise steeply once again.

Assistance. The multilateral UN–FAO World Food Program marked its tenth anniversary in May

Table III. Survey of Retail Food Prices in Selected Cities, Mid-September 1973

In U.S. dollars per pound, converted at current exchange rates

City	Boneless sirloin steak	Boneless chuck roast	Pork chops	Ham, canned	Bacon, sliced, pkged	Cheese (Cheddar, Edam, Gouda)	Butter	Broilers, whole	Eggs, large, doz.	Tomatoes	Onions, yellow	Apples	Oranges, per doz.	Bread, white
Bonn, W.Ger.	3.69	2.38	2.20	5.98	2.46	1.48	1.41	0.84	1.03	0.19	0.09	0.33	1.23	0.45
Brasília, Braz.	.74	.59	1.34	1.67	2.29	1.82	.72	.69	.70	.24	.59	.12	.68	.20
Brussels, Belg.	3.16	1.78	1.82	3.35	1.15	1.18	1.38	1.04	1.13	.29	.13	.27	1.45	.22
Buenos Aires, Arg.	.69	.38	.43	2.43	1.16	.91	.96	.37	.50	.29	.38	.17	*	.24
Canberra, Austr.	2.09	1.13	1.28	2.25	1.61	1.28	.87	1.13	1.08	.74	.30	*	.60	.31
Copenhagen, Den.	4.04	1.67	2.37	2.18	2.14	1.51	1.38	1.58	1.24	.94	.31	.40	2.10	.39
London, Eng.	2.75	1.30	1.30	1.25	1.59	.75	.51	.58	.89	.24	.17	.22	1.44	.15
Ottawa, Ont.	1.77	1.08	1.58	1.80	1.24	1.02	.74	.78	.90	.33	.13	.16	.97	.21
Paris, France	2.54	1.40	2.01	2.46	2.84	1.25	1.41	.90	1.17	.20	*	.34	1.37	.39
Rome, Italy	2.77	2.25	*	*	1.61	1.11	1.51	1.03	.89	.20	.20	.32	*	.24
Stockholm, Swed.	4.42	2.04	2.21	2.29	2.37	1.64	1.18	1.28	1.23	.53	.26	.48	1.38	.61
The Hague, Neth.	3.24	2.20	2.07	*	2.82	1.30	1.29	.78	1.08	.32	.27	.25	1.51	.17
Tokyo, Jap.	12.83	5.99	2.57	3.66	3.42	1.35	1.58	1.03	.61	.40	.19	.81	6.11	.36
Washington, D.C.	2.29	1.49	1.79	2.00	1.39	1.27	.95	.71	.88	.39	.19	.39	1.07	.25
Median	2.76	1.58	1.82	2.27	1.88	1.28	1.24	.87	.97	.31	.20	.30	1.38	.25

Note: Items may vary by quantity and type. Different marketing practices may distort some prices.
*Not available.
Source: U.S. Department of Agriculture, Foreign Agricultural Service, *Foreign Agriculture* (Oct. 8, 1973).

1973. During its existence, $1.2 billion worth of commodities, transportation, and related services had been delivered to 548 development projects in 88 less developed countries. WFP resources in 1971–72 amounted to $249 million, of which 72% was in commodities and 28% was in cash and services. Pledges for the WFP for 1973–74 were targeted at $340 milion, and more than $285 million in services, cash, and commodities had been promised by May. The WFP was reported to be sponsoring some 300 projects benefiting more than 11 million people through programs of human resource development (welfare and education), infrastructure development (housing, transport, and community development), and productive projects (land development, agrarian reform, crop and fishery production, and forestry development).

Emergency aid figured prominently in both multilateral and unilateral food assistance programs in 1972–73. Some of the more prominent examples included disaster assistance for earthquake victims in Nicaragua, famine relief for sub-Saharan Africa and certain East African regions, and assistance to Bangladesh, where the effects of civil war were compounded by three years of poor harvests, floods, and other natural disasters. Probably the most impressive aid program in 1973 came in response to the drought that affected over 200,000 sq.mi. in the African interior. Appeals in late 1972 resulted in the shipment of some 600,000 tons of grains by mid-1973, including U.S. shipments of over 150,000 tons of grain sorghum and corn. An FAO report indicated that total food aid represented approximately 15% of official development assistance in 1971. Among donor countries, the U.S. provided 75% of total food aid, followed by Canada (15%), Australia, West Germany, and Japan.

By late summer 1973, the extraordinary need to increase food assistance produced a proposal within the FAO for the creation of a world food security system. The proposal contemplated an expanded food assistance program in the immediate future, together with a coordinated international program to provide for adequate food reserves in sufficient amounts to prevent famine, ensure development, and prevent violent price fluctuations in the world market. The proposal was presented at the September meeting called to discuss the world wheat situation.

The USDA reported that some 15.2 million Americans received food aid in 1973 through food stamp and food distribution programs for needy families. In addition, 2.7 million schoolchildren participated in government-assisted school lunch programs. The total cost of food assistance programs in the year ended June 30, 1973, was reported at slightly more than $4 billion, including $1.4 billion for a wide variety of child nutrition programs; $97 million for the Special Milk Program; $2.2 billion for the Food Stamp Program; and $306 million for direct distribution of food to needy families and institutions. Despite increases in government-assisted food programs in 1973, a study by the Senate Select Committee on Nutrition and Human Needs in early May reported that more than 12 million Americans continued to be malnourished;

"AGRICULTURAL RESEARCH MAGAZINE"

A single subsoil application of herbicide to this cornfield has prevented the growth of witchweed that would otherwise have destroyed the crop. The new technique is made possible by a soil-layering machine, developed by the USDA, that permits the application of herbicides in an established crop and allows for the use of herbicides the crop might not normally tolerate.

the report charged that rising food prices had reduced the effectiveness of federal programs.

With stocks of U.S. grains reduced by heavy commercial demand, the amounts available for shipment under the Food for Peace Program (Public Law 480) were cut by an estimated 40–50% in 1973–74. Supplies available for distribution by voluntary agencies were reduced by an estimated 30 to 40% from a year earlier. Projected shipments of food aid under Title II of the program were valued at $198 million for 1973–74, compared with $403.7 million shipped in 1971–72. In late September, Secretary of State Henry Kissinger told a congressional committee that current allocations of commodities for Public Law 480 programs "will severely limit the capacity of the U.S. to respond to disaster situations."

Marketing and Manufacturing. The value of shipments by U.S. food manufacturers and processors was expected to rise about 6% in 1973, to a total of $99.8 billion. The biggest increases were 19% in the value of cheese, 17% for condensed and evaporated milk, and 10% for chocolate and cocoa products. Shipments by meat and poultry processors, the largest single segment of the food-processing industry, were valued at $29.2 billion, 6% more than in 1972.

According to USDA reports, the marketing bill for U.S. farm products in 1972 totaled $77.2 billion, an increase of slightly more than 2% over 1971. Components included $3.4 billion in profits before taxes, $37.4 billion in labour costs, and $36.4 billion in other costs. Processors accounted for 34.7% of the total; wholesalers for 13.3%; retailers for 29%; and eating places for 23%. Retailers reported sharply reduced profits before taxes in 1972: $266 million, compared with $555 million a year earlier.

In January 1973 the U.S. Food and Drug Administration announced comprehensive and far-reaching changes in food labeling regulations, designed to provide consumers with specific information about the nutritional value of packaged and processed foods. The new regulations required full nutritional labeling on any product for which nutritional claims were made in advertising. It was expected that, although labeling for most foods would remain voluntary, competitive pressures would result in label information on the calorie content and protein, carbohydrate, and fat content. A USDA study of nearly 13,000 shoppers in Ohio found that open dating of perishable food products had reduced the incidence of complaints about spoiled or stale foods by 50%. At the same time, a study of Maryland supermarkets revealed that low-income consumers seldom used unit-pricing.

Following a ten-year effort to create a body of internationally adopted food standards, a substantial number of countries in 1973 accepted the standards developed by the FAO/World Health Organization Codex Alimentarius Commission. Some 60 standards dealing with a variety of canned and processed foods had been submitted to member countries for acceptance.

NORTH AMERICA

United States. *Crops.* The high productive capacity of U.S. farms was again demonstrated in 1973 under somewhat adverse conditions. All crop production rose to a record high index of 119 (1967 = 100), 6 points above the previous record set in 1972. In considerable part this resulted from the official emphasis on planting more acres, utilizing some 25 million ac. that had been previously restricted. There was some drought in the Southwest and the Pacific Northwest. May rains were excessive, especially in the Midwest, sodden fields were planted late, and some late planting or replanting was required in river floodplains and where frost damage occurred. Except for sugar beets and soybeans, yields per acre tended to fall slightly below those of 1971 or 1972. Boxcar shortages continued to be a problem, and scattered fuel shortages appeared as the energy crisis worsened in the fall. Farmers were among those given priority when the government began allocating certain types of fuel in October.

Food-grain production (wheat, rye, and rice) rose 12% to an indicated 57.5 million tons; the production index was 112, compared with only 101 in 1972. The record 1,727,000,000-bu. wheat crop was harvested from 53,718,000 ac., compared with 47,301,000 ac. the previous year. Of the total, winter wheat accounted for 1,291,463 bu., durum for 85,106,000 bu., and spring wheat other than durum for 350,916,000 bu. The spring wheat planting season came late enough for farmers to take advantage of eased acreage restrictions. More than half the crop, some 970 million bu., consisted of hard red winter wheat. The soft red winter wheat crop of 162 million bu. was short, largely

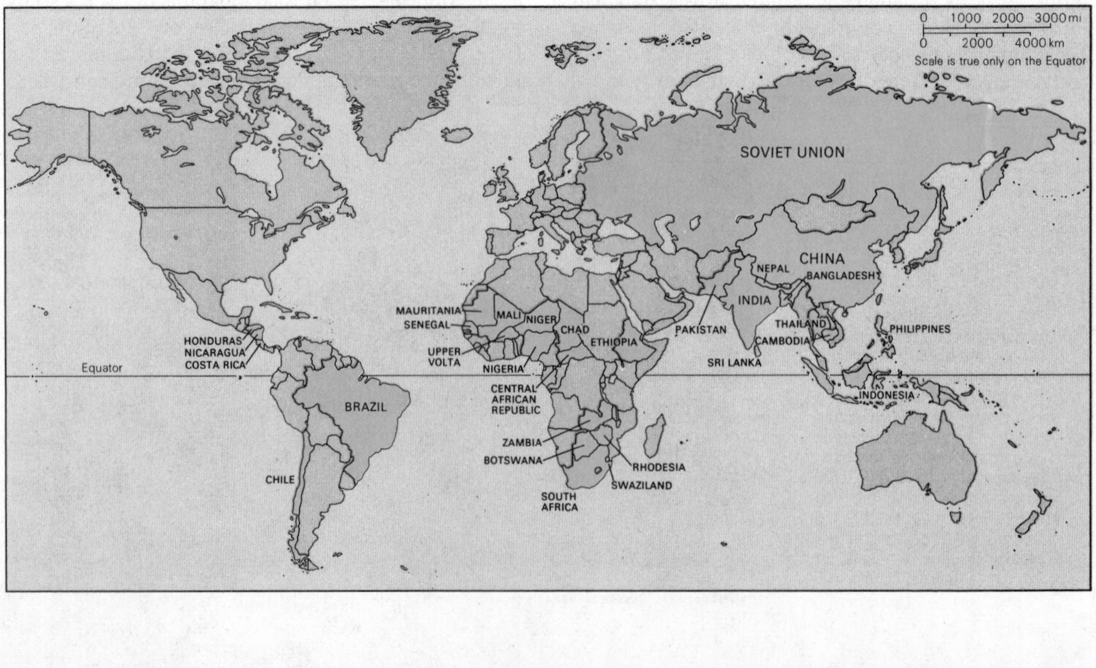

Coloured areas indicate countries where adverse weather led to major agricultural reverses during the first three quarters of 1973. These, together with localized setbacks elsewhere, led to food shortages and worldwide agricultural price inflation.

because wet fields in the Midwest could not be planted in the autumn of 1972. White wheat, both winter and spring, was somewhat affected by drought. The rye crop was indicated at 25,506,000 bu., compared with 29,536,000 bu. the previous year. Rice production was estimated at 95,203,000 cwt., 12% more than in 1972 and the second largest crop on record.

Production of feed grains (corn, sorghum, barley, and oats) was more abundant in all categories. Record corn and sorghum crops were harvested, and the total for the four grains was some 208 million tons, also a record and 4% more than in 1972. Corn was regarded as crucial, not only because of export demand but also because of its close relationship with the livestock economy and hence with inflation and meat shortages. Heroic efforts were made to increase acreage, and 61,479,000 ac. were planted, compared with 57,229,000 ac. the previous year. The yield of 92.4 bu. per ac. was off from the 1972 record of 96.9 bu., but the total crop was indicated at 5,678,141,000 bu., 2% more than in 1972. Sorghum grain production of 971,105,000 bu. was 18% above the 1972 crop. Oat and barley production rose slightly to 702,280,000 bu. and 429,111,000 bu., respectively.

Hay and forage were somewhat affected by the breaking up of land for corn. The indicated index of 103 was slightly below 1972 and 1971. Probable production of all hay was set at 129,501,000 tons, with alfalfa constituting about 60% of the total. With prices high and the government requesting increased plantings, acreage planted to soybeans rose 23% and a record 1,575,000,000-bu. crop was in sight in November. Production of the four oilseed crops (soybeans, cottonseed, peanuts, and flaxseed) added up to a record 4.7 million tons, 19% above 1972. Peanut production was forecast at a record 3,389,000,000 lb., and the flaxseed crop amounted to 15,904,000 bu., compared with 13,909,000 bu. in 1972. Cottonseed production fell 2% to an estimated 5.3 million tons.

The production index for all sugar crops was 124, compared with 139 in 1972. Sugar-beet production fell 12% to an estimated 2.5 million tons, and sugarcane was down 1% to 8,745,000 tons. In a year of very high prices, the cotton crop was smaller, with an index of 176, compared with 181 in 1972. Acreage harvested fell to 12,370,000 ac., but yield rose by 5 lb. per ac.

Tobacco production was estimated at 1,780,000,000 lb., 2% more than in 1972. Production of flue-cured tobacco, prominent in the export market, totaled 1,145,925,000 lb., 13% above a year earlier. Burley was down 17%, while all cigar types rose to 60,022,000 lb. from 53,257,000 lb. in 1972.

WIDE WORLD

U.S. Agriculture Secretary Earl L. Butz answers a question during a Washington press conference called Aug. 11, 1973, to brief newsmen on new crop subsidy legislation.

Production of seven principal processing vegetables was forecast at 10 million tons, 6% above 1972. Only green peas, which were off 4%, failed to exceed the previous crop. Fall potato production was forecast at 253.8 million cwt., 2% more than in 1972; at 50.4 million cwt., the fall crop in the eastern states was down 2%. Sweet potatoes were indicated at 12,486,000 cwt., almost exactly the same as in 1972. Dried beans and peas were both short crops; beans fell to 16.3 million cwt., against 18,015,000 cwt. in 1972, and dried peas totaled only 1,706,000 cwt., compared with 2,103,000 cwt. a year earlier.

The pecan crop was indicated at 262 million lb., 43% larger than the poor crop of 1972 and 6% more than in 1971. Production of filberts, walnuts, and almonds was also higher. Deciduous fruits generally provided larger crops than in 1972, though some areas were hard hit by frost early in the year. The commercial apple crop was forecast at 6,025,200,000 lb., compared with 5,810,000,000 lb. in 1972. Peaches totaled 2,645,600,000 lb., and pear production, at 709,400 tons, was well above the small 1972 crop of 608,330 tons. Plums and prunes for canning rose sharply to 75,000 tons. Sweet cherries were much more abundant in 1973, but tart cherries, hit by late frost, were indicated at 85,000 tons, compared with 135,000 tons in 1972. The large grape harvest of 3,826,000 tons included 900,000 tons of wine varieties from California. The cranberry harvest was indicated at 2,120,000 bbl.

Preliminary citrus estimates included an orange crop of 192.2 million boxes, the second largest crop on record. Grapefruit was indicated at a record 65.8 million boxes, but lemons were down 3% and tangerines were moderately lower.

Table IV. Cotton Production of the Principal Producing Countries

In 000 480-lb. bales net

Country	Indicated 1973*	1972	Average 1966–70	Average 1960–64
Argentina	640	580	460	552
Brazil	2,900	2,950	2,680	2,235
China	7,000	6,500	7,780	5,040
Colombia	595	625	527	335
Egypt	2,400	2,400	2,187	2,037
Greece	620	635	440	337
India	5,400	5,150	4,830	4,741
Iran	1,000	955	636	494
Mexico	1,550	1,790	1,980	2,206
Pakistan	2,900	3,225	2,364	1,656
Peru	390	320	427	632
Spain	250	225	312	427
Sudan	1,100	900	1,019	675
Syria	700	735	666	656
Turkey	2,300	2,495	1,844	1,091
U.S.S.R.	11,500	11,200	9,540	7,370
United States	13,123	13,702	9,629	14,795

*Preliminary.
Source: U.S. Department of Agriculture, Foreign Agricultural Service.

Table V. Orange (Including Tangerine) Production in Principal Producing Countries

In 000 metric tons

Country	1972*	1971	Average 1960–64
Algeria	451	445	402
Argentina	1,029	976	743
Brazil	2,400	2,760	964
Greece	480	390	274
Israel	1,244	1,145	592
Italy	1,581	1,760	1,099
Japan	3,648	2,896	1,373
Mexico	1,270	1,114	842
Morocco	854	821	555
South Africa	545	514	500
Spain	2,511	2,179	1,835
Turkey	535	510	305
United States	9,263	7,889	5,231

*Preliminary.
Source: U.S. Department of Agriculture, Foreign Agricultural Service.

World Production and Trade of Principal Grains

In 000 metric tons

	Wheat			Barley			Oats			Rye			Corn (Maize)			Rice		
	Production		Imports— Exports+	Production		Imports— Exports+	Production		Imports— Exports+	Production		Imports— Exports+	Production		Imports— Exports+	Production		Imports— Exports+
	1948–52 average	1972	1969–72 average	1948–52 average	1972	1969–72 average	1948–52 average	1972	1969–72 average	1948–52 average	1972	1969–72 average	1948–52 average	1972	1969–72 average	1948–52 average	1972	1969–72 average
World total	171,647	339,813	−57,142* +49,547*	59,022	148,521	−8,974* +9,408*	61,208	51,459	−1,380* +1,404*	37,729	28,238	−c.570* +c.750*	139,651	303,577	−27,441* +29,880*	167,479	296,768	−7,109* +7,285*
EUROPE																		
Austria	348	863	−32 +c.5	210	977	−76	274	255	−29	343	402	−3*	120	726	−56	—	—	−39*
Belgium	525	950	−1,114† +207†‡	244	639	−784† +64†‡	483	249	−73†	221	c.73	−9† +2†‡	3	c.17§	−1,374† +423†	—	—	−54† +15†‡
Bulgaria	1,776	3,582	−227‡ +224‡	332	1,427	−64‡	148	75	−1‡	240	21	—	720	2,974	−42‡ +274‡	37	60	−6‡
Czechoslovakia	1,493	c.4,200	−1,152*	1,046	c.2,500	−156* +38‡	961	c.850	−1‡	1,110	c.530	−81‡	316	c.540	−161‡	—	—	−80‡
Denmark	285	602	−5 +35	1,708	5,590	−154 +245	922	638	−25 +14	365	162	−19	—	—	−244	—	—	−7‡
Finland	263	463	−21* +89‡	201	1,140	−15‡ +10‡	718	1,245	+24‡	201	116	−14	—	—	−14	—	—	−16‡
France	7,791	18,123	−414* +4,262*	1,534	10,416	−3‡ +2,980*	3,392	2,463	+117*	573	331	+31*	452	8,610	−456* +2,916*	46	52	−109 +13
Germany, East	1,243	2,744	−1,703‡ +12‡	593	2,592	−508‡	1,188	890	−3‡	2,516	1,904	−70‡	5	c.14§	−363‡	—	—	−38‡
Germany, West	2,669	6,608	−2,433 +1,133‡	1,402	5,997	−2,433 +350	2,523	2,887	−480 +12	3,066	2,914	−73 +135	20	564	−2,749 +156	—	—	−161 +22‡
Greece	894	1,773	−42* +31‡	211	864	−15‡	119	107	—	47	c.9	—	225	579	−269*	39	74	−2‡ +6‡
Hungary	1,909	4,087	−240‡ +484‡	654	803	−34‡ +10‡	216	66	−2‡	732	173	−5‡ +25‡	2,068	5,542	−1‡ +154‡	40	61	−20‡ +1‡
Ireland	327	c.251	−150	163	c.955	−89 +1‡	616	c.151	−10	4	c.1	—	—	—	−170	—	—	−3‡
Italy	7,170	9,412	−1,371 +205	258	388	−1,121	495	461	−206	123	50	—	2,306	4,802	−4,474 +14	723	751	−3‡ +292
Netherlands, The	324	673	−1,501* +575*	201	340	−179* +136*	419	140	−91* +79*	455	151	−36* +49*	26	c.4§	−2,396* +426‡	—	—	−67* +21‡
Norway	58	c.10	−381	109	522	−140 +4‡	170	268	—	2	5	−33*	—	—	−97	—	—	−6‡
Poland	1,833	5,147	−1,369	1,061	2,750	−823* +98*	2,238	3,260	−1‡ +11‡	6,374	8,149	−64‡ +54‡	4	c.13§	−255‡	—	—	−67
Portugal	499	585	−278	96	55	−40‡	124	71	—	162	167	—	421	517	−496	114	163	−23‡
Romania	2,778‖	c.6,100	+525¶	412‖	c.720	—	369‖	c.150	—	177‖	c.55	—	2,495‖	c.8,800	+456‡	35‖	c.66	−32¶
Spain	3,625	4,563	−1‡ +405‡	1,909	4,358	−61 +137‡	519	440	+40‡	482	263	—	520	1,921	−2,189 +4‡	280	346	+55
Sweden	677	1,150	−33 +244	231	1,883	−7* +156‡	804	1,629	−1* +306	258	363	−5‡ +57	—	—	−31	—	—	−12‡
Switzerland	260	400	−457	55	168	−420	68	27	−170	34	55	−23	6	c.100	−204	—	—	−28‡
U.S.S.R.	31,035	85,800	−942‡ +5,339‡	6,354♀	36,800	+626‡	13,005♀	14,000	+8‡	17,812	9,600	+197‡	5,751‖	9,800	−401‡ +264‡	202♀	1,600	−325‡ +6‡
United Kingdom	2,397	4,760	−4,617 +8‡	2,061	9,238	−922 +62	2,852	1,255	−22 +60‡	52	20	−18‡	—	—	−3,095 +6‡	—	—	−129
Yugoslavia	2,171	4,862	−201* +2‡	323	487	−74‡ +1‡	286	267	−9‡	248	120	—	3,078	7,906	−5‡ +226*	5	c.35§	−41‡
ASIA																		
Burma	4	c.50‡	—	—	—	—	—	—	—	—	—	—	30‖	73§	+10*	5,481	7,560	+667*
Cambodia (Khmer Rep.)	—	—	—	—	—	—	—	—	—	—	—	—	57	80	+48‡	1,635	1,927	+119*
China	15,913	c.32,000§	−4,090‡	c.12,360	c.19,200§	+1‡	c.1,540	c.2,500	—	—	—	—	c.14,082	c.29,500§	−15¶ +2‡	55,950δ	c.101,000	−5¶ +850¶
India	6,087	26,477	−2,830*	2,384	2,501	—	—	—	—	—	—	—	2,165	c.5,300	−33¶	33,383	c.59,000	−266 +21‡
Indonesia	—	—	—	—	—	—	—	—	—	—	—	—	1,535δ	2,269	+155¶	9,441δ	19,500	−780‡
Iran	1,879‖	4,500	−1¶	767	1,009	—	—	—	—	—	—	—	6δ	c.35§	—	424	c.1,200	−2¶
Iraq	448	2,625	−349* +7‡	722	980	+59‡	—	—	—	—	—	—	14	c.5§	−2‡	203	268	−1‡ +1‡
Japan	1,375	264	−4,628*	2,020	324	−770*	119	c.66	−127*	6	c.1	−82*	57	c.30§	−5,505* +4‡	12,736	15,450	−29* +497‡
Korea, South	c.139	241	−1,499	c.846	1,965	−59‡	4	—	—	36	c.18	—	14	c.65§	−164‡	c.3,385	5,472	−700‡
Lebanon	51	c.50	−307*	25	c.10§	−98* +1¶	2	c.2	—	—	—	—	12	c.1	−81‡ +1¶	—	—	−23‡
Malaysia	—	—	−305‡	—	—	—	—	—	−6‡	—	—	—	8	c.11§	−158‡	670□	1,909	−342‡ +5‡
Pakistan	3,664	6,891	−c.600*	134	c.95	—	—	—	—	—	—	—	381	760	−c.5‡	1,194	c.3,600	+c.150*
Philippines	—	—	−587	—	—	—	—	—	−3‡	—	—	—	695	1,973	−13‡	2,767	4,958	+1‡
Syria	761	1,808	−327	321	710	−29‡ +163*	6	2	−1‡	—	—	—	31	c.8	—	13	—	−35‡
Thailand	—	—	−55‡	—	—	—	—	—	—	—	—	—	31	1,700	+1,551*	6,846	11,800	+1,439
Turkey	4,770	12,085	−508	2,270	3,700	—	326	390	—	500	740	—	747	1,060	—	109	203	−8‡
Vietnam, South	—	—	—	—	—	−4¶	—	—	—	—	—	—	30δ	c.31§	−82¶	2,395□	6,215	−342
AFRICA																		
Algeria	996	1,692	−421¶	808	720	—	137	39	+10¶	—	—	—	6	c.4§	−8¶	—	c.5§	−2¶
Egypt	1,111	1,616	−1,342	123	107	—	—	—	—	—	—	—	1,378	2,417	−61	971	c.2,600	+647*
Kenya	101	c.210§	+34‡	8	c.13§	—	5	c.4§	—	—	—	—	574◇	1,665	−7‡ +97‡	c.6	28§	−1‡ +2‡
Morocco	786	2,184	−381	1,483	2,466	−3¶ +133¶	51	c.20	+1¶	4	c.3	—	302	368	−2¶ +34¶	8δ	c.45§	+10‡
South Africa	555	1,615	−61‡	41‖	36	−8‡	79‖	103	−2‡	10‖	7	−2‡	2,629	9,630	−256‡ +1,143*	c.6	c.2▲	−82* +2‡
Tunisia	452	914	−348* +3‡	218	236	−38‡	14	35	—	—	—	—	—	—	−8‡	—	—	−1‡
NORTH AND CENTRAL AMERICA																		
Canada	13,443	14,514	+11,030	4,245	11,287	+2,565*	6,220	4,630	+135*	469	344	+161*	388	2,657	−459 +5‡	—	—	−45‡
Mexico	534	1,879	+127*	160	294	−1¶	47	34§	−3¶	—	—	—	3,090	c.9,000	−262* +366*	173	c.420	−11‡
United States	31,065	42,041	−24 +16,762[+]	5,843	9,221	−251 +915	18,970	10,088	−32 +158	524	750	−12 +42	74,308	141,053	−48 +15,910[+]	1,925	3,863	−10‡ +1,809
SOUTH AMERICA																		
Argentina	5,175	8,100	−196‡ +1,819*	656	880	+125*	743	566	+153*	526	690	+15*	2,839	5,860	+5,128*	137	294	+87‡
Bolivia	37	62§	−31‡	39δ	69§	—	2δ	c.11▲	—	—	—	—	163□	293§	—	20δ	c.80§	—
Brazil	498	c.800	−1,952	15	c.26	−37*	9	c.27	−20*	17	c.20	—	5,841	c.14,000	−2‡ +1,136*	2,921	c.7,600	+105*
Chile	928	1,195	−263*	79	139	+10‡	80	111	—	5	12	—	68	283	−255‡	75	67§	−8‡
Colombia	124	90	−294*	50	110	−34¶	—	—	−8¶	—	—	—	753	970	−2¶ +5¶	248	c.940	+8‡
Peru	146	141	−667	208	c.160	−13	c.2	c.1	−1‡	2	c.1	—	275	643	−4‡ +1‡	191	477	−18‡
Uruguay	469	180	+68¶	23	28	−1¶ +2¶	44	57	—	—	—	—	141	141	—	41	128	+58‡
Venezuela	5	c.1	−660*	—	—	—	—	—	−8*	—	—	—	303	737	−110‡	41	128	−2‡ +35
OCEANIA																		
Australia	5,161	6,613	+7,456	531	1,660	−15‡ +1,059	560	562	+360	12	c.20	—	126	214	−1‡	63	252	−2‡ +135
New Zealand	139	420	−40*	49	315	—	49	54	—	—	—	—	10	65§	—	—	—	−3¶

Note: (—) indicates quantity nil or negligible; (c.) indicates provisional or estimated. *1969–71 average. †Belgium-Luxembourg economic union. ‡1969–70 average. §1971. ‖Average of 4 years. ¶1969. ♀1950. δAverage of 3 years. □Average of 2 years. ◇1948. ▲1966. [+]Including foreign aid shipments.

Sources: FAO *Monthly Bulletin of Agricultural Economics and Statistics*; FAO *Production Yearbook 1971*; FAO *Trade Yearbook 1971*.

(M. C. MacDONALD)

Livestock. Record high prices for livestock and meats in 1973 resulted partly from an unexpected but moderate reduction in market supplies but chiefly from unprecedented consumer demand. Meat boycotts, severe weather, muddy feedlots, price ceilings on red meats, and rising feed costs were all part of the picture. There were some 122 million head of cattle and calves on farms and ranches on Jan. 1, 1973, over 4 million head more than a year earlier and 12.6 million head more than in early 1968, when the current expansion began. Further buildup was anticipated in 1973, though cow slaughter during the first half of the year was somewhat higher than in 1971 and 1972. The calf crop was about 4% above 1972. Choice feeder steer calves at Kansas City brought an average of $64 per hundredweight in July, whereas choice-fed steer prices at Omaha for the same month averaged $48.05. This negative spread, combined with high and rising feed prices, was cause for concern to feedlot operators, and replacements were down 11% during the second quarter. Prices did not move up very much after the removal of price ceilings in September, then actually relaxed as more cattle moved to market.

The total number of milk cows declined 2% from a year earlier as a result of high prices for slaughter and high feed costs. Milk production was expected to be down more than 1% from the 1972 total of 120,300,000,000 lb. Farmers received an average of $7.92 per hundredweight for fluid market milk during September, $1.35 more than a year earlier.

Hog producers altered their early intentions to increase production in 1973, apparently in response to sharply higher feed prices, disaffection with retail price ceilings, and growing uncertainties in the livestock and feed market. Instead of rising 6%, farrowings in the December 1972–May 1973 period remained about the same as a year earlier. Unfavourable weather in late winter and early spring reduced the number of pigs saved, and by June the crop was reported to be down 6%. One result was that during part of July and August barrows and gilts topped the fed cattle market at Omaha; during the last week of July they averaged some $51.50 per hundredweight, $23 above a year earlier and $11 above the preceding month. They were not fed to heavier weights, and yielded an average of about 17 lb. of lard, compared with 30 lb. per hog in the early 1960s. The corn–hog price ratio continued to be favourable, at a level of more than 20 to 1. Feed and protein meal supplies were expected to be available at somewhat lower prices in 1973–74, and a rush to buy feeder pigs began.

The 1973 lamb crop declined 9% to 11.2 million head. There were 6% fewer ewes on hand for the January inventory, and unfavourable weather at lambing time resulted in further losses. Prices were favourable but not as strong as for beef and pork. Wool prices were excellent, but it was doubtful whether this would be sufficient to reverse the declining trend of sheep production.

The nation's egg-laying flock averaged some 285 million hens in mid-1973, down 5% from a year earlier and the fewest since 1960. Egg production through August totaled 123 million cases, 7.5 million cases below the comparable period of 1972. Prices to producers fluctuated wildly as a result of high demand, smaller supplies, and controls; in August, they reached the highest level in many years. Hatchery production of broiler-type chicks declined about 2% from the 3,100,000,000 raised in 1972. Outbreaks of Newcastle disease were especially severe in California, but the final quarantines were removed in August. Turkey production was expected to total a record 132 million birds. Honey prices rose above 40 cents per pound (wholesale), although the 1973 U.S. crop was estimated at a high 240,830,000 lb.

Farm Prices, Costs, Income, and Finances. In September 1973 prices received by U.S. farmers stood at a composite index of 191, compared with 129 a year earlier. The index for all crops was 183, up from 117 in 1972. Livestock and products rose from 138 in September 1972 to 198 a year later, with prices of meat animals up sharply from 152 to 218. Food prices soared and pushed living costs to record levels; in August 1973 it cost $135.10 to buy goods and services that cost $100 in 1967. During August the price of food rose 6.1% on a seasonally adjusted basis, the greatest increase in any one month since seasonal ad-

Table VI. Honey Production in Specified Countries

In 000 lb.

Country	1972*	Average 1964–68
Argentina	50,300	61,288
Australia†	44,621	41,366
Austria	4,400	11,394
Brazil	13,900	16,876
Bulgaria	16,000	7,932
Canada	50,599	41,884
Chile	15,430	12,937
China	35,502	29,837
Czechoslovakia	17,000	13,497
France	22,046	30,393
Germany, West	26,450	24,074
Greece	21,391	17,910
Guatemala	8,206	5,145
Hungary	16,800	14,427
Italy	13,404	16,316
Japan	13,227	16,043
Mexico	85,098	68,036
New Zealand	12,540	10,986
Poland	22,046	16,076
Romania	18,000	15,291
Spain	19,908	22,084
Turkey	36,073	25,386
U.S.S.R.	236,000	462,525
United Kingdom	8,267	7,514
United States	214,584	222,649
Yugoslavia	7,866	8,073
World total	1,049,719	1,243,951

*Preliminary.
†Crop year beginning July of previous year.
Source: U.S. Department of Agriculture, Foreign Agricultural Service.

Hatchery workers in Ranger, Ga., dump live baby chicks in drums to be suffocated. Rising prices for soybeans, the principal chicken feed, could not be recovered on the poultry market because of 1973 U.S. government price policies.

UPI COMPIX

justments were first computed in 1947. Meat, poultry, and fish prices together rose 16.4% (seasonally adjusted) and were 40.7% higher than in August 1972.

The parity index of production costs paid by farmers for commodities and services, interest, taxes, and wages was 150 in September, compared with 128 a year earlier. The index for feeder livestock was 195, while feeds rose to 178 from 108 a year earlier. Farm machinery, interest, taxes, and wage rates all increased during 1973. A total of 4,989,700 workers were employed on farms in October 1973. At that time the per-hour wage rate without board or room averaged $1.97, 8% above a year earlier, and the rate per month with house and other allowances was $395, up from $363. Sales of farm machinery rose.

The revised parity ratio, an overall measure of farmers' purchasing power, rose to 127 from 101 a year earlier. Farmers received about 44% of the "all food" market basket at midyear, compared with 40% in 1972. Through the second quarter of 1973 the index of retail food prices stood at 138.6, while the more inclusive consumer price index was 131.5. Based on the first six months of the year, gross farm income was projected at about $80 billion for 1973. Farm production expenses were forecast at about $57 billion and farmers' realized net income at approximately $23 billion, compared with $19 billion in 1972. In 1972, 10% of all farms had sales valued at $40,000 or more, whereas 1,070,000 farms, or 36.2% of the total, had sales of less than $2,500.

The estimated value of farm assets in 1973 was $370.6 billion, up from $339.2 billion a year earlier; real estate accounted for $251.4 billion. The average value of farm real estate per acre rose 13% during the year ended March 1, 1973. Farm debt also continued its long upward trend; mortgage debt rose to $33.9 billion from $31.3 billion and short-term debt (excluding Commodity Credit Corporation loans) to $38.1 billion from $35.6 billion.

Trade and Stocks. U.S. farm-product exports in fiscal 1973 advanced a remarkable 60% in value to an all-time high of approximately $12.9 billion. Grains and grain products accounted for over half the increase in value, and soybeans and products for one-fourth. Only dairy products and vegetable oils fell below the value of fiscal 1972 shipments. In total, farm exports accounted for the output of 65 million ac., or one of every five acres harvested.

Agricultural imports into the U.S. also rose sharply, advancing 21% to a new record of $7,320,000,000, but only 6% was accounted for by increased volume. Led by beef and veal, supplementary imports rose 19% to $4,707,000,000. Complementary imports were up 21%, with big increases in coffee, cocoa and products, and raw silk.

U.S. stocks of agricultural products in late 1972 had seemed so large that official restrictions were continued on wheat production and efforts were made to reduce feed-grain acreage. Even in 1973, major U.S. stocks seemed seriously depleted not in relation to probable domestic demand but only in relation to possible crisis demand from other areas. For example, soybean carry-over stock in September 1973 was 60 million bu., the smallest since 1966. Nevertheless, with a large new crop almost assured, export controls on soybeans, cottonseed, and related products, imposed in June when prices reached $11 a bushel, were officially lifted as of October 1.

Legislation and Administration. Government action in 1973 was highlighted by passage of the Agriculture and Consumer Protection Act, which set national farm policy through 1977. Its most radical departure from previous legislation was its provision for a new system of price guarantees for wheat, feed grains, and cotton. The new legislation contemplated that farmers' prices would be determined by market forces and that deficiency payments would be made only if prices fell below the target price. Total payments under the new act were limited to $20,000 per person, as compared with a limit of $55,000 per crop under the previous program. The production adjustment authority was continued, although the secretary of agriculture had announced there would be no set-aside acres for 1974-crop programs. The Rural Environmental Conservation Program, a long-term, cost-sharing conservation program, was established to replace the Rural Environmental Assistance Program (REAP) and the Water Bank program.

Public Law 480 was extended for four years, with the proviso that no agricultural commodities could go to North Vietnam unless Congress specifically authorized assistance to that country. The secretary of agriculture was ordered to establish disaster reserve inventories of up to 75 million bu. of wheat, feed grains, and soybeans. Several controversial amendments were made to the Food Stamp Program. Con-

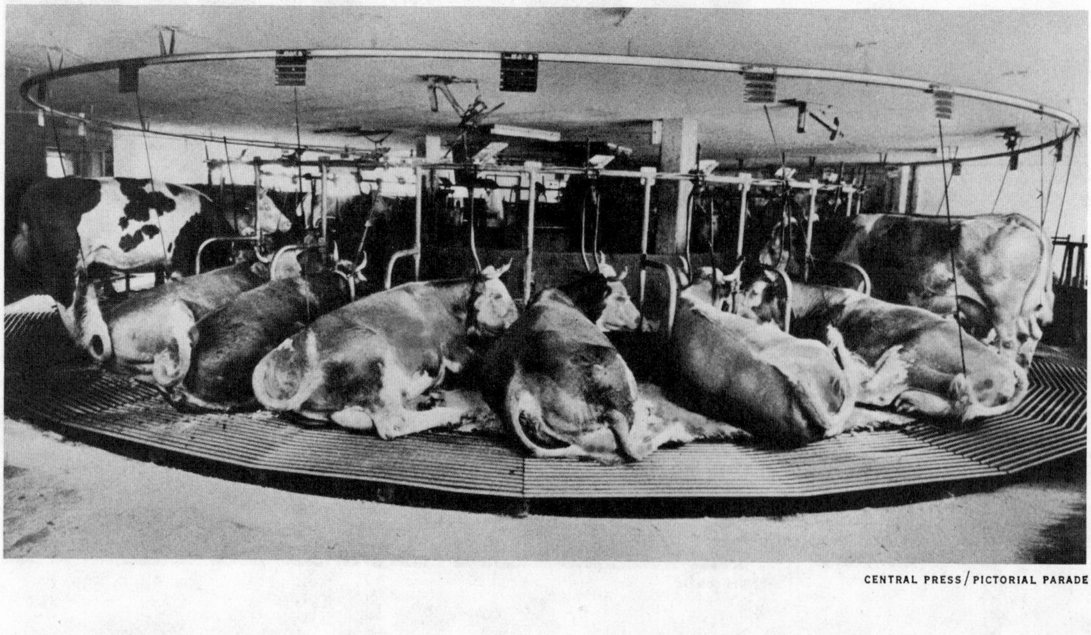

Contented cows on a farm at St. Ursanne, Switz., share a "merry-go-round" stable. Their owner, likewise contented, claimed the new arrangement had reduced his labour by 50%.

CENTRAL PRESS/PICTORIAL PARADE

Table VII. Poultry Meat Production in Selected Countries*

In 000,000 lb.

Country	1972†	1971	1970	Average 1955–59
Austria	100	98	89	4
Belgium-Luxembourg	239	246	248	95
Canada	976	945	980	428
Denmark	185	176	174	58
France	1,389	1,279	1,235	511
Germany, West	576	600	569	172
Greece	183	165	147	36
Italy	1,691	1,471	1,334	215
Japan	1,369	1,183	1,074	—
Netherlands, The	730	712	679	96
Poland	351	305	282	109
Spain	725	702	697	—
United Kingdom	1,494	1,357	1,243	455
United States	11,040	10,531	10,433	5,480

*On ready-to-cook basis (70% of live weight).
†Preliminary.
Source: U.S. Department of Agriculture, Foreign Agricultural Service.

Table VIII. Egg Production in Specified Countries

In 000,000

Country	1972*	1971	1970
Argentina	3,396	3,120	2,952
Australia	3,011	2,909	2,635
Belgium-Luxembourg	4,450	4,344	4,413
Brazil	10,290	10,092	9,714
Canada	5,609	5,876	5,888
Czechoslovakia	4,050	3,996	3,733
France	11,800	11,500	11,400
Germany, East	4,460	4,504	4,442
Germany, West	16,143	15,378	15,377
Hungary	3,300	3,475	3,280
Italy	10,612	10,390	11,070
Japan	30,400	31,067	29,975
Mexico	7,100	6,800	6,570
Netherlands, The	4,421	4,367	4,644
Poland	7,476	7,080	6,941
Romania	4,200	3,984	3,537
U.S.S.R.	48,300	45,100	40,700
United Kingdom†	14,652	14,916	15,084
United States	69,492	70,152	68,532

*Preliminary.
†Year beginning June 1 of year shown.
Source: U.S. Department of Agriculture, Foreign Agricultural Service.

Table IX. Milk Cows and Milk Production in Specified Countries

Country	Number of milk cows in 000			Milk production in 000,000 lb.		
	1972*	1971	Average 1961–65	1972*	1971	Average 1961–65
Australia	2,566	2,600	3,190	15,748	16,133	15,244
Austria	902	911	1,122	7,352	7,255	6,743
Belgium	1,025	1,031	1,024	8,322	7,961	8,664
Canada	2,211	2,255	2,930	17,709	17,775	18,404
Denmark	1,122	1,105	1,428	10,558	10,051	11,713
France	7,500	7,350	9,409	64,374	60,933	54,162
Germany, West	5,442	5,489	5,852	47,376	46,661	45,368
Greece	1,018	988	434	3,238	3,076	1,159
Ireland	1,895	1,782	1,373	8,639	8,132	6,458
Italy	3,165	3,214	3,448	21,164	20,613	21,872
Japan	1,111	1,139	717	10,884	10,626	5,976
Netherlands, The	1,970	1,890	1,701	20,002	18,466	15,578
New Zealand	2,255	2,195	2,007	13,820	13,521	12,302
Norway	414	414	567	4,004	4,012	3,666
Sweden	740	729	1,180	6,552	6,347	8,446
Switzerland	873	869	926	7,343	7,011	6,837
United Kingdom	4,696	4,515	4,202	29,985	28,074	24,791
United States	11,710	11,842	16,195	120,278	118,532	125,660

*Preliminary.
Source: U.S. Department of Agriculture, Foreign Agricultural Service.

gress rejected the administration's proposal that the aged, blind, and disabled no longer be eligible for food stamps, since the Supplemental Security Income program provided for cash payments instead. Food stamp eligibility was extended to drug addicts and alcoholics in approved programs. The administration took a number of actions to expand supplies, including suspension of meat import quotas early in the year. Wide and erratic fluctuations in the commodities futures markets (particularly in grains) prompted Congress to begin investigating their operations.

Canada. Canadian farmers experienced one of their best years in 1973, despite some transportation difficulties. Demand was strong for the grains of the Prairie Provinces and the products of the flourishing livestock industry. Farming expenses increased, but gross incomes also rose sharply.

The Canadian Wheat Board recommended that the western area in wheat be increased by about 30%, but wheat acreage as a whole rose only 16%. Dry weather in July and an August frost did some damage, and an August survey indicated that Canada's wheat crop would be about 604.4 million bu., 13% above the 533 million bu. of 1972 but 2% below the 1962–71 average. As of July 31, stocks were only 366 million bu., down 37% from a year earlier and 42% below the ten-year average. It appeared that exports would be below the 798 million-bu. record of 1972–73. In October a new wheat deal with China was announced, calling for up to 224 million bu. over a three-year period beginning January 1974. The initial price for wheat delivered to elevator set a new high of Can$2.25 per bushel.

As of mid-August the barley crop was estimated at 484 million bu., down 7% from 1972. The prospective oat harvest was 333 million bu., 11% above a year earlier. Oilseed crops were somewhat reduced; rapeseed acreage declined 2% and the harvest, initially estimated at 55.3 million bu., might fall lower because of August frost. Flaxseed acreage rose 17%, but the crop was down from 9 million bu. to 8.6 million bu. Sunflower acreage was down about 40%. Oilseed exports rose rather sharply in 1972–73; rapeseed exports totaled 1,247,000 tons.

In August the Canadian government put cattle, beef, hogs, and pork under export control for an indefinite period. Sales of cattle and calves accounted for about one-fourth of all farm cash income. Slaughter for 1973 was expected to be 4–6% higher than in 1972. Herds were still being increased, particularly in western Canada. Exports of feeder cattle to U.S. feedlots totaled 56,688 head in 1972, the highest level since 1968. Hogs totaled about 7 million head in March 1973, 2% below a year earlier. Early farrowings in 1973 declined about 2% but spring and summer farrowings were expected to be up as much as 4%.

WESTERN EUROPE

The first year of the enlarged EEC saw much discussion and no little criticism—especially of spiraling expenditures and the administration of funds by EEC institutions. With consumer food costs rising, massive export subsidies designed to dispose of agricultural surpluses came under fire, much of it aimed at a 200,000-ton butter sale to the U.S.S.R. at a subsidy cost of over $1,800 per metric ton. A request for 880 million units of account (one unit equal to U.S. $120 to $125) in the new budget was largely to cover the cost of disposing of the butter surplus, as well as some wheat and olive oil surpluses and higher support prices in 1973–74.

Production in 1973 was generally good, with surpluses in dairy products and some grains. Grain production in Western Europe was forecast at about 131 million metric tons but, because of expanded consumption, 1974 imports were expected to surpass the 1973 net of approximately 25 million metric tons. Increased wheat imports were forecast, especially of durum. Coarse grain production showed some improvement. France was anticipating a record corn crop, and record grain production was indicated for West Germany.

In February the U.K., Ireland, and Denmark took the first steps toward changing from their comparatively liberal agricultural systems to the more protective EEC system. Bad weather and lower acreage reduced Ireland's 1972–73 grain crop to 1.3 million metric tons, 13% below the previous year. About 70% of the total was barley, which was expected to support an expanding livestock industry. Grain imports, especially of corn and sorghum, rose markedly.

Storms at harvest time lowered the U.K. wheat crop from an estimated 5 million tons to about 4,560,000 tons and the barley crop from an estimated 9.5 million tons to about 8,930,000. The rapeseed crop rose sharply to about 26,000 long tons from 13,000 long tons in 1972. It had been an insignificant crop as recently as 1968, and the high EEC intervention price

—about 35% above that received by U.K. producers—appeared to have been a factor in encouraging planting.

High prices cut the cost of the 1972–73 agricultural support program in the U.K. from an early estimate of £400 million to £270 million. Most fresh foods were exempted from price controls under Stage One of the government's anti-inflation program, and by February 1973 the Food Price Index showed a 10% increase over the preceding 12 months and a 6.6% increase over the preceding 6 months. More strict Stage Two controls were imposed in February; prices on processed foods could be raised only if higher costs of raw materials made operations uneconomic for manufacturers of semiprocessed foodstuffs. Increases were soon granted on some meat products, however, and in March they were permitted on eggs and some additional meat products, including bacon.

Red meat production in the EEC countries was off somewhat in 1972, although world production rose 1%, from 144,300,000,000 lb. in 1971 to 146,000,000,000 lb. Australia and Eastern Europe showed the largest increases. The European beef shortage and higher prices continued into the second half of 1973. For the original Six, fat cattle prices in 1972 rose about 38% and wholesale beef prices were up about 28%. In the U.K. fat cattle prices rose 55% and beef prices, 44%. In an effort to increase beef production, the EEC authorized premium payments to certain owners of dairy herds who converted to meat production. An outbreak of swine vesicular disease in the U.K. was blamed on illegally imported pork. There were more than 80 outbreaks after the first incident, and 43,000 pigs were destroyed. Outbreaks in several other European countries were reported. (*See* VETERINARY MEDICINE.)

World production of milk increased about 2% over 1971, but in Western Europe the magnitude of increase was closer to 4% and that area again was a principal surplus producer. Despite high internal prices and concern about rising living costs, the EEC agricultural policy for poultry and most other products remained unchanged; imports were limited and exports subsidized. Export subsidies were also retained on several selected types of fresh fruits and nuts. As of June 1973, the subsidy for oranges was eliminated and peaches were added to the list.

A record West German grain crop of 21 million metric tons was harvested in 1973 from 13 million ac., 47,000 ac. less than in 1972. Mixed feed production in West Germany rose 8% to a record 10.7 million tons, and mixed feeds for cattle and calves increased by 17%. It was expected that 9 million to 10 million metric tons of soft wheat would be denatured for feedstuffs in Western Europe in 1973–74. A special levy arrangement in effect since 1967 for feed grains imported into Italy by sea was to be progressively reduced by 1977, placing Italy's prices on a plane with those of other EEC members. Adverse spring weather reduced Italy's 1973 almond harvest to an estimated 8,000 short tons (kernel-weight basis), the smallest crop in decades, but prospects for the filbert crop were outstanding.

The 1973–74 Spanish citrus crop was estimated at 3.3 million metric tons, 22% above the previous year. Export shipments from the 1972–73 crop exceeded 1.8 million tons. Olive oil production for 1973–74 was expected to rise at least 9%; consumption of olive oil declined, although consumption of seed oil, mostly soybean oil, rose 13%. Oilseed support prices were increased, and growers received a 50% subsidy on seed used in planting. Weather damage during the bloom period reduced Spain's almond crop to about 44,000 tons. The U.S. imported 175 tons of Spanish table grapes for the first time in 38 years. Spain began an all-out effort to increase domestic livestock production, including substantial imports of breeding stock and feed grains.

Deciduous fruit production in Greece was estimated to be 10–20% more abundant than in 1972, but prospects for nonirrigated vine crops were diminished by extremely high temperatures during a short period in July. Acreage planted to sugar beets was increased by 18%.

Portugal's 1973 processing-tomato crop was estimated at 1 million metric tons, 20% more than in 1972. Processors were paying growers about U.S. $23.60 per short ton for first-quality tomatoes. In 1972, 27% of Portugal's exports of tomato paste went to the U.S.

EASTERN EUROPE AND THE U.S.S.R.

Eastern Europe. Early indications were that the 1973 wheat crop in Eastern Europe might approximate the 30.5 million tons of 1972, with larger crops in the north offsetting smaller production in the southern countries. Feed-grain production was expected to surpass the 54.8 million-ton record crop of 1972. Nevertheless, imports of as much as 5 million tons of wheat and 3.2 million tons of feed grains might be required.

Poland appeared likely to reap an excellent grain harvest. Sown acreages were increased some 10 to 20% over 1972, and a minimum of 21 million tons was forecast. Even so, as much as 3 million tons of grain would have to be imported in fiscal 1974, partly to provide high-quality bread wheat and durum but mostly to serve the thriving livestock industry. Based on favourable yield reports, estimates of the 1973 grain crop in Czechoslovakia indicated that it might surpass the 1971 record of 8.8 million tons.

East Germany continued to shift emphasis from grain culture to intensive livestock production. By 1971 the grain area on state and collective farms had declined to 2,321,000 ac. from a prewar base of 3,150,000 ac. At the same time, the number of cattle had reached 5,292,000 head, hogs 9,995,000 head, and poultry 43,342,000. Private lands had largely been reorganized into state and collective farms. Recent data

Table X. Eastern European Production, Consumption, and Net Trade of Grains, Oilseed Feeds, and Meat

In 000 metric tons

Item	Grains*			Oilseed feeds†			Meat‡		
	Northern countries§	Southern countries‖	Total East Europe	Northern countries§	Southern countries‖	Total East Europe	Northern countries§	Southern countries‖	Total East Europe
Production									
Average, 1966–70	30,435	40,032	70,467	496	855	1,351	3,508	2,401	5,909
Projected 1975	36,815	47,837	84,652	596	1,208	1,804	4,339	3,177	7,516
Projected 1980	41,426	52,856	94,285	658	1,548	2,206	4,973	3,769	8,742
Consumption									
Average, 1966–70	36,460	38,417	74,877	1,492	1,253	2,745	3,487	2,005	5,492
Projected 1975	43,401	45,192	88,593	2,460	1,955	4,415	4,235	2,633	6,868
Projected 1980	47,081	50,184	97,265	3,196	2,602	5,798	4,865	3,193	8,058
Net trade¶									
Average, 1966–70	−6,025	1,615	−4,410	−996	−398	−1,394	21	396	417
Projected 1975	−6,586	2,645	−3,941	−1,864	−747	−2,611	104	544	688
Projected 1980	−5,655	2,675	−2,980	−2,538	−1,054	−3,592	108	576	684

*Includes wheat, rye, buckwheat, rice, corn, barley, and oats.
†All oilseeds used in animal feeding, in oil-meal equivalent.
‡Beef and veal, pork, mutton and lamb, and poultry, in carcass-weight equivalent.
§Czechoslovakia, East Germany, and Poland.
‖Bulgaria, Hungary, Romania, and Yugoslavia.
¶Minus indicates net imports.
Source: U.S. Department of Agriculture, Foreign Agricultural Service, *Foreign Agriculture* (July 30, 1973).

indicated that state farms averaged 2,189 ac. and collective farms, 1,500 ac. The agricultural sector contributed about 10.7% of the net national income, employed about 985,000 people, and represented about 12.6% of total employment.

Yugoslavia's 1973 grain production was estimated at 13.4 million tons, compared with 13.6 million tons in 1972; wheat accounted for all of the decline. Imports would continue at about the 1972 level. Early, unofficial estimates placed Yugoslavia's 1973 tobacco crop at 159 million lb., up 10% from the 145 million lb. of 1972.

U.S.S.R. No agricultural event of 1972–73 did more to disturb world markets, cause inflation, and use up the non-Communist world's food reserves than the shortfall of grain and other crops of the U.S.S.R. in 1972. By the same token, no other event of 1973 did as much to ease the world food situation, at least temporarily, as the strong recovery in Soviet agriculture to record or near-record levels. The Soviet Union's gross 1973 grain crop was estimated at 195 million metric tons, almost equal to the planned level of 197.4 million tons. In contrast, 1972 grain production had been 168 million tons.

Data published by the U.S.S.R. showed that agricultural production in 1972 was about 4.5% less than the record level of 1971. Crop production was down 9% compared with 1971; grain was down 7%, potatoes 16%, sunflower seed 11%, vegetables 8%, and fibre flax 8%. Cotton production rose 2.8% and sugar beets, 4.8%. Livestock fared better, with a decline of less than 1%. Cattle numbers rose 1.6%, meat 2.3%, and eggs 7.1%; hog numbers fell 6.9%, sheep numbers 0.7%, and wool production 2.3%.

A new grain production target for the current five-year plan called for 214 million tons of grain in 1975, compared with an earlier goal of 205 million–210 million tons. Despite feed-crop problems in 1972 and some consequent lowering of meat, milk, livestock, and dairy goals for 1973, marketing appeared to have increased somewhat, at least during the first half of the year.

Communist countries produced an estimated 18.1 million bales of cotton in 1972–73, down from 18.8 million bales a year earlier; an increase in the U.S.S.R. was offset by a decline in China. The U.S.S.R. continued to expand irrigation, mostly to increase cotton acreage. Cotton production also fell in non-Communist countries outside the U.S., to approximately 27.6 million bales from 27.9 million. World cotton output in 1972–73 was estimated at 59.5 million bales from 83.1 million ac.

In June 1973 the U.S. and the U.S.S.R. signed an agreement on cooperation in the field of agriculture, designed to expedite the exchange of agricultural information and to provide for cooperation in research and technology for crops, soils, livestock, and machinery and equipment. Much of the implementation, under a joint committee on agricultural cooperation, would devolve on two working groups, one on agricultural economic research and information and another on agricultural research and technological development.

LATIN AMERICA

Latin America's agriculture in 1973 may have recouped some of the losses suffered as a result of adverse weather a year earlier, but corn and wheat crops in the northern countries, as well as the important coffee crop in Brazil, failed to reach previous levels. Sugar crops improved throughout the region, and important gains in soybean output were reported in Brazil. Better grain harvests in Argentina promised some recovery for the livestock industry, but drought and political and economic difficulties continued to plague Chile. Livestock industries throughout the continent were buoyed by a strong export market, and many countries took measures to divert supplies from domestic consumption.

Mexico. Wheat production for 1973 was estimated at 1.9 million metric tons, continuing a downward trend from the 1969 peak of 2.2 million tons, but the greatest deficit was in corn. Poor weather cut production to an estimated 8.1 million tons, necessitating imports of about 1 million tons from the U.S. Sugar production rose 13% to an estimated 2,853,000 metric tons, and coffee production rose 9% to 3.7 million bags (60 kg. each). However, midyear estimates indicated a 1973 cotton crop only marginally higher than the 1,720,000 bales (480 lb. each) produced a year earlier.

Retail food prices rose sharply in April, following a March announcement by Pres. Luis Echeverría that the peso would be devalued to maintain parity

KEYSTONE

Farmers wash jute in the Demra area, near Dacca, Bangladesh. Clean jute fibres dry on the bank at right before being transported to market.

"FOREIGN AGRICULTURE"

Chinese agricultural workers prepare corn for export to Japan. China's agricultural trade with Japan had shown steady growth since World War II, and it was expected to increase as diplomatic ties were strengthened.

with the U.S. dollar. In late March Mexico City butcher shops closed to protest rising beef prices, which they attributed to "middlemen and manipulators." The minister of agriculture reported that there were at least 26 million head of cattle in Mexico, and it was suggested that cattlemen were withholding supplies from the domestic market. Exporting firms were ordered to sell one pound of beef to the domestic market for each pound exported, and export quotas for feeder cattle in the year beginning Sept. 1, 1973, were reduced by 200,000 head.

Central America. Widespread drought in the latter half of 1972 reduced total agricultural output in Central America by an estimated 3%; only Costa Rica and El Salvador registered modest gains. Honduras was hardest hit, with a 16% decline in crops only slightly offset by a 4% increase in livestock output. The important corn crop for the six-country region fell from 1,827,000 metric tons in 1971 to 1,325,000 tons, resulting in a steep increase in imports. Rice production fell sharply, except in Honduras. Sugar production for 1972–73 was forecast at 936,000 metric tons, a modest increase over a year earlier. With substantially larger cotton crops in Guatemala and Honduras, total output for the region was estimated at 1.2 million bales. Coffee production throughout the region declined, however. By midyear Guatemala had quarantined 122 coffee farms in an attempt to prevent a spreading infestation of the coffee bean borer. Food supplies in earthquake-ravaged Nicaragua continued to be uncertain.

South America. The economic boom in Brazil was not matched in the agricultural sector. Even so, total agricultural output rose an estimated 3.1%, permitting a 40% increase in agricultural exports. Brazil's farmers harvested a record 1973 soybean crop, estimated at 4.8 million tons, and the strong export market encouraged farmers to increase acreage; tenant rents in soybean areas doubled. Excessive rains in Rio Grande do Sul sharply lowered the 1972–73 wheat crop from the record 2.4 million metric tons harvested a year earlier. The corn crop was estimated at 14.3 million metric tons, compared with 12.9 million tons in 1971–72; at midyear the government required farmers to increase corn acreage in order to qualify for soybean crop loans. At 3 million bales, cotton production was slightly below 1971–72 but 12% above the 1966–70 average. Plantings declined as farmers in São Paulo and Paraná switched to soybeans and sorghum. Cattle slaughter in federally inspected plants in Rio Grande do Sul rose 50% in 1972, and similar increases were reported for São Paulo and Mato Grosso. Beef exports were cut back 30% in 1973 in order to increase domestic supplies and curtail inflation.

The 1973 Brazilian coffee harvest was expected to yield 23.7 million bags, the eighth consecutive crop to fall below annual needs of about 27 million bags. The 1972 frost in Paraná was the major factor in the reduced production, but coffee rust, which had spread to all producing areas, also contributed. Midyear forecasts of the 1973–74 world coffee crop pointed to production of 66,117,000 bags (132.3 lb. each), 9% less than in 1972–73. Exportable production from the 1973–74 crop would be 45.8 million bags, substantially below estimated world import demand of 54 million bags, and a sharp reduction in world surplus stocks would be required to supply the world market. New York wholesale prices rose; Santos 4s (Brazil) averaged 54.4 cents per pound in 1972, compared with 46.1 cents in 1971, and reached 65 cents in April 1973. In April the International Coffee Agreement was extended for a two-year period to Sept. 30, 1975, but without any provisions relating to export quotas and limitations, indicator prices, or trade control mechanisms. Price and export control mechanisms under the previous agreement had been suspended in December 1972, and the conditions that brought about the suspension—a sharp reduction in surplus stocks

Table XI. Centrifugal Sugar Production in Principal Producing Countries

In 000 metric tons, raw value

Country	1972-73	1971-72	Average 1963-64–1967-68
Argentina	1,295	991	1,109
Australia	2,735	2,649	2,078
Brazil	6,268	5,388	4,141
China	2,474	1,932	1,269
Colombia	821	790	491
Cuba	5,500	4,388	5,017
Czechoslovakia	779	700	975
Denmark	342	325	357
Dominican Republic	1,270	1,138	705
France	2,980	3,202	2,054
Germany, East	640	520	690
Germany, West	2,214	2,344	1,931
India	4,459	3,830	3,338
Indonesia	700	680	633
Iran	625	580	288
Italy	1,278	1,240	1,245
Jamaica	396	384	482
Mauritius	686	624	629
Mexico	2,853	2,520	2,168
Netherlands, The	756	837	596
Peru	945	921	782
Philippines	2,209	1,817	1,577
South Africa	1,915	1,865	1,354
Spain	832	971	547
Taiwan	783	746	917
Turkey	815	910	673
United Kingdom	961	1,179	937
U.S.S.R.	7,977	7,995	9,123
United States	5,828	5,317	4,890
U.S. dependencies*	240	270	773
Yugoslavia	427	421	425
World total	75,697	70,308	62,464

*Puerto Rico and Virgin Islands of the U.S.
Source: U.S. Department of Agriculture, Foreign Agricultural Service.

Table XII. Coffee Production (Green) in Principal Producing Countries

In 000 bags, 132.2 lb. each

Country	1973-74*	1972-73	1971-72	Average 1964-65–1968-69
Angola	3,600	3,500	3,400	3,140
Brazil	16,000	25,500	23,600	21,440
Cameroon	1,125	1,250	1,250	1,054
Colombia	8,500	8,200	7,200	7,860
Costa Rica	1,420	1,335	1,350	1,135
Ecuador	1,000	1,000	1,100	968
El Salvador	2,300	2,100	2,600	2,028
Guatemala	2,000	2,100	2,600	2,028
India	1,600	1,500	1,200	1,199
Indonesia	2,300	2,500	2,250	2,000
Ivory Coast	4,000	5,000	4,400	3,605
Malagasy Republic	1,000	1,000	965	948
Mexico	3,900	3,700	3,400	2,810
Peru	1,000	1,030	1,030	866
Philippines	890	850	835	725
Tanzania	800	800	850	788
Uganda	2,900	2,850	2,850	2,707
Venezuela	1,150	1,100	950	783
Zaire	1,450	1,350	1,300	965
Total North America	13,117	12,648	12,904	10,801
Total South America	28,803	36,983	34,036	32,097
Total Africa	19,593	20,709	19,774	17,131
Total Asia and Oceania	5,604	5,642	5,030	4,466
World total	66,117	75,982	71,744	64,494

*Second estimate (September 1973).
Source: U.S. Department of Agriculture, Foreign Agricultural Service.

and the opposition of importing nations to high world coffee prices—continued to dominate the trade. The International Coffee Organization was to prepare a new agreement for consideration by the Coffee Council by Dec. 31, 1974. However, coffee-producing countries announced their determination to organize their own marketing organization.

Argentina in 1972–73 appeared to have recovered from serious drought that reduced output a year earlier. Feed-grain output rose to an estimated 15.9 million metric tons from only 9.5 million tons, and the wheat crop was forecast at 7.5 million tons, compared with 5.7 million tons in 1972–73. Prospects for a further increase in wheat production were dashed, however, by poor planting conditions for the 1973–74 crop. Cattle slaughter was expected to exceed that of 1972, when an estimated 10.1 million head were slaughtered to produce 2.2 million tons of beef (carcass-weight equivalent). Domestic consumption continued to be restricted by a decree that permitted restaurants and butcher shops to sell beef only in alternate weeks.

Uruguay's agriculture also showed overall improvement in 1973. The 1972–73 corn harvest rose sharply to 205,000 metric tons and sugar production was up 22%. The 180,000-ton wheat harvest was disappointing, however, and imports on the order of 250,000 tons were expected. Wool output rose marginally, but high wool prices induced farmers to retain sheep for wool production; sheep slaughter in 1972 fell 32%. Chile suffered further reverses in 1973, as political dislocation combined with drought and inflation to reduce crop production as much as 20%. Total red meat production in 1973 probably remained at 1972 levels, but these were 26% below 1971. Chile's consumer price index rose 163% in 1972 and food prices increased 243%. In October the new military government received assurances of a $24 million credit from the U.S., permitting importation of 120,000 tons of badly needed wheat.

Colombia's agricultural production rose 5.7% in 1972–73. The 1972–73 rice crop was more than 10% above a year earlier and cottonseed output rose more than 20%. Corn production fell 20% as a result of drought in 1972, but sugar production rose 4% and coffee output, 14%. Cattle numbers reached 21,420,000 head in 1973. Peru experienced a 4% decline in output in 1972–73; heavy rains and flooding reduced crops in coastal areas, and adverse weather in the highlands affected potato production. Red meat production in 1972 was reported at 390.2 million lb., an increase of 3% over a year earlier. Bolivia and Ecuador suffered slight reverses. Poor weather reduced Bolivia's potato crop about 12% and held most crops to 1971–72 levels. Banana production in Ecuador rose slightly. Venezuela suffered from both excess rainfall and drought, and per capita output fell an estimated 7%.

The Caribbean. Production throughout most of the Caribbean countries improved in 1972–73. Efforts to diversify agriculture centred on livestock and poultry production, in large measure financed by international development agencies. Lack of growth in Cuba's livestock industry was indicated by the government's announcement in early March of a reduction in the meat ration. The important Cuban sugar harvest was reported at 5.5 million metric tons, a 25% increase over the drought-damaged 1971–72 crop. In the Dominican Republic a further gain in sugar output raised production to a record 1,270,000 metric tons, and Barbados and Jamaica also registered increases. World sugar production in 1972–73 rose nearly 8% to a record 75,697,000 metric tons, but this was still insufficient to meet consumption requirements. As a result, it was expected that about a million tons of carry-over stocks would be needed to supplement production in the 1973–74 trade year. World stocks at the end of the 1972–73 year were estimated at about 18 million tons, and the tightened supply situation was reflected in the rise in world prices to 9.86 cents per pound in July 1973. The International Sugar Agreement expired at the end of 1973, but the supply situation raised doubts as to whether agreement on quota levels and price ranges could be reached in the near future.

AFRICA

By late 1973 a reduction in overall agricultural output in Africa appeared likely. Although several regions reaped impressive 1972–73 harvests, these gains were offset by widely scattered drought in other areas. Moderate to good grain crops were reported in the north and in East Africa, but sharply reduced corn crops in South Africa, Rhodesia, and Malawi and moderate declines elsewhere may have lowered the combined output of wheat, corn, barley, and rice by more than 10%. Production of important export crops was generally higher than a year earlier, and improved world prices raised foreign exchange earnings. Events of 1973 were dominated by the severe drought along the southern edge of the Sahara Desert, which caused untold suffering and dislocation among the largely nomadic populations and decimated cattle herds throughout the region. Agricultural programs continued to stress self-sufficiency in food production, but per capita supplies increased in only a few countries.

Northern Africa. Morocco's grain production, estimated at 4.4 million metric tons in 1972–73, was a near record; wheat was up 10%, and barley rose to 1,744,000 metric tons. However, insufficient rains in the early growing period reduced prospects for the 1973–74 grain crop to 3,010,000 tons, forcing the government to consider a substantial increase in imports. Algeria's 1972–73 wheat crop was estimated at 1,350,000 tons, compared with 1.1 million a year earlier, and production of 800,000 tons in Tunisia was a third above 1971–72. Olive production declined

"FOREIGN AGRICULTURE"

Brazilian workers mix soybean meal and grains for poultry rations. Once a relatively insignificant soybean producer, Brazil in 1972 trailed only the U.S. in exports of the oilseed and its products.

Table XIII. World Cocoa Production in Leading Areas*

In 000 metric tons

Area	Forecast 1973-74	1972-73	1971-72	Average 1963-64–1967-68
North and Central America	91.7	75.7	95.5	77.3
Dominican Republic	39.0	25.7	41.5	30.8
Mexico	29.0	29.0	30.0	20.7
South America	308.6	242.7	264.0	237.2
Brazil	210.0	160.0	165.4	146.1
Ecuador	55.0	43.0	58.0	48.4
Africa	977.0	1,037.0	1,165.6	981.0
Ghana	370.0	420.0	464.0	445.4
Nigeria	245.0	264.0	265.0	241.7
Ivory Coast	180.0	181.0	224.0	131.1
Cameroon	115.0	103.0	123.0	86.2
Asia and Oceania	42.7	37.0	44.1	31.9
Papua New Guinea	27.0	22.0	30.0	20.3
World total	1,420.0	1,392.4	1,569.2	1,327.4

*Crop year, October 1 to September 30.
Source: U.S. Department of Agriculture, Foreign Agricultural Service.

Table XIV. Tea Production in Principal Producing Areas

In 000 metric tons

Area	Forecast 1973	1972*	1971	Average 1965–69
World total†	1,223.7	1,188.0	1,116.0	1,002.7
Asia and Oceania	1,032.6	1,005.2	964.8	890.3
Bangladesh	27.0	23.5	12.5	28.5
India	465.0	453.0	433.3	384.6
Indonesia	50.0	48.3	48.2	40.6
Japan	95.0	94.8	92.9	84.1
Sri Lanka	223.0	213.5	217.8	223.1
Taiwan	27.0	25.1	27.0	23.5
Turkey	45.0	46.5	33.6	23.9
U.S.S.R.	70.0	70.0	68.6	56.0
Africa	159.3	150.1	117.8	88.8
Kenya	58.0	53.3	36.3	26.8
Malawi	22.5	20.7	18.6	15.6
Mozambique	20.0	18.7	16.5	13.9
Uganda	22.0	23.4	18.0	12.7
South America	31.8	32.7	33.4	23.6
Argentina	23.0	24.0	25.0	16.5

*Preliminary.
†Excluding China.
Source: U.S. Department of Agriculture, Foreign Agricultural Service.

throughout the northwestern countries, although good moisture conditions, combined with an upturn in the production cycle, were expected to raise Tunisia's olive oil production in 1973–74 to a level equal to the 1971–72 record. An early estimate put Morocco's citrus production for 1972–73 at 878,250 metric tons, an increase of 4% above a year earlier; Algeria's citrus crop was unchanged at about 400,000 tons. Total agricultural production in Egypt rose about 3% in 1972. Grain production totaled an estimated 6,920,000 metric tons; corn production rose to 2,550,000 tons; and rice output was estimated at 2.6 million tons. Egypt planned to export 470,000 tons in 1973, mostly through trade agreements with the U.S.S.R., Eastern Europe, Cuba, and Bangladesh. Cotton production for 1972–73 was reported at 2.4 million bales, an increase from 2,340,000 bales a year earlier. Cotton production in Sudan in 1972 declined to an estimated 900,000 bales.

Sub-Sahara. Agricultural production in the nations on the southern reaches of the Sahara suffered a devastating setback in 1973. The drought that affected Mauritania, Mali, Niger, Chad, Upper Volta, and Senegal was reported to be the worst since 1913. Production in Mali fell from an index of 103 (1961–65 = 100) for 1971–72 to 92; Niger's production fell from 109 to 91; and Senegal's from 111 to 72. Production of sorghum and millet in Niger was estimated at 900,000 metric tons, 25% below the poor showing of a year earlier, while production of sorghum and millet in Senegal, estimated at 322,000 tons, was only slightly more than half the level of 1970–71. Per capita food production in Mali and Niger was two-thirds below 1961–65 levels.

The dimensions of the disaster unfolded slowly, beginning with an FAO report in September 1972 indicating that severe shortages were in prospect for the six-nation region. By mid-January the shortfall in grain production among the six nations was estimated at about 250,000 metric tons. In April a task force of UN livestock specialists undertook a program to minimize loss of livestock. Estimates of the drought's effects were varied. One report stated that 6 million of the region's 22 million people faced starvation, and that 80% of Mali's livestock and 50% of Niger's had died. An FAO report in May indicated losses of 30 to 40% among Mauritania's 2.1 million head of cattle. The FAO report cited failure to market livestock in sufficient numbers to maintain balance with feed supplies as a cause of the situation. Overgrazing of the savanna's fragile environment had exacerbated drought conditions and reduced feed and food supplies to dangerously low levels.

Throughout the summer, shipments of relief supplies were moved into the region. Commitments of half a million tons of grain and other food were reported. However, the logistics of moving such quantities were complicated by lack of access to many parts of the region, and shipping and port facilities in donor countries were in heavy demand due to the unusually active agricultural trade. Neither Chad nor Niger had a rail system, and rains in May and June made roads impassable. In some cases, grain had to be airlifted into remote regions. In early August the FAO reported that the situation was under control but that aid would have to continue into 1974. It was doubtful that large numbers of people had died as a direct result of starvation, although it was acknowledged that several thousands had died from cholera and measles. Another report indicated that as many as two million nomadic people were totally dependent

Fresh oranges, a major South African export, compete with U.S. citrus sales to the European Economic Community. South Africa enjoys a seasonal advantage in shipping fresh fruits to northern markets.

"FOREIGN AGRICULTURE"

on relief food supplies for their survival, and some observers feared that the drought had doomed the economies of the six nations. By late summer, however, there were some encouraging signs as rains in many parts of the region allowed the planting of millet and sorghum.

West Africa. Agriculture in the West African nations showed moderate improvement in 1972–73, but with the populations growing at about 2.5%, per capita production in Nigeria, Cameroon, Ivory Coast, and Ghana fell about 1%. Corn production in Nigeria, Ivory Coast, Ghana, and Cameroon rose fractionally, but Nigeria's sorghum and millet crops were reduced by drought in the north. Production of cassava throughout the region showed moderate improvement. Nigeria's 1972–73 peanut harvest was estimated at 1,145,000 metric tons, an increase of more than a third over the previous year. Ivory Coast palm oil output for 1973 was forecast at 120,000 tons. Expansion of rice, corn, and coffee in Zaire raised total agricultural output fractionally above 1971–72.

African cocoa production for 1972–73, at an estimated 1,037,000 tons, was 11% below a year earlier, largely because of insufficient moisture. World cocoa production was reported at slightly less than 1.4 million metric tons, well under the record 1971–72 crop of 1,569,200 tons. Lower supplies and higher prices had been expected to reduce grindings in 1973, but by midyear it was evident that the opposite was true. The FAO forecast total world grindings in 1973 at 1,598,000 metric tons, an increase of 4% over 1972. In July trade sources reported that world cocoa bean stocks were at their lowest levels in 15 years, and spot cocoa prices in New York reached record highs. It was generally conceded that in the U.S. the ten-cent candy bar would be a thing of the past by 1974. After 16 years of negotiations, the International Cocoa Agreement was signed on Jan. 15, 1973, and was scheduled to go into operation in the 1973–74 (October–September) cocoa season. Signatories included countries accounting for 70% of world cocoa imports and more than 90% of exports. The U.S. was not a signatory. The three-year agreement provided a mechanism for maintaining cocoa prices within a range of 23 to 32 cents per pound through a system of export quotas and buffer stocks. Because of the world supply situation, prospects for its success in the near future were not bright.

East Africa. Total output improved somewhat in the East African countries in 1972–73. Gains in productivity were recorded for Ethiopia, Kenya, Zambia, and Malawi, and production held to 1971–72 levels in Uganda and Tanzania. Even so, an October 1973 report by the United Kingdom Disasters Emergency Fund indicated that between 100,000 and 150,000 persons in government-administered refugee camps in Ethiopia had died of starvation and that as many as two million faced death as a result of severe drought. Corn production appeared to be down, with small gains in Ethiopia and Uganda offset by reduced production in Kenya, Zambia, and Malawi. Kenya's corn crop was reported at 1.3 million metric tons, 13% below 1971–72. Tea production rose about a third in Kenya and 30% in Uganda. Slaughter of cattle and sheep in Kenya increased 6 and 28%, respectively. At 300,000 bales, cotton production in Tanzania was about equal to 1971–72, while the Ugandan cotton crop, at 325,000 bales, was down from 345,000 bales produced a year earlier. The important Ugandan coffee crop was about equal to the previous year's output. Kenya continued to encourage expansion of cashew production.

AUTHENTICATED NEWS INTERNATIONAL

Veterinary officials in Dar es Salaam, Tanzania, inspect cattle for shipment to southern regions of Mtwara and Lindi. Beef cattle were new to the south, where tsetse fly and tick-borne diseases had long discouraged livestock breeding.

World production of hard fibres—sisal, henequen, and abaca—rose slightly more than 1% in 1972 from the small harvests reported a year earlier. Production of an estimated 1,269,400,000 lb. of sisal reflected declines in the important East African producing countries, where drought continued to affect output. Tanzanian production, at 346 million lb., was 13% less than a year earlier. World production of henequen totaled 363 million lb. in 1972, and abaca production was estimated at 166.5 million lb. Stocks of hard fibres were reported to be virtually depleted, and prices rose to unprecedented levels.

Southern Africa. Total output of crops in South Africa had risen 5% in 1971–72, but the country might have suffered a setback in 1972–73. Wheat production in 1971–72 was a record 1,670,000 metric tons, and South Africa became a net exporter of wheat in 1972. A slight reduction was forecast for 1972–73, however, while lack of rainfall throughout most of the growing season was expected to reduce the 1972–73 corn crop to an estimated 4,319,000 tons, more than 50% below the near-record 9,483,000 metric tons of 1971–72. Grain sorghum production fell in 1971–72, and the South African Maize Board raised producer prices for corn and grain sorghum in early 1973.

Table XV. Production of Meats in Principal Producing Countries

In 000,000 lb., carcass-weight basis

Country	Beef and veal 1972*	Beef and veal 1971	Beef and veal Average 1963–67	Pork (excluding lard) 1972*	Pork (excluding lard) 1971	Pork (excluding lard) Average 1963–67	Mutton, lamb, and goat meat 1972*	Mutton, lamb, and goat meat 1971	Mutton, lamb, and goat meat Average 1963–67
Argentina	4,856.8	4,446.7	5,054.0	465.2	540.6	429.6	207.7	389.4	374.8
Australia†	2,574.7	2,308.8	2,108.2	428.7	400.5	277.2	2,108.3	1,819.7	1,321.4
Belgium-Luxembourg	597.5	615.1	504.8	1,102.3	1,041.5	564.6	2.7	3.3	5.8
Brazil	4,453.3	4,023.4	3,198.0	1,422.3	1,293.6	1,120.2	127.0	125.9	114.6
Canada	1,977.0	1,929.1	1,792.4	1,400.0	1,511.0	1,048.6	20.5	19.0	25.8
Colombia	1,001.1	1,063.3	819.8	190.1	184.1	143.2	8.4	8.3	8.2
Denmark	376.1	429.5	398.8	1,688.3	1,685.4	1,562.2	2.6	3.1	3.6
France	3,207.7	3,527.4	3,219.2	3,062.2	2,989.5	2,620.4	291.0	293.2	245.2
Germany, West	2,621.3	3,033.6	2,598.4	5,225.0	5,207.3	4,153.6	24.3	26.5	26.6
Italy	1,815.3	1,791.9	1,398.0	1,197.3	1,135.6	939.0	94.8	101.6	84.8
Japan	650.4	606.4	405.8	1,697.6	1,652.8	882.8	2.0	1.9	4.0
Mexico	1,552.1	1,344.4	1,090.4	818.4	647.3	491.8	116.8	119.3	130.6
Netherlands, The	604.7	709.4	605.6	1,631.6	1,672.2	1,030.2	23.1	24.9	18.4
New Zealand	...	878.1	643.2	...	95.0	92.8	...	1,243.2	1,064.8
Poland	...	1,174.6	966.4	...	1,999.9	1,874.8	...	51.1	53.0
South Africa	1,200.0	1,111.1	1,024.4	193.6	172.9	122.4	293.1	476.0	289.6
Spain	683.4	714.5	435.6	1,064.8	1,047.2	739.8	308.6	304.2	283.6
U.S.S.R.	11,481.7	11,276.6	8,478.0	8,679.2	8,214.2	6,250.2	2,094.4	2,094.4	2,167.2
United Kingdom	2,003.7	2,095.8	1,958.0	2,224.3	2,285.5	1,900.4	483.8	506.2	563.4
United States	22,851.0	22,450.0	19,649.6	13,654.0	14,795.0	12,000.2	542.0	554.0	686.4
Yugoslavia	681.1	656.0	551.2	1,036.2	1,086.7	885.4	141.1	131.7	111.4

*Preliminary.
†Year ending June 30.
Source: U.S. Department of Agriculture, Foreign Agricultural Service.

Wool production in 1972 declined to 250.2 million lb. Heavy world demand and high prices throughout 1972–73 raised exports of wool by an estimated 40% in volume and 50% in value. Under the new wool marketing program, which came into effect in the 1972–73 season, the Wool Board acquired the entire wool clip at a set floor price. South Africa's 1972–73 sugar production was a record 1,915,000 metric tons, an increase of nearly 3% above the 1971–72 record. Prospects for the 1973–74 sugar harvest appeared favourable, as the Natal belt escaped the severe drought that affected other crops. Higher production of oilseeds was attributed to the legalization of the manufacture and sale of yellow margarine. The South African pack of deciduous fruit was down 2% in 1973. Rhodesia's 1972–73 corn crop was severely affected by drought, and output fell to an estimated 617,000 metric tons, far below the 1,542,000 tons harvested a year earlier.

MIDDLE EAST AND THE INDIAN SUBCONTINENT

Middle East. By early summer it appeared that the 1973 grain harvest would be sharply below the good crop of 1972. The principal grain crops, wheat and barley, were expected to total 2.7 million tons less than in 1972. Production had been halved in some areas, and imports would be required.

In Turkey rains relieved the drought and imports of grain might be avoided (600,000 tons had been exported in 1972–73). Turkey produced an unusually large 1973 filbert crop, perhaps approaching the record 265,000 tons (in-shell basis) of 1970. Announced support prices were 30.3 to 31.3 U.S. cents per pound, an increase of 14 to 17% over rates for the 1972 crop; when revalued exchange rates were taken into account, however, it amounted to only 6%. For the second consecutive year a large almond crop of about 9,000 short tons (kernel weight) was indicated. Exports were projected at 2,000 tons of shelled sweet almonds, 750 tons of shelled bitter almonds, and 40 tons of unshelled almonds.

Israeli agriculture was disrupted by the outbreak of war in October. The trend in Israel had been toward vertical integration of farming, processing, and marketing, in an effort to fight cost inflation, expand exports of high-value crops, and overcome rigid domestic price controls on some important products.

Ford Foundation specialists continued to seek ways to expand Middle Eastern food crops. Much of this centred in the Arid Lands Development Program (ALAD), based in the Bekka Valley of Lebanon. The main goal of the program was to help the countries of the area increase farm production through adaptive research, improved production technology, and development of production and research capacity in local institutions. Initial emphasis had been on basic cereal crops, forage crops and legumes, and sheep.

Syria's tobacco crop, mostly of the Oriental type, was expected to be at least 10% below 1972; acreage had been reduced because of drought conditions at planting. Oil-rich Kuwait was reported to be a growing market for fast-service fried chicken, with broilers imported from Western Europe and the U.S. Iraq borrowed $40 million from the World Bank to help finance a grain storage project at the port of Umm Iuasr. Iran was not affected by drought, and prospective yields were about the same as in 1972. Wheat imports were projected at 700,000 tons and barley at about 250,000 tons. Early forecasts indicated a 9,000-ton almond crop, up from 8,000 tons recorded in 1971 and 1972. Seven livestock and forage experts from the U.S. accepted an 18-month assignment to help develop Iran's agricultural economy.

Indian Subcontinent. Pakistan's program to modernize and diversify farm production, financed largely by cotton export profits, had raised agricultural output to record levels in 1972, but in 1973 drought and then floods took a heavy toll. With the cotton crop severely damaged by floods, a temporary ban was imposed on exports. Earlier, export duties had been sharply increased twice, not only on raw cotton but on textile goods as well. In September Pakistan nationalized the vegetable oil industry.

The monsoon in India was about on time, giving promise of a good harvest despite early drought and some flooding. The government wheat procurement program obtained only 4.2 million metric tons in the spring, against a target of 8.1 million tons. Some imports would be required, in addition to the 1.7 million tons purchased early in 1973. India's 1972–73 peanut crop totaled 3,927,000 metric tons (in-shell basis), more than 36% below the previous crop. Acreage was reduced by 8.4%, but drought was largely responsible for the sharp decline. The monsoon was much more favourable in the summer of 1973, and unofficial estimates for the 1973–74 crop ranged from 4.7 million to 5.2 million metric tons (in-shell basis). Peanut meal exports were expected to reach 600,000 tons in 1973, 250,000 tons below the 1972 volume.

Estimates of India's 1973 cashew crop were revised downward to 88,000 short tons (raw nut basis), compared with earlier forecasts of 105,000 tons. Imports from Africa were expected to decline to 180,000 tons in 1973, compared with 212,000 tons in 1972. With supplies short, prices rose rapidly. The 1973 world tea crop was expected to set a new record of 1,220,000 metric tons (excluding China); India continued to be the leading producer.

Obtaining and distributing sufficient food supplies remained a major problem for Bangladesh, especially during the "starvation months," September through November. Import requirements of about 1.4 million tons were projected for the last half of 1973, a 9% reduction from actual distribution in the same period of 1972.

FAR EAST

Rice shortages persisted throughout 1973. Production in 1972 had fallen about 8% to 103 million tons (milled basis), or about 89 kg. per capita. Total rice imports to the Far East rose to 4.7 million tons in 1972, and any increase in imports in 1973 apparently would have to come from the U.S., since reserves in all Far Eastern countries had been sharply reduced. Much would depend on the main harvest late in 1973.

Following the drought-reduced 1972 food-grain crop of 215 million tons (including miscellaneous grains and potatoes), the Chinese farm work force was mobilized and considerable progress was reported. Early harvests were said to be "good," but the more important late harvest was not yet accounted for. In any case, China continued to buy grains, especially wheat, from the West. Early indications were that grain imports would probably exceed the 6.2 million metric tons of 1972–73, and there were unconfirmed reports of large contracts for U.S. wheat and corn, as well as Canadian wheat. Tobacco in unusual amounts was purchased from the U.S.

Main-crop production in South Korea was down in

1972, but the Koreans did harvest an all-time record 115,934 metric tons of tobacco. Acreage had been increased by about 12% following the announcement of higher prices. South Korea's agriculture, adjusting to rapid industrialization, set new records in both imports and exports, the latter involving silk, tobacco, meat, and horticultural products. Higher grain imports reflected poor production in 1972, especially of rice, as well as some increase in emphasis on livestock. South Korea had become an important producer and exporter of canned mushrooms; 1973 goals of 29,643 metric tons produced and 10,331 tons exported seemed likely to be reached. The Korean Economic Planning Board agreed to use $141 million in foreign loans to finance rural development projects and to buy fishing boats.

Japan announced that its program to reduce rice production would be discontinued for 1974 in view of the current world food situation; stocks had been lowered to 500,000 tons from 7 million tons three years earlier. Farmers were to be permitted to grow as much rice as they wanted, but they would still be encouraged to shift to fruit and vegetable crops. Japanese domestic production of wheat and barley declined to 434,000 metric tons in 1972–73. Increased production was encouraged by a 14% increase in prices to domestic producers. Plans for a larger, modern beef industry were thwarted to a degree by strong demand and high prices, which induced farmers to slaughter cattle as soon as possible. The sizable herd base included 1.8 million female dairy cattle and 900,000 female beef cattle, but the female dairy herd had declined 1% between 1971 and 1972 and the female beef herd by 11%. Japanese cooperatives bought 1,150 young steers from Australia, to be fed for about a year in Japan before slaughter.

In August a serious rice shortage was reported in the Philippines, following two successive poor crops brought on by floods, drought, disease, and civil disturbance. Attempts were made to purchase as much as 400,000 tons on world markets, but traditional suppliers were unable to fill the orders. Some 40,000 tons were to come from Japan, and the purchase of 150,000 tons of corn from Thailand and the U.S. was authorized. Demand for wheat and flour continued strong.

Related to the struggle for increased production was the land reform program announced by Pres. Ferdinand Marcos in September 1972, affecting about a million tenant farmers and covering about 4.9 million ac., of which 741,000 ac. were cornlands and the remainder rice lands. All tenant farmers were to become owners of "family-sized farms" by July 1975, defined as 12.3 ac. of nonirrigated land or 7.4 ac. of irrigated land. Landowners would not retain more than 17.3 ac. of land under cultivation. Land values were set at 2% of the value of the average harvest of three normal years preceding the decree. Payment would be in 15 annual installments at 6% interest, and the government indicated that it would provide credit and technical assistance. Exports of copra and coconut oil during the first half of 1973 were down 8% to 487,700 metric tons (oil basis) from a year earlier. A further decline of 200,000 tons was projected for 1973 as a result of sparse rainfall. The Philippines' first flue-cured tobacco auction market opened in May, with prices ranging from 37 to 54 U.S. cents per pound.

Taiwan, a net importer of agricultural products, inaugurated a $50 million agricultural development program effective through 1974 to bolster its faltering agricultural sector. Target production of white asparagus for export was set at 4.5 million cases, 57% of which was earmarked for West Germany. Production of green asparagus for freezing was estimated at 4,000 tons in 1973, and production of canned mushrooms for export in 1972–73 amounted to about 62,000 metric tons or 3.4 million standard cases.

Of the small amount of the world rice crop traded in international markets in 1972, Thailand accounted for almost 30%, or a record of more than 2.1 million tons. Drought reduced the 1972–73 rice crop to 11.8 million tons, 13% below the previous year, and indications were that 1973 exports would be only half as large. Exports were largely banned in June, but farmers produced a record large second rice crop of 300,000 tons, and very preliminary estimates set the major harvest of the December crop at 14 million tons. The 1973 corn crop was estimated at 2.5 million tons, nearly double the 1972 crop and well above the 1971 record of 2.2 million tons; 1973–74 exports were expected to surpass 2 million tons.

OCEANIA

Australia. Total production of all grains in Australia in 1972–73 fell 27% from the 14,250,000 metric tons of the previous season. Virtually all supplies had been committed when the crop year began. Farmers increased acreages 6% over a year earlier, but serious drought reduced yields 30% below 1971–72 averages. The wheat harvest was down 25% to an estimated 6,357,000 metric tons, and it was predicted that by November 1973 stocks would be drawn down to no more than 300,000 tons. In May the government virtually eliminated restrictions on the 1973–74 wheat crop. The government's hope that farmers would raise plantings to 11.2 million ha. was apparently not realized, however; the Bureau of Census and Statistics estimated planted acreage for the 1973–74 crop at 9,470,000 ha., and reports of drought in northern producing areas and excessive rains in New South Wales and Victoria suggested that it might fall even lower.

Total feed-grain production in Australia in 1972–73 fell 37% from a year earlier as a result of sharply reduced harvests of barley and grain sorghum. The barley crop was down 45% and sorghum, 25%. The small corn crop was estimated at 210,000 metric tons. The rice harvest yielded a record 310 000 metric tons, and strong world demand led the New South Wales government to expand production for 1973–74. Rice

"FOREIGN AGRICULTURE"

Australian workmen prepare finished beef for export. Australia surpassed Argentina as the world's largest supplier of beef and veal and was investing heavily in lot-fed production.

A.F.P./PICTORIAL PARADE

A French fisherman cleans his net after a fruitless day in the English Channel. Industrial pollution from a British chemical factory was blamed for reducing fish supply in the area.

exports in 1972–73 were estimated at 105,000 tons, second only to the 1971–72 record. The combined acreage of oilseed crops fell about 50% in the 1972–73 crop year, and oilseed production was forecast at about 220,000 tons, compared with 330,000 tons in 1971–72. Early prospects for a record cotton harvest failed to materialize, as a severe insect infestation reduced output to some 150,000 bales.

Livestock numbers continued their upward trend in 1972–73, although it was expected that strong export demand and high meat prices might temporarily interrupt the long-term growth rate. Cattle numbers at midyear were given as 29,741,000 head, an increase of 8% over 1972. Hogs numbered 3,263,000 head, and sheep numbers rose about 4%, to a reported 170 million head. Total production of red meat in 1973 was expected to equal or slightly exceed 1972 levels. Indications were that beef and veal production would rise 20% to 3,400,000,000 lb. Expanded slaughter early in the year was related to drought in Victoria and New South Wales, but it continued in response to the rapid rise in prices. Production of lamb and mutton in 1973 was expected to decline 28% as a result of rising wool prices.

Wool production in 1973 was estimated at 1,625,000,000 lb., slightly less than in 1971–72. Exports in the first eight months of the 1972–73 season (June–May) totaled 1,180,000,000 lb. valued at U.S. $880.8 million, representing an 11% increase in volume and a 130% increase in value over the June–May period of 1971–72. Japan, the EEC, and the U.S. accounted for the bulk of wool exports. World wool production in 1973 fell for the fourth consecutive year. The 1973 wool clip was forecast at 5,659,000,000 lb., a 17% reduction from a year earlier. However, the decline, which resulted from low world wool prices in 1970 and 1971, appeared to be slowing as major producing countries began to rebuild flocks. Prices of Australian and New Zealand wool in London rose from U.S. $1.01 per pound in June 1972 to U.S. $2.63 in June 1973.

New Zealand. New Zealand farmers continued to expand livestock production in 1972–73. Drought conditions, which reduced slaughter weights early in the year, were offset by high prices received for meat. Beef production for export in 1972–73 was indicated at some 455 million lb., 11% more than in 1971–72; the U.S. market was expected to account for about two-thirds of the total. The sheep industry was in its second year of recovery; sheep numbers rose to an estimated 60.5 million head from 59.9 million head in 1972, in spite of drought in late 1972 and early 1973 that forced some increase in slaughter. Wool production for 1972–73 was down 4% to an estimated 650.4 million lb. Wool prices averaged 86 U.S. cents per pound, against 43 cents in 1971–72, and sales by the Wool Marketing Corporation totaled 442.5 million lb. for a return of U.S. $398.5 million.

Butter production for the year ended Sept. 30, 1972, rose 10% to 528 million lb., while cheese output, at 228 million lb., was down slightly. Earnings from exports of dairy products in 1972–73 fell 17% from a year earlier, to an estimated U.S. $344 million. New Zealand's minister of agriculture was unsuccessful in his attempt to obtain relief from the EEC from the loss of earnings caused by the devaluation of sterling. The U.K. market for New Zealand's dairy products continued to shrink; only 40% of dairy exports went to the U.K. in 1971–72, compared with 47% in the previous year and 77% a decade earlier.

(JOHN KERR ROSE; HARVEY R. SHERMAN)

FISHERIES

During 1973 the world's fisheries continued their transition into what might be remembered as the race for protein. Country after country signified its wish—or intention—to extend its jurisdiction over a wider area of coastal waters. Claims and proposals ranged from 30 to 200 mi., and all had the same aim—to corner, or to conserve, the resources of fish and shellfish (and minerals) of the continental shelf or beyond.

Behind these actions were the ever expanding, far-ranging fishing fleets of the U.S.S.R., Japan, Poland, and other flotilla fishing nations and, to a lesser but still significant extent, the distant-water freezer fleets of Europe. Despite the growing acceptance of fishing quotas, such as that agreed on by the International Commission for North Atlantic Fisheries (ICNAF), more and more nations decided to claim the right to control their own resources. Some, such as Argentina, made it clear that this meant expanding the fishery to match the resource and allowing foreign fishing only on a joint-venture basis.

Another reason for this apparent epidemic of limit claims was the imminence of the law of the sea conference, scheduled to begin in Caracas, Venezuela, in June 1974. The support of extended limits by such nations as Canada and Australia, as expressed at the February 1973 Vancouver conference, implied the possibility of a completely new concept of fishery conservation and management by coastal nations.

A major confrontation between Britain and West Germany on the one hand and Iceland on the other occupied much of the year. It was set off by Iceland's claim to a 50-mi. limit of control—covering most of its continental shelf—in defiance of a ruling by the International Court of Justice at The Hague. Iceland offered Britain a catch quota of 117,000 tons per annum. while the British proposed 145,000 tons—25,000 tons lower than the quota suggested by the International Court. The cutting of trawl wire by Icelandic gunboats was countered by escort vessels—civil and naval—from Britain, which continued to fish. In October the parties finally agreed on a compromise of 130,000 tons, but not before a Communist Icelandic fisheries minister had attempted to make political capital and Iceland had threatened to close the NATO airport at Keflavik. (*See* ICELAND.)

The importance of the whole question of access to foreign fishing grounds centred on the certainty that a general swing toward the "continental shelf concept" would accelerate the obsolescence of hundreds of big trawlers representing an investment of many millions of dollars. Equally, it could seriously affect the supply of fish to industries built on the concept of free availability. Determined to stay ahead of the game, big fishing nations were negotiating joint fishing enterprises with fish-rich countries. Japan and the U.S. were moving into Oceania, the U.S.S.R. into Mauritania and possibly the Indian Ocean, and West Germany into Argentina. Fisheries research vessels of the Soviet bloc were offering to explore the fishing grounds of nations that lacked their own fleets and facilities.

Peru's fishing crisis continued. Oceanographic changes related to the Humboldt Current had caused the failure of the anchoveta fishery, which had made Peru the world's top fishing nation and leading fishmeal producer. Anchoveta fishing began again on a limited scale at the end of the summer, but not before a diversification program into food fishing had been set in motion. (*See* OCEANOGRAPHY.)

In Europe the EEC was settling down to rationalize its fisheries regulations following the accession of its new members. Norway, afraid for the security of its fishing limits, had voted against membership, but in the light of subsequent trade–tariff problems, the decision was regretted by some Norwegian fishing interests.

Table XVI. World Fisheries, 1971*

Country	Catch in 000 metric tons	Value in U.S. $000
Peru	10,611.4	...
Japan	9,894.5	...
U.S.S.R.	7,336.7	...
China	6,880.0	...
Norway	3,074.9	237,939
United States	2,766.8	643,200
India	1,845.0	341,900
Thailand	1,571.6	260,600
Spain	1,498.7	...
Denmark	1,400.9	141,652
Canada	1,289.2	186,324
Indonesia	1,249.7	...
Chile	1,179.2	...
United Kingdom	1,107.3	254,710
South Africa	1,084.1	...
Korea, South	1,073.7	282,826
Philippines	1,049.7	650,835
Korea, North	800.0	...
France	741.7	315,394
Iceland	684.9	...
Taiwan	650.2	208,758
Vietnam, South	587.5	...
Poland	517.7	...
Brazil	515.4	...
Germany, West	507.6	122,900
Portugal	498.4	...
Burma	442.7	86,065
Pakistan	416.5	...
Mexico	402.5	95,052
Italy	391.2	251,752
Malaysia	390.3	114,460
Angola	368.4	...
Germany, East	323.1	...
Netherlands, The	321.2	93,585
Vietnam, North	300.0	...
Senegal	239.8	48,345
Sweden	237.1	47,320
Argentina	229.0	...
Morocco	228.7	18,691
Ghana	220.4	...
Faeroe Islands	207.1	...
Tanzania	199.1	...
Cambodia (Khmer Republic)	171.1	...
Nigeria	155.8	...
Others†	3,739.2	...
World total†	69,400.0	...

*Excludes whaling.
†May include statistical discrepancy.
Source: United Nations Food and Agriculture Organization, *Yearbook of Fishery Statistics*, vol. 32.

Table XVII. Whaling: 1971-72 Season (Antarctic); 1971 Season (Outside the Antarctic)

Number of whales caught

Area and country	Fin whale	Humpback whale	Sei whale	Minke whale	Sperm whale	Total	Percentage assigned under quota agreement*
Antarctic: pelagic (open sea)							
Japan	1,252	...	4,320	3,013	126	8,711	58.5
Norway	...	...	3	...	...	3	2.2
U.S.S.R.	1,431	3	1,133	8	3,240	5,815	39.3
Total	2,683	3	5,456	3,021	3,366	14,529	100.0
Outside the Antarctic							
Japan	608	...	2,707	...	5,991	9,576†	...
U.S.S.R.	190	...	304	...	8,079	9,211†	...
South Africa	64	...	10	...	2,068	2,143†	...
Peru	37	...	415	...	1,321	1,773	...
Australia	...	...	...	...	860	860	...
Canada	418	20	235	...	37	710	...
Iceland	208	...	240	...	106	554	...
Others	44	4	24	...	890	965*	...
Total	1,569	24	3,935	...	19,352	25,792*	...

*Antarctic only.
†Includes others (Bryde's, right, and blue whales).
Source: The Committee for Whaling Statistics, *International Whaling Statistics*.

The often delicate relations between U.S. and Latin-American fishing interests were not helped during the year by the registration of a new U.S. tuna boat under the Dutch flag in Curaçao—said to be a flag of convenience that would provide access to the yellowfin tuna, otherwise barred to U.S. vessels observing catch restriction regulations. If the scheme proved watertight, and others followed suit, the whole question of foreign registry in Latin-American countries might have to be reviewed. It was significant, however, that this particular vessel, the 206-ft. "Mariner," was registered with a Dutch-owned company that had links with the vessel's owners—yet another indication that fish-seeking nations would have to buy in to good fishing areas in the future. (H. S. NOEL)

See also Alcoholic Beverages; Commercial Policies; Commodities, Primary; Cooperatives; Food Processing; Gardening; Industrial Review; Prices; Tobacco.

ENCYCLOPÆDIA BRITANNICA FILMS. *Midwest—Heartland of the Nation* (1968); *Problems of Conservation—Soil* (1969); *Problems of Conservation—Our Natural Resources* (1970).

Albania

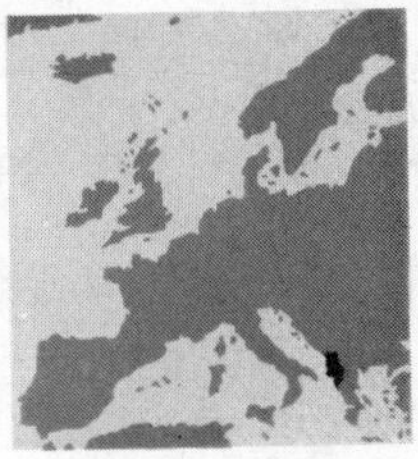

A people's republic in the western Balkan Peninsula, Albania is on the Adriatic Sea, bordered by Greece and Yugoslavia. Area: 11,100 sq.mi. (28,748 sq.km.). Pop. (1973 est.): 2,315,000. Cap. and largest city: Tirana (pop., 1970 est., 171,300). Language: Albanian. Religion: Muslim, Orthodox, Roman Catholic. First secretary of the Albanian (Communist) Party of Labour in 1973, Enver Hoxha; president of the Presidium of the People's Assembly, Haxhi Leshi; chairman of the Council of Ministers (premier), Mehmet Shehu.

Enver Hoxha's traditional policy of hostility toward the U.S.S.R. and the U.S. was badly shaken when China, his great protector, emerged from its isolation, entering the road to détente with the U.S. "imperialists" while the latter eagerly received the leader of the Muscovite "revisionists." Nevertheless, rejecting any change in his course, Hoxha refused to send an Albanian delegation to the Conference on Security and Cooperation in Europe.

At the same time Hoxha launched a campaign to prevent any weakening of the hard ideological line he had pursued at home since 1961. Young people especially came in for criticism. An article in the

Aircraft:
see Defense; Industrial Review; Transportation
Air Forces:
see Defense

Tirana newspaper *Bashkimi* attacked their "mode of dressing, hairstyle, and unworthy behaviour." At the July plenary meeting of the party Central Committee, Hoxha criticized Soviet arguments in favour of coexistence between East and West and warned his people that the "revisionist Kremlin czars" were out to undermine the foundations of Communism. Many members of the party hierarchy were sacked, among them Fadil Pakrami, a veteran member of the Central Committee and president of the National Assembly, Todi Lubonja, a member of the Presidium of the National Assembly, many officials of the Albanian Youth Movement, and almost all the leading figures in the Albanian Writers' Union.

Among Communist countries, Albania was also odd man out in its total hostility to all religions. Hoxha's argument was that all three religions practiced in Albania before World War II (Roman Catholicism, Greek Orthodoxy, and Islam) had collaborated with hostile neighbours. The Roman Catholic cathedral at Shkoder was transformed into a meeting hall; a café and beer hall replaced an Orthodox church in Durres; and the mosque of Tirana was padlocked and derelict. On April 28, 1973, Radio Tirana announced that a Roman Catholic priest, Fr. Stefan Kurti, had been shot as a spy serving the Vatican, Great Britain, and the United States. Roman Catholic sources had reported that he was executed for performing a baptism.

Commercial exchanges between Albania and the West remained modest. Trade with Italy was greatest, with a 1972 turnover of U.S. $16,250,000. West Germany occupied second place with $4.5 million.

(K. M. SMOGORZEWSKI)

ALBANIA

Education. (1969–70) Primary, pupils 506,683, teachers 17,915; secondary, pupils 22,375, teachers 961; vocational and teacher training, pupils 36,525, teachers 941; higher (including University of Tirana), students 23,180, teachers 827.

Finance. Monetary unit: lek, with (Sept. 17, 1973) an official exchange rate of 4.15 leks to U.S. $1 (free rate of 10 leks = £1 sterling) and a noncommercial (tourist) rate of 10.25 leks to U.S. $1 (free rate of 24.70 leks = £1 sterling). Budget (1970 est.): revenue 5,247,000,000 leks; expenditure 4,937,000,000 leks.

Foreign Trade. (1964) Imports 4,906,000,000 leks; exports 2,996,000,000 leks. Import sources: China 63%; Czechoslovakia 10%; Poland 8%; East Germany 5%. Export destinations: China 40%; Czechoslovakia 19%; East Germany 10%; Poland 10%. Main exports: fuels, minerals, and metals (including crude oil, iron ore, chrome ore, and copper chemicals) 54%; foodstuffs (including vegetables, wine, and fruit) 21%; tobacco; wool.

Transport and Communications. Roads (motorable; 1960) 3,100 km. Motor vehicles in use (1960 est.): passenger 1,900; commercial (including buses) 3,400. Railways: (1970) 201 km.; traffic (1969) 220.4 million passenger-km., freight 230 million net ton-km. Shipping (1972): merchant vessels 100 gross tons and over 18; gross tonnage 57,001. Shipping traffic (1970): goods loaded *c.* 2.1 million metric tons, unloaded *c.* 670,000 metric tons. Telephones (Dec. 1963) 10,150. Radio receivers (Dec. 1971) 165,000. Television receivers (Dec. 1971) 2,500.

Agriculture. Production (in 000; metric tons; 1972; 1971 in parentheses): corn *c.* 300 (*c.* 270); wheat *c.* 250 (*c.* 230); oats *c.* 16 (*c.* 15); cotton, lint (1971) *c.* 8, (1970) *c.* 6; sugar, raw value *c.* 19 (*c.* 18); potatoes (1971) *c.* 150, (1970) *c.* 121; wine *c.* 10 (*c.* 10); tobacco *c.* 13 (*c.* 13). Livestock (in 000; Dec. 1971): sheep *c.* 1,600; cattle *c.* 440; pigs *c.* 160; goats *c.* 1,300; poultry (Oct. 1970) *c.* 1,800.

Industry. Production (in 000; metric tons; 1970): crude oil 1,480; lignite 606; petroleum products (1969) 748; chrome ore (oxide content; 1971) 230; iron ore *c.* 400; copper ore (metal content) 7; cement 360; electricity (kw-hr.) 898,000.

Alcoholic Beverages

Beer. World beer production increased again in 1972, rising by some 4.7% to a total of almost 690 million hectolitres (hl.). The increase was lowest in Western Europe. In Eastern Europe production rose 6%, in North America 5.2%, Central and South America 8.3%, Asia 8.7%, Africa 19.8%, and Australia and Oceania 2.6%. Thus there was an overall tendency for the highest relative increases to occur in areas where consumption was lowest. In absolute terms, however, the picture was quite different: of 31 million hl. in increased production, Europe accounted for some 10 million, the Americas for 13 million, Asia 3.8 million, Africa 3.4 million, and Australia 500,000.

Almost a quarter of the total increase was attributable to the U.S., the world's largest producer; U.S. output rose 7.3 million hl. to 156.8 million hl. West Germany and the U.K. both reported increases of around 1 million hl., bringing their totals to 91.1 million and 57.7 million hl., respectively. In the U.S.S.R., where strenuous efforts were being made to expand the brewing industry, production rose 4 million hl. to 46 million hl. Japan's output of 34.2 million hl. was 3.6 million hl. above the preceding year.

In most Eastern European countries and many less developed countries, total output was still determined solely by production capacity. In Western Europe, there was often considerable surplus capacity—as much as 15–20% of the total in some sectors of the West German industry.

In countries where the development of individual brewing concerns was determined primarily by their competitiveness, there was an increasing tendency for large firms to grow even larger while smaller concerns found it more and more difficult to maintain their position in the market. Even though a small business might offer competitive prices and quality and have the advantages of a local distribution network and simpler administration, it could nevertheless be forced out of the market by a selective price-cutting campaign. While the tendency toward concentration had previously been regarded as a more or less natural and beneficial progression, the activities of some of the giant concerns were increasingly seen as a threat to freedom and competition within the industry. The subject aroused heated controversy in West Germany and other highly industrialized countries. Antitrust measures were strengthened and extended, but their overall effect was limited. An argument against overconcentration that appealed particularly to public opinion was the fact that mergers and take-overs seldom led to better beer, or even cheaper beer, for the individual consumer.

In the U.S. the four largest concerns—Anheuser-Busch, Schlitz, Pabst, and Coors—further illustrated the trend toward expansion among the giants and stagnation among the smaller concerns. In 1972 the "big four" achieved a combined output of 79.5 million hl., more than half of the total U.S. production. Anheuser-Busch alone produced 35 million hl., over 20% of the U.S. total and about 2% of the world total. In several European countries a single firm accounted for more than 50% of the market—for example, Carlsberg-Tuborg in Denmark, Heineken-Amstel in The Netherlands, and Pripp in Sweden—while in a number of others, including France and Belgium, a single group controlled more than 25% of the market. Within the extended EEC, Dortmunder Union/Schultheiss (W. Ger.), Bass Charrington (U.K.), Allied Breweries (U.K.), and Heineken (Neth.) achieved outputs of more than 10 million hl. The trend toward large international groupings in Europe was illustrated by the take-over of the French Brasserie de l'Espérance by Heineken and the acquisition of a majority holding in the Stern Brauerei-Carl Funke group (W.Ger.) by Watney's (U.K.) (TILMAN SCHMITT)

Spirits. As living standards rose so, in general, did the demand for potable spirits. Producers continued to concentrate on the U.S., European, Australian, and Hong Kong markets. Sales rose in Japan and South America, but most African markets continued to be regarded as difficult. Such traditionally spirits- (and beer-) drinking countries as the U.K. were starting to drink much more wine, while traditional wine-drinking countries like France consumed more spirits. Japan was beginning to realize its great potential as a market for spirits: restrictions on imports of bottled spirits had been liberalized in 1972, and this, together with a lower tax rate, resulted in a sharp rise in imports.

Concern was expressed in Britain over the implications of a proposed Alcohol Regime for the EEC, which was, however, under review. The proposals took no account of the special needs of Scotch whisky or British gin, and it was feared they might restrict importation of cereals used in Scotch whisky from traditional suppliers outside the EEC. A further difficulty loomed late in 1973 when it appeared that Scotch whisky production might be cut back as a result of Britain's fuel crisis.

Whisky sales in the U.K. home market surpassed the record set in the 1920s. A record 167 million proof gallons of whisky were distilled in 1972, but exports declined slightly to 68.7 million gal., worth £227.9 million. Shipments to the U.S. fell 10% to 31.9 million gal.; France took 3.2 million gal. (up 1.8%), followed by West Germany (down 5% to 3 million gal.). Japan became the second largest export market in 1973; during the first seven months of the year exports to Japan rose 228% in volume to 3.6 million gal.

World sales of cognac in 1972–73 were down slightly as a result of sharp price increases originating at production level and fluctuations in currency rates. Heavy buying by firms seeking to increase stocks also forced prices upward, and there was a shortage of old cognacs. Permission was given to plant 20,000 ha. of new vineyards, which were to come into operation in 1979. Higher cognac prices helped sales of the lower priced and less well known French Armagnac brandies and French grape brandies. World vodka sales rose 28 to 30% in 1972; one prediction was that by 1980 vodka sales would be half those of gin, compared with one-quarter in 1973. (COLIN PARNELL)

Apparent consumption of distilled spirits in the U.S. in 1972 reached a record 391.9 milllion gal., 2.8% above 1971. Per capita consumption rose 1.6% to 1.89 gal. Twenty-seven areas of prohibition in six states were eliminated in 1972 by local option. Five states lowered the drinking age below 21 in 1973, and three lessened or removed the ban on serving liquor on election days. Consumer expenditures for alcoholic beverages in 1972 totaled $25.7 billion, compared with $24.2 billion in 1971. The U.S. federal excise tax on spirits remained at $10.50 per proof gallon. Collections of the tax on alcoholic beverages totaled $5,149,513,473 in fiscal 1973, or 31.1% of all excise taxes collected. U.S. agents seized 2,589 stills producing illicit spirits in fiscal 1973, 392 less than in 1972.

PETERSON—VANCOUVER SUN/ROTHCO

"When everything is driving us to drink . . . it's damned unfair of France to raise wine prices again . . . ."

Table I. Estimated Consumption of Beer in Selected Countries

In litres* per capita of total population

Country	1969	1970	1971
Germany, West	135.74	141.14	144.41
Belgium†	140	140	140
Cze choslovakia	135.1	139.9	...
Australia‡	120.4	123.1	125.8
Luxe mbourg	124.6	127	123.8
New Zealand	111.3	114.9	...
Denmark	102.24	108.52	...
United Kingdom	98.4	101.1	104.7
Germany, East	92	95.7	102.2
Austria	99	98.7	101.8
Canada§	71.2	73.8	78.4
Switzerland	77.1	78.1	...
United States	67.5	70	71.9
Ireland§	61.9	67.1	...
Netherlands, The	51.76	57.38	62.36
Hungary	54.2	59.4	60
Sweden	58.4	57.6	57.4
Finland	52.2	48.8	49.4
France	40.7	41.3	41.9
Venezuela	39	40	...
Norway	34.71	36.76	39.24
Spain	32	38.5	39
Bulgaria	36	35	35
Colombia	35	34	...
Poland	30.4	31.4	33.7

*One litre = 1.0567 U.S. quarts = 0.8799 imperial quart.
†Including so-called "household beer."
‡Years ending June 30.
§Years ending March 31.

Table II. Estimated Consumption of Potable Distilled Spirits in Selected Countries

In litres* of 100% pure spirit per capita of population

Country	1969	1970	1971
Poland	3.4	3.2	3.5
Germany, West	2.75	2.97	3.32
Hungary	2.33	2.7	3
United States	2.83	2.87	2.91
Yugoslavia	3	2.9	...
Spain	2.5	2.84	2.8
Germany, East	2.5	2.6	2.8
Sweden	2.6	2.65	2.5
Canada†	2.23	2.41	2.49
Iceland	1.92	2.23	2.41
Romania	2.2	2.4	...
Czechoslovakia	2.2	2.36	...
France‡	2.22	2.3	2.23
Luxembourg	1.1	1.9	2.2
Netherlands, The	1.88	2.04	2.11
Finland	1.6	1.8	2.1
Switzerland	2.12	1.85	...
Italy	1.6	1.7	1.7
Cyprus	1.47	1.51	1.6
Norway	1.48	1.56	1.59
Belgium	1.08	1.32	1.56
Austria	1.2	1.4	1.5
Ireland†	1.3	1.45	...
Peru	1.7	1.4	...
South Africa	1.11	1.33	1.14

†Years ending March 31.
‡Including alcohol- and wine-based aperitifs and liqueur wines.

Table III. Estimated Consumption of Wine in Selected Countries

In litres* per capita of total population

Country	1969	1970	1971
Italy	115.2	112	111
France†	112	107	108
Portugal	98.5	92.5	91.1
Argentina	88.5	91.8	85.3
Spain	62.5	61.5	60
Chile	46.6	43.9	...
Switzerland‡	40.8	41.9	...
Luxembourg	32	37	40.9
Greece	40	40	40
Austria	31	31.1	39.8
Hungary	38.5	37.7	38
Yugoslavia	28.3	26.9	...
Uruguay	26	26	...
Romania	25	23.1	...
Germany, West	15.9	16.9	20.7
Bulgaria	21.2	18.6	19.3
Czechoslovakia	13.2	14.6	...
Belgium	12.1	13.9	14.5
U.S.S.R.	12	11.2	11.5
South Africa	9.4	9.17	10.28
Australia§	8.2	9.1	8.7
Cyprus	8.2	8.2	8.2
Sweden	5.8	6.4	7
Poland	5.6	5.6	6.2
Denmark	5.13	5.91	...

†Excluding cider (c. 20 litres per capita annually).
‡Excluding cider (c. 7.3 litres per capita 1969–70).
§Years ending June 30.

Source: Produktschap voor Gedistilleerde Dranken, *Hoeveel alcoholhoudende dranken worden er in de wereld gedronken?*

A total of 859,151,755 gal. of distilled spirits were produced in the U.S. in fiscal 1973, 12.4% more than in 1972; this included some not used for beverages. Whiskey production fell 11.3% to 111,978,861 tax gallons. Production of light whiskey, distilled at higher than 160 proof, fell 25.9% to 23,151,864 tax gallons, and some brands were removed from the market.

Total U.S. bottlings rose 3.5% in 1972 to 337,016,-777 gal.; whiskey accounted for 192,730,846 gal. or 57.1% of the total. Bourbon whiskey continued as the largest selling spirit in the world, with sales amounting to 78,235,652 gal. Vodka sales rose 11.2% to 62,832,-529 gal., and gin increased 0.4% to 36,677,131 gal. The swing to larger bottles continued; quarts increased 10.8% and half gallons, 32.5%.

Total imports of spirits into the U.S. fell 1.9% in 1972, to 100,155,883 tax gallons with a value of $537.6 million. Imports of Canadian whiskey rose 10.6% to 38,477,919 tax gallons, while Scotch fell 9.8% to 48,-992,718 tax gallons. The percentage of bulk to total whiskey rose from 38.1 to 41.8% for Canadian and from 28.4 to 31.8% for Scotch. Tequila imports increased 47.2% to 1,655,468 gal.

In Canada public revenue from alcoholic beverage taxes rose 26.8% to Can$1,102,641,000 in fiscal 1972. Consumption of spirits in the same year climbed 14% to 28,952,000 imperial gallons. Production rose 2.6%; imports, 20.6%; and exports, 4%. (JULIUS WILE)

Wine. World production of wine in 1973 was estimated at 325 million hl., an increase of about 16% over 1972. European production was 265 million hl., or 81.5% of the world total, while EEC countries accounted for 153 million hl., or 47% of the total. Almost all wine-producing countries experienced better harvests, and quality was also high in most countries.

At 72 million hl., the French harvest was one of the most abundant on record. In general the wines were of good quality, average alcoholic content, and low acidity. Bordeaux production was up 40% and quality was comparable to that of 1970. Beaujolais promised to be a great vintage. In Champagne the harvest rose above the high level of 1972, and the wine was of excellent quality.

The Italian harvest exceeded 70 million hl., about 10 million hl. above the previous year, but quality was generally below average except in some regions of central and southern Italy. Spanish wine production was some 26% above the 1972 level, and there was also some improvement in quality, which had been below average in 1972. Among other wine-growing countries, Portugal produced 9.5 million hl., an increase of 14% over 1972; West Germany 10 million hl. (+34%); the U.S.S.R. 31 million hl. (+3%); Yugoslavia 7 million hl. (+1.2%); and Algeria 7 million hl. (+22%).

Fine wines continued to fetch very high prices at auction. In London both Christie's and Sotheby's reported record receipts for 1972–73. In France the authorities investigated alleged frauds involving the sale of large quantities of mixed wine labeled as Bordeaux. (PAUL MAURON)

The U.S. grape crop of 1973 totaled 3.8 million tons, 1.2 million tons greater than that of 1972 but well below the 1965 record of 4.3 million tons. California's 3.5 million-ton crop accounted for most of the increase. In terms of quality, the California wines of 1973 were expected to win good to excellent marks when they reached the market. The weather was favourable in upstate New York, but the crop size was limited because the vines had not fully recovered from the damage done by the extraordinarily inclement weather of the previous year.

U.S. wineries turned a record 2.6 million tons of grapes into wine and brandy in 1973. More than 900,-000 tons of wine-variety grapes went into the crushers, easily a record but one that seemed destined to be short-lived as new plantings came into production in the next few years. The recent interest in setting out new vineyards continued through 1973. California added 58,000 ac. to set a post-repeal high of 611,000 ac. for the state. Wine grape plantings outside California also made gains, with major emphasis on French-American hybrids. During fiscal 1973, 25 new wine-producing premises were licensed by the federal government, bringing the total to 495.

A record 349 million gal. of wine went into U.S. consumption channels in fiscal 1973. California-produced wine accounted for 246 million gal., or 70% of the total; other states shipped 50 million gal., and foreign countries contributed the remaining 53 million gal. While Western European nations were the main source of imported wine, increasing amounts reached the U.S. from Eastern Europe, Latin America, Africa, Australia, New Zealand, and Asia.

U.S. consumption by wine classifications for fiscal 1973 was as follows: table wine, 185 million gal.; dessert wine, 72 million gal.; special natural wine, 59 million gal.; sparkling wine, 23 million gal.; and vermouth, 10 million gal. These totals included fruit and berry wine, classified according to alcoholic content. (IRVING H. MARCUS)

Algeria

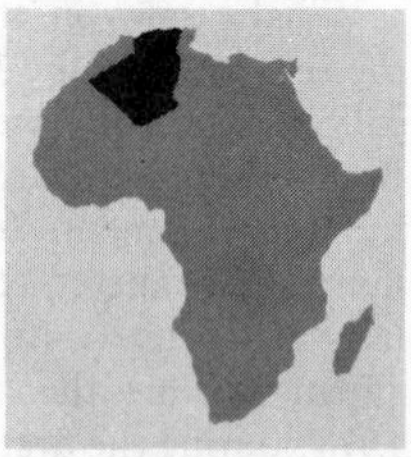

A republic on the north coast of Africa, Algeria is bounded by Morocco, Mauritania, Mali, Niger, Libya, and Tunisia. Area: 896,588 sq.mi. (2,322,164 sq.km.). Pop. (1971 est.): 14,643,700. Cap. and largest city: Algiers (département pop., 1970 est., 1,839,000). Language: Arabic, Berber, French. Religion: Muslim. President in 1973, Col. Houari Boumédienne.

Austerity was still the rule for Algeria in 1973, despite the promise that the country's hydrocarbon industry gave for the future. The public sector of the economy was stated to be at "peak performance," and state investment in development projects was greatly increased. Investment during the first four-year plan period totaled $8.4 billion, one-third more than had been originally proposed.

After setting an example for other Arab oil-producing countries in 1971 by taking over a majority holding in foreign-owned oil exploration companies, Algeria again took the lead in 1973 by raising the price of crude oil to $5 a barrel in September (although the Gulf producers were soon to go beyond this price level in the early days of the fourth Arab-Israeli war). This arbitrary price change did not deter customers. Not only could Algeria count on ready markets for its crude oil and heavy advance demand for its natural gas, due to be developed in the second half of the decade, but it had no difficulty finding financing for its development plans in Western Europe and the U.S. Consortium loans were raised in London, New York, and on the Eurodollar market, not only to finance the oil and gas industry but also to meet the financial requirements of the current and development budgets.

ALGERIA

Education. (1972–73) Primary, pupils 2,244,844, teachers (public only) 51,461; secondary, pupils 278,-843, teachers (public only) 9,892; vocational, pupils 57,422, teachers (public only) 3,391; teacher training, students 7,128, teachers (public only) 542; higher (including 2 universities), students 26,522.

Finance. Monetary unit: dinar, with (Sept. 17, 1973) a free rate of 3.82 dinars to U.S. $1 (9.22 dinars = £1 sterling). Gold, SDRs, and foreign exchange, central bank: (June 1973) U.S. $438 million; (June 1972) U.S. $404 million. Budget: total revenue (1971 est.) 7.5 billion dinars; expenditure (1972 est.) 5.5 billion dinars.

Foreign Trade. (1971) Imports 5,737,000,000 dinars; exports 3,603,000,000 dinars. Import sources (1970): France 42%; West Germany 10%; U.S. 8%; Italy 7%. Export destinations (1970): France 54%; West Germany 13%; U.S.S.R. 5%. Main exports: crude oil 66%; wine 14%.

Transport and Communications. Roads (1971) 75,967 km. Motor vehicles in use (1971): passenger 147,100; commercial (including buses) 84,700. Railways: (1971) 3,951 km.; traffic (1972) 1,014,000,000 passenger-km., freight 1,531,000,000 net ton-km. Air traffic (1971): 634 million passenger-km.; freight 4,360,000 net ton-km. Shipping (1972): merchant vessels 100 gross tons and over 40; gross tonnage 132,-756. Shipping traffic (1970): goods loaded *c.* 40.6 million metric tons, unloaded *c.* 4.2 million metric tons. Telephones (Dec. 1971) 199,000. Radio receivers (Dec. 1969) 700,000. Television receivers (Dec. 1969) *c.* 100,000.

Agriculture. Production (in 000; metric tons; 1972; 1971 in parentheses): wheat 1,692 (1,235); barley 720 (340); oats 39 (36); potatoes 260 (*c.* 260); dates (1971) *c.* 110, (1970) *c.* 100; figs (1970) 66, (1969) 24; oranges (1971) *c.* 450, (1970) 487; tomatoes (1971) *c.* 100, (1970) 118; onions (1970) *c.* 38, (1969) *c.* 38; tobacco (1971) 7.3, (1970) 7.3; olive oil *c.* 15 (*c.* 25); wine *c.* 830 (825). Livestock (in 000; Nov. 1971): sheep *c.* 8,500; goats (1970) *c.* 2,100; cattle *c.* 863; asses *c.* 300; horses *c.* 120; camels *c.* 175.

Industry. Production (in 000; metric tons; 1971): iron ore (53–55% metal content) 3,144; phosphates (oxide content) 491; crude oil (1972) 50,048; natural gas (cu.m.; 1970) 2,838,000; electricity (excluding most industrial production; kw-hr.) 1,901,000.

Stability and assured markets for its main products gave Algeria a cachet in the financial world that other less developed countries might well envy.

Algeria's foreign policy was defined early in the year as being based on a desire to play a responsible role, as a member of the third world, in solving international problems. Although this role did not extend to resumption of diplomatic relations with the U.S., Algeria did seek a closer association with Western Europe, both through renegotiation of its status in relation to the EEC and through an attempt to take an active part in the Conference on Security and Cooperation in Europe.

Algeria's love-hate relationship with France continued. In July Abdel-Aziz Bouteflika paid the first visit ever made by an Algerian foreign minister to Paris. He indicated that the "special relationship" between Algeria and France was at an end and that, in the future, the two countries should treat each other as equals. The cordiality that flowed from Bouteflika's visit was quickly marred by a series of incidents involving Algerians working in France. The 382,000,-strong Algerian work force was to have been augmented by 25,000 a year, but after what appeared to be mob reaction against the resident Algerian communities in Marseilles, Paris, Toulouse, and elsewhere, all emigration to France was suspended in September and Franco-Algerian relations became distinctly cool.

President Boumédienne continued to be a somewhat distant observer of—but a frequent commentator on—the Arabs' predicament in the Middle East. When war broke out in October he sent air force units to assist the Egyptians and himself flew to Moscow (as he had also done at the time of the 1967 conflict) to act as a spokesman for the Arabs with the Kremlin leaders. Later he visited Egyptian Pres. Anwar as-Sadat.

In September President Boumédienne had presided at the opening in Algiers of the fourth summit conference of nonaligned nations, at which 57 heads of state were present. The Algerian delegation was largely responsible (in the absence of any permanent secretariat) for the formulation of the conference's resolutions, and these markedly reflected President Boumédienne's view that the main division in the world was between the industrialized powers and the third world. Boumédienne warned the conference that the détente between the Soviet Union and the U.S. threatened to become "a source of tension in the relations between the privileged world and the rest of humanity." It was up to the third world's peoples and leaders to "provoke a radical transformation in the present situation by counting above all on their potentialities and by mobilizing all their human and material resources for the benefit of their countries." In view of Arab oil policy, such talk could no longer be dismissed as empty rhetoric, a fact that was underlined by the summit meeting of Arab leaders held in late November at the Palace of Nations just outside Algiers. The 15 kings, sheikhs, and presidents in attendance confirmed their use of the oil boycott to influence Western policy in the Middle East. Summing up, Boumédienne noted that "the economic, political and military weapons are now in the hands of the Arabs." (*See* ENERGY.)

At home President Boumédienne once more tried to instill a new spirit into Algeria's sole political organization, the National Liberation Front. Despite changes in its leadership, it still failed to rally any popular enthusiasm for participation in decision-making and the administration of policy. President Boumédienne constantly toured the provinces, initiating several major development schemes. But the Algerian people, deprived of a political voice for so long, seemed reluctant to express themselves now, at a time when boom days seemed just around the corner.

(PETER KILNER)

Yasir Arafat (centre), head of the Palestine Liberation Organization, speaks at the fourth summit conference of nonaligned nations held during September 1973 in Algiers.

A.F.P. / PICTORIAL PARADE

Andorra

An independent principality of Europe, Andorra is in the Pyrenees Mountains between Spain and France. Area: 179 sq.mi. (464 sq.km.). Pop. (1972): 21,425. Cap.: Andorra la Vella (commune pop., 1972, 8,534). Language: Catalan (official), French, Spanish. Religion: predominantly Roman Catholic. Co-princes: the president of the French Republic and the bishop of Urgel, Spain, represented by their *veguers* (provosts) and *batlles* (prosecutors). An elected Council General of 24 members elects the first syndic; in 1973, Julià Reig-Ribó.

In the December 1972 elections for the chief executives of the country, Julià Reig-Ribó and Marc Villa-Riba had been elected first syndic and second syndic, respectively. Their terms of office would extend for three years and they could be reelected for a second term only.

The public budget for 1973 amounted to $8 million. Tourism continued to be a major source of revenue and foreign exchange. Prices in the principality remained considerably below those in France and Spain, attracting many visitors for the summer season. The two main centres of Andorra la Vella and Les Escaldes drew most of the visitors. Skiing continued to develop, and the centre of La Massana, in particular, was thriving. (ROBERT D. HODGSON)

ANDORRA

Education. (1969–70) Primary, pupils 1,850, teachers 63; secondary, pupils 804, teachers 48.

Finance and Trade. Monetary units: French franc and Spanish peseta. No income tax, death duty, or customs; public treasury is funded by a 3% levy on gasoline and liquor. Foreign trade (1972): imports from France Fr. 247,527,000 (U.S. $48.4 million), from Spain 1,577,640,000 pesetas (U.S. $24.5 million); exports to France Fr. 7,957,000 (U.S. $1.6 million), to Spain 45,199,000 pesetas (U.S. $700,000). Tourism (1972) *c.* 2 million visitors.

Communications. Radio receivers (Dec. 1969) 6,000. Television receivers (Dec. 1969) 1,700.

Agriculture and Industry. Production: cereals, potatoes, tobacco, wool. Livestock (in 000; 1971): sheep *c.* 25; cattle *c.* 3; horses *c.* 1.

Antarctica

During 1973 Argentina, Australia, Chile, France, Japan, New Zealand, South Africa, the U.K., the U.S.S.R., and the U.S. continued their scientific assault on Antarctica and surrounding waters from over 40 stations on the continent and outlying islands. Of the 12 Antarctic Treaty nations, only Belgium and Norway did not maintain bases, although they engaged in programs of other countries.

The Executive Committee of the Scientific Committee on Antarctic Research (SCAR) of the International Council of Scientific Unions met in Cambridge, Eng., July 9–11. It considered reports from its ten working groups; future symposia on scientific findings; liaison with other international scientific bodies; relationships with Antarctic Treaty consultative activities; problems of conservation, pollution, tourism, extraction of natural and mineral resources, and a proposal for the disposal of nuclear waste materials in ice sheets. The proposal for nuclear waste disposal had been rejected by international scientists, who felt that the data needed to predict possible outcomes were not available.

Aluminum: *see* Mining

American Literature: *see* Literature

Anglican Communion: *see* Religion

Angola: *see* Dependent States

Scientists concluded that Antarctica has been covered with ice for at least 20 million years. Consistent with the theory of continental drift, they found that Australia broke away from the polar continent some 50 million years ago and since then has been drifting northward at a rate of two to three inches a year. Serious discussion was started on the subject of harvesting large icebergs from Antarctica as sources of fresh water for arid regions of South America and Australia. The Ross Ice Shelf was considered a likely source.

Scientific Programs. Unusually severe sea ice conditions and persistent poor weather seriously restricted summer research programs and logistic activities throughout Antarctica, especially the resupply of bases and construction of facilities. The July mean temperature at Sanae Station rose to 10° F, a virtual heat wave in the midst of the Antarctic winter.

Argentina. Argentina engaged in a broad range of research studies at its six permanent stations on the Antarctic Peninsula and at General Belgrano Station on the continent. Four Americans, a Swede, an Englishman, and a Chilean worked from a temporary summer site on Deception Island, studying the effects of several recent volcanic eruptions on the life and geology of the area.

Australia. The Australian National Antarctic Research Expedition launched research programs at four bases in Antarctica. A traverse party went from Casey Station to a point 45 mi. S, near the summit of Law Dome, taking glaciologic and meteorologic observations along the way. A second traverse headed toward Vostok Station for a distance of 187 mi. A transponder beacon, supplied by the French, was placed on an iceberg for tracking by the French EOLE-1 satellite. Underwater biological surveys were conducted at Mawson Station, and a large rookery of petrels was discovered 88 mi. to the east.

Chile. Biological, oceanographic, and terrestrial studies were carried out at and around the three permanent stations situated on the Antarctic Peninsula. The ship "Yelcho" escorted the badly damaged oceanographic research vessel "Calypso" from the U.S. Palmer Station, across Drake Passage, to the Argentine port of Ushuaia.

France. A wide range of studies were conducted at Dumont d'Urville Station in Victoria Land, with lesser activities in the sub-Antarctic Kerguelen and Crozet islands. French and Soviet scientists, in a joint program, successfully launched 20 upper atmosphere research rockets at the Kerguelen Islands. The glaciologic traverse to Vostok Station, which was started in 1972, was continued as part of the International Antarctic Glaciological Project. After covering 450 mi., with observations of ice thicknesses and properties taken every 6 mi., the traverse was terminated short of its goal due to exceptionally rough terrain and poor weather. With the help of Japan, New Zealand, the U.K., and the U.S., ten transponders were placed on icebergs for the purpose of tracking drift by the EOLE-1 satellite. The information would be useful in determining the little-known winter ocean circulations near the continent.

Japan. For the fourth consecutive year, the icebreaker "Fuji" encountered thick sea ice and was unable to reach Syowa Station. The 40 men and cargo of the 14th Japanese Antarctic Research Expedition were transported 40 mi. from ship to station by helicopter. Upper atmosphere sounding rockets were launched from Syowa Station. Two winter supply trips were made to Mizuho Camp, a small inland station 6,765 ft. above sea level, situated about 185 mi. SW of Syowa. Two glaciologists wintered over at the camp where they engaged in thermal drilling and studies of snow and ice cores.

New Zealand. As in the past, research activities were focused at or near Scott Base and in the nearby Dry Valley area. Ornithologic and meteorologic observations were made at the sub-Antarctic Campbell Island Station. Altogether 200 persons, including one woman, participated in the summer program, one of the largest ever launched to Antarctica by New Zealand. Six New Zealanders were transported by U.S. helicopters from Scott Base to the top of Mt. Erebus, a 12,450-ft. active volcano, where they collected gas and rock samples. Nine persons took part in the joint New Zealand-Japan-U.S. Dry Valley Drilling Project, which was expected to continue for three years.

After their trimaran sailboat became caught in the ice near Cape Bird, four New Zealanders were marooned for six days on drifting ice in the Ross Sea before being rescued by helicopters. They suffered from frostbite and survived by eating penguins and huddling inside hastily built ice shelters.

South Africa. The 14th South African National Antarctic Expedition was launched when the research ship "RSA" sailed in early January for the main Sanae Base in western Queen Maud Land. Field tests of a new tracked vehicle, built in South Africa, were begun. The enclosed vehicle, which carried scientific equipment and had seating and sleeping facilities for three persons, would be used especially for the radio-echo sounding program. Weather and upper air observations were continued on Marion Island.

United Kingdom. The British Antarctic Survey research program was focused largely at its seven permanent stations on the Antarctic Peninsula and outlying islands. Halley Bay Station, the only British station on the continent, was located at the eastern part of the Weddell Sea. Repeated collapse of ice cliffs in Halley Bay made relief of the station by the ship "Bransfield" a hazardous ordeal. Cargo was finally unloaded onto a glacier 35 mi. S of the station.

Four geologists studied the structure and stratigraphy of southern Alexander Island. Glaciologic, geophysical, and geologic studies, along with topographic surveys, were conducted at Stonington Island and Fossil Bluff. Reindeer studies were continued on South Georgia Island, where a new glaciologic laboratory was opened. Two automatic weather stations were placed on nearby Hodges Glacier.

Specimens representing two years' research work in the Antarctic were lost from the "Bransfield" on her voyage home. After a controversy between scientists and crew, the ship's captain ordered the crew to refrain from cooling their beer in the refrigerator that housed scientific specimens. The following night someone forced open the lock on the refrigerator door, removed the samples, and threw them overboard. The loss was estimated at around $50,000.

After 26 years with the British Antarctic Survey, Sir Vivian Fuchs retired as director. He was succeeded by Richard Laws.

U.S.S.R. More than 200 persons participated in the 18th Soviet Antarctic Expedition. The research program was carried out at six permanent stations, several field sites, offshore islands, and on three ships at sea. Attempts to establish a seventh permanent station, Russkaya, at Cape Burks on the Hobbs Coast of Marie Byrd Land, were only partially successful. Bad weather and unfavourable sea ice conditions prevented the research and supply ship "Ob" from penetrating closer than 200 mi. from the Hobbs Coast. The ship's helicopters transported huts, food, and equipment to the site, but completion of the station was postponed until the following year.

A 400-mi. tractor-train traverse was made from Mirnyy Station toward the South Pole. Despite poor weather, scientists were able to make glaciologic, magnetic, and radar sounding observations; instruments were left imbedded in the ice to record long-term changes in ice movement and properties.

Soviet factory trawlers were sent into Antarctic waters to harvest the shrimp-like crustaceans known as krill and convert them into protein-rich paste. Because krill are at the centre of the marine food chain, scientists expressed concern that excessive harvesting might irreversibly harm the rich ecosystems in Antarctic seas.

United States. Over 148 investigators carried out 41 research projects. Most of the work was done at McMurdo, Hallett, Amundsen-Scott South Pole, Siple, and Palmer stations; field parties were placed in southern Victoria Land, Lassiter Coast, and the South Shetland, South Georgia, and Auckland islands. The icebreakers "Glacier" and "Burton Island" supported oceanographic observations, and the crew of the "Glomar Challenger" drilled 16 holes into the sea floor in Antarctic waters.

Preliminary analysis of three cores from the Ross Sea showed evidence of gaseous hydrocarbons, suggesting the likely presence of gas and oil accumulations. Core analyses of two holes drilled in the Dry Valleys were correlated with those from the Ross Sea. Geologic reconnaissance studies on the Lassiter and Black coasts showed that the mountains there are part of a belt that rings the Pacific basin. The "Glacier" recovered two of the four current meters placed on the bottom of the Weddell Sea in 1968; the meters provided winter data from the Weddell Sea for the first time. The "Burton Island" penetrated the pack ice off Oates and George V coasts to conduct a seal census. Preliminary results showed a mean density of approximately four seals per square mile, two less than in a similar survey in the Amundsen and Bellingshausen seas in 1971–72. A new base, Siple Station, was completed in Ellsworth Land despite bad weather. Four scientists remained at the station for the winter to conduct upper atmosphere studies. After several years of operation, the nuclear power plant at McMurdo Station was closed due to numerous malfunctions and its pollution potential. Henceforth, diesel oil would be used to power McMurdo Station, the largest in the Antarctic.

Other Developments. In a single-handed attempt to circumnavigate the Antarctic continent in his 32-ft. steel sloop "Ice Bird," the Australian David Lewis encountered severe storms in the Drake Passage that capsized his ship, causing serious damage. He was barely able to reach Palmer Station, where he pulled alongside underwater explorer Jacques Cousteau's oceanographic research vessel "Calypso." The "Calypso" had also suffered severe ice damage during Cousteau's aborted attempt to spend about a year in Antarctic waters studying animal life. The tourist ship "Lindblad Explorer" made two trips from Buenos Aires, Arg., to the Antarctic Peninsula. A Spanish-Argentine company announced plans to start tourist cruises in the 1973–74 summer season.

A grant of $50,000 was made by the U.S. National Science Foundation to the Antarctic Centre of the Canterbury Museum, Christchurch, N.Z. For many years, Christchurch had been the departure point for numerous exploration and research parties going to Antarctica. Mary Alice McWhinnie, professor of biological sciences at De Paul University, Chicago, and Sister Mary Cahoon were selected to be the first U.S. women scientists to winter over in Antarctica. The two biologists, along with a Polish exchange scientist, would study the krill. McWhinnie made her first Antarctic cruise aboard the research ship "Eltanin" in 1962 and had served as chief scientist on several subsequent voyages. (LOUIS DEGOES)

See also Oceanography.

Anthropology

The year 1973 was not one of startling new ideas but, rather, one that saw refinement of approaches developed in the preceding decade. There continued to be an increasing emphasis on interdisciplinary research in all areas of anthropology—archaeology, physical anthropology, cultural anthropology, and linguistics. The interest generated in recent years in a more practical, problem-centred type of anthropology was finding expression more and more in studies of urban and ethnic problems, development and modernization, medical and applied anthropology, and in cross-cultural studies of child development, education, and cognition. Current funding policies tended to encourage this type of research, along with studies of women and population research of all kinds.

Increased intra- and interdisciplinary sophistication was basically responsible for the controversy over the so-called new archaeology and new ethnography. The archaeologists, now collaborating with cultural anthropologists, botanists, geologists, zoologists, ethologists, systems theorists, and many others as well, had developed new methods and techniques for making inferences about the past. More sophisticated use of mathematical and statistical procedures had led to the rise of computer simulation studies.

In a scene reminiscent of "Hamlet," archaeologist Wilburn Cockrell examines the skull of a young Indian retrieved from an underwater cave near North Port Charlotte, Fla. The skull was believed to be the oldest human remains ever found in the eastern U.S.

UPI COMPIX

The single most talked about item among those interested in early man was the large-brained skull from Lake Rudolf, Kenya, reported in 1972 by Richard Leakey, with a date of between 2.6 million and 3 million years ago. The most striking feature of this skull was its cranial capacity of 800 cc, far larger than that of any hominid of the same or even closely succeeding time ranges. On the basis of this fossil, it was suggested that the genus *Homo* was contemporaneous with the known australopithecines, rather than having evolved from one or another of them, as had been argued previously. Various artifacts had come from the same deposits, but they were not found in direct association with the skull. Not all authorities were satisfied that either the dates or the inferences were correct.

The new ethnography resulted from the merging of traditional cultural anthropology with modern linguistic techniques. This gave rise to a new interest, usually called ethnoscience, which held promise—according to its practitioners, at least—of cross-cultural understanding at levels hitherto believed impossible. The focus here was on the classificatory schemes and cognitive categories of the people being studied, rather than those imposed by Western scientists. This was related, in turn, to the structural anthropology of Claude Lévi-Strauss, which deals with "fundamental structures of the mind." It was also related to yet another new interest, symbolic anthropology, which attempted to deal with cultures as systems of significant symbols necessary for human evolution and survival.

Contrary to what might be assumed, this increased interdisciplinary collaboration had actually helped to maintain anthropology as the most comprehensive of all the disciplines dedicated to the study of man. This was so despite the tendency for the subfields within anthropology itself to fractionate administratively as a result of their exceedingly rapid growth after World War II. A new, more comprehensive view of man and culture seemed to be emerging, variously described as biological anthropology, behavioural anthropology, behavioural evolution, or even Darwinian anthropology. In the words of one of its earliest proponents, A. I. Hallowell, it represented "a conjunctive approach to human evolution [in which] the organic, psychological, social, and cultural dimensions of the evolutionary process are taken into account as they are related to underlying conditions that are necessary and sufficient for a human level of existence." This was a blending of the best anthropological theory with that of many other disciplines. It might well be the single most distinguishing feature of contemporary anthropology.

The Tasaday, the tiny Stone Age population discovered in Mindanao in the Philippines in 1971, reported the birth of a baby girl, increasing by at least that much their doubtful chances for survival. Discovery of a similar small group, with no previous outside contact with other peoples, was reported from the Brazilian Amazon, but the facts of this discovery were not yet clear.

An unusual development in cultural anthropology was the presence of two books by anthropologists, both published in 1972, on the 1973 best-seller lists—*Journey to Ixtlan* by Carlos Castaneda (*see* BIOGRAPHY) and *The Mountain People* by Colin Turnbull.

continued on page 89

THOUGHTS ON THE POTENTIAL OF MANKIND

By Colin M. Turnbull

The Ik, formerly known as the Teuso, are a remnant of a once prosperous and self-sufficient group of hunter-gatherers who roamed a vast mountainous region now divided among Uganda, Sudan, and Kenya. For over two generations they have faced increasing deprivation as political and economic factors forced them into a semisedentary existence in the barren mountains of Uganda's northeastern corner, the least hospitable part of their former homeland. There are no previous studies or records to tell us exactly how the present situation came about, but at the time my own studies began in 1964, what was left of the Ik were facing the constant threat of starvation. Even when starvation was not a reality, the shortage of food was acute enough to kill off any but the strongest. In response, the Ik had developed a completely individualistic, asocial, and loveless society.

The layman might well question the point of my two-year study. Would the time and money not have been better spent in trying to do something for the people? It was a question I often asked myself as I watched people die around me. Since then a colleague (Joseph A. Towles) has returned to Uganda, and in 1971 he found the Ik holding their own. Far from being entirely good news, however, the implications of their continued survival are far-reaching and frighteningly relevant to our own situation in the Western world. If justification for such studies is needed, it surely lies in such relevance.

Although this seems somewhat callous, I should point out that the social anthropologist is concerned primarily with social systems, not with people. This does not mean he is without feelings. Indeed, he *should* have them, and it is precisely this conflict between his own humanity and the detachment his discipline demands that makes fieldwork so difficult and treacherous and ultimately so rewarding. So, putting personal feelings aside for the moment, we find that the study of the Ik financed by the Department of Anthropology of the American Museum of Natural History in New York City reveals a frightening human potential for unsociality that forces us to question our most basic concepts about the nature of humanity.

A Suggestive Parallel. In *The Mountain People,* I described the situation among the Ik, my own reactions to them, and how, to a considerable extent, I became increasingly like them myself. At the end I suggested that certain parallels could be drawn with Western society. I meant no more than a suggestion, but the reactions were immediate and sometimes violent. Some saw it as a prophecy of doom and gloomily accepted it as proven. Others, also taking it to be a conclusion rather than a suggestion, dismissed it as an unscientific and unwarranted generalization.

One colleague, normally restrained and meticulous, was moved to dismiss virtually the whole book as systematic falsification. In his tirade he fell into academic and procedural traps that any first-year student would have avoided. Yet to me his reaction was highly significant because of his own specialized training in avoiding precisely these pitfalls of selectivity, assumption based on personal conviction, imputation of motive, and use of unchecked data. What had happened to him was to some extent what had happened to me in the field. Our painstakingly sought-after objectivity simply became impossible.

I do not think that the book or the Ik situation calls for either uncritical acceptance or denial. But the data, isolated as they are, do demand that we take a long, hard, and entirely new look at ourselves and our humanity. The fact that the Ik represent one isolated case is really irrelevant, for, however singular, it shows that human society and humanity itself have a potential we had never thought possible. If it can happen once, it can again.

Basically, what the Ik tell us is that man is not the social animal we always thought him to be. His prime concern is his individual survival, and sociality is merely a means to that end. In any reasonably balanced economic and ecological situation, sociality is by far the most effective survival technique. But under certain circumstances—and the Ik circumstance is one—sociality can become dysfunctional and actually prove a threat to the survival not only of the individual but also of the group.

We have no right to dismiss the Ik situation because we do not face starvation (though that could well come about). Even a brief look at some of our newer stated values should give us pause, because they are sometimes in direct conflict with our most basic value of sociality. Emphasis on the individual good is found in all phases of life. It is being given much more prominence than the shared, social good, which is relegated to the realm of the ideal.

The Ik Solution. Ik children, from the age of three, are independent of their parents, who thereafter give them neither food and shelter nor affection. The latter may seem the hardest to believe, but it is a necessary corollary of the former, for what is affection, let alone love, if it is not accompanied by giving and receiving? The Ik parents, far from being cruel or inhuman, are merely consistent and logical. Not having enough to guarantee their own survival, they are faced with a choice. If they share what they have, it will be insufficient for anyone, perhaps leading to the death of the entire family. If each parent consumes what little he or she has, at least *they* may survive.

By the age of three, each child has learned that survival is an individual matter. If he finds food he does not think of sharing it with his brothers and sisters, still less with the parents who

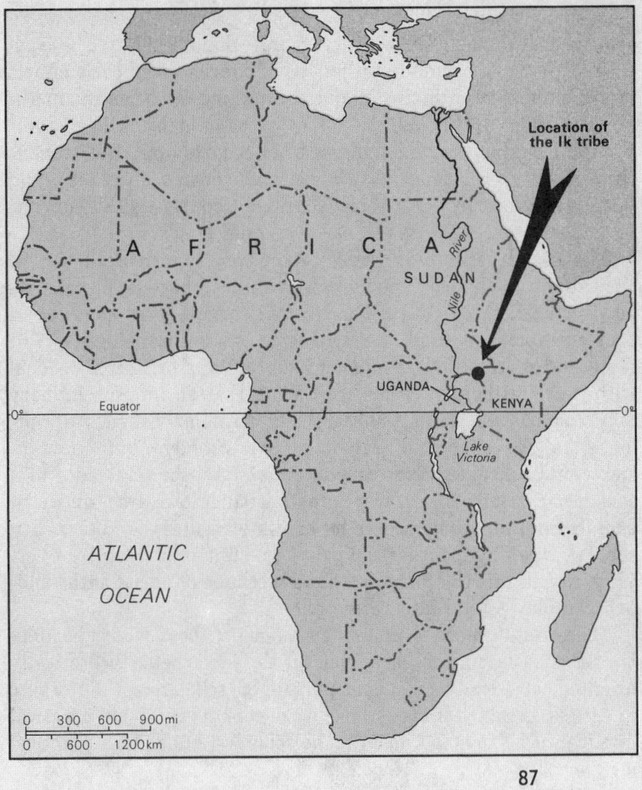

Colin Turnbull, professor of anthropology at Virginia Commonwealth University, has published four books, including The Mountain People *(1972), a report on his experiences with the Ik tribe.*

threw him out. The strongest survive, and since the young teenagers are the strongest, they have the greatest chance of survival, thus ensuring that, even as the weaker children die off, others are born. Thus the group continues to exist at a minimal number. The teen-age breeding group is not only alive but relatively plump and healthy, while the young children and older people (anyone above *25* is old) may be little better than living skeletons.

At first, living among the Ik, one is not aware of starvation. It is only when a village is abandoned that one sees those who are left because they do not have the strength to move. Otherwise, the victims die unseen in their huts and their bodies are surreptitiously removed, or else, more usually, they hobble away to die in the open or die while off on the arduous daily search for food and water.

It is difficult to keep track of such "disappearances," and I was in the field for some time before I realized that starvation was a reality that surrounded me. Only then did I begin to see that the Ik mother was not as heartless as she seemed when she abused her child, not only denying it affection but actually watching with amusement as it hurt itself. But she was quite without love, and by such actions she was keeping herself that way and teaching the child that same vital lesson: that in Ik society love is dysfunctional. By three the Ik child must have learned to rely on nobody, to expect nothing, and to give nothing. And the most important part of that lesson is the denial of love, for therein lies the only way to the denial of mutuality, to the success of individualism in its purest form. Is it not individualism that we honour so highly in Western society, that we teach in our schools and in our games and even use as a yardstick of respectability and success? If, in looking at the Ik and their seemingly inhuman way of life, we see, however dimly, a shadowy reflection of ourselves, we should pursue the nagging self-questioning that must arise. What if our survival, like that of the Ik, lies in a similarly individualistic system of values? We already honour the "self-made man," "rugged individualism," and "self-reliance." Could this be leading us in the same direction of non-sociality and lack of concern for others?

Anthropology and Society. But let us leave such uncomfortable thoughts aside for a moment and consider some other implications of the Ik experience. To my mind it is highly questionable whether social anthropology belongs in the sciences, where it is generally placed, or among the humanities, particularly when one considers its origins in the thought and practical social concern of the 17th- and 18th-century moral philosophers. The successors of those founding fathers have concentrated their efforts on developing scientific techniques of inquiry and scientific methods for ordering the results. Today we have highly refined tools for the examination and analysis of social systems. But what is the validity of a science that has lost all touch with reality, and what is the morality of a social scientist who has lost all concern for society, except as a means of earning a living?

In these days of overspecialization we cannot be all things. We cannot be philosophers as well as anthropologists, nor can we be psychiatrists or educationists or historians. Nor can we expect members of those disciplines to be anthropologists. But more and more study groups and conferences organized to deal with practical human issues are finding that an interdisciplinary approach has enormous advantages. By bringing a variety of outlooks and approaches to bear on a single problem, quite new insights may be gained. It is easy to understand the reluctance of a social scientist to be drawn into the dangerous area of social engineering, for of all people he knows how little he knows. But scholars working together can gain a much more perceptive overview, and in this the techniques and methods of social anthropology can play a vital integrative role.

There is still more than enough room for those whose particular talents lie in the direction of the detached, theoretically oriented, classically academic pursuit of scholarship. But there is also a great need for those who seek to find its practical application. They, too, need to be scholars, but with a practical

COLIN M. TURNBULL

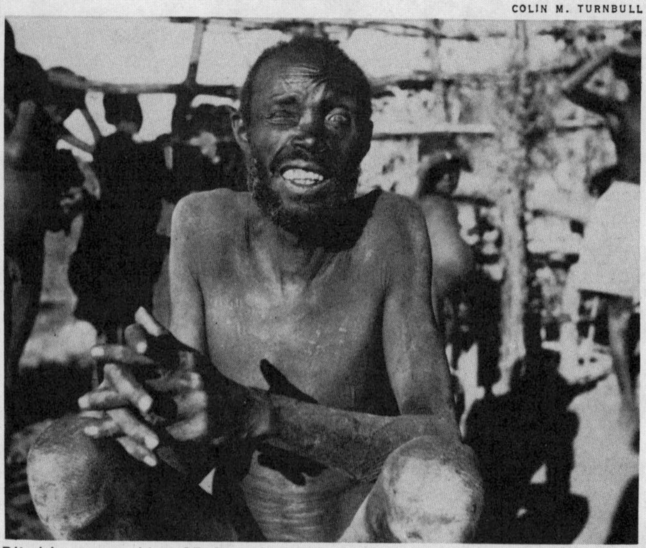

Blind Logwara, old at 25. The old people, like Logwara, accept their impending fate with remarkable ease, since they have always known it would be.

rather than a theoretical orientation. They must be able to communicate (as many theoreticians cannot) with those who are responsible for men's destinies in the practical world of affairs.

The old days of the all-around scholar are gone; there is simply too much to cope with. But that is no reason for forcing such limitations on students who have no intention of becoming professional scholars, and far too many curricula are designed as if their only goal were the production of yet more professionals. Even in many liberal arts programs, the student—who is, after all, probably going to be a businessman, an administrator, a civil servant, or that increasingly rare animal, a housewife—is put through a series of exercises designed to persuade him that he should be a historian, a philosopher, or an economist.

What is there for the individual who will not be any of these things but who needs to know how to face life and to find in it some meaning and purpose? Where there is no sense of meaning and purpose, "rugged individualism" becomes the only refuge, because the only purpose we can recognize is our own survival and success. Surely scholars have as much duty to talk to laymen as to talk to each other. Yet scholarship today implies not merely knowing everything possible about one's own narrow field; it has come to imply knowing nothing of anything else. Because of this attitude, university teachers fail to communicate with students outside the lecture and tutorial situation. The fault lies no more with the teachers than it does with the students; it lies within the system.

The Scholar's Responsibility. The situation of the Ik raises more personal questions for the scholar as well. What can he do about such a situation, and what should he do? What are his responsibilities to the Ik? And what are his responsibilities to the general public if he feels that this or any other situation he has studied has significance beyond the scholastic world?

In both my recent field trips, among the Ik and, more recently, in the Ituri Forest of Zaire, I worked among people in the throes of involuntary social change. In both cases, the governments concerned were anxious to deal with the situation as best they could, and they were more than ready to discuss the problems. In Uganda, however, the government was occupied with massive internal unrest, and I was able to do little more than submit a report and intercede on a few specific issues.

In Zaire the government was devoting all its energies to consolidating the new nation and was actively seeking to improve the lot of all its peoples. That allowed time and opportunity for organizing an interdisciplinary conference, financed by the Wenner-Gren Foundation for Anthropological Research, in which both the government administration and various areas of scholarship were represented. In terms of scholarship, the result was rewarding, as members of each discipline gained new insights through contact with members of others. But, in practical terms, if the government of Zaire had not been willing to listen and discuss, then the scholarship expended, the research done, would have been an empty thing. Every university has a potential for this kind of interaction, and the greater success seems to lie with those universities that address themselves to practical problems. It is a mark of the extraordinary fragmentation of life today that a university *can* remain aloof from public affairs. This in itself is a typically Ik-like attitude.

It is relatively easy to apply scholarship when one is given the opportunity we were given in Zaire. It is immensely exciting in both academic and personal terms and goes far toward solving the moral problems facing a scholar with half a social conscience. It raises other problems, of course, for one can never foresee all the results of one's plans or even of discussing them. One can never be sure that a government will not use such information for its own purposes. Even that uncertainty does not justify noninvolvement, however; it merely demands added caution. But the problem for the social anthropologist remains: how does he relate his experience to his own world, to his own community?

Seeing Ourselves. In the case of the Ik we are faced with the fact of how they live, with the nonsocial system they have developed to enable them to survive. Whereas most anthropological studies prompt little more than structural comparisons with our own society, the Ik evoke an intensely personal response. The comparison with ourselves is there without our having to make it. It stares us in the face when we read of city dwellers looking on impassively as someone is mugged or murdered. It comes home to us when we bypass a drunk lying in the street, avert our eyes from an accident, or choose to give to this beggar and not that one. It is there to some extent when we send our children away to summer camp, having earlier disposed of them in day schools, and when our children in turn place us in old people's homes when we can no longer fend for ourselves.

The solution the Ik have found to their particular situation is the denial of sociality, the denial even of love. If we perceive so many similarities between our attitudes and theirs, should we not look at our own system to see if it is demanding that we, too, sacrifice sociality? We may not have lost all kindness and compassion and love, but increasingly and, it seems, systematically, we are being compelled to suppress them. It would appear, then, that the social anthropologist has an obligation to put this hypothesis to the test and to apply his techniques and methods to a study of his own society. The sociologist, of course, has long been concerned with contemporary social issues, but in a more fragmented way, without the special kind of overview that the social anthropologist can bring.

We cannot dismiss the Ik as an aberration. They are what they have to be in order to survive, an example of yet another facet of the infinite diversity of humankind. It is not a facet that many of us would opt for; yet a sober appraisal of the facts of Ik life and the facts of our own existence brings a nagging conviction that this is where we are heading. The difference, a vital one, is that the Ik are already there, compelled to be what they are by their utter deprivation.

The danger we face comes not from deprivation but from abundance, from a multiplicity of choices. For us society has become so vast as to be almost meaningless. In self-defense we limit our social horizons, restrict our sense of social responsibility, and ultimately opt for the simplest way out and call it rugged individualism. Abundance, technology, and the cash economy make such isolation possible. The pressures of contemporary living, urban dwelling, and the consequent high density of population make it necessary. The shift in our professed values indicates that we are preparing ourselves for an increasingly isolated, individualistic future. But the Ik provide us with a unique opportunity to see what this could mean. It is to be hoped that there is still time to find a happier alternative.

continued from page 86

Both were highly controversial, within the profession and without, the first because of questions relating to its authenticity and its literary rather than scientific character, the latter because of Turnbull's attempt to generalize from a small, rapidly disappearing group of Africans to American society in general. (*See* Special Report.)

For the first time in many years, there were more professional anthropologists in the U.S. than there were available positions. At the same time, cutbacks in various federal programs had reduced the amount of research and training funds and thus the number of jobs. To create further problems for anthropology, a number of countries, most notably India but also including Fiji and various African nations, announced restrictions on the number of outside researchers to be allowed into their countries and on the kinds of research they would be permitted to conduct. With anthropologists already suspect in a number of South American nations and with many American ethnic minorities becoming increasingly hostile to researchers, there was a growing concern that anthropology must somehow change its image.

The discussion of professional ethics, which had begun two or three years earlier, continued to occupy the attention of anthropologists. Particular concern was expressed during the year about policies of ethnocide and forced relocation, continued racism and sexism, the continued illegal trade in antiquities, and the need for protecting confidentiality of sources, conserving nonhuman primates, and furthering open employment procedures.

Joseph B. Casagrande of the University of Illinois at Urbana became president of the American Anthropological Association, succeeding Anthony F. C. Wallace of the University of Pennsylvania. The United States, the American Anthropological Association, and the University of Chicago were hosts in September for the ninth International Congress of Anthropological and Ethnological Sciences, the largest and most successful to date. Three anthropologists were elected to the National Academy of Sciences: Clifford Geertz of Princeton University, Robert F. Heizer of the University of California at Berkeley, and Anthony F. C. Wallace. This brought the number of anthropologists in the Academy to 23.

Scientists at Detroit's Wayne State University study a remarkably preserved male mummy, believed to be 2,600 years old, in an effort to learn about diseases in ancient Egypt.

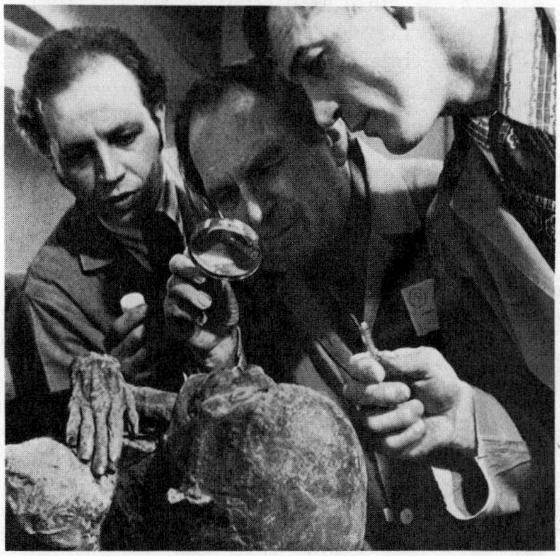

UPI COMPIX

The *American Anthropologist,* the official organ of the American Anthropological Association, divided its functions, and a new journal, the *American Ethnologist,* would be published in addition to it. The change was considered necessary to keep up with the increased volume of publication and also to better serve the various subdivisions of anthropology. Several other new journals and newsletters were started. Among the most notable were *Language and Society* (first published in 1972); *ETHOS; Medical Behavioral Science; Human Ecology* (1972); and *Urban Anthropology* (1972). (LEWIS LEROY LANGNESS)

See also Archaeology.

ENCYCLOPÆDIA BRITANNICA FILMS. *Sentinels of Silence* (1973).

Archaeology

Eastern Hemisphere. What would probably be remembered as the archaeological event of 1973 was a rather sordid cloak-and-dagger tale of the purchase of a Greek vase. The Metropolitan Museum of Art, New York City, reportedly paid $1 million for a broken but restored krater, painted by the master Euphronius about 500 B.C. The museum claimed the vase reached it through a chain of international dealers (such men often act as "fences" for illicitly acquired antiquities). The Italian government claimed the vase had been found north of Rome several years earlier and was exported illegally. There was little doubt that the sum paid for the Euphronius vase raised the already inflated values placed on such antiquities, or that it would give additional stimulation to destructive clandestine digging. (*See* MUSEUMS AND GALLERIES.)

No particularly startling methodological aids to archaeology were reported. The study of the molecular structural sequence of changes in amino acids after an organism dies might lead to a new age-determination method, valuable for the time span earlier than the range of radioactive carbon dating but later than the range of the potassium-argon method. Along with a general increase in archaeological news items coming out of China was the publication of the first listing of radiocarbon age determinations made by the Chinese Academy of Sciences laboratory. Of particular interest were the series that appeared to put the beginnings of the Yang Shao early village horizon as early as 4000 B.C.

The journal *American Antiquity,* which had concerned itself primarily with New World archaeology, introduced—in a section called "Current Research"—brief notes on Old World archaeological fieldwork. A new French journal, *Paleorient,* concerned with the pre- and protohistory of the Near East, also appeared.

Demeter, ancient Greek goddess of the fruitful earth, in the first gold representation ever uncovered. Soviet archaeologists found the 2,300-year-old sculpture in a Scythian burial mound in the Ukrainian S.S.R., and believe it to be part of a necklace.

NOVOSTI/SOVFOTO

Pleistocene Prehistory. In Europe interest continued to shift toward work on open settlement sites, in contrast to work in caves and the image that Pleistocene man was inevitably a cave dweller. Such long-known eastern European open sites as Dolni Vestonice and Pavlov in Czechoslovakia continued to be excavated, while perhaps half the news items on the Paleolithic of western Europe also pertained to open settlement sites. An important late Magdalenian settlement at Gönnersdorf in the Rhine Valley was being cleared.

Considerable archaeological fieldwork on the Pleistocene of Africa continued, mainly in South Africa, Ethiopia, and Kenya. The current status of the eastern Asian Paleolithic was surveyed at a Montreal symposium organized by Fumiko Ikawa-Smith.

The Near East. Once again, archaeological work in this region was disrupted by war, as hostilities between the Arabs and Israelis broke out in October. Reports earlier in the year indicated that more work had been done on the predynastic (early village) range in the Sudan than in Egypt proper. At Luxor a study of the Temple of Khonsu by the Oriental Institute of the University of Chicago yielded important iconographic information on the later pharaohs of the New Kingdom. A new study of the alignment of the Great Pyramids suggested the possibility that their present declination from true north might be due to continental drift since the time of their building. Important work on the early village range and its antecedents had been undertaken in Sinai by James Phillips and in northern Galilee by the French under Jean Perrot and Monique Lechevalier. An Israeli effort under B. Mazar cleared a Philistine temple at Tell Qasile.

The major archaeological efforts in Syria had been pointed toward completing the salvage of sites along the Euphrates River before the flood pool rose behind Meskene Dam. Fourteen different foreign teams took part, and the yield of evidence ranged from about 9000 B.C. to Byzantine times. After several years' interruption, the Oriental Institute had resumed excavation on the great city site of Nippur in Iraq. Various important artifacts and cuneiform tablets were recovered. Robert McC. Adams also had resumed his trail-breaking surface surveys, and a British team under D. Kirkbridge-Helbaek had resumed its clearance at the early village site of Um Dabaghiyah in upper Mesopotamia.

Iran's political stability and remoteness from the Arab-Israeli conflict continued to make it a desirable area for archaeological fieldwork. U.S., British, Canadian, French, West German, and Italian teams, as well as Iranians, were active. The Royal Ontario Museum's work at Godin Tepe yielded a cache of proto-Elamite tablets. At Susa a French expedition under Jean Perrot recovered a portion of a greater-than-life-size statue of Darius I, and it was hoped that the head and shoulders might still be found. The base carried the names (in Egyptian hieroglyphics) of peoples of the different Persian provinces. Marizio Tosi, director of the Italian work at the mound of Sharh-Sokta near the Afghan frontier, identified the shops of various craftsmen.

The authoritative *American Journal of Archaeology*'s yearly collection of news items from Turkey noted a broad spectrum of activities, from Paleolithic to Byzantine in time range, by Turkish and foreign scholars. Important salvage work continued in the area to be covered by the flood pool of the Keban Dam. Ufuk Esin established the presence of the Halafian painted pottery style at Tulin, and a West German expedition under Harald Hauptmann made a broad clearance of Hittite and earlier levels on Norsuntepe. South of the Keban, at Cayonu, Halet Cambel and R. J. Braidwood resumed work for the Joint Istanbul-Chicago Prehistoric Project, with significant architectural clearances in early village levels. The long series of campaigns by the West Germans at Bogazkoy and the Turks at Kultepe continued, with particular attention given to the architectural and town-plan aspects of these great historic sites. The largest synagogue known outside of Israel was partially reconstructed by U.S. archaeologists at Sardis.

The Greco-Roman Regions. The continuing work of Indiana University's team, under Thomas Jacobsen, at the Franchthi cave in the Peloponnesus was adding whole new chapters to late Greek prehistory. The cave yielded evidence of almost continuous human occupation from at least 20,000 B.C. to about 3000 B.C. Obsidian, from the island of Melos, began to appear in the Franchthi sequence at about 7000 B.C., thus providing an early instance of seaborne commerce. More frescoes came from the Aegean island of Thera, where they had been sealed in place by a volcanic eruption around 1500 B.C. Pumice from the Thera eruption was found by the Minnesota Messenia Expedition on the Greek mainland. George Mylonas, in reviewing evidence of the destruction of Mycenae about 1100 B.C., concluded that civil strife and not the Dorian invasion was the cause.

The detailed work of the various foreign academies in Athens and Rome continued. Life-size statues of a young man and a girl, attributed to the sculptor Ariston, were found near Athens. More evidence of Roman viticulture was recovered from the remains of a large vineyard at Pompeii. The remains of a Roman galley, loaded with statues and marble blocks, were located near the entrance to the Bosporus in the Black Sea. A Herodian palace was cleared near Bethlehem, and more Roman catacombs were encountered in Istanbul. Well-preserved traces of documents and clothing were found in a garrison fort next to Hadrian's Wall in northern England.

Late Prehistoric and Historic Europe. The report on the large prehistoric village of Ouroux, in southern Burgundy, appeared, with many details of the cultural and environmental circumstances under which early agricultural settlements appeared in France. Excavations under Bohumil Soudsky continued at the well-preserved village site of Bylany in Czechoslovakia. The Heuneburg, evidently an early Iron Age palace in the upper Danube Valley, was being cleared, as was a German burial mound with well-preserved wooden tools and beams that were being utilized to extend the European tree-ring chronology.

Africa and Asia. In southern Africa there was increasing concentration on the region's remarkable series of rock paintings, which date from at least 1,500 years ago to the present. In western Africa A. Fagg excavated a settlement in which, for the first time, Nok figurines were found in situ. There appeared to be a gratifying increase of archaeological interest in the post-Paleolithic of most of Africa, but the general picture was not yet clear.

Political circumstances discouraged U.S. work on most of the Asian mainland, although French and Italian archaeologists were active in Pakistan and West Germans in Mongolia. In Pakistani Baluchistan, A. H. Dani recovered materials important to the understanding of the origins of the Harappan (Indus Valley) civilization. An intensive archaeological survey in Gujarat, India, was undertaken by Gregory Possehl, with the cooperation of H. D. Sankalia, director of the Deccan College Post-Graduate and Research Institute. Chinese archaeological journals reappeared after a six-year interruption. They contained, among other items, the radiocarbon determinations already noted, which indicated greater antiquity for early agricultural sites in China than had been assumed. More discoveries of remarkably rich royal tombs, from several different dynasties, were reported. Archaeologists were very active in Japan. The Takamatsu tomb find in Nara, yielding a stone coffin and wall paintings, was dated to the 7th–8th century A.D. Chester Gorman, who had previously reported evidence of very early agricultural activity from Spirit Cave in Thailand, located and sampled various other sites; new evidence of food-plant usage was recovered.

(ROBERT J. BRAIDWOOD)

KEYSTONE

This striking Mithras relief is among remains of the ancient Roman town of Interoisa, unearthed at Dunaujvaros, Hungary, by archaeologists of the local museum.

Western Hemisphere. Recent legislation affecting investigation and preservation of archaeological resources, the rise of public interest in archaeology, and the growing awareness of archaeologists on the part of living descendants of pre-Columbian New World inhabitants contributed to a newly awakened self-consciousness within the profession. In 1973 the American Association of Museums adopted a resolution affirming that public display of human skeletal material must reflect concern for human dignity and not be done simply to satisfy the curiosity of visitors. In California the investigation of archaeological remains on the site of the proposed governor's mansion outside Sacramento aroused considerable political interest when Indian groups opposed the excavation of an ancient cemetery. Similar resistance to archaeological fieldwork had arisen within several Indian communities, but in other cases archaeologists and Indians worked in cooperation, facilitating surveys such as those conducted by the University of Colorado within the Southern Ute Reservation and by the Museum of Northern Arizona within the Navajo Reservation.

Archaeological research interests in 1973 focused on reconstructions of prehistoric environments and on questions concerning the location of archaeological sites, the emergence of social ranking and stratification, and the development and functioning of exchange systems. Problems of sampling methodology and computer use continued to receive emphasis, as did technical studies of trade materials. James B. Griffin, University of Michigan, reported that neutron activation studies had identified the Yellowstone Park region as the source of obsidian found in Hopewell sites in the Upper Mississippi Valley. Separate obsidian studies by Robert N. Jack, University of California at Berkeley, Thomas L. Jackson, California State University, San Francisco, and Jonathan E. Ericson, University of California at Los Angeles, identified sources and dispersal routes for obsidian employed in prehistoric California and Nevada.

A number of independent studies contributed information regarding exchange systems in Meso-

Antimony:
see Mining

Arab Emirates:
see United Arab Emirates

Arabia:
see Bahrain; Kuwait; Middle Eastern Affairs; Oman; Qatar; Saudi Arabia; United Arab Emirates; Yemen, People's Democratic Republic of; Yemen Arab Republic

Arab League:
see Middle Eastern Affairs

america. Charles C. Kolb, Bryn Mawr (Pa.) College, identified unworked marine shell recovered from sites in the Teotihuacán Valley, central Mexico, as coming from Panamanian and Caribbean coastal zones and suggested that a small social group served as middlemen in shell importation. Mark Harlan, California State University, Los Angeles, employed ceramic evidence to arrive at tentative definitions of several distinct trading spheres in prehistoric Mesoamerica, while turquoise was utilized by Phillip C. Weigand, State University of New York, Stony Brook, and colleagues to determine prehistoric trade routes in Mesoamerica and the Southwest. Michael P. Simmons, California State College, San Bernardino, traced the use of imported volcanic ash as a tempering agent for ceramics in Northern Yucatán.

Archaeoastronomy. An origin for the previously enigmatic Mesoamerican 260-day ritual calendar was proposed by Vincent H. Malmstrom, Middlebury (Vt.) College, who noted that 260 days mark the interval between zenithal sun positions at about latitude 15° N. Malmstrom proposed that the Late Preclassic ceremonial centre of Izapa, situated at this latitude in the Pacific lowlands of southwestern Mexico, was the most likely place for the origin for the ritual calendar, although Copán, at the same latitude in the highlands of eastern Honduras, later became the principal astronomical centre of the Classic Maya. Archaeoastronomy was a major theme at a summer meeting in Mexico City sponsored by the Consejo Nacional de Ciencia y Tecnologia and the American Association for the Advancement of Science.

Far North. A multidisciplinary research project reported by Jean S. Aigner, University of Connecticut, conducted geologic, ecological, biomedical, and archaeological studies on southwestern Umnak Island, Alaska. Early Aleut occupation was worked out relative to a series of geomorphic events, including the melting of an ice cap 600 m. thick about 11,000 years ago, changes in sea level, and erosion of land surfaces and filling of bays, as well as a catastrophic eruption of Okmok volcano around 8,000 years ago and a brief glacial period approximately 3,000 years ago.

Edwin S. Hall, Jr., and Robert A. McKennan, State University of New York, Brockport, reported an archaeological survey conducted at Old John Lake near Arctic Village in the eastern Brooks Range. The 42 sites discovered were mostly chipping stations, although short-term campsites associated with caribou hunting were also found. The analysis of several hundred stone implements from a series of hunting lookouts around Old Crow Flats, northern Yukon Territory, was reported by W. N. Irving, University of Toronto. Absent or significantly rare were tools attributable to Paleoindian traditions, the Arctic Small Tool tradition, and the late prehistoric Kutchin, suggesting that these cultures did not use lookouts as part of their hunting strategy.

Continental United States. Claire M. Cassidy, University of Minnesota, reported a comparative study of nutrition and general health based on skeletal remains from two prehistoric cultures. The hunter-gatherer population from Indian Knoll in western Kentucky was healthier and suffered significantly less from malnutrition than the farming population from Hardin Village in eastern Kentucky. The findings indicated that, contrary to popular assumption, the stable food supply afforded by farming does not ensure good nutrition or health. The population growth often noted for farming groups may lead to depletion of available game, thus lowering intake of quality protein.

Cynthia Irwin-Williams, Eastern New Mexico University, directed archaeological investigations at Salmon Ruins, an 11th-century Pueblo settlement on the San Juan River in the Four Corners region of the Southwest. In Nevada, Richard Brooks and Robert York, Nevada Archaeological Survey, reported on a reconnaissance conducted in the Spring Mountains. Prehistoric sites were predominantly surface camps, stone circles, and scatters of lithic debris with datable material suggesting utilization between 1500 B.C. and A.D. 1200.

Mesoamerica. Although funding cuts drastically reduced the overall scope of Mesoamerican archaeological investigations, there was a general increase in the work conducted by local institutions. The Instituto Nacional de Antropología e Historia de México continued investigations at Tlapacoya, directed by Lorena Mirambell, and salvage excavations at the La Angostura Dam, directed by Jorge Gussinyer, as well as numerous other projects. Groups from the University of Yucatán, the Centre for Mayan Studies at the University of Mexico, and Monumentos Prehispánicos cooperated in the investigation of Comalcalco on the Seco River in the lowland state of Tabasco. The Foundation for Latin American Anthropological Research (Rhode Island) was granted a four-year concession by the Instituto de Antropología e Historia of Guatemala to conduct multidisciplinary studies in the El Petén rain forest.

Central America. A joint effort of the British Museum and the University of Cambridge attacked a number of archaeological and ecological problems in northern Belize (British Honduras). Under the direction of Norman Hammond, Centre of Latin American Studies, Cambridge, the 1973 phase of the project focused on Protoclassic remains in the Mayan lowlands and their relationship to the emergence of the Classic period. Anthony J. Ranere, University of California at Davis, and the Smithsonian Tropical Re-

KEYSTONE

Buried in the A.D. 79 eruption of Mt. Vesuvius, this courtyard fountain is part of a villa in hitherto legendary Oplontis. The villa was uncovered by Italian archaeologists just five miles from Pompeii.

search Institute conducted excavations at four stratified rockshelters and an open campsite in the upper Chiriquí River canyon in Panama, representing a cultural sequence 7,000 years long. Payson D. Sheets, University of Pennsylvania, reported an investigation of lithic tools and debris from the Barriles chiefdom, dated *c.* A.D. 300, of Chiriquí Province, Panama.

South America. Mario Sanoja and Iraida Vargas, Universidad Central de Venezuela, developed a long cultural sequence based on investigations carried out in the lowlands of eastern Venezuela along the lower Orinoco River. L. Kaplan, University of Massachusetts, Thomas F. Lynch, Cornell University, and C. E. Smith, Jr., University of Alabama, reported the recovery of fully domesticated beans (*Phaseolus vulgaris* and *Phaseolus lunatus*) from the dry deposits of Guitarrero Cave in the Callejón de Huaylas, Peru, within a context that was radiocarbon dated between 10,000 and 7,700 years ago. These were the oldest cultivated beans yet discovered in the New World. S. G. Stephens, North Carolina State University, Raleigh, and M. Edward Moseley, Harvard University, reported cotton remains from four archaeological sites in central coastal Peru that dated about 4,500 to 3,000 years ago. Analysis indicated they were a primitive form of *Gossypium barbadense* that differed little from present-day wild forms of the same species.

Preliminary results were reported for a project conducted by a field party of the University of California at Davis, directed by D. L. True, in the Tarapaca region of northern Chile. Although a number of sites lacked projectile points and were characterized by large bifaces and cobble tools, no radiocarbon dates supporting great antiquity were obtained. In Bolivia, Carlos Ponce Sanginés, Centro de Investigaciones Arqeológicas en Tiwanaku, directed investigation and restoration of the temple of Kalasasaya, while in Argentina the Museo de la Plata continued excavation and restoration at the urban centre of Tastil and initiated a similar project at the urban centre in the Calchaquí Valley. (DAVID A. FREDRICKSON)

See also Anthropology.

ENCYCLOPÆDIA BRITANNICA FILMS. *Sentinels of Silence* (1973).

Architecture

The Sydney Opera House, surely one of the most eagerly anticipated buildings of the 20th century, finally opened in October 1973. Designed by the Danish architect Jørn Utzon in the mid-1950s, the new opera house was world famous even before construction began because of its fantastic structure of giant concrete shell vaults that seemed to express movement and dynamism. The building, which included an opera theatre, concert hall, and drama theatre, cost A$100 million. The podium was of concrete cast at the site, while the famous shells forming the roof were of precast concrete ribs in Y-sections. (*See* AUSTRALIA.)

The energy crisis seemed likely to have an effect on architecture. The sealed-off glass tower, which had come to dominate the urban landscape in recent years, was described as "fantastically inefficient," relying entirely on air conditioning because the windows could not be opened; also, the glass walls were particularly poor insulators, adding to both heating and cooling costs.

The appearance of a new book, *Five Architects*, with an introductory essay by Colin Rowe, was a significant contribution to contemporary architectural thought for its crystallization of one branch of architectural design and theory. In discussing the work of five architects who designed in a style that had been termed, among other things, the "New International Style" and "Neo-Corbusianism," the book grouped together designers working independently and showed how they formed a definite school or movement. The five architects were John Hejduk, Michael Graves, Peter Eisenman, Richard Meier, and Charles Gwathmey. The work described in the book comprised 11 private houses. All five designers were working toward a kind of abstract geometric purity of form divorced from the specific character of the popular environment. In evolving this new movement, they derived their inspiration from the work of Le Corbusier in the 1920s, adapting his vocabulary of white surfaces, clean-cut windows, metal railings, flat roofs, and roof gardens. Rejecting the school of design that had searched for increasing complexity and variety of form, they were striving instead toward a pristine simplicity. While the five all worked in New York, they had kindred spirits in other places. In 1972 the English magazine *Architectural Design* carried an article on "The Neo-Purist School of Architecture" which described the work of a similar group of British designers whose idols were Le Corbusier, Walter Gropius, Ludwig Mies van der Rohe, and the De Stijl group of Dutch designers of the 1920s. This loosely linked British group included Christopher Cross, Jeremy Dixon, Michael Gold, and Edward Jones, all working with the Milton Keynes Development Corp. on a project to design a new town for Buckinghamshire.

Housing. In the U.S. a housing development by Werner Seligmann and Associates could also be fairly described as "New International Style." The New York State Urban Development Corporation's Scattered Site Housing at Ithaca drew on projects of the 1920s and 1930s by Le Corbusier, Gropius, Mies van der Rohe, J. J. P. Oud, and others for its inspiration. The project comprised a series of linked white flat-roofed units built on a hillside overlooking Ithaca, each having its own private outdoor space, cross-ventilation, carpets, and well-fitted bathrooms, despite the limitations imposed by a cost limit of $24 per sq.ft. The project maintained a human scale with a density of 15 units to the acre.

Another solution to low-cost housing was provided in London by the Brunswick Centre on the site of the old Foundling Hospital in Bloomsbury. Twelve years

"THE ARCHITECTURAL PRESS"

London's Brunswick Centre, rising on the site of the old Foundling Hospital in Bloomsbury, rejects the high-rise uniformity of earlier housing developments.

after the original plans were submitted only half the project had been realized, and substantial changes had been made in the design. Designed by Patrick Hodgkinson, it was conceived as a reaction against the high-rise tower-block slabs of housing of the 1950s. The scheme provided one of the first low-rise, high-density solutions to housing and would ultimately provide 560 housing units, 80 shop and office units, and 925 parking places. The controversial development was made up of a series of setback concrete-supported levels, and a greenhouse-like effect was created by the floor-to-ceiling glass cage provided for each living space. It seemed likely that the concrete, at first left raw and gray, would eventually be painted cream like the surrounding Georgian terraces, as Hodgkinson had originally intended.

In West Berlin, the "Märkisches Viertel" housing project was criticized as it neared completion. After nine years of construction the scheme provided homes for 50,000, together with a shopping centre and four schools. More than a dozen different architects were involved in an attempt to achieve variety in the building. Their solution was to provide high-density housing in tall buildings of varying forms, and the scheme attracted much debate on both its architectural and sociological implications. Residents were not all satisfied with the tall blocks, and some complained of a feeling of isolation.

An apartment project in Japan by Sachio Otani featured 14-story buildings in the form of inverted Ys with enormous interior halls. The buildings were part of a new housing development for 130,000 people in the Kawasaki and Kanagawa prefecture redevelopment scheme. Apartments in the stepped-back structures were approached by access galleries.

In Leningrad, U.S.S.R., the Institute for Experimental Projects designed a demountable house unit for use in the Soviet Union's far north. The units could be moved by rail and clipped together into hexagonal clusters on the site.

At the more lavish end of the housing scale, the new residence for the president of Israel was completed in Jerusalem. Designed by Aba Elhanani, who won the national competition for the project, the building was in three parts—reception wing, presidential office, and private residence—and managed to achieve a somewhat reticent monumentality appropriate to its environment and function.

Commercial Buildings. When the American Institute of Architects held its annual convention in San Francisco in May, one of the most remarked upon new buildings was the 840-room Hyatt Regency Hotel which opened during the convention. Designed by John Portman and Associates, who were responsible for similar Hyatt projects in Houston, Chicago, and Atlanta, the new hotel overlooked the waterfront and was part of Embarcadero Center. Its most spectacular feature was the interior lobby, a vast skylighted space 300 ft. long, 170 ft. wide, and 170 ft. high—high enough to allow full-size trees to grow in its interior garden and undoubtedly one of the great interior spaces of the decade.

Architects Kallmann and McKinnell, best known for their Boston City Hall, designed a new bank building for the Boston Five Cents Savings Bank. Situated in a historic area of Boston opposite the old South Meeting House, the new glass-fronted building formed one side of a triangular plaza. Despite its large size it managed to be a positive asset to the urban scene. The bank occupied an awkward wedge-shaped site, and the interior was dominated by a long banking hall 27 ft. high and 100 ft. long.

The new Bank of Ireland headquarters in Dublin, completed in the summer of 1972, was designed by architect Ronald Tallon of Michael Scott and Partners. The two curtain-walled glass buildings in the style of Mies van der Rohe made a nice contrast with the Georgian structures surrounding the site. The larger of the buildings housed public services of the bank, while the smaller accommodated the bank's own internal services. The structure of reinforced concrete had bronze cladding and brown tinted antisun glass on the exterior.

A new commercial complex for Minneapolis, the IDS Center, was designed by architect Philip Johnson with John Burgee. The $100 million complex consisted of four buildings: a 51-story office tower, a 19-story hotel, an 8-story office block, and a 2-story store. These were grouped around a glassed-in central space known as the Crystal Court. The complex tied in with Minneapolis' aerial "skyway" walkway system. The court itself was an inner "room" full of activity that also served as a lobby for the hotel. Mirrored glass was used for both the tower and the hotel.

In Texas, the first terminal of the new Dallas-Fort Worth Regional Airport opened in the fall of 1973. The new airport was being built on a 17,500-ac. site between the two cities. Plans had been drawn up by architects Hellmuth, Obata & Kassabaum with Brodsky, Hopf & Adler along with Geren and Harrell & Hamilton. The terminals were to be arranged in a horseshoe with plenty of space for car parking. Final completion was not scheduled until the year 2001.

An office building for West German radio, designed by Hentrich-Petschnigg and Partners in Cologne, was composed of a series of thin slabs, each slightly offset from the other and each a different height to allow maximum use of natural light. Three smaller buildings completed the group.

Colleges, Libraries, and Museums. A number of schools and universities boasted new arts centres in 1973. At Wallingford, Conn., the new Paul Mellon Center for the Arts, designed by I. M. Pei, formed a gateway between two preparatory schools: Choate and Rosemary Hall. The latter, a girls' school, had moved from Greenwich, Conn., to link up with all-male Choate in 1971, and the new arts centre was conceived as a link between the historic boys' campus and the new girls' campus yet to be built. The complex consisted of two buildings bisected diagonally by a curving pathway that ended in a broad staircase. In-

In a juxtaposition that spans 78 years, Boston Public Library's new wing complements the old building, one of the city's most cherished landmarks. The work of Philip Johnson and John Burgee, the new wing opened in September 1973.

JOYCE DOPKEEN—THE

side were a lounge area, theatre, art study rooms, and practice rooms. In all, there were six levels, including a partially underground auditorium.

The Musical Arts Center at Indiana University, Bloomington, designed by Woollen Associates of Indianapolis, included an opera house and various teaching "lofts." The centre was more or less symmetrically massed, though the concrete structure was criticized by some as too assertive. The small central opera house seated 1,460 and provided a well-equipped working theatre with intimate surroundings.

Schweitzer Associates of Winter Park, Fla., were responsible for the design of the new Ludd M. Spivey Fine Arts Center for Florida Southern College, Lakeland. The new centre had to harmonize with the famous campus designed by Frank Lloyd Wright. The centre contained classrooms for the visual and performing arts, administration space, a gallery, and a 300-seat theatre. The construction was of concrete block walls, poured concrete floors, and a steel-decked roof covered with beige concrete outside.

A new campus for Bryant College was completed on a 220-ac. site near Providence, R.I. The $17 million complex by J. Robert Hillier Architects/Planners was designed to accommodate 1,200 resident and 1,000 day students. The main building was located at the crest of a hill and consisted of two squares joined at two corners by a vast domed area that was the central focus of the campus, both practically and symbolically.

In Oxford, Eng., a new residential building for Keble College by Ahrends, Burton and Koralek was praised for its harmony with the fine original buildings of the college designed by William Butterfield, one of the most colourful of English Victorian architects. The building was to provide 89 study bedrooms, 13 fellows' rooms, and 2 fellows' apartments as well as lecture rooms, common rooms, squash courts, etc. The small quadrangle formed by the new block was linked to the old by a long, thin screen building. Construction was of load-bearing brickwork with concrete floors and roofs. The yellow-buff handmade bricks and brown-tinted glass echoed the warm effect of the ornate red brick Victorian buildings.

After a long delay the design for the John F. Kennedy Library at Cambridge, Mass., was finally announced and a model put on display. The library, which was expected to open in three years, consisted of a glass-enclosed pyramid 85 ft. high, partially surrounded by a low curved building that would house the presidential archives and Harvard University's Institute of Politics. The cost of the library was expected to be $27 million.

The Nathan M. Pusey Library was being built underground at Harvard University. Designed by Hugh Stubbins and Associates, the library was planned to cover 87,000 sq.ft. with two levels completely underground and the third slightly above ground. A landscaped plaza would cover the top.

A new branch of Antioch College at Columbia, Md., opened, housed in a giant air-supported "bubble." Designed by Charles Tilford and Rik Ekstrom and built by students over a three-year period, the air structure was part of Antioch's continuing experimental approach to education. The bubble, which covered 180 sq.ft., cost only $179,000. Students at the School of Building of the University of New South Wales, Sydney, Austr., completed a multistory air-supported building 20 ft. high and 13 ft. in diameter. The structure was surrounded by a membrane of polyvinyl chloride. Other institutions exploring the growing field of air-structures included Harvard, the University of Minnesota, LaVerne (Calif.) College, and South Dakota State University.

AUTHENTICATED NEWS INTERNATIONAL

The dramatic Hyatt Regency Hotel in San Francisco, opened in May 1973, stands opposite the famous Ferry Building in Embarcadero Center. Interior rooms open on a vast, skylighted lobby featuring restaurants and shops.

The North Jutland Museum of Arts in Ålborg, Den., was completed late in 1972 to designs by Elissa and Alvar Aalto and Jean-Jacques Baruel. In the central gallery, 25 m. long, a series of beams and shields diffused the daylight to create a remarkable feeling of luminosity, and there was lavish use of Carrara marble throughout the brick and concrete structure.

Other Buildings. A large sports complex for Chamonix, France, was designed by French government architect Roger Taillibert. Composed of a series of dome-shaped concrete shells, the sports centre would eventually cover a total of 775,000 sq.ft. The complex, of which the sports centre and Olympic pool buildings were already open, would eventually include museums, hotels, and a ski school.

Near Hamburg, W.Ger., the world's first all-plastic lighthouse was completed. The tower, 15 m. high and with a wall thickness of 15 mm., functioned completely automatically. (SANDRA MILLIKIN)

See also Cities and Urban Affairs; Engineering Projects; Environment; Historic Buildings; Housing; Industrial Review.

ENCYCLOPÆDIA BRITANNICA FILMS. *The Medieval Mind* (1969).

Arctic Regions

In the North American Arctic, the dominant questions in 1973 concerned the environmental, economic, and social effects of pending resource development. These questions were intertwined with the growing energy debate in Canada and the U.S. and, in Canada, with a growing sense of economic nationalism. As the year ended it was clear that the vast northern resources would not be fully developed until at least some of these issues had been resolved.

Arctic Regions

In the face of the worsening energy crisis in the U.S., Congress hastily passed a bill that appeared to clear the way for construction of the long-delayed trans-Alaska oil pipeline, and Pres. Richard Nixon signed the measure on November 16. In September the governor of Alaska had announced that work on the pipeline could begin by 1974. (*See* ENVIRONMENT.) Two groups were competing for the rights to transport natural gas from the North Slope. Canadian Arctic Gas Study Ltd., a consortium of over 20 Canadian and U.S. companies, proposed building a 48-in. gas pipeline down the Mackenzie River. El Paso Natural Gas Co. was proposing an 800-mi., 42-in. gas pipeline from the North Slope to a point somewhere in south-central Alaska, where the gas would be liquefied for transshipment. Late in the year two consulting firms independently confirmed estimates of proven and potential gas reserves of 55 trillion cu.ft. in the Mackenzie River Delta and the shallow waters of the Beaufort Sea, plus substantial reserves beyond the shallow water area.

Thousands of unexpected claimants were discovered in a worldwide search for Eskimos, Aleuts, and Indians eligible to share in the $962.5 million Alaska Native Claims Settlement Act. When Congress authorized appropriations in 1971, it was estimated 55,000 to 60,000 natives would share in the settlement, but in 1973 it appeared that the number might go as high as 80,000. Over 170 villages were tentatively declared eligible to participate as profit or nonprofit businesses able to hold, invest, manage, and distribute lands, funds, and other assets. After the enrollment was completed, nearly 40 million ac. of Alaska land would be conveyed to the Alaska Native Corporations.

Midway through the year the Canadian government announced its intention to negotiate Indian and Eskimo claims and to settle outstanding treaty commitments. It was estimated that payments of more than $3 billion would be made eventually, exclusive of land allocations. In September the Northwest Territories Supreme Court ruled that the Indian Brotherhood had sufficient interest in 400,000 sq.mi. (about one-third of the territory) to allow it to file a legal statement of interest against the title. The Brotherhood's claim was based on treaties signed in 1899 and 1921. Although the court did not decide who owned what land, its ruling was a clear warning that titles in the area might not be clear. The decision was historic in that it acknowledged the validity of aboriginal rights that the Canadian government had never officially recognized. Meanwhile, the approximately 2,500 Indians in the Yukon Territory asked for $100 million in royalties and a large amount of land in settlement of their claims.

In January, the Canadian government announced the ten-year Northwest Transportation Plan. Key recommendations included establishing a final railway strategy for the Yukon, economic studies of the Mackenzie Basin, and paving of parts of the Alaska Highway. Late in the year the Arctic Institute of North America released a major report on the development of Arctic marine commerce to the year 2000. If a marine system was developed to supplement planned pipelines, as many as 21 to 33 icebreaking oil tankers with capacities of 245,000 deadweight tons would be needed for operations from offshore terminals north of Alaska to the U.S. East Coast. Arctic ore carrier operations would require three to seven bulk carriers to transport fluorite and copper to the U.S. mainland and coal to Japan.

Two U.S. companies and the Soviet government announced plans to bring natural gas from Siberia to the U.S. by 1979. The plans called for the movement of 2,000,000,000 cu.ft. of natural gas per day through 2,000 mi. of pipeline from Yakutsk, in northeastern Siberia, to the Pacific port of Vladivostok. From there it would go to the U.S. West Coast in tankers especially equipped to keep the gas in liquid form at very low temperatures. Total cost of the project would be in the $4 billion range.

In a daring attempt to extend the regular shipping season of the northern sea route, a Soviet convoy of nine ships, including five icebreakers, successfully completed a historic 800-mi. voyage from Norilsk on the Yenisei River to Murmansk on the Barents Sea during January. Normally the ice-infested seaway route was open only from July to November. The Soviet Union announced the opening of the first Arctic nuclear power station, located in the Kola Peninsula. The station would provide power to mines and industries in the Murmansk region.

It was estimated that as many as 24,000 mining claims might be recorded in the Yukon and Northwest Territories during 1973 as soaring gold prices brought renewed interest in gold mining. With gold prices pushing $100 an ounce, sluicing the long-deserted creeks that feed the Klondike River was again becoming a profitable enterprise. The rebound in the hunt for gold came on the 75th anniversary of the Klondike gold rush. The Canadian minister of northern development announced an agreement with the provincial government of British Columbia for acquisition of its share of the historic Chilkoot Trail, to be included in a new Klondike Gold Rush International Historic Park. The U.S. government previously had designated its portion of the trail as part of the park. The Chilkoot Trail was a major route into the goldfields in 1898. Also inaugurated for the anniversary of the gold rush was a special brand of liquor, Yukon Hootch, produced solely for distribution by the territorial government. Yukon Hootch was a brew of Canadian and imported rums said to have originated during gold rush days in an Indian village that was known as Hootchinoo.

Scientists studying the Alaska fur seals believed the herds numbered 10,000 fewer than they should according to previous population estimates. The decline was blamed on oil pollution of the sea and a reduction in the food supply through overharvesting of bottom fish by certain Pacific nations. An agreement to protect polar bears was signed late in 1973 by the five circumpolar countries, Canada, Denmark, Norway, the Soviet Union, and the U.S.

The Canadian government announced construction of a new research laboratory at Igloolik, the main Eskimo settlement in the Foxe Basin area of the Northwest Territories. In September a Soviet expedition began a sea voyage to an unexplored part of the Arctic Ocean to establish a new winter laboratory on a drifting iceberg, reported by Tass to be located on the 79th parallel in the eastern sector of the Arctic Basin. The expedition was the third in the Soviet Union's "Polar Experiment" program, which was concerned with collecting data to improve forecasting of ice and weather conditions. In March, Soviet and U.S. ships completed an unusual joint research project on ice and weather patterns in the Bering Sea. The experiments were conducted under a weather satellite agreement signed by the two countries in 1971.

(KENNETH DE LA BARRE)

Areas:
see Populations and Areas; *see also the individual country articles*

Argentina

The federal republic of Argentina, occupying the southeastern section of South America, is bounded by Bolivia, Paraguay, Brazil, Uruguay, Chile, and the Atlantic Ocean. It is the second largest Latin-American country, after Brazil, with an area of 1,072,157 sq.mi. (2,776,888 sq.km.). Pop. (1972 est.): 23,392,000. Cap. and largest city: Buenos Aires (pop., 1970, 2,972,453). Language: Spanish. Religion: mainly Roman Catholic. Presidents in 1973, Lieut. Gen. Alejandro Agustín Lanusse and, from May 25 to July 13, Héctor Cámpora; interim president from July 13 to October 12, Rául Lastiri; president after October 12, Juan Domingo Perón.

Domestic Affairs. General elections were held as planned on March 11, 1973, thereby marking the end of the "Argentine Revolution" and, at the same time, of more than seven years of military rule. To the surprise of many local and foreign observers, Héctor Cámpora—the personal choice of Juan Perón (*see* BIOGRAPHY) as presidential candidate for the Frente Justicialista de Liberación alliance of parties (Frejuli) —won a resounding victory.

The electoral procedure had been established in the hope that ultimately it would work to block the election of a Peronista president or government. Indeed, prior to the elections, most commentators believed that the Frejuli presidential candidate would probably win the first ballot but would never poll the 50%-plus-one-vote majority required for immediate election. Subsequent events showed that these prognostications were incorrect. Cámpora came so close to obtaining the required number of votes for immediate election (49.6%), and his nearest rival, the Radical Party (Unión Cívica Radical) leader, Ricardo Balbín, was so far behind (21.3%) that it immediately became obvious to President Lanusse that a second ballot would serve no purpose.

A major factor in the success of the Peronistas at the polls was undoubtedly the magnetic personality of Perón and his ability to weave an electoral web not only around the disparate Peronista groupings but also former president Arturo Frondizi, thereby ensuring the support of dissident radical votes. With Héctor Cámpora and Vicente Solano Lima—both staunch conservatives—as presidential and vice-presidential candidates, the Frejuli alliance was thus able to draw votes from practically every part of the political spectrum. The Frejuli victory was also reflected in the fact that the alliance won all provincial governorships except in Neuquén and Santiago del Estero and an overwhelmingly strong position in Congress.

President Cámpora took office on May 25 and soon concentrated on submitting the various legislative proposals to Congress that would form the framework of the new economic strategy. Diplomatic links were immediately established with Cuba, North Korea, and East Germany. Soon, however, it became increasingly obvious that President Cámpora was finding it extremely difficult to weld together the many groupings within Frejuli and even within the Peronista Party itself. Subversive activities escalated, and conflicts between opposing groups of left-wing and right-wing Peronistas became more acute. At the end of June, Cámpora took a firm stand against the guerrilla groups, notably against the Ejército Revolucionario del Pueblo (ERP).

Having condemned the actions of the guerrillas, President Cámpora surprised many Argentines by announcing on July 13 that he and his vice-president, Solano Lima, had resigned from their respective offices in order that the path might be clear to enable Perón to assume his rightful position as president of Argentina. New elections for the presidency and vice-presidency were announced for September 23, and Perón and his third wife, María Estela Martínez de Perón (Isabelita), accepted the Justicialista Party's nomination. The elections resulted in a massive victory for Perón and his wife, who together polled 62% of the votes. Ricardo Balbín obtained only 24%. Perón and his wife took office as president and vice-president, respectively, on October 12.

Perón's electoral victory was marred by an upsurge of subversive activities. José Rucci, secretary-general of the Confederación General de Trabajo (CGT) and one of Perón's most loyal supporters, was murdered on September 25 by an extremist organization, reportedly the ERP. After Rucci's death, Perón moved strongly against the left. Not only were the extremist and terrorist groups condemned but the decision was also taken that all Marxist elements be eliminated from government and from the Justicial-

WIDE WORLD

Juan Perón, after 17 years in exile, returned to Argentina in June 1973. Despite some violent reaction, the people once again elected him president.

ARGENTINA

Education. (1970) Primary, pupils 3,465,499, teachers 186,720; secondary (1969), pupils 211,537, teachers 31,947; vocational (1969), pupils 519,079, teachers 71,583; teacher training (1969), students 194,190, teachers 25,702; higher (including 15 main universities), students 369,912, teaching staff 18,114.

Finance. Monetary unit: peso, with (Sept. 17, 1973) a free rate of 5 pesos to U.S. $1 (12.05 pesos = £1 sterling) and a financial rate of 9.98 pesos to U.S. $1 (24.05 pesos = £1 sterling). Gold, SDRs, and foreign exchange, central bank: (March 1973) U.S. $144 million; (March 1972) U.S. $278 million. Budget (1970 est.): revenue (total) 10,642,000,000 pesos; expenditure 8,016,000,000 pesos (capital expenditure 4,368,000,000 pesos). Gross national product: (1969) 79,820,000,000 pesos; (1968) 68,320,000,000 pesos. Money supply: (April 1973) 41,010,000,000 pesos; (April 1972) 24,580,000,000 pesos. Cost of living (Buenos Aires; 1963 = 100): (April 1973) 1,308; (April 1972) 744.

Foreign Trade. (1971) Imports 8,579,000,000 pesos; exports 7,968,000,000 pesos. Import sources: U.S. 22%; West Germany 12%; Brazil 11%; Japan 8%; Italy 6%; U.K. 6%. Export destinations: Italy 15%; U.S. 9%; The Netherlands 9%; Chile 7%; Spain 7%; U.K. 7%; West Germany 7%; Brazil 6%. Main exports: meat 24%; corn 19%.

Transport and Communications. Roads (1971) 220,332 km. Motor vehicles in use (1970): passenger 1,550,000; commercial 750,000. Railways: (1971) 39,546 km.; traffic (1972) 12,183,000,000 passenger-km., freight 12,284,000,000 net ton-km. Air traffic (1971): 2,700,000,000 passenger-km.; freight 66,550,000 net ton-km. Shipping (1972): merchant vessels 100 gross tons and over 343; gross tonnage 1,401,075. Telephones (Dec. 1971) 1,828,000. Radio receivers (Dec. 1970) 9 million. Television receivers (Dec. 1970) 3.5 million.

Agriculture. Production (in 000; metric tons; 1972; 1971 in parentheses): wheat 8,100 (5,440); corn 5,860 (9,930); sorghum (1971) 4,784, (1970) 4,068; barley 880 (553); rye 690 (256); oats 666 (475); potatoes 1,340 (1,958); sugar, raw value 1,300 (996); linseed 330 (316); sunflower seed 828 (830); cotton, lint 90 (84); oranges (1971) 1,255, (1970) 1,092; apples 512 (424); wine 1,999 (2,178); tobacco 65 (62); beef and veal 2,203 (2,017); cheese 202 (193); wool (1971) 91, (1970) 98; quebracho extract (1971) 79, (1970) 91. Livestock (in 000; June 1972): cattle *c.* 52,000; sheep *c.* 43,600; pigs *c.* 4,300; horses (1971) *c.* 3,600; poultry (1971) *c.* 55,000.

Industry. Fuel and power (in 000; metric tons; 1972): coal 676; crude oil 22,009; natural gas (cu.m.) 6,182,000; electricity (excluding most industrial production; kw-hr.) 20,555,000. Production (in 000; metric tons; 1972): cement 5,451; crude steel 2,106; cotton yarn (1971) 94; nylon, etc., yarn and fibres 39; passenger cars (including assembly; units; 1971) 196; commercial vehicles (including assembly; units; 1971) 56.

G. SIPAHIOGLU—LIAISON

Young Argentines swarming at a political rally demonstrate their support of Juan Perón. Signs also display their enduring reverence for his second wife, Eva.

ista Party itself. One of the first victims was Rodolfo Puiggros, rector of the University of Buenos Aires, who was asked to resign. Nevertheless, terrorism continued, not all of it emanating from the left. In late October Pablo Marcelo Fredes, a leftist union leader, became the sixth assassination victim in a little over a month. In November a U.S. automobile company executive was ambushed and assassinated, together with his three bodyguards.

The Economy. The economy made reasonable progress in 1973, and a gross domestic product growth rate of about 6% was expected for the year as a whole. The Cámpora and Lastiri administrations were successful in checking the rate of inflation in the three months to the end of August, the index of consumer prices declining by 2.2%. In the final quarter of the year, however, shortages of some foodstuffs developed.

The budget deficit continued to be a serious problem and reflected the country's general inflationary climate. The Ministry of Treasury and Finance stated that the budget deficit for 1973, initially estimated at 6.9 billion pesos and later revised to 21 billion pesos, would finally total 31.3 billion pesos.

A month before submitting his resignation, Cámpora announced an economic and social program that had been previously worked out and agreed on by the CGT and the Confederación General Económica (CGE). Although Perón was expected to make some changes in the plan, the basic guidelines were likely to remain unaltered. The principal objectives of the program were the redistribution of incomes in favour of the low-income groups; the redistribution of public revenues and expenditure; financial reorganization and economic reactivation; and achieving increased efficiency in the marketing systems.

(WILLIAM BELTRÁN)

Art Exhibitions

Armies:
see Defense

Art:
see Architecture; Art Exhibitions; Art Sales; Dance; Literature; Museums and Galleries; Theatre

"Treasures of Chinese Art" was the title of the most celebrated art exhibition of 1973. Shown in Paris in the spring and summer and then in London in the fall and winter, the show was assembled by China in an effort to promote better understanding between the Chinese people and people in other parts of the world. The show offered the first opportunity for Westerners to see the fruits of archaeological excavations made in China since 1949. The emphasis was on objects discovered since the start of the Cultural Revolution in the mid-1960s.

The various art objects on display had been buried for periods ranging from 600 to 7,000 years. The most spectacular exhibits were those taken from the double tomb of the imperial Prince Liu Sheng and his wife Princess Tou Wan. The tomb was discovered in 1968 at Man-ch'eng, about 150 km. SW of Peking, and dates from the Han dynasty (late 2nd century B.C.). The 2,800 objects found in the tomb included many gold-inlaid bronze pieces. The priceless jade suits that clothed the bodies were made from pieces of jade varying in size and sewn together with fine gold links. Jade was believed by the ancient Chinese to be life-giving. The princess' jade suit had 2,156 plates of the precious stone.

Spectacular as it was, the Chinese exhibition was not the only one in 1973 to contribute to wider understanding between distant nations and peoples. "Impressionists and Post-Impressionists from the U.S.S.R." was a show of 41 paintings lent to various U.S. museums, including the National Gallery of Art in Washington, D.C., the Art Institute of Chicago, and the Los Angeles County Museum of Art, by the Soviet Union. All the great names in modern art were represented, including Matisse (seven canvases), Monet, Pissarro, Gauguin, Van Gogh, Braque, Picasso, and Cézanne. The paintings came from the collections of two great museums in the U.S.S.R., the Hermitage Museum in Leningrad and the Pushkin Museum in Moscow. The works had been collected before the 1917 Revolution by Ivan Morozov and Serge Shchukin, two well-known Russian art connoisseurs. Shchukin was one of Matisse's greatest patrons, and the brilliant "Nasturtiums with the Dance," one of the works in the exhibition, was painted by the French artist especially for him.

There were many shows in 1973 devoted to works of modern art, as 20th-century painting continued to attract the interest of museum-goers. In Avignon, France, the first posthumous exhibition of work by the great Pablo Picasso was mounted at the Chapelle du Palais des Papes in late spring. The show included 201 canvases painted between October 1970 and Picasso's death in April 1973 (*see* OBITUARIES). The subject matter of many of these late works was childhood, and the exhibition was notable for its gentle and peaceful atmosphere.

The Solomon R. Guggenheim Museum in New York City held its largest-ever exhibition, a retrospective devoted to the work of the French artist Jean Dubuffet, with 145 paintings, 115 drawings, and 40 "Hourloupes." The same show was seen in Paris at the Grand Palais in the fall. Also in Paris, the Musée de l'Orangerie mounted a retrospective of the work of the Lithuanian-born artist Chaim Soutine, who made France his adopted home. It included about 100 paintings from collections in France and the U.S. Many of them were the brightly coloured expressionistic canvases for which Soutine was famous.

Edward Burra, one of the better known English surrealist painters, whose work was noted for its satirical quality, was the subject of a retrospective at the Tate Gallery in London in the spring. The exhibition included paintings and some theatre designs, covering half a century of the artist's work. Walter Sickert, the best known of the English Impressionists, was the subject of a well-thought-out exhibition at the gallery of the Fine Art Society in Bond Street, London. The show was planned to coincide with a new book on Sickert and was the most important exhibition devoted to his work since 1960.

In the summer the Haus der Kunst in Munich, W.Ger., mounted a large exhibition devoted to the work of the modern French painter Raoul Dufy. It emphasized his development from the early Fauve period of 1905 through the later influence of Cubism on his decorative linear style. Ninety paintings by Renoir were on view at the Art Institute of Chicago. The canvases dated from 1862 to 1919 and gave visitors a chance to reassess the work of this leading French Impressionist painter so loved for his delightful portraits of women and children.

The Arts Council exhibition at the Hayward Gallery in London in the late summer and fall, "Pioneers of Modern Sculpture 1890–1918," included works by Renoir, Tatlin, Epstein, Archipenko, and others. Over 50 sculptors were represented by more than 200 pieces. Two exhibitions in West Germany were devoted to painters of the German Expressionist movement. At the Haus der Kunst in Munich, a show celebrating the centenary of Lyonel Feininger's birth included the most important of his canvases. Feininger left Germany in 1936 and settled in New York, where his work was to achieve considerable popularity. Emil Nolde was the subject of an exhibition at the Kunsthalle, Cologne, where many of his boldly coloured, emotional canvases were on view.

In the U.S., interest in the work of domestic artists continued to be strong and traveling shows devoted to the work of Winslow Homer and Andrew Wyeth drew large crowds. Other shows examined broader subjects. The Indianapolis (Ind.) Museum of Art mounted the first exhibition to document the theme of religion in American art. There were 123 paintings and sculptures on view representing biblical events and characters. Included were works by such diverse artists as John S. Copley, Thomas Eakins, and Benjamin West, as well as anonymous folk artists and American primitives.

"The Arcadian Landscape: Nineteenth-Century American Painters in Italy" was the title of a show organized by the University of Kansas Museum of Art. It included works by Thomas Cole, George Loring Brown, and Washington Allston and endeavoured to show the influence of Italy on American landscape painters of the 19th century. At the Worcester (Mass.) Art Museum, an exhibition of 40 works of American portraiture emphasized the 19th-century painters who carried on the tradition of such eminent earlier portraitists as Gilbert Stuart.

An exhibition of paintings by George Luks, known for his satirical depictions of down-and-out characters, was mounted in April and May at the Munson-Williams-Proctor Institute in Utica, N.Y. Luks, one of the leading social realists of early 20th-century American painting, worked in such a broad, wet, painterly fashion that he was sometimes referred to as the Frans Hals of American art. A retrospective exhibition devoted to the art of the painter Frederic Remington, known for his pictures of Western scenes in the 19th century and for his portraits of American Indians, was put together by the Amon Carter Museum of Western Art at Fort Worth, Tex.

Two exhibitions were devoted to the art of the Eskimos. "The Far North: 2,000 Years of American Eskimo and Indian Art" was first shown at the National Gallery in Washington and then during the summer at the Anchorage Historical and Fine Arts Museum in Alaska. The show included a large wooden frog from the Sitka National Monument, as well as objects lent by the Soviet Union. The show was also seen in Portland, Ore., and in Fort Worth, Tex. An exhibition of 400 carvings covering 2,800 years of Eskimo art, organized by the Canadian Eskimo Arts Council, was seen in the U.S. exclusively at the Philadelphia Museum of Art. In 1972 the show had toured Europe, including London, Paris, Leningrad, and Copenhagen. The works ranged from 800 B.C. to the present day and reflected daily Eskimo life.

Aspects of architecture provided subjects for worthwhile exhibitions in 1973. At Vicenza, Italy, an exhibition of drawings by Andrea Palladio, a 16th-century architect whose work could be seen in Vicenza and the surrounding countryside, included models and plans as well as drawings. Many of the exhibits were lent by the Royal Institute of British Architects in London. Palladio's work inspired the great 17th-century English architect Inigo Jones. The 400th anniversary of Jones's birth was marked by an exhibition at the Banqueting House, Whitehall, in London. The title of the show was "The King's Arcadia: Inigo Jones and the Stuart Court." Included were over 400 books, paintings, drawings, manuscripts, and masque designs. Jones was as well known in his own time for his theatre designs as for his architecture, and the exhibition in London was successful in delineating both aspects of his career.

At the Victoria and Albert Museum in London, an exhibition entitled "Marble Halls" concentrated on Victorian secular architecture. It was planned as a complement to the exhibition of Victorian church art held at the same museum in the winter of 1971–72. The show, mounted in the fall, included splendidly coloured drawings and models of houses, commercial buildings, hotels, and civic buildings, many from the museum's own collection. An American Victorian architect known for his flamboyance was the subject of an exhibition at the Philadelphia Museum of Art. Frank Furness (1839–1912) was best known in Philadelphia as the architect of the Pennsylvania Academy. The young Louis Sullivan worked in his office for a time.

"The Arts and Crafts Movement in America," organized by the Art Institute of Chicago and Princeton University, concentrated on the style of furniture and decorative arts in the late 19th century as shown in the work of a small but important group of architects and designers. The 300 or so exhibits included many objects never before on public view. A large part of the show was devoted to designers of the Prairie School, including Frank Lloyd Wright.

CENTRAL PRESS/PICTORIAL PARADE

A curious viewer inspects "Asparagus Garden," a bronze sculpture by William D. Figg, on display at the Royal Academy's summer exhibition in London.

JACK MANNING—THE NEW YORK TIMES

A mural by Marvin Johnson was one of the works of inmates of New York City's House of Detention (the Tombs) exhibited in 1973.

Frank Lloyd Wright was also the subject of "An Architect and His Client: Frank Lloyd Wright and Francis W. Little," an exhibition held at the Metropolitan Museum of Art, New York City. The show included furniture, drawings, leaded glass, correspondence, and photographs relating to Northome, a house designed by Wright for the Little family in 1912–14. The living room from Northome was to become part of the museum's permanent collection. It would be housed in the new American wing to be opened in 1976, the U.S. bicentennial year.

It was becoming more and more difficult to stage large loan exhibitions of old master paintings because of the reluctance of museums and private collectors to face the risks involved. Graphic arts were more easily available, however, and provided material for some interesting shows. The National Gallery in Washington held an exhibition of Italian prints that coincided with the appearance of the gallery's catalog of its own collection of engravings. In many cases the exhibition included different impressions of the same print from different collections, enabling the viewer to compare print states.

"Le dessin italien sous la Contre Réforme" was the title of a show of about 100 drawings held at the Pavilion de Flore of the Louvre in Paris. The drawings, from the Louvre's own collection, covered the period from 1563 to *c.* 1630 and included work by Federico Barocci and Ludovico Carracci. The Staatgalerie, Augsburg, W.Ger., celebrated the 500th anniversary of the birth of Hans Burgkmair with an exhibition of his paintings and engravings.

In Paris the Musée Carnavalet mounted a charming exhibition in the fall entitled "Éventails—Actualités—Vie Parisienne," consisting of items selected from the museum's collection of 900 fans. The popular fans, dating from the 18th and 19th centuries, reflected political events and personalities of the day. Included was a replica of a fan given to Mme Bonaparte (Napoleon's mother) by the city of Paris in 1798.

The Vassar College Art Gallery, Poughkeepsie, N.Y., prepared a show of paintings and calligraphy by the 17th-century Chinese painter Chu Ta (*c.* 1626–1705). It was only the third exhibition in the U.S. to be devoted to a single Chinese historical painter, and was the first to be devoted to Chu Ta. All the works were lent by U.S. collections, and the show included exquisite hanging scrolls and a painted fan. The paintings were later seen at the New York Cultural Center.

The Iveagh Bequest, Kenwood, London, mounted a pioneer loan exhibition of paintings and drawings of P. J. de Loutherbourg. De Loutherbourg was born in Strasbourg but worked in England from 1771, becoming a royal academician in 1781. At one time he was engaged by the actor David Garrick to design scenery for the Drury Lane Theatre. The exhibition included an actual working half-scale model of de Loutherbourg's famous *Eidophusikon* or miniature theatre.

"A Flower from Every Meadow" was the title of an exhibition of Mogul paintings shown at Asia House Gallery in New York City and later in San Francisco and Buffalo, N.Y. The colourful Indian miniatures, dating from 1500 to 1900, were all lent by U.S. collections, a testimony to the growing interest in that subject in recent years. (SANDRA MILLIKIN)

See also Museums and Galleries; Photography.

ENCYCLOPÆDIA BRITANNICA FILMS. *The Artist at Work—Jacques Lipchitz Master Sculptor* (1968); *Henry Moore—The Sculptor* (1969); *Siqueiros—"El Maestro"* (1969); *Richard Hunt—Sculptor* (1970); *Interpretations* (1970); *Textiles and Ornamental Arts of India* (1973).

Art Sales

The 1972–73 art auction season took everyone by surprise, not least the auctioneers. Inflation had become an international disease and currency realignments were commonplace; the result was a spiral in art prices far exceeding the marginal adjustments that caused it. Both Sotheby's and Christie's in London reported a 70% rise in turnover, and other auctioneers were not far behind. While business had doubtless increased, higher prices were the main contributing factor.

The most remarkable feature of the year was probably the Japanese invasion of London, Paris, and New York and their equally sudden withdrawal later in the year. Japanese buyers became the dominant force in sales of Oriental ceramics and works of art and in sales of Impressionist and modern painting. On one day in March Japanese buyers openly accounted for 111 of 379 lots of Oriental porcelain at Sotheby's and 106 out of 210 lots of Japanese works of art at Christie's. A Chinese 14th-century underglaze red bowl reached £85,000, a blue-green Korean bottle £40,000, and a Ming double-gourd vase £31,000.

Including commission bids, Christie's calculated that 80% of their March Impressionist sale went to Japan, with a Renoir portrait of Madame Mithouard doubling pre-sale expectations to reach £157,500. In New York a new auction record for a 20th-century American painting was broken by the work of a Japanese expatriate, hitherto considered a minor artist, on March 14; this was "Little Joe with Cow" by Yasuo Kuniyoshi, which reached $220,000. In Paris a Ming vase topped the Fr. 1 million mark.

On May 2, however, Sotheby Parke-Bernet's sale in New York of superb Impressionist paintings from the collection of Norton Simon attracted not a single Japanese bid. Nevertheless, a still life of tulips by Cézanne and a still life of fish by Manet each soared to $1.4 million.

Sales in the U.S. demonstrated such a burgeoning of interest in America's own art and antiques that Parke-Bernet had begun to hold special "American Weeks." In October 1972 a mahogany corner chair in Puritan Chippendale style became the most expensive chair in the world when it fetched $85,000, and a new record for an American painting was established by Thomas Anshutz' "Steelworkers—Noontime," which brought $250,000.

The surprise success in this field was the sale in March of the Edith G. Halpert collection of early 20th-century American painting. Georgia O'Keeffe ousted Roy Lichtenstein with a new record for a living American artist when her "Poppies" made $120,000. However, the record was regained by the Pop and Abstract Expressionist artists on October 18, when Jasper Johns's "Double White Map" brought $240,000 at the New York Parke-Bernet auction of the Robert C. Scull collection, a price that also surpassed that paid for the Kuniyoshi earlier in the year.

A new development in Paris involved the high prices paid for the finest Art Deco furniture. At the Doucet sale in November 1972, a sofa in rosewood, ivory, and mohair by Marcel Coard reached Fr. 150,000, a four-leaf lacquer screen by Eileen Gray Fr. 170,000, and a red lacquer cabinet by Pierre Legrain Fr. 89,000; a four-footed ivory table by Clement Rousseau went to the Metropolitan Museum of Art, New York City, for Fr. 70,000.

In New York, Paris, and London, sales of post-World War II paintings, generally concentrating on the American school, developed and flourished. In Paris, Maître Binoche, which had pioneered contemporary sales, was joined by both Laurin and Loudmer, the Éspace Cardin providing a perfect setting for these sales.

In fact, the boom year affected almost every sector of the art market. In November 1972 John Partridge, a London dealer, paid £125,000 for a single gun, a flintlock fowling piece made by Pierre le Bourgeois for Louis XIII. In December the set of 100 Picasso etchings known as the Vollard Suite doubled salesroom expectations to reach £94,500. In the same month a pair of jewel-like Fra Angelico panels brought £230,000, a Goya portrait £160,000, a rare Georges de La Tour, "The Beggars' Brawl," £399,000, and "The Backgammon Players" by Hendrik Terbrugghen £199,500.

In November 1972 and April 1973, a huge collection of ancient coins were sold by Sotheby's in Zürich, Switz., on behalf of the Metropolitan Museum of Art. The museum was criticized for selling, but prices more than doubled expectations.

New high levels were also reached in prices paid for 19th-century paintings of all nationalities: Turner's "Bonneville, Savoy" made £180,000 at Sotheby's in June 1973; "Easter Morning" by Caspar David Friedrich made £57,750 at Christie's in May; and a "Winter Landscape" by Andreas Schelfhout made 360,000 guilders at Mak van Waay, Amsterdam, in February.

An 18th-century Augsburg silver-mounted table and pair of matching torchères made £190,000 at Sotheby's and a pair of solid silver chandeliers £115,000 at Christie's. An Aelbert Cuyp landscape also made £609,000 at Christie's. Following the news of Picasso's death, an impression of his famous print "Le Repas Frugal" sold for SFr. 465,000 at Kornfeld and Klipstein in Bern, Switz. (GERALDINE NORMAN)

Book Sales. Christie's turnover from sales of books and manuscripts during the 1972–73 season, at £760,000, was more than double the previous season's total of £320,000. Sotheby's London salesrooms, with a considerably higher turnover of £2,550,000, achieved a more modest increase over their 1971–72 total of £2,460,000.

ALLEN GREEN—VISUAL DEPARTURES

Loving collaboration by graffiti "all stars" produced a 30-ft. mural, on display at New York City's Razor Gallery. The assertive signatures in the section shown bespeak reformed graffitists whose raw talent may yet produce the next art craze.

Among the more important items sold in 1973 was the Old Hall manuscript of medieval English music, dating from the early 15th century. Put up for sale at Sotheby's by St. Edmund's College, Old Hall Green, Ware, in July, it failed to reach the reserve of £68,000 but was afterward bought privately for the British Museum Library at an undisclosed figure. Another early English item of outstanding interest was a copy, in contemporary calf binding, of the first printed edition (1532) of Chaucer's complete works, for which the U.S. dealer John Fleming paid £23,000 at Sotheby's in November. In Paris a magnificently illustrated 15th-century Flemish book of hours, *Heures à l'usage de Rome,* from the collection of Robert Danon, was sold for Fr. 240,000 at the Hôtel Drouot.

A three-day sale of children's books and juvenilia at Sotheby's in February, which included first editions of Beatrix Potter, A. A. Milne, G. A. Henty, and Jean de Brunhoff, brought in a total of £30,312. *A Manual for Parents, to which is added a little book for children* (1660), by Thomas White, fetched £500; a first edition of *The Comic Adventures of Old Mother Hubbard and Her Dog* (1805–06) went to a U.S. buyer for £360; and a presentation copy of the first edition of Lewis Carroll's *Alice's Adventures Under Ground* (1886) was bought for £220. In July the autographed manuscript of Daisy Ashford's *The Young Visiters* realized £1,900.

A letter written by Lenin during his Swiss exile to the Petrograd committee of the Bolshevik Party, one of the items in a sale at Sotheby's of autograph letters, documents, and music, was bought by a private New York buyer for £4,200. Forty letters written by Mme Germaine de Staël-Holstein to the dowager duchess of Devonshire during 1813–17 fetched £2,400.

In one of a new series of sales from the Sir Thomas Phillipps collection, also at Sotheby's, the Italian State Archives in Rome acquired for £15,000 letters and documents of the duke of Montemar, commander in chief of the Spanish forces in Italy (1733–37).

At Christie's, in June, a first edition copy of George Herbert's *The Temple* (1633) fetched £5,800 and a manuscript copy of *The Pricke of Conscience* (late 14th century), £4,200. Items in an August sale at Christie's included a copy of Ackermann's *Microcosm of London* (1808–10), with 104 aquatint plates (£1,600), and a fourth-edition copy of Goya's *Los Desastres de la Guerra* (£1,600).

At a sale of 19th-century and modern first editions at Sotheby's in July, £3,000 was paid for Lord Esher's copy of Oscar Wilde's *The Sphynx.* In Paris, at the Danon sale in February, Gustave Flaubert's *Madame*

WIDE WORLD

A world auction record for the purchase of a Picasso was set at Sotheby's in London on July 3, 1973. New York dealer Stephen Hahn paid $675,000 for the painting entitled "Le Mort (La Mise au Tombeau)."

Bovary (1857), in a contemporary English half-calf binding, fetched Fr. 18,000. The copy had been given by Flaubert to Joseph Méry, a well-known writer of the day, and bore the inscription "In hommage from an unknown admirer."

Early atlases, Americana, and travel books continued to find a ready market. At Sotheby's in March, Moses Pitt's *English Atlas* (vol. 1–4, 1680–83) went for £2,600 and Alexander Gardner's *Photographic Sketchbook of the War* (Washington; 1865–66) for £1,500. In June five autograph letters (1709–17) from Increase Mather in Boston to Sir William Ashurst fetched £2,000.

Astronautics

The U.S. space program continued its annual decline during 1973. The National Aeronautics and Space Administration (NASA) requested $3,016,000,000, and Congress voted appropriations of $3,002,100,000, enough to sustain ongoing programs but not enough to start new ones. With an eye toward an even leaner future, the space agency decided to concentrate its resources on keeping the space shuttle development as near to schedule as possible and to cancel some of its unmanned scientific satellites and long-range research programs. In doing so, the agency announced that it was getting out of the communications satellite field altogether and suspending all work on nuclear propulsion development. In addition, it canceled its research on a quiet, experimental, short takeoff and landing aircraft and drastically cut back its high-energy astronomy satellite program.

NASA was also faced with the problem of what to do with some very expensive, leftover hardware from the Apollo program. This included two Saturn V launch vehicles worth $345 million, two Saturn IB launch vehicles and associated components worth $120 million, and three Apollo spacecraft valued at $195 million.

On March 1, 1973, astronaut James A. Lovell, Jr., left the space program and retired from the U.S. Navy as well. At the time of his departure, he had accumulated almost 30 days in space. Astronaut Thomas P. Stafford was promoted to the rank of brigadier general in the U.S. Air Force on Dec. 1, 1972, becoming the youngest officer with flag rank in any of the three services.

France's space program also experienced uncertainty because of the status of European Space Research Organization (ESRO) and European Launcher Development Organization (ELDO) programs. These directly affected the activity at that nation's launching site at Kourou, French Guiana. Constructed at a cost of $102 million in the late 1960s, the range had been planned to become a launch site for ELDO's booster rockets as well as French launch vehicles. With the demise of ELDO's Europa II launch vehicle and no Europa III in sight, the range was expected to be hard pressed for business in the near future. Concerning France's future in space, French Minister of Defense Michel Debré said in late October 1972 that his country might be forced to undertake its own, independent program. He said that four years of attempting to put together a unified European program in ESRO had yielded nothing but frustration.

In the field of international relations in space exploration, U.S. Pres. Richard Nixon made a significant policy statement on Oct. 9, 1972. He said that the launch facilities of the U.S. would be made available to other countries on a cost-reimbursable basis for launching their own satellites for peaceful purposes. Some restrictions were placed on communications satellites, however.

Manned Spaceflight. Easily the most dramatic event in manned space flight for 1973 was Skylab, the only U.S. experiment in large, manned space stations scheduled for the remainder of the century. Launched on May 14 from John F. Kennedy Space Center by a Saturn V rocket, the huge unmanned workshop was in trouble slightly more than a minute after lift-off. Telemetry from the vehicle indicated that something drastic had happened. At that point in its upward thrust into orbit, the micrometeorite shield protecting the orbital workshop had ripped away from the craft. In so doing, the shield took with it one of the two large solar cell panels and jammed the other, preventing it from deploying and providing electric power to Skylab.

Engineers and technicians at the George C. Marshall Space Flight Center in Huntsville, Ala., and the Lyndon B. Johnson Space Center in Houston, Tex., went to work immediately on saving the Skylab and its mission. Almost at the same time, a board of inquiry appointed by James C. Fletcher, NASA administrator, began an investigation of the incident. The board was headed by Bruce T. Lundin, director of NASA's Lewis Research Center in Cleveland, O. According to the report, made on July 19, the cause of the malfunction was "absence of sound engineering leadership." The fault lay in a lack of communications between the various engineering disciplines involved in the design of the shield.

While the board was deliberating, those working on the problem of saving Skylab had decided that the best solution lay in devising a shade to cover the side of the space station facing the sun, since the major problem was to control the buildup of temperatures within the craft. Several designs were proposed and tested at the Marshall Space Center.

The astronaut crew of Charles Conrad, Joseph Kerwin, and Paul Weitz joined the team of technicians working at the Marshall Space Center. On May 22 they practiced deploying a huge solar parasol designed and built in only six days at the Johnson Space Center. Their training took place in a large water tank at the Marshall Space Center in which a replica of the Skylab permitted them to perform tasks in simulated weightlessness.

On May 25 Conrad, Kerwin, and Weitz were launched from Cape Kennedy by a Saturn IB vehicle to rendezvous with the Skylab. After several futile attempts to free the stuck solar cell panel, the crew-

Asbestos: *see* Mining

Association Football: *see* Football

men realized that they did not have the proper tool. Then followed 3 hours and 20 minutes of frustrating attempts to dock their spacecraft with the Skylab. Once docked, the crew slept for 7 hours after having been awake and very busy for almost 22 hours.

After awakening, Kerwin checked for the presence of toxic gases that might have been generated by the high temperatures within the orbital workshop. Finding none, the crew entered it and deployed the 6.7 m. by 7.3 m. (22 ft. by 24 ft.) parasol through an airlock on the side of the Skylab.

During their first two weeks in orbit the astronauts were plagued by a shortage of electrical power and had to cancel some of their scientific experiments. On June 7 Conrad and Kerwin emerged from the Skylab for a three-hour work session on its exterior. Using a special tool, Kerwin finally succeeded in freeing the solar cell panel. During the intense labour his heart rate climbed to 150, while Conrad's rose only to 110.

With the panel free and Skylab therefore receiving more power, the crew began a period of catching up on the delayed scientific and engineering experiments. Working as long as 18 hours per day, they accomplished far more than ground controllers thought possible. The fact that they adapted so quickly to weightlessness accounted in large part for their ability to get so much work done.

On June 15 the astronauts started arrangements for their return to the earth. After an uneventful return journey, splashdown took place in the Pacific Ocean on June 22. Physical examinations of the astronauts showed them to be in remarkably good condition after 28 days of weightlessness. They reported that despite all the problems aboard the laboratory they had managed to complete 88% of the man-hours allotted to the Apollo Telescope Mount, 88% of the time planned for earth resources experiments, 90% of the biomedical experiments, and 90–95% of the time scheduled for the experiments provided by 19 high school students across the U.S.

On July 28 astronauts Alan Bean, Owen Garriott, and Jack Lousma lifted off from the Kennedy Space Center aboard a Saturn IB booster for the third Skylab mission, planned for 59 days. Their Apollo spacecraft was crammed to nearly the maximum lift-off weight with extra supplies. It weighed 6,084 kg. (13,410 lb.), the maximum permissible being 6,125 kg. (13,500 lb.).

No sooner had the launch taken place than the astronauts noted trouble with their Apollo spacecraft. Oxidizer was leaking from a small rocket engine used to control the craft's attitude. The engine was shut down, and the leak stopped. However, on August 2, five days later, another leak was found in a similar engine on the opposite side of the Apollo. In preparation for an aborted mission, workers at Cape Kennedy rushed the next Saturn IB launch vehicle and Apollo spacecraft into position for a rescue mission. Later events, however, proved that the Apollo could be operated in an alternate mode and that the rescue would not be necessary.

Unlike the first crew, which took only a few days to adapt to weightlessness, the second crew required almost a week. They were nauseated and dizzy to the point of not being able to perform their tasks. Once adapted, however, they made up for lost time.

On August 24 astronauts Lousma and Garriott spent 4½ hours outside the Skylab performing various jobs. They replaced a "six pack" of faulty gyroscopes with good ones brought up from earth with them, deployed a new sun shield, and replaced the film in the cameras of the Apollo Telescope Mount. Physicians monitoring the second crew found that they reached a plateau in their physical deconditioning prior to 28 days. At that time they began gaining back a portion of lost weight. There was no recurrence of the nausea and dizziness.

As their 59-day mission progressed, the three astronauts amazed both doctors and mission controllers in Houston. Their capacity for work seemed to be limitless. The crew accomplished all their assigned tasks and then asked for more. When their mission ended with a splashdown in the Pacific on September 25, Bean, Garriott, and Lousma had not only gotten the Skylab in shape for its next crew but they had even done some of their work for them. Because the astronauts had run out of things to do, the ground controllers told them to start performing some of the experiments that had been scheduled for the next mission.

The fourth (third manned) Skylab mission began November 16 when Gerald Carr, William Pogue, and Edward Gibson were lifted off by a Saturn IB from the Kennedy Space Center. After a series of rocket maneuvers the astronauts, all newcomers to space flight, guided their Apollo spacecraft to a rendezvous with the Skylab, thereby beginning an 84-day mission in space. The launching had been postponed six days because of cracks in the Saturn; all eight of the rocket's tail fins had to be replaced.

The Soviet Union launched two manned missions during the year. In September Lieut. Col. Vasily Lazarev and civilian engineer Oleg Makarov spent two days in space in Soyuz 12, checking out the modifications made since the tragic crash of Soyuz 11 in 1971. Maj. Pyotr Klimuk and engineer Valentin Lebedev orbited the earth for eight days in Soyuz 13 in December to demonstrate the craft's readiness for a joint flight with the U.S.

Earlier, on April 3, the U.S.S.R. had launched a Salyut space station into orbit. On April 14, before a manned Soyuz craft could reach it, the space station suffered a catastrophic malfunction or internal explosion. Parts ripped from it, and the craft began tumbling in orbit. Western engineers believed that the craft's attitude-control system probably malfunctioned and caused the huge ship to tumble at angular velocities, which eventually tore it apart.

Progress was made during the year on the joint U.S.-U.S.S.R. Apollo/Soyuz Test Project, to be flown

During a "fly around" inspection of the Skylab, an astronaut snapped this picture of the U.S. space station with the earth as a backdrop. One of the solar panels did not extend, an indication of the various malfunctions that beset the mid-1973 mission.

UPI COMPIX

Major Satellites and Space Probes Launched Sept. 30, 1972–Sept. 30, 1973

Name/country/launch vehicle/scientific designation	Launch date, lifetime*	Physical characteristics				Experiments	Orbital elements			
		Weight (kg.)†	Shape	Diameter (m.)†	Length or height (m.)†		Perigee (km.)†	Apogee (km.)†	Period (min.)	Inclination to Equator (degrees)
Molniya 2/U.S.S.R./A IIe/1972-075A	9/30/72	1,247 (2,750)	Cylinder with conical ends and six panels	1.6 (5.25)	4.2 (13.78)	Communications satellite	517 (321)	38,987 (24,227)	700.5	65.4
Radcat/U.S./Atlas F Burner 2/1972-076A	10/2/72	220 (485)	Cylinder	3.05 (10)	12.19 (40)	Radar calibration target	729 (453)	749 (465)	99.5	98.4
(No name)/U.S./Atlas F Burner 2/1972-076B	10/2/72	726 (1,600)	Cylinder	‡	‡	Radiation-study satellite launched piggyback with Radcat	729 (453)	750 (466)	99.5	98.4
Big Bird 4/U.S./Titan IIID/1972-079A	10/10/72 1/8/73	11,340 (25,000)	Cylinder with conical ends	3.63 (11.9)	15.33 (50.3)	Military photoreconnaissance satellite	167 (104)	257 (160)	88.7	96.3
Molniya 1/U.S.S.R./A IIe/1972-081A	10/14/72	1,000 (2,205)	Cylinder with conical ends and six panels	1.6 (5.25)	3.4 (11.15)	Communications satellite	702 (436)	39,654 (24,641)	717.8	65.5
ITOS-D(NOAA 2)/U.S./Delta/1972-082A	10/15/72	312 (688)	Rectangular box with three panels	1.2 (3.94)	1 (3.28)	Improved Tiros weather satellite (OSCAR 6, amateur radio satellite, launched piggyback)	1,451 (902)	1,457 (905)	114.9	101.7
Meteor 13/U.S.S.R./A I/1972-085A	10/26/72	‡	Cylinder with two panels	1.5 (4.92)	5 (16.4)	Weather satellite	864 (537)	893 (555)	102.5	81.2
Anik 1/Canada/Delta/1972-090A	11/9/72	544 (1,200)	Cylinder	1.71 (5.6)	1.52 (5)	First Canadian domestic communications satellite	35,780 (22,234)	35,791 (22,241)	1,436	0.1
Explorer 48/U.S./Scout/1972-091A	11/15/72	186 (410)	Cylinder with four panels	0.55 (1.8)	1.29 (4.23)	Small astronomy satellite launched for the U.S. by Italy from the San Marcos site	443 (275)	630 (391)	95.4	1.9
ESRO 4/ESRO/Scout/1972-092A	11/22/72	115 (254)	Sixteen-sided polygon	0.76 (2.5)	0.3 (0.99)	Joint European scientific research satellite in upper atmospheric physics	241 (150)	1,135 (705)	98.5	91
Intercosmos 8/U.S.S.R./B I/1972-094A	11/30/72 3/4/73	1,100 (2,425)	Octagon and octagonal pyramid with eight panels	1.1 (3.61)	2.5 (8.2)	Eastern bloc scientific satellite to investigate ionospheric physics	199 (124)	590 (367)	92.4	70.9
Molniya 1/U.S.S.R./A IIe/1972-095A	12/2/72	1,000 (2,205)	Cylinder with conical ends and six panels	1.6 (5.25)	3.4 (11.15)	Communications satellite	555 (345)	39,797 (24,730)	717.7	65
Apollo 17/U.S./Saturn V/1972-096A	12/7/72 12/19/72	21,188 (46,710)	Cylinder with conical ends	3 (9.84)	9 (29.53)	Final U.S. manned exploration of the moon	Landed on the moon December 11			
Nimbus 5/U.S./Delta/1972-097A	12/11/72	715 (1,576)	Torus with triangular superstructure and two panels	3.35 (11)	3.05 (10)	Weather satellite	1,093 (679)	1,105 (687)	107.2	99.9
Molniya 2/U.S.S.R./A IIe/1972-098A	12/12/72	1,250 (2,756)	Cylinder with conical ends and six panels	1.6 (5.25)	4.2 (13.78)	Communications satellite	470 (292)	39,297 (24,419)	4,005	65.3
Aeros/W.Ger./Scout/1972-100A	12/16/72	127 (280)	Cylinder	0.91 (2.99)	0.74 (2.43)	Scientific satellite to investigate physics of the upper atmosphere	222 (138)	854 (531)	95.3	96.9
Luna 21/U.S.S.R./Proton/1973/001A	1/8/73 6/4/73	838 (1,848)	Hemispheroid with eight wheels	2.13 (7)	0.74 (2.43)	Deployed unmanned lunar roving vehicle Lunokhod 2, which performed lunar surface exploration	Landed on the moon January 15			
Molniya 1/U.S.S.R./A IIe/1973-007A	2/3/73	1,000 (2,205)	Cylinder with conical ends and six panels	1.6 (5.25)	3.4 (11.15)	Communications satellite	528 (328)	39,826 (24,748)	717.7	65
Prognoz 3/U.S.S.R./1973-009A	2/15/73	845 (1,863)	Domed cylinder with four panels	2.44 (8.01)	5 (16.4)	Scientific probe of interplanetary space to measure gamma and X-radiation and magnetic fields	590 (367)	200,000 (124,280)	5,783	65
Big Bird 5/U.S./Titan IIID/1973-014A	3/9/73 5/19/73	11,340 (25,000)	Cylinder with conical ends	3.63 (11.9)	15.33 (50.3)	Military photoreconnaissance satellite	157 (98)	265 (165)	88.6	95.6
Meteor 14/U.S.S.R./A I/1973-015A	3/20/73	‡	Cylinder with two paddles	1.5 (4.92)	5 (16.4)	Weather satellite	882 (548)	903 (561)	102.6	81.2
Salyut 2/U.S.S.R./Proton/1973-017A	4/3/73 5/28/73	18,960 (41,800)	Cylinder	4 (13.12)	10 (32.8)	Aborted manned space station	249 (155)	269 (167)	39.7	51.5
Molniya 2/U.S.S.R./A IIe/1973-018A	4/5/73	1,250 (2,756)	Cylinder with cone and six panels	1.6 (5.25)	4.2 (13.78)	Communications satellite	525 (326)	39,828 (24,749)	717.7	65.2
Pioneer 11/U.S./Atlas Centaur/1973-019A	4/5/73	258 (569)	Hexagon with parabolic antenna	1.22 (4)	2.9 (9.5)	Scientific investigation of Jupiter	Solar system escape trajectory			
Copernik 500 (Intercosmos 9)/U.S.S.R.–Poland/B I/1973-022A	4/19/73	1,100 (2,425)	Octagon and octagonal pyramid with eight panels	1.1 (3.61)	2.5 (8.2)	Scientific satellite; radio spectrograph made in Poland	199 (124)	1,518 (943)	102.1	48.4
Anik 2/Canada/Delta/1973-023A	4/20/73	544 (1,200)	Cylinder	1.71 (5.6)	1.52 (5)	Communications satellite	35,604 (22,124)	35,709 (22,190)	1,430.7	0.1
Cosmos 557/U.S.S.R./A II 1973-026A	5/11/73 5/22/73	6,000 (13,228)	Sphere with cylinder	3.1 (10.17)	10.7 (35.1)	Unmanned checkflight of Soyuz spacecraft	214 (133)	243 (151)	89.01	51.2
Skylab/U.S./Saturn V/1973-027A	5/14/73	90,607 (199,752)	Cylinder with five solar cell panels	6.6 (21.65)	36 (118.1)	Over 270 biomedical, astrophysical, and engineering experiments in near-earth orbit	423 (263)	440 (273)	93.2	50
Skylab 2/U.S./Saturn IB/1973-032A	5/25/73 6/22/73	6,033 (13,300)	Cylinder with conical ends	3.8 (12.47)	10.9 (35.76)	Carried first crew to Skylab				
Meteor 15/U.S.S.R./A I/1973-034A	5/29/73	‡	Cylinder with two panels	1.5 (4.92)	5 (16.4)	Meteorological satellite	852 (529.4)	896 (556.8)	102.4	81.2
Explorer 49/U.S./Delta/1973-039A	6/10/73	200 (442)	Rectangular polygon with four solar cell panels and four antennas, each 230 m. long	‡	‡	Radio astronomy probe in orbit about the moon	1,053 (654)	1,066 (662)	221.9	38.7
Molniya 2/U.S.S.R./A IIe/1973-045A	7/11/73	1,247 (2,750)	Cylinder with conical ends and six panels	1.6 (5.25)	4.2 (13.78)	Communications satellite	441 (274)	39,284 (24,411)	705	65.4
Big Bird 6/U.S./Titan IIIC/1973-046A	7/13/73	11,340 (25,000)	Cylinder with conical ends	3.63 (11.9)	15.33 (50.3)	Military photoreconnaissance satellite	155 (96)	268 (167)	88.7	96.2
Mars 4/U.S.S.R./Proton/1973-047A	7/21/73	900 (1,984)	Cylinder with two panels	1.1 (3.61)	3.1 (10.17)	Scientific probe of Mars	On trajectory to Mars			
Mars 5/U.S.S.R./Proton/1973-049A	7/25/73	900 (1,984)	Cylinder with two panels	1.1 (3.61)	3.1 (10.17)	Scientific probe of Mars	On trajectory to Mars			
Skylab 3/U.S./Saturn IB/1973-050A	7/28/73 9/25/73	6,084 (13,410)	Cylinder with conical ends	3.8 (12.47)	10.9 (35.76)	Carried second crew to Skylab				
Mars 6/U.S.S.R./Proton/1973-052A	8/5/73	‡	Cylinder	‡	‡	Scientific probe of Mars	On trajectory to Mars			
Mars 7/U.S.S.R./Proton/1973-053A	8/9/73	‡	Cylinder	‡	‡	Scientific probe of Mars	On trajectory to Mars			
Intelsat 4/U.S./Atlas Centaur/1973-058A	8/23/73	706 (1,556)	Cylinder	2.4 (7.87)	2.8 (9.19)	Communications satellite	35,538 (22,083)	35,926 (22,324)	1,440	0.4
Molniya 1/U.S.S.R./A IIe/1973-061A	8/30/73	1,000 (2,205)	Cylinder with conical ends and six panels	1.6 (5.25)	3.4 (11.15)	Communications satellite	463 (288)	36,665 (22,783)	718.4	65.3
Soyuz 12/U.S.S.R./A II/1973-069A	9/27/73 9/29/73	6,600 (14,550)	Sphere and cylinder	3.1 (10.17)	10.7 (35.1)	Manned test of improved Soyuz spacecraft	202 (126)	231 (144)	88.69	51.58

*All dates are in universal time (UT).
†English units in parentheses: weight in pounds, dimensions in feet, apogee and perigee in statute miles.
‡Not available.

(MITCHELL R. SHARPE)

in 1975. Between Oct. 9–18, 1972, U.S. astronauts and space scientists met with their counterparts in the Soviet Union to continue planning for the project. Astronaut Tom Stafford, commander of the Apollo spacecraft for the mission, spent 1½ hours flying the Soyuz simulator at the Yuri Gagarin Training Center for Cosmonauts near Moscow. Later, in November, both countries announced that the Soyuz would be launched from the Soviet Union on July 15, 1975, and that the Apollo would follow from Kennedy Space Center within five days.

Unmanned Satellites. Clearly the satellite of the year was one launched in July 1972. ERTS 1, the Earth Resources Technology Satellite, provided a veritable flood of information about the earth throughout 1973. The applications of the information it provided far exceeded the expectations of the scientists and engineers who had designed the craft. An aerial photograph of Lake Champlain was introduced into a court suit as evidence that a large paper company was polluting that body of water. Another picture showed that Great Salt Lake is really Great Salt Lakes. The railroad bisecting it actually made it into two distinct lakes. Other pictures proved that the rate of erosion in canyons in southern Arizona has been greater during the past 80 years than it was in the previous 10,000 years. Photographs of Wyoming taken in one day produced a map that would have required earthbound geographers 20 years to compile.

Congress responded to this success by demanding a second ERTS satellite. Rep. James W. Symington (Dem., Mo.) of the House space committee said, "This satellite can save us hundreds of millions of dollars in the placing of highways and pipelines alone."

On the international scene, the Soviet Union proposed to ESRO that it launch, at no cost, that organization's next HEOS satellite in 1974. In exchange, it asked for greater participation in ESRO programs in the future. The offer also took some of the magnanimity out of President Nixon's earlier offer to provide launching services to other countries at cost.

ESRO turned down an offer from NASA to participate in its Venus orbiter project. However, ESRO did propose another joint program with NASA. Scheduled for 1977 was an International Sun-Earth Physics Satellite program (ISEPS). As envisioned by ESRO, ISEPS would consist of "mother and daughter" satellites, with the "mother" being provided by NASA and the "daughter" being developed by ESRO. The two satellites would be launched by a single booster provided by NASA.

Japan announced that it hoped to have the technological capability of launching its own communications satellite by its own booster in 1975 or 1976. Likewise, India announced that it hoped to orbit its own communications satellite with an all-Indian launch vehicle by 1982. Late in October 1972 China signed a contract with Western Union International, Inc., of the U.S. to construct a third communications satellite ground receiving station near Peking.

Canada's and the world's first entirely domestic communications satellite, Anik 1, was launched on Nov. 9, 1972, by a Delta vehicle from Cape Kennedy. The 544-kg. (1,200-lb.) satellite had the capability of transmitting more than 5,000 two-way telephone conversations or 12 colour television channels. Anik 2 was launched on April 20, 1973.

Military satellites as usual accounted for the major portion of all launchings during the year. In February the U.S. Air Force received the first model of an improved early warning satellite. Several of the new satellites were being readied to supplement the two currently in geosynchronous orbit over the Indian Ocean and Panama.

In March the U.S. Air Force admitted that it had been operating its own meteorological satellites. It also announced that pictures and data from these satellites would be made available to civil weather bureaus upon request. Since the resolution of the cameras in the military satellites was superior to that in the civil craft, the demand was expected to be great. Also, the Air Force's computerized data processing was much faster than the system used by the civil weather service.

Interplanetary Probes. Mars became the target for an unprecedented number of probes during the year. Mariner 9, which had entered into orbit around Mars on Nov. 13, 1971, finally completed its mission on Oct. 27, 1972. During its 698 orbits of the planet, the probe sent back to the earth 7,329 pictures of its surface, enough for a complete map of Mars.

At a meeting in Moscow from January 29 to February 2, members of the Academy of Sciences of the U.S.S.R. and their counterparts from NASA made some interesting agreements with respect to Mars. The Soviets promised to make available to the U.S. data from their Mars 2 and 3 probes in exchange for pictures made by Mariner 9. The data exchange was made on April 15. Material supplied by the Soviets assisted U.S. scientists in selecting the landing sites for the Viking soft-lander, to be launched in 1975.

Taking advantage of the opportune "launch window," the U.S.S.R. fired a volley of four probes toward Mars. Mars 4 was launched on July 21, 1973, followed by Mars 5 on July 25. They were scheduled to rendezvous with the planet in February 1974. On August 5 the Soviets astounded Western space scientists by sending yet another probe, Mars 6, to the planet. It was expected to reach its destination in the third week of March 1974. Mars 7 was then launched on August 9. Both Mars 6 and 7 carried a Stereo 5 solar spectrometer provided by French scientists.

Later, Roald Sagdeyev, director of the Soviet Space Research Institute, publicly stated that one of these craft would attempt a soft landing on Mars. In fact, most likely two would make the attempt, Mars 4 and 5. They would transmit data and pictures to the orbiting Mars 6 and 7 for relay to the earth.

Pioneer 10, the U.S. probe en route to Jupiter,

Skylab pilot Jack R. Lousma performs an experiment in the space station's forward compartment during the July 28 to Sept. 25, 1973, mission.

COURTESY, NASA

cleared its first hurdle on February 14. It emerged unscathed from the 280 million-km. (175 million-mi.)-wide asteroid belt between Mars and Jupiter after traveling through it for seven months. During the period, four small telescopes aboard the probe spotted between 100 and 200 sizable "chunks of debris" within several miles of the craft. On December 3 the spacecraft survived the planet's intense radiation to pass within 81,000 mi. of Jupiter, transmitting colour pictures and scientific data to the earth. Eventually, it would pass beyond the solar system.

Pioneer 11, launched on April 5, entered the asteroid belt on August 18 and was due to emerge on March 12, 1974. The probe was to swing past Jupiter in early December of the same year. On November 3 Mariner 10 was launched on a mission that would take it past Venus to Mercury.

The moon was visited by another Soviet probe on January 16. Launched on January 8 from Tyuratam, Luna 21 went into a lunar orbit on January 12 and stayed there for over three days. On January 16 it landed inside the crater Le Monnier on the eastern edge of the Sea of Serenity, about 180 km. (112 mi.) north of the landing site of Apollo 17. Taken to the moon by Luna 21 was the unmanned moon rover Lunokhod 2, an improved version of Lunokhod 1.

After five periods of exploration Lunokhod 2 for some unknown reason ceased functioning on June 4. However, during its brief life on the moon, it covered 3½ times the distance traveled by the earlier robot explorer. It also sent back to the earth more than 80,000 pictures of the lunar surface, including 86 panoramic views. On March 16 the U.S. delivered rock and soil samples from Apollo 16 and 17 to the U.S.S.R. in exchange for lunar samples earlier received from Luna 16 and 20 probes.

On June 10 the last scheduled U.S. lunar probe in this century was launched from Cape Kennedy by a Delta booster. The mission of the probe, Explorer 49, was to measure galactic and solar radio noise at extremely low frequencies, which had been previously unmonitorable because of interference generated in the earth's atmosphere. Placing the probe in a lunar orbit allowed the moon to shield it from interference when passing between the craft and the earth.

Launch Vehicles and the Space Shuttle. As 1972 ended, two significant events concerning launch vehicles took place. In the U.S. the government authorized the first major sale of U.S. space boosters to a foreign nation, approving the purchase by Japan of the two-stage Delta. The Japanese planned to add a third stage that they would develop themselves in order to produce their own national launch vehicle.

The second event took place at Brussels on December 20, when the European Space Conference agreed to a four-point program expected to have wide-ranging effects on European space technology. They included: the merging of ESRO and ELDO into a European Space Agency (ESA), which took place Aug. 1, 1973; the integration of various national space projects into a single joint European space project; the accomplishment of two special, multinational projects—Spacelab as a European contribution to the post-Apollo program of the U.S. and the development of the L3S space carrier vehicle of the French as a standard launch vehicle; and the improvement in efficiency of various national satellite programs without compromising a 1971 decision by ESRO to develop an applications satellite exclusively for European use.

In September 1973 the first Titan IIIE was rolled out at the Kennedy Space Center. The new launch vehicle consists of a Titan IIIC core and solid-propellant strap-ons but with a Centaur upper stage. It would be the only large space booster in the U.S. inventory until the space shuttle became available, hopefully in the early 1980s. Capable of placing 15,426 kg. (34,000 lb.) into a circular, low-earth orbit and 3,630 kg. (8,000 lb.) into earth-escape trajectories, the Titan IIIE was scheduled to be used to launch the two Viking Mars probes in 1975.

Work moved ahead on the space shuttle. On November 13, 1972, the program requirements review by NASA cleared the way for Rockwell International, the prime contractor for the shuttle orbiter vehicle, to begin development of the reusable space booster. The company suggested changes in design that would reduce the weight of the vehicle and cost of production, which were accepted by NASA.

Despite this progress, however, NASA's continuously shrinking budget meant the development of the space shuttle would be slowed perceptibly. Cuts in the fiscal year 1973 and reductions in requested funds for fiscal 1974 meant, among other things, that the first manned orbital test flight would slip from a planned date of March 1, 1978, until at least the end of that year. (MITCHELL R. SHARPE)

See also Astronomy; Defense; Industrial Review; Meteorology; Telecommunications; Television and Radio.

ENCYCLOPÆDIA BRITANNICA FILMS. *Man Looks at the Moon* (1971); *Space Exploration: A Team Effort* (1973); *Controversy over the Moon* (1973).

Two cosmonauts who would participate in the 1975 joint U.S.-Soviet space mission practice transfer from spacecraft to rescue raft. Valery N. Kubasov sits at right, Aleksey A. Leonov is standing alongside two frogmen. Water rescue was new to the Soviets, who had parachuted all of their spacecraft to earth.

TASS/SOVFOTO

Astronomy

Globular Clusters. Globular clusters are roughly spherical aggregates of 10^4–10^7 stars and are believed to be among the oldest objects in the Milky Way. The ratio of heavy elements to hydrogen varies widely from cluster to cluster. For some clusters, mainly those far from the galactic centre, this ratio is less than 0.01 of the solar value of the ratio, while for some of the more metal-rich clusters it is more nearly 0.1 to 0.2 of the solar value.

When each star in a globular cluster is represented by a point in a plot of luminosity versus temperature, the stars are confined to tightly restricted regions in the diagram by the processes going on within the stars themselves. Stellar evolution theory gives a fairly successful description of the luminosity-temperature diagram; however, one region, the horizontal branch, remains poorly understood. This horizontal branch (HB) represents a collection of evolved stars that all appear at about the same luminosity (hence horizontal) but are distributed unevenly over a wide range in temperature. HB stars are generally believed to be the next evolutionary stage after the cool red giant phase: when helium begins to burn at the centre of a red giant, the star loses a significant fraction of its mass (according to the theory) and evolves rapidly to the hotter but less luminous horizontal branch.

Two serious problems arose in the theory of the horizontal branch. First, researchers did not understand why the HB in an individual cluster extends over such a wide range in temperature. The second problem concerned distribution along the horizontal branch. For most metal-weak clusters the HB stars are mainly at the hot end of the HB, while for the metal-rich clusters they are mainly at the cool end, and that much is understood from the theory. However, a few clusters that by all indications are metal-weak have mainly cool horizontal branch stars, thus demonstrating that metal abundance alone does not determine the distribution of stars along the HB. For some years, the helium abundance was thought to be the second independent variable, but this later seemed unlikely because determination of the helium abundance in a wide range of objects yielded a remarkably uniform value. Recently, observations showed that the nitrogen abundance may vary independently of the other heavy elements. F. D. A. Hartwick and D. Vanden Berg (University of Victoria, B.C.) demonstrated theoretically that a relative overabundance of nitrogen by a factor of less than ten could explain the HB distribution in the anomalous metal-weak clusters.

Solar Neutrino Problem. During the year the search continued for a solution to a problem in the theory of stellar interiors. The nuclear reactions that burn hydrogen to helium in the central regions of stars produce two neutrinos for every helium atom formed. Having negligible interaction with the stellar material, the neutrinos escape directly into space. Therefore, the observation of neutrinos from the sun would provide the first direct evidence about the nuclear reactions taking place at its centre. In particular, it would provide a sensitive indicator to the central temperature of the sun.

For some years, R. Davis, Jr. (Brookhaven National Laboratory, Upton, N.Y.), has been carrying out a solar neutrino detection experiment based on the reaction

$$\nu_{\text{solar}} + {}^{37}\text{Cl} \rightarrow e^- + {}^{37}\text{A}$$

where νsolar is a neutrino from the sun and e^- is an electron. The experiment used 100,000 gal. of cleaning fluid (C_2Cl_4) as a detector, and was located at 4,850 ft. underground in a South Dakota gold mine. The number of interactions in a 50–100-day period was typically less than 100, and the detection of ^{37}A was 95% efficient. The experiment was capable of recording only those solar neutrinos with energies greater than 0.814 MeV, which effectively limited it to one branch of the proton-proton chain of nuclear reactions at work in the sun. Only an upper limit to the solar neutrino flux was established, and this was less than one-sixth of that predicted by theoretical solar models.

After many unsuccessful attempts to solve the problem through simple changes in the solar models, astronomers had to resort to what W. Fowler (California Institute of Technology) called "desperate explanations." One, proposed by Fowler and also by V. Fetisov and Y. Kopysov (Lebedev Physical Institute, Moscow), was that there exists a previously unknown resonance in the ^{3}He + ^{3}He nuclear reaction which would enhance it at the expense of the ^{3}He + ^{4}He branch; the latter reaction produces the neutrinos recorded in the Davis experiment. On the other hand, F. Barker (Australian National University) demonstrated that such a level would require very extreme properties indeed, while P. Parker (Yale University) reviewed the nuclear physics involved in the problem and claimed that uncertainties in the physics could no longer provide an explanation.

Another desperate solution suggested by Fowler was the intermittent mixing of the solar centre. Such mixing would introduce new hydrogen fuel into the burning regions and thereby lower the central temperature, leading to a dramatic reduction in the flux of detectable neutrinos. Were this mixing to occur at intervals of about 2.5×10^8 years, the associated changes in solar luminosity might also explain the earth's ice ages. Many astronomers investigated the effects of such mixing on actual solar models. Contrary to expectations, the effect was complicated, with the neutrino flux rising at first and then falling sharply. It seemed possible, by mixing about 50% of the sun's mass, to achieve a neutrino flux below the Davis limit while still maintaining the observed solar luminosity and the present estimate of the solar system age; however, this explanation made it necessary to assume that the present epoch is at the minimum of the solar neutrino flux. Furthermore, the fluctuations in solar luminosity would produce temperature changes of some tens of degrees at the earth, which seemed too large for agreement with the geologic record.

Element Abundances in Galaxies. It seemed clear from observations that the helium-to-hydrogen abundance ratio is roughly the same for a great variety of objects, both galactic and extragalactic. On the other hand, the heavy element abundances vary widely, even from galaxy to galaxy. A. Sandage (Hale Observatories) studied the colours of some elliptical and lenticular galaxies covering a wide range in intrinsic luminosity. He found that the ratio of ultraviolet to blue light increases smoothly as the luminosity decreases, almost certainly indicating that the mean metal abundance is lower for the low-luminosity galaxies. S. Faber (Lick Observatory) and H. Spinrad (University of California, Berkeley) measured some metallic lines in galaxy spectra, and showed directly that the line strengths decrease with decreasing galaxy luminosity. The reason for this apparent change of metal abundance with luminosity (and therefore with galaxy mass) was not understood.

Chemical abundance gradients also occur within individual galaxies. The outer parts of the halo component in spiral galaxies have fewer heavy elements than the disk component, by a factor of 10–100; this was known for many years. Recently, astronomers found evidence that the abundance changes within the disk itself. V. Rubin and associates (Carnegie Institution of Washington) observed ionized gas regions in the Andromeda galaxy, and found that the intensity ratio of the nitrogen forbidden emission lines to the hydrogen emission lines changes by a factor of 10 between the galaxy centre and points in the disk at a radius of 15 kiloparsecs (4×10^{22} cm.). This change suggested an abundance decrease of about a factor of

Eclipses, 1974

June 4	Moon, partial (begins 2:24 P.M.*), visible Australia, Cen. and S. Asia, Africa, Cen. and S. Europe, E. S.America, S. Atlantic O., Indian O.
June 19	Sun, total (begins 9:34 P.M.*), visible Madagascar, Indian O., Indonesia, Malaysia, Australia, parts of Antarctica, extreme S. New Zealand
Nov. 29	Moon, total (begins 7:26 A.M.*), visible Arctic, N.W. N. America, N. Pacific O., Asia, N.E. Europe, N.E. Africa, Indian O., Australia, New Zealand
Dec. 13	Sun, partial (begins 9:04 A.M.*), visible N. America except extreme N.W., extreme N. S. America, N. Atlantic O., S. Greenland, extreme W. Europe

Equinoxes and Solstices, 1974

March 20	Vernal equinox, 7:07 P.M.*
June 21	Summer solstice, 1:38 P.M.*
Sept. 23	Autumnal equinox, 4:59 A.M.*
Dec. 22	Winter solstice, 12:57 A.M.*

Earth Perihelion and Aphelion, 1974

Jan. 4	Perihelion, 91,404,000 mi. (147,096,000 km.) from the sun
July 5	Aphelion, 94,511,000 mi. (152,096,000 km.) from the sun

*U.S. Eastern Standard Time.

Source: *The American Ephemeris and Nautical Almanac for the Year 1974*, Washington, D.C., 1972.

G. SIPAHIOGLU—LIAISON

For the century's longest eclipse of the sun on June 30, 1973, scientists rushed to Kenya's Lake Rudolf, a prime observation site. Kenyans (right) are informed of the event through government publications. The movement of the moon across the sun's disk as shown below took 195 minutes.

UPI COMPIX

2 for nitrogen and oxygen relative to hydrogen, with increasing radius. Again, the reason for this abundance variation was not known: it may well be produced very early in the galaxy's life.

Universal Microwave Radiation Field. Observations at wavelengths between 3.3 mm. and 73 cm. showed that there is a background radiation field, uniform over the sky. Its spectrum over this wavelength range is like that of a black body at 3° K, and it is widely believed to be dilute radiation left over from the high-temperature phase early in the life of the expanding universe. However, the possibility remained that this background radiation is just the integrated flux from a large number of discrete sources.

To test this possibility, several observers measured the fine-scale uniformity of the microwave background. Y. Parijskij (Leningrad Special Astrophysical Observatory) found no fluctuations above the 0.8×10^{-4}° K level at 2.8 cm. wavelength, on scales of 3 arc minutes to 1°. P. Boynton (University of Washington, Seattle) and R. Partridge (Haverford College) observed at 3.5 mm. wavelength with an angular resolution of 80 arc seconds, and again found no variations greater than 0.004° K. These demonstrations argued against the discrete source model.

X-ray Astronomy. There is an isotropic component of the extraterrestrial X-ray and gamma-ray flux in the energy range 0.25 keV to 100MeV, and its isotropy suggests an extragalactic origin. (Isotropy is the exhibition of properties with the same values when measured along axes in all directions.) The popular model for this radiation is that it comes from Compton scattering of the universal microwave radiation photons (the 3° K background) by relativistic electrons (those moving near the speed of light) leaking out of galaxies. (In Compton scattering a part of the electron's energy is transferred to the photon, with a consequent gain in frequency.) R. Cowsik and E. Kobetich (University of California, Berkeley) calculated the shape of the background X-ray energy spectrum in this model, and found differences from the observed spectrum. They interpreted these differences as possible evidence for a hot intergalactic gas at a temperature of about 3×10^{8}° K and density of about 3×10^{-6} atoms cm^{-3}; this density is high enough to close the universe if the present estimate for the Hubble constant (which measures the rate of expansion of the universe) is correct.

However, K. Brecher (MIT) argued that the Compton model for the isotropic X-ray background can in fact give a reasonable representation of the X-ray spectrum, depending on the energy spectrum of the electron energies. The problem of the origin of the high-energy X-ray background is very important, because it bears so directly on the existence or nonexistence of a hot intergalactic medium; this, in turn, can indicate whether the universe is closed or open.

The low-energy (less than about 0.3 keV) X-ray background flux, on the other hand, is not isotropic. A. Davidsen and associates (U.S. Naval Research Laboratory, Washington, D.C.) showed that it correlates with galactic latitude and with the galactic neutral hydrogen distribution. P. Gorenstein and W. Tucker (American Science and Engineering) argued that there is no evidence for any substantial extragalactic contribution to the low-energy X-ray background; if it arises from galactic sources, then the scale height of their distribution perpendicular to the galactic plane is about 800 parsecs, and this identifies them with the old disk population of the Milky Way.

Ultraviolet Astronomy. The ultraviolet region of the spectrum (wavelengths less than 3000 Å) is particularly valuable for studies of hot matter and of molecules. It is not accessible to ground-based telescopes because the earth's atmosphere does not transmit ultraviolet light, and so satellite or rocket-borne equipment is needed. D. Morton and associates (Princeton University) showed from rocket observations that resonance lines of some elements in the ultraviolet spectra of the hot stars ζ Oph and ξ Per are shifted by about 1,000–2,000 km/sec. toward shorter wavelengths, indicating a high-velocity outflow of matter from those stars. L. Spitzer and associates (Princeton University) observed the ultraviolet lines of interstellar molecular hydrogen in the spectra of several stars by means of a spectrometer carried on the Copernicus satellite. For 11 stars with significant interstellar reddening, the fraction along the line of sight of total hydrogen in H_2 molecules was greater than 0.1, while for 8 out of 9 unreddened stars the fraction was less than 10^{-7}. This probably showed how the H_2 molecules in dust clouds are protected from stellar ultraviolet light, which would otherwise dissociate the molecules.

J. Holberg and associates (University of California, Berkeley) observed the Coma cluster of galaxies with a rocket-borne detector, and were able to place a tight upper limit on the Lyman-α radiation flux from the cluster. This appeared to rule out the presence of a hot (2×10^{4}° K to 3×10^{5}° K) ionized gas, which many astronomers had invoked to make the cluster gravitationally stable against the random motions of the individual galaxies. There could still be enough undetected cool neutral hydrogen to stabilize the cluster, according to N. Smart, or the galaxies themselves may be much more massive than was believed, as J. Ostriker suggested.

Instruments and Techniques. Detailed mapping of individual radio sources is essential in order to deal with many problems in radio astronomy. This can be done with precision dishes (limited in practice to a resolution of about 1 arc minute), by lunar occultation observations (these depend on the moon passing in front of the radio source and so are limited to sources near the ecliptic), and by aperture synthesis. In the last mentioned two or more small aerials are moved to occupy the positions of elements of a much larger aerial, in order to achieve the resolution of the larger aerial. During the year two major new aperture synthesis radio telescopes went into operation. At the Mullard Radio Observatory (Cambridge, Eng.), the 5-km. telescope has a resolution of 2 arc seconds at a wavelength of 6 cm., close to the resolu-

Athletics:
see Baseball; Basketball; Bowling and Lawn Bowls; Boxing; Cricket; Cycling; Football; Golf; Hockey; Ice Skating; Rowing; Skiing; Sporting Record; Swimming; Tennis; Track and Field Sports

tion of large optical telescopes. In The Netherlands, the Westerbork radio telescope produced spectacular radio maps of nearby spiral galaxies.

The Mayall telescope at the Kitt Peak (Ariz.) National Observatory was dedicated in June and went into operation in October. With a diameter of 158 in., it became the world's second largest optical telescope. (KENNETH C. FREEMAN)

Kohoutek. Late in December astronomers awaited the arrival of Comet Kohoutek, which was expected to create a bright visual display in the January 1974 night sky soon after sunset. On January 5 the comet would come within 75 million mi. of the earth. A variety of airborne and ground-based instruments were used to photograph and obtain data on Kohoutek.

UFOs. An upsurge in reported sightings of unidentified flying objects (UFOs) took place late in the year, especially in southern and eastern areas of the U.S. Two men in Pascagoula, Miss., claimed that they had been taken aboard a fish-shaped craft by three creatures with crab-claw hands who examined and then released them. Other reports told of a flying-V formation of lights near Rochester, N.Y., and "strange creatures with weirdly shaped heads" stopping cars and scratching at windows along the Mississippi Gulf Coast. However, the U.S. Federal Aviation Administration, whose radar network covered 90% of U.S. airspace above 24,000 ft. and somewhat less at lower levels, said that it had detected nothing unusual.

Soviet scientists said that they had detected unusual radio signals from space and were not willing to rule out the possibility that they came from another civilization. The signals were transmitted in pulses after definite intervals, lasted for several minutes, and were repeated several times a day.

See also Astronautics; Seismology.

Australia

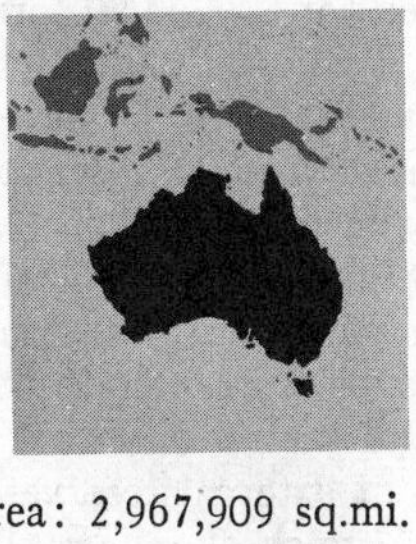

A federal parliamentary state and a member of the Commonwealth of Nations, Australia occupies the smallest continent and, with the island state of Tasmania, is the sixth largest country in the world. Area: 2,967,909 sq.mi. (7,686,849 sq.km.). Pop. (1973 est.): 13,154,722. Cap.: Canberra (pop., 1971, 141,575). Largest city: Sydney (metro. pop., 1971, 2,725,064). Language: English. Religion: (1971) Church of England 31%; Roman Catholic 27%; Methodist 8.6%; Presbyterian 8.1%. Queen, Elizabeth II; governor-general in 1973, Sir Paul Hasluck; prime minister, Gough Whitlam.

Domestic Affairs. Following its election victory of Dec. 2, 1972, the new Australian Labor Party (ALP) government of Gough Whitlam gave immediate attention to aboriginal welfare. On Jan. 10, 1973, the Cabinet granted A$12 million to be spent by the states on the advancement of the aboriginal people. Most of the money was spent in Queensland. On February 4 the government provided a further A$3 million for Western Australian aboriginals. In keeping with the spirit of the worldwide environmental movement, the ALP government banned the export of all kangaroo products. During January the responsible minister, Sen. Lionel Murphy (*see* BIOGRAPHY), protected 310 other species, including the crocodile, the swamp tortoise, the helmeted honey eater, the western ship bird, parakeets and parrots, wallabies, kangaroo rats, Tasmanian tigers, bandicoots, and wombats.

On Dec. 26, 1972, Albert Grassby, minister of immigration in Whitlam's new ministry, had announced that the number of immigrants to be admitted to Australia in 1972–73 would be reduced to 110,000 from the figure of 140,000 fixed by the McMahon government. (William McMahon had retired from the leadership of the Liberal-Country Party [LCP] immediately after the election and had been succeeded by Billy Snedden.) Immigration was to be synchronized with Australia's labour needs and coordinated with regional development plans. Until the employment situation improved, careful control of the type and number of immigrants was necessary. Grassby admitted that too many immigrants were dissatisfied with Australia and were leaving the country. To try to stem the outward flow, immigrants were to be given special assistance in their first years of settlement. In April the House of Representatives withdrew the privileges of British immigrants whereby they had become eligible for citizenship after one year, compared with three for other immigrants.

Grassby said it was the ALP government's aim to end invidious racial considerations in the selection of

continued on page 111

AUSTRALIA

Education. (1970) Primary, secondary, and vocational, pupils 2,768,233, teachers 120,041; teacher training, students 39,853; higher (at 15 universities only), students 116,778, teaching staff 7,371.

Finance. Monetary unit: Australian dollar, with (Sept. 17, 1973) an official rate of A$0.67 to U.S. $1 (free rate of A$1.62 = £1 sterling). Gold, SDRs, and foreign exchange, reserve bank: (June 1973) U.S. $5,932,000,000; (June 1972) U.S. $4,396,000,000. Federal budget (1972–73 est.): revenue A$9,290,000,000; expenditure A$6,835,000,000 (plus payments to states A$2,455,000,000). Gross national product: (1971–72) A$32,340,000,000; (1970–71) A$32,390,000,000. Money supply: (March 1973) A$7,038,000,000; (March 1972) A$5,774,000,000. Cost of living (1963 = 100): (Jan.–March 1973) 145; (Jan.–March 1972) 137.

Foreign Trade. (1972) Imports A$4,317,400,000; exports A$5,421,100,000. Import sources: U.S. 21%; U.K. 20%; Japan 16%; West Germany 7%. Export destinations: Japan 28%; U.S. 13%; U.K. 10%; New Zealand 5%. Main exports (1971–72): wool 12%; meat 11%; wheat 9%; iron ore 8%; nonferrous metals 6%; coal 5%; nonferrous metal ores 5%.

Transport and Communications. Roads (1970) 884,656 km. (including 141,400 km. main roads). Motor vehicles in use (1971): passenger 4,315,700; commercial (including buses) 1,058,750. Railways: (government; 1971) 40,269 km.; freight traffic (1971–72) 25,260,000,000 net ton-km. Air traffic (1971): 9,682,000,000 passenger-km.; freight 255,143,000 net ton-km. Shipping (1972): merchant vessels 100 gross tons and over 370; gross tonnage 1,184,010. Shipping traffic (1972): goods loaded 116,920,000 metric tons, unloaded 22,347,000 metric tons. Telephones (Dec. 1971) 4,157,000. Radio licenses (Dec. 1972) 2,763,000. Television licenses (Dec. 1972) 2,880,000.

Agriculture. Production (in 000; metric tons; 1972; 1971 in parentheses): wheat 6,613 (8,510); barley 1,660 (3,065); oats 562 (1,277); sorghum 1,228 (1,070); corn 214 (230); rice 252 (301); potatoes 747 (747); sugar, raw value 2,801 (2,794); apples 389 (443); oranges (1971) *c.* 296, (1970) 343; wine 276 (251); wool, greasy 874 (886); milk 7,310 (7,320); butter 191 (196); beef and veal 1,321 (1,102); mutton and lamb 865 (905). Livestock (in 000; March 1972): sheep 162,939; cattle 27,894; pigs 3,198; horses (1970) 456; chickens (1971) *c.* 23,100.

Industry. Fuel and power (in 000; metric tons; 1972): coal 59,930; lignite 24,011; crude oil 15,575; natural gas (cu.m.) 3,189,000; manufactured gas (cu.m.) 6,399,000; electricity (kw-hr.) 62,766,000. Production (in 000; metric tons; 1972): iron ore (65% metal content) 63,716; bauxite 14,440; pig iron 6,550; crude steel 6,803; zinc 295; aluminum 206; copper 139; lead 180; tin 7; nickel concentrates (metal content; 1971) 33; sulfuric acid 1,954; cement 4,936; cotton yarn 25; wool yarn 29; gold (troy oz.; 1971) 672; silver (troy oz.) 23,406; passenger cars (including assembly; units) 367; commercial vehicles (including assembly; units) 79. Dwelling units completed (1972) 145,000.

SPECIAL REPORT

AUSTRALIA AND NEW ZEALAND: NEW TRADING PATTERNS

By Gordon Bruns

During 1973, Australia and New Zealand achieved further progress toward economic maturity and closer relations with other countries, especially their Pacific neighbours. Fortunately, world trade trends favoured them. Their produce was required in the developed nations, and there was a growing realization that the less developed countries should be helped to expand their trade in order to further their own social and political progress as well as to contribute to international prosperity.

Australia and New Zealand are well placed geographically to take advantage of the growing trading power in the majority of the less developed nations. These countries are located in Africa, Asia, South America, and Oceania, continents that border an area of the globe of which Australasia is the centrepoint. Politically, the new Labour governments in Australia and New Zealand were taking positive steps toward friendship with the less developed countries while retaining strong trade ties with older, richer nations around the Pacific—the U.S., Canada, and Japan—and with each other. Events that typified this new outlook included diplomatic recognition of China by both Australia and New Zealand and Australia's plans for a treaty of commerce with Japan and a trade agreement with North Korea.

Strong International Accounts. Australia and New Zealand both enjoyed buoyant international trading in 1973, with favourable balances on current account, capital inflows for at least part of the year, and rising reserves of foreign exchange. They experienced the luxury of revaluing their currencies more than once in 1973. For countries traditionally anxious about reserves, often having to deflate to protect them, this was a new era. Australia used its newfound strength to cut tariffs by 25% in 1973 to counter inflation. In September, when troubled by shortages of goods and excess money, New Zealand revalued its currency by 10%, restricted exports of fish and some types of meat and other animal products, diverted some meat export proceeds to a stabilization fund, allowed more car imports, and granted an extra NZ$70 million of import licenses.

Thus, at a time when their trading partners were of growing economic strength and even greater potential, these two countries became able to patronize world trade more generously, so as to obtain greater flows of goods and services in return for their own exports, and on improving terms of trade. A general statement of policy was: "Convert relatively unrewarding reserves into the goods and services which satisfy the community's standards of living and help check inflation."

As the nearby developing markets—such as the Pacific Islands, Indonesia, Papua New Guinea, Malaysia, and China—expanded their industry and world spending, Australia and New Zealand could afford to accept their produce in return for a variety of goods and services—food, fibre, metals, machinery, tourist attractions, and numerous other services.

Diversified Markets. While they stood to gain from the cheap produce and growing demand of their less developed neighbours, Australia and New Zealand maintained important trade links with older markets. By means of deliberate policy, both began diversifying when Britain decided to join the European Economic Community. The prevailing trend was summarized by the following changes in Australia's trade from 1958–59 to 1971–72: Britain's share of its exports fell from 32 to 9%, the U.S. share rose from 8 to 13%, and Japan's from 13 to 28%; Britain's share of Australia's imports fell from 39 to 21%, the U.S. share rose from 14 to 22%, and Japan's from 4 to 16%. The pattern for New Zealand was similar. Africa and South America were not yet important, but they might well become major targets of Australian-New Zealand marketing in the future.

Open Door Closed. Australia has been noted for its large-scale immigration program, which provided additions of nearly 1% to the population annually over the postwar years and almost equaled the natural increase at times. Similarly, foreign capital was welcome, and although exchange controls persistently refused to guarantee in advance the freedom to repatriate capital, the foreign component represented 10–15% of Australia's total investment up to the end of 1972.

During 1972 and 1973, however, migrant and capital inflows were both trimmed as a means of checking inflation, which had begun to worry Australia at the beginning of the 1970s. Previously, Australia had judged, mainly on strategic grounds, that population growth should be maintained.

Australia had had bouts of inflation before, notably in the 1950s, but at that time lacked the strength in its external finance to veto foreign capital. In September 1972, however, a veto was placed on foreign loans of less than two-year terms, and Australians were allowed portfolio investment (buying of securities) abroad for the first time in many years. Direct investment (purchase of physical assets) has long been permitted, mainly in neighbouring countries, because it provides substantial earnings to offset the heavy cost of servicing the foreign capital invested in Australia.

The Foreign Companies (Takeovers) Act of September 1972 empowered the government to screen any foreign take-over offer for Australian company shares of stock, defined as a purchase that would bring a single foreign holding up to 15% of the total shares issued (or 40% in all foreign hands). This power was used to prevent a number of take-overs during 1973.

In December 1972, the new Australian Labor Party government subjected loans of more than two years' duration to a 25% deposit at the nation's central bank (interest-free), which virtually stopped that form of capital inflow. At the same time, a unilateral revaluation of currency was made.

All these measures tended to encourage overseas payments (imports and capital outflow) and check receipts, thus slowing the growth of external reserves. They were followed by further steps in 1973 to check inflows. In February, when the U.S. dollar depreciated 10% (most of Australia's external trade is in U.S. dollars), the Australian dollar retained its gold parity, thus appreciating. In September it was appreciated unilaterally an additional 5%.

Anti-Internationalism. Subsequent to the financial moves, Australian government leaders expressed stronger antiforeign attitudes, stating that they would prevent foreign ownership of the mining industry rising above the then-estimated 62%. Foreign applicants for mining exploration permits were screened, and the entry of capital for property development was embargoed. An inquiry was proposed on multinational corporations, to report whether their Australian activities should be subject to licensing and other conditions.

In summary, there were promising signs that the Australian and New Zealand governments were more prepared than their predecessors to reduce trade barriers against their neighbours, being less beholden than before to manufacturers and exporters and more keen to reap the gains of foreign trade. At the same time, they showed an inconsistency of attitude, both economic and political, in barring foreign capital and management, and their accompanying technologies.

Gordon Bruns is chief economist of the ANZ Banking Group, Ltd.

continued from page 109

immigrants. He declared that the ALP would not set one family against another because of the colour of their skins. He described the LCP administration as having practiced a "White Australia" policy. McMahon had set a limit of 10,000 nonwhite immigrants a year, all of whom had had to pay their own way. Grassby said that in the future non-Caucasians applying for assisted passage would be judged on their qualifications and on the likelihood of their blending into Australian society. This meant that coloured New Zealand citizens from that country's Polynesian possessions would be admitted on the same basis as white New Zealanders.

Foreign Affairs. Until November 1973, when he turned the foreign affairs post over to Sen. Donald R. Willesee, Whitlam acted as both prime and foreign minister. On Dec. 5, 1972, he had begun reassessing foreign policy with the general intention of creating an Australia that would be "less militarily oriented and . . . which will enjoy a growing standing as a distinctive, tolerant, cooperative, and well-regarded nation, not only in the Asian and Pacific regions, but also in the world at large." (*See* Special Report.) Part of the trend toward developing a distinct national identity involved the cutting of several ties with the United Kingdom. On Dec. 7, 1972, Whitlam canceled the Commonwealth of Australia's New Year's Honours List, which had been prepared by McMahon. On Feb. 13, 1973, the Cabinet agreed to delete the reference to the queen from Australia's oath or affirmation of allegiance. Attorney-General Lionel Murphy was dispatched to London to supervise the ending of the constitutional link under which appellants dissatisfied with Australian legal decisions could appeal to the British Privy Council.

On the positive side, Australia moved closer to New Zealand in the diplomatic sphere. Whitlam visited Wellington in January for talks with his New Zealand counterpart, Norman Kirk. After the first meeting between the two new Labor prime ministers, a joint communiqué was issued which revealed their foreign policy preoccupations. Both nations called on France to abandon its nuclear testing program in the Pacific. Subsequently, they successfully appealed to the International Court of Justice at The Hague for a legal embargo on French nuclear testing, which the French government ignored. By May ships flying the French flag had been banned indefinitely from Australian ports by the Australian Seamen's Union; the ban also applied to ships serving French territories in the Pacific. Whitlam agreed to refuel the New Zealand frigate "Otago" when it sailed to the French test zone, and the Australian naval tanker "Supply" was dispatched accordingly.

Since the withdrawal of Australian troops from Vietnam between August 1971 and February 1972, relations with the United States had entered a new phase. Whitlam declared that he would maintain friendly relations with the U.S. "in a spirit of mutual respect and trust," but he looked to a sharing of viewpoints in fields other than defense. In February the government had obtained U.S. agreement to Australian joint control over the naval communications station at North-West Cape, Western Australia. The base was primarily a link between the Pentagon and U.S. Poseidon submarines in the Indian Ocean. The U.S. also agreed to consult further about Pine Gap and Nurrungar, both parts of the early warning system. ALP policy opposed foreign ownership of bases on Australian soil, but the government claimed that these particular sites were not parts of weapons systems.

The most striking international developments concerned Australia's relationships with Communist governments. Australia had recognized the People's Republic of China on Dec. 21, 1972, when the respective ambassadors in Paris signed a joint communiqué that provided for the establishment of full diplomatic relations. Australia acknowledged that Taiwan was a province of China and agreed to remove its ambassador from Taiwan before Jan. 25, 1973. Diplomatic relations were established with North Vietnam in February. Whitlam visited China in November.

Australian-Yugoslav relations improved markedly after their low ebb in 1972, when Croatian émigré terrorists of the Ustashi movement were alleged to have been given training and asylum in Australia, and Yugoslav property in Sydney was bombed. The prime minister of Yugoslavia, Dzemal Bijedic, visited Australia in March. He was closely guarded during his visit, since about half the 165,000 Yugoslavs who had emigrated to Australia after 1945 were Croatians. Whitlam was able to tell Bijedic personally that in the future firm action would be taken to detect, suppress, and expel Croatian extremists known to be operating in Australia. As part of the crackdown, Attorney-General Murphy, accompanied by federal police, raided the headquarters of the Australian Security and Intelligence Organization in Melbourne in search of files relating to Ustashi activities.

Whitlam visited Indonesia in February at which time he addressed the Indonesian Parliament. In June he visited India, where he assured Prime Minister Indira Gandhi that Australia under the ALP was even more determined than before to be a truly Asian nation, not merely an outpost of Western culture and influence. Whitlam and Mrs. Gandhi agreed that the Indian Ocean "should be free from international tensions, great-Power rivalry, and military escalation."

Following a three-day visit to the U.K. by Australian Defense Minister Lance Barnard (*see* BIOGRAPHY) in June, it became clear that the Australian government was not to be dissuaded from the intended reduction in its military commitment to Singapore and Malaysia. It proposed to withdraw Australia's only battalion and battery, involving about 800 men, from Singapore by early 1974, although some support troops were to remain to strengthen the British force on the island. Withdrawal of Australian Mirage jets and the 1,500 men at the Butterworth base on Penang was not to take place before Malaysia had attained "air capability," probably around 1975.

Economic and Social Affairs. Prime Minister Whitlam attempted to reshape the Australian economy by a series of reforms, beginning on Dec. 22, 1972, with the upward revaluation of the Australian dollar by 4.85% in terms of its relationship to the U.S. dollar. At the same time, he announced new measures to control capital inflow with a variable deposit scheme. Borrowers were required to deposit a proportion of overseas borrowings, fixed at 25%, with the Central Reserve Bank. No interest would be paid on the deposits, which would be held frozen until repayment of the borrowings. The new restrictions on capital inflow were in line with the desire of the Australian government to reduce foreign ownership of assets in Australia and to prevent assets from being bought cheaply. A further 5% revaluation of the Australian dollar relative to the U.S. dollar was announced Sept. 9, 1973.

CAMERA PRESS / PICTORIAL PARADE

Gough Whitlam, prime minister since December 1972, stressed a new and broader foreign policy for Australia.

Whitlam's decision to revalue the dollar was made in response to inflation. Prices in Australia had risen by over 7% annually in 1971 and 1972, and it was argued that imported inflation had been responsible for at least a part of the pressure on domestic price levels. The main problem about revaluation was that it was likely to hit vulnerable sectors of the economy exporting to highly competitive world markets, such as the dried fruit and canning industries. The mining industry, most of whose export contracts were written in U.S. dollars, also stood to lose heavily. Finally, for some of the protected domestic manufacturing industries, revaluation was equivalent to a sharp cut in import tariffs.

Whitlam also faced the danger that damage to particular industries or agricultural sectors could increase the national unemployment level beyond the figure of 150,000 anticipated for June 1974. In order to avert this, the government planned to introduce selective compensation measures. In July 1973 the ALP made a 25% cut in import tariffs. James F. Cairns, the overseas trade minister, said that the government would make sure that price cuts resulting from lower tariffs would be passed on to the public, resulting in a saving of more than A$800 million to Australian consumers.

In August Treasurer Frank Crean announced the first Labor budget in 24 years. It massively increased spending on social welfare, urban development, and education, removed investment incentives in the mining industry, and placed a tax on old-age pensions. Outlays would increase by 18.9% over 1973–74 to A$12,168,000,000, while receipts were to rise by 20.6% to A$11,481,000,000. Spending on education was increased from A$404 million to A$834 million, the largest single increase. Social security benefits were raised by A$1.50 a week; pensions were to be taxable following abolition of the means test, with adequate measures being taken to "protect those wholly or largely dependent on pensions from detriment."

Part of the new social welfare program involved the establishment of a national health service. The basic change in the administration of the health service was the replacement of the many health insurance companies by a single government organization. Under the LCP the private organizations had been subsidized to the extent of A$61 million. Labor's new scheme was said to be likely to cost A$59 million, with the money to be raised by a levy of 1.35% on taxable incomes, an increase in motor vehicle third party insurance premiums, and a levy on workers' compensation contributions. Doctors bitterly opposed the scheme, which was to begin in July 1974.

In December 1972 the arbitration court had accepted in principle the idea of equal pay for men and women doing equal work. The president of the Australian Council of Trade Unions, Robert Hawke, welcomed the court's decision, but was disappointed at the plan to phase in the changes slowly. Not until the end of 1975 were all women in Australia to be paid at the same rate as men doing the same jobs.

Whitlam's plans received a severe check in May and June. On May 17 the Senate threw out the ALP's electoral bill, which had provided that the number of eligible voters should not be more than 10% above or below the average number of voters in each electorate, and that electoral commissioners should no longer consider disabilities arising from remoteness or sparseness of population. On June 6 the Senate rejected the Industrial Law Reform bill.

During September 3–7 a constitutional convention, including federal, state, and local leaders, met at Sydney to review the Australian constitution for the first time since its adoption in 1901. Four committees were formed to study specific proposals, and the convention was expected to convene again in 1974. During the convention, Prime Minister Whitlam appealed to the premiers of the states to delegate to the federal government power to control prices, hitherto a state prerogative. South Australia, Western Australia, and Tasmania agreed, but New South Wales and Victoria gave only qualified approval and Queensland refused. As a result, the prime minister announced on September 26 that a referendum would be held December 8 on the issue of federal control of prices and incomes. The results of the referendum, however, constituted a setback for Whitlam. Some 65% of those voting opposed giving the federal government control over incomes, and approximately 55% rejected federal control of prices.

On January 26 Whitlam announced that a small group of established writers and composers would be invited to compose a new national anthem to replace "God Save the Queen." At the same time, the government established a new Council for the Arts which was to administer state support for cultural activities.

The Sydney Opera House. A further stimulus to the nation's cultural life was provided with the opening in the fall of the majestic Sydney Opera House. This unique structure of sloping, white, sail-like roofs, jutting into Sydney Harbour from Bennelong Point, had taken A$100 million, almost 20 years, and unprecedented technical ingenuity to complete. The idea of an opera house had first been put forward in 1954. Competitive designs were sought from architects the world over, and in 1957 the 38-year-old Danish architect Jørn Utzon was announced as the winner.

Construction was begun in March 1959. The roof structures were originally designed to be elliptical paraboloids of thin concrete poured into molds on the site. This idea was eventually dropped and, instead, thick arching concrete ribs were cast on the ground and assembled on top of each other. Work on the roofs alone took eight years. After long disagreement with engineers and officials over materials, methods, and fees, Utzon finally resigned as the Opera House architect in February 1966 and was replaced by a panel.

The completed complex consisted of theatres, a

The distinctive Opera House, opened at last in October 1973, occupies a commanding site on Bennelong Point in Sydney Harbour.

AUSTRALIA INFORMATION SERVICE

concert hall, concert rooms, and facilities for conventions, social affairs, art exhibitions, films, wining, dining, and strolling; it could accommodate almost 7,000 persons. The three sets of roof shells contained about 2,000 panes of glass in more than 700 different sizes, covering 1.5 ac. in all; one sheet alone weighed almost half a ton. The Sydney Opera House was expected to become Australia's most famous single tourist attraction. (A. R. G. GRIFFITHS)

See also Dependent States.

Austria

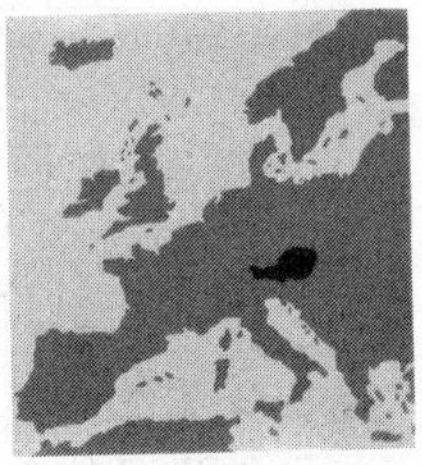

A republic of central Europe, Austria is bounded by West Germany, Czechoslovakia, Hungary, Yugoslavia, Italy, Switzerland, and Liechtenstein. Area: 32,375 sq.mi. (83,850 sq.km.). Pop. (1973): 7,550,000. Cap. and largest city: Vienna (pop., 1971, 1,614,841). Language: German. Religion (1971 est.): Roman Catholic 91%. President in 1973, Franz Jonas; chancellor, Bruno Kreisky.

During 1973 Austria continued to pursue a policy of neutrality, coupled with strenuous efforts to promote international harmony between nations, but these were hampered at times by unforeseen incidents that temporarily soured relations between Austria and various other states.

At the beginning of October, Chancellor Kreisky found himself at the centre of an international controversy after Arab guerrillas had seized three Jewish emigrants from the U.S.S.R. arriving in Vienna en route to Israel. As a condition for the hostages' release, the guerrillas demanded closure of Schönau Castle, the Austrian transit camp for Soviet Jewish emigrants, which received as many as 150 new arrivals every day. The chancellor's decision to accede to this demand provoked a storm of protest from many parts of the world. However, despite a personal visit by Israeli Prime Minister Golda Meir, who also made an impassioned speech on the subject to the Council of Europe in Strasbourg, as well as a plea from U.S. Pres. Richard Nixon, Chancellor Kreisky, himself of Jewish extraction, refused to alter his decision. Nevertheless, Soviet Jewish emigrants continued to pass through Austria at an undiminished rate, even during the Arab-Israeli war in October. The government closed Schönau Castle in December, but a government spokesman said emigrants who could not go on to Israel immediately would be cared for at the Red Cross centre at Wöllersdorf.

Austria's general policy of active neutrality was particularly apparent on the occasion of its becoming a nonpermanent member of the UN Security Council on Jan. 1, 1974. Efforts were also made to promote Austria's position as a centre for international conferences of all kinds. In the first half of the year talks were held in Vienna between NATO and Warsaw Pact countries with a view to mutual and balanced force reductions (MBFR) in Europe. At the beginning of the year, an agreement was signed for the establishment of another international organization in Austria—the International Institute for Applied Systems Analysis, which set up its headquarters at Laxenburg near Vienna. In order to provide facilities for as many international conferences and institutions as possible, the government decided to go ahead with its plans for a UN City, despite the escalating cost of the project.

In December 1972 mutual recognition had been achieved between Austria and North Vietnam and East Germany. In March 1973 the Austrian and Czechoslovak foreign ministers agreed on the establishment of a commission on border incidents. However, late in the year two air incidents in which Austrian aviation enthusiasts lost their lives strained relations between the two countries. Relations with Yugoslavia continued to be hampered by incidents in the mixed-language territory of Carinthia. Following an international agreement in the fall of 1972, bilingual place name signs were provided in the region. When these were repeatedly dismantled or painted over by groups of self-styled "patriots," Yugoslavia protested to the Austrian government on behalf of the 25,000-strong Slovene minority. The Austrian government hoped to be able to settle the dispute by means of a special commission to deal with the problem.

During the year preliminary studies were completed with a view to the comprehensive reform of Austrian penal and family law. Proposals for the relaxation of

AUSTRIA

Education. (1971–72) Primary, pupils 974,510, teachers (1970–71) 44,512; secondary, pupils 151,235, teachers (1970–71) 9,484; vocational, pupils 233,437, teachers (1970–71) 10,689; teacher training, students 12,816, teachers (1970–71) 1,184; higher (including 6 universities), students 62,871, teaching staff 8,928.

Finance. Monetary unit: schilling, with (Sept. 17, 1973) a free rate of 17.83 schillings to U.S. $1 (42.97 schillings = £1 sterling). Gold, SDRs, and foreign exchange, central bank: (June 1973) U.S. $2,738,000,000; (June 1972) U.S. $2,346,000,000. Budget (1972 rev. est.): revenue 113,389,000,000 schillings; expenditure 122,820,000,000 schillings. Gross national product: (1971) 415.7 billion schillings; (1970) 373.9 billion schillings. Money supply: (May 1973) 99.4 billion schillings; (May 1972) 86,340,000,000 schillings. Cost of living (1963 = 100): (May 1973) 151; (May 1972) 140.

Foreign Trade. (1972) Imports 120,576,000,000 schillings; exports 89,747,000,000 schillings. Import sources: EEC (Six) 58% (West Germany 42%, Italy 7%); Switzerland 7%; U.K. 6%. Export destinations: EEC (Six) 39% (West Germany 22%, Italy 10%); Switzerland 11%; U.K. 8%; U.S. 5%. Main exports: machinery 21%; iron and steel 11%; textile yarns and fibres 8%; timber 6%; chemicals 6%; paper and board 5%. Tourism (1970): visitors 9,588,000; gross receipts U.S. $1,276,000,000.

Transport and Communications. Roads (1971) 95,388 km. (including 552 km. expressways). Motor vehicles in use (1971): passenger 1,325,000; commercial 128,000. Railways: state (1971) 5,898 km., private (1970) 636 km.; traffic (state only; 1972) 6,668,000,000 passenger-km., freight 9,817,000,000 net ton-km. Air traffic (1972): 476 million passenger-km.; freight 6,076,000 net ton-km. Telephones (Dec. 1971) 1,547,000. Radio licenses (Dec. 1971) 2,160,000. Television licenses (Dec. 1971) 1,586,000.

Agriculture. Production (in 000; metric tons; 1972; 1971 in parentheses): wheat 863 (974); barley 977 (1,016); rye 402 (448); oats 255 (284); corn 726 (721); potatoes 2,341 (2,717); sugar, raw value 359 (272); apples 156 (243); wine 260 (181); meat (1971) 437, (1970) 414; timber (cu.m.; 1971) 12,400, (1970) 11,800. Livestock (in 000; Dec. 1971): cattle 2,499; sheep 112; pigs 3,445; chickens 12,140.

Industry. Fuel and power (in 000; metric tons; 1972): lignite 3,755; crude oil 2,478; natural gas (cu.m.) 1,964,000; electricity (kw-hr.) 29,366,000 (58% hydroelectric in 1971); manufactured gas (Vienna only; cu.m.) 628,000. Production (in 000; metric tons; 1972): iron ore (30% metal content) 4,132; pig iron 2,847; crude steel 4,069; magnesite (1971) 1,556; aluminum 204; copper 23; lead 10; zinc 17; cement 6,346; paper (1971) 1,074; nitrogenous fertilizers (N content; 1971–72) 232; cotton yarn 23; woven cotton fabric 19; wool yarn 12; rayon and synthetic fibres (1971) 106.

the abortion laws aroused strong opposition, particularly in Roman Catholic circles. Discussions also continued on the question of greater participation by workers in managing companies. From July 1 the age of majority was reduced from 21 to 19. In August the government brought forward its proposals for the reform of the radio and television service, despite strong resistance from the opposition, which saw them as a threat to freedom of information. Other subjects that continued to arouse controversy were the federal Army, the distribution of free schoolbooks, and preliminary studies for the democratization and modernization of higher education.

The economy continued to flourish, with full employment and a growth rate of 6%. Prices rose at a rate of some 7%, however, necessitating a continuation of price control measures. A policy of restraint on both prices and wages was agreed upon by the various interests involved. The revaluation of the West German mark was accompanied by two revaluations of the Austrian schilling, by 2.25% in March and 4.8% in July.

The amalgamation of the four state-owned iron and steel companies to form a giant enterprise employing over 75,000 people became final in the spring. Amalgamations in various other industries were also planned. (ELFRIEDE DIRNBACHER)

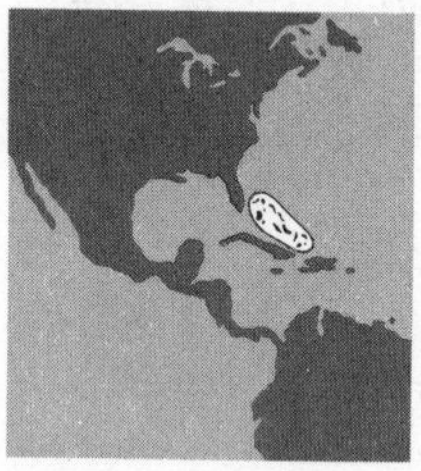

Bahamas

On July 10, 1973, the Bahamas achieved independence as a parliamentary state. A member of the Commonwealth of Nations, the Bahamas comprise an archipelago of about 700 islands in the North Atlantic Ocean just southeast of the United States. Area: 5,382 sq.mi. (13,925 sq.km.). Pop. (1973 est.): 189,000. Cap. and largest city: Nassau (urban area pop., 1970, 101,503). Language: English (official). Religion (1970): Baptist 28.8%; Anglican 22.7%; Roman Catholic 22.5%; Methodist 7.3%; Saints of God and Church of God 6%; others and no religion 12.7%. Queen, Elizabeth II; governors-general in 1973, Sir John Paul and, from August 1, Sir Milo B. Butler; prime minister, Lynden O. Pindling.

Following an independence conference held in London in December 1972, the Bahamas ended its colonial status under Britain, which had lasted since the early 17th century, and declared its independence on July 10, 1973, joining the Commonwealth as its 32nd full member. In September 1972 Lynden O. Pindling (*see* BIOGRAPHY), prime minister since 1967, and his mainly black Progressive Liberal Party (PLP) had won 60% of the popular vote on a platform of immediate independence.

The opposition Free National Movement (FNM), a merger of the United Bahamian Party with dissident PLP members, had questioned the timing of independence. Considerable opposition was also expressed from Abaco, an Out Island (population some 6,500) with a large white minority mostly descended from American loyalist settlers. They expressed the wish to remain British and threatened to secede.

Bahamian prosperity continued after independence, albeit on an uneven basis. While the growth of tourism was reported to be leveling off in 1972, an annual 1.5 million tourists continued to account for 71% of the country's gross national product, 60% of its total revenue, and two-thirds of its labour force. The PLP's White Paper on independence stated bluntly that "the government's policy is that of maintaining the tax-haven status of the country" (a majority of the Bahamas' 14,000 firms were foreign-owned), but the question of whether independence was compatible with the future safety of foreign capital remained. Some firms and investments were said to be leaving for such areas as the Cayman Islands.

(SHEILA PATTERSON)

BAHAMAS

Education. (1969–70) Primary, pupils 35,169, teachers 1,542; secondary, pupils 16,236, teachers 499; vocational, pupils 399, teachers 40; teacher training, students 113, teachers 18; higher, students 252, teaching staff 40.

Finance and Trade. Monetary unit: Bahamian dollar, with (Sept. 17, 1973) a free rate of B$1 to U.S. $1 (B$2.42 = £1 sterling). Budget (1971 est.): revenue B$107.2 million; expenditure B$106.5 million. Foreign trade (1972): imports B$487,258,000 (29% from U.S., 13% from U.K.); exports B$342 million (82% to U.S., 7% to Puerto Rico). Main exports: petroleum products 78%; pharmaceuticals 9%; cement 5%. Tourism (1971): visitors 1,397,000; gross receipts U.S. $278 million.

Transport and Communications. Shipping (1972): merchant vessels 100 gross tons and over 144; gross tonnage 205,862. Telephones (Dec. 1971) 47,000. Radio receivers (Dec. 1969) 125,000. Television receivers (Dec. 1964) *c.* 4,500.

Bahrain

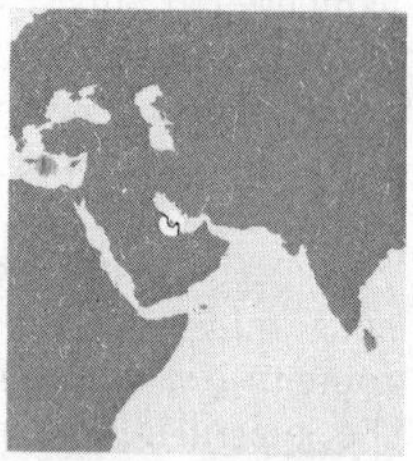

An independent constitutional monarchy (emirate), Bahrain consists of a group of islands in the Persian Gulf, lying between the Qatar Peninsula and Saudi Arabia. Total area: 256 sq.mi. (662 sq.km.). Pop. (1973 est.): 228,792. Cap.: Manama (pop., 1973 est., 93,162). Language: Arabic (official), Persian. Religion (1971): Muslim 95.7%; Christian 3%, others 1.3%. Emir in 1973, Isa ibn Sulman al-Khalifah.

Bahrain took an important step in its political evolution in 1973 with the approval by the Constituent Council on June 2 of a 108-article constitution, intended to replace the 400-year-old rule of the emir and his family by a form of democratic government. The constitution stated that Islam was the official religion and Arabic the language of the state; it provided for women's suffrage and free compulsory education and medical treatment for all citizens. It placed restrictions on the granting of concessions for the island's natural resources. The constitution, which could not

BAHRAIN

Education. (1969–70) Primary, pupils 36,612, teachers 1,547; secondary, pupils 12,144, teachers 728; vocational, pupils 907, teachers 103; higher, students 310, teaching staff 40.

Finance and Trade. Monetary unit: Bahrain dinar, with (Sept. 17, 1973) a free rate of 0.40 dinar to U.S. $1 (0.95 dinar = £1 sterling). Budget (1972 est.): revenue 26.5 million dinars; expenditure 25,750,000 dinars. Foreign trade (1972): imports 100,102,000 dinars; exports (excluding oil) 32,292,000 dinars. Import sources: U.K. 21%; Japan 15%; U.S. 13%; China 7%; Australia 6%; West Germany 5%. Export destinations: Saudi Arabia 51%; Dubai 7%; Kuwait 7%; Iran 6%; Qatar 6%. Main exports: crude oil and petroleum products.

Industry. Production (in 000; metric tons; 1971): crude oil 3,760; petroleum products 12,475.

Automobile Industry:
see Industrial Review; Transportation

Automobile Racing:
see Motor Sports

Aviation:
see Defense; Transportation

Balance of Payments:
see Payments and Reserves, International

Ballet:
see Dance

be altered for five years, also provided for a National Assembly which would include the members of the Cabinet and 30 members elected by popular vote. Elections were held on December 7.

The island continued its steady development as a commercial and communications centre for the Persian Gulf. In June the Organization of Arab Petroleum Exporting Countries (OAPEC) approved the building of a giant dry dock in Bahrain at an estimated cost of $250 million. An aluminum atomizing plant was opened during the year.

Despite the discreetly pro-Western stance of the emir's government, Bahrain participated in the Arab oil boycott during and after the October Arab-Israeli war. In June an important agreement was reached with Kuwait providing for close coordination in trade, economy, and finance. (PETER MANSFIELD)

Bangladesh

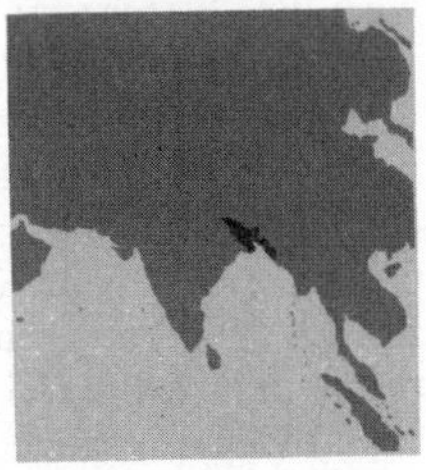

An independent republic and member of the Commonwealth of Nations, Bangladesh is bordered by India on the west, north, and east, by Burma in the southeast, and by the Bay of Bengal in the south. Area: 55,126 sq.mi. (142,776 sq.km.). Pop. (1973 est.): 74.6 million. Cap. and largest city: Dacca (pop., 1971 est., 799,601). Language: Bengali. Religion: Muslim 80%, with Hindu, Christian, and Buddhist minorities. Presidents in 1973, Abu Sayeed Choudhury and, from December 24, Muhammad Ullah; prime minister, Sheikh Mujibur Rahman.

With the holding of a general election in March 1973, four months after the adoption of the country's first constitution by the Constituent Assembly in the previous November, Bangladesh was well embarked on the path of democratic socialism. As Prime Minister Sheikh Mujibur Rahman put it, the adoption of the constitution barely 11 months after liberation was probably a record for a newly independent nation. The general election, which resulted in a landslide victory for Sheikh Mujib's Awami League Party, gave an element of political stability to the country, which still faced formidable problems of reconstruction.

The constitution provided for the establishment of a parliamentary democracy with a president as constitutional head of state, an executive headed by a prime minister, and a separate judiciary. The unicameral legislature of 300 members was to be elected for a five-year term. The preamble enshrined the high ideals of socialism, secularism, democracy, and nationalism. The socialism Bangladesh hoped to achieve would be different from that followed by the U.S.S.R., China, Yugoslavia, or Romania. In the words of Sheikh Mujib, "Bangladesh is to evolve its own socialist system to serve its peculiar needs."

The authors of the constitution, while borrowing heavily from other major democratic constitutions of the world, seemed to have avoided some of the difficulties inherent in the Indian constitution. As in India, the constitution was clear on the right of the government to acquire property, but there was no provision for compensation. The Bangla constitution also specified that an elected member who voted against his party in Parliament or resigned from it was to lose his seat. This was designed to prevent the floor-crossing common in the Indian Parliament.

The election was more a personal victory for the prime minister than a vindication of the policies of the Awami League or some of Mujib's colleagues, against whom charges of personal enrichment and corruption were freely aired. The Awami League captured 292 of the 300 seats in the poll, which was marred by violence. Mujib himself hailed the victory as an endorsement of his internal and external policies and said his next task was to "emancipate the people from hunger and misery." The election acted as a damper on the opposition political leaders, especially the National Awami Party chief, nonagenarian Maulana Bhashani, who called for a nationwide revolt against the government for its failure to curb rising prices.

Mujib's external policies showed remarkable success. In August 1973 he journeyed to Ottawa, Ont., to attend his first Commonwealth heads of government conference, and in September he took part in the summit meeting of nonaligned nations in Algiers. By June over 100 governments had granted recognition to Bangladesh, although it was still being denied acceptance by Pakistan and China as well as entry into the United Nations. However, the Indo-Pakistani agreement signed in New Delhi in August opened the door for eventual recognition by Pakistan.

The agreement, in which Bangladesh was an "invisible partner," was reached after long and arduous negotiations in New Delhi, Rawalpindi, and Dacca. It provided for the three-way exchange of over 90,000 Pakistani prisoners of war held in India, the more than 200,000 Bengalis stranded in Pakistan, and a "substantial number" of Pakistani nationals in Bangladesh. Bangladesh agreed to postpone any decision on the delicate issue of a war crimes trial for 195 Pakistani prisoners, at least until the repatriations were completed. It would then be discussed by Pakistan and Bangladesh on the basis of "sovereign equality," which indicated that Pakistani recognition of Bangladesh was not far off. There were also strong indications that Bangladesh might ultimately decide to drop the idea of a war crimes trial altogether, paving the way for an end to an era of confrontation between the countries of the subcontinent.

Bangladesh's economy continued to be plagued by shortages. Peter Jackson, coordinator of UN relief operations, predicted that the country would be short 2.5 million tons of wheat and rice during 1973, but he believed the worst was over and that there was no danger of famine. Food-grain output in 1973 was offi-

Jubilant supporters of Mujibur Rahman gather around him at a rally held during Bangladesh's first election campaign.

G. SIPAHIOGLU—LIAISON

BANGLADESH

Education. (1972–73) Primary, pupils *c.* 7 million; secondary, pupils *c.* 1,030,000; vocational, pupils *c.* 176,000; primary, secondary, and vocational, teachers *c.* 36,000; higher (including 4 universities), students *c.* 16,500.

Finance. Monetary unit: taka, with a free rate (Sept. 17, 1973) of 7.75 taka to U.S. $1 (18.69 taka = £1 sterling). Foreign exchange (Aug. 1972 est.) U.S. $170 million. Budget (1972–73 est.): revenue 2,916,000,000 taka; expenditure 2,184,000,000 taka (development budget 3,183,000,000 taka). Cost of living (Dacca; 1963 = 100): (April 1973) 276; (April 1972) 180.

Foreign Trade. (1972) Imports 1,027,700,000 taka; exports 2,273,186,000 taka. Export destinations (jute only; 1970–71): U.K. 14%; Belgium-Luxembourg 8%; West Germany 5%; France 5%. Main exports: jute products *c.* 54%; jute *c.* 35%; leather *c.* 5%.

Transport and Communications. Roads (1970) *c.* 24,000 km. (including 3,900 km. with improved surface). Motor vehicles in use (1970): passenger 21,500; commercial (including buses) 14,500. Railways (1969): 2,858 km.; traffic 3,319,000,000 passenger-km., freight 1,570,000,000 net ton-km. Navigable waterways (1972) *c.* 8,000 km. Shipping (1972): merchant vessels 100 gross tons and over 39; gross tonnage 28,888. Shipping traffic (1971): goods loaded 825,000 metric tons, unloaded 3,501,000 metric tons. Radio licenses (March 1969) 531,000.

Agriculture. Production (in 000; metric tons; 1972; 1971 in parentheses): rice *c.* 14,490 (14,670); wheat *c.* 100 (112); sugar, raw value *c.* 320 (*c.* 650); jute 1,192 (761); tea 23 (12). Cattle (1971–72) *c.* 26,000,000.

Industry. Production (in 000; metric tons; 1969–70): steel 177; cement 54; jute fabric 589; cotton yarn 48; paper 79.

cially estimated at 12,680,000 tons, compared with 9.7 million tons in 1972. It was hoped that, with generous food grants from friendly countries in response to a UN appeal and purchases abroad, the government would be able to overcome the crisis. Commodity prices had risen by 120% since liberation, and the price of rice, the staple food, had doubled in six months. The rise in prices was mainly due to the fall in production and the abnormal increase in money in circulation—about 80% more than in 1970.

The government found it difficult to cope with the law and order situation. The response to its appeal for the surrender of illegal arms remained poor. According to the latest estimate there were 80,000 illegal weapons in the hands of the people. The June–August period witnessed an average of seven murders a day in Dacca and other towns and in the country.

Finance Minister Tajuddin Ahmed presented the new government's budget in April. Revenue was estimated at 3,740,300,000 taka and expenditure at 2,950,300,000 taka, leaving a surplus of 790 million taka. Ahmed also submitted a separate budget for rehabilitation and reconstruction amounting to 5,250,300,000 taka. The government expected to obtain 3,520,000,000 taka in foreign aid to help meet the costs of the development and reconstruction program. Estimates for the first five-year plan were still on the drawing board, but the development plan for 1973–74 called for an outlay of 5,250,000,000 taka in the public sector and 1.5 billion taka in the private sector.

The United States and India had been the major sources of aid in 1972, providing U.S. $320 million and $248 million, respectively. India also continued its assistance for rebuilding Bangladesh's communications network and provided export outlets for its products, mainly jute and tea. Total aid received during 1972 had amounted to $1.1 billion.

Despite the problems, there were signs that Bangladesh was recovering from the ravages of the 1971 war and the occupation by Pakistani armed forces. According to J. Burke Knapp, senior vice-president of the World Bank, Bangladesh had made a "remarkable economic recovery within a short time."

President Choudhury resigned unexpectedly on December 24, announcing that he found the office too limiting. He was succeeded by the speaker of the Parliament, Muhammad Ullah. (GOVINDAN UNNY)

Barbados

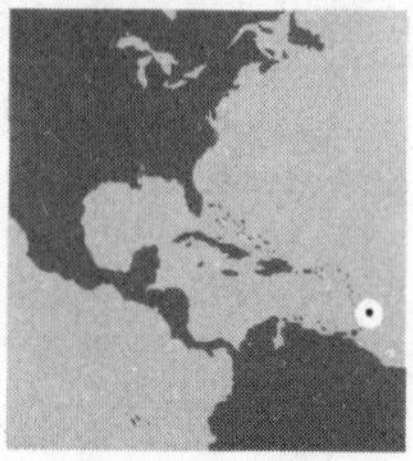

The parliamentary state of Barbados is a member of the Commonwealth of Nations and occupies the most easterly island in the southern Caribbean Sea. Area: 166 sq.mi. (430 sq.km.). Pop. (1972 est.): 241,296, 91% Negro; 4% white; 4% mixed. Cap. and largest city: Bridgetown (pop., 1970, 8,789). Language: English. Religion: Anglican 53%; Methodist 9%; Roman Catholic 4%; Moravian 2%; others 32%. Queen, Elizabeth II; governor-general in 1973, Sir Winston Scott; prime minister, Errol Walton Barrow.

Barbados continued politically stable in 1973 under the government of Errol Barrow. In July the island, with Jamaica, Guyana, and Trinidad and Tobago, signed the Chaguaramas Treaty to establish a Caribbean Community and common market. Some moves were also made to open up closer contacts with Cuba, and joint discussions were held with other states in the area on forms of association with the EEC.

On May 31 the prime minister presented a budget designed to stimulate local agriculture, industrial production, and interregional trade. Tariffs were increased on 376 items, including imported food and drink. Current expenditure was estimated at ECar$140.5 million and current revenue at ECar$120.7 million. The economy had had a real growth rate of less than 1% during 1972.

Tourism continued to grow. Figures for visitors to the island totaled 210,500 in 1972, the most significant increase being from the U.S. and Canada, but the steady increase from the U.K. and Europe also continued. As the island's principal industry, tourism employed approximately 20,000 people and contributed about 25% of Barbados' foreign exchange currency. In ten years there had been a shift in the island's image from that of a millionaire's playground to a year-round holiday resort. (SHEILA PATTERSON)

BARBADOS

Education. (1969–70) Primary, pupils 40,338, teachers 1,215; secondary, pupils 25,788, teachers 942; vocational, pupils 1,199, teachers 64; higher, students 645, teaching staff 67.

Finance and Trade. Monetary unit: East Caribbean dollar, with (Sept. 17, 1973) a free rate of ECar$1.99 to U.S. $1 (official rate of ECar$4.80 = £1 sterling). Budget (1971–72 est.): revenue ECar$97,442,000; expenditure ECar$98,838,000. Foreign trade (1972): imports U.S. $141,694,000; exports U.S. $44,810,000. Import sources: U.K. 27%; U.S. 19%; Canada 10%; Trinidad and Tobago 8%. Export destinations: U.K. 35%; U.S. 13%; Windward Islands 11%; Trinidad and Tobago 5%; Leeward Islands 5%. Main exports (1971): sugar 30%; molasses 8%; rum 5%. Tourism (1969): visitors 138,000; gross receipts (1970) U.S. $32 million.

Agriculture. Sugar production, raw value (in 000; metric tons; 1972) *c.* 110, (1971) *c.* 132.

Banking:
see Money and Banking
Baptists:
see Religion

Baseball

The Oakland Athletics, a team thriving on talent and controversy, repeated as world champions of baseball in 1973. They beat the New York Mets, 5–2, in the decisive seventh game of the World Series. The climax to a long, unpredictable baseball season took on an added dimension when Oakland manager Dick Williams announced his resignation even while the A's were celebrating their second successive title.

As in 1972, the World Series went the full seven games and both pennant play-offs required the five-game limit. Oakland stopped the Baltimore Orioles, 3–0, in the crucial fifth game for the American League flag on Jim "Catfish" Hunter's five-hitter. The Mets and Tom Seaver whipped the Cincinnati Reds, 7-2, in their showdown for National League honours.

The World Series took an unprecedented turn in the second game. Substitute second baseman Mike Andrews of the A's committed two costly 12th-inning errors and in so doing incurred the wrath of Charles O. Finley, the Oakland owner (*see* BIOGRAPHY). Finley, in effect, attempted to "fire" Andrews by placing him on the disabled list, a move that incited considerable protest among Andrews' teammates. Commissioner Bowie Kuhn then rejected Finley's request and reinstated Andrews, who received a standing ovation from a New York crowd when he came in to pinch-hit in the fourth game. After the Series Kuhn fined Finley a reported $7,000 for misconduct.

For baseball and humanity, the year 1973 began on a note of grief. Roberto Clemente, a veteran National League star, died in a plane crash off the shores of his native Puerto Rico on Dec. 31, 1972. Clemente was involved in a mercy mission on an aircraft loaded with relief supplies for earthquake victims in Managua, Nicaragua. Only two months earlier, the 38-year-old Clemente, who had played 18 years for the Pittsburgh Pirates, had emerged as the 11th player in the major leagues to collect 3,000 hits. Clemente was the complete ballplayer, offensively and defensively, and he annexed four National League batting championships along with his .318 lifetime average. In an extraordinary special election Clemente was named to baseball's Hall of Fame in March. Normally a five-year period must elapse between the end of a player's active career and his entrance into the Hall of Fame.

Atlanta's Henry Aaron dominated the individual headlines by hitting 40 home runs to pull within one of Babe Ruth's record 714. The 39-year-old Aaron slammed his 713th on September 29 in Atlanta. Another of the game's superstars, Willie Mays of the Mets, retired at the end of the World Series. Mays, 42, played in the major leagues for 22 years, most of that time with the Giants, and hit 660 homers, third behind Ruth and Aaron.

With his blazing fastball, Nolan Ryan of the California Angels established a new major league strikeout record and pitched two no-hitters. Ryan struck out 383, surpassing the 382 of former Dodger star Sandy Koufax. His no-hitters were against Kansas City and Detroit. The only other major league pitchers to hurl two no-hitters in one season were Johnny Vander Meer of Cincinnati in 1938, Allie Reynolds of the New York Yankees in 1951, and Virgil Trucks of Detroit in 1952. Other no-hitters during the year were registered by Steve Busby of Kansas City, Jim Bibby of Texas, and Phil Niekro of Atlanta.

WIDE WORLD

Hank Aaron watches his 712th career home run head for the left field stands in a game against the Astros at Houston on Sept. 22, 1973. Aaron ended the season with 713 home runs, one short of Babe Ruth's record.

Dick Allen of the Chicago White Sox became the highest paid baseball player in history when he signed a three-year contract calling for a reported total of $675,000. Injuries, however, plagued Allen most of the season. In October Lee MacPhail, general manager of the New York Yankees, was elected president of the American League. He succeeded Joe Cronin, who became the league's chairman of the board.

The American League, in an effort to improve the offense and increase attendance, used the designated hitter rule in 1973. The National League did not. The rule allowed a team to bat an extra player for the pitcher without removing that pitcher from the game. The American League scored an average of 8.55 runs

Final Major League Standings, 1973

American League
Eastern Division

Club	W.	L.	Pct.	G.B.	Balt.	Bos.	Det.	N.Y.	Mil.	Clev.	Cal.	Chi.	K.C.	Minn.	Oak.	Tex.
Baltimore	97	65	.599	—	—	7	9	9	15	12	6	8	8	8	5	10
Boston	89	73	.549	8	11	—	3	14	12	9	7	6	8	6	4	9
Detroit	85	77	.525	12	9	15	—	7	12	9	5	7	4	5	7	5
New York	80	82	.494	17	9	4	11	—	8	11	6	4	6	9	4	8
Milwaukee	74	88	.457	23	3	6	6	10	—	9	7	9	4	8	4	8
Cleveland	71	91	.438	26	6	9	9	7	9	—	7	5	2	7	3	7

Western Division

Club	W.	L.	Pct.	G.B.	Oak.	K.C.	Minn.	Cal.	Chi.	Tex.	Balt.	Bos.	Clev.	Det.	Mil.	N.Y.
Oakland	94	68	.580	—	—	10	4	12	12	11	7	8	9	5	8	8
Kansas City	88	74	.543	6	8	—	9	8	12	11	4	4	10	8	8	6
Minnesota	81	81	.500	13	14	9	—	8	9	12	4	6	5	7	4	3
California	79	83	.488	15	6	10	10	—	8	11	6	5	5	7	5	6
Chicago	77	85	.475	17	6	6	9	10	—	13	4	6	7	5	3	8
Texas	57	105	.352	37	7	7	6	7	5	—	2	3	5	7	4	4

National League
Eastern Division

Club	W.	L.	Pct.	G.B.	N.Y.	St.L.	Pitt.	Mon.	Chi.	Phil.	Atl.	Cin.	Hou.	L.A.	S.D.	S.F.
New York	82	79	.509	—	—	10	13	9	7	9	6	4	6	5	8	5
St. Louis	81	81	.500	1½	8	—	8	10	9	9	6	6	7	4	8	6
Pittsburgh	80	82	.494	2½	5	10	—	12	12	10	5	5	6	2	8	5
Montreal	79	83	.488	3½	9	8	6	—	9	13	6	4	6	5	7	6
Chicago	77	84	.478	5	10	9	6	9	—	10	5	8	6	5	7	2
Philadelphia	71	91	.438	11½	9	9	8	5	8	—	6	4	5	3	9	5

Western Division

Club	W.	L.	Pct.	G.B.	Cin.	L.A.	S.F.	Hou.	Atl.	S.D.	Chi.	Mon.	N.Y.	Phil.	Pitt.	St.L.
Cincinnati	99	63	.611	—	—	11	10	11	13	13	4	8	8	8	7	6
Los Angeles	95	66	.590	3½	7	—	9	7	15	9	7	7	7	9	10	8
San Francisco	88	74	.543	11	8	9	—	7	10	11	10	6	7	7	7	6
Houston	82	80	.506	17	7	11	11	—	7	10	6	6	6	7	6	5
Atlanta	76	85	.472	22½	5	2	8	11	—	12	7	6	6	6	7	6
San Diego	60	102	.370	39	5	9	7	8	6	—	5	5	4	3	4	4

Tie—Atlanta 1, Los Angeles 1.
Source: *The Sporting News.*

WIDE WORLD

The Oakland A's Jim "Catfish" Hunter delivers a pitch on his way to a five-hit, 3–0 victory over the Baltimore Orioles in the fifth and final game of the American League play-off at Oakland, Oct. 11, 1973.

per game as compared with 8.31 in the National League. The American League had averaged 6.93 runs per game in 1972 and 7.72 in 1971. The American League's overall batting average was .259, while the National League posted .254. In 1972, the Americans had averaged .239 and the Nationals .248. The American League enjoyed its greatest season at the gate, 13,443,016, a gain of 2,004,478 over strike-plagued 1972. The National League achieved its second-best attendance mark ever, 16,679,175, up 1,149,445 over the previous year. Together, according to unofficial figures from *The Sporting News,* the two leagues posted an all-time record attendance total of 30,122,191. The previous high was 29,193,417 in 1971.

The Hall of Fame at Cooperstown, N.Y., added the names of Clemente, pitcher Warren Spahn, outfielder Monte Irvin, first baseman George ("Highpockets") Kelly, pitcher Mickey Welch, and umpire Billy Evans.

Major Leagues. The National League East provided perhaps the most bizarre finish in baseball history. The unique possibility of a five-way tie for first existed until the final scheduled day of the regular season on September 30, and only when Yogi Berra's New York Mets won a makeup game from the Cubs in Chicago the next day was the logjam completely broken. The Mets, mired in last place on August 30, finished strongly to edge St. Louis by 1½ games, Pittsburgh by 2½, Montreal by 3½, and the Cubs, early-season pacesetters, by 5. Cincinnati also used a blistering stretch run to outlast Los Angeles by 3½ games for National League West honours.

New York Mets pitcher Jon Matlack is doubled off first base in the opening game of the 1973 World Series at Oakland on Oct. 13, 1973. Gene Tenace is the Oakland A's first baseman in the game, won by the A's 2–1.

UPI COMPIX

In the American League, Oakland and Baltimore captured division titles with room to spare. The A's finished six games ahead of runner-up Kansas City in the West. The Orioles dominated Boston by eight in the East.

The American League play-offs began with a 6–0 triumph by Baltimore over Oakland behind the five-hit pitching of Jim Palmer. Four runs by the Orioles in the first inning knocked out Oakland starter Vida Blue. In the second game the A's retaliated by hitting four home runs off Baltimore's Dave McNally and triumphing 6–3. Sal Bando, third baseman of the A's, hit two homers. The A's then pulled ahead by winning the third game 2–1 when Bert Campaneris hit a home run in the 11th inning to end a pitchers' duel between Ken Holtzman of the A's and Mike Cuellar of the Orioles. Baltimore evened the series by rallying from a 4–0 deficit to win 5–4, sparked by catcher Andy Etchebarren's home run in the seventh inning. Oakland won the final game and league championship 3–0 as "Catfish" Hunter pitched a five-hitter.

Cincinnati gained the first victory in the National League play-offs with a 2–1 victory over the Mets. Pete Rose and Johnny Bench each hit home runs to gain the victory for pitcher Jack Billingham. New York came back in the second game to win 5–0 as Mets pitcher Jon Matlack allowed only two hits. The third game resulted in a 9–2 victory for the Mets, a fistfight between Rose and Bud Harrelson of the Mets, and riotous behaviour on the part of the New York fans. They hurled beer cans and bottles onto the field at Rose, and the game had to be halted until order was restored. Rose gained revenge in the fourth game as his 12th-inning home run won for the Reds 2–1. Clay Carroll was the winning pitcher, in relief. The Mets then won the series and the National League crown 7–2 behind the pitching of Tom Seaver.

Oakland began the defense of its world championship by using two unearned runs to beat the New York Mets, 2–1, in the first game of the World Series at the Oakland Coliseum. With the designated hitter rule banned in Series play, the A's were forced to return to conventional-type baseball, but it worked to their advantage when pitcher Ken Holtzman doubled to trigger a two-run third-inning uprising. Holtzman then scored as second baseman Félix Millán erred on Bert Campaneris' grounder. Campaneris stole second and scored what proved to be the decisive run on Joe Rudi's single. Holtzman pitched five innings and got the win. Rollie Fingers and Darold Knowles checked the Mets in relief over the final four innings. The losing pitcher was Matlack.

The second game lasted 4 hours and 13 minutes—the longest in World Series history—and the Mets finally emerged from the incredible 12-inning marathon with a 10–7 triumph. Willie Mays, earlier beset by defensive and base-running problems, atoned in full measure by singling home the first of four Mets' runs in the 12th. Three more scrambled across on two errors by second baseman Mike Andrews. The A's, guilty of five errors in all, had sent the game into overtime at 6–6 by scoring twice with two out in the bottom of the ninth, then scored once and loaded the bases before surrendering in the 12th. A record-tying 11 pitchers saw action. The winner on the strength of a superb six-inning relief job was Tug McGraw, while the loser was Fingers. Cleon Jones and Wayne Garrett homered for New York.

The Series switched to Shea Stadium in Flushing, N.Y., for the third game. Oakland won, 3–2, this time in 11 innings, to grab a 2–1 lead in games. The winning run was set up in the top of the 11th when Ted Kubiak walked and reached second on Mets' catcher Jerry Grote's passed ball. Campaneris singled to score Kubiak. New York, paced by Garrett's lead-off home run off Hunter, got its two runs in the first inning. But even though Mets' ace Seaver struck out 12, Oakland still managed to tie the game at 2–all with single runs in the sixth and eighth to set the stage for Campaneris. The win went to Paul Lindblad, and the loss to Harry Parker.

It was Matlack against Holtzman in the fourth game, and the Mets prevailed, 6–1, to deadlock the Series again. Rusty Staub slammed a three-run home run as New York drove Holtzman from the mound in the first inning. Staub drove in another pair with a bases-loaded single in the fourth. Matlack surrendered only three hits in the eight innings that he worked.

Airtight pitching by Jerry Koosman and reliefer McGraw carried the Mets past Oakland and Vida Blue, 2–0, in the fifth game, thereby boosting New York into the Series driver's seat, three games to two. Koosman allowed only three hits in $6\frac{1}{3}$ innings. McGraw finished up without allowing a hit. John Milner's single behind Jones's double in the second inning produced the first run for the Mets. Don Hahn's triple drove in the other run in the sixth.

Oakland returned to its home grounds and won the sixth game, 3–1, as Hunter outdueled Seaver to tie the Series at three games each. A pair of run-scoring doubles by Reggie Jackson in the first and third innings spearheaded the A's. Hunter, who yielded four hits over $7\frac{1}{3}$ innings, needed and obtained relief help from Knowles and Fingers when the Mets tallied their lone run in the eighth.

Oakland took it all in the seventh game, 5–2. It was Holtzman over Matlack, and Holtzman launched the decisive four-run third inning for the A's with his second double of the Series. Campaneris then followed with Oakland's first home run of the Series. After Rudi singled, Jackson homered. Holtzman lasted into the sixth inning, when he was rescued by Fingers after the first Mets' run. The other New York run was scored on an error by first baseman Gene Tenace with two out in the ninth. That miscue brought the tying run to the plate, but Knowles, setting an all-time record by pitching in all seven games, came on to record the final out. Jackson was named most valuable player of the Series.

Minnesota's Rod Carew hit .350 to win the American League batting championship. Reggie Jackson of Oakland led in home runs with 32 and in runs batted in with 117.

Twelve pitchers reached the 20-game mark in the American League. Wilbur Wood of the Chicago White Sox posted the most wins, 24. Detroit's Joe Coleman registered 23, and Baltimore's Jim Palmer, 22. Oakland came up with three 20-game winners: Hunter, Holtzman, and Blue. Others were Ryan and Bill Singer of California, Paul Splittorff of Kansas City, Jim Colborn of Milwaukee, Luis Tiant of Boston, and Bert Blyleven of Minnesota.

The National League batting title went to Cincinnati's Pete Rose, who hit .338. Willie Stargell of Pittsburgh set the pace in home runs with 44 and in runs batted in with 119. Dave Johnson of Atlanta broke the record for home runs by a second baseman with 43.

Ron Bryant of San Francisco with 24 was the lone 20-game winner in the National League. Jack Billingham of Cincinnati and Seaver of the Mets won 19 apiece. Relief expert Mike Marshall of Montreal appeared in a record 92 games.

Most valuable player awards went to Pete Rose in the National League and Reggie Jackson in the American. Cy Young awards for outstanding pitching were won by Jim Palmer in the American League and Tom Seaver in the National. Gary Matthews, an outfielder for San Francisco, was named National League rookie of the year; the American League honoured Baltimore outfielder Al Bumbry. Gene Mauch of the Montreal Expos was manager of the year in the National League, and Baltimore's Earl Weaver won in the American. At their winter meeting in Houston, National League owners approved shifting the San Diego Padres to Washington, D.C., in 1974, although no official decision had been made by the end of 1973.

The National League defeated the American League, 7–1, in the 44th annual All-Star game at Royals Stadium in Kansas City, Mo. It was the 10th win in the last 11 games for the National Leaguers and ran their overall record to 25–18–1. Bobby Bonds of San Francisco slammed a two-run homer and added a double to become the game's most valuable player. Johnny Bench of Cincinnati and Willie Davis of Los Angeles also hit home runs for the Nationals. The winning pitcher was Rick Wise of St. Louis, while the loser was Minnesota's Bert Blyleven.

Amateur. Southern California won the National Collegiate Athletic Association baseball title for the fourth consecutive year. The Trojans edged Arizona State, 4–3, in the championship game at Omaha, Neb. Southern California had reached the finale with a storybook 8–7 win over Minnesota. The Gophers led, 7–0, after eight innings only to have the Trojans score 8 runs in the ninth. A record 63,356 fans watched the 14-game tournament. In Little League play Tainan City of Taiwan won the World Series by defeating Tucson, Ariz., 12–0. Tainan's Huang Ching-huy pitched a no-hitter. (JACK BRICKHOUSE)

Japanese. The Tokyo Yomiuri Giants, making history in Japanese professional baseball, captured the Central League title for a record ninth consecutive season and then defeated the Osaka Nankai Hawks in the post-season Japan Series for their ninth consecutive Series championship. In the best-of-seven-games Series, played in Osaka and Tokyo, the Giants beat the Nankai Hawks 4 games to 1.

"Just to hear you cheer like this for me and not be able to do anything about it makes me a very sad man," said 42-year-old Willie Mays at a retirement ceremony in New York City's Shea Stadium on Sept. 25, 1973.

WIDE WORLD

The 1973 season, however, proved to be one of the hardest yet for the Giants, who started in disastrous fashion. They could only manage to place fourth at the end of the first half of the 130-game season in late July. They finally shot into the lead on August 31 but fell again to second place behind the Osaka Hanshin Tigers on October 10. The Tigers maintained a half-game lead going into the final game of the season against the Giants in Osaka on October 22. Behind the stellar four-hit pitching of southpaw Kazumi Takahashi (23–13) the Giants mauled the Tigers 9–0 and clinched the title with 66 victories, 60 losses, and 4 ties. First baseman Sadaharu Oh of the Giants (*see* BIOGRAPHY) became the third Central League player to win the triple crown in batting with a .355 average, 51 home runs, and 114 runs batted in.

The Pacific League adopted the split-season system for the first time in 1973, deciding the league champions in a best-of-five play-off series between the winners of the first and second legs of the 130-game season. The Nankai Hawks of Osaka, who won the first leg, defeated the second-leg champion Hankyu Braves of Nishinomiya three games to two. The Braves were shooting for their third consecutive title in the six-club league.

Hankyu outfielder Tokuji Nagaike, who had the league's most runs batted in at 109 and captured the home run title with 43, failed to take the triple crown when he finished fourth in the batting average race with a .313. That title went to his teammate, first baseman Hideji Kato, with a .337. (HISASHI UNO)

Basketball

United States. *Collegiate.* Of all the honours won by the University of California at Los Angeles (UCLA) basketball team in 1973, the most important —and impressive—was the national championship, the Bruins' seventh in a row. While achieving that, the Bruins managed to do something even they had not done before. They broke the collegiate record of 60 consecutive victories and pushed it to 75 before the season ended.

Only one question troubled Coach John Wooden as UCLA marched through its 30-game schedule: whether his star junior centre, 6-ft. 11-in. Bill Walton, would turn professional after the season. Once the Bruins had throttled Memphis State for the National Collegiate Athletic Association (NCAA) title, Walton announced that he would play for UCLA in 1974.

UCLA spent most of 1973 bettering its own records, among them winning the NCAA tournament for the ninth time in ten years, boosting its tournament winning streak to 36 games, and improving its record for the decade to 381–15. The most significant record the Bruins broke was the University of San Francisco's streak of 60 straight victories, set in the mid-1950s. UCLA accomplished that by crushing Notre Dame 82–63 in a rugged game. Interestingly enough, the Irish had been the last team to defeat the Bruins, the victory coming in an 89–82 upset in 1971.

UCLA triumphed with athletes who were able to play at any pace, skilled at the full-court press (always the trademark of a Wooden-coached team), and mature though young. Leading the team was Walton, who was voted the country's top player by college coaches for the second year in a row. He averaged 20 points and 14 rebounds per game. His offensive help came mainly from junior forward Keith Wilkes. Two junior guards, Greg Lee and Tommy Curtis, got the ball to the scorers.

North Carolina State fielded the only other undefeated team in major college basketball. But talk of how the Wolfpack, with its 27–0 record and its sophomore star, David Thompson, would do against UCLA remained just that. Champion of the Atlantic Coast Conference, North Carolina State was banned from post-season competition by the NCAA because of recruiting violations.

That left the chances of any school upsetting the Bruins slimmer than ever. Certainly none of the three teams—Memphis State, Providence, and Indiana—to reach the semifinals with UCLA came heralded as a dynasty-wrecker.

Providence emerged from the Eastern Regionals with a 103–89 victory over Maryland. The keys to the Friars' success were Ernie DiGregorio, a 6-ft. sleight-of-hand artist, and 6-ft. 9-in. Marvin Barnes.

Steve Downing led Indiana out of the Mideast Regionals with a 75–69 victory over Marquette and a 72–65 victory over perennially tough Kentucky. These triumphs inspired Hoosier supporters to wonder how strong their team would have been with George McGinnis. After starring with Indiana as a sophomore in 1971, McGinnis joined the Indiana Pacers of the professional American Basketball Association.

After failing to reach the top ten in either major press association poll, the Memphis State Tigers raced easily through the Midwest Regionals. They opened by beating South Carolina 90–76 as centre Larry Kenon scored 34 points and grabbed 20 rebounds. Guard Larry Finch hit for 32 points against Kansas State to prove Memphis State's power and potential in a 92–72 romp. The Tigers continued their great leap forward against Providence in the semifinals at St. Louis. After Barnes suffered a knee injury, they came from nine points behind to a 98–85 win.

UCLA reasserted its ability to play at any speed in the Western Regionals. Arizona State chose to run with them and got run out of the game 98–81. San Francisco had other ideas after a 77–67 upset of Long Beach State, a team many believed would pose a major challenge to UCLA. The Dons played a stalling game until, with UCLA trailing 16–9, Walton decided he had had enough. Two baskets and two blocked shots by the Bruins' centre put UCLA on its way to victory, 54–39.

Indiana, which started two freshmen, made things uncomfortable for UCLA in the semifinals until Downing, a high-scoring senior centre, fouled out midway through the second half. A 70–59 win put the Bruins in the finals against Memphis State.

The final game was primarily a showcase for the extraordinary talents of Walton. While UCLA was gaining an 87–66 victory that grew close only briefly in the first half, Walton sank 21 of 22 shots from the field and scored 44 points to break by two the NCAA finals record set by Gail Goodrich of UCLA eight years earlier. Walton also got 13 rebounds. He was named the tournament's most valuable player for the second straight year.

In all the commotion over UCLA, it was easy to forget the National Invitational Tournament (NIT) and its champion, Virginia Tech. The NIT's championship game was as thrilling as the NCAA's was not. Virginia Tech defeated Notre Dame 92–91 when guard Bobby Stevens tipped in his own desperation shot as the final buzzer sounded.

Los Angeles produced the two leading major college

Major College Champions, 1973

League	Team and location
Eastern (Ivy)	Pennsylvania (Philadelphia)
Yankee	Massachusetts (Amherst)
Atlantic Coast	North Carolina State (Raleigh)
Southeastern	Kentucky (Lexington)
Southern	Furman (Greenville, S.C.)
Ohio Valley	Austin Peay (Clarksville, Tenn.)
Big Ten	Indiana (Bloomington)
Mid-American	Miami (Oxford, O.)
Big Eight	Kansas State (Manhattan)
Missouri Valley	Memphis State (Tenn.)
Southwest	Texas Tech. (Lubbock)
AAWU (Pacific Eight)	UCLA (Los Angeles, Calif.)
Western Athletic	Arizona State (Tempe)

scorers in the country, William (Bird) Averitt of Pepperdine, who averaged 33.9 points a game, and freshman Raymond Lewis of Los Angeles State, whose average was 32.9. The defending scoring champion, Dwight Lamar of Southwestern Louisiana, dropped to sixth with a 28.9 average.

Elton Hayes of Lamar Tech., in Beaumont, Tex., became the nation's most accurate shooter from the field by sinking 146 of 222 shots for a .658 percentage. From the free-throw line, the best shooter was Donald Smith of the University of Dayton, who fashioned a .910 percentage by converting 111 of 122 penalty shots.

Kermit Washington of American University, in Washington, D.C., led the country in rebounding with an average of 20.4 a game. He also averaged 20 points a game and thus became only the seventh player in collegiate basketball history to average better than 20 points and rebounds a game for his career.

The 6-ft. 8-in. Washington and Walton of UCLA topped the Associated Press All-American team. Joining them were DiGregorio of Providence, Thompson of North Carolina State, and Ed Ratleff of Long Beach State.

Kentucky Wesleyan had to go overtime to defeat Tennessee State 78–76 and win the championship of the NCAA's college division, limited to smaller schools. Guilford College, of Greensboro, N.C., upset the powerful University of Maryland-Eastern Shore 99–96 in the first all-eastern final in the 36-year history of the tournament of the National Association of Intercollegiate Athletics.

Professional. Intelligent team defense and opportunistic offense, both built around the resurgence of centre Willis Reed, gave the New York Knickerbockers the National Basketball Association (NBA) championship in 1973. Refusing to play any style but their own, the Knickerbockers overcame the Baltimore Bullets, the Boston Celtics, and finally the Los Angeles Lakers, the defending champions, on their way to the title they had last won in 1970.

New York entered the play-offs as the second-place team—by 11 games—in the NBA's Atlantic Division. The Boston Celtics had won the division, and if Reed, a 6-ft. 9-in. strong man hobbled by tendinitis in his knees, continued to play as erratically as he had during the regular season, there seemed no reason why Boston should be denied the finals and, given decent breaks, the championship. But Reed regained his speed and mobility at a most opportune time for New York. He began scoring and rebounding the way he had before his knee injuries when he was 1970's most valuable player.

The transformation began against Baltimore and its burly centre, Wes Unseld. Once the Knicks got past the Bullets, Dave Cowens, the trigger of Boston's fast break, stood in Reed's way. The Celtics had been successful enough during the year to come within one of shattering the record Los Angeles had established for victories during the season, 69 in 1972.

The Boston-New York series went the full seven games, but Boston's demise began in the third game when John Havlicek, one of the game's best and most versatile performers, wrenched his right shoulder badly. Meanwhile, Cowens was neutralized by Reed while Walt Frazier of New York and Jo Jo White of Boston were dueling to a standoff in the backcourt. Forwards Dave DeBusschere and Bill Bradley and reserve Phil Jackson gave the Knickerbockers the strength elsewhere that the Celtics could not summon. The score of the seventh game was 94–78 for New York.

The play-offs in the West opened with a monumental surprise as the Golden State Warriors upset the Milwaukee Bucks, who were considered a major threat to Los Angeles. To accomplish that, Golden State limited the Bucks to fewer than 100 points in each of the four games it won. Clyde Lee averaged 17 rebounds a game, while 6-ft. 9-in. Nate Thurmond held Milwaukee's Kareem Abdul-Jabbar to 27 points a game and forced him to shoot just 43% from the field, 12 percentage points below his average.

To get at Golden State, Los Angeles had to defeat the Chicago Bulls, who forced the Lakers to the full seven games. The final game was played in Los Angeles, where Chicago's old play-off jinx—the Bulls had lost 18 straight games on the road in post-season competition—struck again, and the Lakers won 95–92.

Los Angeles had an easier time with Golden State, whose energy dissipated in the face of the Lakers' persistent pressure at both ends of the floor. Jerry West, Gail Goodrich, and Jim McMillian took turns blasting away at the Warriors, and Los Angeles won the best-of-seven series, four games to one.

It was in the championship series that New York's Reed reached his peak, while the Lakers had to watch West limp to the sidelines repeatedly with a strained hamstring. In addition to that, Los Angeles committed 104 turnovers in the series, including 12 in the third

UPI COMPIX

The New York Knicks' Dave DeBusschere leaps high for a rebound during the sixth NBA play-off game with the Boston Celtics on April 27, 1973. The Knicks lost the game but went on to win the Eastern Division title, four games to three.

quarter of the final game, and 7-ft. 2-in. Wilt Chamberlain failed for the most part to take an active part in the Lakers' offense. Offensively, Reed, Frazier, Bradley, DeBusschere, and Earl Monroe set the pace as New York won the series, four games to one, and the NBA championship. Reed was named the most valuable player in the play-offs.

For the regular season, though, there was no question that Cowens, who led Boston back to respectability and more, was most valuable. He received 444 points in balloting among players. The runners-up were Jabbar, Nate Archibald of Kansas City-Omaha, Chamberlain, and Havlicek. Bob McAdoo, a forward for the Buffalo Braves, was selected as the NBA's rookie of the year. Archibald, a 6-ft. 1-in. guard, led NBA scorers by averaging 34 points a game. He also led in assists with an 11.4 average. For the second straight year, Chamberlain topped the league's rebounders (with an 18.6 average) and field-goal shooters (with a .727 percentage). Rick Barry of Golden State sank 358 of 397 free throw attempts to establish a league-leading .902 percentage.

As the 1974 season approached, Chamberlain of Los Angeles jumped to the San Diego Conquistadors of the rival American Basketball Association (ABA) as a player-coach. He signed a three-year contract for a reported $600,000 a year.

Attendance in the NBA was 5,852,081, slightly below the 1972 figure. The Baltimore Bullets, always a questionable franchise even when they fielded the best of teams, were moved to Largo, Md., a suburb of Washington, D.C., at the season's end. Their name was changed to the Capital Bullets.

The Indiana Pacers won their second ABA championship in two years by defeating the Kentucky Colonels four games to three in a best-of-seven series. Leading the Pacers was George McGinnis, a 6-ft. 8-in. forward.

The NBA produced the ABA's most valuable player, Billy Cunningham, who played seven seasons with the Philadelphia 76ers before jumping to the Carolina Cougars. Cunningham, a 6-ft. 7-in. forward who averaged 24.1 points and 12.1 rebounds a game, made the league all-star team along with Julius Erving of Virginia, Artis Gilmore of Kentucky, Warren Jabali of Denver, and Jimmy Jones of Utah. Brian Taylor, a guard with the New York Nets, was named the ABA's rookie of the year. The leading scorer in the league was Erving, who averaged 31.4 points a game. Gilmore led in rebounding (17.6 a game) and two-point field-goal percentage (.560). Tops in three-point field-goal percentage was Glen Combs of Utah, who hit on 51 of 134 attempts. Bill Keller of Indiana made .870 of his free-throw attempts to become the ABA's best in that department.

UCLA centre Bill Walton stretches to steal the ball from Soviet player Aleksandr Belov in a game between the Soviet and U.S. national teams on April 29, 1973. The U.S. won 83–65 in the first of a six-game match that ended with the U.S. on top four games to two.

UPI COMPIX

League attendance dropped slightly to 2,294,495 from 1972's record 2,436,826. The Dallas franchise, which drew an ABA low of 80,038, was shifted to San Antonio once the season ended.

Mike Storen, former general manager of the Colonels and the Pacers, was named as the fourth commissioner in the six-year history of the ABA. He succeeded Robert Carlson, who resigned after little more than a year on the job. (JOHN SCHULIAN)

World Amateur. In the men's European championships in September 1973, the two preliminary pools were played off in Badalona and Barcelona in Spain with the final rounds in Barcelona. In Badalona the U.S.S.R. was undefeated; it was followed by Czechoslovakia and Turkey, the surprise of the Badalona rounds being the poor showing of Poland. In the Barcelona group Yugoslavia was undefeated, followed by Spain and Italy. The final rounds produced a number of startling results. Perhaps the greatest upset ever in European basketball occurred in the semifinal when Spain beat the U.S.S.R. 80–76. At the 1972 Olympic Games Spain had occupied 11th place while the U.S.S.R. had taken the gold medal. The architect of this victory was Renato Buscata, who was making his final appearance before retiring. Just 34 years old and only 5 ft. 9 in. in height, this "little man" destroyed the U.S.S.R. team with outside shooting that was impressively accurate (89%).

The final contest was played off between Yugoslavia and Spain, and the result was almost a foregone conclusion. The Spaniards were unable to come back after the physical and emotional strain of the semifinal match against the U.S.S.R., and although only 11 points separated the teams (78–67) at the final whistle, Yugoslavia was a convincing winner. Spain finished second, and the U.S.S.R. third.

During the championships the Fédération Internationale de Basketball Amateur became concerned about the increased physical contact, much of it intentional, and decided that a rule change was necessary. Thus, a new article was to be added to the international rules, to the effect that, after the tenth player foul by a team in a half, subsequent fouls by that team would each be penalized by two free throws, with the right of option remaining. It was hoped that the increased penalty would clean up the game.

The 13th European women's championships were staged at Varna, Bulg., during October 1972. The championships were not really necessary to find out the strongest women's team in Europe, for it was without doubt the U.S.S.R., and once again this team demonstrated its complete supremacy in Europe by defeating every opponent convincingly. Bulgaria placed second, followed by Czechoslovakia and France.

In the 1972–73 edition of the European cups, Italian champion Ignis (Varese) retained the Champions' Cup when it beat the Red Army team TSSKA (Moscow) 76–71. This was the third time Ignis had won

Beekeeping:
see Agriculture and Fisheries

Beer:
see Alcoholic Beverages

the cup. In the men's Cup-Winners' Cup Spartak (Leningrad) beat Yugoplastika (Split) 77–62. Predictably, the world-famous Soviet women's club Daugava Riga won the women's Champions' Cup; this gave it a total of ten consecutive wins in the 13-year history of the cup. In the women's Cup-Winners' Cup it was again the U.S.S.R. that carried off the honours when Spartak (Leningrad) beat Slavia VS (Prague) from Czechoslovakia. (K. K. MITCHELL)

Behavioural Sciences

The behavioural sciences continued to look inward during 1973. Questions about the sociology of sociology, the role of psychology, and ethical considerations with regard to human research increased. At the American Psychological Association's annual meeting in Montreal, Donald Hebb of McGill University complained that the data explosion had caused the discipline to sink into specialization. "It is bad not to see the woods for the trees," he warned, "but it is worse not even to see a real tree because you are lost in the bushes, the undergrowth of insignificant detail and so-called replications, the trivial, the transient, the papers that haven't an idea anywhere about them." Hebb argued that psychology as a science is self-limiting, and that mixing it up with artistic and literary ways of examining human behaviour—a gentle jab at the humanists—would deter both.

Theodore Newcomb of the University of Michigan, in his retirement address at the Walgreen Conference on Education for Human Understanding held in his honour, took the opposite view from Hebb, stating that a "joint exploration of values" by humanists and scientists should solve the value conflicts between the two groups. He based his remarks on a study of psychology students and how they deal with the dual roots of psychology—"a discipline which deals with people, including oneself, subjectively and yet also requires 'objective' scientific methods of inquiry." Newcomb found that the students believed in both science and human values, and that a large majority agreed that psychology should teach people how to be objective but should also put them in touch with their own feelings.

Ethical Problems. There was much talk about the ethics of human research, and some action. Concern ranged from the appropriateness of psychosurgery to modify the behaviour of individuals prone to violence or other socially undesirable acts to the legitimacy of deceiving experimental subjects in order to get innocent reactions, untainted by anticipation of what the experimenter expects. The American Psychological Association wrestled with revised human research standards, while the U.S. Department of Health, Education, and Welfare proposed regulations to protect the rights of human subjects in behavioural, social, and biomedical research that it funded.

In the U.K., Roger Jowell told the British Association for the Advancement of Science that sociological researchers must balance their right to know against the individual's right to privacy. Professional codes of practice are not enough, he argued, since they are drawn up by professionals to protect their reputations rather than the public's rights. Jowell suggested that every survey should include a "Charter of Respondent's Rights," spelling out what individuals should demand as rights and safeguards before parting with information about themselves or others.

Suicide. Suicide studies in the U.S. and Great Britain revealed different patterns but many of the same problems. Drugs were the favourite means of suicide in every Western country except the United States, where firearms held a slim but diminishing lead. Nancy Allen, a suicide prevention expert at UCLA, reported that among Californians, suicide was increasing most among the young, blacks, and females. In the 15–24 age group, the California suicide rate had more than doubled since 1960, making suicide the second-highest cause of death at that age, as it was in the 25–34 group. The black suicide rate jumped from 4.4 per 100,000 to 10.4, compared with a white increase from 16.6 to 19.9.

While suicide in the U.S. as a whole increased slightly after 1960 (10.6 to 11.1), the British rate dropped sharply (11.7 to 8). Erwin Stengel, president of the International Association for Suicide Prevention, attributed part of this to a technological change. Gas had long been the leading method of suicide in England and Wales, but when appliances were converted during the 1960s from highly toxic coal gas to detoxicated gas or methane, people turned to drugs and other means. Stengel also credited some of the drop to the Samaritans, the largest suicide prevention agency in the world.

Sleep and Dreams. Interesting work on sleep and dreams was done on both sides of the Atlantic. The Association for the Psychophysiological Study of Sleep reported on research that confirmed some old beliefs and contradicted others. For example: rocking helps babies sleep, and caffeine keeps one awake; but people who live close to airports do not get so accustomed to the noise that it does not bother them (residents adjacent to Los Angeles International Airport obtained 45 minutes less "useful sleep" each night than did people living several miles away), and animal species that sleep a lot are not the ones that live a long time (a study of 40 animal species found a negative correlation between life-span and sleep quotas when metabolic rate and brain weight were allowed for).

In France neurosurgeon Michel Jouvet of the Université Claude Bernard revealed a revolutionary theory of dreaming: dreams are a means of programming behaviour; of practicing, in advance, vital behaviour patterns before the life-or-death situation is encountered. This, he asserted, is why instinctive acts are near-perfect: they have been practiced in dreams. Jouvet planned a series of tests with animals and

At Southern Illinois University, Mrs. Jean Roth proclaims on July 20, 1973, that she must be married before August 15 for inheritance purposes. She said she would pay $50,000 to any man who remained her husband for one year. The 30 men who signed up found that they had become part of a sociology experiment.

UPI COMPIX

people to test his theory further. He intended working with people who take large doses of inhibitors that suppress all dreaming, looking systematically at subtle differences in their behaviour as compared with people who dream normally. He expected that no dreaming would diminish personality, making non-dreamers less individualistic.

Sex Research. Danish criminologist Bert Kutchinsky released data indicating that the open sale of pornography in Denmark resulted in a decline in sex crimes. Kutchinsky, director of the Institute of Criminal Science at the University of Copenhagen, found a decrease in sex crimes against both women and children. Rape, which accounted for 4% of the nation's sex offenses, remained stable. But from 1959 to 1970 exhibitionism declined 66%, indecency 56%, and cases of peeping dropped from 99 to 5 per year. Kutchinsky believed that his research ruled out any explanation for the decrease other than the legal availability of pornography.

In the U.S., Eugene Levitt and Albert Klassen of the Indiana University Institute for Sex Research discovered that the much-heralded sexual revolution had not affected sexual attitudes very much. When a national cross-section of 3,000 adults was asked about prostitution, masturbation, pre- and extramarital sex, and homosexuality, they objected most to extramarital intercourse and homosexual relations without love, both of which were disapproved of by 86%. Premarital intercourse between an adult male and a woman he loved (47%) and masturbation (48%) were the least disapproved.

Influence of Television. The effects of television, particularly on children, continued to be heavily researched. Educational Testing Service reported a survey of 8,000 viewers and nonviewers of the children's educational show "The Electric Company." Children were tested before they saw the series, at school or at home, and retested after seeing the shows. Reading skills showed a significant improvement, particularly among children who watched at school. The children scored higher in 17 of 19 categories of reading skills than a control group of children who did not see the shows. Race, nationality, and sex had no effect on achievement.

Psychologist George Gerbner of the Annenberg School of Communications at the University of Pennsylvania kept a violence index on U.S. television shows. His 1973 index showed a decline in the number of violent characterizations but an increase in the rate of violent episodes; the number of victims for each violent character was the highest in six years.

Gerbner's study of television and cultural indicators found that people who often watched television perceived social reality differently from those who seldom watched and even more differently from people who did considerable reading of newspapers. Those who watched a considerable amount of television consistently overestimated the percentage of the world population comprising U.S. citizens, the number of Americans employed as professionals and managers, and, most significantly, the incidence of violence and their chances of encountering it in real life. Sex, age, and education made no significant difference in these beliefs. (PATRICE DAILY HORN)

See also Medicine: *Special Report.*

ENCYCLOPÆDIA BRITANNICA FILMS. *Operation Bootstrap* (1968); *Heritage in Black* (1969); *The House of Man, Part II—Our Crowded Environment* (1969); *View from the People Wall: A Statement About Problem Solving and Abstract Methods* (1973).

Belgium

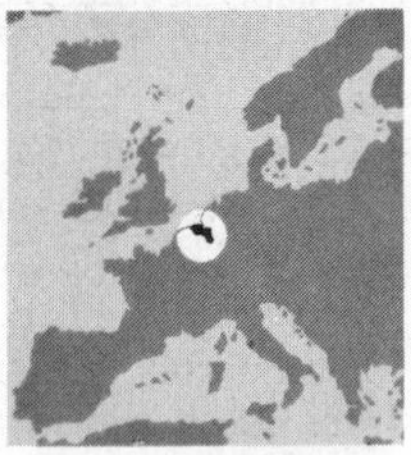

A constitutional monarchy on the North Sea coast of Europe, Belgium is bordered by The Netherlands, West Germany, Luxembourg, and France. Area: 11,781 sq.mi. (30,514 sq.km.). Pop. (1972 est.): 9,726,850. Cap.: Brussels (pop., 1972 est., 155,567). Largest city: Antwerp (pop., 1972 est., 220,296). Language: Dutch, French, and German. Religion: predominantly Roman Catholic. King, Baudouin I; prime minister from Jan. 26, 1973, Edmond Leburton.

The second government of Gaston Eyskens lasted only ten months. Unable to muster the two-thirds majority in Parliament to give effect to the paragraph in the new constitution providing for regionalization of the country, the prime minister tendered his resignation on Nov. 22, 1972. Edmond Leburton (*see* BIOGRAPHY), co-chairman of the Socialists, was invited to form a new government on December 13.

BELGIUM

Education. (1968–69) Primary, pupils 1,018,334, teachers (1967–68) 47,902; secondary, pupils 309,137, teachers (1967–68) 40,074; vocational, pupils 518,709, teachers (1966–67) 47,956; teacher training, students 19,759, teachers (1967–68) 6,089; higher (4 universities; 1969–70), students 69,634, teaching staff (1967–68) 5,489.

Finance. Monetary unit: Belgian franc, with (Sept. 17, 1973) a free rate of BFr. 36.45 to U.S. $1 (BFr. 87.87 = £1 sterling). Gold, SDRs, and foreign exchange, central bank: (June 1973) U.S. $4,449,000,000; (June 1972) U.S. $3,289,000,000. Budget (1972 est.): revenue BFr. 360,635,000,000; expenditure BFr. 367,195,000,000. Gross national product: (1971) BFr. 1,419,000,000,000; (1970) BFr. 1,294,000,000,000. Money supply: (Dec. 1972) BFr. 530 billion; (Dec. 1971) BFr. 465 billion. Cost of living (1963 = 100): (June 1973) 151; (June 1972) 141.

Foreign Trade. (Belgium-Luxembourg economic union; 1972) Imports BFr. 686.9 billion; exports BFr. 707.9 billion. Import sources: EEC (Six) 64% (West Germany 24%, France 19%, The Netherlands 17%); U.K. 6%; U.S. 6%. Export destinations: EEC (Six) 68% (West Germany 25%, France 20%, The Netherlands 19%, Italy 5%); U.S. 6%. Main exports: iron and steel 17%; chemicals 12%; textile yarns and fabrics 12%; motor vehicles 11%; machinery 11%.

Transport and Communications. Roads (1971) 92,158 km. (including 572 km. expressways). Motor vehicles in use (1971): passenger 2,128,000; commercial 216,000. Railways: (1971) 4,144 km.; traffic (1972) 8,168,000,000 passenger-km., freight 7,454,000,000 net ton-km. Air traffic (1972): 3,093,000,000 passenger-km.; freight 233,123,000 net ton-km. Shipping (1972): merchant vessels 100 gross tons and over 224; gross tonnage 1,191,555. Shipping traffic (1972): goods loaded 32,454,000 metric tons, unloaded 54,338,000 metric tons. Navigable inland waterways in regular use (1971) 1,536 km. Telephones (Dec. 1971) 2,180,000. Radio licenses (Dec. 1971) 3,497,000. Television licenses (Dec. 1971) 2,203,000.

Agriculture. Production (in 000; metric tons; 1972; 1971 in parentheses): wheat 950 (915); barley 639 (590); oats 249 (281); rye *c.* 73 (88); potatoes 1,524 (1,623); apples *c.* 238 (272); sugar, raw value *c.* 667 (*c.* 844); pork 508 (463); beef and veal 256 (266); milk (1971) *c.* 3,750, (1970) 3,749; fish catch (1971) 60, (1970) 53. Livestock (in 000; Dec. 1971): cattle 2,643; pigs 3,925; sheep 66; horses 60; chickens (May 1971) *c.* 43,000.

Industry. Fuel and power (in 000; 1972): coal 10,510 metric tons; manufactured gas (1971) 2,979,000 cu.m.; electricity 36,908,000 kw-hr. Production (in 000; metric tons; 1972): pig iron 11,777; crude steel 14,538; copper 328; lead 105; zinc 257; tin 3.9; sulfuric acid 2,466; cement 7,089; cotton yarn 67; cotton fabrics 74; wool yarn 87; woolen fabrics 44; rayon and acetate yarn and fibres 33.

He took it on himself to bring the Liberals into the government in order to obtain a constitutional majority, thereby forming a tripartite coalition of Socialists, Social Christians, and Liberals. The new Cabinet, made up of 22 ministers and 14 secretaries of state, was sworn in on January 26. The three coalition parties were represented by 15 Social Christians, 13 Socialists, and 8 Liberals.

Proposals on regionalization, a revision of the 1958 School Pact, the allotment of funds for regional development, and free choice for parents in the Voer region to send their children to either a Dutch- or French-language school were among the items on the program. First reaction to this tripartite government came from Brussels Liberals, who formed a new "Democratic and Pluralistic Liberal Party." The dissidents were opposed to any limitation of the area of the Brussels region to the existing agglomeration of 19 communes.

The Flemish and Walloon Liberals were willing to assume government responsibility on condition that the proposed regions would get regional assemblies as well as an executive with real power. While the government worked on concrete proposals for regionalization, a parliamentary commission also examined the subject. Prime Minister Leburton had promised to adopt any commission proposals if the coalition parties agreed to them. The Flemish and Walloon parties clearly intended to give regionalization an outspoken federalist orientation.

Tension followed a government decision to implement the linguistic legislation of 1963, providing for an equal number of Dutch- and French-speaking top officials in the administrations of the 19 Brussels communes by September 1. Parliament nevertheless passed new legislation to this effect. A decree by the Flemish Cultural Council making compulsory the use of Dutch in all social contacts in industry established in the Dutch-speaking part of Belgium was loudly decried by French-speaking circles. Legislation providing for the extension of the 1958 School Pact led to hard bargaining between the coalition partners and ultimately to a compromise. The pact had abolished fees in all primary and secondary schools, including those operated by religious denominations.

Minister of Defense Paul Vanden Boeynants submitted plans for a gradual reduction of compulsory military service to six months. A professional Belgian Army would be put at NATO's disposal. In April Parliament decided to grant indemnities, the so-called credit hours, to young workers completing their education outside normal working hours.

The arrest of a Namur gynecologist charged with illegal abortions led to a series of demonstrations. Amendments to the existing legislation on abortion were proposed by the Liberal justice minister, Herman Vanderpoorten, but were rejected as too far-reaching by the Social Christians and as too timid by the Socialists. Belgium's Roman Catholic bishops in an official statement on April 6 opposed any change in the legislation. Meanwhile, Parliament abolished articles in the Penal Code prohibiting advertisements for contraceptives.

Rising prices prompted a series of strong anti-inflationary measures and sharper price controls. Public spending was checked and the 1974 budget limited to BFr. 472.7 billion, which would not require new taxes. Leftists seized on the inflation to stir up labour unrest, paralyzing Ghent harbour for several weeks.

The creation of a state-run Iranian-Belgian Refining and Marketing Company (Ibramco), in which Belgian interests were represented by three Socialist public officials, led to further friction among the coalition partners when the existence was revealed of a secret contract concluded early in December 1972 by the outgoing minister of economic affairs, Henri Simonet. The Socialists were determined to have a state-run refinery near Liège, a first step toward nationalization of the entire energy sector.

Leburton reshuffled his Cabinet in October. Two ministers and seven secretaries of state were dropped and one secretary of state was added, reducing the membership to 28. Among those resigning was Edouard Anseele, the leading Socialist in the Cabinet.

In late November, Belgium followed The Netherlands' lead by imposing a ban on Sunday driving as a fuel-conservation measure. (JAN. R. ENGELS)

Bhutan

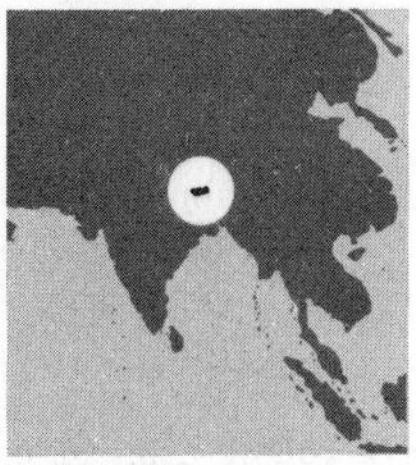

A monarchy situated in the eastern Himalayas, Bhutan is bounded by China, India, and Sikkim. Area: 18,000 sq.mi. (47,000 sq.km.). Pop. (1973 est.): 1,129,000. Official cap.: Thimphu (pop., approximately 10,000). Administrative cap.: Paro (population unavailable). Language: Dzongkha (official). Religion: approximately 75% Buddhist, 25% Hindu. Druk gyalpo (king) in 1973, Jigme Singye Wangchuk.

Bhutan, which had secured entry into the UN in 1971, received further international recognition in 1973 when it was admitted as a full member to the summit conference of nonaligned nations, held in Algiers in September.

The late king Jigme Dorji Wangchuk, who had died in July 1972, was officially cremated according to Buddhist custom in a colourful ceremony in October of that year. Indian Prime Minister Indira Gandhi, the main foreign dignitary present, assured the new king, Jigme Singye Wangchuk, of India's continued support and cooperation. Indian assistance to the Himalayan state was markedly increased with the decision to give Rs. 330 million of the Rs. 350.5 million outlay scheduled for the country's third five-year plan. UN assistance was also promised, though on a lesser scale. Under an agreement signed in New Delhi, India, the UN Development Program would provide U.S. $2.5 million during a four-year period.

Two major irrigation schemes, in the Lobeysa area and the Sandrup Jongkhar subdivision, were completed in January, providing irrigation facilities to a total of 3,100 ac. The popular revolt in neighbouring Sikkim against its chogyal (king) in April had no apparent effect on the generally peaceful atmosphere in Bhutan. The northern borders with Chinese-held Tibet were calm. (GOVINDAN UNNY)

BHUTAN

Education. (1968–69) Primary, pupils 12,601, teachers 275; secondary, pupils 2,559, teachers 141; vocational, pupils 153, teachers 14; teacher training, students 62, teachers 7.

Finance and Trade. Monetary unit: Indian rupee, with (Sept. 17, 1973) a free rate of Rs. 7.76 to U.S. $1 (official rate of Rs. 18.71 = £1 sterling). Budget (1971–72): revenue Rs. 27.5 million; expenditure Rs. 69.1 million. Third five-year development plan (1971–76) total expenditure (est.) Rs. 350.5 million (including *c.* Rs. 330 million from India). About 95% of external trade is with India. Main exports (1963–64): timber Rs. 1,250,000; coal Rs. 220,000.

Benelux: *see* Belgium; Luxembourg; Netherlands, The
Bermuda: *see* Dependent States
Beverages, Alcoholic: *see* Alcoholic Beverages
Bicycling: *see* Cycling
Biochemistry: *see* Life Sciences

Biography 1973

The following is a selected list of men and women who influenced events in 1973.

ABPLANALP, ROBERT HENRY

It was said in business circles that Robert Abplanalp would like to be known as "the father of modern aerosols," but if he was known to the general public at all in 1973, it was as one of Pres. Richard Nixon's closest friends.

Not least among the president's many troubles during the year was the unprecedented attention given to his personal finances. The money spent on his properties, down to the flower beds, was spelled out to the penny amid accusations—none proved—that he might have used GOP campaign funds to pay for his private property. To squelch these reports, the White House disclosed in May that Abplanalp had loaned the president a $625,000 down payment on the presidential retreat in San Clemente, Calif., and that Abplanalp now owned about three-quarters of the estate. Abplanalp paid $1,249,000 for 20.1 ac. of the 26-ac. walled compound in December 1970, leaving Nixon 5.9 ac. and the large, Spanish-style residence.

Abplanalp (pronounced AB-plan-alp) was a college dropout credited with having developed the valve that made the aerosol industry possible. More than half the valves used in the aerosol industry were made by Precision Valve Corp., of which Abplanalp was president, board chairman, and sole owner. His friendship with Nixon began shortly after the 1960 presidential election, when he wrote Nixon a letter saying he would like to meet him. The politically conservative Abplanalp once described Nixon as a "real intellectual," but their friendship was said to be based on a mutual interest in sports and deep-sea fishing rather than politics. Abplanalp owned two Bahamian islands, Grand Cay and Walker's Cay, where Nixon was a frequent guest. He was the lesser known of Nixon's two millionaire friends, the other being Charles ("Bebe") Rebozo.

Abplanalp, a millionaire many times over, was born in the Bronx, New York, on April 4, 1922. After attending local schools and Fordham Preparatory School, he went to Villanova (Pa.) University where he studied mechanical engineering for three years. He entered the Army in 1943, returned in 1946, and three years later designed what is considered to be the first workable aerosol valve that could be mass produced. He founded Precision Valve Corp. that same year in Yonkers, N.Y. (ROBERT A. SIGNER)

Spiro Theodore Agnew

TONY KORODY—SYGMA

AGNEW, SPIRO THEODORE

On Wednesday, Oct. 10, 1973, Spiro T. Agnew made history of a kind that he undoubtedly never had envisioned when he achieved the second-highest office in the United States. In a brief statement, submitted to U.S. Secretary of State Henry A. Kissinger in accordance with federal statute, Agnew resigned as the nation's 39th vice-president. He was the second person in the country's history to quit the office—John C. Calhoun having resigned on Dec. 28, 1832—and the only one to quit under duress.

That same day Agnew made a dramatic, surprise appearance in U.S. District Court in Baltimore, Md. Standing before Judge Walter E. Hoffman, he pleaded no contest to a single federal count of failing to report on his income tax return $29,500 in income that he had received in 1967, while governor of Maryland. Acknowledging that he knew the plea amounted to a felony conviction, Agnew declared that he was not guilty of any other illegal activity and was resigning only because it was in the national interest. The judge fined Agnew $10,000 and sentenced him to three years' unsupervised probation, but he told Agnew that he would have sent him to prison if it were not for a personal appeal by the U.S. attorney general.

Agnew's downfall began on Aug. 2, 1973, when U.S. Attorney George Beall of Baltimore informed the vice-president that he was being investigated in connection with accusations of extortion, bribery, and income tax violations. After declaring at first that he would not discuss the investigation, Agnew called the first of two television sessions to denounce as "damned lies" newspaper reports about the charges against him. Then, in speeches across the country, he repeatedly sounded the theme of his innocence and his intention to "stay and fight."

Even after the plea in Baltimore and his resignation, Agnew asserted his innocence of other wrongdoing and his anger at what he called "scurrilous and inaccurate reports" in the press. He appealed to the Maryland Bar Association not to disbar him from the practice of law, a decision still under consideration at the year's end.

Agnew was born Nov. 9, 1918, in Baltimore, the son of a Greek immigrant to the U.S. who had shortened his name from Anagnostopoulos. He studied chemistry at Johns Hopkins University and later attended the University of Baltimore, where he earned a law degree after service in World War II. He was elected Baltimore County executive in 1962 and governor of Maryland in 1966. Running with Richard Nixon on the Republican ticket, he was elected vice-president in 1968 and again in 1972. (ROBERT A. SIGNER)

ANNE ELIZABETH ALICE LOUISE, PRINCESS, and PHILLIPS, CAPT. MARK ANTHONY PETER

The marriage between Princess Anne and Capt. Mark Phillips, celebrated in Westminster Abbey on Nov. 14, 1973, with brilliant ceremony and televised around the world, was undoubtedly the most notable royal event of the year. Not even Prime Minister Edward Heath's declaration of a national state of emergency on the eve of the wedding, in view of a rapidly worsening economic situation, could dim the colourful pomp and circumstance of the occasion.

The engagement had been widely expected and was formally announced on May 29. To devoted royalty watchers, the fact that Princess Anne had fallen in love with a commoner probably seemed especially romantic; to others this circumstance appeared an appropriate symbol of the less formal style increasingly adopted by the royal family. The couple had been brought together through their joint interest and prowess in competitive horsemanship, a sport in which both had achieved international status. They first met at a social gathering after the 1968 Mexico Olympic Games, at which Captain (then Lieutenant) Phillips was a reserve rider. Both were members of the British team that won the three-day event at the 1971 European championships at Burghley, Eng., Princess Anne becoming individual European champion. Afterward Captain Phillips went on to become a member of the winning British team at the 1972 Munich (W.Ger.) Olympics. Princess Anne, largely because of the indisposition of her most experienced horse, Doublet, was not included in that team or the one sent to Kiev in the U.S.S.R. for the European championships in September 1973. Defending her title there as an individual rider, she withdrew because of a strained shoulder suffered in a fall.

Princess Anne, the only daughter of Queen Elizabeth II and Prince Philip, was born on Aug. 15, 1950, at Clarence House, London, and educated at Benenden School, near Grassbrook in Kent. She began to carry out public engagements early in 1969, made various state visits abroad with her parents and her brother Prince Charles, and went alone to Hong Kong (1971) and Ethiopia (February 1973).

Captain Phillips was born at Tewkesbury in Gloucestershire on Sept. 22, 1948. Educated at Marlborough College and the Royal Military Academy, Sandhurst, he followed his father into the Queen's Dragoon Guards. On his mother's side he was descended from a Lutheran German family, a branch of which moved to England early in the 19th century. (STEPHANIE MULLINS)

ASH, ROY

In December 1972 he was the president of Litton Industries, well known in the world of industry and high finance but largely obscure to the general public. By January 1973 Roy Ash was front page news. Indeed, rarely had a top-level government official assumed office amid so much controversy. Most of it resulted from the heavy-handed silencing of a minor government official who thought Ash was a poor choice for director of the Office of Management and Budget.

Ash was named to the sensitive post by Pres. Richard Nixon in late November 1972. Then, on December 19, Gordon Rule, a civilian Navy procurement officer, told the House-Senate Joint Economic Committee that Ash would be the wrong man for the job because he had been in charge of Navy contracts involved in a cost overrun dispute. Rule was demoted two days later (though he eventually got his old job back). Meanwhile, Ash's background was subjected to intense congressional scrutiny.

Ash rode out the storm only to be involved in new controversy during 1973 over the administration practice of impounding rather than spending congressionally authorized funds. Along with his administration colleagues, he worked successfully for passage of the trans-Alaska oil pipeline bill. At the same time, he said a $10 billion federal commitment for research into energy sources over the next decade would make the nation self-sufficient in energy terms. He was widely criticized late in the year for his earlier predictions that the Middle East war and Arab fuel cutbacks would scarcely affect the U.S.

Ash was born in Los Angeles on Oct. 20, 1918, and received his master's degree in business administration in 1947 from Harvard. In 1949 he went to the Hughes Aircraft Co. under the tutelage of Charles B. Thornton, then assistant general manager. In 1953 Ash and Thornton were squeezed out of Hughes by Noah Dietrich, Howard Hughes's longtime partner. Both men moved into the management of a new firm called Litton Industries, Inc., the core of which was a small electronics firm in San Carlos, Calif., owned by Charles V. Litton. They bought out Litton, and the firm prospered in the market expansion of the '60s with a variety of government contracts and mergers.

(BILL GRANGER)

BAKER, HOWARD HENRY, JR.

The newest glamour boy among political figures in 1973 was Sen. Howard H. Baker, Jr., a Tennessee Republican who soared into public awareness as vice-chairman of the U.S. Senate Select Committee to Investigate the 1972 Presidential Campaign Activities, popularly known as the Watergate committee. Baker's popularity became so high as the committee's televised hearings progressed that a July Harris survey discovered that he had outpolled Sen. Edward M. Kennedy of Massachusetts in a hypothetical presidential election.

Such notice was to be expected of an ambitious, presentable politician whose ties with public life were many: his grandfather was a judge; his father was a U.S. congressman for 13 years; and his wife, Joy, was the daughter of the late Senate Republican leader from Illinois, Everett M. Dirksen.

Baker, the first Republican to be elected to the U.S. Senate from Tennessee since Reconstruction, carefully crafted for himself a reputation as a moderate senator who was acceptable to most elements of the population. Though the first wave of his popularity appeared to have crested at year's end, it was widely assumed that he was interested in the 1976 Republican nomination for the presidency and that he would be molding his public image, and senatorial record, with that end in mind during the next two years.

Baker's posture on the Watergate committee was indicative of the care—some said ambivalence—with which he was proceeding. In his questioning of former attorney general John Mitchell, for example, he would ask such questions as what were Mitchell's "perceptions" of the nature of the presidency. But never did he inquire deeply into Mitchell's startling testimony that, although he was an intimate adviser and friend to the president, Nixon never asked him about the Watergate scandal after the news broke; that tack was left to the Democrats.

Baker was born Nov. 15, 1925, in Huntsville, Tenn. He was sent to school in Chattanooga, Tenn., and studied engineering at the University of the South in Sewanee, Tenn., and at Tulane University, New Orleans, La. He joined the U.S. Navy during World War II and was discharged in 1946 as a lieutenant junior grade. In 1949 Baker earned a law degree from the University of Tennessee.

After a number of years as a trial lawyer, Baker began showing an interest in electoral politics. In 1966 he was elected to the Senate seat once held by Estes Kefauver. In 1972 he was reelected by a margin of more than 270,000 votes, a stunning victory for a Southern Republican. (ROBERT A. SIGNER)

NORMAN PARKINSON—CAMERA PRESS/PICTORIAL PARADE

Princess Anne and Capt. Mark Phillips

Howard Henry Baker, Jr.

UPI COMPIX

BARNARD, LANCE HERBERT

As Australian deputy prime minister and minister for defense in 1973, it fell to Lance Barnard to defend the somewhat isolationist "fortress" philosophy of Australia's new administration. The very modest defense allocation programs of previous governments were now replaced by positive cutbacks, following Australia's withdrawal from the Vietnam war. Conscription was abolished and Army strength reduced from 45,000 to 31,000, with further reductions planned for 1973–74. At the same time, the government was committed to independence for Papua New Guinea, which became self-governing on Dec. 1, 1973, and was determined not to intervene in the island's internal affairs. Barnard stated that no deterioration was foreseen in Australia's strategic environment that would involve commitment to military operations in defense of the country's security or strategic interests.

In view of this attitude the intention to withdraw Australian troops from Singapore was understandable, although not appreciated by the U.K. or New Zealand. A subject of equal contention within the country was the degree of Australian control over several U.S. nuclear weapons communications stations based in Australia.

Barnard's ability to handle his extensive portfolio (overseas defense, Navy, Army, Air Force, and supplies) was questioned by left-wing Victoria Labor Party leaders. They opposed the decision to retain any Australian presence in Singapore, considered Barnard's statements promising to press for greater control of the U.S. bases inadequate, and accused him of being under the influence of Sir Arthur Tange, head of the Defense Department. Prime Minister Gough Whitlam defended his deputy in the face of further attacks from opposition leader Billy Snedden.

Born in Launceston, Tasmania, on May 1, 1919, Barnard was elected to the House of Representatives in 1954 as Labor Party member for Bass, Tasmania, and became party spokesman on defense, supply, and repatriation. He was a member of the Joint Parliamentary Committee on Foreign Affairs (1967–69), state president of the Tasmanian branch of the Australian Labor Party, and a member of the party's federal executive.

(R. J. M. DENNERSTEIN)

BATES, ALAN

With splendid performances in such motion pictures as *Georgy Girl* (1965) and *Women in Love* (1968), Alan Bates made his mark as a leading film actor during the 1960s. Despite many stage appearances during the same period, however, it was not until 1973 that he was acclaimed as a star of the English-speaking stage. Recognition came principally for his brilliant playing in the title role of Simon Gray's *Butley,* first in London (1971), then in New York (1972). For his performance as the bisexual college lecturer whose chief aim in life seems to be to preside at the demolition of his own life, Bates in 1973 received the New York critics' accolade with the Drama Desk Award and the Antoinette Perry (Tony) Award for the best dramatic performance on Broadway by an actor.

Bates first won notice as an actor in roles that demanded the "new style" of acting associated with the antiheroic plays of the late 1950s. It was a style not without pitfalls. Actors, perforce abandoning the traditional, bloodless approach of the drawing-room-and-French-windows school in favour of the feeling-from-the-gut stance, too often succeeded only in serving up crude offal in place of cured ham. Bates, however, brought a steady intelligence to his work that—along with an unusual sensitivity for the shifting moods of a scene—appeared certain to keep his star in the ascendant.

Born in Allestree, Derbyshire, Eng., on Feb. 17, 1934, Alan Bates studied at the

Royal Academy of Dramatic Art and played in provincial repertory theatre for a year before joining the English Stage Society and appearing in a revival of John Osborne's *Look Back in Anger* (London, Moscow, and New York). Later stage performances included Mick in Harold Pinter's *The Caretaker* (London and New York; film version in 1963), the title role in *Richard III* and Ford in *The Merry Wives of Windsor* (both at Stratford, Ont.), and Andrew Shaw in David Storey's *In Celebration* (London). But it was as a film actor that he became best known: a modest part in *The Entertainer* (1960) was followed by starring roles in numerous films, including *A Kind of Loving* (1962), *Zorba the Greek* (1965), *Far from the Madding Crowd* (1967), *A Day in the Death of Joe Egg* (1970), and *The Go-Between* (1970). (DAVID HATELY)

BEAME, ABRAHAM DAVID

A man with a penchant for the middle of the political road, Abraham Beame was elected mayor of New York City on Nov. 6, 1973, by a commanding margin. His 58% of the vote as the Democratic Party candidate was all the more notable since he had three major opponents: Republican John Marchi, Liberal Albert Blumenthal, and Conservative Mario Biaggi. Also elected by comfortable margins were Beame's running mates, Paul O'Dwyer as City Council president and Harrison Goldin as controller.

Beame was born in London March 20, 1906, and emigrated to Manhattan as a boy. He attended City College of New York and was graduated cum laude. A certified public accountant, he taught high school for a time and then accounting courses at Rutgers University on a part-time basis. Normally holding down at least two jobs at once, he was nonetheless active in Brooklyn politics. He became a leader of the Madison Democratic Club and a frequent delegate to national Democratic Party conventions.

A party loyalist, he was named assistant budget director by Mayor William O'Dwyer in 1946. When he became budget director, according to the *New York Times,* he "negotiated all city labor contracts for the next ten years without a strike." Beame then ran for city controller and held the office for one term. In 1965 he campaigned for mayor, but lost to Republican John Lindsay, the man he succeeded in 1973. Beame had to defeat three other candidates in a primary election to gain his spot on the Democratic ticket.

In private life Beame achieved success as an investment counselor, bank director, and a civic activist who did extensive work for charitable organizations. He became New York's 104th mayor and, despite the city's large Jewish population, the first Jew to hold that office. (PHILIP KOPPER)

BENITES, LEOPOLDO

"He is of the old school, his words do not wound, he is a man of integrity," commented one of his fellow diplomats on Sept. 18, 1973, the day Leopoldo Benites of Ecuador became the 28th president of the UN General Assembly. An old hand at the UN, Benites had represented his country there since 1960.

Benites was born on Oct. 17, 1905, the son of a physician, and he grew up in Guayaquil, where he went to school. He would say much later that the Jesuits at the university taught him an old Latin saw that he had lived with all his life: "Suaviter in mondo; fortiter in re." He said it roughly translates to "be soft in form, strong in substance." After schooling in both Ecuador and Uruguay, he served as a member of the constituent assembly in his country and helped draft the current constitution of Ecuador.

During the 1930s, Benites wrote for *El Universo,* a Guayaquil newspaper, and got in trouble with the government because of some of his political articles. He spent eight months in a prison in the western part of Ecuador and, while there, wrote a biography of Capt. Francisco de Orellana, the discoverer of the Amazon River.

After World War II, Benites became his country's representative to Uruguay. He went to the UN for the first time in 1952 as a representative of Ecuador and served as ambassador to Bolivia from 1954 to 1956. He served in Argentina briefly in 1956 and then headed the embassy in Uruguay again until 1960.

Before assuming his UN office, Benites took a long vacation at his home in Ballentina and went on a diet. Rested and ten pounds lighter, he returned to New York in September and plunged into the rough-and-tumble of international politics. Just three weeks after taking office, he chaired a tumultuous General Assembly meeting in which South Africa's credentials were rejected because of that country's apartheid policies. (BILL GRANGER)

BERNSTEIN, CARL, and WOODWARD, ROBERT

They were an unlikely pair to shake a government. One of the two young *Washington Post* reporters was a clean-cut Ivy Leaguer, the other a long-haired state university dropout. But in 1973 their relentless exposure of the Watergate scandal swept away one of the most elaborate cover-ups in U.S. political history and won their paper a Pulitzer Prize for distinguished public service in journalism.

Carl Bernstein and Robert Woodward

ROLAND FREEMAN—MAGNUM

Robert Woodward, the senior member of the team, was born March 26, 1943, in Geneva, Ill., and grew up in Wheaton where his father was a Republican county judge. He graduated from Yale in 1965, served five years in the Navy, and worked six months for a Maryland weekly before joining the *Post.* The other half of the by-line belonged to Carl Bernstein. Born Feb. 14, 1944, in Washington, D.C., he dropped out of the University of Maryland after three years and worked—among other jobs—as copyboy at the *Washington Evening Star.* When he was assigned to Watergate, he had been at the *Post* less than a year.

On June 17, 1972, five men, equipped with electronic bugging devices, were caught breaking into Democratic National Committee headquarters in Washington's Watergate building complex. Woodward, a member of the *Post*'s District of Columbia staff, was assigned to what at first appeared to be a routine police story. Before long he had found traces that seemed to lead higher up and got permission to investigate further. Bernstein, who had been covering local stories in Arlington, Va., also smelled a bigger story and asked for the assignment.

Slowly but persistently, using the reporter's time-honoured techniques of knocking on doors and ringing telephones, the two developed their sources. When the dimensions of the story began to emerge, some *Post* executives thought it should be transferred to the prestigious national staff, but editor Ben Bradlee stayed with his two young reporters.

Their first big story established a direct connection between contributions to Pres. Richard Nixon's reelection campaign and the Watergate burglars. Other exclusive page one stories followed, each adding to suspicions that the scandal reached deeply into the White House and the Committee to Reelect the President. In the end, having broken the biggest scandal since Teapot Dome, they received a public apology from Ron Ziegler, the White House press secretary, whose months of official denials had suddenly become "inoperative."

(ROBERT A. SIGNER)

BERTOLUCCI, BERNARDO

With some notable exceptions—including, perhaps, Chaplin, Hitchcock, and Orson Welles—few film directors have impressed their identity on the cinema-going public as a whole. In 1973, however, it was difficult to ignore the name of the young Italian director Bernardo Bertolucci because of the notoriety that built up around his film *Last Tango in Paris,* with its explicit scenes and language in the story of a love affair between a middle-aged American (Marlon Brando) and a young French girl (Maria Schneider) in Paris.

Bertolucci was born in Parma, Italy, in 1941, the son of poet Attilio Bertolucci and his Australian-born, Irish-Italian wife, and grew up in a cosmopolitan atmosphere. His leap to status as an international celebrity came comparatively late in a career that began 11 years earlier when, at the age of 21, he made his first feature film, *La Commare Secca*—evidently under the influence of Pier Paolo Pasolini's tale of Roman low life, *Accattone!,* on which Bertolucci worked as an assistant. The same year he published a collection of poems, *In cerca del mistero,* which won for him the Viareggio poetry prize.

In his second film, *Prima della rivoluzione* ("Before the Revolution"; 1964), awarded the Young Critics' Prize at the Cannes Festival, he treated the theme that was to be recurrent in his work (down to the bourgeois heroine of *Last Tango*)—that of the young person trying to escape from his class and family background, but always, seemingly, drawn back. In *Prima della rivoluzione* the young hero joins the Communist Party but returns to his middle-class family. *The Spider's Stratagem* (1970) and *The Conformist* (1971) dealt with heroes caught in problems of conscience in Fascist Italy of the 1920s and 1930s.

With these films and the virtuoso handling of *Last Tango,* Bertolucci had clearly progressed to a period of mastery and assurance, escaping from the uncertainties of the preceding period, when he made a pretentious doppelgänger story, *Partner* (1968), strongly influenced by French "new wave" director Jean-Luc Godard, and scripted one of the best-known "spaghetti westerns," *Once Upon a Time in the West.* (DAVID ROBINSON)

BORDABERRY AROCENA, JUAN MARÍA

In 1973 Uruguay, once called the "Switzerland of South America," appeared to be going the way of its larger neighbours, Argentina and Brazil. A "soft coup" by the military in February left Pres. Juan Bordaberry his title and office, but took away his powers and forced him to accept a Security Council consisting of handpicked civilians and top-ranking military officers. In addition, Bordaberry promised the military he would carry out 19 political and economic reforms, including curbing inflation, instituting land reforms, and putting an end to political corruption. In June the military completed its take-over when Bordaberry dissolved Congress and replaced it with a Council of State, headed by himself but dominated by the generals.

Uruguay's problems with the military had begun several years earlier when former president José Pacheco Areco called on the Army to combat the left-wing Tupamaro terrorist organization. No larger than the Montevideo fire department in 1960, the Army grew steadily in size and power, using tactics that effectively destroyed the Tupamaros, but drawing criticism from such international bodies as the World Council of Churches. Bordaberry, who had continued Pacheco's reliance on the military, supported its repressive methods on the ground that "severe" cross-examination of prisoners yielded information that enabled the government to prevent worse ills.

Born in Montevideo on June 17, 1928, into one of the major landowning families in Uruguay, Bordaberry won his first political victory in 1962, when he gained a Senate seat as a Blanco Party candidate. Breaking with the Blancos in 1965 because of their support for the collegiate system of government, Bordaberry favoured the 1966 referendum that switched the nation to a one-man presidency and continued his political career as a Colorado. He was minister of agriculture when he was picked to run for the presidency in 1971 as an alternative should incumbent President Pacheco lose a plebiscite permitting him to serve another term. Pacheco failed in his attempt, and Bordaberry, appealing to fears of Communism and ignoring Uruguay's increasing economic and social problems, won the subsequent election by a tiny margin of 10,000 votes. (DONALD J. KLIMOVICH)

BRADLEY, THOMAS

On July 1, 1973, former city councilman and ex-cop Thomas Bradley became the first black mayor of Los Angeles, defeating three-term incumbent Sam Yorty in a dramatic reversal of his unsuccessful 1969 campaign. Ironically, Bradley's qualifications for mayor of the nation's third largest city were essentially the same in 1969 as in 1973. A moderate liberal, he appeared to be the coolest and most conscientious of three black city council members, having spent most of his adult life concerned with law and city government. During the years he served as councilman for Los Angeles' racially mixed 10th district he proposed a number of changes he felt would improve the city's police department. But, despite the fact that Bradley attracted supporters of all ages, sexes, and races, fearful memories of the 1965 Watts riots were stirred by Yorty's allegations that Bradley was "anti-police" and would undermine law and order.

Bradley's 1973 campaign was based on his image of moderation and a theme of government responsive to social change. His issues included a sorely needed rapid transit system, environmental protection, curtailment of city growth, law and order, and finally the mayor's much publicized absenteeism. This time, Yorty's racial alarmism missed the mark. The voters vindicated Bradley's 1969 decision to try again, "not for personal reasons, but to put down the theory that black men can't win."

Thomas Bradley was born Dec. 29, 1917, on a cotton plantation in the small town of Calvert, Tex. When he was seven his parents settled in Los Angeles, where his father worked as a Pullman porter and his mother as a domestic. Bradley won an athletic scholarship to UCLA, where he was a football and track star, and then joined the Los Angeles police force, serving 21 years and rising to the rank of lieutenant. He attended Southwestern Law School in the evenings and earned an LLB in 1956. Five years later he went into private law practice, and in 1963 he became the first black man elected to the City Council.

Bradley's first important action as mayor was to seek federal assistance for a $4 billion rapid transit system. Other priority projects were controlling street crime, long-range planning to limit the city's population to four million people, and reviving the city's core by attracting private investment. (DONALD J. KLIMOVICH)

BRANDT, WILLY

Only months after his convincing victory in the 1972 federal election, West German Chancellor Willy Brandt in 1973 faced a growing challenge from the left wing of his Social Democratic Party (SPD), spearheaded by the Young Socialists. But he repulsed the challenge and at the party conference in April was reelected chairman for a further two-year term by 404–20.

Brandt's troubles were not over, however, and throughout the year he met criticism for lacking qualities of leadership. Inflation continued at a high rate; there was a wave of unofficial strikes in the metalworking industry; and the final phase of the policy of closer ties with Eastern Europe ran into difficulties. In August he postponed a visit to Prague to sign the treaty normalizing relations between Czechoslovakia and West Germany because of differences concerning the latter's right to represent West Berlin institutions through its Prague embassy. However, Brandt eventually visited Prague on December 11 to sign the treaty, after a compromise had been reached.

Discord with the United States following Bonn's refusal to facilitate U.S. arms deliveries to Israel in October led Brandt to assure Pres. Richard Nixon of his appreciation of the need to preserve the solidarity of the Western alliance. But in addressing the European Parliament in Strasbourg in November, he reflected EEC members' frustration over their negligible influence in the Middle East crisis when he put forward plans for hastening European political union. "We can and will make Europe," he said. "America and other countries . . . must take this for granted."

Born Herbert Ernst Karl Frahm in Lübeck on Dec. 18, 1913, Brandt changed his name on fleeing to Norway as a political refugee in 1933. After World War II he returned to West Germany as a Norwegian citizen but resumed West German nationality and in 1949 was elected to the Bundestag. He was governing mayor of West Berlin (1957–66), became chairman of the Social Democratic Party in 1964, and served as foreign minister and vice-chancellor in the SPD–Christian Democratic Union coalition. He became chancellor in 1969 and in 1971 was awarded the Nobel Peace Prize. (NORMAN CROSSLAND)

BREZHNEV, LEONID ILICH

For Soviet Communist Party leader Leonid I. Brezhnev, 1973 was another year of energetic diplomatic activity. With the prime objectives of maintaining détente with the West, strengthening the solidarity of the socialist bloc, and securing Soviet influence

J. M. VINCENT—CAMERA 5

KOROLEV—STERN / BLACK STAR

Leonid Ilich Brezhnev and Willy Brandt

Thomas Bradley

in the third world against Chinese encroachments, he paid visits to West Germany, the United States, Poland, East Germany, Czechoslovakia, France, Bulgaria, and India. He also presided over a meeting of foreign ministers of Warsaw Treaty countries in Moscow in January and a reunion of the party leaders of Comecon (Council for Mutual Economic Assistance) countries at his summer residence at Oreanda, Crimea, in July.

At his meeting with West German Chancellor Willy Brandt at Bonn in May, Brezhnev admitted that it was not easy for the Soviet people and their leaders to open a new page in Soviet-West German relations, because memories of the last war were still alive; equally, he recognized that it was not a simple matter for Brandt and his government to sign the 1970 treaties with the U.S.S.R. and Poland, because the cold war had a force of inertia, to overcome which required a certain effort. In Washington in June he expressed his conviction that Soviet-U.S. relations were assuming a "maximum stability" of "irreversible character" reflecting "permanent principles" of Soviet foreign policy that rested on the support of the Soviet people. However, speaking in Sofia, Bulg., in September, when the development of West Germany's relations with Eastern Europe had reached a temporary stalemate, Brezhnev admitted that "the struggle between socialism and capitalism continues in international affairs."

The main purpose of Brezhnev's visit to India in late November was to counteract China's growing influence among the nonaligned and less developed nations. While in New Delhi, Brezhnev made proposals for an Asian collective security conference.

Brezhnev was born Dec. 19, 1906, at Kamenskoye (later Dneprodzerzhinsk) in the Ukraine, and joined the Communist Party in 1931. He was elected to succeed Nikita S. Khrushchev as first secretary of the Communist Party of the Soviet Union (CPSU) by a plenary meeting of the Central Committee on Oct. 14, 1964. In April 1966 he was reappointed as general secretary (restoring the title abandoned after Stalin's death). On April 9, 1971, the 24th congress of the CPSU reelected him for a further five years. (K. M. SMOGORZEWSKI)

BUÑUEL, LUIS

When Jean-Paul Sartre refused the 1964 Nobel Prize for Literature, Luis Buñuel, congratulating him, said he would love the opportunity to make a similar gesture. In 1973 the veteran Spanish film director had his chance but did not take it. When his film *Le Charme discret de la bourgeoisie* (*The Discrete Charm of the Bourgeoisie*) won the Academy Award for the best foreign film of the year, he explained that what would once have been an antisocial act had become a publicity stunt.

His continuing assumption that antisocial acts are a matter of duty proved that, at 73 (he was born in Calanda, Spain, Feb. 22, 1900), Buñuel's revolutionary anarchy was no less violent than half a century before, when he arrived in Paris from Madrid and immediately found his spiritual kinship with the Surrealists. *Discrete Charm,* a social farce strongly charged with Surrealist spirit and symbols, finally established the septuagenarian artist as one of the most sought-after commercial directors in the world—an ironic climax to a career that had seen long periods of neglect and had been single-mindedly dedicated to anarchic opposition to every kind of Establishment.

In 1928 Buñuel collaborated with Salvador Dali on the first true Surrealist film, *Un Chien andalou.* His next film, *L'Age d'or* (1930), a full-length Surrealist feature, aroused such anger among reactionary elements that the theatre where it was shown was wrecked. There followed a long period of obscurity during which he worked in pre-Civil War Spain, in Hollywood, and in the Film Department of the Museum of Modern Art, New York City.

In 1947 he settled in Mexico, and with *Los olvidados,* a bitter tragedy of Mexican slum life that won the 1951 Cannes Festival Grand Prix, assumed his place in the front rank of film artists. In 1958 came the first of the major works of Buñuel's maturity, *Nazarin,* followed in 1961 by *Viridiana,* which won the Cannes Grand Prix and was promptly banned in Spain where it had been made. *El ángel exterminador, Le Journal d'une femme de chambre, Simón del desierto, Belle de jour,* and *Tristana* followed. *Belle de jour* brought Buñuel the 1967 Venice Grand Prix and his first spectacular international commercial success.

(DAVID ROBINSON)

BUTZ, EARL LAUER

Earl Butz, the farmer's friend and cantankerous defender of "free enterprise" in the agricultural marketplace, continued in 1973 to be one of the most visible and newsworthy of all secretaries of agriculture. He was widely criticized during the summer for permitting the Soviet Union to purchase wheat from the U.S. at bargain prices in 1972—the deal turned out to be less than a bargain for the U.S. when 1973 brought high prices and food shortages.

The spreading Watergate investigation also tainted the feisty secretary when word was leaked to the press that Butz was under scrutiny for allegedly applying political pressure in a questionable case. The allegations included charges that Butz had tried to stop a Federal Trade Commission investigation into the 1969 acquisition of United Vintners, Inc., a California grape growing group, by Heublein, Inc. Butz denied the charges and the investigation was still unfinished at year's end.

Butz was born in Albion, Ind., on July 3, 1909, and received his agriculture degree in 1932 from Purdue University at Lafayette. After studying at the University of Chicago in 1936, he worked as a farmer before joining the Purdue faculty as professor of agricultural economics. He was dean of agriculture at Purdue from 1957 to 1967, and dean of the school for continuing education in 1968.

He had served as an assistant secretary of agriculture during the Eisenhower years, and returned to Washington to run the department in 1971. His insistence that consumers had been paying too little for food products made him an immediate hit with farmers, despite some critics' claims that his policies favoured "agribusiness" over the family farm.

The mutual admiration society deteriorated in 1973, however, as Butz took the blame for a series of economic disasters that hurt both farmer and shopper. A long, wet fall in 1972 and a wet spring in 1973 slowed crop production, and the massive Soviet wheat deal came under increasing scrutiny; what had been surplus in 1972 was shortage in 1973. Still, at year's end, Butz was again on the attack, blaming food shortages on price controls (which he had opposed) and confidently predicting that the U.S. would be able to feed the world by the end of the century. (BILL GRANGER)

CAMERA PRESS/PICTORIAL PARADE

Luis Buñuel

CARL XVI GUSTAF

"For Sweden—with the times" was the motto chosen by Sweden's new king, 27-year-old Carl XVI Gustaf, when he took the oath of office at Stockholm's Royal Palace on Sept. 19, 1973. He succeeded his grandfather, King Gustaf VI Adolf, who had died on September 15 at the age of 90 (*see* OBITUARIES). It was a case of the world's oldest king being succeeded by the world's youngest.

Carl Gustaf's accession occurred when the future role of the Swedish monarchy was in the process of being radically altered. According to new constitutional laws adopted by the 1973 spring session of the Riksdag (parliament), the formal status of the king was to be changed, leaving him with only representative and ceremonial duties. Under the existing constitution, the king still played a formal role in the administration of the country; for example, he presided over councils of state, signed government decisions, commanded the armed forces, and appointed someone to form a new government in the event of the current administration resigning. The new laws, which would not become effective before Jan. 1, 1975, would relieve the king of all these duties, leaving him with a solely symbolic function.

Carl Gustaf Folke Hubertus was born on April 30, 1946, the only son of Gustaf Adolf's eldest son, Prince Gustaf Adolf, who died in an air crash in 1947. He became crown prince of Sweden in 1950 when his grandfather acceded to the throne. Carl Gustaf was educated at a mixed boarding school in Sigtuna near Stockholm and matriculated in 1966, after which he served two years in the armed forces, being commissioned as a naval officer in 1968. He also studied at military cadet schools, the University of Uppsala, and in France. An enthusiastic sportsman, he was a proficient yachtsman, skier, and marksman.

The new king (who is unmarried) had spent a large part of his time in recent years studying the structure of Swedish society. He visited and worked with municipal and governmental bodies, industrial enterprises, national organizations, Parliament, and the church. He also traveled abroad, working at a bank in London and studying the United Nations in New York. These activities were combined with an increasing responsibility for official duties and representation. (ALAN WILSON)

CASTANEDA, CARLOS

Mystic or scholar, Carlos Castaneda was an enigma and a demicelebrity, the author of a best-selling trilogy involving a modern Don Juan very unlike the classical paradigm. "I was having car trouble. Don Juan told me to talk to my car and make it an extension of myself. I said, 'Come on, don Juan, it's just a machine! . . .' He said, 'The car operates from power and under power. It is the power you must talk to.' I did, and my car is now a warrior's car. It's just a stupid Volkswagen, like anybody else's, but if I run out of gas, it's in front of a gas station."

The *Harper's* writer who recorded that story noted that Castaneda's concerns were not always so commonplace, a fact well known to the uncounted college-age readers who devoured paperbound editions of *The Teachings of Don Juan: A Yaqui Way of Knowledge, A Separate Reality: Further Conversations with Don Juan,* and *Journey to Ixtlan: The Lessons of Don Juan.*

Behind the books—which had been debunked in some quarters as fraudulent fiction and even more heatedly defended as revolutionary fact—lay an anthropologist's research into Mexican-American Indian culture and the use of native psychoactive plants, such as the peyote cactus. In 1960 Castaneda was getting a head start toward doctoral work at UCLA when, in a small Arizona town, he met the man he called Don Juan Matus (*i.e.,* John Smith) in an attempt to conceal his identity and save him from publicity. Don Juan led Castaneda on an odyssey into the "mystical" Indian vision of reality. Descriptions of the weird and awesome psychedelic events that followed were probably responsible for the books' underground popularity.

Attempts by other scholars and critics to assess Castaneda by conventional criteria were bound to be frustrating. He said, for instance, that "To ask me to verify my life by giving you my statistics is like using science to validate sorcery. It robs the world of its magic." Consequently, Castaneda concealed his past. *Time* magazine deduced that he was born in Peru on Christmas Day in 1925 (ten years earlier than he admitted, and in a different country) and that he had studied at the National Fine Arts School in Lima before going to the United States in 1951 to pursue his education.

(PHILIP KOPPER)

CHAPIN, SCHUYLER

"My dear," the French teacher-composer Nadia Boulanger told the young Schuyler Chapin, "you haven't any talent." It was a hard sentence for a youth who loved music, but there is room in the music world for many people besides performers. And in May 1973 Chapin, after a long apprenticeship in such positions, became general manager of New York City's Metropolitan Opera.

Chapin had not expected to be the man in charge at the Met. When Sir Rudolf Bing retired in 1972, after 22 years as general manager, Göran Gentele of the Royal Swedish Opera was named to succeed him and Chapin was to be Gentele's assistant manager. But Gentele was killed in an automobile accident in July 1972. With the season rapidly approaching, Chapin was appointed acting general manager for 1972–73.

Although he had never been a boss before, he held the company together during the emergency and improved morale in the process. A firm believer in the star system, he nevertheless chose to use resident singers, some from the New York City Opera, rather than import European stars on short notice. He picked Gentele's assistant stage director, Bodo Igesz, to direct a new production of *Carmen,* in collaboration with Leonard Bernstein. His reward for a job well done came with the permanent appointment in the spring.

Chapin took over the Met at a time when it, like many musical organizations, faced a shortage of funds. He was forced to cancel a new production of *Don Giovanni,* although four other new productions were still scheduled. Unlike Sir Rudolf, whose dictatorial methods were legend, he preferred cooperation to command and listening to talking. For the first time in many years, the Met reverted to the European system of partnership between the general manager and the musical director, in this case Rafael Kubelik.

Chapin was born in New York City on Feb. 13, 1923. A self-admitted "very bad student," he quit school to become a page boy at NBC. After service in World War II, he worked at NBC for a time and then, returning to music, was tour manager for Jascha Heifetz, Midwest booking manager for Columbia Artists Management, and supervisor of Columbia Masterworks. Before becoming associated with the Met, he was vice-president in charge of creative services at New York's Lincoln Center for the Performing Arts. (DANIEL MILLER)

CHILDERS, ERSKINE HAMILTON

Inaugurated head of state of the Republic of Ireland for a seven-year term on June 25, 1973, Erskine Childers became the republic's fourth president and the second Protestant to hold that office. The inauguration ceremony was preceded by an ecumenical service in St. Patrick's Church of Ireland Cathedral, attended by William Cardinal Conway and the Roman Catholic archbishop of Dublin. This was in marked contrast to the previous inauguration of a Protestant president—that of Douglas Hyde in 1938—when separate religious services were held.

The occasion crowned a career in public life that had begun with Childers' election to the Dail (Irish parliament) in 1938. As a member of successive Fianna Fail administrations, he was for many years the only Protestant in an otherwise Roman Catholic Cabinet, and during the troubles in Northern Ireland this made his a strongly conciliatory voice. He was a staunch supporter of former prime minister Jack Lynch at the time of the Cabinet crisis over the alleged importation of arms in the spring of 1970, and he continued the policy of peaceful reconciliation during his campaign for the presidency.

Childers was born in London, Eng., in 1905 and was given the same Christian name as his father, who became a leading figure in the struggle for Irish independence, was minister for publicity in the Republican government of 1919, and was executed on Nov. 24, 1922. The son was educated in England and read history at Trinity College, Cambridge. He returned to Ireland in 1932 and became advertising manager of the *Irish Press,* the newly founded newspaper owned by the De Valera family. Following his political debut in 1938, he became a junior minister in 1944 and was later minister for posts and telegraphs (1951–54), of lands, forestry, and fisheries (1957–59), of transport and power (1959–69), and minister for health and deputy leader of the Fianna Fail Party from 1969 until the defeat of the Lynch government in February 1973.

(BRUCE ARNOLD)

CHI PENG-FEI

Chou En-lai's role as the supreme internationalist and embodiment of Chinese diplomacy had tended to keep the Foreign

WREN DE ANTONIO—NANCY PALMER PHOTO AGENCY

Erskine Hamilton Childers

Chi Peng-fei

KEYSTONE

Ministry in Peking in the background. The Cultural Revolution added to the process by subjecting foreign minister Chen Yi to severe criticism. Chi Peng-fei, officially named as Chen Yi's successor upon that official's death in 1972, had since filled with distinction the vacuum left by the latter, and in 1973 he gained the limelight in the West as a dedicated Chinese negotiator.

Born in Shensi Province in 1910, Chi graduated as a military doctor and enlisted in the Kuomintang (Nationalist) Army. In 1931 he defected to the Communists and worked in the Revolutionary Military Council's medical department during the Long March. In the late 1930s he served as a political commissar in various army units. He began his diplomatic career in 1950, a year after the Communists came to power.

As the Chinese envoy involved for long in Eastern European, North Korean, and Mongolian relations, Chi became a close foreign policy associate of Premier Chou En-lai. In the mid-1950s, when Chou was foreign minister as well as premier, Chi became a vice-foreign minister directly responsible to Chou. In fact, Chi was very much one of "Chou En-lai's boys," mobilized to revamp the post-Cultural Revolution Foreign Ministry for the détente era.

Chi's familiarity with European affairs made him in 1973 a key element in China's diplomatic efforts to win friends in Europe. In meetings with British and French leaders, he personally canvassed support for the Chinese line that Western Europe must be cautious in dealing with the Soviet Union. There was, however, little evidence to suggest that the Chinese arguments were creating any impact in Europe.

Essentially Chi Peng-fei was a professional diplomat and career officer. He had no personal power base in any region, including his own native province of Shensi, or in the party or the Army. Therefore, he did not figure as a major element in Peking's power structure. (T. J. S. GEORGE)

COCKFIELD, SIR (FRANCIS) ARTHUR

One of the least enviable jobs in inflation-ridden Britain went to Sir Arthur Cockfield, who in March 1973 was appointed chairman of the Price Commission set up as part of the machinery to police the government's counterinflationary policies. It brought into the centre of the public stage a man with remarkable qualifications for the job but one largely unknown to the general public. Yet, before he went to the Price Commission, Cockfield had been one of the principal architects of the revolution in the tax system that was being brought about by the Heath government. Since 1970 he had been adviser on taxation policy to the chancellor of the Exchequer. Before that, when the Conservatives were in opposition, he had worked behind the scenes with Iain Macleod, then "shadow" chancellor, on fiscal reform, and was credited with many of the ideas that were to be embodied in the new tax structure.

It was as a taxation expert that Cockfield made his name when still a young man. Born Sept. 28, 1916, he attended the London School of Economics and in 1938 joined the Inland Revenue. By the age of 29, he had become its director of statistics and intelligence. Soon after the end of World War II he tired of government work and moved into business, joining Boots (Britain's biggest pharmaceutical manufacturers and retailers). He became the firm's finance director in 1953 and, in 1961, managing director, only to leave the company in 1967 (with a parting payment of £55,000). Subsequently he remained in the background of affairs—though in 1968–69 he was president of the Royal Statistical Society. He was well known to Conservative political leaders for his work as taxation adviser to the government, and his knowledge of finance and of the retail trade made him a natural choice to police price control. Though his personal style was unspectacular, his intellectual grip and relaxed, humorous lucidity reinforced his reputation. In a year when the pressure on prices was inexorably upward, he was able to claim in the Price Commission's second report that, by restraining price increases, the commission had saved consumers more than £300 million. (HARFORD THOMAS)

COOKE, (ALFRED) ALISTAIR

Commissioned to do a television documentary series on the United States that took two years and any amount of money to make, Alistair Cooke chose to call it "America." "I thought it was a pretty catchy little title," he said afterward. One of the most celebrated journalists of his time, Cooke operated with consummate success in three media: newspapers, radio, and television. In all three he was, in fact, playing the same role—that of reporter. He might have become an actor—no doubt a successful one, for at Cambridge University he took a leading part in the theatre clubs that breed many professional actors, and he was given a Commonwealth Fund fellowship to study theatre direction at Yale. Instead he turned to newspapers, to broadcasting (which gave some scope for his actor's talent), and to a lifetime involvement with the United States.

Cooke was born on Nov. 20, 1908, in Salford, near Manchester, and grew up in the celebrated Lancashire seaside town of Blackpool, but the United States became his first love, and in 1941 he took U.S. citizenship. His English roots and his American adoption shaped his work as a journalist. He had been brought up in the home territory of the *Manchester Guardian* (later *The Guardian*), and in 1948 he became its chief correspondent in the U.S. In the same year he started his weekly "Letter from America" that for more than two decades was one of the best known BBC radio programs.

Cooke's writing and broadcasting revealed a meticulous judgment in the selection of small, even seemingly trivial detail to establish a substantial point, a fastidious choice of words disguised by the informality of his approach, and a deep yet unpretentious knowledge of American life and history. He brought the same qualities to his television work, winning two Emmy Awards as writer and narrator of the "America" series, which was published in book form in 1973. Few journalists had been so showered with academic awards, among them honorary degrees from the universities of Manchester and Edinburgh and the Benjamin Franklin Medal of the Royal Society of Arts. In 1973 he was made an honorary knight-commander of the Order of the British Empire—honorary because his U.S. citizenship precluded his adopting foreign titles. (HARFORD THOMAS)

COSGRAVE, LIAM

Prime minister of Ireland as successor to Jack Lynch after the general election of February 1973, Liam Cosgrave was nicknamed "Little Liam." Although not particularly small physically, he had a precise, clipped manner, a sober, bank-manager style of dress, and a contained, reserved attitude as a politician that caused the name to stick. He was a conservative man, with strong—even rigid—views on law and order, an equally rigid attitude toward loyalty or lack of it in his supporters, and an unswerving sense of his own political destiny: that of following in his father's footsteps as the country's leader.

His father, W. T. Cosgrave, was president of the Executive Council and head of the government of the Irish Free State during the first ten years of its existence (1922–32). Liam, the elder son, was born in Templeogue, County Dublin, in April 1920. He was educated for the law and called to the Irish bar in 1943, the year in which he entered the Dail (Irish parliament). In 1948, when the first interparty government replaced Eamon De Valera's Fianna Fail regime, which had been in power for the previous 16 years, Cosgrave became parliamentary secretary to the *taoiseach* (prime minister) and to the minister for industry and commerce. It was a short-lived administration, going out of power after three years, in 1951. But it was back again in 1954 for another three years, at which time Cosgrave became minister for external affairs and led the first Irish delegation to the United Nations General Assembly in 1956.

Cosgrave succeeded James Dillon as leader of the Fine Gael party—the second largest political party in the country and the principal party in the 1973 coalition—in 1965. He made no dramatic impact as leader then or in the succeeding years, tending to leave public statements, policy thinking, and general party direction to others. But there was never any equivocation about his leadership, and he was skillful and ruthless in maintaining loyalty and disciplining those who represented a challenge to his position. (BRUCE ARNOLD)

COX, ARCHIBALD

Crisis brought Archibald Cox to Washington in 1973. The soft-spoken, crew-cut law professor was named as special prosecutor in the Watergate scandal, with the task of seeking evidence, presenting it to a special grand jury, and prosecuting wrongdoers. But the manner of his leaving created an even greater crisis that seemed finally to have convinced Pres. Richard Nixon that Watergate would not "go away."

Cox was appointed by his former Harvard Law School student Elliot Richardson (*q.v.*) when the Senate demanded an independent special prosecutor with impeccable creden-

Chief Dan George

WIDE WORLD

tials as the price of confirming Richardson's appointment as attorney general. Richardson promised him job security and the cooperation of the executive branch, but from the start Cox and the White House were at odds. When the Senate Watergate committee turned up evidence that crucial presidential conversations had been recorded, Cox asked for the tapes and was refused. He went to court and obtained a favourable ruling from Judge John Sirica (*q.v.*).

Some said Cox's far-flung investigations had come too close to the White House. Others said he was insubordinate—as a member of the Department of Justice he was, technically at least, a servant of the president. In any case, Nixon apparently decided that Cox must go, and when Cox refused to accept a presidential compromise on the tapes, Nixon ordered Richardson to fire him. Richardson refused and submitted his resignation. His deputy, William Ruckelshaus, also refused and was fired himself. The deed was finally done by Robert Bork, the solicitor general. But the public outcry that followed the "Saturday night massacre" caught the White House by surprise. Three days later Nixon offered to turn the tapes over to Judge Sirica, and he subsequently embarked on an extensive campaign of fence-mending. On November 14 a federal judge ruled that Cox had been fired illegally, but the case was moot. Cox no longer wanted the job.

Cox was born May 17, 1912, in Plainfield, N.J. He earned his law degree from Harvard in 1937 and worked for a year as law clerk for the highly respected Judge Learned Hand. At the age of 34 he became one of Harvard's youngest professors, and he continued to teach there except for five years when he served as U.S. solicitor general in the administrations of John F. Kennedy and Lyndon Johnson.

CRAIG, WILLIAM

The most outspoken and least flexible of Northern Ireland's intransigent right-wing leaders in 1973 was William Craig, leader of the Ulster Vanguard Movement. Craig epitomized the loyalist Protestant opinion that had split the once all-powerful Unionist Party and made possible the power-sharing that brought into being in November 1973 the Northern Ireland executive. His movement, together with Ian Paisley's Democratic Unionist Party and Harry West's newly formed Ulster Unionist Assembly Party, made up the group in the Assembly opposed to power-sharing, to the Council of Ireland, and to the involvement of the Republic of Ireland in Northern Ireland affairs.

Craig had been minister for home affairs in the autumn of 1968, during the growing wave of civil rights demonstrations. Much of the trouble centred on Londonderry, a city of unemployment and community tensions. On November 13, Craig, to Prime Minister Terence O'Neill's horror, put a one-month ban on processions within the city walls. The ban was flouted, but peacefully, and O'Neill was forced to move on his reform package for the province. This made impossible the continued support of the right wing of his party, and made inevitable Craig's dismissal, on December 11.

Craig was thus released from the ambiguities of trying to resolve his own hard-line views with the reforms imposed by the British government. However, it was not until February 1972, after 13 civilians were killed during a demonstration in Londonderry and less than a month before direct rule was imposed by Westminster, that Craig, in collaboration with Billie Hull, leader of the Loyalist Association of Workers in Belfast, formed the Ulster Vanguard Movement.

Craig was born on Dec. 2, 1924, and educated at Dungannon Royal School, Larne Grammar School, and Queen's University, Belfast. After serving in the British Royal Air Force (1943–46), he qualified as a solicitor in 1952. In 1960 he was elected to the Stormont Parliament as Unionist member for the Larne constituency. He was chief whip for the Unionist Party (1962–63) and then, successively, minister for home affairs (1963–64), local government (1964), development (1965–66), health (1966–68), and then home affairs again in 1968.

(BRUCE ARNOLD)

DAN GEORGE, CHIEF

An American Indian movie star, Chief Dan George had been an actor for 13 years when he went on tour in 1973 in the stage play *The Ecstasy of Rita Joe,* a contemporary drama about Indians. Remarkably, he had been a construction worker for 23 years before becoming an actor, and a stevedore for 27 years before that.

A fullblooded Ts-Lall-Watte (meaning "inland") Indian, Chief Dan George was born in 1899 and lived most of his life near Vancouver, B.C. While a son of his was working for a television company, a white actor cast as an old Indian in a television play fell sick. The son suggested that the director hire a "real, old Indian" to stand in, and Chief Dan George thus made his acting debut. Ultimately, that led to his appearance in Arthur Penn's well-received film of 1971, *Little Big Man.* He played Old Lodge Skins, the patriarch to Dustin Hoffman's young protagonist. During the production, the old man said that Hoffman told him, "'I never did have a grandfather.' Then asked if he could call me grandfather and I said 'Any time son. I already have 36 grandchildren, I might as well have 37.'" His appearance as the aging sage won two major critics' awards, though he said, "I really didn't feel I should be given credit for the part. I was an Indian chief for 12 years so I really didn't have to do much acting."

While he was on tour in *The Ecstasy of Rita Joe,* Indian militants took over Wounded Knee, S.D. Asked his views of the events, the chief told an interviewer, "The complete story, I never got it. I don't like to hurt nobody's feelings, but according to my people when there was trouble between two tribes, we sat down and talked. . . . Now they load their rifles and try to settle it by shooting each other." (PHILIP KOPPER)

DAUD KHAN, MOHAMMAD

A stocky figure with shaven head and a reputation for ruthlessness, Mohammad Daud Khan, a member of the Afghan royal house, staged a coup in 1973 that transformed the monarchy into a republic, with himself as president. The constitutional change was probably the condition of support given to Daud by young army officers. In the night of July 16–17 ministers close to King Mohammad Zahir Shah (who was at that time undergoing mud-bath treatment on the island of Ischia) had their houses surrounded, and tanks took up positions in Kabul. The only resistance came from the king's son-in-law, Maj. Gen. Abdul Wali, commander of the Kabul military region. Wali was expected to face trial, together with other personalities including Mohammad Hashim Maiwandwal, prime minister during 1965–67. On Oct. 1, 1973, Radio Kabul reported that Maiwandwal had hanged himself in prison.

Broadcasting on July 17 from Kabul in Pashto, the people's language, Daud declared that the old "corrupt system" of government had been abolished and replaced with a "republican system," in accordance with "the genuine spirit of Islam." He also referred to the problem of Pakhtunistan, the Pathan-inhabited region straddling the frontier between Afghanistan and Pakistan. The frontier, following the British-established Durand Line of 1893, places the 12 million Pathan people in two countries.

Daud Khan was born in Kabul on July 18, 1909, a member of the Barakzai dynasty established in 1826. Educated at Habibia College and in France, he was appointed governor-general of Kandahar in 1932 by his uncle King Mohammad Nadir Khan (assassinated in 1933). In 1939 he was made commander of the army corps stationed in Kabul and from 1946 to 1953 (with an interval in 1948 as ambassador to France) was minister of defense. In September 1953 he became prime minister, stressing in his foreign policy friendly relations with the U.S.S.R. Zahir Shah, his cousin and brother-in-law, forced him to resign in March 1963 and about two years later introduced a new constitution that barred members of the royal family from all political activity.

(K. M. SMOGORZEWSKI)

DEAN, JOHN WESLEY, III

Testifying on nationwide television before the U.S. Senate Select Committee to Investigate the 1972 Presidential Campaign Activities (the Watergate committee), John W. Dean III accused Pres. Richard Nixon of being involved in the cover-up of the Watergate scandal. Dean's testimony was especially dramatic because only a few months earlier he had been the confident,

Archibald Cox

UPI COMPIX

John Wesley Dean III

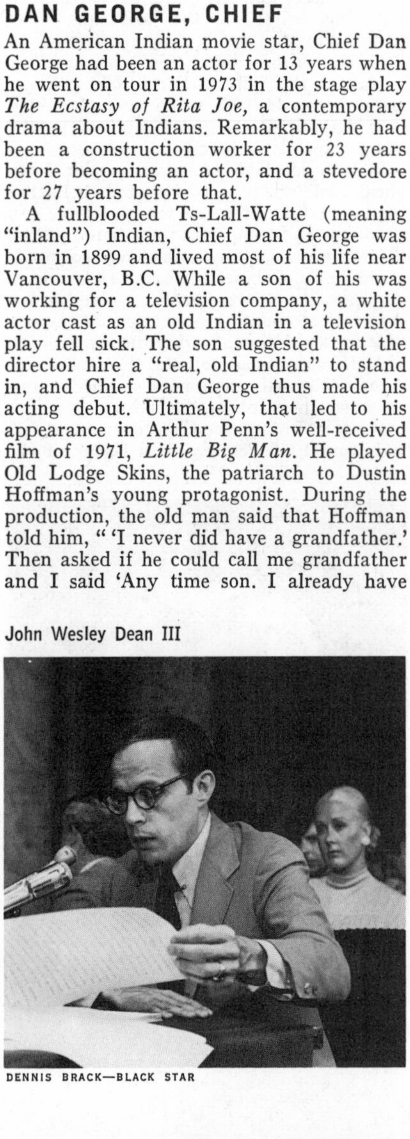

DENNIS BRACK—BLACK STAR

clean-cut counsel to the president and had even been identified once as the man who presumably had directed Nixon's first internal investigation of the Watergate break-in. By the time of the hearings Dean's world had collapsed around him. He was requested to submit his resignation by President Nixon on April 30, and at 34 years of age he seemed to have reached a dead end.

In a droning voice and looking out at the committee members through horn-rimmed glasses, Dean testified that it was his impression that President Nixon had been involved in the cover-up but that the president "did not realize" how deeply he was involved. Dean said that he had told Nixon the details of the cover-up as early as March 21, 1973, four weeks before Nixon told the nation that he had learned startling new information about the case.

In all, Dean contradicted Nixon on four key points: that the president knew about the cover-up; that Nixon had discussed an offer of executive clemency for Watergate defendants; that the president knew about cash payments to defendants in the case; and that he never really investigated the cover-up but acted, with H. R. Haldeman and John D. Ehrlichman, "to protect themselves against the unraveling of the cover-up." In a lengthy "rebuttal" analysis submitted to the committee by the White House staff, Dean was accused of being "the principal actor in the Watergate cover-up."

None of the accusations was proved as 1973 turned into 1974, and in October 1973 Dean pleaded guilty to a charge of conspiracy to obstruct justice. Shortly afterward, a three-judge federal panel suspended Dean from practicing law in the District of Columbia, the first step in disbarment proceedings.

Dean became the president's legal counsel only five years after graduating from Georgetown University Law School. A native of Akron, O., and a graduate of Staunton Military Academy, he attended several colleges before earning a master's degree in public administration at American University. He worked for less than a year with the Washington law firm of Welch and Morgan, but was fired when he drew up an application for a television channel while preparing a competing application for himself and some friends. In 1970 he joined the White House staff as counsel to the president. (ROBERT A. SIGNER)

DEN UYL, JOOP MARTEN

The appointment by Queen Juliana of Joop den Uyl as prime minister of The Netherlands in May 1973 marked the change in the strength of the country's political parties brought about by the November 1972 general election. The balance of power in the election had swung away from the three parties of the centre toward the cooperative left-wing parties—den Uyl's Labour Party, the Democrats '66, and the Radical Political Party.

Den Uyl's government planned an ambitious program of social reform. But by an irony of fate it found itself having to cope, after less than six months in office, with the drastic consequences of the total oil embargo placed on The Netherlands by the Arab countries in October because of Dutch friendliness toward Israel. Thus, the "new quality of life" that den Uyl had proffered the Dutch people threatened to be a general lowering, rather than an enhancement, of living standards. On December 1, with fuel economy measures promising a cheerless winter ahead, den Uyl appeared on television to exhort the nation to concert its efforts to "win the cold war."

Born in Hilversum, Neth., on Aug. 9, 1919, Joop den Uyl studied economics at the University of Amsterdam, graduating in 1942. He worked in the Ministry of Economic Affairs and then entered journalism, becoming editor of the newspaper *Het Parool* and the weekly *Vrij Nederland*. In 1949 he became director of the scientific bureau of the Labour Party. His political career began in 1953 when he was elected as a Labour Party representative to the Amsterdam city council.

In 1956 den Uyl entered the national political scene when he was elected to Parliament as a Labour Party representative. An ambitious and competent politician, in April 1965 he was appointed minister of economic affairs in the Cabinet of Joseph Cals, and in that capacity he was deeply involved in the problems of energy supply. He was responsible for legislation affecting the exploitation of North Sea gas and oil and the consequent industrial transformation of southern Limburg, which involved the closing down of coal mines. In 1966 the Cals government fell, and from 1967 den Uyl was leader of the Labour Party and the main spokesman of the opposition parties in Parliament. (DICK BOONSTRA)

EKANGAKI, NZO

"It would be reasonable to think that the time has come for our Arab brothers to use the oil embargo as a weapon against the white regimes." These words of Nzo Ekangaki, addressing the ministerial council of the Organization of African Unity (OAU) in Addis Ababa, Eth., Nov. 20, 1973, emphasized the position of political influence he derived from his appointment (June 14, 1972) as OAU secretary-general—top post in the pan-African hierarchy. Following the break of most OAU members with Israel, the council was discussing ways of enlisting reciprocal Arab support against the white supremacist regimes of southern Africa.

Prior to his OAU appointment Ekangaki had held ministerial posts in the government of Cameroon, first as deputy foreign minister (1962–64) and later as minister of labour and social welfare. He proved himself a dynamic and effective politician and gained a reputation as a versatile technocrat. He was also a subtle diplomat who could be extremely tough in the difficult situations that abounded during his two years at OAU headquarters in Addis Ababa. He then had to hold the balance not only between the organization's French- and English-speaking members but also (before the massive shift to alignment with the Arabs) between its pro-Arab and pro-Israeli members, as well as between the conservative and radical wings of pan-Africanism.

Born in the former British trust territory of the Cameroons in 1934, Ekangaki was educated in Protestant mission schools in Nigeria and entered the University of Ibadan. He then went to Oxford, where he studied English literature, history, and arts. After graduating he became a civil servant for a year, and then in 1960 went to the University of Bonn, in West Germany, where he took a degree in political science and diplomacy. After completing his schooling he turned to politics, for which he had acquired a taste as a militant student leader, and in 1961 was elected to the Cameroon Legislative Assembly. In 1966 he became a member of the Political Bureau of the nation's ruling party. (COLIN LEGUM)

ERVIN, SAMUEL J., JR.

For most of the nation, 1973 was the year in which tall, jowly Sen. Sam J. Ervin, Jr.,

UPI COMPIX

Joop Marten den Uyl

WIDE WORLD

King Faisal

FRED WARD—BLACK STAR

Samuel J. Ervin, Jr.

became as familiar a figure on television as the stars of "All in the Family" or "Bonanza." Ervin, the 77-year-old chairman of the Senate Select Committee to Investigate the 1972 Presidential Campaign Activities—popularly known as the Senate Watergate committee—presided over the nationally televised Watergate hearings, in which former top officials of the White House and Nixon reelection committee came forward to answer questions about the 1972 burglary and bugging of Democratic Party headquarters and related matters. By the summer's end he was something of a cult figure, even to being featured on T-shirts.

His eyebrows dancing, his soft voice slurred by a Southern accent and frequent spasms of indignation, Ervin lashed away in an effort to force answers from reluctant witnesses or to lecture those with whom he disagreed. "The divine right of rulers perished in America with the Revolution and it doesn't belong to White House aides," he admonished once during an early showdown with Pres. Richard Nixon over the president's refusal to permit his aides to testify publicly before the committee.

And yet Ervin was no radical. A strict interpreter of the U.S. Constitution, the North Carolina Democrat had always stood with the South's segregationist bloc on racial matters. He was often cited as the Senate's foremost constitutional expert, and, although he liked to tell listeners that he was merely a "country lawyer," those who knew his background pointed out that he was a graduate of Harvard Law School.

Ervin was born in Morgantown, N.C., on Sept. 27, 1896, and studied at the University of North Carolina, from which he received a bachelor's degree in 1917. He was admitted to the bar in that state in 1919, but enrolled instead at Harvard, earning a law degree in 1922. During World War I Ervin enlisted as a private and was twice wounded and twice cited for gallantry.

A onetime state legislator and member of North Carolina's Democratic executive committee, Ervin served for six years as an associate justice of the North Carolina Supreme Court. In June 1954 he was appointed to the U.S. Senate to replace Clyde R. Hoey, who had died. Later that year he was elected to the seat, and he was subsequently reelected three times. Late in 1973 he announced that he would not run again.

(ROBERT A. SIGNER)

FAISAL IBN 'ABD-AL-'AZIZ

King Faisal of Saudi Arabia emerged in the 1970s as one of the most influential political figures in the Arab and Islamic worlds because of his position as protector of the Holy Places of Islam and his immense and growing oil wealth. In September 1973 he was partly instrumental in bringing about the rapprochement between Egypt, Jordan, and Syria that preceded the outbreak in October of the fourth Arab-Israeli war. However, Faisal's close association with the United States, regarded as Israel's principal ally, was a growing embarrassment, and he was reluctantly placed in the position of having to carry out his threat to use Saudi Arabia's key position in the world oil industry as a political weapon to undermine support for Israel. With other Arab leaders he embargoed all shipments of oil to the U.S. and The Netherlands, and he announced an immediate 10% reduction in Saudi oil production. As the year ended, the oil policy was being orchestrated in an effort to provide maximum diplomatic dividends while preventing formation of a united front among the oil-consuming nations.

Born in 1905 as the second son of the great King 'Abd-al-'Aziz ibn Saud, the unifier of Arabia, Faisal was in 1927 appointed governor of the Hijaz, recently conquered from the Hashimite King Hussein, and entrusted with its integration into the Saudi kingdom. On Ibn Saud's death in 1953 and the succession of Faisal's elder brother, Saud, Faisal became crown prince, prime minister, and foreign minister. In 1958, as a result of Saud's financial mismanagement and unsuccessful interference in Arab politics, the royal princes and Saudi religious leaders ('Ulama') conferred full powers in the conduct of internal and foreign affairs on Faisal, who instituted a variety of reforms that restored the country's financial position. However, his power struggle with Saud continued until 1964, when the Supreme Council of 'Ulama' deposed Saud and proclaimed Faisal king.

In his political outlook Faisal was an Islamic traditionalist who ruled his country autocratically. In some social matters, however, he was less conservative and he encouraged the education of women. In foreign policy he was a strongly anti-Zionist Arab nationalist and an equally strong anti-Communist. In the 1960s he concentrated on opposing radical republican forces in the Arabian Peninsula, especially in Yemen, and in forming an Islamic Front of conservative, anti-Soviet elements in Arab and Muslim states. This brought him into sharp conflict with Pres. Gamal Abd-an-Nasser of Egypt. His influence grew after Nasser's death in 1970, and he succeeded in forging a close relationship with Nasser's successor, Pres. Anwar as-Sadat.

(PETER MANSFIELD)

FIGGURES, SIR FRANK EDWARD

When it became clear in 1972 that the British government would have to take drastic and unusual steps to curb inflation, one of the most influential advisers in the behind-the-scenes discussions set up by the Heath government with industry and the trade unions was Sir Frank Figgures. A civil servant and diplomat of wide experience, Figgures was subsequently chosen to head the Pay Board, which had the potentially explosive duty of policing the statutory restraints placed on increased earnings during the pay pause and Stages Two and Three of the counterinflationary program. Figgures was chosen not only for his experience but also for his conviction that there must be some form of tripartite agreement on the management of the economy among government, industry, and the trade unions if there was to be any hope of price stability.

Born March 5, 1910, Figgures might have had a distinguished career as a lawyer, which was his calling in the 1930s, but after World War II (when he served on Earl Mountbatten's headquarters staff in Burma) he joined the Treasury in 1946. Events drew him into the diplomatic side of international economic affairs, working for the Organization for European Economic Cooperation as director of trade and finance, and later, after another five-year period at the Treasury, as secretary-general to the European Free Trade Association (EFTA). By 1965 he was back in the Treasury, reaching the rank of second permanent secretary, in charge of home and overseas finance. He then moved on to the National Economic Development Office as director-general, a post that found him in daily contact with the leaders of industry and the trade unions. Figgures brought to the Pay Board not only exceptional experience in negotiation but also a reputation for bluff, direct plain speaking, a combination that saw him through the first months of wages restraint with unexpectedly little controversy. (HARFORD THOMAS)

FINLAY, A(LLAN) MARTYN

For those who practice politics rather than their professions the opportunity seldom occurs to advance both at the same time. But for A. Martyn Finlay, a New Zealand barrister who became minister of justice and attorney general in his country's third Labour government (elected November 1972), there was professional advancement too when in 1973 he appeared before the World Court at The Hague to argue New Zealand's case for an injunction to restrain France from testing nuclear devices in the Pacific. Granting of the injunction was not expected to—nor did it—deter the French, but it was a step toward influencing French public opinion against contaminating other parts of the world.

The court's verdict was a more apparent victory for Finlay than anything he was able to achieve through administration of his portfolio at home, where, despite promising public pronouncements, he was slow to produce legislative reforms. Measures to provide for enlargement of the scope of prison parole boards in reviewing sentences earlier and more often were expected; the ten-year-old pioneering periodic detention system was used further; licensing laws were reported on as a prelude to further liberalization; and public attitudes toward abortion and drug law reform were sampled. All this only pointed to some testing of viewpoints going on between the liberal minister and his more conservative prime minister, Norman Kirk.

As fifth-ranking minister and one whose impetuosity of tongue had previously led to embarrassments, Finlay was watched with interest, particularly in his task of converting the prime minister to some of his own attitudes. Kirk looked singularly unmoved, and was responding instead to ministers like Joe Walding (ranked 17, dealing with overseas trade and deputizing in foreign affairs) and Colin Moyle (ranked 11 and wrestling with agriculture).

Finlay was born in Dunedin on Jan. 1, 1912, and was educated locally, later obtaining a doctorate at London University. From 1946 he represented various Auckland constituencies in Parliament, and was later a decisive Labour Party president.

(JOHN A. KELLEHER)

FINLEY, CHARLES O.

When millionaire insurance executive Charles Finley bought the foundering Kansas City Athletics baseball club in 1960, there were some who believed that he was simply another rich man seeking an expensive hobby. They could not have been more wrong. Not only did he become a working owner, to such an extent that he faced more player revolts and near revolts than anyone else in baseball history, but he also stamped his personality on the team and even the game itself. Acting as his own general manager, hiring and firing ten field managers in 12 years, Finley seemed to thrive on controversy.

Born in Birmingham, Ala., on Feb. 22, 1918, Finley rose from labourer to foreman in the Gary (Ind.) works of the U.S. Steel Corp. In 1945 he formed his own insurance brokerage firm, which eventually became one of the largest in the Middle West. Profits from the firm paid for the baseball team, which was moved to Oakland in 1968, and the California Golden Seals hockey team.

But with ownership Finley also insisted on control, to a degree virtually unique in present-day sports. Every detail of operation was initiated by, or cleared through, him. When he ordered the Athletics to dress in orange and gold uniforms with white kangaroo shoes, some of the players were almost too embarrassed to take the field. He did not back down, and later other teams adopted multicoloured uniforms. When he offered a small bonus to players who grew moustaches, the 1972 A's took on the appearance of fugitives from the Federal League.

Amusing as some of the antics were, there was a darker side to Finley as autocrat. Players who criticized or spoke out against him often found themselves traded or released. Mike Andrews, who made two errors that cost the A's the second game of the 1973 World Series, suddenly found himself on the disabled list. Baseball commissioner Bowie Kuhn fined Finley a reported $7,000 for the incident. A's manager Dick Williams quit after the Series and announced that he planned to sign with the New York Yankees, but Finley, after saying on TV that he would release Williams from the last two years of his contract, later reneged and was upheld by American League president Joe Cronin.

Despite the aura of controversy, Finley must have been doing something right. When the A's defeated the New York Mets in seven games in the 1973 World Series, they became the first team to win back-to-back world championships since the New York Yankees in 1961 and 1962. (DONALD J. KLIMOVICH)

FITT, GERARD

Leader since 1970 of Northern Ireland's Catholic Social Democratic and Labour Party, Gerry Fitt held the unswerving belief that socialism was the best—perhaps the only—antidote to sectarianism in the province. His appointment as deputy chief of the Northern Ireland executive confirmed him as one of the province's key figures. Power in the executive, formation of which was announced by the U.K. government on Nov. 21, 1973, was shared among the Unionist (Protestant) and Catholic parties.

Fitt had entered the former Stormont Parliament in 1962, and in the 1966 U.K. general election he was elected to Westminster as member for Belfast West. His maiden speech at Westminster, against all convention, dragged into the open the inequalities between Northern Ireland and the rest of the U.K. and sounded a solemn warning of what might be expected if the simple demands of one-man, one-vote; fair housing; and greater equality in employment were not acted upon. It was a significant verbal warning shot in the traumatic cycle of events that followed.

During the campaigns for civil rights, the marches, and the riots, Fitt remained levelheaded, unbigoted, and courageous. In the Derry march of Oct. 5, 1968, he was bloodied by police batons, and the incident was seen on television screens around the world. Stoutly opposed to violence, he bent all his efforts at Westminster, during the worsening days of 1969–71, toward achieving reforms and political initiatives that would offset the growing strength of militant extremism.

Fitt was a product of the Belfast working class. He was born April 9, 1926, in the city's dockland, one of six children of a Belfast council worker who was also secretary of the local branch of the Labour Party. His father died when he was eight. He went to work at 14, first as a barber's assistant, then as a cabin boy in the merchant navy. After convoy duties throughout World War II, he gave up the sea in 1953 and began a career in politics for which he had prepared himself as a sailor by extensive reading. His first political work was as agent for Jack Beattie, a Stormont MP who won the Belfast West seat at Westminster in the 1951 U.K. general election. He then took part in local government politics and in 1958 was elected to the Belfast City Council.

(BRUCE ARNOLD)

FORD, GERALD

The longtime conservative Republican minority leader of the U.S. House of Representatives, Gerald Ford was suddenly catapulted to national prominence in 1973 when Pres. Richard Nixon nominated him as vice-president following the resignation on October 10 of Spiro Agnew (*q.v.*). Ford, of Grand Rapids, Mich., immediately told the world that he had no intention of running for president in 1976 if his nomination as vice-president was confirmed. The Senate and House closely scrutinized his background in an extended series of public hearings because, as one Senate leader put it, "Jerry Ford may just become the next president of the U.S." On November 27 the Senate voted 92–3 in favour of confirmation and the House followed suit 387–35 on December 6. Immediately after the House vote, Ford was sworn in as the nation's 40th vice-president.

Ford, whose conservative politics and antibusing stands made him anathema to many liberal and black groups, had been well-liked by most of his colleagues in the House. A football star during his college days at the University of Michigan, he had a reputation of personal integrity.

Ford was born Leslie King in Omaha, Neb., on July 14, 1913. When he was an infant, his parents were divorced and his mother moved to Grand Rapids, where she married Gerald Ford, Sr. Ford adopted the boy and gave him his name. After graduating from the University of Michigan, Ford obtained a law degree from Yale University. He was admitted to the Michigan bar in 1941 and then served in the U.S. Navy from 1942 until the end of World War II.

In 1948 he ran for Congress from his Grand Rapids district and bucked the Democratic tide to win election. Pres. Lyndon Johnson in 1963 named him a member of the Warren Commission, which was charged with the investigation of the assassination of Pres. John F. Kennedy. Ford's estimation in the eyes of his Republican colleagues steadily rose, and he was elected minority leader of the House in 1965, a position he still held in 1973.

During the middle 1960s, he and the late Sen. Everett M. Dirksen (then Republican leader in the Senate) publicized the GOP point of view in a series of feisty, often funny, press conferences that came to be known as the "Ev and Jerry Show" and brought the Michigan congressman national prominence. (BILL GRANGER)

Gerald Ford

WIDE WORLD

FOSSE, ROBERT LOUIS

Choreographer-director Bob Fosse seemed to be everywhere on the entertainment scene in 1973. He won two Antoinette Perry (Tony) awards for directing and choreographing the Broadway musical *Pippin* and an Academy Award for directing the film version of *Cabaret*. At the same time he was working on a film version of the stage show *Lenny,* based on the life of the late comedian Lenny Bruce—partly out of affection for Bruce but also "because I want to see if I can handle a heavy . . . story." In the planning stage was a Broadway musical based on an old play, *Chicago,* which would star Fosse's estranged wife, Gwen Verdon.

At the top of his profession at the age of 46, Fosse had been in show business for 37 years. He was born in Chicago on June 23, 1927. His father was a vaudevillian and a member of a four-man act in which Bob's uncle also performed. Bob took dancing lessons at the age of nine and soon began appearing at local fraternal clubs with a friend in an act called the Riff Brothers. As a teen-ager he worked as a single in burlesque. After World War II he performed in the road companies of several Broadway shows, then went to Hollywood for a number of films.

His first break as a choreographer came when he was allowed to direct 45 seconds of *Kiss Me, Kate*. Handed the script for *The Pajama Game,* he choreographed it into a smash hit, remembered, among other numbers, for the sizzling "Steam Heat." His later credits included *Damn Yankees* (1955), *Bells Are Ringing* (1956), *New Girl in Town* (1957), *Redhead* (1959), and *How to Succeed in Business Without Really Trying* (1961). He played the lead in the New York City Center revival of *Pal Joey* (1961 and 1963) and was choreographer and co-director for *Little Me* (1962).

Although his 1973 awards were by no means his first (he won Tonys for *The Pajama Game, Damn Yankees, Redhead, Little Me,* and *Sweet Charity*), they gave him the prestige and leverage to direct films and plays with a much-needed measure of independence. Following his tremendous success with *Cabaret,* he planned to concentrate on films. "I want to do something that lasts," he said. "I want to do something I can really like." (DANIEL MILLER)

FRANJIEH, SULEIMAN

In May 1973 Lebanon's Pres. Suleiman Franjieh had to handle one of the most dangerous crises in the country's history when severe fighting broke out between Palestinians living in Lebanon and the Lebanese Army. Heavy casualties were suffered on both sides and President Franjieh declared a state of emergency, but a civil war was narrowly avoided and a compromise agreement reached with the Palestinian guerrilla leaders. A grave new danger arose with the outbreak of the Arab-Israeli war in October, but Franjieh and his government succeeded in keeping Lebanon out of the fighting.

Franjieh was elected president by the National Assembly in August 1970 by 50 votes to 49, the smallest majority in the republic's history. He was opposed by followers of former president Fuad Chehab but was supported by both right- and left-wing elements. Born June 14, 1910, a member of the influential Maronite Christian clan of Zgharta in northern Lebanon, Franjieh entered the family business after completing his studies in Beirut and soon showed his financial and business ability. In 1960 Franjieh decided to enter political life by taking over the parliamentary seat traditionally held by his family, his elder brother Hamid having retired because of ill health in 1956. He held ministerial posts in the Cabinets headed by Saeb Salam (1960–61), Abdullah Yafi (1968), and Rashid Karami (1969–70). As minister of economy in the Karami government he acquired a reputation as a shrewd and forceful negotiator with the oil companies.

On becoming president Franjieh did much to restore stability and business confidence, which had suffered severely under his predecessor. Although he was conservative and a strong believer in Lebanese independence within the Arab world, his government established reasonably friendly relations with the other Arab states. However, his relations with Syria underwent severe strain as a result of the May 1973 crisis, the Syrians suspecting his real objective to be outright suppression of the Palestinian movement in Lebanon. (PETER MANSFIELD)

GENEEN, HAROLD SYDNEY

As chairman and chief executive officer of International Telephone and Telegraph Corp., Harold S. Geneen was the controlling genius behind the eighth largest industrial concern in the U.S. and the biggest of all multinational conglomerates. Under Geneen's management, ITT had consistently published impressive earnings reports and appeared immune to attack—until it suddenly became the focus of suspicions that it was tampering with both domestic and foreign politics.

ITT's problems began shortly after the 1970 settlement of an antitrust suit by the U.S. Justice Department, when the corporation was ordered to divest itself of several companies but was allowed to retain the valuable Hartford Fire Insurance and Casualty Co. Geneen had barely finished assuring uneasy stockholders that the divestitures had actually resulted in profits when publication of a secret memo allegedly written by ITT lobbyist Dita Beard aroused speculation concerning the relationship between the favourable antitrust settlement and financial support of the Republican national convention by ITT-owned Sheraton Hotels. While this matter was still under investigation, ITT was accused of attempting to initiate and underwrite the cost of CIA intervention in Chile, where its interests appeared threatened. Salvador Allende subsequently nationalized ITT's telephone company holdings.

Born in Bournemouth, Eng., Jan. 22, 1910, Harold Geneen was brought to the U.S. by his parents in 1911 and became naturalized in 1918. After graduating from New York University in 1934, he worked as an accountant and held upper-management positions with several companies before coming to ITT. In the years after he took control of ITT in 1959, the corporation, once chiefly concerned with overseas telecommunications systems, made a rapid and voracious series of domestic acquisitions. In the process of consuming over two hundred companies, ITT's internal revenues rose to an estimated \$8.5 billion, and Geneen's annual salary of \$812,494 made him one of the highest paid corporate executives in the United States in 1972.

His identity merged with that of the corporation. He had no hobbies or interests outside of business; he traveled only on ITT business on ITT jets, and was reputed to work 19 hours a day. Throughout the conglomerate, a constant flow of detail moved upward to Geneen, enabling him, it was said, to develop countermeasures to problems before they occurred. He was succeeded as president Jan. 1, 1973, by Francis J. Dunleavy. At 63, Geneen was two years away from mandatory retirement, but observers predicted he would remain, working to mold ITT into an enduring corporate structure stamped in his own image.

(DONALD J. KLIMOVICH)

GISCARD D'ESTAING, VALÉRY

Although by 1973 Valéry Giscard d'Estaing had been France's minister of economy and finance for some eight years, at 47 he was the youngest among potential candidates for the presidency in succession to Georges Pompidou (*q.v.*). He was also a veteran among them, for as early as 1965 he had been hoping to succeed Charles de Gaulle. Two elements in his brilliant and precocious career (he was a *député* at 29 and a secretary of state at 32) characterized this outsider in the race for the Élysée.

First, Giscard was generally thought of as the most effective administrator of France's prosperity. Since 1959 he had spent 13 years in the Ministry of Economy and Finance, first as secretary of state until 1962, then as minister, with a single break of one year (1967–68) during which he was president of the finance committee in the National Assembly. He was seen as an expert among experts, admired for his amazing intellect, cool and relaxed temperament, self-assurance, and determined energy. These qualities were fully tested in 1973, when the government's economic and social policies were threatened by the pressures of inflation and the energy crisis.

Second, Giscard was not only an unrivaled technician but also a political animal. He was leader of the Independent Republicans, a group associated with the Gaullists in the governmental majority, and his ambition was to unite under him all the moderates and liberals currently dispersed in the reformist centre, the Gaullist Union des Démocrates pour la République (UDR), and the conservative right. These two aspects of his political personality allowed him to play a double role and to appear to the public both as an active statesman and as an often critical and sometimes independent or even hostile associate of Gaullism in power. Of course, this duality would have to be reconciled if he were one day to be elected to the presidency—for which he would need the support of Gaullist voters. Nonetheless, his originality and authority made him one of the two or three most influential men in French public life.

Giscard was born in Koblenz, Ger., on Feb. 2, 1926. Educated at the Lycée Janson-de-Sailly in Paris, at the École Polytechnique, and at the École Nationale d'Administration (1949–51), he became an inspector of finances in 1954 and was elected *député* for Puy-de-Dôme in 1956.

(PIERRE VIANSSON-PONTÉ)

GOWON, YAKUBU

Nigeria's head of state emerged in 1973 as a spokesman for the entire African continent. Yakubu Gowon addressed the UN General Assembly as chairman of the Organization of African Unity; he attended the summit conference of nonaligned nations in Algiers; he identified his country with the more militant African attitudes on southern Africa; he also strongly supported the creation of a single economic community for West Africa, a policy that was not popular with the French government; he gave only reluctant support to African negotiations for some independent link with the EEC but rejected the idea of associate status; he paid his first state visit to Britain in 1973; and he led the Nigerian delegation to the Commonwealth conference in Ottawa. At home, he continued to consolidate his personal supremacy, while encouraging public debate on Nigeria's return to civilian rule in 1976.

Robert Louis Fosse

FRANK EDWARDS—FOTOS INTERNATIONAL/ PICTORIAL PARADE

Harold Sydney Geneen

WIDE WORLD

Yakubu Gowon

WIDE WORLD

When Gowon took power in August 1966, he was an obscure lieutenant colonel, not yet 32, and completely apolitical. Faced almost immediately with the Ibo attempt to secede into a Biafran republic, Gowon won the respect even of his military opponents by his humanitarian conduct during the bloody civil war. It was largely due to his personal influence that, when the war suddenly ended in January 1970, a remarkable reconciliation became possible between victor and vanquished.

Gowon was born in 1934 of Christian parents belonging to the minority Pankshin tribe on the Benue Plateau. He was educated by Christian missionaries before attending a government secondary school. On leaving school he joined the Army and was chosen for officer training in Britain. He was the first Nigerian to be appointed as adjutant to a battalion, and he served twice with the UN forces in the Congo (1960–61, 1962). Promotion followed quickly, first to the rank of lieutenant colonel and later as adjutant general of the Nigerian Army. During the first army coup in January 1966 Gowon played a leading role in helping to maintain discipline among the troops. When the second coup occurred in August 1966, he was chosen as the head of the federal military government and commander in chief of the armed forces. (COLIN LEGUM)

GRECHKO, ANDREY ANTONOVICH

On Oct. 11, 1973, within a week of the outbreak of the new Arab-Israeli war, the Soviet minister of defense, Marshal Andrey A. Grechko, attended a ceremony in Warsaw marking the 30th anniversary of the birth of the Polish People's Army. It thus fell to Grechko to make one of the first Soviet ministerial references to the event—appropriately enough, since he had been responsible for organizing the massive rearmament of the Arab armies after the previous war in 1967, the year he was named defense minister.

In his speech Grechko said that "in the imperialist countries there are influential circles which would like to return to the . . . cold war," that it was these circles that had engineered a new war, compelling the Arab nations to take up arms again to repel the Israeli aggressors. "In these conditions," he went on, "the U.S.S.R. . . . and other countries of the socialist community consider as their immensely important duty to continue in improving their military collaboration, in increasing their political vigilance and the fighting readiness of their armed forces."

A week later Grechko was honoured on his 70th birthday with the award of a second Gold Star medal "for his great services to the Communist Party and the Soviet state." He had received his first Gold Star medal, with the title of Hero of the Soviet Union, in 1958.

Grechko was born on Oct. 17, 1903, at Golodayevka (later Kuibyshevo), Rostov region, the son of a peasant. He left school in 1919 to join the 1st Cavalry Army under S. M. Budenny (*see* OBITUARIES), in which he rose to squadron commander. By 1939–40, during the Soviet-Finnish war, he was chief of staff of a cavalry division, and during World War II he commanded successively the 12th, 47th, 18th, 56th, and 1st Guards armies. After the war he commanded the Kiev military district, becoming in June 1953 commander in chief of Soviet forces in East Germany. In November 1957 he was recalled to Moscow to serve as first deputy minister of defense, and from 1960 until becoming chief minister in 1967 he was also commander in chief of Warsaw Pact forces. A full member of the Central Committee of the Communist Party of the Soviet Union from 1961, Grechko was elected a full member of the Politburo on April 27, 1973. (K. M. SMOGORZEWSKI)

GRIVAS, GEORGIOS

An ambitious Greek Army officer with a predilection for conspiracy, Georgios Grivas had become famous in the 1950s, under his nom de guerre "Dighenis," as leader of EOKA (Ethniki Organosis Kypriakou Agonos, or National Organization of Cypriot Struggle), whose aim was to end British rule in Cyprus by means of a terrorist campaign. That aim was eventually achieved in 1960, but conflict between the Greek and Turkish communities over the new constitution continued, and in 1973 Grivas, a staunch champion of *enosis* (union of Cyprus with Greece), was once again in the news, this time as an opponent of Archbishop Makarios, president of the island republic since its independence. Several attempts on Makarios' life during the year were attributed to followers of Grivas, while in September the latter alleged that gunmen had been sent from Greece "to capture or kill" him.

Following the independence struggle, Grivas had first reappeared in Cyprus in June 1964, three months after a UN peacekeeping force had been established on the island under conditions of virtual civil war. Makarios appointed him to command the Greek-Cypriot National Guard, but communal violence continued, and in 1967, in order to ease tension with Turkey, the Greek government recalled him. In 1971 Grivas returned secretly to Cyprus, and it was suggested that Makarios might be willing to offer him a ministerial post if he were to accept the principle of independence rather than *enosis*. In September 1973 Grivas declared that Cyprus would be lost to Greece if Makarios continued his current policies.

Grivas was born at Trikomo, near Famagusta, Cyprus, on March 23, 1898. He took Greek nationality and joined the Officer Cadets' School in Athens, being commissioned in 1919. He took part in the Greek invasion of Turkey (1920–22) and later graduated from the Greek Staff College and the École Supérieure in Paris. A major in 1938, he fought against the Italian invasion of Greece (1940–41). Demobilized as lieutenant colonel, he remained in Greece under German occupation and organized a right-wing royalist resistance group. A failed candidate in the Greek elections of 1946 and 1950, he returned to Cyprus in 1952. (K. M. SMOGORZEWSKI)

GROMYKO, ANDREY ANDREYEVICH

Senior member of the world's fraternity of foreign ministers and a full member of the Central Committee of the Communist Party of the Soviet Union (from 1956) and the Politburo (April 27, 1973), Andrey A. Gromyko made two major statements on Soviet foreign policy in the course of his worldwide diplomatic journeyings in 1973. On July 3, in Helsinki, Fin., he opened the first stage of the Conference on Security and Cooperation in Europe. He won this honour over the 35 foreign ministers present not by seniority or by ballot but by having one of his officials rise early to ensure that his (Gromyko's) name headed the list. His opening address included a draft of the principles governing relations between states that the U.S.S.R. would like to see endorsed. "It is especially important," he said, "that the principles of peaceful coexistence should be used in full measure in a Europe crossed from north to south by the visible borderline between two social worlds."

NICHOLAS TSIKOURIAS—GREEK PHOTO AGENCY/KEYSTONE

Georgios Grivas (left)

ALAIN DEJEAN—GAMMA

Andrey Andreyevich Gromyko

On September 25, speaking in New York before the UN General Assembly, Gromyko stated that the period of tension in the world was receding while the movement toward détente and economic cooperation was growing. Convinced that the world was at a "turning point," he proposed that the five nuclear powers all agree to cut their defense budgets by 10%.

Gromyko was born on July 6, 1909, at Staryye Gromyki, Belorussia, into a peasant family. An economist by education, in 1939 he became head of the American division of the People's Commissariat of Foreign Affairs and counselor at the Soviet embassy in Washington, where he succeeded Maksim Litvinov as ambassador in August 1943. After attending the Dumbarton Oaks and San Francisco conferences that preceded formation of the UN, in April 1946 he became permanent Soviet delegate to the UN Security Council. He became deputy foreign minister in 1946, was ambassador to the U.K. from June 1952 to April 1953, and on Feb. 15, 1957, succeeded D. T. Shepilov as foreign minister. (K. M. SMOGORZEWSKI)

GUY, THEODORE W.

In late May, two weeks after Pres. Richard Nixon's banquet honouring 566 returned prisoners of the Vietnam war, Air Force Col. Theodore W. Guy filed charges against eight enlisted men who had been confined with him in a prison camp near Hanoi, accusing them of misconduct, failure to adhere to military discipline, and collaborating with the enemy. Acting on his own initiative after attempts to discourage him were reportedly made by both civilian and military Pentagon officials, Guy seemed to repudiate the official atmosphere of forgiveness established by former secretary of defense Melvin R. Laird. The secretaries of the Army and Navy reluctantly convened an investigation to determine whether the charges were sufficient to warrant court-martial proceedings against the eight in spite of the "mitigating circumstances" of having spent almost five years in prison camps after being captured in South Vietnam.

A career officer with 20 years in the U.S. Air Force, 44-year-old Theodore Guy of Tucson, Ariz., was piloting an F-4 fighter-bomber over Laos in 1968 when his plane was shot down. After his capture, he was taken to a prison camp, where 108 American and other prisoners, both military and civilian, were interned. As senior officer, he set up a chain of command at the POW camp, and though most of his time was spent in solitary confinement, Guy, who had the code name "Moses," issued orders by tapping in code on the walls of his cell. During this time he reinforced his reputation as a strict adherent of military discipline by exhibiting bravery and leadership in spite of frequent brutal beatings by prison guards. He ordered that public antiwar statements by prisoners were to taper off and then desist completely; later, he said that those orders were not obeyed by the eight accused collaborators.

The eight men publicly denied the charges; one, Marine Sgt. Abel Larry Kavanaugh, shot and killed himself on June 27, the day before he was to report to Camp Pendleton, California, his request for a discharge having been denied. After his death, the secretaries of the Army and Navy announced that Guy's charges were based on hearsay and circumstantial evidence and that prosecution would mean a long and bitter trial that would probably result in acquittal. Although the Army said that five of the accused soldiers would not be allowed to reenlist, further investigations were brought to an end.

(DONNA ZIMMERMAN)

HAIG, ALEXANDER

By the middle of 1973, the administration of U.S. Pres. Richard Nixon (*q.v.*) had been so scarred by the Watergate scandal that there was a need to graft a new complexion onto it. So, on May 4, President Nixon named Gen. Alexander M. Haig, Jr., to replace H. R. Haldeman as White House chief of staff in a reorganization that also brought in former secretary of defense Melvin Laird as a presidential adviser. But the new openness in the White House promised by these moves failed to materialize. Laird planned to leave in early 1974. Haig, though less rigid than his predecessor, appeared to lack Haldeman's influence.

Haig was considered the new breed of army officer, half militarist and half diplomat. In 1969, he was hired by Henry A. Kissinger, then Nixon's national security adviser, and he soon became Kissinger's deputy. He managed Kissinger's 120-man staff for four years and was so trusted by Kissinger that he sometimes filled in for the future secretary of state at White House briefings.

On Jan. 4, 1973, Haig, who had been made a four-star general in September 1972, was appointed vice-chief of staff of the Army. He bade farewell to Kissinger and the White House staff, thinking the move was permanent. But it lasted barely five months. By August 1 Haig had retired from the Army after 26 years of service and begun a new career.

Haig was born in Philadelphia on Dec. 2, 1924. He attended Notre Dame University for a year in 1943 and then won a wartime appointment to the U.S. Military Academy, where he was graduated in 1947. He served on the staff of Gen. Douglas MacArthur during the Korean War. During the early days of the war in Vietnam, Secretary of Defense Robert McNamara kept Haig in Washington as a special assistant. Haig finally got to Vietnam for two years in 1966 and commanded first a battalion and then a brigade in combat. He was seriously wounded and had several close brushes with death. During his military career, he earned the Distinguished Service Cross, the Silver Star, the Bronze Star, and the Air Medal.

(BILL GRANGER)

Alexander Haig

WIDE WORLD

HAMMER, ARMAND

In the spring of 1973, 75-year-old Armand Hammer, a nonpracticing physician with a 50-year history of amiable and lucrative business dealings with Soviet officials, once again pulled off cultural and industrial coups. Hammer, the chairman of Occidental Petroleum Corp., loaned part of his extensive art collection to the U.S.S.R. in exchange for the first exhibition of Soviet-owned Western Impressionist and Postimpressionist paintings to be shown in the U.S. In April he announced the largest commercial agreement in the history of U.S.–Soviet trade: a multibillion-dollar barter of Soviet ammonia and urea for U.S. fertilizer. Under other agreements, Occidental would trade and furnish technical assistance in several additional areas, including the exploration, production, and marketing of crude oil and natural gas.

The grandson of a Russian émigré whose family made and lost a shipbuilding fortune, Hammer was born in New York City on May 21, 1898. While still a medical student at Columbia, Armand, with his brothers, took over the nearly bankrupt family pharmaceutical business in 1918 and parlayed it into his first million. He still managed to rank among the top ten in his class but, impatient with the six-month wait before his internship began, he sold his pharmaceutical interests and went to Russia to combat a typhus epidemic. Convinced that starvation among the Russian people was imminent, he bartered surplus U.S. wheat for furs, hides, and caviar. Lenin was impressed with his business talents and he was given industrial and sales concessions. His pencil factory was still in operation in the U.S.S.R. in 1973.

In 1930 Hammer sold his enterprises to the Soviets and returned to the U.S., where he made more millions in the liquor and livestock businesses. After a brief retirement, in 1957 he financed two wildcat oil strikes for tiny Occidental Petroleum Corp. He subsequently bought a controlling interest in the company, and during the next decade its net worth rose from $125,000 to many millions of dollars. In the 1970s, however, Occidental fell into a deep profit slump. In 1971 the company lost $88 million on a poorly timed tanker fleet charter; Libya severely cut the company's oil production and export levels in 1972 and nationalized 51% of its Libyan holdings a year later. During a series of meetings with Soviet officials in Moscow in July, Hammer announced, "I have a great debt to the Russian people, and though I am an old man . . . I will pay it." A successful repayment would also have enormous benefits for Occidental.

(DONALD J. KLIMOVICH)

HARRIS, THOMAS A.

Though Thomas A. Harris, M.D., published *I'm OK—You're OK* in 1969, it took three years for the book to catch fire and a fourth to make his name a household word in some intellectual neighbourhoods. By 1973 the book had sold more than one million copies in hardcover, had been on the *New York Times* best-seller list for more than a year, and had a huge paperback sale.

Harris' thesis in the book is that within each individual are three distinct role-playing personality facets: child, adult, and parent, terms that have special meanings in Harris' context of transactional analysis. In the ideally adjusted mature person, the adult aspect of the personality is the rational, self-controlled master of the reactionary, negativistic parent and of the fun-loving, sexual, inventive child. When people converse or communicate in a "transaction," Harris posits, things go awry if their subpersonalities don't mesh—if one's child reacts to another's parent facet, for instance, or vice versa.

Invented by the late Eric Berne, M.D., this general and pragmatic approach to emotional anatomy threatened to eclipse Freudian analysis. One reason for this was that Freudian theory stresses the importance of psychosexual development in a person's formative years, matters that only seem to sort themselves out after three to five years of two-to-five-times-a-week sessions between patient and analyst. Transactional analysis, which is usually conducted in group sessions with a leader and perhaps a dozen participating subjects, has had some success in relieving painful symptoms.

Harris himself had been an orthodox psychiatrist for most of his career. Born in Mineola, Tex., in 1910, he trained at Temple University Medical School and was, for a time, psychiatric chief of the Navy Bureau of Medicine and Surgery. While practicing in Sacramento, Calif., in 1957, he heard Berne address a medical meeting. "This wasn't just another paper, but indeed a blueprint of the mind, which no one had constructed before, along with a precision vocabulary, which anybody could understand, to identify parts of the blueprint. This vocabulary has made it possible for two people to talk about behavior and know what is meant," he wrote.

(PHILIP KOPPER)

HAYDEN, MELISSA

When Melissa Hayden announced that she would retire from the New York City Ballet at the end of the 1973 summer season, company director George Balanchine paid her the ultimate compliment. To honour her contributions to the company, he created *Cortège hongrois* especially for her. The work was premiered in May, and she danced it at her farewell performance on September 1 at Wolf Trap Farm Park near Washington, D.C.

She was born Mildred Herman on April 25, 1923, in Toronto. After beginning her ballet training with Boris Volkoff in Toronto, she moved in 1945 to New York City. There she joined the corps de ballet at Radio City Music Hall and continued her ballet studies, with Anatole Vitzak and Ludmila Shollar and at the School of American Ballet. She danced with Ballet Theatre (now American Ballet Theatre) and toured South America with Ballet Alicia Alonso before joining the New York City Ballet in 1949. She returned to Ballet Theatre in 1953 but rejoined the New York City Ballet in 1955 and remained with them until her retirement. In 1952 she appeared in the Charlie Chaplin film *Limelight,* doubling for Claire Bloom in the dance sequences.

Among the best known of the ballets in which she performed were *The Cage, Medea, Agon, The Firebird, Stars and Stripes,* and *A Midsummer Night's Dream.* She was one of the first dancers to appear on television, and she pioneered the lecture-demonstration program in the New York City public schools. She also appeared in guest performances with the National Ballet of Canada, London's Royal Ballet, and many regional companies in the U.S. and Canada. Among the awards she received were the 1962 *Dance Magazine* and Albert Einstein Woman of Achievement awards and the 1973 Handel Medallion, New York City's highest cultural award. After her retirement from the New York City Ballet, she became artist in residence at Skidmore College in Saratoga Springs, N.Y. (BARBARA W. CLEARY)

HEATH, EDWARD RICHARD GEORGE

In his third year as prime minister of the United Kingdom, Edward Heath found himself managing a prices and wages freeze, followed by what were called Stage Two and Stage Three of a counterinflation program that involved a substantial degree of intervention in the economy. There was more than a little irony in this situation. Heath had led the Conservatives to victory in the 1970 general election on a program that promised instant action on rising prices and a return to the free market economy.

Like most other countries, Britain had been hit by a tidal wave of inflationary pressures that forced the Heath government to abandon much of conventional Conservative ideology. With prices rising at an unprecedented pace and earnings held down by statutory restraints, it was not surprising that opinion polls showed a deep decline both in support of the Conservative Party (which at one possibly freakish moment fell into third place behind Labour and Liberals) and in Heath's own personal standing. Toward year's end, with Britain already feeling the effects of the Arab oil embargo, Heath's worries were compounded by a head-on confrontation with the country's coal miners over wage claims.

Yet Heath's leadership of the Conservative Party was not seriously challenged (attacks on him by Enoch Powell enjoyed no more than fringe support). If anything, the difficulties of 1973 confirmed his personal qualities of determination and fixity of purpose in battling through unfavourable political weather. His political consistency was demonstrated by his unwavering belief that Britain's future lay in Europe and his success in securing British membership in the EEC, effective January 1. He defended intervention in economic affairs, saying, "I never have been a laissez-faire Tory at any time in my life." Indeed, he was increasingly critical of some aspects of capitalist society, showing considerable impatience with industry's neglect of capital investment and, in a much-quoted phrase, referring to certain City scandals as "the unpleasant and unacceptable face of capitalism."

Heath was born at Broadstairs, Kent, on July 9, 1916, the son of a carpenter who later became a builder, and went via the local grammar school and a scholarship to Oxford University. First elected to Parliament in 1950, he rapidly advanced in the Conservative Party, being given the influential post of chief whip in 1955. He was elected leader of the Conservative Party in 1965. (HARFORD THOMAS)

HERNÁNDEZ COLÓN, RAFAEL

The fourth elected and youngest governor of Puerto Rico, Rafael Hernández Colón took office Jan. 2, 1973, after defeating incumbent governor Luis Ferré by a surprisingly large number of votes. He was an advocate of continuing commonwealth status, mainly because he believed that independence or statehood would result in economic chaos and political ruin, and his overwhelming victory appeared to be a popular rebuttal of Ferré's statehood platform. During his campaign, the protégé of Popular Democratic Party founder and former governor Luis Muñoz Marín attacked the Ferré government's inability to cope with the island's chronic social and economic problems of rising inflation and unemployment, unequal distribution of wealth, inadequate housing, overpopulation, and drug abuse.

Born Oct. 24, 1936, in Ponce, the second largest Puerto Rican city, Hernández Colón grew up in comfortable surroundings as the son of Rafael Hernández Matos, a successful lawyer who served as a Supreme Court judge from 1957 through the 1960s. Graduating from Johns Hopkins University in 1956, he attended law school at the University of Puerto Rico and later practiced law in Ponce and joined the Popular Democratic Party. He was appointed attorney general in 1965 and ran successfully for the Senate in 1968 in spite of a seemingly disastrous split within his party. Becoming party president in 1969, he accomplished both the reconstruction of the party and the paying off of its $6 million debt.

After taking office Hernández Colón applied himself to the island's discouraging economic picture, which included problems in the major industries of sugar and tourism. But in July a series of violent strikes by employees of the government-owned power company, firemen, and the Electrical Workers Union crippled numerous hotels and factories, causing layoffs of 19,000 members of the labour force. After firemen refused to obey a court order to return to work, Hernández Colón called out the National Guard to take over firefighting equipment and safeguard power company installations. This action provoked severe criticism and protest demonstrations by the pro-independence Socialist and Independence parties. (DONNA ZIMMERMAN)

HOVING, THOMAS PEARSALL FIELD

As New York Mayor John Lindsay's park commissioner in the 1960s, Tom Hoving had been largely responsible for the "fun city" image the Lindsay administration projected. So in 1967, when he became the youngest director in the history of the Metropolitan Museum of Art, it was widely assumed that he would bring some much-needed liveliness to that venerable institution. Liveliness the museum had in 1973, as it found itself in the eye of two storms that rocked the art world.

One concerned a Greek vase decorated by the painter and potter Euphronius, purchased by the Met for over $1 million. "The histories of art will have to be rewritten," Hoving said in 1972 when he announced the acquisition. The first chapter of the revision appeared in February 1973, when the *New York Times* reported that the vase had apparently been stolen and smuggled out of Italy, reaching the Met through a series of shadowy deals.

The other controversy involved deaccessioning. Since 1972 the Met had sold or traded some 50 of 211 paintings willed to it by Adelaide de Groot. The Met had also been considering for public sale a number of famous works, among them Picasso's "Woman in White." In the case of the de Groot legacy, critics charged that Hoving had disposed of important works to raise cash but had tried to conceal it by making special arrangements with favoured dealers. A further factor was that Mrs. de Groot had indicated she wanted her pictures to either remain at the Met permanently or be given to other museums.

In neither case were Hoving and the Met engaging in practices unique to them. Some critics said there was hardly a museum in the U.S. that did not have some valuable antiquity acquired through questionable channels. Deaccessioning had been debated for years, defended by some as the logical way to cull a museum's collection, attacked by others as a raid on the public patrimony. At midyear the Met announced new procedures designed to provide greater disclosure of its transactions, but the argument showed no signs of abating. Essentially, the lines were drawn between the museum establishment—of which Hoving, despite his much-publicized populism, was a part—and the new view of museums as belonging to—and answerable to—the public.

Born in New York City, Jan. 15, 1931, Hoving first became interested in art when he was a student at Princeton. He joined the Met staff in 1959 and was curator of medieval art before entering the Lindsay administration in 1966. (DANIEL MILLER)

HOWE, SIR (RICHARD EDWARD) GEOFFREY

Sometimes spoken of as the most brilliant man in the British Cabinet, Sir Geoffrey Howe, in 1973 still only in his 40s, was eyed as a likely future prime minister. It was the kind of reputation that a politician can find dangerous and even damaging to his prospects. Nevertheless, Howe had already had a big hand in shaping some of the most important changes made by Edward Heath's government. As solicitor general he had been concerned with the drafting and successful passage of the legislation for Britain's entry into the European Economic Community, and he also worked on the Industrial Relations Act, 1971. Then, as Britain's first minister for trade and consumer affairs, from November 1972, he masterminded the Fair Trading Act, with its provisions for consumer protection.

AUTHENTICATED NEWS INTERNATIONAL

Melissa Hayden

BRUCE DAVIDSON—MAGNUM

Thomas Pearsall Field Hoving

With such a record it was not surprising that the prime minister should bring Howe into the Cabinet even though he was not in charge of a department of his own but was one of a number of ministers at the Department of Trade and Industry. What was particularly significant was that Howe should echo many of Heath's views about fairness and openness in the economy and in the processes of government.

Born Dec. 20, 1926, Howe made a career in the law for some years after leaving Cambridge University. He was briefly a member of Parliament in the 1960s (1965–66), and did not secure the safe Conservative seat of Reigate until 1969. But from his Cambridge days he had been continuously and prominently active in Conservative politics, and was one of the principal creators of the Bow Group, an intellectual gathering of younger Conservatives with reformist leanings; he became managing director and then editor of the group's magazine *Crossbow,* which made a considerable impact on Conservative thinking. Among his special interests as a lawyer were racial discrimination, discrimination against women, and the legal rights of young people.

(HARFORD THOMAS)

HUSSEIN IBN TALAL

In October 1973 King Hussein of Jordan made the difficult decision to involve his country in the fourth Arab-Israeli war and sent troops to the Syrian front. He had hesitated, having previously made it clear that Jordan would not join another war against Israel because it would be disastrous and because he still hoped to recover lost Jordanian territory by diplomatic means. But pressure from other Arab countries—including Egypt and Syria, with which he had just been reconciled—overcame his reluctance. His relations with the Palestinian guerrillas and the Arabs of the West Bank had remained strained since the civil war of 1970. His proposals made in March 1972 for a federal state to include the East and West banks of the Jordan and to be known as the United Arab Kingdom, with a regional government for the West Bank, had been almost unanimously denounced by other Arab states.

Jordanian troops did not take part in the initial attack by the Egyptians and Syrians in the October 1973 war, and Hussein remained on the fringe of subsequent discussions among Arab leaders. He did not attend the Arab summit meeting in Algiers in November. On December 19 he visited Pres. Hafez al-Assad of Syria in Damascus in a vain effort to persuade him that Syria should take part in the Geneva peace talks, at which Hussein was represented by his prime minister, Zaid ar-Rifai.

Born in Amman on Nov. 14, 1935, Hussein was educated in England at Harrow School and the Royal Military Academy at Sandhurst. In 1951 his grandfather, King Abdullah, was assassinated before his eyes, and he became king the following year after his father, King Talal, had been declared mentally ill. Although receptive to new ideas, Hussein maintained strong convictions concerning his family's hereditary right to rule. Of proved personal courage, he sometimes showed rashness and haste in his political decisions, and his strongly pro-Western sympathies caused him frequent difficulties with his Palestinian subjects and other Arab nations. Even apart from constant border troubles with Israel and the disastrous involvement in the 1967 war, which lost half his country's territory to Israeli occupation, his reign was turbulent, with frequent internal unrest. His relations with Egypt, Syria, and Iraq were highly erratic. Only with the Saudi Arabian monarchy did he maintain consistently friendly ties, and he depended heavily on Saudi and U.S. financial aid. (PETER MANSFIELD)

HERBERT SPENCER—MAGNUM

King Hussein

JOBERT, MICHEL

After working for ten years in the shadow of Georges Pompidou, Michel Jobert emerged into the limelight after the 1973 general election as France's minister of foreign affairs. His career, with its sudden transition from obscurity to prominence, paralleled that of Pompidou himself, who after nearly ten years as Charles de Gaulle's confidential adviser was promoted overnight to premier, eventually succeeding de Gaulle as president. The comparison was all the more striking since both had served as director of the presidential cabinet, and up to the time of their appointment both were as influential in political circles as they were unknown to the general public. It was not surprising, therefore, that Jobert was among those most strongly favoured to succeed Pierre Messmer as premier when the latter came under strong attack at the end of the year for deficient leadership in the face of domestic unrest and international difficulties.

A former colleague of Pierre Mendès-France, Jobert was not a Gaullist. Spare and stern in appearance, short of stature and anything but verbose, after 25 years in financial administration and ministerial departments he had the reputation of a top civil servant, a man of files and dossiers with little or no experience of public life. As a minister, however, he quickly gained authority and proved himself an effective public speaker in Parliament and in international debate—notably when he crossed swords with U.S. Secretary of State Henry A. Kissinger, at the December meeting of NATO foreign ministers, over the failure of the U.S. to consult its allies at the time of the U.S. alert during the Middle East conflict.

Michel Jobert was born in Meknès, Morocco, Sept. 11, 1921, the son of an agricul-

tural expert. A former pupil of the École Nationale d'Administration, he became *conseiller-maître* in the Court of Accounts. During 1952–61 he served in various ministries. He joined Pompidou in 1963 during the latter's premiership and became assistant director and then director of his cabinet (1966), general secretary to the presidency (1969), and finally foreign minister (April 1973).
(PIERRE VIANSSON-PONTÉ)

KATZIR, EPHRAIM

On May 24, 1973, Ephraim Katchalski was formally inaugurated as Israel's fourth president, in succession to Zalman Shazar, and hebraized his name on taking office. As the candidate of the ruling Labour Party, he had been elected by secret ballot of the Knesset on April 10, receiving 66 votes against 41 for Ephraim Urbach, candidate of the National Religious Party.

Although Katzir had held no political office before, and despite the fact that his presidency bestowed no executive power, he made it clear that he did not intend to remain silent on affairs of state. He saw it as his task to project the intellectual, moral, and spiritual values of the state, and he intended to make every effort to close the wide gap in education and social well-being between Oriental and Western Jews, and to promote understanding between Israeli Jews and their Arab neighbours.

As a scientist, Katzir was particularly concerned with the role of the scientific community, which annually spent about 2½% of Israel's gross national product on research and development. He commented: "No decent scientist can escape the feeling that science has sometimes misused its findings. One must find ways to protect society from this." "Scientists . . . must make an earnest and continuing effort to understand politics, economy, the structure of society, even though they are not and should not be decision-makers."

Ephraim Katzir was born in Kiev, Russia, on May 16, 1916, and was brought to Palestine by his parents when he was nine. After graduating from the Hebrew University of Jerusalem, he became an assistant in the university's department of theoretical and macromolecular chemistry (1941–45). During this period he was also a research fellow at Columbia University, and was active in the preindependence underground Jewish army, Haganah, to which he became scientific adviser. In 1949 he was appointed acting head of the department of biophysics in the Weizmann Institute of Science at Rehovot, later becoming its director. A recognized authority on proteins, in 1966 he became the first Israeli to be elected to the U.S. National Academy of Sciences. He was chief scientific adviser to the Israeli Ministry of Defense (1966–68).
(R. J. M. DENNERSTEIN)

KAUNDA, KENNETH

Because of tribal strains, political violence at home, and pressures on his nation's borders, Pres. Kenneth Kaunda of Zambia in 1973 fell into line with most of the African continent and imposed single-party rule on his country. He adopted a constitutional approach to "one-party democracy" similar to that pioneered by his neighbour Pres. Julius Nyerere of Tanzania. Kaunda was inevitably reelected to the presidency for a third term in the general election of December 5, winning 80% of votes cast. However, nowhere did the turnout exceed 52.2% of eligible voters, and in some places it fell as low as 18.1% (compared with 77% in the 1968 election). Whether this was through apathy or protest was hard to tell. Several days later the president announced that, for the first time, his new government would contain members of the armed forces, in order to give genuine representation to all sectors of the Zambian community.

Following the closing of the border with Rhodesia in January, Kaunda successfully appealed to the UN for international economic and diplomatic support. In September Kaunda and Nyerere celebrated completion of the first stage of the Chinese-built Tanzam railway to the border between their two countries.

Kaunda's crusade on racial questions was dictated partly by his belief in nonracial societies and his personal philosophy of nonviolence, and partly by the strategic location of his country. His "humanitarianism," elevated into a state philosophy, was strongly influenced by his mission-school upbringing in Bomba Province, where he was born in 1924. Trained as a teacher, at 21 he joined the African National Congress which spearheaded the independence movement in Northern Rhodesia. He helped found the United National Independence Party, which became the ruling party after Zambian independence in 1964, with himself as its first president. In 1968 he helped formulate the Lusaka Manifesto, signed by 14 east and central African states, which offered a nonviolent program for constitutional change in white-ruled states of southern Africa through peaceful negotiations. The failure of this move led Kaunda to throw in his lot with the "liberation movements" and thereby involved Zambia in direct military confrontation with its neighbours.
(COLIN LEGUM)

KELLEY, CLARENCE MARION

When Clarence M. Kelley became director of the U.S. Federal Bureau of Investigation in July 1973, he had two tough acts to follow. J. Edgar Hoover, who served as FBI director for more than 40 years, had made the bureau the most widely respected agency of the federal government. But under L. Patrick Gray, who succeeded Hoover as acting director after the latter's death in May 1972, the FBI's morale and public image suffered. Much of the damage stemmed from Gray's admission that he had destroyed materials bearing on the Watergate case. Kelley's primary mission, then, was to restore confidence in and within the bureau.

In a series of interviews, Kelley described how he intended to achieve this goal. "For 40 years the FBI had excellent management based on the strengths of one man, Mr. Hoover," he told the *Christian Science Monitor*. "The strength I will bring will be to put into effect . . . good, fresh managerial and general operational procedures."

In a *U.S. News & World Report* interview, he acknowledged that "An immediate problem is to restore the stature—the image—of the agency and repair what damage may have been done to its morale by recent events, such as Watergate."

Clarence M. Kelley was born Oct. 24, 1911, in Kansas City, Mo. He served as an FBI agent in five different cities and as an assistant agent in charge of the bureau's field offices in Houston, Tex., Seattle, Wash., and San Francisco. At the time of his retirement from the FBI in 1961, Kelley was the special agent in charge of the bureau's field office in Memphis, Tenn.

Kelley's next job was chief of police of his native Kansas City. "I don't believe in such activities as police round-ups or vigilantes," he told an interviewer from that city. "I do subscribe to the theory that society has to place some restrictions on the police. . . . But the pendulum can swing too far the other way, and there is no question that police activity can be hampered by too severe an interpretation of constitutional rights." Kelley's view of his job evidently appealed to Pres. Richard Nixon. At Kelley's swearing-in ceremony in Kansas City on July 9, the president said that "a man who has been good for Kansas City will be very good for America."
(RICHARD L. WORSNOP)

KING, BILLIE JEAN

For several years Billie Jean King battled the old-guard arbiters of professional tennis

Billie Jean King

EPOQUE/PICTORIAL PARADE

Kenneth Kaunda

RUSSELL REIF—PICTORIAL PARADE

to win for women the same prerogatives and purses that men enjoyed. She was a successful bargainer partly, no doubt, because she and several like-minded women professionals played spectacular tennis that filled stadiums with old fans and new ones.

By 1971 the argument was moot, as Mrs. King became the first professional sportswoman to win $100,000 in a year, a feat she repeated in 1972. But it took an acknowledged male chauvinist to make her a superstar and give her the chance to earn at least $100,000 in a single evening's match—win, lose, or draw. The man, Bobby Riggs, had swept Wimbledon, winning the men's singles, men's doubles, and mixed doubles. But that took place in 1939, four years before Mrs. King was born Billie Jean Moffit in Long Beach, Calif. Ironically, Riggs too had complained about the hidebound traditionalists of tennis, claiming they had kept him off the prestigious Davis Cup team temporarily because he lacked a gentleman's airs.

At 55, Riggs had not competed in tournaments for many years. But when women started attracting real attention, he saw an opportunity to get back into tennis whites. "You insist that top women players provide a brand of tennis comparable to men's," he declared. "I challenge you to prove it. I contend that you not only cannot beat a top male player, but that you can't beat me, a tired old man." Australian star Margaret Court was the first to respond. In May Riggs defeated her 6–2, 6–1, and it was Mrs. King's turn to challenge.

Partly because of Riggs's energetic promotion, public interest in the match grew. A television network paid $750,000 to broadcast the prime-time event from the Houston (Tex.) Astrodome. An estimated 50 million Americans watched on television and the Astrodome itself drew more than 30,000 persons, the largest crowd ever to attend a tennis match.

Before the match, Riggs offered Mrs. King a three-foot Sugardaddy (a lollypop). She responded with a live pig, gift-wrapped. Soon after play began Mrs. King took control and never relinquished it, winning 6–4, 6–3, 6–3. Her triumph was another in a string that began with junior competition victories in 1958. Her first major win came at Wimbledon in 1966. (PHILIP KOPPER)

KOHL, HELMUT

Prime minister of Rhineland-Palatinate, one of West Germany's ten *Länder,* or states, Helmut Kohl was elected chairman of the Christian Democratic Union (CDU), the main opposition party in the Bundestag (federal parliament), on June 12, 1973. He succeeded Rainer Barzel, who resigned both from that post and from leadership of the joint parliamentary party of the CDU and the Christian Social Union (CSU).

Clarence Marion Kelley

WIDE WORLD

Kohl's election was unopposed, and he polled a large majority of the votes cast, but in spite of this degree of support, few considered him to be the party's new messiah. His election did not necessarily mean that he would be a candidate for the post of chancellor. That choice would be made not only by the CDU but also by the CSU, led by the powerful Franz Josef Strauss. Strauss, though he professed support for Kohl after the latter's election, had once referred to him as a "carpet slippers politician from the provinces."

Known as the "black giant" because of his bulk and swarthy complexion, Kohl had a good record as an administrator and reformer in his own state, but his abilities were known to relatively few people beyond the borders of the cozy Rhineland-Palatinate. He described himself as a middle-of-the-road politician—"certainly not a leftist." He was regarded as ambitious, but not unpleasantly pushing, although he had rated his chances too highly in 1971 when he stood for the chairmanship against Barzel and was defeated by 344 votes to 174. Little was known about his views on foreign policy. He described himself as a firm supporter of Western European integration and said that a CDU-CSU government would have to respect the treaties concluded with the Soviet Union, Poland, and East Germany.

Born into a Catholic family at Ludwigshafen on April 3, 1930, Kohl was educated at the universities of Frankfurt am Main and Heidelberg and took a degree in law. He joined the CDU at 17 and was elected to the state Landtag in 1959, becoming prime minister ten years later. He had been a member of the CDU national executive committee for many years and in 1969 was elected deputy chairman. (NORMAN CROSSLAND)

KORUTURK, FAHRI

Elected to the presidency of the republic by the Turkish Parliament on April 6, 1973, after 14 inconclusive ballots, Fahri Koruturk had all the qualities needed in a compromise candidate. A retired admiral, he had a military background like all former presidents but one. He was not, however, the favourite candidate of the military establishment. He had been placed on the retired list after the coup of May 27, 1960, and had not, therefore, been a beneficiary of military intervention in politics. As an independent senator, nominated by the outgoing president, Cevdet Sunay, he had had five years' parliamentary experience. He had spent many years in foreign posts and was on record as a supporter of NATO. His concern for social and economic progress, coupled with a military emphasis on law and order, stood him in good stead at a time when the left wing was gaining ground in Turkish politics, while the right-wing majority was deeply divided.

Fahri Koruturk was born in Istanbul in 1903 and was educated at the Naval School, from which he graduated in 1923. Much of his early military career was spent watching the Axis powers. Appointed to the intelligence department of the general staff in 1934, he served as Turkish military attaché in Rome, Berlin, and Stockholm between 1935 and 1943. He then returned home and proceeded to work his way up the promotion ladder, reaching the top in 1957 when he became commander of the Navy, with the rank of full admiral.

His experience in totalitarian countries stood him in good stead in 1960 when, after his retirement, he was appointed ambassador in Moscow. The Soviet government was then trying to repair its relations with Turkey by renouncing the territorial claims advanced by Stalin and offering economic help and even a measure of support for Turkey's stand over Cyprus. Koruturk helped shape Turkey's cautious response, giving away little and carefully scrutinizing the teeth of gift horses. A posting to Madrid followed before he retired from his second career and emerged as an elder statesman. His appointment to the Senate in 1968 recognized both his services and his status as a respected adviser. (ANDREW MANGO)

PICTORIAL PARADE

Kris Kristofferson

KRISTOFFERSON, KRIS

Drifter, songwriter, author, Golden Gloves boxer, army brat, celebrity, Kris Kristofferson won a reputation as an actor to watch in 1973 with the release of *Blume in Love.* In it he stole the protagonist's wife and the show from George Segal, a widely regarded dramatic and comedic star. Kristofferson was also acclaimed for his starring role in *Pat Garrett and Billy the Kid* (1973) and had previously been seen in Dennis Hopper's *The Last Movie* (1971) and had played the title role in *Cisco Pike* (1971), but his portrayal of a pot-smoking, guitar-playing, welfare-cheating, romantic, and fast-fisted civvie-of-fortune in *Blume in Love* was his most memorable role to date. One reason, perhaps, was that the character and the actor had some things in common.

Kristofferson was born just before World War II, the son of a career military aviation officer who retired from the U.S. Air Force as a major general. Much of his youth was spent around Brownsville, Tex.; then he attended Pomona (Calif.) College and studied as a Rhodes scholar at Oxford. In England he encountered a rock music promoter who dubbed him "Kris Carson" and prodded him onto the concert circuit—an experience he recalled as "really awful."

He returned to the U.S., married, entered the Army, and became a helicopter pilot. He was later assigned to teach English literature at West Point but never reported for duty. "I bailed out again and landed in Nashville." In that Tennessee city, the spiritual and recording capital of country and western music, he supported himself as a bartender and janitor and practiced a pastime he had first tried at 11: writing songs.

His first commercial venture was "Vietnam Blues" in 1965. Later came "For the Good Times," "Me and Bobby McGee," which was first recorded by Roger Miller and later by Janis Joplin, "Help Me Make It Through the Night," and "Sunday Mornin' Comin' Down," which won him the coveted Song of the Year award of the Nashville

Country Music Association in 1970. While acting, he continued to pursue his career as a singing composer with rare dedication. Once, when he was appearing in a Toronto coffeehouse, he persuaded the management to return the $3 admission fee to the patrons because he felt he had performed poorly.
(PHILIP KOPPER)

KÜNG, HANS

In the decade after Pope John XXIII convoked the Second Vatican Council (1962–65) to "let some fresh air into the Church," the Rev. Hans Küng had exerted significant theological leadership in the progressive wing of Roman Catholicism. His growing influence was accompanied by growing conflict with Vatican conservatives, and the conflict came to a head on July 5, 1973.

An irresistible force (Küng's historical and theological objections to papal infallibility) met an immovable object (the church's century-old dogma that the pope cannot err or teach error when he defines a doctrine of faith or morals). Neither gave way.

On July 5 the Sacred Congregation for the Doctrine of the Faith published its "Declaration in Defense of the Catholic Doctrine on the Church Against Certain Errors of the Present Day." The document was, in part, the Vatican's reply to Küng's book *Infallible? An Inquiry*. Catholics were warned to reject Küng's ideas. At the same time, he was ordered to submit to the doctrine as redefined in the statement or come to Rome for "examination."

Küng disregarded the order at first. Later, in what might have been an opening for a détente, he met with church officials directing the investigation of his theories. "I was always ready to go to Rome," he explained, "but under fair conditions, not as a defendant who had no right to examine the record, no way of choosing his own counsel, and no possibility of appeal."

The debate resulted in a new book in 1973, *Fallible?* (a symposium by various experts and Küng's summing up). In this book Küng went on to develop more fully his idea of the "indefectibility" of the church, the principle "of the Church being maintained in the truth despite all errors" by popes, prelates, and theologians. Once the stumbling block of infallibility was eliminated, Küng argued, all Christian churches could share in the conviction that God does and will continue to preserve his saving truth through the whole Church of Christ.

Born March 19, 1928, in Sursee, Switz., Küng studied at the Pontifical German College and the Pontifical Gregorian University in Rome and received a doctorate in sacred theology from the Catholic Institute at the Sorbonne in Paris. He was ordained a priest in 1954. In 1963 he became professor of dogmatic theology and director of the Institute for Ecumenical Research at the University of Tübingen, W.Ger. (DAVID MEADE)

LAURIN, LUCIEN

Canadian-born Lucien Laurin's long career as jockey and trainer was climaxed in 1973 when a horse he had trained, Secretariat, won Thoroughbred racing's Triple Crown: the Kentucky Derby, the Preakness, and the Belmont Stakes. Secretariat was the first Triple Crown winner since Citation in 1948 and only the ninth in 91 years.

With principal owner Penny Tweedy and jockey Ron Turcotte, Laurin completed a triumvirate that brought fame to Meadow Stable in Doswell, Va. Meadow Stable had come close to the Triple Crown in 1972, when Riva Ridge won the Derby and the Belmont. Secretariat completed the job in style, setting a new record in two of the three races.

Lucien Laurin was born in 1912 in Montreal and spent 12 years as a jockey before beginning a second career training horses in New England. He trained Quill, the champion two-year-old filly of 1958, and Amberoid, winner of the 1966 Belmont. After joining A. B. ("Bull") Hancock's Claiborne Farm in 1966, he saddled Dike to win the Wood Memorial.

In 1971 he succeeded his son Roger as trainer at Meadow Stable when the younger Laurin resigned to join Ogden Phipps's stable. He began training Secretariat for his apprenticeship as a two-year-old; "Big Red," as he was nicknamed, lost his first race at Aqueduct because of an accident at the starting gate, but he won his next nine starts and was named horse of the year—

KEN REGAN—CAMERA 5

Lucien Laurin

an unusual honour for so young a colt. Perhaps his most impressive performance was in the Belmont, at $1\frac{1}{2}$ mi. the longest track in the country. Bold Ruler's sons were supposed not to have staying power, and Laurin admitted he was worried when Secretariat took an early lead. But the big chestnut went on to win by 31 lengths, setting a new American record in the process. Late in the race Laurin had turned to Mrs. Tweedy and said, "To lose it now, he'll have to fall down."

Early in the year Secretariat had been syndicated for stud at over $6 million, and his racing career ended in October with a victory in the Canadian International Championship. His lifetime record was 16 wins in 21 starts, and his earnings totaled $1,316,808. "I never saw Man o' War," said the man who was instrumental in developing him, "but I did see Citation . . . and I thought he was a really great horse. . . . I may be prejudiced, but I have to say my horse is greater." (DANIEL MILLER)

LEBURTON, EDMOND JULES ISIDORE

When he presented his mammoth 36-member Socialist-Social Christian-Liberal government on Jan. 26, 1973, Socialist Party cochairman Edmond Leburton achieved a major political ambition. Belgium's new prime minister had taken the reins of government from the Social Christians, who had been the majority partner with the Socialists in the coalition that had ruled since 1968. Leburton had contributed to the downfall of Gaston Eyskens' government in September 1971, and, although the Social Christian-Socialist coalition under Eyskens had been preserved after the elections that November, there had been no doubt that Leburton favoured another formula. When Eyskens resigned in November 1972, he seemed to be the logical successor.

Always a man with a clear view of the problems, Leburton was not easily roused by the community passions that had shaken the country during the past decade, and had not hesitated to speak out against federalism, which he regarded as a step toward the ultimate division of the country into two or three more or less autonomous parts. He did not, however, view regionalization as a prelude to federalization.

Elected as co-chairman of the Socialist Party in January 1971, he watched with growing apprehension Eyskens' vain efforts to push through regionalization despite his

Maharaj Ji

SYGMA

lack of the necessary two-thirds majority in Parliament. Realizing that it could be achieved with the Liberals in a tripartite government, Leburton first set out to overcome his own party's aversion to the Liberals. However, he himself, as prime minister, had to contend with strong Flemish Social Christian opposition because of his sketchy knowledge of Dutch, the language of the majority of the Belgian population.

Born at Lantremange, now part of Waremme (Liège Province), on April 18, 1915, Leburton became a master of social and political science at Liège University before entering the Ministry of State Insurance. Mayor of his hometown since 1947, he earned himself the nickname "station-master of Waremme" when he personally stopped the trains on the main line between Brussels and West Germany during the big strikes of 1960–61. Only 31 when he first entered Parliament, he had been a member of several coalition governments. (JAN R. ENGELS)

LEWIS, DAVID

In August 1972 Canada's socialist New Democratic Party became a recognizable political force when, in an unprecedented sweep to power, it ended 20 years of Social Credit Party rule in British Columbia. Three months later the NDP solidified its victory on the national level by gaining enough seats in the new House of Commons to create a balance of power between Prime Minister Pierre Trudeau's Liberal Party and Robert L. Stanfield's Progressive Conservative Party. For the first time since its founding convention in 1961, the NDP was in a position to use its parliamentary voting bloc as a bargaining tool to accomplish some of its political goals. The man most responsible for these gains was party leader David Lewis.

By maintaining strict party discipline, Lewis was able to concentrate on such issues as "corporate rip-off" and unemployment, forcing both Liberals and Conservatives into defensive positions without pressing alternative socialist economic policies that would alienate conservative voters. During a deliberately austere campaign, Lewis constantly criticized the government's protective attitude toward foreign-dominated big businesses that benefit from government incentive programs and tax loopholes. Contrasting himself with both Trudeau and Stanfield, who came from rich families, Lewis attacked Trudeau's policy of tolerating a certain amount of unemployment as a curb against inflation: "My background was such that never . . . could I adopt a deliberate policy of creating unemployment. . . . I still vividly recall my father walking the streets looking for work."

David Lewis was born June 23, 1909, in Swislocz, Pol., now part of Soviet Belorussia. His father was a leatherworker and active socialist who emigrated with his family to Montreal when David was 12. Lewis attended McGill University in Montreal and Oxford University in England as a Rhodes scholar. While a practicing labour lawyer, he became involved in the Co-operative Commonwealth Federation, forerunner of the NDP, and after four defeats he was elected to the House of Commons in 1962. In 1971 he emerged as national party leader at an NDP convention polarized between conservative trade unionists and leftist "Waffles"; many who might otherwise have voted against Lewis supported him in preference to the far left.

(DONALD J. KLIMOVICH)

LOUD FAMILY

"Once upon a time in Santa Barbara, California, the American dream came true," wrote *America* magazine of the William C. Loud family. "The handsome father at 50 is prosperously self-employed; the mother at 45 is attractive and bright. . . . Their five children travel widely. Their eight-room ranch house includes a view of the ocean, four cars, a horse, two dogs and a swimming pool." But this apparently ideal situation contained such stuff as nightmares are made on, a fact that was disturbingly apparent when "An American Family" was broadcast over National Educational Television.

The series was produced for WNET, New York, by Craig Gilbert, who said, "If I film one American family over a long period, I will expose the myths . . . that are American and apply to all of us." The Louds agreed to be the family, and Gilbert, carrying *cinéma vérité* to perhaps its greatest extreme yet, spent seven months and $1.2 million filming the family in its intimate moments. Disturbingly, the resulting 12 hour-long installments seemed to show life imitating soap opera. Pat and Bill's 20-year marriage broke up; their oldest son, Lance, was revealed as a homosexual; a fire came within inches of destroying the house; daughter Delilah (15) began her sex life; and Bill's business went downhill. Everything was there, down to the devastating indolence of son Grant (17), the passivity of 18-year-old Kevin, and 13-year-old Michelle's pimples.

Many questions were left unanswered. Was this really the American Dream with a worm at its core? Was there some basic flaw in the family that led it to agree to be filmed in the first place? Did the camera, however unobtrusive, act as a catalyst that brought long-festering sores into the open? And, if so, was this ethical? As the year ended, the Louds themselves, after a brief fling of interviews and talk-show appearances, were picking up the pieces of their lives in relative obscurity.

Anthropologist Margaret Mead called the series debut "as important . . . as . . . the invention of . . . the novel," and Merle Miller, in *Esquire,* called it "this year's *Rashomon.*" In any case, it certainly showed that television had come a long way since "Howdy Doody." (PHILIP KOPPER)

MAHARAJ JI

Called by his followers a "Perfect Master," only one of whom can be alive at any given time, a 15-year-old boy guru from India, Maharaj Ji, toured the world in 1973 to bring world peace by giving to his listeners "inner peace through spiritual knowledge." He opened the U.S. leg of his travels with an appearance in New York City on July 28 and then visited several other cities before climaxing his trip with "Millennium '73," a three-day event in the Houston (Tex.) Astrodome. Along the way, in a much publicized incident, he was hit in the face with a cream pie in Detroit. (In Paris, in September, he retired under a hail of paper darts from ribald French students.)

Although his followers claimed a rising tide of enthusiasm for Maharaj Ji, attendance during the tour was generally disappointing. This was especially true in Houston, where only about one-fourth of the 66,000-seat Astrodome was filled each day. Undaunted, the guru's followers, who reportedly numbered six million, claimed that he would rule the world by the end of the 1970s.

Maharaj Ji was born Dec. 10, 1957, at Prem Nagar in India. The son of Shri Hansji Maharaj, also a "Perfect Master," he was named Pratap Singh Rawat. His father, who founded the Divine Light Mission, died when the boy was eight. At that time, according to Maharaj Ji, "A voice came to me saying, 'You are he, you are the one to continue.' . . . So they crowned me with the crown of Rama and Krishna and put the saffron mark of succession on my forehead." He then took the names Shri Guru Maharaj Ji and Balyogeshwar ("child god").

Maharaj Ji decided to take his message of inner peace outside of India in 1970. He made his first appearance in the West in 1971 at a pop music festival in Glastonbury, Eng., arriving in a white Rolls Royce and taking the stage to deliver a *satsang* ("truth-giving") for five minutes before the microphone was shut off. His first American appearance took place in 1972 in the Colorado mountains.

Although many of his followers called Maharaj Ji "lord of the universe" and "god incarnate," the young guru stated, "I am a humble servant of God, trying to establish peace in the world."

MARCOS, FERDINAND EDRALIN

Completing his second four-year term as president of the Philippines in 1973, Ferdinand Marcos, the last democratically elected leader in Southeast Asia, showed no inclination to lift the martial law he invoked in 1972 to "save the Republic" from leftist subversion. Following Manila-area bombings and an alleged terrorist attempt on his life, Marcos declared martial law to preserve civil order, combat bureaucratic waste and corruption, curb inflation, and begin long overdue economic reforms.

Postponing the plebiscite set for early 1973 on a new constitution that would change the Philippines from a presidential to a parliamentary system allowing him to serve more than two terms, Marcos organized "citizens' assemblies" in every town and village and, according to the resulting open voting, was given a mandate to sustain martial law for up to seven years. Shortly afterward, he pushed through a constitutional amendment enabling him to remain in power indefinitely.

Citing the need for the creation of a "New Society" in the Philippines, Marcos fired thousands of civil servants, closed down pornographic movies and gambling casinos, and granted amnesty to those who cooperated with his program to decrease the vast number of privately owned firearms. He committed himself to breaking the power of the oligarchs, but in 1973 the promised land reform program was barely under way with no concrete decisions made as to how it would be carried out.

Marcos was born in northern Luzon on Sept. 11, 1917, but lived in Manila after 1925, when his father was elected to Congress. He attended law school at the University of the Philippines. During World War II he survived the Bataan "death march" and eight days of torture as a prisoner of the Japanese, eventually escaping to become a guerrilla leader.

Marcos served in the House of Representatives as a Liberal Party member from 1949 to 1959 and was elected to the Senate in 1959 by the largest plurality ever achieved in any Philippine election. Switching to the Nationalist Party, he ran for president in 1965 against incumbent Pres. Diosdado Macapagal, whose Liberal campaign Marcos had managed in 1961. Following an expensive and bitter campaign, Marcos won and was inaugurated on Dec. 30, 1965.

(DONALD J. KLIMOVICH)

MEIR, GOLDA

"You cannot win peace by sacrificing small nations." With that message Golda Meir expressed the bitterness of Israel toward the end of a fateful 1973. At the beginning of an election year the prime minister's chief problems on the home front had been a dangerously high rate of inflation, the highest taxes in the non-Communist world, a 10% decline in Western immigration, a current account deficit of £625 million (later almost to double), and a £2,000 million foreign debt.

In January Mrs. Meir attended the Socialist International in Paris and later became Israel's first prime minister to have an audience with the pope. In June she welcomed West German Chancellor Willy Brandt (*q.v.*) on a state visit, and later that month, just before her 75th birthday, reluctantly accepted Labour Party candidacy for the expected October election.

On October 1 Mrs. Meir appealed to the Council of Europe not to bow to terrorism or political blackmail following Austria's decision under threat to close a transit camp for Jews emigrating from the Soviet Union. Five days later, on the Jewish high holy day of Yom Kippur, Egypt and Syria launched a concerted attack across the cease-fire lines. The prime minister announced to a shocked nation that the government had known of the impending attack, and she defended its decision not to take preemptive measures. Europe's reaction, following the severance of diplomatic ties by many African states, was a bitter blow. At an emergency meeting of the Socialist International in November, Mrs. Meir blamed Britain and France in particular for an eagerness to sacrifice Israeli blood for Arab oil.

On November 13, Menachem Begin, head of the opposition Gahal party, called for the prime minister's resignation, accusing her of having failed to inform the Cabinet of the critical border situation prior to the war. Her answer to the challenge from the right was that "We regard the cease-fire and progress toward peace as preferable to a further victory." In the election, postponed until December 31, the Labour Party was returned, though with a reduced majority, and Mrs. Meir remained prime minister.

Golda Meir was born in Kiev, Russia, on May 3, 1898. Her family emigrated to Milwaukee, Wis., in 1906, where she was educated at Teachers' Seminary. She settled in Palestine with her Russian-born husband in 1921. Her increasing involvement in politics led to the directorship of the political department of the Jewish Agency for Palestine in 1946. She was minister of labour (1949–56), foreign minister (1956–66), and secretary-general of Mapai (the Labour Party) until July 1968. She became Israel's fourth prime minister after the death of Levi Eshkol in February 1969.

(R. J. M. DENNERSTEIN)

MURPHY, LIONEL KEITH

As an experienced legal expert, Lionel Murphy seemed a natural selection for the office of federal attorney general following Labor's victory in the 1972 Australian elections. There his characteristic decisive vigour often led him to act with impetuosity rather than caution. His most dramatic action was to lead a police raid on the headquarters of Australia's Security and Intelligence Organization (ASIO) on March 15 and 16, 1973.

ARNOLD SACHS—PICTORIAL PARADE

Golda Meir

Murphy raided ASIO because of his grave concern for the safety of Yugoslav Premier Dzemal Bijedic, who was visiting Australia at the time. The attorney general suspected that ASIO had not given the government sufficient information about the activities of Croatian nationalists living in Australia who might be plotting to assassinate Bijedic. He was in more hot water in April, when he kept to himself for too long the news that the Yugoslav government had secretly executed three naturalized Australians of Croatian birth who had entered Yugoslavia on a terrorist mission. During the year he announced the preparation of a national environmental legal code, in addition to more immediate government action to protect endangered wildlife. He attended the International Court of Justice at The Hague in May to present Australia's case against French nuclear tests in the Pacific.

Murphy was born in Sydney on Aug. 31, 1922, the son of an Irish immigrant. He was educated both in science and law at Sydney University and was called to the bar in 1947, becoming a queen's counsel in 1960.

He first became prominent in the labour movement in the immediate post-World War II years, when he acted as advocate for left-wing trade unions who were fighting to avoid being taken over by Catholic activists. He was particularly active in the civil liberties area, and in 1963 was elected to the executive of the International Commission of Jurists. Elected as senator for New South Wales in 1962, he was opposition leader in the Senate from 1967 and in that capacity was often critical of party policy. Characteristically, he attacked party leader Gough Whitlam's statement that Labor should not press for an immediate troop withdrawal from Vietnam, at the time when party moderates looked for electoral popularity. "Principles," Murphy declared, "are not like clothing, to be changed whenever it seems convenient." (A. R. G. GRIFFITHS)

MURRAY, LIONEL

Traditionally, the general secretary of the British Trades Union Congress rises inside the organization. That was the pedigree of the last four: Lord Citrine, Sir Vincent Tewson, George Woodcock, and Vic Feather. It was also traditional that they should be known with informality by the first name they actually used. So when Lionel Murray was elected unopposed to the post of general secretary in September 1973, it was as Len Murray that he was known, and it was as a backroom official of the TUC that he had made his reputation. He was, in fact, not at all well known to the public when he took over, though he had been on the TUC staff for more than 25 years.

By origin a working-class trade unionist, the son of a farm worker, Murray was also an intellectual, with a first class honours degree from Oxford University in politics, philosophy, and economics. Though quiet and reticent, he established during his years in the TUC that he was no lightweight. The office of general secretary of the TUC is somewhat enigmatic and its actual power is arguable, for British trade unions are reluctant to give up any of their own independence to a central organization or a single spokesman. Nevertheless, Murray would be the man to lead TUC delegations in discussions with the government and with industry on economic policy—and at a time when tripartite talks on incomes, prices, and other aspects of economic policy had become standard practice. He held the trade unions' conventional views of the undesirability of wage restraint, but was probably more sympathetic than some of his colleagues to ideas for worker participation in experiments in industrial democracy. He took over with a possible 14 years in office until retiring age, a long enough span to show whether the TUC could establish more emphatic leadership of the trade union movement.

Murray was born at Hadley, Shropshire, on Aug. 2, 1922. After World War II, in which he was wounded in the Normandy fighting in 1944, he taught school for a time but gave it up because he found he could not control children. He then went to Oxford and after graduating joined the Economic Department of the TUC in 1947, heading the department from 1954 to 1969 when he became assistant general secretary.

(HARFORD THOMAS)

NAMGYAL, PALDEN THONDUP

Palden Thondup Namgyal, *chogyal* (king) of Sikkim, a small Himalayan state under India's protection, barely avoided being overthrown in April 1973 when a violent popular uprising shook his kingdom. The dissidents demanded electoral and administrative reforms and an end to his "despotic" rule. Timely intervention by the Indian Army helped the *chogyal* keep his crown, but he was forced to concede new democratic reforms and increased Indian supervision over the affairs of his state. His young son, Crown Prince Tenzing Kunzang Jigme Namgyal, a student at Oxford, was hastily packed off to England after being involved in a shooting incident against demonstrators in the capital city of Gangtok. The *chogyal* and his American wife were accused of plotting against India, but the Indian government discounted these reports. The *chogyal* visited New Delhi in September to assure India of his continuing loyalty.

Born in April 1923, the *chogyal* belonged to a line of rulers dating back to the early 17th century. Palden Thondup Namgyal was said to be an incarnation of an earlier *chogyal* and the reincarnation of a famous lama from Kham (eastern Tibet). The second son of Maharaja Sir Tashi Namgyal, who died in 1963, the *chogyal* was initially trained as a monk and was the spiritual head of the Phodong and Rumtek monasteries. He received his early education in Darjeeling and Simla in India, and was about to go abroad for more studies when his elder brother, the Maharajkumar, was killed in a British Royal Air Force plane accident.

As heir apparent, Palden Thondup was trained at the administrative college in Dehra Dun, India, and returned to Sikkim to become one of his father's advisers and subsequently president of the State Council. He led the Sikkimese delegation that negotiated the 1950 treaty with India. A noted scholar in Tibetology, the *chogyal* was president of the Maha Bodhi Society of India and established the Namgyal Institute of Tibetology in Gangtok in 1958. He was formally proclaimed maharaja of Sikkim on Dec. 5, 1963. His first wife, by whom he had two sons and a daughter, died in 1957. Six years later he married Hope Cooke, of New York, in an elaborate Buddhist-style wedding in Gangtok. (GOVINDAN UNNY)

NICKLAUS, JACK

Dominating his sport as few others had ever dominated theirs, Jack Nicklaus set a major new record in golf in 1973. His victory in the Professional Golfers' Association (PGA) tournament in August was his 14th in a major championship event, beating Bobby Jones's long-standing mark of 13. At the end of the 1973 season Nicklaus' victories in the major tournaments included four in the Masters, three each in the U.S. Open and the PGA, and two each in the British Open and the U.S. Amateur.

Before his PGA triumph Nicklaus had played strongly in the major tournaments in 1973 but had not been able to win. He tied for third in the Masters at Augusta, Ga., tied for fourth in the U.S. Open at Oakmont, Pa., and finished fourth in the British Open at Troon, Scot. However, in the PGA, held at Canterbury Country Club near Cleveland, Nicklaus played steady and consistent golf to shoot a seven-under-par 277 and win the tournament by four strokes. The victory was all the more convincing because the tricky greens and hazardous fairways at Canterbury were not ideally suited to Nicklaus' style of play.

Having broken one of Bobby Jones's major records, Nicklaus was ready to set his sights again on a second. This was the grand slam in golf: victory in the same year in the Masters, U.S. Open, PGA, and British Open. No one had been able to accomplish this feat since Jones in 1930 won that year's version of the grand slam: the U.S. Open and Amateur and the British Open and Amateur.

Nicklaus was born Jan. 21, 1940, in Columbus, O. He began playing golf at the age of 10 and at 13 shot a 69 over the 7,095-yd. course at the Scioto Country Club. While attending Ohio State University, he won his first major tournament, the U.S. Amateur, in 1959. He turned professional in 1961 and the next year won his first U.S. Open. His earnings in 1972 totaled a single-season record of $320,542. (DANIEL MILLER)

NIXON, RICHARD MILHOUS

The many recorded crises of Richard Nixon paled into relative insignificance in 1973 as the president of the United States reeled through a year of almost continuous turmoil. His troubles seemed to come in spasms: Watergate, the economy, the energy crisis—and always back to Watergate. And although there were triumphs, notably the achievement of U.S. withdrawal from Indochina and the return of U.S. prisoners of war, they were dimmed by the later problems at home.

The good news came early in the year. President Nixon went on nationwide television on January 23 and announced, "We today have concluded an agreement to end the war and bring peace with honor in Vietnam and Southeast Asia." The president said that all U.S. prisoners of war would be released within 60 days of the cease-fire, which would go into effect on January 27, and that all U.S. military forces would be withdrawn.

Watergate and other scandals were the heaviest burdens. While all around him the men he had handpicked were resigning under fire or facing indictment on criminal charges—including his vice-president, two former Cabinet members, and the two top White House aides—President Nixon spasmodically but vigorously struggled to bolster his credibility. But despite his continued protestations of innocence, each statement seemed only to trigger new questions and doubts.

The worst point in the year for Nixon almost certainly was the weekend of October 20–21, when he fired special Watergate prosecutor Archibald Cox (*q.v.*) in a controversy over the president's tape recordings of his Watergate-related private conversations. As a result, Nixon was forced to accept the resignations of his highly esteemed attorney general, Elliot Richardson, and Richardson's top deputy, William Ruckelshaus.

Afterward, for the first time, members of the Democratic and Republican leadership in the House of Representatives and many other public officials began to talk seriously and publicly about impeaching Nixon. By the next Tuesday, reflecting the public and congressional pressure, Nixon yielded. He agreed to obey a federal court order to surrender the White House tapes to U.S. District Judge John J. Sirica (*q.v.*).

These troubles dominated most other events, at home or abroad. To be sure, there were the settlement with the Soviet Union of the latest Arab-Israeli war, and his meetings with Soviet Communist Party leader Leonid I. Brezhnev in Washington and French Pres. Georges Pompidou in Iceland. But although there were some successes, it was not, in total, a happy year for Richard Nixon.

Born Jan. 9, 1913, in Yorba Linda, Calif., Nixon was graduated from Whittier College and the Duke University Law School. After serving in the Navy during World War II, he was elected a U.S. representative from California in 1946, a senator in 1950, and vice-president in 1952. In 1960 Nixon lost the presidential election to John F. Kennedy, but he returned in 1968 to defeat Hubert H. Humphrey and repeated the victory in 1972 against George McGovern.

(ROBERT A. SIGNER)

OH, SADAHARU

In the 38-year history of Japanese professional baseball, 33-year-old slugger Sadaharu Oh, the first baseman of Tokyo's Yomiuri Giants, became the third player to win the triple crown in the Central League during the 1973 season. His 51 home runs, batting average of .355, and 114 runs batted in contributed greatly to bringing the Giants their ninth consecutive championship.

The way to the triple crown was not an easy one even for Oh, who was praised as "one of the best batters in Japanese baseball history." His long-dreamed-of goal was realized only after playing for 14 years.

Born May 20, 1940, in Tokyo, Oh attracted much attention for his unusual talent

Richard Milhous Nixon

UPI COMPIX

Jack Nicklaus

KEN REGAN—CAMERA 5

as a batter and pitcher during his high-school days and was a driving force in bringing the championship to his team in the National High-School Baseball Tournament. His first few years with the prestigious Giants were not satisfactory, however, partly because he was placed in the difficult position of continuing his training as both a pitcher and a batter. Only in recent years was he able to concentrate on batting.

Oh first demonstrated his hitting ability during his fourth season when his batting coach, Hiroshi Arakawa, advised him to switch batting styles. On the day that he did so, Oh hammered out two home runs. After that he hit more than 40 home runs for eight straight years, setting a Japanese record of 55 in 1964. His home run total at the end of 1973 was 585. In addition, Oh was named the league's most valuable player six times, won the batting title four times, and captured the crown in the category of runs batted in eight times.

Oh's achievements were due not only to his inherent gift but also to his continuous training. When he went into a slump, he tried hundreds of "swings" after a game on a tatami mattress, often using a Japanese sword instead of a bat. Oh believed this exercise to be very effective in attaining mental concentration.

Asked about his future aim, Oh firmly said, "What I have in mind is to catch up with Babe Ruth's home run record, and then outdistance Hank Aaron, who will be sure to outrun Babe Ruth."

(RYUSAKU HASEGAWA)

ORTOLI, FRANÇOIS-XAVIER

Taking office as president of the European Commission, the supreme policymaking body of the EEC, in January 1973, François-Xavier Ortoli was immediately faced with the task of drawing up concrete proposals for putting into practice the new European policies outlined at the October 1972 Paris summit conference of the nine EEC member and prospective member countries. In the past, as a member of the French government in various capacities, he had stressed the need for bilateral and multilateral cooperation within the Community; now he was dedicated to the idea that Europe must play a decisive part in world affairs.

The Community's relations with the U.S., and in particular the need for joint consultations, were the theme of Ortoli's talks with Pres. Richard Nixon in Washington on Oct. 1, 1973—one of several personal diplomatic interventions on behalf of the EEC made by Ortoli during the year. Before the month was out, as a result of the Middle East war and the Arab oil embargo, he was to see U.S.-EEC relations brought to their lowest level, while the self-interest of some EEC members, notably France and Britain, severely strained the Community's internal cohesion.

Born in Ajaccio, Corsica, on Feb. 16, 1925, Ortoli was raised and educated in Indochina. During World War II he took part in resistance against the Japanese, and afterward went to the École Nationale d'Administration in Paris. After serving in the private offices of several ministers, in May 1958 he took up his first appointment with the European Commission—as director general for the internal market. In 1966, after a spell as director of the cabinet to Georges Pompidou (then premier), he was appointed commissioner-general for the French five-year plan, and as such initiated the fifth plan. There followed a number of ministerial posts, ending with industrial and scientific development from 1969 until his appointment as a Commission representative in October 1972, with the understanding that he would replace Sicco Mansholt as president in 1973.

(DEREK PRAG)

Lynden Oscar Pindling

AUTHENTICATED NEWS INTERNATIONAL

OULD, DADDAH, MOKHTAR

In 1973 Pres. Mokhtar Ould Daddah of the Islamic Republic of Mauritania enhanced a rising reputation in Africa by adopting increasingly militant attitudes in international affairs. Having withdrawn Mauritania from the Francophone Common Organization of Africa, Malagasy, and Mauritius and then from membership in the franc zone, following sharp criticism of French policy in Africa, he took the country further along the road of active involvement with the Muslim world by joining the Arab League and by applying for membership in the Maghreb Union with Morocco, Tunisia, and Algeria. On the occasion of a visit by Tunisian Pres. Habib Bourguiba in December, the two heads of state reaffirmed their support for the independence of Spanish Sahara and called for a referendum there under UN auspices. Meanwhile, on the domestic front, Ould Daddah had to contend with the catastrophic effects of a severe drought that Mauritania and the other sub-Saharan countries suffered in 1973.

Ould Daddah was born on Dec. 25, 1924, at Boutilimit in the south of Mauritania, the son of a prominent Islamic religious leader of the Ould Biri clan. He went to the Sons of Chiefs' School and the Interpreters' School. After working for six years as an interpreter he completed his secondary and higher education in France, graduating from the Law School and the National School of Oriental Languages in Paris. On his return home as a lawyer in 1955, he joined the Mauritanian Progressive Union (UPM) and quickly established himself as a rising nationalist politician. Two years later he was elected to the Territorial Assembly of French West Africa, and in 1959 to the French National Assembly in Paris. When in that year Mauritania became an autonomous republic within the French Community, Ould Daddah was its first premier.

The young republic's extreme poverty was considerably alleviated in 1963 by the discovery of rich iron ore deposits at Zouerate and of copper at Akjouit. Apart from the difficult economic conditions of the mainly nomadic Maures, or Moors, his main problem was reconciliation of the conflicting cultural and ethnic interests of the Muslim Maures and the predominantly Christian Negroes of the south. However, he determinedly introduced Arabic as the national language and encouraged the pursuit of Islamic sources of culture. (COLIN LEGUM)

PAHLAVI ARYAMEHR, MOHAMMED REZA

"The industrial world will have to realize that the era of their terrific progress and even more terrific income and wealth based on cheap oil is finished." So stated the ruler of petroleum-rich Iran, Shah-in-shah Mohammed Reza, after a meeting of the Persian Gulf oil ministers late in 1973.

Throughout the year Mohammed Reza worked to gain greater benefits for the oil-producing countries. In July Iran signed a new 20-year agreement with a consortium of Western nations. The agreement initiated a seller-buyer relationship between Iran and the oil companies and gave Iran control over all field operations. Although Iran did not participate in the cutback of oil shipments to the West begun by the Arab producing states during the Arab-Israeli war in October, it did play a leading role in increasing the price of crude oil. At a conference in Teheran in December the posted price of a barrel of crude was doubled.

Earlier in the year the shah had attracted worldwide attention by his major buildup of his country's military forces. Iran and neighbouring Iraq remained hostile over conflicting interests in the Persian Gulf and also because of Iraq's support of secessionist movements in Pakistan. Mohammed Reza met with U.S. Pres. Richard Nixon in July to discuss shipments of U.S. arms to his country in order to maintain stability in the area.

Born in Teheran on Oct. 26, 1919, Mohammed Reza was the eldest son of Reza Shah Pahlavi, commander of the Persian Cossack Brigade, who founded the new dynasty in December 1925. Succeeding to the throne when his father abdicated on Sept. 16, 1941, the new shah-in-shah began his reign with British and Soviet troops (and later those of the U.S.) virtually occupying large areas in the north and southwest of the country. After World War II, however, the Allied troops were withdrawn and the nation gradually returned to normal. Mohammed Reza was married in 1939 to Princess Fawzieh of Egypt (divorced 1948) and in 1951 to Soraya Bakhtiari (divorced 1958); neither of these marriages produced an heir to the throne. In December 1959 he married Farah Diba, the daughter of an Iranian Army officer. A crown prince, named Reza, was born in Teheran on Oct. 31, 1960.

(K. M. SMOGORZEWSKI)

PATRICK, TED

On Aug. 6, 1973, in Manhattan Criminal Court, Ted Patrick was acquitted of charges of assault and illegal detention in a decision that augured well for this 43-year-old black crusader's unusual cause. A Christian himself, he had been making a career of "rescuing" young converts to the ascetic, usually fundamentalist, and often communal sects that had sprung up on the fringes of the Jesus Movement. According to one press report, Patrick had been personally involved in the "deprogramming"—as he called it—of 138 persons affiliated with 68 different religious organizations.

The criminal charges stemmed from the undisputed fact that Patrick had helped Mr. and Mrs. Eugene Voll in an attempt to kidnap their 20-year-old son Daniel. The young man had joined the New Testament Missionary Fellowship, dropped out of Yale, and moved to New York where the fellowship had its headquarters, rejecting, in the process, his family's ethic and influence. His former roommate, who had renounced his new religion after being deprogrammed by Patrick, testified at the trial that converts to the group were urged to sever ties with their families. It was the roommate's parents who had recommended Patrick to the Volls when they found they were unable to reach Daniel by themselves. The acquittal was based on a section of the New York penal code that permits otherwise criminal conduct if it is "necessary as an emergency measure to avoid imminent private injury" and on the fact that Daniel was a minor at the time of the kidnap attempt.

Patrick believed that the sects he opposed gained a nearly hypnotic "mind control" over their young converts, effectively preventing them from exercising free choice. He acted only at the behest of parents or other relatives. His aim was to separate the converts from their fellows and "deprogram" them, a process that consisted largely of marathon Bible-reading sessions in which Patrick attempted to point out that the tenets of the proselytizers actually ran counter to Scripture.

Patrick was born and raised in Chattanooga, Tenn. He was active in organizing Bible courses for inmates of hospitals, jails, and orphanages and continued this work while he was in the Air Force. Subsequently he settled in San Diego, Calif., where he was active in black community politics. In 1968 he was credited with helping keep the peace in the San Diego ghetto after the Watts riots in Los Angeles. He later served as a community relations adviser to California Gov. Ronald Reagan. (PHILIP KOPPER)

PERÓN, JUAN DOMINGO

Surprising those who thought Argentina might be ready for Peronism without Perón, Pres. Héctor Cámpora stepped down only 50 days after taking office "in order to restore to General Perón the mandate that was taken from him unjustly." Eighteen years after being overthrown, the aging ex-dictator returned to power in an election held Sept. 23, 1973.

Born Oct. 8, 1895, in Buenos Aires, Juan Perón began his rise to power as one of a group of career army officers who overthrew the corrupt government of Pres. Ramón S. Castillo in 1943. Accepting at first the relatively minor post of secretary of labour and social welfare, within two years Perón also became vice-president and minister of war. When it became apparent he would make a bid for power on the strength of support by the *descamisados* ("shirtless ones"), Perón was checked by a liberal coup in 1945. But, having retained control of the Army and police force and aided by his second wife, Eva, he successfully campaigned for president and assumed office in June 1946.

Embarking on a program of social welfare called *justicialismo,* Perón improved the lot of the workers through wage increases and fringe benefits, and by building for them hospitals, schools, and resorts. While he was nationalizing banks and railroads and encouraging industrialization and public works programs, his wife Eva acted to ensure his popularity and create her own image, that of "little madonna," by dispensing more than $100 million to the poor each year through the Eva Perón Foundation, the sole charitable agency allowed in Argentina. At the same time, Perón jailed his liberal opponents, muzzled the press, and almost completely eliminated civil liberties. The once-prosperous nation approached economic ruin through mismanagement and corruption. His support faded and, ousted by a military coup in 1955, he was exiled and eventually settled in Spain.

The governments that followed did not succeed in improving economic conditions or in creating a spirit of national unity, and, when Perón was allowed to return to Argentina for the first time in 1972, Peronism was viewed as a means of controlled reunification. More than a million people turned out to welcome Perón on his official return in June 1973, but—in what was perhaps an omen of things to come—it was marred by violence between rival Peronist factions. (DONALD J. KLIMOVICH)

PINDLING, LYNDEN OSCAR

On July 10, 1973, the Commonwealth of the Bahamas became the sixth black-ruled sovereign nation in the Western Hemisphere, achieving the goal set ten years before by Prime Minister Lynden Pindling and other black Bahamians in the self-government movement. Twelve days of celebrations, highlighted by the lowering of the Union Jack in Nassau and the raising of the new black, gold, and aquamarine banner, marked the end of more than 250 years of colonial rule under Great Britain.

In the six years during which he had headed the Bahamian government, Pindling, a London-educated lawyer, had expanded educational and employment opportunities for black Bahamians, who made up 85% of the population. A pragmatist, Pindling said, "Our government has no intention of killing the goose that lays the golden egg." If Pindling's bahamianization program caused some disgruntled whites to leave, it had not affected the Bahamas' rich tourist trade, which accounted for more than 60% of the islands' revenues. He also showed no inclination to begin levying corporate and income taxes on foreign investors who had found a haven in the country.

Pindling was born March 22, 1930, in the impoverished Over the Hill section of Nassau. His father's grocery store prospered well enough to allow Lynden to attend the University of London, where he earned a law degree in 1952. Returning to Nassau in 1953, he was admitted to the Bahamian bar, joined the mainly black Progressive Liberal Party, and was elected to the House of Assembly in 1956. The PLP formed the first organized opposition to the United Bahamian Party, which had kept economic and political power securely in the hands of white merchant politicians known as the "Bay Street Boys." Under Pindling's leadership, the PLP forced Great Britain to grant the Bahamas, in 1964, a ministerial government and a one-man, one-vote constitution.

On April 27, 1965, a day known in the Bahamas as "Black Tuesday," a PLP member was expelled from the House of Assembly for talking too long. Declaring that, since there was no law in the assembly, power should be returned to the people, Pindling picked up the 165-year-old gold mace that symbolized parliamentary authority and threw it out a window into the street, where thousands of Bahamians were singing "We Shall Overcome." Gaining independent support after the elections of 1967, Pindling was sworn in as premier with an all-black Cabinet. In 1972, campaigning on a platform of immediate independence, he won a sweeping reelection victory. (DONALD J. KLIMOVICH)

PINOCHET UGARTE, AUGUSTO

Throughout his life Gen. Augusto Pinochet had steered clear of politics—until the fateful week in September 1973 when Santiago, Chile, was wracked with gunfire, tanks attacked in the streets, the presidential palace was strafed, and Salvador Allende, the first Marxist president freely elected in the Western world, was killed. Within four days of the first military coup in Chile in 46 years, army commander in chief Pinochet became dictator of Chile.

The quiet-spoken but tough-talking strong man had spent most of his life writing on purely military subjects, teaching in military school, and doing articles on geography. After the coup he became the man who imposed an around-the-clock curfew, rounded up political enemies, and broke off diplomatic relations with Cuba.

"He never spoke about politics," said one former student after the coup. "We never knew where he stood." Allende had named Pinochet to succeed Gen. Carlos Prats González as army chief a month before the coup, hoping that Pinochet would remain neutral in Allende's continuing squabbles with the Chilean political right.

Pinochet was born Nov. 25, 1915, in Valparaiso, the same city where Allende was born. He was made an officer of the Army in 1936 after graduating from the nation's military school. In 1956 he was named military attaché to the Chilean embassy in Washington, D.C. He also visited the U.S. Southern Command at the Panama Canal in 1965, 1968, and 1972. In 1968 Pinochet was promoted from colonel to general. He was named army chief of staff in 1972, a year before being given the commander's position.

During riots in 1972, Allende had declared Santiago a military zone and placed it under the protection of Pinochet. At that time, Pinochet had said he hoped the Army would never have to go into the streets to restore order because "the Army, unlike the police, goes out to kill." (BILL GRANGER)

Mohammed Reza Pahlavi Aryamehr

CAMERA PRESS/PICTORIAL PARADE

HENRI BUREAU—SYGMA

Georges Pompidou

WIDE WORLD

Elliot Lee Richardson

WIDE WORLD

Dixy Lee Ray

Annemarie Proell-Moser

A.F.P./PICTORIAL PARADE

POMPIDOU, GEORGES

For Pres. Georges Pompidou of France 1973 was a bad year, both personally and in domestic politics; and while his considerable diplomatic activity served to bolster his international prestige, it brought few concrete results. At the personal level, Pompidou, a robust 62-year-old fond of the good life, was severely shaken by ill health, the effects of which were strikingly apparent at his meeting (May 31–June 1) in Iceland with U.S. Pres. Richard Nixon. The typically Gaullist mania for secrecy led him to cover up his ailment, but its evident existence inevitably encouraged political maneuvering among possible successors.

Although the Gaullists and their allies won the general election in March, they lost many seats to the left-wing opposition. The latter, encouraged despite internal squabbles between the Communists and Socialists, switched from the defensive to the attack. At the same time, the ruling party was divided, orthodox Gaullists accusing Pompidou of betraying the spirit of Gaullism while its moderate and centrist coalition allies threatened to break away. Worsening inflation, industrial unrest, lack of progress in liberalization of the state-controlled broadcasting system (ORTF) and reform of abortion law, and revelations of official "bugging" activities (notably in the case of the satirical weekly *Le Canard enchaîné*) all led to growing dissatisfaction with the government. In December Pompidou defended his premier, Pierre Messmer, against calls for the latter's replacement, but his own authority dwindled to the point where the weekly *Valeurs Actuelles* published his picture with the caption "Is he still there?"

There was some consolation for Pompidou in the year's round of summit meetings, which emphasized his important place in the international arena. Apart from his meeting with Nixon, he was visited in Paris by Soviet party leader Leonid I. Brezhnev, had meetings on several occasions with U.K. Prime Minister Edward Heath, West German Chancellor Willy Brandt, and other EEC heads of government, and visited Chairman Mao Tse-tung in China and Emperor Haile Selassie in Ethiopia. On his initiative an EEC summit meeting convened in Copenhagen on December 14–15 (*see* EUROPEAN UNITY).

Pompidou was born on July 5, 1911, at Montboudif in the Cantal. After a career in teaching he became director of Charles de Gaulle's cabinet and, in 1962, premier. He was elected president in 1969.

(PIERRE VIANSSON-PONTÉ)

PREUS, JACOB A. O.

Before 1958 the Rev. Jacob A. O. ("Jack") Preus, pastor and teacher in a small Lutheran sect, was a conservative thorn in the side of the huge Lutheran Church-Missouri Synod. Then he joined the faculty of the synod's Concordia Theological Seminary at Springfield, Ill. In a little over a decade he was president of the synod, second largest of the three main Lutheran denominations in the U.S., and by mid-1973 he had so consolidated his power that dissidents were calling him "Pope Jacob the First."

J. A. O. Preus viewed with alarm what he considered real and present dangers in the church: doctrinal permissiveness, a tendency by Missouri Synod congregations toward fellowship with other, more liberal Lutherans, and outright heresy of many teachers and pastors. He rose to the top of the 2.8-million-member denomination in the eruption of a long-simmering dispute over how the Bible should be interpreted, particularly in the synod's main seminary, Concordia at St. Louis, Mo.

Elected president of the synod in 1969 as leader of a well-organized conservative wing, Preus soon launched an investigation of the seminary, charging most of the faculty with teaching false doctrine. The conflict reached its climax at the synod's 50th regular biennial convention, July 6–13, 1973, in New Orleans, La. Preus, running for reelection, warned the 1,100 delegates that the church was at a "doctrinal crossroads" where they would be forced to make their stand on whether the Bible is the "inerrant word of God." Preus and his supporters virtually swept all elective offices. The convention also adopted "A Statement of Scriptural and Confessional Principles" which had been formulated by the president as his personal set of beliefs.

Later, Preus tried to alleviate fears that the "Statement" would be used as the sole test of orthodoxy. However, the Concordia board of control voted to suspend the seminary's president, the Rev. John H. Tietjen, although the suspension was delayed for legal reasons.

Preus was born Jan. 8, 1920, in St. Paul, Minn., and attended Luther College, Decorah, Ia., Luther Seminary in St. Paul, and the University of Minnesota. Ordained in 1945 in the former Evangelical Lutheran Church, he left a year later for the smaller and more conservative Norwegian Synod. He joined the Springfield seminary in 1958 and became its president in 1962. (DAVID MEADE)

PROELL-MOSER, ANNEMARIE

The first woman to win the World Alpine Ski Cup three times, Annemarie Proell of Austria sustained through three consecutive seasons, 1971–73, an exceptionally high quality of form and technique, to become widely regarded as the outstanding female racer in skiing history. Only one predecessor, Marielle Goitschel of France, possibly could be ranked in the same class.

Miss Proell (Mrs. Proell-Moser, following her 1973 marriage) first claimed attention in 1969, when, as a 15-year-old two inches shorter than her eventual 5 ft. 6 in., she was runner-up in a World Cup downhill race at Saint-Gervais, France. A year later she gained a bronze medal in the world championship downhill at Val Gardena, Italy. In 1971, only her third international season, she won the World Cup series with a dominating run of impressive victories not previously equaled and received the Martini Golden Skier award from the International Association of Ski Journalists. Her biggest disappointment came when, as clear favourite in the 1972 Winter Olympic Games at Sapporo, Japan, she suffered two defeats, in the downhill and giant slalom, both from the then relatively unknown Swiss schoolgirl Marie-Thérèse Nadig. But her two silver medals in these events, with fifth place in the slalom, gained her the consoling overall world championship title, decided concurrently. She went on to retain the World Cup in 1972 and 1973. At Val d'Isère, France, on December 6, she easily won the first big race of the new season, the Criterium of the First Snow.

Miss Proell was born March 27, 1953, one of eight children of a Salzburg farmer. Her gently amiable personality and evidently small-boned physique belied a tenacious courage and strength not essential for slalom skiers but musts for a great downhill competitor. A notably versatile performer, she had the ability to place high frequently in the slalom and giant slalom, but her forte was downhill, and she registered consistent successes in this event regardless of varying course conditions and orders of start. Her pronounced forward lean and smooth, hip-swinging *wedeln* style were typically Austrian, no doubt handed down from the technique adopted throughout the nation in the 1960s under the leadership of Toni Sailer.

(HOWARD BASS)

QADDAFI, MUAMMAR AL-

With his fervent Arab nationalism, Pres. Muammar al-Qaddafi of Libya had provided the chief impulse for the federation of Libya, Syria, and Egypt, approved by national referenda in 1971. His relations with other Arab states were poor. He was hostile to King Hussein (*q.v.*) of Jordan for his treatment of the Palestinian guerrillas, and had called King Faisal (*q.v.*) of Saudi Arabia "nothing but an oil merchant." His Islamic piety also made him critical of pro-Soviet Arab regimes, though he was equally anti-American.

In August 1972 Qaddafi persuaded Egypt's Pres. Anwar as-Sadat (*q.v.*) to agree to a merger of their two countries. The following April, complaining of shortcomings in the Libyan revolution's domestic progress, he launched his own "cultural revolution," requiring a purge of anti-Islamic and anti-Arab elements and principles and the election of popular committees at every level of society. When Sadat refused to be hurried into total union, Qaddafi launched an abortive march on Cairo but was forced to accept a tepid compromise.

Whether or not Sadat had made Qaddafi aware of his planned October offensive against Israel, when it came Qaddafi dissociated himself from it, though he later claimed to have supplied both planes and tanks and lamented their belated arrival on the battlefront. He remained implacably hostile to any reconciliation between Arab and Jew, and argued for an all-out long-term war. He refused to attend the November Arab summit meeting in Algiers, and at the end of the year he called for revolt in any Arab country that tried to conclude a unilateral peace.

Born in a Bedouin tent in the desert south of Tripoli in 1942, the austere Captain Qaddafi was almost unknown until he led the 1969 coup against King Idris, becoming thereafter a colonel and commander in chief of Libya's armed forces as well as chairman of the Revolutionary Command Council. In January 1970 he also became prime minister and defense minister. In July 1972 he relinquished the premiership to Abdul Salam Jalloud but as president of the RCC continued to dominate the regime. While his brand of revolutionary nationalism had much in common with the Nasserism of the 1950s, Qaddafi's religious and social conservatism was more extreme. Among his first acts had been the banning of alcohol, the enforced use of Arabic on all street signs, and the eradication of the Jewish and Italian communities. (PETER MANSFIELD)

RAY, DIXY LEE

Perhaps the most powerful woman in the U.S. government in 1973 was a zoologist who lived in a house trailer and had specialized in the study of invertebrates. Dixy Lee Ray, in February 1973, was named chairman of the Atomic Energy Commission, the agency charged with the development and application of nuclear energy, from weapons manufacture to medical science.

Observers predicted her tenure might be controversial if not stormy. Committed to equal job opportunities for minorities, she remarked, "If it hadn't been for the women's liberation movement, I doubt the president would have appointed me. I was appointed because I was a woman and that's all right with me." One of her first acts was to name David Jenkins, a black, as her top aide.

She was determined to make other changes in the AEC. Before a closed session of the congressional Joint Atomic Energy Committee, she apparently won the first round in a battle to create a newly independent AEC Division of Reactor Safety Research. The move was applauded by environmentalists who felt that developers of nuclear reactors could not reasonably be expected to police their own safety measures as stringently as an independent office. This was not to brand her as a renegade. She was committed to the increased use of nuclear energy as a power source and to the development of atomic tools in medicine.

Born in Tacoma, Wash., Sept. 3, 1914, Dixy Lee Ray graduated from Mills College, Oakland, Calif., in 1937, and taught high school in Oakland. After earning her doctorate from Stanford in 1945, she joined the University of Washington faculty, becoming associate professor in 1957. As a zoologist, she was involved in "ecology" long before that cause became popular. At various times she was a Guggenheim fellow, a member of the President's Task Force on Oceanography, a special consultant to the director of the National Science Foundation, and chief scientist aboard a research ship in the Indian Ocean taking part in a cooperative international science project.

After the World's Fair in Seattle, Wash., she took over some of its buildings as head of the Pacific Science Center, an organization dedicated to improved public understanding of science. She also launched a weekly television program for laymen. In August 1972 she became the first woman to be appointed to a full term on the AEC when she succeeded commissioner Wilfrid Johnson.

(PHILIP KOPPER)

RICHARDSON, ELLIOT LEE

In a U.S. administration badly tainted by the burgeoning Watergate scandal, Elliot Richardson had the reputation of being one man, at least, who was above reproach. Only recently moved from the Department of Health, Education, and Welfare to Defense in Pres. Richard Nixon's post-election Cabinet reshuffle, he was named to the sensitive post of attorney general on April 30, 1973, in one of several Nixon moves designed to restore confidence in the government. Thus the shock was all the greater when, on October 20, he resigned rather than fire special Watergate prosecutor Archibald Cox (*q.v.*).

As attorney general, Richardson had been in the odd position of presiding over an investigation of the administration by the Department of Justice, which was, constitutionally, a part of that administration. Before the Senate would confirm his nomination to Justice, Richardson had to agree to appoint an impartial federal prosecutor to investigate Watergate, and the promises of job security he gave to Cox were a prime reason he felt he could not fire him. Cox had become embroiled in a struggle with the White House over access to tapes of presidential conversations. While this was going on, a Justice Department investigation of kickback scandals in Maryland had led to the resignation of Vice-Pres. Spiro Agnew (*q.v.*) because of his alleged activities when he was governor of that state.

Richardson had often told friends and interviewers that a *Harvard Law Review* man can do any job well. A Boston aristocrat whose father, grandfathers, several uncles, and two brothers had become physicians in the Bay State, he was born in Boston on July 20, 1920, graduated from Harvard College and Harvard Law School, and served in the Army in World War II. He began his government career as an assistant to U.S. Sen. Leverett Saltonstall (Rep., Mass.), was appointed assistant secretary of HEW in 1957, and served as acting secretary for four months in 1958. In 1959–61 he served as U.S. attorney in Boston and gained notice as the prosecutor of Bernard Goldfine, a figure in administration scandals of the Eisenhower era. He was elected lieutenant governor and later state attorney general in Massachusetts, then returned to Washington in 1969 as undersecretary of state. He was appointed secretary of HEW in 1970.

RIZZO, FRANK LAZARRO

The controversial "law and order" mayor of Philadelphia was elected in November 1971, pledged to clean up corruption in city government, attract more industry, and "make the streets safe." But in 1973 his administration faced severe problems. An unprecedented 48-day strike by the teachers' union resulted in the mayor's having to accept financial terms far beyond the means of a school board already $71 million in debt. Democratic City Committee Chairman Peter J. Camiel accused Rizzo of starting a campaign of harassment against him after Camiel rejected a secret deal in which he would be allowed to choose architectural firms for city projects in return for allowing Rizzo to pick the Democratic candidate for district attorney. Rizzo denied Camiel's allegations, and both men agreed to take lie-detector tests. The polygraph results indicated Camiel was telling the truth; Rizzo failed on six key questions.

Born in Philadelphia on Oct. 23, 1920, Rizzo was the son of an Italian immigrant who served 41 years on the city's police force and reached the rank of sergeant. In 1938 Rizzo dropped out of high school in his senior year and joined the U.S. Navy. Returning to Philadelphia after his medical discharge a year later, he joined the police force as a patrolman in 1943. During his 24-year rise through the ranks to police commissioner in 1967, Rizzo earned a reputation for fearlessness.

While Rizzo was serving as police commissioner of the fourth largest city in the U.S., Philadelphia became the lowest ranking major city in street crimes and civil disorders, according to statistics filed with the FBI. The racial riots of other large cities were averted in Philadelphia. Rizzo also played an important role in integrating the city's police force.

Rizzo defeated Republican candidate W. Thacher Longstreth in the race for mayor in November 1971 by campaigning as the "toughest cop in America." Rizzo's support came chiefly from blue-collar and middle-class whites, and his election was seen by some as evidence of a "blue power" backlash against blacks that would further polarize a socially troubled city.

During his term as mayor, Rizzo kept his promise not to raise taxes and decreased the exodus of businesses from the city. The problems of 1973 seemed to erode much of his once-solid popularity, but some observers believed that the hard-core supporters who elected him mayor would remain unshaken in their faith that "Rizzo means business."

(DONALD J. KLIMOVICH)

ROUNDTREE, RICHARD

The best known, most imitated private eye in the U.S. in 1973 was John Shaft—the most "supercool" of the supersleuths to come out of the black adventure films. Shaft's third movie, *Shaft in Africa,* was released and assured of success; Shaft T-shirts became highly prized in Ethiopia, where the latest exploits of the "black James Bond" were filmed; and black detectives, including Shaft himself, joined the television mystery series parade in regular rotation with the slovenly, seemingly bumbling cops, Western marshals a-sea in the big city, and crafty, urbane insurance investigators.

That Shaft had "simply needed doing," as his white creator, Ernest Tidyman, said, was obvious. But the stereotype of the role, which called for little more than an athletic physique and a collection of glib lines to throw out between episodes of violence, could hardly have achieved status within "the honourable line of hard-boiled nice guys" without some acting skill to give it a life of its own. Actor Richard Roundtree had the tough-friendly visage of the James Cagney-Humphrey Bogart tradition and the skill to carry off the brash, wisecracking role that contrasted with his own personality. For Roundtree was a true product of the great show business tradition: years of bit parts, work with community theatre groups, roles in documentaries and commercials, and even modeling had ended with his surprise choice over much better established black actors for the Shaft part.

"Tree" was born in New Rochelle, N.Y., in 1942; his father was a garbage collector and caterer and his mother a housekeeper, making them "upper lower middle class." He played football at Southern Illinois University until, tired of the battering even a 6 ft. 2 in. 200-pounder had to take, he concentrated on dramatics, dropping out of college in his sophomore year. The lean years that followed ended when he "answered the cattle call" of tryouts for the soon-to-be-celebrated Shaft role. "I know Shaft is a fantasy person, a fictional person," he said, but on the screen he appears as "a black man who for once is a winner," like Richard Roundtree.

RUMOR, MARIANO

When the leading Italian political party, the Christian Democrats, decided at its annual conference in June 1973 to jettison its centre coalition with the Liberals and revert to a centre-left coalition with the Socialists, the choice of Mariano Rumor to lead the new alliance followed naturally. He was, perhaps, the only man trusted by all four parties of the new coalition (Social Democrats and Republicans as well as Socialists and Christian Democrats). He had already been premier from December 1968 to July 1970 (with an interruption in March), and more recently, as minister for home affairs, had successfully checked the increasing political violence. His first task on resuming the premiership was to halt inflation. This he hoped to achieve with a series of financial measures, including a severe price freeze and a tax reform that would take effect from Jan. 1, 1974.

Rumor was born in Vicenza on June 16, 1915. After graduation from Padua University he became a teacher. During World War II he served as an officer in the artillery, and in 1943 he joined the partisans to fight against the Fascist and German forces. In 1945 he became a member of the Christian Democratic Party, and a year later was chosen by the district of Verona as a deputy to the assembly charged with forming the new republican constitution. He entered Parliament in 1948.

After serving as undersecretary for agriculture in the governments of Alcide De Gasperi and Giuseppe Pella, in 1954 he was elected deputy secretary of his party. During 1959–63 he was minister for agriculture under the successive governments of Antonio Segni, Fernando Tambroni, and Amintore Fanfani, and his name was linked with the so-called "green plan" to develop agriculture in Italy. For five months in 1963–64 he was minister for home affairs under Giovanni Leone, during the difficult times of the Alto Adige (South Tirol) terrorism and the Vaiont Dam disaster in which more than 1,500 persons were killed. Made secretary-general and then political secretary of the party, he became premier for the first time in 1968, supported initially by the Christian Democrats alone, then by the parties of the centre-left coalition.

(FABIO GALVANO)

SADAT, ANWAR AS-

On Oct. 6, 1973, Egypt's Pres. Anwar as-Sadat strode boldly out of the shadow of his dead mentor, Gamal Abd-an-Nasser, and, growing hourly to heroic proportions, crossed the Suez Canal to liberate Arab honour and amaze a complacent world. Dreams of revolutionary pan-Arabism were discarded for uncharacteristic realism. Following the expulsion of his Soviet ally, Sadat reestablished diplomatic relations with the United States, leaving many Egyptians bewildered. Instead of realizing the much-heralded union with Muammar al-Qaddafi's Libya, the president looked to where the real power lay, in Saudi Arabia and the Persian Gulf, in the form of vast and, to the West, vital oil and foreign currency reserves.

By forging an axis with Saudi King Faisal (*q.v.*) and persuading him to lead an oil embargo against Israel's allies in return for Egyptian and Syrian armed action, Sadat shook the foundations of the Western world. The British and French, former colonialists, became humble supplicants overnight; the U.S., less directly affected, was still forced to reconsider its relations with Europe, the Soviets, the Arabs, and Israel; and the Israelis became ever more isolated.

Although in theory union with Libya would have given Egypt's 35 million people an annual oil income of £1,000 million, the personal cost to Sadat of embracing the Islamic fanatic Qaddafi (*q.v.*), who himself had designs on Egypt, was too high. In late August, with Sadat's prestige at its zenith, Qaddafi was left to "whistle at vacancy" in Cairo, while Sadat toured Saudi Arabia, Syria, and Qatar. At the Arab summit in Algiers in November, Sadat gained the required support for a "negotiated" settlement —involving Israel's total withdrawal from all Arab territories occupied in the 1967 war and the establishment of the "full national rights of the Palestinian people."

Born Dec. 25, 1918, in the al-Minufiyah Governorate of the Nile Delta, Sadat graduated from the Cairo Military Academy in 1938. During World War II he plotted to evict the British from Egypt and was captured in 1942, but later escaped into hiding. In 1950 he joined Nasser's Free Officers, and after the 1952 revolution held various high offices culminating in the vice-presidency (1964). He became acting president on Nasser's death and was elected president in a national plebiscite on Oct. 15, 1970.

(PETER MANSFIELD)

SAKHAROV, ANDREY DMITRIEVICH

In its September 1973 issue, the *Kommunist,* the ideological organ of the Central Committee of the Communist Party of the Soviet Union, published a vehement attack on a physicist who had been once described as the father of the Soviet hydrogen bomb, Andrey D. Sakharov. He was described as a man who "with fanatical obstinacy continues his activity directed against international détente, and the elimination of war threat." His support, according to *Kommunist,* came from abroad among the "professional anti-Soviet and anti-Communist agitators who had begun to fan out to the utmost his hysterical pronouncements." The Sakharov case, concluded *Kommunist,* was serious because he had become "a tool in the enemy's hands."

Although in the forefront of dissent since 1966 and a co-founder of the unofficial Human Rights Committee in the Soviet Union, Sakharov was practically unknown in the West until the *New York Times* of July 22, 1968, published the English translation of his 10,000-word essay under the title "Thoughts About Progress, Peaceful Coexistence and Intellectual Freedom." Its basic theses were that "the division of mankind threatens it with destruction" and that "intellectual freedom is essential to human society." Among the chief dangers facing mankind, he saw the perpetuation of "intellectually simplified, narrow-minded mass myths" that make nations a prey to hysteria and the dogmatism of "cruel and treacherous demagogues." Departing from Communist orthodoxy, he challenged the Marxist prediction of an inevitable breakdown of capitalism as a result of internal contradictions.

Defying an official warning against foreign contacts, Sakharov gave Swedish television an interview that was filmed secretly in Moscow and whose text was published on July 3, 1973, in the Stockholm newspaper *Dagens Nyheter.* On August 21 he received a group of foreign correspondents and the full text of this press conference was published in *The Times* of London of September 5. On that occasion Sakharov warned the West against the dangers of a sham détente, a détente without democratization in the Soviet Union. On November 29 he told correspondents that he had sought permission to visit the U.S., although aware that he might not be able to return.

Andrey Dmitrievich Sakharov was born May 21, 1921. He graduated with honours in physics from Moscow University in 1942. In 1953 he became the youngest scientist ever to be elected a full member of the Soviet Academy of Sciences. From 1948 to 1956 Sakharov was engaged in research connected with nuclear weapons.

(K. M. SMOGORZEWSKI)

SCHLESINGER, JAMES RODNEY

Adding to his reputation as one of the Nixon administration's iron men, James R. Schlesinger took office as secretary of defense on July 2, 1973. He thus became the third man to head the Pentagon within a six-month period. He had served since February 1973 as director of the Central Intelligence Agency and, before that, as chairman of the U.S. Atomic Energy Commission.

On July 16 Schlesinger admitted that Air Force B-52 bombers had been secretly bombing Cambodia in 1969 and 1970, while the U.S. was publicly proclaiming its respect for that country's neutrality in the Vietnam war. In a letter delivered to Sen. Stuart Symington (Dem., Mo.), Schlesinger said that the bombing raids were "fully authorized" by senior military and civilian officials and that "special security precautions" were taken to avoid public disclosure of the raids due to the sensitive diplomatic situation.

The Cambodian bombing raids had taken place while Melvin R. Laird was secretary of defense, but it fell to Schlesinger to explain and defend them. Earlier, as CIA director, Schlesinger had been obliged to explain the agency's alleged involvement in the cover-up of the Watergate break-in and in the burglary of the office of Daniel Ellsberg's psychiatrist—events that had occurred while Richard Helms headed the CIA.

On August 3 Schlesinger announced that military commanders had been ordered to end "all combat activities" in Cambodia and Laos at midnight August 14. The commanders were directed, however, to continue "unarmed" reconnaissance flights "for the purpose of gathering intelligence."

Schlesinger was born Feb. 15, 1929, in New York City. After obtaining B.A., M.A., and Ph.D. degrees from Harvard, he joined the University of Virginia faculty in 1955 as an assistant professor of economics. In 1963 Schlesinger moved on to the Rand Corporation as a senior staff member, specializing in strategic analysis. One month after the Nixon administration took office, Schlesinger accepted an appointment as assistant director of the Bureau of the Budget. Among his accomplishments in that post was the trimming of about $6 billion from the budget of the Department of Defense. He became chairman of the Atomic Energy Commission in July 1971. (RICHARD L. WORSNOP)

SÉGUY, GEORGES

As secretary-general of France's most powerful labour organization, the Confédération Générale du Travail (CGT), Georges Séguy was the country's leading trade union figure. During 1973, with France bedeviled by industrial strife, racial disturbances involving foreign workers, and a high rate of inflation, his was a voice frequently heard in public debate. As he was also a leading member of the French Communist Party (PCF), the party's political activities and trade union demands were closely linked. CGT membership numbered 2.5 million, and Séguy and his party colleagues could count on the support of every fourth voter and every sixth employee among the French population.

Alert and rosy cheeked, Séguy offered a smiling face and reassuring image to the country. He described the CGT as "a vast, quiet strength" and did his best to avoid the upheavals in which leftist elements and the country's other big trade union federation (Confédération Française Démocratique du Travail) sometimes tried to involve him. Although an enemy of capitalism and an unflinching Marxist, separated only by differences of role and personality from Georges Marchais, the PCF political leader, Séguy played the card of dialogue with the regime and subordinated his desire to pave the way for revolution to improvement of the living standards of working people. Nevertheless, one of his 1973 pronouncements was sufficiently revolutionary in tone to raise hackles in government quarters and to cause disquiet among the Socialists, partners of the PCF in the 1973 election. Speaking at a CGT gathering in Paris in September, he said that the workers' struggle might create a situation whereby "without waiting for another election" the left might come to power.

Born in Toulouse in 1927, the son of a railwayman, Séguy began work in the printing trade at 15. As a PCF member from 1942, he took an active part in resistance against the German occupation of France. He was arrested and deported to Mauthausen, and on his return at the end of World War II he began his career as a trade union official. In 1961 he became secretary-general of the railway workers' union and in 1967 rose to leadership of the CGT. Meanwhile, he became a member of the PCF Central Committee in 1954 and from 1956 was a member of its Political Bureau.

(PIERRE VIANSSON-PONTÉ)

SHAW, TAN SRI RUNME and RUN RUN

The Western world's discovery of the Hong Kong cinema and the stylized conventions of the kung fu Chinese wrestling melodrama —with its shamelessly contrived stories and balletic hand-to-hand fighting—came a little late in the career of the Shaw brothers, Southeast Asia's major producers of films. As long ago as 1924 Tan Sri Runme Shaw (born Shanghai, 1901), newly arrived in Hong Kong as an immigrant from China, had established their first movie theatre. By 1973 Runme and his younger brother Run Run (born Singapore, 1907) were, respectively, chairman and president of one of the biggest entertainment empires in the world. With Runme operating from Singapore and Run Run from Hong Kong, the company owned a chain of more than 140 movie theatres and had production studios in Hong Kong, Singapore, and Kuala Lumpur, Malaysia. Opened in 1960, Run Run Shaw's Movietown in Hong Kong occupied two million square feet and had a dozen sound stages, its own laboratories, and high-rise apartment houses for personnel. Hong Kong alone had 200 artists under contract and 3,000 employees. The remaining Shaw production enterprises employed another 5,000. Annual production of the combined studios was approximately 40 films, with about 10 in production at any one time. The movies achieved great popularity in the U.S. during 1973.

The firm's other interests extended to banking, property, and brewing. The brothers were notable philanthropists, and the Shaw Foundation donated millions of dollars annually to schools, hospitals, and charities. Appropriately laden with honours, the brothers were said to live the lives of great moguls, their privacy closely guarded. In the summer of 1973 *The Times* of London reported the death of Runme Shaw. This proved to be untrue, a misunderstanding that arose from reports of the death of another Shaw brother, Runde, who was in fact unconnected with the film industry.

(DAVID ROBINSON)

SHULTZ, GEORGE PRATT

For U.S. Treasury Secretary George P. Shultz, 1973 was a year of retreat and frustration. The erratic performance of the economy forced Shultz to abandon his positions on interest rates, economic controls, and support of the dollar in international money markets. At midyear he was reported on the verge of resigning. But he remained in his post and, in fact, took on additional duties as a special economic adviser to Pres. Richard Nixon. At year's end, as the administration attempted to cope with the energy crisis, he was reportedly one of those opposing gasoline rationing.

James Rodney Schlesinger

WIDE WORLD

When four major banks raised their prime lending rate from 6 to 6.25% on February 2, Shultz and Federal Reserve Board Chairman Arthur Burns led a partially successful administration campaign to rescind the increase. Six months later, however, Shultz gave his blessing to a prime lending rate of 9.25%. Shultz was one of the principal architects of the liberalized Phase Three economic program that took effect in January, but within three months it was evident that the voluntary approach to wage-price controls was not working. On June 13 President Nixon ordered a freeze on a wide range of consumer prices and announced that Shultz and Cost of Living Council Director John Dunlop would prepare new wage-price policies that would impose "tighter standards." The result was Phase Four, unveiled on July 18. Shultz declined to make any predictions about its success. "It is desirable to be a little humble," he said. He rejected pleas to intervene directly when the dollar was plunging to new lows in early June but promised strong action to deal with inflation. A month later he joined Burns in announcing that the U.S. had intervened in New York foreign exchange markets to support the dollar and that "active intervention" would continue "at whatever time and in whatever amounts are appropriate."

Shultz was born Dec. 13, 1920, in New York City. He served the Eisenhower, Kennedy, and Johnson administrations as an economic consultant and was dean of the University of Chicago Graduate School of Business from 1962 until his appointment as secretary of labour in 1969. In addition to heading the Labor and Treasury departments, he also served as director of the Office of Management and Budget.

(RICHARD L. WORSNOP)

SIHANOUK, NORODOM

In 1973, his third year of exile in Peking, Cambodia's former head of state, Prince Norodom Sihanouk, bounced back to the threshold of power. His rebel forces were able to strike at the Cambodian capital, Phnom Penh, at will, and he himself won diplomatic advantage at the conference of nonaligned nations in Algiers in September. In a sensational exploit, he secretly visited guerrilla-held areas in Cambodia in March. Clearly reflecting his position of strength, Sihanouk was publicly refusing to meet U.S. Secretary of State Henry A. Kissinger, where a year earlier he had been angling for such an invitation. In December he scored further diplomatic success when China and 32 other nations called for the UN representation of the U.S.-supported Lon Nol government to be replaced by that of Sihanouk's Peking-based "royal government of Khmer national union" (GRUNK).

Sihanouk repeatedly affirmed that once the Khmer Rouge established themselves in Phnom Penh his own leadership would be nominal and even transitional. Given the ferocity with which he fought the Khmer Rouge when he was in power, this was logical. But, given his recognized genius for maneuvering, no one could be sure.

One of Southeast Asia's most colourful leaders, Sihanouk, born in Phnom Penh on Oct. 31, 1922, became king at 18, selected by the French, who thought he would be their pliant instrument. Four years later, however, Sihanouk began a systematic campaign for Cambodia's independence, achieving it through peaceful negotiation in 1953. Following the 1954 Geneva agreement, early in 1955 he formed the Socialist People's Community Party, whose program was overwhelmingly approved in a referendum; shortly afterward he abdicated in favour of his father, Norodom Suramarit, and became prime minister (and also, in characteristic style, foreign minister and permanent representative to the UN). When his father died in 1960, Sihanouk again became head of state (not king) and remained so until ousted by the Lon Nol coup in 1970. Disproving expectations that he would settle for a quiet life in France, he set up GRUNK in Peking and vigorously campaigned on behalf of the Khmer Rouge underground and against the Lon Nol regime.

(T. J. S. GEORGE)

SIMPSON, O(RENTHAL) J(AMES)

The outstanding performer in U.S. professional football in 1973 was O. J. Simpson. The Buffalo Bills' running back set a new single-season rushing record of 2,003 yd., breaking Jim Brown's mark of 1,863.

In 1969–71 the former University of Southern California star, winner of the Heisman Trophy, did little to justify the $350,000 that the Buffalo Bills were paying for four years of his services. The fault was not all Simpson's, however. Unlike some college superstars, he was playing regularly and reasonably well. But the Bills were a mediocre team at best. With a porous defense and a barely passable offensive line, they were constantly forced into playing catch-up ball. Given that kind of team, it is little wonder that people were asking: "Whatever happened to O. J. Simpson?" By 1972, however, Simpson began to come into his own.

Born in San Francisco on July 9, 1947, O. J. Simpson could have been another casualty of that city's Hunter's Point ghetto. His parents were separated, and his mother, a hospital worker, had little time to devote to her three children. Indeed, Simpson did have brushes with the police. Two things seem to have turned him around. First, he recognized that he had extraordinary athletic ability. Second, he had an early realization of the importance of material things, and he began to understand that the first could help to achieve the second.

A poor student in high school, Simpson was ignored by recruiters from four-year colleges. Somewhat reluctantly, he enrolled in the City College of San Francisco, where his grades improved and his track and football talents began to attract attention. At the end of two years, he was getting offers from schools throughout the country. Simpson chose Southern California, and in his first year ran 1,541 yd. in leading the Trojans to a national championship. In 1968 he gained 1,709 yd. and scored 22 touchdowns, setting a National Collegiate Athletic Association record.

The Buffalo Bills drafted Simpson and, after some touchy negotiations with his financial adviser, signed him to a four-year contract worth almost $100,000 annually. Then began the years of frustration. However, in 1972 the Bills named Lou Saban coach, and the fortunes of O. J. and the team turned upward. Saban geared his offense to Simpson's talents and was rewarded when O. J. rushed for 1,251 yd. to lead the National Football League; in doing so, he also set a new single-game record of 250 yd. on the ground.

(DONALD J. KLIMOVICH)

SINDERMANN, HORST

In October 1973 Horst Sindermann became premier of East Germany, ranking after Communist Party Secretary Erich Honecker in a collective leadership that also included former premier Willi Stoph as ceremonial head of state. This last post—more precisely that of chairman of the Council of State—had been left vacant by the death on August 1 of Walter Ulbricht (*see* OBITUARIES). Two months later, on October 2, the party's Central Committee decided that Stoph, a former protégé of Ulbricht and rival of Honecker, should succeed Ulbricht, while Sindermann, then first deputy premier, should replace Stoph. These changes were duly approved by the People's Chamber on October 3.

Sindermann, a dynamic and popular 58-year-old Communist, never shared Ulbricht's dreams of a German confederation and always sustained the idea of *Abgrenzung,* that is, total separation of the two German states. A sophisticated realist and a good organizer, he was also a fluent, cogent speaker well able to explain the party's problems. Characteristically, in his inaugural speech as premier he stressed the ever growing satisfaction of the material and cultural needs of the East German people.

Sindermann was born in Dresden on Sept. 5, 1915. As a member of the Communist Youth League he was arrested in 1933 by the newly ensconced Nazi authorities and given a nine-month jail sentence. Arrested again in 1935, he was imprisoned at Waldheim jail and later in the Sachsenhausen and Mauthausen concentration camps until 1945. After the collapse of the Third Reich, Sindermann was appointed editor of Soviet-licensed Communist local newspapers in Dresden and later in Chemnitz (renamed Karl-Marx-Stadt). From 1950 to 1953 he edited the Halle *Freiheit,* which he transformed into one of the few readable newspapers of East Germany. He was transferred to East Berlin in 1954 to become head of the propaganda section of the party's Central Committee. His rise in the party was rather slow because Ulbricht disliked him, and not until the sixth party congress in 1963 was he elected a full member of the Central Committee. A full member of the Politburo from 1967, he was appointed first deputy premier in May 1971, shortly after Ulbricht had been forced to resign from the post of first secretary.

(K. M. SMOGORZEWSKI)

SIRICA, JOHN JOSEPH

In March 1973 John J. Sirica, chief judge of the U.S. District Court for Washington, D.C., provided the catalyst for a series of disclosures that rocked the nation. His handling of the trial of seven men indicted for the 1972 burglary of national Democratic Party headquarters in Washington's Watergate complex opened a Pandora's box of troubles for the administration of Pres. Richard Nixon.

Throughout the trial Judge Sirica expressed impatience with the prosecution's handling of the case against G. Gordon Liddy and James W. McCord, Jr. Prior to being sentenced, McCord wrote Sirica a letter claiming that he and the others were under "political pressure to plead guilty and remain silent." Sirica delayed sentencing McCord until he had a chance to hear the full story, a strong hint to the other defendants that cooperation might affect the sentences he meted out. While none of the other six spoke out, the McCord letter and Judge Sirica's comments did serve to focus public and congressional attention on the Nixon reelection campaign.

Sirica's involvement in Watergate did not end with the conviction of the original "Watergate seven." What had begun as a case of political espionage evolved into a profound constitutional crisis when, on August 29, the judge ordered President Nixon to surrender tape recordings of White House conversations sought by then special prosecutor Archibald Cox. In October the president, so anxious to preserve executive privilege that he had fired Cox and accepted

Stephen Sondheim

"THE TIMES," LONDON/PICTORIAL PARADE

Margaret Hilda Thatcher

KEYSTONE

Sir Georg Solti

ERICH LESSING—MAGNUM

the resignation of his attorney general, agreed to deliver the tapes.

After finding that a part of one tape had been obliterated, Sirica ordered that the others be examined for "any evidence of tampering." He then listened to the tapes and upheld Nixon's claims of executive privilege on all or parts of three of them, turning five over to the new special prosecutor, Leon Jaworski.

The son of an immigrant Italian barber, Sirica was born in 1904 in Waterbury, Conn., and grew up in New Orleans and Jacksonville, Fla. He enrolled in Georgetown University Law School and supported himself through occasional boxing matches. An active Republican, he made countless campaign speeches for Alf Landon in 1936 and Wendell Willkie in 1940. In 1957 Pres. Dwight Eisenhower appointed him to the federal bench, and in 1971, by virtue of seniority, he became chief judge for the District of Columbia. (DONNA ZIMMERMAN)

SOLTI, SIR GEORG

The 1973–74 season of the Chicago Symphony Orchestra was delayed by a musicians' strike, but when it finally opened, with musical director Sir Georg Solti at the baton, there was no sign of discord. Once again, critics acclaimed what the London *Daily Telegraph* had called "the finest orchestra in the world."

This was a relatively new experience for the Chicago Symphony. It had attained national prominence under Fritz Reiner in the '50s, but after Reiner's death nothing seemed to jell. Critics fumed, recording contracts evaporated, and, symphonically speaking, Chicago was not even the Second City.

All that changed when Solti arrived in 1969. By the spring of 1971, when the orchestra made a triumphal European tour, he had brought it new international prestige. Annual concerts in New York received standing ovations, and the subscription series in Chicago was perennially sold out. It was, as Solti said, a musically happy marriage. Since the days of Theodore Thomas and Frederick Stock, Chicago had been a romantic orchestra, and Solti, acclaimed for his performances of Wagner, Mahler, and Bruckner, was a romantic conductor. "That is our secret!" he told *Time* magazine. "At a time when everybody is doing exactly the opposite, we are unafraid to be romantic."

Solti first achieved fame as an opera conductor. Born in Budapest, Hung., on Oct. 21, 1912, he entered the Franz Liszt Academy at 13, then studied piano with Ernst von Dohnanyi and composition with Zoltan Kodaly at the Budapest Academy. At 18 he began a long apprenticeship with the Budapest Opera, making his debut with a 1938 performance of *The Marriage of Figaro*.

When World War II broke out, Solti, a Jew, settled in Zürich, Switz., where he spent the war years as a concert and chamber pianist. After the war he was musical director at three major European opera houses: Munich (1946–52), Frankfurt (1952–60), and the Royal Opera House, Covent Garden (1961–71). At Frankfurt alone he scheduled 44 new productions, and his recording of Wagner's complete Ring brought worldwide acclaim. In addition to his duties at Chicago, he was principal conductor of the Orchestra de Paris and principal music adviser of the London Philharmonic Orchestra and Covent Garden. A British citizen, he was knighted in 1972.

(DANIEL MILLER)

SONDHEIM, STEPHEN

The imminent death of the Broadway musical had been predicted for years. One of those doing his best to keep it alive—and achieving considerable success in the process—was 43-year-old Stephen Sondheim, who in 1973 won an Antoinette Perry (Tony) Award for the music and lyrics of *A Little Night Music*. Most critics agreed that he was responsible for the three finest musicals of the 1970s, the others (for which he also won Tonys) being *Company* (1970) and *Follies* (1971). At the end of March, Broadway saluted him with a gala, "A Tribute to Stephen Sondheim," at which such stars as Angela Lansbury, Alexis Smith, and Jack Cassidy sang 40 of his songs.

In *A Little Night Music,* Sondheim transformed Ingmar Bergman's 1955 film comedy, *Smiles of a Summer Night,* into a dazzling comic-dramatic musical. Written entirely in 3/4 time or multiples thereof, the show featured a variety of ensemble pieces, including contrapuntal duets and trios, a quartet, and a double quintet. Unlike the more satiric and bittersweet *Follies* and *Company, A Little Night Music* was predominantly tender and witty. Like Sondheim's other works, it dealt with its subject in a complex and sophisticated manner, dramatizing various states of love in a turn-of-the-century setting.

Stephen Sondheim admitted to a lifelong passion for craft in general and for the craft of theatre in particular. Born in New York City, March 22, 1930, he began to play the piano at four and took lessons at the age of seven. His parents were divorced when he was ten, and he and his mother moved to a farm in Doylestown, Pa. The famous lyricist Oscar Hammerstein was a neighbour and family friend, and, when Sondheim asked his opinion of a school show he had written, Hammerstein began instructing him in the principles of constructing a Broadway show and streamlining a song.

Sondheim majored in music at Williams College, Williamstown, Mass., and later studied with the composer Milton Babbitt. He considered himself a composer first, despite his brilliance as a lyricist. He wrote the words for *West Side Story* (1957) and *Gypsy* (1959), and both words and music for *A Funny Thing Happened on the Way to the Forum* (1962). (DANIEL MILLER)

STEINER, JULIUS

A former Christian Democratic Union (CDU) member of the West German Bundestag (federal parliament), Julius Steiner in 1973 was the central figure of an inquiry in Bonn into allegations of political corruption. Steiner had disclosed to the magazine *Quick* that he had accepted a bribe of DM. 50,000 ($19,500) to abstain from voting in a vital parliamentary ballot in 1972. The affair became known in the press as the "Bonn Watergate."

Steiner was one of two opposition deputies who had abstained when, on April 27, 1972, the Christian Democrats proposed a "constructive motion" of no confidence in the federal chancellor, Willy Brandt. This was a constitutional device that enabled the Bundestag to dismiss the head of government if a majority of its members agreed on the election of a successor. The attempt to replace Brandt as chancellor with the then opposition leader, Rainer Barzel, failed by two votes.

According to Steiner, the bribe had been paid to him by Karl Wienand, parliamentary business manager, or chief whip, of Brandt's Social Democratic Party. This Wienand denied. The parliamentary committee of inquiry, which started its investigations in June, was confronted with a mass of conflicting evidence and made little progress, but it was established that Steiner became richer by DM. 50,000 immediately after the no-confidence vote had taken place.

Steiner was born in Stuttgart on Sept. 18, 1924. After war service he studied philosophy, theology, and history. He held a number of posts as business consultant, and admitted to the inquiry that he had worked as a double agent for the East and West German intelligence services. He was a prominent member of the CDU in Baden-Württemberg for many years, but as a member of the Bundestag during 1969–72 he attracted little attention and once said that he felt bitter because Barzel had taken no notice of him. In assessing the "Bonn Watergate," Steiner's character and mental and physical condition had to be taken into account. He had had heart trouble and had been suffering from stress, and his statements were seldom models of lucidity.

(NORMAN CROSSLAND)

THATCHER, MARGARET HILDA

Although the most reviled minister in a Tory Cabinet might well be expected to be the industrial relations minister, in Edward Heath's government that distinction almost certainly belonged to Margaret Thatcher, secretary of state for education and science. Some of the actions held against her, such as the withdrawal in 1970 of free milk from schoolchildren over the age of seven, were, no doubt, part of general retrenchment policies rather than the specific work of Mrs. Thatcher's department. The basic cause of her unpopularity with the Labour opposition and teachers was that she arrived in office in time to prevent the completion of Labour's plans to amalgamate grammar and secondary modern schools into comprehensive schools. Mrs. Thatcher was determined to maintain a diversity of educational establishments (including private, fee-paying schools) in order, in her view, to provide parents with adequate choice and children with schools that would best develop their varying abilities. In her opponents' view, choice was available only to a well-off minority. Another controversial matter within the scope of her administration was the charging of admission fees to museums and galleries—a measure narrowly approved by Parliament in November and due to take effect on Jan. 2, 1974.

Incisive in argument and swift to seize upon telling points in debate, polite, and imperturbable, Mrs. Thatcher was probably one of the most active British education ministers since World War II. She gave special attention to teacher training and primary schools, and set up inquiries into problems of violence, truancy, vocational guidance, school meals, and transport. On one issue that arose in 1973 she did succeed in improving her standing with the teaching profession: in November she acceded to demands that teachers' pension contributions be reduced to 6% of salary.

Born at Grantham, Lincolnshire, on Oct. 13, 1925, Margaret Thatcher was educated at Kesteven and Grantham Girls' School, and at Somerville College, Oxford. A research chemist, she also studied law. Conservative MP for Finchley, North London, from 1959, she was joint parliamentary secretary to the Ministry of Pensions and National Insurance, and, while the Conservatives were in opposition, shadow minister of education. (STEPHANIE MULLINS)

THORPE, (JOHN) JEREMY

Under the leadership of Jeremy Thorpe, Britain's Liberal Party enjoyed a run of sensational by-election victories during 1972 and 1973, raising the number of Liberal members in the House of Commons from 6 to 11. Thorpe had been elected party leader in 1967, taking over from Jo Grimond, who in his ten years of leadership had reestablished the party's claim to be a significant political force. After the 1970 general election, in which Liberal strength in the Commons fell back from 13 to 6, the quality of Thorpe's leadership came in for criticism, but by the autumn of 1973 he had confirmed his hold on the party.

Thorpe was an appropriately youthful leader of a party that had more than the average quota of young MPs and the liveliest young rank-and-file membership of any party. Born April 29, 1929, and educated in the U.S. and at Eton College and Oxford, he was elected to Parliament in 1959 for North Devon, a seat in a somewhat conservative part of rural England which he managed to hang onto through successive general elections by uncomfortably small majorities.

It was not surprising that Thorpe should look to politics for a career, for both his father and maternal grandfather had been MPs—as Conservatives. But Thorpe's instincts were radical. At the 1973 meeting of the Liberal Assembly he said the party was "unashamedly in favour of redistributing wealth in this country to secure a decent standard of living for all our people." This was not a new development, in that the Liberals in Grimond's time had presented themselves as the "radical alternative." But Thorpe himself was sometimes criticized as too conventional and traditionalist. This was partly because his manner was somewhat dandyish and his style somewhat theatrical, so much so that some of his critics complained that he was a playboy. But this was to misjudge his fundamental seriousness. When he clashed with the turbulent Young Liberals, it was on a fundamental issue; Thorpe uncompromisingly upheld the commitment to parliamentary democracy at a time when some of the Young Liberals were attracted by ideas of direct action.

(HARFORD THOMAS)

ULLMANN, LIV

Starring in a costly Hollywood spectacular in the old-time manner, appearing on the cover of *Time* magazine, succeeding to a role that Greta Garbo had made seemingly inimitable nearly 40 years before, and generally finding herself in 1973 one of the most sought-after film actresses in the world left Liv Ullmann serenely unimpressed. "At 33 I am much too old to be swept off my feet or to deceive myself with the illusions of stardom. Of course it's a lot of fun."

She was born in 1939, in Tokyo, where her Norwegian father was working as a civil engineer. The family later joined the refugee Norwegian colony in Toronto; and not until 1946, after World War II and following her father's death, did she arrive in Oslo. At 17 she was taken by her mother to London to study drama. Returning home to Norway, she was, however, turned down by the State Theatre School, and went into repertory. An overnight success in *The Diary of Anne Frank* had already confirmed her as one of the most popular actresses in the country when Ingmar Bergman took her to Sweden to star in *Persona* (1966), largely on account of her resemblance to Bibi Andersson, who co-starred with her. While sharing Bergman's life and bearing his daughter, the actress worked with him on three more films, *Hour of the Wolf* (1968), *The Shame* (1968), and *A Passion* (1970). Following their domestic parting, she made her most memorable appearance in a Bergman film in *Cries and Whispers,* the New York film critics' choice for the best movie of 1972.

Two films directed by Jan Troell, *The Emigrants* and *The New Land* (both 1972), based on the epic novels of Vilhelm Moberg, proved to be the biggest box-office success ever achieved for Swedish movies, both at home and abroad; her role in *The Emigrants* earned Ullmann a nomination for an Academy Award. International film offers followed fast: in Britain she appeared in the title role of *Pope Joan* (1972); in the U.S. in the musical version of James Hilton's *Lost Horizon* (1972). In 1973 the leading role in *Forty Carats* was rewritten for her, and the film was chosen for a "royal premiere" in London; she co-starred in *Zandy's Bride;* and then returned to Britain to play the role of Queen Christina of Sweden in Anthony Harvey's *The Abdication,* based on the early period of Christina's exile in Rome.

(DAVID ROBINSON)

VESCO, ROBERT L.

Once known as the boy wonder of international finance, Robert Vesco in 1973 became known instead as an elusive multimillionaire, a key figure in a monumental financial scandal that led to the indictments of two former Nixon Cabinet members. Wanted by both the U.S. and the Swiss governments, Vesco lived a harried but regal life in Costa Rica and the Bahamas, both of which declined on juridical grounds to grant extradition requests.

Vesco's troubles began with an extensive investigation by the U.S. Securities and Exchange Commission. The SEC accused him and 41 other persons or companies of violating securities laws and of defrauding four foreign mutual funds managed by Investors Overseas Services (IOS), a mutual fund empire that Vesco once controlled, of $224 million. Vesco was also indicted twice in 1973 in connection with $250,000 in illegal contributions to Pres. Richard Nixon's reelection campaign.

All but $50,000 of that money was delivered on April 10, 1972, in a black suitcase filled with $100 bills, to former secretary of commerce Maurice Stans, who was then the chairman of the Finance Committee to Re-elect the President. The money was turned over to Stans three days after a federal law went into effect requiring contributions to be reported to the government and disclosed publicly. Also, the money was contributed at the same time that the SEC was examining Vesco's financial dealings, leading to the suspicion that the donation was intended to influence the inquiry.

On May 10, 1973, a federal grand jury in New York City indicted Vesco, Stans, former U.S. attorney general John Mitchell, and Harry L. Sears, a onetime New Jersey campaign director for President Nixon. The indictment accused the four men of conspiring to obstruct justice in connection with the SEC investigation and conspiracy to commit fraud. Vesco never appeared at the arraignment, and warrants were issued for his arrest.

Vesco was born on Dec. 4, 1935, in Detroit. A onetime auto mechanic, he was said to have designed a popular aluminum grille for the Oldsmobile before leaving Detroit for New York's business world. In 1965 he took control of two small companies, merged them, and quickly raised their annual earnings from zero to $4.7 million. In 1971 he purchased IOS, whose assets once topped $1 billion.

(ROBERT A. SIGNER)

VONNEGUT, KURT, JR.

It was a very good year for Kurt Vonnegut, Jr. In 1973 his latest novel, *Breakfast of Champions,* threatened to become a perennial on the best-seller list; he was appointed distinguished professor (of English) at City College of New York; and he was elected to the National Institute of Arts and Letters, the nation's most prestigious honour society in the arts.

But it was also Vonnegut's 50th year and, in what he claimed was the same spirit of

Liv Ullmann

WIDE WORLD

Robert L. Vesco

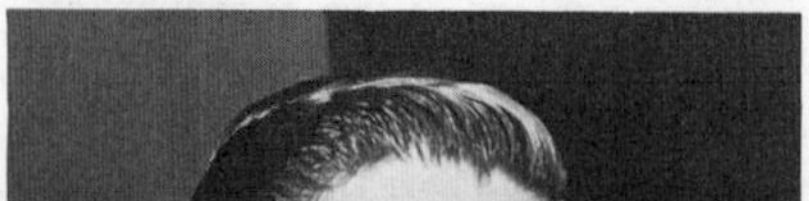

WIDE WORLD

John Barrington Wain

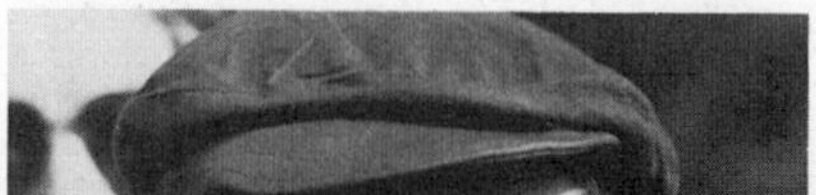

"THE TIMES," LONDON/PICTORIAL PARADE

cleansing that had led Tolstoy and Jefferson to free their slaves, he said he was setting all of his characters free. *Breakfast* did show a shift in approach in that for the first time Vonnegut dealt with a character who actually goes mad. Previously it had been Vonnegut's world that was mad. Whether his characters would stay at liberty remained to be seen: after the 1969 publication of *Slaughterhouse-Five,* he had announced he would never write another novel.

Vonnegut was born Nov. 11, 1922, in Indianapolis, Ind. He entered Cornell University to study biochemistry in 1940, transferred to Carnegie Tech, and then was drafted into the Army for World War II. Serving in the infantry in Europe, he was captured by the Germans and taken with other prisoners to Dresden. "It was the first fancy city I'd ever seen. . . . Then a siren went off—it was Feb. 13, 1945, and we went down two stories under the pavement into a big meat locker. . . . When we came up the city was gone," destroyed by a massive Allied air attack.

After the war Vonnegut attended the University of Chicago and then went to work in public relations for the General Electric Co. in Schenectady, N.Y., which provided grist for his first novel, *Player Piano.* Later works included *The Sirens of Titan, Mother Night, Cat's Cradle,* and *God Bless You, Mr. Rosewater.*

Then came *Slaughterhouse-Five,* a madcap, gloomy, clever, and persuasive recall of his Dresden experience with science-fiction overtones. A spectacularly antiwar novel, it elevated Vonnegut to folk-hero status on the campus circuit as a lecturer. His one failure in recent years was a play, *Happy Birthday, Wanda June,* which closed in New York, partly because of a newspaper strike, in 1970. But otherwise, as Vonnegut himself put it, "I'm in the dangerous position now where I can sell anything I write."

(PHILIP KOPPER)

WAIN, JOHN BARRINGTON

Well known in Oxford for his informal poetry seminars—more often than not held in the King's Arms pub in Hollywell—the 48-year-old British poet, novelist, and critic John Wain was elected in May 1973 for the traditional five-year term as Oxford University's professor of poetry. He succeeded Roy Fuller in a post previously held by such other distinguished poets as W. H. Auden (*see* OBITUARIES), C. Day-Lewis, and Robert Graves.

Eight candidates were up for election, with Stephen Spender (213 votes) emerging as runner-up to Wain (231 votes). The official duties of the poetry professor are light, but Wain announced that he would take his new position seriously and that he would devote 5 of his 15 obligatory lectures to considering the work submitted to him by undergraduates and young graduates. He would also continue his pub seminars, which would now be subsidized by the modest stipend that the 256-year-old office carried with it.

John Barrington Wain was born at Stoke on Trent on March 14, 1925, and graduated from Oxford. He first came to prominence in 1953 with a novel, *Hurry on Down* (U.S. title *Born in Captivity;* 1954). Before the end of the 1950s he had also established himself as a poet, with *A Word Carved on a Sill* (1956), and as a literary critic, with *Preliminary Essays* (1957), for which he won the 1958 Somerset Maugham award.

Along with poets such as Kingsley Amis and Robert Conquest, Wain was at first associated with the so-called University Wits of the 1950s, but he never became a "fashionable" poet. His poetry often risked sentimentality in its celebration of human interdependence, but more often it achieved poignant insights into human feelings and emotions. Some critics held that his collection *Weep Before God* (1961) contained his finest work. His fiction had a strong narrative drive that rendered it splendidly accessible to the general reader. His novels included *The Contenders* (1958), *A Travelling Woman* (1959), *Strike the Father Dead* (1962), *The Young Visitors* (1965), and *A Winter in the Hills* (1970). As a critic who dared to make moral as well as imaginative judgments, he was lucid and forthright. He was above all an honest writer.

(DAVID HATELY)

WANG HUNG-WEN

The tenth Chinese Communist Party congress in August 1973 took the world by surprise; it was unannounced until it was over, and it was so short as to prompt speculation that differences of opinion in the top hierarchy were still serious. But the biggest surprise of all was the appearance on the threshold of ultimate power in China of an almost unknown personality. Ranked immediately after Mao Tse-tung and Chou En-lai and billed as a deputy chairman of the party and member of the Politburo and its nine-man Standing Committee was Wang Hung-wen.

Of Wang's importance, there was no doubt. Official photographs showed him sitting at Mao's right hand. He wore an army uniform, indicating that his authority extended beyond civilian jurisdiction. He made a speech that, along with Chou En-lai's political report, was the only one to be published by the Chinese media.

Nevertheless, an air of mystery hung about this new star in the Chinese galaxy. Initially, he was described as 35 or 36 years old, but later indications were that he was nearer 40. He was also reported as a Shanghai man of working-class origin. The Communist press in Hong Kong took up the cue to speculate that he was the son of Communist martyr Wang Hsia-ho who died shouting "Long live the Chinese Communist Party" before a Nationalist firing squad in 1949. But subsequently there were suggestions that he was in fact born in Kirin Province in northeastern China and was a well-educated and cultivated man.

Wang certainly served his political apprenticeship in Shanghai. He was reputedly a textile worker there and won recognition through his unusual organizing ability. During the Cultural Revolution he came to prominence by organizing two million workers on the side of Mao and against "capitalist-roaders" in the party. By 1972 he was the third ranking party official in Shanghai, a significant position considering Shanghai's preponderant influence in national affairs since the Cultural Revolution.

Wang's rather ostentatious elevation to the top at the party congress, official efforts to stress his ideal revolutionary background, and above all his youth were seen as evidence of his being groomed for possible supreme power after the Mao–Chou leadership had passed on.

(T. J. S. GEORGE)

Wang Hung-wen

G. SIPAHIOGLU—LIAISON

WATT, HUGH

When in November 1972 New Zealand voters sent their National Party government packing after 12 years of unbroken rule, they were conscious of how the old conservatives had faded but had mostly been retained in office. There had been a much greater mortality or dismissal rate in the Labour Party opposition, so that when it came back to power only one minister from 12 years earlier returned to Cabinet rank. He was Hugh Watt, who once again became minister of works and was also given the highly sensitive labour, works, and development brief and the post of deputy to Prime Minister Norman E. Kirk.

Watt, 60 compared with Kirk's 49 and an average Cabinet age of 48, was looked to for maturity, and he supplied it in such assignments as a visit to Paris to put to Pres. Georges Pompidou New Zealand's case against French nuclear testing in the Pacific. But the 12 years from one Labour administration to the next had been a long time, and Watt showed hesitation and a lack of authority in his dealings with organized labour; he seemed barely able to keep a grasp on the reins of government when Kirk was out of the country. More and more it began to look as though Watt was in his post not so much for the strength he would bring to it as to provide a buffer between the party leader and the more lean and hungry types with their eye on the top job. It also seemed that Watt was being rewarded for the key role he had played in the overthrow of the previous party leader, former finance minister Arnold Nordmeyer, and for his subsequent loyalty to Kirk.

Born in 1912 in Perth, Western Australia, Watt was two when the family moved to New Zealand. From Remuera (Auckland) Primary and Seddon Technical College, he signed as an engineering apprentice, established his own sheet-metal and engineering business, and entered politics as a member of the Auckland Harbour Board. After serving on the national executive of the Labour Party, he won a parliamentary seat in 1953, at a by-election, and was promoted to the Cabinet four years later. Ill health had taken him out of the running for the party leadership when it passed from Walter Nash to Nordmeyer and subsequently to Kirk. Watt's main attributes were a warm personality, a good speaking style for small occasions, and common sense.

(JOHN A. KELLEHER)

WOODWARD, ROBERT: *see* BERNSTEIN, CARL.

See also Nobel Prizes.

Bolivia

A landlocked republic in central South America, Bolivia is bordered by Brazil, Paraguay, Argentina, Chile, and Peru. Area: 424,162 sq.mi. (1,098,581 sq.km.). Pop. (1972 est.): 5,195,000, of whom more than 50% were Indian. Language: Spanish (official). Religion (1971 est.): Roman Catholic 94.5%. Judicial cap.: Sucre (pop., 1971 est., 69,800). Administrative cap. and largest city: La Paz (pop., 1971 est., 850,000). President in 1973, Col. Hugo Banzer Suárez.

President Banzer's main task throughout 1973 was that of maintaining a workable balance within the coalition of the Falange Socialista Boliviana (FSB), the Movimiento Nacionalista Revolucionario (MNR), and the armed forces. The hostility that existed between the right-wing FSB and the left-wing MNR continued during the year, with some members of the former wishing to isolate the MNR within the group if not to oust it altogether. Most notable of these was Carlos Valverde, erstwhile minister of health and secretary-general of the FSB, who, having taken issue with the leadership on this matter, led an attempted coup in August. He was allowed to escape to Paraguay. Twice in 1973, Banzer undertook complete Cabinet reshuffles to preserve the alliance. In June he announced that elections were to be held in 1974; late in the year he said he would not be a candidate for reelection.

In May former colonel Andrés Selich, who was instrumental in bringing Banzer to power in 1971 and was then abruptly dismissed, was discovered plotting with right-wing army officers to overthrow the government. He subsequently died at the hands of his interrogators. Other attempts planned by army officers, including the commander in chief, Gen. Joaquín Zenteno, were aborted at an early stage. In November the government announced that a plot had been foiled with the arrest of three politicians, including Julio Prado Salmon, who had been dismissed from the post of minister of economy and planning on October 5.

On another front the government met with open opposition from the miners who, despite the ban imposed in 1971 on the Centro de Obreros Bolivianos, reconstituted this organization. Social discontent persisted throughout the year since wage increases were frozen until October and the cost of living rose very quickly. At the end of September, a plot allegedly being devised by labour union leaders was discovered, resulting in their arrest and a subsequent strike by 30,000 workers in protest.

In May in the El Alto district police shot and killed two members of the National Army of Liberation, the group formed by the martyred "Che" Guevara. The dead were identified as Monica Ertl, a 35-year-old German-born Bolivian wanted for the murder of the Bolivian consul general in Hamburg in April 1971, and Osvaldo Ucasqui, an Argentine national. The Bolivian consul general had apparently been murdered for his alleged part in the death of Guevara.

Banzer continued his policy of encouraging foreign investment, and during the first half of the year an estimated $600 million was invested in the country. A loan of $42 million was granted by the Inter-American Development Bank to Yacimientos Petrolíferos Fiscales Bolivianos (YPFB) for the construction of two oil refineries, and several other loans were received from international organizations and governments for the improvement of roads, railways, and the water supply. The government concluded the agreement whereby it would pay $13.4 million to United States Steel Corp. and Engelhard Minerals & Chemicals Corp. for Mina Matilde, a zinc and lead mining property nationalized in 1971.

One potential setback of great significance to the Bolivian economy was the liquidation of the Williams Harvey tin smeltery at Kirkby, Eng., which processed approximately 8,000 tons of tin yearly. However, an outlet for this amount was found at Capper Pass, England's other tin smeltery, which was owned by Rio Tinto-Zinc Corp. Plans were announced during the year for the expansion of the metallurgical complex at Vinto, including tripling the tin smelting capacity.

In response to the hydrocarbons law of March 1972, two foreign companies, Union Oil and Occidental Boliviana, applied for and were granted concessions for oil exploration. Meanwhile, YPFB made new discoveries of natural gas, at Vilgue and at Campo Palometas. (PHILIPPA HUGHES)

BOLIVIA

Education. (1970) Primary, pupils 661,423, teachers 24,073; secondary, pupils 192,435, teachers 7,837; vocational, pupils 11,491, teachers 915; teacher training, students 10,948, teachers 497; higher (including 8 universities; 1969), students 27,352, teaching staff 2,727.

Finance. Monetary unit: peso boliviano, with an official rate (Sept. 17, 1973) of 20 pesos to U.S. $1 (free rate of 48.23 pesos = £1 sterling). Gold, SDRs, and foreign exchange, central bank: (June 1973) U.S. $72.6 million; (June 1972) U.S. $54.5 million. Budget (1973 est.) balanced at 2,917,000,000 pesos. Gross national product: (1971) 12,865,000,000 pesos; (1970) 11,810,000,000 pesos. Money supply: (March 1973) 2,256,600,000 pesos; (March 1972) 1,769,-400,000 pesos. Cost of living (La Paz; 1963 = 100): (Dec. 1972) 197; (Dec. 1971) 160.

Foreign Trade. (1971) Imports U.S. $171,283,000; exports U.S. $268.5 million. Import sources: U.S. 31%; Japan 16%; Argentina 10%; U.K. 5%. Export destinations: U.K. 46%; U.S. 28%; Japan 6%; Argentina 6%. Main exports: tin 31%; zinc 5%; tungsten 5%.

Transport and Communications. Roads (1971) 25,637 km. Motor vehicles in use (1970): passenger *c.* 19,200; commercial (including buses) *c.* 28,800. Railways: (1971) 3,524 km.; traffic (1970) 271 million passenger-km., freight 326 million net ton-km. Air traffic (1971): 145.6 million passenger-km.; freight 2,599,000 net ton-km. Telephones (Jan. 1972) 44,000. Radio receivers (Dec. 1968) 1,350,000.

Agriculture. Production (in 000; metric tons; 1971; 1970 in parentheses): corn 293 (283); wheat 62 (53); barley 69 (62); potatoes 655 (655); cassava (1970) 221, (1969) 213; oranges 71 (68); sugar, raw value (1972) *c.* 96, (1971) 123; rubber (exports) 3 (3). Livestock (in 000; Oct. 1971): sheep *c.* 6,900; cattle *c.* 2,300; pigs *c.* 1,000; horses *c.* 300; asses *c.* 680; goats *c.* 2,500; llamas *c.* 1,500.

Industry. Production (in 000; metric tons; 1971): crude oil 1,714; electricity (kw-hr.) 830,000 (82% hydroelectric in 1969); cement (1969) 80; gold (troy oz.) 21; other metal ores and concentrates (exports; metal content) tin 30, lead 27, antimony 12, zinc 42, tungsten (oxide content) 2.6, copper 7.5, silver 0.21.

Biological Sciences: *see* Life Sciences

Biophysics: *see* Life Sciences

Birth Statistics: *see* Vital Statistics

Boating: *see* Motor Sports; Rowing; Sailing

Bonds: *see* Savings and Investment; Stock Exchanges

Books: *see* Art Sales; Literature; Publishing

Botanical Gardens: *see* Zoos and Botanical Gardens

Botany: *see* Life Sciences

Botswana

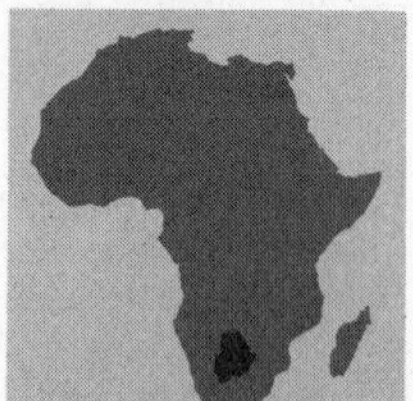

A landlocked republic of southern Africa, Botswana, a member of the Commonwealth of Nations, is bounded by South Africa, South West Africa, and Rhodesia. Area: 222,394 sq.mi. (576,000 sq.km.). Pop. (1971 est.): 608,000, almost 99% African. Capital: Gaborone (pop., 1971, 17,718). Largest city: Francistown (pop., 1971, 18,613). Language: English (official) and

WIDE WORLD

Nomadic Bushmen of Botswana hunt for food in traditional fashion. As game and natural water became increasingly scarce, primitive Bushmen were driven to beg or steal from local farmers.

Tswana. Religion: Christian 60%; animist. President in 1973, Sir Seretse Khama.

The escalation of guerrilla activities during 1972–73 emphasized Botswana's delicate position, with its political sympathies oriented toward black Africa but economically dependent on South Africa. While the new U.S. Agency for International Development road from Kazungula to Nata expressed the determination to expand links with the north, the vast new mining developments linked the country even more securely than before to the technical abilities of the white-dominated south.

The 1973–76 development plan, for which Britain had agreed to provide capital aid of £8.1 million and technical assistance, committed the government to the strategy of getting large and rapid returns from the capital-intensive mining developments of outside companies, and then using the proceeds to promote labour-intensive industries by the Botswana Enterprises Development Unit, and for rural development. The population explosion in the work force, with 10,000 leaving school each year, was not absorbed either in agriculture or by the South African labour market. An appropriation of R 55 million was made for the development plan, the greater part for the Shashi copper-nickel project. (MOLLY MORTIMER)

BOTSWANA

Education. (1970) Primary, pupils 83,002, teachers 2,275; secondary, pupils 3,905, teachers 197; vocational, pupils 1,009, teachers 124; teacher training, students 283, teachers 32.

Finance and Trade. Monetary unit: South African rand, with (Sept. 17, 1973) an official rate of R 0.67 to U.S. $1 (free rate of R 1.62 = £1 sterling). Budget (1972–73 est.): revenue R 22,924,000; expenditure R 23,526,000. Foreign trade (1971–72): imports R 60 million (65% from South Africa in 1966); exports R 33 million (18% to South Africa in 1966). Main exports (1967): meat 42%; hides and skins 18%; meat extract 14%; other meat products 11%; live cattle 5%.

Agriculture. Production (in 000; metric tons; 1971; 1970 in parentheses): sorghum 73 (8); corn 17 (5). Livestock (in 000; 1971): cattle 1,832; sheep 370; goats 1,015; poultry 234.

Bowling and Lawn Bowls

The finals of the World Cup (singles tournament for amateur bowlers) of 1972 were played in December in Hamburg, W.Ger. For the first time the tournament organizers included a women's division. The local elimination rounds had started in 40 countries in May; in December in Hamburg there was a parade of 16 women and 36 men from different countries. In the men's finals Ray Mitchell of Canada won by 18 pins in a three-game match against Loreto Maranan of the Philippines, 550–532. In the women's finals Irma Urrea of Mexico met Oy Sri-Saard of Thailand and with her greater experience of tournament pressure defeated her young opponent 591–537.

At the second Asian Zone Championships of the Fédération Internationale des Quilleurs (FIQ)—the world governing body of bowling—in Malaysia in August 1972, bowlers from Singapore took all first places in the men's division and the Philippines team took all but one in the women's division. The results were: *men:* teams of five, Singapore, 5,670; teams of three, Singapore, 3,447; doubles, Singapore, 2,290; singles (six games), Singapore, 1,251; singles (12 games), Singapore, 3,236. *Women:* teams of four, Philippines, 4,192; teams of three, Philippines, 3,208; doubles, Philippines, 2,176; singles (six games), Japan, 1,178; singles (12 games), Philippines, 2,261. Early in October, 14 European countries sent their best five-man teams to West Berlin to compete over one weekend for the "Cup of Europe, Memorial Emilio de Miguel." From the early rounds of the tournament (one-game matches, round-robin) it was evident that West Germany, Great Britain, and Italy were the leaders, the West Germans eventually winning by two points over both Great Britain and Italy, with France fourth. The best player was Jean Pierre Horn of France, who averaged 211 over the 13 games.

The year ended with the European Bowling Championships during September 1973 in Dublin. The traditional 14 countries participated. As many as 15 new tournament records were bowled during the week, 8 marks being set by men and 7 by women. In the men's division the Swedish octet set two new marks, 1,651 for a team high game and 12,304 for a high series. Individually, Lasse Hedqvist of the Swedish team bowled a new record of 1,740 for eight games. Two days later, the quintet from Finland set new marks for one-game, three-game, and six-game totals in the competition for teams of five players. The two remaining records were bowled by René Ferrie of France (the European all-events champion of 1965), 269 in one game, and by Ulf Lönngren of Sweden, 670 in the three-game series. Of the seven records in the women's division five were scored by Sweden and the remaining two by Great Britain's team of five: of these the high game of 470 in the doubles' competition by Doris Hagelin and Mary Ann Lando and the new 24-game all-events record of 4,528 by Gerda Nylund, also from Sweden, were most noteworthy. The winners were: men's teams of eight, Sweden, 12,304; men's teams of five, Finland, 5,862; men's doubles, Norway, 2,403; men's individual all-events (28 games), Arne Strøm, Norway, 5,716; women's teams of four, Sweden, 4,534; women's teams of five, Great Britain, 5,483; women's doubles, Sweden, 2,304; women's individual all-events (24 games), Gerda Nylund, Sweden, 4,528. (YRJÖ SARAHETE)

United States. While the professional bowlers were collecting most of the headlines as usual in 1973, Elvin Mesger, a 57-year-old shipping room supervisor from Sullivan, Mo., extended one of the most remarkable records in tenpins by bowling his 25th perfect game in sanctioned competition. Mesger rolled his most recent 300 score in a league match in St. Louis, Mo., where he was employed. His 25 easily set the record for 300s in league or tournament play, with George Billick of Old Forge, Pa., in second place with 17.

In Professional Bowlers Association (PBA) action, Don McCune of Munster, Ind., won tournaments in Winston-Salem, N.C., Milwaukee, Wis., and Los Angeles, Fresno, and Redwood City, Calif., appearing certain to earn bowler-of-the-year honours. McCune, a long-time regular on the PBA tour, had finished first in only two professional tournaments prior to 1973. Among those conceded an outside chance of overtaking McCune in the remaining PBA events was Don Johnson of Akron, O., who finished strongly in 1972 and captured the bowler-of-the-year crown as a result. Johnson also won the honour in 1971. The richest event on the PBA schedule, the $125,000 Firestone Tournament of Champions, in Akron, was won by Jim Godman of Lorain, O., who defeated Barry Asher, Costa Mesa, Calif., 224–200, in the nationally televised final game.

At the American Bowling Congress (ABC) tournament in Syracuse, N.Y., the winners in the Classic Division (for professionals) were: team, Stroh's Beer, Detroit, Mich., 3,050; doubles, Bobby Cooper, Houston, Tex., and George Pappas, Charlotte, N.C., 1,339; singles, Nelson Burton, Jr., St. Louis, Mo., 724; all-events, Jimmy Mack, Paramus, N.J., 1,994. Triumphing in the Regular Division were: team, Thelmal Masters, Louisville, Ky., 3,118; doubles, Jamie Brooks and Jimmy Paine, Houston, Tex., 1,337; singles, Ed Thompson, Denver, Colo., 762; all-events, Ron Woolet, Louisville, Ky., 2,104. Dave Soutar of Kansas City, Mo., won the Masters Tournament, held on the lanes used by the ABC Tournament, by capturing all seven of his four-game matches. Soutar topped Dick Ritger of Hartford, Wis., 849–718, in the final.

Las Vegas, Nev., for the first time was the site of the Women's International Bowling Congress (WIBC) meet. A record total of 48,220 women from 50 states and 5 foreign countries competed during the 107 days that the WIBC meet was held at Showboat Lanes. The Open Division champions were: team, Fitzpatrick Chevrolet, Concord, Calif., 2,897; doubles, Dotty Fothergill of North Attleboro, Mass., and Millie Martorella of Rochester, N.Y., 1,238; singles, Bobbie Buffaloe, Costa Mesa, Calif., 706; all-events, Toni Calvery, Midwest City, Okla., 1,910. At the WIBC Queens Tournament, also in Las Vegas, Fothergill was the winner for the second consecutive year, defeating Judy Cook of Grandview, Mo., 804–791.

Left-hander Mike McGrath of El Cerrito, Calif., bowls to a surprise victory in the Bowling Proprietors Association of America U.S. Open at New York City's Madison Square Garden, March 10, 1973.

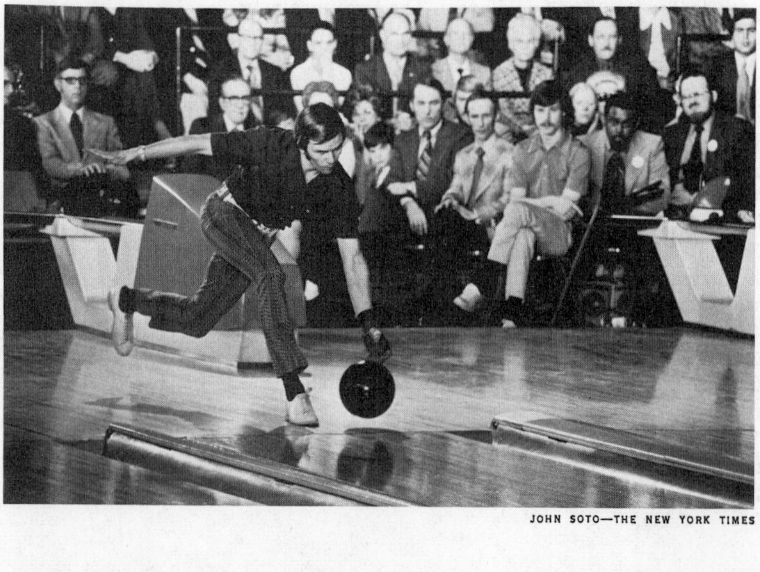

JOHN SOTO—THE NEW YORK TIMES

The largest prize in bowling again was the award given in the annual Petersen Classic, an event open to both men and women, held at the Archer-35th Recreation lanes in Chicago, Ill. George Wade, manager of a bowling centre in Steubenville, O., won $36,195 by totaling 1,728 for eight games.

In October the PBA banned the practice of "soaking" or softening plastic balls with solvents, which according to a PBA spokesman had reached "epidemic proportions" on the tour. A soaked ball permitted the bowler to exercise greater control and thus gave him an unfair advantage. In addition, the solvents used were flammable and potentially dangerous.

Duckpins. The 1973 National Duckpin Tournament was held at the T-Bowl Lanes in Newington, Conn. The winners in the men's division were: team, Dudley Excavating, Washington, D.C., 2,063; doubles, Larry Shepley and Tom Ramsburg, Frederick, Md., 901; singles, Fred Belliveau, Norwich, Conn., 466; all-events, Keith Dashno, Newington, Conn., 1,332. Women's division: team, Parkville Majors, Baltimore, Md., 1,902; doubles, Rola Ough and Miki Irish, Manchester, Conn., 799; singles, Agnes Claughsey, Hebron, Conn., 435; all-events, Nancy Brindle, Providence, R.I., 1,214. Mixed teams (three men, two women): 4 A's and a B, East Providence, R.I., 1,894. Mixed doubles: Patsy Stroessner and Robert Stroessner, Baltimore, Md., 866. (JOHN J. ARCHIBALD)

Lawn Bowls. International lawn bowls in 1973 was dominated by the competition at the South African Games, staged at Berea Park, Pretoria. Inevitably, political considerations resulted in the absence of several bowls-playing nations, notably New Zealand and the Australian women. Teams from 14 countries entered, and during the 11 days more than 10,000 spectators watched the play. England had the winning team, its men and women both winning the trophies for best overall performances. Yet the only English bowler to win a gold medal was Mavis Steele in the women's singles. Undoubtedly, Willie Wood of Scotland, winner of the men's singles gold medal, proved the man of the tournament. A 34-year-old automobile mechanic, he said little, smiled often, and played with immense skill and tenacity.

In Britain, Scotland continued its monopoly of the home International Team Championship for the ninth year in succession, though it suffered a defeat by England. The English Bowling Association was pursuing policies intended to attract young men to the game. These included imposition of an unspoken, yet definite, upper age limit of 50 for the England team, and only one man over that age was selected. Sponsorship led to the scheduling of a 25-and-under national tournament for 1974, as well as one for "senior citizens." Both were to offer substantial prizes.

David Bryant won the British Isles Championship (for the third time) from a field that included world champion Maldwyn Evans (Wales), whose form slumped badly in 1973. Bryant also won the English Singles Championship for the third year in succession. (C. M. JONES)

Boxing

George Foreman (U.S.) became the new heavyweight champion of the world in January 1973 by stopping Joe Frazier (U.S.) in two rounds at Kingston in Jamaica, where the championship was staged for the first time. In his only other contest during 1973, Foreman knocked out José Roman (P.R.) in one round in Tokyo. Muhammad Ali remained the big attraction of world boxing. Though Ali had not held the title since 1967, he was watched by millions on television when clearly outpointing European heavyweight champion Joe Bugner (Eng.) over 12 rounds at Las Vegas, Nev. He then lost a controversial decision to Ken Norton (U.S.), at San Diego, Calif. Norton also succeeded in breaking Ali's jaw and putting him out of action for several months. Ali proved his courage by refusing to quit despite the injury, and reversed the decision against Norton six months later. Ali took part during the year in one more fight, in which he outpointed Dutch champion Rudi Lubbers in Jakarta, Indon. Frazier won a victory on points over Bugner in a 12-round contest.

Bob Foster (U.S.), veteran world light heavyweight champion, retained his title with two victories on points against Pierre Fourie (S.Af.) at Albuquerque, N.M., and in Johannesburg. The second contest made boxing history because it was the first between a black and a white opponent allowed in South Africa.

Carlos Monzón (Arg.) retained the world middleweight championship by outpointing Emile Griffith (U.S.) and Jean-Claude Bouttier (France). Koichi Wajima (Jap.) retained the junior middleweight crown: he drew with Miguel de Oliveira (Braz.), outpointed Ryu Sorimachi (Jap.), and stopped Silvano Bertini (Italy) in 12 rounds.

Veteran José Nápoles (Mex.) kept the welterweight championship by knocking out Ernie López (U.S.) in seven rounds in Los Angeles and outpointing Roger Menetrey (France) at Grenoble, France, and Clyde Gray (Can.) in Toronto. Among the junior welterweights Antonio Cervantes (Colombia) remained World Boxing Association (WBA) champion, scoring a win on points over José Márquez (P.R.) and stopping Nicolino Loche (Arg.) in ten rounds, Alfonso Frazer (Panama) in five, and Carlos Giménez (Arg.) in five. Bruno Arcari (Italy) retained the World Boxing Council (WBC) version of the title when he knocked out Jurgen Hansen (Den.) in five rounds.

Roberto Durán (Panama) held off all challenges to the WBA lightweight title with wins inside the distance against Jimmy Robertson (U.S.) in five rounds, Hector Thompson (Austr.) in eight rounds, and Ishimatsu Susuki (Jap.) in ten. The WBC championship was retained by Rodolfo González (U.S.), who stopped Rubén Navarro (U.S.) in nine rounds and Antonio Puddu (Italy) in ten. Kuniaki Shibata (Jap.) took the WBA junior lightweight title from Ben Villaflor (Phil.) with a win on points and repeated this victory a month later. In a third meeting Villaflor regained the title with a first-round knockout. In between, Shibata scored another title win by outpointing Víctor Echegaray (Arg.). Ricardo Arredondo (Mex.) retained the WBC title by outpointing Apollo Yoshio (Jap.) and stopping Morito Kashiwaba (Jap.) in six rounds.

Eder Jofre, veteran Brazilian and former bantamweight champion, took the WBC featherweight crown with a win on points over José Legra (Spain) in Brasília, Braz. This followed Legra's successful defense of the title against Clemente Sánchez (Mex.) with a ten-round win. Jofre later retained the championship, stopping former world champion Vicente Saldívar (Mex.) in four rounds. Ernesto Marcel (Panama) retained the WBA version by stopping Antonio Gómez (Venez.) in 12 rounds and S. Nemeto (Jap.) in 9.

Romeo Anaya (Mex.) captured the WBA bantam-

WIDE WORLD

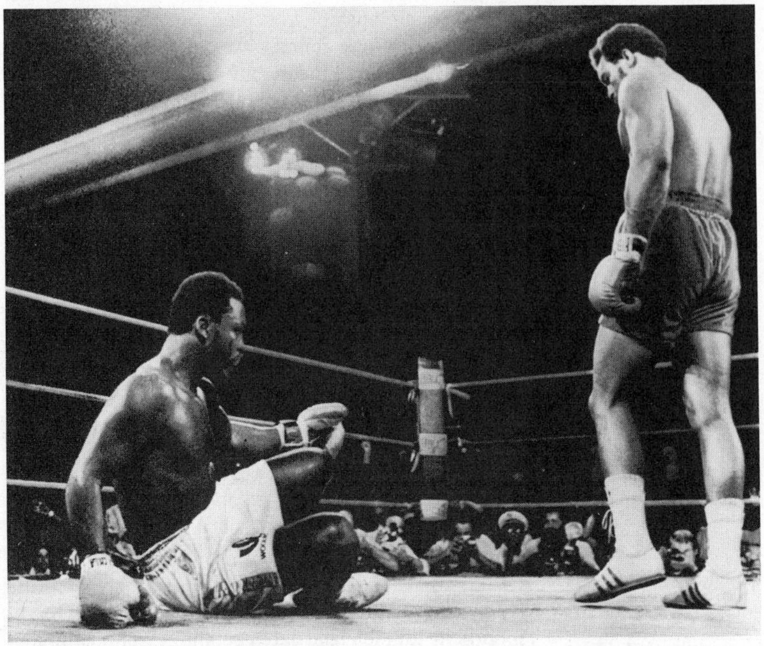

Challenger George Foreman stands over world heavyweight champion Joe Frazier in the first of several knockdowns that won Foreman the title in the second round of the Jan. 22, 1973, bout.

Boxing Champions

As of Dec. 31, 1973

Division	World	Europe	Commonwealth	Britain
Heavyweight	George Foreman, U.S.	Joe Bugner, Eng.	Danny McAlinden, N.Ire.	Danny McAlinden, N.Ire.
Light heavyweight	Bob Foster, U.S.	John Conteh, Eng.	John Conteh, Eng.	John Conteh, Eng.
Middleweight	Carlos Monzón, Arg.	Elio Calcabrini, Italy	Tony Mundine, Austr.	Bunny Sterling, Eng.
Junior middleweight	Koichi Wajima, Jap.	Jacques Kechichian, France	Charkey Ramon, Austr.	Larry Paul, Eng.
Welterweight	José Nápoles, Mex.	Roger Menetrey, France	Clyde Gray, Can.	John H. Stracy, Eng.
Junior welterweight	Bruno Arcari, Italy* Antonio Cervantes, Colombia†	Toni Ortíz, Spain	Hector Thompson, Austr.	Des Morison, Jamaica
Lightweight	Rodolfo González, U.S.* Roberto Durán, Panama†	Antonio Puddu, Italy	Percy Hayles, Jamaica	Ken Buchanan, Scot.
Junior lightweight	Ricardo Arredondo, Mex.* Ben Villaflor, Phil.†	Lothar Abend, W.Ger.	...	...
Featherweight	Eder Jofre, Braz.* Ernesto Marcel, Panama†	Gitano Jiménez, Spain	Bobby Dunne, Austr.	Evan Armstrong, Scot.
Bantamweight	Rafael Herrera, Mex.* Arnold Taylor S.Af.†	Johnny Clark, Eng.	Paul Ferreri, Austr.	Johnny Clark, Eng.
Flyweight	Betulio González, Venezuela* Chartchai Chionoi, Thailand†	Fernando Atzori, Italy	Henry Nissen, Austr.	John McCluskey, Scot.

*World Boxing Council champion.
†World Boxing Association champion.

weight championship, knocking out Enrique Pinder (Panama) in three rounds. Anaya then beat Rogelio Lava (Mex.) and Pinder, but later was knocked out in 14 rounds and lost his title to Arnold Taylor (S.Af.) in Johannesburg. The WBC bantamweight championship was kept by Rafael Herrera (Mex.), who stopped Rodolfo Martínez (Mex.) in 12 rounds and later outpointed Venice Borkorso (Thailand). After Masao Ohba (Jap.) knocked out Chartchai Chionoi (Thailand) in 12 rounds in Tokyo, the WBA flyweight title became vacant, but it was later won by Chionoi, who stopped Fritz Chervet (Switz.) in four rounds. Chionoi retained the crown by outpointing Susumu Hanagata (Jap.). After Borkorso had retained the WBC flyweight title with a win on points against Erbito Salavarria (Phil.) in Bangkok, this version also became vacant until Betulio González (Venezuela) outpointed Miguel Canto (Mex.).

In Europe Bugner kept the heavyweight championship by outpointing Lubbers and Bepi Ros (Italy), both fights taking place in London. John Conteh (Eng.) took the European light heavyweight title from Rudi Schmidtke (W.Ger.), stopping him in 12 rounds in London and later retaining the championship against Chris Finnegan (Eng.).

Tom Bogs (Den.) won the vacant European middleweight championship, outpointing Fabio Bettini (Italy); he then retained the title, outpointing Mario Lamagna (Italy). The championship later became vacant and was captured by Elio Calcabrini (Italy) with a win on points over Bunny Sterling (Eng.). Carlos Durán (Italy), after retaining the junior middleweight title against Hans Orsolics (Aus.), lost the championship when stopped by Jacques Kechichian (France) in nine rounds. Menetrey retained the welterweight crown with wins against Sandro Lopopolo (Italy) in 13 rounds and against José González (Spain) in 15 rounds. Toni Ortíz (Spain) took the junior welterweight title from C. Kamaci (Turkey).

Puddu retained the lightweight crown, stopping Dominique Azzaro (France) in one round. Lothar Abend (W.Ger.) kept the junior lightweight title, stopping Jean de Keers (Belg.) in one round. The vacant featherweight title was captured by Gitano Jiménez (Spain). Johnny Clark (Eng.) became bantamweight champion, outpointing Franco Zurlo (Italy). After Chervet retained the flyweight crown against John McCluskey (Scot.), the title became vacant. It was later won by Fernando Atzori (Italy) from D. Cesari (France). (FRANK BUTLER)

Brazil

A federal republic in eastern and central South America, Brazil is bounded by the Atlantic Ocean and all the countries of South America except Ecuador and Chile. Area: 3,286,470 sq.mi. (8,511,965 sq.km.). Pop. (1973 est.): 101,706,000. Principal cities (pop., 1970): Brasília (cap.) 271,570; Rio de Janeiro 4,251,-918; São Paulo 5,924,612. Language: Portuguese. Religion: Roman Catholic 93%. President in 1973, Gen. Emílio Garrastazú Médici.

Political Affairs. The outstanding political event of the year and one that absorbed the country's attention for some time was the announcement on June 18 by President Médici of his choice for his successor in the presidency after the termination of his five-year term of office on March 15, 1974. The question had been debated in private for many months, but such discussions had been repeatedly discouraged by the president. In fact, in a message to the federal Congress on March 31, 1972, he declared that it was imperative to avoid disturbing the nation with premature discussion of the presidential succession.

When the Congress convened on March 1, 1973, President Médici in his message announced that he planned soon to submit his draft law on the electoral college, which, under the 1967 constitution, was to meet Jan. 15, 1974, to elect the new president and vice-president for the next five-year term. He added that there would thus be plenty of time to discuss and solve the presidential succession problem. Members of the opposition party (Brazilian Democratic Movement, MDB), whose powers were mostly limited to debating, tried to wrest the initiative away from the government by introducing their own bills on the

BRAZIL

Education. (1969) Primary, pupils 12,294,343, teachers 438,928; secondary, pupils 2,689,442, teachers 176,625; vocational, pupils 602,016, teachers 51,312; teacher training, students 337,917, teachers 37,336; higher (including 44 official universities), students 346,824, teaching staff 39,188.

Finance. Monetary unit: cruzeiro, with a free rate (Sept. 17, 1973) of 6.13 cruzeiros to U.S. $1 (14.78 cruzeiros = £1 sterling). Gold, SDRs, and foreign exchange, official: (March 1973) U.S. $4,355,000,000; (March 1972) U.S. $1,951,000,000. Budget (1972 est.) balanced at 32,177,000,000 cruzeiros. Gross national product: (1972) 296,566,000,000 cruzeiros; (1971) 231,546,000,000 cruzeiros. Money supply: (March 1973) 68,040,000,000 cruzeiros; (March 1972) 47,987,000,000 cruzeiros. Cost of living (São Paulo; 1963 = 100): (May 1973) 1,686; (May 1972) 1,464.

Foreign Trade. Imports (1972) 28,060,000,000 cruzeiros; exports 23,580,000,000 cruzeiros. Import sources (1971): U.S. 29%; West Germany 13%; Japan 7%; U.K. 6%. Export destinations: U.S. 26%; West Germany 9%; Italy 7%; Argentina 7%; The Netherlands 6%; Japan 5%. Main exports: coffee 25%; iron ore 6%.

Transport and Communications. Roads (1971) 1,138,444 km. (including 52,900 km. paved roads). Motor vehicles in use (1970): passenger 2,324,300; commercial (including buses) 696,200. Railways (1971): 31,773 km.; traffic 11,232,000,000 passenger-km., freight 17,358,000,000 net ton-km. Air traffic (1972): 5,959,000,000 passenger-km.; freight 265,-562,000 net ton-km. Shipping (1972): merchant vessels 100 gross tons and over 444; gross tonnage 1,884,537. Shipping traffic (1972): goods loaded 45,160,000 metric tons, unloaded 39,290,000 metric tons. Telephones (Dec. 1971) 2,145,000. Radio receivers (Dec. 1971) 5.8 million. Television receivers (Dec. 1971) 6.5 million.

Agriculture. Production (in 000; metric tons; 1972; 1971 in parentheses): corn *c.* 14,000 (14,307); rice *c.* 7,600 (6,593); cassava (1970) 29,464, (1969) 30,-074; sweet potatoes (1971) *c.* 2,210, (1970) 2,134; wheat *c.* 800 (2,132); cotton, lint 672 (499); coffee *c.* 1,500 (1,795); cocoa (1971–72) 204, (1970–71) 182; bananas (1970) *c.* 6,396, (1969) *c.* 6,023; oranges (1971) 3,580, (1970) 3,344; sisal (1971) 190, (1970) 190; tobacco *c.* 240 (*c.* 245); peanuts *c.* 950 (894); sugar, raw value *c.* 6,350 (5,730); dry beans *c.* 2,400 (2,500); soybeans *c.* 3,350 (1,977); beef and veal *c.* 1,900 (*c.* 1,900); rubber *c.* 26 (*c.* 24); timber (cu.m.; 1970) 169,800, (1969) 165,600; fish catch (1970) 515, (1969) 493. Livestock (in 000; Dec. 1971): cattle *c.* 97,500; horses *c.* 9,000; pigs *c.* 67,000; sheep *c.* 24,500; goats (1970) 14,700; chickens *c.* 278,000.

Industry. Fuel and power (in 000; metric tons; 1972): crude oil 8,259; coal (1971) 2,498; natural gas (cu.m.) 1,242,000; electricity (kw-hr.; 1971) 50,988,000 (85% hydroelectric). Production (in 000; metric tons; 1972): pig iron 5,299; crude steel 6,520; iron ore (metal content; 1970) 20,400; bauxite (1969) 362; manganese ore (metal content; 1971) 1,150; gold (troy oz.; 1971) 157; cement (1971) 9,803; asbestos (1968) 345; wood pulp (1970) 741; paper (1970) 1,081; passenger cars (including assembly; units) 437; commercial vehicles (including assembly; units) 177.

electoral college and other matters relating to the presidential election.

The 1967 federal constitution had provided for the indirect election of the nation's president and vice-president by an electoral college that was to meet for that purpose on January 15 of the year when the presidential term was to expire. However, the constitution did not provide for the composition and functions of the college. This was left to be determined later in a complementary law.

On June 18 President Médici sent to the Congress his proposed bill on the electoral college. A special committee of 11 senators and 11 deputies was appointed by the Congress the following day to consider and report on the proposal.

Drafted by the minister of justice, the bill specified that the electoral college would include the 310 deputies and the 66 senators of the present national Congress and 125 delegates to be selected by the state assemblies. The college would meet at Brasília in the building of the national Congress on Jan. 15, 1974, to elect by absolute majority the new president and vice-president from among the candidates selected and duly registered by the only two legal parties permitted to function in Brazil. The college was forbidden to consider any question other than the election of the new president and vice-president.

Although about 40 amendments to the bill were introduced by the special committee, mostly by opposition party members, all except two minor ones were rejected. The president's bill became law in August.

After secret consultations with the military leaders of the regime and with his intended candidate, President Médici announced also on June 18 that his successor would be Gen. Ernesto Geisel, a chief executive of Petrobrás, the government-owned national petroleum corporation. Geisel, the son of a German immigrant, had occupied important positions in the Army and in the civil service. He was considered to be conservative, strongly nationalist, hard-working, and a capable administrator. In 1944 he attended the U.S. Army Command and General Staff College at Ft. Leavenworth, Kan. In 1967 he left active military service in order to become a member of the Supreme Military Tribunal, a position which he resigned in 1968 to join Petrobrás. If elected, Geisel would be the first president of Brazil since the revolution of 1964 to assume office under the current constitution and not as an emergency measure.

On June 25 the leader of the government party, ARENA, announced in Brasília that Médici had selected Gen. Adalberto Pereira dos Santos as his candidate for the vice-presidency. At the time, Santos was serving as the president of the Supreme Military Tribunal.

As provided by the constitution, ARENA held its national convention at Brasília on September 15. As expected, the convention endorsed Geisel and Santos as its candidates for president and vice-president, respectively. General Geisel, in a talk before the convention, declared that, if elected, his government would be inspired by the principle of "development and security." A week later, on September 22, the MDB nominated its candidates: Ulysses Guimarães, a member of Congress, for president and Barbosa Lima Sobrinho for vice-president.

The Economy. The U.S. Federal Reserve Board chairman, Arthur F. Burns, was said to have called Brazil's growth during the previous five years "one of the great economic miracles of our time." Brazilian leaders, however, insisted that it was no miracle but only the result of hard work and intelligent economic and financial planning. In 1972 Brazil's gross national product (GNP) was estimated at $50 billion, nearly double what it was in 1964. In 1971 the nation's rate of growth was reported to have been 11.3%, according to an economic report prepared by the World Bank. Brazilian exports, which in 1972 had reached almost $4 billion, were expected to attain a value in 1973 of from $4.5 billion to $5 billion.

The annual growth rate of inflation was estimated at 15% at the end of 1972. It had been 24% in 1967–68 and 144% for a period during 1964. The administration hoped that it would not exceed 10% by 1974.

In large measure this phenomenal spurt of growth was due to six main factors, according to a special edition on Brazil published by *The Economist.* These included: neutralization of the inflation by appropriate government measures; promotion of exports, especially of manufactured goods; promotion of private investments in certain undeveloped areas; the increase in private savings with what was called "monetary correction"; continued confidence on the part of foreign investors; and large investments in basic industries as well as in electric power production, road construction, and port facilities.

The government's policy of granting incentives to investors included a deduction of up to 50% in income tax payments for those who invested part of their income in certain undeveloped areas (the Northeast and the Amazon). Inducements were also granted to exporters of manufactured goods. The monetary correction policy was adopted mainly to compensate salaried workers for the depreciation of their purchasing power due to the decline in value of the cruzeiro. It also aimed at promoting savings by the periodic readjustment of their value in proportion to price level changes.

To help exporters compete in foreign markets a policy of periodic readjustment of the cruzeiro's exchange rate was adopted by the financial authorities. The rate was 6.130–6.165 to U.S. $1 in the early part of December 1972; this was increased shortly thereafter to 6.180–6.215. In February 1973, for the first time in years, and due to the U.S. dollar devaluation, the rate was decreased to 5.995; but in April it became 6.100–6.160 and on July 9 it was announced as 6.09–6.13.

WIDE WORLD

Gen. Ernesto Geisel was chosen in June 1973 by Brazil's leaders to succeed to the presidency after Gen. Emílio Médici's term of office ended in March 1974.

Brazil's first executive transport planes, the sophisticated Bandeirantes, under construction at São José dos Campos.

MARVINE HOWE—THE NEW YORK TIMES

During the period two valuable windfalls came to the assistance of Brazil's agriculture, which had not generally kept pace with industry. As a result of poor sugarcane and sugar-beet crops in the Soviet Union and Cuba, Brazil was enabled to sell large quantities of sugar to other countries. Under an agreement with China 240,000 metric tons were to be exported to that country during 1973; this was the third sale since the middle of 1972. To the Soviet Union, Brazil sold 690,000 tons and to Japan 300,000 tons to be delivered in the period of 1974–78. A sale of 400,000 tons to France was announced in September.

The other windfall was the result of the curtailment of soybean exports by the U.S. government. As a consequence, Brazil's production of soybeans was enormously increased. It was officially estimated that the crop would reach five million metric tons in 1973. In mid-1973 an agreement was announced with Japan for the sale to that country of 2.5 million tons in 1974 for an estimated $1 billion. (RAUL D'ECA)

Bulgaria

A people's republic of Europe, Bulgaria is situated on the eastern Balkan Peninsula along the Black Sea, bordered by Romania, Yugoslavia, Greece, and Turkey. Area: 42,823 sq.mi. (110,912 sq.km.). Pop. (1971 est.): 8,565,000. Cap. and largest city: Sofia (pop., 1971 est., 910,242). Language: chiefly Bulgarian.

BULGARIA

Education. (1969–70) Primary, pupils 1,064,200, teachers 48,140; secondary, pupils 102,795, teachers 6,242; vocational, pupils 274,836, teachers 17,045; teacher training, students 157, teachers 6; higher (including 3 universities; 1970–71), students 89,331, teaching staff 7,125.

Finance. Monetary unit: lev, with an official exchange rate of 0.97 lev to U.S. $1 (2.46 leva = £1 sterling) and a tourist rate of 1.65 lev to U.S. $1 (4.18 leva = £1 sterling). Budget (1972 est.): revenue 6,526,000,000 leva; expenditure 6,514,000,000 leva.

Foreign Trade. (1971) Imports 2,456,000,000 leva; exports 2,551,000,000 leva. Main import sources (1970): U.S.S.R. 52%; East Germany 9%; Czechoslovakia 5%. Main export destinations (1970): U.S.S.R. 54%; East Germany 9%. Main exports (1970): machinery 29%; tobacco and cigarettes 13%; metals 7%; wines and spirits 6%; clothing 6%.

Transport and Communications. State roads (1971) 35,608 km. (including 2,397 km. main roads). Motor vehicles in use: passenger (1969) *c.* 17,000; commercial (1961) *c.* 20,000. Railways: (1971) 4,231 km.; traffic (1972) 6,701,000,000 passenger-km., freight 15,813,000,000 net ton-km. Air traffic (1971): 313 million passenger-km.; freight 5,850,000 net ton-km. Shipping (1972): merchant vessels 100 gross tons and over 149; gross tonnage 741,986. Telephones (Dec. 1971) 534,000. Radio licenses (Dec. 1971) 2,305,000. Television licenses (Dec. 1971) 1,181,000.

Agriculture. Production (in 000; metric tons; 1972; 1971 in parentheses): wheat 3,582 (3,095); corn 2,974 (2,518); barley 1,427 (1,253); sunflower seed 494 (462); dry beans *c.* 68 (65); tomatoes 816 (721); grapes 933 (1,059); apples 340 (344); tobacco *c.* 142 (120); meat (1971) 335, (1970) 320. Livestock (in 000; Jan. 1972): sheep 10,127; cattle 1,379; goats (1971) 335; pigs 2,806; horses 159; asses (1971) 305; poultry (1971) 34,102.

Industry. Fuel and power (in 000; metric tons; 1972): lignite 26,865; coal 384; crude oil 248; electricity (kw-hr.) 22,171,000. Production (in 000; metric tons; 1972): iron ore (32% metal content) 3,204; manganese ore (metal content; 1971) 12; copper ore (metal content; 1971) 37; lead ore (metal content; 1971) 102; pig iron 1,561; crude steel 2,121; copper (1970) 38; lead (1971) 102; zinc (1971) 78; cement 3,911; sulfuric acid 514; soda ash (1971) 301; cotton yarn 78; cotton fabrics (m.) 322,000; wool yarn 26; woolen fabrics (m.) 28,000.

First secretary of the Bulgarian Communist Party in 1973 and chairman of the Council of State, Todor Zhivkov; chairman of the Council of Ministers (premier), Stanko Todorov.

Two state visits to Bulgaria by Soviet leaders in 1973 implied some difficulties between Moscow and its strategically and militarily important Warsaw Pact ally. The Bulgarian leadership seemed disturbed by Soviet efforts to lure Yugoslavia back into the fold, and particularly by the Kremlin's apparent acceptance of President Tito's view of the Macedonian issue.

At the beginning of July, Nikolay V. Podgorny, chairman of the Presidium of the Supreme Soviet, was a guest of the Bulgarian government. In September Leonid I. Brezhnev, general secretary of the Communist Party of the U.S.S.R., was presented in Sofia with the insignia of the Order of Georgi Dimitrov and the Gold Star of Hero of the Bulgarian People's Republic. "To us Bulgarians," said Chairman Zhivkov on that occasion, "the behest of the great Dimitrov—to cherish Bulgarian-Soviet friendship as our dearest possession, a friendship which is as vital to us as the sun and air to a living creature—has long assumed the character of a sacred pledge." Replying, Brezhnev reminded the Bulgarians that the U.S.S.R. had helped them to build 180 major enterprises and assured them that another 150 would be built under the current five-year plan.

"The great Dimitrov," Bulgaria's first premier after World War II, had not only accepted the fact that Macedonia was one of the six member republics of the Yugoslav federation but had agreed with Tito that a greater South Slav federation uniting Yugoslavia and Bulgaria should be formed. Stalin had severely rebuked Dimitrov for supporting such a plan and had sent Tito outside the pale of Communist society. Although that occurred in the late 1940s, the memories of these and even older events (as for instance the 1878 Russian plan for a Greater Bulgaria) still lingered in Sofia. Bulgarians did not recognize Macedonians as a separate nationality and considered them as a branch of the Bulgarian ethnic group. The Skopje, Yugos., newspaper *Nova Makedonija* complained in July that the Macedonian minority in Bulgaria had lost its rights. In September, at the Plovdiv International Trade Fair, the Bulgarian authorities seized Macedonian journals from the Yugoslav pavilion.

On December 12, in Sofia, Bulgarian Foreign Minister Lyuben Petrov and Gunther van Well, representing West Germany, signed preliminary documents establishing diplomatic relations between their two countries. Bulgaria was thus one of the last Eastern European nations to normalize relations with Bonn.

Economically, Bulgaria was making remarkable progress. The turnover of its foreign trade in 1972 amounted to more than $2.3 billion; four-fifths of this exchange was with the Soviet-bloc countries, and more than 50% was with the Soviet Union. In 1972 Bulgaria exported approximately 6 million tons of goods and imported more than 20 million tons, but the value of the exports and imports was practically equal. The Soviet Union supplied the total Bulgarian imports of coal, 82% of cellulose, 77% of crude oil, 75% of pig iron, and 70% of wool. Foodstuffs, drinks, and tobacco represented 40% of Bulgarian exports, but the proportion of domestically made machinery going abroad had risen from 13.6% in 1960 to 30.4% in 1971. On Nov. 10, 1972, an important Polish-Bulgarian cooperative agreement was signed in Sofia

Bridge:
see Contract Bridge
Bridges:
see Engineering Projects
British Commonwealth:
see Commonwealth of Nations; *articles on the various member states*
British Honduras:
see Dependent States
Broadcasting:
see Telecommunications; Television and Radio
Brunei:
see Dependent States
Buddhism:
see Religion
Budgets, National:
see Government Finance
Building and Construction Industry:
see Engineering Projects; Housing; Industrial Review

stipulating joint construction at the Varna shipyards of 24 tankers of 100,000 deadweight tons each. During his visit to London in February Andrey Lukanov, Bulgarian deputy minister of foreign trade, said that his country had no intention of applying for membership in the International Monetary Fund and the World Bank; neither would Bulgaria approach the European Economic Community for trade preferences. (K. M. SMOGORZEWSKI)

Burma

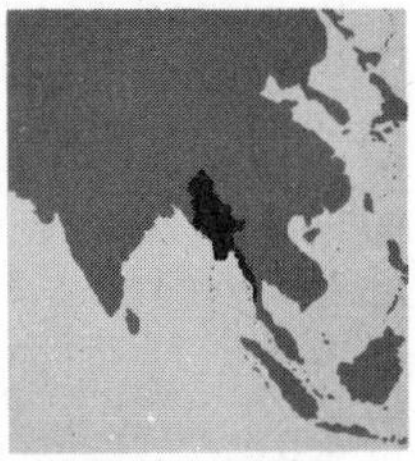

A republic of Southeast Asia, Burma is bordered by Bangladesh, India, China, Laos, and Thailand. Area: 261,789 sq.mi. (678,034 sq.km.). Pop. (1973 est.): 29.1 million. Cap. and largest city: Rangoon (metro. pop., 1971 est., 1,844,000). Language: Burmese. Religion (1970): Buddhist 85%. Chairman of the Revolutionary Council and prime minister in 1973, U Ne Win.

After months of "public debate," the third and final draft of Burma's socialist constitution was approved with minor alterations by the Central Committee of the Burma Socialist Program Party (BSPP), headed by Chairman U Ne Win. Ne Win informed the committee that more than eight million people from various walks of life had shown interest in the third draft, which had been explained to them by trained cadres of the BSPP. The constitution, which was to be proclaimed in March 1974, passed through two more stages before becoming law—approval by the BSPP's second congress in October and ratification by the majority of voters in a referendum in the second half of December.

One of the main items on the agenda of the BSPP congress was to make arrangements for the general election under the new constitution, to be held during Jan. 15–31, 1974. The BSPP's confidence was indicated by the fact that party cadres began working for the election long before the December referendum. More than 500,000 "deputies" were to be elected to the People's Congress and the people's councils at state, divisional, town, and village levels. The BSPP, the sole political party allowed by the constitution, would nominate all candidates, and the chances of "opposition" or rebellious elements creeping in were almost nil.

U Ne Win was expected to complete the handing over of "power to the people" by March 2, 1974, the 12th anniversary of his seizure of power from former prime minister U Nu. The occasion was to be marked by large-scale festivities and, as a special gesture, an amnesty of political prisoners was expected. However, the actual power structure in Burma was not likely to change with the proclamation of the constitution or the election of the People's Congress, since Ne Win was certain to be elected its president.

The Burmese economy remained stagnant as BSPP leaders and their followers concentrated on constitution-making. Adding to their worries was the steep fall in rice production, from 2.2 million tons in 1971–72 to an estimated 1.5 million tons in 1972–73. Lethargy among the farmers and drought conditions contributed to the decline. In an address to the fifth BSPP Central Committee meeting in February, Ne Win said "rice production has fallen. Despite this there is enough for the whole country. Only surplus will be exported." In the following month rice exports were suspended.

The government also launched a campaign to unearth hoarded rice, cooking oil, and other essential foodstuffs. About 500 people, described as "economic insurgents," were arrested in a single week in January in Rangoon and other towns. Foreign exchange reserves, already at a record low in the previous year, were almost gone, and the government was subsisting purely on foreign aid. In July the International Development Association announced two credits totaling U.S. $33 million for rehabilitation of the state-run railways and the inland water transport system. Canada gave 7,500 tons of wheat in March. Japanese assistance amounting to $20.5 million was promised for setting up a new petroleum refining plant near Rangoon, in addition to continuing help in drilling for offshore oil.

The insurgent menace was as much a problem as in previous years, though the threat from U Nu and his rebel followers was eliminated with his departure from Bangkok to the U.S. U Nu's flight from Bangkok also helped to improve relations between Burma and Thailand. The most serious incident occurred in April when two Soviet technical experts were kidnapped by insurgents in Shan state. The Burmese Army launched a large-scale operation against the insurgents in May and killed about 25, but the remainder escaped with their Soviet captives. For the first time the death sentence was passed on a rebel leader, 66-year-old Thakin Soe, chief of the Burmese Communist Party (Red Flag), who was found guilty of taking up arms against the government. (GOVINDAN UNNY)

BURMA

Education. (1969–70) Primary, pupils 3,328,000, teachers 65,326; secondary, pupils 692,290, teachers 21,814; vocational, pupils 4,080, teachers 393; teacher training, students 3,245, teachers 255; higher, students 45,891, teaching staff 2,310.

Finance. Monetary unit: kyat, with (Sept. 17, 1973) a free rate of 5 kyats to U.S. $1 (12.05 kyats = £1 sterling). Gold, SDRs, and foreign exchange, official: (Jan. 1973) U.S. $49.7 million; (Jan. 1972) U.S. $55.8 million. Budget (1972–73 est.): revenue 8,734,000,000 kyats; expenditure 9,702,000,000 kyats. Gross national product: (1967–68) 9,796,000,000 kyats; (1966–67) 8,588,000,000 kyats.

Foreign Trade. (1972) Imports 690.6 million kyats; exports 611.4 million kyats. Import sources (1971): Japan 30%; West Germany 9%; U.K. 8%; India 8%; China 7%. Export destinations (1971): Sri Lanka 12%; India 11%; Japan 10%; Singapore 8%; West Germany 5%; Philippines 5%. Main exports: rice 36%; teak 27%; oilcakes 8%.

Transport and Communications. Roads (1972) *c.* 25,000 km. (including *c.* 13,700 km. all-weather). Motor vehicles in use (1970): passenger 29,800; commercial (including buses) 31,000. Railways (1971): 3,098 km.; traffic 2,382,000,000 passenger-km., freight 829 million net ton-km. Air traffic (1971): 154 million passenger-km.; freight 2,159,000 net ton-km. Shipping (1972): merchant vessels 100 gross tons and over 40; gross tonnage 54,877. Telephones (Dec. 1971) 27,000. Radio licenses (Dec. 1971) 423,000.

Agriculture. Production (in 000; metric tons; 1972; 1971 in parentheses): rice 7,560 (8,178); rubber (exports) *c.* 7 (*c.* 7); sesame *c.* 102 (*c.* 102); peanuts *c.* 520 (485); dry beans *c.* 140 (*c.* 140); cotton, lint *c.* 17 (16); jute *c.* 50 (65); tobacco 52 (41); sugar, raw value *c.* 243 (*c.* 238); timber (cu.m.; 1971) 15,900, (1970) 15,600. Livestock (in 000; March 1972): cattle *c.* 7,200; buffalo 1,640; pigs (1971) *c.* 1,340; goats (1971) *c.* 610; sheep *c.* 185; chickens (1971) *c.* 13,500.

Industry. Production (in 000; metric tons; 1971): crude oil 823; electricity (excluding most industrial production; kw-hr.) 541,000; cement (1972) 197; lead concentrates (metal content; 1970) 4.1; zinc concentrates (metal content; 1970) 3.7; tin concentrates (metal content) 0.5.

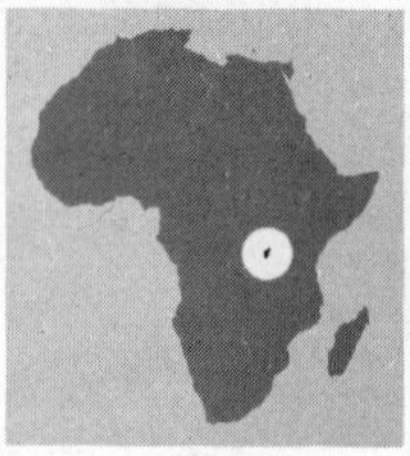

Burundi

A republic of eastern Africa, Burundi is bordered by Zaire, Rwanda, and Tanzania. Area: 10,747 sq.mi. (27,834 sq.km.). Pop. (1972 est.) 3.4 million, mainly Hutu, Tutsi, and Twa. Cap. and largest city: Bujumbura (pop., 1970 est., 110,000). Language: Kirundi and French. Religion (1964): Roman Catholic 51%; Protestant 4%; animist 45%. President in 1973, Michel Micombero; prime minister until June 6, Albin Nyamoya.

Civil warfare between the 85% Hutu majority and the ruling Tutsi continued to trouble Burundi in 1973. In March, while a number of political detainees were being released on President Micombero's order, an alleged rebel Hutu ambush of an army patrol provoked an attack by Burundian forces, including French-piloted aircraft, on several Tanzanian villages, resulting in the deaths of 41 Burundian refugees and 33 Tanzanian villagers. Though at first denying any frontier crossing, Burundi officials finally visited the area and offered apologies and compensation to Tanzania on April 3.

In May a second Hutu attack, apparently by insurgents who had fled to Tanzania, Zaire, and Rwanda, led to a wave of repression supported by the Unity and National Progress Party Youth Wing. Fighting in the south resulted in thousands of refugees pouring over into Tanzania from Mabanda and Kiofi, causing the Tanzanian government to send a border commission to the area in June. Fresh fighting occurred between Tanzanian and Burundian forces on the border at Ngina on July 13. Tanzania claimed that since May 1972 it had received more than 35,000 refugees from Tutsi repression. It demanded the promised compensation for the Tanzanian dead in previous raids, and dockworkers in the Tanzanian port cities of Dar es Salaam and Kigoma, which normally handled 85% of Burundi's trade, organized a boycott.

President Micombero tightened his personal control internally by the removal of moderate Prime Minister Albin Nyamoya on June 6. Arms shipments were received from Libya. Diplomatic relations with Israel were severed on May 16.

On July 22, following threats from President Micombero to resort to force unless a solution to the dispute with Tanzania was found, an agreement was reached. Burundi again promised to compensate Tanzania and to prevent further hostilities on its side, while Tanzania promised to restore normal relations and to end its trade boycott.

Although the boycott ended the following day, Burundian officials expressed concern about the aftereffects of the blockade. Large quantities of coffee were still awaiting delivery in Bujumbura Harbour, and it was expected to take weeks to clear the backlog of goods. European buyers had generally agreed not to cancel orders despite the delay, but U.S. buyers had not all answered government requests. Up to 80% of the country's 18,000 tons of coffee exports had previously gone to the U.S.

Almost 25% of Burundi's 1973 budget was allocated to defense. While joining the Common Organization of Africa, Malagasy, and Mauritius (OCAM) in negotiations with the EEC, the government accepted $12.6 million from the European Development Fund for agricultural development, in particular for a tea processing plant at Teza, and for tea cultivation.

After talks between a UN delegation and representatives of the Institute for Scientific Research in Central Africa at Bakavu in Zaire, it was agreed that Burundi, Zaire, Tanzania, and Zambia would form a regional fishing-research project. A research base was to be established at Bujumbura.

(MOLLY MORTIMER)

BURUNDI

Education. (1969–70) Primary, pupils 182,444, teachers 4,877; secondary, pupils 3,701, teachers 328; vocational, pupils 2,264, teachers 230; teacher training, students 2,892, teachers 214; higher (including University of Bujumbura), students 397, teaching staff 90.

Finance. Monetary unit: Burundi franc, with (Sept. 17, 1973) a free rate of BurFr. 81.40 to U.S. $1 (BurFr. 196.21 = £1 sterling). Gold, SDRs, and foreign exchange, central bank: (June 1973) U.S. $19,690,000; (June 1972) U.S. $17,920,000. Budget (1971 est.) balanced at BurFr. 2,121,000,000.

Foreign Trade (1972) Imports BurFr. 2,736,000,000; exports BurFr. 2,305,000,000. Import sources: Belgium-Luxembourg 16%; Tanzania 16%; France 9%; West Germany 8%; Japan 5%. Export destinations: U.S. 62%; West Germany 6%. Main exports: coffee 85%; cotton 5%.

Agriculture. Production (in 000; metric tons; 1971; 1970 in parentheses): corn *c.* 200 (182); cassava (1970) 1,577, (1969) 1,024; sweet potatoes (1970) 1,082, (1969) 874; millet 22 (34); sorghum 53 (96); dry beans *c.* 300 (349); dry peas *c.* 36 (34); coffee (1972) *c.* 20, (1971) 24; cotton, lint 3 (3). Livestock (in 000; Dec. 1971): cattle *c.* 680; sheep (1970) *c.* 240; goats 412.

Business Review:
see Economy, World

Butter:
see Agriculture and Fisheries

Cambodia

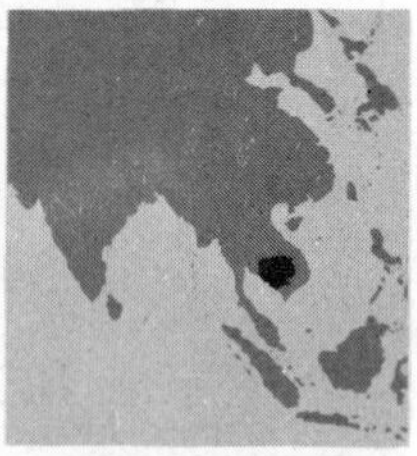

A republic of Southeast Asia, Cambodia (officially known as the Khmer Republic) is the southwest part of the Indochinese Peninsula. Area: 69,898 sq.mi. (181,035 sq.km.). Pop. (1973 est.): 7,190,000, including (1962 est.) Khmer 93%; Vietnamese 4%; Chinese 3%. Cap.: Phnom Penh (pop., 1971 est., 479,300). Language: Khmer (official) and French. Religion: Buddhist. President in 1973, Gen. Lon Nol; premiers, Hang Thun Hak until April 17, In Tam from April 17 to December 7, and, from December 26, Long Boret.

In 1973 U.S. bombing of Cambodia ended, under orders of Congress rather than of Pres. Richard Nixon. Although there was an immediate intensification of ground fighting, an eventual peace settlement was thought to be a matter of months away.

On May 31 the U.S. Senate voted overwhelmingly to cut off funds for U.S. bombing of Cambodia, only to be vetoed by Nixon. A compromise was eventually hammered out, with the administration agreeing to end all bombing over Cambodia on August 15.

During the fighting that raged just before and after the bombing halt, the Communist forces convincingly proved once again that they could, if they wanted, take Phnom Penh city. But their volatile campaigns gave no clue to their overall military strategy.

The last year of direct involvement by the U.S. in the Cambodian war brought the Nixon administration many embarrassing moments. One came when a federal district court in Brooklyn, N.Y., ordered a bombing halt in Cambodia by July 27 on the ground that the U.S. Congress had never authorized any form of war in Cambodia and that President Nixon was

CAMBODIA
Education. (1969–70) Primary, pupils 989,464, teachers 23,864; secondary, pupils 119,988, teachers 5,292; vocational, pupils 5,789, teachers (1967–68) 464; teacher training, students 1,005, teachers (1966–67) 104; higher (including 9 universities; 1968–69), students 11,094, teaching staff 1,200.
Finance. Monetary unit: riel, with (Sept. 17, 1973) a free rate of 195 riels to U.S. $1 (470 riels = £1 sterling). Budget (1971 est.) balanced at 18.7 billion riels.
Foreign Trade. (1971) Imports 4,346,000,000 riels; exports 825 million riels. Import sources (1970): France 23%; Japan 22%; West Germany 6%; U.K. 5%; Saudi Arabia 5%; U.S. 5%. Export destinations (1970): Hong Kong 18%; France 15%; Japan 14%; Senegal 11%; Singapore 10%; West Germany 7%. Main exports (1970): rice 46%; rubber 14%.
Transport and Communications. Roads (1970) *c.* 11,000 km. Motor vehicles in use (1971): passenger 26,400; commercial (including buses) 11,100. Railways: (including some sections not in operation; 1972) 552 km.; traffic (1971) 90 million passenger-km., freight 10 million net ton-km. Air traffic (1971): 32.4 million passenger-km.; freight 660,000 net ton-km. Inland waterway (Mekong River; 1970) *c.* 1,400 km. Telephones (Jan. 1972) 8,000. Radio receivers (Dec. 1968) 1 million. Television receivers (Dec. 1969) 50,000.
Agriculture. Production (in 000; metric tons; 1972; 1971 in parentheses): rice 1,927 (2,732); corn 80 (121); rubber *c.* 9 (*c.* 11); bananas (1970) 134, (1969) 134; dry beans (1971) 18, (1970) 20; jute *c.* 6 (*c.* 8). Livestock (in 000; Dec. 1971): cattle *c.* 2,100; buffalo *c.* 700; pigs *c.* 1,000.

therefore acting unconstitutionally. Supreme Court Justice William O. Douglas later confirmed the ruling, although eventually the administration was saved by the rest of the Supreme Court.

Another embarrassment was a quick succession of bombing errors in Cambodia in August in two mistaken raids that killed civilians and Cambodian soldiers in and around the key ferry town of Neak Luong. Errors apart, many questioned the validity of intensified saturation bombing when the Nixon administration had agreed to halt all bombing on August 15.

Perhaps the gravest embarrassment of all was the revelation, first made by a former U.S. Air Force officer, that B-52s had been secretly ordered to bomb Cambodia at a time when the U.S. government was publicly denying any such activity. Further denials—and more revelations—followed. In September a Pentagon White Paper admitted the White House had approved, raid-by-raid, a total of 2,875 clandestine B-52 bombing strikes in Cambodia four years previously and had kept them secret.

With a deadline for the bombing halt set, the U.S. seemed anxious to devise a face-saving peace formula. There was even talk of Henry Kissinger going to Peking for the purpose. But instead the Chinese ambassador to the UN merely visited President Nixon in San Clemente, Calif. In Peking Prince Norodom Sihanouk (*see* BIOGRAPHY) scornfully announced that he would not be available for talks with Kissinger. When Pres. Lon Nol's foreign minister, Long Boret, suggested peace negotiations with the rebel forces, Sihanouk rejected the idea "with scorn and disgust." He said Nixon only had a "tiny door" through which to pull out of the Cambodian mess: direct negotiations with the insurgent Khmer Rouge—if the Khmer Rouge agreed to it. Sihanouk's toughness represented a marked change from his position in May when he offered to open talks with the U.S. if Washington halted air raids and withdrew its military personnel.

Peace efforts were not helped by the confusion that prevailed on the domestic political scene in Cambodia. In February the presidential adviser in charge of "reconciliation and national concord," In Tam, resigned on the ground that he enjoyed no freedom of action. A month later military police announced that former deputy premier Lieut. Gen. Sisowath Sirik Matak had been placed under strict house arrest. An air force officer and son-in-law of deposed Prince Sihanouk staged an assassination attempt on Lon Nol by bombing his palace on March 17, killing 47 people but failing to hit the president. The officer escaped to Peking, but a wave of arrests followed. A second such attempt was made in November.

The sudden proposal in March for new elections was one of the ways in which the government, under growing U.S. pressure, tried to create a favourable atmosphere for negotiations with the rebels. On April 17 Lon Nol abruptly announced the resignation of the government. It took a month for a new 24-member coalition Cabinet to be formed. In Tam was named the new premier on May 11. The maneuver was believed to have been arranged by the U.S. to broaden the base of the Lon Nol Cabinet and get other non-Communist leaders of Cambodia into the administration. As a further move to strengthen the government, the U.S. successfully got the president's influential but unpopular brother, Brig. Gen. Lon Non, out of the country into virtual exile in May.

Nothing, however, seemed to shore up the government's ebbing strength. Lon Nol's reported assurance to a U.S. presidential emissary that he would agree to negotiate with Sihanouk only worsened the position for him when Sihanouk ridiculed the idea. On May 29, Ieng Sary, a prominent Cambodian Communist leader and special envoy of the National United Front of Cambodia, announced rebel determination to fight on until final victory and claimed that 80% of the country and a population of 5.5 million (out of a total of about 7 million) were under Communist control.

Early in December, Algeria, China, and 31 other countries began a campaign in the UN General Assembly to expel the Lon Nol government and seat instead that of Prince Sihanouk. The U.S., along with

WIDE WORLD

A Cambodian trooper watches as smoke billows from a suspected enemy position, bombed by U.S. Air Force jets, 10 mi. NW of Phnom Penh.

WIDE WORLD

Cambodian soldiers search a father and son captured in Ang Snuol following a rout of Communist occupying forces.

Japan, Thailand, Malaysia, and several other Asian countries sought to block the move. Their efforts proved successful as the assembly voted 53–50 to defer the issue until 1974. On December 7 Premier In Tam offered his resignation to Lon Nol, stating as his reason the lack of cooperation by several of his Cabinet officers. In Tam had previously offered to resign in October, but Lon Nol had refused. This time, however, he accepted the resignation, and on December 26 appointed Foreign Minister Long Boret, who had successfully defended Cambodia's UN seat. At the same time, the Cabinet was reshuffled.

Early in the year, the planning ministry prepared a modest $155 million plan to rebuild Cambodia's economy in the first two years after a signed peace. This was done in the burst of optimism before the January Vietnam cease-fire agreement. But the later deterioration of the government's military and political positions made the plan an academic exercise.

The economic devastation of the country was dramatized by some facts officially announced early in the year: half the nation's farmland had been abandoned; rice production was down to two-fifths of the prewar level and because 80% of the working population used to be employed in rice fields, the bulk of them were now unemployed; 700,000 Cambodians had become refugees; and the population was increasingly dependent on direct U.S. assistance, which, in the first quarter of the year, was running at $350 million annually. (T. J. S. GEORGE)

Cameroon

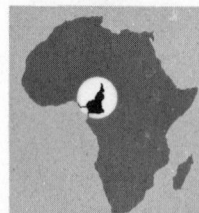

A republic of west equatorial Africa on the Gulf of Guinea, Cameroon borders on Nigeria, Chad, the Central African Republic, the Congo, Gabon, and Equatorial Guinea. Area: 179,557 sq.mi. (465,054 sq.km.). Pop. (1973 est.): 6,090,000. Cap.: Yaoundé (pop., 1972 est., 190,000). Largest city: Douala (pop., 1972 est., 252,000). Language: English and French (official), Bantu, Sudanic. Religion: mainly animist; some Christian and Muslim. President in 1973, Ahmadou Ahidjo.

In the sphere of foreign affairs the most important events of 1973 were the revision of cooperation agreements concluded with France at the time of Cameroon's accession to independent status in 1960, an official visit by President Ahidjo to China, and Cameroon's decision to withdraw from the Common Organization of Africa, Malagasy, and Mauritius (OCAM). Domestic affairs during the year were characterized by an atmosphere of calm and stability, and the main event of 1973 was the election of a new National Assembly on May 18.

In February the Cameroonian leaders announced that they had officially informed the French government of their country's desire for a revision of the texts governing arrangements for cooperation between Cameroon and the former colonial power. The 12 texts involved were duly amended or modified on September 25 following negotiations in Paris.

In March President Ahidjo was received in Peking as the official guest of Chinese Premier Chou En-lai, exactly two years after Cameroon's recognition of the Communist regime there. An agreement on economic and technical cooperation was signed at the close of Ahidjo's visit, providing among other things for a loan from China of $17 million.

President Ahidjo took the opportunity of a visit to Dakar in July to inform Senegalese Pres. Léopold Sédar Senghor, with whom he had close personal links, of his country's intention to withdraw from OCAM. Disappointed with the operation of an organization which he regarded as "ineffective," President Ahidjo was also at pains to demonstrate his desire to maintain a certain distance between his country and France, with which OCAM had maintained close relations. Nevertheless, he was agreeable to his country remaining a member of the various technical and specialist bodies of OCAM.

The legislative elections of May 18 resulted predictably in the winning of all 120 seats in the Cameroonian National Assembly by candidates put up by the country's only legal political party, the Cameroonian National Union. (PHILIPPE DECRAENE)

CAMEROON

Education. (1969–70) Primary, pupils 888,435, teachers (including preprimary) 18,972; secondary, pupils (1971–72) 65,305, teachers 1,964; vocational, pupils (1971–72) 21,447, teachers 913; teacher training, students 3,852, teachers 275; higher, students 2,030, teaching staff 210.

Finance. Monetary unit: CFA franc, with (Sept. 17, 1973) a parity of CFA Fr. 50 to the French franc and a free commercial rate of CFA Fr. 212.55 to U.S. $1 (CFA Fr. 512.25 = £1 sterling). Federal budget (1972–73 est.) balanced at CFA Fr. 52.7 billion.

Foreign Trade. (1972) Imports CFA Fr. 76,420,000,000; exports CFA Fr. 55.7 billion. Import sources (1970): France 50%; West Germany 8%; U.S. 8%. Export destinations (1970): France 31%; The Netherlands 23%; West Germany 12%; U.S. 10%. Main exports (1971): coffee 25%; cocoa 23%; timber 8%; aluminum 7%.

Transport and Communications. Roads (1971) 55,992 km. (including 6,968 km. main roads). Motor vehicles in use (1970): passenger 32,400; commercial (including buses) 32,400. Railways: (1971) 839 km.; traffic (1972) 199 million passenger-km., freight 308 million net ton-km. Telephones (Jan. 1972) 22,000. Radio receivers (Dec. 1969) c. 210,000.

Agriculture. Production (in 000; metric tons; 1972; 1971 in parentheses): corn c. 320 (c. 355); sweet potatoes (1971) 359, (1970) 328; cassava (1970) 930, (1969) 902; coffee c. 90 (c. 88); cocoa (1971–72) 112, (1970–71) 112; bananas (1970) c. 125, (1969) c. 120; peanuts c. 215 (209); rubber (exports) 15 (13); cotton, lint c. 22 (16); millet and sorghum (1971) 426, (1970) 312; palm kernels c. 57 (58); palm oil c. 58 (56); timber (cu.m.; 1971) c. 7,300, (1970) c. 7,200. Livestock (in 000; Dec. 1971): cattle c. 2,200; pigs c. 350; sheep c. 1,150; goats c. 2,700; chickens (1970) c. 8,700.

Industry. Production (1971): aluminum 51,000 metric tons; gold 100 troy oz.

Canada

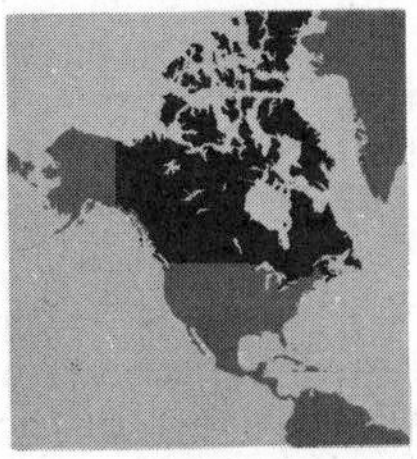

Canada is a federal parliamentary state and member of the Commonwealth of Nations covering North America north of conterminous United States and east of Alaska. Area: 3,851,809 sq.mi. (9,976,139 sq.km.). Pop. (1973 est.): 22,125,000, including (1971) British 44.6%; French 28.7%; other European 23%; Indian and Eskimo 1.4%. Cap.: Ottawa (pop., 1972 est., 613,315). Largest city: Montreal (metro. area pop., 1972 est., 2,760,469). Language (mother tongue, 1971): English 60.1%; French 26.9%; others 13%. Religion (1971): Roman Catholic 46.2%; Protestant 42.1%. Queen, Elizabeth II; governor-general in 1973, D. Roland Michener; prime minister, Pierre Elliott Trudeau.

Canada was governed by a minority administration during 1973 following the indecisive results of the federal election on Oct. 30, 1972. In the election the Liberal Party led by Trudeau had captured only 109 of the 264 seats in the House of Commons, while the principal opposition party, the Progressive Conservatives, won 107 seats. Thus during 1973 the balance of power lay with the socialist New Democratic Party (NDP), holding 31 seats. The life of the Trudeau government depended upon its proposing policies that would earn NDP backing while working to regain the favour of the voters. In the first of these tactics it was successful during 1973, but there was doubt whether the Liberals had managed to create the new consensus of support they sought.

Paradoxically, although the Canadian economy showed exceptional growth in 1973, economic problems provided the chief challenge to the Trudeau government. Unemployment declined steadily for the first half of the year, and the government could claim that its policies had assisted in creating an unprecedented number of new jobs. But inflation and a dramatic rise in the cost of living haunted the government and dictated most of its legislative activity. In this respect the government was unlucky, for inflation was a worldwide phenomenon, and the Canadian experience had been remarkably good in recent years. Nevertheless, increases in living costs (1.3% in August alone, a 22-year record) came as an ugly shock to Canadians. From August 1972, the Canadian consumer price index had risen 8.3% with the food component increasing at nearly double that rate.

Domestic Affairs. With the House of Commons sitting for almost ten months in 1973, the government was under continuous attack during the first session of Canada's 29th Parliament. The opposition parties seized every opportunity to move motions of no confidence in the Trudeau administration. The first formal test came on January 9, just five days after the new session began. It was precipitated by the Conservatives and was defeated, 154–104, by a coalition of the Liberal, NDP, and Social Credit parties. Although the lineup of parties differed in later votes, the Liberals always obtained sufficient support from the opposition groups to maintain themselves in office.

The most dangerous moment for the Trudeau government came after May 29, when it introduced a measure providing for a reduction in the tax on profits earned by corporations engaged in manufacturing or processing. This change, which had been proposed by Finance Minister John Turner as a job-creating incentive in his budget of May 1972, had not been enacted by the previous Parliament. During the fall election campaign David Lewis (*see* Biography), the NDP leader, had angrily described the proposal as an excuse for "a corporate ripoff." The "moment of truth," which commentators had predicted for the government over this issue, failed to occur. Turner neatly modified his proposal to win Conservative support. He introduced corporate tax reductions of nine percentage points but offered to provide an interim report on the efficacy of the tax cuts by April 1, 1974. If 60 members of Parliament wished to debate the matter at that time, the government would allow the House to decide whether to eliminate the tax reductions or to continue them. This expedient met Conservative wishes, the party lined up behind the Liberals to defeat the NDP attack, and the tax change later became law.

Other major legislation in 1973 was directed toward dealing with inflation. Turner's budget of February 19 attempted to balance the task of spurring the economy with the need to avoid fueling inflationary pressures. Called the "family budget" by the finance minister, it provided for a 5% reduction in the rate of personal income tax (really a 2% decrease, since an additional 3%, resulting from a previous budget, had gone into effect on January 1) and increased personal exemptions. Turner also borrowed an idea from Conservative leader Robert Stanfield by announcing that an inflation factor would be built into personal exemptions in the future so that tax concessions would not be nullified by constant rises in the price level. The universal old-age pension was increased to $100 a month as of April 1, while increases were provided in government allowances for war veterans and disadvantaged groups. The federal sales tax of 12% on "near foods," such as candy and soft drinks, was abolished, and the tariff on imported foods was reduced. (In September the tariff on imported live cattle and beef and veal was reimposed as U.S. beef began flooding into Canada in response to U.S. price-control policies.)

Throughout the year the government moved to restrict the export of scarce commodities in order to relieve the pressure on prices. Oilseeds and vegetable oil products were put under export controls on June 30, and beef followed on August 13. The attempt to shield the Canadian economy from U.S. demands was

U.S. war resisters in Canada read of Vietnam cease-fire in January 1973 at a Montreal coffeehouse.

UPI COMPIX

CANADIAN PRESS

Queen Elizabeth reviews the Royal Regiment of Canada on her arrival at Toronto International Airport, June 25, 1973, for a ten-day tour of four provinces.

most clearly seen in the field of oil and natural gas exports. In March crude oil exports to the U.S. were cut back 3.7% from the supply requested by U.S. refineries, and on June 15 temporary controls were imposed on sales of gasoline and heating oils. The latter move resulted from the revelation that in the first four months of 1973 gasoline exports to the U.S. had been 50 times larger than in the same period of 1972. Seeking a voluntary freeze on Canadian crude oil prices until January 1974, the Trudeau government imposed an export tax of 40 cents a barrel on Alberta crude moving to Chicago in order to bring its price into line with average U.S. prices. The rationale was not a desire to restrict exports to the U.S. but an attempt to isolate Canadian oil prices from more rapidly rising U.S. price levels.

A new Canadian oil policy, announced on September 4, indicated that the U.S. could not look to Canada for a solution to its energy shortage. In 1973 Canada was exporting about 1.1 million bbl. of crude oil a day to the U.S. It was also supplying, from its own wells, domestic requirements from British Columbia to Ontario and importing almost as much as it exported in order to serve the needs of Quebec and the Maritime Provinces. As the U.S. shortage grew, American refineries began requesting supplies from Canada almost half again as large as previous deliveries. These additional amounts could not be provided because of limited pipeline capacity and because it was felt that eastern Canada was dangerously dependent on foreign suppliers. The Arab-Israeli conflict of October, which placed Arab oil exports to Canada in jeopardy, showed that there was a sound basis for this concern. Thus the new oil policy announced by Energy Minister Donald Macdonald envisaged the extension of the major Alberta–Toronto pipeline into the area east of the Ottawa River, thus assuring security of supply for eastern Canada. This would also mean, however, that Canada would be unable to increase its oil exports to the U.S. in any significant sense.

On November 1, with the oil situation worsening, the government raised the export tax on crude oil to $1.90 a barrel, effective in December. The purpose of the new tax was to allow Alberta to obtain higher international prices for its oil exports while holding down the price for its sales in Ontario and western Canada. The September freeze on oil prices was relaxed to allow an immediate increase in gasoline and heating oil prices in eastern Canada to match the escalating costs of oil imported from Venezuela and the Middle East.

In September the Trudeau government afforded disadvantaged groups further relief. Universal old-age pensions, paid to 1.8 million Canadians, were to be increased in October to $105.30 from $100 a month and were to be revised every quarter, depending on the cost-of-living index. The guaranteed income supplement, paid to about one million indigent pensioners, was also raised. A 2% ceiling on cost-of-living increases in government pensions and registered pension plans was removed. Family allowances, paid on a scale depending on the age of the child, were to be substantially increased, although the higher payments would be considered part of taxable income.

The first session of the 29th Parliament met for three periods during 1973. The first began on Jan-

continued on page 172

CANADA

Education. (1969–70) Primary, pupils 3,841,040, teachers (including preprimary) 163,513; secondary, pupils 1,505,571, teachers 100,791; vocational (excluding Quebec), pupils 307,300; higher (including 45 main universities), students 562,648, teaching staff (full-time university only) 21,840.

Finance. Monetary unit: Canadian dollar, with a free rate (Sept. 17, 1973) of Can$1.01 to U.S. $1 (Can$2.44 = £1 sterling). Gold, SDRs, and foreign exchange, official: (June 1973) U.S. $5,682,000,000; (June 1972) U.S. $5,891,000,000. Budget (1971–72 est.): revenue Can$12,260,000,000; expenditure Can$14,841,000,000. Gross national product: (1972) Can$102,940,000,000; (1971) Can$93.4 billion. Money supply: (April 1973) Can$21,980,000,000; (April 1972) Can$19,810,000,000. Cost of living (1963 = 100): (May 1973) 144; (May 1972) 134.

Foreign Trade. (1972) Imports Can$20,396,000,000; exports Can$20,816,000,000. Import sources: U.S. 66%; EEC (Six) 6%; Japan 6%; U.K. 5%. Export destinations: U.S. 67%; U.K. 6%; EEC (Six) 5%. Main exports: motor vehicles 24%; metal ores 7%; nonferrous metals 6%; timber 6%; newsprint 6%; crude oil 5%; wheat 5%.

Transport and Communications. Roads (1971) 831,065 km. (including 2,765 km. expressways). Motor vehicles in use (1971): passenger 6,967,200; commercial (including buses) 1,856,000. Railways: (1971) 74,106 km.; traffic (1972) 3,289,000,000 passenger-km., freight 179,026,000,000 net ton-km. Air traffic (1971): 15,459,000,000 passenger-km.; freight 485,933,000 net ton-km. Shipping (1972): merchant vessels 100 gross tons and over 1,235; gross tonnage 2,380,635. Shipping traffic (1972): goods loaded 97,664,000 metric tons, unloaded 61,604,000 metric tons. Telephones (Dec. 1971) 10,253,000. Radio receivers (Dec. 1971) 16,850,000. Television receivers (Dec. 1971) 7,610,000.

Agriculture. Production (in 000; metric tons; 1972; 1971 in parentheses): wheat 14,514 (14,412); barley 11,287 (13,099); oats 4,630 (5,606); rye 344 (557); corn 2,657 (2,946); potatoes 1,880 (2,224); rapeseed 1,300 (2,155); linseed 483 (567); tobacco 83 (102); butter 136 (134); cheese 113 (109); beef and veal (1971) *c.* 918, (1970) 899; pork (1971) *c.* 690, (1970) 608; timber (cu.m.; 1970) 121,500, (1969) 121,800; fish catch (1971) 1,289, (1970) 1,389. Livestock (in 000; June 1972): cattle 13,657; sheep 845; horses 354; pigs 7,150; poultry 101,099.

Industry. Labour force (June 1973) 9,327,000. Unemployment: (May 1973) 5.3%; (May 1972) 6.2%. Index of industrial production (1963 = 100): (1972) 169; (1971) 159. Fuel and power (in 000; metric tons; 1972): coal 15,808; lignite 2,977; crude oil 76,700; natural gas (cu.m.) 91,011,000; electricity (kw-hr.) 237,627,000 (74% hydroelectric in 1971). Metal and mineral production (in 000; metric tons; 1972): iron ore (shipments; 55% metal content) 38,859; crude steel 11,860; copper ore (metal content) 709; nickel ore (metal content; 1971) 267; zinc ore (metal content) 1,279; lead ore (metal content) 377; aluminum (1971) 1,002; asbestos (1971) 1,489; gold (troy oz.) 2,030; silver (troy oz.) 46,707. Other production (in 000; metric tons; 1972): wood pulp 16,743; newsprint 7,857; sulfuric acid 2,749; synthetic rubber 196; passenger cars (units) 1,154; commercial vehicles (units) 320. Dwelling units completed (1972) 232,230.

SPECIAL REPORT

CANADIAN CULTURAL NATIONALISM

By Robert Fulford

The rise of cultural nationalism has been one of the striking aspects of life in English-speaking Canada during the early 1970s. If this surprises visitors to the country and those who hear of it from a distance, it also surprises many older Canadians. Certainly no one predicted that it would appear so suddenly and in so many fields at once, reaching into everything from legitimate theatre to popular music.

The development of economic nationalism was, by comparison, predictable. There had been many indications that Canadians were becoming dissatisfied with the extent to which foreign corporations, mainly U.S.-owned, control the Canadian economy. But in the arts, as late as the mid-1960s, there were few signs of articulate discontent. English-speaking Canada imported most of what its people read, watched, listened to, and talked about, and for the most part English-speaking Canada seemed content. This was not true in Quebec and never had been. Protected by the French language, Quebec culture thrived as an independent entity. It is in English-speaking Canada that the change has taken place.

The New Canadian Presence. It would be a mistake to overestimate this change. American-made television still dominates the airwaves in Canada, even on the government-owned Canadian Broadcasting Corporation. In the movie theatres the Hollywood product remains the staple, and on paperback racks and magazine stands American publications still vastly outnumber the Canadian. There is no evidence that the American presence is substantially diminished, and no real possibility that it will be in the foreseeable future. But beside the American presence there is now a separate Canadian presence. It is still fragile and much worried-over, and it appears to need the support of government regulations and subsidies. Nevertheless, its existence is more evident than at any previous time in this century.

In the theatre, for instance, the change has been remarkable. In the early 1960s Canadian theatre people thought themselves fortunate if they produced half a dozen new plays across the country in a season; a decade later each season brings scores of new plays in Toronto alone. There are, at any given moment, half a dozen theatre companies devoted mainly to producing new plays by Canadians. In 1970, when the Factory Theatre Lab in Toronto announced that it would run a regular schedule consisting entirely of new Canadian plays, the idea seemed faintly ridiculous. But the company found not only good scripts and enthusiastic audiences; it also found imitators. Soon the established theatres were under heavy pressure to discover playwrights of their own or borrow those already unearthed by the new little theatres.

Until 1967 book publishing in Canada was dominated by eight or ten branches of New York and London firms, and by only three Canadian companies. In 1967 a new company, the House of Anansi Press, was started by two young writers in Toronto. From the beginning its intentions and outlook were nationalistic, and it proved to be only the first of a dozen or so companies that set out to promote Canadian authors. Through zealous lobbying, these firms helped make support of a native publishing industry a priority of government cultural policy. The federal government now provides subsidies for Canadian-owned book publishers in the form of grants and book purchases, especially for use in schools and libraries.

Government initiatives play an even larger role in the mass media. In broadcasting the government has taken a more nationalistic line than at any point since the 1930s. The Canadian Radio-Television Commission, which regulates broadcasting, compelled both the CBC and the private television stations to increase the number of Canadian-produced programs shown in prime time, and after 1970 it forced radio stations to give a substantial percentage of their air time to records by Canadian performers or composers—a ruling that transformed the Canadian recording industry. The Canadian Film Development Corporation, another federal agency, invested some Can$10 million in Canadian feature movies, though this policy proved much more successful in Quebec than in English-speaking Canada.

Fending Off the American Giant. All this is to protect Canadian culture against America, more than anything else. American culture is perceived by Canadian artists and intellectuals as imperialistic. It may be unintentionally imperialistic, but the effect on Canada is the same as if a cultural invasion had been carefully planned in Washington. American culture, from school textbooks to girlie magazines, floods the Canadian scene. American entrepreneurs of the arts come into Canada with enormous advantages. The words and images they produce are generally interesting because of the importance of their subject: the United States itself. They send their products to a world market, whereas Canadians, whose products are of interest mainly to other Canadians, sell in a much smaller market, with all the limitations that implies. Canadians have always allowed government a larger role in their lives than Americans have, and they tend to see the job of offsetting this cultural disadvantage as a natural one for the government.

Not all Canadians regard the new mood as ideal. Some established publishers and writers find the nationalistic publishers bumptious, and some of the established theatre people feel the same way about the new wave of directors and playwrights. Anti-Americanism, which in the past has often reflected the meanest side of the Canadian spirit, is seen as a grave danger; picketing a public art museum for hiring an American curator (that happened in 1972 in Toronto) is widely regarded as, at best, a breach of Canadian good taste. Moreover, there are some who believe that certain branches of American cultural organizations have proved, by their interest in Canadian creative work, that they are valuable to the Canadian scene.

Deciding why cultural nationalism arose at this particular time may require more historical perspective than we now have. Certainly it mirrors, to some extent, Americans' growing distrust of their own national assumptions. Certainly it also reflects a widespread Canadian disillusionment with American foreign policy, particularly in Asia. Possibly it is a natural parallel to the resentment Canadians feel about American ownership of the most important sectors of the Canadian economy.

In some sense this cultural nationalism may be an outgrowth of that most curious experience, the celebration in 1967 of the hundredth anniversary of the Canadian confederation. That year-long party left Canadians with mixed feelings—a giddy sense of accomplishment about Expo 67 combined with a certain puzzlement over just what was being celebrated so feverishly. Possibly, a generation from now, historians will decide that the cultural nationalism of the early 1970s was merely a natural part of the maturation process every country works through on its way from colonial status to full independence. One may hope they will also find that this period produced art of permanent value.

Robert Fulford is editor of Saturday Night *magazine, a syndicated columnist for the* Toronto Star, Ottawa Citizen, *and* Montreal Star, *and author of several books.*

continued from page 170

uary 4 and lasted 132 sitting days until July 27, a month more than the normal session. It was recessed during August but had to be called back on August 30 to deal with a national railway strike. This concerned 56,000 nonoperating railway workers who began rotating strikes in late July and a general strike on August 23. In a 12-hour session ending on September 1, the House of Commons passed a bill ordering the workers back to their jobs and providing for arbitration of their demands on wages and working conditions. Minimum wage increases were guaranteed in the bill, the amount being set by a Conservative amendment to the government's measure which won the support of the NDP.

Although rail traffic was soon restored throughout the country, the opposition parties forced the government to keep Parliament in session until September 21 to consider anti-inflation strategies. At the autumn session, beginning on October 15, the suspension of capital punishment was continued for another five years; the ban on the death penalty did not apply to convicted killers of police or prison guards. Other bills passed by the 1973 Parliament included tougher security measures to restrain airplane hijackers and a measure authorizing the sale of commemorative coins and stamps to assist in financing the 1976 Olympic Games at Montreal. A new Immigration Act proclaimed on August 15 gave persons presently living in Canada as illegal immigrants a chance to come forward and apply for landed status. About 50,000 persons registered with the immigration authorities as a result of this measure.

There were no federal by-elections in 1973, and standings in the House of Commons remained unchanged throughout the year. The Liberals formed the largest party with 109 seats, the Conservatives held 107, the New Democratic Party 31, and the Social Credit Party 15. There were two independents, one of them being the speaker of the House, Lucien Lamoureux.

Progress was slow in the delicate task of working out a new balance of powers between the central government and the provinces. A number of meetings were held, the most significant being the Western Economic Opportunities Conference in Calgary, Alta., July 24–26. Here the premiers of the four Western provinces sat down to discuss their economic grievances with 13 federal Cabinet ministers led by Prime Minister Trudeau. The West felt that national policies, particularly in transportation, encouraged the region to concentrate on raw materials to be sent to the factories of the industrialized East. The federal ministers responded with a number of positive steps. They agreed to review allegedly discriminatory freight rates, to provide more information to the provinces on railway operation costs, and to freeze existing freight rates for an 18-month period. They also promised to join with the provinces in a $157 million program to improve the prairie road network.

Most importantly, they accepted the contention of the Western premiers that federal banking laws should be amended to allow provincial governments to own shares in banks. Thus a province such as British Columbia, with its own federally chartered private bank, would be allowed to own up to 25% of the capital stock of the institution. Although provincial participation would have to be reduced to 10% over a ten-year period, this concession represented a significant breach in the federal government's exclusive jurisdiction over banking.

While the four premiers expressed satisfaction at the results of the Calgary meeting, federal fence-mending suffered a setback in early September when Ottawa imposed the special export tax on Alberta oil going to the U.S. Claiming that this tax would inhibit development and investment in the Alberta oil industry, Premier Peter Lougheed bitterly attacked the Trudeau government for failing to consult on such an important measure. Earlier, Lougheed's plan to set up a two-price structure for Alberta natural gas, announced in November 1972, had provoked a quarrel with Ontario, a prime customer. The Ontario government claimed that having one price for Alberta and another for the rest of Canada would undermine the Canadian national economy.

Two provincial elections were held in 1973. In Manitoba Edward Schreyer's NDP government, first elected in 1969, won a solid victory. The party gained 2 seats, for a total of 31 in a 57-seat legislature. The Conservatives and Liberals each won one seat, bringing their totals to 21 and 5, respectively. A much more decisive result occurred in Quebec on October 29, when Premier Robert Bourassa's Liberals captured 102 of the 110 seats in the National Assembly. In office since 1970, the Liberals were challenged by a confident Parti Québécois, advocating the separation of Quebec from the Canadian federation and its creation as an independent state. The PQ had made a strong effort to capture the support of Quebec's intellectuals and youth, but the election results showed that most voters preferred the experience and financial caution of the Liberals, who had presented four budgets since taking office without increasing taxation. More importantly, there was substance to Bourassa's claim that the results indicated a decided preference on the part of the residents of Quebec to remain within the federal system. The Liberals' popular vote increased from 45 to 55%. The PQ vote also increased, from 23 to 30%, but the party won only six seats, one less than in 1970. The once mighty Union Nationale, which dominated Quebec from 1944 to 1960, failed to elect a single member, while the Créditistes dropped from 12 to 2.

Foreign Affairs. The largest international conference ever to be held in Canada took place August 2–10, when the 19th meeting of Commonwealth heads of government was held in Ottawa. Some 700 delegates representing 32 countries came together for a series of intensive discussions on problems of administration

Prime Minister Pierre Trudeau welcomes Mexican Pres. Luis Echeverría (left) to address the Canadian Parliament, March 30, 1973.

WIDE WORLD

and world politics. Queen Elizabeth II, in her capacity as head of the Commonwealth, visited Ottawa for six days during the conference, the first time she had done so for a Commonwealth meeting outside Britain. (This was the queen's second visit to Canada in 1973; she made a ten-day tour of four provinces from June 25 to July 5.) Observers remarked that the discussions in Ottawa were largely free from the divisive tensions that had marred the last conference at Singapore in January 1971. (*See* COMMONWEALTH OF NATIONS.)

Canada experienced a brief and unsatisfactory involvement in the troubled affairs of Vietnam in 1973. In a gesture of practical support for the January 23 cease-fire agreement, it accepted membership on the four-power International Commission of Control and Supervision and sent 290 military personnel and external-affairs officers to begin service on January 29. The initial commitment was for 60 days, subsequently lengthened for another three months after Mitchell Sharp, the secretary of state for external affairs, paid a visit to Vietnam in mid-March. At the Geneva conference ending on March 2, Sharp pressed for the establishment of a political authority other than the belligerents to which the ICCS could report. He failed to gain this objective, and Canadian insistence that reports of the commission be impartial and made public was not accepted by Hungary and Poland, two of the other members of the body. On May 29 Sharp regretfully gave notice that by July 31 Canadian membership on the commission would have to come to an end. (*See* VIETNAM: *Special Report.*)

Another Canadian participation in a peacekeeping operation began in November in the Middle East, when the UN set up an emergency force to move into the Suez Canal area following the Arab-Israeli war. Canada was asked to provide signals and supply some maintenance services, movement control, and postal facilities for the force, expected eventually to total about 7,000 men. An advance party of 11 men arrived in Egypt on November 5, and between November 11 and 19, 480 Canadians took up their places. Poland, a Warsaw Pact nation, was designated to share logistic support duties with Canada; it provided engineering units that were gradually built up to match the Canadian contribution. Two and a half weeks of intensive discussion at the UN, ending November 23, produced an agreement whereby 600 more Canadians were to be flown to Egypt to assist in the support role. Canada also provided vehicles, trailers, signal equipment, and aircraft to carry out its functions in the tense Middle East war zone.

Prime Minister Trudeau undertook a successful visit to China in October to cement the good relations that had existed since diplomatic recognition occurred in 1970. It was his third visit to China since the Communist revolution, the first two having occurred while he was a private citizen. He held a number of meetings with Premier Chou En-lai, during which a wide-ranging discussion on world politics took place. The highlight of the visit was a long meeting with the aged Chairman Mao Tse-tung, which the Chinese reported as being held in "a friendly atmosphere."

Trudeau brought back a number of bilateral agreements, the most important of which provided for the exchange of consuls between China and Canada, an unprecedented concession to a Western country. This move was expected to improve communications between the 100,000 Chinese Canadians and their relatives in China. Other agreements established most-favoured-nation trading arrangements between the two countries and set up the machinery whereby Chinese physicians could instruct their Canadian colleagues in acupuncture analgesia. Days before the prime minister's arrival in Peking, Canada and China signed another wheat agreement in which Peking promised to buy up to 224 million bu. of wheat over a three-year period.

Canadians received the news of the appointment of a new governor-general on October 5. He was to be Jules Leger, a long-time career diplomat and former journalist, currently Canadian ambassador to Belgium and Luxembourg. He was a brother of Paul-Emile Cardinal Leger, who had retired as archbishop of Montreal to take up missionary work in Cameroon. Leger, the fourth native-born Canadian to be appointed to the office, would succeed Roland Michener in mid-January.

Just seven months after the death of Lester B. Pearson on Dec. 27, 1972, Pearson's predecessor as Liberal Party leader, Louis S. St. Laurent, prime minister from 1948 to 1957, died in Quebec City at the age of 91. (*See* OBITUARIES.)

The Economy. The Canadian economy moved ahead strongly in 1973, enjoying its greatest real improvement since 1966. A 7% gain in real growth was anticipated, bringing the gross national product to about $116 billion for the year. The advance resulted from a number of factors: a booming U.S. market for Canadian exports, markets in other countries that became more accessible as the Canadian dollar floated downward, and strong domestic demand. Business inventories were built up at a higher rate than normal, and housing starts were above average. The economy, in fact, needed to be braked, a requirement that led to five increases in the bank rate between April and September alone.

Exports, going mostly to the U.S. and the EEC, totaled $17,810,000,000 for the first nine months of 1973, a gain of 25.9% over the previous year. Imports for the same period stood at $16,722,000,000 (preliminary), a gain of 23.5%, and came, in descending order, from the U.S., Japan, and Britain. Canadian wheat stocks fell to their lowest point in 20 years, reflecting the worldwide grain shortage. Fortunately, the Canadian wheat harvest, estimated at 622 million bu., was better than average, and the country made a number of major sales abroad.

Although jobs were created in large numbers during 1973, the labour force grew even more rapidly. Thus the rate of unemployment, seasonally adjusted, rose to 6% in September after having declined for the first six months of the year. Unemployment was disturbingly high in the 14–24 age group, although there were some shortages of experienced and skilled workers. The combination of high rates of inflation and unemployment continued to baffle the government's economic policy makers.

Federal government revenues, as outlined in the budget by Finance Minister Turner on February 19, were expected to reach $18 billion for the fiscal year 1973–74. Budgetary expenditures were predicted at $18,970,000,000, leaving a deficit of approximately $975 million. In a period of strong economic growth and price inflation, these figures could only be regarded as tentative. In the 1972–73 fiscal year, for instance, Turner had predicted a deficit of $450 million, but the budgetary position turned out to be roughly in balance by the end of the year. (D. M. L. FARR)

ENCYCLOPÆDIA BRITANNICA FILMS. *The Legend of the Magic Knives* (1970).

Canadian Literature: *see* Literature

Canals: *see* Transportation

Canning Industry: *see* Food

Catholic Church: *see* Religion

Cattle: *see* Agriculture and Fisheries

Cave Exploration: *see* Speleology

Cement: *see* Mining

Census Data: *see* Populations and Areas; *see also the individual country articles*

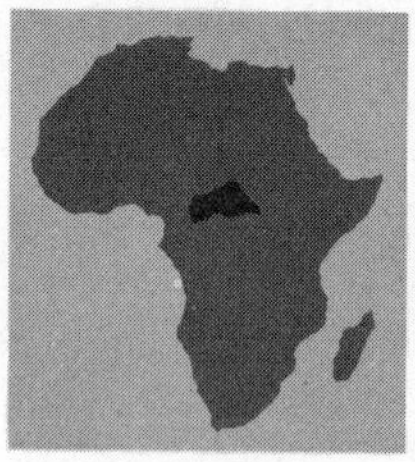

Central African Republic

The landlocked Central African Republic is bounded by Chad, Sudan, Congo, Zaire, and Cameroon. Area: 240,377 sq.mi. (622,577 sq.km.). Pop. (1971 est.): 1,637,000. Cap. and largest city: Bangui (pop., 1968, 298,579). Language: French (official). Religion: Protestant, about 40%; animist and Catholic, about 30% each. President and premier in 1973, Jean-Bédel Bokassa.

President Bokassa announced in April that a plot to overthrow his government had been discovered and that former minister of public works, transport, and housing Auguste M'Bongo had been placed under house arrest. M'Bongo had been dismissed from the government earlier in the month in the course of one of the president's Cabinet reshuffles. According to President Bokassa, M'Bongo had unsuccessfully attempted to bribe the deputy commander in chief, Gen. Jean-Claude Mandaba, to join him in an attempt to overthrow the government. The president also stated that M'Bongo had been involved in an attempted coup in 1967 but had been "forgiven" on that occasion. In June, after being accused of complicity in the affair, France replaced its ambassador in Bangui. The ultimate fate of M'Bongo remained unclear.

A seven-point agreement on economic aid and technical cooperation was signed with the Swiss Union for Cooperation with Centrafrica, an association of Swiss commercial, industrial, and banking concerns aimed at organizing and extending economic relations with the Central African Republic and ultimately with neighbouring states having close economic ties with that country. The agreement provided for Swiss aid for development projects in return for the right to exploit various natural resources and the country's tourist potential.

Projects covered by the agreement included studies for the construction of a hydroelectric power station on the Lobaye River, modernization of the capital's telephone and telex networks, and equipment and staff training for the republic's social and sanitary services. In return, the Central African government agreed to the Swiss Union's projects for exploiting copper deposits, prospecting for tin in the Yalinga area, and for the construction of a timber factory—for which 20 local citizens would be trained in Switzerland—as well as for the development of tourist potential in the northern part of the country. Swiss aid to agriculture would cover cotton, tobacco, coffee, and peanut production, truck farming, and the raising of livestock.

(PHILIPPE DECRAENE)

CENTRAL AFRICAN REPUBLIC

Education. (1970–71) Primary, pupils 178,550, teachers (1969–70) 2,757; secondary, pupils 9,540, teachers (1970–71) 359; vocational, pupils 1,420, teachers (1969–70) 130; teacher training (1969–70), students 249, teachers 25. The University of Bangui was founded in 1970.

Finance. Monetary unit: CFA franc, with (Sept. 17, 1973) a parity of CFA Fr. 50 to the French franc and a free commercial rate of CFA Fr. 212.55 to U.S. $1 (CFA Fr. 512.25 = £1 sterling). Budget (1972 est.) balanced at CFA Fr. 11,680,000,000.

Foreign Trade. (1971) Imports CFA Fr. 9,753,000,000; exports CFA Fr. 9,539,000,000. Import sources: France 61%; West Germany 6%; U.S. 5%. Export destinations: France 56%; Belgium 12%; Israel 9%. Main exports: diamonds 35%; coffee 23%; cotton 23%.

Agriculture. Production (in 000; metric tons; 1971; 1970 in parentheses): cassava *c.* 1,000 (*c.* 1,000); peanuts *c.* 85 (85); sweet potatoes *c.* 47 (*c.* 47); bananas *c.* 170 (*c.* 170); coffee *c.* 12 (10); cotton, lint *c.* 18 (20). Livestock (in 000; 1970–71): cattle *c.* 480; pigs *c.* 56; sheep *c.* 66; goats *c.* 530; chickens *c.* 1,100.

Industry. Diamond production (1971) 468,000 metric carats.

Central America:
see Latin-American Affairs; *articles on the various countries*

Ceylon:
see Sri Lanka

Chad

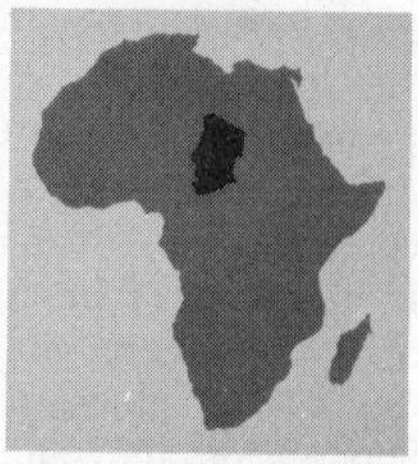

A landlocked republic of central Africa, Chad is bounded by Libya, the Sudan, the Central African Republic, Cameroon, Nigeria, and Niger. Area: 495,752 sq.mi. (1,284,000 sq.km.). Pop. (1973 est.): 3,869,000, including Saras, other Africans, and Arabs. Cap. and largest city: N'Djamena, until Nov. 28, 1973, known by its former French name, Fort-Lamy (pop., 1973 est., 193,000). Language: French (official). Religion (1964): Muslim 41%; animist 30%; Christian 29%. President and premier in 1973, Ngarta (formerly François) Tombalbaye.

For Chad 1973 was characterized by deteriorating relations with France, a general reorientation of foreign policy, and continued difficulties at home. In February and April, President Tombalbaye paid official visits to various Middle Eastern nations. On the earlier occasion he claimed that the aircraft in which he was traveling had been threatened by Israeli Phantom jets while flying over the island of Cyprus. In May an agreement was signed between Chad and China, and in July Chad withdrew from the Common Organization of Africa, Malagasy, and Mauritius (OCAM).

The government in July denounced French interference in the country's internal affairs. On various occasions during the year French nationals were imprisoned or expelled from the country. The country's sole political party, the Chadian Progressive Party, was dissolved by the president in August, and a new party, the National Movement for Cultural and Social Revolution, was created. Also in August, a leading opponent of Tombalbaye's government, Outel Bono, was assassinated in Paris under mysterious circumstances. The Chadian authorities denied involvement in the murder.

In September, after making verbal attacks on various members of the French government, President Tombalbaye went so far as to accuse French Pres. Georges Pompidou of planning armed intervention in his country's affairs. A campaign for the abolition of French names in Chad led to Fort-Lamy being re-

CHAD

Education. (1970–71) Primary, pupils 183,250, teachers (public only; 1968–69) 2,542; secondary, pupils 9,267, teachers (1969–70) 313; vocational, pupils 495; teacher training (1969–70), students 504, teachers 33.

Finance. Monetary unit: CFA franc, with (Sept. 17, 1973) a parity of CFA Fr. 50 to the French franc and a free commercial rate of CFA Fr. 212.55 to U.S. $1 (CFA Fr. 512.25 = £1 sterling). Budget (1970 est.): revenue CFA Fr. 11.8 billion; expenditure CFA Fr. 13.5 billion. Cost of living (Ndjamena; 1963 = 100): (Dec. 1972) 155; (Dec. 1971) 155.

Foreign Trade. (1971) Imports CFA Fr. 17,220,000,000; exports CFA Fr. 7,787,000,000. Import sources: France 77%; West Germany 5%; The Netherlands 5%. Export destinations: France 46%; West Germany 25%; Italy 9%; Belgium-Luxembourg 7%. Main export cotton 68%.

named Ndjamena and President Tombalbaye abandoning his former Christian name of François in favour of that of Ngarta.

Chad was one of the six West African states severely affected by drought, although the confused domestic situation made it difficult for observers to determine its extent. (*See* AGRICULTURE AND FISHERIES.) (PHILIPPE DECRAENE)

Chemistry

Physical and Inorganic. *Application of Liquid Crystals to Electro-Optical Displays.* Liquid crystals had long been characterized by the property of not melting sharply on heating but, instead, changing initially to a turbid liquid, which became clear and isotropic only at a considerably higher temperature. Owing to the ability of their molecular aggregates to undergo reorientation and alignment, these organic materials found increasing application in display devices; when subjected to relatively small electric fields, they produced striking optical effects. Liquid crystals found wide application in optical display devices for electronic instruments such as digital voltmeters, desk calculators, clocks, and watches.

Nematic liquid crystals, in which the long axes of the molecules are statistically distributed in a particular direction but in which the centres of gravity and the short axes are randomly placed, were most commonly used in liquid crystal displays. Nematic liquid-crystal compounds, such as derivatives of benzalaniline, stilbene, diphenylacetylene, or azobenzene, were employed in three different types of optical displays involving dynamic scattering, memory effects, and induced alignment.

Dynamic scattering devices required a thin film of sample in which the liquid was more or less transparent for sections up to a few micrometres in thickness. The application of an electric field across the thin film caused the molecular dipoles to rotate and assume a position parallel to the applied field, giving rise to a short pulse of scattered light. Continued application of the electric field caused ions to be injected and propelled through the liquid crystal medium. The nature of these ions and their mechanism of operation remained largely uncertain, but the end result was to produce a strong turbulence in the liquid crystal, which, being anisotropic, formed a large number of optical scattering centres. The film consequently changed its appearance from transparent to the semi-opaque character of frosted glass.

Optical displays with memory effects were produced by the addition of a small amount of cholestric liquid crystal to the usual dynamic scattering material. This brought about a semi-permanent optical scattering state that persisted for several weeks after the supply voltage had been removed but that could be reversed by the application of an alternating-current field.

Field Desorption Mass Spectrometry. The underlying principle in field desorption mass spectrometry involved inserting a specially designed, activated, field ion emitter, on which the material for analysis had been deposited, into the ionization chamber of a mass spectrometer. Molecular ions were generated when electrons were stripped from the sample in an environment of high electrical field potential under high vacuum conditions. The beam of molecular ions was

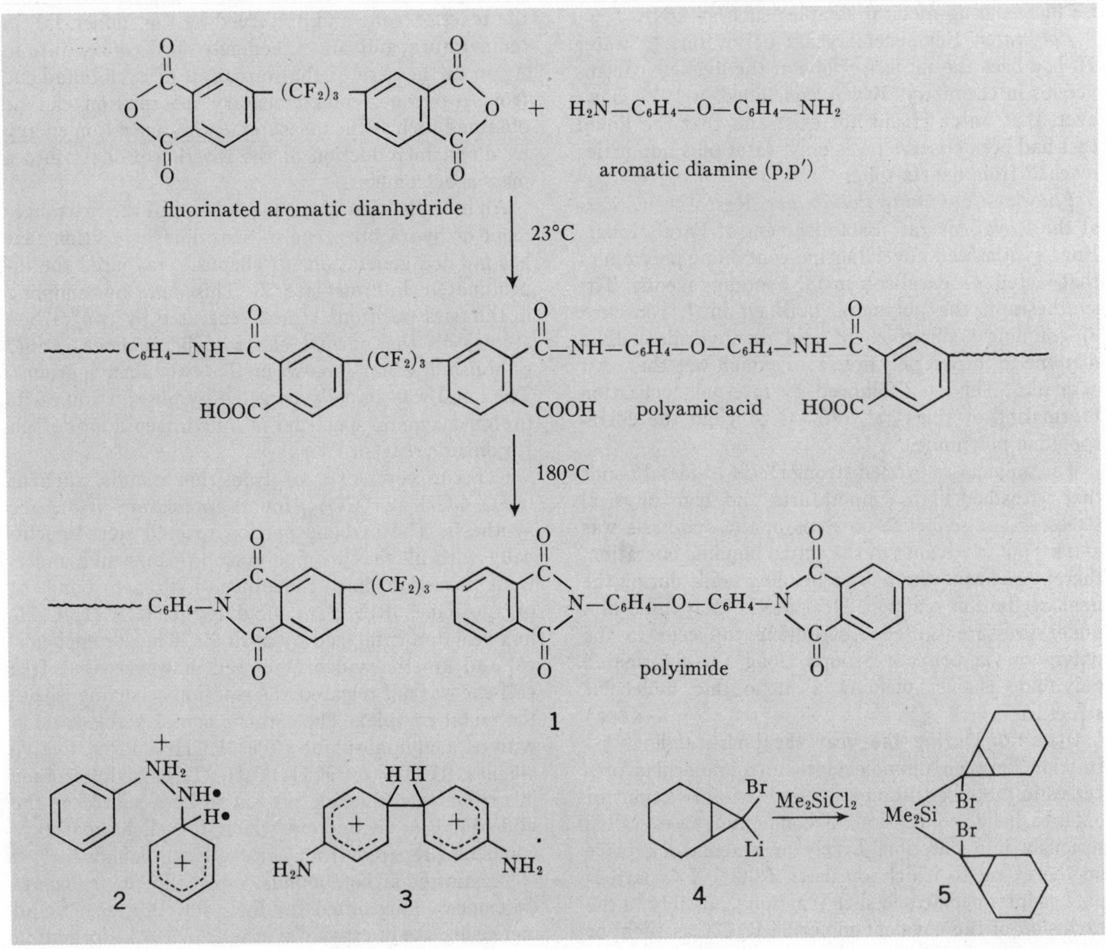

Cheese:
see Agriculture and Fisheries
Chemical Industry:
see Industrial Review

COURTESY, WAVE ENERGY SYSTEMS, INC.

Raymond Boucher of Wave Energy Systems checks a test sample treated with a new rapid sterilization process that employs ultrasonic waves and a chemical sterilant. Described as ten times faster than other methods, the process will benefit manufacturers of food packages and of plastic disposables for hospitals.

magnetically focused onto a sensitized photographic plate or electrical ion detector.

The method produced primary molecular ions as opposed to a variety of secondary ionic species from conventional electron impact-mass spectrometry. The resultant spectra were consequently much simpler and easier to interpret. Additional advantages included the use of nanogram (one-billionth of a gram) amounts of material for analysis, and the applicability to high-molecular-weight, low-vapour-pressure compounds. Field desorption mass spectrometry was applied to the analysis of pesticide molecules and, in conjunction with pyrolytic techniques, showed considerable promise in analyzing medical samples such as DNA.

Polywater. For several years polywater, or water II, had been the subject of one of the liveliest controversies in chemistry. It was concluded in 1973, however, that water II did not exist and that the liquid that had been observed was only water plus impurities leached from quartz tubes.

Fluorine-Containing Polyimides. Research workers at the Royal Aircraft Establishment at Farnborough, Eng., synthesized novel fluorine-containing polyimides that acted as excellent metal-bonding agents. The synthesis of the polymers, outlined in **1,** consisted of coupling a dicarboxylic acid dianhydride with a diamine to form a polyamic acid, which was then cast as a film. This was followed by internal cyclization (formation of rings) at 180° C to yield the corresponding polyimide.

The polyimides formed strong metal-to-metal bonds that withstood high temperatures and high physical stresses. The sequence of steps in the synthesis was carried out in advance of the actual bonding operation, thereby reducing the risk of forming voids during the final cyclization reaction. Heating the polyimide film under pressure caused crosslinking to occur in the polymers via pendant groups along the fluorinated polyimide chains, yielding a monolithic molecular structure. (J. A. KERR)

Organic. During the year the long-standing distinction between unimolecular and bimolecular processes in the substitution and elimination reactions of organic halides and similar compounds was called seriously into question. Lively argument took place on the extent to which ion pairs, $R_3C^+ X^-$, participate as intermediates in such reactions, possibly to the exclusion of the covalent molecule R_3CX as such, or to the exclusion of the free carbonium ion R_3C^+, which, it was claimed, is rarely formed. As a further complication, ion pairs may be "intimate," when the two oppositely charged ions are actually in contact, or "solvent-separated," when the two ions, though maintained in close association by electrostatic attraction, have solvent molecules inserted between the positive and negative centres. It was suggested that the overall result of a particular reaction would depend in a subtle and complex way on the relative importance of a large number of competing pathways, involving the formation of intimate ion pairs, their conversion to solvent-separated ion pairs, and the disappearance of both by reversion to starting material, interconversion, and reaction with external nucleophiles as well as solvent. Some of these processes may allow retention or inversion of configuration at the carbonium ion centre, though in many cases one or the other is predominant, as described in the classical theory of Sir Christopher Ingold.

The development of two techniques, based on contrasting principles, for the preparation and observation of short-lived and reactive species was noted. The matrix isolation technique depended on the "freezing" of a reaction product in an inert solid such as argon at −253° C, in which it is generated from a suitable precursor. The protolysis of α-pyrone or pyridine in such a matrix gave rise to the extrusion of carbon dioxide or hydrogen cyanide, respectively, the resulting cyclobutadiene being characterized spectroscopically. On the other hand, flash vacuum thermolysis is a development of the well-known technique of pyrolysis, one of the earliest ways of obtaining new organic compounds. The reactive species in this case was formed at a high temperature, but was at once removed from the reaction zone and preserved by the sudden fall in temperature and an exceedingly low concentration. Again in the case of the formation of cyclobutadiene from α-pyrone, complementary information can be obtained such as the measurement of ionization energy by direct introduction of the reaction product into a mass spectrometer.

An investigation of the mechanism of the rearrangement of hydrazobenzene to benzidine, a reaction that has puzzled generations of chemists, favoured the diprotonated intermediate **2**. This ion, by coupling in the para positions (those separated by two carbon atoms) ih the normal electrophilic manner, would establish the bond between the two phenyl groups. The ion **3** was actually detected by observation of its proton magnetic spectrum in a hydrogen fluoride/sulfur dioxide reagent.

Carbene complexes of transition metals, such as $C_6H_5(OCH_3)Cr(CO)_5$, found application in organic synthesis. The carbene portion reacted stereospecifically with alkenes to give cyclopropanes and underwent insertion into the silicon-hydrogen bond of organosilanes R_3SiH to yield $R_3SiCH(OCH_3)C_6H_5$ in a reaction catalyzed by pyridine. The stereochemical and kinetic evidence showed, however, that free carbene was not released, the reaction occurring within the metal complex. The carbene complex also reacted with triphenylphosphine ylides, $RCH = PPh_3$, to give alkenes, $RCH = C(OCH_3)C_6H_5$. Triphenylphosphine in carbon tetrachloride proved to be a source of the ylide $Ph_3P = CCl_2$ from which 1, 1-dichloroalkenes could be prepared from carbonyl compounds.

Organosilicon compounds, especially polysiloxanes (silicones), long noted for their stability, also found increasing use in organic synthesis in 1973. Formation of the organosilyl ether from hydroxyl compounds and trimethylchlorosilane or, more particularly, *t*-butyldimethylchlorosilane was recommended for the protection of hydroxyl groups in compounds sensitive to both acid and base so that other synthetic transformations could be carried out. Subsequent removal of the protective silyl group was achieved by treatment with tetra-*n*-butyl ammonium fluoride in tetrahydrofuran, or by reduction with lithium tri-*t*-butoxy aluminum hydride. Trimethylsilyl cyanide was found to be a useful replacement for hydrogen cyanide in the addition reaction to many carbonyl compounds. The formation of siloxy cyanides $R_2C(OSiMe_3)CN$ was catalyzed by zinc iodide.

The first examples of silacyclopropanes were reported. Compound **5** was obtained by reaction between dimethyldichlorosilane and the bromolithium reagent **4,** followed by ring closure with magnesium.

(J. C. YOUNG)

Chess

Bobby Fischer (U.S.), who wrested the world title from Boris Spassky (U.S.S.R.) in 1972, played not a single match or tournament game during 1973. Nevertheless, the Fischer-Spassky match gave impetus to chess throughout the world as more people took up the game and more events were organized and sponsored.

In August 1972 at Atlantic City, N.J., Walter Browne (U.S.) won the U.S. open championship. First in the tenth Rubinstein Memorial Tournament at Polanica Zdroj, Pol., was J. Smejkal (Czech.). Former world champion M. Tal (U.S.S.R.) was a convincing first in the International Tournament at Sukhumi, U.S.S.R., and went on to win the 40th U.S.S.R. championship at Baku. The annual Tschigorin Memorial Tournament, held at Kislovodsk, U.S.S.R., was won by L. Polugayevsky (U.S.S.R.). Two international tournaments were also held in Yugoslavia: A. Lein (U.S.S.R.) was first at Novi Sad and at Sombor first place went to 18-year-old Soviet master A. Belyavsky.

The strong international tournament held at San Antonio, Tex., ended in a triple tie between A. Karpov (U.S.S.R.), T. Petrosian (U.S.S.R.), and L. Portisch (Hung.). There was a triple tie, too, in the Palma de Mallorca, Spain, tournament between O. Panno (Arg.), Smejkal, and V. Korchnoy (U.S.S.R.).

Over the turn of the year 1972–73 Bent Larsen (Den.) was the first-prize winner at the annual Hastings Congress Premier Tournament. In February 1973 a play-off in Chicago of the tie between R. Byrne, L. Kavalek, and S. Reshevsky that had taken place in the previous year's U.S. championship went in favour of Byrne. E. Geller (U.S.S.R.) was first in a strong tournament in Budapest, Hung., and Tal once more played fine chess to win first prize $1\frac{1}{2}$ points ahead of Polugayevsky at Tallinn, U.S.S.R. At the tenth Capablanca Memorial Tournament at Cienfuegos, Cuba, V. Smyslov (U.S.S.R.) won first prize. An international tournament in Bucharest, Rom., was won by M. Taimanov (U.S.S.R.), and first prize in the Las Palmas, Canary Islands, International Tournament in April was shared by Petrosian and Leonid Stein (U.S.S.R.). Later in 1973 Stein was to die of a heart attack in Moscow at the age of 38. Smejkal was

Miguel Cuellar (right) of Colombia plays U.S.S.R.'s Viktor Korchnoy during June 1973 Interzonal Tournament in Leningrad, scheduled to determine qualifiers for 1974 elimination. The winner in 1974 would challenge world chess champion Bobby Fischer the following year.

TASS/SOVFOTO

Ruy Lopez (from a Soviet team match-tournament in Moscow, 1973)

White	Black	White	Black
A. Karpov	B. Spassky	A. Karpov	B. Spassky
1 P—K4	P—K4	18 B—Q3	P—Kt3(c)
2 Kt—KB3	Kt—QB3	19 Q—B2	KKt—Q2
3 B—Kt5	P—QR3	20 QR—Q1	B—Kt2
4 B—R4	Kt—B3	21 P×P	P×P
5 O—O	B—K2	22 P—B4	P×P(d)
6 R—K1	P—QKt4	23 B×BP	Q—K2(e)
7 B—Kt3	P—Q3	24 B—Kt3	P—QB4
8 P—B3	O—O	25 P—QR4	P—B5(f)
9 P—KR3	Kt—Kt1(a)	26 B—R2	B—QB3
10 P—Q3	QKt—Q2	27 P—R5	B—R5
11 QKt—Q2	B—Kt2	28 Q—B1	Kt—QB1(g)
12 Kt—B1	Kt—B4	29 B×RP	B×R
13 B—B2	R—K1	30 R×B	Kt—Q3(h)
14 Kt—Kt3	B—KB1	31 B×B	K×B
15 P—QKt4	QKt—Q2	32 Q—Kt5	P—B3
16 P—Q4	P—R3	33 Q—Kt4(i)	K—R2
17 B—Q2(b)	Kt—Kt3	34 Kt—R4	resigns(j)

(a) Thus far as in the famous tenth game of the World Championship match at Reykjavik, Ice., in 1972; then Fischer replied 10 P—Q4, but Karpov prefers a closer line. (b) The alternative is 17 B—Kt2, intending an eventual P—QB4, when the bishop would bear down on the enemy king side. (c) At San Antonio (1972) Gligoric played 18 . . ., R—B1 against Karpov but after 19 Q—B2, Q—Q2; 20 QR—Q1, White had the advantage. (d) If 22 . . ., P—QB4; 23 BP×P, P—B5; 24 B×BP, R—QB1; 25 B×Pch, K×B; 26 Q—Kt3ch, with a winning attack for White. (e) He should have played 23 . . ., Kt×B, since now the bishop escapes exchange and becomes a thorn in Black's side. (f) 25 . . ., P×P is bad because of 26 P—R5. (g) No better is 28 . . ., B×R; 29 R×B, Kt—R5; 30 B×P, B×B; 31 Q×B, when White's attack is irresistible. (h) A mistake that loses quickly; correct was 30 . . ., R—R2 though White would still have had the advantage after 31 B×B, K×B; 32 Q×P. (i) Threatening 34 R×Kt, Q×R; 35 Kt—B5ch. (j) If 36 . . ., P—Kt4; 37 Kt—B5, or if 36 . . ., R—KKt1; 37 B×P, R—Kt2; 38 Kt—B5, Kt×Kt; 39 Kt×Kt, P×Kt; 40 Q—R5 mate.

Q. P. King's Indian Defense (played in the World Junior Championship at Teesside, Eng., 1973)

White	Black	White	Black
R. Dieks	A. J. Miles	R. Dieks	A. J. Miles
1 P—QB4	P—KKt3	16 R—Q1	Q—R4
2 Kt—KB3	B—Kt2	17 P—Kt3	Kt(B5)—K4
3 P—Q4	Kt—KB3	18 Q—Kt2	Kt×Ktch
4 P—KKt3	O—O	19 B×Kt	Q—K4
5 B—Kt2	P—Q4	20 QR—B1(d)	Kt—Q5
6 P×P	Kt×P	21 B—Kt2	B—Kt5
7 O—O	Kt—QB3	22 P—B4	Q—B3
8 P—K4	Kt—Kt3	23 P—K5(e)	Q—Kt3
9 P—Q5(a)	Kt—R4	24 Kt—Q5(f)	Kt—K7db.ch
10 Kt—B3	P—QB3	25 K—R1	Q—B7
11 P×P	Kt×P(b)	26 R×R	R×R(g)
12 B—B4	B—K3	27 Q—Q2	B—B6
13 Q—B1	Kt—B5	28 Kt—K3	R—B8
14 B—R6	R—B1(c)	29 B×B(h)	Q—Kt8ch
15 B×B	K×B	resigns	

(a) Forced; 9 B—K3 would be bad on account of 9 . . ., Kt—B5 when Black would gain the advantage of two bishops. (b) White has been playing for equality and a draw. The natural result is that the initiative passes into Black's hands. (c) And not 14 . . ., B×B; 15 Q×B, Kt×P; because of 16 Kt—KKt5. But now White's queen is uncomfortably placed vis-à-vis the enemy rook. (d) If 20 Kt—R4, Q×Q; 21 Kt×Q, Kt—Kt5 and Black exerts strong pressure on the queen side. (e) After 23 R—Q2, Kt—B6ch is very strong, but the next move prepares a blunder. (f) Now comes a very pretty and instructive finish. (g) He could also have won by Kt×Pch and Q×Q, but he has a more pleasing finish in mind. (h) Now he is mated; but also hopeless is 29 R×R, Kt×Pch; 30 P×Kt, Q×Q, etc.

first in an international tournament at Luhacovice, Czech., in May 1973. The second West German championship at Dortmund ended in a triple tie between U. Andersson (Swed.), J. Hecht (W.Ger.), and Spassky. West Germany was first at the Clare Benedict International Team Tournament at Gstaad, Switz., half a point ahead of England. A double-round international tournament at Hilversum, Neth., ended in a tie for first prize between Geller and L. Szabo (Hung.).

The first of the two interzonal tournaments in the cycle of world championship events was held in June in Leningrad. The top three, who qualified for the 1974 candidates' event, were Karpov and Korchnoy ($13\frac{1}{2}$) and Byrne ($12\frac{1}{2}$); among those who failed to qualify were Tal and Larsen. The second interzonal was held at Petropolis, Braz., in July and August. H. Mecking (Braz.) was first, but there was a triple tie for the next place between Geller, Polugayevsky, and Portisch: this tie was resolved by a play-off at Portoroz, Yugos., won by Portisch; he and Polugayevsky, who was second, were the two extra qualifiers. The European Team Championship finals at Bath, Eng., in July were won by the titleholders, the U.S.S.R., ahead of Yugoslavia and Hungary. The IBM International Tournament in Amsterdam ended in a tie for first place between Petrosian and Planinc (Yugos.). Belyavsky won the World Junior Championship Tournament that was held at Teesside, Eng.; second and third places went to two English players, A. Miles and M. Stean. The British championship at Eastbourne resulted in a tie between M. Basman and W. Hartston. The Northern Open Championship held at Grena, Den., was won by Larsen. Tal was first at the international tournament at Sochi, U.S.S.R., in September 1973, a point ahead of Spassky; but Spassky made a comeback at the very strong Soviet championship in Moscow in October. (HARRY GOLOMBEK)

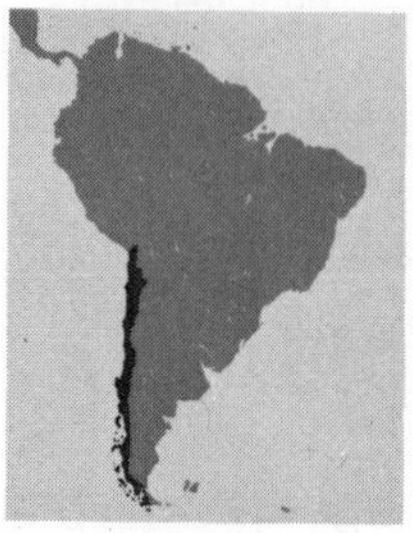

Chile

A republic extending along the southern Pacific coast of South America, Chile has an area of 292,257 sq.mi. (756,945 sq.km.), not including its Antarctic claim. It is bounded by Argentina, Bolivia, and Peru. Pop. (1973 est.): 10,228,767. Cap. and largest city: Santiago (metro. pop., 1973 est., 3,435,854). Language: Spanish. Religion: predominantly Roman Catholic. President until Sept. 11, 1973, Salvador Allende Gossens; president of the four-man military junta from September 13, Gen. Augusto Pinochet Ugarte.

UPI COMPIX

Santiago riot police fire tear gas into fleeing crowd of student demonstrators during Aug. 24, 1973, protests against the government of Pres. Salvador Allende.

CHILE

Education. (1970) Primary, pupils 2,043,032, teachers (public only; 1969) 35,588; secondary (1969), pupils 178,887, teachers 11,900; vocational (1969), pupils 85,987, teachers 8,600; teacher training (1969), students 2,895; higher (8 universities), students 96,000, teaching staff (1965) 8,835.

Finance. Monetary unit: escudo, with (Sept. 17, 1973) a multiple exchange rate system having a basic rate of 75 escudos to U.S. \$1 (180 escudos = £1 sterling) and other rates varying from 25 escudos to 890 escudos to U.S. \$1. Gold, SDRs, and foreign exchange, central bank: (March 1972) U.S. \$193.1 million; (March 1971) U.S. \$341.2 million. Budget (1972 est.): revenue 43,273,000,000 escudos; expenditure 40,689,000,000 escudos. Gross national product: (1971) 119,069,000,000 escudos; (1970) 90,799,000,000 escudos. Money supply: (Feb. 1973) 65,822,000,000 escudos; (Feb. 1972) 23,401,000,000 escudos. Cost of living (Santiago; 1963 = 100): (March 1973) 2,548; (March 1972) 899.

Foreign Trade. Imports (1971) U.S. \$980 million; exports (1970) U.S. \$1,246,900,000. Import sources (1970): U.S. 33%; West Germany 10%; Argentina 10%; U.K. 5%. Export destinations: West Germany 20%; Japan 17%; U.S. 13%; U.K. 12%; Italy 8%; France 6%; Argentina 6%. Main exports: copper 73%; iron ore 6%.

Transport and Communications. Roads (1971) 70,701 km. Motor vehicles in use (1970): passenger 177,025; commercial 134,900. Railways (1971): 9,757 km.; traffic (principal railways only) 2,481,000,000 passenger-km., freight 2,718,000,000 net ton-km. Air traffic (1972): 1,142,000,000 passenger-km.; freight 55,169,000 net ton-km. Shipping (1972): merchant vessels 100 gross tons and over 134; gross tonnage 382,013. Telephones (Dec. 1971) 393,000. Radio receivers (Dec. 1970) 1.4 million. Television receivers (Dec. 1970) 500,000.

Agriculture. Production (in 000; metric tons; 1972; 1971 in parentheses): wheat 1,195 (1,368); barley 139 (114); oats 111 (112); corn 283 (258); potatoes 733 (836); rapeseed 78 (82); dry beans 83 (72); sugar, raw value *c.* 150 (193); apples *c.* 98 (*c.* 93); wine *c.* 526 (525); beef and veal *c.* 170 (*c.* 170); wool (1971) *c.* 13, (1970) *c.* 13; timber (cu.m.; 1971) 8,200, (1970) 7,600; fish catch (1970) 1,179, (1969) 1,095. Livestock (in 000; 1971–72): cattle *c.* 3,000; sheep (1970–71) *c.* 6,800; pigs *c.* 1,200; horses *c.* 430.

Industry. Production (in 000; metric tons; 1972): crude oil 1,615; coal 1,328; electricity (kw-hr.; 1971) 8,524,000; iron ore (65% metal content) 8,653; pig iron 486; crude steel (ingots) 581; copper (1971) 468; nitrate of soda (1971) 829; manganese ore (metal content; 1971) 10; iodine (1971) 2.6; molybdenum (metal content; 1971) 6.3; gold (troy oz.; 1970) 64; silver (troy oz.; 1971) 5,369; woven cotton fabrics (m.) 85,000; fish meal (1971) 263.

At 4:30 A.M. on Sept. 11, 1973, the armed forces of Chile and the paramilitary national police force overthrew the Marxist-dominated constitutional government of President Allende (*see* OBITUARIES). Before noon Allende died in the national palace, La Moneda, after refusing surrender demands from army and air force units that had periodically attacked the palace throughout the morning. Resistance by partisans of the Unidad Popular coalition of Communist and Socialist parties, which had ruled Chile tenuously since the 1970 election, was crushed by the 90,000-man uniformed forces. Overnight, Chile was converted from a turbulent leftist democracy into a rightist authoritarian state.

The coup was the first experienced by Chile in 49 years. The armed forces struck hard at any conceivable opposition, outlawed all political activity, arrested more than 6,000 suspected extremists, abolished the constitution, and severed relations with the Soviet Union, Cuba, and other Marxist countries. At the same time, they immediately made overtures to reinstate the nation in the good graces of the U.S. and other countries from which friendship, investment, aid, and recognition were sought.

There were many motives behind the armed forces

intervention, not least of which was the economic chaos that had sent Chile from crisis to crisis throughout the nearly three years of Allende's government. On September 11 Chile was bankrupt, with a nearly worthless currency, debts of more than $3 billion, an empty treasury, a deteriorating economy, and no international credit except from the socialist bloc. The country had endured a series of crippling strikes, the worst being that of the independent truck drivers. Demonstrations had become almost a daily fact of life in Santiago and other large cities, while the farmers had lost incentive to produce for fear of either legal nationalization or illegal seizure by peasants. The officer corps claimed it was finally moved to action by the discovery of Plan Zeta, an alleged Marxist plot to murder 20,000 nonleftists. The military, traditionally apolitical in Chile, was also disillusioned with the confusion and unrest and viscerally opposed to Allende's anti-U.S., pro-Soviet attitude.

Allende had won the Sept. 4, 1970, election with less than 37% of the vote. He did not win control of the legislature, however, so the Marxist executive branch was continually at odds with a Congress dominated by the opposition parties. Nevertheless, Allende was determined to socialize Chile while at the same time retaining the democratic political form of government. Some of his reforms were initially popular. He expropriated the U.S.-owned copper companies, ordered wage increases of up to 40%, froze prices, and ordered production doubled. When Chile exhausted its financial reserves and began defaulting on international debts, credit sources dried up and shortages of food, fuel, and other basic necessities of life became standard. The inflation rate had exceeded 300% in the last year of Allende's government.

The armed forces struck first in the port city of Valparaiso before dawn on September 11. Following a carefully drawn plan, they seized all public buildings, communications facilities, airports, and border points. In Santiago martial law was declared, and tanks and infantry units surrounded La Moneda. Allende was offered a chance to give up, but he and his personal bodyguard rejected the ultimatum. The new government issued evidence that he committed suicide with a weapon given to him by Cuban Prime Minister Fidel Castro, although his followers claimed he was murdered.

The junta then moved to arrest all known Marxist activists in the country, including several hundred foreigners. Estimates of the number of persons killed varied widely. A curfew from 10 P.M. to 6 A.M. was put into effect, and only anti-Allende newspapers and radio-TV stations were permitted to operate.

The opposition Christian Democrats, the conservative groups, and the Radicals took no part in the military uprising or the new government. Former president Eduardo Frei Montalva, a Christian Democrat and probably the most popular politician in Chile, remained aloof. Coincidentally, Nobel laureate Pablo Neruda, who had been the Communist Party presidential candidate in 1970, died of natural causes in the first week of the revolution (*see* OBITUARIES). Most of the members of Allende's 21 Cabinets were seized in the first hours of the coup and sent to a naval prison at Dawson Island in the Strait of Magellan. The National Stadium of Santiago was also used as a detention centre.

The junta, headed by General Pinochet (*see* BIOGRAPHY), installed an almost entirely military Cabinet, but civilian experts were assigned to draw up economic plans and a new constitution. The junta announced that it would honour all Chile's debts and indicated that it wanted foreign investment and assistance. In return, it intended to compensate private owners of nationalized property. Austere economic measures were instituted.

The military regime had no known timetable for holding elections or announcing the future political structure of the nation. (JEREMIAH A. O'LEARY)

CAMERA PRESS/PICTORIAL PARADE

Chile's new military junta assembles following September anti-Marxist coup. From left: Adm. José Toribio Merino Castro, junta president Gen. Augusto Pinochet Ugarte, Air Force Comdr. Gen. Gustavo Leigh Guzmán, and commander of the armed police Gen. César Mendoza Duran.

China

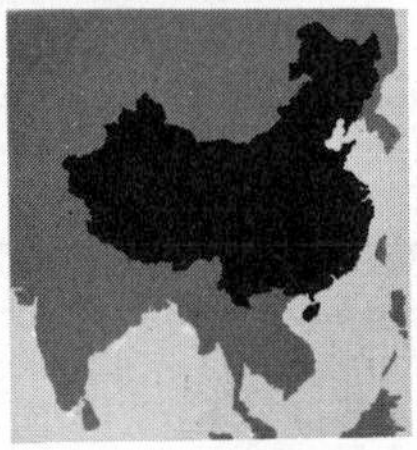

The most populous country in the world and the third largest in area, China is bounded by the U.S.S.R., Mongolia, North Korea, North Vietnam, Laos, Burma, India, Bhutan, Sikkim, Nepal, Pakistan, and Afghanistan. From 1949 the country has been divided into the People's Republic of China (Communist) on the mainland and on Hainan and other islands, and the Republic of China (Nationalist) on Taiwan (*see* TAIWAN). Area: 3,691,500 sq.mi. (9,561,000 sq.km.), including Tibet but excluding Taiwan. Pop. of the People's Republic (1972 United Nations est.): 800,720,000 (however, official estimates originating in the People's Republic total only about 700 million). Cap.: Peking (metro. pop., 1970 est., 7,570,000). Largest city: Shanghai (metro. pop., 1970 est., 10,820,000). Language: Chinese (varieties of the Mandarin dialect predominate). Chairman of the Communist Party in 1973, Mao Tse-tung; premier, Chou En-lai.

In 1973 China returned to political stability and normalcy in internal and external affairs with the durable Premier Chou as the chief architect and executor of policy in the name of Chairman Mao and his doctrine of proletarian dictatorship. Chou's policy of peaceful coexistence with countries having different social systems won the Peking government recognition as the legitimate government of all China by the great majority of countries of the world. In contrast to the rapid success in foreign policy, however, the rebuilding and reconstruction of party and government organs after the convulsion of the Cultural Revolution, 1965–69, which involved the adoption of a new party charter and a new state constitution, proved to be tortuous and slow. Nevertheless, developments during the year pointed to further movement away from

continued on page 182

Child Welfare:
see Education; Social Services

CHINA'S FOREIGN POLICY IN AN ERA OF DÉTENTE

By Richard Harris

Any consideration of détente among the world's competing powers must start by abandoning the assumption that the foreign policy of Communist governments differs fundamentally from those of all others. All governments have a primary concern with the security of their countries. Talking in private, all foreign ministers will start by expressing their fears and will then justify their actions accordingly.

A necessary proviso in considering China, however, is that the Western concept of the nation-state must also be set to one side. For centuries China was the largest, richest, most cultivated country at the centre of its own world, operating a tributary system by which smaller states acknowledged its supremacy. While the China of today knows that this era vanished a century ago, it should not be surprising if the instincts bred in Chinese minds over a millennium are still sometimes operative.

Another proviso about the China that came into being with the Communist victory in 1949 must be recalled a quarter of a century later. At that time, Chinese emotions had been worked on for half a century by the power of foreign imperialism. Chinese sovereignty had been invaded. Peripheral territories that had been part of the Chinese family had been filched from China during a time of weakness. The first task was thus to bring such territories back under Chinese authority and to restore frontiers satisfying to Chinese sentiment. In Sinkiang and Tibet China succeeded, but in the case of Taiwan it was foiled by the unforeseen circumstances of the Korean War.

Second only to national security, therefore, this unfulfilled objective of a united and untrammeled China has been the main interest of Chinese action since 1949. Arguably, China's active interest in world revolution in the late 1950s and early 1960s sought to harness this force so as to weaken China's main enemy, the United States, and thereby to serve China's national purpose rather than any specifically Communist end.

Changing World View. In 1973 China's view of the world was very different. By 1964 hopes of any alliance with the Soviet Union had been abandoned, while fears of the U.S. were reaching a new peak because of American involvement in Vietnam. China had no wish to intervene in that war: far from it; but there was anxiety, especially in 1965, lest some U.S. attack might make direct confrontation with China inevitable.

These calculations of national security were reinforced by a Maoist view of the world that still saw the principal contradiction as that "between the U.S. imperialists and the national liberation struggles of the third world." The Sino-Soviet dispute had grown more heated in this emotional ambience. In China's view the Soviet Union was not giving to the struggles in the third world the support it should; on the contrary, Nikita S. Khrushchev's visit to U.S. Pres. Dwight D. Eisenhower in 1959 marked the beginning of a process of détente by which growing friendship between the U.S.S.R. and the U.S. would leave the Americans free in their confrontation with China.

Richard Harris is deputy foreign editor of The Times *of London and a noted Sinologist.*

Two events in 1968 marked China's further departure from this world view of imperialists confronting revolutionaries, a view defined by ideology rather than by power. The first was U.S. Pres. Lyndon B. Johnson's decision in March 1968 not to run again for the presidency. To the Chinese this decision was a turning point in the U.S. commitment to Vietnam. It marked the admitted failure of U.S. policy to achieve its ends in the Vietnam war. The Chinese were fortified in their calculation of this failure by the strong student antiwar movement in the U.S., then at its peak, and even more by the revolutionary potential of the Black Power movement. Chinese hopes of a new relationship with the U.S. were still concealed by an expressed glee and contempt for these signs of failure. The U.S. was in its "death throes," and Chairman Mao Tse-tung duly issued a personal statement on the political significance of the Black Power movement. Nevertheless, at this time the seeds were first sown that flowered into the Nixon visit of 1972 and the policy of détente.

The other climacteric in Chinese thinking in 1968 was the Soviet-organized invasion of Czechoslovakia in August. The bitterness between the two countries was by then irreparable. Ugly scenes in Peking and in Moscow had already accompanied the xenophobic temper of China's Cultural Revolution, which had begun in 1965. Now, as a result of the Czechoslovakian intervention, the Soviets were dubbed "social-imperialists" and "new czars." China's fears of an actual Soviet preemptive strike against its nuclear sites became acute overnight. Soviet leader Leonid I. Brezhnev's utterance about "limited sovereignty" in reference to Eastern Europe drew fierce attacks from Peking lest China's newly recovered sovereignty in border areas be undermined.

The result was to drain away much of the ideological content of the China-U.S.S.R. dispute and to substitute full-scale concern with national security. Two rival and hostile Communist powers had now become bitter enemies, each calculating the other's military strength and the use that might be made of it. China's fears were now such that the security offered by a détente with the U.S. as a counterbalance against the U.S.S.R. probably became a factor in Peking's thinking.

But the Chinese were not likely to rush into contact with Washington until the signs of a new U.S. attitude had become unmistakable. The first message to the Chinese from U.S. Pres. Richard M. Nixon, in 1969, needed tangible backing by U.S. action in the Far East before the avowed U.S. withdrawal could be confirmed. Meanwhile, the visit to Washington in November 1969 by Prime Minister Eisaku Sato of Japan alarmed China with its reference to Taiwan and South Korea as being within the area of security interest of the Japanese. The U.S. invasion of Cambodia to expel North Vietnamese troops in April 1970 was another move against possible détente, damaging hopes of a U.S. withdrawal. Not until the South Vietnamese drive into southern Laos early in 1971 were the Chinese satisfied about U.S. intentions, since in this case the slowing of the drive of the South Vietnamese Army did not bring out supporting action from its protector. The Chinese concluded that the South Vietnamese really were going to have to fight their own battles in the future.

Thereafter, the invitation to the U.S. table tennis team and the Henry Kissinger visit to Peking began paving the way for peaceful coexistence between the Chinese and the Americans. In this matter China also had a direct nationalist objective apart from counterbalancing Soviet power. The return of Taiwan to the sovereignty of the mainland was still an unfulfilled aim. A China united and free of all foreign influence, for which all Chinese had longed, depended especially on the return of Taiwan (an island ceded in 1895 to Japan after the ignominious defeat of China); and the more so because U.S. support sustained on the island a rival government which by its continued existence challenged the sovereignty of the regime in Peking.

The opportunity of reaching a settlement over Taiwan remained an objective of even greater importance than the withdrawal of U.S. power from the mainland of Asia. Of course, the two were intimately interlinked, but Chinese revolutionary interest in Vietnam was trivial by comparison with its nationalist concern over Taiwan.

Development of Détente. The containment of the Soviet Union and the détente with the U.S. have, therefore, been the twin themes of Chinese policy since 1969. That year saw serious incidents on the Sino-Soviet frontier. The Chinese, profiting by their fears to mend a country torn by the upheaval of the Cultural Revolution, frantically started a campaign of "preparation for war," digging air-raid shelters and rallying Chinese opinion against the Soviet threat. While the serious danger was diverted by a meeting between premiers Aleksey N. Kosygin and Chou En-lai at Peking's airfield in September 1969, no resolution of the border problems or of the substantial military confrontation followed. Indeed, fears of a Soviet preemptive strike against China rose again to a new peak in the summer of 1973.

In 1969 China's interest in Europe became much more active and pointed. The European Economic Community was a potential independent force that had before been welcomed (thanks to French influence) as a body resisting U.S. domination but which was now looked on as a force to resist Soviet expansion. In particular, the Chinese saw the election of Britain's Conservative government in 1970, led by Edward Heath, as ensuring British membership in the EEC and a stiffening of Western European attitudes to the U.S.S.R. China now wanted U.S. troops to stay in Europe and looked favourably on NATO.

The other country of urgent interest to China in the new situation was Japan. The election of Kakuei Tanaka as leader of the governing Liberal-Democratic Party in 1972 promised fruitful relations between Peking and Tokyo. The Chinese were quick to drop their reiterated fears of Japanese militarism and to welcome Tanaka to Peking before Soviet attempts to appease Japan took the country beyond China's reach.

With the U.S. and Japan represented in Peking, China in the early 1970s found itself occupying one corner of a quadrilateral of power, the other corners being filled by the U.S., Japan, and the Soviet Union. Any shift in relations between any two of these four necessarily affected the relations of the rest. China had thus moved decisively away from a world of ideology into a world of power, and in consequence its old interest in Africa and Latin America declined. Nevertheless, the ideological mantle had not been cast off. China's revised world view—of which the first outlines were apparent in 1968—defined two superpowers, the U.S. and U.S.S.R., whose habit it was to dominate or intrude on the national independence of smaller states. "We must not fail to see," said Chi P'eng-fei, the Chinese foreign minister, in 1973, "that certain big powers have not abandoned their hegemony and expansionist policy of aggression. From the Middle East to South Asia, from the Persian Gulf to the Indian Ocean, in Asia, Africa, and Latin America, as in the whole world, they are intensifying their expansion and rivalry."

This was said in Teheran, and it was a mark of China's priorities that its friendship with Iran and Pakistan in that part of the globe aimed to counter Soviet expansion. Not that China would not wish also to improve relations with India so that the links India, Afghanistan, and Bangladesh had with the Soviet Union would also be counterbalanced. For further evidence of China's dominant concern with the Soviet Union across the whole Eurasian landblock, its friendly relations with Greece may be cited. The countries had different social systems, the Chinese admitted when welcoming a Greek minister in Peking, but both had "encountered foreign aggression and oppression and were determined to resist it."

Given China's fear of Soviet attack and the cautious, slow, and still slightly suspicious détente with the Americans, the question to be asked is: how fixed are these attitudes? Despite harsher definitions of U.S. imperialism in the context of the Chinese Communist Party's tenth congress, 1973 saw no change in China's basic policy of détente with the U.S. or in the confrontation with the U.S.S.R. Both rest on geographic factors irrespective of political change. A U.S. military withdrawal from the Far East necessarily puts the Pacific Ocean between the two countries, thus much reducing the area of possible conflict. No such belt or buffer stands between China and the Soviet Union. The Mongolian People's Republic on China's northern border looks to Moscow for support and modernization, and that commitment is unlikely to change. So even if one may expect some amelioration of Sino-Soviet relations after Mao Tse-tung's personal involvement in the struggle is removed, it is not easy to forecast conditions in which their long frontier will become stable and peaceful. Also, it would be very surprising indeed if their common Communist affiliation ever again serves to bridge the vast historical and cultural gap that divides the U.S.S.R. from China.

Waning Internationalism. Such prospects emphasized the divergence between nationalism and internationalism. The international aspirations of a revolutionary China were much more marked in the 1950s and 1960s than they were in 1973. While China welcomes admiration from other countries for its preeminent revolutionary achievements, the stress on self-help colours all its relations with third world countries. They must not only liberate themselves by their own efforts but their revolutionary progress must match their own conditions. In effect, this amounts to admitting that just as Mao Tse-tung's great achievement was to adapt Marxism to China's revolutionary nationalist needs, so African or Latin-American or Asian countries must adapt Chinese doctrines in accordance with their own conditions of nationalist development.

Such divergent paths between nationalism and internationalism have afflicted revolutionary movements ever since 1917. They present China with an underlying conflict springing from a much longer historical perspective. The traditional system by which smaller tributary states acknowledge China's superiority (formally, if not by conviction) has left in the Chinese psyche a strong impulse toward universalism. China was a country very much open to world contacts and influences under the T'ang (618–906), but certainly since the advent of the Ming dynasty in 1368 it has lived in its own world and looked on outsiders as inferiors who should respect and learn from it.

China's membership in the United Nations poses new questions. Can China now settle down to the working of an international system of nearly 140 equal nation-states—albeit China is one of the five permanent members of the UN Security Council? Alternatively, is China as a revolutionary power inherently hostile to the stability the UN seeks to attain? Or, yet again, will China's purpose in the UN be to use the organization primarily for its own nationalistic ends?

No conclusive answer to these questions may emerge for many years. It seems unlikely that China's phase of international revolutionary enthusiasm will determine its behaviour at the UN. Similarly, China's readiness to accept a system of equal nation-states has strong instincts working against it. Insofar as China stands forth as a leader of the smaller powers this is done in its own nationalist interest, not in any direct concern to devise a new world system.

What must be emphasized is that China's Communist revolution is no more than the fulfillment of its nationalist revolution. Mao Tse-tung as the progenitor of this phase is the first man to domesticate Marxism-Leninism in the context of Chinese history. Further steps in reestablishing an essential Chineseness will be the most likely actions in China following his death. A Chinese foreign policy that can give effect to any universalistic assumptions is thus still far away, although the instincts are observably there.

China's concern begins with the still-unfulfilled establishment of absolute independence—the recovery of Taiwan and (although these present lesser problems) of Hong Kong and Macau. Coupled with this is the security of China's frontiers, behind which the task of modernizing the country can be pursued. All of China's military preparations are entirely defensive. China disdains the role of a great power and could not attain such power for several decades even if it were an aspiration.

continued from page 179

internal political extremism and to an emphasis on moderation and pragmatism.

Internal Politics. The long-expected tenth congress of the Chinese Communist Party, the sovereign and policymaking body in the political system, was finally held in strict secrecy on August 24–28 without prior public announcement and with little fanfare at its conclusion. Nevertheless, the convocation of this congress, following two great purges of Mao's political opponents, consummated the prolonged and devious struggle for leadership and power initiated by the Cultural Revolution against "revisionism."

Before the congress two significant preparatory measures in reconstructing the party and government structures were rapidly enacted early in 1973: (1) the reestablishment of defunct mass organizations and (2) political rehabilitation of cadres. The Communist Youth League, the Trade Union Congress, and the Women's Federation, all of which had fallen into disuse during the Cultural Revolution, were resurrected, partly to counter the military influence. As the date drew nearer to the calling of the tenth party congress the process of rehabilitation became intensified, and a campaign was begun to reconcile all divergent groups in order to bring back to government service the badly needed experienced administrators. Scores of ranking officials and thousands of cadres who had been denounced as "revisionists" or "capitalist roaders" during the Cultural Revolution were restored to good standing and given jobs. The restoration of Teng Hsiao-ping, former secretary-general of the party and the second-ranking villain of the Cultural Revolution, to the rank of deputy premier in April without fuss or explanation was a significant event. Other former Politburo members were similarly restored.

The main functions of the tenth party congress were: (1) to denounce Lin Piao and others allied to him in his coup attempt; (2) to restore the shattered structure of the party by filling the numerous vacancies in its Central Committee and the Politburo; and (3) to reaffirm existing foreign and domestic policies that had undergone important changes since the ninth congress. Although the convocation of the five-day congress was officially concealed until a communiqué was issued on August 29, it constituted a major political event.

David Bruce, centre foreground, leader of the first U.S. diplomatic mission to Communist China, steps into China from Hong Kong on May 14, 1973.

WIDE WORLD

CHINA

Education. Primary (1959–60), pupils 90 million, teachers (1964) *c.* 2.6 million; secondary (1958–59), pupils 8,520,000; vocational (1958–59), pupils 850,000; teacher training (1958–69), students 620,000; higher (1962–63), students 820,000.

Finance. Monetary unit: jen min piao or people's bank dollar, also called the yuan, with (Sept. 17, 1973) an official exchange rate of 0.38 yuan to Hong Kong $1 (1.66 yuan = U.S. $1; 4.66 yuan = £1 sterling). Gold reserves (1972 est.) U.S. $2,250,000,000. Budget (1960 est., latest published) balanced at 70,020,000,000 yuan. Gross domestic product (1970 est.) U.S. $130 billion.

Foreign Trade. (1971) Imports *c.* U.S. $2.2 billion; exports *c.* U.S. $2.3 billion. Import sources: Japan *c.* 27%; Canada *c.* 9%; West Germany *c.* 6%. Export destinations: Hong Kong *c.* 24%; Japan *c.* 14%; Singapore *c.* 6%. Main exports: textiles and clothing; metal ores; fruit and vegetables; meat products; hides and skins.

Transport and Communications. Roads (1970) *c.* 800,000 km. (including *c.* 300,000 km. all-weather). Motor vehicles in use (1970): passenger *c.* 60,000; commercial *c.* 400,000. Railways: (1970) *c.* 35,000 km.; traffic (1959) 45,670,000,000 passenger-km., freight 265,260,000,000 net ton-km. Air traffic (1960): 63,882,000 passenger-km.; freight 1,967,000 net ton-km. Inland waterways (including Yangtze River; 1970) *c.* 150,000 km. Shipping (1972): merchant vessels 100 gross tons and over 286; gross tonnage 1,181,179. Telephones (1951) 255,000. Radio receivers (Dec. 1965) *c.* 11.5 million. Television receivers (Dec. 1969) *c.* 300,000.

Agriculture. Production (in 000; metric tons; 1971; 1970 in parentheses): rice *c.* 106,000 (*c.* 105,226); corn *c.* 29,500 (*c.* 30,000); wheat *c.* 32,000 (*c.* 31,000); barley *c.* 19,200 (*c.* 19,000); potatoes *c.* 36,000 (*c.* 35,000); soybeans (1972) *c.* 11,570, (1971) 11,741; peanuts 2,678 (2,772); dry peas *c.* 3,400 (*c.* 3,300); cotton, lint 1,411 (1,649); jute 502 (514); rapeseed 1,017 (992); sugar, raw value (1972) *c.* 4,790, (1971) *c.* 4,749; tobacco *c.* 797 (*c.* 806); tea *c.* 200 (*c.* 200); pears *c.* 920 (*c.* 920); oranges *c.* 790 (*c.* 856); timber (cu.m.; 1970) 170,800, (1969) 166,900; fish catch (1971) 6,880, (1970) 6,255. Livestock (in 000; 1970–71): cattle *c.* 63,300; sheep *c.* 71,000; pigs *c.* 223,000; goats *c.* 57,500; buffalo *c.* 29,400; horses *c.* 7,200; asses *c.* 11,650.

Industry. Fuel and power (in 000; metric tons; 1972): coal (including lignite) *c.* 350,000; coke (1970) 18,000; crude oil 30,000; electricity (kw-hr.; 1960) *c.* 58,500,000. Production (in 000; metric tons; 1971): iron ore (metal content) 27,000; pig iron 27,000; crude steel (1972) 23,000; lead *c.* 100; copper *c.* 100; aluminum (1970) *c.* 130; tungsten concentrates (oxide content) *c.* 10; cement *c.* 10,000; salt *c.* 15,000; sulfuric acid (1966) *c.* 2,500; phosphates (oxide content; 1970) 1,200; nitrogenous fertilizers (N content) 1,840; cotton yarn (1968) 1,453; cotton fabrics 9,000; paper 4,161.

According to the communiqué, a total of 1,249 delegates were elected to the congress through "an extensive and democratic process" and representing "the opinions of the masses both inside and outside the Party." The congress was presided over by Chairman Mao, who reportedly made no speech. Premier Chou delivered the political report, which pledged to carry out all of Chairman Mao's policies and outlined China's policy in opposing the hegemony of the two superpowers, the United States and the Soviet Union. Wang Hung-wen (*see* BIOGRAPHY), a young militant leader of worker groups in Shanghai, was chosen to submit the draft of the party constitution, which deleted the provision on Lin Piao's role as Mao's successor and made no provision for a successor. Other provisions in the old constitution reflecting the cult of Mao were dropped, giving a new emphasis on the collective leadership of the party. Both the political report and the draft constitution were unanimously adopted.

In the strongest possible terms, the Congress denounced and expelled Lin Piao, Mao's former heir-apparent who had died in a plane crash in 1971 while apparently fleeing the country, and his principal collaborator, Ch'en Po-ta. Compared with the old Central Committee of 279 (170 full and 109 alternate), the 195 full members and 124 alternates elected by the congress to the new Central Committee had fewer members from the military and a notably larger number of women. The pro-Soviet faction appeared to be routed, while scores of persons who played a role in the rapprochement with the U.S. were promoted to membership on the Central Committee. The Central Committee unanimously elected Chairman Mao, five vice-chairmen (Chou En-lai, Wang Hung-wen, K'ang Sheng, Yeh Chien-ying, and Li Te-sheng), and Chang Ch'un-ch'iao as secretary-general.

At its first meeting, the Central Committee chose its Politburo of 21 full and 4 alternate members. Of the 25 members, 16 had belonged to the old body. Included in the new membership were three striking additions: Wang Hung-wen, Wei Kuo-ching, political boss in Kwangsi Chuang Autonomous Region and leader of a minority people, and Ch'en Yung-kuei, head of a model commune in Shansi Province. As the first of the five vice-chairmen, Premier Chou's commanding leadership was fully recognized, although there was no clear indication that he had been given any formalized status as Mao's deputy.

Economic Development. In spite of notable industrial progress, China's economy remained basically agricultural. Natural calamities caused by drought and floods resulted in an estimated reduction of grain output from 250 million tons in 1971 to 215 million tons in 1972. A second straight year of floods and drought made the farm outlook for 1973 rather dim. In the face of these adverse conditions, the government gave economic priority to increased grain production. To cope with the problem of food shortages, millions of tons of wheat and other grains were imported, mainly from Australia, Canada, and the U.S. According to a U.S. Department of Agriculture report, China bought 755,000 bales of U.S. cotton in 1973 for delivery through 1974.

Some relaxation of emphasis on ideology and doctrine took place on the production front. More importance in the communes was being given to labour output, and as a bonus to encourage factory workers to perform well a small additional wage called a living allowance was added.

Foreign Relations. Premier Chou's new lines of foreign policy, initiated with the Sino-American Ping-Pong match and followed by U.S. Pres. Richard Nixon's "journey to Peking for peace" and a rapid reconciliation between China and Japan, brought a fundamental change in the international relationship in the Pacific area. It also thrust China into the arena of great power diplomacy as an advocate of the cause of the third world. Ideologically, while Peking continued to uphold "proletarian internationalism" and its "three antis" (anti-imperialism, antirevisionism, and antireactionaries), it moved to improve relations, in particular, with the U.S., Japan, and Western Europe, in order to offset the threatening shadow of the Soviet Union.

These lines of foreign policy were endorsed by the party congress. Chou's report to the congress urged the Chinese people to strengthen their unity with all countries subjected to imperialist aggression and control in order to "form the broadest united front against . . . neo-colonialism, and in particular, against the hegemonism of the two superpowers—the U.S. and the U.S.S.R." The declaration of 1973 as the "year of Europe" and the convocation of the European security conference to promote détente in Europe would turn Soviet attention eastward toward China. The congress's specific denunciation of the Soviet Union in bitter and harsh terms clearly indicated that Peking considered the U.S.S.R. as a greater threat to China than the U.S. However, the policy of rapprochement with the U.S. was not openly praised but only tacitly approved by the congress.

The widened activities in foreign affairs were reflected in the increasing numbers of Chinese diplomatic, military, economic, and cultural missions dispatched to various parts of the world, in the numbers of foreign delegations and missions visiting China, and in the continued increase in the number of countries recognizing the Peking regime. In the first half of 1973 a total of 230 Chinese missions were sent abroad, compared with 106 groups in all of 1972. Foreign Minister Chi P'eng-fei (*see* BIOGRAPHY) headed a special mission to Britain and France in June.

Small boats from Kiangsu Province harvest sea cultures and algae, used for food and medicine, in the sea off Tungshan, eastern China.

KEYSTONE

UPI COMPIX

Plentiful meat supplies in Shihchiachuang market appear to support official claims that China's food production is rising.

On his return trip Chi discussed matters of common concern with Iran's foreign minister and was granted an audience by the shah. He also visited Pres. Zulfikar Ali Bhutto in Pakistan.

During the year heads of government paying state visits in Peking included Pres. Georges Pompidou of France, Pres. Ahmadou Ahidjo of Cameroon, Pres. Mobutu Sese Seko of Zaire, and Canadian Prime Minister Pierre Trudeau. They all received an audience with Chairman Mao. The list of countries establishing diplomatic relations with Peking had increased to 90 in December 1972 when Australia and New Zealand quickly extended recognition following the electoral victories of the Labour parties in the two countries. In March 1973 diplomatic relations were established between Spain and China.

China and Western Europe. Peking's relations with London and Paris steadily improved following the visits to Peking by the British foreign secretary and the French foreign minister in late 1972. Subsequently, Chinese students came to Britain and France for language and technical training. Following talks between China's minister for foreign trade, Pai Hsiang-kuo, and British Prime Minister Edward Heath in January in London, a large British trade fair was opened in Peking in March. It was reported that during Sino-British talks Peking renewed its proposal for some official representation in Hong Kong, but Britain was evidently reluctant.

At Premier Chou's invitation President Pompidou, the first EEC head of state to visit China, arrived in Peking on September 11 for a week to discuss Chinese-French economic and cultural affairs and the problem of relations among the major powers, including the sensitive issue of European détente. Peking felt concerned that if Western Europe relaxed its guard, the Soviet Union would put more pressure on the Chinese-Soviet border. In a joint communiqué President Pompidou and Premier Chou declared that they were against all hegemony. The week-long visit was marked by cordiality, but no new initiative in Sino-French relations was announced.

Sino-Soviet Relations. Ideological dispute and rivalry for leadership in the Communist world as well as mutual suspicion and fear between the two Communist giants apparently influenced China and the U.S.S.R. to seek accommodation with all the major powers of the West. Both Peking and Moscow were openly critical and suspicious of each other's relations with the U.S. However, the rapprochement of both with the U.S. facilitated the conclusion of direct U.S. military intervention in Vietnam, and when the peace settlement was signed in Paris on January 27 both Peking and Moscow hailed it as an important step forward in international affairs.

Sino-Soviet relations showed some improvement following the return to China in January of the Soviet ambassador and the arrival there of Leonid Ilichev, the head of the Soviet delegation, for border talks. The Joint Commission on the Navigation of Boundary Rivers resumed its sessions, which ended in March without any agreement. On the border question the Soviet decision early in 1973 to replace with Russian names the original Chinese names for towns in an area seized by the czarist empire in 1858–60 infuriated the Chinese. The boundary negotiations again became stalled as Moscow refused to make any concession in accepting Peking's position that the existing frontiers were based on the "unequal treaties" enacted during czarist days.

On June 27 Peking fired its 15th nuclear explosion since 1964, and Moscow showed concern about Peking's growing nuclear power. It was reported that the Soviet forces stationed on the Sino-Soviet frontiers had been increased. Shortly before the opening of the party congress, Moscow chose to escalate polemics against Peking. Soviet leader Leonid I. Brezhnev, speaking at Alma-Ata in central Asia, launched a sharp criticism of Peking's leadership under Mao for following a policy of anti-Sovietism and subversive activity against the socialist countries. In an apparent reference to Brezhnev's speech, Premier Chou declared in his report to the congress that Soviet accusations of Chinese opposition to the relaxation of world tensions "are above all meant for the monopoly Capitalists." However, on November 10, on the eve of the 56th anniversary of the 1917 Bolshevik Revolution, Peking sent a message to Moscow expressing the hope of reestablishing good relations between the two countries through a peaceful solution of their border problem.

Sino-Japanese Relations. Six months after Prime Minister Kakuei Tanaka's visit to Peking and the formal establishment of diplomatic relations in September 1972, China and Japan exchanged ambassadors. There then followed a steady expansion of cultural and commercial contacts and negotiations on trade, fisheries, and aviation.

China took the initiative in strengthening diplomatic ties with Japan in order to counter Soviet influence in the Far East and to further isolate Taiwan from the international community. Consequently, Peking ceased to denounce the U.S.-Japan security treaty, the U.S. military presence in Japan, and the accelerating rearmament of Japan. Concerning the status of Taiwan, China succeeded in forcing the Japanese government to surrender the former Nationalist Chinese embassy to its use. Japanese news companies with correspondents in Peking were compelled to enter into written agreements with Chinese authorities not to pursue any policy that might be regarded as hostile toward China. However, aviation talks became deadlocked over Peking's refusal to have its planes share Japanese airports with the Chinese Nationalists and Japan's unwillingness to sacrifice its lucrative air connections with Taiwan for the sake of less profitable

continued on page 186

EDUCATION AFTER THE CULTURAL REVOLUTION

By Edward H. Levi

Education in the People's Republic of China has responded to the conflicting pressures of promoting socialist ideals on the one hand and producing highly trained specialists on the other. At an early period, Chairman Mao Tse-tung pressed for a close relationship between factory and farm work and schooling. Half work-half study schools set up on a nationwide scale in 1958 were a manifestation of this influence. Today universities run factories and send their students to factories. Fu-t'an University, for example, runs an experimental electronics factory and a quartz factory and assembles parts for computers. The efforts of the Ministry of Education and the Ministry of Higher Education in the 1950s in support of uniform standards, a nationwide entrance examination, high quality education, and the restriction or elimination of accelerated schools with lower standards were reversed by Chairman Mao in 1958. When similar efforts were made in the early 1960s, Mao again reversed them through the Cultural Revolution, beginning in 1965.

Political indoctrination has been a matter of primary importance. Education is regarded as the tool of the state to be used for the benefit of the ruling masses. Despite criticism of the Soviet Union's emphasis on technology in education, the direction of education is toward vocational and practical ends. Official doctrine has it that research must be for practical purposes, although it is recognized that for some scientific research it may not be possible to see immediate results.

Expansion and Adjustment. In this setting, a large, expanding system of primary schools and middle schools (very roughly corresponding to U.S. high schools) is being created. In 1973 Chih Chun, deputy head of the Science and Education Group under the State Council, reported that there were 127 million children in primary schools and 36 million in middle schools, five or six times the number in primary schools before liberation and 22 times the number in middle schools. Based on various estimates, it appears that about 7.5% of the relevant age group attended middle school in 1956, about 21% in 1966, and possibly more than 30% in 1973. Though it has been said that primary education is not yet universal in rural areas, and though educational opportunity narrows at the middle school level, the achievement is still impressive. The goal appears to be universal education through the first two, possibly three, years of middle school.

The thrust for expansion at the higher education level was stopped for four years by the Cultural Revolution and its aftermath. Student enrollment was thought to have gone from 117,000 in 1949 to 820,000 in 1962, but higher education institutions were closed during the Cultural Revolution, and they have reopened slowly. In general, students were not admitted until 1970. Peking University, which had 10,000 students before the Cultural Revolution, had 4,300 in 1972. It was "loosely estimated" in June 1973 that the number of new students entering colleges and universities would be at the level of 100,000 for 1973–74. But there was apparently strong pressure for more rapid expansion and the figure released by Peking in September showed that more than 153,000 students had enrolled.

An emphasis on primary and middle schools, not as preparatory to college education, is in line with the long-standing position of Chairman Mao. So is the effort to cut down the number of years occupied by the standard curriculum. Primary education has been reduced from six to five years and middle school education from six to four years. A reduction from five to three years has taken place at the college or university level, although some slight reversal of this trend is now appearing. At some universities the number of required undergraduate courses has been cut in half, with offerings in the social sciences and humanities particularly limited.

The Changing Student Body. A determined effort has been made since 1949 to give preference in higher education to children of peasants and workers. It has been stated that prior to 1949 there were no children of workers among the student body at Peking University. In 1958 peasants and workers are said to have comprised only 19.5%. At present, it is reported that more than 90% are of worker, peasant, or soldier origin.

In general, for all institutions of higher learning, political correctness and peasant, worker, or soldier origin are essential, although not necessarily sufficient, qualifications for entry. All students, after middle school graduation, must work in the country or in a factory for two or three years and some work as many as five. After this, they may be recommended by the "masses" (peers) in their work unit for admission to a university. This recommendation must be approved by the "leadership" of the unit. A recommended student may be rejected by a university on the basis of an examination, although this is a matter of continuing controversy.

Some slight relaxation in emphasis on worker and peasant origin may be seen in new provincial directives to universities issued in 1973. These state that "after guaranteeing the rights of workers and peasants and their sons and daughters to priority admission to schools, attention should be paid to enrolling sons and daughters from the exploiting classes who have truly performed well and who can be educated."

In universities, faculty, consulting with students, are revising courses and creating new textbook materials. Efforts have been made to get away from rote instruction. Open book examinations have been encouraged, and students are urged to link their studies with investigations into factories, communes, or the docks.

There is some indication that, among those students who excel in fields where academic work or research is especially desired, some will be selected to go through advanced apprenticeship at the various research institutes, either within the universities or in the Chinese Academy of Sciences. Such a development would not be unexpected and would be rather easy to administer in a society where all have assigned places.

A Peking University student learns how oscilloscopes are made in one of the school's dozen workshops. Technical courses reflect Chinese emphasis on education for vocational and practical purposes.

UPI COMPIX

Edward H. Levi, president of the University of Chicago, visited China during 1973.

continued from page 184

flights to Peking. In August the two nations decided to bypass the aviation issue and concentrated on the negotiation of a new trade agreement. After two weeks of bargaining the two agreed on the principle of most-favoured-nation treatment for each other and on the establishment of a joint committee to supervise their mutual trade.

Sino-U.S. Relations. After President Nixon's visit to China in 1972 and following the signing of the Vietnam peace settlement in January 1973, Sino-U.S. relations were free from serious tension. Foreign Minister Chi P'eng-fei attended the International Conference on Vietnam in Paris February 26–March 2, and on the eve of the conference began private talks with then-U.S. Secretary of State William P. Rogers on matters of improving relations, which Henry A. Kissinger had discussed with Premier Chou during an earlier trip to Peking.

In the wake of the Vietnam settlement Kissinger visited China from February 15 to 19 for the fifth time since June 1971 to hold talks with Premier Chou. Mao's apparent approval of and Peking's jubilation over the results of Kissinger's visit indicated that a wide range of subjects had been discussed, including the new peaceful order in Asia and enlarged contacts and economic cooperation in the development of China's faltering agriculture and offshore oil resources. Upon Kissinger's return to Washington a joint communiqué was issued on February 22, which announced the joint commitment to bring about a normalization of relations by carrying out "a complete program of expanding trade as well as scientific, cultural and other exchanges" and by the establishment of liaison offices in Peking and Washington.

At a press conference on February 22, Kissinger stated that the U.S. would continue to maintain diplomatic relations with the Nationalist government on Taiwan, and that the level of U.S. troops on Taiwan was not a subject of negotiation with Peking. As a sign of goodwill China released John Downey, agent of the U.S. Central Intelligence Agency who had been in a Chinese prison for 21 years, as well as two military prisoners (Lieut. Comdr. Robert J. Flyn and Maj. Philip E. Smith) who had been held in China since 1967 and 1965, respectively.

With the establishment of the liaison offices in April, Sino-U.S. relations entered a new stage. David Bruce, the head of the U.S. mission, arrived in Peking on May 14 and immediately met with Premier Chou. Less than 24 hours after his arrival in Washington to head the Chinese liaison office on May 29, Huang Chen, seasoned diplomat and Peking's first ambassador to France, was received by President Nixon.

During the year the exchange of visits by cultural, scientific, medical, journalistic, commercial, and athletic groups and individuals was accelerated.

A further visit to China by Kissinger, his first after his appointment as U.S. secretary of state, was postponed from late October to November 10 because of the Middle East crisis. During his three-day stay in Peking, Kissinger held extensive discussions with Premier Chou and Chairman Mao, and in a joint communiqué on November 14, China and the U.S. agreed to take further steps toward diplomatic recognition by maintaining contact at "authoritative levels" and broadening the function of the liaison offices, presumably to include consular, trade, and information services.

(HUNG-TI CHU)

See also Taiwan.

Christian Church (Disciples of Christ): *see* Religion

Christianity: *see* Religion

Christian Science: *see* Religion

Chromium: *see* Mining

Churches of Christ: *see* Religion

Church Membership: *see* Religion

Church of England: *see* Religion

Church of Scotland: *see* Religion

Cigars and Cigarettes: *see* Tobacco

Cinema: *see* Motion Pictures

Cities and Urban Affairs

During 1973 the problems with which urban officials, decision makers, and citizens were confronted remained primarily the same as in past years: traffic congestion; inner city decay; lack of sufficient housing for low-income families; garbage and trash collection and disposal; air, water, and noise pollution; how to stretch insufficient revenues to attempt to meet continuing demands for more and better services; finding means whereby planning and implementation activities could best be coordinated externally, with other governmental units, as well as internally—in short, the whole range of subject matter that makes up a living, changing, urban environment.

Predictions of doom to the contrary and despite the slowness of change and the magnitude of the crisis, cities had not completely broken down. That they continued to function, however imperfectly, was a result of the introduction of new technology and management techniques, changing attitudes of higher governments toward the distribution of resources and responsibilities among government levels, and pressures from local citizens for improved conditions. It was due also to all the people who willingly accepted the challenge of keeping them going, and who often received little recognition for it: elected and appointed officials, mayors, city managers and council chairmen, councillors and aldermen, and engaged citizens.

A Tale of Five Cities. Despite the multifarious facilities of the "age of communication," cities, whether located in different continents or even in the same region, were often unaware of each other's activities in combating common problems. At the international level, an attempt to breach the information gap existing between mega-cities was made at the end of 1972, when the leaders of five world cities gathered in Tokyo on November 28–30.

Moscow. Vladimir F. Promyslov, chairman of the Executive Committee of the Moscow City Soviet of Working People's Deputies—in effect Moscow's mayor—said that protection of the environment was his city's chief concern. A new general plan for the Moscow metropolitan area provided for a polycentric layout, whereby eight planning zones would be linked together and with the city centre. The development of peripheral areas was being encouraged by limitations on the location of productive enterprises and on further population growth in the central area. New factories were being grouped in 65 production zones, centred on existing enterprises. Over the past ten years, moreover, in an effort to reduce air pollution, 300 industrial enterprises had either been rebuilt or relocated out of the city.

Within the past decade the housing stock of Moscow had doubled and the average living space increased by 50%. A new water supply source was being constructed, and measures were being taken to utilize industrial waste and to develop closed-cycle production processes. Whereas solid wastes and garbage were being disposed of by dumping, the rate at which their amounts were increasing indicated that industrial methods would soon have to be employed. As yet 3% of the population was not serviced with sewers. Public transportation was well developed and (with Moscow automobile registrations still not exceeding 250,000) would continue to be the main means of moving people within the city for many years to come.

London. In metropolitan London, stated Sir Desmond Plummer, leader (until April 1973) of the Greater London Council (GLC), there was a need to forecast population trends more effectively so as to be able to ensure the availability of financial and physical resources for improvements. One of the critical needs of London was for more housing to take the place of aging, overcrowded dwellings that were in need of demolition. Surplus population was being encouraged to relocate in the new expanding towns outside the city, to which London was giving financial and material help in order to construct housing built to modern standards. Incentives were also being given to industries to relocate outside Greater London, thereby relieving congestion, reducing air pollution, and providing employment opportunities in other areas. At the same time, there was a need to ensure that the outflow was not so great that the economic future of the metropolis was threatened.

Because many people, and particularly younger ones, were moving to suburban areas where there was more open space and modern housing but were continuing to work in the city, the GLC was extending public transportation lines. By encouraging commuters to leave their cars at home, the council hoped that traffic congestion, particularly during peak travel hours, would be considerably decreased, along with noise, air pollution, and the pressure for ever more parking facilities on space that could be put to better use.

Like most cities, Greater London saw the lack of finances as a major problem. Several new sources of revenue were under consideration, one being the levying by the central government of a "super rate" on commercial and industrial property. The GLC was examining the advantages and disadvantages of several other taxes, *e.g.,* on tourists, sales, and payrolls, and, to help finance roads and the transportation system, was considering a transfer of money received from motor vehicle taxes.

Paris. Continuous growth and sprawl were the problems with which Paris was coping, reported Raoul R. Moreau, secretary-general of the Prefecture of the Paris Region. Between 1954 and 1970 the population in the region increased by one million, and density in the city centre was extremely high. In order better to guide the future evolution of the metropolitan area, a master plan for remodeling and urbanizing the Paris Region had been adopted in 1965. This called for future development along two preferential axes, one in the north and one in the south, parallel with the Seine River. Along these axes, at approximately 20 mi. from Paris, five new towns were to be built, each to be self-supporting and containing between 300,000 and 500,000 people.

Decongestion would also be sought by encouraging the dispersal of economic activities throughout the region, to be implemented by means of special fees and permits. This would help to diminish work–residence distances and thus reduce the number of commuters, but it would still be necessary to extend the public transportation network and to modernize equipment. More roads and expressways were also needed to provide better access to social service and recreational facilities. Efforts were to be directed toward reducing air and noise pollution as well as the despoliation of forests.

The master plan called for the establishment of a regional real estate agency to undertake large-scale buying, servicing, and resale of land that the local government wished to protect for specific purposes. Better controls on real estate would not merely keep land and infrastructure costs under control, but the concentration of activities in the centre could also be reduced, commuting distances lessened, and more freedom of choice made available for locations of housing and renewal projects.

Since implementation of the plan began, there had been a balance between in- and out-migration, an annual total of 10,000 industrial jobs were dispersed to the provinces, and new towns began to emerge. With the removal of the wholesale food market, Les Halles, to Rungis, renovation began on its former 20-ac. site in the heart of Paris. The work, to be carried out in several phases, included extending the rapid transit lines to connect the area with the suburbs, putting the road system underground, with access roads on the periphery, and restoring some former streets as pedestrian throughways. The space above ground would be freed from traffic and would feature areas of intensive activity, separated from areas of quiet. Between the surface and the underground traffic arteries, there would be a series of commercial, cultural, and sports installations of various types. The centre of the area would contain office buildings, with the remainder of the space being devoted to antique dealers' galleries, large hotels, and several housing developments.

Flanked by commercial buildings, the pedestrian mall under construction is part of Denver's Skyline Project, intended to revive the late-19th-century heart of the city.

GARY SETTLE—THE NEW YORK TIMES

Tokyo. Ryokichi Minobe stated that Tokyo was seeking means to alleviate such enduring problems as insufficient parks and housing and river-water pollution. In addition, it faced the new challenges of reducing air pollution caused by increasing numbers of motor vehicles and by the disposal of new kinds of waste products such as those from the plastic and petrochemical industries. Past emphasis on national economic growth meant that priority had been given to investment in roads, harbours, communications, and industrial water systems, while facilities such as libraries, sewerage systems, reasonably priced dwellings, and open space had had to take second place.

The critical situation with regard to pollution in metropolitan Tokyo had led to the establishment of the Environment Agency in 1971. The ten-year pollution control program which it drew up was aimed at drastically reducing photochemical smog, lead poisoning resulting from auto exhausts, cadmium poisoning, and waste pollution. In conjunction with this, thought was being given to restricting the use of automobiles within the central city. To fight the "garbage war" resulting from an imbalance between volume and disposal facilities, eight new incinerator plants were to be built. The ten already in existence incinerated 40% of the garbage produced, the remainder being used as landfill. The latter means of disposal had proved unsatisfactory, and authorities intended to incinerate all garbage produced within the Tokyo region.

Traffic congestion was aggravated by the distance between the dwellings on the outskirts and places of employment in the city centre, which, due to the high cost of land, was used primarily for commercial purposes. It was therefore necessary not only to limit office development in the centre but also to extend public transport facilities to the suburbs and to exercise firmer controls over land use in general.

An underlying cause of Tokyo's problems was the lack of autonomy to determine priorities, provide services, and raise revenue. As the country's capital, the city was closely supervised by the national government, which further restricted its activities by establishing ad hoc administrative bodies to deal with projects in various fields and thus complicated even more the already difficult task of coordinating planning and implementation activities.

Residents of Copenhagen bid farewell to their popular mounted police during a final appearance in the streets of the Danish capital.

KEYSTONE

New York. Mayor John V. Lindsay of New York City, speaking of urbanization in the U.S., described a development that was at the root of the worldwide urban crisis. Since 1790 the United States had changed from a rural society in which only 5.1% of the population lived in urban places to one in which 73.5% were urban dwellers, and the latter figure was expected to rise to 90% by the end of the century.

Under the U.S. federal form of government, American cities were creatures of the state in which they were located. For the most part controlled by rural and suburban-based legislators, state governments continued to exercise firm controls over all aspects of urban affairs, and cities could not modernize their organizational structure, change their boundaries, set work rules for local employees, or levy taxes without state approval. At the same time, cities had been given new tasks by the federal government, particularly in social welfare, but insufficient funds to carry them out effectively. It was, therefore, being proposed that the 26 U.S. cities with more than 500,000 people be chartered by the federal government as "national cities." Instead of having to work through their states, they could deal directly with the federal government with regard to trade, finance, and social welfare services. While there was little likelihood of such a proposal being adopted in the foreseeable future, the federal government acknowledged its responsibility for ensuring a better balance between the tasks that cities were required by law or public demand to undertake and the resources with which they could do so by initiating a program of revenue sharing with cities and states. This was only a small start, but urban leaders hoped that it might prove to be the opening wedge in attaining a better overall distribution of responsibilities and funds among all levels of government.

An urgent concern of the New York City administration was to improve public transportation. The subway system was being extended and modernized, efforts were being made to improve the bus system linking downtown with outlying areas, and the movement of merchandise was being consolidated and deliveries reorganized. Computer-controlled traffic signals were being installed to reduce rush-hour congestion, and in one of the oldest parts of Manhattan, the Wall Street business district, pedestrian malls were inaugurated. Despite the budgeting of huge sums for these transportation improvements, many people still had to be wooed away from the private automobile. To this end, studies were being made of new "people moving" devices, such as maxi-taxis and mini-buses, to complement the existing subway and bus system.

Need for Housing. The other cities of the world, both large and small, with few exceptions, were also experiencing the pains of rapid growth coupled with the illnesses of age. In particular, they were in need of housing, especially for low-income families. The slums in industrialized countries, the *favelas* in Brazil, the *bidonvilles* in northern Africa, and the squatter settlements in Asia all emphasized this need. While shelter was a basic necessity of life, economic, cultural, and racial barriers often denied a large proportion of city dwellers any freedom of choice in this respect.

In the less developed countries, where resources were particularly limited, "sites and services" schemes had been initiated by central governments to help provide permanent housing for people living in temporary huts. For a small monthly payment families were given leasehold or freehold rights to a plot of land on which they might build any kind of home they desired. In some instances, basic public facilities such as water and sanitation were provided; in others, there might also be paved roads, electric lighting, telephone service, markets, cultural and educational facilities, and police and fire services. Some governments also provided mass-produced building components for a small monthly payment. The United Nations, which firmly supported the "sites and services" scheme, estimated that the combined cost of land and materials should not exceed 10–15% of a family's monthly earnings.

The experiment proved successful where residents had a steady source of income and land was readily available, as was often the case in Latin America. Elsewhere, however, particularly in Asia, employment opportunities for migrants to the cities were limited and any income had to be spent entirely on staying alive. Moreover, land was usually at a premium and the number of people involved so great that the cost of more than the minimum services would be prohibitive. In these instances, the primary need was for a roof overhead, which might even have to be provided by the government, in conjunction with water and sewerage facilities. Simple though it might be, this was nevertheless better than the conditions under which many of the recipients had previously been living.

In Eastern Europe, housing was financed primarily by the state, by economic enterprises, or by cooperative societies. In Poland, for example, cooperatives had become the principal homebuilders, although about half of all urban housing was still owned by the state. Housing cooperatives and private investors in single-family dwellings in urban areas received land on a 99-year leasehold from the state, which had an automatic option on land to be used for buildings and could buy or expropriate it at fixed prices, usually lower than the market price. This abolished land speculation—a major cause of the housing shortage in other countries. The cost to the cooperative for the leasehold would be approximately 2% of the value of the land, and it might also receive state loans for construction. In the case of tenants' cooperatives these might be as high as 80–84% of costs, with no interest charges. Beginning in 1972 members were able to buy their own homes, and owners' cooperatives might also receive state loans on favourable terms.

Cooperative societies were becoming an increasingly frequent means of providing housing in the cities of the developed countries, particularly where land was limited and prices were high. In the U.S. they provided luxury dwellings in renewed city centres, while in The Netherlands, for example, they were a normal means of providing middle-class, multiple-family housing. In The Netherlands, as in many other countries of Europe, the provision of low-cost housing formed part of the government's ongoing program, with annual targets being set for the number of dwellings to be completed. Despite these and all other programs, however, the demand for housing still outstripped supply. Increased population, rising standards, limited land, high land and building prices, general economic conditions—all contributed and all had to be considered if the right of every citizen to a decent home was to become a reality and not an empty slogan.

The Australian government announced in August that it planned to spend A$33 million to develop new

WIDE WORLD

A high-rise apartment building in the background and demolition of the structure at right signal the decline of Hong Kong's Cat Street trading area, long a mecca for bargain-hunting tourists.

cities within the next several years. The largest share, A$9 million, was to go to Albury-Wodonga on the Murray River at the border of New South Wales and Victoria. The projected population for Albury-Wodonga was 300,000.

Leisure. Ironically, while many people in many parts of the world still had to devote all their time and energy just to staying alive, in other countries cities faced the problem of providing the facilities and activities to enable citizens to make meaningful use of their leisure. Increasing leisure as a consequence of sophisticated technology and the concomitant urbanization was forcing city administrators and decision makers to take a closer look at this aspect of urban life. Many people clearly had little idea of

World's 25 Most Populous Cities*

		City proper		Metropolitan area	
Rank	City and country	Most recent population	Year	Most recent population	Year
1	Tokyo, Japan	8,875,103	1973 estimate	22,082,044	1970 census
2	New York City, U.S.	7,847,100	1972 estimate	16,206,841	1970 census
3	Osaka, Japan	2,857,181	1973 estimate	14,885,005	1970 census
4	London, U.K.	7,353,810	1972 estimate	12,762,370	1971 census
5	Shanghai, China	...	...	10,820,000†	1970 estimate
6	Ruhr, West Germany‡	—	—	9,813,000	1970 estimate
7	Paris, France	2,461,000	1972 estimate	9,282,981	1968 census
8	Mexico City, Mexico	2,902,969	1970 census	8,589,630	1970 census
9	Buenos Aires, Argentina	2,972,453	1970 census	8,352,900	1970 census
10	Los Angeles, U.S.	2,836,400	1972 estimate	8,351,266	1970 census
11	São Paulo, Brazil	5,924,612	1970 census	8,139,705	1970 census
12	Peking, China	...	...	7,570,000†	1970 estimate
13	Moscow, U.S.S.R.	7,151,000	1972 estimate	7,300,000	1972 estimate
14	Rio de Janeiro, Brazil	4,251,918	1970 census	7,092,627	1970 census
15	Calcutta, India	3,148,746	1971 census	7,031,382	1971 census
16	Chicago, U.S.	3,666,957	1970 census	6,714,578	1970 census
17	Nagoya, Japan	2,073,520	1973 estimate	6,574,847	1970 census
18	Bombay, India	...	...	5,970,575†	1971 census
19	Cairo, Egypt	5,139,000	1970 estimate	5,925,400	1970 estimate
20	Seoul, South Korea	...	...	5,525,262†	1970 census
21	Manila, Philippines	1,435,507	1973 estimate	5,100,959	1973 estimate
22	Jakarta, Indonesia	...	...	4,576,009†	1971 census
23	Tientsin, China	...	...	4,280,000†	1970 estimate
24	Wu-han, China	3,000,000	1970 estimate	4,250,000†	1970 estimate
25	Leningrad, U.S.S.R.	3,620,000	1972 estimate	4,066,000	1972 estimate

*Ranked by population of metropolitan area.
†Municipality or other civil division within which a city proper may not be distinguished.
‡A so-called industrial conurbation, within which a single central city is not distinguished.

how to use their increasing amount of leisure time for the benefit both of themselves and of their society. This was particularly true of those who had grown up in a culture where the work ethic dominated and leisure was regarded as a luxury or as a necessary consequence of completing one's productive life, an attitude reinforced by educational systems whose main aim had been to prepare young people for entry into the country's work force. Not that recreational activities were ignored, of course, either by schools or by the cities themselves, as witness the libraries, museums, art galleries, sports halls, swimming pools, parks, camping sites, and other facilities that they provided for their own citizens and for visitors from elsewhere. Mention should also be made of the many voluntary organizations whose efforts had immeasurably added to the knowledge and enjoyment of children and adults.

Ideas and attitudes, however, were changing. Many thoughtful people had become disillusioned with what they saw as the consequences of an emphasis on productive activities to the exclusion of social, cultural, and environmental values: a deteriorating environment; an increasingly widening gap between the "haves" and the "have-nots"; antisocial behaviour by young people not only in rundown neighbourhoods with few facilities but also in more affluent areas, where the quality of life was equally impoverished; a countryside eaten up by second homes and trailer camps, with sites of natural beauty becoming overcrowded and destroyed; and people bored and dissatisfied because they did not know what to do with their free time. At the same time, there was a growing awareness of those groups in society upon whom leisure had been forced, often against their will—older people, handicapped people, and those whose skills were no longer needed in a rapidly changing world; they, too, needed meaningful activities and an opportunity to be part of the mainstream of local life. In short, many people were seeing the necessity for a more positive, creative attitude toward the use of leisure time. In seeking help to effect this change, they turned increasingly to their governments, particularly on the local and regional levels.

In June elected and appointed local and higher governmental officials from throughout the world gathered at Lausanne, Switz., under the auspices of that city and the International Union of Local Authorities, to discuss the responsibility of local government in the "age of leisure." Expenditure for this purpose, they concluded, must not be regarded as a luxury but as a necessity, in the interests of a healthy society. Although there would never be sufficient resources to do everything that needed to be done, much could be achieved at negligible cost by enlisting local enthusiasm and participation. There was a need to bring together different levels of government and different types of local authorities with other social, political, and professional groups and to tackle jointly a number of problems: the impact of leisure on the environment, and the provision of recreational facilities for city dwellers without overwhelming unspoiled rural areas and smaller towns and without blurring the respective identities of city and countryside.

Intelligent research was needed into the whole question of leisure time. It could no longer be assumed that the purpose of leisure was idle relaxation after a day's strenuous activity; indeed, there might well be a need for leisure facilities to stimulate people and to draw them out of passivity into active participation both in the improvement and maintenance of the environment and in the planning and implementation of communal services and facilities. Cities, moreover, should make more imaginative use of existing facilities such as city halls and schools, which from the outset should be designed and located as multipurpose structures. At the same time, urban governments should ensure that citizens become aware of the facilities available and are encouraged to make the fullest use of them.

To help ensure that the age of leisure did not become the age of boredom, the conference concluded that cities should begin at once to draw up long-term plans for the provision of facilities for social contact, physical recreation, and cultural and intellectual stimulation, aimed at all ages and physical conditions. This would require the diversion of funds from other purposes, but it would be well worthwhile if the result were a happier, more fulfilled citizenry whose horizons had been extended to include an ever wider range of people, events, and skills. (IULA)

Structure. The 1972 *Census of Governments* reported that there were still more than 78,000 governments in the U.S., of which only 51 were federal and state. Although this was substantially below the 1957 level of over 102,000, it still indicated the chaotic nature of local government structure in the nation. Moreover, although the trend toward the consolidation of school districts was clear—they decreased from 50,454 to 15,781 between 1957 and 1972—the creation of special districts to provide local services increased from 14,424 in 1957 to 23,885 in 1972. The number of townships, municipalities, and counties remained about the same during the decade. The continuing creation of special units documented the inability of

Under construction on Roosevelt Island in New York City's East River, this moderate-income project is part of an urban development designed to house 18,000 persons. The Queensboro Bridge is in the background.

MEYER LIEBOWITZ—THE NEW YORK TIMES

inherited and outmoded local governmental structure to cope with the ever growing need for public services at the local level—a need generated by the increasing complexity, interdependence, and vulnerability of 20th-century urban civilization.

Hopeful developments arising from efforts to come to grips with serious urban problems included the increasing concern and activities of state governments and the augmented role of county governments in facing up to local needs. In a study by Michael C. LeMay of the University of Wisconsin analyzing state action in respect to local government from 1965 to 1970, the evidence revealed a trend toward greater state attention to urban problems. As measured by legislative activity, 21 states were "highly" or "moderately" active, 8 "moderately" inactive, and 17 "inactive."

Of the 46 states that cooperated in the study the number that were legislatively active with regard to major urban problems were as follows: on air pollution and control, 45; on sewage treatment and disposal, 30; on mass transit, 26; on metropolitan functional authority, 25; on open space programs, 17; on neighbourhood parks, 13; and on slum fire insurance, 11. In the vital area of state financial support to urban areas, 44 states provided support of housing and urban renewal; 22 made changes in state aid to education; 16 increased per capita aid to local government; 12 assisted urban job incentive boards; and 8 helped to finance urban renewal credit.

Beginning in 1965 states had become more involved in air pollution control, urban housing and renewal, metropolitan planning commissions, sewage treatment and disposal, and mass transit. In these areas stimulation was provided by grants-in-aid by the federal government. Less involvement occurred in areas involving metropolitan functional authorities, state aid to education, urban development corporations, metropolitan study commissions, and open space programs. The lowest levels of involvement were in increasing per capita aid to local governments, neighbourhood parks, slum fire insurance, urban job incentive boards, and state credit for urban renewal, all areas of either limited or no federal incentives. The increasing involvement of state government in urban affairs undoubtedly reflected the trend toward increased representation in state legislatures of urban areas.

Another study, undertaken by Henry J. Pratt of Wayne State University, analyzed the role of county governments in urban affairs. Focusing on 11 county governments in a Southern (Atlanta-five counties) and a Northern (Detroit-six counties) metropolitan area, the analyses revealed that county governments were assuming a more significant role in urban, and especially suburban, affairs. Although, in accordance with the "Southern tradition," Atlanta counties were an important element in the state political system and, in accordance with the "'Northern pattern," Detroit county governments were of lesser importance to municipalities, townships, and villages, in both regions county governments had become increasingly important in intergovernmental relationships, especially in regard to suburban affairs.

For the 1972 fiscal year, as reported by the U.S. Bureau of the Census, U.S. municipalities spent $43.3 billion, $1.4 billion in excess of total revenues of $41.9 billion. Total expenditures increased by 10.9% over fiscal 1971, while total revenues increased by 12.2%. The gap between expenditures and revenues decreased by $300 million. Taxes imposed by the cities yielded $17 billion, about half of all general city revenues. Property taxes remained the predominant source, accounting for $10.9 billion, or about two-thirds of the tax yield. State governments provided $8.4 billion to municipalities, and additional moneys from the federal government and from other local governments (mostly counties) raised the total revenues from all intergovernmental sources to $11.4 billion, more than one-fourth of total revenue from all sources. Total intergovernmental revenue increased by 17.9% over fiscal 1971, intergovernmental revenue from state governments increased by 13%, and from the federal government by 34.8%. Thus, intergovernmental sources provided 27.3% of all local government revenue in fiscal year 1972, as compared with 25.9% in fiscal 1971.

Education. Especially significant in respect to local finances was the U.S. Supreme Court decision of March 21, 1973, which reflected the constitutional challenge to the traditional way of financing state public school systems through local property taxes. The court, in a 5 to 4 decision, crushed the growing movement to achieve reform in education in behalf of underprivileged groups by judicial means. In consequence, financial inputs per child for public school education, because they depend principally on local property taxes, would continue to vary by school district in accordance with its property tax revenues. The court held that spending patterns for public education do not violate the Fourteenth Amendment's guarantee of equal protection of the laws. It ruled that education is not a fundamental constitutional right; that residents in poor areas with low taxable wealth are not constitutionally entitled to the level of public school education in more affluent districts; and that state laws are not void just because their benefits fall unevenly.

The effect of the Supreme Court decision was to leave the devising of a more equitable funding of public education to the states. Justices Thurgood Marshall and William O. Douglas, in their dissenting opinion, called the majority decision "a retreat from our historic commitment to equality of educational opportunity." Although the judicial road to reform

Former U.S. chief justice Earl Warren congratulates Thomas Bradley after swearing him into office as the first black mayor of Los Angeles on July 1, 1973. A past police lieutenant and city councilman, Bradley defeated 12-year incumbent Sam Yorty.

WIDE WORLD

KEYSTONE

London's metropolitan police demonstrate their latest weapon against traffic congestion: a hydraulic lifting vehicle that can remove an illegally parked car in less than three minutes.

of educational financing appeared to be closed for the time being, it seemed certain that pressures would continue to be exerted to assure that all children in the nation including those in urban slums received the opportunity of acquiring the skills that would enable them to assume the obligations as well as the rights of U.S. citizenship.

If the decision had gone the other way, educational funding in every state but Hawaii would have been affected in that more affluent districts would have had to help pay for educational services in poorer districts. In light of the growing importance of education as preparation for "urbanism as a way of life," the decision delayed the achievement of equality of educational opportunity for the children of the disadvantaged in the nation. This inequality, as in the past, undoubtedly was a major cause of social unrest among U.S. minority groups—disproportionately concentrated in the inner cities.

Social Unrest and Crime. Social unrest in urban America erupted into violent forms of behaviour—riots, arson, shootings, looting, etc.—especially during "long hot summers" of the late 1960s. In recent years large-scale manifestations of violence dwindled in number, as the alienation and hostility of minority groups found less violent channels.

Violence, however, did not disappear from the urban scene in the U.S. New tactics and techniques evolved for its continuation by "urban guerrillas." In its *Law Enforcement Bulletin*, July 1973, the FBI published an article on "Trends in Urban Guerrilla Tactics," referring to the growing literature on urban guerrilla warfare. Attacks on police remained the chief tactic of the "revolutionary executioners." During 1972, 11 police officers were killed and 43 wounded in incidents in which responsibility for the action was claimed by revolutionary or guerrilla groups or individuals. Major objectives of urban guerrillas were the acquisition of guns from murdered police officers and the acquisition of money from bank robberies.

Bombings were another frequently used tactic, especially by the Weather Underground, formerly the Weatherman. During 1972 the U.S., according to the FBI, experienced 1,507 bombings and 455 attempted bombings. The results included 25 deaths, 176 injuries, and about $8 million in damaged property. Of the bombings 43% took place in cities with more than 250,000 inhabitants. The West experienced 40% of the bombing incidents, with California having 28% of the total.

For all cities in the U.S. (4,585 cities with 121.7 million inhabitants) the total crime index declined by 25%. This net decline, however, was the result of a 1.4% increase in violent crime and a 3.1% decrease in property crime. The six cities with one million or more persons registered a decrease of 11.8% in the total crime index, a 4.1% decrease in violent crime, and a 14.1% decrease in property crime. In contrast, rural areas reported a 4.4% increase in the total crime index, a 9.2% increase in violent crime, and a 3.8% increase in property crime; and suburban areas reported a 2% increase in the total crime index, an 11.5% jump in violent crime, and a 1.2% rise in property crime. In general, the larger the population of an area the greater was the decrease both in violent and property crime.

It must be borne in mind, however, that whether the decreases in the larger cities were the result of the special efforts to reduce crime motivated by federal programs or represented changes in completeness of reporting remained a moot question. No less an authority than the then U.S. attorney general, Elliot L. Richardson, called attention during the year to the deficiencies of available crime statistics. Moreover, various studies showed that the crimes reported to the police constitute only about half of the crimes committed, as revealed by general population surveys of the victims of crime.

Growth Policies. Related to the incidence of crime are the growth policies of cities. A federally funded study by the National League of Cities and the United States Conference of Mayors severely criticized those city economic policies aimed at increased growth and which assumed growth as a major objective. The study urged cities to concentrate more on living conditions, especially of the low-income population. The study stated: "By promoting developments that largely ignore the requirements of lower economic groups, many cities have improved their position as producer of goods. . . . They have increased significantly the amount of income they generate, but they still have the woes, and attendant expenses, of the unemployed and the underemployed. Thus, they have growth but many of these same cities remain 'sick' as places to live."

The study also faulted cities for specific policies: "Many city governments which deplore the flight of the middle class and wring their hands of the burden of the underprivileged on the city's budget are nonetheless pursuing courses of action which increase job opportunities for the suburbanites and further decrease any viable job opportunities for the lower skilled and less educated people who populate the welfare rolls and are overrepresented in the crime statistics."

(PHILIP M. HAUSER)

See also Architecture; Crime; Environment; Historic Buildings; Housing; Law; Transportation.

ENCYCLOPÆDIA BRITANNICA FILMS. *Operation Bootstrap* (1968); *Problems of Conservation—Air* (1968); *The House of Man, Part II—Our Crowded Environment* (1969); *Manuel from Puerto Rico* (1969); *The South: Roots of the Urban Crisis* (1969); *Chicano from the Southwest* (1970); *The Garbage Explosion* (1970); *The Industrial City* (1970); *Linda and Billy Ray from Appalachia* (1970); *The Rise of the American City* (1970); *What Is a Community?* (1970); *Jesse from Mississippi* (1971); *Noise—Polluting the Environment* (1971); *Turn off Pollution* (1971); *Our Changing Cities: Can They Be Saved?* (1973); *The Image of the City* (1973).

Civil Rights:
see Race Relations

Clothing:
see Fashion and Dress; Furs

Coal:
see Energy; Mining

Cobalt:
see Mining

Cocoa (Cacao):
see Agriculture and Fisheries

Coffee:
see Agriculture and Fisheries

Coinage:
see Philately and Numismatics

Colleges:
see Education

Colombia

A republic in northwestern South America, Colombia is bordered by Panama, Venezuela, Brazil, Peru, and Ecuador and has coasts on both the Caribbean Sea and the Pacific Ocean. Area: 439,735 sq.mi. (1,138,914 sq.km.). Pop. (1973 est.): 23,209,300. Cap. and largest city: Bogotá (pop., 1973 est., 2,825,400). Language: Spanish. Religion: Roman Catholic (91%). President in 1973, Misael Pastrana Borrero.

The improvement in the political situation following the municipal and departmental elections in April 1972 was maintained in 1973 and accompanied by satisfactory economic progress, particularly in the external sector. The only noteworthy political event of the year was the abrupt resignation in June of Carlos Lleras Restrepo from the leadership of the Liberal Party. Lleras had previously formally proposed to the Conservatives that both parties should select a "national" candidate and voluntarily continue the National Front agreement, due to expire in 1974, whereby Liberals and Conservatives alternate in the presidency every four years. The left-wing faction of the Liberal Party and the supporters of Lleras' former foreign minister Alfonso López Michelsen, however, bluntly refused to accept Lleras' political plan. Lleras promptly resigned from the party leadership but made it known that if he was chosen as presidential candidate of the Liberal Party he would accept the nomination. Lleras was in fact rejected by the Liberals in favour of Michelsen. The planned April 1974 elections were likely to represent a straight battle for popular support between the traditional parties, with the National Popular Alliance, led by former dictator Gustavo Rojas Pinilla and his daughter María Eugenia Rojas, creating more of a nuisance than a threat to either of the two principal candidates.

COLOMBIA

Education. (1968) Primary, pupils 2,733,432, teachers 100,629; secondary, pupils 407,966, teachers 39,056; vocational, pupils 191,573, teachers 22,328; teacher training, students 54,527, teachers 5,441; higher (including 16 state universities; 1969), students 85,339, teaching staff 10,730.

Finance. Monetary unit: peso, with (Sept. 17, 1973) a free rate of 22.90 pesos to U.S. $1 (55.18 pesos = £1 sterling). Gold, SDRs, and foreign exchange, central bank: (June 1973) U.S. $463 million; (June 1972) U.S. $214 million. Budget (1973 est.) balanced at 25,433,000,000 pesos. Gross national product: (1970) 127 billion pesos; (1969) 108,280,000,000 pesos. Money supply: (June 1970) 19,640,000,000 pesos; (June 1969) 15,737,000,000 pesos. Cost of living (Bogotá; 1963 = 100): (May 1973) 313; (May 1972) 238.

Foreign Trade. (1972) Imports 18,409,000,000 pesos; exports 12,896,000,000 pesos. Import sources (1971): U.S. 42%; West Germany 11%; Japan 7%; U.K. 5%. Export destinations: U.S. 37%; West Germany 16%; The Netherlands 5%; Spain 5%. Main exports: coffee 73%; crude oil 5%.

Transport and Communications. Roads (1971) 45,100 km. (including 20,017 km. main roads). Motor vehicles in use (1971): passenger 165,000; commercial 86,555. Railways (1971): 3,509 km.; traffic 282 million passenger-km., freight 1,151,000,000 net ton-km. Air traffic (1971): 2,182,000,000 passenger-km.; freight 82,967,000 net ton-km. Shipping (1972): merchant vessels 100 gross tons and over 54; gross tonnage 231,994. Telephones (Dec. 1971) 856,000. Radio receivers (Dec. 1971) 2,250,000. Television receivers (Dec. 1971) 891,000.

Agriculture. Production (in 000; metric tons; 1972; 1971 in parentheses): corn 970 (915); rice *c.* 940 (841); wheat 90 (49); barley 110 (112); potatoes 652 (1,084); cassava (1970) 1,200, (1969) 950; soybeans *c.* 140 (130); coffee 680 (661); bananas 348 (351); cotton, lint *c.* 152 (111); cane sugar, raw value *c.* 830 (744); sugar, panela *c.* 730 (*c.* 700); palm oil 37 (36); tobacco 36 (38). Livestock (in 000; Dec. 1971): cattle 22,400; sheep *c.* 1,750; pigs *c.* 3,900; goats (1970) 928; horses (1970) 1,123; poultry (1970) 38,188.

Industry. Production (in 000; metric tons; 1972): crude oil 10,143; natural gas (cu.m.; 1970) 1,464,000; coal (1970) 3,317; electricity (kw-hr.; 1971) 8,500,000; crude steel 275; gold (troy oz.; 1971) 190; salt (1971) 638; cement 2,990.

WIDE WORLD

Club-wielding Bogotá police drive off striking bus drivers who were demonstrating for higher wages on Oct. 1, 1973.

On the economic front the inflationary pressures of the first quarter of 1973 intensified in subsequent months despite the government's attempts to check the rise in prices. During the first eight months of the year the cost-of-living index for workers rose by 15.8%, compared with 8.7% in January–August 1972. By the end of September 1973 the money supply was reported to have risen by 25.2% on an annual basis, compared with 18.4% a year earlier. Faced with this growing inflationary problem, in October Minister of Finance Luis Fernando Echavarría decided to reduce government expenditures by 10%; the public investment plan was to be revised, and expenditure on nonpriority public works projects would be either reduced or canceled.

Apart from inflation the economy progressed satisfactorily, particularly in the external sector where exports of nontraditional products such as meat, textiles, seafood, beans, grains, and fishing vessels continued to expand rapidly. Indeed, one of Colombia's major current achievements was the gradual reduction of the country's dependence on coffee and oil as its principal exports. This was the result of a vigorous export promotion by the government, which provided for generous tax incentives, financing, and technical aid to exporters of the nontraditional products.

The healthy external position was reflected in the fact that the balance of exchange transactions recorded a surplus of $110.6 million in the period Jan. 1–Sept. 8, 1973, compared with a deficit of $28.7 million in the corresponding period of 1972. Total exports during the year were valued at $682 million (nontraditional exports $328.3 million), compared with $532.6 million ($254.8 million) in 1972. Imports were valued at $398.5 million ($396.5 million in the period Jan. 1–Sept. 8, 1972). A further indicator of the strong external accounts position was the fact that gross international reserves totaled $509.4 million as of Sept. 11, 1973, compared with $392.6 million on Dec. 31, 1972.

The short- and medium-term prospects for the economy continued to be satisfactory and were reflected in the ease with which Colombia was capable of obtaining foreign credits from both private and international sources. Colombia's debt servicing burden was comparatively light in 1973, estimated at about 13% of foreign exchange earnings, and was well below the 17% ratio generally considered to be the tolerable limit. (WILLIAM BELTRÁN)

Commercial Policies

The significant acceleration in the growth of international trade that had developed in 1972, following the upswing in economic activity in the U.S. and the subsequent strengthening of demand in other industrial countries, continued in 1973. As the pressure of demand increased and became more uniform in nearly all industrial countries, the major trade disequilibriums that had developed in the preceding year gradually narrowed. Trends prevailing in the early months of the year indicated a continuing improvement of the U.S. trade balance and the disappearance of Japan's trade surplus.

Against this background, it was not surprising that hardly any countries made use of new import restrictions or controls for the purpose of safeguarding monetary reserves or protecting industries. The "trade war" that had threatened a short time earlier was defused by the boom, as well as by active preparations for international trade negotiations. Instead of curbing imports, governments found themselves in 1973 in the unaccustomed position of having to control or prohibit exports of essential commodities in short supply, a phenomenon that had not been seen since the Korean War.

Export Controls. Soaring commodity prices on world markets reflected growing demand, generated by the high level of economic activity in most industrial countries. They were given added impetus by fears of impending shortages and the price effects of further inflation. By midyear exports of some commodities from major producing countries rose beyond expected levels, and drastic action was sometimes taken to curb them. The most notable case was the embargo on soybean and cottonseed exports introduced by the U.S. at the end of June to protect domestic consumers and traditional overseas customers against the upsurge of overseas demand that threatened to exhaust reserve stocks. The embargo was almost immediately replaced by a system of "validated licenses," and the effect was a 50% reduction in exports of soybeans and derivatives. The export licensing controls applied to more than 40 agricultural commodities in the categories of edible oils, animal fats, and livestock feeds. In the face of vehement foreign protests, the curb on soybean exports was subsequently relaxed, especially for beans intended for human consumption as against those destined for animal feed and industrial use. All these controls were lifted at the beginning of October.

The U.S. export controls introduced in early July also applied to iron and steel scrap, an action urged by the domestic steel and foundry industries in the face of sharply rising prices. Similar action was taken by Canada in August. To meet anticipated shortages in some parts of the country, the U.S. in March relaxed quota restrictions on petroleum imports. As a result, imports of crude oil and petroleum products increased considerably in 1973. By fall the world faced acute oil shortage problems caused by the politically motivated production and export cuts introduced by the Arab countries.

Multilateral Negotiations. These trade controls and restrictions, however, did not deter the major trading nations from pursuing the long-term goals of trade liberalization and reordering the world trading system. Early in 1972 the U.S., the EEC, and Japan had called for a comprehensive review of international trade relations. Following this lead, a large number of countries announced at a GATT (General Agreement on Tariffs and Trade) Council meeting their intention to initiate a new round of multilateral trade negotiations in the following year. This was reaffirmed at the annual meeting of the contracting parties to GATT in November 1972. Many less developed countries expressed their interest and desire to participate in the preparations. They took the position, however, that before they could commit themselves to take part in the negotiations they would need a clearer view of the "techniques and modalities" that would be used.

The contracting parties agreed to set up a preparatory committee with the task of analyzing and interpreting the essential facts of the situation, developing methods and procedures, and promoting attainment of the necessary conditions under which the negotiations could take place. It was decided that a ministerial-level meeting of the participating countries should be held in September 1973 to consider the preparatory committee's report, set up a trade negotiations committee, and provide the necessary guidelines for the negotiations.

Between January and July the preparatory committee laboured against a background of monetary uncertainties and drastically changing world trading conditions caused by inflation, rising prices, and acute shortages of essential materials. The unpropitious circumstances limited the scope of its real contribution. Apart from taking stock of the fact-finding and analytical work that had been achieved by various GATT technical committees and working groups and recording divergent views on various aspects of the planned negotiations, the committee managed to produce a draft declaration in which certain important points of contention were, of necessity, left unsettled.

The Tokyo Declaration. The ministerial meeting opened in Tokyo on September 12 and was attended by representatives of ministerial or comparable level from 102 countries. On September 14 the meeting closed with the adoption of what came to be called the Tokyo Declaration. The essential points of the declaration may be analyzed briefly.

In accordance with the basic direction that the world trading system had followed since World War II, it was laid down that the negotiations should aim at achieving the expansion and ever greater liberalization of world trade and contributing to economic growth through progressive dismantling of obstacles to trade and improvement of the international framework for the conduct of trade. While these high-sounding words were totally unexceptionable, some of the passages that followed appeared to have been so carefully worked out as to betray an effort to ac-

Colonies:
see Dependent States
Comecon:
see Soviet Bloc Economies
Commerce:
see Commercial Policies; Economy, World; Merchandising; Trade, International

commodate divergent and even opposing positions. Thus the declaration called for coordinated efforts to solve the trading problems of all participating countries in an equitable way and laid down that the negotiations should be considered as one undertaking, whose various elements should move forward together. At the same time, it was provided that the negotiations would aim to include an approach that, while in line with the general objectives of the negotiations, should take account of the special characteristics and problems in the agricultural sector.

In the face of significantly different attitudes on the proper way to reduce tariff barriers, the declaration urged the use of "appropriate formulae of as general application as possible." The way was thus open for the general elimination of industrial tariffs, the harmonization of disparate tariffs, a linear reduction of limited dimensions, and so on. Along with the general aim of reducing, eliminating, or regulating nontariff trade barriers, the declaration also provided for exploring the possibilities of using the "sector approach" to trade liberalization, to which certain major trading nations attached great importance.

Much of the hard bargaining in the corridors at Tokyo was devoted to ironing out a difference that had been left unresolved by the preparatory committee. This related to the timing of the trade negotiations in relation to negotiations on a new world monetary system. European countries, particularly France, which once wanted to separate trade bargaining from the monetary talks, had begun to be apprehensive over the possibility of further dollar devaluation. While the U.S. was discovering the comforts of a cheap dollar, the French advanced the view that the trade negotiations could enter a concrete phase only if the grid of parities agreed upon in March was maintained. Subsequently, the EEC shifted from defending monetary parities to requiring parallel efforts in the trade and monetary fields and to making progress in the trade negotiations conditional upon "the existence of prospects of establishing a durable and fair monetary system."

The Tokyo Declaration, as finally agreed upon, met the European position part way by noting that "the efforts which are to be made in the trade field imply continuing efforts to maintain orderly conditions and to establish a durable and equitable monetary system." On the other hand, it was equally recognized that the intended liberalization of trade should facilitate the orderly functioning of the monetary system.

The Tokyo Declaration differed markedly from previous GATT documents in the inordinately large portion of its language devoted to strengthening the negotiating position of the less developed countries. One of the general aims of the negotiations was said to be the securing of additional trade benefits for less developed countries. Specifically, the trade negotiations would aim at improving the conditions of access for products of interest to those countries and ensuring stable, equitable, and remunerative prices for primary products. Tropical products would be given special and priority treatment. The principle of nonreciprocity in negotiations between developed and less developed countries, an established principle in GATT, was reaffirmed. The importance of maintaining and improving the Generalized System of Preferences granted by developed countries to less developed countries, as well as the need for special measures and the importance of providing special, differential, and more favourable treatment for less developed countries, were recognized. Special attention was to be given to the trade interests of the least developed countries.

One of the basic objectives of the negotiations was to improve the framework for the conduct of world trade—to revamp a system that had become increasingly inadequate and irrelevant. The task was an urgent one, but a number of obstacles stood in the way of its attainment.

One appeared to have been overcome with the conclusion of a four-year arrangement covering trade in textiles, agreed to by 50 countries on December 20. Industrial countries had long been obsessed with the fear that imports of particular lines of products from low-cost countries would disrupt their domestic markets and injure their industries. The North American countries and many European nations placed great stress on the importance of ensuring orderly marketing, especially with regard to textiles. The international cotton textiles arrangement, which legalized protective measures that would otherwise be in conflict with GATT provisions, was due to expire at the end of 1973, and the U.S. administration in particular had forcefully demanded a new multinational arrangement to govern trade not only in cotton textiles and clothing but in wool and synthetic fibre products as well. By and large, the U.S. succeeded in its aims; the new arrangement covered all three types of textiles and apparel and contained more safeguards for importing countries than had been the case in the old agreement. It did, however, remove one barrier to multilateral negotiations, since the official U.S. position had been that the textiles question must be settled first.

Still at issue was the question of compensation for damages caused to the trade of the U.S. and certain other countries by the enlargement of the EEC. The so-called Art. XXIV:6 negotiations were likely to be drawn out, and the underlying conflict was apt to be further complicated by new agreements negotiated in 1972–73 between the EEC and Austria, Iceland, Portugal, Norway, Sweden, Finland, and Switzerland which provided for duty reductions between the partners, although these would not involve Art. XXIV:6 procedures. Serious controversy had also arisen in connection with preferential agreements between the EEC and associated African and Mediterranean countries. Discussions opened in October with a view to "enlarging, enriching and strengthening" the association arrangement, with the inevitable effect of antagonizing third countries.

The U.S. Trade Law. In addition to these hurdles, the U.S. administration's lack of juridical negotiating authority would make concrete negotiation impossible. The agreement reached in GATT in 1972 indicated an intention to begin the negotiations in 1973 "subject to such internal authorization as may be required." The U.S. took the position that negotiations could begin before the trade law was enacted, but the EEC insisted that this would serve no useful purpose.

The matter had been pending in the U.S. Congress since the spring of 1973. On April 10 Pres. Richard M. Nixon transmitted to Congress a proposed text for a "Trade Reform Act." The purpose of this legislation was said to be to help the U.S. negotiate for "a more open and equitable world trading system," deal effectively with market disruption and unfair competitive practices, manage U.S. trade policy more efficiently and effectively in dealing with balance of payments and inflation problems, and take advantage of new trade opportunities while enhancing the contribution that trade can make to the development of poorer countries. Under the proposed act, the U.S. administration would have, among other things, authority to increase or decrease customs tariffs without limit, modify the system of customs valuation, and reduce, remove, or harmonize nontariff barriers or other distortions in international trade in implementation of agreements. The act would grant authority to the administration for five years to participate in the Generalized System of Preferences, subject to specified conditions and limitations. The bill was passed by the House of Representatives on December 11, with amendments that would deny government-backed credits and most-favoured-nation treatment to the U.S.S.R. unless Soviet emigration policy was eased. The Senate was scheduled to begin consideration of the bill early in 1974.

Also in April, the EEC Commission forwarded to the Council of Ministers a memorandum containing its suggestions on the Community's position in the trade negotiations. The objectives of the negotiations, in the Commission's view, were to consolidate and continue the liberalization of international trade on the basis of reciprocity and mutual advantage and to improve the opportunity of the less developed countries to participate in the expansion of world trade in order to ensure a better equilibrium between developed and less developed countries. The suggestions related to the reduction of tariffs, the reduction and regulation of nontariff barriers, and negotiations in the agricultural sector. With regard to the less developed countries, the Commission's recommendation was to achieve a coherent body of measures and a balanced contribution by industrialized countries.

Intentions and Reality. Nearly two years after the leading nations had agreed, amid the ruins of the postwar trading and monetary system, that they ought to work out new rules, the process of world trade negotiations thus finally started in September 1973, although significant momentum would not be gained until much later. In the meantime, however, emerging shortages and the ensuing export-control measures had seriously brought into question the relevance of the original aims of the negotiations—to reduce protectionism and to improve access to markets. The central issue now was no longer one of industrial or even agricultural protection but one of scrambling for the limited supplies of foodstuffs and essential materials such as oil.

The irony was that after nearly 20 years of hammering at European trade barriers against agricultural imports, the U.S. should have found it necessary to embargo its exports of soybeans and other farm products to the European market. In July U.S. spokesmen continued to advance arguments reconciling traditional policy objectives, as reflected in the trade bill and directives concerning the upcoming trade negotiations, with the need for international action to deal with the new situation. By October, however, the U.S. had diversified its policy interests by proposing a UN conference to produce guidelines on maintaining adequate food supplies. The multilateral trade negotiations would go on, but the unwieldy machinery that had been set in motion might well be found to be heading toward obsolete objectives.

(CONSTANT CHUNG-TSE SHIH)

See also Agriculture and Fisheries; Commodities, Primary; Development, Economic; Trade, International.

Commodities, Primary

Although the energy crisis caused the most immediate concern among the rich industrialized nations of the world in 1973, the year also brought clear indications that the availability of many primary products besides petroleum would, in the future, be affected by the determination of producing countries to retain full control over the exploitation of their natural resources. In some cases producers of a particular commodity acted in concert to obtain better terms, as when Morocco (the world's largest supplier), Senegal, and Tunisia raised the prices of their phosphate rock by 300%, and it was forecast that similar producers' alliances might develop to control the supply of such commodities as rubber, pepper, jute, copper, and tin.

Trends in World Production. For the first time since World War II, world agricultural production declined slightly in 1972. Fishery production also decreased, by about 1%, but the output of forest products rose approximately 2%. Thus, the combined world output of agricultural, fishery, and forest products in 1972 was about the same as in 1971 (*see* Table I).

Unfavourable weather, particularly drought, was mainly responsible for the reduction in world agricultural output. This drop, in the face of a world population growth of 2%, led to a 3% decline in world per capita food production. By the end of 1972 a precarious balance had developed between supply and demand for food, and world prices rose sharply. The 1973–74 season opened with stocks at levels so low that there was little assurance that world food supplies would be adequate to meet world demand if output was below normal in one or two major producing areas. Large surplus stocks of grain were no longer available in North America to cushion unexpected reductions in

Table I. Indexes of World Production of Agricultural, Fishery, and Forest Products

1961–65 average=100

Item	1968	1969	1970	1971	1972*
Total production	116	117	120	124	124
Agriculture	116	117	120	124	123
Fisheries†	127	130	135	136	134
Forestry†	109	112	114	116	119
Population	110	112	114	117	119
Per capita total output	105	104	105	106	104
Agriculture	106	104	105	107	104
Fisheries	115	116	118	116	113
Forestry	99	99	100	99	99

*Preliminary.
†Excluding China.
Source: Food and Agriculture Organization of the United Nations, *The State of Food and Agriculture* (1973).

Table II. Indexes of World Production of Certain Raw Materials

1963 average=100

Raw material	1968	1969	1970	1971	1972
Coal*	105	106	108	107	109
Crude petroleum	147	158	173	183	190
Cement	138	145	152	160	169
Pig iron†	139	150	156	154	163
Crude steel	137	148	153	149	161
Copper (smelter)‡	120	131	137	133	149
Zinc‡§	133	144	140	132	144
Lead‡§	114	128	131	124	133
Tin‖	128	124	124	127	130
Aluminum‡§	155	174	188	200	209
Natural rubber	124	138	143	141	144

*Including coal equivalent of brown coal and lignite.
†Including ferroalloys.
‡Excluding the U.S.S.R., East Germany, and North Korea.
§Excluding Czechoslovakia and Romania.
‖Excluding the U.S.S.R. and Eastern Europe.
Source: United Nations, *Monthly Bulletin of Statistics* (November 1973).

output, while the amount of reserves required to guarantee minimum world security was growing in line with population and consumption. The margin of safety, therefore, was steadily shrinking.

Meanwhile, many less developed nations continued to be extremely vulnerable to shortages. A good illustration was the sub-Saharan zone of Africa where, as a result of prolonged drought, famine threatened more than six million people. International emergency relief measures were being coordinated by the Food and Agriculture Organization on behalf of the UN in close cooperation with national governments and multilateral organizations.

Long-term trends in agricultural production in the less developed countries were also of considerable concern. The strategy for the Second UN Development Decade called for a 4% average annual increase in the agricultural output of the less developed countries if they were to play their full potential role in economic and social development. This target contrasted sharply with the 1% gain in these countries in 1971 and the stagnant position in 1972. Although the annual rate of growth of 2.8% during 1961–71 represented a considerable achievement, a much greater and more sustained effort was needed in agriculture in most less developed countries.

Preliminary indications were that world production (excluding Communist Asia) of food, fibres, and tobacco in 1973 rose about 6% to a new record high. Improved weather was largely responsible, and the Asian monsoon was particularly favourable. The most noticeable production increases occurred in the U.S., Canada, the Soviet Union, India, Latin America, and Oceania. Also, world food production (again excluding Communist Asia) in 1973 rose to a new high, with per capita output of food about equal to the record set in 1971. Total production rose about equally in the developed countries. But with their population increasing much faster, the less developed countries had smaller rises in per capita food production.

Markets for most fishery products in 1972 were characterized by strong demand for declining supplies and consequent record price levels. World fish production in 1972 was estimated at 55.8 million metric tons, more than 10% below 1971. The most drastic change occurred in Latin America, where output was down 47%.

While many less developed countries continued to make progress in expanding their fisheries, a severe decline in the production of Peru—the country that had become the world's largest producer in the 1960s—more than offset the net increase in the rest of the world. Frequently, lower catches were due to measures in traditional fishing grounds that were taken to rebuild many of the depleted stocks. These measures took the form of area and species quotas, permanent or temporary closings of fisheries, protection of spawning grounds, and regulations to prevent the taking of fish below a certain size and weight or which had not yet spawned. In Peru, for example, fishing for the species that provides raw material for fish meal had to be suspended for extended periods.

Although starting slowly, 1972 proved to be a very good year for forest products. Demand began to outstrip supplies and price increases were considerable, particularly in the U.S. An exception was pulpwood, of which there were large stocks. (*See* FORESTRY.)

For other primary commodities, excluding agricultural, fishery, and forest products, production increased during 1972. This was particularly true for pig iron, crude steel, copper, zinc, lead, and aluminum (*see* Table II). These increases largely reflected booming economies in most industrialized countries. Strong demand for these commodities continued into 1973, and shortages of copper, lead, zinc, tin, and aluminum occurred.

Prices and Terms of Trade. Trends in primary commodity prices during recent years are shown in Table III. While there was some variation among the different products, price rises that began in 1972 generally continued into 1973. With the exception of aluminum, copper, copra, peanuts, and natural rubber, average prices of the commodities listed increased markedly in 1972 and many of them exploded in 1973.

Continuing to gain momentum, the value of world exports of agricultural, fishery, and forest products in 1972 increased by 14%, up from a 5% rise in 1971. Although earnings from both fishery and forestry products expanded rapidly (both by 13%), growth in the value of agricultural exports was responsible for most of the increase. The high rate of inflation in 1972, particularly in the developed countries, eroded the real value of agricultural export earnings. Also, the currency revaluations relative to the U.S. dollar affected the terms of trade and import capacity of many less developed countries.

A major share of the increased export earnings accrued to the developed countries, as in other years of trade expansion, boosting their share in world agricultural trade from 59% in 1971 to 61% in 1972. In spite of the notable advance registered by the less developed countries in 1972, compared with virtually no increase in 1971, their share in world agricultural trade again declined, although marginally, to less than 32%.

In 1972 many countries reported a substantial increase in the volume and an even higher increase in the value of their fishery trade. Imports reached record levels in the U.S. and Japan, the two major markets for fishery products.

While world trade in pulpwood declined about 17% in 1972, trade in coniferous logs rose by 20% and in broad-leaved logs by about 8%, both to record levels. The main feature of trade in coniferous logs was the sharp recovery of Japanese buying.

Commodity Policies. *National Policies.* Following the overthrow of the government of Pres. Salvador Allende Gossens in Chile, which had nationalized the copper industry in that country, the succeeding military government attempted to rectify the conditions that caused the decline of production in the Chilean copper mines. Its success was shown by a rise of copper production in October 1973 to nearly 67,000 metric tons, up from an average of 47,400 tons per month for the first nine months of 1973.

In the United States, Pres. Richard Nixon on Aug. 10, 1973, signed into law a new farm bill providing a "target price" support plan for grains and cotton for four years beginning Jan. 1, 1974. This law replaced a system of price supports and cash payments for diverting cropland from production.

Under the new law supports of $2.05 per bushel for wheat, $1.38 per bushel for corn, and 38 cents per pound for cotton would be set for 1974 and 1975 crops. A farmer would sell his crops in the free market for whatever they would bring. If his average prices fell below the legally established targets—which were well under current market prices—the U.S. Department of Agriculture would pay him the difference, with the total cash payment limited to

Table III. Changes in International Prices of Selected Major Commodities

Commodity, unit, country of origin, and market	Wholesale price in U.S. dollars 1965	1970	1971	1972	July 1973
Aluminum (100 lb.) Canada	24.50	27.90	28.40	26.80	27.30*
Beef (100 lb.) U.S. (N.Y.)	29.61	41.32	42.51	49.76	66.11
Butter (100 lb.) New Zealand (London)	40.10	33.31	46.43	54.92	47.09
Cocoa (100 lb.) Ghana (N.Y.)	18.15	33.26	25.64	30.55	90.02
Coffee (100 lb.) Brazil (N.Y.)	44.78	53.94	45.17	50.74	68.87
Copper (100 lb.) U.K. (London)	58.72	64.17	49.02	48.56	91.71
Copra (100 lb.) Philippines (London)	10.27	10.13	8.53	6.38	14.21
Cotton (100 lb.) Egypt (Liverpool)	51.18	62.60	61.72	65.29	85.23
Hides (100 lb.) U.S. (Chicago)	14.00	12.90	14.50	29.60	36.30
Jute (short ton) Bangladesh (N.Y.)	300.00	310.00	321.00	334.00	337.00
Lead (100 lb.) U.K. (London)	14.39	13.78	11.46	13.69	21.30
Newsprint (short ton) Canada (Quebec)	116.10	131.30	134.60	140.50	143.00
Peanuts (100 lb.) Nigeria (London)	9.37	10.41	11.44	11.40	21.90
Petroleum (bbl.) Venezuela (La Cruz)	2.80	2.80	2.80	3.21	3.77
Rice (100 lb.) U.S. (New Orleans)	8.30	8.60	8.70	9.80	15.30
Rubber (100 lb.) Malaysia (Singapore)	22.88	18.44	15.06	15.05	34.45
Sugar (100 lb.) Caribbean (N.Y. for exp.)	2.12	3.76	4.52	7.52	9.81
Tea (100 lb.) Sri Lanka-India (N.Y.)	54.00	45.80	48.70	50.70	48.70
Tin (100 lb.) Malaysia (Penang)	172.20	163.00	154.70	166.70	204.10
Tobacco (100 lb.) U.S. (U.S.)	59.40	80.61	73.23	80.03	82.62
Wheat (bu.) Canada (Fort William)	1.80	1.70	1.75	1.93	3.49
Wool (100 lb.) U.S. (Boston)	63.40	46.60	35.10	48.80	87.50
Zinc (100 lb.) U.K. (London)	14.11	13.40	13.98	17.13	38.13

*June 1973.
Source: International Monetary Fund, *International Financial Statistics.*

$20,000 per farmer. The bill did provide for restrictions on crop output that could be imposed in the event of real or threatened surpluses.

Even with the prospective huge expansion in farm production, demand, in the opinion of some experts, would be strong enough to keep market prices above the new target levels at least through 1975, thereby eliminating subsidy payments on major crops during the next two years. Even the more conservative observers expected subsidy payments on 1974 crops to drop to $500 million or less from an estimated $2.8 billion on 1973 crops.

In an effort to prevent European food prices from rising to the higher world levels and to keep EEC farmers from shipping their produce to more profitable markets abroad, the EEC invoked export taxes on most grains and sugar. It banned outright exports of durum wheat, including processed durum wheat products such as spaghetti. Having taxed these exports, the EEC removed its corresponding import taxes, but outside suppliers such as the U.S. had become less interested in the EEC market because they could often get higher prices elsewhere.

Bolstered by a record grain harvest, the Soviet Union in December 1973 decided to reorganize its agricultural system in order to spur the modernization of Soviet agriculture. In addition, the reorganization was expected to improve the quality of Soviet rural life and to strengthen Communism in the countryside. To carry out the changes, the Soviet government planned to rely on economic incentives, which had proved effective in pilot programs, rather than on administrative actions.

Late in December Brazil announced that beginning in January 1974 it would raise the price of its exported coffee and also reduce the amount of exports. Green coffee was scheduled to increase from 60 cents per pound to 68 cents by June, and instant coffee would show comparable gains. Brazil planned to export only 5.1 million 132-lb. bags of green coffee during the first six months of 1974, compared with 9.1 million bags for the first half of 1973.

International Policies. The International Coffee Organization, meeting in London on April 14, adopted a resolution extending the 1968 International Coffee Agreement (ICA) for two years until Sept. 30, 1975. This extension, however, deleted all the economic provisions contained in the 1962 and 1968 agreements relating to export quotas and limitations, indicator prices, and export control mechanisms (such as certificates of origin and reexport, and export and transit stamps).

Common Market:
see Commercial Policies; European Unity

Thus, on Oct. 1, 1973, the beginning of the 1973–74 marketing year, the world coffee market was freed from the ICA's artificial restraints. The ICA was acting only as a centre for compiling and disseminating statistical information on coffee, and as a forum for the negotiation of a new ICA with economic provisions more attuned to the evolving world coffee situation.

In the absence of economic clauses in the ICA, the 17-member Inter-African Coffee Organization (IACO) in late July met to formulate its own concerted policy on sales of Robusta coffee. Reflecting their conviction that a quota system was needed in marketing coffee, the IACO members—which produced about 23% of the world's coffee and 90% of the world's total Robusta coffee—agreed to limit their sales of Robusta coffee to 11 million–13 million bags (1 bag = 132.3 lb.) during the 1973–74 coffee year. This was an effort to raise prices, which, the IACO members claimed, had been adversely affected by devaluation of the U.S. dollar.

On August 30 about 30 world coffee producers, in an attempt to secure "reasonable prices," agreed to withhold 5.5 million bags of coffee (10% of the average exports of 1970–72) from the market in the 1973–74 coffee year. These producers, accounting for about 80% of world coffee production, expected to supply the market with 52.5 million bags out of estimated 1973–74 import needs of 56.5 million bags.

Like coffee, sugar would also be traded on a free basis in 1974. The UN Sugar Conference, which convened in Geneva in September, failed to negotiate a new International Sugar Agreement (ISA) with economic provisions to replace the pact that expired Dec. 31, 1973. While quotas under the former ISA were suspended for both calendar years 1972 and 1973, there was a supply commitment on a member-to-member basis. Such deliveries, which were mainly below the world price of sugar, were particularly valuable to the recipient countries. In 1974 there would be no such shipments. Meanwhile, the International Sugar Organization (ISO) was to be maintained. Its council would decide when the circumstances were propitious to convene a new UN sugar conference.

Following 16 years of negotiations and consultations, the International Cocoa Agreement became effective June 30, 1973. Although the agreement would be operative for the 1973–74 season (October 1–September 30), it was not likely to have an opportunity to prove its effectiveness during this period in view of the short supply of cocoa. Although not a member of the pact, the U.S., the world's largest consumer of cocoa, was expected to cooperate with the International Cocoa Council in supplying statistical information on trade and prices. The aim of the cocoa agreement was to stabilize prices within a range of 23 cents to 32 cents per pound by means of a system of export quotas that would be reduced as prices fell and a buffer stock from which sales would be made when prices approached the upper end of the range.

Initial basic export quotas were allocated according to each country's highest production since the 1964–65 crop year. These annual quotas, totaling 1,467,300 metric tons, were divided as follows: Ghana, 580,900; Nigeria, 307,800; Ivory Coast, 224,000; Brazil, 200,600; Cameroon, 126,000; and Togo, 28,000. They were to be automatically revised at the end of the first quota year, with the revised quotas to apply for the remaining life of the three-year agreement.

At the annual meeting of their governing board in Paris on Nov. 15–16, 1973, the four member nations (Chile, Peru, Zaire, and Zambia) of the Intergovernmental Council of Copper Exporting Countries (CIPEC) laid down the foundation for a more active organization and moved to consolidate its ties with the Organization of Petroleum Exporting Countries (OPEC). Avoiding political difficulties, such as the breaking of diplomatic relations by Zambia as a protest against the military coup in Chile, they reaffirmed their goal to "continue aid and assistance to each other in the face of all emergencies." CIPEC in 1972 provided about 40% of world copper production and about 80% of world copper exports.

Ending three days of talks in Vienna, representatives from the world's 12 major oil-exporting countries agreed that world oil prices must be increased. At this meeting of OPEC, it was decided to restrict supplies and sell on a free market, a development that could double current oil prices. The 12 countries involved—Abu Dhabi, Algeria, Ecuador, Indonesia, Iran, Iraq, Kuwait, Libya, Nigeria, Qatar, Saudi Arabia, and Venezuela—exported 85% of the world's crude oil. Most of these nations raised their prices sharply at the year's end. (*See* ENERGY.)

(NORMAN R. URQUHART)

See also Agriculture and Fisheries; Commercial Policies; Development, Economic; Food Processing; Mining; Payments and Reserves, International; Trade, International.

Commonwealth of Nations

The 19th Commonwealth heads of government conference, held in Ottawa, Ont., in August 1973, proved the largest to date, with all 32 full members attending (the Bahamas accounting for an increase of one over the 1972 total). The conference reflected the flexibility of the association and the fluidity of world politics, and, in the words of the communiqué, "greatly strengthened the Commonwealth." The main opening sessions of the conference dealt with changing world power relations and emphasized the value of the Commonwealth as a unique worldwide association of medium and small nations. The Nuclear Test Ban Declaration, which might have confronted Britain (as the only nuclear power and member of the EEC present) with Australian and New Zealand protests against French Pacific tests, was confined to generalities, since Singapore's Prime Minister Lee Kuan Yew pointed out that the Chinese bomb was even nearer to Singapore and Canada remembered the U.S. tests near its own border.

Africa. Although African members insisted on a special conference session on southern Africa, moderate views prevailed, largely because of the conciliatory influence of Gen. Yakubu Gowon of Nigeria. U.K. Prime Minister Edward Heath, whose view that Britain had as much right to an independent foreign policy as other members appeared to be accepted, clearly set out British official views on southern Africa, declaring it illogical to support détente with Communist states over one ideological conflict while deploring dialogue in southern Africa over another. He regarded any great power fight over South West Africa (Namibia) as unrealistic, and, although the British government supported peaceful methods of achieving self-determination, in the final communiqué it reserved its position concerning aid for "humanitarian" ends, since such assistance could be converted to military use.

The final communiqué of the conference also expressed concern at the lack of any Rhodesian settlement. Prime Minister Heath stated that since the Commonwealth saw this as a British responsibility, British policy took precedence. Rhodesia had itself to find a solution acceptable to Africans and others. Neither a Commonwealth force nor a constitutional conference would be acceptable to black or white Rhodesians.

Pres. Kenneth Kaunda's creation of a one-party "participatory democracy" in Zambia, giving himself dictatorial financial and detention rights, did not increase sympathy for him within the Commonwealth. Nor did his take-over later in the year of overseas copper assets in contravention of a 1969 agreement, although this action only followed that of Ghana, Nigeria, and Uganda in turning the nationalization screw against externally controlled industry. Although the construction of the TanZam railway was ahead of schedule, it showed little sign of improving Zambia's economy or of countering indebtedness to China. The trans-African road system, under development by a Western consortium at an estimated cost of £300 million, progressed with 1,600 km. from Addis Ababa to Nairobi and 6,400 km. from Nairobi to Lagos planned. Due for completion by 1977, it was seen as not only of economic value but as a salve to East African conflicts, exacerbated by Uganda's brutal regime, which had caused loss of life and embarrassment to its neighbours. Its callous expulsion of its Asians, condemned at the Commonwealth conference, caused repercussions far beyond Britain to Asia and Fiji, whose multiracial society (with an Indian immigrant majority) suffered disturbing symptoms.

Asia. The Asian Commonwealth, in the aftermath of the Vietnam and Indo-Pakistani wars, took stock of East-West détente, finding small comfort in the neutrality of ASEAN (Association of Southeast Asian Nations) in the face of growing Chinese influence, and in some of the new policies of the Commonwealth.

Australian Attorney General Lionel Murphy (left) chats with Kamal Hossain, Bangladesh minister of law and parliamentary affairs, at the opening session of the Commonwealth law ministers meeting in London on Jan. 16, 1973.

CENTRAL PRESS/PICTORIAL PARADE

Australia's new Labor Party government, which announced its intention to withdraw its combat forces from Commonwealth defense in Singapore and from the 1973 SEATO (Southeast Asia Treaty Organization) exercises, propounded a left-wing, pro-third world policy, out of line with Britain, Malaysia, Singapore, and New Zealand. New Zealand, whose protest of the French Mururoa nuclear tests expressed its responsibilities in the Pacific, took a leading part in the fourth meeting of the South Pacific Forum in Western Samoa in April, attended by the prime ministers of New Zealand, Australia, Fiji, Nauru, Tonga, Western Samoa, and the Cook Islands.

Canada and the Caribbean. Canada performed much the same services for the Caribbean as did New Zealand in the South Pacific as leader of the western Commonwealth of six multiracial democracies. Its own American Indian and French minorities gave it strength and understanding for its increasing role as a bridge between English- and French-speaking Africa. Canada also was the leading financial contributor to the Commonwealth ($180 million a year including 40% of the whole Commonwealth Fund for Technical Cooperation). As host to the 1973 Commonwealth conference, its central role and support for a regenerated Commonwealth proved vital.

Economic Affairs. Economic aspects of the Commonwealth received considerable attention at the 19th conference. Multinational corporations were examined in terms of economic nationalism and of their acceptance by host countries. The conference agreed with Caribbean claims that reciprocity between unequals was an economic contradiction, and the suggestion of Commonwealth preferences, even without Britain, was debated. Commonwealth economic ties were felt to be far from illusory, and a permanent economic bureau at the secretariat for channeling inter-Commonwealth aid was set up; likewise, a Commonwealth Development Bank was to be considered at the finance ministers' meeting in Dar es Salaam, Tanzania, in October.

The July 25 Brussels meeting of less developed countries (which included 22 from the Commonwealth) concerning relationships with the EEC was followed by ministerial negotiations in October, with a view to agreements to take effect in 1975. Commonwealth Africa, led by Nigeria, questioned the whole pattern of economic relationships, which left it as a supplier of raw materials without control over price or market. Eight principles of negotiation were laid down by African finance ministers at Abidjan, Ivory Coast, in May. They included, in particular, nonreciprocity and a guarantee of stable and equitable EEC markets. Commonwealth Asia, with its 700 million population, was concerned with access to U.K. markets; neither Pacific nor Caribbean Commonwealth countries were reassured over the EEC import policy concerning sugar, despite the promise of 1.4 million tons as a permanent minimum to be accepted by the Community. The 13 Commonwealth sugar-producing countries formed a standing committee in March to act as a united front against European pressure for expansion in the production of sugar beets, which can be grown in Europe itself.

The Commonwealth continued to account for about one-fifth of total world trade. Intra-Commonwealth trade accounted for about one-quarter, with Britain as the main customer for most members. Of the U.K. total of £1.4 billion in trade with Africa, about £800 million was estimated to come from black Africa and the rest from the southern part of the continent. Though trade with black Africa was increasing, with Nigeria as the most important partner, such factors as the relative returns and the political instability in many black African nations continued to tip the economic balance in favour of the south. Increased interest in intra-Commonwealth aid and trade was particularly marked in Canada, whose trade with other members more than doubled between 1963 and 1973 and whose aid steadily increased. Official aid increased by more than 25% in 1972 over 1971 to Can$500 million.

Commonwealth professional and technical bodies numbered more than 1,000, each holding annual conferences in various Commonwealth countries. The Commonwealth Parliamentary Association and Commonwealth Press Union both functioned in London in 1973, while the latest organization, the Commonwealth Youth Programme, was brought into being at Lusaka, Zambia, in January. Recognizing that more than half its 850 million people were under 25 years of age, the Commonwealth provided Youth Service awards and increased educational opportunities with a budget of £1 million. (MOLLY MORTIMER)

See also articles on the various political units.

Communications: *see* Telecommunications; Television and Radio

Communist Parties

Some notable successes for the Communist movement in 1973 were counterbalanced by some frustrating setbacks. The achievements of the revolutionary forces in Indochina were consolidated through negotiated settlements, but the experiment in parliamentary revolution in Chile was brutally suppressed. There was a general aura of harmony among many of the Communist states, but Sino-Soviet polemics escalated. Major efforts by Communists to achieve an international détente were offset to some degree by a revival of mistrust and confrontation.

In many ways, the policy of the Communist Party of the Soviet Union contributed directly to this contradictory picture. Following a pattern that had developed over the preceding several years, the Soviet leadership attempted simultaneously to pursue a foreign policy of détente and peaceful coexistence, a domestic policy with a strong emphasis on continued ideological war against bourgeois ideas and dissent, a popular front policy of rallying all leftist and progressive forces of the world, and a policy of strengthening unity within the world Communist movement and condemning those, particularly the Maoists, who sought to divide it.

Contradictions in Soviet Policy. In the spring Soviet party leader Leonid I. Brezhnev's authority within the Soviet leadership appeared to receive a significant boost (*see* BIOGRAPHY). At its April plenary session, the Central Committee of the Soviet Communist Party gave full approval to Brezhnev's recent conduct of international relations and to alterations in the composition of the Politburo that appeared to enhance the general secretary's position. At the same time, the fact that the three men promoted to full membership in the Politburo included not only Foreign Minister Andrey A. Gromyko but also Defense Minister Andrey A. Grechko and secret police chief Yuri V. Andropov indicated that Brezhnev's attempts to promote détente and trade with the West would be more than matched by efforts to ensure a high level of military preparedness and internal control.

After the April plenary session, Brezhnev personally set about carrying his "peace program" to the West. In May he traveled to West Germany and in June to the U.S., where, with a great show of amiability, he and Pres. Richard Nixon signed accords designed to foster cooperation and trade. Brezhnev's personal diplomacy was also evidenced in his discussions with French Pres. Georges Pompidou in Minsk in January and in Paris in June and in his less-than-successful talks with Prime Minister Kakuei Tanaka of Japan in Moscow in October. At the same time, the Soviet Union and its allies pressed ahead with their effort to reduce the tensions and expenses of the cold war and to stabilize the postwar division of Europe at the 35-nation Conference on Security and Cooperation in Europe and, somewhat less eagerly, at the 19-nation conference on mutual and balanced force reductions (MBFR) in central Europe.

The Soviet determination to limit the spirit of détente to formal state relations caused particularly great difficulties. For example, the Soviet desire for a speedy conclusion to the European security conference, to be followed by a summit meeting in 1973, was frustrated in large measure by their own unwillingness to make concessions on the free flow of people and information between states. Some of the worst restrictions on the emigration of Soviet Jews were relaxed at the time of Brezhnev's visit to the U.S., and, later, Soviet jamming of certain Western radio stations was ended, but Soviet leaders were unwilling to go further.

In March the party began a long-prepared-for purge. Throughout the first half of the year, as increasingly severe measures were taken against prominent dissidents, the image of the Brezhnev regime inevitably became tarnished in the West. In late summer the prominent Soviet physicist and civil rights advocate Andrey D. Sakharov (*see* BIOGRAPHY) warned the West that conditionless provision of technological and economic aid to the Soviet Union would merely strengthen its military power and facilitate its repressive policies. Amid a concerted Soviet press campaign against Sakharov and following the much publicized trial of dissidents Pyotr P. Yakir and Viktor A. Krasin, Nobel Prize-winning author Aleksandr I. Solzhenitsyn came to Sakharov's defense and bitterly assailed Western liberals who failed to denounce oppression in Communist countries. The harassment of Sakharov, Solzhenitsyn, and others contributed to some second thoughts about the conditions for Soviet-U.S. trade and meaningful détente on the part of the U.S. Senate and several Western leaders. It also tended to interfere with efforts by Communists in various countries to form popular fronts.

If the Soviet Union's internal policy seemed to counteract its encouragement of popular fronts, however, its policy of promoting an international popular front of all anti-imperialist forces, symbolized by the year-long preparations for the World Congress of Peace Forces in Moscow in October, tended to run counter to its policy of détente with the U.S.

Even in the Middle East, where the Soviets had provided extensive military, technical, and economic assistance, some Arab nationalist leaders openly expressed the fear that détente was an imperialist conspiracy. Then, when war broke out in the Middle East in October, the Soviet leaders faced the reverse side of the dilemma: that their desire to unite all anti-imperialist forces in a popular front threatened to undermine their efforts toward détente.

But the worst problem involved in the Soviet efforts to provide leadership for the world revolutionary movement continued to be China. Early in the year, at the time of the Vietnam peace negotiations, Soviet criticism of the Chinese was reduced in an apparent attempt to maintain a semblance of Communist unity. In June Brezhnev offered the Chinese a nonaggression treaty, and the two powers did manage to sign an agreement on air service between Moscow and Peking and a trade treaty. However, throughout this time Soviet authorities were also changing the Chinese names of Siberian towns and rivers to Russian ones and encouraging settlement close to the Chinese border. In early August, the Soviet press resumed its full-scale attack on the Maoists and in late August, on the eve of the tenth congress of the Chinese Communist Party, Brezhnev began a series of speeches denouncing the "frantic anti-Sovietism" of the Chinese leaders. At the congress, Chinese Premier Chou En-lai responded in kind.

Communist Governments of Europe. The Chinese Communists were not alone in their distrust of détente. Even some of the Soviet Union's closest allies in Eastern Europe seemed to fear that the U.S.S.R. was negotiating with the West at their expense. Nevertheless, in general 1973 was a year of comparative harmony within the Soviet bloc, as the various Communist governments followed the Soviet example both in seeking to improve their own relations with the West and in voicing their hostility to the penetration of bourgeois ideas.

There were, however, some significant differences among the various Eastern European governments. In almost opposite ways, Romania and Hungary were the most nonconformist. Romania continued to demonstrate that peculiar combination of conservatism at home and recalcitrant nationalism and independence in its dealings with its Communist neighbours

Children carrying hammer-and-sickle insignia leave an April 1973 Communist rally staged in Rome to protest alleged rightist violence.

WIDE WORLD

that had characterized its behaviour for almost a decade. Hungary, in contrast, tended to be quite conformist in its foreign relations and the most liberal of the Soviet bloc nations in its internal policy. In 1973, however, this nonconformity began to be reduced somewhat. In the ideological sphere, indications of a tightening up included a crackdown on sociologists and a new tendency to view Western ideas and even tourism with suspicion.

Since their respective crises in 1970 and 1968, the governments of Poland and Czechoslovakia had been trying to rebuild support, largely on the basis of popular economic well-being. There were indications in 1973 that both had succeeded to some degree. An amnesty for those who had fled Czechoslovakia after 1968 was announced, and there were reports that some of the job discrimination against liberals who had been dropped from the party after 1968 had been ended. A similar confidence that economic improvements had won back popular support could be seen to underlie the Polish government's decision to reduce press censorship.

The tenth World Festival of Youth and Students, held in East Berlin in August, met in a far more relaxed atmosphere than had been evident at the ninth festival, held in Bulgaria in 1968. In part, this reflected the differences in political sophistication and development between East Germany and Bulgaria. In 1973 East Germany emerged fully on the international scene; the treaty normalizing relations with West Germany was ratified, diplomatic relations had been established with 84 countries by midyear, and East Germany became a member of the UN. Nevertheless, the East German leaders were extremely wary of détente, an attitude that was reinforced by the continued penchant of some East German citizens to escape to the West. Politically, party chief Erich Honecker seemed to have consolidated his leadership position; in October Premier Willi Stoph was moved into the largely honorary post of chairman of the State Council. For the traditionally loyal Bulgarian Communists, probably the most important event of the year was Brezhnev's visit in October.

The subversive influence of bourgeois attitudes was also an issue in the two European Communist states that were not in the Soviet bloc. Faced with growing economic problems, nationality conflict, and dissent, Yugoslav President Tito had called for a new crackdown on dissident intellectuals and for ideological revitalization of the League of Communists. This campaign continued throughout 1973 at varying levels of intensity. With the tenth party congress scheduled for early 1974, the revitalization drive took on the appearance of a succession struggle in which Stane Dolanc, the secretary of the League's executive bureau, appeared to be in the ascendancy. Attacks on U.S. policy contributed to the impression that Yugoslavia was moving in a pro-Soviet direction. In contrast, Albania remained China's sole Communist ally in Europe.

Communism in Asia. The central event of 1973 for the Chinese Communists was the rather undramatic tenth party congress in late August. Preceded throughout the year by the rehabilitation of officials who had been purged during the Cultural Revolution, the congress appeared to represent a victory for the moderate and pragmatic policies of Premier Chou. It certainly was a setback for the extreme left-wing faction, since its main representative, Mao Tse-tung's wife, Chiang Ch'ing, failed to gain reelection to the Standing Committee of the Politburo. Although there were some indications even after the congress that Chou's position was not secure, the only surprising change within the top leadership was the appointment of the young and relatively unknown Wang Hung-wen (*see* BIOGRAPHY) to the Standing Committee.

The Sino-Soviet dispute presented Asian Communists with both dilemmas and opportunities for maneuver. The Mongolian People's Revolutionary Party remained firmly tied to the Soviet Union. On the other hand, Prince Norodom Sihanouk, head of the Cambodian government-in-exile in Peking, generally lent his support to the policies of his hosts. Sihanouk's situation became somewhat more complex in October, when, as his chances of returning to power increased, the Soviet Union finally recognized his National Union Front as the legitimate government of Cambodia.

The North Vietnamese Communists had become skilled in maintaining amicable relations with both sides in the Sino-Soviet dispute. Top-level North Vietnamese party and governmental leaders traveled during the summer not only to Peking and Moscow but also to Eastern Europe, Mongolia, and North Korea, where they received fresh promises of continued support. A similar stance was maintained by the Pathet Lao. After agreement was reached with the Laotian government on the terms for a coalition government, both Chinese and Soviet transport were involved in bringing Pathet Lao forces to the capital. Kim Il Sung's regime in North Korea was also successful in this regard. Both China and the U.S.S.R. backed Kim's proposal for peaceful Korean unification.

Among the nonruling Communist parties of Asia, the Sino-Soviet dispute caused particular difficulties for the pro-Moscow but rather nationalist Japanese Communists. China at its party congress reiterated its support for Japanese claims to the four southernmost Kuril Islands held by the Soviet Union, while Brezhnev, in his October meeting with Tanaka, agreed only to continue discussions looking toward an eventual peace treaty.

Communism in Latin America. The most dramatic reversal for the generally pro-Moscow Communists in Latin America was the military coup d'etat that overthrew Pres. Salvador Allende's Popular Unity Coalition government in Chile in September. This resulted not only in the death of Allende, the execution or imprisonment of a number of the supporters of his government, including Communist Party leader Luis Corvalón, and the outlawing of all Marxist parties, but also in repressive actions against the many foreign revolutionaries who had sought asylum in Chile. Earlier in the year, the military in Uruguay had in essence seized power and, in its effort to suppress the Tupamaro urban guerrillas, had forced the dissolution of the Congress, the suspension of civil liberties, and the banning of radical parties including the Communists.

In the generally bleak picture in Latin America, the situation of the Communists in Argentina was the exception. One of the first measures of the new Peronist government was to repeal the anti-Communist law and to legalize the party. Although the Peronists continued to combat Marxist (in some cases Trotskyite) guerrilla terrorists and Juan Perón later called for a "war on Marxism," the Communist Party was able to hold a party congress in August and subsequently agreed to support the election of Perón as president. In May the new Argentine government also recognized

Membership of the Major Communist Parties of the World*

Countries with a membership of 2,000 or more persons

Country	Membership
Albania	87,000†
Argentina	70,000
Australia	3,900
Austria	25,000
Bangladesh	2,500
Belgium	12,500
Bolivia‡	3,200
Brazil‡	7,000
Bulgaria	700,000†
Burma‡	§
Chile	120,000
China	28,000,000†
Colombia	11,000
Cuba	125,000†
Cyprus	13,000
Czechoslovakia	1,200,000
Denmark	6,000
Finland	49,000
France	400,000
Germany, East	1,909,800†
Germany, West	35,000
Greece‡	28,000
Guadeloupe	3,000
Hungary	724,000†
India	166,000
Iraq‡	2,000
Israel	2,000
Italy	1,596,000†
Japan	320,000
Korea, North	1,600,000†
Laos	13,000
Lebanon	2,500
Malaysia‡	2,000
Mexico	5,000
Mongolia	58,000†
Nepal‡	5,000
Netherlands	10,000
Norway	2,500
Paraguay‡	3,500
Peru	3,200
Philippines‡	8,000
Poland	2,270,000†
Romania	2,260,000†
Spain‡	5,000
Sri Lanka (Ceylon)	4,000
Sudan	7,500
Sweden	17,000
Switzerland	3,000
Syria‡	3,000
U.S.S.R.	14,700,000†
United Kingdom	29,000
U.S.	§
Uruguay‡	22,000
Venezuela	8,000
Vietnam, North	1,100,000
Vietnam, South‡	§
Yugoslavia	1,025,000†

*Estimated from figures available December 1972.
†Official claim.
‡Communist Party illegal.
§No estimate available.
Source: U.S. Department of State, Bureau of Intelligence and Research, "World Strength of the Communist Party Organizations" (July 1973).

Fidel Castro's Cuba after an 11-year break, and in August it extended $200 million in credits to Cuba—moves that were warmly welcomed at a time when the Castro regime was primarily engaged in institutionalizing the revolution. (DAVID L. WILLIAMS)

See also China; Czechoslovakia; Defense; Soviet Bloc Economies; and articles on various countries.

Computers

The most significant event in 1973 for the computer industry was the decision in favour of the Telex Corp. in its antitrust suit against International Business Machines Corp. (IBM). In the decision, Judge A. Sherman Christensen of the U.S. District Court in Tulsa, Okla., awarded Telex damages of $352.5 million and enjoined IBM from engaging in certain pricing and leasing practices and from withholding information on certain technical specifications—actions that had impaired the ability of competitors to design and market equipment for use with IBM computers. It was the first time IBM had lost a major court case.

In the same decision, Judge Christensen found Telex guilty of stealing trade secrets from IBM through the improper use of copyrighted materials and through the hiring of former IBM employees to work on similar projects at Telex. In this decision, resulting from a countersuit filed by IBM, Telex was required to pay IBM $21.9 million, to return or destroy the copyrighted material, and to stop hiring former IBM employees except with court approval.

On October 9 Judge Christensen stated that he had made "substantial error" in calculating the amount that IBM must pay Telex. After four more days of hearings the judge on November 10 reduced the amount to $259.5 million and also lifted the injunctions against IBM. IBM then appealed the decision before the U.S. Appellate Court in Denver, Colo. At year's end five other companies had sued IBM separately on grounds similar to those of Telex.

In a separate case, Control Data Corp., which had also sued IBM under the antitrust laws, settled out of court. The settlement included a payment by IBM to Control Data of $60 million and transfer of the Service Bureau Corp., an IBM subsidiary, to Control Data. Later in the year, Control Data began to integrate the services and facilities of SBC into its own computer service network, called Cybernet.

As one condition of the settlement, Control Data destroyed a computerized index to an extensive file of IBM documents that could have been used as evidence had the case come to trial. The destruction caused considerable criticism by the industry, and by the U.S. Department of Justice, which had hoped to obtain the use of the index in its own antitrust suit against IBM. The Justice Department suit was scheduled for trial in October 1974.

At the end of 1972, the U.S. Supreme Court rejected an appeal on an attempt by two employees of Bell Laboratories, part of American Telephone and Telegraph Co. (AT & T), to patent a computer program. The program provided a means of translating numbers from one system of notation to another; the U.S. Patent Office had rejected the patent application and the Court of Customs and Patent Appeals had overruled the Patent Office. The Supreme Court then overruled the appeals court, describing the program as an idea and therefore not patentable.

The decision, however, was far from definitive. It called for Congress to redefine the patent rules, which had not been updated to account for the inventiveness that some computer programs contain. Congress, however, took no action in 1973.

UPI COMPIX

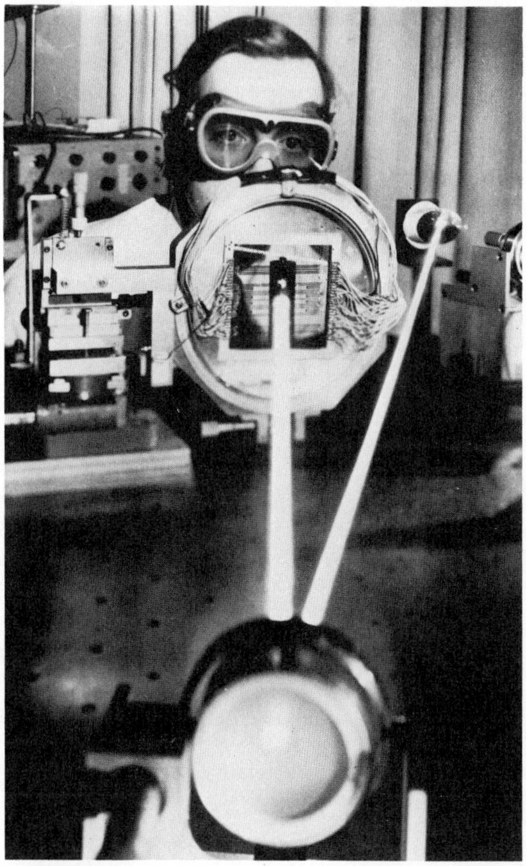

Wilber C. Stewart at the RCA Laboratories in Princeton, N.J., observes a laser beam illuminating a hologram in the demonstration of an experimental holographic optical computer memory.

Late in October Control Data and the Soviet Union signed a ten-year agreement to cooperate in the design and development of advanced computer technology. It was the first long-term agreement in the computer field between a U.S. firm and the Soviets and might eventually lead to joint manufacturing operations.

In 1973 a mushrooming growth took place in the use of small electronic calculators—some for desktop use and some small enough to fit into a pocket. At the beginning of the year many of these sold for about $100; by the year's end similar models, all capable of the four basic arithmetic operations, were going for $60 to $70, and one new model was being offered for $30. Hewlett-Packard Co., which had earlier introduced a higher-priced model for use by engineers and scientists, with more than the usual complement of functions, brought out a similar unit for business and financial users in 1973.

A private company, Telenet Communications Corp., prepared to build and operate a commercial data communications network using the packet-switching concept. With this concept, special processors serve as interfaces between the user and the network and transmit data in 1,000-bit "packets" to assure error-free transmission and to simplify routing. Slated to become president of Telenet was Lawrence G. Roberts, who was the architect of Arpanet, the packet-switching network developed by the Advanced Research Projects Agency (ARPA) of the U.S. Department of Defense. Another company, Packet Communications Inc., had similar plans; it was established by former employees of Bolt, Beranek & Newman, Inc., which had developed the packet-switching processors for Arpanet and then operated the network for the Department of Defense.

In Europe, Siemens AG in West Germany, Compagnie Internationale pour l'Informatique in France, and N. V. Philips Gloeilampenfabrieken in The Netherlands, three of Europe's four largest computer firms, agreed to collaborate in a joint effort to meet the formidable competition offered by IBM in Europe. The lone holdout, Britain's International Computers Ltd., was expected to join the group later, and sponsors hoped eventually to lure some of IBM's U.S. competitors into the group, which was named Unidata. However, Honeywell Bull, a French company which was two-thirds owned by Honeywell Inc. of the U.S., was not permitted to join the group unless the U.S. firm reduced its share of the company to less than half.

In Japan, a similar combination of the country's six largest computer firms, Hitachi, Tokyo Shibaura, Oki Electric, Fujitsu, Mitsubishi, and Nippon Electric, into three or perhaps two groups was being promoted by the government, which also indicated plans to begin selling Japanese computers in the U.S. within two or three years.

Technology. Microprocessor designs and markets began to multiply during 1973. Microprocessors, functionally corresponding to the central processing unit of large computers, are relatively low-performance processors with four- to eight-bit word lengths built in the form of a single integrated circuit, not particularly large or complex. In 1973 they sold for $50 to $100, depending on the particular design and the volume ordered; in conjunction with read-only and read-write semiconductor memory circuits, input-output connections, and appropriate programming, they can perform functions usually carried out by digital logic networks. However, they are much more flexible than the digital networks because the program can be changed more easily than the logic can be rewired.

Semiconductor memories in general, and metal oxide semiconductor (MOS) memories in particular, developed into a significant portion of the computer main-memory market, primarily with several versions of a 1,024-bit integrated circuit. But during the year a few 4,096-bit versions from several manufacturers began to appear on the market in small volume. Semiconductor memories first became acceptable when their cost fell to levels competitive with those of the older ferrite-core and other magnetic memories. Quadrupling the capacity of a single circuit promised to cut the cost even further, and so, as the 4,096-bit units went into large-scale production, they threatened the core memory market even more.

A research scientist adds an "atom" to the model of an amorphous film structure from which high-density magnetic bubble memories can be made. The upright objects represent the film's magnetic anisotropy, an essential characteristic for the creation of bubble memories.

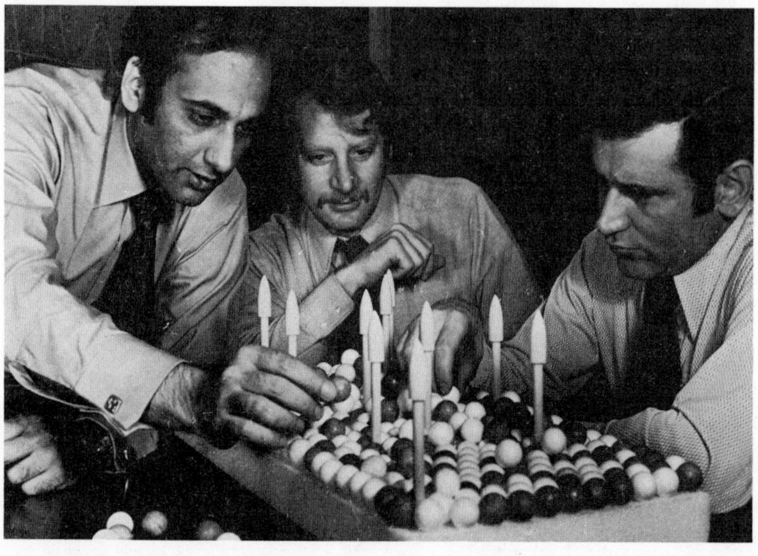

Meanwhile, new semiconductor technologies were being developed. One group of IBM researchers disclosed that it had built an 8,192-bit MOS memory on one chip; another IBM project developed a bipolar cell design with an area of only 1.1 square mils (1 square mil = 0.000001 sq.in.), corresponding to more than 16,000 bits of bipolar memory on an ordinary chip; and a third research group, also at IBM, used electron-beam lithography to produce memory cells of only one-eighth square mil in area. Meanwhile, Texas Instruments Inc. developed a 4,096-bit shift register made with charge-coupled devices, a semiconductor technology with great promise for fast bulk memories.

Though there was much work in semiconductor technology, magnetic cores were not being ignored. Several makers of core memories began to reexamine an old idea, storing more than one bit in a core. If successful, this technique would substantially increase storage density yet require only a minimal increase in the cost of electronics and stringing the cores. One approach was to use partial switching—switching only the inner part of a toroidal (doughnut-shaped) core with a current pulse in which the amplitude and duration can be closely controlled.

At Bell Laboratories, where the magnetic bubble memory was first developed, a 1.1-megabit bubble memory was put together from 56 chips 200 mils square and carrying 20,000 bits each in an epitaxial garnet film. Meanwhile, scientists at IBM's research laboratory disclosed a method for making magnetic bubble memories out of a film of amorphous material. The method suggested that much faster data rates and storage densities would be feasible than could be attained with the previously used crystalline materials, and that amorphous films were demonstrably easier to prepare.

Developments in peripheral equipment included almost simultaneous announcements by IBM and Storage Technology Corp. of magnetic-tape systems with data stored at 6,250 bits per linear inch of tape (bpi). Several other manufacturers, including Telex and Control Data Corp., followed with announcements of their own within the next few months.

Applications. An audio-response time-shared computer was installed at the Protestant Guild for the Blind, Watertown, Mass., to help blind persons type correspondence, proofread manuscripts, and do bookkeeping work. The typewriter keyboard transmits the typed data to the computer, where they are recognized and translated into spoken words that either tell the typist what he has typed or respond to a command. The computer can also generate typed copy, Braille copy, or a voice recording of the input data.

In Washington, D.C., tests began on a computerized bus priority system that would let a bus driver hold a green traffic light for himself and expedite bus traffic during rush hours. The system includes a switch on the bus's steering column, a transmitter in the bus, an antenna embedded in the pavement, a circuit module in the traffic light controller, and a central computer that correlates bus signals with overall traffic conditions.

WIDE WORLD

Picture editing by computer: editors can view photos on a TV screen (upper left) and then recrop and transmit them by using a cursor on an electronic board (foreground).

A computer-controlled gasoline filling station opened in suburban Los Angeles. A terminal in the station accepts either cash or a credit card and dispenses the amount of gasoline requested—unless the credit card has been stolen. Then it keeps both the card and the gasoline.

The U.S. Customs Service began testing an anti-smuggling computer network at key points where highways cross the Canadian and Mexican borders. At each port of entry, an agent would enter the license number of an approaching car on his keyboard, and by the time the car pulled up to the booth he would have information about any previous offense in which the car was used. Terminals at these ports were connected to a pair of large computers in San Diego, Calif., and in Washington, D.C., that maintained the data base.

The U.S. Federal Aviation Administration began experimenting with a voice-answer-back system, built by the Univac division of Sperry Rand Corp., that generates advisory messages for airplane pilots from data picked up by radar. Radar, for example, might detect two airplanes near one another; when this information is fed into the computer, the voice-answer-back unit transmits a message to one pilot about the proximity of the other. It can also warn a pilot of his approach to a mountain peak or a television transmitting tower. Eventually, it could be expanded to air traffic control applications, telling pilots specifically what to do instead of just warning them of a dangerous situation.

In a new system developed in Sweden, computers can recognize photographs on identification cards. The cards must carry three photos—full-face, three-quarters, and profile, with lines drawn on the back to outline the main facial characteristics, such as the curve of the nose or a deep wrinkle. Full recognition requires only 200 to 250 bits of data, many fewer than were used by previously attempted systems.

(WALLACE B. RILEY)

ENCYCLOPÆDIA BRITANNICA FILMS. *What Is a Computer?* (1971); *A Computer Glossary* (1973).

Congo

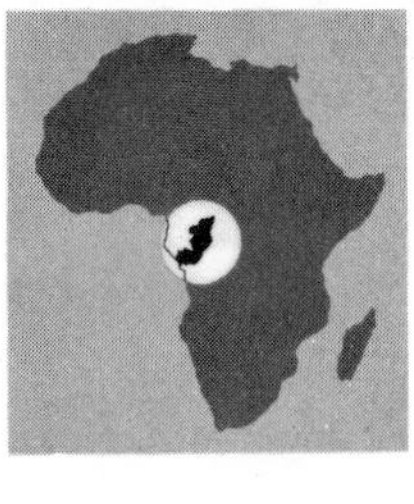

A people's republic of equatorial Africa, the Congo is bounded by Gabon, Cameroon, the Central African Republic, Zaire, Angola, and the Atlantic Ocean. Area: 132,000 sq.mi. (342,000 sq.km.). Pop. (1972 est.): 1,148,000, mainly Bantu. Cap. and largest city: Brazzaville (pop., 1971 est., 175,000). Language: French (official) and Bantu dialects. Religion: mainly animist, with a Christian minority. President in 1973, Maj. Marien Ngouabi; prime minister from August, Henri Lopes.

The atmosphere of political unrest that had characterized Congolese domestic affairs since the deposing a decade earlier of the country's first president, Fulbert Youlou, persisted throughout 1973. In February, after issuing warnings to the Army and to the population about the "dangers" of treason, President Ngouabi announced the discovery of a plot against the state in which Minister of Information Sylvain Bemba and former prime minister Pascal Lissouba were alleged to have conspired with leftist leader Ange Diawara to overthrow the government. The president also announced to a mass meeting of the Congolese Army that the country's police force was to be disbanded immediately and its duties taken over by the Army.

Diawara succeeded in avoiding arrest, only to be killed a few weeks later in a skirmish. As a result of the alleged conspiracy some 40 people were arrested and brought to trial, including several French teachers. After several adjournments the trial took place in April. The French nationals among the accused, however, were released before the conclusion of the proceedings on orders from President Ngouabi. Bemba received a suspended sentence of three years' imprisonment, while Lissouba was "given the benefit of the doubt" and acquitted. Of the remaining accused conspirators, nine were acquitted, ten were given suspended sentences, and others received sentences ranging from one year to life, together with four death

CONGO

Education. (1971–72) Primary, pupils 260,534, teachers 3,800; secondary, pupils 37,430, teachers 672; vocational, pupils 4,086, teachers (1969–70) 317; teacher training (1969–70), students 583, teachers 34; higher (1969–70), students 1,786, teaching staff 103.

Finance. Monetary unit: CFA franc, with (Sept. 17, 1973) a parity of CFA Fr. 50 to the French franc and a free commercial rate of CFA Fr. 212.55 to U.S. $1 (CFA Fr. 512.25 = £1 sterling). Budget (1972 est.) balanced at CFA Fr. 21.8 billion.

Foreign Trade. (1971) Imports CFA Fr. 24.1 billion; exports CFA Fr. 11,760,000,000. Import sources (1969): France 57%; West Germany 8%; U.S. 7%. Export destinations (1969): West Germany 17%; The Netherlands 14%; France 14%; Belgium-Luxembourg 8%; South Africa 6%; U.K. 6%; Israel 5%; Italy 5%. Main exports: timber 56%; diamonds 7%.

Transport and Communications. Roads (1971) *c.* 11,000 km. (including 310 km. with improved surface). Motor vehicles in use (1968): passenger 7,200; commercial 5,600. Railways (1971): 801 km.; traffic 146 million passenger-km., freight 534 million net ton-km. Air traffic (1971): 82 million passenger-km.; freight 7,837,000 net ton-km. Telephones (Dec. 1971) 11,000. Radio receivers (Dec. 1970) 65,000. Television receivers (Dec. 1971) 1,900.

Agriculture. Production (in 000; metric tons; 1971; 1970 in parentheses): cassava *c.* 450 (*c.* 450); coffee 1.9 (2); peanuts *c.* 20 (20); sugar, raw value *c.* 122 (*c.* 98); palm kernels *c.* 2.6 (1.8); palm oil *c.* 6 (*c.* 5.7). Livestock (in 000; 1970–71): sheep *c.* 60; cattle *c.* 32; pigs *c.* 38.

sentences in absentia. Underground rebel movements continued to be a source of harassment to the Congolese authorities, and there were a number of clashes between government forces and rebels.

In June general elections and a constitutional referendum were held, although only single candidates from the country's sole legal political party were put up. Nevertheless, the new constitution was approved by 411,272 votes to 118,311—figures that suggested a degree of electoral freedom uncommon in that part of the world. In August Henri Lopes was appointed prime minister, the country's sixth in ten years.

October brought more evidence of unrest. Col. Yhomby Opango was dismissed from his post as Army chief of staff, and seven men accused of assassinating a labour-union leader were sentenced to 20 years of forced labour. (PHILIPPE DECRAENE)

Consumer Affairs

The increasing effect of the consumer movement on the market and the growing acceptance of the consumer interest as a distinct factor in social planning and political life were evidenced in 1973 by a larger volume of national legislation in areas closest to the consumer, such as product labeling and description. The same growing strength enabled consumer activists and consumer organizations to expand their range of activities. While the evaluation and comparison of products and services remained basic features of almost all consumer groups, they were joined by a concern to speak out for the individual in many situations where his essential weakness adversely affected his interests at the hands of industry or the state.

In 1973, for example, consumerists were active in investigating and attempting to control the activities of multinational companies and in such areas as international air fares, the packaging and worldwide marketing of pharmaceutical drugs, and environmental issues, particularly noise pollution. In the less developed countries, consumer organizations took the lead in campaigning against food shortages, high prices, and adulteration. This broadening of the concept of consumer affairs made it progressively more difficult to define. Nevertheless, the cycle of consumer campaign—legislation—market impact—increased consumer awareness stood out more clearly than ever before.

"Poor chap, wiped out overnight—freezer defrosted."

ULUSCHAK, EDMONTON JOURNAL, CANADA; ROTHCO

Intergovernmental Organizations. At the international level, the widening recognition of the consumer interest found expression at the 29th session of the UN Commission on Human Rights, held at Geneva from February to April 1973. The commission emphasized that "people must know and assert their rights as consumers if they are to get maximum benefit from the development process." It considered the four most important of these rights to be: the right to safety; the right to be adequately informed about products and services and the conditions of sale; the right to choose among alternative goods of satisfactory quality at fair prices; and the right to be heard in the decision-making process of government.

The direct representation of consumers at the UN level through the International Organization of Consumers Unions (IOCU) was strengthened in 1973. IOCU's permanent representative to the Economic and Social Council was appointed chairman of the new NGO (nongovernmental organizations) Committee on Development, established to enable nongovernmental organizations in consultative status with the UN to fulfill their responsibilities in relation to the Second UN Development Decade.

In May the UN secretary-general reported on plans to carry out a broad investigation into "the impact of multinational corporations on the development process and on international relations." A specially appointed panel of experts held hearings in September and November, with a third session to follow in the spring of 1974. The president of IOCU appeared before the second session and presented evidence of how multinational companies flout consumers' rights.

The Food and Agriculture Organization of the UN announced in August that by midyear the joint FAO/World Health Organization Codex Alimentarius Commission had adopted 64 international food standards, 42 of which had been circulated among governments. In 1973 IOCU, representing consumers at the Codex Commission, submitted detailed proposals on food labeling, minimum and average weight, and foods for special dietary uses. Consumers' representatives were also associated with the formulation of an international standard for a system of shoe sizing—to be known as Mondopoint—issued in 1972 by the International Organization of Standardization (ISO). In June the International Standards Steering Committee for Consumer Affairs urged ISO to issue a directive on a guide for the preparation of standard methods of measuring the performance of consumer goods.

In Paris the Committee on Consumer Policy of the Organization for Economic Cooperation and Development (OECD) continued its general review and exchange of information and experience concerning consumer policies in OECD member countries. The Council of Europe's Working Party (No. 2) on Consumer Education and Information was engaged in completing its studies of adult education and information and undertook a further study of consumer representation in official bodies.

In April the Parliamentary Assembly of the Council of Europe adopted a Consumer Protection Charter for recommendation to member states. The 28-article charter defined basic principles for a comprehensive consumer protection policy founded on international standards and designed to ensure certain minimum guarantees for all European consumers. The Assembly also announced its intention to consider the possibility of drawing up a European convention on consumer protection.

Within the EEC, a number of steps were taken to strengthen representation of the consumer at the level of the EEC Commission. These included the direct allocation of responsibility for consumer interests to a vice-president of the Commission; the establishment of a separate Division for Consumer Affairs within the EEC; the allocation of around U.S. $2.5 million by the Commission to promote the interests of consumers; and the appointment of three consumer representatives to the Economic and Social Committee. Consumer representation in the EEC was further reinforced by the establishment in May of a permanent office and secretariat in Brussels by the Bureau Européen des Unions de Consommateurs (BEUC), an affiliate of IOCU.

World Consumer Movement. Many reforms relating to the consumer had stemmed directly from the activities of consumer organizations. In the U.K. the Criminal Justice Act (effective from Jan. 1, 1973), which empowered the courts to award compensation to a consumer who had suffered as a result of proven misdescription of goods, followed a test case brought by the British Consumers' Association. In India a boycott of the open sugar market, organized in January by the Consumer Guidance Society of Bombay in an effort to keep prices down, led, according to the *Bombay Times,* to the government's releasing an additional supply of sugar. Other "shoppers' strikes" organized by consumer organizations against prices made themselves felt in several countries, including Israel and Jamaica. In Brussels the consumer representatives on the Economic and Social Committee of the EEC were able to include, in a directive on the safety of cosmetics, a declaration reflecting the view of consumer organizations that only ingredients proven to be safe should be permitted.

The organized consumer movement achieved further advances in growth during 1973, in terms of both membership in established associations and the formation of new groupings. The *Consumers Directory,* published by IOCU in July, listed 129 organizations in some 50 countries—an increase of nearly 15% over the previous year. Consumer organizations were listed for the first time by Barbados, Greece, Guam, Guyana, Montserrat, and St. Lucia, while additional organizations were established in the U.K., Australia, West Germany, Malaysia, Nigeria, and Switzerland. IOCU admitted six new members during 1973, raising its membership to 88 organizations from more than 40 countries. Membership in individual organizations also continued to show a steep upward trend. For example, the Consumentenbond (Neth.) reported 430,000 members, compared with 330,000 the previous year; the Consumers' Institute of New Zealand rose to 100,000 from 65,000; and Stiftung Warentest, West Germany, to 311,000 from 150,000.

National Developments. In many countries, pressure for consumer reform centred on product labeling and description, particularly of prepackaged food, and on unsafe products or practices. There was also some reflection at the national level of the growing concern over multinational companies and environmental pollution. Other concerns that became prominent during the year included consumer credit and control of undesirable commercial practices; several countries, for example, introduced legislation and litigation against the "pyramid sales" schemes that had become notorious by the end of 1972. (*See* MERCHANDISING.)

In the U.K. the Fair Trading Act, which came into effect in September, established a director general of fair trading and a Consumer Protection Advisory Committee with members drawn from business, weights and measures enforcement bodies, and consumer organizations. Under the act, the director general and the committee could lay an order before Parliament prohibiting or controlling any trade practice (including advertising practices) considered to be against the consumers' economic interest.

In August the U.K. minister of trade and consumer affairs announced plans for a network of consumer advice centres to be set up by local authorities, on the pattern of the experimental centre opened by the British Consumers' Association in 1969. In September the minister announced new measures to outlaw pyramid selling schemes, and in October a new procedure was adopted to enable consumers to bring small claims (up to £75) in the county courts.

In Sweden, where the National Board for Consumer Policies came into being on January 1, small claims were the subject of a bill to simplify procedures in civil cases. Norway's first consumer ombudsman and market court, patterned after the Swedish model, also came into effect on January 1. In Australia discussions began in mid-1973 with a view toward establishing a national commission for consumer affairs to coordinate federal activities in the field. Ireland proposed to establish consumer consultative councils for public enterprises.

Strong legislative measures to extend and/or control the labeling and description of consumer goods were introduced in many countries. In the U.K. the Labelling of Food Regulations, 1970, which came into effect on January 1, compelled manufacturers and retailers to give far more information about both prepacked and nonprepacked food and ruled out the "small print" on many food labels. In February the government decided to apply the recommendations of the Food Standards Committee to make date marking of foods compulsory by 1975. The Weights and Measures (Unit Pricing) Bill was introduced, requiring that goods be marked with the price per unit of measure. Other countries that introduced similar legislation included Australia, New Zealand, Norway, Sweden, Switzerland, West Germany, Canada, and the U.S.

Consumer organizations continued to campaign for greater protection by the state against unsafe or hazardous products. Legislation to this end was introduced in 1973 in several countries, notably the U.K., Canada, the U.S., Norway, Sweden, and Switzerland. The main areas covered by such legislation were medicinal drugs, electrical goods, cars, alcohol and tobacco products, flammability, and food additives. The problem of noise came under mounting attack by consumer organizations, and in 1973 a number of provisions were introduced to counter this, notably in Norway, France, and the U.K.

Pressure for greater control of consumer credit was strongest in the U.S. and the U.K. where the recommendations of the Crowther Committee led in 1973 to the introduction of a bill to control lending and license credit reference bureaus. West Germany, Sweden, and Ireland were the scene of major government efforts to investigate or control multinational companies, monopolies, and restrictive practices.

(JOHN CALASCIONE)

UPI COMPIX

General Motors demonstrated the elasticity of an experimental bumper system in March 1973. Top, a car traveling at 5 mph nears a pole. Centre, the entire bumper system deforms on impact. Bottom, almost as soon as the car backs away the bumper restores itself.

Congregational Churches: *see* Religion

Conservation: *see* Environment

Construction Industry: *see* Engineering Projects; Housing; Industrial Review

UPI COMPIX

Members of the National Consumers Congress picket the White House on April 18, 1973, to protest the high cost of meat. Several of the women brandish meat bones, which they say is all they can afford to buy.

In the U.S. the consumer interest was becoming increasingly organized. The Consumer Federation of America represented nearly two hundred local and state consumer associations, while Consumers Union had approximately two million subscribers and took an interest in consumer affairs beyond the rather restricted one of consumer testing. In addition, spokesmen for organized labour, women's groups such as the American Association of University Women, and groups concerned with health and nutrition had increased their consumer activities. All had been strengthened by the newly aroused interest in the environment and the quality of life as represented by such groups as the Sierra Club and the Wilderness Society.

The problems of the consumer were certainly much more general than the traditional "consumer interests" would indicate. One that was brought forcefully to the attention of consumers in 1973 was that of rising prices. The increase in food prices was of special concern to consumers in the low-income category, since the largest percentage of their expenditure went for food. To these individuals the price rise represented a serious erosion of real income and caused a severe strain on already low income-maintenance programs.

The full meaning of the energy crisis for the consumer was not yet known. As 1973 ended, cutbacks and rationing of gasoline and heating oil loomed as the most immediate worries. In the long run, however, energy shortages meant shortages in the whole range of consumer goods, and the government had only begun to tackle the question of priorities. The affluent society began to look less so, and the problems of affluence, which had underlain at least part of the consumerist movement, might well cease to be a major concern. (*See* ENERGY.)

That time had not yet arrived, however. Short-term and intermediate consumer credit amounted to $169,148,000,000 in July. This represented an increase since January of approximately $12 billion, indicating that consumers were continuing to borrow despite rising interest charges. In 1973 various credit interests continued to urge passage of the Uniform Consumer Credit Code in state legislatures. The code admittedly did eliminate some objectionable credit practices, but it was generally opposed by consumer organizations because it would permit a rise in the maximum interest rates for various types of credit. Some half-dozen states had passed it, despite the opposition.

No-fault automobile insurance was another subject of interest to consumer groups. Under the no-fault principle, the individual experiencing an automobile accident would be paid by his own insurance coverer for automobile and property damage and personal injury to himself and anyone riding in his automobile. No longer would it be necessary to go through a long, tedious legal process to determine who was responsible for the accident. Proponents insisted that no-fault would permit a reduction in insurance premiums by reducing the costs of litigation, which currently accounted for about 16% of the premium dollar.

Consumer groups generally favoured federal legislation, while insurance interests preferred state legislation. The trial lawyers' associations strongly opposed federal action and favoured some state legislation. The consumer groups insisted that true no-fault insurance must provide for payment for loss by the insured's insurance company, limit rights to additional compensation, be compulsory, and restrict the right of insurance companies to cancel or fail to renew insurance policies. However, some advocates of the rights of the low-income consumer were skeptical about state plans. Their concern was that, if the insurance was compulsory, the poor would find the additional cost prohibitive. If it was not compulsory, they would lack coverage and would be unable to recover even when they were not at fault. (*See* INSURANCE.)

The popularity of mobile homes as permanent residences was increasing rather rapidly in the U.S. In recent years new mobile homes had equaled 25% of conventional single- and multifamily housing starts. However, the more conventional type of housing was regulated by building codes that did provide some minimum structural standards. This did not hold for mobile homes transported in interstate commerce, although some standards for sanitation and utilities had been established by local and state governments.

Another problem for mobile home owners concerned their rights as tenants in a mobile home court, especially with regard to the landlords' seemingly unlimited ability to order an individual to vacate. The mobile home owner pays an entry fee in addition to regular monthly rent, and it was alleged that some landlords ordered tenants to leave in order to secure more vacancies and hence more initial fees. An article in *Consumer Reports* (July 1973) stimulated action on the state level to limit this power. Maine, New York, Minnesota, and New Hampshire passed new legislation regulating trailer court practices.

Legislation regulating warranties passed the U.S. Senate. Meaningless and untruthful warranties had been a consumer problem for many years. The legislation would set minimum standards for warranties and manufacturer performance under them. The administration of warranties would be under the Federal Trade Commission (FTC). Other consumer legislation introduced into Congress in 1973 included a truth in savings bill that would make clear to consumers the true annual rate of interest on savings accounts; a food labeling act that would require disclosure of grade and nutritional value and the latest date before spoilage; a truth in advertising act; a bill to provide a consumer education program in the Office of Education; a bill under the Federal Trade Commission Act allowing class actions in cases of consumer fraud; a bill to require durable consumer goods to bear a label indicating the life expectancy of the product; and a bill mandating open dating of perishable foods.

Another bill of potentially major importance introduced during the year was the Consumer Protection Act of 1973, which would establish a federal Consumer Protection Agency charged with representing the consumer interest at legislative and regulatory commission hearings. Two versions of the bill were introduced, one of which would allow the agency to present information only at formal hearings while the other would permit it to enter informal proceedings as well.

A number of bills relating to the energy crisis would have far-reaching effects on consumers. The Emergency Energy Act would give the president sweeping powers, including the power to implement fuel rationing and allocation programs. Attempts to compromise House and Senate versions of the bill broke down over the questions of limiting windfall profits for the oil industry and congressional approval of various presidential actions, and further consideration of the measure was postponed until Congress reconvened in January 1974. On December 10 the Senate passed an energy conservation measure requiring, among other things, "truth in energy" labels on cars and major appliances showing their approximate annual operating costs and stickers on cars giving the expected gas mileage. However, the bill was opposed by the administration on the ground that it would fragment federal energy-conservation efforts.

In other matters of consumer interest, the Office of Interstate Land Sales Registration, established in the Department of Housing and Urban Development in 1969 to bring some order into this business and provide some protection for the consumer, adopted a set of regulations that took effect Dec. 1, 1973. The vitamin habit was almost as American as apple pie, and for many years a rather casual attitude had existed concerning vitamin sales. Increasing evidence that vitamin overdoses were possible led the Food and Drug Administration to issue new regulations on the sale, labeling, and promotion of vitamins and mineral supplements. (DAVID HAMILTON)

See also Advertising.

Contract Bridge

Tournament bridge had made no distinction between professionalism and amateurism in the past, but in the course of 1973 it became necessary to give the topic closer consideration, particularly with regard to the organization of tournaments and exhibition matches, and the formation of an association of professional contract bridge players. In the U.S. a standing committee had the question of special tournaments for professional players under review; but it was only in the U.S. that the practice of expert players' partnering with the less expert on a professional basis had been a widespread one. In 1973, however, the prize money on the Riviera circuit in May, June, and July totaled some $250,000 (£100,000), and there were signs on both sides of the Atlantic that commercial interests could find a publicity value in promoting tournaments featuring top players, with the result that for the first time such players could regard the prize money trail as justifying their complete commitment. No one person had done more to create this interest in public competitive contract bridge than the film actor Omar Sharif, who professed that he filmed for a few months each year to earn the wherewithal to indulge his passion for playing tournament bridge. The World Bridge Federation recognized his contribution by appointing him honorary chief commentator at future world championships.

At the same time one pair, Giorgio Belladonna and Benito Garozzo, members of the late Italian Blue Team, who were world champions from 1957 until their retirement in 1969, added to the glamour of the game with a series of performances that established them as the world's outstanding partnership. When the Blue Team disbanded, Garozzo and Belladonna decided that their future lay in bridge. In 1973 they competed again in the Bermuda Bowl competition, the official world championship, representing Italy in a team with Pietro Forquet, a third member of the former Blue Team, and Benito Bianchi, Giuseppe Garabello, and Vito Pittala, three players making their first appearance in a world championship match. In the final, Italy met the defending champions, the American Aces, a professional team representing the United States and brought into being by Ira Corn, a bridge-playing millionaire industrialist from Texas. After 32 boards of the 128-board final the match was effectively over. Italy led by the staggering score of 124–6. After 96 boards the Italians led 294–101 with their third pair, Garabello and Pittala, not having played a board; this pair was introduced for the last session when the Italians, playing in lighter vein,

NORTH
♠ A K 7 4
♥ K J 9 4 3
♦ A Q J
♣ 8

WEST
♠ 10 9 6
♥ A 10 2
♦ 9 7
♣ J 6 5 4 3

EAST
♠ Q J 8 2
♥ 8 7 6
♦ 2
♣ A K 9 7 2

SOUTH
♠ 5 3
♥ Q 5
♦ K 10 8 6 5 4 3
♣ Q 10

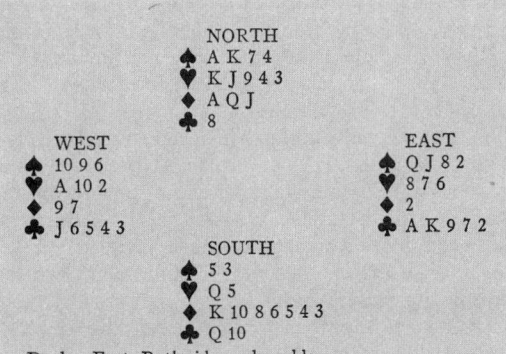

Dealer, East. Both sides vulnerable.

The first time the hand was played, Jacoby and Wolff for the U.S., pressing for points, reached six diamonds in an uncontested auction. A club was led and there was no way to avoid losing a further trick to the ace of hearts. The second time, when Forquet sat North and Bianchi South, the auction was:

East Goldman	South Bianchi	West Blumenthal	North Forquet
Pass	Pass	Pass	1 ♣
Pass	1 ♦	Pass	1 ♥
Pass	3 ♦	Pass	3 ♠
Pass	4 ♥	Pass	6 ♥
Pass	Pass	Pass	

Forquet and Bianchi were a relatively unpracticed partnership but had agreed on a form of the Precision Club bid. One club was forcing, one diamond negative, and one heart natural; three diamonds, by their methods, should have shown a positive hand, in spite of the original one diamond bid, with a 4-4-4-1 distribution and a singleton spade. Bianchi had forgotten the convention but Forquet had remembered. Forquet's bid of three spades asked for controls, with an ace counting as two and a king as one. Again Bianchi had forgotten and four hearts, which he intended as a simple sign-off, in fact showed five controls—and Forquet had remembered. Goldman, on lead, had also remembered. Reviewing the bidding he decided that North surely had a singleton club and South a singleton spade and that his best defense was to prevent a cross-ruff game. He led a trump, hoping to enter later with his club trick to lead a second trump. Blumenthal won with the ace, tried to guess which ace his partner might hold, and, guessing wrongly, returned a spade. Needless to say, it was not by these haphazard methods that the Italians had built up their commanding lead.

lost ground for a final result of 333–205. The Italians outplayed the American Aces, but the most astonishing hand of the match was one on which an uncharacteristic misunderstanding produced the Italians' largest positive swing (*see* box).

Belladonna and Garozzo had achieved so much that it was difficult to find a new challenge. They found one by choosing as their teammates in the Italian team for the European championship four young players, all unproved in the international arena—Arturo Franco, Soldano de Falco, Antonio Vivaldi, and Rodolfo Pedrini. In a 23-nation tournament they won by more than two and a half matches and left the firm impression that with Belladonna and Garozzo in their lineup, at least 12 other teams could have taken the title.

The Italian women retained their European championship and Italy, therefore, remained champions of Europe and of the world in both the open and the women's series. (HAROLD FRANKLIN)

Cooperatives

During 1973 important changes took place in the cooperative movements of West Germany, The Netherlands, and the United Kingdom. The West German cooperative wholesale society was converted into a public company in order to provide better opportunities to raise capital for expansion. CO-OP Nederland, the apex organization of the Dutch consumer movement, was sold to a private enterprise, together with a number of retail societies that had vested their management in CO-OP Nederland. The six remaining independent societies formed a new national organization called CO-OP Holland. The engagements of the Scottish Cooperative Wholesale Society were transferred to the Cooperative Wholesale Society at the end of June. The new organization, with an annual turnover in excess of £700 million, now served the whole of the United Kingdom.

A cooperative and producer marketing section was set up within the Canadian Ministry of Agriculture to support agricultural cooperatives and to develop proposals for new federal programs of direct assistance to cooperatives in collaboration with representatives of the cooperative movement. The first national convention of the Australian cooperative movement was held in Canberra in August in order to promote closer collaboration among cooperatives in Australia. The first cooperative congress was held in Suva, Fiji, in August, endorsing the constitution of the Fiji cooperative union for the territory. Following the successful establishment of five pilot rural electric cooperatives in various states of India, it was proposed to expand the experiment during the fifth five-year plan. A group of cooperative banks from West Germany, The Netherlands, Austria, Denmark, Finland, and France set up a full-fledged merchant banking subsidiary in London in August.

A progress report on the "Promotion of the Cooperative Movement During the Second United Nations Development Decade" was submitted to the 54th session of the UN Economic and Social Council in May. The International Labour Organization (ILO) pledged continuing support to the growth and better functioning of cooperatives in less developed countries. The joint committee for the promotion of aid to cooperatives (Copac), on which the International Cooperative Alliance (ICA), the ILO, the UN Food and Agriculture Organization (FAO), and UN Social Development Division were represented, met several times during the year.

The International Cooperative Alliance. In February UN Secretary-General Kurt Waldheim, receiving the Executive Committee of the ICA in New York, stated that the UN was increasingly recognizing the cooperative movement as an instrument that could effectively raise the living standards of the peoples of the third world and pledged the support of the UN and its agencies to the implementation of future cooperative projects.

The ICA Central Committee met in Budapest, Hung., in October. The main theme was "International Cooperative Enterprises—Prospects and Problems." Papers presented dealt with international cooperative efforts in the field of fertilizers, international collaboration in the field of petroleum and oil, financial aspects of international cooperative enterprises, and joint international cooperative productive enterprises in the Nordic countries. The meeting also received a report on the first stage of the Cooperative Development Decade. The constitution of the advisory group on international training was approved.

In March an auxiliary ICA committee was set up with the object of promoting consumer information, protection, enlightenment, and education. A meeting of ICA research officers held in Vienna in June dealt with communicating with the cooperative consumer. The working party on the cooperative press discussed the role of cooperators in the defense of the environment in Geneva in October.

Educational activities carried out by the ICA Regional Office for Southeast Asia included a seminar on cooperative management in the Philippines in January, and one on cooperative credit in Japan in April. In Tokyo in October Asian top-level cooperative leaders discussed cooperative agricultural development, legislation, and autonomy. A coordinator for cooperative aid to Bangladesh, jointly financed by the Oxford Committee for Famine Relief (Oxfam) and the ICA, was appointed in May for a period of two years. The International Technical Assistance Department of the Netherlands Ministry of Foreign Affairs agreed to finance a research officer at the ICA Regional Office for East and Central Africa for two years.

The Latin American Technical Institute for Cooperative Integration (Latici) established a research and training centre in Aruba, Netherlands Antilles, in April and assisted in the opening of a number of consumer stores in Venezuela. A project on educational techniques and material for use in less developed countries, made possible by a grant arranged by the Cooperative League of the U.S., was initiated.

INTER-COOP, the ICA committee representing wholesale and retail interests, discussed international collaboration in the field of production at its meeting in Budapest in October. Representatives of cooperative productive enterprises manufacturing chocolate and confectionery, toiletries, and flour met during the year to discuss the joint purchasing of raw materials. Purchasing groups dealing with fresh fruit and vegetables and car accessories met for the first time. The International Cooperative Housing Development Association decided to establish a European office.

Membership and Trade. At the end of 1973, the number of cooperative federations in membership with the ICA totaled 165 in 62 countries. The latest available statistics showed an increase in the number of member cooperative societies from 564,398 in 1970 to 624,900 in 1971. Membership within these societies rose from 281 million to 305 million during the same period. The largest membership was reported from the U.S.S.R. (60.5 million), followed by India (59.3 million) and the U.S. (45.2 million). Of the total membership, the greatest proportion was in consumer societies (40.89%), followed by credit societies (29.67%), agricultural societies (18.30%), miscellaneous societies (6.22%), building and housing societies (2.66%), workers' productive and artisanal societies (1.66%), and fisheries societies (0.60%).

A five-point program of cooperative collaboration was agreed between the Cooperative League of the U.S. and the National Cooperative Council of India. An agreement of collaboration in the fields of education and training and the promotion of trade was signed between the General Cooperative Union of Iraq and the Central Cooperative Council of Czechoslovakia. The Polish and Japanese cooperative movements agreed to promote trade between the two countries. Further collaboration between Canadian and Japanese cooperators was discussed in Canada at the end of June. (LOTTE KENT)

Costa Rica

A Central American republic, Costa Rica lies between Nicaragua and Panama and has coastlines on the Caribbean Sea and the Pacific Ocean. Area: 19,652 sq.mi. (50,898 sq.km.). Pop. (1973 est.): 1,867,045, including white and mestizo 97.6%. Cap. and largest city: San José (pop., 1972 est., 217,772). Language: Spanish. Religion: predominantly Roman Catholic. President in 1973, José Figueres Ferrer.

The governing National Liberation Party nominated Daniel Oduber Quirós, formerly president of the Senate, to run against Tréjos Escalante, the candidate of the National Unification Party, in the presidential elections to be held in February 1974. The remaining opposition parties had been expected to form an electoral alliance, but they failed to reach agreement, and each party submitted its own candidate.

President Figueres came in for severe criticism as a result of his proposal, in October 1972, to create a tax haven for multinational companies in Costa Rica, following which the U.S. financier Robert L. Vesco (*see* BIOGRAPHY) took up residence there. Vesco was wanted in the U.S. in connection with alleged swindles involving $224 million, and it was generally believed that Figueres' relationship with him would damage the National Liberation Party's chances of victory in the coming elections.

During 1973 Costa Rica's economic development policy continued to be centred on improvements to basic productive facilities. Particular attention was paid to port development projects as a result of the inability of existing facilities to cope with the country's increasing foreign trade. It was announced in May that a total of $19 million was to be invested in the construction of a new port in Caldera Bay at a site recommended by a Japanese technical mission that had visited the country in 1972. Japan was to supply a loan of $14.5 million for the project, which would comprise three docks with full port facilities such as transportation, electrical, and telephone services; warehouses; and a railroad.

WIDE WORLD

Costa Rican families, with the few possessions they can carry, flee from the area struck by an earthquake in April 1973.

The government, the Instituto Costarricense de Electricidad, the U.S.S.R., the World Bank, and the Aluminum Company of America agreed to study the establishment of a hydroelectric plant and an aluminum smelter, and as a result work was to begin early in 1974 on the construction of a large dam using the waters of the Arenal River and Lake Arenal. This project, representing a first step toward the development of the nation's bauxite resources, was expected to provide about 20,000 new jobs and improve flood control and irrigation facilities.

One important precondition for the restructuring of the Central American Common Market (CACM) was the reduction in Costa Rica's trade deficit, which, at

COSTA RICA

Education. (1969–70) Primary, pupils 339,558, teachers 11,460; secondary, pupils 49,438, teachers 2,935; vocational, pupils 5,757, teachers 445; higher, students 11,384, teaching staff (universities; 1968–69) 678.

Finance. Monetary unit: colón, with (Sept. 17, 1973) an official rate of 6.62 colones to U.S. $1 (16.11 colones = £1 sterling) and a free rate of 8.60 colones to U.S. $1 (20.74 colones = £1 sterling). Gold, SDRs, and foreign exchange, central bank: (June 1973) U.S. $35,820,000; (June 1972) U.S. $31,950,000. Budget (1971 est.): revenue 1,210,119,000 colones; expenditure 1,242,897,000 colones. Gross national product: (1971) 6,808,000,000 colones; (1970) 6,357,000,000 colones. Money supply: (April 1973) 1,688,600,000 colones; (April 1972) 1,361,800,000 colones. Cost of living (San José; 1963 = 100): (Jan. 1973) 130; (Jan. 1972) 122.

Foreign Trade. (1972) Imports 2,475,900,000 colones; exports 1,845,100,000 colones. Import sources: U.S. 33%; Japan 11%; Guatemala 8%; West Germany 7%; Nicaragua 7%; El Salvador 6%; U.K. 5%. Export destinations: U.S. 40%; West Germany 12%; Nicaragua 6%; Guatemala 6%; El Salvador 5%. Main exports: bananas 26%; coffee 25%.

Transport and Communications. Roads (1970) 18,742 km. (including *c.* 3,250 km. all-weather and 665 km. of Pan-American Highway). Motor vehicles in use (1971): passenger 43,400; commercial (including buses) 26,400. Railways (1971): 799 km.; traffic *c.* 57 million passenger-km., freight *c.* 13 million net ton-km. Air traffic (1971): 199 million passenger-km.; freight 9,440,000 net ton-km. Telephones (Jan. 1972) 68,000. Radio receivers (Dec. 1971) 130,000. Television receivers (Dec. 1971) 120,000.

Agriculture. Production (in 000; metric tons; 1972; 1971 in parentheses): coffee *c.* 100 (*c.* 100); bananas (1970) 1,100, (1969) 967; sugar, raw value 211 (178); dry beans *c.* 15 (*c.* 14); cocoa (1971–72) 3.4, (1970–71) 3.9; palm oil 22 (22). Livestock (in 000; 1971–72): cattle *c.* 1,630; horses *c.* 112; pigs *c.* 190.

Industry. Electricity production (1971) 1,148,000,000 kw-hr. (90% hydroelectric).

Copper:
see Mining

Corn:
see Agriculture and Fisheries

Cosmetics:
see Fashion and Dress

$124.3 million in 1971, accounted for more than half of CACM's deficit with the rest of the world. In this regard, various measures were taken to control imports and to seek new export markets, especially in the U.S.S.R. and Japan. As a result, the trade deficit was reduced to $99.8 million in 1972. In an attempt to improve the situation further, Congress in 1973 studied a proposal to grant fiscal incentives to exporters of nontraditional goods. This proposal was of particular importance in view of the drought that seriously affected basic grains and other agricultural products during the year.

In 1972 the gross domestic product rose in real terms by 5.3%, representing a slight improvement over the 1971 growth rate of 4.9%. It was hoped that the establishment of the Costa Rican Development Corporation and the implementation of the five-year development plan for 1974–78 would enable Costa Rica to enjoy an even higher growth rate in the near future. (ANNE PARSONS)

Cricket

All six test-playing countries took part in 1972–73 in the busiest season ever, England playing four series, Pakistan three, Australia, West Indies, and New Zealand two each, and India one. Some rubbers were of five matches and others of three.

India v. England. England, captained for the first time by a Welshman, A. R. Lewis, lost a five-match series 1–2 to India, led by A. L. Wadekar. For England, Lewis, A. W. Greig, and K. W. R. Fletcher made centuries, but all batsmen were bemused by the spin of B. S. Chandrasekhar, B. S. Bedi, and E. A. S. Prasanna, who shared 70 wickets. For India, F. M. Engineer and G. R. Viswanath made centuries.

England won the first test match at New Delhi by 6 wickets: India 173 (S. Abid Ali 58, G. G. Arnold 6 for 46) and 233 (E. D. Solkar 75, Engineer 63, D. L. Underwood 4 for 56); England 200 (Greig 69 not out, Chandrasekhar 8 for 80) and 208 for 4 (Lewis 70 not out, Greig 40 not out). India won the second test at Calcutta by 28 runs: India 210 (Engineer 75) and 155 (S. A. Durani 53, Greig 5 for 24); England 174 (Chandrasekhar 5 for 65) and 163 (Greig 67, Bedi 5 for 63, Chandrasekhar 4 for 42). India won the third test at Madras by 4 wickets: England 242 (Fletcher 97 not out, Chandrasekhar 6 for 90) and 159 (M. H. Denness 76, Bedi 4 for 38, Prasanna 4 for 16); India 316 (Mansur Ali Khan 73, P. I. Pocock 4 for 114) and 86 for 6 (Pocock 4 for 28). The fourth test at Kanpur was drawn: India 357 (Wadekar 90, S. M. Gavaskar 69, Mansur Ali Khan 54, C. M. Old 4 for 69) and 186 for 6 (Viswanath 75 not out); England 397 (Lewis 125, J. Birkenshaw 64, Fletcher 58, Chandrasekhar 4 for 86). England, needing to win the fifth test at Bombay to even the series, just failed, and the match was drawn: India 448 (Engineer 121, Viswanath 113, Wadekar 87, Durani 73) and 244 for 5 declared (Engineer 66, Gavaskar 67); England 480 (Fletcher 113, Greig 148, A. P. E. Knott 56, Chandrasekhar 5 for 135) and 67 for 2.

Barbara Bevege, New Zealand's opening bat, drives the ball to the boundary during a match against England at Chiswick, London, on June 16, 1973. It was the opening day of the first Women's World Cup cricket series.

KEYSTONE

Australia v. Pakistan. Meanwhile, Pakistan under Intikhab Alam was being beaten 0–3 by Australia, led by I. M. Chappell. Six Australians and three Pakistanis made centuries in the three-match rubber.

Australia won the first test at Adelaide by an innings and 114 runs: Pakistan 257 (Wasim Bari 72, Intikhab 64, D. K. Lillee 4 for 49) and 214 (Sadiq Mohammed 81, A. A. Mallett 8 for 59); Australia 585 (I. M. Chappell 196, R. W. Marsh 118, R. Edwards 89). Australia won the second test at Melbourne by 92 runs: Australia 441 for 5 declared (I. R. Redpath 135, G. S. Chappell 116 not out, Marsh 74) and 425 (J. Benaud 142, A. P. Sheahan 127, G. S. Chappell 62); Pakistan 574 for 8 declared (Majid Khan 158, Sadiq Mohammed 137, Intikhab 68, Mushtaq Mohammed 60, Zaheer Abbas 51, Saeed Ahmed 50) and 200 (Intikhab 48, Majid Khan 47). Australia won the third test at Sydney by 52 runs: Australia 334 (Redpath 79, Edwards 69, Sarfraz Nawaz 4 for 53) and 184 (Salim Altaf 4 for 60, Sarfraz 4 for 56); Pakistan 360 (Mushtaq 121, Asif Iqbal 65, Nasim ul Ghani 64, G. S. Chappell 5 for 61) and 106 (Zaheer 47, M. H. N. Walker 6 for 15).

New Zealand v. Pakistan. Pakistan found New Zealand under B. E. Congdon easier opponents. Intikhab won the toss in all three tests and Pakistan won the rubber 1–0. There was much magnificent batting by Sadiq, Majid, Mushtaq, and Asif, the last two having a partnership of 350 in the second test, which was ultimately won by the spin of Intikhab (11 for 130) and Mushtaq (7 for 64) on a dusty field. For New Zealand, B. R. Hastings and R. E. Redmond, in his first test, made centuries; wicket-keeper K. J. Wadsworth made five catches in the first innings of the first test and ten in the series, a New Zealand record; B. R. Taylor became the second New Zealand bowler to take 100 test wickets, and Hastings and R. O. Collinge set a new world record for the tenth wicket of 151.

The first draw was at Wellington: Pakistan 357 (Sadiq 166, Majid 79, Taylor 4 for 110) and 290 for 6 declared (Majid 79, Sadiq 68, Intikhab 53 not out); New Zealand 325 (M. G. Burgess 79, Hastings 72) and 78 for 3. The Pakistan victory, by an innings and 166 runs, was won at Dunedin: Pakistan 507 for 6 declared (Mushtaq 201, Asif 175, Sadiq 61); New Zealand 156 (Intikhab 7 for 52) and 185 (V. Pollard 61, Mushtaq 5 for 49). The other draw was at Auckland: Pakistan 402 (Majid 110, Mushtaq 61, Saleem 53 not out, Taylor 4 for 86) and 271 (Mushtaq 52); New Zealand 402 (Hastings 110, Redmond 107, Collinge 68 not out, G. M. Turner 58, Intikhab 6 for 127) and 92 for 3 (Redmond 56).

Pakistan v. England. Pakistan then went home and drew all three tests with England. Slow pitches assisted spin bowlers on both sides. Intikhab gave up the captaincy in favour of Majid, and the latter, Mushtaq, Asif, and Sadiq all made centuries. For England D. L. Amiss, who had failed against India, made centuries in the first two tests and 99 in the third.

The first test was at Lahore: England 355 (Amiss 112, Fletcher 55, Denness 50) and 306 for 7 declared (Lewis 74, Greig 72, Denness 68); Pakistan 422 (Sadiq 119, Asif 102, Mushtaq 66) and 124 for 3 (Talat Ali 57). The second test was played at Hyderabad: England 487 (Amiss 158, Fletcher 78, Knott 71) and 218 for 6 (Greig 64, Knott 63 not out); Pakistan 569 for 9 declared (Mushtaq 157, Intikhab 138, Asif 68, Pocock 5 for 169). The third draw was played at Karachi: Pakistan 445 for 6 declared (Majid 99, Mushtaq 99, Sadiq 89, Intikhab 61) and 199 (N. Gifford 5 for 55, Birkenshaw 5 for 57); England 386 (Amiss 99, Lewis 88, Fletcher 54) and 30 for 1.

West Indies v. Australia. Australia, after defeating Pakistan at home, went to the Caribbean and beat the West Indies 2–0 in a five-match rubber. For the first time in 18 years and 80 tests, G. S. Sobers was not on the West Indies team on account of injury, and R. B. Kanhai took over the captaincy. Seven centuries were made by Australian batsmen, and the fast-medium Walker on his first tour took 26 wickets. Lillee, the scourge of English and Pakistani batsmen, played in only the first test because of a back injury. Kanhai, C. H. Lloyd, and M. L. C. Foster made centuries for the West Indies, and the veteran off-spinner L. R. Gibbs took 26 wickets.

The first test, at Kingston, Jamaica, was drawn: Australia 428 for 7 declared (Marsh 97, K. D. Walters 72, Edwards 63) and 260 for 2 declared (K. R. Stackpole 142, Redpath 60); West Indies 428 (Foster 125, Kanhai 84, L. G. Rowe 76, Walker 6 for 114) and 67 for 3. The second test, at Bridgetown, Barbados, was also drawn: Australia 324 (G. S. Chappell 106, Marsh 78, I. M. Chappell 72) and 302 for 2 declared (I. M. Chappell 106 not out, Walters 102 not out, Stackpole 53); West Indies 391 (Kanhai 105, R. C. Fredericks 98, D. L. Murray 90, Walker 5 for 97) and 36 for no wicket. Australia won the third test, at Port of Spain, Trinidad, by 44 runs: Australia 332 (Walters 112, Redpath 66, G. S. Chappell 56) and 281 (I. M. Chappell 97, Gibbs 5 for 102); West Indies 280 (Kanhai 56, A. L. Kallicharran 53) and 289 (Kallicharran 91, Fredericks 76, O'Keeffe 4 for 57). Australia won the fourth test at Georgetown, Guyana, by ten wickets: West Indies 366 (Lloyd 178, Kanhai 57, Walters 5 for 66) and 109; Australia 341 (I. M. Chappell 109, Walters 81, G. S. Chappell 51) and 135 for no wicket (Stackpole 76 not out, Redpath 57 not out). With the rubber decided, the fifth test, at Port of Spain, was drawn: Australia 419 for 8 declared (Walters 70, Edwards 74, I. M. Chappell 56, Marsh 56) and 218 for 7 declared; West Indies 319 (Fredericks 73, Lloyd 59, Walker 5 for 75, T. J. Jenner 5 for 90) and 135 for 5.

England v. New Zealand. England, captained again by R. Illingworth at home, beat New Zealand 2–0, with one drawn, but the bare statistics hide a dramatic rubber in which New Zealand just failed to win the first two tests and lost the third. Centuries were scored for New Zealand by Congdon (2), Pollard (2), and Burgess, and for England by G. Boycott, Amiss, Fletcher, and Greig.

England won the first test at Trent Bridge, Nottingham, by 38 runs: England 250 (Boycott 51) and 325 for 8 declared (Greig 139, Amiss 138 not out); New Zealand 97 (Greig 4 for 33) and 440 (Congdon 176, Pollard 116, Arnold 5 for 131). New Zealand then played a drawn match at Lord's, London: England 253 (Greig 63, Boycott 61, G. R. J. Roope 56) and 463 for 9 (Fletcher 178, Boycott 92, Amiss 53, Roope 51); New Zealand 551 for 9 declared (Congdon 175, Burgess 105, Pollard 105 not out, Hastings 86, Old 5 for 113). England won the third test at Headingley, Leeds, by an innings and 1 run: New Zealand 276 (Burgess 87, Pollard 62) and 142 (Turner 81, Arnold 5 for 27); England 419 (Boycott 115, Fletcher 81, Illingworth 65, Collinge 5 for 74).

England v. West Indies. West Indies under Kanhai proved much tougher opposition, winning a short series in England 2–0. Glorious cricket, almost entirely by the West Indies, emphasized the current dearth of first-class cricketers in England, and at the end of the series Illingworth was deposed from the captaincy after a long and honourable reign in favour of Denness for a forthcoming tour of the West Indies. Five West Indians made centuries and only one Englishman, F. C. Hayes in his first test. The Essex all-rounder K. D. Boyce took 19 wickets for the West Indies, and Sobers, returning to test cricket, made 150 not out at Lord's, took 6 catches, and bowled beautifully in all 3 tests. Arnold (15 wickets) was easily England's best bowler.

West Indies won the first test at the Oval, London, by 158 runs: West Indies 415 (Lloyd 132, Kallicharran 80, Boyce 72, Arnold 5 for 113) and 255 (Kallicharran 80, Sobers 51). England 257 (Boycott 97, Boyce 5 for 70) and 255 (Hayes 106 not out, Boyce 6 for 77). The second test at Edgbaston, Birmingham, was drawn: West Indies 327 (Fredericks 150, B. D. Julien 54) and 302 (Lloyd 94, Sobers 74, Kanhai 54); England 305 (Boycott 56 not out, Amiss 56, Fletcher 52) and 182 for 2 (Amiss 86 not out). West Indies won an overwhelming victory in the third test at Lord's by an innings and 226 runs: West Indies 652 for 8 declared (Kanhai 157, Sobers 150 not out, Julien 121); England 233 (Fletcher 68) and 193 (Fletcher 86 not out).

County Cricket. For only the second time, Hampshire won the English county championship, beating Surrey by 31 points. Northamptonshire finished third and Kent fourth. Kent won two of the one-day competitions, beating Worcestershire by 39 runs in the final of the Benson and Hedges Cup and Yorkshire by 6 points in the John Player League. The Gillette Cup was won for the first time by Gloucestershire, which defeated Sussex in the final by 40 runs. Turner (Worcestershire and New Zealand) became the seventh batsman, and the first since 1938, to score 1,000 runs before the end of May, and he ended the season 400 runs ahead of all rivals. He was the only man to make more than 2,000 runs during the season. M. C. Cowdrey (Kent) became the 16th batsman in all cricket to score 100 first-class centuries. Two bowlers took more than 100 wickets, B. S. Bedi (Northamptonshire and India, 105) and P. Lee (Lancashire, 101).

National Cricket. In Australia, Western Australia won the Sheffield Shield; in South Africa, Transvaal won the Currie Cup; in New Zealand, Wellington won the Plunket Shield; in the West Indies, Guyana won

Cotton:
see Agriculture and Fisheries; Industrial Review

Council for Mutual Economic Assistance:
see Soviet Bloc Economies

Council of Europe:
see European Unity

Credit and Debt:
see Government Finance; Money and Banking; Payments and Reserves, International

the Shell Shield. In India, Bombay won the Ranji Trophy, West Zone won the Duleep Trophy, and State Bank of India took the Moin-ud-Dowlah Cup. In Pakistan, Karachi Blues won the B.C.C.P. Patron's Trophy (formerly the Ayub Trophy), and Pakistan Western Railways gained the Qaid-i-Azam Trophy.

(REX ALSTON)

Crime

Trends in Crime and Criminology. Few countries could report very optimistically about the state of crime in 1973. Acts of politically motivated violence exacted a rising toll of deaths and injuries. The Northern Ireland conflict spilled over into the United Kingdom with random bomb attacks on public buildings in London and other metropolitan areas. Before full-scale war between Arabs and Israelis erupted in October, the combatants' underground forces fought one another in Europe and North America. An Israeli diplomat was shot to death in Washington, D.C., while a number of Arab terrorist leaders were killed in a commando raid by Israelis in Beirut. Italian police thwarted an attempt by Arabs to use a ground-to-air missile to shoot down an Israeli civilian jet as it approached Rome airport. In the Sudan, Palestinian guerrillas killed two U.S. officials in an effort to secure the release of imprisoned colleagues. In Argentina a number of labour leaders supporting newly elected Pres. Juan Perón were assassinated.

Aerial hijackings seemed to be on the wane in 1973, with vastly improved security procedures at the world's major airports, estimated to cost the airlines at least $300 million a year, largely credited with the overall reduction. (*See* TRANSPORTATION.) Apart from the mounting price of these and other crime prevention measures, rampant inflation in many nations produced new patterns of criminality. As the cost of art objects escalated—the Metropolitan Museum of Art, New York City, reportedly paid $1 million for an ancient vase and bid $3.5 million for a statue—the prospects for quick cash killings by thieves became extremely good. The problems of preventing theft and destruction of important relics were exacerbated by these economic developments. Among others, the magnificent remains of the ancient Mayan civilization in Guatemala and Mexico were systematically decimated. Within Europe, Italy's recurrent problem of art theft and smuggling became more serious—in one 48-hour period police reported recovery of 68 Etruscan relics stolen by grave robbers, the seizure by customs officers of eight valuable paintings, including one attributed to Raphael, and the theft from an isolated village church of a painting by Tiepolo valued at more than $1 million.

Spiraling food prices, particularly for meat, resulted in a startling increase in cattle and sheep rustling. In Australia rustlers were said to be removing truckloads of cattle and sheep from ranches, while in the U.S. thieves used helicopters to round up cattle. Similarly, as fuel shortages became critical at the end of the year, petroleum products became prime targets for theft, and the appearance of black-market gasoline was reported. Official concern over the ease with which thieves disposed of ill-gotten goods was expressed at hearings of the U.S. Senate Small Business Committee in May, where witnesses stressed the vital role played by the criminal receiver, or fence.

The role of the fence also received attention from researchers presenting papers at the fifth National Conference on Teaching and Research in Criminology, held at Cambridge University in July. Another major topic at this conference was the recent and dramatic increase in reported incidents of forcible rape, particularly in the U.S., where during the 1960–72 period the rate had more than doubled from 9.5 per 100,000 population to 22.3 per 100,000 (43 per 100,000 females), outstripping all other categories of violent crime.

The latest Federal Bureau of Investigation figures indicated that in the U.S. violent crimes as a group increased only 1% in calendar year 1972 over 1971. Forcible rape was up 11%, aggravated assault up 7%, and homicide up 4%, while the crime of robbery declined 3%. Combining all major offense categories, crime rates in the U.S. in 1972 showed a 2% decrease, the first such reduction for many years. However, victimization surveys indicated that actual crime rates were considerably higher than reported rates.

Victims of crime were the major subject of consideration at the first International Symposium on

LARRY MORRIS—
THE NEW YORK TIMES

Patrolman Richard Buggy, impersonating an easy "mark," shuffles along near Columbia University in New York City. When muggers attack, a backup team sweeps in to make the arrests.

Victimology, held in Jerusalem in September under the joint sponsorship of the International Society of Criminology, Israeli government authorities, and several Israeli universities. Among resolutions adopted by the conference was one recommending that all nations should, as a matter of urgency, give consideration to the establishment of state systems of compensation for victims of crime. Some success was reported in 1973 with new methods of preventing the experience of becoming a crime victim.

Automobile antitheft devices, such as steering column locks, were said to have made a substantial impact on the level of car thefts, which were reported to have declined in the U.S. for the first time in 60 years, despite a record jump in the total number of car registrations. Juveniles, however, continued to be responsible for a disproportionate amount of crime, and observers noted that very young children were increasingly becoming involved in criminal activities. Police in Melbourne, Austr., for example, charged a nine-year-old boy with stealing an automobile. A nine-year-old girl became the youngest person ever to be tried in a Scottish criminal court (and spared on appeal), for stabbing and wounding a playmate with a knife. The 13-year-old boy positively identified as the robber of a Buffalo, N.Y., bank in February 1973 was described by police as the youngest person ever accused of armed bank robbery in the U.S.

Women were involved in a larger proportion of crimes in 1973 than in previous years. Five-year arrest trends (1967–72) in the U.S., for example, revealed that arrests of women under the age of 18 increased 62% while arrests of men under 18 rose 21%. While most arrests of women in the U.S. and other countries were for offenses of theft, such as shoplifting, greater female participation in crimes of violence (many of them associated with narcotics use) was also apparent.

Homicides, justified and unjustified, resulting from the use of firearms continued to rise at an alarming rate in many parts of the world. In the U.S. in 1972 two-thirds of all homicides involved firearms, mostly cheap handguns called "Saturday night specials," which remained widely available despite persistent attempts to control their production and sale.

The U.S. courts came under increasing attack for what was termed laxity of judicial administration. In a major review, a National Advisory Commission on Criminal Justice Standards and Goals suggested sweeping reforms of the entire U.S. system of criminal justice. Among its many recommendations were the establishment of a maximum period from arrest to trial of 60 days in felony cases and 30 days in misdemeanours and adoption of policies limiting the number of jurors to fewer than 12 but more than 6 in all but the most serious criminal cases. The commission's recommendations provoked immediate controversy, which seemed likely to continue as the extensive reports on police, community crime prevention, courts, corrections, and the criminal justice system produced by five task forces of the commission became widely available. The commission concluded that the U.S. could and should reduce "high fear" crimes—murder, rape, aggravated assault, robbery, and burglary—committed by strangers, by 50% in ten years.

Attempts in other countries to combat high fear crimes often centred around movements to impose very severe penalties, including capital punishment, on offenders. Such severity was reported to have had little effect in deterring blood feuds in Kosovo Province, Yugos. The usual pattern for these feuds was for the killer, often designated by tribal leaders, to encounter his victim in a public place and, after firing a fusillade, to turn himself over to the police to accept punishment, to run away being regarded as dishonourable.

Another form of honour killing was said to be under attack in Beirut, Lebanon, where the penal code incorporated a custom permitting a man to slay a female member of his family who "dishonoured" the family through sexual misconduct. A man who choked his 15-year-old daughter to death because she "flirted with boys" was released from prison on a presidential pardon after serving nine months of a seven-year sentence.

The capital punishment issue continued to stir emotions and discussion during 1973. The guillotining in late 1972 of two men in France added fuel to the debate throughout Europe. The two executions were the first to take place in France since Pres. Georges Pompidou came to office in June 1969. In not commuting the men's sentences, Pompidou was believed to have been influenced by strong sympathy for their victims' families, pressure for the death penalty from corrections officers, and the results of opinion polls showing well over half of the French population to be in favour of capital punishment. Similar and rising levels of public support for the death penalty were reported elsewhere. In the U.S. more than 20 states introduced or passed legislation reimposing the death penalty for a variety of crimes of violence involving aggravating circumstances, such as the killing of a police officer or elected official. The constitutionality of this legislation remained to be tested before the U.S. Supreme Court.

(DUNCAN CHAPPELL)

Notable Crimes and Criminal Trials. By late 1973 seven persons had received prison sentences for their involvement in the break-in, during the 1972 U.S. presidential campaign, at the Democratic Party offices in the Watergate buildings in Washington, D.C.; at least five persons who had been connected with the White House or the Nixon reelection effort had pleaded guilty to or were under indictment for a variety of charges related to the break-in or to attempts to hide it; and the acting director of the FBI had had to ask that his nomination for the permanent post be withdrawn and later to resign altogether. The case against two men charged with revealing secret Pentagon documents in 1971 had been dropped and four persons, including a former White House chief adviser, were under indictment for, or had pleaded guilty to, criminal activities that had forced the mistrial. Two former Cabinet members had been indicted along with others in a New Jersey case that was alleged to involve secret contributions made to the Nixon campaign in exchange for a favourable handling of a securities fraud case, and several major U.S. corporations faced court dates for having made illegal political contributions. And, as if this were not enough, a federal investigation into corruption in Maryland politics had led the vice-president of the United States to resign and plead no contest to a charge of income tax evasion. (*See* UNITED STATES: *Special Report.*)

At the state level, by Jan. 9, 1973, when a federal grand jury in Newark, N.J., charged a former state treasurer, John A. Kervick, with having extorted money from a consulting engineering concern, 59 other past and present New Jersey officials had been convicted or were awaiting trial on charges brought since September 1969 by the U.S. attorney's office in Newark. On May 21, 1973, six former high officials of

Atlantic City, N.J., were sentenced to prison terms for conspiracy to extort money from contractors. Two of those sentenced were former mayors William T. Somers and Richard Jackson. A former U.S. congressman from New Jersey, Cornelius E. Gallagher, was fined and sentenced to prison in Newark on June 15 for income tax evasion.

In Chicago on February 19, U.S. court of appeals judge and former Illinois governor Otto Kerner was convicted on a variety of charges stemming from a race track stock deal in which Kerner, while governor, had netted $140,000. Convicted with Kerner was Theodore Isaacs, the state revenue director when Kerner was governor. Also in Chicago, on March 7, Cook County Clerk Edward J. Barrett, a powerful figure in Illinois Democratic politics for over 40 years, was found guilty on 16 charges in connection with irregularities in the purchasing and insuring of voting machines.

As if to assure Europeans that the United States was not unique in suffering corruption in high places, a series of bourgeois scandals interspersed the more respectable crimes of murder, rape, robbery, and politically motivated violence that had become the staple reading of the urban industrial consumer in 1973. In West Germany *Quick* magazine pointed the finger at Julius Steiner (*see* BIOGRAPHY), a former Bundestag deputy, for allegedly accepting money for abstaining in a vote of no confidence in the Willy Brandt government in 1972. Further allegations involved other deputies, and in June the government decided to appoint a committee of inquiry.

Those insular British readers who viewed continental Europeans with mistrust had their suspicions seemingly confirmed when a Lille, France, court sentenced a West German, two Frenchmen, and a Belgian to a total of nine years in prison for fraudulently labeling maize (corn) shipped to West Germany as destined for Britain and Denmark (before those countries had joined the EEC) in order to obtain special EEC subsidies on cattle feed exported to non-EEC countries. In October a number of Bordeaux wine shippers, including members of four leading firms, were arrested and charged with falsifying their wares by blending cheap wines from other districts with genuine (*appellation contrôlée*) wines of Bordeaux.

In Italy in early April, 27 persons were being held without bond in Rome and Milan on charges of unlawful wiretapping. Newspapers reported that various private and governmental spy rings had been "bugging" telephones for various political and economic interests and for foreign governments. A Roman magistrate, Luciano Infelisi, was investigating charges that police and the fiscal crime agency, Guardia di Finanza, had used illegal wiretaps. This last charge was denied in the Chamber of Deputies by Justice Minister Guido Gonella, who conceded that the police had purchased a number of electronic surveillance devices. The bugging controversy took on further dimensions in November when a device was found in the office of the magistrate heading a judicial inquiry into charges that Montecatini Edison, Italy's largest firm, had, prior to 1970, maintained a fund to subsidize politicians and other influential persons.

But if the British were beginning to feel self-satisfied with respect to their probity and sobriety, they were to be slightly shaken by revelations involving ministers and members of the BBC.

In May two men tried to sell compromising photographs of Lord Lambton, undersecretary of state for the Royal Air Force, to the newspaper *News of the World*. On May 22, after police had interviewed Lord Lambton and asked whether he had been subject to blackmail by the husband of a prostitute, who had taken photographs of them together, Lambton resigned. On May 24 it was announced that Earl Jellicoe, lord privy seal and leader of the House of Lords, had also resigned over similar connections with call girls. Police and security services were concerned that no material on persons in high office should fall into the hands of any hostile foreign power, making such persons vulnerable to blackmail. Soon after, Norma Levy, a woman involved with Lord Lambton, appeared in court on a charge under the Sexual Offences Act, 1956, and was granted bail of £10,000. In Spain a warrant was issued for the arrest of her husband, Colin Levy, whom Spanish police charged with attempting to murder his wife.

In July BBC disc jockeys, producers of television commercials, and others were involved in another scandal involving prostitution, as well as bribery and attempted murder. Janie Jones, a singer, was accused of attempting to interfere with witnesses, controlling prostitutes, and offering them to people in the entertainment industry as an inducement to play records on radio and television. Several clients were blackmailed. Miss Jones was also accused of trying to drug her former husband.

On June 23 John Poulson, former head of a bankrupt firm of architects, and William G. Pottinger, secretary of the Department of Agriculture and Fisheries for Scotland, were charged with conspiring to obtain government contracts by corrupt means. The police investigation into 20 tons of Poulson's files was expected to last several years and to net a number of other corrupt officials and businessmen. In 1972 the then home secretary, Reginald Maudling, had resigned because of a previous connection with Poulson's firm.

Of the numerous mass murder cases that received headlines in 1973 perhaps the most bizarre was the one that came to light in Houston, Tex., following the slaying on August 8 of electrician Dean Allen Corll. A 17-year-old boy, Elmer Wayne Henley, Jr., reportedly told police he shot Corll after a quarrel during a paint sniffing and sex party, and then he and David Owen Brooks, 18, related a weird tale of receiving from $5 to $200 for recruiting boys for Corll who, over a three-year period, had tortured them, forced them into homosexual acts, and murdered them. By August 14 officials had uncovered 27 bodies buried in South Texas locations, most of which were of young boys with no police records.

In Washington, D.C., on the afternoon of Jan. 18, 1973, eight men invaded a house donated to the Hanafi Muslims by professional basketball player Kareem Abdul-Jabbar. Four of the victims were shot to death and three children were drowned in a bathtub. Two surviving women were hospitalized for gunshot wounds. Hamaas Abdul Khaalis, the Hanafi leader, arrived at the house during the murders. He foiled attempts on his life and the assassins fled.

In California, on November 8, Sacramento police arrested Douglas Gretzler, 22, of New York City and Willie L. Steelman, 28, of Lodi, Calif., one day following the execution-style shooting deaths of two couples, their four children, and a friend in Victor, Calif. In the next few days police linked the two men with at least 18 murders in California and Arizona, including the nine in Victor, in the sixth mass murder case in California in four years.

Several California murder cases ended in convictions in 1973. On January 18 a Sutter County jury convicted labour contractor Juan V. Corona of murdering 25 itinerant farm workers whose mutilated bodies had been found buried in the peach orchards of Yuba City in the spring of 1971. In Santa Cruz in August Herbert W. Mullin, 26, was convicted of having killed ten persons, and on November 8 Edmund Emil Kemper III, 24, was found guilty of murdering his mother, her best friend, and six student hitchhikers, several of whom had been dismembered. The two Santa Cruz cases accounted for 18 or 19 murders that had occurred in the scenic oceanside area in 16 months. Both men had had long histories of confinement in mental hospitals. On July 2 Gourgen M. Yanikian, an Armenian engineer who had emigrated to the U.S. in 1946 and become well known in the Santa Barbara area, was convicted of murder in the shooting deaths of the Turkish consul general and vice-consul general to Los Angeles. Yanikian's attorney contended that his client suffered from "diminished mental capacity" from brooding over the massacres of 26 members of his family in Turkey and the U.S.S.R. in 1915 and thereafter.

On September 6 a former United Mine Workers union president, W. A. Boyle, who already faced a five-year prison term for misusing union funds, was arrested in Washington, D.C., and charged with murder in the December 1969 killings in Clarksville, Pa., of an insurgent union official, Joseph A. Yablonski, his wife and daughter. The arrest of Boyle, and of William J. Turnblazer, a UMW district president who was charged the same day with complicity in the case, brought to nine the number of persons linked with the murder, which a Pennsylvania warrant charged Boyle had been planning as early as June 1969, after Yablonski announced his plans to oust Boyle as union president. Boyle was hospitalized on September 24 after taking an overdose of barbiturates, but was later deemed mentally competent to stand trial.

On the morning of Sunday, January 7, Mark Essex, a 23-year-old navy veteran being trailed by police, slipped into a downtown New Orleans hotel and began firing a rifle. In the next 12 hours three policemen, two hotel guests, and a hotel employee were killed and ten policemen and two firemen wounded while the sniper held them at bay from the hotel roof. Late in the evening Essex was killed by police fire from a helicopter. Convinced that there had been more than one sniper, police continued their siege of the building for most of the next day. The rifle found on the hotel roof had been used to kill a New Orleans police cadet and wound a patrolman on New Year's Eve.

A case with a touch of mystery struck the headlines in March when a 29-year-old British schoolteacher and poet, Jeremy Cartland, and his father, John Basil Cartland, were the victims of a night attack as they slept in their camper by the roadside in southern France. The father was stabbed and battered to death with an ax; the son awoke to see a figure trying to open their car trunk and was then knocked unconscious from behind; the camper was set on fire. After protracted interrogation by the French police, Jeremy Cartland returned to England. Letters received at the BBC's Paris office from "A Friend of Britain" suggested that the elder Cartland's death was related to his having worked for British Intelligence during World War II. The French police shifted their search for clues to the U.K. but, failing to produce anything, on May 17 charged Jeremy Cartland with his father's murder. He strongly denied the charge. The French Ministry of Justice later dropped extradition proceedings and handed over the evidence to Britain's director of public prosecutions.

WIDE WORLD

Greek police check the bloody debris at Athens International Airport transit lounge after Arab terrorists attacked with hand grenades and submachine guns on Aug. 5, 1973.

In one of France's most controversial murder cases in recent years, Jean-Pierre Flahaud, 17, was formally charged on April 19 with the slaying in April 1972 of Brigitte Dewevre, whose body was discovered in a vacant lot in Bruay near the villa of Pierre Leroy, a notary and the city's richest citizen. Leroy and his mistress were arrested and released three months later, after a court ruled that the investigating magistrate, Henri Pascal, had been biased when he ordered the two held in preventive detention. Pascal was dismissed from the case and Flahaud led a march in protest. Subsequently, Flahaud was sent to a reformatory for stealing a car and while there, according to police, confessed to the murder.

George Henry Ince was tried in May, accused of the killing of housewife Mrs. Muriel Patience. Ince and an accomplice were alleged to have entered the Patiences' Essex home in November 1972 intending to rob the family's adjoining restaurant. Mrs. Patience and her daughter Beverley returned home and discovered the intruders; Patience soon joined them, and all three were held at gunpoint while Ince allegedly demanded the safe key, then shot Mrs. Patience through the head, bound her husband and daughter, whom he shot through the back, and attempted to shoot Patience through the head, actually chipping out a piece of his ear instead. On November 27 Beverley Patience picked Ince out of a lineup while Patience picked out another man. In the trial the jury failed to agree on a majority verdict and a new trial was ordered. In the second trial the wife of a notorious criminal, Charles Kray, serving a ten-year jail sentence, told the court that Ince had been with her on the night of the murder and Ince was found not guilty of any charge. In July detectives announced the discovery of the murder weapon in a mattress found in the Lake District, and articles from the Patience home buried in a field. In August a John Brook and Nicolas De'Clare Johnson were accused of Mrs. Patience's murder.

Horst Mahler, 37, arrested in 1971 in connection with activities of the West German Baader-Meinhof urban guerrilla group, was sentenced to 12 years in prison in February. In July a Karlsruhe court sentenced Carmen Roll, 24, to four years in prison for membership in the same group. At London's Central Criminal Court in January sentences totaling 58 years were passed on members of the Tibbs family and its associates for attempted murder, wounding, blackmail, and conspiracy to pervert the course of justice. Unfortunately the gang, which had used all manner of violence to impose its will on an area of East London, had so many enemies in Britain's prisons that housing it would not be easy.

The largest mass murder trial in Japanese history was held up five times when five members of the Japanese Red Army guerrilla group resisted all attempts to get them into court from their cells. The trial involved 17 deaths, 14 of which were of Red Army troops tortured and executed by colleagues in an internal purge. In January the chief spokesman of the group, Tsuneo Mori, committed suicide in his cell, apparently out of remorse at having surrendered. Hijackings, bomb attacks, and bank robberies were among the group's main activities.

California corrections officials acknowledged in May that a vicious struggle for power waged between two rival Mexican-American gangs was responsible for frequent killings, knifings, and terrorism throughout the state's 12 prisons and 16 work camps. One organization, El Mexicano Encarcelado (The Imprisoned Mexican), nicknamed the Mexican Mafia, had turned to the use of hired killers in fighting off the challenge of the newer, smaller, but equally vicious New Family. At stake in the struggle was the long-time domination of the Mexican Mafia in most of the prison rackets, including the smuggling and sale of narcotics, gambling, three-for-one loan sharking, the auctioning off of youthful new arrivals to homosexuals, and the corruption of "boss cons" and guards to obtain choice job assignments and other favours. The New Family was also challenging the Mexican Mafia's growing power outside prison in the crowded areas where members released from prison had moved to take over the narcotics trade and a variety of protection rackets.

BARTON SILVERMAN—THE NEW YORK TIMES

Hostages are helped down from a rooftop after their daring escape from gunmen who were attempting to rob an adjoining sporting goods store in Brooklyn, N.Y. The gunmen later surrendered, some 47 hours after entering the store on Jan. 19, 1973.

In June an unusually violent gang war was reported under way in San Francisco's famed Chinatown. In a little more than two years, 15 youths had been killed, two of them gunned down on the streets within the space of a few days in June. Police officials attributed the killings to young immigrants from Hong Kong, who reputedly formed the nucleus of gangs that competed for control of Chinatown rackets. Chinatown insiders pointed to overcrowded slum conditions in the area, which housed most of San Francisco's 65,000 Chinese residents. City officials were also disturbed because the area was a prime tourist attraction.

In Stockholm, Sweden, on August 23, Jan-Erik Olsson, 32, an escaped prisoner armed with a submachine gun, seized four bank employees, three women and a man, and held them hostage in a vault of the main office of the Kreditbanken when police foiled his attempt to rob the bank. During negotiations that followed, the police agreed to demands to free Clark Olofsson, 26, who was serving a life sentence for murder, and to allow him to join Olsson in the bank and to pay a ransom of $650,000. During the next four days, as millions of Swedes watched on national television, policemen got into the bank and slammed the vault door shut, locking the six inside, and offered to provide a getaway car if the hostages were released. Olsson insisted upon keeping at least two of the hostages. When the police announced a plan to pour sleeping gas into the vault, Olsson told the officers he had the hostages tied in such a way that they would strangle themselves if affected by gas. Finally, on August 28, policemen stormed the vault behind clouds of tear gas and apprehended the two gunmen.

Four men were jailed in January for London's biggest bank theft ever, involving £3 million in cash and jewelry taken from Lloyd's Bank in Baker Street in September 1971. Five other men were still being sought. Police complained that some of the gang's take was probably resting safely in another bank deposit. The tunnel into the Lloyd's Bank had taken two weeks to dig and was described as a "magnificent piece of engineering."

An oak coffin containing the body of Marshal Henri-Philippe Pétain, the man who organized the French defense of Verdun in World War I, was stolen in February from a tomb on the Ile d'Yeu. A blue pickup truck containing the coffin was located several days later in Paris. (VIRGIL W. PETERSON; X.)

Law Enforcement. Following investment of millions of dollars on research and development, particularly in the U.S., law enforcement officers began to benefit substantially from the computer age. In the U.K. police phased in a new national computer; in Australia police forces began integrating records for transfer to a unified computer system; in the U.S. at the FBI, whose new permanent director, Clarence Kelley (*see* BIOGRAPHY), was sworn in July 9, a computerized criminal history file began providing a documented record of an individual's contacts with the criminal justice system based on arrests for serious or significant crimes. This new file supplemented the National Crime Information Center (NCIC), a computerized index of serialized stolen property and wanted persons serving all 50 states, the District of

Columbia, and the Commonwealth of Puerto Rico.

The FBI's computerization of files was not without its critics. Massachusetts, for instance, refused to provide criminal history files until adequate safeguards were developed to prevent their unlawful use. Of particular concern to civil libertarians in all countries was the establishment of checking procedures to ensure that data placed in computers were accurate. Suggestions included the right of individuals with files to examine their contents for reliability. Further questions about whether personal freedoms were being abridged were raised noisily in the U.S. after federal drug agents staged several illegal no-knock raids in Illinois (*see* DRUGS AND NARCOTICS) and when the Central Intelligence Agency acknowledged that it had trained men from domestic police forces in such matters as the handling of explosives, the organization of intelligence files, and the detection of wiretaps, all areas that the CIA claimed did not violate the law that barred the CIA from participation in domestic law enforcement activities.

Identification and subsequent successful prosecution of drinking drivers remained a problem for the police forces of many nations. Roadside breath testing of motorists by British police, introduced into English life by the Road Safety Act, 1967, came under close research scrutiny. While the number of automobile casualties had, at first, decreased, the act's deterrent power quickly declined because of an unexpectedly small number of arrests. Modifications of the 1967 act were under review.

Relieving police of many of the more mundane chores of traffic enforcement formed the focus of several projects in the U.S. An experimental program diverting adjudication of less serious traffic violations from criminal courts to administrative tribunals began in Seattle, Wash. Earlier tests in New York City suggested these hearings saved substantial amounts of the time spent by police in court. Another study revealed that in New York City an arresting officer required 9 hr. 40 min. to process a criminal case that took his counterpart in Oakland, Calif., only 45 min.; many of the administrative steps after actual arrest in Oakland were performed by civilian employees, and in Oakland neither the victim nor the officer had to be present at arraignment.

The role of women in policing attracted renewed attention in the U.S. when the results of an ongoing study of women assuming police patrol duties in Washington, D.C., suggested no substantial diminution of patrol effectiveness and general public and male police acceptance of this expanded female police role. In fact, it was a Louisville, Ky., policewoman, Martha Green, who was credited with subduing the gunman in January in the last airplane hijacking attempt reported in the U.S. in 1973. European police forces, in contrast, frequently used women in investigative work. In 1970 North Rhineland-Westphalia, the largest of West Germany's ten Länder (states), began using policewomen trained in judo, karate, and pistol shooting in general detective work. In Israel women had long been used in both crime detection and patrol work, and 90% of the traffic police were women. These Israeli traffic police were generally regarded as the best in the world and had assisted with the training programs in the U.K., Japan, France, and many less developed countries. In many European countries policewomen were also used extensively in administrative jobs. In contrast, the FBI in 1973 had 24 women among its 8,500 agents.

The use of violence by and against police remained a sensitive issue in many countries, and particularly in the U.K., where the usually unarmed London police were involved in some rare gunplay. Two officers on a special guarding assignment that permitted them to be armed shot and killed two masked Asian youths who invaded and terrorized the Indian high commissioner's office in central London with imitation guns. These killings and later bombing attacks by Irish terrorists sparked intense debate both in and outside Parliament concerning the arming of police. U.S. experience with massive police weaponry no doubt contributed to continued opposition to the idea; in New York City alone in 1971 police shot 314 suspects, while in more than three years British officers wounded 3 and killed 3 suspects.

UPI COMPIX

W. A. ("Tony") Boyle, former United Mine Workers president, was arrested on Sept. 6, 1973, and charged with ordering the murder of union leader Joseph A. Yablonski and his wife and daughter. A few weeks later Boyle attempted suicide.

In South Africa the killing by police of 11 blacks and the wounding of 16 more during disturbances at the Western Deep Levels gold mine at Carltonville, Transvaal, produced national and international criticism. The shooting was the most extensive act of police violence in South Africa since the Sharpeville incident more than a decade earlier. An inquest in October found that the police had acted under provocation.

The killing and wounding of police officers by criminals was an equally contentious topic. In the U.S. 112 local, county, and state law enforcement officers were killed during 1972, 14 fewer than in the previous year. A new and disturbing trend, however, was the increasing number of officers slain from ambush. The FBI *Uniform Crime Reports* revealed that ambush attacks on officers in the U.S. resulted in an estimated 600 assaults in 1972 in which 14 officers were killed. In Oakland, Calif., for example, two officers in a police helicopter were killed when their craft crashed after being fired on by unknown gunmen. The number of assaults on police was estimated to be 61,800, or 15 per 100 officers. The British Police Association began publishing colour photographs of the results of serious assaults on officers, stimulating substantial public backing for police.

This was in considerable contrast to police problems in New York 17 years before, when that city's longest and costliest police manhunt was seeking the "Mad Bomber." No one was killed in at least 37 explosions set by George Metesky as he carried out a 16-year vendetta against the Consolidated Edison Co., his former employer. Metesky, who was finally arrested in 1957, was released from prison in December 1973.

Research indicated that police intervention in domestic disputes frequently resulted in an explosive situation producing the likelihood of injury to police and citizens. The use of specially trained and staffed family crisis intervention units in many U.S. and European police forces seemed to be reducing this injury rate substantially. So, too, did intensive training of police officers in the proper handling of tense and difficult crowd control problems.

Minority representation in police departments remained a delicate subject in U.S. cities. A federal judge directed that half the police vacancies opening up in Bridgeport, Conn., be filled with blacks and Puerto Ricans until those minorities made up 15% of the 485-member force, and a federal court of appeals in Philadelphia upheld a court order requiring the police department to hire one black officer for every two white ones. In August the U.S. Justice Department filed lawsuits in the U.S. district courts of Chicago and Buffalo, N.Y., that charged the police departments of those cities with discrimination against blacks, Spanish-surnamed persons, and women in their employment practices. The two suits were the first brought to enforce the employment discrimination section of the Civil Rights Act of 1964 and the equal employment opportunity regulations of the department's Law Enforcement Assistance Administration.

Scandal struck several major police departments in 1973. On January 31 New York City Police Commissioner Patrick V. Murphy disclosed that 398 lb. of heroin and cocaine (about one-fifth of all the narcotics seized by the New York City police between January 1961 and December 1972) had been stolen from the department. The New York State Commission of Investigation held public hearings in September on alleged widespread corruption in the Albany Police Department, including organized burglaries, larcenies, and thefts of public funds.

In Chicago numerous police officers, including Capt. Clarence E. Braasch, one of the department's top-ranking officers, were convicted for extorting money from tavern owners. The number of citizens' complaints against members of the Philadelphia Police Department dropped slightly in 1972, but the number of officers who resigned, were reprimanded, or suspended rose.

Louisiana Attorney General William Guste made public a report on July 10, 1973, that asserted that the police who were called to the Southern University campus at Baton Rouge on Nov. 16, 1972, were overarmed and underdisciplined. Two black students had been killed by a blast of buckshot as they fled police tear gas during a campus demonstration. Information obtained in a reopening of Justice Department investigations into the 1970 shootings at Kent (O.) State University, in which four students were killed, was presented to a federal grand jury in December.

(DUNCAN CHAPPELL; VIRGIL W. PETERSON)

International Criminal Police Organization. Interpol, with an affiliate membership of 117 countries, held its 42nd General Assembly in Vienna, Oct. 2–9, 1973, marking the 50th anniversary of its inception in that city. A major topic of concern was the future relationship of police forces of the EEC countries. Although one school of thought favoured direct links between forces, even to the extent of creating a European equivalent of the FBI, the general secretary, Jean Nepoté, strongly disputed this view. The real need, as he saw it, was for an expansion of Interpol and a radical speedup in information dispersal through the use of computers. This was not yet possible on the current budget of SFr. 4.3 million. The question of political crime remained a contentious one, as Interpol's constituent members spent more and more of their resources combating it.

Rubble strewn about at King's Cross Station, London, after an IRA terrorist bomb exploded there on Sept. 10, 1973.

EPOQUE/PICTORIAL PARADE

Other topics discussed at the assembly included international illicit drug traffic in 1972, international currency counterfeiting in 1972, the connections between currency counterfeiting and other types of crime, theft of cultural property and art works, police foot patrols in urban areas, and the powers and duties of the police relating to the search of persons and premises and the seizure of property. To mark the 50th anniversary, the general secretariat produced a commemorative brochure describing Interpol's activities from 1923 to 1973.

In 1972 a total of 178,431 messages (including 720 general broadcasts and 2,290 zone broadcasts) were carried over the Interpol radio network, an increase of 11% over 1971. Intense activity by the national central bureaus (NCBs) during the year, involving the exchange of 126,119 items of information, led to 1,597 arrests. Between June 1972 and June 1973 the general secretariat examined 22,733 cases resulting in 1,177 arrests; 10,695 items of information were supplied to NCBs, and 571 persons were the subject of international notices.

In accordance with long-standing tradition, Interpol followed the work of the UN Commission on Narcotic Drugs in Geneva. It also took part in EEC efforts to harmonize laws on illicit drug traffic, was represented at conferences in Canada, Mexico, and Italy on the prevention of unlawful interference with international civil aviation and also at the meetings of the Council of Europe's committee on crime problems, at the Arab League conference on juvenile delinquency, and at the International Criminology Conference.

See also Law; Museums and Galleries; Prisons and Penology; Race Relations; United Kingdom.

ENCYCLOPÆDIA BRITANNICA FILMS. *Our Community Services* (1969).

Cuba

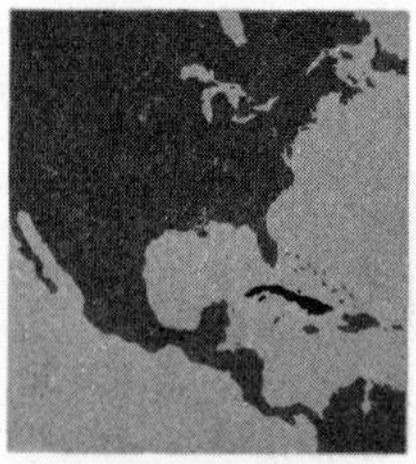

The socialist republic of Cuba occupies the largest island in the Greater Antilles of the West Indies. Area: 42,827 sq.mi. (110,922 sq.km.), including several thousand small islands and cays. Pop. (1972 est.): 8,750,000, including (1953) white 72.8%; mestizo 14.5%; Negro 12.4%. Cap. and largest city: Havana (pop., 1970, 942,348). Language: Spanish. Religion: predominantly Roman Catholic. President in 1973, Osvaldo Dorticós Torrado; prime minister, Fidel Castro.

During 1973 Prime Minister Castro's position as Cuba's national leader remained unshaken. There were signs, however, that the Central Committee of the Cuban Communist Party was gaining greater influence over policymaking, and Castro acknowledged this in a speech on July 26 celebrating the 20th anniversary of the attack on the Moncada barracks that began his rise to power. The most important political event of the year was the introduction in September of a new judicial system that had been under study since 1971. The principal body of the new system was the Tribunal Supremo Popular, the four chambers of which were to deal with criminal offenses, civil and administrative offenses, crimes against state security, and military offenses. Below these were the Tribunales Provinciales Populares, dealing with cases that warranted sentences of up to six years' imprisonment.

Relations with the Soviet Union and other Eastern European states continued to grow closer. Early in January details were announced of an agreement signed in Moscow late in 1972 that made available massive Soviet economic and financial aid to Cuba. It provided for the refinancing of the Cuban debt to the Soviet Union, which was estimated to be over $4 billion, excluding military aid; no repayments were required until 1986, and they were then to be spread over 25 years. The U.S.S.R. also agreed to trade a specified amount of goods with Cuba during 1973–75 and to make available credit for any imbalance incurred by Cuba during this period. The agreement also provided for a substantial increase in prices paid for purchases from Cuba of nickel and sugar, and a loan of about $330 million, to be repaid as of 1976 at a low rate of interest, to help finance the development of the production of sugar, other agricultural products, and nickel, and also transport, telecommunications, electric power, and oil refining.

In April important agreements were signed with Poland and Czechoslovakia: Poland was to export to Cuba increased quantities of capital goods and to furnish technical assistance for the shipbuilding industry and the modernization of sugar mills; Czechoslovakia was to supply transport equipment in return for Cuban exports of primary products. Meanwhile, in September Castro attended the summit meeting of nonaligned nations in Algiers—where he was outspoken in his praise of the Soviet Union—and later in the month visited North Vietnam. Earlier in the year, an agreement was signed with China providing for trade during 1973.

Cuba had some success in strengthening its ties with other Latin-American countries. Diplomatic links were restored with Argentina on May 28, and in August the two countries signed an agreement providing for the purchase of Argentine goods valued at $200 million over an eight-year period. Late in 1972 Guyana, Barbados, Jamaica, and Trinidad and Tobago all established diplomatic relations with Cuba. In July an agreement was signed for the purchase from Peru of fishing vessels to a value of $20 million–$30 million. On the other hand, Cuba lost its closest friend in the region when the government of Pres. Salvador Allende Gossens in Chile was overthrown in September.

Cuba maintained efforts to improve economic relations with Western European countries and Japan. Sweden agreed to provide aid amounting to $15 million to finance educational projects between 1973 and 1975. A French firm signed a contract to supply 100 tractors to agricultural cooperatives. On March 1 the Banco Nacional de Cuba established a wholly owned subsidiary in London.

Relations with the U.S., which had continued to apply the trade embargo in force since the early 1960s, remained strained and were exacerbated by the Chilean coup, U.S. complicity in which was alleged by Cuba. Nevertheless, following the spectacular hijacking of a Southern Airways jetliner with 31 passengers and crew aboard to Havana in November 1972, the Cuban government offered to negotiate an antihijacking agreement with the United States. A nonretroactive five-year agreement was signed in February 1973 under which both countries undertook to prosecute air and sea pirates where they landed for theft, illegal entry, or other crimes, rather than to send them home again; and the hijacked plane or ship, passengers, and crew were to be returned promptly, as well as any funds extorted.

There were indications of improvement in the economy. The formulation of economic policy had become more pragmatic, largely as a result of Soviet pressure; measures adopted since 1970 to improve productivity were clearly taking effect. The 1972–73 sugar crop amounted to 5.5 million tons, compared with 4.2 million tons in 1971–72, and the 1973–74 harvest was estimated at about 6 million tons; a record area was planted and steps were taken to increase mechanization. The minister of basic industries, Joel Domenech, announced in January that production by heavy industries was expected to reach a value of about $450 million in 1973, compared with $380 million in 1972; installed capacity was to be increased by 19%. Domenech also forecast that output by light industries would be valued at $600 million, 8.5% more than in 1972. The 1973 fish catch was expected to exceed the record 139,000 tons of 1972. Up to mid-September there was a significant rise in production of foodstuffs and consumer goods, and as a result rationing of cigarettes was ended and rations of beef, pork, fish, vegetables, leather goods, and clothing were increased.

(ROBIN CHAPMAN)

CUBA

Education. (1969–70) Primary, pupils 1,427,607, teachers 52,008; secondary, pupils 174,700, teachers 13,409; vocational, pupils 60,332, teachers 4,780; teacher training, students 31,619, teachers 1,543; higher (at 3 universities), students 31,035, teaching staff 4,036.

Finance. Monetary unit: peso, with (Sept. 18, 1972) an official rate of 0.83 peso to U.S. $1 (free rate of 2 pesos = £1 sterling). Budget (1966) balanced at 2,718,000,000 pesos.

Foreign Trade. (1970) Imports 1.3 billion pesos; exports 1,043,000,000 pesos. Import sources: U.S.S.R. 53%; France 5%. Export destinations: U.S.S.R. 51%; Japan 10%; Czechoslovakia 5%. Main exports (1966) sugar and products 85%.

Transport and Communications. Roads (1972) 13,343 km. (including 1,144 km. of the Central Highway). Motor vehicles in use (1969): passenger c. 71,000; commercial (including buses) c. 31,000. Railways: (1971) 14,797 km. (including 9,439 km. plantation); traffic (1970) 1,130,000,000 passenger-km., freight 1,625,000,000 net ton-km. Air traffic (1971): 537 million passenger-km.; freight 10,963,000 net ton-km. Shipping (1972): merchant vessels 100 gross tons and over 267; gross tonnage 398,030. Telephones (Dec. 1971) 275,000. Radio receivers (Dec. 1971) 1,338,000. Television receivers (Dec. 1968) c. 575,000.

Agriculture. Production (in 000; metric tons; 1972; 1971 in parentheses): rice c. 400 (c. 400); corn c. 115 (c. 115); cassava c. 220 (c. 220); sweet potatoes (1971) c. 260, (1970) 250; sugar, raw value 4,400 (5,924); coffee c. 28 (c. 28); oranges (1971) c. 140, (1970) 138; tobacco c. 54 (c. 27). Livestock (in 000; 1971–72): cattle c. 7,300; pigs c. 1,450; sheep c. 300; goats c. 83.

Industry. Production (in 000; metric tons; 1969): crude oil 206; petroleum products c. 5,300; electricity (kw-hr.; 1970) 4,072,000; chrome ore (oxide content; 1967) c. 11; manganese ore (metal content; 1968) 20; nickel ore (metal content; 1971) 36.

Cycling

Although by 1973 the Union Cycliste Internationale had cleared the way for cycling competition between amateurs and professionals, administrators of amateur

Crops:
see Agriculture and Fisheries
Currency:
see Money and Banking
Cybernetics:
see Computers

and professional bodies for various reasons were still reluctant to allow the two categories to meet in major competition. This was regretted as much by the public as by the cyclists themselves: in Poland enthusiasts claimed that their amateur hero Ryszard Szurkowski was as good as all-conquering Belgian road star Eddy Merckx, while in France track experts were confident that world amateur sprint champion Daniel Morelon would beat his professional counterpart, Robert Van Lancker of Belgium, in three races out of five.

Merckx began the season with his usual rush. By mid-April he had, in eight weeks, won the seven-day Tour of Sardinia and five one-day "classics": Het Volk, Gent–Wevelgem, and Liège–Bastogne–Liège (all in Belgium); Amstel Gold Race (The Netherlands); and Paris–Roubaix (France). During the same period, however, he suffered two major defeats in multistage races: the eight-day Paris–Nice—won for the second year in succession by veteran Frenchman Raymond Poulidor—and the "Catalan Week" (Spain), taken by Luís Ocana of the host country. Merckx then won the first two big multistage races, each lasting three weeks, the tours of Spain and Italy. Runners-up were the host nations' own stars, Luís Ocana and Felice Gimondi, respectively. Considering the ease with which he had triumphed, it was thought that Merckx would line up for the Tour de France in July in an attempt for the "triple," a feat never yet performed. Merckx, however, did not enter the event, leaving the way clear for Ocana to win.

On September 2 the "big three"—Merckx, Ocana, Gimondi—figured in a dramatic climax to the season on a hilly road circuit near Barcelona, Spain. Together with Freddy Maertens (Belg.) they were well ahead of the field, and it was clear that one of them must be the new world champion. All evidence of previous form pointed to Merckx as probable winner of the final sprint, but the victory went to 30-year-old Gimondi, followed by Maertens and Ocana.

Other professional races and winners were: Nice–Genoa, Marino Basso (Italy); the five-day Tyrrhenian–Adriatic and Milan–San Remo, Roger de Vlaeminck (Belg.); Tour of Flanders, Eric Leman (Belg.); Tour of Belgium, Leif Mortensen (Den.); Flèche Wallonne and Zürich championship, Andre Dierickx (Belg.); Bordeaux–Paris, Enzo Mattioda (Italy); the four-day Dunkirk, Freddy Maertens (Belg.); Tour of Switzerland, José Manuel Fuente (Spain); Dauphiné Libéré, Ocana; Paris–Brussels, Merckx; Paris–Tours, Rik Van Linden (Belg.); Grand Prix des Nations time trial and Tour of Lombardy, Merckx.

Ole Ritter pumps his way to a new world record in the one-hour motor pace at Copenhagen on June 28, 1973. Ritter covered 76,813 m., beating Ettore Castoldi's old record by 130 m.

NORDISK PRESSEFOTO/PICTORIAL PARADE

Polish amateur star Szurkowski was also in early good form, though not with the brio of Merckx. After finishing second to compatriot Stanislav Szozda in the 12-day Tour of Algeria in March, he built up form gradually for the Prague–Warsaw–Berlin "Peace Race." In this 14-day test Szurkowski reversed the Algerian placings to beat Szozda and win the event for the third time, also leading Poland to an easy team victory. In other national stage events Piet Van Katwijk (Neth.) won the Tour of Britain in which Sweden won the team race. In Sweden and The Netherlands honours went to home riders Bernt Johansen and Fedor den Hertog. Olympic silver medalist Clive Sefton (Austr.) took the Scottish Milk Race, while in Ireland Doug Dailey (U.K.) was best. In the Tour de l'Avenir (amateur Tour de France), Giambattista Baronchelli (Italy) was a deserved though suffering winner, having crashed heavily four days from the finish. He had previously won the amateur Tour of Italy.

Baronchelli was perhaps the only rider who could have given Szurkowski a real race in the world amateur road championship at Barcelona in September, but his injuries prevented his taking part. Szurkowski won decisively. A few days earlier, also in Spain, Szurkowski and Szozda, with compatriots Lis and Mytnik, had won for Poland the 100-km. road team time trial championships.

In the world track championships at San Sebastian, Spain (August 22–September 1), Hugh Porter (U.K.) won the professional pursuit title for the fourth time in six years and the victory of Sheila Young (U.S.) ended a 15-year domination of the women's sprint by Soviet riders. Although technically winners, the four U.K. riders took only silver medals in the 4,000-m. team pursuit championship. They accepted the decision to award the title to West Germany whose entire team crashed 50 m. from the finish line when comfortably in the lead. (J. B. WADLEY)

Cyprus

An island republic and a member of the Commonwealth of Nations, Cyprus is in the eastern Mediterranean. Area: 3,572 sq.mi. (9,251 sq.km.). Pop. (1972 est.): 645,000, including Greeks 77%; Turks 18%. Cap. and largest city: Nicosia (metro. pop., 1972 est., 118,000). Language: Greek and Turkish. Religion: Greek Orthodox 77%; Muslim 18.3%. President in 1973, Archbishop Makarios III.

The winter of 1972–73 saw continuing conflict between the Greek Cypriots supporting the cause of *enosis* (union with Greece) under the guidance of Gen. Georgios Grivas (*see* BIOGRAPHY) and the Greek Cypriots aligned with the policies of Archbishop Makarios. Underlying the guerrilla activities that General Grivas and his adherents carried out against the established regime in Cyprus was a growing fear that the long-sustained talks designed to resolve the differences separating the Greek and Turkish communities on the island might be moving at last toward a successful outcome—an outcome that would render dubious indeed the prospect of a future union between Cyprus and Greece.

NICHOLAS TSIKOURIAS—GREEK PHOTO AGENCY/KEYSTONE

Archbishop Makarios III, proclaimed president for a third five-year term on Feb. 8, 1973, inspects a Cypriot Army commando division upon his arrival at the parliament building.

Since his return to Cyprus, General Grivas had gathered around himself a hard core of Greek Cypriots dedicated to *enosis*. He also established a political organization to represent his aims (the Committee for the Coordination of the Enosis Struggle) and to disseminate propaganda through pamphlets and news sheets. His guerrillas often raided quarries, warehouses, and police stations in order to secure arms, explosives, and radio equipment. These raids were especially numerous in the Limassol area (a stronghold of pro-Grivas influence) during spring 1973.

To oppose Grivas' campaign, Makarios relied chiefly on the resources of government available to him. He recruited an elite force loyal to his cause (the Tactical Police Reserve) and endeavoured to remove from the police and National Guard elements believed to favour Grivas' aspirations. Perhaps his main resource was the visible prosperity which, under his conduct of affairs, Cyprus had known in recent years. This prosperity did much to ensure for Makarios the approval of a large majority among the Greek Cypriots—a majority so pronounced that Grivas did not venture, through a candidate of his own choice, to contest the presidential election in February. Makarios was returned unopposed for a third term as head of state.

Shortly thereafter, however, Makarios encountered serious opposition within the Greek Orthodox Church. Three dignitaries of the church, the bishops Anthimos of Kitium, Yennadios of Paphos, and Kyprianos of Kyrenia, had criticized Makarios on the ground that his secular duties as president of the republic conflicted with his religious duties as ethnarch of the Greek Orthodox Church of Cyprus. At a meeting held in Limassol in April, the three bishops declared Makarios deposed from his spiritual office. A synod of the Eastern Orthodox churches, convened at Nicosia in July under Patriarch Nicholas of Alexandria and including representatives of the patriarchates of Antioch and Jerusalem, in turn dethroned the three bishops, depriving them of all ecclesiastical authority. At the same time the synod declared that Makarios, as president, had not acted against the true spirit of the Scripture or of Greek Orthodox canon law.

A new wave of guerrilla violence affected much of Cyprus during the summer months. How far Grivas' arm was able to reach became clear when, late in July, his men kidnapped Christos Vakis, Makarios' minister of justice. Vakis was eventually set free at the end of August. With the intensification of violence came reports—vigorously denied by Grivas—that two attempts had been made to assassinate Makarios. In September Grivas announced that there was evidence of an assassination scheme directed against himself, and in October it was stated that yet another attempt had been made against Makarios. Meanwhile, the talks between the Greek Cypriot and the Turkish Cypriot communities, renewed at intervals throughout the year, seemed once more to be almost at an impasse.

(V. J. PARRY)

CYPRUS

Education. (Greek schools; 1971–72) Primary, pupils 64,974, teachers 2,208; secondary, pupils 40,339, teachers 1,731; vocational, pupils 4,640, teachers 313; higher (1969–70), students 580, teaching staff 48. (Turkish schools; 1965–66) Primary, pupils 16,700; secondary, vocational, and teacher training, pupils 7,600.

Finance. Monetary unit: pound, with (Sept. 17, 1973) a free rate of C£0.35 to U.S. $1 (C£0.83 = £1 sterling). Gold, SDRs, and foreign exchange, monetary authorities: (June 1973) U.S. $332.7 million; (June 1972) U.S. $304 million. Budget (1972 est.): revenue C£42,311,000; expenditure C£36,029,000.

Foreign Trade. (1972) Imports C£120,690,000; exports C£51.3 million. Import sources: U.K. 28%; Italy 8%; West Germany 7%; U.S. 6%; France 6%; Greece 5%; Japan 5%. Export destinations: U.K. 41%; West Germany 7%. Main exports: citrus fruit 24%; potatoes 14%; copper 10%.

Transport and Communications. Roads (1970) 8,699 km. Motor vehicles in use (1971): passenger 63,300; commercial (including buses) 15,800. Air traffic (1972): 254 million passenger-km.; freight 3,428,000 net ton-km. Shipping (1972): merchant vessels 100 gross tons and over 394; gross tonnage 2,014,675. Telephones (Dec. 1971) 48,000. Radio licenses (1971) 174,000; television licenses 58,000.

Agriculture. Production (in 000; metric tons; 1972; 1971 in parentheses): barley 69 (112); wheat (1971) 90, (1970) 43; grapes *c.* 185 (185); potatoes 175 (200); oranges (1971) 169, (1970) 92; grapefruit (1971) 57, (1970) 37; olives *c.* 15 (15). Livestock (in 000; 1971–72): sheep 460; cattle 33; pigs 112; goats 365.

Industry. Production (in 000; metric tons; 1971): asbestos 28; copper ore (exports; metal content) 16; chromium ore (oxide content) 19; cement (1972) 545; electricity (excluding most industrial production; kw-hr.; 1972) 715,000.

Czechoslovakia

A federal socialist republic of central Europe, Czechoslovakia lies between Poland, the U.S.S.R., Hungary, Austria, and East and West Germany. Area: 49,373 sq.mi. (127,876 sq.km.). Pop. (1973 est.): 14,572,350, including (1970 est.) Czech 65%; Slovak 29%. Cap. and largest city: Prague (pop., 1972 est., 1,083,717). Language: Czech and Slovak (official). General secretary of the Communist Party of Czechoslovakia in 1973, Gustav Husak; president, Ludvik Svoboda; premier, Lubomir Strougal.

Internationally, the most interesting aspect of Czechoslovak policy in 1973 involved relations with West Germany. On May 30 a compromise agreement was at last reached on the 1938 Munich agreement, which had forced Czechoslovakia to surrender the Sudetenland and which was now to be declared null and void, although the moment at which this condition of nullity was to be achieved was left to the varying interpretation of each side. However, the treaty normalizing relations and exchanging diplomatic representation between West Germany and Czechoslovakia

WIDE WORLD

Ludvik Svoboda signs the constitutional oath of the presidency at Prague after his unanimous reelection by the Federal Assembly on March 22, 1973.

remained unsigned for some months. West German Chancellor Willy Brandt had intended to go to Prague for the signing in September, but canceled his visit because the Czechoslovaks, putting the narrowest possible interpretation on the 1971 four-power agreement on Berlin, refused to concede West Germany's right to exercise consular representation on behalf of institutions located in West Berlin. Eventually, it was agreed that further negotiations would be held on the subject, and the treaty was finally signed by Brandt and Premier Strougal on December 11.

This hesitancy on the part of Prague may have been connected with a growing awareness of the ideological consequences of détente. Czechoslovakia was taking part in the Conference on Security and Cooperation in Europe, but on June 20 the Communist Party weekly *Tribuna* emphasized that "the dialectics of peaceful coexistence consist in the fact that we must negotiate with bourgeois representatives and conclude political agreements and compromises, but ideologically there can be nothing sacred for us in them." On the other hand, at the end of June a small group of anonymous Czech intellectuals, who had obviously been active in the reform movement in 1968, issued a statement claiming that genuine European cooperation could only be achieved "when all countries are open to new ideas."

Throughout 1973 Czechoslovakia was reasonably successful in extricating itself from the relative isolation within the international community that had followed the crushing of the '68 reform movement by Warsaw Pact forces. In April Czechoslovakia was visited by Harold Wilson, leader of the British Labour Party. At the time of Wilson's visit, the Czechoslovak authorities released the Rev. David Hathaway, a British clergyman of the Pentecostal Church, who had been sentenced to two years' imprisonment in October 1972 on a charge of trying to smuggle contraband Bibles into the country. In July the U.S. secretary of state, William P. Rogers, came to sign a consular convention and used the opportunity to ask the Czechoslovak government to release 31 citizens who had been denied permission to emigrate to the U.S. to join their families. In September the U.S. and Czechoslovakia resumed negotiations in Prague on outstanding financial issues. In December Husak paid a six-day official visit to India, Czechoslovakia's second most important third world trading partner.

Fences in Eastern Europe were also mended. The Romanian party leader, Nicolae Ceausescu, one of the most determined critics of the 1968 invasion, came to Prague on an "unofficial" friendship visit in March. The Czechoslovak foreign minister went to Belgrade, Yugos., in the spring to prepare for the October visit of party leader Husak.

Secret negotiations with the Vatican dealt with relations between church and state, especially the question of filling a number of vacant bishoprics. By March agreement had been reached on the appointment of four new bishops.

At home, the retreat from 1968 continued. The Husak regime tried to compensate for the continuing repression of intellectual freedoms by raising the material standard of living. In this respect it was markedly successful. In 1972 gross national income increased by 5.8% (0.8% in excess of target) and industrial production by 6.4% (1% in excess of target). Despite a serious housing shortage, the cost of living was kept reasonably steady. On the other hand, there was a serious manpower shortage in industry.

While the regime obviously tried to achieve a certain degree of legitimacy by improving the material aspects of life, it certainly did not relax the strict political and social controls imposed after 1968. The amnesty proclaimed in February 1973, on the 25th anniversary of the seizure of power by the Communist Party, was not extended to political offenders, although persons who had left the country illegally in 1968 were included provided they returned before the end of 1973.

The resignation of Miloslav Bruzek as minister of culture in the Czech regional government and his replacement by President Svoboda's son-in-law, Milan Klusak, in May gave rise to hopes that some of the pressures on writers and other intellectuals might be relaxed, but there was little change. Indeed, a systematic purge of libraries went on throughout the year. The most alarming development concerned proposals for the reform of the penal code, put forward in the spring: the police were to have the right to conduct searches without a warrant and to confiscate mail; the choice of defense counsel was to be controlled by the state; the maximum penalty for political crimes was to be raised from 15 to 25 years' imprisonment; and discipline in prisons was to be strengthened. When Leonid I. Brezhnev, the general secretary of the Soviet Communist Party, came to Prague in February to participate in the celebration of 25 years of Communist rule and to receive the Order of the White Lion, he seemed satisfied with the degree of "normalization" achieved by the Husak regime. (OTTO PICK)

CZECHOSLOVAKIA

Education. (1971–72) Primary, pupils 1,939,590, teachers 97,204; secondary, pupils 120,124, teachers 7,095; vocational and teacher training, pupils 279,978, teachers 16,241; higher (including 6 main universities), students 128,124, teaching staff 16,030.

Finance. Monetary unit: koruna, with (Sept. 17, 1973) an official exchange rate of 5.60 koruny to U.S. $1 (13.80 koruny = £1 sterling) and a tourist rate of 13.43 koruny to U.S. $1 (30.91 koruny = £1 sterling). Budget (1971 est.): revenue 219,021,000,000 koruny; expenditure 212,632,000,000 koruny.

Foreign Trade. (1971) Imports 28,870,000,000 koruny; exports 30,090,000,000 koruny. Import sources: U.S.S.R. 34%; East Germany 12%; Poland 7%; West Germany 6%; Hungary 5%. Export destinations: U.S.S.R. 32%; East Germany 11%; Poland 8%; Hungary 6%; West Germany 6%. Main exports (1969): machinery 36%; motor vehicles 10%; iron and steel 9%; chemicals 5%.

Transport and Communications. Roads (1971) 145,975 km. Motor vehicles in use (1971): passenger 918,200; commercial (including buses) 207,100. Railways (1971): 13,296 km. (including 2,595 km. electrified); traffic 18,983,000,000 passenger-km., freight (1972) 65,909,000,000 net ton-km. Air traffic (1972): 1,199,000,000 passenger-km.; freight 19,008,000 net ton-km. Shipping (1972): merchant vessels 100 gross tons and over 13; gross tonnage 103,049. Telephones (Dec. 1971) 2,112,000. Radio licenses (Dec. 1971) 3,825,000. Television licenses (Dec. 1971) 3,187,000.

Agriculture. Production (in 000; metric tons; 1972; 1971 in parentheses): wheat *c.* 4,200 (3,878); barley *c.* 2,500 (2,851); oats *c.* 850 (902); rye *c.* 530 (619); corn *c.* 540 (524); potatoes 4,968 (4,621); sugar, raw value *c.* 734 (*c.* 714); beef and veal (1971) *c.* 370, (1970) 362; pork (1971) *c.* 590, (1970) 586. Livestock (in 000; Jan. 1972): cattle 4,349; pigs 5,935; sheep 932; poultry 38,238.

Industry. Index of industrial production (1963 = 100): (1972) 211; (1971) 180. Production (in 000; metric tons; 1972): coal 27,536; brown coal 85,566; electricity (kw-hr.) 51,344,000; iron ore (30% metal content) 1,581; pig iron 8,377; steel 12,725; cement 8,056; sulfuric acid 1,189; nitrogenous fertilizers (N content; 1971) 366; phosphate fertilizers 331; cotton yarn 121; cotton fabrics (m.) 572,000; woolen fabrics (m.) 55,000; rayon and acetate yarn and fibres 71; nylon, etc., yarn and fibres 42; passenger cars (units) 154; commercial vehicles (units) 37. New dwelling units completed (1972) 114,516.

Dahomey

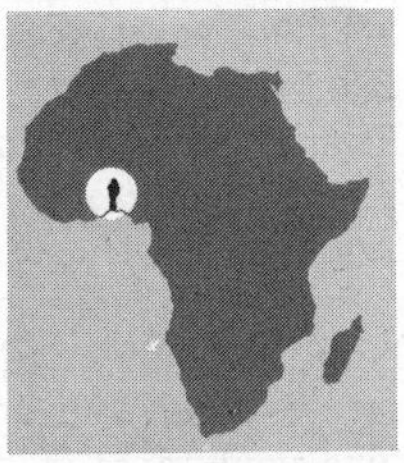

A republic of West Africa, Dahomey is located north of the Gulf of Guinea and is bounded by Togo, Upper Volta, Niger, and Nigeria. Area: 43,475 sq.mi. (112,600 sq.km.). Pop. (1972 est.): 2,835,000, mainly Dahomean and allied tribes. Cap.: Porto-Novo (pop., 1971 est., 90,000). Largest city: Cotonou (pop., 1971 est., 152,000). Language: French and local dialects. Religion: animist, with Christian and Muslim minorities. President in 1973, Maj. Mathieu Kerekou.

In March President Kerekou announced the discovery of a plot against the government involving several members of the armed forces. Former president Alphonse Alley was arrested and brought to trial, accused of plotting both the overthrow of the military government that had taken power in October 1972 and the assassination of a number of its members. He was sentenced to 20 years' imprisonment for his part in the conspiracy. Two other officers received similar sentences, and two more men, one of them a civilian, received sentences of ten years' hard labour for "active complicity." Another three received sentences of five years' imprisonment for "passive complicity" in not denouncing the plot to the authorities.

The announcement of the discovery of the plot led to violent anti-French demonstrations in Cotonou during which the windows of the French embassy were smashed and the walls daubed with slogans. Despite the fact that relations between Dahomey and France had suffered a considerable deterioration since Kerekou's seizure of power, the behaviour of the demonstrators was immediately condemned by the government.

The general reorientation of the country's foreign policy, which had remained somewhat in abeyance during the early months of the new military regime, continued to develop in a broadly progressive direction. In January an agreement was reached with China whereby the Chinese would make available a major loan to the Dahomean government. In April, Dahomey withdrew from the Francophone West African Economic Community, retaining only observer status. President Kerekou justified the decision on the grounds that certain Dahomean views had not been sufficiently taken to heart and that in any case the grouping of states according to whether the colonial language had been French or English was an outmoded concept. Later in the month he announced that he had no wish to damage relations with France but rather desired to develop cooperation agreements in keeping with the new situation. (PHILIPPE DECRAENE)

DAHOMEY

Education. (1971–72) Primary, pupils 186,000, teachers (1968–69) 3,565; secondary, pupils 27,000, teachers (1968–69) 634; vocational, pupils 2,000, teachers (1968–69) 102; teacher training, students 2,553; higher, students 600, teaching staff 52.

Finance. Monetary unit: CFA franc, with (Sept. 17, 1973) a parity of CFA Fr. 50 to the French franc and a free rate of CFA Fr. 212.55 to U.S. $1 (CFA Fr. 512.25 = £1 sterling). Budget (1973 est.): receipts CFA Fr. 12,391,000,000; expenditure CFA Fr. 13,192,000,000.

Foreign Trade. (1971) Imports CFA Fr. 21 billion; exports CFA Fr. 11,650,000,000. Import sources (1969): France 39%; The Netherlands 7%; U.S. 6%; West Germany 5%. Export destinations (1969): France 36%; Nigeria 13%; The Netherlands 13%; U.S. 10%; West Germany 8%; Japan 5%. Main exports: palm products 34%; cocoa 24%; cotton 19%.

Agriculture. Production (in 000; metric tons; 1972; 1971 in parentheses): corn *c.* 190 (216); cassava (1970) 736, (1969) 681; sweet potatoes (1971) *c.* 610, (1970) 605; millet and sorghum (1971) 68, (1970) 60; dry beans *c.* 25 (25); peanuts *c.* 70 (65); cotton, lint *c.* 22 (20); palm kernels *c.* 55 (*c.* 70); palm oil *c.* 42 (*c.* 49); cocoa (exports) (1971) 19, (1970) 7; coffee *c.* 2 (2.5). Livestock (in 000; 1970–71): cattle *c.* 590; sheep *c.* 580; pigs *c.* 370.

Dance

Distinctions between ballet companies and modern dance groups continued to disappear in 1973, so that it was difficult in many instances to classify a given group as "ballet" or "modern." Ethnic dance attractions were also on the increase. Large companies with elaborate stagings and small groups and soloists performed in cities, towns, and universities in the U.S. and most major Western countries. Among the ethnic theatre arts groups and simpler folk dance units performing outside their own countries in 1973 were, from the Caribbean, the Jamaican National Dance Theater and the Trinidad Folk Company; from India, the Kathakali Dancers, the Chhau Dancers of Bengal, and many recitalists; from Korea, the Mansudai National Dance Company and the Little Angels; from Poland, the Mazowsze Dance Company; the Georgian State Dance Company from the U.S.S.R.; the Mahalli Dancers from Iran; the Bayanihan Dance Company from the Philippines; the Ballet Folklorico from Mexico; the Gulbenkian Ballet from Portugal; and units from Spain, Ecuador, Japan, Indonesia, Israel, Yugoslavia, Romania, Pakistan, Haiti, and several nations in Africa.

For the U.S. theatre of dance, the major news of 1973 was the return of Martha Graham to the dance scene following a series of illnesses. Although she announced her total retirement as a dancer, Miss Graham not only reestablished a daily teaching schedule at her school in New York City but also created two new works for her reconstituted company's Broadway season, *Mendicants of Evening,* incorporating lines from St. John Perse's "Chronique," with an electronic score by David Walker and decor by Fangor, and *Myth of a Voyage,* with music by Alan Hovhaness and decor by Ming Cho Lee. The Graham repertory also included a revival of the four-act *Clytemnestra,* with Mary Hinkson and Pearl Lang (guest artist) alternating in the title role, previously danced exclusively by Miss Graham.

At least 50 modern dance performer-choreographers, many with supporting groups, were active in presenting programs in the U.S., all featuring new dance compositions. Among major participants were the Repertory Dance Theater of Utah, the José Limón Dance Company, the Alvin Ailey City Center Dance Theater, Pilobolus, the Juilliard Dance Ensemble (including some ballet as well as modern at its concerts), ChoreoConcerts, the Dance Theater Workshop, and companies headed by Alwin Nikolais, Murray Louis, Merce Cunningham, Paul Taylor, Erick Hawkins, Louis Falco, Charles Weidman, Mary Anthony, Rudy Perez, Chuck Davis, Ze'eva Cohen, Yvonne Rainer, Dan Wagoner, and Deborah Hay. Carmen de Lavallade added two historic solos to her contemporary repertory, *The Incense* (1906) and *The Yogi* (1908), dances created and performed for 60 years by Ruth St. Denis.

Dairy Products: *see* Agriculture and Fisheries

Dams: *see* Engineering Projects

The New York City Ballet, resident company of the New York State Theater and with George Balanchine as its artistic director, drew its repertory in large measure from the 30 ballets given by the company in 1972 at its mammoth Stravinsky Festival. New ballets for 1973 included two by Jerome Robbins, *An Evening's Waltzes* (Prokofiev) and *Four Bagatelles* (Beethoven), and a *pièce d'occasion,* Balanchine's *Cortège Hongrois* to music of Aleksandr K. Glazunov and created especially for ballerina Melissa Hayden (*see* BIOGRAPHY) on the occasion of her retirement from the company. Edward Villella, a principal male dancer with the New York City Ballet, choreographed *Salute to Cole* (Cole Porter) for the Philharmonic Promenades given in Philharmonic Hall, which was located only a few feet from the State Theater enabling Villella to dance in both theatres on the same nights. The opening of the 1973–74 season was delayed by a 24-day strike of the dancers. The musicians, who were negotiating, agreed to begin the season without a contract, but it was believed they might strike at the start of the profitable Christmas season run of *The Nutcracker,* and the dancers struck to enforce their demand for a guaranteed season. Both disputes were settled in time for *The Nutcracker* to open.

The American Ballet Theatre, official dance company of the Kennedy Center in Washington, D.C., featured in its repertory a new production of an evening-long ballet, *Tales of Hoffmann* (Offenbach), choreographed by Peter Darrell. The ballet was staged especially for Cynthia Gregory. The repertory also featured Lar Lubovitch's new *Scherzo for Massah Jack* and major revivals of Agnes de Mille's *Three Virgins and a Devil* (Ottorino Respighi) and Antony Tudor's *Undertow* (William Schuman).

The City Center Joffrey Ballet, resident company of the New York City Center 55th Street Theater, featured a new production of Sir Frederick Ashton's *The Dream* (Shakespeare-Mendelssohn), marking the first time that this popular ballet had been danced by a company other than Britain's Royal Ballet. *The Moor's Pavane,* choreographed by José Limón to music of Henry Purcell and with costumes by Pauline Lawrence (Mrs. Limón), had long been considered a modern dance classic (it was first done in 1949) and one that ballet companies found could be danced successfully. Added to the Joffrey repertory in 1973, it became an immediate hit. The Joffrey also went to great pains and expense to restage a ballet classic from the Diaghilev era, *Parade* (1917), with choreography by Leonide Massine, music by Erik Satie, book by Jean Cocteau, and scenery and costumes by Pablo Picasso. Massine himself directed the Joffrey revival. The company also featured two new works by the avant-garde choreographer Twyla Tharp: *Deuce Coupe,* with music by the Beach Boys, dancers from both the Joffrey and Tharp troupes, and fresh graffiti at every performance sprayed on moving panels by nine youngsters from the US GUYS Graffiti Group; and *As Time Goes By* (third and fourth movements of Haydn's Symphony No. 45). Other novelties included Robert Joffrey's first new choreography in several years, *Remembrances* (Wagner), Eliot Feld's *Jive* (Morton Gould), and the company's first staging of Jerome Robbins' *Interplay* (Gould).

Ballet visitors from abroad included members of the Bolshoi Ballet in divertissements and, for the first time in the U.S., students from Moscow's Bolshoi Dance Academy, plus recent ballet competition prizewinners Nadezhda Pavlova and Vyacheslav Gordeyev. The Stuttgart Ballet performed John Cranko's production of *Swan Lake,* in addition to the U.S. premieres of Cranko's *Initials R.B.M.E.* (Brahms), *L'Estro Armonico* (Vivaldi), and *Traces* (Mahler). The National Ballet of Canada, with Rudolf Nureyev as guest star, also toured the U.S.

Major dance films, both movies and television videotapes, included three involving Nureyev: *I Am a Dancer, The Sleeping Beauty* (with the National Ballet of Canada), and *Don Quixote* (with the Australian Ballet). *American Ballet Theatre: A Close-Up in Time* was a television special dealing exclusively with that group. *First Position,* a movie focusing upon young ballet aspirants, made use of American Ballet Theatre School facilities.

Summertime dance events were presented by the Jacob's Pillow Dance Festival at Lee, Mass., and the American Dance Festival at Connecticut College, New London, Conn. New works given at the festivals included a solo, *In Nightly Revels* (J. S. Bach), with choreography by Peter Darrell, created especially for Dame Margot Fonteyn at Jacob's Pillow. In New York, in celebration of the 85th birthday and 60-year career of the impresario Sol Hurok, an S. Hurok Gala was held at the Metropolitan Opera House. The Handel Medallion, New York City's highest cultural award, was presented to Hurok by Mayor John V. Lindsay.

(WALTER TERRY)

BERNARD GOTFRYD—NEWSWEEK

The rhythm of their graceful movements caught in a triple exposure, Danuta Kisiel-Drzewinska and Stefan Niedzialkowski of the Polish Mime Ballet Theatre perform a sensuous pas de deux typical of this group's powerfully emotional repertory. The company toured the U.S. in 1973.

MARTHA SWOPE

Left, in a scene from the Martha Graham Dance Company's "Clytemnestra," Daniel Maloney (top), Yuriko Kimura, and Bertram Ross strike a solemn pose over Pearl Lang in the title role. Below, Martha Graham at curtain call. The troupe performed for two weeks in New York City during May 1973.

In Britain, the Royal Ballet's main company at Covent Garden continued to include work by the contemporary U.S. choreographer Glen Tetley. Apart from Tetley's *Laborintus* (Berio), in which Nureyev, Seymour, and other artists showed that classically trained dancers could take to modern forms as if born to them, Kenneth MacMillan's *Triad* (Prokofiev), and Ashton's *The Walk to the Paradise Gardens* (Delius), the 1972–73 season was largely devoted to revivals. From the repertory of the New York City Ballet Robbins revived *Requiem Canticles* (Stravinsky), and three works from Balanchine were *The Prodigal Son* (Prokofiev), *Agon* (Stravinsky), and *The Four Temperaments* (Hindemith). MacMillan mounted a new production of *The Sleeping Beauty* (Tchaikovsky), the fourth in the company's history, principally for a tour of Brazil in the summer of 1973.

The Royal Ballet New Group managed to develop its repertory considerably despite spending most of its time on tour. Following the success of his *Grand Tour* (Coward), Joe Layton presented *O. W.* (Walton), based on the theme of Oscar Wilde's life and trial. New creations included MacMillan's *The Poltroon* (Rudolf Maros), Ronald Hynd's *In a Summer Garden* (Delius), and David Drew's *Sacred Circles* (Shostakovich). Revivals new to the company were Hans van Manen's *Tilt* (Stravinsky) and *Twilight* (John Cage) and Balanchine's *Allegro Brillante* (Tchaikovsky).

Despite continual tours to the British provinces, several extended overseas trips, and London seasons in three different theatres, London Festival Ballet managed to create an almost entirely new repertory. To its existing full-length classics *The Sleeping Beauty* and *Giselle,* Beryl Grey had added a new production of *Swan Lake* based on the original Petipa-Ivanov. New creations included Barry Moreland's *Summer Solstice* (John Field) and *In Nomine* (Peter Maxwell Davies), Ronald Hynd's *Mozartiana* (Mozart-Tchaikovsky), and Peter Darrell's *La Peri* (Dukas). Revivals taken into the repertory included Massine's *The Three Cornered Hat* (Falla) and *Gaité Parisienne* (Offenbach), Antony Tudor's *Echoing of Trumpets* (Martinu), Ben Stevenson's *Three Preludes* (Rachmaninoff), and August Bournonville's *Conservatoire,* revived by Mona Vangsaa. Galina Samsova and André Prokovsky were no longer permanent members of the company, although they would return as guests from time to time, having formed an independent concert group—the Samsova-Prokovsky New London Ballet—which had been touring the world.

Ballet Rambert extended its touring both in the English provinces and overseas. It continued to extend its repertory for area presentation on the many thrust stages being built throughout Britain, particularly in universities. New works created for these stages included an hour-long one by Christopher Bruce, *There Was a Time* (Brian Hodgson), based on the relationship of gods and mortals in the cause and effect of the Trojan war. New works taken into the regular repertory included Lar Lubovitch's *Considering the Lilies* (Bach) and Jonathan Taylor's *Listen to the Music* (Anthony Hymas).

London Contemporary Dance Theatre, as well as giving seasons at The Place in London, toured regularly in the provinces where Robert Cohan's full-evening *Stages* was enormously popular; the company also made a three-month tour of South America. Creations included Cohan's *People* (Bob Downes), which combined his *People Alone* and *People Together* in a full-evening work, his *Mass* (Vladimir Rodzianko), in which the dancers also sang, and Flora Cushman's *Scalene Sequence* (Berio). The company and the London School of Contemporary Dance also gave regular workshop programs from which a number of interesting choreographers were beginning to emerge. Strider, the new group formed by Richard Alston, still partly attached to The Place, also gave regular performances in the experimental field.

Possibly the most interesting feature of the dance scene in Britain was the way in which the two regional companies, Scottish Theatre Ballet in Glasgow and Northern Dance Theatre in Manchester, had developed their work and settled down as integral parts of the artistic life in their respective areas. Scottish Theatre Ballet produced the last act of Ivanov's *The Nutcracker* (Tchaikovsky), intending to revive the full work by the end of 1973. Toer van Schayk created *Ways of Saying Bye Bye* (Purcell-Poptie). Revivals included Fokine's *Carnaval* (Schumann) and Tudor's *Soirée Musicale* (Rossini-Britten). The "Tangents" workshop program produced several new works including Peter Cazalet's *Some Bright Star* (Pink Floyd and others), Peter Darrell's *Variations on a Door and a Sigh* (Pierre Henry), and Alston's *Balkan Sobrani* (Stravinsky-Francaix-Fukushima). Scottish Theatre Ballet also formed a splinter group, Ballet for Scotland, to tour small towns and villages. Northern Dance Theatre had its first full-length ballet when Laverne Mayer created *Cinderella* (Robert Stewart). Other creations included Jonathan Thorpe's *The Wanderer and His Shadow* (Brahms) and John Haynes's *Within Walls* (Soler). Revivals were Walter Gore's *The Night and Silence* (Bach) and *Hoops* (Poulenc) and Jooss's *The Green Table* (Cohen).

Each year saw more and more visiting companies in Britain. In the 1972–73 season these included the National Ballet of Canada and the Toronto Dance Theatre, and several companies from the U.S., among them the Murray Louis Dance Company, Merce Cunningham and Dance Company, Dan Wagoner and

MARTHA SWOPE

KEYSTONE

Rudolf Nureyev sways on the shoulders of another dancer during a frolicsome scene from "The Prodigal Son," presented by the Royal Ballet in London during January 1973.

Dancers, the Paul Taylor Dance Company, and the Alvin Ailey Dance Theater.

In France the Paris Opera Ballet, with its new administrator, Rolf Liebermann, had entered a period that might well prove the most adventurous in its illustrious history. In addition to new productions of two of its greatest romantic classics, Pierre Lacotte's *La Sylphide* and Alicia Alonso's *Giselle,* a strong contemporary repertory was also being developed. One of the most imaginative programs given during 1973 was one in which five different choreographers (John Butler, Janine Charrat, Felix Blaska, Serge Keuten, and Carolyn Carlson) created nine works in a "Homage to Varèse," each work using music by this most original and influential modern composer. Programs devoted to a single composer were an important feature of the principal French modern ballet company, Ballet-Théâtre Contemporain, now based at Angers. The company had its greatest success with two such programs, one devoted to Stravinsky and the other to Stockhausen.

The main event in West Germany was the emergence of an important choreographer in John Neumeier with the Ballet of the Frankfurt State Theatre, where among other works he created new versions of *Le Sacré* (Stravinsky), *Daphnis and Chloë* (Ravel), and *Don Juan* (Gluck). The Stuttgart Ballet continued as one of the most important companies in continental Europe and a full-length work on *The Taming of the Shrew* created by John Cranko (*see* OBITUARIES) was extremely successful, as was his production of *Swan Lake.* Tragedy hit the company when Cranko died while on a plane returning from a New York season in the summer of 1973.

In Denmark, the Royal Danish Ballet enlivened its traditional repertory, mainly works by Bournonville, with two works by Flemming Flindt—*The Triumph of Death* and *Felix Luna*—which reflected more modern tendencies, including a certain amount of nudity.

The Netherlands Dance Theatre extended its Hans van Manen repertory with *Opus Lemaître* (Bach), *Grosse Fuge* (Beethoven), and *Tilt.* Otherwise the accent was on young American creators, including a work entitled *Sunday Papers* (John Herbert McDowell) by Cliff Keuter. (PETER WILLIAMS)

See also Music; Theatre.

Danish Literature:
see Literature

Deaths:
see Vital Statistics;
see also biographies of prominent persons who died in 1973, listed under Obituaries

Debts, National:
see Government Finance

Defense

In 1973 the military implications of Henry A. Kissinger's pentagonal balance of power between the U.S., the U.S.S.R., China, Japan, and Europe became clearer. That the balance of nuclear deterrence was primarily a bilateral Soviet-U.S. understanding was underlined by their June 22 Agreement on the Prevention of Nuclear War, which stressed their determination to prevent their political détente from being threatened by improvements in their strategic weapons systems or by the emergence of additional nuclear powers. Thus, although China was acquiring a nuclear strike force sufficient to deter a disarming counterforce strike by the U.S.S.R., and while France and Britain were upgrading their nuclear forces, these powers could use their nuclear arms only to deter a Soviet strike by the threat of one strike against Soviet cities. Contrary to earlier U.S. predictions, nuclear proliferation had left the superpowers' technological supremacy in nuclear weapons unaffected, while strengthening their determination to preserve the status quo.

The limitations of superpower influence were underlined by the end of U.S. involvement in the Indochina war with the signing of the Vietnam peace treaty on Jan. 27, 1973, and the cessation of U.S. bombing in Cambodia on August 15. The U.S. failure to halt the North Vietnamese attempt to dominate Indochina indicated the difficulties facing either superpower if it tried to intervene directly in local military confrontations, difficulties also experienced by the U.S.S.R., which had been unable to use its alliances with Egypt and India to exercise significant influence over either power. Since China remained unable to project meaningful conventional power beyond its borders and Japan continued to be an economic giant but a military pigmy, third world countries seemed likely to be left to find their own military balances.

In the chief remaining area of superpower conflict, the Middle East, the U.S. continued to supply arms to Israel and to build up Iran in order to secure increasingly vulnerable oil supplies. The U.S.S.R. countered by arming Egypt and Syria and encouraging the oil-producing states to use their economic power to lessen U.S. support for Israel. But both superpowers were avoiding, in the Middle East or elsewhere, any risk of a military clash with potential for escalation. The October Middle East war was a classic example of confrontation by proxy. (*See* Special Report.)

In the one area where the superpowers were still in military confrontation, Europe, they were seeking to broaden the 1972 strategic arms limitation talks (SALT I) agreement into a multilateral arrangement guaranteeing the political status quo. Hence the interlocking complex of negotiations comprising the second round of Soviet-U.S. strategic arms negotiations, SALT II; the 35-nation Conference on Security and Cooperation in Europe; and the 11-power talks on mutual and balanced force reductions (MBFR).

In the SALT II negotiations, resumed on March 12, the U.S. and U.S.S.R. were seeking to develop their temporary SALT I agreement, extending to 1978, into a more lasting and comprehensive set of limitations on the strategic arms race. Since both superpowers were building up to the maximum levels allowed by SALT I, it seemed probable that SALT II would function, like its predecessor, chiefly as a forum in which both sides could exchange information on force deployments and technical developments, limiting their political effects and elucidating areas where the two powers could agree on the number and capabilities of particular weapons systems. Whether such agreement would, or could, constitute restraint seemed doubtful, given the extent of the asymmetries between the Soviet and U.S. force structures and the problems of comparing different weapons systems. For example, the U.S. had sought a complete ban on mobile intercontinental ballistic missiles (ICBMs), which it was not interested in developing, whereas the Soviets, who were developing a mobile ICBM, had opposed such a ban. The U.S., on the other hand, had rejected any limits on strategic bombers, in which it had superiority. Any agreed limits, therefore, would probably start from the planned U.S. force level for 1979 of about 250 strategic bombers, with the new B-1 replacing the B-52 and FB-111A. The U.S.S.R. might agree not to deploy more than an equivalent number of its new Backfire bombers if they were developed.

But there seemed little hope of agreement except where technological developments and economic constraints appeared likely to produce comparable types and levels of forces. The Soviet flight testing of an advanced multiple independently targeted reentry vehicle (MIRV) system in the summer, plus the impossibility of verifying whether a MIRV was deployed or not, meant that a MIRV ban was no longer feasible. Overall limits on payloads would continue to be impossible as long as the U.S.S.R. continued to prefer ICBMs larger than those of the U.S., although SALT I's ceiling of 313 very large Soviet ICBMs (primarily the SS-9) might set a precedent where the two sides could put together suitable bargaining packages.

Such packages were unlikely in research and development, since neither limitations nor verification seemed possible, or in antisubmarine warfare (ASW) and antiaircraft (AA) defense, where the U.S. and Soviet forces had different purposes. The U.S. saw ASW in terms of defending supply lines to Europe in time of war, while the U.S.S.R. had developed an ASW force to act against U.S., British, and French submarine-launched ballistic missile (SLBM) systems. AA defense had been cut back in the U.S. to less than 500 fighters and 800 surface-to-air missiles (SAMs) because of the minimal Soviet bomber threat, while the Soviet AA system had been expanded to over 3,000 interceptors and 10,000 SAMs to deal with both U.S. strategic bombers and the forward based systems (FBS) for delivering nuclear weapons from Western Europe to Eastern Europe and the U.S.S.R. Indeed, FBS seemed likely to become the most important subject for discussion in SALT II.

The European NATO countries saw FBS as symbols of U.S. willingness to risk nuclear war in defense of Western Europe, since the Soviets were expected to take out FBS with nuclear weapons in the event of a major conflict, thereby bringing the U.S. strategic deterrent into action. Whether this reasoning was correct was less important than its acceptance by NATO's European members, who would see any reduction in FBS as lowering the credibility of the U.S. guarantee. For the same reason the U.S.S.R. would seek bilateral restraint on FBS deployment. Any such restraint was largely meaningless in a military sense, because what constituted an FBS depended on whether it was defined in terms of capability or intention. Moreover, by any definition, FBS were deployed in large numbers, 800–1,700 for NATO versus about 1,800 for the Warsaw Pact, with even larger numbers available for reinforcement. The problems of defining anything more than symbolic but politically important restraints on this single class of weapons system suggested that the MBFR negotiations would also be likely to produce symbolic rather than substantive force reductions on an agreed basis.

DISARMAMENT

In one sense, the institutionalization of SALT represented a major achievement for the Geneva disarmament discussions, which had always urged the establishment of effective communication between the superpowers. But it left the 26-nation Conference of the (UN) Committee on Disarmament (CCD) with little to do. The superpowers could conduct their own negotiations in private, and the U.S. and U.S.S.R. increasingly used their powers as joint chairmen of the CCD to secure its approval of their bilateral agreements while minimizing discussion of their failure to restrain the strategic arms race.

This failure was emphasized by the continued inability of the superpowers to agree on a comprehensive nuclear test ban. Both the U.S. and the U.S.S.R. had actually increased their annual rate of nuclear testing since the 1963 treaty banning nuclear tests in the atmosphere, while France and China, which had refused to sign the treaty, both continued atmospheric testing. The failure of the partial test ban to create a climate of restraint made a comprehensive ban more important from the arms-control viewpoint, but neither the U.S. nor the U.S.S.R. seemed to desire it. As neither wished to appear to favour nuclear tests, they took refuge in their 1963 positions, the U.S. demanding seven annual on-site inspections of suspicious events (possible nuclear test explosions) while the U.S.S.R. argued that such inspections were meaningless but said it might accept three. Increasing evidence that both sides could unilaterally verify observance of a comprehensive ban embarrassed the U.S. more, since it was the side that insisted on inspection, but the U.S.S.R. had not exploited its advantage for fear the U.S. might drop its inspection requirements, forcing the U.S.S.R. to find new reasons for its rejection of a comprehensive ban.

The SALT I agreements had been based on limits representing the maximum effort the superpowers were prepared to put into the strategic arms race, preventing the race from getting any faster rather than slowing it down. After a year of SALT I, both sides seemed intent on racing at the maximum speed it permitted. The U.S.S.R. had 1,527 of the allowed 1,618 ICBMs deployed, and three new types, the SS-16, SS-17, and SS-18, were being tested. Both the SS-17 and SS-18 had been tested with multiple reentry vehicles (MRVs) and were designed for the MIRV system finally tested in the summer. First estimates suggested that the greater throw-weight of Soviet missiles would be utilized to carry either more or heavier MIRVs than the U.S. Minuteman III ICBM—an expectation that had clearly set the basis for Soviet ICBM ceilings in SALT I. Deployment of the SS-17 and SS-18 would bring overall Soviet ICBM strength to the allowed level of 1,618, probably within a year.

The Soviet concentration on ICBMs at the expense of SLBMs was reversed by the U.S. Its ICBM program was limited to installing 550 Minuteman III missiles with MIRV by 1975, increasing the protection of missile silos against nuclear attack, and setting up a Command Data Buffer system to provide rapid

ICBM retargeting. The U.S. retained its qualitative lead in SLBMs, with 320 Poseidon SLBMs deployed and the conversion of a further 11 submarines to Poseidon scheduled for completion by 1975–76. Future development was concentrated on the 4,600-mi.-range Trident I SLBM with MIRV, due to become operational in late 1978. It now appeared that Trident could be deployed in Poseidon-carrying submarines or in the confusingly named Trident (carrying) submarine, also scheduled to become operational in 1978. Indications were that the U.S. would make use of the provision in the interim agreement that allowed it to replace the 54 Titan ICBMs, nearing obsolescence, with Trident SLBMs, giving the U.S. 1,000 out of the permitted 1,054 ICBMs and the allowable maximum of 710 SLBMs.

Antiballistic missile (ABM) systems were not yet being built up to the SALT I maximum of two deployment areas, each with 100 missiles. The Soviet Galosh ABM with a range of 200 mi. and a nuclear warhead in the megaton range was still deployed around Moscow in four sites (64 launchers), but resumption of work on uncompleted complexes suggested that an improved, longer-range ABM was scheduled for deployment. The U.S. Safeguard ABM, defending ICBM silos at Grand Forks, N.D., was to become operational in 1974, using long-range Spartan missiles and short-range Sprint missiles, but interest was shifting to a more economical defense of ICBM silos using only short-range Sprint-type missiles in a system known as Site Defense (formerly Hard Site). No ABM deployment around Washington, D.C., seemed contemplated.

Against the background of these energetic weapons acquisition programs, the CCD's requests for restraints in the arms race seemed largely irrelevant, especially since many of its third world members were equally active in acquiring conventional arms. Debate centred around the comprehensive test ban and clarification of the prohibitions against chemical warfare in the Geneva Protocol of 1925. The withdrawal of the U.S. from the Vietnam war made less pressing the question of whether its use of riot-control agents and herbicides there violated the protocol. This issue partly explained U.S. refusal to ratify the protocol, despite Canada's initiative in announcing that it would agree, on a reciprocal basis, not to allow the use of such agents by its armed forces. This approach avoided the question of whether or not such use was banned under the protocol, the major obstacle to any agreed interpretation of the protocol by its signatories.

Canada, along with The Netherlands, Japan, and Sweden, also developed a distinction between supertoxic agents, the so-called nerve gases, and toxic agents, chemical weapons of the type used in World War I. Most toxic agents were also used for industrial purposes, making a ban on their production for military use impossible to enforce. It was hoped that a treaty might be drawn up preventing the production of supertoxic agents, which could be verified with some degree of assurance, while prohibiting preparations for the military use of toxic agents. Unfortunately the difficulties of verification, combined with continuing Soviet development of chemical weapons, made the chance of any substantive progress minimal.

NATO

The opening of negotiations on MBFR had brought to the surface the most divisive single issue in NATO, the credibility of the U.S. guarantee to defend Western Europe against political pressure from the U.S.S.R. This guarantee had always been symbolized by the U.S. forces in Western Europe, and if MBFR meant equal reductions in the 4 U.S. and 31 Soviet divisions in Europe, the Western Europeans could only lose. Any such reductions would be unmutual and unbalanced, leaving the U.S.S.R. stronger militarily and, more important, politically.

Since the principal Western objective in MBFR was greater security at less cost, the two main types of reduction sought were qualitative—in those weapons most suitable for surprise attack—and quantitative—overall force reductions that would not increase the existing Soviet superiority enough to encourage an attack. Preliminary talks on MBFR had indicated that, for purposes of negotiation, the NATO-Warsaw Pact military balance would be divided into two parts: the U.S. and Soviet forces stationed outside their territories and the indigenous forces of their allies, chiefly those on the Central Front (the U.K., France, and West Germany for NATO and East Germany, Hungary, Poland, and Czechoslovakia for the Pact). Even so, any numerical comparisons would still underestimate the geographic and organizational asymmetries. Because of its geographic position, the U.S.S.R. could return troops more quickly to Central Europe than could the U.S., and it could do so with none of the domestic difficulties that would face any NATO government reinforcing its troops in time of a crisis.

As far as organization was concerned, it had always been accepted that the Pact benefited from uniform Soviet equipment and training. Now, however, it appeared that the Soviet force structure was more suited to a European war than the U.S. model used by NATO. The Pact had fewer men per division (9,000–10,000 as against 15,000), but it had 64 divisions in Central Europe as against NATO's 24. To prevent NATO from developing its greater military potential in wartime, Soviet strategy aimed at a quick conventional victory, with formations being used until they were destroyed and then replaced by similar units. This was more suited to a blitzkrieg than the U.S.-NATO system of maintaining units large enough to sustain considerable casualties and still function, permitting the replacement of losses on an individual basis.

Despite these asymmetries, the Western European powers had moved toward suggesting a package involving a 14% cut in U.S. forces in Europe, including the Mediterranean, and in Soviet troops in East Germany, Poland, and Czechoslovakia—reductions of 45,000 and 60,000 men, respectively. There would be an accompanying 7% drop in other ground forces in West Germany, principally 4,000 British troops, and a 7% cut in the East and West German armies and those of the other Central Front powers. The Western Europeans hoped that these or similar reductions would forestall a unilateral U.S. troop reduction for economic reasons.

The most likely qualitative restraints were on the numbers or deployment of main battle tanks. These were easily countable and of more use to an attacker, the more so because specialized antitank weapons like the U.S. helicopter-launched TOW missiles were replacing the tank as the main antitank weapon. However, tanks were also the weapons for which NATO's numerical inferiority was most pronounced, and its members tried to offset this by qualitative superiority. Attempts to determine the relative force capabilities of the NATO and Pact armoured formations and thus arrive at figures for asymmetrical but balanced reductions had been largely unsuccessful.

The initial outcome of the MBFR negotiations thus seemed likely to be a fairly rapid agreement on simple percentage reductions in manpower and tanks on the Central Front, with NATO accepting, as multilateral, reductions that would probably have been made unilaterally in any case. Ironically, the chief result would be to make the rapid use of tactical nuclear weapons against a Pact attack more likely, particularly since the U.S. was developing a new generation of extremely clean, low-yield weapons. Currently NATO had some 7,000 tactical nuclear weapons in the 20–100 kiloton range, all under U.S. control, against about 3,500 larger-yield weapons under Soviet control in the Pact area.

Even allowing for the difference between quantitative and qualitative estimates of the NATO-Pact balance, however, there were indications that the main problem for the U.S. and its allies would be in securing agreed positions within the alliance on what assessments of the military balance would be regarded as most relevant for the purpose of negotiations. Nor was the solution made easier by the evident strain within the alliance resulting from U.S. failure to consult its NATO partners during the October Middle East war, especially with regard to its worldwide troop alert. At the December NATO meeting in Brussels, French Foreign Minister Michel Jobert complained that Europe had been brushed aside by the superpowers during the Middle East crisis. Underlying this, as the Arab program of oil boycotts and cutbacks began to take effect, was Europe's feeling that it was being made to suffer for a U.S. policy in which it had had no part. At the same time, the U.S. indicated displeasure because its allies were not giving it full support at a critical time. France's new draft covering the security aspects of a proposed Atlantic declaration, which appeared to move closer to U.S. views in some respects, contained a pledge that the allies would keep each other fully informed vis-à-vis East-West relations.

UNITED STATES

With the end of direct U.S. involvement in the Vietnam war and the cessation of bombing in support of Cambodian forces, the major issue for U.S. defense policy became the extent to which congressional unwillingness to meet the rising costs of all-volunteer armed forces and their weapons systems would impair the nation's ability to preserve a stable strategic deterrent and maintain its overseas commitments. Although less was heard of the so-called military-industrial complex, a majority in Congress reflected their constituents' feelings that military spending had enjoyed too high a priority for too long in a country facing growing internal crises, and that Congress had allowed its supervisory authority over the military to be eroded. The decision of the traditionally pro-military Senate Armed Services Committee to cut $100 million from Air Force funding for the B-1 strategic bomber, $29.3 million from naval procurement, and 156,100 troops typified the new climate. So did passage, over a presidential veto, of the War Powers Act limiting the president's ability to wage undeclared war.

Although the Senate had passed, as an amendment to its approval of the SALT I agreements, a stipulation that the U.S. must not accept a position of inferiority in any future arms limitation agreement, the U.S. strategic forces were an obvious target for cutbacks in funding. These forces accounted for about $7.4 billion out of the $81.1 billion fiscal 1974 defense budget, with the Trident submarines estimated at $1 billion each. Moreover, the apparent stability of the nuclear balance suggested that the deployment of new deterrent systems could be delayed without endangering U.S. security. The Air Force was particularly vulnerable, since its B-1 bomber seemed to owe its existence as much to Air Force determination to preserve the manned bomber as to any clear military rationale. Furthermore, the idea of using airpower to support U.S. allies without incurring significant U.S. casualties appeared increasingly suspect as the full costs of the air war in Vietnam became evident. The U.S. had suffered 4,240 airmen killed, lost 3,706 planes and 4,866 helicopters, and spent $16 billion to drop 7.4 million tons of bombs, and had still been unable to win a victory.

Revelations of a clandestine B-52 bombing campaign in Cambodia, conducted for 14 months in 1969 and 1970 at a cost of $1.5 billion and deliberately concealed from the Senate by the Defense Department, forced the president to end U.S. bombing in support of the Cambodian government on August 15. But suspicions that airpower could all too easily be used by the president in violation of legislative restraints were not appeased. Other cuts in the Air Force included a reduction of the Aerospace Defense Command (ADC) following testimony to the Senate that the existing system offered no effective barrier to Soviet bombers attempting a surprise attack. Over the Horizon (OTH) radar, in combination with the new Airborne Warning and Control System (AWACS) and the F-15 Eagle fighter, offered a more effective defense, but one that the Senate would fund only slowly. Meanwhile, the 585 interceptors of the ADC were reduced to 500. The strategic bomber force was to be reduced by the disbandment of two squadrons of B-52Ds, leaving 117 in service, plus 240 B-52 G/Hs in 16 squadrons and 66 FB-111As in 4 squadrons. For the rest of the 1970s the Air Force would continue its reorientation to support of land forces.

Like the Air Force, the Navy had been relatively successful in recruiting enough volunteers to meet its

continued on page 234

"Business is booming!"

PETERSON—VANCOUVER SUN/ROTHCO

THE OCTOBER WAR

By Robert J. Ranger

The fourth Arab-Israeli war started with a surprise attack by Egypt's Pres. Anwar as-Sadat and Syria's Pres. Hafez al-Assad on Israel, launched on Oct. 6, 1973. Partly because this was Yom Kippur, the most sacred day in the Jewish religious calendar, and partly because there had been no political and little military warning of the attack, Israel took 72 hours to reach full mobilization strength. The thin Israeli forces covering the frontiers with Egypt and Syria were driven back, forcing Israel to launch counterattacks, first against the Syrians, who were driven to within 20 mi. of Damascus by October 17, and then against the Egyptian bridgehead on the east bank of the Suez Canal.

The Egyptians' failure to advance on the passes to Israel in the Sinai meant that their eventual attack on October 14 was defeated. This was followed by a brilliant Israeli penetration of the Egyptian lines south of Ismailia, and by October 22 Israeli forces were established in strength on the west bank of the canal. They destroyed Egyptian surface-to-air missile (SAM) sites and rear formations while swinging south to cut off the Egyptian 3rd Army and threaten Cairo. The Arabs called for a cease-fire, which was agreed on October 22 but was almost immediately breached as Israel surrounded the 3rd Army on October 23. The final positions, with Israeli troops on the west bank of the canal and Egyptian forces on the east bank, seemed too unstable to be held for long, forcing both sides to negotiate a lasting peace settlement at discussions that began in Geneva in December.

The Arabs had obtained their political objectives of challenging the boundaries, favourable to Israel, that had been established after the 1967 Arab-Israeli war and of reestablishing Arab self-respect through a successful limited war against Israel. The Arabs had been aided by a massive Soviet airlift of supplies during the fighting. This broke previous superpower understandings on crisis management, compelling the U.S. to resupply Israel. A direct superpower confrontation was barely avoided, but U.S. Secretary of State Henry A. Kissinger's rapid negotiation in November of cease-fire terms agreeable to the superpowers and their client states left the diplomatic initiative with the U.S.

Tactically, the greatest lesson of the October war was the success of the new Soviet SA-6 missile against the Israeli Air Force and of Soviet antitank missiles against Israeli armour, suggesting that the aircraft/tank combination that had dominated the battlefield since World War II might be threatened. Nevertheless, the war had again demonstrated Israel's qualitative superiority in conventional weapons, enabling it to defeat the larger armed forces of the Arabs despite a much criticized decision by Israeli Prime Minister Golda Meir and Defense Minister Moshe Dayan not to secure the advantages of a preemptive strike.

The Opening Phase. The prewar military balance gave Israel, when fully mobilized, an army of 275,000, with 400 M-48 Patton tanks, 250 Ben Gurions, 200 Ishermans, and 100 TI-67s (captured Soviet T-54/55s), all with 105-mm. guns, plus 600 Centurions and 150 M-60s. The Egyptian Army of 260,000 had 1,650 T-54/55, 100 T-62, and 100 T-34 medium tanks, while Syria's 120,000-man army had 900 T-54/55 and 240 T-34 medium tanks. This gave Egypt and Syria combined 380,000 men to Israel's 275,000 and 3,000 tanks to Israel's 1,700. The Israeli Air Force of 20,000 men had 95 F-4E Phantoms and 35 Mirage III-B/C fighter-bomber interceptors, plus 160 A-4E/4 Skyhawk and 23 Mystère IV-A fighter-bombers and 24 Barak and 18 Super-Mystère B-2 interceptors. The Egyptian and Syrian air forces included some 300 aircraft in reserve for want of trained pilots, but nominally they totaled 180 MiG-17 and 110 Su-7 fighter-bombers with 410 MiG-21 interceptors. Egypt's air defense network was based on 130 SAM sites, each with 6 SA-2 and SA-3 launchers for use against high- and low-level attacks, plus SA-6s and SA-7s and 23-, 37-, 57-, and 85-mm. mobile antiaircraft guns for defense against low-level attacks. Both sides had light naval forces with missile-carrying fast patrol boats. Israel used its 12 Saar-class patrol boats, with Gabriel missiles, to attack the Syrian ports of Latakia and Baniyas, which received incoming Soviet supplies.

Jordan and Iraq both came to the support of Syria after the war started, although they were not able to throw in all their forces. These amounted to 68,000 men and 420 medium tanks for Jordan, with a small air force of 32 Hunter fighter/ground-attack planes and 20 F-104A interceptors. Iraq had 90,000 men, 900 T-54/55 tanks, and an air force of 60 Su-7s, 90 MiG-21s, and 30 MiG-17s. The Libyan Air Force of 35 Mirage III-B/E and 9 F-5A interceptors was thought to have intervened in support of Egypt.

This numerical superiority meant that the Arabs' best tactics would be a limited advance into Israeli-held territory, remaining within the 20-mi. range of their air defense systems while forcing Israel to engage in relatively static battles of attrition rather than the mobile armoured battles in which it excelled. The initial Arab attacks thus involved a Syrian advance with 500 tanks and two infantry divisions against an outnumbered Israeli defense along the Damascus–al-Qunaytirah road. Simultaneously, the Egyptians launched a long-rehearsed crossing of the Suez Canal, between al-Qantarah and Suez. The 2nd Army of about 25,000 men and 200 tanks moved across in the northern sector between al-Qantarah and the Great Bitter Lake and the 3rd Army of 20,000 men and 200 tanks in the southern sector between the Bitter Lakes and Suez. The Israelis' Bar-Lev line was quickly pierced; it was thinly held and was intended only to identify a major attack, unless heavily reinforced.

Counterattack. The failure of the Israeli government to order mobilization until just before the war broke out created a major domestic political dispute. It was hard to explain, except on the assumption that Israel had underestimated the Arabs' military capabilities, especially the morale of their troops, and assumed they would be as easily defeated as in the 1967 Six-Day War. In fact, the Arabs proved in 1973 to be much more formidable opponents, able to take considerable losses and still keep on fighting. Within the first week Arab casualties were estimated at 12,000 dead and wounded, mostly in a major tank battle on the Syrian front. There Jordanian and Iraqi forces had joined the Syrians, giving them over 300 tanks as reinforcements. These were committed to battle against the now-mobilized Israelis, who had knocked out the computers controlling the Syrian air defense network. By October 17–18 the Syrians were defeated, having lost some 50% of their tanks and 30% of their aircraft. The Israelis advanced within artillery range of Damascus, destroying an Iraqi armoured division en route.

Meanwhile, the Egyptians had built up their forces on the east bank and had destroyed the 190th Israeli Armoured Brigade and most of its 200 tanks, which mounted the first Israeli counterattack. This revealed the vulnerability of Israeli aircraft to the Soviet-supplied SA-6, used for the first time in the October war and so less vulnerable to electronic countermeasures devised by the U.S. and Israel against the older SA-2s and 3s. The Egyptians also used the SA-7 (Strella), carried by infantrymen, as was the Snapper antitank missile. Both were used in large quantities, with the Soviet airlift replacing munitions as they were used.

Robert J. Ranger is assistant professor of political science at St. Francis Xavier University, Antigonish, Nova Scotia, and a long-time contributor to the Britannica Book of the Year.

Israel retreated to the passes into the Sinai Desert about 30 mi. east of the canal, leaving some five mechanized and two armoured Egyptian divisions in possession of a bridgehead about 10 mi. deep into the Sinai. Following a conservative strategy, these forces did not try to seize the passes, although a rapid advance might have succeeded. Instead, they chose to build up their strength until they could advance on a broad front.

This delay gave the Israelis time to defeat the Syrians and shift their forces to the Sinai front, where on October 17 they defeated the Egyptian attempt to advance. During the Israeli counterattacks, they discovered a weak link between the Egyptian 2nd Army in the north and the 3rd Army in the south and established a bridgehead with some 200 tanks and 15,000 troops on the west bank of the canal, destroying the Egyptian SAM network and forcing the Egyptian Air Force to engage in dogfights that ended in Israeli victories. The Egyptian high command reacted too slowly to the Israeli counterattack along the southern part of the canal, partly because the Israelis had held the Egyptian 2nd Army's attention with a cautious frontal attack by 30,000 Israeli troops and 200 tanks. This enabled the Israelis, on October 20, to execute the classic breakout from a bridgehead of armoured warfare, led by Maj. Gen. Ariel Sharon, popularly known as the Israeli Patton. By October 22 Israeli forces were within 50 mi. of Cairo, having defeated all Egyptian attempts to dislodge them, and had captured intact SA-6 missiles.

With Soviet assistance, Egypt secured a cease-fire on October 22, before the 3rd Army was cut off, but its attempts to break out on October 23 led to renewed fighting that ended with the 3rd Army being encircled by Israeli forces. A further cease-fire, supported by both the U.S. and the U.S.S.R., was successful. UN peace observation forces were interposed between the Arabs and Israelis. Beginning October 28 the Egyptians and Israelis negotiated directly (for the first time since 1956) on an exchange of the 8,301 prisoners of war held by Israel and the 241 held by Egypt. This was carried out in the third week of November. Both sides suffered casualties proportionately heavier than those of the U.S. in Vietnam; the Israelis had 4,100 killed and wounded to Egypt's 7,500 and Syria's 7,300. The fate of the surrounded 3rd Army seemed to depend on the negotiations for a lasting peace. Syria initially refused to consider such negotiations or a POW exchange.

Pause or Peace? The October war provided the maximum incentive for a negotiated peace that would leave Israel with secure and defensible frontiers while allowing the Egyptians and Jordanians to regain some of their territory lost in the 1967 war. The two superpowers would have to underwrite, implicitly or explicitly, any such settlement, which would probably involve the presence of a UN peacekeeping force of 7,000 lightly equipped troops to supervise any demilitarized areas. Both the U.S. and U.S.S.R. could be expected to pressure their allies into reaching such a settlement, since the superpowers appeared to have barely avoided a direct confrontation between their military forces on October 25. The Soviets had supported an Egyptian request for a joint U.S.-U.S.S.R. peacekeeping force to underwrite the first cease-fire, and when the U.S. rejected this proposal the Soviets indicated they might unilaterally place their forces in Egypt. With some seven airborne divisions, totaling 49,000 men, equipped with armour and artillery and supported by the augmented Mediterranean squadron with naval infantry (marines), the U.S.S.R. certainly had the capability to intervene. The U.S., therefore, on the advice of Kissinger and Defense Secretary James R. Schlesinger, ordered a Defense Condition Three, a precautionary alert of U.S. troops, with special readiness for the 82nd Airborne Division at Ft. Bragg, North Carolina, and all strategic forces, including B-52 bombers.

This alert was criticized in the U.S. as an attempt by Pres. Richard M. Nixon to divert attention from the Watergate scandal (*see* UNITED STATES), but subsequent analysis of the available evidence suggested a possible Soviet intervention. The U.S.S.R. was already mounting a major air- and sea-lift of munitions to Egypt and Syria, using its 15 giant Anatov An-22 transports. The U.S. had countered by supplying additional Phantoms to Israel via a staging base in the Azores and by airlifting supplies, using 72 of the much criticized C-5A transports which, however, proved very successful. These outside supplies partly offset wartime losses, estimated at 840 tanks and 107 aircraft for Israel, against 421 aircraft and 1,775 tanks for Egypt and Syria.

The NATO allies' refusal to permit U.S. aid to Israel from bases in their territories was understandable in view of the Western European countries' dependence on Arab suppliers for 80% of their oil. However, it produced sharp reminders from the U.S. that European support was expected for a policy that served the interests of NATO as a whole. The disarray in the Atlantic alliance encouraged the Arabs to hope that their reduction in oil supplies to states supporting Israel would produce a swing in diplomatic opinion against Israel. This certainly occurred, but the U.S. remained committed to support of the existence of Israel —though not its conquests, as Kissinger put it—if only because the U.S. could not afford to be seen giving in to economic blackmail. Nevertheless, the long-term effects of a continued Arab oil blockade of NATO and Japan would be so serious that Israel seemed unlikely to be able to resist pressure to make a reasonable offer of frontiers acceptable to the Arabs.

The real danger seemed to be that the Arabs, having regained their self-respect, might be tempted to demand unacceptable concessions by Israel, hoping the U.S.S.R. would be forced to support these demands. Ironically, the overriding lesson of the October war was the inability of either superpower to control its smaller allies, who remained able, in the Middle East, to threaten the superpower détente with disputes of marginal concern to the real interests of the U.S. or the U.S.S.R.

Paradoxically, this also increased the chance that peace in the Middle East might be nearer as a result of the largest conventional war, in terms of armoured forces, since World War II.

UPI COMPIX

UN peace observation forces enter the Israeli-occupied city of Suez in Egypt on Oct. 28, 1973, the same day that Egyptian and Israeli negotiators began discussing prisoner exchanges.

A.F.P./PICTORIAL PARADE

The French Mirage F-1 soars on its maiden flight, Feb. 15, 1973.

continued from page 231

needs, and it retained a slightly larger share of the defense budget (35%) than the other two services. Nevertheless, it was experiencing difficulty in securing funding for its fourth nuclear carrier, the CVN-70. Its second nuclear carrier was commissioned, and it had, in addition, eight Forrestal/Kitty Hawk-class large attack carriers, with 80–90 aircraft, and six smaller Midway- and Hancock-class carriers with 70–80 planes. Fleet deployment was changing with the end of the Vietnam war. The 7th Fleet (western Pacific) was being run down to strengthen the 3rd Fleet (eastern Pacific), which would provide the major force for intervention in the Persian Gulf. The 6th Fleet (Mediterranean) remained at its normal level of 2 carriers, 17 surface combat vessels, and 1 amphibious group, while the 2nd Fleet (Atlantic) had increased to 4 carriers and 63 surface combat vessels. The five new landing helicopter assault ships intended to exploit the vertical envelopment techniques developed in Vietnam were 23 months behind schedule; the first was due for delivery in March 1975 if the Navy could settle its dispute with Litton Systems, Inc., over cost overruns. A tough line on overruns was also evident in the Navy's insistence that Grumman Aerospace Corp. build 48 more F-14 Tomcat fighters at the contract rate of $16.8 million each, despite Grumman's claim that this would involve a loss of $105 million. The Marine Corps recruited its authorized strength of three 19,000-man divisions with 550 combat aircraft.

The Army's predictable difficulties in recruitment, which fell 15% short of the target, made it difficult to estimate how many of its active divisions were really operational. With the U.S. withdrawal from Vietnam, the 7th Army in West Germany became the major overseas force, comprising four divisions (two armoured and two mechanized infantry), one mechanized infantry brigade, and two armoured cavalry regiments. Congressional critics of this force, led by Sen. Mike Mansfield, contended it was larger than necessary for the performance of its function of a hostage. However, dual-based units, kept in the U.S. but with most of their equipment stockpiled in West Germany, would actually cost more, since they would have to be returned to West Germany for training. Nor would there be a substantial saving in foreign exchange, since the total cost of U.S. forces in Europe not covered by offset payments was only about $1.7 million per year. Advocates of substantial U.S. troop reductions in Europe also overlooked the extent to which these had been carried out: from the 1962 peak of 434,000, the number had dropped to 300,000.

The only other substantial army deployments outside the continental U.S. were one infantry division of 20,000 men, scheduled for reduction, in South Korea and one division in Hawaii. Within the continental U.S., the main active unit was the Strategic Reserve of one Tricap (triple-capable) division, one infantry, one air-mobile, and one airborne division, though most of these units were not at full strength. Recruiting problems could reduce total army personnel from its current strength of 801,000 to 730,000, of which 15% (120,000) would, by Pentagon ruling, be combat soldiers. This was not enough to meet the nondraft goal of 11 divisions at an average strength of 15,000 men, and the U.S. could be forced to adopt the two-tier system of a small regular force supplemented by reservists who could be activated quickly. The existing U.S. Reserve structure was too cumbersome and underequipped to do this, although the Army National Guard, with an authorized strength of 402,300 and an actual strength of 386,700, could provide, given time, two armoured, one mechanized, and five infantry divisions as well as making good shortfalls in regular units.

The major problem facing the U.S. armed forces was whether they could change from the structure evolved in the 1960s—forces nominally equipped to fight a limited war in Asia and a major war in Europe but actually preoccupied with an Asian war and able to fight in Europe only if allowed to mobilize on the World War II model. What were required were forces able to fight a major war in Europe and intervene in a limited conflict in the Middle East.

The U.S. defense establishment was further weakened by a rapid turnover of senior policymakers. Secretary of Defense Melvin R. Laird had efficiently implemented the military aspects of the Nixon-Kissinger doctrine of limited U.S. responsibility from 1969 to January 1973, but later in 1973 he joined the White House staff, as did Gen. Alexander M. Haig, Jr., after less than a year as Army vice-chief of staff. Elliot L. Richardson, confirmed as defense secretary in January, became attorney general in May, leaving the new secretary, James R. Schlesinger (*see* BIOGRAPHY), in a politically weak position.

U.S.S.R.

Despite formal recognition of the Soviet sphere of control in Eastern Europe by the U.S. and West Germany and a desire to exploit political détente to secure Western financial and technical resources, the Soviet

Union continued a program of heavy military spending. Soviet defense spending was estimated at $81 billion–$85 billion out of a net material product of $439 billion, or roughly 7.5% of NMP. Soviet objectives appeared to include the achievement of as great a superiority in strategic forces as was possible under SALT I, giving the U.S.S.R. a psychological advantage in SALT II; quantitative superiority in conventional forces in Western Europe, creating a favourable bargaining position in MBFR; and the capability to intervene to further Soviet interests on its borders, especially in the Middle East. This suggested both a reaction against the U.S.S.R.'s historical position of inferiority vis-à-vis the U.S. and a realization that growing pressures in the West for a reduction in defense spending, coupled with an often uncritical acceptance of détente, could create situations where the existence of superior Soviet forces would produce opportunities for political gains.

The U.S.S.R.'s emphasis on increasing its strategic nuclear delivery forces could be explained as an effort to achieve qualitative and therefore psychological parity with the U.S., especially in terms of immunity from a surprise attack or preemptive strike—now politically less likely but technically more feasible. It was harder to explain the buildup of Soviet nuclear systems and conventional forces for use against Western Europe in purely defensive terms. These forces were far larger than would be needed for defense or deterrence, especially since the U.S.S.R. no longer relied on its ability to conquer Western Europe as a deterrent to a U.S. strike against it. The Soviets still maintained a force of 500 SS-4 medium-range ballistic missiles (MRBMs) and 100 SS-5 intermediate-range ballistic missiles (IRBMs) deployed from 1959–61 onward, and an added 100 SS-11 ICBMs, configured for short range and greater payloads, were sited within IRBM-MRBM fields, mostly near the western border. Of the Tactical Air Force's 4,500 aircraft, about half were oriented against Western Europe.

Soviet military doctrine rejected the Western concept of an initially limited use of tactical nuclear weapons, escalating into a major nuclear exchange only after a pause for negotiation, in favour of a major strike by Soviet tactical nuclear forces against NATO bases. The larger yield of Soviet nuclear weapons made them less suitable for a limited exchange, but this stated policy also served to exploit Soviet conventional superiority. Soviet deployment and aid to its Pact allies certainly suggested a desire to retain the capability for a rapid conventional victory against Western Europe.

The nominal strength of the Soviet Army remained at 107 motorized rifle, 50 tank, and 7 airborne divisions, with the effective units concentrated in Eastern Europe, European U.S.S.R., and the Sino-Soviet border area. In Eastern Europe there were 31 divisions, including 12 tank divisions with 7,850 medium tanks. The T-54/55 tank was being replaced by the T-62, while a new medium tank, the M-1970, and a new light tank were beginning production. In European U.S.S.R. there were 40 motorized rifle and 14 tank divisions in categories 1 (combat ready) and 2 (not requiring major reinforcement in time of war), plus a further 10 motorized rifle and 7 tank divisions in category 3 (requiring major reinforcement in time of war). The Sino-Soviet border area had absorbed about 37 infantry and 8 tank divisions, split evenly between categories 1, 2, and 3. This suggested that the Soviets were not expecting any sudden outbreak of hostilities with China.

Pact forces had remained about the same size for nearly a decade but had been extensively modernized. In approximate order of effectiveness, they were: East Germany, two tank and four motorized rifle divisions; Poland, five tank, six motorized rifle, one airborne, and one amphibious assault divisions; and Hungary, one tank and two motorized rifle divisions. Czechoslovakia's five tank and three motorized divisions were imposing on paper but of doubtful political reliability. Pact naval forces added significantly to Soviet capabilities for a rapid sea and air advance in the Baltic.

The Soviet Navy continued its steady expansion. A 40,000-ton aircraft carrier was launched, designed to operate vertical/short takeoff and landing (V/STOL) aircraft and helicopters, primarily for ASW but also to give greatly superior protection against aircraft or surface-to-surface missiles (SSMs). Average deployments reflected the differing tasks assigned to the various fleets. The Northern Fleet of 45 major surface combat ships and 170 submarines was designed to counter U.S. missile-carrying submarines while protecting those of the U.S.S.R. and, in wartime, covering a Soviet advance into northern Norway. The Baltic Fleet of 52 major surface combat vessels and 43 submarines was intended to secure the Baltic for the U.S.S.R. in time of war. The Black Sea Fleet provided the overpublicized Soviet Mediterranean squadron from among its 63 major surface combat vessels and 31 submarines, a relatively small force given its wartime task of suppressing the U.S. and French SLBM-carrying submarines and knocking out the carriers of the U.S. 6th Fleet.

Paradoxically, the heavy Soviet investment in military hardware had rendered the U.S.S.R. less sensitive to its adverse effects on the states it was intended to impress, and there were signs that this military overkill was becoming counterproductive. Egyptian Pres. Anwar as-Sadat showed no signs of reversing his 1972 decision to expel the majority of Soviet advisers, and Col. Muammar al-Qaddafi of Libya was nearly as hostile to the Soviets as to the West. Elsewhere, Cuba remained a reliable, if expensive, protectorate. The distribution of Soviet instructors and advisers outside the Pact area suggested that Soviet influence had increased less than the West had feared. Meanwhile, within Western Europe and, to a lesser extent, the U.S., continued Soviet stress on military superiority was generating a more cautious approach to détente.

The U.S.S.R.'s decision to resupply the Arab states during the October Middle East war emphasized these contradictions in its defense policy. By reequipping the Arabs, the U.S.S.R. had implicitly committed itself to supporting them in any future war, rather than using the threat of cutting off supplies to restrain them. Yet the U.S.S.R. seemed unlikely to make any substantive gains from Arab successes while its actions jeopardized the Soviet-U.S. relationship. It appeared that, like the U.S. in Vietnam, the U.S.S.R. was becoming a prisoner of its own military machine, with the availability of forces creating pressure for a foreign policy that facilitated their use.

UNITED KINGDOM

The major issues in U.K. defense policy in 1973 were the future of Britain's nuclear deterrent, the continued presence of its troops in Northern Ireland, and its attitude to the MBFR-European security debate. The

CAMERA PRESS/PICTORIAL PARADE

A French balloon carries a crated nuclear device scheduled for explosion in the atmosphere over Mururoa Atoll in the Pacific Ocean.

August report of the House of Commons Committee on Estimates on Britain's deterrent force, comprising four SSBN nuclear-powered submarines each carrying 16 Polaris A-3 missiles, reopened the debate on whether these should be retained, modernized with MIRV warheads, or replaced by Poseidon missiles in improved submarines. The committee recommended the retention of the existing Polaris, equipped with improved MRVs. The purchase of Poseidon missiles was rejected as too expensive, as was the acquisition of additional missile-carrying submarines, but the absence of reliable cost figures made it hard to justify the acceptance of an expensive deterrent system that might prove inadequate unless it was upgraded.

The need for the U.K. and France to coordinate their nuclear policies was largely ignored, although this was vital if they were to receive maximum U.S. aid in strengthening their nuclear forces to provide a substitute guarantee of escalation as U.S. troops withdrew from Western Europe. So was the imbalance between procuring only four Polaris submarines and the commissioning of additional nuclear-powered hunter-killer submarines to provide a total of six in 1974. The need for the U.K. to build a tactical missile system comparable to the French Pluton or U.S. Lance was also ignored. But the committee did help to focus attention on the problems facing a Western Europe with substantially fewer U.S. troops.

The civil war in Northern Ireland continued. Britain maintained an average of 15,000 soldiers there, including 3,500 from the British Army of the Rhine (BAOR)—a drop of 7,000 from the previous year. (*See* United Kingdom.)

The U.K. defense budget reflected British opposition to the MBFR negotiations as a cover for bilateral U.S.-U.S.S.R. agreements on troop reductions, and to the European security conference as a Soviet device to secure multilateral legitimization of its Eastern European empire without making corresponding concessions. At £3,365 million, the budget represented 4.6% of gross national product (GNP), the highest percentage in Western Europe. Overseas commitments had been reduced to a minimum, with two brigades (half consisting of Gurkha battalions) in Hong Kong, one infantry battalion group in Singapore, one Gurkha battalion in Brunei, and one infantry battalion in Gibraltar. The BAOR had been brought up to its full strength of 54,900 men, composed of 3 divisions with 5 armoured brigades (out of the U.K. total of 13 armoured regiments), 1 mechanized and 2 artillery brigades, and 2 armoured reconnaissance regiments. The land element of the U.K. Mobile Force, intended primarily to reinforce the BAOR, comprised one division and four infantry and one parachute brigades, plus the Special Air Service regiment. The two Army aviation wings were acquiring long-overdue helicopter capability.

The Royal Air Force, now geared to its primary role of army support, had only minor deployments overseas apart from West Germany. The six Vulcan medium bomber squadrons had been transferred from a strategic strike role to one of tactical support and interdiction as part of RAF Strike Command, but could still carry thermonuclear weapons. Rapid airlift from the U.K. to West Germany could be provided by four strategic and seven tactical transport squadrons, the latter equipped with the U.S. C-130 Hercules heavy transport.

Although the Royal Navy remained the third largest in the world, with 78 major surface combat vessels, it seemed likely to shrink in the face of rising costs and a decreasingly relevant role. The one remaining aircraft carrier, HMS "Ark Royal," carried only 12 Buccaneer S Mk 2 strike bombers and 12 F-4K Phantom interceptors, plus 6 Gannet early-warning aircraft. Thus it could offer only very limited protection against threats from long- and short-range SSMs, air-to-surface missiles, and submarines. Yet without air cover it was difficult to see how any landing force could survive in a sophisticated combat environment. The Navy's ASW vessels were mostly too large to risk combat with missile-equipped opponents and lacked any SSMs comparable to those in the Soviet and U.S. navies. The two cruisers had Seacat SAMs and the nine destroyers had Seaslug I and Seacat II SAMs, except for one with Ikara ASW missiles. Of the 35 general purpose frigates, 12 mounted Seacat and one Ikara; all had one ASW helicopter, as did 9 of the 20 ASW frigates. Nevertheless, the 8,000-man Royal Marines could represent a significant deterrent if landed before an attack started, and it was decided to add 100 Lynx helicopters to the Fleet Air Arm.

FRANCE

France's continued testing of miniaturized thermonuclear warheads for its SLBMs at Mururoa Atoll in the Pacific brought the total of French nuclear tests to 45. The 1973 test series aroused widespread protest, especially from New Zealand and Australia, but fears of danger from radioactive fallout were regarded by the French government as excessive and insufficient to warrant halting tests that were part of a $15 billion weapons program. This program had already produced 36 Mirage IV-A strategic bombers with a 2,000-mi. range, carrying a 150-kiloton nuclear weapon similar to the warheads on France's 18 SSBS S-2 IRBMs. Both would receive improved thermonuclear warheads, probably in the 500-kiloton range, as these became available. Two missile-carrying nuclear submarines were operational in mid-1973, as was the Pluton tactical missile system.

The French government's belief in the need for an independent nuclear deterrent as a *taux d'ennui* ("nuisance tax") against a possible Soviet threat to which the U.S. might not respond was strengthened by what the French saw as a too uncritical acceptance of détente by the U.S. France demonstrated its opposition to the MBFR negotiations by indicating it would not reduce its forces as a result of the talks, and it continued to refrain from military participation in NATO.

Nevertheless, French defense spending was held down to $8.4 million, only 3.1% of GNP as compared with 3.5% in 1969. The Army of 332,400 included 216,000 conscripts; proposals designed to eliminate student exemptions aroused some domestic opposition, although their effect would be to make the draft more socially equitable. With the French withdrawal from Chad and a sharp reduction in the 3,000-man force in the Malagasy Republic, overseas forces consisted of only two battalions in the French Territory of the Afars and Issas, about 4,000 troops elsewhere in Africa, two battalions in the Pacific territories, and one battalion in the Caribbean. Growing resentment in French-speaking Africa against France's neocolonial role meant that it would be increasingly difficult for the *force d'intervention* (renamed the Strategic Reserve) to be used in propping up pro-French governments.

Of the five mechanized divisions in the *force de manoeuvre,* two were still in West Germany under bilateral agreements. The remaining three divisions were deployed close to the Franco-West German border. Reequipment continued, giving France an effective armoured force. The territorial defense force (Défense Opérationnelle du Territoire or DOT) numbered 52,000 men in 2 alpine brigades, 21 infantry battalions, and 3 armoured cavalry and 1 artillery regiments. These formed a cadre for mobilization of 450,000 reservists, bringing DOT up to 80 battalions if sufficient time were allowed.

The Air Force began to receive the jointly produced Anglo-French Jaguar fighter-bombers. They joined the two squadrons of Mystère IV-As, part of the Tactical Air Force designed to support the *force de manoeuvre.* As in most other tactical-support air forces, the fighter-bomber was replacing the old combination of interceptors and bombers. The Air Defense Command was mainly intended to defend the *force de frappe*'s 36 Mirage IV-A bombers and the 12 KC-135 tankers. The Air Transport Command retained a modest airlift capability.

Like the U.K., France had traditionally maintained a large navy whose role seemed less and less likely to justify its expense. If a major war broke out, the ASW forces of 12 destroyers would be of use only in screening Atlantic convoys and in tracking Soviet hunter-killer submarines in the Mediterranean. France retained a limited capability to land amphibious forces, but the Naval Air Force of two Etendard IV-M fighter-bomber squadrons and two F-8F Crusader interceptor squadrons could provide air cover only against very limited opposition. The provision of carrier-borne ASW helicopter squadrons was also a diminishing asset as Soviet SLBMs increased in range, so that their submarines no longer had to patrol close to NATO coasts.

France remained a major arms supplier. Sales included 180 AMX-30 medium tanks to Spain, Exocet naval SSMs to Turkey, 14 Mirage V fighters to Abu Dhabi, 30 AMX-30s to Saudi Arabia, 4 Roland SAM units and 30 SA-341 Gazelle helicopters to Brazil, an unknown number of Mirage fighters to Iran, and 142 AMX-30s and 20 AMX-155 self-propelled guns to Venezuela. French supremacy in this field was being challenged, however, by a major increase in U.S. arms sales, often on terms amounting to aid, as part of the Nixon Doctrine and by Britain's adoption of the French policy of selling arms without regard to their intended use as long as the price was paid.

WIDE WORLD

Chinese women fliers of the People's Liberation Army observe as one of their colleagues demonstrates with a model airplane.

NORTHERN EUROPE

With the admission of West and East Germany as separate members of the UN on September 18, West German Chancellor Willy Brandt's *Ostpolitik* reached its logical conclusion: the formal acceptance of the existence, as he put it, of two German states but one German nation. At the same time, Soviet recalcitrance concerning the normalization of West German relations with Eastern Europe emphasized the changing nature of West Germany's defense problem. The original threat had been one of Soviet military action against West Germany. Now the U.S.S.R. was using its military strength to secure recognition of its sphere of control in Eastern Europe (a goal largely achieved) and to obtain economic and political concessions from a West Germany increasingly unsure that the U.S. would guarantee its security in any eventuality short of major war and doubtful of its own capabilities for self-defense.

The report of the commission on the Bundeswehr's structure reflected the problems faced by West Germany and other NATO members in maintaining armed forces able to provide political security and military deterrence in an era of rapidly rising manpower costs and public indifference or hostility to the military. The immediate stimulus to reform in West Germany was the fact that the increasing numbers of men who would be called up under the existing universal conscription would require an expansion of the Army or a reduction in the length of service from the existing 15 months, about the minimum necessary for effective training.

The commission recommended calling up only those conscripts required to maintain existing force levels. Economies would be made by maintaining fewer combat units at full strength and more cadre units, on the Soviet model. The Army would have a peacetime strength of 472,000, with 24 full-strength and 12 cadre-strength brigades. Territorial Army defense units would constitute a separate reserve force. Even so, these forces could be equipped only if the level of defense spending was raised from the current 3.2% of GNP to 3.5% by 1981.

This would still leave West Germany with the largest army in NATO. Its existing 334,000 men (183,500 conscripts) provided 13 armoured, 12 armoured infantry, 3 motorized infantry, 2 mountain, and 3 airborne brigades organized in 12 divisions and 2 tank regiments. Reequipment with the West German Leopard tank continued, with 2,200 in service plus 1,050 M-48A2 Patton tanks. The Air Force continued to replace its F-104G Starfighters with F-4 Phantoms. The 168 G-91 light fighter/ground-attack planes were retained, as were 72 Pershing nuclear-capable SSMs with warheads in U.S. custody.

A U.S. Navy senior fire-control technician views a test target on one of the Aegis system's console displays, which visually provide data on aircraft targets, as well as instructions for fire control. Aegis was the Navy's latest fleet air-defense system.

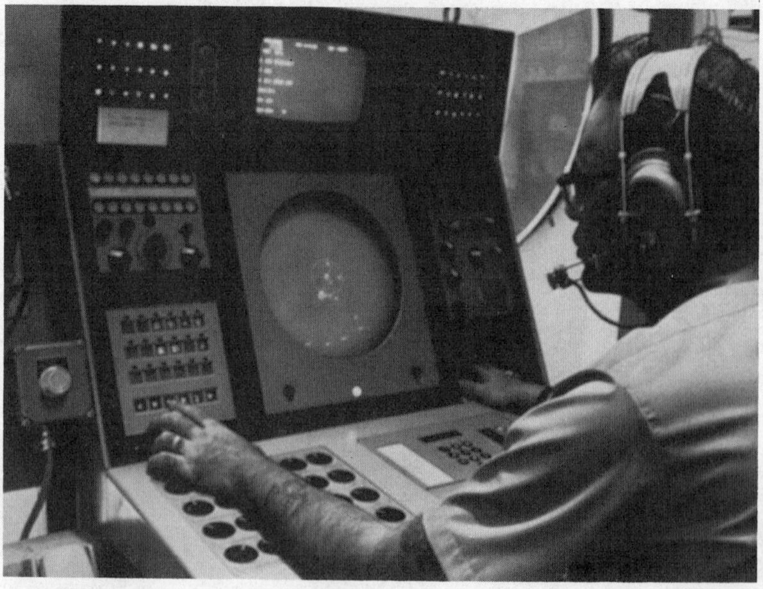

UPI COMPIX

The Navy was keeping its 72 F-104Gs in service but was replacing its 23 S-58 SAR helicopters with 20 SH-3D Sea King Mk-41s. It had comparatively few vessels for its task of retaining control over the mouth of the Baltic and protecting the Danish coast. If maintained at current levels but with greater efficiency, they would be able to offer an effective conventional forward defense sufficient to halt any but a major Soviet attack. However, West Germany, like its Western European partners in NATO, rejected the new U.S. view that a prolonged conventional defense could be offered, stressing instead the importance of the U.S. retaining a credible willingness to use tactical nuclear weapons.

West Germany's commitment to maintain its defense forces contrasted strongly with Denmark's cuts under the 1973 Defense Bill establishing a four-year-plan for the armed forces. Defense spending was only 2.2% of GNP, and even this was regarded as too high by Danish politicians anxious to forestall extremist pressures for Denmark's withdrawal from NATO. The Defense Bill envisaged a very lightly manned five-brigade Army, with a covering force of 13,000 men and a reserve of 65,000 men. Naval forces would drop to 5,760 men, and the Air Force would have 6,570 men. In contrast, a Netherlands commission of civilian and military experts recommended that the Dutch defense effort be increased from 3.5% of GNP in 1972 to 4.25% between 1973 and 1976.

The report of the 1970 Swedish Commission on National Defense, issued on Jan. 14, 1972, had emphasized that, like other industrial democracies, Sweden could meet the rising costs of defense either by raising the percentage of GNP spent on defense, which would be unacceptable to the public, or by altering the force structure. Accordingly, the commission had recommended that Sweden concentrate on resisting a conventional attack through a total defense effort, providing local defense of major targets supplemented by mobile forces for counterattack.

FAR EAST

In Kissinger's pentagonal balance, China and Japan were seen as the bases of the evolving South and East Asian centre of power. The U.S.S.R. would be unable to gain substantial influence there, though it was compelled to tie down considerable conventional forces on the Sino-Soviet border. At the same time, the U.S. would reap the advantages of disengaging itself from direct involvement on the Southeast Asian mainland.

China's significance became clearer if its military strength, likely to remain far below that of the superpowers, was compared with that of other powers in the area. As long as Japan remained determined to minimize its defense spending, China would be the dominant political and military power in the region. This would not be because of its nuclear weapons, which were barely sufficient to deter the U.S.S.R., or because of its massive conventional armies, which were unable to move much beyond China's borders, but because its sheer size and political unity made it so much stronger than its potential rivals, notably

Approximate Strengths of Regular Armed Forces of the World

Country	Military personnel in 000s: Army	Navy	Air force	Warships: Aircraft carriers (CV)/ cruisers (CA/CL)	Submarines*	Destroyers/ frigates	Total major surface combat vessels	Jet aircraft: Bombers†	Fighters	Tanks‡	Defense expenditure as % of GNP
I. NATO											
Belgium	65.0	4.6	20.0	—	—	—	—	80 FB	36	482	2.0
Canada	33.0	14.0	36.0	—	4	22	22	50 FB	66	32	1.9
Denmark	24.0	6.3	9.5	—	6	6	6	48 FB	80	250	2.2
France§	332.4	69.0	102.0	3 CV, 2 CA	19, 2 FBMS	42	47	30 B, 225 FB, 36 SB	150	820	3.1
Germany, West	334.0	37.0	104.0	—	8	17	17	388 FB	60	3,250	2.9
Greece	120.0	18.0	22.0	—	7	13	13	128 FB	54	650	4.1
Italy	306.5	44.5	76.5	3 CA	9	18	27	135 FB	90	1,200	2.7
Luxembourg	0.5	—	—	—	—	—	—	—	—	—	0.8
Netherlands, The	70.0	20.0	22.2	—	6	18	18	90 FB	36	885	3.5
Norway	18.0	8.0	9.4	—	15	5	5	80 FB	29	158	3.2
Portugal	170.0	18.0	16.0	—	4	12	12	60 FB	40	100	5.1
Turkey	365.0	40.0	50.0	—	15	14	14	162 FB	72	1,400	3.6
United Kingdom‖	177.0	89.0	103.5	3 CV, 2 CA	22, 6 N, 4 FBMS	71	78	150 B, 300 FB	150	900	4.6
United States‖	997.5	564.0	691.6	15 CV, 5 CA, 4 CL	24, 60 N, 41 FBMS	134	221	1,400 FB, 438 SB	1,240	...	7.2
II. WARSAW PACT											
Bulgaria	120.0	10.0	22.0	—	2	—	—	66 FB	144	2,000	...
Czechoslovakia	150.0	—	40.0	—	—	—	—	168 FB	252	3,400	4.1
Germany, East	90.0	17.0	25.0	—	—	2	2	—	303	2,000	5.3
Hungary	90.0	0.5	12.5	—	—	—	—	—	108	1,500	2.7
Poland	200.0	25.0	55.0	—	5	4	4	48 B, 144 FB	432	3,400	4.0
Romania	141.0	8.0	21.0	—	—	—	—	—	220	1,700	1.7
U.S.S.R.	2,000.0	475.0	550.0	26 CA, 3 CL	195, 35 N, 34 FBMS, 20 BMS, 51 SSM	180	212	400 B, 3,000 FB, 140 SB	4,000	33,600	...
III. OTHER EUROPEAN											
Albania	30.0	3.0	5.0	—	4	—	—	—	84	85	...
Austria	48.3	—	3.7	—	—	—	—	38 FB	—	273	1.0
Finland	34.0	2.5	3.0	—	—	3	3	—	47	...	1.5
Ireland	9.6	0.4	0.6	—	—	—	—	—	3	—	...
Spain‖	210.0	44.0	39.0	1 CV, 1 CA	6	24	30	140 FB	—	370	1.8
Sweden	51.2	11.9	11.7	—	22	11	11	150 FB	165	...	3.6
Switzerland	29.5	—	4.5	—	—	—	—	240 FB	30	560	1.8
Yugoslavia	200.0	20.0	20.0	—	5	1	1	180 FB	132	1,256	5.3
IV. MIDDLE EAST AND MEDITERRANEAN; SUB-SAHARAN AFRICA; LATIN AMERICA¶											
Algeria	55.0	3.5	4.5	—	—	—	—	115 FB, 30 B	35	400	2.0
Egypt	260.0	15.0	23.0	—	12	5	5	180 FB, 30 B	210	2,000	20.2
Iran	160.0	11.5	44.0	—	—	7	7	144 FB	—	920	6.2
Iraq	90.0	2.0	9.8	—	—	—	—	96 FB, 8 B	120	1,000	8.8
Israel♀	11.5/275.0	3.5/5.0	15.0/20.0	—	3	1	1	343 FB, 10 B	42	1,700	18.2
Jordan	68.0	—	4.6	—	—	—	—	32 FB	20	420	17.4
Lebanon	14.0	—	1.0	—	—	—	—	8 FB	10	60	...
Libya	20.0	2.0	3.0	—	—	1	1	—	44	221	2.6
Morocco	50.0	2.0	4.0	—	—	1	1	24	24	120	2.8
Saudi Arabia	36.0	1.0	5.5	—	—	—	—	36 FB	35	25	8.9
Sudan	37.0	0.6	1.0	—	—	—	—	17 FB	20	150	7.4
Syria	120.0	2.0	10.0	—	—	—	—	120 FB	200	1,170	11.5
Ethiopia	40.9	1.4	2.2	—	—	—	—	12 FB, 4 B	15	50	2.0
Nigeria	150.0	3.0	4.0	—	—	3	3	12 FB, 3 B	—	—	2.0
S. Africa	10.0	2.5	5.5	—	3	8	8	95 FB, 18 B	50	120	2.5
Zaire	49.0	—	0.8	—	—	—	—	—	15	—	2.0
Argentina	85.0	33.0	17.0	1 CV, 3 CA	4	10	14	22 FB	—	120	1.8
Brazil	130.0	43.0	35.0	1 CV, 2 CA	4	17	24	—	16	190	2.2
Chile	32.0	10.0	18.0	3 CA	2	7	10	—	29	76	4.6
Colombia	50.0	7.2	6.0	—	2	5	5	—	18	—	1.3
Cuba	90.0	6.5	12.0	—	—	2	2	—	215	600	6.2
Mexico	54.0	11.2	6.0	—	—	10	10	12 FB	—	—	0.7
Peru	39.0	8.0	7.0	3 CL	4	7	10	15 B	24	60	3.2
V. FAR EAST AND OCEANIA¶											
Australia	33.1	17.4	22.8	1 CV	4	13	14	60 FB, 12 B	24	143	3.6
Bangladesh	17.0	0.5	0.4	—	—	—	—	—	13	—	...
Burma	135.0	7.0	7.6	—	—	1	1	—	—	—	2.9
Cambodia	180.0	3.4	3.8	—	—	—	—	—	—	—	...
China‖δ	2,500.0	180.0	220.0	—	40	15	15	500 FB, 400 B	3,100	1,500	...
India	826.0	30.0	92.0	1 CV, 2 CL	4	18	18	316 FB, 80 B	420	1,700	3.0
Indonesia‖	250.0	39.0	33.0	—	10	12	12	32 B	27	—	3.0
Japan	180.0	41.4	44.6	—	13	43	43	120 FB	250	520	0.9
Korea, North	408.0	17.0	45.0	—	3	—	3	328 FB, 70 B	130	380	24.9
Korea, South‖	590.0	16.7	25.0	—	—	8	8	165 FB	20	750	4.6
Laos	72.0	—	1.7	—	—	—	—	—	—	—	11.0
Malaysia	46.5	4.8	4.7	—	—	2	2	18 FB	—	—	6.8
New Zealand	5.5	2.9	4.3	—	—	4	4	24 FB	—	—	1.8
Pakistan	300.0	10.0	17.0	—	3	6	6	222 FB, 10 B	6	850	8.6
Philippines	19.3	12.2	11.2	—	—	1	1	16 FB	24	100	1.2
Taiwan‖	395.0	38.0	80.0	—	—	30	30	90 FB	93	800	7.2
Thailand‖	125.0	20.0	35.0	—	—	4	4	11 FB	20	—	4.0
Vietnam, North	565.0	3.2	10.0	—	—	—	—	8 B, 100 FB	70	105	21.5
Vietnam, South‖	477.0	45.0	50.0	—	—	9	9	248 FB	—	...	17.4

Note: Data exclude paramilitary, security, and irregular forces. Naval data exclude vessels of less than 100 tons standard displacement. Figures are for July 1973.
*Nuclear hunter-killers (N); fleet ballistic missile submarines (FBMS); ballistic missile submarines, short-range (BMS); long-range cruise missile submarines (SSM).
†Medium and heavy bombers (B), fighter-bombers (FB), and strategic bombers (SB).
‡Medium and heavy tanks (31 tons and over).
§French forces were withdrawn from NATO in 1966, but France remains a member of NATO.
‖Includes Marine Corps.
¶Sections IV and V list only those states with significant military forces. Figures for Middle East are pre–October war.
♀Second figure is fully mobilized strength.
δApproximate.
Sources: International Institute for Strategic Studies, 18 Adam Street, London, *The Military Balance 1973–1974, Strategic Survey 1972.*

India. China's relative superiority was further enhanced by Chairman Mao Tse-tung's combination of an aggressive verbal policy with a cautious, even conservative, action policy.

In terms of strategic stability, China's acquisition of an effective nuclear deterrent was preferable to its possession of a deterrent so small that the U.S.S.R. might be tempted to consider a preemptive nuclear strike. China's nuclear force comprised 15–20 IRBMs, some in soft sites aboveground but some in hardened emplacements or silos, plus about 50 MRBMs. With these, together with some 100 Tu-16 medium bombers and 300 F-9 fighters for tactical missions, the Chinese could hope to deliver most of their rapidly growing nuclear stockpile on the major cities of Asian U.S.S.R. An improved, multistage IRBM with a range of 3,500 mi., sufficient to hit Moscow, was reportedly ready for deployment, and an ICBM 20% larger than the Soviet SS-9 was apparently under development.

The People's Liberation Army (PLA) remained primarily oriented toward a "people's war"; 120 of its 150 divisions were infantry units, but more sophisticated equipment, including Type-59 medium, Type-62 light, and Type-60 amphibious tanks and armoured personnel carriers, was becoming available. China remained divided into 11 military regions, with the PLA concentrated in the coastal provinces, the Yangtze and Yellow river basins, Peking and Manchuria, and on the Sino-Soviet border. There were 20,000–30,000 construction troops and engineers in the northern border regions of Laos and North Vietnam.

The reshuffle of the Politburo following the tenth Communist Party congress suggested that the moderate faction in the Army remained ascendant, with the Army's role in administration declining from its post-Cultural Revolution peak. No replacement for the late Lin Piao was appointed, leaving the PLA without a defense minister, chief of staff, or air force commander. Nevertheless, China's forces seemed adequate to deter a Soviet nuclear strike, ensure that its border territories were in friendly hands, and support pro-Chinese Communist parties farther afield.

In contrast, Japan's fourth five-year defense plan for the fiscal years 1972–76 envisaged only modest increases over the 1973 defense budget of $3,530,000,000, representing a mere 0.9% of GNP. Japan would be given the capability of resisting a major attack for ten days, allowing time for the U.S.-Japanese security treaty to be invoked or, if the U.S. failed to respond, for Japan to surrender and avoid civilian losses. New prominence was given to the Army's role in combating a major foreign-inspired domestic insurgency. The Army would remain at 180,000 men, providing 1 mechanized division and 12 infantry divisions of 7,000–9,000 men, plus 1 airborne, 1 artillery, 1 helicopter, and 1 mixed brigade. The Air Self-Defense Force would be significantly improved, with its 120 F-86F Sabre ground-attack planes, 150 F-104J Starfighters, and 80 Sabre interceptors being replaced by 120 F-4EJ Phantoms. The Navy, which was expected to defend Japan's sea lanes, was being reinforced to provide a total of 54 destroyers and 15 submarines.

Even so, it was stressed that these forces could only counter indirect aggression or repel small-scale direct aggression; otherwise, Japan would remain dependent on the U.S. guarantee. On the other hand, such modest forces seemed adequate for Japan's needs, since it was unlikely to be threatened by China. Indeed, Japan seemed to be thinking more in terms of cooperation between Japanese capital and Chinese resources to develop the potentially unlimited Chinese market. Japan was also unlikely to try to protect its large investments elsewhere in Southeast Asia or its oil supplies from the Persian Gulf by military action.

If the Sino-Japanese strategic relationship was to be characterized by the irrelevance of either side's military forces to their political relations, the reverse was true of North and South Korea. Their tentative steps toward détente had foundered on mutual suspicions, but this seemed unlikely to lead to hostilities, since their forces balanced each other out. North Korea had an army of 408,000 as against the South's 560,000. Though both navies were geared to coastal duties, the North's could prove superior. The North also enjoyed a considerable qualitative air superiority, but these disadvantages for South Korea were more than balanced by the U.S. guarantee. Since attack from the North seemed improbable, the U.S. felt able to replace its one division of 20,000 men by a smaller force, with arrangements for rapid reinforcement of U.S. air power if necessary.

Three British destroyers maneuver in a major demonstration of British maritime power arranged for the defense ministers of NATO countries. The exercise took place off the east coast of Scotland.

KEYSTONE

SOUTHEAST ASIA

When the U.S. ceased bombing operations in support of the Cambodian government on August 15, it ended a decade of U.S. combat activity in Southeast Asia. It had incurred 45.940 dead and 303,475 wounded and had expended $138 billion in military aid in the second Indochina war while securing in the Jan. 27, 1973, Paris agreement with North Vietnam only the return of the 540 U.S. prisoners of war and a nominal cease-fire in Vietnam. North Vietnam continued political and military action aimed at giving it control over Cambodia and South Vietnam.

The more obvious military lessons of the war were the limitations of airpower using conventional bombs, the inability of a conscript army equipped to fight a Korean- or European-type war to defeat an opponent prepared to accept losses totaling an estimated 926,541 killed, and, most importantly, the apparent invincibility of the guerrilla soldier. Yet, in retrospect, the Vietnamese war of 1963–73 may have been the guerrilla's last major victory. The second Indochina war was basically a war of decolonization, in which the U.S. had come to assume the military role of the previous colonial power, France. That the North Vietnamese government was Communist was a heritage of the first Indochina war (1948–54), when the most efficient and ruthless opponents of the French had been the local Communists. Their subsequent support by the U.S.S.R. and Communist China owed less to Communist ideology than to the Soviet interest in involving the U.S. in a war it could not win and China's desire to end any U.S. presence on the mainland of Southeast Asia.

Ironically, the most important lesson for these three powers was their relative inability to influence the course of local struggles for power. A unified Communist Indochina seemed unlikely to benefit the U.S.S.R. and likely to resist Chinese efforts to influence Vietnamese politics. Strategically, the Vietnam war had demonstrated the irrelevance of the area to the real interests of the superpowers.

On paper, the military balance seemed to favour the governments of South Vietnamese Pres. Nguyen Van Thieu and Cambodian Pres. Lon Nol. South Vietnam's army of 460,000 men provided 11 infantry and 1 airborne divisions, plus 7 independent armoured cavalry regiments. Paramilitary forces included 285,000 Regional Forces, 250,000 Popular Forces, 1.4 million in the People's Self-Defense Force (militia), and 35,000 in the Police Field Force. Cambodia had an army of 180,000 men organized in 9 static and 3 mobile divisions, 300 infantry battalions, 1 tank regiment, and 12 field artillery batteries. Against these forces, in a war where armour was of little use, North Vietnam had a 564,750-man army of 15 infantry divisions, each 12,000 strong, one artillery division of 10 regiments, 3 armoured regiments, and 12 antiaircraft artillery regiments. The 46 SAM battalions, each with six SA-2 launchers, were part of an extremely sophisticated Soviet-supplied air-defense network that had made U.S. air attacks far more costly than the damage they inflicted on a decentralized, underdeveloped economy. The North Vietnamese and Cambodian navies were minuscule, but South Vietnam had 45,000 men tied up in its navy trying to keep its waterways open. (*See* VIETNAM.)

The extent of North Vietnam's superiority in effective, rather than paper, soldiers was evident from its ability to deploy 60,000 men in Laos, 40,000 in Cambodia, and 145,000 in South Vietnam, despite the peace settlement's provision for the withdrawal of foreign military forces. North Vietnam's strategy involved switching its military effort from South Vietnam to Cambodia, while securing its political hold on the northern half of South Vietnam. That North Vietnam was continuing the conflict was clear from the failure of the International Commission of Control and Supervision established by the Paris peace settlement. (*See* VIETNAM: *Special Report.*)

In Laos the agreement whereby the nominally neutralist Prince Souvanna Phouma remained as premier, with his half brother Prince Souphanouvong, leader of the North Vietnamese-supported Pathet Lao, as first deputy premier, reflected the Communist forces' control over most of the country. Pathet Lao forces, estimated at 40,000, were integrated with 60,000 regular North Vietnamese troops controlling the eastern half of Laos and most of the north. The outnumbered Royal Lao forces consisted of an army of 72,000 organized into 24 mobile and 33 garrison infantry battalions, with 4 battalions of artillery and a small air force. In Cambodia the end of U.S. air support for Lon Nol's regime left an estimated 20,000 Communist forces besieging the capital, Phnom Penh; defending it were about 75,000 troops, of whom some 12,000 were regarded as effective. North Vietnam could therefore expect to be in control of Laos, Cambodia, and most of South Vietnam within a few years, although how complete its control over Laos and Cambodia would be remained open to question.

For the time being, at least, Thailand remained a base for the U.S. 7th Air Force with 40,000–50,000 U.S. personnel. Thai armed forces amounted to only 125,000 men in an army of four divisions, with a navy of 20,000, including 6,500 marines, and an air force of 35,000 maintaining 160 combat aircraft.

The U.S. had supplied sufficient equipment to make Taiwan impregnable. The defense budget of $700 million, representing a drop from 9.8 to 7.2% of GNP, still provided an army of 350,000, composed of 12 well-equipped infantry and 2 armoured divisions. The Taiwanese Air Force was comparable to South Korea's or Japan's.

INDIA AND PAKISTAN

The August 1973 India-Pakistan agreement on the repatriation of prisoners of war and an exchange of populations between Pakistan and Bangladesh resolved the problems left outstanding by the July 3, 1972, Simla accord formalizing the cease-fire that had followed the December 1971 war. India agreed to release the over 90,000 Pakistani prisoners captured in the war and persuaded the Bangladesh government to postpone its plans to try 195 Pakistanis in Indian custody for alleged wartime atrocities. In return, Pakistani Prime Minister Zulfikar Ali Bhutto promised to permit 160,000 Bengalis living in Pakistan to emigrate to Bangladesh, if they wished, while accepting an undetermined number of Bangladesh's 260,000 Bihari Muslims, regarded by the Bangladesh government as Pakistani collaborators. India had failed to use the POWs to secure formal Pakistani recognition of Bangladesh, though this was brought closer by Pakistan's direct negotiations with Bangladesh on the issues of the alleged war criminals and the number of Biharis to be transferred to Pakistan. Unfortunately this balanced settlement of the 1971 war did little to ease the continuing Indo-Pakistani confrontation, with the result that both countries maintained larger armed forces than they could afford.

India, the victor in the 1971 war, faced the greater problems, notably the threat of military involvement in domestic politics as civil unrest and pressures for regional autonomy increased. Paradoxically, the chances of such involvement were made greater by the prospect of an indefinite military stalemate with Pakistan on the eastern frontier, relative success in containing guerrilla movements among the Nagas, and the lack of any potential political or military gains that might tempt China to repeat its 1962 punitive expedition. The need to guard against these three possible dangers necessitated maintaining large armed forces, unlikely to be employed in fighting an external enemy but facing a growing threat to internal security.

The defense budget of $2,386,000,000 for 1973–74 represented a nominal increase of $500 million over the previous year because of alterations in exchange rates, but in actuality it fell from 3.4% of GNP to 3%. The Army had decreased slightly, to 826,000 men, divided into 11 mountain divisions to deter a Chinese attack and 14 infantry and 2 armoured divisions for use against Pakistan and general-purpose duties. The Air Force had been brought up to about its prewar strength. The order of 17 HS 748 maritime reconnaissance aircraft and 3 Sea King ASW helicopters suggested that India wished to develop a surveillance capability over the Indian Ocean.

Pakistan had also sought to restore its armed forces to their prewar strength though with less success. The 1972–73 defense budget of $433 million represented a rise from 7.9% of GNP to 8.6%, about three times the Indian level. The Air Force had only 10 U.S.-built Canberra bombers (32 in 1971), 20 Mirage IIIEP fighter-bombers (32), 90 F-86 Sabre fighter-bomber interceptors (112), and 6 F-104A/B Starfighter interceptors (12). Fresh supplies of Sabres and MiG-19s had kept the ground-attack force at about 112. Nevertheless, the Pakistani Air Force was no longer able to threaten India on two fronts and seemed unlikely to offer serious opposition to India in the future.

The Army's numerical strength had increased to 300,000, providing 12 infantry divisions instead of 10 the previous year, but there were still only 2 armoured divisions with 850 medium tanks against India's 1,700. Pakistan had 900 guns, mostly 25 pounders, compared with 3,000 for India. The effective Pakistani Navy remained at three submarines, two fast frigates, and four elderly destroyers, offering no challenge to India's naval superiority.

AFRICA SOUTH OF THE SAHARA

While the conventional military balance remained overwhelmingly favourable to the white-dominated regimes in South Africa, Rhodesia, and the three Portuguese states of Guinea, Angola, and Mozambique, all three governments felt increasingly threatened by the various African guerrilla movements. These movements continued to receive Soviet and Chinese antipersonnel weapons. Though still divided among themselves, they appeared to be gaining some support among the African population, at least along the Zambezi River which continued to be the scene of small-scale clashes. (*See* AFRICA: *Special Report*.) Paradoxically, the apparent improvement in the guerrillas' position was counterproductive in that it led to increasing cooperation among the white regimes.

Outside the white-dominated countries, African armies generally were relatively small infantry forces supported by a few armoured vehicles and light ground-attack aircraft whose primary role was to assure government dominance of the capital. Gen. Idi Amin was able to control Uganda's population of 10,750,000 with forces of 12,600 men, 12 medium tanks, about 50 armoured personnel carriers, and 21 combat aircraft because he had removed all officers whose loyalty was suspect and rewarded the ordinary soldiers with pay and loot. He could threaten Tanzania with these limited forces because its army of 10,000 was even more poorly equipped. The only African countries with significantly larger forces were Zaire, with 49,000 men and no armoured vehicles, and Nigeria, with an army of 150,000. Ethiopia had a well-trained army of 41,000 and paramilitary forces of 20,400 men. These forces were engaged in containing the Eritrean Liberation Front—about 2,000 hard-core guerrillas who received aid from adjoining Sudan. The Sudanese Army of 37,000, with about 150 tanks, was sufficient to deter Ethiopian strikes at guerrilla bases. But, compared with these forces, even Rhodesia's modest army of 3,500 regulars and a 10,000-man reserve was a force of some significance.

In Rhodesia, the Zambian-based Zimbabwe African National Union and Zimbabwe African People's Union had been unable to cooperate in the Joint Front for the Liberation of Zimbabwe. Rhodesian forces continued to destroy most guerrilla units crossing from Zambia, and the guerrillas suffered a significant political setback when Zambian forces killed two Canadian tourists on Rhodesian territory. Rhodesia still had not reached a formal settlement with the U.K. over its unilateral declaration of independence, but it remained largely unaffected by the few sanctions still being imposed. Spares for its British-equipped forces clearly had been obtained.

Portuguese Guinea, isolated among its African neighbours on the coast of West Africa, appeared to be the most vulnerable of Portugal's territories. Some 27,000 troops were stationed there, confronting the African Party for the Independence of Guinea and Cape Verde. However, PAIGC had been considerably weakened when its leader, Amilcar Cabral, was killed in an internal power struggle. Farther south, in Angola, similar feuding made it unlikely that the newly established United Supreme Council of the Popular Liberation Movement and the Revolutionary Government in Exile would be able to threaten any major population centres or inflict serious losses on the 55,000 Portuguese troops who controlled most of the countryside.

Portugal maintained 55,000 troops in Mozambique, where they were protecting the Cabora Bassa Dam in Tete district against an estimated 6,000 guerrillas. The Mozambique Liberation Front remained at odds with the rival Mozambique Revolutionary Committee, however. Portuguese Premier Marcello Caetano's state visit to the U.K. in July was marred by allegations, made by Roman Catholic priests, of a Portuguese massacre of about 400 Africans at the village of Wiriyamu. The Portuguese denied the story, although a South African paper reported in September that a Portuguese government inquiry had confirmed that a massacre had taken place. In any case, the possibility of such incidents on both sides seemed high. Portugal was adopting a version of the strategic hamlets policy used by the U.S. in South Vietnam; some two million of Mozambique's nine million inhabitants were to be moved into settlements or *aldeamentos,* outside of which free fire zones would be established. Guerrilla attacks in Manica e Sofala district, containing the road and rail links between the Rhodesian capital of Salisbury and the Portuguese port of Beira, caused more concern to Rhodesia and South Africa than to Portugal. Portuguese defense expenditure had dropped to 5.1% of GNP ($425 million) from 5.9% in 1969. This provided 137,000 troops for the overseas territories, with two half-strength divisions, totaling 33,000 men, as training cadres. The 18,000-man Navy provided coastal patrols for the overseas territories. Air support was adequate by African standards, despite reliance on a heterogeneous collection of elderly aircraft.

The South African Air Force, by far the best in Africa, included 9 Canberra and 13 Buccaneer light bombers, 44 Mirage III fighter-reconnaissance aircraft, and about 300 MB 326M Impala light attack planes. The Army of 10,000 regulars had 100 Centurion Mk 5 and 20 Comet medium tanks, plus 800 armoured cars. There were 80,000 reserves in the Citizen Force and 75,000 commandos organized as a home guard. South Africa was still able to buy military equipment, chiefly from France but also from the U.K. and Italy, and was nearly self-sufficient in ammunition and small arms. The defense budget had increased marginally to a modest 2.5% of GNP.

(ROBERT J. RANGER)

See also Astronautics.

Denmark

A constitutional monarchy of north central Europe lying between the North and Baltic seas, Denmark includes the Jutland Peninsula and 100 inhabited islands in the Kattegat and Skagerrak straits. Area (excluding Faeroe Islands and Greenland): 16,629 sq.mi. (43,070 sq.km.). Pop. (1972 est.): 4,994,335. Cap. and largest city: Copenhagen (pop., 1971 est., 805,331). Language: Danish. Religion: predominantly Lutheran. Queen, Margrethe II; prime ministers in 1973, Anker Henrik Jørgensen and, from December 19, Poul Hartling.

During 1973 Denmark's most pressing problems continued to be economic. Dissatisfaction with the ever increasing burden of taxation and the lack of any apparent improvement in the country's perennially troubled economy were clearly responsible for the emergence of the Progress Party and the resignation of the government following December 4 elections in which the government and the principal opposition parties all suffered setbacks.

It was generally agreed that the severe shortage of labour was due to overconsumption of both labour and other resources by the public sector, and warnings were issued to government departments. Meanwhile, the Social Democratic minority government, with the support of the leftist Socialist People's Party, passed new social legislation providing compensation for any wage-earner who lost income as a result of illness. The final cost of the scheme remained to be seen, but estimates suggested several billion kroner. Adding to the inflationary pressures, a two-year collective agreement signed in April, which ended the country's worst labour crisis in almost 40 years, provided for a 7½% wage increase plus automatic cost of living adjustments and a reduction in the workweek; at the height of the crisis some 260,000 workers were either on strike or locked out.

In Denmark, as in Norway and Sweden, the parliamentary balance of power was extremely delicate. The ruling Social Democratic Party, with its ally the Socialist People's Party, commanded a majority of only one seat. Wage claims made any effective savings policy difficult to establish, and it seemed that no party wished to be responsible for introducing the tough legislation that was needed. The budget for 1973–74 showed increases of some 13% for the state and more for the local authorities and regions.

These developments provided added impetus for the emergence of a new political movement, the Progress Party. The founder of the movement, Mogens Glistrup, a Copenhagen tax lawyer and adept tax avoider to whom the authorities had so far failed to impute illegal evasion, put forward a very simple scheme for the solution of all Denmark's economic ills. His plan involved the abolition of personal income tax, the reduction of administrative bureaucracy to a minimum, and the transfer of large numbers of civil servants to productive labour. Within a very short time, public opinion polls showed that Glistrup's party commanded the support of up to 26% of the electorate.

Meanwhile, every new savings policy was criticized

WIDE WORLD

Thousands of demonstrators take to the streets of Copenhagen to protest the NATO ministerial meeting in that city on June 14, 1973. Some of the signs say: "NATO attacks Icelandic fishermen with warships."

as a disguised tax increase, and the government's latest finance plan showed a 30% rise in public spending over two years. The consumer price index for April–June rose at an annual rate of 10%, while labour consumption in the public sector showed a similar gain. Local authorities complained that the government gave them ever more duties to perform while refusing to provide the funds needed to carry them out. A building and construction standstill in the public sector was imposed during the summer in the hope of releasing labour for industry, but complaints about the manpower shortage continued. Moreover, the high cost of government housing and soaring rates of land taxation brought allegations that many families would be forced out of their homes unless drastic action was taken. All these problems were mentioned by Prime Minister Anker Jørgensen in his opening speech to the Folketing (parliament) in October. Shortly before this the prime minister had reshuffled his Cabinet, appointing several new ministers known for their leftist views.

Early in November, Erhard Jakobsen, a Social Democratic member of the Folketing, announced that he was defecting from the Social Democrats to form his own Centre Democratic Party, although he planned to vote with the government on key issues. Jakobsen was absent, however, on November 8, during a key vote on a tax measure; the government lost, and elections were called for December 4.

The results left the Social Democrats as the largest party in the Folketing, but the number of seats they held fell from 70 to 46. At the same time, the Socialist People's Party won 11 seats, down from 17, and the nonsocialist opposition parties won a total of 58 seats, compared with 88 before the election. The Progress Party obtained 28 seats, second only to the Social Democrats. Jakobsen's new Centre Democrats obtained 14 seats; the Christian People's Party, 7; the Communists, 6; and the single-tax Justice Party, 5. On December 5 Prime Minister Jørgensen submitted his resignation to Queen Margrethe. On December 12 the police were granted judicial authority to seize documents relating to stock transactions from Glistrup's office in a first move to expedite possible charges of tax evasion and fraud. A week later, on December 19, a minority Liberal Cabinet took office under Poul Hartling, the party leader and a former foreign minister.

Government proposals to bring about "economic democracy" were a major source of controversy during the year. The plans, which included worker participation in management and the establishment of a central fund to which firms would be obliged to contribute, were designed to give workers considerable influence on company management and a large stake in the capital created by their labour.

EEC membership seemed to be paying off. In the first half of the year the value of Danish exports to other EEC countries rose by over 30%, with a 42% increase in agricultural exports, although to a large extent this was due more to price rises than to increases in quantity. (STENER AARSDAL)

DENMARK

Education. (1970–71) Primary, pupils 527,401; secondary, pupils 177,629; primary and secondary, teachers 44,500; vocational (1969–70), pupils 171,629; higher (including 4 universities), students 82,367, teaching staff (1968–69) 8,956.

Finance. Monetary unit: Danish krone, with (Sept. 17, 1973) a free rate of 5.71 kroner to U.S. $1 (13.76 kroner = £1 sterling). Gold, SDRs, and foreign exchange, central bank: (June 1973) U.S. $1,054,800,000; (June 1972) U.S. $715.7 million. Budget (1972–73 est.): revenue 45,895,000,000 kroner; expenditure 42,902,000,000 kroner. Gross national product: (1971) 127,290,000,000 kroner; (1970) 116,650,000,000 kroner. Money supply: (March 1973) 38,370,000,000 kroner; (March 1972) 32,910,000,000 kroner. Cost of living (1964 = 100): (May 1973) 177; (May 1972) 163.

Foreign Trade. (1972) Imports 35,335,000,000 kroner; exports 30,791,000,000 kroner. Import sources: EEC (Six) 33% (West Germany 19%; France 5%); Sweden 16%; U.K. 12%; U.S. 7%; Norway 5%. Export destinations: EEC (Six) 22% (West Germany 12%); U.K. 19%; Sweden 15%; U.S. 8%; Norway 7%. Main exports: machinery 22%; meat and meat products 14% (including bacon 5%); chemicals 7%; dairy products 6%; fish 5%.

Transport and Communications. Roads (1971) 63,925 km. (including 240 km. expressways). Motor vehicles in use (1971): passenger 1,147,300; commercial 215,200. Railways: state (1971) 1,995 km.; private (1970) 538 km.; traffic (state only; 1971) 3,637,000,000 passenger-km., freight (1972) 1,926,000,000 net ton-km. Air traffic (including Danish part of international operations of Scandinavian Airlines System; 1971): 1,651,000,000 passenger-km.; freight 72,702,000 net ton-km. Shipping (1972): merchant vessels 100 gross tons and over 1,331; gross tonnage 4,019,927. Shipping traffic (1971): goods loaded 7,373,000 metric tons, unloaded 30,589,000 metric tons. Telephones (including Faeroe Islands; Dec. 1971) 1,798,000. Radio licenses (Dec. 1971) 1,628,000. Television licenses (Dec. 1971) 1,375,000.

Agriculture. Production (in 000; metric tons; 1972; 1971 in parentheses): wheat 602 (586); barley 5,590 (5,458); oats 638 (704); rye 162 (150); potatoes 703 (750); sugar, raw value *c.* 337 (324); apples *c.* 110 (115); butter 136 (124); cheese 122 (120); pork 814 (815); beef and veal 190 (230); fish catch (1971) 1,401, (1970) 1,226. Livestock (in 000; July 1972): cattle *c.* 2,650; pigs (1971) 8,626; sheep (1971) 57; horses *c.* 50; chickens *c.* 18,500.

Industry. Production (in 000; metric tons; 1972): pig iron 124; crude steel 498; cement 2,870; nitrogenous fertilizers (1971–72) 75; phosphate fertilizers 97; manufactured gas (cu.m.) 380,000; electricity (net; kw-hr.; 1971) 17,540,000. Merchant vessels launched (100 gross tons and over; 1972) 904,800 gross tons.

Dentistry:
see Medicine

Dependent States

Western dependent territories continued to receive hostile attention from Communist propaganda, either directly or via bodies such as the UN or the Organization of African Unity (OAU). Nonetheless, Japan found it simpler to obtain the return of Okinawa from the U.S. than a share of its former Kuril Islands from the Soviet Union, both possessed in 1945. The attitude was epitomized in the directives of the UN Fourth Committee and of the Oslo International Conference for the Support of Victims of Colonialism and Apartheid in Southern Africa in April, openly directed at NATO forces deployed in the Atlantic and Indian oceans. These directives finally wiped out the theory of self-determination enshrined in the UN Charter but now held to be nonapplicable where suitable. Such was the case in Gibraltar, where, despite the overwhelming choice of the people, Spain, supported by the UN, declared that time had run out for British sovereignty, and also in the Falklands, where despite the April declaration by the British government that no transfer of sovereignty could be made against the wishes of the people, the new Peronist government in Argentina stated that it would "eradicate this anachronistic colonial situation."

A more dangerous doctrine was preached by the OAU regarding its right to recognize and aid any minority group it chose as the true representatives of the people, whether or not a local government had been democratically chosen. This assumed right was put into practice by both the UN and the OAU in the case of the Canary Islands, Spanish Sahara, and southern Africa. It was most blatantly expressed in the case of the British Seychelles, where the minority Seychelles People's United Party (SPUP) was recognized by the OAU, after being twice defeated by majority one-man, one-vote elections in favour of James Mancham's Seychelles Democratic Party, which had chosen continued association with Britain.

British dependent territories, containing about six million people living mainly in small Caribbean and Pacific Islands, proceeded toward independence within the Commonwealth in orderly fashion with increasing participation in technical and economic associations. The main problem remained the possible proliferation of tiny states that would not be viable but would be unwilling to accept special Commonwealth status on the model of Nauru.

Africa. *French Africa.* During his January visit to the French Territory of the Afars and Issas (French Somaliland), Pres. Georges Pompidou reaffirmed that the territory would remain French in accordance with the 1967 referendum and would be defended against pro-Somali and pro-Ethiopian secessionists. The visit strengthened the position of Ali Aref Bourhan, president of the governing council, who welcomed French support and complained bitterly of illegal immigration and of "foreign interference," notably the support given by the OAU and UN to dissident groups wishing to usurp the legally elected government. He suggested that the French troops that had recently evacuated Malagasy be brought to Afars and Issas. Despite this, the opposition showed itself locally through the Popular African League (LPA), and outside the area through the Front for the Liberation of the Somali Coast (FLSC). The secretary-general of the FLSC, Aden Robleh Awale, participated in the Algiers conference of nonaligned states, and proclaimed his movement's solidarity with the aims of the LPA militants.

Portuguese Africa. The Portuguese Army in Mozambique claimed heavy losses among Mozambique Liberation Front (Frelimo) guerrilla forces in 1973, and in spite of the involvement of 55,000 troops there was a widespread feeling of optimism. Portugal's decision to force economic independence on its overseas territories had resulted in a shortage of many imported goods and an urgent need for foreign investment to maintain economic development. Yet bankers and businessmen were confident that the need would be met. Construction work on the Cabora Bassa Dam was ahead of schedule; the increasing cost of the project owed more to inflation than to guerrilla activities.

Elections were held in March to the legislative assemblies in all Portuguese African territories. In both Mozambique and Portuguese Guinea control of the assemblies fell to locally born people, though this meant whites as well as blacks. The significance of this, at least in its external appearance, was that guerrillas were now fighting against largely self-governing states rather than against a foreign government.

Mozambique captured public attention in July as the result of a report in a British newspaper that a large-scale massacre of Africans by Portuguese troops had taken place in December 1972 in the village of Wiriyamu in the Tete district. The report originated with a Roman Catholic priest, Father Adrian Hastings, who claimed to have received his information from Spanish missionaries operating in the country. The report immediately preceded a visit to Britain by Premier Marcello Caetano of Portugal and so became the occasion of demonstrations and protests against the Portuguese leader. The Portuguese government denied the accusation, but criticisms persisted and the Army was subsequently accused of committing various other atrocities. Sweden reacted by proposing an immediate UN investigation into the Wiriyamu incident and by promising to increase its aid to Frelimo from £200,000 to £400,000. Portugal announced in August a new white settlement scheme for the four northern districts of Mozambique.

CENTRAL PRESS/PICTORIAL PARADE

Sir Edwin H. C. Leather signs the oaths of office as the new governor of Bermuda. Seated beside him is Chief Justice Sir John Summerfield, and behind are other dignitaries and members of Sir Edwin's family.

In January Amilcar Cabral, the Moscow-backed leader of the African Party for the Independence of Guinea and Cape Verde (PAIGC), was assassinated in Conakry in the Republic of Guinea (*see* OBITUARIES). Aristide Pereira was elected to succeed him as secretary-general of the party. In September the PAIGC declared the independence of Guinea-Bissau, claiming that guerrilla forces controlled three-quarters of the country. A number of African countries, together with Yugoslavia, extended recognition to the new state, and the liberation committee of the OAU agreed to send £100,000 in financial assistance. On October 22 the UN General Assembly officially recorded "the aggression of Portuguese Forces against the state of Guinea (Bissau)." Portugal dismissed the proclamation of independence, which had been anticipated for some weeks, as a "propaganda stunt." Meanwhile, Agostinho Neto, president of the Popular Movement for the Liberation of Angola (MPLA), had visited Yugoslavia in February and was promised continuing support from the Yugoslav Communist Party. Later in the year a delegation of Frelimo leaders visited East Germany before going on in August to West Germany, where they were received by Willy Brandt's Social Democratic Party.

South Africa. In a report published in May based on exchanges between UN Secretary-General Kurt Waldheim and South African Foreign Minister Hilgard Muller, Waldheim concluded that the South African position on South West Africa (Namibia) was "still far from coinciding with that established in resolutions of the United Nations concerning Namibia."

Zambia's chief UN delegate, Paul Lusaka, who was also president of the UN Council for Namibia, in June expressed pessimism about the possibility of future contacts between the South African government and the UN. In June the South African government appeared to make a major concession (following the previous year's Ovamboland strikes) by pledging itself to the full independence of South West Africa within ten years. This did not satisfy the Namibian Africans. Six members of the South West African People's Organization (SWAPO) youth league were arrested at Easter; with others, the leader of the opposition Democratic Cooperative Development Party, Johannes Nangutuuala, was detained, accused of undermining state security in leading a march to the office of the Ovamboland chief executive in order to forestall any move toward the granting of only a limited autonomy to Namibia. He was later publicly flogged.

Spanish Africa. Spanish claims to Gibraltar were undermined by the fact that Spain itself still held enclaves in Africa, one of which, Spanish Sahara, with its valuable Bu Craa phosphate deposits, was subject to the conflicting claims of Algeria, Morocco, and Mauritania. A Spanish Saharan "assembly" presented a petition requesting a referendum administered by Spain and declaring a renewed allegiance to Spain and the right to become self-governing without external interference. Spain agreed to the referendum request, but the entire petition was rejected by Mauritania on the ground that it had been offered by the chiefs of the nomad tribes who were not representative of the colony's people. The three African states in May decided to recognize Morehob (an anti-Spanish terrorist group) as the legal representatives of Spanish Sahara and asked the OAU and UN for recognition. The OAU, casting its anticolonial net ever wider, had already decided to recognize the Canary Islands as "an integral part of Africa" and the MPAIAC, a left-wing group, as the true representatives of the islands. This was mainly a move against NATO bases on the islands and Las Palmas, which handled South African passages.

Caribbean. Notable trends in the Caribbean region were an increased desire for political independence, a keener concern with Caribbean neighbours, and a growing interest in the area by Venezuela, Colombia, and such outsiders as China and Japan. In view of the possible withdrawal from the area of Great Britain and The Netherlands, the United States was concerned over the future of the region, notably in relation to its interests in bauxite and oil refineries and to the question of recognition of Cuba. The creation of more mini-states, possibly under one-man rule, was an additional cause for concern.

Fragmentation had already begun with the breakup of the British West Indies Federation in 1962. The West Indies Act of 1967 set up six "associated states" with full autonomy except for defense and foreign relations, but the principle was breached by the secession of Anguilla from St. Kitts in 1970. In 1973 Premier Eric Gairy of Grenada obtained British approval for full independence in February 1974. This was achieved despite evidence of widespread local opposition to the move, resulting toward the end of the year in communal violence and threats of a general strike.

In the other five associated states, St. Lucia, St. Vincent, St. Kitts-Nevis, Antigua, and Dominica, popular pressures for full independence regardless of viability were intensified by Gairy's initiative though each had grave political and economic problems. In St. Vincent, the attorney general was fatally shot in May, and in June the Antigua Freedom Fighters blew up the residence of the minister of home affairs.

On June 1 British Honduras became Belize, following the passing of a surprise bill by George Price's ruling People's United Party. The opposition had claimed that such a change would play into the hands of Guatemala, which claimed the country under that name, but Price declared that the constitutional relationship with the U.K. would remain the same. Thinly veiled U.S. support for the Guatemalan claim was linked by some reports with the Gulf Oil Corp.'s operations in the Petén jungle just over the Belize border in Guatemala.

The Netherlands was proposing to loosen its ties with the Netherlands Antilles and Surinam, to the point of full independence within a few years. A general strike and public disorders in Surinam in January and February contributed to the decision. Tensions within the Antilles federation were underlined by elections in August, which revealed great dissensions between the islands, vulnerable to Venezuelan annexation because of the oil deposits off Aruba.

The U.S. government suffered some embarrassment over the future of the Panama Canal Zone when the UN Security Council met in Panama City during March. Faced with a situation where the government of Panama, supported by 13 of the 15 council mem-

WIDE WORLD

Demonstrators burn photographs of Sikkim's royal couple, King Palden Thondup Namgyal and his American-born queen, Hope Cooke, at Gangtok in April 1973. Indian Army forces were called in to quiet the demonstrators, who were demanding popular government.

bers, demanded instant U.S. withdrawal despite a valid treaty, the U.S. found no alternative to the use of its veto. Fears were expressed on the U.S. side that a unilateral nationalization and neutralization (meaning the end of a U.S. military presence), demanded by Gen. Omar Torrijos of Panama, would be to the detriment of world shipping.

Indian Ocean. *French Dependencies.* The possibility of France reannexing the island of Mayotte in the Comoros diminished after the December 1972 elections replaced Prince Said Mohamed Jaffar's administration with the new Ahmed Abdallah government. The new regime demanded independence, and was backed by MOLINACO, the national liberation movement based in Dar es Salaam that was aiming at making the Comoros the 42nd African state. Negotiations between Abdallah and Bernard Stasi, French minister of overseas départements and territories, in June resulted in an agreement for independence in 1978 for the four islands. Mayotte, however, demanded continued French connections, while MOLINACO wanted immediate independence for the 280,000 peoples of mixed race on Grande Comore, Anjouan, Mayotte, and Mohéli, regardless of the fact that they were not economically viable without aid. Some French troops taken from the Malagasy Republic were redeployed on Réunion.

British Dependencies. The chief minister of the Seychelles, James Mancham, toured Africa early in the year, complaining of gross interference in the internal affairs of the islands by the OAU. However, Guy Simon, leader of the opposition, continued to draw support from the liberation committee based in Tanzania, which favoured federation, even though the majority of Seychellois preferred their European to African heritage. The new civilian airport built with British aid of £5 million on Mahé had created a lively tourist trade, and in 1973 further grants of £2,274,000 went toward ensuring an adequate water supply for the growing population of 60,000.

Pacific. *British Pacific Territories.* Hong Kong's remarkable prosperity continued undeterred by allegations of corruption from within or by China's growing influence without. While an ever rising number of Chinese refugees arrived in the colony (more than 3,000 known, during the first half of 1973), more concern was felt over the possible focus of subversion that would result if Peking's demand for official representation in Hong Kong were met. Though China no longer needed Hong Kong as its window on the West, the colony continued to provide vital foreign exchange: in 1972 China took £246 million, exporting to the colony only £4 million. Though Hong Kong was leased to the U.K. in perpetuity, the eventual loss to China of the New Territories, leased until 1997, would make the island's existence apart from China impossible.

French Pacific Territories. The 1973 series of nuclear tests was the most eventful of the seven carried out by France in the Pacific, although it consisted of five relatively weak explosions. The establishment of a security zone of 60 nautical miles around Mururoa Atoll did not prevent lively criticism of the government's nuclear policy, both within France and abroad.

From May 16 the Australian labour unions refused to handle any trade with France, a measure they did not rescind until September 26. In June the International Court of Justice at The Hague requested France to abstain from any testing that might be of danger to Australia, while two months later Deputy Prime Minister Hugh Watt of New Zealand (*see* BIOGRAPHY) declared that his government was considering breaking diplomatic relations with France.

While political tensions in New Caledonia seemed in the process of easing, the island's economic difficulties rose to the fore. These centred above all on the fall in the market price of nickel, the territory's resource, and on the fact that Le Nickel, the company that dominated the local economy, considered that it was being taxed too heavily at so unfavourable a time. The government had not yet decided definitely to award concessions on the nickel deposits in the south of the island to the Canadian INCO and the U.S.-French Freeport-Aquitaine companies, which still awaited authorization to commence exploitations.

Australian External Territories. In Papua New Guinea, part Australian and part trust territory, not only did Bougainville continue to agitate for federation with the Solomons, but New Britain and Papua itself also spoke of secession. Independence continued to be almost forced on the territory by an Australian government anxious not to have a colonial image. The chief minister of New Guinea, Michael Somare, suggested that the date of independence following the start of formal self-government on Dec. 1, 1973, be left flexible, and Internal Finance Minister Julius Chan stated that it should be deferred until sufficient experience in self-government had assured stability; already numbers of expatriate civil servants and businessmen had left and the Chinese community expressed fears for its future. Australia pledged to continue its considerable aid, currently £75 million annually, until at least 1977, but viability continued to depend on the presence of adequate personnel to develop the country's considerable resources.

U.S. Territories. American Samoa (East) refused by referendum in November 1972 to elect its own governor and become self-governing by 1974, although a provisional date of 1976 was set. Samoan leaders, recognizing their high standard of living, free entry into the U.S., and the fact that their budget was underwritten by the U.S., showed no signs of preferring immediate independence and a possible linkup with Western Samoa, where Eastern Samoa would be very much a junior partner.

Guam, although also supported by the U.S., decided that the 1975 South Pacific Games were beyond its pocket. The local legislature, alarmed at increased economic penetration by Japan and Taiwan, including 90% control of the growing tourist trade, decided that there must be 25% local participation in all economic enterprises. The return of Japanese economic interests to the one-time Japanese League of Nations mandate of Micronesia became increasingly evident, particularly in tourism and transport.

Following the breakdown of the 1972 talks with the Micronesian joint committee over its demand for total independence as opposed to the U.S. preference for some guarantee of continued presence, a seventh round of talks took place early in 1973. New proposals were made whereby the Mariana group, with administrative headquarters at Saipan, opted for a close and permanent association with the U.S., either with Guam or along Puerto Rican lines. This, though not agreeable to the Micronesian Congress, appeared to be the only way of resolving stalemate and ending the unique strategic trusteeship.

Indian Protected State (Sikkim). A popular uprising in Sikkim in April led to tighter control over the kingdom's affairs by India and a whittling down of the powers held by the chogyal (king), Palden Thondup Namgyal (*see* BIOGRAPHY). An agreement, signed in May by the chogyal, the Indian representative, and leaders of the three major political factions, provided for new elections on the basis of one-man, one-vote and a concentration of supervisory powers in the hands of the Indian-nominated chief executive. The accord was hailed by all but was clearly a temporary solution as other demands, including increased autonomy and a democratic government with the chogyal as a figurehead, were not conceded. The chogyal visited New Delhi in September to work out a formula for the pending general election. During the visit he also attempted to reassure Indian leaders of his desire to maintain harmonious relations between the two countries.

(PHILIPPE DECRAENE; KENNETH INGHAM; MOLLY MORTIMER; SHEILA PATTERSON; GOVINDAN UNNY)

See also African Affairs; Portugal; South Africa; United Nations.

ANTARCTIC, THE

Claims on the continent of Antarctica and all islands south of 60° S remain in status quo according to the Antarctic Treaty, to which 17 nations are signatory. Formal claims within the treaty area include the following: Australian Antarctic Territory, the mainland portion of French Southern and Antarctic Lands (Terre Adélie), Ross Dependency claimed by New Zealand, Queen Maud Land and Peter I Island claimed by Norway, and British Antarctic Territory, of which some parts are claimed by Argentina and Chile. No claims have been recognized as final under international law.

AUSTRALIA

CHRISTMAS ISLAND

Christmas Island, an external territory, is situated in the Indian Ocean 875 mi. NW of Australia. Area: 52 sq.mi. (135 sq.km.). Pop. (1972 est.): 2,741. Cap.: The Settlement (pop., 1971, 1,300).

COCOS (KEELING) ISLANDS

Cocos (Keeling) Islands is an external territory located in the Indian Ocean 2,290 mi. W of Darwin, Austr. Area: 5.5 sq.mi. (14 sq.km.). Pop. (1972 est.): 637.

NEW GUINEA

New Guinea, a trust territory administered with the Territory of Papua, consists of the northeastern part of the island of New Guinea, the Bismarck Archipelago, and several other nearby islands. Area: 92,160 sq.mi. (238,693 sq.km.). Pop. (1971 est.): 1,795,602. Cap.: Port Moresby, Papua (pop., 1971, 66,244).

Education. (1969) Primary, pupils 149,026, teachers 4,736; secondary, pupils 10,672, teachers 501; vocational, pupils 2,870, teachers 190; teacher training, students 1,230, teachers 142.

Finance and Trade. Monetary unit: Australian dollar, with (Sept. 17, 1973) an official rate of A$0.67 to U.S. $1 (free rate of A$1.62 = £1 sterling). Budget: *see* Papua. Foreign trade (1970–71): imports A$184,069,000; exports A$86,738,000. Import sources: Australia 49%; Japan 19%; U.S. 12%. Export destinations: Australia 37%; U.K. 21%; U.S. 15%; Japan 12%; West Germany 6%. Main exports: coffee 24%; cocoa 16%; copra 13%; copra oil 9%; timber 7%.

Transport. Shipping (1972): merchant vessels 100 gross tons and over 50; gross tonnage 26,186.

Agriculture. *See* Papua.

Industry. Production (in 000; troy oz.; 1971): gold 23; silver 17.

NORFOLK ISLAND

Norfolk Island, an external territory, is located in the Pacific Ocean 1,035 mi. NE of Sydney, Austr. Area: 14 sq.mi. (36 sq.km.). Pop. (1972 est.): 1,694. Cap. (de facto): Kingston.

PAPUA

Consisting of the southeastern part of the island of New Guinea and several offshore island groups, Papua, an external territory, is governed in an administrative union with the Trust Territory of New Guinea. Area: 86,100 sq.mi. (222,998 sq. km.). Pop. (1971 est.): 671,384. Cap.: Port Moresby (pop., 1971, 66,244).

Education. (1969) Primary, pupils 64,368, teachers 2,059; secondary, pupils 5,597, teachers 297; vocational, pupils 1,281, teachers 98; teacher training, students 464, teachers 62; higher (University of Papua and New Guinea), students 1,201, teaching staff 154.

Finance and Trade. Monetary unit: Australian dollar. Budget (Papua New Guinea; 1971–72): revenue A$200,118,000 (including A$69,875,000 grant by Australian government); expenditure A$199,363,000. Foreign trade (1970–71): imports A$67,495,000; exports A$15,194,000. Import sources: Australia 56%; Japan 11%; U.S. 10%; U.K. 5%. Export destinations: Australia 74%; Japan 9%; U.K. 7%. Main exports: copra 18%; rubber 14%.

Agriculture. Production (Papua New Guinea; in 000; metric tons; 1972; 1971 in parentheses): copra *c.* 136 (*c.* 141); rubber (exports) *c.* 6.2 (6); cocoa 29 (29); coffee (1971) 28, (1970) 28; timber (cu.m.; 1969) 4,100, (1968) 4,000. Livestock (in 000; March 1971): cattle *c.* 80; pigs *c.* 7; poultry *c.* 300.

DENMARK

FAEROE ISLANDS

The Faeroes, an integral part of the Danish realm, are a self-governing group of islands in the North Atlantic about 360 mi. W of Norway. Area: 540 sq.mi. (1,399 sq.km.). Pop. (1972 est.): 38,731. Cap.: Thorshavn (pop., 1970 est., 10,726).

Education. (1971–72) Primary, pupils 5,555; secondary (1970–71), pupils 1,564; primary and secondary, teachers (1966–67) 299; vocational, pupils 1,131, teachers (1966–67) 88; teacher training, students 94, teachers (1966–67) 12; higher, students 39.

Finance and Trade. Monetary unit: Danish krone, with (Sept. 17, 1973) a free rate of 5.71 kroner to U.S. $1 (13.76 kroner = £1 sterling). Budget (1971–72 est.): revenue 105,376,000 kroner; expenditure 104,839,000 kroner. Foreign trade (1971): imports 301,052,000 kroner; exports 278,708,000 kroner. Import sources: Denmark 71%; Norway 11%; U.K. 5%; Sweden 5%. Export destinations: Denmark 21%; U.S. 17%; U.K. 13%; Italy 12%; Spain 9%; West Germany 7%. Main exports fish and products 92% (including fish meal 9%).

Transport. Shipping (1972): merchant vessels 100 gross tons and over 133; gross tonnage 42,166.

Agriculture and Industry. Fish catch (metric tons; 1971) 207,000, (1970) 208,000. Livestock (in 000; Dec. 1970): sheep 64; cattle 3. Electricity production (1971–72) 76 million kw-hr. (74% hydroelectric).

GREENLAND

An integral part of the Danish realm, Greenland, the largest island in the world, lies mostly within the Arctic Circle. Area: 840,000 sq.mi. (2,175,600 sq.km.), 84% of which is covered by ice cap. Pop. (1971 est.): 50,000. Cap.: Godthaab (pop., 1970, 7,478).

Education. (1970–71) Primary, secondary, and vocational, pupils 10,417, teachers 710; teacher training, students 58, teachers (1967–68) 3.

Finance and Trade. Monetary unit: Danish krone. Budget (1970 est.) balanced at 55,165,000 kroner. Foreign trade (1971): imports 452,759,000 kroner (91% from Denmark, 7% from The Netherlands); exports 139,343,000 kroner (75% to Denmark, 23% to U.S.). Main exports: fish products 84%; fur skins 5%; cryolite 5%.

Agriculture. Fish catch (metric tons; 1971) 38,000, (1970) 40,000. Livestock (in 000; Nov. 1970): sheep 33; reindeer 3.

Industry. Production (in 000; metric tons; 1971): coal 16; cryolite (1968) 67; electricity (kw-hr.) 86,000.

FRANCE

AFARS AND ISSAS

The self-governing overseas territory of Afars and Issas is located on the Gulf of Aden between Ethiopia and Somalia. Area: 8,900 sq.mi. (23,000 sq.km.). Pop. (1971 est.): 97,000. Cap.: Djibouti (pop., 1970 est., 62,000).

Education. (1969–70) Primary, pupils 7,639, teachers 259; secondary, pupils 887, teachers 45; vocational, pupils 219, teachers 15; teacher training, students 14, teachers 9.

Finance. Monetary unit: Djibouti franc, with (Sept. 17, 1973) free rates of DjFr. 170 to U.S. $1 and DjFr. 40 to 1 French franc (DjFr. 410 = £1 sterling). Budget (1971 est.) balanced at DjFr. 2,487,000,000.

Foreign Trade. (1971) Imports DjFr. 9,248,000,000; exports DjFr. 1,133,000,000. Import sources: France 51%; Ethiopia 11%; U.K. 6%; Japan 5%. Export destination France 43%. Main exports: leather, shoes, cattle, coffee.

Transport. Ships entered (1969) vessels totaling 5,142,000 net registered tons. Shipping traffic (1971): goods loaded 90,000 metric tons, unloaded 895,000 metric tons.

COMORO ISLANDS

The self-governing overseas territory of the Comoro Islands is in the Indian Ocean approximately midway between the northern tip of Madagascar and the mainland of Africa. Area: 863 sq.mi. (2,235 sq.km.). Pop. (1971 est.): 280,000. Cap.: Moroni, Grande Comore (pop., 1970 est., 14,000).

Education. (1971–72) Primary, pupils 16,660, teachers (1969-70) 235; secondary, pupils 1,466, teachers (1969–70) 60.

Finance and Trade. Monetary unit: CFA franc, with (Sept. 17, 1973) a parity of CFA Fr. 50 to the French franc and a free commercial rate of CFA Fr. 212.55 to U.S. $1 (CFA Fr. 512.25 = £1 sterling). Budget (1972 est.) balanced at CFA Fr. 1,498,000,000. Foreign trade (1971): imports CFA Fr. 2,834,000,000; exports CFA Fr. 1,572,000,000. Import sources (1965): France 47%; Malagasy 17%; Cambodia 10%; Thailand 7%; Argentina 6%. Export destinations (1965): France 47%; U.S. 26%; Malagasy 6%. Main exports (1968): essential oils 42%; vanilla 35%; copra 17%.

FRENCH GUIANA

French Guiana is an overseas département situated between Brazil and Surinam on the northeast coast of South America. Area: 34,750 sq.mi. (90,000 sq.km.). Pop. (1972 est.): 50,400. Cap.: Cayenne (pop., 1967, 19,668).

Education. (1969–70) Primary, pupils 7,962, teachers 262; secondary, pupils 2,030, teachers 96; vocational, pupils 895, teachers 42.

Finance and Trade. Monetary unit: local franc, at par with the French (metropolitan) franc (free "commercial" rate Fr. 4.25 = U.S. $1, Fr. 10.24 = £1 sterling; free "financial" rate Fr. 4.32 = U.S. $1, Fr. 10.40 = £1 sterling). Budget (1972 est.) balanced at Fr. 144 million. Foreign trade (1971): imports Fr. 219,914,000 (69% from France, 8% from U.S.); exports Fr. 14,788,000 (79% to U.S., 6% to France, 5% to Guadeloupe, 5% to Martinique). Main exports: shrimps 75%; timber 7%.

FRENCH POLYNESIA

An overseas territory, the islands of French Polynesia are scattered over a large area of the south central Pacific Ocean. Area of inhabited islands: 1,261 sq.mi. (3,265 sq.km.). Pop. (1971): 119,168. Cap.: Papeete, Tahiti (pop., 1971, 25,342).

Education. (1971) Primary, pupils 30,660, teachers (1969) 952; secondary, pupils 5,457, teachers (1969) 281; vocational, pupils 876, teachers (1969) 69; teacher training (1969), students 69, teachers 4.

Finance. Monetary unit: CFP franc, with (Sept. 17, 1973) a parity of CFP Fr. 18.18 to the French franc and a free commercial rate of CFP Fr. 77.30 to U.S. $1 (CFP Fr. 186.27 = £1 sterling). Budget (1971) balanced at CFP Fr. 3,112,000,000.

Foreign Trade. (1971) Imports CFP Fr. 14,-073,000,000 (59% from France, 15% from U.S.); exports CFP Fr. 1,749,000,000 (87% to France). Main exports (1969): coconut oil 10%; vanilla 5%. Tourism: visitors (1971) 63,200; gross receipts (1968) U.S. $9 million.

GUADELOUPE

The overseas département of Guadeloupe, together with its dependencies, is in the eastern Caribbean between Antigua to the north and Dominica to the south. Area: 687 sq.mi. (1,780 sq.km.). Pop. (1971 est.): 332,000. Cap.: Basse-Terre (pop., 1967, 15,458).

Education. (1969–70) Primary, pupils 69,-419, teachers (including preprimary) 2,229; secondary, pupils 21,715; vocational, pupils 3,805; secondary and vocational, teachers 1,230; teacher training, students 234, teachers 10; higher, students 376, teaching staff (1968–69) 8.

Finance and Trade. Monetary unit: local franc, at par with the French (metropolitan) franc. Budget (1970 est.) balanced at Fr. 421 million. Foreign trade (1971): imports Fr. 692,-710,000 (72% from France, 6% from U.S.); exports Fr. 231,015,000 (76% to France, 16% to U.S.). Main exports: sugar 56%; bananas 31%; rum 9%.

MARTINIQUE

The Caribbean island of Martinique, an overseas département, lies 24 mi. N of St. Lucia and about 30 mi. SE of Dominica. Area: 431 sq.mi. (1,116 sq.km.). Pop. (1973 est.): 344,000. Cap.: Fort-de-France (pop., 1967, 99,051).

Education. (1969-70) Primary, pupils 68,437, teachers (including preprimary) 2,799; secondary, pupils 30,313; vocational, pupils 1,740; secondary and vocational, teachers 1,656; teacher training, students 127, teaching staff 6; higher, students 1,673, teaching staff (1966–67) 21.

Finance and Trade. Monetary unit: local franc, at par with the French (metropolitan) franc. Budget (1972 est.) balanced at Fr. 392 million. Foreign trade (1971): imports Fr. 860,-881,000 (74% from France); exports Fr. 188,-902,000 (95% to France). Main exports: bananas 49%; rum 16%; fruit conserves 9%; sugar 8%; petroleum products 7%.

NEW CALEDONIA

The overseas territory of New Caledonia, together with its dependencies, is in the South Pacific 750 mi. E of Australia. Area: 7,366 sq.mi. (19,079 sq.km.). Pop. (1973 est.): 124,715. Cap.: Nouméa (pop., 1973 est., 57,000).

Education. (1970) Primary, pupils 24,676, teachers 940; secondary, pupils 3,745, teachers 251; vocational, pupils 1,346, teachers 127; teacher training, students 41, teachers 26; higher, students 85, teaching staff 13.

Finance. Monetary unit: CFP franc. Budget (1971 est.): revenue CFP Fr. 9,990,000,000; expenditure CFP Fr. 9,699,000,000.

Foreign Trade. (1971) Imports CFP Fr. 23,-530,000,000; exports CFP Fr. 19,033,000,000. Import sources (1970): France 64%; Australia 17%; East Germany 7%. Export destinations: Japan 54%; France 40%. Main exports: ferronickel 43%; nickel 33%; nickel castings 23%.

Industry. Production (in 000; 1971): nickel ore (metal content; metric tons) 149; electricity (kw-hr.) 1,272,000.

RÉUNION

The overseas département of Réunion is located in the Indian Ocean about 450 mi. E of Madagascar and 110 mi. SW of Mauritius. Area: 970 sq.mi. (2,512 sq.km.). Pop. (1973 est.): 470,-800. Cap.: Saint-Denis (pop. 1972 est., 98,000).

Education. (1971–72) Primary, pupils 107,-754, teachers 4,507; secondary and vocational, pupils 32,271, teachers 1,422; teacher training, students 500, teachers (1969–70) 19; higher, students 625, teaching staff (1966–67) 26.

Finance and Trade. Monetary unit: CFA franc. Budget (1972) balanced at CFA Fr. 67,-250,000,000. Foreign trade (1971): imports CFA Fr. 48,125,000,000 (64% from France, 8% from Malagasy); exports CFA Fr. 12,092,000,000 (83% to France, 14% to Italy). Main exports: sugar 83%; essences 8%.

SAINT PIERRE AND MIQUELON

The self-governing overseas territory of Saint Pierre and Miquelon is located about 15 mi. off the south coast of Newfoundland. Area: 93 sq.mi. (242 sq.km.). Pop. (1972 est.): 5,650. Cap.: Saint Pierre, Saint Pierre.

Education. (1969–70) Primary, pupils 880, teachers 38; secondary, pupils 283, teachers 32; vocational, pupils 83, teachers 13.

Finance. Monetary unit: CFA franc. Budget (1971 est.) balanced at CFA Fr. 831 million.

Foreign Trade. (1971) Imports CFA Fr. 3,-117,000,000; exports CFA Fr. 1,381,000,000 (including CFA Fr. 698,000,000 ship's stores). Import sources: Canada 57%; France 32%. Export destinations (excluding ship's stores): Canada 60%; U.S. 32%; France 8%. Main exports (excluding ship's stores, 82% of which were petroleum products): livestock 59%; fresh fish 34%.

WALLIS AND FUTUNA

Wallis and Futuna, an overseas territory, lies in the South Pacific west of Western Samoa. Area: 98 sq.mi. (255 sq.km.). Pop. (1971 est.): 9,000. Cap.: Mata Utu, Uvea (pop., 1969, 566).

INDIA

SIKKIM

This protected kingdom is bordered by China, Bhutan, India, and Nepal. Area: 2,744 sq.mi. (7,107 sq.km.). Pop. (1972 est.): 202,000. Cap.: Gangtok (pop., 1968 est., 9,000).

Education. (1972) Primary and secondary, pupils *c.* 19,000.

Finance and Trade. Monetary unit: Indian rupee, with (Sept. 17, 1973) a free rate of Rs. 7.40 to U.S. $1 (Rs. 17.06 = £1 sterling). Fourth five-year development plan (1971–76) Rs. 201 million; development aid from India (1971–72) *c.* Rs. 35 million. Foreign trade mainly with India. Main exports: cardamon, oranges, potatoes, apples.

NETHERLANDS, THE

NETHERLANDS ANTILLES

The Netherlands Antilles, a self-governing integral part of the Netherlands realm, consists of an island group near the Venezuelan coast and another group to the north near St. Kitts-Nevis-Anguilla. Area: 385 sq.mi. (996 sq.km.). Pop. (1972): 223,196. Cap.: Willemstad, Curaçao (pop., 1960, 43,547).

Education. (1971–72) Primary, pupils 37,884, teachers 1,245; secondary, pupils 11,570, teachers 529; vocational, pupils 476, teachers 13; teacher training (1966–67), students 311.

Finance. Monetary unit: Netherlands Antilles guilder or florin, with (Sept. 17, 1973) a free rate of 1.79 Netherlands Antilles guilder to U.S. $1 (4.32 Netherlands Antilles guilders = £1 sterling). Budget (1970 est.): revenue 95,840,000 Netherlands Antilles guilders; expenditure 86,-121,000 Netherlands Antilles guilders. Cost of living (Curaçao; 1963 = 100): (Feb. 1973) 122; (Feb. 1972) 118.

Foreign Trade. (1970) Imports U.S. $791,-391,000; exports U.S. $675,582,000. Import sources: Venezuela 61%; U.S. 12%; The Netherlands 5%. Export destinations: U.S. 52%; Canada 9%; Puerto Rico 5%. Main exports petroleum products 94% (from crude oil imports, accounting for 84% of imports).

Transport and Communications. Roads (1971) 1,183 km. (Curaçao 541 km.; Aruba 380 km.; Bonaire 209 km.; St. Maarten 53 km.). Motor vehicles in use: passenger (1969) 33,400; commercial (1968) 3,700. Shipping traffic (1970): goods loaded 42,203,000 metric tons, unloaded 49,293,000 metric tons. Telephones (Dec. 1971) 28,000. Radio receivers (Dec. 1971) 120,000. Television receivers (Dec. 1970) 32,000.

Industry. Production (in 000; metric tons; 1971): petroleum products *c.* 38,200; natural phosphates (oxide content; exports; 1970) 109; electricity (kw-hr.; 1969) 1,256,000.

SURINAM

A self-governing integral part of the Netherlands realm, Surinam is on the northern coast of South America bounded by French Guiana, Brazil, and Guyana. Area: 70,060 sq.mi. (181,455 sq.km.). Pop. (1973 est.): 403,000. Cap.: Paramaribo (pop., 1971, 102,300).

Education. (1964–65) Primary, pupils 71,397, teachers 2,052; secondary, pupils 10,252, teachers 463; vocational, pupils 1,430, teachers 78; teacher training, students 1,583, teachers 150; higher, students 667, teaching staff 74.

Finance. Monetary unit: Surinam guilder or florin, with (Sept. 17, 1973) a free rate of 1.79 Surinam guilder to U.S. $1 (4.32 Surinam guilders = £1 sterling). Budget (1972 est.): revenue 183 million Surinam guilders; expenditure 222 million Surinam guilders.

Foreign Trade. (1971) Imports 237 million Surinam guilders; exports 287 million Surinam guilders. Import sources (1970): U.S. 42%; The Netherlands 19%; U.K. 9%; Japan 8%; West Germany 7%. Export destinations: U.S. 39%; West Germany 15%; The Netherlands 11%; Norway 8%; Italy 8%. Main exports (1968): bauxite and alumina 70%; aluminum 16%; rice 5%.

Transport and Communications. Roads (main; 1970) 1,335 km. Motor vehicles in use (1970): passenger 16,200; commercial 3,500. Railways (1971) 54 km. Shipping traffic (1970): goods loaded *c.* 4.8 million metric tons, unloaded *c.* 1,080,000 metric tons. Telephones (Dec. 1971) 12,000. Radio receivers (Dec. 1971) 95,000. Television receivers (Dec. 1971) 31,000.

Agriculture. Production (in 000; metric tons; 1971; 1970 in parentheses): rice *c.* 122 (*c.* 122); oranges *c.* 12 (*c.* 12); grapefruit *c.* 6 (*c.* 6); sugar, raw value *c.* 12 (*c.* 12); coffee (1972) *c.* 0.2, (1971) *c.* 0.2; bananas *c.* 25 (*c.* 25). Livestock (in 000; January 1971): cattle *c.* 45; goats *c.* 5; sheep *c.* 3; pigs *c.* 11.

Industry. Production (in 000; metric tons; 1971): bauxite 6,717; aluminum 55; gold (troy oz.; 1970) 1.1; electricity (kw-hr.) 1,362,000 (72% hydroelectric in 1968).

NEW ZEALAND

COOK ISLANDS

The self-governing territory of the Cook Islands consists of several islands in the southern Pacific Ocean scattered over an area of about 850,000 sq.mi. Area: 93 sq.mi. (241 sq.km.). Pop. (1971): 21,317. Seat of government: Rarotonga Island (pop., 1971, 11,437).

Education. (1969) Primary, pupils 5,870, teachers 310; secondary, pupils 959, teachers 69; teacher training, students 27, teachers 7.

Finance and Trade. Monetary unit: New Zealand dollar, with (Sept. 17, 1973) an official rate of NZ$0.68 to U.S. $1 (free rate of NZ$1.63 = £1 sterling). Budget (1970 actual): revenue NZ$1,917,000 (excluding subsidy of NZ$2,375,-000 for 1970–71); expenditure NZ$4,618,000. Foreign trade (1971): imports NZ$5,766,000 (64% from New Zealand, 7% from U.K., 6% from Australia in 1969); exports NZ$2,692,000 (95% to New Zealand in 1969). Main exports (1967): fruit juice 51%; clothing 22%; citrus fruit 9%; copra 6%.

NIUE ISLAND

The territory of Niue Island is situated in the Pacific Ocean about 1,500 mi. NE of New Zealand. Area: 100 sq.mi. (259 sq.km.). Pop. (1973 est.): 4,419. Capital: Alofi (pop., 1971, 1,045).

Education. (1969) Primary, pupils 1,308, teachers 69; secondary, pupils 525, teachers 29; vocational, pupils 19, teachers 5; teacher training, students 5.

Finance and Trade. Monetary unit: New Zealand dollar. Budget (1971–72): revenue NZ$980,000 (excluding subsidy of NZ$1,140,-000); expenditure NZ$2,024,000. Foreign trade (1970): imports NZ$748,000; exports NZ$194,-000. Bulk of trade is with New Zealand. Main exports: passion fruit 18%; copra 14%; honey 8%.

Dependent States

TOKELAU ISLANDS

The territory of Tokelau Islands lies in the South Pacific about 700 mi. N of Niue Island and 2,100 mi. NE of New Zealand. Area: 4 sq.mi. (10 sq. km.). Pop. (1972 est.): 1,599.

NORWAY

JAN MAYEN

The island of Jan Mayen, a Norwegian dependency, lies within the Arctic Circle between Greenland and northern Norway. Area: 144 sq.mi. (373 sq.km.). Pop. (1973 est.): 37.

SVALBARD

A group of islands and a Norwegian dependency, Svalbard is located within the Arctic Circle to the north of Norway. Area: 23,957 sq.mi. (62,050 sq.km.). Pop. (1973 est.): 3,026.

PORTUGAL

ANGOLA

The self-governing state of Angola is located on the southwestern coast of Africa, bordered by Zaire, Zambia, and South West Africa. Area: 481,350 sq.mi. (1,246,700 sq.km.). Pop. (1971 est.): 5,714,662. Cap.: Luanda (pop., 1970, 475,-328).

Education. (1970–71) Primary, pupils 440,-985, teachers 10,065; secondary, pupils 43,174, teachers 2,603; vocational, pupils 12,620, teachers 1,023; teacher training (1968–69), students 1,147, teachers 108; higher, students 2,088, teaching staff 225.

Finance and Trade. Monetary unit, Angola escudo, at par with the Portuguese escudo, with a free rate (Sept. 17, 1973) of 23.30 escudos = U.S. $1 (56.20 escudos = £1 sterling). Budget (1972 est.) balanced at 10,239,000,000 escudos. Foreign trade (1972): imports 10,689,000,000 escudos; exports 13,915,000,000 escudos. Import sources: Portugal 23%; U.S. 13%; West Germany 12%; U.K. 9%; France 6%; Japan 6%; Italy 5%. Export destinations: Portugal 26%; U.S. 16%; Canada 12%; Japan 10%. Main exports: coffee 28%; crude oil 25%; diamonds 11%; iron ore 7%.

Transport and Communications. Roads (1971) 72,323 km. Motor vehicles in use (1971): passenger 102,000; commercial (including buses) 31,700. Railways: (1971) 3,049 km.; traffic (1972) 270 million passenger-km., freight 4,268,-000,000 net ton-km. Ships entered (1971) vessels totaling 9,273,000 net registered tons. Shipping traffic (1972): goods loaded 13,050,000 metric tons, unloaded 1,620,000 metric tons. Telephones (Dec. 1971) 30,000. Radio receivers (Dec. 1971) 100,000.

Agriculture. Production (in 000; metric tons; 1972; 1971 in parentheses): corn *c.* 430 (404); dry beans *c.* 65 (*c.* 65); sugar, raw value *c.* 87 (87); coffee *c.* 215 (228); cotton, lint *c.* 20 (36); sisal (1971) *c.* 53, (1970) 68; palm kernels *c.* 13 (13); palm oil *c.* 40 (*c.* 38); fish catch (1970) 368, (1969) 419. Livestock (in 000; Dec. 1971): sheep 184; goats 878; cattle 2,994; pigs 342.

Industry. Production (in 000; metric tons; 1971): crude oil 5,722; cement 529; iron ore (60–65% metal content) 6,160; manganese ore (metal content) 9.4; diamonds (metric carats; 1971) 2,167; salt 90; fish meal 51; electricity (kw-hr.) 742,000.

CAPE VERDE ISLANDS

The Cape Verde Islands, an overseas province, form an archipelago in the eastern Atlantic Ocean about 380 mi. off the coast of Senegal. Area: 1,557 sq.mi. (4,033 sq.km.). Pop. (1971 est.): 271,864. Cap.: Praia, São Tiago (pop., 1970, 21,494).

Education. (1970–71) Primary, pupils 45,103, teachers (1968–69) 589; secondary, pupils 2,805, teachers (1968–69) 149; vocational, pupils 369, teachers (1968–69) 23.

Finance and Trade. Monetary unit: Cape Verde escudo, at par with the Portuguese escudo. Budget (1970 est.): revenue 196 million escudos (extraordinary receipts 127.7 million escudos); expenditure 170 million escudos (extraordinary expenditure 123 million escudos). Foreign trade (1971): imports 573,984,000 escudos (52% from Portugal, 21% from Angola); exports 45,638,000 escudos (62% to Portugal, 15% to U.S., 5% to Guinea). Main exports: bananas 16%; fish products 13%; fish 12%.

Transport. Ships entered (1970): vessels totaling 7,815,000 net registered tons. Shipping traffic (1971): goods loaded 45,000 metric tons, unloaded 425,000 metric tons.

MACAU

The overseas province of Macau is situated on the mainland coast of China 40 mi. W of Hong Kong. Area: 6 sq.mi. (16 sq.km.). Pop. (1972 est.): 253,425.

Education. (1968–69) Primary, pupils 24,732, teachers 934; secondary, pupils 7,020, teachers 475; vocational, pupils 1,555, teachers 93; teacher training, students 68, teachers 18.

Finance and Trade. Monetary unit: patacá, with a free rate of *c.* 5.10 patacás to U.S. $1 (*c.* 12.30 patacás = £1 sterling). Budget (1971 est.) balanced at 73.4 million patacás. Foreign trade (1971): imports 480,112,000 patacás; exports 324,019,000 patacás. Import sources: Hong Kong 65%; China 27%. Export destinations: West Germany 17%; Hong Kong 16%; Angola 13%; France 12%; Portugal 11%; U.S. 7%; Mozambique 5%. Main exports: textiles 64%; chemicals 7%.

Transport. Shipping traffic (1971): goods loaded 63,000 metric tons, unloaded 329,000 metric tons.

MOZAMBIQUE

Mozambique, on the southeastern African coast, is a self-governing state bounded by Tanzania, Malawi, Zambia, Rhodesia, South Africa, and Swaziland. Area: 308,642 sq.mi. (799,380 sq. km.). Pop. (1971 est.): 8,356,097. Cap.: Lourenço Marques (pop., 1970, 354,684).

Education. (1967–68) Primary, pupils 485,-045, teachers 6,274; secondary, pupils 12,658, teachers 720; vocational, pupils 15,346, teachers 836; teacher training, students 1,061, teachers 104; higher, students 904, teaching staff 192.

Finance and Trade. Monetary unit: Mozambique escudo, at par with the Portuguese escudo. Budget (1972 est.) balanced at 8.9 billion escudos. Foreign trade (1971): imports 9,639,000,-000 escudos; exports 4,613,000,000 escudos. Import sources: Portugal 26%; South Africa 15%; West Germany 9%; U.K. 8%; U.S. 7%; Japan 5%; Iraq 5%. Export destinations: Portugal 37%; U.S. 13%; South Africa 9%; Angola 5%. Main exports: textiles 19%; sugar 15%; cashew nuts 14%; tea 6%; copra 5%.

Transport and Communications. Roads (1970) 37,106 km. Motor vehicles in use (1970): passenger 77,800; commercial (including buses) 18,300. Railways (1970): 3,703 km.; traffic 315 million passenger-km., freight 2,957,000,000 net ton-km. Ships entered (1970) vessels totaling 15,461,000 net registered tons. Shipping traffic (1971): goods loaded 11,153,000 metric tons, unloaded 5,263,000 metric tons. Telephones (Jan. 1972) 30,000. Radio receivers (Dec. 1971) 100,-000.

Agriculture. Production (in 000; metric tons; 1972; 1971 in parentheses): corn 430 (310); cotton, lint *c.* 52 (*c.* 40); sisal (1971) *c.* 29, (1970) *c.* 29; sugar, raw value *c.* 370 (325); copra *c.* 65 (65); bananas *c.* 25 (*c.* 25); tea *c.* 20 (17). Livestock (in 000; Dec. 1971): cattle *c.* 2,150; sheep *c.* 230; goats *c.* 870; pigs *c.* 260.

Industry. Production (in 000; metric tons; 1971): petroleum products 730; cement 421; electricity (kw-hr.) 551,000.

PORTUGUESE GUINEA

The African overseas province of Portuguese Guinea has an Atlantic coastline on the west and borders Senegal on the north and Guinea on the east and south. Area: 13,948 sq.mi. (36,125 sq.km.). Pop. (1971 est.): 485,754. Cap.: Bissau (pop., 1970, 71,169).

Education. (1971–72) Primary, pupils 34,-125, teachers 803; secondary, pupils 2,657; vocational, pupils 500; secondary and vocational, teachers 158.

Finance and Trade. Monetary unit: Guinea escudo, at par with the Portuguese escudo. Budget (1970 est.): revenue 333 million escudos; expenditure 308 million escudos. Foreign trade (1972): imports 866,843,000 escudos (57% from Portugal, 8% from Italy, 5% from U.K., 5% from Japan); exports 69,035,000 escudos (88% to Portugal). Main exports: peanuts 70%; coconuts 8%.

Agriculture. Production (in 000; metric tons; 1971; 1970 in parentheses): peanuts *c.* 65 (*c.* 65); rice *c.* 35 (35); palm kernels (exports) *c.* 7.3 (6.8); palm oil *c.* 8 (*c.* 8). Livestock (in 000; 1970–71): cattle *c.* 270; pigs *c.* 150; sheep *c.* 65; goats *c.* 175.

PORTUGUESE TIMOR

Portuguese Timor, an overseas province consisting of the eastern portion of the island of Timor and the exclave of Oé-Cussé in the western portion, is located about 300 mi. N of Australia. Area: 5,763 sq.mi. (14,925 sq.km.). Pop. (1971 est.): 621,767. Cap.: Dili (pop., 1970, 6,730).

Education. (1970–71) Primary, pupils 32,-873, teachers (1968–69) 541; secondary, pupils 278, teachers (1968–69) 23; vocational, pupils 625, teachers (1968–69) 22; teacher training (1968–69), students 114, teachers 8.

Finance and Trade. Monetary unit: Timor escudo, at par with the Portuguese escudo. Budget (1970 est.): revenue 221 million escudos; expenditure 203 million escudos. Foreign trade (1971): imports 203,280,000 escudos; exports 121,132,000 escudos. Import sources: Portugal 26%; Singapore 13%; Australia 13%; Macao 12%; Mozambique 10%; Japan 10%; U.K. 5%. Export destinations: Belgium-Luxembourg 25%; Denmark 16%; The Netherlands 16%; U.S. 11%; Singapore 9%; Portugal 8%; West Germany 8%. Main exports: coffee 85%; copra 6%.

Agriculture. Production (in 000; metric tons; 1971; 1970 in parentheses): corn *c.* 18 (*c.* 18); rice *c.* 15 (*c.* 15); sweet potatoes *c.* 7 (*c.* 7); copra *c.* 2.4 (*c.* 2.4); coffee *c.* 5 (*c.* 5). Livestock (in 000; 1971): cattle *c.* 61; sheep *c.* 38; goats *c.* 220; pigs *c.* 230; buffalo *c.* 124; horses *c.* 101.

SÃO TOMÉ AND PRÍNCIPE

The overseas province of São Tomé and Príncipe lies in the Gulf of Guinea off the west coast of Africa. Area: 372 sq.mi. (964 sq.km.). Pop. (1971 est.): 74,445. Cap.: São Tomé (pop., 1970, 17,380).

Education. (1970–71) Primary, pupils 9,081, teachers 271; secondary, pupils 1,463, teachers 73; vocational, pupils 112, teachers 34.

Finance and Trade. Monetary unit: Guinea escudo, at par with the Portuguese escudo. Budget (1971 est.): revenue 173 million escudos; expenditure 185 million escudos. Foreign trade (1971): imports 221,164,000 escudos; exports 197,860,000 escudos. Import sources (1970): Portugal 51%; Angola 23%; The Netherlands 5%; West Germany 5%. Export destinations (1970): Portugal 34%; The Netherlands 32%; West Germany 12%; Denmark 7%; U.S. 5%. Main exports (1970): cocoa 80%; copra 11%.

Agriculture. Production (in 000; metric tons; 1971; 1970 in parentheses): copra *c.* 6 (4.5); bananas *c.* 2 (*c.* 2); cocoa 10 (10); palm kernels (exports) *c.* 2.5 (2.2); palm oil *c.* 1 (1). Livestock (in 000; Dec. 1970): cattle *c.* 3; sheep *c.* 2; pigs *c.* 3; goats *c.* 1.

SOUTH WEST AFRICA (NAMIBIA)

South West Africa has been a UN territory since 1966, when the General Assembly terminated South Africa's mandate over the country, renamed Namibia by the UN. South Africa considers the UN resolution illegal and has stated that it is determined to continue its jurisdiction over the area. Area: 318,261 sq.mi. (824,296 sq.km.). Pop. (1970): 746,328. National cap.: Windhoek (pop., 1970, 61,260). Summer cap.: Swakopmund (pop., 1970, 5,681).

Education. (1970) Primary and secondary, pupils 129,927, teachers 3,790.

Finance and Trade. Monetary unit: South African rand, with (Sept. 17, 1973) an official rate of R 0.67 to U.S. $1 (free rate of R 1.62 = £1 sterling). Budget (1969–70): revenue R 53,-818,000; expenditure R 54,476,000. Foreign trade included in the South African customs union. Main exports: diamonds and other minerals (1970) R 130 million; karakul pelts (1967) R 14 million.

Agriculture. Production (in 000; metric tons; 1971; 1970 in parentheses): corn *c.* 12 (*c.* 12); millet *c.* 13 (*c.* 13); butter *c.* 2 (*c.* 2); beef and veal c. 65 (c. 62). Livestock (in 000; 1970–71): cattle c. 2,550; sheep c. 4,100; goats c. 1,750; horses c. 37; asses c. 58.

Industry. Production (in 000; metric tons; 1971): lead ore (metal content) 73; zinc ore (metal content) 49; copper ore (metal content) 26; tin concentrates (metal content) 1; silver (troy oz.) 1,415; diamonds (metric carats) c. 1,900; electricity (kw-hr.; 1963) 188,000.

SPAIN

SPANISH SAHARA

Spanish Sahara is a province in northwest Africa, bordered by Morocco, Algeria, Mauritania, and the Atlantic Ocean. Area: 102,703 sq.mi. (266,000 sq.km.). Pop. (1972 est.): 91,000. Cap.: El Aaiún (pop., 1970, 24,519).

Education. (1971–72) Primary, pupils 4,019, teachers (1969–70) 69; secondary, pupils 1,500, teachers (1969–70) 63.

Finance and Trade. Monetary unit: Spanish peseta, with (Sept. 17, 1973) a free rate of 56.82 pesetas to U.S. $1 (136.95 pesetas = £1 sterling). Budget (1972 est.) balanced at 1,215,000,000 pesetas (mainly aid from Spain). Foreign trade (1970): imports 388.3 million pesetas; exports negligible.

Agriculture and Industry. Livestock (in 000; 1970–71): camels 61; goats 162; sheep 21. Electricity production (1971) 8,350,000 kw-hr. Phosphate exports began in April 1972.

UNITED KINGDOM

ANTIGUA

The associated state of Antigua, with its dependencies Barbuda and Redonda, lies in the eastern Caribbean approximately 40 mi. N of Guadeloupe. Area: 171 sq.mi. (412 sq.km.). Pop. (1970): 70,000. Cap.: Saint John's (pop., 1960, 21,396).

Education. (1970–71) Primary and secondary, pupils 22,000, teachers (1963–64) 470; higher (1963–64), students 50, teachers 3.

Finance and Trade. Monetary unit: East Caribbean dollar (ECar$1.99 = U.S. $1; ECar$4.80 = £1 sterling). Budget (1972 est.): revenue ECar$24.3 million; expenditure ECar$32.5 million. Foreign trade (1968): imports ECar$39,248,000; exports ECar$5,780,000. Import sources (1967): U.S. 29%; U.K. 23%; Trinidad and Tobago 10%. Export destinations (1967): Canada 21%; U.S. 9%; U.K. 5%; Puerto Rico 5%. Main exports (1967) petroleum products 85%. Tourism (1971) 68,000 visitors.

BELIZE (formerly British Honduras)

Belize, a self-governing colony, is situated on the Caribbean coast of Central America, bounded on the north and northwest by Mexico and by Guatemala on the remainder of the west and south. Area: 8,866 sq.mi. (22,963 sq.km.). Pop. (1971 est.): 124,000. Cap.: Belmopan (pop., 1973 est., 5,000).

Education. (1969–70) Primary, pupils 31,080, teachers 1,212; secondary, pupils 3,629, teachers 230; vocational, pupils 267; teacher training, students 80, teachers 6; higher, students 89, teaching staff 14.

Finance and Trade. Monetary unit: Belize dollar, with (Sept. 17, 1973) a free rate of Bel$1.66 = U.S. $1 (Bel$4 = £1 sterling). Budget (1972 est.) balanced at Bel$29,846,000 (including U.K. development grants of Bel$8 million). Foreign trade (1969): imports Bel$49,351,000; exports Bel$28,080,000. Import sources: U.S. 34%; U.K. 25%; Jamaica 8%; The Netherlands 6%. Export destinations: U.S. 36%; U.K. 27%; Mexico 20%; Canada 9%. Main exports: sugar 34%; oranges and products 9%; grapefruit and products 6%; clothing 5%; lobster 5%; timber 5%.

BERMUDA

The colony of Bermuda lies in the western Atlantic about 570 mi. E of Cape Hatteras, North Carolina. Area: 21 sq.mi. (53 sq.km.). Pop. (1971 est.): 52,610. Cap.: Hamilton, Great Bermuda (pop., 1970, 2,060).

Education. (1969–70) Primary, pupils 8,198, teachers 335; secondary, pupils 3,898, teachers 250; vocational, pupils 346, teachers 37.

Finance and Trade. Monetary unit: Bermuda dollar, at par with the U.S. dollar (free rate of Ber$2.41 = £1 sterling). Budget (1972–73 est.): revenue Ber$50,207,000; expenditure Ber$48,393,000. Foreign trade (1971): imports Ber$108,478,000 (excluding Ber$79,306,000 for free-port area); exports Ber$91,575,000 (including Ber$849,000 domestic). Import sources: U.S. 45%; U.K. 22%; Canada 12%. Export destinations (drugs and medicines only): U.K. 25%; Australia 19%; The Netherlands 16%; France 12%; Japan 7%. Main exports (domestic) drugs and medicines 82%. Tourism (1971): visitors 319,000; gross receipts U.S. $97 million.

Transport and Communications. Shipping (1972): merchant vessels 100 gross tons and over 48; gross tonnage 813,586. Telephones (Dec. 1971) 32,000. Radio receivers (Dec. 1970) 38,000. Television receivers (Dec. 1970) 17,000.

BRITISH INDIAN OCEAN TERRITORY

Located in the western Indian Ocean, this colony consists of the Chagos Archipelago and the islands of Aldabra, Desroches, and Farquhar. Area: 85 sq.mi. (221 sq.km.). Pop. (1972 est.): 350. Administrative headquarters: Victoria, Seychelles.

BRITISH SOLOMON ISLANDS

British Solomon Islands is a protectorate in the southwestern Pacific east of the island of New Guinea. Area: 10,983 sq.mi. (28,446 sq.km.). Pop. (1972 est.): 173,510. Cap.: Honiara, Guadalcanal (pop., 1971 est., 13,350).

Education. (1970) Primary, pupils 21,270, teachers 885; secondary, pupils 1,042, teachers 64; vocational, pupils 248; teachers 23; teacher training, students 110, teachers 11.

Finance and Trade. Monetary unit: Australian dollar. Budget (1971 est.) balanced at A$12,513,000 (including A$1,878,000 development aid). Foreign trade (1971): imports A$13,858,000 (35% from Australia, 26% from Japan, 15% from U.K., 6% from U.S.); exports A$9,273,000 (58% to Japan, 12% to Australia, 12% to The Netherlands, 7% to West Germany, 5% to U.K.). Main exports: copra 41%; timber 36%; fish 13%.

BRITISH VIRGIN ISLANDS

The colony of the British Virgin Islands is located in the Caribbean to the east of the U.S. Virgin Islands. Area: 59 sq.mi. (153 sq.km.). Pop. (1970): 10,298. Cap.: Road Town, Tortola (pop., 1970, 2,183).

Education. (1970–71) Primary, pupils 1,718; secondary, pupils 865; primary and secondary, teachers 139.

Finance and Trade. Monetary unit: U.S. dollar (free rate at Sept. 17, 1973, of U.S. $2.41 = £1 sterling). Budget (1971 est.): revenue U.S. $6,991,000; expenditure U.S. $7,985,000. Foreign trade (1970): imports U.S. $10,224,000 (51% from U.S., Puerto Rico, and U.S. Virgin Islands, 23% from U.K.); exports U.S. $65,000 (94% to U.S. Virgin Islands). Main exports: fish 40%; motor vehicles (reexports) 21%; sheep 6%; bananas 5%.

BRUNEI

Brunei, a protected sultanate, is located on the north coast of the island of Borneo, surrounded on its landward side by the Malaysian state of Sarawak. Area: 2,226 sq.mi. (5,765 sq.km.). Pop. (1972 est.): 141,497. Cap.: Bandar Seri Begawan (urban area pop., 1972 est., 75,663).

Education. (1969–70) Primary, pupils 27,580, teachers 1,203; secondary, pupils 16,587, teachers 655; vocational, pupils 79, teachers 8; teacher training, students 541, teachers 31.

Finance and Trade. Monetary unit: Brunei dollar, with (Sept. 17, 1973) a free rate of Br$2.34 to U.S. $1 (Br$5.65 = £1 sterling). Budget (1972 est.): revenue Br$226 million; expenditure Br$154 million. Foreign trade (1970): imports Br$265,122,000; exports Br$292,063,000. Import sources: U.S. 20%; U.K. 18%; Singapore 17%; Malaysia 6%. Export destination Malaysia (Sarawak) 98%. Main export crude oil 95%.

Agriculture. Production (in 000; metric tons; 1971; 1970 in parentheses): rice c. 8 (c. 8); rubber (exports) c. 0.3 (0.3). Livestock (in 000; Dec. 1970): cattle 3; pigs c. 13; goats 1.

Industry. Production (1971): crude oil 6,341,000 metric tons; natural gas 220 million cu.m.

CAYMAN ISLANDS

The colony of the Cayman Islands lies in the Caribbean about 170 mi. NW of Jamaica. Area: 100 sq.mi. (259 sq.km.). Pop. (1971 est.): 11,300. Cap.: George Town, Grand Cayman (pop., 1970, 3,975).

Education. (Public only; 1969–70) Primary, pupils 1,203, teachers 39; secondary, pupils 551, teachers 30.

Finance and Trade. Monetary unit: Cayman Islands dollar, with (Sept. 17, 1973) a free rate of CayI$0.83 to U.S. $1 (CayI$2 = £1 sterling). Budget (1972 est.): revenue CayI$3,702,000; expenditure CayI$3,266,000. Foreign trade (1971): imports CayI$9,055,000; exports CayI$475,000. Main export turtle meat. Tourism: visitors (1971) 24,000; gross receipts (1969) c. CayI$2.4 million.

Transport. Shipping (1972): merchant vessels 100 gross tons and over 38; gross tonnage 26,172.

DOMINICA

The associated state of Dominica lies in the Caribbean between Guadeloupe to the north and Martinique to the south. Area: 289 sq.mi. (750 sq.km.). Pop. (1972 est.): 71,793. Cap.: Roseau (pop., 1970, 9,949).

Education. (1969–70) Primary, pupils 15.904, teachers (1963–64) 459; secondary, pupils 4,954; vocational, pupils 154; teacher training, students 19.

Finance and Trade. Monetary unit: East Caribbean dollar. Budget (1971 est.): revenue ECar$17,007,000; expenditure ECar$17,541,000. Foreign trade (1970): imports ECar$31,514,000; exports ECar$11,810,000. Import sources (1969): U.K. 33%; U.S. 15%; Trinidad and Tobago 11%; Canada 10%; The Netherlands 6%; West Germany 5%. Export destination (1969) U.K. 84%. Main exports (1969): bananas 73%; essential oils 6%; fruit juices 5%.

FALKLAND ISLANDS

The colony of the Falkland Islands and Dependencies is situated in the South Atlantic about 500 mi. NE of Cape Horn. Area: 6,150 sq.mi. (15,930 sq.km.). Pop. (1972): 1,957. Cap.: Stanley (pop., 1972, 1,079).

Education. (1971) Primary and secondary, pupils 417, teachers (1970) 37.

Finance and Trade. Monetary unit: Falkland Island pound, at par with the pound sterling (free rate at Sept. 17, 1973, of FI£0.41 = U.S. $1). Budget: (1972–73 est.) revenue FI£433,000; expenditure FI£479,000. Foreign trade (1971): imports FI£607,000; exports FI£731,000. Main export wool.

GIBRALTAR

Gibraltar, a self-governing colony, is a small peninsula that juts into the Mediterranean from southwestern Spain. Area: 2.25 sq.mi. (5.80 sq.km.). Pop. (1972 est.): 29,254.

Education. (1971–72) Primary, pupils 3,821, teachers 175; secondary, pupils 1,397, teachers 96; vocational, pupils 74, teachers 17.

Finance and Trade. Currency: Gibraltar pound, at par with the pound sterling. Budget (1972–73 est.): revenue Gib£5,374,000; expenditure Gib£5,183,000. Foreign trade (1971): imports Gib£9.5 million (49% from U.K., 21% from EEC); exports Gib£1.2 million (31% to EEC, 16% to U.K.). Tourism (1971) 132,000 visitors.

Transport. Shipping (1972): merchant vessels 100 gross tons and over 11; gross tonnage 21,375. Ships entered (1971) vessels totaling 10,872,000 net registered tons. Shipping traffic (1971): goods loaded 8,000 metric tons, unloaded 316,000 metric tons.

GILBERT AND ELLICE ISLANDS

The Gilbert and Ellice Islands colony is scattered over an area of more than two million sq.mi. in the western Pacific Ocean. Area: 283 sq.mi. (734 sq.km.). Pop. (1973 est.): 62,000. Seat of government: Tarawa Atoll (pop., 1968, 12,642).

Education. (1970) Primary, pupils 14,570, teachers 546; secondary, pupils 622, teachers 44; vocational, pupils 337, teachers 16; teacher training, students 112, teachers 16.

Finance and Trade. Monetary unit: Australian dollar. Budget (1970 est.): revenue A$4,-

356,000; expenditure A$3,329,000. Foreign trade (1970): imports A$3,917,000 (60% from Australia, 11% from U.K. in 1968); exports A$7,-460,000 (63% to Australia, 24% to New Zealand, 12% to U.K. in 1968). Main exports (1968): phosphates 84%; copra 14%.

GRENADA

Grenada, a West Indian associated state, includes the island of Grenada and its dependency, the southern Grenadines. Area: 133 sq.mi. (344 sq.km.). Pop. (1971 est.): 96,000. Cap.: Saint George's (pop., 1969 est., 8,644).

Education. (1970–71) Primary, pupils 30,355, teachers 800; secondary, pupils 3,039, teachers 129; vocational, pupils 985, teachers 20; teacher training, students 57, teachers 12.

Finance and Trade. Monetary unit: East Caribbean dollar. Budget (1971 est.) balanced at ECar$35,613,000. Foreign trade (1970): imports ECar$44,080,000; exports ECar$10,497,000. Import sources (1968): U.K. 33%; U.S. 10%; Canada 10%; The Netherlands 5%. Export destinations (1968): U.K. 64%; West Germany 10%; The Netherlands 9%; U.S. 5%. Main exports (1968): bananas 40%; nutmegs 25%; cocoa 21%; mace 7%.

GUERNSEY

Located 30 mi. W of Normandy, France, Guernsey, together with its small island dependencies, is a crown dependency. Area: 30 sq.mi. (78 sq.km.). Pop. (1971): 53,734. Cap.: St. Peter Port (pop., 1971, 16,303).

Education. (1971) Primary and secondary, pupils 9,056.

Finance and Trade. Monetary unit: Guernsey pound, at par with the pound sterling. Budget (1971): revenue £9,222,000; expenditure £6,780,000. Foreign trade included with the United Kingdom. Main exports: tomatoes, flowers, stone. Tourism (1971) 237,000 visitors.

HONG KONG

The colony of Hong Kong lies on the southeastern coast of China about 40 mi. E of Macau and 80 mi. SE of Canton. Area: 403 sq.mi. (1,040 sq.km.). Pop. (1973 est.): 4,159,900. Cap.: Victoria (pop., 1971, 520,932).

Education. (1971–72) Primary, pupils 757,-151, teachers (1969–70) 22,444; secondary and vocational, pupils 290,578, teachers (1969–70) 9,952; higher (1969–70), students 19,874, teaching staff 1,992.

Finance. Monetary unit: Hong Kong dollar, with (Sept. 17, 1973) a free rate of HK$5.12 = U.S. $1 (HK$12.36 = £1 sterling). Budget (1972–73 est.): revenue HK$3,704,000,000; expenditure HK$3,657,000,000.

Foreign Trade. (1972) Imports HK$21,971,-000,000; exports HK$19,575,000,000. Import sources: Japan 23%; China 18%; U.S. 12%; U.K. 7%. Export destinations: U.S. 33%; U.K. 12%; West Germany 8%; Japan 7%. Main exports: clothing 32%; electrical equipment 11%; textile yarns and fabrics 11%; toys 7%. Tourism (1971): visitors 907,300; gross receipts U.S. $267 million.

Transport and Communications. Roads (1970) 976 km. Motor vehicles in use (1971): passenger 110,200; commercial (including buses) 34,200. Railways (1971) 35 km. Shipping (1972): merchant vessels 100 gross tons and over 97; gross tonnage 457,924. Ships entered (1971) vessels totaling 28,674,000 net registered tons. Shipping traffic (1972): goods loaded 3,821,000 metric tons, unloaded 12,293,000 metric tons. Telephones (Dec. 1971) 692,000. Radio receivers (Dec. 1970) 694,000. Television receivers (Dec. 1971) 444,000.

ISLE OF MAN

The Isle of Man, a crown dependency, lies in the Irish Sea approximately 35 mi. from both Northern Ireland and the coast of northwestern England. Area: 221 sq.mi. (572 sq.km.). Pop. (1972 est.): 56,038. Cap.: Douglas (pop., 1971, 20,389).

Education. (1971–72) Primary, pupils 4,916; secondary, pupils 3,139; vocational, pupils 2,173.

Finance and Trade. Monetary unit: pound sterling. Budget (1972–73 est.): revenue £14,-075,000; expenditure £14,929,000. Foreign trade included with the United Kingdom. Main exports: fish products, metal ores, tweeds. Tourism (1972) 500,000 visitors.

JERSEY

The island of Jersey, a crown dependency, is located about 20 mi. W of Normandy, France. Area: 45 sq.mi. (117 sq.km.). Pop. (1971): 72,-629. Cap.: St. Helier (pop., 1971, 28,135).

Education. (1970–71) Primary, pupils 5,400; secondary, pupils 3,245.

Finance and Trade. Monetary unit: Jersey pound, at par with the pound sterling. Budget (1971): revenue £18,906,000; expenditure £13,-940,000. Foreign trade included with the United Kingdom. Main exports: potatoes, tomatoes. Tourism (1971) passengers arrived by sea 251,-000, by air 604,000.

MONTSERRAT

The colony of Montserrat is located in the Caribbean between Antigua, 27 mi. NE, and Guadeloupe, 40 mi. SE. Area: 40 sq.mi. (102 sq.km.). Pop. (1972 est.): 13,076. Cap.: Plymouth (pop., 1971 est., 1,400).

Education. (1970–71) Primary, pupils 2,684, teachers 115; secondary, pupils 232, teachers 16; vocational (1969–70), pupils 12, teachers 1; teacher training (1969–70), students 12, teachers 3.

Finance and Trade. Monetary unit: East Caribbean dollar. Budget (1972–73 est.): revenue ECar$3,729,000; expenditure ECar$5,121,000. Foreign trade (1971): imports ECar$8,558,000; exports ECar$100,400. Main exports: fruit and vegetables 51%; tires 27%; cotton 21%.

PITCAIRN ISLAND

The colony of Pitcairn Island is in the central South Pacific, 3,200 mi. NE of New Zealand and 1,350 mi. SE of Tahiti. Area: 1.75 sq.mi. (4.53 sq.km.). Pop. (1973): 69. Cap. (de facto): Adamstown.

ST. HELENA

The colony of St. Helena, including its dependencies of Ascension and Tristan de Cunha islands, is located in the Atlantic off the southwestern coast of Africa. Area: 119 sq.mi. (308 sq.km.). Pop. (1971 est.): 6,562. Cap.: Jamestown (pop., 1969 est., 1,600).

Education. (1968–69) Primary, pupils 773, teachers 36; secondary and teacher training (1969–70), pupils 410, teachers 33.

Finance and Trade. Monetary unit: pound sterling. Budget (1971–72 est.; 15-month period): revenue £954,709; expenditure £853,255. Foreign trade (1970): imports £472,500 (61% from U.K., 28% from South Africa in 1968); exports £200 (73% to U.K., 20% to South Africa in 1968).

ST. KITTS-NEVIS-ANGUILLA

This associated state consists of the islands of St. Kitts and Nevis; Anguilla was under direct British administration. Area: 135 sq.mi. (350 sq.km.). Pop. (1970, excluding Anguilla): 45,457 (Anguilla about 5,500). Cap.: Basseterre, St. Kitts (pop., 1970, 13,055).

Education. St. Kitts-Nevis (1969–70): primary, pupils 11,435, teachers 325; secondary, pupils 2,692, teachers 115; vocational, pupils 1,250, teachers 15. Anguilla (1969–70): primary, pupils 1,351, teachers 67; secondary, pupils 486, teachers 10.

Finance and Trade. Monetary unit, East Caribbean dollar. Budgets: (St. Kitts-Nevis; 1971 rev. est.) revenue ECar$12 million, expenditure ECar$22.8 million; (Anguilla; 1967 est.) balanced at ECar$600,000 (U.K. development aid *c.* ECar$240,000 per year). Foreign trade (St. Kitts-Nevis; 1970): imports ECar$22,-427,000; exports ECar$8,290,000. Import sources (1969): U.K. 28%; Canada 14%; U.S. 14%; Trinidad and Tobago 10%; Barbados 5%. Export destinations (1969): U.K. 76%; Canada 10%. Main exports (1969): sugar and preparations 88%; (Anguilla only) postage stamps, salt.

ST. LUCIA

The Caribbean island of St. Lucia, an associated state, lies 24 mi. S of Martinique and 21 mi. NE of St. Vincent. Area: 238 sq.mi. (616 sq.km.). Pop. (1971 est.): 103,000. Cap.: Castries (pop., 1964 est., 5,100).

Education. (1969–70) Primary and secondary, pupils 25,571, teachers 854; teacher training, students 90, teachers 12.

Finance and Trade. Monetary unit: East Caribbean dollar. Budget (1971 est.): revenue ECar$18,345,000; expenditure ECar$18,546,000. Foreign trade (1969): imports ECar$41.5 million; exports ECar$16,543,000. Import sources: U.K. 31%; U.S. 14%; Trinidad and Tobago 12%; Canada 13%; Netherlands Antilles 6%; Barbados 5%. Export destinations: U.K. 86%; Barbados 7%. Main exports: bananas 86%; copra 7%. Tourism (1971): visitors 33,000; gross receipts (1969) ECar$7.2 million.

ST. VINCENT

St. Vincent, including the northern Grenadines, is an associated state in the eastern Caribbean about 100 mi. W of Barbados. Area: 150 sq.mi. (389 sq.km.). Pop. (1972 est.): 90,000. Cap.: Kingstown (pop., 1970, including suburbs, 23,-645).

Education. (1969–70) Primary, pupils 36,089, teachers 843; secondary, pupils 3,004, teachers (1968–69) 92; vocational, pupils 225, teachers 3; teacher training, students 288, teachers 25.

Finance and Trade. Monetary unit: East Caribbean dollar. Budget (1971 est.) balanced at ECar$25,047,000. Foreign trade (1969): imports ECar$23.8 million; exports ECar$7.5 million. Import sources: U.K. 32%; Trinidad and Tobago 15%; Canada 11%; U.S. 9%; Netherlands Antilles 5%. Export destinations: U.K. 62%; Trinidad and Tobago 14%; U.S. 8%; Barbados 7%. Main exports: bananas 55%; arrowroot 14%.

SEYCHELLES

The colony of Seychelles consists of a group of about 80 islands scattered over 400,000 sq.mi. in the western Indian Ocean northeast of Madagascar. Area: 107 sq.mi. (278 sq.km.). Pop. (1973 est.): 56,534. Cap.: Victoria, Mahé (pop., 1972 est., 14,000).

Education. (1972) Primary, pupils 10,074, teachers (1970) 381; secondary and vocational, pupils 2,514, teachers (1970) 120; higher (1970), students 87, teaching staff 7.

Finance and Trade. Monetary unit: Seychelles rupee, with (Sept. 17, 1973) a free rate of SRs. 5.53 to U.S. $1 (official rate of SRs. 13.33 = £1 sterling). Budget (1971 est.): revenue SRs. 31,170,000; expenditure SRs. 31,813,000. Foreign trade (1970): imports SRs. 55,924,000; exports SRs. 11,878,000. Import sources: U.K. 44%; Kenya 8%; The Netherlands 7%; South Africa 6%. Export destinations: India 42%; U.S. 17%; U.S.S.R. 6%; U.K. 5%. Main exports: copra 50%; cinnamon bark 36%.

TURKS AND CAICOS ISLANDS

The colony of the Turks and Caicos Islands is situated in the Atlantic southeast of the Bahamas. Area: 193 sq.mi. (500 sq.km.). Pop. (1972 est.): 6,000. Seat of government: Grand Turk Island (pop., 1970, 2,287).

Education. Primary, pupils (1970) 1,615, teachers (1969) 82; secondary (1969), pupils 227, teachers 15.

Finance and Trade. Monetary unit: Jamaican dollar with (Sept. 17, 1973) a free rate of Jam$0.91 to U.S. $1 (par value of Jam$2.20 = £1 sterling). Ordinary budget (1969 actual): revenue Jam$1,363,000; expenditure Jam$1,367,-000. Foreign trade (1969): imports Jam$993,-000; exports Jam$216,000. Main exports: crayfish 96%; salt 4%.

UNITED KINGDOM and FRANCE

NEW HEBRIDES

The British-French condominium of the New Hebrides is located in the southwestern Pacific about 500 mi. W of Fiji and 250 mi. NE of New Caledonia. Area: 5,700 sq.mi. (14,800 sq.km.). Pop. (1972 est.): 86,000. Cap.: Vila (pop., 1972 est., 8,500).

Education. (1970) Primary, pupils 18,250, teachers 778; secondary, pupils 541, teachers 50; vocational, pupils 143, teachers 12; teacher training, students 100, teachers 9.

Finance. Monetary units: Australian dollar and New Hebridean franc, with a free rate (Sept.

17, 1973) of NHFr. 69 = U.S.$1 (NHFr. 166 = £1 sterling). Condominium budget (1972 est.) balanced at A$5,004,000. British administration budget (1972–73 est.) balanced at A$3,911,000. French administration budget (1972 est.) balanced at A$4,975,000.

Foreign Trade. (1971) Imports A$18,142,000; exports A$12,849,000. Import sources: Australia 39%; France 16%; Japan 12%; U.K. 7%. Export destinations: U.S. 37%; France 34%; Japan 18%; New Caledonia 7%. Main exports: fish 51%; copra 33%.

Agriculture. Copra production (metric tons; 1972) *c.* 28,000, (1971) *c.* 34,000.

UNITED STATES

AMERICAN SAMOA

Located to the east of Western Samoa in the South Pacific, the unincorporated territory of American Samoa is approximately 1,600 mi. NE of the northern tip of New Zealand. Area: 76 sq.mi. (197 sq.km.). Pop. (1972 est.): 28,000. Cap.: Pago Pago (pop., 1970, 2,451).

Education. (1969–70) Primary, pupils 7,957, teachers 356; secondary and vocational, pupils 2,122, teachers 119.

Finance and Trade. Monetary unit: U.S. dollar. Budget (1970 est.) revenue $24.8 million (including U.S. grant $17 million). Foreign trade (1972): imports $19,557,000 (91% from U.S. in 1970); exports $41,369,000 (95% to U.S. in 1970). Main exports (1970): canned tuna 90%; pet food 5%.

CANAL ZONE

The Canal Zone is administered by the U.S. under treaty with Panama and consists of a 10-mi.-wide strip on the Isthmus of Panama through which the Panama Canal runs. Area (land only): 362 sq.mi. (964 sq.km.). Pop. (1970): 44,198. Administrative headquarters: Balboa Heights (pop., 1970, 232).

Education. (1969–70) Primary, pupils 8,626, teachers 369; secondary and vocational, pupils 5,952, teachers 264; higher, students 1,186, teaching staff 70.

Finance. Monetary unit: U.S. dollar (Panamanian balboa is also used). Budgets: (Canal Zone government; 1972) revenue $54.5 million, expenditure $53 million; (Panama Canal Company; 1972) revenue $183.4 million, expenditure $182.6 million.

Traffic. (1971–72) Total number of ocean-going vessels passing through the canal 13,766; total cargo tonnage 109.2 million; tolls collected U.S. $98.8 million. Nationality and number of commercial vessels using the canal: Liberian 1,700; Japanese 1,533; British 1,472; Norwegian 1,239; U.S. 1,165; West German 937; Panamanian 898; Greek 766; Netherlands 524; Swedish 410; Danish 382.

GUAM

Guam, an organized unincorporated territory, is located in the Pacific Ocean about 6,000 mi. SW of San Francisco and 1,500 mi. E of Manila. Area: 209 sq.mi. (541 sq.km.). Pop. (1970): 84,996. Cap.: Agana (pop., 1970, 2,119).

Education. (1969) Primary (including preprimary), pupils 17,618, teachers 650; secondary, pupils 9,607, teachers 491; higher, students 2,125, teaching staff 100.

Finance and Trade. Monetary unit: U.S. dollar. Budget (1970 est.): revenue $57.7 million (including U.S. grants $6.3 million); expenditure $48.9 million. Foreign trade (1971): imports $115 million; exports $3.8 million. Tourism (1971) 119,000 visitors.

Agriculture and Industry. Main crops: corn, sweet potatoes, cassava, lemons. Industrial production (1969): stone 593,000 metric tons; electricity (1971) 798 million kw-hr.

PUERTO RICO

Puerto Rico, a self-governing associated commonwealth, lies about 885 mi. SE of the Florida coast. Area: 3,421 sq.mi. (8,860 sq.km.). Pop. (1972 est.): 2,824,700. Cap.: San Juan (pop., 1972 est., 471,558).

Education. (1969–70) Primary (including preprimary), pupils 481,700, teachers 14,960; secondary and vocational, pupils 261,850, teachers 9,580; higher (including 3 universities), students 56,681, teaching staff *c.* 3,500.

Finance. Monetary unit: U.S. dollar. Budget (1970–71): revenue $1,172,000,000; expenditure $1,098,000,000. Gross domestic product: (1970–71) $5,464,000,000; (1969–70) $4,857,000,000. Cost of living (1963 = 100): (April 1973) 137; (April 1972) 132.

Foreign Trade. (1971) Imports $2,884,000,000 (75% from U.S.); exports $1,736,000,000 (92% to U.S.). Main exports (1968–69): clothing 21%; petroleum products 9%; chemicals 9%; electrical machinery and equipment 8%; cigars 6%; shellfish 5%; sugar 5%. Tourism (1971): visitors 1,095,000; gross receipts U.S. $235 million.

Transport and Communications. Roads (1972) 10,546 km. Motor vehicles in use (1970): passenger 499,800; commercial (including buses) 102,600. Telephones (Dec. 1971) 356,000. Radio receivers (Dec. 1969) 1,625,000. Television receivers (Dec. 1969) 410,000.

Agriculture. Production (in 000; metric tons; 1971; 1970 in parentheses): sweet potatoes 22 (21); bananas (1970) 114, (1969) 113; coffee (1972) *c.* 12, (1971) 10; sugar, raw value (1972) *c.* 267, (1971) *c.* 291; tobacco 2.5 (3); pineapples (1970) 57, (1969) 49; oranges 32 (29); grapefruit 10 (9). Livestock (in 000; Jan. 1972): cattle 542; pigs 198; chickens 4,373.

Industry. Production (in 000; metric tons; 1971): cement 1,791; sand and gravel (1969) 8,557; stone (1969) 6,337; electricity (kw-hr.) 9,156,000.

TRUST TERRITORY OF THE PACIFIC ISLANDS

The Trust Territory islands, numbering more than 2,000, are scattered over 3 million sq.mi. in the Pacific Ocean from 450 mi. E of the Philippines to just west of the International Date Line. Area: 707 sq.mi. (1,831 sq.km.). Pop. (1972 est.): 114,645. Seat of government: Saipan Island (pop., 1972 est., 10,745).

Education. (1971–72) Primary, pupils 29,917, teachers (1969–70) 1,210; secondary and vocational, pupils 6,447, teachers (1969–70) 273; teacher training (1968–69), students 971, teachers 55.

Finance and Trade. Monetary unit: U.S. dollar. Budget (1972 est.): revenue $73.6 million (including U.S. grant $9.4 million); expenditure $49 million. Foreign trade (1972): imports *c.* $30 million (50% from U.S., 28% from Japan in 1968); exports $2.6 million (57% to Japan in 1971). Main exports (1971): copra 55%; fish 30%; meat, fruit, and vegetables 8%.

Agriculture. Production (in 000; metric tons; 1971; 1970 in parentheses): copra *c.* 15 (*c.* 16); bananas *c.* 2 (*c.* 2). Livestock (in 000; June 1972): cattle 13; pigs 17; goats 6; poultry 151.

VIRGIN ISLANDS

The Virgin Islands of the United States is an organized unincorporated territory located about 40 mi. E of Puerto Rico. Area: 133 sq.mi. (344 sq.km.). Pop. (1970): 62,468. Cap.: Charlotte Amalie, St. Thomas (pop., 1970, 12,220).

Education. (1969–70) Primary (including preprimary), pupils 12,800, teachers 500; secondary and vocational, pupils 4,800, teachers 330; higher, students 1,425, teaching staff 40.

Finance and Trade. Monetary unit: U.S. dollar. Budget (1970 actual): revenue $105 million; expenditure $94,757,000. Foreign trade (1971): imports $551.9 million (41% from U.S. in 1970); exports $327.1 million (93% to U.S. in 1970). Main exports: petroleum products, watches, rum, fish. Tourism (1968–69): visitors *c.* 1.1 million; gross receipts *c.* $100 million.

Industry. Production: stone (1969) 373,000 metric tons; electricity (1971) 621.1 million kw-hr.

Development, Economic

In 1970 the UN had proclaimed the Second Development Decade, designed to focus world attention on the needs of the less developed countries. In the three years that followed, however, development problems appeared to have become more acute. Many old problems—population growth, unemployment, income inequalities, environmental deterioration—remained. At the same time, new ones arose: international monetary crises, food shortages, energy crises, and worldwide inflation. (*See* ENERGY; PAYMENTS AND RESERVES, INTERNATIONAL.)

The relationship of social equity to economic growth was receiving increasing attention, particularly in the low-income countries where a majority of the world's population lived. The benefits of development had not reached the poorest 40% of the population in the less developed countries. At the annual meeting of the World Bank in Nairobi, Kenya, in September 1973, the World Bank president, Robert S. McNamara, called on the less developed countries to redirect their policies with a view toward helping the poorest groups. For its part, the World Bank planned to give more attention to rural development, with increasing emphasis on agricultural lending.

Poverty and massive unemployment were intimately linked, but the means for attacking unemployment were severely limited. The drift from rural areas to urban centres continued, depriving the farms of skilled workers before the urban centres could employ them productively. Industrialization has advanced rapidly in many less developed countries, but it had failed to generate sufficient employment. A 10–25% unemployment rate was common.

The prices of some of man's principal food commodities reached historic highs in the international markets in 1972–73. Most serious was the reduction in world grain production, aggravated by the demand for meat in the higher income countries and the consequent expansion of coarse-grain requirements for feeding livestock. Since 1960 world grain reserves had fluctuated from a high of 115 million metric tons to a low of 100 million metric tons, representing only 7% of annual world grain consumption. Stocks of wheat in the exporting countries had fallen to their lowest level in 20 years. Stocks of other grains, including rice, had been depleted in both exporting and

Table I. Selected Economic Indicators for Less Developed and Industrialized Countries, Regional Summary

Region	Total GDP	Agricultural production	Manufacturing production	Population	GDP per capita	Total gross investment	Gross investment	Savings
	Average annual real rates of growth (%)						Shares in GNP (%)	
Less developed countries*								
1961–67	5.2	2.7	7.8	2.4	2.7	6.6	18.9	16.2
1971	6 0	1.8	8.2	2.4	3.5	7.8	19.8	16.3
1972†	5.8	—0.9	...	2.4	3.3	...	...	...
Africa								
1961–67	3.9	2.2	9.1	2.5	1.4	5.4	16.9	13.8
1971	5.5	2.6	10.1	2.5	2.9	10.7	20.2	15.1
1972†	5.4	1.0	...	2.6	2.7	...	...	...
Southern Europe								
1961–67	6.9	3.6	10.4	1.5	5.3	9.6	24.4	21.2
1971	6.8	3.0	9.3	1.5	5.2	8.6	23.6	20.7
1972†	8.2	0.3	...	1.4	6.7	...	...	...
East Asia								
1961–67	6.0	2.9	10.8	2.5	3.4	12.8	16.4	11.7
1971	7.4	3.6	12.5	2.6	4.6	6.8	20.8	17.2
1972†	5.4	2.7	...	2.6	2.7	...	...	...
Middle East								
1961–67	7.2	5.4	9.1	3.0	4.1	7.0	19.5	14.3
1971	9.4	1.5	12.2	3.0	6.2	12.1	21.6	12.9
1972†	9.9	9.0	...	3.0	6.8	...	...	...
South Asia								
1961–67	3.7	1.6	6.3	2.4	1.4	3.9	16.1	12.9
1971	2.9	—0.1	4.1	2.2	0.7	3.1	14.6	12.0
1972†	0.6	—5.6	...	2.1	—1.5	...	...	...
Western Hemisphere								
1961–67	5.1	3.3	5.7	2.9	2.1	4.8	19.0	17.8
1971	6.5	2.5	7.5	2.9	3.5	7.6	19.7	17.1
1972†	6.6	1.2	...	2.8	3.7	...	...	...
Industrialized countries‡								
1961–67	5.1	2.3	6.0	1.2	3.8	6.0	21.9	22.5
1971	3.9	2.4	2.9	1.0	3.0	2.3	23.9	24.5
1972†	5.5	1.9	...	0.9	4.6	...	...	...

*Less developed countries (75 countries and territories covering approximately 96% of GDP of all less developed areas with market economies): Africa—Algeria, Angola, Cameroon, Egypt, Ethiopia, Gabon, Ghana, Ivory Coast, Kenya, Libya, Malagasy Republic, Malawi, Mali, Mauritius, Morocco, Niger, Nigeria, Southern Rhodesia, Senegal, Sudan, Tanzania, Togo, Tunisia, Uganda, Upper Volta, Zaire, Zambia (coverage 91%); south Asia—Bangladesh, Burma, India, Pakistan, Sri Lanka (coverage 100%); east Asia—Hong Kong, Indonesia, South Korea, Malaysia, Philippines, Singapore, Taiwan, Thailand, Vietnam (coverage 98%); southern Europe—Cyprus, Greece, Portugal, Spain, Turkey, Yugoslavia (coverage 100%); Western Hemisphere—Argentina, Bolivia, Brazil, Chile, Colombia, Costa Rica, Dominican Republic, Ecuador, El Salvador, Guatemala, Guyana, Haiti, Honduras, Jamaica, Mexico, Nicaragua, Panama, Paraguay, Peru, Trinidad and Tobago, Uruguay, Venezuela (coverage 99%); Middle East—Iran, Iraq, Israel, Jordan, Lebanon, Syria (coverage 78%).
†Preliminary.
‡Industrialized countries: Australia, Austria, Belgium, Canada, Denmark, Finland, France, Germany, Iceland, Ireland, Italy, Japan, Luxembourg, The Netherlands, New Zealand, Norway, South Africa, Sweden, Switzerland, United Kingdom, United States.
Source: World Bank.

Table II. Trade Balance of Less Developed Countries
In U.S. $000,000,000

Item	1967	1968	1969	1970	1971	1972
Less developed countries						
Exports (f.o.b.)	43.8	47.3	53.7	60.3	68.3	80.5
Imports (c.i.f.)	49.7	53.8	59.7	67.8	78.0	87.1
Trade balance	−5.9	−6.5	−6.0	−7.5	−9.7	−6.6
Excluding less developed countries of southern Europe*						
Exports (f.o.b.)	39.4	43.2	48.4	54.1	60.8†	71.5†
Imports (c.i.f.)	41.6	45.2	49.7	55.7	64.1†	71.1†
Trade balance	−2.2	−2.0	−1.3	−1.6	−3.3	.4
Excluding southern Europe and major petroleum exporters‡						
Exports (f.o.b.)	29.8	32.5	37.1	41.6	44.5	59.2§
Imports (c.i.f.)	36.9	39.8	43.9	49.7	57.1	64.1§
Trade balance	−7.1	−7.3	−6.8	−8.1	−12.6	−4.9

*Greece, Portugal, Spain, Turkey, Yugoslavia.
†Estimate.
‡Iran, Iraq, Kuwait, Libya, Saudi Arabia, Venezuela.
§Estimate for Venezuela based on first quarter data. Estimate for Libya based on data for first two quarters. Data for Saudi Arabia not available.
Source: International Monetary Fund, *International Financial Statistics*.

Table III. Total Official and Other Flows of Long-Term Financial Resources (Net)* from DAC Countries to Less Developed Countries and Multilateral Agencies by Country
In U.S. $000,000

Country	Official flows 1969	1970	1971	1972	Other flows 1969	1970	1971	1972	Total flows 1969	1970†	1971†	1972†
Australia	175	202	202	271	57	179	328	153	232	381	530	425
Austria '	15	19	12	18	66	77	81	94	81	96	93	112
Belgium	116	120	146	193	141	189	171	198	257	309	317	391
Canada	245	346	340	462	119	280	412	524	364	626	752	986
Denmark	54	59	74	96	97	27	64	24	151	86	138	120
France	955	1,006	1,075	1,320	755	863	548	753*	1,710	1,869	1,623	2,073*
Germany, West	579	599	734	808	1,449	888	1,181	906	2,028	1,487	1,915	1,714
Italy	130	147	183	104	718	535	688	435	848	682	871	539*
Japan	436	458	511	611	827	1,366	1,629	2,114	1,263	1,824	2,140	2,725
Netherlands, The	143	196	216	310	226	261	389	343	369	457	605	653
Norway	30	37	42	63	45	30	23	—7	75	67	65	56
Portugal	58	39	99	115*	40	30	48	48*	98	69	147	163*
Sweden	121	117	159	198	91	112	84	74*	212	229	243	272*
Switzerland	29	30	28	64	90	107	217	109*	119	137	245	173*
United Kingdom	431	447	562	609	715	832	1,007	1,086	1,146	1,279	1,569	1,695
United States	3,092	3,050	3,324	3,349	1,733	3,204	3,543	4,005	4,825	6,254	6,867	7,354
Total	6,609	6,872	7,707	8,592	7,169	8,980	10,413	10,866	13,778	15,852	18,120	19,458

*Provisional.
†Including grants by voluntary agencies.
Source: OECD, Development Assistance Committee.

importing countries, and the remaining levels of stocks no longer constituted an adequate buffer against serious crop failure in one or more major producing areas. The assistant director general of the UN Food and Agriculture Organization (FAO) noted that the danger of straining world food supplies as a whole, hypothetical in 1971, had become real in 1973. Food prices rose in less developed and developed countries alike, in some cases by nearly 20%. Burdensome everywhere, these price increases had their greatest effect in less developed countries, where a larger proportion of income is spent on food.

With population expanding at an annual rate of 2%, merely maintaining current per capita consumption levels would require a doubling of food production over the next generation. To meet the nutritional needs of a growing population and the escalating demands of persons with higher incomes, it was estimated that agricultural output would have to be raised at an average annual rate of 4% at least well into the 1980s. By comparison, the rate of increase in 1972 was 1%. The often-expressed fears of world food shortages were becoming more credible. Clearly, worldwide policies were needed, and the crucial issue was how the world as a whole would face up to the problem.

In terms of world priorities, defense expenditures continued to make first claim on the resources of many governments, overshadowing such major civilian programs as public education and public health. International development assistance remained very small compared with defense expenditures. The UN continued to urge that human, material, and financial resources be concentrated on civilian purposes, but this was not yet the practice of most countries.

Multinational Corporations. The term multinational corporation refers to an enterprise that controls assets in two or more countries. Of the ten largest multinational corporations in 1973, eight were based in the U.S. In 1971 the production (value added) of each of these top ten was in excess of $3 billion, greater than the individual gross national product (GNP) of over 80 countries. Forty percent of the activities of multinational corporations were concentrated in manufacturing and 29% in petroleum.

The role of multinational corporations had become a major issue in economic and social development. They often played a useful role in transferring needed capital and technology to less developed countries, but their activities had given rise to serious questions concerning their effect on the economic and social development of low-income countries, as well as their intrusion into those countries' domestic affairs. According to a UN report, *Multinational Corporations in World Development*, about two-thirds of the activities of multinational corporations took place in developed market economies. Nevertheless, the re-

Table IV. Average Terms of Official Development Assistance Loan Commitments

Country	Average maturity (years) 1971	1972	Average interest rate (%) 1971	1972
Total DAC countries	29.1*	...	2.8*	...
United States	35.7	37.1	2.9	2.6
United Kingdom	23.6	23.3*	1.1*	0.2*
France	17.7	15.3	4.0	4.1
Germany, West	29.6	28.9	2.0	2.6
Italy	15.8	11.4*	4.4	5.6*
Japan	22.1	21.2	3.5	4.0

*Provisional.
Source: OECD, Development Assistance Committee.

port noted, the presence of such a corporation in a less developed country has much greater relative significance than would be the case in a developed country. The UN was conducting a study of the effect of multinational corporations on both global development and international relations. The aim, according to the UN secretary-general, was to set up "accepted standards of behaviour and a measure of international accountability."

Growth. In 1972 the combined gross domestic product (GDP) of the less developed countries grew at a rate of 5.8%, slightly higher than the average rate in 1961–67 but below the 1971 level. (*See* Table I.) Thus, even though population growth in 1972 did not exceed the 1971 rate, the rate of growth of GDP per capita was slightly lower in 1972 than in 1971. As always, there were wide regional differences. The rate of growth of GDP per capita in South Asia was a minus 1.5% in 1972, while in southern Europe it was 6.7%.

For all countries, the rate of increase in agricultural output was 1% lower in 1972 than in 1971. In the less developed countries agricultural production fell by nearly 1% after registering a gain of close to 2% in the preceding year. Among the crops of particular significance to the less developed countries, cereals, cocoa, and wool declined while tea, coffee, and sugar showed gains.

World Trade. Measured in current U.S. dollars, world trade expanded by more than a sixth between 1971 and 1972. This was almost twice the average rate of increase recorded in the 1960s and well above the 12% gain of the previous year. It raised the total value of world exports to $400 billion for the first time. However, inflation and exchange rate changes had raised the average unit value of traded goods by almost 10%. This meant that the volume of world trade rose by about 8%, the average rate of growth in the 1960s.

The value of exports from the less developed countries in 1972 was markedly higher than in 1971. (*See* Table II.) The largest increase in volume was in exports from southern and southeastern Asia. A similar improvement was achieved by Latin America, with the exception of Chile, Jamaica, Uruguay, and Venezuela. With supplies of most primary commodities rising only modestly and demand strengthening, export prices on the average were up between 11 and 12%. This played a major role in increasing the export earnings of less developed countries. Imports rose less than exports in most of the primary-producing regions.

Savings and Investment. Domestic savings financed 82% of total investment in less developed countries. As indicated in Table I, on the average, 16% of GNP had been saved, despite the very low per capita income. The average savings rate of 22–24% in the industrialized countries was less impressive, since per capita income was much higher. The inflow of foreign capital continued to enable the less developed countries to achieve investment rates higher than the savings rates. Nevertheless, investment rates were much higher in the developed countries, indicating that the gap between poorer and richer nations would continue.

There were wide differences in the savings/investment picture among less developed countries as well as between developed and less developed countries. In Africa, for example, the savings/investment ratio was far below that in the Western Hemisphere.

Population Growth and Employment. Another marked difference between the developed and less developed countries was the rate of population growth. For the less developed countries it had remained around 2.4%, as compared with about 1% in the developed countries. If the current rate of growth was maintained, the world's population would double by the year 2006.

The concomitant increase in the working-age population would have serious implications for countries with prevailing high rates of underemployment and unemployment. A UN report, *The Demographic Situation in the ECAFE Region,* stated that the urban proportion of the population in Asia and the Far East would increase from the 1970 total of 25% to 44% in the year 2000. This was an alarming prospect, since problems of unemployment were most acute in urban areas. Nevertheless, there was little coordination between population programs and other development plans, and achievements in population restraint still lagged far behind national objectives. The UN was preparing for a world population conference in 1974, under the leadership of Antonio Carrillo-Flores of Mexico.

External Sources of Finance. In 1972 the level of total financial flows from the member countries of the Development Assistance Committee (DAC) of the Organization for Economic Cooperation and Development (OECD) to the less developed countries was slightly higher than in 1971. (*See* Table III.) The total of $19,458,000,000 was less than 1% of the total GNP of the industrialized countries. The U.S. was still the largest contributor, providing over $7 billion, although its contribution was far below the UN target of 1% of GNP. There was a significant increase in the contributions of Japan, France, and Canada.

Total net official development assistance from DAC countries rose by 12% to $8.6 billion, measured at current exchange rates and prices, but the 12% nom-

Table V. External Public Debt Outstanding and Debt Service Payments for Less Developed Countries*

In U.S. $000,000

Year	Total	Africa	East Asia†	Middle East‡	South Asia	Southern Europe§	Western Hemisphere‖
Debt outstanding, Dec. 31							
1968	54,315	9,019	6,295	4,364	12,666	5,601	16,369
1969	60,174	9,688	7,776	5,018	13,654	6,368	17,671
1970	69,310	10,865	9,217	7,022	14,942	6,965	20,297
1971—Total (at Dec. 31, 1971, exchange rates)	79,218¶	11,922	11,217	8,899	15,929	8,196	23,052
Disbursed	58,345	8,355	7,900	5,582	13,203	5,914	17,388
Undisbursed	20,872	3,566	3,316	3,316	2,726	2,282	5,663
Service payments during							
1968	4,525	596	286	334	595	503	2,211
1969	4,997	682	387	452	689	542	2,246
1970	6,012	791	625	634	736	697	2,527
1971	6,789	913	731	847	758	814	2,725

Note: Items may not add to totals due to rounding.

*Includes the following countries: Africa—Botswana, Burundi, Cameroon, Central African Republic, Chad, Congo, Dahomey, Egypt, Ethiopia, Gabon, Ghana, Ivory Coast, Kenya, Lesotho, Liberia, Malagasy Republic, Malawi, Mali, Mauritania, Mauritius, Morocco, Niger, Nigeria, Rhodesia, Rwanda, Senegal, Sierra Leone, Somalia, Sudan, Swaziland, Tanzania, Togo, Tunisia, Uganda, Upper Volta, Zaire, Zambia, plus the East African Community; east Asia—Indonesia, Malaysia, Philippines, South Korea, Singapore, Taiwan, Thailand; Middle East—Iran, Iraq, Israel, Jordan, Syria; south Asia—Afghanistan, Bangladesh, India, Pakistan, Sri Lanka; southern Europe—Cyprus, Greece, Malta, Spain, Turkey, Yugoslavia; Western Hemisphere—Argentina, Bolivia, Brazil, Chile, Colombia, Costa Rica, Dominican Republic, Ecuador, El Salvador, Guatemala, Guyana, Honduras, Jamaica, Mexico, Nicaragua, Panama, Paraguay, Peru, Trinidad and Tobago, Uruguay, Venezuela.

†Does not include publicly guaranteed private debt of the Philippines estimated at $439 million in 1971.

‡Does not include undisbursed portion of the debt of Israel for the years 1967–70.

§Does not include nonguaranteed debt of the "social sector" of Yugoslavia contracted after March 31, 1966.

‖Debt outstanding of Brazil includes some nonguaranteed debt of the private sector to suppliers and excludes the undisbursed portion of suppliers' credits and of bilateral official loans except for those owed to the U.S. government.

¶Includes $5,134,000,000 of loans payable in multiple currencies and $4,197,000,000 undisbursed on World Bank loans which are shown at book value. For both of these, information on the currencies to be repaid was not available.

Source: World Bank.

inal increase corresponded to a real increase of only 1%. The net flow of official development assistance represented only 0.34% of the combined GNP (at market prices) of the donor countries, compared with 0.35% in 1971. The largest contributor was the U.S., but its contribution in relation to its GNP had fallen from 0.37% in 1968 to 0.29% in 1972. During the same period, Canada's contribution rose from 0.26 to 0.44%.

The total net flow of official and private financial resources increased by about $1.2 billion to about $19.5 billion, or slightly more than 7%, mainly reflecting the devaluation of the U.S. dollar. After adjusting for price increases, the real volume of total flows in 1972 was estimated to have fallen by about 3%. The net flow of total official and private financial resources in relation to donors' GNP declined from 0.82% in 1971 to 0.77% in 1972. Export credits (official and private) fell from $3.4 billion to $2.1 billion and multilateral portfolio investment declined to $620 million from $770 million.

The average maturity of official U.S. loan commitments rose in 1972, approaching the 1970 level of 37.4 years. In the case of Italy, average maturity fell to 11.4 years and of France, to 15.3 years. Differences were also observed for interest rates; Japan's and Italy's rose while those of the U.S. and the U.K. declined.

The World Bank Group approved development assistance totaling $3,555,000,000 during the year ended June 30, 1973. The figure fulfilled the goal of providing twice as much assistance in 1969–73 as in the previous five years. Lending by the International Development Association (IDA) was almost 36% higher than in fiscal 1972; 70% of IDA resources had been channeled to the poorest countries. Aggregate gross commitments by IDA reached $5,907,000,000 as of June 30, 1973. Disbursements during the year totaled $493 million, compared with $261 million in fiscal 1972. Aggregate disbursements to June 30, 1973, were $3,215,000,000, including a $485 million adjustment that reflected devaluation of the U.S. dollar. The third replenishment of the association's resources, effective on Sept. 22, 1972, provided $2.5 billion for the three years ending in mid-1974. Negotiations were under way to replenish IDA resources to the level of $1.5 billion per year beginning in mid-1974, for a total of $4.5 billion over three years.

External Public Debt. The external public indebtedness of the less developed countries was estimated at $79.2 billion as of the end of 1971, an increase of about 14% over the previous year. (*See* Table V.) Approximately $21 billion of this was still undisbursed. Western Hemisphere nations held the largest single bloc of external debt: $23 billion, with service payments exceeding $2.7 billion, South Asia was next, but the service payments were much lower because most of the debt had been incurred on "developmental" terms.

Overall, debt service payments rose by more than 11% in 1972. To avoid difficulties in servicing their external debt, the less developed countries needed to increase their export earnings, as well as to obtain long-term assistance on easier terms. Rising prices for primary products would help to provide the exchange, but many less developed countries did not have these relatively scarce resources. India, for example, had to import such commodities from other less developed countries. For these countries, the need for external capital inflows would continue to be large, though many were trying to decrease their dependence on official development assistance, particularly from national agencies. This might well require major changes in development objectives and policies; *e.g.*, greater reliance on labour-intensive industries and more emphasis on rural development.

(IRVING S. FRIEDMAN)

See also Agriculture and Fisheries; Commodities, Primary; Industrial Review; Inter-American Affairs; Investment, International.

Gross National Product per Capita of Less Developed and Selected Developed Countries, 1960 and 1971

GNP at market prices in 1971 U.S. dollars

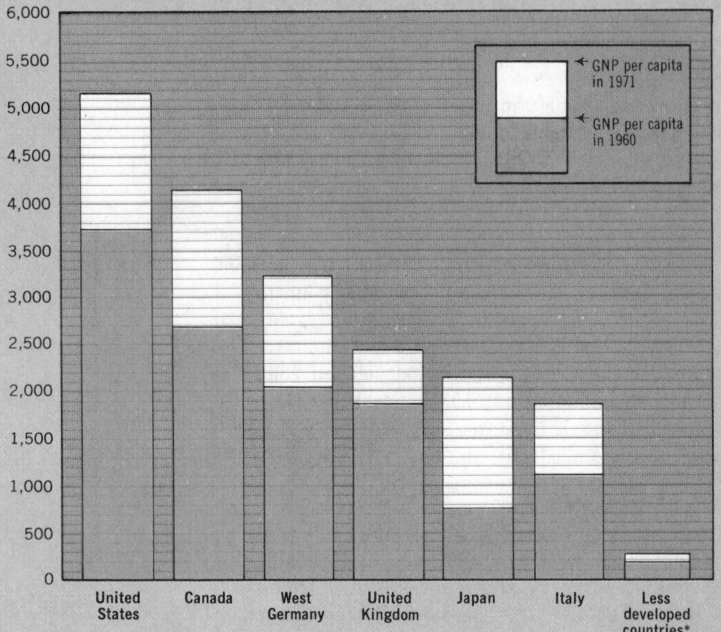

*Data for 79 countries.
Source: International Bank for Reconstruction and Development.

Net Flow of Financial Resources from DAC Countries to Less Developed Countries and Multilateral Agencies in Relation to Gross National Product in 1958-72

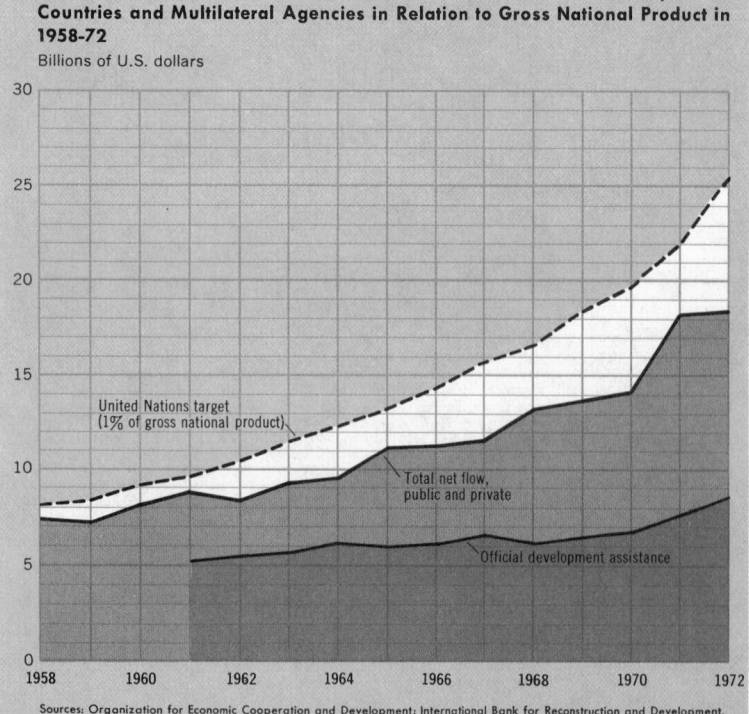

Billions of U.S. dollars

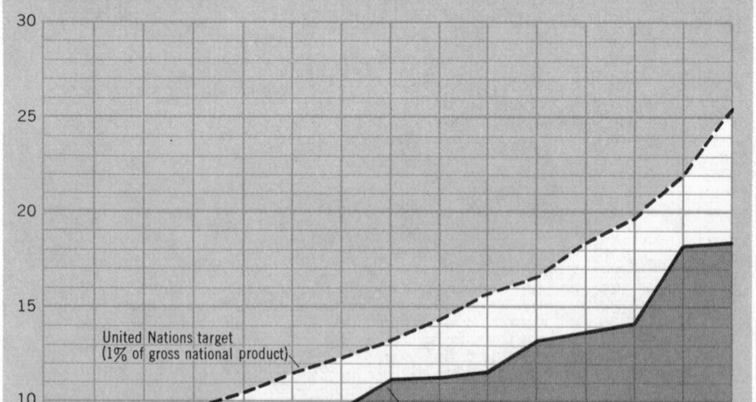

Sources: Organization for Economic Cooperation and Development; International Bank for Reconstruction and Development.

Disasters

The loss of life and property in disasters during 1973 included the following. (*See also* METEOROLOGY.)

AVIATION

Jan. 22 Kano, Nigeria. A Royal Jordanian Airways Boeing 707 jetliner, chartered by Nigeria Airways and carrying Muslim pilgrims home from a trip to Mecca, Saudi Arabia, crashed and burst into flames as it landed in dense fog at the Kano airport; of the 205 passengers and crew members aboard 176 perished (equaling the record number of fatalities to date).
Jan. 29 Northern Cyprus. Egyptian Soviet-built Ilyushin-18 turboprop airliner, en route to Nicosia, Cyprus, from Cairo, struck the side of a rocky mountain peak and killed all of the 38 persons aboard.
Feb. 19 Prague, Czechoslovakia. Soviet national airline Aeroflot Tupolev-154 trijet, completing the regular morning flight from Moscow, smashed into the ground and burst into flames as it came into the Prague International Airport; 66 of the 100 persons aboard were killed.
Feb. 28 Szczecin, Pol. A Polish Air Force Soviet-built Antonov-24 turboprop carrying several top Polish and Czechoslovakian security officials crashed near the Szczecin airport and killed all 15 persons aboard.
March 3 Moscow. Bulgarian Balkan Airlines Ilyushin-18 turboprop flying from Sofia, Bulg., to Moscow plunged into a deep snowbank and burned near the village of Skhodnya as it came in for a landing at Moscow's Sheremetyevo Airport; all 25 persons aboard died.
March 5 Nantes, France. Two Spanish jetliners, an Iberian twin-engine DC-9 and a Spantax Convair 990 charter plane, collided in the sky 29,000 ft. over Nantes; the DC-9 fell in flames killing all 68 persons aboard; the Convair 990 made a landing with all its 108 passengers and crew members safe.
March 19 Central Highlands, South Vietnam. South Vietnam national airline Air Vietnam four-engine DC-4 prop plane, en route from Saigon, crashed as it approached the Ban Me Thuot airport; at least 58 persons died.
April 10 Hochwald, Switz. British Invicta charter plane, a four-engine Vanguard turboprop, en route from Bristol, Eng., with a group of women on a one-day holiday trip to Switzerland, cracked up when a wing hit a tree as it approached the Basel airport during a heavy snowstorm; 107 of the 145 persons on board the plane perished.
April 12 Sunnyvale, Calif. U.S. Space Agency Convair 990 laboratory aircraft collided with a U.S. Navy P-3 Orion antisubmarine patrol plane in midair about 300 ft. above a Sunnyvale golf course and both plunged to earth in flames; 16 men died, a Navy crewman survived.
May 31 New Delhi, India. An Indian Airlines Boeing 737 jetliner, en route from Madras, burst into flames and crashed into a residential area moments before a scheduled landing at Palam Airport; 48 persons aboard the plane were killed, the other 17 received injuries.
June 2 São Luís, Braz. A Brazilian Cruzeiro do Sul airlines Caravelle jet crashed in a landing attempt at the São Luís airport killing all 23 persons aboard.
June 3 Paris. Soviet Tupolev-144 civilian supersonic airliner exploded in midair during a demonstration flight at the Paris International Air Show at Le Bourget Airport with the flaming wreckage falling on the town of Goussainville; seven villagers on the ground perished as did all six crewmen aboard the plane.
June 20 Puerto Vallarta, Mex. An Aeroméxico DC-9 jet, on a flight from Houston, Tex., to Mexico City, smashed into a mountainside near the resort town of Puerto Vallarta killing all 27 persons aboard.
July 11 Saulx-les-Chartreux, France. Brazilian Varig Airlines Boeing 707, nearing the end of a 6,000-mi. flight from Rio de Janeiro, caught fire and plopped into a vegetable patch just short of Paris' Orly Airport; 122 of the 134 persons aboard the plane died in the smoke and fire, 12 survived.
July 22 Papeete, Tahiti. A U.S. Pan American Boeing 707 heading for Los Angeles plunged into the sea moments after takeoff from the Papeete airport; only one passenger of the 79 passengers and crew members aboard the plane survived.
July 23 St. Louis, Mo. U.S. Ozark Air Lines twin-engine Fairchild 227 turbojet slammed into a St. Louis suburban area as it approached the runway in a thunderstorm at Lambert Airport; 37 of the 45 persons aboard were killed.
July 31 Boston. A Delta Air Lines jetliner on a flight from Burlington, Vt., crashed while landing in a dense fog at Boston's Logan International Airport. The DC-9 came in over the harbour, hit an earthen embankment, and disintegrated in flames; of the 89 persons aboard, only one survived with serious burns and injuries.
Aug. 13 La Coruña, Spain. A Spanish Caravelle airliner arriving from Madrid exploded and crashed into several houses after striking treetops near the fogbound La Coruña airport; none of the 85 passengers and crew survived.
Aug. 27 Bogotá, Colombia. A Colombian Lockheed Electra turboprop airliner crashed into a hill and burned shortly after taking off from Bogotá; none of the 40 persons aboard survived.
Aug. 28 Madrid. A U.S. Air Force C-141 StarLifter cargo jet on a flight from Athens to Torrejon air base near Madrid hit a low hill as it approached to land, then exploded in flames as it struck the ground; of the 24 who died, some were children and military wives; one navigator survived.
Sept. 11 Titograd, Yugos. A French-built Caravelle aircraft belonging to Yugoslav Airlines crashed into a mountain as it was approaching the Titograd airport after a flight from Skoplje, Macedonia; all 42 aboard were killed.
Oct. 12 Near Requena, Peru. A Sikorsky helicopter carrying 15 geologists and technicians in search of oil reserves crashed in the Peruvian jungle; four survivors were rescued after two days.
Oct. 13 Moscow. A Soviet airliner, probably a Tupolev-104, crashed at a Moscow airport after completing a flight from Tbilisi, U.S.S.R.; 28 persons were reported killed.
Dec. 11 Mount Sitkin Island, Alaska. A C-118 U.S. Navy Reserve transport plane crashed into a mountain about 25 mi. from Adak Naval Air Station; all of the ten aboard died.
Dec. 22 Tangier, Morocco. A French-built Caravelle twin-jet airliner, under charter by the Belgium Sabena Airlines and flying from Paris to Casablanca via Tangier, crashed into a mountain in stormy weather near the coastal town of Tétouan, 30 mi. SE of Tangier; none of the 99 passengers and 7 crewmen survived.

FIRES AND EXPLOSIONS

Jan. 13 Kampala, Uganda. Flames burst from an overturned gasoline truck when a lighted cigarette was dropped into the leaking fuel; 10 persons were burned to death, 70 others were hospitalized.
Feb. 2 Eagle Grove, Ia. A cafe and several other downtown buildings were destroyed by fire following a gas explosion; 14 persons died as a result of the blast.
Feb. 10 Staten Island, N.Y. Explosion in a huge 287-ft. circular storage tank for liquefied gas caught members of a repair and cleaning crew in a hail of concrete and flaming debris, killing 40 workmen; damage to the tank and equipment was set at $31 million.
March 10 Neufmesnil, France. Flames swept through a family home and killed 10 of the 13 children in the family; the parents and three other children escaped with injuries.
Sept. 1 Copenhagen. In the worst such disaster in Denmark's history, an early morning fire destroyed the 74-year-old Hafnia hotel, a city landmark that fire officials had several times warned was a firetrap; fire, smoke, falling debris, and desperate leaps from windows and roof killed 35 foreign tourists.
Sept. 29 Hoboken, N.J. An early morning fire swept through four tenements in a predominantly Puerto Rican area of the city, killing ten and injuring six; some 50 others were rescued.
Nov. 29 Kumamoto, Jap. In the worst such disaster in Japanese history, a fire swept through the seven-story Taiyo Department Store, blinding and choking thousands of shoppers as it raced from the third floor up the stairwells and toward the roof; 103 bodies were recovered, many of them burned beyond recognition.
Dec. 13 Tachov, Czechoslovakia. A faulty heating system caused a violent explosion that demolished a dormitory where teen-aged apprentice workers were sleeping; about 80 died.
Dec. 17 Near Quito, Ecuador. A can of gasoline, dropped on the floor of a crowded bus, exploded into flames when a passenger lit a match; 23 persons were burned to death.

MARINE

Jan. 6 Off Sabang, Sumatra. Cyprus oil tanker, the 20,000-ton "Anson," quickly sank after colliding with the 15,000-ton Liberian tanker "Atlantic Faith" in foggy weather about 120 mi. offshore; ten crewmen from the "Anson" were lost and presumed dead.
Jan. 8 Posadas, Arg. Explosion and fire on board a ferryboat crossing the Paraña River with 61 passengers returning from

Rescue workers surround the smoldering remains of a Brazilian jetliner that crashed just short of Orly Airport near Paris on July 11, 1973. Of 134 persons aboard, 122 were killed.

LIAISON

a gambling casino on the Paraguay side brought death to 16 persons; another 23 were missing and presumed dead.
Jan. 25 Off South Korea. A 76-ton Korean ferryboat feeling its way through dense fog ran aground and sank; many among the 100 passengers were believed drowned.
Feb. 7 SE of Tasmania. Japanese tuna boat, the "Nissan Maru No. 8," was wrecked as it ran aground about 25 mi. S of Brunia; 21 fishermen were lost and presumed dead, one survivor clung to a rock and was rescued.
Feb. 21 Rangoon, Burma. A crowded ferryboat collided with the Japanese freighter "Bombay Maru" in the Rangoon River; an estimated 200 persons died when the ferry sank.
March 22 SE of Cape May, N.J. Norwegian freighter, the 541-ft. "Norse Variant," foundering in stormy Atlantic seas with two flooded cargo holds sank moments after the crew abandoned ship; of the 30 seamen aboard 29 perished, one was rescued from a life raft.
May 5 SE of Dacca, Bangladesh. Carrying about 300 passengers, the riverboat "Ghazi" was rammed astern by another launch, the "Dirghirpir Express," and sank almost immediately; at least 250 persons aboard the "Ghazi" were believed to have perished, the other boat left the scene with about 50 of its passengers injured.
May 17 Near Magwe, Burma. Burmese government-owned vessel, the "Tawpan," sank in the Irrawaddy River drowning more than 100 persons.
May 19 Off Port Judith, R.I. U.S. party boat "Comet" on a day-long fishing trip tipped over in a choppy sea and broke in two; 12 persons died in the chilly waters, 5 were missing and presumed dead, and 11 survived.
June 2 Off Staten Island, N.Y. Steering-gear failure on the U.S. "Sea Witch" apparently caused the big container ship to ram into the Belgian oil tanker "Esso Brussels" as it rode at anchor in the Narrows of New York Harbor; fires were set off in both ships bringing death to 16 persons.
June 16 Bay of Bengal. A motor launch carrying 150 members of a wedding party was caught in a gale, capsized, and sank in the bay off Chittagong, Bangladesh; 31 persons drowned.
June 25 Off Cape Guardafui, Somalia. Indian cargo and passenger vessel, the 5,973-ton "Saudi," foundered in heavy seas and was abandoned; 105 persons died or were missing and presumed dead in the shark-infested waters off East Africa's "horn."
June 27 S of Cebu, Phil. A Philippine interisland ship with 400 passengers aboard struck a coral reef and sank; at least 20 persons perished.
July 16 SE of Manila. The "Mactan," carrying about 700 passengers from the southern Philippines to Manila, sank near a small island during a typhoon; two bodies were recovered and most of the 35 missing were believed drowned.
Oct. 28 Río de la Plata estuary, Arg. The "Ushuaia," an Argentine navy transport, collided with an Argentine cargo vessel about 90 mi. from Buenos Aires shortly after midnight. Of the 89 persons aboard the "Ushuaia," 24 were missing and believed drowned when the vessel sank in a narrow channel of the estuary.
Dec. 19 NW of Vancouver Island, B.C. The 10,000-ton Liberian freighter "Oriental Monarch" lost power and sank in heavy seas during a Pacific storm while carrying grain from Japan to Portland, Ore.; rescue ships that first spotted only empty lifeboats, rafts, and floating life jackets later recovered 27 bodies; 13 other crew members were presumed dead.
Dec. 24 Gulf of Guayaquil, Ecuador. The heavily overloaded ferryboat "Jambeli," making its way from Puerto Bolívar to Guayaquil, capsized in converging currents near Puná Island; at least 191 drowned, 142 were rescued, and an undetermined number were unaccounted for.

Mangled vehicles are strewn in a long row on the New Jersey Turnpike near Kearny, Oct. 24, 1973. At least 9 persons were killed and more than 40 injured in the series of pileups blamed on fog and on dense smoke from a nearby dumping ground.

WIDE WORLD

MINING AND TUNNELING

Feb. 8 Johannesburg, S.Af. It was reported that an underground fire in the nearby West Drienfontein gold mine had killed at least 26 miners.
March 18 Dhanbad, India. A series of gas explosions in a coal mine brought death to at least 50 miners.
May 5 Changsong, South Korea. Six mine cars transporting miners into the coal pits went out of control and tipped over killing 18 workers and injuring 18 others.
June 28 Near Johannesburg, S.Af. A surfacing mine cage rammed into steel girders of the hoisting machinery and killed 16 men.
Dec. 19 Orkney, S.Af. Tons of falling rock at the Vaal Reefs gold mine trapped workers more than a mile underground; though 3 were rescued, 9 died and little hope was held out for nearly a dozen others because of the intense heat and shortage of oxygen.

MISCELLANEOUS

Feb. 23 Andhra Pradesh State, India. Poisoning from drinking liquor sold in a store at Suryapet accounted for the deaths of at least 60 persons, more than 500 others became ill.
March 2 Baileys Crossroads, Va. Collapse of a partly constructed 24-story condominium building killed 14 workmen and injured 34 others.
Aug. 20 Sudan. A wild elephant, attacking a Sudanese village near the Zaire border, killed 11 persons, injured 3 others, and destroyed 10 homes.
Oct. 18 Ipoh, Malaysia. A gigantic piece of limestone, loosened by heavy rains and nearby blasting, went hurtling down a hillside and into a cluster of squatters' shacks; 40 or 50 persons were killed outright or buried alive.
Late November Mozambique. A large quantity of methyl alcohol was washed ashore in drums and mistakenly drunk as whisky; 58 deaths were confirmed but hundreds were believed to have succumbed.

NATURAL

Jan 1–6 Sicily. Storms lashing the island of Sicily and southern Italy with high winds and torrential rains claimed 24 lives and left 5,000 persons homeless; damage amounted to more than $360 million.
Jan. 5 Uttar Pradesh and Bihar states, India. Bitter two-week cold wave brought death to at least 115 persons.
Jan. 10 San Justo, Arg. Three-minute tornado with 100-mph winds wrecked buildings in the town and surrounding farmland killing 60 persons and injuring more than 300 others.
Jan. 17 Iberian Peninsula. A severe 70-mph storm hit the coasts of Spain and Portugal stirring up 45-ft. waves that sank dozens of boats, leveled harbour installations, and left at least 19 persons dead or missing.
Jan. 31 Tecomán, Mex. An earthquake struck Mexico's Pacific coastal area and killed 17 persons, hundreds of others were injured.
March 26 East central Brazil. Flooding along the Caratinga River caused at least 20 deaths; thousands of persons were left homeless and damage amounted to $16 million.
April 7 Tunisia. Late March and early April floods brought wide devastation to town and countryside leaving 86 persons dead and 33 missing; an estimated 6,000 homes were destroyed and 10,000 head of cattle lost.
April 9 Midwest U.S. A 24-hour storm battered a three-state area and churned up Lake Michigan into huge waves that pounded 28 mi. of lakefront causing nearly $600,000 in damage to breakwaters and shorelines; 26 deaths were attributed to the tempest.
April 12 Faridpur District, Bangladesh. More than a dozen villages were struck by a 90-mph wind and rainstorm that killed possibly up to 200 persons, injured about 15,000 others, and left 10,000 more homeless.
April 14 Guanacaste Province, Costa Rica. An earthquake centring near the village of Tilarán near the Nicaragua border killed at least 16 persons.
April 29 Mississippi Valley, U.S. Persistently rising waters of the Mississippi and its tributaries finally crested at St. Louis, Mo., after flooding 6,350,000 lowland acres S of the city, washing out farms and homes, bridges, roads, and levees; flood-related accidents caused at least 16 deaths.
May 26–28 South central U.S. Severe weekend rainstorms and tornadoes wreaked havoc over 11 states with Alabama and Arkansas declared disaster areas; 48 persons died, hundreds were injured, and damage to buildings and to inundated newly planted crops was in the millions.
June 26 San Antonio de Prado, Colombia. Rubble from a landslide buried three homes in which 16 persons perished.
July 8 Near Guadalajara, Mex. A cloudburst in the mountains poured floodwaters over the fishing towns of Ocotlán, San Pedro Itzican, and Mazcola on the shores of Lake Chapala; at least 30 persons died and 27 others were injured.
July 14–15 Northern Italy. Heavy weekend rainstorms drenched the Italian Riviera area touching off floods and landslides that resulted in 14 deaths.
July West central Africa. A seven-year period of near universal drought in the sub-Sahara countries of Senegal, Mauritania, Mali, Upper Volta, Niger, and Chad destroyed crops, decimated cattle, and threatened to cause one of the worst famines of the century; no accurate death toll could be made, but food and other supplies rushed from many parts of the world averted a catastrophe of calamitous proportions.

UPI COMPIX

At Orizaba, Mex., a woman sits among the ruins of her home after a massive earthquake that killed three of her children on Aug. 28, 1973. The quake took at least 600 lives and left about 4,000 injured.

August Northern Indian subcontinent. Prolonged monsoon rains along the entire Himalayan mountain range caused rampaging rivers to overflow their banks and engulf entire towns in Pakistan, Bangladesh, and the Indian states of Uttar Pradesh, Assam, and Bihar; thousands died, millions were made homeless, and property damage was estimated in the hundreds of millions of dollars; thousands of square miles of farmland were inundated, huge quantities of stored crops were washed away, and numerous bridges, railroad tracks, and roads were destroyed.
August Iripuato, Mex. Severe flooding caused by prolonged rains that fell over wide areas of Mexico killed an estimated 200 persons and made 150,000 homeless; national crop losses of sorghum, maize, and cotton were valued at more than $100 million.
Aug. 28 States of Puebla, Veracruz, and Oaxaca, Mex. An earthquake measuring 6.4 on the Richter scale occurred along the Zacomboxo Fault in central Mexico killing at least 600 persons (the highest such toll ever recorded in Mexico), injuring about 4,000, and destroying or severely damaging 10,000 buildings.
Sept. 30 Ethiopia. The United Kingdom Disasters Emergency Fund estimated that between 100,000 and 150,000 Ethiopians had already starved to death because of severe drought over the past two years; because there were no crops and because most of the country's cattle had died, the toll in human casualties could rise to a million or more unless the situation was alleviated in the immediate future.
Oct. 12 Central U.S. Unusually heavy rains and severe flash flooding from Nebraska to Texas took the lives of at least 11 persons; some 35 others were reported missing.
Oct. 19–21 Southern Spain. Torrential night rains that caused widespread flash flooding in the provinces of Granada, Almería, and Murcia brought death to at least 500 persons as homes collapsed, roads gave way, and communication facilities toppled; damage was estimated at $400 million.
Nov. 10–11 South Vietnam. Typhoon rains pouring down on Binh Dinh and neighbouring provinces washed out bridges, destroyed homes, damaged crops, and ruined harvested grains; at least 60 persons died and about 150,000 were forced to flee their dwellings.
Nov. 18–24 Philippines. A typhoon and heavy monsoon rains flooded Cagayan Valley and many towns in the southern islands, bringing death to 54 persons and damaging crops, roads, bridges, and thousands of homes.
Dec. 9 Bangladesh. A cyclone striking the southern coast capsized at least 200 fishing boats; many of the 1,000 missing fishermen were feared drowned.
Dec. 13 Qafsah, Tunisia. Surging floodwaters brought on by torrential rains smashed into a school and swept 45 children to their deaths; no immediate estimate could be made of other deaths or damage throughout the country.
Dec. 17 U.S. Atlantic seaboard. A severe weekend snow and ice storm stretching from Maine to Georgia cut off power supplies to hundreds of thousands of homes and left at least 20 dead.
Dec. 23 Eastern and northern India. A cold wave that continued for several weeks in the state of Bihar claimed 146 lives; similar fatalities were reported in Delhi and neighbouring areas.

RAILROAD

Feb. 1 Medjez-Sfa, Algeria. A train running down a slope 50 mi. from the Tunisian border crashed and killed 35 persons; 30 others were injured.
Feb. 16 Megara, Greece. A passenger train jumped the tracks and overturned killing at least 10 persons and injuring 17.
March 16 Las Villas Province, Cuba. Derailment of a Santiago de Cuba–Havana passenger train as it crossed a bridge near Santa Clara caused one car to fall into the river; 24 of the 400 passengers were killed, 31 others injured.
Dec. 19 Ealing, Eng. A crowded express commuter train returning to Oxford from London with Christmas shoppers left the tracks, plowed into an embankment, and overturned; 14 of the 600 aboard were killed and 40 injured.

TRAFFIC

Jan. 14 Zonguldak, Turk. Blinded by heavy snow the driver of a bus steered over a cliff; 16 occupants of the bus died, 25 others were injured.
Jan. 21 Suva, Fiji. Bus carrying a group of wedding guests collided with another bus killing 15 guests, mostly women and children; another 48 guests were injured.
Jan. 29 Near Cordoba, Arg. A bus fell into a 90-ft. ravine and killed 11 persons, 25 others received injuries.
Jan. 30 Kecskemet, Hung. Traveling over a crossing, a bus was rammed by a passenger train; 24 persons died, 20 more were severely hurt.
Feb. 15 Uvita, Colombia. A bus burst into flames as it fell to the bottom of a ravine and brought death to 20 persons and injured 6 others.
March 12 Baquedano, Chile. Head-on crash of two buses in Chile's worst traffic accident to date accounted for the deaths of 45 persons with another possible 50 hurt.
March 18 Barrie, Ont. A fiery 32-car pileup on Highway 400 killed 12 persons in one of Canada's worst road accidents.
May 2 Near Salvador, Braz. Out of control on a rural road after hitting a donkey, an overloaded bus crashed head-on into a truck killing 39 persons, 13 of whom were children.
May 3 Dacca, Bangladesh. A bus waiting for a ferry to take it across the Bansi River rolled off the dock and into the river drowning at least 52 persons, 8 others scrambled out of the bus before it went under.
May 16 Kyongju, South Korea. As an overloaded bus attempted to cross some railroad tracks it was struck by a train and hurled into a stream; 23 persons, mostly high-school students, were killed, and more than 60 others were hurt.
June 10 Near Buenos Aires, Arg. Caught on the train tracks, a standing bus was rammed by a train and dragged 100 ft.; 13 persons died, 30 were injured.
June 21 Pindamonhangaba, Braz. Multiple crash involving four buses, five trucks, three trailers, and six cars occurred in a thick fog on Brazil's busiest highway; a group of pilgrims on their way to a holy shrine on Corpus Christi Day were among the 14 fatalities resulting from the pileup.
July 2 Alwar, India. A bus attempting to ford a swollen stream stalled in the swirling waters; two differing high-caste groups of passengers refused to share the single rescue rope brought out from shore and stayed on the bus, which was swept downstream with the loss of 78 lives, 8 persons survived.
July 9 Bogor, Indon. Colliding with another bus, a crowded bus veered off the road and into a river killing 18 persons and injuring 33 others.
July 15 Japalpur, India. Crashing through a collapsing bridge, a bus fell into the Kopra River killing 31 of 40 passengers.
July 22 Iran. A bus speeding around a curve in northeast Iran hit a pedestrian, crashed through a bridge guardrail, and plunged into a river; of the 48 persons who died, 22 were children.
Aug. 17 Monterrey, Mex. A highway bus collided with a car and trailer truck on the Monterrey–Monclova highway sending 18 persons to a fiery death and seriously injuring 40 others.
Sept. 21 Isparata, Turk. An open truck careened off a highway and overturned, hurling 23 farmers who were on their way to market to their deaths and seriously injuring 4 others.
Sept. 26 New South Wales, Austr. Brake failure caused a tourist bus to roll backward and down a mountainside in the Australian Alps before plunging into a hydroelectric dam; 18 elderly persons from Adelaide were killed and 21 injured.
Sept. 29 Guadalajara, Mex. A bus traveling from Tepic to Mexico City collided with a truck near Guadalajara; 22 persons were killed and 16 injured.
Oct. 24 Kearny, N.J. A spectacular chain-reaction crash involving 65 vehicles on the New Jersey Turnpike killed 9 persons and injured more than 40; dense fog and smoke from burning garbage a mile from the highway had reduced visibility to almost zero.
Oct. 29 Nagpur, India. A bus traveling in the Chanda district of Nagpur, central India, plunged into a rain-swollen river drowning 30 persons.
Nov. 3 Sacramento, Calif. A Greyhound bus carrying 43 passengers to Reno's gambling casinos was totally demolished when it crashed head-on into a highway abutment near Sacramento; 13 were killed, 31 injured.
Nov. 20 San Nicolás Coatepec, Mex. A drunken driver lost control of a bus overloaded with religious pilgrims as it moved along a twisting mountain road about 70 mi. SW of Mexico City and sent it plunging into a ravine 150 ft. below; 15 persons died, most of them children, and 43 others were injured.

Disciples of Christ: *see* Religion
Diseases: *see* Medicine
Divorce: *see* Vital Statistics
Docks: *see* Transportation

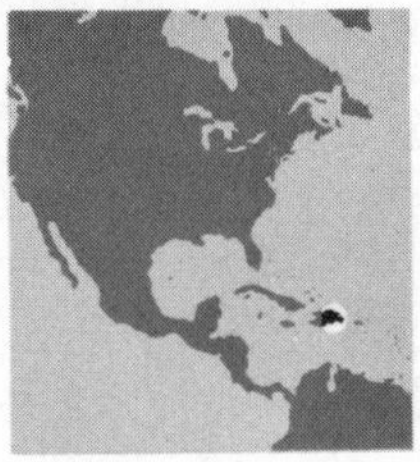

Dominican Republic

Covering the eastern two-thirds of the Caribbean island of Hispaniola, the Dominican Republic is separated from Haiti, which occupies the western third, by a rugged mountain range. Area: 18,658 sq.mi. (48,323 sq.km.). Pop. (1972 est.): 4,304,873, including (1960) mulatto 73%; white 16%; Negro 11%. Cap. and largest city: Santo Domingo (pop., 1972 est., 768,887). Language: Spanish. Religion (1971 est.): Roman Catholic 92%. President in 1973, Joaquín Balaguer.

On February 5 the government announced that a small band of guerrillas had landed on the south coast about 70 mi. W of Santo Domingo. An armed clash took place the next day between the guerrillas and government troops, with at least one rebel killed before the others fled into a wooded mountain area. The government charged that the guerrillas had come from Cuba to help prepare a coup against President Balaguer under the leadership of former president Juan Bosch. Bosch denied any connection with the group.

With President Balaguer proclaiming "Labor and Tourism Year," the republic ushered in 1973 on the upswing of a continued economic boom. High prices for the better than average sugarcane harvest and the higher income from other agricultural products over the past year had an advantageous effect on the economy. Economic trends in 1973 were favourable, although annual economic growth was expected to ease to about 8–9%. The government's budget projected a surplus of 141 million pesos on current account, with capital expenditures at 141 million pesos plus 11 million pesos for unclassified expenditures.

Midyear projections of export earnings showed a rise over the previous year of 10%, reflecting increases of 9% in receipts from sugar exports and of nearly 50% from ferronickel. Preliminary foreign trade statistics indicated that exports during the first six months of 1973 were valued at $236 million, compared with $172 million in the first half of 1972. Import demands and investment service payments were also expected to rise by about 10%. Notwithstanding, the overall balance of payments situation for 1973 was expected to permit net international reserves to rise by about 7 million SDRs (Special Drawing Rights, or "paper gold"). Early in 1973, the Dominican Republic eliminated completely payment arrears on import collections and letters of credit, which at the end of 1972 amounted to 7 million SDRs.

Planned public sector investments for 1973 continued to reflect the national strategies and priorities outlined in the government's development plan for 1970–74. Of a total public sector investment of nearly 480 million pesos in 1971–74 (80% financed from public sector savings), investment allocations were as follows: 20% each for transportation and energy, 17% for agriculture including irrigation, and 14% each for housing, water, and sewer works.

Within the total planning framework, special importance was attached to the role of agriculture, as the strengthening of this sector, particularly in areas other than sugar, was viewed as essential for future industrial growth and fuller employment. The Special Agricultural Development Fund (FEDA) established in September 1971, together with various action programs to increase production within the peasant farm sector of selected priority regions, was formally restructured as the Integrated Agricultural Development Program (Pidagro).

Sizable investments in tourism were prompted by both the more relaxed political climate and the government's concerted drive to bolster that sector of the economy. In July it was announced that a tourist complex would be built at Manzanillo, in the northwest near the Haitian border, at a cost of $73.2 million. A joint venture of the government and a U.S. firm, it was to include an airport and extensive recreational facilities.

(GUSTAVO ARTHUR ANTONINI)

DOMINICAN REPUBLIC

Education. (1969–70) Primary, pupils 726,398, teachers (including preprimary) 12,584; secondary, pupils 97,501, teachers 4,183; vocational, pupils 4,636, teachers 231; teacher training, students 570, teachers 58; higher, students 18,817, teaching staff 1,319.

Finance. Monetary unit: peso, at parity with the U.S. dollar, with a free rate (Sept. 17, 1973) of 2.41 pesos to £1 sterling. Gold, SDRs, and foreign exchange, central bank: (June 1973) U.S. $40.7 million; (June 1972) U.S. $31.1 million. Budget (1971 actual): revenue 276 million pesos; expenditure 294.1 million pesos. Gross national product: (1971) 1,604,200,000 pesos; (1970) 1,446,300,000 pesos. Money supply: (May 1973) 225.8 million pesos; (May 1972) 182 million pesos. Cost of living (Santo Domingo; 1963 = 100): (May 1973) 132; (May 1972) 116.

Foreign Trade. (1972) Imports 369.6 million pesos; exports 347.4 million pesos. Import sources: U.S. 52%; Japan 13%. Export destinations: U.S. 65%; Japan 8%; The Netherlands 6%; Spain 5%. Main exports: sugar 48%; coffee 9%; tobacco 8%; cocoa 5%.

Transport and Communications. Roads (1970) *c.* 6,250 km. Motor vehicles in use (1971): passenger 44,800; commercial (including buses) 23,800. Railways (1971) *c.* 1,700 km. Telephones (Jan. 1972) 56,000. Radio receivers (Dec. 1971) 165,000. Television receivers (Dec. 1970) *c.* 100,000.

Agriculture. Production (in 000; metric tons; 1972; 1971 in parentheses): rice *c.* 200 (*c.* 207); corn *c.* 45 (*c.* 45); sweet potatoes (1971) *c.* 108, (1970) *c.* 107; cassava (1970) *c.* 170, (1969) 170; dry beans *c.* 30 (*c.* 32); peanuts *c.* 92 (*c.* 84); sugar, raw value *c.* 1,238 (*c.* 1,131); oranges *c.* 58 (*c.* 58); bananas (1970) *c.* 275, (1969) *c.* 267; cocoa (1972–73) 36, (1971–72) 41; coffee *c.* 41 (*c.* 43); tobacco *c.* 24 (*c.* 23). Livestock (in 000; June 1972): cattle *c.* 1,200; sheep *c.* 86; pigs *c.* 1,400; horses *c.* 160; chickens *c.* 7,500.

Industry. Production (in 000; metric tons; 1971): bauxite 1,032; cement 593; electricity (kw-hr.) 1,052,000.

Dominican Army officers view the body of Col. Francisco Caamaño Deñó, alleged guerrilla leader, killed in a clash with government forces in February 1973.

WIDE WORLD

Drama:
see Motion Pictures; Theatre

Dress:
see Fashion and Dress; Furs

Drugs and Narcotics

Parental hysteria of the 1960s over their offspring's use of "pot" (*Cannabis sativa,* or marijuana) and "acid" (LSD) had diminished in 1973, and the myth that marijuana and other drugs of dependence were substitutes for alcohol throughout the younger generation had been dispelled. But the public continued to equate the abuse of illicit drugs, particularly heroin, with crimes of burglary, robbery, rape, and homicide. The drug abuse profile for 1973, therefore, was characterized by public demand, political pressures, and the use of political power as a major force in efforts to control traffic in narcotics and other dangerous drugs. Emphasis on harsher penalties for possession of drugs, as well as for their sale and barter, was again on the upswing, even in the face of a growing mass of data indicating that reliance on the system of criminal justice as a deterrent to drug dependence had little chance of success.

Perhaps the most significant document to be published in the field in 1973 was the second and final report of the National Commission on Marihuana and Drug Abuse, titled *Drug Use in America: Problem in Perspective.* Supported by four volumes of documentary evidence, this report was undoubtedly the most comprehensive presentation of the disparate points of view within the American psyche that continued to block efforts to achieve a national, much less a governmental, policy vis-à-vis the use and abuse of drugs.

The Scope of the Drug Problem. The latest available figures furnished by countries reporting to the International Narcotics Control Board (INCB) showed that in 1971 world production of opium reached 1,388 tons (1,157 tons in 1970), a maximum not attained since the end of World War II. India had its best postwar harvest: 883 tons, 64% of the grand total. Iran, with 222 tons, almost trebled its production in relation to 1970 (78 tons) and became the second largest producing country, replacing the U.S.S.R., which was third with a harvest of 144 tons (227 tons in 1970). In Turkey, the fourth and last major opium producer, progress in yield improvement made possible a harvest of 134 tons as against 51 tons in the previous year. Turkey, however, had decided to discontinue its opium production after the 1972 harvest and to replace the cultivation of opium poppy with other cash crops. Some 1,096 tons of opium went into the manufacture of 110 tons of morphine, the bulk of which (90%) was converted into codeine.

In Peru 9,900 tons of coca leaf were produced, the highest figure reported since 1957. Bolivia, the other producing country, did not furnish information to the board on its production and utilization of coca leaf in 1971. Almost all of Peru's production was used for nonmedical purposes, only nine tons (3%) being used for the manufacture of cocaine.

The INCB reported that in 1972 the pattern of drug abuse broadly followed the trends observed in recent years. There had been expansion in volume, in geographic extent, and in the number of persons affected. In particular there had been a disturbing increase in the misuse of heroin, and cocaine had reappeared on the illicit market. Although part of the misuse appeared to be experimental and therefore ephemeral in character, the enlargement of the "drug culture" clearly had continuing implications for the moral, physical, and economic health of the community. Governments and local communities had reacted to these developments by strengthening countermeasures at local, national, and international levels. Intensified operations against illicit traffic had achieved striking success.

The U.S. government, for example, spent $808 million in 1973 for prevention, treatment, and enforcement, up from $81 million in 1969. More than 2,000 special agents were investigating criminal activity, compared with 300 approximately ten years before. In two years, the number of federally funded treatment programs had increased from 36 to 360, and the number of patients in those programs had climbed from 16,000 to 72,000. State and local programs increased their treatment load to 150,000, with federal support.

There was no way to estimate accurately the total number of heroin users in the U.S., but federal authorities indicated that the number of addicts may have decreased from 625,000 in 1972 to 400,000. The Drug Enforcement Administration estimated that in New York City in 1972 there were more than 300,000 narcotics addicts, a figure estimated to have dropped in 1973 to 274,000.

Even though the size of the problem was a statistical puzzle, there were gauges on which to base conclusions that the drug problem had lessened in some areas. One of these was the availability of heroin, cocaine, and marijuana. In the 1973 fiscal year, federal narcotics agents seized 309 lb. of heroin in the domestic market, as compared with 995 lb. seized the year before. Seizures of cocaine fell from 443 lb. to 239 and of marijuana from 27,827 lb. to 26,953.

The reduced availability of heroin had caused its price to triple since 1969 and its purity to drop to a low of 2% in some markets. Another, although very rough, indicator was the rate of serum hepatitis, since hepatitis is frequently transmitted by sharing unsterile hypodermic needles. In 1972 the rate was only a fifth of the 1971 rate. Even though the heroin problem was apparently decreasing, federal agencies estimated that by the end of 1973 they would have spent $551 million in treatment and prevention and $257 million in law enforcement.

A new and more subtle problem, according to Robert L. DuPont, director of the Special Action Office for Drug Abuse Prevention, was a shifting trend

UPI COMPIX

Joyous demonstrators chant "smoke that joint" after the Ann Arbor, Mich., City Council repealed a $5 marijuana law in July 1973. Their mood is not shared by two councilmen in the foreground.

from heroin as a drug of choice to a wide range of stimulants and depressants. "Non-opiate polydrug abusers are less predictable, much like alcohol abusers, and are, therefore, harder to trace and draw into treatment." Principal new drugs of abuse were "downers" (barbiturates) and stimulants, including a wide range of amphetamines, many of them available on the commercial market.

Reports on Marijuana. Increasingly sophisticated data on the extent, patterns, and social context of use of marijuana in the U.S. and other countries, on preclinical research, and on the effects of *Cannabis* on man were being published. In the U.S. the first report of the marijuana commission, published in 1972, and 1971 and 1972 annual reports to Congress by the secretary of health, education, and welfare, entitled *Marihuana and Health,* were followed by the 1973 edition of *Marihuana and Health* and the final report of the commission.

From the HEW report, it was evident that marijuana had become the drug of choice of at least 24 million persons, the larger number of whom used it experimentally. Males were twice as likely to use marijuana as females, and the rate of use was highest among college students (54%, an overall increase of 12% from 1971 figures). In the past, it was frequently suggested that, for many, marijuana use might supplant alcohol use, thus reducing the severity of the alcohol problem. It now appeared that alcohol use was a typical concomitant of *Cannabis* use. Among 1973 college populations, the drugs used, from most frequently to least, were beer, wine, hard liquor, lower potency marijuana, higher potency marijuana, hashish, and, in diminishing frequency, LSD and other drugs. Heroin use in this group was extremely uncommon.

Studies of use by adolescents showed that the teenager's use of marijuana was closely correlated with its use by his friends. Additionally, drug use by children was related to drug use by parents. When both parents used such drugs as alcohol, tobacco, and other psychoactive drugs, there was greater likelihood that their children would use marijuana. The probability of drug use was also associated with such factors as lack of family cohesiveness, use of other medications, and less parental emphasis on self-control. The sources of information on drugs most commonly mentioned by children between the ages of 11 and 17 were television, parents, friends, and other students.

Animal research continued to be an important source of increased knowledge about the implications of *Cannabis* used by humans. Perhaps the most important finding during the year was that both synthetic delta-9-tetrahydrocannabinol (THC), the principal active ingredient responsible for marijuana's psychic effects, and natural marijuana—even when given in relatively high doses over extended periods—apparently have no deleterious effects on pregnancy, fetal development, or the newborn. There was no way, however, of being certain that *Cannabis* when used in combination with other drugs might not produce adverse effects that might not occur when it was used alone. In animals, THC increases the depressant effects of barbiturates, and yet it also enhances the stimulating effects of amphetamines. The clinical implications of these findings as they relate to human use were not clear, although such an effect might be a factor in multiple drug use.

The commission on marijuana's final report, published in March, recommended that possession of marijuana for personal use should no longer be an offense, but that marijuana possessed in public should remain contraband and be subject to summary seizure and forfeiture. The casual distribution of small amounts of marijuana without payment, or for small payment not giving the seller any profit, should also cease to be an offense. The purpose of this and similar recommendations made in other countries, such as Canada, was to draw a distinction between marijuana and the hard drugs, and a similar sharp distinction between the private user and the professional drug trafficker. In support of its recommendations the commission said:

> Marijuana clearly is not in the same chemical category as heroin insofar as its physiological and psychological effects are concerned. In a word, cannabis does not lead to physical dependence. No verification has been found of a causal relationship between marijuana and subsequent heroin use. No objective evidence of specific pathology of brain tissue has been documented. This fact contrasts sharply with the well established brain damage of alcoholism. A careful search has revealed not a single human fatality in the U.S. proven to have resulted solely from ingestion of marijuana. . . . In all its studies, the Commission found no evidence of chromosome, teratogenic (birth defects), or mutagenic effects due to cannabis commonly used by man.

The commission also emphasized the current political, social, legal, and clinical dilemmas surrounding marijuana use. It pointed out that, paralleling the dramatic increase in the use of marijuana and other illicit drugs during the 1960s, there was an increased awareness that "enforcement of stringent possession laws enacted a social cost which exceeded the cost of drug use itself." Penalties for possession were quickly and substantially reduced under the Comprehensive Drug Abuse Prevention and Control Act of 1970 and various state laws, so that by 1973 possession for personal use was "a misdemeanor for marijuana in 44 states, for depressants in 26 states, for stimulants in 23 states, for hallucinogens in 20 states, and for the narcotics (opiates and cocaine) in 13 states."

Related to these developments was a growing leniency toward first offenders that often included "conditional discharge of first-time possession offenders before a formal adjudication of guilt" and "the increasing use of the criminal justice system to refer drug users, particularly drug-dependent persons, to treatment services." The commission felt that such policy changes indicated that "public opposition to drug abuse no longer carries the strong moral overtones characteristic in the early days of this century," and that, as a result of this "loss of moral certainty . . . , in the search for a new basis for policy, the issue most debated is the appropriate role of the criminal justice system."

Government Activities. There appeared to be an increasing public belief, at least in the large cities, that narcotic addiction and crime were inseparable. So, at the time when public acceptance of drug treatment programs had reached its highest point, when federally funded programs to train professionals and paraprofessionals in the field of drug abuse were beginning to show positive results, and when drug research findings were being translated into more effective treatment modalities, U.S. Pres. Richard M. Nixon indicated his rejection of the less punitive provisions of the 1970 federal drug legislation and the position taken by the commission. In March, the same month in which the commission report was published, Nixon forwarded to the Congress proposed "reforms" revoking the changes in the 1970 legislation. The president's proposals included higher maximum penalties for drug possession as well as for traffickers and mandatory minimum penalties in a wide range of drug-related offenses. The Congress, as 1973 came to a close, had not translated these proposals into statutes.

In the state of New York, however, Gov. Nelson Rockefeller and the legislature cooperated to write into law, with the passage of the Controlled Substances Act, court procedures and legal penalties that dismayed opponents of punitive penalties (including police officers and judges, as well as treatment personnel). Although the legislature rejected Rockefeller's initial proposal for a mandatory death penalty for any illicit distribution, the new statute established mandatory penalties, brought into being a new court system with the appointment of district judges whose sole task was to hear drug-related cases, and cut deeply into the traditional discretionary role of the bench.

The relative power of what was known as the "law and order" group within the U.S. Department of Justice during President Nixon's first term of office diminished to some extent in 1973. But it could only be assumed to be a temporary hiatus brought about by other concerns and other priorities within that beleaguered department.

The marijuana commission had been critical of the federal drug efforts, citing bitter jurisdictional rivalries between the Justice Department's Bureau of Narcotics and Dangerous Drugs (BNDD) and the Treasury Department's Bureau of Customs and describing the White House agency that was to oversee federal antidrug efforts as a failure. The commission proposed that a new superagency modeled after the Atomic Energy Commission be created. Instead, Nixon submitted an executive reorganization order, which became effective July 1, consolidating all drug enforcement efforts into a single agency within the Justice Department. The new Drug Enforcement Administration absorbed the BNDD, the Justice Department's Office of Drug Abuse Law Enforcement, the Office of National Narcotics Intelligence, and 500 special customs agents.

On June 29 John E. Ingersoll resigned as director of BNDD, which he had headed since 1968, charging the White House with interfering in the agency's affairs and criticizing especially DALE, formed 18 months before, whose agents, he said, detracted from BNDD efforts and were unprofessional in their conduct. Ingersoll cited specifically the raids made by a group of federal and local narcotics officers under DALE supervision on two Collinsville, Ill., homes. During the raids, made on April 23 on uncorroborated tips, doors were knocked in, property ransacked and damaged, and the families subjected to physical abuse and obscenities by shabbily dressed men who did not identify themselves until the middle of the raids. No narcotics were found. A later survey by the *New York Times* indicated that numerous "mistaken, violent, and often illegal" raids had occurred throughout the U.S. during the last three years. At least four deaths had been attributed to these raids. In August a federal grand jury indicted 12 undercover narcotics agents, eight of them federal officers, on charges stemming from the investigation of the Collinsville raids and four others in southern Illinois in April. Earlier John R. Bartels, acting head of the new combined enforcement agency, was reported to have issued new guidelines to federal agents that prohibited entry without search warrants except when approved by Bartels or his deputy. He also ordered agents to wear attire that would "invite confidence" and limited use of weapons to self-defense.

Administrative reorganizations also occurred within the Department of Health, Education, and Welfare in 1973, the results of which were yet to be demonstrated. Effective Oct. 1, 1973, a new agency was created within HEW—the Alcohol, Drug Abuse, and Mental Health Administration (ADAMHA)—containing as coequals a newly created National Institute of Drug Abuse, the National Institute on Alcohol Abuse and Alcoholism, and the National Institute of Mental Health.

In Britain a new law, the Misuse of Drugs Act, 1971, which went into force on July 1, 1973, followed the tendency to make a sharp distinction between the unlawful possession of drugs and the unlawful supply of drugs. Penalties prescribed for the unlawful manufacture of, trafficking in, or smuggling of drugs like opium, heroin, methadone, morphine, and LSD, and of soft drugs such as marijuana and the amphetamines, were up to 14 years' imprisonment or an unlimited fine, or both. But the mere possession of *Cannabis* still carried a possible five-year prison sentence, or an unlimited fine, or both. The new law, thus, fell very far short of the wish of the reformers to take the use of marijuana outside the reach of the criminal courts. In September, however, the lord chancellor, addressing the annual meeting of the Magistrates Association in London, told his audience that individual *Cannabis* users should be treated with "becoming moderation."

The Council of Europe also recommended that while member states should mount a vigorous and cooperative effort aimed at suppressing the production and distribution of illicit drugs, drug users should be treated with understanding, and that "unless alternative methods are inappropriate, drug abusers, in particular minors, first offenders, and offenders who are not launched on a criminal career, should not be imprisoned." Meanwhile, The Netherlands remained the Mecca of the pot-smoking generation, and while the use of the drug was illegal, the authorities showed such tolerance that a houseboat from which the hippie population of Amsterdam could obtain supplies remained unmolested, with *Cannabis* plants flourishing on its deck, despite the fact that the boat was moored on a canal opposite a police station.

New York City authorities restrain a narcotics suspect, as part of a group of 89 alleged drug dealers arrive for processing at police headquarters on April 16, 1973.

UPI COMPIX

Research and Treatment. The unsatisfactory state of scientific understanding of the drug problem was well reflected by the report of a World Health Organization study entitled *Youth and Drugs,* which recorded no significant advances in treatment, prevention, or even the experimental evaluation of the results of drug use. While the harmful effects of drugs like heroin, morphine, cocaine, the amphetamines, and the barbiturates were reasonably well known and agreed upon, dispute still centred around the likely risks run by users of LSD and *Cannabis.* The result of a two-year survey at the George Washington University Medical Center, published at the end of 1972, suggested that LSD does damage chromosomes and that its use by pregnant women may give rise to the birth of abnormal babies, although the researchers pointed out that this effect could have been the result of impurities in the LSD used by the subjects.

As a result of experiments on mice, Swiss workers at the Institute of Cancer Research, Lausanne, suggested that pot smoking might carry a greater risk of lung cancer than the use of tobacco, but this opinion did not take into account the fact that the true tobacco addict may get through 40 or more cigarettes a day, whereas the pot smoker inhales comparatively tiny amounts of smoke. Experiments reported from Switzerland and New Zealand seemed to show that marijuana may seriously affect attention and reaction times and that this effect may persist for over 24 hours, so that use of the drug may present a serious driving hazard.

Overall, present evidence suggested that marijuana use could result in psychiatric complications under some circumstances. Such complications, including acute panic and psychotic reactions, appeared to be commoner in those with previous histories of psychological difficulties or in those taking larger doses than usual. Chronic *Cannabis* intoxication, according to *Marihuana and Health,* could be a problem in much the same way that chronic alcoholism is, although there was little basis for certainty about the comparative risk each of the drugs might pose under conditions of equal social acceptability.

The misuse of medicinal drugs, such as the amphetamines and barbiturates, continued at a high level, both because of their illegal distribution and because of overprescribing by physicians. At the annual meeting of the British Medical Association doctors were urged to voluntarily restrict their use of such agents (and of tranquilizers). This reflected a worldwide tendency within the medical profession.

In line with research efforts in the U.K., the smoking of *Cannabis* and *Cannabis* resin for research purposes was made legal in June, after which institutes would be able to seek government permission to use their premises for such experiments. The new Misuse of Drugs Act imposed drug controls to prevent addicted doctors from getting supplies for their own use. Physicians would henceforth have to keep a register of drugs administered or prescribed to addicted patients. They would also be obliged to notify the Home Office when they suspected a patient of being addicted to a controlled drug.

A team of Swedish pharmacologists at the Karolinska Institutet in Stockholm reported development of the first reliable test for detection of low levels of marijuana in human blood. They were able, by gas chromatography and mass spectrometry methods, to measure THC at levels as low as half a billionth of a gram. Although application of the technique was hampered by its extreme sophistication, such measurements could have significant bearing on the investigation of road accidents.

(DONALD W. GOULD; CHRISTOPHER JOHN TRAIN; STANLEY F. YOLLES)

Earthquakes: *see* Disasters; Seismology
Eastern Orthodox Churches: *see* Religion
Ecology: *see* Environment; Life Sciences

Economics

A 1973 survey of the economics literature by Michael Lovell of Wesleyan University, Middletown, Conn., showed that economic knowledge had doubled every 14 years during the preceding century (*Journal of Economic Literature,* March 1971). His index of production of economic knowledge was the number of articles published in professional journals. Whether each new journal article should be counted as a "contribution to knowledge" was, however, more questionable in economics than in such disciplines as biology, chemistry, and physics. Although controversy abounded in all fields of knowledge, experiments in the biological and physical sciences could be replicated and validated by other scientists. The appeal to facts, the test of any scientific hypothesis, differed in economics because the relevant environment was subject to rapid change.

Disagreement among economists was richly illustrated in 1973 by John Kenneth Galbraith, who in his presidential address to the American Economic Association flayed his fellow economists for sanctioning a principle of economics that excluded, through the doctrine of market competition, the issue of economic and political power (*American Economic Review,* March 1973). He developed this theme more fully in a book, *Economics and the Public Purpose.* Galbraith criticized the "conventional wisdom" for assuming that prices, wages, and profits are determined primarily by the market. The reality, according to Galbraith, is that the market dominates only a minority sector of the total U.S. economy. In the larger "planning sector," 2,000 giant corporations dominate the market, administering prices and, jointly with labour unions, administering wages. Galbraith saw the crux of the inflation problem in this power structure. Pecuniary rewards of the corporate bureaucracy—what Galbraith called the technostructure—are more closely related to the volume of sales than to profits earned for the passive shareholders.

In contrast with Galbraith, whose writings were probably more widely read than those of any other living economist, his successor as president of the American Economic Association, Kenneth J. Arrow, was known as an economists' economist. Arrow shared the 1972 Nobel Prize for Economics for an esoteric mathematical welfare theory understandable by only a handful of economists and mathematicians. Yet the problems that preoccupied Arrow were by no means lacking in general significance.

During 1973 Arrow participated in a reexamination of the philosophical foundations of economic theory occasioned by John Rawls's *A Theory of Justice* (1971), one of the few noneconomics books of recent years to have a significant impact on economic thinking. The implications of Rawls's theory related to numerous economic issues, including taxation, savings, time preference, negative income taxes, and, above all, the time-honoured subject of inequalities in the distribution of income and wealth. His theory was strongly egalitarian. Inequality is justified only to the extent that it is necessary to improve the well-being of the least advantaged (poorest) members of society. For economists, Rawls's work opened new vistas by providing a nonutilitarian basis for welfare economics. In contemporary economic thought, his theory of justice bore some analogy to that of Plato and Aquinas for the economics of earlier ages.

Simon Kuznets, in his Nobel lecture on "Modern Economic Growth: Findings and Reflections," pointed to the inequality of income among nations (*American Economic Review,* June 1973). He found that the one-third of the world's population living in economically advanced nations enjoyed a per capita domestic product of $1,900 (in 1965, at market prices), compared with only $120 for the two-thirds of the world's population in economically less developed countries. Even allowing for deficiencies in measurement, this 16 to 1 difference was vast, and it was not decreasing. When great inequalities within the less developed nations were taken into account, along with the inequalities between the advanced and the less developed nations, Rawls's egalitarian principle of justice was violated on a massive scale throughout the world.

The awarding of the Nobel Prize for Economics to Wassily Leontief for his pioneering work in developing input-output analysis recognized the importance of a technique that had been applied to such diverse topics as the labour composition of foreign trade, the economics of disarmament, national and regional planning, and economic forecasting. Input-output analysis gives operational meaning to the theory of general economic equilibrium, according to which everything affects everything else in a system of mutual interdependence. One of Leontief's former students, Clopper Almon, used a computer-based input-output model to forecast, in 1973, a sluggish 2.6% average annual growth of the U.S. economy through 1985.

Simulation was another computer-based technique that came into wider use during 1973. An article in the July 1973 issue of *The Review of Economic Studies,* "A Duopoly Simulation and Richer Theory: An End of Cournot," employed a computer-simulated model in an attempt to give a definitive solution to one of the oldest problems of economic theory. In 1838 a French economist, Antoine Augustin Cournot, published the classical "solution" to the duopoly problem; that is, the determination of price and output in a market with only two sellers. The authors of the 1973 article contended that no single, definitive solution can result from duopoly; the specific solution depends on the conditions and numerical specification in any particular duopoly case. They concluded: "Finally, the Cournot question should be considered dead, and analytic attempts to answer it or to expand it should be abandoned as a waste of time" (p. 365). Old issues in economic theory never die easily, however, and one could safely predict that the Cournot question would be back in the journals in the form of further "contributions to knowledge."

(DUDLEY DILLARD)

See also Nobel Prizes.

Economy, World

The United States, Western Europe, and Japan experienced in 1973 a troubled boom—a boom that, with an unsustainable speed of expansion, brought with it a strong increase in the already high rate of inflation. The governments tried to cool off the boom, which began to weaken just at the time when, in October, the Middle East crisis imposed new constraints on industrial nations in two fell swoops: a sharp rise in oil prices and cuts in supply. As the year ended, the disappearing boom hit the industrial world with a vengeance for, unlike earlier years when Western Europe and Japan were in expansionary phases during recessions in the U.S., all three industrial parts of the world accelerated together in 1972 and early 1973 and, from the midyear on, began to slow down together. They no longer led and lagged each other, they moved as if synchronized. This convergence in cyclical trends threatened to accentuate the recessionary tendencies throughout the world, especially since the oil crisis appeared to be superimposed on them. In this environment, inflationary *and* recessionary, there arose a deep concern, especially in Western Europe and in Japan, about social and political tensions that might emerge from rising unemployment and from the struggle to distribute whatever increases there might be, real or imaginary, in national income.

The Troubled Boom. Output of goods and services —the real gross national product (GNP)—in seven major industrial countries taken together rose by nearly 7% during 1973; this growth rate compared with somewhat less than 6% in 1972 and an average of close to 5% during the preceding ten years (*see* Table I). But the fast rate of growth was overshadowed by accelerating inflation, averaging about 6.5% in all of the seven countries, as against 4.4% in 1972 and 3.4% during the preceding decade (*see* Table II). The second half of the year, however, brought a turnaround, with the rate of GNP growth in the aggregate down to a 4% annual rate from 8% in the first half.

The cyclical upswing in economic activity had begun in the U.S. and Canada in early 1971 and had gradually appeared in most other industrial countries during 1972. In the first half of 1973 almost the entire industrial world outside the U.S.S.R., China, and the

Table I. Growth of Real Gross National Product

Country	Annual percent changes 1960–71	1972	1973
Japan	11.1	9.6	11.0
Canada	4.9	5.8	7.3
United Kingdom	2.9	3.0	6.8
France	5.8	5.5	6.3
West Germany	4.9	3.0	6.3
United States	3.9	6.1	6.0
Italy	5.5	3.5	5.3
Seven major countries	4.8	5.8	6.8
Spain	7.2	8.3	7.5
Australia	5.0	2.4	6.0
Austria	4.9	6.4	6.0
Belgium	4.9	4.9	6.0
Finland	5.2	6.8	6.0
Ireland	4.0	3.0	6.0
Switzerland	4.6	5.7	4.8
Denmark	4.8	5.0	4.5
Sweden	4.3	2.1	4.3
Netherlands, The	5.3	4.4	4.0
Norway	5.0	4.3	4.0
All industrial countries	4.8	5.7	6.8
Of which:			
Europe	4.9	4.3	6.0

Source: Adapted from OECD, *Economic Outlook* (December 1973).

Table II. Price Trends in Industrial Countries*

Country	Annual percent increases 1960–71	1972	1973
United States	2.8	3.2	5.3
United Kingdom	4.2	6.7	5.8
West Germany	3.6	6.1	6.3
Canada	3.0	4.6	6.5
France	4.4	5.7	7.0
Japan	4.8	4.6	10.5
Italy	4.4	6.0	11.0
Major countries	3.4	4.4	6.5

*As measured by deflators of gross national product.
Source: Adapted from OECD, *Economic Outlook* (December 1973).

countries in their spheres of influence peaked together; among the major industrial nations, the only country where output accelerated in the second half of 1973 was Italy, which had started to expand relatively late from a situation of widespread underutilization of industrial capacity. These trends in the output of goods and services as a whole were also reflected in the movement of industrial production (*see* Chart 1).

The upswing in the industrial economies brought about a reduction in unemployment in the U.S. as well as in several European countries, especially Italy. But unemployment tended to remain higher in many countries than in earlier boom periods.

Even before the oil crisis it came to be realized that cheap and plentiful supplies of energy could not be taken for granted. Other scarcities had appeared in mid-1973—metals, steel, industrial materials, paper, wool, cotton, etc. In the U.S. capacity utilization of major materials industries (basic metals, paper and pulp, textiles, etc.) was, by mid-1973, at the highest level recorded since World War II.

Thus, the shortages and capacity bottlenecks that appeared at the peak of the business cycle were a new fact of economic life. For the U.S., Western Europe, and Japan had long acted as if the rate of economic growth were determined by changes in productivity and the size of the labour force, and had tended to take natural resources for granted. Since World War II, governments were preoccupied to "manage" demand to ensure—or, at least, to attempt to ensure—that demand would keep up with supply. They sought, more often than not, to expand demand and to redistribute national income. The big lesson of 1973 was that constraints on supply—materials, industrial capacity, and, of course, labour—became vital.

Table III. Industrial Countries Ranked by Price-Cost Performance

Item	Percent change in 1973*	1972	1971
Consumer prices			
United States	5.5	3.3	4.3
France	7.1	5.9	5.5
Canada	7.1	4.8	2.9
West Germany	7.2	5.7	5.2
United Kingdom	8.8	7.1	9.4
Japan	10.2	4.5	6.1
Italy	10.5	5.7	4.8
Earnings in manufacturing			
United States	6.6	6.2	6.6
Canada	8.1	7.7	9.1
West Germany	10.0	8.8	13.7
United Kingdom	12.2	13.5	11.4
France	12.9	11.3	11.2
Italy	19.1	10.5	13.5
Japan	20.0	15.4	14.4
Output in manufacturing			
United States	11.1	8.6	−0.2
United Kingdom	10.3	1.9	−0.3
France	9.9	6.4	6.0
Canada	8.7	6.8	5.0
Japan	8.2	7.4	2.7
West Germany	7.3	6.2	4.5
Italy	5.9	2.2	−3.2
Wage costs per unit of output in manufacturing (expressed in national currencies)			
Japan	1.0	4.9	11.3
United States	1.9	1.7	2.7
France	3.5	4.0	4.9
Canada	3.7	2.9	2.1
West Germany	4.8	3.6	8.1
United Kingdom	5.1	8.2	7.5
Italy	11.4	5.9	12.8
Wage costs per unit of output in manufacturing (expressed in U.S. dollars)			
United States	1.9	1.7	2.7
United Kingdom	2.2	11.2	9.1
Canada	3.2	5.0	5.6
Italy	11.5	12.4	13.8
France	13.8	13.9	5.3
Japan	14.1	20.6	15.0
West Germany	24.8	13.3	13.4

*1973 to date, compared with the same period of 1972.
Source: Adapted from OECD, *Economic Outlook* (December 1973).

Inflation in a Setting of Recession. Another problem shaping up in 1973 was that the tide of inflation became a flood just when the industrial economies were displaying recessionary tendencies. The rate of increase in the general price level—the so-called GNP deflator—in seven major industrial countries reached an estimated 8.5% during the second half of 1973; for the year as a whole, as already noted, the average worked out to 6.5% (*see* Table II). In the U.S. the GNP deflator during the second half of the year surged to 7%; for the year, it was 5.25%—a dramatic rise from 3.2% in 1972 and the average of 2.8% during the ten years ended 1971. At the close of 1973 the general price levels in the seven major countries were rising at the fastest rates since the Korean War boom at the beginning of the 1950s.

Consumer prices rose even more than general price levels (*see* Chart 2 and Table III, which shows at a glance where countries stood relative to one another). In a number of countries, the underlying trend of

Table IV. Depreciation of Money

Country	Indexes of value of money (1962=100) 1967	1972	Annual rates of depreciation (percent) '62–'72*	'71–'72	'72–'73†
Industrial countries					
United States	91	72	3.2	3.2	5.6
Sweden	80	63	4.5	5.8	6.1
Luxembourg	86	71	3.3	5.0	6.1
Belgium	84	69	3.7	5.2	6.5
Australia	88	71	3.3	6.0	6.5
France	85	65	4.2	5.5	6.6
Canada	88	72	3.2	4.6	6.7
Austria	84	68	3.8	5.9	6.7
West Germany	87	73	3.2	5.4	6.7
Norway	82	61	4.9	6.7	6.9
New Zealand	84	61	4.9	6.4	7.0
Netherlands, The	79	59	5.1	7.3	7.4
Switzerland	83	67	3.8	6.2	7.6
Denmark	75	56	5.7	6.1	7.8
United Kingdom	85	62	4.7	6.6	8.1
South Africa	86	70	3.5	6.1	8.8
Spain	67	51	6.6	7.6	9.3
Italy	79	65	4.1	5.3	9.3
Portugal	83	54	5.9	9.7	9.5
Finland	75	57	5.4	7.2	9.5
Ireland	82	56	5.5	8.0	9.9
Japan	76	57	5.5	4.6	10.0
Greece	88	77	2.6	4.1	10.2
Turkey	72	44	7.9	13.3	10.6
Iceland	60	33	10.5	9.0	14.8
Less developed countries					
Morocco	89	79	2.3	3.6	0.6
Venezuela	94	83	1.9	3.0	3.5
Honduras	89	77	2.6	5.0	4.1
South Korea	46	27	12.4	10.6	4.6
Iraq	93	76	2.7	5.0	5.0
Philippines	76	51	6.6	9.3	5.8
Peru	61	40	8.8	6.7	5.9
Iran	93	79	2.3	6.1	6.9
Taiwan	93	75	2.8	4.7	7.1
Ecuador	82	60	4.9	7.3	8.8
Thailand	89	80	2.2	3.8	9.6
Mexico	87	70	3.5	4.9	9.8
Guatemala	100	94	0.7	0.5	10.2
Paraguay	89	76	2.7	8.4	11.5
Jamaica	89	64	4.4	5.6	12.5
India	62	52	6.3	4.8	12.9
Pakistan	80	63	4.5	8.1	14.0
Israel	75	54	6.0	11.4	15.3
Singapore	91	87	1.4	1.8	15.3
Yugoslavia	48	28	3.2	4.6	16.6
Colombia	48	31	11.0	12.5	19.4
Bolivia	75	60	5.2	6.1	20.9
Brazil	10	4	27.8	14.1	25.7
Argentina	30	10	20.4	36.9	42.2
Chile	25	5	25.3	43.8	54.7

Note: Depreciation of money is measured by rates of decline in the domestic purchasing power of national currencies (as computed from reciprocals of official cost-of-living or consumer price indexes), not by rates of price inflation. For example, a rate of inflation of 100% is equivalent to a 50% rate of depreciation of the buying power of money.
*Compounded annually.
†Based on average monthly data available for 1973 compared with corresponding period of 1972.

price inflation was, of course, obscured by price controls.

Because of the weight of food in consumer spending, food price increases had a greater effect than other increases in wholesale prices on consumer price developments. A further twist to consumer prices was inevitable as the effects of sharp rises in wholesale prices and primary commodity prices—food, petroleum, nonferrous metals, and agricultural raw materials—fed through more fully into consumer prices.

The common influence of world commodity prices was, thus, a basic factor behind the similarity of rates of price inflation in individual countries. Another factor contributing to inflation was the excess of dollar liquidity stemming, up to mid-1973, from U.S. balance of payments deficits. Exchange rate changes also contributed to rising prices. But purely domestic factors exerted a decisive influence everywhere. These domestic factors included the expansion of credit to the private economy; government deficit spending and intervention in the economy to influence economic development and redistribution of income; and the fact that rising taxation increased costs and prices directly, and that tax increases were met with larger wage demands and cuts in personal savings. Finally, and most critically, inflation was exacerbated by the interaction of prices and wages in the struggle of various groups of society to redistribute real or imaginary increases in national income. In the U.S., where initial increases in real wages were moderate, the especially sharp rise in food prices worked its way through the economy by accelerating the demands by wage earners to readjust wages in order to preserve and, indeed, to improve upon earlier real gains. Major labour contracts in 1973 provided for escalation clauses linked to the cost of living.

The rise in wage costs was uneven (*see* Table III). The U.S. had the best ranking; but the favourable impact on unit labour costs of rapid productivity growth during the upswing tended to diminish during the economic slowdown in the second half of the year. Furthermore, price-wage controls, which seemed to have helped in 1972 and early 1973 to hold wage settlements down to relatively moderate levels, gradually became less effective. Finally, as just mentioned, escalation clauses in labour contracts were bound to push the wage structure upward as time passed.

Wage costs per unit of output as expressed in terms of the U.S. dollar (*see* Table III, bottom) worked out greatly to the U.S. advantage. They reflected not only the relatively moderate rise in U.S. unit costs, but also the depreciation of the dollar relative to other currencies—a process (*see* PAYMENTS AND RESERVES, INTERNATIONAL) that resulted in an improvement in the price competitiveness of U.S. goods in export markets as well as at home. At the year's end, it is true, the dollar's competitive advantage was reduced, since the effective exchange rate of the dollar against other currencies (on a trade-weighted basis) had improved sharply from early July when the dollar had reached its all-time low.

Money depreciated disastrously (*see* Table IV). In the U.S. the average rate of depreciation of the dollar was 5.8%, up from 3.2% in 1972. At the rate of depreciation in 1973, the dollar would lose one-half of its buying power in only 12 years. Not too surprisingly, transactions involving a time duration were increasingly expressed in terms that sought to eliminate the effect of inflation. Many union contracts negotiated in 1973 had escalator clauses tied in to changes in the consumer price index. New legislation provided for higher social security benefits to accommodate increases in the cost of living. Variable annuity retirement and life insurance policies spread rapidly, but—since they were tied to the stock market, which did very poorly (*see* STOCK EXCHANGES)—they offered no protection against inflation in 1973. More savings seem to have been diverted toward real assets, such as land, houses, works of art, etc. In this context, the soaring price of gold, which reached $127 an ounce in late June, was significant. Attempts to flee from money into real assets could not fail to reduce

CHART 1.

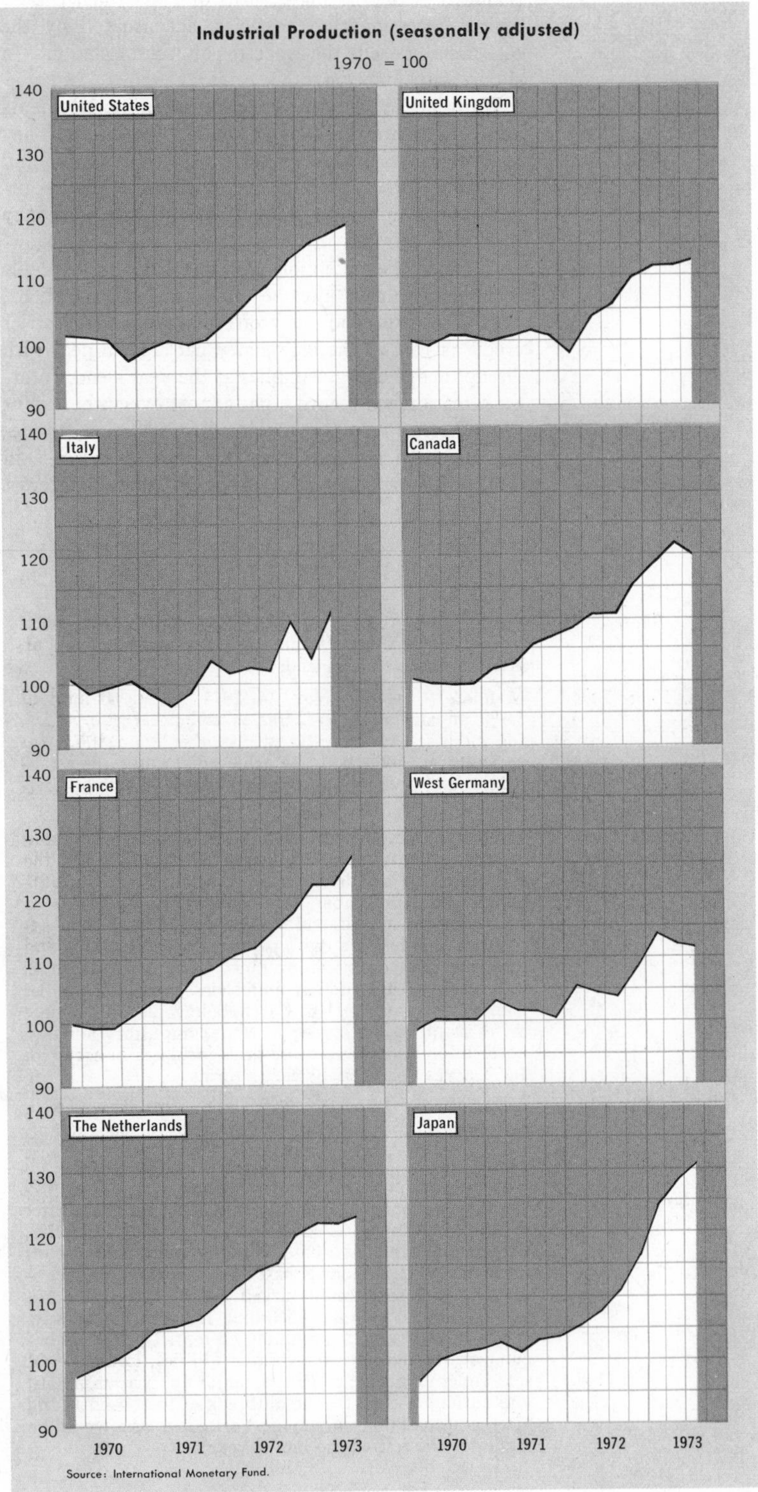

Source: International Monetary Fund.

the efficiency, and increase the instability, of the economy.

Cooling the Boom. How to slow down the inflation became an even more perplexing question in 1973 than in earlier years. No government sought to reduce the pressure of aggregate demand for goods and services to a degree severe enough to slow down inflation at the cost of a slowdown in the economy. Most governments were unwilling to accept slower economic growth as the price to be paid for less inflation—an attitude rationalized by pointing toward the experience during the 1970–71 recession that, despite the slack in the economy, did little to counter inflation. The difficulties of combating inflation were compounded in the closing months of 1973 when the incipient recessionary tendencies, accentuated by the oil crisis, raised the spectre of "slumpflation"—a slump with inflation.

Until late in the year, government pronouncements and policies were aimed at cooling the boom. They centred around monetary restraint, fiscal restraint, and price-wage-profit restraint. Everywhere, the main burden fell on monetary policy. The growth of money supply decelerated in the U.S., but—despite a slowdown from the exceptionally rapid rates in 1972—it remained high in Europe, especially in the U.K., which, however, took new direct measures to restrict credit as part of the emergency package to deal with disruptions in energy supplies at the year's end. Interest rates reached record highs almost everywhere. But when interest rates are corrected for inflation (by deducting from nominal rates the rate of increase in GNP deflators shown in Table II), "real" interest rates remained low in the major countries, with the possible exception of the U.K.

Fiscal policy became restrictive in only a few countries. In the U.S. strict control of expenditures and rapidly rising tax revenues stimulated by the boom brought the federal budget from a substantial deficit in the fiscal year ended June 1973 to a moderate deficit anticipated for 1973–74—a deficit the size of which depended, in the absence of new taxation, on the degree of slackening in economic activity for the remainder of the fiscal year. West Germany raised direct and indirect taxes in May 1973 and temporarily abolished depreciation allowances; this move restricted new housing starts and private plant and equipment expenditures. In December these steps were partly rescinded. Japanese fiscal policy, strongly expansionary in 1972, switched to a moderately restrictive stance. Elsewhere, fiscal policy moved from expansionary to neutral—but not restrictive—postures. In the U.K. the government budget deficit, which was large, was slashed in December as part of the package to deal with the energy and balance of payments crises; capital programs were cut drastically, tax rates were raised on substantial capital gains from land or buildings and on high incomes.

Controls on prices, wages, and profits had a checkered history in 1973. In the U.S. and in the U.K., governments practiced formal and comprehensive controls on prices and incomes (wages, salaries, dividends, rents, and other incomes). In the U.S. controls had been adopted in August 1971 and in the U.K. in November 1972; but the two approaches were similar in that each began with a freeze to allow time to work out legislation and regulation.

The evolution of price-wage-profit controls in the U.S.—two freezes and four phases that left prices spiraling upward nearly three times as fast as in the months immediately prior to the beginning of controls—is traced in the accompanying box. Controls led to distortions and scarcities by reducing or removing incentives to produce many product lines and expand capacity, and by diverting goods into exports in search of higher world market prices. For practical or political reasons, the continental European countries did not have recourse to formalized controls of prices, wages, and profits, but the informal surveillance was reinforced. Only in West Germany did the government refrain from direct controls, hopefully relying on severe monetary and fiscal restraint.

Primary Producers Cash in on the Industrial Boom. As the U.S., Western Europe, and Japan expanded and inflated together and the prices of foodstuffs, agricultural raw materials, and metals practically doubled from mid-1972 on, countries producing primary commodities cashed in on the boom in the industrial world. The scramble for foodstuffs and industrial raw materials became a hard fact of economic life. Furthermore, as the year ended, oil producing countries began to cash in dramatically on the worldwide shortage of energy. Obviously, not all nations outside the industrial world benefited from the boom. The gap between the countries exporting crops and raw materials and those that had no such resources widened still further.

The vigorous upswing in the demand for wheat and other agricultural commodities and the sharp spurt in their prices also benefited the U.S. and Canada; for the U.S., they were the single biggest factor in rectifying the balance of foreign trade. But, outside North America, the beneficiaries were numerous and scat-

U.S. Price-Wage-Profit Controls

Phase One — First freeze, Aug. 15, 1971. Wages, prices, and rents frozen for 90 days. "Voluntary" restraints applied on interest rates and dividends.

Phase Two — Mandatory controls, Nov. 14, 1971. A general limit of 5.5% on annual wage increases and a target of 2.5% for increases in domestic prices other than those for agricultural products, to be achieved through the establishment of profit-margin ceilings. A 4% ceiling on dividend increases.

Phase Three — Voluntary compliance, Jan. 11, 1973. The 5.5% limit on wage increases, the 2.5% target for price rises, and the 4% ceiling on dividend increases retained; but profit-margin limitation liberalized somewhat, the range of exceptions broadened, and the program to be to some extent self-administered, with prior approval for wage and price increases dropped for most industries (the food, health, and construction industries remaining under mandatory controls). In March ceiling placed on meat prices at prevailing levels; in May compulsory advance notification reintroduced for price increases in excess of 1.5% a year planned by larger firms.

Phase 3½ — Second freeze, June 13, 1973. Only prices frozen, with raw agricultural products continuing to be exempt. Wages, interest, and dividends remaining under Phase Three rules; but rents exempted.

Phase Four — Mandatory controls, Aug. 12, 1973. Cost increases after 1972 allowed to be passed through only dollar for dollar, with maintenance of Phase Three restrictions on profit margins. Wage standards of Phase Two and Three remaining in force; unions urged not to exceed a 6.2% average annual increase, including fringe benefits. Raw agricultural products remaining exempt. Decontrols begun with exemption of regulated utilities, lumber, coal sold under long-term contracts, major nonferrous metals, and automobiles (after the outbreak of the oil crisis and after assurance that only modest price increases would be made for the rest of the model year).

tered throughout the world: Australia gained from wheat, wool, and metals; New Zealand from meat and wool; Indonesia, Malaysia, and Singapore from rubber and tin; South Africa from metals; Zaire, Zambia, Peru, and Chile from copper (copper, which provides 80% of Chile's foreign exchange earnings, kept the country solvent); Pakistan from cotton; Brazil, Colombia, Cameroon, and Ghana from coffee and cocoa. The gains from sugar went to many countries. Since most primary producing countries do the bulk of their trade with the U.S. or the U.K., they sold their commodities at world prices in dollars or in sterling—prices that rose as the two currencies slipped. The end result of these trade, price, and foreign-exchange developments was reflected in the rise of monetary reserves of governments and central banks during the 12 months ended September 1973: $1.6 billion for Australia, New Zealand, and South Africa to a total of $8.7 billion in September 1973; and $8.6 billion for all less developed countries other than the oil producing countries of the Middle East, Libya, Ecuador, and Venezuela to an aggregate of $27.6 billion in September 1973.

The oil producing countries just enumerated added $2.8 billion to their official monetary reserves from October 1972 through September 1973, when these reached $12.9 billion. In October, as already mentioned, the oil producing countries doubled petroleum prices, and in December they boosted them again. The cost of Persian Gulf crude was, thus, brought to a level five times that of December 1972. Supply and price became less matters of market forces and more matters for political negotiation among governments.

The rise in the price of oil mercilessly hit other less developed countries, especially those that did not enjoy the bonanza of the world commodity boom because they had no crops or raw materials to export. The gap between the more developed primary producing countries and the world's poor was widened in 1973 visibly and flagrantly. The growth rate of these 25 "least developed" countries had fallen in 1972 below its already low level of 1971.

The Predicaments of the Communist Countries. The Soviet Union and other countries in Central and Eastern Europe also had their share of economic difficulties. Following a marked slowdown in 1972, the U.S.S.R. had a good year in 1973. The high spot was the harvest—after the disaster in 1972 that had necessitated huge purchases of wheat in the U.S., Canada, and Australia. The harvest success tended, however, to overshadow other problems: the great shortage of storage and transport capacity, and fundamental reorganization of Soviet agriculture under which collective farms, jointly owned by members and selling their produce to the state, would be replaced by state farms, *i.e.,* businesses capable of producing efficiently and handling produce from planting or rearing through to canning. The transformation was resisted by collective farm workers who would be separated from their private plots; since there were in 1973 more collective than state farms, the change would take time and large amounts of capital.

Soviet industry exceeded official targets in 1973. Official announcements failed to recall, however, that targets had been slashed in 1972. Reportedly, industrial output rose by 7.3% in 1973, exceeding the revised target of 5.8% for the year; but the original target had been 9%. Similarly, national income rose less than had been originally targeted. Significantly, it was publicized that light industry, which produces

CHART 2.

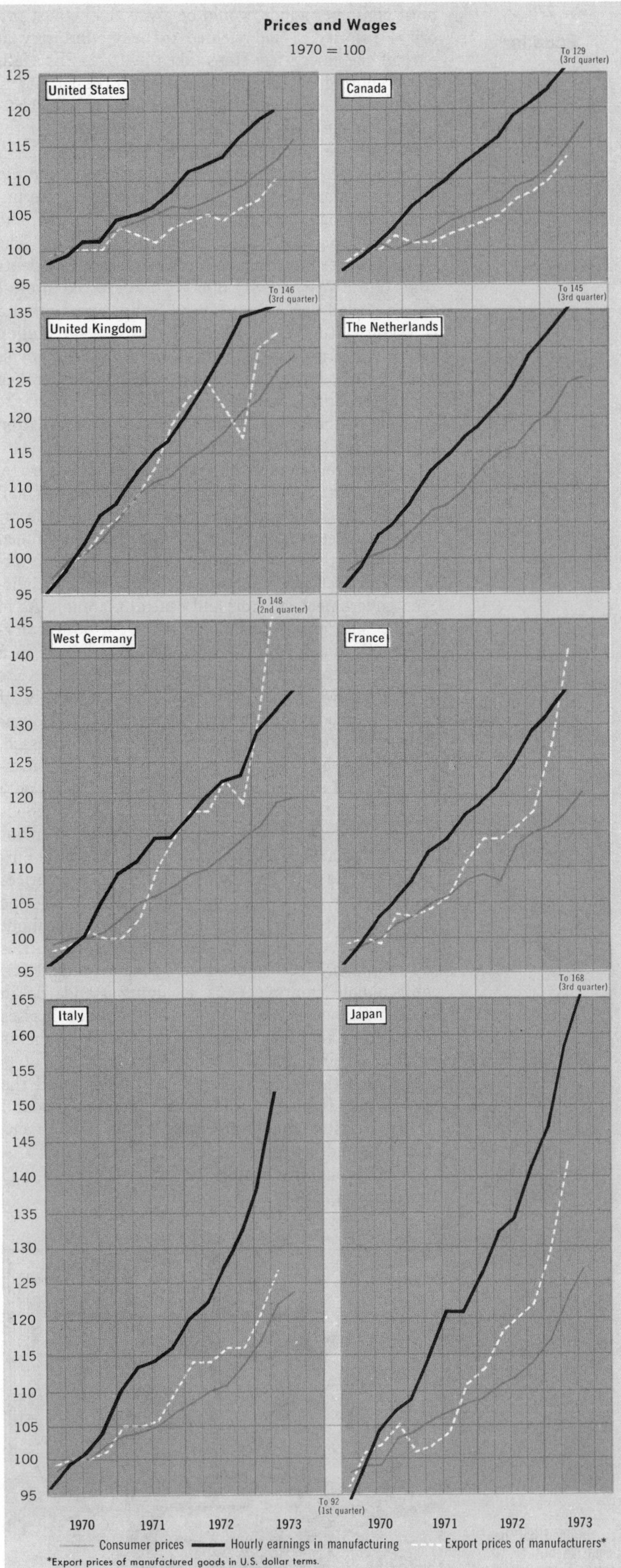

*Export prices of manufactured goods in U.S. dollar terms.
Sources: International Monetary Fund; National Institute for Economic and Social Research (London).

most consumer goods, would be given the highest priority—priority it had yielded to heavy industry as part of the emergency steps taken in 1972. Shortfalls were reported for oil and natural gas. Productivity in industry was reported to have increased by only 1.5% in each of the years 1971 and 1972, well short of the 3.7% average planned for the five years 1971–75.

Against this background, the Soviet Union sought in 1973 even more intensely than in earlier years to import technology from the U.S., Western Europe, and Japan. Forging U.S.-Soviet links proved difficult. The U.S.S.R. agreed to the settlement of Lend-Lease debts from World War II—$11 billion *plus* deferred interest over a period up to the year 2001; but apart from a U.S. Agriculture Department credit of $500 million for three years to help finance extraordinary Soviet wheat purchases in 1972, official credits were stalled by congressional opposition, which also linked the granting to the U.S.S.R. of the most-favoured-nation clause to the treatment of Soviet Jews.

In other countries of Central and Eastern Europe, the year was also marked by reports of progress and setbacks, ups and downs in productivity, and the attractions of consumer societies. The shifts continued back and forth between cautious changes in the interests of productivity and economic efficiency and tightened government controls and central planning. As in the U.S.S.R., excess demand persisted for both everyday goods and luxuries because no government in a Communist country had the courage to keep the pace of wages down to the slow growth in the supply of consumer goods. But since prices were controlled, inflation appeared only where it could not be suppressed, as evidenced by long queues, black markets, and massive personal savings usable, for the most part, only when a permit was obtained to buy such scarce goods as cars. Loss of faith in money and the debasement of money as a work incentive were the inevitable outcome. Yet, Eastern Europe's success in keeping prices steady helped avoid—except in Poland in 1970—the social unrest that inflation threatened to bring about in 1973 in several of the Western European countries and in Japan. Because of steady prices, gradual but unmistakable improvements in living standards in Eastern Europe became more visible for the masses of people—a fact that made it easier for governments to justify their conduct of economic affairs.

In China the grain harvest in 1973 surpassed the 1971 record. Industry had its mix of good results and bottlenecks stemming from shortages of equipment, materials, and low productivity. Like the Soviet Union, China sought to acquire Japanese, European, and American technology and wanted trade.

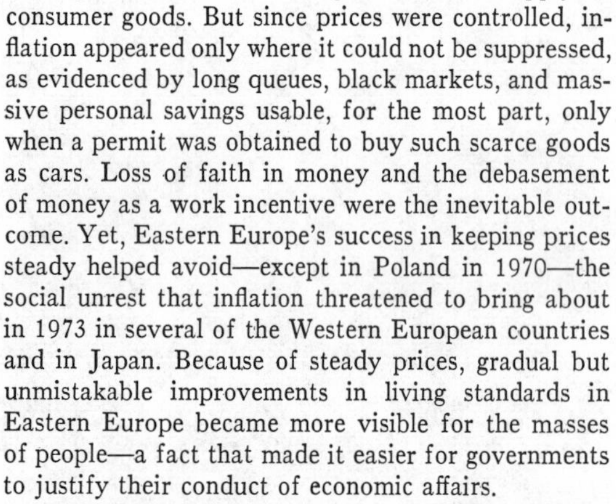

"... finally I had no alternative but to turn to crime to maintain my habit ... eating."

NORRIS—VANCOUVER SUN/ROTHCO

Crisis and Opportunity. The Chinese word for crisis, as scholars tell us, is composed of two symbols—one representing danger and the other opportunity.

Economically and monetarily, the danger for the Western world (and this includes Japan) in late 1973 was the unaccustomed threat of recession *and* inflation. Such a condition could no longer be dealt with by allowing the recession to run its course to get rid of inflation. Governments discarded recession as a cure, for obvious social and political reasons. But they faced an agonizing choice. One way out was to cool the economy gradually through moderate monetary and fiscal policies, with more modest employment goals and economic growth targets than those demanded by the people and urged by the politicians in the last decade. The other way out was to restimulate the economy through persistent monetary and fiscal expansion until a breakthrough would be achieved and inflation overcome through more growth of output and productivity, as the U.K. government tried in 1973.

Persistent monetary and fiscal stimulation carries with it the danger of controls on prices and incomes, on allocation of materials, and, indeed, controls over the entire economic life. A slide further into state intervention and control ultimately does nothing to improve productivity and economic efficiency, as the experience of Eastern Europe amply demonstrates. But encroaching on economic freedoms inexorably leads to the loss of political freedoms as well. It is a sad irony to have to recall these elemental truths at the close of the year that was the 250th anniversary of the birth of Adam Smith. (MIROSLAV A. KRIZ)

See also Economics; Employment, Wages, and Hours; Income, National; Industrial Review; Labour Unions; Prices; Profits; Savings and Investment; Trade, International.

Ecuador

A republic on the west coast of South America, Ecuador is bounded by Colombia, Peru, and the Pacific Ocean. Area: 109,483 sq.mi. (283,561 sq. km.), including the Galapagos Islands (3,075 sq.mi.). Pop. (1973 est.): 6,819,500. Cap.: Quito (pop., 1973 est., 599,900). Largest city: Guayaquil (pop., 1973 est., 924,086). Language: Spanish, but Indians speak Quechuan and Jivaroan. Religion: mainly Roman Catholic. President in 1973, Brig. Gen. Guillermo Rodríguez Lara.

In March 1973 Ecuador became the sixth member of the Organization of American States (OAS) Security Commission, a group frequently denounced by the ill-fated Allende regime in Chile as aimed at the suppression of Communism. Other members were the United States, the Dominican Republic, Costa Rica, Colombia, and Guatemala.

The government's chief claims to legitimacy rested on its advocacy of reform and its sentencing of corrupt members of previous regimes to terms of imprisonment. During the first week of January Defense Minister Víctor Aulestia was dismissed, and shortly afterward the Texaco-Gulf Oil consortium was ordered to hand back half the areas it had acquired under concessions granted by the deposed government of José Velasco Ibarra. Both events were considered a victory for the nationalists.

ECUADOR

Education. (1969–70) Primary, pupils 975,480, teachers 25,137; secondary, pupils 120,860, teachers 9,714; vocational, pupils 55,659, teachers 3,643; teacher training, students 18,163, teachers 1,064; higher (including 7 universities), students 31,921, teaching staff 2,454.

Finance. Monetary unit: sucre, with (Sept. 17, 1973) an official rate of 25 sucres to U.S. $1 (free rate of 59.84 sucres = £1 sterling). Gold, SDRs, and foreign exchange, central bank: (June 1973) U.S. $177.1 million; (June 1972) U.S. $92.5 million. Budget (1971 est.): revenue 4.2 billion sucres; expenditure 5 billion sucres. Gross national product: (1971) 42,640,000,000 sucres; (1970) 34,490,000,000 sucres. Money supply: (May 1973) 7,758,000,000 sucres; (May 1972) 5,915,000,000 sucres. Cost of living (Quito; 1965 = 100): (May 1973) 160; (May 1972) 144.

Foreign Trade. (1972) Imports U.S. $326.5 million; exports U.S. $311.1 million. Import sources: U.S. 43%; Japan 12%; West Germany 10%; U.K. 6%. Export destinations: U.S. 37%; Japan 19%; West Germany 11%; Chile 5%; Colombia 5%. Main exports: bananas 38%; coffee 14%; cocoa 7%.

Transport and Communications. Roads (1972) 18,345 km. Motor vehicles in use (1970): passenger 27,000; commercial (including buses) 36,400. Railways (1970): 990 km.; traffic 85 million passenger-km., freight 56 million net ton-km. Air traffic (1971): 209 million passenger-km.; freight 5,018,000 net ton-km. Telephones (Dec. 1971) 150,000. Radio receivers (Dec. 1970) 1.7 million. Television receivers (Dec. 1970) 150,000.

Agriculture. Production (in 000; metric tons; 1972; 1971 in parentheses): corn *c.* 220 (261); barley *c.* 100 (69); potatoes *c.* 350 (*c.* 370); rice *c.* 190 (150); cassava (1971) *c.* 420, (1970) *c.* 410; dry beans *c.* 30 (*c.* 30); bananas (1970) 4,137, (1969) 5,834; coffee *c.* 54 (*c.* 66); cocoa (1972–73) 53, (1971–72) 60; oranges *c.* 195 (*c.* 195); sugar, raw value *c.* 280 (*c.* 249); cotton, lint *c.* 7 (*c.* 5). Livestock (in 000; 1971–72): cattle *c.* 2,550; sheep *c.* 1,900; pigs *c.* 1,370; horses *c.* 250; chickens *c.* 5,500.

Industry. Production (in 000; metric tons; 1971): petroleum products 1,271; crude oil (1972) 3,835; electricity (kw-hr.) 1,050,000; cement 482; gold (troy oz.; 1970) 8.5; silver (troy oz.) *c.* 70.

The oil consortium sought compensation for the loss of 500,000 ha., but the government refused to pay. Following the dollar devaluation of February, the price of Ecuadorian oil was raised from $2.60 to $2.90 a barrel. In June Ecuador applied for membership in the Organization of Petroleum Exporting Countries (OPEC) but was not accepted until November. It again raised the oil price, to $3.60 a barrel. Under a 20-year agreement signed with the Texaco-Gulf group in August Ecuador was to receive almost 80% of the consortium's gross profits from petroleum exports plus the right to buy 51% of total production. On October 17, with the Arab oil boycott creating worldwide shortages, the oil price was raised to $5.33.

Despite talk of progressive reform there were still over a million people living on subsistence doles of $16 per month, and the government remained reluctant to upset the oligarchy. There was a one-day strike of 3,000 policemen in Quito in January and further labour unrest in Quito and Guayaquil in September; in June more than 15,000 peasants met in Guayas Province to urge the implementation of the government's proposed land reform scheme. A version of this appearing in a local newspaper aroused vociferous resentment from landowners. The government indicated that no immediate action was contemplated.

Demands from opposition groups for a return to constitutional rule and general elections brought a sharp negative reaction from President Rodríguez in late July. The armed forces, he declared, would not serve under "disreputable" political parties or tolerate opposition to its work. A new coalition of opposition groups—the Frente para la Restauración de la Democracía—was formed after meetings in Quito in July among politicians, labour union leaders, and students. The country's small Communist Party held aloof, claiming that the Frente was an alignment of bourgeois interests. The Frente possibly hoped to exploit the differences between pro-Brazilian and pro-Peruvian factions within the government, while the government itself hoped that its growing oil revenues (which had multiplied money reserves sixfold in 14 months) could finance its five-year plan (1972–77) and reap sufficient popularity to forestall any further coups.

The five-year plan emphasized the need for social improvements and called for anti-inflation measures to counter the rise in domestic prices, to increase food supplies, and to neutralize the demand that was expected from increased domestic purchasing power as petroleum exports rose. Industrial reforms and the prospects of an enlarged market offered by Andean Group membership combined to bring about renewed interest in industrial development, although the chief interest still centred on the petroleum industry. The Trans-Andean pipeline had been completed in June 1972, and exports of petroleum reached 250,000 bbl. a day by October 1973, by which time total exports were estimated at 74.5 million bbl. Plans for the construction of the state oil refinery at Esmeraldas continued, and bids for its construction were under consideration. (MICHAEL WOOLLER; X.)

Education

The illiteracy of approximately 30% of the world's population over 15—almost 800 million people—continued to be the major challenge to educators in 1973, and since the number of adult illiterates was rising steadily it seemed likely to remain so for at least another two decades. Although more people were receiving a basic education, in many of the less developed countries population growth was overtaking the output of the schools. While many of these countries had sizable education budgets—and most of those that had achieved independence since World War II had long since committed themselves politically to the principle of increased prosperity through universal literacy, and thus to high educational expenditure—UNESCO statistics showed in 1973 that all too often they applied their budgets in a way that was least rewarding educationally and that the richer countries were still pulling steadily ahead. Thus in 1960 the developed world was spending 3.7% of its gross national product on education, and the less developed, 2.4%. By 1970 the gap had widened to 5.4% as against 3.2%. Moreover, in many countries the distribution of educational investment was equally misguided. UNESCO data showed that in the developed world the ratio of primary-secondary-higher education spending was approximately 1:3:10. In the less developed world it was 1:25:1,000. The practical consequence of this in agricultural economies was to reinforce the tendency for people to leave their villages for nonmanual work in the towns and to seek some form of higher education, which the economy was not geared to utilize.

The problems were not, however, confined to less developed nations. In the developed industrial countries of Europe the college population (in universities, technical institutes, and colleges of education) had risen from 8.6 to 17% of the total age group during the period 1960–70 and was still rising. The consequences for employment of this enormous increase

Ecumenical Movement: *see* Religion

ensured that the secondary stage (grade 5 and upward in U.S. terms) continued to occupy a central place in educational discussion and policymaking in 1973, despite the fact that most educators had come round to the view that greater priority was needed for the primary stage.

In the U.S. approximately $96.7 billion was spent on governmental and privately funded educational efforts for 59 million students, according to the U.S. Office of Education. About 30% of the nation's population was involved in education, stated Commissioner John R. Ottina, who claimed that education had become the country's largest activity in terms of the number of people involved and the dollars expended. Approximately 8% of the gross national product was spent on education.

The Canadian Teachers' Federation released a report, "New Goals, New Paths," in July, the product of three years of research. The study concluded that almost everyone in Canada was criticizing schools for failing to meet the needs of their students but that no government consensus existed on how to improve the situation. As the report stated, "The most clear-cut conflict is between the right wing and the left wing in educational thought, that is to say, between those who would keep the present structure with occasional modifications and those who would dismember it, or at least loosen it up and give it new direction."

Nursery and Primary Education. In the U.K. the Conservative government determined to invest more, proportionately, in primary schools. The government's White Paper *A Framework for Expansion*, published in December 1972, promised a building program for primary schools that would replace or improve, at the very least, the approximately 1,500 schools built before 1902. It was also announced that nursery school for three- and four-year-olds (compulsory schooling began at five) should be made available without charge to all children whose parents desired them to have it. In 1973 this policy came under attack from two sides. First, the Labour Party opposition held that the demand for nursery school would be far higher than the government had assumed and that, in fact, as many as three-quarters of all three-year-olds would attend nursery classes if given the opportunity. Second, Lady Plowden, chairman of the committee that produced the Plowden report on primary education in 1967 (*Children and Their Primary Schools*), took the view that it would be much more satisfactory to invest money in educating the parents of nursery school children rather than on the nursery schools themselves. Speaking to the Pre-School Playgroups Association at Edinburgh on April 7, she said, "Our most vital task is to raise the quality of the mother-child relationship in the home."

Elma Lewis observes a drum class at her School of Fine Arts in the heart of Boston's Roxbury ghetto. In 23 years the school developed from a dance class into a multimillion-dollar cultural arts centre.

WIDE WORLD

This view did not receive a favourable response from teachers, though it evidently commanded support in other countries, notably the U.S. and also Czechoslovakia, where in 1973 admission to nursery schools at age two was instituted. The Czechoslovakians also took steps to reinforce their somewhat draconian method of mother education. A working mother was allowed 26 weeks paid leave on 90% pay, and for a second child about $20 a week for two years, but if she failed to attend the "consultative centres," which provided medical and educational advice, she forfeited these family allowances.

Beginning at the age of two weeks, most children in Brookline, Mass., began to receive intensive examinations and tests to prepare them for better grades six years later. The program, funded by the Carnegie and Robert Wood Johnson foundations, was designed to determine over a period of five years whether or not complete tests of mental and physical development and subsequent efforts to help parents perform their role better could lead to better grades. It was to be made available to families of all socioeconomic classes.

In The Netherlands, too, the new government elected in 1973 directed educational expenditure toward primary schools and away from higher education. A major project was set in motion to unite infant and junior schools involving 2 million children and 150,000 schools. The aim was to allow children to begin school at the age of 4 and remain in the same school until the age of 12 before transfer to the secondary stage. The Dutch educational budget for 1974 was increased to a record level of approximately $5.6 billion, about 27% of the total budget.

Set against this background, the additional $1,450,000,000 to be spent by the Indian government on primary education in the fifth five-year plan due to start in April 1974 seemed seriously inadequate. It was nevertheless more than had been spent by the central government on primary education since 1951. The intention of the five-year plan was to educate all children between the ages of 6 and 11 and 75% of those between 11 and 14 by 1979. This meant enrolling approximately 12 million children in the 6–11 age group between 1974 and 1979 and about half that number in the 11–14 group. There was little optimism about the prospects of achieving this, as wastage in Indian schools was very high. In 1973 statistics showed that out of every 100 children entering class 1, only 40 reached class 5 and 25 reached class 7; the dropouts lived chiefly in the villages.

In other less developed countries, however, the outlook was more promising. In Tanzania, for example, it was announced in Parliament in June that free primary schooling, originally planned for 1984, would be introduced in 1973 despite the additional cost involved.

Secondary Education. According to UNESCO calculations, secondary education throughout the world was still growing faster than was primary. However, the great improvement in quantity had been no guarantee of quality. A survey of 63 countries conducted by UNESCO early in 1973 showed that almost all had anxieties about the mismatch between education and the needs of employers. Thus, the U.S. replied to the UNESCO questionnaire: "About 50%

of our high school students are in the so-called general track which prepares them neither to go to college nor to enter a job. Nearly 2.5 million students leave . . . each year without adequate preparation for careers."

The National Commission on the Reform of Secondary Education, after a year of visiting U.S. secondary schools, painted a picture of declining growth, stabilized and therefore older teaching staffs, restricted money, increased student violence, excessive student absenteeism, and absence of lasting effects of the curriculum innovations of the 1960s. In its report, the commission criticized attempts to keep dropouts in school and encouraged high schools to develop different ways for students to earn diplomas, increase student rights, and utilize television more extensively. The commission seemed to favour students spending time in the working world, without the excessive protection built into current work laws.

A panel chaired by James S. Coleman suggested that 16-year-olds receive education vouchers adequate for four years of college education and usable anytime during their lifetime at any bona fide educational agency. In its report *Youth in Transition*, the panel concluded that schools serve well in only one way—cognitive development—but do not assist youth in their transition into adulthood (*see* Special Report).

In an effort to understand the impact that education has upon the young, the U.S. Office of Education began a $1.2 million National Longitudinal Study of the nation's secondary-school graduating class of 1972. The 104-item study involved approximately 18,000 graduates from about 1,200 public, private, and church-related schools. Plans were to do a follow-up study of the graduates every year for six to eight years to determine the extent to which they succeeded in attaining their plans and goals.

The concern that secondary education was not an adequate preparation for working life was not confined to countries with a capitalist system. Evidence quoted in the leading Soviet educational journal *Sovietskaya Pedagogika* demonstrated the kind of mismatch between job aspirations and the requirements of society that was only too familiar in the West. Thus, for example, in the Kemerovo region the official "plan" had determined that 56% of the tenth-grade pupils would leave school and enter productive employment. In fact, in a survey of 20,000 tenth graders, only 17.8% expressed any desire or intention of doing so. Similarly, a survey was carried out among 976 senior pupils in the town of Elektrostal in the Moscow region to discover their attitude to the 29 occupations—chiefly manual—upon which the town's economic life depended. Over one-third of the pupils said that they were not in the least attracted by these jobs. Not one of them wished to be forgehand, concrete layer, or plasterer, while 117 wished to become physicians.

The solution proposed by Soviet educators was, again, a familiar one in the West: to involve schools much more in the world of work and, where possible, to give boys and girls industrial and commercial experience while still at school. This had become particularly important in view of the universal tendency for pupils to leave school later and for this trend to be reinforced by raising compulsory school-leaving ages to 16 or higher. In the U.K., where the school-leaving age was raised to 16 for the 1972–73 school year, a Work Experience Act was passed by Parliament in June. This amended previous legislation that had prevented boys and girls under school-leaving age from working in industrial enterprises, even when the sole object was to obtain work experience.

The diplomatic détente between the U.S. and China led to a considerable reawakening of interest in the progress of education in the latter, particularly as the Chinese seemed to have recovered from the cataclysmic effects on education of the Cultural Revolution. This interest was shown, for example, at the 34th session of the biennial conference of the International Bureau of Education in Geneva in September, when 350 delegates from more than 60 countries held a nine-day meeting on future trends in education. They seemed generally to agree that China's attempts to end artificial social divisions between nonmanual and manual work and to abandon pay differentials were worth close observation. (*See* CHINA: *Special Report*, "Education After the Cultural Revolution.")

In Europe, the nearest to the Chinese example was Albania, where in 1973 the government introduced a rule that all pupils must spend one year in manual work after leaving school before going on to further education. Judging from the evidence presented at the Geneva meeting, no other country seemed yet to have been willing to go that far. Most had compromised by introducing a strong vocational element into the schools, or by legislation such as that adopted in the U.K. to encourage schools to send individuals or groups of children to places of work. In Guinea, a system of comprehensive secondary schools, known as *centres d'enseignement révolutionnaires,* was developed, at which pupils spent about 50% of their time on vocational training, all with the declared aim of "integrating school into life."

The difficulty so often was to encourage pupils to go into vocational education, as academic-style courses held greater prestige. In Qatar, students were actually paid an allowance in order to attract them into vocational and technical education. In secondary school systems where there was rigid classification of students by ability, a larger proportion of course time was being taken up by vocational studies, notably in Colombia, Nigeria, and in parts of Canada. But in countries with genuinely comprehensive schools, especially in Sweden, the choice of a vocational course was being postponed until 16 or later. It was evident, too, that Arab countries with a strong Islamic tradition and heavy emphasis on abstract theory found the development of vocational education particularly difficult. In 1973, for example, 90% of all secondary pupils in Jordan were in the academic stream, leading to a hopeless mismatch with manpower requirements. As in most other Arab countries, this led to a shortage of personnel at middle management and technician levels.

In Libya, the most recent Arab country to attempt a great leap forward, it was official policy to place more emphasis on developing vocational schools. Nonetheless, it became evident in 1973—the year of the "merger" between Libya and Egypt (in principle if not in practice)—that the Libyan system was more or less in line with that of Egypt, *i.e.*, primary school from 6 to 12, middle or preparatory school from 13 to 15, and secondary from 15 upward. Figures disclosed in 1973 showed that in Libyan towns approximately 50% of 15-year-old boys went on to further education, 45% to secondary schools, and the rest to teacher training colleges or vocational schools. The prospects for girls were much poorer: only about half were going to primary schools and less than one-quarter to the middle schools. This reflected the patriarchal nature of Muslim society, especially in rural areas. Nonethe-

UPI COMPIX

A graduate student at the Massachusetts Institute of Technology demonstrates a new tactual map designed for blind students. The map, termed a breakthrough in mapmaking for the blind, provides campus geography in relief and information in braille.

World Education

Most recent official data

Country	1st level (primary)			General 2nd level (secondary)			Vocational 2nd level			3rd level (higher)			Literacy	
	Students (full-time)	Teachers (full-time)	Total schools	Students (full-time)	Teachers (full-time)	Total schools	Students (full-time)	Teachers (full-time)	Total schools	Students (full-time)	Teachers (full-time)	Total schools	% of population	Over age
Afghanistan	614,790	14,796	3,249	147,221	6,446	687	8,476	678	36	9,447	1,014	19	8.	15
Albania	555,300	18,944	1,374	32,867	7,157	46	50,072	1,205	85	25,500	926	5	71.	9
Algeria	2,244,844	51,461	7,139	278,843	9,892	422	12,870	3,933	259	26,522	...	15	67.	9
Angola	434,370	9,786	4,418	43,174	2,603	159	14,898	1,064	86	2,187	250	3	30.	...
Argentina	3,671,451	198,610	25,311	404,668	58,120	1,647	602,869	80,037	2,517	51,870	8,857	704	91.5	15
Australia	1,806,791	63,366	8,354	956,210	51,546	2,456	180,000*	...	216	111,219	9,652†	120	...	...
Austria	609,262	...	4,110	516,483	24,439	1,922	81,621	7,199	495	70,971	8,476	34	99.	15
Bangladesh	6,000,000	124,146	30,446	1,700,000	63,000	5,983	11,300	887	86	45,014	3,073	68	22.7	15
Bolivia	748,506	27,046	8,887	86,365	4,116	383	8,114	1,060	80	37,692	3,026	16	39.8	15
Botswana	81,662	2,467	294	5,564	288	15	1,888	204	25	100	18	2	10.6	15
Brazil	12,812,029	457,406	146,136	4,562,126	336,212	8,707	...	...	...	561,397	61,111	586	68.0	10
Bulgaria	1,025,921	49,775	3,739	109,173	6,891	304	293,226	18,252	571	115,113	8,736	51	91.4	8
Burma	3,198,670	71,136	18,299	813,144	25,461	1,748	8,735	756	35	54,502	3,827	20	68.3	8
Cambodia	989,464	22,465	5,699	119,988	3,990	172	6,834	604	108	9,162	1,205	9	54.1	10
Cameroon	754,101	14,703	3,450	65,360	2,719	191	21,547	961	134	3,559	322	11	12.	15
Canada	3,975,575	271,823‡	16,710‡	1,814,155	‡	‡	...	...	...	501,274	44,657	345	95.	14
Chad	183,250	2,313	714	9,212	298	31	1,278	70	8	—	—	—	5.2	15–24
Chile	1,980,906	35,588§	7,302	178,887	7,374§	461	92,014	6,571§	276	52,937	...	8	83.6	14
China‖	90,000,000	...	...	8,520,000	...	...	1,470,000	...	...	820,000	...	...	40.	...
Colombia	3,282,387	93,980	31,901	688,746	21,511	2,457	103,745	3,963	358	109,639	5,304	45	78.5	15
Congo	244,160	3,793	895	30,371	697	56	3,969	344	36	1,788	117	4	30.	...
Costa Rica	356,171	12,109	2,530	78,224	...	121	7,679	462	19	17,366	1,275	5	84.7	15
Cuba	1,852,714	68,699	15,474	222,481	16,734	498	67,850	6,920	163	34,398	...	4	...	...
Czechoslovakia	1,939,590	97,204	10,747	112,676	7,095	340	212,668	16,241	661	102,251	16,030	37	99.6	15
Denmark	548,300	33,700	2,700	227,600	15,700	...	100,000	3,000	120	78,000	7,800	100	100.	10
Dominican Republic	820,215	14,752	4,916	122,565	2,131	933	7,544	460	8	20,183	1,098	10	67.2	15
Ecuador	975,480	25,137	7,472	194,682	14,421	720	...	...	...	33,562	2,298	15	69.6	10
Egypt	3,740,551	96,693	8,415	1,146,704	41,038	1,705	274,688	15,689	261	192,605	9,886	106	26.3	14
El Salvador	531,309	13,501	2,891	60,870	2,635	300	26,183	588	114	9,695	599	9	49.0	15
Fiji	126,331	3,911	627	18,094	720	73	1,530	151	25	754	90	1	81.	14
Finland	379,611	17,310	4,311	417,523	14,994	1,135	105,141	6,048	744	61,778	6,563	25	100.	15
France	4,853,725	212,388	61,500	3,643,034	295,203	7,502	867,546	2,928	3,419	781,596	...	...	100.	7
Germany, East	2,675,695	147,453	5,587	55,064	...	291	496,510	14,897	1,240	113,665	...	54	100.	15
Germany, West	6,888,669	221,065	24,811	2,417,868	112,890	4,691	1,932,267	39,757	6,081	777,890	...	3,361	100.	15
Greece	919,067	29,011	9,097	458,771	14,277	900	85,322	450	348	97,130	3,458	49	85.8	10
Guatemala	509,502	14,639	5,322	60,710	5,566	408	20,333	...	...	17,171	867	...	37.9	15
Honduras	376,966	10,437	4,143	33,392	2,516	110	1,778	272	13	3,639	183	4	47.3	10
Hong Kong	725,172	21,829	1,214	243,214	9,700	288	16,680	...	36	15,559	1,699	7	80.9	10
Hungary	1,043,600	64,004	5,197	346,543	13,687	540	196,583	3,772	382	90,857	10,778	55	98.2	10
India	39,033,000	994,513	398,951	32,647,000	1,129,620	114,567	231,000	16,548	2,593	856,000	72,715	2,933	33.3	15
Indonesia	13,219,490	338,077	68,047	1,411,402	85,024	5,657	540,337	49,575	2,928	117,974	8,998	40	39.	15
Iran	3,230,776	75,641	26,024	1,400,213	34,360	4,918	68,137	2,238	331	97,338	3,639	105	22.8	15
Iraq¶	1,297,756	54,979	6,260	353,114	14,338	1,033	19,015	1,250	68	42,930	1,318	39	22.	15
Ireland	526,765	16,499	4,163	201,128	...	893	3,754	...	83	26,218	...	67	100.	15
Israel	525,453	26,631	1,719	74,244	4,901	337	72,234	4,687	347	73,720	...	...	91.0	14
Italy	4,891,454	228,998	38,083	2,840,087	247,521	11,068	983,302	84,860	4,162	678,845	9,437	77	91.6	7
Ivory Coast	535,039	11,572	2,311	77,188	2,359§	118	1,088	139	8	3,572	189§	2	20.	...
Japan¶	9,696,133	381,591	24,325	6,987,953	433,040	14,204	1,572,729	...	1,426	1,638,121	99,231	961	99.9	15
Jordan♀	326,111	8,521	1,048	109,028	4,971	768	3,548	237	11	6,604	309	16	43.8	15
Kenya	1,675,919	53,536	6,657	161,910	7,106	949	10,731	682	36	6,534	756	6	43.	15
Korea, South	5,692,285	107,259	6,269	2,243,198	56,086	2,368	428,212	14,897	563	232,182	12,052	155	88.5	13
Kuwait	88,299	4,580	159	82,235	6,452	160	2,872	663	10	3,339	152	5	59.8	10
Laos	273,678	7,747	3,347	7,917	370	22	4,908	380	12	523	101	3	34.3	15
Lebanon	203,725§	14,763§	735§	73,995§	2,763§	47§	23,617	...	249	42,784	2,759	13	88.	...
Lesotho	176,404	4,006	1,085	8,873	391	40	1,162	121	23	511	...	1	58.4	15
Liberia	120,245	3,384	889	15,494	918	195	1,277	66	5	1,109	164	3	23.6	5
Libya	467,204	18,840	1,869	67,161	5,093	299	14,365	1,406	106	8,220	414	11	27.	6
Malagasy Republic¶	1,004,445	14,881	6,055	107,781	5,181	535	9,213	759	126	5,293	307	10	39.5	15
Malawi	333,102	7,546	...	10,930	545	...	1,330	162	...	987	147	1	42.	15
Malaysia	1,769,296	55,870	6,346	663,769	25,145	1,135	16,745	757	74	20,000	1,614	23	58.0	10
Mali	218,416	6,265	873	2,823	197	10	4,358	281	24	628	107	4	20.	15
Mauritius	155,624	5,078	360	52,378	1,747	130	688	81	10	1,530	84	2	61.6	12
Mexico	9,248,290	201,453	46,010	1,219,792	80,331	4,530	364,550	29,191	1,107	247,637	17,103	374	76.2	9
Morocco	1,231,936	34,882	1,609	313,414	21,633	...	7,075	...	...	15,148	638	...	11.2	15
Mozambique	496,381	6,607	4,095	17,831	1,150	91	2,754	292	25	1,145	213	9	...	...
Nepal	449,141	18,250	7,256	96,704♂	5,257♂	1,041♂	♂	♂	♂	17,390	1,110	49	11.5	10
Netherlands, The	1,540,790	56,439	9,116	626,442	40,900	1,528	429,546	40,400	2,054	191,163	19,100	355	100.	15
New Zealand	519,276	19,163	2,579	190,709	10,482	391	—	—	—	35,385	3,786	29	100.	15
Nicaragua	314,425	8,154	2,115	54,139	1,578	185	6,945	429	44	11,618	694	6	57.6	15
Nigeria	3,515,827	103,152	14,902	310,054	14,091	895	45,959	2,702	225	8,617	1,533	6	25.	15
Norway	386,496	18,239	2,991	253,060	17,729	912	57,310	5,405	598	49,757	5,442	108	100.	15
Pakistan	3,887,500	96,731	44,637	2,075,485	71,940	5,893	34,897	2,914	193	272,942	10,525	421	16.3	5
Panama	305,651	10,689	2,127	65,833	3,366	81	33,003	1,673	131	18,492	990	2	79.4	10
Papua New Guinea	227,699	7,381	1,658	24,335	1,079	71	7,951	602	91	853	178	1	24.1	10
Paraguay	444,894	15,304	2,587	55,797	5,793	560	3,069	948	44	7,224	618	2	74.4	15
Peru	2,562,695	64,004	20,034	547,316	21,863	1,451	127,207	6,333	414	41,633	2,175	124	61.1	15
Philippines	6,968,978	243,821	40,823	1,719,386	46,689	3,883	106,099	6,507	625	651,514	40,093	728	72.	10
Poland	4,841,300	206,700	23,796	451,100	21,800	884	1,829,700	74,700	9,344	229,000	38,200	88	95.7	7
Portugal	988,559	30,444	16,586	328,354	19,552	1,623	160,250	10,845	488	51,510	3,111	62	66.5	15
Puerto Rico	497,836	14,304§	1,623	278,365	9,348§	622	16,168	253§	65	54,113	2,250	8	99.9	10
Rhodesia	792,103	19,861	3,708	63,037	3,352	200	6,663	335	32	2,712	308	6	28.6	16
Romania	2,650,880	135,089	14,899	236,366	16,107	532	297,063	18,809	858	103,171	14,488	...	100.	8
Rwanda	404,357	7,153	2,003	9,298	...	177	2,006	...	85	755	136	4	23.	15
Saudi Arabia	482,312	19,879	2,212	81,263	4,671	421	15,509	1,237	71	8,230	969	6	10.	...
Singapore	346,041	11,893	410	170,099	7,974	124	6,388	740	11	11,992	805	4	74.	10
South Africa	3,801,219	86,275	13,661	486,651	21,255	1,337	64,203	2,818	253	85,579	12,313	64	...	...
Soviet Union	49,229,000	2,522,000	169,500	4,421,000	...	4,260	2,425,000	...	...	4,597,000	...	805	99.7	...
Spain	4,942,306	162,607	133,500	1,332,986	60,794	3,140	430,248	19,966	1,171	242,131	17,847	135	90.1	15
Sri Lanka	2,110,306	95,281‡	6,971	439,501	‡	1,660	11,513	895	39	11,813	1,417	4	82.6	10
Sudan	610,798	12,986	3,352	190,749	9,020	1,210	2,983	251	23	11,833	1,002	12	17.4	10
Sweden	673,306	67,150	3,942	587,250	21,037	800	—	—	—	111,029	6,600	40	100.	15
Syria	845,130	23,431	5,261	281,254	14,310	813	13,203	1,557	61	38,132	...	4	44.	...
Taiwan	2,459,743	61,178	2,337	1,105,766	43,700	780	216,905	8,512	171	243,755	12,270	99	81.6	15
Tanzania	856,213	18,160	4,705	41,178	2,130	114	...	...	...	1,767	...	1	15.	...
Thailand	6,228,469	192,318	30,933	666,755	28,064	1,705	178,866	12,044	278	63,940	8,448	26	82.3	10
Togo	257,885	4,271	983	24,595	778	72	2,712	228	16	880	...	1	10.5	...
Tunisia	935,725	19,421‡	2,205	195,296	‡	154	...	...	...	9,858	528	13	32.2	10
Turkey	5,268,811	159,599	40,383	1,263,802	33,619	2,933	186,225	10,688	563	180,689	10,703	81	54.7	6
Uganda	786,899	24,032	2,937	53,887	2,341	159	6,243	501	31	4,018	470	2	31.	15
United Kingdom	6,180,998	239,936	28,544	3,914,707	227,533	6,544	344,011	62,120	898	334,837	40,868□	228	100.	...
United States	35,800,000	1,288,000	80,172◇	15,510,000♂	1,030,000♂	27,342♂	♂	♂	♂	8,220,000	620,000	2,556	99.	14
Venezuela	1,981,582	58,869	10,591	530,795	...	1,018	—	—	—	100,000	...	35	77.1	10
Vietnam, South	2,910,872	54,721	8,377	840,953	25,132	1,078	22,018	1,464	60	68,649	1,570	14	80.	...
Yemen (Aden)	134,522	4,316	872	16,631	769	81	891	102	12	110	13	1	10.5	...
Yugoslavia	2,833,838	121,435	13,868	188,539	39,129	436	234,085	9,394	723	295,398	16,783	273	80.3	10
Zaire	3,088,011	69,999	4,756	185,370	2,516	646	67,864	3,232	557	12,363	1,386	32	15.	15
Zambia	777,873	16,491	2,628	60,051	2,779	110	3,878	164	18	1,934	...	2	34.3	5

*Includes part-time and correspondence. †Excludes teacher training. ‡Data for primary include secondary. §Public only. ‖Latest official (1958, except higher, 1962).
¶Data do not apply to a single year. ♀East Bank only. ♂General includes teacher training and vocational.
□Excludes general education teachers in private 3rd level institutions in Northern Ireland. ◇Includes 1,780 combined primary and secondary schools.

less, partly under the influence of the growing feminist movement in Egypt, the education of girls was slowly beginning to show progress throughout the Arab world.

In Israel a 25% increase in the education budget was announced for fiscal 1973. This was partly done in order to restructure the basic 12-year system. It was decided to allow free compulsory schooling to cover all pupils to the age of 14, and this was scheduled to reach 16-year-olds by 1977. This, it was hoped, would assist in the integration of Israel's Jewish population of North African and Asian origin with those drawn from the West. Approximately 60% of Israel's Jewish population under 18 were of North African or Asian origin, but from a 60% share of attendance in primary schools their proportion declined steadily to a 10% share of university places. Conscious attempts to integrate these Jews with those of Western origin extended even to widespread busing to schools.

Without doubt the country where secondary education showed signs of the biggest breakthrough in 1973 was Australia. Education had been an important issue in the December 1972 elections, and so when the first national Labor Party government in 23 years took office it was under an obligation to make some tangible changes. The new minister of education announced that approximately A$660 million would be invested in education over two years by the federal government. This followed the recommendations of the interim committee of the Australian Schools Commission, which produced its report—known as the Karmel Report, after its chairman, Peter Karmel—in May. As a result, the government decided in August to eliminate or reduce federal aid to some of the wealthier private Protestant schools, while spending large sums on the development of public and, more controversially, Roman Catholic parochial schools. This policy met with criticism from several quarters. Middle-class Protestant parents protested that their schools were receiving no aid (these included schools such as Geelong Grammar in Victoria, which was attended by Britain's Prince Charles), while left-wing critics seized on the fact that Catholic parochial schools would receive federal aid almost as though they were government schools, although the funds would be distributed by the various Catholic education authorities.

In France, which had been nervous about its secondary schools since the troubles of 1968, the new minister of education, Joseph Fontanet, announced that he would carry out a wide public consultation with a view to formulating proposals for a complete reform of secondary education. This culminated in a three-day meeting at the end of November of some 600 French educators and the appointment of an independent commission of 11 people to report on its conclusions. The survey carried out by the French minister of education revealed some unexpected findings. Parents were asked if they wished to see the school-leaving age extended beyond 16. Only 6% wished to see it raised to 18, while 52% actually wanted it reduced to 14. It was generally believed that most of those who favoured a lower school-leaving age were thinking in terms of their children going on to an apprenticeship or some other form of full-time vocational training.

In large measure, these attitudes reflected widespread discontent with the content of school programs. Much the same was true of Italy, where there was evidence of much unrest in secondary schools. Indeed, in June, the government presented a bill in Parliament to reform the highly specialized secondary schools serving the 14–18 age group, the intention being to broaden their program and provide more options. The legislation also earmarked approximately $1.6 billion for urgent school building to overcome the chronic shortage of classrooms. In the U.K. there were also criticisms—which had been growing over a number of years—concerning the narrow specialism in the 16–18 age group ("the sixth forms") when pupils normally concentrated on three subjects (generally related ones, such as mathematics, chemistry, and physics). There was fairly widespread agreement among teachers on the need to broaden programs at that level. The main objectors were the universities, which feared that if the specialisms were abandoned standards would fall. However, the biggest single issue in England was the Conservative government's policy of resisting the development of comprehensive schools and favouring the continuation of grammar (academic college preparatory) schools wherever possible. This led to sharp differences of opinion between the minister of education, Mrs. Margaret Thatcher (*see* BIOGRAPHY), and the local education authorities responsible for running the system.

The enactment of a new law on national education —the first for 15 years—in the Soviet Union in July reflected not so much educational needs as those of the manpower planners and the Communist Party. The emphases in the statutes, due to come into force on Jan. 1, 1974, were on the education of highly qualified specialists (notably in mathematics and cybernetics, computer design, and automation) and on imparting a better grasp of Marxist-Leninist theory. Together with the second requirement, stress was laid on the need to nurture personal attributes such as high moral character and sound political consciousness.

In South America there was little sign of radical change. In Argentina the 1969 reform program envisaged a grand restructuring of the system and radical changes in curricula, but in practice there was little tangible progress. Similarly, in Chile the government of Salvador Allende, up to the time of its overthrow in September, did little to carry forward the reforms already embarked upon by the previous government.

continued on page 278

Mrs. Richard Nixon, herself a former teacher, looks on as 1973 Teacher of the Year Jack Ensworth explains the White House award ceremony to his deaf-mute mother, April 18, 1973.
The National Teacher of the Year Award, oldest ongoing national award program for classroom teachers in the U.S., is sponsored by "Encyclopædia Britannica," the "Ladies' Home Journal," and the Council of Chief State School Officers.

NATIONAL EDUCATION ASSOCIATION PUBLISHING

SPECIAL REPORT

AMERICA QUESTIONS ITS SCHOOLS

By Thomas Fraser Pettigrew

Do schools make a difference? The question would not have been raised even in the early 1960s. But by 1973 the issue was being debated throughout the United States, given wide media coverage, and even used as the title of a featured article in the March 1973 issue of *The Atlantic*. What lay behind this sudden questioning of America's schools? And what were the dimensions of the debate?

Why the Questioning? The early 1970s were a generally unsettled period. Many of the country's deepest values and beliefs were under review and attack, not just those involving education. Even so, doubts about the value of schooling were surprising, for America's belief in education was both deep and long standing. Schools were believed to be the means by which deserving citizens advanced themselves and their children. Schools were often thought to be the secret behind America's enormous economic growth and affluence. And the idea of public education as a right constituted a leading U.S. contribution to democratic theory.

Yet the issue emerged prominently in 1973. Basically, this came about because social scientists challenged traditional educational assumptions and these challenges received attention from both policymakers and journalists. Four trends thus coalesced: increased sophistication of social science theory and research; increased attention by policymakers to social science, especially in education; increased mass media coverage of policy-relevant social science; and increased concern over the education of black Americans.

The social sciences had advanced markedly in the preceding three decades. While not yet definitive, they had developed to the point of being worth serious consideration in the determination of public policy. To be sure, limited use had been made of social science in earlier periods. Presidents since Franklin Roosevelt had utilized public opinion surveys; the Supreme Court's 1954 ruling against de jure public school segregation had cited social science sources; and government had long sought the advice of economists. But it was during the '60s that social science came into style in Washington. Often the new prominence involved unrealistically high expectations of what social science in its current state could do.

In particular, help was sought in the areas of education and race relations. In Title IV of the 1964 Civil Rights Act, Congress called for a national study of the inequality of educational opportunity. Two years later, a massive report was issued, popularly known as the Coleman Report after its chief author, James Coleman, a leading sociological methodologist then at Johns Hopkins University. This sociological analysis represented a watershed in the history of educational research and the beginning of America's current questioning of its schools.

Only a handful of reporters appeared at the news conference marking the issuance of the Coleman Report by the U.S. Office of Education in July 1966. But once the policy implications of the report's findings became known, the mass media began to view the report and similar social science publications as constituting an important, continuing news story. Their often intense coverage made reexamination of the schools a public, not just a scholarly, issue. Unfortunately, few journalists were sufficiently familiar with social science to avoid distortions, and this contributed to the uninformed nature of much public discussion of the issue.

Interwoven with these trends was the national concern over public school desegregation. Black Americans, too, hold the traditional belief in the central importance of public education, and they made it the initial target of the civil rights movement. Thus it was not surprising that Congress first called for national educational research in a civil rights act. Nor was it surprising that the nation's concern over schools was often confused with such issues as busing and hereditarian claims of the intellectual "superiority" of Caucasians.

The Principal Reports. Five major reports and numerous evaluations of specific programs fueled the current controversy. The first, the Coleman Report (officially called *Equality of Educational Opportunity*), was prepared by the U.S. Office of Education. It delved into a variety of issues, but the debate centred on chapters 2 and 3, dealing with elementary and secondary school facilities and pupil achievement.

Congress, educators, and the researchers themselves had all assumed that there were vast discrepancies in facilities, services, curricula, and staff between schools attended largely by minority children and those serving majority children. These discrepancies, it was thought, constituted the chief denial of "equal educational opportunity" to minority pupils. But the report's results, based on questionnaires from a national sample of about 4,000 schools, indicated that the differences in resources money can buy were not as great as had been believed. Black children were somewhat more likely to be in schools without accreditation, physics laboratories, gymnasiums, or college preparatory curricula, but the contrasts were not nearly as large as had been expected.

So the Coleman Report turned its attention to the correlates of student achievement in the 1st, 3rd, 6th, 9th, and 12th grades. The data for this complex analysis came from approximately 645,000 public school pupils and 60,000 staff members. Not surprisingly, the report found that the social class background of the children constituted the major correlate of achievement test scores. The unexpected finding was that the most significant school correlate of the scores was the social class climate of the student body. Put bluntly, children of all backgrounds tend to do better in schools with a predominantly middle-class milieu, and this trend is understandably stronger in the later grades when the full force of peer-group influence is felt.

Though challenged more than any other finding in the report, this "social class climate" effect had been found in three earlier studies and was verified by later research. Thus, equality of educational opportunity appears to be more a function of whom one goes to school with than of purchasable resources. In terms of policy, this indicates the need for social class integration of education, a return to America's original model of "the common school."

The racial significance of this conclusion becomes clear when one recalls that only about 40% of black Americans are "middle-class" in terms of education, income, and occupation, compared with about 65% of white Americans. Apart from strictly racial factors, then, extensive desegregation would be needed to provide black pupils with predominantly middle-class school settings. On these grounds alone, black children in interracial classrooms would be expected to achieve more than comparable black children in all-black classrooms, and these expectations received support in the Coleman data.

In 1967 a second major report appeared that focused more specifically on racial desegregation of schools. Issued by the U.S. Commission on Civil Rights, *Racial Isolation in the Public*

Thomas Fraser Pettigrew is a professor of social psychology at Harvard University. He is the author of A Profile of the Negro American *and* Racially Separate or Together?

Schools provided the first of many reanalyses of Coleman's data together with numerous new investigations. The commission confirmed the Coleman Report's finding that black academic performance is higher in classrooms with a white majority. It also showed that the performance of white pupils in "more-than-half" white classrooms averages just as high as that of comparable children in all-white classes. Further, these test score benefits were found more often in truly "integrated" schools than in racially tense "desegregated" schools.

While important, high scores on achievement tests are certainly not the only goal of education. Indeed, many advocates of integrated education argue for it solely in terms of the need for diverse contacts as preparation for the interracial world of tomorrow. The Coleman and Commission on Civil Rights reports spoke to this issue, too. Coleman found that whites who attend public school with blacks are the least likely to prefer all-white classrooms and all-white "close friends," and this effect is strongest among pupils who began their interracial education in the early grades. In a special survey of Northern adults, the commission discovered that blacks who attended desegregated schools are more likely to send their children to such schools and to hold white-collar jobs than previously segregated blacks of comparable origins. Similarly, white adults who experienced biracial education differ from whites who did not in their greater willingness to reside in interracial neighbourhoods, to have black friends, and to have their children attend interracial schools.

Just four months after the Coleman Report was issued, a faculty seminar, organized at Harvard University by Daniel P. Moynihan and the author, brought together professionals ranging from pediatricians to constitutional lawyers to probe the Coleman Report in detail. The published result, *On Equality of Educational Opportunity* (1972), was edited by Frederick Mosteller and Moynihan. Though data errors caused by haste were found in the original analysis, the Harvard seminar's intensive reexamination did not substantially alter Coleman's principal conclusions.

The U.S. Office of Education issued its own reanalysis of the Coleman data, *A Study of Our Nation's Schools,* in 1972. Dealing specifically with differences between schools in motivation, attitudes, and achievement, it also confirmed Coleman's chief conclusions and provided further support for the policy of balancing student bodies by both social class and race. In addition, it emphasized the influence of schools on their students, since some observers had misconstrued the Coleman Report to mean that "schools do not make a difference."

The final major report, Christopher Jencks's *Inequality,* appeared in 1972 and received as much attention as the Coleman Report itself. Jencks was not primarily concerned with equality of educational opportunity, the focus of the other reports. Rather he strove to discover whether education played a role in reducing income inequality in the United States—an important, but different, issue.

Jencks concluded that educational opportunities are far from equal, but that inequality in test scores would not be reduced by more than a fourth even if economic status and the amount and quality of schooling could be equalized. He agreed with Coleman that "redistributing resources will not reduce test score inequality"; that school desegregation by race and social class have the largest educational effect on test score differences; and that "the most important determinant of educational attainment is family background." Though he found occupational status strongly related to educational attainment, Jencks still noted "enormous" differences among people with the same amount of formal schooling. But it was Jencks's economic conclusions that gained widespread attention: "Neither family background, cognitive skill, educational attainment, nor occupational status explains much of the variation in [white] men's incomes." Wealth, he speculated, may be largely determined by "luck" and "personality."

Public attention also centred on the book's policy recommendations. Jencks advocated more diversified educational programs, centralized educational financing, and job rotation. But his principal recommendations focused on reducing income inequality. Only economic measures, not educational equality, Jencks insisted, would reduce the nation's vast income inequality.

A Brief Evaluation. All five of these reports analyzed Coleman's data and must be evaluated in light of the limitations of Coleman's work. Critics emphasize four of these. First, the Coleman study, though massive, measured American education at only one moment in time, and therefore resembles a snapshot rather than a motion picture. Second, it could measure and evaluate only what existed in the nation's public schools in the fall of 1965 and not their unrealized potential. Third, roughly a third of the districts chosen for the sample refused cooperation. This sample loss was not random, but was heavily weighted toward those systems that most defied racial change. Finally, a survey cannot take into account possible selection biases involved in choosing schools. Thus, black children in interracial schools may score higher partly because aspiring parents with bright offspring make an effort to enroll them in such schools.

All these criticisms indicate genuine problems. Yet hypotheses drawn from the report's chief conclusions were largely substantiated by smaller studies that overcame many of these difficulties. The three reanalyses sponsored by the Civil Rights Commission, the Harvard seminar, and the Office of Education further clarified the results, problems, and policy implications of the original report. Only the commission study tested Coleman's conclusions with new research. In each case, the Coleman result was upheld or even enhanced.

The Jencks volume, however, enlarged the scope of the controversy by focusing on income inequality. To evaluate this work, a distinction must be made between three different "Jencks reports." The first consists of ingenious data analyses confined largely to the footnotes and appendices. The second, Jencks's interpretation of these results, is provocative but often removed from the actual findings. The third is the mass-media vulgarization. The often-ignored analyses represent an important contribution; the text is intriguing but debatable; and the journalistic distortions are largely an obfuscation.

Jencks's conclusion that economic reforms will do more to lessen income disparities than educational reforms is obvious enough, but his other major conclusion, that education has little to do with later economic success, is open to challenge. His analyses focus on white males alone; his arguments conflict with other types of data and analyses; and his emphasis on "luck" and personality is mere speculation. Much of what is called "luck" is probably the result of "knowing the right people." Such influence networks are related not only to family ties but to school contacts as well. This is probably why racially integrated schooling is more beneficial for blacks in terms of getting college training and good jobs than in terms of immediate test scores. "Luck" may well relate to schooling in ways Jencks does not consider.

The mass media played the determining role in shaping the public's conception of these reports. Few who debate them have actually read them. The Harvard seminar and Office of Education publications are relatively unknown because the media ignored them. But the coverage of *Inequality* reveals the problem. "Harvard Proves Schools Fail" blared a typical headline. Such distortions suggest that the mass media need newspeople as sophisticated in the social sciences as space reporters are in astronautics.

America should regularly question its schools but, to be informed and productive, this questioning will require three things: more detailed experimentation that concentrates on process as well as effects; more accurate mass-media coverage; and an administration willing to support innovation and change when they are indicated without primary regard to its ideological position.

continued from page 275

There was much talk, however, of the *escuela integrada,* a concept widely discussed elsewhere in Latin America. The *escuela integrada* was intended to be an all-embracing educational institution that could include nursery schools on the one hand and diverse and profuse forms of adult education on the other.

Research. The principal research document of 1973 was the second major project of the International Association for the Evaluation of Educational Achievement (IEA). (The first, an international study of achievement in mathematics, was published in 1967.) The second project involved nearly 10,000 schools in 19 countries, the object being to pinpoint cross-national variations in attainment in science, literature, and reading comprehension at the ages of 10, 14, and 18. Few of the findings were clear-cut; the academic high-fliers—the top 5%—had very similar scores in each country. It was clear that although school was an essential ingredient in achievement it was far from being the only one.

Another set of research findings of some educational significance was published in the U.K. in August, financed by the Columbia Broadcasting System Inc. This was a study of the effect of television violence on teen-age boys, conducted by an Australian, W. A. Belson, and his team at the London School of Economics and Political Science. The initial research concentrated on the incidence of violence itself. This showed that in London among boys aged 12 to 17 as many as 12% indulged in violent behaviour, approximately double the figure previously assumed in England by educators working with delinquent children.

The recently publicized theory that intelligence measurable by test scores is largely inherited was challenged in March by Leon Kamin of Princeton University. He said that studies cited by University of California psychologist Arthur R. Jensen are weak. Jensen had claimed that up to 80% of the variations in IQ test scores could be traced to individual genes. Speaking at a symposium brought together by the Southern Regional Council, Kamin said that he feared genetic inheritance studies might be used to curtail compensatory programs.

At a sixth-grade open classroom in Lawrence Township, N.J., children in the foreground take tests while those in the background participate in a reading session. The student at centre works on a large paper saucer to be used for the roof of a classroom planetarium.

WIDE WORLD

Rep. Albert H. Quie (Rep., Minn.) introduced an amendment to Title I, Elementary and Secondary Education Act of 1965, to require that U.S. federal funds be distributed to the states on the basis of demonstrated need for remedial programs in reading and mathematics. Aid would be based on achievement levels such as those determined by the National Assessment of Educational Progress (NAEP). The first reassessment of NAEP test data collected in 1969–70 was undertaken, under the auspices of the Education Commission of the States.

Higher and Adult Education. It seemed clear by 1973 that higher education was not going to occupy the limelight in the 1970s that it had enjoyed in the 1960s. In most countries there was talk of containing the expansion of higher education in one way or another, although the very fact that secondary education had expanded and would continue to do so meant inevitably that more and more students would expect to receive higher education and that the most that governments could do was to prevent numbers from expanding as rapidly as in the recent past. The most radical reform plan to appear during the year was in Sweden, the report of the much-publicized "U68" commission. The plan proposed the unification of all higher education; that is to say, there should be no hierarchy of institutions according to prestige, and technical institutes and colleges of education should be regarded as having the same status as universities. Second, students would be expected to have a vocational purpose in mind in their higher education, the intention being to prevent the purposeless continuation of such schooling simply for its own sake. The plan was a long-term one, but it seemed clear that if it were put into operation successfully it would mark the sharpest change in higher education policy in any European country since World War II.

The other major reform proposed on higher education in Europe was a good deal more modest and pragmatic. This was the Report on Adult Education in England and Wales, produced by a committee under the chairmanship of Sir Lionel Russell and known as the Russell Report. It proposed that spending on adult education (that is to say, nonvocational, part-time education of adults in the main) should be increased from 1% of the educational budget, as it was in 1973, to 2% by 1980. Also recommended was the establishment of national and local development councils to help organize adult education.

Meanwhile, in France a far more radical scheme for adult education, begun in 1972–73, ran into some difficulties. The scheme provided for a system of study leave for wage-earners. As many as 10,000 wage-earners, for example, attended approximately 100 courses organized for them by the universities of Paris during the 1972–73 academic year. The intention was that by 1976–77 about 2% of the total labour force, 450,000 men and women, would be released to receive some form of continuing training and education. The cost of the training was to be met by a levy equal to 0.8% of the annual wages bill of all firms employing more than 100 people, rising to 2% by 1976. Inevitably, the scheme required a small army of administrators, estimated at at least 2,400—and the difficulty encountered in 1973 was that the levy was insufficient to permit the establishment of this administrative structure.

That faculties of colleges and universities change

slowly was revealed in the American Council on Education publication on teaching faculties in 1972–73, a report by Alan E. Bayer. The August publication reported an increase of less than 1% of blacks and women on U.S. college faculties over the past five years. Although colleges were under pressure to implement "affirmative action programs" in staffing, blacks constituted 2.9% in 1972–73, while women faculty members reached a 20% level.

A Ford Foundation-funded study, sponsored by the Association of American Colleges and American Association of University Professors, claimed that unless abuses are removed and major reforms undertaken tenure as it is now practiced cannot survive. One major change advocated was the use of evaluations of teaching effectiveness in determining tenure.

In June the Carnegie Commission on Higher Education noted that higher education tends to change primarily in response to changes in the society and to the impact of society on the campus itself. The chairman, Clark Kerr, said that higher education in the U.S. in recent years had undergone its greatest time of troubles since the founding of Harvard in 1636 but that it generally was on the road to recovery. Two reforms were advocated: greater reliance on the doctor of arts in teaching degree, based on the teaching competence rather than research skills, and the provision of a three-year option for students who want to complete their studies quickly. The commission estimated that 10–15% of students now enrolled should not be in college. The panel expected college enrollments to drop 5–10% between 1980 and 1990.

Student unrest, although it attracted far less publicity than in previous years, was nonetheless fairly widespread, ranging from protests by women students at the University of Libya at Tripoli against the compulsory wearing of headscarves to rent strikes by students in the U.K. protesting the inadequate level of annual maintenance grants. Among the more serious examples of university protest were disturbances in Turkey, where there was strong resistance to the University Reform Law that came into effect on July 7. This gave security forces the right to enter any university at will and led directly to the resignation of several prominent professors. In Mexico, too, there was major interference by the judiciary with the university authorities, and during the summer the Federal Judicial Police moved into several university campuses to arrest students.

Desegregation. In the U.S. the courts were active in cases involving school desegregation. The Supreme Court rejected a lower federal court ruling that the largely black Richmond (Va.) city schools and the schools of predominantly white surrounding counties be combined. In the Detroit-Wayne County (Mich.) area Judge Stephen Roth, of the U.S. District Court in Detroit, mandated approximately $3 million worth of school buses to carry out the integration of the 65% black Detroit system and the 80% white school population of adjoining districts. Final legal disposition of the case remained uncertain.

The U.S. Department of Health, Education, and Welfare (HEW) was ordered by a federal judge to cut off federal aid to school systems in 17 states after their failure to comply with the desegregation requirements established by the department. In the Denver case the Supreme Court indicated that in Northern states, where segregation was never legally mandated, action had to be taken to break up de facto school segregation resulting from segregated housing patterns. This was the first Supreme Court ruling in a major Northern school district segregation case, perhaps ranking in importance with the 1954 Brown decision outlawing the separate-but-equal principle that had permitted dual white and black school systems and the 1971 Swann decision that recognized busing as a means of securing desegregation.

In Alexandria, Va., a federal district judge ruled that private schools cannot deny admission to blacks because of their race. As the basis for his decision, which affected 395 private schools in seven Southern states, the judge cited a civil rights law of 1866. In July the U.S. Commission on Civil Rights reported that its study of ten communities in various stages of desegregation indicated that integration was substantially improving the quality of education. (*See* RACE RELATIONS.)

Finance and Administration. The proposal by U.S. Pres. Richard Nixon for the 1974 fiscal year contained a reduction from 1973 of about $1 billion from health, education, and poverty programs. The president's strategy for federal education efforts was "revenue sharing" to replace categorical aid-to-education programs. Education aid amounting to $2,770,000,000 would be funneled from the federal government to the states. The second major strategy was consolidation of all categorical programs into the "Better Schools Act." Some 32 existing programs would be incorporated into five main categories controlled to a considerable extent by the states. Congress objected to this proposal, however, and seemed more likely to enact an extension of the Elementary and Secondary Education Act with relatively minor adjustments, such as a combination of existing titles and possibly a provision for granting aid based on learning deficiencies as well as existing poverty criteria.

The U.S. Congress opposed many of the Nixon administration's educational proposals and passed appropriations exceeding those requested by the administration. The president, in turn, refused to spend much of the money. In November, in a class-action suit brought by the state of Pennsylvania, a U.S. District Court judge ordered the release of $380 million in impounded funds originally appropriated for the nation's elementary and high schools.

The U.S. Office of Education demanded that 150 all-men or all-women's colleges explain why sex discrimination in admissions had not been eliminated. The institutions were located in 33 states and included many of the nation's most prestigious colleges.

Thomas K. Glennan, Jr., director of the National Institute of Education (NIE), defended the progress made by NIE in becoming totally operational since its establishment in 1972, noting that three years are needed in creating either elaborate technological systems and/or education and social science research. Faced with 3,000 proposals for funding amounting to $250 million, NIE funded 206 at $11.3 million. NIE expenditures totaled $106.5 million of the $110 million that had been appropriated. Funding for the new fiscal year was cut to $75 million by Congress.

The muddied property tax situation within the states of the U.S. was clarified when the Supreme Court ruled 5–4 in late March that financing of public schools with local property taxes is constitutional and is not discriminatory against the poor. Prior to the Supreme Court ruling, suits had been brought in 27 states to support the claim that equalized spending must be brought about in all school districts within a state.

In a June decision the U.S. Supreme Court upheld

a state's right to charge higher college fees to nonresident students. The court by a 6–3 vote also ruled that Connecticut laws cannot permanently block students who ultimately might want to qualify for resident status and thus for resident fees.

Although approximately 10,500 Roman Catholic schools remained in operation in the U.S. in 1973, the National Catholic Educational Association reported a 20% student decline over the past six years, to less than 10% of all students in schools. The U.S. Supreme Court continued to reject efforts in several states to aid parochial systems, directly or indirectly.

Although there were widely publicized teacher surpluses in selected fields of specialization and declining enrollments in teacher education programs, efforts were made continuously to upgrade teacher education. The U.S. National Education Association (NEA) suggested that about 670,000 more positions were needed for the nation's schools: to reduce class size and teaching loads, to provide special education, to provide more kindergarten and nursery school programs, and to reinstate programs and services cut back since 1969.

In September 693,000 students were out of school in the U.S. because of teacher strikes, which were reported in a number of states. The largest school system affected was that of Detroit, where the teachers remained on strike for six weeks before agreeing to arbitration. (JOEL L. BURDIN; TUDOR DAVID)

See also Libraries; Medicine; Motion Pictures; Museums and Galleries.

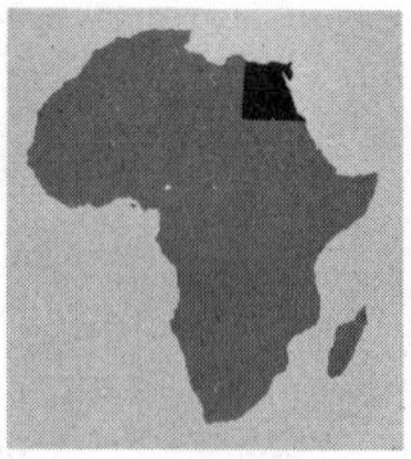

Egypt

A republic of northeast Africa, Egypt is bounded by Israel, Sudan, Libya, the Mediterranean Sea, and the Red Sea. Area: 386,900 sq.mi. (1,002,000 sq.km.). Pop. (1972 est.): 34,839,000. Cap. and largest city: Cairo (pop., 1971 est., 5,139,000). Language: Arabic. Religion: Muslim 93%; Christian 7%. President in 1973, Anwar as-Sadat; prime ministers, Aziz Sidky and, from March 26, Anwar as-Sadat.

For Egypt 1973 was a momentous year as President Sadat (*see* BIOGRAPHY) and his government decided to break the 1967 cease-fire agreement and launch a full-scale offensive across the Suez Canal on October 6, the Jewish high holy day of Yom Kippur, to recover Sinai from Israeli occupation. The attack was coordinated with a similar Syrian move in the Golan Heights. Various indications of Egypt's intentions had been given earlier in the year, as Sadat and his senior representatives said on several occasions that Egypt had no alternative to going to war because the U.S. supported the Israeli occupation of Arab territory and the Soviet Union refused to supply Egypt with offensive arms; since Egypt refused to engage in any negotiations until there was a complete Israeli withdrawal, all diplomatic efforts to achieve a settlement had failed. Nevertheless, Egypt's offensive surprised many observers because Sadat had already postponed it many times (possibly as a ploy to relax the Israeli guard). Also, Egypt's diplomatic offensive (*see* below) was producing results. It seemed likely that Sadat feared that the U.S.-Soviet détente would lead to an imposed settlement, backed by immense world pressure, in which Egypt would be obliged to give up territory. He was determined at all costs to prevent this. It was thus a political, as well as a military, preemptive strike, following as it did hard on the Israeli Cabinet's acceptance of a program advanced by Israel Galili, a Cabinet minister, for the occupied territories. (For an account of the military operations, *see* DEFENSE: *Special Report.*)

After some extremely heavy tank fighting, a cease-fire was accepted on the Sinai battlefront on October

Egyptian troops rejoice as they plant their flag atop a bunker on the Bar-Lev line east of the Suez Canal in October 1973.

WIDE WORLD

EGYPT

Education. (1970–71) Primary, pupils 3,740,551, teachers 96,693; secondary, pupils 1,149,803, teachers 41,292; vocational, pupils 271,638, teachers 13,401; teacher training, students 25,526, teachers 2,113; higher (including 6 universities), 227,463, teaching staff 4,570.

Finance. Monetary unit: Egyptian pound, with (Sept. 17, 1973) an official rate of E£0.43 to U.S. $1 (E£1.04 = £1 sterling) and a tourist rate of E£0.63 to U.S. $1 (E£1.52 = £1 sterling). Gold, SDRs, and foreign exchange, central bank: (May 1973) U.S. $206 million; (May 1972) U.S. $173 million. Budget (1971–72 est.): revenue E£1,920 million; expenditure E£2,000 million. Gross national product: (1969–70) E£2,927 million; (1968–69) E£2,657 million. Money supply: (May 1973) E£1,064.4 million; (May 1972) E£843.7 million. Cost of living (Cairo; 1963 = 100): (March 1973) 153; (March 1972) 153.

Foreign Trade. (1972) Imports E£381.4 million; exports E£358.8 million. Import sources (1971): West Germany 12%; France 9%; U.S. 8%; Italy 7%; U.K. 6%; U.S.S.R. 5%; India 5%. Export destinations (1971): U.S.S.R. 35%; East Germany 5%. Main exports: cotton 45%; cotton yarn 12%; rice 7%; cotton fabrics 5%.

Transport and Communications. Roads (1970) *c.* 50,000 km. (including *c.* 22,000 km. with improved surface). Motor vehicles in use (1971): passenger 141,500; commercial (including buses) 34,700. Railways: (1970) 5,175 km.; traffic (1970–71) 6,772,000,000 passenger-km., freight 3,340,000,000 net ton-km. Air traffic (1971): 955.9 million passenger-km.; freight 18,081,000 net ton-km. Shipping (1972): merchant vessels 100 gross tons and over 127; gross tonnage 242,745. Telephones (Dec. 1968) *c.* 365,000. Radio licenses (Dec. 1971) 4.5 million. Television licenses (Dec. 1970) 529,000.

Agriculture. Production (in 000; metric tons; 1972; 1971 in parentheses): corn 2,417 (2,342); wheat 1,616 (1,729); barley 107 (76); sorghum 831 (854); potatoes *c.* 460 (451); rice *c.* 2,600 (2,534); sugar, raw value *c.* 535 (*c.* 515); tomatoes (1971) 1,637, (1970) 1,553; onions (1971) 582, (1970) 452; dry broad beans (1971) 296, (1970) 277; dates (1971) 340, (1970) *c.* 355; oranges (1971) 809, (1970) 639; lemons (1971) 74, (1970) 83; grapes *c.* 128 (122); cotton, lint 520 (510); cheese *c.* 190 (*c.* 190). Livestock (in 000; 1971–72): cattle *c.* 2,130; sheep *c.* 2,040; goats *c.* 1,150; buffaloes *c.* 2,100; asses *c.* 1,350; camels *c.* 130; chickens *c.* 25,000.

Industry. Production (in 000; metric tons; 1971): cement 3,921; iron ore (metal content; 1970) 227; crude oil (1972) 10,630; phosphates (oxide content) 574; salt 398; cotton yarn 171; cotton fabrics (1970) 101; electricity (kw-hr.; 1970) 7,591,000.

22. Almost immediately, fighting broke out again, and Egypt accused Israel of breaking the cease-fire in order to strengthen the spearhead its army had established on the west bank of the Suez Canal, enabling it to encircle Egypt's 3rd Army and the town of Suez. After a spectacular whirlwind visit to Cairo by U.S. Secretary of State Henry A. Kissinger in early November, during which diplomatic relations between Egypt and the U.S. were reestablished after six years, a tentative breakthrough to a possible peace was reached when Egyptian and Israeli generals met on the west bank of the Suez Canal and in face-to-face talks agreed on an exchange of prisoners and the resupply of food and medicine to Egypt's beleaguered 3rd Army. (Israel held around 8,000 Egyptian prisoners, and Egypt held well over 200 Israelis.) The exchange began on November 14. Egypt participated in the Middle East peace conference that started in Geneva on December 21. After the opening round, Egypt and Israel met for secret talks concerning the Suez front. (*See* MIDDLE EASTERN AFFAIRS.)

Foreign Relations. Relations with the U.S.S.R. had remained cool since the expulsion of the Soviet military advisers in July 1972, and in May 1973 Sadat said in a press interview that the U.S.S.R. was playing big-power politics at Egypt's expense. Egypt was alarmed at the possible consequences of the U.S.-Soviet détente, symbolized by the visit of Soviet leader Leonid I. Brezhnev to Washington, D.C., in June. Despite Egypt's declared skepticism about the results of its diplomatic initiatives, these continued throughout the year. The foreign minister, Sadat's personal representative Hafez Ismail, and the Arab Socialist Union secretary-general among them visited scores of world capitals, and Sadat himself attended the summit meeting of the Organization of African Unity (OAU) in Addis Ababa, Eth., in May and the Algiers summit meeting of nonaligned nations in September. This diplomatic offensive produced some positive results. West German-Egyptian relations improved markedly, and the West German foreign minister, Walter Scheel, visited Cairo in May. In black Africa an increasing number of states adopted an anti-Israeli position. But it was especially in the Arab world that Sadat forged new political links. Egypt moved notably closer to Saudi Arabia and the other conservative oil-producing states. Also in September, after a summit meeting in Cairo with King Hussein of Jordan (*see* BIOGRAPHY) and Pres. Hafez al-Assad of Syria, the quarrel with Jordan was patched up and diplomatic relations were immediately restored. Egypt received promises of increased financial aid from Saudi Arabia, and one of the consequences of the rapprochement was the willingness of King Faisal (*see* BIOGRAPHY) to threaten and then to implement the withholding of oil to reduce Western support for Israel.

A negative aspect of Egypt's new alignment was a cooling in relations with Libya, Saudi Arabia's chief critic among the Arab states. Early in the year it had been assumed that the planned merger of Egypt and Libya would take place in September, but it became apparent after Sadat's visit to Libya in June that Egypt was having second thoughts. Libyan leader Col. Muammar al-Qaddafi (*see* BIOGRAPHY) paid an unexpected and prolonged visit to Cairo between June 22 and July 9 during which he openly criticized "liberal" aspects of Egypt's social and political life but urged that the merger should take place as planned. He failed to persuade the Egyptians, and, when he organized a mass march of Libyans to Cairo to try to force Egypt's hand, President Sadat had the march stopped before it reached Alexandria and declared that Egypt would not be bullied into union. However, he aimed to preserve the principle of union and sent some senior ministers to Tripoli. In August they produced a plan for a union by stages and for the immediate formation of a joint constituent assembly, with 50 members for each country, to draft a constitution and nominate a president, to be approved by a referendum. The plans also provided for the exchange of resident ministers and the formation of a Supreme Planning Council. However, the rift between Cairo and Tripoli was clear when Qaddafi said that he had not agreed to Egypt's strategy against Israel in October. The Libyan embassy in Cairo was closed, at least temporarily, in December.

Domestic Affairs. Early in 1973 the Sadat regime had to face rising discontent that was a direct consequence of the prolonged "no peace, no war" situation. University students, who had demonstrated in December 1972, rioted again in early January 1973 and five universities and 20 colleges were closed; 120 were arrested, including 21 nonstudents. The People's Assembly was asked to investigate the trouble and, although both the right and left were blamed, the onus was clearly placed on the left. Some left-wing intellectuals, including several of Egypt's most prominent journalists and writers, were dismissed from the Arab Socialist Union, which meant that they were prevented from practicing as journalists though their salaries were still paid. A clear move to the right was seen in the rise to prominence of the "rural bourgeoisie," exemplified by the growing influence of the speaker of the People's Assembly, Hafez Badawy. On February 11 Cairo University students again demonstrated, calling for the release of those arrested. Although the government acted firmly to suppress the demonstrations, a move toward compromise was noted in the publication of a manifesto by 900 "moderate" students supporting the key demands of the demonstrators but denouncing extremist agitators. On February 26 about one-third of the arrested students were released.

One of the main student demands was that the country should be put on a proper war footing, as had been promised. On February 11 Prime Minister Sidky announced a war budget that included the freezing of salaries and other measures, but he was subjected to strong criticism both inside and outside Parliament over shortages and maladministration. On

Egyptian Pres. Anwar as-Sadat peers through a telescope during a June 1973 visit to a front-line Sinai position. Using binoculars is Gen. Ahmed Ismail, Egypt's defense minister.

WIDE WORLD

March 26 Sidky resigned, and President Sadat himself took over as prime minister. He appointed four deputy ministers, all from the former Cabinet.

The Economy. In April various measures were announced to increase food supplies to the poorer sections of the population. During the summer, moves were made toward creating a more market-oriented economy. Trade and currency restrictions were relaxed, and measures were introduced to encourage the investment of foreign capital and guarantee it against nationalization. On August 1 a "parallel" exchange market alongside the official exchange was established. Egypt's debts to various countries were rescheduled and several new foreign loans secured.

In January plans were announced to increase Egypt's industrial production by E£164 million to E£1,820 million, but military expenditure required cuts in a number of long-term investment projects. Oil production in 1972 was declared to have risen to 19 million tons from 14.6 million tons in 1971, and an important new oil field was found in the Gulf of Suez during 1973. On February 1 Egypt joined the Organization of Arab Petroleum Exporting Countries (OAPEC). Soviet oil exploration teams were withdrawn from the Siwa area of the Western Desert, and in October the contract for the Suez–Alexandria oil pipeline (SUMED) was awarded to the U.S. Bechtel Corp. instead of the French-led Western European consortium that had been negotiating for it for two years. Financing would be organized by U.S. banks but with an expected Saudi-Kuwaiti 50% participation. The contract was signed in Cairo on December 14. (PETER MANSFIELD)

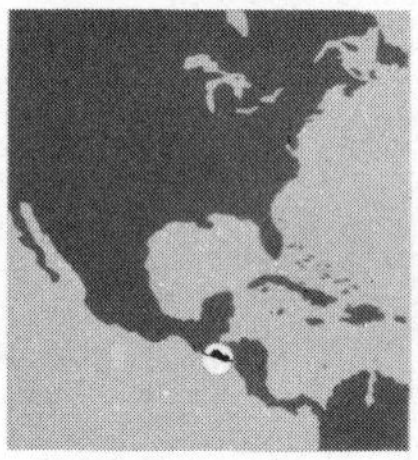

El Salvador

A republic on the Pacific coast of Central America and the smallest country on the isthmus, El Salvador is bounded on the west by Guatemala and on the north and east by Honduras. Area: 8,098 sq.mi. (21,975 sq.km.). Pop. (1972 est.): 3,649,197. Cap. and largest city: San Salvador (pop., 1972 est., 387,489). Language: Spanish. Religion: Roman Catholic. President in 1973, Col. Arturo Armando Molina.

Economic matters dominated events in El Salvador in 1973. The adverse economic effects resulting from the war with Honduras in 1969 had lessened over the years, and by the beginning of 1973 the outlook was favourable for coffee, cotton, and sugar despite drought conditions that resulted in an estimated one-third production cut for coffee, El Salvador's major source of export earnings. The drought also created shortages of corn (maize), rice, and beans, all staples in the Salvadorean diet, and increased the prices of these items. To conserve urban water supply during the drought period, the government allowed the capital to turn on its water only one hour each day. The overall effect of the drought, however, was to bring a pause but not a halt to the country's upward economic development.

El Salvador continued to improve its trade balance in spite of the loss of its traditional Central American trading partner, Honduras, after the 1969 war. This was achieved by greatly reducing imports of beans, gaining self-sufficient status in the growing of corn, rice, and sorghum, and increasing export earnings of cotton, sugar, beef, and shrimp. The lifting of exchange controls in February further improved the nation's trade balance.

EL SALVADOR

Education. (1969–70) Primary, pupils 516,875, teachers 13,491; secondary, pupils 57,533; vocational, pupils 27,250; secondary and vocational, teachers 3,430; higher, students 8,151, teaching staff 537.

Finance. Monetary unit: colón, with (Sept. 17, 1973) a par value of 2.50 colones to U.S. $1 (free rate of 6.05 colones = £1 sterling). Gold, SDRs, and foreign exchange, central bank: (June 1973) U.S. $106.9 million; (June 1972) U.S. $84.1 million. Budget (1972 actual): revenue 316.6 million colones; expenditure 367.7 million colones. Gross national product: (1971) 2,656,000,000 colones; (1970) 2,544,000,000 colones. Money supply: (May 1973) 394.6 million colones; (May 1972) 347.6 million colones. Cost of living (1963 = 100): (April 1973) 114; (April 1972) 109.

Foreign Trade. (1972) Imports 691.4 million colones; exports 683.2 million colones. Import sources: U.S. 31%; Guatemala 17%; Japan 13%; West Germany 8%; Costa Rica 5%. Export destinations: West Germany 20%; U.S. 18%; Guatemala 17%; Japan 13%; Costa Rica 8%; Nicaragua 6%. Main exports: coffee 39%; cotton 14%.

Transport and Communications. Roads (1971) 10,733 km. (including 625 km. of Pan-American Highway). Motor vehicles in use (1970): passenger 35,900; commercial (including buses) 20,900. Railways (1970) 623 km. Telephones (Jan. 1972) 41,000. Radio receivers (Dec. 1971) 350,000. Television receivers (Dec. 1971) 125,000.

Agriculture. Production (in 000; metric tons; 1972; 1971 in parentheses): corn *c.* 395 (377); rice *c.* 46 (*c.* 45); sorghum (1971) 156, (1970) 147; dry beans *c.* 35 (*c.* 33); coffee *c.* 150 (159); sugar, raw value 203 (107); cotton, lint *c.* 75 (69). Livestock (in 000; 1971–72): cattle *c.* 1,265; pigs *c.* 420; horses *c.* 65; poultry *c.* 8,000.

Industry. Production (in 000; metric tons; 1971): cotton yarn 5.5; cement (1972) 218; electricity (kw-hr.) 743,000.

The government's commitment made in the wake of the 1969 war to improve the social and economic lot of Salvadoreans made some tangible advancement in the public sector in 1973. A five-year development plan (1973–77) was announced, which, if fulfilled, would result in an almost threefold increase in public sector investment. The plan emphasized energy, water, roads, health, and educational facilities. To meet the nation's continuing energy requirements, the government announced in January that it would spend approximately $80 million on a hydroelectric project, Cerrón Grande, on the Lempa River.

The major events in domestic politics were the arrest in February of approximately 100 left-wing labour union leaders and politicians after the government's alleged uncovering of an international terrorist plot led by El Salvador's Communist Party, and, in October, the first resignations in President Molina's Cabinet, those of Economy Minister Salvador Sánchez Aguillón and Agriculture Minister Enrique Álvarez Córdova. In foreign politics, several talks were held with Honduras in 1973 with the hope of achieving a signed peace treaty some time in 1974.

(ALLEN D. BUSHONG)

Employment, Wages, and Hours

In late 1972 and early 1973 it became apparent that the world was recovering from the slump of the early 1970s and was enjoying a strong boom in economic activity as well as suffering from accelerating price inflation. As expansion proceeded, labour shortages became an increasing constraint. A United Nations survey on economic growth in Europe over the past two decades showed how economies coped with this problem in the past. Table I ranks countries in order

Eggs:
see Agriculture and Fisheries

Eire:
see Ireland

Electrical Industries:
see Energy; Industrial Review

Electronics:
see Computers

of growth rates and shows that industrial market economies have grown at widely different rates, ranging from 2.5% annually in Ireland to 6.2% per year in West Germany, with an annual overall average of 4.3%. The rates of growth of the labour force were fairly similar in most of these countries, so that much of the difference in growth rates was due to differences in the growth of labour productivity, which ranged from 2.2% per year in the United Kingdom and 2.3% annually in the United States to 5% annually in West Germany, Italy, and Austria. In turn, the growth of labour productivity depended largely on increasing the quality and the quantity of the country's stock of fixed capital; Table I indicates that, with the exceptions of Norway, Finland, and Italy, a close correspondence existed between the proportion of output that a country devoted to investment and its increase in labour productivity.

Comparing the centrally planned economies with the industrial market economies, the former on the average experienced considerably higher rates of growth of output. This could be ascribed to higher rates of growth of both employment and labour productivity. However, investment ratios in those countries were similar to those of the industrial market economies, and much of the faster growth was connected with an improved overall use of resources, particularly in the shift of labour from agriculture to industry.

Tables II and III permit an interesting comparison of growth patterns within the industrial sector among the two groups of countries (excluding the U.S. and Switzerland). The same industries in both groups were fast- or slow-growing, and, on the average, the industries in the centrally planned economies grew 1½ times faster than the industries in Western Europe. But it is significant that this difference was not due to differences in productivity growth (which was in fact slightly lower in the centrally planned economies) but to the very large differences in the growth rates of manufacturing employment made possible by the movement of labour from agriculture to industry in the centrally planned economies. As this source of industrial employment dwindled, these economies came under pressure to maintain their growth rates either by more investment or through continuous improvements in industrial efficiency.

Employment and Unemployment. The bottom of the recent world slump was reached in 1971. Employment growth in industrial market economies slowed down considerably while the level of manufacturing employment even declined on average (Table IV). There were thus large increases in unemployment, especially in Western Europe and in the U.S. By contrast, employment in the third world and in centrally planned economies continued to grow satisfactorily on average.

Third World Economies. Growth of employment and changes in recorded unemployment continued to be variable, with expansion in employment in some countries leading to encouraging declines in unemployment but with other countries suffering continuing increases in unemployment (Tables IV and V). India's agricultural production was affected by drought in the second half of 1972, and shortages caused considerable rural-urban migration and a subsequent rise in urban unemployment. Food prices rose in consequence by more than 16% in 1972 with an adverse effect on real wages. The resulting level of industrial disputes upset the government's attempts to obtain better industrial relations through new methods of wage settlements. In 1973 the government was contemplating some form of incomes policy to supplement its industrial relations measures.

In Chile unemployment continued to fall in 1972 as the government determinedly pursued its policies of expanding output both through a redistribution of income to the lower-paid workers and through investment in the public sector. In 1972 unemployment in the Greater Santiago area was down to 3% of the labour force, compared with 8.3% in 1970. The effect of the military coup in 1973 was uncertain at the year's end.

Industrial Market Economies. In the more developed economies the slump of 1970–71, which caused large increases in unemployment, continued into the first part of 1972, with declines in manufacturing employment and rises in general unemployment (Tables IV and VI). However, in the latter part of 1972 and early 1973 worldwide economic expansion again took place, and employment rose while unemployment fell. These trends had seemed likely to continue, but the energy crisis brought about by the cutbacks in Middle Eastern oil production late in the year was expected to affect the industrialized nations adversely.

In the U.S. manufacturing employment rose in 1972 and still more strongly in 1973, with corresponding declines in unemployment. This expansion was associated with a large increase in private consumption due to a reduced rate of private saving. Unemployment, which had stood at nearly 6% of the civilian labour force in 1971, had declined to 4.8% by June 1973, comprising 4.3% for whites and 8.5% for blacks and representing an absolute decline of about 750,000 persons. Canadian employment and unemployment followed a pattern similar to that in the U.S. and for similar reasons. However, in Canada the labour force was growing rapidly at about 4.9% in 1972 so that

Table I. Growth of Total Output, Employment, and Labour Productivity, and Investment as a Percentage of Output

Annual compound % changes 1950–69:

Country	Gross domestic product (1963 prices)	Employment	Labour productivity	Investment as a percentage of output 1950–69
Industrial market				
Germany, West	6.2	1.2	5.0	27.0
Italy	5.4	0.4	5.0	22.1
Austria	5.0	0.1	5.0	26.2
France	5.0	0.4	4.6	23.7
Netherlands, The	5.0	1.1	3.9	26.0
Finland	4.4	0.9	3.5	27.3
Switzerland	4.2	1.6	2.5	23.9
Norway	4.1	0.3	3.7	32.0
Sweden	4.1	0.3	3.8	24.4
Denmark	4.0	1.1	2.8	21.0
United States	3.7	1.4	2.3	18.9
Belgium	3.5	0.4	3.1	22.4
United Kingdom	2.7	0.5	2.2	17.5
Ireland	2.5	−0.7	3.2	21.9
Unweighted average	4.3	0.6	3.6	23.9
Centrally planned				
U.S.S.R.	7.6	2.0	5.5	17.8
Romania	7.2	0.9	6.2	24.2
Bulgaria	6.9	0.5	6.4	22.4
Yugoslavia	6.2	0.8	5.4	29.0
Poland	6.1	1.8	4.2	19.7
Germany, East	5.7	0.4	5.3	16.9
Czechoslovakia	5.2	1.2	4.0	17.4
Hungary	4.8	1.0	3.8	21.0
Unweighted average	6.2	1.1	5.1	21.1

Note: Investment ratios include dwellings, and are for 1950–68 in the case of centrally planned economies (except Yugoslavia) and 1960–69 for Ireland.

Source: United Nations, *Economic Survey of Europe in 1971: Part I: The European Economy from the 1950s to the 1970s* (1972).

reductions in unemployment for a given expansion of output were low. The government successfully operated special projects to tackle unemployment, especially the Winter Job Expansion Plan, which created more than 160,000 temporary jobs. This, together with an expanded worker-training scheme, had a beneficial effect not only on the level but also on the structure of unemployment.

Unemployment in the U.K. reached a peak of 3.9% of the labour force in March 1972 and thereafter declined, slowly at first but substantially by mid-1973. Employment in manufacturing continued to decline because of the existence of spare capacity in industry, which also depressed industrial investment. Employment in construction expanded rapidly as house building rose. Unfilled job vacancies rose strongly from 187,000 in the second quarter of 1972 to 383,000 in the second quarter of 1973.

In France unemployment was much slower to respond to increases in manufacturing output, but this might have been due partly to improvements in recording and registering unemployment. However, part of the explanation might also lie in the recent expansion of the labour force as a result of natural growth and from rises in the participation ratio for women. Net immigration of workers into France declined by one-third in 1972, and toward the end of the year the extra jobs began to catch up to the supply of labour so that unemployment began to fall.

Italy's longest postwar recession, during which investment (particularly residential construction) declined substantially, began to end in 1973. Unemployment continued to rise, despite a virtual halt to the exodus of labour from agriculture (which averaged more than 250,000 workers a year after 1960). During the slump there was substantial disguised unemployment as women voluntarily withdrew from the labour force. Although there were signs of expansion in 1973, particularly in industrial production, authorities feared that wage increases might preclude any early improvement in unemployment; in 1973 this totaled more than 700,000 persons.

Table II. Growth in the Manufacturing Industries of Western Europe

Annual compound % changes 1958–69

Industry	Volume of output	Employment	Labour productivity	Average earnings	Unit labour costs	Prices
Chemicals and rubber	9.3	1.8	7.4	8.2	0.8	−0.4
Other manufacturing	6.5	1.1	5.3	7.3	2.1	1.4
Metal-using	5.3	1.7	3.6	7.6	4.0	2.6
Metal-making	4.4	0.2	4.2	7.3	2.9	0.5
Food processing	4.4	0.1	4.3	8.8	4.6	2.7
Textiles and light industry	4.2	−0.7	5.0	8.5	3.7	2.6
Total manufacturing (weighted average)	5.5	0.5	4.8	8.1	3.3	2.0

Note: In Table II and Table III the growth of output, etc., refers to growth in the output of each country's industry added together. The countries are those in the first part of Table I, excluding the U.S. and Switzerland. Average earnings include employers' social security payments.
Source: United Nations, *Economic Survey of Europe in 1971: Part I: The European Economy from the 1950s to the 1970s* (1972).

Table III. Growth in the Manufacturing Industries of Eastern Europe*

Annual % change 1958–69

Industry	Volume of output	Employment	Labour productivity	Fixed capital	Fixed capital per employee
Chemicals	13.0	6.7	5.9	13.4	6.3
Metal-using	12.4	5.6	6.5	9.4	3.6
Other manufacturing	9.3	3.0	6.1	7.8	4.6
Metal-making	8.2	3.1	4.9	9.5	6.2
Food processing	6.4	3.1	3.1	7.4	4.1
Textiles and light industry	5.5	2.0	3.4	7.4	5.3
Total manufacturing (weighted average)	8.6	3.8	4.5	9.0	5.0

*Countries include: Bulgaria, Czechoslovakia, Hungary, Poland, and the Soviet Union.
Source: United Nations, *Economic Survey of Europe in 1971: Part I: The European Economy from the 1950s to the 1970s* (1972).

Centrally Planned Economies. The growth of manufacturing production in the centrally planned economies was, on the whole, slightly less rapid in 1972 than in 1971 (Table VII), although employment growth continued at roughly the same rates. A major feature of 1972 was that the Soviet economy was badly affected in 1972, first by a very severe winter that destroyed much of the wheat crop and dislocated industrial production, and second by a summer drought that reduced agricultural production still further. Consequent large Soviet purchases of wheat, feed grains, and soybeans had a considerable impact on the world prices of those commodities and so affected the cost of living throughout the world. As a consequence of all this, Soviet national income per capita rose by only 3.7% in 1972, about half the rate of the previous year.

Czechoslovakia's growth rate continued to be satisfactory despite increasingly critical shortages of labour and high labour turnover. Czechoslovakia began trying to recruit labour from neighbouring Comecon countries and was negotiating with Yugoslavia. As part of a long-term plan to increase the labour force, family allowances were raised, and in April 1973 couples under the age of 30 with low earnings became eligible for loans of up to 30,000 crowns (about £1,000 or $2,430), with the debt to be reduced by 2,000 crowns on the first birthday of the first child and by 4,000 crowns on the first birthday of each additional child. In the face of continuing labour shortages and labour turnover, earnings rose quite rapidly. Incipient price inflation was curtailed by a price freeze in mid-1972.

Wages. *Industrial Market Economies.* On the average the rates of both wage and price inflation increased as economic activity expanded, but the rate of growth of real wages fell (Table VIII). The sharpest wage and price increases occurred in countries such as Japan and Italy that had no form of price or incomes policy. The effects of such policies in other countries must therefore be seen as restraining the rate of inflation below what it would otherwise have been.

The main cause of rising prices in 1972 and 1973 was the rising world price of food; at the beginning of 1973 food prices were rising three times faster than nonfood prices. This was partly caused by very large Soviet purchases of wheat and feed grains in 1972, but was also partly due to the expansion in the industrial market economies that placed a strain on limited supplies of "luxury" foods, such as meat, which are always sensitive to demand from rising levels of income.

In the U.S. rising prices of food and other agricultural produce were the immediate cause of an almost complete 60-day freeze imposed on prices in June 1973 by Pres. Richard M. Nixon. Earlier in the year there had been a number of legal price increases, after the Phase Two system of mandatory price controls had been relaxed and replaced by the largely voluntary system of Phase Three. The administration's wage policy had been effective in restraining the rate of wage increase, and the policy stood its test well by leading to only moderate wage settlements in the 1973 round of wage negotiations. Phase Four of the administration's policy was designed to hold wage increases to 9.5% annually plus 0.2% for fringe benefits. Price increases might compensate partly for cost increases, but profit margins might not be increased at all.

In the U.K. the prices and wages freeze of November 1972 was extended to the beginning of April, when

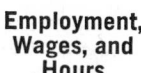

Demanding more building-trade jobs and contracts for minorities, pickets demonstrate before a construction site in the Bedford-Stuyvesant neighbourhood of Brooklyn, N.Y., in January 1973.

THE NEW YORK TIMES

it was replaced by Stage Two. This phase permitted limited price increases and annual wage adjustments not exceeding £1 a week plus 4%, estimated for male employees to be equivalent to about £2.30. This amounted to a 7% annual increase for the median wage earner, and ranged from about 9% for the lower-paid to about 6% for the higher-paid. Although the increase in average earnings between the second quarters of 1972 and 1973 showed a substantial rise due to the six-month increase of 8% from May to November 1972, between then and April 1973 the increase was only 1½%. The rate of price inflation accelerated during the freeze because of rapidly rising food and import prices, and there was thus a marked drop in the rate of increase of real wages. In October 1973 the government announced Stage Three, to operate from November for one year. This permitted wage increases of either 7% or £2.25, but with limited "flexibility" margins in order to improve the use of manpower or to compensate for "unsocial" working hours or regional differences in the cost of living. These margins could add 2 or 3 percentage points to wage settlements.

In France price inflation became worse during 1972, especially after price control measures were relaxed in March and the rise in hourly wage rates accelerated. In December various anti-inflationary measures were introduced, chiefly a cut in the rates of the value-added tax to reduce prices to the consumer prior to the elections of March 1973. The legal minimum wage was raised by 19.5% in 1972, and additional increases were promised during the election campaign. The price control policy was being used to keep France's rate of inflation 1% below that of its European partners.

In West Germany inflation continued at a rapid rate, and in consequence wage settlements backed by strikes or threats of strikes in 1973 showed higher rates of negotiated annual increases, averaging about 12%. The government resorted to traditional policies of managing demand by means of higher taxes and cuts in spending by public authorities.

Third World Economies. Price inflation in the third world rose in 1972, partly in response to the higher rates of price inflation in industrialized countries, a trend likely to continue, and partly because of the much higher rate of inflation in Chile. Chilean prices rose by 78% in 1972 as the government policy of stimulating industrial growth encountered bottlenecks of supply. Due to substantial redistribution of land ownership, agricultural production was disrupted and actually fell by 8% in 1972, thus causing food prices to double. Food imports were increased to maintain the balance of supply, but this put a severe strain on Chile's reserves of foreign exchange. In order to finance its program of expansion, the government was operating on a large budget deficit, spending more than it received in taxes and so adding further upward pressure on prices. The government rejected the conven-

Table IV. Employment, Unemployment, and Population

Changes for 1971 over 1970 (%)

Country	Employment: General	Employment: Manufacturing	Numbers unemployed	Population
Third world				
Chile	...	−5.6	−20.0	1.5
India	2.5*	...	23.5	2.2
Korea, South	1.4	−5.3	2.5	1.9
Philippines	10.9	0.1	...	2.9
Puerto Rico	2.7	1.4	10.6	1.8
Sierra Leone	1.3*	−6.8	−15.6	...
Singapore	10.5	17.0	−25.1	1.9
Zambia	6.5	11.6	0	2.9
Average	5.1	1.8	−3.4	2.2
Industrial market				
Australia	1.9	1.0	17.3	2.2
Austria	2.8	3.0	−11.0	1.0
Belgium	1.0	0.3	−0.6	0.1
Canada	2.5	−1.0	11.5	1.3
France	0.1*	0.5	29.0	1.0
Germany, West	−0.1	−0.7	23.6	1.1
Italy	−0.4	2.0	−0.3	0.6
Japan	0.4	0.8	8.5	1.2
Netherlands, The	0.5	−1.0	33.6	1.2
Norway	...	...	−2.4	0.5
Sweden	0.2	−2.9	71.2	0.8
United Kingdom	−1.6	−3.4	29.3	0.3
United States	0.7	−3.9	22.1	1.1
Average	0.7	−0.4	17.8	1.0
Centrally planned				
Bulgaria	2.2	1.2	...	0.6
Czechoslovakia	1.3	1.6	...	0.6
Germany, East	1.3	0.4	...	−0.1
Hungary	0.6	−0.3	...	0.3
Poland	2.8	3.1	...	0.9
Romania	...	6.1	...	1.1
Yugoslavia	4.8	5.3	...	1.0
U.S.S.R.	1.9	1.6	...	1.0
Average	2.1	2.4	...	0.7

*Nonagricultural sector.
Source: United Nations, *Monthly Bulletin of Statistics* (September 1973).

tional solutions of freezing wages and cutting government expenditure and initiated instead a policy of direct food rationing. However, this solution was only partly successful, and the continued acceleration of price inflation was accompanied by growing food shortages (aggravated by a truck owners' strike against the government). All this formed the background to the military coup on September 11.

During 1972 wage and price inflation accelerated in Greece as the economy continued to operate near the limit of full capacity. Under the pressure of a tight labour market, wages continued to rise rapidly. At the end of 1972 the government cut back credit and public spending and announced stricter measures of price control. Despite these measures prices continued to rise, and in the first quarter of 1973 the government increased minimum wages substantially to compensate for higher food prices.

In South Korea the main problem for economic policy in 1972 concerned the high rate of price inflation. In August Pres. Park Chung Hee announced a price freeze and restraints on wage increases. Prices subsequently fell slightly, and this was expected to make the proposed wage policy easier to enforce. However, in 1973 the South Korean economy, like all others, continued to suffer from rising world prices of food and raw materials.

Hours. Two conflicting forces affected weekly hours of work in manufacturing in industrial countries. On the one hand, successful labour union demands for a reduction in the required length of the working week were becoming very common. This was due in part to

Table V. Unemployment: Third World

Changes over previous years (%)

Country	1972	1971
Burma	20.2	17.8
Chile	−30.1	−20.0
Cyprus	−11.6	1.4
Ghana	72.3	11.5
Greece	−21.5	−37.8
Guatemala	−6.1	0
Guyana	−23.8	−14.1
India	28.8	23.5
Korea, South	5.9	2.5
Malaysia, West	2.3	−7.2
Malta	28.8	36.2
Mauritius	...	46.1
Morocco	...	−16.8
Nigeria	6.3	6.7
Puerto Rico	6.7	10.6
Sierra Leone	−15.3	−15.6
Singapore	−4.2	−25.2
Sri Lanka	4.8	10.2
Surinam	−10.4	−57.3
Trinidad	...	0
Zambia	18.6	0
Average	4.0	−1.3

Source: United Nations, *Monthly Bulletin of Statistics* (September 1973).

Table VI. Employment and Unemployment in Manufacturing: Industrial Market Economies

Changes over previous years (%)

Country	Employment 1973*	Employment 1972	Unemployment 1973*	Unemployment 1972
Canada	4.7	1.7	−8.6	1.8
United States	5.0	2.2	−11.4	−3.1
Japan	1.0	−2.6	−8.8	6.8
Australia	1.0†	−1.4	−16.1	41.2
Austria	2.4	2.3	−25.6	−5.7
Belgium	...	−3.1	4.9	22.5
Denmark	4.3	0	−30.6	1.0
Finland	0.3	1.9	−5.4	16.3
France	2.0	0.5	−1.4	12.8
Germany, West	0.6	−2.1	3.8	31.4
Ireland	2.6†	0	−8.3	14.3
Italy	−0.1†	−1.3	18.6	14.4
Netherlands, The	...	...	4.3	74.2
Norway	−2.0	...	−5.4	21.3
Sweden	1.1	−0.7	−0.7	6.4
United Kingdom	−1.1†	−3.9	−28.1	10.2
Average	1.6	−0.5	−7.4	16.6

*Second quarter 1973 over second quarter 1972.
†First quarter 1973 over first quarter 1972.
Source: Organization for Economic Cooperation and Development, *Main Economic Indicators* (October 1973).

Table VII. Output, Employment, Wages, and Prices: Centrally Planned Economies

Change in 1972 over 1971 (%)

Country	Manufacturing production	Manufacturing employment	Average earnings in manufacturing	Consumer prices
Bulgaria	8.4*	2.2	3.9	...
Czechoslovakia	18.5	...	4.8†	−1.6
Hungary	6.1	−0.8	4.5	3.3
Poland	10.8	3.8	5.4	−0.1
U.S.S.R.	6.8	1.5‡	3.7§	...
Yugoslavia	7.9	5.6	16.7	16.8

*Industrial sector.
†First quarter 1972 over first quarter 1971.
‡Estimated by applying productivity growth of 5.2% to output growth.
§Change in per capita income.
Sources: United Nations, *Monthly Bulletin of Statistics* (September 1973); Economic Intelligence Unit, *Quarterly Reports* on individual countries.

Table VIII. Money and Real Wages in Manufacturing and Consumer Prices: Industrial Market Economies

Changes over previous years (%)

Country	Money wages 1973*	Money wages 1972	Real wages 1973*	Real wages 1972	Prices 1973*	Prices 1972
Canada	9.5	7.3	2.1	2.5	7.3	4.8
United States	7.1	6.6	1.6	3.2	5.5	3.3
Japan	21.8	15.6	10.3	10.6	10.5	4.5
Australia	8.9†	9.4	3.1†	3.3	5.6†	5.8
Austria	7.9	12.2	0.6	6.1	7.3	5.7
Belgium	15.8†	14.3	8.4†	8.4	6.9†	5.5
Denmark	11.4†	12.2	3.8†	5.2	7.3†	6.6
Finland	13.9†	13.9	4.4†	5.9	9.1†	7.6
France	...	11.2	...	5.0	7.1	5.9
Germany, West	9.8	8.8	1.9	2.9	7.7	5.7
Ireland	14.2†	14.7	3.7†	5.5	10.1†	8.7
Italy	24.2	10.4	11.8	4.4	11.1	5.7
Netherlands, The	10.5	12.5	2.2	4.4	8.1	7.8
Norway	9.4†	8.9	2.1†	1.3	7.2†	7.6
Sweden	7.2	15.0	0.5	8.5	6.6	6.0
Switzerland	8.4	8.2	0.2	1.4	8.2	6.7
United Kingdom	12.6	12.9	3.0	5.3	9.4	7.1
Average	12.0	11.4	3.7	4.9	7.9	6.2

*Second quarter 1973 over second quarter 1972.
†First quarter 1973 over first quarter 1972.
Source: Organization for Economic Cooperation and Development, *Main Economic Indicators* (October 1973).

Table IX. Money and Real Wages in Manufacturing and Consumer Prices: Third World

Changes over previous year (%)

Country	Money wages 1972	Money wages 1971	Real wages 1972	Real wages 1971	Prices 1972	Prices 1971
Barbados	...	8.2	...	0.6	11.8	7.5
Chile	...	42.2	...	18.4	78.0	20.1
El Salvador	...	2.1	...	1.8	1.7	0.4
Greece	9.6	8.8	5.1	5.6	4.3	3.0
Guatemala	0	0	−0.5	0.5	0.5	−0.5
Korea, South	17.8	20.0	5.1	5.7	12.1	13.5
Malawi	18.0	5.0	13.6	−2.9	3.9	8.1
Puerto Rico	7.0	6.3	3.7	1.9	3.1	4.3
Sri Lanka	...	2.2	...	−0.5	6.4	2.7
Venezuela	7.1	6.4	3.6	3.6	3.4	2.7
Average	9.9	10.1	5.1	3.5	12.5	6.2

Source: United Nations, *Monthly Bulletin of Statistics* (September 1973).

Table X. Weekly Hours of Work in Manufacturing

Country	1972	1971	Absolute change
Industrial countries			
Austria	36.4	37.0	−0.6
Canada	40.0	39.7	0.3
Finland	38.2	38.5	−0.3
France*	44.6	45.1	−0.5
Germany, West	42.7	43.0	−0.3
Ireland	42.2	42.1	0.1
Japan	42.3	42.6	−0.3
Netherlands, The	...	43.8	...
Norway	34.4	34.8	−0.4
Switzerland	44.4	44.6	−0.2
United Kingdom	44.1	43.6	0.5
United States	40.6	39.9	0.7
Czechoslovakia	43.7	43.7	0
U.S.S.R.	...	40.4	...
Average	41.1	41.3	−0.1
Third world			
El Salvador	...	47.5	...
Greece	44.6	44.1	0.5
Guatemala	46.1	46.3	−0.2
Korea, South	...	54.3	...
Puerto Rico	36.4	37.2	−0.8
Average	42.4	45.9	−0.2

*All activities.
Sources: United Nations, *Monthly Bulletin of Statistics* (September 1973); Organization for Economic Cooperation and Development, *Main Economic Indicators* (October 1973).

the fact that the high rates of income tax caused workers to benefit more from a reduction in hours than from an equivalent increase in pretax income, and in part it was also due to the formal incomes policies that prescribed a limit to increases in weekly wages without specifying anything about the hours of work required for that wage; this had the effect of permitting increases in hourly wages through a reduction of hours. On the other hand, as economic expansion encounters the constraint of labour shortages, the amount of overtime being worked rises, thus increasing weekly hours of work. The net effect depends on which force predominates. Economic expansion in the U.S., Canada, and the U.K. caused a rise in weekly hours in 1972, but in other industrial countries, whose economies were also expanding, reductions were of greater effect. (D. A. S. JACKSON)

See also Economics; Economy, World; Income, National; Industrial Review; Prices.

ENCYCLOPÆDIA BRITANNICA FILMS. *The Industrial Revolution—Beginning in the United States* (1968); *The Rise of Labor* (1968); *The Industrial Worker* (1969); *The Rise of Big Business* (1970); *The Progressive Era* (1971).

Energy

A shortage of energy became a problem of major proportions in many parts of the world during 1973. Especially hard hit were Western Europe and Japan. The United States suffered somewhat less, but the situation there was worsening at the end of the year.

The fuel supply problem was caused basically by the continuing rapid growth in the demand for energy, especially in the form of petroleum products, and the absence of a comparable increase in oil refining capacity. Oil consumption in Western Europe, for example, rose sevenfold from 1956 to 1973. The situation was greatly exacerbated late in 1973 when most of the petroleum-producing nations of the Middle East cut back production 5% in retaliation for U.S. support of Israel during the Arab-Israeli war in October. At that time, the Organization of Arab Petroleum Exporting Countries (OAPEC) embargoed oil shipments to the U.S. and The Netherlands, a ban later extended to Portugal, Rhodesia, and South Africa.

The seriousness of the problem was underlined by the fact that in 1973 Western Europe depended on the Middle East for more than 70% of its oil and Japan relied on the region for over 80% of its supply. The U.S. was much less dependent on imported oil, but the embargo nonetheless had a considerable impact. Late in December it was revealed that about 770 million gal. of oil had leaked into the U.S. from Arab countries since the beginning of the embargo, which undoubtedly helped ease the situation.

The shortages began to be felt early in the year in the U.S. During the summer season of vacation driving, local gasoline supplies dwindled in many parts of the country. In some localities service stations ran out of gasoline for several days at a time. Throughout the country, stations limited the quantity of gasoline a customer could purchase, shortened their hours of operation, or closed entirely on weekends. All users of propane and the "distillate" fuels—kerosene, jet fuel, diesel oil, and home heating oil—began to find them increasingly difficult to secure. By October the situation was so serious that the government instituted mandatory allocation programs for these fuels.

As fuel consumers, the electric utilities also experienced supply difficulties. Summer heat waves strained total capacity to the limit as the industry strove to keep up with record electricity use caused by air conditioning. By means of voltage reductions, more serious actions, such as the cutting off of power to selected areas, were averted. In the Pacific Northwest, however, an area that traditionally relied on hydroelectric power, a record drought reduced river flows to such low levels that service to large power users, such as aluminum plants, was severely curtailed and the state of Washington declared an emergency.

In response to these problems the U.S. government devoted much attention to energy throughout the year. In April Pres. Richard Nixon proposed legislation authorizing increased offshore drilling for oil and removed limitations on oil imports. He followed this in June with a 7% reduction in federal government energy consumption in the ensuing 12 months. In September Nixon urged states and cities to relax their air pollution regulations in order to permit the use of fuels with higher sulfur content and thus ease the supply tightness in home heating oil. He also stated that the licensing procedure for nuclear-power plants would be speeded up.

After the Arab oil embargo the U.S. government took stronger actions. Late in November President Nixon announced a 15% cut in supplies of gasoline to wholesalers and reductions of home heating oil that amounted to 15% for residences, 25% for commercial users, and 10% for industry. He urged retail gasoline stations to close from 9 P.M. Saturday to 12:01 A.M. Monday, and a drastic reduction in promotional, display, and ornamental lighting. As of Jan. 6, 1974, the nation would go on daylight saving time for two years, a move that was expected to conserve electricity. In December Congress passed legislation that required the states to lower their maximum speed limit to 55 mph or lose federal highway funds, a policy that caused considerable protest by truck drivers.

Gasoline rationing had been expected by many observers, but it was not imposed in the U.S. in 1973. On December 27 William Simon, director of the recently established Federal Energy Administration, announced that a standby gasoline-rationing system had been devised; it could be put into operation as early as March 1, 1974. At the same time, Simon increased the 1974 fuel allocations to commercial and general aviation over previously announced figures, and predicted an overall national fuel shortage of 2.7 million bbl. per day for the first three months of 1974. He had earlier asked U.S. motorists to limit themselves voluntarily to ten gallons of gasoline per week. (*See* UNITED STATES.)

Many critics in the U.S. believed that the energy crisis had been deliberately contrived by the large oil companies in the interest of greater profits. The firms denied this charge, but late in the year it appeared that the government was planning an investigation of their assets.

Conservation efforts began taking a toll on various sectors of the U.S. economy. Sales of standard-sized automobiles, which traditionally achieved relatively poor gasoline mileage, declined sharply in December. Consequently, the automobile manufacturers laid off thousands of workers for varying periods of time. Airlines were forced to cancel flights, resulting in layoffs of pilots and other personnel. An obvious victim was the tourism industry, which began to feel the effect of gasless Sundays.

Other nations were also compelled to enact fuel-saving measures. Sunday driving was banned in many parts of Western Europe, and Sweden began to ration electricity. The Japanese government in November asked the public and major industries to reduce their energy consumption by 10%. Prime Minister Pierre Trudeau announced in November that Canada would begin rationing petroleum at the wholesale level, and he urged his countrymen to reduce consumption voluntarily.

Perhaps the hardest hit nation was Great Britain. There, bans on overtime work by coal miners, electric power workers, and railway engineers were added to the oil cutback to create a condition of crisis. On November 13 Prime Minister Edward Heath declared a state of national emergency and reduced the supply of energy to the public and industry by 10%. A month later Heath underscored the severity of the situation by placing most of the nation on a three-day workweek as of Dec. 31, 1973. Television broadcasting hours would be shortened, and some industries were to receive only 65% of their previous allotment of power.

As would be expected, severe price rises accompanied these shortage conditions. During the year the oil-producing nations of the Persian Gulf (Iran, Iraq, Saudi Arabia, Kuwait, Qatar, and Abu Dhabi) increased the cost of a barrel of crude oil by 470% to over $11, and other oil countries followed suit. This caused prices of all petroleum products to rise, gasoline in the U.S. increasing to 45–55 cents per gallon at the year's end.

The high prices were expected to have a considerably adverse effect on the economies of the consuming nations. Large trade deficits were expected, and increasing unemployment was feared in Western Europe and Japan. Consequently, when OAPEC decided late in December to increase oil production 10% (retaining the embargo against the U.S. and The Netherlands), many of the consuming countries continued to impose austerity measures, in hopes of minimizing their trade deficits. Expected to be severely hurt by the higher prices were less developed countries that were beginning to industrialize and needed fuel but did not have the resources to pay the increased bill.

There were other developments of note in the international oil industry during the year. Despite agreements previously worked out specifying a timetable for gradual acquisition of 51% ownership by members of the Organization of Petroleum Exporting Countries (OPEC) of foreign producing companies within their borders, the pace of acquisition speeded up abruptly. In March Iraq and Iran nationalized all oil companies operating within their borders. In September Libya took over 51% of the ownership of all foreign operations in its territory, and in November Saudi Arabia announced plans to speed up the timetable for similar 51% ownership. In September the Canadian government announced a major change in national oil policy. Traditionally, Quebec and the Maritime Provinces had relied on Venezuela and the Middle East for their oil supplies; henceforth, they were to be supplied with Canadian oil via an extension of the pipeline from the Ottawa Valley to Montreal. The effect would be to curtail seriously the quantity of Canadian oil available for export to the U.S.

Large discoveries continued to be made in the British and Norwegian sectors of the North Sea, and the first offshore production in the Mediterranean Sea began from a field in Spanish waters. In February a new record-size tanker of 483,000 deadweight tons began operation, and it was announced that an order had been placed for a ship of 706,000 tons. Arrangements were completed for the beginning of a $400 million oil pipeline project to replace the Suez Canal.

A new precedent was set in technical cooperation between the U.S. and the U.S.S.R. with an agreement by the two countries to begin trading data, hardware, and research personnel in the field of magnetohydrodynamics (MHD). The purpose of the joint effort was to be to develop a practical application of the advanced MHD concept to the production of electricity from coal. (BRUCE C. NETSCHERT)

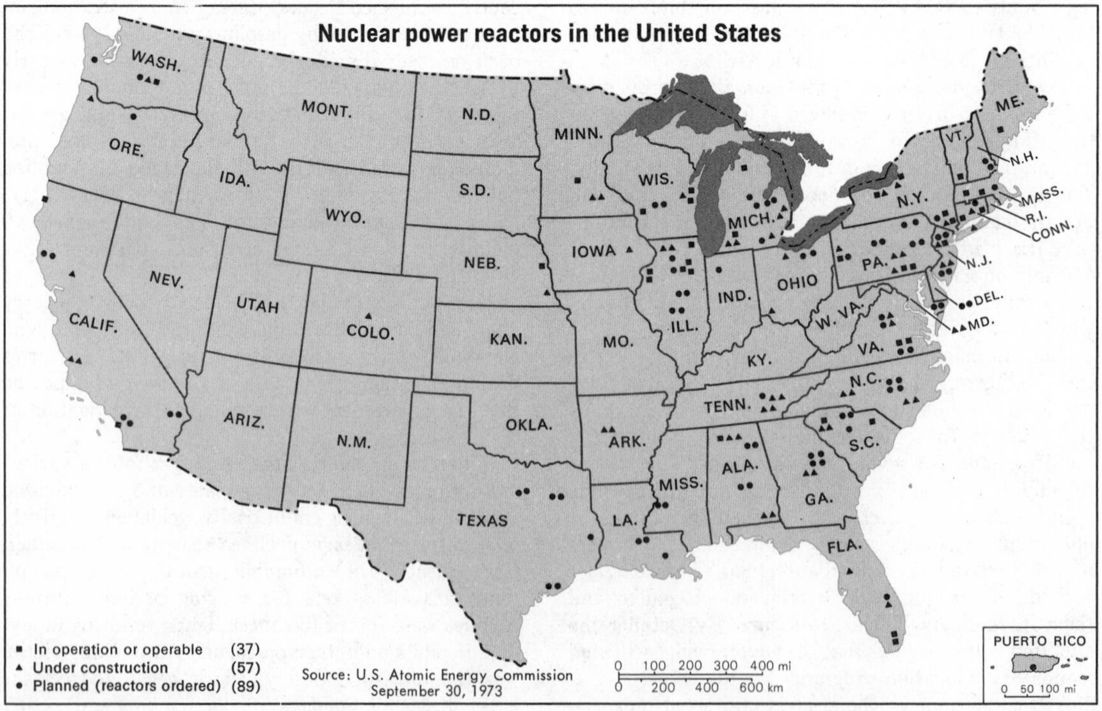

THE U.S. ENERGY CRISIS

By James Ridgeway

The energy crisis facing the United States may best be understood as operating on two levels. On the first are the recent temporary shortages of fuel oil, gasoline, and natural gas, exacerbated by the Arab oil boycott following the Arab-Israeli war late in 1973. These temporary dislocations suggest that fuels are harder to find, are located farther away from their end use, and are in greater demand than they used to be. Moreover, they should be taken as signals of what can happen if the situation continues.

For on the second level is a real long-term shortage of fuel that will probably become critical within the next century, because the amount of fossil fuel is finite and man is using it up quickly. The world's economy is based on fossil fuels—coal, oil, and natural gas. According to geologist M. King Hubbert, fossil fuels will last only a few centuries longer. Hubbert says that most of the earth's remaining coal will be extracted between 2000 and 2400, that 80% of all oil in the U.S. will be used up in 65 years from 1934 to 1999, and that for natural gas the peak production "will probably be reached between 1975 and 1980."

The fuel situation is exacerbated by the demand for energy. Production of electrical energy doubles every ten years. While the U.S. and Europe have dominated the world in consumption of fuels until recently, other countries in Africa and Asia are now beginning to demand an equal share of resources.

The production, distribution, and use of energy fuels increasingly is the business of the oil industry. Worldwide, seven companies control two-thirds of the oil and dominate the refining, transportation, and marketing of petroleum and natural gas products. In the U.S. petroleum companies produce a sizable amount of coal and uranium and are engaged in the manufacturing of chemicals, petrochemicals, nuclear fuel, and, in some instances, in the construction of nuclear power plants. Perhaps most important, the large petroleum companies are the only source of information available to the government on the extent of mineral fuel resources.

Demands by Producing Nations. In part, the "energy crisis" is a reflection of political and economic pressures that were exerted on the oil industry after 1950 and the industry's efforts to cope with resulting changes. After the Suez crisis of 1956, the Iranian Parliament wrote an oil law, which for the first time recognized and encouraged the concept of joint ventures between foreign producers and the producing country in the Middle Eastern oil fields. Until that time, the big oil companies essentially went into the Middle Eastern countries and paid the governments a small price or royalty for every barrel of oil they took out.

When other nations followed Iran's lead, the major Anglo-American oil companies realized that the rules of the oil game in the Middle East were changing. Not only would they be called on to pay more money, but increasingly they would also be asked to cede control of oil operations to the producing countries; those countries would then be asking for participation in the profits gained from marketing the products.

As a result of this changing situation, the oil industry determined to diversify its holdings. The major companies spread their search for oil into Southeast Asia, in the shallow seas off Indonesia, near Indochina, and extending south to Australia. They moved actively in Alaska, and then into the Canadian Arctic. They stepped up a campaign in the United States for increased drilling on the outer continental shelf. But most important, they bought into the coal industry, took a major position in uranium, and branched out into nuclear energy.

Natural Gas Shortage. Actually, the widely publicized "energy crisis" can best be understood as a series of crises, not all of them obviously connected to one another. Probably the most important involves the alleged shortage of natural gas. Gas supplies about one-third of all energy in the U.S. It is basically a clean fuel and because of the stiff air pollution standards formulated in the late 1960s came into great demand. In particular, electric utilities, which previously had burned air-polluting sulfurous coal, sought gas.

Most of the natural gas in the U.S. is produced by major oil companies from fields in the South and Southwest and is transported to market by interstate pipeline firms. In the future, most gas for the U.S. will come from wells located beneath the sea in the Gulf of Mexico off Louisiana.

The U.S. Supreme Court ruled in 1954 that the U.S. government, through the Federal Power Commission (FPC), must regulate the price that the interstate pipeline companies pay for natural gas to the industry producers. Subsequent attempts at regulation were resisted by the producers, who claimed that their economic incentive to drill would thereby be cut off. After another Supreme Court decision regulation efforts began in 1968, and by 1969 gas reserve figures published by the industry began to decline. Government attempts to investigate these figures were resisted by the industry, and in 1971 the FPC accepted the industry figures as truth, agreed that there was a gas shortage and an "energy crisis," and said that the price of gas should be made higher so as to offer additional incentives to companies that searched for new deposits. Thus, the price at the wellhead for gas off the shore of Louisiana was raised from 18½ cents per thousand cubic feet (Mcf) to 26 cents per Mcf. Statistics for 1972 suggest that the price increase had an unusual effect on the industry: more successful gas wells were reported in that year, but, oddly, gas reserves continued to decline.

In June 1973, James T. Halverson, director of the Bureau of Competition of the U.S. Federal Trade Commission (FTC), testified before U.S. Sen. Philip Hart's antitrust subcommittee that there was "serious under-reporting" of reserves by natural gas producers to the Federal Power Commission. He went on to say that the procedures for reporting reserves by the American Gas Association "could provide the vehicle for a conspiracy among the companies involved to under-report gas reserves."

While the FTC experts were reporting their findings to Senator Hart, the FPC was granting yet another price rise to the natural gas producers, one that would lift the price from 26 to 45 cents per Mcf. Both the FPC and the White House also sought to persuade Congress and the courts to deregulate the price of gas. If those moves succeeded, the price of gas would rise even higher, possibly doubling within a few years. It is worth pointing out that as of late 1973 the FPC's incentive program had more than doubled the price of natural gas in two years without any indication that the industry had discovered new supplies of gas.

But the price rise affected the structure of the industry in other ways. As the price of natural gas climbed, the oil companies began to take a more active interest in synthetic gas, made from naphtha or coal. If the price of natural gas rises to a high enough level, synthetic gas becomes profitable and is likely to be introduced to ease the "energy crisis."

In the U.S. the major synthetic projects involved changing coal into a gas that can be intermingled with natural gas in the pipeline system. The technology is complex with certain problems unresolved, but the profitability from the producers' point of view seems to be clearly established. Therefore, these coal gasification projects, about 200 of which were planned west of the Mississippi, were expected to go forward. Coal gasification

---

James Ridgeway's most recent book is The Last Play: The Struggle to Monopolize the World's Energy Resources *(1973).*

requires large quantities of strip mine coal and of water, along with the construction of expensive plants. Consequently, it will lead to large-scale development of the huge untapped coal resources in the western mountain states with an attendant decline in their existing agricultural economy and a tremendous strain on the already scarce water resources of the region.

What began, therefore, as an effort by the oil industry to ward off federal regulation of the gas business may now result in a more wide-ranging reorganization of the energy business. The use of coal to make gas will result in an enormous relocation of capital resources throughout the nation. It will require moving the coal industry out of Appalachia, leaving behind stripped hills, impoverished people, and the United Mine Workers, an important political adversary. (The UMW is poorly organized in the West.) Billions of dollars in capital investments will be needed for pipelines and synthetic-gas plants, and the basic economy of the mountain states will be changed from agriculture to mining.

Gasoline and Fuel Oil. If the controversy over natural gas is at the base of the energy crisis, for most people the "crisis" was translated into higher prices for gasoline in the summer and fuel oil in the winter, and a threat of scarcity in both cases. These shortages stemmed in part from the embargo placed on oil shipments to the U.S. by the Middle Eastern nations after the Arab-Israeli war in October, but also seemed to involve distribution problems. The industry says that it does not have the refinery capacity to meet demand, and that it has been blocked by environmentalists and others in attempts to expand existing refineries or build new ones. It also claims that there was a shortage of crude oil, again because of demand. This shortage was eased by elimination of oil import quotas in 1973 but again became acute after the Middle East embargo.

Independent refiners claimed that their plants were working at below capacity because the major oil companies would not sell them crude oil. Independent gasoline station owners complained that while the major companies refused to sell them gasoline because of the shortage, they were setting up their own discount brands of gasoline to compete with the independents.

In general, it appears that fuel scarcities may crop up here and again over the next few years because of distribution problems. Also, it seems clear that the price of fuel will continue to rise. In part that is because of the growing reliance by the U.S. on Middle Eastern oil at a time when oil exporters were raising prices and the Arab countries were using oil as a political weapon. It is also true because the oil companies will be seeking to make greater profits from refining and marketing than they once did since their traditional profits from production of crude oil were sharply reduced by the producing nations.

Solutions. Technical developments conceivably can ease the "crisis." The U.S. Atomic Energy Commission (AEC) and the administration of U.S. Pres. Richard Nixon take the position that safe, inexpensive supplies of nuclear energy offer a solution to the crisis. But nuclear power has not grown as fast as the AEC had predicted. In part, that is due to attacks and lawsuits brought by conservationists; their actions help to postpone building the plants, thereby adding to the eventual costs. In addition, the AEC is faced with serious scientific questions concerning catastrophic accidents should the radioactive core of a power plant melt and break out of its protective covering.

The U.S. government initiated a program through the Tennessee Valley Authority (TVA) to build and test a breeder reactor, which supposedly will supply large quantities of inexpensive nuclear power and conserve uranium. But construction of the plant has been delayed, and environmentalists protest its construction because of its danger.

While the federal government without question will promote the development of atomic energy, it seems that the real political and economic consequences of the energy crisis will be seen in a growing reliance on coal as a base for synthetic fuel. That will lead to a virtual reorganization of the energy business, and a change in the economy of the western mountains as well as Appalachia. The U.S. has an estimated 400 years' worth of coal left, most of it in the mountain states.

In addition, the oil industry wants to drill for oil in the Atlantic Ocean off the east coast of the U.S. In his budget message in the spring of 1973, President Nixon for the first time proposed to increase the lease sales on the outer continental shelf, scheduling for first consideration a tract off the east coast of Florida. This marks the first time that exploration and production of oil and gas will take place in the Atlantic Ocean. Observers expect that the government, under pressure from the oil industry, will allow increased drilling activity in the Atlantic, opening up areas off Delaware, Maryland, the Carolinas, and Georgia. The likelihood of finding gas and oil is good because Mobil discovered large gas wells at Sable Island off the east coast of Canada.

While the western mountains and Appalachia will be changed by the energy crisis, so too will the Atlantic seaboard. If oil and gas are discovered, a new industry will take its place in the already crowded industrial corridor of the eastern seacoast.

Perhaps the most hopeful, though little emphasized, technical solution to the energy crisis lies in solar energy—a safe, nonpolluting, plentiful, and inexpensive source of energy. Solar power was used during the early part of this century for heating water in southern and western areas of the U.S. and is in use today in Israel, Australia, and Japan. A December 1972 report by the U.S. National Science Foundation and National Aeronautics and Space Administration (NASA) says that solar energy can be introduced into widespread use today. The report estimated that solar-generated power could replace half the energy now used to heat and cool buildings, and concluded that "solar energy is received in sufficient quantity to make a major contribution to the future U.S. heat and power requirements." If successful programs could be established, building and heating systems could reach public use in 5 years, cooling systems in 6–8 years, synthetic fuels made from organic materials in 5–8 years, and electricity production in 10–15 years.

Another potential source of clean, safe energy, geothermal power, now supplies electricity to parts of the U.S., Soviet Union, Japan, New Zealand, Mexico, Italy, and Iceland. Power plants utilizing underground supplies of steam and hot water to generate electricity have been located over large reservoirs of hot water, such as those beneath the Imperial Valley floor in California. With advances in deep-drilling techniques, man may be able to tap geothermal energy anywhere on earth, producing pollution-free energy at low costs.

It is unlikely that any single technical solution will solve the energy crisis—whether it be the development of nuclear energy, solar power, coal gasification, or another source. There seems to be considerable agreement within the U.S. Congress, the federal administration, and even by leaders in the oil industry that the long-term situation can only be dealt with by a reorganization of the nation's political economy. That probably means initiating an energy conservation program while at the same time setting off on a vigorous research effort aimed at developing sources of power that can replace fossil fuels.

In 1972 the staff of the President's Office of Emergency Preparedness produced a plan for an energy conservation program which indicated that large amounts of energy could be saved if freight were handled by trains rather than trucks, if the growth of the airline industry were curtailed, if better insulation standards were applied to new buildings, and if mass transit were introduced into urban areas. It seems likely that the U.S. will begin to move soon in one or another of these areas. Mass transit slowly is beginning to win favour in Congress, where its development in the past was blocked by rural, Southern committee members who were not interested in the problems of large cities. But a changeover in handling freight and a curtailment of the airline business will require arduous pressure if they are ever to be accomplished.

COAL

World hard coal production in 1972 amounted to an estimated 2,208,000,000 metric tons, an increase of 24 million over 1971. As in 1971, there were increases in the U.S.S.R., China, Poland, and Australia. U.S. coal production regained its upward momentum after being interrupted by a prolonged strike at the end of 1971.

In Western Europe production dropped 13.5%, but Eastern European production (including the U.S.S.R.) showed an increase of 2.9%. China, with an output estimated at 400 million metric tons, an increase of 20 million, remained the world's third largest producer. New deposits announced in 1973 were thought to bring China's reserves up to 1.5 trillion metric tons.

U.S.S.R. Production increased more rapidly in 1972 than in previous years, with a gain of 15 million metric tons, to 500 million metric tons, over 30% of it produced by surface operations. A record 219 million metric tons was produced in the Donets Basin region. Lignite production remained at about the same level as 1971, at 155 million metric tons.

New facilities, with an annual capacity of 18 million metric tons of ungraded coal, came into production during the year. The U.S.S.R., with estimated exploitable reserves exceeding 500,000,000,000 tons, planned to provide 1,000,000,000 metric tons annually by the turn of the century.

United States. In 1972, 590 million short tons of bituminous coal and lignite were produced, an increase of almost 7% over the 1971 level of 552.2 million short tons, despite labour disputes and work stoppages. Anthracite production continued to decline with a reduction of about 19% to 7.1 million short tons.

With other fuels in increasingly short supply, it appeared likely that many environmentalist restrictions on the mining and use of coal would be eased. Discovery of a large low-sulfur coal deposit amounting to an estimated 200,000,000,000 metric tons in the Powder River Basin in Wyoming and Montana was announced, and several electric utilities expressed interest in building the world's largest power station complex to develop the deposit. Research into the gasification of coal continued, with several large projects announced during the year. Exports in 1972 remained at about the same level as 1971, at 57 million short tons.

European Economic Community (EEC). In 1972 the five EEC coal-producing nations suffered further reductions in output. With a total of only 145.8 million metric tons of hard coal, the decline in production within the Community averaged 12.1%. Belgium produced 10.5 million metric tons, 459,900 less than in 1971. France showed a decrease of 3,250,000 metric tons, and Italy fell by 105,300 to 151,000 metric tons. The Netherlands, still planning to phase out production by 1975, suffered a 22% reduction to 2.8 million metric tons. West German production fell more than 7% to 102.8 million metric tons.

United Kingdom. Production recovered rapidly after the seven-week miners' strike, which ended in February 1972 and accounted for a loss of 26 million long tons. Output per manshift reached a record level of 48.6 cwt. in the last week of the 1972–73 financial year, and the average of 45.8 cwt. for the whole year was a 9% improvement over the previous 12 months.

National Coal Board (NCB) deep-mined output was 129.8 million long tons, compared with 109.2 million tons in the previous 12-month period. Open-pit operations produced 10.1 million long tons, a slight gain over the previous year and a level that the NCB proposed to maintain for some time.

Despite continued restrictions on coal exports in the early months of the year, coal shipments in 1972–73 increased 200,000 long tons to 2.3 million long tons. Solid fuel imports dropped from 5.5 million long tons in 1971–72 to 3.5 million long tons in 1972–73.

In an effort to extricate the NCB from the difficult financial situation created by the miners' strike and the resultant pay increases, the government announced plans to inject nearly £1.2 billion into the coal industry. Eight collieries closed during the year due to the exhaustion of economic reserves, and manpower in the industry decreased by 10,400 during 1972–73. In November 1973 miners started a ban on overtime. (*See* UNITED KINGDOM.)

An inrush of water at Lofthouse Colliery on March 21, 1973, resulted in the deaths of seven men. The fatality rate for 1972–73 showed a reversal of the previous downward trend, though casualties per 100,000 manshifts were slightly below 1971–72.

Poland. Hard coal production again rose in 1972, reaching 151 million metric tons, an increase of 4% over 1971. Lignite production reached 38 million metric tons and was expected to expand to about 100 million metric tons by the mid-1970s. Hard coal production was planned to expand to 167 million metric tons by 1975. Poland remained second only to the U.S. in coal exports with 33 million metric tons of hard coal and 4.1 million metric tons of brown coal and lignite, an increase of 3 million metric tons over 1971.

India. In 1972 coal production increased to 73.5 million metric tons, compared with 69.2 million in 1971. The industry remained beset by financial and technical difficulties. Nationalization of 464 coal mines producing noncoking coals was announced in January 1973. This followed the earlier nationalization of 214 coking mines in 1972, the takeovers being steps toward the complete nationalization of India's approximately 800 mines. By the end of the five-year plan in 1978–79 the coal requirements of the country were expected to rise to 141 million metric tons. Nationalization seemed one way of providing the capital investment needed to achieve this goal.

Japan. During 1972 production dropped by 16% to 28.1 million metric tons of hard coal, and it remained cheaper to import. Imports for 1972 at 49,277,985 metric tons were 2.3 million metric tons more than in 1971, but less than the record 50.2 million metric tons of 1970. Imports from Australia, Japan's chief supplier in 1972, were 20,560,000 metric tons of bituminous coal, almost 4 million metric tons more than in 1971. Imports from the U.S., Japan's second largest supplier, fell from 18,489,565 to 16,544,045 metric tons.

Concern was expressed during 1972 over the rapid decline of Japan's indigenous coal industry. The Coal Mining Council, an advisory body to the Ministry of International Trade and Industry, submitted a report on long-term coal policy, which proposed that a minimum demand of 20 million metric tons be created.

Africa. Of an estimated output of 62.7 million metric tons in 1972, 58,440,000 were produced by South Africa and 2.8 million by Rhodesia. South African bituminous production of 57.1 million metric tons showed a modest gain of 280,000 metric tons, but anthracite production fell by more than half a million to 1,840,000 metric tons. The anxieties expressed in 1971 over the actual amount of workable reserves were still to be resolved. New contracts with West Germany and Japan amounted to about three million metric tons a year for South Africa.

Australia. Coal exports expanded sharply during the fiscal year 1971–72, rising to 21.4 million long tons, a gain of 15.3% over the previous year. Japan received 17.9 million long tons, up by 2 million tons. The bulk of the remaining exports were to Western European countries, with the U.K. the biggest customer. Queensland's exports exceeded those of New South Wales for the first time. Total production of black coal was 53 million long tons, up by 4.7 million long tons from the 1971 figure, and brown coal production from Victoria reached 24 million long tons, one million long tons over 1971. Domestic consumption of coal and lignite increased by 820,000 long tons to 32 million long tons. To satisfy Australia's growing export trade, several large mines were brought into production in 1972.

Canada. Production of all types of coal in 1972 reached a record 21 million short tons, representing a 13.5% increase over the 1971 figure. Canada's exports reached a record 9 million short tons, 7.8 million of this to Japan, despite transport difficulties. British Columbia showed a gain of 25% to 6 million short tons, stimulated by the Japanese export trade. Alberta recorded a modest increase, and the other three coal-producing provinces, New Brunswick, Nova Scotia, and Saskatchewan, remained at about their 1971 levels.

In a survey of Canada's energy reserves published in 1973, the country's coal deposits were estimated at 120,000,000,000 short tons. Prospects for the industry were good, with annual production expected to reach 23 million short tons in 1973 and 30 million short tons by 1975. (R. J. FOWELL)

ELECTRICITY

By 1973, in a world consuming in excess of five trillion kw-hr. of electricity annually, nuclear power was capable of providing just 582,000,000,000 kw-hr., nearly half of that within the U.K. Consumption of electricity rose in mid-1972, and world production in 1972 was 6.5% higher than in 1971. Eight countries that annually produced more than 100,000,000,000 kw-hr., the U.S., the U.S.S.R., Japan, West Germany, the U.K., Canada, France, and Italy, accounted for 76% of the world's total.

Conventional thermal stations still produced approximately 75% of the world's electricity, with an additional 23% being provided by hydroelectric installations. Coal-burning power stations were still predominant, although more stations switched to fuel oil. However, even before events in the Middle East played havoc with fuel costs, a kilowatt-hour cost more to produce in an oil-burning power station than in a nuclear power station.

Nuclear Electric Power. Nuclear energy provided far less electricity than had been predicted earlier. Delays in the commissioning of power stations were one reason for this, and public opposition another. Switzerland, the U.S., and Sweden met with most difficulty in getting nuclear power stations, thereby running the risk of a crisis in electricity production in the fairly near future. The Swiss government even prepared plans to ration electricity should nuclear power stations not be in use by 1975.

Nuclear electricity seemed the only hope of providing the massive quantities of power

Installed Capacity and Production of Electric Power in Selected Countries, Dec. 31, 1971

Political division	Hydroelectric power: Operating plants: Installed capacity (000 kw.)	Hydroelectric power: Operating plants: Production (000,000 kw-hr.)	Total electric power: Installed capacity (000 kw.)	Total electric power: Production (000,000 kw-hr.)
World	...	...	...	5,222,500
Afghanistan*	185.4	321*	210.9	326*
Algeria†	340	322	639	1,901
Angola	212	605	320	742
Argentina	709	1,528	7,103	23,623
Australia	3,864	11,766	14,436	57,099
Austria	5,658	16,778	8,229	28,748
Belgium	66*	156	6,769*‡	31,597§
Bolivia	171†	...	252†	830
Brazil	10,244	43,274	12,670	50,988
Bulgaria	826	2,170	4,481	21,016
Burma	103*	...	258*	541‖
Cameroon	193	1,139	221	1,169
Canada	30,601	160,984	46,676‡	216,472§
Chad‖¶	—	—	29.5	48
Chile	1,068	4,397	2,133	8,524
Colombia	...	...	2,700*	8,750*
Costa Rica	182	1,035	250	1,148
Cuba	—	—	941*‖	4,072*‖
Czechoslovakia	1,531	2,684	11,696	47,237
Denmark	9	24	5,057	17,540
Ecuador	105	440	328	1,050
Egypt	2,448*‖	4,705*‖	4,357*	7,591*
El Salvador	108‖	712	207	743
E hiopia‖	91.4	...	137.4	585♀
Finland	2,285	10,499	5,398	20,842
France	15,459	48,726	41,494‡	148,998§
Gabon‖	—	—	16.0♁	114
Germany, East	679	1,251	13,339‡	69,420§
Germany, West	4,842	14,054	53,976‡	253,792§
Ghana	912*	2,909	...	2,944
Greece‖	1,040	2,646	2,695	10,615
Guatemala	...	...	177†	780*
Honduras	...	...	92□	310*
Hong Kong‖¶	—	—	1,573	5,574
Hungary	20	94	2,932	14,990
Iceland	284‖	1,540‖	394◇	1,602▲
India*	6,386	25,258	16,126‡	60,382§
Indonesia*‖	312	1,225	657	2,084
Iran	800‖	2,679	2,807	8,309
Ireland	219*‖	705*‖	...	6,334
Israel	—	—	1,410‖	7,639
Italy	15,280	40,019	36,050‡◇	124,860§▲
Jamaica	16*‖	126‖	356†♀	1,637
Japan	20,176	86,849	76,480‡◇	385,612§▲
Ken/a‖	71	319	186	555
Korea, South	340‖	1,319‖	2,908	10,952
Lebanon‖	246*	839	421*	1,375
Liberia	37.5*	242*	224.0*	650
Libya‖¶	—	—	168	508
Luxembourg	932‖	1,069‖	1,157	2,329
Malagasy Republic	...	129‖	58.0†	266
Malaysia:				
Malaya	293‖	1,046	866*	3,574
Sabah¶	—	—	46.4‖	100‖
Sarawak¶	—	—	46.2	121
Mauritius	26.0	51	68.7	148
Mexico	3,320	14,518	7,873◇	31,322▲
Morocco	300*‖	1,498‖	466*	2,085
Mozambique	114*‖	242	355*	551
Netherlands, The¶	—	—	11,447‡	44,904§
New Zealand‖	3,271	12,971	4,093◇	15,194▲
Nicaragua	...	...	170.2*	649
Nigeria	...	1,574	805	1,820
Norway	12,783*	62,647	12,910*	62,930
Pakistan*‖	666	2,914	2,398‡	7,068§
Panama	15.2*‖	82*‖	198.4*	956*
Peru	...	...	1,685*	5,324*
Philippines	549*	2,524‖	2,176*	7,111‖
Poland	820	1,920	14,814	69,887
Portugal	1,937	6,146	2,735	7,815
Rhodesia	705	5,622	1,192	6,800
Romania	1,905	4,495	8,334	39,454
Singapore‖¶	—	—	704	2,585
South Africa	...	...	...	52,717
Spain	11,054	32,283	19,018‡	61,917§
Sri Lanka (Ceylon)	195	834	281	900
Sweden	11,065	52,027	16,118‡	66,549§
Switzerland	9,630	29,488	10,890‡	32,785§
Syria	—	—	418	1,049
Thailand	451*‖	1,787*‖	1,336*	4,977‖
Tunisia	28‖	50‖	269	887
Turkey	876	2,501	2,645	9,781
Uganda‖	150	813	154	817
U.S.S.R.	133,448	126,099	175,365‡	800,360§
United Kingdom	2,158	4,311	72,119‡	256,098§
United States	56,586	269,580	386,701‡◇	1,717,521§▲
Uruguay‖	236	1,470	503	2,289
Venezuela	...	...	3,298	13,589
Vietnam, South‖	...	...	531*	1,215*
Yugoslavia	4,265	15,644	7,925	29,509
Zaire	...	...	...	3,718
Zambia	180*	...	364*	1,168

1970. †1969. ‡Includes nuclear (in 000 kw.): Belgium 11; Canada 1,570; France 2,301; Germany, East 75; Germany, West 962; India 420; Italy 670; Japan 1,336; Netherlands 55; Pakistan 125; Spain 460; Sweden 12; Switzerland 700; U.S.S.R. 2,031♀; U.K. 5,607; U.S. 8,687. §Includes nuclear (in 000,000 kw-hr.): Belgium 57*; Canada 3,988; France 8,743; Germany, East 404; Germany, West 5,812; India 2,417*; Italy 3,365; Japan 8,010; Netherlands 405; Pakistan ...; Spain 923*; Sweden 90; Switzerland ...; U.S.S.R. ...; U.K. 26,937; U.S. 37,899. ♀Provisional. ♁1967. □1968. ◇Includes geothermal (in 000 kw.): Iceland 2; Italy 402; Japan 31; Mexico 4; New Zealand 192; U.S. 203. ¶Thermal only. ‖Public sector only. ▲Includes geothermal (in 000,000 kw-hr.): Iceland 12; Italy 2,664; Japan 236; Mexico 1; New Zealand 1,174; U.S. 548.

Source: United Nations. (F. H. SKELDING)

needed to satisfy ever increasing consumption. Demand was not likely to diminish, and even the oil companies showed an interest in the opportunities offered by the nuclear industry. In Italy the Ente Nazionale Idrocarburi (ENI) operated a nuclear power station, and in the U.S. Tenneco joined with Westinghouse Electric Corp. to construct floating nuclear power stations in Florida. Gulf, another U.S. oil company, began building high-temperature reactors (HTR). Gulf also linked up with Europe, showing an interest in a West German firm looking into the construction of an HTR, and, together with various French enterprises, joining a group that planned to begin construction of an HTR in June 1974.

Graphite gas and advanced gas reactors still provided more than 50% of total nuclear electric generating power. HTRs and fast-breeder reactors would not be widely available for 15 or 20 years. Pressurized-water (PWR) and boiling-water reactors (BWR) had been greatly improved in the U.S., which, with enrichment factories built during World War II for the production of nuclear weapons and now converted for peacetime use, had large amounts of enriched uranium for use at home and elsewhere.

France and West Germany made an agreement with the U.S.S.R. for supplies of enriched uranium, but supplies were not assured since such agreements were often temporary. Uranium enrichment plants in the U.S. would not fully supply the needs of the West until 1980 or 1982. Supplies of enriched uranium would be vital in the future, and it seemed that Japan might be asked to help out. Western Europe would achieve independence only when one or several enrichment factories to meet the bulk of its needs functioned on the continent.

Two possible enrichment techniques were under study: gaseous diffusion and centrifugation. In June the Association for Enrichment by Centrifugation was formed by the U.K., The Netherlands, West Germany, Australia, Belgium, Canada, France, Italy, Japan, Spain, and Sweden. Those countries wishing to experiment with gaseous diffusion had earlier formed themselves into another group, known as Eurodif, and planned to construct a factory using techniques developed at Pierrelatte, in France. France, Italy, Belgium, Spain, the U.K., West Germany, and The Netherlands were all involved, but in 1973 the U.K., The Netherlands, and West Germany left the group.

Euratom negotiated with the U.S. to purchase sufficient enriched uranium to charge ten power stations of 800 to 1,000 Mw. capacity. However, the U.S. conditions, which included a stipulation that payment should be made some ten years in advance of delivery of the fuel, proved too restricting and demanding. Euratom then approached the French Commissariat of Atomic Energy (CEA) for supplies. Agreement was reached, but it seemed unlikely that the factory at Pierrelatte would be able to supply the quantities required, and some other solution was needed to Europe's problems. To this end, France, West Germany, Belgium, Spain, Italy, and Switzerland formed a research association in May.

In the U.S. 34 reactors with a total capacity of 37,453 Mw. were ordered in 1972. Sales to September 1973 showed a slight drop, with a total of about 35,000 Mw. Five companies combined to order six identical reactors, with a total capacity of nearly 7,000 Mw., from Westinghouse, thus saving about 20% on the cost price.

Also in the U.S. Westinghouse was chosen to build the first prototype fast-breeder reactor, of 350 to 400 Mw. capacity, to be located at Oak Ridge, Tenn. However, pressure from a group of scientists caused the project to be abandoned on the ground that it might prove detrimental to the environment and to the health of the population.

In the U.K. the remaining two nuclear reactor construction companies amalgamated in 1973 to form a single group. The new company was capable of competing with the U.S. giants, but the problem of choosing a reactor for future use was no nearer a solution. However, in April the Central Electricity Generating Board (CEGB) was given authority to build several types of reactor at Sizewell, in Suffolk.

In France the five reactors under construction, with a total capacity of 4,000 Mw., were all of the pressurized-water type. For financial reasons Électricté de France (EDF) had not accepted the first proposals made by the French company that held a license to build light boiling-water reactors. However, agreement was reached in June, when EDF placed on order two BWRs, each of 995-Mw. capacity. A 925-Mw. PWR had been on order since the beginning of the year. The 250-Mw. prototype fast-breeder reactor at Marcoule, named Phénix, received 1,400 tons of sodium in January, thus assuring its cooling.

With nuclear power capacity of 2,200 Mw., West Germany was third in line in Europe, after the U.K. (5,300 Mw.) and France (2,700 Mw.). However, several nuclear power stations were under construction, and when those began operating West Germany could well take the lead. In Italy, where three nuclear power stations were in use in 1973, a fourth was being built at Caorso on the Po River, and bids were out for a fifth. Three nuclear power stations were in operation in Spain, where six PWRs were put on order in 1972.

Japan's sixth nuclear reactor was under construction at Shimana, near Hiroshima, and in the U.S.S.R. a nuclear power station of 440-Mw. capacity began operations on the Kola Peninsula—the first to function north of the Arctic Circle.

Thermoelectricity. Conventional thermal power stations still provided three-quarters of the world's electricity. Renewed interest was shown in coal, and several U.S. enterprises proclaimed their intention of replacing projected nuclear facilities with coal-burning stations, which could be put into commission far more quickly. In the U.K. the government announced plans to subsidize the coal mining industry to increase coal consumption in power stations to 65 million tons a year. In West Germany 75% of the electricity was produced by stations burning combustible solids. Several stations to burn lignite were under construction in Greece, and in Australia the Victoria State Electricity Commission decided to reinforce the lignite-burning equipment in the Yallourn region.

Hydroelectricity. The Iron Gate on the lower course of the Danube River was probably the last massive hydroelectric project to be completed in Europe. Production was to be shared equally between Romania and Yugoslavia.

In April 1973 Brazil and Paraguay agreed to the construction of Sete Quadras on the Paraná River. It was not certain whether Argentina, which had other projects in the region, would object to the choice of site at Itaipu. In New South Wales, Austr., the second group of Tumut 3 (250 Mw.) went into operation in October 1972, and four additional identical groups were planned.

In France the three groups of the Le Châtelard-Vallorcine power station, part of the Franco-Swiss Emmasson project, went into use. Annual production of the station was designed to be 324 million kw-hr. The

AUTHENTICATED NEWS INTERNATIONAL

Scientist William Brown plugs a diode into model of an antenna array, designed to receive microwave energy beamed to earth from an orbiting satellite. The model was developed as part of a NASA-funded program to find ways to capture solar energy and convert it into electrical current.

West Khantayka power station on the Taymyr Peninsula (440 Mw.), with an annual production of about 2,000,000,000 kw-hr., came into operation in the U.S.S.R.

(LUCIEN CHALMEY)

GAS

In the U.S., lack of incentive to explore for natural gas reached general public attention in 1973 by its effect—a shortage of the fuel itself—but then was overshadowed by shortages of oil and oil derivatives. As in years past, a move toward deregulation of the natural gas industry was begun and, indeed, was set in motion by the Federal Power Commission (FPC) in September for a six-month period. This move to add incentive for exploration was immediately challenged in the courts on the ground that it would lead to increased prices, the dilemma the industry had been facing for several years.

Deregulation had been proposed earlier in the year for gas discovered from the beginning of 1973. A doubling of the 26 cents per thousand cubic feet (Mcf) regulated price was estimated by proponents, a cost to U.S. consumers of $50 billion over 20 years. The FPC did double the regulated price on newly discovered Permian Basin gas to 35 cents per Mcf from 16.5 cents. Permian accounts for 15% of U.S. gas.

Two previous attempts by Congress to deregulate gas prices had been vetoed by Pres. Harry S. Truman in 1948 and by Pres. Dwight D. Eisenhower in 1956. A threat to the regulatory powers of the Natural Gas Act of 1938 was also squelched by the U.S. Supreme Court in 1954.

The principle on which deregulation is opposed is that the fuel is a basic commodity and must be regulated to assure a fair price to the consumer. Otherwise, its use at a fair price may be endangered by the cornering of the market by a few proprietors. The argument has been that the regulated fair price has been too low and therefore unprofitable.

Fogging the air in 1973 were further indications that the actual amount of available gas may well have been concealed. A Federal Trade Commission (FTC) study revealed that reported discoveries on company books were as much as ten times the amount reported to the American Gas Association (AGA), whose estimates had previously been relied upon by the FPC. An FTC attempt to open company gas books publicly was being considered in the courts.

Consumers also faced the situation wherein the AGA continued to delay for a fourth year approval of a device that would cut consumer gas bills by one-quarter to one-third. The device, approved in Canada, requires for practical reasons AGA sanction before contractors consider themselves legally safe in making installations.

As to government policy, Congress beat down an attempt to allow all five FPC commissioners to come from industry and leave consumers unrepresented at the agency. The White House emphasized the urgency of the fuel shortage, establishing in December the Federal Energy Administration to deal with the problem. The public was called on to conserve fuel in a variety of ways; the main effect on gas consumption was the requirement to turn down thermostats.

Better foreign relations brought about agreements with the Soviet Union for the U.S. to import $10 billion—two billion cubic feet (Bcf) daily—of natural gas to both U.S. coasts in the last quarter of the century. U.S. firms involved in the agreement included Occidental Petroleum, El Paso Natural Gas, Texas Eastern, Tenneco, and Brown & Root, Inc.

A similar import contract with Algeria—doubled over 1972 to 2 Bcf daily—ran into opposition from environmentalists strongly opposed to the building of a mile-long pier and gas terminal at Cove Point on Chesapeake Bay to receive the fuel. Environmentalists also continued to challenge the reversal of court rulings by Congress that had the effect of allowing pipeline construction at a cost to the environment. Environmentalists failed to prohibit a nuclear explosion aimed to free 300 Mcf of gas at Rio Blanco, Colo. A similar experiment in 1969, Project Rulison, was found by the University of Colorado to have been an economic failure that contaminated the environment.

Future potential reserves were estimated by the Potential Gas Committee at 1,146 Tcf (trillion cubic feet), though some estimates reached 6,600 Tcf. AGA reported 266.1 Tcf of proved reserves Jan. 1, 1973, down 4.6% in a year. The U.S. Department of the Interior estimated that deregulation would increase supplies up to 2.2 Tcf in 1975 and 5–8.1 Tcf in 1985, with 1980 prices at 36–76 cents per Mcf.

Canada hedged its participation in the U.S. market by citing U.S. exploitation and domination. Indeed, it made moves of retaliation by attempting to move into U.S.-owned resources and to limit Canadian production. For the first time, the U.S. imported more than 1 Tcf from Canada.

(JOSEPH J. ACCARDO)

In the U.K., North Sea gas production reached record levels again in 1973, with average daily usage reaching almost 3.5 Bcf a day. More than 90% of all gas supplied in Britain in 1973 was based on North Sea supplies, and at the end of the year about ten million customers had had their appliances converted to use it directly. The remaining 3.5 million gas users were supplied with town gas manufactured largely from natural gas. Conversion was still proceeding at a high level and was expected to be virtually complete by 1976.

On the gas supplies front, the biggest news during the year was an agreement be-

Electrical Power Production of Selected Countries, 1972

By source

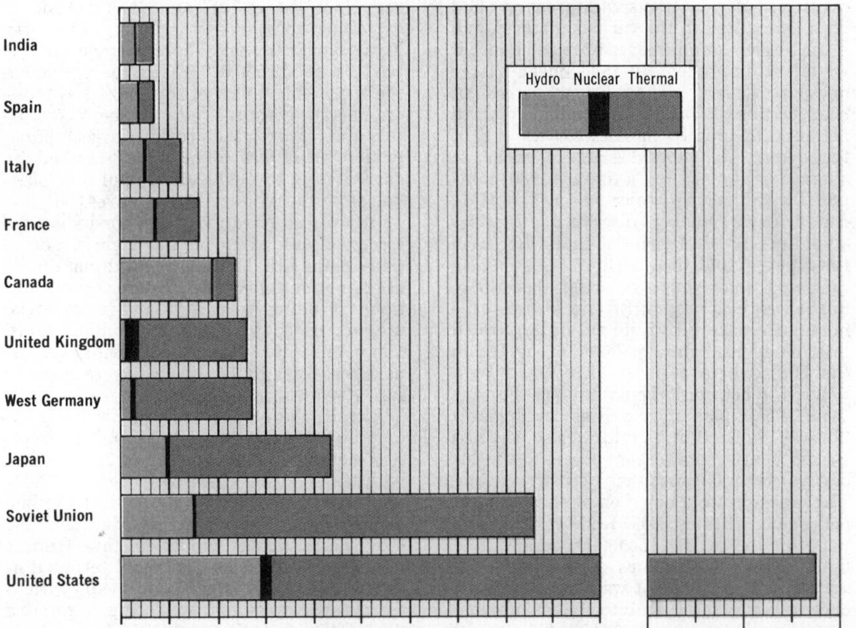

Sources: United Nations, *Monthly Bulletin of Statistics; World Energy Supplies, 1961-1970.*

tween the British Gas Corp. and the largely French-owned Total Group for the entire output of the latter's Frigg field. One of the largest discoveries yet made in the North Sea, the field straddles the median line dividing the British and Norwegian continental shelves. The agreement was awaiting Norwegian government ratification at the year's end. Production from the field was expected to build up to at least 1.4 Bcf by the end of the 1970s.

On shore, large developments were necessary in order to connect the new supplies into the existing transmission system. A terminal was to be built at St. Fergus near Peterhead, Aberdeenshire, where the gas would be brought ashore, treated, and passed into new pipelines to enter Britain's national network. Altogether, about 750 mi. of new pipelines were to be laid.

Negotiations were proceeding at the end of the year with several exploration groups that had found gas in the southern or northern basins of the North Sea. Moreover, there was optimism that the increased pace of exploration would reveal further discoveries of natural gas, either associated with oil or on its own. Reinforcing this optimism, the first commercial gas find to the west of Britain, 20 mi. off Cork, was announced at the end of the year. It is in the Irish sector of the continental shelf, and discussions were proceeding between the successful group and the Irish government on its exploitation. Further exploration was expected in 1974 on the U.K. side of the Irish Sea, and interest was being expressed in the Western Approaches of the Atlantic Ocean, the English Channel, and the area east of the Shetlands.

Success from all this activity would be very welcome. Earlier in the year the British Gas Corp. announced that it was having to turn away large industrial fuel users seeking gas supplies and that it might not be able to renew some existing contracts when they expired. This situation had been reached because all the North Sea gas expected under existing supply contracts with producers had been committed in the various markets, and if these sales commitments were to be met it would be imprudent to take on any large new customers. The Frigg agreement changed this situation and did allow forward planning to proceed in sales for the end of the decade. It allowed sales to reach an average of about 5 Bcf a day by 1980, compared with the long-projected 4 Bcf by 1975. But without further discoveries, supplies would necessarily remain at that 5 Bcf level for a period and then decline.

Should that situation arise, then there might well be a need in Britain for the technology to make substitute natural gas. Such technology had already found a market in the U.S., where a dozen plants had been ordered to help ease the natural gas shortage there. These plants, as well as earning millions of dollars in royalties, also enabled British contractors to gain access to the lucrative U.S. chemical-engineering market. The processes were based on naphtha, a light petroleum distillate, as feedstock, though naphtha itself was in such short supply as to limit further installations of this kind. Research and development was therefore being encouraged in the U.K. into the use of other feedstocks, heavier oils, and coal.

The work on coal seemed to represent the wheel going full circle as far as gas supplies were concerned. At the end of the 1950s almost all gas in Britain was based on coal, but by 1973 only a handful of coal-gas works were left, and all were scheduled to shut down as production stations. One, however, gained a new role, as an international centre for research into the use of coal for gas making. There, 2.5 million cu.ft. of substitute natural gas a day, based on coal as raw material, were being made for the first time. Interest in the process was stimulated by the energy crisis.

The world's largest liquid natural gas (LNG) plant was officially opened in the first half of 1973. The £100 million complex was in Brunei and was designed to supply 5 million tons of LNG per year to Japan over the next 20 years. The first shipment was made at the end of 1972.

In Australia the government decided to build a national pipeline grid to supply natural gas to all the mainland states, the Capital Territory, and the Northern Territory. The grid was to be linked to the Cooper Basin field, the Palm Valley field in central Australia, and the offshore Northwest Shelf fields. More than 5,000 mi. of pipeline were to be built at a cost of A$600 million to A$1 billion.

Agreement was reached on the development of New Zealand's big Maui field, off Taranaki Province in the North Island, after three years of negotiations. The field was discovered in 1969, is ten miles offshore, and has estimated reserves of 5 Tcf. In the short term all the gas was to be used to generate electricity, starting in 1978.

Gas production in the Soviet Union in 1973 was expected to reach 235,800,000,000 cu.m., 6.7% over the previous year. Production was expected to rise in the fields in Soviet Central Asia, in Tyumen (West Siberia), and in the Komi area of the far north. But these increases would be partly offset by the continued decline in some old-established and geographically more convenient regions, such as the northern Caucasus and the Ukraine. Production from the Orenburg region, within the Ural-Volga area, was due to start during the year and build up to approximately 15,000,000,000 cu.m. a year.

Established Soviet Union reserves were put at 20 trillion cu.m. Most are in outlying areas, presenting severe production and transportation difficulties. The Soviets were actively enlisting U.S. and Japanese aid in exploiting these reserves during the year. Most significant was the agreement to export up to 20,000,000,000 cu.m. a year to the U.S., using a fleet of some 20 LNG tankers operating from a port in the Vladivostok area. There, the world's largest liquefaction plant was to be built, supplied by gas traveling through 2,000 mi. of new pipeline from the Yakutsk gas reserves.

Iran placed export markets for its gas reserves, estimated to be the highest potentially in the Middle East, at third place in its list of national priorities. Internal consumption, including industrial and commercial use, accounted for about 120 million cu.ft. a day, but this was expected to rise over the next ten years to 1.6 Bcf a day to account for 37% of the country's needs.

Algeria, the first country in the LNG export business, continued to expand its overseas markets during the year. A 25-year deal with the U.S. was expected to begin in 1976, with the full contract volume of 10 billion cu.m. a year being reached the following year. Nine tankers would operate from a vast new liquefaction plant and terminal at Arzew. An even larger agreement with a European consortium was being negotiated during the year. It would involve 15,500,000,000 cu.m. a year, over a 20-year period, going to West Germany, France, Belgium, Austria, and Switzerland. Deliveries were due to start in 1978.

World primary energy requirement figures, issued by the Oil Committee of the Organization for Economic Cooperation and Development, showed that the need for gaseous fuels was expected to increase by 6.2% per year during the 1970s. The 923 million metric tons (oil equivalent) in 1970 were expected to rise to 1,697,000,000 in 1980. Western Europe's share was forecast to rise from 70 million to 231 million tons at an average annual rate of 11.9%, North America's from 598 million to 870 million tons (3.8% per year), Japan's from 4 million to 14 million (14.5% per year), and the rest of the world from 251 million to 582 million (8.8% per year). (x.)

PETROLEUM

In 1973, another eventful year for the oil industry, the consuming countries experienced a tightening supply-demand relationship. The gravity of the situation was disputed and the reasons for it varied, but the reality of an energy "gap" if not a "crisis" was admitted and was emphasized by the ever increasing cost of crude oil and products.

The problem had several aspects. The failure of U.S. domestic production to match increasing consumption led to growing dependence upon the Middle East supplies, coupled with a lack of refining capacity to cope with the increased demand. By late 1973 the U.S. depended on imports for one-third of its oil supplies. The second aspect involved the increasing use of oil as a political weapon, particularly in the context of the Arab-Israeli confrontation. In October, with war raging in Sinai, the Arab oil-producing states banned all exports to the U.S.

Meeting in Geneva in May, ministers of the Organization of Petroleum Exporting Countries (OPEC) and representatives of more than 20 Western oil companies reached agreement on a new formula for adjusting oil prices in accordance with currency parity changes. For the future, prices would be adjusted monthly, instead of quarterly as previously, in the light of the daily movement of currencies against one another. For those countries whose currencies were revalued against the dollar the agreement made little difference.

Another major agreement concluded during the year involved Iran and the oil consortium. The existing Consortium Agreement was voluntarily abrogated, and the National Iranian Oil Co. assumed responsibility for all internal operations with a guarantee that prices for its oil and products would not fall below those achieved under the earlier participation arrangements. In return, the companies composing the consortium were guaranteed a privileged position as buyers of Iranian oil with "an assurance of security of supply" for 20 years. In October, Iraq nationalized the assets of U.S. companies in the Basrah Petroleum Co. Ltd. Libya concluded agreements with some oil companies for a 51% participation, and in October nationalized those companies that did not voluntarily accept nationalization. Saudi Arabia indicated in November that it planned to speed up the timetable for acquiring 51% ownership in the oil companies operating within its borders.

As a result of OPEC demands made in September, the 1971 Teheran Agreement—hoped to produce stability for five years—would be revised. Arabian Light 34°, which cost $1.80 per barrel at the end of 1970, had risen to $3.066 per barrel in August 1973, and Libyan 40° rose from $2.20 per barrel to $4.582. Pressures on prices, supplies, and security prompted discussions among the ma-

BEHRENDT—HET PAROOL, AMSTERDAM/ROTHCO

jor consuming countries, with Japan taking a leading part.

Outside the Middle East, operating conditions in the North Sea stretched existing technology to its limits as exploration reached 600 ft. below sea level. Estimates in June told of a possible production of 70 million–100 million metric tons in the 1980s. A new field with a potential output of 300,000 bbl. per day was found in December. Indonesian crude oil production increased significantly to 394.8 million bbl.

World production in the first half of 1973 increased by approximately 9.7% more than in the corresponding period of 1972. The increase was the highest ever recorded in volume, and production averaged 55 million bbl. daily. Middle East production rose by 19%.

Reserves. At the beginning of 1973 the total world proved and probable oil reserves increased to 672,700,000,000 bbl., compared with 641,800,000,000 bbl. for the previous year. The Western Hemisphere share was 85,500,000,000 bbl., falling to 12.6% of the total, and that of the Eastern Hemisphere was 587,200,000,000 bbl., a rise to 87.4%. The Middle East accounted for the largest share of the world reserves, 355,300,000,000 bbl., 53.3%, while the U.S.S.R., Eastern Europe, and China further decreased to 14.9%, and the U.S. to 6.2%.

Production. During 1972 world crude oil production increased by 5.4% to 52,925,000 bbl. a day. The increase in 1971 had been 5.6%. The Middle East continued to dominate production with an increased share of 34.2%, 17,975,000 bbl. a day, including a 27.8% increase from Saudi Arabia to 5,735,000 bbl. and only a 10.9% increase from Iran to 5,050,000 bbl. U.S. production, at 9,450,000 bbl. a day, dropped to 18% of the world total. Venezuelan production was 3,285,000 bbl. a day in 1972, 6.6% of the total, a decrease of 9% from 1971. Nigerian production, at 1,815,000 bbl. a day, 3.4% of the total, showed only an 18.9% increase over 1971, compared with 40.2% in the previous year. Libya registered the greatest percentage drop in production, 19.8%, to 2,210,000 bbl. a day. Canada, Trinidad and Tobago, Indonesia, and South America recorded increased production.

Consumption. World consumption of petroleum in 1972 was 52,695,000 bbl. a day, an increase of 8% over 1971. Japanese demand, at 4.8 million bbl. a day, increased 8% over the previous year. The U.S. remained the largest single consuming nation at 15,980,000 bbl. a day in 1972, a 7.9% increase over 1971 and 30% of the world total. Western European consumption in 1972 was 14,205,000 bbl. a day, an increase of 7.4% over 1971 and 27.1% of the world total. Spain's increase at 14.2% and France's at 11.2% were above the general average but in line with their respective general annual increases over 1967–72. The largest increase took place in Southeast Asia, which at 16.9% was double the general average.

Nearly two-thirds of European imports and 80% of Japan's requirements came from the Middle East. Two-thirds of the Caribbean exports continued to go to the U.S. In 1972 the U.S. consumed 6,960,000 bbl. a day of gasolines, 3,935,000 bbl. of middle distillates, and 2.3 million bbl. of fuel oil. In Japan fuel oil was the major product consumed, whereas in West Germany and France the consumption of middle distillates predominated.

Imports of oil into the U.S. from the Middle East continued to rise: 475,000 bbl. a day in 1972, compared with 390,000 bbl. a day in 1971 and 175,000 bbl. a day in 1970. This increased dependence caused a serious shortage in the U.S. when Middle Eastern supplies were curtailed during and after the Arab-Israeli conflict in October 1973.

Refining. World refining capacity in 1972 was 59,425,000 bbl. a day, an increase of 7.1% over 1971. The capacity of the Western Hemisphere was 21,670,000, Western Europe 17,140,000, the Middle East 2,415,000, and the U.S.S.R., Eastern Europe, and China 9,550,000 bbl. a day. Capacity in the U.S. continued to decline, accounting for 22.6% of the world total.

Transportation. The world tanker fleet at the beginning of 1972 totaled 193.9 million tons deadweight (dw.), a slightly reduced increase of 18.6% over 1972. The pattern of ownership showed little variation from the previous three years. Liberia with 50.2 million tons dw. had 26% of the total, followed by the United Kingdom with 13%, Japan with 12%, and Norway with 10%. New building in progress and on order at the end of 1972 totaled 120.7 million tons dw., of which 75% was accounted for by vessels of 205,000 tons dw. or greater.

Petrochemicals. The availability and cost of feedstock pressed heavily on the petrochemical industry. After a period of expansion in Europe, overproduction led to a decline in realized prices. By midyear, however, a renewal of demand put considerable pressure on ethylene production, and attempts were made to harmonize future investment with anticipated demand.

(R. W. FERRIER)

See also Engineering Projects; Industrial Review; Mining; Transportation.

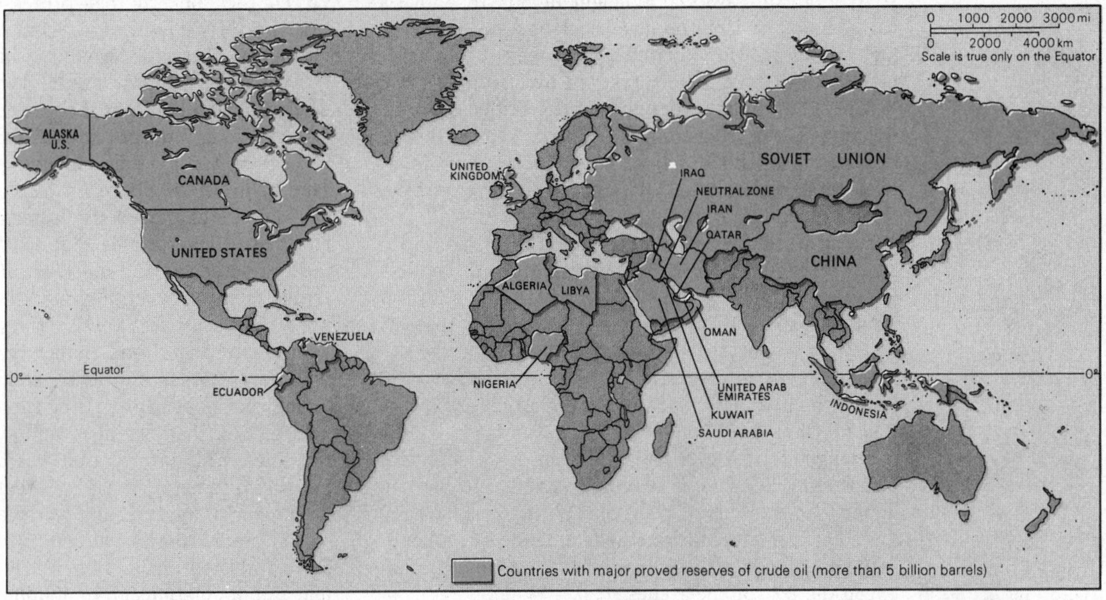

Engineering Projects

Bridges. *Suspension Bridges.* In 1973 Turkey's Bosporus bridge, designed by Freeman Fox & Partners of London and built by an Anglo-West German consortium, opened to traffic at the end of October. With a 3,524-ft.-long central span, it was the fourth longest suspension bridge in the world and the longest outside the United States. Crossing the Bosporus between Ortakoy in the west and Beylerbeyi in the east, and joining the Asian and European sections of Istanbul, the bridge became the first link between Asia and Europe south of the Black Sea in nearly 2,500 years, since Darius I of Persia lashed galleys together to form a bridge across the Bosporus.

The Turkish General Directorate of Highways anticipated that approximately 22,000 vehicles per day, carrying 100,000 people, would use the bridge, with its six traffic lanes and two pedestrian footways, and that it would have a substantial effect on urban commuting patterns. The entire cost, about $36 million, had been financed by the Turkish government, which hoped to recoup its investment within four to six years.

In the U.K., work began on foundations for a bridge over the River Humber, near Hull, which would have a central suspended span of 4,580 ft. This would be the longest span suspension bridge in the world, taking first place from the Verrazano-Narrows Bridge in New York.

Cable-Stayed Bridges. In Austria, two cable-stayed bridges over the Danube River were put into service. The Linz bridge had four spans, two of 197 ft., one of 236 ft., and one of 705 ft. The 748-ft. suspended span of the Hainburg bridge, near the Czechoslovakian frontier, carried a 44-ft.-wide roadway. From the top of its 253-ft.-high pylon the view extended to Bratislava, where a similar bridge had recently opened.

In Belgium construction was completed on the first cable-stayed bridge across the Meuse, between Heer and Agimont. The deck, concrete on twin steel girders, crossed a 407-ft. main span.

Roadway Girder Bridges. In West Germany, work continued on the 2,888-ft. Jagsttalbrücke, with a main span of 492 ft., scheduled to be in service by 1974. The bridge was designed to carry the Heilbronn–Würzburg expressway at a height of 262 ft. above a valley north of Heilbronn. A steel box girder, 17 ft. high and 35 ft. wide, carried a 98-ft.-wide orthotropic plate with the overhang supported by struts.

More traditional in design was the bridge over the Arkansas River, near Little Rock, Ark. About 5,000 ft. long and with a main span of 430 ft., it was formed of two metal girders set 33 ft. apart and covered by a concrete deck.

Other Metal Bridges. In the U.S., a metal arch with a record (1,700 ft.) span to cross a gorge on the New River east of Charleston, W.Va., was under construction. In Japan, a bowstring bridge with a span of 640 ft. was put together near Tokyo, loaded onto a pontoon, and transported across approximately 250 mi. of the open Pacific to its final destination in the Bay of Ohnours. There, advantage was taken of the outgoing tide to lower the bridge onto its supports. The deck, which was of striking elegance, included an upper boom of two transversely inclined arches, joined at their summit like the two handles of a handbag, and a lower ribbing that acted as a tie beam between the feet of the arches.

Marking continued preference in the U.S. for large triangulated structures, work began on a viaduct with a total length of 1.6 mi. to cross the port at Baltimore, Md. The main structure had three spans of lattice girders, the outer spans 720 ft. long and the central one 1,200 ft. long.

Prestressed Concrete Bridges. In the U.K., the Tyneside Bridge, crossing the River Tyne, with a main span of 541 ft., would be when completed the largest cable-stayed railway bridge in prestressed concrete to date. In Austria, the Melk Bridge across the Danube River, 50 mi. W of Vienna, opened to traffic in December 1972. The bridge had two large central spans, each 623 ft., between two bankside spans of 253 ft. each. It consisted of a box girder, constructed by successive corbeling of voussoirs molded on the spot, which varied in height from 35 ft. on the piers to 16 ft. at the centre of the span.

In the Dominican Republic, work continued on the largest prestressed span in the Americas (623 ft.), which crossed the Río Higuamo between Santo Domingo and San Pedro de Macoris. The deck was formed of a triple-web box girder, with a 59-ft.-wide plate carrying four traffic lanes.

When very large deck areas were required, the use of prefabricated voussoirs saved both money and time. The bridge over the Sofia River, in the northwest of the Malagasy Republic, with a deck divided into three sections by two articulations (to facilitate expansion), was constructed in this manner. The method was also used in two structures in France. The Calix viaduct at Caen, 3,400 ft. long, had a main span of 512 ft. The 53-ft.-wide plate was carried on two independent box girders 32 ft. high at the supports. The Saint-Cloud viaduct near Paris crossed the Seine, following a curve 1,180 ft. in radius, and then overpassed the roadway along the Left Bank. The deck, a four-web box girder 67 ft. wide and 12 ft. high, had the appearance of a long ribbon unwinding (length about 3,600 ft.) and freed a main span of 334 ft. over the river.

In Canada, the bridge over the Bear River, near Digby, N.S., used a similar method of construction. Remarkable for the complexity of its ground plan, this bridge had eight spans, two of 200 ft. and six of 265 ft., and was of constant height throughout.

(ROBERT CHAUSSIN)

Buildings. In 1973, leading architectural engineers voiced the concern that professionals in their field were not giving adequate attention to environmental problems. These concerns were identified with a need to evaluate a broad range of factors relating to the design of buildings and their orientation and location. For example, students at the University of Florida's College of Architecture and Fine Arts worked with the faculty in an extensive project to evaluate from an environmental perspective alternative land uses for all areas of the state of Florida. They analyzed existing and potential land use in the state in terms of such things as the characteristics of the soil, water supply, waste disposal, air pollution, existing and planned highways, mineral and timber resources, recreational and park needs, industrial and economic developments, and population. Using these and other relevant data inputs, they classified and evaluated all areas of the state. This information was then drawn together in composite maps, and all of the information was programmed for analysis and retrieval.

Writing in the *Architectural Forum,* Richard G. Stein reported on his research into the energy problem and its relationship to building design, orientation, and location. He estimated, for example, that by the elimination of sealed windows and the use of untreated outdoor air during temperate seasons, the heating and air conditioning needs in office buildings could be reduced substantially. He observed that the energy used for all lighting purposes in office buildings could be cut 50% and noted also that changes in structural design could produce significant savings in energy.

Fred Durbin reported in *Architecture Plus* that in the U.S. the use of appropriate measures could save 15–25% on energy consumption in the existing 68 million buildings and from 35–50% in new buildings without sacrificing the quality of their usefulness. In his analysis he stressed the importance of examining the increase in initial costs of construction in relation to the building's total lifetime costs. While initial construction costs of a building may be higher as a result of an energy-saving design in the construction features, lower lifetime costs will result. Durbin also suggested the use of total energy systems instead of inefficient utility plants, pointing out that such systems were already in use in several locations in the U.S. These included a housing development of 5,680 units in New York, a 24-story housing complex in Brooklyn, an apartment complex in Missouri, and garden apartments in Indianapolis.

Some of the plans for urban renewal in 1973 revealed the broad interdisciplinary nature of such undertakings and also the need to obtain approval from many diverse groups in order to accomplish the planners' goals. In *Architecture Plus,* there was a report on a plan by a young architect named Ada Karmi-Melamede to convert Second Avenue in New York City's Manhattan into a beautiful underground city of shops, boutiques, restaurants, and pedestrian walkways and malls. The planning of this project encompassed goals that were to take advantage of the city's population density, integrate existing transportation, and create a multipurpose environment where residential, commercial, and business functions could interact in a coordinated way. Sketches of her plan revealed the many factors that would have to be evaluated by all of the people involved in the decision-making process.

Plans to consider not only the physical environment but also the cultural and social aspects of the environment were revealed in a comparatively modest project in Far Rockaway, a community located near Kennedy Airport in New York City. The designer sought to build a school that would be appropriate to the neighbourhood of two- and three-story houses and six-story apartment buildings. The architect, Victor Lundy, wanted the buildings to provide the students with the opportunity to relate to the sky, the sun, the time of day, and the weather. He designed a structure that provided classroom light in part by skylights that he created by offsetting each floor from the one below. He also sought to keep the four-story structure "in scale with the 'village' atmosphere of the neighborhood and site."

While essentially all cities throughout the world were experiencing the continued construction of tall buildings designed to meet pressing space needs, it was obvious that these structures were failing to meet many other needs. There were extensive reports during the year of large skyscrapers nearing completion that could only add to the environmental problems of population congestion and the wasteful use of resources. These enormous structures were designed to create a pleasant environment within at great expense to the environment without. (CARTER C. OSTERBIND)

Dams. *Europe.* The Spanish Soria arch dam (height 427 ft., crest length 487 ft., volume 277,000 cu.yd.) on the Soria River was completed in 1972. Dams under construction in Spain in 1973 included: the Guadalhorce-Guadalteba rockfill dam on the Guadalhorce River; the Cobre rockfill dam on the Arroyo Rejondillo; the Mediano concrete gravity dam on the Cinca River; the Tous rockfill and concrete dam on the Júcar River; the Riaño double-curvature arch dam on the Esla River; the La Baells double-curvature arch dam on the Llobregat River; and the Lanuza double-curvature arch dam on the Gallego River.

The Sainte-Croix arch dam (height 312 ft., crest length 453 ft., volume 66,700 cu.yd., storage 623,577 ac-ft.) on the Verdon River in France was under construction. In Switzerland, the Gigerwald arch dam (height 482 ft., crest length 1,401 ft., volume 602,000 cu.yd., storage 27,154 ac-ft.) on the Tamina River and the Mapragg concrete gravity dam (height 245 ft., width at foundation 180 ft., storage 3,821 ac-ft.), also on the Tamina downstream from the Gigerwald dam, were under construction.

In the United Kingdom, work proceeded on the Scammonden earthfill dam (height 260 ft., crest length 2,050 ft., volume 5,630,000 cu.yd., storage 6,840 ac-ft.) on the Black Brook, Leicestershire. The Tarnita arch dam (height 292 ft., crest length 784 ft., volume 170,000 cu.yd., storage 57,510 ac-ft.) on the Somesu Cald River was under construction in Romania, while in Bulgaria the Belmeken Lake dam (height 328 ft., storage 110,000 ac-ft.) neared completion. Water from the reservoir would supply a chain of hydroelectric stations with a total capacity of 2,000 Mw.

In the Soviet Union, construction continued on the Nurek earth and rockfill dam (height 1,040 ft., crest length 2,390 ft., total volume about 76 million cu.yd., storage 8.4 million ac-ft.). The reservoir was to supply a power station of 2,700-Mw. capacity, and the third of its generators went into operation early in 1973. The plant was scheduled to be completely operational in 1977.

UPI COMPIX

Two levels of traffic patiently await the ceremonial opening of the Sembonmatsu Bridge, in Osaka, Japan, Oct. 31, 1973. The eyeglasses-shaped structure is more than 1,000 ft. long and 120 ft. above mean water level.

Asia. In India, construction proceeded on the Thein concrete gravity dam (height 482 ft.) on the Ravi River. The Rampanga earth and rockfill dam (height 397 ft., crest length 2,051 ft.) on the Kalagarh River in Uttar Pradesh neared completion. It would be the highest such structure in India.

In Thailand work continued on the Sirikit earth and rockfill dam (height 338 ft., volume 13,097,500 cu.yd., storage 7,296,429 ac-ft.) on the Nan River. Japan had several dams under construction, including the Takase and Nanukura rockfill dams (height 577 and 410 ft., respectively) on the Takase River, both of the centre-core type, which would create upper and lower reservoirs of the Takase pumped-storage plant (1,280-Mw. capacity). Built in an earthquake zone, each dam had a maximum core thickness of half its height, with an allowance for sufficient water tightness and stability during earthquakes.

North and South America. There were more than 28,000 dams in the United States by 1972. Construction began on the Oregon rock and earthfill dam (height 227 ft., crest length 3,700 ft. including the gates spillway) on the upper Rogue River, about 26 mi. NE of Medford, Ore. Two generators were to provide a capacity of 4,900 kw. Also under construction was the Chivor rockfill dam (height 778 ft.) on the Bata River, Colombia, to be completed in 1975. In Canada, the Bighorn rockfill dam (height 300 ft., crest length 1,400 ft.) on the North Saskatchewan River in Alberta was completed late in 1972. The dam incorporated an extensive concrete cutoff wall reaching 200 ft. below the river bed and extending 25 ft. above this level to form part of the impervious central core.

In South America, construction continued on the Marimbondo earthfill dam (height 295 ft., crest length 11,970 ft., volume 24,328,000 cu.yd., storage 5,184,000 ac-ft.) on the Río Grande in Brazil and on the Collipulli earthfill dam (height 246 ft., crest length 1,180 ft., volume 2,485,000 cu.yd., storage 210,780 ac-ft.) on the Malleco River in Chile.

Australia. The Talbingo rockfill and earth-cored dam (height 535 ft., crest length 2,303 ft., volume 19 million cu.yd., storage 7,496 ac-ft.) on the Tumut River in New South Wales was inaugurated in November 1972. The reservoir fed the Tumut 3 power station. Construction started on the Dartmouth earth and rockfill dam (crest length 2,300 ft., volume 20.3 million cu.yd., storage reservoir 3 million ac-ft.) on the Mitta Mitta River, in northeast Victoria, scheduled for completion in 1978.

Africa. In Morocco, the Mansour Eddahbi arch dam (height 230 ft., volume 209,300 cu.yd., storage 455,285 ac-ft.) on the Oued Draa (watercourse) and the Youssef Ben Tachfine earthfill dam (height 297 ft., crest length 2,198 ft., volume 4,840,000 cu.yd., storage 252,030 ac-ft.) on the Oued Massa were completed in

Major World Dams Under Construction in 1973*

Name of dam	River	Country	Type†	Height (ft.)	Length of crest (ft.)	Volume content (000 cu.yd.)	Gross capacity of reservoir (000 ac-ft.)
Auburn	American (N. Fork)	U.S.	A	685	4,150	6,000	2,300
Balimela	Sileru	India	E	230	15,200	29,600	3,100
Beas	Beas-Indus	India	E	435	6,400	45,800	6,600
Bilanadi Tank	Bilanadi	India	EG	105	2,320	26,907	51
Cabora Bassa	Zambezi	Mozambique‡	A	561	994	667	51,900
Carters Lake	Coosawattec	U.S.	E	450	2,050	14,300	475
Chirkeyskaya	Sulak	U.S.S.R.	A	764	1,109	1,602	2,252
Chivor	Bata	Colombia	ER	778	919	14,126	661
Cochiti	Rio Grande	U.S.	E	251	28,200	41,100	513
Emosson	Barberine	Switzerland	A	590	1,818	1,400	182
Fierze	Drin	Albania	E	518	1,312	916	2,124
Gran Suarna	Navia	Spain	A	499	1,150	882	567
Hasan Ugurlu	Yesilirmak	Turkey	ER	574	1,427	11,827	874
Idikki	Periyar	India	MA	561	1,201	609	1,182
Ilha Solteira	Paraná	Brazil	EG	291	20,300	35,741	17,172
Inguri	Inguri	U.S.S.R.	A	892	2,513	4,967	891
Itaipu	Paraná	Brazil-Paraguay	EG	558	26,717	36,624	23,511
Jocassee	Keowee	U.S.	E	437	1,950	11,600	1,160
Keban	Euphrates	Turkey	RG	679	3,598	19,600	25,110
Kölnbrein	Malta	Austria	A	650	1,969	2,093	162
Las Portas	Camba	Spain	G	498	1,587	977	609
Libby	Kootenai	U.S.	G	446	2,240	4,200	5,850
Marimbondo	Grande	Brazil	EG	295	11,970	24,328	5,184
Melones, New§	Stanislaus	U.S.	ER	625	1,600	15,970	2,400
Mratinje	Piva	Yugoslavia	A	722	879	971	713
Nader Shah	Marun	Iran	R	574	1,050	9,940	1,313
Nagarjuna Sagar	Krishna	India	EG	407	15,257	73,575	9,165
Nurek	Vakhsh	U.S.S.R.	E	1,040	2,390	75,864	8,424
Oymapinar	Manavgat	Turkey	A	607	1,181	739	243
Patia I	Patia	Colombia	R	755	1,540	26,000	11,200
Sayano-Shushenskaya	Yenisei	U.S.S.R.	A	794	3,504	11,916	25,353
Sterkfontein	Nuwe Jaanspruit	South Africa	E	292	10,007	20,274	2,156
Tachien	Tachia	Taiwan	A	591	951	562	188
Takase	Takase	Japan	EG	577	1,115	13,996	62
Tarbela	Indus	Pakistan	ER	486	9,000	186,000	11,100
Toktogul	Naryn	U.S.S.R.	A	705	1,476	3,480	15,800
Ukai	Tapi	India	EG	226	16,165	33,375	6,089
Ust-Ilim	Angara	U.S.S.R.	EG	344	11,695	11,382	48,100
Warm Springs	Dry Creek	U.S.	E	318	2,999	32,438	245
Zeyskaya	Zeya	U.S.S.R.	G	377	2,318	3,139	55,452
MAJOR WORLD DAMS COMPLETED IN 1972 AND 1973*							
Charvakskaya	Chirchik	U.S.S.R.	ER	551	2,506	24,983	1,620
Dworshak	Clearwater (N. Fork)	U.S.	G	717	3,287	6,500	3,453
Gokcekaya	Sakarya	Turkey	A	525	1,542	850	737
Jayakwadi	Godavari	India	E	120	32,493	15,409	2,110
Kanev	Dnepr	U.S.S.R.	E	82	52,950	49,520	2,125
Kapchagay	Ili	U.S.S.R.	E	164	7,741	10,338	22,761
Khantaika	Khantaika	U.S.S.R.	RE	213	21,058	2,452	16,743
Krasnoyarsk	Yenisei	U.S.S.R.	G	407	3,493	5,685	59,425
Mica	Columbia	Canada	R	800	2,600	42,000	20,000
Reza, Shah Kabir	Karun	Iran	A	656	1,247	1,570	2,351

*Having a height exceeding 492 ft. (150 m.); or having a total volume content exceeding 20 million cu.yd. (15 million cu.m.); or forming a reservoir exceeding 12 million ac-ft. capacity.
†Type of dam: E=earth; R=rock fill; A=arch; G=gravity; MA=multiple arch.
‡Mozambique is a Portuguese possession.
§Replacement of present dam.

(T.W. MERMEL)

1972. In Zaire, the Shongo buttress dam (height 172 ft., crest length 1,969 ft., volume 321,000 cu.yd.) on the Zaire River was inaugurated in November 1972. Construction continued in Mozambique on the Cabora Bassa arch dam (height 561 ft.) on the Zambezi River, which was founded on the gorge's excellent gneiss rock. A power station on the right bank was designed to house five generating units. The Kossou earth and rockfill dam (height 190 ft., crest length 4,922 ft., volume 6,890,000 cu.yd.) on the Bandama Blanc River in the Ivory Coast was completed. In Zambia, work started on the Itezhitezhi earth and rockfill dam (height 213 ft., volume 10,725,000 cu.yd.) on the Kafue River, part of the second stage of the Kafue River development project and scheduled for completion in 1978. (ALDO MARCELLO)

Roads. The main road-building development during recent years was the international cooperation in the planning and building of great continental networks of roads linking cities of one country to those of another. Latest plans were for the Trans-African Highway, which was to stretch across six countries, from Lagos in Nigeria on the west coast to Mombasa, Kenya, on the east. The road would pass through Cameroon (660 mi.), Central African Republic (820 mi.), Kenya (570 mi.), Nigeria (530 mi.), Uganda (410 mi.), and Zaire (960 mi.). The Trans-Sahara Road (1,800 mi.) was also planned, and three-quarters of the Trans-West African Highway (total length 6,300 mi.) was already open.

The Asian Highway Network, more than 40,000 mi. in total length, included 41 routes, with about one-quarter of the total planned mileage in India. Countries linked by the network were Afghanistan, Bangladesh, Burma, Cambodia, India, Indonesia, Iran, Laos, Malaysia, Nepal, Pakistan, Singapore, Sri Lanka, Thailand, and South Vietnam.

India announced the planning of an additional 2,238 mi. to the India National Highway System. This would include a west coast road, a road linking this with the port of Marmagoa, and a direct highway from Mangalore on the west coast to Madras on the east coast.

The Pan-American Highway System was eventually to be about 14,000 mi. long, linking all the major capital cities in the Americas. When complete, it would be possible to drive from Fairbanks in Alaska to the southern tip of South America at Tierra del Fuego. Completion was expected by 1977. In South America, the system would take in Argentina, Bolivia, Brazil, Colombia, Chile, Ecuador, Paraguay, Uruguay, Venezuela, and Peru. The U.S. Interstate System was designed to link with Canadian and Mexican highways, and with the Pan-American Highway System. Bilateral agreements of cooperation, signed in 1971 by the governments of Colombia, Panama, and the U.S., allowed contracts to be let for the last link of the Pan-American Highway, the Darien Highway in Panama. Major routes within the Pan-American System included the Marginal Forest Highway (4,847 mi.) and the Trans-Amazon Highway (3,107 mi.).

Brazil's road-building program was designed to be associated with the Pan-American Highway. About half of the main coastal highway, BR-101, was completed in 1973 with another one-third under construction. The highway, linking Natal to Osório, would be 2,596 mi. long. Another section of the Trans-Amazon Highway, 777 mi. between Estreito and Itaituba, was opened. The Immigrants' Highway between São Paulo and Santos, although only 36.8 mi. long, was thought to be one of the boldest engineering achievements in the world.

The first privately built expressway in France, 42 mi. between Paris and Chartres, was opened. A 10-mi. section of the A9 expressway between Nîmes and Remoulins was completed and the next section, from Remoulins to Orange, was under construction. The Pont-à-Mousson–Metz section of the Nancy–Thionville expressway was put into service. The four-lane ringway around Paris opened, as did the first expressway link between Paris and another European capital, the 183-mi. highway to Brussels. The French government adopted a plan for a National Highway Network, to comprise more than 17,000 mi.

In the U.K., more than 1,000 mi. of expressway were in use. The M1 expressway, linked to the M5 and the M6 by the Midlands Link expressway, included the Gravelly Hill Interchange, one of the largest of its kind in Europe. A through expressway route, 303 mi. long, ran via M1 and M6 from London to north of Carlisle. The M4 expressway from London to South Wales; the southern extension of the M5 that linked it with the M4, providing 285 mi. of expressway from north of Carlisle to Bristol; and the first section of the M3 London–Basingstoke expressway all opened.

Italy opened the Adriatic Motorway from Bologna in the north to Canosa in the south (390 mi.), which joined the Naples–Bari freeway. Elsewhere in Europe, a 20-mi. section of the Ljubljana–Trieste expressway between Vrhinka and Postojna in Yugoslavia, two sections in the province of Steiermark in Austria, a 13-mi. section of the Southern expressway, and a 3-mi. section of the Pyhrn expressway were all completed during the year. In the U.S., a bill was passed allowing money in the Federal Highway Trust Fund to be spent on mass transit facilities. (R. S. MILLARD)

Tunnels. Throughout the world increasing concern for the environment, coupled with pressure for continual improvement in communication and living standards, maintained the boom in underground engineering. In Japan, a 19-km. railway tunnel linking Honshu and Kyushu islands under the Kammon Strait was under construction; 9.6 m. wide, it was mainly being

UPI COMPIX

The World Trade Center, its twin towers soaring 1,350 ft. above New York City, was dedicated on April 5, 1973.

driven by using a bottom heading method with a 10-cm. layer of gunite applied immediately behind the face. Chemical grouting from a pilot tunnel was used for controlling the water. Work was scheduled for completion in late 1974. Another massive project in Japan, estimated to be completed by mid-1975, was the 2.8-km. Wangan-Sen Highway tunnel, designed to carry a six-lane highway under the principal shipping channel in Tokyo Bay. The underwater section would be the first reinforced concrete submersed tube tunnel in Japan and probably the largest in the world.

The largest tunneling project in Europe, the 3.3-km. Elbe tunnel at Hamburg, W.Ger., was expected to be opened at the end of 1974. Work began in May 1968, and the tunnel attracted considerable worldwide interest because of the problems that had to be overcome and the consequent variety of construction methods used on the site, including open-cut, immersed tube, and shield driven tunnels. In Stuttgart work was in progress on the first phase of a massive extension to the rapid transit system that would ultimately require 15 km. of new tunnels and 19 underground stations. Of particular interest was a new method of using concrete at the site in conjunction with steel H beams placed in bored holes to support ground during excavation of the open-cut sections. Plastic foam was used in a novel application to prevent adhesion of the concrete to the steel.

In Paris, a 7-m.-diameter tunneling machine was in use to bore a 4.7-km. section of an extension to the Chatelot–Gare-de-Lyon Métro line. Also in Paris the underground works associated with the urban renewal at La Défense on the western side of the city continued to attract considerable interest in view of the convergence and crossover of four major roads and a section of the regional underground network.

In Switzerland the largest tunneling machine in the world was in use on the Huttegg portion of the Sedisberg Highway tunnel. The tunnel consisted of two parallel bores, each 12.2 m. in diameter and 2,070 m. long. The machine weighed 450 tons and had a 3,950-kw. electrohydraulic system.

In the U.K. interest centred on the government's proposal—approved by Parliament in October—to proceed, in conjunction with France, with the Channel Tunnel project. Trial borings on both sides of the Channel were to begin in 1974; in the U.K. this would involve sinking a shaft at Shakespeare Cliff near Dover and driving a 4-m.-diameter, 2-km.-long test tunnel under the Channel. Total cost of the project by estimated completion in 1980 was put at £846 million.

Following approval from the Department of the Environment, work was to begin in the spring of 1974 on a major rock tunneling project forming a 32-km.-long aqueduct linking the River Tees to the River Tyne. The tunnel was to form part of the Kielder scheme, the largest reservoir project in the U.K.

In São Paulo, Braz., completion of civil engineering work on the subway was planned for 1974. Tunneling continued, using compressed air under very difficult conditions; a tunneling machine was being used on one drive. In the United States work was in progress on a 1½-mi.-long two-lane tunnel between Norfolk and Hampton, Va. Costing approximately $50 million, this was the second immersed tube under Hampton Roads. Construction involved sinking 15,000-ton steel tube tunnel sections in 36.5 m. of water.

(DAVID A. HARRIES)

ENCYCLOPÆDIA BRITANNICA FILMS. *The Mississippi System: Waterway of Commerce* (1970).

England:
see United Kingdom

English Literature:
see Literature

Entertainment:
see Dance; Motion Pictures; Music; Television and Radio; Theatre

Entomology:
see Life Sciences

Environment

The worldwide debate about man's relationship with his environment became more overtly political in 1973. Environmentalists turned their attention to the exploitive nature of the relationship between rich and poor nations and found themselves moving much closer to those seeking radical reforms, nationally and internationally. There was also a growing governmental awareness of the need to minimize the disruptive effects of human activity, an awareness that led the UN General Assembly to adopt the Declaration on the Human Environment agreed upon at the 1972 UN Conference on the Human Environment in Stockholm. At the same session the General Assembly established a new UN agency, the United Nations Environment Program (UNEP), which was charged with operating the global Earthwatch monitoring system.

In the main, however, it was the condition of the global environment itself and the world's incapacity to organize the exploitation of its resources that compelled governments to pause and consider. Certain predictions made in 1972 in such documents as *The Limits to Growth* and "A Blueprint for Survival" appeared to be coming true, despite earlier reassurance from the more complaisant laissez-faire optimists. During the year a major famine and an energy crisis were complicated by a new flare-up in the Middle East.

Exceptionally large wheat purchases by the U.S.S.R. in 1972 had depleted world grain reserves. This, combined with heavy buying by other countries that, like the U.S.S.R., had been stricken by prolonged drought, left world grain stocks at their lowest level since the end of World War II. For the first time in many years world food supplies were dependent on the current year's production. The UN Food and Agriculture Organization warned that another such misfortune before the damage had been made good would create a very grave shortage indeed.

In the drought-stricken areas, tens of millions of people faced starvation. The drought extended across the northern edge of the Northern Hemisphere monsoon belt, from Central America through Africa (the Sahel belt) to Asia. Climatologists calculated that it was caused by a southward shift in the monsoon belt itself and that the monsoons were unlikely to return to their former position in the 20th century. (*See* AGRICULTURE AND FISHERIES.)

"Ah, the sounds of spring—geese coughing overhead on their way north."

ULUSCHAK, EDMONTON JOURNAL, CANADA/ROTHCO

Unlike the food shortage, the energy crisis had nothing to do with any imminent exhaustion of the world's petroleum reserves, but it did underline the dependence of the industrial nations on petroleum, and especially on the petroleum of the Middle East. The U.S. found itself short of refining capacity and thus unable to meet the rising demand from domestic sources at competitive prices. It was forced onto the world market as a buyer, and almost overnight a buyer's market became a seller's market. The Organization of Petroleum Exporting Countries (OPEC) was quick to exploit the new situation, first by raising prices and then by limiting exports. The U.S. experienced sporadic gasoline shortages throughout the spring and summer, and on October 2 it was announced that formal allocation of fuel oils would be introduced. Then, in October, with the eruption of hostilities in the Middle East, Arab producers began a cutback of oil shipments that threatened to make the "energy crisis" a reality. Oil exports to the U.S., The Netherlands, Portugal, Rhodesia, and South Africa were stopped, and shipments to Western Europe and Japan were reduced. The affected countries introduced a variety of fuel-saving measures, including lower speed limits and bans on Sunday driving, while the Netherlands and Sweden made plans to begin gasoline rationing early in 1974. In the U.S. Pres. Richard Nixon asked Congress for wide-ranging powers to deal with the situation and, in the interim, urged the public to conserve energy on a voluntary basis. (*See* ENERGY.)

INTERNATIONAL COOPERATION

An agreement between the U.S. and the Soviet Union to cooperate on a number of projects of an environmental nature began to be implemented in June 1973. Major efforts would concern air pollution by motor transport and industry, the protection of nature and the establishment of reserves, and the protection of freshwater lakes from pollution.

The first session of the governing council of UNEP was held in June in Geneva. In September most of the staff, including Executive Director Maurice Strong, moved to Nairobi, Kenya. There was widespread concern that the difficulty and high cost of communications from Kenya to the decision-making centres of the world would make it impossible for UNEP to function effectively. The UNEP budget was $100 million spread over five years, but by the end of 1973 it appeared unlikely that the first year's entitlement of $20 million would be subscribed in full.

Fifty-eight countries were represented on the UNEP governing council at the time of the move from Geneva. The council agreed on general policy objectives at its first session. In accordance with the Action Plan agreed at Stockholm and approved by the General Assembly, these were:

1. To provide, through interdisciplinary study of natural and man-made ecological systems, improved knowledge for an integrated and rational management of the resources of the biosphere, and for safeguarding human well-being as well as ecosystems.
2. To encourage and support an integrated approach to the planning and management of development, including that of natural resources, to achieve maximum social, economic, and environmental benefits.
3. To assist all countries, especially developing countries, to deal with their environmental problems and to help mobilize additional financial resources for the purpose of providing the required technical assistance, education, training, and free flow of information and exchange of experience, with a view to promoting the full participation of developing countries in the national and international efforts for the preservation and enhancement of the environment.

The full program, with an anticipated expenditure of $5.5 million for the Earthwatch Program, was submitted for approval to the 28th session of the UN General Assembly, which began on September 18.

In December, at UN headquarters, the organizational meeting was held to prepare for the conference on the law of the sea, scheduled to begin June 20, 1974, in Caracas, Venezuela. The aim of the conference was to make new international law governing the exploitation of ocean resources and to control the dumping of pollutants in international waters. At a conference on marine pollution, held in London in October, it appeared that most countries were moving toward a much more stringent attitude.

In August the Council of Europe published its long-awaited European Soil Charter. The charter recognized that "soil is one of humanity's most precious assets" and that it is "a limited resource which is easily destroyed." The charter laid down 12 principles for soil conservation and good management, and called for proper inventories to be made of soils in order to facilitate better planning and higher standards of husbandry. It would serve as a recommendation to member governments as they formulated policies.

June 5, which the United Nations designated as World Environment Day, passed almost unnoticed in most countries.

URBAN ENVIRONMENT

In the world's major cities, too many people continued to press on too few resources. The panacea that mass production had first seemed to provide was rapidly turning into a nightmare as manufacturers felt compelled to export to each other more and more of the planet's nonrenewable resources, metamorphosed into automobiles, heavy trucks (in which to carry yet more nonessentials), and aircraft. Although most people accepted the need for such symbols of progress as new airports, none wanted them near his own home.

In the U.K. government plans to proceed with the Concorde supersonic airliner, the environmentalist's bête noire, encountered strenuous opposition from

WIDE WORLD

A jet airplane makes its landing approach over an expanse of marshy wilderness at the Everglades airstrip near Miami, Fla. Environmentalists prevented the site from becoming a major airport.

the Labour and Liberal parties and from economists. However, as the economic arguments against the aircraft strengthened, the environmental one weakened, as it was shown that large fleets of aircraft flying in the stratosphere were unlikely to have any significant adverse effect on the ozone belt.

In spite of the government's declared determination to go ahead with its Maplin airport-seaport complex east of London, at year's end it seemed likely that the project would be abandoned in favour of the Channel tunnel. Maplin was opposed by environmentalists, local groups, economists, airlines, and the opposition political parties, and a vigorous anti-Maplin campaign was mounted.

One definite success for the environmentalist lobby (specifically the Conservation Society) came with a reinterpretation by the government of the Highways Act, 1959. In previous public inquiries into road plans for proposed developments, objectors had not been permitted to question the need for roads that had been planned as part of the government's expressway program. The change made it possible to relate the expressway program to an overall concept of transport and energy needs and so to challenge it.

In reaction to a 1972 report from the Department of the Environment recommending drastic cuts in the country's rail network, the Conservation Society joined with the rail unions and British Rail management in "Transport 2000," a group formed to combat the plan with a comprehensive transport policy for Britain. The Transport 2000 plan was adopted by the Liberal Party at its assembly in September.

The Conservation Society was also successful in persuading the Liberal Party to adopt its policy for energy. Thus the Liberal Party became the first British political party to collaborate closely with a radical environmental society and the first party to adopt comprehensive plans for transport and energy. Environmentalists had long urged the need for both as part of an "ecological" approach to national planning.

A two-year-long campaign by Friends of the Earth against a plan for mining copper in the Snowdonia National Park reached a climax when Rio Tinto Zinc announced in April that it was abandoning the project because it was not economically feasible. Widely acclaimed as an environmentalist victory, the statement was received more cautiously by Friends of the Earth, which pointed out that a rise in world prices for copper could change the situation. To the environmentalist, victories were never permanent; defeats were.

Legislation was passed with the aim of reducing emissions of carbon monoxide by 30% and of hydrocarbons by 10% for all motor vehicles first used on or after October 1. The government also announced a program for phased reduction of the lead content in gasoline and held discussions within the EEC on a common standard. According to *Which?*, the journal of the Consumer's Association, the British population was in danger of slow lead poisoning.

During a London heat wave in August there was a buildup of photochemical smog, one of the most dangerous forms of air pollution. This contradicted the view of British automobile manufacturers that clean air standards proposed in the U.S. were irrelevant to the British situation because, according to them, Britain had insufficient sunlight to cause photochemical smog. The smokeless zone policy continued, and by June 30, 59.9% of the "black areas" in England were covered by smoke-control orders.

In May the National Radiological Protection Board published a report stating that the dosage of man-made atomic radiation received by the population was one-hundredth of that from natural radiation. The highly radioactive wastes from nuclear reactors in the U.K. were stored in liquid form in double-walled stainless steel tanks, on sites covering, in all, less than one acre. The ultimate intention was to transform these liquid wastes into solid matter for longer-term storage. The sites would have to be supervised for several centuries.

An environmental protection bill introduced in Parliament in the fall contained regulations aimed at limiting the effects of noise in urban areas, chiefly from industry. Local authorities would be empowered to control noise output within a statutory decibel limit. Noise readings would be measured at factory fences, levels set, and owners prohibited from increasing noise without permission. Fines of £200 for ignoring a first warning, plus £100 for each further day of infringement, could be levied. The proposed legislation followed recommendations from the Noise Advisory Council's Scott Report on Neighbourhood Noise. Findings of the Institute of Biology revealed in September that noise could be a direct cause of illness, ranging from nausea to fatal brain tumours.

In Vienna, Austrian conservationists and the press spearheaded a powerful campaign against a plan to construct university buildings in a central park. Mayor Felix Slavik, who supported the plan, resigned over the issue. Other similarly unpopular schemes included an extension to Schechat Airport, new expressways through woodlands, and a nuclear power station on the Danube. (MICHAEL ALLABY)

Dead trees jut starkly before a petroleum refinery in the Bashkir A.S.S.R. Like capitalist countries, the Soviet Union faces surging environmental problems.

EASTFOTO

In the U.S. the environment ceased to be a "motherhood" issue in 1973. As growing gasoline and fuel oil shortages gripped the nation, environmentalists and new antipollution regulations were charged with a variety of sins, including low gas mileage, the shortage of oil refineries, and delays in construction of nuclear power plants. Other factors were primarily responsible in most of these cases. For example, increased weight and air conditioning cut gas mileage more than emission-control devices. Still, the energy crisis did stem in part from environmental concerns. Clean air regulations were limiting the use of high-sulfur coal and oil. "Clean" fuels—natural gas, low-sulfur coal and oil—were in great demand, but supplies were tight. There was still widespread public support for cleaning up pollution, but that support was facing severe strains.

In mid-October the Environmental Protection Agency (EPA) began to issue final transportation-control plans for 37 major U.S. cities, designed to cut down vehicle traffic so that primary federal health-related air standards could be met by 1975 or 1977. The plans included such controversial measures as restricted and higher-cost downtown parking, establishment of car pool systems, and exclusive bus lanes.

A Supreme Court decision handed down in June banned "significant" deterioration of air quality in areas where the atmosphere already met federal standards. The decision meant that the EPA would have to reject any state clean air plan that allowed such degradation. Thus, polluting industries would not be allowed in unpolluted rural areas, even though they met national standards.

In mid-April then-EPA administrator William Ruckelshaus put off from 1975 to 1976 the deadline for installing catalytic converter devices on all new cars, though tough interim standards were established. Catalytic converters were designed to reduce polluting emissions by 90%. At the same time, the EPA asked Congress to ease the stringent nitrogen oxide standard for car exhausts. In November, however, the new EPA administrator, Russell Train, announced that he had decided to go ahead with the 1975 deadline.

With low-polluting fuels in short supply, the government in September asked hard-pressed states to consider the temporary waiver of air standards so that high-sulfur coal and oil could be used, though the EPA indicated that the states would have to carry out strong conservation efforts before waivers would be granted. The emergency energy bill requested by the president to deal with the energy crisis included more far-reaching relaxations of air-pollution controls. Although the bill was not passed before Congress adjourned at year's end, the House and Senate did agree on a one-year delay in implementing auto-emission standards, suspension of federal, state, and local clean air standards through November 1974 where "clean" fuels were not available, allowing the EPA to require industrial and power plants to convert to "dirty" fuels to save natural gas and low-sulfur coal, and extension of exemptions from the Clean Air Act until Jan. 1, 1979, if necessary.

As the costs of improving the nation's air became more evident, various industries and some legislators began asking whether the standards were too strict. Congress authorized a National Academy of Sciences study to evaluate the health risks of air pollution. During a preliminary conference in October, scientists conceded that they lacked definitive knowledge about links between dirty air and disease. Pending more far-reaching research, however, they tended to support present standards.

Health and safety became a prime issue for the Atomic Energy Commission (AEC). Challenges by environmentalists led to a long series of hearings on the adequacy of the emergency core-cooling system in nuclear power plants—a final-resort safety device that would flood an overheating reactor core with water in case of a major breach. The hearings brought to light serious questions among top AEC experts as to whether the system would work effectively. While the commission was reviewing the testimony, it opted for conservatism by ordering most existing plants to run at less than full power.

There were other signs that the AEC, under its new chairman, Dixy Lee Ray (*see* BIOGRAPHY), was becoming more responsive to environmentalist and citizen concerns. In June the agency moved quickly to comply with an appeals court order to file an environmental impact statement on the entire breeder reactor program. In the same month it ordered creation of a new safety research division; critics had maintained that keeping all safety activities within the Division of Reactor Development constituted an inherent conflict of interest. In September, for the first time, the AEC refused a construction permit for a nuclear power plant because the location, on an island in the Delaware River, was too close to major population centres.

After a series of legislative battles, congressional backers of mass transit finally obtained passage of a bill that would allow big cities to spend their revenues from the Highway Trust Fund (from gasoline and tire excise taxes) for rail mass transit, beginning in fiscal 1976. In return, however, powerful congressional highway interests won approval of a new priority primary highway system that could run up to 10,000 mi. Under pressure of growing fuel shortages, Congress passed and President Nixon signed, on November 16, a bill authorizing construction of the trans-Alaska pipeline. Environmentalists had successfully delayed the pipeline for nearly three years in the courts. Earlier in the year the Supreme Court had upheld an appeals court decision halting construction because the project violated an obscure 1920 law limiting the width of pipeline rights-of-way. The bill revised the right-of-way limitation, authorized the secretary of the interior to grant exceptions, and declared it was the will of Congress that there be no further judicial consideration of the issues. It was uncertain whether the environmentalists would mount another court challenge. Meanwhile, construction at last seemed about to proceed. (SAMUEL R. IKER)

THE NATURAL ENVIRONMENT

There was a growing realization in 1973 that the world's future had to be linked to the planned safeguarding and use of its renewable resources. This implied a searching reevaluation of what were, to all intents and purposes, the world's long-term, inexhaustible assets such as solar energy, rainfall, and soil fertility.

A European Ministerial Conference on the Environment was held in Vienna on March 28–30, attended by delegations from all 17 member states of the Council of Europe, plus 7 observer countries. Discussions concentrated on nature and wildlife conservation; planning and management of the natural environment, including recreation areas; and information, education, and training in the natural environment field. Among many problems thought to require international cooperation, the conference highlighted the protection and maintenance of natural landscape types, characteristic of Europe's original environment.

Such advanced techniques as remote multispectral sensing from high above the planet were being applied on the first earth resources satellite, ERTS-1, launched by the U.S. in July 1972. The satellite, which was equipped with a four-channel multispectral scanner, passed over the same area on the earth every 18 days, thereby registering all seasonal changes for later computer analysis. The cost and complex technology of remote sensing limited its application to the richer countries, although it was the poorer and less developed lands that were in greatest need of its results. The UN sought ways to spread the knowledge it provided. The Apollo Skylab manned satellite, launched by the U.S. in May, significantly extended the range of the Earth Resources Experiment Program. (*See* ASTRONAUTICS; GEOLOGY.)

Land Conservation. In an address entitled "Humanizing the Earth," delivered to the 139th annual meeting of the American Association for the Advancement of Science at the end of December 1972, René J. Dubos, professor emeritus of Rockefeller University, New York City, reviewed the whole story of man's effect on his native planet. Man, he reminded his hearers, augmented the natural physical and biological diversification of the world by "altering the physical characteristics of the land, changing the distribution of living things, and adding human order and fantasy to the ecological determinism of nature." But many of man's interventions had proved catastrophic. "Countries which were most flourishing in antiquity are now among the poorest in the world."

The severe drought that struck the countries along the southern fringe of the Sahara reminded the governments of the countries involved of the great desert's constant threat to expand southward. As grasslands on the borders of the sandy waste were damaged by overgrazing, the loosened sand grains drifted before the winds, extending the useless zone. The nomad herdsmen were obliged to migrate south, intensifying the pressures on yet more marginal land. Technical measures were known that could reverse this trend, such as the planting of shelterbelts or husbandry designed to raise more fodder with minimum water use, but they proved difficult to adopt among peoples who measured their wealth in livestock. Moreover, political divisions made it virtually impossible to present a united front to the advancing sand dunes.

As an example of what had been achieved elsewhere, the Western Australian Forests Department claimed a victory over the enormous sand dunes that had long menaced coastal forests and farms near the Donnelly, Warren, and Meerup rivers. The white, lime-rich soil became free to move after unrestricted grazing, and deliberate midsummer burning around the year 1900 had destroyed the natural protective cover of heaths and short grasses. Under the strong southwest winds blowing off the Southern Ocean, sand dunes had built up into vast wastes, over 200 ft. deep and covering many square miles. Such dunes could advance hundreds of yards in one season and increase in depth by 10 ft. a year. They could bury valuable karri and jarrah forests up to 200 ft. tall. The remedy, both cheap and simple, was the persistent and well-planned planting of marram grass, assisted by the encouragement of native scrub. Both forms of vegetation checked wind speeds at ground level and halted sand-grain movement. Control of grazing, however, was the first essential step. (HERBERT L. EDLIN)

Land use emerged as a key issue in the U.S. In June the Senate passed (for the second time) land-use legislation that would require states to draw up, within three years, planning procedures that included preparation of a land resources inventory and methods of identifying and inventorying critical environmental areas, key facilities, and large-scale developments. The bill would also order states to set up programs to control recreational land sales abuses. However, efforts to include sanctions that would force states to act were defeated.

The Senate followed up this bill in September with a tough strip-mining measure. Under the bill, before mining operators could obtain permits they would have to submit approved reclamation plans and post large bonds to ensure that restoration of the stripped land would be carried out. The most far-reaching provision: strip miners would have to restore the area to its "approximate original contour."

In a decision that might have wide-ranging effects on the conservation effort, the U.S. Supreme Court in December ruled that lakeshore property owners could not bring a class action against a polluter unless it could be established that each member of the affected class has suffered damage amounting to at least $10,000, the minimum needed to bring suit in a federal court.

A number of states acted to preserve environmentally precious areas. New Jersey followed Maine, Delaware, Georgia, and California by reclassifying its coastline to prevent the ravages of poor development. Maine reserved 400,000 ac. of state-owned land for new parks, recreation areas, and wildlife reserves. New York adopted a law to protect tidal wetlands. Another New York law put 3.7 million ac. of privately owned land in the Adirondacks under land-use restrictions.

Seven states, Iowa, Maryland, Michigan, Ohio, Pennsylvania, South Carolina, and Virginia, approved legislation to control sediment from agricultural and construction activity that was polluting their lakes and rivers. Oregon passed a new land-use law designed to discourage rather than attract new industry. Oregon's ban on nonreturnable bottles, which had reduced litter along the state's highways by 80%, was emulated by Washington and Vermont. (SAMUEL R. IKER)

Water Conservation. Work began in northern Quebec on the world's largest hydroelectric scheme. Known as La Grande Complex, it would eventually involve over 50,000 sq.mi. of land in the wilderness east of Hudson Bay. The La Grande River was to be dammed at four points, and three neighbouring rivers were to be diverted to add to its flow. One, the Grand Baleine or Great Whale River, formerly flowed west into Hudson Bay; another, the Opinaca, went southwest into James Bay; while the third, the Caniapiscau, crossed the territory northward to Ungava Bay in the far north. Ten natural and artificial lakes would feed generators with a combined output of 9,000 Mw.

In Mozambique Portuguese forces protecting the vast Cabora Bassa Dam project on the Zambezi River were struck repeatedly by guerrilla forces opposed to white domination. These Frelimo fighters aimed their attacks mainly at supply routes. Their purpose was not to destroy the dam, which would be a great economic asset if and when they achieved independence.

Soviet authorities took an unusual step to safeguard the valuable fishery in the small Sea of Azov, an inlet of the Black Sea connected to it by the three-mile-wide Kerch Strait. Formerly, the Sea of Azov had received large volumes of fresh water from the Don and Kuban rivers; its salinity was very low, and this favoured the breeding of food fish. However, irrigation and hydroelectric projects on the tributary rivers led to a reduced flow of the Sea of Azov's brackish water into the Black Sea. In fact, a reverse flow occurred; the enclosed sea's salinity increased and the fishery declined. By building a dam across the Kerch Strait, the Soviets hoped to control tidal flows and so to reduce the Sea of Azov's salinity.

In mid-Siberia the Soviet authorities were enforcing strict antipollution measures to protect Lake Baikal, the largest fresh-water lake in the world. Over a mile deep and 400 mi. long, it was reputed to hold one-fifth of all the fresh water on earth and nourished a peculiar fauna developed in age-long isolation, including a kind of salmon called the omoul. Industrial developments along the Selenga River and the sinking of cut logs had led to pollution, while the cold climate, with freezing temperatures over eight months of the year, had hampered normal microbial breakdown of waste materials.

A World Intercommunal Conference for the Protection of the Mediterranean, attended by about 200 delegates, was held at Beirut, Lebanon, in June. André Chaudière, a French town-planning expert, described the Mediterranean as a "man-sick" sea and said it was heading for the same lifeless condition as Israel's famous Dead Sea. The Beirut Charter, signed at the conference, called for joint action by all the countries with Mediterranean shorelines to prevent further pollution.

Mediterranean problems had been highlighted in January by the Corsican "red mud" scandal. This material, a waste product of titanium extraction, was being dumped into the sea, at a rate of 3,800 tons each night, by the Italian Montedison company near Follonica on the coast of Tuscany. The firm asserted that it was harmless. Corsican fishermen, however, maintained their fishing grounds were being ruined, and the company undertook to install a treatment plant.

Writing in the British scientific journal *Nature,* V. P. Starr of the Massachusetts Institute of Technology and A. H. Oort of Princeton University predicted the development of long-term drought conditions in Western Europe. They claimed that the mean temperature of the atmosphere had fallen by 0.6° C between 1958 and 1963, with a corresponding decrease in atmospheric humidity. This was causing a decrease in "atmospheric vigour" and a retreat of winds and pressure belts toward the Equator. The westerly winds that brought Europe its rainfall had consequently lessened in force. Sea ice advancing toward the shores of Iceland and cores drilled in the Greenland ice field gave supporting evidence of this trend.

In Israel a severe drought led to the realization that the country's total water reserves were at the danger level. Its one substantial source of fresh water, the Jordan River, flowed into the Sea of Galilee, the only sizable reservoir. From there, the waters were dispatched through the National Water Channel to irrigate the farming settlements of the Negev, which produced fruit and vegetables for both internal use and export. The residue sank through the soil to feed wells, important as local water supplies. But the intensive character of modern kibbutz farming filled this otherwise valuable reserve with surplus nitrates and pesticides, rendering it unsuitable for drinking water or even, in the forseeable future, for further irrigation. The National Committee on the Environment warned the government that stringent water planning was essential.

TERESA ZABALA—THE NEW YORK TIMES

San Francisco resident Norman Babkirk, sitting at a filled-in marsh area, is one of a group of bay watchers who report illegal dumping in San Francisco Bay. Dumping was partly to blame for reducing the bay from 700 sq.mi. in 1850 to about 400 sq.mi. today.

In the U.S. the complex provisions of the 1972 Federal Water Pollution Control Act were being implemented only slowly. The EPA was still in the process of working out guidelines to govern the discharge of pollutants. It seemed clear that meeting the guidelines would cost industry more than had been thought originally. At the same time, results of a survey disclosed in September showed that estimates of state waste-water treatment requirements had escalated dramatically. The states estimated their investment needs over the next 27 years at some \$60 billion. A 1971 survey had projected a figure of around \$18 billion.

In a controversial decision, the EPA had banned the use of DDT except in special circumstances. The ruling was based on the conclusion that DDT, because of its persistence in the food chain and in human and animal fat, presented long-range hazards. Unfortunately DDT was being replaced with other pesticides that, while less persistent, were toxic and involved hazards in use. Federally aided research efforts were under way to develop effective biological pest-control methods. (HERBERT L. EDLIN)

Wildlife. In January Norman Myers visited Ethiopia on behalf of the International Union for Conservation of Nature and Natural Resources (IUCN). His report, published in *Oryx,* journal of the Fauna Preservation Society (FPS), indicated that the trade in leopard and cheetah skins still flourished, in spite of protection and the moratorium recommended by the International Fur Trade Federation. Skins came not only from Ethiopia, but also from Kenya, Somalia, Sudan, Uganda, and more distant countries. The trade in the entire region was difficult to regulate because of the protection it received from senior officials.

A similarly depressing report came from P. R. O. Bally, who visited Somalia on behalf of the World Wildlife Fund (WWF). He found the country devastated by overgrazing to supply cattle to Saudi Arabia. Lions, leopards, cheetahs, serval, caracal, hyenas, and even the larger vultures had been killed off by government-organized poisoning. From Rhodesia came news that 19 black rhinoceroses moved from the Zambezi valley, where they had been in danger from poachers, had established themselves in the Gona-re-Zhou reserve and that at least seven young had been born.

March saw the culmination of many years of work by the IUCN to control the trade in wildlife threatened with extermination. At a conference in Washington, D.C., convened by the U.S. government, 80 nations settled the text of a Convention on International Trade in Endangered Species of Wild Fauna and Flora. The convention established a system of permits to regulate the trade not only in endangered animals and plants but also in their derivatives. Animals and plants subject to the convention were listed in three appendices. Those in Appendix I, the most at risk, were subject to especially strict control and were not to be moved between countries unless both exporting and importing states were satisfied that the transfer would not be detrimental to the survival of the species and that the animal or plant would not be used commercially. Appendix II regulated traffic in less threatened species, and Appendix III governed species in need of local conservation. Provision was made for alterations in the species lists.

During the conference Assistant Secretary of the Interior Nathaniel P. Reid described how the U.S., with the aid of Canadian, Mexican, Brazilian, and other governments, had broken up the largest ring of traffickers in illegal animal skins ever uncovered. U.S. Fish and Wildlife Service agents discovered that during the period Jan. 1, 1971, to May 31, 1972, Vesely-Forte Inc. had done over $5 million worth of business involving purchase or sale of 30,068 ocelot, 46,181 margay, 15,470 otter, 5,644 leopard, 1,867 cheetah, 1,939 jaguar, 468 puma, and 217 giant otter skins. This represented about half the U.S. trade in spotted cats. The U.S. added 17 Australian species, including all the large kangaroos, to its list of animals whose importation was forbidden.

From April 1, use of the gin trap became illegal throughout Great Britain; until then its use against foxes had been legal in Scotland. The Royal Society for the Protection of Birds (RSPB) continued its 1971 campaign against the illegal pole trap, designed to catch any bird landing on it by the leg and used especially against birds of prey. The July issue of the RSPB magazine *Birds* reported that 130 pole traps had been discovered. Because of the difficulty of proving who actually set the traps, only 22 prosecutions were launched, 18 of them successful. In May the RSPB had announced the purchase of Copinsay, with the aid of the WWF and others. This 210-ac. island off the coast of Orkney, with its fine cliffs and seabird colonies, had been bought as a memorial to the internationally famous ornithologist James Fisher.

Three schoolboys don gas masks to protect themselves from pollution and stench while taking a gondola ride in Venice, Italy. They may have been reacting to an official order for workers at a nearby construction site to wear gas masks.

UPI COMPIX

In June the British government, following a recommendation of the FPS, banned the importation of baleen whale products. The importation of sperm whale oil remained legal, however, despite the availability of satisfactory substitutes. During the same month the International Whaling Commission, meeting in London, rejected a U.S. proposal to implement the ten-year ban on whaling, recommended by the 1972 UN Conference on the Human Environment. In July the Badger Act, supported by the Council for Nature and others, became law in Great Britain, giving belated protection to this increasingly harassed animal. From Feb. 1, 1974, no badger was to be taken or killed without a license from the Nature Conservancy Council, except with the written permission of the landowner. Taking badgers for sport, for their pelts, or as pets was prohibited. This was designed to stop the growing commercialization of badgers; the old ones were being killed for their skins while the young were sold as pets.

In July a Tobago firm, Mariculture, announced the first known success in breeding the green turtle from captive stock, as distinct from the hatching of eggs collected in the wild. After two wild-caught males were introduced into Mariculture's ponds, 4,000 eggs were laid and incubated artificially. This might be the only way to preserve the sea turtles, which were much in demand for their eggs, meat, and shells. All turtle species were endangered; in Hawaii George H. Balazs of the Institute of Marine Biology pointed out that in 1963 commercial fishermen had produced 380 lb. of turtle meat for sale, while in 1972 the amount was 25,583 lb.

In Seville, Spain, in September, tens of thousands of birds at the 17,000-ac. Doñana Nature Reserve, established by the WWF in 1963, were killed by a highly poisonous chlorate pesticide, thought to have been banned by the government. It was suspected that the compound had been sprayed on neighbouring rice paddies to fight mosquitoes. (C. L. BOYLE)

See also Cities and Urban Affairs; Life Sciences.

ENCYCLOPÆDIA BRITANNICA FILMS. *Problems of Conservation—Air* (1968); *The House of Man, Part II—Our Crowded Environment* (1969); *Problems of Conservation—Forest and Range* (1969); *Problems of Conservation—Minerals* (1969); *Problems of Conservation—Water* (1969); *The Garbage Explosion* (1970); *Problems of Conservation—Our Natural Resources* (1970); *Problems of Conservation—Soil* (1970); *Problems of Conservation—Wildlife* (1970); *A Field Becomes a Town* (1970); *The Aging of Lakes* (1971); *Turn off Pollution* (1971); *Poison Plants* (1972); *The Great Lakes* (1972); *The Environment: Everything Around Us* (1972); *Buffalo: An Ecological Success Story* (1972); *Controversy over Industrial Pollution: A Case Study* (1973); *The Ways of Water* (1973); *Noise: Polluting the Environment* (1973).

Equatorial Guinea

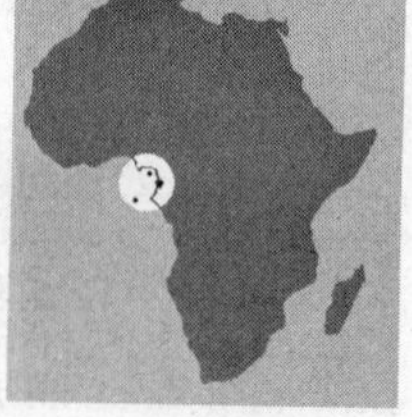

The African republic of Equatorial Guinea consists of Río Muni, which is bordered by Cameroon on the north, Gabon on the east and south, and the Atlantic Ocean on the west; and the offshore islands of Macías Nguema Biyogo (until 1973 called Fernando Po) and Pagalu

EQUATORIAL GUINEA

Education. (1966–67) Primary, pupils 38,395, teachers 504; secondary, pupils 2,343, teachers 40; teacher training, students 130, teachers 28.

Finance and Trade. Monetary unit: ekpwele, at par with the Spanish peseta, with (Sept. 18, 1973) a free rate of 56.82 ekpwele to U.S. $1 (136.95 ekpwele = £1 sterling). Budget (1969–70 est.): revenue 712.5 million ekpwele; expenditure 1,139,000,000 ekpwele. Foreign trade (1966): imports 1,278,000,000 ekpwele (58% from Spain in 1965); exports 1,817,000,000 ekpwele (97% to Spain in 1965). Main exports (1965): cocoa 44%; coffee 21%; timber 19%.

Agriculture. Production (in 000; metric tons; 1972; 1971 in parentheses): sweet potatoes *c.* 27 (*c.* 27); bananas *c.* 12 (*c.* 12); cocoa 24 (23); coffee *c.* 6.9 (*c.* 6.9); palm kernels (exports) *c.* 2 (*c.* 2); palm oil *c.* 4 (*c.* 4). Livestock (in 000; 1970–71): sheep *c.* 29; cattle *c.* 3; pigs *c.* 6; goats *c.* 7; chickens *c.* 78.

(formerly Annobón). Area: 10,830 sq.mi. (28,050 sq.km.). Pop. (1971 est.): 289,000. Cap. and largest city: Malabo (formerly Santa Isabel), on Macías Nguema Biyogo (pop., 1970 est., 19,341). Language: Spanish. President in 1973, Francisco Macías Nguema.

The third national congress of the Party of National Unity was held in Bata, July 9–13, 1973, under the chairmanship of President Nguema. Deploring separatist tendencies which had become apparent on the island of Macías Nguema Biyogo, the congress decided that under a new constitution, replacing that of 1968, no further distinction would be made between the various islands and the mainland province of Río Muni. The administration of Macías Nguema Biyogo would be reorganized, with more mainland officials posted to the island and more islanders posted to the mainland.

An agreement between Nigeria and Equatorial Guinea providing personal security, annual leave, improved rations, and increased pay for Nigerian workers on the Macías Nguema Biyogo plantations expired in February. Nigeria's federal commissioner for labour, Chief Anthony Enahoro, visited Equatorial Guinea to investigate alleged infringements of the agreement, and on July 18 a Nguema government spokesman announced that Nigeria had suspended further cooperation in recruitment of Nigerian workers pending results of a government inquiry.

President Nguema expressed "profound gratitude" to the Spanish government after it had intercepted a Spanish ship, the "Albatross," at Punta de Afrecife in the Canary Islands on January 16. The ship was carrying a group of anti-Nguema mercenary soldiers to Equatorial Guinea. They were all returned to their departure points in Europe. An alleged opposition plot to overthrow the government met with hundreds of arrests in late summer. (R. J. M. DENNERSTEIN)

Ethiopia

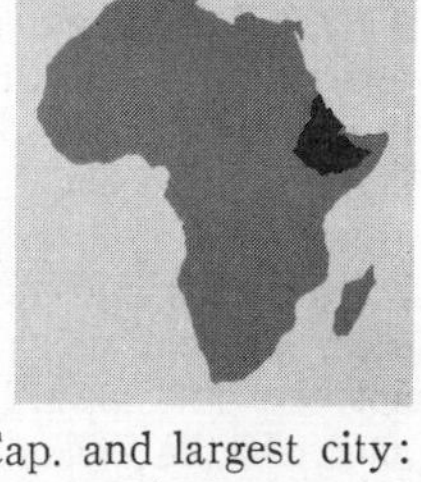

A constitutional monarchy of northeastern Africa, Ethiopia is bordered by Somalia, Afars and Issas, Kenya, Sudan, and the Red Sea. Area: 471,800 sq.mi. (1,221,900 sq.km.). Pop. (1973 est.): 26,461,200. Cap. and largest city: Addis Ababa (pop., 1972 est., 912,090). Language: Amharic (official) and English. Religion: mainly Ethiopian Orthodox (Coptic), with Muslim and animist minorities. Emperor, Haile Selassie I; prime minister in 1973, Aklilu Habte-wold.

The fact that Ethiopia faced severe drought in 1973 had been known since June–September 1972, when the annual heavy rainy season failed to materialize in the Ethiopian highlands. Millet, corn, and sorghum crops could not be planted in the most seriously affected regions in Shoa Province and throughout Welo and Tigre provinces. By May, when rumours of the gravity of the situation were heard in Addis Ababa, to the south of the affected area, total crop failure had led to the loss of 80% of the cattle in the region and a smaller loss in camels. By November at least 50,000 persons had died in six months of drought and a UN report indicated the total might reach 100,000. Failure to seek sufficient relief early in the crisis—which could have been expected from earlier observations that mean monsoon rainfall had declined in recent years from 165 to 100 mm. per year and from the severity of drought conditions elsewhere in the sub-Saharan region—was laid to the reluctance of the proud Ethiopian peoples to admit the seriousness of the conditions. Ethiopia seemed unwilling to acknowledge that the situation was out of control and to therefore risk the loss of tourist income. Major relief efforts, expected to continue for at least a year, were under way by year's end.

Ethiopia's trade deficit, which early in 1972 had been the largest on record, was turned in 1973 into an overall trade surplus for the first time since 1957. One aspect of the changing trade scene was the significant expansion of trade with China since Haile

ETHIOPIA

Education. (1970–71) Primary, pupils 655,500, teachers (1969–70) 11,964; secondary, pupils 135,300, teachers (1969–70) 3,971; vocational, pupils 6,200, teachers (1969–70) 508; teacher training, students 2,800, teachers (1969–70) 131; higher, students 4,500, teaching staff (1969–70) 503.

Finance and Banking. Monetary unit: Ethiopian dollar, with (Sept. 17, 1973) a par value of Eth$2.07 to U.S. $1 (free rate of Eth$5 = £1 sterling). Gold, SDRs, and foreign exchange, central bank: (June 1973) U.S. $155.3 million; (June 1972) U.S. $72.5 million. Budget (1972–73 est.): revenue Eth$732 million; expenditure Eth$757 million. Money supply: (June 1973) Eth$500.4 million; (June 1972) Eth$415.5 million. Cost of living (Addis Ababa; 1963 = 100): (June 1973) 150; (June 1972) 134.

Foreign Trade. (1972) Imports Eth$435.6 million; exports Eth$385.4 million. Import sources: Japan 15%; Italy 15%; U.S. 13%; West Germany 10%; U.K. 8%; Iran 7%. Export destinations: U.S. 37%; Japan 8%; West Germany 7%; Italy 6%; Saudi Arabia 6%; Afars and Issas 6%. Main exports: coffee 47%; oilseeds 13%; hides and skins 12%; cereals 7%.

Transport and Communications. Roads (1972) *c.* 23,400 km. (including 8,170 km. main roads). Motor vehicles in use (1972): passenger 31,933; commercial 7,410. Railways (1971): 1,088 km.; traffic (including traffic of Afars and Issas portion of Djibouti–Addis Ababa line) 80 million passenger-km., freight 243 million net ton-km. Air traffic (1972): 430.6 million passenger-km.; freight 16,928,000 net ton-km. Telephones (Dec. 1971) 51,000. Radio receivers (Dec. 1971) 163,000. Television receivers (Dec. 1971) 8,500.

Agriculture. Production (in 000; metric tons; 1972; 1971 in parentheses): barley 1,601 (1,565); wheat 923 (876); corn 1,004 (971); millet, sorghum, and teff (1971) *c.* 2,680, (1970) 2,630; sweet potatoes *c.* 256 (*c.* 254); potatoes *c.* 164 (*c.* 163); linseed *c.* 70 (*c.* 66); sesame *c.* 73 (*c.* 70); sugar, raw value *c.* 130 (*c.* 122); chick-peas *c.* 190 (*c.* 189); dry peas *c.* 130 (*c.* 130); dry broad beans *c.* 145 (*c.* 143); lentils *c.* 110 (*c.* 109); dry beans *c.* 75 (*c.* 74); coffee *c.* 216 (*c.* 215). Livestock (in 000; 1971–72): cattle *c.* 26,450; sheep *c.* 12,900; goats *c.* 11,350; horses *c.* 1,420; mules *c.* 1,450; asses *c.* 3,900; camels *c.* 100; poultry *c.* 47,000.

Industry. Production (in 000; metric tons; 1969–70): cement 175; cotton yarn (1968–69) 10.5; cotton fabrics (sq.m.; 1968–69) 70,000; electricity (kw-hr.) 520,000.

Epidemics:
see Medicine

Episcopal Church:
see Religion

Selassie's visit in 1971. Exports to China reached more than Eth$22 million for 1971–73, producing a favourable balance of about Eth$4.5 million in fiscal 1972.

The summit meeting of heads of state held in Addis Ababa in May during the tenth anniversary celebrations of the Organization of African Unity was the scene of clashes, as tension was renewed between Somalia and Ethiopia and as Libyan representatives sought to undermine Ethiopia's friendly relations with Israel. The subsequent breaking of relations with Israel as a consequence of the Middle East war was not an easy decision for Ethiopia. Also at the conference, the emperor mediated the basis for an accord between Tanzania and Uganda. Later in the year, he attended the conference of nonaligned states in Algiers and made a lightning visit to Moscow and Belgrade. He received official visits from presidents V. V. Giri of India, Mobutu Sese Seko of Zaire, William Tolbert of Liberia, Georges Pompidou of France, Gaafar Nimeiry of Sudan, Idi Amin of Uganda, Siaka Stevens of Sierra Leone, and Makarios of Cyprus, as well as from King Baudouin I of the Belgians.

The fifth general election for the Chamber of Deputies was held in August and the new Parliament had on its agenda measures for reform of land administration that had previously failed to get approval.

(G. C. LAST)

UPI COMPIX

A London resident reads of Britain's entry into the European Common Market on Jan. 1, 1973, after more than ten years of negotiations. Denmark and Ireland became full members on the same day.

European Unity

On Jan. 1, 1973, the European Community of the Six became the Community of the Nine, following the formal accession of the United Kingdom, Denmark, and Ireland. The Six were already the world's largest trading unit; the Nine, with a population of 255 million, became, in addition, the world's biggest producer of steel and motor vehicles, the owner of the world's largest shipping fleet, and one of the world's largest agricultural producers.

Britain's Labour Party decided to take no part in the life of the Community in 1973 and sent no Labour delegates to the European Parliament's sessions in Strasbourg. Throughout the year it maintained its official view that it was not opposed to entry in principle, unlike the Trades Union Congress, but only to the terms negotiated by the British government. Nevertheless, its left wing made its total opposition to the Community very clear. It was strengthened in its attitude by the tendency of the British public to blame the year's massive rise in food and commodity prices on "the Common Market" rather than on world conditions.

The vast free-trade area that the enlarged Community formed with the remaining EFTA countries came into being on April 1, 1973. On that date a 20% cut was made in tariffs between the Six and Ireland on the one hand and Iceland, Sweden, Portugal, and Switzerland on the other. Remaining import duties between the Six and Ireland and these EFTA "nonjoiners," together with Austria (still operating on an earlier interim agreement) and Norway and Finland, who signed free trade agreements with the EEC later in 1973, were being removed gradually, parallel with the timetable for abolishing tariffs between the three new members and the Six. The free trade already achieved between Britain and Denmark and their former EFTA partners was substantially maintained. However, final agreement with Iceland was held up over Iceland's claim to a 50-mi. territorial limit. The value of the Six's exports to the seven EFTA nonjoiners had been $10 billion in 1970, compared with $6 billion to the three new members.

The changes wrought by the arrival of the British—in 1973 at any rate—appeared more superficial than real. The brasher, shriller note of British politics—and a Westminster-style question-time—arrived in the European Parliament's debates, and Britain was much criticized in the continental press for defending its interests too brutally. But there was also understanding of its difficult economic position and the need to impress an increasingly hostile public opinion. By and large, the actual policies of the Community in 1973 showed a remarkable continuity with the past.

The Paris Summit. The Paris summit meeting of heads of state and government of the Nine in October 1972 had set a formidable series of new targets and deadlines, most of which involved the preparation of detailed memorandums by the European Commission. Although the communiqué that it published in the early morning of October 21 contained few concrete decisions, it set out in a single document, for the first time since the Rome treaties of 1957, the vast range of tasks that faced the Community and a timetable for accomplishing them. The Paris summit formally extended the Community's purview to regional and industrial policy and gave new emphasis to social, environmental, and energy policies. It also reaffirmed the intention to go ahead with the second stage of economic and monetary union at the beginning of 1974 and invited the Nine to adopt an "overall policy of development cooperation on a worldwide scale." Political cooperation would be further improved, and the member states would form a "European union" by 1980.

Although the Paris agreement set a timetable for the various stages of its tasks, hoping to provide thereby a framework for "a Europe with a human face," it did not envisage any concrete steps by which this aim could be achieved. There was no timetable for direct election of the European Parliament and no indication as to how the people were to be drawn into greater participation in the development of the Community, as the Nine had solemnly pledged in the communiqué's preamble.

Economic and Monetary Union. The Community's plans for economic and monetary union faced a series of fresh storms in 1973. The pound sterling, floating freely since June 1972, had been expected to rejoin the other currencies in the Community "snake" (a relationship to each other in which the maximum rate variation permitted between any two currencies at any given moment would not exceed 2.25%; the snake operated in a world "tunnel" in which the Community currencies could fluctuate against the dollar by 4.5%). The pound continued to float, however; it was judged by the British government to be too weak to return to a virtually fixed rate without risking deflation and an end to Britain's newly achieved rapid growth. In January an assault on the Italian lira brought that currency out of the snake in order to float. A second dollar devaluation on February 12 did not ease the upward pressure on the West German mark and the Japanese yen. Finally, on March 12, the governments of the six Community countries with strong currencies agreed to float their currencies against the dollar; *i.e.,* to stop jointly supporting the dollar with their currencies. Britain's pound—and Ireland's, pegged to it—and the Italian lira continued to

European Economic Community: *see* Commercial Policies; European Unity

European Free Trade Association: *see* Commercial Policies; European Unity float freely. (Subsequently, two upward revaluations of the mark and one of the Dutch guilder were needed to keep the joint float in being.)

Britain had refused to join the combined float without an infinitely greater Community support fund than the other countries were prepared to finance. The notion of fixed margins as a step to a single Community currency was looking very sick indeed. The common agricultural policy, in particular, was covered over with bits of sticking plaster in the shape of compensatory payments, which covered up the price difference arising from changes in exchange rates.

Nevertheless, the European Monetary Cooperation Fund was formally set up on April 6, 1973, to keep member states' currencies in the 2.25% band, settle debits and credits multilaterally, and operate the Community's short-term credit fund of 1.4 billion units of account (the unit of account equaling the value of the dollar prior to the 1971 devaluation). At the time of the major meeting of finance ministers on October 29–30, however, the Nine were very far from agreement on the next stage. West Germany in particular, supported by The Netherlands and Denmark, regarded it as meaningless to move into the second stage when the main objectives of the first stage—the narrowing of exchange rate margins and parallel progress on aligning economic policies—had not been achieved.

Regional Policy. Among the policies formally brought into the field of Community activity by the Paris summit, one of them, regional policy, was linked particularly closely with economic and monetary union. Without it free movement of people and capital could easily exacerbate the problems of regional poverty and decline affecting particularly the deprived rural regions and the areas of contracting industries. For Britain, it also offered a means of recuperating some of the vast Community expenditure on agriculture, which largely benefited France and The Netherlands.

On May 3 the Commission unveiled its general proposal for regional policy in a memorandum, and added flesh to these bare bones at intervals during the year. In particular, it sent the Council on July 26 a draft regulation to set up the Regional Development Fund agreed on at the Paris summit, and a draft decision to establish a regional development committee to coordinate national policies. The Commission proposed that for the three years 1974–76 the Community should be able to undertake new expenditures of 2.4 billion units of account (roughly £1,200 million) on regional development. The Community's commitment to a regional fund was reiterated at the EEC summit meeting in Copenhagen in December, although there was disagreement as to details. West Germany, in particular, urged a scaling down of the Commission's plans, especially in light of the possible consequences of the energy crisis, while Britain, in view of its own regional problems, supported the earlier, more ambitious proposals.

Industrial Policy. On industrial policy, the Commission produced a memorandum in May setting out proposals intended to give the Community additional means of remaining among the world's leading economic powers. They included: completion by 1977 of the Community's program to eliminate technical barriers to trade; opening-up of the market for public works contracts and purchases; making it possible for viable competitive European enterprises to emerge by facilitating supplies of risk capital and improving the legal and fiscal framework; giving special attention to advanced-technology industries such as computers, aircraft, and telecommunications; helping crisis-struck sectors; and coordinating investment in heavy industries.

The saving of the Euratom program by the skin of its teeth was hardly a good augury for future Community research and development. On February 6 the Council decided on a four-year program costing 160 million units of account—far less, as a Belgian newspaper put it, than the annual cost of supporting olive-oil production in the Community. A feature of the program was that for the first time it contained non-nuclear as well as nuclear projects.

Europe's neglect of its Atomic Energy Community was particularly difficult to comprehend in the light of mounting preoccupation with energy supplies. For years the Commission had been urging a combined energy policy on the member states; in 1972 and 1973 it redoubled its warnings on the Community's growing dependence on imported oil. The insecurity of Europe's oil supplies was strikingly underlined when, following the outbreak of war in the Middle East in October, the Arab oil producers instituted a program of cutbacks in oil shipments to the West and a complete ban on exports to the U.S. and to The Netherlands because of its alleged pro-Israeli stance. The need for coordination in dealing with the energy crisis dominated the summit meeting held December 14–15 in Copenhagen at the instigation of French Pres. Georges Pompidou. The communiqué supported sharing among the Nine in principle, with detailed plans to be prepared by the Commission, but at year's end no firm policy had been agreed. A group of Arab foreign ministers who arrived at the meeting uninvited were admonished that their policy might produce a backlash of European public opinion, although the meeting also produced some indications of sympathy for the Arab position.

Living and Working Conditions. The Commission rapidly produced a document on social policy, presenting its guidelines for a social action program to the public on April 18. They covered virtually everything that anyone had ever thought of as good, from retraining and rehousing to studies covering paid maternity leave, capital accumulation for workers, minimum wages, and the abolition of assembly-line working. The Commission was instructed to submit final —and more discriminating—proposals.

Farm Policy Under Pressure. The oldest and indeed only fully operative common Community policy,

J.-P. BONNOTTE—GAMMA

More than 30,000 farmers gather in Valenciennes, France, in April 1973, to apply pressure to the nine EEC agricultural ministers meeting in Luxembourg. The high-level meeting was called to establish farm prices.

the common agricultural policy, came under heavy pressure during the year. On the one hand, it was heavily assailed, particularly in Britain, as illogical and ill-adapted to the Community's needs, since it subsidized efficient as well as inefficient farmers, burdened consumers with high prices, and kept consumption lower than it need be. Far greater problems were produced, however, by the chaos in the exchange markets. In addition to the compensatory refunds and levies needed to even out the differing price levels between the new member countries and the old, there were complex "monetary compensatory amounts" to counterbalance price reductions and increases produced among the old member states by the changes in exchange rates. A system that would support needy farmers directly through their incomes rather than all farmers through a high price level was advocated by many. France, however, remained adamantly in favour of the existing system and was ready to admit nothing more radical than some modification of the price ratios. The price problem became somewhat academic by late summer, however, when the rapid rise in world food prices had taken all except those for milk products above the Community levels.

Restrictive Practices and Monopolies. There were few fields in which the Commission had the power of decisive action. In one of them—that of restrictive practices and monopolistic abuse by companies—its record was impressive. In December 1972 it had fined 16 sugar-refining companies a total of 9 million units of account for operating a price-fixing cartel. The previous month it had fined Pittsburgh Corning Europe 100,000 units of account for isolating the West German market for cellular glass insulation material and charging prices 40% higher than it charged in the Benelux. The Commission had also fined a French record manufacturer, WEA-Filipacchi, 60,000 units of account for a similar offense that had enabled it to sell records in the West German market at prices 65% higher than in France.

Most important, however, was the Court of Justice's de facto extension of the Commission's powers over concentration in industry. Although it upheld the appeal by the U.S. metal-packaging company, Continental Can Co., against a Commission order to divest itself of a Dutch firm it had taken over (Thomassen en Drijver-Verblifa N.V.), the court confirmed the Commission's thesis that a take-over or merger was in itself an abuse when it "permits only the existence of firms which are dependent in their behaviour on the dominant company." The Commission followed up the decision by sending the Council in July a draft regulation that would give it direct powers to control mergers. (*See* LAW.)

The Community's External Relations. In its external relations, the Community in 1973 faced a number of crucial tests. One was the further round of world trade negotiations under the General Agreement on Tariffs and Trade (GATT), which began in Tokyo in September. The Council wished the negotiations to lead to a significant, harmonized, and reciprocal lowering of industrial customs duties and also of nontariff barriers. The Community was ready with other industrialized countries to improve its system of generalized preferences for less developed countries. The agricultural policy would not be negotiable in its main principles or in its essential machinery, but the Community would consider world agreements for some products.

A second, and perhaps greater, test was the negotiation for a new association agreement linking with the Community not only the previous 18 African associates of the Six, and Mauritius, which joined them in May 1972, but also 24 other countries in Africa, the Caribbean, and the Pacific. Among the main problems to be decided were the amount of development aid to be given by the Community to the less developed countries, whether the latter should grant reciprocal concessions (including "revenue preferences"), and whether there should be any relationship between the less developed countries and the Community. (*See* AFRICAN AFFAIRS.)

During the year the Community continued negotiations with many of the Mediterranean countries, including Spain, Israel, Morocco, Algeria, Tunisia, and Yugoslavia, within the framework of its global Mediterranean policy. Trade pacts were signed with Egypt and Lebanon; the Community's association agreement with Turkey moved into its second stage on January 1; and association with Cyprus went into effect on February 1.

The foreign ministers of the Nine met regularly to concert their views and action on foreign policy, in particular with reference to the Conference on Security and Cooperation in Europe, and their attitude toward the United States.

EFTA. The departure for the EEC of two members, the U.K. and Denmark, did not bring about the demise of EFTA. Meeting in Vienna in November 1972, it had decided to continue and to recruit new members. It decided to bring its statistical methods into line with those of the Community, and greater use of the French language was advocated. The maintenance of free trade in industrial goods between the remaining EFTA countries and the U.K. and Denmark, and the agreement to implement free trade among them and the other seven members of the Community by 1977 were perhaps among the most important of EFTA's achievements.

The Council of Europe. The Council of Europe continued its work in providing a forum for its 17 member states and the machinery for intergovernmental cooperation among them on a wide variety of matters, such as harmonization of legislation on health protection for workers, the preservation of European towns (notably Venice), cultural cooperation, and the repatriation of corpses. (DEREK PRAG)

See also Commercial Policies; Defense; Payments and Reserves, International; Taxation; Trade, International; and articles on the various countries.

Fashion and Dress

With the fashion gap between Europe and the U.S. narrowing and a natural and relaxed mood in clothes becoming more general, there was no doubt that 1973 would go down in international fashion history as the year of blue denim. Worn alike by presidents of companies and their employees, by heads of state, royal princesses, farmers, truck drivers, Black Panthers, and film stars, blue jeans had become the most patent class-leveling garment ever known in the West and second only in the entire world to the Chinese worker's blue cotton uniform.

Since Levi Strauss turned out his first pair of blue jeans in San Francisco during the gold rush, the firm he founded had spread its factories all over the U.S. and now claimed to be the world's largest ready-to-wear concern. Levi's jeans ranked third on the list of

Evangelical Churches: *see* Religion
Exchange Rates: *see* Payments and Reserves, International
Exhibitions: *see* Art Exhibitions; Museums and Galleries; Photography
Expeditions, Scientific: *see* Antarctica; Arctic Regions; Mountaineering; Oceanography; Speleology
Faeroe Islands: *see* Dependent States
Falkland Islands: *see* Dependent States
Farming: *see* Agriculture and Fisheries

internationally smuggled goods, right after alcohol and cigarettes and just before drugs. Smuggled or stolen, blue jeans brought high prices on the black market. The highest price was said to be paid in the U.S.S.R.—$90 a pair. Denim cotton material still came from the U.S. exclusively, but rival firms had been set up in Europe to make the jeans. France alone produced three million pairs in 1973, and the number-one client was the United States!

Plain or patched, embroidered with naïve flowers and butterflies or appliquéd with metal stars, studs, and eyelets to form scattered or regular designs, pale blue denim jeans, blousons, jumpsuits, and skirts crowded city streets and summer resorts. A wider leg-cut marked the 1973 brand, and there was a switch in emphasis from thigh hugging to bottom cupping. In St. Tropez, France, where bare tops were de rigueur, mini-jeans were worn for swimming.

Drifting away from the previously emphasized "poor look," jeans were effectively dressed up with neat classic shirts, fancy jerkins, halter tops, or waist-length knitted tops with deep ribbed welts and puffed sleeves reminiscent of the 1940s. T and tank shapes were still popular, however, usually with bold letters across front or back spelling out brand names of such products as cigarettes, cars, and soft drinks. T or sweat shirts emblazoned with the names of American colleges were a fad among European youth. For a more feminine approach, girls turned to soft blouses: in cheesecloth with a dairymaid-type drawstring neckline flirtatiously dipping off one shoulder, in flower-sprigged lawn, moss crepe, wrinkled cotton crepe, or Liberty prints, but always gathered, frilled, and low necked.

Manufacturers and retailers did their best to bring back the skirt, at first without the slightest success. Pants remained standard all winter. Under fluffy, long-haired fur coats, they formed the basic street look. When spring came, the trousered silhouette with its new, bottom-cupping cut was topped with a wide-brimmed Texan hat. Sometimes the look was completed with high-heeled sandals, but more often with the inevitable clumsy clogs. Soles were thicker than ever, allowing only a hasty shuffle when it came to street crossing and often landing the unfortunate wearer in the hospital with a sprained or broken ankle. The craving for height-enhancing shoes was well established, but the very high and straight Spanish heel, nearing four inches, got the better of clogs for autumn. It flattered the leg and induced a return of the skirt.

Meanwhile, in the spring, everyone waited for the dress revival announced in the fashion magazines. Then, suddenly, came the change overnight. Tiring of jeans, young girls appeared in long bias-cut skirts, ending just above the ankle, still in pale blue denim but with spiral patchwork inserts in printed cotton. An alternative was the equally long skirt in country cottons, flared or gathered and often with a frill on the hem. In France these skirts were often worn with T shirts or more romantic see-through white embroidery blouses. Large, floppy hats with cabbage roses and ribbon trim completed the flower girl look. In Paris the Flea Market was the place to piece together such outfits. In Britain, Laura Ashley, a Welsh firm with outlets in London and several country shops, produced inexpensive models with a country flavour, smock-shaped or waisted and long sleeved.

Older women wore blue denim jeans by day too, but they showed a definite tendency toward a more pulled-together look, with an accent on accessories. Classic British tailor-mades and knits were back in high fashion, with Donegal tweeds, sporty checks, herringbone, and small caviar designs used for well-made suits and pantsuits. They were worn with classic shirts and the still favoured layered look of shirt plus long-sleeved (or sleeveless) V-necked pullover, plus matching cardigan, all adorned with striping and brightly coloured geometric patterns. Pleated skirts in matching designs were often a substitute for pants. Jackets appeared in blazer, hacking, or blouson shapes.

For sportswear the legendary cardigan appeared in many updated forms. The cabled "cricket" version, in white or pale beige bordered with several rows of bright stripes, came in for summer. For winter there were heathery mixtures and deep earthy tones in all-over jacquard patterns. Heavy knitted or crocheted jackets, longer and longer, more and more slouchy, with low pockets, self-shawl collar and belt plus long matching stole, were the junior's choice for a first autumn buy. Paris haute couture endorsed this fad and enhanced it with sumptuous fox fur trimming, but gave it a slimmer cut.

When it came to dresses, everyone played for safety in the summer with pleated and printed shirtwaists, worn with a matching or plain jacket with tailored collar and lapels. The freshest touch was provided by Yves Saint Laurent's white linen jacket, perfectly tailored and worn over a multicoloured print silk dress with pleated skirt. For after dark wear, dress shapes became more fluid and more sophisticated. Hems were on the move again, dropping downward to hide the knees. Following the lead of British designer Jean Muir, slinky, silk jersey shapes appeared, clinging to the body and often baring backs for evening.

The news that F. Scott Fitzgerald's book *The Great Gatsby* was being adapted to the screen in the U.S. produced an immediate reaction in the fashion world. The "Great Gatsby" look was launched for autumn, with the soft, low-waisted, slightly bloused silhouette of the jazz age. Another influential figure for fashion designers was Sarah Miles as she appeared in the film *The Hireling*—a fragile silhouette that inspired Sonia Rykiel, the gifted Paris knitwear designer, to make her dark mohair ensembles with soft, long-drawn-out jackets or cardigans and short, knotted, knitted scarves, worn with narrow, mid-calf-length skirts.

The autumn silhouette was divided between this lean and measured look and the full, swirling, but unconstructed shape, of which the unlined cape was one example. One of the prettiest cape outfits was from the Saint Laurent boutique: in heather-shaded speckled tweed, worn with an amethyst knitted cardigan and flannel trousers, jacquard knit gloves, a plain wool etamine scarf, and crocheted bonnet, all in beautifully blended shades.

With the knitwear fad came the tweed revival. Knit and tweed often combined happily. Tweed was just the right material for the more bulky and flared autumn silhouette, with wide gored skirts ending at mid-calf or gathered coats with back fullness and low armholes, such as Kenzo made for Jap. In most cases tweed designs remained small, discreetly speckled or checked, or with tone-on-tone knobs. There was quite a bit of herringbone pattern too, often in rust and beige and trimmed with red fox. Back-flaring coats with raglan sleeves and deep armholes, cut very much on the raincoat style, were worn loose or pulled in at the waistline with a self-fabric or leather belt. Pants appeared in the same discreetly patterned tweeds, matched to the overcoats. Straight, fairly wide, cuffed

The 1973 designer collections included Yves Saint Laurent's jeans pants suit and boa scarf (above right), his wool jersey skirt and sweater trio (below), and Givenchy's classic cotton satin coat and dress ensemble (above left).

TOP, A.F.P./PICTORIAL PARADE; OTHERS, PICTORIAL PARADE

or not, with crease or without, they just uncovered the shoe tip.

There was, however, a definite feeling for getting out of pants by night and into something more feminine and glamorous. As just below the knee seemed to be the most popular hemline level for day, so just above the ankle looked right for after-dark dresses and suits. Black velvet and black lacquered satin made evening suits look somewhat younger than dresses. They had softly belted jackets and skirts to just above the ankle, with barely enough ease for walking. They were worn with soft chiffon blouses, black on black or white on black, or with white crinkled satin. Sheer black stockings and high-heeled bracelet shoes completed the Merry Widow look. A veiled hat and an occasional black ostrich feather boa added the last touch, just for the fun of it.

Knitwear, the season's standby, could hardly be left out of the evening scene. It arrived with the addition of metal and Lurex threads, in the form of long glittering cardigans, accompanying dresses or evening pants in soft crepes. The glitter could be gold or silver, but bright firework colours had an equal appeal. In London, John Bates, director and designer of Jean Varon and Capricorn, noted for his sexy, frilly evening dresses for the young, was bent on bringing back the small waist. A high cummerbund and fat, puffy sleeves were his means of producing the desired effect.

Commenting on the above-ankle skirt length for evening, Paris designers held that it was the only way of getting women out of pants. But many women said that this was merely wishful thinking on the designers' part. Pants were far too practical to give up.

Cosmetics and Hairstyles. The "Roaring Twenties," Scott Fitzgerald, and the "Great Gatsby" look influenced cosmetics as well as clothes. Helena Rubinstein christened her spring makeup line "Jazz." The lipsticks, which varied from copper to pinkish red and frosted pink, bore such evocative names as "Shimmy," "Fox Trot," and "One Step."

Spring makeup, natural and fruity by day, heightened by a touch of blusher in warm copper tones, reflected a healthy look showing the effects of good care combined with exposure to sun and fresh air. For evening a more daring look appeared, along with the feeling for more femininity and glamour. There was a tendency to "paint your face" for special occasions.

Emulsions and creams helped to preserve the suntan. Hydroregulating creams, used to regularize the moisture content of all types of skins, were stressed at Helena Rubinstein with "Moisture Response," at Estée Lauder with "Performance Cream," and at Revlon with special "Hydrating Prescriptions" containing fruit and plant ingredients. Elizabeth Arden's "Flawless Finish," applied with a damp sponge, aimed at a transparent makeup in various tints of beige.

Blue denim could hardly be left out of cosmetics for spring and summer. London's Biba introduced an entire "Denim Range," including everything from face gloss, eye colour, and powder to mascara and nail polish. Next came a light denim "Powder Tint/Watercolour set" with two shades of denim "Powder Tint," a cream "Powder Tint," and a dark denim "Watercolour."

For spring, lips echoed the golden complexion, in shades of ripe melon and romantic red at Estée Lauder and "Clearly Coral" for blonds and "Pimento" for brunettes at Elizabeth Arden. For autumn, Mary Quant advocated rusty brown, copper red, and lilac pink with, respectively, "Hot Hennâ," "Gingerbread," and "Bed of Roses." Guerlain turned to "Mahogany" and "Brick."

Cosmetics picked up the autumn fashion colours, forest green, plum, burnt orange, and camel beige. Revlon harmonized eyes, lips, and nails, the last two in toasted shades of toffee, honey, pink, and plum; eye makeup included forest green. Mary Quant introduced "Windsor Brown," "Thundergray," and a gray-green note with "Highland Fling," all in the "Jeepers Peepers" eye-shadow line.

For evening, eye shadow became iridescent and scintillating. Arden's "18 Karat Collection" with "Ultra Frost" sprinkled gold dust on eyelids, and Rubinstein's "Diamond Eyes" added flakes of glitter that mirrored the light.

London streets provided the wildest look in hair styles during the summer. A short boyish cut, sported by girls and boys, was heightened by fronts dyed in such exotic colours as orange, green, or pale blond. In more civilized circles the "Great Gatsby" look gained ground for autumn, with short, frothy curls at Alexandre and Vidal Sassoon and a short, neat cut at Carita, reminiscent of Van Dongen portraits. Softly waved, longer hair was the favourite of those who were nostalgic for the Hollywood of the 1930s.

(THELMA SWEETINBURGH)

Men's Fashions. Simplicity of line, elegance in styling, strong colours, no gimmicks; this proved to be the most profitable formula for men's fashion in 1973. The British Menswear Guild described the look of the year as one of "easy elegance in comfortable clothes." Other countries reported a return to the classical and romantic look and a trend away from the "hippie" styles of recent years. The easy-to-wear ready-to-wear suit, with at least one and a half centuries of tradition behind it, again became the focal point of men's fashion. At IMBEX in London, SEHM in Paris, SAMIA in Turin, Italy, the International Men's Fashion Week in Cologne, W.Ger., and at other important trade fairs the emphasis was clearly on suits and suitings.

This overchecked worsted suit was made especially for the 15th World Congress of Master Tailors held in London. The tailoring is the work of Hawes and Curtis Ltd.

INTERNATIONAL WOOL SECRETARIAT

A return to simplicity and elegance was also the theme of the 15th World Congress of Master Tailors, held in London during August 26–September 1. Styling in both ready-to-wear suits and tailored suits continued to be mostly single-breasted. Lapels were at their widest on ready-to-wear models; pocket flaps were deeper, buttons bigger, and jackets tended to be shorter. Pants continued to be wide at the bottoms, usually with deep cuffs. Tailored suits were more classic, featuring a clean, uncluttered silhouette and many more single-breasted, one-button styles, no flaps on jacket pockets and no cuffs on the pants, which were slim-fitting.

In suit materials, flannels gave some ground to fancy worsteds and woolens in country or rustic colours. With the possible exception of West Germany, where brown was the first fashion shade, gray continued to be the most popular colour. For informal occasions jackets in check patterns and overchecks, sometimes with vests (waistcoats), were combined with plain pants in the same ground colour, or the pants might be checked and the jacket plain.

Shirts had much more white. Colours were lighter and stripes and checks were discreet, while bold block stripes became less popular. Ties, still wide, were in more subdued patterns and softer, often self-colours. The bow tie remained fashionable.

There was less elegance in footwear styles. Thick soles and high heels, bold eyelets, and speckled laces were the choice of the younger man.

(STANLEY H. COSTIN)

See also Furs.

Fiji

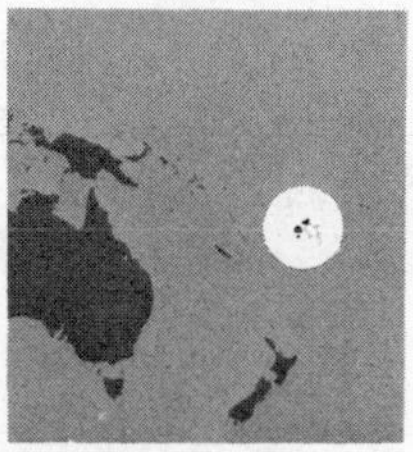

An independent parliamentary state and member of the Commonwealth of Nations, Fiji is an island group in the South Pacific Ocean, about 2,000 mi. E of Australia and 3,200 mi. S of Hawaii. Area: 7,055 sq.mi. (18,274 sq.km.), with two major islands, Viti Levu (4,011 sq.mi.) and Vanua Levu (2,137 sq.mi.), and several hundred smaller islands. Pop. (1973 est.): 564,000. Cap. and largest city: Suva (pop., 1971 est., 63,172). Language: English, Fijian, and Hindi. Religion: Christian and Hindu. Queen, Elizabeth II; governor-general in 1973, Sir Robert Foster; prime minister, Ratu Sir Kamisese Mara.

Despite the severe damage caused by Hurricane Bebe in October 1972, economic growth continued during 1973 at an annual rate of 6.2%. A record trade deficit of F$66 million for the year ended in August was mostly covered by invisible earnings from tourism and the inflow of overseas capital. Sugar production fell, but higher prices increased export earnings. Real output in manufacturing and processing rose about 5% and in building and construction about 14%. Industrial unrest and strikes by building, airline, and sugar workers reflected the increased cost of living, due partly to food shortages and the unpopularity of a prices and incomes policy to curb inflation. The government passed drastic and controversial antistrike legislation.

Control of the sugar industry passed to the Fijian government. Negotiations for a new five-year international sugar agreement at Geneva proceeded satisfactorily. Fiji participated in the Brussels meeting of countries associated or eligible for association with the EEC, and the question of Fiji's association was considered in the light of a study by the South Pacific

Feed Grains: *see* Agriculture and Fisheries

Field Hockey: *see* Hockey

FIJI

Education. (1971) Primary, pupils 126,331, teachers (1970) 3,717; secondary, pupils 18,094, teachers (1970) 598; vocational, pupils 1,172, teachers (1970) 92; teacher training, students 358, teaching staff (1970) 34; higher (University of the South Pacific), students 1,062, teaching staff 104.

Finance and Trade. Monetary unit: Fiji dollar, with (Sept. 17, 1973) a free rate of F$0.78 to U.S. $1 (F$1.89 = £1 sterling). Budget (1972 est.): revenue F$56.5 million; expenditure F$54.1 million. Foreign trade (1972): imports F$232 million; exports F$105 million. Import sources: Australia 37%; New Zealand 16%; U.K. 11%; Japan 10%; Singapore 6%. Export destinations: U.K. 18%; Australia 15%; U.S. 14%; New Zealand 10%. Main exports (1971): sugar 68%; coconut products 8%; gold 5%. Tourism (1971): visitors 152,000; gross receipts (1970) U.S. $27 million.

Transport and Communications. Roads (1971) *c.* 2,400 km. Railways (1971) *c.* 700 km. Shipping (1972): merchant vessels 100 gross tons and over 20; gross tonnage 4,839. Ships entered (1971) vessels totaling 2,137,000 net registered tons; goods loaded (1971) 618,000 metric tons, unloaded 685,000 metric tons. Telephones (Dec. 1971) 20,000. Radio licenses (Dec. 1971) 52,000.

Agriculture. Production (in 000; metric tons; 1971; 1970 in parentheses): sugar, raw value 322 (361); sweet potatoes *c.* 17 (*c.* 16); cassava *c.* 90 (*c.* 86); copra 28 (28); bananas (exports) *c.* 3 (3). Livestock (in 000; Sept. 1971): cattle *c.* 130; pigs *c.* 27; horses *c.* 27.

Industry. Production (in 000; 1971): cement (metric tons) 78; gold (troy oz.) 89; electricity (kw-hr.) 179,000.

Bureau for Economic Cooperation established by the South Pacific Forum in Suva in November 1972. The need for trade rather than aid was stressed by the prime minister at the meeting of heads of Commonwealth governments in Ottawa. (MARY BOYD)

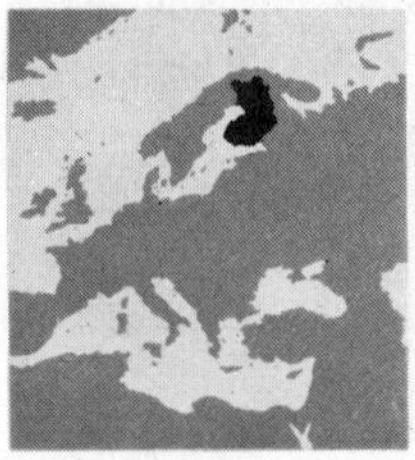

Finland

The republic of Finland is bordered on the north by Norway, on the west by Sweden and the Gulf of Bothnia, on the south by the Gulf of Finland, and on the east by the U.S.S.R. Area: 130,128 sq.mi. (337,032 sq.km.). Pop. (1973 est.): 4,636,000. Cap. and largest city: Helsinki (pop., 1972 est., 507,654). Language: Finnish, Swedish. Religion (1970): Lutheran 92.5%. President in 1973, Urho Kaleva Kekkonen; prime minister, Kalevi Sorsa.

During 1973 the question of whether to sign the EEC free trade agreement initialed in 1972 continued to cause major upheavals in Finnish political life and led indirectly to President Kekkonen's reelection by means of a special parliamentary bill. The agreement, which provided for the progressive abolition of customs duties on industrial goods, was finally signed in Brussels on October 5.

Earlier in the year, in order to safeguard its policy of neutrality and, in particular, to dispel any Soviet misgivings about Finland's relationship with the EEC, Finland became the first non-Communist state to sign a technical cooperation treaty with Comecon. The agreement would have no effect upon tariffs or other foreign trade restrictions.

The third phase of Finland's general reorganization of trading relations with Europe as a whole got under way officially on August 15, when negotiations began in Helsinki between Finland and Bulgaria with a view to the progressive abolition of tariffs and other trade barriers. These were followed by similar negotiations with Hungary, Czechoslovakia, and Poland. Three other Eastern European states—East Germany, Yugoslavia, and Romania—expressed interest in the possibility of similar talks.

Finance, International: *see* Development, Economic; Economy, World; Money and Banking; Payments and Reserves, International

There was much debate on the question of Soviet attitudes to the EEC issue. Late in 1972 three Scandinavian newspapers had published the text of a secret report on talks held between President Kekkonen and Soviet party leader Leonid I. Brezhnev at Zavidovo near Moscow earlier in the year. According to the report, Kekkonen had stressed that he could personally guarantee that the agreement with the EEC would have no negative effects on relations with the U.S.S.R. The Soviet reply was that if the EEC offer made mathematical sense it was nonetheless politically incorrect, and that Finland should wait. Investigations into the source of the news leak led to the resignation of the trade and foreign trade minister, Jussi Linnamo, and the head of the Presidential Office, Antero Jyraenki, after a report of the attorney general had stated that they and former minister for industry Seppo Lindblom had passed secret information to unauthorized persons.

In December 1972 President Kekkonen had announced that he no longer regarded himself as bound by his earlier pledge to continue in office when his third six-year term expired in 1974, saying that he had lost the trust of the Soviet leaders due to the leakage of the secret report. This was interpreted by some as a tactical move to hasten interparty negotiations on

FINLAND

Education. (1970–71) Primary, pupils 416,966, teachers 21,201; secondary, pupils 323,615, teachers 17,519; vocational, pupils 105,058, teachers (1969–70) 9,841; teacher training (1969–70), students 1,660, teachers 391; higher (including 11 universities), students 58,615, teaching staff 6,022.

Finance. Monetary unit: markka, with (Sept. 17, 1973) a free rate of 3.70 markkaa to U.S. $1 (8.91 markkaa = £1 sterling). Gold, SDRs, and foreign exchange, central bank: (June 1973) U.S. $505.7 million; (June 1972) U.S. $735.3 million. Budget (1973 est.) balanced at 14,961,000,000 markkaa. Gross national product: (1972) 52,840,000,000 markkaa; (1971) 47,170,000,000 markkaa. Money supply: (Feb. 1973) 4,757,000,000 markkaa; (Feb. 1972) 4,539,000,000 markkaa. Cost of living (1963 = 100): (June 1973) 183; (June 1972) 165.

Foreign Trade. (1972) Imports 13,114,000,000 markkaa; exports 12,082,000,000 markkaa. Import sources: Sweden 17%; West Germany 17%; U.S.S.R. 12%; U.K. 12%. Export destinations: U.K. 18%; Sweden 17%; U.S.S.R. 12%; West Germany 10%; U.S. 5%. Main exports: paper 25%; machinery 11%; timber 9%; wood pulp 8%; clothing 6%; ships 6%; plywood 5%.

Transport and Communications. Roads (1972) 72,927 km. (including 130 km. expressways). Motor vehicles in use (1972): passenger 818,044; commercial 121,499. Railways: (1971) 5,968 km.; traffic (1972) 2,580,000,000 passenger-km., freight 6,508,000,000 net ton-km. Air traffic (1972): 935.3 million passenger-km.; freight 27,270,000 net ton-km. Navigable inland waterways (1971) 6,674 km. Shipping (1972): merchant vessels 100 gross tons and over 402; gross tonnage 1,630,473. Telephones (Dec. 1971) 1,290,000. Radio licenses (Dec. 1971) 1,791,000. Television licenses (Dec. 1971) 1,076,000.

Agriculture. Production (in 000; metric tons; 1972; 1971 in parentheses): wheat 463 (443); barley 1,140 (1,054); oats 1,245 (1,424); rye 116 (132); potatoes 716 (803); sugar, raw value *c.* 86 (65); butter 83 (84); timber (cu.m.; 1971) 43,000, (1970) 45,100; fish catch (1970) 81, (1969) 87. Livestock (in 000; June 1972): cattle 1,835; sheep 155; pigs 1,093; horses 60; chickens 9,910.

Industry. Production (in 000; metric tons; 1972): iron ore (66% metal content) 852; pig iron 1,183; crude steel 1,456; copper 38; cement 1,976; plywood (cu.m.; 1971) 657; cellulose (1971) 3,921; mechanical wood pulp (1971) 2,008; chemical wood pulp (1971) 4,238; newsprint 1.491; other paper and board (1971) 3,117; electricity (kw-hr.) 26,279,000; manufactured gas (cu.m.) 47,000.

his reelection. After being reelected in 1968, Kekkonen had said that he would not stand for election again. Early in 1972, however, he had indicated that he was willing to continue in office but would not campaign as a candidate. After complicated interparty negotiations and heated debates in Parliament, the necessary special legislation was passed on Jan. 18, 1973, by 170 votes to 28 with one abstention. The bill, the second of its kind in Finnish history—Field Marshal Carl Gustav Mannerheim had been elected by Parliament during World War II—extended the president's current mandate for a further four years, until 1978.

The year also saw the fulfillment of Finland's patient efforts in the first phase of the Conference on Security and Cooperation in Europe. After 198 days of preconference bargaining at a technical school near Helsinki, the 35-nation conference finally assembled on July 3 at the ultramodern Finlandia House conference centre. Following five days of speeches and celebrations, a somewhat hazy resolution was formulated and the foreign ministers returned home. The conference was continued at expert level in Geneva, beginning on September 18.

For many years Finland had maintained an attitude of extreme caution on the question of the various divided states of the world. However, on Dec. 8, 1972, an agreement was signed on the establishment of diplomatic relations with East Germany. A similar agreement with West Germany was signed on Jan. 7, 1973, and the two came into force simultaneously. During the heavy bombing of North Vietnam in December 1972, Finland recognized the Hanoi government but maintained that the situation in the south was "too unclear to justify recognition." On June 2, 1973, an agreement was reached on the establishment of diplomatic relations with North Korea, followed by a similar agreement with South Korea on August 24.

On October 2 world-famous long-distance runner Paavo Nurmi died at the age of 76 (*see* OBITUARIES).

(ILMARI SUNDBLAD)

The largest fire in Finland's history broke out on May 23, 1973, when three oil tanks exploded at the Ykspihlaja fuel storage site near the west coast town of Kokkola.

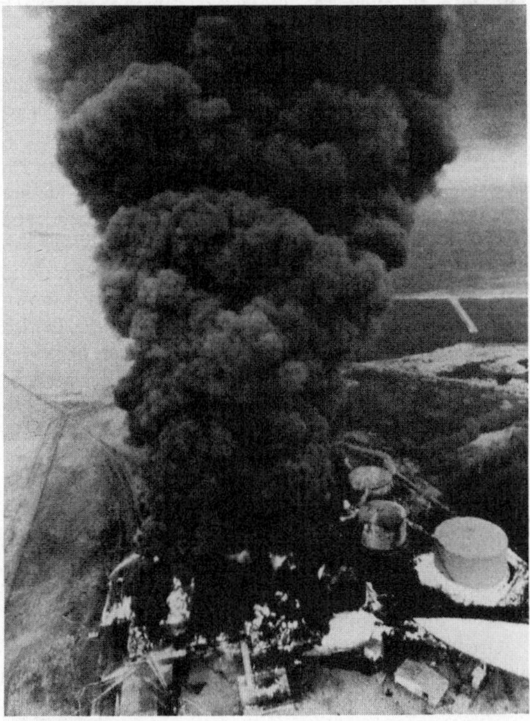

WIDE WORLD

Food Processing

The U.S. Food and Drug Administration (FDA) in 1973 introduced legislation concerning nutrient labeling, other measures to prevent consumer deception, and regulations to restrict the claims made in regard to vitamin, mineral, and other supplements. Because of several cases of botulism from canned foods, the FDA ordered a review of canning and made new regulations on processing. The U.S. and Norway restricted the use of nitrates and nitrites. The FDA introduced regulations prohibiting the industrial use of polychlorinated biphenyls (PCBs) in heat exchangers and for other purposes in animal feeds and food-processing plants. It also established temporary safe tolerances for PCBs in packaging materials. The FDA removed saccharin from the GRAS (Generally Recognized as Safe) list pending further investigation, and Japan banned it; however, European specialists, after reviewing the evidence, concluded that restrictions were not justified. Canadian authorities issued proposals for new regulations on nitrates and nitrites in cured meats, minimum protein requirements for certain meat products, and minimum nutritional requirements for simulated meat products based on spun or textured vegetable protein.

The Swedish Agency for Administrative Development drew up detailed proposals for the world's first environmental data bank with a view toward collecting comprehensive information on environmental hazards. It would embrace factory discharges, environmentally dangerous substances, food additives, nuclear power risks, aircraft noise, and "hard-to-explain phenomena," such as sudden deaths of fish, insect infestations, and injuries sustained by seabirds. A computer would note early warning signals in the case of a potential hazard. The British authorities were confronted with the dual problem of updating various regulations and of harmonizing these with existing EEC regulations. Amendments pertaining to cheese, antioxidants, colouring matters, lead and arsenic, and heat-treated milk were proposed. Work was undertaken at a British research institute on alternative flour improvers in view of an EEC proposal to ban chlorination. It was established that heating whole wheat and subsequently milling it to a predetermined particle size achieved the desired characteristics without chemical treatment.

Production Technology. French technologists developed a process for canning vegetables whereby the evacuated cans were directly heated by gas flames to the sterilizing temperature, held for some minutes, and water-cooled; improved quality was claimed. U.S. scientists overcame the problem of high costs and shortage of skilled labour in the oyster industry by the novel use of a laser beam to destroy the adhesive layer between the muscle and the shell without causing heat damage. The cost of fruit sorting and examination for internal quality defects was cut as a result of a new type of photometer introduced by workers at the U.S. Department of Agriculture (USDA).

A Swiss company invented a new absorption technique to replace chocolate conching, thereby reducing the processing time from 72 hours to 20 minutes. A U.S. firm eliminated starch molds for making the cream centres of chocolates by casting these in metal molds coated with a nonadhesive fluorinated hydrocarbon.

Fires:
see Disasters; Insurance

Fisheries:
see Agriculture and Fisheries

Floods:
see Disasters; Engineering Projects

A British research institute investigated microwave baking and showed that bread of good texture could be made from soft English wheat instead of imported strong wheat. The institute estimated that imports could be cut by 800,000 tons if the English wheat were used for half the nation's needs.

Removal of the protein from cheese whey by ultrafiltration was successfully accomplished by several U.S. firms and a Danish company. Commercial plants to apply the technique were commissioned in the U.S., Denmark, France, and New Zealand; a Swiss company developed fermentation processes for the production of proteins from the deproteinized whey.

The use of enzymes that are chemically attached to the surface of membranes of porous resins, the so-called immobilized enzymes, attracted much attention from workers in many countries because this method proved superior to previous methods of enzyme treatment. It was mainly used in the degradation of starch to dextrins, maltodextrins, and glucose and for the isomerization of glucose to fructose. A new and more economical method for the continuous production of such syrups was developed at a British university utilizing an advanced immobilized enzyme system. A process was also reported by Peruvian scientists for the continuous conversion of cassava to glucose syrup, also using an immobilized enzyme system. Another novel application of enzymes was the decaffeination of coffee by a *Penicillium* enzyme.

A British meat-research institute reported upon a comprehensive analysis of weight losses at all stages from preslaughter starvation through butchering, freezing, cold storage, vacuum packing while in display cabinets, and thawing. The effects of curing and smoking were also investigated. Several large meat complexes with processing facilities, cold storage, and organized distribution systems were established in Iran. An automated factory for the slaughter of 12,000 hogs daily and 1,600 head of cattle per week was commissioned in The Netherlands with the object of converting a substantial part of the output to vacuum-packed fine cuts for wholesale distribution. A factory was constructed in the U.S. for the completely automated continuous production of skinless frankfurter sausages at the rate of 12,000 lb. per hour.

The shortage of glass bottles in Britain caused a number of dairies to change over to paper and plastic containers in spite of the traditional attachment to glass. A British research group with support from the Ministry of Agriculture began a three-year study on the packaging of fruit and vegetables in glass. Reported to be the first comprehensive research of its kind ever undertaken, it set out to examine all aspects of glass packaging of field crops. A new type of clear vinyl film that is resistant to puncture was introduced in the United States for the vacuum packaging of meat cuts.

Irradiation. Reports were presented at the second International Symposium on Food Irradiation in Bombay on the irradiation of soybeans during sprouting to reduce the oligosaccharide content and thereby diminish the incidence of flatulence. Details were given of toxicological tests on irradiated wheat, shrimps, enzyme-inactivated beef, cornstarch, strawberries, mushrooms, and chicken. No toxicity was demonstrated with any of these items.

Researchers in Thailand demonstrated that the shelf life of many tropical and subtropical fruits could be extended sufficiently by irradiation to facilitate marketing overseas. It was reported that one of the best uses of irradiation was to extend the market life of vegetables, and clearance was given for the human consumption of irradiated potatoes in Canada, Denmark, Israel, Japan, The Netherlands, Spain, the U.S., and the Soviet Union and for irradiated onions in Canada and Israel. The efficacy of grain irradiation was reported to be superior to that of chemical insecticides with the additional advantage that treatment could be carried out after sealing the container. Irradiated wheat and flour received clearance in Canada, the U.S., and the Soviet Union.

Fisheries. Ocean scientists of the U.S. and the Soviet Union met during the year to discuss the depletion of many species of fish and what action should be taken. Fish on experimental farms in Scotland were successfully raised from egg to marketable size, and progress was made in rearing turbot, lemon sole, cod, pollack, and gray mullet after capture at sea. A French fisheries-research institute began the artificial rearing of bass from the larvae with only moderate losses.

The green turtle farm established in 1968 at the Grand Cayman Islands successfully bred turtles for the first time in captivity. The Soviet research institute for the poultry industry developed a feed for broilers that proved superior to fish meal. It was made from Antarctic krill, a crustacean that had increased substantially since the depletion of whales and for which reserves were estimated at 1,800,000,000 tons. A new £1,250,000 herring-processing factory, claimed to be the most modern in the world, began operation in Scotland.

New Foods. Really new foods are a rare phenomenon since there is very little that is edible that has not been consumed by one community or another. The only true ones that have appeared recently are those derived from novel proteins not previously consumed by man. But on a broader basis there was much new development with a view to increasing the consumption of nutritious foodstuffs of limited acceptability in their native condition. Many new or revised convenience foods and snacks were introduced as part of the competitive growth process of the food industry and also to meet the increased demand for snack foods.

There was a proliferation of fermentation processes for the production of microbial proteins from a wide range of substrates, including petroleum, natural gas, sulfite liquor, cassava, carob, molasses, cheese whey, starch, and many food industry wastes. A Finnish research institute developed a process for the production of fungal protein from paper industry wastes and planned to produce 100,000 tons per year. A Swedish company developed an ingenious fermentation process using two yeasts growing in symbiosis to break down and ferment starchy wastes. Invented by a British firm was a novel process for the conversion of North Sea gas to methanol, which was then fermented to yield microbial protein of high nutritive value. Negotiations were started with some Middle East oil-producing companies to convert the massive quantities of gas burned off at the wellheads to methanol and subsequently to protein. Only the yeast-derived proteins grown on natural substrates proved acceptable as food, and so most efforts were directed toward using the microbial proteins as animal feed to achieve increased meat production.

Great activity took place in the development of proteins and protein concentrates from many sources such as oilseeds and even some grains. From oats

WIDE WORLD

Jean Mayer (seated at table, centre), of the School of Public Health, Harvard University, testifies before the Senate Select Committee on Nutrition and Human Needs in March 1973. The committee was investigating experts' warnings to ban child-oriented TV ads for nonnutritional sugary breakfast cereals.

a protein concentrate was obtained suitable for the fortification of foods and beverages. Researchers in the U.S. began an investigation of tannery wastes with a view to producing products suitable for human use. A substantial feeding trial was organized in India to test the acceptability and nutritive value of leaf protein produced according to a technique developed at a British research institute.

The growing demand for meat coupled with high prices accelerated the wider penetration and acceptance of textured vegetable protein preparations as meat extenders for institutional feeding and for domestic use. The U.S. government authorized their use for the school lunch program. There were substantial technological improvements to the texture of these meat substitutes, and flavour manufacturers devoted much effort to the development of new types of meat flavourings to improve taste acceptability. According to a U.S. market-research organization, protein ingredients used to supplement foods totaled 970 million lb. in 1972, of which textured vegetable proteins accounted for 52 million lb.

Because of the international importance of bread, work continued on its production from nonwheat flours and wheat flours supplemented with other protein additives such as soy or cottonseed proteins. USDA researchers overcame many of these problems by the use of sugar esters, and satisfactory bread, containing 20% protein, was made from an admixture of wheat, corn, sesame, and soybean flours. A U.S. firm introduced a fortified loaf for toasting, two slices of which contained the nutritional equivalent of a six-ounce glass of milk, one egg, and two slices of bacon. Another firm introduced a frozen, pan-ready mini-loaf of 12 buttered slices.

Snack foods based upon textured vegetable proteins appeared in many interesting guises, including imitation mushrooms, a seafood extender complying with U.S. requirements for school lunches, a range of precooked beef preparations extended with textured vegetable proteins and other protein additives for institutional feeding. A novel deep-fried snack consisted of chopped soybeans and onions in batter.

A Swiss company introduced a protein supplement based on wheat, soybeans, and chick-peas supplemented with the amino acid methionine, and a Dutch organization developed an acceptable product based on equal parts of dried fish and yam flour. One U.S. firm introduced a boil-in-bag snack consisting of brown rice in beef stock, while another introduced deep-fried rice fingers flavoured with onion, celery, and garlic.

The high price and scarcity of milk proteins stimulated much work on milk replacers and extenders based on vegetable proteins. Progress was made in the recovery of cheese whey proteins, and these found many uses as supplements for fortifying beverages and baby foods. Various other innovations in the dairy industry included the introduction of a chocolate-coated milk bar; a range of fruit preparations, which, when added to cold milk, thickened rapidly to form a creamy dessert; and new types of yogurt, especially the extension of low-fat varieties in Europe. The Australian government licensed throughout the world the new technology for the production of butterfat and beef that contained much polyunsaturated fat, based on the use of protected polyunsaturated fat included in the cattle feed.

Improvements in deboning techniques made possible the introduction in Britain of kipper fingers as an alternative to whitefish fingers. A U.S. firm developed a novel seafood product, tasting like shrimp, from a species of fish plentiful in the Gulf of Mexico. The British White Fish Authority in cooperation with a university research unit developed a new line of fish recipes for institutional catering.

Several years of discussions concerning the better utilization of wild game from Africa culminated in the introduction of a line of canned game products following the establishment of a slaughterhouse in the Kruger National Park. Other innovations included, in the U.S., sweet-potato chips, deep-fried batter-dipped pineapple chunks, and a line of frozen omelettes. A British company introduced a novel line of nutritious dried soups for use as snack meals by simply adding the contents of a packet to a cup of hot water. (H. B. HAWLEY)

See also Agriculture and Fisheries; Commodities, Primary; Prices.

ENCYCLOPÆDIA BRITANNICA FILMS. *Produce—From Farm to Market* (1968); *Milk: From Farm to You* (1973).

Football

Association Football (Soccer). While the European, Asian, American, and African competitions evoked their usual interest and fervour, additional excitement was provided during 1973 by the qualifying rounds for the World Cup finals, to be held in West Germany during the summer of 1974. Before the end of October 1973 several countries had qualified as potential finalists to join defending champion Brazil and host West Germany in the finals. There were some notable casualties along the way, including Israel, which had traveled to the Mexico finals in 1970; Hungary, previous winners of the trophy; Northern Ireland; and England, unexpectedly ousted by Poland. The U.S.S.R. was disqualified because it refused to play in Chile on the ground that the National Stadium had been used as a detention centre after the September coup.

Also during 1973 the persistent problem of hooliganism among spectators at matches in many parts of the world and strikes and threats of strikes by players in both South America and Europe darkened the football scene. Clubs in many countries experienced a decline in attendances at matches, and many laid the blame for this on the swing toward increasingly defensive play and the "disappearance" of wingers, on crowd violence, and on the escalating prices of admission. Suggestions were put forward as to means of halting this drop in spectators and improving the game. More emphasis was laid on scoring, and more leagues operated the goal difference method of separating teams of equal points as opposed to the goal average system; that goals by the visiting team should count double in all competitions was also debated. In England, to make the Football League more competitive, the number of clubs promoted and relegated to a lower rank among each of the top three divisions was increased from two to three, to take effect immediately at the end of the 1973–74 season. Several established players retired: centre half Jack Charlton and forward Bobby Charlton of England, Brazilian centre forwards Pelé (Edson Arantes do Nascimento) and Tostão (Eduardo Andrade), and goalkeeper Gordon Banks (England).

Tottenham Hotspurs' goalie, assisted by Steve Perryman, clears the ball during a Norwich attack in the League Cup Final at Wembley Stadium, London, on March 3, 1973. The Spurs won 1–0.

KEYSTONE

European Cup. Ajax of Amsterdam completed a hat trick of victories in this competition on May 30 in Belgrade, Yugos., by beating Juventus from Turin, Italy, in an entertaining struggle. Horst Blankenberg effectively settled the final after four minutes, when he sent a long pass through the Italians' defense and Johnny Rep, a late choice for the Dutch team, leaped high to head the ball past the twisting Italian goalkeeper, Dino Zoff, for what proved to be the only score of the match. Ajax did not rest on its laurels but persisted in attacking throughout the game and harassed the Juventus defense before 95,000 in the Red Star Stadium. The famed Juventus rearguard, which adopted a man-to-man marking system, was never allowed to get into its stride by the tremendous volume of shots that the Ajax forwards, superbly led by Johan Cruyff, unleashed. Little was seen of the Juventus attack until the second half when the Italians had two good chances to score. Then, José Alatafini found the Dutch goalkeeper, Heinz Stuy, diving at his feet when he was clear, and an inaccurate clearance by Blankenberg struck Gianpietro Marchetti but the ball was easily held by Stuy. Yet, for all their pressure, the men from Amsterdam could not increase the score.

In the semifinals Ajax had eliminated the Spanish champions Real Madrid, winning both legs with an aggregate score of 3–1, while Juventus triumphed over Derby County of England by winning 3–1 at home and sharing a goalless draw in the second leg.

European Cup-Winners' Cup. As with the European Cup, this trophy was won in the final by a single goal, again scored in the opening four minutes. Luciano Chiarugi hammered in a free kick to give AC Milan victory over Leeds United and end a three-year British reign. The Italian club became the first to win this competition twice, having also triumphed five years earlier against SV Hamburg. The final contest, in the Kaftant-zaglion Stadium, Salonika, Greece, on May 16 was marred when violence flared in the closing minutes, and Norman Hunter (Leeds) and Riccardo Sogliano (Milan) were put out of the game. A storm had preceded the kickoff, and steady rain during the match marred much of the play; the teams, too, were below normal strength. Leeds, though the persistent attackers, did not win, AC Milan owing its success in large measure to a brilliant display by goalkeeper William Vecchi. He defied all that the English club could throw at him during a second half of hectic but vain bombardment.

In the semifinals AC Milan had defeated Sparta Prague of Czechoslovakia 2–0 on aggregate, and Leeds had beaten Hajduk Split of Yugoslavia 1–0 on aggregate.

UEFA Cup. British domination of the UEFA Cup tournament continued for the sixth consecutive time, when Liverpool beat Borussia Mönchengladbach 3–2 on aggregate over a two-leg final during May. In the first match, at Liverpool on May 10 (delayed 24 hours because a torrential rainstorm had halted the first attempt after 27 minutes), Liverpool's manager, Bill Shankly, brought in Welsh cap John Toshack to add height to his attack. The move paid off handsomely. Toshack headed on to Kevin Keegan for each of the first two goals, and England cap Larry Lloyd moved forward from his centre-back position to score the third as Borussia failed to snap out of its ultra-defensive setup. Those three goals were not the only shocks for the West Germans in this leg, for Wolfgang Kleff had to save a penalty shot by Keegan and other efforts were too close for German comfort. In the second half, Borussia also received a penalty shot, but goalkeeper Ray Clemence managed to turn it away.

In the second leg, at Mönchengladbach two weeks later, the shoe was on the other foot. Borussia did almost all the attacking, and Liverpool had to defend, often desperately, to keep the West Germans from scoring. Heynckes put the Mönchengladbach team back in the game at the Bokelberg Stadium when he scored twice in the opening 40 minutes. The first goal came on the half hour after an inaccurate back-pass by Ian Callaghan; the energetic Bernd Rupp snapped it up and then crossed the ball for Heynckes to drive home. Though Günter Netzer initiated most of the Germans' attacks, it was Rupp who had a hand in the second goal. He moved down on the left and let the ball roll on, and Heynckes kicked it hard into the net clear of Clemence. Yet despite the wiles of the Borussia men, Liverpool managed to contain their efforts and hold out for victory, though not without a few alarms.

In the semifinals Liverpool had defeated the defending champions, compatriots Tottenham Hotspur (2–2 aggregate), on the away goals rule—when the score is tied after the two games, then those goals scored away from home count double—and Borussia had put out the Dutch team Twente Enschede 5–1 on aggregate.

Inter-Continental Cup. The trouble-strewn Inter-Continental Cup tournament saw the trophy return to Europe when Ajax of Amsterdam beat Independiente of Buenos Aires 4–1 over two legs. The first was held in the Argentine capital on September 6, and, as was usual in these encounters, the game was played scrappily and was spattered with fouls. The Dutch went ahead after a goal by star forward Cruyff, but he left the field with a bad leg injury after 25 minutes. The tactics of the Argentines were so rough that at one stage the Ajax captain, Piet Keizer, warned the referee that he would take his team off for good at half time if an Independiente player deliberately kicked an opponent again. The game continued, but, with the Dutch pulling back into defense and the Argentines' attack being weak, thrills were few. Independiente managed to tie the score a few minutes before the end of the game. In the return match in Amsterdam, three weeks later, the game was even-tempered and, in its more orthodox attacking style, Ajax soon gained the upper hand over its South American rivals. Two goals by Rep and one by Johan Neeskens brought a 3–0 victory.

British Isles Championship. England once more won the British Isles tournament but was far from impressive in doing so, and its performance roused no terror in the hearts of other prospective World Cup finalists. True, England beat the other three United Kingdom countries and only conceded one goal, to Northern Ireland, but its attack could not be measured in the same terms as those of, for example, Brazil and West Germany.

In the opening pair of matches, England took on Northern Ireland at Goodison Park, Liverpool, since the political climate in Northern Ireland made it unwise to stage the game there. Two goals by Martin Chivers (Tottenham Hotspur) were enough to see England through, even though Northern Ireland scored on a penalty shot taken by Dave Clements (Sheffield Wednesday), one of the stars of the Irish side. After that the game deteriorated to such an extent that the crowd of less than 30,000 showed their displeasure by clapping slowly. Meanwhile, at Wrexham, Wales was defeated by Scotland 2–0—George Graham (Manchester United) scored both goals—in a game more marked by robust effort than skill, though Derek Parlane (Glasgow Rangers) at 19 caused his more experienced shadowers more than enough difficulties with his flair and dash.

Three days later England, with a performance vastly superior to its first, won 3–0 over Wales in a less-than-half-filled Wembley Stadium, London, the scorers being Chivers, his Spurs club colleague Martin Peters, and Mike Channon (Southampton). The following night at Hampden Park, Glasgow, Northern Ireland gave England a boost on its way to the title by beating Scotland 2–1. Again the Irish owed much to the ability and drive of Clements and young Trevor Anderson (Manchester United). The Scottish defense looked very fallible, and even by using two substitutes, David Hay (Celtic) and Billy Bremner (Leeds United), Scotland failed to swing the match, though managing a late goal by Ken Dalglish (Celtic).

In the first of the final pair of matches, at Wembley, England defeated the Scots, but only because Peter Shilton (Leicester City) brought off a magnificent one-handed save from Dalglish in the dying minutes, permitting an earlier goal by Peters to decide the game. With a much-changed team the Scots produced a far better performance, particularly in midfield.

On the same day, before only 4,946 spectators at Goodison Park, Northern Ireland firmly handed Wales the last-place wooden spoon when Bryan Hamilton (Ipswich) drove home the only goal from outside the penalty area after a free kick in the 13th minute. Wales showed some improvement from its two earlier performances but still finished with no victories in the tournament. (TREVOR WILLIAMSON)

Rugby. *Rugby Union.* The main event of the 1972–73 period was the full-length tour of the British Isles and France by the New Zealand All Blacks. This tour was to have been followed by a major tour of New Zealand by the South African Springboks, but the New Zealand government refused to allow such a tour to take place because of a fear of disruptive demonstrations against the South African government's policy of apartheid.

The All Blacks, whose tour extended from Oct. 29, 1972, to Feb. 10, 1973, beat Wales 19–16 at Cardiff, Scotland 14–9 at Edinburgh, and England 9–0 at Twickenham; then they were held to a draw, 10–10, by Ireland in Dublin and were defeated 13–6 by France in Paris. They had a close game against Wales, largely because their scrummaging was relatively weak, but thereafter they improved this aspect of their play so that against England and Scotland they were never in the same amount of difficulty. Ireland's exceptionally strong and experienced scrummaging kept the issue of this match in doubt until the final goal-kick, Barry McGann, the Irish standoff half, narrowly failing with a conversion kick that would have won the match for Ireland. The All Blacks' match against France was the last of the tour, and by this time they had lost their freshness. At the same time, the French played positive attacking rugby based on the sudden, swift combination of their captain, Walter Spanghero, at no. 8 and Max Barrau, their scrum half.

The All Blacks, captained by Ian Kirkpatrick from wing forward, had an overall playing record of 23 wins, 5 losses, 2 ties, points for 568, and points against 254. They thus had a slightly less impressive record than any of their six predecessors on tour in Britain. They were beaten in only the second match of the tour by the Llanelli club, and in the eighth match North-West Counties beat them 16–14, thus becoming the first English noninternational side ever to beat a touring team from New Zealand. The All Blacks' other three defeats were by Midland Counties West, 16–8, by the Barbarians, 23–11, and by France. The game against the Barbarians, played at Cardiff, was memorable for the superb running and passing of the Barbarians, captained by John Dawes, the man who had led the Lions to their victories in New Zealand in 1971. Keith Murdoch, one of the All Blacks' prop forwards, was sent home during the tour as a unique disciplinary measure by the manager, Ernie Todd. Murdoch was involved in an incident in a Cardiff hotel on the night following the Welsh international match, the 11th of the tour.

For the first time in the history of the home international championship, the 1973 event ended in a tie between all the competing countries. Moreover, each of the five countries won both its home matches. The French were the first to show form, defeating Scotland 16–13 in Paris. Wales then gained an expected victory over England, 25–9, in Cardiff, but Welsh progress was halted at Murrayfield, where Scotland won 10–9. Ireland began with a sound 18–9 success over England in Dublin, but England upset form by subsequently defeating France 14–6 at Twickenham. The sequence of home wins continued, Scotland beating Ireland 19–14 at Murrayfield, Wales defeating Ireland 16–12 in Cardiff, and England topping Scotland 20–13 at Twickenham. The last two matches seemed to give France a great chance of winning the championship, but, after duly winning at home against Wales, 12–3, the French were beaten 6–4 by Ireland in Dublin.

Scotland during the 1972–73 season celebrated the 100th anniversary of the founding of the Scottish Rugby Union with two separate occasions. In October 1972, players from all four home countries took part in a match at Murrayfield in which a combined Scotland and Ireland team defeated a combined England and Wales team 30–21. Then in March and April 1973, players from the leading rugby countries of the world gathered in Scotland for three special events. In the first of these, at Murrayfield, Scotland achieved a victory, 27–16, over a team composed of players from New Zealand, South Africa, Australia, and France. In the second, at Galashiels, a similarly composed team from overseas beat a Scottish Districts team 43–8. The third of these special events was the first international seven-a-side tournament ever held. The countries taking part in this tournament at Murrayfield were Scotland, Ireland, Wales, England, France, New Zealand, and Australia. In addition, the president of the Scottish Rugby Union raised a team that included South Africans and Scots. The tournament was won by England, which beat Ireland 22–18 in the final.

French and Scottish players leap for the ball during the first match of the Five Nations Tournament in Paris, Jan. 13, 1973. France won 16 to 13.

A.F.P./PICTORIAL PARADE

Wales made a five-match tour of Canada in May and June, scoring more than 30 points in each of its games. Wales, captained by Gareth Edwards from scrum half, toured with a full-strength team except for two players who were not available. In the only international match of the tour Wales beat Canada 58–20 in Toronto.

England was scheduled to make a three-week tour of Argentina in August and September, but this was canceled because of threats by Argentine guerrilla organizations to kidnap England players. In place of this tour England visited Fiji and New Zealand. Captained by John Pullin from hooker, England beat Fiji 13–12 at Suva, lost its three provincial games in New Zealand, but beat the All Blacks 16–12 in the only test match in New Zealand. Meanwhile, Romania took England's place as tourists in Argentina, losing 15–9 and 24–3 at Buenos Aires.

The annual meeting of the International Board, held in Edinburgh at the time of the Scottish centenary celebrations, produced three important alterations in the laws of the game. First, the value of a try was increased from three points to four. Second, a fumble was not to be considered a knock-on provided the player recovered the ball before it touched the ground. Third, there must be a gap of one yard between players of the same team at a line-out, and this gap must be maintained until the ball has touched either the ground or a player taking part in the line-out.

Rugby League. The main Rugby League event of 1972–73 was the World Cup competition held in France in October and November 1972, the competing countries being France, Great Britain, Australia (the defending champions), and New Zealand. France opened the tournament by beating New Zealand 20–9, and then Great Britain won a fast and exciting game against Australia 27–21. In the next two matches Great Britain and Australia firmly established themselves as the two strongest teams in the competition: Great Britain beat France 13–4, and Australia defeated New Zealand 9–5. This impression was confirmed when Great Britain next beat New Zealand 53–19 (the highest score the British team had ever reached in international competition) and Australia won from France 31–9. Therefore, the final, at Lyons, was between Great Britain and Australia. This match ended in a draw, 10–10, after extra time, but Great Britain was declared winner of the World Cup because of its superior scoring record in the earlier matches.

(DAVID FROST)

U.S. Football. The Miami Dolphins gained the championship of the National Football League for the second straight year when they defeated the Minnesota Vikings 24–7 in the Super Bowl on Jan. 13, 1974, in Houston. Not since Green Bay in 1967–68 had a team won two Super Bowls in a row. Notre Dame was ranked first among the college teams.

College. Tradition-rich Notre Dame, with its first undefeated team in 25 years, emerged as the 1973 national collegiate champion after a season in which at least four other schools had legitimate chances for the honour. The crown went to the Fighting Irish after they defeated Alabama 24–23 on a field goal by Bob Thomas in the dying moments of the Sugar Bowl. Outstanding members of Coach Ara Parseghian's team were quarterback Tom Clements, running backs Eric Penick and Art Best, and defensive tackle Steve Niehaus.

Alabama won 11 consecutive games for Coach Paul ("Bear") Bryant before losing in the Sugar Bowl and finishing fourth in the Associated Press rankings. Notre Dame's other chief opposition for the national title came from Ohio State, Penn State, and Oklahoma. Second-ranked Ohio State crushed Southern California 42–21 in the Rose Bowl, but its undefeated season was tainted by a controversial 10–10 tie with Michigan in the game to determine the Big Ten champion. When the league's athletic directors voted to send Ohio State to the Bowl, they were scorned by critics who believed that Michigan, which also was unbeaten, had been passed over because of an injury to its starting quarterback.

Despite a perfect season that included a 16–9 win over Louisiana State University in the Orange Bowl, Penn State was voted only the fifth-best team in the country due mainly to a mediocre schedule. The nation's most appealing team may well have been third-ranked Oklahoma, which was completely overlooked before the season when recruiting violations cost it a star quarterback and barred it from Bowl games after the 1973 and 1974 seasons. But first-year Coach Barry Switzer took an offense built around a running quarterback, Steve Davis, and a defense anchored on the line by the Selmon brothers—Lucious, Dewey, and LeRoy—and marched the Sooners to 10 victories and 1 tie in 11 games. Michigan was ranked sixth in the Associated Press poll, followed by Nebraska, Southern California, and Arizona State and Houston, which tied for ninth.

John Cappelletti, who gained 1,522 yd. and scored 17 touchdowns during the regular season, became the first Penn State player to win the Heisman Trophy, the symbol of the country's top college player. The Outland Trophy for the best lineman went to offensive tackle John Hicks of Ohio State.

The leading rusher in the country was Mark Kellar, a senior fullback from Northern Illinois, who gained 1,719 yd. Tony Dorsett of Pittsburgh, Cappelletti, Archie Griffin of Ohio State (1,428 yd.), and Roosevelt Leaks of Texas (1,415) trailed Kellar. Tailback Jim Jennings of Rutgers tallied 128 pt. on 21 touchdowns and 2 extra points to lead the nation in scoring.

A strong throwing arm enabled quarterback Jesse Freitas of San Diego State to lead the country in total offense with an average of 263.7 yd. per game as well as in many passing categories. About the only one he failed to achieve was touchdown passes, which went to Arizona State's Danny White with 28. Jay Miller of Brigham Young University was the top pass catcher with 100.

Arizona State led the nation in team scoring by averaging 44.6 pt. a game and in total offense by averaging 565.5 yd. per contest. Alabama set national records by rushing for 748 yd. and collecting 833 yd. in total offense while ravaging Virginia Tech 77–6. The best defensive teams were Ohio State, which allowed just 4.3 pt. a game, and Miami of Ohio, which yielded an average of only 177.4 yd. each game.

Penn State relied on its 11–0 regular-season record to win the Lambert Trophy as the top major college team in the East for the third consecutive year and the tenth in the past 13. Dartmouth won the Ivy League championship, which it had held all or part of for five straight years. Kevin Rogan, a senior quarterback making his first varsity start, engineered Yale to a 35–0 victory over Harvard in the 90th meeting between the two schools. In the other major traditional contest in the East, Navy smashed Army 51–0 in their 74th meeting. The University of Connecticut won the Yankee Conference.

Powerful Alabama experienced no trouble winning all eight of its Southeastern Conference games and the league title. North Carolina State led the Atlantic Coast Conference with a 6–0 record. East Carolina won the Southern Conference, and Western Kentucky did likewise in the Ohio Valley.

The Big Ten ended with Ohio State and Michigan in a tie for first. The rugged Big Eight produced not only Oklahoma but Nebraska, which won 11 games, including a 19–3 whipping of Texas, the Southwest Conference champion, in the Cotton Bowl. Miami of Ohio used its stubborn defense to gain the Mid-American Conference title and win all ten of its regular-season games. Tied for the Missouri Valley Conference championship were Tulsa and North Texas State, with 5–1 league records.

In a pair of neighbourly rivalries, Southern California edged UCLA to win the Pac-8 championship, and Arizona State did the same to Arizona in the Western Athletic Conference.

While the National Football League was experiencing difficulty in maintaining attendance, the crowds at college football games were increasing for the 20th consecutive season. National Collegiate Sports Services listed the total as 31,282,540, roughly a 1% increase over the 30,828,802 who walked through the turnstiles in 1972.

Professional. For many the main interest and excitement in the National Football League in 1973 came not from Miami and Minnesota but from O. J. Simpson (*see* BIOGRAPHY), an extraordinary running

WIDE WORLD

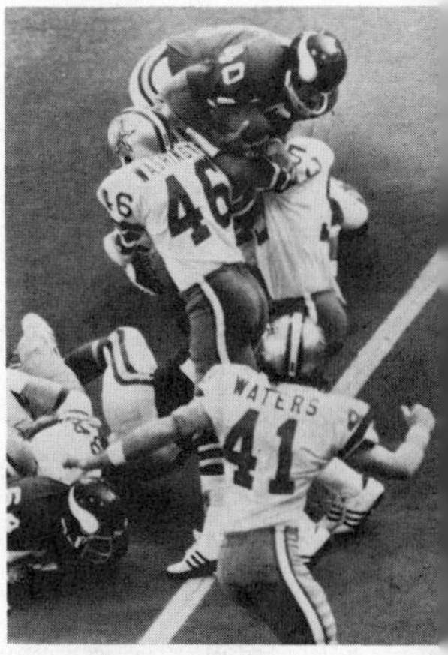

Dallas Cowboys Mark Washington (46) and John Babinecz (53) upend Minnesota Vikings' punt returner Charlie West in the National Football Conference championship game on Dec. 30, 1973, at Irving, Tex. The Vikings won 27–10.

UPI COMPIX

Ohio State fullback Pete Johnson skips across the goal line for one of the three touchdowns he scored as the Buckeyes overwhelmed Southern California 42–21 in the Rose Bowl, Jan. 1, 1974.

NFL Final Standings and Play-offs, 1973

	W	L	T
AMERICAN CONFERENCE			
Eastern Division			
Miami	12	2	0
Buffalo	9	5	0
New England	5	9	0
Baltimore	4	10	0
New York Jets	4	10	0
Central Division			
Cincinnati	10	4	0
*Pittsburgh	10	4	0
Cleveland	7	5	2
Houston	1	13	0
Western Division			
Oakland	9	4	1
Denver	7	5	2
Kansas City	7	5	2
San Diego	2	11	1
NATIONAL CONFERENCE			
Eastern Division			
Dallas	10	4	0
*Washington	10	4	0
Philadelphia	5	8	1
St. Louis	4	9	1
New York Giants	2	11	1
Central Division			
Minnesota	12	2	0
Detroit	6	7	1
Green Bay	5	7	2
Chicago	3	11	0
Western Division			
Los Angeles	12	2	0
Atlanta	9	5	0
New Orleans	5	9	0
San Francisco	5	9	0

*Fourth qualifier for play-offs.

Play-offs

American semifinals
Miami 34, Cincinnati 16
Oakland 33, Pittsburgh 14

National semifinals
Minnesota 27, Washington 20
Dallas 27, Los Angeles 16

American finals
Miami 27, Oakland 10

National finals
Minnesota 27, Dallas 10

Super Bowl
Miami 24, Minnesota 7

back for the Buffalo Bills. On a snowy December day in New York's Shea Stadium, the acrobatic, 212-lb. Simpson burst for seven yards against the New York Jets and thus became the sport's first rusher to gain more than 2,000 yd. in one season. In all, it took him a record 332 carries to gain 2,003 yd. and break the mark of the Cleveland Browns' Jim Brown, who had run for 1,863 yd. a decade before. While proving he was everything he had appeared to be in his Heisman Trophy-winning career at Southern California, Simpson established a spate of other records: he gained 200 or more yards in three different games, he put two of those games back to back, he rushed for 250 yd. in one game, and he carried the ball 39 times in another. As final testimony to the magnitude of his performance, Simpson enabled Buffalo to become the first team to run for more than 3,000 yd.

Miami, the defending world champions, lost only two regular-season games as Coach Don Shula marched the Dolphins to a third straight Super Bowl with the same mechanical precision that achieved their unprecedented 14–0 record in 1972. Miami got through the American Conference play-offs by eliminating the Cincinnati Bengals 34–16 and the Oakland Raiders 27–10. The Bengals failed to stop the running of Eugene ("Mercury") Morris, who gained 106 yd., and the passing combination of quarterback Bob Griese to wide receiver Paul Warfield, which accounted for two touchdowns. Against Oakland, which had halted the Dolphins' regular-season winning streak at 18 with a 12–7 victory early in the year, Griese was content to hand the ball to Larry Csonka and let him run for 117 yd. and three scores. In both games, as they had all season, centre Jim Langer and guard Larry Little distinguished themselves on offense, while linebacker Nick Buoniconti and safety Dick Anderson did likewise on defense.

Minnesota arrived at the Super Bowl via the steady play of Fran Tarkenton, a quarterback demeaned throughout his statistically impressive career as a loser, and an aging defense enjoying what may have been its last moment of greatness. The Washington Redskins welcomed the Vikings to the National Conference play-offs by giving them a 27–20 victory. In one 65-second span early in the fourth quarter, Tarkenton turned Washington mistakes into touchdown passes of 28 yd. and 6 yd. to John Gilliam.

The Vikings then matched the Dallas Cowboys bumble for bumble in the National Conference championship game but hung on to win 27–10. Tarkenton and Gilliam teamed up for a 54-yd. scoring bomb; rookie star Chuck Foreman ran for a touchdown; and cornerback Bobby Bryant iced the victory by scoring on a 63-yd. pass interception. All the while, defensive linemen Alan Page, Carl Eller, Gary Larsen, and Jim Marshall were playing as they had done in the days when they were renowned as Minnesota's "Purple People Eaters."

In the Super Bowl Miami dominated the game throughout to defeat Minnesota 24–7. Dolphin fullback Larry Csonka was the individual star of the contest, scoring two touchdowns and setting a Super Bowl record by rushing for 145 yd. He credited Miami's offensive line for opening the holes to make his runs possible. The other Miami scores came on a touchdown run by Jim Kiick and a 28-yd. field goal by Garo Yepremian. Tarkenton scored Minnesota's only touchdown on a 4-yd. run.

Dallas and Washington emerged from the National Conference's Eastern Division with identical 10–4 records, each beating the other once, but the Cowboys gained the role of champions by outscoring the Redskins in their two meetings and forcing George Allen's veteran team to become a wild-card entry in the play-offs. The Dallas offense was as lively as ever, thanks largely to quarterback Roger Staubach and running back Calvin Hill, while the defense, primarily tackle Bob Lilly, began to creak with age. Injuries hampered runner Larry Brown and quarterbacks Billy Kilmer and Sonny Jurgensen of Washington, but linebacker Chris Hanburger anchored a defense that kept the Redskins in contention.

Out of the Western Division of the National Conference came the Los Angeles Rams, who under new Coach Chuck Knox lost only two games and those by a total of three points. The Rams boasted the NFL's premier long-pass combination in quarterback John Hadl and wide receiver Harold Jackson. They fleeced Dallas for four touchdowns in an early-season game, but the Cowboys gave them just one pass in the play-offs and won 27–16.

Cincinnati beat Pittsburgh twice, and when both teams finished the season with 10–4 records the Bengals became the American Conference's Central Division champions and the Steelers the conference's wild-card team. The keys to the Bengals' success were the running of Essex Johnson and rookie Charles ("Boobie") Clark and the defense of tackle Mike Reid. Oakland knocked the Steelers from the play-offs 33–14, gaining revenge for Pittsburgh's controversial 13–7 victory over them in 1972.

In his first year as Oakland's first-string quarterback, Ken Stabler was the league's most accurate passer with a 62.7% completion rate. Staubach of Dallas and Roman Gabriel of Philadelphia each threw 23 scoring passes to tie for the league lead in that department. Philadelphia's Harold Carmichael caught an NFL high of 67 passes, 9 of them for touchdowns. The league's highest-scoring player was Larry Brown of Washington, who had 14 touchdowns.

Perhaps the most telling statistics in the NFL involved the kickers. Ten of them scored more than 100 pt., with David Ray of Los Angeles amassing a league-leading 130. The 18th-best kicker, who had 76 pt., would have been the third-leading scorer among regular players. As more and more coaches decided not to gamble on long touchdown passes in favour of the more certain three points from a field goal, fans and writers began to protest. Some suggested reducing the value of field goals.

O. J. Simpson darts for yardage during the Buffalo Bills' 34–14 win over the New York Jets at Shea Stadium in New York City, Dec. 16, 1973. Simpson smashed the single-season rushing record, and became first player to gain over 2,000 yd. in a season.

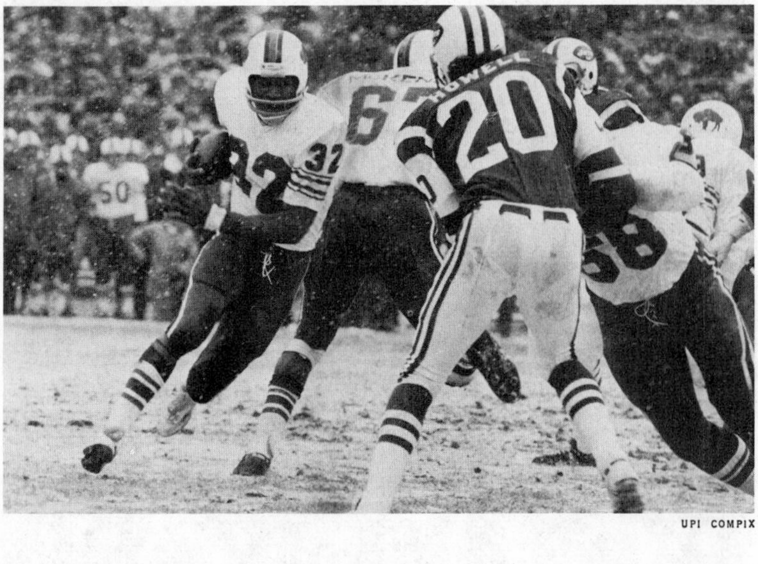

UPI COMPIX

The most tangible evidence that professional football was beginning to fall from favour was the first decrease in attendance in almost two decades. It dropped from a record 10.8 million in 1972 to barely more than 10 million. And one of the reasons for that was television, which had done so much to make the game the most popular in the country. Congress abolished the right of teams to black out home games sold out for three or more days in advance, and many fans responded by staying away and watching on television even though they had tickets. For the 182 regular-season games, there were 1,016,565 absent ticket-holders, an increase of 63% over 1972.

To compound the NFL's worries, plans for the new World Football League were being readied by Gary Davidson, a proven success at starting professional basketball, hockey, tennis, and soccer leagues. The WFL would be international, would alter the rules to increase scoring, and would seek to lure disgruntled NFL players along with college and Canadian stars.

Canadian Football. A lineman who played offense as well as defense and a quarterback who was not supposed to play at all combined talents to lead the Ottawa Rough Riders to the Canadian Football League (CFL) championship. Fittingly, neither tackle Charlie Branch nor veteran Rick Cassata performed any better all season than in the 22–18 Ottawa win over the Edmonton Eskimos that clinched the Grey Cup, the league's victory symbol. Branch emerged as the game's outstanding player, while Cassata deftly mixed runs with spot passes to set up touchdowns by backs Jim Evenson and Rhome Nixon. The championship substantiated beyond a doubt the faith of Ottawa Coach Jack Gotta, who had refused to let the Rough Riders management release Cassata before the season began.

Although never allowed to break free in the championship game, split end George McGowan of Edmonton was named the regular season's outstanding performer by Canadian football writers. Ray Nettles, a middle linebacker for the British Columbia Lions, was voted the outstanding lineman, and the rookie-of-the-year award went to Montreal Alouettes wide receiver Johnny Rodgers, who won the Heisman Trophy in U.S. college football in 1972. (JOHN SCHULIAN)

Forestry

A new forest inventory carried out by the Food and Agriculture Organization (FAO) of the United Nations revealed that forests cover 9,170,000,000 ac., 28% of the world's land area. This was 2,470,000,000 ac. less than in the last forest inventory, conducted in 1963, but FAO hastened to explain that the forest land had not diminished to that extent; rather, the new survey was more precise. Of this forest land, one-third supported softwoods (coniferous trees) and two-thirds supported hardwoods. Most of the softwood acreage was in the U.S.S.R., with 1,366,000,000 ac., and in North America, with 1,087,000,000 ac. Of the 425 million ac. of softwoods in the rest of the world, about half were in Europe. Latin America had the largest area of hardwood forest, with 1,831,000,000 ac., followed by Africa, with 1,700,000,000 ac., and Asia (exclusive of the U.S.S.R.), with 1,690,000,000 ac.

The seventh World Forestry Congress was held in Buenos Aires, Arg., in October 1972, and was attended by more than 2,000 forestry leaders representing 87 countries. The foresters addressed themselves to the question of how to accelerate economic and social progress while maintaining the quality of the environment. Noting that the gap between developed and less developed nations continued to widen in forestry, as in other sectors, and that some of the world's largest forest resources lay in countries where economic and social development lagged, the congress called for proper exploitation of those resources, both to raise living standards and to help meet the world's need for forest products. It was pointed out that this could be accomplished while not merely maintaining but enhancing the quality of the environment. The congress also noted that developing trends in supply and demand for forest products on a worldwide basis did not indicate either a feast or a famine. Based on known world forest inventories and estimates, there appeared to be a sufficient supply of raw wood to meet total world demand through at least the year 2000. This assumed that the vast resources of the tropical areas would be utilized.

China, which was well represented at the Forestry Congress, joined the FAO as of April 1973. Figures reported in FAO statistics in the past about China had had to be unofficial, but as of 1973 China would report to the organization as one of the requirements of membership. The still-unofficial figures for 1973 were that China had only 7% of its land forested. But in spite of its necessarily small timber production to meet the needs of its 800 million population, China was self-sufficient in the forestry area. This was partly due to a low level of use and partly because bamboo, which was plentiful, supplemented the demand for timber and was substituted for it for almost all uses.

It was estimated that in addition to the land already forested about one-third of the remaining land in China was suitable for growing trees. In recent years China made many attempts at afforestation, some of which failed due to floods and droughts. A new five-year plan started in 1971 called for the afforestation of ten million hectares a year (1 hectare = 2.47 ac.). Along the old course of the Yellow River, a forest belt about 500 km. long and 25 km. wide was created, and similar schemes were carried out in the Haiho and Sinkiang basins.

The gap between developed and less developed nations showed up clearly in world production and trade figures. Preliminary estimates of world roundwood production (excluding fuelwood) for 1972 indicated a total of 1,327,000,000 cu.m., a 2% increase over 1971. About 87% of this production took place in the industrialized countries, particularly the Soviet Union, the U.S., Canada, and Japan. This was only a slightly lower percentage than in the early 1960s, when it was 90% (1961–65 average). World production of sawn wood also continued to grow at a rate well above the trend. Trade in coniferous logs showed the greatest increase, rising by 20%, while trade in hardwood logs increased by 8%. Both were record levels. World trade in pulpwood fell about 17% in 1972, attributed to the fact that Western Europe drew on its inventory. Prices rose for all forest products except pulpwood, which had a price ceiling on it in the U.S. and of which there were large stocks in Europe.

In North America, production of industrial roundwood showed a substantial increase, mainly in coniferous sawlogs, veneer logs, and pulpwood. The increased production of softwoods was needed for new housing programs in the U.S., Canada, and Japan. Softwoods were the lumber of choice for most housing needs. The U.S. increased its shipments of coniferous logs

UPI COMPIX

A forestry worker measures the diameter of a 120-foot-tall larch to calculate how much lumber it will yield. U.S. lumber production in 1973 was expected to be only slightly lower than the record-setting 1972 yield.

Foreign Aid: *see* Development, Economic

Foreign Exchange: *see* Payments and Reserves, International

Foreign Investments: *see* Investment, International

and sawn wood to Japan. In several areas of the U.S., availability of fresh logs was insufficient to keep pace with demand. The increased demand contributed to higher prices and supply problems. By the end of 1973 prices of softwood logs were bid up to triple the previous levels.

North American prices were so much higher in 1972 than those in Western Europe that Canada's exports to Europe fell by 17%, to 1.2 million cu.m., the lowest volume in many years, while its shipments to the U.S. rose by 21%, to a record 19.9 million cu.m. As a result, the U.S. ended up importing (net) about 11% of its total timber products. A panel on timber and the environment, appointed by U.S. Pres. Richard Nixon, submitted its report in April 1973 and recommended that the U.S. Forest Service should increase its timber sales in order to meet domestic needs—51% of the nation's softwood inventory was in national forests.

Forest Service timber sales had fallen off in recent years because of a contest over the use of national forest lands. Citizen groups and preservationist organizations contended that national forests should be used for recreation and for wilderness experiences and that timber harvesting interfered with those uses.

Britain declared 1973 to be "Tree Planting Year," and in honour of the event, the government issued a nine-penny stamp depicting Queen Elizabeth II and the native oak, *Quercus robur*. The government made available grants of up to 75% of cost to stimulate tree planting. (IRENE MC MANUS)

See Environment; Industrial Review.

ENCYCLOPÆDIA BRITANNICA FILMS. *The Coniferous Forest Biome* (1969); *Problems of Conservation—Forest and Range* (1969); *Problems of Conservation—Our Natural Resources* (1970).

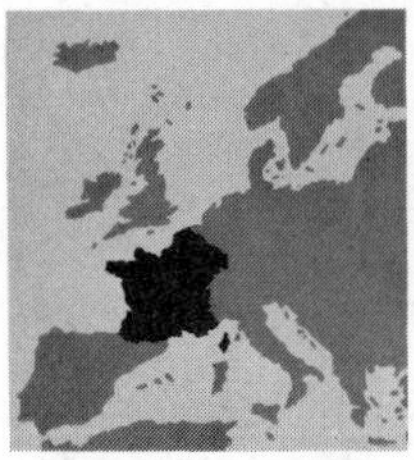

France

A republic of Western Europe and head of the French Community, France is bounded by the English Channel, Belgium, Luxembourg, West Germany, Switzerland, Italy, the Mediterranean Sea, Monaco, Spain, Andorra, and the Atlantic Ocean. Area: 210,038 sq.mi. (543,998 sq.km.), including Corsica. Pop. (1973 est.): 52 million. Cap. and largest city: Paris (pop., 1972 est., 2,461,000). Language: French. President in 1973, Georges Pompidou; premier, Pierre Messmer.

The main event of 1973 was the general election in March. While the ruling parties succeeded in retaining a majority in Parliament, the recently united leftist opposition and particularly the Socialists under François Mitterrand gained a great deal of ground, leading Premier Pierre Messmer's new government to contemplate more wide-ranging reforms than might otherwise have been the case.

Domestic Affairs. In a television broadcast in February, Pres. Georges Pompidou (*see* BIOGRAPHY) himself entered the political arena, presenting the forthcoming general election as a duel between the left and "all the others" and repeating what he had said at his press conferences on Sept. 21, 1972, and Jan. 9, 1973; namely, that the French people need not expect him to support the Socialist-Communist conspiracy.

The majority of opinion polls carried out during the six months prior to the elections had suggested that the leftist union presented a serious threat to the ruling majority. In the elections the left did not gain control but the voting on March 4 and 11 certainly brought sweeping changes in the makeup of the new National Assembly, with a change of incumbent in no less than 174 of the 490 seats and a reduction of almost 100 seats for the outgoing majority coalition, the Union des Républicains de Progrès (URP). In addition to the erosion of its total parliamentary strength from 372 to 275 seats, the balance within the coalition underwent a considerable modification at the expense of the Gaullist group, the Union des Démocrates pour la République (UDR). While the UDR remained the dominant group within the bloc, it no longer had an absolute majority by itself. (*See* POLITICAL PARTIES.)

As the voting figures showed, a very small majority in terms of votes brought a far more substantial advantage to the ruling group in terms of seats in the National Assembly. The Reform Movement of Jean Lecanuet and Jean-Jacques Servan-Schreiber suffered from the same disadvantage as the left in this respect, gaining some 3 million votes but no more than 31 seats, only one above the minimum required to form a group in the National Assembly. The disparity was due in part to overrepresentation of the least populated areas and also to factors tending to produce somewhat artificial effects in the context of the two-round majority ballot system. On the whole it might be said that the elections showed a marked increase in support for the left at the expense of the majority but that the balance of power between right and left remained roughly the same as in 1967. A number of younger candidates were elected to the assembly, 26 of them under 35 and the youngest under 30. On the other hand, while women formed the majority (52%) of the electorate they still represented only a tiny fraction of the National Assembly.

The New Messmer Government. On March 28 Premier Messmer formally submitted his government's resignation to President Pompidou as required by the constitution, but was invited by the head of state to continue his functions. The second Messmer government to be appointed by President Pompidou was, nevertheless, to show profound changes in composition. The new government was appointed in three stages: the premier (April 2), the 21 Cabinet ministers (April 5), and finally the 16 secretaries of state.

Five ministers had voluntarily left the first Messmer Cabinet even before the formation of the second. Maurice Schumann and René Pleven were defeated in the elections and resigned from the Ministries of Foreign Affairs and Justice, respectively, and Edgar Faure, minister of state for social affairs, resigned his portfolio when he was elected president of the National Assembly on April 2. Jacques Duhamel, minister of cultural affairs, had resigned for health reasons, and Michel Debré had resigned his post as defense minister.

The new government was composed as follows: premier, Pierre Messmer (UDR); justice, Jean Taittinger (UDR); foreign affairs, Michel Jobert (nonparliamentary); interior, Raymond Marcellin (Independent Republicans, IR); defense, Robert Galley (UDR); economy and finance, Valéry Giscard d'Estaing (IR); education, Joseph Fontanet (Centre Démocratie et Progrés, CDP); regional planning, Olivier Guichard (UDR); administrative reform, Alain Peyrefitte (UDR); environment, Robert Poujade (UDR); cultural affairs, Maurice Druon (nonparliamentary); agriculture, Jacques Chirac (UDR); industrial development, Jean Charbonnel (UDR); commerce and small traders, Jean Royer (no affiliation); relations with Parliament, Joseph Comiti

Formosa:
see Taiwan

(UDR); labour, Georges Gorse (UDR); public health, Michel Poniatowski (IR); transport, Yves Guéna (UDR); information, Philippe Malaud (IR), later Jean-Philippe Lecat (UDR); posts and telecommunications, Hubert Germain (UDR); overseas départements and territories, Bernard Stasi (CDP); ex-servicemen, André Bord (UDR).

A striking feature of the new Cabinet was the appointment to the foreign affairs post of Michel Jobert (*see* BIOGRAPHY), who was replaced at the General Secretariat of the Elysée Palace by Edouard Balladur. In this appointment and that of Maurice Druon as minister of cultural affairs, President Pompidou followed in the footsteps of Charles de Gaulle in appointing nonparliamentarians to important Cabinet posts. Moreover, in appointing his principal adviser on foreign affairs to the Ministry of Foreign Affairs, the president as it were reminded his government that foreign affairs remained the privileged area of the presidency as it had been in the time of de Gaulle. Two women also joined the government for the first time: Suzanne Ploux, a member of the UDR Central Committee, as secretary of state for education, and Marie-Madeleine Dienesch as secretary of state for public health and social security.

Regional Elections. By the time the "cantonal" elections for the new-style regional assemblies provided for in the local government legislation of July 1972 took place in September, the French people seemed to have become more than a little "election-weary," 46.6% abstaining in the first round and 45.8% in the second. The left continued to show a marked increase in support, although the general increase in the number of seats as a result of the new legislation meant that all parties could boast an increase in the number of seats won.

Parliament. A great deal had been expected from the first session of the new National Assembly, which ended on June 30, and the necessity for a renewal of Parliament had been much talked about during the election campaign. Certainly the new Parliament's debates on a wide range of controversial topics suggested that the assembly was beginning to reestablish itself as a national forum for debate. Nevertheless, many of the changes were purely technical rather than political, and the executive continued to show a certain degree of contempt for the legislature.

On the left, Georges Marchais continued to exercise considerable authority as head of the Communist Party, and in June François Mitterrand was reelected first secretary of the Socialist Party. Mitterrand was already regarded as the obvious candidate for the left in the 1976 presidential elections. As for the majority, it was widely thought that if President Pompidou did not stand for reelection Valéry Giscard d'Estaing (*see* BIOGRAPHY), who had given up his position as president of the Independent Republicans to devote himself to his duties as finance minister, would be the most likely candidate. In the meantime, the end of the spring parliamentary session was marked by the dissolution of two extremist political movements: the right-wing Ordre Nouveau and the left-wing Ligue Communiste. At the beginning of the year an ombudsman had been appointed to try to improve relations between the government and its citizens, in the person of the much respected elder statesman Antoine Pinay.

The autumn session was marked as usual by the debate on the draft budget adopted by the Council of Ministers in September. The budget for 1974, which was distinguished by the fact that it balanced,

A.F.P. / PICTORIAL PARADE

Huge artificial harbour between Le Havre and Etretat, shown here under construction in August 1973, was designed to receive 500,000-ton tankers.

involved provisions for a more equitable distribution of the income tax burden and the closing of certain loopholes that had allowed various forms of tax avoidance and evasion to take place. In particular, the notorious "Pinay" state loan, which had carried in addition to its 3.5% interest rate a one-third exemption from death duties, was eliminated by the government, and a new loan was issued known as the "Giscard," which bore interest at 4.5% and was likewise linked to gold but which conferred no exemption from death duties on its holders. This particular measure had long been demanded by the opposition parties, the "Pinay" having been regarded by the left as a particularly scandalous form of state-aided tax avoidance.

Shortly after Parliament reassembled on October 2, a bill was brought in defining the rights of small traders and artisans in relation to the development of large-scale enterprises. The bill, which was passed by 302 votes in favour and none against (but with 180 abstentions, including the Socialist and Communist deputies), was a personal triumph for the minister for commerce and small traders, Jean Royer, a man of considerable political ambition who was also mayor of Tours.

Industrial Relations and Economy. While inflation remained the first concern of the government, French workers were concerned with problems of employment and working conditions as well as with those of wages and purchasing power. On October 29 the leader of the Confédération Générale du Travail (CGT), Georges Séguy (*see* BIOGRAPHY), called for a halt to rising prices. This was followed the next day by a government call for a halt to the inflationary process and for a series of economic measures, which led to a flood of strikes. Anxious not to curb the expansion of the French economy, the government decided to postpone the strict measures it had contemplated to slow down the inflationary spiral. Early in December, however, stringent credit control measures were introduced.

The most spectacular industrial dispute was the one at the Lip watch factory in Besançon, in which the company's relatively small number of employees refused to lose their jobs when the company went into liquidation as a result of bad management. Within a short time the employees had taken over the factory and decided to run the watch-manufacturing concern on their own account. This action brought enthusiastic praise from Edmond Maire, head of the huge Confédération Française Démocratique du Travail (CFDT). Massive demonstrations in support of the Lip workers in September, the fourth month of the dispute, brought representatives from overseas labour movements as well as from all the French labour unions, and what had been a relatively small dispute at the outset rapidly acquired the dimensions of a major national event. The efforts of Henri Giraud, the government mediator, to reestablish the firm on a new basis failed when the workers insisted on a guarantee of employment as an essential part of any agreement.

Other sectors affected by industrial unrest were the metallurgy industry, the French National Railways, and the Renault factories which underwent a month-long strike in the spring. Also in the spring thousands of young people took part in massive but orderly protests in Paris against the Debré law on compulsory military service and other student grievances. The leaders of the CGT and CFDT had earlier published a long joint declaration reaffirming their solidarity with the Renault workers as well as with the students in their "common struggle against capitalist society." Toward year's end Messmer came under heavy attack for ineffective leadership. His position was further threatened by revelations early in December of the attempted bugging allegedly by Ministry of Interior agents of the offices of the satirical weekly *Le Canard enchaîné*.

Foreign Affairs. In his press conference on September 27—the ninth in his term of office—Pompidou again stressed foreign affairs, thus confirming this as the particular concern of the president. This was emphasized by his meetings, in the space of under six months, with U.K. Prime Minister Edward Heath (twice), West German Chancellor Willy Brandt (also twice), Soviet party leader Leonid I. Brezhnev, U.S. Pres. Richard Nixon, Japanese Prime Minister Kakuei Tanaka, the Chinese leaders, the president of Italy, Pres. Muammar al-Qaddafi of Libya, Pres. Habib Bourguiba of Tunisia, and the energy and oil ministers of Algeria and Saudi Arabia, respectively.

French policies and aspirations remained broadly the same as previously, including the policy of an independent French nuclear deterrent. Nuclear tests continued in the Pacific despite widespread protests both in France and throughout the world, although there were plans for future tests to take place underground rather than in the atmosphere to reduce the level of atmospheric pollution. President Pompidou thus remained true to de Gaulle's precepts in the matter of French independence in this regard. Moreover, his appearance of physical and intellectual vigour throughout the press conference served to dissipate rumours concerning his health.

In January President Pompidou made his fourth trip to Africa, visiting Djibouti, capital of the French Territory of Afars and Issas, and Ethiopia. Later in the year a "summit" conference of French-speaking black African states took place in Paris to discuss the future of cooperation agreements with France. Neither Mauritania nor the Malagasy Republic, both of which left the franc zone in 1973, showed any interest in this conference of African leaders, which was expected to meet about once a year.

On November 16 and 17 Pompidou visited London for further talks with Edward Heath, following those that had taken place in Paris in May. During the course of the visit an agreement relating to the construction of a tunnel under the English Channel was signed.

The most spectacular of Pompidou's foreign voyages, however, was undoubtedly his visit to China, September 11–17. The French president received a very warm welcome both from the government and from the Chinese people and was received by Chairman Mao Tse-tung and Premier Chou En-lai. Nevertheless, the shadow of the U.S.S.R. loomed large in the background, and President Pompidou replied to Chinese references to the hegemony of the superpowers by reaffirming France's desire for the relaxing of tensions and greater international agreement as well as for increased cooperation in Europe.

The president's summer meeting in Iceland with U.S. Pres. Richard Nixon was largely a follow-up to the Azores meeting in December 1971, the talks centring on the question of the U.S. dollar. At Pompidou's meeting with Brezhnev a few weeks later in

FRANCE

Education. (1971–72) Primary, pupils 7,339,000, teachers (full time only; 1969–70) 220,295; secondary, pupils 3,643,000; vocational, pupils 824,000; secondary and vocational, teachers (full time; 1969–70) 248,934; teacher training (1969–70), students 31,228, teachers (full time only) 2,309; higher (including 23 universities), students 811,000, teaching staff (1969–70) 31,039.

Finance. Monetary unit: franc, with (Sept. 17, 1973) a free "commercial" rate of Fr. 4.25 to U.S. $1 (Fr. 10.24 = £1 sterling) and a free "financial" rate of Fr. 4.32 to U.S. $1 (Fr. 10.40 = £1 sterling). Gold, SDRs, and foreign exchange, official: (June 1973) U.S. $10,998,000,000; (June 1972) U.S. $8,941,000,000. Budget (1971 actual): revenue Fr. 173,576,000,000; expenditure Fr. 174,740,000,000. Gross national product: (1971) Fr. 904.2 billion; (1970) Fr. 820.2 billion. Money supply: (Feb. 1973) Fr. 278,980,000,000; (Feb. 1972) Fr. 248,830,000,000. Cost of living (1963 = 100): (June 1973) 156; (June 1972) 145.

Foreign Trade. (1972) Imports Fr. 136,190,000,000; exports Fr. 133,250,000,000. Import sources: EEC 56% (West Germany 22%, Belgium-Luxembourg 11%, Italy 10%, The Netherlands 6%); U.S. 8%; U.K. 5%. Export destinations: EEC 49% (West Germany 21%, Belgium-Luxembourg 11%, Italy 11%, The Netherlands 5%); U.K. 5%; U.S. 5%; Switzerland 5%. Main exports: machinery 18%; motor vehicles 11%; chemicals 10%; textiles 8%; iron and steel 7%; cereals 5%. Tourism (1971): visitors 14.7 million; gross receipts U.S. $1,583,000,000.

Transport and Communications. Roads (1972) 789,172 km. (including 2,172 km. expressways). Motor vehicles in use (1972): passenger 13,920,000; commercial 1,890,000. Railways: (1971) 35,277 km.; traffic (1972) 43,093,000,000 passenger-km., freight 68,493,000,000 net ton-km. Air traffic (1971): 14,023,000,000 passenger-km.; freight 556,197,000 net ton-km. Navigable inland waterways in regular use (1971) 7,192 km.; freight traffic 13,773,000,000 ton-km. Shipping (1972): merchant vessels 100 gross tons and over 1,390; gross tonnage 7,419,596. Telephones (Dec. 1971) 9,546,000. Radio licenses (Dec. 1971) 16,025,000. Television licenses (Dec. 1971) 11,655,000.

Agriculture. Production (in 000; metric tons; 1972; 1971 in parentheses): wheat 18,123 (15,360); rye 331 (289); barley 10,416 (8,950); oats 2,463 (2,539); corn 8,610 (8,970); potatoes 7,966 (9,021); rice 52 (80); rapeseed 722 (650); sunflower seed 85 (74); tomatoes 490 (534); onions 168 (*c.* 190); apples 2,829 (3,362); pears 500 (588); flax fibre 46 (53); sugar, raw value *c.* 2,913 (*c.* 3,198); wine 5,854 (6,133); tobacco 47 (43); beef and veal *c.* 1,530 (*c.* 1,690); pork 1,540 (1,492); milk (1971) 32,575, (1970) 31,820; butter *c.* 516 (442); cheese *c.* 828 (767); fish catch (1971) 742, (1970) 764. Livestock (in 000; Oct. 1971): cattle 21,803; sheep 10,115; pigs 11,386; horses 524; poultry (1970) *c.* 186,000.

Industry. Index of production (1963 = 100): (1972) 173; (1971) 160. Fuel and power (in 000; 1972): coal (metric tons) 29,763; electricity (kw-hr.) 160,080,000; natural gas (cu.m.) 7,432,000; manufactured gas (cu.m.; 1971) 6,492,000. Production (in 000; metric tons; 1972): iron ore (32% metal content) 54,246; bauxite 3,254; pig iron 19,002; crude steel 24,054; aluminum 505; lead 160; zinc 262; cement 30,066; cotton yarn 255; cotton fabrics 199; wool yarn 148; wool fabrics 64; rayon, etc., filament yarn 47; rayon, etc., staple fibre 81; nylon, etc., filament yarn 97; nylon, etc., staple fibre 122; sulfuric acid 4,033; petroleum products (1971) 97,960; nitrogenous fertilizer (1971–72) 1,401; phosphate fertilizer (1971–72) 1,500; potash fertilizer (1971–72) 1,797; passenger cars (units) 2,993; commercial vehicles (units) 335. Merchant shipping launched (100 gross tons and over; 1972) 1,128,900 gross tons.

France, it was decided to arrange another meeting early in 1974 in the U.S.S.R.

The outbreak of a new war in the Middle East led to heated debates on the subject of aid to the parties involved. The gasoline crisis, caused by the curtailment of oil shipments from the Middle East, became a major preoccupation in France along with what Pompidou regarded as the Soviet-U.S. "condominium" in the Middle East. In view of these problems Pompidou took the initiative in calling for an EEC summit meeting in December with the aim of strengthening Community links in facing the problems of inflation and the fuel crisis. On December 19 Jean Blancard was appointed to take charge of all matters affecting fuel and energy.

At the NATO council of foreign ministers at Brussels in December, Jobert clashed with U.S. Secretary of State Henry Kissinger, charging that the Soviet-U.S. agreement in June on the prevention of nuclear war undermined U.S. nuclear protection of Western Europe. Jobert claimed that his point was proved during the Middle East war in October when the U.S. placed its forces on worldwide precautionary alert without informing its NATO allies. Kissinger denied the charges, stating that Jobert's claim was a "misrepresentation" of the U.S.-Soviet agreement.

(JEAN KNECHT)

Furs

With fashion taking a renewed interest in furs in 1973, the industry throughout most of the Western world enjoyed one of its best years in decades. Retail sales of fur apparel advanced sharply over the previous year, which also had shown substantial gains. Strong endorsement of furs by couturiers and fashion leaders overcame any resistance that might have developed to substantially higher prices. As the winter season approached its peak, the problem facing furriers was not finding customers but, rather, finding merchandise.

After many years of poor business and attrition, the U.S. industry experienced its second consecutive good year. According to American Fur Industry, the central trade association, stores sold about $425 million worth of furs in 1973, almost 30% more than in 1972. Even this was considered a conservative figure, since it was derived from reports by manufacturers who paid a levy on their sales for industry promotion. Allowing for price increases of 20 to 30%, unit sales still showed impressive gains.

Nevertheless, the New York fur trade, heart of the U.S. fur industry, continued to shrink because of attrition. Union chief George Stofsky, head of the Furriers Joint Council, listed only 5,600 workers in 1973, compared with 7,500 three years earlier. The reverse was true in other parts of the world. Fur industries flourished and expanded in Scandinavia, West and East Germany, Greece, and Italy. Even in the Orient, where fur manufacturing was relatively unknown, interest in furs and the craft itself began to develop. Japan, with its newfound affluence, entered the international market as a strong buyer of both skins and finished apparel. Factories were established in Tokyo and other major cities, and experienced craftsmen were brought from the U.S. and Europe to train new workers. Plants also were established in such low-wage areas as South Korea, Taiwan, and Hong Kong, many of whose products were imported into the U.S.

Furs from China began entering the U.S. for the

WIDE WORLD

A long Eskimo parka, featuring a fur-trimmed hood, was among the creations of the Yves St. Laurent ready-to-wear 1973 winter collection.

first time since 1951. The pelts of many varieties of Chinese lamb, kid, and other furs were imported and played an important part in the "fun fur" scene. Many of these furs also were manufactured outside the U.S. to take advantage of lower wage rates, thus enabling them to be retailed in direct competition with conventional cloth coats.

Because of the strong international demand, prices of virtually all kinds of furs advanced sharply during the year. The biggest increases were in such long-haired furs as lynx and fox, with some of the best Russian lynx bringing as much as $600 per pelt at the July auction in Leningrad. Coats of Russian lynx were retailing for more than $10,000.

Prices of ranched mink, the most popular of the luxury furs, also rose 30% or more. This reflected not only the demand from established world markets and the entry of Japanese buyers but also a drop in worldwide mink production. It was estimated that fewer than 16 million pelts were put on the market. (This did not include several million produced in the U.S.S.R. and kept for domestic consumption.)

Mink production in 1973 was statistically slightly higher. However, while 5% more female mink were bred in the U.S., and the average litter size remained approximately the same (3.5), the number of kits raised to maturity actually declined, the result of economies attempted through feed substitutions and adverse weather conditions. The U.S. Department of Agriculture reported that 901,000 females were bred, compared with 858,000 the previous year. The USDA also estimated that only 1,379 ranches were producing mink in the U.S. at the beginning of 1973, compared with 1,615 a year earlier. Samuel Bleiweiss of the Emba Mink Breeders Association said ranchers did well in 1973, many of them for the first time in several years. For those who planned to remain in business, most of the profits would go toward paying off debts and refurbishing ranches and equipment that had fallen into disrepair during the lean years.

As in 1972, the spring and fall auctions of Alaska sealskins were dominated by European buyers, who purchased an estimated 95% of the nearly 100,000 pelts offered. The prices paid were 20–30% over 1972

French-Canadian Literature: *see* Literature
French Community: *see* Dependent States; *articles on the various member states*
French Guiana: *see* Dependent States
French Literature: *see* Literature
Friends, Religious Society of: *see* Religion
Frozen Foods: *see* Food Processing
Fruit: *see* Agriculture and Fisheries
Fuel and Power: *see* Energy

levels and ranged as high as $201 per skin. These were pelts taken from adult bachelor seals, considered by U.S. Department of Commerce experts as surplus in the herds based on the Pribilof Islands.

(SANDY PARKER)

See also Fashion and Dress.

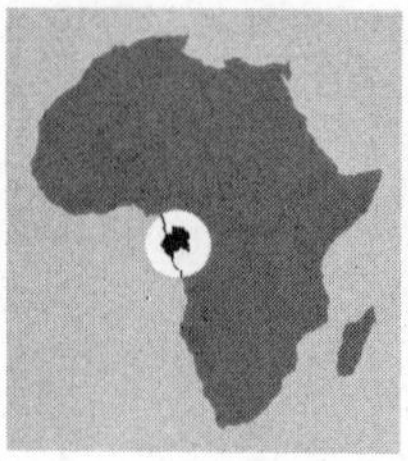

Gabon

A republic of western equatorial Africa, Gabon is bounded by Río Muni, Cameroon, the Congo, and the Atlantic Ocean. Area: 103,347 sq.mi. (267,667 sq. km.). Pop. (1970): 950,009. Cap. and largest city: Libreville (pop., 1970, 105,080). Language: French and Bantu dialects. Religion: traditional tribal beliefs; Christian minority. President in 1973, Omar Bongo.

On Feb. 25, 1973, President Bongo, together with the 70 parliamentary candidates fielded by the country's sole political party, was reelected with more than 99% of the votes cast, the electoral turnout being stated officially as 100%. Two Cabinet reshuffles took place during the year. In March the number of Cabinet portfolios was increased from 24 to 26 and Georges Rawiri was appointed minister of state for foreign affairs. In October the number was further increased to 29, and the president added foreign affairs to the portfolios he already held, naming Rawiri as his assistant in this field.

In foreign affairs President Bongo's most compelling need was to find new sources of finance for the controversial trans-Gabon railway. To this end he undertook a tour of European capitals in May, discussing the matter with French Pres. Georges Pompidou as well as EEC leaders in Brussels. After a further discussion in July, President Pompidou agreed to a substantial increase in the French commitment. Relations with the ex-colonial power, nevertheless, were not all sweetness and light. Negotiations for the revision of cooperation agreements between the two countries opened in Libreville in November and were completed in Paris in December.

On October 29 Gabon broke off diplomatic relations with Israel. This decision, tending to align Gabon more closely with general black African policy, was not entirely unexpected as on September 30 the president had solemnly announced his conversion to the Islamic faith. Nevertheless, it marked a complete about-face in attitude. In June the president himself had stated that diplomatic relations with Israel would not be broken off.

(PHILIPPE DECRAENE)

GABON

Education. (1971–72) Primary, pupils 105,600, teachers (1970–71) 2,230; secondary, pupils 9,387, teachers (1969–70) 322; vocational, pupils 1,733, teachers (1969–70) 156; teacher training, students 231, teachers (1968–69) 22; higher, students 172.

Finance. Monetary unit: CFA franc, with (Sept. 17, 1973) a parity of CFA Fr. 50 to the French franc (free commercial rate of CFA Fr. 212.55 = U.S. $1; CFA Fr. 512.25 = £1 sterling). Budget (1972 est.) balanced at CFA Fr. 19,524,000,000.

Foreign Trade. (1971) Imports CFA Fr. 26,810,-000,000; exports CFA Fr. 51.8 billion. Import sources: France 56%; West Germany 9%; U.S. 6%; Cameroon 5%. Export destinations: France 44%; Netherlands Antilles 10%; West Germany 9%; U.S. 7%; Cameroon 5%. Main exports (1970): crude oil 41%; timber 32%; manganese 10%; plywood 7%.

Transport and Communications. Roads (1972) 6,119 km. Motor vehicles in use (1970): passenger 7,100; commercial 5,800. Railways (1972) 372 km. Telephones (Dec. 1970) 7,000. Radio receivers (Dec. 1970) 62,000. Television receivers (Dec. 1970) 1,200.

Agriculture. Production (in 000; metric tons; 1972; 1971 in parentheses): corn *c.* 2 (*c.* 2); coffee *c.* 0.9 (*c.* 0.6); cocoa 5 (5); bananas *c.* 10 (*c.* 10); timber (cu.m.; 1971) 3,200, (1970) 3,200. Livestock (in 000; 1970–71): cattle *c.* 4; pigs *c.* 5; sheep *c.* 54; goats *c.* 60.

Industry. Production (in 000; metric tons; 1971): crude oil 5,785; manganese ore (metal content) 952; electricity (kw-hr.) 114,000.

Gambia, The

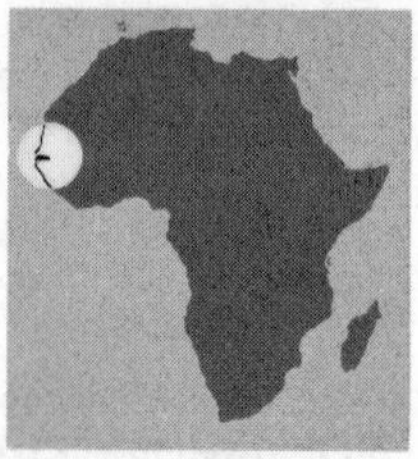

A small republic and member of the Commonwealth of Nations, The Gambia extends from the Atlantic Ocean along the lower Gambia River in West Africa and is surrounded by Senegal. Area: 4,467 sq.mi. (11,569 sq. km.). Pop. (1973): 494,279, including (1963) Malinke 40.8%; Fulani 13.5%; Wolof 12.9%; Diola 7%; Soninke 6.8%; non-African 1.9%. Cap. and largest city: Banjul (named Bathurst until April 24, 1973; pop., 1973, 39,476). Language: English (official). Religion: predominantly Muslim. President in 1973, Sir Dauda Jawara.

The Gambia continued to tread a diplomatic path between Senegal and Sierra Leone in 1973. After his 1972 visits to Europe and Taiwan, President Jawara opened the new year with a series of West African visits to Guinea, Sierra Leone, and Senegal, while in February Pres. William R. Tolbert, Jr., of Liberia celebrated Independence Day at Bathurst (later renamed Banjul). Both presidents deplored the assassination in January of Amilcar Cabral (*see* OBITUARIES), leader of the independence movement in Portugal's West African territories. They agreed to give all assistance to the peoples of Guinea (Bissau) and the Cape Verde Islands in their struggle for "their legitimate goals."

At the eighth Sene-Gambian ministers' meeting in March, progress was noted in the joint development of the Gambia basin under the supervision of the Sene-Gambian secretariat. But while President Jawara spoke warmly of "progressive economic integration," the meeting concluded that political unity required "careful thought" and could only be seen in the context of West African regionalism and a joint relationship with the EEC.

Despite the resignation of the vice-president because of his brother's smuggling in Senegal with the use of government vehicles, the stability of the government and its small opposition United Party was maintained. The dalasi was revalued upward from 5 to 4 to £1 sterling on March 19. Efforts continued to end the country's economic dependence on peanuts.

(MOLLY MORTIMER)

GAMBIA, THE

Education. (1970–71) Primary, pupils 16,867, teachers 690; secondary, pupils 5,178, teachers 328; vocational, pupils 181, teachers 18; teacher training, students 149, teachers 12.

Finance and Trade. Monetary unit: dalasi, with (Sept. 17, 1973) a free rate of 1.66 dalasis to U.S. $1 (par value of 4 dalasis = £1 sterling). Budget (1972–73 est.): revenue 19,652,000 dalasis; expenditure 19,-986,000 dalasis. Foreign trade (1972): imports 49,-530,000 dalasis; exports 37,380,000 dalasis. Import sources: U.K. 29%; Japan 12%; China 11%. Export destinations: U.K. 40%; France 20%; Italy 15%; Portugal 13%. Main exports: peanuts and products 94%.

Gardening

Air pollution caused increased damage to food crops grown by farmers and gardeners during 1973. Howard E. Heggestad of the U.S. Department of Agriculture (USDA) Agricultural Research Service, Beltsville, Md., estimated losses for the year at nearly $1 billion. The air pollutants of most concern to horticulturists were ozone, peroxyacetyl nitrate, sulfur dioxide, and fluoride. In the United States the major pollutant affecting plants was ozone, chiefly from motor vehicle exhaust.

Plant pathologists at Michigan State University found that air pollution was responsible for heavy damage to potato crops in that state, causing premature death of vines and a reduction in yield and tuber size. Agricultural Research Service scientists at Raleigh, N.C., learned that yield loss in corn caused by air pollution might be greater than previously realized. Golden Midget sweet corn, grown experimentally in field exposure chambers of clear plastic film, suffered visible injury at ozone levels that were lower than those commonly found in many of the large urban areas.

Insect pests threatened forests in several parts of the U.S. The gypsy moth was found as far south as Georgia and as far west as Minnesota. Millions of acres of trees in New England, New Jersey, New York, and Pennsylvania had been killed or severely damaged by this insect. Authorities believed it could survive any place in the U.S., but the major immediate concern was for the valuable commercial oak forests in the Appalachian and Ozark mountains and possibly in some parts of the Great Lakes region. Elsewhere, a massive outbreak of tussock moths in the fir forests of the Pacific Northwest was threatening more than 800,000 ac. of timberland. The spruce budworm continued to do tremendous damage to spruce and balsam fir forests of Maine and the Canadian provinces of New Brunswick and Quebec.

A disease known as lethal yellowing, believed to be caused by a microorganism and spread by an unknown agent, was killing coconut palm trees in the Miami and Fort Lauderdale areas of Florida. Randy McCoy, Florida State University plant pathologist, said that if the disease continued to spread at the current rate all the coconut palms in Dade County would be destroyed by 1980. A mysterious disease of unknown origin threatened to destroy 60% of Florida's citrus trees. It seemed to affect only citrus growing on rough lemon rootstock, and was most prevalent among groves of sweet oranges, especially Valencias.

Two poinsettias with exceptional tolerance to air pollution were released by the Agricultural Research Service Plant Genetics and Germplasm Institute, Beltsville. Ruff & Ready is a vigorous, compact, tough, easy-to-grow, and long-lasting brilliant red plant. Trulypink is a large, deep salmon-pink plant that keeps well and produces pink progeny. A coloured Easter lily with a distinctive fragrance was developed by University of Minnesota horticulturists. The flower is shaped like the white Easter lily, but it is light pink on the outside with a pale yellow throat and yellow bands on the interior segments. Four new hybrid impatiens, Sprite, Cheers, Arabesque, and A'Flame, were released by the Agricultural Research Service. They were selected primarily for their bright, highly contrasting foliage colours and for their potential use as container-grown ornamental foliage plants.

A new potato variety, Hudson, was introduced by the New York (state) Agricultural Experiment Station. It was resistant to golden nematode infestation and had produced yields averaging 616 bu. per ac. Seed would be available in 1974. A new passiflora, Incense, developed by the USDA Plant Introduction Station, Miami, Fla., had potential value for home cultivation in Florida and similar areas. It bears large, fragrant, violet-coloured flowers and edible olive-coloured fruit.

Three roses won All-America awards for 1974: Perfume Delight, a fragrant, clear pink hybrid tea hybridized by O. L. Weeks; Bahia, an orange-tinged pink floribunda hybridized by Walter E. Lammerts; and Bon-Bon, a fragrant pink and white bicolour floribunda hybridized by William Warriner.

(TOM STEVENSON)

A British association of rose breeders was formed with the aim of improving the relationship between breeders and growers. The first of its selection trials, to be held annually at members' nurseries, began during the year. Initial judging would take place in 1974 and the rose trade would be informed of the winners in the spring of 1975, in time to build up stocks for release to the public in 1976.

Patrick Dickson of Northern Ireland won the 1973 Golden Rose of The Hague, Neth., with Scarlet Queen Elizabeth. His Red Planet won the German International Rose Trials award for the best hybrid tea, and Mala Rubenstein, described as a camellia-rose, won the Uladh trophy at the Northern Irish Rose trials for the best hybrid tea and the most fragrant rose for 1973. The best floribunda was Picasso, raised by Sam McGredy IV, who emigrated to New Zealand from Northern Ireland during the year. An Afro-French marigold called Showboat, raised in Britain by Sutton and Sons Ltd., was the first flower to win all three major seed awards—All America, All Britain, and Fleuroselect (all Europe). Showboat is an F_I triploid, early flowering with deep yellow, carnation-type flowers.

A chemical that accelerates the ripening of tomatoes, especially toward the end of the season, was being used on an increasing scale in the U.K. Commercially called Ethrel E, it was a growth-regulating chemical containing ethephon (2-chloroethyl-phosphonic acid). Other uses for which it had been officially approved were to separate black currants from the plant in harvesting, to improve the colour of apples, and for defoliating roses.

The British seed firm of A. L. Tozer Ltd. introduced Cheltenham Mono, a monogerm beet seed for precision sowing. The seed had taken 14 years to develop. Two Dutch seed firms, Den Berg Seeds and Enza-Zaden, were introducing tomato cultivars resistant to mosaic virus and to *Fusarium* and *Verticillium* wilts. Resistance to greenback and to two or three strains of leaf mold (*Cladosporium*) was also claimed.

The blanched leaves produced from the crowns of chicory forced in darkness were widely used in salads in Europe and were becoming popular in England. The Institute for Vegetable Research at Grossbeeren, E.Ger., evolved an industrial method of forcing chicory in pure water held in shallow containers that could be piled one on top of another. It was grown at a temperature of 14°–18° C and was ready for cutting in 24–28 days.

(J. G. SCOTT MARSHALL)

See also Agriculture and Fisheries; Life Sciences.

Garment Industry:
see Fashion and Dress; Furs

Gas Industry:
see Energy

Genetics:
see Life Sciences; Medicine

Geography

A continuing awareness of the significance of territorial dimensions for many of man's activities spurred U.S. federal legislation that would build upon geographic knowledge, methodologies, and research techniques. Passage of the Land Use Policy and Planning Assistance bill was expected to provide innumerable opportunities for geographers to contribute their skills to the development of state land use plans. Geography has a rich tradition of substantive contributions in inventorying, classifying, and interpreting the dynamics of land use, beginning with the Michigan Land Economic Survey in 1920. Imagery provided by the instruments aboard the ERTS-1 and Skylab spacecraft was expected to complement aerial photographs and field surveys in the preparation of state plans after the federal legislation became operational.

Geography enrollments in U.S. colleges and universities reached the 750,000 mark in 1973, an 86% increase since 1963 compared with a 62% increase in overall college and university enrollments. The strength of geography at the college level might be attributed in part to the increasing significance of geographic research not only to the environmental movement but also to other contemporary problem areas such as urbanization, population growth, transportation, technological innovation, and housing.

At the annual meeting of the Association of American Geographers (AAG) in Atlanta, Ga., in April, a record number of participants attended sessions ranging from the traditional topical sessions on economic, social, and political geography to the president's session dealing with the geographers' participation in "The Question of Survival." The research findings were characterized by the use of sophisticated statistical and mathematical analyses, providing new insights into contemporary issues. Past association president Edward Taaffe called upon the geographers to focus their considerable analytical skills on man-environment relations and on regional geography and away from arcane techniques focusing on trivial issues.

In November the National Council on Geographic Education held its annual meeting in Washington, D.C. The council emphasized geography as effective environmental education and provided three days of workshops, field trips, paper sessions, and discussion groups designed to enrich environmental education through geographic techniques, methods, and ideas.

The National Geographic Society continued to sponsor a broad spectrum of research and publications. It sent a team to cover the January 23 eruption of Eldfell (also called Kirkjufell), Iceland's newest volcano, which covered the island of Heimaey near Vestmannaeyjar, Iceland's fifth largest town.

Research and education were advanced by a number of significant geographical projects, among which were the Assessment of Research on Natural Hazards, a two-year project at the University of Colorado supported by the National Science Foundation (NSF); continuing research on urban problems of major metropolitan areas in the U.S., supported by the NSF and sponsored by the AAG; and a pioneer program in varied approaches to teacher-role development in graduate geography programs currently under way at six graduate geography centres in the U.S., also sponsored by the AAG with NSF support. To be released early in 1974 was a volume on *Perspectives on Environment,* containing essays on geographic approaches to environmental problems, published by the AAG.

The AAG's Commission on College Geography published resource papers on using radar imagery in climatological research, on man and environment, the urban health care crisis, and visual blight in the U.S. The association also expected to publish studies on interurban systems and regional economic development, values in geography, the underdevelopment and modernization of the less developed nations, and citizen participation, advocacy, and dissent in planning. In preparation also was a study on the black ghetto of Philadelphia. (SALVATORE J. NATOLI)

See also Antarctica; Oceanography.

ENCYCLOPÆDIA BRITANNICA FILMS. *Earth: Man's Home* (1970).

Geology

Greater changes in the earth sciences took place during the 1960s and early '70s than had occurred in the entire previous century. In 1973 this rapid pace of change continued as discoveries provided new information about the moon and planets, the deep-sea floor, and the origin and early history of the earth. Problems of earthquake prediction, of the environment, and of future resources of energy and metals attracted great interest.

The Moon and Mars. Results from the six manned Apollo landings on the moon, which ended with the splashdown of Apollo 17 on Dec. 19, 1972, showed that the moon probably has a crust 60 km. (35 mi.) thick and a mantle 1,000 km. (620 mi.) thick covering a core of partially molten silicate rock. This core is far less active than that of the earth, and most of the observed small moonquakes originate at the base of the mantle along two great belts, each 1,000 km. in length. These resemble the circum-Pacific belts of earthquakes on the earth.

The Apollo 16 and 17 missions landed on the lunar highlands, which appear to viewers on the earth as the brighter parts of the full moon. The rocks there are largely anorthosite, consisting chiefly of complex sodium, calcium, and aluminum silicates called feldspars. Formed between 4,500,000,000 and 3,900,000,000 years ago, these rocks were broken by meteoric impact and then recemented. By contrast, the smoother, darker, and less disturbed maria, which earlier Apollo missions had investigated, are largely covered with darker lavas of a basaltic composition. These rocks are richer in iron and magnesium than in feldspars and were formed 3,700,000,000 to 3,100,000,000 years ago, after most of the meteorites that form craters had fallen. The orange volcanic rocks discovered on the Apollo 17 mission, which were at first thought to be evidence of recent volcanism, turned out to be as old as the other lavas.

During the year ended October 1972, the U.S. space probe Mariner 9 was in orbit around Mars and telemetered 7,300 television pictures back to the earth. These covered the whole planet. Analysis and publication of the results showed that the changing reddish patterns on Mars are due to the transport of huge quantities of dust during periodic sandstorms, the progress of one of which was observed. Stream patterns apparently formed by flowing water were identified in the equatorial zone. Under the observed conditions on Mars liquid water would immediately freeze or evaporate, but evidence suggests that the Martian polar caps contain ice as well as solid carbon dioxide snow. Speculation suggests that storms may sometimes so distribute dust that it could lead to the absorption of solar heat and the melting of both caps. If so, the vapour pressure of water may be raised enough for liquid water to condense in the warmest regions of the planet and form streams.

These results, along with the continued investigation of meteorites, which appear to be fragments of a few small planetary bodies, demonstrated that the earth is not unique but is one of a graded family of planets, all formed about 4,600,000,000 years ago. A different approach to determining the earth's origins was to study the oldest rocks on earth. Revised age estimates in 1973 showed that the oldest known are feldspathic gneisses in Greenland, of 3,700,000,000 and not 3,900,000,000 years, as earlier believed. A growing school of thought believed that the earth's atmosphere and oceans were formed early and have not changed greatly during its history.

Plate Tectonics and Sea-Floor Spreading. The concept of plate tectonics, which is that the surface of the earth consists of a few rigid plates moving relative to one another along belts marked by earthquakes, originated in 1968. In 1973 it continued to attract great attention. Much of the evidence for plate tectonics was found in the phenomenon of sea-floor spreading. Deep-sea drilling from the research ship "Glomar Challenger," with more than 200 holes drilled and cored in the ocean floor, supported the view that the mid-ocean ridges are young and spreading so that progressively older rocks are found ever farther away from them toward continental margins.

Considerable debate was raised over the suggestion that many ocean ridges, such as the Hawaiian Islands, are trails of volcanic rock left behind as plates moved over nearly stationary sources of lava. One phase of the argument was whether the Mid-Atlantic Ridge is underlain by a continuously upwelling limb of a system of convection currents, or whether plumes or jets of heated rock are slowly rising like vertical pipes under such volcanic islands along the ridge as Jan Mayen, Iceland, the Azores, Ascension, Tristan, and Bouvet, and whether these and similar plumes constitute the mechanism that drives the plates about.

Another remarkable discovery was the realization that a widespread change in the pattern and direction of sea-floor spreading which occurred during Cretaceous time about 100 million years ago coincided with the end of a more rapid rate of spreading along the ridge system, which was of the same length then as today. If the earlier rate of spreading was as rapid as indicated, it suggests a rate of release of energy in the earth at that time about double that of today. The significance of this was not yet understood.

Another matter under active discussion concerned evidence of the beginning of plate movements. One suggested line of evidence was provided by the overlapping of plates of continental crust, such as is considered to have occurred when India was overridden by another part of Asia to uplift the Tibetan plateau. Accounts of travelers, supported by evidence of craters and calderas seen on the Earth Resources Technology Satellite (ERTS) pictures, suggest extensive volcanism in Tibet. Geophysical evidence and calculations support the view that the concentration of crustal radioactivity caused by doubling the thickness of plates should produce partial melting in the lower plate to explain the Tibetan volcanics. Geologists proposed that large areas of metamorphic rocks in Precambrian shields, such as the Grenville province extending from the Adirondacks to Labrador in North America and the Mozambique province in Africa, represent the lower of two plates, which was formerly overridden but has now been uplifted and exposed by erosion. These areas are believed to show depletion in the more siliceous elements, which rose to the surface and are now found in recent volcanics such as those in Tibet.

U.S. GEOLOGICAL SURVEY

A mammoth sinkhole near Montevallo, Ala., is one of at least 1,000 created in the central Alabama area in the past 15 years. Lowering of the water table is blamed for the growing sinkhole problem in many Appalachian regions that lie over porous limestone or dolomite.

The investigation since the mid-1960s of hot brines rich in base metals in deep pools along the axis of the Red Sea led some geologists to believe that mid-ocean ridges are a common site for such deposits. They noted that the copper deposits on Cyprus were possibly formed along such a ridge that was subsequently lifted above the sea. Others believed the source of the Red Sea brines to be the action on the adjacent continental rocks of evaporites formed from seawater on the sea's floor. These scientists pointed to the absence of ores in Iceland, which definitely lies on a mid-ocean ridge. A clearer case can be made for the association of ores with subduction zones, along which one plate is overriding another beneath young mountains and island arcs; evidence for this is found in the manner in which ores of different metals occur in belts parallel with subduction trenches in the Andes, Japan, and the Philippines.

Volcanoes and Earthquakes. As in every year, natural disasters occurred. One of the most spectacular was the eruption starting January 23 of Eldfell (also called Kirkjufell), a volcanic cone on Heimaey not far from the 1963–67 eruption of Surtsey, Iceland. Residents of the island successfully diverted some of the lava away from their houses and harbour by bulldozing ash and by chilling lava with hoses.

In 1973 for the first time there were reports of phenomena that seemed to present the possibility of predicting earthquakes. It was noted that the velocity at which seismic body waves were transmitted through the area around the San Fernando, Calif., earthquake of Feb. 9, 1971, had fallen for 3½ years before the event but had returned to normal just before the earthquake occurred. Some geologists believed that the longer the time during which the velocity falls the larger will be the magnitude of the subsequent event. Verification of this relationship would provide a method of predicting the onset and probably the magnitude of earthquakes.

ERTS. A new aid in assessing the features and resources of the earth's surface was promoted by the Earth Resources Technology Satellite, which circled the earth 14 times a day in a polar orbit 920 km. (570 mi.) high. Four scanning systems on the satellite telemetered complete coverage of the earth every 18 days in four wavelength bands in the green, red, near infrared, and farther infrared portions of the spectrum. Linear features, faults, and other structures were revealed particularly clearly, and glaciers, glacial deposits, dunes, craters, lava flows, polluted water, and other features were also well shown in many places. Many institutions undertook programs to assess the value to geologists of this new and powerful system for scanning the earth. (J. TUZO WILSON)

See also Antarctica; Astronautics; Energy; Mining; Oceanography; Seismology; Speleology.

ENCYCLOPÆDIA BRITANNICA FILMS. *How Solid Is Rock?* (1968); *Reflections on Time* (1969); *Heartbeat of a Volcano* (1970); *How Level Is Sea Level?* (1970); *Ecology of a Hot Spring* (1972); *Controversy over the Moon* (1973); *Earthquakes: Lesson of a Disaster* (1973); *Geyser Valley* (1973); *Glacier on the Move* (1973).

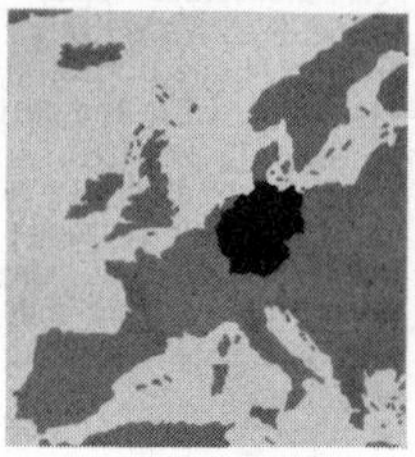

Germany

A country of central Europe, Germany was partitioned after World War II into the Federal Republic of Germany (Bundesrepublik Deutschland; West Germany) and the German Democratic Republic (Deutsche Demokratische Republik; East Germany), with a special provisional regime for Berlin. Germany is bordered by Denmark, The Netherlands, Belgium, Luxembourg, France, Switzerland, Austria, Czechoslovakia, and Poland and the North and Baltic Seas.

Federal Republic of Germany. Area: 95,980 sq.mi. (248,587 sq.km.). Pop. (1972 est.): 61,774,900. Provisional cap.: Bonn (pop., 1972 est., 278,778). Largest city: Hamburg (pop., 1972 est., 1,766,200). (West Berlin, which is an enclave within East Germany, had a population of 2,062,600 in 1972.) Language: German. Religion (1970): Protestant 49%; Roman Catholic 44.6%; Jewish 0.05%. President in 1972, Gustav Heinemann; chancellor, Willy Brandt.

In 1973 both German states entered the United Nations, following conclusion of the Basic Treaty between East and West Germany in which Bonn accepted the existence of two states while maintaining there was still but one German nation. At home the efforts of the federal government were concentrated on fighting inflation.

Domestic Affairs. With the cost of living rising some 8% over 1972, in May the government introduced measures to reduce spending power, including a 10% nonrepayable surcharge on income tax paid by medium- and high-income groups, an 11% tax on investments, and big cuts in public spending. Inflation was the basic cause of a wave of unofficial strikes in the metalworking industry, principally in North Rhine-Westphalia. In most cases employers gave in to demands for pay increases. Many of the strikers were foreign workers, most of whom were in either unskilled or semiskilled jobs and, therefore, among the lowest paid. On November 23 further recruitment of foreign (non-EEC) workers was prohibited following the Arab oil boycott and the likelihood of increased unemployment.

The program to restore economic stability had already been undermined by an influx of foreign currencies into West Germany. Within the space of 12 trading days in June the Bundesbank had to buy European currencies worth DM. 4 billion to maintain the rates of exchange within limits agreed in March when seven other European countries—five members of the EEC plus Norway and Sweden—had agreed to take part in a joint float against the dollar. On June 29 the mark was revalued upward by 5.5%. This meant that in the previous four years its value in relation to the dollar had increased by no less than 55%.

In June a parliamentary committee of inquiry was appointed to investigate allegations that bribes were offered or paid to persuade opposition deputies to abstain from voting against the government in crucial parliamentary divisions in 1972. The main allegation concerned a former Christian Democratic Union (CDU) deputy, Julius Steiner (*see* BIOGRAPHY), who claimed that DM. 50,000 had been paid to him by Karl Wienand, the parliamentary business manager of the Social Democratic Party (SPD). This Wienand denied.

CDU leader Rainer Barzel announced his resignation in May. The immediate reason was his party's decision—against his advice—to oppose West German membership in the UN, but it was clear that one of the motives of this vote was to challenge Barzel's leadership. It had long been expected that he would have to pay for his party's 1972 election defeat. The joint parliamentary party of the CDU and its Bavarian sister party, the Christlich-Soziale Union (Christian Social Union, or CSU), rejected by a vote of 101–93 Barzel's recommendations to support the bill that would enable the government to make formal application for UN membership. His opponents said West German entry was not desirable since it would be followed by East German membership, and East Germany should not be admitted because it constantly violated the UN Covenant on Human Rights by shooting people who were trying to flee to the West.

Shortly afterward, Barzel announced that he would not seek reelection as chairman of the CDU, thus renouncing his leadership of the party not only in Parliament but also in the country. He was succeeded by two men: Karl Carstens, formerly state secretary in the Foreign Ministry and head of the Chancellery when Kurt Georg Kiesinger had been chancellor of the "grand coalition" (1966–69), became floor leader of the CDU/CSU parliamentary party; at a special CDU conference in June Helmut Kohl (*see* BIOGRAPHY), the minister president (premier) of the Rhineland-Palatinate, was elected chairman of the party.

Chancellor Brandt (*see* BIOGRAPHY) had reason to feel pleased with the result of the SPD congress in Hanover in April. He succeeded in preserving party unity—by either containing or integrating left-wing rebels—and avoided decisions that would have strained relations with his coalition partner, the Free Democratic Party.

Foreign Affairs. The Basic Treaty with East Germany was ratified in the Bundestag on May 11 by a majority of 51 votes. There was a majority of 244 in favour of West German membership in the UN, which meant that it was supported by almost 100 opposition deputies. With the completion of the ratification procedure, four new crossing points were set up on the East-West German border to enable some 6.5 million West Germans living in the border areas to visit the other side 30 days a year. Many thousands took advantage of this opportunity but the number of visitors dropped sharply in November when the

German Literature:
see Literature

East German authorities doubled the minimum amount of money that had to be exchanged for East German marks at the border.

The ratification of the Basic Treaty created a good atmosphere for the visit to Bonn in May of the Soviet Communist Party leader, Leonid I. Brezhnev, the first Soviet politician of this rank to visit West Germany. A considerable part of the discussions between Brezhnev and Brandt was devoted to economic and industrial cooperation. Brezhnev offered the prospect of long-term cooperation in the exploitation of Soviet raw materials with the aid of West German technology and capital. An agreement to this end was signed, but was couched in somewhat vague terms; later in the year there were expressions of disappointment from Moscow that the agreement had not yet produced practical results. There was a general feeling in Bonn that the Soviet leader had overestimated the possibilities of economic and industrial cooperation between the two countries. Even so, Brandt later described the Brezhnev visit as one of the outstanding political events since World War II. In the communiqué on the Brandt-Brezhnev talks it was stated that both countries had agreed to observe strictly the 1971 four-power agreement on Berlin, and this was taken by Bonn as a sign that the Soviets in the future would not raise objections to West Germany's representing West Berlin in international agreements.

But difficulties were soon to arise over the question of the consular representation of West Berlin by the West German embassies in Eastern Europe. Negotiations for a treaty between West Germany and Czechoslovakia, under which the two countries would establish diplomatic relations, were delayed when the Czechoslovaks raised objections to Bonn's demand that the West German embassy in Prague should fully represent West Berlin in consular matters. The Czechoslovaks agreed that the embassy should represent the citizens of West Berlin, but not the city's courts and other institutions, since to do so would violate the Berlin agreement. Because of this, Brandt canceled a visit to Prague in September to sign the treaty. A suggested compromise, reached when West German Foreign Minister Walter Scheel visited Moscow in November, provided that the West Berlin courts should deal directly with the courts of the Eastern European countries, thus bypassing the West German embassies. The final treaty, signed when Brandt visited Prague on December 11, included an exchange of notes in which both sides agreed to use the Moscow formula as the basis for further negotiations. Negotiations also proceeded toward treaties with Hungary and Bulgaria, which had adopted a common attitude toward the problem on Moscow's instructions.

Relations between Bonn and Washington became strained during the October Middle East war when the West German government told the U.S. not to send arms to Israel from U.S. bases in West Germany. This step was taken after disclosures that two Israeli ships laden with U.S. war matériel had sailed from Bremerhaven for Haifa. The West German government was strongly criticized by U.S. spokesmen for failing to cooperate in maintaining the balance of power in the Middle East. Bonn's attitude was based on its policy of neutrality in the area, although the West German government reiterated that it regarded Israel's right to exist as incontestable. Although the

KEYSTONE

Soviet party leader Leonid I. Brezhnev (right) and West German Chancellor Willy Brandt review troops, May 22, 1973, the last day of Brezhnev's state visit in Bonn.

GERMANY: Federal Republic

Education. (1970–71) Primary (including special), pupils 6,678,730, teachers 207,224; secondary, pupils 2,233,337, teachers 103,986; vocational, pupils 2,177,364, teachers 49,597; higher (including 43 universities), students 636,617, teaching staff (1968–69) 36,438.

Finance. Monetary unit: Deutsche Mark, with (Sept. 17, 1973) a free rate of DM. 2.41 to U.S. $1 (free rate of DM. 5.81 = £1 sterling). Gold, SDRs, and foreign exchange, central bank: (June 1973) U.S. $30,986,000,000; (June 1972) U.S. $21,894,000,000). Budget (federal; 1973 est.): revenue DM. 116.4 billion; expenditure DM. 120,390,000,000. Gross national product: (1971) DM. 758.8 billion; (1970) DM. 685.6 billion. Money supply: (May 1973) DM. 125.2 billion; (May 1972) DM. 115.3 billion. Cost of living (1963 = 100): (June 1973) 144; (June 1972) 133.

Foreign Trade. (1972) Imports DM. 128,150,000,000; exports DM. 148,910,000,000. Import sources: EEC 49% (France 14%, The Netherlands 14%, Italy 11%, Belgium-Luxembourg 10%); U.S. 8%. Export destinations: EEC 40% (France 13%, The Netherlands 10%, Italy 8%, Belgium-Luxembourg 8%); U.S. 9%; Switzerland 6%; Austria 5%; U.K. 5%. Main exports: machinery 32%; motor vehicles 14%; chemicals 12%; iron and steel 7%.

Transport and Communications. Roads (1972) 418,600 km. (including 5,258 km. of autobahns). Motor vehicles in use (1972): passenger 16,324,000; commercial 1,220,000. Railways: (1971) federal 29,268 km. (including 8,954 km. electrified), other 3,570 km.; traffic (1972) 39,065,000,000 passenger-km., freight 64,865,000,000 net ton-km. Air traffic (1972): 10,452,000,000 passenger-km.; freight 700,684,000 net ton-km. Navigable inland waterways in regular use (1971) 4,369 km.; freight traffic 44,991,000,000 ton-km. Shipping (1972): merchant vessels 100 gross tons and over 2,546; gross tonnage 8,515,669. Telephones (Dec. 1971) 15,246,000. Radio licenses (Dec. 1970) 19,622,000. Television licenses (Dec. 1971) 17,673,000.

Agriculture. Production (in 000; metric tons; 1972; 1971 in parentheses): wheat 6,608 (7,142); rye 2,914 (3,029); barley 5,997 (5,774); oats 2,887 (3,037); potatoes 15,036 (15,174); apples 1,211 (1,955); sugar, raw value *c.* 2,265 (2,342); wine 686 (555); milk 21,432 (21,156); butter 490 (462); cheese *c.* 550 (*c.* 500); beef and veal 1,169 (1,340); pork 2,352 (2,363); fish catch (1971) 508, (1970) 613. Livestock (in 000; Dec. 1971): cattle 13,612; pigs 19,985; sheep 850; horses used in agriculture 265; chickens 100,298.

Industry. Index of production (1963 = 100): (1972) 163; (1971) 157. Unemployment: (1972) 1.1%; (1971) 0.8%. Fuel and power (in 000; metric tons; 1972): coal 102,471; lignite 110,416; crude oil 7,099; coke (1971) 37,537; electricity (kw-hr.) 274,774,000; natural gas (cu.m.) 17,688,000; manufactured gas (cu.m.) 17,238,000. Production (in 000; metric tons; 1972): iron ore (28% metal content) 4,826; pig iron 32,222; crude steel 43,705; aluminum 739; copper 398; lead 273; zinc 493; cement 42,614; sulfuric acid 4,740; cotton yarn 222; woven cotton fabrics 189; wool yarn 87; rayon, etc., filament yarn 70; rayon, etc., staple fibre 88; nylon, etc., filament yarn 316; nylon, etc., fibre 324; nitrogenous fertilizer (1971–72) 1,321; phosphate fertilizer (1971–72) 943; potash fertilizer (1971–72) 2,376; synthetic rubber 337; plastics and resins 5,450; passenger cars (units) 3,514; commercial vehicles (units) 302. Merchant vessels launched (100 gross tons and over; 1972) 1,632,000 gross tons. New dwelling units completed (1972) 661,000.

government reluctantly participated in the joint European declaration on the Middle East that reinterpreted UN Security Council Resolution 242 of November 1967, as the Arab oil embargo began to take effect at the end of the year, Brandt strongly urged his EEC partners to face the crisis together.

(NORMAN CROSSLAND)

West Berlin. Addressing a committee of the West Berlin City Assembly on September 25, a senior official of the city administration gave a glowing picture of the way the regulations for West Berliners wishing to visit East Berlin, in force since June 4, 1972, were working. About five million visits of West Berliners to East Berlin and East Germany had been registered. (On October 26 East German First Secretary Erich Honecker told an audience of high party functionaries that in 1972 visitors from West Germany and West Berlin had totaled 7.5 million and that the estimate for 1973 was 10 million.)

But there was evidence in the autumn that pointed to a change in climate. The growing number of escapes from East Germany via the autobahn, organized partly by commercially motivated escape organizations in West Berlin and West Germany, led to mounting protests by East German authorities, culminating in a much publicized trial of three escape organizers who, on November 5, received sentences ranging from 7 to 11½ years' imprisonment. Also on November 5 the East German press published an ordinance of the minister of finance doubling the minimum daily amounts of currency to be exchanged into East German marks to DM. 10 for visitors to East Berlin and to DM. 20 for those visiting elsewhere in East Germany.

In an interview published in *Neues Deutschland* on November 1, Honecker demanded that the West German "presence" in West Berlin be reduced. He insisted that the 1971 Berlin agreement spoke of connections between West Germany and West Berlin and not of links or ties. The remarks were published while West German Foreign Minister Scheel was in Moscow working out the compromise solution to the Berlin problem.

German Democratic Republic. Area: 41,768 sq. mi. (108,178 sq.km.). Pop. (1972 est.): 17,011,343. Cap. and largest city: East Berlin (pop., 1972 est., 1,089,874). Language: German. Religion (1950): Protestant 81.3%; Roman Catholic 11%. First secretary of the Socialist Unity (Communist) Party (SED) in 1973, Erich Honecker; chairmen of the Council of State, Walter Ulbricht to August 1 and, from October 3, Willi Stoph; presidents of the Council of Ministers (premiers), Stoph and, from October 3, Horst Sindermann.

Europe and the world witnessed the virtual peaceful settlement of World War II on Sept. 18, 1973, when the General Assembly of the United Nations accepted East Germany as a member, along with West Germany and the Bahamas. This had become possible once the treaty between East Germany and West Germany had gone into force on June 21, after the two states had exchanged official notification of ratification. The treaty had been signed on Dec. 21, 1972.

The ratification gave formal expression to the concept of the existence of two German nations—at least in the eyes of the East German leadership. Earlier, in June, Erich Honecker, first secretary of the Socialist Unity Party, said as much to the party's Central Committee. The fact that the two states shared a common language and cultural tradition did not mean that they belonged to the same nation. He gave the example of Britain, Australia, and the United States, which were not one nation. And Foreign Minister Otto Winzer, in his speech to the UN General Assembly on October 1, said that his fellow countrymen had chosen the socialist system of government "forever." Because of the differences between East Germany and West Germany, unification of the two countries would never be possible. These words were clearly intended as a rebuttal to a speech made earlier by West German Chancellor Brandt in New York in which he said that unification would be West Germany's aim.

Peter Florin, first deputy foreign minister, was appointed the permanent East German representative at the UN. Before becoming a full UN member, East Germany had been accepted to membership in the World Health Organization on May 8.

Walter Ulbricht, the architect of East Germany, died on August 1, a few weeks after his 80th birthday; he had been seriously ill since suffering a stroke on July 19 (*see* OBITUARIES). Despite his justified reputation as a ruthless Stalinist, Ulbricht had proved to be more pragmatic than he was given credit for, especially after Stalin's death. His ability to adapt himself to, and indeed to anticipate, changes in Soviet policy, both domestic and foreign, was quite remarkable. His funeral on August 7 was attended by presidents Nikolay V. Podgorny of the U.S.S.R., Ludvik Svoboda of Czechoslovakia, and Nicolae Ceausescu of Romania. The absence of most of the leaders of the Communist parties of the Warsaw Pact

GERMANY: Democratic Republic

Education. (1971–72) Primary, pupils 2,570,504; secondary, pupils 57,278; primary and secondary, teachers (1969–70) 134,000; vocational, pupils 603,010; teacher training (1969–70), students 25,233; vocational and teacher training, teachers (1969–70) 20,115; higher (including 7 universities), students 152,375, teaching staff (1966–67) 14,200.

Finance. Monetary unit: Mark of Deutschen Demokratischen Republik, with (Sept. 17, 1973) an official exchange rate of M. 1.78 to U.S. $1 (nominal rate of M. 6 = £1 sterling). Budget (1971 est.): revenue M. 80,222,000,000; expenditure M. 79,141,000,000. Net material product: (at 1967 prices; 1972) M. 120.1 billion; (1971) M. 113.6 billion.

Foreign Trade. (1972) Imports M. 22,851,000,000; exports M. 23,931,000,000. Import sources: U.S.S.R. 38%; West Germany 10%; Czechoslovakia 10%; Poland 6%; Hungary 5%. Export destinations: U.S.S.R. 38%; West Germany 10%; Czechoslovakia 9%; Poland 9%; Hungary 6%. Main exports (1970): machinery 38%; transport equipment 11%.

Transport and Communications. Roads (1971) *c.* 160,000 km. (45,620 km. main roads, including 1,464 km. autobahns). Motor vehicles in use (1971): passenger 1,268,000; commercial 198,000. Railways: (1971) 14,525 km. (including 1,370 km. electrified); traffic (1972) 19,931,000,000 passenger-km., freight 44,710,000,000 net ton-km. Air traffic (1971): 1,073,100,000 passenger-km.; freight 29,719,000 net ton-km. Navigable inland waterways in regular use (1971) 2,100 km.; freight traffic 2,331,000,000 ton-km. Shipping (1972): merchant vessels 100 gross tons and over 436; gross tonnage 1,198,365. Telephones (Dec. 1971) 2,165,000. Radio licenses (Dec. 1971) 6,016,000. Television licenses (Dec. 1971) 4,649,000.

Agriculture. Production (in 000; metric tons; 1972; 1971 in parentheses): wheat 2,744 (2,490); rye 1,904 (1,754); barley 2,592 (2,286); oats 890 (807); potatoes 12,140 (9,412); sugar, raw value *c.* 587 (*c.* 530); rapeseed *c.* 220 (196). Livestock (in 000; Dec. 1971): cattle 5,293; sheep 1,607; pigs 9,995; goats 112; horses used in agriculture 106; poultry 43,343.

Industry. Index of production (1963 = 100): (1972) 171; (1971) 161. Production (in 000; metric tons; 1972): lignite 248,400; coal (1971) 857; petroleum products (1971) 12,108; manufactured gas (cu.m.; 1971) 4,480,000; electricity (kw-hr.) 72,906,000; iron ore (25% metal content) 264; pig iron 2,151; crude steel 5,630; cement 8,880; potash (oxide content; 1971) 2,426; sulfuric acid 1,045; synthetic rubber 132; cotton yarn (1971) 67; rayon filaments and fibres (1971) 157; passenger cars (units; 1971) 134; commercial vehicles (units; 1971) 28.

countries was a formal acknowledgment of the change in his status after he had lost the post of first secretary of the SED in May 1971.

The new leadership team headed by Honecker, who had been handpicked by Ulbricht, underwent the necessary reshuffle on October 3 along expected lines. Willi Stoph, chairman of the Council of Ministers since 1964, was elected chairman of the Council of State while Horst Sindermann (*see* BIOGRAPHY) took Stoph's place. Honecker, of course, retained his post as the party's first secretary and, thus, leadership of the Politburo; but the special position of Ulbricht as both first secretary and chairman of the Council of State was ended.

The total membership of the Politburo remained at 16. Following the Soviet model, Gen. Heinz Hoffmann, minister of defense, was elected a full member; previously he had only been a member of the Central Committee. New candidate members were Werner Felfe and Konrad Naumann, first SED district secretaries for Halle and Berlin, respectively; Gerhard Schürer, chairman of the State Planning Commission; Inge Lange, in charge of the Central Committee department dealing with women; and Joachim Herrmann, editor of *Neues Deutschland.*

Günter Mittag, who remained a member of the Politburo, had been relieved of his duties as Central Committee secretary for economic questions and was appointed to the post of first deputy to the chairman of the Council of Ministers. Bernhard Quandt, first SED district secretary for Schwerin, was elected to a membership in the State Council. Heinz Kuhrig, state secretary in the Ministry of Agriculture, was elected minister, replacing the late Georg Ewald.

According to figures released in October prior to party elections, SED membership totaled 1.9 million, 55.6% of whom were shown as workers. Of those who joined the party in 1972, roughly 80% had been workers.

A new decree on publicly owned enterprises that went into force on May 1, while not introducing fundamental changes, clearly reflected the trend toward renewed centralization of economic decision-making. An ordinance of the Council of Ministers promulgated in October revealed a similar approach. It considerably strengthened the position of the State Planning Commission by authorizing its chairman to issue instructions to ministers and others in charge of central authorities. Hitherto the commission had not possessed this power.

Because the Vatican was unable to agree to the complete reorganization of diocesan districts demanded by East German authorities during the summer, Julius Cardinal Döpfner, chairman of the conference of German bishops, was refused entry to East Germany on October 26. The cardinal had been invited to attend the 200th anniversary of St. Hedwig Cathedral in East Berlin; he received news about the ban imposed on him while concluding a four-day visit to Poland.

(S. E. SCHATTMANN)

Ghana

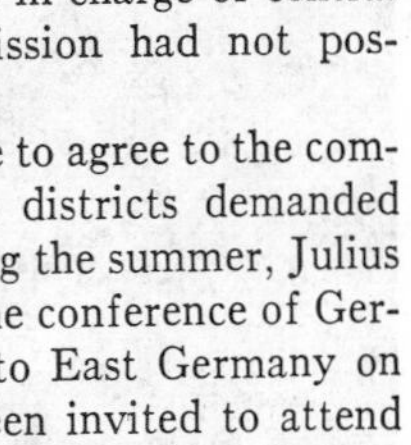

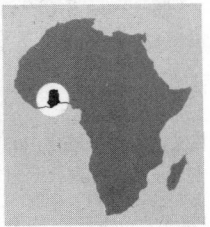

A republic of West Africa and member of the Commonwealth of Nations, Ghana is on the Gulf of Guinea and is bordered by Ivory Coast, Upper Volta, and Togo. Area: 92,100 sq.mi. (238,500 sq.km.). Pop. (1973 est.): 9,190,000. Cap. and largest city: Accra (pop., 1970, 564,194). Language: English (official); local Sudanic dialects. Religion (1960): Christian 43%; Muslim 12%; animist 38%. Chairman of the National Redemption Council in 1973, Col. Ignatius Kutu Acheampong.

The military regime of the National Redemption Council felt strong enough at the beginning of 1973 to commute death sentences imposed on participants in the July 1972 plot against the government. By July the last of the thousand-odd imprisoned members of the banned Progress Party had been released, including Gen. Akwasi Afrifa (still under house arrest) and J. H. Mensah, former finance minister. The prohibition on public meetings was maintained. Industrial strikers were tried by military tribunal under the Subversion Decree, which was extended to include profiteering.

Colonel Acheampong made no move toward civilian rule during the year, and in several speeches he indicated that civilian government was not necessarily identical with democracy or responsive to the wishes of the people. On January 13, the anniversary of the revolution, the NRC published a 19-page Charter of Redemption, which included seven aims: (1) one nation, one folk, one destiny; (2) total manpower development and employment; (3) revolutionary self-discipline; (4) self-reliance; (5) service to the people; (6) patriotism and international brotherhood; (7) total mobilization of spirit, intelligence, and willpower.

GHANA

Education. (1970–71) Primary, pupils 1,389,804, teachers 46,960; secondary, pupils 52,852, teachers 2,899; vocational, pupils 12,169, teachers 578; teacher training, students 16,478, teachers (1968–69) 1,275; higher (including 3 universities), students 4,759, teaching staff 833.

Finance. Monetary unit: new cedi, with (Sept. 17, 1973) a free rate of 1.15 cedis to U.S. $1 (2.78 cedis = £1 sterling). Gold, SDRs, and foreign exchange, official: (June 1973) U.S. $174 million; (June 1972) U.S. $76 million. Budget (1972–73 rev. est.): revenue 386 million cedis; expenditure 329 million cedis. Gross domestic product: (1970) 2,571,000,000 cedis; (1969) 2,328,000,000 cedis. Money supply: (March 1973) 437.5 million cedis; (March 1972) 335.9 million cedis. Cost of living (Accra; 1963 = 100): (Dec. 1972) 203; (Dec. 1971) 180.

Foreign Trade. (1971) Imports 452,250,000 cedis; exports 337,380,000 cedis. Import sources: U.K. 24%; U.S. 15%; West Germany 12%; Japan 8%; Nigeria 5%. Export destinations: U.S. 20%; U.K. 18%; U.S.S.R. 14%; West Germany 9%; Japan 8%; The Netherlands 6%. Main exports: cocoa 60%; timber 10%.

Transport and Communications. Roads (1971) 30,960 km. Motor vehicles in use (1970): passenger 36,500; commercial (including buses) 27,000. Railways: (1970) 953 km.; traffic (1971) 448 million passenger-km., freight 293 million net ton-km. Air traffic (1972): 135,440,000 passenger-km.; freight 2,668,000 net ton-km. Shipping (1972): merchant vessels 100 gross tons and over 74; gross tonnage 166,183. Telephones (Jan. 1972) 49,000. Radio receivers (Dec. 1971) 750,000. Television receivers (Dec. 1971) 20,000.

Agriculture. Production (in 000; metric tons; 1972; 1971 in parentheses): corn *c.* 360 (384); cassava (1970) 1,596, (1969) 1,320; sweet potatoes (1971) 909, (1970) 1,642; millet and sorghum (1971) 292, (1970) 179; rice *c.* 70 (*c.* 70); peanuts *c.* 105 (102); cocoa (1972–73) 417, (1971–72) 470; palm oil *c.* 60 (*c.* 60); timber (cu.m.; 1970) 10,700, (1969) 9,200; fish catch (1971) 220, (1970) 171. Livestock (in 000; 1971–72): cattle *c.* 600; sheep 1,449; pigs *c.* 350; goats *c.* 780.

Industry. Production (in 000; 1971): gold 698 troy oz.; diamonds 2,562 metric carats; manganese ore (metal content) 224 metric tons; bauxite 329 metric tons; electricity 2,944,000 kw-hr.

On July 3 a Prohibition of Rumours decree was published in Accra, under which the circulation of rumours or false reports was made liable to fines of up to 1,000 cedis and up to three years' imprisonment. Also in July, Colonel Acheampong reported the arrest of a number of chiefs in the Volta Region for attempting to incite secession and the merger of their peoples with Togo; they were later released but were warned not to allow themselves to be manipulated by politicians. Former prime minister Kofi Busia was allegedly behind the unrest.

The government achieved a record in its trade surplus and currency reserves as the 1973 cocoa crop proved both large and, because of a world shortage, more lucrative than ever; the main crop sold at about £640 per ton. Ghana's future continued to depend largely on cocoa, since overseas investors remained wary following the unilateral debt repudiation of 1972. Following NRC publication of its investment and participation policy, increasing state control and nationalization developed along lines similar to those advocated by the late Ghanaian leader Kwame Nkrumah. The mineral negotiating committee reached agreement with the British Aluminum Co. for 55% government control, retrospective to January 1973. Similar minimum equity participation was set out for overseas-controlled timber, oil, and fertilizer interests. Agreements covering Lonrho's Ashanti Goldfield Corp. interests and Consolidated African Selection Trust's diamond interests called for compensation for fixed assets by an independent valuation apparatus appointed by the government.

In March China agreed to renew a 40 million cedi loan originally granted during the Nkrumah regime. Only 5 million cedis of the loan had been used at the time of Nkrumah's overthrow in 1966. The loan was interest-free and carried a ten-year moratorium and a 20-year repayment period.

Early in the year a decree was published extending territorial waters to 30 nautical miles. In March a permanent joint commission with Togo was established as a first step toward West African economic cooperation. This followed the Economic Commission for Africa meeting at Accra, which emphasized the need for the Organization of African Unity to present a united front in negotiations with the EEC.

(MOLLY MORTIMER)

Golf

The golfing year of 1973 was memorable for three outstanding performances. When Jack Nicklaus (*see* BIOGRAPHY) won the Professional Golfers' Association (PGA) tournament at Canterbury Country Club near Cleveland, O., he brought his total of major championship victories to 14, one more than Bobby Jones had achieved. John Miller won the U.S. Open at Oakmont, Pa., with a final round of 63, the lowest ever achieved in that tournament, and Tom Weiskopf at last began fulfillment of a superb talent with victory in the British Open at Troon, Scot., after a remarkable sequence of successes in U.S. tournaments. Later, he won the World Series of Golf at Akron, O.

Nicklaus once again was the dominating figure wherever he played. For the sixth time, and the third in succession, he headed the official money-winning list with $308,362; this brought his lifetime total to $2,012,068, nearly $400,000 ahead of Arnold Palmer, and made him the first golfer to earn $2 million. During the season he won seven tournaments, two more than Weiskopf. If third place in the Masters and fourth in the U.S. and British Opens were disappointing by his standards, his victory by four strokes over Bruce Crampton of Australia in the PGA was a commanding gesture of his continuing supremacy. During the year Crampton, with four tour victories and as many second-place finishes, became the first non-U.S. golfer to pass the $1 million mark in winnings. Renowned as a consistent money earner rather than a winner of tournaments, Crampton had by far his most successful season.

After years as a highly consistent player with an unenviable habit of narrowly failing to win, Tommy Aaron gained his first major triumph in the Masters at Augusta, Ga. An opening 68 gave him the lead over Nicklaus and Masashi Ozaki of Japan, but rounds of 73 and 74 set him back. After the third round Peter Oosterhuis of England took the lead, three strokes ahead of J. C. Snead. Oosterhuis' great round of 68 was the lowest of the day, and the golfing world wondered whether he would join Gary Player (S.Af.) as the only non-U.S. competitor to win the Masters. In the final round Oosterhuis remained in contention until he took a six at the 15th, while Aaron shot a 68 to edge Snead by one stroke. Rain beset the U.S. Open at Oakmont, Pa., and the great course was not the fearsome test of nerve and touch expected of it. The greens were easy-paced and holding, and the Open was locked in uncertainty with John Schlee, Lee Trevino, Weiskopf, Palmer, and others within a stroke of each other midway through the final round. Then Miller, whose third round of 76 had left him six shots off the pace, exploded from the pack. Opening with four birdies, he scored 32 for the first nine holes before the other leaders realized what was happening and then shot home in 31 to win the tournament by one stroke from Schlee. Not since Billy Casper in 1966 had the champion come from so far behind.

For some years Miller had played strongly in the major events, and he and Weiskopf almost made a private match of the contest for the British Open at

Jack Nicklaus sinks a long putt during the final round of the PGA championship in Cleveland. Nicklaus won the match, racking up the 14th major golf title of his career.

WIDE WORLD

Gibraltar: *see* Dependent States
Glass Manufacture: *see* Industrial Review
Gold: *see* Mining; Payments and Reserves, International

Troon. After three rounds Weiskopf led Miller by one stroke; Bert Yancey was five behind and no other player was within seven strokes. Weiskopf played a beautiful, composed last round of 70, giving nothing away, and it was just as well he did so, for Neil Coles produced a great 66 to join Miller in second place. Nicklaus, starting nine behind, mounted one of his thunderous late charges for a 65, but the burden of a bad third round was too great. The course played slow and easy in gray, damp weather, and Weiskopf's total of 276 equaled Palmer's British Open record set on the same course in 1962. In November at Marbella, Spain, Miller and Nicklaus won the World Cup for the U.S., with South Africa second and Taiwan third. Miller was the leading individual player, four strokes ahead of Nicklaus and Lu Liang-Huan of Taiwan.

Although U.S. teams retained the Ryder Cup in the match against Great Britain and Northern Ireland at Muirfield, Scot., and regained the Walker Cup they had lost at St. Andrews, Scot., in 1971, both contests were closely fought. The home side at Muirfield made a strong start, winning the morning foursomes $2\frac{1}{2}$–$1\frac{1}{2}$ and three of the afternoon four-ball matches. This form of golf, introduced ten years earlier, had always strongly favoured the Americans, but the British, who recently had approached these encounters with much greater confidence, were splendidly served by Tony Jacklin, Oosterhuis, Brian Barnes, Bernard Gallacher, Maurice Bembridge, and Brian Huggett. Jack Burke, the U.S. captain, who had led the only side to lose (1957) since 1933, was a worried man that evening. Changing his pairings for the next day, he brought Nicklaus and Weiskopf together. They won twice, and with Casper and Trevino unbeaten, the foundation of U.S. recovery was laid though the teams were still even going into the 16 singles matches on the last day. Inevitably, the U.S. team with its immensely powerful vanguard had the edge from the outset. Huggett, Jacklin, and Oosterhuis alone won matches for Britain. The final margin of 19–13 was a fair statement of the difference between the sides.

No one gave the British much of a chance of retaining the Walker Cup at Brookline, Mass., against the youngest team ever to represent the United States, but the contest was far closer than a 14–10 result suggests. Facing a seemingly hopeless task of needing to win six of the eight singles on the last afternoon, the British actually were leading in all of them after the first nine holes. Had Marvin Giles not halved with Charles Green by making a wonderful birdie on the last hole, the contest would have been extremely close. As it was, Danny Edwards, who with Giles was the most accomplished American, defeated Trevor Homer 2 and 1, and Marty West beat Michael King in the decisive matches. The following week Giles lost his U.S. National Amateur title when he was beaten in the semifinal by Craig Stadler of California, who had a comfortable 6 and 5 victory over David Strawn in the final. The British Amateur Championship was won by Dick Siderowf (U.S.), who beat Peter Moody 5 and 3 in the final at Porthcawl, Wales.

Apart from Jacklin, Coles, and Oosterhuis, who won eight between them, the British golfers made a moderate showing in European professional events. Charles Coody (U.S.) won twice, including the year's biggest prize, £15,000 in the John Player Classic. The season ended with the Piccadilly championship which Gary Player won for the fifth time, beating Graham Marsh of Australia at the 40th hole.

In women's golf Kathy Whitworth and Judy Rankin headed the U.S. professional scene, but Susie Berning retained the Women's Open with her third victory in the event, a number surpassed only by Betsy Rawls and Mickey Wright. The U.S. Women's Amateur was won by Carol Semple, who beat Ann Sander, champion three times previously, in the final. Although Michelle Walker, the outstanding British golfer, lost the British title she had held for two years to Ann Irvin, she won the English championship and turned professional in the late summer.

Introduced during the year was a golf club that had a graphite shaft. Some players believed it improved their distance and accuracy, but others disagreed.

(P. A. WARD-THOMAS)

Government Finance

During 1973 demand-management policies in almost all major industrial countries shifted from lending support to the economic expansion to a braking stance. The cumulative effects of expansionary actions taken in 1971–72, which generally had been underestimated, contributed to exceptionally high rates of economic growth in early 1973, coupled with an acceleration in inflation rates virtually unprecedented since the Korean War. Accordingly, the overriding policy concern in 1973 was the achievement of a reduction in inflationary pressures.

Toward the end of the year, cuts in oil supplies from the Middle East added a further dimension to national policy problems. In many countries, oil shortages, together with price increases by the producing countries, were thought to be adding to inflationary pressures. Some countries tightened demand-management policies further. In other countries the uncertainties created by the oil situation, combined with already diminishing rates of economic growth, were thought to be sufficiently severe to lead either to a postponement of further restrictive measures or to some actual relaxation of anti-inflationary policies.

United States. In 1972 the administration of Pres. Richard Nixon had pursued a deliberately stimulative fiscal policy, especially in the first half of the year. This, together with an expansionary monetary policy, contributed to rapid economic growth, which appeared to be accelerating in the last months of 1972. Fearing that the economy was approaching full employment at too rapid a pace, the administration called for a slowdown in the growth of nominal gross national product (GNP) in order to reduce the inflationary pressures of excess demand. Thus, the fiscal 1974 budget, issued in January 1973, proposed a more restrictive fiscal policy. The standard fiscal measures for fighting excess demand are increases in tax rates and/or reductions in the growth of federal expenditures. However, in the 1972 election campaign President Nixon had taken a stand against further tax increases. Thus, the administration proposed to achieve a more restrictive fiscal policy by holding down spending.

The proposed reduction in fiscal stimulus was reflected in the budget projection of a $24.8 billion deficit in the ongoing fiscal year, followed by a $12.7 billion deficit in fiscal 1974. To ensure that federal spending did not exceed the $268.7 billion figure recommended in the budget for fiscal 1974, the president requested that Congress establish a rigid spending ceiling. Assuming that spending was held to this ceiling, the administration estimated that the official full-employment budget, a measure of fiscal stimulus, would move from a $2.3 billion deficit in fiscal 1973 to a $300 million surplus in fiscal 1974. (The full-employment budget is an estimate of the budget posture that would exist at a hypothetical level of full employment.)

In the budget issued in January 1973, the administration also reaffirmed a $250 billion limitation on federal outlays for the ongoing fiscal year. A number of costly spending bills had already been enacted, including a 20% Social Security benefit hike and the landmark revenue-sharing program. To offset these increases, the administration suggested reductions in a large number of spending programs. Additional savings were to be achieved by deferring payments for such programs as revenue sharing until the next fiscal year and by increasing proprietary receipts, including sales of financial and real assets.

To reduce outlays for enacted spending programs, the administration stated that it would "impound" appropriated funds as necessary. Official reports to Congress from the Office of Management and Budget showed that the total of impounded funds at the end of June 1973 amounted to nearly $8 billion. Although earlier administrations had also followed this practice, the constitutional authority for it was a matter of controversy and challenges were mounted in the courts. The federal government reportedly lost in a majority of the lower court decisions, but the issue seemed unlikely to be resolved completely until the cases reached the Supreme Court.

The only significant tax law change in calendar 1973 was the sharp hike in Social Security taxes in January. This increase, which produced about $11 billion in additional federal receipts in 1973, was legislated several months before the release of the fiscal 1974 budget, but it was consistent with the administration's plan to adopt a more restrictive fiscal policy. However, significant tax stimulus was forthcoming in the spring of 1973 due to a sharp increase in personal tax refunds—nearly $8 billion higher than in the spring of 1972—as a result of overwithholding of personal taxes in 1972. The overwithholding, which was unintended, resulted from the failure of taxpayers to adjust their declared exemptions for withholding purposes when the Treasury Department adopted a new withholding schedule in January 1972. Apparently, most taxpayers failed to adjust their exemptions in 1973; substantial overwithholding continued throughout the year, and personal tax refunds were expected to be exceptionally large again in the spring of 1974.

The realized budget deficit in fiscal 1973, which ended on June 30, 1973, was $14.3 billion, about $10.5 billion less than had been projected. A number of factors combined to produce this large forecast error. Apparently the limitations on spending were more successful than anticipated, because federal outlays were $3.3 billion less than had been estimated by the administration. Total receipts in fiscal 1973 were $7.2 billion above the January estimate, with individual and corporate income taxes accounting for most of the difference. The administration's forecast had underestimated the increases in personal income and corporate profits that accompanied the rapid economic expansion and the high rate of inflation experienced in the last half of the fiscal year. The high rate of inflation also necessitated upward revision in the estimate of the full-employment surplus. In fact, estimates of full-employment receipts for fiscal 1974 were raised by about $7 billion. Thus, a significant portion of the projected shift in the full-employment budget surplus from fiscal 1973 to fiscal 1974, shown in the table, reflects inflation rather than discretionary policy.

Summary of the U.S. Federal Budget

In $000,000,000

Item	Fiscal year ending June 30 1972 actual	1973 actual	1974 estimate*
Budget receipts	208.6	232.2	270.0
Budget outlays	231.9	246.5	270.0
Actual surplus or deficit (—)	—23.2	—14.3	—
Full-employment budget surplus or deficit (—)	—3.9	1.0	10.0

*Source: Testimony presented to the House Ways and Means Committee on Oct. 18, 1973, by Roy L. Ash, director, Office of Management and Budget. The full-employment surplus was estimated by the author.

West Germany. The broadening of the economic expansion in West Germany in 1972 led to a shift in budgetary policy from a strongly expansionary to a progressively restrictive stance. The budget proposals for 1973 were only mildly restrictive, projecting federal expenditures to rise at the expected rate of growth of overall GNP and admonishing the *Länder* (states) and local authorities to adopt a similar guideline for their expenditure plans. In February 1973, however, these proposals were augmented by a number of fiscal measures designed to moderate the rise of demand and, particularly, to restrain the rise in prices. To keep public expenditures within the projected limits, the proceeds of these stabilization measures were to be frozen at the Bundesbank. By May it became clear that economic activity was expanding even faster than had been anticipated at the beginning of the year, and a second stabilization package was introduced. The new measures were aimed primarily at limiting private investment expenditures and at a further reduction in government spending at all levels.

During the year fiscal policy turned out to be rather more restrictive than had been anticipated, as inflation itself raised tax revenues well above earlier expectations. This was so partly because, in contrast with preceding periods of economic expansion, local authority expenditures in 1973 did not rise in line with the increase in tax revenues. Toward the end of the year it became evident that the rate of growth of domestic demand had begun to slow considerably. However, very little, if any, slowing in the rate of inflation was observable, causing the authorities to declare a continued need for tight demand-management policies. Accordingly, in November the Financial Planning Council agreed that budgets at all levels of government would need to remain stability-oriented.

Signs that demand in certain sectors of the economy might be severely affected by the oil crisis, on top of an already weakening general demand situation, caused the government to lift some of the anti-inflationary measures at the end of November. The 11% tax on new investment expenditures was abrogated, and accelerated depreciation allowances on investment goods as well as favourable depreciation terms for residential building were restored. At the same time, the government retained the credit ceilings planned for public budgets for 1974, indicating that moderation of inflation rates would remain a primary policy concern.

United Kingdom. Demand-management policies in the United Kingdom in 1972 had been unequivocally expansionary. Fiscal policy, with the help of an easy monetary policy, was designed to produce a rise in GNP about two percentage points above what it would have been otherwise. During the second half of 1972 economic activity became progressively more buoyant and unemployment diminished rapidly. Despite productivity increases that were well above long-term averages, price inflation continued to be a matter of primary concern. However, a desire to maintain the longer-term move toward a higher underlying growth rate motivated the government not to use demand-management instruments to combat price increases. Instead, the government adopted a comprehensive wage-price policy.

In submitting his budget for 1973–74 in March 1973, the chancellor of the Exchequer declared that he had based his budget on two major considerations: inflation had to be contained; and reduction in the rate of economic growth might have a counterproductive effect on the pace of inflation because prices and wages could be controlled more easily under conditions of expanding incomes. Budgetary policy was designed to have a neutral effect on aggregate demand. Expenditures of the public sector were projected to rise by 13% in nominal terms, somewhat less than in 1972 and considerably less in real terms. Because of the faster growth in incomes, revenues were expected to rise more rapidly than in 1972, but not as fast as expenditures.

The borrowing requirement of the public sector as a whole was projected to rise from about £3,000 million in 1972–73 to a record £4,400 million in 1973–74. The chancellor stressed that there would be a surplus on current account and that the increase in the borrowing requirement mainly reflected a shift in the timing of indirect tax receipts associated with the adoption of the value-added tax (VAT) on April 1, 1973. But, recognizing that the massive borrowing needs of the public sector might have undesirable inflationary effects, the chancellor proposed a number of measures designed to encourage increased private sector holding of public debt.

The budget confirmed that the introductory rate of VAT would be 10% and that the new unified personal income tax system—replacing a dual rate system consisting of a standard and a surtax—would have an initial basic rate of 30%.

During the year the exceptionally high rate of economic expansion registered in the first quarter of 1973 moderated, but labour became scarce in certain sectors and the underlying rate of price increase accelerated. The oil crisis was superimposed on this situation. Although theoretically Britain should have been relatively little affected by cutbacks in oil supplies because of the availability of coal as an alternative source of energy, labour unrest in the coal and transport industries brought about an emergency situation. As a result, the government took a number of drastic measures including massive public expenditure cuts. The chancellor explained the latter measure by saying that the emergency situation would cut supplies more than demand and that, therefore, it would be appropriate to reduce the claim on resources made by the public sector by significant amounts.

Japan. In Japan, as elsewhere, demand-management policies became progressively restrictive during 1973. The major share of restrictive action fell on monetary policy, however, as the government attempted to preserve its longer-term objective of expanding the share of resources devoted to infrastructure investments.

The budget for fiscal 1973 was formulated against a background of rapidly rising economic activity and price pressures. Accordingly, general account expenditures were slated to rise at only two-thirds of the rate registered in the preceding year—by 18%, as compared with a rise of 27% in fiscal 1972. At the same time, the rise in expenditures under the Fiscal Investment and Loan Program (FILP) was projected to slow from an increase of 21% to 14%. The usual cut in personal income taxes, however, was preserved.

As inflationary pressure increased and inflation rates spiraled upward, the government decided to moderate the effect of public demand on the private sector by postponing the placement of government contracts in May and again in June. In August further postponements were announced. The supplementary budget for fiscal 1973, drafted in the fall of 1973, asked for a substantial amount of additional appropriations, but these were mainly to cover increased salary and transfer payments and did not include additional real spending plans.

The oil crisis, which was expected to affect Japan more severely than most other countries, further complicated Japan's management problems. Because of feared shortfalls in output, prices received an additional upward impetus. The government stated that it was prepared to risk creating recessionary tendencies in the economy in order to combat price inflation. A stabilization package was announced toward the end of the year aimed at achieving price stability in 1974. To moderate price increases directly, public utility rates were frozen and planned increases in railway fares were postponed. Under the budget retrenchment policy included in the package, public works expenditures would be held to the same level registered in fiscal 1973. In particular, construction projects planned for 1974 were to be deferred indefinitely.

Canada. In contrast with some other countries, the Canadian economy appeared less buoyant toward the end of 1972 than had been anticipated earlier in the year. Unemployment remained very high, and business investment appeared not to be expanding to the extent expected. At the same time, however, the rate of inflation had been accelerating since mid-1972. The federal budget for the 1973–74 fiscal year was thus designed both to reduce unemployment and to counteract inflation. The emphasis on the expansionary side in the budget was placed on revenue-reducing rather than on expenditure-increasing measures.

During the first half of 1973, economic growth accelerated considerably, as did the rate of inflation. As a result, budget revenues also grew faster than had been estimated. But higher-than-expected spending, coupled with the effects of an anti-inflation package adopted in September 1973, probably more than offset the larger revenue outturn. This anti-inflation program was designed to provide direct relief from the effects of inflation rather than to damp down demand. It linked old-age pensions and the guaranteed income supplements to quarterly changes in the consumer price index and introduced subsidies for bread and milk prices. Government statements indicated that budgetary policy would remain expansionary, albeit less so than in 1972 and 1973, with the main thrust aimed at a reduction in unemployment as well as in inflation rates.

(HELLA B. JUNZ; WILLIAM J. BEEMAN)

See also Economics; Economy, World; Payments and Reserves, International; Taxation.

Greece

A republic (proclaimed June 1, 1973) of Europe, Greece occupies the southern part of the Balkan Peninsula. Area: 50,944 sq.mi. (131,944 sq.km.), of which the mainland accounts for 41,227 sq.mi. Pop. (1972 est.): 8,896,000. Cap. and largest city: Athens (pop., 1971, 867,023). Language: Greek. Religion: Orthodox. King until June 1, 1973, Constantine II, in exile since Dec. 14, 1967; regent until June 1, Georgios Papadopoulos; presidents, Georgios Papadopoulos from June 1 and, after November 25, Phaidon Gizikis; prime ministers, Georgios Papadopoulos, Spyridon Markezinis after October 1, and Adamantios Androutsopoulos after November 25.

Greece, which began 1973 as a monarchy without a sovereign and was for six months a "presidential parliamentary republic" without a parliament, ended the year under undisguised military leadership. Georgios Papadopoulos, the ex-artillery colonel who engineered the military take-over of Greece in 1967, staged another coup d'etat on June 1, 1973, to abolish the monarchy and become president of the new republic. The move to proclaim a republic was not unexpected. It was prompted not by ideology but by a political deadlock that occurred as a result of increasing domestic and external pressures. The deadlock, which obsessed Papadopoulos, was caused by his evident lack of popular support and also by the refusal of exiled King Constantine to cloak the regime's intended 1974 "elections" with respectability.

The continued ostracism of the Greek dictatorship from the Western community proper, combined with growing student agitation and rampant inflation and social unrest at home, increased the need for drastic action. The target date for the abolition of the monarchy had originally been set for some time in October. But an abortive plot by naval officers and civilians in May, aimed at forcing the regime to restore full constitutional rule by commandeering ships and occupying an Aegean island, was seized on as a perfect pretext for this action.

Since the beginning of the year the domestic situation had been dominated by growing student unrest, evidently politically motivated but with many reasons for being: inadequate university facilities, tight government controls, secret police surveillance on campuses, and rigging of union elections. Agitation was first countered with repressive police tactics combined with a law depriving protesters of academic deferments from military duty. Between the end of February and mid-May the military police rounded up more than 80 lawyers, intellectuals, professors, and student leaders and held them without charges or trial, in an effort to emasculate the student movement. This was combined with orders to newspapers to stop printing student news. The senate of Athens University resigned en masse.

The economic crisis was less spectacular but far more disturbing. Police measures, employed through 1972 to control prices in the naive hope of sparing Greece the effects of worldwide inflation, naturally backfired: commodity shortages induced more hoarding and a hasty revision of the government's expansionary credit policies. This was combined with a gradual relaxation of price controls, which, however, came too late. Inflation hit back with a vengeance, especially as Greece committed the cardinal error on February 14 of maintaining the drachma parity to the devalued dollar. Price controls on vital items created a black market. Within the first nine months of 1973 the Greek imports bill, at $2.8 billion, was up by 64%, and the trade deficit increased by 74% to $1,960,000,000. The official cost-of-living index had soared by 19.3% in the 12 months ended in September 1973, and labour unions were asking for 40% increases in minimum wages.

In foreign affairs, the agreement to provide homeport naval facilities that the regime signed on January 8 with the U.S. 6th Fleet came under strong congressional fire in Washington, revealing the tenacity of antiregime feelings inside the U.S. At the same time, the EEC continued to deny associate status to Greece, which created additional difficulties after the EEC Six became the Nine. Many countries improved commercial relations with the Greek regime, but the Western political-diplomatic ostracism continued.

It was against this background that Papadopoulos took his dramatic constitutional action to end the monarchy. When the navy plot was discovered and thwarted on May 22–23, a regime spokesman called it "an operetta." It took the regime a few days to realize that the plot gave it the best pretext for setting its plans in motion.

On June 1 Papadopoulos, in a nationwide broadcast, openly charged King Constantine with plotting subversion. He announced a "Cabinet act" abolishing the monarchy and proclaiming a "presidential parliamentary republic" with himself as provisional president. He promised a nationwide referendum in two months and parliamentary elections by the end of 1974. A July 29 national referendum on the issue of converting Greece into a republic and sanctioning Papadopoulos as president until 1981, held with the district of Athens still under martial law and with full denial to opponents of the regime to campaign against it, produced a 77.2% vote in favour.

GREECE

Education. (1969–70) Primary, pupils 948,097, teachers 28,128; secondary, pupils 418,617, teachers 12,659; vocational, pupils 103,202; higher (including 5 universities), students 72,616, teaching staff 2,693.

Finance. Monetary unit: drachma, with (Sept. 17, 1973) a par value of 30 drachmas to U.S. $1 (free rate of 72.15 drachmas = £1 sterling). Gold, SDRs, and foreign exchange, central bank: (June 1973) U.S. $1,061,700,000; (June 1972) U.S. $698.9 million. Budget (1973 est.): revenue 79,550,000,000 drachmas; expenditure 103,750,000,000 drachmas. Gross domestic product: (1972) 368.6 billion drachmas; (1971) 321.5 billion drachmas. Money supply: (Dec. 1972) 75,880,000,000 drachmas; (Dec. 1971) 63,640,000,000 drachmas. Cost of living (1963 = 100): (May 1973) 140; (May 1972) 127.

Foreign Trade. (1972) Imports 70,440,000,000 drachmas; exports 26,113,000,000 drachmas. Import sources: EEC 46% (West Germany 20%, Italy 11%, France 8%); Japan 8%; U.K. 7%; U.S. 6%. Export destinations: EEC 48% (West Germany 21%, Italy 10%, France 8%, The Netherlands 6%); U.S. 10%. Main exports (1971): tobacco 13%; cotton 8%; chemicals 7%; aluminum 7%; textiles, yarns, and fabrics 7%; fresh fruit 6%; dried fruit 6%. Tourism (1971): visitors 1,981,300; gross receipts U.S. $305 million.

Transport and Communications. Roads (1972) 35,512 km. (including 11 km. expressways). Motor vehicles in use (1972): passenger 301,937; commercial 130,234. Railways (1971): 2,571 km.; traffic 1,635,000,000 passenger-km., freight 748 million net ton-km. Air traffic (1972): 2,964,900,000 passenger-km.; freight 46,533,000 net ton-km. Shipping (1972): merchant vessels 100 gross tons and over 2,241; gross tonnage 15,328,860. Telephones (Dec. 1971) 1,230,000. Radio receivers (Dec. 1969) 1,184,000. Television receivers (Dec. 1969) 86,000.

Agriculture. Production (in 000; metric tons; 1972; 1971 in parentheses): wheat 1,773 (1,905); barley 864 (780); oats 107 (113); corn 579 (549); potatoes 683 (*c.* 700); rice 74 (68); tomatoes (1971) 1,049, (1970) 920; apples *c.* 240 (239); oranges (1971) 395, (1970) 450; lemons (1971) 125, (1970) 134; sugar, raw value *c.* 137 (*c.* 155); cotton, lint 125 (121); olive oil *c.* 255 (*c.* 211); wine *c.* 490 (507); raisins (1971) *c.* 150, (1970) 168; currants and sultanas (1971) 167, (1970) 168; figs (1970) *c.* 130, (1969) *c.* 130; tobacco 85 (88). Livestock (in 000; Dec. 1970): sheep 7,535; cattle 952; goats 4,130; pigs 446; horses 232; asses 358; chickens *c.* 24,500.

Industry. Production (in 000; metric tons; 1972): lignite 11,318; electricity (excluding most industrial production; kw-hr.) 12,035,000; petroleum products (1971) 5,211; bauxite 2,435; magnesite (1971) 900; cement 6,287; cotton yarn 49.

KEYSTONE

Georgios Papadopoulos (right) is sworn in as president of the Greek Republic during a religious ceremony in Athens Cathedral on Aug. 19, 1973.

On August 19 the president took the oath of office in Athens Cathedral. In his inaugural speech he announced: a general amnesty for all politically motivated offenses after 1967, including the navy plot; grace for Alexandros Panagoulis, the man who was sentenced to death after trying to assassinate him in 1968; and an all-civilian Cabinet by October to prepare and hold "impeccable" elections in 1974. Martial law was lifted from Athens, forcing the military police to release all its prisoners. The decision to demilitarize the regime, including the ousting of 11 fellow-junta members who held Cabinet posts, caused ominous rumblings among his erstwhile coup partners.

The new prime minister, Spyridon Markezinis, was generally regarded as possessing the economic and political talent so desperately needed to face the looming economic crisis and the social unrest that was already manifesting itself in labour strikes staged for the first time since the 1967 coup. The new government's first move was to end price controls in order to please the producers and the traders. On October 19 the drachma was revalued by 10% relative to the dollar, in order to induce hoarders to sell out. While it could be argued that these moves tended to create a favourable psychological climate, the energy crisis then hit Greece, adding new price increases for fuel and electricity and stringent fuel-saving restrictions.

To preempt a resumption of student agitation, the government released 107 student leaders drafted for military service, promised to let the student unions hold fair elections under judicial supervision, and granted them other academic claims. But after a memorial service for the former liberal leader Georgios Papandreou on November 5, crowds leaving the Athens cemetery chanting antiregime slogans were brutally attacked by the police.

On November 13 students seized the National Technical University of Athens after being refused union elections. They set up a radio station and called on the people of Athens to join the revolt. Students and workers took to the streets and fought troops throughout the capital, and the government called out tanks and troop carriers for a show of force that resulted in at least 13 deaths. The revolt spread to Patras and Salonika before order was reimposed.

On November 25 the Greek people awoke to discover a new ruler in power. Papadopoulos had been placed under house arrest at about 5 A.M. in an army coup aimed at steering the nation back to the "original ideas of the 1967 revolution" and away from "an electoral travesty." Lieut. Gen. Phaidon Gizikis, whose appointment as chief of the armed forces in August 1972 Papadopoulos had prevented, was sworn in as the new president. The new prime minister was Adamantios Androutsopoulos, formerly minister of the interior. In an immediate purge 13 generals were compulsorily retired. The curfew was lifted, the armed forces left the streets of the capital, and politicians placed under house arrest by the Papadopoulos regime were set free. A new constitution was promulgated on December 17. (MARIO MODIANO)

Guatemala

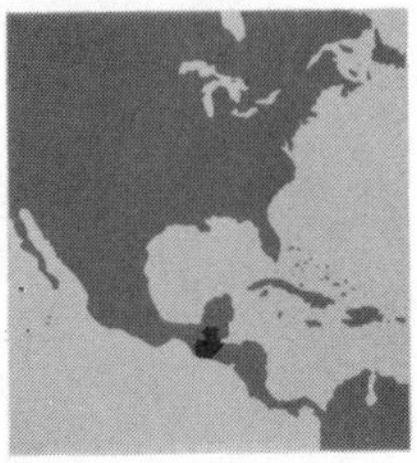

A republic of Central America, Guatemala is bounded by Mexico, Belize, Honduras, El Salvador, the Caribbean Sea, and the Pacific Ocean. Area: 42,042 sq.mi. (108,889 sq.km.). Pop. (1972 est.): 5,603,840. Cap. and largest city: Guatemala City (pop., 1972 est., 819,440). Language: Spanish, with some Indian dialects. Religion: predominantly Roman Catholic. President in 1973, Carlos Manuel Arana Osorio.

Although the opening years of the Arana administration had been characterized by intense guerrilla activity, Guatemala enjoyed a period of relative calm through 1973, with violence being the exception rather than the rule. Social unrest arose, however, as a result of the government's inability to control a 25% inflation rate. Dissatisfaction was expressed through strikes that affected production, particularly in the public sector. In view of the elections due on March 3, 1974, the government felt obliged to take corrective measures, and a new salaries law for public employees was passed, permitting a wage increase every two years and providing for a higher budget allocation for the civil service. This, however, did nothing to alleviate the grievances of 2,000 striking teachers, whose wage claims (for a 50% increase) had been denied. Their strike gained the support of the labour unions and students, who combined to form the Frente Nacional de Unidad Popular. The street demonstrations that followed were violently suppressed. A compromise agreement was finally reached, but the significance of the strike lay in the political awareness it created and the concerted action that resulted.

Three separate and unidentifiable groups of bodies were discovered during the year; presumably, these were Communist opponents murdered in the violence of 1972. A Cuban news agency in February quoted a kidnapped Guatemalan policeman as stating that eight missing leaders of the Guatemalan Communist Party (Partido Guatemalteco del Trabajo), who had disappeared in September 1972, had been tortured and then thrown from an air force plane into shark-infested waters off the Pacific coast. An original plan to drop them into a volcano reportedly had been abandoned because of bad weather.

Right-wing congressional deputy Hector Solís Juárez was shot dead in June. He had been accused of assassinating left-wing leader Víctor Rodríguez in 1970.

Gen. Eugenio Kjell Laugerud resigned as defense minister in January on being chosen as the presidential candidate of the ruling coalition of the Partido Institucional Democrático (PID) and the Movimiento de Liberacion Nacional (MLN) for the 1974 elections. President Arana declared that he would use "all the might that goes with holding power" to ensure Laugerud's election. By the end of the year both op-

Great Britain: *see* United Kingdom

Greek Orthodox Church: *see* Religion

Greenland: *see* Dependent States

Gross National Product: *see* Economy, World; Income, National

GUATEMALA

Education. (1969–70) Primary, pupils 489,565, teachers 13,662; secondary, pupils 41,292, teachers 4,583; vocational, pupils 11,784, teachers 1,380; teacher training, students 7,569; teaching staff 1,008; higher (including 4 universities), students 14,151, teaching staff 771.

Finance. Monetary unit: quetzal, at par with the U.S. dollar, with a free rate (Sept. 17, 1973) of 2.41 quetzales to £1 sterling. Gold, SDRs, and foreign exchange, central bank: (June 1973) U.S. $203.7 million; (June 1972) U.S. $100.6 million. Budget (1972 est.) balanced at 250.9 million quetzales. Gross domestic product: (1971) 2,001,000,000 quetzales; (1970) 1,904,000,000 quetzales. Money supply: (June 1973) 236.5 million quetzales; (June 1972) 193.3 million quetzales. Cost of living (Guatemala City; 1963 = 100): (May 1973) 123; (May 1972) 108.

Foreign Trade. (1972) Imports *c.* 315.6 million quetzales; exports *c.* 346.7 million quetzales. Import sources: U.S. 36%; El Salvador 14%; Japan 9%; West Germany 9%; Costa Rica 5%. Export destinations: U.S. 31%; El Salvador 12%; West Germany 10%; Costa Rica 9%; Japan 9%; Nicaragua 5%. Main exports: coffee 34%; cotton 9%; meat 6%; bananas 5%.

Transport and Communications. Roads (1971) 11,230 km. (including 830 km. of Pan-American Highway). Motor vehicles in use (1970): passenger 42,600; commercial (including buses) 24,400. Railways: (1971) 868 km.; freight traffic (1970) 106 million net ton-km. Air traffic (1971): 85 million passenger-km.; freight 5,490,000 net ton-km. Telephones (Dec. 1971) 44,000. Radio receivers (Dec. 1968) 559,000. Television receivers (Dec. 1970) 72,000.

Agriculture. Production (in 000; metric tons; 1972; 1971 in parentheses): corn 726 (719); cotton, lint *c.* 83 (*c.* 81); cane sugar, raw value 192 (198); sugar, panella *c.* 45 (*c.* 45); dry beans 65 (63); coffee 133 (133); bananas (1971) *c.* 80, (1970) *c.* 80. Livestock (in 000; March 1972): cattle *c.* 1,660; sheep *c.* 520; pigs *c.* 800; poultry *c.* 9,800.

Industry. Production (in 000; metric tons; 1970): cement 251; petroleum products (1971) 782; lead ore (metal content) 1.1; zinc ore (metal content; 1971) 0.5; electricity (kw-hr.) *c.* 780,000.

position parties had replaced civilian with military candidates. Gen. Efraín Ríos Montt (43), director of the Inter-American Centre of Military Studies in Washington, represented the Frente Oposicion Nacional, and Col. Ernesto Píaz Novales the Partido Revolucionario.

In April Congress authorized the creation of a Trade and Industry Zone at the port of Santo Tomás de Castilla on the Atlantic coast, to provide work for 15,000 persons. A preferential trade agreement with Mexico was sanctioned.

Prospects for the economy were encouraging, with official estimates of the 1973 growth rate at 7%, compared with 6% in 1972. The strength of the economy was reflected in a move taken by the authorities in February to remove all foreign exchange controls, following a trade surplus of $28 million in 1972.

(ANNE PARSONS)

Guinea

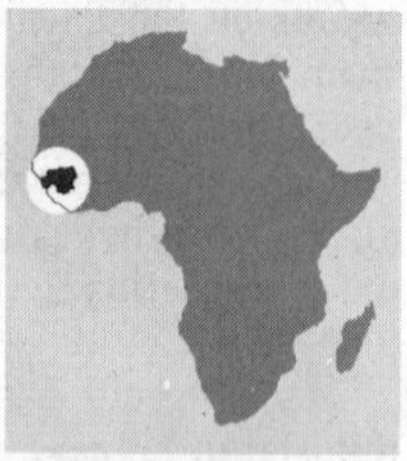

A republic on the west coast of Africa, Guinea is bounded by Portuguese Guinea, Senegal, Mali, Ivory Coast, Liberia, and Sierra Leone. Area: 94,925 sq.mi. (245,856 sq. km.). Pop. (1972 est.): 4,109,000. Cap. and largest city: Conakry (pop., 1967 est., 197,267). Language: French (official). Religion: mostly Muslim. President in 1973, Sékou Touré; premier, Louis Lansana Beavogui.

Government reshuffles and denunciations of foreign plots against President Touré's regime continued to be a constant feature of Guinean life. However, the most important event to take place in Conakry during 1973 was undoubtedly the assassination on January 20 of Amilcar Cabral (*see* OBITUARIES), leader of the anti-Portuguese nationalist movement, the African Party for the Independence of Guinea and Cape Verde (PAIGC). An enlarged revolutionary committee of the PAIGC was convened to try the alleged assassins of Cabral, whose funeral took place with due ceremony on February 1. However, within a short time the Conakry authorities had turned their attention to denouncing the alleged disunity of the anti-Portuguese nationalist movement—an attitude regarded by many observers as a bid by Touré for its leadership—and the exact circumstances of Cabral's death remained obscure.

In August and December Cabinet reshuffles and purges in the country's sole political party testified to the almost pathological fear of conspiracies against him that seemed permanently to haunt Touré. In March, April, and August, he announced over the radio the discovery of new plots to invade the country allegedly being hatched abroad by Guinean exiles with the connivance of various foreign states including France, the Ivory Coast, and Senegal. Following Touré's August accusations, Senegal broke off diplomatic relations with Guinea in September.

The Guinean president's constant accusations against France prevented any normalization of relations between the two governments in 1973, though fairly cordial relations were maintained between the Guinean leaders and the French opposition.

(PHILIPPE DECRAENE)

GUINEA

Education. (1968–69) Primary, pupils 167,340, teachers (1965–66) 3,990; secondary, pupils 33,448, teachers (1965–66) 567; vocational, pupils 5,334, teachers (1965–66) 261; teacher training, students 2,954, teachers (1965–66) 52; higher, students 942, teachers (1965–66) 95.

Finance. Monetary unit: sily (which replaced the Guinea franc at the rate of 10 Guinean francs per sily on Oct. 2, 1972), with an official rate (Sept. 17, 1973) of 20.46 sily to U.S. $1 (free nominal rate of 49.30 sily = £1 sterling). Budget (1971–72 est.) balanced at GFr. 27.8 billion.

Foreign Trade. (1971) Imports GFr. 22.2 billion; exports GFr. 14 billion. Import sources: France 26%; U.S. 17%; U.S.S.R. *c.* 12%; Italy 9%; West Germany 5%. Export destinations: Norway 24%; West Germany 22%; Spain 18%; Cameroon 11%; Switzerland 8%; U.S. 6%; Poland 8%. Main exports (1962): aluminum 60%; bananas 10%; palm products 7%; coffee 6%; iron ore 6%.

Guyana

A republic and member of the Commonwealth of Nations, Guyana is situated between Venezuela, Brazil, and Surinam on the Atlantic Ocean. Area: 83,000 sq.mi. (215,000 sq.km.). Pop. (1972 est.): 754,000, including (1970) East Indian 51%; African 30.7%; mixed 11.4%; Amerindian 4.4%. Cap. and largest city: Georgetown (pop., 1970, 66,070). Language: English (official). Religion: Protestant, Hindu, Roman Catholic. President in 1973, Arthur Chung; prime minister, Forbes Burnham.

On July 4 Forbes Burnham joined the prime min-

Guiana:
see Dependent States; Guyana

Guided Missiles:
see Defense

Guinea, Portuguese:
see Dependent States

GUYANA

Education. (1969–70) Primary, pupils 129,527, teachers 4,328; secondary, pupils 52,618, teachers 1,933; vocational, pupils 2,639, teachers 101; teacher training, students 654, teachers 36; higher, students 1,085, teaching staff (1968–69) 110.

Finance. Monetary unit: Guyanan dollar, with (Sept. 17, 1973) a free rate of Guy$2.16 to U.S. $1 (official rate of Guy$5.21 = £1 sterling). Budget (1972 est.): revenue Guy$226 million; expenditure Guy$225 million.

Foreign Trade. Imports (1972) Guy$299 million; exports (1971) Guy$298.4 million. Import sources: U.K. 19%; U.S. 16%; Trinidad and Tobago 18%; Japan 5%. Export destinations: U.K. 22%; U.S. 20%; Canada 8%; Trinidad and Tobago 6%. Main exports: bauxite 32%; sugar 27%; alumina 14%; rice 7%.

Agriculture. Production (in 000; metric tons; 1972; 1971 in parentheses): rice *c.* 194 (137); sugar, raw value *c.* 329 (*c.* 375); cassava (1971) *c.* 12, (1970) *c.* 12; oranges *c.* 10 (*c.* 10). Livestock (in 000; 1970–71): cattle 258; sheep 99; goats 37; pigs 82.

Industry. Production (in 000; 1971): electricity 337,000 kw-hr.; bauxite 4,235 metric tons; diamonds 48 metric carats.

isters of Jamaica, Trinidad and Tobago, and Barbados in signing the Chaguaramas Treaty introducing the first stage of the Caribbean Common Market and Community (Caricom). On July 16 his People's National Congress swept back into power with a two-thirds majority in Guyana's National Assembly, though there were widespread allegations of election rigging. Cheddi Jagan's Marxist People's Progressive Party gained 14 seats.

Prime Minister Burnham repeated election assurances that his party was not interested in dictatorship and would maintain civil liberties and the independence of the judiciary. He would, however, use his two-thirds majority to abolish appeals to the British Privy Council and to extend the franchise to 18-year-olds. In late July the three opposition parties categorically rejected the results of the election and announced that they would not take their seats.

The worst drought since 1966 adversely affected both the sugar and rice crops, each showing a decline from 1972 totals. Bauxite production was up, and timber exports were being promoted. The five-year development plan (1972–76) envisaged the expenditure of Guy$1,150,000,000 aimed at achieving self-sufficiency in food, clothing, and housing; economic diversification; promotion of labour-intensive activities; and opening up of the interior. The UN Development Program was to provide more than Guy$10 million over that period in technical assistance and pre-investment studies. Guyana seemed to have held down inflation better than other Caribbean countries, with a 9% rise in the cost of living during 1967–71. (SHEILA PATTERSON)

Haiti

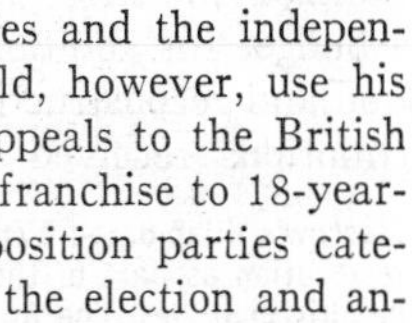

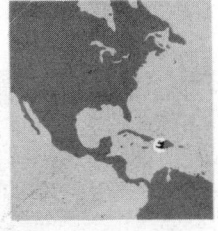

The Republic of Haiti occupies the western one-third of the Caribbean island of Hispaniola, which it shares with the Dominican Republic. Area: 10,714 sq.mi. (27,750 sq.km.). Pop. (1971): 4,243,926, of whom 95% are Negro. Cap. and largest city: Port-au-Prince (pop., 1971, 419,947). Language: French (official) and Creole. Religion: Roman Catholic; Voodooism practiced in rural areas. President in 1973, Jean-Claude Duvalier.

HAITI

Education. (1968–69) Primary, pupils 291,000, teachers 6,700; secondary, pupils 27,600, teachers 1,700; vocational, pupils 6,400, teachers 400; teacher training, students 230, teachers 60; higher (University of Haiti), students *c.* 2,000, teaching staff 183.

Finance. Monetary unit: gourde, with (Sept. 17, 1973) a par value of 5 gourdes to U.S. $1 (free rate of 12.06 gourdes = £1 sterling). Gold, SDRs, and foreign exchange, central bank: (June 1973) U.S. $20.8 million; (June 1972) U.S. $15.1 million. Budget (1972–73 est.) balanced at 157 million gourdes. Cost of living (Port-au-Prince; 1963 = 100): (March 1973) 168; (March 1972) 132.

Foreign Trade. Imports (1972) *c.* 520 million gourdes; exports *c.* 350 million gourdes. Import sources: U.S. 56%; Japan 8%; Canada 6%; France 5%. Export destinations: U.S. 72%; France 8%; Belgium-Luxembourg 5%. Main exports (1971): coffee 40%; bauxite 14%; sugar 7%; essential oils 7%.

Transport and Communications. Roads (1971) 3,157 km. (including 286 km. with improved surface). Motor vehicles in use (1970): passenger 11,600; commercial 1,500. Telephones (Jan. 1972) 5,000. Radio receivers (Dec. 1971) 85,000. Television receivers (Dec. 1970) 11,000.

Agriculture. Production (in 000; metric tons; 1972; 1971 in parentheses): coffee *c.* 25 (25); sugar, raw value *c.* 70 (*c.* 68); corn (1971) 257, (1970) 252; millet (1971) 215, (1970) 211; bananas (1971) 190, (1970) 189; sisal *c.* 27 (27). Livestock (in 000; 1970–71): pigs *c.* 1,800; cattle *c.* 960; goats *c.* 1,400; sheep *c.* 80.

Industry. Production (in 000; metric tons; 1971): cement 75; bauxite (exports) 715; electricity (excluding most industrial production; kw-hr.) 101,000.

Haiti enjoyed political stability and made considerable economic progress in 1973. President Duvalier strengthened his position during the year by removing potential rivals from the Cabinet and reorganizing the command structure of the armed forces. In January, Roger Lafontant was dismissed from the Ministries of Interior and Defense; he had been appointed to the posts in November 1972 following the enforced resignation of Luckner Cambronne. Lafontant was reported to have been gradually infiltrating supporters into key positions in the administration, with a view to eventually making a bid for the presidency. In August, Marie Denise, the president's sister, was forced to leave Haiti after she had made attempts to attract support among officers for a coup to seize power. Also in August, the Cabinet was reorganized:

A group of Haitians, described as revolutionaries, seek asylum at Mexico City Airport on Jan. 24, 1973. They were flown there after the release of the U.S. ambassador to Haiti and the consul general, who were held captive in Port-au-Prince while three of the Haitians bargained for the release of the others.

UPI COMPIX

Emmanuel Bros, a civil servant, was appointed minister of finance, and former ministers in Cabinets of the late president, François Duvalier, along with representatives of other factions, were appointed to lesser positions. In the same month committed supporters of the Duvalier family were appointed as commanders of the Army and Navy and as police chief in Port-au-Prince. In July, an explosion and fire of unknown origin gutted the presidential palace in Port-au-Prince.

Urban guerrillas were active between January and June. On January 23, the U.S. ambassador to Haiti, Clinton Knox, and the U.S. consul general were kidnapped, but they were released 18 hours later following payment of a ransom of $70,000 and the release of 12 political prisoners, who were flown to Mexico City. A series of bomb explosions took place in Port-au-Prince in June. In September a "Marxist-oriented" guerrilla invasion in the Baie Saint-Nicolas area was beaten off by a Haitian coastal patrol.

The general improvement of the economy during recent years continued in 1973. A rise in gross domestic product, in real terms, of 7% was forecast for 1973, against 6.5% in 1972 and 5.7% in 1971. The upswing in industrial production and the tourist boom that began in 1971 gathered momentum. There was a sharp increase in public investment during the year, and considerable private investment was made in hotels and in factories to supply light industrial products to the U.S. market. Exports of agricultural products, especially coffee, increased in both volume and value between January and September. Haiti cleared outstanding arrears on its external debt by May.

International financial institutions and foreign countries demonstrated renewed confidence in Haiti's economic prospects. In January the U.S. Agency for International Development appointed a representative to Haiti for the first time since 1963 and approved a loan of $3.5 million to finance road-building projects. In June the International Monetary Fund granted a 12-month standby credit of $4.8 million to the government. The Inter-American Development Bank made available in August a loan of $22 million to help finance the building of a highway in southern Haiti. In June France and Haiti signed a ten-year agreement for economic and technical cooperation; France was to grant aid equivalent to $1,250,000 in 1973 and more in 1974; the French government guaranteed investments by their nationals against expropriations by Haiti. In August West Germany gave a similar guarantee to its investors. (ROBIN CHAPMAN)

Historic Buildings

The General Conference of UNESCO, at its 17th session in October–November 1972, adopted two international instruments concerning the preservation of cultural property. The first was a convention concerning the protection of the world's cultural and natural heritage, which 20 nations would have to ratify or adhere to before it came into force. The second was a recommendation concerning the protection of the cultural and natural heritage at the national level. The conference also authorized preliminary studies on the feasibility of international instruments on: (1) the exchange of original objects and specimens among institutions of different countries; and (2) the preservation of historic quarters and historic cities in a modern environment. Both studies were to be carried out during 1973–74.

Three international campaigns to safeguard monuments were in the news during 1972–73. That concerning Philae in Egypt was the last project of the international Nubian campaign, of which the preservation of Abu Simbel was the best-known objective. The temples of Philae, dedicated to the cult of Isis and Osiris, were situated on an island formed in the reservoir between the Aswan Dam and the High Dam. It was decided to dismantle the temples and to re-erect them on the island of Agilkia a few hundred yards to the south. Construction of the coffer dam surrounding Philae was under way. After the site had been drained, the temples would be dismantled and transferred to Agilkia, which was being landscaped to resemble ancient Philae.

On April 13, the Italian Parliament passed the necessary legislation to float a loan of more than $500 million for the safeguarding of Venice. The funds would be used for such purposes as the construction of gates at the entrance of ship canals; the restoration of several monuments and improvement of old habitations; the construction of an aqueduct; and sewage disposal. In cooperation with the Italian government, UNESCO issued a booklet, *Venice Restored,* listing palazzos and houses that could be taken over by a government or by institutions for restoration.

The third international campaign was for the preservation of Borobudur, a Buddhist shrine in Indonesia probably built in the late 8th century. On August 10, at a ceremony attended by members of the diplomatic corps and senior government officials, President Suharto officially launched the restoration works on the shrine. The Executive Committee of Borobudur authorized the first payments and, at the same time, a budget for additional studies to refine the restoration and reconstruction program. In addition to contributions received from several governments, two

Moscow's dilapidated 17th-century Znamensky Cathedral is under restoration as part of the city's plan to restore some of its historic churches. The Rossiya Hotel looms in the background.

WIDE WORLD

Harbours: *see* Transportation
Harness Racing: *see* Horse Racing
Hay: *see* Agriculture and Fisheries
Health: *see* Medicine
Hebrew Literature: *see* Literature
Highways: *see* Engineering Projects; Transportation
Hinduism: *see* Religion

national committees (The Netherlands and Japan) had been raising funds, and committees were being established in the U.S., Switzerland, and West Germany.

The Council of Europe's campaign to preserve Europe's architectural heritage officially opened in July in Zürich. Its goals included: (1) stimulating the people of Europe to become interested in and to care for the preservation of old buildings; (2) bringing together professionals, administrators, and political leaders to stimulate their interest in the problem and to work out common solutions. A number of European countries not members of the Council, including Poland, Portugal, Spain, and Yugoslavia, were also participating in the campaign, which was to culminate in the celebration of European Architectural Heritage Year in 1975.

In the U.S. the National Endowment for the Arts established a program called "City Options," inviting individuals or organizations to apply for grants (a maximum of $10,000 to individuals and matching grants up to $50,000 to nonprofit groups, universities, and governmental units) to preserve a city's past or to carry out a study of new developments or other alternatives that would contribute to the enhancement of a community's physical setting.

One of the most intriguing projects to be launched in a U.S. city was a variation of the Homestead Act (originally enacted in 1872 and granting federal land to settlers provided that they cultivated or lived on it for five years). The city of Wilmington, Del., offered ten dilapidated homes, whose titles had lapsed over the years through nonpayment of taxes, in an open lottery. The winners had to repair them to meet city ordinances within 18 months and live in them for three years, after which they would receive titles to the houses. The city of Philadelphia had adopted similar legislation and planned to hold its first lottery in the fall of 1973, and Boston and Baltimore, Md., were considering similar measures. The projects were carried out in cooperation with local banks and other financing institutions.

Concern was once more expressed about plans to alter the U.S. Capitol in Washington, D.C. The House of Representatives, by a narrow margin, decided to appropriate the funds required to extend the west front of the building approximately 80 ft. in order to provide an additional 285 offices as well as meeting rooms and an auditorium. The National Trust for Historic Preservation and the American Institute of Architects were among those to register disapproval. The AIA proposed, instead, an underground building on the south side of the Capitol as a more aesthetically pleasing and less expensive solution. On July 19, 1973, the Senate rejected the House views and voted unanimously against the extension. Instead it authorized $18 million to restore the west front and $15 million for underground offices.

In September 1972 the Canadian government announced the formation of Heritage Canada, modeled on the National Trusts of the U.K. and U.S. A nonprofit organization with membership open to all, it was authorized to acquire, through purchase, gifts, or bequests, cultural and natural property of historical and national value. The government provided an initial endowment of $12 million.

In London, after a two-year campaign, sufficient funds were raised for the restoration of Christopher Wren's masterpiece, St. Paul's Cathedral, the survival of which was threatened by weakened foundations. In addition, an anonymous donor provided capital funds valued at £1 million to ensure normal repairs and maintenance in the future. The area surrounding St. Paul's was to become a pedestrian precinct. To the southwest, an attractive area of narrow, twisting lanes and old buildings previously zoned for redevelopment was rezoned for preservation to retain the historic ambience of the cathedral.

In Belgium progress was made toward preserving the historic city of Bruges. The city was an important commercial and political centre in the 13th–15th centuries, but silting of the river and harbour facilities and changes in political fortunes had turned it into a sleepy town during the 16th–19th centuries, contributing to the preservation of medieval buildings. In recent years, with the expansion of industry, the Bruges–Ghent canal had become polluted, adding to the city's malaise. In December 1972, however, water from this canal was diverted and fresh spring water introduced into the city's canal system. As a result of this and the introduction of modern methods of sewage disposal, the canals became clear once more as the accumulated, contaminated silt was dredged away.

In Moscow the Society for the Preservation of Architectural, Historical, and Cultural Monuments protested strongly against a project to change Moscow into a "model Communist city." If carried out, the plan would involve destruction of buildings along the western entrance to Red Square, including such outstanding gems as the 175-year-old Maly, Russia's oldest theatre. The Kremlin would be retained as the hub of the city, from which would radiate 16 broad boulevards, of necessity condemning many other architectural landmarks.

The winding down of the war in Southeast Asia had repercussions on the need to repair or restore monuments damaged during the conflict. In South Vietnam the project given first priority was the restoration of the Imperial Citadel of Hue, while in Laos it was Wat Phou. In Cambodia, the fighting was concentrated around the capital city of Phnom Penh, and the country's most famous monuments, at Angkor, remained a quiet zone. At the autumn 1972 session of the General Conference of UNESCO, a resolution was adopted authorizing preliminary studies for an overall program to restore sites and monuments in the event of peace being reestablished.

In Pakistan the government organized an international symposium in February to mark the 50th anniversary of the beginning of archaeological excavations in Mohenjo-Daro. Many notables took part in the symposium including Pres. Zulfikar Ali Bhutto, who opened the proceedings. Later, in October, the Executive Board of UNESCO approved a project to launch an international campaign to safeguard the site. The government agreed to provide a third of the cost.

In Nepal a UNESCO-aided project was under way to restore the royal palace of Hanuman Dhoka, the oldest part of which was constructed in the 18th century. The building, though dilapidated, was characterized by outstanding examples of Nepalese carving and architectural detail. Worshipers still came daily to the shrine of the "Dancing God" found in one of the 14 courtyards of the palace, where the Shah kings were traditionally crowned. Restoration of the palace would also contribute to economic development as it would become one of the central attractions for the country's growing tourist industry.

(HIROSHI DAIFUKU)

See also Architecture; Museums and Galleries.

Historical Studies: *see* Literature

Hockey

Professional Ice Hockey. The 1972–73 professional hockey season was quite ordinary, except for the fact that more teams claimed to be big-league than ever before. The National Hockey League (NHL) remained a congress of 16 clubs, but planned to expand to 18 with the addition of Washington, D.C., and Kansas City in 1974–75. The World Hockey Association (WHA), a defiant rival, began play in 12 North American cities. Not one of the WHA franchises made money and the result was considerable shifting of locations—the Miami Screaming Eagles never got off the ground until they became the Philadelphia Blazers, who subsequently became the Vancouver (B.C.) Blazers; the Ottawa Nationals were a box-office failure in Canada's capital and became the Toronto Toros.

Clarence Campbell remained president of the NHL for the 27th successive season, but Gary Davidson resigned the presidency of the WHA. Davidson, a lawyer from Santa Ana, Calif., organized the WHA in 1971, presided over its first struggles, and then quit to organize the World Football League. Dennis Murphy, who had been general manager of the Los Angeles Sharks, became interim president in November.

On the ice, the Montreal Canadiens won their fourth Stanley Cup in the last six seasons in the NHL. They dismissed the Buffalo Sabres and the Philadelphia Flyers in preliminary play-offs, and then beat the Chicago Black Hawks four games to two in the finals.

Ken Dryden, the Montreal goalkeeper, won the Vezina Trophy as the best NHL player at his position. Before the 1973–74 season began, Dryden abruptly abandoned the Canadiens because they refused to renegotiate his contract upward from $80,000 a year. After his Montreal contract expires on Oct. 1, 1974, he expected to join the Toronto Toros of the WHA.

The New England Whalers, based in Boston, lost only 3 play-off games in 15 to certify their regular-season dominance of the WHA. They defeated the Winnipeg Jets, coached by former NHL star Bobby Hull, four games to one in the final round for the AVCO World Cup, sponsored by a finance company.

The WHA intended to match the NHL in expansion in 1974–75, with new franchises in Cincinnati and Indianapolis. The battle for talent inspired competitive bidding that inflated salaries beyond profitable limits for several teams. Unofficial negotiations toward a merging of the leagues failed to gain the approval of a majority of the teams in the NHL.

The frantic search for talent reached dramatic lengths when the Houston Aeros of the WHL recruited Gordie Howe, for 25 years a superstar with the Detroit Red Wings of the NHL before his retirement in 1971. Howe's two sons, juniors under NHL rules, were also signed by the Aeros. (R. H. BEDDOES)

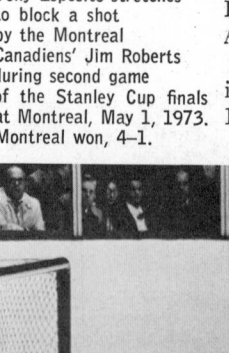

Chicago Black Hawk goalie Tony Esposito stretches to block a shot by the Montreal Canadiens' Jim Roberts during second game of the Stanley Cup finals at Montreal, May 1, 1973. Montreal won, 4–1.

UPI COMPIX

Table I. NHL Final Standings, 1972–73

	Won	Lost	Tied	Goals	Goals against	Pts.
EAST DIVISION						
Montreal Canadiens	52	10	16	329	184	120
Boston Bruins	51	22	5	330	235	107
New York Rangers	47	23	8	297	208	102
Buffalo Sabres	37	27	14	257	219	88
Detroit Red Wings	37	29	12	265	243	86
Toronto Maple Leafs	27	41	10	247	279	64
Vancouver Canucks	22	47	9	233	339	53
New York Islanders	12	60	6	170	347	30
WEST DIVISION						
Chicago Black Hawks	42	27	9	284	225	93
Philadelphia Flyers	37	30	11	296	256	85
Minnesota North Stars	37	30	11	254	230	85
St. Louis Blues	32	34	12	233	251	76
Pittsburgh Penguins	32	37	9	257	265	73
Los Angeles Kings	31	36	11	232	245	73
Atlanta Flames	25	38	15	191	239	65
California Seals	16	46	16	213	323	48

Table II. WHA Final Standings, 1972–73

	Won	Lost	Tied	Goals	Goals against	Pts.
EAST DIVISION						
New England Whalers	46	30	2	318	263	94
Cleveland Crusaders	43	32	3	287	239	89
Philadelphia Blazers	38	40	0	288	305	76
Ottawa Nationals	35	39	4	279	301	74
Quebec Nordiques	33	40	5	276	313	71
New York Raiders	33	43	2	303	334	68
WEST DIVISION						
Winnipeg Jets	43	31	4	285	249	90
Houston Aeros	39	35	4	284	269	82
Los Angeles Sharks	37	35	6	259	250	80
Alberta Oilers	38	37	3	269	256	79
Minnesota Fighting Saints	38	37	3	250	269	79
Chicago Cougars	26	50	2	245	295	54

Amateur Ice Hockey. Twenty-two nations took part in the 40th world amateur ice hockey championships during March and April. The six leading teams contested the title in Group A in Moscow, each playing the others twice. With convincing form on home ice, the U.S.S.R. recaptured the title from Czechoslovakia to gain a tenth victory in 11 years. The Soviet skaters emphasized supremacy by winning all their matches, a feat last achieved six years previously, and by being the first to score 100 goals. Outstanding were the Soviets' first-string forward trio, Vladimir Petrov at centre between Boris Mikhailov on the right wing and Valeri Kharlamov on the left.

Sweden and Czechoslovakia were next best, the Swedes winning a close battle between the two for the silver medal, while Finland and Poland placed fourth and fifth. The Swedes, with an effective defense but weak shooting, produced an outstanding player in defenseman Borje Salining. The best goalkeeper was Jiri Holecek of Czechoslovakia, with brilliant anticipation and superb catching. West Germany, winning only one game and losing nine, was relegated to Group B. East Germany, winner of Group B, moved up to Group A.

The East Germans did well to pin the U.S. to second place in the Group B contest at Graz, Aus. Eight nations competed, each playing the others once. The order after East Germany and the U.S. was Yugoslavia, Romania, Japan, Switzerland, and Austria,

Norm Beaudin of the Winnipeg Jets (right) shoots the puck past New England Whalers' goalie Al Smith during fifth game of the WHA finals at Boston on May 6, 1973. Jets' player-coach Bobby Hull hampers the goalie's effort. The Whalers won the game 9–6, to capture the AVCO World Cup.

WIDE WORLD

with last-place Italy failing to collect a point. Norway gained promotion to Group B in place of Italy by winning in Group C, played in The Netherlands. The host country finished second followed by Hungary, Bulgaria, China, France, Denmark, and Great Britain. It was an unhappy reentry for the British after a two-year absence, and demonstrated that the U.K. lacked rinks actively encouraging the game.

The Canadians declined to compete for a fourth successive year, and there was little prospect of a change in attitude. Canada had insisted on being allowed to include professional players, but the International Ice Hockey Federation's congress in Moscow reversed a previous decision to allow some professionals by 27 votes to 3, the only countries still voting for open world championships being Canada, Sweden, and the U.S. (HOWARD BASS)

Field Hockey. The number of national associations affiliated with the International Hockey Federation rose to 70 in 1973, and international events and tours multiplied. The second World Cup, in Amsterdam in August and September, drew teams from Argentina, India, Japan, Kenya, Malaysia, New Zealand, and Pakistan to challenge the leading teams of Western Europe. The champion club of England, Hounslow, reached the final stage of the European championship in the first appearance of an English club in this competition. League hockey was strongly reinforced in England by the establishment of the Truman South League, comprising 200 clubs organized in six county areas. Indoor hockey, played on a hard surface approximately 40 yd. by 20 yd., took on a new dimension with the advent of the first European indoor championship, held in Paris in February.

Surprisingly, first place in the World Cup did not go to Pakistan, the defending champions, nor to West Germany, the 1972 Olympic titlists, nor to India, which had led the world for so long. Instead, The Netherlands triumphed after overcoming West Germany and India in the semifinal and final rounds, respectively: each time The Netherlands won on penalty strokes after five periods of extra time. India, which placed second, was perhaps the team that gave most pleasure to most people through their delightful ball play and elusive bodywork. West Germany did not quite work itself up to the fine pitch of effort achieved in the Olympic Games a year before, but it did defeat Pakistan 1–0 in the play-off for third place. Pakistan lacked precision and polish, having had to rebuild its team because of the suspension of all the players who took part in the 1972 Olympic finals. Spain defeated England 3–0 for fifth place.

All the U.K. countries and Ireland expanded their international programs. England played nine international matches, excluding the World Cup games. Wales, Scotland, and Ireland did not take part in the World Cup, but Wales visited Kenya and Ireland went to South Africa. Scotland had the best record in the contests among the countries of the British Isles, beating both England and Ireland and drawing with Wales.

In the European outdoor championships the winner was Sports Club 1880 of Frankfurt (W.Ger.), which beat Utrecht Kampong (Neth.) 2-1. In the annual women's hockey international at Wembley Stadium, London, England was defeated by Ireland (the tournament winners) but won its games against Scotland and Wales, who played to a tie against each other. Ireland, Scotland, and Wales each played one international against a continental country: Ireland defeated Belgium, while The Netherlands and Belgium defeated Scotland and Wales, respectively.

In August and September, England took part in the eight-nation women's jubilee tournament of the Royal Netherlands Hockey Association, held in Amsterdam concurrently with the men's World Cup. West Germany finished first, The Netherlands second, New Zealand third, and England fourth. On the last day of the tournament, the International Hockey Federation (FIH), to which all the men but not all the women players belonged, announced that it had decided "to go its own way about women's hockey without taking into consideration any longer the International Federation of Women's Hockey Associations." The FIH wished to establish its right to speak for the whole game and to embrace all men's and women's national associations. The IFWHA then announced that its international tournament in Scotland in 1975 would be a world championship. Since the FIH intended to hold a women's World Cup in 1974, the argument between these two international bodies seemed likely to intensify. (R. L. HOLLANDS)

Table III. World Amateur Ice Hockey Championships

GROUP A	Won	Lost	Tied	Goals	Goals against	Pts.
U.S.S.R.	10	0	0	100	18	20
Sweden	7	2	1	53	23	15
Czechoslovakia	6	3	1	48	20	13
Finland	3	6	1	24	39	7
Poland	1	8	1	14	76	3
West Germany	1	9	0	19	82	2

Hogs:
see Agriculture and Fisheries

Holland:
see Netherlands, The

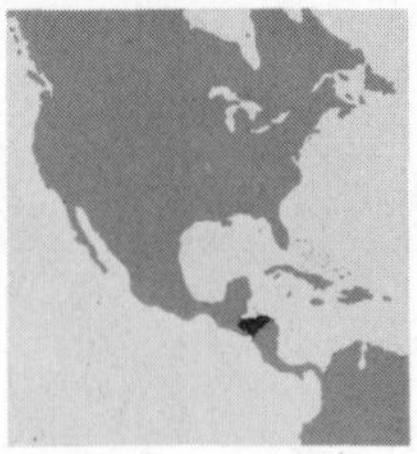

Honduras

A republic of Central America, Honduras is bounded by Nicaragua, El Salvador, Guatemala, the Caribbean Sea, and the Pacific Ocean. Area: 43,277 sq.mi. (112,-088 sq.km.). Pop. (1973 est.): 2,781,400, including 90% mestizo. Cap. and largest city: Tegucigalpa (pop., 1972 est., 310,214). Language: Spanish; some Indian dialects. Religion: Roman Catholic. President in 1973, Gen. Oswaldo López Arellano.

Honduras' slow economic recovery from the disastrous aftermath of its 1969 war with El Salvador was severely impeded by a prolonged drought during the first half of 1973, the worst experienced throughout Central America in 50 years. Honduras, along with Costa Rica, was hardest hit. Drinking water had to be rationed in many areas of the country, and by April drought conditions were such that the government declared a state of national emergency. Production of basic grains declined, and other farm products had to be imported, further worsening an already unfavourable balance of trade. Having withdrawn from the Central American Common Market (CACM) in 1971, Honduras began to seek out bilateral free-trade agreements within the region. In March two such agreements were concluded, with Guatemala and Nicaragua. Negotiations to achieve a similar accord with Costa Rica continued.

The government embarked on a $13.3 million program to expand and modernize agriculture. Of this amount $9.2 million came from an Inter-American Development Bank (IDB) loan to Honduras' national development agency, the Banco Nacional de Fomento (BNF), early in 1973. The loan aided in financing a credit program designed to assist small- and medium-scale farmers, along with ranchers and cooperatives, and to increase production of grains, fruits, vegetables, and oilseed crops, as well as hogs, poultry, and dairy and beef cattle.

Attempts to restore formal diplomatic relations between Honduras and El Salvador, which were severed by the 1969 war, continued to be made in 1973. These efforts were considered the first serious peace negotiations since 1969. In August, representatives of the two nations met for two days at the headquarters of the Organization of American States (OAS) in Washington, D.C., where they agreed to meet with a Mexican-appointed mediator in Mexico City on September 15. This was followed in October by lower-level negotiations in Mexico City, while President López and Pres. Arturo Armando Molina of El Salvador met concurrently in neighbouring Guatemala. It was hoped that a peace treaty could be signed early in the new year, but at year's end no significant progress had been made. Talks were scheduled to resume in April 1974.

(ALLEN D. BUSHONG)

HONDURAS

Education. (1969–70) Primary, pupils 392,670, teachers 10,614; secondary, pupils 28,524; vocational, pupils 6,761; teacher training, students 4,572; secondary, vocational, and teacher training, teachers (1968–69) 2,689; higher (1968–69), students 3,459.

Finance. Monetary unit: lempira, with (Sept. 17, 1973) a par value of 2 lempiras to U.S. $1 (free rate of 4.82 lempiras = £1 sterling). Gold, SDRs, and foreign exchange, central bank: (June 1973) U.S. $44,860,000; (June 1972) U.S. $28,340,000. Budget (1972 est.) balanced at 268 million lempiras. Gross domestic product: (1972) 1,598,000,000 lempiras; (1971) 1,509,000,000 lempiras. Money supply: (March 1973) 217,190,000 lempiras; (March 1972) 179,710,000 lempiras. Cost of living (Tegucigalpa; 1966 = 100): (June 1973) 123; (June 1972) 115.

Foreign Trade. (1972) Imports 386.6 million lempiras; exports 391.7 million lempiras. Import sources: U.S. 52%; Venezuela 10%; Japan 9%; West Germany 5%. Export destinations: U.S. 51%; West Germany 14%; Canada 9%. Main exports: bananas 42%; coffee 14%; timber 14%.

Transport and Communications. Roads (1969) 5,185 km. (including 153 km. of Pan-American Highway). Motor vehicles in use (1970): passenger 18,800; commercial (including buses) 16,900. Railways (1971) 1,007 km. Air traffic (1972): 174.5 million passenger-km.; freight 3,283,000 net ton-km. Shipping (1972): merchant vessels 100 gross tons and over 58; gross tonnage 74,030. Telephones (Dec. 1971) 17,000. Radio receivers (Dec. 1970) 147,000. Television receivers (Dec. 1971) 25,000.

Agriculture. Production (in 000; metric tons; 1972; 1971 in parentheses): corn *c.* 300 (354); coffee *c.* 36 (*c.* 39); sorghum *c.* 50 (47); sugar, raw value *c.* 120 (*c.* 113); dry beans *c.* 60 (*c.* 60); bananas (1971) *c.* 1,400, (1970) 1,280; cotton, lint *c.* 3 (*c.* 3); beef and veal *c.* 50 (*c.* 48). Livestock (in 000; 1971–72): cattle *c.* 1,710; pigs *c.* 830; chickens *c.* 7,000.

Industry. Production (in 000; metric tons; 1971): silver 0.11; gold (troy oz.; 1970) 2.5; lead ore (metal content) 16; zinc ore (metal content; exports; 1969) 8.4; electricity (kw-hr.; 1970) 310,000.

Honduras, British:
see Dependent States

Hong Kong:
see Dependent States

Horse Racing

Thoroughbred Racing. *U.S.* The 1973 Thoroughbred racing season in the U.S. belonged to Secretariat. The first Triple Crown (Kentucky Derby, Preakness, and Belmont) winner in 25 years and three-time conqueror of top-quality older horses, Meadow Stable's home-bred Virginian, trained by Lucien Laurin (*see* BIOGRAPHY), was unanimously acclaimed three-year-old champion, grass course champion, and, for the second consecutive season, horse of the year. He equaled or broke five track records, including one U.S. and one world record. Veteran turf observers called him "horse of the century," while others went still further and named him the best Thoroughbred of all time.

A large, powerful, perfectly proportioned chestnut colt with three white stockings and a white star on his forehead, Secretariat thrilled millions in his television appearances and gave rise to a huge army of followers. The week preceding his attempt at Belmont Park for the Triple Crown he made the front covers of three national magazines, *Time, Newsweek,* and *Sports Illustrated.*

Secretariat was defeated three times during the season. He finished third to entrymate Angle Light and Sham in the Wood Memorial, second to the older Onion in the Whitney Stakes, and second to the older Prove Out in the Woodward Stakes. His only other defeats, at two years old, were a fourth in his racing debut and a disqualification after a victory in the Champagne Stakes that caused him to be placed second.

The son of Bold Ruler-Somethingroyal, by Princequillo, began his quest of the Triple Crown classics before a crowd of more than 134,000 at the Kentucky Derby in Louisville. Because of his shocking defeat in the Wood Memorial, the colt went to the post at odds of 3–2, the last time his odds would be higher than 1–2. Running the first sub-two-minute race in Kentucky Derby history, Secretariat was timed in 1 min. 59.4 sec. for 1¼ mi. while defeating Santa Anita Derby winner and second choice Sham by 2½ lengths.

Secretariat again defeated Sham by the same margin in the Preakness at Baltimore, where a probable malfunction of the electric timer denied him another track record. Then came the Belmont Stakes and Secretariat's triumph by an incredible margin of 31 lengths. He quickly overpowered Sham, who finished far out of the money, and reached the final pole in U.S. record time of 2 min. 24 sec. for 1½ mi.

The $250,000 Marlboro Cup, also contested at Belmont Park, found Secretariat facing six top-rated older opponents including stablemate Riva Ridge, himself holder of a world record, Cougar II, Onion, Annihilate 'Em, Kennedy Road, and Key to the Mint. The seven starters together had won 63 stakes and a total of $4,539,335. Secretariat, in one of his finest races, stalked Riva Ridge to the final turn and then broke through in the stretch under his regular jockey, Ron Turcotte, to defeat his stablemate by 3½ lengths in the world record time of 1 min. 45.4 sec. for 1⅛ mi. Proving his versatility, the champion ended his career with two easy victories over older adversaries in races over grass courses: the 1½-mi. Man o'War at Belmont Park and the Canadian International Championship at Woodbine, his only start outside the U.S.

The Canadian victory marked Secretariat's 16th triumph in 21 career starts and climaxed the most lucrative season ever recorded by any Thoroughbred. In 1973 Secretariat earned $860,404 to break Damascus' mark of $817,941 established during his three-year-old campaign in 1967. Secretariat, syndicated for a world-record $6,080,000 for 32 shares early in the year, was retired to Claiborne Farm in Kentucky in mid-November with total earnings of $1,316,808. This placed him fourth behind horses who had raced longer and oftener: Kelso ($1,977,896), Round Table ($1,749,869), and Buckpasser ($1,462,014).

Another Meadow Stable horse, the four-year-old Riva Ridge, was acclaimed best older competitor in the consolidated poll of the Thoroughbred Racing Associations' board of selection, the *Daily Racing Form,* and the National Turf Writers Association. Riva Ridge, also retired to stud at season's end, won three stakes, including the Brooklyn Handicap in a world record clocking of 1 min. 52.4 sec. for 1³⁄₁₆ mi. The son of First Landing-Iberia, by Princequillo, ended his career with earnings of more than $1 million.

Elmendorf Stable horses swept honours in the two-year-old divisions. The colt Protagonist (Prince John-Hornpipe, by Hornbeam) started slowly and ended strongly with victories in divisions of the Cowdin and Champagne stakes and in the Laurel Futurity. Most important triumphs for the filly Talking Picture (Speak John-Poster Girl, by Nasrullah) came in the Schuylerville, Adirondack, Spinaway, and Matron.

H. T. Mangurian, Jr.'s Desert Vixen (In Reality-Desert Trial, by Desert Chief) dominated the three-year-old filly division with seven consecutive stakes victories. They included a season-ending 8½-length decision over older rivals, including Susan's Girl, in the nine-furlong Beldame at Belmont Park.

Fred W. Hooper's Susan's Girl (Quadrangle-Quaze, by Quibu), divisional champion at three years old in 1972, was voted best older filly or mare. Her victories included the Delaware and Spinster handicaps.

The three-year-old colt Shecky Greene (Noholme II-Lester's Pride, by Model Cadet), Joseph Kellman's winner of nine races, was acclaimed sprint champion. The Sheppard Stable's five-year-old Athenian Idol (Alcibiades II-Dotty's Dream, by Francis S.) was first in the steeplechase and hurdle classification. Other winners included: breeder, Meadow Stud; owner, Meadow Stable; trainer, H. A. Jerkens; jockey, Laffit Pincay, Jr.; and apprentice jockey, Steve Valdez. Pincay became the first jockey whose mounts won more than $4 million in purses.

(JOSEPH C. AGRELLA)

Canada. Distinguished visitors provided two of the major highlights of the Canadian racing season in 1973. In June, Queen Elizabeth II attended the 114th running of the Queen's Plate, at Woodbine in Toronto. The rich and prestigious event was won by Stafford Farm's appropriately named Royal Chocolate. Plate day attendance was 40,137 and wagering totaled $2,166,056, both figures new one-day records for Canadian racing. In October, U.S. Triple Crown winner Secretariat visited Woodbine, to end his remarkable racing career by winning the Canadian International Championship.

Royal Chocolate could only manage a third-place finish in Fort Erie's Prince of Wales Stakes, the second leg, after the Queen's Plate, of the Canadian Triple Crown for three-year-olds. However, his stablemates Tara Road and Good Port finished first and second, to give Stafford Farm an unprecedented sweep in a classic event. The trio was heavily favoured to take top money in the final Triple Crown event, the

Jockey Ron Turcotte turns to view the distant field as he rides Secretariat to victory in the Belmont Stakes at Belmont Park, N.Y., on June 9, 1973.

UPI COMPIX

Breeders' Stakes at Woodbine, but Tara Road and Good Port were edged by H. Tenenbaum's Come In Dad, while Royal Chocolate finished unplaced.

Beset by a multitude of infirmities, courageous Come In Dad wrote an incredible rags-to-riches story in a few short months. Claimed for $3,250 in his first start of the year, in June, he went on to win three stakes events and emerge as the leader of the three-year-old colt division before injury stopped him in October.

W. P. Gilbride's Square Angel, a daughter of Quadrangle, assumed leadership among three-year-old fillies when she triumphed over North America's 1972 filly champion, La Prévoyante, in the Canadian Oaks. Toward the end of the season, however, Mrs. J. A. McDougald's late-developing Musketeer Miss defeated Square Angel in two important tests.

Eastern-based three-year-olds dominated the major Western Canadian classics in 1973. Kinghaven Farm's Wing Span captured the Canadian Derby in Edmonton, while Bo-Teek Farm's Zaca Spirit won the rich Manitoba Derby in Winnipeg. The Quebec Derby in Montreal went to J. L. Levesque's La Prévoyante, a week before the Buckpasser filly suffered her stunning defeat in the Oaks.

The most exciting runner to emerge from the ranks of two-year-olds was Lord Durham, from E. P. Taylor's Windfields Farm. After finishing second in his debut, the good-looking son of Damascus launched a series of impressive victories that prompted owner-breeder Taylor to declare him the best prospect he had produced since North American champion Northern Dancer. Among two-year-old fillies, Douglas Banks's Trudie Tudor was a standout with five stakes victories.

Mrs. A. W. Stollery's Kennedy Road, a Canadian champion at ages two, three, and four, topped the handicap division at age five, although most of his season was spent in California, where he won four major stakes events. W. P. Gilbride's five-year-old Lord Vancouver, by George Royal, won a major U.S. turf event and two Canadian grass stakes, while six-year-old Twice Lucky was a multiple stakes winner again for owner-breeder Conn Smythe.

Sandy Hawley rode 503 winning horses to break Bill Shoemaker's record and become the first North American jockey with more than 500 victories in a single season. It was Hawley's third North American riding championship in four years. (ERIC A. ASTROM)

Europe and Australia. Trainer Fred Winter brought four strong favourites to the Cheltenham meeting in March, the climax of the 1972–73 National Hunt season in England. They were the Australian horse Crisp for the 2-mi. Champion Steeplechase, Killiney for the Totalisator Steeplechase, speedy Bula for the Champion Hurdle, and Pendil for the Gold Cup Steeplechase; it was a shock when none succeeded except Killiney, who broke a shoulder in a subsequent race and had to be destroyed. In the two most important of these races, Comedy of Errors won the Champion Hurdle, and, in a thrilling finish, The Dikler, whose courage had always been suited to Cheltenham's stiff course, held off Pendil in the Gold Cup by a short head.

The Grand National Steeplechase, run in fast time, also produced a spectacular finish when Crisp, carrying the top weight of 168 lb., led soon after the start to 100 yd. from the finish where he was caught by Red Rum carrying 149 lb. Toward the end of the year the imminent possibility of the sale of Aintree racecourse for a building development put the future of the Grand National in jeopardy. In other major steeplechase events the Hennessy Gold Cup was won by Charlie Potheen; the King George VI Steeplechase by Pendil; the Whitbread Gold Cup Steeplechase was abandoned because of fog; the Schweppes Gold Trophy hurdle race was won by Indianapolis; and the Irish Sweeps Hurdle was taken by Captain Christy. Ron Barry was National Hunt champion jockey.

The outstanding feature of flat racing in 1973 in both Britain and France was the superiority of the three-year-old fillies to the colts. In France, Allez France and Dahlia and, in England, Mysterious and Jacinth were outstanding. Also, at the very end of the season Hurry Harriet from Ireland made her mark with a superbly close-timed victory over Allez France in the Champion Stakes at Newmarket, these two leaving 12 top-class colts and 2 other fillies trailing behind them. Meanwhile, a filly, Lady Berry, had won the Prix Royal Oak, the French St. Leger, for the first time since 1929.

The Two Thousand Guineas and One Thousand Guineas were won on rain-soaked going respectively by Mon Fils and Mysterious (who went on to win the Oaks and the Yorkshire Oaks) from Jacinth; on good ground the Irish colt Thatch afterward excelled at a mile, with victories that included the St. James's Palace Stakes at Royal Ascot, the July Cup at Newmarket, and the Sussex Stakes at Goodwood from Jacinth, while Jacinth herself took the Coronation Stakes at Royal Ascot. A substandard Derby was won by Morston, not only trained by Arthur Budgett but also bred and owned by him and running for only the second time in his life, from Cavo Doro and Freefoot; a tendon injury prevented Morston from ever running again. The St. Leger, also substandard, was won by Peleid.

In the French classics, the equivalents of the Two

Dahlia, ridden by W. Pyers, pulls away from the field to win the King George VI and Queen Elizabeth Stakes at Ascot, Eng., on July 28, 1973.

KEYSTONE

Thousand and One Thousand Guineas were won by Kalamoun and Allez France, respectively; the Prix du Jockey Club (Derby) by Roi Lear from his compatriot Tennyson; and the Prix de Diane (Oaks) by Allez France from Dahlia, in record time. The Irish Two Thousand and One Thousand Guineas were won by Sharp Edge and Cloonagh, respectively; the Irish Sweeps Derby by Weaver's Hall; and the Irish Oaks by Dahlia. The Italian Derby was taken by Cerreto and the Italian Oaks by Ora Maggiore, who went on to place second to the French horse Sang Bleu in the Gran Premio del Jockey Club in Milan. The West German Derby was won by Athenagoras, who later ran second to the French Acaccio d'Aguilar in the Preis von Europa.

The Ascot Gold Cup and the Prix du Cadran, its French equivalent, were both won by the good French stayer Lassalle, who also won the Prix Gladiateur, but among the older horses the four-year-old colt Rheingold was most outstanding: he took the John Porter Stakes at Newbury, the Prix Ganay at Longchamp, the Hardwicke Stakes at Royal Ascot, and the Grand Prix de Saint-Cloud. Though unexpectedly beaten by Dahlia in the King George VI and Queen Elizabeth Stakes and third to Moulton and Scottish Rifle in the Benson and Hedges Gold Cup at York, Rheingold crowned the season with a victory over Allez France in Europe's most valuable race, the Prix de l'Arc de Triomphe. Rheingold was afterward sold for more than £1 million and retired to stud in Ireland. He had become Europe's highest stakes winner, having earned nearly £300,000 in nine races over three seasons. Tennyson won the Grand Prix de Paris. Roberto, winner of the 1972 Derby by a short head from Rheingold, took the Coronation Cup at Epsom in fast time from Attica Meli (who later won the Doncaster Cup) but was withdrawn from two subsequent races because of a soft track and disappeared from the racing scene not long after failing in the King George VI and Queen Elizabeth Stakes.

The three-year-old Sandford Lad was probably the best sprinter in Europe, his victories including the King George Stakes at Goodwood and the Nunthorpe Stakes at York; Boldboy, Rapid River, and the Irish filly Abergwaun also were fast. Among leading British two-year-olds were Giacometti (Gimcrack Stakes and Champagne Stakes), Habat, and Welsh Harmony, but their form did not measure up to that of the French horses Nonoalco (Prix Morny and Prix de la Salamandre) and Mississipian (Grand Criterium, from Nonoalco) and Irish trainer V. O'Brien's Cellini (Dewhurst Stakes) and Apalachee (Observer Gold Cup, from Mississipian).

In England, W. Carson was again champion jockey, and the Australian jockey W. Williamson, noted for his quiet and effective style, retired. Sandown Park racecourse, with a new grandstand, was reopened in September.

Gala Supreme, ridden by Frank Reys, beat favoured Glengowan to win the A$153,000 Melbourne Cup, Australia's premier event. Two weeks earlier Gala Supreme had finished second in the A$114,000 Caulfield Cup to the New Zealand mare Swell Time.

(R. M. GOODWIN)

Harness Racing. New names and faces dominated the championship scene in North American harness racing in 1973, at least as far as horses were concerned. Among drivers, the familiar figure of Hervé Filion ruled supreme again, for the sixth straight year in races won and fourth straight in earnings.

Three horses towered above all others. The four-year-old pacing stallion Sir Dalrae won 15 straight races, posted 17 winning miles in two minutes or faster, just one short of the all-time record set in 1972 by Albatross, and was named harness horse of the year. While Sir Dalrae captured honours among older horses, two phenomenal juvenile fillies, the two-year-old trotter Starlark Hanover and the two-year-old pacer Handle With Care, rewrote harness racing's record books.

Starlark Hanover, a daughter of Hickory Smoke and the Star's Pride mare Stardel Hanover, won an unprecedented 21 of 22 starts for trainer-driver Dave Wade and owners Constance and Courtney Foos, Jr., of Malvern, Pa. She trotted a mile in 2 min. 1 sec. over a $\frac{5}{8}$-mi. track, a world record for two-year-old fillies; won $145,478, more than any two-year-old trotting filly in history in a single season; and closed her campaign by defeating 11 colts and the filly Noble Florie in the $52,536 Harriman Trot at Yonkers Raceway.

Handle With Care, meanwhile, was recording an equally impressive season for trainer-driver William Haughton and owner Irving Liverman of Montreal. The fleet daughter of Meadow Skipper and the Hillsota mare Lady Emily raced undefeated through 17 starts, eclipsing the old consecutive winning record of 16 straight set in 1970 by the filly Thimble. In doing so she earned $141,124, most ever by a juvenile pacing filly.

Despite the accomplishments of these precocious fillies, centre stage went to Sir Dalrae. In winning 20 of 26 races he earned more than $300,000 for owner Bill Smith of Los Angeles and trainer-driver Jim Dennis. His victories included a mile in 1 min. 56 sec., making him the fastest harness horse of the year along with the brilliant three-year-old pacer Armbro Nesbit, who recorded the same time in winning the $53,525 Western Pace against older horses at Hollywood Park. Sir Dalrae's record mile came in the first leg of Harness Tracks of America's U.S. Pacing Championship, a new event in 1973 contested over the $\frac{5}{8}$-mi. track at Sportsman's Park in Chicago, the $\frac{1}{2}$-mi. track at Roosevelt Raceway in New York, and the 1-mi. track at Hollywood Park. Sir Dalrae won all three legs, each carrying a $50,000 purse, and picked up an additional $10,000 bonus for accomplishing the sweep. Sir Dalrae had started his racing career as a trotter at two but was converted to pacing when he showed limited ability at the trotting gait.

While Starlark Hanover established herself as the sport's finest two-year-old trotter of either sex, Handle With Care shared two-year-old pacing honours with several top colts. Boyden Hanover, trained and driven by George Sholty, was the fastest of the division with winning miles in 1 min. 58.2 sec. on a 1-mi. track and 2 min. 0.4 sec. on a $\frac{1}{2}$-mi. track. Southampton V took divisional speed honours on the $\frac{5}{8}$-mi. tracks with a 1 min. 59.6 sec. performance for Hervé Filion.

Although there were clear-cut champions in the two-year-old ranks, the battle for supremacy among three-year-olds—both trotters and pacers—produced fierce competition and saw the major classics of the sport won by ten different horses. In trotting, Flirth won the coveted $144,710 Hambletonian and $103,495 Colonial, driven by Ralph Baldwin; Knightly Way captured the $101,563 Dexter Cup for John Simpson, Jr.; Tamerlane won the $93,242 Yonkers Futurity in the fourth start of his life for Charles Clark before going lame and being retired; and Arnie Almahurst took the

UPI COMPIX

Ralph Baldwin drives Flirth to victory in the Hambletonian at Du Quoin, Ill., on Aug. 29, 1973.

$64,174 Kentucky Futurity for Joe O'Brien, driving for regular trainer-driver Gene Riegle. Flirth's 1 min. 57.2 sec. Hambletonian mile was the fastest of the year by a trotter.

The pacing division was equally fragmented, with Armbro Nadir winning Canada's $130,000 Prix d'Ete under Nelson White's guidance; Valiant Bret the $122,732 Messenger Stakes for Lucien Fontaine; Melvin's Woe the $120,000 Little Brown Jug for Joe O'Brien; Armbro Nesbit the $101,200 Shapiro for O'Brien; Smog the $100,000 Cane Pace for Vernon Dancer; and Ricci Reenie Time the $86,780 Adios for Harold Dancer, Jr. Speed honours in the division went to Armbro Nesbit, who won the Western Pace in 1 min. 56 sec., and Armbro Nadir, who posted 1 min. 56.2 sec. in taking the Prix d'Ete.

Among older pacers, Sir Dalrae stood alone for much of the year, pressed closest in several starts by Bye Bye Max, who came within a neck of beating him in the $50,000 Roosevelt Raceway leg of the U.S. Pacing Championship. At the season's end, however, a new star flashed onto the scene at Hollywood Park in Invincible Shadow, a four-year-old Shadow Wave-I'm It colt from the Vancouver stable of John F. Graham. Purchased at Hollywood Park for only $5,500 a year earlier after electrocardiograms had indicated a heart condition, Invincible Shadow developed into a late 1973 sensation for 28-year-old trainer-driver Jim Miller and capped his campaign by defeating 12 of the world's best pacers in the $114,100 American Pacing Classic at $1\frac{1}{8}$ mi.

When the world's best trotters met in August in North America's richest harness race, the $150,000 Roosevelt International at a mile and a quarter, one of the year's closest races resulted. Delmonica Hanover and Spartan Hanover, representing the U.S., finished 1–2 in a tight three-horse battle with the French champion Une de Mai third.

Among drivers, Hervé Filion again monopolized the honours. Although he did not approach his world record of 605 victories in a single season, set in 1972, he did win more than 400 races during the year, the fifth time he had done so. No other North American driver had ever won 400 in one season. Filion also won the money-winning championship by a wide margin, his fourth consecutive national title in that category.

A major development during the year was the widespread use of the revolutionary single-shaft sulky. More than 50 two-minute miles were recorded by horses pulling the new device, which has only one arching shaft that is fastened to the horse at a single point above the shoulders rather than by shafts on each side. Although it produced some exceptionally fast times, including a world record of 1 min. 57.4 sec. by the pacing gelding Starboard Butler over the $\frac{1}{2}$-mi. track at Maywood Park in Chicago, the new design came under heavy criticism from many drivers who considered it unsafe and was barred at a number of tracks during the season. (STANLEY F. BERGSTEIN)

In New Zealand the top money winner in 1972–73 was the New Zealand Cup winner Globe Bay with $39,470, just ahead of the Auckland Cup winner Royal Ascot with $36,665. The New Zealand Derby went to Willie Win, and the Great Northern Derby to Speedy Guest. Maurice Holmes was the season's leading driver. In Australia the Lord Mayor's Cup at Melbourne went to Adios Victor from Nicotine Prince and Simpsonic. In Perth, James Eden won the $50,000 Cup final from Yankee Rhythm and Dark Adair. Hondo Hanover won the Inter-Dominion Championship in Sydney by a head from Royal Ascot. Top two-year-old performer was Flying Heel (by Bravado Hanover) and champion three-year-old was Paleface Adios (by Deep Adios), whose best performance was at 1 min. 59 sec. for the mile. Leading driver of Australia was Brisbane-based Brian Pelling.

Europe was the scene of the World's Driving Championship in 1973, contested by eight drivers from the United States, Canada, Australia, New Zealand, and four European countries. Twenty races were held in France, Austria, Italy, and West Germany and drew record crowds. The winner was Ulf Thoresen of Norway, from Jack Smolenski (N.Z.) and Hervé Filion (Can.).

Une de Mai, heading toward her second million dollars, won the $25,000 Prix Buenos Aires in Paris before leaving for the Roosevelt International in the U.S. Fantastic Buffet II won six races in succession and set a 2 min. 0.2 sec. record before being beaten at Vincennes over 2,325 m. in a race that set a track record of 2 min. 0.6 sec. The $70,000 Prix de l'Étoile was won by Catharina.

The German Trotting Derby, raced in Berlin for $37,500, was won by Agami. Toscar won both the $43,000 Prix de Hamburg and the $35,000 Recklinghausen Trophy. The $40,000 Deutschland Pokal went to German-bred Robbyono. In Brussels the five-year-old championship went to Swedish invader Tim Cross. The Swedish Trotting Derby of $48,000 was won by Pom Chips, driven by Sören Nardin, who won his tenth Derby. The Jarlsberg Grand Prix in Norway was taken by Baron Pels, which had won the four-year-old Scandinavian championship the previous month. In Finland the Trotting Derby for four-year-olds at Helsinki was won by Star Speed. Outstanding Italian trotter Latest Record, bred in the United States, won the $35,000 Campionato Europeo and also the Premio d'Europa. The top race in Britain, at Musselburgh, Scot., was won by Saunders Leopard over Smokila.

European stables were purchasing trotting yearlings each year at the American sales as well as buying brood mares in foal, and it was noticeable that the interbreeding of these American mares with successful European sires was producing trotters that were often able to hold their own in the international trotting races in America. The breeding of harness horses in Britain was improving, and noted U.S. trainer Stanley Dancer visited England and Wales and purchased eight pacers early in 1973. British sales also received a boost when Saunders Pearl set up a string of wins at the end of the previous season. (NOEL SIMPSON)

Horticulture: *see* Gardening

Hospitals: *see* Medicine

Housing

For many Western countries, late 1972 and early 1973 was the period when attention turned from the physical problems of housing—slums and substandard buildings—to the problems of the housing market—finance, allocation, and costs. There were staggering increases in the costs of housing, and many people who under normal circumstances had found little difficulty in meeting these costs were now either hard-pressed or completely unable to do so. The supply of available housing took a turn for the worse, and for the first time in many years developed countries were faced with a situation in which increasing numbers of their population were becoming homeless. For the less developed countries, the primary problem of housing remained, as it had been for many years, that of trying to meet the excess demand from an ever growing population.

Supply and Demand. Any review of current events and trends in the housing field must attempt some international comparisons of construction performance. The usual strictures about international comparisons must apply: that records are kept differently in different countries and that strictly comparable definitions do not exist. Therefore, the figures given in the tables and the comparisons made between them are necessarily inexact.

Table I shows the average monthly dwelling construction performance in 28 countries for the first part of 1973, compared with the same figures for all of 1971 and 1972. The monthly averages for 1973 were calculated over a shorter time period and are therefore subject to error. Additionally, in some countries construction performance during the winter months provides an underestimate of performance over the whole year. The figures, which are based on UN data, should therefore be treated with caution.

Table I. Dwelling Construction in Early 1973, Compared with 1971 and 1972

Country	Monthly average (early 1973)	Monthly average 1971	Monthly average 1972	New or total*	Type of measure
Australia	11,686	11,796	12,124	Total	Buildings completed
Canada	18,107	16,769	19,352	New	Buildings completed
Czechoslovakia	14,201	9,152	9,543	New	Buildings completed
Denmark	4,542	4,181	4,167	New	Buildings completed
Finland	1,340	4,200	4,175	Total	Buildings completed
Germany, East	9,100	6,342	9,800	Total	Buildings completed
Germany, West	27,452	46,249	55,057	Total	Buildings completed
Ireland	1,856	1,249	1,736	Total	Buildings completed
Italy	9,913	28,771	20,014	New	Buildings completed
Japan	156,323	121,980	150,632	Total	Buildings started
Korea, South	7,483	6,393	5,314	Total	Building permits issued
Kuwait	533	495	419	New	Building permits issued
Morocco	1,695	...	1,516	Total	Building permits issued
Netherlands, The	12,307	11,462	12,751	New	Buildings completed
New Zealand	2,879	1,983	2,500	New	Building permits issued
Norway	3,632	3,399	3,634	Total	Buildings completed
Panama	402	...	291	New	Building permits issued
Poland	11,900	15,883	12,600	Total	Buildings completed
Portugal	2,456	3,001	2,384	New	Buildings completed
Puerto Rico	2,165	2,066	2,089	New	Building permits issued
South Africa	1,099	1,265	1,119	New	Private buildings completed
Spain	12,469	15,922	15,868	Total	Buildings completed with state aid only
Sweden	8,253	8,932	8,670	New	Buildings completed
Switzerland	2,273	2,257	2,315	New	Buildings completed
Turkey	16,135	12,529	13,827	Total	Building permits issued
U.K.	25,581	30,290	27,648	New	Buildings completed
U.S.	191,037	173,700	198,200	New	Buildings started
Yugoslavia	1,861	2,995	3,390	Total	Buildings completed

*New dwellings plus conversions, extensions, etc.

Table II. Average Monthly Dwelling Construction in Early 1973 as a Percentage of the Mid-1972 Population

Country	Percentage	Country	Percentage
Australia	0.090	New Zealand	0.099
Canada	0.083	Norway	0.092
Czechoslovakia	0.098	Panama	0.026
Denmark	0.091	Poland	0.036
Finland	0.029	Portugal	0.028
Germany, East	0.053	Puerto Rico	0.077
Germany, West	0.045	South Africa	0.005
Ireland	0.062	Spain	0.036
Italy	0.018	Sweden	0.102
Japan	0.146	Switzerland	0.035
Korea, South	0.023	Turkey	0.044
Kuwait	0.059	U.K.	0.046
Morocco	0.011	U.S.	0.091
Netherlands, The	0.092	Yugoslavia	0.009

Though the countries that showed a decrease in average monthly construction performance in 1973 as against 1972 exceeded those showing an increase, the overall picture for early 1973 was not so poor as was that for early 1972 when compared with 1971. Allowing for the underestimate likely to be shown by these figures, 1973 showed a general upturn in housing construction over the previous years. The downward trend of the past few years was halted in many countries and reversed in some.

The picture was not a uniform one, however. Australia, Finland, West Germany, Italy, Poland, South Africa, Spain, Sweden, the U.K., and Yugoslavia all showed a decrease in average monthly dwelling construction as compared with both 1971 and 1972. In some, the decrease was dramatic: Finland produced 68% fewer houses per month in 1973 as against 1971 and 1972 (though this might partly be accounted for by low winter construction rates in 1973); West Germany and Italy both produced 50% fewer houses than in 1972; and Yugoslavia declined 45%.

Among the countries that, on the other hand, showed an improved construction performance over both 1971 and 1972 were Czechoslovakia, Denmark, Ireland, Japan, South Korea, Kuwait, New Zealand, Puerto Rico, and Turkey. The countries showing the greatest increases were Czechoslovakia (49% over

continued on page 355

This fanciful complex of apartment buildings, under construction in Créteil, near Paris, bears the name "Les Choux," meaning "the cabbages."

KEYSTONE

PUBLIC HOUSING: A TALE OF TWO COUNTRIES

By John Edwards

The governments of both the United States and Great Britain have recognized the need for decent and adequate housing for all their people. They have, therefore, instituted diverse forms of government intervention in the free play of the housing markets. The most direct and explicit means of such intervention is public housing—housing provided and subsidized by, and remaining in the ownership of, the state. Other forms of government intervention do exist in both countries in the form of various housing subsidies, but in the U.S. they are negligible and in Britain so recent (having been introduced by the Housing Finance Act, 1972) as to be as yet untried.

In Britain, the term "public housing" is confined to housing financed and provided by local housing authorities, which are also elected local government bodies. In the U.S., however, all federally assisted housing, whether provided by local authorities or not, is popularly described as "public," though strictly speaking there is a real and significant difference between public housing that remains in the ownership of local housing authorities and other federally subsidized housing that does not.

While public housing in Britain in 1973 constituted a significant proportion of the total housing stock, it made an almost negligible contribution to the total dwelling units in the U.S. The relative proportions are shown in Table I.

Public housing in Britain started in 1919. In the U.S. it is much younger, having begun only in 1937. Nevertheless, the great differences in the extent of public housing in the two countries are not a product of history alone. In Britain, the proportion of public housing in the total stock has increased until today it approaches one-third. In the U.S., there has likewise been an increase in the proportion of publicly owned dwelling units, but it has been a very small one, so that after 36 years of the Public Housing Program it still constitutes only about 2% of the total stock. Quite clearly, then, there are large and fundamental differences in public housing policies and programs to be explained.

Aims of Public Housing. The almost complete cessation of home construction during World War I left Britain with an acute housing shortage and a stock of aging and inadequate dwellings. Those who suffered most from this situation and from the inability of private developers to provide adequate housing at reasonable rents were the lower income groups. It was in response to this situation that the concept of public housing developed, whereby local authorities were charged with the task of providing accommodations for the less well-off. While it is still true today that the public housing tenant is characterized by having a lower income than his house-owning counterpart, it is not the case that public housing in Britain remains exclusively for the lower-paid. There are, for example, no upper income limits for eligibility, as in the U.S. Indeed, since public housing accounts for almost one-third of all the residential stock (far more in some areas), its function quite clearly cannot be restricted to that of providing solely for the "working classes." Public housing in Britain today is best seen not as the reserve of the poor, but as an alternative to home ownership.

In the U.S., by contrast, the aim of public housing has always been and still is to provide accommodation for the poorest section of the population. However, the stimulus for public housing programs came as much from a need during the depression years to create employment as it did from a desire to provide for the housing needs of the poor. Despite this confusion of manifest and latent aims of the program, public housing has explicitly retained the function of providing accommodation for the poor—to the extent of imposing upper income limits on residents.

As with the British government, the U.S. has embodied its housing responsibilities and objectives in an all-embracing and perhaps rather grandiose statement: the preamble to the Housing Act of 1949 stated the official government policy as that of eventually achieving "a decent home and suitable living environment for every American family."

While "a decent home for every . . . family" remains the aim of both governments, the means adopted to achieve it have differed markedly.

Administration of Public Housing. *United States.* The Public Housing Program in the U.S. began with the Housing Act of 1937. This placed the responsibility for developing, owning, and managing subsidized low-rental housing with independent local government agencies—the local housing authorities. The 1937 act was, however, enabling legislation and did not make it a statutory duty of local jurisdictions to provide public housing. Nevertheless, by 1973 there were approximately 2,500 local housing authorities in the U.S. managing more than one million units. Because the enabling legislation is framed in fairly broad terms, there are considerable variations in the circumstances under which public housing programs are established. For example, some state laws require local government approval of specific sites, while others require local support by means of voters' referenda.

Notwithstanding the relative freedom with which public housing programs may or may not be established, the requirements to be met, once a decision has been made in principle, are numerous and complex. Two such requirements are that a local housing authority cannot receive federal assistance without the approval of both its local government and the appropriate local office of the Department of Housing and Urban Development (HUD), and, since 1954, that public housing cannot be built in areas that do not have a HUD-certified "Workable Program for Community Improvement."

Britain. The Housing and Town Planning Act of 1919 required that local government authorities survey the housing needs in their area and take steps to meet these needs, with special attention to the "working classes." Unlike the U.S. legislation, this was a statutory requirement placed by the central government on all local housing agencies. Since that day, there has been a steady growth in the proportion of all dwellings that are publicly owned, though this is accounted for by the decline in the private rental sector as well as by the continuing construction of public housing. By 1973 there were approximately 1,500 local housing authorities in the U.K., most of which, by U.S. standards, owned and managed a large number of units. In addition to the normal local authority housing, a relatively small but growing amount of public housing is provided by New Town Development corporations under the New Town legislation.

Unlike the practice in the U.S., public housing in Britain has not been confined to the poorer sections of the community, although in areas with a housing shortage some means has always been adopted of allocating dwelling units to those "in most need." This is normally accomplished by a form of "points

John Edwards is a research fellow of the University of Southampton; in 1973 he was involved in the British government's Urban Programme, aimed at alleviating problems of urban deprivation. He is the author of Social Patterns in Birmingham.

Table I. Public Housing as % of Total Housing Stock in the U.S. and the U.K.

United States		United Kingdom*	
Year	Percent	Year	Percent
1949	0.4	1951	18
1961	1.1	1961	29
1970	1.7	1972	31

*Includes New Towns housing.

Table II. Public Housing Starts in the U.S. and the U.K.

	United States		United Kingdom	
Year	Total number of public housing starts	Public housing starts as % of all housing starts	Total number of public housing starts	Public housing starts as % of all housing starts
1969	32,800	2.2	138,427	48.2
1970	35,400	2.4	120,346	44.8
1971	32,300	1.5	109,199	37.1
1972*	10,500	0.9	...	...

*First six months.

scheme," whereby families on the waiting list gain points for such factors as length of residence in the area, condition of their present accommodations, and family size.

The Housing Finance Act of 1972 instituted a new system under which local housing authorities are required to charge a "fair rent" (market rent) for all their units. In theory, this should make the units self-sufficient over a period of time, enabling central government subsidies to be withdrawn in stages. The immediate effect of such a system, however, is a considerable rise in public housing rents, and any hardship this may cause is to be alleviated by means of rent rebates to be awarded to a tenant subject to a test of his qualifications. The principle behind the new system is to "subsidize families and not dwellings."

Achievements. On any numerical measure of production in public housing, U.S. achievements have been negligible when compared with those of Britain. However, given the relative status of public housing in the two countries, this is not surprising. Table II shows both the total volume of public housing starts in the U.S. and Britain during 1969–72 and the share of public housing in all housing starts.

Apart from the purely statistical achievement, the success or otherwise of the public housing programs of the two countries must be measured against their aims. It could be said that in Britain public housing has more than fulfilled its initial claim of providing decent accommodations for those who could not afford to compete on the open markets. It is now a permanent and integral part of the British housing system. It is not without its critics, however. While it is true that public housing has provided for the poorer sections of the population, there is a relatively small but growing number of households in areas with a housing shortage whose needs it does not meet. The inflexibility with which it is managed in some areas adds to the problem.

In the U.S., on the other hand, the public housing program has been noted for its failures rather than its achievements. Public housing has failed to gain a foothold in the U.S. housing system and by and large remains unpopular. During the past two years it has faced its greatest financial crisis, resulting from a cutback in the federal operating subsidies that had been introduced to compensate local housing authorities for the extra burden imposed by the Brooke Amendment of 1969. This legislation set rent ceilings for welfare families so that they would not spend more than 25% of their income on rent. While this measure was welcome to the many who had to commit a very high proportion of their income to rent, it created severe financial problems for some local housing authorities.

It is perhaps the general unpopularity of public housing programs that is the main cause of their lack of success in the U.S. The requirement of local government approval of sites, along with that of the "Workable Program," have proved to be major stumbling blocks to growth and expansion.

continued from page 353

1972), South Korea (41%), Panama (38%), and Kuwait (27%).

A better, though still crude, measure of the relative achievements of different countries was the average monthly construction figures expressed as a percentage of the total population. Though population figures do not necessarily provide an accurate guide to housing need, Table II gives some indications of relative performance. Dwelling construction figures are for early 1973, while population figures reflect mid-1972.

Probably the greatest shortage in dwellings was in Latin America. In 1961 the UN estimated that the housing shortage there was approximately 20.3 million dwellings. The intervening decade, far from seeing a reduction in this shortage, added to the problem. One measure of it was the situation in Colombia, where at the 1973 rate of dwelling construction it would take 20 years to meet present housing needs, not accounting for the inevitable increase in demand.

Another aspect of the demand and supply equation, which continued to be crucial in 1973, was the rapid increase in the demand for houses in the large cities of many countries. The continuing and increasing shift in population from rural to urban areas created an insatiable demand for houses in the cities and left many vacant and unwanted houses in the rural areas.

Housing Standards. For many countries the need to provide a very large number of dwellings, very quickly and very cheaply, meant that little attention could be paid to housing standards. Nevertheless, there was in 1973 a continuing concern over the size of the dwellings being provided and the amenities that went into them. In some countries there was a reaction against the monotonous blocks of small, cheap apartments that necessity had dictated in the past.

In some countries, concern about housing standards progressed beyond the dwelling itself, and centred on the provision of aesthetically pleasing dwelling environs. In The Netherlands, for example, where minimum dwelling standards had been the rule for some time, subsidies were made available for housing that experimented with improved standards within the dwelling and more pleasing environs outside.

Organization and Finance. The housing markets in a number of countries were in a state of flux in late 1972 and early 1973, and this situation was reflected in increased governmental concern about the organization and finance of housing. The increased burden put upon the state by heavy building programs in a number of Eastern European countries led to an attempt to shift some of the financial burden of housing onto the people. Thus, in both Hungary and Czechoslovakia there were moves to encourage owner occupation of houses, and in Poland the trend away from direct state-aided housing to housing cooperatives continued. In The Netherlands, 1973 saw the beginning of the shift away from direct government subsidies for dwelling construction to the subsidization of rents for poorer households. Similar moves were made in the U.K., where the new Housing Finance Act came into operation. This represented a major change in the means by which public housing in Britain was to be financed. (*See* Special Report.)

Allied to this fundamental change in the finance of public housing in Britain was a greater emphasis on housing cooperatives and housing associations. The U.K. was not alone in this new emphasis, and it may be said that 1973 was the year when housing cooperatives came into their own as possible major providers

THOMAS HOPKER—THE NEW YORK TIMES

New apartments in Seefeld in the Austrian Tirol welcome their tenants. Mass tourism and the condominium movement were blamed for rapid building development in the picturesque Alpine region.

of housing. They had been a significant part of the total housing effort in Scandinavian countries for some time, but in 1973 they expanded into a number of other countries, including Poland, The Netherlands, France, Turkey, East Germany, and even in Latin America. In this growing trend toward nonstate but nonprofit housing, the U.S. stood out as the exception, cooperative housing never having gained a foothold there. Indeed, 1973 saw the narrowing of the housing markets in the U.S. with the almost complete cessation of new public housing. In some parts of the U.S. condominium housing, in which the individual bought his apartment much as he would buy a single-family dwelling and obtained equity in it, was increasing in popularity. Since this market was largely restricted to middle- and upper-income groups, the construction of condominiums in cities and, in some cases, the conversion of older rental buildings into condominiums seemed likely to tighten the lower-income housing market still further.

Costs. If there was one overriding issue in the housing field in 1973, it was the phenomenal rise in the cost of housing in many developed countries. Escalating costs in The Netherlands confined the owner-occupation of houses to the well-to-do; house prices in London continued to rocket, doubling and sometimes tripling in price over a two-year period. The results of this upheaval left their mark in a number of countries. The straightforward provision of more houses appeared a simple matter compared with the seemingly intractable problem of providing housing of the right quality in the right place and at a price that people could afford.

Whether any successful measures could be found to deal with this situation remained to be seen, but there were indications in 1973 that some Western governments recognized the need to intervene more fully in the housing markets (by encouraging housing cooperatives, controlling housing and office developments, and initiating integrated housing and social welfare programs for the decaying inner areas of cities). Ironically, 1973 also saw the cessation of much direct state financial aid to housing. (JOHN EDWARDS)

See also Architecture; Cities and Urban Affairs; Economy, World; Environment; Industrial Review; Money and Banking.

ENCYCLOPÆDIA BRITANNICA FILMS. *Equality Under Law—The California Fair Housing Cases* (1969); *The House of Man, Part II—Our Crowded Environment* (1969); *The Image of the City* (1973).

Hungary

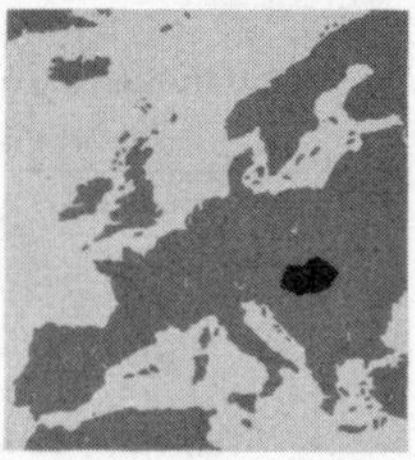

A people's republic of central Europe, Hungary is bordered by Czechoslovakia, the U.S.S.R., Romania, Yugoslavia, and Austria. Area: 35,920 sq.mi. (93,032 sq.km.). Pop. (1973 est.): 10,415,626, including (1970) Hungarian 95.8%; German 2.1%. Cap. and largest city: Budapest (pop., 1973 est., 2,038,787). Language (1970): Magyar 95.8%. Religion (1956): Roman Catholic 67%; Protestant 27.3%; Orthodox 2.5%; Jewish 1.5%. First secretary of the Hungarian Socialist Workers' (Communist) Party in 1973, Janos Kadar; president of the Presidential Council (chief of state), Pal Losonczi; president of the Council of Ministers (premier), Jeno Fock.

On an official visit to Finland in September 1973, Janos Kadar, asked by Finnish television what headway Hungary had made since 1956, replied that the political atmosphere at home was good and the country's international position very satisfactory. Kadar complimented Finland for its part in convening the Conference on Security and Cooperation in Europe and emphasized that political détente necessitated the scaling down of military confrontation.

HUNGARY

Education. (1971–72) Primary, pupils 1,070,000, teachers 63,432; secondary and vocational, pupils 351,536, teachers 13,594; higher (including 18 universities), students 86,311, teaching staff 10,312.

Finance. Monetary unit: forint, with (Sept. 17, 1973) an official exchange rate of 9.39 forints to U.S. \$1 (22.63 forints = £1 sterling) and a noncommercial rate of 24.87 forints to U.S. \$1 (58.38 forints = £1 sterling). Budget (1972 est.): revenue 213 billion forints; expenditure 216 billion forints. National income (net material product): (1971) 294.3 billion forints; (1970) 272.4 billion forints.

Foreign Trade. (1972) Imports 34,093,000,000 forints; exports 35,583,000,000 forints. Import sources (1971): U.S.S.R. 34%; East Germany 11%; Czechoslovakia 8%; West Germany 6%; Poland 5%. Export destinations (1971): U.S.S.R. 35%; East Germany 10%; Czechoslovakia 8%; Poland 7%; Italy 6%; West Germany 5%. Main exports (1971): machinery 20%; transport equipment 11%; chemicals 8%; fruit and vegetables 6%; meat 5%; iron and steel 5%; livestock 5%; clothing 5%.

Transport and Communications. Roads (1972) 109,315 km. (including 158 km. expressways). Motor vehicles in use (1972): passenger 340,202; commercial 100,374. Railways: (1971) 8,664 km.; traffic (1972) 14,041,000,000 passenger-km., freight 19,432,000,000 net ton-km. Air traffic (1971): 321 million passenger-km.; freight 7,564,000 net ton-km. Telephones (Dec. 1971) 873,000. Radio licenses (Dec. 1971) 2,543,000. Television licenses (Dec. 1971) 1,943,000.

Agriculture. Production (in 000; metric tons; 1972; 1971 in parentheses): corn 5,542 (4,674); wheat 4,087 (3,922); rye 173 (182); barley 803 (785); oats 66 (91); rice 61 (67); potatoes *c.* 1,350 (1,488); sugar, raw value *c.* 326 (262); tomatoes (1971) 383, (1970) 293; rapeseed *c.* 70 (71); sunflower seed *c.* 140 (151); dry peas *c.* 107 (106); apples *c.* 620 (621); pears *c.* 90 (89); wine *c.* 430 (429); tobacco 17 (16); beef and veal (1971) *c.* 180, (1970) 184; pork (1971) *c.* 400, (1970) 316. Livestock (in 000; March 1972): cattle 1,901; pigs 7,353; sheep 2,271; horses 204; chickens (1971) 66,148.

Industry. Index of production (1963 = 100): (1972) 164; (1971) 156. Production (in 000; metric tons; 1972): coal 3,671; lignite 22,171; crude oil 1,977; natural gas (cu.m.) 4,085,000; electricity (kw-hr.) 16,317,000; iron ore (25% metal content) 694; pig iron 2,069; crude steel 3,273; bauxite 2,356; cement 2,969; sulfuric acid 566; nitrogenous fertilizer (1971–72) 377; phosphate fertilizer (1971–72) 174; cotton yarn 56; wool yarn 14; commercial vehicles (units) 12.

More significant were Kadar's declarations to the leading Finnish daily newspaper *Helsingin Sanomat*. Without mentioning Soviet criticism of the Hungarian New Economic Mechanism (NEM) in 1972, he said that since that reform had been introduced on Jan. 1, 1968, the national economy had developed in a more planned and balanced manner. "We have no intention," he said, "of changing the basic principles of the Hungarian economic reforms."

Indeed, the first five years of the NEM had witnessed a growth of 32.4% in public consumption, 32.1% in real incomes, and 16.6% in the values of real wages and salaries, while the corresponding indices for 1963–67 had been 25.3%, 26.2%, and 8.7%, respectively. Industrial production had risen more slowly, the rate of the annual increase having dropped from an average 6.8% in 1963–67 to 5.7%. This, Hungarian economists claimed, was not the result of any shortcoming in the NEM but simply mirrored the attempts of factories to adjust their production more closely to existing requirements.

The lessons of the first five-year period of the NEM were that the centralized system of control was no longer able to direct and supervise the whole economy; on the other hand, the enterprises and management were unable to adapt themselves continuously and flexibly to changing market demands. The need for some improvements in the system was obvious.

In a speech on March 20, 1973, Premier Fock told Parliament that the planning of the national economy must be learned by experience. On June 29 a new State Planning Commission was set up by the Council of Ministers, with the task of improving economic planning and coordinating the work of various economic bodies. Gyorgy Lazar, formerly minister of labour, was appointed deputy premier and chairman of the new commission. The NEM lost a strong supporter on September 18 when Deputy Premier Peter Valyi died after falling into a pit of red hot ingots at the Lenin metalworks in Miskolc, north Hungary.

Recognizing the nationalistic feelings of the Hungarian people, Kadar authorized the celebration of the 125th anniversary of the March 1848 revolution and the 150th birthday of its poet, Sandor Petofi. At the same time, he attempted to meet the demands of "proletarian internationalism" by expelling from the Hungarian Socialist Workers' Party the sociologist Andras Hegedus and the philosophers Janos Kis and Mihaly Vajda, who had been questioning the party's power monopoly.

From July 10 to 13 Kadar visited Yugoslavia's President Tito on Brioni Island. It was their first meeting since the 1968 invasion of Czechoslovakia, which Tito had condemned and in which Hungary had been forced to participate. Hungary, however, was the first Comecon country to change from a barter system of trading to convertible payments, a move that favoured the expansion of Hungarian–Yugoslav trade and economic cooperation.

French Premier Pierre Messmer and Michel Jobert, the foreign minister, paid an official visit to Budapest in July, the first such visit since World War II. Both sides expressed a desire to improve trade and industrial cooperation. The first round of talks between West Germany and Hungary on establishing diplomatic relations ended on August 16 in a deadlock over representation of West Berliners' interests, but by the end of the year considerable progress was made and a treaty was expected to be formalized in 1974.

(K. M. SMOGORZEWSKI)

Iceland

Iceland is an island republic in the North Atlantic Ocean. Area: 39,769 sq.mi. (103,000 sq.km.). Pop. (1972 est.): 210,775. Cap. and largest city: Reykjavik (pop., 1972 est., 83,977). Language: Icelandic. Religion: 98% Lutheran. President in 1973, Kristjan Eldjarn; prime minister, Olafur Johannesson.

On Jan. 23, 1973, the Eldfell (also called Kirkjufell) volcano on Heimaey, one of the Westmann Islands off Iceland's southern coast, erupted, cutting the island almost in two and forcing the 5,000 or so inhabitants to take to their boats. A few hours after a mile-long rift had opened up, the new ash and lava mountain began to arise and it soon covered part of the township of Vestmannaeyjar on Heimaey, an important fishing centre. For some time there seemed a danger that lava would fill the harbour and permanently end all economic activity on the island, but the lava flow was sufficiently cooled and diverted by pumping seawater onto it. Eventually the major part of the town was saved, and with the volcano gradually subsiding many inhabitants returned late in 1973.

The "cod war" that had begun in 1972 continued throughout most of the year, with a number of clashes between Icelandic gunboats and British trawlers protected by contingents of the Royal Navy; to a lesser extent the dispute also involved the West German government. Iceland showed no sign of abandoning its claim to a 50-mi. fisheries limit, and indeed called attention to the growing number of nations that were claiming or aiming for 200-mi. limits. Iceland's continued membership in NATO was called into question, and it appeared likely that diplomatic relations with

ICELAND

Education. (1968–69) Primary, pupils 27,356, teachers 1,319; secondary, pupils 15,675, teachers 1,229; vocational, pupils *c.* 5,000, teachers 548; teacher training, students 909, teachers *c.* 97; higher (at Reykjavik University), students 1,302, teaching staff 150.

Finance. Monetary unit: króna, with (Sept. 17, 1973) a free rate of 89.16 krónur to U.S. $1 (free rate of 214.87 krónur = £1 sterling). Gold, SDRs, and foreign exchange, central bank: (June 1973) U.S. $86.3 million; (June 1972) U.S. $64.7 million. Budget (1971 est.): revenue 13,260,000,000 krónur; expenditure 13,530,000,000 krónur. Gross national product: (1971) 52.5 billion krónur; (1970) 42.4 billion krónur. Money supply: (June 1973) 9,555,000,000 krónur; (June 1972) 7,157,000,000 krónur. Cost of living (Reykjavik; 1963 = 100): (May 1973) 323; (May 1972) 274.

Foreign Trade. (1972) Imports 20,422,000,000 krónur; exports 16,698,000,000 krónur. Import sources: U.K. 15%; West Germany 14%; U.S. 8%; Denmark 10%; Sweden 7%; Norway 6%; The Netherlands 6%; U.S.S.R. 6%. Export destinations: U.S. 31%; U.K. 11%; West Germany 9%; Portugal 5%; Denmark 5%; Italy 5%; Switzerland 5%. Main exports: fish and products 74%; aluminum 16%.

Transport and Communications. Roads (1972) 11,137 km. Motor vehicles in use (1971): passenger 46,737; commercial 5,706. There are no railways. Air traffic (1972): 1,939,600,000 passenger-km.; freight 20,001,000 net ton-km. Shipping (1972): merchant vessels 100 gross tons and over 301; gross tonnage 130,561. Telephones (Dec. 1971) 75,000. Radio licenses (Dec. 1970) 62,000. Television licenses (Dec. 1971) 42,000.

Agriculture. Production (in 000; metric tons; 1971; 1970 in parentheses): potatoes 11 (5); hay *c.* 410 (289); milk 122 (117); mutton and lamb 11 (12); fish catch 685 (734). Livestock (in 000; Dec. 1971): cattle 59; sheep 786; horses 37; poultry 178.

Industry. Production (in 000): electricity (public supply only; kw-hr.; 1972) 1,767,000; aluminum (metric tons; 1971) 41.

Hurricanes:
see Disasters; Meteorology

Hydroelectric Power:
see Energy; Engineering Projects

Ice Hockey:
see Hockey

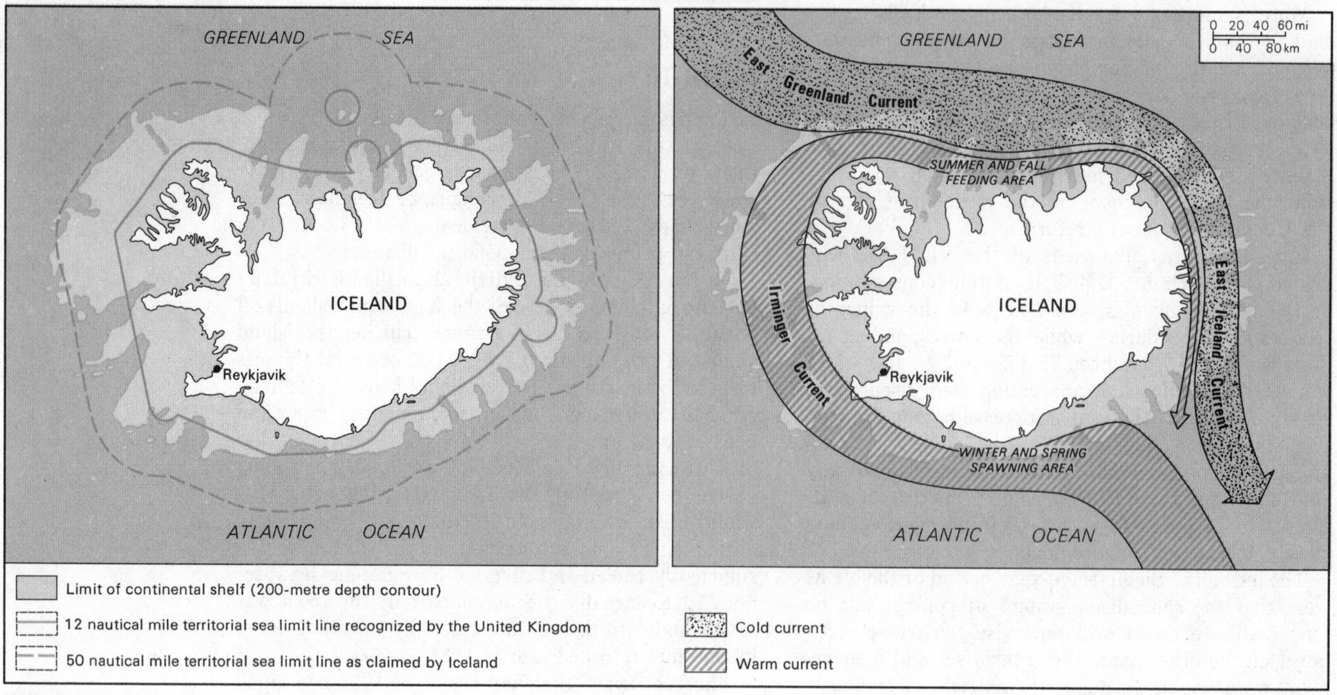

Iceland's unilateral extension of its territorial waters from 12 to 50 mi. was intended to cover the continental shelf (left) and, hence, the rich fisheries of cod and herring in the warm current over the shelf (right).

Britain would be severed. However, in mid-October Prime Minister Johannesson visited London for talks with U.K. Prime Minister Edward Heath, as a result of which a preliminary agreement was reached. It was expected to ease the situation over the next two years, during which time the UN international conference on the law of the sea was to meet. The agreement, signed on November 13, allowed restricted British trawling within the 50-mi. limit until 1975. It was based on an annual British catch of 130,000 tons (some 54,000 tons below recent catches) and the fleet was limited to 68 large vessels and 71 smaller ones.

Early in October, Iceland and the U.S. began formal talks, in Washington, concerning Iceland's demand that the 1951 defense pact be revised. Under the agreement, U.S. forces were permitted to use Keflavik air base on behalf of NATO. Details of the talks were not made public, although it was believed Iceland had suggested moving NATO operations to Greenland or Scotland.

A major hydroelectric power project was under way in the south of Iceland which would meet the growing consumption of power and also provide energy for a ferrosilicone plant at Hvalfjördhur in the west, which was to be run jointly by Union Carbide of the U.S. and the Icelanders. High and rising prices for fish in the U.S. had a favourable effect on the economy.

(VALDIMAR KRISTINSSON)

Ice Skating

Two major developments in 1973, each revolutionary by skating standards, affected long-standing traditions in international figure and speed competitions. A momentous alteration to the figure-skating rules abolished the judging of the compulsory six figures and free skating on a 50–50 ratio. Instead, the number of compulsory figures was reduced to three, worth 40% of the total marks, while, in addition to the normal free skating, a program of six prescribed free-skating elements was introduced. Speed skating, previously a wholly amateur sport, had some of its best talent made ineligible for its world championships when about 20 top racers broke away to form a professional league. Skating's continuing worldwide expansion was typified by the appreciable increase of electrically frozen rinks in the U.S. to 1,200 and by an industrial award to a British manufacturer for exporting more than a million skates in a year.

A total of 120 skaters from a record 22 nations took part in the world ice figure and dance championships at Bratislava, Czech., on February 27–March 3. On his home rink, Ondrej Nepela ended his amateur career with a third successive men's victory. Clearly inspired by local support, the Czechoslovakian was at his best in a thrilling jump combination of double axel, double loop, and double Salchow. But Nepela was closely challenged by Sergey Chetverukhin, the Soviet runner-up, who scored the highest marks in the free skating. Jan Hoffmann of East Germany kept the bronze medal from John Curry, whose fourth place was the highest reached by a British skater in 34 years. Seven triple Salchow jumps were seen in the men's event.

Karen Magnussen, competent in all departments, became the first Canadian since 1965 to win the women's title. She excelled with a great double axel and a clever combination of split, reverse split, axel, and double loop jumps. Janet Lynn outpointed her in the free skating, but the U.S. skater was too far behind after the compulsory figures to do better than finish as runner-up over Christine Errath of East Germany.

A performance of rare technical quality, half of it without music because the record stopped, made Aleksandr Zaitsev and Irina Rodnina the new pair champions. They showed remarkable coordination after less than a year in partnership. It was the ninth consecutive victory for the U.S.S.R., the fifth for Miss Rodnina, and the first for her partner. Aleksey Ulanov, Miss Rodnina's partner in her four previous victories, was runner-up with his wife, Ludmila Smirnova, and Uwe Kagelmann and Manuela Gross of East Germany finished third. The ice dance title was retained by Aleksandr Gorshkov and Ludmila

JOHN SOTO—THE NEW YORK TIMES

Bill Lanigan (right) battles Barth Levy to regain the national speed skating championship during competition at Cantiague Park, N.Y., March 11, 1973.

Pakhomova, their fourth successive win for the Soviet skaters after an always threatening West German challenge from Erich and Angelika Buch. An all-British duel for the bronze medal was clinched by Glyn Watts and Hilary Green, who narrowly outpointed Peter Dalby and Janet Sawbridge.

The world ice speed-skating championship for men was won by a Swede, Göran Claesson, at Deventer, Neth., on February 17–18. He won both the long-distance events, 5,000 m. and 10,000 m. A Norwegian, Sten Stensen, was overall runner-up and a Dutchman, Piet Kleine, placed third, Stensen took the 1,500 m., and Bill Lanigan of the U.S. finished first in the 500-m. sprint. The previous overall champion, Ard Schenk of The Netherlands, was among a much missed elite group whose eligibility ceased when they signed professional contracts.

Atje Keulen-Deelstra of The Netherlands retained her overall title in the women's world championship at Strömsund, Swed., February 24–25. Tatjana Shelekova was runner-up for the U.S.S.R., and another Dutch girl, Trijnie Rep, finished third. Mrs. Keulen-Deelstra proved best in the 1,000 m., Sheila Young of the U.S. won the 500-m. sprint, and the longer distances, 1,500 m. and 3,000 m., were gained by Galina Stepanskaya of the U.S.S.R. and Sippie Tichelaar of The Netherlands, respectively. Separate world sprint titles for men and women were won by Valery Muratov (U.S.S.R.) and Miss Young at Oslo on February 3–4.

Olympic figure skating star Janet Lynn of Rockford, Ill., makes her professional debut with the Shipstads & Johnson Ice Follies in Los Angeles, Sept. 5, 1973.

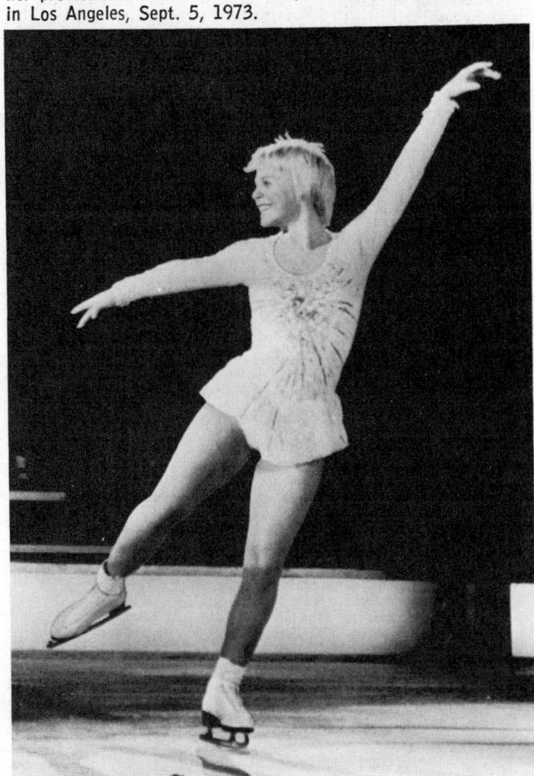

WIDE WORLD

Two world records were bettered and another equaled during the year. Lasse Efskind of Norway set a new time of 1 min. 17.6 sec. for the 1,000 m. The same day, January 13, at Davos, Switz., he became the fourth skater to clock 500 m. in 38 sec. A week later, also at Davos, Miss Young lowered the women's 500-m. mark to 41.8 sec. (HOWARD BASS)

Income, National

The world economy grew faster in real terms (*i.e.,* after allowing for price changes) in 1972 than in any year since 1968, and at a rate above the long-term trend. The International Monetary Fund (IMF), in its *Annual Report, 1973,* estimated the growth rate as 5.6% in 1972, compared with 3.9% in 1971, 3.5% in 1970, and an annual average of 5% for the decade 1960–70. Growth rates increased for both the developed and the less developed groups of countries. (*See* Table III; information about individual countries is given in Table I.)

Estimates published by the Organization for Economic Cooperation and Development (OECD) in *Economic Outlook* (December 1973) and similar estimates made by the European Commission suggested that this increase had been sustained or increased in the developed countries in 1973. The improvement was most substantial for the United Kingdom, West Germany, Ireland, and Luxembourg. While these estimates were based on the latest available evidence, they should be regarded as provisional, although similar estimates for previous years proved reasonably reliable in most cases.

Experience was more varied among the less developed countries. Brazil, Ecuador, Iran, and Syria recorded growth rates of 10% or more in 1972. Preliminary UN Statistical Office estimates published in the "World Economic Survey 1972" suggested that a number of other countries had also achieved 10% growth rates, namely, Algeria, Botswana, Gabon, Hong Kong, Mauritius, Qatar, Saudi Arabia, Senegal, and Tunisia. Growth rates in Israel (listed in Table I) and in the Dominican Republic, Malawi, Mauritania, Rhodesia, Singapore, and Swaziland (UN estimates) were at least 8% but under 10%. Countries with growth rates of at least 6% but under 8% included Fiji, Guatemala, Kenya, South Korea, Mexico, Pakistan, and Panama (Table I) and Bolivia, Colombia, Lebanon, Nigeria, Sierra Leone, and Togo (UN estimates). Countries with growth rates of at least 5% but under 6% included Malaysia and Paraguay (Table I) and the Congo, Costa Rica, Egypt, Ethiopia, Gambia, Haiti,

Table I. Growth of Real Gross National Product, 1960–73

Country	Annual % change 1960–70	% change from preceding year 1971	1972	1973*
Industrial countries				
Austria	4.8	5.2	6.4	6
Belgium	5.0	3.7	4.9	6
Canada	5.2	5.6	5.8	7¼
Denmark	4.9	3.6	5.0	4½
France	5.8	5.0	5.5	6¼
Germany, West	4.9	2.8	3.0	6¼
Italy	5.6	1.4	3.5	5¼
Japan	11.1	6.3	9.6	11
Luxembourg	3.4	0.7	3.9	6¾
Netherlands, The	5.3	4.3	4.4	4
Norway	5.0	4.9	4.3	4
Sweden	4.6	0.3	2.1	4¼
Switzerland	4.6	4.3	5.7	4¾
United Kingdom	2.8	1.6	3.0	6¾
United States	4.0	2.8	6.1	6
Other developed areas				
Australia	5.0	4.4	5.8	6¾
Finland	5.2	2.1	6.8	6
Greece	7.6	7.3	10.0	...
Iceland	4.4	9.9	7.3	...
Ireland	4.2	3.0	3.0	6
Malta	5.3	1.3	...	...
New Zealand†	3.9	2.5	4	...
Portugal	6.3	5.9	...	...
South Africa‡	5.8	3.6	4.0	...
Spain	7.5	4.6	8.3	7½
Turkey	5.6	9.2	6.7	...
Centrally planned economies§				
Albania	9.2	...	...	...
Bulgaria	7.7	7.0	7.0	...
Czechoslovakia	4.3	5.2	5.7	...
Germany, East	4.3	4.5	5.7	...
Hungary	5.6	6.6	5.1	...
Poland	6.1	8.1	10.1	...
Romania	8.6	12.9	10.0	...
U.S.S.R.	7.1	5.6	4.0	...
Yugoslavia	6.3	8.9	4.4	...
Less developed areas				
Argentina	4.2	3.7	...	...
Bolivia	5.6	3.8	...	...
Brazil	6.0	11.3	10.5	...
Chile	4.3	8.3	...	...
Cyprus	6.1	12.1	...	...
Dominican Republic	4.6	9.9	...	...
Ecuador	5.0	8.0	10.0	...
El Salvador	5.2	4.6	...	...
Ethiopia	4.7¶	4.8	...	...
Fiji	7.0¶	7.5	6.0	...
Guatemala	5.3	5.6	6.4	...
Haiti	1.0	5.7	...	...
Honduras	4.9	4.3	4.3	...
India†	3.8	...	...	...
Iran†	8.8	13.7	15.1	...
Israel	8.6	9.8	9.9	...
Jamaica	5.0	1.7	...	...
Kenya	6.6¶	7.3	6.6	...
Korea, South	9.3	9.8	7.3	...
Malawi	5.4¶	14.8	...	...
Malaysia	6.1	4.8	5.8	...
Mexico	7.1	3.4	7.5	...
Nicaragua	7.3	5.7	...	...
Pakistan‖	3.9	5.8♀	6.5♀	...
Panama	8.1	8.8	7.4	...
Paraguay	4.5¶	4.6	5.3	...
Peru	5.2	5.9	...	...
Philippines	4.8	5.8	4.6	...
Puerto Rico‖	7.4	8.9	...	...
Rhodesia	5.1¶	9.3	...	...
Sri Lanka	4.9	1.4	...	...
Syria	6.8	11.8	13.7	...
Thailand	7.9	6.3	3.9	...
Tunisia	4.2	9.2	...	...
Uganda	4.6¶	1.7	...	...
Uruguay	1.4	0.5	0	...
Venezuela	5.6	4.4	3.5	...

*OECD estimates, based on incomplete data.
†Financial year beginning April 1 (March 21 for Iran).
‡Includes Namibia.
§Growth of material product. *See* text for discussion of comparability with other figures.
‖Financial year beginning July 1.
¶Ethiopia, 1961–70; Paraguay, 1962–70; Uganda, 1963–70; Kenya, Malawi, 1964–70; Fiji, Rhodesia, 1965–70.
♀Excludes Bangladesh.
Sources: Publications of the United Nations, the OECD, and the International Monetary Fund; various national sources.

Table II. Total and Per Capita Gross Domestic Product and National Income

Country	Year	Gross domestic product U.S. $000,-000,000	Gross domestic product U.S. $ per capita	National income U.S. $000,-000,000	National income U.S. $ per capita
Industrial countries					
Austria	1972	20.6	2,750	18.4	2,450
Belgium	1972	35.8	3,690	32.6	3,360
Canada	1972	105.0	4,810	92.5	4,230
Denmark	1972	20.9	4,200	19.2	3,840
France	1972	198.7	3,840	177.5	3,430
Germany, West	1972	260.2	4,220	230.6	3,740
Italy	1972	117.7	2,170	108.1	1,990
Japan	1972	294.1	2,750	256.5	2,400
Luxembourg	1972	1.3	3,740	1.1	3,070
Netherlands, The	1972	45.8	3,440	42.1	3,160
Norway	1972	14.5	3,700	12.3	3,140
Sweden	1972	41.7	5,140	37.9	4,670
Switzerland	1972	29.5	4,600	26.9	4,200
United Kingdom	1972	150.7	2,700	137.9	2,470
United States	1972	1,159.0	5,550	1,040.0	4,980
Other developed areas					
Australia	1971–72*	42.1	3,270	38.1	2,960
Finland	1972	13.4	2,900	12.0	2,600
Greece	1972	12.3	1,380	11.8	1,320
Iceland	1971	0.6	2,880	0.5	2,490
Ireland	1972	5.4	1,810	5.1	1,700
New Zealand	1971–72†	7.3	2,560	6.7	2,360
Portugal	1971	6.8	790	6.4	750
South Africa‡	1972	19.9	840	17.4	730
Spain	1972	46.6	1,350	43.0	1,250
Turkey	1972	16.4	440	15.9	430
Less developed areas					
Africa					
Algeria	1971	4.3	290	4.3	290
Egypt	1970–71*	13.5	400	13.0	390
Ethiopia	1971	1.9	70	1.8	70
Ghana	1970	2.2	260	2.1	240
Ivory Coast	1971	1.6	360	1.5	340
Kenya	1972	1.0	830	1.0	810
Libya	1972	4.9	2,340	3.8	1,850
Morocco	1971	3.7	240	3.6	240
Mozambique	1963	1.0	150	1.0	150
Nigeria	1969	5.2	100	4.5	80
Rhodesia	1971	1.6	300	1.5	270
Sudan	1970–71*	1.8	120	1.7	110
Tanzania§	1971	1.4	100	1.3	90
Tunisia	1971	1.6	310	1.5	290
Uganda	1971	1.5	140	1.4	140
Zaire	1972	2.8	120	2.3	100
Zambia	1972	1.7	390	1.5	340
Caribbean and Latin America					
Argentina	1970	24.4	1,050	22.7	980
Brazil	1972	51.2	520	48.2	490
Chile	1971	9.9	1,100	8.8	980
Colombia	1970	8.7	410	7.7	370
Costa Rica	1972	1.2	630	1.1	580
Dominican Republic	1971	1.6	390	1.5	360
Ecuador	1972	2.1	320	1.9	300
El Salvador	1972	1.2	310	1.1	290
Guatemala	1972	2.2	400	2.0	370
Honduras	1971	0.8	300	0.8	300
Jamaica	1972	1.0	520	0.9	460
Mexico	1972	41.1	780	38.9	740
Panama	1972	1.3	860	1.2	760
Peru	1971	6.8	480	6.1	440
Puerto Rico	1971–72*	6.2	2,230	5.4	1,920
Uruguay	1972	2.4	810	2.4	800
Venezuela	1971	11.6	1,080	9.9	920
Asia, Middle East					
Iran	1972–73†	17.4	570	14.9	490
Iraq	1969	3.1	340	2.5	280
Israel	1972	7.1	2,300	6.2	2,010
Kuwait	1971–72†	4.0	4,670	3.1	3,590
Lebanon	1970	1.5	530	1.5	520
Saudi Arabia	1970–71*	4.7	620	3.3	440
Syria	1972	2.0	300	1.9	290
Asia, East and Southeast					
Burma	1967–68‖	2.1	80	2.0	70
Hong Kong	1972	4.1	1,000	...	...
India	1969–70†	49.1	90	46.2	90
Indonesia	1971	9.4	80	8.6	70
Korea, South	1972	9.9	300	9.1	280
Malaysia¶	1971	3.3	370	3.1	350
Nepal	1969–70♀	0.9	80	0.9	80
Pakistan♂	1971–72*	9.7	180	...	...
Philippines	1972	8.6	220	7.5	190
Singapore	1972	2.7	1,270	2.7	1,230
Sri Lanka	1971	2.2	175	2.1	162
Taiwan	1971	6.2	440	5.8	400
Thailand	1972	7.4	200	6.9	190
Vietnam, South	1972	3.3	170	3.3	170

*Year beginning July 1.
†Year beginning April 1 (March 21 for Iran).
‡Includes Namibia.
§Former Tanganyika only.
‖Year ending September 30.
¶Western Malaysia only.
♀Year ending July 15.
♂Excludes Bangladesh.
Sources: Publications of UN, OECD, and IMF; official national sources.

Table III. Growth of World Output 1960–72

Percent changes in real GNP

Country group	Annual averages 1960–70	1960–65	1965–70	Change from preceding year 1968	1969	1970	1971	1972
Industrial countries*	4.8	5.2	4.5	5.7	4.8	2.5	3.5	5.5
Primary producing countries	5.7	5.6	5.8	5.9	7.0	6.4	5.6	5.9
More developed areas†	6.4	7.1	5.6	5.1	7.2	5.7	5.2	5.4
Less developed areas‡	5.5	5.1	5.8	6.2	6.9	6.6	5.7	6.1
World (excluding centrally planned economies, except Yugoslavia)	5.0	5.3	4.7	5.7	5.4	3.5	3.9	5.6

*Includes Canada, United States, Japan, France, West Germany, Italy, the United Kingdom, Austria, Belgium, Denmark, Luxembourg, The Netherlands, Norway, Sweden, and Switzerland.
†Includes Australia, Finland, Greece, Iceland, Ireland, Malta, New Zealand, Portugal, South Africa, Spain, Turkey, and Yugoslavia.
‡Includes other IMF member countries not included in the lists above.
Source: International Monetary Fund, *Annual Report* (1973).

Indonesia, Kuwait, Morocco, Namibia, Nicaragua, Peru, Somalia, Sudan, Upper Volta, and Zambia (UN estimates). In the group having growth rates of at least 3% but under 5% were Honduras, Philippines, Thailand, and Venezuela (Table I) and Angola, Argentina, Bangladesh, Burma, Cameroon, Chad, El Salvador, Ghana, Guinea, Ivory Coast, Jordan, Lesotho, Liberia, the Malagasy Republic, Mozambique, Niger, Tanzania, Trinidad and Tobago, and Zaire. Countries that grew by less than 3% included Uruguay (Table I) and Afghanistan, Bahrain, Burundi, Chile, Dahomey, India, Jamaica, Laos, Mali, Nepal, Oman, Rwanda, Sri Lanka, Uganda, and South Vietnam (UN estimates). UN estimates suggested that a number of less developed countries experienced a decline in real output (a negative growth rate), namely, Barbados, Cambodia, the Central African Republic, Guyana, Iraq, and Libya.

Comparisons between Eastern European and other countries are difficult because the former exclude from national income accounts certain "unproductive services," such as public administration and personal and professional services. If such items were included, the growth rates in those countries would probably be somewhat lower than those recorded in Table I. The U.S.S.R., Hungary, Romania, and Yugoslavia showed growth rate declines in 1972 as compared with 1971, while Czechoslovakia, East Germany, and Poland had increases.

Table II shows the latest available figures for gross domestic product (GDP) and national income, on both a total and a per capita basis, in more than 70 countries, converted from national currencies to U.S. dollars. The concept of gross domestic product is designed to measure the value of total domestic production; it is the sum of all final domestic current expenditures by consumers and public authorities, investment expenditures (in both fixed capital and inventory), *plus* exports of goods and services, *less* imports of goods and services. The concept of national income is related to GDP. National income is the sum of GDP *plus* the factor income from abroad (payments such as interest and dividends arising in one country and paid to residents of another country), *less* an allowance for the depreciation of the country's stock of fixed capital for the year being considered. Defined in these ways, GDP and national income are said to be measured in terms of market prices. The table includes all countries that had a national income of $1 billion or more in 1970.

The national figures have been converted to U.S. dollars at current exchange rates. Two important qualifications must be made about this procedure. First, the use of current exchange rates determined for foreign trade and payments purposes may not adequately reflect differences in the purchasing power of the various national currencies. For most countries the exchange rates used are the "trade conversion factors" published by the IMF in *International Financial Statistics* (from October 1973 onward), which are averages of the effective exchange rates for international trading. Second, the figures in national currencies are themselves estimated in a variety of ways, and there are differences in definitions used among various countries. In particular, some countries adopted the new UN system of national accounts, in which the precise definitions of certain of the concepts used differ somewhat from the system of national accounts still in use in most countries. Although the per capita figures given have been rounded to the nearest $10 to avoid a spurious appearance of accuracy, it is still unwise to place much reliance on small differences between countries. The net effect of the devaluations and currency floats of recent years was to reduce the size of GDP and national income for the United States and United Kingdom in relation to most other countries. On this basis, the U.S. economy was about four times the size of Japan's economy and between seven and eight times the size of the U.K. economy.

(M. F. FULLER)

See also Economy, World.

India

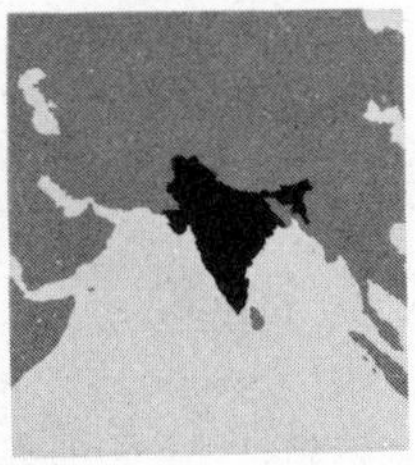

A federal republic of southern Asia and a member of the Commonwealth of Nations, India is situated on a peninsula extending into the Indian Ocean with the Arabian Sea to the west and the Bay of Bengal to the east. It is bounded (east to west) by Burma, Bangladesh, China, Bhutan, Sikkim, Nepal, and Pakistan; Sri Lanka lies just off its southern tip in the Indian Ocean. Area: 1,261,810 sq.mi. (3,268,090 sq.km.), including the Pakistani-controlled section of Jammu and Kashmir. Pop. (1973 est.): 574,216,000; Indo-Aryans and Dravidians are dominant, with Mongoloid, Negroid, and Australoid admixtures. Cap.: New Delhi (pop., 1971, 301,801). Largest cities: Calcutta (metro. pop., 1971, 7,031,382) and Greater Bombay (metro. pop., 1971, 5,970,575). Language: Hindi and English (official). Religion (1971): Hindu 82.7%; Muslim 11.2%; Christian 2.6%; Sikh 1.9%; Buddhist 0.7%; others 0.9%. President in 1973, Varahagiri Venkata Giri; prime minister, Mrs. Indira Gandhi.

For India 1973 was a year of soaring prices, intense economic hardship, and political troubles in many states. The decline in self-confidence was checked only by the bounty of the monsoon, the traditional dispenser of India's destiny. In foreign affairs, however, Mrs. Gandhi's government retained most of its élan and took important initiatives to solve subcontinental problems.

The Economy. The wheat crop of the winter of 1972 did not prove as plentiful as expected, in spite of large expenditures on special agricultural programs. In a situation of growing shortages, the government took over the wholesale trade in wheat. Without the requisite administrative drive, procurements fell far below the targets. The resolve not to seek concessional supplies from abroad, combined with the pressure on wheat in the North American markets, prevented resort to the large-scale imports of earlier years. Although the public distribution system was expanded, especially in towns and drought-hit areas, the releases of stocks were slowed down during the summer months. Vast sums of money were also spent on relief programs in the states of Maharashtra, Gujarat, and Rajasthan. At the peak some nine million people were employed on public works. All this led to a sharp rise in prices.

Fortunately the monsoon rains of June–October were uniformly good in all regions, and indeed proved to be the best in years. With brightening crop prospects and improvement in hydroelectric power production, prices, which had reached their peak in August, showed some decline. Even so, on October 6 the wholesale price index stood 21.2% higher than on October 7 of the previous year. Wholesale food prices were 21.2% higher and those of industrial raw materials 53.6% higher. The dramatic announcement by the Soviet Union on September 29 that it would provide India with two million metric tons of grain on loan improved hopes of bringing prices in check. An important consequence of the harrowing experience in food management was the government's decision, reached in September, to defer taking over the wholesale trade in rice.

Net bank credits to the government in September 1973 were Rs. 15,990,000,000 higher than a year earlier. In August the government announced several measures to reduce public expenditure and curb the volume of deficit financing (which in the fiscal year 1972–73 amounted to a record Rs. 8,280,000,000). The bank rate was raised to 7%. The economic crisis led to (and was aggravated by) widespread industrial strikes. Particularly crippling were strikes by power plant employees in several states. New Delhi was paralyzed early in November by a city-wide strike protesting shortages and high prices.

The budget of the union government for 1973–74 envisaged income of Rs. 50,810,000,000 (after new taxes amounting to Rs. 2.5 billion), expenditure of Rs. 47,520,000,000, capital receipts of Rs. 24.6 billion, and capital expenditure of Rs. 28,740,000,000, leaving a deficit of Rs. 850 million.

In January the planning commission received approval for a fifth five-year plan. It provided for development expenditure of Rs. 533,500,000,000 during 1974–79 (of which Rs. 372,500,000,000 was to be in the public sector) to achieve an annual growth rate of 5.5% and to provide a greater volume of the people's basic needs. The principal targets for the fifth plan were: food grains 139.9 million metric tons, cotton cloth 10,703,000,000 m., coal 141.2 million metric tons, steel 9.4 million metric tons, cement 26.8 million metric tons, petroleum products 36 million metric tons, and power 129,300,000,000 kw-hr.

Early in the year the government took over the management of 711 noncoking coal mines. Parliament formally passed the Coal Mines Nationalization Act in May.

Sir Christopher Soames, vice-president of the Commission of the European Communities, visited Delhi in September. In talks with senior Indian officials, he expressed the view that any loss of duty-free access to the traditional British market for a variety of Indian goods would be more than offset by planned reductions of EEC tariffs. India was pressing for quota-free and duty-free entry into Europe for its jute and coir products, but there appeared to be no chance of more than a 60% reduction in tariffs. The U.K., which annually received 10% of Indian exports, had been by far the biggest importer of Indian goods among EEC members.

Domestic Affairs. In January there was serious rioting in Andhra Pradesh over the *mulki* rules (which gave some transitional safeguards in education and public appointments to people of the former dominion of the nizam of Hyderabad). The ministry resigned and the state was brought under president's rule. The exit of legislators from the Congress Party in Orissa led to a constitutional crisis, and that state also passed under president's rule on March 3. Disgruntled policemen of the Provincial Armed Constabulary flouted orders in Lucknow (where they joined student strikers to set fire to the university) and other parts of Uttar Pradesh in May. The military had to disarm them. To help restore order the ministry resigned,

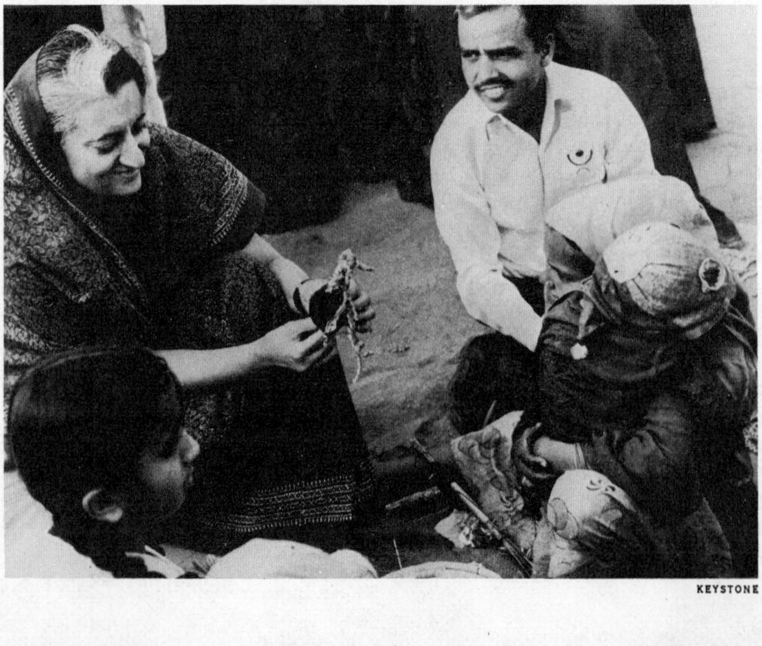

KEYSTONE

Prime Minister Indira Gandhi admires a doll made by children of Dera Mandi, a village near New Delhi, during ceremonies to mark the opening of the nation's first children's home.

DONALD KIRK—CHICAGO TRIBUNE

Women relief workers near Poona carry baskets of dirt to a dam being built to capture monsoon rain water. Drought severely reduced food supplies in the region which neighbours Bombay.

and central rule was imposed on the state on June 13.

Two other state Cabinets fell in June as a result of factional fighting in the Congress—those of G. Oza in Gujarat and Kedar Pandey in Bihar. New governments were formed under Chimanbhai Patel and Abdul Ghafoor, respectively. It was only by a determined assertion of the Congress leadership that crises were averted in Madhya Pradesh and Mysore. By a similar exercise of will, Mrs. Gandhi persuaded the leaders of both regions of Andhra Pradesh to accept a six-point plan to resolve their differences within the framework of a unified state. President's rule was ended in December and a new government formed under J. Vengal Rao.

At the national level, there was a confrontation between the executive and the judiciary. Ironically, this came several days after the Supreme Court had averted a collision with Parliament by upholding, 9–4, the power of Parliament to abridge even the fundamental rights guaranteed by the constitution, thus sustaining the legality of the Constitution (24th Amendment) Act. However, the majority ruling that art. 368 (dealing with the power to amend the constitution) "does not enable Parliament to alter the basic structure or framework of the Constitution" had the effect of retaining the court's right of judicial review. The judgment was the last judicial act of the chief justice, S. M. Sikri, who retired April 25.

The government appointed A. N. Ray to the post, whereupon three judges who were senior to him in the court (J. M. Shelat, K. S. Hegde, and A. N. Grover) resigned in protest at being bypassed. Calling the appointment an executive effort to undermine the independence of the judiciary, the Bar Council of India strongly deplored this departure from the practice of appointing the seniormost judge as chief justice, as well as the failure to consult the outgoing chief justice. In an acrimonious debate in Parliament, the government spokesmen asserted the government's right to consider the social philosophy of judges.

Earlier, on February 4, Mrs. Gandhi had reshuffled her council of ministers, giving the home portfolio to Uma Shankar Dikshit and inducting D. K. Barooah, Bhola Paswan Shastri, K. Raghuramiah, and L. N. Mishra into the Cabinet. The minister for steel and mines, Mohan Kumaramangalam, died in an air crash in Delhi on May 31. A brilliant left-wing lawyer, he was the main exponent of the government's position in the court controversy. (*See* OBITUARIES.)

Dayanand Bandodkar, the chief minister of Goa, Diu, and Daman, died on August 12, and Barkatullah Khan, chief minister of Rajasthan, on October 11. Shashikala Kakodkar, daughter of Bandodkar, became the new chief minister of Goa, Diu, and Daman, and Hari Deo Joshi headed the government of Rajasthan. The year also saw the elevation of Gen. Sam Manekshaw as the country's first field marshal and the appointment of Lieut. Gen. G. G. Bewoor, Air Chief Marshal O. P. Mehra, and Adm. S. N. Kohli as chiefs of staff of the Army, the Air Force, and the Navy.

The name of the state of Mysore was changed to Karnataka on November 1, and that of the union ter-

INDIA

Education. (1971–72) Primary, pupils 78 million, teachers (1970–71) 1,602,515; secondary and vocational, pupils 8.4 million, teachers (1970–71) 523,341; teacher training (1965–66), students 177,607, teachers 13,460; higher (including 86 universities), students 2,540,000, teaching staff (1970–71) 119,000.

Finance. Monetary unit: rupee, with (Sept. 17, 1973) a free rate of Rs. 7.76 to U.S. $1 (official rate of Rs. 18.71 = £1 sterling). Gold, SDRs, and foreign exchange, official: (March 1973) U.S. $1,219,000,000; (March 1972) U.S. $1,194,000,000. Budget (1971–72 actual): revenue Rs. 39,851,000,000; expenditure Rs. 40,097,000,000. Gross national product: (1969–70) Rs. 365.6 billion; (1968–69) Rs. 328.4 billion. Money supply: (May 1973) Rs. 97,330,000,000; (May 1972) Rs. 84,080,000,000. Cost of living (1963 = 100): (April 1973) 204; (April 1972) 179.

Foreign Trade. (1972–73) Imports Rs. 17,967,000,000; exports Rs. 19,569,000,000. Import sources: U.K. 13%; U.S. 13%; Japan 9%; West Germany 9%; Iran 7%; U.S.S.R. 6%; Canada 6%. Export destinations: U.S.S.R. 16%; U.S. 14%; Japan 11%; U.K. 9%; Bangladesh 8%. Main exports: jute manufactures 13%; leather 9%; tea 8%; cotton fabrics 6%; iron ore 6%.

Transport and Communications. Roads (1972) 1,021,819 km. (including 28,819 km. main roads). Motor vehicles in use (1972): passenger 646,463; commercial 346,000. Railways: (1971) 59,969 km.; traffic (1970–71) 118,309,000,000 passenger-km., freight 127,407,000,000 net ton-km. Air traffic (1972): 4,556,000,000 passenger-km.; freight 151,350,000 net ton-km. Shipping (1972): merchant vessels 100 gross tons and over 412; gross tonnage 2,649,677. Telephones (Dec. 1971) 1,293,000. Radio licenses (Dec. 1970) 11,747,000. Television licenses (Dec. 1971) 49,000.

Agriculture. Production (in 000; metric tons; 1972; 1971 in parentheses): wheat 26,477 (23,832); rice *c.* 59,000 (64,100); barley 2,501 (2,784); corn *c.* 5,300 (5,026); millet (1971) 9,106, (1970) 12,074; sorghum (1971) 7,753, (1970) 8,188; potatoes *c.* 4,750 (4,807); cassava (1971) 5,216, (1970) 5,214; tea *c.* 452 (*c.* 432); chick-peas 5,106 (5,247); bananas (1970) *c.* 3,000, (1969) 3,105; sugar, raw value 3,437 (4,131); tobacco 409 (362); rapeseed and mustard seed 1,451 (1,975); linseed 510 (474); peanuts *c.* 4,500 (5,712); cotton, lint 1,127 (1,258); jute 876 (1,023). Livestock (in 000; 1971–72): cattle *c.* 176,750; sheep *c.* 43,000; pigs *c.* 4,790; buffalo *c.* 54,800; goats *c.* 68,500; poultry *c.* 117,500.

Industry. Production (in 000; metric tons; 1972): coal 74,766; iron ore (61% metal content) 35,194; pig iron (1971) 6,740; crude steel 6,654; electricity (excluding most industrial production; kw-hr.) 64,202,000; aluminum 179; cement 15,747; cotton yarn 972; woven cotton fabrics (m.; 1971) 7,356,000; petroleum products (1971) 17,744; sulfuric acid 1,131; caustic soda 395; gold (troy oz.; 1971) 118; manganese ore (metal content; 1971) 670.

ritory of Laccadive, Amindivi, and Minicoy into Lakshadweep. The strength of the Lok Sabha (House of the People) was raised to a maximum of 545 under the Constitution (31st Amendment) Bill. Another important bill that was introduced was designed to discourage defection by legislators by requiring that a legislator who changed parties should seek reelection. In the southern state of Tamil Nadu, the breakaway Anna DMK challenged the power of the ruling DMK (Dravida Munnetra Kazhagam) and scored an impressive victory in the parliamentary by-election in the Dindigul constituency.

In Sikkim, officially an Indian protectorate, there was a popular rising in April, and the chogyal vested governmental functions in an Indian administrator. He also signed an agreement with leaders of political parties to usher in full responsible government. (*See* DEPENDENT STATES.)

Foreign Affairs. The impressive victory of Sheikh Mujibur Rahman in the general election in Bangladesh in March was received with satisfaction. Several agreements were reached to strengthen economic cooperation with that country. In July, India and Bangladesh evolved an agreed approach toward Pakistan over problems remaining from the 1971 war. Mrs. Gandhi's special emissary, P. N. Haksar, visited Pakistan later in July, and talks continued in New Delhi in August between him and Aziz Ahmed, Pakistan's minister of state. On August 28 an agreement was reached between the two countries, to which Bangladesh gave its concurrence. Pakistan undertook to return all Bengalis and simultaneously to accept all Pakistanis from Bangladesh. India, in turn, was to repatriate the Pakistani prisoners of war and civilian internees (numbering over 90,000). Pakistan and Bangladesh were to meet directly to discuss what additional number of people Pakistan would take after a substantial number of non-Bengalis had been repatriated to Pakistan. In the meantime, Bangladesh offered not to proceed with the proposed war crimes trial of 195 prisoners of war; the agreement also provided for tripartite discussions on the question of these 195. The first group of prisoners left India for Lahore on September 19.

Relations with the U.S. improved. The new U.S. ambassador, Daniel Patrick Moynihan, initiated discussions with the Indian government to settle the accumulated U.S. commodity loans under Public Law 480. In September, New Delhi clarified that it did not intend to restrict the number of U.S. scholars who would be admitted to India. The External Affairs Ministry noted several faint signs that China might be considering an improvement of relations with India, although it was still puzzled by Peking's generally "negative attitude." For the first time since 1962, China's vice-minister attended India's Republic Day function at the Peking mission. A senior Chinese diplomat had also been appointed to the Chinese mission in New Delhi.

Economic ties with the Soviet Union were further strengthened. During Soviet party leader Leonid I. Brezhnev's visit in late November, a 15-year development agreement was signed providing for a significant increase in Soviet economic aid. Mrs. Gandhi participated in the conference of nonaligned nations in Algiers in September. In the fourth Arab-Israeli war, which broke out in October, India followed its traditional policy of extending support to the Arab position. (H. Y. SHARADA PRASAD)

See also Bangladesh; Pakistan.

Indonesia

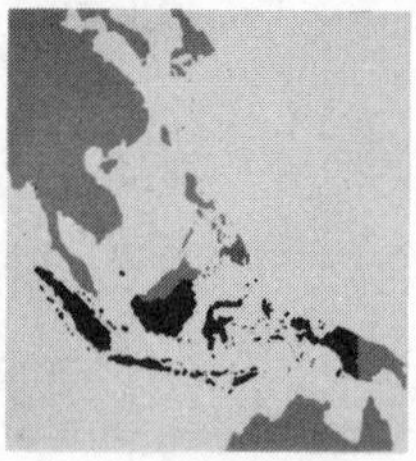

A republic of Southeast Asia, Indonesia consists of the major islands of Sumatra, Java, Kalimantan (Indonesian Borneo), Celebes, and Irian Jaya (West New Guinea) and approximately 3,000 smaller islands and islets. Area: 782,658 sq.mi. (2,027,087 sq.km.). Pop. (1973 est.): 125.7 million. Cap. and largest city: Jakarta (pop., 1971, 4,576,009). Language: Bahasa Indonesian (official); Javanese; Sundanese; Madurese. Religion: mainly Muslim; some Christian, Buddhist, and Hindu. President and prime minister in 1973, General Suharto.

Domestic Affairs. On March 22 the 920-member People's Consultative Congress (MPR), which met once every five years to elect the country's leadership and set "the broad lines of the policy of the state," unanimously reelected Suharto to a second consecutive five-year term as president and elected Sultan Hamengku Buwono IX of Jogjakarta, central Java, as vice-president. Suharto's reelection by acclamation was expected. After assuming de facto control in 1965, he retrieved the country from political and economic chaos, made peace with Indonesia's neighbours, and launched the country's first five-year-plan. Upon his reelection, Suharto reshuffled the Cabinet and relinquished his post as minister of defense, appointing Gen. Maraden Panggabean, a Sumatran and Christian, as his replacement. The post of vice-president had been vacant for 17 years, ever since Muhammad Hatta, the country's first vice-president, resigned in 1956 in protest against Sukarno's moral corruption, alliance with the Communists at home and abroad, and increasingly authoritarian rule.

A development with sensitive undertones was the "Bandung Affair," a racial outburst that occurred in August when thousands of Indonesian students rampaged against the Chinese minority in Bandung, the capital of West Java. Hundreds of Chinese shops, homes, and other buildings were looted or damaged. The riot was touched off by a traffic accident involving a Chinese and an Indonesian. Troops were summoned to restore order. Suharto publicly deplored the incident, authorized the Army to act to prevent a recurrence, and reiterated the government's policy of integration of different ethnic communities. The incident mirrored the continuing hostility between the largely impoverished Malay majority and the Chinese minority, which exercised economic leverage out of proportion to its size.

Perhaps the most important political development was the government's submission to Parliament of a marriage bill that would meet the demands of feminist groups and codify the marriage laws inherited from the colonial period. These laws had set different standards for marriages involving Muslims, Indonesian Christians, Europeans, Chinese, and Indonesians who are neither Muslim nor Christian. The bill, which was being debated as the year closed, gave rise to tensions between the republic's secular leadership and the orthodox Islamic community, which claimed to represent about 85% of the population. Nominally, most Indonesians consider themselves Muslim, making Indonesia the largest Islamic state in the world. Orthodox Muslims denounced the bill as "disguised christianization." For example, it would provide women rights not permitted by Islamic law such as initiating divorce. Underlying the parliamentary debate was a profound political issue, the conflict between the secular republic established by the modern nationalist movement in the struggle for independence and the desire of some orthodox Muslims for creation of an Islamic state.

The Economy. Indonesia's economy experienced its first setback under Suharto in early 1973 when a severe drought affected the winter 1972 rice crop. As a result, the cost of living index rose by 26%, compared with an annual 3% in recent years. Suharto ordered a crash program of rice imports, and by midyear the rice situation had stabilized. The imports from China, upward of 500,000 tons, raised eyebrows since diplomatic relations between Peking and Jakarta had been frozen since 1967 when Indonesia accused China of involvement in the 1965 Communist coup attempt. The government also increased the floor price of rice to stimulate production and set up a stockpiling program against future disasters. By the end of 1973 the rice outlook had improved.

As evidence of foreign confidence in the economy, the Inter-Governmental Group on Indonesia (IGGI), a consortium of 12 donor countries and international agencies, pledged Indonesia $760 million worth of assistance for the year. Despite the impact of the drought, the gross national product continued to increase at an impressive annual rate of 7%. Crude oil production alone reached a record 1.4 million bbl. per day, making Indonesia the largest oil producer in the Far East. Indonesian oil assumed even more importance with the Arab oil cutback in the fall. Lieut. Gen. Ibnu Sutowo, head of the state-owned oil enterprise, indicated that his country planned an aggressive exploration program and that production could double in the next few years.

Foreign Affairs. Indonesia won international recognition of its leadership role among the non-Communist powers of Southeast Asia when it joined Canada, Hungary, and Poland as a member of the International Commission of Control and Supervision (ICCS). The body was established in Vietnam under the terms of the Paris peace accord. (*See* VIETNAM: *Special Report*.) Indonesia's membership reflected a shift of power in Asian affairs.

Among foreign visitors during 1973, the most important was Prime Minister Lee Kuan Yew of Singapore, whose city-state opposite Sumatra largely consisted of people of Chinese racial heritage. By 1972 Indonesia had restored intimate relations with all of its neighbours except Singapore. The most important factor affecting relations between the two was a disposition on the part of Indonesians to regard Singaporeans not so much as Singaporeans but as Chinese. Against this background, the Lee-Suharto exchange acquired significance and did much to clear the air between the two countries. Indeed, the two leaders discovered that they shared mutual foreign policy objectives in Southeast Asia. Neither Suharto nor Lee attended the conference of heads of state of nonaligned nations at Algiers in September, although both countries were represented by their foreign ministers.

JAMES P. STERBA—THE NEW YORK TIMES

Children fill the entrance to their home of bamboo and cardboard in Jakarta. City officials estimated that three-fourths of the dwellings in this fast-growing urban centre are "inadequate and unsafe."

Without fanfare, Indonesia signed several border accords during the year, including an agreement with Singapore that delineated their sea border in the Straits of Singapore; "a memorandum of understanding" with Australia, which clarified the border between the Indonesian province of Irian Jaya and the Australian-administered territory of Papua New Guinea which was expected to attain independence in 1974–75; and an agreement with Malaysia and Thailand covering a contiguous sea frontier at the northern passageway of the strategic Straits of Malacca. The accords emphasized the about-face in Indonesian foreign policy under Suharto, as compared with Indonesia's "policy of confrontation" in the last days of the Sukarno regime.

(ARNOLD C. BRACKMAN)

INDONESIA

Education. Primary (1969–70), pupils 12,802,415, teachers 323,218; secondary (1968–69), pupils 1,121,181, teachers 81,620; vocational (1968–69), pupils 358,833, teachers 35,462; teacher training (1968–69), students 130,361, teachers 12,385; higher (1967–68), students 192,416, teaching staff 21,309.

Finance. Monetary unit: rupiah, with (Sept. 17, 1973) an official rate of 415 rupiah to U.S. $1 (free rate of 1,001 rupiah = £1 sterling). Gold, SDRs, and foreign exchange, central bank: (April 1973) U.S. $627 million; (March 1972) U.S. $347 million. Budget (1973–74) balanced at 862.4 billion rupiah. Gross domestic product: (1971) 3,697,000,000,000 rupiah; (1970) 3,340,000,000,000 rupiah. Money supply: (Jan. 1973) 476,180,000,000 rupiah; (Jan. 1972) 317.9 billion rupiah. Cost of living (Jakarta; 1963 = 100): (May 1973) 93,104; (May 1972) 74,186.

Foreign Trade. (1972) Imports U.S. $1,438,100,000; exports U.S. $1,533,900,000. Import sources: Japan 35%; U.S. 15%; West Germany 8%; Singapore 6%. Export destinations: Japan 49%; U.S. 15%; Singapore 8%; The Netherlands 5%. Main exports: petroleum and products 47%; timber 14%; rubber 12%; coffee 5%.

Transport and Communications. Roads (1972) 84,891 km. Motor vehicles in use (1972): passenger 277,210; commercial 131,175. Railways: (1970) 7,891 km.; traffic (1968) 3,884,000,000 passenger-km., freight 655 million net ton-km. Air traffic (1972): 1,253,800,000 passenger-km.; freight 22,452,000 net ton-km. Shipping (1972): merchant vessels 100 gross tons and over 513; gross tonnage 618,589. Telephones (Dec. 1971) 230,000. Radio receivers (Dec. 1970) 13,796,000. Television receivers (Dec. 1971) 95,000.

Agriculture. Production (in 000; metric tons; 1972; 1971 in parentheses): rice 19,500 (20,190); corn 2,269 (2,632); cassava (1970) 10,451, (1969) 11,034; sweet potatoes (1971) 2,154, (1970) 2,175; sugar, raw value *c.* 1,130 (1,045); tea *c.* 72 (72); copra *c.* 740 (*c.* 730); soybeans 515 (475); palm oil (estates only) *c.* 264 (248); peanuts 455 (467); coffee *c.* 210 (188); tobacco *c.* 70 (75); rubber *c.* 840 (811); fish catch (1971) 1,250, (1970) 1,249. Livestock (in 000; Dec. 1971): cattle *c.* 7,500; pigs *c.* 2,630; sheep *c.* 3,760; horses *c.* 600; buffalo *c.* 2,700; goats *c.* 7,000; chickens *c.* 67,000.

Industry. Production (in 000; metric tons; 1972): crude oil 63,339; coal 178; tin concentrates (metal content) 22; bauxite 1,283; electricity (excluding most industrial production; kw-hr.; 1970) 2,084,000.

Industrial Review

In 1972 industrial activity was buoyant: world manufacturing production rose by about 6½%, more than twice as fast as in 1971. This upturn was mainly due to greatly improved conditions in the United States, where booming activity followed the previous year's stagnation, but in practically all industrial countries the growth of manufacturing was higher than a year before. According to UN estimates, manufacturing in the less industrialized countries expanded faster than in the industrial countries.

Personal consumption remained the main source of demand; consumers' expenditure and private housing increased their shares in gross national product in almost all countries. Other private investment rose relatively fast in North America but still fairly slowly in Western Europe and Japan, although faster than in 1971. Stockbuilding also recovered, particularly in the U.S., but was a less powerful expansionary factor than might have been expected in a period of accelerating economic growth.

This pattern of demand differed considerably from the 1971 situation, and the change was reflected in production in the Organization for Economic Cooperation and Development (OECD) countries. There was a renewed rise of about 6% in the production of base metals, which had fallen more than 3% in 1971. Output of metal products rose similarly, following two years of stagnation. The production of chemicals also accelerated quite markedly; but the textiles and clothing industries, whose output had declined in 1970 and then recovered strongly in 1971, grew only very moderately, and the rate of increase of the food-beverages-tobacco sector was the lowest in some ten years.

The general upswing continued during the first half of 1973. Through the end of June total output, in terms of the gross national products, was approximately 7% greater than it had been in the previous 12 months, and the rise from the first half of 1972 to the same period in 1973 was even higher. The growth of manufacturing production was on the order of 10% or more on either basis of comparison. The cyclical peak of this boom, however, seemed to have been passed by the early autumn of 1973. There were signs of a slowdown in production in the U.S. and the U.K. about midyear. In many of the industrial countries, certainly in West Germany and France, limitations on capacity, both labour and equipment, appeared liable to brake the advance. Finally, many countries adopted restraining measures of various kinds in order to ease inflationary pressures and avoid "overheating" their economies, factors that were to have increasing impact over the following 12 months.

The original target of the U.S. administration, aiming at a 6% growth of the economy in 1972, was comfortably exceeded. Buoyant demand for consumer goods, a strong recovery in manufacturing investment, lively residential building activity, and the rebuilding of inventories were the main generators of expansion, and the deficit on the federal budget for 1972–73 was an important stimulative factor. By mid-1973—partly as the outcome of various measures taken in defense of the international position of the dollar, such as higher interest rates and reduced liquidity—the rate of growth had slowed down, affecting all sectors of demand for industrial products. Late in the year production was again adversely affected by the growing energy crisis, which was touched off by the refusal of Arab oil-producing nations to ship petroleum to the U.S. because of its support of Israel.

In Canada, industrial output was boosted by all categories of demand, especially by business investment. The Economic Council of Canada set for 1973–75 steeper targets than the achievements in the previous decade; these involved a 6% growth rate of the economy, with correspondingly faster progress of manufacturing output, and it seemed that for 1973 this target would be reached or exceeded.

Japanese industry recovered in 1972 from its previous temporary setback. The growth of real incomes stimulated private consumption; the availability of credit to both the corporate and private sectors at historically low interest rates, with the bank rate at 4¼% in the second half of 1972, contributed much to the increased investment of the nonmanufacturing sector and to the boom in residential construction. For some

Table I. Index Numbers of World Production, Employment, and Productivity in Manufacturing Industries
1963 = 100

Area	Relative importance		Production			Employment			Productivity*		
	1963	1972	1970	1971	1972	1970	1971	1972	1970	1971	1972
World†	1,000	1,000	151	154	164	...	...	...	...	...	...
Industrial countries	876	862	150	152	162	...	...	...	...	...	...
Less industrialized countries	124	138	158	171	184	...	...	...	...	...	...
North America‡	480	434	139	139	151	...	...	...	...	...	...
Canada	28	28	149	155	164	116	115	117	128	135	140
United States	452	406	139	139	149	114	110	112	122	126	133
Latin America§	49	57	164	178	192	...	...	...	...	...	...
Mexico	8	10	188	196	212	...	...	...	...	...	...
Asia ‖	88	127	212	220	237	...	...	...	...	...	...
India	16	14	135	139	148	...	...	...	...	...	...
Japan	55	100	264	277	297	120	121	121	220	229	245
Pakistan	3	...	186	164	...	...	...	...	...	...	...
Europe¶	350	347	149	152	160	...	...	...	...	...	...
Austria	7	8	154	164	179	101	104	106	152	158	169
Belgium	11	11	144	148	158	107	107	...	135	138	...
Denmark	6	6	149	153	160	108	110	110	138	139	145
Finland	4	5	166	165	185	115	119	121	144	139	153
France	51	55	154	162	177	100	100	102	154	162	173
Germany, West	89	89	156	158	164	107	106	108	146	149	152
Greece	2	3	186	204	231	117	125	130	159	163	177
Ireland	1	1	154	160	167	116	114	115	133	140	145
Italy	36	33	151	146	151	107	110	108	141	133	140
Netherlands, The	12	13	166	172	181	100	99	...	166	174	...
Norway	4	4	143	148	151	110	...	...	130	...	...
Portugal	2	2	182	176	203	...	...	...	...	...	...
Spain	12	19	210	218	255	125	127	...	168	172	...
Sweden	14	13	151	150	154	99	96	96	153	156	160
Switzerland	10	9	142	146	150	95	93	91	149	157	165
United Kingdom	73	58	127	127	131	100	97	93	127	131	141
Yugoslavia	13	16	174	191	206	119	125	132	146	153	156
Rest of the World♀	33	35	...	...	...	...	...	...	...	...	...
Australia	14	12	139	142	143	119	120	119	117	118	120
South Africa	5	5	159	163	167	155	161	164	103	101	102
Centrally planned economies♂	...	...	178	193	207	...	...	...	...	...	...

*This is 100 times the production index divided by the employment index, giving a rough indication of changes in output per person employed.
†Excluding Albania, Bulgaria, China, Czechoslovakia, East Germany, Hungary, Mongolia, North Korea, North Vietnam, Poland, Romania, and the U.S.S.R.
‡Canada and the United States.
§South and Central America (including Mexico) and the Caribbean islands.
‖Asian Middle East and East and Southeast Asia, including Japan.
¶Excluding Albania, Bulgaria, Czechoslovakia, East Germany, Hungary, Poland, Romania, and the U.S.S.R.
♀Africa, the Middle East, and Oceania.
♂These are not included in the above world total and consist of Albania, Bulgaria, Czechoslovakia, East Germany, Hungary, Poland, Romania, and the U.S.S.R.
Sources: UN *Monthly Bulletin of Statistics;* U.K. National Institute of Economic and Social Research, *Economic Review.*

Table II. Manufacturing Production in the U.S.S.R. and Eastern Europe
1963=100

Country	1970	1971	1972*
Bulgaria†	218	237	257
Czechoslovakia	158	184	218
Germany, East	154	162	172
Hungary	153	163	173
Poland	180	195	216
Romania	226	253	283
U.S.S.R.	178	192	205

*Provisional.
†General (all industries).
Source: UN *Monthly Bulletin of Statistics.*

time industrial investment remained sluggish because of excess capacity. It picked up, however, during 1973 to the extent that some large companies, including automobile manufacturers, were requested by the government to cut back their capital commitment in view of the inflationary pressures and shortages of skilled labour. Monetary and fiscal restraints were also introduced and were expected to slow down the very fast industrial growth. Japan was also affected late in 1973 by the cutbacks in Arab oil shipments.

In the spring of 1972 the manufacturing industry of the U.K. started to recover quite rapidly from its decline in 1971, and its output at the end of the year was running $8\frac{1}{2}\%$ higher than a year before; this progress continued in 1973, the growth reaching more than 10% at an annual rate toward midyear. Rapidly rising consumption in the private and public sectors, higher investments, and exports contributed to the boom, the exports benefiting from the gradual devaluation of the pound sterling. After midyear, the very fast progress slowed down, though the growth rate still exceeded the previous longer-term trend. The effects of the oil crisis and industrial disputes threatened to reduce industrial output drastically at year's end.

In France expansion continued uninterrupted through 1972 and 1973, though toward the middle of the latter year bottlenecks in capacity became more widespread. High consumers' expenditure and soaring exports induced industrialists to livelier investment activity toward the end of 1973.

Italian industry recovered only very slowly from its serious recession in 1971. Its growth in 1972 was about 3%, half of that in the late 1960s. The somewhat outdated industrial structure, a long period of flagging investment, and a recurrence of strikes were all responsible for this, apart from the slow recovery of domestic demand. By mid-1973 growth appeared to be accelerating, led by private consumption, somewhat revived investment, and exports, aided by devaluation of the lira.

Manufacturing industries of most smaller European countries expanded in 1972, and the prospects in each of those countries were for equal or faster growth in 1973. Spanish industry grew at a rate of 17% in 1972, following 4% in 1971, and Belgian industry doubled its growth rate; Austrian, Danish, and Dutch industries also increased their output faster than in the previous year. There was no change in the growth of Swiss production, and the growth rates in Norway and Yugoslavia lagged behind 1971, though in the latter at a high level. In the three countries where output fell in 1971 growth was resumed; in Finland and Portugal it was at a rate above 10%, while Sweden had a more moderate 3%.

Outside Europe some of the less industrialized countries such as India and Mexico succeeded in doubling the rate of growth of their manufacturing in 1972. South African industry advanced only moderately, whereas in Australia there was hardly any expansion.

Manufacturing in the U.S.S.R. continued to expand rapidly, at about 7% in 1972, although this rate was slightly lower than in 1971. Progress in Bulgaria, Hungary, and East Germany, at 6–8%, was comparable to that in 1971, whereas in Poland and Romania it accelerated, exceeding 10%. The fastest advance among the centrally planned economies was in Czechoslovakia at $18\frac{1}{2}\%$.

The generally expanding output, as well as the labour-saving equipment that had gradually been installed to reduce the effect of rising wage costs, resulted almost everywhere in higher productivity. In the major industrial countries output per hour worked in manufacturing rose faster in 1972 than in 1971, with the exception of the U.S. where this advance was fractionally slower. (G. F. RAY)

D.P.A./PICTORIAL PARADE

This giant blast furnace at the Peine-Salzgitter steelworks, Ilsede, W.Ger., was activated during 1973, with a capacity of 2,500 tons of raw iron per day. An elaborate system of dust filters helps meet environmental requirements, and sound absorbers muffle operating noise.

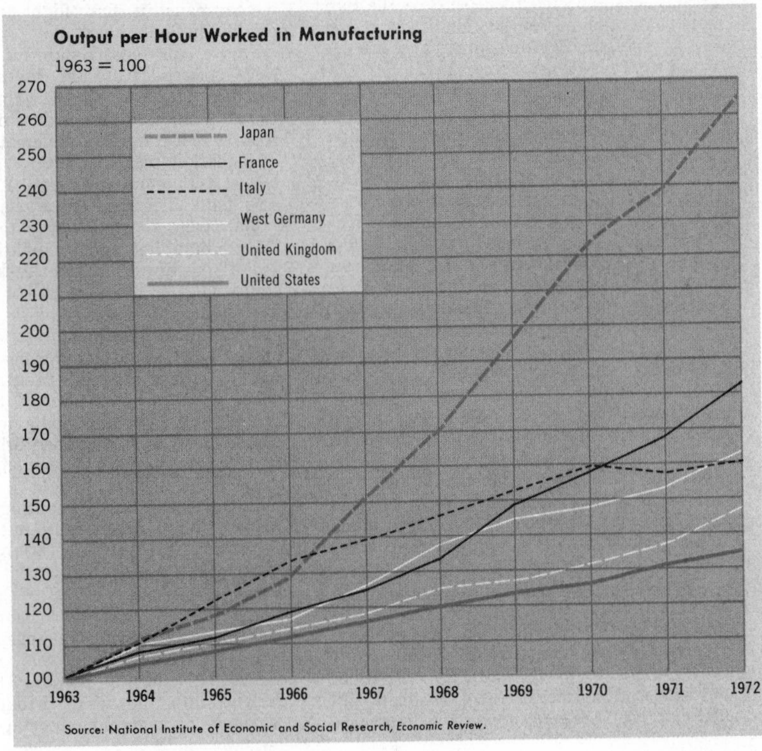

AEROSPACE

Recovery in the U.S. aerospace industry, a feature of 1972, leveled out in 1973. U.S. extrication from the war in Vietnam could be expected to have a further dampening effect. The European situation also remained rather static. Britain's annual aerospace sales, based on the first six months' figures, could be the highest ever, but France's two major manufacturers, Dassault and Aérospatiale, were reorganized on a firmer commercial footing, following poor 1972 figures.

The supersonic transport (SST) programs of Britain, France, and the U.S.S.R. remained the spearheads of aerospace programs. In September, the Anglo-French Concorde SST was the feature attraction at the opening of the Dallas-Fort Worth (Tex.) airport, and it then flew a full load of U.S. government and airline management officials from Washington to Paris in $3\frac{1}{2}$ hours, which augured well for its commercial introduction. Production of 16 aircraft and the purchase of long-lead time components for an additional six was authorized. Various improvements suggested by the manufacturers were being considered by the British and French governments at the year's end.

The Soviet Tu-44 SST suffered a setback when a preproduction aircraft broke up and crashed at the Paris Air Show in June. Aeroflot was understood to have 30 on order, and might eventually operate as many as 75.

The Boeing 747, McDonnell Douglas DC-10, and Lockheed TriStar remained the prestige planes. Boeing announced in September that it would go ahead with a new, short-fuselage "Jumbo," designated the 747SP (Special Performance), to meet an order for ten from Pan American World Airways. Designed for long-haul routes with low traffic density, such as New York-Tokyo, it could affect sales of the long-range versions of the existing trijets, the McDonnell Douglas DC-10-30 and the Lockheed L-1011-LR.

Launching of the long-range L-1011-2LR TriStar was expected to depend on the two main potential customers, British Airways and Air Canada. Britain's interest lay in sales of the uprated Rolls-Royce (1971) RB. 211 engine, of 48,000-lb. thrust, which was under development for this aircraft.

The DC-10 Twin, a two-engined version of the DC-10, emerged. Like the long-range TriStar, it awaited sufficient orders (minimum 30) to justify a go-ahead in production, at which time it could challenge Europe's big twin-engined transport, the A-300B Airbus. Plans for another competitor in this field, the 200-seat Europlane, a joint venture of British, West German, Swedish, and Spanish firms, were shelved.

During the summer, Boeing revealed details of its projected family of two-, three-, and four-engined 7X7 airliners, 1980s replacements for the 707, 727, and DC-8. Manufacture of these aircraft was to be shared with Italy and Japan. Sales of the Boeing 727, the world's most-built commercial jet transport, continued vigorous, and the 7X7 was temporarily shelved. Continued popularity of the 727 might also depress the market for the DC-10 Twin.

New power plants became almost as important as the aircraft themselves; 1973 was notable for the clarification of the "ten-(metric) ton" engine, a 25,000-lb. thrust power plant to power the 7X7 and other new-generation medium-size airliners. In October, the U.S. government sanctioned the use of General Electric F101 components (designed for the U.S. Air Force's new B-1A swing-wing bomber) as the basis of France's Snecma CFM56. Pratt & Whitney announced its equivalent JT10D project in June, with Motoren Turbinen Union of West Germany and Fiat of Italy as prospective partners. Rolls-Royce (1971) plans were based on the RB-235 design, though no international partners appeared to be in sight. In Britain, the Hawker Siddeley HS.146, was launched in September, with 50% British government support.

The F-14 financial crisis that threatened to put Grumman out of business came to a head during the spring, but an acceptable formula was worked out that should eventually make the swing-wing fighter—a direct replacement for the McDonnell Douglas Phantom—a profitable venture. All the new U.S. military aircraft were larger, exhibiting a level of technology superior to anything under way in Europe, and prospective F-14 and McDonnell Douglas F-15 customers were already in view. Technical developments included two lightweight fighters, the Northrop YF-17 and the General Dynamics YF-16, the aerodynamically advanced short-take-off-and-landing McDonnell Douglas YC-14, and the Boeing YC-15 transports.

The Anglo-French Jaguar entered service with the air forces of Britain and France. There were firm planning contracts for 400 Jaguars, and some industry observers believed that they might sell abroad as widely as the Hunter and Mirage III. Increasing importance attached to the Anglo-French Adour power plant, designed specially for the Jaguar and also selected for Japan's Mitsubishi T-2 trainer and Britain's HS.1182 Hawk.

Britain's Harrier remained the only vertical take-off and landing (VTOL) aircraft in service, a big breakthrough coming in August when Spain placed an order for eight Harriers, to be bought through the U.S. Marine Corps. U.S. interest in VTOL continued with the experimental supersonic XFV-12A fighter sponsored by the U.S. Navy, the Bell tilt-rotor XV-15 financed by NASA and the Army, and the Sikorsky S-69, which made its first flight in August but crashed in September.

One of the most significant new ideas to have emerged from the Vietnam war was the RPV (Remote Piloted Vehicle), used for the unmanned reconnaissance of North Vietnam, which proved both versatile and cheap. The market was difficult to assess, but all major U.S. companies had a stake in the new field. The RPV idea seemed likely to extend from reconnaissance to remote-controlled bombing and air-fighting, with the "pilot" sitting at a safe desk, and RPVs could well be the next major development in military aviation.

The most important industrial space event of the year was the agreement by Europe to take on the Spacelab program associated with the U.S. space shuttle. Spacelab, the means whereby the shuttle would become transformed into a manned orbiting laboratory, was a much lower-keyed project than the U.S. Skylab, but would provide Europe with the means of participating in U.S. technology and of eventually putting its own astronauts into orbit. (MICHAEL WILSON)

AUTOMOBILES

Many exceptional international developments presented new challenges to the automobile industry during 1973, ranging from the formal entry of Britain, Denmark, and Ireland into the EEC through the early warnings of a gasoline shortage in the U.S. in the spring to the crisis in oil supplies resulting from the Arab-Israeli war in the fall. Nevertheless, the production of cars and commercial vehicles in the U.S. showed a phenomenal advance (averaging nearly 19%) during the first eight months of 1973, compared with 1972, and smaller but significant gains were made by vehicle manufacturers in Canada, West Germany, France, and Sweden. Due mainly to a frequent dislocation of production schedules by strike action and absenteeism, the output of cars and commercial vehicles decreased by about 5% in the U.K. during the first half of 1973, and importers reaped the major benefit from a concurrent boom in demand. Industrial strife had an even more crippling effect upon vehicle production in Italy. The Japanese motor industry again registered a strong advance in output, but in Australia only a small gain was recorded.

A continuing paradox was that the general strengthening in the demand for cars and trucks occurred through a year when the attack upon all forms of road transport was intensified everywhere by ecologists supported, in varying degrees, by governmental agencies concerned with road safety, pollution, and noise. The threatened scarcity and increasing cost of liquid fuels (even before the October crisis) strongly influenced customer preferences in the choice of a car, especially in the U.S. where models of small and intermediate size accounted for a much higher proportion of total sales than in previous years. This trend accelerated following Pres. Richard Nixon's call for voluntary fuel-saving measures in November. Toward year's end American Motors, which specialized in small cars, was the only major U.S. manufacturer to report increased sales. Ford, General Motors, and Chrysler all announced layoffs, and many big-car plants curtailed production or were shut down; some were to be converted to small models, demand for which was outrunning supply. Reports indicated that the bottom had dropped out of the market for big used cars, and trade-in values of large models plummeted.

In the U.S., as in Europe, there was a strong demand for what might be termed an upgraded small car that was as well-equipped, as luxuriously furnished, and nearly as quiet at expressway cruising speeds as the larger cars. Usually based to a varying extent upon the body shell and/or mechanical parts of a lower priced model, these deluxe variants offered a comparably low operating cost at the penalty of a higher purchase price. Many desirable features and accessories, traditionally offered as options at extra cost, were included in the specifications and recommended price of cars of this class, which widened their appeal to buyers formerly accustomed to larger models. New examples of this trend, announced in the fall, were Ford's Mustang II in the U.S. and General Motors subsidiary Vauxhall's Magnum in the U.K.: two very different variations on an increasingly important theme. Another interesting development from GM was the announcement, in the U.S., of a high-performance engine option for the Vega with a special four-valve aluminum-alloy head developed by Cosworth in England.

One practical improvement that was widely adopted for 1974-model engines in the U.S. was motivated by the knowledge that federal emission standards would, before long, require consistent engine performance for 50,000 mi. As no conventional ignition system (using a mechanically operated contact-breaker) could give such service, the "breakerless" type of electronic ignition system became a standard fitting on a wider range of engines than in 1971–72. No change in the U.S. federal emission standards had to be met for the 1974 model year, but a slightly more severe requirement was enforced by California. The Canadian government announced in the fall that it did not propose to adopt the much more stringent restrictions that the U.S. government intended to impose after 1975.

Among the larger U.S. cars, one of the few new models was the Matador coupe (from American Motors), which had sweeping, uncomplicated contours bearing a strong resemblance to European styling. Chrysler changed the external sheet metal on many of the larger models but did not make any drastic alteration to their appearance. GM continued to hold the lead in the styling of attractive roofs and rear quarters for their large Chevrolet, Pontiac, Oldsmobile, and Buick coupes, with small side windows (of various geometric patterns) located at each side, behind the doors. An important innovation during the year was a new radical tire designed by GM engineers for manufacture by five of the leading tire companies.

Two entirely new European passenger-car models introduced during 1973 were the Austin Allegro (British Leyland) and the Opel Kadett (GM), each designed to compete in the most important sector of the "volume" market comprising cars appreciably larger than the "mini" class. The Allegro followed the traditional Austin front-drive transverse-engine configuration but was a little larger and decidedly more sophisticated in design and style than the 1100/1300 Austin series that it would eventually supersede. The principal innovation was a "Hydragas" suspension in which compressed nitrogen replaced steel springs. The Opel Kadett, of similar size, was much more conventional in its engineering design and appearance. It was expected to prove an acceptable successor to the previous and highly successful Kadett model. In the U.K., Vauxhall's new Magnum was basically a Viva but with a much more luxurious interior decor and equipment; British Ford pursued a similar policy by broadening the highly successful Cortina range with the introduction of the "200 E," a luxury model with attractive seating, interior trim, and instrumentation.

Other new European models of special significance were the Fiat 126 and the Volkswagen Passat: the former an updated, roomier, and more powerful version of the little rear-engine air-cooled Fiat 500 and the latter a considerably larger front-drive car in which the major mechanical units (and many of the body stampings) were derived from the higher-priced Audi "80" model introduced about a year earlier. In general, the European car manufacturers followed a policy of improving their existing models rather than embarking upon entirely new ventures, although in some cases (such as the 4½-litre range introduced by Mercedes Benz in the spring) the changes were extensive. In the sports car field, Porsche offered a larger engine equipped with a new Bosch "K-Jetronic" fuel injection system, and British Leyland installed a 3½-litre V-8 engine in the MGB sports car. Citroën announced its long-expected Wankel engine option for the GS model in August; the engine proved to be a two-rotor design and went into production at the new Comotor plant in the Saar, which was specially built and equipped for the purpose. Part of the Wankel "package" was a semi-automatic transmission.

A British innovation of particular interest was the Dunlop Denovo "Total Mobility" tire, fitted to a two-piece rim (without the usual well, or channel) so that the tire cover remained in place when deflated. In combination with other design innovations, the tire enabled the driver to retain control in the event of a blowout and could be run while flat at speeds up to 50 mph (and for a distance of 100 mi.) without damage or appreciable loss of steering control. Another British tire company (Avon) retained a well-base rim but closed the channel with a hoop of spring steel, after fitting the tire, so that the cover could not escape when deflated. The kind of channel required was appropriate to the costly light alloy type of wheel (used on many European sports cars) but could not be formed in a conventional steel wheel.

The efforts already being made by the original members of the EEC to harmonize the multiplicity of national regulations affecting the design and operation of motor vehicles (both cars and trucks) became even more tangled but, at the same time, received new impetus from the accession of the U.K. to the Community in January. Wide differences in many of these regulations had become an increasingly serious barrier to international trucking and an obstacle to export sales of both cars and commercial vehicles. In addition to primary considerations affecting safety, the environmental issues involved in exhaust pollution, noise, and the maximum permissible weights and dimensions of commercial vehicles all received urgent attention.

At the Frankfurt am Main, W.Ger., motor show, held in September after an interval of some years, the three leading British truck producers (British Leyland, Bedford, and Ford) all exhibited new models designed to take advantage of the progressive reduction in tariffs that was to occur in EEC countries during the next four years. Conversely, leading continental makers such as Sweden's Volvo and West Germany's Mercedes Benz were increasing their marketing efforts in the U.K. Increasing attention to driver comfort in the layout of cabs and controls was a noticeable European trend in heavy vehicle development. "Antilock" braking systems designed to ensure a straight-line stop even on treacherous road surfaces was one of several projected U.S. federal standards that were also being actively studied in Europe.

The Japanese government, which announced an intention to adopt the U.S. program with regard to antipollution regulations, gave immediate effect to incentives (in the form of reductions in tax) to buyers of new cars having specific antipollution equipment; it also gave similar encouragement for the conversion of existing cars. Honda announced that it had successfully developed its "CVCC" stratified charge system for a V-8 engine, following earlier research based on a smaller four-cylinder model. This approach continued to attract wide interest among engineers as a means for meeting future emission requirements without the sacrifice of economy in fuel consumption that other methods entailed. Fiat disclosed that it was working on another type of stratified charge engine.

Early in 1973 Datsun launched a new small car named the Violet, to supersede the Bluebird model, with optional 1,428-cc. and 1,595-cc. four-cylinder engines. The Mitsubishi Motor Corp., in which Chrysler participated, countered with a new Lancer range, also with engine options. At midyear, Mazda introduced an RX-4 model that was somewhat larger, more luxurious, and costlier than the RX-3, but used the same two-rotor Wankel engine. Toyota, claimed to rank third in size among the world's motor vehicle manufacturers, expected to build 2.3 million passenger cars and trucks in 1973.

A new high-performance model based on the HQ series was announced by GM-Holden in Australia early in the year. Called the Monaro GTS, it was offered with a choice of three V-8 engines ranging up to 5.7 litres in displacement. Ford scored a success with a six-cylinder version of the Cortina, using the Falcon engine, and brought out a new, large, and powerful LTD model (overall length, 204 in.). British Leyland developed the P.76, a special passenger car to compete in Australia with the Holden, the Ford Falcon, and the Chrysler Valiant. It had a choice of either a 2.6-litre six-cylinder or a 4.4-litre V-8 engine, both being somewhat enlarged versions of comparable power units made by BL in the United Kingdom.

(MAURICE PLATT)

Table III. Production and Exports of Motor Vehicles by the Principal Producing Countries

In 000 units

Country	1970 Passenger cars	1970 Commercial vehicles	1971 Passenger cars	1971 Commercial vehicles	1972 Passenger cars	1972 Commercial vehicles
Production						
United States	6,550.2	1,733.4	8,583.7	2,088.0	8,828.2	2,482.5
Japan	3,178.7	2,110.4	3,717.9	2,092.9	4,022.3	2,272.1
Germany, West	3,527.9	314.4	3,696.8	285.9	3,521.5	294.5
France	2,458.0	292.0	2,694.0	316.3	2,992.9	335.3
United Kingdom	1,641.0	457.5	1,741.9	456.2	1,921.3	408.0
Italy	1,719.7	134.5	1,701.1	116.0	1,732.4	107.4
Canada	937.2	250.2	1,096.1	276.0	1,154.5	319.9
U.S.S.R.	344.0	572.0	518.0	612.0	730.0	649.0
Australia	391.9	81.8	391.2	78.9	366.6	81.2
Sweden	279.0	31.2	287.4	29.7	317.9	33.0
Other countries	1,412.3	520.7	1,604.9	559.1	1,857.7	490.6
World total	22,439.9	6,498.1	26,033.0	6,911.0	27,445.5	7,473.7
Exports						
Germany, West	1,934.5	177.7	2,155.9	163.2	2,097.6	167.0
France	1,061.3	65.9	1,148.6	65.4	1,240.0	69.7
Japan	788.9	306.1	1,299.4	479.7	1,407.3	547.5
Canada	733.2	430.9	822.3	390.7	979.4	372.7
United Kingdom	690.3	172.3	721.1	194.7	627.5	139.9
Italy	632.1	38.9	640.2	40.3	659.1	40.6
United States	285.0	92.7	386.6	99.1	410.2	119.9
Sweden	186.5	24.0	212.5	23.4	195.2	23.7

Source: British Society of Motor Manufacturers and Traders, *The Motor Industry of Great Britain.*

BUILDING AND CONSTRUCTION

Expenditures for new construction in the U.S. during 1973 were estimated at over $130 billion, compared with the previous record outlay of $123.8 billion in 1972. The exact amount was uncertain because of the sharp decline in housing that occurred in August and September, and it was expected that housing starts would drop even further during the remainder of the year.

In January housing starts had reached a peak of 2,497,000 units at a seasonally adjusted annual rate. By August, with mortgage money becoming extremely scarce, the annual rate had dropped to 2,045,000 units. However, there was a large backlog of commitments, and it was anticipated that outlays for labour and equipment would continue strong throughout the year. It appeared that the total number of housing units started during 1973 would fall below the 1972 figure of 2,378,000 units but would still be slightly over two million.

At the beginning of 1973 the U.S. government placed a freeze on the housing subsidy programs, and the secretary of housing and urban development was instructed to find a less expensive way of obtaining adequate housing for low-income families. Various alternatives were explored, but no one clearly defined program emerged. The main action by the president involved a short-term program of easing the existing tight mortgage credit situation. There was a widely expressed view that the president wished to get the government out of the housing business.

In 1973, as in the three preceding years, mobile homes continued to be an important part of the U.S. housing market. Shipments of mobile homes were equal to over 20% of all housing starts in 1972, and the proportion was expected to be greater in 1973. The purchase of mobile homes rose rapidly during the year, and commercial banks and finance companies made credit readily available for this purpose. As of the end of 1973, mobile home owners in the U.S. had an aggregate obligation on mobile homes amounting to over $10 billion. The continuing inflationary trend in building costs made the mobile home an increasingly important type of low-cost housing.

While total outlays for construction in the U.S. in 1973 were expected to be approximately $7 billion greater than in 1972, much of the increase was attributable to inflation. On a constant dollar basis, it appeared that construction in 1973 would be close to the 1972 level of $89 billion. The U.S. Department of Commerce composite construction cost index was 139 (1967 = 100) for 1972, having moved from 135 in January to 144 in December. By August 1973 the index had reached 153, and the upward movement appeared likely to continue during the remainder of the year. Uncertainty concerning the government's monetary and fiscal policies and its housing policies made prediction of the price level difficult. The Department of Commerce price index of new one-family houses sold had risen from 131 (1967 = 100) in 1972 to 144.1 in the second quarter of 1973.

According to the U.K. National Institute of Economic and Social Research's *Economic Review,* combined national output in Western Europe in 1973 was higher than anticipated as a result of the widespread continuation of favourable business conditions. Italy was still plagued by a low level of investment, however, and efforts to stimulate construction through public works programs were not successful.

Building activity continued at a high level in Canada in 1973. However, in Canada, as in other parts of the world, spiraling inflation was creating problems in all areas of economic activity. In Australia housing starts, after rising sharply in 1972 and early 1973, showed signs of leveling off because of shortages of materials and labour and a reduction in available finances. The New Zealand economy expanded rapidly during the year, and business confidence was high. Investment in plant and equipment was up, and housing construction expanded strongly. An increase in public investment was planned in South Africa, but private investment in plant and equipment was not expanding. In Japan housing was up 34% in 1973.

(CARTER C. OSTERBIND)

CHEMICALS

Demand for products of the chemical industry, which was high throughout 1972, continued to climb during the first three quarters of 1973. Plants were operating at a high rate of capacity. Chemical prices were rising, and industry profits improved considerably. The problem of overcapacity that had plagued the industry in earlier years disappeared, and the industry and its customers found themselves in the position of coping with a broad range of shortages.

In the U.S., shipments of chemicals and allied products increased to $57,437,000,000 in 1972, according to the Department of Commerce. That represented a 10.7% increase over the $51,872,000,000 value of shipments in 1971. For the first six months of 1973, shipments totaled $33,898,000,000, higher by 18.4% than the $28,617,000,000 registered for the corresponding period of 1972. The U.S. Department of Labor's index of prices of chemicals and allied products averaged 104.2 (1967 = 100) in both 1971 and 1972. It rose during the first half of 1973 and was 110.8 in July. This represented a weighted index for a diverse group of chemicals, however. Thus, the price index for industrial chemicals dropped from 102.1 in 1971 to 101.2 in 1972 and then went up in the first half of 1973, reaching 103.4 in July. By contrast, the price index for inedible fats and oils declined from 133.5 in 1971 to 115.8 in 1972 and then soared through the first part of 1973 to reach 263.2 in July.

Chemical production set records. The U.S. Federal Reserve index of production for chemicals and allied products rose from 126.4 (1967 = 100) in 1971 to 139.6 in 1972. It continued the trend through the early part of 1973 and was 151.3 in July (seasonally adjusted). Production of resins (the basis for plastics) reached a new high in 1972 when it surpassed 23.6 billion lb., according to a preliminary estimate of the Society of the Plastics Industry.

The U.S. chemical industry continued to make a significant contribution to the country's balance of trade. The U.S. Department of Commerce reported chemical exports of $3,836,000,000 in 1971 and chemical imports for the same year of $1,612,300,000. In 1972 exports rose to $4,132,900,000, and imports to $2,014,800,000. Exports for the first six months of 1973 were $2,609,800,000, while imports were $1,225,700,000. Thus, the U.S. chemical trade surplus dropped from $2,223,700,000 in 1971 to $2,118,100,000 in 1972. But it recovered to $1,384,100,000 for the first half of 1973.

Against this background of heavy demand and firm prices, chemical companies in the U.S. were planning impressive increases in expenditure for new capacity. The McGraw-Hill fall survey of preliminary plans for capital spending in 1973 indicated that chemical companies planned to boost their spending in 1974 by 33% to $5,510,000,000.

Despite the strong economic climate and prevailing optimism, the chemical industry was facing a number of short- and long-term problems. For instance, it was a heavy user of electrical energy and fuel. The petrochemical segment depended upon petroleum products—natural gas, natural gas liquids, and refinery products—for raw materials. The already clouded outlook for energy worsened during the third quarter of 1973 as a result of the Arab-Israeli war and the subsequent ban on petroleum shipments to the U.S. by Arab nations. The chemical industry was facing up to a winter of uncertainty with regard to its ability to maintain operations in some plants. Delays in deliveries of equipment and structural materials and a possible shortage of engineering manpower also cast some doubt on the ability of the industry to carry out its expansion plans on schedule.

Because of differences in definitions for "chemical industry" in various countries and sharp fluctuations in the value of currencies, it was all but impossible to make a meaningful comparison of sales of chemical industries around the world. In general, however, they were flourishing while facing the same sort of problems and prospects as the U.S. industry.

Illustrative of the changes in currency was the situation in West Germany. The mark was worth 25 cents in 1969 and 31 cents in 1972. By the third quarter of 1973, it had gone as high as 43 cents. The country was experiencing cost increases in items such as labour. The Association of German Chemical Employers reported the hourly wage rate in 1968 was $2 per hour, less than half the comparable rate in the U.S. of $4.17 per hour. By 1973, however, the figure for West Germany was $5.87 per hour, while that for the U.S. had risen only to $5.71 per hour.

Despite this situation West German chemical companies made solid gains. Exports, which accounted for 36% of total chemical sales in 1968, were expected to make up 39.5% of sales in 1973. The country was looking toward a chemical export level that would surpass $10 billion for the first time. And although imports were growing even faster than exports, the country still expected a chemical trade surplus of $4.2 billion for 1973.

In Japan the chemical industry had shown remarkable growth, largely because of its ability to export. But throughout 1972 the country was beset with problems of overcapacity. In 1972, according to preliminary figures, chemical companies produced about $11 billion of product but sold only $9.5 billion. Capacity increases were not significant during 1973, and demand was coming into better balance with supply. The chemical industry, moreover, finding that yen revaluations were making the exporting of chemicals more costly, was seeking to invest considerable sums outside of Japan. Major projects revealed during 1973 indicated that chemical investment abroad would be $500 billion by 1980.

In the U.K. the chemical industry was having a record year. Indications by the third quarter were that chemical sales for 1973 would approximate $13.5 billion, a 12.8% increase over 1972. That would make it second only to West Germany among European chemical producers. The problem that was facing British producers was the government's wage-price freeze. That policy, according to British chemical men, meant that prices in some countries in Europe were 40% higher than the corresponding prices in the U.K. By the third quarter of 1973, chemical prices in the country had risen only 1%.

The industry was trying to offset that by stepping up its chemical exports at the higher prevailing prices on the world market. Indications were that chemical exports in 1973 would amount to $3,050,000,000, approximately 20% more than in 1972. However, imports were rising at an even faster rate, expected to be 25% over 1972.

Détente with the Soviet Union became an important strategy for the U.S. during 1973, and some industry observers believed that the policy could involve major changes in the chemical industries of Western countries. One of the early results of the new willingness to exchange was a $400 million a year agreement between the U.S.S.R. and Occidental Petroleum. The agreement called for Occidental to supply superphosphoric acid, technology, and equipment in exchange for ammonia, urea, and potash.

(DONALD P. BURKE)

ELECTRICAL

An EEC business survey carried out in the first half of 1973 reported that the production outlook for electrical equipment had improved over the previous year. Similarly, the Liaison Group for the European Engineering Industries (ORGALIME) reported improved conditions following the slowdown that had begun around 1971. However, the upturn was not expected to be at as fast a rate as that between 1968 and 1970.

Inflationary strains and currency fluctuations had badly distorted world trade statistics since 1971, making it difficult to judge accurately the performance of the electrical industry. However, the latest annual reports of the major electrical manufacturers provided some economic indicators.

General Electric Co. reported a 9% increase in sales in 1972 and a 14% increase during the first six months of 1973. GE's president, R. H. Jones, set a target of earnings improvement in 1974 "despite the predicted slowdown in the United States economy." He noted that the company's backlog of orders increased steadily in 1973 and by October stood at a record $12 billion. The two main West German companies slightly improved their performances in 1973 compared with 1972. AEG (Allgemeine-Elektrizitäts-Gesellschaft) expected 1973 sales to rise by 12% and Siemens by 10%. It was believed that the expected increases would be due to a rise in consumer expenditure, and that increases in sales of capital goods were likely to be slow but could improve in 1974. In France, Compagnie Général d'Electricité recorded a 16.5% increase in sales turnover in 1972 and forecast a 17% increase in 1973. The Swiss Brown, Boveri group had a modest turnover increase of 2.6% in 1972. In Britain, GEC's turnover ($2,650,000,000 in 1971) increased by 5% in 1972. The Swedish Allmänna Svenska Elektriska Aktiebolaget (ASEA) sales showed a 24% increase in 1972 compared with 1971. Matsushita of Japan reported a 9.5% increase in sales in 1972 and expected a 16% increase in 1973.

Good growth prospects for French electrical companies were forecast in a mid-1973 report by U.K. stockbrokers James Capel & Co. They were, however, cautious in their forecasts on the prospects for British companies and pessimistic about the West German market. One significant factor in Capel's recommendation of French companies was the dramatic rate of increase in capital investment since the late 1960s, which had resulted in an 11.7% per annum increase in output per employee in the French electrical industry. This compared with annual increases in output per employee of 2.6 and 6.3% in West Germany and Britain, respectively.

Domestic appliances and power station equipment accounted for the majority of orders placed in 1972–73. Demand for industrial equipment was low. In Europe, a survey showed that British households were falling behind many continental households in appliance ownership. More homes in West Germany, Sweden, and The Netherlands had home laundry equipment and refrigerators than British homes, but there were proportionally more television sets in Britain than in any other European country.

Long-term prospects for electrical heating appliances improved steadily, particularly in the U.S. In 1973 the Tennessee Valley Authority (TVA) began promoting the installation of electrically operated heat pumps. The heat pump was a practical energy conservation device that worked in the opposite way from a refrigerator, extracting large quantities of low-grade heat from outside a building and supplying smaller quantities of high-grade heat for use inside the building. A domestic heat pump should deliver about twice as much energy, in the form of high-grade heat, as it consumes in electricity. TVA believed that a change to electric space heating should be publicly encouraged in view of the U.S. energy crisis.

Electric storage batteries continued to receive the attention of research laboratories throughout the world because of their importance to the development of electric cars. But in all industrialized countries, the major research and development expenditure concentrated on equipment for electricity generation and power transmission. If expected future growth in the demand for electric power was to be satisfied and environmental problems were to be overcome, more powerful generators and transmission circuits would be required.

The superconducting generator was one of the more important developments. At the Massachusetts Institute of Technology, a large (2 Mva) development machine with a superconducting rotor was built in 1973, following successes with an experimental (40 kva) generator. Previously, it had been thought to be impossible to refrigerate the rotor, and machines with superconducting stators had been developed. The MIT machine had two major advantages. No iron was required for magnetic flux, and there was no need to insulate each conductor from the earth. Second, better utilization of the transmission lines was possible because of higher dynamic stability. The MIT superconducting generator design was thought to be competitive with current sizes of conventional machines, and the margin would increase as machine sizes increased.

(T. C. J. COGLE)

GLASS

European container manufacturers were hard pressed to keep customers supplied in the first half of 1973, and there were reports of increased profitability in the flat-glass industries. The handmade sector of the Swedish glass industry recovered after several years of crisis, reporting a 25% increase in output in 1972.

Container manufacturers in the U.S., Japan, and Europe continued to be involved in environmental disputes. Environmentalists preferred returnable containers for beer and soft drinks to the nonreturnable variety, and a differential deposit system favouring returnable containers was introduced in a few areas of the U.S. and Canada. Emission of toxic fumes from chimney stacks and noise were two other areas where the glass industry had to reexamine its processes for environmental reasons.

The glass industries of the U.K., Ireland, and Denmark gained a representation on the Comité Permanent, the organization through which glass manufacturers had contact with the EEC Commission, and were thus involved in discussions aimed at harmonization in certain aspects of marketing throughout the EEC.

Pilkington Brothers Ltd. announced worldwide availability of a reflection-free glass for instrumentation. The glass, introduced as a safety measure, had a textured surface without loss of clarity. The West German firm Carl Zeiss announced an improved mechanical design for light microscopes, replacing the gallows type that had been in use since the mid-19th century. In the U.S. three Bell Laboratories introduced a method of fabricating efficient light-carrying fibres from a single material. The fibre comprised a tube, a solid inner rod, and a supporting plate for the rod, all manufactured from identical low-light-loss glass, with the solid rod as the light-carrying centre core of the fibre. Photochromic glass, which automatically darkens as light increases, became popular for ophthalmic use, particularly sunglasses. Both Corning Glass Works and the U.K. company Chance-Pilkington announced a new line of photochromic glasses.

Corning International Corp. and Saint Gobain (France) exchanged their minority interests in the French companies Électro-Réfractaire and Sovirel. Corning also purchased James A. Jobling & Co. (U.K.) from Thomas Tilling Ltd.; Corning's existing manufacturing facilities included Sovcor SA in France, manufacturers of electronic components, and Corning Nederlandse Fabrieken BV, makers of glass ceramic ovenware. Saint Gobain extended its interests in Europe, taking control of the Belgian company Glaceries Réunies, and showed interest in the U.K. market through being listed on the London Stock Exchange. The U.S. Owens-Illinois, with the Australian Consolidated Industries, took controlling interest in a new glass-container plant opened in Jakarta, Indon., in February 1973.

A glassworks for both automatic and handmade glassware neared completion in Hyderabad. Said to be the largest glassworks in India, it was built with Hungarian support. In Malta the Chinese government was building a factory for ornamental glass, and in Israel, Koor Phoenicia Glass Works, in partnership with Glaverbel of Belgium, completed a project for the manufacture of sheet glass, at least half of which would be exported to the U.S.

A bizarre use of glass was reported from Vancouver Island, B.C. A certain George Plum built himself a castle from the bottles left by visitors. His preference was for those of a certain English gin. (CYRIL WEEDEN)

IRON AND STEEL

Boom conditions prevailed for the international iron and steel industry in 1973, accompanied by a marked degree of inflation. However, much of the industry was affected by international monetary adjustments, while for some producers the enlargement of the EEC constituted an event of profound significance.

Recovery from the deep depression of 1971 had accelerated during the latter part of 1972. World steel output in 1972 totaled 629 million metric tons, an increase of 8.2%, and world production of crude steel in 1973 was estimated to have risen a further 10% to some 690 million metric tons. The industry was able to exploit capacity based on investments made during the previous period of strong demand in 1969–70. Even so, lack of productive capacity proved to be the chief limiting factor. Shortages, acute in some cases, were widespread.

There were inflationary increases in raw material and labour costs during the year, and steel prices on the international market rose substantially. But in some cases, prices charged on domestic markets were restrained by government intervention, and although most companies experienced some improvement in profits, overall there was no evidence that the adverse profit trend in steel was being reversed.

Repeated upheavals among international currencies during the year brought sudden and arbitrary changes in the relative competitiveness and profitability of exports. This created especially difficult situations for producers in countries whose currencies were upvalued. The voluntary restraint arrangements in the U.S. market, first established at the beginning of 1969 and renewed and developed in 1972, were maintained. However, because of world steel shortages, high prices prevailing in other markets, and the effects of the depreciation of the dollar, the U.S. market was less attractive to Japanese and European Coal and Steel Community (ECSC) exporters, and the agreed tonnages were not attained in 1973.

On April 1 tariff cuts were made between the original six EEC members and the three new member countries, reducing duties on industrial products, including steel, to 80% of the basic levels. A further 20% reduction was to take place on Jan. 1, 1974.

Steel production in the U.S. was estimated in the neighbourhood of 135 million metric tons in 1973, an increase of some 12%. With demand for consumer durables particularly strong, domestic steel shipments were expected to set records, while imports appeared likely to decline by at least 15%. Shortages were experienced in many areas. Capital expenditure by steel companies, having fallen in both 1971 and 1972, probably rose by more than 35% in 1973, without, however, regaining the 1970 level.

The Japanese steel market was subject to severe overheating during the year. Crude steel output was expected to rise almost 25% to a level approaching 120 million metric tons, but shortages of labour and of such services as water and electricity prevented further expansion, so that heavy home demand could not be fully satisfied. "Spot" prices for all products rose to levels last attained in 1957.

Crude steel output in the enlarged EEC was estimated at 150 million metric tons in 1973, an increase of 8.6% over 1972. During 1972 the steel industries of the original six members of the ECSC had experienced some increased activity, but in 1973 demand broadened and intensified, first in the consumer goods sector and then in the equipment and construction sectors as well. Shortages developed and prices rose.

U.K. entry into the EEC entailed conformity with the Treaty of Paris (1951) by which the ECSC had been established in 1952. ECSC steel products were accordingly excluded from the legislation embodying Stage Two of the U.K. government's anti-inflation program, and U.K. prices for ECSC steel products were raised by almost 10% in the spring. Further increases were made in the fall, but prices on the British market remained substantially below the levels prevailing in the rest of the ECSC for virtually all products.

Production in the U.S.S.R. and in Eastern Europe continued to rise. Soviet crude steel output was expected to reach some 130 million metric tons in 1973, 5 million metric tons more than in 1972. The increase was attributable both to more intensive exploitation of existing capacity and to the commissioning of new plant.

(TREVOR MACDONALD)

MACHINERY AND MACHINE TOOLS

The worldwide demand for machinery and machine tools was extremely good in 1973. The trend that started in 1972, after a depressed period of several years, presented a bright outlook for all of 1973.

World demand for farm machinery was accelerated by the higher prices for farm products and the need to increase production to meet the demand. Many U.S. firms found exceedingly high demand for their products in the large wheat-producing countries of Canada, Argentina, Australia, France, and the U.S. Japanese manufacturers of farm machinery had a very good year and increased their competition in the world market.

The extensive worldwide search for oil in 1973 brought about new developments in machinery for that type of exploration. In addition to producing the conventional drilling machinery, manufacturers were devoting much research to new equipment for offshore oil exploration. Companies were working on projects that could replace offshore oil platforms with equipment and machinery that would be installed on the ocean floor. Should this research prove successful, manufacturers of this type of equipment might experience a sales boom in the near future as pressures increased in the search for new sources of oil.

Pollution-control machinery remained in great demand in 1973 as the U.S. Environmental Protection Agency's regulations caused companies and other agencies to appropriate large capital expenditures to remedy pollution problems. Throughout the world attention was focused on these problems, and manufacturers of this equipment should continue to find good markets.

U.S. machine tool orders for the third quarter of 1973 exceeded any previous period since 1956, when combined metal-forming and metal-cutting tool statistics

Table IV. World Production of Pig Iron and Blast Furnace Ferroalloys
In 000 metric tons

Country	1968	1969	1970	1971	1972
World	376,320	407,420	426,030	423,060	445,790
U.S.	80,540	86,620	83,320	74,110	81,110
U.S.S.R.	78,790	81,630	85,930	89,260	92,300
Japan*	46,400	58,150	68,050	72,740	74,050
Germany, West	30,310	33,760	33,630	29,990	32,000
United Kingdom	16,700	16,650	17,670	15,420	15,310
France	16,450	18,210	19,220	18,350	19,010
China*†	15,500	16,000	16,000	19,000	21,000
Belgium	10,370	11,210	10,840	10,390	11,780
Italy*	7,840	7,780	8,330	8,530	9,420
Canada*	7,600	6,770	8,280	7,810	8,470
India	7,290	7,190*	6,900	6,670	7,080
Czechoslovakia*	6,920	7,040	7,620	8,070	8,360
Poland	6,640	7,030	7,300	7,500	7,810
Australia*	5,290	5,800	6,150	6,130	6,490
Luxembourg*	4,310	4,870	4,810	4,590	4,670
South Africa*	3,830	3,930	3,930	4,010	4,400
Brazil	3,350	3,700	4,200	4,690	5,290
Romania	2,990	3,490	4,210	4,380	4,890
Netherlands, The*	2,820	3,460	3,590	3,760	4,280
Spain*	2,780	3,330	4,160	4,830	5,930
Sweden*	2,490	2,500	2,610	2,570	2,350
Austria*	2,470	2,820	2,960	2,850	2,850
Germany, East	2,330	2,100	2,000	2,030	2,150
Hungary	1,650	1,760	1,840	1,990	2,060
Mexico*	1,600	1,700	1,660	1,690	1,900
Yugoslavia*	1,200	1,200	1,270	1,510	1,810
Bulgaria*	1,080	1,120	1,200	1,330	1,520

*Pig iron only.
†Estimated.
Source: British Steel Corporation.

Table V. World Production of Crude Steel
In 000 metric tons

Country	1968	1969	1970	1971	1972	1973 Year to date	1973 No. of months	Percent change 1973–72
World	529,000	574,000	595,000	581,000	629,000	...	...	...
U.S.*	119,260	128,150	119,310	109,270	120,750	90,760	8	+14.7
U.S.S.R.	106,530	110,310	115,880	120,640	126,000	65,000	6	+ 4.2
Japan	66,890	82,170	93,320	88,560	96,900	77,910	8	+26.4
Germany, West	41,160	45,320	45,040	40,310	43,700	32,620	8	+13.6
U.K.	26,280	26,850	28,320	24,180	25,320	20,000	9	+ 8.4
France	20,410	22,510	23,770	22,860	24,050	16,450	8	+ 5.5
Italy	16,960	16,430	17,280	17,450	19,810	12,990	8	− 0.4
China†	15,000	16,000	18,500	21,000	23,000	...	...	...
Belgium	11,570	12,830	12,610	12,440	14,530	10,430	8	+10.9
Poland	11,010	11,250	11,750	12,690	13,480	7,010	6	+ 4.2
Czechoslovakia	10,560	10,800	11,480	12,090	12,730	7,710	7	+ 3.6
Canada	10,210	9,350	11,200	11,040	11,860	8,860	8	+10.9
Australia	6,600	7,030	6,840	6,750	6,750	4,920	8	+16.4
India	6,450	6,560	6,280	6,100	6,860	4,680	8	+ 4.2
Sweden	5,090	5,320	5,500	5,270	5,260	3,650	8	+ 9.9
Spain	5,080	5,980	7,390	8,020	9,530	7,110	8	+16.8
Luxembourg	4,830	5,520	5,460	5,240	5,460	3,940	8	+ 8.8
Germany, East	4,700	4,820	5,050	5,350	5,750	...	...	...
Brazil	4,450	4,920	5,390	6,000	6,570	4,600	8	+ 7.2
Romania	4,320	5,540	6,520	6,800	7,400	...	...	...
South Africa	4,050	4,620	4,760	4,880	5,340	3,750	8	+ 6.5
Netherlands, The	3,710	4,720	5,030	5,080	5,570	3,740	8	+ 1.5
Austria	3,470	3,930	4,080	3,960	4,070	2,820	8	+ 5.1
Mexico	3,260	3,470	3,880	3,820	4,360	3,140	8	+11.6
Hungary	2,900	3,030	3,110	3,110	3,270	1,660	6	+ 1.2
Yugoslavia	2,000	2,220	2,230	2,450	2,590	1,380	6	+ 7.6
Argentina	1,560	1,690	1,820	1,910	2,110	1,400	8	+ 3.9
Bulgaria	1,460	1,510	1,800	1,950	2,120	1,300	7	+ 3.3

*Excludes production of independent foundries.
†Estimated.
Sources: British Steel Corporation; International Iron and Steel Institute.

were first tabulated. In the first nine months total domestic and foreign orders were $1,910,000,000, compared with $948.4 million for the same period in 1972. This nine-month figure surpassed any yearly totals except for 1966.

In 1973 U.S. manufacturers benefited by sales to Eastern European countries and with the devaluation of the dollar were able to compete more favourably in other foreign markets. The dollar devaluation also gave U.S. manufacturers an advantage because imported machines were relatively more expensive than in past years. Another favourable factor was the lifting of many U.S. government controls on machine tool exports. The National Machine Tool Builders' Association announced in September that agreement with the Soviet machine tool industry had been reached for exhibitions of U.S. machine tools in the Soviet Union. In return, the association planned to assist Soviet builders in exhibiting their tools at the 1974 International Machine Tool Show in Chicago.

The high rate of domestic orders in the U.S. could be attributed to several factors. Modernization in industries was stimulated by the investment tax credit and the asset depreciation guidelines. The shortage of skilled labour in many plants necessitated the use of improved new machines to increase production. An additional favourable factor foreseen by machine tool builders was a growing demand for new equipment because of the increasing age of many machines that needed replacement. Therefore, capital investments should continue to stimulate the market into 1974.

Ultrasonic metal forming, developed by a British firm, was a new development in 1973 that promised to be a significant improvement for draw ironing operations. Ultrasonics Ltd. in Yorkshire, Eng., produced the equipment, which reduces the friction between the workpiece and dies by transmitting a high-frequency cyclic motion to the workpiece.

Electrical-discharge machine sales increased significantly in 1973. New machines were designed for a wider range of production applications, and it was anticipated that 1973 would show a 40% sales growth over 1972. The metalworking industry was offered an advanced electrochemical machining method, developed and patented by General Electric Co. The electrostream process produced more precise, smaller, and deeper drilling operations than other processes permitted. It was especially effective in drilling metals too hard for conventional methods to machine.

Orders of machinery and machine tools in 1974 could only be adversely affected if the worldwide energy crisis caused companies to start cutbacks in anticipation of production dislocations. In the U.S. it was anticipated that there would be a 7% increase in general industrial machinery production in 1974. (ORLAND B. KILLIN)

NUCLEAR INDUSTRY

Enrichment of uranium was the big news of 1973 in the nuclear industry. The development program sponsored by the British, Dutch, and West German governments reached the point where the joint company set up to market enrichment services could now negotiate with customers. Plants being built would utilize the centrifuge technique. The technique offered greater flexibility in plant construction and operation than the diffusion process used in the U.S. Another European effort, sponsored by the Eurodif group, aimed to construct a diffusion enrichment plant using a French design. South Africa's enrichment program remained secret.

Sharing technology with another country might solve U.S. problems. The Canadian company Brinco Ltd. proposed using its James Bay hydroelectric development project to supply cheap electrical power for a U.S.-designed diffusion plant. Canada, like Australia, had large quantities of uranium. Japan expressed willingness to help finance a plant anywhere since it would need enrichment in the future. The Soviet Union also offered spare capacity and signed a contract with the largest West German utility, RWE (Rheinisch-Westfälisches Elektrizitätswerk AG), and with other German utilities.

Gulf Oil of the U.S. and Shell Oil of the U.K. and The Netherlands merged nuclear interests. Shell would take a half interest in Gulf Energy and Environmental Systems, which had orders for six high-temperature gas-cooled reactor (HTGR) units as well as the Fort St. Vrain prototype plant. The race for Western Europe's first prototype fast breeder reactor (FBR) ended. France's Phénix plant went into operation on August 31, followed by a British plant in Scotland at the end of 1973. The Phénix project's phenomenal success was expected to lead to the construction of two commercial plants of 1,300 Mw. capacity, one in France and the other in West Germany. The U.S. breeder program finally got under way with the awarding of the primary contract to Westinghouse Electric Corp. The program was about two years behind the West German-Benelux project, SNR-300. Fusion reactor development received a major impetus from two directions. The U.S. Atomic Energy Commission (AEC) proposed advancement of its program by five years, and the EEC Commission approved the building of a large experimental facility in the U.K.

In the U.S., the start-up of the first units of over 1,000 Mw. and the ordering of at least six plants to be built on floating platforms and located within man-made barrier reefs about three miles from the Florida shore (to be built by a company jointly owned by Westinghouse and Tenneco Corp.) were features of 1973. The start-up of the first prototype high-temperature gas-cooled reactor (HTGR), built by Gulf General Atomic Inc., was also expected. A recurrent problem with Westinghouse pressurized water reactor (PWR) fuel, that of fuel rod flattening, again surfaced. The AEC was not satisfied with General Electric's explanation as to why the problem was irrelevant to its own boiling water reactor (BWR) fuel, and so restricted the operation of ten BWRs.

Other significant events included the ordering of six identical units by one utility, and an order for several identical units by a group of utilities. Advantages included standardization of components, design, and experience, and accompanying cost savings. The AEC's attempt to allow private industry access to its enrichment technology met with poor response from industry, largely because of advances made in centrifuge enrichment technology in Europe.

The U.K. made a major attempt to revitalize its nuclear industry, which had had no new orders for nuclear plants since 1967. The government set up a single company, the National Nuclear Corp., both to build nuclear plants and to enter the fiercely competitive international marketplace. The new Nuclear Power Advisory Board had the task of choosing a reactor type to be built by the new company. A decision was expected by early 1974, and there was talk of ordering a U.S. light-water reactor. In West Germany Kraftwerk Union's virtual monopoly in reactor construction ended when an order was placed with a joint company of Deutsche Babcock & Wilcox AG and Brown, Boveri & Cie AG, utilizing a B. & W. (U.S.) design.

In France, which had started building light-water reactors, first orders had gone to Framatome to build PWRs under a Westinghouse license. A second supplier chosen by the national utility Électricité de France, Compagnie Générale d'Électricité, was scheduled to build BWRs under a General Electric license.

Canada made a notable breakthrough. The Canadian reactor system (Candu), which had suffered from many technical problems, was vindicated as the four units of Canada's first commercial plant became operational. That success helped Canada to win an important export order, for a Candu plant in Argentina. The Ontario government planned to build approximately 10,000 Mw. of Candu capacity during the 1970s and early 1980s, and other provinces also showed interest.

After several years of controversy in Switzerland, two contracts were placed. The long-suspended Leibstadt project was awarded to a joint Brown, Boveri & Cie and General Electric consortium, and the contract for the Gosgen site went to Kraftwerk Union. Local community opposition was slowly appeased. Japan suffered increased opposition to nuclear power, although most projects continued uninterrupted. However, the nuclear ship "Mutsu" was prevented by local fishermen from starting sea trials.

One Spanish utility finally ordered a BWR from General Electric. Finland ordered two Soviet 440 Mw. units (Novovoronezh type) for the state-owned utility, and a private group of utilities ordered a BWR from the Swedish manufacturer ASEA-ATOM. In Sweden, nuclear power became a political issue, with the main opposition party calling for a moratorium on the future power program until all safety issues had been fully satisfied. Taiwan ordered two General Electric BWRs.

The less developed countries, long promised nuclear power by the rest of the world, were still not much closer to acquiring it in 1973, although both Pakistan and India made significant headway.

(RICHARD W. KOVAN)

PAINTS AND VARNISHES

The paint industry entered 1973 with some foreboding. Toward the end of 1972 a number of important raw materials had begun to show sharp price rises. At first these were mainly the natural products such as shellac and castor oil, but the movement spread to such vital commodities as titanium dioxide and organic solvents, and left the industry facing the prospect of greatly increased costs.

The growth of powder coatings proved sufficient to attract those major paint manufacturers who did not already have a stake in the market. The introduction of polyester, acrylic, and polyurethane types to complement the well-established epoxy powders gave promise of expanding the market at the expense of conventional industrial finishes. Since powder coatings do not cause pollution, the process was speeded by worldwide concern over the environment.

Output of paints and varnishes in the U.K. increased 4–5% in volume and 11% in value in 1972. The largest increases (over 10% in value) were in decorative emulsion paints and in industrial cellulose and oil-synthetic paints. There was no growth in oil-synthetic paints for decorative use, and the distemper market continued to decline. Official U.K. statistics, compiled from returns from establishments employing 25 or more persons, showed total sales of £230.7 million, compared with £207.9 million for 1971. Total sales for the industry were estimated at £250 million. The number of employees in the U.K. paint industry at mid-1972 was about 31,000, a decrease of only 1–2% compared with a decline of 5% over the previous two years.

The picture was similar in most other EEC countries. In France total sales, at 795,000 tons, showed a 6% increase, and decorative paints had their best year since 1967. The value of sales reached Fr. 2,430,-000,000, a gain of 11%. French paint imports from the original six EEC countries were 2.5 times the level of exports, while sales to the U.K. were 63% more than in 1971. Paint makers in Italy, suffering from slackness of the economy and higher labour costs, nevertheless achieved a gain of 4% by volume, attributable partly to the high consumption per capita (14 kg., compared with 12 kg. in Switzerland and Belgium) and partly to stockpiling by householders before the introduction of the value-added tax.

The U.S. paint industry enjoyed a reasonably successful year in 1972, with sales expanding 6% by volume to 927.2 million gal. and 6.3% by value to $3,010,300,000. The main gains were achieved in industrial coatings, up 7.2% by volume.

In Finland, where the preceding year had been marked by severe labour disputes, the industry was able to increase prices for the first time since 1967. Sales rose a remarkable 26.7% in value. Paint sales in South Africa reached a record 80 million litres, worth R 68 million. Plascon-Evans, with 44% of the market, had an enviable 25% return on capital. Powder coatings were reported to have "caught on splendidly."

International trends during 1972 included the growing popularity of emulsion paints and powder coatings and the rising cost of raw materials. In the U.K. emulsion paints accounted for approximately £28 million of the £50 million retail paint market. The ICI (Imperial Chemical Industries Ltd.) Dulux brand was still leading with some 28% of the market, but its share was eroded by the Crown Plus Two brand (Reed Group), which at 17.3% had surpassed the Berger brands Magicote and Brolac (14%). The Woolworth household brand (Donald Macpherson) held 10%. Total advertising expenditure reached £2.3 million, with 80% spent on television. (LIONEL BILEFIELD)

PAPER AND PULP

World production of paper and paperboard increased by nearly 7% in 1972, to a total of some 141 million metric tons. The increase exceeded the long-term average annual gain of about 5%, reflecting sharply improved business conditions in the principal world markets.

The upturn followed two years of relatively slow growth. In 1971 production rose by less than 2% and in 1970, by just slightly more than 2%. In both years there was a substantial surplus of productive capacity for some products, such as newsprint and pulp. This caused curtailments in output, some mill closures, and large reductions in earnings, especially in North America and Europe.

The change for the better, which became apparent by the spring of 1972, was surprisingly swift. By year's end, pulp and paper manufacturing facilities in general were fully occupied, and demand and supply for the major products had come approximately into balance. This situation continued through 1973, and there was evidence of shortages in some parts of the world. A severe U.S. newsprint shortage resulted largely from a strike in Canadian mills.

The recession in 1970–71 slowed expansion in manufacturing capacity, and growth was still relatively moderate in 1973. In the U.S., the largest producing nation, paper and paperboard capacity was expected to increase by only 2.4% annually during 1974–76, compared with an average annual increase of 3.8% in 1956–73. In second-ranking Canada, productive capacity for wood pulp would rise by about 3.2% annually in 1972–75, and paper and paperboard by 2.8%, compared with average gains of 4.2% and 3.8%, respectively, in 1952–72. By late 1973, with recovery in the industry well advanced and prices on the rise, it appeared that expansion was once again gathering speed. However, two years or more are required to build a new pulp and paper mill or to complete major expansion of an existing one.

By far the largest portion of pulp and paper manufactured throughout the world in 1972 was produced and consumed in the same country. Nevertheless, exports totaled over 40 million tons, with Canada and Scandinavia accounting for the biggest single shares, each about one-third.

Some significant trends were becoming apparent. One was the gradually increasing need of Western Europe to supplement its own large production with imports from America, chiefly in the form of wood pulp, newsprint, and packaging papers and paperboards. Another involved the increasing import requirements of Japan, the world's third largest pulp and paper manufacturer and second largest consumer. Having virtually reached the limit of expansion based on its own softwood forest resources, Japan was importing raw wood, wood pulp, and paper in growing quantities. It was also investing substantially in pulp-manufacturing plants overseas. Still a third trend was the continuing effort to increase pulp and paper production and exports in many of the countries of Asia and Latin America.

Of the total world production of 141 million metric tons of paper and paperboard in 1972, North America accounted for 65 million tons, Europe for 48 million, Asia for 23 million, Latin America for 4 million, and Africa for 1 million. Environmental issues continued to be a matter of concern. In the U.S. the paper industry spent more than $400 million on pollution-abatement projects during 1972, with similar expenditures expected in both 1973 and 1974.

(GORDON MINNES)

PETROLEUM PRODUCTS

World consumption of petroleum and its products continued to expand at a rapid rate in 1973 and brought with it ominous signs of demand outrunning supply in the United States, Japan, and Europe. One measure of the world's appetite for petroleum products was the steady increase in oil production worldwide. For the first seven months of 1973 world oil production established new records by averaging more than 55 million bbl. daily. This was a gain of nearly 5.8 million bbl. daily, or 11.7%, over output during the same period of 1972. The increase was more than twice the gain from 1971 to 1972, which averaged 5.3%.

The major source of this new production was the Middle East, which showed phenomenal increases in oil shipments. In 1972 the Middle Eastern nations produced slightly more than 18.1 million bbl. daily, a gain of 10.7% over 1971. But in 1973, until the cutbacks during and after the Arab-Israeli war in October, production was running at the rate of 21.3 million bbl. daily for a 23% increase.

The leading producing nation in the Middle East was Saudi Arabia, which until the war increased its output by 35% to exceed 7.6 million bbl. daily in 1973. Other major Middle Eastern producing countries and their output in the first seven months of 1973 included: Iran, 5.8 million bbl. daily; Kuwait, 3.1 million; Iraq, 1.9 million; and Abu Dhabi 1.3 million.

Outside the Middle East, the two dominant oil producers were the United States and the Soviet Union. Although the U.S. remained the top oil-producing nation, its output was on the decline while that of the U.S.S.R. was rising. U.S. production in 1972 averaged about 9.5 million bbl. daily, while the Soviet Union averaged 7.9 million. In the first seven months of 1973, however, U.S. production declined to 9.2 million bbl. daily and Soviet output increased to 8.2 million. Other countries with major oil production included Venezuela, 3.4 million bbl. daily in 1973; Libya, 2.3 million; Nigeria, 1.9 million; Canada, 1.8 million; Indonesia, 1.2 million; and Algeria, 1.1 million.

Demand for petroleum products in the U.S. in mid-1973 was more than 3,100,000,-000 bbl., or an average of 17.4 million bbl. daily, about a 6% increase over a year earlier. Gasoline continued to dominate the list of petroleum products with a demand of nearly 1,200,000,000 bbl., an increase of 5.4%. Distillate fuel oil demand was 583 million bbl., up only 3.6%; and residual fuel oil consumption was 519 million bbl., an increase of 11.2%. Because demand in the U.S. exceeded supply by nearly 6 million bbl. daily, imports of crude oil and products in the first half of 1973 were running at an average of 5,970,000 bbl. daily.

The imports represented an increase of 30% over the corresponding period of 1972, with the larger volumes of the gain coming from Africa and the Middle East. Although Canada and Latin America remained the major sources of U.S. imports, Western Hemisphere sources were believed nearly at maximum ability to supply the U.S. As a result, nearly two-thirds of the added imports in 1973 came from the Eastern Hemisphere. Therefore, when the Arab nations cut off their oil shipments to the U.S. in October because of its support of Israel, U.S. authorities expected serious shortages of gasoline and other fuels to occur.

This need to import an increasing amount of its petroleum requirements was one factor in a growing fuel crisis in the U.S. but was by no means the only one. U.S. consumers in the winter of 1972–73 and the summer of 1973 had close calls with possible fuel shortages that threatened to slow down industry and commerce and drastically alter living habits.

The basic reason for the problem was that petroleum product demand in the U.S. increased steadily over the last decade while the ability of the nation to supply its energy needs with petroleum remained static or declined. The growth in demand was accentuated after 1970 by new air pollution regulations affecting industrial and automotive fuels. The regulations penalized coal because of its high sulfur content and a large amount of fuel oil for the same reason, putting an extra demand burden on natural gas and low-sulfur distillate and residual fuel oils. At the same time, antipollution devices on U.S. automobiles and low-lead requirements for gasoline added to petroleum demand.

This was the situation in late 1972 when an abnormally early siege of cold weather in the Middle West put a heavy demand on supplies of distillate and residual heating oils and on propane used for rural heating and crop drying. Shortages appeared in many areas, causing some factories and schools to close and also threatening power-generating plants. A serious situation was averted early in 1973 by unusually warm weather, which sharply lowered demand for fuels.

A similar shortage, this time of gasoline, was predicted for the summer of 1973; and early in the driving season there were reports of service stations rationing their customers. But a crisis never occurred, although some rural areas served by independent distributors and some regions at the ends of distribution channels ran low. Americans evidently restricted their summer driving, and the industry increased its supply both at home and from abroad.

Thus the Arab boycott of oil shipments to the U.S. in the fall was superimposed on an already touchy situation. U.S. Pres. Richard Nixon asked Congress for sweeping emergency powers to deal with the "energy crisis" and urged users to voluntarily limit consumption in the meantime. Although the administration insisted that gasoline rationing would be used only as a last resort, many observers believed it was inevitable. In Western Europe and Japan, far more dependent than the U.S. on Middle Eastern oil, a variety of fuel-saving measures were instituted to cope with cutbacks in shipments to those countries. Late in the year the Arab producers announced they were easing restrictions on shipments to Europe and Japan, but at the same time they raised prices drastically—a step followed to a greater or lesser degree by other exporting countries. There were allegations of stockpiling, leaks in the Arab boycott, and diversion of supplies from one country to another by the oil companies, but at year's end the situation remained unclear.

(WILFRED A. BACHMAN)

PLASTICS

Unexpected expansion of demand for plastics was a major—but not the only—factor causing the shortages for which 1973 was notable. During the year the industry was severely frustrated by its inability to meet the booming demand for so many of its products.

The situation was new to the industry's experience. Individual plastics materials had been in short supply from time to time, but in 1973 the problem was universal, almost unforeseen, and large in scale, with most plastics affected. Polystyrene was in the worst position, although other styrenic plastics and all those relying on aromatic feedstocks were in jeopardy. The cause was not a shortage of capacity for polystyrene, or even for styrene monomer; rather, it lay with the oil industry.

For years antiknock properties in high-octane gasoline had been achieved by the addition of lead compounds. These now came under attack on environmental grounds, and were banned in some countries. The alternative was to add aromatics; hence less benzene became available for styrene production. Additional refinery capacity to make good the shortfall of aromatics was not available, since the erection of new refineries had also become difficult because of environmental considerations. A return to a balance between supply and demand in benzene, and hence polystyrene, was not expected for several years. Naphtha, the feedstock for the "oil crackers" that produce ethylene and other olefins, essential materials for many plastics, was also in tight supply during 1973. Again, shortage of refinery capacity—not of crude oil—appeared to be the root cause. However, these problems were greatly exacerbated by the cutback in oil exports imposed by the Arab oil producers after the outbreak of war in the Middle East in October. By year's end the supply position for all materials was chaotic and steadily deteriorating.

Technical problems with the new large plants also played a part in the shortages. At one point during the year, major vinyl chloride, or PVC, plants in West Germany, Japan, and the U.K. were all shut down simultaneously. An inevitable consequence was a very sharp rise in prices over and above general inflationary trends. In the U.K. plastics materials manufacturers made strong representations requesting relief from statutory price controls. They claimed that inability to get an adequate return on their operations could throttle investment and adversely affect the entire future of the British plastics industry. Plastics converters suffered worst of all. With supplies rationed, they were unable to meet orders from final users, and some smaller concerns had to close.

Total plastics consumption in 1973 was considerably higher than in 1972. Every ton of material that could be made was sold. In the U.K. growth in demand was estimated at 20% over the year. A proportion of this could not be met, however, and the market probably expanded by about 17%, much more than in several years. Output was 1,850,000 metric tons. Total Western European production for 1973 was estimated at 15 million metric tons, compared with 13 million in 1972. Major contributions came from West Germany, with about six million metric tons, and from France and Italy, each with more than two million metric tons. Average European plastics growth in 1973 neared 15%. Plastics output in the U.S., the world's largest producer, also expanded by some 15%, against a similar background of booming demand and tight supply, to reach approximately 12.5 million metric tons. Total world production of plastics in 1973 was probably about 38 million metric tons.

The year saw no slowdown in the pace of innovation. At Interplas in London, the main European plastics exhibition, the usual crop of modifications to existing materials and completely new, specialized engineering-type polymers were displayed. Many claimed fire resistance (a crucial theme) or resistance to high temperatures, combined with ease of processing, as salient features. Developments in processing and machinery were also shown. Among basic methods of plastics conversion, injection-molding machines revealed increased attention to process control to eliminate variables, while in extrusion equipment the emphasis was on higher productivity.

In 1973, however, most public attention was focused on fire resistance. The tragic August fire at the Summerland recreation centre on the Isle of Man, U.K., a structure making wide use of plastics, was the subject of intense investigation. Much remained unknown about the behaviour of plastics in fires and about the mechanisms of major fires in general. The first British chair of fire engineering was established in 1973 at the University of Edinburgh.

For the future, the price of plastics would inevitably continue to rise sharply, along with those of oil and of energy in general. Chemicals and plastics used only a small proportion of world oil production, and endemic shortages seemed unlikely. Nevertheless, with other basic materials—wood, paper, leather, ferrous and nonferrous metals—rapidly becoming scarce and expensive, plastics in the future would have to be directed into those applications where their clear superiority over alternative materials made the higher price worth paying. When oil supplies eventually began to run out, the overall needs of the market might dictate priority use for such applications rather than for energy. (ROBIN C. PENFOLD)

PRINTING

The printing industry achieved improved profit figures in 1973. Respected names disappeared as mergers and take-overs continued. In Switzerland overinvestment was blamed for the take-over of the Bucher Printing Works, Lucerne, by Ringier & Cie of Zofingen. In Britain, where the trend to larger firms was reversed, the number of printing houses with fewer than 20 employees rose. No new or revolutionary systems were introduced during the year.

Electronic colour scanners continued their penetration of the industry. Largest selling of the new generation of scanners was the Crosfield Magnascan from Britain. West German manufacturer Dr.-Ing. Rudolf Hell introduced a budget version of the Chromagraph DC digital scanner having only five fixed enlargement ratios. Several European newspapers announced complete computerization of their typesetting operations. At Periodica of Brussels, two Digiset cathode-ray-tube (CRT) typesetters were linked to optical reading equipment. In Sweden, Esselte Norstedt and Almquist and Wiksell merged, forming Scandinavia's largest printing group; it claimed Europe's most advanced phototypesetting system, using Digiset and Linotron.

New York consultant Edward McSweeney estimated micrographics sales in the U.S. at $1 billion–$1.5 billion by 1975. Economic full-colour micrographic reproduction would absorb a sizable chunk of traditional printing revenues. The Grendon Trust took over the Monotype Corp. and introduced a new Monophoto 400 phototypesetting machine. CRT phototypesetting machines dropped in price, with new machines from Compugraphic, Sun, and MGD Graphic Systems. In Britain, Linotype-Paul reported a new, compact machine to compete with the U.S. machines. The end of 1973 saw the *Los Angeles Times* change entirely to phototypesetting. In Norway, the country's oldest newspaper, *Addresseavisen* of Trondheim, became the first European user of the Photon CRT 700 phototypesetting system.

Photopolymer printing plates made news. The Grace Letterflex system was sold in Europe, first in The Netherlands and then in Britain. West Germany's BASF Nyloprint reported sales of photopolymer plates to Spain and Japan, while Japanese APR plates came to Europe. In the U.S., where Dynaflex plates gained ground, Lee Enterprises planned to build a plant to make Japanese plates under license. However, the *Los Angeles Times,* with a weekly plate requirement of 25,000, announced a changeover to a new plate based on polypropylene and molded from conventional etched magnesium plates.

Among newspapers, the web offset versus

rotary letterpress controversy continued. The Scottish *Daily Record* (110,000 copies a day, entirely filmset) reported that offset and letterpress were about equal in cost but that offset offered improved quality. The West German Springer Group adopted all-web offset production of newspapers, but the *Frankfurter Rundschau* reported that web offset was too costly and ordered Albert Color-Star news rotaries. *Gazet van Antwerpen* installed the first newspaper rotary with giant Jumbo cylinders. Makers were König & Bauer of West Germany.

Some West German magazine printers went over completely to electronic engraving on Helio-Klischographs. Several rotogravure presses with electrostatic ink transfer-assist devices, which print more smoothly on rough and cheap papers, were installed. The U.S.S.R. introduced a Mega electronic engraving machine for textile rollers. An electronic colour scanner from Dainippon of Japan, for textile and wallpaper printing, permitted separation of 14 or more colours.

Compact web offset presses sold well; Sweden installed 14 GDR Polygraph machines in an 18-month period. Albert of West Germany claimed the largest sales of compact commercial web offset machines. U.S.–British MGD Graphic Systems, with West German MAN, dominated the newspaper market. Japanese press makers sold little to the West, although smaller machines, such as Komori, achieved improved sales in North America, South America, and Europe.

The introduction of the West German Roland 800 series of sheet-fed offset machines made four-colour printing of 10,000 sheets an hour realistic. MAN's new range of G-MAN offset machines had a similar capability. A Roman printer, Fraire, successfully combined two processes, sheet-fed offset on Nebiolo machines and screen process on Argon machines, both Italian-made. The Netherlands and Austria reported special-purpose screen-printing machines with up to four colour units for wallpaper printing.

Printers unexpectedly faced a threatened paper shortage. Forecasts of future requirements had been underestimated, and newspaper advertising had boomed, while in the U.S. the situation was compounded by a strike in Canadian paper mills. Forests must grow before new paper supplies can be created. Finland made long-term arrangements with the Soviet Union for the development of Siberian forests, and Japanese industrialists discussed paper production in the U.S.S.R. Ever rising costs of paper, postage, and transport led printers to reconsider their plans for new equipment and to take a fresh look at letterpress and rotogravure for printing on lighter weight papers.

(W. PINCUS JASPERT)

SHIPBUILDING

As of July 1973, statistics showed that the world total in contracted tonnage, at 105,316,423 gross registered tons (grt), had passed 100 million tons for the first time. Work in hand involved more than 2,000 steamships and motor vessels totaling 26,550,507 grt, and 2,280 ships on order but not yet started totaled 78,765,916 grt.

The top ten shipbuilding countries held orders for new tonnage totaling 92,972,920 grt. Japan, with 46,091,817 grt, had the largest order book, followed by Sweden with 9,262,407 grt, the U.K. with 6,891,101 grt, and West Germany with 6,736,405 grt. Orders in France, Norway, Denmark, Italy, and Spain, including U.S. orders to Spanish shipyards, totaled 5,446,625 grt. In the U.S. itself the figure was 3,202,930 grt.

Tankers accounted for 71% of the total order book, with 74,735,732 grt. Bulk carriers accounted for 18.5% and general cargo for 5.1%, while container-ship tonnage on order represented 18.9% of the general cargo figure. Of the 412 ships of more than 100,000 grt on order, 34 were motor vessels. There were 119 tankers on order in the 260,000- to 280,000-ton-deadweight (dw.) class and 26 vessels in the over-400,000-ton-dw. class. By July the average building price of a 250,000-ton-dw. tanker was about £25 million. The cost of a fast 30,000-ton-dw. container ship with 2,000 containers exceeded £16 million.

There had been a remarkable upsurge in shipbuilding in the U.S. By mid-1973 U.S. yards had orders for 91 vessels totaling 5,273,000 tons dw. The U.S. Merchant Marine Act of 1970 had called for 300 new vessels in ten years and made provision for a shipbuilding subsidy to encourage owners to build vessels in domestic yards for U.S. registration. The growing U.S. order book included fast container ships, LASH ("lighter aboard ship") vessels (designed to load, carry, and discharge huge lighters loaded with containers or general cargo on pallets or in crates), tankers, ore carriers, and liquefied natural gas (LNG) carriers.

The hoped-for spate of orders for 125,000-cu.m.-capacity LNG carriers had not materialized. There had been a slow but steady growth in orders, however, nearly all of them tied to large financial projects involving U.S. and Japanese interests. There were seven designs for LNG tankers, with the membrane self-supporting tank and the special spherical tank the most popular. The first LNG vessel from Moss-Rosenberg of Norway, a spherical-tank design, was delivered to a British owner in October 1973. The second such vessel would also be able to carry ethylene, but with LNG as the cargo it would be possible to use the boil-off from the cargo as fuel for the main diesel engine. LNG vessels fell into a specialized category that included chemical carriers. Many more of the latter were now on order, including 1,017 in French yards, 544 in Japan, and 538 in Norway.

As shipbuilding overhead—particularly labour costs—continued to escalate, more support was given to new shipyards in the less developed countries, such as Brazil and South Korea. The five major shipyards in Brazil had a total annual capacity of over one million tons, and two of the yards would soon be able to build 400,000-tonners. In South Korea there would be nine shipyards in operation by 1978. New shipyards were under construction in Spain and in Portugal, where the Lisnave organization, operating one of the largest ship repair complexes in the world, was building a new yard at Setúbal to construct tankers of up to 750,000 tons dw.

During 1973 Howaldtswerke-Deutsche Werft, in West Germany, announced plans to increase the size of vessel it could build to 500,000 tons dw. At yards in Sweden, Norway, and the U.K. specializing in giant tankers, extra crane capacity was installed to speed production. The existing 800-ton Goliath crane at Harland and Wolff Ltd., Belfast, N.Ire., was joined by a second, larger crane.

(W. D. EWART)

TEXTILES AND FIBRES

Textile Industry. In 1973 the spinning, weaving, knitting, and allied industries were at the threshold of still more important advances. Streamlined processes involving higher speeds, fewer machines and operatives, more automation, and far greater diversity of end products were in prospect. Continually escalating demand applied relentless pressures on practically all manufacturing capacities. Through the year supply, demand, and distribution were often greatly at variance, leading to periodic fluctuations whereby some mill closures and short workweeks were quickly followed by frantic efforts to obtain maximum production. The new Arab-Israeli war in October raised serious questions concerning the availability of raw materials and energy.

In Britain the year closed on a brighter note from the point of view of investment and production potential. The labour situation was unsatisfactory, however, largely because of a shortage of young recruits to the industry. Another disturbing factor was that Lancashire-type fabrics were being severely hit by cheap imports from continental Europe and the Far East.

Courtaulds Northern Spinning Division placed orders for over £2 million worth of cotton-type machinery with Platt International. This included the latest type ring frames and open-end spinning machines. Courtaulds also ordered 384 Swiss Sulzer looms for its new Londonderry, N.Ire., factory. Platt International introduced several improvements in its line of heavy-denier twisting machinery.

ICI (Imperial Chemical Industries Ltd.) announced plans to increase its production of Terylene (Dacron) staple fibre by about 10,000 tons a year at its Wilton plant. British Enkalon opened a new technical centre in Leicester to evaluate yarns and develop new fabrics and other end products. Interknit, Britain's first exhibition of knitwear machinery and accessories in many years, was held in Granby Halls, Leicester. It aroused encouraging interest in the wide range of specialties available.

More nonshrink polypropylene tapes were being consumed in the carpet trades, and polypropylene-jute combinations were gaining favour for such applications as backings and sackings. Novelty spun yarns were also increasingly used in traditional carpet-manufacturing techniques. An impressive range of new yarn speed meters, slub detectors, and tension meters was introduced. A new line of bench-mounted electronic tensile testers gave an accurate load-readout system, eliminating inertia and friction problems.

A Czech machine for stitch-bonded fabrics for floor coverings became available in widths up to 4.2 m., and a 5.5-m. version was expected. In a new Swiss cloth batcher, the speed and tension of the drive system were controlled by oil pressure, accurately predetermined for every type of fabric. A U.S. solvent dyeing system, in five variations, became available to firms throughout Europe. A Japanese automatic colour separator, said to be a breakthrough, was designed to pick up any colour from a multicolour design or drawing. A Spanish firm introduced an automatic carriage for screen printing on long tables.

(ALFRED DAWBER)

Natural Fibres. *Cotton.* World demand soared during the 1972–73 season, and prices advanced to the highest levels in many years. This strength was all the more remarkable because production in the two previous seasons had far exceeded all records. Global consumption of cotton also reached a new peak. World carry-over stocks at the end of the season were some 10% higher than a year earlier but remained below the minimum desirable level.

Total supply reached almost 80 million

bales, while consumption exceeded 57 million bales. A major factor was the failure of the Chinese crop, which led China to purchase some 1.8 million bales from the U.S. In addition, severe floods in the growing areas of the southern U.S. and in Pakistan interfered with output at a time when production prospects were becoming more encouraging. Growers had increased world plantings by 5.6 million ac. in two years, and record yields gave a further lift to production. Improved harvesting methods contributed to the third successive record crop in the Soviet Union.

Cotton consumption reached a new record for the ninth consecutive year, with much of the increase going into blended yarns with synthetic fibres. Fabric supplies remained tight in many countries despite high levels of mill activity. Prices were greatly affected by the pressure on production and the keenly competitive supply situation. The Liverpool index of average values, after falling to a low of 31½ cents per pound in September 1972, advanced to 38½ cents by the beginning of 1973 and to 56½ cents by midyear. Over the next two months it rose in a series of sharp jumps to 83 cents, and 88½ cents was posted in mid-October.

World stocks at the beginning of the 1973–74 season were estimated at 22 million bales, representing little more than 4½ months' supply. No significant improvement was anticipated in the immediate future, and observers predicted that world production could fall by as much as a million bales in the current season. Some dampening of the consumption expansion was anticipated as a result of high prices and anti-inflationary measures in many countries. Competition from man-made fibres was restrained by the tight supply of chemical intermediates, but blending of natural and synthetic fibres gained potential with the development of improved mixing procedures.

Although world consumption had risen by about 3.5 million bales over the last five seasons, aggregate use in North America and Western Europe had declined by nearly 1.3 million bales. Consumption by these two traditional textile-manufacturing centres fell to 27.5% of the world total in the 1972–73 season, against 31.6% five years earlier. The comparable gain in Asia and Oceania was 2.3 million bales, but the rate of gain was fastest in Africa (30%) and South America (20%). (ARTHUR TATTERSALL)

Silk. The raw silk market took a startling turn during 1973, leading to a situation that might prove crucial to the future of silk consumption on its current scale. The background to this situation lay in Japan's transformation, since the mid-1960s, from the world's foremost supplier of raw silk into a buyer of silk material wherever it was available. Europe had turned to China for supplies, and in spite of initial problems a good and steady trade was established. China maintained its price with only minor upward adjustments.

The first major upward movement—of 10%—had come in January 1970. This dampened demand but did not prove disastrous. A far greater disaster was an attempt to redress the position by a 5% reduction in February 1971. Far from stimulating demand, it frightened off buyers, who deferred purchases in anticipation of a possible further decline. Business fell in 1971 in all countries except Japan, where the domestic market continued to thrive at a price level very much above that of China. The situation inevitably brought a flow of reexports of Chinese silk to Japan, at guaranteed profits to the merchants.

In August 1972 China instituted a series of price increases designed to bridge the gap between its own selling price and that being paid in Japan. Taking the August 1972 level as 100, by January 1973 the index had risen to 118½. Europe proved able to absorb these additional costs, the Japanese market rose freely, and European reexports continued. But then came a rise of 37%, bringing the price level to 162 in February.

World inflation was rife, and all commodity values soared to new levels. Silk consumers in the West set about accustoming themselves to the new plateau, and they might well have done so had not, less than two months later, in April, the Chinese announced an increase of a further 30%, bringing the price level to 211. Thus raw material costs had more than doubled within eight months.

The reaction was immediate. Steps were taken to dilute the silk content of what had been traditional silk fabrics, and buying was brought to a standstill. In August, China reduced prices by 10%, to the level of 190, but, as in 1970, this maneuver appeared to have served as a deterrent rather than a stimulus. At the same time, strength seemed to have forsaken the Japanese market, and at the end of the year the future of the world's silk trade was uncertain. (PETER W. GADDUM)

Wool. The 1972–73 wool selling season was an unprecedented boom period for many wool growers. Production was lower as a result of uneconomic prices received in the 1970–71 season and the first half of 1971–72. This, in turn, had caused many farmers to produce other commodities as alternatives to wool. At the same time consumption increased following a general recovery in world trade and an upturn in the textile cycle. There were also continuing signs of a preference for wool as a fibre, although this was eventually checked in some fields by rising prices. Assisting and accelerating this rising price trend was an increase in world commodity prices over a very wide field, as well as currency changes that created confusion and led to more intensive covering purchases in a rising market than might otherwise have developed.

Production of wool in the 1972–73 season was estimated by the Commonwealth Secretariat at 1,484,000 metric tons, clean basis. As a result of resistance to high prices, consumption in 1973 was expected to be lower than the 1,598,000 metric tons estimated to have been consumed in 1972, while world wool production was expected to rise, if only slightly. Thus, while demand put considerable pressure on supplies in the 1972–73 season and led to a contraction of stocks in all leading producing and consuming countries except Japan, the 1973–74 season was showing signs of corrective tendencies. These were confirmed by a downward price trend, especially in the merino wool section, which experienced its highest recorded peak prices in 1973.

Wool prices had risen continuously since late 1971. The peak for merino wool was reached in March 1973, when the Australian Wool Corporation's price for 64s-count wool reached 590 cents (Australian) per kilogram. Prices subsequently declined sharply, by 200 cents in two weeks, but for the remainder of the 1972–73 season they maintained a high level in the region of 400 cents per kilogram and only gradually declined as the 1973–74 selling season got under way during the last four months of 1973. Crossbred prices in New Zealand did not rise to such extremes and maintained relative stability on the high March basis.

While wool producers were less pessimistic than in recent years, there was some anxiety on the wool-using side that, in the long term, higher prices, and particularly the extreme fluctuations of 1972–73, might damage wool's prospects compared with synthetic fibres. A Commonwealth Secretariat analysis showed that in the second quarter of 1973 virgin wool represented 39% of all materials consumed at the carding stage in seven major consuming countries, compared with 45.3% a year earlier.

(H. M. F. MALLETT)

Man-Made Fibres. In 1973 the surplus output of man-made fibres that had been a feature of 1972 was absorbed, and there was a serious shortage of virtually every fibre. The situation was totally different from that of the previous year, with manufacturers seeking supplies from virtually every corner of the world. Nevertheless, the double jersey knitters and warp knitters showed no appreciable improvement in their trade setup, and prices remained depressed with clear evidence of overcapacity, particularly in Britain, the U.S., France, and West Germany. Shortages became even more acute following an explosion in Japan that destroyed about 10% of that country's nylon raw material. In Britain the collapse of a tower at the main nylon raw material plant made matters even more difficult, while in West Germany there was a setback when one company lost a high proportion of its phenol capacity following an accident.

The price of wool rose to such levels that many who had never considered using man-made fibres before were forced to seek alternatives in order to maintain their competitive position—a trend that was likely to last for some years to come. Once the synthetic fibres were established, it seemed unlikely that they would ever again be displaced by natural fibres, even if the latter fell in price. This had been evident in the carpet trade and in the manufacture of men's and women's suitings.

In nylon production there were advances in the development of variants, such as fibres with special dye affinities. These could be used in a fabric that would dye to different colours, or shades, in a single dyebath. Specialized nylons were also under development, including a new high modulus nylon with strength properties greater than those of steel and another similar to silk.

A British fibre producer announced plans to make textiles by the spun-bonded process, using heterofil fibres of his own invention. Research continued in the development of a wide range of flame-resistant materials, a matter that became more urgent with the introduction of regulatory legislation in the U.S. Linked with this work, a number of companies embarked on the development of new high-performance organic and inorganic fibres.

With textiles becoming progressively more expensive, efforts were concentrated on the development of such products as nonwoven textiles requiring a minimum of labour, as well as composite materials in which such substances as flexible foam could be used as substitutes for the more expensive and heavier cloths. (PETER LENNOX-KERR)

See also Advertising; Agriculture and Fisheries; Alcoholic Beverages; Cooperatives; Economy, World; Employment, Wages, and Hours; Energy; Food Processing; Forestry; Housing; Labour Unions; Merchandising; Metallurgy; Mining; Prices; Rubber; Television and Radio; Tobacco; Toys and Games; Trade, International.

Insurance

More than 13,000 private insurance companies in the Western world achieved a total annual growth rate of nearly 10% in 1973. Sales exceeded $150 billion of premium income, with North America accounting for three-fifths of the global market and Western Europe for one-fourth. Japan entered the ranks of world leaders, displacing West Germany as number two in total insurance sales. The U.K. maintained its number four position, and increased trade prospects were noted within the new nine-member EEC resulting from the entry of the U.K., Ireland, and Denmark.

Life Insurance. The ratio of life insurance in force to national income, a basic measure for comparing the significance of insurance in different parts of the world, was in excess of 100% in eight nations: Canada (184%), the U.S. (176%), Sweden (156%), New Zealand and Japan (149%), Australia (131%), The Netherlands (127%), and the U.K. (113%). In general, the North American and Western European countries led in the use of life insurance for family and business security. Japan, however, ranked second to the U.S. in the dollar amount of total life insurance in force. Canada ranked third, the U.K. fourth, and West Germany fifth.

WIDE WORLD

Raymond L. Dirks, an insurance analyst who uncovered alleged fraud at Equity Funding, answers newsmen's queries during a May 14, 1973, press conference at Lincoln Center, New York City.

As an example of the importance of insurance within a single country, in Canada the amount of life insurance purchased in 1973 exceeded $20 billion, for a total of more than $150 billion in force. More than 11 million policyholders owned life insurance, which was several million more persons than paid income taxes in that year. Assets of $21 billion were invested mostly in the private sector, primarily in bonds and mortgages, with about one-fifth of the funds invested in the U.S.

In the U.S. two out of every three persons were covered by life insurance, for a total approaching $1.8 trillion. Income of U.S. life insurance companies rose to nearly $65 billion, including life, health, and annuity premium income of almost $50 billion. This premium income represented slightly less than 4% of total disposable income, a level that had been quite stable for 20 years.

By mid-1973 company assets had risen to approximately $250 billion, of which about two-thirds was invested in bonds and mortgages. Some concern was expressed over the relatively rapid growth of policy loans, which would probably exceed the 1972 total by 20–25%. This increase was encouraged by policy-guaranteed loan rates of 5–6% during the credit crunch and by higher interest earnings.

Life insurance purchases in the U.S. during the year were in excess of $230 billion. About three-fourths was bought on an individual basis through agents and one-fourth on a group basis, chiefly through employers. Recent studies of life insurance purchases through regular or "ordinary" agents showed that over half the contracts sold were for $10,000 or more. Special family plans covering all members of a family accounted for 16% of purchases. More than 40% of all nongroup life insurance was term insurance, and 60% was of the permanent type. Group insurance usually was based on one-year renewable term insurance. Males purchased about 70% of the policies and 85% of the life insurance bought during the year.

Among the developments of major concern to the U.S. life and health insurance industry during 1973 were federal proposals for national health insurance and for private pension funding and vesting requirements. A federal pilot program to test the impact of national health insurance on the cost and availability of medical care was initiated during the year. The $30 million program, to be administered by the Office of Economic Opportunity, would enroll up to 2,300 families in four cities during a two-year period. Three experimental insurance models would be tested, with terms of three to five years, after which their effect could be evaluated.

Action on these topics was expected in 1974. Another concern was the Equity Funding Corp. of America scandal, which surfaced in March. To obtain needed cash, the company had invented policyholders and then sold the fictitious policies to reinsurers. Investigators had some difficulty determining the extent of the fraud since, among other things, computer tapes had been altered to hide the evidence. It appeared, however, that millions of dollars of the company's listed assets were nonexistent, and its stock, once valued at $80 a share, became virtually worthless. A large number of insurance companies, banks, and brokerage houses stood to lose as a result of their dealings with Equity, but it was believed that the company's genuine policyholders would probably be covered. Twenty former Equity executives and employees and two auditors were indicted in November.

Service records for some 20 million veterans fueled the flames at the Military Personnel Records Center in St. Louis, Mo. Included in the destruction were data essential to settling claims before the Veterans Administration.

WIDE WORLD

Information Science and Technology: *see* Computers

ROTHCO/RENAULT—MCCLATCHY NEWSPAPERS, CAL.

"GET OUT. WE WANT TO TALK TO YOU!"

A report from the Committee on Corporate Social Responsibility of U.S. life insurers recommended ending the urban investment program because of changing government priorities and support. The six-year-old program had encouraged $2 billion of investments in blighted urban areas. Another 5.9% increase in Social Security benefits in 1973, following a 20% hike in 1972, resulted in benefit increases totaling more than 70% over five years. Medicare costs continued to grow in 1973. Basic hospital and medical protection was provided to more than 21 million older citizens, and in July these benefits were extended to totally disabled persons and their dependents.

Property and Liability Insurance. No disasters occurred in 1973 comparable to the late 1972 earthquake in Nicaragua, which caused about 6,000 deaths. However, floods in Asia and droughts in Africa were severe, and an August earthquake in Mexico was the longest ever recorded there. Record spring floods occurred in the Mississippi River valley, and by June storm-insured losses there exceeded $320 million, more than the entire 1972 total of weather-related insured losses in the U.S. Memorial Day week saw a record number of tornados in 21 states, causing $75 million of insured damage, and a catastrophic fire that destroyed an estimated $50 million industrial complex in Chicago. In July a spectacular multimillion-dollar fire raged for two days in the top floors of the Military Personnel Records Center in St. Louis, Mo. Some 20 to 25 city blocks were involved in a fire in the Boston suburb of Chelsea in October and a multimillion-dollar fire in the heart of the business district of Indianapolis, Ind., took place in early November. U.S. fire insurance losses in 1973 exceeded $3 billion, involving nearly three million buildings. The British Insurance Association reported fire insurance losses at about $270 million, approximately the same as in previous years despite soaring fire losses resulting from Northern Ireland bombing incidents.

U.S. property and liability insurance underwriting profits appeared certain to decline from the record level of $1.1 billion in 1972. Results for the first six months of 1973 indicated a 10% increase in sales volume, to an approximate annual level of $40 billion. However, only a disappointing underwriting profit of less than $200 million was earned by mid-1973. Preliminary estimates for the U.K. also anticipated decreasing underwriting profits as compared with the early years of the decade.

In the U.S. the federal government maintained its pressure on the states to enact "no-fault" automobile insurance, under which damages suffered by the insured are paid by his own company, up to a fixed level, regardless of how they were caused. A small but growing group of insurers were backing federal minimum guidelines for state laws on no-fault motor vehicle insurance, as advocated by the American Insurance Association. These included State Farm, Reliance, Aetna, Aetna Life and Casualty, Royal-Globe, and the Crum and Forster companies. One of the advantages of no-fault was said to be the lowering of insurance costs, although early experience with no-fault plans in Massachusetts and Florida showed mixed results. Several other states, including New York and Michigan, adopted no-fault laws in 1973, but their provisions varied widely and it was impossible to say whether or how much they would reduce the number of traditional tort liability lawsuits. An Illinois court decision declaring that state's no-fault law unconstitutional seemed likely to slow adoption of such plans in other states. In Canada, where no-fault automobile insurance plans had been operational for several years, a substantial market change was scheduled for 1974 when an automobile insurance monopoly would take effect in British Colombia.

An encouraging note was sounded by FBI reports showing that serious property crimes in the U.S. had fallen 2% in the first half of 1973. Changes in state workmen's compensation laws continued at a record pace; many conformed to recent recommendations of a national commission advising minimum disability income benefits, full medical care, and reduced exemptions from the work accident and sickness laws. The attention of insurers and employers was being directed to the problem of responsibility for hazards uncovered by federal inspections under the Occupational Safety and Health Act (1970) and the 1973 requirements of the Consumer Product Safety Act. Both of these laws appeared to be of growing importance in promoting loss-prevention activities throughout U.S. industry. (DAVID L. BICKELHAUPT)

See also Cooperatives; Disasters; Industrial Review; Social Services.

International Organizations

The following table shows the membership of the world's sovereign states in various international organizations in 1973. The growing realization that political and economic problems transcended international boundaries led to a proliferation of international organizations after World War II. Of these, the UN and its specialized agencies (some of which, such as the ILO and the UPU, antedated the war) aimed at least theoretically at universality. The World Bank, originally established to provide help to war-devastated nations, turned more and more in succeeding years toward concentration on the problems of economic development. Organizations with more restricted membership included regional political groupings (OAS, OAU), military alliances (NATO, the Warsaw Pact), and organizations with a primarily economic orientation (EEC, Comecon). Such groupings as the Colombo Plan were chiefly vehicles for channeling aid from the developed to the less developed countries.

Inter-American Affairs: *see* Latin-American Affairs; *articles on the various countries*

International Bank for Reconstruction and Development: *see* Development, Economic

International Criminal Police Organization: *see* Crime

International Law: *see* Law

International Monetary Fund: *see* Payments and Reserves, International

Membership in International Organizations, December 1973

Country	UN 1	FAO 2	IMCO 3	IAEA 4	ICAO 5	ILO 6	IBRD 7	IDA 8	IFC 9	IMF 10	ITU 11	UNESCO 12	UPU 13	WHO 14	WMO 15	GATT 16	CE 17	LAS 18	OAS 19	OPEC 20	OCAS 21	C-Plan 22	Comecon 23	Euratom 24	ECSC 25	EEC 26	EFTA 27	IDB 28	LAFTA 29	OECD 30	CN 31	WIPO 32	NATO 33	OCAM 34	WTO 35	CFA 36	OAU* 37	SPC 38
Afghanistan	●	●		●	●	●	●	●	●	●	●	●	●	●	●							●																
Albania	●			●							●	●	●	●	●																							
Algeria	●	●	●	●	●	●	●	●		●	●	●	●	●	●			●		●												●					●	
Argentina	●	●	●	●	●	●	●	●	●	●	●	●	●	●	●	●			●									●	●			●						
Australia	●	●	●	●	●	●	●	●	●	●	●	●	●	●	●	●						●								●	●	●						●
Austria	●	●		●	●	●	●	●	●	●	●	●	●	●	●	●	●										●			●		●						
Bahamas	●						●			●																					●							
Bahrain	●	●			●		●			●		●		●				●																				
Bangladesh				●	●	●	●	●		●	●	●		●	●	●						●									●							
Barbados	●	●	●		●	●				●	●	●	●	●	●	●			●									●			●							
Belgium	●	●	●	●	●	●	●	●	●	●	●	●	●	●	●	●	●							●	●	●				●		●	●					
Belorussia	●			●		●					●	●	●	●	●																	●						
Bhutan	●												●									●																
Bolivia	●	●		●	●	●	●	●	●	●	●	●	●	●	●				●									●	●									
Botswana	●	●					●	●		●	●		●		●																●						●	
Brazil	●	●	●	●	●	●	●	●	●	●	●	●	●	●	●	●			●									●	●			●						
Bulgaria	●	●	●	●	●	●					●	●	●	●	●								●									●			●			
Burma	●	●	●	●	●	●	●	●	●	●	●	●	●	●	●	●						●																
Burundi	●	●			●	●	●	●		●	●	●	●	●	●	●																					●	
Cambodia	●	●	●	●	●	●	●	●		●	●	●	●	●	●							●																
Cameroon	●	●	●	●	●	●	●	●		●	●	●	●	●	●	●																●		●		●	●	
Canada	●	●	●	●	●	●	●	●	●	●	●	●	●	●	●	●						●						●		●	●	●	●					
Central African Rep.	●	●			●	●	●	●		●	●	●	●	●	●	●																●		●		●	●	
Chad	●	●			●	●	●	●		●	●	●	●	●	●	●																●		●		●	●	
Chile	●	●	●	●	●	●	●	●	●	●	●	●	●	●	●	●			●									●	●			●						
China	●			●	●	●	●	●	●	●	●	●	●	●	●																							
Colombia	●	●		●	●	●	●	●	●	●	●	●	●	●	●				●									●	●									
Congo (Brazzaville)	●	●			●	●	●	●		●	●	●	●	●	●	●																●				●	●	
Costa Rica	●	●		●	●	●	●	●	●	●	●	●	●	●	●				●		●							●										
Cuba	●	●	●	●	●	●					●	●	●	●	●	●			●				●									●						
Cyprus	●	●		●	●	●	●	●	●	●	●	●	●	●	●	●	●														●	●						
Czechoslovakia	●	●	●	●	●	●					●	●	●	●	●	●							●									●			●			
Dahomey	●	●			●	●	●	●		●	●	●	●	●	●	●																●		●		●	●	
Denmark	●	●	●	●	●	●	●	●	●	●	●	●	●	●	●	●	●							●	●	●				●		●	●					
Dominican Rep.	●	●	●	●	●	●	●	●	●	●	●	●	●	●	●	●			●									●				●						
Ecuador	●	●	●	●	●	●	●	●	●	●	●	●	●	●	●				●									●	●									
Egypt	●	●	●	●	●	●	●	●	●	●	●	●	●	●	●	●		●														●					●	
El Salvador	●	●		●	●	●	●	●	●	●	●	●	●	●	●				●		●							●										
Equatorial Guinea	●		●		●		●	●		●	●		●																								●	
Ethiopia	●	●		●	●	●	●	●	●	●	●	●	●	●	●																						●	
Fiji	●	●					●	●		●	●		●	●								●									●	●						●
Finland	●	●	●	●	●	●	●	●	●	●	●	●	●	●	●	●														●		●						
France	●	●	●	●	●	●	●	●	●	●	●	●	●	●	●	●	●							●	●	●				●		●	●					●
Gabon	●	●		●	●	●	●	●	●	●	●	●	●	●	●	●																●		●		●	●	
Gambia, The	●	●					●	●		●				●		●															●						●	
Germany, East	●											●											●									●			●			
Germany, West	●	●	●	●	●	●	●	●	●	●	●	●	●	●	●	●	●							●	●	●				●		●	●					
Ghana	●	●	●	●	●	●	●	●	●	●	●	●	●	●	●	●															●						●	
Greece	●	●	●	●	●	●	●	●	●	●	●	●	●	●	●	●														●		●	●					
Guatemala	●	●		●	●	●	●	●	●	●	●	●	●	●	●				●		●							●										
Guinea	●	●			●	●	●	●		●	●	●	●	●	●																						●	
Guyana	●	●			●	●	●	●	●	●	●	●	●	●	●	●															●							
Haiti	●	●	●	●	●	●	●	●	●	●	●	●	●	●	●	●			●									●				●						
Honduras	●	●	●		●	●	●	●	●	●	●	●	●	●	●				●		●							●										
Hungary	●	●	●	●	●	●					●	●	●	●	●	●							●									●			●			
Iceland	●	●	●	●	●	●	●	●	●	●	●	●	●	●	●	●	●										●			●		●	●					
India	●	●	●	●	●	●	●	●	●	●	●	●	●	●	●	●						●									●	●						
Indonesia	●	●	●	●	●	●	●	●	●	●	●	●	●	●	●	●				●		●										●						
Iran	●	●	●	●	●	●	●	●	●	●	●	●	●	●	●					●		●										●						
Iraq	●	●		●	●	●	●	●	●	●	●	●	●	●	●			●		●																		
Ireland	●	●	●	●	●	●	●	●	●	●	●	●	●	●	●	●	●							●	●	●				●		●						
Israel	●	●	●	●	●	●	●	●	●	●	●	●	●	●	●	●																●						
Italy	●	●	●	●	●	●	●	●	●	●	●	●	●	●	●	●	●							●	●	●				●		●	●					
Ivory Coast	●	●	●	●	●	●	●	●	●	●	●	●	●	●	●	●																●		●		●	●	
Jamaica	●	●		●	●	●	●		●	●	●	●	●	●	●	●			●									●			●							
Japan	●	●	●	●	●	●	●	●	●	●	●	●	●	●	●	●						●								●		●						
Jordan	●	●		●	●	●	●	●	●	●	●	●	●	●	●			●														●						
Kenya	●	●		●	●	●	●	●	●	●	●	●	●	●	●	●															●	●					●	
Korea, South		●	●	●	●		●	●	●	●	●	●	●	●	●	●						●																
Kuwait	●	●	●	●	●	●	●	●	●	●	●	●	●	●	●	●		●		●																		
Laos	●	●			●	●	●	●		●	●	●	●	●	●							●																
Lebanon	●	●	●	●	●	●	●	●	●	●	●	●	●	●	●			●														●						
Lesotho	●	●					●	●	●	●	●	●	●	●																	●						●	
Liberia	●	●	●	●	●	●	●	●	●	●	●	●	●	●																							●	
Libya	●	●	●	●	●	●	●	●	●	●	●	●	●	●	●			●		●																	●	
Liechtenstein				●							●		●																			●						
Luxembourg	●	●		●	●	●	●	●	●	●	●	●	●	●	●	●	●							●	●	●				●		●	●					
Malagasy Rep.	●	●	●	●	●	●	●	●	●	●	●	●	●	●	●	●																●		●		●	●	
Malawi	●	●			●	●	●	●	●	●	●	●	●	●	●	●															●	●					●	
Malaysia	●	●	●	●	●	●	●	●	●	●	●	●	●	●	●	●						●									●							

*Membership was extended November 1973 to the revolutionary government of Guinea-Bissau, which was not internationally recognized as a state.

Membership in International Organizations, December 1973

Country	UN 1	FAO 2	IMCO 3	IAEA 4	ICAO 5	ILO 6	IBRD 7	IDA 8	IFC 9	IMF 10	ITU 11	UNESCO 12	UPU 13	WHO 14	WMO 15	GATT 16	CE 17	LAS 18	OAS 19	OPEC 20	OCAS 21	C-Plan 22	Comecon 23	Euratom 24	ECSC 25	EEC 26	EFTA 27	IDB 28	LAFTA 29	OECD 30	CN 31	WIPO 32	NATO 33	OCAM 34	WTO 35	CFA 36	OAU 37	SPC 38
Maldives	●	●	●								●		●	●								●																
Mali	●	●		●	●	●	●	●		●	●	●	●	●	●																	●					●	
Malta	●	●	●		●	●				●	●	●	●	●		●	●														●	●						
Mauritania	●	●	●		●	●	●	●	●	●	●	●	●	●	●	●																●				●	●	
Mauritius	●	●			●	●	●	●	●	●	●	●	●	●	●	●															●			●			●	
Mexico	●	●	●	●	●	●	●	●	●	●	●	●	●	●	●				●									●	●			●						
Monaco				●							●	●	●	●																		●						
Mongolia	●					●					●	●	●	●	●								●															
Morocco	●	●	●	●	●	●	●	●	●	●	●	●	●	●	●			●														●					●	
Nauru											●		●																									●
Nepal	●	●			●	●	●	●	●	●	●	●	●	●	●							●																
Netherlands, The	●	●	●	●	●	●	●	●	●	●	●	●	●	●	●	●	●							●	●	●				●		●	●					
New Zealand	●	●	●	●	●	●	●		●	●	●	●	●	●	●	●						●								●	●	●						●
Nicaragua	●	●			●	●	●	●	●	●	●	●	●	●	●	●			●		●							●										
Niger	●	●		●	●	●	●	●		●	●	●	●	●	●	●																●		●		●	●	
Nigeria	●	●	●	●	●	●	●	●	●	●	●	●	●	●	●	●				●											●	●					●	
Norway	●	●	●	●	●	●	●	●	●	●	●	●	●	●	●	●	●										●			●		●	●					
Oman	●	●					●			●	●	●	●	●				●																				
Pakistan	●	●	●	●	●	●	●	●	●	●	●	●	●	●	●	●						●										●						
Panama	●	●	●	●	●	●	●	●	●	●	●	●	●	●	●				●									●										
Paraguay	●	●		●	●	●	●	●	●	●	●	●	●	●	●				●									●	●									
Peru	●	●	●	●	●	●	●	●	●	●	●	●	●	●	●	●			●									●	●									
Philippines	●	●	●	●	●	●	●	●	●	●	●	●	●	●	●							●										●						
Poland	●	●	●	●	●	●					●	●	●	●	●	●							●									●			●			
Portugal	●	●		●	●	●	●		●	●	●		●	●	●	●											●			●		●	●					
Qatar	●	●			●	●	●			●		●	●	●				●		●																		
Rhodesia											●				●	●																●						
Romania	●	●	●	●	●	●	●			●	●	●	●	●	●	●							●									●			●			
Rwanda	●	●			●	●	●	●		●	●	●	●	●	●	●																		●			●	
San Marino													●																			●						
Saudi Arabia	●	●	●	●	●		●	●	●	●	●	●	●	●	●			●		●																		
Senegal	●	●	●	●	●	●	●	●	●	●	●	●	●	●	●	●																●		●		●	●	
Sierra Leone	●	●		●	●	●	●	●	●	●	●	●	●	●	●	●															●						●	
Singapore	●		●	●	●	●	●		●	●	●	●	●	●	●	●						●									●							
Somalia	●	●			●	●	●	●	●	●	●	●	●	●	●																						●	
South Africa	●			●	●		●	●	●	●	●		●	●	●	●																●						
Spain	●	●	●	●	●	●	●	●	●	●	●	●	●	●	●	●														●		●						
Sri Lanka (Ceylon)	●	●	●	●	●	●	●	●	●	●	●	●	●	●	●	●						●									●	●						
Sudan, The	●	●		●	●	●	●	●	●	●	●	●	●	●	●			●																			●	
Swaziland	●	●					●	●	●	●	●		●																		●						●	
Sweden	●	●	●	●	●	●	●	●	●	●	●	●	●	●	●	●	●										●			●		●						
Switzerland		●	●	●	●	●					●	●	●	●	●	●	●										●			●		●						
Syria	●	●	●	●	●	●	●	●	●	●	●	●	●	●	●			●														●						
Taiwan																																						
Tanzania	●	●			●	●	●	●	●	●	●	●	●	●	●	●															●	●					●	
Thailand	●	●		●	●	●	●	●	●	●	●	●	●	●	●							●										●						
Togo	●	●			●	●	●	●	●	●	●	●	●	●	●	●																●		●		●	●	
Tonga																															●							
Trinidad and Tobago	●	●	●		●	●	●	●	●	●	●	●	●	●	●	●			●									●			●	●						
Tunisia	●	●	●	●	●	●	●	●	●	●	●	●	●	●	●			●														●					●	
Turkey	●	●	●	●	●	●	●	●	●	●	●	●	●	●	●	●	●													●		●	●					
Uganda	●	●		●	●	●	●	●	●	●	●	●	●	●	●	●															●	●					●	
Ukraine	●			●		●					●	●	●	●	●																	●						
United Arab Emirates	●				●	●	●			●	●	●		●				●		●																		
United Kingdom	●	●	●	●	●	●	●	●	●	●	●	●	●	●	●	●	●					●		●	●	●				●	●	●	●					●
United States	●	●	●	●	●	●	●	●	●	●	●	●	●	●	●	●			●			●						●		●		●	●					●
Upper Volta	●	●			●	●	●	●		●	●	●	●	●	●	●																●		●		●	●	
Uruguay	●	●	●	●	●	●	●		●	●	●	●	●	●	●	●			●									●	●			●						
U.S.S.R.	●		●	●	●	●					●	●	●	●	●								●									●			●			
Vatican City				●							●		●																			●						
Venezuela	●	●		●	●	●	●		●	●	●	●	●	●	●				●	●								●	●									
Vietnam, South		●		●	●	●	●	●	●	●	●	●	●	●	●							●										●						
Western Samoa										●				●																	●							●
Yemen (Aden)	●	●			●	●	●	●		●	●	●	●	●	●			●																				
Yemen (Sana)	●	●		●	●	●	●	●	●	●	●	●	●	●	●			●																				
Yugoslavia	●	●	●	●	●	●	●	●	●	●	●	●	●	●	●	●																●						
Zaire	●	●		●	●	●	●	●	●	●	●	●	●	●	●	●																●					●	
Zambia	●	●		●	●	●	●	●	●	●	●	●	●	●	●																●	●					●	

UN **1** United Nations.
FAO **2** Food and Agriculture Organization of the United Nations.
IMCO **3** Intergovernmental Maritime Consultative Organization.
IAEA **4** International Atomic Energy Agency.
ICAO **5** International Civil Aviation Organization.
ILO **6** International Labour Organization.
IBRD **7** International Bank for Reconstruction and Development.
IDA **8** International Development Association.
IFC **9** International Finance Corporation.
IMF **10** International Monetary Fund.
ITU **11** International Telecommunication Union.
UNESCO **12** United Nations Educational, Scientific, and Cultural Organization.
UPU **13** Universal Postal Union.
WHO **14** World Health Organization.
WMO **15** World Meteorological Organization.
GATT **16** General Agreement on Tariffs and Trade.
CE **17** Council of Europe.
LAS **18** League of Arab States (Arab League).
OAS **19** Organization of American States.
OPEC **20** Organization of Petroleum Exporting Countries.
OCAS **21** Organization of Central American States.
C-Plan **22** Colombo Plan for Co-operative Economic Development in South and South-East Asia.
Comecon **23** Council for Mutual Economic Assistance.
Euratom **24** European Atomic Energy Community.
ECSC **25** European Coal and Steel Community.
EEC **26** European Economic Community.
EFTA **27** European Free Trade Association.
IDB **28** Inter-American Development Bank.
LAFTA **29** Latin American Free Trade Association.
OECD **30** Organization for Economic Cooperation and Development.
CN **31** Commonwealth of Nations.
WIPO **32** World Intellectual Property Organization.
NATO **33** North Atlantic Treaty Organization.
OCAM **34** Common African, Malagasy, and Mauritian Organization.
WTO **35** Warsaw Treaty Organization.
CFA **36** African Financial Community.
OAU **37** Organization of African Unity.
SPC **38** South Pacific Commission.

Investment, International

The total value of international investment in 1972 and 1973 was higher than in 1971. Direct investment (the purchase of productive assets) was at a level similar to the previous year (about $13 billion), but there was a marked increase in portfolio investment (the purchase of foreign securities). The latter consists of many sales and many purchases of securities, and the net value of sales minus purchases is recorded in each case. This type of investment is very sensitive to interest rate differences between countries and to expectations of changes in exchange rates, and it was for these reasons that the flow of portfolio investment rose as it did in 1972. Foreign investment in U.S. and West German securities reached record levels of $4.4 billion and DM. 8.7 billion, respectively.

The continued high rate of international investment throughout the 1960s and into the 1970s led to the rapid expansion of multinational companies. In recent years increasing concern was expressed about the activities and the impact of such firms. Some critics believed that their activities should be controlled, but few specific proposals were forthcoming. Figures were quoted concerning the extent to which domestic industries were dominated by foreign firms, and consequently some people saw multinational companies as a threat to national sovereignty and the ability of governments to control domestic industry. The possibility of the development of worldwide near-monopolies in which consumers would be denied the benefits of competition was also foreseen. On the other hand, others saw multinational companies as a very efficient means of spreading the benefits of modern technical progress and of breaking down national barriers and the frictions associated with them.

There was no consensus, but it was clear that the question of multinational companies would occupy the thoughts of many economic and financial experts throughout the world for the next few years.

Investment:
see Investment, International; Savings and Investment; Stock Exchanges

United States. The rate of foreign investment by U.S. companies and residents was slightly lower in 1972 than in 1971, at $8.5 billion compared with $9 billion. Decreases were recorded in both direct and portfolio investment. During the first half of 1973 there was a very substantial increase in direct investment but a further marked decline in portfolio investment (Table III).

Table III. U.S. Investment Abroad

In $000,000

Item	1968	1969	1970	1971	1972	1973*
Direct investment						
New funds	3,209	3,271	4,410	4,943	3,404	6,366*
Reinvested profits	2,175	2,604	2,948	3,157	4,521	...
Total	5,384	5,875	7,358	8,100	7,925	...
Portfolio investment	1,133	1,494	942	909	614	154*
Total	6,517	7,369	8,300	9,009	8,539	...

*First half year, seasonally adjusted; at annual rate.
Source: U.S. Department of Commerce, *Survey of Current Business.*

At the end of 1972 the total value of U.S. foreign assets amounted to $117 billion, of which direct investments accounted for $94 billion and portfolio investments for $23 billion (Table I). Of the direct investments, about one-third of the assets were in Europe and a little over one-quarter in Canada; since 1965 the shares of these two areas had been reversed, reflecting the increased attention paid by U.S. corporations to the rapidly growing markets in Europe.

Although direct investment in 1972 was somewhat below the level of 1971, it was sufficiently large to bring about a 9% increase in the total value of assets held overseas; this rate was similar to the average of the previous five years. A marked change took place in the financing of U.S. direct investment in 1972. In many previous years a large part had been financed by the outflow of new funds from the U.S., but in 1972, for the first time since 1955, reinvested profits financed more than half the new investment. This was largely due to the 1971 devaluation of the dollar, which increased the dollar value of foreign currency earnings and reduced the amount of foreign currency earnings necessary to maintain a reasonable growth in repatriated profits. It can be seen in Table II that the sharp increase in the amount of reinvested profits was not at the expense of repatriated earnings. In addition, the U.S. government's Foreign Direct Investment Program was encouraging new foreign borrowing to offset partially the effect of capital flows on the balance of payments.

Direct investment in foreign manufacturing industries accounted for half of the 1972 investment, a larger proportion than in recent years. The continued rapid growth in demand for oil and petrochemicals resulted in foreign investment in petroleum of $2.3 billion, a rate which, although slightly lower than in 1971, was considerably above the average of $1.4 billion recorded in 1968–70.

A regional breakdown of U.S. investment is given in Table I. Investment in Canada increased by $400 million in 1972, due to more manufacturing investment. The rate of investment in Europe was about 10% lower, with a particularly sharp decline in the U.K. where investment in both petroleum and manufacturing was almost $200 million lower than in 1971. A large part of the increased investment in the early part of 1973 was in Europe.

The reduced rate of U.S. portfolio investment abroad in 1972 was attributable to net sales of foreign company securities, amounting to $500 million, compared with a small net purchase in 1971; this reduction in holdings by U.S. investors was particularly noticeable in securities of European firms. New issues in the U.S. of foreign bonds continued at a similar

Table I. U.S. Foreign Assets, Investment, and Earnings by Region, 1972

In $000,000

Area	Value of assets at end of year			Investment during year			Earnings		
	Direct	Portfolio	Total	Direct	Portfolio	Total	Direct	Portfolio	Total
Canada	25,784	12,622	38,406	1,747	679	2,426	2,236	972	3,208
Latin America	16,644	1,333	17,977	879	45	924	1,532	532	2,064
Western Europe	30,715	2,807	33,522	2,959	−533	2,426	3,685	465	4,150
Japan	2,222	876	3,098	371	29	400	345	244	589
Other countries	13,933	2,512	16,445	1,476	273	1,749	4,112	357	4,469
International organizations and unallocated	4,733	2,098	6,831	495	121	616	476	126	602
Total	94,031	22,248	116,279	7,925	614	8,539	12,386	2,697	15,083

Source: U.S. Department of Commerce, *Survey of Current Business.*

Table II. U.S. Investment Earnings

In $000,000

Item	1968	1969	1970	1971	1972	1973*
Direct investment						
Repatriated profits	4,973	5,658	6,001	7,295	8,004	10,022*
Reinvested profits†	2,049	2,470	2,788	3,004	4,382	...
Total	7,022	8,128	8,789	10,299	12,386	...
Portfolio investment						
Total income	1,949	2,267	2,597	2,556	2,697	3,310*
Total earnings	8,971	10,395	11,386	12,855	15,083	...

*First half year, seasonally adjusted; at annual rate.
†Excluding interest but before deducting foreign withholding taxes.
Source: U.S. Department of Commerce, *Survey of Current Business.*

Table IV. Foreign Investment in U.S.

In $000,000

Inflow of funds	1968	1969	1970	1971	1972	1973*
Direct investment	319	832	969	−67	160	1,456*
Portfolio investment	4,389	3,112	2,190	2,282	4,335	4,514*
Total	4,708	3,944	3,159	2,215	4,495	5,970*
Total earnings†	2,231	3,686	4,143	3,059	3,379	4,364*

*First half of year, seasonally adjusted, at annual rate.
†Excluding undistributed profits.
Source: U.S. Department of Commerce, *Survey of Current Business*.

Table V. U.K. Investment Abroad

In £000,000

Item	1965	1969	1970	1971	1972	1973*
Direct investment†						
New funds	141	228	209	329	294	...
Reinvested profits	167	321	308	316	398	...
Total	308	549	517	645	692	870
Portfolio investment‡	−94	34	112	77	715	130
Oil and miscellaneous	154	96	144	153	72	130
Total	368	679	773	875	1,479	1,130

*Estimate based on first half of year.
†Excluding oil.
‡Net disinvestment in 1965.
Sources: *U.K. Balance of Payments, 1973; Economic Trends.*

rate in 1972, about $1.5 billion. Net sales of existing bonds in 1971 were replaced by modest purchases in 1972, and despite increased redemptions of mature bonds, total investment in bonds increased to $1.1 billion. In the first half of 1973 a similar pattern prevailed, with net sales of foreign company securities being offset by purchases of newly issued bonds to give a very modest figure for total portfolio investment.

Foreign investment in the U.S. increased very sharply in 1972 from the abnormally low level of 1971 and almost reached the record inflow of 1968. Much of this increase was due to foreign portfolio investment, but in the first half of 1973 there was a rapid expansion in foreign direct investment. A small net outflow of direct investment from the U.S. had occurred in 1971, but, as Japanese subsidiaries ceased the large transfers of funds to their parent companies, there was a small net inflow of foreign funds in 1972. The major inflow of funds came from EEC and Canadian companies. The inflow of direct investment funds increased very sharply in the first half of 1973, with U.K. and Japanese companies, in particular, building up their assets.

Portfolio investment in the U.S. by foreign investors in 1972 reached the 1968 record level, with a particularly large inflow of $1.9 billion in the fourth quarter alone. Foreign purchases of Eurobonds newly issued by U.S. corporations increased from $800 million to $2 billion. The buoyant U.S. stock market attracted foreign investors, who purchased $2.5 billion of U.S. company stocks in 1972; Western European investors increased their purchases from $700 million to $2.2 billion in 1972. This high inflow continued during the first half of 1973, although purchases of Eurobond issues declined.

United Kingdom. There was a very large increase in foreign investment by the U.K. in 1972 to a level about 70% higher than in 1971 (Table V). Provisional figures for the first half of 1973 suggested that the total investment in 1973 would show a marked drop from the very high level of 1972 but would still be well above other recent years. Portfolio investment accounted for the major part of the increase in 1972; there was a modest increase in direct investment, and a decline in the oil and miscellaneous category. The year 1973, however, saw a sharp drop in portfolio investment but marked increases in the other two groups.

The geographic distribution of U.K. foreign direct investment is shown in Table VI, where the recent importance of investment in other EEC countries can be seen. A feature of 1972 was the increased share of investment being directed toward sterling area countries.

In 1971 slightly more than half of the direct investment was financed by new funds, but in 1972 a much larger proportion was financed by the reinvestment of profits earned abroad. Much of the investment in 1973 was financed either by reinvestment of profits or by borrowing overseas. The latter method reduces the effect of foreign investment on the balance of payments at the time, although it does mean that in future years interest payments have to be made to the foreign stockholders.

British portfolio investment abroad rose to record levels in 1972, partly influenced by the desire of British investors to hold assets in a currency less likely than the pound sterling to depreciate. Much of this portfolio investment was in EEC countries and to a lesser extent in U.S. securities. The level of investment was more than £700 million, compared with an average of only £70 million in the years 1969–71. The peak rate was reached in the second quarter of 1972. Thereafter, there was a steady decline until by the second quarter of 1973 there were net sales of foreign securities by British investors.

Earnings on British international investments continued their steady increase in 1972 (Table VII). A marked increase occurred in the fourth quarter of 1972, associated with the depreciation of the pound, and continued into 1973. Earnings in the first half of 1973 were more than 30% higher than in the corresponding period of 1972.

Foreign investment in the U.K. fell sharply in 1972 from its abnormally high level in 1971, which had been the first year in which foreign investment in the U.K. had exceeded U.K. investment abroad (Table VIII). The year 1972, however, restored the traditional pattern of the U.K. as a capital exporter. Foreign investment in the U.K. rose again in 1973 and in the first half of the year was almost as large as British investment abroad. A feature of foreign direct investment in the U.K. in 1972 was the unusually large proportion that was financed by reinvested profits; the flow of new funds totaled only £90 million.

Foreign portfolio investment in the U.K. declined by more than £100 million in 1972. Foreign purchases of British government stocks and of new issues of U.K. company securities abroad increased substantially, but there was no borrowing abroad by British nationalized industries in 1972. In addition, foreign purchases of U.K. company shares fell from £100 million in 1971 to only £6 million in 1972. In the first half of

Table VI. U.K. Direct Investment and Earnings: by Region*

In £000,000

Area	Investment 1969	Investment 1970	Investment 1971	Investment 1972	Earnings 1969	Earnings 1970	Earnings 1971	Earnings 1972
North America	89	178	152	...	136	141	158	...
Latin America	21	13	22	...	33	32	29	...
EEC	105	71	244	...	83	93	94	...
EFTA	14	21	4	...	17	22	20	...
Others	7	12	41	...	37	37	41	...
Total nonsterling area	236	295	463	390	306	325	342	395
Total sterling area	313	222	182	302	344	359	351	419
Total	549	517	645	692	650	684	693	814
Of which less developed countries (included above)	147	134	133	145				

*Excluding oil companies.
Source: *U.K. Balance of Payments, 1973.*

Table VII. U.K. Investment Earnings

In £000,000

Item	1965	1969	1970	1971	1972	1973*
Direct investment†						
Repatriated profits	233	329	376	377	416	...
Reinvested profits	167	321	308	316	398	...
Total	400	650	684	693	814	1,096
Portfolio investment	158	161	171	166	166	186
Oil and miscellaneous	434	527	533	612	605	736
Total earnings	992	1,338	1,388	1,471	1,585	2,018

*First half of year, seasonally adjusted, at annual rate.
†Excluding oil.
Sources: *U.K. Balance of Payments, 1973; Economic Trends.*

Table VIII. Foreign Investment in U.K.

In £000,000

Item	1965	1969	1970	1971	1972	1973*
Direct investment†						
New funds	79	187	168	254	90	...
Reinvested profits	118	132	171	174	253	...
Total	197	319	339	428	343	300
Portfolio investment	−38	136	73	368	259	430
Oil and miscellaneous	67	218	303	391	230	320
Total	226	673	715	1,187	832	1,050

*Estimate based on first half of year.
†Excluding oil.
Sources: *U.K. Balance of Payments, 1973; Economic Trends.*

1973 new issues abroad by U.K. companies, by nationalized industries, and, for the first time, by local authorities, together with resumed foreign purchases of company shares, pushed the inflow of portfolio investment to a record level.

Other Industrial Countries. Data on foreign investment by, and in, other industrial countries is given in Table IX. These flows are recorded in national currency units because recent changes in exchange rates mean that it is no longer appropriate to measure such flows in terms of the U.S. dollar.

Belgium. The main feature of Belgian international investment in 1972 was the large increase in portfolio investment by Belgium over the 1971 figure, which itself had been quite large. Belgian investors were encouraged in their purchase of foreign securities by the high yields offered, by the increased issue of Eurobonds, and by the generally good performances of foreign stock exchanges. Belgian direct investment declined slightly in 1972, and foreign direct investment in Belgium dropped by BFr. 5 billion to a level similar to that in 1970. The overall effect of all these changes was a very large increase in the net outflow of funds from Belgium.

West Germany. The net inflow of long-term capital into West Germany reached record levels of almost DM. 14 billion in 1972. West German direct investment continued at a rate similar to 1971 but there was a further increase in foreign direct investment in the nation to DM. 3.7 billion, compared with only DM. 1.5 billion in 1970. This increased inflow was attributed to the enlargement of the EEC, and it was noticeable that the U.S. increased its investment by DM. 1.5 billion. It was, however, in portfolio investments that the most dramatic changes took place. In order to avoid uncertainties associated with other currencies, there was a strong demand from foreign investors to acquire mark assets. In the first seven months of 1972 alone foreign purchases of West German fixed-interest securities amounted to DM. 6.5 billion. In order to check this inflow, the acquisition by foreigners of domestic bonds was made subject to authorization under the Foreign Trade and Payments Act in June 1972. The inflow ceased, and in the last five months of the year there were net sales of such bonds amounting to DM. 800 million. Foreign purchases of West German shares of stock and investment fund units, which had been approximately DM. 500 million in 1970 and 1971, accelerated to DM. 3 billion in 1972, and in February 1973 the authorization requirement for bond purchases was extended to cover shares also.

The capital inflow was further increased by large sales of foreign securities by West German investors, who sold DM. 4.2 billion foreign mark bonds in 1972. These sales reached a peak in the third quarter of 1972 after the restrictions on foreign purchases of West German securities, suggesting that West German residents wished to acquire foreign funds by selling DM. bonds. There was considerable foreign demand for these foreign DM. bonds from nonresidents seeking mark assets; these bonds, unlike those issued by West German residents, were not liable to the 25% coupon tax. The magnitude of these sales resulted in an appeal by the Bundesbank to West German financial institutions for restraint, and in the final quarter of the year the inflow of funds was only DM. 200 million, compared with DM. 8.5 billion in the preceding three quarters. The various restrictions reduced the net inflow of portfolio investment, but the total inflow of DM. 12.7 billion was extremely large by any standards.

Italy. The Italian pattern of international investment also shifted from direct to portfolio in 1972. Italian direct investment declined 50% in 1972, partly due to a sharp fall in the financing of oil exploration. On the other hand, Italian purchases of international bonds rose sharply, accounting for much of the large increase in Italian foreign portfolio investment.

The Netherlands. Direct foreign investment by Dutch companies increased from the relatively low level of 1.6 billion guilders in 1971 to 2 billion guilders in 1972, while foreign investment in The Netherlands declined slightly. Although sales of Dutch shares increased by 300 million (with strong U.K. demand more than offsetting U.S. sales), the inflow of foreign portfolio investment was sharply reduced. At the same time Dutch investors increased their purchases of foreign securities, with U.S. shares and bonds being particularly popular. Overall, there was a net outflow of capital of 1.5 billion guilders in 1972, compared with a similar inflow in the previous year.

(A. G. ARMSTRONG)

Table IX. Other OECD Countries' International Investment, 1971–72

In billions of national currency unit

Country	1971 Direct	1971 Portfolio	1971 Total	1972 Direct	1972 Portfolio	1972 Total
Belgium						
Outflow	8.8	26.1	34.9	7.6	37.1	44.7
Inflow	21.8	5.5	27.3	16.6	8.0	24.6
Net	−13.0	20.6	7.6	−9.0	29.1	20.1
France						
Outflow	...	...	6.8	...	...	7.6
Inflow	...	...	8.0	...	...	8.1
Net	...	...	−1.2	...	...	−0.5
West Germany						
Outflow	2.7	−0.5	2.2	2.8	−4.0	−1.2
Inflow	3.2	2.0	5.2	3.7	8.7	12.4
Net	−0.5	−2.5	−3.0	−0.9	−12.7	−13.6
Italy						
Outflow	250	118	368	125	410	535
Inflow	325	70	395	365	30	395
Net	−75	48	−27	−240	380	140
The Netherlands						
Outflow	1.6	1.4	3.0	2.0	2.2	4.2
Inflow	2.0	2.6	4.6	1.8	0.9	2.7
Net	−0.4	−1.2	−1.6	0.2	1.3	1.5

Sources: Annual Reports of International Monetary Fund, Bank for International Settlements, and national banks.

See also Development, Economic; Payments and Reserves, International; Trade, International.

Iran

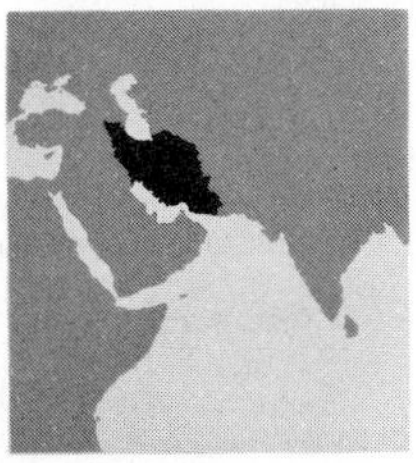

A constitutional monarchy of western Asia, Iran is bounded by the U.S.S.R., Afghanistan, Pakistan, Iraq, and Turkey and the Caspian Sea, the Arabian Sea, and the Persian Gulf. Area: 635,932 sq.mi. (1,647,064 sq.km.). Pop. (1972 est.): 30,820,000. Cap. and largest city: Teheran (pop., 1972 est., 3,858,000). Language: Farsi Persian. Religion: (1966) Muslim 96%; Christian, Jewish, and Zoroastrian minorities. Shah-in-shah, Mohammad Reza Pahlavi Aryamehr; prime minister in 1973, Emir Abbas Hoveida.

The nationwide support that had secured an overwhelming majority in the Majlis for the New Iran Party in the 1971 general elections continued throughout 1973. Under Prime Minister Hoveida the party's program of social and economic reform made steady progress, and the advances achieved in improved communications and in the promotion of rural reconstruction through agricultural cooperatives became a matter of national pride. This was illustrated in October when certain passages in a British television program devoted to Iran were taken to reflect adversely on Iranian domestic and foreign policies and on the part played by Shah Mohammad Reza Pahlavi (*see* BIOGRAPHY) in framing them. Resentment was so intense that the BBC's offices in Teheran were closed.

After protracted negotiations, a new 20-year oil agreement with the consortium of Western countries, replacing the agreement of 1954, was concluded in July. It had the effect of initiating a plain seller-buyer relationship between Iran and the oil companies and of giving Iran control over field operations. These operations, along with all facilities and installations previously worked by the consortium, were vested in the National Iranian Oil Company, which planned to use its new powers to ensure the fuller application of advanced recovery methods for the extraction of crude oil and the exploitation of natural gas. The consortium agreed to provide technical staff and expert knowledge through a new service company, which was to be registered under Iranian law. The company was to operate for an initial period of five years, after which it could be terminated if the National Iranian Oil Company so decided.

Iran did not participate in the cutback of oil shipments to the West instituted by the Arab producing states during the Arab-Israeli war in October, although it was said to be under some pressure from the Arab countries. However, it was not slow to take advantage of the resulting energy crisis. At a series of secret auctions, Iranian crude was sold at prices that in some cases surpassed $17 a barrel, and Teheran was the scene of a meeting of Persian Gulf oil ministers at which it was agreed to double the posted price to approximately $11.65. "The industrial world," the shah told a news conference, "will have to realize that the era of their terrific progress and even more terrific income and wealth based on cheap oil is finished."

In foreign affairs, the government pursued the traditional Iranian policy of cultivating friendly relations both with the great powers and with the nations in the south Asian region. Iraq remained hostile. The interests of the two countries conflicted in the Persian Gulf where, since October 1972, Iran had had friendly diplomatic relations with the United Arab Emirates. A fresh source of friction emerged when Iraq, with Soviet support, gave encouragement to secessionist movements in the western provinces of Pakistan. Iran saw a double danger in these movements. They would weaken Pakistan, its firm ally and partner in the Regional Cooperation for Development. Furthermore, the campaign for a "Free Baluchistan," if successful, would open the way for direct Soviet access from central Asia to the Arabian Sea ports along Pakistan's southern coast. In Iran's view, these were well placed to afford facilities for the strengthening of the Soviet maritime presence in the Persian Gulf region.

The apprehensions expressed by Iran on all these matters were sympathetically viewed at the meeting of the council of ministers of the Central Treaty Organization (CENTO), held in Teheran in June. Concerted programs of cooperation in the fields of communications, technical aid, and military planning between the constituent countries and friendly Western nations were carried to further stages. Iran had steadily increased the power and weaponry of its armed forces, and its influence as a stabilizing factor in the CENTO region had attained new importance. In February it was announced that Iran had ordered $2 billion worth of arms from the U.S.

In October, 12 Communist filmmakers were arrested and charged with plotting to kidnap the shah and his family as hostages for the release of political prisoners. (L. F. RUSHBROOK WILLIAMS)

IRAN

Education. (1969–70) Primary, pupils 2,916,266, teachers 89,320; secondary, pupils 897,443, teachers 25,890; vocational, pupils 23,335, teachers 2,165; teacher training, students 9,275, teachers 505; higher (including 8 universities), students 67,268, teaching staff 6,103.

Finance. Monetary unit: rial, with (Sept. 17, 1973) a free rate of 66.80 rials to U.S. $1 (161 rials = £1 sterling). Gold, SDRs, and foreign exchange, central bank: (June 1973) U.S. $1,130,000,000; (June 1972) U.S. $810 million. Budget (1971–72 actual): revenue 256.5 billion rials; expenditure 302.8 billion rials. Gross domestic product: (1970–71) 852.1 billion rials; (1969–70) 772.5 billion rials. Money supply: (April 1973) 230,290,000,000 rials; (April 1972) 165,090,000,000 rials. Cost of living (1963 = 100): (June 1973) 137; (June 1972) 128.

Foreign Trade. (1972) Imports 182,570,000,000 rials; exports 222.5 billion rials. Import sources: U.S. 23%; West Germany 17%; Japan 13%; U.K. 12%; Italy 6%; France 5%. Export destinations: Japan 34%; Italy 9%; West Germany 9%; The Netherlands 8%; U.K. 7%; U.S. 5%. Main export crude oil 86%.

Transport and Communications. Roads (1972) 43,442 km. Motor vehicles in use (1972): passenger 354,800; commercial (including buses) 101,300. Railways (1971): 4,509 km.; traffic 1,991,000,000 passenger-km., freight (1972) 3,363,000,000 net ton-km. Air traffic (1971): 727 million passenger-km.; freight 11,739,000 net ton-km. Shipping (1972): merchant vessels 100 gross tons and over 88; gross tonnage 180,659. Telephones (Jan. 1971) 307,000. Radio receivers (Dec. 1968) 2.5 million. Television receivers (Dec. 1969) 250,000.

Agriculture. Production (in 000; metric tons; 1972; 1971 in parentheses): wheat 4,400 (3,700); barley 1,009 (800); rice *c.* 1,200 (*c.* 1,100); sugar, raw value *c.* 657 (*c.* 638); dates (1971) *c.* 280, (1970) *c.* 310; grapes *c.* 650 (648); raisins *c.* 60 (*c.* 60); tea *c.* 20 (*c.* 21); tobacco *c.* 20 (16); cotton, lint *c.* 190 (*c.* 147). Livestock (in 000; Oct. 1971): cattle 5,516; sheep *c.* 36,000; goats *c.* 12,500; horses (March) *c.* 380; asses (March) *c.* 2,000; chickens *c.* 31,000.

Industry. Production (in 000; metric tons; 1971–72): cement 2,850; coal 600; crude oil (1972) 248,277; lead concentrates (metal content; 1970–71) *c.* 23; chrome ore (oxide content; 1970–71) *c.* 145; electricity (kw-hr.) 8,309,000.

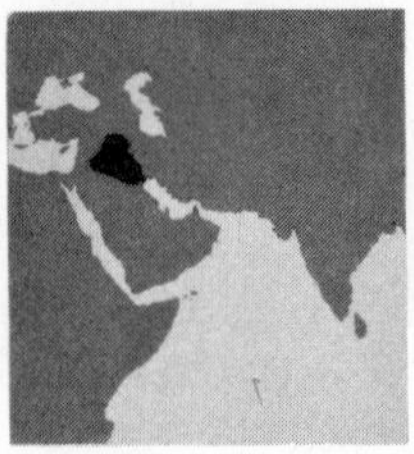

Iraq

A republic of western Asia, Iraq is bounded by Turkey, Iran, Kuwait, Saudi Arabia, Jordan, Syria, and the Persian Gulf. Area: 168,927 sq.mi. (437,522 sq.km.). Pop. (1973 est.): 10,210,000, including Arabs, Kurds, Turks, Assyrians, Iranians, and others. Cap. and largest city: Baghdad (pop., 1970 est., 2,183,760). Language: Arabic. Religion: mainly Muslim, some Christian. President in 1973, Gen. Ahmad Hassan al-Bakr.

In 1973 Iraq retained its rather isolated place in the Middle East despite military aid to Syria in the October war against Israel. Internally, the Baathist-dominated regime maintained firm control despite one serious attempted coup within its ranks and rumbling discontent among the Kurdish minority. On February 10 a severe crisis with Pakistan arose when a large cache of arms was discovered in the Iraqi embassy in Islamabad. The Iraqi ambassador was expelled, and it was later reported that the arms had been intended for rebels in the Iranian sector of Baluchistan. Relations with Iran continued to be bad, and frequent border clashes occurred. Iraqi suspicions that Iran was supplying the Kurds with arms were confirmed by Kurdish leader Mustafa al-Barzani in a press interview in June. The dispute with Kuwait in March, caused by Iraq's occupation of a police post on Kuwaiti territory, was not resolved despite Arab mediation, although a more serious clash was avoided.

There were some signs that Soviet-Iraqi relations were cooling because of the Soviet-Iranian rapprochement, and in August the Soviet and Czechoslovakian cultural centres in Baghdad were closed. However, in October it was reported that the Soviets had supplied Iraq with supersonic bombers of a type that had not been sent to a non-Communist country before. When Egypt and Syria attacked Israel on October 6, the Iraqi government first nationalized the U.S. and Dutch interests in the Basrah Petroleum Co. and then sent 18,000 troops with tanks and aircraft to fight alongside the Syrians. They were withdrawn a few days after the cease-fire, despite Syrian protests. President Bakr refused to attend the Arab summit conference at Algiers in November. Iraq joined the other Arab oil producers in boycotting oil shipments to the U.S. and The Netherlands, but it planned to increase oil production rather than cutting back. According to Iraqi spokesmen, the government's position was that indiscriminate use of the oil weapon would hurt countries friendly to the Arab cause.

Members of Iraq's Revolutionary Command Council march in the funeral procession of Defense Minister Hammad Shihab, slain in a coup attempt July 1, 1973.

WIDE WORLD

IRAQ

Education. (1969–70) Primary, pupils 1,040,968, teachers 48,290; secondary, pupils 302,611, teachers 10,114; vocational, students 9,994, teachers 1,022; teacher training, students 3,625, teachers 198; higher (including 5 universities), students 36,736, teaching staff 1,652.

Finance. Monetary unit: Iraqi dinar, with (Sept. 17, 1973) an official rate of 0.296 dinar to U.S. $1 (free rate of 0.714 dinar to £1 sterling). Gold, SDRs, and foreign exchange, central bank: (June 1973) U.S. $1,104,100,000; (June 1972) U.S. $686 million. Budget (1971–72 actual): revenue 514,680,000 dinars; expenditure 534,760,000 dinars. Gross national product: (1969) 961.9 million dinars; (1968) 899.3 million dinars. Money supply: (April 1973) 274.3 million dinars; (April 1972) 235.1 million dinars. Cost of living (Baghdad; 1963 = 100): (June 1973) 129; (June 1972) 124.

Foreign Trade. (1972) Imports 234.7 million dinars; exports 356.7 million dinars. Import sources: U.S.S.R. 12%; France 10%; U.K. 9%; Spain 5%. Export destinations: France 22%; Italy 18%; Greece 8%; U.K. 6%; Brazil 5%; Australia 5%. Main export crude oil 93%.

Transport and Communications. Roads (1971) 12,840 km. Motor vehicles in use (1971): passenger 53,460; commercial 42,290. Railways: (1970) 2,528 km.; traffic (1970–71) 467 million passenger-km., freight 1,310,000,000 net ton-km. Air traffic (1972): 252,750,000 passenger-km.; freight 2,683,000 net ton-km. Shipping (1972): merchant vessels 100 gross tons and over 41; gross tonnage 121,399. Telephones (Jan. 1971) 120,000. Radio receivers (Dec. 1970) 1.7 million. Television receivers (Dec. 1971) 500,000.

Agriculture. Production (in 000; metric tons; 1972; 1971 in parentheses): wheat 2,625 (822); barley 980 (432); rice 268 (307); tomatoes (1971) 383, (1970) 220; dates *c.* 330 (*c.* 330); sesame *c.* 12 (*c.* 8); linseed *c.* 12 (6); tobacco *c.* 10 (*c.* 10); cotton, lint 16 (14). Livestock (in 000; 1971–72): sheep *c.* 14,500; cattle *c.* 2,000; goats *c.* 2,600; buffalo *c.* 300; camels *c.* 220; horses *c.* 130; asses *c.* 600.

Industry. Production (in 000; metric tons): crude oil (1971) 83,775; cement (1969) 1,381; electricity (excluding most industrial production; kw-hr.; 1970) 2,115,000.

On July 1 a coup led by Director of Internal Security Nazem Kazzar and aimed at the assassination of President Bakr was foiled by the regime's strong man, Vice-Pres. Saddam Takriti, but led to the death of the defense minister, Hammad Shihab, and wounding of the interior minister, Saadun Ghaidan, whom Kazzar had taken as hostages. Kazzar and 35 of his associates were executed, and it was revealed that Kazzar had wielded considerable independent power and been responsible for much of the violent repression inside Iraq. In mid-July amendments to the constitution gave important new powers to the president, who had formerly been regarded as a figurehead in contrast to the vice-president. On July 26 President Bakr took over the defense ministry.

On July 17 an agreement to form a nationalist front was announced with a supreme committee that would have a Baathist chairman, 8 Baathist members, 3 Communists, 3 members of the Kurdish Democratic Party, 1 Progressive Nationalist, and 1 Independent Democrat. The Communists joined at once, but despite Baathist overtures the KDP was hesitant and there were persistent reports throughout the summer of Kurdish discontent. The Kurds accused the Baghdad government of bad faith in carrying out its 1970 agreement with the Kurdish minority. On September 28 Baghdad Airport was closed and a curfew imposed after a series of brutal and mysterious murders in the capital.

The Iraqi economy received an important boost when, after prolonged negotiations, agreement was reached with the Iraq Petroleum Co. (IPC), which Iraq had nationalized in June 1972. Iraq was to pay the company compensation in the form of 109.5 million bbl. of crude oil. IPC would waive its objections to the Iraqi Law 80 of 1961 which confiscated most of IPC's concession area and also pay $338 million in back royalties. The government announced that as a result Iraq would receive 460 million dinars in revenues in 1973, 540 million dinars in 1974, and 647 million dinars in 1975, compared with 300 million dinars in 1971. On August 27 an agreement was announced with Turkey for the building of a 1,050-km. oil pipeline from Kirkuk to the Turkish port of Dortyol. (PETER MANSFIELD)

Ireland

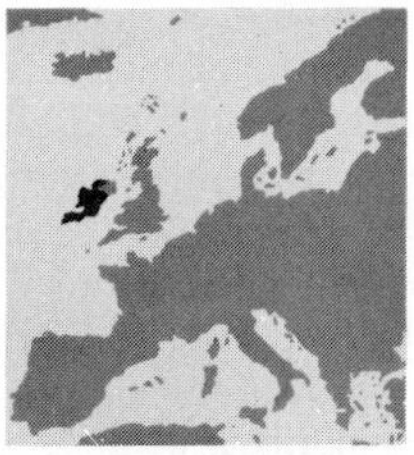

Separated from Great Britain by the North Channel, the Irish Sea, and St. George's Channel, the Republic of Ireland shares its island with Northern Ireland to the northeast. Area: 27,136 sq.mi. (70,282 sq.km.), or 83% of the island. Pop. (1972 est.): 3,014,000. Cap. and largest city: Dublin (pop., 1971, 567,866). Language: English (80%) and Gaelic. Religion: predominantly Roman Catholic (95%). Presidents in 1972, Eamon de Valera and, from June 25, Erskine Childers; prime ministers, John Lynch and, from March 14, Liam Cosgrave.

In 1973, for the first time in 16 years, power changed hands in the republic with the election of a coalition government under Liam Cosgrave (*see* BIOGRAPHY), leader of Fine Gael. The election was announced on February 5 by Jack Lynch, prime minister since 1966, who sought to reestablish a clear majority for his Fianna Fail party following various defections from it. He based his election campaign on security, law and order, and his policy for Northern Ireland.

The following day, February 6, the two opposition parties, Fine Gael and Labour, came together in a coalition agreement with a policy based on bread-and-butter issues such as housing, prices, and employment. Voter turnout in the February 28 election was 75%, the highest since the 1933 general election. Fianna Fail gained 69 seats, the coalition 73, and there were 2 independents. The changeover of government was achieved more by the effective use of transfer voting under the proportional representation system than by any dramatic swing in public attitude. The new coalition alliance of a traditional conservative party with the main left-wing socialist party achieved its success largely on the basis of personalities, such as Conor Cruise O'Brien (who became minister for posts and telegraphs in the new administration) and Garret FitzGerald (the new foreign minister).

In the presidential election in May, the two main parties put forward candidates Tom O'Higgins (Fine Gael) and Erskine Childers (Fianna Fail), and the campaign was fought on party lines. On May 30 Childers (*see* BIOGRAPHY) was elected for a seven-year term. He succeeded Eamon de Valera, who retired after more than half a century of political life, 21 years as prime minister, and 14 years as president.

The dominant issues, both before and after the elections, were Northern Ireland, the involvement of the republic, and the relationship of the Dublin and Westminster governments. On March 8 the new prime minister, Liam Cosgrave, held his first meeting with the British prime minister, Edward Heath. Their discussions centred on the British White Paper on Northern Ireland, which was published on March 20. The gravity of the situation facing both leaders was emphasized by bomb explosions in the centre of London on the day of their meeting.

In April, Foreign Minister FitzGerald paid a visit to Belfast, and on June 11 the prime minister made an important policy speech on Northern Ireland, the theme of which was conciliation. This, however, received a setback as the so-called "Littlejohn affair" unfolded, following the sentencing, on August 3, of the two Littlejohn brothers for a £67,000 robbery in Dublin. At their trial and afterward, it developed that there had been collaboration between the brothers and the British government in ineffective attempts at spying in Ireland. The revelations, admitted by the British government, damaged Anglo-Irish accord, and the situation was aggravated when the coalition government engaged in controversial exchanges with former prime minister Lynch on the extent to which his government had known of the Littlejohn affair. Lynch claimed that he had forgotten an important document, and his memory lapse was exposed by the government. He threatened resignation as opposition leader but was persuaded by his party to stay on. The episode hinted at an unacceptable level of British-Irish security collaboration and damaged relations all round.

To some extent these were mended by the deter-

IRELAND

Education. (1969–70) Primary, pupils 513,805, teachers 16,613; secondary, pupils 148,197, teachers 9,842; vocational (1967–68), pupils 83,206, teachers 5,595; higher (1968–69), students *c.* 25,660, teaching staff (1967–68) *c.* 1,370.

Finance. Monetary unit: Irish pound, at par with the pound sterling, with a free rate (Sept. 17, 1973) of U.S. $2.41 = £1 sterling. Gold, SDRs, and foreign exchange, official: (June 1973) U.S. $988 million; (June 1972) U.S. $1,001,000,000. Budget (1972–73 est.): revenue £622 million; expenditure £650 million. Gross national product: (1971) £1,897 million; (1970) £1,663 million. Money supply: (June 1973) £495.6 million; (June 1972) £436.8 million. Cost of living (1963 = 100): (May 1973) 189; (May 1972) 169.

Foreign Trade. (1972) Imports £844.9 million; exports £644.5 million. Import sources: U.K. 51%; U.S. 8%; West Germany 8%. Export destinations: U.K. 61%; U.S. 9%; West Germany 5%. Main exports: meat 15%; livestock 13% (cattle 11%); textiles and clothing 10%; dairy produce 7%; machinery 6%; chemicals 5%. Tourism (1971): visitors 1,692,000; gross receipts U.S. $185 million.

Transport and Communications. Roads (1971) 87,202 km. Motor vehicles in use (1971): passenger 418,100; commercial 44,528. Railways: (1971) 2,189 km.; traffic (1972) 818 million passenger-km., freight 499.8 million net ton-km. Air traffic (1972): 1,622,900,000 passenger-km.; freight 80,023,000 net ton-km. Shipping (1972): merchant vessels 100 gross tons and over 97; gross tonnage 182,319. Telephones (Dec. 1971) 324,000. Radio licenses (Dec. 1971) 615,000. Television licenses (Dec. 1971) 486,000.

Agriculture. Production (in 000; metric tons; 1972; 1971 in parentheses): potatoes *c.* 1,300 (*c.* 1,330); oats *c.* 151 (207); barley *c.* 955 (992); wheat *c.* 251 (377); sugar, raw value *c.* 186 (*c.* 188); milk (1971) *c.* 3,700, (1970) 3,634; butter (1971) 75, (1970) 73; cheese (1971) 34, (1970) 29; beef and veal (1971) *c.* 340, (1970) 337; pork (1971) *c.* 147, (1970) 144; fish catch (1971) 74, (1970) 79. Livestock (in 000; Dec. 1972): cattle 5,946; sheep 2,835; pigs 1,007; horses *c.* 120; chickens 9,143.

Industry. Index of production (1963 = 100): (1972) 168; (1971) 161. Production (in 000; metric tons; 1972): coal 74; cement 1,470; electricity (excluding most industrial production; kw-hr.) 6,675,000; manufactured gas (cu.m.) 257,000; beer (hl.; 1969–70) 3,751; wool fabrics (sq.m.) 5,400; rayon, etc., fabrics (sq.m.) 7,400.

English-born Erskine Childers, the second Protestant to be elected president of Ireland, won over his Catholic opponent in May 30 elections. Officials reported heavy election turnouts despite IRA pleas for a boycott of the polls.

WIDE WORLD

WIDE WORLD

Outgoing president of the Irish Republic Eamon de Valera, oldest head of state in the world, leaves Parliament in Dublin after a sentimental final visit, June 24, 1973.

mination of the British to establish an executive in Northern Ireland in which Protestants and Catholics would share power. The historic visit of Prime Minister Heath to Ireland for nine hours of talks with Cosgrave on September 17 was followed, in December, by the marathon meeting at Berkshire, Eng., at which Cosgrave, Heath, and representatives of Northern Ireland reached agreement on the North's future. Dublin recognized that the North's link with Britain could not be changed unless a majority in the North agreed, and both Britain and the republic were to deposit solemn pledges on the North's status with the UN. A Council of Ireland was to be set up, including seven members of the Dublin government and seven members of the Northern executive, although its exact functions remained somewhat vague. The accord, which represented a triumph for the moderates, cleared the way for establishment of the Protestant-Catholic coalition in the North early in 1974.

The historic decision was made to establish diplomatic relations with the Soviet Union, and a joint statement was issued by the foreign ministers of both countries at the UN on September 29. Ireland's first year as a member of the EEC benefited Irish farmers substantially, but it produced difficulties with rising costs and serious uncertainty about employment as falling tariffs threatened the survival of industries that had grown up under protectionist policies. After a spate of industrial mergers and acquisitions, the government introduced a Restrictive Practices (Amendment) Bill to the Dail in February.

In his first major speech on the economy after his election, the prime minister in April pledged the government to the fair implementation of price controls while doing everything possible to encourage free competition and investment from abroad. He laid particular stress on the need to curb inflation, which was running at $8\frac{1}{2}$–10% annually. Key provisions in the May budget included record increases in social welfare benefits and higher duties on cigarettes, spirits, and beer. The value-added tax was removed from most food items, although VAT rates were increased for cars, hardware, and electrical goods. On June 7 Minister for Labour Michael O'Leary announced the creation of a National Economic Council to advise the government in the context of EEC membership.

Continued friction and judicial severity marked the relationships between the new government and the extremist organizations in the country. The first confrontation occurred on March 28, within a fortnight of the formation of the Cabinet, when the "Claudia," a West German vessel bringing illegal arms into the country, was arrested off the south coast. The owner of the ship claimed that it should have been carrying 100 tons of arms, although only 5 tons, including Soviet-made weapons, were recovered. The arms were thought to have come from Tripoli, Libya. (Col. Muammar al-Qaddafi had claimed that he was aiding the Irish Republican Army.) Joe Cahill, former commander of the Belfast brigade of the IRA's Provisional wing, was among six men arrested on board. He was sentenced to three years' imprisonment.

Further arrests of militants were made during the year, but on October 21 David O'Connell, leader of the Provisional IRA, escaped arrest when crowds overturned a police car at the Mansion House, Dublin, in a diversionary action. O'Connell had slipped disguised into the annual Sinn Fein convention and delivered the annual message of the IRA leadership. On October 31 a brilliantly executed rescue of three top IRA men from the Mountjoy Prison, Dublin, took place with the aid of a hijacked helicopter.

The former Roman Catholic archbishop of Dublin, John Charles McQuaid, symbol of church conservatism in the country, died in April at the age of 78. The distinguished novelist Elizabeth Bowen also died (*see* OBITUARIES). (BRUCE ARNOLD)

See also United Kingdom.

Ireland, Northern: *see* United Kingdom

Iron and Steel: *see* Industrial Review; Mining

Islam: *see* Religion

Israel

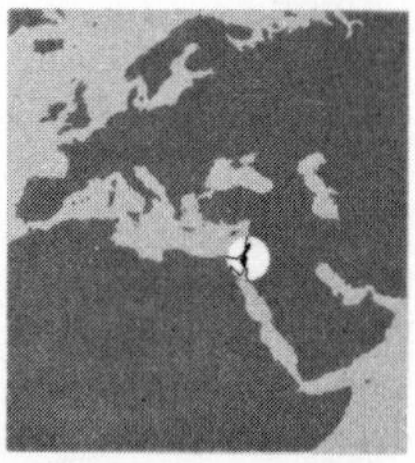

A republic of the Middle East, Israel is bounded by Lebanon, Syria, Jordan, Egypt, and the Mediterranean Sea. Area (not including territory occupied in the June 1967 war): 7,992 sq.mi. (20,700 sq.km.). Pop. (1973 est.): 3,249,000. Cap.: Jerusalem (pop., 1972 prelim., 304,500). Largest city: Tel Aviv-Yafo (pop., 1972 prelim., 362,900). Language: Hebrew and Arabic. Religion: predominantly Jewish. Presidents in 1973, Schneor Zalman Shazar and, from May 23, Ephraim Katzir; prime minister, Mrs. Golda Meir.

The year 1973 brought war to Israel. Even before the end of 1972, the nation's internal political problems were overshadowed by growing tension on the Syrian frontier, which had been sparked by a military clash on November 9 followed by a nine-hour battle on November 21 when aircraft, armour, and artillery were engaged. These incidents appeared to have more than local implications when the Syrian defense minister, Mustafa Tlass, was invited to Moscow for talks with Soviet Defense Minister Andrey A. Grechko on December 6. Fighting on the Syrian border was renewed on December 27 and continued intermittently until Jan. 8, 1973, when it erupted into a daylong battle during which the Syrian authorities appealed for the intervention of all Arab states. Thus, it was an uneasy beginning to the new year that confronted Prime Minister Golda Meir (*see* BIOGRAPHY).

The 25th anniversary of Israel's renewed independence was also the tenth year since the withdrawal of David Ben-Gurion from the premiership; the end of the first decade of the post-Ben-Gurion style of government by Levi Eshkol and Mrs. Meir. But the essence of this extraordinary year was that—for the first nine months—Mrs. Meir's administration froze all change and development despite attempts by Defense Minister Moshe Dayan to introduce a new initiative on the occupied territories. The tragic shooting down by Israel of a civilian Libyan airliner with 113 persons on board in February came at a time when the Israeli government was anxious to win renewed international understanding in response to what officials in Jerusalem described as "Sadat's peace offensive." In support of Israel's position, Mrs. Meir attended a meeting of the Socialist International in Paris in January, had an audience with Pope Paul VI at the Vatican on January 15, a meeting at Geneva with the president of the Ivory Coast, Félix Houphouët-Boigny, one of Israel's oldest and staunchest friends (who nevertheless severed diplomatic relations in November), on January 17, and on March 1 paid a private visit to U.S. Pres. Richard Nixon in Washington. Mrs. Meir had found unexpectedly strong support for Israel's position in Washington, where Egyptian Pres. Anwar as-Sadat's special envoy, Hafez Ismail, had preceded her and had emphasized Egypt's unyielding stand for total Israeli withdrawal and substantial but unspecified additional Israeli concessions to meet Palestinian demands.

It was this encounter in Washington that was to be a decisive element in Mrs. Meir's attitude on all questions of foreign policy that concerned relations with the Arab countries. Basing its outlook on what it described as "the soundest possible information," which showed conclusively that President Sadat (*see* Biography) would not make peace and would not recognize Israel until he could dictate the terms of a settlement, Israel's government reached the conclusion that there was no chance of any kind of acceptable settlement for at least five years. Moreover, any territorial concessions by Israel would serve only to strengthen the Arabs in preparation for their next war against Israel. This then set the course of Israel's defense and foreign policies—and also shaped the general state of mind that pervaded every sector of Israeli society: that time was on the side of Israel and that it could now concern itself with the economic well-being of the country and pay more attention to social problems that had been gravely neglected. The military balance and the defense situation were no longer considered serious difficulties. Warning voices on the political fringe went largely unheeded. More significant was the position taken by General Dayan, who urged that Israel should seek "to exchange some of its military security for political security."

This alternative of Dayan's to a standpat policy became the central issue of debate inside the ruling Labour Party in the preparation of its platform for the general election. At the party's decisive meeting on April 12 a compromise solution that largely favoured Dayan's position was proposed, but it was not until August that the party leadership accepted it.

Meanwhile, more urgent preoccupations demanded attention. Attacks by Palestinian terrorists had greatly increased since the end of 1972. On Jan. 9, 1973, the Jewish Agency headquarters in Paris was bombed, and on April 9 the apartment of the Israeli ambassador in Nicosia, Cyprus, and an El Al Israel Airlines plane at Nicosia airport were attacked. But these were only the outward indicators of a worldwide battle that had been joined. Mrs. Meir had herself authorized a counterattack against the terrorist organizations, and on April 10 Israeli Army commando units raided Beirut, Lebanon, killed three Palestinian leaders associated with the terrorist attacks, and destroyed a headquarters of the Democratic Popular Front.

WIDE WORLD

An Israeli woman army officer supervises target practice for three female recruits in March 1973. Although subject to conscription, Israeli women were banned from active battle zones.

Only much later did it become known that Israel's armed forces had been on a major alert during the spring because, in April, Israeli intelligence had reported that the Egyptian military buildup on the Suez Canal was such that an imminent attempt to cross the canal had to be expected. Mrs. Meir obliquely warned the country on April 28 that Israel had to be ready for a resumption of hostilities. However, the expected attack did not take place. The Israelis believed that this was due to U.S. intervention with the Soviet Union and the resultant pressure on President Sadat not to embark on what all concerned considered a suicidal folly. (The Egyptians later maintained that the April-May preparations had been a bluff to confuse the Israelis when the real attack came.)

All the same, the attack that did not materialize was to have a traumatic effect on Israel's military establishment, especially that concerned with intelligence evaluation. It had been the fourth such warning by Israel's secret intelligence service in four years, and already in June a new warning was addressed to the military leaders to the effect that President Sadat was determined to go to war in the autumn of 1973. It was a documented and detailed warning, but it was not accepted. The warnings multiplied and increased in intensity. At the beginning of October, the Israeli Air Force was placed on alert, but not the armoured forces or the reserves. Three inquiries from the U.S. in the week before October 6 about reports it had received of Egyptian and Syrian preparations for an attack on Israel were also discounted on the strength of evaluations by Israel's military intelligence specialists, a body quite distinct from the secret service.

Intelligence evaluations notwithstanding, Egypt and Syria did attack at 2 P.M. local time on Saturday, October 6—Yom Kippur, the Day of Atonement, the most sacred occasion in Israel's religious calendar. As it turned out, the country was more unprepared psychologically than militarily. Precisely what happened became a matter of dispute not only among the political parties but also among some of the principal senior officers involved. In response to public pressure, the government appointed a high-level judicial inquiry into the state of Israel's preparedness. Dayan offered to resign; Mrs. Meir rejected the offer but Dayan came under sustained attacks.

In regard to the war itself, Dayan had the last word: the assault, on a scale unimagined—the Arab armies attacked with approximately 5,000 tanks, as many as Hitler had used for the invasion of the Soviet Union in 1941—was halted within 48 hours and the tide turned despite the heavy infusion of Soviet aid for the Arab forces. When the fighting ended after the third cease-fire on October 25, Israel was within 30 mi. of Damascus and within 50 mi. of Cairo (although Dayan claimed that both Egypt and Syria were better equipped at the end of the war than at the beginning). (For an account of the military operations, *see* DEFENSE: *Special Report*.)

This war, like all previous Arab-Israeli conflicts, ended politically inconclusively. On the initiative of the Soviet Union and the United States there was to be yet one more attempt at a political solution, this time in peace talks held in Geneva from December 21. (*See* MIDDLE EASTERN AFFAIRS.)

The Israeli public approached the December 31 general election in a mood of deep misgiving. The country was largely isolated diplomatically, 27 African nations and Cuba having severed relations by year's end, while France, Britain, and Japan moved closer to the Arabs when threatened with a loss of Middle Eastern oil. In the election Mrs. Meir's Labour Party retained control of Parliament but lost about five seats to the opposition parties.

ISRAEL

Education. (1970–71) Primary, pupils 459,949, teachers (1969–70) 26,547; secondary, pupils 65,132; vocational, pupils 62,617; teacher training, students 5,449; secondary, vocational, and teacher training, teachers (1969–70) 12,657; higher (including 4 universities; 1969–70), students 49,076, teaching staff (universities only) *c.* 4,650.

Finance. Monetary unit: Israeli pound, with (Sept. 17, 1973) a par value of I£4.20 to U.S. $1 (free rate of I£10.12 = £1 sterling). Gold, SDRs, and foreign exchange, central bank: (June 1973) U.S. $1,387,-400,000; (1972) U.S. $1,079,900,000. Budget (1971–72 est.): revenue I£10,167 million; expenditure I£11,-583 million. Gross national product: (1971) I£23,328 million; (1970) I£18,949 million. Money supply: (June 1972) I£5,075 million; (June 1971) I£3,889 million. Cost of living (1963 = 100): (June 1973) 207; (June 1972) 171.

Foreign Trade. (1972) Imports I£7,966 million; exports I£4,821 million. Import sources: U.S. 20%; U.K. 19%; West Germany 12%; Italy 7%; Belgium-Luxembourg 6%; France 5%. Export destinations: U.S. 19%; U.K. 10%; West Germany 9%; The Netherlands 6%; Japan 5%; Hong Kong 5%; Switzerland 5%; France 5%. Main exports: diamonds 37%; citrus fruit 11%; chemicals 8%; clothing 6%; fruit preparations 5%.

Transport and Communications. Roads (1972) *c.* 9,300 km. (including 3,300 paved). Motor vehicles in use (1972): passenger 201,130; commercial 82,500. Railways: (1971) 793 km.; traffic (1972) 387.8 million passenger-km., freight 421.5 million net ton-km. Air traffic (1972): 3,355,900,000 passenger-km.; freight 103,326,000 net ton-km. Shipping (1972): merchant vessels 100 gross tons and over 99; gross tonnage 698,068. Telephones (Dec. 1971) 584,000. Radio receivers (Dec. 1971) 660,000. Television licenses (Dec. 1971) 345,000.

Agriculture. Production (in 000; metric tons; 1971; 1970 in parentheses): wheat 195 (125); barley 18 (14); sorghum 21 (11); potatoes *c.* 130 (137); oranges 1,106 (938); grapefruit 361 (284); grapes (1972) *c.* 70, (1971) 67; sugar (1972) 28, (1971) 32; tomatoes 162 (159); olives (1972) *c.* 20, (1971) 13; bananas (1970) 61, (1969) 53; cotton, lint (1972) *c.* 40, (1971) 37; fish catch 28 (24). Livestock (in 000; Dec. 1971): cattle 263; sheep 184; goats 134; poultry 9,750.

Industry. Index of production (1963 = 100): (1972) 254; (1971) 228. Production (in 000; metric tons; 1972): cement 1,545; electricity (kw-hr.) 8,477,-000; salt (1971) 79; potash (oxide content; 1971) 569. New dwelling units completed (1971) 38,000.

Earlier in the year Pres. Zalman Shazar had retired and Ephraim Katzir, a noted scientist, was elected as Israel's fourth president (*see* BIOGRAPHY). On December 1, David Ben-Gurion, Israel's first prime minister, died at the age of 87 (*see* OBITUARIES).

(JON KIMCHE)

ENCYCLOPÆDIA BRITANNICA FILMS. *Israeli Boy: Life on a Kibbutz* (1973).

Italy

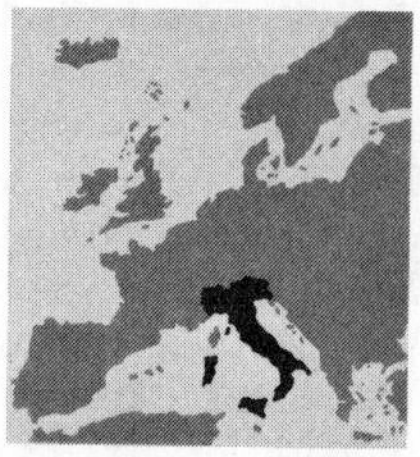

A republic of southern Europe, Italy occupies the Apennine Peninsula, Sicily, Sardinia, and a number of smaller islands. On the north it borders France, Switzerland, Austria, and Yugoslavia. Area: 116,313 sq.mi. (301,250 sq.km.). Pop. (1972 est.): 54,345,000. Cap. and largest city: Rome (pop., 1971, 2,799,836). Language: Italian. Religion: predominantly Roman Catholic. President in 1973, Giovanni Leone; premiers, Giulio Andreotti until June 12 and, from July 8, Mariano Rumor.

Domestic Affairs. Italy returned to a centre-left coalition government in 1973, with the participation of Christian Democrats, Socialists, Social Democrats, and Republicans. The change had its origins in the national congress of the Christian Democrats in June. Under the leadership of the newly elected secretary, Amintore Fanfani, the party decided to abandon the centre coalition experiment that had been conducted by Premier Giulio Andreotti with the support of the Liberal Party. Andreotti resigned on June 12, but the crisis was only a formal one; the road, in fact, had already been paved for a return to power of former premier Mariano Rumor (*see* BIOGRAPHY). On June 20 he was asked by President Leone to form a new government. He achieved this on July 7, after a Socialist decision to renew the party's support of a centre-left coalition, and was sworn in July 8. On July 18 the Senate approved the new government, and two days later the Chamber of Deputies followed suit.

The immediate program of the Rumor government was to stop inflation and put an end to the social and political unrest that had troubled Italy since the beginning of the year. In January three bombs had exploded in Milan, and a student was later killed by police during a demonstration at that city's Luigi Bocconi University of Economics and Commerce. In April, Angelo Mangano, a police inspector who was conducting inquiries into Mafia activities, was wounded by five bullets. A few days later a bomb thrown by right-wing extremists killed a policeman in Milan, and on April 16 two sons of right-wing leader Mario Mattei died in a blaze at their Rome apartment. On May 17 a bomb exploded in front of the Milan police headquarters, killing 3 people and wounding 43. Union unrest added to the general disorder, although workers' demands were gradually met and the situation seemed to ease during the summer.

A telephone tapping scandal, which had been brought to light in Rome, Milan, and other major Italian cities, resulted in the arrest on March 23 of Tom Ponzi, head of the largest Italian private detective firm. In April Parliament approved a bill prescribing up to three years' imprisonment for the violation of telephone secrecy.

A series of kidnappings kept the police busy. Indus-

Italian Literature: *see* Literature

trialist Pietro Torrielli was set free after payment of a 1,250,000,000 lire ransom. Seven-year-old Mirko Panattoni was returned to his parents in June after being held for 17 days, and in July, after a long wait, a San Marino doctor, Italo Rossini, and his daughter Rosella were freed by their kidnappers. J. Paul Getty III, grandson of the oil tycoon, was held prisoner for some five months until his father paid a ransom rumoured at almost $3 million. Mystery also surrounded the reappearance in Rome of U.S. newsman Jack Begon, who was allegedly kidnapped by the Mafia.

A cholera epidemic broke out in southern Italy at the end of August. First detected in Naples, it soon spread to Bari and other centres. Hundreds were stricken, and 19 persons died in Naples, 7 in Bari, and 5 elsewhere. The cause of the outbreak seemed to be infected seafood imported from North Africa.

The problem of pollution was faced with new urgency all over the country. In January labour inspectors prescribed the use of gas masks for workers in Marghera, near Venice. A Montedison plant in Scarlino, near Follonica, was closed in September because of its constant pollution of the sea by a poisonous substance that came to be known as red mud. The substance reached as far as the coast of Corsica, causing an uproar in the French island. In April the government approved a long-term, 1,000,000,000,000 lire program for the defense of the environment.

Foreign Affairs. The Middle East problem, which erupted in a new war between Israel and the Arab countries in October, was the focal point of Italian diplomacy throughout the year. In January Israeli Prime Minister Golda Meir was in Rome, where she had long discussions with President Leone and Premier Andreotti before meeting Pope Paul VI. Further Italian contacts with the Israeli government occurred on March 26, when Foreign Minister Giuseppe Medici visited his counterpart, Abba Eban, to discuss the possibility of reopening the Suez Canal. That the Italian efforts for peace in the Middle East were fruitless was demonstrated by the new war.

West German Pres. Gustav Heinemann visited Rome on March 21 and held long discussions with President Leone. Leone was a guest, on October 1, of French Pres. Georges Pompidou, completing this top-

WIDE WORLD

Italian Premier Giulio Andreotti leaves the presidential offices in Rome after presenting his resignation to Pres. Giovanni Leone, June 12, 1973.

level interchange between Italy, France, and West Germany. The new relationship with China was underlined by Medici's visit to Peking, where he had a series of meetings with Premier Chou En-lai.

The Economy. The widening of the EEC in January was welcomed enthusiastically. However, the introduction of the value-added tax (VAT) to replace previous forms of taxation on the production and sale of goods, bringing Italy into line with EEC tax policy, was unpopular and highly criticized. Even from the government's point of view the new system proved disappointing. Income in the first seven months fell short of expectations by 293 million lire.

In January, for the first time, a two-tier exchange rate system was introduced on currency markets. The so-called commercial lira was to be pegged to a fixed parity, whereas the financial lira would be allowed to fluctuate. A crisis in February, however, forced the closure of the money markets, and both lire were permitted to fluctuate after the further devaluation of the dollar. Throughout the year the lira had to be sustained by various interventions. By June nearly U.S. $10 billion had been borrowed for that purpose from various sources. In July, however, the lira gave clear signs of renewed strength.

The new centre-left government's first action to check inflation and the price spiral came on July 24, with the freezing of prices and of rents for families with an annual income less than 4 million lire. Twenty-

ITALY

Education. (1971–72) Primary, pupils 4,954,341, teachers 232,616; secondary, pupils 2,762,161, teachers (1969–70) 206,971; vocational, pupils 988,211, teachers 86,846; teacher training, students 206,545, teachers 18,465; higher (including 38 universities), students 845,567, teaching staff 43,087.

Finance. Monetary unit: lira, with (Sept. 17, 1973) a free rate of 564 lire to U.S. $1 (1,359 lire = £1 sterling) for the commercial (*valutaria*) rate and 600 lire to U.S. $1 (1,443 lire = £1 sterling) for the financial rate. Gold, SDRs, and foreign exchange, official: (June 1973) U.S. $5,634,000,000; (June 1972) U.S. 6,081,000,000. Budget (1972 est.): revenue 13,318,900,000,000 lire; expenditure 15,695,700,000,000 lire. Gross national product: (1971) 62,913,000,000,000 lire; (1970) 58,212,000,000,000 lire. Money supply: (Dec. 1972) 46,336,000,000,000 lire; (Dec. 1971) 37,160,000,000,000 lire. Cost of living (1963 = 100): (June 1973) 158; (June 1972) 141.

Foreign Trade. (1972) Imports 11,244,000,000,000 lire; exports 10,815,000,000,000 lire. Import sources: EEC 45% (West Germany 20%, France 16%, The Netherlands 5%); U.S. 8%. Export destinations: EEC 45% (West Germany 23%, France 14%); U.S. 10%. Main exports: machinery 24%; motor vehicles 9%; textiles, yarns, and fabrics 7%; chemicals 7%; footwear 5%; fruit and vegetables 5%. Tourism (1971): visitors 10,485,500; gross receipts U.S. $1,882,000,000.

Transport and Communications. Roads (1971) 287,447 km. (4,615 km. expressways in 1972). Motor vehicles in use (1972): passenger 12,475,000; commercial 986,000. Railways: (1971) 20,116 km.; traffic (1972) 35,370,000,000 passenger-km., freight 17,097,000,000 net ton-km. Air traffic (1971): 9,502,000,000 passenger-km.; freight 323,704,000 net ton-km. Shipping (1972): merchant vessels 100 gross tons and over 1,684; gross tonnage 8,187,323. Telephones (Dec. 1971) 10,322,000. Radio licenses (Dec. 1971) 12,068,000. Television licenses (Dec. 1971) 10,344,000.

Agriculture. Production (in 000; metric tons; 1972; 1971 in parentheses): wheat 9,412 (9,994); corn 4,802 (4,528); barley 388 (373); oats 461 (488); potatoes 3,002 (3,268); rice 751 (862); dry broad beans 348 (349); onions 421 (468); sugar, raw value *c.* 1,195 (1,233); tomatoes 3,068 (3,424); wine 5,919 (6,421); olives 1,920 (3,210); oranges 1,777 (1,766); lemons 728 (818); apples 1,873 (1,698); pears 1,526 (1,706); peaches (1971) 1,249, (1970) 1,127; figs (1971) 176, (1970) 198; tobacco 84 (79); cheese (1971) *c.* 465, (1970) *c.* 460; beef and veal 755 (812); pork 541 (515). Livestock (in 000; Jan. 1972): cattle 8,611; sheep 7,846; pigs 8,196; goats 976; horses, mules, and asses 655; poultry *c.* 110,000.

Industry. Index of production (1963 = 100): (1972) 152; (1971) 146. Unemployment: (1972) 3.6%; (1971) 3.1%. Fuel and power (in 000; metric tons; 1972): lignite 863; coal 250; crude oil 1,153; natural gas (cu.m.) 14,142,000; manufactured gas (cu.m.) 2,926,000; electricity (kw-hr.) *c.* 135,000,000. Production (in 000; metric tons; 1972): iron ore (50% metal content) 616; pig iron 9,616; crude steel 19,689; aluminum 157; zinc 158; lead 62; cement 33,459; cotton yarn 146; rayon, etc., filament yarn 68; rayon, etc., staple fibre 105; nylon, etc., filament yarn 133; nylon, etc., fibres 187; nitrogenous fertilizers (1971–72) 1,034; sulfuric acid 3,073; petroleum products (1971) 110,647; passenger cars (units) 1,732; commercial vehicles (units) 107. Merchant vessels launched (100 gross tons and over; 1972) 949,000 gross tons. New dwelling units completed (1972) 240,000.

one groups of articles, mainly food, were pegged at their July 16 level for a three-month period, to the end of October. Special tribunals were formed to punish transgressors promptly and severely. Industrial goods could be increased in price only by permission of the Ministerial Price Board, and this procedure would have to be followed for any food price increases between November and July 31, 1974. The results were immediate. The rise in the cost of living decelerated suddenly, and for the eight months from January to August it was limited to 7.3%. Late in the year gasoline and heating oil prices rose in response to the Arab oil-production cutback, and a series of fuel-saving measures were introduced, including lower speed limits and a ban on Sunday driving.

Other economic statistics were encouraging. By July unemployment had been reduced to 3.1% (against 3.7% in July 1972), and industrial production in the first eight months was 7.2% above the same period of 1972. The trade balance, however, showed a deficit of 1,877,000,000,000 lire by August, and the balance of payments deficit for the first eight months amounted to 378 billion lire, compared with 108.3 billion lire for the same period a year earlier. The national budget for the fiscal year 1974 forecast a deficit of 8,606,000,000,000 lire.

In September a new direct taxation system was announced, with effect from Jan. 1, 1974. The new tax, to be levied directly on salaries, would replace the income tax, local tax, and house tax. Although lower in percentage than previous taxes, it would provide a greater public income because it could be administered more efficiently. (FABIO GALVANO)

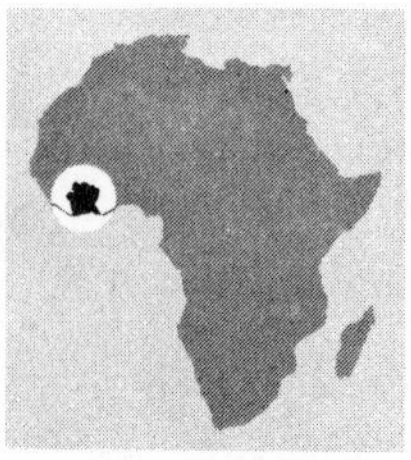

Ivory Coast

A republic on the Gulf of Guinea, West Africa, the Ivory Coast is bounded by Liberia, Guinea, Mali, Upper Volta, and Ghana. Area: 123,483 sq.mi. (319,822 sq.km.). Pop. (1972 est.): 4,530,000, including about 15,000 Europeans. Cap. and largest city: Abidjan (pop., early 1970s est., 650,000). Language: French and local dialects. Religion: animist 65%; Muslim 23%; Christian 12%. President and premier in 1973, Félix Houphouët-Boigny.

After a decade of domestic stability, the announcement in June 1973 that a plot to overthrow the government had been discovered came as a political bombshell. President Houphouët-Boigny announced in June that a military coup had been planned by certain members of the armed forces with the aim of overthrowing the government and assassinating the president and other high officials. According to the president, the coup was to have taken place on Aug. 7, 1974, the 14th anniversary of independence.

A dozen officers were arrested and brought to trial in Abidjan. During the trial the alleged ringleader, Capt. Ernest Sio Koulahou, was accused of the ritual sacrifice of five foreign fishermen to ensure the success of the plot. On August 1, seven of the accused were condemned to death for their part in the conspiracy and four others sentenced to life imprisonment. However, the discovery of the plot was not followed by any major increase in security precautions.

In September, a year after the last attempt at reconciliation between the presidents of the Ivory Coast and Guinea, Pres. Sékou Touré of Guinea renewed his attacks on Houphouët-Boigny and accused him, along with other governments, of plotting the overthrow of the Guinean government. Breaking his usual policy of silence in the face of such allegations, Houphouët-Boigny announced that he had no further interest in reconciliations with Touré, since they invariably produced no lasting results.

The country's economic expansion continued throughout the year. A major inter-African conference held in Abidjan in April with the aim of providing some concrete content for the West African Economic Community established in June 1972 approved a budget and resulted in the signing of ten protocols.

Ivory Coast foreign policy continued to be oriented toward solidarity with the West. This was clearly illustrated in January, when a meeting took place in Geneva between Houphouët-Boigny and Israeli Prime Minister Golda Meir, and in October, when the Ivory Coast president paid an official visit to the U.S. However, diplomatic relations with Israel were broken off in November. (PHILIPPE DECRAENE)

IVORY COAST

Education. (1969–70) Primary, pupils 464,817, teachers 10,094; secondary, pupils 53,267, teachers 1,910; vocational, pupils 4,794, teachers 402; teacher training, pupils 1,615, teachers 95; higher, students 3,755, teaching staff 208.

Finance. Monetary unit: CFA franc, with (Sept. 17, 1973) a parity of CFA Fr. 50 to the French franc (free commercial rate of CFA Fr. 212.55 = U.S. $1; CFA Fr. 512.25 = £1 sterling). Gold, SDRs, and foreign exchange, central bank: (April 1973) U.S. $124.2 million; (April 1972) U.S. $105 million. Budget (1972 est.) balanced at CFA Fr. 68.2 billion. Money supply: (March 1973) CFA Fr. 115,440,000,000; (March 1972) CFA Fr. 100,920,000,000.

Foreign Trade. (1972) Imports CFA Fr. 114,320,000,000; exports CFA Fr. 139,540,000,000. Import sources: France 50%; West Germany 7%; U.S. 6%; Italy 5%. Export destinations: France 30%; West Germany 14%; U.S. 14%; Italy 10%; The Netherlands 6%. Main exports: coffee 26%; timber 23%; cocoa 16%.

Agriculture. Production (in 000; metric tons; 1972; 1971 in parentheses): corn 300 (280); sweet potatoes (1971) 1,555, (1970) 1,572; cassava (1970) 540, (1969) 532; rice *c.* 410 (385); millet (1971) *c.* 42, (1970) 37; peanuts 42 (42); coffee *c.* 270 (268); cocoa (1971–72) 200, (1970–71) 180; bananas (1970) 179, (1969) 172; palm kernels 24 (19); palm oil 81 (61); cotton, lint 25 (20); rubber 14 (14); timber (cu.m.; 1971) 9,400, (1970) 8,900. Livestock (in 000; 1971–72): cattle *c.* 412; pigs *c.* 169; sheep *c.* 875; goats *c.* 760; poultry *c.* 8,000.

Jamaica

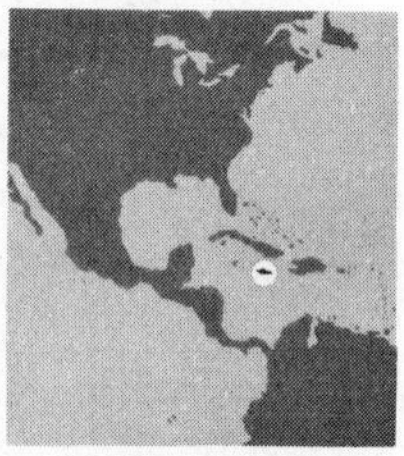

A parliamentary state within the Commonwealth of Nations, Jamaica is an island in the Caribbean Sea about 90 mi. S of Cuba. Area: 4,244 sq.mi. (10,991 sq.km.). Pop. (1973 est.): 1,968,000, predominantly Negro, but including Europeans, Chinese, Indians, and persons of mixed race. Cap. and largest city: Kingston (pop., 1972 est., 157,483). Language: English. Religion: Christian, with Anglicans and Baptists in the majority. Queen, Elizabeth II; governors-general, Sir Clifford Campbell until Feb. 28, 1973, Sir Herbert Duffus (chief justice acting as interim governor-general), and, from June 27, Florizel Glasspole; prime minister, Michael Manley.

During 1973 some of the euphoria generated by the previous year's landslide victory of the People's National Party under Michael Manley was inevitably dissipated as the magnitude of Jamaica's economic and

JAMAICA

Education. (1969–70) Primary, pupils 384,129, teachers (including preprimary) 7,491; secondary and vocational, pupils 60,693, teachers 2,414; teacher training, students 2,201, teachers 143; higher, students 2,687, teaching staff 287.

Finance. Monetary unit: Jamaican dollar, with (Sept. 17, 1973) a par value of Jam\$0.91 to U.S. \$1 (free rate of Jam\$2.20 = £1 sterling). Budget (1972–73 est.): revenue Jam\$283 million; expenditure Jam\$374 million.

Foreign Trade. (1972) Imports Jam\$493,170,000; exports Jam\$300,760,000. Import sources: U.S. 39%; U.K. 19%; Canada 7%; Venezuela 7%. Export destinations: U.S. \$43%; U.K. 21%; Norway 8%; Canada 5%. Main exports: alumina 40%; bauxite 23%; sugar 12%.

Agriculture. Production (in 000; metric tons; 1972; 1971 in parentheses): sweet potatoes *c.* 160 (*c.* 160); cassava *c.* 10 (*c.* 10); sugar, raw value 384 (396); bananas (1971) *c.* 150, (1970) *c.* 145; oranges (1971) *c.* 73, (1970) *c.* 87; grapefruit (1971) *c.* 20, (1970) *c.* 23; copra *c.* 19 (*c.* 21). Livestock (in 000; 1971–72): cattle *c.* 270; goats *c.* 380; pigs *c.* 200; sheep *c.* 13.

Industry. Production (in 000; metric tons; 1972): bauxite 12,890; cement 431; petroleum products 1,670; electricity (kw-hr.; 1971) 1,637,000.

social difficulties was again recognized. These included long-standing unemployment and underemployment, overpopulation, illiteracy, sharply rising food prices, worsening public services, and a deterioration in the balance of payments. To these were added rising middle-class fears of "Communistic" moves in internal and external policies (mainly aimed at closer links with nonaligned and third world states) and, at the same time, a revival of agitation among the young theoretical Marxists at the University of the West Indies.

Cornerstones of the May budget (Jam\$460 million) were to be a new thrust in agriculture (with increased production, self-reliance, and the bringing into production of idle land) and a breakthrough in industry (an oil refinery and petrochemical project, expansion of the tourist industry, and restructuring of industrial incentives).

In June the police and Defence Force launched massive operations to crush the rising wave of violent crime, especially among juveniles. In the fall pay rises for police and military totaling Jam\$4 million were announced. (SHEILA PATTERSON)

Japan

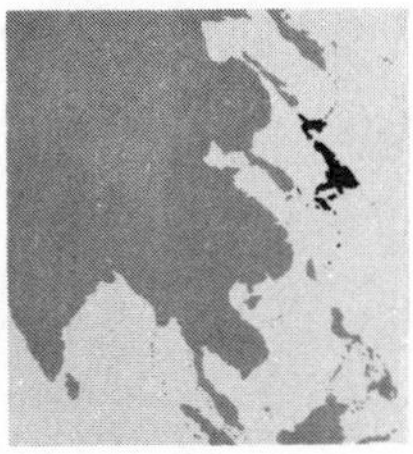

A constitutional monarchy in the northwestern Pacific Ocean, Japan is an archipelago composed of four major islands (Hokkaido, Honshu, Kyushu, and Shikoku) and minor adjacent islands. Area: 145,711 sq.mi. (377,389 sq.km.). Pop. (1973 est.): 107,790,000. Cap. and largest city: Tokyo (pop., 1973 est., 8,775,103). Language: Japanese. Religion: primarily Shinto and Buddhist; Christian 0.5%. Emperor, Hirohito; prime minister in 1973, Kakuei Tanaka.

Domestic Affairs. In August the Organization for Economic Cooperation and Development offered a succinct analysis of the Japanese economy in 1973: a marked upswing in economic activity despite severe revaluation of the yen; a "remarkable decline" in Japan's trade surplus; and a sharp rise in prices on the domestic front. According to the Economic Planning Agency, gross national product in fiscal 1972 (April 1972–March 1973) reached 95,224,800,000,000 yen and per capita national income was figured at \$3,022. The economy grew at a nominal 17.4% (11.5% discounted for rising prices). Gold and foreign exchange reserves reached an all-time high of \$19.1 billion in February but fell sharply in September, to \$14.8 billion on October 1. Meanwhile, according to the Prime Minister's Office, the consumer price index rose 8.8% to 119.1 in the first six months of 1973 (1970 = 100).

At year's end, however, the Japanese economy faced what some observers described as its worst crisis since World War II as the result of the Arab cutback in oil shipments begun during the October Arab-Israeli war. Japan was the world's second largest oil consumer, after the U.S., but unlike that country it was totally dependent on oil imports, of which over 80% came from the Middle East and more than 40% from Arab producers. Thus the 5% per month cutback in shipments to Japan announced by the Arabs was in itself serious, but in the confused situation following the Arab action, some crude from non-Arab suppliers was being diverted from Japan to other customers. Although projections differed, there was general agreement that this could mean increased inflation, shortages, and a drastic reduction in the Japanese economy's rate of growth.

On November 16 the government announced an emergency program for rationing oil and electric power to industry and urged voluntary conservation by the consuming public. A week later the Cabinet issued a statement favourable to the Arab cause, with the result that Japan was exempted from the 5% cut in Arab oil shipments in December. With further reductions scheduled in the new year, however, Prime Minister Tanaka declared a state of emergency, and an energy restriction program was announced that would lower industrial use of oil and electricity by 20% beginning Jan. 1, 1974.

Meanwhile, Deputy Prime Minister Takeo Miki, on a tour of the Middle East, made several statements urging Israel to withdraw from occupied Arab territory and promising substantial Japanese aid to Arab states. Subsequently, Japan was reclassified by the Arabs as a "friendly" country and exempted from the January cutback. Implementation of the emergency program was postponed, with a final decision to be made by January 10. It was still unclear how much oil would actually reach Japan and, in any case, the huge increase in the price of crude announced by

Leftist political workers satirize the policies of Prime Minister Kakuei Tanaka during pre-election campaign for seats in the Tokyo Metropolitan Assembly. The male mime at centre represents Tanaka.

ROBERT TRUMBULL—THE NEW YORK TIMES

Persian Gulf producers was sure to aggravate inflation. Also uncertain was the reaction of the U.S., Japan's chief trading partner and chief ally, which showed little sign that it would approve further anti-Israeli moves.

The oil crisis came at a time when Prime Minister Tanaka was facing considerable public dissatisfaction, especially over inflation. According to an *Asahi Shimbun* opinion poll, the percentage of those who approved of the government fell from 62 to 27% in ten months. Following Japan's general election in December 1972, party representation in the Diet was as follows (seats before the election in parentheses): House of Representatives (lower house), Liberal-Democrats (LDP) 271 (297), Japan Socialists (JSP) 118 (87), Japan Communists (JCP) 38 (14), Komeito (KMT) 29 (47), Democratic Socialists (DSP) 19 (29), independents 16 (3), (total 491); House of Councillors, LDP 136, JSP 62, JCP 10, KMT 23, DSP 12, independents (including Niin Club) 6, vacancies 3 (total 252). Tanaka was reelected prime minister by the Diet, and formed his second Cabinet. He retained Masayoshi Ohira as foreign minister and nominated several powerful LDP faction leaders.

On January 15 the government agreed on a general account budget of 14,284,073,000,000 yen ($46.4 billion), up 24.6% from 1972. The budget featured increases in social security and public works expenditures. It was not until February 19, however, that opposition parties agreed to renew discussion of it. It finally passed intact in late March, but the Diet continued to be hampered by confrontations between the majority LDP and the opposition. On July 24 deliberations again came to a halt after the LDP unilaterally decided on a second 65-day extension of the session; the decision was made in a lower house plenary session that was not attended by the opposition. On August 16 an agreement was reached to clear three major bills in question: legislation to raise Japan National Railways fares, a proposal to establish an experimental university in Tsukuba, and a measure providing for the buildup of defense personnel. On September 28 the Diet ended its 280-day session, having exceeded the previous record of 230 days set in 1951.

The Cabinet was reshuffled in November following the death of Finance Minister Kiichi Aichi. In a move that some observers believed might signal a more stringent anti-inflationary policy, Tanaka named one of his chief rivals, Takeo Fukuda, to the finance post. Other major ministers, including Ohira, were retained.

The LDP made an unexpectedly good showing in the by-election for the Tokyo Metropolitan Assembly, held on July 8. Although the LDP remained the largest party with 51 seats, the three-party "progressive" coalition that backed Gov. Ryokichi Minobe retained a majority in the 125-seat body.

On March 20 the Kumamoto District Court ordered the Chisso chemical company to pay 937 million yen in damages to 138 patients and relatives who had suffered from "Minamata disease." (*See* LAW.)

The future expansion of Japan's Self-Defense Forces (SDF) was called into question. After a four-year-long dispute, the Sapporo District Court on September 7 ruled that the SDF violated art. 9 of the constitution. The specific controversy revolved around the government's right to construct a missile base at Naganuma, Hokkaido. Prime Minister Tanaka promised an appeal.

In March the Cabinet adopted a five-year basic socioeconomic plan (1973–77) entitled "Toward a Dynamic Welfare Society." The guidelines pointed toward limitation of environmental disruption, preservation of natural surroundings, promotion of a comfortable life with emphasis on social security and quality of education, and, simultaneously, support of international economic cooperation.

Foreign Affairs. The 1973 edition of the Foreign Ministry's diplomatic Blue Book stated that Japan should operate a "balanced" foreign policy in today's multipolar world. This meant maintaining a "close relationship" with the U.S. while, at the same time, promoting "friendly ties" with China and the Soviet Union and further developing the "traditional relations" with the countries of Asia, Oceania, and Europe.

Trade and financial indices had come to dominate the "close relationship" between Japan and the U.S. Even with earlier revaluation of the yen, the trade imbalance early in 1973 was running over $4 billion annually in Japan's favour. William D. Eberle, U.S. presidential trade representative, warned that Japan must adopt more effective measures to reduce the surplus. On February 3, amid the latest dollar crisis, the Bank of Japan bought nearly $300 million at the

JAPAN

Education. (1969–70) Primary, pupils 9,403,193, teachers 362,986; secondary, pupils 7,399,361; vocational, pupils 1,833,786; secondary and vocational, teachers 443,490; higher (including 7 main state universities), students 1,631,319, teaching staff 145,608.

Finance. Monetary unit: yen, with (Sept. 17, 1973) a free rate of 265 yen to U.S. $1 (free rate of 639 yen = £1 sterling). Gold, SDRs, and foreign exchange, official: (June 1973) U.S. $14,532,000,000; (June 1972) U.S. $15.3 billion. Budget (1972–73) balanced at 11,421,000,000,000 yen. Gross national product: (1971) 78,960,000,000,000 yen; (1970) 70,985,000,000,000 yen. Money supply: (May 1973) 35,776,000,000,000 yen; (May 1972) 27,418,000,000,000 yen. Cost of living (1963 = 100): (June 1973) 178; (June 1972) 160.

Foreign Trade. (1972) Imports 7,228,980,000,000 yen; exports 8,806,070,000,000 yen. Import sources: U.S. 25%; Australia 9%; Iran 6%; Indonesia 5%; Canada 5%. Export destination U.S. 31%. Main exports: machinery 24% (telecommunications apparatus 8%); motor vehicles 14%; iron and steel 13%; ships 8%; textile yarns and fabrics 8%; chemicals 6%.

Transport and Communications. Roads (1972) 1,037,605 km. (including 888 km. expressways). Motor vehicles in use (1972): passenger 12,531,000; commercial 9,820,000. Railways: (1971) 27,919 km.; traffic (1972) 301,491,000,000 passenger-km., freight 60,265,000,000 net ton-km. Air traffic (1972): 13,695,000,000 passenger-km.; freight 593,426,000 net ton-km. Shipping (1972): merchant vessels 100 gross tons and over 9,433; gross tonnage 34,929,214. Telephones (Jan. 1972) 29,828,000. Radio receivers (Dec. 1971) 23,281,000. Television receivers (March 1971) 23 million.

Agriculture. Production (in 000; metric tons; 1972; 1971 in parentheses): rice 15,450 (14,139); wheat 264 (440); barley 324 (503); sweet potatoes (1971) 2,041, (1970) 2,564; potatoes 3,537 (3,273); sugar, raw value *c.* 450 (441); tea *c.* 94 (93); onions (1970) 1,587, (1969) 1,723; tomatoes (1971) 851, (1970) 790; apples 1,003 (1,007); oranges (1971) 2,834, (1970) 2,814; grapes 269 (246); pears *c.* 450 (441); tobacco *c.* 142 (149); pork 886 (844); timber (cu.m.; 1971) 46,900, (1970) 49,800; fish catch (1971) 9,943, (1970) 9,351; whale and sperm oil (1971–72) 26, (1970–71) 70. Livestock (in 000; Feb. 1972): cattle *c.* 3,684; sheep *c.* 25; pigs (1971) 6,904; goats *c.* 160; horses *c.* 125; chickens (1971) 172,226.

Industry. Index of production (1963 = 100): (1972) 290; (1971) 270. Fuel and power (in 000; metric tons; 1972): coal 28,097; crude oil 715; natural gas (cu.m.) 2,693,000; manufactured gas (cu.m.; 1971) 5,042,000; electricity (kw-hr.) 414,291,000. Production (in 000; metric tons; 1972): iron ore (55% metal content) 1,344; pig iron 75,797; crude steel 96,899; petroleum products (1971) 181,000; cement 66,333; cotton yarn 555; woven cotton fabrics (sq.m.) 2,256,000; rayon, etc., filament yarn 119; rayon, etc., staple fibres 393; nylon, etc., filament yarn 503; nylon, etc., fibres 614; sulfuric acid 6,690; cameras (units) 5,318; radio receivers (units) 76,833; television receivers (units) 14,300; passenger cars (units) 4,022; commercial vehicles (units) 2,276; motorcycles (units) 3,566. Merchant vessels launched (100 gross tons and over; 1972) 12,835,000 gross tons. New dwelling units started (1972) 1,808,000.

virtual floor price of 301.10 yen = $1 to support the U.S. dollar. On February 13, after the U.S. had unilaterally devalued the dollar by 10%, the Japanese government announced that it would float the yen. By February 19 the value of the dollar had settled at the 264.40 yen level, a de facto revaluation of 16.49%.

On April 24 Japan formally notified the U.S. of its decision to cancel the plan for Emperor Hirohito and the empress to visit America. A crowded schedule was cited as an excuse, but Japanese newspapers reported opposition pressure against any "political" use of their majesties. The government itself was uneasy over Pres. Richard Nixon's difficulties in the Watergate affair.

The prime minister and the president met in Washington on July 31 and August 1. The Japanese press reported that the talks centred on trade and economic problems and involved hard bargaining. The Japanese-U.S. tie was supposed to be a key factor in Asian stability, the press editorialized, yet scarcely a year passed without a crisis of confidence, the most recent having been caused by the U.S. embargo on soybean exports. As usual, the Tanaka-Nixon communiqué did not emphasize these difficulties. The two leaders expressed satisfaction with the continuous dialogue, recognized the greatest transoceanic commerce between two nations in history, and promised to exert their best efforts to supply each other with essential materials. The U.S.-Japan security treaty was defined as an important factor in the stability of East Asia, and the U.S. promised to maintain an adequate level of deterrent forces in the region. The U.S. supported Japan's hope for a permanent seat on the UN Security Council. President Nixon reaffirmed the standing invitation to their majesties to visit America, and Prime Minister Tanaka expressed the hope that the president and Mrs. Nixon might visit Japan before the end of 1974. In a speech to the National Press Club in Washington, Tanaka was less diplomatic. "In enterprises of this scope, not even the United States, with all its might, can unilaterally solve the problems, nor should we expect it to do so."

On the eve of President Nixon's visit to Peking in 1972, it had appeared that Japan might profit from Soviet reaction. Indeed, the U.S.S.R. had indicated a willingness to begin conversations looking toward the long-awaited peace treaty. Tokyo even entertained hopes of settling the outstanding issue, the status of the so-called northern territories (the southern Kuril Islands occupied by the U.S.S.R. since the war). Early in 1973, however, an ominous change appeared in the Soviet attitude. Normalization of relations between Tokyo and Peking in 1972, Moscow charged, constituted a conspiracy between Japan and China aimed at the U.S.S.R. The newspaper *Pravda* further denounced Japan's fiscal 1973 defense appropriations as running counter to the general trend of international détente. When Japan's ambassador to Moscow, Kinya Niizeki, arrived in Tokyo early in August to brief the foreign minister in preparation for Tanaka's forthcoming visit to Moscow, he reported that the Soviet Union sought credit and technical know-how for the cooperative development of oil and gas resources in Siberia. On August 25, however, the prime minister stated publicly that settlement of the northern territories issue was a prerequisite to a peace treaty.

On September 26, Prime Minister Tanaka left Tokyo for a 16-day European tour, including stops in France, Britain, and West Germany, as well as the Soviet Union. In the first ten days, he strengthened his hand for negotiations with the Soviet leaders by reaching significant agreements on energy: with France, on joint development of enriched uranium; with Britain, on exploitation of North Sea oil resources; and with West Germany, on the establishment of a joint energy commission. In his talks with Soviet party leader Leonid I. Brezhnev and Premier Aleksey N. Kosygin, however, the prime minister encountered Soviet intransigence over the territorial issue. At a news conference in Moscow, Tanaka spoke with a frankness unknown to Japanese diplomacy. "The question has been on the agenda for 25 years," he said. The communiqué covering the talks nonetheless spoke of the "friendly atmosphere." After his return to Tokyo, Foreign Minister Ohira took a softer line, stating that Moscow had agreed to continue discussion of the territorial issue.

UPI COMPIX

Japanese housewives scrutinize increasingly precious beef in a Tokyo department store. By August 1973, prices for prime beef had reached $23.76 a pound.

Although contacts between Japan and China had increased, relations between Tokyo and Peking remained relatively low-key. On February 1 China formally opened its temporary embassy at the Hotel New Otani in Tokyo, and on February 8 Heishiro Ogawa was appointed Japan's first ambassador to the People's Republic. Ogawa said that his priority would be to conclude an aviation agreement. Early in April, however, talks on this subject became stalled, partly because of disagreement over existent Japan-Taiwan routes. Chinese Ambassador Chen Chu arrived in Tokyo on March 27.

Despite the slow pace of diplomacy, Sino-Japanese trade for the first half of 1973 totaled $871.5 million, an increase of 66% over the corresponding period of 1972. Steel for China's five-year plan accounted for half of Japan's exports, while textile products made up almost half of its imports. Over $1.6 million worth of Chinese crude oil was imported into Japan for the first time. On August 17 the two countries opened talks on a bilateral trade pact designed to replace the successive one-year semigovernmental memorandum trade agreements.

The most spectacular diplomatic developments, however, occurred in Japan's relations with South Korea. In 1965, amid considerable opposition on both sides of the Korea Strait, Japan had normalized its relations with South Korea. In August, just after the Tanaka-Nixon meeting, Foreign Minister Ohira had said that the U.S. military presence in Japan made "a great military contribution" to the security of Korea. On August 10 the *Korean Herald* revealed that South Korea and four allies (Japan, the U.S., Britain, and Australia) had reached agreement on two draft resolutions to deal with the Korean question before the forthcoming UN General Assembly. Later, Tanaka informed the Diet that Japan would support membership for both North and South Korea in the UN.

On the heels of these promising developments came news of a bold political kidnapping in Tokyo. Apparently (the details were not at all clear), Kim Dae Jung, who had opposed Gen. Park Chung Hee in the 1971 South Korean presidential election and was living in self-imposed exile, was visiting friends at the Hotel Grand Palace. On August 8, according to Tokyo police, he was seized by five men and taken away by car. As Kim himself later recounted the incident, he was taken by speedboat out of Japanese waters and through the extremely strict Korean maritime security lines. On August 13 he turned up at his home in South Korea, available for guarded interviews by the press but in effect under house arrest.

On August 20 the government published a letter from South Korean Prime Minister Kim Chong Pil expressing his deep regret over the affair. He said his government "was endeavouring to learn the truth of the matter . . . so that you will be satisfied with the result." Japanese newspapers openly, and Seoul residents somewhat more covertly, speculated that only a skilled, well-funded organization could have carried out the kidnapping across national boundaries. The finger of suspicion pointed at the ubiquitous South Korean CIA. Furthermore, on September 15, Tokyo police revealed that the South Korean embassy's first secretary had registered at the hotel the night before the kidnapping, was a prime suspect in the abduction, and had left Japan without notice.

On August 24 the Japanese government announced its decision to postpone ministerial-level consultations with South Korea scheduled for September 7–8. On October 26 the South Korean regime released Kim from house arrest. Ambassador Torao Ushiroku in Seoul agreed to relay to Tokyo Korea's proposal that the case be settled by diplomatic compromise, and in November Prime Minister Kim journeyed to Tokyo to apologize publicly for the affair. The ministerial meeting was held without fanfare in late December. The communiqué issued at its close was vaguely worded, but it was reported that Japan had almost halved its aid to South Korea, from some $170 million to about $90 million.

Elsewhere in Asia, Japan established diplomatic relations with North Vietnam while explaining that its attitude toward South Vietnam would remain unchanged. (ARDATH W. BURKS)

Jordan

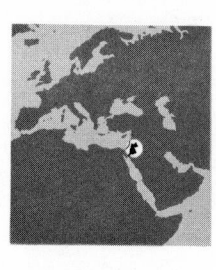

A constitutional monarchy in southwest Asia, Jordan is bounded north by Syria, northeast by Iraq, east and south by Saudi Arabia, and west by Israel. Area (including territory occupied by Israel in the June 1967 war): 36,832 sq.mi. (95,394 sq.km.). Pop. (1972 est.): 2,497,000. Cap. and largest city: Amman (pop., 1973 est., 565,000). Language: Arabic. Religion (1961) Muslim 94%; Christian 6%. King, Hussein I; prime ministers in 1973, Ahmed al-Lawzi and, from May 26, Zaid ar-Rifai.

The outbreak of the fourth Arab-Israeli war on Oct. 6, 1973, confronted King Hussein (*see* BIOGRAPHY) with an increasingly painful choice—to enter the war and risk defeat and an end to his dynasty, or to wait on the sidelines and risk political upheaval afterward. Eventually, he decided to hedge his bets by sending troops to the Syrian front without opening a third front along the Jordan River. Prime Minister Rifai headed the Jordanian delegation to the Middle East peace conference that opened in Geneva in December. (*See* MIDDLE EASTERN AFFAIRS.)

There had been signs during the summer that Jordan was moving out of its isolated position in the Arab world. Regular high-level contacts with Egypt began in June, and the visit to Amman of the Syrian defense minister at the end of August led to a summit meeting in Cairo in September between Hussein, Pres. Anwar as-Sadat (*see* BIOGRAPHY) of Egypt, and Pres. Hafez al-Assad of Syria. Egypt agreed to restore diplomatic relations at once, and Syria followed in October. The war brought clearly into the open the conflicting claims of the king and Yasir Arafat, head of the Palestine Liberation Organization, to represent the Palestinian Arabs. In November Hussein suggested to Egypt and Syria that they accept Jordan's claim to sovereignty over the West Bank and East Jerusalem; once this was accepted, the West Bank population could decide their fate through a plebiscite.

On February 13 a group of Palestinian guerrillas headed by a leading member of al-Fatah, known as Abu Daoud, had been arrested after entering Jordan from Syria and were tried by a military court on charges of aiming to overthrow the government. The death sentences passed on Abu Daoud and others were commuted after strong mediation efforts by other

JORDAN

Education. (1969–70) Primary, pupils 259,388, teachers 6,433; secondary, pupils 85,289, teachers 3,757; vocational, pupils 2,801, teachers 171; higher (including University of Jordan), students 4,463, teaching staff 368.

Finance. Monetary unit: Jordanian dinar, with (Sept. 17, 1973) a free rate of 0.322 dinar to U.S. $1 (0.777 dinar = £1 sterling). Gold, SDRs, and foreign exchange, central bank: (June 1973) U.S. $307.7 million; (June 1972) U.S. $223.9 million. Budget (1973 est.) balanced at 149 million dinars. Gross national product: (1970) 226 million dinars; (1969) 231.4 million dinars. Money supply: (June 1973) 132,320,000 dinars; (June 1972) 110,520,000 dinars. Cost of living (Amman; 1967 = 100): (June 1973) 137; (June 1972) 126.

Foreign Trade. (1972) Imports 97,740,000 dinars; exports 17 million dinars. Import sources: U.S. 17%; West Germany 9%; U.K. 9%; Lebanon 5%; Japan 5%. Export destinations: Saudi Arabia 17%; Kuwait 13%; Syria 13%; Lebanon 12%; Iraq 12%; India 11%; Japan 5%. Main exports (1971): phosphates 20%; tomatoes 10%; oranges 7%.

Transport and Communications. Roads (1972) 5,861 km. Motor vehicles in use (1972): passenger 17,223; commercial 6,490. Railways (1969) 480 km. Air traffic (1972): 209,890,000 passenger-km.; freight 4,828,000 net ton-km. Telephones (Dec. 1971) 33,000. Radio receivers (Dec. 1971) 410,000. Television receivers (Dec. 1971) 61,000.

Agriculture. Production (in 000; metric tons; 1972; 1971 in parentheses): wheat 211 (168); barley 34 (26); lentils (1971) 21, (1970) 5; tomatoes (1971) 137, (1970) 137; olives *c.* 32 (*c.* 17); oranges (1971) *c.* 25, (1970) 50; lemons (1971) *c.* 10, (1970) 14; figs (1971) 2.9, (1970) 3; grapes (1970) 26, (1969) 14; bananas (1971) 4, (1970) 8; olives *c.* 15 (*c.* 25); tobacco *c.* 2 (*c.* 2). Livestock (in 000; 1971–72): cattle 39; goats *c.* 360; sheep *c.* 690; camels 17; asses *c.* 45; chickens *c.* 2,000.

Industry. Production (in 000; metric tons; 1971): phosphate 651; cement 419; electricity (kw-hr.) 187,000.

Arab leaders. On May 26 Zaid ar-Rifai, a former senior political adviser to the king and ambassador to Britain, formed a new government to replace that of Ahmed al-Lawzi, who had entered the hospital. Nine of the new 19-member Cabinet were from the West Bank. On May 30 the new government raised restrictions on Jordanian citizens traveling to the Israeli-occupied West Bank. In February King Hussein visited the U.S. with Queen Alia, and his relations with the U.S. remained friendly. U.S. financial aid to Jordan was maintained. Of the Arab states, Saudi Arabia continued its subsidy; that from Kuwait was resumed in mid-October; while Libya's remained cut off since the fighting with the Palestinian guerrillas in 1970.

Although precariously balanced, the Jordanian economy expanded in 1973. Industrial production in the first half of the year was 18% above the first half of 1972. However, a severe summer drought caused restrictions on exports of foodstuffs, and the Egyptian blockade of the Bab el-Mandeb straits, while aimed against Israel, severely affected the port of Aqaba. A project to irrigate 29,000 ac. and settle 130,000 people in the Jordan Valley "to form a barrier to Israeli expansion" was announced, with the cost of £37.3 million to be financed jointly by the World Bank, West Germany, and the U.S. On April 1 it was announced that women would have the right to vote in elections and sit in the lower house of Parliament. (PETER MANSFIELD)

Kenya

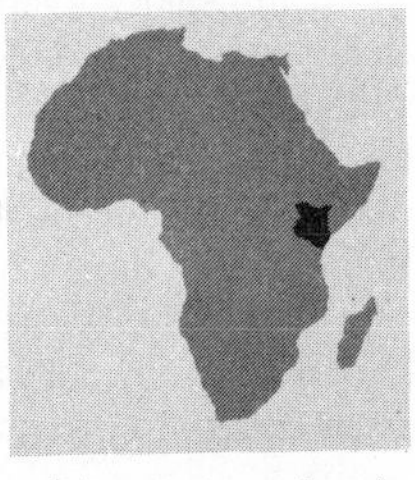

A republic and a member of the Commonwealth of Nations, Kenya is bordered on the north by Sudan and Ethiopia, east by Somalia, south by Tanzania, and west by Uganda. Area: 224,960 sq.mi. (582,646 sq.km.), including 5,172 sq.mi. of inland water. Pop. (1973 est.): 12,482,000, including (1969) African 98.1%; Asian 1.5%. Cap. and largest city: Nairobi (pop., 1973 est., 629,000). Language: English and Swahili. Religion (1962): Christian 57.8%; Muslim 3.8%. President in 1973, Jomo Kenyatta.

The issue that attracted most attention throughout 1973 was africanization. Early in the year both President Kenyatta and Vice-Pres. Daniel Arap Moi publicly stressed the importance of increasing African control of the economy. While insisting that non-Africans must expect to share with their fellow African citizens the profits they had derived from the country, President Kenyatta reaffirmed that this did not mean that people's property would be snatched away from them. As an indication of the lines along which the policy was to be implemented, the minister of tourism announced that beginning in 1974 noncitizens operating tourist and travel agencies would have to become minority stockholders in their enterprises with citizens; at about the same time Arap Moi urged insurance companies to support projects submitted to them by Africans.

The British government became anxious about the effects of the policy in January when it was announced that 418 notices to leave Kenya had been served on noncitizens. Fearing a repetition of the drastic expulsion of Asians holding British passports by Pres. Idi Amin of Uganda, the British home secretary, Robert Carr, stated that similar action by Kenya would be unacceptable. His remark caused indignation in Kenya, but Britain's fears were quickly allayed and an offer of an additional £17 million in aid to Kenya over the following three years was announced in March, £7 million of which was earmarked for the continued transfer of British mixed farms to Kenyan ownership.

In July the Asian question was revived when another 1,000 notices to leave before December 31 were given to noncitizen traders. It was thought that Britain in 1974 would have to increase Kenya's share of the 3,500 immigration vouchers issued annually to heads of families wishing to enter Britain. About the same time, the government said that all secretarial jobs must also be africanized by the end of the year except where the retention of non-Africans was in the national interest.

In January Kenya offered assistance to help Zambia overcome difficulties arising from the closing of the Rhodesian border. Relations with Uganda were less friendly. During the early part of the year the government was deeply concerned for the safety of Kenyans employed in Uganda by the East African Community, many of whom were said to be fleeing to Kenya. After consultations between presidents Kenyatta and Julius Nyerere of Tanzania in February, the two leaders reaffirmed their determination to uphold the East African Community in spite of their differences with Uganda. There was, consequently, considerable satisfaction when it was announced at the meeting of the East African Legislative Assembly in June that

KENYA

Education. (1970–71) Primary, pupils 1,427,589, teachers 41,479; secondary, pupils 126,855, teachers 5,881; vocational, pupils 2,136, teachers 143; teacher training, students 8,017, teachers 575; higher (at University of Nairobi), students 1,226.

Finance. Monetary unit: Kenyan shilling, with (Sept. 17, 1973) a free rate of KShs. 6.92 to U.S. $1 (KShs. 16.68 = £1 sterling). Gold, SDRs, and foreign exchange: (June 1973) U.S. $291.1 million; (June 1972) U.S. $159.6 million. Budget (1972–73 est.): revenue KShs. 2,720,000,000; expenditure KShs. 2,640,000,000. Gross national product: (1971) KShs. 12,324,000,000; (1970) KShs. 11,326,000,000. Cost of living (Nairobi; 1963 = 100): (June 1973) 132; (June 1972) 124.

Foreign Trade. (Excluding trade with Tanzania and Uganda; 1972) Imports KShs. 3,534,000,000; exports KShs. 1,911,000,000. Import sources: U.K. 21%; Japan 10%; West Germany 10%; U.S. 7%; Iran 8%. Export destinations: U.K. 21%; West Germany 10%; The Netherlands 7%; U.S. 6%; Zambia 5%. Main exports: coffee 27%; tea 18%; petroleum products 12%; meat 5%.

Transport and Communications. Roads (1972) 43,278 km. Motor vehicles in use (1972): passenger 67,500; commercial 61,570. Railways: (1970) 2,069 km. (operated under East African Railways Corp., serving Kenya, mainland Tanzania, and Uganda with a total of 5,895 km.); traffic (total East African; 1966) 4,529,000,000 passenger-km., freight (1971) 4,418,-000,000 net ton-km. Air traffic (East African Airways Corp., including Tanzania and Uganda; 1972): 860.3 million passenger-km.; freight 27,108,000 ton-km. Telephones (Dec. 1971) 85,000. Radio receivers (Dec. 1969) 500,000. Television receivers (Dec. 1970) 16,000.

Agriculture. Production (in 000; metric tons; 1972; 1971 in parentheses): corn 1,665 (c. 1,400); wheat (1971) c. 210, (1970) 205; coffee c. 61 (60); tea 53 (36); sugar, raw value c. 105 (135); sisal (1971) c. 50, (1970) 48; cotton, lint c. 5 (c. 5); fish catch (1971) 35, (1970) 34. Livestock (in 000; May 1972): cattle c. 9,200; sheep c. 3,500; pigs c. 70; goats c. 4,000; camels (1970) 516; chickens (1970) 13,586.

Industry. Production (in 000; metric tons; 1971): salt 43; soda ash 161; cement 794; electricity (excluding most industrial production; kw-hr.; 1972) 661,000.

Japanese Literature:
see Literature

Jazz:
see Music

Jehovah's Witnesses:
see Religion

Jewish Literature:
see Literature

Journalism:
see Publishing

Judaism:
see Israel; Religion

Kashmir:
see India; Pakistan

normal relations had been restored between Uganda and Tanzania. In the meantime, Kenya had been worried by the activities of a number of religious sects inside the country, and in April a ban was imposed on Jehovah's Witnesses and six other sects and societies that were said to be a danger to stability.

Kenya's financial position remained satisfactory, and in March the West German government offered £3.6 million in aid to improve water supplies to towns for irrigation purposes and road construction. Later in the year, Sweden promised a loan of £4.2 million to finance a five-year program to control foot-and-mouth disease and an additional £700,000 for a rural electrification scheme. (KENNETH INGHAM)

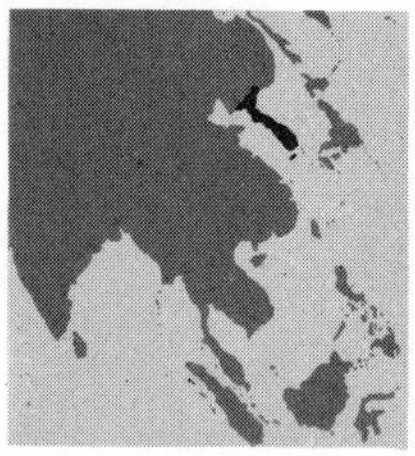

Korea

A country of eastern Asia, Korea is bounded by China, the Sea of Japan, the Korea Strait, and the Yellow Sea. It is divided into two parts at the 38th parallel.

Direct talks between the two Koreas continued during 1973 but there was no progress toward what South Korea's Pres. Park Chung Hee called "the daybreak of a great achievement—a prosperous, unified fatherland." The July 1972 joint declaration of rapprochement had, among other things, banned mutual slandering and defaming. But in January 1973 public denunciations started. On January 26, North Korea charged that South Korean aircraft had violated its airspace. However, Red Cross officials of the two countries met—in Pyongyang in March and in Seoul in May—to discuss ways of reuniting ten million families separated as a result of the Korean War. Political talks also took place when the Coordinating Committee set up under the 1972 declaration met in Pyongyang in March and again in Seoul in June. Apart from providing the two sides with a platform to state their respective cases, these meetings achieved little. The North was of the opinion that the South should either ease or abolish its anti-Communist law and education before detailed peace negotiations began. The South branded this demand as political and maintained that mutual trust must first be built up through economic, social, and cultural exchanges.

A side effect of direct North-South contacts was the decision by the UN Commission for the Unification and Rehabilitation of Korea to disband itself. The commission argued that both Koreas had accepted the bilateral talks as the primary forum for reunification efforts. North Korea's spirited pleas for the disbanding of the UN (military) Command did not, however, meet with any response.

In further developments on the UN front, North Korea obtained "observer" status in the world body. But attempts to get the two Koreas seated in the UN ran into further polemics. Under reported United States advice, South Korea dropped its objection to the North's admission and sought two UN seats for the two Koreas, citing the case of the two Germanys as a precedent. The North, for its part, rebuffed the idea of separate admissions on the ground that it would perpetuate the division of the country; it proposed the entry into the UN of a single "Confederal Republic of Koryo" (an ancient name for Korea), pending reunification. This position contrasted with Pyongyang's successful efforts to establish diplomatic ties with several countries already having relations with Seoul, thereby promoting the concept of separate representation.

Republic of Korea (South Korea). Area: 38,022 sq.mi. (98,477 sq.km.). Pop. (1973 est.): 32,711,000. Cap. and largest city: Seoul (pop., 1970, 5,525,262). Language: Korean. Religion: Buddhist; Confucian; Tonghak (Chondokyo). President in 1973, Gen. Park Chung Hee; prime minister, Kim Chong Pil.

An unusually eventful 1973 was ushered in by the inauguration (on Dec. 27, 1972) of Park Chung Hee's fourth presidential term. Under a 1969 constitutional amendment, Park, in power since 1961, should have been out of office at the end of his third term. But on inauguration day, a new constitution was promulgated that ended the Western-style democracy South Korea had known since 1948 and gave Park a new six-year term and the option to serve an indefinite number of terms.

Elections to the National Assembly were held on Feb. 27, 1973. The constitution provided for 146 elected seats, with an additional 73 seats to be filled by Park. In the elections the ruling political party, the Democratic Republicans, took 73 seats, while the opposition New Democratic Party obtained 52 seats,

KOREA: Republic

Education. (1971–72) Primary, pupils 5,807,448, teachers 103,756; secondary (1969–70), pupils 1,441,700, teachers 36,653; vocational, students 337,919, teachers 23,051; higher (including 27 universities), students 162,669, teaching staff 8,194.

Finance. Monetary unit: won, with a free rate (Sept. 17, 1973) of 399 won to U.S. $1 (961 won = £1 sterling). Gold, SDRs, and foreign exchange, central bank: (June 1973) U.S. $886.7 million; (June 1972) U.S. $597.1 million. Budget (1972 est.): revenue 715,610,000,000 won; expenditure 748,250,000,000 won. Gross national product: (1972) 3,840,600,000,000 won; (1971) 3,151,600,000,000 won. Money supply: (March 1973) 573.1 billion won; (March 1972) 355.6 billion won. Cost of living (1963 = 100): (June 1973) 317; (June 1972) 314.

Foreign Trade. (1972) Imports 981,660,000,000 won; exports 637,650,000,000 won. Import sources: Japan 41%; U.S. 26%. Export destinations: U.S. 47%; Japan 25%. Main exports (1971): clothing 29%; textile yarns and fabrics 13%; plywood 12%; electrical machinery and equipment 6%.

Transport and Communications. Roads (1972) 40,634 km. (including 655 km. expressways). Motor vehicles in use (1971): passenger 67,600; commercial (including buses) 70,800. Railways (1971): 5,448 km.; traffic 8,750,000,000 passenger-km., freight (1972) 7,086,000,000 net ton-km. Air traffic (1971): 749 million passenger-km.; freight 39,070,000,000 net ton-km. Shipping (1972): merchant vessels 100 gross tons and over 446; gross tonnage 1,057,408. Telephones (Dec. 1971) 755,000. Radio receivers (Dec. 1970) 4,012,000. Television licenses (Dec. 1970) 418,000.

Agriculture. Production (in 000; metric tons; 1972; 1971 in parentheses): rice 5,472 (5,556); wheat 241 (322); potatoes 459 (600); barley 1,965 (1,857); sweet potatoes 1,901 (*c.* 2,000); soybeans *c.* 250 (222); onions (1971) 162, (1970) 153; apples *c.* 210 (*c.* 220); grapes *c.* 42 (34); tobacco *c.* 94 (63); fish catch (1971) 1,074, (1970) 934. Livestock (in 000; Dec. 1971): cattle *c.* 1,250; pigs (1970) 1,121; goats *c.* 95; chickens (1970) 23,477.

Industry. Production (in 000; metric tons; 1972): coal 12,403; iron ore (50% metal content) 414; steel 585; cement 6,485; tungsten concentrate (oxide content; 1971) 2.8; kaolin (1971) 124; fluorite (1971) 51; limestone (1970) 9,937; gold (troy oz.; 1971) 30; silver (troy oz.; 1971) 1,511; electricity (excluding most industrial production; kw-hr.) 11,839,000.

KOREA: Democratic People's Republic

Education. (1970–71) Primary, secondary, and vocational, pupils *c.* 3 million, teachers *c.* 100,000; higher, students 214,000, teaching staff (1964–65) 9,013.

Finance and Trade. Monetary unit: won, with (Sept. 17, 1973) an official exchange rate of 0.96 won to U.S. $1 (2.14 won = £1 sterling). Budget (1972 est.) balanced at 7,373,000,000 won. Foreign trade (excluding trade with China; 1966): imports *c.* U.S. $126.5 million (68% from U.S.S.R., 6% from France); exports *c.* U.S. $148,742,000 (62% to U.S.S.R., 15% to Japan, 7% to Czechoslovakia). Main exports (1964): metals 50%; minerals 12%; farm produce 11%.

Agriculture. Production (in 000; metric tons; 1972; 1971 in parentheses): rice *c.* 2,700 (*c.* 2,800); corn *c.* 1,800 (*c.* 1,800); barley *c.* 275 (*c.* 275); potatoes *c.* 1,000 (*c.* 1,000); fish catch (1964) 770, (1963) 640. Livestock (in 000; Dec. 1971): cattle *c.* 750; pigs *c.* 1,400; sheep *c.* 200; goats *c.* 175.

Industry. Production (in 000; metric tons; 1971): coal *c.* 25,000; iron ore (metal content; 1970) 4,014; pig iron 2,500; steel (1970) 2,180; lead (1970) 55; zinc (1970) *c.* 90; magnesite (1971) 1,724; cement (1970) 4,010; electricity (kw-hr.; 1965) 13,300,000.

with 2 seats going to the Democratic Unification Party and 19 to independents. Park could expect that with the combined support of his party and the nominees he would have firm control of the assembly.

The return to constitutional formalities did not remove the widespread impression that the spirit of the martial law suddenly proclaimed the previous October was still at large. In July, for example, a government decree restricted outdoor meetings in major cities.

Hints of some trouble behind the scenes were confirmed by the announcement in April that Maj. Gen. Yoon Pil Yong, former head of the capital garrison command, had been sentenced to 15 years in prison on corruption charges. The general, dismissed secretly a month earlier, had been a confidant of President Park and was linked with persistent rumours of a power struggle among Park's closest aides. Nine other officers also received prison terms at the same court-martial.

To all appearances these sentences were part of a purge at the top that included the twin props of the Park government, the military and the high-powered South Korean Central Intelligence Agency. Among those reportedly arrested was the inspector general of the agency, Lee Choi Kol, a cousin of its director and reputedly South Korea's second most powerful man, Lee Hu Rak. There was speculation as to whether this meant a downgrading of Lee Hu Rak's own influence.

The South Korean CIA as a whole came in for widespread denigration in August when it was implicated in the kidnapping of a well-known opposition leader and former presidential candidate, Kim Dae Jung. Five Koreans abducted Kim from Tokyo, where he had been living in voluntary exile since the imposition of martial law, and smuggled him back to Seoul with visible cuts and bruises. Although the South Korean government officially denied any involvement in the affair, the kidnapping led to strained relations between Seoul and Tokyo. (*See* JAPAN.)

In the first week of October the first open resistance to the government in a year erupted in Seoul. Some 400 National University students demanded an end to "police-fascist rule" and called for a restoration of civil rights. The government arrested more than 200 students and others were expelled from the university, but the disorders continued through the fall. On December 3 the Cabinet resigned and a new one was named; Kim Chong Pil was retained as prime minister, but Lee Hu Rak was not reappointed, suggesting that the sudden reshuffle was intended to appease the demonstrators.

Although hit by inflation, the South Korean economy remained generally buoyant during the year. The Economic Planning Board reported that the growth rate for 1972 was 2.1% lower than that of the previous year. The target for 1973 was set in January at 9.5% but in August the board said a 12% growth rate would be achieved and the government would take measures to prevent the economy from overheating.

Democratic People's Republic of Korea (North Korea). Area: 46,800 sq.mi. (121,200 sq.km.). Pop. (1972 est.): 14,680,000. Cap.: Pyongyang (metro. pop., 1970 est., 1.5 million). Language: Korean. Religion: Buddhist; Confucian; Tonghak (Chondokyo). General secretary of the Korean Workers' (Communist) Party, president, and chairman of the Council of Ministers (premier) in 1973, Marshal Kim Il Sung.

As coincidence would have it, North Korea like South Korea promulgated a new constitution at the end of December 1972. It enabled Kim Il Sung to become president as well as premier. Apparently designed for the era of coexistence with the South, the constitution abandoned previous insistence on Seoul being the capital of all Korea and declared North Korea "an independent socialist state" with its capital at Pyongyang.

All through 1973 the preoccupation of the government seemed to be to make a big international showing. It established new links with a series of countries, including the Scandinavian countries and Australia. The crowning success came when it was admitted to the World Health Organization in May and automatically obtained observer status in the UN.

Relentlessly pursuing the reunification slogan, the Supreme People's Assembly took the unusual step in April of addressing a letter to the U.S. Congress. The letter said, "It is time the U.S. should remove the obstacles lying in the way of Korea's peaceful reunification" and "refrain from instigating the South Korean authorities to make Koreans fight Koreans." U.S. reaction to the move was that Pyongyang was trying to take advantage of congressional sentiment in favour of reducing U.S. troop levels overseas. In an October interview, Kim Il Sung questioned why "the U.S., after all its failures in Asia, continues to invest hundreds of millions of dollars in a handful of rich individuals like Park . . . when there are plenty of sound political personalities in the South." On the whole Kim in 1973 projected the image of a man gaining strength and friends, while his rival in the South was beset with domestic opposition and dwindling support abroad. (T. J. S. GEORGE)

WIDE WORLD

Plainclothes and uniformed police break up a student rally on the campus of Seoul National University, Oct. 2, 1973. More than 200 students were arrested during a week of demonstrations demanding abolition of the South Korean Central Intelligence Agency and other government reforms.

Kuwait

An independent emirate, Kuwait is on the northwestern coast of the Persian Gulf between Iraq and Saudi Arabia. Area: 6,880 sq.mi. (17,818 sq.km.). Pop. (1973 est.): 862,200. Cap.: Kuwait (pop., 1973, 93,050). Largest city: Hawalli (pop., 1973, 125,310). Language: Arabic. Religion (1970): Muslim 94.7%; Christian 4.6%. Emir in 1973, Sheikh Sabah as-Salim as-Sabah; prime minister, Crown Prince Sheikh Jabir al-Ahmad al-Jabir as-Sabah.

In 1973 Kuwait maintained its independent line among the Arab states. It kept close ties with Saudi Arabia and signed wide-ranging cultural and economic agreements with Bahrain (June 19) and the United Arab Emirates (June 30). It also retained good re-

Khmer Republic: *see* Cambodia

UPI COMPIX

In an extraordinary session held Oct. 17, 1973, in Kuwait, ministers from the six largest Persian Gulf oil-producing companies announce a price increase for crude oil of 17%. Unhappy Western customers, they suggested, could buy their oil elsewhere.

lations with Egypt and Syria, although it refused to accept the cease-fire that followed the October Arab-Israeli war. As a member of the Organization of Arab Petroleum Exporting Countries, it participated in that organization's program of embargoes and cutbacks of oil shipments to Western countries and Japan.

In March an acute crisis arose with Iraq when Iraqi troops occupied a police post at Sameta 2.5 mi. inside Kuwaiti territory but dominating the Iraqi port of Umn Qasr. A serious clash was avoided, but talks between the two sides, which continued until late August, failed to reach any final agreement.

In June it was revealed that the National Assembly had decided to spend approximately $1.2 billion to build a new armed force for the nation. In 1973 Kuwait's military consisted of 7,000 men, 80 aging tanks, and 20 jet fighters.

Oil output in 1972 was just under 3 million bbl. a day, a 2.8% increase over 1971. In the 1973–74 budget estimated oil revenues of 589 million dinars marked a 7% increase from 1972–73. In January the government signed an agreement with the British Petroleum and Gulf Oil companies providing for Kuwait's 25% participation in the Kuwait Oil Company but the National Assembly refused ratification. Finally, in December, the government introduced a bill providing for complete nationalization of the entire oil industry operating in Kuwait.

(PETER MANSFIELD)

KUWAIT

Education. (1970–71) Primary, pupils 57,414, teachers 2,813; secondary (including intermediate), pupils 63,729, teachers 4,586; vocational, pupils 1,387, teachers 317; teacher training, students 2,103, teachers 348; higher (1969–70), students 1,713, teaching staff 158.

Finance. Monetary unit: Kuwaiti dinar, with (Sept. 17, 1973) a par value of 0.296 dinar to U.S. $1 (free rate of 0.698 dinar = £1 sterling). Gold and foreign exchange, official: (June 1973) U.S. $554.9 million; (June 1972) U.S. $363 million. Budget (1972–73 est.) balanced at 415 million dinars. Money supply: (March 1973) 179.4 million dinars; (March 1972) 140.3 million dinars.

Foreign Trade. (1972) Imports 262.2 million dinars; exports 931.7 million dinars. Import sources: Japan 18%; U.S. 13%; U.K. 11%; West Germany 8%; France 5%; Italy 5%. Export destinations: Japan 18%; U.K. 14%; France 13%; The Netherlands 12%; Italy 10%; Singapore 5%. Main exports (1971) petroleum and products 96%.

Industry. Crude oil production (1972) 151,146,000 metric tons.

Labour Unions

The activities of labour unions have to be seen in the context of the general economic and political affairs not only of the countries where they operate but also of the wider international community. The extension of the EEC and the activities of multinational firms in different ways both gave an international complexion to what are frequently insular activities. Indeed, multinational firms created a relatively rare link between unions in developed and less developed countries. Insofar as internal economic and political affairs are concerned, they also bear heavily on union activities. The year 1973 was one of international monetary crisis with sharp internal repercussions, of internal inflationary crisis, and of energy crisis. In all of these, labour unions either played a part or were perceived by governments as having played a part. The situation, in general, further demonstrated the increasing intervention of governments in industrial relations.

Industrialized Countries. The year began in the U.S. with Pres. Richard Nixon announcing, on January 11, Phase Three of his anti-inflation program. Acting under the authority of the amended Economic Stabilization Act of 1970, Nixon ended mandatory wage and price controls except in the "problem areas" of food, health care, and construction industries. The new program was largely voluntary. Under it the guideline for annual wage increases remained at 5.5%. Firms employing 5,000 workers or more had to file quarterly reports on wage increases instead of seeking permission from the Pay Board to pay them. Firms with 1,000 to 5,000 employees merely had to keep a record of wage changes, while all other firms were free of any obligations. It was clear at the beginning of the year that the voluntary nature of Phase Three would be tested, for 1973 was scheduled to be a peak year for wage bargaining, with negotiations affecting at least 4.7 million workers. In 1973, for the first time in two decades, negotiations in the transportation, automobile, and several other key industries had to operate in a setting of government pay controls.

In the middle of January the International Brotherhood of Teamsters negotiated new contracts with 170 major vegetable growers, covering 30,000 field workers. The contracts were for the remainder of a five-year agreement negotiated in 1970, and were part of the Teamsters' campaign to retain negotiating rights against the pressure of the United Farm Workers under the presidency of César Chávez, who had led the long and bitter struggle to organize the migrant grape pickers in California. On January 3 Chávez announced that his union would picket California lettuce growers and many of the nation's supermarkets to force the growers to sign labour contracts. The next day in federal court in San Francisco the United Farm Workers filed two suits for damages against the Teamsters and the growers. The suits claimed the defendants conspired against blacks, Chicanos, and Filipinos in the 1970 settlements and that they gave growers and shippers unilateral control over workers. The California Supreme Court had ruled on Dec. 29, 1972, that the 1970 agreement had been concluded without determining whether the field-workers supported the Teamsters and that, therefore, the United Farm Workers was free to organize field-workers.

This interunion dispute was intensified in March when the Teamsters signed a two-year agreement with the National Farm Labour Contractors Association covering 150,000 California field hands. Then in April the Teamsters announced contracts with 15 table-grape growers, contracts which the United Farm Workers claimed covered its members. The AFL-CIO sided with the United Farm Workers in this struggle and donated $1.6 million to it.

During the first half of 1973 the strike situation in the U.S. was only marginally more intense than during the same period in 1972. The federal government imposed a 90-day cooling-off period in the Long Island Railroad strike on January 17. Milwaukee County employees in January staged the largest public employee strike ever to be held in Wisconsin. At about the same time, 26,000 teachers in Chicago and 13,000 in Philadelphia struck for improved pay. The bargaining round in the petroleum refining industry was delayed by a strike against Shell Oil Co. in five states in January after the company had refused to accept provisions the union had gained from other major refiners. The strike lasted four months. Rubber workers settled on a three-year contract with the Goodyear Tire & Rubber Co. in April, but the 10,000 employees of B. F. Goodrich Co. went on strike in May after rejecting a similar contract. Trans World Airlines was grounded by a 41-day strike of cabin attendants in November and December.

In the main, however, settlements in the U.S. were reached without major strikes. An "experimental negotiating agreement," designed to avert crisis bargaining and stockpiling in the steel industry, was reached between the United Steelworkers of America and the steel industry coordinating committee, consisting of ten of the major steel producers in the U.S. The agreement provided for binding arbitration in the 1974 negotiations and prohibited national strikes or lockouts to support bargaining positions. In March 15 railroad unions and the railroad companies reached an agreement granting 10.7% increases in wages and benefits over 18 months. There were settlements without strikes between the Teamsters and the Trucking Employers, Inc., covering 400,000 over-the-road and local cartage drivers; between the General Electric Co. and its two largest unions; in the U.S. Postal Service with over 600,000 employees; and in the ladies' garment industry with 40,000 workers. The United Auto Workers, however, struck the Chrysler Corp. in September. After a brief walkout wages and pensions were increased over three years, and the union won concessions on the key issue of voluntary overtime. Settlements at General Motors and Ford followed a similar pattern.

The British government also confronted the problem of inflation with a three-phase anti-inflation policy. The Counter-Inflation Bill, introduced on Nov. 6, 1972, enabled the government to forbid any increase in pay, prices, charges for services, rents, and dividends above the level prevailing before November 6. The standstill was to last for 90 days from the passing of the bill. In fact it lasted until March 31, a period of nearly five months, when Stage Two began. In the second phase a limit for pay increases of £1 per week plus 4% of the pay bill of the group of workers concerned, with an upper limit of £250 per year for any individual, was permitted. During the pay freeze period there were disputes among schoolteachers and hospital workers, but in the main the major unions had either reached wage settlements prior to November 6 or were not ready to press final claims.

There were substantial strikes against the conditions of Stage Two, but surprisingly none involved the traditionally militant groups. The coal miners, for example, accepted the Stage Two proposals even though they fell far short of the miners' demands. Dockworkers and automobile workers also accepted the proposals after some minor protests. The government, instead, experienced strong resistance from civil servants, gas workers, and hospital ancillary workers, none of whom had any previous experience of strike activity. A one-day strike of civil servants was held on February 27, while in March there were strikes among different groups of civil servants lasting up to two weeks. On April 3 the main union involved, the Civil and Public Services Association, decided reluctantly to call off the program of strike action. Negotiations continued throughout January in the gas industry, but on February 14 an official policy of strike action began. In March the gas workers accepted by ballot an offer, which, in fact, was largely in line with government policy. Hospital ancillary workers, most of whom were women, voted by a large majority to strike in February. By mid-March strike action was being taken at 299 hospitals, while an additional 800 were affected by other forms of industrial action. The strike escalated, and demonstrations were held by trades councils to support the strikers. It ended in April when the unions accepted a slightly improved offer over that which was originally made.

The General Council of the Trades Union Congress took an exceptional step on March 28 by inviting all affiliated unions to hold a "day of national protest and stoppage" on May 1 and, regardless of the legal consequences, to give assistance to unions taking action in conflict with Stage Two. It was estimated that about 1.6 million workers were involved in stoppages on May Day.

On November 7 the government introduced Stage Three of its policy with a maximum permitted pay

LONDON DAILY EXPRESS/PICTORIAL PARADE

A sedate but angry civil servant makes his stand before London's Somerset House as members of the Civil and Public Services Association walked off their jobs to attend meetings protesting a government freeze on wage increases, Jan. 10, 1973.

increase of 7%, or £2.25 per week. It was followed, within five days, by a ban on overtime work by the National Union of Mineworkers. On November 13 the government invoked the Emergency Powers Act to cope with the fuel situation caused by the ban and the Middle East oil crisis. A month later it announced the introduction of a three-day working week throughout industry from December 31. (*See* UNITED KINGDOM.)

In Britain the government's pay policy was one of two major causes of industrial disputes, the other being the Industrial Relations Act. Though the Trades Union Congress maintained its opposition, the main difficulty was the refusal of the Amalgamated Union of Engineering Workers to recognize any of the institutions set up by the act. Throughout December 1972 there were numerous strikes by engineering workers against a fine of £50,000 imposed by the National Industrial Relations Court. Numerous minor issues later arose concerning judgments by the Industrial Relations Court and decisions of unions to deregister under the act. The Amalgamated Union of Engineering Workers, with 1.5 million members, again confronted the Industrial Relations Court in November when it refused to pay a fine of £75,000, imposed for defying a court order to end a strike involving about 20 workers. Widespread strike action against the court decision started on Monday, November 5, and continued on successive Mondays in November.

As in Britain, labour unions on the continent of Europe were involved in various types of activity as a result of an intensification of international and domestic pressures. About 14 million Italian workers went on a token strike on January 12 against the government's economic policies. A breakdown in the annual wage negotiations between unions organizing petroleum workers in Belgium and the Belgium Employers' Federation in January resulted in a strike that quickly produced oil shortages and involved a royal decree to maintain oil supplies. Austrian teachers staged a one-day national strike on February 15, demanding higher salaries. Then in The Netherlands, where strikes are relatively uncommon, a wave of them occurred in the steel, engineering, and shipbuilding industries during March. The right to strike had never been established in Dutch law, and the courts had the power to order unions to call off strikes. Denmark, with a history of industrial peace similar to The Netherlands, also experienced a sharp rise in the incidence of industrial unrest when unofficial protests began in the shipyards in March, after the state labour mediator ordered the postponement of a strike for 14 days. Later in the month about 250,000 workers, representing two-thirds of the industrial labour force, were either on strike or locked out for three weeks in the nation's biggest work stoppage since 1936. The dispute was settled in April, with workers gaining higher wages and a shorter workweek.

Late evening workers at a Detroit Chrysler plant prepare for a midnight strike as talks between union and company negotiators break down. Deadline for agreement to a new contract was 11:59 p.m., Sept. 14, 1973.

UPI COMPIX

A long dispute began in France when air traffic controllers went on strike in February for higher pay and the legal right to strike. The government substituted military air traffic controllers for the strikers in Paris at the end of February, but this was regarded as being provocative and the military personnel were withdrawn. Most controllers returned to work late in March as negotiations continued. A strike of automobile workers at the Renault plant began about the same time. Approximately 80% of those on strike in the body-pressing works were foreigners, mainly Algerians, Portuguese, and Spaniards. On March 29 the Renault company laid off 7,000 men at Billancourt, near Paris, as the strike spread to other Renault plants. By April 18 about one-half of the 90,000 workers employed by the firm were either on strike or laid off. The strike, initiated by low-paid groups, concerned the wage structure and job grades in the firm. It ended early in May with management agreeing to consider the workers' demands.

The dispute that attracted most attention in France during the year was that at the Lip watch factory in Besançon, where on April 17 the workers not only occupied the premises but also produced watches in defiance of a decision to end production. The workers were supported by the national trade union bodies, the Confédération Générale du Travail (CGT) and the Confédération Française Démocratique du Travail (CFDT), and by the Communist and Socialist parties, and for almost four months managed to continue their occupation. On August 14, 3,000 armed paramilitary police expelled the workers, provoking a number of sympathetic strikes but without settling the issue. The outstanding question toward the end of the year was how many layoffs among the 1,300 employees the workers' representatives would accept.

Industrial relations in West Germany continued in 1973 to show signs of conflict. Newspaper production was stopped in April for the first time since 1952 when the IG Druck und Papier union, which represented nearly 200,000 printing workers, led a series of strikes for higher pay. In May air traffic controllers began a go-slow campaign that had a serious impact on internal German flights and lasted well into the autumn. Difficulties in getting wage rises to meet the high cost of living in West Germany led to a breakdown of negotiations between the IG Metal trade union and employers in September. The negotiations were accompanied by a wave of unofficial strikes, particularly in the automobile industry.

The issues of recent years that had dominated industrial relations in Japan carried over into 1973.

Local and national public service employees were denied the right to strike under the Public Corporation and National Enterprise Labour Relations Law, yet those workers were effectively organized and regularly defied the law. A consequence of this defiance was that many workers faced disciplinary action. Such action imposed a heavy burden on the unions because they took care of the living expenses of the workers who were dismissed and compensated workers who suffered salary cuts. On account of disciplinary action against railway workers in 1971, the two railway unions, Kokuro and Doryokusha, had financial losses amounting to over $20 million. The government had suggested in 1972 that it might amend the act, but later changed its mind. The railway unions, along with unions organizing other transport workers, held a general strike of transport workers over wages on April 27 that totally crippled Japan's public transport service. On the same day, the government agreed to give serious consideration to an alteration in the strike law.

The struggle for free trade unionism continued in Spain. The year began with the trial of 25 workers alleged to have led a shipyard strike the previous March during which 2 workers were killed and 36 injured when the police opened fire. Other shipyards experienced sitdown strikes in February: a lockout was then imposed and some strikers were arrested and fined large sums. The strikes at one time spread to 20,000 other workers in the province of Biscay. A striking building worker was killed by police fire on April 3 in Barcelona.

The tendency to improve trade union unity was expressed in various ways. A new European trade union confederation was founded on February 9 in Brussels with affiliates from 15 countries. The confederation represented the interests of the International Confederation of Free Trade Unions and excluded bodies affiliated to the World Federation of Trade Unions. The activities of multinational firms were a source of interest throughout the year, and an international trade union conference on them was held in Brussels in February. A second conference, held in Tokyo in October, recommended consumer boycotts against the Farah Manufacturing Co. in the United States, which, despite an 18-month strike, refused to recognize trade unionism, and the Brook Bond Co. with respect to the wages it paid its employees on tea plantations in Sri Lanka.

Less Developed Countries. Confrontation between labour unions and governments in the less industrialized countries were commonplace in 1973, but the centre stage was occupied by black workers and the South African government. A wave of spontaneous strikes began in October 1972 with a walkout by stevedores in Durban. The issues were wages and conditions of work, and they evoked much international publicity. Comparisons were made between black and white workers, and it was revealed that about 80% of the black African workers earned wages that put them below the poverty line. On January 9 strikes involving approximately 60,000 Africans broke out, affecting about 100 firms and halting municipal services in Durban. The police arrested more than 250 strikers. On May 22 the South African government published a bill to give black workers a limited right to strike for the first time in 30 years. However, a wide variety of black workers would not be allowed to strike, and the government had the authority to extend the list. Before a strike could be called legally a lengthy procedure of negotiation and conciliation had to be completed. Early in September, 11 African miners were killed and 27 wounded by the police at Carletonville, where migrant miners were striking.

In Uruguay and Chile unions were involved in unsuccessful action against military take-overs. At the end of June a national strike was called in Uruguay against a military-backed coup. Workers occupied some factories, and no newspapers were published. Hundreds of union officials were arrested, and troops dislodged workers from the factories by force. The military junta that overturned the democratically elected government of Pres. Salvador Allende in September also suppressed labour unions in Chile and dissolved the Chilean national labour union centre.

The leaders of the Bangladesh labour union federation, the Jatyo Sramik League, urged the Bangladesh government late in 1972 to alter the policy that denied the right to strike in the public sector. A new law on associations in Turkey aroused union protests because it made it impossible for unions to release news or arrange press conferences. Two officials of the Turkish Energy, Water and Gas Workers' Federation were arrested in February for issuing a press statement. Unions in the Fiji Islands protested in April because of the government's intention to introduce restrictive labour laws.

During the summer a conflict occurred between the government of Upper Volta and the Upper Volta Organization of Free Trade Unions that resulted in the imprisonment of 17 trade union officials. A strike by 600,000 plantation workers in Sri Lanka in mid-September ended after only 24 hours when employers agreed to arbitration by the labour minister. On the initiative of the Organization of African Unity a new pan-African trade union organization, called the Organization of African Trade Union Unity, was established in April. (V. L. ALLEN)

See also Employment, Wages, and Hours; Race Relations.

ENCYCLOPÆDIA BRITANNICA FILMS. *The Rise of Labor* (1968); *The Industrial Worker* (1969); *The Rise of Big Business* (1970); *The Progressive Era* (1971).

Laos

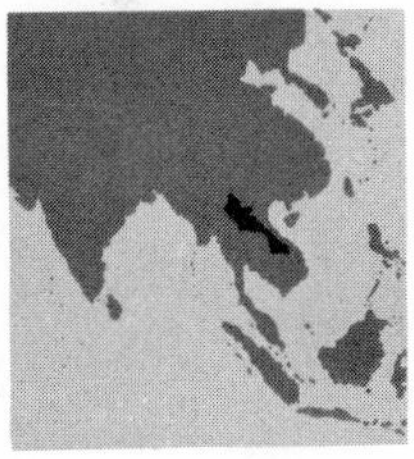

A constitutional monarchy of Southeast Asia, Laos is bounded by China, North and South Vietnam, Cambodia, Thailand, and Burma. Area: 91,400 sq.mi. (236,800 sq.km.). Pop. (1972 est.): 3,106,000. Administrative cap. and largest city: Vientiane (pop., 1973, 176,637). Royal cap.: Louangphrabang (Luang Prabang; pop., 1970 est., 25,000). Language: Lao (official); French and English. Religion: Buddhist; tribal. King, Savang Vatthana; premier in 1973, Prince Souvanna Phouma.

After two decades of war, peace came to Laos in 1973. On February 21, amid the popping of champagne corks, the Laotian government and the Pathet Lao signed an accord that provided for: a cease-fire freezing all troops in place; withdrawal of all foreign troops within 90 days; a new provisional coalition government to be formed within 30 days; and the establishment of a national political consultative council, which would organize general elections at a date to be fixed.

However, during the period immediately following the cease-fire agreement there was a severe intensification of the fighting. Government soldiers and the irregular forces operating under the sponsorship of the U.S. Central Intelligence Agency fell back under determined Communist offensives in the central and southern sectors. U.S. warplanes resumed limited bombing in Laos, in response to a request from Premier Souvanna Phouma, who declared "we have been tricked" by the Communists.

As with the fighting immediately before the cease-fire pact, the post-pact operations were interpreted as the result of attempts by one side or the other to consolidate positions in key areas. By March the fighting began tapering off and the adversaries started serious negotiations for the establishment of a viable peace.

But the differences over the future government were too serious to be resolved within the 30-day limit set by the cease-fire agreement. The main arguments were over Pathet Lao demands that the post of a vice-premier be created and allocated to it to offset the retention of premiership by Prince Souvanna Phouma; that the four key portfolios of foreign affairs, defense, interior, and finance be equally divided; and that the capital cities of Vientiane and Louangphrabang be neutralized by on-site stationing of equal numbers of government and Pathet Lao troops.

After five months of bargaining, agreement was reached by the end of July. It provided for two deputy premierships, the first to be obligatorily held by the Pathet Lao if the premiership went to the Vientiane side; the defense, interior, and finance ministries were to go to the Vientiane side and foreign affairs to the Pathet Lao. Altogether, each side was to have five ministries with two to be held by neutralists. Neutralization of Vientiane and Louangphrabang was to be effected by the introduction of Pathet Lao troops into the cities and the integration of Pathet Lao policemen into the national police force.

Rightists in Vientiane had strong objections to the agreement, which, therefore, remained formally unsigned. The terms of the agreement were generally considered favourable to the Pathet Lao, despite the fact that the interior and defense portfolios were to be held by the Vientiane side. Vientiane's generals, most of whom identified with the entrenched rightist establishment, had strongly opposed the stationing of Pathet Lao regulars in the two cities. But the agreement allowed almost exactly the number of Communist troops originally demanded by the Pathet Lao. Earlier public statements by Souvanna Phouma that he would retire sooner than expected reinforced the impression of a Pathet Lao victory, for it was widely believed that their leader, Prince Souphanouvong, would succeed his half brother as premier.

Suddenly, on August 20, an attempt was made to overthrow the government at Vientiane. The coup was staged by Thao Ma, a 43-year-old former commander of the Air Force, in exile since a previous military revolt in 1966. Slipping into Vientiane from Thailand, Thao Ma and a handful of other exiled officers succeeded in commandeering four or five T-28 aircraft and an armoured car and in recruiting some supporters by offering $5 to each recruit. In a matter of hours the coup was over. After dropping a bomb or two on army headquarters, Thao Ma's plane, hit by ground fire, crash-landed at the airport. An hour later he was dead—executed, according to some informed sources. Some of the other coup leaders also were executed, but some escaped. There was great speculation as to whether the right-wing establishment in Vientiane had any liaison with the coup group, but no evidence of a link was available. The failure of the coup, however, was seen as evidence of lack of popular support for rightist maneuvers.

For a while the rightists in the Cabinet kept putting pressure on Souvanna Phouma, who at one stage threatened to resign. But the coup had strengthened Pathet Lao demands for effective neutralization of the capital cities. Prince Souvanna eventually succeeded in patching up his differences with the rightists. On September 14 the full political and military settlement was finally signed.

Souvanna Phouma set October 11 as the date for forming the new coalition. The right-wing-controlled National Assembly was to recess on that day. But on October 3 the Assembly resolved to extend its session for another month to allow the new Cabinet to be formed. The delay in establishing the government was attributed to technical hitches—the Pathet Lao had not yet finalized the names of their Cabinet ministers—but observers believed that much more hard bargaining might be needed before the coalition became a reality.

Among the immediate problems that would face the new coalition Cabinet was a looming economic crisis. The winding down of U.S. military spending and other changes in the nature of the U.S. commitment to Laos affected the Vientiane government, which was dependent almost entirely on U.S. financial aid for its economic survival. The international monetary crisis also had its impact. In June experts forecast a budget deficit of about 15 billion kip (U.S. $25 million) for the 1973–74 fiscal year—more than 50% of the draft budget itself.

A special problem that peace brought to Laos was the possibility of an intensified struggle among Communist powers for influence in the country. While the main contestants were China and the Soviet Union, a subtler tussle between China and North Vietnam was also under way. It was believed that U.S. advice to Souvanna Phouma was to befriend China. Prince Souvanna did make several public statements in support of China. In October the Vientiane government accepted a Soviet offer of aircraft to fly Pathet Lao officials to Laos from North Vietnam. Immediately China also offered a "helping hand" in arranging the airlift—and Laos agreed.

LAOS

Education. (State; 1970–71) Primary, pupils 217,889, teachers 6,529; secondary, pupils 7,050, teachers 436; vocational, pupils 1,092, teachers 196; teacher training, students 3,340, teachers 408; higher, students 509; teaching staff 133.

Finance. Monetary unit: kip, with (Sept. 17, 1973) an official exchange rate of 600 kip to U.S. $1 (free rate of 1,447 kip = £1 sterling). Budget (1972–73 est.): revenue (excluding foreign aid) 8,008,000,000 kip; expenditure 22,808,000,000 kip (including defense expenditure of 11,322,000,000 kip).

Foreign Trade. (1971) Imports (excluding gold) 19,740,000,000 kip; exports (excluding reexports of gold) 795 million kip. Import sources: Thailand 42%; France 20%; U.S. 13%; Japan 13%. Export destinations: Thailand *c.* 66%; Singapore 9%; Philippines 9%; U.S. 6%; Hong Kong 5%. Main exports: tin 49%; timber 48%.

Transport and Communications. Roads (1971) 7,231 km. (including 2,489 km. all-weather). Motor vehicles in use (1971): passenger 12,100; commercial (including buses) 2,100. Air traffic (1971): 20 million passenger-km.; freight 440,000 net ton-km. Telephones (Dec. 1971) 2,000. Radio licenses (Dec. 1971) 51,000.

Agriculture. Production (in 000; metric tons; 1972; 1971 in parentheses): rice 780 (812); corn *c.* 25 (*c.* 25); coffee *c.* 2.6 (*c.* 2.8); tobacco *c.* 4 (*c.* 4). Livestock (in 000; 1971–72): cattle *c.* 435; buffalo *c.* 940; pigs *c.* 1,200; chickens *c.* 12,000.

Industry. Production (in 000; 1971): tin concentrates (metric tons) 1.6; electricity (excluding most industrial production; kw-hr.) 16,128.

Within the Pathet Lao hierarchy a group of "hard-liners" was reported to be emerging, generally backing close liaison with China. North Vietnam, on the other hand, seemed to consider Laos and Cambodia as its areas of special interest. Diplomatic reports suggested that China's maneuvers were aimed at preventing both Moscow and Hanoi from gaining further influence in Indochina. Peace or war, Laos seemed destined to remain an arena of big-power conflict.

(T. J. S. GEORGE)

Latin-American Affairs

U.S. Relations with Latin America. There was no U.S. initiative in 1973 toward Latin America to improve relationships or to formulate policies. The administration of U.S. Pres. Richard M. Nixon, mainly concerned with domestic matters arising from the Watergate affair, otherwise gave priority to improving relationships with the U.S.S.R. and China, and from mid-October it was preoccupied with the Middle East crisis. Nevertheless, any threats to U.S. hegemony over the region were dealt with no less firmly than before.

The lack of a U.S. response to calls from Latin America for new policy initiatives was demonstrated at the meeting of the Organization of American States (OAS) held in Washington, D.C., April 4–15. The then U.S. secretary of state, William P. Rogers, rejected a demand by several Latin-American countries that the sanctions imposed against Cuba in 1962 be lifted. The U.S. also gave only qualified support to a motion put forward by Chilean, Peruvian, and Uruguayan delegates that the structure of the OAS be reexamined. On two other topics U.S. delegates abstained: a demand for greater control over the activities in Latin America of multinational companies, and a request that the U.S. not sell off its strategic stockpiles of minerals such as lead, zinc, and copper, as this would endanger the exports of such countries as Bolivia, Chile, and Peru.

The U.S. also largely opposed a document agreed on by delegates at the 15th session of the UN Economic Commission for Latin America (ECLA), held in Quito, Ecuador, March 23–30. The document expressed concern over the slow rate of economic development in Latin America and the comparative lack of cooperation that the region had been receiving from the developed world; it therefore called for automatic refinancing, under certain circumstances, of Latin America's external debt, and criticized the continuance of Latin America's large trade deficit with the U.S. and the protectionism and tendency toward self-sufficiency shown by the EEC. The document was subsequently submitted for debate at the UN General Assembly.

The Nixon administration's comparative neglect of Latin America was demonstrated further by conflicting statements in September by Secretary of State Henry Kissinger. Before the Foreign Relations Committee of the U.S. Senate, Kissinger said that the region would be high on the list of concerns of the State Department. However, in a speech at the UN General Assembly shortly afterward, he made no mention of Latin America, although every other area of the world was referred to.

Early in June a report issued by the Inter-American Committee of the Alliance for Progress criticized U.S. policies toward Latin America, particularly the reduction in financial and economic aid in recent years. The document noted that Nixon's pursuit of worldwide monetary and trade objectives made it more difficult for the U.S. to achieve a special relationship with Latin America. It also urged the U.S. administration to adopt measures to permit an increase in Latin-American exports to the U.S.

In July the U.S. administration pressed Congress to lift all restrictions on arms sales to Latin America; Congress had previously imposed a limit of $100 million on the value of these sales, but it was later increased by $50 million, at presidential discretion. The principal purchasers of arms in Latin America (Argentina, Brazil, Chile, Colombia, Peru, and Venezuela) had turned increasingly to Western Europe for supplies; between 1967 and 1972, Latin-American countries spent $1.7 billion on weapons, of which Europe supplied 75% and the U.S. only 13%. The U.S. was, therefore, concerned that it was losing one of its chief means of exerting influence in Latin America.

There was a great improvement in U.S. relations with Chile following the overthrow of the Marxist administration of Pres. Salvador Allende (*see* OBITUARIES) by a military coup in mid-September. The new government was quickly recognized by the U.S., a number of European countries, Argentina, and Brazil, but the U.S.S.R. and most of the Eastern European countries broke off diplomatic links. In October the Inter-American Development Bank (IDB) granted a loan of $65 million for a hydroelectric project; this was the first loan granted by the bank to Chile since the Allende government took office late in 1970. The new Chilean government announced that it was prepared to reopen talks with U.S. copper companies on compensation for assets expropriated since 1971. The removal of Allende was greeted with relief by the U.S.; it had been alarmed over rapidly growing Soviet influence in Chile.

Relations with Peru also improved during the year, and it was reported in September that U.S. aid would be resumed; in that month the World Bank made available a loan of $25 million for agricultural projects, its first in three years. The U.S. regarded Peru as one of the most stable countries in Latin America; most U.S. companies nationalized since 1968 had been paid some compensation, and negotiations were under way to settle other claims.

The U.S. greeted with caution the return of Gen.

ROBERT TROSTLE—KEYSTONE

Hortensia Allende, widow of the former Chilean president, is greeted solemnly on her arrival in Mexico, Sept. 16, 1973.

Juan Perón (*see* BIOGRAPHY) to power in Argentina on October 12. Washington accepted, however, that a Peronist government, supported by a majority of the population, was the only government with the authority to carry out policies to permit an economic revival.

There were no signs of a rapprochement between the U.S. and Cuba, despite the signing of an antihijacking agreement by the two countries in February. On the other hand, there were growing indications that Venezuela was considering recognizing the Castro regime. In September, the Venezuelan minister of youth, Rodolfo José Cardenas, visited Havana; this was the first official visit to Cuba by a member of the Venezuelan government since diplomatic relations were broken off in 1962. Venezuela had been the leading proponent among Latin-American countries of an accommodation with Cuba. Argentina restored diplomatic links with Cuba in May; and in August it granted a loan of $200 million to finance the purchase by Cuba of Argentine-made agricultural equipment and trucks.

Inter-American Development Bank. The IDB held its 14th annual meeting in Kingston, Jamaica, in May. It was reported that in 1972 the bank's lending volume was higher than in any other year; it granted 52 loans amounting to $807 million, against $657 million in 1971. Commentators, however, expressed doubts about its future. U.S. Secretary of the Treasury George Shultz stated at the meeting that U.S. congressional support for the bank was uncertain, and some Latin-American delegates expressed dissatisfaction over political discrimination in granting loans. There was heated but inconclusive debate at the meeting on extension of membership to Japan and European countries.

Regional and Subregional Integration. The Latin American Free Trade Association (LAFTA) showed no enthusiasm for regaining the dynamism of the early and mid-1960s. There was a round of official meetings during the year, but no decision of importance rose from them.

The Andean Group (Bolivia, Chile, Colombia, Ecuador, and Peru) emerged during 1973 as by far the most promising of the groupings among Latin-American countries working toward eventual economic integration. As of January 1 duty reductions were made on 2,370 items included within the common customs tariff of the group. Peru, Colombia, and Chile applied a 10% tariff cut on trade among themselves and a 30% reduction on imports from Ecuador and Bolivia, which, after a 40% cut in 1972, left tariffs against those countries at only 30% of their original levels.

In April the Colombian Congress ratified the Cartagena Agreement, which set out the policy decisions of the Andean Group, and agreed to abide by further decisions made by the group. In March it was announced that Colombia was to receive loans totaling $95 million from the Andean Development Corporation (CAF) between 1973 and 1975.

On February 13 Venezuela joined the group as its sixth member. The announcement of Venezuela's membership marked the culmination of a notable diplomatic exercise by Pres. Rafael Caldera, who visited the Andean countries and Argentina during nine days in February before reaching Peru for the signing of the Consensus of Lima, the document formalizing Venezuelan accession. Venezuelan membership, which surprised few observers, was expected by experts to have profound consequences for the future development of the group, especially with regard to trading patterns and the development of industries. The Caracas government made the decision basically because of its growing awareness that the nation's crude oil reserves would near exhaustion by the end of the century and that it was therefore imperative to find other outlets and markets to help speed up the process of diversification and expansion of the economy.

Mexico and Brazil took a growing interest in the development of the Andean Group during the year. In December 1972 the Mexican government granted an initial loan of $5 million, with the possibility of further increases, to the CAF to help finance the purchase of Mexican goods and services; it also agreed to invest $1 million in a preinvestment fund to finance feasibility studies for future projects. In June and July the Brazilian foreign minister, Mário Gibson Barbosa, visited Bolivia, Colombia, Ecuador, and Peru; joint communiqués that were published after the visits established that trade and technical cooperation between Brazil and those countries were to be considerably increased.

There were signs of a revival in the Central American Common Market (CACM; El Salvador, Honduras, Nicaragua, Guatemala, and Costa Rica). Late in 1972 a group of experts from the Permanent Secretariat of Central American Economic Integration (SIECA) completed a study which reached the conclusion that prospects for the future growth of the Central American countries depended on closer integration and that this could be achieved only through the concept of an economic community, somewhat in the European style. Taking evident inspiration from Europe, and possibly from the Andean Group, the SIECA experts recommended the establishment of a Council of Ministers, on which each country's interests would be represented, and a Permanent Committee to defend and promote the interests of the CACM as a whole. The ministers of finance and economy of the member countries approved the study in December 1972 and agreed to appoint a reviewing committee by Jan. 1, 1973, but the committee was not formally established until June.

Honduras remained outside the CACM during 1973 though retaining formal membership. Some experts considered, however, that the country would eventually return to the community; it had already signed bilateral trade agreements with Guatemala, Nicaragua, and Costa Rica. There was some improvement in relations between Honduras and El Salvador, which had been severely strained following the war of June 1969.

Bilateral Relations. Following a meeting in Brasília on April 26–27 of Pres. Emilio G. Médici of Brazil and Pres. Alfredo Stroessner of Paraguay, an agreement was signed to establish the Itaipu hydroelectric project, which on completion was to be one of the largest in the world. A binational enterprise known as Itaipu was to be established by Eletrobras of Brazil and ANDE of Paraguay, with an initial capital of $100 million. The Paraguayan share of $50 million was to be financed by a Brazilian loan over 60 years at 6.5% annual interest. When finished, the capacity of the complex, on the Rio Paraná, was to be 10.7 million kw. at a total cost of $2.4 billion; the first stage was due for completion by 1980.

In October Argentina and Paraguay reached agreement on the construction of two hydroelectric plants on the Rio Paraná. The first complex, on the Yacyreta-Apipe islands, was to cost $1 billion and was to have a capacity of 3.3 million kw. The Paraguayan govern-

VON HEDEMANN—ROTHCO

"I've never heard of it."

ment agreed to call for feasibility studies for a second plant at Corpus.

Economic ties between Mexico and Brazil grew closer in 1973. A mission headed by the Mexican secretary of commerce and industry, Carlos Torres Manzo, visited Brazil in July. Another Mexican mission visited Brazil in October to negotiate joint ventures in civil engineering and to produce fertilizers, insecticides, pesticides, and tempered glass.

In April Brazil and Bolivia agreed in principle to lay, at a cost of $100 million, a 1,350-mi. pipeline to carry natural gas from Santa Cruz in Bolivia to the Paulinia refinery in the Brazilian state of São Paulo. An additional agreement signed in the same month established that Brazil was to provide financial and technical assistance for the building of a large iron and steel mill at Puerto Suárez on the Brazilian frontier.

It was announced in October that a joint Colombian-Brazilian company was to be established to develop coal deposits near Cúcuta, Colombia, with reserves estimated at 30,000,000,000 to 40,000,000,000 tons. The coal was to be transported by rail to Cartagena and then shipped to Brazil to supply a planned steel plant to be built in the state of Pará in Amazonia.

(ROBIN CHAPMAN)

ENCYCLOPÆDIA BRITANNICA FILMS. *Siqueiros: "El Maestro" (March of Humanity in Latin America)* (1969); *The Mexican-American Speaks: Heritage in Bronze* (1973); *Venezuela: Oil Builds a Nation* (1973).

Law

Court Decisions and Related Developments. During 1973 courts throughout the world were occupied with cases involving abortion, family law, censorship, labour relations, and the environment. In addition, the U.S. federal courts were the focal points of a constitutional crisis occasioned by criminal charges made against Vice-Pres. Spiro Agnew and by questions concerning executive privilege, separation of powers, and other matters stemming from the alleged reluctance of Pres. Richard Nixon to cooperate with the Senate committee investigating the Watergate affair and with the special prosecutor in the case in his efforts to bring criminal charges against some individuals allegedly involved in that affair and related incidents.

Abortion. In the companion cases of *Roe* v. *Wade* and *Doe* v. *Bolton,* the U.S. Supreme Court struck down the antiabortion statutes of Texas and Georgia. Legal scholars felt that these decisions also effectively nullified similar statutes in 29 other states which made it a crime to procure or attempt an abortion except on medical advice for the purpose of saving the life of the mother. The court held, however, that the states have legitimate interests in the health of the mother and in protecting fetal life after viability, and that they may pass laws that are narrowly drawn to implement these interests. In this respect, the court said that statutes that except from criminality only a lifesaving procedure on behalf of the mother, without regard to the stage of pregnancy and without recognition of the other interests involved, are too broad to pass constitutional muster.

The court suggested that valid statutes must recognize that different interests come into play depending on the stage of the pregnancy. During the first trimester (*i.e.,* three months of pregnancy), maternal mortality occurs less frequently because of an abortion than in normal childbirth. As a result the state cannot pretend to be protecting the mother's health by proscribing abortions. Nor can it claim a right to protect the unborn child, because the fetus is not viable. Consequently, during this time, the pregnant woman and her doctor must be given an absolute right to make the decision on abortion.

During the second and third trimesters, however, medical evidence shows that the mother's health is somewhat threatened by an abortion. Thus the states, in promoting the interest in the health of the mother, may, if they choose, regulate the abortion procedure during these stages in ways that are reasonably related to maternal health; for example, by setting up requirements as to the qualifications of the person who is to perform the abortion and the facilities in which it is to be performed. The states also may implement their legitimate interest in potential life by prohibiting abortions after the fetus becomes viable, except where necessary to preserve the life of the mother. "Viability," said the court, "is usually placed at about seven months (28 weeks) but may occur earlier." It is the time at which the fetus has the capability of meaningful life outside the mother's womb.

A similar approach was proposed by the Danish government. It sponsored legislation that would enable all women to obtain a free abortion during the first 12 weeks of pregnancy. During this stage of pregnancy, the decision on abortion would be left to the individual woman, with no obligation to obtain the consent of her husband or, in the case of an unmarried girl, of her parents. After the 12th week, however, important qualifications on the woman's right to have an abortion would be imposed. Liberalized abortion statutes were proposed or enacted in several other countries.

Family Law and Women's Rights. The Supreme Labour Court of Spain ruled that Maria de los Angelos could become Spain's first female bullfighter. In a controversial case that was much publicized in Spain, she successfully appealed a decision of the Spanish Bullfighters' Union denying her a license on the sole ground that she was a woman.

The West German Cabinet approved a draft bill that would change the divorce law radically and improve women's rights. The draft would eliminate the concept of "grounds" for divorce and substitute the single rule that a divorce may be granted if there has been a "breakdown" of the marriage. A marital breakdown would be deemed to have occurred if the spouses had lived apart for a year or more and both wanted a divorce or if one partner had lived apart from the other for three years and sought a divorce.

The U.S. Supreme Court held in the case of *Gomez* v. *Perez* that a state may not invidiously discriminate against illegitimate children by denying them legal rights that are accorded to children generally. The

Latin-American Literature: *see* Literature
Latter-day Saints: *see* Religion

WIDE WORLD

Vice-Pres. Fouad Ammoun (right) of the International Court of Justice reads the court's decision in the Australian-French dispute over France's nuclear tests in the South Pacific, June 22, 1973. By an 8–6 vote, the court called on France to refrain from nuclear testing in the area pending a final decision.

case held that a state may not constitutionally grant a legitimate child a judicially enforceable right to support from its natural father and at the same time deny that right to an illegitimate child.

Censorship. The issue of censorship came before the courts in several countries, and some surprising judicial decisions were handed down. For example, the legal community was amazed when the Spanish Supreme Court ruled that the possession of Communist tracts was not necessarily illegal. The decision overturned a lower court judgment that two men were guilty of "illegal propaganda" on account of possessing a number of Communist-inspired books and pamphlets. The court accepted the defense that the literature in question dealt only with Communist doctrine and with disputes among Communists and did not refer specifically to Spain.

The Federal Constitutional Court of West Germany upheld the validity of a federal law giving the government power to review the importation of films whose content tended to threaten the basic free democratic order. The exact meaning of the decision was not clear, however, because the court stressed the fact that the kind of censorship envisaged by the federal law was only "preliminary" in nature in most cases. This aspect of the decision tended to suggest to some legal scholars that the statute might be invalid in cases where facts showing more rigid censorship could be established.

Once again the U.S. Supreme Court was called upon to decide whether allegedly obscene material is protected by the First Amendment to the Constitution and, if not, what standards must be followed in suppressing it. In *Miller* v. *California* the court, by a 5–4 decision, gave these answers: obscene material is not protected by the First Amendment and it may be suppressed if (1) the average person, applying contemporary community standards, would find that the work, taken as a whole, appeals to the prurient interest, (2) the work depicts or describes, in a patently offensive way, sexual conduct specifically defined by the applicable state law, and (3) the work, taken as a whole, lacks serious literary, artistic, political, or scientific value.

The case made two important changes in the law. First, it rejected the "utterly without redeeming social value" test that it had used to define obscenity in the past, and second, it held that a jury is not required to apply "national standards" in making its determination under the three guidelines stated above as to whether a particular work is obscene. Rather, juries could now measure the essential factual issues of "prurient appeal" and "patent offensiveness" by the standards prevailing in their own community. In this connection, Chief Justice Warren Burger, in the majority opinion, stated that, "It is neither realistic nor constitutionally sound to read the First Amendment as requiring that the people of Maine or Mississippi accept public depiction of conduct found tolerable in Las Vegas or New York City."

In December, the court agreed to hear the appeal of a Georgia theatre manager who had been convicted under a state obscenity law for showing the motion picture *Carnal Knowledge,* which had received considerable critical acclaim. This raised the possibility that the court might further clarify its new ruling on obscenity, although the Georgia case also involved the question of whether the new guidelines could be applied retroactively, since the conviction took place before the Miller decision had been handed down.

Labour Law. The rights of employees were improved by court decisions in the West Indies, the U.K., and the U.S. A West Indian case, *Antigua Trades and Labour Union* v. *Walter,* held that a paid union officer could not be summarily dismissed by his union. The court held that the right to notice would be implied into the contract of employment and that dismissal without notice would be a breach of that contract entitling the victim to damages.

The Court of Appeal of Great Britain broadly construed the new British Industrial Relations Act to protect workers who were notified of dismissal before the act came into effect. The act, relating in large part to unfair dismissals, was held to apply to workers who were notified of dismissal before the act came into force if the expiration of the notice came at a time when the act was in effect. The decision resulted in compensation being given to a number of employees who were notified of discharge just before the new act went into effect in an attempt by employers to get rid of certain marginal or undesirable employees under the less rigorous requirements of the previous labour laws.

A U.S. court found a union guilty of an unfair labour practice in fining union members who resigned during a strike and then returned to work. The court held that a union loses control over a member once he lawfully resigns from membership.

Searches and Seizures. The U.S. Supreme Court, in upholding, 6–3, the convictions of two men who had been searched and charged with possession of narcotics after being arrested for minor traffic violations, considerably broadened the power of the police to search persons without a warrant. Previously, officers in such cases had been confined to frisking the suspect for weapons or for evidence of the crime for which the arrest had been made. This rule continued to apply in cases where there was no probable cause for making the arrest, but the majority held that "no additional justification" was needed to search the subject of a valid custodial arrest thoroughly for further incriminating evidence.

The Environment. Two important cases were decided in Great Britain and Japan. In Great Britain a shipping company registered in London was fined more than £2,500 ($6,250) by the Central Criminal Court for discharging oil in a prohibited area off Nova Scotia. The prosecution, initiated by the Department of Trade, was the first of its kind to be brought in a British criminal court.

An extremely large damage judgment was granted by a district court in Japan against a prominent fertilizer producer. The court awarded 937 million yen ($3,530,000) to 138 residents of Minamata who were poisoned and otherwise injured by waste materials pumped into the coastal waters of southwestern Japan by the fertilizer company some 20 years earlier. The decision, the fourth important case in which Japanese residents had won substantial awards against industrial polluters, was believed by legal scholars to be the largest award of its kind ever rendered in any country. The company announced that it would not appeal.

The U.S. Supreme Court held that the federal Admiralty Extension Act did not preempt the law of shipping so as to preclude the various states from enacting antipollution legislation related to oceangoing vessels. The case involved the Florida Oil-Spill Prevention and Pollution Control Act, which provided for the recovery of cleanup costs and damages from waterfront oil-handling facilities and ships using such facilities.

Constitutional Crisis. A constitutional crisis of major dimensions occurred in the U.S. as the result of unrelated legal actions involving Vice-President Agnew and President Nixon. The "Agnew case" began with a routine investigation by George Beall, U.S. attorney for the state of Maryland, into payments ("kickbacks") allegedly made by building contractors to Maryland public officials to influence the awarding of contracts. When the investigation was started, there was no suspicion that Vice-President Agnew was in any way implicated, but as it unfolded, evidence was produced that possibly showed his involvement in certain kickbacks made when he was county executive of Baltimore County and later governor of Maryland.

When rumours of this evidence were reported in the press, Agnew hotly denied the story, charging that he was being tried by the press and that leaks to the news media had resulted in the creation of a climate in which he could not get a fair trial. He officially requested the U.S. House of Representatives to conduct a full, public inquiry that would give him the opportunity to exonerate himself. This request for impeachment proceedings was coupled with a contention that the Constitution prevented the indictment of the vice-president while he remained in office, and that, therefore, the only public forum open to him was the House itself.

Some legal scholars thought the vice-president's request to be heard by the House was designed to put pressure on President Nixon to use his good offices to suppress the Maryland investigation. It was speculated that Nixon, because of his own difficulties stemming from Watergate, would not like to have on the lawbooks a decision by the U.S. Supreme Court as to whether a high government official could be indicted while in office, and would not like to resuscitate the long-dead impeachment machinery of the House. In any event the House refused Agnew's request, and the case suddenly came to a close when he pleaded "no contest" to a charge of income tax evasion. In return for this plea and the right to publish certain information pertaining to misconduct, the government recommended that no jail sentence be imposed. The vice-president resigned from office and the court sentenced him to three years of unsupervised probation and fined him $10,000.

The plea of "no contest" left Agnew technically free to continue to argue that he was innocent, and shortly after he resigned, he vigorously defended himself on national television. His resignation brought into play for the first time the recently ratified 25th Amendment to the Constitution, which provides that "whenever there is a vacancy in the office of vice-president, the president shall nominate a vice-president who shall take office upon confirmation by a majority vote of both houses of Congress." Pursuant to this amendment, President Nixon nominated Rep. Gerald Ford of Michigan, who was subsequently confirmed.

President Nixon's legal problems were closely related to the so-called Watergate investigation, an inquiry by a special Senate committee into abuses that allegedly occurred in the 1972 presidential campaign and illegal efforts to cover up that wrongdoing. (*See* UNITED STATES.) In the course of the Senate hearings it was revealed that the White House routinely tape recorded conversations between the president and others. Because there was conflicting evidence before the committee as to the president's knowledge of the alleged abuses, the tapes of his various conversations were considered to be important evidence. A special prosecutor, Harvard law professor Archibald Cox (*see* BIOGRAPHY), brought into office to prosecute in the criminal courts those suspected of illegal activities in connection with the Watergate affair, also wanted the tapes as essential evidence for his prosecutions.

President Nixon refused to surrender the tapes on the ground that it would be unconstitutional for him to do so. He opined that the office of president was constitutionally privileged to withhold confidential information, arguing that any other rule would inhibit the free flow of discussion and seriously cripple the presidency. He based his argument on the "separation of powers" principle of the Constitution. Rejecting this argument, both the special prosecutor and the committee brought action in the federal district court in Washington, D.C., to compel the president to hand over the tapes.

Judge John Sirica (*see* BIOGRAPHY) decided that the tapes should not be delivered to the Senate committee but held that the special prosecutor was entitled to them, assuming they contained no material relating to national defense. To resolve this matter, he ordered the tapes turned over to him for a determination as to whether or not they should ultimately be delivered to the special prosecutor. In making this decision, Judge Sirica rejected the constitutional claim of the president that the tapes could not be delivered to another branch of the government. The president appealed, but the Court of Appeals essentially affirmed Judge Sirica. The case was not appealed to the Supreme Court. Some legal scholars believed this was because of the strong possibility that the four Nixon appointees to the court might recuse themselves from the hearing on the ground that their participation in the case could lead to charges that they had not acted with proper judicial propriety. The president, it was thought, would have virtually no chance of winning in the Supreme Court if only the five non-Nixon appointees were to hear the case.

In the event, President Nixon worked out a compromise whereby he would turn over the tapes to Sen. John Stennis (Dem., Miss.), who, in turn, would make a summary of their contents for the use of the special prosecutor and the Senate committee. Senators Sam Ervin and Howard Baker, the chairman and vice-chairman of the committee, agreed, but Cox threatened to bring a proper action in the courts to determine whether or not the president was in contempt for his refusal to follow Judge Sirica's order. President Nixon responded by summarily discharging Cox. Cox's immediate superior, Attorney General Elliot Richardson, resigned (*see* BIOGRAPHY), and a public outcry stimulated an investigation by the House as to whether impeachment proceedings should be brought against the president. While this was going on, President Nixon reversed his former position and agreed to release the tapes to Judge Sirica. After the tapes were delivered, it was discovered that two important conversations had apparently not been taped and that one tape contained an erasure of about 18 minutes' duration. The president's personal secretary, Rose Mary Woods, testified that she might inadvertently have caused part of the erasure, but the matter was unclear. On December 17 President Nixon allowed to become law, without his signature, a bill giving Judge Sirica's court jurisdiction over the Senate committee's subpoenas, and the following day the committee voted to subpoena nearly 500 tapes and documents. Meanwhile, the House Judiciary Committee began investigating the various charges against the president in the first step toward possible impeachment proceedings, and the special prosecutor's office continued its work under the newly appointed Leon Jaworski, a former president of the American Bar Association.

(WILLIAM D. HAWKLAND)

International Law. *International Court of Justice.* After several years of almost complete inactivity, the court had four cases on its files during 1973: the U.K. and Germany versus Iceland, Australia and New Zealand versus France, Pakistan versus India, and an advisory opinion on UN staff conditions. However, the two European respondent states, Iceland and France, not only contested the court's jurisdiction (which had happened before) but also boycotted the court's proceedings without even arguing the jurisdiction issue before it. This was particularly disturbing, since the Western European countries had given the most support to the court in the past.

In the Icelandic case, relating to the unilateral extension of Iceland's exclusive fishery limits to 50 mi. offshore, the court on July 12 renewed its interim order of August 1972 imposing provisional protective measures that would allow British and West German

Former Watergate special prosecutor Archibald Cox prepares to testify before the Senate Judiciary Committee on Oct. 29, 1973. The committee sought information on his surprise dismissal by President Nixon Oct. 20, in a dispute over subpoenaed tape recordings.

WIDE WORLD

fishermen to continue to take fish from the disputed waters. The Icelandic government continued to disregard the order, however, and its gunboats engaged in systematically cutting away the nets of British trawlers, unless prevented by one of the two British frigates stationed on the spot. In October the British and Icelandic governments agreed to end the "cod war," but settlement of the issues awaited the international conference on the law of the sea (*see* below).

The French case involved nuclear tests made by France in French Polynesia. The plaintiff governments complained of the danger of radioactive fallout. The court issued a form of interim injunction on June 22, which France ignored, and the tests were subsequently carried out. A security zone of 60 mi. of high seas was unilaterally proclaimed around the test area, and a New Zealand frigate with a Cabinet minister on board sailed to the edge of the zone in protest. Private protest vessels that sailed inside the zone (but not into French territorial waters) were forcibly boarded and temporarily impounded by French naval units. Proceedings on the substantive issues were continuing before the court, despite the respondent's boycott.

The only actual judgment of the court during the year was its advisory opinion of July 12 on the *Applications for Review of Judgment 158 of the United Nations Administrative Tribunal.* This was the first time the court had been called upon to review a decision of the UN Administrative Tribunal under art. 11 of the tribunal's statute. Having held that the Committee on Applications for Review of Administrative Tribunal Judgments was an "organ of the UN" entitled to request an advisory opinion under art. 96 of the UN Charter, the court rejected the claim of a former UN Development Program official that the tribunal had not fairly adjudicated his claims.

The Pakistani government asked the court to postpone consideration of its request for interim protective measures to enjoin transfer of Pakistani prisoners of war to Bangladesh for war crimes trials, since negotiations on the subject were about to begin. The court complied by order of July 13, and the negotiations subsequently took place. (*See* INDIA.)

The court nominated Judge Gunnar Lagergren (Swed.) to act as arbitrator in a dispute over oil from nationalized fields in Libya. His award held that, since due compensation had not been paid to the previous owners, the nationalization was not in accordance with the rules of international law. Proposals for payment of a small compensation were subsequently made by Libya.

The Sea. As could be seen from the cases involving Iceland and France, maritime affairs were extremely sensitive. The UN conference on the law of the sea, which it was hoped would settle most of the issues, was to have been held in 1974 in Santiago, Chile, but the new military government of Chile indicated that that country could not be the host until 1975. The conference was then moved to Caracas, Venezuela, where it was scheduled to open June 30, 1974. The preliminary meeting was held at UN headquarters in New York early in December.

Meanwhile, the unilateral extension of territorial waters or fishery limits continued. A new development, based on Uruguay's extension in 1969, was the concept of the "patrimonial sea," which had so far taken the form of a 200-mi. territorial water belt with the inner 12 mi. being treated as true territorial waters and the coastal state exercising a monopoly of economic activity in the remaining 188 mi. This Uruguayan principle was approved by the Inter-American Juridical Committee in Rio de Janeiro, Braz., at the beginning of 1973 and by the African states in preparatory studies for the law of the sea conference. Territorial waters were extended by Guinea to 130 mi., by Tanzania to 50 mi., and by Ghana to 30 mi.; fishery limits were extended by Pakistan to 50 mi. and by Gabon to 150 mi. (*i.e.,* 50 mi. beyond the existing 100-mi. territorial sea), and future extensions were announced by Australia to 200 mi. and by Finland and Sweden to 12 mi. In September seven states agreed on national quotas outside the Faeroes' exclusive fishing zone in order to preserve stocks.

The North East Atlantic Fisheries Commission adopted a recommendation to ban high seas fishing for salmon from 1976 (a similar ban was already in force for the northwest Atlantic). In September a convention was signed setting up a Baltic Fisheries Commission. Also in September, an agreement on pollution was signed by the Baltic coastal states in Gdansk, Pol. The 15 countries subscribing to the Convention on Pollution from Rivers and Outfalls in North West Europe met in Paris, December 13–19, and agreed that formal ratification of the convention should take place in February 1974. An international sea lane safety convention signed in London in October 1972 would institute compulsory sea lanes by 1976; in July 1973 the first British prosecution was brought against a skipper who had ignored the existing lanes in the Dover Strait.

The question of the ocean floor continued to be discussed in the UN Sea Bed Committee, but definite action awaited the law of the sea conference. It was reported, however, that at least two heavily capitalized expeditions were being prepared to start dredging for manganese nodules on the floor of the Pacific, whether the issue was regulated or not. Lateral shelf boundaries were ratified between Finland and Sweden and, following the 1969 judgment of the International Court of Justice, between West Germany, The Netherlands, and Denmark.

Human Rights. The Soviet Union adhered to the UN International Covenant on Civil and Political Rights. Switzerland signed, and France announced ratification of, the European Convention on Human Rights. There was some concern, however, that the U.K. might not renew its acceptance of the right of individual petition in January 1974; there had been a dramatic increase in cases involving that country, mostly arising out of the Northern Ireland "troubles" and the immigration restrictions applied to U.K. citizens from overseas.

Commercial Law. In September the European Patent Convention was signed in Munich, W.Ger. It provided for a unified European system of patent application to run parallel with national systems, and would be supplemented in the spring of 1974 by an EEC patent convention creating a single Community patent. In Vienna in June three new conventions were signed on the international registration of trademarks, international classification of trademarks, and protection of printers' type faces. The Convention for the Protection of Producers of Phonograms against Unauthorized Duplication of their Phonograms came into force in April, and almost simultaneously the U.S. passed legislation giving copyright protection to recordings for the first time. The U.S.S.R. adhered to the Universal Copyright Convention and thus for the first time came into the world copyright system. Satisfaction at this step was quickly tempered, however,

UPI COMPIX

Daniel Ellsberg and his wife Patricia leave the Los Angeles Federal Building, May 11, 1973, following dismissal of the government's case against Ellsberg and Anthony Russo in connection with release of the Pentagon papers. U.S. District Court Judge William M. Byrne dismissed the case on the basis of "unprecedented" violation of the defendants' rights by the government.

by the realization that this would be used to hinder the publishing abroad of Soviet underground writings.

The Council of Europe passed a Consumer Protection Charter. (*See* CONSUMER AFFAIRS.) Decisions in the field of competition law included the long-awaited judgment of the EEC Court of Justice in the Continental Can case, in which the court upheld the European Commission's right to control mergers by a firm in a dominant position. This decision led directly to the introduction of an EEC draft regulation on merger control that appeared to subject even certain supply contracts to merger authorization. In the Boehringer case, the EEC Court of Justice held that there was no double jeopardy in an antitrust case in which the EEC Commission and a U.S. court had both convicted and fined the same defendant for the same participation in the same cartel, since the laws that had been infringed were different. The EEC Commission fined a U.S. firm, Commercial Solvents Corp., not for having a de facto world monopoly of an essential drug ingredient but for refusing to supply it to a rival Italian manufacturer who wanted to produce the drug itself. In the U.K. the Monopolies Commission concluded that the Swiss firm Hoffmann-La Roche had been overcharging for its popular tranquilizers Librium and Valium. The government ordered a reduction in price and repayment of money allegedly overpaid in the past, while the company resisted by applying a little-used parliamentary procedure. The U.K. action sparked a spate of investigations in other European countries, where even higher prices were charged for the two drugs, and by the EEC Commission.

Tort Law. New Zealand legislation providing strict liability, covered by compulsory social security-type insurance, for all personal injuries caused at work or by motor vehicles was extended to cover such injuries wherever and however caused. While this aspect of strict liability had been making but slow progress in Europe and the other developed countries, its relevance to newly introduced drugs was much in the news. The Oslo Court of Appeal dismissed an action for damages brought against the manufacturers of contraceptive pills in the case of a woman who had been taking them and who died of a thrombosis; the court ruled that there had been no negligence and that the principle of strict liability in such cases was not an established part of Norwegian law. Later in the year the first of a series of similar cases was brought in Sweden using the same arguments. In the U.K. the Thalidomide case, involving the birth of deformed children to women who took the drug during pregnancy, reached a climax after some ten years of desultory negotiation when the manufacturers made proposals for financial compensation that were generally acceptable. Instrumental in attaining this conclusion was a series of articles published and nearly published in *The Sunday Times.* (*See* PUBLISHING.)

(NEVILLE MARCH HUNNINGS)

See also Cities and Urban Affairs; Crime; Environment; Race Relations; United Nations.

ENCYCLOPÆDIA BRITANNICA FILMS. *Equality Under Law—California Fair Housing Cases* (1969); *Free Press vs. Fair Trial by Jury—The Sheppard Case* (1969); *The Schempp Case—Bible Reading in Public Schools* (1969); *United States Supreme Court: Guardian of the Constitution* (2nd ed., 1973).

Lebanon

A republic of the Middle East, Lebanon is bounded by Syria, Israel, and the Mediterranean Sea. Area: 3,950 sq.mi. (10,230 sq.km.). Pop. (1970 est.): 2,126,-325, excluding (1972) 191,000 Palestinian and other refugees. Cap. and largest city: Beirut (pop., 1970 est., 475,000). Language: Arabic. Religion: Christian majority with strong Muslim minority. President in 1973, Suleiman Franjieh; prime ministers, Saeb Salam until April 10, Amin Hafez from April 20 to June 14, and, after July 8, Takieddin as-Solh.

Lebanon did its best to remain out of the war that Egypt and Syria launched against Israel in October 1973. On October 9, Israeli Phantom jets destroyed an important radar station near al-Baruk, and on October 18 a number of undersea explosions cut the Beirut-Marseilles submarine telephone cable. The same day five Arab gunmen seized 40 hostages in Beirut's Bank of America and demanded $10 million toward the Arab war effort. Lebanese security forces broke the siege, killing two gunmen during a battle in which the guerrillas slew one of their captives. The Lebanese Army did not interfere with the estimated 400 Palestinian guerrillas operating in southern Lebanon. Attempts by the guerrillas to cross into Israel from southern Lebanon were repulsed, although rocket attacks on Israeli kibbutzim intensified as the war went on.

The country had already survived a serious threat to its fragile unity, provoked by an Israeli commando raid on Beirut on April 10 and the killing of three Palestinian leaders. Tension rose as the Palestinians accused the Lebanese authorities of offering no resistance to Israel. Prime Minister Salam resigned when his demand for the resignation of the army commander in chief was refused, and Amin Hafez was appointed to succeed him. Shortly after Hafez formed his government, violence erupted between the Army and Palestinians, causing scores of casualties. President Franjieh (*see* BIOGRAPHY) declared a state of emergency. On May 17 Hafez reached an agreement with the guerrilla leadership that allowed the emergency regulations to be entirely removed by May 23, but his leadership remained ineffective and he was replaced by a more traditional politician, Takieddin as-Solh, who formed a government on July 8.

The damage to Lebanon's prosperous economy was severe—especially for the tourist sector—and the government estimated total losses at £200 million. One serious consequence was Syria's closing of its borders with Lebanon on May 8 in protest against Lebanese actions against the guerrillas. They remained closed, despite mediation efforts, until August 17, causing serious disruption for Lebanon's exports.

Apart from the effects of the Palestinian-Lebanese crisis, there were other signs of social and economic discontent—among tobacco farmers in the south demanding increased prices and teachers in government schools demanding higher wages. Muslims and Christians also clashed over a proposal to introduce a Monday–Friday workweek, Muslim leaders demanding that Friday as well as Saturday should be a holiday and Christian businessmen claiming that a four-day workweek would be economically disastrous. However, the overall trend of the Lebanese economy was expansive. Building activity and bank deposits steadily increased, and the industrial sector assumed growing importance in the country's traditionally service-based economy. Probably the most significant development was Beirut's emergence as an international financial centre. During the year loans were arranged in Lebanese currency through Lebanese banks for Iran, Algeria, India, the French state-owned Renault concern, and the World Bank.

(PETER MANSFIELD)

LEBANON

Education. (1969–70) Primary, pupils 450,499; secondary, pupils 145,710; primary and secondary, teachers 32,178; vocational, pupils 2,198, teachers 508; teacher training, students 2,967, teachers 423; higher (including 4 universities), students 38,519, teaching staff 1,918.

Finance. Monetary unit: Lebanese pound, with a free rate (Sept. 17, 1973) of L£2.54 to U.S. $1 (L£6.12 = £1 sterling). Gold, SDRs, and foreign exchange, central bank: (June 1973) U.S. $894.6 million; (June 1972) U.S. $592.9 million. Budget (1973 est.) balanced at L£1,065 million. Gross domestic product: (1970) L£4,866 million; (1969) L£4,565 million. Money supply: (April 1973) L£2,345 million; (April 1972) L£2,059 million. Cost of living (Beirut; 1966 = 100): (May 1973) 116; (May 1972) 114.

Foreign Trade. (1971) Imports L£2,510 million; exports L£973 million; transit trade L£2,430 million. Import sources: U.S. 11%; West Germany 11%; France 10%; Italy 9%; U.K. 7%; Japan 5%; Iraq 5%. Export destinations: Saudi Arabia 15%; Kuwait 11%; Syria 10%; Iraq 9%; Libya 9%; Jordan 5%. Main exports: fruit and vegetables 13%; precious stones 6%; machinery 12%; textiles and clothing 10%; chemicals 10%; transport equipment 7%. Tourism (1971): visitors 1,603,300; gross receipts U.S. $175 million.

Transport and Communications. Roads (1971) 7,400 km. Motor vehicles in use (1971): passenger 146,300; commercial 15,600. Railways: (1971) 374 km.; traffic (1972) 5,010,000 passenger-km., freight 32,110,000 net ton-km. Air traffic (1972): 1,221,000,-000 passenger-km.; freight 271,824,000 net ton-km. Shipping (1972): vessels 100 gross tons and over 70; gross tonnage 116,571. Telephones (Dec. 1971) 300,-000. Radio receivers (Dec. 1971) 605,000. Television receivers (Dec. 1971) 300,000.

Agriculture. Production (in 000; metric tons; 1972; 1971 in parentheses): wheat *c.* 50 (*c.* 50); sugar, raw value *c.* 30 (*c.* 27); tomatoes (1971) *c.* 75, (1970) *c.* 75; grapes *c.* 95 (*c.* 90); olives *c.* 40 (*c.* 55); figs *c.* 13 (*c.* 13); bananas (1971) *c.* 30, (1970) *c.* 30; oranges (1971) *c.* 203, (1970) *c.* 205; lemons (1971) *c.* 65, (1970) *c.* 85; apples *c.* 130 (*c.* 150); tobacco *c.* 7.3 (*c.* 7.3). Livestock (in 000; 1970–71): cattle *c.* 84; goats *c.* 318; sheep *c.* 218; poultry *c.* 17,800.

Industry. Production (in 000; metric tons; 1972): cement 1,626; petroleum products (1971) 1,908; electricity (excluding most industrial production; kw-hr.) 1,547,000.

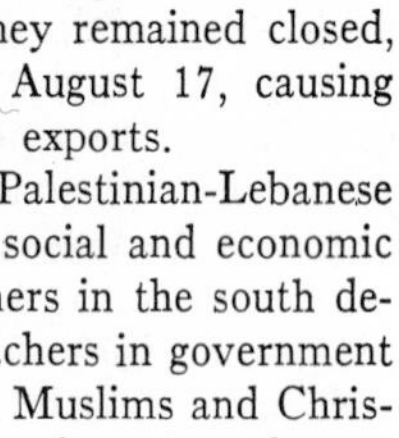

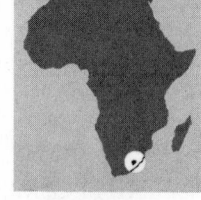

Lesotho

A constitutional monarchy of southern Africa and a member of the Commonwealth of Nations, Lesotho is completely surrounded by South Africa. Area: 11,720 sq.mi. (30,355 sq.km.). Pop. (1973 est.): 1,130,600. Cap. and largest city: Maseru (pop., 1972 est., 18,-

Law Enforcement:
see Crime

Lawn Bowls:
see Bowling and Lawn Bowls

Lawn Tennis:
see Tennis

Lead:
see Mining

LESOTHO
Education. (1968) Primary, pupils 179,386, teachers (1967) 3,065; secondary, pupils 4,141, teachers (1967) 152; vocational, pupils 511, teachers (1967) 44; teacher training, students 675, teachers (1967) 47; higher (University of Botswana, Lesotho, and Swaziland), students (Lesotho only; 1971) 218.
Finance and Trade. Monetary unit: South African rand, with (Sept. 17, 1973) an official rate of R 0.67 to U.S. $1 (free rate of R 1.62 = £1 sterling). Budget (1971–72 est.): revenue R 10.3 million; expenditure R 11.3 million. Foreign trade (1971): imports R 27,-997,000; exports R 2,197,000. Main exports: cattle 28%; mohair 15%; wool 15%; diamonds 11%; peas and beans 9%; wheat 6%. Most trade is with South Africa.
Agriculture. Production (in 000; metric tons; 1971; 1970 in parentheses): corn *c.* 80 (*c.* 40); wheat *c.* 70 (*c.* 60); sorghum *c.* 60 (30); wool *c.* 2.2 (2.2); meat 24 (24). Livestock (in 000; Sept. 1972): cattle *c.* 560; goats *c.* 1,000; sheep *c.* 2,200.

800). Language: English and Sesotho (official). Religion: Roman Catholic 38.7%, Lesotho Evangelical Church 24.3%, Anglican 10.4%, other Christian 8.4%, non-Christian 18.2%. Chief of state in 1973, Paramount Chief Moshoeshoe II; prime minister, Chief Leabua Jonathan.

In March 1973 Chief Jonathan announced a return to party politics and the setting up of an interim assembly to draft a new constitution. The assembly was to consist of nominated members, chosen from lists drawn up by the various parties and by the king on Chief Jonathan's advice, and also of the nation's 22 principal chiefs and others of distinguished national service. Although 20 seats were offered to the main opposition, the Basutoland Congress Party, its leader, Ntsu Mokhehle, refused cooperation unless he was offered equal partnership and the right to choose his own members; however, deputy leader Gerard Ramoreboli and the majority of the party took the oath of office. Their subsequent expulsion from the party by Mokhehle split the opposition and strengthened Chief Jonathan and his Basuto National Party. The assembly, opened by King Moshoeshoe II, underlined Chief Jonathan's diplomatic dilemma of remaining on friendly terms with South Africa, on which Lesotho depended, while supporting black Africa. The three-year-old state of emergency was lifted on July 25.

Lesotho remained closely dependent economically on South Africa, although new labour-intensive factories and tourism were being encouraged. In January the nation endured the worst drought in its history, and corn was imported from South Africa to stave off starvation. (MOLLY MORTIMER)

Liberia

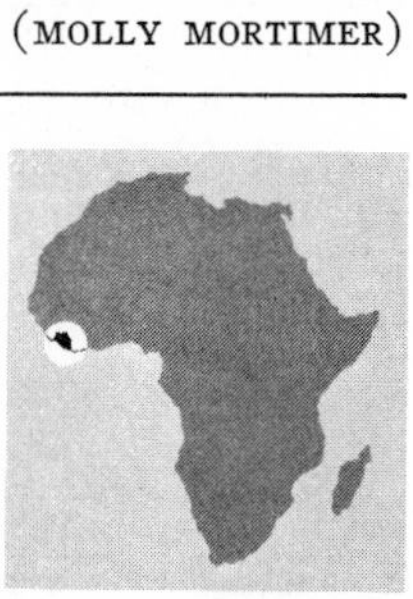

A republic on the west coast of Africa, Liberia is bordered by Sierra Leone, Guinea, and Ivory Coast. Area: 43,000 sq.mi. (111,400 sq.km.). Pop. (1973 est.): 1,677,000. Cap. and largest city: Monrovia (pop., 1970 est., 150,-000). Language: English (official) and tribal dialects. Religion: mainly animist. President in 1973, William R. Tolbert, Jr.

President Tolbert pressed ahead in 1973 with his plan to "liberianize" his country's economy. Because of the long-standing "open door" policy on foreign in-

LIBERIA
Education. (1970–71) Primary, pupils 120,245, teachers 3,384; secondary, pupils 15,493, teachers 918; vocational, pupils 887, teachers 66; teacher training, pupils 390, teachers 32; higher, students 1,109, teaching staff 164.
Finance. Monetary unit: Liberian dollar, at par with the U.S. dollar, with a free rate (Sept. 17, 1973) of L$2.41 to £1 sterling. Budget (1971 actual): revenue L$69.9 million; expenditure L$62.5 million.
Foreign Trade. (1972) Imports L$178.7 million; exports L$244.4 million. Import sources (1971): U.S. 32%; West Germany 10%; U.K. 9%; Japan 8%; The Netherlands 8%. Export destinations (1971): U.S. 22%; West Germany 18%; The Netherlands 15%; Italy 13%; Japan 11%; France 5%; Belgium-Luxembourg 5%. Main exports: iron ore 72%; rubber 15%.
Transport and Communications. Roads (1971) *c.* 6,500 km. (including *c.* 2,000 km. main state roads). Motor vehicles in use (1970): passenger 14,800; commercial (including buses) 8,400. Railways (1970) 493 km. Shipping (1972): merchant vessels 100 gross tons and over 2,234 (mostly owned by U.S. and other foreign interests); gross tonnage 44,443,652. Telephones (Jan. 1972) 3,000. Radio receivers (Dec. 1970) 155,000. Television receivers (Dec. 1970) 6,500.
Agriculture. Production (in 000; metric tons; 1971; 1970 in parentheses): rice 91 (138); cassava *c.* 370 (*c.* 370); rubber (exports) *c.* 74 (83); palm kernels (exports) *c.* 15 (*c.* 13); palm oil *c.* 41 (*c.* 41); cocoa (1971–72) 1.8, (1970–71) 1.8; coffee 4.5 (5.1). Livestock (in 000; August 1971): cattle *c.* 30; pigs *c.* 83; sheep *c.* 156; goats *c.* 140.
Industry. Production (in 000; 1971): iron ore (metal content; metric tons) 16,728; diamonds (exports; metric carats) 739; electricity (kw-hr.) 650,-000.

vestment, the nation's economy was controlled largely by overseas interests. The four large iron mines and several rubber plantations that formed the base of the economy were all foreign-owned, and foreigners held most of the top-paying jobs. In addition, expatriate Lebanese controlled retail trade.

As a result, Tolbert pushed for the replacement of foreigners with Liberians in responsible positions at foreign-owned concerns. But his freedom to maneuver seemed severely limited. For example, early in the year, Minister of Information and Tourism G. Henry Andrews implied in a letter that the Lebanese business community could be expelled from Liberia, just as Asian businessmen were expelled from Uganda in 1972. For this statement Andrews was immediately dismissed by President Tolbert. "There is strong feeling here among the young people, often shared by the old, against the Lebanese control of parts of the economy," said Stephen A. Tolbert, the Liberian minister of finance and younger brother of the president. "It is not an easy problem to tackle." He added that he did not want to see a vacuum created in the business community, which would occur if the Lebanese departed.

In another approach to liberianization, the Tolbert administration launched a campaign to raise $10 million from native Liberians for a series of self-help programs. By the spring of 1973, after nine months of fund-raising efforts, approximately $4.5 million in voluntary contributions had been collected. Shortly thereafter, there were ground-breaking ceremonies throughout the country for the construction of farm-to-market roads, schools, hospitals, and clinics.

President Tolbert continued his campaign to encourage greater efficiency in government. "I have made a public pronouncement," he declared, "that any minister of government who was not at his desk on the occasion of my morning visits to his ministry, or would not fully justify his absence, would be relieved of his portfolio." Tolbert demonstrated that he meant what he said when he dismissed George Flamma Sherman, his education minister, in April. Sherman was absent when Tolbert paid a surprise visit to the education ministry at 8 A.M. (RICHARD L. WORSNOP)

Libraries

In 1973, the year after International Book Year, the production and use of books was well maintained, although about 30% of the world's population still produced some 70% of the world's publications. There was, however, a growing tendency to supply information on audiovisual media, such as slides synchronized with lectures on magnetic tape (tape-slide sets), computer-output microfilm (COM), and ultrafiche.

There was a growing demand for quicker and more complete access to information, making the international standardization of library techniques ever more urgent. For example, in both East and West Germany efforts were made to change from the old "Prussian Instructions" for cataloging to new rules based on the International Federation of Library Associations (IFLA)-UNESCO Cataloguing Conference of 1961; new rules were published in East Germany.

At the annual General Council of the IFLA, held at Grenoble, France, in August, the main theme was universal bibliographic control (UBC). This idea was the logical outcome of the "shared cataloging" promoted in recent years by the U.S. Library of Congress, by which each nation was to catalog its own book production in its national bibliography for the benefit of all nations. UBC aimed at perfecting such a system and persuading every national bibliography to introduce it. To ensure uniformity, IFLA's cataloging committee developed the "international standard bibliographic description" (ISBD).. Simultaneously, the national bibliographies of many countries were putting their affairs into better order; in France by the amalgamation in 1972 of *Biblio* and the *Bibliographie de la France,* and in the U.S.S.R. by further development of the "book chambers" (*Knizhnye palaty*) of each union republic as centres for national bibliographies.

A parallel tendency was the increase in financial support given to information and documentation systems by governments in many countries. The West German government provided DM. 530 million for its "promotion program for information and documentation" during 1973–76. In the U.K. the Office for Scientific and Technical Information (OSTI) received £902,000 for payments and research grants in 1973–74, £80,000 of which was earmarked for an experimental national information network. In the international field UNESCO pursued its International Information System on Research in Documentation (ISORID).

Meanwhile, access to information was accelerated by the introduction and spread of mechanical devices. In the U.K. alone there were 138 libraries using computerized systems for at least part of their work, while in Bochum, W.Ger., a new building for the almost entirely automated University Library was completed. At the University of Grenoble, France, the library produced its catalogs by computer. On-line computer systems were introduced. An example was Retrospec, based on the "inspec" system of the Institution of Electrical Engineers, London, which supplied on-line information on computer and control engineering to all users with access to a "teletype" compatible data terminal; this gave retrospective information for three years. Another new device was the Plessey "library pen" data-capture system, a light-sensitive device that read and recorded numbers and codes on magnetic tape for compiling lists or statistics. Some 400 were ordered for Swedish libraries. The device was already popular in the U.S. and the U.K.

There was a growing tendency to form national networks for libraries and information, such as DANDOK in Denmark, TINFO in Finland, NORINDOK in Norway, and SINFDOK in Sweden, with NORDOK to coordinate information services for all Scandinavia. In West Germany Bibliotheksplan '73 was the blueprint for a national library network, while in Italy plans were being developed for decentralized regional networks. An international colloquium on the planning of national library buildings, sponsored by IFLA, UNESCO, and the Associazione Italiana Biblioteche, was held in Rome in September to coincide with the opening of the new building of the Biblioteca Nazionale Centrale. Plans and photos of 23 recent national libraries and seven extensions were exhibited. Notable were the newly completed National Library of Serbia at Belgrade, Yugos.; the almost completed National Science Library in Ottawa, Ont.; the National Library of Iceland, Reykjavik; a planned national library for Nigeria at Lagos; the third block of the storage library of Versailles, France; and the storage library under construction at Khimki, outside Moscow, U.S.S.R., for the Lenin Library.

Some advances in the public library field were the opening of the central library in Hamburg, W.Ger.; the achievement of direct lending in the Pas-de-Calais, France, from a model central lending library with mobile libraries; the opening of a new central library at Caen, France; and the opening of the vast new building for the Central Public Library in Birmingham, Eng. A tendency appeared to amalgamate popular with scholarly reference libraries, exemplified by the libraries at Arnhem, Neth., and at Nürnberg and Lübeck, W.Ger. In Munich, W.Ger., important progress was made in the library service to factories and offices, based on and organized by the city library and serving over 7,000 employees in factories and other institutions.

The U.S.S.R. signed the Universal Copyright Convention in May, thus ending a long period of literary piracy. West Germany followed the example of the Scandinavians by passing an amendment to its copyright law establishing, from Jan. 1, 1973, the legal right of authors to demand a financial contribution from libraries for lending their works. Discussions continued throughout the year on the best method of calculating, collecting, and distributing the libraries' contribution to authors. (ANTHONY THOMPSON)

ENCYCLOPÆDIA BRITANNICA FILMS. *Library of Congress* (1969).

Libya

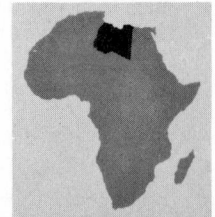

A socialist republic on the north coast of Africa, Libya is bounded by Egypt, Sudan, Tunisia, Algeria, Niger, and Chad. Area: 675,000 sq.mi. (1,749,000 sq.km.). Pop. (1972 est.): 2,082,000. Cap. and largest city: Tripoli (pop., 1970 est., 264,000). Language: Arabic. Religion: predominantly Muslim. Leader of the Revolutionary Command Council in 1973, Col. Muammar al-

Qaddafi; prime minister, Maj. Abdul Salam Jalloud.

The early part of 1973 was overshadowed by the tragic destruction on February 21 of a Libyan airliner over the Sinai desert. Israeli fighters shot down the Boeing 727, killing 108 passengers and crew after it had inadvertently flown into a sensitive military area and refused to land after warning shots. The action hardened Libyan opinion against Israel and unexpectedly brought tension to the surface vis-à-vis the Egyptian community in Benghazi, since many Libyans felt that retaliatory action should have been taken by Egypt.

Qaddafi's (*see* BIOGRAPHY) commitment to union with Egypt remained strong, although the testing experiences of the year did bring him to criticize his ally. Unofficial estimates suggested that more than 250,000 Egyptians were living in Libya in 1973, a significant proportion of the Libyan population. Qaddafi ignored the uneasiness felt by educated Libyans concerning Egyptian participation in the country's affairs and appealed to the masses through his "cultural revolution," proclaimed in mid-April, to support the policy of full economic and political union with Egypt. Opposition to the union was also strong in Cairo, and September 1, the supposed date of union, passed with no union proclaimed. Nor did Qaddafi's speeches in Egypt during the summer bring any concessions from Egyptian Pres. Anwar as-Sadat (*see* BIOGRAPHY). On occasion Qaddafi's words provoked skepticism concerning his Islamic policies, especially where these might affect women's rights in the more liberal, urbane Egypt.

LIBYA

Education. (1970–71) Primary, pupils 350,225, teachers 12,804; secondary, pupils 8,441, teachers 902; vocational, pupils 3,088, teachers 331; teacher training, students 5,377, teachers 463; higher (1969–70), students 3,663, teaching staff *c.* 320.

Finance. Monetary unit: Libyan dinar, with (Sept. 17, 1973) a par value of 0.296 dinar to U.S. $1 (free rate of 0.714 dinar = £1 sterling). Gold and foreign exchange, central bank: (June 1973) U.S. $2,709,900,000; (June 1972) U.S. $3,141,900,000. Budget (1971 actual): revenue 730 million dinars (including petroleum revenue of 629 million dinars); expenditure 490 million dinars (including development expenditure of 166 million dinars). Gross national product: (1971) 1,298,000,000 dinars; (1970) 1,113,000,000 dinars. Money supply: (March 1973) 442.6 million dinars; (March 1972) 353.4 million dinars. Cost of living (Tripoli; 1964 = 100): (March 1973) 147; (March 1972) 140.

Foreign Trade. (1972) Imports 343.2 million dinars; exports 966,310,000 dinars. Import sources: Italy 26%; West Germany 9%; France 8%; U.K. 8%; U.S. 6%; Japan 5%. Export destinations: West Germany 26%; Italy 21%; U.K. 14%; France 10%; U.S. 7%; Trinidad and Tobago 5%. Main export crude oil 99%.

Transport and Communications. Roads (with improved surface; 1970) *c.* 5,200 km. (including 1,822 km. coast road). Motor vehicles in use (1970): passenger 100,100; commercial (including buses) 45,400. Air traffic (1971): 269 million passenger-km.; freight 3,429,000 net ton-km. Ships entered (1970) vessels totaling 4,381,000 net registered tons; goods loaded (1971) 127,188,000 metric tons, unloaded 3,094,000 metric tons. Telephones (Dec. 1971) 42,000. Radio licenses (Dec. 1971) 90,000. Television licenses (Dec. 1971) 2,000.

Agriculture. Production (in 000; metric tons; 1972; 1971 in parentheses): barley 150 (32); wheat (1971) 18, (1970) 21; potatoes (1971) 23, (1970) 10; tomatoes 143 (131); olives 100 (5); dates (1971) 66, (1970) 49. Livestock (in 000; 1970–71): goats 1,141; sheep 2,284; cattle 109; camels *c.* 120; asses *c.* 96.

Industry. Production (in 000; metric tons): salt (1970) 11; crude oil (1972) 106,267; electricity (Tripolitania; excluding most industrial production; kw-hr.; 1971) 508,000.

C. CHAUVEL—SYGMA

A hijacked Japan Air Lines plane bursts into flames on the Benghazi, Libya, airfield minutes after the release of 137 persons, held hostage for three and a half days by terrorists. The jumbo jet was seized over The Netherlands at the start of a flight to Tokyo.

Meanwhile, the balance of financial influence in the Middle East shifted very much in favour of Saudi Arabia, which became at once the most respected of U.S. oil suppliers and the chief supporter of Egypt, allowing the latter to deal independently of Libya. Qaddafi joined with other Arab oil producers in reducing petroleum output and cutting supplies to the U.S. during the Arab-Israeli war of October. He also threatened to deprive Europe of oil in order to exert pressure on the U.S. Libya's position in the October conflict was clear. Qaddafi was not in favour of its timing or of the limited aims of those who conducted it, preferring Israel's annihilation. He provided financial support and sent a number of Mirage aircraft, thereby breaking his contract with France and embarrassing the French government. Nevertheless, the strains in the Libya-Egypt relationship were pointed up in early December when Qaddafi closed the Libyan embassy in Cairo and called the staff home for "consultation." Later in the month, in an interview with a Lebanese magazine, he called for a popular revolt in Egypt to prevent any peace settlement with Israel.

At home, Libya continued to press the oil companies for control of its petroleum industry. Characteristically, Libya pursued a policy outside the agreements reached by the Persian Gulf producers (and outside its own agreements), and took a new direction by pressing U.S. oil interests in Libya for the first time. In June the Libyan government nationalized Nelson Bunker Hunt's 50% interest in the Sarir field (the other half, operated by British Petroleum Co., was nationalized in 1971). By August, Occidental's Armand Hammer (*see* BIOGRAPHY) had yielded to a 51% take-over, and on September 1, Libya announced the 51% nationalization of all the remaining oil companies operating in the country. In mid-September the Organization of Petroleum Exporting Countries (OPEC) indicated that there would be a collective response to any Western boycott of Libyan "nationalized" oil. In this atmosphere it came as a surprise in late October that Libya should indicate a preparedness to offer compensation to British Petroleum. The amount suggested was, however, less than 15% of the $750 million valuation by BP. The more than threefold rise in oil revenues since 1969 made it possible for Libya to build huge currency reserves abroad, and these gave the nation important leverage over the continued stability of the world monetary situation. (J. A. ALLAN)

Liechtenstein

A constitutional monarchy between Switzerland and Austria, Liechtenstein is united with Switzerland by a customs and monetary union. Area: 62 sq.mi. (160 sq.km.). Pop. (1972 est.): 22,300. Cap. and largest city: Vaduz (pop., 1972 est., 4,200). Language: German. Religion (1970): Roman Catholic 90.1%. Sovereign prince, Francis Joseph II; chief of government in 1973, Alfred Hilbe.

The free trade association with the EEC, which had been unanimously approved by the Landtag (parliament) on Nov. 29, 1972, became effective Jan. 1, 1973. Liechtenstein, although not originally a member of the European Free Trade Association (EFTA), adhered to that agreement as a result of its 50-year customs agreement with Switzerland.

On February 11 the all-male electorate of Liechtenstein again rejected a constitutional amendment to grant women the vote. The referendum had been supported by all major political parties and by the government. Nevertheless, the margin of defeat was greater than in 1971. Over 86% of the eligible voters went to the polls and, of the 3,801 valid votes, 2,126 were against and 1,675 for women's suffrage. Liechtenstein, as a result, remained the only European state with an all-male electorate.

Liechtenstein intermediaries were implicated in the sale, in April, of three 12-year-old jets by a West German airline to Rhodesia, despite UN sanctions.

(ROBERT D. HODGSON)

LIECHTENSTEIN

Education. (1970–71) Primary, pupils 2,412, teachers 89; secondary, pupils 664, teachers 48; vocational, pupils 859, teachers 29.

Finance and Trade. Monetary unit: Swiss franc, with (Sept. 17, 1973) a free rate of SFr. 3 to U.S. $1 (SFr. 7.24 = £1 sterling). Budget (1972 est.): revenue SFr. 67,330,000; expenditure SFr. 67,590,000. Exports (1971) SFr. 372 million. Export destinations (1970): Switzerland 34%; EEC 33%. Main exports: metal manufactures, furniture, pottery. Tourism (1971): visitors 74,000; gross receipts *c.* SFr. 18 million.

Life Sciences

To the general biologist the most interesting developments of 1973 were those concerned with the control of biological processes, ranging from large-scale control of the environment to small-scale control of cellular activities. At the cellular level control could be either intra- or extracellular. The former was based on the complex interactions of the genes and other cellular components; concerning these, notable contributions were made during the year to the "punctuation" of the genetic code and to the role of the protein coat surrounding the chromosomes. Typical of the extracellular control mechanisms were the action of auxin on the outside of plant cell membranes resulting in release of RNA polymerase from the inside of the membrane, thus stimulating cell activity, or, in growing animal cells, the action of a hormone at a specific receptor site on the outer surface leading to release of cyclic AMP from the inner surface which stopped cell division. The type of communication between the outer and inner surfaces of the membrane that these processes required was studied especially in relation to the familiar sodium pump by which exchange of sodium and potassium between the cell and its environment takes place. Such studies resulted in a revision of the current oversimplified model of the cell membrane.

Cell-membrane based control mechanisms analogous to these were studied with respect to a very wide range of problems including pollination in plants, the transformation of normal into cancerous cells and vice versa, immunology, virology, pharmacology, cell growth and differentiation, whether in slime fungi or in vertebrate embryos, and in transmission across nerve synapses including those involved in memory and other brain functions. Control of hormone production by specific releasing factors from the pituitary and control of these in turn by the brain continued to be the subject of considerable research. New possibilities for controlling crop productivity were raised by the work of Zelitch and others on the relations between photorespiration and the fixation of atmospheric CO_2 and by various approaches toward increasing nitrogen fixation by the introduction of nitrogen-fixing bacteria, or their genes, into root cells of nonleguminous plants.

Control of humanity and its environment is essential for civilization and increasingly so as the pace of social change quickens. Investigations such as those listed above were therefore among the most important scientific activities taking place. Unfortunately the possibilities of evil through wrongly directed controls were often more obvious than those for good. Emotional (sometimes fully justified) reports about such matters as medical abuse of drugs, brainwashing, brain surgery, test-tube babies, vivisection, factory farming, etc., coming at a time of widespread disillusionment with scientific technology in general, resulted in serious public reaction against such research. Other factors contributed to this. Control of the environment involved economic and political issues at all levels from local to international, and ill-judged intervention by nonscientific self-styled "ecologists" tended to bring the whole subject into disrepute. The intervention of distinguished nonbiological scientists into biological matters sometimes added to public confusion. Oversimplified deductions from intelligence-measuring data were fallaciously applied to problems of race, class, and education. Important progress in studies of the biochemical precursors of life was assumed to give authority to dogmatic pronouncements about the evolution of living organisms and even of intelligence on other worlds in total disregard of the well-established principles of biological evolution, thus blurring the distinction between science and fantasy.

The year's significance in the history of science could be judged in part by new contributions to knowledge and in part by the changing ideas and public attitudes that determined the conditions for future progress, especially insofar as these affected the rising generation of potential scientists. Judged by the former of these criteria, 1973 was a good year, but judged by the second there were grounds for anxiety. More hopeful, however, were improvements in the teaching of the life sciences in several countries and improvements not only in the numbers, popularity, and technical quality of film and television productions dealing with living plants and animals but also in the quality of their scientific content.

(HAROLD SANDON)

Life Insurance: *see* Insurance

BOTANY

In the past few years it had become possible to strip plant cells of their surrounding wall and to maintain the resulting protoplasts in viable states. Such protoplasts might be made to regenerate entire plants or be fused together to form hybrid cells. A combination of these techniques led in 1973 to the fusion of protoplasts from different species of tobacco, followed by the generation from the hybrid cells of entire, fertile hybrid tobacco plants. These parasexually-produced plants appeared to be identical to the hybrids formed by normal sexual reproduction. Such techniques held considerable potential not only for plant breeding but also for understanding mechanisms involved in plant development.

Another spectacular area of research was opened by the discovery that foreign genes can be incorporated into plant cells in such a way that the genetic information is expressed and that the plant cells can use the gene products for growth and reproduction. Cultured cells of sycamore, tomato, or *Arabidopsis* are unable to utilize either lactose or galactose as energy sources and, therefore, cannot grow if one of these is the sole sugar source. Certain strains of bacteria, however, contain genes that allow them to utilize lactose or galactose. When viruses that had incorporated either of these specific bacterial genes into their DNA were added to the plant cells, the cells acquired the capacity to utilize the corresponding sugars by producing the necessary enzymes coded for by the bacterial genes. This capacity was passed on to the descendants of these cells, indicating that the "transformation" or "transgenosis" might be permanent. The possibility that specific pieces of genetic information could be incorporated into cells from which whole plants could be regenerated now had to be seriously considered.

The composition, structure, and mode of extension of plant cell walls were related aspects of plant structure and development that had never been satisfactorily explained. The recent use of advanced techniques of enzyme degradation and biochemical analysis had led to an extensive chemical characterization of primary cell walls. It was now clear that primary walls are composed of no more than six or seven major structural components, including cellulose. Based on the chemical composition and the nature of the association between the different components, a model of cell wall structure was proposed. One interesting feature of this model was that xyloglucan, one of the wall components, is hydrogen-bonded to cellulose; it was suggested that disruption of these hydrogen bonds would allow a molecular "creeping" to occur that would result in cell-wall extension. This hypothesis was attractive in view of the revival of interest in the idea that the auxin effect on cell wall extension results from a drop in the pH of the cell wall. Any change in pH might be expected to alter the hydrogen-bonding properties of the wall components. Recent experiments indicated that auxins can interact with the plasma-membrane of the cell and may affect ion transport across the membrane. In this way the pH outside the membrane, *i.e.,* at the cell wall, could be influenced.

The plasma-membrane might be the primary site of auxin action not only for the "loosening" of the cell wall but also for its effect on RNA and protein synthesis. A recent set of experiments showed that treatment of plasma-membranes with auxins resulted in the release of a factor that increases the activity of RNA polymerase; in this way transcriptional patterns in the cell could be affected. It should be stressed that an assumption that all auxin effects can be explained on the basis of interactions at the surface membrane was still premature.

Recent geologic ideas on continental drift stimulated interest in the centre of origin of the flowering plants. The Smith-Takhtajan hypothesis, that the angiosperms originated in the region including Southeast Asia and Australasia, was challenged on the ground that in the early Cretaceous, at the time when the angiosperms are thought to have arisen, Southeast Asia and Australasia were much farther apart than they are today. If, indeed, these two continental plates became juxtaposed only after the angiosperms had evolved, the region that today includes both cannot have been the centre of origin. The large number of primitive families found in this region would then be explained on the basis of two separately diverging floras being brought together at the point recognized as Wallace's line. It was hoped that more accurate dating of continental movements and of the time of origin of the angiosperms would resolve this conflict; it was clear, however, that phytogeographers had to recognize the role of continental drift in determining plant distributions. (PETER L. WEBSTER)

See also Gardening.

MARINE BIOLOGY

In 1973 the International Council for the Exploration of the Sea completed 71 years of existence. Founded when personnel and facilities for marine research were scanty, the council had succeeded in stimulating a wide range of marine biological activities and had pioneered conservation of particular fish and whale stocks. Antarctic baleen whales had been exploited for 50 years, and conservation measures had been in operation for about half that time. Nevertheless, in 1964 catches of right whales were three times the sustainable yield and the blue and humpbacked whales were approaching commercial extinction. With new measures in 1965, some improvement was achieved with

UPI COMPIX

A worker near Miami, Fla., loads coconut palm trees on a truck to be hauled away. Scientists blamed a microorganism, spread by an unknown agent, for the lethal "yellowing disease" that threatened nearly a million coconut palms in the state.

these and with sei whales, but fin whale stocks remained seriously depleted.

Ongoing effects of the building of the Suez Canal indicated that 30 species of Red Sea fish, comprising 21% of the commercial catches, were in the eastern Mediterranean, and that species were still arriving. Reduced freshwater discharge in the Nile Delta owing to the completion of the Aswan High Dam permitted a westward extension of immigrant Red Sea species to Libya and Tunisia. Long-term studies of post-larval fish in the English Channel indicated that, after the decline in the 1930s–50s, recovery began in 1965 and was continuing. This probably related to changed hydrographic conditions bringing more nutrient-rich water from the Atlantic into the English Channel and southern North Sea, following declining mean sea temperatures around Britain since 1960.

In the fish-rearing field, plaice sperm were kept viable when stored for 315 days at −196° C, thus opening up more possibilities for selective breeding. Laboratory plaice fed with diethylstilbestrol showed increased weight gain, although some work suggested that this substance might be carcinogenic. Methods were invented for rearing turbot larvae, while newly metamorphosed turbot were discovered to be easy to manage, suffering no damage or ill effects from handling and crowding. Progress was also made in rearing larval scallops (*Pecten maximus*) and, in Portugal, larval scampi (*Nephrops norvegicus*) were reared to metamorphosis for the first time. A ten-year study of a flat-fish nursery ground showed that the sand meiofauna (that which would pass through a 0.5-mm. sieve) did not contribute energy to the higher elements of the food chain and was separate from the main energy path from phytoplankton through zooplankton to fish.

The surface movement of upwelling cold water had been hard to detect from ships, but new techniques involving colour-enhanced infrared photography from satellites were being applied. Areas such as that off West Africa were usually turbid and showed the shallowest vertical migrations by the organisms of the so-called sonic scattering layers. Vertical migration was greatest in areas of greatest ocean transparency, such as the Sargasso Sea, emphasizing the role of light in contributing to these migrations. Newly hatched phyllosoma larvae of the crayfish *Palinurus* had a very low threshold of light sensitivity, which presumably enabled the larvae to reach the surface from great depths at night. Such light sensitivity was a possible explanation of midnight sinking of larvae by negative phototaxis on moonlit nights. Light also appeared to control position maintenance in Chesapeake Bay estuaries by the cladoceran *Podon.* They appeared at the surface by day and in deeper water at night, spending approximately equal periods alternately in seaward-flowing surface water and inward-flowing bottom water.

Sea anemones, normally considered to show a very limited behavioural repertoire, were shown to exhibit intraspecific aggression. Aggregations of the North American species *Anthopleura elegantissima* were normally composed of asexually reproducing individuals of a single clone. Groups of anemones of mixed clonal origins were found to reaggregate into isolated clonal groups and contacts between genetically different individuals initiated elaborate aggressive behaviour often resulting in mutual damage. In the elucidation of some outstanding problems of substrate recognition at settlement by the motile larvae of the sessile polychaete *Spirorbis spirorbis,* scanning electron microscope studies showed that the larvae produced mucous attachment threads. The extent of thread adhesion was thought to be a possible determinant of substrate attractiveness, and the abundance of threads a stimulus to gregarious behaviour. Gregariousness and territoriality in *Spirorbis* might therefore be more reliant on mechanical stimuli associated with thread adhesion than on chemical recognition of surfaces, important in barnacles. In the high-latitude barnacle *Balanus balanoides,* which spreads southward in Britain in cold years, resistance to frost at low tide was related to a winter increase of glycerol in the body tissues.

Amphioxus moves forward and backward equally effectively. This was explained by a new interpretation of the function of the notochord, previously thought to be a passive, elastic support for body muscles. It probably functions as a muscular hydrostatic skeleton capable of changes in stiffness by altering its internal fluid pressure at the anterior or posterior ends, depending on whether the head or tail is leading. Hydrodynamic factors were shown to present important advantages for obligate schooling fish, since endurance increased 2–6 times in schools compared with isolated individuals. Swimming efficiency was enhanced when swimming in diamond-shaped patterns, any one fish swimming in the forward component of the vortices of the two fish ahead of it. Fish avoided swimming directly behind one another, where the backward components of the vortices were created. Symbiotic associations were reported for British wrasses, the corkwing being observed to suck the parasitic isopod *Gnathia* from mackerel, plaice, and pink bream. Pink bream "invited" cleaning attentions by adopting a stationary, head-down posture.

A new species of a remarkable deepwater isopod (*Anuropus*) was collected in an unusual way from the gut of fish among the regurgitated food of the waved albatross on its only known breeding place in Galápagos. Atlantic eels had previously been taken at sea as they migrated to oceanic spawning grounds, but in 1973, for the first time, the New Zealand eel *Anguilla diefenbachii* was taken at sea. Discovery of more complete specimens of Pogonophora, whose setae were studied electron microscopically and histochemically, now related them to a protostomatous, annelid-like ancestor rather than to deuterostomatous echinoderm-chordate forms to which they had previously been assigned. (ERNEST NAYLOR)

MOLECULAR BIOLOGY

Biochemistry. To really know about the chemistry of life, the biochemist needed to study the properties of enzymes and to try to understand their great specificity, such that each generally enhances the rate of only a single type of reaction. Another impetus for studying single enzymes was the fact that many diseases can be traced to malfunctions of specific enzymes. Until recently the isolation of an enzyme was based upon trial-and-error methods, using procedures that were time-consuming, difficult, and yielded only small amounts of the enzyme. Biochemists had long dreamed of fractionating enzymes not on the basis of such incidental characteristics as size, charge, or solubility but on the basis of the distinguishing ability of each particular enzyme to bind a particular substrate. If that substrate could be tightly coupled to an insoluble support and if a mixture of enzymes were then exposed to that specially prepared support, only the enzyme that binds to the coupled substrate would stick. With the other enzymes washed away, the desired enzyme could be liberated from the support by treatment with a solution of its substrate or by any change in conditions that temporarily suspended its affinity for the substrate. Because such manipulations could be performed with apparatus already developed for chromatography and because the separations depend upon the specific affinity between enzyme and substrate, this method was called affinity chromatography.

A few fortunate cases that illustrated the power of affinity chromatography spurred the search for generally applicable methods. Such methods now included the coupling of specific substrates, inhibitors, or coenzymes to a variety of insoluble supports including cellulose, polystyrene, polysaccharide gels, and even glass beads. The methods usually incorporated the attachment of the substrate to the support by way of a long flexible arm, to overcome steric problems and provide the reach needed to allow close approach of the substrate and an active site that might be located in a crevice or pocket on the surface of the enzyme. Many enzymes had been purified easily and in good yield, and affinity chromatography methods were being extended to the purification of hormones and antibodies as well. The person most closely responsible for the flowering of the use of affinity chromatography was Pedro Cuatrecasas, formerly at the U.S. National Institutes of Health, Bethesda, Md., later at Johns Hopkins University.

It was also becoming increasingly clear that working with dilute solutions of pure enzymes served to mask a complexity of behaviour that was dependent upon the association of one protein with another. Such associations, which were now seen to markedly modify the properties of enzymes, were certainly favoured by the conditions that pertain inside cells. Protein-protein interactions had already been studied, to some degree, as the basis of the binding of antigen to antibody or of trypsin inhibitor to trypsin, but studies involving enzymes were relatively new.

An example illustrating the trend concerned the genome of the virus T_4, which, when it gets into the bacterium *Escherichia coli,* modifies the biochemical machinery of the host cell. The result of this subversion is that the cell then makes new virus particles rather than new bacteria. One of the many changes that accompany such a virus infection is a modification of an enzyme whose function is the activation of the amino acid valine so that it may subsequently be incorporated into proteins. This enzyme, called valyl-t RNA synthetase, is changed in several respects as a consequence of the viral infection. These changes, which include an increase in stability, in electrophoretic mobility, and in molecular weight and a change in catalytic specificity, were studied by Frederick C. Neidhardt and his co-workers (University of Michigan). They found that the modification of this enzyme was caused by its association with another protein that was synthesized only after infection by the virus. This viral protein, which associates with the host enzyme and, thus, changes its properties, was called the tau factor. The tau factor was purified and found to be a small protein with a molecular weight of 10,000. Similar associations between proteins, with attendant changes in their catalytic and physical properties, were observed to occur on numerous occasions in normal cells. (IRWIN FRIDOVICH)

UPI COMPIX

Ellis L. Yochelson of the U.S. Geological Survey studies one of the largest fossil snails ever collected. About 425 million years old, this seven-inch member of the Maclurite family of snails was found near Lander, Wyo., where it once lived in a shallow sea.

Biophysics. The application of new dyes and staining techniques and of standard biophysical techniques to whole chromosomes led to new molecular information about chromosomes, revolutionized mammalian cytogenetics, and led to significant technical breakthroughs in medical genetics. The male Y chromosome could be made to fluoresce brightly in human cells when stained with quinacrine mustard or quinacrine dihydrochloride (a common antimalarial drug). As shown by Pearson, Voss, and Babrow (Oxford), this fluorescence, visible as a small bright dot even in the nuclei of cells in which the chromosomes are not condensed, made possible the sexing of cells at any time during their cell cycle and provided an improved method for determining the genetic sex of a fetus during pregnancy.

Quinacrine staining techniques had even greater significance for human cytogenetics, because all chromosomes could be stained specifically and each chromosome identified by its particular fluorescent-banding pattern. These possibilities were greatly expanded by recent developments in Giemsa dye staining techniques for chromosomes, which no longer required the use of fluorescent microscopy. In cytogenetic studies of laboratory mammals the use of the quinacrine fluorescent technique by D. A. and O. J. Miller and their associates (Roche Institute of Molecular Biology) made possible the first complete identification of each of the 20 chromosome pairs of mice. By the use of fluorescent banding, groups of linked genes were identified as bands on the same chromosome. In addition, the accidental translocation of groups of bands from a chromosome in one strain of mice to a different chromosome in a second strain was observed.

Banding techniques were already being used to examine the kinds of chromosomal changes appearing in human malignancy. J. D. Rowley (University of Chicago) identified a chromosomal abnormality in chronic myelogenous leukemia, by both quinacrine fluorescence and Giemsa staining. The disease is associated with a shortened chromosome *22*, and Rowley observed additional fluorescing material, with banding that corresponded to the region normally present in chromosome *22*, at one end of chromosome 9. A fuller understanding of this and other specific chromosomal changes might prove vital to the solution of many cancer problems.

From a comparison of the different staining patterns with different dyes, D. E. Comings and his colleagues (City of Hope National Medical Center, California) concluded that the dyes do not differentially stain different DNA regions, but rather reflect an uneven distribution along the chromosome of nonhistone proteins. By using another DNA dye, feulgen, they showed that dye-binding is not proportional to the DNA packing concentration along the chromosome.

By measuring buoyant densities and using autoradiographic techniques, C. J. Bostock, D. M. Prescott, and F. T. Hatch at the University of Colorado and the Lawrence Livermore Laboratory, California, studied density changes in DNA molecules from synchronized kangaroo rat cells. They found that euchromatic DNA regions had high buoyant densities, which was characteristic of DNA rich in the bases guanine and cytosine. Heterochromatic DNA regions had low buoyant densities and, therefore, were rich in adenine and thymine. Furthermore, this heterochromatic DNA occupied regions around the centromeres. Centromeric DNA is known to contain highly repetitive, "satellite" DNA sequences that differ in their chromosomal proteins from less repeated sequences at other locations. These results provided the first evidence that proteins in chromosomes may be segregated according to chromosomal function. The true function of heterochromatic DNA remained unknown; however, according to Hatch and J. A. Mazrimus of the Lawrence Livermore Laboratory, it seemed to be important for supragenic functions of the chromosome, such as recombination and translocation.

Chromosome banding techniques were also coupled with other recently developed, powerful techniques for in vitro cultivation and fusion of somatic cells, leading to spectacular progress in studies of human chromosomes. Hybrid cells could be formed when two quite different cell lines were mixed together and cocultured. Thus it is possible, for example, to fuse a single human cell to a single mouse cell. Membrane fusion, which usually occurred only rarely, was enhanced by treatment of the cells with inactivated Sendai virus or with lysolecithin, and fusion of the two parental cells gave rise to a binucleate heterokaryon. After the first mitosis many of the heterokaryons formed mononucleate daughter cells containing chromosomes from both parents, which could be subcultivated for further analysis.

For physicochemical experiments, it was necessary to select hybrids from mixed populations, and J. Littlefield (Harvard Medical School) devised a method of enzyme complementation for this purpose. Mutant cell lines, each deficient in a different enzyme, were selected. These mutants could survive individually only if the missing enzyme were supplied exogenously. However, hybrids of the two lines that had both deficiencies complemented by enzymes produced from normal chromosomes supplied by the other parent survived. Confirmation that these cells were indeed hybrids was obtained by studying particular enzymes and proteins from these cells. Although similar, the enzymes of mice and men usually differ slightly in amino acid sequence and can be distinguished by electrophoretic methods. Using such a method, F. Ruddle and his associates (Yale University) confirmed that the hybrid enzymes were those expected.

In some hybrid cells, such as man-mouse or man-Chinese hamster cells, there was a slow but continual loss of human chromosomes during cell cultivation. The loss of human chromosomes was variable in number and combination, leading to the formation of cells and clones of a variety of types. In these clones, however, the remaining human chromosome constitution might be maintained for many generations. Conditional lethal rodent mutant cells were extremely useful in assigning genes to surviving chromosomes. If, for example, mutant rodent cells could not synthesize the enzyme thymidine kinase, then mouse-human hybrids survived only if they carried the human chromosome number 17, which specifies this enzyme. In this way, genetic characters were localized to specific human chromosomes.

Using these techniques, Ruddle, his associates, and many other investigators assigned approximately 30 genetic markers to 14 human autosomal chromosomes and to the female sex (X) chromosome. The development of a detailed human genetic map not only appeared possible but seemed to be only a matter of time. With such a map and present cloning techniques, it should be possible to provide extremely reliable genetic counseling. A detailed human map also was expected to elucidate the common evolutionary origins of man and the primates. Human chromosomes 11 and 12 are similar to those in primates in size, centromere position, and banding patterns. This correspondence was thought to be consistent with the occurrence of a common primordial polyploid event in the early primate genome. (H. E. KUBITSCHEK)

Genetics. Spiegelman and his co-workers (Columbia University) continued their studies of the self-replicating viral-derived RNA molecule. They were able to isolate a variant form that was 218 nucleotides long and that could duplicate itself 12 trillion times in 20 minutes in a test tube. The sequence of this molecule revealed extensive internal pairing of nucleotides to form hairpin loops, which were thought to be involved in interactions of this molecule with the protein enzyme that brings about its duplication. This finding showed that the informational content of the RNA molecule resides in the secondary structure as well as in the primary sequence of nucleotides. It would make possible further characterization of this self-duplicating molecule under different selective conditions in a test tube. These studies would help to show the possible evolutionary pathways that self-duplicating macromolecules have taken to form the informational core of living things.

Another achievement involving sequencing of informational macromolecules was announced at the 13th International Genetics Congress by Maziel and Gilbert (Harvard University). They succeeded in purifying the operator region of the *lac* operon, a group of related genes involved in lactose utilization. The genes of an operon are regulated coordinately by the operator gene, which interacts with a repressor protein to shut off template activity of the operon. When the repressor is removed, template activity resumes and gene products are made.

To understand regulation at the molecular level required knowing the exact sequence and structure of the operator region. This was determined by using

continued on page 422

CIVIL RIGHTS FOR ANIMALS?

By Robert McHenry

The idea that some animals may be capable of speechlike communication, may indeed one day come to be acknowledged as rational, raises the question: "Do animals have civil rights?" The question would doubtless strike most people as absurd, or worse.

Still, the possession of civil rights is not subject to popular opinion or preference. Those who have civil rights have them, regardless of whether their rights are recognized by others or not. Rights cannot be legislated into or out of existence, and the attempt to do so would be as vain and futile as that fabled action of the Indiana legislature, which in the last century passed a bill that, on the basis of a bit of biblical exegesis performed by one of the honourable representatives, provided that the value of pi would thenceforth be reckoned at precisely three and would be so taught in the common schools of the state.

Very well, then, just what do I mean by "civil rights" in speaking of them as possibly being possessed by animals? To begin with, I do not mean natural rights. The classic definition of natural rights was given by John Locke, who wrote that men are free "to order their actions and dispose of their persons and possessions as they think fit, within the bounds of the law of nature." It is immediately clear that animals embody, even personify, natural rights. It would not be too farfetched to claim that the example of the animals—the gamboling lamb, perhaps, or the soaring eagle, or the she-wolf defending her pups to the last—actually inspired the very notion of natural rights. "Free as a bird," isn't it? Moreover, much of what we believe we know of the law of nature we have inferred from the observed behaviour of animals.

Civil rights are usually understood to be those propositions that define the terms of the mutual respect among all its members that is fundamental to a just and orderly civil society. What has that to do with animals? It would be foolish to suggest that the "community" of nature is somehow analogous to a civil human society; nature, "red in tooth and claw," as Tennyson vividly if somewhat one-sidedly summed it up, simply is no setting for such ethical maxims as "Thou shalt not kill."

Civil or not, the lives of nature's creatures are already well regulated by that same law of nature, and no speculating on our part as to whether there are imbedded in them relations that we might call "rights" will alter the pattern an iota. The naming of names in such a case is quite useless.

Rather, if the notion of rights is to have any application to the wider realm of nature, it will have to be in a form that comprehends the relations between man, on the one hand, and the rest of nature on the other. Note that this is no ad hoc division of creation, but one with a considerable weight of tradition behind it; "man and nature," or "man against nature," or "man over nature" is a dichotomy so long and fully established in life and thought that there can be no objection to exploring what amounts to its obverse.

Robert McHenry is editor of the Britannica Roundtable, *a quarterly publication of the Encyclopædia Britannica Society.*

Seen in this light, then, the question "Do animals have civil rights?" becomes instead "What respect, if any, is owed by man to nature's other creatures?"

The possibility that some animals may partake, in degree, of the light of reason suggests one ground for man's respect. Surely a fellow rational creature can expect of us treatment on a fairly lofty plane? It may well be that current researches will prove, not that *2* or *5* or *11* other species besides man possess rational faculties while the rest, as we have always suspected, do not, but rather that rationality is simply not the all-or-nothing matter we have believed. Perhaps it is distributed—spread out, so to speak—through creation, thicker here and thinner there. Perhaps there is no sharp dividing line between the rational and the brute portions of creation. This does not mean that we ought to expect much in the way of intelligent conversation from the average earthworm, but merely that we ought not to dismiss him out of hand as a moron.

Another basis on which we might build our respect for nature's other creatures is the very fact mentioned earlier, that they have taught us through their lives the meaning of natural rights, of freedom. Might we not go further and imitate the animals in certain other ways? There is in nature little armed robbery, little mass murder, very little mugging, and simply no organized crime whatever. Indeed, the necessities of mealtime aside, animal society appears to be a good deal safer than human. And compared with the vicissitudes, the "thousand natural shocks" of life as we know it, the kingdom of nature would seem a veritable Eden.

In the last few years we have all been reading that many of our old assumptions about nature were wrong and that in our foolhardiness we have done serious, perhaps fatal injuries to her. Wolves, we now learn, seldom attack livestock and never attack man, but they are very good at keeping down other kinds of vermin that, in sufficient numbers such as occur when there are too few wolves, have truly destructive capacities. For decades we have been hounded by Smokey the Bear and his ilk to be ever vigilant against forest fires; now we learn that it is this prudish refusal to allow the thousands of naturally occurring small fires to run their courses—clearing off and helping enrich the forest floor and allowing, for example, the sequoia seed to germinate—that makes possible the terrible crown fires that completely and permanently destroy thousands of acres of forest in a flash. What we are finding out, in short, is that we—man—are not necessary for the continued proper functioning of nature. Nature does quite well without us. Every change we make, every "improvement" in the running of things, is quite likely to show up sooner or later as a first-class foul-up. And it will be expensive, too.

This problem of bumbling interference in nature might be solved, or at least alleviated, by a healthy dose of respect for nature and her creatures. Whether you believe they are rational or not, you must admit that they know their business. Aldo Leopold wrote *25* years ago of "changing the role of *Homo sapiens* from conqueror of the land-community to plain member and citizen of it," and this fits in rather neatly with our question about civil rights. Whether animals have them or not, I don't know; neither do I know if I *really* have them. I do know that through his history man has learned, slowly and painfully and often only incompletely, that it is best to act as though civil rights were real; we are now faced with accepting the further necessity of acting as though the rest of nature also had a claim on our respect and forbearance. Thus does enlightened self-interest give rise to an ethical standard, and the more clearly we perceive the one, the more easily will we adhere to the other.

It is unlikely that the acceptance of the idea of civil rights for animals would lead to the kind of legal wrangling we are accustomed to in our own parochial human affairs, but perhaps it should. Imagine the fun of watching the Supreme Court deliberate the merits and demerits of *Ex parte Canis lupus.*

continued from page 420

the purified DNA operator region as a template to synthesize RNA copies. The increased quantity of purified RNA molecules made possible sequence determination. Once the RNA sequence was known, then DNA sequence could be determined because of nucleotide pairing specificity. The operator DNA region proved to be a double-stranded molecule 27 nucleotide pairs in length that retained its specificity for the protein repressor. The operator gene contained self-complementary sequences, which meant that internal nucleotide pairing could lead to hairpin loop formation. It was this secondary loop structure that was thought to be responsible for the specificity of the interaction between the DNA operator and the protein repressor. Sequencing of operator genes from mutants with altered operator function would reveal the nature of this interaction and the basis of this regulatory system.

One aspect of DNA replication was its mode, the form the replicating DNA entity takes, in contrast to its mechanism, which is concerned with the molecular means whereby DNA is synthesized. The bacterial DNA virus lambda had been reported to replicate both bidirectionally as a closed loop, theta mode, and also as a rolling circle, sigma mode. At first these reports appeared contradictory, but now it seemed they were both true. On entering a cell the lambda chromosome, which is a linear, double-stranded DNA molecule, circularizes. It then replicates by the theta mode. At some point, for as yet undetermined reasons, the theta mode of replication stops and replication continues by the sigma mode. It was learned that the sigma mode of replication is necessary for packaging the lambda DNA molecule into the protein coat to form a mature, infectious virus particle. Mutants of lambda had been obtained that would not replicate according to this sigma mode and would not form mature virus particles. These mutants must be maintained as a part of the bacterial host genome. Other modes of DNA replication were reported for viruses and for DNA-containing, subcellular organelles such as mitochondria. It appeared that these modes of replication were dictated by the life-style of the organelle or organism in question.

The number of repair systems available indicated that repair of damage to DNA is most important to a cell. The overall mechanisms of three such systems were well understood but the identity of the enzymes involved at each step was still being worked out. This had immediate interest to molecular geneticists in general because DNA polymerases involved in repair processes had been confused with those responsible for DNA replication. Hanawalt (Stanford University) found that a second of the three known DNA polymerases from the bacterium *E. coli* is responsible for repair of damaged DNA. Polymerase I, isolated by Kornberg (Stanford University), was now known to have a repair function. Hanawalt showed that polymerase II was also involved in a repair process. DNA polymerase III was known to be involved with replication, but the possibility that the other polymerases might also comprise backup enzymes for replication needed to be considered.

The repair systems were all highly efficient and unlikely to make errors when repairing damaged DNA. Yet, it was a common observation that agents or treatments that damage DNA usually are mutagens and also carcinogens. Witkin (Rutgers University) discovered yet another repair system in the bacterium *E. coli* that was error prone and could account for the mutants produced after damaged DNA is repaired. This error-prone system was inducible, that is, it only functioned when damage to DNA was greater than could be handled by the repair systems that are always present and functioning.

The importance of functioning repair systems to humans was documented by Cleaver (University of California), who showed that the inherited syndrome for xeroderma pigmentosum is the result of a faulty excision repair system. Individuals with this condition are extremely sensitive to sunlight and develop extensive skin tumours that often become lethal. Another question first raised by Evans (Edinburgh, Scot.) that lent relevance to studies on repair was the possibility that among the more than one trillion cells that make up the human body there are mutants that are altered in some of their repair systems. The role of these altered cells in viral acceptance and induction or oncogenesis was unknown.

(JAMES C. COPELAND)

ZOOLOGY

Some interesting studies relating animal behaviour to metabolism were reported in 1973. The first known case of hypothermia in a temperate species of bird was described by W. A. Calder and J. Boose in the Colorado broad-tailed hummingbird, *Selasphorus platycercus*. The bird's temperature was determined by embedding thermistors and thermocouples in synthetic eggs and connecting them to recording potentiometers. All previous studies had shown that sitting hummingbirds did not become hypothermic during incubation. In the present study, the temperature of the eggs fell gradually during one of the nights, from a high of 31° C down to a low of 6.5° C. It was assumed that the temperature of the hen was slightly higher than the lower temperature during the hypothermia. The egg temperature stabilized at the lower temperature, even though the air temperature went lower, then rose to normal before sunrise. Cooling of the eggs as a result of movement of the hen was ruled out and it was concluded that this was a case of true hypothermia. A similar situation existed in the case of the Andean hill star, *Oreotrochilus estella*, which is capable of maintaining a body temperature of 7° C on the cold Andean high plateau. This was the minimum body temperature from which spontaneous arousal had been observed.

Another interesting study pertinent to energy metabolism was carried out by C. R. Taylor and V. J. Rowntree, who showed that primates consume the same amount of energy running on two legs as they do on four legs. They trained two chimpanzees (*Pan troglodytes*) and two capuchin monkeys (*Cebus capucinus*) to run on a treadmill either on two or on four legs. All animals were fitted with ventilated masks and their steady-state oxygen consumption was measured while they ran at various speeds. There was no measurable difference in the amount of oxygen consumed at any speed on two or four legs. The observed cost of locomotion in the chimp was about 50% higher than would be predicted from the relationship between the cost of running and body size for true quadrupedal animals. The results showed that cost or efficiency of bipedal versus quadrupedal locomotion should not be used in arguments about the relative advantages or disadvantages conferred by bipedal locomotion on man.

The converse of the hummingbird hypothermia was

found in studies with leatherback turtles, *Dermochelys coriacea,* on the Atlantic coast by W. Frair *et al.* A long-standing question had centred about how these turtles manage thermally in northern waters where they migrate, although they do not nest north of Florida. It was felt that their northward movement might be a regular migration associated with feeding on jellyfish. It was found that the deep body temperature of a large turtle was 18° C above the Nova Scotia water temperature where it was captured. It was felt that this differential was caused by the retention of muscular heat, due to large size (417 kg.). Another turtle was found to cool far less rapidly than its tank water, suggesting the value of this heat retention for adaptation to cold. Similar situations had been encountered in other endothermic animals. Thus, the Indian python could maintain its body temperature some 7° C above ambient by muscular contractions at brooding time. Skipjack tuna (1.64 kg.) were reported in 1971 to be commonly 9° C warmer than their environment and large bluefin tuna (181–363 kg.) could be as much as 21.5° above their ambient temperature. It was felt that the pigmented dorsal surface of these animals could serve for absorption of solar radiation in the open sea. The length of time that such a differential can be maintained was unknown.

Another behaviour pattern resulted in better accommodation of the organism to its substrate. F. Chia reported why juvenile sand dollars (*Dendraster excentricus*) selectively ingest heavy sand grains and store them in an intestinal diverticulum. The resulting weight change assists in maintaining position in shifting sands. The smaller the juvenile, the more sand it contained proportionally. There was evidence for selective accumulation of sand grains; iron oxide, though it constituted only 9% of the sand, made up 78% of the diverticular sand.

Other studies dealt with interactions between animals, at both species and organism level. P. B. Moyle studied the effect of the long-term introduction of bullfrogs (*Rana catesbeiana*) on the indigenous frog species in the San Joaquin Valley region of California and concluded that bullfrogs are driving the others out. Bullfrogs were introduced between 1914 and 1920 and spread throughout the state. At 72% of the 95 sites sampled in the Sierra Nevada foothills, bullfrogs were the most frequently encountered frog species. The study showed dramatically the effect of introducing a large, vigorous species on the smaller, indigenous species of the area, when this is accompanied by the effects of human activity.

In a study demonstrating sex reversal in a coral-reef fish, D. R. Robertson found that males control this process in a Great Barrier Reef species of "cleaner fish," *Labroides dimidiatus,* which removes ectoparasites from the skin of other fishes. It had been shown that there are far more females than males in this species (protogyny), and that all the males are secondarily derived from females. Each male, the largest, oldest fish, has a harem of three to six mature females and several immature individuals. For about a half hour after the death of the male, the dominant female continues as an aggressive female, but then proceeds from neutral behaviour to aggressively male display within about one-half hour to two hours. This is followed by male courtship and spawning, which takes one to four days to appear. The biological significance of protogyny had been debated. Some felt that an excess of females should enhance fecundity; others that inbreeding could result, because of the reduced number of genotypes available for recombination, with resultant better adaptation to specific, local conditions.

A dramatic report in the field of reproduction involved the laboratory synthesis of a unisexual "species" of fish, *Poeciliopsis monachalucida,* which occurs in northwestern Mexico as a result of the hybridization of two true species, *P. monacha* and *P. lucida.* It consists only of females, and thus cannot be regarded as a true species. Such "species" were known from no fewer than nine genera of cold-blooded vertebrates, but R. J. Schultz was the first to report the successful synthesis of one of them in the laboratory. The problem in the development of the hybrids results from the large size of the embryo in relation to the yolk, which can cause the heart to lie outside of the yolk sac. The number of hybrids that survive is then reduced because of yolk-sac rupture, premature abdominal wall closure, or predation. Those that do survive are all females, as in nature, because the female sex-determining mechanism is "stronger" in *P. monacha* than in *P. lucida.* Marker genes proved that Schultz's fish were true hybrids; they were intermediate between their parents in many characters.

(RONALD R. NOVALES)

Entomology. Following the 1972 U.S. ban on the general use of DDT, in 1973 warnings continued of the danger of other contact insecticides. Charles F. Hammer of Georgetown University, Washington, D.C., pointed out that heptachlor, far from leaving few toxic residues as had been supposed, was converted by ultraviolet light into the relatively stable heptachlor epoxy ketone, three times as toxic as the original compound to both houseflies and mice. P. P. Jaques of the Canadian Department of Agriculture, Ontario, reported a way of lessening dependence on insecticides. He found that mixtures of methomyl with a virus preparation were more effective than either agent alone in controlling cabbage looper and cabbage worm. He also found that a preparation of *Bacillus thuringensis* could be more effective against these pests than formulations containing chemical insecticides.

J. F. Longworth and co-workers at the Unit of Insect Virology, Oxford, and at the Animal Virus Research Organization, Pirbright, found unexpectedly that domestic animals and deer in the U.K. had natural antibodies to a virus isolated from a moth, *Gonometa,* that was thought to occur only in East Africa. How the U.K. animals could have become sensitized to the virus was a mystery, since it indicated that this or a closely similar virus must have gained regular access to the animals. And for the first time an insect virus had been indicated as a potential pathogen of mammals.

Leading the field in interest as potential replacements for neurotoxic chemical insecticides such as DDT were the synthetic analogues of juvenile hormone (JH). Natural JH controlled the development of insects and later affected mating behaviour and egg laying. If an insect was treated with JH at the wrong time in its life history it could fail to develop into a reproductively competent adult. Although natural JH was nonspecific, synthetic analogues had proved highly specific and of low toxicity to forms of life other than insects. The only remaining problem was to find analogues that would work at economically low rates of application.

Encouraging was the report by James Wright and George Spates of the U.S. Department of Agriculture that they had found a JH analogue that would prevent

WIDE WORLD

A once-in-17-years visitation of cicadas occurred in parts of the U.S. in the spring of 1973. Here an adult emerges from its old skin.

adult development of the stable fly *Stomoxys* but that left unaffected a parasitic wasp. *Stomoxys* caused millions of dollars worth of damage annually in the U.S. by putting cattle off their feed. Of even greater significance was the indication that JH analogues might affect pests but not their parasitic enemies. On the other hand, Edgardo D. Gomez and colleagues at the Scripps Institution of Oceanography, La Jolla, Calif., found that one JH analogue at as little as 0.01 part per million prevented barnacles from attaching themselves. Although this discovery was considered of possible use in formulating marine antifouling agents, it also opened up the possibility that, as pollutants, JH analogues might have untoward effects on marine life.

Another approach to insect control was the use of the "sex pheromones" (by which females attract males), either to trap and destroy males in lures or to confuse populations of insects to such an extent that successful matings seldom occurred. Previous research had revealed surprisingly that different species often produce the same chemical attractant. Milton C. Ganyard, Jr., and U. Eugene Brady of the University of Georgia found that the same compounds could attract males of species of moths so different as to be classified in different superfamilies. They pointed out that while such substances would be of potential use against a broad spectrum of pests, they might, by the same token, affect nontarget species. On the other hand, R. S. Kaae and colleagues at the University of California at Riverside found that although males of two moths, *Autographia californica* and *Trichoplusia ni,* were both attracted by the same pheromone, *A. californica* would enter lures when the compound was being released at a lower rate than could trap *T. ni.* In other words, different rates of release by the females might be sufficient to maintain the "reproductive isolation" of the two species.

Dutch elm disease is caused by a fungus carried by beetles—*Scolytus* in Europe and *Hylurgopinus* in North America. Usually the disease in Europe is relatively mild, causing little more than 30% leaf drop, from which the tree recovers. But occasionally outbreaks occur in Europe in which trees die within two weeks of the initial attack. John Gibbs and C. M. Brasier of the U.K. Forestry Commission explained that there were two strains of the fungus, a slow-growing "waxy" strain and a more deadly, fast-growing "fluffy" strain. Normally only the waxy strain was found in Europe and the fluffy was confined to North America, but timber reaching Southampton from Canada in 1971 contained beetles carrying the fluffy strain, thereby starting an outbreak of the killer disease in the U.K. that continued into 1973.

Paul A. Opler of the University of Costa Rica claimed the first authentic records that traced the ancestry of modern species of moths as far back as the mid-Miocene period (some 20 million years ago). The more primitive of the families of moths were leaf miners, and Opler discovered *Nepticula* mines in fossil leaves of the Miocene ancestor of *Quercus wislizenii* that were indistinguishable from those made by extant *N. variella* on the present-day tree. The great stability of the ecological relationship between insect and plant was thereby also demonstrated. (PETER W. MILES)

Ornithology. Cosmetic coloration in birds is by any standards extremely rare, a handful of the 8,600 species in the world using coloured preen oil to enhance their visual effect. All the more surprising, therefore, was Y. Uchida's discovery that the Japanese crested ibis changes its colour by a previously unknown type of cosmetic coloration. As the bird approaches the breeding season, its plumage changes from white to gray. This was found to result from the daubing of a black substance produced by the naked face of the ibis onto the feathered shoulder region after bathing. The reverse change from gray to white occurs at the time of the next molt.

In a new close study of the well-known nesting method among hornbills, in which the female is sealed into the nest hole, A. C. Kemp found that young were successfully reared from about 90% of hornbill nests. He concluded that freedom from nest predation must be the chief advantage of the sealed-in nesting method, since parallel studies on hole-nesters of similar size but of different (nonhornbill) species that did not "seal in" showed that success rates of eggs laid to young fledged were only about 35%.

In an important paper R. S. Payne reviewed the problem of how owls locate their prey. Payne's work demonstrated that barn owls can locate food animals, such as small mammals, in total darkness with an error of less than 1% in both horizontal and vertical planes, using only the sense of hearing. To this end, the owl's ears are anatomically asymmetrical.

G. T. Crosby, in an up-to-date review, outlined one of the most extraordinary range expansions known for any bird. The cattle egret is a bird that in very recent times crossed the Atlantic to the New World, probably from North Africa utilizing the northeast trade winds. The species was established in South America in 1930, and by 1970 had spread throughout South America, the West Indies, and the eastern United States. Its most recent presence on the west coast of the U.S. was due to a northward extension of range from Central America and Mexico.

The Greenland breeding stock of the barnacle goose spends the winter in Scotland and in Ireland. The population between 1957 and 1963 doubled from 12,000 to 24,000. However, the number wintering in Ireland remained stable during this period at about 4,500. Differential breeding success of the Scottish and Irish winterers in different parts of Greenland was believed to account for this.

The Finnish ornithologist S. Sulkava showed that holes in winter snow that might have been attributed

Liquors, Alcoholic:
see Alcoholic Beverages

to small mammals had in fact been made by tiny burrowing birds like arctic redpolls, which in very cold winter weather dig snow burrows for themselves for the night.

A study of the magellanic penguin of southern South America, the least studied of the world's 18 species, revealed that its population was probably to be numbered in tens of millions of birds, ranging from Argentina through Tierra del Fuego and into Chile. A highly detailed scientific film was made of the species' breeding biology.

B. Bertram's studies of that popular cagebird the Indian hill mynah, renowned for its ability to imitate human speech, showed perhaps surprisingly that in the wild the species is *not* given to copying either human speech or the vocalization of other species of birds.

A species of bird entirely new to science was described by K. C. Parkes and C. B. Keplar from Puerto Rico. It was named the Elfin Woods warbler (*Dendroica angelae*).

Two papers by the British ornithologist David Lack on the birds of two West Indian islands were the last to be published during his lifetime. Lack's prodigious output and breadth, depth, and originality of scientific thought made him easily one of the most outstanding ornithologists of all time. Lack died in April 1973.

An important and original international ornithological meeting brought together at Slimbridge, Eng., over 50 "phoenicopterologists"—students of flamingos—from 20 different countries. Discussions centred on the population distribution and ecology of the six species of wild flamingo. The maintenance in captivity of these bizarre birds with their highly specialized feeding requirements was also discussed, including in particular the problem of keeping captive flamingos the correct colour.

Edited by Janet Kear of the Wildfowl Trust, *The Swans* was a synthesis of exceptional grace and accuracy of what is known of one of the most romantic and interesting of bird groups. Thirteen phonograph records under the title *The Peterson Field Guide to the Bird Songs of Britain and Europe* were published by the Swedish broadcasting corporation. They presented the voices of nearly 500 species. The work was the first attempt to bring together in one continuous reference the bird voices of an entire continent, and was easily the most ambitious work of its kind ever published. Academic Press published the first two volumes of a new important and wide-ranging work, *Avian Biology,* edited by Donald S. Farner and James R. King. The first volume was concerned primarily with systematics, population biology, and ecology; the second, with anatomy and physiology. Another work of meticulous scholarship was Charles Vaurie's impeccably produced *Tibet and Its Birds.*

(JEFFERY BOSWALL)

See also Environment; Medicine; Oceanography.

ENCYCLOPÆDIA BRITANNICA FILMS. *Insect Parasitism—The Alder Woodwasp and Its Enemies* (1968); *The Ears and Hearing* (2nd ed., 1969); *Muscle: Chemistry of Contraction* (1969); *Muscle: Dynamics of Contraction* (1969); *Muscle: Electrical Activity of Contraction* (1969); *The Origin of Life—Chemical Evolution* (1969); *Radioisotopes: Tools of Discovery* (1969); *Theories on the Origin of Life* (1969); *Succession on Lava* (1970); *The Nerve Impulse* (1971); *Seed Dispersal* (3rd ed., 1971); *Investigating Hibernation* (1972); *A Bird of Prey: The Red Tailed Hawk* (1972); *World of Close-Up* (1973); *How Do They Move?* (1973); *Some Friendly Insects* (1973); *What Do They Eat?* (1973); *Where Does Life Come From?* (1973); *Cactus: Adaptations for Survival* (1973); *Cactus: Profile of a Plant* (1973); *Let's Find Life* (1973); *Nematode* (1973).

Literature

The 1973 Nobel Prize for Literature was awarded to the Australian novelist Patrick White, who was cited for "an epic and psychological narrative art which has introduced a new continent into literature." (*See* NOBEL PRIZES.)

Keeping abreast of the cultural van in any one country proved yearly more difficult, but to stay tuned in to anything but the best-seller lists from other countries demanded the cultivation of very sensitive antennae. "Any strengthening of literary entente between countries is overwhelmingly dependent on the quality and quantity of translations," noted *The Times Literary Supplement.* So one of the best pieces of news was that the German Institute and Britain's National Book League had formed a working committee that would seriously explore the possibility of establishing a permanent exchange to promote likely marriages between authors, publishers, and translators. If anything were to come of it, and the scope of such a service were to be extended to include other-language partners, no little encouragement would be needed from editors of the literary pages in finding space for well-informed reviews.

Otherwise, the general reader read what he could buy, and during the year it became increasingly apparent that the economic facts of publishing life were precluding the easy availability of all but the hottest properties, especially in fiction (*see* PUBLISHING). Nor was it only the reader who suffered. Anthony Burgess quoted the horror story of the year, of the new author whose first novel was duly published but, thanks apparently to the eagerness of a machine that calculates the number of "unsold" copies, the entire printing was dispatched to the pulping machines, without the writer ever seeing a copy or having it exposed to a hostile critic.

The memoir and the diary, often written with an eye on posthumous publication, confirmed their status in 1973 as perhaps the most widely read and eagerly discussed forms—at least in newspaper serializations. Evelyn Waugh perhaps made the biggest splash ("The Private Diaries of Evelyn Waugh," edited by Michael Davie and serialized in *The Observer Magazine*). Biography sometimes seemed to be confusing itself with historical fiction, a situation that led inevitably to the observation that Norman Mailer, in his inventive biography of Marilyn Monroe, should be discredited with the word of the year: "factoid." Its monstrous overtones were apt enough, since by it he apparently meant any statement that might or might not be verifiable, but the underlying truth of which the biographer had no very great anxiety (or time) to determine.

Outstanding literary figures who died during 1973 were: the Chilean poet Pablo Neruda, who was awarded the Nobel Prize for Literature in 1971; the Anglo-American poet W. H. Auden; and the English philologist J. R. R. Tolkien, author of *The Lord of the Rings* trilogy. (*See* OBITUARIES.) (DAVID HATELY)

AMERICAN

Fiction. Whether their setting was Berlin or Lower Manhattan, American novels of recent months reaffirmed in different ways not merely similar aspirations but a common, grotesque vision of despair, violence, and apocalypse. The violence was of a special kind.

PICTORIAL PARADE

Kurt Vonnegut's "Breakfast of Champions," a "comic novel of despair," appeared in 1973.

It was absurd in the sense that no meaning or value could be assigned to it. Its function was to turn men into things, pressing the human form downward toward the robots of Thomas Pynchon and Kurt Vonnegut, Jr. (*see* BIOGRAPHY), and the insect people of William Burroughs.

Hardly any novel of the last decade approached Pynchon's *Gravity's Rainbow* in scope, ambition, and achievement. It seemed, in fact, the apotheosis of the mid-century American novel: an exploration, celebration, and dramatization of paranoia and the imagery of impending destruction. For Pynchon the additional comic horror of the Faustianism peculiar to the 20th century is that it can no longer be located in the mad heroics of individuals. It is instead part of the bureaucratic enterprise, of the technological systems that have set history on an irreversible course. Pynchon's "science" and knowledge of gravity serves as a check against the tendency of his fantasy to be private and cultish, and his imagination is strong enough to clarify his world so that there is less need for the "explanations" that might leaden so much of his fiction. There are some imaginations for which this balance is precisely what is needed: there are few Kafkas; as a matter of fact there are few Pynchons.

Breakfast of Champions is Vonnegut's own parody of Vonnegut. Absurd insignificant detail becomes the major fictional technique as he deliberately emphasizes his view of man's obscenely inflated opinion of himself caught in his materialistic nightmare. Science-fiction writer Kilgor Trout, a minor figure in previous novels, is the major one here. One of his stories causes Pontiac dealer Dwayne Hoover to go mad: the one free man in the universe is surrounded by human robots created for the pleasure of God, who wants to see how he chooses to act toward them. The absurdity of Vonnegut's comic view of despair hides a horror that must be tempered with laughter to be endured.

Sci-fi horror-erotica continued with William Burroughs' *Exterminator!*, a savage work peopled with ubiquitous insects masquerading as men, junkies and cops, pitchmen and pushers, crummy doctors and brave freedom fighters. Here was the author of *Naked Lunch* at his withering, surrealistic best.

One of the more remarkable and successful works of the year was theologian Arthur A. Cohen's second novel, *In the Days of Simon Stern,* a work as dense and felicitous as a Brueghel painting. Simon Stern is a complex theological hero designed to assume all the sins of Judaism's revolutionary messianic perspective and expiate them with incisive passion; the hero founds the Society for the Rescue and Resurrection of the Jews to save survivors from the Nazi death camps.

Sexism and transvestitism were burlesqued in Thomas Berger's *Regiment of Women.* The year is 2125 and women rule the world in this ferocious Swiftian satire of the rigid roles with which society and language encrust mankind. Philip Roth was in mostly fine seriocomic fettle in *The Great American Novel.* His grotesque World War II baseball team, the Ruppert Mundys, is composed of dwarfs, amputees, and other 4-Fs who are condemned to a season of away games.

Money, the hoi polloi, the ideal of status, and the clash of power and principle became the objects of fantasy in *Facing the Lions,* a wryly humorous Washington novel by *New York Times* journalist Tom Wicker. This was a superior political novel about a senator's try for the presidency and its alcoholic aftermath. Prolific Joyce Carol Oates contributed *Do with Me What You Will,* a stylized and symbolic novel of crime and punishment revolving around the passive adventures of a virginal heroine who innocently slays her lover. Thomas McGuane's *Ninety-Two in the Shade,* a novel of Camus-like brilliance, tells the story of a young fishing guide in Key West in competition with his ultimate murderer. In the tradition of *True Grit* and *Butch Cassidy,* Marc Norman's *Oklahoma Crude* tells the story of a stubborn, strong-willed woman who thinks she hates men and a likable conman who thinks he has no scruples. They take each other on in one of the more appealing love stories of the year.

Much in evidence were urban-jungle books, such as Joseph Wambaugh's *The Onion Field,* a "factual novel" owing much to Truman Capote that depicts the senseless murder of a Los Angeles policeman. John Godey's *The Taking of Pelham One Two Three* was a tautly suspenseful novel about a hijacked subway train and New York City in the grip of desperate men.

An important posthumous work was *Recovery* by poet John Berryman, prizewinning author of *Dream Songs.* Berryman required that the poet suffer strikingly painful and gruesome experiences and put these into verse or prose in all their detail. His unfinished novel is fiction struggling to become truth; the hero is an alcoholic former professor embarked upon an irresistible descent into hallucination and death.

Two major short story collections also appeared. John Cheever's *The World of Apples,* his first collection in nine years, deals with the disruptions in family life and marriage caused by lack of love, misunderstanding, or temporary insanity (usually caused by lack of love) in one of the partners. Bernard Malamud's *Rembrandt's Hat* was his first collection in ten years, and an event worth waiting for. Each of the eight new stories is touched by wistful and ironic humour and beautifully bold fantasy that transforms daily experience into art.

History, Biography, and Belles Lettres. The best political and social histories should register the norms, values, aberrations, and monumental absurdities of the age, and should employ a language so original that even the limpest clichés are revivified as basic truths. The histories written in 1973 were not of that sort. If anything, they were partisan and polemical.

The concluding volume of Daniel Boorstin's trilogy *The Americans: The Democratic Experience* appeared, carrying the story from the Civil War onward. Boorstin's focus in this big, rambling book is on the growth of business and the development of technology, the latter of which he contends created the momentum for the contemporary "everywhere community" with "befuzzled" boundaries and indefinite rules for citizenship.

In a sometimes vigorous, sometimes bland collection, *The World of Nations,* one of the most influential young "revisionist" historians, Christopher Lasch, explored the "bankruptcy" of the liberal establishment within the context of an antiprogressive view of U.S. history. Kirkpatrick Sale came closer to the mark with *SDS,* a weighty history of a movement that emerged from the anti-Communist League for Industrial Democracy and ended in flaming collapse in a Greenwich Village bomb factory.

An illuminating political history could doubtless have been constructed out of the atom-spy trial of Julius and Ethel Rosenberg, but Louis Nizer's best-selling *The Implosion Conspiracy,* filled with smug and routine pieties about the American legal system's infallibility, was not it. *The New Populism* by former Oklahoma senator Fred Harris was similarly disappointing; it followed his earlier *Now Is the Time* in attacking the unequal distribution of wealth and the problems that result from it. Equally unimpressive was *The Coming of Post-Industrial Society* by sociologist Daniel Bell, who summarized major theories of industrial and postindustrial life and offered a forecast of the future stratification of society.

John Kenneth Galbraith was well received, as always, with *Economics and the Public Purpose,* an attempt to reach the general reader with a summation of the problems of the U.S. economy. Drawing largely on his earlier books, especially *The Affluent Society* and *American Capitalism,* Galbraith argued for change, and although his prescriptions were far-ranging, they were not at all new. Far more interesting and topical was *The Living Presidency* by Emmet John Hughes, a journalist and experienced presidential aide who showed how the office brings out the best in some men, reduces others, and tempts an ill-starred few to overreach themselves. Also in the category of enjoyable popular history, Colin Simpson's *The Lusitania* offered a shattering exposé of political cynicism, arrogance, and expediency among high British and U.S. officials in the story of a ship, on a collision course with a U-boat.

Unexpected conjunctions also abounded in Gerald Hawkins' *Beyond Stonehenge,* a venture in astro-archaeology. With the help of computers, Hawkins tried to discover whether other ancient sites besides Stonehenge were built in purposeful alignment with the planets, and found impressive evidence that they were.

More down to earth was *Lesbian Nation: The Feminist Solution* by Jill Johnston, an immensely well-argued addition to the literature of feminist liberation and of radical analyses of society. The *Village Voice* columnist redefines "lesbian" as a generic term for feminist activism and the goal of the separate state and argues for lesbian nationalism as the only means to the liberation of women.

By far the most sensational biography of the year was the immensely praised and damned *Marilyn* by Norman Mailer. Mailer had already embodied different aspects of the Marilyn Monroe image in the characters of Lulu Meyers and Elena Esposito in *The Deer Park.* In the more mawkish word flights of *Marilyn,* when Mailer lets his fascination with Hollywood sex cloud his vision, *The Deer Park* seems to be returning, a shade too purple. Called by Mailer a "novel biography," *Marilyn* is filled with Rabelaisian "factoids" and riddled with Mailerisms ("the cameraman . . . was the altar at which actors' prayers were laid"). The focus is frequently unclear; and although one is not quite sure whether this portrait of "everyman's love affair with America" owes more to Marilyn Monroe or to Mailer's imaginative abilities, the character plays on the emotions like the protagonist of some richly satisfying novel.

CARLOS SANTOS—RAPHO GUILLUMETTE

John Kenneth Galbraith, economist and diplomat, offered wry summation of problems plaguing the U.S. economy in "Economics and the Public Purpose," published in 1973.

Less entertaining, perhaps because of its subject, but nonetheless a commendable contribution to the social and literary history of the 1950s and 1960s was *Kerouac,* a disturbing biography by Ann Charters, revealing Jack Kerouac, beatnik par excellence and artist.

Barbara Howar's *Laughing All the Way* caused some stir, not so much for its literary value as for its disclosures of scandal in high life; it is the story of a Southern girl-next-door who grew up to become the Johnson administration's leading chandelier swinger. More basically political was the memoir *Revolutionary Suicide* by Huey Newton. Well thought out as an apology for the Black Panthers, the book ends up expounding an explicit existentialism and pragmatism that seems a retreat from Newton's earlier theories of revolutionary practice. Less rewarding than Joseph Lash's *Eleanor and Franklin,* but nevertheless fascinating as a testament to oedipal pain and recrimination, was *An Untold Story: The Roosevelts of Hyde Park.* In it Elliott Roosevelt and James Brough offered sketches of the Roosevelts' life from 1916 to 1932, with belaboured stress on unverifiable if "intimate" revelations.

Contributions to the literature of pop culture included Myra Friedman's *Buried Alive,* an analytical, detailed, and rich biography of singer Janis Joplin told with compassion—a tragicomical tale of highs, lows, drugs, sex, and loneliness, ending in accidental death. Pop culture relies heavily on cop books and Mafia books. With the Knapp Commission's investigation into police payoffs in New York City, the writer had a new vein to work—the cops as the mafia. Such was the stuff of *Serpico,* Peter Maas's melodrama in

WIDE WORLD

Playwright Jason Miller, whose "That Championship Season" won the Pulitzer Prize, receives word of the award in New York City, May 7, 1973.

the true-to-life style of "the cop who defied the system."

In the general area of belles lettres, although difficult to describe and impossible to categorize, was *Closing Time,* another tour de force by Norman O. Brown, one of the most controversial modern literary thinkers. Employing a notational method of paralleling passages from Giambattista Vico's *New Science* and James Joyce's *Finnegans Wake,* Brown achieves enigmatic, though always provocative, effects. From within the same dense aura of the avant-garde's critical perspective, John Cage offered a new collection of "essays" called *M: Writings '67–'72,* which were fun, frustrating, tuneful, and often polyphonic assemblages of dadaist rhythms and "mesostics" (acrostics read down the middle, not on the edge). But perhaps the most impressive contribution of the year was *Bright Book of Life: American Novelists and Storytellers from Hemingway to Mailer* by Alfred Kazin. Kazin charts the contemporary frequencies of the fictional spectrum, concentrating mostly on women writers, black and Jewish novelists, and the literature of the South.

Poetry. Despite the large number of new collections by younger poets, 1973 was a season in which outstanding middle-aged poets, many celebrated as modern masters, continued to display their considerable range of subject matter and skills. The major publication event was the appearance of three volumes of visions and revision by Robert Lowell. Overwhelming the reader with its range and virtuosity was *The Dolphin,* a continuation of the *Notebook* poems, containing 103 new poems "all muscle, youth, intention" organized as a cycle of love sonnets with a full-scale plot revolving around the question: can twice-married poet find happiness as husband of titled divorcée 15 years his junior and the mother of three children? The answer, predictable enough in the context of Lowell's pervasive despair, is no. The famed confessional mode, inaugurated by Lowell's beautiful *Life Studies* (1959), reaches its point of no return. *History,* with over 360 poems, 80 of them new and the rest revised, is charged and claustrophobic, steaming with grandeur. *For Lizzie and Harriet,* 67 old poems, all revised, is on the end of 20 years of marriage.

Robert Bly's *Sleepers Joining Hands* contained mature and ardent poems that sought to discern the whole meaning of the dominion of life and death over America; similarly focused was Allen Ginsberg's *The Fall of America,* showing the poet at midpoint and middle age, his friends dead, the world tasted, turning to observe the metaphysical geography of America. Lawrence Ferlinghetti, at 53, was still as dynamic and verbose as when he began writing poetry. In *Open Eye, Open Heart,* his concerns were politics, love, loneliness, ecology, and women, his rhythms rough and colloquial, the contexts often surreal. Muriel Rukeyser's *Breaking Open* was a fine collection of common sense poems by one of the country's foremost older poets.

The Anonymous Lover, John Logan's fifth volume, contained an unusual sequence of poems on Hawaii and two superb long ones: "New Poem," on his marriage, and the tragicomic tour de force "Heart to Heart Talk with My Liver." Irving Feldman was brilliant in *Lost Originals,* a collection equally given to dream and elegy and to the whole wry fable-making Talmudic tradition. And *Writings to an Unfinished Accompaniment* showed prolific religious poet W. S. Merwin at the peak of his powers, with his themes still deprivation, fragmentation, mystical silence, and the search for visionary purity.

Well-received volumes by younger poets included Joyce Carol Oates's *Angel Fire,* often approaching the bitter genius of Sylvia Plath; Alice Walker's *Revolutionary Petunias and Other Poems,* depicting three stages in the life of a black woman, and evocative of Gertrude Stein; and Victor Hernandez Cruz's *Mainland,* which combined the images and imagery of Puerto Rico and New York. (FREDERICK S. PLOTKIN)

CANADIAN

English Language. Most of the best Canadian novels in 1973 dealt in some manner with the current Canadian scene. In *The Vanishing Point* by W. O. Mitchell, for example, teacher and Indian agent Carlyle Sinclair becomes profoundly involved with the residents of the Paradise Valley Indian Reserve in southwest Alberta. Power, compassion, authentic dialogue, wry humour, and a sensuous evocation of nature characterize this moving work. Clark Blaise in *A North American Education* provided insight and irony in short stories that explored a young man's search for identity and survival. Austin Clarke's *Storm of Fortune* combined lilting dialogue and memorable characters with realism and stinging bitterness to portray the impact of an alien culture on West Indian immigrants to English Canada. Erstwhile doctoral student Jeremy Sadness, hero of Robert Kroetsch's *Gone Indian,* records his quest for a mythical identity on tapes sent to his professor. Rudy Wiebe in *The Temptations of Big Bear* portrayed the tense atmosphere of the Louis Riel uprisings and Big Bear's efforts to maintain his people's dignity in the face of the white man's intervention. Richard B. Wright's *In the Middle of a Life* was an eloquent and acute observation reflecting the comedy, sadness, and absurdities of the crises besetting an urban, middle-class, middle-aged man.

The printing in book form of many collections by relatively unknown Canadian poets who formerly relied upon literary magazines and the underground press was notable in 1973. Among the first volumes was Shirley Gibson's *I Am Watching,* in which very personal, moving love poems combined with recurring images of violence and pain. *Lovers and Lesser Men* by Irving Layton was full of the anger and love with which one associates this major Canadian poet. In *Crusoe: Poems Selected and New,* Eli Mandel gave vent to his passion for words, history, and intricate meanings. Al Purdy's 11th volume of poetry, *Sex and Death,* gained particular power in his acute, often bitter, reflections upon his worldwide travels. *The Dance Is One,* F. R. Scott's eighth book of verse, was a satisfying sampler of one of Canada's older poets including a previously unpublished narrative poem about the Mackenzie River. John Metcalf edited an excellent anthology, *The Speaking Earth,* which struck a good balance between new and established poets.

Selected and edited by James A. MacNeill and Glen A. Sorestad, *Tigers of the Snow: 18 Canadian Short Stories* was the best of several collections published in 1973. The pieces evoked a true sense of time and place whether set on the prairie, beside the ocean, or in a large town, as in stories by Sinclair Ross, Don Bailey, and Hugh Garner.

Survey: A Short History of Canadian Literature by Elizabeth Waterson was a personal, rather than inclusive, look at 18th–20th-century writers. Robert Weaver and William Toye edited *The Oxford Anthology of Canadian Literature,* in which a brief taste of each writer's work, be it poetry, drama, or prose, is preceded by a solid biographical and critical sketch. An impressive group of contributors under Toye's general editorship produced the *Supplement to The Oxford Companion to Canadian History and Literature* covering 1967–73.

Dialogue and Dialectic by the Alice Theatre Workshop was an anthology of short Canadian plays with political overtones. *Encounter,* containing Canadian drama from four media, was edited by Eugene Benson of the University of Guelph. Rolf Kalman issued the second volume of a *Collection of Canadian Plays* containing William Fruet's highly praised *Wedding in White,* about family life in the Prairies during World War II, and plays of such establishment writers as Hugh Garner and Mavor Moore. Michael Hollingsworth's *Strawberry Fields,* brilliant and often brutal, was published by Playwright's Co-op, Toronto, a group formed in 1972. On the West Coast, Peter Hay's Talon Books issued *Ashes for Easter and Other Monodramas,* created by David Watmough from intensely personal memories of his Cornish childhood and life in Europe and North America. Useful dramatic criticism and commentary on the growth of Canadian theatre included Mavor Moore's introduction to the works of George Ryga, James Reaney, Robertson Davies, and Gratien Gélinas, in *Four Canadian Playwrights.* Betty Lee's *Love and Whiskey* contained an enlightening commentary on the early years of the Dominion Drama Festival.

The plight of Canada's native peoples received attention. In her autobiography, *Halfbreed,* Maria Campbell, a Métis from Saskatchewan, portrayed her rejection by both whites and Indians in childhood and adolescence and her later activity in the movement for native rights. In *One Woman's Arctic* Sheila Burnford described a year spent in a remote outpost. *Wilderness Man: The Strange Story of Grey Owl* was Lovat Dickson's biography of Archie Belaney, a champion of Canadian wild nature and the Indians. *Mike: The Memoirs of the Right Honourable Lester B. Pearson, Vol. 2, 1948–1957,* edited by John A. Munro and Alex I. Inglis, recorded Pearson's involvement in the formation of NATO, the cold war, and other events of those years.

Collections and essays on Canadian political science included *Home Country* by Peter Newman and *Greenpeace and Her Enemies,* in which James Eayrs maintained his reputation as a foremost writer on political matters. Abraham Rotstein's essays in *The Precarious Homestead* discussed various aspects of the Canadian identity problem.

The Royal Canadian Mounted Police was the subject of many books during 1973, its centennial year. In *Maintain the Right,* British journalist Ronald Atkin's excellent study of the Mounties' first quarter century, the men are not always the romantic heroes of fiction, but they are commended for their bravery and fairness in establishing law on the Canadian frontier. This traditional image is convincingly challenged by Lorne and Caroline Brown in *An Unauthorized History of the RCMP,* which shows how the Mounties were used by government agencies to settle civil strife. Similarly, in *Tundra,* while Farley Mowat is impressed by the courage of various European adventurers who first penetrated Arctic lands, he also decries their destruction of the delicate northern environment and pleads that the area be restored and preserved as a sanctuary from the technological age.

(H. C. CAMPBELL)

French Language. Many interesting works of French-Canadian, or "québécoise," literature were published during 1973. Perhaps the most outstanding was Réjean Ducharme's *L'Hiver de force.* Among noteworthy novels were: *Un Joualonais, sa joualonie* by Marie-Claire Blais; *C't'à ton tour, Laura Cadieux* by dramatist Michel Tremblay; *Le Deux-millième Étage* by Roch Carrier; *Oh Miami, Miami, Miami* by Victor-Lévy Beaulieu; *Mariaagélas* by Antonine Maillet; *Louve Storée* and *Sexe-fiction,* both by Emmanuel Cocke, who died during the year in India; *Adéodat I* by André Brochu; *Un Voyage* by Gilles Marcotte; *Les Fous d'amour* by Adrien Thério; *Monsieur Isaac* by Gilles Racette and Normand de Bellefeuille; and *Axel et Nicholas* by André Carpentier.

In the field of poetry the following titles were published: *Variables* by Michel Beaulieu, who won the Études Françaises award for this work; *Pulsions,* also by Michel Beaulieu; *La Main au feu,* collected poems from 1949 to 1968 by Roland Giguère; *Poésies I,* collected poems from 1958 to 1962 by Yves-Gabriel Brunet; *Nouveaux Poèmes* by Gilles Constantineau; *Les Ecrits de Zéro Legel* and *Novembre* by Gilbert Langevin; *Le Pays saint* by Luc Racine; and *Cri de terre* by Raymond LeBlanc.

Among dramatic works published were: *Hosanna* by Michel Tremblay; *Le Tabernacle à trois étages* and *Le Procès de Jean-Baptiste M.* by Robert Gurik; *La Vie exemplaire d'Alcide Ier* by André Ricard; *Oeuvres dramatiques* by Réal Benoit, the novelist, who died in 1972; *Anthologie du théâtre québécois, 1606–1970,* compiled by Jan Doat; *Dossier en théâtre québécois,* a bibliography; and two sketches by Dominique de Pasquale, several comedies by Jean Barbeau, and three farces by Jean-Claude Germain and his group.

A variety of other works were published, among them: the complete works of Nérée Beauchemin, poetry and prose; new editions of the Jesuit *Relations* and *Journal; Lignes québécoises,* a series issued by the University of Montreal Press and including short stories of Desrosiers, Saint-Denys-Garneau, Guèvremont, Aquin, and Ferron; *Indépendances,* essays by Pierre Vadeboncoeur; *Du Fond de mon arrière-cuisine* by Jacques Ferron; and *Le Joual de Troie* by Jean Marcel. (LAURENT MAILHOT)

GLYDENDALSKE BOGHANDEL NORDISK FORLAG

Danish poet Ole Wivel's memoirs, "Romance for Valdhorn," offered an insider's view of postwar literary movements.

DANISH

Particularly interesting in Danish literature were Ole Wivel's memoirs, *Romance for Valdhorn* (late 1972), written by an outstanding postwar poet who was at the centre of the literary movements of his day. In the same genre Aase Hansen, at 80, remembered her childhood in *Klip af et Billedark.*

Ingeborg Johansen, author of a number of sensitive novels in recent years, continued with *Joaweski* (1972), the story of a young woman's fruitless visit to her brother in a lonely forest area of Estonia. Grethe Heltberg's monologue *Vi lukker om lidt* (1972) dealt in the best Danish tradition with human motivation and responsibility. While expressing tolerance toward unthinking action, it showed the misery resulting from capitulation to impulses and emotions divorced from ethical standards.

Willy-August Linnemann continued his family saga from Schleswig in *Forkynderen* (1972), sober, realistic, well told, and not without humour. Likewise realistic in approach was Christian Kampmann's *En tid alene,* dealing with loneliness and the need for contact in young and old alike. In 1972 Klaus Rifbjerg produced two characteristic novels, *R. R.* and *Brevet til Gerda,* the latter another of his portrayals of middle-class Danish mentality, and in 1973 he wrote a new roman à clef, *Spinatfuglene.* Leif Panduro's *Amatørerne* looked at mental attitudes in contrasting generations, a tragicomic mixture typical of its author. Of Henning Ipsen's three novels from 1972 and 1973 *Kysten ved Nab* was the best, ingeniously constructed and dealing with a gentle man's reaction to historical and contemporary violence.

The work of some of the younger authors was more experimental. Svend-Åge Madsen, awarded the Danish Academy's prize in 1972, published *Dage med Diam eller Livet om Natten,* a many-faceted novel on the necessity of choosing without being able to see the implications. Scarcely less complex was Henning Mortensen's *Nattelegram til Xerophyte,* a series of reflections, with quotations from everything from the Koran to pornographic literature. The difficulty of fitting into ordinary life emerged again in Sven Holm's *Syg og munter* (1972), where the "hero" is finally judged to be mad because he cannot adapt.

One who had adjusted was Tove Ditlevsen. In *Min nekrolog og andre skumle tanker* she gave direct expression to the wisdom derived from the experience of a disastrous marriage.

In *S.,* Frank Jæger wove a fantasy around the love affair between King Christian VII's English-born queen, Caroline Matilda, and the court physician, Count von Struensee. History played its part, too, in Karl Bjarnhof's *Støv skal du blive,* a biographical study of Niels Stensen (Nicolaus Steno) that read like a novel. The Danish exponent par excellence of the documentary novel, Thorkild Hansen, published, in the fall of 1972, his *Vinterhavn,* the diaries he kept while working in Canada on his Jens Munk study of 1965. (W. GLYN JONES)

ENGLISH

Prose. A year that saw the death of W. H. Auden, the 70th birthday of Cyril Connolly, another arbiter of English literary taste in his time, and the little-remarked 20th anniversary of the once influential magazine *Encounter* ought to look like some sort of watershed. However, if this was true at all of the English literary scene in 1973, it was so only in the sense of it seeming a backward-looking year, full of an uneasy nostalgia that no doubt reflected the general mood of escapism in the face of the inexorably rising barometer of inflation and so many economic and political gale warnings. What was truly remarkable in 1973 was the quantity and quality of the output of fiction: it was as if all the last decade's concerned debate about the state of the novel, and all the anxious increase in patronage through prizes and Arts Council grants, had suddenly begun to take effect —so much so that reviewers were actually to be found complaining in print about having to divide their attention among so many decent things. Of the score or so of British novelists with serious critical reputations, only two—William Golding and Anthony Burgess—failed to bring out a new work of fiction.

The great Bloomsbury revival subsided a little, its chief manifestation being *Portrait of a Marriage,* Nigel Nicolson's account, at once filially affectionate and totally unreticent, of the amorous and social eccentricities of his parents, Harold Nicolson and Vita Sackville-West. Apart from some embarrassment at the ardours of Vita's grandest passion (for Violet Trefusis), reviewers generally were not much put out by the details of a bisexuality which, after all, was only the general Bloomsbury sexual "style" raised to the nth degree. What did seem unnerving was the Nicolsons' bizarre social snobbery—what Frank Kermode called the "isolative cruelty" of class prejudice in a story in which "nobody outside the circle counts" (though "intellectuals were called 'souls' and accepted provided they 'have some breeding and a gun' ").

One of the year's gains was some refinement of the terms of the running debate about pornography and moral standards in contemporary literature generally. This came out of the discussion of Ian Robinson's *The Survival of English,* in which the author argued that the health of the language was the crucial index of the health of the culture, and attempted to demonstrate that in Britain in the 1970s both were chronically sick. Poets, theologians, and politicians, he concluded, were now unable to find language adequate to express the meanings of love for man, God, or country. Many critics thought his exercise in practical criticism on the language of *The New English Bible* particularly devastating, and approved the attack on a vulgar notion of Lord Longford and his new moral rearmers: the point being not that pornography *causes* depravity, but that pornography *is* depravity. His case against the language of modern politics and journalism was less secure. That this language was often evasive and manipulative was not in doubt. But here Robinson's own standards became vague and nostalgic. As *The Guardian's* reviewer pointed out: "There is an historic catastrophism working behind his argument, the assumption that change generally means decline, that lurks and is not fully stated." Nevertheless, Robinson's book seemed likely to improve the level of a difficult debate.

Fiction. It was the year in which Patrick White won the Nobel Prize and Graham Greene once more did not. Each produced new novels, neither of which much altered the more or less established view of their gifts, though White's *The Eye of the Storm* conveyed a sense of disgust with most of his characters and humanity in general that seemed disturbingly strong even for a novelist who had never been exactly optimistic about the human condition. With Graham Greene's *The Honorary Consul,* the characters, setting, and ambience seemed so familiar as to make one wonder for a moment whether it might not be a kind of self-parody. Spoiled priest, boozy English expatriate, enigmatic policeman, burnt-out case, all were on stage in the South American sector of Greeneland, grappling with God, sex, politics, and their variously crippled souls, and disclosed, as *The Times Literary Supplement* (*TLS*) reviewer said, "in a voice that after all these years has become as familiar as a hangover." But they develop formidably around the business of a political kidnapping (an event that makes one think more in terms of nature imitating art than of parody), and that inimitable voice articulates formidable arguments with God's ways to man, over the eternal dilemmas of love and honour, and (not at all incidentally) for the political relevance of the novelist's art. The book should be counted among its author's successes.

Patrick White's new novel, however, should not; and for all the recognition of his creative vitality and psychological penetration, this seemed to be the verdict. Partly it was the complaint, which had grown with his recent novels, that he had overreached his considerable talents. Paul Bailey, writing in the *Observer,* found that this story of a household devoured by a psychically voracious mother, now on her deathbed but refusing to die, "far from meriting comparisons with Tolstoy and Shakespeare, seems . . . to have more in common with a Visconti film. There is the same enormous accomplishment, the same operatic over-emphasis, the same constant straining after the Big Effect." Critics with more tolerance of or taste for White's baroque rhetoric felt that the weight of sheer misanthropy overbalanced *The Eye of the Storm* in a way that put it out of the class of such earlier achievements as *Voss* and *Riders in the Chariot.*

There were other disappointments. Richard Hughes's *The Wooden Shepherdess,* the second volume, awaited for over a decade, of a projected trilogy dealing with the world between the wars, failed to show the outline of a structure that could carry through the fascinating enterprise launched in *The Fox in the Attic.* It was a very English enterprise, seeking to illuminate the guilty innocence of the English political imagination, but creating images of that innocence with great tenderness. In this second installment there was again counterpointed with the sentimental education of the English hero vivid night-flashes from the other world, the world of Hitler's imagination that was meanwhile coming into being in Germany, but it became increasingly difficult to see how these insights and rich re-creations of historical moments were to be integrated into something artistically whole and coherent.

There were more problems with structure (and tone, and ear) in *As If by Magic,* in which Angus Wilson breathlessly conducted two converging moral pilgrimages through large tracts of the underdeveloped world. John Bayler, while admiring the energy, found that all this tearing about did "no good at all to the texture of the prose"; Martin Amis in the *New Statesman* thought much of the writing frankly scruffy, and sharply disposed of one possible interpretation of its form: "Nothing in *As If by Magic* is experimental—except for routine eng.-lit. coltishness and a periodic uncertainty as to what the hell's going on—yet one suspects Wilson is using the tag merely to widen his pitying smile should anyone be gauche enough to raise questions of motivation and probability." With David Storey's *A Temporary Life* the trouble seemed to be that the pressures, real or merely fashionable, that so many novelists now felt against writing in a way that might be called naturalistic had diverted his gifts of acute social and psychological awareness into allegorizing and obliquity: the result was impressive but wrong. There were regrets, too, that Kingsley Amis should be letting himself off so easily with a period-piece detective story like *The Riverside Villas Murder.*

In the spring Iris Murdoch and Muriel Spark produced novels as rich and strange as any of their earlier works. *The Black Prince* was not only the most complex set of sexual algebra Miss Murdoch had yet devised; it involved also an intricate debate on the nature of her fictions as well as a story of almost best-sellerish romance. Muriel Spark's *The Hothouse by the East River* was well described by Gabriel Pearson in his *Guardian* review: "a vision of damnation where the abruptly slain, like ghosts in some modern Noh drama, live out with decreasing solidity the hallucinations of their might-have-beens . . . a queer mirror where metaphor and fact chillingly reverse their relations." Susan Hill increased her growing reputation with a set of stories also much concerned with death (*A Bit of Singing and Dancing*), and in *The Summer Before the Dark* Doris Lessing traveled further down the Laingian path she had been treading in her last three novels, liberating a middle-aged housewife into self-doubt and setting her on the purgatorial way of self-discovery, dissolving a whole, apparently full life in one summer of crisis. Mrs. Lessing also produced an excellent sifted collection of her short stories, as did her fellow expatriate from southern Africa, Dan Jacobson (*Inklings*).

It was a year rich in fantasy, the most benign thing in this line being Michael Frayn's *Sweet Dreams,* which devised utopias fit for the very nicest ex-Cambridge trendies: intelligently funny and rather self-indulgent, like most of his novels. Maureen Duffy's *I Want to Go to Moscow,* with its very literary Cockney criminal blowing up animal research labs and liberating mink farms, was both more poetical and more robust.

The most whole-hogging fantast was the poet Peter Redgrove, whose *In the Country of the Skin* was a dissolving sequence of surrealist visions prompted by the author's experience of numerous insulin shock comas in late adolescence. Redgrove had developed a peculiarly English kind of surrealism and produced many images and pages of great beauty and mad logic. "I am the world telling its story to itself," one of his voices claimed; whether he communicated enough of his private world for the book to be placed in the tradition of the novel was less certain, even though Redgrove was awarded *The Guardian*'s 1973 fiction prize.

The Siege of Krishnapur, J. G. Farrell's appallingly vivid working up of an incident in the Indian Mutiny, was chosen for the 1973 Booker Prize for fiction. Another award winner was *Catholics,* Brian Moore's 1972 novella about an Irish last stand against a Rome of the near future whose church has been humanized literally beyond belief (W. H. Smith Prize). Piers Paul Read's *The Upstart,* Shiva Naipaul's *The Chip-Chip Gatherers,* and William Trevor's *Elizabeth Alone* all sustained their authors' reputations, and a new reputation was made with the very respectful reviews given to Beryl Bainbridge's *The Dressmaker,* a slice of wartime life in working-class Liverpool re-created with marvelous economy, accuracy, and atmospheric bloom. Two good first novels were *Stone,* Forbes

HUTCHINSON PUBLISHING GROUP

English poet Dannie Abse, whose controversial "Funland and Other Poems" was published in 1973.

Bramble's unsentimental account of a boyhood in the Scottish highlands, and Mark Ellis' myth-haunted account of a voyage up an African river, *Bannerman.* There was also a welcome for Sir Cecil Parrott's new and unexpurgated translation of Jaroslav Hasek's *The Good Soldier Svejk.* But the pleasure least alloyed, as so often in the last decade or so, came from the latest, the penultimate, installment of Anthony Powell's great novel sequence. *Temporary Kings* brought time and his large cast up to the late 1950s and into the television age, installed Widmerpool in the House of Lords as a life peer, and had as its memorable climax a great gathering of freeloading culture-vultures in Venice.

Biography, History, Letters. Politicians' and journalists' memoirs were thick as leaves in the autumn season. Most affectionate respect was paid to the final volume of Harold Macmillan's enormous set, *At the End of the Day,* and most attention to the second of Malcolm Muggeridge's *Chronicles of Wasted Time, The Infernal Grove.* "The best and most revealing of the lot," the *TLS* reviewer thought of Macmillan's last installment, which packed in the Cuban missile crisis, the Vassall and Profumo affairs and other domestic political mayhem, as well as insights into the major economic and social changes that were beginning to emerge in the Britain of the early 1960s. Wonderfully fluent and funny, like almost all his writing, Muggeridge's liberality with the acid evidently began to get on the critics' nerves as they read easily through his account of the end of the awful '30s in Geneva, Calcutta, and Fleet Street and of the pomposities and lunacies of the Ministry of Information and the secret service during World War II. "I have never found any difficulty in understanding how irritating I can be to other people" was characteristic and disarming, but not disarming enough. "A diet of constant denigration," wrote the well-disposed Arthur Marshall in the *New Statesman,* "ends by turning the stomach."

Two other senior journalists, Louis Heren of *The Times* in *Growing Up Poor in London* and J. D. Pringle, another old *Guardian* hand, in *Have Pen: Will Travel,* produced thoughtful, well-written, and less disapproving memoirs of their lives and work over something like the same period, while the evidence of Claud Cockburn's *The Devil's Decade* ought to have been an antidote to fashionable nostalgia for the '30s, but no doubt added to it instead. David Leitch's *God Stand Up for Bastards,* with its rudely candid sketches of Prince Philip, Nikita Khrushchev, and Lord Thompson, his former employer, was a highly enjoyable account of more recent work in the trade by a bright young practitioner. For the politicians, Leo Abse (*Private Member*) produced some amusing Freudian interpretations of British politics and its practitioners, and in *Journey into Silence* another Labour member of Parliament, Jack Ashley, described movingly how he coped with the total deafness that afflicted him soon after the promising start of his career in the House of Commons.

Lost leaders of both parties were the subjects of the two major political biographies of the year. Nigel Fisher's of the Tory *Iain Macleod,* who died in 1970, was a clear and accurate portrait of "the most intelligent member of the Stupid Party," as Michael Foot once saluted him. Foot's own final volume of his two-decker study of *Aneurin Bevan* was acclaimed variously as "a classic of historical literature" (David Marquand) and even as "the best political biography in the English language" (Hugh Delargy), although Marquand wondered if the author might not have resisted more firmly the temptation to make Bevan so absolutely a Bevanite.

It was an important year for Marxist studies in England, with David McLellan's biography of *Karl Marx,* the first full-scale study in English for nearly half a century, and the launching of the Marx Library with an excellent edition of the *Grundrisse* by Penguin, for some years now Britain's leading radical publishing house. Raymond Williams' *The Country and the City* was a substantial example of the English school of cultural criticism, outlining the whole history of a literary tradition central to the English imagination and commenting shrewdly on its political implications. Something closer to the continental tradition was to be found in an absorbing account of *Wittgenstein's Vienna* by Allan Janik and Stephen Toulmin. The most elegantly written and widely discussed work of sociology was *The Symmetrical Family,* by Michael Young and Peter Willmott, full of information on how the English middle-class way of life was changing and intelligent speculation about future change.

In historical studies the field was dominated by a massive two-volume study of how the Victorians lived during a period of great cultural change, *The Victorian City: Images and Realities,* edited by H. J. Dyos and Michael Wolff. Two of the more impressive biographical studies were Brian Inglis' of *Roger Casement* and Antonia Fraser's *Cromwell* which drew praise from Christopher Hill as "an admirable corrective to popular stereotypes of the killjoy Puritan, the ruthless dictator."

The most stimulating literary criticism was to be found in Donald Davie's *Thomas Hardy and British Poetry,* an odd but powerful attempt to alter the received view of the modern tradition of English poetry (Hardy, not Yeats, is the crucial progenitor), and Malcolm Bradbury's *Possibilities,* working toward a new poetics of the novel. Richard Ellmann's *Golden Codgers* was a set of biographical speculations—on the problems of biography in general and on particular problems posed by the interaction of "life-and-works" for students of Ruskin, Wilde, Gide, and the Eliots, both George and T. S.—while Brigid Brophy posed problems for her readers by writing *Prancing Novelist: . . . in Praise of Ronald Firbank* in a mode as idiosyncratic and dandified as Firbank's own. For his 70th birthday Cyril Connolly presented *The Evening Colonnade,* a collection of those sharply elegant essays and reviews that had occupied too much of his time since the end of his magazine *Horizon* and *The Unquiet Grave,* and Auden took his leave with a similar collection called *Forewords and Afterwords.* J. R. R. Tolkien left an unpublished work, "The Silmarillion." (W. L. WEBB)

Poetry. If 1973 was unremarkable for the discovery of any exceptional new talent, it certainly presented a large number of young and previously unknown writers with the opportunity of publishing their poetry, if only in booklet form. It was, however, distinctly noticeable that most of the new poets were introduced to the public by small presses devoted to poetry rather than by the firmly established publishing companies, which appeared to be unduly cautious in confining themselves to poets already on their lists.

The predominant tone, whatever the style adopted —and there was considerable variety in form and treatment—was one of pragmatic realism, throwing emphasis upon the virtues of frankness, forbearance, and healthy skepticism. Perhaps the poets were inclined to be a little too skeptical, and too conscious of their own limitations in the face of the complexities of modern life, to take strong positive lines or allow themselves free rein in articulating their deepest feelings. *Behind Heslington Hall* by Cal Clothier, for instance, was characterized by delicacy of approach and descriptive precision, but somehow skirted gently around the subjects without coming to grips with the basic material. In *Powers* Michael Fried left so much to the imagination of his readers that if he had been any more taciturn he might easily have relapsed into complete silence; as it was, his poem "Offshore" was limited to 12 words, all but one of them monosyllables. The same combination of delicacy and linguistic skill was to be discerned in Michael Schmidt's *It Was My Tree,* though this poet had the advantage of being able to draw upon a Mexican background, which added strength and colour to his work.

To Have Eyes by Geoffrey Holloway and *Walk Down a Welsh Wind* by Tony Curtis were impressive first collections. Despite his determination "not to sentimentalize the view," Holloway exhibited a natural tenderness in the pieces featuring members of his own family, giving his ironic sense of humour free play, and he wrote with vigour about the changing seasons, cricket, and people. Curtis, equally precise, concerned himself with personal experience caught in time, "then taken and held out of time to stand as statement, story, revelation, or picture." Perhaps the most intriguing of the new poets was Paul Muldoon, whose *New Weather* seemed to owe something, in choice of background, to the influence of Seamus Heaney without being in any way derivative. Muldoon demonstrated an individual outlook as well as a quite extraordinary capacity for changing the apparently casual into something cryptically menacing.

The established poets were well represented with volumes by Edwin Brock, Patric Dickinson, Geoffrey Grigson, Seamus Heaney, Thomas Kinsella, Brian Patten, Peter Redgrove, Anne Ridler, and many others. Although Martin Booth had published only one volume (but several booklets) prior to 1973, he had already earned himself a reputation as a poet of rich potentiality. His second volume, *Coronis,* containing his ambitious long poem "On the Death of Archdeacon Broix," confirmed the promise of his earlier work with its control of form and language and its adventurous approach to major themes. *Funland and Other Poems* by Dannie Abse aroused a good deal of controversy and not a little animosity. It was divided into two sections, the first largely a continuation of his previous genre, the second consisting of a sequence of nine poems, "Funland," using "the metaphor of a mental institution to develop a comic, but surrealistic and disturbing, view of the modern world," which some critics welcomed as a new development of significance. No doubt as a result of his return to England, D. J. Enright turned his attention from the Far East to produce, in *The Terrible Shears,* a series of autobiographical poems about his childhood and youth in Leamington in which he captured all its moods in an extremely amusing manner. Sydney Tremayne's *Selected and New Poems* provided clear evidence of this poet's descriptive gifts and his remarkable skill in the deployment of language and images.

The year was enlivened by some interesting anthologies, among which were *The Oxford Book of Twentieth-Century English Verse* chosen by Philip Larkin, *Poetry of the Committed Individual* edited by Jon Silkin, *London Between the Lines* compiled by John Bishop and Virginia Broadbent, and *African Voices* selected by Howard Sergeant. *The New Oxford Book of English Verse* edited by Helen Gardner finally appeared in 1972, replacing the Quiller-Couch revised selection of 1939. (HOWARD SERGEANT)

FRENCH

Fiction. The French Academy's Grand Prix du Roman was awarded to a classical writer of established reputation, Michel Déon, for *Un Taxi mauve,* a novel with a strong Irish flavour whose highly original and vividly portrayed characters and atmosphere of mystery were reminiscent of *Wuthering Heights.* The most widely praised of the year's novels was Christine de Rivoyre's *Boy,* which portrayed the adored son of a great Basque family as seen through the marveling eyes of his young niece and a parlourmaid. Abandoning the style and methods of the avant-garde, Suzanne Prou received the Prix Renaudot for a perfectly turned novel in the traditional form, *La Terrasse des Bernardini,* peopled with elderly provincials who seemed on the surface to be living out their lives in peace and tranquillity far from the mainstream of life —but only on the surface. The richest of the novels published during the year was, nevertheless, Paul Gadenne's posthumous masterpiece *Les Hauts-Quartiers,* which told the story of an intellectual of high moral principles forced to live a petty existence as a subtenant in various situations and to be more or less taken advantage of by just about everyone he meets. The author, who died in 1956, accomplished this excellent psychological dissection with an admirable economy of style and language. A similar theme was taken up by Guy Rohou, a writer with very much the same type of literary talent, in *Gris Tourterelle.*

The return to a more economical, polished style was also evident among a number of young writers. The tone of Philippe de Saint-Robert's *La Même Douleur démente,* for example, was close to that of Montherlant. In *Un Prince* Henry Bonnier portrayed a village community and the failure of the man who saw himself in the role of its ideal ruler. Didier Decoin's *Ceux qui vont s'aimer* was set in Athens under Roman rule,

A.F.P./PICTORIAL PARADE

Barricaded by piles of his autobiographical work "Souvenirs pour demain," French actor and director Jean-Louis Barrault accepts congratulations on award of the Prix Dagneau, in Paris, April 24, 1973.

while Simonne Jacquemard's erudite *La Thessalienne* drew its inspiration from Greece in the time of Alcibiades and Michel Dard's rich and masterly *Juan Maldonne,* which won the Prix Fémina, was set in Istanbul. François Clément's *Naissance d'une île* was rather like a latter-day *Robinson Crusoe,* while Bernard de Kerraoul chose Central America for *Le Temps de l'imposture* and, in *Les Nouveaux Territoires,* Jacques Lanzmann converted his hero to Zen and transported him to Asia.

Intellectuality gave way to more carnal preoccupations in Patrick Grainville's *La Lisière,* in which three couples, one a pair of adolescents, showed a veritable obsession with their own and others' bodies. The Prix Goncourt went to the Swiss writer Jacques Chessex for *L'Ogre,* which portrayed a son who had been stifled by his father to the point of committing suicide after the latter's death. There was also some fine writing to be found in a number of books inspired by the subject of childhood. Michel Bataille's *Les Jours meilleurs* captured the sadness of a bastard child with gentle humour. In Camille Bourniquel's *L'Enfant dans la cité des ombres* a druggist dabbles in spiritualism while his son wanders the ancient quarters of Paris, and in *Le Soleil du désert* André Dhôtel's youthful characters drift about as though in a dream. A kidnapping incident formed the basis of Joseph Majault's captivating *Virginie ou le premier matin du monde,* while Patrice du Boucher's *La Bande du Parc Monceau* was a terrifying documentary of completely corrupted and amoral adolescents.

The populist genre continued to find able practitioners with Clément Lépidis' *L'Arménien,* Jean-Marie Paupert's *Mère Angoisse,* René Fallet's sharply comic *Le Braconnier de Dieu,* and Raymond Jean's *La Ligne 12.* The action of Michèle Perrein's *Le Buveur de Garonne* stemmed from the provincial bourgeoisie, but it was clear that the author's sympathies lay with the common people and they remained the most successfully portrayed characters.

In *L'Été fracassé* Louis Gardel portrayed with tact and sensitivity the breakdown of a great French family in Algiers after the Algerian secession, while Anne Loesch's *La Grande Fugue* dealt with the same events in a far less restrained idiom. In *Les Bonheurs de la guerre* Roger Rabiniaux portrayed the book's main character at Vichy as both a politician and a modern Don Juan. The journalist Lucien Bodard published his first novel, *Monsieur le consul,* a vivid and compelling description of life in China, where he had been born, which won unanimously the Prix Interallié.

Other talented writers turned to the sphere of fairy tales and the supernatural. Works in this genre included J. de Bourbon-Busset's *Le Lion bat la campagne,* Maurice Pons's *Mademoiselle B.,* Jean Cayrol's *Histoire de la mer,* Jean Moal's *Les Grands Fonds,* and Jean Mistler's *Le Naufrage du Monte-Christo.* The last two were set in Britanny, as were Henri Queffélec's *La Cache éternelle* and *À fonds perdu.*

Works by foreign authors writing in French included a first novel, *Le Solitaire,* from the academician and dramatist Eugène Ionesco and two new novels, *Le Roi miracule* and *Mission terminée,* by the Cameroonian Mongo Beti. C. V. Gheorghiu's *L'œil américain* was a savage attack on the methods for progress set up in the less developed countries.

Claude Simon, the leading figure of the old avant-garde, showed even more virtuosity than previously in his *Triptyque,* while Michel Butor's *Intervalle* centred on the possibilities involved in a brief chance reunion of a man and a woman for a few hours. J.-M. Le Clezio's *Les Géants* was an impassioned indictment of the modern world, a torrent of words evoking the horrors of hell. *La Lettre au vieil homme* was an attempt by Dominique Rolin to psychoanalyze the feelings between parents and children, not without a certain amount of obscenity. Tony Duvert's *Paysage de fantaisie,* which gained the Prix Médicis, portrayed children in a sadomasochistic world rich in sexual images, while the subject of Monique Wittig's book was contained in its title, *Le Corps lesbien.* In a single uninterrupted stream of dialogue in which the speakers became confused with one another, Bernard Noël's *Les Premiers Mots* seemed to be attempting to find the reasons for the suicide of a painter, while Marcel Moreau adopted a similarly psychophysical but considerably less obscure approach in *L'ivre Livre,* which consisted of two separate texts: *Egobiographie tordue* and *Les Feux de l'ébriété.* These authors attracted a considerable amount of enthusiasm and attention from a certain number of critics while being largely ignored by others, including the public.

Best sellers in 1973 were Guy des Cars's *Le Donneur,* which made the best of a highly amusing idea, Jean Lartéguy's *Enquête sur un crucifié,* about Vietnam, Pierre Rey's *Le Grec,* which dealt with shipowners and other millionaires, and René Barjavel's *Le Grand Secret,* which postulated the existence of an elixir of eternal life.

Nonfiction. Topicality had become almost a sine qua non for the success of a book. The large number of visits to China by various heads of state had, thus, made the subject a potential gold mine, and there was no shortage of literature on the subject in 1973. Almost a dozen books were written about China in French alone, quite apart from translations of foreign works that appeared in France. Firmly established at the head of the list was government minister Alain Peyrefitte's best-selling *Quand la Chine s'éveillera.* In *La Médaille de sang* Serge Groussard provided a monumental and disturbing minute-by-minute account of the events and the persons involved in the massacre of the Israeli athletes at the Munich Olympics.

L'Histoire secrète des Français à Londres de 1940 à 1944 by André Gillois recalled the lives and activities of those who worked with Charles de Gaulle in London for the French resistance movement under difficult conditions in World War II, while Roger Bruge's *Faites sauter la ligne Maginot* provided a meticulous, impressively documented account of the troubled history of that fortification from 1925 onward and rehabilitated the reputation of the French forces involved.

Considerable enthusiasm was evident among editors and readers for works dealing with the periods before, during, and after the French Revolution. One of the best of these was Claude Manceron's *Les Vingt Ans du roi,* a vivid portrait of Louis XVI and other figures whose activities or attitudes influenced the events of 1789.

The worldwide reputation enjoyed by French cookery was also well looked after by a number of writers. André Castelot's *L'Histoire à table* provided a wealth of anecdotes and recipes to delight both the gastronomic and the literary palate, while Jean-Paul Aron's *Le Mangeur du XIXème siècle* gave an account of eating places, both exalted and unpretentious, that survived the vicissitudes of wars and revolutions. Another tempting publication in the culinary sphere was James de Coquet's *L'Appétit vient en lisant.* Meanwhile, following the removal of the famous central market of Paris, a fascinating and well-researched history of the quarter was provided by R. Héron de Villefosse in his study *Les Halles de Lutèce à Rungis.*

Joel Schmidt provided a compelling study of the social, political, and economic role of slaves in ancient Rome with *Vie et mort des esclaves,* while Georges Duby of the Collège de France provided two further works in the new historical method in which sociological and economic factors loom larger than single famous individuals or events, *Le Dimanche de Bouvines* and *Hommes et structures du Moyen-Age.*

One of the year's most notable biographies was Paul Guth's *Mazarin,* in which the petulance of the hero's character was extremely well portrayed despite allegations of overindulgence by some critics. In a more mystical vein was Gérard Mourgue's *François d'Assise, Poète de la sainteté,* while Maurice Toesca's *Alfred de Vigny ou la passion de l'honneur* was a slightly romanticized but nevertheless faithful study of the tortured life of the poet.

André Malraux had already become the French writer subjected to the largest number of studies during his own lifetime, and 1973 brought further contributions. Following upon the excellent biography by R. Payne, translated from the English, Jean Lacouture's *André Malraux* succeeded with admirable virtuosity and irony in linking the subject's political and literary actions. *Ce que je sais de Soljenitsyne* by Pierre Daix was a study of the works of Soviet novelist Aleksandr Solzhenitsyn and a plea for the individual that brought its Communist author the opprobrium of his party.

Two other much praised works were *Monsieur Proust* by Céleste Albaret, who had been the great writer's servant for eight years, and *Les Cahiers de la petite dame* by Maria Van Rysselberghe, a remarkable day-to-day journal written while she was living in close contact with André Gide. Marcel Arland's *Proche du silence* told in limpid prose of important moments in his life and his relations with great writers, while Gabriel Delauney's reflections in *Le Piéton des nuages* showed both wisdom and boldness. *Questions à la littérature* by Jean-Louis Curtis was a brilliant satire on the avant-garde and literary fashions, and Robert Kanters' *L'Air des lettres* surveyed the whole contemporary literary universe with a not unhumorous eye. Pierre de Boisdeffre's *Les Écrivains de la nuit* provided a very thorough study on Baudelaire, Kierkegaard, Montherlant, and others. Henri Guillemin's *Précisions* showed the author's usual forthright and stimulating manner, although in his treatment of the 17th to 19th centuries he seemed at times more concerned with his own pet hates than with historical objectivity. Jean Bernard's *Grandeur et tentations de la médecine* had considerable success with both critics and the public despite its serious topic. A posthumous work by Henry de Montherlant, to whom Jean Dutourd dedicated his pungent and witty *Carnet d'un émigré,* entitled *Mais aimons nous ceux que nous aimons?,* provided an account of the great man's youthful love life.

Three works found particular favour with the general public for their wit and the savageness of some of their attacks: *À Pleines Dents,* in which J. Luis de Vilallonga spared neither himself nor the great ones of this world; Philippe Bouvard's *Un Oursin dans le caviar,* which subjected the vedettes of Paris to the same treatment; and *Ces Messieurs du Canard,* in which Jean Egen recalled some of the attacks of the famous French satirical journal *Le Canard enchaîné* on the political figures of the century.

Poetry. Very little poetry would see the light of day at all but for the magazines that exist specifically for the purpose, some of them ephemeral, others more lasting, such as *Points et Contrepoints, Betelgeuse, Les Cahiers du Soleil,* and the more recent *Formes et Langage.*

The year's poetic output included Georges-Emmanuel Clancier's melancholy but unsentimental *Peut-Être une demeure,* Philippe Soupault's bold yet lyrical *Poèmes et poésies,* and François Pradelle's *Les Naïves Amours,* which recalled the flavour of the medieval pastoral. In Jean Loisy's *Le Double Jeu,* dominated by an atmosphere of metaphysical doubt, the poet took up each of his poems in prose and proved captivating in both media. Katia Granoff's *Méditerranée* was enriched by magnificent illustrations to a text that abounded in themes of art and history. A sense of mystery pervaded Pierrette Sartin's *Le Destin accepté.* Among the extremely avant-garde of the "Tel Quel" group, Denis Roche's *Le Mécrit* was hermetic to the point of being accessible only to initiates, while Michel Deguy's *Tombeau de Du Bellay* was not a study of the Pléiade poet but a play of images around memories.

Given the scarcity of readers, prizes were the poet's consolation. The Max Jacob went to Hubert Juin for *Le Cinquième Poème,* the Guillaume Apollinaire to Marc Alyn, the French Academy's Grand Prix to André Frénaud, and the Grand Aigle d'Or to Eugène Guillevic.

Deaths during the year included those of Alexandre Arnoux, Roland Dorgelès, the philosopher Jacques Maritain, Gabriel Marcel, and academician Vladimir d'Ormesson (*see* OBITUARIES). His nephew Jean d'Ormesson, dramatist André Roussin, and anthropologist Claude Lévi-Strauss were elected to the Academy in 1973. (ANNIE BRIERRE)

GERMAN

West German, Austrian, and Swiss. The shift from fiction to the documentary novel continued. Manfred Franke's *Mordverläufe* was a montage of documents on the pogrom of Nov. 9–10, 1938, in a small industrial town that united the impressions of an eight-year-old boy with historical evidence to produce a terrifying portrait of prejudice. More privately, Peter Härtling's *Zwettl* juxtaposed the author's experiences during 1945–46 with what actually happened. Lothar-Günther Buchheim's popular *Das Boot* was a tremendously gripping autobiographical account of a submarine expedition of 1941. Making no concessions to ideology, it punctuated minute descriptions of daily routine with vivid evocations of helplessness in a storm and under attack.

More apparently literary were substantial novels by Wolfgang Hildesheimer (*Masante*) and Walter Höllerer (*Die Elephantenuhr*), although both almost completely eschewed a story basis. *Masante* found its narrator in an isolated inn at the edge of the desert looking for "a story which would be worth telling." It consisted of countless, often fragmentary anecdotes, told with Hildesheimer's characteristic blend of melancholy and humour. *Die Elephantenuhr*, too, was a novel about the impossibility of writing a novel. Only Thomas Mann ever quite succeeded in merging the cerebral and the narrative form; Höllerer's novel remained abstract and forgettable, although doubtless much would be written on it. Gerold Späth had no qualms about novel-writing. *Stimmgänge* was a picaresque novel about an organ maker. It revealed a fertile imagination and, especially, a virtuoso control of language—but also a complete lack of thought.

Writers who managed to reconcile ideas and a story were Siegfried Lenz, in his best-selling *Das Vorbild*, and Martin Walser, in the final part of his Anselm Kristlein trilogy, *Der Sturz*. The former, highly competent in its construction but marred by an inappropriate narrative standpoint, provided fascinating vignettes of contemporary German society. *Der Sturz* was a more depressing affair in which middle-class society at the end of its tether is forced by the need to "earn money" into ever more degrading postures. Almost all of the Kristleins' acquaintances are killed or commit suicide. The family is disintegrating. Only a revolution might help, but this remained a vague implication.

All these novels were exclusively bourgeois. Even Walser did not present more than a caricature of the working classes. Simultaneously, however, there appeared a rash of politico-social novels in which the everyday lives of industrial workers were presented in straightforward, realistic detail. Most notable was Max von der Grün's *Stellenweise Glatteis*, an account of a strike over the "bugging" of workers' conversations and the failure of the trade union to support its members. Here, refreshingly, were the "real" problems of West German society. Michael Scharang's more limited *Charly Traktor* described in simple and convincing language a semiskilled worker's inarticulate struggle against exploitation. More "modernist" in technique was Wolfgang Hermann Körner's *Katt im Glück*. A study in alienation, it showed Katt wandering aimlessly through Berlin until he joins a strike over a dismissed secretary and, at last, finds his identity. Christine Spöcker's play *Das Geldmensch* showed the rise and fall of Adele Spitzeder, whose bank ruined thousands of investors when it crashed in 1872. Clearly influenced by Peter Weiss, its jingly verses gained from the remarkable concreteness of their Bavarian dialect.

Siegfried Lenz, best-selling West German novelist, published "Das Vorbild" in 1973.

HOFFMANN & CAMPE VERLAG

Notable collections of short stories were Eva Zeller's *Der Turmbau*, which included an unforgettable confrontation of a progressive liberal housewife with an asocial unmarried mother ("Wer ist das Opfer von wem?"), and Jürg Federspiel's absurdist *Paratuga kehrt zurück*.

The usual crop of light novels included Johannes Maria Simmel's inevitably best-selling *Die Antwort kennt nur der Wind*, Oliver Hassenkamp's *Erkenntnisse eines etablierten Herrn*, and Gudrun Pausewang's *Aufstief und Untergang der Insel Delfina*. More interesting were Fanny Morweiser's *La vie en rose*, an English type of thriller with grotesque characters and misty settings, and Ulf Miehe's *Ich hab noch einen Toten in Berlin*, an exciting story of armed robbery with some splendid evocations of the seedier parts of Berlin. Walter Vogt's *Der Wiesbadener Kongress* was a tedious satire on hospital doctors. More thought-provoking was Walter R. Fuch's *Der Hundeplanet*, a science-fiction novel that raised interesting questions of language and intelligence and the probable outcome of any discovery of extraterrestrial civilizations.

Important collections of poems were Peter Huchel's *Gezählte Tage*, Marie Luise Kaschnitz' *Kein Zauberspruch*, and Erich Fried's *Die Freiheit den Mund aufzumachen*. Günter Herburger's *Operette* was disappointing, the programmatic simplicity of his diction merely underlining the banality of his themes. More interesting were the aphoristic poems of J. P. Stössel's *Friedenserklärung* on the absurdity and inhumanity of Western society.

Belles lettres were represented by Peter Bamm's best-selling reminiscences, *Eines Menschen Zeit*, Hans Habe's *Erfahrungen*, and Friedrich Dürrenmatt's *Dramaturgisches und Kritisches*. Important posthumous works included Carl Einstein's *Die Fabrikation der Fiktionen*, Heimito von Doderer's *Divertimenti*, and above all Bertolt Brecht's *Arbeitsjournal 1938–1955*.

East German. A new generation of writers seemed to be emerging, one that took its country and political system for granted and could, therefore, write about its own reality without having to justify itself either to the party or to the West. A corresponding relaxation on the part of the authorities was apparent. Helga Schütz consolidated her reputation with a collection of short stories, *Das Erdbeben bei Sangerhausen*. The most notable publication, however, was Ulrich Plenzdorf's *Die neuen Leiden des jungen W.* Written with great verve in the jargon of the "pop generation," it described the brief career of a young hippie who, like Goethe's Werther, comes to grief as much through his own inadequacies as through society's—there is no suggestion that the capitalist West would have been preferable. Jurek Becker's *Irreführung der Behörden* was more conventionally written. The story of a writer who owes his success to his increasing readiness to conform, it presented no facile solution to the tension between "authorities" and individual.

In this it differed markedly from more traditional works like Margarete Neumann's *Der grüne Salon,* which portrayed in terms reminiscent of Adalbert Stifter the programmatic submission of the eccentric to the collective. In the second part of Erwin Strittmatter's *Der Wundertäter* (Part I appeared in 1957), the picaresque hero Stanislaus passes through various sections of postwar society until he learns to appreciate proletarian life. Filled at times with platitudinous observations on art and life, it was, nevertheless, more relaxed and ironic about its hero's development than one might have expected. Anna Seghers' three stories in *Sonderbare Begegnungen,* on the other hand, were disappointing, notable mainly for an attack on Franz Kafka in the third. An important autobiography from the older generation was *Memoiren* by the political scientist Jürgen Kuczinski, with its revealing subtitle, "J.K.'s education to a Communist and scientist."

Finally, a reminder that all was not yet relaxed in the East. Wolf Biermann published *Für meine Genossen,* a collection of political poems and songs, and *Deutschland: ein Wintermärchen,* a long satirical poem on divided Germany. Biermann, a Communist living in East Germany, could still publish only in the West. (J. H. REID)

ITALIAN

Literary awards sometimes seem to be justified more by an author's earlier work than by his latest book. This was perhaps true in the case of Carlo Sgorlon, whose novel *Il trono di legno* won the 1973 Campiello Prize. Sgorlon was no realist; nevertheless, the dream world described in his earlier books was just as convincing as a real-life experience. His latest novel had a less dreamlike content, being about a young man's search for his own origins and identity. The story, however, unfolded in the fabulous atmosphere of some remote northern Italian villages, which the precise references to real places and events in the rest of the world conspired to make even more fabulous and remote. The novel was like a naif painting: in the very fact that it somehow failed to be a credible representation of life lay its subtle and captivating charm. The only way in which a book can come to life, be it realistic or not, is by stimulating and enlivening the reader's imagination. This was certainly true of Italo Calvino's *Le città invisibili.* On the surface it looked like a further step away from his early realistic beginnings; yet the emblematic quality of his descriptions of nonexistent towns and the poetic powers of his style endowed the book with a depth of vision far beyond that of his previous stories. Another remarkable novel was Giorgio Saviane's *Il mare verticale,* a summing-up of the whole spiritual and cultural development of mankind as if it were experienced by a single protagonist moving backward and forward from prehistory to the present day. For such a dauntingly ambitious project it was quite successful, lacking neither intellectual substance nor a strong narrative rhythm.

It was a vintage year for established writers. Whatever one might think of Carlo Cassola's *Monte Mario,* it was certainly a best seller. *Pavana* confirmed Franco Cordero's reputation as a subtle and merciless investigator of human corruption. Like many a writer with a Roman Catholic background, Cordero was fascinated by evil; but unlike a true religious moralist he did not find its roots so much in individual consciences as in the whole warped structure of social relationships. Natalia Ginzburg's latest novel (*Caro Michele*) and comedies (*Paese di mare*) dealt perceptively and often movingly with men's inability to relate to each other, but in a rather lighthearted vein in which wit and slickness were achieved at the expense of depth and characterization. Leonardo Sciascia's crisp and terse stories *Il mare colore del vino,* containing some biting indictments of the Sicilian way of life, marked a welcome change from the vague and noncommittal tone of his most recent novel (*Il contesto,* 1971). *Sulla soglia* by Gianna Manzini and *Amore e Psiche* by Raffaele La Capria, on the other hand, made many concessions to woolliness and obscurity, as if they were indispensable ingredients of self-analysis and introspection. From her early unsentimental observation of the mother-son relationship, Lalla Romano moved on to an oversentimentalized view of the grandmother-grandson relationship; *L'ospite* was a piece of fawning baby worship in the worst Italian tradition.

Among the newcomers to literature, Armando Tagliavento gave, in *Tra fascisti e germanesi,* a powerful evocation of the last violent weeks of World War II in Italy, and in *La marchesa e i demoni* Maria Luisa Marsigli painted a terrifying picture of an Italian mental hospital, confirming one's worst suspicions that the use of psychiatry as an instrument of repression extended also to the so-called free world. Music critic Luigi Magnani wrote an interesting reconstruction of Beethoven's personality seen through an imaginary diary by his unruly nephew (*Il nipote di Beethoven*).

In *A quale tribù appartieni?* Alberto Moravia collected various essays on Africa written over the previous decade. His cold objectivity occasionally reflected a certain lack of sympathy and understanding. Hazy general assumptions about "Black Africa" were often used as a basis for particular assertions that, therefore, did not carry sufficient conviction. Of course, generalizations are unavoidable in books of this kind, but they should be the end and not the methodological framework of analysis, a point well taken by Umberto Eco in his collection of articles *Il costume di casa,* which would undoubtedly be welcomed by all students of Italian culture and society.

For those wishing to keep up with contemporary Italian poetry there was the *Almanacco dello Specchio.* The first two issues (for 1972 and 1973) included, together with many interesting translations of non-Italian poets, much original work by Vittorio Sereni, Bartolo Cattafi, Claudio Villa, Alessandro Peregalli, Paolo Universo, Cesare Garboli, Domenico Naldini, Ferdinando Camon, and Luciano Marrucci, to mention but a few. In *Questo muro* Franco Fortini collected poems written between 1962 and 1972; his usual vigour appeared tempered by a hint of pessimism and disillusionment. A similar mood also pervaded parts of Pier Paolo Pasolini's *Trasumanar e organizzar,* which contained many works smacking more of ideological manifestos than of poems. Although *Scem-*

pio e lusinga by Libero De Libero followed *Di brace in brace* (1971), it was in fact a collection of earlier poems written between 1930 and 1956 in which the echoes of Italian hermetic tradition blended well with the rural images of his native Ciociaria. After a lifetime of prose-writing Marino Moretti turned once more to poetry; literary historians would find it interesting to compare his most recent poems, *Le poverazze,* with the verse he published about half a century before. (GIOVANNI CARSANIGA)

JAPANESE

Monthly magazines continued to play their remarkable role in the Japanese literary scene, with no less than five important ones wholly devoted to serious literature in 1973. These high-quality commercial monthlies contained criticism, poetry, and serialized novels, but their main emphasis was on short stories. Another remarkable feature was the *bungei-jihyo,* or monthly literary survey of short stories in the newspapers, which provided sensitive appreciation and critical evaluation. These facts proved that the short story was not at all a lost art in Japan. In addition, one of the important rituals for *Bungeika-kyokai* (Japan Society of Writers) was the publication of annual anthologies, usually containing more than 20 "best short stories." The current anthology, misleadingly titled *Literature in 1973* (not 1972), included contributions to this subtle and sensitive art by Tatsuo Nagai, Junnosuke Yoshiyuki, Tan Konuma, Tsundeko Nakasato, and Taeko Tomioka, all of whom showed that they were the literary descendants of the traditional haiku and tanka poets. This tradition of sensibility and craftsmanship was also true of Komao Furuyama, winner of the Akutagawa Prize of 1970, whose novelette *Chisana Shigai-zu* ("A Small Map of the Town") was remarkable for the curious but effective mixture of the narrator-hero's nostalgic attachment to his lost home in Korea and his detached, almost ironic attitude toward the collapse of the Japanese empire that was the cause of his loss.

Two historical novels, *Goshirakawain* ("The Ex-emperor Goshirakawa") by Yasushi Inoue, a senior writer, and *Haikyosha Yurianusu* ("Julian the Apostate") by Kunio Tsuji, a young author, made an interesting pair, in both technique and setting. The former consisted of four objective eyewitness reports on the central character, while the latter was remarkable for its broad historical perspective and colourful evocative description. There were three impressive novels with contemporary settings, all by women novelists. Chiyo Uno's *Aru Hitori no Onna no Hanashi* ("The Story of a Woman") was autobiographical and closely related to the "poetic diary" genre initiated by the court ladies of the 11th century. Ineko Sata's *Juei* ("Shadow of Trees") had a sociopolitical theme and was set in Nagasaki. Taeko Kono's *Somu* ("Double Dreams") was an avant-garde tour de force of erotic fantasy that could not be acclaimed as wholly successful but was curiously effective.

Notable works of literary criticism and biography were *Watakushi no Sakka Hyoden* ("Literary Biographies") by Nobuo Kojima, *Mori, Ogai* by Masakazu Yamazaki, *Uno Koji* by Tsutomu Minakami, and *Tanizaki Junichiro* by Shogo Nomura. The sensational best sellers of the year were Sawako Ariyoshi's novel *Kokotsu no Hito* ("Man of Infatuation") and Sakyo Komatsu's *Nippon Chinbotsu* ("Submersion of Japan"), which depicted Japan's final sinking under the sea. (SHOICHI SAEKI)

JEWISH

Hebrew. Hebrew literature again showed vigour in most genres, as it had for the 25 years since the establishment of Israel. During the year death came to A. Shlonsky, a pioneering modernist poet, and to the formidable dean of Hebrew novelists, H. Hazaz, whose *Even ha-Shaot* was his last work. Also during the year Nobel laureate S. Y. Agnon's posthumous volume *Ir Umeloah* appeared. The prolific A. Megged published a novel, *Mahbarot Avitar,* and a collection of stories, *Hazot ha-Yom. Ke-Ishon ha-Ayin* was A. Applefeld's novel on the estrangement problem of the Jew, while R. Ben-Yosef, a young U.S. author, contributed a novelette on "finding oneself," *ha-Derech Hazara.* Another young storyteller's volume was *Logaat ba-Mayim Logaat ba-Ruach* by A. Oz. Two volumes of short stories were *Merkava Lailit* by I. Yoaz-Kast and *Ir Sheain bah Mistor* by Y. Orpaz. B. Tamuz' distinctive collection *Angoxil* appeared, as did D. Zalka's sensitively drawn *Etz Habasun.* A novel attracting some attention was *ha-Isha Hagdola min ha-Hahalomot* by Y. Kenaz.

An important scholarly event was the publication of a new translation from the Arabic by Y. Ibn Shmuel of Yehuda Halevi's seminal work *Sefer Hakuzari.* Of significance was the late B. Z. Dinur's new volume of monumental documentary history of the Jews in the Diaspora, *Yisrael ba-Golah. Ha-Mahazot shel M. H. Luzzatto* was Y. David's comparative study of the dramas of the "father of modern Hebrew literature." Coincidentally, the first volume of A. Ashman's collected plays, *Mahazot,* reintroduced a pioneer playwright. Critical and timely essays were *Dapai Pinkas* by Sh. Zemach and D. Sdan's *Pulmus ve-Shaveh Pulmus.* Indirectly related were two volumes of a series edited by A. D. Shapir on the writings of the veteran critic D. Frishman and of former Israeli Pres. Z. Shazar. I. Cohen's exhaustive monograph *Y. Steinberg: ha-Ish ve-Yezirato* dealt with a forerunner of modern Hebrew poetry, while the poet S. Halkin was honoured with a volume of studies on his 75th birthday.

More or less contemporary in concept were A. Gilboa's poems *Ayalah Eshlach Otha* and D. Rabikovich's *Kol Mishbareha ve-Galeha.* A selection of the religiously imbued poems by the late Y. Z. Rimon, *Shirim,* edited by Z. Luz, appeared, as did *Kol Shirai Y. Lamdan,* the complete writings of a foremost "national" Hebrew poet. H. Lenski was represented by a selection, *Yalkut Shirim,* and Y. Bat-Miriam by a distinguished volume, *Bain Chol ve-Shemesh.* R. Adi's *Emor Pelayim* was linguistically interesting. The only books by American Hebrew authors were *ha-Meziut ha-Aheret,* a second volume of disquisitions by the recently deceased poet A. Zeitlin, and G. Preil's collected poems in a mainly contemporary vein, *Mitoch Zeman ve-Nof,* both published in Israel. (GABRIEL PREIL)

Yiddish. Immigration of readers and writers from the U.S.S.R. and elsewhere in 1973 enhanced Israel's role as a centre of Yiddish literature, and an expansion of printing facilities enabled Tel Aviv to outrank New York in the number of Yiddish titles published during 1972. The most important event was Max Weinreich's posthumous *History of the Yiddish Language* in four volumes, published in New York by the Yivo Institute for Jewish Research, which Weinreich had co-founded. Other works published posthumously included Abraham Joshua Heschel's two-volume *Kotzk, In the Struggle for Truthfulness* and

Abraham Menes' collection of essays *Sabbath and Holidays, Self-Search and Redemption During the Jewish Year.* While Eliyahu Lippiner depicted in *Marranos and Apostasy* the trials and tribulations of Jews in Portugal during the Middle Ages and of early Jewish settlers in Brazil, modern times were dealt with in Vladimir Grossman's *World-Jewry and World-Politics (1914–1973)* and in Paul L. Goldman's *In Step with the Times.* Books of personal reminiscences were numerous and included historian N. Blumenthal's *Retrospects,* M. Pulover's *Arrarat, Types of Lodz and Yard Singers,* Lifshe Schechter-Widman's *A Full Life,* S. Shichatov's *Years of Battle and Struggle,* M. Tabachnik's *Rungs on the Road of My Life,* and S. Tennenbaum's *In the Kaiser's Winery.*

The 25th anniversary of Israel's independence was marked by several anthologies, among them J. Papiernikov's *Jerusalem in Yiddish Song; Almanac of Yiddish Writers in Jerusalem,* edited by Joseph Kerler; and S. Rollansky's *In a Land of Your Own.* A general anthology of Yiddish prose and poetry was Joseph Kage's *We Are Here,* printed in Montreal. Herz Grossbard compiled a selection of the writings of humourist and poet Moshe Nadir.

In fiction there were more collections of short stories than full novels. Of particular interest were S. Apter's *When the Kuntzenmacher Will Come,* the third and fourth volumes of B. Demblin's *A Strange World,* A. Karpinowitz' *A Day of War,* Joseph Okrutni's *Deaf Territory,* L. Olitzky's *Vohlynian Jews,* Joel Perel's *The Morningstar Shines Again,* David Rodin's *A Curious Girl from Brooklyn,* Yekhiel Schreibman's *Days and Moments,* and Isaiah Spiegel's *The Crown.*

Essays and literary criticisms were few in quantity but important in quality. Isaac Goldkorn's *Literary Etudes* presented 32 essays on Yiddish and other writers, and Rivkah Kopeh's *Intimate with the Book* dealt with authors of various eras and schools. Two previously unpublished works of the late critic Samuel Niger were the second volume of *Yiddish Writers of the 20th Century* and *From My Diary.* The greatest accomplishment in the field of translation came from Montreal, where S. Dunsky's annotated translation of *Midrash Rabba Shir Hashirim* appeared.

(MOSHE STARKMAN)

LATIN-AMERICAN

Only in the dark times of the 19th century was the Latin-American reality so little conducive to literature as in 1973. In varying degrees throughout the continent the increasing power of the military, terrorism, censorship, inflation, and paper shortages limited editorial plans and reduced the size of the reading public. Never in recent times had Latin America been so isolated or had it been so difficult in one country to acquire books published in a neighbouring one.

All these problems appeared minor compared with what occurred in Chile, where the vast majority of the writers had taken part in the programs of Pres. Salvador Allende, and where in two years the state publishing house, Quimantu, had published five million books. The coup of Sept. 11, 1973, marked the end of the cultural life; many writers unable to seek political asylum were apprehended and tortured. Pablo Neruda, the foremost poet of the language, left upon his death seven unpublished books and one volume of memoirs; his last work, *Incitación al nixonicidio y alabanza de la revolución chilena,* presents, in tercets of great combative efficacy, a poetic testimony of the Allende years. *Poesía joven de Chile,* edited by Jaime Quezada, showed that the new poets had not committed aberrations of socialist realism but had, nevertheless, participated in the daily debate. A vision of the forces that opposed change was found in *Tres novelitas burguesas* by José Donoso. The liveliest reflections of the tensions in private life were found in Antonio Skármeta's short stories, *Tiro libre.*

Naturally, soldiers and guerrillas were the main characters of the Latin-American novels of 1973, among which might be included *The Honorary Consul,* in which English novelist Graham Greene almost gave the scenario of a kidnapping that took place in Mexico a few days after his book was published. A delirious, stereotyped version of the theme was *El secuestro del general* by Demetrio Aguilera Malta, an Ecuadorean who acquired fame in the '30s for his novels of denunciation.

Of much more literary importance was *El libro de Manuel,* even though in it Julio Cortázar did not surpass *Hopscotch* or his admirable stories. A group of Argentines in Paris kidnap an international agent and two of them compile an album of news clippings of insurrection and repression so that when their newborn son Manuel grows up he will have a mirror of their horrible world. Cortázar experiments with changing points of view and with a new prose that is anti-academic as well as colloquial and poetic. If in his last poems Neruda fought rightists and ultraleftists equally, Cortázar sincerely supports the overthrow of the established order, but expresses his fear of "the ants of the good side, the fascists of the revolution."

Gabriel García Márquez donated the $10,000 Books Abroad Prize to the political prisoners of his country, Colombia. He announced he would no longer write novels because *One Hundred Years of Solitude* had taken him 10 years and he had already spent 15 preparing an imaginary biography that was expected to be published in 1974. Jorge Luis Borges won Mexico's Alfonso Reyes Prize and published only one book, in English, *Borges on Writing,* edited by N. T. di Giovanni and others. His friend and collaborator Adolfo Bioy Cesares was celebrated in French criticism as a modern *maître du fantastique* and confirmed his title with an uncommon novel, *Morir al sol.*

In the best Latin-American novel of 1973, *Pantaleón y las visitadoras,* there are two intertwined stories, one of a self-proclaimed saint who announces the end of the world and wishes to save souls through crucifixions, and another of a captain to whom the Peruvian Army entrusts the mission of inducting a group of prostitutes (the *visitadoras*) to prevent the rape of native women by soldiers stationed in the Amazon jungle. All this was told by Mario Vargas Llosa through humorous military dispatches, bureaucratic notes, letters, radio programs, sermons, and news, presented with the greatest seriousness and objectivity. Humour, a new element in Vargas Llosa, made this brutal criticism of the establishment more poignant. The *tristes tropiques* never appeared so sad as in this novel.

The Buenos Aires Affair (original title) was Manuel Puig's third novel and, along with *Betrayed by Rita Hayworth* and *Heartbreak Tango,* was acquiring a wide audience in English. Puig once again succeeded in what appeared impossible, the marriage of the experimental novel and popular literature.

The great Uruguayan novelist Juan Carlos Onetti made a brief addition to the saga of Santa María, his imaginary city that was in reality both Montevideo and the world, in *La novia robada*. Increasing recognition of Onetti, after years of disregard, was found in a volume of essays, *Onetti,* edited by Jorge Rufinelli. The most noteworthy first novel was *Los hijos del orden,* whose author, Luis Urteaga Cabrera, was introduced in the excellent anthology *Narrativa peruana* compiled by Abelardo Oquendo. Cabrera described with great force the rebellion in a prison for juveniles. The theme of child imprisonment also appears in *Un oscuro día de justicia* by the Argentine Rodolfo Walsh. Confrontation between conservatives and liberals in Mexican Catholicism gave rise to *Redíl de ovejas* by Vicente Leñero. The hellish opposites of Acapulco appear in *Se está haciendo tarde* by José Agustín. The Mexican Revolution's death was symbolized by Agustín Yáñez in *Las vueltas del tiempo.*

The brightest Spanish-American poetry in 1973 came from Colombia: *Summa de Magroll el Gaviero,* written by Alvaro Mutis since 1948 and portraying a world of corruption and death where the only light emerges from the enjoyment of words. Mutis turned from poems in prose to the poetrylike stories of *La mansión de Araucaíma.* Equally worthy of attention for what they did and promised were the 20-year-old Peruvians whom José Miguel Oviedo presented in *Estos trece.* Ernesto Cardenal personalized Ezra Pound's style to write the *Canto nacional* of his tragic Nicaragua. Poetry of note in Uruguay included Ulalume González de León's *Plagio* and Enrique Fierro's *Mutaciones.* In Mexico poets José Emilio Pacheco and Gabriel Zaid, who presented *Irás y no volverás* and *Práctica mortal,* respectively, also edited the most important Mexican book of the year: *El otoño recorre las islas,* the poetic works of José Carlos Becerra from 1961 to 1970. Octavio Paz wrote the prologue to the Becerra volume and added *Veinte poemas* by William Carlos Williams to Spanish poetry. He attracted a great deal of attention with the publication in English of *Alternating Current* and *The Other Mexico,* while three works in Spanish confirmed him as an author of brilliant and transparent prose.

With the publication of the collective volume *América Latina en su literatura,* edited by César Fernández Moreno, the Latin-American complaint of the lack of critical works was partially dispelled. At least a dozen other critical works were published, including *Cómo leer a Vallejo* by the Peruvian Alberto Escobar, *Función de la novela* by the Cuban Julieta Campos, and *Mito y poesía* and *Contracorrientes* by two Spanish-born Mexicans, Ramón Xirau and Tomás Segovia.

The publishing industry would do well to give some thought to Gabriel Zaid's invective against the bibliographic explosion in *Los demasiados libros.* Demonstrations of the technological superiority of books over newer media and technical treatises on other aspects of reading are concluded with a biblical warning to authors: "[Your book] is cellulose and unto cellulose it will return." (SALVADOR BARROS)

Brazilian. The most effective book published in Brazil in 1973 was Afonso Arinos de Melo Franco's historical study of the life and administration of Pres. Rodrigues Alves and of the First Republic and its link to the empire. Outstanding in the field of poetry was *Manino Antigo,* in which Carlos Drummond de Andrade gave continuity to *Boitempo.* Amorous poetry succeeded the epic poetry of *Anga* in Carlos Nejar's eighth book, *Casa dos Arreios.* Álvaro Pacheco presented *Tempo integral.*

In fiction, in the novel *O caso Morel,* Ruben Fonseca confirmed and enlarged his reputation as a storyteller, already disclosed in his tales. Resende Filho returned to the novel with *Túmulo,* and Clarice Lispector brought out two books, a novel, *Água Viva,* and the tales of *Imitação da Rosa.* Sérgio Sant'Anna published *Notas de Manfredo Rangel, o Reporter,* while Antonio Celso produced another novel, *Girassol de Ouro,* which, like *O Nó Cego* by Geraldo França de Lima, evokes life in the interior of Minas Gerais state. *O Fim de Tudo* consolidated Luis Vilela's reputation as a tale writer. The most important memoir produced in 1973 was *Uma Vida e Muitas Lutas* by Juarez Távora. (ANTONIO CARLOS DA ROCHA VILLAÇA)

NORWEGIAN

Documentary material figured prominently, providing two very different best sellers: Per Hansson's *Hvem var Henry Rinnan?,* the life story of the leading Norwegian agent provocateur during the German occupation, and Dagfinn Grønoset's *Anna i ødemarka,* a low-keyed report of the hardships of a poor woman tilling an isolated croft in the wilds. Wartime sabotage of the Røros railway was excitingly retold by Asbjørn Øksendal in *Operasjon Lapwing,* while Tor Obrestad's documentary novel *Sauda! Streik!* was based on a wildcat strike at the U.S.-owned Sauda smelting works in 1970. Taped conversations about death provided material for Finn Carling's moving book *Resten er taushet.* Recent political events were elucidated in the memoirs of two former prime ministers, socialist Einar Gerhardsen's *I medgang og motgang* and conservative John Lyng's *Vaktskifte.* The first volume of Tim Greve's biography *Fridtjof Nansen* incorporated much new material on the years 1861 to 1904.

Pungent satire of modern bureaucracy was provided in Fredrik Skagen's witty novel *Papirkrigen.* Science fiction was impressively represented by Jon Bing's *Scenario,* and Sigrun Krokvik followed the outstanding *Bortreist på ubestemt tid* with another spellbinder, *Kikkeren.* Ernst Orvil showed his usual unique handling of the Norwegian language in a collection of short stories, *Balanse,* while Johan Borgen gave free rein to his imagination in *Den store havfrue,* where the story was told by a television screen. Various aspects of feminism were dealt with in the nine short stories of Bjørg Vik's *Kvinneakvariet.* Bjørg Berg's novel *Bendiks datter* gave a colourful picture of life in a farming and fishing community, while a fervently religious Pentecostal milieu in East Oslo formed the background to Tor Edvin Dahl's *Guds tjener.* The 15-year-old hero of Knut Faldbakken's *Insektsommer* finds himself enmeshed in a web of erotic tensions, while Terje Stigen's *Min Marion* was a touching and humorous account of a love affair between two handicapped people. Stigen also showed himself a master of the essay with *Norsk rapsodi.* Violent clashes between heathen and Christian attitudes provoked dramatic events in Felix Thoresen's *Langferd mot vest* and a 16th-century farming community formed the background to Vera Henriksen's *Blåbreen.*

Collected poems by Inger Hagerup, Rolf Jacobsen, and Tarjei Vesaas (d. 1970) dominated the poetic scene, while Paal Brekke's *Aftenen er stille* dealt with the dead life of an old people's home and Espen Haavardsholm's *Grip dagen* was a poetic diary of the year of Norway's "no" to the EEC.

Johan Vogt's *Aksel Sandemose. Minner, brev, betraktninger* was a portrait based on close personal friendship. Allen Simpson's *Knut Hamsuns Landstrykere* analyzed Hamsun's novel *Vagabonds,* while

Bjørn Hemmer's *Brand, Kongs-emnerne, Peer Gynt* was a perceptive analysis of three Ibsen plays.

(TORBJØRN STØVERUD)

SOVIET

In 1973 the Soviet regime intensified its efforts to suppress and discredit the "dissident" movement, of which a number of writers well known in the West formed an influential arm; however, the reasoning behind the moves, at a time of increased genuflections toward Soviet-West détente, was open to question. In late summer, during the trial of former dissidents Pyotr Yakir and Viktor Krasin, the Nobel Prize-winning novelist Aleksandr I. Solzhenitsyn—whose works were banned in the Soviet Union and who was implicated by Yakir's testimony—told Western press correspondents that he had received death threats and that, in the event of his sudden death or mysterious disappearance, he had made arrangements for the hitherto unpublished "main body" of his works.

In September Solzhenitsyn announced he had circulated in *samizdat* (self-published) form two chapters of a revision of *The First Circle,* published (in an unauthorized version) in the West in 1968. This formed a preliminary challenge to a newly established "copyright agency," formed to handle transactions between the Soviet Union and Western publishers following the former's signing of the Geneva Universal Copyright Convention on May 27 (*see* PUBLISHING). A far more serious challenge, one that also set back the Soviet image abroad, came in December with the surprise publication in Paris of *The Gulag Archipelago,* a copy of which had been seized by the Soviet secret police in September. Solzhenitsyn's first nonfiction publication, the work documented the oppression and terror of the Soviet labour camp system, for which Gulag is the Russian acronym, using the reports of 228 persons who, like himself, had been among the victims and survivors of the camps that dotted the U.S.S.R. like islands between 1918 and 1956.

In November English-speaking readers were able to read a firsthand report of the "liberalization" of Soviet culture that followed the years Solzhenitsyn's work covered. This account, by Solzhenitsyn's close friend the biochemist Zhores Medvedev (currently living in London), was titled *Ten Years After Ivan Denisovich.* Although chiefly about the novelist, it was also welcomed for its information about other participants in events, notably the former editor of *Novy Mir,* poet Aleksandr Tvardovsky (d. 1971). During the year the seventh volume of *Literaturnaya Ensiklopediya* made its delayed appearance—without the expected, officially compiled biographical entry on Solzhenitsyn.

Other dissident writers in the news during 1973 included Andrey Amalrik, best known in the West for his essay "Will the Soviet Union Survive Until 1984?" Due to finish a three-year prison sentence in May for "slandering the state," Amalrik was immediately rearrested on the same charge and jailed for a further three years (the sentence was later commuted to exile in Magadan province). In June Andrey Sinyavsky—arrested in 1965 along with Yuli Daniel for publishing "anti-Soviet" literature in the West—was granted an exit visa and in August reached Paris, where he had recently been elected a professor at the Sorbonne. His reflections noted during his years in prison camp, *A Voice from the Chorus,* were published (in Russian) later in the year.

In August the Soviet Writers' Union confirmed that

HENDRICK SMITH—THE NEW YORK TIMES

Aleksandr Solzhenitsyn, dissident author and Nobel laureate, with his wife, Natalya, and son Yermolai in Moscow.

the novelist Vladimir Maksimov had been expelled from its number. The same month its journal, *Literaturnaya Gazeta,* launched a virulent attack on the West German Nobel Prize winner Heinrich Böll, who had criticized the Soviet Union for putting obstacles in the way of genuine cultural exchanges. (Böll's criticisms were the more embarrassing since his antifascist, antiwar writings were enormously popular in the Soviet Union.) In February the same journal had brought sharply to task poet Yevgeny Yevtushenko, accusing him of abusing his talent by writing insincere, insignificant, journalistic verses and of plagiarism. Yevtushenko's reply was conspicuously lame.

In March Soviet writers were reminded at a plenary meeting of the Writers' Union that the rich variety of the country's social, economic, and cultural life provided the broadest scope for imaginative composition. New novels about Soviet workers included *Midday on the Sunny Side* by Vadim Kozhevnikov, *Industrial Ballad* by M. Kolesnikov, and *An Ordinary Month* by I. Shtemler. *Engineers* by Ukrainian novelist Y. Shovkoplyas was about the building up of socialist industry during the first five-year plan (1928–32). *The Emelyanovs* by V. Kukushkin centred on a Leningrad-district steelworker's family in the 1900–17 period. F. Abramov's *Roads and Crossings* was a novel of the Soviet peasantry in the 1950s.

Books with a World War II background included volume four of *Blockade,* telling of Stalin the wise wartime leader and showing the modest side of the dictator. This was by Aleksandr Chakovsky, editor of *Literaturnaya Gazeta.* Others were *Live Till Dawn,* a study of patriotism by Belorussian writer V. Bykov; *Five Hours to Immortality* by Y. Pilyar, about military heroism; and *Last War* by V. Roslyakov, who returned in this book to the theme of young people growing up in wartime.

Ethical and psychological problems were at the heart of *The Brother's Return* by V. Amlinsky; *Fortune Smiles* by Akhto Levi; and *Spring Hypocrisies* by V. Tendryakov. *The Balance* by V. Marchenko, *The White Antelope* by Daghestan writer Abu-Bakar, and *The Glybukhinsky Wood-Goblin* by D. Eremin all dealt with man and his environment.

Autobiography flourished in 1973. Outstanding were V. Katayev's *Broken Life, or Oberon's Magic Horn,* set at the beginning of the 20th century and describing a child's growing awareness of the world around him; and a further installment of Vera Ketlinskaya's *Evening. Windows. People,* in which the author's memories of the civil war and of her youth were linked by reflections on the fate of people she had known. Marietta Shaginyan, the well-known authority on Lenin, published a third volume of her memoirs, *Man and Time.*

Historical novels also enjoyed great success, especially *Marfa-Posadnitsa* by D. Balshov, about the widow of the head of ancient Novgorod; *Mithridatus* by V. Polupudov, set in ancient Crimea; and *The Wreck,* third part of A. Nurpeisov's trilogy *Blood and the Poet,* about the Kazakh people in World War I and the civil war.

Science fiction and adventure stories appeared in *Science Fiction, Issue 12, On Land and at Sea, Brigantine, Adventures, 1972–73,* and in many other collections. Poetry was represented by new work from several poets including F. Alieva, K. Kuliev, and Yevtushenko. Perhaps the most remarkable addition to Soviet literary criticism was a collection of Dostoevsky's comments on art, gathered together for the first time in *F. M. Dostoevsky on Art.*

In early November the death was reported of Vsevolod Kochetov, novelist and editor. (x.)

SPANISH

The best Spanish novels and shorter fiction remained firmly in the hands of Latin-American writers living and working in Spain. Late in 1972 Gabriel García Márquez issued an interim collection of shorter pieces, *La increíble y triste historia de la cándida Eréndira y de su abuela desalmada,* published simultaneously in four cities, a measure of success perhaps unprecedented in Spanish writing. The stories, burgeoning with colonial ripeness, were products of an authentically myth-making mind.

The first printing of expatriate Peruvian Mario Vargas Llosa's *Pantaleón y las visitadoras* ran to 100,000 copies, a remarkable achievement in a not very literate Spain. (See *Latin-American,* above.) Censors "disauthorized" the original cover printed for the book, a reproduction of a painting by Carlos Mensa, and a substitute had to be printed.

The Sephardic presence was ever more consciously being expressed in Spain. There were two books replete with Hebrew symbols (and characters) by the Argentine-born Marcos Ricardo Barnatán: *Arcana mayor,* a collection of glosses on the Tarot, and *Gor,* an impressionistic development of personal myth; both books were heavy with cabbalistic association. The "unconscious" Jewish presence in Spain (the Jewish strain become Catholic) was most notably expressed in Américo Castro's work on suppressed Judaism in Spanish history, and the first posthumous collection of his essays, *Españoles al margen,* compiled by Pedro Carrera Eras, was published.

Camilo José Cela produced a nihilistic surrealist "novel" infinitely titled *oficio de tinieblas 6 o novela de tesis para ser cantada por un coro de enfermos para adorno de la liturgia con que se celebra el triunfo de los bienaventurados y las circunstancias de bienaventuranza que se dicen . . . ,* to cite but half, organized—or atomized—into 184 sections. The youngest author of a notable fiction work during the year was Javier Marías, whose *Travesía del horizonte* narrated a violent marine adventure from a mysteriously moral, and perhaps existentially meaningless, point of view.

An anthology of texts compiled and translated by an economist, a historian, a theologian, and a psychologist, *Alquimia y ocultismo,* served to place the medieval proselytizer and Arabist Ramon Llull squarely among the alchemists. A rare and exotic book of verse written from exile in Paris was Agustín García Calvo's *Sermón del ser y no ser.*

The prestigious Premio de la Crítica went to Gonzalo Torrente Ballester for *La saga/fuga de J B,* regarded by some critics as the best novel to appear for a decade. (ANTHONY KERRIGAN)

SWEDISH

The death of Vilhelm Moberg (*see* OBITUARIES), author of the epic novel suite *Utvandrarna* (*The Emigrants*), in August 1973 came shortly after the appearance of *Otrons artiklar,* a collection of challenging essays. The journalist, author, and playwright Birger Norman published socially and politically perceptive articles in *Vinkelskott,* while *Du skulle gråta om du visste . . .* by Marit Paulsen and Sture Andersson surveyed an oppressed and exploited group—women office cleaners. In *Snälla kuratorn* Lennart Frick's main character was a "trendy" social worker whose professionalism masked a past failing; both milieu and jargon were convincing. Documentary in nature, 86-year-old Tora Dahl's *När jag var sjuk* described lucidly how it felt to be helpless in the hospital machine, while Bosse Gustafson's *U* was a thinly veiled exposure of the supposed perfidies of the military machine and P. C. Jersild's *Djurdoktorn,* a tale of inhuman bureaucracy in a fictional state veterinary institute.

In time for the 600th anniversary of Sweden's only saint came *Birgitta i Rom,* the final volume of Sven Stolpe's biography of this extraordinary woman. F. J. Nordstedt studied early Christian sources, including William Cureton's manuscript *The Apostle Addais' Teaching,* to produce *En syrisk saga,* an imaginative work on the legendary correspondence between Jesus and King Abgar of Edessa. Lars Gyllensten added to his impressive output with *Grottan i öknen,* a major work restating the story of St. Anthony.

World War II figured in three novels: in *Bönder och herrar,* the expatriate Greek author Theodor Kallifatides ironically but affectionately described his people, the war, and the German occupation; in *Dalarö 1941,* Ole Söderström explored human passions and uncertainties; in *Vallmo höst* Håkan Boström gave a moving and lyrical picture of the war through the eyes of a child and of the Suez and Hungarian crises through those of an adolescent. Birgitta Trotzig's major novel *Sjukdomen* was a psychologically and stylistically complex study of a father's guilt feelings being visited on his son. In Sven Delblanc's *Stenfågel,* a sequel to *Åminne,* tragedy predominated in a rural setting. Lars Gustafsson's *Yllet* and Per Gunnar Evander's *Det sista äventyret* both had schoolmaster heroes.

Kung Mej och andra dikter showed that ten years after his debut poet Lars Norén was going from strength to strength. Kjell Espmark's *Samtal under jorden* and Elsa Grave's *Mödrar som vargar* were pleasing contributions in an otherwise meagre year. (KARIN PETHERICK)

See also Libraries; Philosophy; Theatre.

ENCYCLOPÆDIA BRITANNICA FILMS. *Bartleby by Herman Melville* (1969); *Dr. Heidegger's Experiment by Nathaniel Hawthorne* (1969); *The Lady, or the Tiger? by Frank Stockton* (1969); *The Lottery by Shirley Jackson* (1969); *Magic Prison* (1969); *My Old Man by Ernest Hemingway* (1969); *James Dickey: Poet* (1970); *The Deserted Village* (1971); *The Lady of Shalott* (1971); *The Prisoner of Chillon* (1971); *Shaw vs. Shakespeare—Part I: The Character of Caesar; Part II: The Tragedy of Julius Caesar; Part III: Caesar and Cleopatra* (1971); *The Greek Myths* (1972); *Walt Whitman: Poet for a New Age* (1972); *Look in the Answer Book* (1972); *The Crocodile by Fyodor Dostoyevsky* (1973); *The Secret Sharer by Joseph Conrad* (1973); *John Keats: His Life* (1973); *John Keats: Poet* (1973).

Livestock and Animal Products: *see* Agriculture and Fisheries

Lumber: *see* Forestry

Lutherans: *see* Religion

Luxembourg

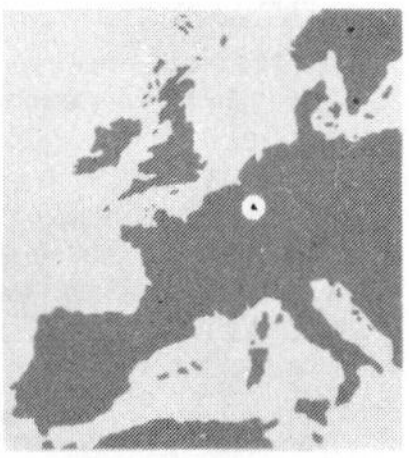

A constitutional monarchy, the Benelux country of Luxembourg is bounded on the east by West Germany, on the south by France, and on the west and north by Belgium. Area: 999 sq.mi. (2,586 sq.km.). Pop. (1972 est.): 348,200. Cap. and largest city: Luxembourg (pop., 1972 est., 78,000). Language: French, German, Luxembourgian. Religion: Roman Catholic 97%. Grand duke, Jean; prime minister in 1973, Pierre Werner.

In September 1972, Mrs. Madeleine Frieden-Kinnen, minister of public health, family, and youth affairs, resigned. Subsequently, Camille Ney was named minister of agriculture; Jean-Pierre Buchler assumed the Family Ministry; Education Minister Jean Dupong took over the Youth Affairs post; and Jacques Sauter became the cultural affairs minister.

Pursuant to its examination of the tangled affairs of financier Robert Vesco (*see* BIOGRAPHY), the U.S. Securities and Exchange Commission charged that $224 million of the Vesco mutual funds' assets had been transferred to Vesco-controlled banks in Luxembourg and the Bahamas. Regulatory officials of Canada, the U.S., and Luxembourg announced on June 29, 1973, that the four mutual funds of Vesco's Investors Overseas Services (IOS) would be liquidated. The IOS chairman, Milton F. Meissner, had been arrested in Luxembourg on June 28.

On Jan. 5, 1973, Luxembourg recognized the government of East Germany. Earlier, relations had been established with China after a break with Taiwan.

The national statistical office announced that, after a year of "quasi-stagnation," the Luxembourg economy in 1972 had entered a new phase of expansion. Industrial production grew 4.2%, while steel alone gained 4.8%. Prices, however, continued to rise and the economy was troubled by inflationary pressures.

(ROBERT D. HODGSON)

LUXEMBOURG

Education. (1969–70) Primary, pupils 36,035, teachers 1,758; secondary, pupils 8,689, teachers 629; vocational, pupils 9,347, teachers 690; higher, students 422, teaching staff 120.

Finance. Monetary unit: Luxembourg franc, at par with the Belgian franc, with (Sept. 17, 1973) a free rate of LFr. 36.46 to U.S. $1 (LFr. 87.87 = £1 sterling). Budget (1973 est.): revenue LFr. 16,791,-000,000; expenditure LFr. 17,033,000,000. Gross domestic product: (1972) LFr. 57.5 billion; (1971) LFr. 52.9 billion. Cost of living (1963 = 100): (June 1973) 145; (June 1972) 136.

Foreign Trade. *See* BELGIUM.

Transport and Communications. Roads (1972) 4,460 km. Motor vehicles in use (1972): passenger 111,000; commercial 9,300. Railways: (1971) 271 km.; traffic (1972) 261.8 million passenger-km., freight 782.9 million net ton-km. Air traffic (1971): 119 million passenger-km.; freight 234,000 net ton-km. Telephones (Dec. 1971) 87,000. Radio licenses (Dec. 1971) 167,000. Television licenses (Dec. 1971) 73,100.

Agriculture. Production (in 000; metric tons; 1972; 1971 in parentheses): wheat *c.* 38 (39); oats *c.* 37 (38); rye *c.* 5 (6); barley *c.* 54 (53); potatoes (1971) 59, (1970) 68; wine *c.* 10 (10). Livestock (in 000; May 1972): cattle 192; sheep 3; pigs 95; chickens 316.

Industry. Production (in 000; metric tons; 1972): iron ore (30% metal content) 4,116; pig iron 4,670; crude steel 5,458; electricity (kw-hr.) 2,220,000; manufactured gas (cu.m.; 1971) 15,000.

Malagasy Republic

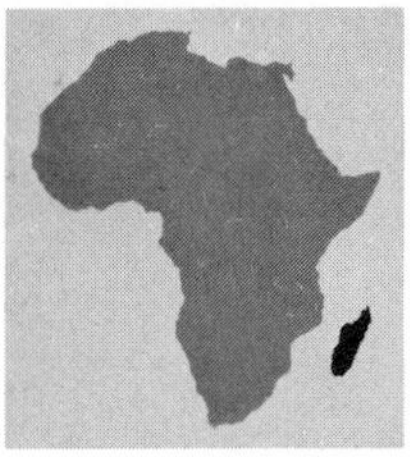

The Malagasy Republic occupies the island of Madagascar and minor adjacent islands in the Indian Ocean off the southeast coast of Africa. Area: 226,442 sq.mi. (586,486 sq.km.). Pop. (1973 est.): 7,140,000. Cap. and largest city: Tananarive (pop., 1972 est., 366,-530). Language: French and Malagasy. Religion: Christian (approximately 50%) and traditional tribal beliefs. Head of government in 1973, Gen. Gabriel Ramanantsoa.

The new leadership under General Ramanantsoa, who had come to power in 1972, continued to revise the whole direction of Malagasy foreign policy. In June 1973 new cooperation agreements were signed with France; in August the Malagasy Republic withdrew from the Common Organization of Africa, Malagasy, and Mauritius (OCAM); and in October diplomatic relations with Israel were broken.

On June 4 representatives of the French and Malagasy governments signed eight new cooperation agreements in Paris. The negotiations, which opened in January, had been lengthy and difficult and had been suspended several times, notably when the republic withdrew from the franc zone in May.

An important element in the agreements related to the departure of French ground and air forces stationed on the island by September 1. On the agreed date, French troops were posted elsewhere. Military installations were handed over to the Malagasy authorities, though the naval base at Diégo-Suarez was to remain available for use by the French for a further two years. In June a reorganization of French military deployments in the whole area was carried out.

In the absence of any act of settlement, French citizens would in the future be regarded as "foreigners."

MALAGASY REPUBLIC

Education. (1971–72) Primary, pupils 938,000, teachers 14,400; secondary (1968–69), pupils 94,104, teachers 4,158; vocational, pupils 9,000, teachers (1968–69) 494; teacher training, students (1968–69) 2,627, teachers (1964–65) 118; higher, students 7,000, teaching staff 260.

Finance. Monetary unit: Malagasy franc, at par with the CFA franc, with (Sept. 17, 1973) a parity of MalFr. 50 to the French franc (free commercial rate of MalFr. 212.55 = U.S. $1; free rate of MalFr. 512.25 = £1 sterling). Gold, SDRs, and foreign exchange: (June 1973) U.S. $67.2 million; (June 1972) U.S. $52 million. Budget (1972 est.) balanced at MalFr. 52.5 billion.

Foreign Trade. (1972) Imports MalFr. 51,753,000,-000; exports MalFr. 41,864,000,000. Import sources: France 54%; West Germany 9%; U.S. 6%. Export destinations: France 40%; U.S. 18%; Malaysia 6%; Réunion 6%; Japan 5%. Main exports: coffee 28%; vanilla 9%.

Transport and Communications. Roads (1970) 26,937 km. (8,595 km. main roads in 1972). Motor vehicles in use (1970): passenger 48,900; commercial 31,100. Railways: (1971) 884 km.; traffic (1972) 191.8 million passenger-km., freight 205.1 million net ton-km. Air traffic (1972): 283.5 million passenger-km.; freight 11,157,000 net ton-km. Telephones (Dec. 1971) 28,000. Radio receivers (Dec. 1970) 540,000. Television receivers (Dec. 1970) 3,200.

Agriculture. Production (in 000; metric tons; 1972; 1971 in parentheses): rice *c.* 1,925 (1,873); corn (1971) 118, (1970) 109; cassava (1970) 1,218, (1969) 1,253; sweet potatoes (1971) 344, (1970) 350; potatoes (1971) 108, (1970) 94; dry beans *c.* 50 (*c.* 52); bananas (1971) 344, (1970) 212; peanuts *c.* 45 (40); sugar, raw value *c.* 125 (115); coffee *c.* 60 (58); tobacco (1971) 5.7, (1970) 4.9; sisal (1971) 25, (1970) 26. Livestock (in 000; Dec. 1971): cattle *c.* 10,000; sheep *c.* 500; pigs *c.* 540; goats *c.* 920; chickens *c.* 11,500.

Machinery and Machine Tools: *see* Industrial Review

Madagascar: *see* Malagasy Republic

Magazines: *see* Publishing

Thus, 13 years after Malagasy independence, French nationals were subject for the first time to entry and exit visa requirements. This led many people to speak of 1973 as the year of the second—and real—restoration of Malagasy independence.

At home General Ramanantsoa faced persistent unrest and a deterioration in the economic and social situation. Disturbances in January at the port of Tamatave, which had been the scene of violent rioting in December 1972, were followed in February by violent protests in Diégo-Suarez and Majunga. As a result of these disturbances, several members of the previous government were arrested, including former finance minister Victor Miadana and former minister of information and tourism René Rasidy. A total of 28 prison sentences were imposed. In July a French national was expelled for alleged conspiracy. Opposition from the left was as active as that from the right, and in July the extremist left-wing leader Manandafy Rakotonirina was sentenced to two years' imprisonment for taking part in a banned demonstration.

Elections to the National Popular Development Council in October brought little change in the political complexion of the government, though several leading figures, including Malagasy Socialist Union leader André Resampa, were not reelected.

(PHILIPPE DECRAENE)

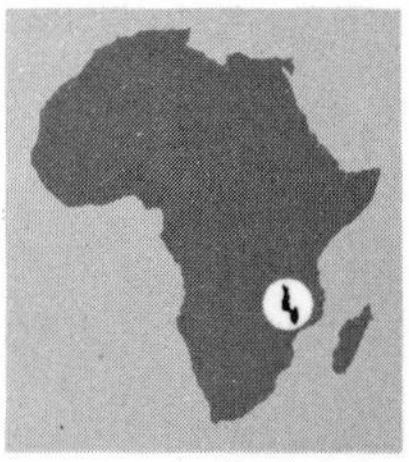

Malawi

A republic and member of the Commonwealth of Nations in east central Africa, Malawi is bounded by Tanzania, Mozambique, and Zambia. Area: 45,747 sq.mi. (118,484 sq.km.). Pop. (1972 est.): 4,666,000. Cap.: Zomba (pop., 1971 est., 20,000). Largest city: Blantyre (pop., 1971 est., 169,000). Language: English (official) and Nyanja (Chichewa). Religion: predominantly traditional beliefs. President in 1973, Hastings Kamuzu Banda.

MALAWI

Education. (1968) Primary, pupils 333,876, teachers 8,564; secondary, pupils 9,283, teachers 508; vocational, pupils 536, teachers 53; teacher training, students 1,085, teachers 119; higher (University of Malawi), students (1971) 1,087, teaching staff 140.

Finance. Monetary unit: kwacha, with (Sept. 17, 1973) a free rate of 0.83 kwacha to U.S. $1 (par value of 2 kwachas = £1 sterling). Gold, SDRs, and foreign exchange, official: (June 1973) U.S. $49,460,000; (June 1972) U.S. $34,080,000. Budget (1972–73 est.): revenue 53.3 million kwachas; expenditures 56.2 million kwachas.

Foreign Trade. (1972) Imports 102,832,000 kwachas; exports 63,710,000 kwachas. Import sources: U.K. 29%; Iran 14%; Rhodesia 11%; Japan 8%. Export destinations: U.K. 37%; Zambia 11%; Rhodesia 9%. Main exports: tobacco 39%; tea 19%; peanuts 11%.

Transport and Communications. Roads (1971) 10,721 km. Motor vehicles in use (1972): passenger 12,700; commercial 10,100. Railways: (1971) 584 km.; traffic (1972) 74.2 million passenger-km., freight 217.8 million net ton-km. Air traffic (1972): 54.4 million passenger-km.; freight 724,000 net ton-km. Telephones (Dec. 1971) 14,000. Radio receivers (Dec. 1970) 90,000.

Agriculture. Production (in 000; metric tons; 1972; 1971 in parentheses): corn *c.* 1,150 (*c.* 1,100); cassava (1971) *c.* 145, (1970) *c.* 144; sweet potatoes (1971) *c.* 46, (1970) *c.* 45; sugar, raw value *c.* 60 (34); peanuts (1971) *c.* 180, (1970) *c.* 152; tea *c.* 21 (19); tobacco *c.* 25 (22); cotton, lint *c.* 9 (*c.* 9). Livestock (in 000; 1971–72): cattle *c.* 450; sheep *c.* 120; goats *c.* 640; pigs *c.* 145; poultry *c.* 8,000.

Industry. Production (1972): electricity (public supply) 174 million kw-hr.; cement 74,000 metric tons.

Malawi began 1973 in an optimistic mood with regard to its financial position. Linked to the triumph of balancing the budget without foreign aid was the hope that before long the prospect of doubling the gross domestic product would be realized. This hope was mainly based on a reassuring growth in the production of the country's three major crops, peanuts, tobacco, and tea, though there were also signs of a valuable increase in the tourist trade. Funds for development would still be needed from abroad, but careful economic management continued to encourage foreign investment. Malawi continued to look to the Western powers to provide the bulk of the assistance needed, and in March the government became the first of the Commonwealth countries to ask for associate membership in the EEC.

Hastings Kamuzu Banda, president of Malawi since it became a republic in 1966, dictated hemlines and hairstyles as well as more significant matters in the affairs of the central African country.

WIDE WORLD

On the political front the situation was less cheerful. Toward the end of 1972 a number of foreign residents, including journalists and senior government officers, had been expelled. Journalists were again in trouble in May 1973 when eight Africans were detained without trial, apparently for sending abroad news reports of fighting between Portuguese and Malawi forces on the border with Mozambique; Joseph Wadda, director of news programs for the Malawi Broadcasting Corporation, was later deported. Shortly afterward the last white journalists resigned and left the country. The university, too, felt the weight of the president's displeasure. A number of white foreign students were deported, while others, including the newly elected chairman of the students' union, were detained by security police. Earlier in the year the government had turned its attention once again to the Jehovah's Witnesses, many thousands of whom had returned from a temporary exile in Zambia where they had fled to escape persecution in 1972. More than 20 of their leaders were arrested for refusing to take out Malawi Congress Party cards, and many others were again subject to persecution. As a result, refugees once more began to stream into Zambia and also into Mozambique. In March Aleke Banda, who had been one of the country's prominent ministers, was dropped from the Cabinet, suspended from duty, and deprived of all party rights and privileges for giving information to a Zambian newspaper that resulted in an article suggesting that he was the chosen successor to President Banda.

(KENNETH INGHAM)

Malaysia

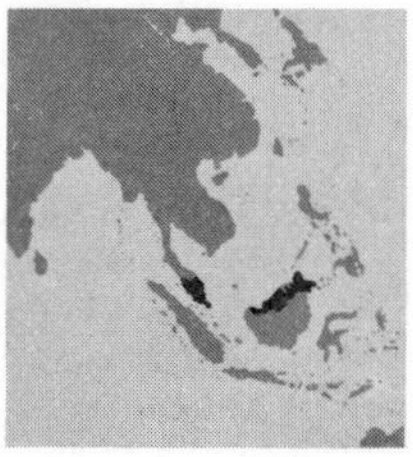

A federation within the Commonwealth of Nations comprising the 11 states of the former Federation of Malaya, Sabah, and Sarawak, Malaysia is a federal constitutional monarchy situated in Southeast Asia at the southern end of the Malay Peninsula (excluding Singapore) and on the northern part of the island of Borneo. Area: 127,316 sq.mi. (329,747 sq.km.). Pop. (1973 est.): 10,920,000. Cap. and largest city: Kuala Lumpur (pop., 1970, 451,810). Official language: Malay. Religion: Malays are Muslim; Indians mainly Hindu; Chinese mainly Buddhist, Confucian, and Taoist. Supreme head of state in 1973, with the title of *yang di-pertuan agong,* Tuanku Abdul Halim Mu'azzam Shah ibni al-Marhum Sultan Badlishah; prime minister, Tun Abdul Razak.

Malaysia in 1973, the tenth anniversary of federation, enjoyed political stability and a booming economy. On January 1 the ruling Alliance of the United Malays National Organization, the Malaysian Chinese Association, and the Malaysian Indian Congress entered into a coalition with the Pan Malayan Islamic Party, giving the government a comfortable two-thirds (112 out of 144) majority in the House of Representatives. The Cabinet was reshuffled on August 13 and the number of ministers increased from 20 to 24. Ismail bin Dato Abdul Rahman died on August 2 (*see* OBITUARIES) and was replaced as deputy prime minister by Hussein bin Dato Onn.

In the ten months to August 1973 six offshore oil and natural gas strikes were announced; the deposits were in commercial quantities and the oil of low sulfur content. The government decided to reassess its relations with the nine oil companies operating around Malaysia's shores and began to draw up a comprehensive oil policy. The minister for industry, Dato Taib Mahmud, expressed the government's general approach: "We do not want to siphon out all our oil at the quickest possible rate. Our oil policy must be such as to give us maximum economic and social benefits in the long term." The government was considering production-sharing agreements with the oil companies on the Indonesian model. The country was already self-sufficient in oil, producing 100,000 bbl. daily, and the government was optimistic that by 1980 Malaysia would be a fairly important oil exporter. Although Malaysia was able to meet its oil needs from its own resources, the Arab oil-producing countries listed it as one of the "friendly" nations that

MALAYSIA

Education. *West Malaysia.* (1969) Primary, pupils 1,369,376, teachers 44,987; secondary, pupils 512,212, teachers 19,726; vocational, pupils 12,632, teachers 407; higher (including 3 universities), students 15,017, teaching staff 1,129. *East Malaysia:* Sabah. (1971) Primary, pupils 113,570, teachers (1969) 4,655; secondary, pupils 33,427, teachers (1969) 1,071; vocational (1969), pupils 180, teachers 20; teacher training (1969), students 730, teachers 50. *East Malaysia:* Sarawak. (1970) Primary, pupils 144,007, teachers 4,404; secondary, pupils 35,459, teachers 1,424; vocational, pupils 343, teachers 28; teacher training, students 269, teachers 55; higher, students 430.

Finance. Monetary unit: Malaysian dollar, with (Sept. 17, 1973) a par value of M$2.32 to U.S. $1 (free rate of M$5.58 = £1 sterling). Gold, SDRs, and foreign exchange, official: (June 1973) U.S. $1,167,000,000; (June 1972) U.S. $877 million. Budget (1972 est.): revenue M$2,849,000,000; expenditure M$2,825,000,000. Gross national product: (1971) M$12,357,000,000; (1970) M$11,872,000,000. Money supply: (March 1973) M$2,987,000,000; (June 1972) M$2,234,000,000. Cost of living (West Malaysia; 1963 = 100): (Dec. 1972) 114; (Dec. 1971) 109.

Foreign Trade. (1972) Imports M$4,633,000,000; exports M$4,851,000,000. Import sources: Japan 20%; U.K. 11%; U.S. 10%; Singapore 8%; Australia 6%. Export destinations: Singapore 19%; Japan 18%; U.S. 15%; U.K. 6%. Main exports: rubber 27%; tin 19%; timber 18%; palm oil 7%.

Transport and Communications. Roads (1971) *c.* 28,500 km. (including *c.* 22,000 with improved surface). Motor vehicles in use (1971): passenger 308,900; commercial (including buses) 73,300. Railways (1971): 1,775 km.; traffic (including Singapore) 672 million passenger-km., freight 1,108,000,000 net ton-km. Air traffic (apportionment of Malaysia-Singapore Airlines; 1971): 857 million passenger-km.; freight 16,653,000 net ton-km. Shipping (1972): merchant vessels 100 gross tons and over 99; gross tonnage 149,304. Shipping traffic (1971) goods loaded 20,737,000 metric tons, unloaded 8,877,000 metric tons. Telephones (Jan. 1972) 190,000. Radio licenses (Dec. 1971) 439,000. Television receivers (Dec. 1971) 150,000.

Agriculture. Production (in 000; metric tons; 1972; 1971 in parentheses): rice 1,909 (1,809); rubber 1,325 (1,324); copra (1971) *c.* 182, (1970) 176; palm oil *c.* 730 (589); tea (West Malaysia only) *c.* 4 (3.3); bananas (1970) *c.* 355, (1969) *c.* 355; pineapples (1970) 353, (1969) 376; pepper (Sarawak only; 1971) 26, (1970) 24; timber (cu.m.; 1970) 24,000, (1969) 22,300; fish catch (1971) 390, (1970) 365. Livestock (in 000; 1971–72): cattle *c.* 354; pigs *c.* 990; goats *c.* 360; sheep (West Malaysia only) *c.* 40; buffalo (1970–71) 309; poultry (1970–71) *c.* 29,250.

Industry. Production (in 000; metric tons; 1972): tin concentrates (metal content) 77; bauxite 1,076; cement (West Malaysia only) 1,160; iron ore (West Malaysia only; 56% metal content) 529; crude oil (Sarawak only) 4,418; gold (troy oz.; 1971) 5.7; electricity (kw-hr.) 4,190,000.

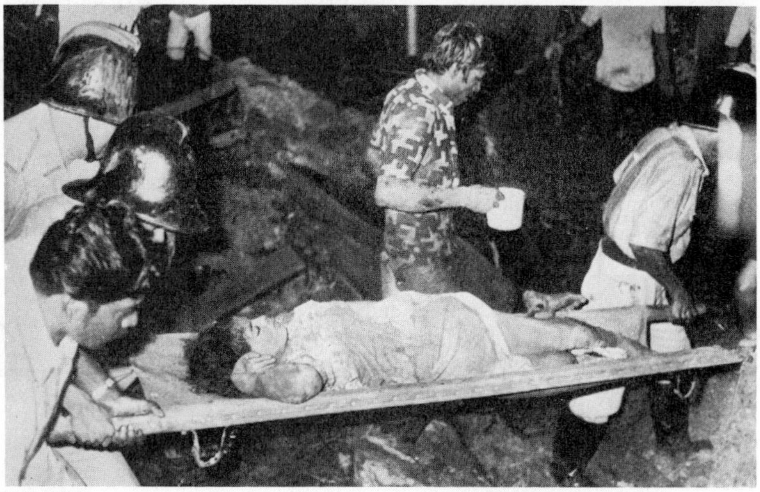

Rescue workers carry an injured Indian from the scene of a landslide in Ipoh, Malaysia, Oct. 18, 1973. At least 27 persons were buried and another 11 bystanders killed when a limestone cliff collapsed on a colony of squatters.

WIDE WORLD

would be exempted from their program of embargoes and cutbacks instituted during the Middle East war in October.

In September a major joint venture was announced between the Malaysian government and three private companies for the construction of one of the largest shipyards in Southeast Asia, to be located in Pasir Gudang and to cost M$100 million. It was to contain two dry docks, of 80,000 and 400,000 deadweight tons capacity, and there would be other facilities for ship repairs and the construction of small craft. Shipbuilding was expected to have a stimulating effect on many other sectors of the economy.

The gross national product (GNP) for 1973 was estimated to have risen by 9% nominally and 6% in real terms. The per capita GNP increased to M$1,200.

On May 8 Malaysia's agreement for the free interchange of Malaysian and Singapore dollars at par was ended; the Malaysian dollar was allowed to float from June 21. The joint stock exchange with Singapore was also terminated in favour of a separate one.

In foreign relations Tun Abdul Razak continued to work for the neutralization of Southeast Asia. On March 12 the government announced Malaysia's withdrawal from the nine-nation Asian and Pacific Council. According to the communiqué, Malaysia saw "no point in belonging to an organization which has done nothing" and wished "to concentrate on cooperation in the Association of Southeast Asian Nations." However, the move was seen as a necessary preliminary to the establishment of diplomatic relations with China. On March 30 Malaysia became the first Southeast Asian state to recognize North Vietnam. An Australian proposal to replace the Asian and Pacific Council with a new grouping of Asian and Pacific states, including China, was rejected by Malaysia in February.

Yugoslavian Prime Minister Dzemal Bijedic visited Malaysia March 15–17. Tun Abdul Razak attended the fourth summit conference of nonaligned nations in Algiers September 5–9.

In April the House of Representatives and the Senate approved a bill whereby Kuala Lumpur, seat of the federal government and state capital of Selangor, was to become a federal territory and capital of the Malaysian federation.

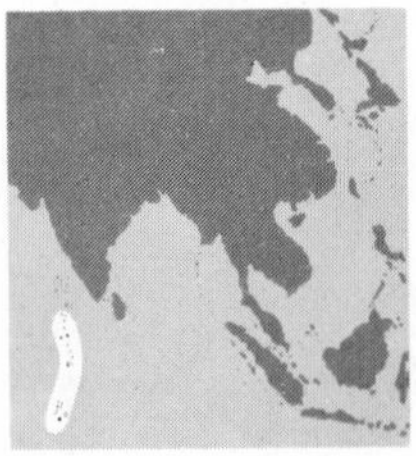

Maldives

Maldives, a republic in the Indian Ocean consisting of about two thousand small islands, lies southwest of the southern tip of India. Area: 115 sq.mi. (298 sq.km.). Pop. (1973 est.): 122,000. Cap.: Male (pop., 1971, 15,129). Language: Divehi. Religion: Muslim. Sultan, Emir Muhammad Farid Didi; president in 1973, Ibrahim Nasir; prime minister, Ahmed Zaki.

Because it had experienced delays in the implementation of a proposed agreement with Sri Lanka, the Soviet Union turned to the Maldives, and in June 1973 the two countries concluded a fisheries agreement. Soviet technical assistance and training of local personnel would be provided; there would be an exchange of technical and scientific information on marine affairs; joint fisheries would be established; and, most important to the U.S.S.R., port facilities would be made available.

The Maldives continued to benefit from Colombo Plan aid, particularly in the field of education. Scholarships abroad were provided by Britain, Canada, New Zealand, Australia, India, and the U.S.; the total number of students studying abroad reached nearly 100. Laboratory equipment at the two secondary schools in Male was provided by Britain, and 83 teachers from overseas were serving in the islands. Nonetheless, a shortage of teachers continued to hamper expansion in primary education, which was largely conducted by Islamic authorities. Arrangements were made with the University of London to hold general certificate of education examinations in Male.

In 1972 the republican constitution (declared in November 1968) was amended to give the prime minister executive powers; the first prime minister appointed by Pres. Ibrahim Nasir in August 1972, Ahmed Zaki, took over administrative responsibility under the president. The Majlis, elected every five years, remained the supreme legislative body. (MOLLY MORTIMER)

MALDIVES

Education. (1970–71) Primary, pupils 648, teachers 29; secondary, pupils 327, teachers 26.

Finance and Trade. Monetary unit: Maldivian rupee, with (Sept. 17, 1973) a nominal free rate of MRs. 6.46 to U.S. $1 (MRs. 15.57 = £1 sterling). Budget (1970) expenditure MRs. 17,289,000. Foreign trade (1970): imports MRs. 11,790,000; exports MRs. 22,986,000. Trade is mainly with Sri Lanka. Main exports (metric tons): fish 5,200; copra 78; shells 49.

Mali

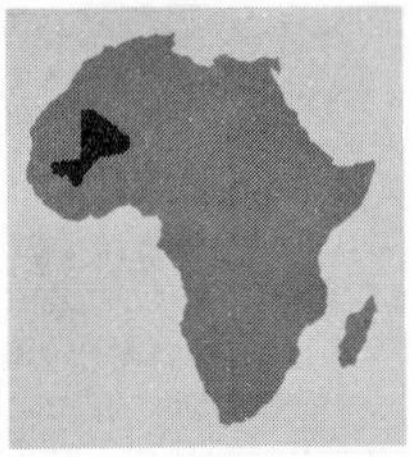

A republic of West Africa, Mali is bordered by Algeria, Niger, Upper Volta, Ivory Coast, Guinea, Senegal, and Mauritania. Area: 478,822 sq.mi. (1,240,142 sq.km.). Pop. (1973 est.): 5,376,400. Cap. and largest city: Bamako (pop., 1969 est., 189,200). Language: French (official); Hamito-Semitic and various tribal dialects. Religion: Muslim 65%; animist 30%. Head of military government in 1973, Col. Moussa Traoré.

During 1973 there were no major events in Malian domestic affairs apart from a Cabinet reshuffle in May which resulted in an increase in the number of portfolios from 12 to 14 and an increase in the number of civilians serving in the government from 6 to 9. In July it was announced that ex-Capt. Yoro Diakité, a former vice-president of the ruling Military Com-

A Malian crew unloads emergency food grains from a U.S. Air Force cargo plane at Timbuktu. The May 1973 flight was one of many relief missions bringing food for the drought-stricken interior.

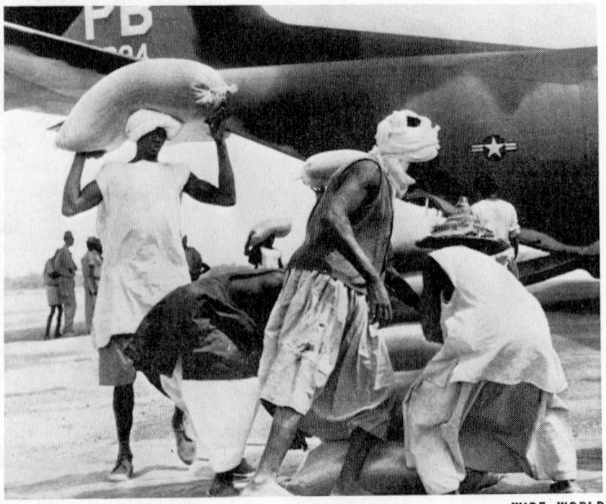

WIDE WORLD

MALI

Education. (1969–70) Primary, pupils 218,416, teachers 6,265; secondary, pupils 2,823, teachers 233; vocational, pupils 2,889, teachers 281; teacher training, students 1,469, teachers 93; higher, students 628, teaching staff 137.

Finance. Monetary unit: Mali franc, with (Sept. 17, 1973) a free rate of MFr. 425 to U.S. $1 (MFr. 1,024 = £1 sterling). Gold, SDRs, and foreign exchange: (June 1973) U.S. $3.5 million; (June 1972) U.S. $4.1 million. Budget (1971 est.): revenue MFr. 23 billion; expenditure MFr. 24.7 billion.

Foreign Trade. (1972) Imports MFr. 35,680,000,000; exports MFr. 17,230,000,000. Import sources: France *c.* 46%; Senegal *c.* 17%; Ivory Coast *c.* 17%; West Germany *c.* 7%. Export destinations: France *c.* 42%; Ghana *c.* 10%; Upper Volta *c.* 8%; U.K. *c.* 8%; Senegal *c.* 7%; Greece *c.* 6%; Belgium-Luxembourg *c.* 5%. Main exports: cotton 38%; peanuts 6%; fish 5%.

Agriculture. Production (in 000; metric tons; 1971; 1970 in parentheses): millet and sorghum 900 (600); rice 150 (138); corn *c.* 80 (*c.* 80); peanuts *c.* 143 (158); sweet potatoes *c.* 71 (*c.* 67); cassava (1970) *c.* 155, (1969) *c.* 150; cotton, lint 25 (25); beef and veal *c.* 50 (*c.* 50); mutton and lamb *c.* 34 (*c.* 33). Livestock (in 000; 1971–72): cattle *c.* 5,600; sheep *c.* 6,000; horses (1970–71) 174; asses *c.* 460.

mittee of National Liberation, had died in prison as a result of a heart attack. In August 1972 Diakité had been sentenced to forced labour for life for his part in an attempted coup on March 9, 1971. Col. Moussa Traoré announced that he had learned "with sadness" of the death of his former comrade-in-arms.

In January Mali broke off diplomatic relations with Israel, and in June Colonel Traoré paid an official visit to Peking which resulted in the signing of an agreement on economic and technical cooperation between China and Mali. Traoré announced that the agreement would allow the realization of a number of important projects in his country, particularly in the sphere of agriculture.

In July, after discreetly conducted negotiations between French and Malian officials, it was announced that cooperation agreements between the two countries had been renewed for another five-year period.

Mali was one of the six West African states severely affected by drought in 1973. The hardest hit of the country's populations were the Tuareg tribes, many of whom emigrated toward the south, particularly into neighbouring Upper Volta, in search of a means of subsistence for themselves and their animals. Exceptional aid was offered to Mali by the developed countries of the world, and a large amount of essential foodstuffs was stockpiled at the port of Dakar in Senegal, awaiting transport by air to the Malian interior. However, while there was no shortage of supplies awaiting distribution, the problems involved in airlifting these to the areas hardest hit by the drought led to considerable delays and to pleas from the Mali government for a speeding up of the operation to prevent further hardship. (PHILIPPE DECRAENE)

Malta

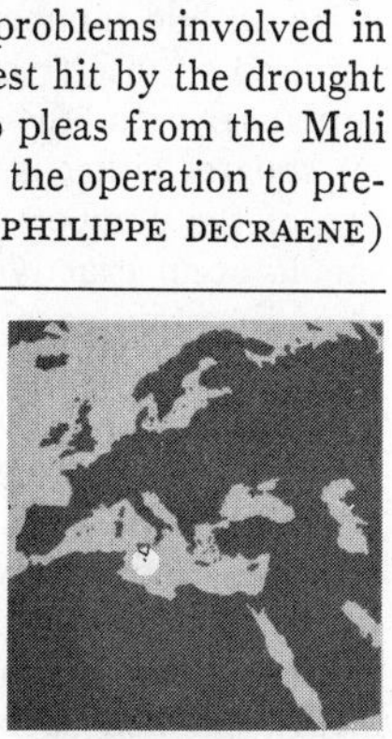

An island in the Mediterranean Sea, between Sicily and Tunisia, Malta is a parliamentary state and a member of the Commonwealth of Nations. Area: 122 sq.mi. (316 sq.km.), including Malta, Gozo, and Comino. Pop. (1972 est.): 318,530. Cap.: Valletta (pop., 1972 est., 15,191). Largest city: Sliema (pop., 1972 est., 21,-

MALTA

Education. (1968–69) Primary, pupils 52,368, teachers (1967–68) 2,494; secondary, pupils 12,074, teachers 886; vocational, pupils 4,911, teachers 467; higher (including Royal University of Malta), students 1,544, teaching staff 223.

Finance. Monetary unit: Maltese pound, with (Sept. 17, 1973) a free rate of M£0.36 to U.S. $1 (M£0.86 = £1 sterling). Gold, SDRs, and foreign exchange, official: (June 1973) U.S. $312.9 million; (June 1972) U.S. $227.4 million. Budget (1971–72): revenue M£43,489,000; expenditure M£39,369,000 (capital expenditure M£12,436,000).

Foreign Trade. (1972) Imports M£67,210,000; exports M£25,721,000. Import sources: U.K. 31%; Italy 19%; West Germany 6%; France 6%; U.S. 5%; The Netherlands 5%; Australia 5%. Export destinations: U.K. 37%; West Germany 16%; Italy 8%; Belgium-Luxembourg 6%. Main exports: clothing 31%; textile yarns and fabrics 11%; rubber products 7%; plumbing fittings 6%; ships 5%. Tourism (1971): 178,700 visitors; gross receipts U.S. $24 million.

Transport and Communications. Roads (1970) 1,200 km. Motor vehicles in use (1971): passenger 45,400; commercial (including buses) 11,200. There are no railways. Air traffic (1972): 119,890,000 passenger-km.; freight 1,896,000 net ton-km. Shipping (1972): merchant vessels 100 gross tons and over 20; gross tonnage 14,641. Ships entered (1971) vessels totaling 1,804,000 net registered tons; goods loaded (1972) 90,000 metric tons, unloaded 845,000 metric tons. Telephones (Dec. 1971) 44,000. Radio licenses (Dec. 1971) 118,000. Television licenses (Dec. 1971) 53,000.

572). Language: Maltese and English. Religion: mainly Roman Catholic. Queen, Elizabeth II; governor-general in 1973, Sir Anthony Mamo; prime minister, Dom Mintoff.

The seven-year development plan published in August 1973 was intended to enable Malta to dispense, after 1979, with the £14 million rent payable annually by Britain and other NATO members for use of the island's naval base. The plan aimed at providing about 20,400 new jobs, mostly in manufacturing. To attain full employment and economic viability, a total investment of M£205 million (at 1972 prices) would be required. The major part of this capital would be made available by domestic savings; the remainder would be financed by loans from the World Bank, China, Italy, Libya, the U.K., and the U.S.

The plan's political objective was that Malta should discard its centuries-old role as a fortress. Malta would disengage itself from power bloc affiliations and dedicate itself to economic and social progress through peaceful collaboration with all nations. In September, at the fourth summit conference of nonaligned nations in Algiers, Malta was admitted to full membership despite the presence on the island of the British and NATO facilities; these, the government explained, were permitted only out of economic necessity. At the Conference on Security and Cooperation in Europe, at Helsinki, Fin., in July, Malta, supported by Spain, proposed that Algeria and Tunisia, which were nonparticipants, be allowed to address the conference. However, no consensus could be reached on the proposal. When the fourth Arab-Israeli war broke out in October, Prime Minister Mintoff declared that the Maltese government would take no sides in the conflict.

On January 8 Radio Malta went on the air for the first time. In March a national airline was formed with the help of Pakistan International Airlines, which was given a 20% stake in the capital. Air service agreements were made with Tunisia and Austria. Tourism during January–August was 39% above the same period in 1972. (ALBERT GANADO)

Manganese:
see Mining

Manufacturing:
see Economy, World; Employment, Wages, and Hours; Industrial Review

Marine Biology:
see Life Sciences

Marriage:
see Vital Statistics

Mathematics

Group theory, Banach spaces, and combinatorial analysis were in the spotlight during 1973, as the ever growing world community of mathematicians continued research at a vigorous pace.

An advance was made in the mathematical study of objects, such as crystals, that possess a high degree of symmetry. Such objects, whose atoms or molecules are arranged in specific geometric patterns called crystal lattices or space lattices, possess a relatively large number of symmetry elements—*i.e.*, they can be reoriented in space, in a relatively large number of ways, such that the new positions of their atoms or molecules are indistinguishable from their original ones. Because the various ways of exhibiting symmetry can be combined algebraically, they can be considered to form mathematical systems called groups—specifically, space groups. Combinations of the various ways of reorienting the crystal lattices can be used to classify these space groups, and it is of interest to find out the total number of combinations in which the symmetry can be maintained and to list them usefully. The problem can be discussed not only in the world of three spatial dimensions in which we live but in fictitious worlds having a smaller or larger number of dimensions (and it is valuable to do so). For dimensions one and two it is easy to find the number of space groups to be 2 and 17, respectively. In dimension three the task is considerably more difficult, but it was accomplished in 1885 by the Russian crystallographer E. Feodorov. The answer is usually given as 230; but the smaller number 219 is the answer if mirror images are ignored. In 1973, with the aid of computation done at Ohio State University, H. Brown, J. Neubüser, and H. Zassenhaus found the number which in four dimensions corresponds to 219: it is 4,783. The larger number corresponding to 230 remained unknown.

There is a question in group theory called the "dimension subgroup problem." Though rather technical to state, it has an important status in group theory. There has been much work on it, and, in particular, several erroneous proofs have been published. To state the dimension subgroup problem, one has to attach two series of subgroups to a group G. The first is the lower central series Z_n. Roughly speaking, Z_n measures in stages the extent to which G departs from commutativity (the property of having elements that combine in such a manner that the result is independent of the order in which the elements are taken). The second series D_n of subgroups is obtained by passing from G to its group ring, making a certain ring-theoretic construction there, and then going back to G. D_n is called the nth-dimension subgroup. That Z_n is contained in D_n is easy; the problem is whether the two are equal. E. Rips, a young mathematician who recently emigrated from the Soviet Union to Israel, found that they are not. He constructed a large group for which Z_4 and D_4 are different.

01	—	45	67	—	—	23
57	02	—	—	—	13	46
—	56	03	12	—	47	—
—	37	—	04	26	—	15
36	14	27	—	05	—	—
24	—	—	35	17	06	—
—	—	16	—	34	25	07

The 7 by 7 Room square develops a problem posed by Australian mathematician T. G. Room.

Banach spaces, invented by the Polish mathematician S. Banach, are infinite-dimensional vector spaces that have been found to be a suitable vehicle for much of modern analysis. One fundamental question raised by Banach in his initial studies was: does every Banach space have a basis? (A basis of a Banach space is a set of elements that generate it economically, in a certain technical sense.) Investigations through the years revealed that all the familiar Banach spaces have bases. Nevertheless, the Swedish mathematician P. Enflo succeeded in constructing a Banach space that has no basis. His construction was promptly simplified by A. M. Davie of Scotland.

Another fundamental question concerning Banach spaces asks whether any continuous linear transformation admits a closed invariant subspace (this amounts to asking whether the transformation can be broken down into simpler constituents). In 1954 it was proved by N. Aronszajn and K. T. Smith that this is true if the transformation is compact (a technical property that asserts that the transformation behaves the way it would if the Banach space were finite-dimensional). In 1973 a much simpler proof was found by the Soviet mathematician M. Lomonosov; moreover, his method yielded much extra information. There were indications that resolution of the fundamental question was in sight.

In the branch of mathematics called combinatorial analysis there are a number of challenging problems of the following kind: determine whether or not it is possible to arrange certain objects into a configuration obeying certain rules. One such conundrum was answered in 1973; it concerns the existence of Room squares. The Australian mathematician T. G. Room proposed the problem in 1955, but it should be added that directors of duplicate bridge tournaments had previously grappled with virtually the same question in arranging the pairing of opposing teams and the assignment of prearranged deals to tables. Let m be an odd number. In an m by m square we are required to insert the numbers 0, 1, . . . , m in accordance with the following rules: each of the m^2 squares either is to be left blank or is to contain two of the numbers; every possible pair of numbers should occur exactly once; and each row and column should contain each of the numbers exactly once. It is easy to argue that for $m = 3$ or $m = 5$ the task is impossible. But for $m = 7$, the array in the figure shows one way of doing it. Is it possible for a larger m? Many mathematicians joined the attack on this problem, and slowly it yielded its mysteries until success had been achieved for every m except the strangely recalcitrant $m = 257$. This last case was finally handled successfully by W. A. Wallis (also Australian), thus completing the proof that there exists a Room square for every odd m larger than 5.

(IRVING KAPLANSKY)

Mauritania

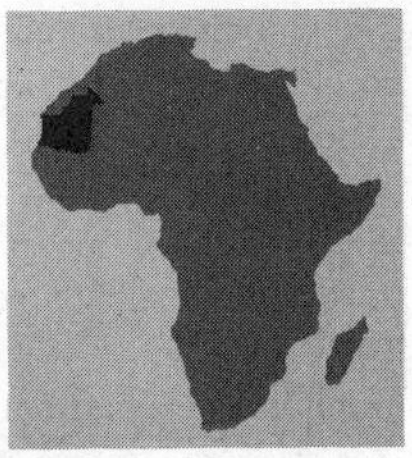

The Islamic Republic of Mauritania is on the Atlantic coast of West Africa, adjoining Spanish Sahara, Algeria, Mali, and Senegal. Area: 398,000 sq.mi. (1,030,700 sq.km.). Pop. (1972 est.): 1,150,700. Cap.: Nouakchott (pop., 1972 est., 55,000). Language: Arabic, French. Religion: Muslim. President in 1973, Moktar Ould Daddah.

After somewhat laborious negotiations, new cooperation agreements were signed between Mauritania and France in February 1973. The agreements covered questions relating to education, scientific research, and the status of French nationals in Mauritania, but no agreement was reached on military questions, or on the vexed question of the Mauritanian monetary system. This had been a source of difficulty since Pres. Moktar Ould Daddah (*see* BIOGRAPHY) had announced in 1972 that he intended to withdraw Mauritania from the franc zone. A new Mauritanian currency, the ouguiya, came into circulation in July, replacing the CFA franc.

A certain degree of political unrest persisted in Nouakchott throughout the year. In April five senior civil servants were suspended after supporting the trade unionist cause. In May the minister of the interior announced that an underground political movement, the National Democratic Movement (MDN), had been in existence since 1968, and that its aim was to overthrow the government. He said the movement involved political dissidents, students who had been expelled from their colleges, and unemployed persons calling themselves variously Communists, federalists, nationalists, or "Kadihines" (proletarians). In October a tract that was circulated in Dakar, Senegal, proclaimed the formation of a Mauritanian Kadihines Party to unite "proletarian" opposition to the government.

At a meeting in Cairo in October, foreign ministers of the Arab League agreed to accept Mauritania as a member.

Mauritania was one of the West African states hit by drought in 1973, and Ould Daddah criticized international opinion for failing to heed his earlier warnings of impending disaster. In June scientists from all over the world flocked to Mauritania to observe a total eclipse of the sun. (PHILIPPE DECRAENE)

MAURITANIA

Education. (1971–72) Primary, pupils 31,945, teachers (1965–66) 1,025; secondary, pupils 3,745, teachers (1963–64) 61; vocational, pupils 234; teacher training (1968–69), students 294.

Finance. Monetary unit: ouguiya (new currency introduced from June 29, 1973), with (Sept. 17, 1973) a parity of 1 ouguiya to 5 CFA francs (free commercial rate of 42.51 ouguiya = U.S. $1; 102.45 ouguiya = £1 sterling). Gold, SDRs, and foreign exchange, central bank: (March 1973) U.S. $10.1 million; (March 1972) U.S. $7.7 million. Budget (1972 est.) balanced at CFA Fr. 10.4 billion.

Foreign Trade. (1971) Imports CFA Fr. 15,780,000,000; exports CFA Fr. 25,129,000,000. Import sources: France 41%; U.S. 18%; U.K. 7%; Senegal 6%; West Germany 5%. Export destinations: France 21%; U.K. 16%; Belgium-Luxembourg 13%; West Germany 12%; Italy 11%; Spain 9%; Japan 8%. Main exports: iron ore 83%; fish 7%; copper ore 4%.

Mauritius

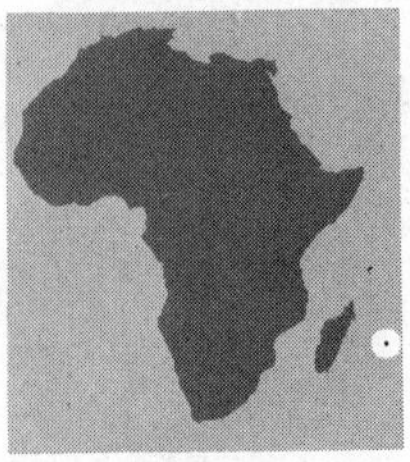

The parliamentary state of Mauritius, a member of the Commonwealth of Nations, lies about 500 mi. E of the Malagasy Republic in the Indian Ocean. Area: 720 sq.mi. (1,865 sq.km.). Pop. (1973 est.): 875,000, including Indian and Pakistani 67%; Creole (mixed French and African) 29%; others 4%. Cap. and largest city: Port Louis (pop., 1971 est., 142,270). Language: English (official). Religion (1962): Hindu 49%; Roman Catholic 32%; Muslim 16%. Queen, Elizabeth II; governor-general in 1973, Sir Abdool Raman Mahomed Osman; prime minister, Sir Seewoosagur Ramgoolam.

Following the death the previous December of Sir Leonard Williams, in March 1973 Sir Abdool Raman Mahomed Osman was appointed governor-general. Mauritius celebrated the fifth anniversary of independence in March amid every sign that Prime Minister Ramgoolam's coalition government had achieved stability and acceptance. Paul Berenger and other detained leaders of the left wing were released and their movement showed signs of severe splintering.

In April Mauritius acted as host to the Common Organization of Africa, Malagasy, and Mauritius (OCAM), during the deliberations of which the most important item was the projected new sugar agreement (Mauritian production being about 700,000 tons a year). Though anxiety remained about the future of sugar following the end of preference within the Commonwealth, free market prices remained high. Government attempts to attract export-oriented industry also began to show results as at least 16 industrial plants in the Export Processing Zone demonstrated that attempts to diversify the country's sugar-based economy were achieving some success, and both unemployment and the birthrate declined. There were marked signs that tourism, trade, and investment, discouraged from the Malagasy Republic by the coup there, were turning to Mauritius; a Club Mediterranée, under construction at Pointe aux Cannoniers in the north of the island, presaged increased tourist trade. A British loan of £5 million on September 27 completed Britain's promised aid for the four-year development plan and was tied to the provision of British goods, services, and technical assistance.

(MOLLY MORTIMER)

MAURITIUS

Education. (1971–72) Primary, pupils 152,331, teachers (1968–69) 4,253; secondary, pupils 45,198, teachers (1968–69) 1,706; vocational, pupils 549, teachers (1968–69) 34; teacher training, students 668, teachers (1968–69) 25; higher (1968–69), students 178, teaching staff 41.

Finance and Trade. Monetary unit: Mauritian rupee, with (Sept. 17, 1973) a free rate of MauRs. 5.53 to U.S. $1 (par value of MauRs. 13.33 = £1 sterling). Budget (1971–72 est.): revenue MauRs. 294 million; expenditure MauRs. 283 million. Foreign trade (1972): imports MauRs. 638.1 million; exports MauRs. 570.8 million. Import sources: U.K. 21%; Japan 9%; Australia 8%; South Africa 7%; Iran 6%; West Germany 6%; Burma 5%. Export destinations: U.K. 56%; Canada 20%; U.S. 9%. Main export sugar 89%. Tourism: visitors (1968) 15,600; gross receipts (1971) U.S. $6 million.

Agriculture. Production (in 000; metric tons; 1972; 1971 in parentheses): sugar *c.* 650 (624); tea *c.* 4.3 (4.1); tobacco (1971) 0.6, (1970) 0.4. Livestock (in 000; April 1971): cattle *c.* 49; pigs *c.* 3; sheep *c.* 3; goats *c.* 68; chickens *c.* 400.

Medicine

The Nobel Prize for Physiology or Medicine was awarded in 1973 to Konrad Lorenz, Nikolaas Tinbergen, and Karl von Frisch (*see* NOBEL PRIZES), three men who had spent their lifetimes investigating the behaviour of animals. The choice of men who had contributed to advances in sociobiology, an admitted departure for the Karolinska Institutet committee, suggested the tardy recognition of a most important truth—that there was value in and an urgent need for an application of the techniques and skills of science to the study of man not just as a person but as a member of a group. Animal studies could be regarded as a valuable step along this path. The most significant advances in medicine during what remained of the 20th century could well be concerned with a greater understanding of how the environment and the conditions of life in a community might be regulated to give men and women the best possible chance of being not only healthy in themselves but also of being healthy members of a stable and rewarding community.

For the time being, however, medicine remained almost wholly concerned with the ills of the person, a preoccupation that, nonetheless, proved productive. Clinical investigators reported progress in treating cancer, cardiovascular and kidney disease, and other illnesses; laboratory researchers increased medicine's understanding of the causes of these and other of man's most persistent health problems; and educators, health administrators, and politicians explored new ways to train physicians and other health professionals and prepare them to utilize medical science's advances. But this progress was not unaccompanied by problems. In the U.S., for example, a cutback in government support of research slowed the rate of scientific exploration and discovery, while a combination of cost-consciousness and apathy hampered efforts to guarantee good health facilities to all citizens. In the U.K. and Australia ethical and moral questions were raised by reported attempts to "create" life in the laboratory. Swedes, meanwhile, began finding fault with their highly socialized health care system. And in the less developed countries, famine and disease stalked, much as they had since the beginning of time.

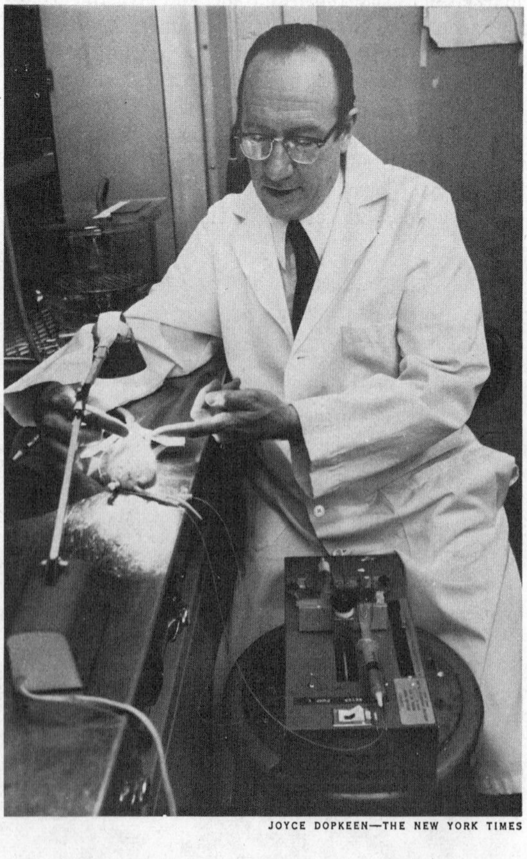

JOYCE DOPKEEN—THE NEW YORK TIMES

Harvard biochemist Robert P. Geyer conducts a transfusion, substituting a totally artificial solution of fluorocarbons and industrial emulsifiers for this experimental rat's real blood.

PROFILE OF PROGRESS

Many of the diseases that once plagued man simply ceased to exist as vaccination and improved sanitation eliminated their causes. Others remained, but as much-attenuated ailments easily controlled by antibiotics. An outbreak of cholera, for example, occurred in Italy in the summer of 1973, causing some concern in neighbouring countries, but it was rapidly brought under control. But the outbreak had been caused by the El Tor strain of the cholera bacillus, which had been spreading into North Africa and Europe from the Middle East since 1971—an infection that, with the conditions of hygiene prevalent in the Mediterranean area, seemed likely to remain in Europe for some time.

Nor did other infectious diseases pose the problems they once had. Plague, typhus, and mosquito-borne ailments like malaria and yellow fever had succumbed to rodent and insect control programs conducted by health agencies in many parts of the world. Smallpox, despite an occasional case, was so rare that various health authorities required immunization only of travelers returning from countries where the disease was endemic or where an outbreak had occurred recently. There was, however, a growing population that was susceptible to the disease, and through which it could spread rapidly if introduced.

Rh disease (erythroblastosis fetalis), which once claimed as many as 5,000 lives a year in the U.S. among babies whose mothers had produced antibodies against the blood type the baby inherited from its father, could now be prevented by vaccines.

Statistical indices reflected Western man's growing freedom from illness. Life expectancy continued to rise in Europe, while both infant and maternal mortality rates moved steadily downward. These numerical guideposts did not always reflect merely the state of medicine in these countries. Sweden's impressive statistics on infant and maternal mortality, for example, were as much the product of a high standard of living, low population density, or lack of intense urbanization as they were of the country's well-organized health-care system. Nor did U.S. figures, which showed the country to be trailing several others in life expectancy and exceeding nearly a dozen in infant mortality, necessarily reflect adversely on the quality of U.S. medicine. They did, however, reflect the low availability of that medical care to the poor.

The U.S. statistics remained unquestionably better than those for many of the world's less developed nations, where disease remained rampant, life expectancy lower and infant mortality higher than in the West. Smallpox, for example, continued to be a problem in most of Africa. So did schistosomiasis, a liver disease caused by snail-carried parasites, which affected an estimated 200 million in tropical countries throughout the world. The World Health Organization (WHO) attributed several thousand deaths to the disease in Africa alone in 1973; the ailment was also common to many parts of South America and the island nations of the Caribbean.

In few parts of the world, however, was health so precarious as it is on the Indian subcontinent. In its annual report, WHO noted that several dread diseases once thought to be under control were once again on the march in this overpopulated, famine-plagued, and war-stricken region. Cholera had long been endemic to India, as well as Southeast Asia and the Malay Archipelago; it was still a serious and constant threat to health. Smallpox had increased sharply in Bangladesh and northern India: in one week, 324 cases of the disease were reported in Calcutta alone. Malaria, successfully controlled until a few years before, had returned to India with a vengeance. More than 1.5 million cases were reported in 1972; half again that number were expected in 1973. Polio was also on the rise and nutritional deficiencies continued unchecked.

Other health problems, many of them possibly avoidable, afflicted those in the more developed nations, where the two main killers were the diseases of the arteries that caused heart attacks and strokes and cancer. The latest figures for the U.K., for example, published in October 1973, revealed that heart attacks had accounted for one quarter of all the deaths in the country during the previous year, and that cancer was the next most frequent cause of death, killing one person out of every five. Influenza, chronic bronchitis, and arthritis and rheumatism accounted for a high proportion of the spells of sickness that kept people away from work, and although bronchitis was peculiarly common in Britain, to the extent that it had been called the "English disease," this broad pattern of the causes of death and sickness was typical of all the industrial nations.

In the U.S. heart disease was expected to claim close to half a million lives during 1973. In West Germany an increase in deaths due to high blood pressure coincided with an increase in caloric intake made possible by a rising standard of living. In Japan a steady rise in heart disease was being attributed to the increase in fat consumption that resulted from a more westernized diet. Two decades before, when the Japanese diet was largely limited to rice, fish, and vegetables, deaths linked to atherosclerosis totaled 34,298 per year; more recently, they exceeded 70,000.

Cancer also seemed to be on the increase, although it had been suggested that much of the rise might be the result of better detection and diagnosis. In the U.S., where cancers of all types were expected to claim more than 349,000 lives in 1973, the incidence of lung cancer, much of it a product of smoking or the inhalation of airborne pollutants, continued to rise. Cancer also appeared to be on the increase in China, where the elimination of infectious disease was enabling more people to survive longer and thus increased the chance of their developing malignancies.

Two other categories of illness were gaining increasing attention. These were iatrogenic illnesses—diseases resulting from the unwanted side effects of treatment (usually by powerful modern drugs)—and diseases caused by pollution of the environment, such as lead poisoning, or cancer following the swallowing or inhalation of such toxic chemicals as asbestos dust. Both medical men and conservationists, for example, had been worried for years about the burial of radioactive wastes in the ground at Broomfield, Colo. In 1973, for the first time, scientists were able to measure radioactive tritium in the town's drinking water and in the urine of local residents. Although no specific ailments had been linked to the substance, doctors were keeping a careful watch on the area and its people. Others were showing concern about other radiation hazards as the more-than-coincidental occurrence of leukemia or radiation sickness in the vicinity of atomic generators increased suspicion that reactor hazards might have been underestimated.

Carbon monoxide and other air pollutants were well known as health hazards. The air in New York City was labeled "unsatisfactory" on more than 50 days in 1972, meaning that the levels of airborne pollutants were too high for safety. Waterborne pollutants also presented problems. Japanese continued to suffer from itai-itai (or "ouch-ouch") disease, a form of cadmium poisoning resulting from the dumping of mine wastes into streams. The discovery in 1973 that water supplies in Duluth, Minn., and 23 other Lake Superior communities contained high levels of asbestos, the result of mining operations in the area, raised concern over whether waterborne asbestos could cause cancer. Airborne asbestos had been linked to the onset of lung cancers 30 years after exposure.

Meanwhile, the threat of disease epidemics was revived in those nations that had become lax about immunization. Although effective vaccines were available to prevent such childhood diseases as diphtheria, measles, German measles, whooping cough, and poliomyelitis, these diseases continued to occur and claim lives. The U.S. Public Health Service's Center for Disease Control in Atlanta, Ga., recorded 2,242 measles cases in the first 24 weeks of 1973, up 10% over 1972. A polio outbreak at a Connecticut private school crippled 12 boys who had either not been vaccinated because of religious conviction or had received insufficient doses of vaccine. Failure to take advantage of immunization programs was, in fact, becoming a problem of increasing concern. John Witte, chief of the immunization branch of the Center for Disease Control, reported that 5 million of the 14 million infants in the U.S. were not inoculated against childhood diseases, and warned parents that this lack of protection endangered not only their children's health but that of others. It did indeed: German measles was responsible for deformities in thousands of U.S. children whose mothers were exposed to the disease during pregnancy and polio for crippling thousands of youngsters.

CLINICAL ADVANCES

Medicine had yet to find "magic bullets," or one-shot cures, for most of the major human ailments. But 1973 did bring remarkable advances in medicine's ability to treat, manage, and control many diseases. Progress was most notable against cancer, heart disease, kidney disease, depression, genetic diseases, leprosy, and in applications of acupuncture techniques.

Cancer. The second leading cause of death, cancer, was still one of the most feared of conditions and continued to be regarded as a virtual death sentence by many of its victims. Despite this gruesome reputation, cancer's grip was considerably loosened by several clinical developments. Surgery, to be sure, continued to offer the quickest way of removing large numbers of malignant cells and, at least in cases where the disease was diagnosed early, carried the best chances for survival. But other methods were gaining greater acceptance in 1973. Radiotherapy, or the use of X-rays to bombard and destroy hard-to-reach cancers, was made more effective by the adoption of neutron therapy. This technique used a cyclotron, or atom smasher, to fire neutrons at a cancer with pinpoint accuracy. London's Hammersmith Hospital had been using a cyclotron successfully for several years; in 1973 researchers at the Massachusetts Institute of Technology and the M. D. Anderson Hospital and Tumor Institute, Houston, Tex., began using similar devices.

Chemotherapy, or drug treatment, also had some new successes. The armamentarium of drugs capable of killing cells at the moment of division increased. Since cancer cells replicate more frequently than normal cells, these drugs tended to hit harder at tumours than at healthy tissue. Used singly or in combination, cytotoxic, or cell-destroying, chemicals proved extremely effective against acute lymphocytic leukemia, a cancer that strikes particularly hard at children. Prior to 1949 only 4% of acute lymphocytic leukemia's victims survived for three years after diagnosis. By 1969 this figure had risen to 30%, and in 1973 half of all children treated chemotherapeutically at major medical centres could be expected to live at least five years. Similar progress had been made against Hodgkin's disease, a cancer of the lymphatic system. The disease, like most cancers, was once considered fatal. Although no one would say categorically that Hodgkin's disease was curable, survivals of seven or eight years were anything but uncommon, and some victims had survived for as long as 15 years.

One of the new drugs under active investigation was ICRF 159, so called because it was discovered in the cancer chemotherapy department of the Imperial Cancer Research Fund laboratories in London by Kurt Hellman and his team. ICRF 159 had first been tested about seven years before because, from its chemical structure, it was thought that it should act as a cytostatic agent, one that interferes with cell division. This ICRF 159 did, but it also proved to have several quite unexpected and very valuable additional properties. Most strikingly it prevented the formation of secondary growths (metastases), those that are established when small groups of cells break away from the main tumour mass and are carried by the bloodstream, or along lymph channels, to distant parts of the body, where they settle down and multiply to form new tumours. It is commonly these secondary growths that kill. Usually the walls of the vessels in a cancer are defective, and it is this that allows cancer cells to be distributed around the body. It appeared that ICRF 159 improves the structure of the minute blood vessels that run through the substance of the parent tumour. This beneficial effect might also be responsible for the fact that the administration of ICRF 159 produced a remarkable increase in the effectiveness of X-ray treatment or of the other anticancer or cytostatic drugs. Blood flow to the tumour might well be so much improved that cytostatic drugs could reach the abnormal cells much more readily, and that oxygen supply would also be improved. The lethal effects of X rays upon dividing cells are much more marked in the presence of ample oxygen.

According to Hellman, the new drug might convert cancer from an acutely dangerous disease to a controlled, chronic condition. Most of the work so far had been done on laboratory animals, but a number of trials on patients were under way, in both Britain and the U.S., to discover whether the laboratory findings could be repeated on patients. The results so far were reported to be encouraging.

Some of the most encouraging progress against cancer was being made in the study and use of the individual's defenses against disease. The healthy body normally recognizes disease-causing microbes as foreign, or "non-self," and produces antibodies to resist, isolate, and destroy them. Because cancer cells are produced by the body itself, they are not always recognized as foreign. Immunologists were using a form of biological judo to trick the body into fighting its cancerous cells by stimulating it to make antibodies against some other ailment. One of the agents being used for this purpose was BCG (Bacillus Calmette-Guérin), a live-bacteria tuberculosis vaccine. By itself, BCG has no cancer-fighting properties. But when it is injected into patients with either natural or acquired immunity to tuberculosis, the immunological memory of the disease is jogged, producing a generalized immune response. In some patients this body activity to repulse bacterial boarders destroys cancer cells as well.

BCG was being used routinely as an adjuvant immunotherapy. Donald Morton of the University of California at Los Angeles (UCLA), for example, used it to boost immune responses in patients with malignant melanoma, a cancer that first appears on the skin and spreads rapidly throughout the body; some of his patients remained symptom-free for two years or more. Georges Mathé, a leading French cancer researcher at the Hôpital Paul-Brousse in Villejuif, administered BCG to patients as part of a two-pronged treatment for lymphoid leukemia, which tends to depress the already-weakened immune system. He first used chemotherapeutic agents to destroy large numbers of cancer cells and then administered BCG to elicit an immune reaction capable of rooting out residual cells.

Other researchers were trying to combat cancer with vaccines. Edmund Klein of Roswell Park Memorial Institute, Buffalo, N.Y., experimented with vaccines made from tumours similar to those of the patient, injecting them into cancer victims in the hope of producing reactions against both the foreign cancers and the patient's own. Loren Humphrey, chairman of the department of surgery at the University of Kansas School of Medicine, in a follow-up on nearly 100 patients who received such homologous vaccines, reported that 20% had had at least partial remission, while three were completely free of disease.

Cancer therapy, whether medical or surgical, could not by itself reduce cancer's death toll, for it could be applied only after the disease was diagnosed. Some forms of cancer could, however, be detected quite early. The Pap test, now a regular part of most routine gynecological examinations, could identify the earliest stages of cervical cancer and was rightly given considerable credit for reducing the mortality from this particular malignancy. But many, indeed most, cancers remained undetected until they were fairly well advanced, thus reducing the chances of dealing effectively with them. Even this situation might be improving, as medical researchers reported that efforts to develop accurate, inexpensive tests to screen for cancers were beginning to pay off. Arnold Leonard of the University of Minnesota School of Medicine developed a simple test for neuroblastoma, a highly malignant tumour that was second only to accidents as a cause of death in children. The test used treated paper strips that could be dipped into a urine sample or placed on a wet diaper. The paper turned orange when it was exposed to the unusual chemicals secreted by up to 80% of the children with neuroblastoma.

One of the most notorious and well established causes of cancer was, of course, cigarette smoking. But this fact seemed to do hardly anything to persuade people to give up the habit. In his annual report on the state of the public health, Britain's chief medical officer at the Department of Health and Social Security, after noting that the reduction in cigarette smoking that had followed reports on its role in lung cancer had been completely lost in 1972, concluded that "the cigarette must be the most lethal instrument devised by man for peaceful use."

At the beginning of its 150th year, the British medical periodical the *Lancet* poured scorn on the idea that air-cured tobacco was any safer than the flue-cured variety. The journal dismissed both the experimental and the statistical evidence in support of this comforting idea. A few weeks later the magazine *New Scientist* carried an article dampening hopes for the early emergence of a safer cigarette. Companies in Britain, West Germany, and the U.S. had been working for almost a decade on the production of a tobacco substitute, but nothing that was demonstrably safer than the natural weed was yet in sight.

Other studies reported during the year confirmed that mothers who smoked during pregnancy gave birth to smaller babies, and that this was probably an effect of the carbon monoxide that they inhaled with their cigarettes. Carbon monoxide combines with hemoglobin, reducing the amount of oxygen that the blood can carry and, therefore, the amount of oxygen that the mother can supply to the developing fetus. However, if these small babies survived the first year of life, they appeared to suffer no permanent harm. Another report suggested that nonsmokers who had to suffer living or working in smoke-filled rooms could inhale the equivalent of one or two cigarettes a day, which might be enough to double their chances of dying from lung cancer. A further study showed that nonsmokers in smoke-filled rooms could suffer significant rises of carbon monoxide in their blood.

Heart Disease. The cause of atherosclerosis—the development of patchy excrescences on the inner walls of arteries, which, by blocking the blood flow, give rise to heart attacks and strokes—remained a major subject for research. Over the years a massive amount of evidence has indicated that saturated or animal fats, and another fatty substance, cholesterol, are often present in excess in patients suffering a heart attack or stroke. For this reason diets in which margarine made from vegetable oils replaced butter, and in which foods like eggs, which contain a large amount of cholesterol, were restricted, had had a considerable vogue. To test the idea that diets can influence the risk of deaths from heart attacks, a number of long-term studies had been mounted. By 1973 papers describing the results of these studies were a regular feature of the medical year.

At the end of 1972 the *Lancet* carried a report from Finland of an experiment involving patients in two mental hospitals near Helsinki. Over a period of 12 years well over 2,000 middle-aged, long-term patients had been given either a cholesterol-lowering or a normal diet. At the end of the sixth year the diets were reversed; those patients who had been on the low-fat diet went onto normal food, and vice versa. The diet appeared to reduce the risk of death from heart attack among the men involved by half or more but, for some reason that the experimenters could not explain, it had a much less marked effect upon the women.

A ten-year study in New Jersey, reported during 1973, had involved 200 younger men, aged between 30 and 50, who had already suffered at least one heart attack. Half the men were placed on a low-fat diet while the others ate what they liked. This study showed that a controlled diet markedly reduced the chances of dying from a second heart attack within ten years of the first, survival among the dieting subjects being 17% better than among the uncontrolled group, and that this effect was most marked among the younger men. The important factor, however, seemed to be the total amount of fatty substances eaten, and not whether these were animal fats or vegetable oils.

While both these studies supported the theory that fats in the diet do influence the occurrence and the course of atherosclerosis in some people, and perhaps particularly in males, they also showed that the role that fats play is complex. Other factors clearly modify whatever damage a high blood-fat level may bring about. For example, several studies published during 1973 emphasized the important part played by smoking. Indeed, one investigation concluded that to stop smoking was possibly the surest way for a person with high blood pressure or high blood-fat level to avoid a heart attack or stroke.

The role of exercise in preventing rapidly fatal heart attacks continued to receive attention. A London team reported that a survey of the physical activities of nearly 17,000 executive-grade civil servants between the ages of 30 and 64 found that the men who regularly undertook spells of really vigorous exercise reduced their chances of developing coronary artery disease (atherosclerosis of the arteries supplying the heart muscle) by about two-thirds. To do the trick the ex-

continued on page 456

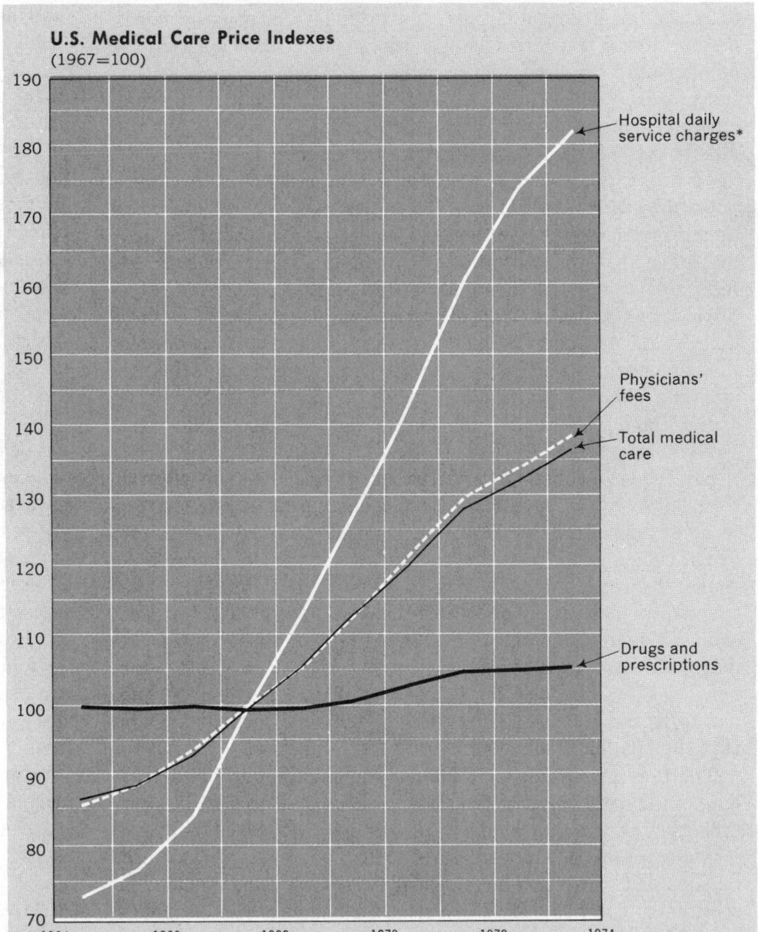

Annual averages except 1973 data are for July.
*From Feb. 1972, hospital daily service charges exclude cost of private rooms, for which separate data are no longer compiled.
Source: U.S. Department of Labor, Bureau of Labor Statistics.

SPECIAL REPORT

MEDICINE AND MADNESS

By Thomas S. Szasz

All too often, the language in which a personal or social problem is couched subtly but inexorably supplies its solution. Nowhere is this more evident than in the field of so-called mental illness.

In earlier times, when "the problem" was witchcraft—that is, when persons who provoked punishment for certain antisocial actions, or who were scapegoated for other reasons, were said to be witches possessed by demons—the solution was exorcism and burning at the stake. Today, when "the problem" is mental illness—that is, when such persons are said to be psychiatric patients suffering from mental diseases—the solution is to imprison them in buildings called hospitals and torture them in the name of treatment. In neither case did the "solution" arise from a hardheaded examination of the difficulty. It is against this background that we must view what is now usually called "the problem of the civil rights of mental patients."

I submit that this problem is primarily linguistic. I do not, of course, mean that it is "just" a matter of semantics or words. Rather, it is a matter of how words are used to shape popular opinion and to justify legal action and political policy. The concepts and terms "mental illness" and "mental patient" combine and confuse two entirely different and, at bottom, contradictory sets of ideas and interventions: disease and cure on the one hand, and deviance and control on the other.

Cure and Control. If we take an unbiased look at the traditional, commonsense meanings of the words "ill" and "insane," we notice that they conjure up two quite different images and refer to two quite different ideas. Illness means there is something wrong with the body of the person said to be ill, whereas insanity means there is something wrong with the behaviour of the person said to be insane. This is why, traditionally, the first idea has led to interventions usually called "treatments" and "cures" and the second to interventions usually called "restraints" and "controls."

Especially in contemporary free societies, there is, for all practical purposes, no such thing as the involuntary medical treatment of adults. The social act of medical treatment comes into being not so much because the patient is sick as because he wants treatment and is willing to submit to it. In short, what ultimately justifies medical treatment is not disease but consent. Conversely, what characterizes involuntary psychiatric diagnosis, hospitalization, and treatment is that each comes into being not because the alleged patient wants or is willing to submit to it, but because someone other than the "patient" claims that the "patient" is "mentally ill."

The present psychiatric situation cannot be understood without some appreciation of the history of psychiatry. Briefly, modern psychiatry began in the 17th century, with the building of insane asylums in which all sorts of troublesome and unwanted persons were incarcerated. Originally, then, psychiatry was "institutional"; it was a kind of extralegal penology. In the course of its 300-year history, and especially during the past century, immense and unceasing efforts have been directed at redefining psychiatric confinement as "hospitalization" and psychiatric control as "treatment."

Perhaps because the best efforts of the most energetic psychiatrists have been devoted to this task—from Philippe Pinel and Benjamin Rush to Sigmund Freud and Karl Menninger—this medicalization of human problems and their coercive control by means of the police power of the state has been amazingly successful. (*See* Szasz, *The Myth of Mental Illness* [1961]; *The Manufacture of Madness* [1970]; *The Age of Madness* [1973].) As a result, no other group in modern history has been so consistently and unrelentingly persecuted, and deprived of their human and constitutional rights, as the insane or so-called mentally ill.

Involuntary and Voluntary Mental Hospitalization. The most important deprivation of human and constitutional rights inflicted on persons said to be mentally ill is involuntary mental hospitalization; that is, the coerced confinement of the person in an institution called a mental hospital. Many thousands of persons are now so confined in the United States, and countless more in other countries. While the precise legal requirements for commitment differ from state to state and from nation to nation, the procedure, in effect, is based on and justified by the closely connected ideas of mental illness and dangerousness. This is exemplified by the traditional American legal formula for commitment, which speaks of the alleged patient as suffering from a "mental disease or disorder" and of being "dangerous to himself or others." Regardless of the legal phraseology in which commitment laws are enshrouded, their implementation depends almost entirely on the ideology that animates the psychiatrists and judges who practice this sort of "medicine." Their ideology has been, quite simply, paternalistic.

"If a man brings his daughter to me from California," a prominent psychiatrist testified before a U.S. Senate committee, "because she is in manifest danger of falling into vice or in some other way disgracing herself, he doesn't expect me to let her loose in my hometown for that same thing to happen" (*Constitutional Rights of the Mentally Ill,* Washington, D.C.: U.S. Government Printing Office, 1961, p. 71). Jurists have held the same view of the problem. In denying damages to a man who had entered a mental hospital voluntarily, was subsequently prevented from leaving, and sued, a Connecticut appeals court judge ruled that "mental patients are often not in a condition to appreciate what is for their own best interests or what their real desires are" (*Roberts* v. *Pain,* 124 Conn. 173, 199 A. 115 [1938]).

Although most of the people committed to mental hospitals against their will are poor or old, many prominent persons have also suffered this fate, both in former times and in our own. King Ludwig II of Bavaria; Mary Todd Lincoln, President Lincoln's widow; U.S. Secretary of Defense James Forrestal; Ernest Hemingway; and the dissident intellectuals in the U.S.S.R.—these are but a few of the famous victims of psychiatric incarceration as a method of social control.

While in many cases persons committed to mental hospitals ostensibly lose only the right to leave the hospital, actually they often lose all their civil rights. They may be declared incompetent to manage their persons and assets; may lose the right to vote, drive a car, or practice their profession; may be subjected to the most brutal and injurious acts—called psychiatric treatments—imaginable to modern man; and are permanently stigmatized as "ex-mental patients."

Although some mental hospitalization is nominally and semantically "voluntary," so-called voluntary mental patients incur many of the same deprivations of civil rights suffered by the involuntarily hospitalized mental patient. Indeed, because voluntary mental hospitalization is always potentially and often actually a covert form of involuntary mental hospitalization—and because this type of hospitalization now involves many more

Thomas S. Szasz is professor of psychiatry, State University of New York Upstate Medical Center, Syracuse, N.Y., and the author of numerous books.

persons than does involuntary mental hospitalization—this psychiatric intervention is perhaps an even greater threat to civil liberties than is involuntary mental hospitalization. Both in fact and by law, voluntary mental patients are treated essentially the same way as involuntary mental patients. Moreover, patients hospitalized voluntarily often enter a psychiatric institution under the threat of commitment. Once confined, they cannot secure their release as can medical patients, and when they insist on release against psychiatric advice, they may be committed by their relatives and physicians. The prisoner status of such patients was openly acknowledged by a 1971 decision of the Supreme Court of Utah, in which the court held "that a voluntary patient at the [mental] hospital is as much 'confined' and has as little freedom as a mentally alert trusty in a jail or prison" (*Emery* v. *State*, 483 P 2d, 1296).

Psychiatric interventions may be invoked against persons accused of crime at every point where the criminal process impinges on the accused. At every such point psychiatry is used to deprive the accused of freedom and dignity in the name of protecting his mental health and treating his mental illness. A person accused of a crime may thus be declared mentally unfit to stand trial and be confined in a mental hospital until he is declared to be fit. Such a person is deprived of the Sixth Amendment guarantee to a speedy and public trial, and may be imprisoned, under psychiatric auspices to be sure, without trial. Ezra Pound was so confined for 13 years. Tens of thousands of Americans have been, and continue to be, so confined, some drawing a psychiatric life sentence for a trivial offense. A defendant allowed to stand trial may plead not guilty by reason of insanity —a plea that may be entered for him by his attorney without his understanding its implications. He may, as a result, draw an indefinite sentence of psychiatric incarceration in lieu of a possible acquittal or a finite prison sentence. Finally, once in jail, a prisoner may be declared psychotic and transferred to a hospital for the criminally insane.

This brief survey does not exhaust all of the ways in which psychiatric interventions are now used as methods of social control—through legislatures and courts, through medical organizations and mental institutions, and last but not least through the personal desire to control others. Our society is shot through with the use of psychiatric incriminations and excuses, from declaring wealthy relatives mentally incompetent or their wills invalid to evading the draft and abortion laws. (*See* Szasz, *Law, Liberty, and Psychiatry* [1963]; *Psychiatric Justice* [1965]; *Ideology and Insanity* [1970].)

Reforms. For centuries, involuntary psychiatric interventions were regarded as things done *for* the so-called patient rather than as things done *to* him. This perspective, which is still the official psychiatric posture, precludes genuine reforms in the mental health field. In recent years, however, increasing numbers of persons, both in the mental health professions and in public life, have come to acknowledge that involuntary psychiatric interventions are methods of social control. With this recognition, the question with respect to psychiatric reforms becomes whether we want to retain such methods and introduce certain safeguards into their use, or whether we want to abolish their use altogether. On both moral and practical grounds, I advocate the abolition of all involuntary psychiatry.

This goal could easily be attained. However, because of our intense devotion to the medical perspective on human problems, efforts to do so may prove to be, at least for the time being, unpalatable and impractical. To attain this goal, we would first have to accept that so-called mental health problems are not medical but human—they are economic, moral, social, and political problems. In other words, mental illnesses are metaphorical diseases.

It is impossible, of course, to understand the metaphorical nature of the concept of mental illness without coming to grips with the literal meaning of the concept of ordinary or bodily illness. When we say a person is ill, we usually mean two quite different things: first, that he believes, or his physician believes, or they both believe, that he suffers from an abnormality or malfunctioning of his body; and second, that he wants, or is at least willing to accept, medical help for his suffering. The term illness thus refers primarily to an abnormal biological condition, the existence of which may be claimed, truly or falsely, by patient, physician, or others. Secondarily, it refers to the social role of patient, which may be assumed or assigned.

The accepted or literal meaning of "illness" is thus an abnormal biological condition; for example, a myocardial infarction. When mere complaints—for example, a person's complaints about his body or about the bodies or behaviours of other persons —are defined as illnesses, we are faced with the metaphorical use and meaning of "illness." In short, bodily illness stands in the same relation to mental illness as a defective television set to a bad television program. Of course, the word sick is often used metaphorically. Comedians tell "sick" jokes, economies become "sick," sometimes even the whole world seems "sick." But only when we call minds "sick" do we systematically mistake and strategically misinterpret metaphor for fact and send for the doctor to "cure" the "illness." It is as if a television viewer were to send for a television repairman because he dislikes the program he sees on the screen. (Szasz, "Mental Illness as a Metaphor," *Nature*, 242:305–307, March 30, 1973.)

To attain the goal of abolishing involuntary psychiatry, we would also have to acknowledge that so-called psychiatric diagnoses, prognoses, hospitalizations, and treatments not explicitly sought by clients for their own use are coerced. In other words, compulsory psychiatry is an exercise in social control, like penology but unlike medicine. And finally, we would have to conclude that involuntary psychiatric interventions violate the protections guaranteed by the Constitution of the United States (and fly in the face of basic principles of human fairness and justice) and must therefore be abolished.

The mere act of speaking about protecting the "civil rights of mental patients" is an injury to their civil rights. To speak of the "civil rights of slaves" implicitly legitimizes the legal distinction between slaves and free men and hence deprives the former of liberties and dignities enjoyed by the latter. Today we accept that this is nonsense: that being a slave means not having any civil rights, or at least having fewer of them than free men. But we still speak of the "civil rights of mental patients." And by so doing we implicitly legitimize the legal distinction between insane patients and sane citizens and hence deprive the former of liberties and dignities that the latter group enjoys.

Not until a free people accept and demand that civil rights be independent of psychiatric criteria, just as they now are independent of religious criteria and are becoming independent of racial and sexual criteria, and not until legislators and jurists deprive physicians, and especially psychiatrists, of the power to exercise social control by means of quasi-medical sanctions, will the civil rights of persons accused of mental illness, or otherwise faced with involuntary psychiatric interventions, be protected.

What would become of psychiatry if involuntary psychiatric diagnoses, hospitalizations, and treatments were abolished? In principle, psychiatry would then become more like any other medical specialty, such as dermatology or ophthalmology—practiced only on voluntary clients. More generally, it would become like any other profession, such as accounting or architecture—contracting for the sale of certain services and products with informed buyers in a free market. In practice, psychiatry would then have to identify and define—as it never has had to before—the services it offers for sale. Clearly, such a change would spell the doom of psychiatry as we now know it. If it survived the change, which seems doubtful, psychiatry would emerge as a system, or as several systems, of applied secular ethics. Hence, its practitioners would find themselves in competition, not with clinicians, but with clerics.

UPI COMPIX

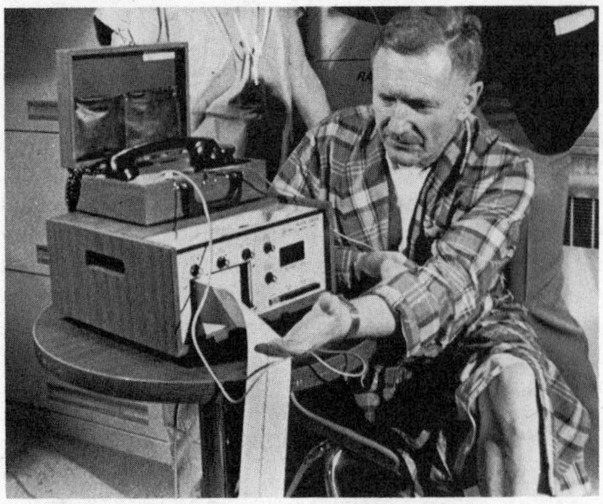

Max Spieler of Nutley, N.J., checks an electrocardiogram report from his nuclear-powered pacemaker. The large machine is for use at home, and allows physicians to monitor heart condition by telephone.

continued from page 453

ercise had to be sufficiently vigorous, had to continue for bouts of not less than 15 uninterrupted minutes, and had to have a "training" effect on the heart and the blood vessels. A particularly interesting finding was that exercise had no effect upon the incidence of a high blood pressure or a high blood fat, but appeared to increase the immunity of the subject to any ill effects of these conditions. Also, vigorous exercise appeared almost to neutralize the malign influence of smoking on vascular disease. This, unfortunately, did not mean that a person could smoke away to his heart's content, because exercise was not going to do anything to reduce the chances of lung cancer.

Another study by members of the same London group (the Medical Research Council's Social Medicine Unit), which also involved civil servants, showed that subjects living in soft water areas had higher average blood pressures, blood cholesterol levels, and heart rates than similar subjects living in hard water towns. Several earlier studies had shown that the residents of soft water areas ran an increased risk of developing coronary artery disease.

A report from an international group organized from Boston, Mass., described the coffee-drinking habits of patients admitted with coronary artery disease to various hospitals in the U.S., Canada, Israel, and New Zealand. The inquiry showed that heart attack victims were accustomed to drinking appreciably more coffee than patients admitted for other conditions. But the investigators admitted that they did not know whether coffee drinking encouraged heart attacks. Perhaps coffee drinkers took more sugar than others, and the sugar was the culprit, but if that was the explanation then tea drinkers should also be more liable to heart attack, and they are not. Perhaps coffee drinkers smoked more cigarettes. Or perhaps their addiction reflected a tense and driving personality of the kind associated by some authorities with an increased risk of heart disease. Earlier work showed that heavy coffee drinkers tended to have higher blood cholesterol levels, and perhaps this was the clue to the Boston findings. In any case, the survey suggested that persons drinking more than five cups of coffee a day had about twice as great a chance of having an acute coronary attack as persons drinking no coffee at all.

Two fascinating theories concerning the actual cause of those excrescences on the walls of the arteries, which are the root of all the heart trouble, came from two different pairs of workers at the Washington University School of Medicine, St. Louis, Mo. Both pairs agreed that the fundamental fault is a local overgrowth of the muscle cells that form the middle layer of the wall of the arterial hosepipe. This muscle allows the artery to dilate or contract according to the needs of the tissue that it supplies. The inner layer of these arteries consists of flat, delicate, pavement-like cells that allow the blood to flow with little friction. But this fragile lining can probably be damaged by the rush of blood through the arteries, and such damage would be more likely at points where arteries branch, and there is a turbulent or rough flow. Damage would also be more likely to happen in people with a high blood pressure, in whom the force of the blood flow is more violent. The idea that such lining damage is the first step in the production of these atherosclerotic patches was supported by the facts that patches are more frequently found at the points where arteries divide, and that they are commoner in people suffering from high blood pressure.

The first of the Washington University teams proposed that something in the blood makes the muscle cells in the middle layer of the arteries grow rather like a wart and push into the cavity of the vessel. The second pair produced quite convincing evidence in favour of the view that these atheromatous plaques are, in fact, small tumours. They believed that one single cell at the site of a patch has mutated (that a fault has occurred within the pattern of its genetic code) so that it begins to reproduce itself somewhat as a cancer would. Both pairs of researchers could be right, to the extent that atherosclerosis might be caused by damage of the artery lining that permits some substance in the bloodstream (perhaps an abnormal ingredient) to promote an excessive growth of the underlying muscle cells. This concept might be one very large step forward in the understanding of the mechanism of atherosclerosis. Such an understanding is the first, and often the most difficult, step in the process of devising an effective prevention of or cure for disease.

In the meantime, transplant surgery, never really regarded as the answer to heart disease, received a further setback. Norman Shumway, a Stanford University heart transplant surgeon with a high success record, reported that atherosclerosis continued in certain patients, rapidly blocking the blood supply to the transplanted organ. But another form of surgery, the coronary bypass, won support as a means of coping with certain heart conditions. The procedure, in which a piece of vein was taken from the leg or elsewhere and used to carry blood around an obstruction in the coronary arteries, had, since its development about ten years earlier, been regarded by many cardiologists as little more than a surgical spectacular. Although there were no accurate figures in 1973 on the number of such operations being performed, there was little question that the bypass was the most frequently tried radical procedure in U.S. hospitals. At the annual meeting of the American Heart Association, researchers from the Cleveland (O.) Clinic, which led the world in use of bypass surgery, showed that patients who had undergone bypass surgery had a life expectancy 15% longer than that of a control group that had been treated medically before the bypass procedure became available.

Heart patients were also aided by improvements in the pacemaker, a miniature device implanted under the skin in the chest cavity that emitted electrical impulses that regulate heartbeat. Most pacemakers were battery operated and had to be recharged regularly under surgical conditions. But in recent months human tests were begun with nuclear-powered pacemakers. These relied on small quantities of a radioactive plutonium isotope, which, as it decayed, generated heat that was converted into electrical energy for the pacemaker. Like the devices they were designed to replace, the new pacemakers were not permanent; they were, however, expected to operate effectively for at least ten years.

Kidney Disease. Kidney failure, the late and irreversible stage of kidney disease, threatened anywhere from 8,000 to 13,000 persons in the U.S. alone each year. Its victims faced certain death unless they could receive regular dialysis, in which the blood was cleansed of most of its impurities by an artificial kidney machine, or obtain a kidney transplant. Most chose the former, not because it was necessarily the better alternative but because it was the more readily available: dialysis was a time-consuming, frequently debilitating process, but transplantable kidneys were in short supply. Steps were being taken, however, to improve both the supply of donor kidneys and the safety of transplant surgery. Improved tissue-matching techniques reduced the incidence of rejection, permitting reductions in the doses of toxic immunosuppressive drugs given to transplant recipients. Better matching also improved chances of successful transplantation. The success rate in a so-called A match, one in which the donor and recipient were identical genetically, as with identical twins, or nearly so, as with a parent and child, had always been high, and remained as high as 90%. But more sophisticated matching improved the success rate with kidneys from non-relatives as well. Indeed, the chance for a "take" with such a transplant was now around 75%. An estimated 2,900 kidney transplants of all types were performed in the U.S. in 1972. Most recipients could lead normal lives and hold regular jobs; several women had successfully conceived and delivered children.

The task of matching donor and recipient was further eased by the presence of a National Kidney Registry, headquartered in New York City, which kept computerized profiles of all patients waiting for kidneys. Through its contacts with hospitals throughout the U.S., it could quickly match a kidney available for transplant with the best recipient and have it flown to the patient's hospital within hours.

Depression. Psychiatrists had long suspected that there was a biochemical basis for severe depression, the acute psychiatric disturbance that Freud termed melancholia. Their suspicions not only led them to new discoveries about depression, but also to new ways of treating it. Researchers at the University of North Carolina School of Medicine had been studying thyrotrophin-releasing hormone (TRH), a substance released by the hypothalamus at the base of the brain that triggers the production in the anterior pituitary of thyrotrophin, or thyroid-stimulating hormone. They found that TRH, for reasons yet to be discovered, also functioned as an antidepressant. In one study, when 18 women suffering from severe depression each received a single shot of TRH, eight experienced prompt though short-term relief. In subsequent studies, ten women responded favourably to TRH when it was administered over a two-week period.

TRH was not the only drug-like substance being studied as a treatment for depression. Recognizing that an increase in the enzyme monoamine oxidase (MAO) is associated with depression, other scientists perfected a class of substances called MAO inhibitors. These did not cure depression, but they could relieve its most acute symptoms while the patient underwent psychotherapy to get at the root of the problem.

Acupuncture. Although an acceptable explanation of how acupuncture works remained elusive, the revival of Western interest in the ancient Chinese medical art of curing illness and relieving pain by means of needles placed in strategic points in the body continued during 1973. Laymen, fascinated as always with something that seemed to offer an easy cure for many ailments, provided a fertile field for quacks and medical entrepreneurs who took advantage of the technique's current popularity. But more scientific minds, recognizing that, whatever the explanation, acupuncture anesthesia actually worked, slowly expanded its clinical applications.

In France, where acupuncture had been practiced for more than a decade, some medical men used acupuncture techniques to treat nerve deafness. Many reported encouraging results in curing cases of nerve deafness, some of which had defied the best efforts of physicians using more conventional approaches. Nonetheless, it could be expected that in medical practice outside of China acupuncture techniques would find increasing use in anesthesia, while their value in treating chronic illness remained questionable.

Genetic Diseases. Physicians continued to be better at diagnosing and predicting genetic diseases than they were at treating them; in most such diseases, the damage was done at the moment of conception, and, given existing skills, was irreparable. But even this might be changing. Work done at the U.S. National Institutes of Health, Bethesda, Md., demonstrated the possibility of enzyme therapy, the replacement of an enzyme whose absence caused the genetic disease. Fabry's disease, an inherited metabolic disorder characterized by the accumulation of a fatty acid derivative called ceramidetrihexoside in the organs and tissues, is caused by a lack of the enzyme galactosidase, which is essential to splitting the ceramidetrihexoside molecule. Past treatment for the disease involved infusions of human plasma and kidney transplants, both of which produced only limited success. But the new treatment, developed by a team of researchers at the Metabolic Neurology Branch of the NIH's National Institute of Neurological Diseases and Stroke, seemed more promising. Highly purified ceramidetrihexoside extracted from human placental tissue was administered intravenously to two patients with the disease. Tests showed that the enzyme was cleared rapidly from the blood and taken up by the liver. This caused the levels of circulating ceramidetrihexoside in both

Two members of Los Angeles County Fire Department's mobile paramedical program provide emergency assistance to a young accident victim.

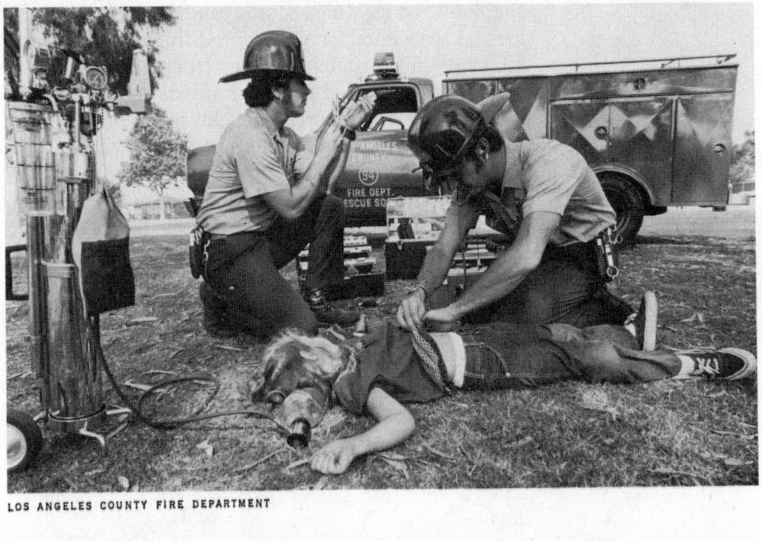

LOS ANGELES COUNTY FIRE DEPARTMENT

patients to drop dramatically, and the disease-causing substance failed to build up in their organs.

The NINDS team's effort was the first successful demonstration that a genetic disease resulting in an enzyme deficiency was treatable by the administration of an enzyme. Most genetic ailments involve errors of metabolism akin to that causing Fabry's disease. The discovery suggested that similar enzyme replacements might be tried with other hereditary ailments.

Leprosy. Rare in the Western world, leprosy remained a threat in parts of Africa and had defied eradication efforts among Middle and Far Eastern peoples. Drugs that attack and destroy the leprosy bacillus had long been used with fair success to control and, in some cases, cure the disease, but a new treatment developed by Soo Duk Lim of Seoul National University, South Korea, and researchers from the University of Minnesota that used the body's own immune responses was both exciting and encouraging. Large doses of white blood cells from volunteer donors with natural immunities to the disease were infused weekly in 14 patients for periods of up to 16 weeks in an attempt to trigger in the patients the manufacture of antibodies against the foreign lymphocytes. The treatment succeeded in switching on the patients' idling immune systems, stimulating their production of antibodies that not only rejected the donor lymphocytes but destroyed the bacilli as well.

MEDICAL RESEARCH

Although medicine had made more progress in the past 25 years than it had in its entire previous history, most physicians admitted there was still much more to be learned. Not only were they still looking for answers to age-old questions, but they also had to try to formulate the right questions to elicit answers to new puzzles. This lack of knowledge tended to stimulate rather than discourage members of the medical research community.

Virology. Viruses, submicroscopic packets of nucleic acids, had been known since 1911 to be capable of causing cancer in animals. Viral causes of human cancers, however, remain to be positively identified. This did not mean that there was any dearth of suspects. In 1973 research findings concentrated on one suspected family, the herpes viruses. Of these, herpes simplex, which was responsible for cold sores, proved, contrary to its name, to be a complex microbe. It is now thought that nearly everyone carries the best-known form of this virus in a dormant state, probably in nerve tissue, until it is activated by fever, sunburn, or nervous tension. A variant form, herpes simplex Type II, which causes painful sores and swellings on the genitals, buttocks, and thighs, was becoming increasingly common among teen-agers and young adults, who acquired it during sexual intercourse. In fact, genital herpes was thought by many to rank second only to gonorrhea as the most common sexually transmitted disease in the U.S.

A new antiviral drug, isoprinosine, could clear up genital herpes, but Type II viruses had also been found in laboratory studies to transform normal cells into cancerous ones, raising speculation that the virus might play a role in human genital cancers. The evidence for this suspicion was more than circumstantial. Type II antibodies, produced in response to the virus, had been isolated from the cells of women with cervical cancer and Albert Sabin, developer of the live-virus polio vaccine, found such antibodies in 56 patients with cancers at various sites and no trace of the virus in 51 patients without cancer. Andre Nahmias and his colleagues at Emory University, Atlanta, Ga., provided other evidence linking the virus to cancer. In a long-term study, the incidence of cervical cancer among 900 women known to have genital herpes was found to be eight times higher than among 600 women who had not had the infection.

Other researchers studied possible methods of viral transmission. The idea that cancer viruses are transmitted from one generation to the next, proposed by Robert Huebner of the National Cancer Institute as part of his "oncogene," or cancer-causing gene, theory, picked up substantial scientific support. In experiments conducted at Jackson Laboratories, Bar Harbor, Me., the crossbreeding of two specially bred strains of mice, one extremely cancer-prone, the other highly tumour-resistant, to observe the rates at which cancers occurred in their offspring proved that proneness to cancer might, in mice at least, be inherited along straight Mendelian lines.

Another group of researchers, meanwhile, established that some cancer viruses may also be transmitted from individual to individual. At New York's Sloan-Kettering Institute for Cancer Research, William Hardy and his colleagues observed that leukemia, which is common in cats, tended to occur in clusters, that is, when one cat in a colony developed the disease, others did also. Further tests, carried out at three major veterinary hospitals, provided convincing evidence that feline leukemia can be transmitted from one animal to another. Blood tests of 1,462 cats from disease-free colonies revealed that only two animals carried the Feline Leukemia Virus (FeLV), while tests of 543 cats from infected colonies showed 177 harbouring the virus. Of the 148 cats from this group that the veterinarians were able to follow, 35, or 23.7%, died within six months from leukemia or FeLV-related anemia. That Hardy's finding might have significance for human cancer studies could be found in reports that Hodgkin's disease tended to occur in population clusters that defied the laws of coincidence, suggesting that, in some cases, the disease might be contagious. An outbreak of leukemia in Illinois raised similar suspicions about that disease.

Immunology. Immunology attracted new attention in 1973 as scientists began to find answers to the many disease problems related to the body's natural defense, or immune system. It was firmly established that two populations of cells, called T cells (because they become differentiated in the thymus, a small organ located just under the breastbone) and B cells (because, in chickens, at least, they originate in an organ called the bursa of Fabricius), recognize foreign cells, identify them as invaders, and call up the production of antibodies that isolate, immobilize, and eventually destroy the attackers. The ability to manufacture antibodies to various antigens, or disease agents, could protect an individual against those agents to which he had already been exposed and, through vaccination, permit the development of an immunological "memory" of antigens not yet encountered naturally. But absence or malfunction of the system could invite disaster. Many researchers believed, for example, that immunological malfunctions play a role in cancer by allowing outlaw cells to replicate unchecked. Autoimmune diseases, in which the individual makes antibodies against some of his own tissues, included lupus erythematosus, which killed several hundred, most of them children, each year, and rheumatoid arthritis, in which the body produces antibodies that destroy its own joint tissues, crippling hundreds of thousands.

Past successes in immunotherapy included the development of a vaccine that could desensitize an Rh-negative woman who had been pregnant with an Rh-positive child and had produced antibodies that could attack as foreign the blood of a future Rh-positive fetus. More recent evidence proved to be a clue to a possible treatment of hereditary combined immunodeficiency disease (CID). Researchers at the University of Minnesota had noted that a child suffering from the disease lacked a specific enzyme, and other scientists confirmed the same deficiency in their patients. They began seeking to determine if replacing the missing enzyme could somehow enable the patients' immune systems to function and, if so, how this enzyme can be replaced. Another new method of dealing with CID clinically was bone marrow transplantation. (Lymphocytes, which fight infection, are produced by bone marrow.) The number of such transplants for immunodeficiencies (bone marrow transplants were also sometimes used to treat leukemia) did not exceed two dozen. The technique might, however, have more regular use if research being carried on by Fritz Bach and colleagues at the University of Wisconsin produced the expected results. Bach found what appeared to be new and better ways to match tissues and overcome incompatibility, which might eliminate, or at least greatly reduce, transplant rejection.

Meanwhile, other researchers worked on developing new vaccines. In France and the U.S. a vaccine made from the red blood cells of cattle and sheep produced antibodies against infectious mononucleosis in nearly all of the subjects tested. It was expected to take at least another year to determine whether definite protection against the disease was provided. Other researchers continued the search for an effective influenza vaccine. The flu virus' apparently infinite capacity to mutate meant that vaccines that worked against one strain were of limited effectiveness against successors. In an attempt to anticipate this phenomenon, a team at the Institut Pasteur in Paris headed by Claude Hannoun put flu viruses through a process of forced evolution in the laboratory in the hope that they would produce a virus that had undergone all the changes that nature can produce in the virus in the next five years. They believed the vaccine developed against this virus would be effective through 1978.

Chalones. There was renewed interest in naturally occurring substances called chalones, which had not attracted much attention when first discovered in 1960 at Birkbeck College in London. Chalones appeared to act as switch mechanisms operating on cell growth. It seemed that each different type of tissue produced its own chalone, and that when the concentration of the appropriate chalone in a particular tissue reached a certain level further cell growth and division were inhibited. For example, if half of the liver is removed the production of liver chalone is also halved, so that its concentration in the circulating bloodstream falls. In response to this the cells in the remaining half of the liver begin dividing at a faster than normal rate until the liver has been restored to its original size. At this point the rate of chalone production will also have been restored to normal, and liver chalone will be present in the blood at a concentration just sufficient to keep the liver cells dividing at a rate adequate for the replacement of dying cells.

Recently, at the University of Helsinki, Fin., T. Rytömaa and K. Kiviniemi experimented on the use of chalones as a cancer treatment. By employing the appropriate chalone they were actually able to cure a type of leukemia in rats, and although there was not sufficient of this particular chalone available to test its effect upon human leukemia, the Helsinki workers showed that the agent prevented the division of human leukemic cells grown in the laboratory.

UPI COMPIX

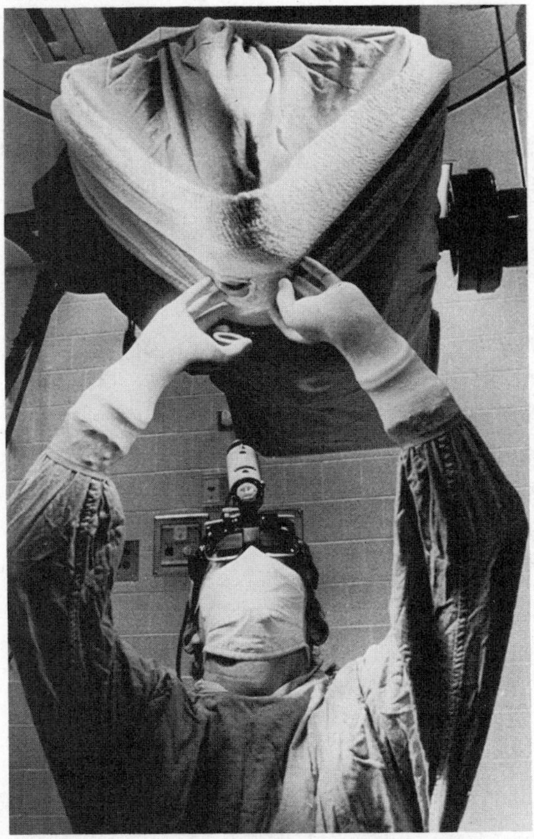

Hal MacKenzie Freeman, retina surgeon at Massachusetts Eye and Ear Infirmary, demonstrates the advantages of his unique operating table. Free to rotate 360 degrees, the table employs gravity to unfold the retina.

Chalones might also find an important role in dealing with the transplant rejection problem, which is largely mediated by the lymphocytes. In the first recorded use of these agents in a patient, Georges Mathé in Paris used the lymphocytic chalone to prevent the rejection of a bone marrow graft. More recently J. Houck of the Children's Hospital, Washington, D.C., also used the lymphocytic chalone to prevent the rejection of skin grafts in mice.

These substances, which appeared to be proteins, or perhaps even smaller polypeptide molecules, were not only nontoxic to the body, but their effect was reversible. That is to say, everything returned to normal when their administration ceased. Moreover, although particular tissues produce their own chalones, it appeared that a chalone from a tissue of one species of animal would be equally effective in controlling the growth of the comparable tissue of an animal of another species. This fact greatly eased the problem (still formidable enough) of preparing chalones in quantities sufficient for the experimental treatment of human disease. Although the history of medicine is littered with examples of apparent breakthroughs that end in disappointment, it appeared in 1973 that chalones might be one of the most rewarding and exciting discoveries since the isolation of penicillin.

Hypertension. Hypertension, or high blood pressure, was a primary cause of 25,000 deaths and many of the more than 1.5 million heart attacks in the U.S. alone each year. The condition, the causes of which were unknown, played a role in kidney problems and

WIDE WORLD

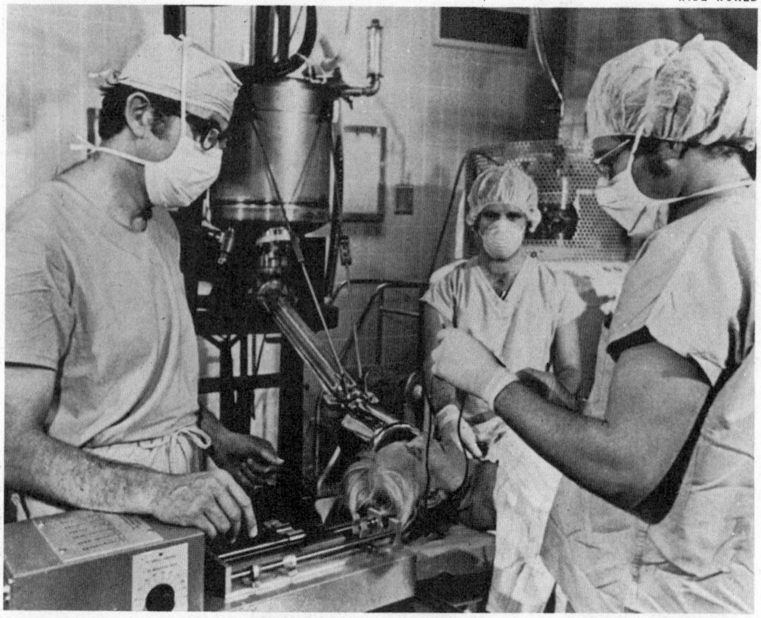

In a successful bloodless surgical technique, developed recently at the University of California, Los Angeles, School of Medicine, a powerful electromagnet (adjacent to the patient's head) concentrates an injected silicone-iron compound at the point of blood supply to a brain tumour. Denied blood, the tumour dissolves in time.

diabetes as well. As many as 25 million, or one out of every eight persons in the U.S., were estimated to have high blood pressure, many without knowing it. A disproportionate number of those thus afflicted were black—a statistic for which there was no suitable medical explanation.

Some 15 drugs on the market could effectively control hypertension, and physicians and public health officials had been carrying out mass screening programs to detect persons with the condition in several cities around the U.S. But at the same time, they were trying to acquire a better understanding of the ailment. Levels of renin, an enzyme produced in the kidneys, were found to increase in certain types of hypertension related to kidney disease and to decrease in other types of hypertension, such as those related to increased activity of the adrenal glands. It was possible that tests for renin levels might be valuable diagnostic tools in recognizing patients with different types of hypertension, thereby permitting the best treatment for their conditions.

Aging. Few things were more puzzling medically than the aging process, that steady deterioration of the body that can begin at any time after the age of 19. The process could be described, but it was not understood, and scientists continued to study it. Alexander Leaf of the Harvard Medical School visited Vilcabamba in Ecuador, Abkhazia in the Georgian S.S.R., and Hunza in the Kashmir, three regions in which living beyond the age of 100 was commonplace. After studying these people, Leaf offered a number of conclusions on longevity. One was that a moderate diet helps avoid such life-shortening ailments as heart disease and diabetes. The diets of people in all three geriatric paradises were low in saturated fats; meat and dairy products accounted for less than 2% of the calories consumed. All three areas were agrarian, and natives were used to prolonged physical labour. Leaf noted that attitudes might also be important in longevity. In all three regions the elderly were held in high esteem and continued to perform such valuable work as tending flocks, caring for grandchildren, or keeping house well past their 100th birthdays. The people in these regions were also relatively free from the pollutants and other hazards that threatened more industrialized man, and unconcerned with many of his worries. They expected to live a long time, regarding 100 years as a normal life span.

Other researchers offered new theories on aging. Leonard Hayflick of Stanford University School of Medicine, for example, wondered whether the body might simply be programmed to self-destruct at a certain time. But he also wondered if this process, which envisions the occurrence of errors in the repeated copying of DNA messages, might be controlled chemically. He was devising a series of experiments aimed at determining whether the finite doubling of the cell is controlled by the DNA in its nucleus or by RNA, the messenger molecule that carries out the DNA's instructions. If the process is controlled from without, he reasoned, it might be altered by drugs.

Nutrition. In several nations of equatorial Africa in 1973, drought left thousands dying of hunger, despite the efforts of international relief organizations to bring in food. In Nigeria, where the scars of civil war had yet to heal, serious protein deficiencies continued to produce cases of kwashiorkor, a wasting disease that hit particularly hard at the young. In Bangladesh, floods wiped out a large part of the country's agricultural production and produced a famine that killed untold thousands. In the West, meanwhile, abundance was more of a problem than famine. Rising standards of living enabled those in industrialized nations to eat better than ever before and contributed to such problems of plenty as atherosclerosis, diabetes, and simple obesity.

Physicians trying to learn exactly how diet affects development uncovered some clues. Medicine had long known that infant malnutrition contributes to mental retardation, but recently a British study showed that maternal malnutrition was responsible for low birth weight among some babies born at term, and a U.S. study showed that infants born to malnourished mothers tended to have a higher incidence of prematurity, with all its attendant problems. The babies tended to be smaller and to lag behind other infants in intellectual development. The reason for this gap was thought to be a lack of brain-building proteins during the critical stages of brain development, 80% of which takes place between conception and two years of age. Growth that fails to take place during this period does not take place at all.

Immunologist Robert Good, of the Sloan-Kettering Institute for Cancer Research, reported that protein deficiencies may also contribute to failures of the immune system. Observations of protein-deprived children in Africa, Egypt, and Israel led to the finding that of the children who have suffered such deprivation since birth, 75% died of infection. Most had failed to develop a key immunoglobulin by the age of six months; many were unable to respond to smallpox and cholera antigens. Good also found considerable rheumatic heart disease among aboriginal children in Australia. He reasoned that "the classical association between pestilence and famine can be better understood" from such findings as these. In addition, work done by William Cooper of Cleveland showed that chronic or moderately severe protein deprivation depresses humoral, or thymus-controlled, immunity. His work led Good to speculate that diet may prove valuable in the control of cancer, which the body battles via the cell-mediated and not the humoral immune system.

Meanwhile, others found ways to overcome some forms of nutritional deprivation. At St. Luke's Childrens Medical Center in Memphis, Tenn., an inexpensive, protein-enriched baby formula was supplied to ghetto mothers along with instructions to feed it to infants. The first class of children thus fed entered school in 1973. Normally children from the Memphis ghettos lagged far behind better-fed children from other parts of the city; the children fed on the dietary supplement, however, were able to keep up with their contemporaries.

Reproduction. Research into methods of preventing conception had advanced enormously in recent years. The Pill remained a preferred method of birth control, despite British studies showing that women who used it ran a slightly higher risk of cerebral stroke than those who did not. Intrauterine devices also won wider acceptance as improvements reduced the problems of cramping, bleeding, and spontaneous expulsion. And from Sydney University in Australia came the announcement that a three-year contraceptive implant was now possible in the form of a pellet of the hormone progestogen combined with a plastic, which could be inserted under the skin.

Vasectomy, or male sterilization, also gained in popularity, particularly in the U.S., where it had been performed on well over three million men. The procedure itself was simple: under local anesthetic the vas deferens, the thin, convoluted tubule that carries the sperm from the testicles to the prostate gland, is severed and its ends are tied back on themselves. But it was not without its problems. For one thing, it must be considered permanent. Although the severed vas had been successfully rejoined in a significant number of cases, fertility was restored in only a handful. Nor was there yet a way to make the operation more easily reversible: tests at New York Medical Center on a device that could be inserted in the sperm ducts and turned on and off by a simple surgical procedure had failed to establish its effectiveness. In addition, although the procedure should have no physiological effect on a man's potency, many men who felt that they were pressured into having vasectomies reported that they became impotent afterward.

One available way of dealing with unwanted pregnancy was the "morning after" pill, diethylstilbestrol, which the U.S. Food and Drug Administration approved as a post-coital contraceptive in cases of rape or medical emergency. But the agency's action proved premature. Researchers noted a high incidence of vaginal cancers in the teen-age daughters of women who had taken DES during pregnancy to prevent miscarriage. Others reported that the drug had caused cancers in animals in whose feed it had been used as a fattener. As a result the FDA qualified its endorsement of DES late in the year and ordered that physicians who prescribed it warn women about its side effects.

Physicians continued to be less successful in their efforts to promote fertility. Hormone drugs prescribed to help overcome inovulation worked in only a limited number of cases and often were too effective in that they caused a woman to release several eggs at once, which when fertilized led to the multiple births that had made newspaper headlines often in recent years. Unfortunately, although the women conceived and delivered as many as seven children at once, the infants were usually born prematurely, and few, if any, survived.

For some years R. G. Edwards, a physiologist at Cambridge University, and Patrick Steptoe, a gynecologist at Oldham General Hospital, had been experimenting with the technique of removing egg cells from a woman's ovary by means of a simple operation, fertilizing them in the laboratory by mixing them with human spermatozoa, and growing the fertilized eggs in a test tube until they became very early human embryos, with the idea that the best of the batch might be reimplanted in the woman's womb, where it would develop to full term and be delivered finally in the natural manner. The stated aim of these efforts was to overcome the difficulty of a woman who could not become pregnant in the normal manner because of a blockage in the fallopian tubes, often the result of an infection, which was a common cause of sterility among women. So far, however, Edwards and Steptoe had not successfully reimplanted a laboratory-fertilized ovum in the mother's womb. Moreover, their efforts had not attracted much official support, and toward the end of 1973 they announced the establishment of the Edwards-Steptoe Research Trust, saying they would launch an appeal for funds to allow them to continue their experiments. A Melbourne, Austr., physician actually tried such an implantation in 1973, but the woman miscarried several days after implantation.

Although this research might suggest the experiments of a Dr. Frankenstein or the efforts of Faust to create Homunculus, the researchers doing the studies were anything but movie-style mad scientists. Most were seriously concerned with helping women to have children although not all were aware of the implications, both ethical and scientific, of their work. But all encountered opposition. The NIH bowed to pressure from church groups and adopted a policy banning all research on aborted fetuses, as well as any studies that are not intended to benefit the unborn.

Vitamin C. During the year a number of reports appeared that seemed to support Nobelist Linus Pauling's claim that people could all do with much more vitamin C than they actually receive. Cedric Wilson of Dublin University claimed that an eight-year study had shown that an intake of about two grams of vitamin C a day, while not preventing colds, reduced the severity of symptoms by some 30–40%. He believed that the catarrhal symptoms of the common cold were associated with a deficiency in the body's defense mechanisms that vitamin C makes good. Similar results were reported from the University of Toronto. The Canadian workers also found that the subjects of their tests taking the vitamin spent some 30% fewer days off work during the trial than their nonvitaminized contemporaries. A report from Czechoslovakia suggested that vitamin C may reduce the level of cholesterol in the blood, and thereby afford some protection against coronary artery disease, and a study at Stanford University School of Medicine showed that very large doses of vitamin C had substantially reduced the amount of insulin required to keep a diabetic patient in a steady state of health.

Public Health. Venereal disease remained a major public health problem in 1973, as cases of gonorrhea, syphilis, and other ailments connected with relaxed sexual attitudes continued to increase around the world. But nowhere was the problem more acute than in the U.S., where the incidence of gonorrhea increased by more than 15%, raising the annual number of new cases reported to 718,401 in the year ended June 30, 1972. Few cases, however, were reported among teenagers, who apparently preferred self-treatment to risking a physician's betrayal of confidence, or from the lower or upper classes, suggesting that actual incidence might be twice that reported. Despite a $16 million federal effort to find and treat the disease, particularly in asymptomatic women, there were no signs that it was receding.

But progress was made toward the control of another serious health problem. A test nearly 100 times more sensitive than existing procedures was developed for detecting hepatitis antigen B in blood. In approving the test the FDA said that its regular use should more than double detection of blood plasma or serum units harbouring hepatitis virus. Since blood transfusions were a significant source of hepatitis infection, widespread use of the test could reduce the incidence of the disease.

A better means was also developed to detect lead poisoning, which could cause mental retardation, crippling, and death in children who ate chips of lead-based paints found in older buildings. Previous tests had been time-consuming and required amounts of blood that could only be drawn by a professional. The new test required only a drop of blood that can easily be obtained by a volunteer, cut the time required for diagnosis to a matter of minutes, and could facilitate mass screening for the ailment. The possibility for such action came none too soon: in the U.S. tests had shown that 5% of urban children under seven had elevated blood lead levels.

HEALTH CARE DELIVERY

The U.S. public's dissatisfaction with both the amount of health care available and the ways in which it was being delivered deepened in 1973. Most health authorities agreed that the U.S. could use a 20% increase in practicing physicians. But, although they had expanded in recent years, U.S. medical schools could accommodate only 13,000 of the more than 45,000 applicants for admission in 1972. With tuition providing only one-third of the $10,000 it cost per student per year, medical schools could not expand further without additional funding. The shortage of places at home had led some 4,000 U.S. students to seek their medical educations abroad. Many of these students had to meet the foreign country's requirements before they could obtain their degrees. In Mexico, for example, they had to work for a year in a rural area, a rule that helped, among other things, to lower the incidence of tuberculosis among Mexican Indians. But it was equally obvious that the talents of those willing to try the tough foreign route were needed. Many hospitals were so short of professional staff that they hired foreign physicians, few of whom spoke English, to run their emergency rooms, places where a knowledge of the language was essential.

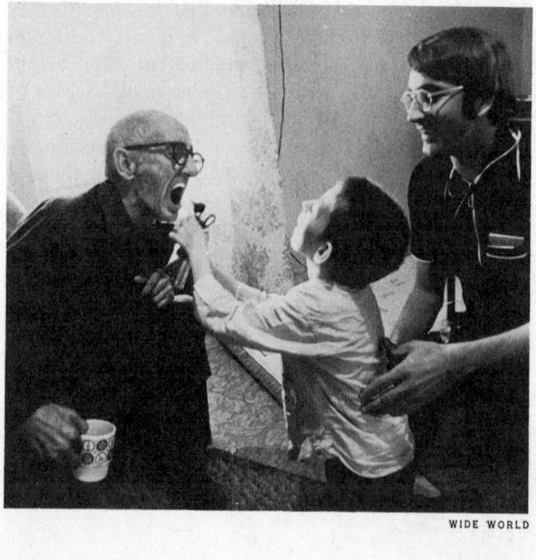
WIDE WORLD

Young Jeff Handshoe of Knott County, Ky., makes mock examination of his father's throat. Dr. Grady Stumbo, right, is visiting Jeff as part of an outreach and screening program of the East Kentucky Health Services Center, a comprehensive rural clinic.

Meanwhile, other steps were being taken to meet steadily increasing demands for health care through the use of allied health professionals. For example, in the U.S. in 1973 there were 1,200 practicing midwives, compared with 400 ten years before. Most were registered nurses and graduates of nurse-midwife programs at such centres as the Yale University School of Nursing and Johns Hopkins School of Hygiene and Public Health. Among the factors explaining this resurgence was the desire of some women's liberationists to avoid male obstetricians and the growing acceptance of home delivery, especially in rural areas. That midwives, properly utilized to handle most deliveries, calling in a physician when delivery was other than routine, could relieve a physician of much work was evident from the European experience. In the U.K., for example, under one of the world's most advanced health care systems, 80% of all births were handled by midwives.

In the U.S.S.R. highly trained paramedical personnel, "feldshers," provided much of the routine preventive care, first aid, and immunization in the country's vast undeveloped areas. Similar use was made in China of specially educated "barefoot doctors" who worked in factories and fields, providing medical care and emergency services when necessary. The idea of making greater use of paramedics was also catching on in the U.S. In Washington, for example, the Medex program recruited former military corpsmen and trained them as physicians' assistants who handled much of the routine work of taking histories, applying bandages, and administering some injections. Paramedics were also being used as ambulance personnel, some of them functioning as members of cardiac emergency crews.

Nurses were demanding—and getting—more responsibility. Specially trained nurses conducted much of the cardiac monitoring in hospitals, handled kidney dialysis, and ran heart-lung machines in surgery. In a program under way in Colorado, nurses provided pediatric care in one section of the state, handling all routine well-baby matters and referring possible cases of illness to physicians for confirmation and treatment. In addition, private-practice nurses, although still a rarity, were becoming more common. Such nurses treated minor injuries, helped patients care for themselves, and helped them decide when they should see a physician.

GENERAL DEVELOPMENTS

In 1973 U.S. politicians and journalists alike wondered what had become of the issue of national health insurance, which had been an "idea whose time had come" two years earlier. It appeared that most people were convinced that they could obtain care when needed, were unenthusiastic about the costs of implementing any of the various health proposals before the U.S. Congress, or had reservations about the concept of national health insurance. Many justly feared the abuses, by both doctors and patients, that such a system could not help but encourage. Many also feared the bureaucratization of medicine. In Sweden, for example, patients complained bitterly of long waits for all but emergency care and railed against indifferent doctors. The doctors, on the other hand, argued that their national system reduced them to mere government employees, stifled initiative, and destroyed interest in the patient as an individual. A number of Swedish doctors threatened to quit, or, if prevented from doing so, to strike.

The U.K. Parliament approved a bill for the reorganization of the National Health Service that, in theory, brought the three major branches of the service into more effective liaison by placing them all under regional authorities responsible to the government for the administration of all health matters within their areas. Many suspected that in practice nothing much would change, but doctors feared that they would have a smaller say in the running of their own affairs.

U.S. medical research, long considered the best, and best-funded, in the world, was seriously slowed in 1973 as the Nixon administration drastically reduced federal funding, especially for new research grants. Also hit were U.S. medical schools, which counted on the government for almost half their operating budgets and were scheduled to get 15% less in the current fiscal year than they had received the year before. The irony of the cutback was that it occurred while the government was also taking a step that most saw as a major one in the direction of socialized medicine. In a masterpiece of political maneuvering, Congress amended the Social Security Act to provide federal support under Medicare for much of the cost of treating patients with end-stage kidney disease. The measure, reluctantly signed by the president to take effect at midyear 1973, meant that for the first time the government had accepted responsibility for a group of patients regardless of age, occupation, or financial status. The impact of the measure could be enormous. With the kidney disease legislation as a precedent, the Congress would find it increasingly difficult to withstand the pressures from other "disease" lobbies demanding subsidized treatment of other expensive yet manageable illnesses.

Once the unchallenged voice of U.S. medicine, the American Medical Association found its membership reduced to 42% of the profession in 1973 and its leadership under sharp attack. At issue was the official position the AMA should take on a section of the Social Security Act of 1972 that ordered groups of physicians to review the validity of every medical decision that involved services to be paid for with federal funds in an effort to eliminate unnecessary expenses. The AMA leadership, backed by the younger and more liberal members, urged compliance with the law. But older and more conservative factions, which one poll estimated reflected the sentiments of two-thirds of all physicians, saw this position as yet another example of the AMA's unwillingness to protect them from government inroads. They pushed the organization to demand repeal of the law or face further loss of members, who would seek redress through unionization. A compromise approved at the AMA's clinical convention in December 1973 ordered the association to work toward amending the legislation to remove its most onerous provisions.

M. G. Candau retired in 1973 as director general of the World Health Organization (WHO) after serving in that office for 20 years. He was succeeded by Halfdan Mahler, a Dane, who had been assistant director general since 1970. The WHO, which sponsored research into many of the diseases, was suited by both organization and character to coordinate efforts to combat disease by disseminating information, handling relief efforts, and enlisting nations to battle the common enemy of illness. To function effectively, however, it needed the full cooperation of every nation. That such cooperation was not always forthcoming was evident in Italy during the cholera outbreak. Italian authorities, fearful of scaring off the tourists upon whom much of the economy depended, minimized the seriousness of the outbreak, which claimed more than 20 lives before it was brought under control. WHO, which might have kept other nations informed about the nature and scope of the disease flare-up and advised them on action to prevent its spread, could only take the Italian government at its word and assist it in obtaining vaccines and medications. (DONALD GOULD; PETER STOLER)

DENTISTRY

During 1973 the National Institute of Dental Research celebrated its 25th anniversary with a two-day special conference in Washington, D.C. The establishment of the NIDR in 1948 had climaxed an eight-year battle by the American Dental Association to obtain federal funds for dental research. Since then, the NIDR budget had risen from an initial $237,000 to $40,333,000 in 1973. Although about 80% of NIDR's total appropriations were spent for extramural research and training activities, the intramural staff had played a pivotal role in advancing research into dental decay and periodontal (gum) disease.

As inflation in the U.S. continued, leaders of the dental profession repeatedly pointed out that the costs of dental care had not risen as rapidly as those of most other health services. In fact, the American Dental Association (ADA) emphasized, dentists' fees during the preceding decade had climbed at a rate slightly below that of the composite cost of all services throughout the economy.

Nevertheless, dental fees had risen over the years, and the profession intensified its efforts to teach the public how the individual patient can effectively reduce his own dental costs while increasing his oral health. Preventive dentistry, encompassing a broad spectrum of approaches including regular dental checkups, sound personal oral hygiene, a sensible diet, and fluoridation, was already practiced by most dentists. A recent survey of dental services indicated that for the first time the volume of preventive care surpassed the volume of repair or restorative care.

About 18 million persons in the U.S. were covered by dental insurance. The growing interest in such programs was exemplified by the 1973 contract between the United Auto Workers and the Chrysler Corp., which provided for a dental insurance program. Nonprofit dental service corporations in 38 states and a number of commercial insurance companies were working with dentists to stimulate preventive care. Subscribers were urged to use these programs for regular dental checkups.

To meet the growing demand for dental care, the profession was taking a hard look at future manpower requirements. On the positive side, the number of dental school graduates had climbed consistently over the preceding several years, resulting in a slight improvement of the dentist-to-population ratio. However, proposed cutbacks in federal funding of educational programs in the health professions had an alarming effect on the future outlook. According to the ADA, the proposed reduction of operating grants and elimination of training grants could put dental schools in a precarious position and jeopardize continuation of even the smallest expansion programs.

Bootleg dentistry—a dental laboratory technician illegally selling low-cost dentures directly to the public—had occurred sporadically in the U.S. for decades. Although these bootleg technicians had generally been kept under close surveillance, there were indications that denturism, as this activity was often called, might be expanding. Bootleg technicians in Canada had succeeded in gaining legal recognition or, where this had not been accomplished, had persuaded the authorities not to take a hard-line approach against them. Patients living near the Canadian border could avail themselves of the services of Canadian denturists, and denturists were reported to be active in Minnesota, Michigan, New York, Idaho, and Texas. The ADA launched a full-scale educational campaign to warn legislators and the public about the serious damage bootleg technicians could inflict on their unsuspecting customers.

Undiscovered cancer of the breast, lung, or kidney sometimes can cause a secondary tumour in the jaws. Since cancer of the jaw may be the first clinical manifestation of a distant malignancy, dentists can help in the identification of such metastatic cancers. This was the opinion of Henry M. Cherrick, a UCLA researcher, who added that metastatic cancer of the jaw does not occur frequently, but dentists should be aware of its significance. Previous statistics showed that the breast, lung, large intestines, prostate, kidney, thyroid gland, and testes, in that order, are most common sites of origin of secondary jaw tumours.

According to Cherrick, however, "With the great increase in the incidence of carcinoma of the lungs, new statistics will probably reveal that carcinoma of the lungs is the most common tumour to metastasize to the jaws." The lower jaw is more frequently afflicted by cancer than the upper jaw, and the most common site is around the lower molar and premolar teeth. The most common symptoms are slight discomfort or pain, followed by numbness of the lip or chin caused by involvement of the lower jaw nerve. Teeth in the affected area may become extruded or roots may become resorbed.

The dental profession was adopting a cautious attitude on the use of acupuncture in dental treatment. The ADA Council on Dental Research declared that, based on present knowledge, the use of acupuncture in the treatment of orofacial pain or as anesthesia in dental procedures was "still considered highly experimental." Calling for a concentrated research effort on this ancient Chinese technique, the council at the same time cautioned dentists against premature use of the method pending further scientific evaluation of its effectiveness and safety.

Speech therapy as well as orthodontic treatment is frequently needed to correct such faulty oral habits as tongue-thrusting. Jeanne M. Goldberger, a Cleveland speech therapist, felt that since a relationship between speech and tongue thrust exists, a speech therapist is the logical person to correct this habit. Tongue thrust, or reverse swallowing, is characterized by the incorrect placement of the tongue between the upper and lower teeth in swallowing and in the rest position. Goldberger noted that 90% of her private practice represented referrals from orthodontists who recognized that the correction of malocclusions (faulty bite) caused by tongue-thrusting would be only temporary unless the habit itself was completely eliminated.

Duane T. DeVore of the University of Maryland suggested that collagen grafts made from calfskin might have some potential value in the replacement of jaw or facial bone lost through accident or oral disease. Collagen, a soft, gelatin-like substance, is the main supportive protein of skin, bone, cartilage, and connective tissue. Reporting to the International Association for Dental Research, DeVore noted that "unlike metal grafts, which usually have to be replaced or removed, collagen grafts should be an immediate, permanent replacement."

Electronic electrosurgery was being used more and more frequently in dentistry to improve the patient's appearance, overcome speech problems, and correct troublesome dentures. Daniel Strong of New York City reported that this cold-cutting technique functions like a scalpel but with no pressure of the instrument against the tissue. "The advantage of using high-frequency current instead of a knife is that there is practically no bleeding." (LOU JOSEPH)

PSYCHIATRY

There was renewed interest in the concept of mental health during the year. The simplest definition included the ability to love well, play well, and work well, and to maintain optimism for the future; these stemmed partially from inner processes provided by healthy genes and salutary early-life experiences, and partially from external social and cultural phenomena. Greater stress was being placed on child development in an effort to determine the factors leading to subsequent health and/or illness, but much was still to be learned.

Within recent years psychiatry had shifted from notions of linear cause and effect and reliance on a single school of thought and a single technical approach. Instead, all schools and techniques were being combined into a field in which each theory and method had an appropriate role. Based on such general systems theory, psychiatry was concentrating on multidisciplinary approaches, in keeping with the recognition that the health–sickness array was based on multiple causes. For example, schizophrenia was not attributed solely to genes, brain damage, poor mothering, bad family communications, or traumatic adult experiences. Each was seen as part of the total picture, participating to one degree or another in the precipitation of the disease.

There had been a shift in the character or expression of psychiatric disease. The dramatic and histrionic psychoses were seen less frequently. Catatonic excitement and stupors were rare; manic episodes were less wild and depressions were quieter. Instead, the most common psychiatric syndromes were more in the shape of introverted, constricted character changes; for example, the so-called borderline syndrome and the narcissistic neuroses. Why these changes should have occurred was unclear. However, many deviances or disturbances are deeply affected by social and cultural factors, which had been undergoing rapid change in the last few decades.

At the same time, there was a growing demand that psychiatry change its focus from the individual, who requires lengthy treatment, to couples, families, groups, and communities, and that psychiatric services be made available to the indigent as well as the rich. One outgrowth of this trend was community psychiatry, an organizational concept oriented toward making the psychiatric resources of a "catchment area" available to all its residents regardless of their ability to pay.

Psychiatry differs from other fields in many ways,

including its vague and unsatisfactory system of classifying diseases. Unlike other medical specialities, it is concerned not only with diagnosis and treatment but with a complicated biopsychosocial system. Because psychiatry can offer no definitive true or false answers, the field is especially vulnerable to faddists and self-appointed lay people of various stripes who offer what they claim are panaceas for psychic difficulties or merely unhappiness. In the 1970s the interest in group therapy had spilled over into a variety of encounter groups, sex groups, sensitivity groups, primal scream groups, and the like that held out hope of better socialization and rapid and cheap cures. Unfortunately, they were not effective for the most part; moreover, there was a high casualty rate of psychoses, especially in groups that had a highly traumatic effect on the participants. Many persons with psychiatric disturbances, but who are by no means psychotic, are miserable and eager for help, but a little push can send them over the line into psychosis.

The modern use of drugs had decreased the population of mental hospitals by over 50%. However, many patients were released prematurely only to return quickly, leading some in the field to speak of the revolving door policy. Many patients ceased taking medication after discharge, and after a year or so many of the medications were no longer effective. The discharged patients needed halfway houses or continued ambulatory care in offices or clinics, and for some long-term hospitalization was the only viable alternative. It was becoming increasingly clear that the current policy of closing state hospitals needed serious reconsideration.

Even more ominous was the toxic nature of the drugs being used for psychiatric patients. For example, the antimanic drug lithium, when used in large amounts over a long period, may produce heart and kidney damage. Phenothiazines, used for schizophrenia, may produce rigidity and tremor.

Considerable excitement had developed during the last year or so over the use of huge quantities of vitamins in the treatment of schizophrenia. Most psychiatrists in the field opposed this "megavitamin" therapy, although it had a number of enthusiastic advocates and at least one organization was devoted to promoting its use. Strong evidence developed in 1973 indicated that huge doses of vitamins do not cure schizophrenia but may act, through the power of suggestion, as a placebo.

Another widely publicized controversy in the field involved psychosurgery. At one time psychosurgery—specifically, prefrontal lobotomy—was widely used as a treatment for severe psychoses and neuroses. It was a mutilating operation in which a punching instrument was used to sever the nerves connecting the frontal lobes with the thalamus, and since the surgical method was imprecise, other brain tissue was sometimes destroyed as well. Many people suffered severe brain damage as a result—although lobotomized patients were usually quieter. In later years the method fell into disrepute and was performed only infrequently. More recently, surgeons involved in the treatment of certain physical diseases developed new and extremely precise techniques, permitting them to work on very highly specific brain areas, and the question arose as to whether these techniques should not also be applied to alleviate psychiatric illnesses. Good results were claimed in some cases, although it was still too early to make a definitive judgment. Meanwhile, since these procedures often involved personality changes, and since they were irreversible, ethical questions were raised regarding their use. Some psychiatrists felt that, at the least, psychosurgery should be more closely controlled and should be used only as a treatment of last resort.

The concept of psychosomatic disease was being reconsidered and expanded. Such diseases as rheumatoid arthritis, migraine, hypertension, peptic ulcer, ulcerative colitis, and asthma were no longer regarded as the result of specific unexpressed emotions evoking a bodily response that, because it is not expressed, becomes destructive. Recent research indicated that the responses of individuals are specifically based on their own genetic and experiential background, no matter what the stimulus or stress. Further, various physical diseases evoke a variety of emotional responses, often before the physician recognizes the presence of the disease, so that the term psychosomatic represents a two-way street.

Another change in definition occurred in response to changes in the social outlook and mores. Following a long campaign by homosexual activist groups, the American Psychiatric Association removed homosexuality per se from its manual of mental disorders, replacing it with "sexual orientation disturbance."

Research in psychiatry remained splintered among various fields, from biogenetics to sociology and anthropology, but some small degree of integration was being effected. The effects of psychotropic drugs had led to renewed interest in the chemistry of various parts of the brain. If this chemistry could be altered in some way, it might be possible to discover specific antidotes for mental illnesses, just as insulin is an antidote for diabetes. In 1973, however, that was still a distant hope. (ROY R. GRINKER, SR.)

See also Drugs and Narcotics; Life Sciences; Social Services; Vital Statistics.

ENCYCLOPÆDIA BRITANNICA FILMS. *The Eyes and Seeing* (1968); *The Work of the Heart* (1968); *Ears and Hearing* (1969); *Muscle: Chemistry of Contraction* (1969); *Muscle: Dynamics of Contraction* (1969); *Radioisotopes: Tools of Discovery* (1969); *Respiration in Man* (1969); *The Nerve Impulse* (1971); *Health (Eye Care Fantasy)* (1972); *Health: Toothache of the Clown* (1972); *Work of the Kidneys* (2nd ed., 1973); *Regulating Body Temperature* (2nd ed., 1973); *Venereal Disease: The Hidden Epidemic* (1973); *Alcohol Problem: What Do You Think?* (1973); *Tobacco Problem: What Do You Think?* (1973); *Intern: A Long Year* (1973).

Merchandising

Two major themes dominated the European merchandising scene throughout 1973: the enlargement of the EEC and the continuing development of large-scale business units.

EEC Expansion. In line with EEC policy, the U.K. introduced the value-added tax (VAT) in April at a basic rate of 10%, the lowest in Europe. Italy, too, had at last fallen into line and introduced VAT in January at a basic rate of 12%. Many people had in the U.K. feared the changeover from purchase tax would be a cataclysmic experience. However, reports from the Board of Customs and Excise, processing the first batch of tax returns, indicated that this was not the case, although there was certainly evidence of misunderstanding of the tax in the large number of incomplete or incorrect returns. Several technical complications were revealed, especially in claims for costs not easily identifiable in normal business activity. Similarly, the need for speed and detail in returning information was not fully appreciated. But,

Mental Health: *see* Behavioural Sciences; Medicine

Proposed design for the Pepsi-Cola bottle to be marketed in the U.S.S.R. Under a contract signed in Moscow, April 19, 1973, Pepsi became the first U.S. consumer product for sale in the Soviet Union.

PEPSICO, INC.

as anticipated, these problems arose almost entirely among small businesses. The larger concerns generally coped very easily.

The entry of the U.K. into the EEC led to a great deal of movement by British firms into Europe aiming to establish a permanent base for future expansion. The most important development was probably the penetration of the French food industry at both manufacturing and distribution levels. The incentives for such investment were substantial, for the food industry in France was still predominantly based on small-scale business units in structurally segmented markets. Consumption of foodstuffs, meanwhile, was growing at three times the rate being experienced in the U.K. The British food industry, with its much greater reliance on large-scale, highly effective units, was not slow to seize the opportunities thus opened up. J. Lyons & Co., Ltd., was just one company that took over or approached a number of French concerns in a variety of food activities. Southland Corp. of Dallas, Tex., with more than 4,000 stores in the U.S. and direct links with the British group of Cavenham Foods, was pushing for outlets in France and West Germany. But it was not just in France or in the food industry that British firms were making their presence felt. For example, Harrods and Miss Selfridge Ltd. moved into Paris; Mothercare, the maternity and infant clothing outlet, moved into Denmark on a very large scale; Marks & Spencer Ltd. was going ahead with its first European store in Brussels, to be ready by 1974; and the Green Shield organization began business in Brussels and Paris.

The reaction in Europe to these moves was mixed. In France the government took a very defensive position. Financial assistance was provided from state funds to encourage mergers between purely French companies. Restrictions were also introduced to curb mergers involving foreign companies. But, of course, the process had not been entirely in one direction. European firms were also penetrating the U.K. Crowsons, a French wholesale food firm, moved in as did the Dutch-West German Makro group of cash-and-carry wholesalers. Movements of firms across the Channel, in both directions, were expected to continue to alter the appearance of the distribution sector in each of the EEC countries for some time to come.

A dispute over the price charged by Hoffmann-La Roche, a Swiss pharmaceutical company, for several of its drugs in the U.K. raised certain issues important to European merchandising. It brought to light once again the price differences that existed between the different members of the EEC for internationally marketed goods. Pharmaceuticals were a prime example of this phenomenon. The EEC Commission was investigating such differences in depth, concentrating in particular on foodstuffs, household appliances, and electrical goods. Some reports indicated that differentials of the order of 50% between any two EEC countries were fairly common. The price of certain vacuum cleaners in France was found to be no less than 95% higher than the price for the same units in West Germany. What emerged from the Commission's investigations and the debate surrounding the Roche affair in the U.K. was that, in general, such differentials were not the consequence of differences in taxation systems or in distribution and marketing costs. Instead, they resulted from differences in the degree to which the distribution sector in each country was able to act as a countervailing power to international manufacturers. Thus, for example, the fact that The Netherlands had a relatively highly concentrated food distribution sector was a prime reason why food prices in The Netherlands were low compared with other EEC countries.

Large-Scale Units. While an expanding EEC dominated the changing direction of marketing activities in 1973, expanding unit size continued to dominate the changing shape of the marketing sector. Various offshoots of the French Carrefour organization were springing up throughout Europe in the form of new "hypermarkets," retail stores with at least 25,000 sq.ft. of selling area. The new stores in Milan, Italy, and Liège, Belg., were approaching three times the size of the unit opened in 1972 by the same organization in Caerphilly, South Wales (which covered an area of 55,000 sq.ft.).

The development of the superstore in the U.K. proceeded during 1973, but relatively slowly compared with most European countries. Controversy over hypermarkets was, indeed, the key feature of the retailing scene in the U.K. Planning permission was the immediate bone of contention, but behind this lay a debate over the effect of superstores on downtown merchants, town centres, and retail competition in general. Clearly, there was a need for controls to protect certain locations from hypermarket development, such as green belts and areas with poor traffic controls. Also, uninhibited development might threaten to generate general overcapacity. But given certain minimum controls, there was no reason why the hypermarket could not be allowed to supersede the self-service supermarket on the grounds of pure retail efficiency. Exploitation of increased disposable incomes through the emergence of new retail outlets did not necessarily imply any enormous redistribution of fixed purchasing power. Studies in both France and West Germany supported the findings of a report by the U.K. stockbrokers Capel-Cure Carden that while, initially, other traders suffered from the arrival of a hypermarket, they soon recovered.

Increasing scale in distribution was occurring throughout Europe. The U.K. lagged behind France and, particularly, West Germany, which had almost 400 hypermarkets. The 160 Institute of Munich, W.Ger., estimated that the substantial increase in the retailing sector's investment (20%) in 1972–73 resulted from superstore development. But a new land development bill was expected to restrict future development in northern West Germany significantly. In Belgium the Magee company, selling domestic appliances, opened three new superstores. The Danish company Magasin du Nord opened the 150,000-sq.ft. "Circle House" complex near Copenhagen. In France during 1972 the number of hypermarkets (25,000–200,000 sq.ft.) had risen from 147 to 209.

Profitability did not always accompany these advances. It was argued in France that more than half the new hypermarkets did not break even. Only 40 hypermarkets were opened in the country in 1973, so perhaps fears of dramatic excess capacity were premature. In The Netherlands the problem of hypermarkets had an interesting twist. Because of drastic labour shortages, further development was seriously handicapped. To tackle the problem several companies joined together to form their own employment agency.

Another interesting insight into the hypermarket debate was the publication of several studies on consumer reactions. Reports from France, West Germany, and the U.K. all indicated that consumers had absorbed the superstores into their established pattern of shopping behaviour. The chief reason given in 1973 for visiting such stores was their lower prices. Convenience, accessibility, and time saving were no longer their principal attractions.

Catalog Stores. One development in the merchandising sector of the U.K. and the U.S. was potentially the most significant single event for some time. Both the enlargement of the EEC and the progress toward large-scale distribution outlets played some part in its inception. In July Richard Tompkins, head of the Green Shield Trading Stamp Co. Ltd., launched Argos, a chain of discount retail outlets handling more than 5,000 items from diamonds to trash cans. The average discount claimed on branded goods was 29.2%. Three hundred outlets were planned by 1976, with a turnover of £100 million. The selling method was based on a substantial catalog from which consumers chose items at home. By visiting an Argos shop, with the guarantee of availability of most items in the catalog, any item chosen could be bought directly across the counter. No sales talk, no ordering, no delays; fireside shopping. EEC regulations limited any future expansion of the Green Shield stamp venture, so the profits were to be directed into setting up the Argos machinery. The scheme reduced the costs of showrooms, packaging, displays, and sales staff, but direct personal sales avoided the anonymity of the mail-order system.

In the U.S. the St. Louis-based May Department Stores Co., the nation's third largest department-store chain, opened 18 catalog stores on the east and west coasts in August. The firm planned to join with Consumers Distributing Co., Ltd., Canada's largest catalog store operator, to open 150 stores throughout the U.S. and Canada in the next few years. Other U.S. firms active in developing catalog stores included Grand Union Co., Giant Food Inc., and Supermarkets General Corp. The only problem envisaged by independent observers was that suppliers might not be able to meet the demands made by customers and that the guarantees of availability would suffer as a consequence.

Pyramid Sales. Two "pyramid sales" concerns in the U.S. came under fire from the federal and state governments and private investors during the year. In a typical organization of this kind, the firm recruits investors who may pay as much as $5,000 for the right to distribute the firm's products by means of door-to-door salesmen. An investor then receives an inventory of the products, but, more important, he gains the right to recruit others to become distributors and to share in the fees that these new recruits pay to the firm and in a percentage of their sales. For those who join a successful pyramid operation in its early stages the profits are often great; however, as the pyramid widens, the newest investors have decreasing opportunities to sell new distributorships and often have difficulty in selling their own inventory.

In the legal action, the Securities and Exchange Commission charged Holiday Magic, Inc., with defrauding 80,000 investors of $250 million. The firm, which had lines of cosmetics, cleaning supplies, food supplements, and oil additives, also faced charges from the Federal Trade Commission, 15 states, and scores of investors. In the other case approximately 900 lawsuits involving $436 million were filed against Glenn W. Turner Enterprises Inc., a holding company. Turner himself was charged with mail fraud, and Koscot Interplanetary Inc., a cosmetic firm that was

UPI COMPIX

Merchants demonstrate outside London's Houses of Parliament, protesting the Shops Act of 1950 which makes it an offense to trade on Sunday.

a major part of the Turner organization, filed for bankruptcy.

Declining Profit Margins. Several retail firms in the U.S. suffered during the year from declines in their margin of profit. Super Valu Stores, Inc., the nation's largest food wholesaler, planned to cope with this problem by entering the field of nonfood retailing. After extensive market research, the discount chain Korvettes announced that it would begin to stress sales of high-fashion clothing and other soft goods, items that were expected to yield greater profits than the firm's traditional appliances and other hard goods. The New York-based department store R. H. Macy & Co. hoped to improve its financial position by upgrading the quality of much of its soft goods and thereby achieving "better fashion appeal."

The Great Atlantic & Pacific Tea Co. (A & P), one of the major food supermarket chains in the U.S., received the first results of its heavily promoted discount operation WEO ("Where Economy Originates"). Although the company's sales for fiscal 1972 increased by over $800 million, the final balance sheet showed a net loss of $51 million. This contrasted with a profit of $14.6 million for fiscal 1971 and was by far the worst year for A & P since it went public in 1958.

(JOHN C. SHOREY)

See also Advertising; Consumer Affairs; Cooperatives; Industrial Review; Prices.

Metallurgy

During 1973 the most pressing problem in metallurgy was pollution control. The growing awareness of the dependence of the United States on either foreign sources or low-grade domestic deposits for ore stimulated developments in extractive metallurgy. Alloy development was largely confined to improvement of perhaps only a single property, such as maximum extrusion speed, without harming others and with a minimum increase in cost.

In extractive metallurgy, control of sulfur dioxide emissions remained basically an unsolved problem.

Merchant Marine: *see* Transportation
Mercury: *see* Mining

Exhaust stacks about 1,000 ft. high were giving some relief, but selective absorption of the sulfur dioxide (SO_2) by liquids or solids seemed to hold the greatest promise of a true solution. To test the citrate liquid adsorption process, equipment was being installed to treat 1,000 cu.ft. per minute of the gas, low in SO_2, that is emitted during lead production. The sulfur was to be recovered as a valuable and easily stored and handled solid. Other tests were being conducted in which the gases containing SO_2 were reacted with various solids, especially lime, in a fluidized bed. Removing the SO_2 without incurring the cost of removing harmless components as well, and converting the sulfur to some form that would not constitute a disposal problem of its own were among the problems that had to be solved.

A plant that would produce aluminum from aluminum chloride neared completion. Aluminum oxide is converted to the chloride, which is then electrolytically reduced to metal and chlorine; these are recirculated in a closed system so no pollution results. Cryolite, the source of fluorine emission in the Hall process of making aluminum, is not used.

Increasing in use were various leaching processes to obtain metals from a variety of sources. Economy and freedom from air pollution were two advantages of these processes. A plant was nearing completion for production of copper by the newly developed Arbiter low-temperature, low-pressure leaching process. Low in capital cost, the process was applicable to small installations. A copper ore containing bismuth, which could not be refined by previous methods, was being successfully treated by the Arbiter process. Waste dumps and low-grade copper ore were usually leached with a solution of dilute sulfuric acid. The copper almost always is recovered from these solutions by precipitation with iron, usually old tin cans. An estimated 15% of the copper produced in the U.S. each year was by this method, which eliminated three tons of scrap cans for each ton of copper produced. Leaching was also the key to economical recovery of metal left in old mill tailings by inefficient extraction methods and also of by-product metals not recovered formerly.

Oxygen and other gases not removed in the refining furnace were being removed from premium steel by blowing argon through the metal while it was held in the ladle. The results were nearly as good as more expensive vacuum degassing. Oxygen added to the argon reacts with any carbon in the steel, yielding carbon monoxide that is removed by the argon and thus producing a product with very low carbon content. Stainless steel made by this method has outstanding corrosion resistance and weldability.

Sulfur in steel, even the 0.02% allowed by many specifications, can seriously reduce the fracture toughness, especially if the sulfide inclusions form long stringers. Magnesium will remove sulfur from steel, but adding this light, low-boiling-point metal to liquid steel was difficult until the discovery that coke impregnated with 45% magnesium could successfully be added and reduce the sulfur to below 0.01%. Misch metal, a mixture of cerium and other rare earth metals, also can both reduce the sulfur in steel and prevent the remaining sulfides from forming stringers. A plant to meet the growing demand for misch metal was under construction.

The production of alloy steel and steel parts by powder metallurgy without melting was expanding rapidly, causing a growing shortage of iron powder. A Swedish company planned to use powder metallurgy to produce 3,400 tons a year of tool steel billets. A new low-alloy air-hardening powder metallurgy steel for parts such as gears avoids distortion and cracking as well as the oil fumes resulting from conventional quenching. Dispersion-hardened copper produced by powder metallurgy became available. It has a combination of strength, hardness, and good conductivity that is retained to higher temperatures than with competitive alloys.

Among the new alloys were: an aluminum alloy that has properties equal to the older alloys but that can be extruded at higher speed and has the potential for a better surface finish; an aluminum alloy with conductivity almost as good as electric conductor grade but with better creep resistance so that less support is required for wiring; a high-chromium-content stainless steel containing molybdenum that is practically immune to the insidious chloride stress corrosion cracking that often causes abrupt failure.

(DONALD F. CLIFTON)

See also Industrial Review; Mining; Physics.

ENCYCLOPÆDIA BRITANNICA FILMS. *Problems of Conservation—Minerals* (1969).

Metals:
see Industrial Review; Metallurgy; Mining

Meteorology

Every year sees some abnormal meteorological occurrences, but 1973 appeared to be unusual in that respect. The most destructive flooding in history occurred in the northern part of the Indian subcontinent while a seemingly endless drought devastated parts of West Africa, breaking all meteorological records for those areas and giving grim witness to man's need for basic knowledge about the causes of climate and atmospheric anomalies. In the U.S. the worst flooding in 200 years took place on many stretches of the Mississippi River, and during the last week in May 111 tornadoes were sighted, the greatest number ever reported within a five-day period. (*See* Table I.)

Research and Development. In the decades following World War II, incredibly large sums had been spent on atmospheric research, including such subjects as long-range weather forecasting, construction of models for climatic changes, and investigation of artificial weather modification. During 1973 these researches continued at a relatively high level, but the tangible results were still far short of the goals envisaged in the 1950s. Perhaps for this very reason, a wholesome maturity in outlook was apparent. Although overall budgets for meteorological research had been reduced from the levels of the late 1950s and early 1960s, there were still sufficient funds for hundreds of reputable research proposals. Expectations of "miracle" solutions to problems of long-range forecasting and weather modification, often expressed a decade or two earlier, gave way to more realistic planning. Viewed from this more rational standpoint, the progress reported during the year was heartening.

In most countries advice and information about the weather were the sole province of the official government meteorological office. Only a few countries—notably Australia, Canada, Great Britain, and the U.S.—encouraged the private practice of meteorology, and it was a much bigger business in the U.S. than in any other part of the world. In 1973, for example, the *Bulletin* of the American Meteorological Society (AMS) contained the professional notices or advertisements of more than 50 independent weather agencies. The AMS had been in the forefront in fostering sound ethical practices and attempting to reduce the number of irresponsible sources of weather advice, but there was still a confusing plethora of weather pronouncements. To assist the public in making more intelligent use of these many weather predictions, the AMS, in the January *Bulletin,* published a revision of its statement on the scope and limitations of forecasting.

A noteworthy event of 1973 was the partial resumption of publication and export of scientific and technical papers and journals by China. Scientific literature had been sharply curtailed during the Cultural Revolution of the mid-1960s. Practically nothing on scientific meteorology came out of China from 1967 through 1972, although daily synoptic weather data and upper air observations were obtained through various channels. It was known that China was operating an extensive and good quality synoptic weather network, and that meteorologists there were continuing research in applied meteorology. Basic research was largely suppressed, but it appeared that a few outstanding meteorological scientists continued their work. Indications in 1973 were that their findings would be published in a year or two.

By far the greatest modern advances in the technology of weather science had been the earth-orbiting satellites, the meteorological radar network, the high-speed electronic computer, and worldwide communications systems. During 1973 there were further refinements in the routine operation of these technological facilities and improvements in the accuracy of weather forecasting, although much remained to be done.

Substantial developments were reported by the various groups and agencies engaged in meteorological research, but there were no major breakthroughs. Most of the work in the field involved improving or refining the advances of the preceding decade. Work continued on plans for extending the data-gathering and analysis programs envisioned in the Global Atmospheric Research Program (GARP), the GARP Atlantic Tropical Experiment (GATE), the First Garp Global Experiment (FGGE), and the Polar Experiment (POLEX). The U.S.S.R. gave special support to POLEX.

Dynamic Meteorology. The ultimate objective of these programs was to obtain sufficient samplings of the state of the atmosphere to enable analysts to deal mathematically with atmospheric mechanics. This effort toward making an exact science of weather forecasting had begun in the 19th century, but the emphasis on it increased greatly after 1940. The 1973 president's address to the Royal Meteorological Society reviewed present and future trends in the analysis of the general circulation of the atmosphere. Among the conclusions was the expectation that, within a few years, meteorologists would be able to simulate the global ocean-atmosphere system over periods representing more than 100 days and over areas extending about 100 km. in the horizontal, with 20 different levels represented in the vertical.

Another preview of the dynamic meteorology of the future was contained in a series of views of the birth and growth of a tropical cyclone over the eastern North Atlantic, as televised by a quasi-stationary weather satellite in orbit over the Equator. While this was not the first example of such observations, it was exceptional in the frequency, clarity, and regularity of the photographs in the sequence. The series was being studied intensively for elements that could be incorporated into the storm and circulation models used in computerized analysis and prediction. A new aspect of such satellite monitoring was an improved method for determining wind speed and direction at cloud level by vectoring cloud identities in successive brief-interval photographs.

WIDE WORLD

Residents of West Alton, Mo., boat their way home to inspect water damage as floodwaters of the Mississippi and Missouri rivers recede in April 1973.

Weather Modification. While rainmaking and other forms of weather modification were still controversial subjects, experimentation in this field was beginning to acquire scientific respectability. Reviews of the field indicated that the U.S. and the U.S.S.R. had conducted the largest number of experiments and given most support to research, and that the U.S.S.R. had reported success in more cases. During the first week in October, an international conference on weather modification was held in Tashkent under the sponsorship of the World Meteorological Organization (WMO) and the International Association of Meteorology and Atmospheric Physics of the International Union of Geodesy and Geophysics. The numerous research papers and field reports presented the findings of leading theoreticians and experienced field operators in various parts of the world. The conference included evaluation of results and estimates of some economic factors. Summaries of the conclusions were to be published by WMO in 1974.

The extent of the Soviet effort was seen in a review published in the AMS *Bulletin* in April. It described the techniques used for hail suppression, provided illustrative diagrams, and summarized successful results said to have been obtained in certain cases. One of the conditions found essential to success in cloud seeding for hail suppression was an abundance of moisture in the lower layers of the air. This condition was present in many of the heaviest hailstorms in the northern region of the Caucasus Mountains, as well as in the high plateau area of the western U.S.

Elsewhere experiments in weather modification took many different forms. Cloud seeding in New York state was conducted under carefully controlled conditions in an effort to test the feasibility of redistributing snowfall so as to alleviate the traffic problems caused by heavy snow accumulation close to the Great Lakes. The results were indecisive and no conclusions could be drawn regarding the dependability of cloud seeding as a routine solution to the

Table I. Selected Weather Headlines, 1973

Date	Place	Kind of weather	Casualties, damage, or nature
Jan.–Oct.	Central U.S.	Tornadoes	New record of 225 tornadoes in the U.S. during June; more than 900 during January–October; 73 deaths and heavy property damage
March 9–May 25	Mississippi River valley	Heavy spring rains and flooding	Flood stage reached along 900-mi. stretch of the Mississippi River; many new high-water records; few deaths but huge property damage
April 8–11	Minnesota and Wisconsin	Snowstorms	Record late date for snowstorms in many localities
April 10–12	Southeastern U.S.	Late below-freezing temperatures	Record low temperatures for April in many southeastern states; severe crop damage
All year	West Africa	Drought	Estimated 10,000 deaths in a seven-year drought in the area extending westward from the Sahara
August	Indian subcontinent	Heavy monsoon rains and flooding	Thousands drowned; heavy property losses; worst flooding on record in areas of Pakistan, India, and Bangladesh south of the Himalayas; devastation in many areas never before flooded
All year	Northern Siberia	Extreme temperature range	Temperatures ranged 155° from 70° below zero F in February to 85° in July
Oct. 10–11	Central U.S.	Heavy rain and flash flooding	Seven drowned; heavy property damage; worst flooding on record in some localities; unusual in October

Table II. Meteorological Space Satellites

Item	ESSA-8	ESSA-9	NOAA-2	ATS-3
Date of launching	12/15/68	2/26/69	10/15/72	11/5/67
Days in operation as of Nov. 1, 1973	1,781	1,708	381	2,187
Average altitude (statute miles)	892	909	901	22,221
Usable photos	...	151,000 (approx.)	Not equipped	25,000+
Cloud analyses, no. of times used	Not equipped	12,000	2,800	...
Vectored for winds, no. of times used	...	...	...	161,000
Storm advisories, no. of times used	...	4,500	1,500	...

Note: ESSA-8, ESSA-9, and NOAA-2 operate in orbits over poles; ATS-3 is in an equatorial orbit.

weather problem involved. Success was achieved in some cases, but the results were not specific and the quantity could not be controlled.

Other experiments also yielded inconclusive results. The seeding of cumulus clouds was tried as a means of precipitating rain during a serious drought in the Everglades region of Florida in the spring of 1973. The conclusion was that, if rainfall was increased at all, the quantity was insufficient to solve the drought problem. In separate seeding operations over Arizona and the California Sierras, an effort was made to initiate precipitation from certain types of clouds and then delay it so as to distribute rain- or snowfall to localities downwind. Considerable success was reported in some operations, especially in augmenting accumulation of moisture for later runoff into irrigation reservoirs.

Despite the uncertainties, the feasibility of "artificial rainmaking" in certain limited circumstances appeared to have been demonstrated, at least to the extent that it could be used routinely under the specified conditions. Results of other kinds of weather experimentation were even less conclusive, although suppression of severe local storms was the subject of intensive research and discussion.

The WMO Centenary. The International Meteorological Organization was established in Vienna in 1873 by the directors of the leading meteorological institutes, then mostly in Europe. The IMO was one of the first international bodies to achieve almost universal membership. During 1947–51 the IMO modified its structure, and in 1951, as the World Meteorological Organization, it became one of the specialized agencies of the UN. Its 1973 centenary was celebrated during September 4–12 in Vienna and Geneva, where the permanent WMO headquarters were located. The celebration included conferences and seminars in which some of the world's foremost atmospheric scientists reviewed recent progress and future prospects of atmospheric research and applied meteorology. Among topics reviewed were the scientific basis for and aims of GARP, WMO's working relationships with the national meteorological services of its member nations and territories, and its continuing coordination of national operations comprising the WWW (World Weather Watch). (FRANCIS W. REICHELDERFER)

See also Astronautics; Disasters; Oceanography.

ENCYCLOPÆDIA BRITANNICA FILMS. *Reflections on Time* (1969); *A Time for Rain* (1973); *A Time for Sun* (1973); *Fog* (1973).

Methodists: *see* Religion

Mexico

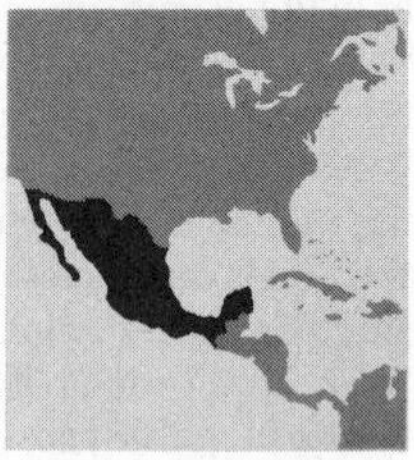

A federal republic of Middle America, Mexico is bounded by the U.S., Belize, and Guatemala. Area: 761,600 sq.mi. (1,972,547 sq.km.). Pop. (1972 est.) 53,230,000, including about 55% mestizo and 29% Indian. Cap. and largest city: Mexico City (pop., 1970, 2,902,969). Language: Spanish. Religion: predominantly Roman Catholic. President in 1973, Luis Echeverría Álvarez.

Foreign Relations. In March and April 1973 President Echeverría visited Canada, the U.K., Belgium, France, the U.S.S.R., and China. The aim of the tour was to continue the administration's policy of improving political and economic ties with countries other than the U.S., to encourage other nations to support the president's proposal for a UN Charter of the Economic Rights and Duties of States (which embodied certain provisions for the development of the third world that must be recognized by less developed countries), and to press for the signing of the Treaty of Tlaltelolco to ban nuclear weapons in Latin America.

During the year Mexico strengthened its relations with the neighbouring countries of Central America by signing a cooperation agreement with Guatemala and, in September, Mexico City was the scene for negotiations to reconcile the problems of Honduras and El Salvador.

On August 28 a violent earthquake struck parts of the states of Puebla, Vera Cruz, and Oaxaca, causing some 500 deaths. Although the earthquake caused considerable damage and came in the wake of torrential rains that caused several hundred fatalities and devastated huge areas of agricultural land, President Echeverría declined all offers of assistance from foreign sources.

Domestic Affairs. Congressional elections held in July were successful in bringing in new, younger deputies as had been the government's intention when it introduced a bill in 1972 to lower the minimum age for deputies and senators. This was in keeping with the objective of the official Partido Revolucionario Institucional (PRI) to modernize its image. Uprisings by university students at both the Universidad Nacional Autónoma de México and at Puebla reflected more clearly the conflict at government level between the modernizing forces and the old guard. They also demonstrated frustration caused by political stagnation, resulting from the fact that there was only one effective party. Left-wing urban guerrilla activities during the year included the kidnapping on May 4 of the U.S. consul general in Guadalajara. He was released on May 7 in exchange for 30 political prisoners who were flown to Cuba. On October 14 the honorary British consul in Guadalajara, kidnapped four days previously, was released after the government refused to fly 51 prisoners to North Korea.

Notable new legislation brought into effect in 1973 included a law to promote Mexican investment and to regulate foreign investment, and a law on the transfer of technology. Both formed part of the government's policy to achieve a more balanced and independent development. The first law, which in effect brought together all previous legislation on the subject, confirmed that foreign investment was welcome when it contributed to the country's development. It specified the economic activities that were reserved exclusively for the state and for Mexicans or Mexican companies. As a general rule foreign investment in any enterprise was limited to 49% of the company's capital, except in cases where the company was set up for export only or where specialist technology, not available in Mexico, was to be used. The second law had been passed in December 1972 in order to attain a more rational use of foreign patents and know-how and to stimulate the development of Mexican technology. The law established a registry to which all Mexican companies using or planning to use foreign technology must submit full details of the contracts.

The Economy. In 1972 the government took steps to reinflate the economy after the recession of 1971 by increasing investment and expenditure and by expanding the money supply. Demand for all goods increased as a result of higher incomes and new employment, and most sectors of the economy responded. While this caused little change in the level of prices during 1972, in 1973 it had a more marked effect. The wholesale price index for Mexico for the first seven months of 1973 showed an increase of 11% over the same period of 1972. On the basis of such figures it was estimated that the rate of inflation for the year as a whole would be as high as 12–15%, compared with a rate of only 5.9% in 1972 and 5.8% in 1971.

Although high rates of inflation were often accepted by less developed countries, and such a rate as Mexico's was far lower than those of Argentina or Chile, it was, nonetheless, the government's intention to contain the current upward trend in prices without impairing the high growth rate of the economy. In August the government published its 16-point plan for controlling inflation. It planned to channel more funds into immediately productive and, therefore, less inflationary areas. From the beginning of the year the administration endeavoured to keep a watch on prices, and anticipated that in the plan even more control would be exercised. As part of the plan to keep prices down, the Compañía Nacional de Subsistencias Populares (Conasupo) began a program for the establishment of 5,000 stores in rural areas. These areas received special attention during 1973: the fact that about half of Mexico's labour force was employed on the land, most of them at subsistence level, made the development of this sector imperative for the growth of the economy as a whole. The 1973 budget provided for greater expenditure on education, especially in rural areas, and considerable new investments were to be made in the agricultural sector, especially in irrigation projects.

The increase in the cost of living obviously eroded purchasing power, particularly of the lower-paid classes. The Confederación de Trabajadores de México (CTM) pressed for wage increases of 33%, as well as for a reduction in working hours. In Septem-

IPI COMPIX

U.S. Consul General Terrance G. Leonhardy, right, is helped from a car in Guadalajara after his release by guerrillas. He had been held hostage for the release of 30 Mexican prisoners.

MEXICO

Education. (1971–72) Primary, pupils 9,127,226, teachers 182,454; secondary, pupils 1,008,205, teachers 71,057; vocational, pupils 359,927, teachers 25,091; teacher training (1969–70), students 59,324, teachers 5,449; higher (including 38 universities; 1969–70), students 188,011, teaching staff (1968–69) 21,087.

Finance. Monetary unit: peso, with (Sept. 17, 1973) a par value of 12.50 pesos to U.S. $1 (free rate of 30.25 pesos = £1 sterling). Gold, SDRs, and foreign exchange, central bank: (April 1973) U.S. $1,175,000,000; (April 1972) U.S. $1,054,000,000. Budget (excluding autonomous agencies; 1972 est.): revenue 27,534,000,000 pesos; expenditure 27,285,000,000 pesos. Gross domestic product: (1971) 455.4 billion pesos; (1970) 418.7 billion pesos. Money supply: (Dec. 1972) 68,240,000,000 pesos; (Dec. 1971) 57,890,000,000 pesos. Cost of living (Mexico City; 1963 = 100): (April 1973) 149; (April 1972) 136.

Foreign Trade. (1972) Imports 36,651,000,000 pesos; exports 23,063,000,000 pesos. Import sources: U.S. 63%; West Germany 8%; Japan 5%. Export destinations: U.S. 66%; Japan 7%. Main exports: metal ores *c.* 9%; cotton 8%; chemicals 7%; sugar 6%; coffee 5%. Tourism (1971): visitors 2,530,700; gross receipts U.S. $1,580,000,000.

Transport and Communications. Roads (1972) 109,230 km. (including 957 km. expressways). Motor vehicles in use (1972): passenger 1,520,100; commercial 592,800. Railways: (1970) 19,835 km.; traffic (1971) 4,362,000,000 passenger-km., freight 22,374,000,000 net ton-km. Air traffic (1971): 3,571,000,000 passenger-km.; freight 45,257,000 net ton-km. Shipping (1972): merchant vessels 100 gross tons and over 216; gross tonnage 416,832. Telephones (Dec. 1971) 1,712,000. Radio receivers (Dec. 1970) 14,005,000. Television receivers (Dec. 1970) 2,978,000.

Agriculture. Production (in 000; metric tons; 1972; 1971 in parentheses): corn *c.* 9,000 (9,302); wheat 1,879 (2,019); sorghum (1971) 2,593, (1970) 2,565; rice *c.* 420 (441); dry beans *c.* 800 (679); tomatoes (1971) 855, (1970) 783; bananas (1971) 1,219, (1970) 1,136; grapes *c.* 225 (219); oranges (1971) 1,610, (1970) 1,650; lemons (1971) 179, (1970) 199; coffee *c.* 222 (186); sugar, raw value *c.* 2,510 (*c.* 2,562); tobacco *c.* 80 (*c.* 83); sisal (1970) 150, (1969) 128; cotton, lint 379 (372); fish catch (1971) 402, (1970) 357. Livestock (in 000; Dec. 1970): cattle 25,124; sheep 5,321; pigs 11,721; horses 5,026; mules 3,603; asses 3,199; chickens *c.* 142,900.

Industry. Production (in 000; metric tons; 1972): cement 8,579; crude oil (1971) 21,412; coal (1971) *c.* 1,500; natural gas (cu.m.) 18,293; electricity (kw-hr.) 34,448,000; iron ore (metal content) 3,052; pig iron 2,676; steel 4,361; sulfur (1971) 1,243; sulfuric acid 1,518; nitrogenous fertilizers (1971–72) 327; lead 141; zinc 79; copper, smelter 76; aluminum 39; manganese ore (metal content; 1971) 96; antimony ore (metal content; 1971) 3.4; gold (troy oz.; 1971) 151; silver (troy oz.) 36,700; cotton yarn (1971) 130; woven cotton fabrics (1971) 116.

ber interim increases of 18% were granted, although wages were not scheduled to be revised until the end of the year. When these were not immediately paid by employers, workers at over 1,000 plants went on strike.

In response to high levels of demand, many industries were working at full capacity and had to undertake expansion programs. These included plans to expand the Tamuin cement plant in order to meet new export demands, Petroleos Mexicanos' plan to build a polyethylene plant, and other projects for the expansion of the chemical, steel, textile, pharmaceutical, and paper industries.

Foreign trade figures showed a growth in exports both in 1972 and in the first six months of 1973, when they amounted to U.S. $1,813,000,000 and U.S. $1,154,000,000, respectively. Imports expanded at an equal rate, totaling U.S. $2,937,000,000 in 1972 and U.S. $1,809,000,000 in the first six months of 1973. The expansion of exports was somewhat constrained by internal demand, but attempts were made to reinforce the export drive. These included the setting up of the government's joint trading companies with Japan and West Germany (Eximin and Exmex), the creation of about seven export consortia that benefited from tax reductions as well as from tax-rebate certificates awarded to exporters, and the establishment of the Fondo Nacional de Equipamiento Industrial, which was to help finance industries that would increase exports or replace imports. Nonetheless, vast investments in Mexican industry were necessary not only to expand this area sufficiently for the trade gap to be narrowed but also to absorb the 700,000 new recruits entering the employment market each year. (PHILIPPA HUGHES)

Middle Eastern Affairs

The Arab-Israeli Dispute. In 1973 the 25-year-old conflict between Arabs and Israelis entered a new phase. On October 6 the uneasy cease-fire that had lasted since August 1970 was broken by major coordinated Egyptian and Syrian offensives against Israeli positions.

The Egyptian and Syrian initiative took most observers by surprise. The "no peace, no war" situation that had endured for six years had appeared stable. In January U.S. Secretary of State William P. Rogers hinted at a new peace initiative and later in the year he repeatedly urged Arabs and Israelis to negotiate, but he discounted any possibility of the U.S. pressing Israel to withdraw by threatening to withhold arms supplies. In early September it was reported that the U.S. would supply Israel with 48 more Phantoms and 36 Skyhawks to maintain the balance against Soviet supplies to the Arab nations.

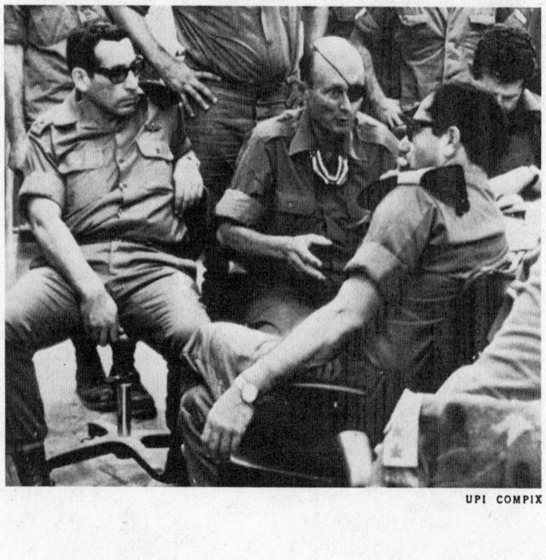
UPI COMPIX

Israeli Defense Minister Moshe Dayan confers with his generals during a meeting in the Sinai on the second day of the Middle East war.

Israel's confidence lay in its military power and its friendship with the United States. It continued its policy of heavy retaliation against military action by Arab troops or Palestinian guerrilla or terrorist actions. Israeli air attacks on Syria in January and on Palestinian guerrilla strongholds in refugee camps in Lebanon in February caused heavy casualties. Israeli spokesmen repeatedly expressed their opposition to the creation of a Palestinian state between East Jordan and Israel. In August plans were announced for the establishment of 35 new Jewish settlements in the occupied (after the 1967 war) territories in addition to the 44 that had already been created. In September the Israeli Labour Party adopted a four-year plan for the development of the territories that broadly reflected Defense Minister Moshe Dayan's desire for their economic absorption just short of annexation.

The appointment in the U.S. of a strong secretary of state in Henry A. Kissinger (*see* NOBEL PRIZES) in August was welcomed by some Arab governments, such as Egypt. Although a Jew, he was not regarded as a Zionist, and reports of a "Kissinger plan" for a Middle East settlement that might be acceptable to the Arabs began to circulate.

By the late summer there were signs that Egyptian Pres. Anwar as-Sadat's (*see* BIOGRAPHY) diplomatic campaign was making progress. It was, therefore, a surprise to most observers that he decided to cross the cease-fire lines on October 6. An important factor was almost certainly the U.S.-Soviet détente, which led to fears of an agreement between the two superpowers to shelve the Middle East problem and freeze the status quo.

After initial successes by Egypt and Syria on October 7–10, Israel, though heavily outnumbered in men and equipment, launched effective counterattacks on both fronts. The Syrian front was stabilized about 20–30 mi. from Damascus, and on the Sinai front the Israelis succeeded in crossing the Suez Canal in the southern sector and establishing a firm bridgehead. Iraq and Jordan sent forces to help Syria, and Moroccan troops already in Syria were engaged. Saudi Arabia, Kuwait, Tunisia, Sudan, and Algeria contributed on a smaller scale. (For an account of the military operations, *see* DEFENSE: *Special Report.*)

A UN Security Council Resolution 338, jointly sponsored by the U.S. and the Soviet Union and passed unanimously on October 22, called for a cease-fire, to be followed immediately by the implementation of Resolution 242 of the Security Council of Nov. 22, 1967 (calling, among other things, for Israel's withdrawal from the occupied territories), in all its parts, and for negotiations "under the appropriate auspices" aimed at establishing a just and durable peace in the Middle East. The cease-fire was accepted by Israel and then Egypt; Syria accepted after 36 hours. Iraq, Kuwait, Algeria, and the Palestinian guerrilla organizations rejected it. Libya, which said at the outset of the war that it had not agreed with Egyptian-Syrian strategy but would provide money, called for a continued all-out war to destroy Israel.

The cease-fire broke down on the Sinai front on October 23 and 24, and when it was finally, if precariously, established on October 25 the Israelis had improved their position by surrounding the town of Suez and cutting off most of Egypt's 3rd Army. After the U.S. had placed its forces on alert in reaction to an alleged threat by the Soviet Union to send troops into the Middle East, the UN Security Council agreed to send an emergency peace force from which all permanent members of the Security Council would be excluded. President Sadat sent his personal envoy, Ismail Fahmy, to Washington, and Israeli Prime Minister Golda Meir (*see* BIOGRAPHY) also arrived for talks with U.S. officials.

As no progress was registered on the key questions of Israel's demand for an immediate exchange of prisoners and Egypt's demand for a return to the October 22 cease-fire lines, a renewed outbreak of fighting seemed increasingly likely when U.S. Secretary of State Kissinger arrived in Cairo on November 6. In his talks with President Sadat, Kissinger succeeded in developing a formula for agreement on implementing the cease-fire resolution that was acceptable, though with initial reservations, to Israel and Egypt. The U.S. and Egypt agreed to reestablish diplomatic relations, which had been broken off in 1967. Prisoner exchanges began, and a peace conference was scheduled for December 21 in Geneva, Switz.

Syria boycotted the peace conference, which was attended by Israel, Egypt, Jordan, the U.S., the U.S.S.R., and the UN. During the first phase of the talks, which lasted for two days, Egypt and Israel agreed to discuss the separation of their troops along the Suez front. Military leaders from the two countries began talks in closed session on this issue on December 26.

By the end of the year it was clear that several essential elements in the Middle East situation had changed. On the military-strategic level the fact that, despite Israel's victories in the second week of the war, the performances of the Arab and Israeli armies were much more evenly matched than in 1956 or 1967 was of major importance. The Egyptian and Syrian armies, massively equipped with Soviet weaponry, showed that they were able to combine the elements of careful planning and surprise, previously a monopoly of the Israelis. In particular, the use of Soviet surface-to-air missiles deprived the Israelis of their unchallenged command of the air, which had been decisive in 1967. In addition, the Arab naval blockade of the Bab-el-Mandeb straits at the southern entrance of the Red Sea effectively cut off the Israeli port of Elath (and Jordan's Aqaba) and, in some views, eliminated the strategic importance of the Israeli occupation of Sharm el-Shaikh.

On the political-economic level the main factors in the situation, which were to some extent interrelated, were the great-power involvement, the Arab use of their oil weapon, and Israel's increasing diplomatic isolation as a result of the Arab oil policy. The Soviet Union began airlifting massive supplies of arms to the Arabs during the first days of the war, and shortly afterward the U.S. began to do the same for Israel. On October 25–26 the two superpowers seemed to be on the verge of confrontation on behalf of their respective clients. However, both were anxious to preserve the détente between them, symbolized by the visit to Washington in June of the Soviet leader Leonid I. Brezhnev. Confrontation was avoided and the Soviet Union acquiesced in Kissinger's peace initiative. A shift in U.S. Middle East policy to one that would be more "evenhanded" between Arabs and Israelis, evidenced by the restoration of Cairo-Washington relations, strengthened the Arab position—especially because the Arab oil embargo had left Israel almost uniquely dependent on U.S. military, economic, and political support. As the Israeli prime minister pointed out, the Arabs now had relations with both superpowers but Israel only had them with the U.S.

The Arab states made more effective use of their oil weapon in the war and its aftermath than had been generally expected. Saudi Arabia, the leading Arab oil producer, had earlier given warning to the U.S. that it would not expand production at the rate required unless the U.S. modified its Middle East policies; the fact that these warnings were ignored spurred the Arab oil states to action. Meeting in Kuwait during the war, they agreed on a plan to cut back output by 5% a month until Israel withdrew from occupied territory and "Palestinian rights" were restored. (These the Arabs refused to define.) They also agreed to try to continue supplies at normal levels to countries whose attitude they regarded as friendly or satisfactory, such as France, Spain, and the U.K., while cutting off exports to those they regarded as biased in favour of Israel—the U.S. and The Netherlands. The Arab reduction in oil output at a time of worldwide energy shortage caused many industrialized countries to introduce restrictions on fuel consumption. The use of the oil weapon caused many governments to modify their policies in favour of the Arabs, although most seemed reluctant to submit to Libya's demands that they should break relations with Israel and supply the Arabs with weapons. The declaration by the nine EEC countries on November 6 (reinterpreting the original UN Resolution 242) was regarded in Israel as strongly favouring the Arabs. In November Saudi Arabia told Japan that if it wanted oil it would have to break off diplomatic relations with Israel. Japan issued a statement favourable to the Arabs and was later reclassified by the Arabs as "friendly."

UPI COMPIX

An Israeli soldier leads a long line of Egyptian prisoners from their previously held position on the west bank of the Suez Canal, Oct. 24, 1973.

Although public opinion in many Western countries still favoured Israel, the growing diplomatic isolation of Israel and its increased dependence on the U.S. were emphasized not only by the EEC countries' attitude but by the anti-Israeli moves of many third world countries. In the 20 months before the war seven African states broke off relations with Israel, and during and immediately after the war they were followed by 16 more; Israel was left with ties with only five African states, including South Africa.

In November, when Kissinger devised his formula for stabilizing the cease-fire, most observers agreed that the possibility of a general peace settlement was greater than it had been for many years. On the one hand, the Arabs had recovered enough of their self-respect to be able to contemplate negotiating with the Israelis. Statements by President Sadat and Pres. Hafez al-Assad of Syria after the initial phase of the war were designed to show the world that their objectives were limited to the recovery of territory lost in 1967. But other statements by Assad and previous ones by Egyptian officials called into doubt their long-term intentions. There were still immense obstacles to a settlement. Mutual mistrust was intense. The Arabs still rejected direct negotiations without other participants. Israel still refused to contemplate giving up any part of Jerusalem. The most uncertain element of all was the extremist Palestinian leadership. Egypt and Syria both insisted that any settlement must provide for the "just rights" of the Palestinians, and most members of the UN took the view that the Palestinians would have to be associated with any permanent peace agreement.

The Palestinian Element. Disagreements between the various Palestinian groups over aims and policy arose early in the year. A meeting of the Palestinian National Congress in Cairo increased the membership in the congress from 155 to 175 and elected a new Palestine Liberation Organization executive in which the former preponderance of the largest guerrilla group, al-Fatah, was reduced. The PLO and Fatah leader Yasir Arafat indicated that they now accepted the principle of equal representation of all Palestinian groups.

Disagreement within the Palestinian movement was over strategy and attitudes toward different Arab governments. Fatah was implicated by the Sudanese government in the Khartoum incident on March 1, when one Belgian and two U.S. diplomats were taken hostage and then assassinated by Palestinian guerrillas; Fatah denied the charge. Fatah also denied responsibility for an attack on passengers at Athens Airport on August 5 and on the Saudi embassy in Paris on September 5. In December five guerrillas killed more than 30 at the Rome airport and then commandeered a plane and bargained with Greece to release two Palestinians awaiting trial. When Greece refused, the hijackers surrendered in Kuwait.

The Palestinian movement suffered a severe blow in the Israeli commando attack on Beirut on April 10, which killed three of its leaders; but one of Israel's prime targets, George Habash, the leader of the Popular Front for the Liberation of Palestine, narrowly escaped capture when the Israelis kidnapped an Iraqi Airways plane over Lebanon on August 10 in the mistaken belief that Habash was a passenger. During the year several prominent Palestinians were assassinated in various European capitals by what were assumed to be Israeli counterterrorist agents.

The various Palestinian groups were fairly united on one point: hostility toward King Hussein (*see* BIOGRAPHY) and the Jordanian government. The moves toward a rapprochement among Jordan, Syria, and Egypt in September were condemned by all except the Syrian-backed Saiqa group.

In the October war the Palestinians acknowledged that they were not directly involved because Egypt's and Syria's objectives were declared limited to recovering their own lost territory. However, President Sadat's insistence that they should be represented at any subsequent peace negotiations and the growing world opinion that they must be a party to any settlement sparked off a debate within the movement. Some of the guerrillas, who were broadly supported by Iraq and Libya, continued to reject any suggestion of Israel's right to exist, but others, realizing that they were in danger of being isolated and abandoned if Egypt, Syria, and Jordan all subscribed to a peace settlement, were prepared to consider taking part in negotiations. The guerrillas did not take part in the first phase of the peace conference in Geneva.

Inter-Arab Relations. In 1973 the Arab states showed a greater capacity for coordinated action than before, despite continuing sharp differences of outlook. The Arab Defense Council met in Cairo January 27–30, and the oil states agreed to increase their military aid to Syria and Egypt. The decision was sharply criticized by Arafat, who said that the Palestinian movement was being starved of funds. The Egyptian war minister, Gen. Ahmed Ismail, was appointed Arab commander in chief on the Egyptian, Syrian, and Jordanian fronts with Israel, but, in the absence of trust and cooperation between Jordan and the rest, the decision remained ineffective.

The situation was transformed by the initiative of President Sadat toward forming a new united Arab front against Israel. This involved moving closer to Saudi Arabia, whose oil resources would be a key element in any effective Arab strategy. Sadat's success in forging new links with Saudi Arabia helped to achieve a rapprochement with Jordan, with Saudi encouragement. This was sealed at the meeting in Cairo in early September of King Hussein and Presidents Assad and Sadat. Jordan did not open a third front against Israel in the October war but contributed troops to the Syrian front.

A military vehicle carrying Egyptian infantrymen crosses the Suez Canal to the east bank early in the Arab campaign.

WIDE WORLD

One of the inevitable consequences of Egypt's alignment with Saudi Arabia was to jeopardize the merger into a single state of Egypt and Libya, Saudi Arabia's strongest critic among the Arab states, which was to have taken place on September 1. Aware that Egypt was moving away from union, Pres. Muammar al-Qaddafi (*see* BIOGRAPHY) of Libya tried to force Sadat's hand by appealing directly to the Egyptian people. These moves failed, and, although a compromise was reached in the form of an agreement on a union in stages, the Libyan regime remained dissatisfied.

Whether King Faisal (*see* BIOGRAPHY) of Saudi Arabia had been consulted on the war by Egypt and Syria remained uncertain, but he cooperated fully with them in supporting their military offensive by restricting output of oil. Since all Arab oil states cooperated—although Iraq placed more emphasis on the need to nationalize U.S. interests in the Arab world—the weapon was more effective than most people had thought possible. Saudi Arabia and the other more conservative oil-producing states were aware that overuse of the oil weapon could be unproductive if it provoked consumer countries into countermeasures, but they declared their readiness to continue restrictions after the war until Israel had withdrawn from all occupied Arab territories and recognized the "legitimate rights of the Palestinians."

The heads of state of 15 Arab nations met in Algeria late in November. They emphasized the continued use of oil as a political weapon and announced embargoes on oil shipments to Portugal, Rhodesia, and South Africa. As a condition for peace in the Middle East, they called on Israel to withdraw from all occupied territories. Late in December the Arab oil ministers decided to increase the flow of oil to most countries but to retain the total embargo against the U.S. and The Netherlands. (PETER MANSFIELD)

See also Energy; articles on the various political units.

Migration, International

An important change in world patterns of migration in recent years had been the decreasing importance of Europe as a supplier of overseas migrants. In the three-year period 1970–72, three traditional countries of immigration, the U.S., Canada, and Australia, considerably increased their intake of extra-European immigrants, and in 1971 and 1972 the U.S. actually accepted more Asians than Europeans. (*See* Table.) The number of Asian immigrants in professional and technical categories was reported to be very high in 1972.

In Canada the majority of immigrants were still coming from Europe, but the percentage had declined from 85.6% in the years 1946–62 to 42% in 1972. Meanwhile Asian immigration to Canada rose from an average of 2.6% in 1946–62 to 19.1% in 1972; African immigration from 0.6 to 6.8%; Latin-American from 0.9 to 3.5%; and "others" (including North American) from 9.3 to 26.8%. The intake from the West Indies in the five years 1967–71 was 52,358, compared with 35,800 in the 22 years after 1946.

The first modest relaxation of the "White Australia" policy had been heralded in 1966 with a statement by the then minister of migration that applications from non-Europeans wishing to settle in Australia would be considered "on the basis of their suitability as settlers, their ability to integrate readily and their possession of qualifications which would be in fact positively useful to Australia." Between 1966 and 1970 Australia gained approximately 11,000 Lebanese and Syrians, 9,000 Indians (with a few Sinhalese), 5,000 Chinese, 6,000 Eurasians, 3,000 other Asians, and 5,000 Mauritians. Of the 2.5 million overseas-born persons in the Australian population in 1970, however, the overwhelming majority (94%) were born in Europe.

The decline in overseas migration from Europe was accompanied by an upsurge of migration from Asian and Latin-American countries. For instance, some 500,000 Filipinos were estimated to be living outside their home country by 1971, the great majority in the U.S. Over 170,000 Japanese emigrated from their home islands in the post-World War II period up to 1971, about half of them to the U.S. and nearly 56,000 to Brazil. Meanwhile, some 600,000 Koreans were reported to be living in Japan despite strict immigration laws to prevent Koreans from entering the country as temporary workers. Increased mobility was reported among the 40 million Chinese living outside mainland China, particularly toward the U.S. and Latin America. In Latin America, Mexicans continued migrating (mainly to the U.S.), as did Chileans (to Argentina) and Colombians (to Venezuela). Another rather special American intracontinental movement was that between Canada and the U.S.; for a long time Canada had been an exporter of migrants to the U.S., but in 1971 the current was reversed, with Canada receiving 23,277 Americans and the U.S. only 12,366 Canadians.

In 1973 there was a further reinforcement in the trend noted the previous year for Western Europe to raise stronger barriers against free movement of migrant workers (other than the free movement of "Community" members within the enlarged EEC and of members of the Nordic community). The overall total of foreign or "guest" workers and their dependents in countries north of the Alps (including Switzerland, Austria, and Sweden) rose appreciably from an approximate 11 million migrants, including dependents, in early 1972 to 7.5 million workers plus a slightly lower number of dependents in 1973. In recent years migrants had increasingly come from outside Europe (Turkey, North Africa). In addition, an increase in migrant workers to fill the worst-paid jobs left vacant by emigrants in traditional Mediterranean labour-exporting countries was noted. Thus Italy had some 40,000 officially registered foreign workers. Spain had an estimated 100,000, including Portuguese, Moroccans, and Algerians (many being illegal immigrants). In Greece, about 30,000 Egyptians, Sudanese, Ethiopians, and Somalis were reported to be working in such industries as mining and hotels and catering.

This whole European movement reflected the transformation of Western Europe's industrialized countries into "post-industrial" societies. This had resulted in a growing aversion among indigenous workers to heavy, dirty or dangerous, low-paid, and low-status jobs, and more recently to jobs involving monotonous assembly-type work or inconvenient working hours. Western European countries had thus become increasingly dependent on the continuing importation of foreign labour for the functioning of crucial sectors of the economy and for the maintenance of their living standards.

The growing doubts felt by governments—for example, that of West Germany—as to the macroeconomic utility of continued demand by employers for immigrant labour were augmented by rising popular

Immigration and Naturalization in the United States

Year ended June 30, 1973

Country or region	Total immigrants admitted	Quota immigrants	Nonquota immigrants: Total	Nonquota immigrants: Family— U.S. citizens	Aliens naturalized
Africa	6,655	4,762	1,893	1,740	1,242
Egypt	2,274	2,007	267	215	248
Asia*	124,160	85,332	38,828	32,486	30,283
China†	17,297	13,652	3,645	3,270	9,056
Hong Kong	4,359	3,753	606	522	...
India	13,124	12,196	928	723	1,210
Iran	2,998	2,019	979	961	578
Japan	5,461	2,158	3,303	2,736	1,599
Jordan	2,450	1,932	518	490	1,006
Korea, South	22,930	15,703	7,227	5,372	3,562
Philippines	30,799	19,962	10,837	9,999	8,149
Thailand	4,941	1,609	3,332	3,029	263
Vietnam, South	4,569	463	4,106	2,437	675
Europe‡	92,870	69,501	23,369	20,507	47,735
Germany, West	6,600	1,878	4,722	4,123	6,670
Greece	10,751	8,452	2,299	2,092	5,423
Ireland	2,000	1,523	477	390	1,771
Italy	22,151	18,859	3,292	2,973	8,902
Poland	4,914	3,874	1,040	902	3,323
Portugal	10,751	9,690	1,061	957	2,671
Spain	4,134	3,031	1,103	896	849
United Kingdom	10,638	5,812	4,826	4,265	7,589
Yugoslavia	7,582	7,042	540	491	2,119
North and Central America	152,788	107,691	45,097	39,030	33,988
Canada	8,951	4,092	4,859	4,040	4,739
Mexico	70,141	43,581	26,560	22,868	5,507
Cuba	24,147	23,063	1,084	328	17,415
Dominican Republic	13,921	10,187	3,734	3,519	1,104
Haiti	4,786	4,345	441	382	1,015
El Salvador	2,042	1,398	644	619	318
Jamaica	9,963	8,242	1,721	1,560	936
Trinidad and Tobago	7,035	5,787	1,248	1,197	486
Oceania	3,255	1,942	1,313	1,129	540
South America	20,335	13,683	6,652	6,061	5,905
Argentina	2,034	1,351	683	581	1,419
Colombia	5,230	3,473	1,757	1,612	1,303
Ecuador	4,139	3,058	1,081	1,023	800
Guyana	2,969	2,412	557	509	315
Total, including others	400,063	282,911	117,152	100,953	120,740

Immigrants listed by country of birth; aliens naturalized by country of former allegiance.
*Includes Turkey. †Taiwan and People's Republic. ‡Includes U.S.S.R.
Source: U.S. Department of Justice, Immigration and Naturalization Service, *1973 Annual Report*.

resistance and resentment on social grounds. The restrictionist and xenophobic feelings noted in 1972 were intensified, notably in France, where incidents of violence (mostly involving Arabs) occurred in the south and southwest.

Britain had curbed growth and immigration for over a decade or more. Switzerland, with the highest concentration of foreigners in Europe (just over 1 million out of a total population of 6.4 million), remained under sustained pressure to limit intake. In West Germany all recruitment after mid-1972 had to be channeled through the federal labour office, and in 1973 the government introduced a program whereby employers would have to show that they had adequate housing, the recruitment fee was raised from $120 to $384 a head, and recruitment was restricted in the main population centres.

After June 1973 France began to date-stamp the passports of foreign tourists as part of a campaign to get illegal immigration (tolerated for many years) under control. The Fontanet Circular, introduced in September 1972, was intended to protect the French labour market, to improve the living conditions of new arrivals, and to simplify residence and work permit procedures. In practice it proved ambiguous and likely to decrease the job and residential security and status of the migrants and to cut them off still further from the rest of the working class. In the densely populated Netherlands, from which half a million Dutchmen had emigrated since 1946, the government was moving toward induced rotation; *i.e.*, the idea of offering incentives to migrant workers to leave after two years. (SHEILA PATTERSON)

See also Refugees.

Military Affairs:
see Defense

Mining

Strong worldwide consumer demand, accompanied by a variety of obstacles to mineral production and distribution, made 1973 the most hectic period for mining in many years. Prices fluctuated irregularly, but mainly with an upward trend; corporate and government indecision hindered mineral exploration and expansion; technology was strained to maintain reasonable economic conditions in the face of strict environmental protection requirements; and labour strikes and political unrest in many countries hampered full use of existing production and processing capacity.

Even more strikingly than in 1972 the disruptive energy shortage dominated public attention. The graveness of the energy situation stimulated a wider fear that other latent mineral resource scarcities might be developing. Speculation distorted commodity markets, alerting government, industry, and the public to the delicate balancing role of raw material supplies in the total economy. This role had been concealed by a steady decline in raw material industry employment. It was overlooked that the shift in employment to service and manufacturing industries had been made feasible by relatively cheaper basic agricultural and mining materials, largely due to improved direct labour productivity in raw material industries.

The second annual report of the U.S. secretary of the interior under the Mining and Minerals Policy Act of 1969 concluded that "Development of our domestic [mineral] resources is not keeping pace with needs." Nine major recommendations for government action were made, including reiteration of a proposed federal Department of Energy and Natural Resources.

Legislative action foundered over environmental and land use issues. In the U.S. new mining laws drafted to replace the basic law of 1872 were debated, but none was enacted. Regulation of surface mining also was strenuously discussed publicly and in Congress. In April Pres. Richard Nixon disclosed plans to cut the mineral inventory in the national stockpile of materials by $4.1 billion. Legislation to authorize a cutback of $900 million was enacted late in the year, and disposals under earlier legislation were stepped up. In May the Department of the Interior transferred enforcement of federal mine safety laws from the Bureau of Mines to the newly created Mining Enforcement and Safety Administration.

An erratic free market for gold peaked in June and again in July at a price of $127 per troy ounce. Subsequently, the price dropped to about $90 per ounce and hovered in the $95 to $105 range. The official U.S. gold price had been raised from $35 to $38 in 1972 and to $42.22 in 1973. In November the U.S. and six European countries terminated the agreement that barred them from selling gold in the free market, causing the virtual end of trading in the official market. The immediate impact of higher prices was to permit profitable mining of lower grade ore at operating mines.

Industry Developments. The pace and direction of mineral resource developments changed in 1973 in response to shifting governmental policies. Australia and Canada had second thoughts about policies supporting mineral resource development, and exploration slowed sharply. Brazil, Zaire, Panama, and, late in the year, Chile, showed a loosening of restraints on mining. In the U.S. the year was marked by controversy and indecision, but there appeared to be a lessening of the adverse public attitude toward mining that had hindered planning in recent years. Mining profits rose sharply due to high prices, particularly for copper and gold.

Arizona was the site of much of the copper mining activity. Development continued rapidly on the underground mine at the large Lakeshore project near Casa Grande. Two 12-ft.-diameter shafts were bored to provide ventilation, and a 4-ft.-diameter service shaft was completed; all were about 1,300 ft. deep. The main mine entries were through two 15° inclines, one of which served as a belt haulageway for ore from the mine to the surface. Near Tucson, The Anaconda Co. and American Metal Climax, Inc., joined in a $200 million project to expand copper production from the Twin Buttes area from 75,000 to 120,000 tons per year. A plant to treat large reserves of oxide ore was also scheduled to be built. Two porphyry deposits discovered by American Smelting and Refining Co. (ASARCO) near Sacaton were being uncovered by stripping overburden, and mining of the ore was scheduled for 1974.

U.S. iron ore mining and processing was marked by mine closings as well as new developments. The Cornwall mine near Lebanon, Pa., was closed in March after a life of 231 years, during which 100 million tons were mined. In the famous Mesabi Range area of Minnesota the Mahoning mine was closed after 80 years of operation. However, a new iron ore open pit was begun nearby at Hibbing, and a $150 million iron-ore pelletizing facility was financed by Bethlehem Steel and Pickands Mather.

An extensive new area of trona beds was developed by Texas Gulf, Inc., in Wyoming, and a $75 million mine and plant was planned to produce one million tons per year of soda ash. A 16-ft.-diameter, 1,500-ft.-deep shaft was sunk to the deposit, on which specially designed mining equipment was tested. Full production was expected to begin in 1976.

The Yogo sapphire mine, discovered in 1895 and operated by a British company until 1927, was being reopened near Utica, Mont. The gem sapphires occurred in an eight-foot dike, which was being drilled and blasted. The oxidized ore decomposed in the air and was washed to free the gemstones. High-quality stones were then sent to Thailand for cutting.

The encouragement of mineral developments that had characterized Canada in recent years lessened noticeably in 1973 as both federal and provincial governments adopted or considered more restrictive mineral land rights, taxation, and securities regulations. The duration and magnitude of a perceptible slowdown in exploration were expected to hinge partly on the extent of government involvement in mining. The shift in policy was highlighted by a bid in July by the Canadian government's Canada Development Corp. to purchase $290 million worth of shares in Texas Gulf, Inc., and increase its holding in the company to 35%. In 1973 Texas Gulf derived about two-thirds of its income from Canada, principally from the rich Kidd Creek mine at Timmins, Ont.

In the Highland Valley area of British Columbia exploration and development continued at a slower pace following the opening in 1972 of the large Lornex open-pit copper-molybdenum mine. Nevertheless, the area maintained its promise of becoming one of the major world copper regions. In a related development, a major copper district was identified in central British Columbia after a ten-year search by Falconbridge. Several promising deposits were disclosed and a large potential area delineated.

KEYSTONE

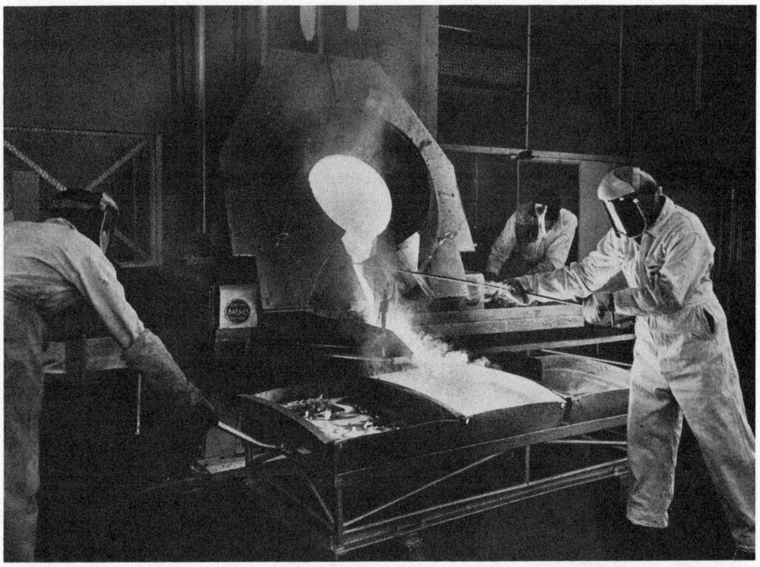

South African workmen draw slag from an electric furnace in a gold mine smelthouse. South Africa was mining previously unprofitable ore in response to soaring world gold prices.

One of the major suspense stories of the year unfolded slowly in Panama at Cerro Colorado as Canadian Javelin continued to enlarge its ore estimates. The company negotiated with the Panamanian government on arrangements to exploit the 2,200,000,000-ton 0.8% copper deposit. Javelin also held discussions with other mining companies to obtain the large-scale financing and technical assistance required. A two-stage plan was announced. Initial ore output would be at a rate of 80,000 tons per day, to be doubled in the second stage. More than 4,000 ft. of continuous mineralization was revealed in one drill hole. Because of the size of projected output it was anticipated that a smelter would be needed in Panama.

Mineral exploration in Brazil, particularly in the northwest, was accelerated as the Brazilian government undertook road building to improve access to this remote area. Airborne side-look radar, infrared, and other reconnaissance techniques were used to identify promising mineral areas. Bauxite, iron ore, and copper attracted interest, but areas showing tin, gold, lead-zinc, other metals, and construction materials also were found and being studied. Emerging in this same area of Brazil was an iron-ore mining and steelmaking venture that might require $1 billion in total expenditures. The iron-ore phase would comprise development of a prospective 18,000,000,000-ton deposit at Serra dos Carajás in Para State.

Copper mining in Chile continued the decline that had set in under the policies of the Marxist government of Salvador Allende. Production also was interrupted by strikes. The overthrow of Allende in September opened the door for a change in policies and a renewal of expansion of the huge Chilean potential for copper production. A clear redirection of policy had not been taken by the end of the year, but at the mines labour unrest was overcome and production rates increased. On December 31 the Peruvian government nationalized the Peruvian holdings of the Cerro de Pasco Corp.

Social and political unrest also were important influences on mining in southern Africa. In January Rhodesia halted road and rail traffic with Zambia, and the dispute between the two nations smoldered throughout the year. Copper mining in Zambia was severely disrupted because imports of mining materials, coal, food, and other items were interrupted; and, consequently, its exports of copper declined. Temporary road transportation was established from Zambia through Tanzania to the port of Dar es Salaam, pending the completion of the Tanzam railway. In September Pres. Kenneth Kaunda (*see* BIOGRAPHY) of Zambia announced plans to further nationalize the large copper industry. Negotiations were started with the companies participating in mining activities. Despite the adverse situation, work progressed on the world's largest solvent extraction plant to recover copper from low-grade and oxidized ores and tailings at Chingala. When completed in 1974, the leach plant was expected to extract 66,000 tons of copper per year from nearly one million tons of material, and total output at the mine was to be increased from 400,000 to 500,000 tons.

In Zaire plans were laid by Gecamines to increase copper output to 600,000 tons per day by 1980. Mines in the western, central, and southern districts were to be expanded. At the Kipushi copper-zinc mine in the south, an 850-m. shaft was completed and lateral mine development begun. The Lubumbashi smelter was to be enlarged from 130,000 to 150,000 tons capacity of blister copper per year. Several other copper projects were at various stages of development in Zaire, and the government's stability attracted exploratory efforts.

The sharp rise in gold prices was a boon to South Africa, the world's leading gold producer. It was accompanied, however, by labour unrest and rising costs that could well erase some of the temporary advantages. Nevertheless, exploration expanded on the famous Witwatersrand gold reef, and older mines had a resurgence as gold in lower grade reef left behind in earlier mining became economically recoverable.

More significant long-term developments in South Africa were plans to build two deep-sea loading ports for iron ore, one at Saldanha on the Atlantic coast and the other the Port St. Croix project near Port Elizabeth on the Indian Ocean. Each involved construction of an 850-km. railway to the mining areas. Saldanha was to receive ore from the Sishen mines, initially at a rate of 15 million tons per year, while St. Croix would handle about 7 million tons of ore from several sources.

In Indonesia a 250-million-ton lateritic nickel deposit in the Halmahera area of the Molucca Islands was investigated by an Indonesian-Japanese firm. Should the situation prove favourable, a ferronickel smelter would be built there. Also in Indonesia, the famous Ertsberg copper mine was officially dedicated in March. Full production was not achieved because of ore transportation trouble, and an additional aerial tramway was to be installed.

Lateritic nickel deposits in Australia and New Caledonia were under development. Construction began on the nickel recovery plant at the $350 million Greenvale project in Australia. In New Caledonia the $275 million Goro project encountered financing difficulties but remained active. The smaller Sommeni project in northern New Caledonia remained similarly alive under limited and uncertain sponsorship.

Technological Developments. A technique developed by the U.S. Bureau of Mines to support the ground around mine openings was similar in principle but superior to rock bolting for many situations. As in rock bolting, a hole is drilled in the wall or roof of the opening. Then a mixture of polyester resin and a hardening catalyst is pumped into the hole along with strands of fibreglass. The mixture hardens quickly, achieving nearly all of its strength in 10 to 15 minutes. The so-called pumpable bolts are more versatile than other advanced types such as conventional steel bolts anchored with cement grout or polyester resin.

An unusual copper mining technique was used at the Big Mike open pit at Winnemucca, Nev. About 400,000 lb. of explosive were used to blast more than half a million tons of oxide ore into the pit. The ore was bulldozed into terraces, and acid water was then sprayed onto it to leach out the copper. Pumps in deep wells were used to circulate the solution and pump it to a precipitation plant. In a somewhat similar operation at the Zonia mine in Arizona approximately 4 million lb. of explosive were used to fracture 2.6 million tons of oxide ore in place for leaching.

Continuing engineering advances in boring machines enabled their successful use in the hard abrasive rocks encountered in gold and platinum mining in South Africa. At the Rustenburg platinum mine a 6-ft.-diameter vertical shaft was bored to a depth of 1,000 ft. in hard norite in 58 days.

Experimental ocean mining technology included a suction dredge to harvest nodules from the ocean bottom at a depth of 2,700 ft. A similar dredge to reach to 20,000 ft. was being designed. An alternative scheme used a submersible barge that would be filled with nodules with an underwater tractor and then refloated. (PAUL FREDERICK YOPES)

Production. In 1973 it was clear that after their usual lag the mineral industries had largely recovered from the world economic recession of 1970–71. The upturn began late in 1972, the last year for which reasonably complete data were available. That year, world production of 51 minerals increased by an average 6.5% (ranging from 45.6% for columbium and tantalum to less than 0.1% for mine zinc), while that of only 21 declined by an average 5.8% (from a 25.1% decline in rutile to 0.3% each in mine output of nickel and peat).

On the basis of incomplete data for the first half of the year, the production of most minerals was expected to rise in 1973. However, widespread labour problems, a wave of nationalism, power shortages, environmental considerations, and distortions of the mineral economy arising from mandatory wage and price controls imposed in several countries might prove to have more or less severely affected production. The general condition of world demand for minerals resulting from the accelerating return to economic normality in 1973 was best seen in mineral prices, many of which reached record highs. Copper wirebar, for example, was well over $1 per pound on the London Metal Exchange (LME) by mid-November 1973, and on the same market zinc reached unheard-of levels in excess of 80 cents per pound. Not only were these prices indicative of shortages in the market generally but they also attracted metal away from its normal markets in the U.S., where producer prices were frozen: copper at 60 cents a pound and zinc at 17.5 cents.

In 1972 the U.S. led the world in the production of 28 minerals, including lead, aluminum (but not bauxite), copper, natural gas, crude oil, molybdenum, phosphate, and uranium (non-Communist countries); the Soviet Union led in 13, including iron ore, pig iron and steel, all forms of coal, chromite, and manganese; Canada in 7, especially nickel; Japan in 5; Australia in 4; Zaire and South Africa in 3 each; Malaysia and Brazil in 2; and six other countries in 1.

Aluminum. World production of bauxite, the primary ore of aluminum, rose 3.7% in 1972 to 65.9 million metric tons. As expected, Australia (14.4 million tons) supplanted Jamaica (12.5 million) in first place. Surinam (6.9 million tons) and the Soviet Union (4.7 million) were next. Aluminum output, however, rose 6.4% to 11 million metric tons. The U.S. remained in first place with 3.7 million tons, followed by the Soviet Union with 1.3 million. Japan (1 million) captured third place from Canada (900,000 tons). Demand for aluminum began to strengthen in the last quarter of 1972 and continued to increase throughout 1973 to such an extent that idle capacity was brought back into production and new plants and expansions were being planned. The entire output of many U.S. producers had been presold for 1974, and a definite shortage of aluminum was evident.

Antimony. World production of antimony in 1972 rose 5.8%, to 68,000 metric tons. There was no change in the relative positions of the leading producers: South Africa (14,568 metric tons), Bolivia (13,144), China (11,791), and the Soviet Union (6,984). U.S. output fell drastically (95%) because of a fire at the Sunshine Mine in Idaho, which accounts normally for about 80% of U.S. production. In general, demand began to strengthen late in 1972 and prices, which had remained stable that year, began to rise slowly, indicating that there was a reasonable balance between supply and demand.

Asbestos. At 3.7 million metric tons, world asbestos output in 1972 was 3.3% above 1971. Canada continued in the lead (1.4 million metric tons), followed as before by the Soviet Union (1.2 million), South Africa (300,000), and China (200,000). Although the market appeared to have held relatively firm and prices steady, several announced new projects failed to materialize (one each in Greece, Mexico, and Colombia). Also, at the end of 1973, Woodsreef Mines Ltd.'s Barraba mine in Australia, which had come into production in 1972, was in serious difficulties that seemed to necessitate either closing or government assistance.

Cement. World cement production in 1972 increased 5.2%, to 637.3 million metric tons. The Soviet Union led with 104.1 million tons, followed by the U.S. (75.9 million), Japan (60.6 million), and West Germany (43.1 million). In the U.S. a long period of overcapacity finally ended. Cement prices firmed and rose, and in 1973 shortages appeared and plans for expansion or new facilities were heard. Much the same situation occurred elsewhere. In the Philippines, for example, cement plants had been working at about half capacity in 1972, but by the end of 1973 the demand for cement from throughout the Pacific Basin exceeded productive capacity.

Chromium. World output of chromium in 1972 declined 1%, to 6.2 million metric tons, due largely to decreased output from the Philippines, which fell from third to sixth place. As usual, the Soviet Union was first (1,850,000 metric tons), followed by South Africa (1,480,000), Turkey (640,000), and Albania (610,000). Supply exceeded demand in 1972, in part perhaps because Rhodesian chromite was available to the U.S. despite the UN sanctions imposed in 1966. Overall, prices reflected this situation, shifting from a range of $24–$46.50 per ton depending upon grade and origin at the end of 1972 to $33–$39 per ton by late 1973.

Cobalt. World mine production of cobalt in 1972 rose 7.1%, to 23,264 metric tons, while output of metallic cobalt fell 9.4%, to 20,271 metric tons. There was no change in the relative ranking of producers, led by Zaire (13,043 metric tons), Zambia (2,053 tons), U.S.S.R. (1,650 tons), and Canada (1,549 tons). Due to economic conditions, demand was poor during most of 1972, and the list price (New York) held steady at $2.45 per pound. Demand improved early in 1973, and the list price rose to about $3.30 by the year's end. The reduction in output in 1972 was partially voluntary (Zaire and Canada) and partially involuntary (an explosion at the Kristiansand cobalt refinery in Norway).

Copper. World mine production of copper in 1972 increased 9.9%, to 6,630,000 metric tons, and smelter output increased 8.3%, to 6,620,000 metric tons. In mine production the U.S. continued to lead (1,510,000 metric tons), but Canada rose from fifth place in 1971 to second in 1972 with 730,000 tons. Chile (720,000) and Zambia (710,000) were third and fourth, and the Soviet Union, formerly second, was fifth (660,000). Canada's rise was due largely to the beginning of production at the new Lornex mine in British Columbia. The Bougainville mine in Papua New Guinea also came into production in 1972, and Ertsberg in Indonesia in 1973. Despite significant increases in world mine capacity, however, 1973 ended with copper in short supply for a variety of reasons. Labour problems, for example, affected output in Canada, Chile, and Yugoslavia during 1973, the main difficulty in Canada being a railroad strike. China and Japan both made unexpectedly large open market purchases, and environmental problems caused cutbacks in smelter production in several countries, including Japan and the U.S. The situation was reflected in copper prices. In 1972 spot wirebar prices ranged from about 46 to 53 cents per pound on the New York Commodities Exchange (COMEX) and 44 to 49 cents on the LME. By the end of 1973, both the LME and COMEX prices were well over $1, but the U.S. producer price was frozen at 60 cents.

Diamonds. Total world output of diamonds in 1972 increased 5%, to 43,160,000 carats, due to an 8.8% rise in the output of industrial diamonds (31,290,000) that offset another decline in gem diamond production, down 3.9% to 11,870,000 carats. Zaire led again with 13,360,000 carats, of which 12,380,000 were industrial stones. The Soviet Union was second in all departments (total 9.2 million, industrial 7.4 million), supplanting South Africa (7.4 million total); the latter, however, remained the leading producer of gem diamonds (3,370,000 carats). Ghana (2,660,000, almost all industrial) was fourth. Botswana, fifth, was a newcomer with 2.4 million carats (2,040,000 industrial) from the newly developed Orapa mine. Demand remained firm, and several price increases after early 1972 reflected more than just currency revaluations.

Gold. In 1972 world gold production again declined, falling 3.8%, to 44,710,000 troy ounces, with no changes in the relative order of major producers: South Africa (29,250,000 troy ounces), U.S.S.R. (6.9 million), Canada (2,080,000), and the U.S. (1,450,000). The free market price remained comparatively stable in 1972, ranging from about $44 to $70 per troy ounce, but in 1973 various monetary disturbances caused it to shoot up to a record $127 per troy ounce on June 5. It remained high until late in the year when, after the U.S. and several European countries announced termination of the two-tier price system, it fell back to between $95–$105 per

The Mountaineer, a strip-mining shovel weighing 2,750 tons, prepares to cross a highway in eastern Ohio's coal country. Before crossing, the giant machine laid down an earthen dike to protect the usually busy highway.

UPI COMPIX

troy ounce. Despite the high prices there was not as much mining as expected, largely because increased costs for labour and supplies militated against the reopening of old mines.

Iron and Steel. World production of iron ore (768.9 million metric tons) declined 1.3% in 1972, while output of both pig iron (452.4 million metric tons) and steel (627.6 million) rose by 5.2 and 8.8%, respectively. This reflected the impact of economic recovery, which was quickly transmitted to the steel industry but did not influence iron ore production until 1973. The Soviet Union (208 million metric tons) continued to lead in iron ore, followed by the U.S. (76.6 million), Australia (63.8 million, up from sixth place in 1971), and France (54.3 million). In pig iron, the Soviet Union (91,610,000) surpassed the U.S. (80.6 million), and they were followed by Japan (72,040,000) and West Germany (31,680,000). The same sequence occurred in steel production: Soviet Union (126 million metric tons), U.S. (120.9 million), Japan (96.9 million), and West Germany (43.7 million). The scope of the economic recovery led to a steel shortage toward the end of 1973.

Lead. In 1972 world mine output of lead rose 2%, to 3,490,000 metric tons, while smelter production at 3,380,000 metric tons was 6.4% above 1971. Relative rankings remained the same as 1971: U.S. (584,000 metric tons mine, 631,000 smelter); U.S.S.R. (456,000 mine, 463,000 smelter), and Australia (385,000 mine, 348,000 smelter). Although the improved economic climate increased lead consumption, the higher prices were more a reflection of currency revaluation than a shortage of metal. In 1972 the U.S. producer price ranged from 14 to 16 cents per pound and from about 10 to 15 cents on the LME (cash). In 1973 the U.S. producer price rose from 14.5 to 16.5 cents, where it was frozen, and LME (cash) varied from about 14 to about 23 cents.

Manganese. Production of manganese in 1972 declined 4.5%, to 20,710,000 metric tons. The leading producers were the Soviet Union (7.8 million metric tons), South Africa (3,270,000), Gabon (1,940,000, up from fifth place in 1971), and Brazil (1,930,000 tons). At the end of 1972 manganese ore was quoted in the U.S. at 63–68 cents per long ton unit. This rose to about 75–85 cents by the end of 1973.

Mercury. At 279,000 flasks, 1972 world mercury production declined 6.5%, a clear reflection not only of a troubled world economy but of the environmental disfavour into which mercury had come. Spain (60,500 flasks) retained the lead among producers, followed by the Soviet Union (50,000 flasks), Italy (41,800 flasks), and China (26,000 flasks). After a three-year decline, mercury prices hit a $145 per flask low in April 1972, from which they recovered to a high of $280. The 1973 range, resulting from deliberately withheld production, was $250–$318.

Molybdenum. World molybdenum production in 1972 was 79,500 metric tons, a 2.6% increase over 1971. The leading producers remained the U.S. (50,900 metric tons), Canada (11,300), and the Soviet Union (8,200). The majority of the increased output was as a byproduct of copper mining, which accounted for nearly half the non-Communist world production.

Nickel. While mine output of nickel in 1972 fell 0.3%, to 633,000 metric tons, smelter production rose to 635,200 metric tons, 2.9% over 1971. Leading mine producers were Canada (232,600 metric tons), the Soviet Union (127,000), and New Caledonia (100,200), while smelter production came from Canada (131,700 metric tons), the Soviet Union (127,000), and Japan (107,900). The decline in mine output was attributed to production cutbacks instituted in 1971 in response to the general recession. Demand improved in 1972, especially toward the end of the year, and continued to strengthen through 1973 as some idled capacity was reactivated. Despite large inventories, prices held firm in 1972 in expectation of a strike in the Canadian industry which never materialized. The range for 1972 was $1.28–$1.40 per pound and for 1973 was $1.40–$1.53.

Phosphate. World production of phosphate in 1972 increased 8.1%, to 94,210,000 metric tons. The U.S. (37,030,000 metric tons) continued in first place, followed as before by the U.S.S.R. (22,520,000), Morocco (14,970,000), and Tunisia (3,390,000). The increased output barely kept pace with growing demand, and the several years of significant overcapacity and industry shakeouts appeared to have ended. U.S. list prices increased about $1 per ton in 1972, and prices strengthened still further in 1973.

Platinum Group Metals. After a 1971 decrease, world production of platinum metals rose 4.4% in 1972, to 4,260,000 troy ounces. No change took place among the leading producers: U.S.S.R. (2,350,000 troy ounces), South Africa (1,450,000), and Canada (400,000). As a result of demand for platinum for use in catalytic automobile exhaust control devices in the U.S., the major primary platinum producers (practically all in South Africa) began planning important, staged increases in productive capacity. Producer prices ranged in 1972 from $110 to $130 per troy ounce and then reached highs of about $160 in 1973.

Potash. At 20,380,000 metric tons in 1972, world potash production rose 3% over 1971. As usual, the Soviet Union led (5.5 million metric tons), followed by Canada (3,750,000) and West Germany (2,840,000). Demand in 1972 and 1973 was progressively stronger, and shipments in 1972 closely equaled production. This did not mean, however, that surplus Canadian productive capacity, which had triggered chaos in the industry in the late 1960s, was yet worked off. Rather, under the system imposed by the Saskatchewan provincial government, output (and price) was controlled, and Canadian producers were operating at about 47% of capacity in 1972 and 52% in 1973. Prices firmed, and the 1973 season brought an average $5 per ton, a 12–14% increase over 1972.

Silver. World production of silver in 1972 rose 0.9%, to 291,390,000 troy ounces. There was a considerable but probably temporary realignment of leading producers. Canada (47 million troy ounces), formerly second, took the lead, followed by Peru (40,190,000, up from fourth), U.S.S.R. (40 million, formerly fifth), and Mexico (37,480,000). The U.S. (37,230,000), formerly first, dropped to fifth place as the result of loss of production due to the disastrous Sunshine mine fire in Idaho. The mine reopened in 1973. Industrial demand for silver strengthened steadily throughout 1972 and 1973 as a concomitant of improved economic conditions, and prices moved generally higher.

Sulfur. World production of sulfur in 1972 in all forms increased 13.5%, to 26,210,000 metric tons. This quantity consisted of approximately 40% from Frasch sulfur (brimstone), 58% recovered sulfur (largely from sour gas), and 2% from sulfur ores. Leading producers were the U.S. (9,370,000 metric tons—all sources), Canada (6,950,000—recovered), and Poland (2,940,000—Frasch and ores). Throughout the period, prices remained severely depressed until 1973, when the two increases initiated by U.S. Frasch producers more or less compensated for increased costs and currency revaluations.

Tin. In 1972 world production of mine tin increased 3.2%, to 239,602 long tons, and smelter output rose 1.5%, to 235,417 long tons. Leading mine producers were Malaysia (75,617 long tons), Bolivia (31,056), and U.S.S.R. (28,000). Producers of smelter tin were Malaysia (89,564 long tons), U.S.S.R. (28,000), and Thailand (21,889). Although production increased in 1972 and probably also in 1973, demand remained static throughout 1972 and only began to pick up late in 1973. As a result, most production went to producer inventory, leading to buffer stock purchases in 1972 under the fourth International Tin Agreement and the imposition of export controls under the agreement from mid-January to mid-September 1973. Beginning in 1971–72, both Indonesia and Bolivia smelted significant portions of their own tin output, at the expense of smelters in The Netherlands and the U.K., respectively. In 1972 the price range in London was approximately $1.59–$1.82 per pound, compared with the New York market of about $1.71–$1.84. In 1973 prices ranged for most of the year between $1.75 and $2.36 in London and $1.78 and $2.49 in New York, but toward the end of the year tin reached a new record of $2.59 in London and $2.66 in New York.

Titanium. World production of titanium minerals (concentrates) declined in 1972, rutile by 25.1%, to 387,800 metric tons, and ilmenite by 3.2%, to 3,250,000 metric tons. The reduction in rutile output was due to liquidation of the Sherbo Minerals operation in Sierra Leone, which left Australia the only significant producer (349,900 metric tons), followed by India (3,400). Canada (830,000 metric tons), formerly third, was the leading producer of ilmenite in 1972. Australia (710,000) was second as in 1971, and the U.S. (620,000) was third rather than first.

Tungsten. World mine production of contained tungsten in 1972 rose 5%, to 38,454 metric tons. The leading producers were China (6,984 metric tons), U.S.S.R. (7,211), U.S. (3,696), and Thailand (3,342). Consumption also increased in 1972, but prices reached a six-year low, largely as a result of excess supplies accumulated during the 1970–71 recession. The London price slid from about $39 per short ton unit (stu) in January 1971 to $31.68/stu in October 1972, but then started to rise, reaching $42–$43/stu late in 1973.

Uranium. Uranium production in the non-Communist world rose 14% in 1972, to 24,700 metric tons of uranium oxide (U_3O_8). Among those countries for which production was known, the U.S. (11,700 tons) was first, followed by South Africa (5,069) and Canada (4,442). Australia developed into a major uranium region with three or four important new mines ready to develop and a growing number of promising new prospects. Uranium prices in 1972, for near term delivery, were about $6–$6.50 per pound of U_3O_8 in the U.S., partially as a result of the stalled nuclear power program. However, as the energy crisis of 1973 developed, prices improved to $7–$10 per pound in the U.S.

Zinc. World mine production of zinc in 1972 grew less than 0.1%, to 5,590,000 metric tons, while smelter output increased 8.5%, to 5,090,000 metric tons. The U.S. (1,280,000 metric tons), U.S.S.R. (650,000), and Australia (500,000) were the leading mine producers. As a result of environmentally caused closings of zinc smelters in the U.S., that country fell from first to third place in smelter production, being supplanted by Japan (810,000 tons) and the U.S.S.R. (650,000). Zinc prices, like those of other metals, were affected directly by various currency revaluations and indirectly by monetary uncertainties. Under controls, the U.S. producer price ranged from 17 to 18.5 cents per pound in 1972 and from 18 to 22 cents in 1973. On the LME in 1972, the range was 16.8–18.2 cents per pound, but on Nov. 4, 1973, the price there reached its record high of 80.5 cents per pound, whereupon trading in zinc was suspended until the end of the year. (FRANK H. SKELDING)

See also Energy; Geology; Industrial Review; Metallurgy.

Missiles:
see Defense

Molecular Biology:
see Life Sciences

Molybdenum:
see Mining

Monaco

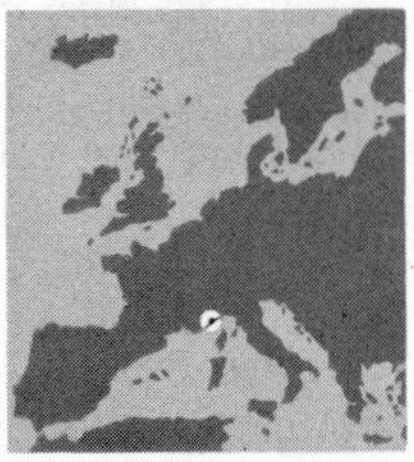

A constitutional monarchy on the northern Mediterranean coast, Monaco is bounded on all land sides by the French département of Alpes-Maritimes. Area: 0.73 sq.mi. (1.89 sq.km.). Pop. (1972 est.): 24,500. Language: French. Religion: Roman Catholic. Prince, Rainier III; minister of state in 1973, André Saint-Mleux.

The principality continued to foster a varied and lively program of cultural affairs, arts, and sporting events in 1973. Tourism, seemingly unhindered by rising prices and monetary problems, remained a major source of revenue and foreign exchange. A brief strike of casino employees occurred in early June, when the 250 workers protested the installation of closed-circuit television cameras in the gaming and private rooms. The cameras were intended to watch the guests at the various gaming tables. The union of casino employees decried the introduction of television as an unacceptable violation of the guests' privacy.

French drivers Jean-Claude Andruet and Michele Petit, in an Alpine Renault, won the controversy-marred 42nd running of the Monte Carlo Rally on Jan. 26, 1973. The Rally had been plagued for years by poor weather. In the '73 race, over 140 cars were declared out of competition when the roads were blocked by a freak blizzard, and disqualified drivers retaliated by physically blocking other parts of the course to prohibit those under way from completing their run. Only the early starters were able to finish.

The principality began preparations for the May 1974 celebration of the 25th anniversary of Prince Rainier's reign. (ROBERT D. HODGSON)

MONACO

Education. (1969–70) Primary, pupils 1,446, teachers 49; secondary, pupils 1,847, teachers 116; vocational, pupils 331, teachers 29.

Finance. Monetary unit: French franc, with (Sept. 17, 1973) a free "commercial" rate of Fr. 4.25 to U.S. $1 (Fr. 10.24 = £1 sterling) and a free "financial" rate of Fr. 4.32 to U.S. $1 (Fr. 10.40 = £1 sterling). Budget (1971 est.): revenue Fr. 220 million; expenditure Fr. 188 million.

Foreign Trade. Included with France. Tourism: visitors (1971) 101,900; gross receipts (1966) U.S. $6.1 million.

Money and Banking

In 1973 domestic monetary problems and policies were profoundly influenced by several international developments. The new structure of fixed exchange rates negotiated in Washington, D.C., in December 1971 proved to be fragile and short-lived. Not only did it leave the U.S. dollar still overvalued, but it was also undermined by events and policies in particular countries in 1972 and early 1973. In consequence, a new exchange crisis of major proportions erupted in early February, causing the U.S. dollar to again be devalued, by 10%, while other major currencies either retained their old parities in terms of gold or SDRs (IMF special drawing rights) or floated. When these adjustments failed to restore confidence, a new breakdown ensued, leading to the launching in late March of a common float by all European Community countries except the United Kingdom, Ireland, and Italy, which felt impelled to float independently. Thereafter, the dollar drifted steadily downward, reaching such a low level by early July that joint official intervention was initiated on a limited, intermittent basis. At that time the dollar began to recover, helped by a strengthening U.S. trade position, and by late 1973 it was again near its levels of the previous February.

Also during 1973 the world economy found itself in the grip of a serious inflation of growing proportions. For the first time since the mid-1950s the expansion of the major industrial countries was closely synchronized. In consequence of parallel reflationary policies earlier, economic activity moved ahead with unexpected speed, with demand inflation being superimposed on an already high rate of cost-push inflation. The generalized expansion, combined with various food and raw material supply problems, caused international commodity prices to soar to levels not experienced since the Korean War. In industrial countries wholesale prices advanced sharply, and consumer prices rose on average by about 8%, compared with 6% in 1972. Wages, too, continued to increase rapidly and accelerated in a number of continental European countries and Japan.

Finally, the October war in the Middle East soon confronted the industrial countries with a critical new problem. The decision of the Arab producers to curtail oil output sharply and increase their prices threatened to disrupt economic activity and give further impetus to inflation. The seriousness of the problem varied according to each country's dependence upon imported oil supplies and the state of its balance of payments, a major uncertainty being the extent and duration of the cuts in supplies. In any event, significant changes in trade, payments, and reserve relationships were inevitable.

Against this background, national authorities adopted a wide variety of anti-inflationary measures during the year. A number of them, including the U.S. and the U.K. but not West Germany and Japan, continued their efforts to achieve workable prices and incomes policies. Fiscal policies helped to restrain demand in a few countries such as the U.S., France, and West Germany but more generally played a neutral or even destabilizing role. Monetary policy was therefore called upon to bear a heavy burden of restraint, and interest rates, particularly those at short term, rose to new high levels in the late summer and autumn. In countries where these changes, together with speculative influences, tended to stimulate unwanted inflows of funds, exchange regulations were made more restrictive.

As suggested by the movement of short-term interest rates, the tightening of monetary policy began about the autumn of 1972. By September 1973 central-bank discount rates had moved to unusually high levels in most countries, particularly in the U.S., France, and the U.K. The rise in long-term interest yields was comparatively moderate in some countries, reflecting liquidity and profits strength and the continuing availability of bank credit, but in others, such as West Germany, The Netherlands, the U.K., and Japan, yields moved upward substantially. Even so, given the high rates of price inflation, "real" interest rates remained low or negative almost everywhere. Nominal interest rates, in other words, were a deceptive indicator of the degree of monetary restraint.

Looking at the monetary aggregates, it may be seen that the growth of the money supply, broadly defined to include time and savings deposits, generally continued at very high rates, though in several countries some slowing down occurred (Table I).

As the winter of 1973–74 approached, stabilization policies were influenced by various crosscurrents. With cost inflation remaining strong, production was increasingly limited by shortages of skilled labour, industrial materials, and, suddenly, energy supplies. Although the spectre of recession began to loom, monetary authorities generally believed that inflation remained the greater danger and for the time being chose continued restraint. However, the likelihood of a supply-induced recession, coupled with more intense cost/price pressures, seemed bound before long to sharpen the dilemma confronting monetary policy.

Eurocurrency and Eurobond Markets. After a short period of relative calm, the Euromarkets came under considerable strain from February 1973 onward. The international currency crisis, together with the monetary squeeze under way in key financial centres, led to a pronounced rise in interest rates on both markets. But, whereas Eurobond issues dropped off sharply from February to August, the growth of Eurocurrency lending accelerated.

In the 12 months to September 1973 Eurocurrency lending by banks of the major European countries increased by over 40%. Several factors accounted for this. The banks, called upon during the crisis to take in large amounts of forward dollars (those to be sold at a specified time in the future), covered themselves by borrowing Eurodollars and selling them at once against other currencies. Second, borrowers showed a strong preference for short-term rather than long-term commitments. Third, public bodies in the U.K. and Italy were officially encouraged to borrow heavily on the Eurocurrency market so as to help finance external deficits. A fourth element was continuing heavy borrowing by less developed countries. In this context, the estimated volume of new syndicated Eurocurrency bank credits rose from $8.5 billion in January–September 1972 to more than $15 billion in the corresponding period of 1973, thus dwarfing the volume of new Eurobond issues.

A notable feature in 1973 was that, despite currency unrest, withdrawals of dollar funds from the market were more than offset by new deposits attracted by the higher interest yield. On the other hand, roughly 80% of the growth of the Eurobanks' foreign currency liabilities in January–June 1973 was in nondollar form. Later in the year the dollar appeared to have resumed its dominant role.

After a record volume in January 1973, Eurobond issues contracted sharply and by August were virtually at a halt. Issues of straight bonds were inhibited by high interest rates, those on dollar bonds having risen from about 7½% in January to 8½% about midyear, and the weakness of the U.S. equity market reduced the attractiveness of convertible dollar bonds. Later in the year, with the dollar stronger and U.S. financial markets somewhat easier, the climate for Eurobond issues improved.

Table I. Rates of Growth of Money plus Quasi-Money

Country	1971 June	1971 Dec.	1972 June	1972 Dec.	1973 March	1973 June	1973 Sept.
United States	13.2	11.4	9.4	11.3	8.8	8.9	7.6
Canada	16.2	16.4	16.9	14.5	12.6	12.1	12.5
Japan	20.6	24.3	22.8	24.7	25.1	24.7	22.9
United Kingdom	10.3	13.5	23.3	27.6	27.9	23.0	27.9
Belgium	9.9	12.8	16.3	17.5	18.9	16.9	16.5
France	19.4	18.2	19.2	18.4	14.8	14.2	13.2
Germany, West	12.7	14.3	13.9	17.0	20.5	18.3	17.7
Italy	14.6	17.1	18.5	18.2	18.5	20.3	21.2
Netherlands, The	8.1	10.2	9.6	11.9	16.3	14.9	19.2

United States. In 1972, although the dollar had been devalued the previous December and economic activity was accelerating vigorously from the early spring onward, monetary policy had remained relatively easy over most of the year. To some extent, it is true, inflation was checked by the mandatory system of price and wage controls and by a declining public-sector deficit. Yet, total net credit expansion in July–December 1972 was disquietingly high, rising as a proportion of gross national product (GNP) to 16.1% from 14.8% in 1971 and 10.4% in 1970.

In November 1972, with growth in production still accelerating, the authorities began to shift toward more active restraint, and in mid-January the official discount rate was raised from 4½ to 5%. These moves were quickly overshadowed by exchange market developments. As fissures had already appeared in the international exchange structure established in December 1971, a new attack on the dollar seemed less a question of "whether" than of "when." The decision in early January to shift to a voluntary prices and incomes policy, coupled with new exchange disturbances in Europe later that month, helped in early February to spark a heavy outflow of funds, which under the circumstances was partly financed by the creation of new credit. After the dollar had again been devalued, the discount rate was raised in late February to 5½%, but the authorities sought, in the interest of the incomes policy, to retard the adjustment of the banks' prime lending rates to market rates. In April the authorities issued guidelines for a system of dual prime rates: a higher one for large corporate borrowers, to be adjusted in line with market conditions, and a lower, fairly stable one for small businesses and farms.

In the spring, with prices rising rapidly and production bottlenecks beginning to appear, monetary policy entered a more restrictive phase. In contrast to similar phases in 1966 and 1969 and in order to avoid disrupting financial markets, emphasis was placed mainly on control of the monetary aggregates, with interest rates being left to adjust freely over a broader range. Thus, in May interest rate ceilings on large certificates of deposit ($100,000 or more), already removed for 30–89-day maturities, were suspended altogether. To reduce distortions in the treatment of different sources of funds, a uniform marginal reserve requirement of 8% was fixed for banks' issues of such certificates and of bank-related commercial paper as well as for their foreign borrowing, chiefly Eurodollars.

Against this background the official discount rate was raised in five steps from 5¾% in early May to 7½% by mid-August, and reserve requirements against demand deposits were increased as of early July. The prime rate for large borrowers was regularly adjusted upward to reach a peak of 10% in early September. At the same time, the commercial banks continued to bid strongly for funds through issues of certificates of deposit, the rates on which rose as high as 11½%. In early September, to discourage this tendency, the Federal Reserve authorities raised the marginal reserve requirement from 8 to 11% for the increase in such deposits since mid-May. Early in December the figure was again reduced to 8%.

In September, after it had been seen that monetary expansion was slowing down, the Federal Reserve backed away from any further tightening of credit. Market participants, misinterpreting official actions as a move toward relaxation, drove down short-term rates well into October, but these rose again late in the year as it became clear that the policy had remained steadfastly restrictive.

Canada. Beginning in late 1972, economic activity accelerated in response to a strengthening of exports, investment, and consumer demand. However, given the scale of unemployment and the scope for continued expansion, monetary policy remained fairly easy, and the budget, presented in February, was aimed at stimulating expansion. By early spring of 1973, however, capacity limitations were beginning to appear, leading the monetary authorities to change course. From April to September the discount rate was increased in five steps from $4\frac{3}{4}$ to $7\frac{1}{4}\%$, and supporting actions, including moral suasion, were taken to moderate the growth of credit, particularly to large business corporations. For both domestic and exchange rate reasons, however, the upward adjustment of Canadian short-term interest rates was until late in the year kept behind the adjustments in financial centres abroad. After midyear the money supply decelerated, but savings deposits grew faster than before. In general, the flow of mortgage funds was well maintained.

Japan. Faced in 1972 with a continuing huge balance of payments surplus, Japan managed by means of stringent exchange controls to avoid the limelight of currency speculation until the U.S. dollar itself came under attack in February 1973. Over this period the growth of official exchange reserves led to a large increase in domestic liquidity, which, in turn, contributed to a strong revival of economic activity from the early autumn of 1972 onward. An upsurge in private demand was reinforced by an expansionary budget policy, the aim of which was to reduce the external surplus by allocating more resources to social welfare and infrastructural uses. The authorities hesitated to tighten monetary policy for fear of inducing further unwanted inflows of funds.

The floating of the yen in February enabled the authorities to change over to a fairly vigorous policy of monetary restraint. The Bank of Japan's discount rate was increased in four steps, to reach 7% by the end of August, and reserve requirements were progressively raised. In addition, the quantitative guidelines for bank lending were applied as of April to local banks and mutual savings banks as well as to city banks, and were gradually tightened during the year. Moreover, as the balance of payments swung around into deficit the authorities intervened in the exchange markets to support the yen, thereby helping to reduce domestic liquidity. To combat inflationary strains, the government also pursued a more cautious public expenditure policy after midyear.

EEC Countries. At the beginning of 1973 the U.K., Ireland, and Denmark formally became members of the EEC. Soon afterward the Community in general was forced into disarray by the international currency crisis, but a strong nucleus of EEC countries (West Germany, France, the Benelux nations, and Denmark), joined by Norway and Sweden, achieved significant success in managing a joint float against other currencies while seeking to keep their own exchange rates within margins of $2\frac{1}{4}\%$. A further cohesive step was taken when the European Monetary Cooperation Fund came into force in April 1973. In combating inflation the EEC countries continued their search for common ground with respect to fiscal and monetary objectives and policies.

The United Kingdom, after a long period of disappointing growth, was engaged by late 1972 in a new experiment in sustained expansion. Large tax reductions and other stimulants to the economy had been introduced the previous spring; the pound sterling had been floated in June 1972; and a statutory prices and incomes policy was brought into force in November of that year. Moreover, reliance on quantitative credit controls had been abandoned in favour of credit control based on competition and interest rates.

In the first months of 1973 this strategy seemed to be yielding good results. Output was expanding buoyantly, and a consumption boom was gradually giving way to higher exports and a long-awaited revival in industrial investment. The pound sterling weathered the international exchange crisis comparatively well, and for a time wages and prices advanced more slowly. On the other hand, the balance of payments was deteriorating, largely because of higher import costs due to the depreciation of sterling after mid-1972 and to the continuing sharp rise in world commodity prices; also, limitations of productive capacity lay ahead. In early March, however, the budget of 1973–74 signaled the government's determination to keep on an expansionary course, this being viewed as a prerequisite to achieving moderation in wage demands. The budget envisaged a public-sector borrowing requirement of £4,400 million, as against £2,900 million and £1,300 million in the two preceding years. Domestically, short-term interest rates, already high, eased from January onward.

About mid-1973 the government's growth policy began to encounter serious difficulties. The weakness of the dollar, together with Britain's deteriorating trade balance and declining interest rates relative to those abroad, brought the pound sterling under considerable pressure. To limit the exchange depreciation, the Bank of England brought about a sharp rise

UPI COMPIX

Londoners read of the U.S. decision to devalue the dollar by 10%, Feb. 12, 1973. The U.S. move was followed by a Japanese decision to allow the yen to float, in an effort to bring about more realistic international exchange rates.

in short-term interest rates in July–August by a call for special deposits and by relaxing the rules governing the discount market's holdings of public-sector paper. In September, moreover, the Bank of England requested the banks to curb their lending for purposes of consumption, property development, and financial transactions.

In the late summer and early autumn the pound sterling stabilized relative to other currencies at about 18% below the level of June 1972. Borrowing abroad by residents was further facilitated, and the government introduced proposals for the next phase of its prices and incomes policy. By November, however, the economy faced an onslaught from all sides: the oil crisis, higher commodity prices, adverse trade results, growing labour unrest, and rapid monetary expansion. The Bank of England raised its minimum lending rate to 13% and made a new call for special deposits. In mid-December the government declared a national emergency and scheduled a three-day workweek for most of industry. New restraint measures included large cuts in public expenditure, an income tax surcharge, a new marginal reserve requirement on deposits, and reimposition of installment buying controls.

In West Germany a previously hesitant recovery turned into a buoyant upswing in the autumn of 1972. Foreign and domestic demand leaped ahead, while prices increased faster and wage pressures were building up. Having earlier introduced insulating measures against capital inflows, the monetary authorities saw scope for greater restraint. From October 1972 to January 1973 the official discount rate was raised in four steps from 3 to 5%, and two reductions in rediscount quotas were announced. Then the exchange crisis of February and early March resulted in huge inflows of funds from abroad and prompted new exchange restrictions.

The government viewed a vigorous attack on inflation as the first priority. The 1973 budget proposals, presented about mid-February, provided for a temporary tax surcharge on corporations and higher personal incomes, for a curtailment of investment grants and of fiscal stimulants to building, and for a large stabilization loan aimed at curtailing the growth of liquidity. In March 1973 the revaluation of the mark by 3% against SDRs, coupled with the launching of the joint European float, provided the basis for still further restraint. In May, shortly after a rise in the discount rate to 6%, the government introduced a sweeping new stabilization package. The tax surcharge was broadened in coverage; a tax of 11% was imposed on new investment; accelerated depreciation allowances on plant and equipment were withdrawn; and government expenditure was cut back.

Monetary policy was turned a notch tighter in late May with a rise in the discount rate to 7% and a suspension of central-bank advances against security. Yields on public-sector bonds quickly moved to above 10%. Fiscal and monetary restraint, together with external strength on trade account, soon produced new upward pressures on the mark, particularly in the joint European float. This led the government to revalue again at the end of June, by 5.5% against SDRs. By late 1973 the expansion of money and credit was slowing down, the external current account remained in surplus, and the rate of increase in consumer prices was again one of the lowest among the industrial countries. In December the 11% investment tax was terminated and accelerated depreciation allowances restored, but monetary policy remained restrictive.

France continued, as in recent years, to achieve an enviable growth record, a main ingredient of which was planning that aimed at maintaining a high rate of growth of investment and productivity. In the summer and autumn of 1972 monetary restraint measures were taken to damp down demand, and in December guidelines were introduced in order to bring about a deceleration of bank lending, any excesses over established ceilings being subject to stiff penalties. As a price stabilization measure, value-added tax rates were reduced, but a 15-year 7% government loan for Fr. 6.5 billion was issued early in 1973 so as to absorb most of the resultant increase in the public's liquidity. In the currency upheavals of February–March 1973, France retained its parity in terms of gold established in December 1971 as well as its dual exchange rate system; it also joined the common European float against the dollar.

In the spring and summer of 1973 the emergence of capacity strains and a faster rise in consumer prices prompted new measures of monetary restraint. Ceiling guidelines on bank credit expansion were made more restrictive; bank reserve requirements on demand deposits were increased; the official discount rate was raised in July and August from 7½ to 9½%; and the central bank suspended certain types of credit facilities available to the money market. In late September, when currency uncertainties within the joint European float were accompanied by a flight from the franc, the discount rate was increased again to 11% and the bank-credit limit for 1973 as a whole was set at 13%, implying a sharp reduction in monetary expansion compared with 1972. After tightening price controls in November, the government introduced in early December a package of stabilization measures, including a deferral of dividends in 1974, an acceleration of direct tax payments during that year, and terms improving the attractiveness of time and savings deposits and Treasury bonds.

Table II. Selected Interest Rates

Country		1971 June	1972 June	1972 Sept.	1972 Dec.	1973 March	1973 June	1973 Sept.
Belgium	A	6.00	4.00	4.00	5.00	5.00	5.50	6.50
	B[1]	2.34	2.00	1.73	3.67	3.15	2.96	5.54
	C	7.35	7.07	6.93	7.18	7.28	7.29	7.71
France	A	6.75	5.75	5.75	7.50	7.50	7.50	11.00
	B[1]	6.45	3.85	3.89	7.32	7.49	7.46	9.73
	C	8.12	7.56	7.61	8.03	8.25	8.36	9.00
Germany, West	A	5.00	3.00	3.00	4.50	5.00	7.00	7.00
	B[2]	4.25	2.75	2.75	4.25	4.75	7.00	7.00
	C	8.20	7.90	7.90	8.60	8.50	9.90	9.60
Italy	A	5.00	4.00	4.00	4.00	4.00	4.00	6.50
	B[2]	5.54	5.54	4.30	4.40	5.50	6.00	7.00
	C	7.11	6.42	6.52	6.74	6.70	6.92	6.88
Netherlands, The	A	5.50	4.00	3.00	4.00	4.00	5.00	6.50
	B[2]	4.51	1.94	1.13	3.19	1.58	3.72	5.87
	C	7.22	7.25	6.39	7.35	6.83	7.75	8.29
Switzerland	A	3.75	3.75	3.75	3.75	4.50	4.50	4.50
	B[1]	1.88	1.38	1.56	4.13	2.50	1.81	3.00
	C	5.38	5.06	4.98	5.27	5.29	5.36	5.79
United Kingdom	A	6.00	6.00	6.00	9.00†	8.50*	7.50*	11.50*
	B[2]	5.60	5.64	6.63	8.31	7.94	6.96	10.94
	C	9.16	9.32	9.54	9.62	10.01	10.15	11.55
United States	A	4.75	4.50	4.50	4.50	5.50	6.50	7.50
	B[2]	4.74	3.91	4.66	5.07	6.09	7.19	8.29
	C	5.94	5.59	5.70	5.63	6.20	6.32	6.42
Canada	A	5.25	4.75	4.75	4.75	4.75	6.25	7.25
	B[2]	3.15	3.58	3.57	3.66	4.29	5.40	6.41
	C	7.30	7.45	7.46	7.12	7.30	7.74	7.72
Japan	A	5.50	4.25	4.25	4.25	4.25	5.50	7.00
	B[1]	6.25	4.39	4.25	4.46	5.18	6.30	8.47
	C	7.95	6.45	6.64	6.75	7.58	7.89	8.66

A=Central bank's discount rate.
B=Money-market rate.
B[1]=Day-to-day money.
B[2]=90-day Treasury bills; one-year bills in the case of Italy.
C=Long-term government bond yield.
*Minimum lending rate as of Oct. 13, 1972.

In Italy a seemingly endemic problem of political and industrial unrest resulted in recent years in severe wage/price inflation, impaired investment incentives, and large capital outflows. Despite vigorous efforts to reactivate the economy economic stagnation persisted and capital outflows became more intense. Seeking to break out of this vicious circle, the authorities introduced in January 1973 separate exchange markets for commercial and financial transactions and retained this separation when the commercial lira itself was floated in February.

From the spring onward an abatement of industrial strife enabled production to rise strongly in response to consumer and export demands. On the other hand, continuing capital outflows and rising world commodity prices sharply depressed the lira, which was kept approximately in line with the U.S. dollar only with the help of large officially sponsored borrowings in the Euromarkets. Worsening inflation and rising interest rates abroad led during the summer to the introduction of a price freeze—unsupported, however, by an incomes policy—as well as to some tightening of monetary policy. The terms governing the banks' recourse to central-bank credit were tightened; a 12% annual growth ceiling was imposed on bank credit to large borrowers; and the banks' lending and deposit rates were progressively raised.

In Belgium economic activity gained renewed momentum in the early autumn of 1972 thanks to a broadly based increase in foreign and domestic demand. However, by the spring of 1973 real growth had slowed down considerably owing to limitations of capacity, though the trend of wages and consumer prices remained fairly favourable by international standards. The government's budget continued to be expansionary, but efforts were made to space out expenditures and to rely mainly on medium- and long-term financing.

The economy's lively demand for bank credit, together with the liquidity impact of a large balance of payments surplus, called forth various measures of monetary restraint. From late 1972 to November 1973, the official discount rate was raised in seven stages from 4 to $7\frac{3}{4}$%; the banks' rediscount quotas were reduced; and measures to limit inflows of funds were further tightened. In addition, the banks and other financial institutions were asked on several occasions to agree to increase their noninterest-bearing cash deposits with the National Bank. In the agreement coming into force in October 1973, moreover, bank credit expansion in excess of certain base levels was made subject to reserve requirements.

In The Netherlands economic revival lagged somewhat behind the cyclical upswing abroad. Cost pressures and official price surveillance tended to hold back the recovery of industrial investment, and public consumption outlays grew only slowly. But with ceilings on bank credit suspended in March 1972 and with interest rates having fallen substantially by the autumn, bank credit to the private sector began rising rapidly in early 1973. Another factor contributing to accelerated monetary growth was the strength of the balance of payments in January–June. In view of the rise in interest rates abroad and of inflationary pressure, the central bank raised its discount rate in five steps from 4% in June to 7% by October. Short- and long-term interest rates increased sharply during the summer, and monetary expansion slowed down. On both external and domestic grounds the guilder was revalued on September 15 by 5%. By early December, however, with the guilder under pressure in the exchange markets, the Nederlandsche Bank raised its discount rate to 8%. (WARREN D. MC CLAM)

WIDE WORLD

Hectic trading that followed the Feb. 12, 1973, U.S. dollar devaluation is reflected in this scene at a Frankfurt, W.Ger., currency dealer's office.

See also Economics; Economy, World; Government Finance; Housing; Investment, International; Payments and Reserves, International; Stock Exchanges.

Mongolia

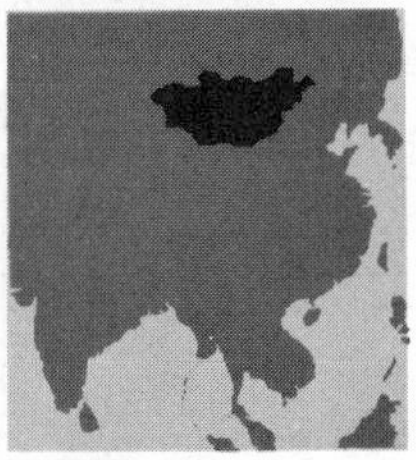

A people's republic of Asia lying between the U.S.S.R. and China, Mongolia occupies the geographic area known as Outer Mongolia. Area: 604,000 sq.mi. (1,565,000 sq.km.). Pop. (1973 est.): 1,340,000. Cap. and largest city: Ulan Bator (pop., 1971 est., 295,000). Language: Khalkha Mongolian. Religion: Lamaistic Buddhism. First secretary of the Mongolian People's Revolutionary (Communist) Party and chairman of the Council of Ministers (premier) in 1973, Yumzhagiyen Tsedenbal.

Relations between Mongolia and China became tense in 1973. In September the Ulan Bator newspaper *Utga Dzohiol Urlag* ("Literature and Art") published a long article containing sweeping charges of border violations and subversions by China, alleging that from 1969 to July 1973 the Chinese Army had orga-

MONGOLIA

Education. (1969–70) Primary, pupils 137,420, teachers 4,362; secondary, pupils 74,344, teachers 3,566; vocational, pupils 8,254; teacher training, pupils 2,239; higher (including University of Ulan Bator), students 7,226, teaching staff (1968–69) 700.

Finance. Monetary unit: tugrik, with (Sept. 17, 1973) an official exchange rate 3.20 tugriks to U.S. $1 (7.11 tugriks = £1 sterling). Budget (1972 est.): revenue 2,136,000,000 tugriks; expenditure 2,124,000,000 tugriks.

Foreign Trade. (1970) Imports *c.* 900 million tugriks; exports *c.* 310 million tugriks. Import sources: U.S.S.R. *c.* 80%; Czechoslovakia *c.* 5%. Export destinations: U.S.S.R. *c.* 70%; Czechoslovakia 9%. Main exports: agricultural raw materials 58%; foodstuffs raw materials 20%; foodstuffs 10%.

Transport and Communications. Roads (1970) *c.* 75,000 km. (including *c.* 8,600 km. main roads). Railways (1971) 1,423 km. Telephones (Jan. 1972) 25,000. Radio receivers (Dec. 1970) 166,000. Television receivers (Dec. 1970) *c.* 20,000.

Agriculture. Production (in 000; metric tons; 1972; 1971 in parentheses): wheat *c.* 300 (316); oats *c.* 30 (*c.* 36); barley *c.* 9 (*c.* 9); potatoes *c.* 23 (*c.* 23). Livestock (in 000; Dec. 1971): cattle *c.* 2,150; sheep *c.* 13,350; goats *c.* 4,250; horses *c.* 2,300; camels *c.* 650.

Industry. Production (in 000; metric tons; 1971): coal 101; electricity (kw-hr.) 568,000.

nized more than 150 maneuvers in the immediate proximity of the Mongolian-Chinese frontier and that Chinese soldiers sometimes had penetrated 10 to 15 mi. inside Mongolian territory. The article was illustrated with a Chinese map of 1952 according to which not only Mongolia but also large stretches of Siberia and Soviet Turkistan, as well as Korea, Indochina, Thailand, and Burma, were described as "immemorial Chinese territories."

The Ulan Bator authorities noted the rehabilitation of Ulanfu, former governor of the Mongolian Autonomous Region of China, who had been disgraced during the Cultural Revolution. Ulanfu was reported as having said at Huhehot that the Mongolian People's Republic was "a Soviet colony."

During 1973 high-level delegations from Czechoslovakia, East Germany, and Bulgaria visited Ulan Bator in June, October, and November, respectively, to coordinate with Mongolia their development plans for 1976–80. A member of the Council for Mutual Economic Assistance (Comecon), Mongolia enjoyed special privileges as a less developed country. Large reserves of coking coal, estimated at three billion tons, were discovered in the southern part of the country.

(K. M. SMOGORZEWSKI)

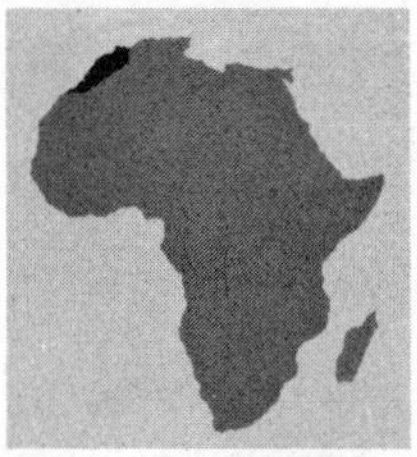

Morocco

A constitutional monarchy of northwestern Africa, on the Atlantic Ocean and the Mediterranean Sea, Morocco is bordered by Algeria and Spanish Sahara. Area: 177,116 sq.mi. (458,730 sq.km.). Pop. (1972 est.): 15,547,000. Cap.: Rabat (pop., 1971, 374,809). Largest city: Casablanca (pop., 1971, 1,506,373). Language: Arabic; Berber. Religion: Muslim. King, Hassan II; prime minister in 1973, Ahmed Osman.

King Hassan made it clear in January 1973 that he saw no future in cooperation with the main political parties in the running of the country. The proposed general election, already postponed since April 1972, was shelved. The king argued that he had the direct support of the people, but the main opposition group, the leftist National Union of Popular Forces (UNFP), replied that he ruled only through royal puppets and the police. Some of the UNFP supporters, barred from constitutional opposition, were prepared to oppose the king by illegal means.

An armed attack on a police post in the Atlas Mountains in March was followed by bomb explosions in Casablanca and other towns. More than 1,000 Moroccans were arrested and the UNFP was banned in Rabat, though not in the rest of the country. UNFP leaders were not detained, but there were many UNFP members among the 16 sentenced to death by the Kenitra military tribunal in August for endangering the security of the state, all but one of whom were executed on November 1. In the aftermath of the August 1972 attempt to kill King Hassan, 11 air force officers were executed in January.

The students of Rabat University started the year with their perennial protests against the educational system, and the National Union of Moroccan Students was suspended after a policeman was killed in clashes with the security forces. Teachers joined in the protests, and less than half the total student enrollment of 16,000 continued their studies.

The Moroccan economy showed signs of improvement, and in May King Hassan launched a new five-year plan (1973–77) that envisaged an annual growth

MOROCCO

Education. (1971–72) Primary, pupils 1,231,436, teachers (1969–70) 33,238; secondary and vocational, pupils 313,424, teachers (1969–70) 13,471; teacher training (1969–70), students 3,622, teaching staff 121; higher, students 15,148, teaching staff (full-time; 1969–70) 571.

Finance. Monetary unit: dirham, with (Sept. 17, 1973) a free rate of 3.96 dirhams to U.S. $1 (9.55 dirhams = £1 sterling). Gold, SDRs, and foreign exchange, central bank: (May 1973) U.S. $254 million; (May 1972) U.S. $240 million. Budget (1972 est.): revenue 5,799,000,000 dirhams; expenditure 6,197,000,000 dirhams. Gross domestic product: (1972) 20,150,000,000 dirhams; (1971) 18,570,000,000 dirhams. Money supply: (March 1973) 7,320,000,000 dirhams; (March 1972) 6,406,000,000 dirhams. Cost of living (Casablanca; 1963 = 100): (April 1973) 120; (April 1972) 121.

Foreign Trade. (1972) Imports 3,572,000,000 dirhams; exports 2,968,000,000 dirhams. Main import sources: France 31%; U.S. 8%; West Germany 7%; Italy 6%; U.K. 5%. Main export destinations: France 33%; Italy 9%; West Germany 9%; Spain 5%; U.K. 5%. Main exports: phosphates 23%; citrus fruit 15%; tomatoes 6%; fish 5%. Tourism (1971): visitors 757,300; gross receipts U.S. $150 million.

Transport and Communications. Roads (1972) 25,231 (including 14 km. expressways). Motor vehicles in use (1971): passenger 242,100; commercial (including buses) 90,500. Railways (1971): 1,756 km.; traffic 549 million passenger-km., freight (1972) 3,032,000,000 net ton-km. Air traffic (1971): 480 million passenger-km.; freight 6,908,000 net ton-km. Shipping (1972): merchant vessels 100 gross tons and over 39; gross tonnage 46,907. Telephones (Dec. 1971) 171,000. Radio licenses (Dec. 1971) 1,002,000. Television receivers (Dec. 1971) 223,000.

Agriculture. Production (in 000; metric tons; 1972; 1971 in parentheses): wheat 2,184 (2,188); barley 2,466 (2,572); corn 368 (390); sugar, raw value c. 235 (c. 222); oranges (1971) 822, (1970) 676; dry peas c. 35 (48); dry broad beans (1971) 243, (1970) 190; wine c. 115 (115); olives c. 250 (450); figs c. 65 (c. 65); dates c. 90 (c. 90); tomatoes c. 250 (c. 250); fish catch (1971) 229, (1970) 256. Livestock (in 000; 1971–72): cattle c. 3,640; sheep c. 18,000; goats c. 8,900; horses c. 400; mules c. 420; asses c. 950; camels (1970–71) c. 230; poultry (1970–71) c. 15,800.

Industry. Production (in 000; metric tons; 1972): coal 547; crude oil 28; cement 1,540; iron ore (55–60% metal content) 235; phosphates (oxide content; 1971) 12,030; manganese ore (metal content; 1971) 80; lead concentrates (metal content) 95; zinc concentrates (metal content) 18; electricity (kw-hr.; 1971) 2,085,000.

rate of 7.5%. Much of the foreign financing for the plan was expected to come from France, the U.S., and West Germany, Morocco's three leading trade partners, but the Soviet Union was also invited to take part in development projects. Major projects completed during the year included the Wadi Inawen Dam, first stage in a large-scale irrigation scheme near Fès; another dam near Agadir in the southwest; and a Soviet-built power station located at Oujda in the northeast.

The nationalization of 600,000 ac. of foreign-owned agricultural land was completed after strong resistance from the foreign landowners, who were mainly French. King Hassan announced that 100 large commercial concerns would be "moroccanized" by mid-1974 and that foreign banks and insurance companies would be similarly taken over by 1975.

Relations with Spain were strained. In March Morocco announced the extension of its territorial waters to 12 mi. and of fishing rights to 70 mi. There were skirmishes with Spanish fishing fleets and, despite formal talks, no agreement was reached with Spain. Regarding Spanish Sahara, the three bordering states of Morocco, Mauritania, and Algeria discussed but did not agree on a common policy; the heads of the three states, meeting at Agadir in July, were, however, able

Mormons:
see Religion

to express a common concern about Spain's hesitation in carrying out a UN resolution on self-determination for the territory.

Throughout the year Morocco kept up a war of words with Libya, whose head of state, Muammar al-Qaddafi, continued to press for King Hassan's overthrow. Toward the Middle East situation King Hassan demonstrated a more positive policy; in May he sent a motorized infantry unit of 1,800 men to serve on the Syrian cease-fire line with Israel "in the coming battle," and, when war did break out in October, these troops were reinforced. (PETER KILNER)

Motion Pictures

For the cinema 1973 seemed an unusually cheerless year almost everywhere. In most areas of the West the economic stress of rising costs and declining audiences seemed ever more acute, and the withdrawal of Metro-Goldwyn-Mayer from film distribution was a terrible blow to morale; in much of the Communist East—but especially in Czechoslovakia and Yugoslavia—a hardening of official attitudes inhibited adventurous or progressive film activity; and even in the emergent areas of Latin America, with mounting political uncertainties, and in Africa there appeared an appreciable slackening of activity.

The year's obituary list, too, was a gloomy one. Headed by two of the cinema's greatest directors, John Ford of the U.S. and the Soviet pioneer and director Grigory Kozintsev, it included Sir Noel Coward, director, actor, writer, and composer; Betty Grable, queen of pinup girls in the 1940s; Anna Magnani, an international symbol of Italian womanhood in all its forms since her memorable performance in Roberto Rosselini's *Open City* (1946); and Edward G. Robinson, an actor who from his appearance as the gangster in the title role of *Little Caesar* had been a mythic figure in the American cinema. Other losses included actors Joe E. Brown, Lon Chaney, Jr., Willy Fritsch, Laurence Harvey, Jack Hawkins, Veronica Lake, Bruce Lee (star of Hong Kong kung fu pictures), Janet Munro, Dennis Price, Robert Ryan, and Claire Windsor; directors Merian C. Cooper (maker of *King Kong*), Wilhelm Dieterle, Mikhail Kalatozov, Jean-Pierre Melville, and Robert Siodmak; writer Adrian Scott; and Ernest Lindgren, founder of Britain's National Film Archive. (*See* OBITUARIES.)

English-Speaking Cinema. *United States.* The year was far from encouraging for the U.S. cinema. Metro-Goldwyn-Mayer, for half a century a universal symbol of Hollywood prosperity and magnificence, announced that it would no longer be involved in distributing films. Explaining the decision, its president, James T. Aubrey, Jr., said that "the bottom has fallen out of the market." Other companies, too, seemed to be feeling the pinch. The new president of Columbia Pictures, David Begelman, announced that Columbia was mortgaging some of its radio stations to pay off debts amounting to approximately $150 million. However, he was less pessimistic than Aubrey about the future: "There is a large enough audience to enable pictures to make a healthy profit," he asserted.

If any general pattern and preoccupation was to be discerned in current U.S. production, it was perhaps a sense of self-examination provoked by an era of national and global anxiety. Although it was too early for the Watergate shock to have had a direct effect upon movie production, a film such as John G. Avildsen's *Save the Tiger,* with its story of a businessman in mounting panic as he feels the once-secure ground of known moral values slipping from under his feet, captured with some accuracy the sense of the major breakdown of the era.

A recurrent form was the definition and exploration of a contemporary hero or antihero in his special social context. Some examples were the folk singer of atrophied sensibilities played by Rip Torn in Daryl Duke's *Payday;* Timothy Bottoms' ambivalent law student in James Bridges' *The Paper Chase;* the ruthlessly and consciencelessly ambitious race driver played by Jeff Bridges in Lamont Johnson's *The Last American Hero;* and the terminally ill second-rate professional baseball player in John Hancock's *Bang the Drum Slowly.*

Other filmmakers seemed to look for elucidation of present dilemmas in projections of a not-too-distant future. George Romero's *The Crazies,* for instance, predicted the horror that might ensue if a bacteriological warfare virus was allowed to escape in a small U.S. town. Both Richard Fleischer's *Soylent Green* and George Lucas' balletically directed *THX 1138* predicted futures far less optimistic than the older type of science fiction conceived. *Soylent Green* foresaw a time of overpopulation, shortage, and breakdown, with distinctions of privilege becoming ever more acute and commodities in such short supply that cannibalism would become an authorized economic policy. *THX 1138* was more concerned with the spiritual effects of a future society in which human beings were kept contented by being withheld from the need or possibility of independent thought and action.

The past, too, was reexamined in the light of either nostalgia or criticism. Several films dealt with the Depression period. Peter Bogdanovich, director of *The Last Picture Show,* made another essay in nostalgia in *Paper Moon,* a picaresque adventure of a middle-aged Bible salesman and a precocious nine-year-old, while Robert Aldrich's *Emperor of the North Pole* illustrated an incident from the violent war of the workless and the employed in the Depression era. *American Graffiti,* directed by George Lucas, depicted in fine detail adolescent behaviour in small-town northern California in 1962.

Hollywood even subjected some of its own most hallowed myths to critical reevaluation. In *The Long Goodbye* Robert Altman faced Raymond Chandler's favourite private eye hero Philip Marlowe—the archetypal romantic hero of the 1940s—with the 1970s, a confrontation shattering to both the hero and the age. Other long-standing Hollywood myths to be assaulted were the glamour of the criminal (undermined in

FOX-RANK

Wily Michael Caine (left) toys with the fancies of his aristocratic rival Lord Olivier in the film "Sleuth." The screenplay by Anthony Shaffer was based on his original award-winning play.

Down and out in Depression America, Ryan O'Neal and his worldly wise daughter Tatum portray two con artists in "Paper Moon," directed by Peter Bogdanovich.

Howard Zieff's thriller parody *Slither*), and the whole opposition of law and disorder in Peter Yates's *The Friends of Eddie Coyle,* where the area between the two was a no-man's-land in which all appeared in the same gray hue.

In the climate of reaction against screen permissiveness and anxiety about possible future attitudes of state authorities, most filmmakers were more restrained in their treatment of sexual matters (though screen violence seemed to have been consistently aggravated). While Ernest Lehman's adaptation of Philip Roth's *Portnoy's Complaint* finally diluted the novel into simple vulgarity, Ralph Bakshi followed *Fritz the Cat* with another "adult" animated feature, *Heavy Traffic,* about trying to survive in the city jungle.

Certain genres proved, as ever, to be durable in the face of changing times and conditions. Notable Westerns were Sydney Pollack's mock-heroic *Jeremiah Johnson;* Robert Aldrich's sparse and antiheroic *Ulzana's Raid;* and Sam Peckinpah's ill-structured but compelling *Pat Garrett and Billy the Kid.* After his triumphant return to form with *Fat City,* John Huston's self-indulgent Western comedy *The Life and Times of Judge Roy Bean* was a disappointment. Representing the occult was *The Exorcist,* which opened in December to mixed reviews and capacity crowds.

The year was not a vintage one for musicals. Norman Jewison's *Jesus Christ Superstar* made a bolder effort than David Greene's *Godspell* to escape its stage origins, but neither director wrested really effective cinematic material from their rock-oratorios. The musical version of *Lost Horizon,* starring Liv Ullmann (*see* BIOGRAPHY) with music by Burt Bacharach, merely aroused regret for the solider virtues and shorter running time of Frank Capra's original 1930s version.

Films by or starring black artists continued to testify to an important market in the U.S. and elsewhere. The year produced a black answer to *Love Story* in Sidney Poitier's mawkish *A Warm December;* another episode in the adventures of the black detective in *Shaft in Africa;* and even a black vampire in William Crain's grisly *Blacula.*

A project that represented a marriage between motion pictures and theatre was American Film Theatre. Produced by Ely Landau, this comprised filmed versions of eight stage plays sold on a subscription series basis and shown in more than 500 theatres throughout the U.S. and Canada. The series began in October and included *The Iceman Cometh* with Lee Marvin, *A Delicate Balance* with Katharine Hepburn, *Three Sisters* with Lord Olivier, *The Homecoming* with Paul Rogers, *Butley* with Alan Bates, *Luther* with Stacy Keach, *Rhinoceros* with Zero Mostel, and *Lost in the Stars* with Brock Peters.

In the annual awards of the U.S. Academy of Motion Picture Arts and Sciences, *The Godfather* and *Cabaret* practically swept the board. *The Godfather* was awarded Oscars for best film, best actor (Marlon Brando), and best screenplay from a work in another medium; *Cabaret* was rewarded for best direction (Bob Fosse; *see* BIOGRAPHY), best actress (Liza Minnelli), best supporting actor (Joel Grey), and best cinematography (Geoffrey Unsworth). The award for the best original screenplay went to Jeremy Larner for *The Candidate;* and for the best supporting actress to Eileen Heckart for her playing in *Butterflies Are Free.* The best foreign-language film was Luis Buñuel's (*see* BIOGRAPHY) *The Discreet Charm of the Bourgeoisie;* the best documentary, *Marjoe,* produced and directed by Howard Smith and Sarah Kernochan; the best animated (short subject) film, *A Christmas Carol,* made in Britain by Canadian-born Richard Williams. A special award was made posthumously to Edward G. Robinson. Marlon Brando caused consternation by refusing his Oscar; he was represented by a young Indian girl who read his statement protesting the treatment of American Indians.

Britain. The year looked no brighter in Britain, with cinema attendances reaching an all-time low, Shepperton Studios in the hands of developers, and Elstree studios threatened as a result of MGM's withdrawal from distribution. The filmmakers' union issued a report strongly urging nationalization of the British film industry, without compensation, and with control in the hands of the workers.

For all that, production continued, and there were some promising debuts. New filmmakers tended to work on literary adaptations. Michael Apted's first feature, *The Triple Echo,* was a stylish adaptation of an H. E. Bates novella about a World War II deserter who disguises himself as a woman; Peter Duffell's *England Made Me* dealt, with somewhat less assurance and style, with an early Graham Greene story; and Alan Bridges shared the Cannes Grand Prix (with the U.S. film *Scarecrow*) for his sensitive handling of a novel by L. P. Hartley, *The Hireling.* Among these debuts, Claude Whatham was exceptional in not treating a literary original; *That'll Be the Day* was a brave attempt to define the style and nostalgia of the 1950s.

The year produced two outstanding films. Lindsay Anderson's *O Lucky Man!* developed the Brechtian "epic" method of *If . . .* and *The White Bus.* The hero, Mick Travis, played by Malcolm McDowell and a close relation to the Mick Travers of *If . . .*, makes a painful pilgrim's progress throughout the length and breadth of contemporary Britain, meeting down-and-outs and industrialists, corrupt officials and latter-day saints, good fortune and ill. If the final scenes remained deliberately elusive, there were some impressive insights and glittering entertainments along the way. The great length of the film apparently proved disconcerting to its distributors, and it was subjected to considerable cutting following its first release in London and its screening as the official British entry at the Cannes Film Festival. Following his earlier *Performance* and *Walkabout, Don't Look Now* confirmed Nicholas Roeg as an outstanding new talent in the

British cinema. The film was based on a story by Daphne du Maurier but transformed its literary original into something authentically of the cinema in its exhilarating visuals and almost tangible atmospheres of menace and fear in an out-of-season Venice.

Commercially, the British cinema's biggest successes during the year were (predictably) an Ian Fleming story, *Live and Let Die,* with a new James Bond—the third—in Roger Moore; and Joseph Mankiewicz's lively screen version of Anthony Shaffer's play *Sleuth,* an expert duologue with Lord Olivier and Michael Caine. Another U.S. director, Fred Zinnemann, adapted rather less successfully Frederick Forsyth's novel about an attempted assassination of Charles de Gaulle, *The Day of the Jackal.*

Other commercial productions included a very pedestrian new account of the love affair of Nelson and Lady Hamilton, *Bequest to the Nation,* and two versions of Ibsen's *A Doll's House,* one by Joseph Losey with Jane Fonda, David Warner, and Trevor Howard, and the other by Patrick Garland with Claire Bloom, Anthony Hopkins, and Sir Ralph Richardson.

Interesting low-budget productions included James Scott's first feature, *Adult Fun,* an espionage drama-fantasy with undertones of metaphysical speculation; Tony Bicat's short, *Skinflicker,* a film within a film, purporting to be an official training film made up of footage shot by a professional pornographer while taking part in a political kidnap and murder; and Bill Douglas' *My Ain Folk,* a feature-length sequel to his autobiographical study of a deprived Scottish boyhood, *My Childhood.*

Canada. Both French- and English-speaking areas of the industry were involved in conscious and successful efforts to develop feature production. Denys Arcand's *Réjeanne Padovani* was outstanding: a Watergate-era tale about high-level official corruption, Arcand claimed that it was in fact inspired by Tacitus' account of the court of Emperor Claudius. It created an atmosphere of sophisticated, sinister elegance quite unlike the vivid realism of Donald Shebib's impressions of poverty in Toronto in the English-speaking *Between Friends* (previously titled *Get Back*), with its story of a rather incompetent gang of would-be bank robbers, whose attempts to escape, through crime, to daydreams of riches are inevitably and brutally frustrated.

Australia. Directed by Bruce Beresford, sometime secretary of the British Film Institute's Production Board in London, *The Adventures of Barry McKenzie* proved the most profitable and exportable film in the cinema history of Australia. Based on a popular underground comic strip about an Australian innocent in the perilous wilds of London, its comedy was recklessly inexpert and incorrigibly ribald, but undoubtedly energetic.

Western Europe. *France.* The French feature cinema continued to be dominated by the "new wave" generation that emerged in the late 1950s and early 1960s. François Truffaut made an attractive tribute to his craft (and, in style and mood, to the spiritual father of the group, Jean Renoir) in *La Nuit Américaine (Day for Night),* while his contemporary, Claude Chabrol, achieved commercial success with two of the highly sophisticated and skilled tales of middle-class murder with which he had become associated: *Juste Avant la Nuit* and *Les Noces Rouges.*

Two other directors from the "new wave" era asserted reaction against the commercial cinema with marathon films shot on substandard 16-mm. stock.

The jackal (Edward Fox) tests the calibration of a rifle made to his specifications and intended for assassination in "The Day of the Jackal," directed by Fred Zinnemann.

Jean Eustache's *La Maman et la Putain* used its 220-minute running time for the kind of leisurely, meticulous development more usually associated with the novel, to record a very contemporary Parisian triangle, all three characters being unimportant and unremarkable except in being exactly observed as products of their times. The everyday frankness of its words and scenes clearly outraged many of the audience at the Cannes Film Festival in May, where the film received a special prize. Jacques Rivette's *Out One Spectre,* whose original running time of 13 hours was cut to 6 for screening in the Berlin Young Film Forum, was a bewildering composition of deliberate mystification and contradiction.

The genre of political drama created by Costa-Gavras in *Z* and *L'Aveu* (*The Confession*) retained its vogue. Gavras himself made *État de Siège* (*State of Siege*), which described the kidnapping by Tupamaros of U.S. political agents, while Yves Boisset's *Plot* was a somewhat speculative recreation of the Ben Barka affair. Claude Faraldo's *Themroc,* one of the few notable feature films by a new director, was a diverting fantasy about one man's reaction to the political malaise. A Parisian worker sets up a cave-man commune in the middle of a Paris suburb, copulating paganly with his converted neighbours and feeding on roasted policemen. Another fantasy of dropping out, Marco Ferreri's *La Grande Bouffe,* provided the cinema scandal of the year with its inspiring images of four men who determine on a suicide pact by gorging themselves to death.

Belgium. André Delvaux followed *Rendez-vous à Bray* with another exercise in atmospheric mystery, *Belle,* in which a dull university professor's staid and settled life is suddenly disrupted by a mysterious pair of beautiful foreigners who, with no common language, lead him into a vortex of passion and finally what seems to be murder.

Switzerland. The remarkable revival of the Swiss feature cinema, following a measure of government support for the industry, continued. Alain Tanner, director of *Charles Mort ou Vif* and *Le Salamandre,* made *Le Retour de l'Afrique,* about a young couple who decide to go to Africa. After they have sold their possessions and thrown a party in their empty apartment, their scheme is frustrated. From shame of ad-

Annual Cinema Attendance

Country	Total in 000	Per capita
Afghanistan	19,200	1.1
Albania	8,400	4
Algeria	28,700	2.3
Angola	2,900	0.5
Argentina	53,900	2
Australia	32,000	3
Austria	32,900	4
Bahrain	1,400	6
Barbados	1,300	5
Belgium	31,500	3
Belize	300	2
Bhutan	200	0.3
Brazil	234,700	3
Bulgaria	109,600	13
Burma	218,000	8
Burundi	100	0.04
Cambodia	20,000	3
Canada	78,900	4
Central African Rep.	500	0.4
Chad	1,300	0.4
Chile	66,500	7
China	4,000,000	6
Colombia	92,800	5
Cyprus	6,100	10
Czechoslovakia	114,800	8
Dahomey	1,200	0.4
Denmark	24,300	5
Ecuador	22,500	4
Egypt	59,700	1.8
Equatorial Guinea	500	1.7
Faeroe Islands	300	7
Falkland Islands	20	10
Finland	11,000	2
France	183,100	4
French Guiana	700	14
Germany, East	91,400	5
Germany, West	167,400	3
Ghana	18,700	2
Greenland	400	11
Guam	500	5
Guatemala	4,600	0.9
Hong Kong	79,400	19
Hungary	79,600	8
Iceland	2,300	12
India	2,190,000	4
Iran	16,400	0.6
Iraq	8,300	1.3
Israel	35,100	12
Italy	600,000	11
Japan	253,000	2.4
Jordan	2,000	0.9
Korea, South	168,400	5
Kuwait	3,800	5
Laos	1,000	0.3
Lebanon	4,700	18
Liberia	900	0.8
Luxembourg	1,500	5
Macau	95,900	23
Malagasy Rep.	4,500	0.7
Malaysia	99,100	9.4
Mali	2,500	0.5
Malta	3,500	11
Mauritius	8,300	10
Mexico	251,500	5
Monaco	100	5
Morocco	18,200	1.3
Mozambique	2,500	0.3
Netherlands, The	30,100	2.3
New Caledonia	700	7
Niger	800	0.2
Norway	15,900	4
Panama	5,000	4
Poland	137,600	4
Portugal	28,000	3
Qatar	500	5
Réunion	1,200	3
Romania	198,800	10
St. Kitts-Nevis-Anguilla	70	1.1
Senegal	5,200	1.5
Sierra Leone	100	0.05
Singapore	28,000	14
Somalia	4,700	1.7
Spain	330,900	10
Sri Lanka	97,700	8
Surinam	1,700	5
Swaziland	100	0.2
Sweden	26,000	3
Switzerland	32,000	5
Trinidad and Tobago	8,400	8
Tunisia	8,000	1.6
Uganda	2,000	0.3
U.S.S.R.	4,651,800	19
United Kingdom	193,000	4
United States	920,600	5
Upper Volta	1,000	0.2
Venezuela	37,700	4
Vietnam, South	25,500	1.4
Western Samoa	500	3
Yemen (San'a')	1,800	0.4
Yugoslavia	86,300	4
Zaire	1,100	0.1

Source: UNESCO, *Statistical Yearbook* (1971).

mitting failure to their friends, they hide in the apartment and make the journey in spirit. Claude Goretta's first cinema feature, *L'Invitation,* was on the surface a gentle account of a visit by the personnel of a small office to the estate of one of their colleagues who had come into a little money. However, the wine and the heat go to their heads and loosen their tongues and libidos, and the rural idyll suddenly becomes a merciless exposé of the anxieties and inhibitions of the Swiss bourgeoisie.

Italy. Ironically, while the official mood in Italy showed a clear reaction in favour of greater reticence and prudery, the year's outstanding successes all depended for their huge box-office attraction on their sexual content. Bernardo Bertolucci's (*see* BIOGRAPHY) *Last Tango in Paris* achieved unprecedented international notoriety and commercial success and was in and out of the Italian courts on a series of obscenity charges. In fact, the sexuality was incidental to his sensitive observation of a middle-aged American and a young girl who meet, and love, anonymously in a vacant apartment in Paris—an intense and meditative vision of private torments dominated by Marlon Brando's performance. The commercial intention of Salvatore Samperi's *Malizia* was more blatant. The film described the crisis precipitated in a middle-class widower's household when an eligible young Sicilian housekeeper takes charge.

Pier Paolo Pasolini's version of *The Canterbury Tales,* having won the 1972 Berlin Golden Bear in its unfinished state, was finally completed and promptly faced with official disapproval and prohibition. Franco Zeffirelli's beautifully picturesque and aimless *Brother Sun, Sister Moon* was a 1970-ish reading of St. Francis of Assisi as a holy hippie, while Gianni Amelio's *La Citta del Sole* was a gentle meditation upon the philosophy of the 17th-century sage Tommaso Campanella.

West Germany. In *The Pedestrian,* Maximilian Schell attempted a philosophical exploration of the problems raised by the case of a rich industrialist accused by a newspaper of Nazi activities during World War II, while Werner Herzog's *Aguirre, the Wrath of God* was an account of a conquistador expedition in search of El Dorado, told in images of mesmeric beauty and through highly stylized performances. Jean-Marie Straub's *A History Lesson* counterpointed Bertolt Brecht's version of the rise of Julius Caesar with images of present-day Rome, while Hans-Jürgen Syberberg's *Ludwig—Requiem for a Virgin King* attempted a portrait of Ludwig II of Bavaria through a deliberately mannered stylization that lost its charm after the first reel or so.

Sweden. Ingmar Bergman's *Cries and Whispers,* which emerged at the end of 1972, proved to be one of the great Swedish director's major works, but the year's box-office success was *The New Land.* This followed *The Emigrants* as the second episode of Jan Troell's adaptation of Vilhelm Moberg's (*see* OBITUARIES) epic novel of emigrants to the New World.

Spain. Alongside rather commonplace commercial production, limited by severe censorship and the exploitation of Spain's labour and location resources by foreign producers, young or radical filmmakers continued to attempt occasional offbeat projects. In *The Spirit of the Beehive,* first-time feature director Victor Erice explored the relationships between the dream world of children and the harsh and unpredictable real world of adults in the period just after the Spanish Civil War. In *Anna and the Wolves,* a more seasoned director, Carlos Saura, presented a rather overschematic allegory of a dominating mother with her three dreadful sons representing, respectively, sex, religion, and the military spirit.

Greece. Despite a distinct decline in standards due to a dramatically falling box office and the pressures of political censorship, at least one film of substance appeared in the course of the year. Theo Angelopoulos' *Days of 36* was a meticulous account of an episode just before the establishment of the Metaxas dictatorship, creating a gripping suspense story out of an apparently simple anecdote.

Netherlands. The year's production was dominated by two documentary films. Louis van Gasteren's *Now Do You Get Why I'm Crying?* achieved riveting horror through its simple observation of a former victim of the World War II concentration camp at Belsen recalling his experiences under the effect of psychiatric drugs. Bert Haanstra's more vaunted *Ape and Super-Ape* proved disappointing, using well-worn nature film to portray some simplistic views of the nature of man. A newcomer to feature direction, Guido Pieters, attracted attention with his experiment in time magic, *The Romantic Agony.*

Eastern Europe. *U.S.S.R.* The long-delayed release in the West of Andrey Tarkovsky's *Andrey Rublev* merely emphasized the period of general aridness through which the Soviet cinema was passing. While studios in Moscow and Leningrad seemed dedicated to the production of formula pictures in the socialist mold, interesting work (unfortunately too little exploited abroad) was being produced in the studios of the national republics. From Kirghiz came Tolomush Okeyev's (now three-year-old) *Bow to the Fire,* a fresh and original reexamination of the collectivization program of the 1930s; from Turkmenistan came *The Daughter-in-Law;* from Moldavia, *Lautari (Wandering Minstrels),* directed by the poet Emil Lotyani; from Georgia, Georgy Shengelaya's *Pirosmani,* a tender reconstruction of the life and times of the Georgian primitive artist; and from Lithuania, V. Zhalakyavchus' *That Sweet Word—Liberty,* winner of the Moscow Festival grand prix.

Poland. The Polish cinema continued to be dominated by Andrzej Wajda. His version of Stanislaw Wyspianski's play *The Wedding* (based on an actual event of 1900: the marriage, more out of demonstration than affection, of a popular poet and a humble peasant girl) was an exhilarating, highly charged affair, discerning beyond the turn-of-the-century incident contemporary references to Poland's situation. Krzysztof Zanussi's *Illumination* was a variation on the theme of his first feature, *Structure of Crystals.* Again the hero is a scientist who discovers through his own personal and professional problems the impossibility of a "scientific" and absolute truth.

Hungary. Hungary seemed still to be recovering from the hiatus caused by the 1972 reorganization of its film industry. Its only notable exhibit at a major film festival was Ferenc Kardos' *Petőfi '73,* a strange celebration of the patriot through a supposed reconstruction of the 1848 revolution by contemporary students. Pal Zolnay's *Photography* was an expansion of a short subject already released, presenting through the adventures of a young itinerant photographer strange dramas and tragedies of Hungarian peasant lives over the past half century.

Czechoslovakia. The country's once outstanding film production continued to be muted by official caution; the year's major effort was concentrated on a costly reconstruction of the Munich confrontation between Nazi Germany and the U.K. and France.

Asia. *Japan.* Yoshishige Yoshida's *Coup d'État* reconstructed the personality of Ikki Kite, a right-wing revolutionary of the 1930s, while Kon Ichikawa's *The Wanderers* reduced to ridicule the old militaristic codes.

India. India looked forward to a new wave and the overthrow of the outmoded (but still popular) star-dominated commercial system as a result of direct government intervention in film production, the first successes of a national film institute, and the enthusiasm of many young artists. Meanwhile, the distinguished Bengali master Satyajit Ray won the Berlin Festival's major award with *Distant Thunder,* describing the reverberations of World War II and the effects of the great rice famine on a remote Bengali village.

Hong Kong. Film production in Hong Kong, dominated by Run Run Shaw (*see* BIOGRAPHY), prospered during the year. A series of action-adventure dramas featuring the martial arts of the Orient, primarily karate and kung fu, enjoyed great popularity, especially in the U.S.

Latin America. *Argentina.* Production was cautious due to the atmosphere of uncertainty preceding the national elections in May, but Leopoldo Torre Nilsson adapted two novels by Roberto Arlt, as *Los Siete Locos.* This was a fantasy about an unlikely band of anarchists whose hopes and delusions are used to illuminate contemporary Argentine aspirations and failures.

Brazil. Government and industrial organization of the film industry placed increasing obstacles in the way of the radical filmmakers of Cinema Novo, though Nelson Pereira dos Santos made an interesting and intermittently successful science fiction allegory, *Who Is Beta?* Arnaldo Jabor's *All Nudity Will Be Punished* employed extremely witty burlesque for a deadly attack upon bourgeois morality.

Mexico. In striking contrast to the general run of cheaply made popular comedies and melodramas, *The Holy Mountain,* by the Chilean-born Alexandro Jodorowsky, was one of the most expensive and extravagant "underground" movies ever made. In a highly decorative adventure in wonderland, seven pilgrims are led by a sage (played by Jodorowsky himself) in search of the secret of the immortals.

Venezuela. The public and critical success of Mauricio Walersstein's *When I Want to Cry I Won't Cry,* an allegory about three young men of contrasted social classes who are born and who die violently on the same days, seemed to encourage official determination to develop the country's film industry.

(DAVID ROBINSON)

Nontheatrical Cinema. The growing international interchange of nontheatrical films became strikingly evident during 1973 in the proliferation of film festivals, competitions, and showings of an international character. The American Film Festival, a long-established national event meeting in New York May 22–26, had an international flavour with the screening of films from Canada, Britain, Yugoslavia, Poland, and other countries, with some of these receiving top awards. A notable example of international teamwork was the winner of the Emily Award, the highest honour of the show. This film, *The Three Robbers,* was a production in animation for Weston Woods Studio, but created in Czechoslovakia.

Two other festival prizewinners were films produced for the British Broadcasting Corporation: *Christians at War* and *The Jesus Trip.* Another international feature of the festival was the initiation of a new award to be conferred in honour of John Grierson, the great British documentarian. This went to Martha Coolidge for *David: Off and On.*

In all, more than 100 film festivals and competitions of an international character were held during the year, with a number of these in specialized fields of interest. Among such events was the meeting of the ninth International Week for Educational and Teaching Films, organized at Brussels by the Belgian Ministry of Education on March 19–23. The 31 participating countries previewed 248 films from 29 nations. Also meeting in Brussels was the sixth International Festival of Scientific and Technical Films.

An estimated 15,710 standard nontheatrical films were produced in the U.S. in 1972. This was only a modest gain of 5% over the previous year. In the school field, 1,320 films were produced, a 4% decline from 1972. Films for government totaled 1,760, a 4% increase, and for business and industry the total was 10,170, an increase of 6%.

This moderate growth in production was matched by the estimates of spending for films and other media. The entire investment for films, filmstrips, projectors, videotapes, and equipment and related products totaled $1,543,000,000, an increase of 8% over 1972.

(JOHN T. BOBBITT; THOMAS W. HOPE)

See also Photography; Television and Radio.

ENCYCLOPÆDIA BRITANNICA FILMS. *Growing* (1969)—a computer-animated film; *Practical Filmmaking* (1972).

Motor Sports

Automobiles. In 1973 Formula One Grand Prix racing airfoils were again modified for safety reasons, and new design requirements were introduced in order to cut down the grave risk of fire after an accident. The Grand Prix Drivers' Association continued to maintain a strict watch on circuit construction and other safety aspects, but unfortunately fatalities still occurred. Financial sponsorship remained available for the Grand Prix competition, and the 1973 season was contested by 12 teams of single-seater road-racing cars, with some 30 drivers.

Team Lotus used two number-one drivers, Emerson Fittipaldi of Brazil and Ronnie Peterson of Sweden, while Ken Tyrrell had Jackie Stewart of Scotland on his team. Stewart clinched the drivers' world championship for the third time before the season was over, scoring 71 points to Fittipaldi's 55 and Peterson's 52, and announced his retirement after the end of the season. By far the majority of the 1973 Grand Prix cars used the well-tried Ford-sponsored Cosworth V-8 engine driving through a Hewland gearbox. In all cases the engines were behind the drivers, in rear-wheel-drive cars. Ferrari, which had a poor year, remained an advocate of the 12-cylinder power unit, as did the British team of BRM; both of these firms built their own engines. A few small newcomers such as Connew and UOP-Shadow dallied with top-class racing, but the awards went to the well-established regulars. Results depended very much on how effective the tires used were, with the usual changes to comply with wet or dry road surfaces before the start of a race.

The season began in Argentina and Brazil. In Brazil the Lotus 72D of Fittipaldi won at 183.86 kph,

Motorboating: *see* Motor Sports
Motor Industry: *see* Industrial Review

WIDE WORLD

Wally Dallenbach in car 62 and Mel Kenyon (along inside wall) pass the overturned and burning car of David ("Salt") Walther in the first lap of the Indianapolis 500, May 28, 1973. A racing official, crouching in foreground, avoids the flames that injured Walther and several spectators.

after setting a fastest lap of 184.877 kph, a new record for the São Paulo circuit. There was not much that Stewart in the Tyrrell 005 could do about this, but he finished second, ahead of Denis Hulme of New Zealand in a McLaren M19. As Fittipaldi had previously won the Argentine Grand Prix for Lotus at Buenos Aires, at 165.688 kph, Lotus was well in the ascendant at this stage. The scene then changed to South Africa, and the Kyalami circuit. There, after a bad practice crash owing to brake failure, Stewart took over teammate François Cevert's Tyrrell and scored a convincing victory at an average speed of 188.526 kph, although it was Fittipaldi who set a new lap record of 191.626 kph. In an exciting finish Peter Revson, driving a McLaren, was second. There was a protest that Stewart had passed while a yellow warning flag was being displayed, and some thought he should have been disqualified.

At Montjuich Park, Barcelona, Fittipaldi did some skillful motoring in the Spanish Grand Prix and gained a victory that was lucky because one of his tires was punctured in the closing stages of the race. He averaged 157.489 kph. Cevert's Tyrrell was second, and the Shadow, driven by George Follmer (U.S.), third. The insistence of the drivers, led by Stewart, on safer circuits and conditions generally resulted in the Belgian Grand Prix's being held at Zolder instead of at Spa. It was a minor event in consequence, won by Stewart at 173.384 kph from teammate Cevert, who took the lap record to 177.850 kph. Third place went to Fittipaldi.

Much more traditional, although run over a revised streets-circuit, was the Monaco Grand Prix. It enabled Stewart to chalk up his 25th Grand Prix victory, and Graham Hill, driving for the Shadow team, to start in his 150th GP race. Stewart was in form, winning at 130.297 kph, chased by Fittipaldi's Lotus, which had made a record lap for the changed course of 133.947 kph. Peterson backed up this effort with third place, the two Lotus cars splitting the Tyrrells of Stewart and Cevert. The competition then traveled to the flat airfield circuit of Anderstorp for the Swedish Grand Prix, where Hulme won, at 165.2 kph, for McLaren, followed by a Lotus 72 driven by Peterson and a Tyrrell by Cevert. The French Grand Prix took place over the Paul Ricard circuit, and Peterson in a John Player-sponsored Lotus 72 managed to win from Cevert and Carlos Reutemann of Argentina. A new lap record for the circuit was made by Hulme at 189.114 kph.

It was the turn of Silverstone instead of Brands Hatch to host the British Grand Prix. The race was marred by a remarkable multiple accident on the opening lap, in which all those involved escaped serious injury but which delayed the start for almost two hours and emphasized how quickly incidents can become tragedy in fast motor races. The race was rerun, and Revson won it for McLaren, at 212.03 kph in an M23 car, from Peterson and Hulme.

The Dutch Grand Prix, run over the tidied-up Zandvoort course, was a sad affair, in which Roger Williamson was burned to death in his overturned March in spite of the brave but unavailing efforts of another driver, David Purley, to free him. The fire-fighting precautions at the course were severely criticized. Stewart won the victory, averaging 134.025 kph, with Cevert second and James Hunt of the U.K. third. Over the punishing Nürburgring the German Grand Prix demonstrated that the Tyrrell was back in winning form and that Stewart was the master. He won at 188 kph backed up by Cevert, with third place going to Jackie Ickx of Belgium in a McLaren M23. Carlos Pace of Brazil in a Surtees TS14 raised the lap record for this arduous 22.8 km. course to 190.6 kph and finished fourth.

At the Austrian Grand Prix at Zeltweg, over the Österreichring, a crowd of over 100,000 saw Peterson (Lotus), Stewart (Tyrrell), and Pace (Surtees) finish in that order, the race averaging 214.850 kph and Pace setting a new lap record of 218.720 kph. Only 11 completed the course. The Italian Grand Prix at Monza was the occasion at which Stewart became world champion; although Stewart placed fourth in the race, Fittipaldi needed to win to oust him from the lead in the championship competition, and this the Brazilian did not do. Peterson triumphed at 211.449 kph with Fittipaldi second. Stewart, however, set a lap record of 218.153 kph.

The season's final events were the Canadian and U.S. Grands Prix. The former, at the Mosport circuit, was a complete shambles, all the cars making pit stops to change tires because a wet start turned into dry weather. This upset the lap scoring, which was further confused when the pace car, going onto the track to lead the race under a new ruling while the debris from an accident was removed, paced the wrong car. The victory was eventually given to Revson, with Fittipaldi second and Jackie Oliver in an AVS-Shadow-Ford third. At the U.S. Grand Prix, richest of the series, at Watkins Glen, N.Y., tragedy struck again, Cevert crashing fatally in practice, probably because of a driving error. Stewart withdrew from the event and announced his retirement soon after the race. Peterson led all the way, winning for JP-Lotus-Ford at 118.055 mph. Hunt finished second, in a March.

The John-Player Lotus team took the manufacturers' world championship, with 92 points, from Tyrrell-Ford (82) and Yardley-McLaren-Ford (58). Ferrari concentrated more on long-distance sportscar racing and won that category, but the Le Mans 24-hour race was a victory for a Matra-Simca, at 202.25 kph, to the delight of the French onlookers.

Among international rallies the Monte Carlo Rally, to be dropped from championship status for 1974, was dominated in 1973 by the Alpine Renault team, which filled the first three places ahead of a Ford Escort RS (out of 298 starters only 51 finished). Alpine Renault won the Morocco Rally from three DS23 Citroëns, the Acropolis Rally from the Fiat 124s, and the TAP (Transportes Aereos Portugueses)

Rally. The tough East African Safari Rally was won by a Datsun 240Z, with another of these Japanese cars of a different type in second place. In the Royal Automobile Club Rally, British Ford Escorts took the first three places, the winning driver being the Finn Timo Makinen. The Polish Rally was run to a high-speed schedule and was won by a Fiat 125 Abarth. A new fixture was the Avon Tour of Britain, in which the best showing was made by James Hunt in the A. J. Rivers Chevrolet Camaro. The Tour of France was headed by a Lancia Stratos.

(WILLIAM C. BODDY)

A particularly tragic edition of the Indianapolis 500, first postponed and then shortened by rain, claimed the life of Art Pollard in practice. Swede Savage and a mechanic were injured during the race; both died later. Also, spectators and Salt Walther, whose father's company sponsored his race car, were injured. Gordon Johncock of Michigan, a teammate of Savage, won the 332.5-mi. race with an average speed of 159.014 mph and earned approximately $236,000. He led 64 of the 133 laps completed in his STP Special, and only Bill Vukovich was in the same lap when the rains came. Rounding out the top five in order were Roger McCluskey, Mel Kenyon, and Gary Bettenhausen. It was the sixth victory at Indianapolis for team manager George Bignotti, who had given Johncock the only Offenhauser engine of its kind in the race.

The deaths and injuries led to a $300,000 modification of the Indianapolis course, probably the oldest auto racing venue in the world, and also to stringent new rules designed to cut speed by the United States Auto Club (USAC), the race's sanctioning body. For 1974 the pits would be widened 40 ft., a new pit entrance was built, the dangerous box seats were removed, and the walls along the straightaway were raised. Those changes, combined with car and fuel modifications, were expected to make the race more palatable to the drivers.

In the two other USAC 500-mi. events that make up the Triple Crown of auto racing, A. J. Foyt won at Pocono, Pa., with an average speed of 144.944 mph when McCluskey ran out of gas on the final laps, and at the California 500 in Ontario, veteran Wally Dallenbach—22 years a racer with no championship victories until 1973—edged Mario Andretti by five seconds, averaging 157.664 mph. McCluskey, at 43 years the oldest champion in USAC history, won the season title in his Hopkins McLaren/Offy by amassing consistently high finishes in a year when there were 10 different winners in 16 events.

USAC reduced the size of the wings on its championship single seaters to 43 in., the same as for the Formula One cars, and instituted a fuel formula designed to cut allowable gallonage for a 500-mi. race from 375 to 280. The club also banned rear-engined sprint cars and demanded that antipollution equipment be left on all its stock cars. Butch Hartman won the stock-car crown for an unprecedented third time; Rollie Beale won the sprint crown after two decades of trying; and Al Unser took the dirt car title.

National Association for Stock Car Auto Racing (NASCAR), the premier late model saloon car circuit in the world, had its own travails, including its first Winston Cup fatality in several years, Joe Frasson. Again, excessive speed was one of the villains, and as a result NASCAR changed carburetor restrictor plate configurations in mid-season. Benny Parsons won the Winston Cup season championship, emblematic of the NASCAR major league crown, but David Pearson was the biggest money winner in his Purolator Mercury.

Pearson won 11 of the 500-mi. events, earning himself close to $250,000 for the season. Ironically, NASCAR's premier race, the Daytona (Fla.) 500, eluded him. It was won for the fourth time by Richard Petty and his STP Dodge. Petty also passed the $100,000 mark in winnings along with Cale Yarborough and Bobby Allison.

Sports Car Club of America (SCCA) had its own problems. One came when Liggett & Myers, which had bankrolled its Formula 5000 series, announced that it was withdrawing from racing after the 1973 season. Another came when a change in the Canadian-American Challenge Cup series, designed to make it more competitive, was not effective. A mid-season switch to two heats attempted to correct this.

Mark Donohue, in the Penske Porsche factory 12-cylinder P910/30, won six Can-Ams to gain the series championship. These included Laguna Seca and Riverside, Calif., Mid-Ohio, Elkhart Lake, Wis., Edmonton, Alta., and Watkins Glen, N.Y. At the end of the season, the 37-year-old engineer announced that he was retiring as a driver to oversee the vast Roger Penske Racing Enterprises.

Meanwhile, SCCA's L&M series showcased a major new star in Jody Scheckter, 23, of South Africa. Driving mostly a Sid Taylor Valvoline Delta Trojan, Scheckter took second to Brian Redman in the Riverside opener and then ran off four victories in a row—at Laguna Seca, Michigan, Mid-Ohio, and Watkins Glen—before Redman in a Steed Lola began a streak of his own with wins at Elkhart Lake, Road Atlanta, Pocono, Pa., and Seattle. Scheckter won $115,200, actually $350 less than Redman, who finished second in the series. Both leaders were powered by Chevrolet. In other SCCA championships, Nissan Motors (Datsun) won the manufacturers rally crown; Peter Gregg of Florida won the Trans-Am title in a Porsche Carrera 911RS, and Chevrolet won the Trans-Am manufacturers' crown.

Fred Offenhauser, a developer of the engine that for 40 years had been a dominant force in U.S. single-seater racing, died at the age of 85.

(ROBERT J. FENDELL)

Motorcycles. Giacomo Agostini, world champion for MV Augusta in the 500-cc road-racing championship for seven years, had to relinquish his title to his new 1973 British teammate, Phil Read; Agostini ended the season by badly damaging a leg at Misano near Riccione, in Italy. He amassed sufficient race points through the series to retain the 350-cc title. The 250-cc world champion was Dieter Braun, riding a Japanese Yamaha, while another Yamaha-mounted rider, Kent Andersson, won the 125-cc championship. Jan de Vries, on a Kreidler, won the 50-cc class, and Karl Enders, after close competition with Siegfried Schauzu, emerged as the sidecar class champion, driving a BMW machine.

In the motocross championships Suzuki lost its hold on the 250-cc class, Håkan Andersson winning on a Yamaha. The 500-cc champion was Roger de Coster of Belgium, on a Suzuki. World speedway champion was Jerzy Szczakiel of Poland.

In the road-racing field, many star riders fulfilled threats they had made after deaths in the 1972 Tourist Trophy races on the Isle of Man and refused to take part in the 1973 series—chief among them Agostini. In the absence of the Italian and others of

1973 U.S. National Motorboat Racing Champions

Inboard

Class	Owner (Champion)
7 Litre (division I)	Howie Benns, Grand Island, N.Y.
7 Litre (division II)	Tony Piazza, Metairie, La.
5 Litre	Gerald L. Bangs, Seattle, Wash.; John P. Stone, Bothell, Wash.
2½ Litre	Terry Turner, Pomona, Calif.
280 Hydro	Thomas E. Baker, Queenstown, Md.
225 Hydro	John Siracusa, Jr., Morgan City, La.
145 Hydro	Ernest Lauber, Jr., Seattle, Wash.
850 Hydro	Harrison P. Quirk, Ypsilanti, Mich.
98 Hydro	Gordy Cole, Seattle, Wash.
44 Hydro	Not scheduled
44 Runabout	Not scheduled
Cracker Box	Danny E. Mang, Hacienda Heights, Calif.
Jersey Speed Skiff	Jack and Judith Lawrence, Lincroft, N.J.
Super Stock	Del Daily, Miami, Fla.
Ski Racing Runabout	Duff Daily, Miami, Fla.
B Racing Runabout	Not scheduled
K Racing Runabout	Julian K. Pettengill, Glendale, Ariz.
E Series Runabout	Not scheduled
F Series Runabout	Not scheduled

Outboard

Class	Driver
A Racing Runabout	Lee F. Sutter, Jr., Waukesha, Wis.
B Racing Runabout	W. J. Parker, E. Gadsden, Ala.
C Racing Runabout	Richard K. Krier, Virginia Beach, Va.
D Racing Runabout	Jerry Simison, Fergus Falls, Minn.
F Racing Runabout	Douglas W. Bindrim, Lindenhurst, N.Y.
C Series Runabout	Bob Murphy, Springfield, Ill.
M Hydro	Ronald R. Anderson, Winneconne, Wis.
A Hydro	Ronald R. Anderson, Winneconne, Wis.
B Hydro	Ray Hardy, Des Plaines, Ill.
C Hydro	Daniel W. Kirts, Elkhart, Ind.
D Hydro	John R. Yale, Meriden, Conn.
F Hydro	William Rucker, Sr., San Lorenzo, Calif.
C Series Hydro	Larry D. Latta, Schaumburg, Ill.

his calibre, racing in many classes was close, and relatively unfamiliar names filled the lists of winners. Main event winners were: 750-cc production race, Tony Jefferies (Triumph); 500- and 750-cc sidecar, Karl Enders (BMW); 350-cc international, Tony Rutter (Yamaha); 250-cc international, Charles Williams (Yamaha); formula 750-cc, Peter Williams (Norton); 500-cc international, Jack Findlay (Suzuki). Winners of the Manx Grand Prix were: 250 cc, D. Arnold; 500 cc, P. Read. Both rode Yamaha machines.

The annual track fixture of the Anglo-American match races—now termed the John Player Transatlantic meetings—were held at Brands Hatch, Mallory Park, and Oulton Park, all in the U.K. The U.S. visitors appeared with powerful Kawasaki and Suzuki three-cylinder two-strokes, reputed to be capable of over 170 mph, and 750-cc Harley Davidsons, and were faced by home riders on twin-cylinder Nortons and three-cylinder Triumphs. Two impressive wins in the last round of the series, at Oulton Park, by Peter Williams (Norton) put the British team ahead at the final tally, with the best individual scores being achieved by Williams and the Canadian Yvon du Hamel (Suzuki), with 84 points each. The "Race of the Year" at Mallory Park, with its first prize of £1,500, was won by Phil Read on the MV 500-3.

(CYRIL J. AYTON)

Motorboating. The 1973 unlimited hydroplane championship was not settled until the last race on the U.S. circuit, when an innovative, tail-winged thunderboat nailed down the title. The boat, "Pride of Pay 'N Pak," raised eyebrows throughout the summer as it won 20 of 28 heats entered, set new qualifying records in 7 of the 9 regattas, and won 4 of them. It also became the first boat in history to exceed 126 mph on a closed course, which requires considerable slowing down on the turns, and proved so durable it failed to finish only one heat.

Driver Mickey Remund mastered the art of moving the radical design around the tight eastern courses and the more open ovals of western waters. He was given command of the new hull by owner Dave Heerensperger. "Pride of Pay 'N Pak" was built largely of honeycomb aluminum, which was extremely light yet sturdy.

A striking feature of the boat was the stern stabilizer. It was a horizontal winglike structure the angle of which could be preset before a race to suit the crew's judgment of wind and water conditions. Its purpose, successfully achieved, was to provide aerodynamic lift. The stabilizer made it possible for Remund to rocket through the turns because of about 400 lb. of lifting force at the stern.

Remund's closest competition came from Dean Chenoweth, driving Bernie Little's "Miss Budweiser." Chenoweth fought Remund down to the wire, winning four races with a combination of skill at the helm and the rocket-like acceleration of his boat. The two men totally dominated the thunderboat circuit. Only Gene Whipp, driving "Lincoln Thrift and Loan," also got into the winner's circle. He won the President's Cup at Washington, D.C., but largely because "Pride of Pay 'N Pak" was hosed down by wake water and stalled.

Remund won at the Miami Champion Spark Plug Regatta in May, the season opener. He repeated at Madison, Ind., Seattle, and Toledo. Chenoweth won at Owensboro, Ky., and Detroit, and took the annual Gold Cup race at Tri-Cities, Wash. He also won the final event, also at Detroit, but surrendered the season championship to Remund by a scant margin of 275 points. Bill Muncey, whose "Atlas Van Lines" won the 1972 title, ranked third in 1973.

The world outboard championships at Lake Havasu, Ariz., were canceled, leaving only one event of international significance. This was the ON Outboard World Championships sanctioned by the Union of International Motorboating (UIM) and open to boats equivalent to the American Power Boat Association Unrestricted S for 100-cu.in. engines. It was held in 1973 at Koblenz, W.Ger. Italian boatbuilder Renato Molinari, driving a Mercury-powered picklefork tunnel hull of his own design and construction, won three of four heats to take the championship. Earlier in the season, he won the European title as well.

Italy's Carlo Bonomi won the world offshore powerboat racing championship after a long and costly campaign on two continents. He dueled all year with British sportsman Don Shead. By late autumn Bonomi had won two races in France and one each in Spain and Sweden. Shead won twice in Italy, and also the prestigious Cowes event in Britain, where Bonomi could do no better than third. The two were only a few points apart going into the final Miami-Nassau race in late October. Beset by poor weather, including a nearby tropical storm, the Nassau race endured postponements for 16 days. When it was finally held, the race went to Bonomi, driving a 36-ft. "Cigarette" with dual Aeromarine engines. (JIM MARTENHOFF)

With 29 of a possible 30 points, Soviet driver Gabtrahman Kadyrov (front) captures his sixth world ice speedway championship at Inzell, W.Ger., March 11, 1973.

UPI COMPIX

Mountaineering

In 1973 in the Himalayas the trend toward climbing of great technical difficulty at high altitudes continued, the numerous Japanese expeditions again being particularly noticeable. In the Alps, and also in New Zealand, much of the novelty was provided by new winter ascents. In the former this was extended to the first winter ascents of major ridges *intégrale* (an ascent following the entire line of the ridge of a main peak over all subsidiary peaks), in addition to such ascents in summer, and especially solo winter ascents.

In the Alps in the late summer of 1972 some of the many new routes made were new lines on Mont Blanc (Miage face and Frêney far-left pillar); the north faces of the Aiguille du Plan, Aiguille de Rochfort, Grandes Jorasses, and Matterhorn; the northeast faces of Mont Blanc de Tacul, Aiguille de Leschaux, and Pigne d'Arolla; the northwest face of the Lyskamm; the south faces of the Aiguille d'Argentière and the Tour Noire; the southeast face of the Piz Badile; and the west face of the Weissmies. There were many new routes in the eastern Alps and the Dolomites. Solo ascents were made of the north ridge of Mont Blanc de Tacul, the Lagarde couloir on the Droites, and the Nant Blanc face of the Aiguille Verte. The Innominata ridge of Mont Blanc was ascended *intégrale,* and the Peuterey ridge and the northeast spur on the north face of the Droites were done solo *intégrale.*

In the winter of 1972–73 many important first winter ascents were made in the Alps, including the north faces of the Meije, Aiguille du Midi, Col du Plan, Pigne d'Arolla, Droites (Couzy-Salzou route), Mont Blanc de Cheilon (Jenkins ridge), Dent Blanche (Bournissen-Pralong route), and Lauterbrunnen Breithorn; the northeast faces of the Grand Combin de Valsorey, Mont Blanc de Cheilon, and Gspaltenhorn; the northwest faces of the Col du Dolent, Mont Dolent (Golay route), and Blanc de Perroc; the south face of the Aiguille Dibona; the southeast faces of the Eiger and the Piz Badile (Via Vera); the east faces of the Gross Grünhorn and the Zumsteinspitze; the west faces of the Petits Jorasses (Bron-Contamine-Labranie route); the Tronchey arête and a new route beside the Walker Spur on the Grandes Jorasses; the northwest ridge of the Piz Ĉengalo; and the south ridge of the Lyskamm (Cresta Solla). Among many noteworthy ascents in the Dolomites the Philipp-Flamm route on the Civetta and the Detassis route on the Brenta Alta may be singled out. In the early summer of 1973 notable events were three important new lines on the west face of the Aiguille Noire de Peuterey.

Many expeditions again visited the Hindu Kush, where the supply of new routes was dwindling and attention was being diverted to new routes on peaks already climbed, and to winter ascents; examples included the first winter ascent of Noshaq and a route up its southwest face, both by Polish expeditions.

In the Himalayas in late 1972 the French climbed the south face of Makalu; the Japanese, the central peak of Annapurna South; and a Japanese-U.S. party, Piutha Hiunchuli. Before the monsoon in 1973 the Italians climbed Everest by the ordinary route; Japanese climbed Yalung Kang, Annapurna II (west ridge), and Pumori (south ridge). A West German party made a new route on Manaslu. Other attempts on Annapurna I, Dhaulagiri I and IV (on which a British climber and a Sherpa lost their lives in November 1973), Lhotse, and Makalu failed. After the monsoon the Japanese failed on the southwest face of Everest and climbed the ordinary route.

In New Zealand in winter 1972 the south face of Douglas was climbed. In the 1972–73 season first ascents were made on Cook, Douglas, Hicks, Tasman, Haast, Elie de Beaumont, and many lesser peaks. In East Africa in 1973 important new routes were made on Mount Kenya and Mawenzi.

In the Alaska-Yukon area in 1972 new routes were made on McKinley, St. Elias, and La Perouse, and in 1973 on Hubbard, Hunter, Silverthrone, and the Devil's Thumb. A traverse was completed from Quincy over Adams to Fairweather. In the Canadian Rockies the north faces of Bryce and Alberta were climbed in 1973, and some first winter ascents were completed in the 1972–73 season, as they were in the Tetons in the U.S.

In Guyana a first ascent of Mt. Roraima (9,219 ft.) was made in November 1973 by a Guyanese and four Britons, two previous attempts having failed. The Andes were visited by expeditions of many nationalities. New routes were climbed on Huascarán, Huantsan, Ojos del Salado, Alpamayo, Chopicalqui, Huandoy, Huaynan Potosí, Nevado Chinchey, Cayesh, and other peaks. In Patagonia Cerro Lautoro, Cerro Mimosa, Cerro Pyramid, and peaks in the Cordillera Darwin were climbed, including new routes on Cerro Fitzroy and Cerro Moreno. (JOHN NEILL)

Museums and Galleries

During 1973 thefts from museums, churches, historic monuments and other public buildings, and private homes, and the pillage of archaeological sites continued to present a grave danger to the cultural heritage of every country. (*See* CRIME.) In Mali in February illegal excavations were discovered in the region of Gourma, on the banks of the Bani and Niger rivers, where several ancient villages rich in bas-relief and terra-cotta figures were known to be situated. Looting of Italy's art treasures continued, with thieves becoming more audacious; at least 6,000 works were known to have disappeared during 1972. Since an uncounted number of the paintings in unguarded and isolated parish churches had never been cataloged, tracing them, if stolen, would be almost impossible.

Security, in all its forms, remained a constant preoccupation for all those responsible for museums and works of art. The General Secretariat of the International Criminal Police Organization (Interpol), for example, compiled a card index of works of art stolen and taken abroad since 1968. There were also encouraging examples of institutions willing to face the restoration of stolen objects that they might have acquired unwittingly. U.S. museums tightened their rules regarding the ethics of acquisition, supported the UNESCO convention on illicit import, export, and transfer, and called for an international art "pool" of surplus art objects from all countries, thus permitting lawful exchanges. However, the financial burden of returning stolen objects that had been acquired in good faith remained a matter of concern.

Funding of museum projects received considerable attention during the year. The Samuel H. Kress Foundation announced grants totaling $380,000 for various U.S. and foreign projects. The National Endowment for the Arts made several grants to U.S. museums, most of them to be used to stage special exhibitions or for cataloging existing collections. The U.S. Senate held hearings during the year on a museum services bill, which would provide $40 million in federal funds for museum functions and services, a considerable increase over the $9 million currently provided to 256 museums.

Plans for new museums included the announcement that the Metropolitan Museum of Art, New York City, would open its new American Museum in 1976 as a part of the U.S. bicentennial celebrations. During the year the M. H. de Young Memorial Museum in San Francisco opened a new gallery of art from Africa, Oceania, and the Americas, and the Wadsworth Atheneum in Hartford, Conn., opened its tactile gallery. The Museum of Modern Art, New York City, opened a space for the documentation and presenta-

Motor Vehicles: *see* Disasters; Industrial Review; Motor Sports; Transportation

Mozambique: *see* Dependent States

Muhammadanism: *see* Religion

Municipal Government: *see* Cities and Urban Affairs

YESHIVA UNIVERSITY

The Mendel Gottesman Library of Yeshiva University, home of the new Yeshiva University Museum, opened April 1, 1973. New York City's newest repository of classical Judaica, the museum comprises 4,000 sq.ft. of display space distributed on three levels of the building.

tion of advanced contemporary works that lend themselves poorly to museum exhibition. Also in New York, the Brooklyn Children's Museum was completed, while in Indianapolis, Ind., a very large expansion of the Children's Museum was announced. The Baltimore (Md.) Museum of Art opened a new downtown facility.

Under construction on an eight-acre site adjacent to the Detroit Institute of Arts was the Detroit Science Center, planned as a parallel to Canada's highly successful Ontario Science Centre. At Cornell University, Ithaca, N.Y., the Herbert F. Johnson Museum of Art by I. M. Pei was opened to replace the Andrew Dickson White Museum of Art, and a new museum opened at the University of California at Berkeley. The J. Paul Getty Museum, a replica of a Roman villa at Herculaneum that was to house ancient sculpture and French decorative arts, was scheduled to open in Malibu, Calif., and in San Francisco the International Museum of Erotic Art was established. In Texas the Fort Worth Art Center Museum and an extension of the Houston Museum of Fine Arts were scheduled to open. The Grandma Moses Schoolhouse Museum opened as an adjunct of the Bennington (Vt.) Museum.

In Canada the Museum of Anthropology at the University of British Columbia received $2.5 million from the government to house its collection of Indian art; the facility would permit the re-creation of an Indian village and the display of massive totem poles. The Montreal Museum of Fine Arts announced a $6 million expansion program. France inaugurated a national Chagall museum in Nice in July, devoted to works by him on biblical themes.

Acquisitions. In late 1972 Thomas P. F. Hoving (*see* BIOGRAPHY), director of the Metropolitan Museum of Art, announced the museum's acquisition of a previously unknown Greek vase (calyx krater) decorated by the Athenian artist Euphronius and executed by the potter Euxitheus. Museum officials said little about how the vase was acquired but left the impression that it had come in nearly perfect condition from a private European collection that had owned it since before World War I. During 1973, however, it was gradually established that the museum had acquired the vase, for approximately $1 million, from an expatriate American art dealer, Robert E. Hecht, Jr., then living in Rome. Hecht maintained he had acted as agent for a Lebanese dealer whose father had obtained the vase in London in 1920 in a trade for coins. The Lebanese said the vase had been kept in a hatbox in fragments, several of which were missing.

Meanwhile, Italian authorities began pursuing information that the vase had been looted from an Etruscan grave site in November 1971 and sold to Hecht, who smuggled it out of Italy along with a cup also attributed to Euphronius, which he later offered for sale to the Metropolitan. Later Italian attempts to link the Metropolitan vase with fragments seized in the home of a bootleg excavator and with evidence given by another one, who said he had been present when the vase was unearthed, were frustrated by the museum's refusal to provide prerestoration pictures of the vase. The museum could maintain that it had acquired the vase legally, since it had been declared with U.S. Customs and brought from Switzerland, which did not prohibit the export of art works.

The fact that the Metropolitan sold a considerable portion of its coin collection to finance the purchase of the vase added fuel to the already heated controversy over the museum's deaccession practices. At midyear the museum issued a "white paper" detailing the various transactions that were being criticized and outlining guidelines for future transactions of this type. Curiously, at the same time the Metropolitan, as well as the National Gallery of Art, Washington, D.C., was reattributing many of its acquisitions. This process involved 300 paintings, nearly 15% of the Metropolitan's European holdings, and led to the downgrading of 14 of its 38 "Rembrandts" to the work of followers and the description of two more as doubtful.

Of the numerous acquisitions by other museums in 1973, only a few were noteworthy. In France 205 acquisitions were reported by the national museums, of which the colossal Amenophis IV bust (gift of the government of Egypt), two small paintings by the Maître de Saint Séverin, one painting by Fra Filippino Lippi, "The Calvary" by David Teniers I, "Le Tricheur" by Georges de la Tour, a portrait of Diderot by Fragonard, a few paintings by Sisley and C. Pissarro, and one Jackson Pollock "Painting" (1948) were of outstanding importance.

In West Germany the Badisches Landesmuseum in Karlsruhe acquired several ivory objects of Arslan Tash from the 9th century B.C.; the Kestner-Museum, Hanover, a notable Roman mosaic; the Bayerische Staatsgemäldesammlungen, Munich, "Madame de Pompadour" by François Boucher, "Flora" by Jean Marc Nattier, "La Marquise de Lorcy" by J. L. David, and the "Apotheosis of Homer" by Salvador Dali; the Museum Folkwang, Essen, "The Lion and the Serpent" by Delacroix, "Rouen Cathedral" by Claude Monet (1894), and "Landscape" by Joan Miró.

The Victoria and Albert Museum, London, acquired important Indian bronzes and Japanese sculptures, and works by Andrea del Verrocchio, J. de Vos, William Blake, J. R. Cozens, and others. The Tate Gallery acquired an interesting painting by Turner, and the Ashmolean Museum, Oxford, acquired works by Hans Holbein, L. Carracci, Isaak van Ostade, and Ruysdael and an important van Gogh, "Restaurant of the Sirène in Asnières." With the aid of a £100,000 grant from the National Art Collections Fund, the National Gallery finally became owner of Titian's "Death of Actéon." Henri Rousseau's "Tropical Storm with Tiger," one of his rare jungle pictures, was purchased at the end of 1972. The British Museum acquired several important Asian objects and sculptures, an Italian manuscript of the 14th century, and a 14th-century medieval clock.

In Eastern Europe the Fine Arts Museum, Budapest, Hung., acquired "Arab Camp" by Delacroix. The National Museum in Poland acquired two Attic amphoras and the Czechoslovakian National Gallery a Henry Moore sculpture. Works by Goya, Vlaminck, Bourdelle, Rouault, Matisse, and Léger were acquired by museums in the U.S.S.R.

The Minneapolis (Minn.) Institute of Arts acquired a paleolithic Venus (200 B.C.); the Toledo (O.) Museum of Art an Egyptian barge with oarsmen of the 11th-12th dynasty (2134–1786 B.C.). The Cleveland (O.) Museum of Art obtained paintings by Baron Gros, Constable, J. F. Millet, and Picasso; the Denver (Colo.) Art Museum a Dégas, a Toulouse-Lautrec, and two works by Renoir; the National Gallery, Washington, D.C., works by Gauguin, Cézanne, H. Rousseau, and Picasso; the Los Angeles County Museum of Art Rembrandt's "The Resurrection of Lazarus" and sculptures by Rodin. Another Rembrandt and a Caravaggio were acquired by the Detroit Institute of Arts. The Toledo Museum of Art was given "The Conversation" by J. A. Watteau, and the Philadelphia Museum of Art acquired portraits by Gainsborough, Raeburn, and Romney and a painting by B. West. The Cincinnati (O.) Art Museum's most notable acquisition was "Samson and Delilah," by Rubens. The Princeton University Art Museum acquired Claude Monet's "Nénuphars" from the famous series of water lilies with a Japanese bridge. A "Still Life" by van Gogh was acquired by the City Art Museum, St. Louis.

Japanese museums acquired several interesting objects including paintings by Jacopo Tintoretto, Millet, and Manet. The Israel Museum, Jerusalem, acquired works by Renoir, Gauguin, Modigliani, Chagall, Vlaminck, Jean Arp, Henry Moore, and Picasso. The National Museum of Fine Arts, Buenos Aires, Arg., acquired paintings by Rubens, van Dyck, Rembrandt, F. Guardi, and Léger. The Australian National Museum in Canberra acquired Jackson Pollock's "Blue Poles" for $2 million, the highest price to be paid for an American painting.

International Cooperation. In December 1973 UNESCO held a ten-day seminar in Lagos, Nigeria, on the role and development of museums in Africa that brought together a group of directors and curators of museums from several English-speaking African countries. The International Committee of the International Council of Museums for museums of archaeology and history met in Budapest, Hung., in June 1973 to discuss theoretical and practical questions on open air archaeological museums and site monuments and their conservation problems.

The UNESCO regional centres in Africa (Jos, Nigeria), Arab countries (Baghdad, Iraq), and Latin America (Mexico City) continued their courses in museography and conservation of the cultural and natural heritage, and the African training centre introduced a course in the conservation of the natural heritage and the protection of environment with the teaching staff provided by the U.S. National Park Service.

The International Centre for the Study of the Preservation and Restoration of Cultural Property in Rome offered a six-month course for architect-restorers, a four-month course in basic conservation of museum objects, and a three-month course in conservation of mural paintings.

(JOSHUA KIND; ANDREW SZPAKOWSKI)

See also Art Exhibitions; Art Sales.

Music

The event of the year was undoubtedly the opening in the fall of the Sydney Opera House. The concert hall (the larger building, originally intended to house opera) was launched with a concert of, rather inappropriately, Wagner, sung by Birgit Nilsson, played by the Sydney Symphony Orchestra, and conducted by Australian-born Charles Mackerras. The smaller house, now designated for opera, was inaugurated with a largely successful production of Sergey Prokofiev's epic *War and Peace* given by the Australian Opera Company and conducted by its musical director Edward Downes. The future of the latter building as a home for opera was in doubt, largely because of the small size of the pit, and there was even talk of the need for a "proper" opera house! The Cleveland Orchestra, under its new musical director, Lorin Maazel, gave a series of satisfying programs in the larger hall, which apparently proved its excellent acoustical properties. (*See* AUSTRALIA.)

Symphonic Music. At the end of 1972 in London there was a festival of Russian music presented by Russian performers, under the title "Days of Russian Music." Dmitry Shostakovich was present; although he did not take part as an executant, his music could be said to dominate the concerts, particularly when compared with that of his younger contemporaries. In October 1972 an International Symposium on the Problems of Graphic Music, held in Rome, dealt with the codification of musical symbols.

The main centenarians of 1973 were Rachmaninoff and Reger. In Great Britain, many of Rachmaninoff's rarely heard works were revived, including his opera *Francesca da Rimini,* broadcast by the BBC, and his choral symphony *The Bells,* conducted by André Previn in a special centenary concert during the summer promenade concerts. Previn, in a recording, also made a good case for Rachmaninoff's Second Symphony in its complete form. Nicolai Gedda brought back many of Rachmaninoff's songs with success at a

Antal Dorati rehearses with the National Symphony of Washington, D.C., during his fourth year as music director. Famed for his skill with failing orchestras, he was credited with renewing the artistic stature of the group.

DENNIS BRACK—BLACK STAR

Queen Elizabeth Hall recital. Reger did not receive such large-scale treatment, except in Bonn, where there was a special series of centenary concerts in mid-March. He wrote so much, performed so much (and, for that matter, ate and drank so much) that his memory was kept very fresh, but more in writing and criticism than in performance. These concerts were, therefore, invaluable for reassessing his worth as a composer. His music provided an incongruous combination of classical conformity and modern (for his time) devices, and the lesser-known pieces, several of them choral, did not suggest that there were great discoveries to be made in his *oeuvre*.

Three new symphonies were given in England. Anthony Milner's first, presented by the BBC Symphony Orchestra at the Festival Hall on January 17, and Peter Wishart's second, given by the New Philharmonia on January 21, were both sound, undemonstrative pieces in a relatively traditional vein. Krzysztof Penderecki's first symphony, given in July both at Peterborough Cathedral and at the King's Lynn Festival and followed by a recording, all performed by the London Symphony under the composer's direction, was more revolutionary in not conforming to true symphonic thinking but nonetheless inventive for that. Penderecki was also represented at the happily revived Gulbenkian Festival at Lisbon in May when his new choral work, *Canticum canticorum Salomonis* (Solomon's Song of Songs), received considerable critical praise.

Pierre Boulez continued his conducting with the New York Philharmonic (which appointed a new general manager, Harold Lawrence, formerly of the LSO) and with the BBC Symphony (where his contract was extended to 1975), and found time to complete ". . . *explosante/fixe* . . . ," a piece, as the title would suggest, of variable length and dimensions. This was performed during the BBC Symphony's tour of Italy in May and also at the London Proms in the summer. Alberto Ginastera's Second Piano Concerto had its premiere at Indianapolis in March, and Stanley Silverman's *King Oedipus,* with a text by Anthony Burgess, who was also the narrator, was first given on May 16 at the Whitney Museum, New York.

Elliott Carter's arresting Third String Quartet was given its first performance at the Alice Tully Hall, New York, on January 23 by the Juilliard Quartet. Marvin David Levy's oratorio *Masada,* written for the 25th anniversary of the founding of the state of Israel, was given its premiere at the John F. Kennedy Center in Washington on October 30. On October 24 at Carnegie Hall, New York, the Buffalo Philharmonic Orchestra, under its musical director, Michael Tilson Thomas, gave a program called *Spectrum,* exploring electronic music. Thomas was also in charge of the concerts at the 27th annual weekend at Ojai, Calif., in June. The Philadelphia Orchestra went on a ten-day tour of China in September. Earlier, in March, the London Philharmonic had been the first foreign orchestra to play in China since the Communist revolution.

Musicians' strikes stalled the opening of the 1973–74 symphony seasons in New York and Chicago amid charges from the musicians that the major U.S. orchestras had conspired to use contract negotiations to demonstrate their plight following failure to get federal funds. The Chicago Symphony, which, with Sir Georg Solti (*see* BIOGRAPHY) as musical director, was being praised as the finest in the U.S., opened its season four weeks late, after its players won a $60-a-week increase over the life of a three-year contract. The New York strike dragged on for six more weeks until the Philharmonic agreed to a package that brought its musicians' wages in line with Chicago's.

Four of the five new works at the Promenade Concerts in London's Albert Hall were by woman composers—Elisabeth Lutyens (*De Amore*), Thea Musgrave (*Viola Concerto*), Nicola LeFanu (*The Hidden Landscape*), and Priaulx Rainier (*Ploërmel*). All, but particularly Lutyens and Musgrave, acquitted themselves well. The Proms again left the Albert Hall for some concerts to visit the Roundhouse (for very modern programs) and Westminster Cathedral for a marvelous account of Monteverdi's *Vespers of the Blessed Virgin* (1610). The series as a whole was again of true festival standard. It included a concert performance by Sadler's Wells Opera of Benjamin Britten's *Gloriana* as a 60th birthday tribute to the composer. Britten underwent a serious operation in the spring but was enough recovered to attend a special birthday concert in late November. On November 1, singer Dietrich Fischer-Dieskau made his London debut as a conductor with the English Chamber Orchestra.

The Concert Hall in Stockholm was refurbished and reopened on January 26 with a performance of Mahler's Eighth Symphony given by the Stockholm Philharmonic under Antal Dorati's baton. Guido Ajmone-Marsan won the Rupert Foundation conducting scholarship in London in March and later also won the Sir Georg Solti Competition in Chicago. Riccardo Muti was appointed principal conductor of the New Philharmonia Orchestra in London. The Oxford University Press celebrated 50 years of music publishing with a series of six concerts in London, Oxford, and Cambridge.

At the Brighton Festival in May, Havergal Brian's Second Symphony had its premiere, although it was many years since its composition, and the San Francisco Orchestra under Seiji Ozawa gave several concerts. At the Bath Festival in May–June Sir Michael Tippett's Third Piano Sonata was given its premiere and much praised. At the Cheltenham Festival, Lennox Berkeley's 70th birthday was celebrated at several concerts; Berkeley also wrote a Sinfonia Concertante for oboe and chamber orchestra that received its first performance in a special birthday Prom. Olivier Messiaen was present at both the English Bach Festival (Oxford and London) in April and at the Cardiff Festival in March. At the Aldeburgh Festival in June new works by Malcolm Arnold, Gordon Crosse, and David Bedford were given.

October 1973 brought the death of the great cellist Pablo Casals, not long after he had dominated the Israel Festival in September with his personal aura and some fine conducting, from a seated position. The year also saw the deaths of composers Gian Francesco Malipiero, Havergal Brian, and Benjamin Frankel (who had just completed his first opera, *Marching Song,* based on John Whiting's play). The ranks of conductors were almost decimated with the deaths of Otto Klemperer, Jascha Horenstein, Paul Kletzki, Hans Schmidt-Isserstedt, and Istvan Kertesz. Violinist Joseph Szigeti and tenor Lauritz Melchior also died. (*See* OBITUARIES.)

Among the books published were two outstanding biographies—John Warrack's *Tchaikovsky* and the third volume of Norman Del Mar's biography of Richard Strauss, which completed a monumentally definitive study of the German composer's life and work. Julian Budden's *The Operas of Verdi,* vol. 1, was an outstanding survey of the composer's work up to and including *Rigoletto.*

Opera. *United States.* At the Metropolitan in November 1972, Charles Mackerras made his Metropolitan Opera debut conducting Gluck's *Orfeo ed Euridice* with Marilyn Horne in the title role. Also in November, Erich Leinsdorf conducted a new production of *Siegfried* with Jess Thomas in the title role and Birgit Nilsson as Brünnhilde. In February Leonie Rysanek appeared with great success in the title role of *Salome.* The 1973–74 season opened in September with a fine revival of *Il trovatore,* conducted by James Levine and with Placido Domingo as Manrico. Domingo made his conducting debut at the beginning of October at the New York City Opera with *La traviata,* after singing Alfredo in the same opera at the Metropolitan the previous week. *Les Troyens* was given for the first time at the Metropolitan on October 22, conducted by its new musical director, Rafael Kubelik. Because of the indisposition of Christa Ludwig, the roles of Cassandra (for which she was scheduled) and Dido were taken by the American mezzo Shirley Verrett. Later Ludwig resumed as Dido. Jon Vickers was Aeneas.

At the New York City Opera an orchestral strike during the first weeks of September forced the company to stage three new productions, Donizetti's *Anna Bolena* (with Beverly Sills in the title role), Strauss's *Ariadne auf Naxos,* and Delius' *A Village Romeo and Juliet,* during a single week in October. The company achieved the feat easily despite the strain on its resources and finances.

Severe financial crisis at the Metropolitan Opera, which projected a $1 million loss for the 1973–74 season, led to cancellation of a new production of *Don Giovanni* and of the company's summer park concerts and Mini-Met program. In the face of an expected $2 million loss for the 1974–75 season, the new general manager, Schuyler G. Chapin (*see* BIOGRAPHY), announced in November 1973 cancellation of the 1975 June Festival and plans to curtail the length of future seasons and of annual employment contracts.

The season of the San Francisco Opera opened on September 7 with a new production of Donizetti's *La Favorita* and continued with *Die Fledermaus,* with Joan Sutherland singing her first Rosalinda, and the first local performance of *Peter Grimes,* with Jess Thomas singing the title role for the first time. The Chicago Lyric Opera opened its season on September 21 with a new production of Donizetti's *Maria Stuarda* with Montserrat Caballé in the title role. That was followed by *Manon,* with Teresa Zylis-Gara in the title role, and by *Siegfried.* Richard Tucker sang Eleazar in Halévy's *La Juive* for the first time on stage for the New Orleans Opera Association on October 20. The Cincinnati Summer Opera Season opened on June 30 with *The Tales of Hoffmann,* with Beverly Sills as all four heroines, a feat also achieved by Joan Sutherland at the Metropolitan in November.

Great Britain. Don Pasquale, the first new production of the 1972–73 season at the Royal Opera House, Covent Garden, was staged amusingly in February by Jean-Pierre Ponnelle with Geraint Evans singing the title role for the first time. A controversial *Don Giovanni,* produced in abstract manner by John Copley, followed on April 18. Sir Georg Solti returned in July to conduct a new production of *Carmen* with Verrett in the title role and Domingo as Don José. The 1973–74 season opened with a visually disastrous new production of *Tannhäuser* finely conducted by Colin Davis. Rudolf Kempe returned in October after an eight-year absence to conduct *Elektra.*

Josephine Barstow sang an unforgettably moving Violetta in the Sadler's Wells Opera's new production of *La traviata* at the Coliseum on March 14. The company presented its first cycle of the complete *Ring* during July and August, conducted by Reginald Goodall. The first new production of the 1973–74 season was Janáček's *Katya Kabanova* in September. This was followed by Penderecki's *The Devils of Loudun,* produced by John Dexter in November, with Barstow again brilliant as Sister Jeanne, and *Maria Stuarda* with Janet Baker in the title role. The Camden Festival presented the first British performance of Verdi's *Stiffelio* in February and followed it with a revival of Offenbach's *Robinson Crusoe.*

Glyndebourne Festival Opera distinguished itself with Peter Hall's thoughtful production of *Le nozze di Figaro* on June 29 and followed that with a new staging by John Cox, in 1920s setting, of Strauss's *Capriccio.* The season had opened at the end of May with the first British performance of Einem's *The Visit of the Old Lady,* also staged by Cox. The Welsh National Opera presented new productions of *Idomeneo* and Bizet's *The Pearl Fishers* (in English) in the autumn. Scottish Opera produced *Tristan und Isolde,* with Helga Dernesch as Isolde, and a memorable *Pelléas et Mélisande.* At the end of August Peter Ustinov produced *Don Giovanni* at the Edinburgh Festival, with Daniel Barenboim conducting his first operatic assignment.

Britten's new *Death in Venice* had its premiere, given by the English Opera Group, at the Aldeburgh Festival on June 16. The production was seen at various European centres, including Venice itself, before it reached Covent Garden in October. Peter Pears sang von Aschenbach; Steuart Bedford conducted; the ballet was choreographed by Sir Frederick Ashton; Robert Huguenin was the boy Tadzio. The work, much of it an interior monologue, was acclaimed by the critics, who, nonetheless, felt that the ballet failed to blend with the rest of the work. Colin Graham was the producer. Graham also produced Tchaikovsky's rarely heard but very beautiful one-act opera *Iolanta* for the English Opera Group at Sadler's Wells Theatre, London, in October, in a double bill with an inventive production of Gilbert and Sullivan's *Trial by Jury.* The New Opera Company gave the first British

TONY ESPARZA

Teruo Ohmura plays a devil dancer in "The Man from the East," a Red Buddha Theatre production. Blending ancient Japanese art and ritual with contemporary rock and mime forms, it depicts 2,000 years of national life, culminating in the destruction of Hiroshima.

performance of Shostakovich's *The Nose* at Sadler's Wells Theatre on April 6 and the first performance of Elisabeth Lutyen's opera *Infidelio,* written nearly 20 years earlier.

Austria. The Vienna Festival in May and June saw an enchanting new production at the Theater an der Wien of *L'elisir d'amore* by Otto Schenk with Reri Grist and Nicolai Gedda in the main roles. At the State Opera there was the first Viennese production of Schoenberg's *Moses und Aron.* The 1973–74 season opened in October with August Everding's restudied production of *Tristan und Isolde,* notable chiefly for the conducting of Carlos Kleiber. Kleiber was probably the most sought-after new conductor of the year, with his recording in Dresden of *Der Freischütz* added to his successes. Earlier in the year Riccardo Muti, another rising star, conducted a new production of *Aida* at the State Opera. At the Salzburg Festival Carl Orff's new opera, *De temporum fine comoedia,* had its first performance in August; it was not well received. The festival's other new production was of *Idomeneo,* conducted by Karl Böhm.

Germany. There were no new productions at the Bayreuth Festival in 1973, but a restudying of Wolfgang Wagner's production of *Die Meistersinger* was presented. At the Munich Festival in July and August there were new productions of *Don Giovanni* and *Pelléas et Mélisande;* the latter was staged by Ponnelle with outstanding success. Wolfgang Brendel and Edith Mathis took the central roles. The regular season included a production of Wolfgang Fortner's *Elisabeth Tudor, Parsifal,* conducted by the musical director, Wolfgang Sawallisch, and, on November 20, the first German performance of Shostakovich's *Katerina Ismailova.* At Hamburg on May 5 there was the first performance of Walter Steffen's *Under Milk Wood,* based on Dylan Thomas' play, and in September a new production of *Don Giovanni.* At Frankfurt in June Anja Silja sang the title role in a new production of *Carmen,* conducted by Christoph von Dohnanyi. On September 9 the Lower Saxon State Opera gave the first performance in German of Britten's *Owen Wingrave,* and on September 29 the Baden State Opera gave the first German performance of Tippett's *The Midsummer Marriage.*

In East Berlin the State Opera gave the first performance of Ernst Hermann Meyer's *Reiter de Nacht* on November 17, and at Leipzig Joachim Herz produced a *Rheingold* with a socialist message.

Italy. The most newsworthy event was the opening on April 10 of the new opera house in Turin with a production by Maria Callas of Verdi's *I vespri Siciliani,* predictably notable for the manner in which the singers were made to act their roles. (Later in the year Callas reappeared as a singer in a number of European recitals with Giuseppe di Stefano.)

Paolo Grassi, the new director of La Scala, Milan, opened his regime with a new production by Franco Zeffirelli of *Un ballo in maschera* on Dec. 7, 1972. *Don Pasquale* followed in January and *Das Rheingold* in March. On May 11 the house presented the first Italian performance of Paul Dessau's *Die Verurteilung des Lukullus.* At Naples on March 4 the premiere of Jacopo Napoli's opera *Dubrowsky II* was given, and on April 12 Giordano's rarely heard *La Cena delle Beffe* was revived. The Rome Opera had an unremarkable 1972–73 season but opened the 1973–74 season with a revival of Rossini's *La gazza ladra,* in a new edition by Alberto Zedda, the scholar and conductor who was restoring all Rossini's scores to their pristine state.

France. The new Rolf Liebermann regime at the Paris Opéra was launched with a production by Giorgio Strehler of *Le nozze di Figaro* in April, although the performance had first been seen at the Royal Opera in Versailles on March 30; Solti was the conductor. This was followed by new productions of Gluck's *Orphée* on April 4 and *Parsifal* on Good Friday. The first new production of the 1973–74 season was the French premiere of Schoenberg's *Moses und Aron* on September 27, also conducted by Solti, followed in November by Gian Carlo Menotti's new production of *La Bohème,* conducted by Aldo Ceccato. On Dec. 15, 1972, the Théâtre de la Musique in Marseilles opened with *Simon Boccanegra,* conducted by the company's new administrator and musical director, Reynald Giovaninetti. *Wozzeck,* a rarity in France, followed on January 26. At the Monte Carlo Festival, Renzo Rosselini's *La Reine Morte* had its premiere on July 7.

Sweden. The bicentenary of the Royal Opera in Stockholm was celebrated by the premiere of Lars Johan Werle's opera *Tintomara* on January 18. At the summer festival at Drottningholm, Georg Joseph Vogler's *Gustav Adolf and Ebba Braha* was revived, produced by Lars Runsten and conducted by Charles Farncombe.

Canada. Opera Canada celebrated its 25th season in September with the first performances of Charles Wilson's *Heloise and Abelard,* a highly effective work produced by Leon Major and conducted by Victor Feldbrill. The company also gave the first Canadian performances of *Götterdämmerung.* In Montreal in September Opera du Quebec called on Zubin Mehta to conduct a new production of *Otello,* with Jon Vickers in the title role. At the National Arts Centre in Ottawa in July, Festival Canada 73 gave a new production of *Don Giovanni* and revived *Così fan tutte* and *La Belle Hélène.* (ALAN BLYTH)

Jazz. Throughout 1973 the jazz world continued to live with the daunting but undeniable truth that, no matter how splendid the noises might be that came from its great masters, there was no sign of a new generation of virtuosi growing into maturity. Although jazz is not quite the exclusively young man's art that popular books and movies like to suggest, it is certainly a music in which complete technical and creative maturity comes at a comparatively young age, and there was now no escaping the ominous fact that for the first time in living memory there was virtually no jazz master of less than 40 years of age. The im-

An experiment in light and tones, "Kyldex I," Nicolas Schoeffer's latest opera performance, opened in Hamburg, W.Ger., in February 1973.

D.P.A. / PICTORIAL PARADE

plications were alarming, for the situation existed where not only was every death of every famous figure analogous to the disappearance of a member of a beleaguered garrison but also where jazz appeared to be no longer a musical activity in the mainstream of musical life.

And yet 1973 was not quite the year of unmitigated gloom that the facts suggest, because, with continuing zest, the aging masters of the jazz world continued to scatter themselves all over the planet in their desire to keep their art well polished. Although the number of European locales capable of making a major jazz concert viable was marginally less than in the past, the movement outward from the United States continued to be both lively and regular. The international nature of jazz had been an accepted fact for some years, but it was interesting that by 1973 potential album sales figures for Japan, which did not exist at all as a jazz market until the late 1940s, were said to have passed the total for all the EEC countries put together. If this was so, one entrepreneur who would surely know how to take advantage of the fact was Norman Granz, the U.S. record maker and concert promoter, who, after a ten-year retirement, returned to the fold with a new catalog. In addition to reissuing priceless pearls from his earlier career, for example, a whole catalog of solo masterpieces by the late Art Tatum, Granz also included various new performances by Ella Fitzgerald (now recovered from her eye operation), Oscar Peterson, and Duke Ellington.

Ellington's career had now arrived at a most curious climax, which was one of the great talking points of the year. After a lifetime of distinctly secular pursuits, Ellington, the great bon vivant of jazz, had in his old age (b. 1899) tended to gravitate more and more to the Christian fervour of his early environment. This tendency manifested itself in a long series of "Sacred Concerts" that took Ellington and his jazz orchestra into the churches and cathedrals of the world to play programs of music, the evangelical intent of which by no means compromised the fierce jazz essence of the performance. Perhaps the most prestigious of these concerts during 1973 was the one that took place in London at Westminster Abbey in October to aid the fund-raising activities of the UN.

There was little indication during the year that the various avant-garde movements had arrived at any significant point of development. Indeed, the silence from some of the lions of contemporary music was faintly disturbing. Perhaps the saddest noncontribution came from the tenor saxophonist Sonny Rollins, the musician best equipped of all to fashion coherence out of the chaotic antiprocedures of avant-garde jazz-making. The incessant soul-searching that had always been a feature of the jazz life could be found in a florid but lovingly compiled biography by Ross Russell of the life of Charlie Parker, *Bird Lives!*

Of the several deaths during the year, the saddest were perhaps those of two founding fathers, Gene Krupa, the drummer most closely associated in the public mind with the extrovert virtuosity of the big band, and Ben Webster, the tenor saxophonist with the sumptuous tone. Krupa, whose bowdlerized biography appeared as a garbled feature movie some years before, was a Chicagoan who graduated from the rough-and-ready small groups of his hometown in the bootleg days to the altogether more suave disciplines of the Benny Goodman band during the ballroom boom of the Roosevelt era. His playing was characterized by a flamboyant technique and a natural gift for dramatizing its execution. But even with all of his crowd-pleasing style, Krupa was one of the great drummers of jazz history. As for Webster, he had begun his career out of Kansas City as a slavish imitator of his greater contemporary Coleman Hawkins. However, his own individuality gradually asserted itself throughout his life, until by the time of his last decade his loss of technical dexterity was more than compensated for by the final flowering of the most beautiful instrumental tone in the history of the saxophone. It was Webster's seductive style that tempted Duke Ellington, in 1934, to increase the size of his saxophone section to accommodate it.

WIDE WORLD

Two generations of Brubecks perform at the Newport Jazz Festival, held in New York City's Central Park, July 1973. Veteran jazz pianist Dave (left) is backed up by his son Chris, at right on trombone.

Other significant deaths in 1973 were those of the New Orleans clarinet virtuoso Albert Nicholas, who had succeeded in sustaining his expertise much longer than was usual for the Louisiana pioneers; Eddie Condon, guitarist and originator of "Chicago style" jazz; pianist and composer Willie (The Lion) Smith; Elmer Snowden, a prominent performer of the 1920s; and DeDe Pierce of the Preservation Hall Jazz Band.

(BENNY GREEN)

Popular. During 1973 popular music remained extrovert and entertaining. The emphasis on presentation strengthened, with styles ranging from the most casual to a theatricality bordering on decadence. Among the personalities dominating the music, Bette Midler stood out as "the first cabaret star of the Beatle generation" (*Melody Maker*). Born in Hawaii, Miss Midler began her career singing in New York clubs, but, on New Year's Eve 1972, with an appearance at the New York Philharmonic Hall, "The Divine Miss M" had arrived. A dynamic personality, she gave vivid performances of songs ranging from "Am I Blue" (1929) to contemporary numbers.

Pop was hitting the newspaper headlines again, mainly through fan-mania. Chief idols were the Osmonds, the Jackson Five, David Cassidy (who gave his first British concerts in March), and Slade, the four-man group from Wolverhampton, Eng., whose loud, cheerful music appealed to the teen-agers. On a more sophisticated level was the Mahavishnu Orchestra, led by the British guitarist Mahavishnu John McLaughlin. This instrumental quintet, which also included Jerry Goodman (violin), Jan Hammer (key-

WIDE WORLD

"It's more or less the decade of the star again," claims rock performer Alice Cooper (foreground with hatchet). His star-like stunts include fake hangings and decapitations, and a male lead with a female name.

boards), Rick Laird (bass), and Billy Cobham (drums), drew its influence from sources including jazz and Eastern music.

One of the brightest new solo stars was David Essex, the cockney singer who rose to fame in the lead of the London production of *Godspell* and won great acclaim for his portrayal of a 1950s teen-ager in *That'll Be the Day*. A much-praised new instrumentalist was guitarist Roy Buchanan. The year saw a peak in the career of Roy Wood, a stalwart of the British music scene since 1967. After several hit singles with The Move, Wood formed the Electric Light Orchestra, and then, early in 1973, Wizzard. This band, which featured brass, was an immediate success. Among the other groups, Genesis attracted much attention with its complex music and striking presentation, and Steely Dan's first two LPs were best sellers. In a lighter vein were 10 CC, whose songs cleverly updated 1960s styles.

One of the year's most distinctive sounds emanated from Philadelphia, where writers Gamble and Huff and producer Thom Bell created "Philly Soul." Among the groups performing in this attractive style, a blend of soul and pop with close-harmony vocals, were the Stylistics and Harold Melvin & The Blue Notes. One of America's top solo soul singers was Al Green. The Tamla Motown organization, settling into its new headquarters in Los Angeles, had another successful year. Motown's musical style was growing more complex, partly because of the work of writer/producer Norman Whitfield. Motown's first venture into films, with Diana Ross playing Billie Holiday in *Lady Sings the Blues,* was a worldwide success, and Miss Ross gained an Oscar nomination for her performance. Leading lady of the singer-songwriters was Carly Simon, who had an international hit early in 1973 with "You're So Vain." Other successful musicians in this genre were John Denver and Gilbert O'Sullivan, and promising new talents included Bonnie Koloc, Linda Lewis, and Clifford T. Ward.

The U.S.-British domination of pop was being challenged by European bands, especially the Dutch quartet Focus. West Germany was rich in progressive groups, such as Faust and Amon Duul, and a "heavy" stream was appearing in Italian pop. West Indian reggae continued to be very popular in Britain, with the Wailers, a Jamaican band, commanding particular respect.

The careers of several established artists, including Lou Reed, Neil Sedaka, Jeff Beck, and British group Status Quo, received new impetus during the year. Country songwriter Kris Kristofferson (*see* BIOGRAPHY) turned to more religious works in his fourth album, "Jesus Was a Capricorn," and became an actor to watch for his performance in the film *Blume in Love*. In January Eric Clapton played a single spectacular "comeback" concert in London. Possible reunions of groups—including the Beatles—were the subject of much speculation. The personnel of pop groups was in a continual state of flux, with splits affecting, among others, Deep Purple, Lindisfarne, and the Everly Brothers. A promising career was tragically ended when Jim Croce was killed in an air crash in September, two months after he had topped the U.S. charts with "Bad Bad Leroy Brown." The Grateful Dead lost their organist, "Pig Pen," and Donald Peers, popular British singer of the 1950s, died in August.

The rock musicals *Godspell* and *Jesus Christ Superstar* appeared as films during 1973, and *Godspell*'s writer Stephen Schwartz had another success with *Pippin*. Possibly the biggest rock-theatre event of 1972–73 was the production by Lou Reizner of The Who's *Tommy,* at London's Rainbow Theatre in December 1972, with an all-star cast including Peter Sellers and Rod Stewart.

A healthy leavening of humour was permeating pop —in the songs of Dr. Hook & The Medicine Show, in the British television comedy show "Monte Python's Flying Circus," which became a favourite with pop audiences, and in the number that gave Chuck Berry the biggest hit of his career by topping both the British and U.S. charts: "My Ding-A-Ling."

Pop musicians were working harder than ever, with long tours very much in vogue. The Rolling Stones were particularly busy, touring Australia, Britain, and Europe to packed houses. After a long tour taking in the U.S., Japan, and Britain, David Bowie dramatically announced his retirement from live performances, but it was not certain whether he would stick to this decision.

An exciting new field was that of black film music, led by Curtis Mayfield whose *Super Fly* score topped the U.S. album charts. Nostalgia was still rife, with particular emphasis on the 1950s, seen in the success of the musical *Grease* and the film *That'll Be the Day*. In the summer of 1973 some of the British stars of the 1960s recreated the "British invasion" of that decade in a U.S. tour. Nevertheless, pop was still looking to the future, pleasing a new generation of fans with its liveliness and variety. (HAZEL MORGAN)

Folk Music. Among 1973's events involving traditional folk music, the Smithsonian Institution's seventh Festival of American Folklife in Washington, D.C., was of special interest for its innovation in showing "Old Ways in the New World." Nearly 50 musicians, singers, and dancers were brought from Croatia (Yugoslavia) especially to demonstrate their tamburitza orchestra tradition, still carried on in the United States. Several Yugoslav-American groups from Chicago, Lackawanna, N.Y., and Elizabeth, N.J., also played. After the nine-day program the visitors traveled to several Yugoslav communities to perform. This focused attention in a new and effective way on the traditional artistic expression of a relatively small ethnic group in the U.S.

In the West folk music research tended to be sponsored privately rather than by government institutions, as it was in Eastern Europe and the third world. Four major exceptions to this rule were: the Canadian Centre for Folk Culture Study in the National Museum of Man, Ottawa; the Musée National des Arts et Traditions Populaires, Paris; the Musée de l'Homme, also in Paris; and, in the U.S., the Smithsonian Institution's Division of Performing Arts, especially its Folklife Program.

The Canadian Centre expanded its activities and staff during 1972–73. Films were made of traditional fiddle-playing in Ontario, and of an Estonian zither player. Studies were made of Gaelic folklore and folk music, and also of Afro-Canadian as well as Bulgarian, Korean, and Polish communities in Ontario.

In Paris, the Ethnomusicology Research Group was founded in 1970 in the Centre of French Ethnology at the Musée National des Arts et Traditions Populaires. On the basis of a corpus of French ethnic musics from France and islands of French culture abroad, the group was establishing an ethnomusicological map of France and relevant localities abroad, and had also worked out a typology of French folk music instruments and a systematic analysis of French folk music. In 1973 the group collected recordings of folk music in the Val d'Aosta (northwestern Italy), the western Pyrenees, Catalonia (Spain), and Louisiana.

Soviet folk music specialists held a six-day congress in Vilnius, Lithuanian S.S.R., in May, devoted to theoretical and practical classification and systematization of folk melodies. The system adopted in the Lithuanian folklore research institute and conservatory was examined and discussed, along with other proposed systems. The meeting was part of a new all-Soviet program in folk music research being developed under the aegis of the Union of Composers of the U.S.S.R. The International Folk Music Council held its 22nd conference in Bayonne, France, in August. Most of those present represented the English-speaking countries and Western Europe, but there were also delegates from Eastern Europe, North and West Africa, the Middle East, and Japan.

In Central Europe the fourth Slovak Ethnomusicological Seminar in September concentrated on the transcription of folk music and dance, and especially on the problems of dealing with instrumental ensembles. A Roundtable on Music Research in Southeast Asia was convened in Manila by the UNESCO National Commission of the Philippines in October to permit both scholars and musicians to discuss methods for comparative music studies. (BARBARA KRADER)

See also Dance; Motion Pictures; Television and Radio; Theatre.

Nauru

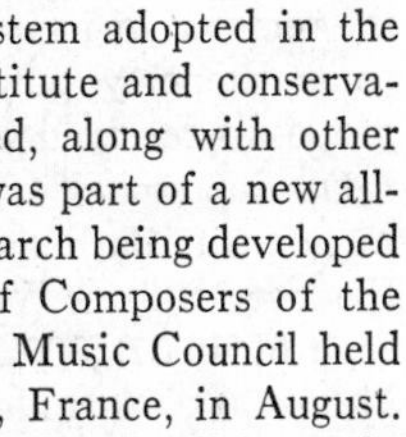

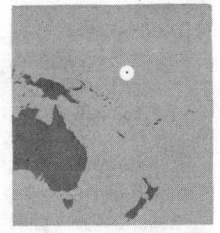

An island republic in the Pacific Ocean, Nauru lies about 1,200 mi. E of New Guinea. Area: 8.2 sq.mi. (21 sq.km.). Pop. (1972 est.): 6,768. Seat of government: Domaneab, Uaboe District. Language: English and Nauruan. Religion: Christian. President in 1973, Hammer de Robburt.

Nauru celebrated five years of independence and prosperity on Jan. 31, 1973. Throughout the year President de Roburt stressed the importance of close friendship with the people of Japan. Japan was a substantial customer for Nauru's phosphate output and provided maintenance for Nauru's shipping line. Osaka shipyards were building Nauru's first large ship, the "Kolle D," of 30,000 tons, at a cost of A$7 million. In January Air Nauru inaugurated a service between Nauru and Kagoshima, Jap.

The Nauruan economy received a boost when the British Phosphate Commission contracted to buy a total of 1,350,000 tons of phosphate rock for Australia and New Zealand for the financial year 1972–73. Initially the contract was for 750,000 tons, with the option of a further 100,000 tons. Before the recession in the world phosphate market, Nauru's sales had run at around two million tons annually.

In March President de Roburt and the prime minister of Tonga, Prince Tu'ipelehake, agreed to cooperate in regional shipping ventures. Both the Nauruan and the Tongan shipping lines agreed to coordinate the routing of ships, the integration of schedules, and the allocation of cargoes to meet consumers' needs. The start of a new monthly cargo-passenger service between New Zealand, Fiji, Tonga, and Samoa was delayed when Nauru's "Enna G" became strike-bound in Wellington, N.Z. (A. R. G. GRIFFITHS)

NAURU

Education. (1970) Primary, pupils 1,465, teachers 94; secondary, pupils 368, teachers 28.

Finance and Trade. Monetary unit: Australian dollar, with (Sept. 17, 1973) an official rate of A$0.67 to U.S. $1 (free rate of A$1.62 = £1 sterling). Budget (1971–72): revenue A$7.5 million; expenditure A$7,720,000. Foreign trade: imports (1970–71) A$4,502,000 (92% from Australia); exports (phosphates; 1968–69) A$24,046,000 (65% to Australia, 24% to New Zealand, 7% to Japan by tonnage).

Industry. Production: phosphates (oxide content; 1970) *c.* 2.2 million metric tons; electricity (1968) 19.3 million kw-hr.

Nepal

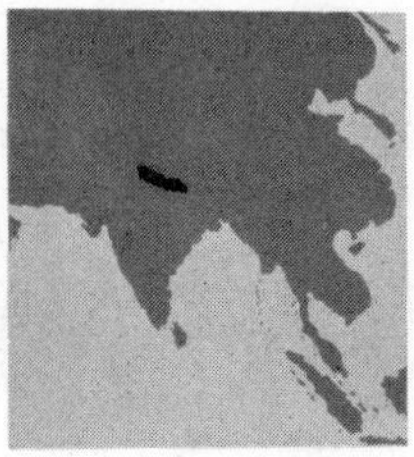

A constitutional monarchy of Asia, Nepal is in the Himalayas between India and Tibet. Area: 54,362 sq.mi. (140,797 sq.km.). Pop. (1971): 11,555,983. Cap. and largest city: Kathmandu (pop., 1971, 150,402). Language: Nepali (official); also Newari and Bhutia. Religion (1971): Hindu 89.4%; Buddhist 7.5%. King, Birendra Bir Bikram Shah Deva; prime ministers in 1973, Kirti Nidhi Bista and, from July 17, Nagendra Prasad Rijal.

A devastating fire, which gutted most of the vast Singha Durbar or Lion Palace (central secretariat) complex in Kathmandu in July 1973, led to the downfall of the 27-month old Kirti Nidhi Bista government and proved an embarrassment to young King Birendra. The new Cabinet, headed by Nagendra Prasad Rijal, chairman of the National Panchayat, included most of the ministers of the Bista government. The worst food crisis in the nation's history, caused by floods and drought, was alleviated through timely food shipments from India and the U.S. The king used a strong hand to put down unrest among extremist student elements and followers of disgruntled politicians.

Namibia:
see Dependent States; South Africa
Narcotics:
see Drugs and Narcotics
NATO:
see Defense
Navies:
see Defense

NEPAL

Education. (1971–72) Primary, pupils 478,743, teachers 11,490; secondary and vocational, pupils 257,245, teachers 3,334; teacher training (1969–70), students 365, teachers (1966–67) 19; higher, students 25,000, teaching staff 1,070.

Finance. Monetary unit: Nepalese rupee, with (Sept. 17, 1973) an official rate of NRs. 10.56 to U.S. $1 (nominal free rate of NRs. 25.45 = £1 sterling). Gold, SDRs, and foreign exchange, central bank: (April 1973) U.S. $110.9 million; (April 1972) U.S. $94.5 million. Budget (1972–73): revenue NRs. 601 million; expenditure NRs. 410 million (excluding development expenditure of NRs. 857 million, partly financed by foreign aid of NRs. 291 million).

Foreign Trade. (1968–69) Imports NRs. 744.3 million (97% from India in 1966–67); exports NRs. 568 million (99% to India in 1966–67). Main exports: food and livestock 45%; crude materials (including timber and jute) 29%; manufactures 24%.

Agriculture. Production (in 000; metric tons; 1972; 1971 in parentheses): rice *c.* 1,754 (2,353); millet and sorghum *c.* 115 (*c.* 115); jute *c.* 55 (58). Livestock (in 000; 1971–72): cattle *c.* 6,400; pigs *c.* 300; sheep *c.* 2,250; goats *c.* 2,300.

Other measures launched during the year included banning the production and sale of marijuana, hashish, and other narcotic drugs, and the state take-over of the jute trade and the distribution of oil and petroleum products.

The economy showed signs of improvement with the foreign exchange reserves for 1971–72 showing an increase of 21.7%. The budget for 1973–74 envisaged a total expenditure of NRs. 1,567,000,000, an increase of 22% over the previous year. Internal revenues, foreign aid, and income through new taxation were expected to yield NRs. 1,280,000,000, leaving a deficit of NRs. 287 million. India continued to be the major foreign aid donor with 50% of the total. Foreign aid estimated for 1973–74 was NRs. 225 million.

Nepal maintained a balanced relationship with India and China during the year, but in October King Birendra and Queen Aishwarya made an eight-day state visit to India that helped to remove some of the "irritants" in Indo-Nepalese relations. The king made his first official visit abroad when he attended the summit meeting of nonaligned nations in Algiers in September. (GOVINDAN UNNY)

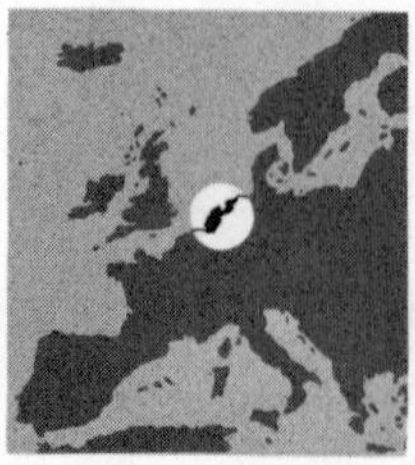

Netherlands, The

A kingdom of northwest Europe on the North Sea, The Netherlands, a Benelux country, is bounded by Belgium on the south and West Germany on the east. Area: 15,892 sq.mi. (41,160 sq.km.). Pop. (1973 est.): 13,387,623. Cap. and largest city: Amsterdam (pop., 1973 est., 791,769). Seat of government: The Hague (pop., 1973 est., 510,360). Language: Dutch. Religion (1971): Roman Catholic 39.6%; Dutch Reformed 23%; no religion 22.4%; Reformed Churches 7%. Queen, Juliana; prime ministers in 1973, Barend W. Biesheuvel and, from May 11, Joop den Uyl.

The most significant event of 1973 was the imposition, during the Arab-Israeli war in the fall, of a ban on the sale of oil by Arab oil-producing countries in retaliation for what they regarded as The Netherlands' traditional friendship with Israel. Dutch Foreign Minister Max van der Stoel believed the Arab boycott of his country was part of a well-prepared plan that took into account the vital importance of Rotterdam in the transport, transit, and refining of crude oil. Two-thirds of West Germany's oil supplies and a large proportion of those of Belgium passed through The Netherlands, and the Arabs obviously hoped to exert pressure on the EEC as a whole. From early November the Dutch government banned all Sunday traffic (except public transport), and gasoline rationing was scheduled to begin Jan. 7, 1974. Prince Bernhard was seen cycling through the streets surrounded by cheering crowds.

On May 11 Queen Juliana had received the 33 ministers and undersecretaries of the government formed by Joop den Uyl (*see* BIOGRAPHY), thus terminating the longest parliamentary crisis in Netherlands history. The main cause of the long duration of the crisis had been the change in the balance of political power in the lower house of Parliament as a result of the elections of Nov. 29, 1972. The three confessional parties, the Catholic People's Party, the Antirevolutionary Party, and the Christian Historical Union, failed to capture a majority in the lower house. The three left-wing parties, Labour, Democrats '66, and the Radical Politicals, became the leading alignment but did not gain a clear majority. The left-wing combination had declared it did not intend to enter into negotiations for a common platform after the elections. The three confessional parties refused to support the left wing unless they could have a substantial say in the formulation of the program of the new government and in the composition of the Cabinet. It took 164 days to reach an agreement that the government's program should be based on the platforms of both combinations, and that the left-wing group should take ten seats in the Cabinet and the confessionals six. The Christian Historical Union rejected this compromise and refused to join such a coalition. On June 23 the confessional parties decided to begin moves toward their integration.

On May 28 the Cabinet made its first public policy statement. The main principles of its policy concerned the removal of inequality by fairer distribution of income, property, power, knowledge, and controls. The proposals received warm trade-union support.

On September 18 Queen Juliana opened the new session of Parliament. The budget, presented by Finance Minister Willem F. Duisenberg, forecast revenue of 49,026,000,000 guilders and expenditures of 51,068,000,000 guilders. The Government Planning Office foresaw a rise in exports but a fall in internal demand, resulting in a deficit in the balance of payments; it also predicted that the number of unemployed for 1973 would increase to as many as 115,000. Prices were expected to rise by 8% and wages by a

Streets of Woudenberg wear a new Sunday quiet Nov. 4, 1973, during the first weekend after The Netherlands announced a ban on Sunday driving because of Arab oil embargoes.

UPI COMPIX

NETHERLANDS, THE

Education. (1971–72) Primary, pupils 1,541,000, teachers (1969–70) 47,841; secondary, pupils 626,000, teachers (1969–70) 36,912; vocational (1969–70), pupils 536,460; teacher training (1969–70), students 10,822, teachers 1,012; higher (including 9 universities; 1969–70), students 211,513.

Finance. Monetary unit: guilder, with (Sept. 17, 1973) a free rate of 2.55 guilders to U.S. $1 (6.14 guilders = £1 sterling). Gold, SDRs, and foreign exchange, central bank: (June 1973) U.S. $5,329,000,000; (June 1972) U.S. $3,792,000,000. Budget (1973 est.): revenue 40,115,000,000 guilders; expenditure 43,081,000,000 guilders. Gross national product: (1971) 127,970,000,000 guilders; (1970) 113,920,000,000 guilders. Money supply: (April 1973) 38,780,000,000 guilders; (April 1972) 33,620,000,000 guilders. Cost of living (1963 = 100): (June 1973) 177; (June 1972) 163.

Foreign Trade. (1972) Imports 55,921,000,000 guilders; exports 53,878,000,000 guilders. Import sources: EEC 57% (West Germany 28%, Belgium-Luxembourg 16%, France 8%); U.S. 8%; U.K. 5%. Export destinations: EEC 64% (West Germany 36%, Belgium-Luxembourg 13%, France 11%, Italy 5%); U.K. 7%. Main exports: chemicals 15%; petroleum products 12%; meat products 10%; textile yarns and fabrics 8%; dairy products 8%; electrical machinery and equipment 7%; machinery (nonelectrical) 6%; iron and steel 6%; transport equipment 6%. Tourism (1971): visitors 2,415,600; gross receipts U.S. $598 million.

Transport and Communications. Roads (1972) 81,406 km. (including 790 km. expressways). Motor vehicles in use (1972): passenger 3,117,400; commercial 346,500. Railways: (1971) 3,147 km. (including 1,645 km. electrified); traffic (1972) 8,114,000,000 passenger-km., freight 3,071,000,000 net ton-km. Air traffic (1972): 7,857,000,000 passenger-km.; freight 479,623,000 net ton-km. Navigable inland waterways (1971): 5,587 km. (including 1,733 km. for ships of 2,000 tons and over); freight traffic 30,429,000,000 ton-km. Shipping (1972): merchant vessels 100 gross tons and over 1,452; gross tonnage 4,972,244. Ships entered (1971) vessels totaling 128.5 million net registered tons; goods loaded (1972) 77,219,000 metric tons, unloaded 232.8 million metric tons. Telephones (Dec. 1971) 3,721,000. Radio licenses (Dec. 1971) 3,719,000. Television licenses (Dec. 1971) 3,211,000.

Agriculture. Production (in 000; metric tons; 1972; 1971 in parentheses): wheat 673 (706); rye 151 (209); barley 340 (373); oats 140 (206); potatoes 5,581 (5,799); tomatoes 365 (346); onions 305 (*c.* 300); apples 400 (520); pears 140 (100); sugar, raw value *c.* 763 (*c.* 838); dry peas 11 (31); rapeseed 45 (33); linseed *c.* 6 (*c.* 7); flax fibre 12 (14); milk 8,940 (8,388); butter 163 (143); cheese 320 (319); eggs *c.* 276 (264); beef and veal 268 (323); pork 743 (758); fish catch (1971) 321, (1970) 301. Livestock (in 000; May 1972): cattle 4,306; pigs 6,233; sheep 592; horses used in agriculture *c.* 100; chickens 58,430.

Industry. Index of production (1963 = 100): (1972) 203; (1971) 188. Production (in 000; metric tons; 1972): coal 2,812; crude oil 1,597; natural gas (cu.m.) 58,419,000; manufactured gas (cu.m.) 795,000; electricity (kw-hr.) 49,550,000; pig iron 4,289; crude steel 5,587; cement 4,029; cotton yarn 44; wool yarn 16; rayon, etc., filament yarn 36; nylon, etc., filament yarn and fibres (1971) 106. Merchant vessels launched (100 gross tons and over; 1972) 752,000 gross tons. New dwelling units completed (1972) 153,000.

minimum of 14%. On September 15 the government announced a 5% revaluation of the guilder.

At the beginning of the year, strikes over wage differentials were organized in several sectors of the economy by the three national trade unions, NVV, NKV, and CNV. At the request of Hoogovens, a big steel corporation, the courts ordered an end to the strikes, but the conflict continued to expand. Eventually, mediation attempts by Minister of Social Affairs Jaap Boersma were successful. In June, however, the biggest national trade union, NVV, refused to take further responsibility for a report of the Social-Economic Council on social and economic measures and walked out of the deliberations.

Also in June, the lower house of Parliament passed a bill approving the European Treaty of Strasbourg, which prohibited pirate radios. This provoked the ire of many young people who enjoyed the broadcasts of the offshore Radio Veronica, and attempts were made to convert Veronica into a legal broadcasting organization.

From August 18 to 25 a 14-member parliamentary delegation, led by the chairman of the lower house, Anne Vondeling, visited China. During the trip, the delegation conferred with Premier Chou En-lai. Earlier in the year, at the invitation of the Supreme Soviet, Princess Beatrix and Prince Claus had made a study-trip to the Soviet Union, where they had talks with Pres. Nikolay V. Podgorny and Minister of Foreign Affairs Andrey A. Gromyko. Nicolae Ceausescu, general secretary of the Romanian Communist Party, visited The Netherlands in April; an official statement emphasized the development of trade and economic, technical, and cultural cooperation. In September Queen Juliana celebrated the 25th anniversary of her accession to the throne. (DICK BOONSTRA)

See also Dependent States.

New Zealand

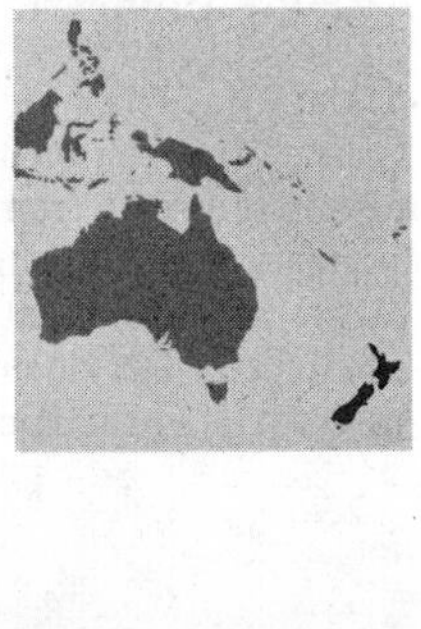

New Zealand, a parliamentary state and member of the Commonwealth of Nations, is in the South Pacific Ocean, separated from southeastern Australia by the Tasman Sea. The country consists of North and South islands and Stewart, Chatham, and other minor islands. Area: 103,736 sq.mi. (268,675 sq.km.). Pop. (1973 est.): 2,974,659. Cap.: Wellington (pop., 1973 est., 140,000). Largest city: Christchurch (pop., 1973 est., 168,000). Largest urban area: Auckland (pop., 1973 est., 578,420). Language: English (official), Maori. Religion (1966): Church of England 33.7%; Presbyterian 21.8%; Roman Catholic 15.9%. Queen, Elizabeth II; governor-general in 1973, Sir Denis Blundell; prime minister, Norman E. Kirk.

The month-old third Labour government, bent on revitalizing New Zealand after 12 years of National Party administration, started 1973 on a wave of goodwill that more than matched its majority in Parliament of 56 seats to 31. Labour went about its work with a relish that seemed to imply that New Zealand had been without a government for some years. Norman Kirk steered it through some controversial issues, such as recognition of China, the banning of a tour of New Zealand by a Springbok (South African) rugby team, the dispatch of a frigate as an unfriendly observer of the French nuclear tests at Mururoa Atoll, and the reorganization of the monolithic New Zealand Broadcasting Corp. But within eight months, inflation, the main enemy of the previous administration, was tearing at Labour's vitals.

It was typical of the style of government that Kirk should return from the Commonwealth conference at Ottawa in August as an acclaimed emerging international statesman, only to be savaged at home for unconvincing handling of industrial and economic crises by his 60-year-old deputy Hugh Watt (*see* BIOGRAPHY). Kirk had succeeded in buttressing Labour against the pre-election charge that it was a one-man band through the development of Minister of Overseas Trade Joseph A. Walding (who had started the dialogue with Peking), the credibility of articulate Martyn Finlay (*see* BIOGRAPHY), the justice minister, the promise of Colin J. Moyle, who had the difficult agriculture portfolio, and the modest confidence of the finance minister, William E. Rowling.

Rowling's first budget, in June, was acclaimed as a "workingman's" easement, providing tax cuts for those on low incomes, a rise in social security benefits, a crippling tax on property speculation, easier financing for home ownership, and the outline for a national

Netherlands Overseas Territories: *see* Dependent States

New Guinea: *see* Dependent States; Indonesia

Newspapers: *see* Publishing

NEW ZEALAND

Education. (1971) Primary, pupils 519,276, teachers 19,163; secondary, pupils 190,709, teachers 10,482; vocational, pupils (including correspondence) 99,037, teachers 960; teacher training, students 9,309, teachers 615; higher (at 7 universities), students 37,305, teaching staff 2,211.

Finance. Monetary unit: New Zealand dollar, with (Sept. 17, 1973) a free rate of NZ$0.68 to U.S. $1 (NZ$1.63 = £1 sterling). Gold, SDRs, and foreign exchange, central bank: (June 1973) U.S. $978 million; (June 1972) U.S. $504 million. Budget (1972–73 est.): revenue NZ$1,866,000,000; expenditure NZ$2,124,000,000. Gross national product: (1971–72) NZ$6,260,000,000; (1970–71) NZ$5,432,000,000. Cost of living (1963 = 100): (2nd quarter 1973) 172; (2nd quarter 1972) 160.

Foreign Trade. (1972) Imports NZ$1,281,400,000; exports NZ$1,477,700,000. Import sources: U.K. 28%; Australia 22%; Japan 13%; U.S. 10%. Export destinations: U.K. 32%; U.S. 15%; Japan 12%; Australia 7%. Main exports (1971–72): meat and meat preparations 29%; wool 17%; butter 13%; cheese 5%; hides and skins 5%. Tourism (1969): visitors 148,100; gross receipts (1971) U.S. $47 million.

Transport and Communications. Roads (1971) 89,345 km. Motor vehicles in use (1971): passenger 941,600; commercial 185,300. Railways: (1972) 4,807 km.; traffic (1971–72) 724 million passenger-km., freight 3,036,000,000 net ton-km. Air traffic (1972): 2,260,100,000 passenger-km.; freight 57,916,000 net ton-km. Shipping (1972): merchant vessels 100 gross tons and over 120; gross tonnage 181,901. Telephones (Dec. 1971) 1,305,000. Radio licenses (Dec. 1971) 713,000. Television licenses (Dec. 1971) 698,000.

Agriculture. Production (in 000; metric tons; 1972; 1971 in parentheses): wheat 420 (324); barley 315 (227); oats 54 (49); potatoes *c.* 325 (*c.* 325); dry peas *c.* 50 (50); tomatoes (1971) 60, (1970) 51; apples 125 (128); wine *c.* 21 (21); milk *c.* 7,320 (6,780); butter 216 (236); cheese 104 (104); mutton and lamb (1971) 558, (1970) 563; beef and veal (1971) 397, (1970) 393; wool (1971) *c.* 236, (1970) 238; timber (cu.m.; 1971) 8,500, (1970) 8,700; fish catch (1971) 66, (1970) 59. Livestock (in 000; Jan. 1972): cattle 8,774; sheep 60,883; horses (1971) *c.* 81; pigs 580; chickens (April) *c.* 5,500.

Industry. Fuel and power (in 000; metric tons; 1972): coal 417; lignite 1,736; crude oil (1971) 100; natural gas (cu.m.; 1971) 301,000; manufactured gas (cu.m.) 128,000; electricity (excluding most industrial production; kw-hr.) 16,957,000. Production (in 000; metric tons; 1972): cement 899; phosphate fertilizers (1971–72) 341; wood pulp (1971–72) 581; newsprint (1971–72) 218; other paper (1971–72) 251.

compulsory retirement scheme. But food costs were so much on the increase that emergency measures to deal with them upstaged the budget. Following a freeze on mutton and fish in April, the government moved again in August, freezing prices for a month and wages until June 30, 1974, then striking at the problem with a 10% revaluation, a ban on some sheepmeat exports to the price-inflated overseas markets, which were forcing up home prices, and a grant of more import licenses to blunt demand. The package seemed to be effective in its first month of operation, although farmers claimed they bore the brunt of it in lost earnings.

Out of all proportion to its impact at home was the international publicity resulting from the dispatch of an observer frigate to Mururoa to back up the interim injunction sought and won against French nuclear tests from the International Court of Justice. New Zealanders had been mildly opposed to French testing, but the national trade union federation stiffened this attitude by blacklisting French transport, and Labour had gone into office pledged to something more than the court action. Greater feeling was involved in the issue of whether the all-white Springbok rugby team should visit. The government created a new policy for New Zealand sports bodies; it would host teams from any country that were fully representative of the country, and not of one of its races.

In a significant first year as prime minister, Kirk received the Australian Labor prime minister, Gough Whitlam, in January, toured Pacific islands, attended the Ottawa conference, and then was received in Washington with rather more enthusiasm than had been shown to Whitlam. If there was embarrassment that the leader of a small country instead of its larger neighbour seemed to be emerging as a South Pacific spokesman, Kirk tried to gloss over it on an official visit to Canberra late in the year.

Notable visitors to Wellington during the year included the Soviet trade minister, Nikolay S. Patolichev, Malaysia's deputy prime minister, Tun Ismail, Prince Bernhard of The Netherlands, and the crown prince and princess of Japan.

In a country not noted for seasonal extremes farmers were hit by summer drought and winter snowstorms, both accounting for huge sheep losses. The August snowstorms were followed by national power shortages when the mainly hydroelectric system tried to cope with extra demand. A new method of power generation was offered in October, when the government bought a $30 million half share in offshore natural gas.

In London Terence H. McCombs, a former schoolteacher and Labour politician, became high commissioner, and new diplomatic posts included Peking, Moscow, Vienna, and Santiago, Chile. But the diplomatic event of the year was the arrival at Wellington in May of the first ambassador of the People's Republic of China, Pei Tsien-chang. Before the year was out there were complaints from other missions alleging that the Chinese waged too positive a propaganda push among students, Maoris, and others.

(JOHN A. KELLEHER)

See also Dependent States.

Nicaragua

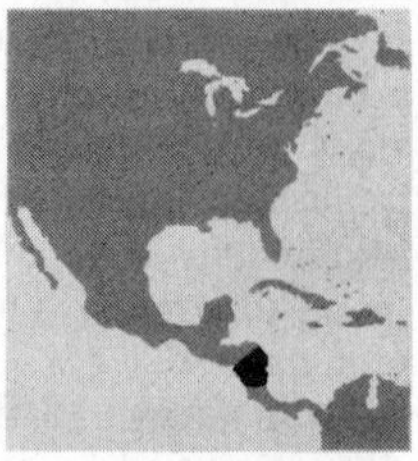

The largest country of Central America, Nicaragua is a republic bounded by Honduras, Costa Rica, the Caribbean Sea, and the Pacific Ocean. Area: 49,759 sq.mi. (128,875 sq.km.). Pop. (1973 est.): 2,019,000. Cap. and largest city: Managua (pop., 1971, 398,514). Language: Spanish. Religion: Roman Catholic. Heads of state in 1973, a triumvirate: Roberto Martínez Lacayo, Alfonso Lovo Cordero, and, until March 1, Fernando Agüero Rocha; after March 1 Rocha was replaced by Edmundo Paguaga Irias.

On March 1, 1973, the National Assembly dismissed Fernando Agüero Rocha, leader of the opposition Conservative Party, from the triumvirate that had ostensibly ruled Nicaragua for a year. Such a leadership was to remain in force until the general election in September 1974, at which time Anastasio Somoza Debayle was expected to regain official rule of the country. The Somoza family had directly or indirectly governed Nicaragua since the 1930s.

Most of the year was spent in taking stock of the damage incurred in the disastrous earthquake that struck Managua on Dec. 23, 1972, and in making efforts to recover from it. According to a UN report a "realistic" fatality figure was 6,000, contradicting an earlier assertion that at least 10,000 had succumbed. The official UN document stated that the quake measured 6.25 on the Richter scale. Approximately 20,000 persons were injured, and 300,000 (well over half the city's population) were left homeless. At least 60% of the fixed investment of more than $1 billion was lost. Of the 78,000 housing units in Managua, 50,000 were destroyed, and many of the remainder were damaged. Commerce was hard hit, the quake destroying or damaging 50% of the city's commercial establishments. Half the nation's gross national product was disrupted, and there was an approximate 39% reduction in government income. Some authorities estimated that it would take about ten years to recover.

Recovery efforts were extensive. Insurance companies operating in Nicaragua paid claims totaling $56 million during the first six months of 1973. Approximately $60 million–$80 million was paid throughout the year. Reconstruction was to be paid for by high cotton export earnings and loans from various international agencies, such as a $20 million (50-year interest free) loan from the International Development Association, mainly to replace schools and the water system. The U.S. provided relief aid of approximately $25 million, and neighbouring Latin-American countries made sizable contributions.

Steps taken by the government to facilitate reconstruction included extension of the workweek from 48 to 60 hours, adoption of a 10% export duty and a two-year rent freeze, abolition of tax exemption for two years, and a levy of one month's wages on public employees for 1973.

Technical assistance from Mexico and the U.S. included a rebuilding plan. Twenty-six housing zones would be constructed around the edge of Managua, each to have its own business district, parks, and services. Connections to downtown would be by streets 325 ft. wide built along geologic faults. The estimated cost for Managua's reconstruction surpassed $100 million. (GEORGE P. PATTEN)

NICARAGUA

Education. (1969–70) Primary, pupils 266,346, teachers (including preprimary) 7,535; secondary, pupils 38,149, teachers 1,671; vocational, pupils 4,221, teachers 297; teacher training, students 3,254, teachers 259; higher (including 2 universities), students 7,682, teaching staff 487.

Finance. Monetary unit: córdoba, with (Sept. 17, 1973) a par value of 7 córdobas to U.S. $1 (free rate of 16.99 córdobas = £1 sterling). Gold, SDRs, and convertible currency, central bank: (March 1973) U.S. $109,670,000; (March 1972) U.S. $89,010,000. Budget (1972 est.) balanced at 793 million córdobas. Gross national product: (1971) 6,271,000,000 córdobas; (1970) 5,771,000,000 córdobas. Money supply: (March 1973) 1,131,600,000 córdobas; (March 1972) 768 million córdobas.

Foreign Trade. (1972) Imports *c.* 1,566,000,000 córdobas; exports 1,662,400,000 córdobas. Import sources: U.S. 34%; Guatemala 9%; Costa Rica 9%; Japan 8%; El Salvador 7%; Venezuela 7%; West Germany 7%. Export destinations: U.S. 33%; Japan 18%; Costa Rica 11%; West Germany 7%. Main exports: cotton 26%; meat 15%; coffee 13%; sugar 6%.

Transport and Communications. Roads (1971) 13,147 km. (including 485 km. of Pan-American Highway). Motor vehicles in use (1970): passenger 34,400; commercial (including buses) 8,900. Railways (1970): 317 km.; traffic 30 million passenger-km., freight 16 million net ton-km. Air traffic (1971): 107 million passenger-km.; freight 1,020,000 net ton-km. Telephones (Jan. 1972) 26,000. Radio receivers (Dec. 1971) 110,000. Television receivers (Dec. 1971) 56,000.

Agriculture. Production (in 000; metric tons; 1972; 1971 in parentheses): corn 236 (236); rice (1971) 74, (1970) 109; sorghum *c.* 60 (*c.* 60); dry beans *c.* 55 (*c.* 57); coffee *c.* 34 (*c.* 42); sugar, raw value *c.* 184 (*c.* 189); cotton, lint *c.* 96 (104). Livestock (in 000; 1971–72): cattle *c.* 2,670; pigs *c.* 630; chickens *c.* 3,000.

Industry. Production (in 000; 1971): cement (metric tons) 99; gold (troy oz.) 107; electricity (kw-hr.) 649,000.

Niger

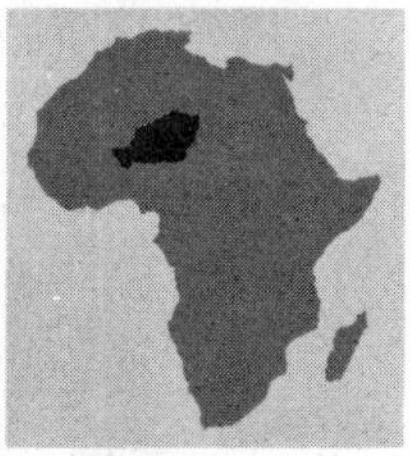

A republic of north central Africa, Niger is bounded by Algeria, Libya, Chad, Nigeria, Dahomey, Upper Volta, and Mali. Area: 489,191 sq.mi. (1,267,000 sq.km.). Pop. (1973 est.): 4,303,900, including (1970 est.) Hausa 53.7%; Zerma and Songhai 23.6%; Fulani 10.6%; Beriberi-Manga 9.1%. Cap. and largest city: Niamey (pop., 1973 est., 121,900). Language: French and Sudanic dialects. Religion: Muslim, animist, Christian. President in 1973, Hamani Diori.

Niger was one of the six French-speaking West African states most gravely affected by drought in 1973, the Agadès region being declared a disaster area by the authorities in Niamey. With the support of his four colleagues in the Conseil de l'Entente (Togo, Ivory Coast, Upper Volta, and Dahomey), Pres. Hamani Diori made increasingly strenuous efforts to mobilize international opinion. On several occasions he demanded a full-scale "Marshall Plan for Africa."

The president once again called for a thoroughgoing revision of his country's cooperation agreements with France. He also wished to see a reform of the statutes of the Central Bank of the States of West Africa, which covered all but two (Guinea and Mauritania) of the French-speaking West African countries.

In the course of a conference on educational reform in the early part of the year, major proposals were put forward for the reorganization and democratization of the country's educational system in order to match it more closely to the nation's cultural values and economic and technical needs. It was agreed that local languages would be used in the early school years, but that a single national language should be used as the language of instruction. Foreign languages would also form an important part of the curriculum, as would modern technological instruction. Professional and technical training centres were envisaged for those wishing to make careers in agriculture, crafts, industry, or commerce. Plans were also advanced for the training of a new kind of teacher who would be able

NIGER

Education. (1970–71) Primary, pupils 88,594, teachers (1968–69) 2,176; secondary, pupils 6,531, teachers (1969–70) 277; vocational, pupils 188, teachers (1969–70) 21; teacher training, students 494, teachers (1969–70) 37.

Finance. Monetary unit: CFA franc, with (Sept. 17, 1973) a parity of CFA Fr. 50 to the French franc (free commercial rate of CFA Fr. 212.55 = U.S. $1; CFA Fr. 512.25 = £1 sterling). Gold, SDRs, and foreign exchange, central bank: (March 1973) U.S. $44.8 million; (March 1972) U.S. $32.2 million. Budget (1971–72 est.) balanced at CFA Fr. 11,886,000,000.

Foreign Trade. (1971) Imports CFA Fr. 14,975,000,000; exports CFA Fr. 10,670,000,000. Import sources: France 39%; West Germany 9%; Ivory Coast 5%. Export destinations: France 70%; Italy 5%; Dahomey 5%. Main exports: peanuts 32%; cattle 16%; peanut oil 9%; cotton 5%.

Transport and Communications. Roads (1972) 6,998 km. Motor vehicles in use (1972): passenger 11,910; commercial 2,200. Telephones (Dec. 1971) 4,000. Radio receivers (Dec. 1971) 150,000.

Agriculture. Production (in 000; metric tons; 1971; 1970 in parentheses): millet 800 (901); sorghum 300 (337); cassava (1970) *c.* 200, (1969) 199; rice 40 (37); peanuts (1972) 270, (1971) 256; dates *c.* 5 (*c.* 5). Livestock (in 000; 1971–72): cattle *c.* 4,400; sheep *c.* 2,800; goats *c.* 6,300.

Nickel:
see Mining

THOMAS A. JOHNSON/THE NEW YORK TIMES

Hungry Hausa children beg a crewman of a Belgian supply plane for food in Tahoua, Niger. By mid-1973 many parts of the southern Sahara country were parched by drought and totally dependent on relief supplies.

to implement the reform program and who would have the necessary skills in teaching modern technology.

Diplomatic relations with Israel were broken off in January. When the fourth Arab-Israeli war broke out in October, the Niger government took a stand in support of the Arab cause. (PHILIPPE DECRAENE)

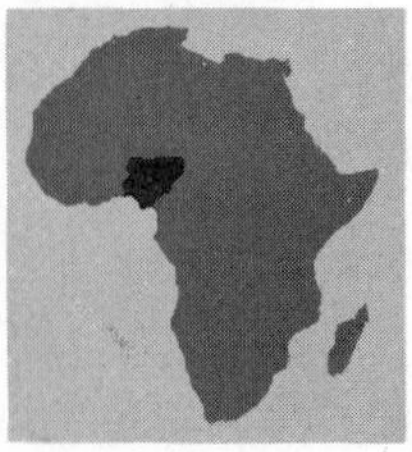

Nigeria

A republic and a member of the Commonwealth of Nations, Nigeria is located in Africa on the north coast of the Gulf of Guinea, bounded by Dahomey, Niger, Chad, and Cameroon. Area: 356,669 sq.mi. (923,768 sq.km.). Pop. (1973 est.): 71,262,000, including: Hausa 21%; Ibo 18%; Yoruba 18%; Fulani 10%. Cap. and largest city: Lagos (pop., 1973 est., 970,262). Language: English (official). Religion (1963): Muslim 47%; Christian 34%. Head of provisional military government in 1973, Gen. Yakubu Gowon.

Nigeria's claim to African leadership as the continent's giant state in terms of population, resources, and land increased with General Gowon's chairmanship of the tenth annual meeting of the Organization of African Unity (OAU) at Addis Ababa, Eth., in May. At the meeting Gowon (*see* BIOGRAPHY) emphasized the need for inter-African cooperation and independence from Europe. The All-Africa Games held in Lagos during January added lustre.

Relations with Britain, cool at first, thawed with British Foreign Secretary Sir Alec Douglas-Home's visit to the largest-ever British trade fair in Lagos in February and warmed with the accolade of a personal invitation from Queen Elizabeth to Gowon to visit London in June, the first such invitation ever extended to a head of state of a Commonwealth country in Africa. Gowon accepted and offered both the queen and Prime Minister Edward Heath return invitations. Emphasizing the value of contact, Gowon lifted his ban on British journalists and urged British support against colonialism as an implicit bargain for Nigerian oil. At the Commonwealth conference in Ottawa in August, the Nigerian leader played an exemplary conciliatory role.

General Gowon's military regime continued to rule without any visible move toward civilian government, promised for 1976. In May Federal Commissioner Gen. Hassan Katsina gave assurances of civilian rule, but they were countered by Minister of Finance A. A. Ayida, who upheld former president Nnamdi Azikiwe's Lagos University speech of October 1972 that suggested a transitional mixed military and senior civil service dyarchy. Under a decree promulgated on July 25, labour union funds might no longer be used to promote political objectives, and it was henceforth an offense for workers to support prospective political candidates. A government commissioner stated that the new law in no way deprived the citizen of his right to form political associations or to belong to political parties when the country returned to civilian rule. A basic political problem remained in the disposal of Africa's largest army, reorganized in February and absorbing a large part of the national budget. In June the new National Youth Corps began conscripting graduates under 30 for their compulsory one year's service.

Because of the controversies that arose during the censuses of 1962 and 1963, the government prepared carefully for the national count in November. General Gowon, launching a publicity campaign in April, emphasized that it was a technical exercise to obtain data for national planning and not for tax assessment. Controversy over centralization continued, as did some pressure for the creation of more states. This was epitomized in resentment over the central educational policy, which covered Nigeria as a whole instead of providing a quota system for the benefit of the North. To counter this an Islam Educational Trust was launched at the beginning of 1973 by the sultan of Sokoto.

The groundwork of Nigerian and African relationships with Europe was laid in London and Brussels during the summer. Nigeria, playing host to 43 countries in Lagos before the Brussels meeting, did not accept any of the three alternatives offered for association but hoped to negotiate trade terms for a united and regionally cooperating Africa.

Nigeria's oil production of some two million bar-

NIGERIA

Education. (1970–71) Primary, pupils 3,515,827, teachers 103,152; secondary, pupils 310,054, teachers 14,091; vocational, pupils 13,645, teachers 845; teacher training, students 32,314, teachers 1,857; higher (universities only; 1971–72), students 17,495, teaching staff 2,628.

Finance. Monetary unit: naira (which replaced the Nigerian pound on Jan. 1, 1973, at the rate of 2 nairas per Nigerian pound), with (Sept. 17, 1973) an official rate of 0.66 naira to U.S. $1 (1.59 nairas = £1 sterling). Gold, SDRs, and foreign exchange, official: (June 1973) U.S. $556 million; (June 1972) U.S. $314 million. Federal budget (1971–72): revenue 1,306,000,000 nairas; expenditure 1,096,000,000 nairas (including 240 million nairas for development). Money supply: (March 1973) 810.7 million nairas; (March 1972) 669.2 million nairas. Cost of living (Lagos; 1963 = 100): (March 1973) 164; (March 1972) 170.

Foreign Trade. (1972) Imports 987.9 million nairas; exports 1,411,500,000 nairas. Import sources: U.K. 29%; West Germany 11%; Japan 10%; U.S. 9%; France 6%. Export destinations: U.K. 17%; U.S. 15%; France 15%; The Netherlands 13%; West Germany 10%. Main exports: crude oil 81%; cocoa 7%.

Transport and Communications. Roads (1971) 89,900 km. Motor vehicles in use (1971): passenger 68,000; commercial (including buses) 44,000. Railways: (1971) 3,505 km.; traffic (1971–72) 963 million passenger-km., freight 1,226,000,000 net ton-km. Air traffic (1971): 280 million passenger-km., freight 7,607,000 net ton-km. Shipping (1972): merchant vessels 100 gross tons and over 56; gross tonnage 99,226. Telephones (Dec. 1971) 87,000. Radio licenses (Dec. 1971) 1.5 million. Television licenses (Dec. 1970) 75,000.

Agriculture. Production (in 000; metric tons; 1972; 1971 in parentheses): millet *c.* 2,800 (*c.* 2,800): sorghum *c.* 3,500 (*c.* 3,500); corn *c.* 1,350 (*c.* 1,220); rice *c.* 550 (580); sweet potatoes (1971) *c.* 13,600, (1970) *c.* 13,500; cassava (1970) *c.* 7,300, (1969) *c.* 6,800; peanuts *c.* 1,100 (*c.* 850); palm oil *c.* 450 (*c.* 500); cocoa (1972–73) 244, (1971–72) 254; cotton, lint *c.* 38 (*c.* 39); rubber (exports) *c.* 51 (50). Livestock (in 000; 1970–71): cattle *c.* 11,600; sheep *c.* 8,100; goats *c.* 23,500; pigs *c.* 840; poultry *c.* 83,000.

Industry. Production (in 000; metric tons; 1972): crude oil 89,777; cement 1,112; tin 6.7; electricity (kw-hr.; 1971) 1,820,000.

rels a day assumed increased importance in international markets as the Arab countries began their program of oil cutbacks and boycotts following the Arab-Israeli war. The country's booming economy was largely dependent on oil (recognized as a wasting asset of about 30 years' duration), currently responsible for the 12% annual rate of growth and for 75% of federal revenues. Moves toward increased local control of petroleum production began in June with a government decree under which Nigeria immediately took over 35% of Shell-British Petroleum share capital, scheduled to rise to 51% by 1982; later demands for an initial 40% of the capital of the Mobil, Gulf, and Texaco operations led to speculation that the government might wish to renegotiate the Shell-BP contract. Nigeria obtained a 12.3% increase in crude oil prices at the Geneva meeting of the Organization of Petroleum Exporting Countries (OPEC) in June, and the posted price was raised substantially late in the year.

(MOLLY MORTIMER)

Nobel Prizes

The Nobel Prize announcements often prompt some grumbling amid the plaudits, but the protests became especially widespread and vigorous when Henry Kissinger and Le Duc Tho jointly won the peace prize in 1973. They were cited for framing the Paris accords that brought an official cease-fire to Vietnam on January 27, an armistice that proved to be a paper truce as continued fighting had claimed about 50,000 lives by the time the prize was announced in October.

Even the two laureates themselves greeted the honour with something less than perfect appreciation. Le Duc Tho, a preeminent member of the North Vietnam Politburo, refused outright to accept the prize, arguing that "peace has not yet really been established" and that the U.S. had waged "a war of aggression against [a reunified] Vietnam." In turn, Kissinger, the world-ranging U.S. troubleshooter who had become secretary of state, announced that the press of business elsewhere would prevent him from attending the award ceremonies in person. An ambassador would represent him.

The dual award was variously greeted in other quarters with anger, disgust, and incredulity. In Paris, *Le Monde* called the matter "a masquerade." In an editorial entitled "Nobel War Prize," the *New York Times* said that the award to the two diplomats "is, at the very least, premature." In Oslo, the dominant Labour Party formally deplored the selections, while two members of the Nobel selection committee protested the majority's choice by resigning. In the U.S. there was speculation that Pres. Richard Nixon, besieged by the Watergate scandal, was miffed at not receiving the award himself; he had been among the twoscore nominees.

In fact, the Kissinger-Le Duc Tho negotiations in Paris were a notable achievement. Meeting in secret over three years, the diplomats found a formula to exchange war prisoners and to end the domestically unpopular involvement of U.S. troops, without making it appear that the U.S. was abandoning an ally. But *U.S. News & World Report* summed up the "built-in irony" of the peace prize being conferred on two "men who successfully negotiated their own nations' short-range goals in Indochina while bringing little or no peace to South Vietnam itself." And the Nobel committee's hope that their aegis might inspire renewed and conclusive peace efforts appeared increasingly vain.

The selection of ten other laureates in literature and the sciences marked some departures from tradition, but hardly radical ones. Three ethologists received the prize for physiology or medicine—the first time that animal behaviourists were so honoured—and the chemistry prize went to two men involved in "pure" chemistry rather than interdisciplinary science. The physiology or medicine award to Konrad Lorenz was criticized because of the racialist views he had espoused during the Nazi period. At the presentation ceremony he said that he now felt deep regret for having held those opinions.

The honorarium for each prize category in 1973 was $122,000, demonstrating the continued improvement in the fortunes of Alfred Nobel's legacy. Baron Stig Ramel's liberal investment policies were responsible for the growth of the estate of dynamite's inventor to an estimated $37 million.

PRIZE FOR PEACE

Henry Kissinger, who succeeded William P. Rogers as U.S. secretary of state in August, was born in Fürth, Ger., on May 27, 1923. His family fled Nazi persecution of Jews in 1938, going first to London and then settling in New York. Kissinger worked his way through high school and had entered a local college to study accounting when he was drafted into the U.S. Army. After intelligence duty in Germany, he entered Harvard University, where he won four scholarships, earned three degrees, and later taught. He worked with the Council on Foreign Relations and wrote influentially on international affairs in the nuclear age.

Though he had counseled another candidate, Kissinger was tapped by Nixon to be a White House assistant after the 1968 election. Among the administration's outstanding achievements, in which Kissinger played a major role, were the opening of diplomatic relations with China and the dramatic improvement of relations with the Soviet Union. In five years Kissinger emerged as a peerlessly effective international conciliator, one who was greatly respected and seemingly endlessly busy. Three weeks after the announcement of the peace prize, he was touring the troubled Middle East, where war had broken out again, and persuading the Arab states and Israel to take the first steps toward a negotiated settlement of their long feud.

The co-winner of the peace prize, Le Duc Tho, was born in what is now North Vietnam in 1912 and joined the anti-French revolutionary youth movement as a teen-ager. By 1929 he was a member of the Indochina Communist Party

UPI COMPIX

Nikolaas Tinbergen, professor of animal behaviour at Oxford University, shared the 1973 Nobel Prize for Physiology or Medicine with two others, all concerned with the study of individual and social behaviour patterns.

UPI COMPIX

Brian Josephson celebrates outside the Cavendish Laboratory at Cambridge University after learning that he shares the 1973 Nobel Prize for Physics with Ivar Giaever of General Electric and Leo Esaki of IBM.

and an effective organizer. Jailed several times by the colonial government, he may have spent World War II in prison, though according to other reports he escaped to join Ho Chi Minh in China. Following the war he was elected to the party's Central Committee and served on its standing committee. He worked in the south during the successful war for independence from the French and later returned north to become a member of the Politburo and secretary of the Vietnam Workers' Party.

PRIZE FOR PHYSIOLOGY OR MEDICINE

A committee of the Karolinska Institutet in Stockholm awarded the prize for physiology or medicine to Konrad Lorenz, Nikolaas Tinbergen, and Karl von Frisch for discoveries "concerning organization and elicitation of individual and social behaviour patterns." While their studies in the young science of ethology involved animals and insects, the results have been extrapolated to human behaviour as well.

Eldest of the trio was Frisch, who was born in Vienna Nov. 22, 1886. After doctoral studies at the University of Vienna and the University of Munich, where he became a zoology professor, he made several discoveries about bees and fish. He proved conclusively for the first time that fish can hear, and bees, he deduced, can distinguish between odours and communicate with each other through a dance language: a scout bee entering its hive moves in a figure eight to announce a distant food source and in a circle to declare a near one. Furthermore, the directional orientation and intensity of his dance indicate the direction of the food and its amount. Frisch demonstrated that the dance patterns are hereditary—bees from one colony cannot dance directions to those from another colony.

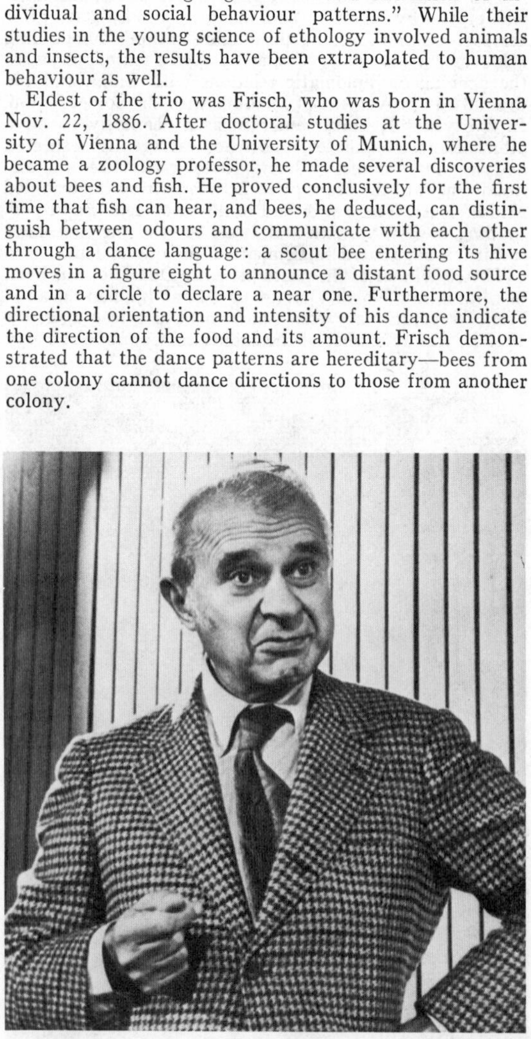

Wassily Leontief, winner of the Nobel Prize for Economics, discusses his theories at a news conference in Cambridge, Mass., Oct. 18, 1973.

WIDE WORLD

Much of Frisch's important work was performed by means of painstaking experiments in the 1920s, 1930s, and 1940s; in 1955 colleagues proved a hypothesis he had suggested 20 years earlier. Five thousand bees flown from France to the Museum of Natural History in New York City continued to conform to a Parisian feeding schedule.

Konrad Lorenz, celebrated as the popular founder of ethology—the study of animal behaviour in natural environments—was born in Vienna Nov. 7, 1903. Son of an orthopedic surgeon, he was steered toward a medical career, studied at Columbia University, and received an M.D. from the University of Vienna in 1928, returning for a Ph.D. in zoology five years later. He taught animal anatomy and psychology and spent four years as a prisoner of the Soviet Union during World War II. After his release the Max Planck Institute built a centre for behavioural physiology for him in Seewiesen, W.Ger.

It was at the centre that Lorenz proved that natural selection imposes some innate behaviour patterns on special animal species. Greylag goslings, for instance, are imprinted to follow the first moving thing they see after hatching. This is usually their mother, but Lorenz substituted balloons, boxes, and even himself to prove his point. *Science News* wrote that his early work inspired research with primates that "has shown that conditions such as isolation or overcrowding can lead to psychotic behavior in adult animals (and humans)." *On Aggression,* Lorenz' most widely read and controversial book, argues that aggression per se is a genetically programmed element in human behaviour.

"One of Nikolaas Tinbergen's most important contributions," the Nobel committee said, "is that he has found ways to test his own and others' hypotheses by means of comprehensive, careful and quite ingenious experiments." Born in The Hague, Neth., April 15, 1907, Tinbergen won a doctorate at the University of Leiden in 1932. According to *Science,* he returned to join the zoology faculty at Leiden when "a seminal meeting with Lorenz in 1936 . . . gave rise to their only joint paper . . . and to more than 30 years of mutual cooperation, criticism, and stimulation that brought the new science of ethology into full flower."

Later Tinbergen, whose brother Jan won the economics prize in 1969, moved to Oxford University, where he established a department of animal behaviour. His work, notably involving the study of seagulls, is described in *The Herring Gull's World, The Study of Instinct,* and *Animal Behavior.* In recent years Tinbergen applied his ethologic theories to human behaviour. Noting that most animals in the wild are deterred from killing their own kind by appeasing gestures or facial expressions on the part of the intended victims, he posited that long-range weapons may have increased man's proclivity for war by freeing him from these natural restraints.

PRIZE FOR CHEMISTRY

"Chemistry for chemists," according to a spokesman for the Swedish Royal Academy of Sciences, was the basis for selecting Ernst Otto Fischer and Geoffrey Wilkinson to win the Nobel Chemistry Prize. In 1951 both read in the journal *Nature* an article about a puzzling synthetic compound called ferrocene. Starting to work independently, they concluded that the material comprised a single iron atom sandwiched between two five-sided carbon rings to form an organometallic molecule. In effect, they explained a previously unknown way in which metals and organic substances can merge. While practical applications of this theoretical work are still scarce, cleaner urban air may be an eventual product. This is because lead may be replaced as a gasoline additive by less toxic metals.

Fischer was born in Munich Nov. 10, 1918. Son of a physics professor at the University of Munich, his own studies were delayed by service in the German Army; he served for a decade in peacetime and throughout World War II. In 1952 he finally received his doctorate from Munich's Technical University, where he became a full professor five years later. From 1959 he headed the university's Institute for Inorganic Chemistry.

Wilkinson, born in England July 14, 1921, was teaching at Harvard University in the early 1950s when he began his investigations of sandwich compounds. In 1955 he returned to the Imperial College of Science and Technology at the University of London, where he himself was trained.

KEYSTONE

Ernst Otto Fischer, head of the Institute for Inorganic Chemistry at Technical University, Munich, W.Ger., shared the 1973 Nobel Prize for Chemistry with Geoffrey Wilkinson, professor of inorganic chemistry at the Imperial College of Science and Technology, London.

PRIZE FOR PHYSICS

The physics prize was awarded for work as practical as the discovery of molecular sandwiches was theoretical. It involved transistors, the often infinitesimally small components that revolutionized electronics by replacing fragile, short-lived, bulky vacuum tubes with tiny, durable, solid components made of semiconductive material. Semiconductor crystals perform in ways that defy the classical rules of physics.

Working for the Sony Corp. in Tokyo, Leo Esaki developed the tunnel diode, which enabled electrical current to do the "impossible" because, as he told a Brussels conference in 1958, electrons can behave either like separate particles or like part of a wavelike chain in order to pass through normally impassable electronic barriers. Norwegian-born Ivar Giaever, in his own words, married "tunneling to superconductivity." Using a sandwich of an insulated piece of superconducting metal and a normal one, he achieved new tunneling effects that led to greater understanding of superconductivity. Then Brian Josephson, a Cambridge University experimenter, calculated the effects if both sides of the sandwich were superconductors. The Josephson effect, an oscillation between the two sides when electrons tunnel in pairs, has been used to measure magnetic fields in space as well as laboratory currents and has achieved previously unattainable accuracy. Half the prize was awarded to Josephson, while Esaki and Giaever divided the remaining half.

Esaki was born in Osaka, Jap., March 12, 1925, and studied at the University of Tokyo, where he earned a doctorate in 1959. By then, as head of an advanced development group at Sony, he had already done the work that won him the prize. He came to the U.S. in 1959 as a consultant to IBM and in 1973 headed a study group at the corporation's Thomas J. Watson Research Center outside New York City. Though residing in the U.S., he retained his Japanese citizenship.

Giaever was born in Bergen, Nor., April 5, 1929. After gaining an electrical engineering degree from the Trondheim Technical High School, he was a patent examiner for his government. In 1954 he emigrated to Canada, where he worked for General Electric, and then transferred to the company's Research and Development Center in Schenectady, N.Y. He earned his doctorate at nearby Rensselaer Polytechnic Institute.

Josephson was a 22-year-old graduate student at Cambridge when he performed the work that won him the prize. Born in Cardiff, Wales, Jan. 4, 1940, he took three degrees at Cambridge, where he became assistant director of research and a reader in physics.

PRIZE FOR LITERATURE

Patrick White "has given the continent of Australia an authentic voice that carries across the world," his Nobel citation read. The first Australian to win the literature prize, White was also the first English-language writer to win in a decade.

Born in London May 28, 1912, he was taken to Australia soon after birth but returned to England for schooling. He earned a degree in modern languages at King's College, Cambridge, in 1935. During World War II he served in the Royal Air Force.

His first novel appeared in 1939 and his latest in 1973. Most of his works focus on people of the Australian outback. In *The Tree of Man,* which describes a dairyman, he said, "I wanted to suggest every possible aspect of life, through the lives of an ordinary man and woman. But at the same time I wanted to discover the extraordinary behind the ordinary." His other novels include *The Eye of the Storm, Happy Valley, The Living and the Dead, The Aunt's Story, Voss,* and *The Vivesector.* He also wrote short stories and plays. His work was compared to that of James Joyce and D. H. Lawrence, whose writings influenced his style, though some Australian critics found him pretentious and unreadable.

PRIZE FOR ECONOMICS

The Bank of Sweden, celebrating an anniversary in 1969, established the Nobel Memorial Prize in Economic Science. Subsequently, it had been awarded to four Americans, three of them Harvard University professors. The 1973 winner was Wassily Leontief from Harvard. Leontief was described as "the sole and unchallenged creator of the input-output technique," a method for studying specific interdependencies within an economy as well as for predicting major trends and the effects of specific events. Using the technique, the effect of a truckers' strike, for instance, can be quantified. Simple in original concept, the technique is complicated in actuality because in order to extrapolate trends or effects, millions of interdependent simultaneous equations must be solved.

By 1973 the technique had been used in 50 countries to study and predict economic trends. The U.S. Department of Commerce made several computer models of the nation's economy using Leontief's process.

Born in Leningrad Aug. 6, 1906, Leontief entered the university there at 15 and earned a doctorate in Berlin seven years later. Having gone to Harvard as an instructor in 1931, he rose to Henry Lee professor of economics and chairman of the elite Society of Fellows.

(PHILIP KOPPER)

Norway

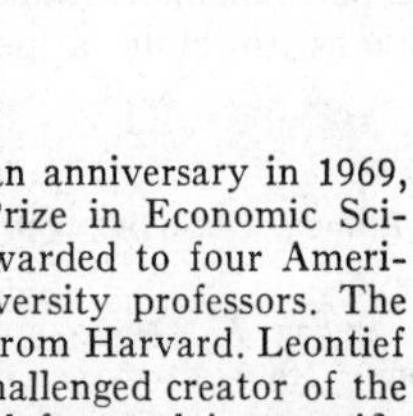

A constitutional monarchy of northern Europe, Norway is bordered by Sweden, Finland, and the U.S.S.R.; its coastlines are on the North Sea, the Norwegian Sea, and the Arctic Ocean. Area: 125,052 sq.mi. (323,886 sq.km.), excluding the Svalbard Archipelago, 23,957 sq.mi., and Jan Mayen Island, 144 sq.mi. Pop. (1973 est.): 3,948,235.

Northern Ireland: *see* United Kingdom

Norwegian Literature: *see* Literature

Nuclear Energy: *see* Defense; Energy; Industrial Review

Numismatics: *see* Philately and Numismatics

Nutrition: *see* Agriculture and Fisheries; Medicine

Nuts: *see* Agriculture and Fisheries

Cap. and largest city: Oslo (pop., 1973 est., 472,609). Language: Norwegian. Religion: Lutheran (96.2%). King, Olav V; prime ministers in 1973, Lars Korvald and, from October 16, Trygve Bratteli.

Throughout most of 1973, Norway was ruled by a three-party anti-EEC "mini coalition" of the Christian People's Party, the Centre (farmers') Party, and the Liberals, formed as a direct result of the popular referendum in September 1972 when the country voted not to join the European Economic Community. With the active support of only about one-quarter of the 150 Storting (parliament) members, the coalition was obliged to pursue middle-of-the-road policies in most fields. It fulfilled its main task, however—the negotiation of a trade pact with the EEC. The pact was signed in Brussels in May, and provided for the gradual reduction of tariffs on industrial goods traded between Norway and the Common Market over a period of four and a half years, with longer transitional periods for certain sensitive products.

The coalition achieved some success in other areas, too. In negotiations with the group led by the Phillips Petroleum Co., which had the development concession for the Ekofisk oil and gas field in Norwegian waters, it secured very favourable terms in return for an agreement to allow oil from the field to be piped to Britain and gas to West Germany. The terms included a 50% stake for Norway in a separate company that would own and operate the gas and oil pipelines, with Phillips owning the other half. Moreover, Phillips agreed to ship back to Norway, at no extra cost, enough natural gas liquids from the field to permit production of 250,000 tons of ethylene a year for 15 years. This would make possible the establishment of a petrochemical industry in Norway. By autumn 1973 plans to build a petrochemical complex based on Ekofisk had been drawn up by the state-controlled industrial concern Norsk Hydro, in cooperation with another leading Norwegian industrial concern, Borregaard. Meanwhile, Norway, in common with other Western European countries, suffered from the effects of reduced oil supplies from Arab countries, and weekend use of automobiles was restricted.

In economic policy the coalition adopted a new approach in its drive to hold down prices. During the spring review of wage rates under the two-year contract concluded in 1972, it managed to persuade the unions to accept only moderate wage increases in return for a government "package" of higher food subsidies and special measures to hold down prices. The government's decision not to devalue the Norwegian krone in February (when the U.S. dollar was devalued) was also partly motivated by anti-inflation considerations.

The worldwide economic revival brought an upsurge in demand for all Norway's exports, and the rapidly expanding offshore oil industry led to increased demand for labour in an already tight labour market. Under these conditions, and with import prices rising, a steady increase in domestic price levels was virtually inevitable. In the 12 months prior to mid-September, prices had risen by 6.7%.

A record number of parties and groups—about 14, some half of which had been founded in the previous ten months or so—put up candidates for the general election in September. Most of the newcomers attracted few votes, but a new antitax party led by an extreme right-winger, Anders Lange, won four seats in the enlarged, 155-member Storting. A newly created "Socialist Alliance" of Communists, Socialist People's Party, and Labour Party dissidents won 16.

Labour, the largest party, suffered severe losses. Its share of the vote fell to 35.5 from 46.6% in the general election four years earlier, and it secured only 62 seats out of 155, compared with 74 out of 150 in the previous Storting. Its losses reflected the strains created when the party's leaders had supported joining the EEC while many of the rank and file had been against it. Of the pre-election coalition partners, Lars Korvald's Christian People's Party increased its parliamentary strength from 14 to 20 seats and the Centre Party from 20 to 21, while the Liberals, who had split into two factions after the EEC referendum, were virtually wiped out.

Despite Labour's losses, Labour and the Socialist Alliance together secured a one-seat majority over the nonsocialist parties in the Storting, and the Labour Party leader, Trygve Bratteli, was given the task of forming a new minority government. It seemed likely that Labour might be forced to adopt more leftist policies than previously in order to retain the backing of the Socialist Alliance—one of whose tenets was opposition to Norwegian membership in NATO.

The decision by the Nobel Committee of the Storting to award the peace prize for 1973 to Henry Kissinger and Le Duc Tho aroused violent controversy in Norway. Two members of the committee who had disagreed with the choice resigned, and many leading political figures condemned the award. A nonparty campaign was launched to award an "alternative" prize to Brazilian Archbishop Helder Camara. (*See* NOBEL PRIZES.)

On July 20 a son was born to Crown Princess Sonja and Crown Prince Harald. Christened Haakon Magnus, he was second in the line of succession to the Norwegian throne. (FAY GJESTER)

NORWAY

Education. (1971–72) Primary (including upper primary), pupils 557,799, teachers 30,899; secondary, pupils 79,542, teachers 4,808; vocational, pupils 66,867, teachers 5,405; teacher training, students 7,939, teachers 735; higher (including 4 universities), students 45,572, teaching staff (1969–70) 4,922.

Finance. Monetary unit: Norwegian krone, with (Sept. 17, 1973) a free rate of 5.52 kroner to U.S. $1 (13.30 kroner = £1 sterling). Gold, SDRs, and foreign exchange, central bank: (June 1973) U.S. $1,497,900,000; (June 1972) U.S. $1,222,100,000. Budget (1973 est.): revenue 26,753,000,000 kroner; expenditure 30,862,000,000 kroner. Gross national product: (1971) 90,190,000,000 kroner; (1970) 80,470,000,000 kroner. Money supply: (June 1973) 22,870,000,000 kroner; (June 1972) 20,260,000,000 kroner. Cost of living (1963 = 100): (June 1973) 172; (June 1972) 159.

Foreign Trade. (1972) Imports 28.8 billion kroner; exports 21,585,000,000 kroner. Import sources: Sweden 19%; West Germany 14%; U.K. 12%; Denmark 7%; U.S. 6%; Japan 5%. Export destinations: U.K. 19%; Sweden 16%; West Germany 13%; U.S. 7%; Denmark 7%. Main exports: ships 16%; machinery 10%; aluminum 9%; fish 8%; iron and steel 7%; chemicals 7%; paper 6%.

Transport and Communications. Roads (1972) 74,177 km. (including 138 km. expressways). Motor vehicles in use (1972): passenger 854,200; commercial 161,600. Railways: (1971) 4,240 km. (including 2,439 km. electrified); traffic (state only; 1972) 1,620,000,000 passenger-km., freight 2,640,000,000 net ton-km. Air traffic (including Norwegian apportionment of international operations of Scandinavian Airlines System; 1972): 2,526,200,000 passenger-km.; freight 90,371,000 net ton-km. Shipping (1972): merchant vessels 100 gross tons and over 2,826; gross tonnage 23,507,108. Ships entered (1971) vessels totaling 16,339,000 net registered tons; goods loaded (1972) 37,493,000 metric tons, unloaded 20,384,000 metric tons. Telephones (Dec. 1971) 1,204,000. Radio licenses (Dec. 1971) 1,204,000. Television licenses (Dec. 1971) 895,000.

Agriculture. Production (in 000; metric tons; 1972; 1971 in parentheses): barley 522 (569); oats 268 (279); potatoes 634 (708); apples (1971) *c.* 50, (1970) 48; milk 1,716 (1,644); butter 20 (19); cheese 56 (54); beef and veal (1971) 56, (1970) 57; pork (1971) 69, (1970) 65; timber (cu.m.; 1971) 9,300, (1970) 7,600; fish catch (1971) 3,075, (1970) 2,980. Livestock (in 000; June 1972): cattle 938; sheep *c.* 1,650; pigs *c.* 700; goats *c.* 80; chickens *c.* 6,000.

Industry. Fuel and power (in 000; metric tons; 1972): crude oil 1,627; coal (Svalbard mines; Norwegian operated only) 455; manufactured gas (cu.m.) 28,900; electricity (kw-hr.) 67,522,000. Production (in 000; metric tons; 1972): iron ore (65% metal content) 3,921; pig iron 1,287; crude steel 916; aluminum 542; zinc 73; copper 26; cement 2,646; sulfuric acid 353; nitrogenous fertilizers (N content: 1971–72) 383; mechanical wood pulp (1970) 1,244; chemical wood pulp (1971) 904; newsprint 534; other paper (1970) 863. Merchant vessels launched (100 gross tons and over; 1972) 829,000 gross tons. New dwelling units completed (1972) 44,000.

Obituaries 1973

The following is a selected list of prominent men and women who died during 1973.

ACKERMAN, EDWARD A., U.S. geographer (b. Post Falls, Ida., Dec. 5, 1911—d. Washington, D.C., March 8, 1973), was a leading authority on water resources and environmental systems. In 1958 he became executive officer of the Carnegie Institution in Washington, held various federal executive and advisory positions, and was an instructor in geography at Harvard University (1940–48) and the University of Chicago (1948–51).

ADRIAN, MAX, British actor (b. Ireland, Nov. 1, 1903—d. Shamley Green, Surrey, Eng., Jan. 19, 1973), whose inimitable voice and style were utilized in a wide variety of roles from revue to the classics, first appeared in a walk-on part at the Globe Theatre, London, in 1927. He portrayed Baron de Charlus in BBC radio's *Proust Reconstructions* and in 1967 put on a one-man show based on the nondramatic writings of George Bernard Shaw.

AIKEN, CONRAD POTTER, U.S. poet and prose writer (b. Savannah, Ga., Aug. 5, 1889—d. Savannah, Aug. 17, 1973), won the Pulitzer Prize in 1930 for *Selected Poems.* Other honours included the National Book Award in 1954, the Bollingen Prize in 1956, the Gold Medal for poetry of the National Institute of Arts and Letters in 1958, and the National Medal for Literature in 1969. Aiken, whose writings were influenced by Sigmund Freud and Henry James, was a close friend of T. S. Eliot and Ezra Pound, but never matched them in popular success.

ALLENDE GOSSENS, SALVADOR, Chilean political leader (b. Santiago, Chile, July 26, 1908—d. Santiago, Sept. 11, 1973), first freely elected Marxist president in the Western Hemisphere, was long active in national politics, particularly as president of Chile's Senate. Allende, presidential candidate of the Unidad Popular, a coalition of left-wing parties, won over two opponents with 36.3% of the vote in the September 1970 presidential elections and was victorious in the required runoff election in the Chilean Congress, where he won 153 of the 200 available votes. He encountered stiff resistance, nevertheless, in achieving his goal of "socialism with a human face." Policies aimed at equalizing income and land distribution were established at the expense of middle-class voters, prompting work slowdowns by professional workers and virulent terrorist activities by the right wing. By October 1972 civil disorders and the withdrawal of international credit had severely damaged the Chilean economy, but in the March 1973 congressional elections the UP won 44% of the vote. Antigovernment terrorism escalated during the summer of 1973 to include the assassination of President Allende's aide-de-camp as well as lesser figures. The death of Allende, during a concerted military attack on the presidential palace, marked the end of Chile's democratic government and was followed by the installation of a military junta.

ALLSOP, KENNETH, British journalist and broadcaster (b. Yorkshire, Eng., Jan. 29, 1920—d. West Milton, Dorset, Eng., May 23, 1973), became known to British television audiences after joining the BBC current affairs series "Tonight" in 1960. From 1965 until 1972 he was a lead commentator on its successor, "24 Hours," and was then seen on "Down to Earth," a series on the environment. He was rector of Edinburgh University (1968–71).

ANCERL, KAREL, Czechoslovakian conductor (b. Tucapy, Bohemia [now Czechoslovakia], April 11, 1908—d. Toronto, Ont., July 3, 1973), became music director and conductor of the Toronto Symphony Orchestra in 1968 after serving for 17 years as director of the Czech Philharmonic.

ANDERSON, SIR DONALD FORSYTH, British shipowner (b. Sept. 3, 1906—d. March 20, 1973), became managing director and chairman (1960–71) of the Peninsular and Oriental Steam Navigation Co., the largest independent shipping concern in the world. He was chairman of the Shipping Federation, joint chairman of the National Maritime Board, and president of the International Shipping Federation (1950–62); president of the British Chamber of Shipping, and chairman of the General Council of British Shipping (1953–54). Under his leadership the British shipping industry in the 1960s entered on a vigorous program of modernization and diversification. He was knighted in 1954.

ARMSTRONG, HAMILTON FISH, U.S. journalist and authority on international politics (b. New York, N.Y., April 7, 1893—d. New York, April 24, 1973), was a founder and managing editor (1922–28) of the quarterly *Foreign Affairs* and the editor from 1928 until his retirement in 1972. An adviser to the U.S. State Department during World War II, Armstrong attended the 1945 San Francisco conference that drafted the United Nations Charter.

ARNOUX, ALEXANDRE, French author (b. Digne, France, Feb. 27, 1884—d. Paris, France, Jan. 5, 1973), was treasurer of the Académie Goncourt, of which he became a member in 1947. His writings span the gamut of literature from poetry to novels, essays, memoirs, travelogues, translations, plays, and filmscripts.

ARTSIMOVICH, LEV ANDREEVICH, Soviet physicist (b. Moscow, Russia, Feb. 25, 1909—d. U.S.S.R., March 1, 1973), was a world leader of research into controlled thermonuclear reactions and overall organizer of physical and astronomical research in the U.S.S.R. At 21 he began work on nuclear and particle physics at the Leningrad Physical-Technical Institute. After World War II he led a successful electromagnetic isotope separation project and in the early 1950s conducted primary investigations into the high temperature state of matter in electrical discharges, leading to the evolution of plasma confinement in "Tokamak" devices (use of which became widespread). Artsimovich was elected to the Soviet Academy of Sciences in 1953.

AUDEN, W(YSTAN) H(UGH), naturalized U.S. poet (b. York, Eng., Feb. 21, 1907—d. Vienna, Aus., Sept. 28, 1973), an outstanding poet whose theme, the striving after virtue and love, was expressed in a variety of metres and forms, usually by appeal to the intelligence. He wrote songs, ballads, light verse, plays, libretti (notably for Igor Stravinsky's opera *The Rake's Progress* [1951]), and also film commentaries and travel books. He began writing poetry at the age of 15, first under the influence of Thomas Hardy and Walter de la Mare and later under that of T. S. Eliot; but the profoundest influence upon his verse was that of Anglo-Saxon and Middle English poetry. His first published book of verse, *Poems* (1930), was an immediate success and was followed by *The Orators* (1932), *The Dance of Death* (1933), *Look Stranger!* (1936), *Another Time* (1940), and by a series of plays written in collaboration with Christopher Isherwood: *The Dog Beneath the Skin* (1935), *The Ascent of F6* (1936), and *On The Frontier* (1938). In 1937 he received the King's Gold Medal for Poetry.

Salvador Allende Gossens

WIDE WORLD

In 1939 Auden went to the U.S. and later took U.S. nationality. His religious development, under the influence of Kierkegaard and Reinhold Niebuhr, was expressed in *New Year Letter* (1941), *For the Time Being* (1944), and *The Age of Anxiety* (1947), for which he was awarded a Pulitzer Prize. Collections of his later poetry include *The Shield of Achilles* (1955), *Homage to Clio* (1960), *About the House* (1966), and *City Without Walls* (1969). He was also a wide-ranging and scholarly critic of literature, whose fresh and illuminating views were exemplified in *The Enchafèd Flood* (1950) and *The Dyer's Hand* (1962). His autobiography, *A Certain World: A Commonplace Book,* was published in 1970. In 1956 he was appointed professor of poetry at Oxford, where in 1972 he settled within the precincts of his old college, Christ Church.

AULAQI, SALEH AL-, Yemenite political leader (b. 1938—d. Aden, April 30, 1973), was foreign minister of Yemen (Aden) since 1969. A former trade union leader at the British Petroleum refinery, secretary of the Labour Federation in Aden, and a prominent member of the National Liberation Front before independence in 1967, he was minister of defense in the country's first Cabinet and later minister of social affairs.

BACH, STEFAN JOSEPH, British biochemist (b. 1898—d. March 22, 1973), a lecturer at the School of Biochemistry, Cambridge (1935–50), and first reader in the biochemistry department of Bristol University until 1965, gained an international reputation for his work on the metabolism of amino acids. He spent many years in cancer research.

BAKER, JOHN HOPKINSON, U.S. naturalist and conservationist (b. Cambridge, Mass., June 30, 1894—d. Bedford, Mass., Sept. 21, 1973), was chief executive officer and president of the National Audubon Society for 25 years until his retirement in 1959.

BARNES, SIDNEY GEORGE, Australian cricketer (b. Queensland, Austr., 1916—d. Dec. 16, 1973), represented his country in first-class test matches during the 1940s. He reached his peak after World War II, forming with Arthur Morris a brilliant first-wicket partnership. During his career in first-class cricket he scored over 8,000 runs and hit 26 hundreds.

BARSACQ, ANDRÉ, French stage designer, director, and theatre manager (b. Theodosia, Crimea, Russia, Jan. 24, 1909—d. Paris, France, Feb. 3, 1973), studied under Charles Dullin at the Atelier Theatre in Montmartre, where he made his debut as designer of an outstanding production of Ben Jonson's *Volpone* (1928). In 1937 he was a co-founder of the Quatre Saisons company, which subsequently played for two seasons at the French Theatre in New York, and in 1940 he succeeded Dullin as director of the Atelier. There he staged a long series of notable productions, particularly of Jean Anouilh's plays, including the controversial wartime *Antigone* (1944).

BATISTA Y ZALDÍVAR, FULGENCIO, Cuban military leader and politician (b. Banes, Cuba, Jan. 16, 1901—d. Guadalmina, Spain, Aug. 6, 1973), was among the leaders of a military coup that installed a new provisional president on Sept. 4, 1933. During the following years Batista was always near the centre of power until his own election as president in 1940. Forbidden by law to run for reelection in 1944, he left Cuba for voluntary exile in Florida when his chosen candidate was defeated at the polls. Anxious to regain power, he returned to Cuba in 1948 and shortly before the 1952 elections seized control of the government. Though his regime was responsible for many social reforms, it was denounced as dictatorial and corrupt. On New Year's Day 1959, when it became apparent that rebel forces under Fidel Castro could not be contained, Batista fled to the Dominican Republic and eventually to permanent exile in Portugal.

BAZZAZ, ABDUL RAHMAN AL-, former Iraqi prime minister (b. Baghdad, Iraq, 1913—d. Baghdad, June 28, 1973), was dean of the Baghdad Law School (1955–56) and president of the Court of Cassation after the coup that ousted the monarchy in 1959. He fell afoul of the president, Gen. Abdul Karim Kassem, in 1960, and after a brief imprisonment retired to Cairo. Early in 1963, after Kassem's murder, he returned to Iraq and began a diplomatic career. In 1964 he also became secretary-general of the Organization of Petroleum Exporting Countries (OPEC). In 1965 he resumed government service until the fall of the Abdul Razzak government in 1967. Forced out of office, he was arrested, and in July 1969 it was announced that he was to be tried with 19 others on a charge of conspiracy to overthrow the government. He was released in 1970.

BEAUMONT, HUGH, British theatrical manager and producer (b. South Wales, March 27, 1908—d. London, Eng., March 22, 1973), was for many years an influential figure in the British theatre world. He was managing director of H. M. Tennent Ltd. and of Tennent Productions Ltd., director of the London Pavilion, and governor of the Shakespeare Memorial Theatre from 1950. He was a member of the National Theatre Board (1962–68).

BEHRMAN, S(AMUEL) N(ATHANIEL), U.S. playwright (b. Worcester, Mass., June 9, 1893—d. New York, N.Y., Sept. 9, 1973), was an acknowledged master of sophisticated comedy, whose more than two dozen plays delighted intellectual audiences with their clever conversation and mordant wit. Behrman's first play appeared in 1927. After moving to Hollywood Behrman prepared more than a dozen scripts, mostly for Fox and M-G-M. Greta Garbo, one of his favourites, starred in *Anna Karenina* (1935), for which Behrman adapted the dialogue from Tolstoi's book, and in *Two Faced Woman* (1942), one of Behrman's original screenplays.

BEMIS, SAMUEL FLAGG, authority on U.S. diplomatic history (b. Worcester, Mass., Oct. 20, 1891—d. Bridgeport, Conn., Sept. 26, 1973), was recipient of two Pulitzer Prizes and a member of the Yale University faculty from 1935 until his mandatory retirement at age 68. In 1927 he received the Pulitzer award for *Pickney's Treaty: A Study of America's Advantage from Europe's Distress* and in 1950 for the biography *John Quincy Adams and the Foundations of American Foreign Policy.*

BEN-GURION, DAVID (David Gruen), Israeli statesman and scholar (b. Plonsk, Russian Poland, Oct. 16, 1886—d. Tel Aviv, Israel, Dec. 1, 1973), prime minister of Israel from its creation in 1948 until 1953 and again from 1955 to 1963, was a founder of the state of Israel and for many Jews its symbol. At 20 Ben-Gurion settled in Palestine as a farm labourer, intent on re-creating a Jewish state. Refusing to accept Ottoman citizenship during World War I, he went to the U.S., where he founded the Labour Zionist party Poale Zion and the pioneer movement Hechalutz. Returning to Palestine as a soldier in the British forces in 1918, he became chairman of the Palestine branch of the Jewish Agency and helped form the Histadrut (the General Federation of Jewish Labour), which was to become the nucleus of the nascent socialist state under the British mandate. In 1930 he founded the Palestine Labour Party (Mapai) and, displacing Chaim Weizmann's quiet diplomacy, was its activist leader until 1965. He formed the Jewish self-defense organization, Haganah, which later became the nucleus of Israel's army. After UN approval of a Jewish state, Ben-Gurion proclaimed the independence of Israel in Tel Aviv on May 14, 1948. Diplomatic recognition was widely granted, first by the U.S. and the U.S.S.R. As the country's first prime minister, Ben-Gurion immediately took over the Ministry of Defense and successfully repelled Arab forces that attacked the fledgling state. At the same time the state settled some 700,000 Jewish refugees from Arab lands, who entered the country largely destitute. In 1953 he resigned and retired to his Negev kibbutz, Sede Boqer, in the southern desert.

In February 1955 he was recalled as defense minister and again became prime minister after the third general election. Acting in cooperation with Britain and France, Ben-Gurion launched the Israeli Army on a five-day campaign that won the Sinai Peninsula in 1956 and gained assurances of free navigation in the Gulf of Aqaba and the stationing of a UN force on the Sinai and Gaza frontiers.

In June 1963 he retired to devote himself to writing and reading. He constantly urged the need for understanding with Israel's Arab neighbours and with the Soviet colossus in the north, but he did not live to see peace.

BENTON, WILLIAM, publisher and chairman of *Encyclopædia Britannica* (b. Minneapolis, Minn., April 1, 1900—d. New York, N.Y., March 18, 1973), who in business, education, and national and international affairs acted with imagination, energy, and sufficient persistence to see many of his innovations become contributions of lasting value.

Raised on homestead land in Montana, he graduated from Yale University in 1921 and entered advertising. With Chester Bowles he founded the agency of Benton and Bowles in 1929 and by 1935, in spite of the Great Depression, had made it one of the six largest firms of its kind in the world.

In 1937 Benton was appointed vice-president of the University of Chicago, having sold his interest in advertising, and there became one of the young administrative officers who gave the university unparalleled vitality under Pres. Robert M. Hutchins. While an officer of the university in 1942, he helped organize the Committee for Economic Development and dedicated himself to the task of acquiring *Encyclopædia Britannica* as a gift to the school. The university accepted the gift in 1943 and committed the management and stock control to Benton, retaining a royalty arrangement that, by 1974, had produced some $46 million in revenue for the university.

In 1945 Benton resigned from the university to become U.S. assistant secretary of state. He organized the first major U.S. program for peacetime international information and educational exchanges, saved the Voice of America broadcasts from threatened extinction, established the United States information offices, and promoted international visits of professors and students. He also led U.S. participation in organizing the United Nations Educational, Scientific and Cultural Organization (UNESCO), which he later served as U.S. representative to its Executive Board with the rank of ambassador for a six-year term that ended in 1969. In 1947 he resigned his State Department post and in 1949 accepted an appointment as U.S. senator from Connecticut. In the Senate, at the height of Sen. Joseph R. McCarthy's power, he led the attack on McCarthyism with a courage unusual in politicians of the time.

Benton was defeated for reelection in the Eisenhower landslide of 1952, and thereafter divided his energies between numerous educational and public interests and the affairs of Encyclopædia Britannica, Inc. In the latter capacity he acquired Encyclopædia Britannica Films (now Encyclopædia Britannica Educational Corp.); published *Great Books of the Western World,* the *Enciclopedia Barsa* in Spanish, and the *Enciclopédia Barsa* in Portuguese; purchased *Compton's Pictured Encyclopedia;* acquired the G. & C. Merriam Co., dictionary publishers, and Frederick A. Praeger, Inc., book publishers; and expanded Britannica's operations throughout the world, establishing sales and editorial branches in many countries.

William Benton's contributions to the 15th edition of *Britannica,* to be published in 1974, were incalculable; very simply, this freshly written and totally restructured new encyclopaedia could not have been created without his unwavering commitment of time and resources.

BERTRAND, JEAN-JACQUES, Canadian politician (b. Ste.-Agathe-des-Monts, Que., June 10, 1916—d. Montreal, Que., Feb. 22, 1973), was premier of Quebec (1968–70) in the Union Nationale administration, after being provincial minister of justice from 1966. One of his first moves as premier was to propose that Canada cease to be a monarchy and become a republic within the Commonwealth of Nations.

BIBESCO, PRINCESS MARTHE, Romanian-born writer who wrote in French (b. Bucharest, Rom., Jan. 28, 1888—d. Paris, France, Nov. 29, 1973), published her first work, *Les Huits Paradis,* at 18. It dealt with her travels in Iran, and was acclaimed by the French Academy. Other books included *Catherine-Paris,* the first modern French novel selected by the U.S. Literary Guild, *Isvor: The Country of Willows, Au bal avec Marcel Proust, La Nymphe d'Europe,* and *Le Confesseur et Les Poètes.* She was a member of the Royal Belgian Academy.

BIKILA, ABEBE, Ethiopian long-distance runner (b. 1927—d. Oct. 25, 1973), was the first African athlete to make his mark in the Olympic Games, winning the marathon in 1960 in Rome (while a member of the household guard of Emperor Haile Selassie) and again four years later in Tokyo, this time breaking the world record five weeks after having had his appendix removed. In 1969 he was paralyzed in a car accident; though confined to a wheelchair, he took up archery and competed in the paraplegic Olympics.

BISHOP, MORRIS, U.S. scholar and author (b. April 15, 1893—d. Ithaca, N.Y., Nov. 20, 1973), whose whimsical verse delighted readers of *The New Yorker* and other publications, wrote highly acclaimed biographies of Pascal, La Rochefoucauld, Ronsard, and Samuel de Champlain; he published more than 400 works in all, 15 of them books. He was associated with Cornell University from 1921, first as a graduate student (Ph.D. 1926), then as an instructor and finally professor of Romance languages. In 1948 Bishop was instrumental in obtaining a position at Cornell for Vladimir Nabokov.

BLACKMER, SIDNEY, U.S. stage, film, and television actor (b. Salisbury, N.C., July 13, 1895—d. New York, N.Y., Oct. 6, 1973), was a founder of the Actors Equity Association, on the executive board of the American Federation of Television and Radio Artists, and president of the Theater Authority, which clears all benefit performances. Blackmer appeared in more than 40 Broadway plays, 200 movies, and numerous television dramas. In 1950 he won the Donaldson and

David Ben-Gurion

William Benton

CAMERA PRESS/PICTORIAL PARADE

Tony awards as best actor of the season for his portrayal of an alcoholic husband in *Come Back, Little Sheba*. His last major film role was in *Rosemary's Baby* (1968).

BONDARENKO, FYODOR, Soviet lieutenant general (b. 1918—d. Moscow, U.S.S.R., Oct. 13, 1973), was commander in chief of Soviet antiaircraft rocket forces. The *Red Star* stated that he died "tragically," and it was later disclosed that he was killed in an air crash in the U.S.S.R. This disclosure was issued apparently in order to silence speculation that he had been killed in an Israeli bombing raid on Syria during the Arab-Israeli war in October.

BONNET, GEORGES ÉTIENNE, former French foreign minister (b. Bassillac, France, July 23, 1889—d. Paris, France, June 18, 1973), was a leading advocate of appeasement of Nazi Germany immediately before World War II and a creator of the Munich agreement of 1938, which prepared the way for Germany to occupy Czechoslovakia. Entering politics in 1924, he served in no less than 12 governments, four times as minister of finance, and was for a time French ambassador to Washington. He became foreign minister in the Radical-Socialist government of Édouard Daladier in April 1938 but was dismissed on the outbreak of World War II. A member of the National Council of the Vichy government, he exonerated himself in political memoirs after the war and was elected a deputy for Dordogne in 1956–58 and for Nontron in 1958, being reelected in 1962.

BONTEMPS, ARNA WENDELL, U.S. poet and critic (b. Alexandria, La., Oct. 13, 1902—d. Nashville, Tenn., June 4, 1973), was a leading figure in the Harlem Renaissance, a black literary movement of the 1920s. He received his B.A. (1923) from Pacific Union College in Angwin, Calif., and his M.A. (1943) from the University of Chicago. He was librarian at Fisk University, Nashville (1943–65), and professor at the University of Chicago (1966–69). In 1969 he was appointed lecturer and curator in the Beinecke Rare Book and Manuscript Library at Yale University, and in 1970 he was named writer in residence at Fisk. Among Bontemps' many works were the anthologies *The Poetry of the Negro, 1746–1949* (1949) and *The Book of Negro Folklore* (1958), both with Langston Hughes; a number of novels including *God Sends Sunday* (1931), *Black Thunder* (1936), *Chariot in the Sky* (1951), and *Great Slave Narratives* (1969); and biographies of Frederick Douglass and George Washington Carver. He was a critic for the *Saturday Review* and *The American Scholar*. Bontemps was awarded the *Crisis* Poetry Prize and the Alexander Pushkin Prize, both in 1926, and the Jane Addams Children's Book Award in 1956.

BOWEN, ELIZABETH DOROTHEA COLE, Anglo-Irish novelist (b. Dublin, Ire., June 7, 1899—d. London, Eng., Feb. 22, 1973), was among the most distinguished writers of her day. Her acute sensibility to place and atmosphere were best expressed in *The Death of the Heart* (1938) and *The Heat of the Day* (1949); the latter and the short stories collected in *The Demon Lover* (1945) portrayed life in London during World War II. Her first novel, *The Hotel,* appeared in 1927 and was followed by *To the North* (1932) and *The House in Paris* (1935). Among her nonfiction writings were *A Time in Rome* (1960) and *Collected Impressions* (1950). She was made a Companion of Literature in 1965.

BOWEN, IRA SPRAGUE, U.S. astronomer (b. Seneca Falls, N.Y., Dec. 21, 1898—d. Los Angeles, Calif., Feb. 6, 1973), was director of joint operations of the Palomar and Mount Wilson observatories in California from 1948 until his retirement in 1964. He joined the staff of the California Institute of Technology in 1921, and while there helped to plan the 200-in. Hale telescope on Palomar Mountain and directed its final testing. Bowen helped design other large telescopes, including the 120-in. reflector at Lick Observatory, California, and the 84-in. reflector at Kitt Peak National Observatory near Tucson, Ariz.

BRASCH, CHARLES, New Zealand poet (b. Dunedin, N.Z., July 27, 1909—d. May 1973), in 1947 launched *Landfall,* a literary journal that gained an international reputation and influenced New Zealand's cultural life.

BRETSCHER, EGON, Swiss-born nuclear physicist (b. Zürich, Switz., May 23, 1901—d. Zürich, April 16, 1973), was head of the nuclear physics division of the Atomic Energy Research Establishment (1948–66) in Britain. From 1939 until 1944 he lectured in nuclear physics at Cambridge University, and thereafter for two years was a member of the British mission to the Los Alamos Laboratory, N.M., where the first nuclear weapons were produced. He headed the AERE chemistry division (1947–48).

BROOKEBOROUGH, BASIL STANLAKE BROOKE, 1st Viscount, prime minister of Northern Ireland, 1943–63 (b. Northern Ireland, June 9, 1888—d. Belfast, N.Ire., Aug. 18, 1973), was an Anglo-Irish aristocrat whose inflexible belief in the Protestant ascendancy helped bring about the bitter violence that prevailed after 1969. He became a senator in the first Northern Ireland Parliament in 1921 but retired the next year in order to become commandant of the Special Constabulary in County Fermanagh. In 1929 he was elected to the constituency of Lisnaskea, which he served through five more general elections until 1968. He was minister of agriculture (1933–41) and of commerce (1941–45).

BROWDER, EARL RUSSELL, U.S. Communist leader (b. Wichita, Kan., May 20, 1891—d. Princeton, N.J., June 27, 1973), was general secretary of the Communist Party of the United States during the years of the party's greatest influence and growth, from 1930 until 1945. A member of various radical movements before World War I, Browder opposed U.S. entry into the war and was jailed for failing to register under the draft law. He became an honorary member of the U.S. Communist Party, legally formed in 1921 as the Workers' Party of America, and headed a trade union delegation of non-Communists to the first congress of the Red International of Labor Unions in Moscow.

After the dissolution of the Communist International (Comintern) during the period of the Soviet-Western alliance against Hitler, the Communist Party in the U.S. was dissolved in 1943 and replaced by the Communist Political Association with Browder as its head. He came under criticism when Moscow resumed its hard anti-Western line after World War II, was ousted as party leader in 1945, and in 1946 was thrown out of the Communist Party.

BROWN, JOE E., U.S. comedian (b. Holgate, O., July 28, 1892—d. Brentwood, Calif., July 6, 1973), whose elastic-mouth grin was his trademark, began a Broadway career in *Listen, Lester* in 1918. After a number of stage successes he turned to motion pictures in 1928, appearing in *Crooks Can't Win*. Brown made over 50 films in all, including *Hollywood Canteen* (1945) and *Some Like It Hot* with Marilyn Monroe (1959).

BRUNOT, ANDRÉ GILBERT FRANÇOIS, French actor (b. Prémery, France, Oct. 3, 1879—d. Paris, France, Aug. 3, 1973), was associated with the Comédie Française in a career spanning over 50 years. Among his roles were Scapin, Figaro, Don César de Bazan, Crespin, and Cyrano de Bergerac. He was professor of dramatic art at the National Conservatory (1934–46) and later joined the Madeleine Renaud–Jean-Louis Barrault company. His films included *Hôtel du Nord, Le Comte de Monte-Cristo, Le Rouge et le Noir,* and *La Nuit blanche.*

BUCK, PEARL COMFORT SYDENSTRICKER (Mrs. Richard J. Walsh), U.S. author (b. Hillsboro, W.Va., June 26, 1892—d. Danby, Vt., March 6, 1973), winner of the Nobel and Pulitzer prizes for literature, spent almost half her life in China and depicted the people and culture of that country in much of her work. As an infant she was taken to China by her missionary parents and was educated by Chinese tutors. At age 16 she entered Randolph-Macon Woman's College in Lynchburg, Va. After graduating in 1914, she returned to China and in 1917 married John Lossing Buck, an agricultural missionary.

Her first fiction piece, *A Chinese Woman Speaks,* appeared in *Asia Magazine* in 1926. *East Wind: West Wind,* her first novel, was published in 1930; it was followed in 1931 by her most widely read book, *The Good Earth,* awarded the 1932 Pulitzer Prize and translated into 30 languages. The screen adaptation starred Paul Muni and Luise Rainer, who received an Academy Award for her portrayal of O-lan. *Sons* (1932) and *A House Divided* (1935) completed *The Good Earth* trilogy. In 1936 Miss Buck published biographies of her mother, *The Exile,* and father, *Fighting Angel.* In all, she wrote more than 85 novels, short stories, children's stories, and nonfiction works. In 1938 she was awarded the Nobel Prize for Literature "for rich and genuine epic portrayals of Chinese life, and for masterpieces of biography."

Deeply interested in children's welfare, in 1949 she founded Welcome House to provide for the children of Asian mothers and U.S. servicemen, and in 1964 organized the Pearl S. Buck Foundation of Philadelphia, also to aid Amerasian youth.

BUCK, TIM, Canadian Communist leader (b. Beccles, Eng., 1890?—d. Cuernavaca, Mex., March 11, 1973), a founder (1921) of the Communist Party of Canada, was head of the party from 1929 until 1972.

BUDENNY, SEMYON MIKHAILOVICH, marshal of the Soviet Union (b. Kozyurin, near Rostov-on-Don, Russia, April 25, 1883—d. Moscow, U.S.S.R., Oct. 27, 1973), son of a Cossack farmer, fought in the Russo-Japanese War (1904–05) and in World War I before joining the Communist side after the Revolution of October 1917. His fame as a soldier grew with successive military campaigns. Budenny joined the Communist Party in 1919 and was inspector of cavalry from 1924 to 1937. When Stalin created the rank of marshal of the Soviet Union for five senior officers, Budenny was one of them. Appointed commander in chief of the southwestern front in June 1941, he disastrously failed to contain the German offensives round Kiev and was relieved of his command, but as a loyal friend of Stalin he escaped the consequences. After World War II Budenny was a much-decorated figurehead. In 1958 he was made a Hero of the Soviet Union and published his autobiography.

BURON, ROBERT GASTON ALBERT, French politician and journalist (b. Paris, France, Feb. 27, 1910—d. Paris, April 28, 1973), was a founder of the Popular Republican Movement (MRP) and a member of many French governments. A lawyer by profession, in 1944 he became general administrator of Radiodiffusion Française. He was MRP deputy for Mayenne (1946–58), and from 1959 to 1962 minister of public works and transport under Michel Debré and Georges Pompidou. He was on the negotiating team at Évian-les-Bains that ended the Algerian war. In 1962 he resigned from the government in protest against Charles de Gaulle's apparent chauvinism. He was president of the Organization for Economic Cooperation and Development (1963–67). He joined the Socialist Party in 1971.

BURROWS, SIR FREDERICK JOHN, British railway worker and governor of Bengal (b. Hert-

Pearl Buck

A.G.I.P./PICTORIAL PARADE

fordshire, Eng., 1887—d. Ross-on-Wye, Eng., April 20, 1973), was elected president of the National Union of Railwaymen in 1942 and attracted the attention of Winston Churchill, who selected him as a Labour delegate to the Soulbury Ceylon constitutional commission in 1945. In 1946 he was appointed governor of Bengal, where he won the trust and admiration of the people and helped make the transition to independence in that region a relatively peaceful one.

CABRAL, AMILCAR, Portuguese Guinean nationalist leader (b. Bafata, Portuguese Guinea, 1926—d. Conakry, Republic of Guinea, Jan. 20, 1973), was secretary-general of the African Party for the Independence of Guinea and Cape Verde (PAIGC), of which he was a co-founder in 1956. He also helped form the Popular Movement for the Liberation of Angola (MPLA). Under his leadership PAIGC in 1963 initiated one of the most successful of the guerrilla campaigns against Portuguese colonial power in Africa and Cabral was widely recognized as one of the continent's ablest political leaders. In 1972, following elections in PAIGC-controlled areas of Portuguese Guinea, he established a Guinean People's National Assembly as a step toward independence. Cabral was assassinated, allegedly by a group of PAIGC malcontents.

CADE, SIR STANFORD (born KADINSKY), British surgeon (b. St. Petersburg, Russia, March 22, 1895—d. Portsmouth, Eng., Sept. 19, 1973), an acknowledged authority on the treatment of cancer by surgery and various forms of radiation, was elected in 1924 to the surgical staff of Westminster Hospital, London, later becoming surgeon to the Radium Institute and Mount Vernon Hospital. In 1927 he collaborated with Arthur Evans in a paper on the treatment of cancer of the tongue by radium. During World War II he served as consulting surgeon to the RAF and in 1940 published the first edition of what became a standard work, *Malignant Disease and Its Treatment by Radium*. In 1949 he was elected to the Council of the Royal College of Surgeons and in 1958 was elected president of the International Cancer Congress held in London.

CALWELL, ARTHUR AUGUSTUS, Australian politician (b. Melbourne, Austr., Aug. 28, 1896—d. Melbourne, July 8, 1973), was Labor opposition leader in Parliament from 1960 to 1967. He entered the House of Representatives in Canberra in 1940 and was appointed Australia's first minister for immigration in 1945. In 1961 he led the Labor Party into the general election against Robert Menzies' Liberal-Country Party and reduced its majority from 32 to 1. In 1966 Calwell suffered a record electoral defeat by Harold Holt.

CAREY, JAMES BARRON, U.S. labour leader (b. Philadelphia, Pa., Aug. 12, 1911—d. Silver Springs, Md., Sept. 11, 1973), was the founder of the 285,000-member International Union of Electrical Workers and its first president. Carey held numerous major positions in labour organizations and served in government posts under Presidents Franklin D. Roosevelt and Harry S. Truman.

CARMICHAEL, LEONARD, U.S. psychologist, educator, and author (b. Philadelphia, Pa., Nov. 9, 1898—d. Washington, D.C., Sept. 16, 1973), was president of Tufts College, Medford, Mass., for 14 years before being named head of the Smithsonian Institution in 1953. He retired in 1964 to join the National Geographic Society as vice-president for research and exploration and remained there until the time of his death. Carmichael brought new vitality and prestige to the Smithsonian by building the Museum of History and Technology and adding two wings to the Museum of Natural History. The lively exhibits that he initiated eventually attracted more than ten million visitors a year. He earlier edited and compiled *Manual of Child Psychology*, a classic in its field. In recognition of his lifelong scholarship, Macrobius A, a bright moon crater, was renamed after him.

CARRERO BLANCO, LUIS, admiral, Spanish Navy (b. Santoña, Spain, March 4, 1903—d. Madrid, Spain, Dec. 20, 1973), longest-standing associate of Gen. Francisco Franco's regime and the most loyal interpreter of his policies, had been named by Franco to succeed him as head of government, which post he took over in June 1973. Carrero was assassinated, allegedly by the Basque underground movement. He became a naval cadet in 1918 and during 1924–26 took part in the Rif war in Morocco. In 1935 he was appointed an instructor at the Naval War School in Madrid. When the Civil War began he went into hiding, emerging in 1937 as a supporter of the nationalists. In 1941 he was brought into Franco's inner circle and became his private secretary. He was made an admiral in 1966. Carrero urged the reinstitution of the Spanish monarchy and the naming of Prince Juan Carlos de Borbón y Borbón as Spain's future king. He also played a part in encouraging Spain's technological development, hoping for the country's eventual closer integration with Europe. He became vice-premier in October 1967. His influence thereafter prevailed to increase censorship, limit political association, stiffen sentences for political offenses, and reaffirm the subservience of the trade unions to government.

CASALS, PABLO (Catalan PAU), Catalan cellist (b. Vendrell, Spain, Dec. 29, 1876—d. Río Piedras, Puerto Rico, Oct. 22, 1973), was a world-famous virtuoso, conductor, and composer. Already able to play several musical instruments at the age of 12, Casals became principal cellist with the Paris Opéra orchestra in 1895 and three years later made his first solo concert appearances in Paris and at the Crystal Palace, London. By 1910 he was accepted as the greatest cellist of his time. In 1919 he formed the Orquestra Pau Casals in Barcelona, but in 1939 went into exile after Franco's victory in the Spanish Civil War. In the late 1940s he refused to play in Britain and the U.S. because they tolerated Franco's regime in Spain; he had already refused to play in Fascist Italy, Nazi Germany, and Stalinist U.S.S.R. He settled at Prades in the French Pyrenees and there organized a music festival. In 1963 he agreed to conduct his oratorio *El Pessebre* (*The Manger*) in Britain's Royal Festival Hall. It was due to Casals that Bach's unaccompanied cello suites, long regarded as mere exercises, came to be recognized for their profound eloquence.

CHANDLER, NORMAN, U.S. newspaper publisher (b. Los Angeles, Calif., Sept. 14, 1899—d. Los Angeles, Oct. 20, 1973), built the *Los Angeles Times* into the nation's second largest newspaper in daily circulation, the largest in advertising, and one of the most influential in forming public opinion. After retiring as publisher in 1960 he continued to oversee the operations of the Times Mirror Co. In later years Chandler confessed in an interview that the *Times* had been biased in favour of Republicans and management during the 1940s and 1950s.

CHANEY, LON, JR. (CREIGHTON CHANEY), U.S. actor (b. Oklahoma City, Okla., Feb. 10, 1906—d. San Clemente, Calif., July 12, 1973), was noted for his movie monster roles. He began his career in 1932, following in the footsteps of his father, Lon Chaney, Sr., who had gained fame in silent films as "the man of a thousand faces." He played the part of Lennie in *Of Mice and Men* (1939) and that of the old marshal in *High Noon* (1952), as well as such weird characters as the Mummy, the Wolf Man, and Frankenstein.

CHARRIÈRE, HENRI, French author (b. Saint-Étienne-de-Ludgarès, Ardèche, France, Nov. 16, 1906—d. Madrid, Spain, July 29, 1973), who in 1931 was convicted of a Paris underworld killing and sentenced to hard labour for life on Devil's Island, the penal colony in French Guiana, achieved a sensational, worldwide literary success in 1969 with the publication of *Papillon*. The book, whose authenticity Charrière defended in the courts, recounted his life as a convict and his eventual escape to Venezuela after numerous unsuccessful attempts. A sequel, *Banco*, and a film based on *Papillon*, which he wrote and directed himself, attracted less attention. Charrière, who always denied his guilt, was accorded an official pardon in 1970.

CHEHAB, FUAD, Lebanese general and politician (b. Jounieh, Lebanon, 1901—d. Beirut, Lebanon, April 25, 1973), was Lebanese president (1958–64). After a successful military career under the French mandate, he was appointed commander in chief of the Lebanese Army in 1945 and held that post for 13 years. In 1952 he headed a stopgap government after the fall of Pres. Bishara al-Khuri. After further troubles in 1958, when U.S. Marines restored order, Chehab was accepted by the rival factions of Pres. Camille Chamoun and Saeb Salam as a "neutral," and under his subsequent presidency peace was restored.

CHESSER, EUSTACE, British psychiatrist, author, and broadcaster (b. Edinburgh, Scot., March 22, 1902—d. London, Eng., Dec. 5, 1973), was an outstanding therapist and a controversial reformer of sexual mores, who championed abortion and homosexual law reform. He wrote more than 30 books, including *Love Without Fear* (1941), a best seller that sold millions of copies in many languages, *Is Chastity Outmoded?* (1960), and *Living with Suicide* (1967).

CICOGNANI, AMLETO CARDINAL, Italian prelate of the Roman Catholic Church (b. Brisighella, Italy, Feb. 24, 1883—d. Vatican City, Dec. 17, 1973), as Vatican secretary of state (1961–69) was second to the pope in the hierarchy of the Roman Catholic Church. He entered Vatican service in 1910, lectured for ten years on canon law, and wrote several classic works on the subject. He was appointed apostolic delegate to the United States in 1933 and held the post for more than 25 years. He became cardinal in 1958.

COBHAM, SIR ALAN JOHN, British aviator (b. London, Eng., May 6, 1894—d. Suffolk, Eng., Oct. 21, 1973), was a pioneer of long-distance flight who brought home to the British Commonwealth the possibilities of air transport. He entered the Flying Corps in 1917 and in 1921 joined Geoffrey de Havilland's new company where he began a succession of long eye-catching flights: 5,000 mi. around Europe; 8,000 mi. across Europe and North Africa; 12,000 mi. through Europe to Palestine, Egypt, along the North African coast, and back through Spain; to the Cape of Good Hope and back; to Australia and back; 23,000 mi. around Africa; and in 1931 a survey flight up the Nile and across the Belgian Congo. During the next four years his flying circus gave many their first thrills of aerial display. He worked out a system for refueling aircraft from aerial tankers which was first used off Ireland in 1939.

CONDON, EDDIE (ALBERT EDWIN CONDON), U.S. jazz guitarist (b. Goodland, Ind., Nov. 16, 1905—d. New York, N.Y., Aug. 4, 1973), was an advocate and exemplar of unscored music played by small jazz bands. He never played solo because he believed that true jazz required spontaneity and multiple sounds. After his first recordings in the 1920s, Condon's music became known as "Chicago style" jazz. During his long career he played with most of the country's leading jazz musicians. His last public appearance was at Carnegie Hall in July 1972 during the Newport Jazz Festival.

COOPER, MERIAN C., U.S. screen director (b. Jacksonville, Fla., Oct. 24, 1895—d. San Diego,

Pablo Casals

UPI COMPIX

Calif., April 21, 1973), creator, co-author, and co-producer of the Hollywood classic *King Kong,* spent three years (1930–33) filming the story of the 50-ft. ape. Cooper's other notable motion picture successes included *Four Feathers* in 1929, *Fort Apache* in 1948, and *The Quiet Man* in 1952.

COSTES, DIEUDONNÉ, French pioneer aviator (b. Septfonds, France, Nov. 4, 1892—d. Paris, France, May 18, 1973), with Maurice Bellonte made the first ever westbound nonstop Atlantic crossing from Paris to New York in 1930. The flight took just over 37 hours in the Breguet "Question Mark." In 1949 Costes was tried by a military tribunal for selling French aircraft secrets to the Germans during World War II; he was acquitted by five votes to four.

COWARD, SIR NOEL, English playwright, composer, actor, director, novelist, and all-round entertainer (b. Teddington, Eng., Dec. 16, 1899—d. Jamaica, West Indies, March 26, 1973), was the author of some 50 plays, revues, and films (including notably *Hay Fever, Bitter Sweet, Private Lives, Cavalcade, Blithe Spirit, Present Laughter, This Happy Breed, In Which We Serve,* and *Brief Encounter*), more than 250 songs, numerous poems, short stories, a novel, and two volumes of autobiography (*Present Indicative; Future Indefinite*). Born into "genteel poverty," Coward made his first public appearance in a children's play in 1909, thereafter playing many juvenile parts until stricken with tuberculosis in 1915. He spent World War I in a labour battalion and in the Artists Rifles. In 1920 he appeared in his own first produced play, *I Leave It to You.* His first great success came with the melodramatic *The Vortex* (about drug-taking) in 1925.

Although his popularity waned somewhat after World War II, Coward appeared in a variety of small film parts, continued to write prolifically, and was enjoying a major revival at the time of his death.

COX, WALLY (Wallace Maynard Cox), U.S. comedian (b. Detroit, Mich., 1924—d. Bel Air, Calif., Feb. 15, 1973), remembered for his performances as Robinson Peepers in the popular "Mr. Peepers" television series of the mid-1950s, a role for which he received the Peabody Award (1953). He was appearing on the TV quiz show "Hollywood Squares" at the time of his death.

CRANKO, JOHN, South African choreographer and ballet director (b. Rustenburg, S.Af., Aug. 15, 1927—d. in flight from Philadelphia to Stuttgart, W.Ger., June 26, 1973), was director of the Stuttgart Ballet from 1961 and ballet director at Munich from 1968. His first ballet, a version of Stravinsky's *The Soldier's Tale,* was produced for Cape Town University when he was 16. In 1946 he came to England, joining the Sadler's Wells Theatre Ballet, of which he became resident choreographer in 1950. Successes there included *Pineapple Poll, The Lady and the Fool,* and *The Prince of the Pagodas;* full-length works for the Stuttgart Ballet, which he made famous, included *Romeo and Juliet, The Taming of the Shrew,* and *Eugene Onegin.* He also staged works for the Paris Opéra and for La Scala, Milan.

CREASEY, JOHN, British writer (b. Southfields, Surrey, Eng., Sept. 17, 1908—d. Wiltshire, Eng., June 9, 1973), was one of the world's most prolific writers of crime fiction, turning out 560 books in 40 years (14 more were still awaiting publication at his death). He left school at 14, was sacked from 25 jobs in seven years, and received 743 publishers' rejection slips before successfully launching his career with *Seven Times Seven* (1932). He used 28 pseudonyms. Among his best-known creations were the Toff, Inspector West, Gideon of the Yard, and the Baron. His novels were estimated to have sold 60 million copies in 23 languages.

DARIN, BOBBY (Walden Robert Cassotto), U.S. pop singer (b. Bronx, N.Y., May 14, 1936—d. Los Angeles, Calif., Dec. 20, 1973), became a budding teen-age idol when his 1958 recording of "Splish Splash," his own composition, sold 100,000 records in three weeks; his 1960 recording of "Mack the Knife" sold 2 million copies and earned him two Grammy awards, for best song and for best new artist of the year. Darin performed in major nightclubs, on television, and in movies, and in 1965 was nominated for an Academy Award for his role in *Captain Newman, M.D.*

DE CASTRO, JOSUE, Brazilian scholar and diplomat (b. Recife, Braz., Sept. 5, 1908—d. Paris, France, Sept. 24, 1973), won international recognition for his efforts on behalf of third world nations. His analysis of the growing disparity between industrialized and less developed nations was set down in two essays: "Geography of Hunger" and "Geopolitics of Hunger." The latter was translated into 24 languages. De Castro occupied the chair of human geography at Rio de Janeiro Federal University from 1939 to 1970, concurrently serving as a member of the Brazilian Parliament (1955–63) and chairman of the United Nations Food and Agriculture Organization (1952–56).

DEKOBRA, MAURICE (Maurice Ernest Tessier), French novelist (b. Paris, France, May 26, 1885—d. Paris, June 2, 1973), author of the best-selling *The Madonna of the Sleeping Cars* (*La Madone des sleepings;* 1927), sold over 10 million copies of his works in more than 30 languages and was for many years the most-read French author in the world. Other books include *Les Mémoires de Rat-de-Cave* (1912), *Orient Express, Serenade to the Hangman* (1929), *The Perfumed Tigers* (1930), *Confucius in a Tail-Coat* (1935), and *Opération Magali* (1951), for which he won the Prix du Quai des Orfèvres.

DE LA BEDOYERE, COUNT MICHAEL, British author and journalist (b. May 16, 1900—d. July 13, 1973), edited the *Catholic Herald* (1934–62) and *Search Newsletter* (1962–68). Among De la Bedoyere's many books were biographies of Lafayette, Washington, St. Catherine of Siena, Baron von Hügel, and St. Francis of Assisi. His *Objections to Roman Catholicism* (1964) reflected his characteristic spirit of questioning.

DIETZE, CONSTANTIN VON, German agricultural economist (b. Gottesgnaden, Ger., Aug. 9, 1891—d. West Germany, March 21, 1973), was a leader of the anti-Nazi "confessing church" before World War II and president of the Synod of the Evangelical Church in Germany (1955–61). First arrested in 1936, he was in 1944 sentenced by the "people's court" to Ravensbrück concentration camp. He became rector of Freiburg University in 1946 and was twice a delegate to the World Conference of Churches. In 1951 he was Carl Schurz memorial professor at the University of Wisconsin.

DODD, THE REV. CHARLES HAROLD, British New Testament scholar (b. Wrexham, Eng., April 7, 1884—d. Goring, Eng., Sept. 22, 1973), was both convener of the New Testament Panel of the New English Bible, whose work was published in 1961, and co-director (with Sir Godfrey Driver) supervising publication of the complete Bible in 1970. A Congregationalist, he was the first non-Anglican professor of divinity (Norris-Hulse chair) at Cambridge University (1935–49). His books include *The Meaning of Paul for To-day* (1920), *The Interpretation of the Fourth Gospel* (1953), and *Historical Tradition in the Fourth Gospel* (1963). Dodd was also a keen numismatist and archaeologist. He was made a Companion of Honour in 1961.

DODDS, SIR (EDWARD) CHARLES, British biochemist (b. Darlington, Eng., Oct. 13, 1899—d. London, Eng., Dec. 16, 1973), emeritus professor of biochemistry, University of London, Courtauld professor of biochemistry and director of the Courtauld Institute of Biochemistry (1927–65), was an outstanding researcher in medical biochemistry, particularly in relation to cancer. He was elected a fellow of the Royal Society in 1942, created a baronet in 1964, and was president of the Royal College of Physicians (1962–66).

DORGELÈS, ROLAND (Roland Lécavelé), French author (b. Amiens, France, June 15, 1886—d. Paris, France, March 18, 1973), president of the Académie Goncourt from 1955, was especially famous for his novel *Les Croix de bois* (1919), based on his wartime experiences.

DREW, GEORGE ALEXANDER, Canadian politician (b. Guelph, Ont., May 7, 1894—d. Toronto, Ont., Jan. 4, 1973), leader of Canada's Progressive Conservative Party from 1948 to 1956. He was premier of Ontario Province from 1943 until 1948 and served as Canada's high commissioner to London from 1957 until 1964.

DUCKWITZ, GEORG FERDINAND, West German diplomat (b. Bremen, Ger., Sept. 29, 1904—d. Bremen, W.Ger., Feb. 16, 1973), was shipping attaché at the German legation in Copenhagen at the outset of World War II. His warning to the Danish resistance movement in September 1943 of Hitler's plans for the imminent deportation of Danish Jews permitted virtually the whole Jewish population of some 6,000 to escape to Sweden. After the war he returned to Copenhagen as West Germany's ambassador (1955–58), headed the eastern division of the West German Foreign Ministry (1958–61), and was ambassador to India (1961–65). As state secretary at the Foreign Ministry (1967–70) he conducted negotiations leading to the treaty between West Germany and Poland.

DUNN, MICHAEL (Gary Neil Miller), U.S. actor (b. Shattuck, Okla., Oct. 20, 1934—d. London, Eng., Aug. 29, 1973), won the Laurel Award and an Academy Award nomination as best supporting actor for his film role in *Ship of Fools* (1964). Because of his height (3 ft. 10 in.), Dunn always played the part of a dwarf. He was also nominated for a Tony Award for his part in *Ballad of the Sad Cafe* (1963), a Broadway play, and for two Emmy awards for his acting on television.

EINZIG, PAUL, naturalized British economic journalist (b. Brasov, Transylvania, Aug. 25, 1897—d. London, Eng., May 8, 1973), was London correspondent of the *Commercial and Financial Chronicle,* New York, from 1945, correspondent (1921), foreign editor (1923), and political correspondent (1939–45) of the London *Financial News,* and political correspondent of the London *Financial Times* (1945–56). He wrote more than 50 books, including *The Theory of Forward Exchange* (1937), *History of Primitive Money* (1949), and an autobiography, *In the Centre of Things* (1960). He was given a high place on Hitler's blacklist.

EISENDRATH, RABBI MAURICE, U.S. religious leader (b. Chicago, Ill., July 10, 1902—d. New York, N.Y., Nov. 9, 1973), as director and from 1946 as president of the Union of American Hebrew Congregations was the main spokesman for Reform Judaism in America. He was the author of *The Never Failing Stream* (1939) and *Can Faith Survive?* (1958).

ELLERMAN, SIR JOHN REEVES, 2nd Baronet, British shipping magnate (b. Dec. 21, 1909—d. July 17, 1973), was director of Ellerman Lines Ltd. and reputedly one of the richest men in England. He took a personal interest in the blind of South Africa and learned Afrikaans and braille in order to correspond with them.

ESCANDE, MAURICE, French actor and theatrical administrator (b. Paris, France, Nov. 14, 1892—d. Paris, Feb. 10, 1973), was associated with the Comédie Française from 1918 and was

Michael Dunn

UPI COMPIX

its director from 1960 to 1970. A professor of dramatic art, he also made more than 50 films. In 1970 he published *Dix années d'activité à la Comédie-Française.*

FADDEN, ARTHUR WILLIAM, Australian statesman (b. Ingham, Austr., April 13, 1895—d. April 1973), was treasurer of the Australian Commonwealth (1940–41 and 1949–58) and prime minister for 40 days in 1941. He guided his country through a period of unprecedented growth, combating both worldwide inflation and the effects of the U.S. recession. He led the Country Party from 1941 until his retirement from the federal Parliament in 1958. Fadden served as acting prime minister on ten separate occasions.

FERRETTO, GIUSEPPE CARDINAL, Italian prelate of the Roman Catholic Church (b. Rome, Italy, March 9, 1899—d. March 17, 1973), was cardinal bishop of Sabina and Poggio Mirteto. Ordained in 1923, he was for a number of years professor of Christian archaeology at the Lateran University, Rome, and professor of sacred liturgy at the Urbanum (College of the Propaganda). In 1958 he was appointed secretary of the Sacred College of Cardinals and consecrated titular archbishop of Sardica. In 1961 he became the most junior of the cardinal priests appointed by Pope John XXIII.

FIRESTONE, HARVEY S., JR., U.S. rubber company executive (b. Chicago, Ill., April 20, 1898—d. Akron, O., June 1, 1973), son of the founder of the Firestone Tire and Rubber Co., served the company for half a century. As chief executive officer from 1946 until 1963, he saw Firestone's sales doubled to $1.3 billion, with 121 plants and facilities in 29 countries. He was the author of *Man on the Move: The Story of Transportation,* published in 1967.

FLACH, KARL-HERMANN, West German politician (b. Königsberg, Ger., Oct. 17, 1929—d. Frankfurt am Main, W.Ger., Aug. 25, 1973), general secretary of the Free Democratic Party (FDP) from 1971, played a leading part in the FDP's 1972 election campaign, as a result of which the party increased its representation in the Bundestag (federal parliament) from 30 to 41 seats. Elected himself, Flach became deputy chairman of the FDP parliamentary party. A journalist by profession, he became editor of the *Frankfurter Rundschau* in 1964.

FORD, JOHN (Sean Aloysius O'Feeney), U.S. movie director (b. Cape Elizabeth, Me., Feb. 1, 1895—d. Palm Desert, Calif., Aug. 31, 1973), cited by the Screen Actors Guild in 1971 as "one of the few giants in motion pictures," won six Academy Award Oscars during his long and prolific career. Though he directed some 130 movies, none of his Oscars was for a Western, a genre that he raised to a high level of artistry. His award-winning features were *The Informer* (1935), *The Grapes of Wrath* (1940), *How Green Was My Valley* (1941), and *The Quiet Man* (1952). Two more Oscars went to Ford for World War II documentaries called *The Battle of Midway* and *December Seventh*. Among his other well-known and highly successful films were *Stagecoach* (1939), *Tobacco Road* (1941), *My Darling Clementine* (1946), *The Fugitive* (1947), *Mister Roberts* (1955), and *The Last Hurrah* (1958). In April 1973 Ford was given the first Life Achievement Award by the American Film Institute. During the ceremony Pres. Richard M. Nixon conferred on Ford the Presidential Medal of Freedom.

John Ford

WIDE WORLD

FORDE, DARYLL, British anthropologist (b. London, Eng., March 16, 1902—d. London, May 3, 1973), professor of anthropology, University of London (1945–69), was director of the International African Institute from 1944 and editor of its journals *Africa* and *African Abstracts.* After studying in California, he held the post of Gregynog professor of geography and anthropology, University of Wales (1930–45); during World War II he worked at the Foreign Office Research Department. He was a contributor and adviser to *Encyclopædia Britannica.*

FRISCH, FRANK FRANCIS ("Frankie"), U.S. baseball player (b. New York, N.Y., Sept. 9, 1898—d. Wilmington, Del., March 12, 1973), known as the "Fordham Flash," in 1919 joined the New York Giants who won four straight National League pennants (1921–24) and two World Series victories (1921, 1922). In 1926 he joined the St. Louis Cardinals to win pennants in 1928, 1930, and 1931. He became player-manager of the "Gashouse Gang" in 1933, the year the team took the World Series. In 1938 he retired as a player and in 1939 as manager of the Cards. He then managed the Pittsburgh Pirates and the Chicago Cubs. Frisch, who was inducted into baseball's Hall of Fame in 1947, had a career average of .316 as a switch hitter.

FRISCH, RAGNAR ANTON KITTIL, Norwegian economist (b. Oslo, Nor., March 3, 1895—d. Oslo, Jan. 31, 1973), a joint winner of the Nobel Prize for Economics (1969), was professor of economics at Oslo University (1931–71), a founder of the Econometric Society (1931), and chief editor of *Econometrica* (1933–55). He received the J. Schumpeter Prize from Harvard University in 1955 and the Antonio Feltrinelli Prize in 1961.

FULLER, ALFRED CARL, U.S. businessman (b. Berwick, Nova Scotia, Jan. 13, 1885—d. Hartford, Conn., Dec. 4, 1973), developed a basement operation into a brush-making enterprise with yearly sales exceeding $130 million. His door-to-door salesmen became such a part of American folklore that in Walt Disney's *Three Little Pigs* the wolf disguised himself as a Fuller Brush Man. Fuller was chairman of the board of the Fuller Brush Co. until 1968.

GAST, PAUL W., U.S. geologist (b. Chicago, Ill., 1930—d. Houston, Tex., May 16, 1973), was chief of the NASA Division of Planetary and Earth Sciences at the Lyndon B. Johnson Space Center at Houston, where he directed the study of lunar geology after the first moon rocks were brought to earth by Apollo 11 in 1969. Gast developed the rubidium-strontium and uranium-lead isotope methods for dating moon rocks. He received the NASA Medal for Exceptional Service in 1970 and its Distinguished Service Medal in 1972, the same year he was awarded the Geochemical Society's Victor Goldschmidt Medal. In 1973 he received the Space Science Award of the American Institute of Aeronautics and Astronautics and Columbia University's James Furman Kemp Medal for distinguished service.

GIMPEL, (ERNEST RICHARD) CHARLES, Anglo-French art dealer (b. France, 1913—d. Cretingham, Suffolk, Eng., Jan. 26, 1973), cofounder in 1946 of the Gimpel Fils art gallery in London, who distinguished himself in the French resistance, was imprisoned in Buchenwald, Auschwitz, and Flossenbürg during World War II, and was a member of Gen. Charles de Gaulle's Compagnons de la Libération. Branches of Gimpel Fils were later opened in Zürich, Switz., and in New York City.

GLOBKE, HANS, German politician (b. Düsseldorf, Ger., Sept. 10, 1898—d. Bonn, W.Ger., Feb. 13, 1973), one of the most controversial figures in post-World War II Germany, was often called the *éminence grise* behind federal Chancellor Konrad Adenauer. He was appointed secretary of state in the Federal Chancellery by Adenauer in 1953 despite his having been a member of the Ministry of the Interior during the Nazi era and having written the commentary to the Nürnberg racial laws, the basis for Hitler's anti-Jewish legislation. He retired with Adenauer in 1963.

GOLDSCHEIDER, LUDWIG, London-based art-book publisher and art historian (b. Vienna, Aus., 1896—d. London, Eng., June 1973), in 1923 became co-founder with Bela Horovitz of the Phaidon Verlag. There he was largely responsible for introducing the first large-sized art books, in 1937, on Botticelli, van Gogh, and the French Impressionists. With the Phaidon Press for 35 years, he edited books on other artists, including Leonardo da Vinci, Michelangelo, El Greco, and Vermeer.

GRABLE, BETTY (Ruth Elizabeth Grable), U.S. film star (b. St. Louis, Mo., Dec. 18, 1916—d. Santa Monica, Calif., July 2, 1973), was the favourite "pin-up girl" of the U.S. armed forces during World War II. She made more than 40 motion pictures, grossing around $100 million for 20th Century-Fox and close to $3 million for herself as one of the highest-salaried women in the U.S. during the mid-1940s. Her pictures included *Million Dollar Legs* (1939), *Tin Pan Alley* (1940), *Down Argentine Way* (1940), *Moon over Miami* (1941), *A Yank in the R.A.F.* (1941), *Pin Up Girl* (1944), *Mother Wore Tights* (1947), and her last, *How to be Very, Very Popular,* in 1955. She was married twice, the second time to bandleader Harry James.

GREEN, HENRY (Henry Vincent Yorke), British novelist (b. near Tewkesbury, Eng., Oct. 29, 1905—d. London, Eng., Dec. 13, 1973), produced in nine novels of poetic realism one of the most original contributions to modern English fiction. His first novel, *Blindness,* begun while he was a pupil at Eton, was published in 1926; those that followed, all dealing evocatively with the sad and comic aspects of the English class structure, included *Living* (1929), *Party Going* (1939), *Caught* (1943), *Loving* (1945), *Back* (1946), *Concluding* (1948), *Nothing* (1950), and *Doting* (1952). He also wrote an autobiography, *Pack My Bag* (1940).

GUSTAF VI ADOLF, king of Sweden (b. Nov. 11, 1882—d. Hälsingborg, Swed., Sept. 15, 1973), succeeded his father in 1950, after 43 years as crown prince. His modesty, scholarship, and interest in his people made him the best-loved figure in Swedish life and confounded the republican intentions of the ruling Social Democrats. During the 1920s he had sponsored a number of archaeological expeditions in Greece and Cyprus, and he spent many years thereafter digging on Etruscan sites north of Rome. In 1905 he married Princess Margaret of Connaught, daughter of the duke of Connaught; after her death in 1920, he married Lady Louise Mountbatten, a sister of Lord Mountbatten of Burma. She died in 1965.

GUTHRIE, RAMON, U.S. poet, painter, teacher, and translator of French works (b. New York, N.Y., Jan. 14, 1896—d. Hanover, N.H., Nov. 22, 1973), received the Marjorie Peabody Waite Award of the National Academy of Arts and Letters (1973) for a book-length poem entitled *Maximum Security Ward,* which was described by the poet-critic Louis Untermeyer as "the evocation of one man's stubborn struggle against extinction." He retired in 1963 after 33 years on the faculty of Dartmouth College.

HACKWORTH, GREEN HAYWOOD, U.S. jurist (b. Prestonburg, Ky., Jan. 23, 1883—d. Washington, D.C., June 24, 1973), an authority on international law, was elected a member of the International Court of Justice at The Hague in 1946 and reelected for a nine-year term in 1952. He served three years as president of the body (1955–58) before retiring in 1961.

HALECKI, OSKAR, Polish historian (b. Vienna, Aus., May 26, 1891—d. White Plains, N.Y., Sept. 17, 1973), graduated from Cracow University in 1913, was professor of Eastern European history at Warsaw University (1918–39), and served on the secretariat of the League of Nations (1921–24); after World War II he emigrated to the United States and taught at Fordham and Columbia universities. Halecki's many historical writings include *A History of Poland* (1943) and *Borderlands of Western Civilization—A History of East-Central Europe* (1963).

HAMILTON (14th Duke of) **AND BRANDON** (11th Duke of), **DOUGLAS DOUGLAS-HAMILTON,** Scottish nobleman (b. Feb. 3, 1903—d. Edinburgh, Scot., March 30, 1973), hereditary keeper of Holyroodhouse and bearer of the crown of Scotland, lord steward of the royal household (1940–64), and chancellor of St. Andrews University from 1948, was also lord high commissioner to the General Assembly of the Church of Scotland (1953–55 and 1958). As a pioneer pilot he was the first man to fly over Mt. Everest. In 1941 Hitler's deputy, Rudolf Hess, parachuted into Scotland in the hope of using Hamilton as an intermediary for peace negotiations.

HANSFORD, S(IDNEY) HOWARD, British Sinologist (b. London, Eng., June 22, 1899—d. Shropshire, Eng., April 1, 1973), was professor of Chinese art and archaeology in the University of London (1955–66, afterward emeritus), head of the Percival David Foundation of Chinese Art, and an honorary fellow of the School of Oriental and African Studies. Apart from his catalog of the Seligman collection of Chinese bronzes, he published a *Glossary of Chinese Art and Archaeology* (1954) and *Chinese Carved Jades* (1968), on which subject he was the foremost Western expert.

HANSON, EMMELINE JEAN, British biologist (b. Derbyshire, Eng., 1919—d. August 1973), director of the Muscle Biophysics Unit, Medical Research Council, from 1970, and professor of biology, King's College, London; was a leading contributor to understanding of muscular contraction. With H. E. Huxley at the Massachusetts Institute of Technology (1953–54), she provided the basis for the "sliding filament" theory of muscle contraction. She was elected a fellow of the Royal Society in 1967.

HAUPTMANN, ELISABETH, German writer (b. Paderborn, Ger., 1897—d. East Berlin, April 20, 1973), for many years was Bertolt Brecht's chief collaborator and editor. She translated the *Beggar's Opera* for him to use as a basis for his *Threepenny Opera,* and introduced him to Arthur Waley's translations of the Japanese nō plays, which provided him with his "school opera," *Der Jasager,* and helped form his ideas of the *Lehrstücke* or didactic cantata. A gifted writer in her own right, she had a hand in much of Brecht's output. She wrote the "Alabama Song" in *Rise and Fall of the Town of Mahagonny.* She was artistic director of the Berliner Ensemble.

HARVEY, LAURENCE (Larushka Mischa Skikne), British actor (b. Joniskis, Lithuania, Oct. 1, 1928—d. London, Eng., Nov. 25, 1973), was long a leading man in the U.K. and Hollywood. Born of a Jewish family, he moved to South Africa as a child and began his acting career in Johannesburg. He went to London in 1946 and was thereafter engaged in a busy film and stage career. His first major role was in *I Am a Camera* in 1955, followed in 1959 by *Room at the Top* and in 1968 by *A Dandy in Aspic.* He made his New York stage debut in Ugo Betti's *The Island of Goats.* He directed and starred in *The Ceremony,* played in Shakespeare and musicals (notably as King Arthur in the London production of *Camelot*), and gave a fine screen performance in *The Manchurian Candidate* in 1962.

HAWKINS, JACK (John Edward Hawkins), British actor (b. London, Eng., Sept. 14, 1910—d. London, July 18, 1973), was best known for his roles as a stoical war hero, for which his rugged bearing and World War II experience as a colonel seemed to fit him. He had acted in such plays as *Autumn Crocus* and *Journey's End* and played many Shakespearean roles before the war, and afterward appeared in such films as *Angels One Five, The Cruel Sea, Malta Story, Ben Hur, Five Finger Exercise,* and *Lawrence of Arabia.* In 1960 Hawkins was troubled with a throat complaint that was later diagnosed as cancer, and in 1966 his larynx was removed by surgery. He took part in several films thereafter, having his voice dubbed.

HAYAKAWA, SESSUE, Japanese actor (b. Honshu, Jap., June 10, 1890—d. Tokyo, Jap., Nov. 23, 1973), after a long career in silent and talking pictures, was nominated for an Academy Award for best supporting actor for his role as a Japanese army officer in *The Bridge on the River Kwai* (1957). He was an ordained Buddhist priest and the author of *Zen Showed Me the Way* (1960).

HESS, WALTER RUDOLF, Swiss physiologist (b. Frauenfeld, Switz., March 17, 1881—d. Zürich, Switz., Aug. 12, 1973), shared the Nobel Prize for Physiology or Medicine in 1949 with Antonio Egas Moniz of Portugal "for . . . discovery of the functional organization of the interbrain as a coordinator of the activities of the internal organs." In 1912 he gave up a successful practice as an ophthalmologist to take up physiology. In 1917 he became director of the physiological institute in Zürich, where he spent 34 years in research and teaching.

HINDLE, EDWARD, British parasitologist (b. Sheffield, Eng., March 21, 1886—d. London, Eng., Jan. 22, 1973), was scientific director of the Zoological Society of London (1944–51) and honorary secretary of the Royal Geographical Society (1951–61). His work helped subdue Kala-Azar disease in China and yellow fever in Brazil and the Congo. From Aleppo he brought back to England two pairs of golden hamsters (*Mesocricetus auratus*) from which modern pets and laboratory animals are descended. A fellow of the Royal Society from 1942, he published papers on numerous subjects and was a contributor to the *Encyclopædia Britannica.*

HOGARTH, WILLIAM, British trade unionist (b. Glasgow, Scot., 1912—d. May 13, 1973), was general secretary of the National Union of Seamen from 1962. He became a seaman at the age of 16 but was soon discharged from his ship as an agitator and spent the next five years on tankers and tramp steamers. During World War II he was a boatswain on troopships, and afterward became a full-time official of the NUS, becoming London district secretary in 1960. In 1967 he led the longest seamen's strike since the war. Politically moderate, he was a member of the Trades Union Congress (TUC) Economic and Nationalized Industries committees. Following the 1971 Industrial Relations Act, the NUS defied TUC policy and through the National Industrial Relations Court obtained a legally closed shop. For this breach the union was suspended from the TUC in March 1972.

HORENSTEIN, JASCHA, Russian-born Jewish conductor (b. Kiev, Russia, May 6, 1898—d. London, Eng., April 2, 1973), was an internationally renowned musician who faithfully interpreted a wide range of composers. He first appeared as an orchestral conductor in Vienna in 1923, conducted the Blüthner concerts in Berlin in 1924, and in 1928 became chief conductor and then musical director of the Düsseldorf Opera. He left Germany in the 1930s and in 1941 settled in the U.S., later traveling widely in Europe.

HORKHEIMER, MAX, German-born philosopher and sociologist (b. Stuttgart, Ger., Feb. 14, 1895—d. Nürnberg, W.Ger., July 7, 1973), began lecturing at Frankfurt am Main in 1925 and became the director of its Institute for Social Research in 1931. He emigrated to the United States in 1934 and took U.S. citizenship in 1940. He was director of New York's Institute of Social Research from 1934. He returned to teach in Germany after World War II. In 1954 he was appointed professor of sociology at the University of Chicago. Among his books are *Eclipse of Reason* (1947) and *Studies in Prejudice* (5 vol.).

HOWICK OF GLENDALE, EVELYN BARING, 1st Baron, British administrator (b. Sept. 29, 1903—d. Alnwick, Northumberland, Eng., March 10, 1973), as governor of Kenya (1952–59) helped crush the Mau Mau uprising. He joined the Indian civil service in 1926, later becoming secretary to the Indian agent-general in South Africa. In 1942 he became governor of Southern Rhodesia and two years later was appointed U.K. high commissioner in South Africa. In 1960 he became chairman of the Colonial Development Corporation and worked with the World Bank to expand agricultural aid to Commonwealth countries.

HUNTINGTON, ANNA HYATT, U.S. sculptor (b. Cambridge, Mass., March 10, 1876—d. Redding, Conn., Oct. 4, 1973), was an artist of international renown whose works, most often featuring horses or other animals, were displayed in some 200 museums and galleries throughout the world. Among her best known works are "Joan of Arc," completed in 1915; a statue of José Martí, a Cuban patriot; "Torchbearers," now in Madrid; statues of Lincoln and Andrew Jackson; and "El Cid," in the possession of the Hispanic Society of America, founded by her husband in 1904.

HUSSEIN, TAHA, Egyptian author and scholar (b. Maghagha, Upper Egypt, Nov. 14, 1889—d. Cairo, Egypt, Oct. 28, 1973), acknowledged to be the greatest literary figure in the modern Arab world, author of some 70 works of literary and cultural studies and fiction. Although he lost his sight at the age of two, Hussein rose to the top of the academic world from an origin in village poverty, and it was under his aegis as minister of education that free universal schooling was introduced in Egypt. In 1914 he went to France, where he studied French, Greek, and Latin and returned home with a Sorbonne doctorate. He was appointed professor of ancient history at the Egyptian University and later became professor of Arabic and dean of the faculty of arts at Fuad I (now Cairo) University. Two days before his death he received the UN Human Rights Prize. His early life is told in his autobiography, *Kitab al-Ayyam* (1929–32; Eng. trans., part i, *An Egyptian Childhood,* 1932, and part ii, *The Stream of Days,* 1943).

INGE, WILLIAM MOTTER, U.S. playwright (b. Independence, Kan., May 3, 1913—d. Hollywood Hills, Calif., June 10, 1973), was the author of the play *Picnic,* which in 1953 won both the Pulitzer Prize for drama and the New York Drama Critics Circle Award. It was adapted for the screen in 1956. In 1962 his screenplay *Splendor in the Grass* won an Academy Award. Inge's other long-run Broadway plays were *Come Back, Little Sheba* (1950; film version, 1953), *Bus Stop* (1955; film version, 1956), and *Dark at the Top of the Stairs* (1957; film version, 1960).

INONU, ISMET, former president of Turkey (b. Izmir [Smyrna], Turk., Sept. 24, 1884—d. Ankara, Turk., Dec. 25, 1973), became a corps commander in World War I, and was afterward the close companion of Mustafa Kemal Ataturk, founder of modern Turkey. He was prime minister from 1923 to 1937. On Ataturk's death in 1938, Inonu was elected president; amid conflicting interests he kept the country on the political and social course set by Ataturk and skillfully maintained its neutrality through most of World War II, joining the Allies in February 1945. Reelected president in 1943 and 1946, he encouraged the formation of a parliamentary opposition, the Democratic Party, which defeated his Republican People's Party in May 1950 when he ceased to be president and led the opposition. But victory in the elections of October 1961 made him prime minister of a coalition government; in more restless times, his government had to survive political crises, an enlargement of the coalition, and revolutionary opposition from radical extremists in the Army (plots in 1962 and 1963). In June 1964 Inonu visited the U.S., Britain, and France to confer with heads of government. In the October 1965 elections, his party was defeated. Inonu relinquished the party chairmanship in 1972.

ISHIBASHI, TANZAN, Japanese economist and politician (b. Yamanashi Prefecture, Sept. 25, 1884—d. Tokyo, Jap., April 24, 1973), was prime minister of Japan during 1956–57, and served as finance minister (1946–47) and minister for international trade and industry (1954–56).

JEANS, URSULA, British actress (b. Simla, India, 1906—d. Hertfordshire, Eng., April 21, 1973), was a favourite of London audiences through a career spanning 40 years, in which she also toured Australia, New Zealand, and South Africa. After an acclaimed performance as Flämmchen in *Grand Hotel* in 1931, she was invited by Tyrone Guthrie to join his first season at the Old Vic, to which she frequently returned. A brilliant leading actress, she played opposite nearly all her major contemporaries in classic and modern plays.

JOHNSON, LYNDON B(AINES), 36th president (1963–69) of the United States (b. Gillespie County, Tex., Aug. 27, 1908—d. San Antonio, Tex., Jan. 22, 1973), was elected vice-president in 1960 and acceded to the presidency upon the assassination of Pres. John F. Kennedy (Nov. 22, 1963). A moderate Democrat and vigorous Senate leader, he signed into law the most comprehensive civil rights legislation since Reconstruction, initiated major social service programs, and bore the brunt of national opposition to his administration's actions in Southeast Asia.

The eldest of five children, Johnson was born in a three-room house in the hills of southwest Texas. Though both his father and grandfather had served in the Texas legislature, the Johnson ranch along the Pedernales River was barren and the family very poor. As a young man he resisted college, preferring to hitchhike around the country taking odd jobs for a living. Eventually he enrolled at Southwest Texas State Teachers College at San Marcos, where he trained as a teacher in three whirlwind years.

His first teaching job, at Sam Houston High School in Houston, Tex., introduced him to Mexican-Americans and, through them, to the problems of minorities. Working tirelessly as a volunteer in state politics, he reaped considerable political benefit as champion of that minority. In 1932 he went to Washington, D.C., as legislative assistant to Richard M. Kleberg, whose congressional campaign he had aided.

Johnson was befriended by the powerful Sam Rayburn, soon to become speaker of the House, and his political career blossomed rapidly. Following two years as director of the National Youth Administration in Texas (1935–37), he ran successfully for Congress at a time when the New Deal administration of Pres. Franklin D. Roosevelt was under heavy conservative attack. Impressed by Johnson's loyalty and astuteness, Roosevelt made him his political protégé, and for the next decade Johnson represented the 10th congressional district of Texas.

In 1948 Johnson narrowly won his bid for a seat in the Senate, where he remained for 12 years, becoming Democratic whip in 1951. During those years he developed his talent for negotiating and reaching accommodation among dissident political forces. By methods sometimes tactful but often ruthless, he created a remarkably disciplined group of Senate Democrats. As majority leader (1955–61), he stressed consensus, and his skilled leadership was largely responsible for passage of the civil rights bills of 1957 and 1960—the first in the 20th century.

By 1960 Johnson's prodigious political talents had made him something of a legend in national politics, and many were surprised when he accepted the Kennedy invitation to join the national Democratic ticket as vice-presidential candidate. However, he campaigned energetically, and many observers felt his presence on the ticket was essential to the Democratic victory. Johnson endured without complaint the relative obscurity of his new office, and found some satisfaction in his duties as chairman of the President's Committee on Equal Employment Opportunity and of the National Aeronautics and Space Council.

It was during a political tour of Johnson's own Texas that Pres. John F. Kennedy was assassinated, thrusting Johnson into the most difficult role of his long political career. In the tempestuous days after the death of Kennedy, Johnson helped to calm national hysteria and ensure continuity in the presidency. Unfavourable comparisons between his folksy Southwestern ways and the sophistication of the previous Eastern-dominated administration proved one of his most trying burdens. Nevertheless, in his first few months in office the new president succeeded in getting Congress to pass important legislation—previously stalled—concerning civil rights, tax reduction, an antipoverty program, and conservation.

In November 1964 Johnson won reelection with an unprecedented popular majority of more than 15 million votes, which he interpreted as an extraordinary mandate to pursue his domestic reform program aimed at creating what he called the "Great Society." As the nation struggled to deal with the problems born of racial hostility, long-term urban decay, and persistent poverty, he succeeded in pushing through an impressive mass of welfare legislation—in medical care for the aged, education, housing and urban development, conservation, and immigration. But the effect of these accomplishments was vitiated by increasing U.S. military involvement in the war in Indochina, which had begun under the previous administration.

Despite specific campaign pledges not to extend hostilities, the president and his advisers—fearful that South Vietnam would fall before "Communist aggression"—steadily increased U.S. intervention. As each new escalation met with fresh enemy response, and as no end to the combat appeared in sight, the president's public support diminished markedly. His gravest criticism came from the "doves," those who favoured an early negotiated settlement of the war. Strident student opposition to both the war and the draft system ,spread to include liberals, intellectuals, and civil rights leaders, while the administration's budget—once geared to the abolition of poverty and injustice—buckled under the strain of wartime spending.

On March 31, 1968, after three of the most turbulent years in U.S. political history, Johnson startled television viewers with a national address that included three announcements: that he had just ordered major reductions in the bombing of North Vietnam; that he was requesting peace talks; and that he would neither seek nor accept his party's renomination. "What we won when all of our people were united must not now be lost in suspicion, distrust, selfishness and politics among our people. . . . Believing this as I do, I have concluded that I should not permit the Presidency to become involved in the partisan divisions that are developing in this political year."

Within four days of his announcement, civil rights leader Martin Luther King, Jr., was assassinated, triggering one of the last waves of urban riots; in the months that followed, Sen. Robert F. Kennedy was also assassinated, and the disastrous August convention of the Democratic Party took place in Chicago. President Johnson neither attended the convention nor participated in his party's unsuccessful attempt to retain the presidency.

In January 1969 he returned home to operate his ranch near Johnson City, Tex., and to write his version of the presidential years, *The Vantage Point* (1971). Less than one week before the signing of an agreement to end the war in Vietnam, Johnson suffered a heart attack at his home and died.

Flanked by his wife (left) and Mrs. John Kennedy, Lyndon Johnson takes the oath of office as president of the United States on board the presidential plane at Love Field, Dallas, Tex., shortly after President Kennedy's assassination on Nov. 22, 1963.

UPI COMPIX

COURTESY, LBJ LIBRARY

UPI COMPIX

UPI COMPIX

COURTESY, LBJ LIBRARY

At one of the high points of his presidency, Johnson addresses the nation before signing into law the Civil Rights Act of 1964 (top, right). His plans for the Great Society increasingly gave way before the country's growing involvement in the war in Indochina. His visits to Vietnam (top, left) were marked by optimism, but opposition at home and abroad (as in the protest in Rome, centre) led to his decision not to seek reelection for a second full term.

JORN, ASGER, Danish painter (b. Vejrum, Jutland, Den., March 3, 1914—d. Copenhagen, Den., May 1, 1973), was a founder of Cobra (an acronym for Copenhagen, Brussels, and Amsterdam), an art movement of "barbarism," influenced by child and folk art, which held together for a brief period after World War II.

KALATOZOV, MIKHAIL, Soviet film director (b. Tiflis, Russia, Dec. 8, 1903—d. U.S.S.R., March 27, 1973), was best known for *The Cranes Are Flying* (1957), a love story set in Moscow during World War II. His early films *The Salt of Svanetiya* and *Nail in a Boot* were frowned on and he spent some years in administration, not directing again until 1939. Among his postwar films were *The Conspiracy of the Doomed, Firm Friends, The First Echelon, The Letter that Was Never Sent,* and *The Red Tent,* a Soviet-Italian production about Umberto Nobile's airship flights to the Arctic.

KATZ, LOUIS NELSON, U.S. researcher specializing in heart diseases (b. Pinsk, Pol., Aug. 25, 1897—d. Chicago, Ill., April 2, 1973), was head of the Cardiovascular Institute at Michael Reese Hospital in Chicago. He pioneered research on the cause of hardening of the arteries and developed clinical electrocardiography. He served as president of the American Physiological Society (1956–57).

KELLY, WALT, U.S. cartoonist (b. Philadelphia, Pa., Aug. 25, 1913—d. Hollywood, Calif., Oct. 18, 1973), was the creator of "Pogo," a cartoon strip that delighted millions of readers for a quarter of a century with its innocent foolishness and gentle satire on politics and society. Pogo, a warmhearted opossum, spoke in humorously garbled language with such friends as Albert the Alligator and Howland Owl, all inhabitants of Okefenokee Swamp. Kelly spent years as a commercial artist and as an animator at Walt Disney Studios before publishing his first "Pogo" cartoons in the *New York Star* in 1948; the strip was eventually syndicated to more than 450 newspapers. Kelly also turned out a dozen "Pogo" books and gave hundreds of lectures. He was named Cartoonist of the Year in 1952.

KENNY, SEAN, Irish stage designer (b. Tipperary, Ire., Dec. 23, 1932—d. London, Eng., June 11, 1973), a highly original designer for the theatre, was responsible for the stage sets used in *Oliver!, Pickwick Papers, Lock Up Your Daughters, Blitz,* and in 32 major West End productions between 1960 and 1970, including Michael Tippett's opera *King Priam* at Covent Garden. He also designed a thrill ride at Canada's Expo 67 and an all-glass underwater restaurant in Nassau, Bahamas.

KERR, ANNE PATRICIA, British progressive (b. March 24, 1925—d. Twickenham, Greater London, Eng., July 29, 1973), was Labour MP for Rochester and Chatham (1964–70) and later chairman of the Women Against the Common Market movement. Mrs. Kerr frequently joined peace marches, protested the sale of warlike toys for children, supported the North Vietnamese in their war with the U.S., and in 1968 was caught up in a riot during the Democratic national convention in Chicago. She had acted in theatre, film, television, and radio before entering politics.

KLEMPERER, OTTO, German-born conductor (b. Breslau, Ger., May 14, 1885—d. Zürich, Switz., July 6, 1973), was an authoritative interpreter of Beethoven, Bruckner, and Brahms and honorary president and principal conductor for life of the New Philharmonia Orchestra. Recommended by Mahler for his first post at the German Opera in Prague in 1907, he was first conductor of the Berlin State Opera (1927–33) before leaving Germany because of Hitler. After directing the Los Angeles Philharmonic (1933–39), Klemperer became a guest conductor in many parts of the world, annually conducting at Britain's Festival Hall (1960–71). He retired from the concert stage in 1972 but continued to make records. Although reared in 19th-century romanticism, Klemperer championed the work of such moderns as Stravinsky, Schoenberg, Hindemith, and Janacek.

KLETZKI, PAUL, Polish-born Swiss conductor (b. Lodz, Pol., March 21, 1900—d. Liverpool, Eng., March 5, 1973), was widely known in Europe, Israel, and the U.S. for his romantic but disciplined interpretations of a wide repertoire. After studying composition and violin in Warsaw and Berlin, he went to Italy and, at the outbreak of World War II, to Switzerland, where he acquired Swiss nationality. In 1954 he was appointed conductor of the Liverpool Philharmonic Orchestra, and later he became conductor of the Dallas, Tex., symphony orchestra.

KOCHETOV, VSEVOLOD, Soviet journalist (b. Novgorod, Russia, 1912—d. Moscow, U.S.S.R., November 1973), was editor in chief of the *Literaturnaya Gazeta* (1955–59), chief channel of expression of the Soviet Writers' Union, of which he was a director. He began his journalistic career in Leningrad and during World War II was a military correspondent. Author of a number of highly conformist novels nostalgic for Stalinism, in 1960 Kochetov assumed editorship of the revue *Oktiabr,* the rival of *Novy Mir.*

KONEV, IVAN STEPANOVICH, marshal of the Soviet Union (b. Vyatka [now Kirov], Russia, 1897—d. Moscow, U.S.S.R., May 21, 1973), one of the outstanding generals of World War II, commanded the second Ukrainian front from 1943. He liquidated ten German divisions in the Korsun salient (part of Gen. Erich von Manstein's 8th Army) and was the first to carry the fighting beyond Soviet frontiers, advancing from the Vistula to the Oder in 1945 and entering Prague after contacting the Americans at Torgau. Afterward he commanded the Soviet forces in Austria and Hungary (1945), succeeded Marshal Georgi K. Zhukov as commander in chief of Soviet ground forces (1946), and was commander in chief of Warsaw Pact forces from 1955 until his retirement in 1960. In 1961 he was temporarily recalled to act as commander in chief of Soviet forces in East Germany.

KOZINTSEV, GRIGORY, Soviet film director (b. Russia, 1905—d. Leningrad, U.S.S.R., May 11, 1973), was best known outside the U.S.S.R. for his productions of *Don Quixote* (1957), *Hamlet* (1964), and *King Lear* (1970). Originally an artist, he turned his attention to the theatre in 1920, forming with Leonid Trauberg the "Factory of the Eccentric Actor." He took up films in 1924, his earliest pictures including *The Adventures of an October Child* (1924), *The Devil's Wheel,* and *The Cloak* (1926). His first major triumph was *New Babylon* (1929), based on events in the Paris Commune. His "Maxim" trilogy—*The Youth of Maxim* (1935), *The Return of Maxim* (1937), and *The Vyborg Side* (1939)—re-created the early idealism of the Revolution.

KRUPA, GENE, U.S. jazz musician (b. Chicago, Ill., Jan. 15, 1909—d. Yonkers, N.Y., Oct. 16, 1973), best remembered for his flashy solos on the drums, first gained prominence with Benny Goodman's band in the 1930s. He later organized his own band and played with many of the leading jazz bands of his era. (*See* MUSIC.)

Gene Krupa

WIDE WORLD

KRUSEN, FRANK HAMMOND, U.S. physician (b. Philadelphia, Pa., June 26, 1898—d. Orleans, Mass., Sept. 16, 1973), regarded by the medical profession as the father of physical medicine and rehabilitation, turned from surgery to problems of physical disabilities while recovering from tuberculosis. His early work was undertaken at Temple University, Philadelphia (1929–35), where he established and directed the department of physical medicine. He returned to Temple in 1963 to head the Krusen Rehabilitation Center. From 1935 to 1963 Krusen was associated with Mayo Clinic in Rochester, Minn. As a result of his successes with World War II amputees, paraplegics, and other seriously wounded persons, the American Medical Association recognized physical medicine as a specialty in 1947. Krusen received numerous awards, among them the Medal for Distinguished Service of the AMA in 1958 and the Eisenhower Medal for outstanding contributions to international understanding in 1969.

KUIPER, GERALD PETER, U.S. astronomer (b. Harencarspel, Neth., Dec. 7, 1905—d. Mexico City, Mex., Dec. 23, 1973), whose analysis of early lunar photos helped determine the Apollo landing sites, was chief scientist in charge of the Ranger spacecraft crash-landing probes of the moon in the mid-1960s.

KUKIEL, MARIAN WLODZIMIERZ, Polish soldier and historian (b. Dabrowa Tarnowska [then in Austrian Poland], May 15, 1885—d. London, Eng., Aug 15, 1973), was one of a phalanx of Polish patriots who, sensing the coming of a European war, resolved in 1908 to form a secret organization as the nucleus of a future national army. In World War I he fought against czarist Russia and, as a brigade commander in the reborn Polish Army, in 1920 against Soviet Russia. In World War II he followed Gen. Wladyslaw Sikorski to London and in 1942 was appointed minister of defense of the Polish government-in-exile. After the war he founded and directed in London the Polish Institute and Sikorski Museum. His postwar writings include *Czartoryski and European Unity* (1955), *History of Partitioned Poland, 1795–1921* (in Polish, 1961), and *General Sikorski* (in Polish, 1970).

KUMARAMANGALAM, MOHAN, Indian politician (b. London, Eng., Nov. 1, 1916—d. New Delhi, India, May 31, 1973), minister of steel and mines from 1971, was one of Prime Minister Indira Gandhi's closest advisers, and a champion of her radical economic policies. Before India's independence he spent almost 25 years in Britain. He was president of the Cambridge Union in 1938 and was called to the bar in 1939. Until the mid-1960s he was an active Communist.

LADOUMÈGUE, JULES RAYMOND, French athlete (b. Bordeaux, France, Dec. 10, 1906—d. Paris, France, March 2, 1973), 19 times an international champion in the 1,500-m. run, broke six world records between October 1930 and October 1931. In 1932 he was disqualified for life by the French athletic federation for breaking the rules of amateurism, and became a sports journalist and broadcaster. In 1956 he won the national prize for sporting literature with his autobiography, *Dans ma foulée.*

LAKE, VERONICA (CONSTANCE OCKELMAN), U.S. actress (b. Brooklyn, N.Y., Nov. 14, 1919—d. Burlington, Vt., July 7, 1973), glamorous film star of the 1940s whose seductive hair style set a new fashion, played in more than 25 pictures. One of her most successful films was *This Gun for Hire,* which she made with Alan Ladd in 1942.

LAUGIER, HENRI, French physiologist and diplomat (b. Mane, France, Aug. 5, 1888—d. Antibes, France, Jan. 19, 1973), was deputy secretary-general of the United Nations (1946–51). He was appointed professor of occupational physiology at the National Conservatory of Arts and Trades in 1930, and in 1937 took up the chair of general physiology at the Sorbonne. In 1940 he visited London, New York, and Canada seeking support for the French government-in-exile. In 1943 Charles de Gaulle appointed him rector of the Algerian Academy. After the liberation of France he became the first director general of cultural relations at the Ministry of Foreign Affairs in Paris. He returned to the Sorbonne in 1951 and retired in 1958.

LAWRENCE, DAVID, U.S. editor and columnist (b. Philadelphia, Pa., Dec. 25, 1888—d. Sarasota, Fla., Feb. 11, 1973), was founder and editor of *U.S. News & World Report* magazine. A lifelong conservative, he began his career as a columnist with the *New York Evening Post* in 1916. In 1926 he founded *U.S. Daily*, a report of federal government activities, which in 1933 was succeeded by *U.S. News*, a weekly. In 1947 Lawrence combined *U.S. News* with *World Report*, another of his publications, started in 1946. Lawrence's Washington columns were syndicated in 1916 and at one time appeared in 300 daily papers. He was the author of a number of books, including *Diary of a Washington Correspondent* (1942), and was one of radio's first political commentators, with a Sunday night broadcast from 1929 until 1933. He received the Presidential Medal of Freedom in 1970.

LAWRENCE, HARRY GORDON, South African politician (b. Rondebosch, S.Af., Oct. 17, 1901—d. Cape Town, S.Af., April 10, 1973), was national chairman of the Progressive Party which he helped found in 1959, along with Helen Suzman and others, after they had broken away from the United Party. A barrister by profession, Lawrence was appointed minister of labour by Gen. J. B. M. Hertzog in 1938. The following year he held portfolios of health and the interior. In 1943 he became minister of welfare and demobilization and in 1947 led the South African delegation to the United Nations.

LAYDEN, ELMER, U.S. football figure (b. Davenport, Ia., May 4, 1903—d. Chicago, Ill., June 30, 1973), was the 160-lb. fullback of the famed "Four Horsemen" backfield of the University of Notre Dame's 1924 national championship team. He later served as football coach and athletic director at Notre Dame (1934–40) and was the first commissioner of the professional National Football League (1941–46).

LEAHY, FRANCIS WILLIAM ("Frank"), U.S. football coach (b. O'Neill, Neb., Aug. 27, 1908—d. Portland, Ore., June 21, 1973), led Notre Dame's "Fighting Irish" through 1941–54 with a 87–11–9 win-loss-tie record. He graduated from Notre Dame in 1931, having played on the last team coached by Knute Rockne. After coaching jobs at Georgetown University (1931), Michigan State (1932), Fordham (1933–38), and Boston College (head coach 1939–41), Leahy became head coach at Notre Dame. Following his coaching career, Leahy wrote a football column for the *Chicago Daily News* and held positions in a number of private industrial concerns. In 1970 he was elected to the College Football Hall of Fame. His career coaching record was 106–12–9.

LEE, BRUCE, U.S. movie actor (b. San Francisco, Calif., 1940—d. Hong Kong, July 20, 1973), whose films set box-office records in Hong Kong and won him instant international popularity, was a karate expert and master of kung fu, one of China's traditional unarmed martial arts. He starred in such movies as *Fist of Fury* (1972), *Enter the Dragon* (1973), and *The Chinese Connection* (1973).

LEE, HAROLD B., U.S. religious leader (b. Clifton, Ida., March 28, 1899—d. Salt Lake City, Utah, Dec. 26, 1973), became president of the Mormon Church in July 1972. He was previously involved in coordinating a wide variety of Mormon activities that ranged from home studies to sports to welfare programs.

LEE, LILA, U.S. actress (b. Union City, N.J., July 25, 1905—d. Saranac Lake, N.Y., Nov. 13, 1973), was one of the great stars of silent films, playing opposite such idolized leading men as Rudolph Valentino in *Blood and Sand* (1922). Her career, which began at age five, also extended to the stage and talking pictures.

LEFEBVRE, JOSEPH CARDINAL, French prelate of the Roman Catholic Church (b. Tourcoing, France, April 15, 1892—d. Bourges, France, April 2, 1973), was archbishop of Bourges (1943–69). He was created cardinal by Pope John XXIII in 1960 after a career that included posts as diocesan director of works, vicar-general, and bishop of Troyes.

LEFÈVRE, THÉODORE JOSEPH ALBÉRIC, Belgian statesman (b. Ghent, Belg., Jan. 17, 1914—d. Brussels, Belg., Sept. 18, 1973), was his country's prime minister from 1961 to 1965 and president of the International Union of Christian Democrats. National president of the Social Christian Party (1950–61), he was responsible for scientific affairs in the Eyskens governments of 1968 and 1972. He was called to the bar in 1940 and during World War II was an active member of the underground. He entered Parliament in 1946. Under his leadership as prime minister, the tax and social security systems were reformed, the expansion of Brussels was limited, and linguistic frontiers were set between Dutch- and French-speaking areas; a start was also made on revision of the constitution.

LEJEUNE, C(AROLINE) A(LICE), British journalist (b. Manchester, Eng., 1897—d. April 1, 1973), doyenne of English film critics, reviewed films for *The Observer* (London) from 1928 until retiring in 1960. Previously she wrote a weekly film column for the *Manchester Guardian* (1922–28). She also wrote for other papers, including the *New York Times*. After World War II she became increasingly out of sympathy with trends in film-making and after retiring she never went to the cinema again. Her books include *Cinema* (1931), an autobiography, *Chestnuts in Her Lap* (1947), and *Thank You for Having Me* (1964).

LEONARD, JACK E. (Leonard Lebitsky), U.S. nightclub comedian (b. Chicago, Ill., April 24, 1911—d. New York, N.Y., May 10, 1973), was noted for his one-line insults of prominent persons.

LIÉNART, ACHILLE CARDINAL, French prelate of the Roman Catholic Church (b. Lille, France, Feb. 7, 1884—d. Lille, Feb. 15, 1973), bishop of Lille (1928–68), played a leading part in the worker-priest movement in France and as head of the Mission de France from 1954 was responsible for the movement's reorganization following the Vatican's decision to recall priest-workers. Though he was the youngest French bishop at the time of his appointment, he was made a cardinal two years later by Pope Pius XI. He was an active participant in the Second Vatican Council.

LITTLER, PRINCE, British theatre proprietor and manager (b. Ramsgate, Kent, Eng., July 25, 1901—d. Sussex, Eng., Sept. 13, 1973), brother of Blanche and Emile in the famous Littler family of theatre management, was chairman and managing director of the Stoll Theatres Corporation, Associated Theatre Properties, and the Theatre Royal, Drury Lane; chairman of Moss Empires and of the London Pavilion; and a director of Associated Television and the Independent Television Corporation. After being resident managers of a theatre owned by his parents, in 1927 he and his sister began sending companies on tour. For many years he presented pantomimes and musicals in London and over 200 pantomimes in the provinces.

LOCKSPEISER, EDWARD, British musicologist (b. London, Eng., May 21, 1905—d. Alfriston, Sussex, Eng., Feb. 3, 1973), was especially renowned for his study *Debussy: His Life and Mind* (1962, 1965). A conductor and composer for some years, Lockspeiser turned to criticism in 1936. He was at one time music editor of *Encyclopædia Britannica*.

Frank Leahy

WIDE WORLD

LÓPEZ CONTRERAS, ELEÁZAR, Venezuelan politician (b. Queniquea, Táchira, Venezuela, May 5, 1883—d. Caracas, Venezuela, Jan. 2, 1973), was president of Venezuela from 1935 until 1941.

LOPUKHOV, FYODOR V., Soviet dancer and choreographer (b. St. Petersburg, Russia, October 1886—d. Leningrad, U.S.S.R., Jan. 28, 1973), whose *Paths of a Ballet Master* (1916, publ. 1925) caused heated controversy in Western ballet circles, first put his ideas for symphonic ballet into practice with the *Dance Symphony* to Beethoven's Fourth Symphony at Leningrad's Little Opera Theatre in 1923. The first attempt at a specifically Soviet revolutionary ballet was his *The Red Whirlwind* of 1924. He also published *Sixty Years in Ballet* (1966) and *Choreographic Confessions* (1971).

LUDLOW-HEWITT, SIR EDGAR RAINEY, British air chief marshal (b. June 9, 1886—d. Wroughton, Wiltshire, Eng., Aug. 15, 1973), as head of Bomber Command (1939–40) planned the first bombing raids on Germany.

MacDONNELL, RONALD MACALISTER, Canadian diplomat (b. Vernon, B.C., May 11, 1909—d. Colombo, Sri Lanka, May 19, 1973), Canada's high commissioner to Ceylon (now Sri Lanka) from 1970, was a career diplomat who joined the Department of External Affairs in 1934. He served as ambassador to the United Arab Republic, Lebanon, and Indonesia and as high commissioner to New Zealand before going to Ceylon.

MACGOWRAN, JACK, Irish actor (b. Dublin, Ire., Oct. 13, 1918—d. New York, N.Y., Jan. 30, 1973), was best known for his memorable interpretations of Samuel Beckett's characters, especially Clov in *End-Game* and Lucky in *Waiting for Godot*. Films in which he appeared include *The Quiet Man, Lord Jim, Tom Jones, Dr. Zhivago, King Lear, Cul de Sac,* and *The Exorcist*. A radio production of Beckett's *Embers*, in which he played the lead in 1959, won the Italia Prize.

MacMILLAN, SIR ERNEST CAMPBELL, Canadian director-composer (b. Mimico, Ont., Aug. 18, 1893—d. Toronto, Ont., May 6, 1973), called the "statesman of Canadian music," directed the Toronto Symphony Orchestra from 1931 until 1956. He was dean of the music faculty of the University of Toronto (1927–52) and principal of the Toronto Conservatory of Music (1926–42). His compositions included "Sketches for String Quartet" and "A Song of Deliverance." He was the editor of *Music in Canada* (1955), the first comprehensive study of Canadian music.

MAGNANI, ANNA, Italian film actress (b. Rome, Italy, March 7, 1908—d. Rome, Sept. 26, 1973), whose portrayals of Italian womanhood reflected the volatile passion and strength of the matriarch, first appeared in films in 1934. Her husband, Goffredo Alessandrini, directed her in *Cavalleria* (1936). *Rome: Open City*, directed by Roberto Rossellini, brought her international fame; she was again directed by him in *The Miracle* and in Jean Cocteau's *La Voix Humaine*. After making *Bellissima* with L. Visconti, she spent some time in Hollywood, making *Wild Is the Wind, The Rose Tattoo* (for which she won an Academy Award), and *The Fugitive Kind*. In 1962 she played the tart-mother in Pier Paolo Pasolini's *Mamma Roma*. In later years she appeared briefly in Federico Fellini's *Roma*, and on Italian television.

MALIPIERO, GIAN FRANCESCO, Italian composer and musicologist (b. Venice, Italy, March 18, 1882—d. Treviso, Italy, Aug. 1, 1973), was professor of the history of music at the University of Padua and a former director of the Conservatorio Musicale, Venice. He edited and published complete works of Vivaldi and Monteverdi and wrote several books on musical subjects. His musical compositions, enriched in inspiration by his studies, include 25 operas, 11 symphonies, 6 piano concertos, and 2 violin concertos. (*See* Music.)

MANSTEIN, FRITZ ERICH VON (Erich von Lewinski), German field marshal (b. Berlin,

Ger., Nov. 24, 1887—d. Irschenhausen, W.Ger., June 10, 1973), 16 members of whose family had been Prussian or Russian generals, was one of the outstanding soldiers of World War II. He played a decisive role in the Polish campaign of autumn 1939 as chief of staff of Gerd von Rundstedt's Army Group; then in France in June 1940 he speeded his infantry to the Loire River. As commander of the 11th Army in the south he captured Sevastopol in July 1942 and in February 1943 recaptured Kharkov. In March 1944 he was removed from command by Hitler and in May 1945 surrendered to the British in western Germany. He was tried in August 1949, was acquitted on the most serious charges, was nevertheless sentenced to 18 years' imprisonment, but was released in 1953 and later advised his government on the organization of the West German Army.

MARCEL, GABRIEL, French philosopher and playwright (b. Paris, France, Dec. 7, 1889—d. Paris, Oct. 8, 1973), known for his development of a Christian form of existentialism of unsystematized Socratic approach, in opposition to the more pessimistic exposition of Jean-Paul Sartre. He taught philosophy at various lycées, becoming a convert to Roman Catholicism in 1929, and later earned his living as a free-lance critic and writer. His writings in translation include the philosophical works *The Philosophy of Existence* (1948) and *The Mystery of Being* (1951), and the plays *Ariadne, Man of God, Increase and Multiply,* and *Broken World.* He held the Grand Prix de Littérature of the French Academy (1948), the Goethe Prize (1956), and was William James lecturer at Harvard University in 1961.

MARITAIN, JACQUES, French Thomist philosopher (b. Paris, France, Nov. 18, 1882—d. Toulouse, France, April 28, 1973), a convert to Roman Catholicism, was the most distinguished interpreter to the 20th century of the philosophy of St. Thomas Aquinas. In 1914 he was elected to the chair of philosophy in the Institut Catholique in Paris. He was lecturing in the U.S. when World War II overtook France and remained in North America to teach at Columbia and Princeton universities and in Toronto. In 1945 Gen. Charles de Gaulle appointed him ambassador to the Vatican. He was awarded the Grand Prix de Littérature of the French Academy (1961) and the Grand Prix National des Lettres (1963). Among Maritain's writings are *L'Evolutionnisme de M. Bergson* (1911), *Art et scolastique* (1920), *Scholasticism and Politics* (1940), *La Primauté du spirituel* (1927), *Existence and the Existent* (1948), and *Le Paysan de la Garonne* (1966).

MASON, EDITH (EDITH BARNES), U.S. lyric soprano (b. St. Louis, Mo., March 22, 1893—d. San Diego, Calif., Nov. 26, 1973), whose international reputation was established and enhanced in Milan, Turin, Salzburg, Rome, Monte Carlo, Paris, and London, sang also at the Metropolitan Opera in New York City but was especially fond of the Chicago Opera, where she was warmly received from 1921 to 1923, and most especially from 1934 to 1942. Mason's voice was praised by critics for its delicate tones and exceptional smoothness.

MATTHEWS, THE VERY REV. WALTER ROBERT, British Anglican clergyman (b. London, Eng., Sept. 22, 1881—d. London, Dec. 4, 1973), dean of St. Paul's Cathedral (1934–67; later emeritus), was an outstanding philosophical theologian who, after five years as a bank clerk, worked his way up the academic ladder while simultaneously holding a rapid succession of curacies. He became chaplain to King George V in 1923. Apart from his work at London and Exeter (where he was dean from 1931 to 1934), he held external lectureships at Oxford and Harvard. He was largely responsible for guarding St. Paul's against destruction during World War II and for its later restoration.

MELCHIOR, LAURITZ, U.S. opera singer (b. Copenhagen, Den., March 20, 1890—d. Santa Monica, Calif., March 18, 1973), was considered the outstanding Wagnerian tenor of his time. He performed at the Metropolitan Opera in New York City from 1926 until 1950, starring in such operas as *Tannhäuser, Lohengrin, Die Walküre, Siegfried, Götterdämmerung, Tristan und Isolde,* and *Parsifal.* He appeared in a number of motion pictures, including *The Stars Are Singing* (1952).

MELVILLE, JEAN-PIERRE (JEAN-PIERRE GRUMBACH), French film director (b. Paris, France, Oct. 20, 1917—d. Paris, Aug. 2, 1973), influenced the French "new wave" of film directors of the late 1950s. He served in the Free French Army during World War II and used his resistance experience in his feature debut, *Le Silence de la Mer* (1947), and in *L'Armée des Ombres* (1969). Among his other films were a noteworthy adaptation of Jean Cocteau's *Les Enfants Terribles, Bob le Flambeur, Deux Hommes Dans Manhattan,* and *Le Samourai.*

MILLIONSHCHIKOV, MIKHAIL DMITRYEVICH, Soviet physicist (b. Russia, Jan. 16, 1913—d. Moscow, U.S.S.R., May 27, 1973), was joint director of the Kurtchatov Atomic Energy Institute and had been a president of the Supreme Soviet of the Russian Federation. Known for his work on turbulence, he was holder of a Lenin Prize and an active member of the international Pugwash movement for fostering contacts between scientists of all nations.

MITFORD, NANCY, British writer (b. November 1904—d. Versailles, France, June 30, 1973), was the daughter of the 2nd Lord Redesdale and the eldest of six gifted and unusual sisters. Nancy Mitford became a well-known novelist through *The Pursuit of Love* (1945) and *Love in a Cold Climate* (1949), with their lively caricatures of her father as "Uncle Matthew." Later she published the popular historical biographies *Madame de Pompadour* (1953), *Voltaire in Love* (1957), *The Sun King* (1966), and *Frederick the Great* (1970). She lightheartedly drew up a code of the social nuances of "U" (upper-class) and "non-U" behaviour.

MOBERG, CARL ARTHUR VILHELM, Swedish novelist (b. Algutsboda, Kronoberg, Swed., Aug. 20, 1898—d. Väddö, Roslagen, Swed., Aug. 8, 1973), was Sweden's best-known and most widely read contemporary author; in the 1970s he reached an international audience when his epic novels of 19th-century Swedish emigration to the United States were made into highly successful films (*The Emigrants, The New Land*). The son of a private soldier of Småland peasant stock, Moberg worked as a provincial journalist in the late 1920s, publishing his first novel, *Raskens,* in 1927. His books conveyed a strong vein of social criticism and he was an indefatigable campaigner for individual rights and against judicial abuses. His forthright opposition to Nazism, at a time when neutral Sweden possibly risked invasion by Germany, was unmistakably expressed in his historical novel *Rid i natt!* ("Ride This Night!"), published in 1941.

MONROE, VAUGHAN, U.S. singer and band leader (b. Akron, O., Oct. 7, 1912—d. Stuart, Fla., May 21, 1973), who introduced his own "Camel Caravan" radio show in 1945, was best known for his versions of the hit tunes "Racing with the Moon," his theme song for many years, and "Ghost Riders in the Sky."

MORIN, RELMAN ("PAT"), U.S. news reporter (b. Freeport, Ill., Sept. 11, 1907—d. New York, N.Y., July 16, 1973), with the Associated Press from 1934, was the recipient of two Pulitzer prizes in journalism. The first award, in 1951, was for his coverage of the Korean War; in 1958 he was honoured for his story of school desegregation in Little Rock, Ark.

NABARRO, SIR GERALD DAVID NUNES, British politician (b. London, Eng., June 29, 1913—d. Broadway, Worcestershire, Eng., Nov. 18, 1973), was a Conservative member of Parliament for Kidderminster (1950–64) and for South Worcestershire (1966–73), and one of the most colourful of backbenchers. His self-written epitaph read: "A splendid moustache, a deep resonant voice, a remarkable memory were among the characteristics of this notorious man. . . . He tried hard, always, but never quite made it." He pressured governments into simplifying the purchase tax system, into passing a Clean Air Act (1955), and into putting health warnings on cigarette packets. He also fought for tax reductions. He was knighted in 1963.

NAISH, J(OSEPH PATRICK) CARROL, U.S. actor (b. New York, N.Y., Jan. 21, 1900—d. La Jolla, Calif., Jan. 24, 1973), a master of dialect, during his 30-year career played character roles representing almost every nationality. His first major part was that of an elderly Chinese in *The Hatchet Man,* with Edward G. Robinson (1932). Other films included *Captain Blood, Beau Geste* (1939), and *A Medal for Benny* (1945), for which he received an Academy Award nomination. Naish starred in the radio-TV comedy series "Life with Luigi" from 1948 until 1953 and later appeared on Broadway in *A View from the Bridge* (1955).

NANSEN, ODD, Norwegian champion of the cause of refugees (b. Lysaker, Nor., Dec. 6, 1901—d. Oslo, Nor., June 27, 1973), son of the explorer Fridtjof Nansen and an architect by profession, who devoted himself to the alleviation of the sufferings of refugees uprooted by two world wars. He founded the Nansen Help Organization in 1936, aided the escape of Norwegians to Sweden after 1940, was himself arrested in 1941 and imprisoned in concentration camps till 1945. Thereafter he was active in Norwegian aid and in 1954 was designated by his government to represent it on the committee of the UN High Commissioner for Refugees. He took a lead in sponsoring the World Refugee years 1960 and 1971 and the European Refugee Campaign of 1966.

NASSER, KAMAL, Palestinian nationalist and poet (b. Bir Zeit, Transjordan, 1928—d. Beirut, Lebanon, April 10, 1973), was a member of the Palestine National Council and from 1968 official spokesman for the Palestine Liberation Organization. A poet, active in pan-Arab politics from his student days, Nasser was exiled from the West Bank of Jordan by the Israelis after the Six-Day War of 1967. He was assassinated in an Israeli commando raid into Beirut.

NEILL, A(LEXANDER) S(UTHERLAND), Scottish educator (b. Forfar, Scot., Oct. 17, 1883—d. Aldeburgh, Suffolk, Eng., Sept. 23, 1973), was a pioneer and champion of free self-development by children and founder of the internationally famous Summerhill School in Suffolk where pupils governed themselves and attendance at lessons was optional. A headmaster of Gretna Green School, and later a teacher at the King Alfred School, Hampstead, Neill moved to Dresden in 1921, and there ran the international department of a school, before founding one of his own in Austria. This school, which he brought to England in 1924, became Summerhill.

NERUDA, PABLO, Chilean poet, diplomat, and political partisan (b. Parral, Chile, July 12, 1904—d. Santiago, Chile, Sept. 23, 1973), referred to as "the poet of enslaved humanity," was awarded the Lenin Prize for Peace and the Nobel Prize for Literature in 1971, during which time he served as Chilean ambassador to France.

Neruda was raised in the frontier lands of southern Chile where he became also a militant anarchist and translated the work of Jean Grave, theorist of Peter Kropotkin's "anarchist communism."

Pablo Neruda

A.F.P./PICTORIAL PARADE

In 1921 Neruda moved to Santiago and in 1923 published his first book, *Crepusculario,* at his own expense. The following year he found a publisher for what was to become his most widely read book: *Veinte poemas de amor y una canción desesperada.* The year 1927 marked the beginning of his long career as diplomat/poet with appointment as honorary consul in Rangoon, Burma. In 1933 he was named Chilean consul in Buenos Aires, Arg., where he began a friendship with the visiting Spanish poet Federico García Lorca. The following year he was transferred to Barcelona and later to Madrid.

However, these years of poetic and political development were interrupted by the outbreak of the Spanish Civil War in 1936. The execution of Lorca, the "blood in the streets," and the imprisonment of his friends all contributed to the development of Neruda's political attitudes reflected in *España en el corazón,* published from the Republican front lines.

Returning to Chile in 1938 as a refugee, Neruda entered a phase of intense poetic production, much of it determined by World War II, and renewed his political activity. When, however, the Chilean government moved to the right, Neruda, a Communist, was forced into hiding. Those clandestine years produced *Canto general,* and forced Neruda to travel extensively. In 1952, after the order to arrest leftist writers and political figures had been withdrawn, he returned to Chile, where he married his third wife, Matilde Urrutia.

During the 20 years of poetry and politics that followed, Neruda articulated the growth and chaos experienced by his continent. His steadfast support of Marxist Salvador Allende (*q.v.*) capped a lifetime devoted to the integration of private and public expression.

NICHOLS, ROY FRANKLIN, U.S. historian (b. Newark, N.J., March 3, 1896—d. Philadelphia, Pa., Jan. 11, 1973), was dean of the Graduate School of Arts and Science of the University of Pennsylvania from 1952 to 1966. In 1949 he received the Pulitzer Prize in history for his distinguished work on the causes of the American Civil War, *The Disruption of American Democracy.* He was the author of other authoritative books on U.S. history, including *The Invention of the American Political Parties* (1967). Nichols was president of the American Historical Association in 1966.

NICHOLSON, NORA, British actress (b. Leamington, Warwickshire, Eng., Dec. 7, 1892—d. London, Eng., Sept. 18, 1973), whose anonymous face and frail, eager figure became known to millions through minor "character roles" portrayed on stage, television (particularly in *The Forsyte Saga*), and film over more than 60 years. She studied under Frank Benson, made her debut at Stratford-on-Avon in 1912 and later joined the original Shakespeare company of the Old Vic. Acknowledgment of her quiet and subtle talent came slowly through such parts as the governess in *The Cherry Orchard,* but was widespread after her spinster role in Wynyard Browne's *Dark Summer* and her portrayal of Margaret in Christopher Fry's *The Lady's Not for Burning* (1949).

NORD, FRIEDRICH FRANZ, U.S. biochemist (b. Budapest, Hung., Aug. 9, 1889—d. Vermont, July 12, 1973), established the concept of cryobiology, the use of low-temperature environments in biological research (1927), and was the first to isolate lignin (1955), the chief component of woody tissue. He was the founder (1941) and editor of *Archives of Biochemistry,* and editor (1939–71) of *Advances in Enzymology and Related Areas of Molecular Biology.*

NURMI, PAAVO JOHANNES, Finnish runner (b. Turku, Fin., June 13, 1897—d. Helsinki, Fin., Oct. 2, 1973), known as the "Flying Finn" and considered by many the greatest runner of all time, won seven individual Olympic gold medals and between 1921 and 1932 broke more than two dozen world records at distances ranging from 1,500 m. to 40,000 m. In 1920 he made his international debut, winning the 10,000-m. track and 10,000-m. cross-country events in the Olympic Games in Antwerp, Belg. In 1923, while holding the world 10,000-m. record, he became the fastest miler with a time of 4 min. 10.4 sec. The next day he set a world three-mile record. On June 19, 1924, in just over one hour, he broke the world records for both 1,500 m. and 5,000 m. The following month he won those events at the Paris Olympics, where, in addition, he won gold medals in the 3,000-m. team race and 10,000-m. cross-country. In the 1928 Olympics in Amsterdam he won the 10,000 m. once more. In 1952 he carried the Olympic torch at the opening of the Games at Helsinki.

OHBA, MASAO, Japanese boxer (b. 1950—d. Tokyo, Jap., Jan. 25, 1973), world flyweight boxing champion, was killed when his sports car smashed into a truck. Ohba won his world title in October 1970 when he knocked out Berkrerk Chartvanchai of Thailand in the 13th round. After turning professional in 1966, he established a career record of 35 victories (including 16 knockouts), 2 losses, and 1 draw; he successfully defended his crown five times.

ORMESSON, COUNT WLADIMIR LEFÈVRE D', French author and diplomat (b. St. Petersburg, Russia, Aug. 2, 1888—d. Ormesson-sur-Marne, France, Sept. 15, 1973), was president of the board of ORTF (French Radio and Television; 1964–68) and a member of the board of the Paris daily newspaper *Le Figaro,* to which he was a contributor from the early 1930s. In 1940 he was appointed ambassador to the Vatican, but was dismissed by Marshal Philippe Pétain and sought by the Gestapo. In 1945 Ormesson was appointed ambassador to Argentina by Gen. Charles de Gaulle and in 1948 he returned to the Vatican, becoming a close friend of Pius XII. He was elected to the French Academy in 1956.

OTTESEN-JENSEN, ELISE, Norwegian-born social reformer (b. Højland, Nor., Jan. 2, 1886—d. Stockholm, Swed., Sept. 4, 1973), was founder and second president of the International Planned Parenthood Federation. She fought long and hard for reform in social mores, and in 1933 she founded the Swedish National League for Sex Education, to promote sex education in schools, establish guidance centres, eradicate illegal abortion, provide free contraceptives, and amend laws on homosexuality. In 1972 she was nominated for the Nobel Peace Prize.

PALOCZI-HORVATH, GEORGE, Hungarian-born British writer (b. Budapest, Hung., 1908—d. London, Eng., Jan. 3, 1973), whose autobiography, *The Undefeated* (1959), tells of two hazardous escapes from Hungary, torture by the secret police, five years in prison, and an active part in the 1956 uprising, left Hungary at the outset of World War II and became a British intelligence agent in the Middle East. Returning to Hungary after the war, he was arrested on charges of espionage and imprisoned until after Stalin's death. Among his writings are biographies of Nikita S. Khrushchev (1960) and Mao Tse-tung (1962), *The Writer and the Commissar* (1960), *The Facts Rebel* (1964), and *Youth up in Arms* (1971).

PAVEL, JOSEF, Czechoslovak politician (b. 1908—d. Prague, Czech., April 9, 1973), was Czechoslovak minister of the interior just prior to the Soviet invasion of Czechoslovakia in August 1968, when he tried to dismantle the network of Soviet agents in the Czechoslovak police and secret service. A battalion commander in the International Brigade in the Spanish Civil War, he was interned in France in 1939 as a Communist and released in 1943. Back in Czechoslovakia, he headed the Security Department of the Central Committee of the Communist Party in 1947, and secured the Communist seizure of power in 1948 as commander of the People's Militia. After serving briefly as deputy minister of the interior, he was arrested and sentenced to 25 years' imprisonment in 1951, but was released in 1955 and given an obscure post. He became minister of the interior under the Alexander Dubcek regime but was prevented from carrying through his intended reforms. He was forced to resign ten days after the Soviet invasion in 1968 and was expelled from the Communist Party in 1970.

PAXINOU, KATINA, Greek tragic actress (b. Piraeus, Athens, Greece, 1904?—d. Athens, Feb. 22, 1973), whose primitive power frequently enthralled huge audiences at Epidaurus, won an Oscar in 1943 for her performance as Pilar in the film version of Ernest Hemingway's *For Whom the Bell Tolls.* After a beginning in opera, her first dramatic role came in 1924 in *La Femme Nue;* she became a leading lady at the Royal Theatre, Athens, playing ancient and modern classics, and in 1939 and 1940 appeared on the London stage before going to the U.S. She returned to Athens in the early 1950s and helped to revive ancient Greek tragedy at the National Theatre.

PEERS, DONALD, Welsh singer (b. Wales, 1909—d. Brighton, Eng., Aug. 9, 1973), popular in the late 1940s and early 1950s with songs like "Powder Your Face with Sunshine," "Faraway Places," and "By a Babbling Brook," his signature tune.

PICASSO, PABLO RUIZ (Y), Spanish painter, sculptor, and engraver (b. Málaga, Spain, Oct. 25, 1881—d. Mougins, France, April 8, 1973), the greatest exponent of the visual arts of the 20th century, credited, with Georges Braque, with the invention of Cubism. He produced an estimated 14,000 paintings and drawings, 100,000 prints, 24,000 book illustrations, and 300 models and sculptural works, radically altered the course of art in his time, and won the unique accolade for a living artist of an exhibition at the Louvre, Paris, to mark his 90th birthday.

The son of a painter, Picasso left the Royal Academy at Madrid with high awards and finally established himself in Paris in 1904. He then began his progress through a succession of styles, beginning with strongly coloured portraits and real-life scenes. Next were scenes of poverty and suffering in his "blue" period of painting of great delicacy, 1901–04. Then, with a lessened interest in emotional qualities, and influenced by Paul Cézanne and African sculpture, he produced "Les Demoiselles d'Avignon" (1907) and introduced a revolutionary exchange of Renaissance perspective for a shifting viewpoint, giving birth to Cubism. A naturalistic and monumental style followed—his "neoclassical" period, during 1918–23—and about 1925 he began the formulation of the astonishing dislocations of features and limbs that marked his work thereafter. In the 1920s he took up sculpture and was to execute powerful works ("Man with a Lamb," 1943–44), while also being influenced by Surrealism. The Spanish Civil War inspired his apocalyptic composition "Guernica" (1937) and the concentration camps of World War II did the same for "The Charnel House" (1945). In 1945 Picasso joined the Communist Party and a preoccupation with humanity's need for peace was reflected in the mural for UNESCO headquarters in Paris (he was awarded the Lenin Peace Prize in 1963). After 1955 he was increasingly absorbed by themes of the artist ("Les Ménines," 1957) and, later, emotions, physical sensations, and old age. Picasso's work in other fields included décors for Sergei Diaghilev's Russian ballets *Parade, Le Tricorne,* and *Pulcinella;* many fine engravings, with technical innovations in lithography; painted ceramics; superb book illustrations; and gay little artifacts made out of any material at hand. During his last years Picasso lived mainly in the Provence region of France, near the sea. All his work expresses his intense concern with the eternal themes of birth, life, love, death, time, and truth, and their special relevance to the creative artist, often in images from classical mythology. Women (he married twice) and children completed his existence.

Pablo Picasso

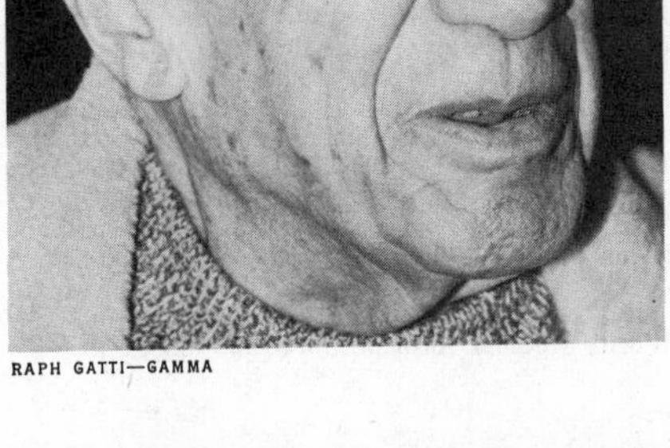

RAPH GATTI—GAMMA

PINCUS, LOUIS ARIEH, Israeli Zionist leader (b. Clocolan, Orange Free State, S.Af., May 21, 1912—d. Jerusalem, July 25, 1973), was chairman of the executive of the Jewish Agency and World Zionist Federation. In 1948 he moved to Palestine, just before the proclamation of the Israeli state. Under Israel's first government he was appointed director general and legal adviser to the Ministry of Transport. He joined the executive of the Jewish Agency in 1961, and succeeded Moshe Sharett as chairman in 1965. In later years he fought for the right of Soviet Jews to emigrate to Israel.

PLOMER, WILLIAM CHARLES FRANKLYN, South African writer born of English parents (b. Pietersburg, S.Af., Dec. 10, 1903—d. Brighton, Eng., Sept. 21, 1973), was associated with the poet Roy Campbell in a radical review *Voorslag*, and caused an outcry with his novel *Turbott Wolfe* (1926) because of its concern with race relations. Travel in Africa, Japan, and Europe bore fruit in short stories and novels, *I Speak of Africa* (1927), *Paper Houses* (stories about Japan, 1929), *The Case Is Altered* (1932) and *The Invaders* (1934), both set in London, and *Museum Pieces* (1952), and in two volumes of autobiography, *Double Lives*. (1943) and *At Home* (1958). He also wrote librettos for Benjamin Britten, and was a notable poet (awarded the Queen's Gold Medal for Poetry in 1963), whose *Collected Poems* (1960) was followed by *Taste and Remember* (1966) and *Celebrations* (1972). Plomer also discovered and edited (3 vol., 1938–40) the remarkable diaries of the Victorian clergyman Francis Kilvert.

POST, MARJORIE MERRIWEATHER, U.S. business executive and philanthropist (b. Springfield, Ill., March 15, 1887—d. Washington, D.C., Sept. 12, 1973), was the grand matron of American high society for some 40 years. Her first involvement in business began at age ten when she started to attend board meetings of the Postum Cereal Co. with her father. When he died in 1914, Miss Post inherited several million dollars and control of the company. By 1929 she and the second of her four husbands changed the company name to General Foods Corp., which marketed a wide variety of products, including some of the first frozen foods. A large part of Miss Post's personal wealth, estimated at $200 million, was bequeathed to public institutions.

PREETORIUS, EMIL, German stage designer and graphic artist (b. Mainz, Ger., June 21, 1883—d. Munich, W.Ger., January 1973), abandoned a career in law for art, in which he was largely self-taught. As an illustrator (one of the *Simplicissimus* group) he strongly influenced German book design. Encouraged by Thomas Mann, he turned to stage design and eventually became head of design at the Festspielhaus, Bayreuth, where his Wagnerian settings were noted for their stylized naturalism. He was also a collector of East Asian art.

PRICE, DENNIS (DENNISTOUN FRANKLYN JOHN ROSE-PRICE), British actor (b. Twyford, Berkshire, Eng., June 23, 1915—d. Guernsey, Channel Islands, Oct. 6, 1973), known to millions for his portrayals of refined villainy. His cool, sardonic style was best seen in *Kind Hearts and Coronets*. Other films included *The Bad Lord Byron, I'm All Right Jack, School for Scoundrels*, and *Wonderful Life*. His New York debut came with *Heartbreak House* in 1959. In 1965 he enjoyed an outstanding success on television as Jeeves, the manservant of P. G. Wodehouse's Bertie Wooster.

PRICE THOMAS, SIR CLEMENT, British surgeon (b. Abercarn, Monmouthshire, Wales, Nov. 22, 1893—d. March 19, 1973), an internationally distinguished pioneer of thoracic surgery, successfully performed a serious thoracic operation on King George VI in 1951. He was civilian consultant in thoracic surgery to the RAF and to the British Army (1946–63) and adviser in thoracic surgery to the Ministry of Health (1946–63), as well as being president of the Association of Surgeons of Great Britain and Ireland, the Society of Thoracic Surgeons, the Royal Society of Medicine, the British Medical Association, and the World Medical Association (1965–66).

RABINOWITCH, EUGENE, U.S. physical chemist and atomic scientist (b. St. Petersburg, Russia, April 27, 1901—d. Washington, D.C., May 15, 1973), was senior chemist (1944–46) on the Manhattan Project that led to the development of the atomic bomb. From 1947 to 1968 he was professor of botany and biophysics at the University of Illinois, Urbana, then he transferred to the State University of New York at Albany as professor of chemistry. In September 1972, on leave from Albany, he joined the Smithsonian Institution, Washington, D.C., to investigate the scientific revolution and its social implications. He was founder (1945) and editor of the *Bulletin of the Atomic Scientists*.

RADFORD, ARTHUR WILLIAM, admiral (ret.), U.S. Navy (b. Chicago, Ill., Feb. 27, 1896—d. Bethesda, Md., Aug. 17, 1973), a much-decorated veteran of three U.S. wars, was promoted to full admiral in 1949. He was then named commander in chief of the Pacific Fleet. Pres. Dwight Eisenhower appointed him chairman of the Joint Chiefs of Staff in 1953, the first navy man to hold the post. In 1957, during his second term in that position, he retired from active duty.

RANKIN, JEANNETTE, U.S. congresswoman (1917–19, 1941–43) from Montana (b. near Missoula, Mont., June 11, 1880—d. Carmel, Calif., May 18, 1973), a militant feminist and social reformer, was the first woman to serve in the U.S. Congress and the only member to have voted against U.S. entry into both World Wars I and II. A Republican, she was elected to the House of Representatives in 1916. She was defeated in her bid for a second consecutive term, but was elected for one more term in 1940.

RENWICK, ROBERT BURNHAM RENWICK, 1st BARON, British businessman (b. Oct. 4, 1904—d. London, Eng., Aug. 30, 1973), was chairman of the Institute of Directors, a long-standing opponent of nationalization, and a pioneer of British commercial television. He was controller of communications at the Air Ministry (1942–45) and chairman of Associated Television (1961–73), and held a number of other directorships.

RICHARDS, DICKINSON W., U.S. physiologist (b. Orange, N.J., Oct. 30, 1895—d. Lakeville, Conn., Feb. 23, 1973), received the Nobel Prize for Physiology or Medicine in 1956 for his work in cardiac physiology that paved the way for open-heart surgery. In 1945 he became director of the First Medical Division at Bellevue Hospital in New York City and in 1947 was appointed Lambert professor of medicine at Columbia University. He retired from both posts in 1961. Richards shared his Nobel Prize with André F. Cournand, also of Columbia, and Werner Forssmann of West Germany. Richards published two books, *Circulation of the Blood: Men and Ideas* (with A. P. Fishman; 1964) and *Medical Priesthoods and Other Essays* (1970).

RICKENBACKER, CAPT. EDDIE (EDWARD VERNON RICKENBACKER), U.S. racing driver, World War I flying ace, and commercial airline executive (b. Columbus, O., Oct. 8, 1890—d. Zürich, Switz., July 23, 1973), gained international fame in three major careers. As racing driver-salesman for the Frayer-Miller Co. he set a world speed record of 134 mph and won seven national championships.

During World War I Rickenbacker was credited with 22 enemy planes and four observation balloons, and he became the most decorated American pilot of the war. In 1934, as general manager of Eastern Air Lines, he set a speed record for passenger planes flying from coast to coast. Under his management the airline made the first profits in aviation history. Rickenbacker bought the airline in 1938; he resigned as president in 1959 and as director and chairman of the board in 1963.

Twice during World War II he made headlines. Though critically injured, he was one of eight survivors (eight others died) of an air crash outside Atlanta, Ga., and in October 1942 was aboard a B-17 that crashed in the Pacific. Capt. Eddie (the name he preferred) was rescued with six others after 22 days on rubber rafts.

Never hesitant to speak his mind, Rickenbacker supported Sen. Joseph McCarthy, advocated severance of diplomatic relations with the Soviet Union, withdrawal from the UN, and the abolition of government subsidies, trade unions, and personal income tax. He wrote three books: *Fighting the Flying Circus, Seven Came Through*, and *Rickenbacker—An Autobiography*.

Edward G. Robinson

UPI COMPIX

ROBINSON, EDWARD G. (EMANUEL GOLDENBERG), U.S. actor (b. Bucharest, Rom., Dec. 12, 1893—d. Hollywood, Calif., Jan. 26, 1973), whose portrayals of movie gangsters set a trend in crime films in the 1930s. His first notable screen success, in the early 1930s classic *Little Caesar*, brought a demand for his appearance in dozens of similar roles, including *Smart Money, Five Star Final, A Slight Case of Murder*, and *I Am the Law*. Later films included *The Cincinnati Kid* (1965) and *Grand Slam* (1968). In all, Robinson made more than 100 pictures during his 50-year career and played in 40 Broadway productions. In March 1973 a special Academy Award was conferred on him posthumously "for his outstanding contribution to motion pictures." An avid art collector, Robinson amassed paintings once valued at $3,250,000.

ROCKEFELLER, WINTHROP, U.S. political and philanthropic figure (b. New York, N.Y., May 1, 1912—d. Palm Springs, Calif., Feb. 22, 1973), grandson of multimillionaire industrialist John D. Rockefeller, was governor of Arkansas from 1967 until 1971. During his governorship he secured passage of the state's first minimum-wage law, introduced extensive prison reforms, and led an industrialization drive in the state that resulted in 600 new plants and 90,000 more jobs. His philanthropies in Arkansas included: $1,250,000 for a model school; financing of civic projects and medical clinics; and contributions to the building of the Arts Center at Little Rock.

RUÍZ CORTINES, ADOLFO, Mexican politician (b. Veracruz, Mex., Dec. 30, 1890—d. Mexico City, Mex., Dec. 3, 1973), while president of Mexico from 1952 to 1958 initiated quiet but forceful measures to remove corruption from government and restore public confidence in the administration.

RYAN, IRENE NOBLETTE (MRS. TIM RYAN), U.S. actress (b. El Paso, Tex., 1903—d. Santa Monica, Calif., April 26, 1973), star of the "Beverly Hillbillies" television series from 1962 through 1971, whose 60-year acting career covered vaudeville, stock, musical comedy, motion pictures, and the Broadway stage, where she last appeared in *Pippin* (1972–73).

RYAN, ROBERT, U.S. actor (b. Chicago, Ill., Nov. 11, 1913—d. New York, N.Y., July 11, 1973), Hollywood "tough guy," played first on Broadway in *Clash by Night* in 1941. Two other Broadway appearances won acclaim, a 1969 revival of *The Front Page* and another revival, *Long Day's Journey into Night*, in 1971. Ryan made his film debut in *Bombardier* in 1943 and went on to make some 90 more pictures, including *Crossfire* (1947) and *The Set-up* (1949), two he considered among his best, and *Executive Action* and *The Iceman Cometh*, both of which were completed in 1973.

ST. LAURENT, LOUIS STEPHEN, Canadian lawyer and politician (b. Compton, Que., Feb. 1, 1882—d. Quebec, Que., July 25, 1973), was Liberal prime minister of Canada from 1948 to 1957.

To underscore Canadian independence, his government eliminated recourse to the Privy Council in London by making the Canadian Supreme Court the highest legal body available to Canadian subjects. Though he was only the second French Canadian to become prime minister, St. Laurent was unsympathetic to the Quebec separatist movement.

SANDS, DIANA, U.S. stage, film, and television actress (b. New York, N.Y., Aug. 22, 1934—d. New York, Sept. 21, 1973), received the Outer Circle Critics' Award for her 1959 role in the stage play *A Raisin in the Sun.* Miss Sands continued on the road to stardom in such stage and film productions as *The Egg and I* (1958), *Tiger, Tiger, Burning Bright* (1962), *The Owl and the Pussycat* (1964), *Two for the Seesaw* (1967), and *An Affair of the Skin* (1963), winning the International Artist Award in 1961, the Theatre World Award in 1963, the Obie Award in 1964, and Tony and Emmy nominations.

SANTOS, RUFINO CARDINAL, Filipino prelate of the Roman Catholic Church (b. Guagua, Pampanga Province, Phil., Aug. 26, 1908—d. Manila, Phil., Sept. 3, 1973), was appointed the first Filipino cardinal by Pope John XXIII in 1960. After his ordination in Rome in 1931, Santos returned to Manila where he was entrusted with ever increasing responsibilities in archdiocesan administration. He was named auxiliary bishop of Manila in 1947 and archbishop in 1953. Santos was a controversial figure, criticized by activist Catholics for his alleged conservative policies, extensive landholdings, and financial control of three Manila banks.

SCHIAPARELLI, ELSA, Italian-born French fashion designer (b. Rome, Italy, Sept. 10, 1896—d. Paris, France, Nov. 13, 1973), used a daring, somewhat surrealistic talent to establish herself as a leading European designer during the 1930s. She was the first to use rough-surfaced fabrics for formal as well as sportswear; the first to use zippers in dressmaking (1935); and the first to use man-made fibres such as nylon. She became a French citizen in 1931. In 1940 she received the Nieman-Marcus Award for distinguished service in the field of fashion design. She published her *Shocking Life* in 1954.

SCHMIDT-ISSERSTEDT, HANS, German conductor (b. Berlin, Ger., May 5, 1900—d. Hamburg, W.Ger., May 28, 1973), was musical conductor of the North West (later North) German Radio Symphony Orchestra from 1945. He was also, from 1954 until 1963, principal conductor of the Stockholm Philharmonic. He conducted memorable performances of Mozart's *Figaro* (at Glyndebourne in 1958) and of Wagner's *Tristan* (at Covent Garden in 1962). He conducted all the major London orchestras and was the chief advocate in West Germany of the music of Michael Tippett.

SENANAYAKE, DUDLEY, Sinhalese politician (b. Ceylon, June 19, 1911—d. Colombo, Sri Lanka [Ceylon], April 12, 1973), was prime minister of his country on three occasions. A barrister by profession, he was appointed minister of agriculture by his father, Prime Minister D. S. Senanayake, in 1947. On his father's death in March 1952, he became Ceylon's youngest prime minister; he was confirmed in office in May after an immediate general election but resigned because of ill health in 1953. In 1958 he returned to politics to head the United National Party, but was shortly defeated by Mrs. Sirimavo Bandaranaike's Freedom Party. In 1965 Senanayake formed a coalition government with five other parties but was defeated again in the 1970 general election.

SERREAU, JEAN-MARIE, French stage director (b. Poitiers, France, April 28, 1915—d. Paris, France, May 22, 1973), helped launch the post-World War II European avant-garde theatre, introducing dramatists like Samuel Beckett, Bertolt Brecht, Jean Genet, Eugène Ionesco, and Max Frisch to the French public. In 1952 he opened the left bank Théâtre de Babylone and a decade later went on to discover "third world" dramatists such as Aimé Césaire and Kateb Yacine; he also introduced Brecht to black Africa, with an African cast.

SEYRIG, HENRI ARNOLD, French archaeologist (b. Héricourt, France, Nov. 10, 1895—d. Neuchâtel, Switz., Jan. 23, 1973), an outstanding Hellenist, was secretary-general of the French School of Archaeology at Athens (1922–29), director of antiquities in Syria and Lebanon (1929–41), cultural attaché to the French embassy in Washington, D.C. (1943–46), and director of the French Institute of Archaeology at Beirut, Lebanon (1946–67). He was also director of French museums (1960–62). He directed the journal *Syria,* in which he published a notable series on Syrian antiquities, and contributed to *Encyclopædia Britannica.*

SHARPLES, SIR RICHARD CHRISTOPHER, British politician (b. Aug. 6, 1916—d. Hamilton, Bermuda, March 10, 1973), governor of Bermuda from October 1972, was murdered, with his aide-de-camp, on the grounds of Government House, Hamilton, by unknown assailants, just six months after the unsolved assassination of the island's commissioner of police. After World War II service with the Welsh Guards, Sharples was Field Marshal Lord Montgomery's military assistant (1951–53) before entering Parliament as Conservative MP for Sutton and Cheam in 1954. He held various posts in the postwar Conservative governments and was minister of state, Home Office, from 1970 to 1972.

SISLER, GEORGE HAROLD, U.S. baseball player (b. Nimisila, O., March 24, 1893—d. St. Louis, Mo., March 26, 1973), called the "perfect ballplayer," spent most of his 15-year professional career as first baseman with the St. Louis Browns. He won the American League batting title in 1920 with .407 and again in 1922 with .420. Eye trouble caused a year's layoff in 1923, but he came back the next season as player-manager of the Browns, hitting .304 that year and .345 in 1925. Sisler went to Washington in 1928, then to the Boston Braves where he finished his major league career in 1930. His lifetime batting average was .340. He was elected to baseball's Hall of Fame in 1939.

SMITH, MILDRED CATHARINE, U.S. publishing executive (b. Smithsport, Pa.—d. Long Island, N.Y., Aug. 30, 1973), was associated with R. R. Bowker Co. and *Publishers Weekly* for some 45 years. She was made a director of Bowker in 1934 and secretary in 1935. In 1962, five years before her retirement, she was named editor in chief of *Publishers Weekly.*

STEICHEN, EDWARD JEAN, U.S. master photographer (b. Luxembourg, March 27, 1879—d. West Redding, Conn., March 25, 1973), emeritus director of the department of photography of the Museum of Modern Art in New York City, abandoned a career in painting for one in photography, which he then raised to the level of a fine art. His first important job (1923) was doing portrait and fashion photography for *Vogue* and *Vanity Fair.*

Though Steichen photographed everything from flowers to cityscapes to insects, his portraits were especially remarkable for their use of soft lighting that conveyed an emotion or mood normally found only in paintings. In 1942, 150 of Steichen's photos, reflecting the spirit and energy of the American people and entitled "Road to Victory," were exhibited at the Museum of Modern Art. The texts that accompanied the photos were contributed by Carl Sandburg, his brother-in-law. In 1955 Steichen selected 503 photos of men, women, and children by 273 photographers for an exhibit called "The Family of Man." It was meant to show the essential oneness of mankind and was viewed by more than nine million persons in 69 countries; in book form it sold more than three million copies. The museum honoured Steichen in 1961 with a one-man exhibit and later established the Edward Steichen Photography Center. His autobiography, *A Life in Photography,* was published in 1963.

STEIN, LEONARD, British Zionist (b. London, Eng., Dec. 12, 1887—d. London, April 23, 1973), was political secretary of the World Zionist Organization (1920–29), honorary legal adviser to the Jewish Agency for Palestine (1929–39), and president of the Anglo-Jewish Association (1939–49). He was a principal lieutenant of Zionist leader Chaim Weizmann, whose letters he edited. He wrote several books on the Palestine problem, and others on taxation, a subject on which he specialized at the bar.

STRANSKY, JAROSLAV, former Czechoslovak minister (b. Brno, Moravia [now Czechoslovakia], Jan. 15, 1884—d. Canvey Island, Eng., Aug. 12, 1973), was a historian and legal expert and had been a member of all the governments of Edvard Benes from 1940, in exile in London and afterward in Prague until 1948, when the Communists took over. He then returned to England and thereafter broadcast regularly for Radio Free Europe.

SUN FO, Chinese politician (b. Kwangtung, China, Oct. 20, 1891—d. Taipei, Taiwan, Sept. 13, 1973), a son of Sun Yat-sen, the founder of the Republic of China, was himself its prime minister from November 1948 to March 1949. Mayor of Canton (1921–25, 1927), a member of the Kuomintang Central Committee in 1926, and thereafter holder of a succession of ministerial posts, he failed in his bid for the vice-presidency of China in April 1948. Regarded as an obstacle to peace, he resigned in 1949. He later lived in France, the U.S., and Taiwan, where in 1965 he became a senior adviser to Pres. Chiang Kai-shek.

SZIGETI, JOSEPH, Hungarian violinist (b. Budapest, Hung., Sept. 5, 1892—d. Lucerne, Switz., Feb. 19, 1973), was an internationally admired virtuoso, distinctive for the purity of his tone and unadorned honesty of style. As well as being a master of the classic repertoire, he gave first performances of the violin concerti of Busoni, Casella, and Hamilton Harty and included in his repertoire works by Prokofiev, Bloch, Bartok, and Stravinsky. He devoted much of his time to teaching and was also a master of transcription.

TINGSTEN, HERBERT L. G., Swedish political scientist (b. Järfälla, Swed., March 17, 1896—d. Dec. 26, 1973), was editor in chief of the influential Stockholm newspaper *Dagens Nyheter* from 1946 to 1960 and was the author of numerous books on political and social problems in Sweden and other countries, including the U.S., West Germany, South Africa, Japan, Israel, and the U.K. An opponent of Socialism, Tingsten believed that Sweden should join the Atlantic alliance.

TITMUSS, RICHARD MORRIS, British scholar and social administrator (b. Bedfordshire, Eng., 1907—d. London, Eng., April 6, 1973), professor of social administration and deputy chairman of the Supplementary Benefits Commission from 1968. During 17 years spent working in an insurance company he wrote three books, *Poverty and Population* (1938), *Our Food Problem* (1939), and *Parents Revolt* (1942), as a result of which he was invited to join a team of historians writing the civil history of World War II. His *Problems of Social Policy* (1950) won him the chair of social administration at the London School of Economics in 1950. His *The Social Division of Welfare* (1956) was the basis of later Labour Party plans for social security reform. *Income Distribution and Social Change* (1962) revealed how untrue it was that income distribution had become less unequal since 1945. A critique of the commercial market in human blood, *The Gift Relationship* (1970), led, in the U.S., to congressional regulation of the private market in blood.

TOLANSKY, SAMUEL, British physicist (b. Newcastle upon Tyne, Eng., Nov. 17, 1907—d. Roehampton, Eng., March 4, 1973), professor of physics at the University of London's Royal Holloway College from 1947, who correctly predicted that the moon's surface would be covered by millions of tiny glassy "marbles" (caused by meteoritic impact or volcanic activity), was among the first scientists chosen to study moon dust brought back by Apollo astronauts.

TOLKIEN, JOHN RONALD REUEL, English author, philologist, and scholar (b. Bloemfontein, S.Af., Jan. 3, 1892—d. Bournemouth, Eng., Sept. 2, 1973), creator of *The Hobbit* (1937) and *The Lord of the Rings* (3 vol., 1954–55), two immensely popular—especially among the young—works of imagination, was professor of Anglo-Saxon (1925–45) and Merton professor of English language and literature (1945–59) at Oxford University. He first achieved fame with his edition of *Sir Gawain and the Green Knight* and his essay *Beowulf: The Monster and the Critics.* He wrote a farce, *Farmer Giles of Ham* (1949), and a great deal of unpublished material including his last book, "The Silmarillion."

TOMALIN, NICHOLAS, British journalist (b. London, Eng., 1931—d. Israel, Oct. 17, 1973), greatly admired for the consistently high quality of his reporting, which, through dispatches in the *Sunday Times,* contributed uniquely to the British people's understanding of the Vietnam war. His last dispatch to the *Sunday Times,* from Israel's northern front during its fourth war with the Arabs, dryly observed that he had just had the honour of being the first Englishman to be bombed by the new Soviet Sukhoi bomber. He was later killed by a Syrian rocket.

TOUREL, JENNIE, U.S. mezzo-soprano (b. Montreal, Que., June 1910—d. New York, N.Y., Nov. 23, 1973), made her operatic debut with the Chicago Civic Opera in 1930. Her first major role was that of Carmen at the Opéra Comique in Paris in 1933. After a number of highly successful seasons in Paris she joined the Metropolitan Opera of New York City. It was in concerts, however, that her extraordinary voice and flawless control created the greatest excitement. She sang under the direction of Toscanini, Koussevitsky, Stokowski, and every other major director who could secure her services. She seemed to have special rapport with Leonard Bernstein, with whom she recorded some of her greatest music.

TREGASKIS, RICHARD, U.S. war correspondent and author (b. Elizabeth, N.J., Nov. 28, 1916—d. Honolulu, Hawaii, Aug. 15, 1973), covered nine wars during his professional career. His *Guadalcanal Diary,* a popular and critical success, was made into a motion picture the year it was published (1943). Tregaskis later won the George Polk Memorial Award for *Vietnam Diary* (1963).

TUGENDHAT, GEORG, Austrian oil pioneer and commentator (b. Vienna, Aus., Feb. 17, 1898—d. London, Eng., April 6, 1973), with Franz Kind in 1936 founded the Manchester Oil Refinery Ltd., the basis of the U.K. domestic oil-refining industry, and, immediately after World War II, Petrochemical Ltd., one of the pioneer companies of the British petrochemical industry. A notable commentator on energy and economic matters, he was an exponent of a cheap fuel policy and warned against dependence on Middle East oil. He was a governor and honorary fellow of the London School of Economics.

ULATE BLANCO, OTILIO, Costa Rican politician (b. 1894—d. San José, Costa Rica, Oct. 27, 1973), was president of Costa Rica from 1949 to 1953 and a former newspaper publisher. When his election in 1948 was contested on the basis of fraud, Congress voted 27 to 19 to sustain the charges. Ulate and six associates were arrested, but all charges were dropped the following day.

ULBRICHT, WALTER, East German statesman (b. Leipzig, Ger., June 30, 1893—d. East Germany, Aug. 1, 1973), chairman of the Council of State of the German Democratic Republic from its creation in 1949, was also until his retirement in May 1971 first secretary of the Socialist Unity (Communist) Party. Ulbricht joined the Socialist youth movement in 1906 and entered the Socialist Party in 1912. After the failure of the Socialist revolution at the end of World War I, he helped form the German Communist Party, returning to Germany, after training in Moscow, to be elected to the Reichstag in 1928. The Communist Party was destroyed by Hitler in 1933, but Ulbricht escaped to Paris, where Stalin appointed him over other Communist exiles as party secretary of the Auslandskomitee. He was sent to Spain in 1936, where he was entrusted with the liquidation of unreliable party members, socialists, anarchists, and anti-Stalinists. He returned to Germany in 1945 and began to establish the framework of a Communist administration; after a revolt of workers in 1953 had provided the last challenge to Ulbricht's regime, complete agricultural collectivization was pushed through in 1960.

The regime was unpopular. Between 1945 and 1961 more than three million of its subjects fled westward, mostly through Berlin. In 1961 Ulbricht directed that a wall be set up to block further escape. Ulbricht then undertook a thorough overhaul of East Germany's economy; to this end he brought in young technocrats and succeeded in raising the standard of living, while retaining political control. Treaties signed between Poland and the Soviet Union and West Germany in 1970 were an acute embarrassment to Ulbricht, who had shown himself hostile to the Czechoslovak reform movement and was committed to "cold war" confrontation.

VAN ZEELAND, (VICOMTE) PAUL, Belgian economist and statesman (b. Soignies, Belg., Nov. 11, 1893—d. Brussels, Belg., Sept. 22, 1973), rescued his country during the Depression when King Leopold III summoned him in 1935 to be prime minister of a coalition government facing national bankruptcy. Van Zeeland's devaluation of the Belgian franc, retention of the gold standard, and thorough reform of the banking and credit structure led to solvency within little more than a year. A scandal at the National Bank forced his resignation in 1937. He was out of office when the Nazis overran Belgium in 1940 and spent most of the war in the U.S., returning home in 1944. In 1949 he became a member of the Belgian Senate and was appointed foreign minister in the Eyskens Christian-Social-Liberal coalition. He played a leading role in the formation of the European Payments Union, Robert Schuman's European Coal and Steel Community, the Council of Europe in Strasbourg, and the Organization for European Economic Cooperation. He also took part in abortive attempts to create a European Defense Community. He was a founder member of the Atlantic Institute and was a lifelong devotee of a united Europe.

VARDINOYIANNIS, NICOS, Greek shipping magnate (b. Episkopi, Crete, 1931—d. Athens, Greece, July 2, 1973), rose to millionaire status through a secret deal with Rhodesia to break the British oil blockade in 1966. He joined the Greek Navy in 1952 and by 1962 was a lieutenant commander, but resigned to make money. He set up a bunkering business in Crete to supply fuel to westbound ships navigating the Suez Canal, later extended it, and in the Rhodesian deal was said to have been paid off with three oil tankers which became the nucleus of a private fleet of over 20 ships. In November 1972 he began operating a £20 million oil refinery west of Athens.

VENEZIS, ELIAS, Greek author (b. Asia Minor, 1904—d. Athens, Greece, Aug. 3, 1973), was a leading figure in contemporary Greek literature, well known abroad through translations of his writings and for his participation in the Council of European Writers.

VIRTANEN, ARTTURI ILMARI, Finnish biochemist (b. Helsinki, Fin., Jan. 15, 1895—d. Helsinki, Nov. 11, 1973), was awarded the Nobel Prize for Chemistry in 1945 for his research into agricultural and nutritive chemistry. He studied in Switzerland, Germany, and Sweden before taking up an appointment at the University of Helsinki in 1924. In 1939 he became professor of biochemistry at the university.

VOISIN, GABRIEL, French inventor (b. Belleville-sur-Saône, France, Feb. 5, 1880—d. Ozenay, France, Dec. 25, 1973), was a pioneer of aviation. He designed flying machines as early as 1900 and in 1904 flew a glider of his own design with frontal elevator and rear rudder. The following year he added a motor to his glider and, with his brother Charles, founded the world's first aircraft factory, at Boulogne-Billancourt. During World War I he produced 10,400 aircraft.

WAKSMAN, SELMAN ABRAHAM, U.S. microbiologist (b. Novaya Priluka, Ukraine, July 22, 1888—d. Hyannis, Mass., Aug. 16, 1973), was awarded the Nobel Prize for Physiology or Medicine in 1952 for his discovery of streptomycin. His long academic career was spent at Rutgers University, New Brunswick, N.J., where he headed the Institute of Microbiology from 1949 to 1958, when he retired.

WALLIS, THOMAS E., British pharmacognosist (b. Islington, London, Eng., 1876—d. Thames Ditton, Surrey, Eng., March 7, 1973), produced three standard textbooks (*Textbook of Pharmacognosy, Practical Pharmacognosy,* and *Analytical Microscopy*) and devised a method of quantitative microscopy by the use of *Lycopodium* spores. He was president of the Royal Microscopical Society (1954–55).

WATTS, ALAN WILSON, British Zen philosopher, writer, and lecturer (b. Chislehurst, Eng., Jan. 6, 1915—d. Mill Valley, Calif., Nov. 16, 1973), was largely responsible for the popularity of Zen among young Westerners during the 1950s and early 1960s. Criticized for personally disregarding traditional Zen ascetic practices, Watts described himself as "somewhat of a disreputable epicurean who has three wives, seven children and five grandchildren." Watts became fascinated with the Orient at an early age and eventually, in search of mysticism, sought out gurus and Buddhists in London. In 1939 he entered Seabury-Western Theological Seminary in Evanston, Ill. He was ordained in the Episcopal Church and served as chaplain at Northwestern University from 1944 to 1950. After leaving the ministry he was totally devoted to Zen until the end of his life. His writings include *The Wisdom of Insecurity* (1951), *Myth and Ritual in Christianity* (1953), *Beat Zen, Square Zen and Zen,* and an autobiography, *In My Own Way* (1972).

WHEELER, JOHN N., U.S. newspaper executive (b. Yonkers, N.Y., April 11, 1886—d. Norwalk, Conn., Oct. 13, 1973), spent a lifetime syndicating the writing of prominent persons before retiring in 1964 as chairman of the North American Newspaper Alliance, Inc. (NANA).

WHITE, PAUL DUDLEY, U.S. physician (b. Roxbury, Mass., June 6, 1886—d. Boston, Mass., Oct. 31, 1973), an international authority on heart disease, became a national figure as cardiologist to Pres. Dwight D. Eisenhower. White obtained his M.D. degree from Harvard Medical School (1911) and later taught there while maintaining a lifelong association with Massachusetts General Hospital. Among the first to employ electrocardiograms for diagnosis of heart disease, he used some 21,000 cardiograms as the basis for one of his many books, *Heart Disease* (1931), a classic in its field.

WHITTAKER, CHARLES EVANS, U.S. jurist (b. near Troy, Kan., Feb. 22, 1901—d. Kansas City, Kan., Nov. 26, 1973), was an associate justice on the U.S. Supreme Court from 1957 until his retirement in 1962. He had earlier been a trial lawyer and a federal judge in the district and circuit courts.

WIGMAN, MARY, German dancer and choreographer (b. Hanover, Ger., Nov. 13, 1886—d. W. Berlin, Sept. 18, 1973), exercised a lasting and creative influence on modern dance, both as a performer and as a teacher. Her stark and sombre dances, often accompanied by drums, gongs, or the flute, aroused great controversy until it was understood that the purpose was "not to entertain but to communicate." Wigman insisted that the dance itself came first and that musical scores be composed as the choreography evolved or after the dance, with its intense, angular movements, was completed. Among her more memorable accomplishments were *Scenes from a Dance-Drama, Totenmal,* and *Le Sacre du Printemps.*

WINTERHALTER, HUGO, U.S. musician (b. Wilkes-Barre, Pa., 1909—d. Greenwich, Conn., Sept. 17, 1973), played with the Dorsey brothers, Count Basie, Vaughn Monroe, and other top bands during the big-band era of the 1940s before turning to musical arrangement. In the 1950s, while music director (1950–63) for RCA Victor, he arranged the music for 11 popular tunes that sold over one million copies each.

YOUNG, MURAT BERNARD ("CHIC"), U.S. cartoonist (b. Chicago, Ill., Jan. 9, 1901—d. St. Petersburg, Fla., March 14, 1973), created the "Blondie" comic strip, which was distributed by King Features Syndicate from its beginning on Sept. 8, 1930. At the time of Young's death, "Blondie" was appearing in 1,623 newspapers in 60 countries.

ZIEGLER, KARL, German chemist (b. Helsa, Ger., Nov. 26, 1898—d. Mülheim-Ruhr, W.Ger., Aug. 12, 1973), was joint holder with Guilio Natta of the 1963 Nobel Prize for Chemistry, awarded for their work in macromolecular chemistry. He was director of the Max Planck Institute for Coal Research, Mülheim-Ruhr (1943–69), and became a foreign member of the Royal Society in 1971.

ZULETA ANGEL, EDUARDO, Colombian jurist and career diplomat (b. Barcelona, Spain, Sept. 12, 1899—d. Miami, Fla., Sept. 26, 1973), presided over the first meeting of the United Nations as an organization when it convened in London on Jan. 10, 1946.

Oceanography

The complex relationship forced upon nations by their common dependence on the natural resources of the oceans emerged as a dominant factor in setting the direction of oceanographic research in 1973. The failure of the Peruvian anchovy fishery and its consequences for a world protein market already suffering from depleted grain stocks was the most dramatic example of such international interdependence, but there were also many instances of international dispute over maritime resources. With many nations laying claim to 200-mi. territorial waters or to priority of resource utilization within such waters, it appeared that the traditional doctrine of freedom of the seas, including free access for research, would continue to be subjected to strong pressures for modification.

Spring of 1972 had witnessed a severe occurrence of the warm El Niño current off the Peruvian coast. The normally cool coastal water coming from below (water so rich in nutrients that this region alone supplies more than 20% of the world's fish catch) was replaced by much warmer water, and the total 1973 anchovy catch fell to less than 20% of that taken in 1971. Fear for the survival of the basic stock itself finally led the Peruvian government to suspend all anchovy harvesting. The extent to which heavy fishing in past years was responsible for this disaster was difficult to estimate, but the weakening of the southeast trade winds, which was believed to have resulted in the failure of coastal upwelling and hence in El Niño, was not an isolated event but was bound up with the entire climate of the globe.

The winter of 1971–72 had been a year of anomalous sea-surface temperature in the North Pacific, and during that year Northern Hemisphere weather also changed markedly. The causal relationship, if any, between these occurrences remained obscure, but their consequences were great. Much of the U.S. experienced a very wet winter while the U.S.S.R. experienced the drought that ultimately led it to make huge purchases of U.S. grain. This pressure on the U.S. grain crop occurred just at the time when, because of the failure of the Peruvian anchovy fishery, livestock owners were turning to the grain-soybean market to feed their animals. The end of this chain of events was not yet in sight.

The role of the oceans in bringing about such fluctuations and the oceans' response to them emerged as basic themes of oceanographic research in 1973. Study of the circulation of the oceans from this viewpoint was the basic purpose of several International Decade of Ocean Exploration (IDOE) projects, including Geosecs, MODE, and CUE.

The first Atlantic phase of the Geosecs (Geochemical Ocean Sections Study) was completed when the research vessel "Knorr," operated by the Woods Hole (Mass.) Oceanographic Institution, put into port on April 4 after a nine-month voyage that took her from above the Arctic Circle to the Weddell Sea off Antarctica. Her first traverse of the Atlantic followed the southward flow of North Atlantic deep water, which is believed to originate in the Norwegian Sea and which is then thought to proceed southward along the western part of the deep Atlantic Ocean. In addition to the usual measurements of temperature, salinity, and oxygen, concentrations of radioisotopes and of particulate matter were examined. Radioisotopes, both natural and man-made, have intrinsic decay rates, and thus serve as timers that record their length of residence in the deep water. The study of particulate matter is important because the vertical distribution of many elements in the ocean is controlled by near-surface biological processes that package these elements into particles that then sink to the sea floor.

Geosecs's Pacific phase began when the research vessel "Melville," operated by the Scripps Institution of Oceanography, La Jolla, Calif., left San Diego on August 22 for a voyage that would take her from the Bering Sea to Antarctica. As in the Atlantic, the ship's track was planned to follow the flow of deep water believed to move along the western edge of the Pacific basin, ultimately filling the deep Pacific. The Atlantic has two major sources of deep water, the Norwegian Sea in the north and the Weddell Sea in the south, whereas the Pacific is supplied only from the Weddell Sea via the circumpolar current. Geosecs scientists therefore expected to see a very different distribution of properties in the North Pacific than in the North Atlantic.

While Geosecs aimed at understanding such currents by showing how they store and transport on a global scale, thus yielding information about such practical matters as the oceanic transport of heat and large-scale dispersal of wastes, MODE (Mid-Ocean Dynamics Experiment) concentrated on detailed examination of the local structure of ocean currents by such direct means as current meter observations and observations of drifting floats. The necessity for such study had been evident since measurements in 1959–60 revealed that the deep flow was rapid and highly irregular, as though composed primarily of a collection of eddies perhaps 100–200 km. (62–124 mi.) wide and taking several weeks to several months to complete a rotation. Similar but larger eddy systems exist in the atmosphere, and they are known to be of crucial importance in the chain of events that establishes the general atmospheric circulation. Whether the role of eddies in the ocean might be similar was one of MODE's underlying concerns.

During 1972 a program of preliminary shipboard and buoy observations had been pursued at the MODE experimental site, an irregularly shaped area

AUTHENTICATED NEWS INTERNATIONAL

This scanning electron microscope picture, magnified 100 times, shows skeletons of various forms of Radiolaria in sediment cores taken from the western Pacific Ocean by the Deep Sea Drilling Project.

roughly 600 km. (373 mi.) across located just southwest of Bermuda. The statistical properties of ocean flow estimated at that time were crucial for the proper design of the main program of fieldwork, which was carried out from March to mid-July 1973 in this region. In all, six ships were involved.

Both Geosecs and MODE were primarily concerned with the deep sea, but three IDOE projects, CUE (Coastal Upwelling Experiment), Norpax (North Pacific Experiment), and GATE (Global Atmospheric Research Program Atlantic Tropical Experiment), dealt with the large-scale interaction between ocean and atmosphere. These experiments were not only oceanographic but climatologic.

Coastal upwelling, the object of study of CUE, occurs especially along the west coast of continents as Equatorward surface winds and the rotation of the earth force surface water seaward and hence bring up (upwell) cold and nutrient-rich water from the depths. Major coastal upwelling areas supply some 50% of the oceans' fish catch, so the understanding that CUE sought was of fundamental economic importance. In the summer of 1973 CUE concentrated its efforts on a shipboard, moored buoy, and aerial study of ocean currents, temperature, and meteorology off the Oregon coast. The previous summer's work had shown that upwelling occurs in discrete events rather than continuously; the 1973 study aimed at further elucidation of the process initiating such events.

CUE was oriented toward understanding how the atmosphere can force ocean upwelling. Norpax and GATE were concerned with the feedback effects which the ocean, driven by the atmosphere, may then exert on the atmosphere. The Norpax experiment arose from the realization that shifts in the patterns of sea-surface temperature in the Pacific Ocean were apparently correlated with Northern Hemisphere climate fluctuations over the past 25 years. The immediate problem facing Norpax was to decide whether these temperature anomalies actually influence the atmosphere or whether they are only passive indicators that reflect the state of the atmosphere.

A new atmospheric diving suit eliminates much of the danger of deep diving, according to its developer. A magnesium alloy encloses the diver at normal atmospheric pressure while his own muscle power works the articulated joints at depths of up to 1,000 ft.

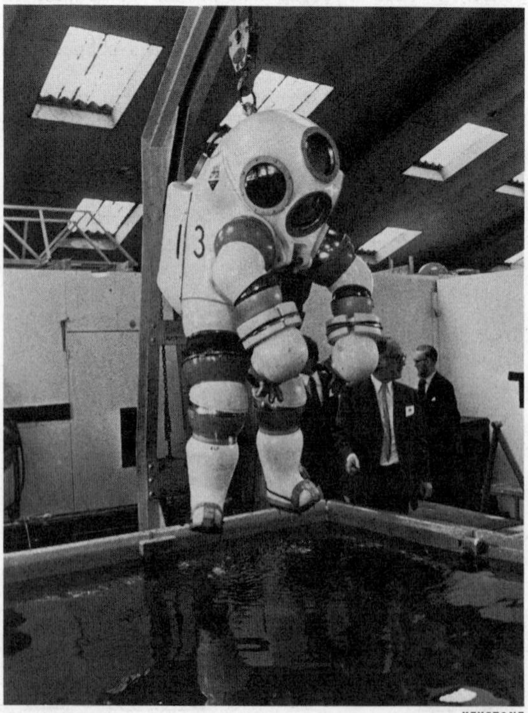

KEYSTONE

The Norpax project planned fieldwork in the winter to begin to study what contributes to the formation of the anomalous ocean temperature field in the North Pacific. Surface effects such as the passage of storms were prime suspects, but there was also the intriguing possibility that deep eddies of the type observed in MODE might distort the prevailing mean north-south temperature gradient into an anomalous temperature field. As Norpax concentrated on the mid-latitude aspect of this problem, GATE planned fieldwork on the tropical Atlantic Ocean for the summer of 1974.

Study of the ocean floor continued in 1973 as the research vessel "Glomar Challenger" took the Deep Sea Drilling Project (DSDP) into Antarctic waters. Among the most interesting results were elucidation of the manner in which the Australian continent split off from Antarctica. Later drilling during 1973 studied the formation of island arcs in the western Pacific. The sediments recovered in the DSDP program have been strongly influenced by the nature of the oceans' circulation at the time of sediment deposition. Thus they constitute a unique record of how oceanic climate changed as continents drifted.

As the readily accessible supply of natural resources became increasingly inadequate, exploration of the sea floor for hydrocarbon and mineral deposits was intensifying. Particular interest was being shown in the so-called manganese nodules, possible sources of a number of scarce minerals. Besides continental margin mapping efforts, pursued by industry and government, deep-sea efforts such as DSDP and the French-American Mid-Ocean Undersea Study (FAMOUS), a detailed study of a portion of the Mid-Atlantic Ridge, were laying the foundation for ultimate understanding of when and where concentrations of minerals occur in nature. (MYRL C. HENDERSHOTT)

See also Antarctica; Geology; Law; Life Sciences; Meteorology.

ENCYCLOPÆDIA BRITANNICA FILMS. *How Level Is Sea Level?* (1970); *The Ways of Water* (1973).

Oman

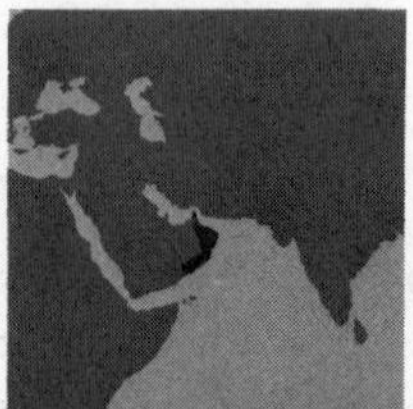

An independent sultanate, Oman occupies the southeastern part of the Arabian Peninsula and is bounded by the United Arab Emirates, Saudi Arabia, the Gulf of Oman, and the Arabian Sea. A small part of the country lies to the north of the rest of Oman and is separated from it by the United Arab Emirates. Area: 82,000 sq.mi. (212,380 sq.km.). Pop. (1972 est.): 700,000 to 750,000. Cap.: Muscat (pop., 1973 est., 15,000). Largest city: Matrah (pop., 1973 est., 18,000). Language: Arabic. Religion: Muslim. Sultan in 1973, Qabus ibn Sa'id.

In 1973 the rebellion in the southwest, led by the Popular Front for the Liberation of Oman and the Arabian Gulf (PFLOAG) and supported from Yemen (Aden), continued, although the sultan's government claimed to be gaining the upper hand. Senior officers in the sultan's army were British, and aid was provided by Iran and Saudi Arabia. (In December Yemen [Aden] alleged that some 30,000 Iranian troops were concentrated in Oman.) Early in the year the government claimed that it had uncovered a plot by members

Oil:
see Energy; Industrial Review
Opera:
see Music
Organization for Economic Cooperation and Development:
see Development, Economic
Organization of African Unity:
see African Affairs
Organization of American States:
see Latin-American Affairs
Ornithology:
see Life Sciences
Orthodox Churches:
see Religion
Painting:
see Art Exhibitions; Art Sales; Museums and Galleries
Paints and Varnishes:
see Industrial Review

OMAN

Finance and Trade. Monetary unit: rial Omani, with (Sept. 17, 1973) an official rate of 0.35 rial to U.S. $1 (free rate of 0.83 rial = £1 sterling). Budget (1972 est.): revenue *c.* 50 million rials; expenditure *c.* 80 million rials. Foreign trade (1972 est.): imports 71 million rials; exports 135 million rials. Import sources: France 45%; U.K. 26%. Export destinations: Japan 33%; France 19%; Denmark 11%; Sweden 9%; Spain 8%; Norway 8%; The Netherlands 6%. Main export (1971) crude oil 99%.

Industry. Crude oil production (1972) 14.1 million metric tons.

of PFLOAG in Muscat to overthrow the regime. Ten of the alleged conspirators were executed in June, and nine others had their death sentences commuted to life imprisonment. Omani-owned ships were banned from sailing to Yemen (Aden), which was alleged to be supplying Chinese arms to the rebels. PFLOAG held a conference in Aden in April.

Sultan Qabus visited Britain, Tunisia, Algeria, and France in July–September. Oman scored a diplomatic success when it was admitted as a full member of the summit conference of nonaligned nations, held in Algiers in September, despite some left-wing opposition. It participated in the Arab cutback of oil shipments to the West.

The development of Oman's primitive economic infrastructure continued, with the construction of new roads and administrative centres in Muscat and Salalah. A National Bank of Oman, the first of its kind in the country, was established with 39% foreign capital. An offshore oil exploration concession was granted to a partnership of U.S. and West German companies, although the previous holder, Wendell Phillips Oil, claimed that its concession was still valid. A concession to explore for copper and nickel in the mountains northwest of Muscat was granted to U.S. and Canadian partners. (PETER MANSFIELD)

Pakistan

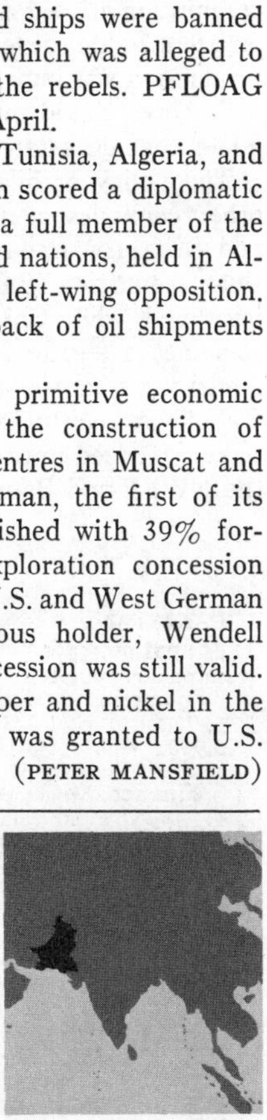

A federal republic, Pakistan is bordered on the south by the Arabian Sea, on the west by Afghanistan and Iran, on the north by China, and on the east by India. Area: 307,374 sq.mi. (796,095 sq.km.), excluding the Pakistani-controlled section of Jammu and Kashmir. Pop. (1972) 64,892,000. Cap. Islamabad (pop., 1972, 77,000). Largest city: Karachi (metro. area pop., 1972, 3,469,000). Language: Urdu and English. Religion: Muslim 90%, Hindu and Christian minorities. Presidents in 1973, Zulfikar Ali Bhutto and, from August 14, Chaudhri Fazal Elahi; prime minister from August 14, Zulfikar Ali Bhutto.

During the first half of 1973, political interest in Pakistan focused on details of the new constitution and relations between the government and the National Awami Party. The NAP commanded a narrow majority in the national and provincial assemblies, in rather incongruous alliance with the right-wing Jamiat-ul-Ulema-i-Islam, and had formed governments in the North West Frontier Province (NWFP) and Baluchistan.

The drafting committee of the National Assembly had reached agreement on a draft constitution on Dec. 21, 1972, and presented its report ten days later, accompanied by dissenting notes demanding new elections after the constitution had been adopted and objecting to restrictions on the procedure for votes of no confidence on future prime ministers. The NAP dissociated itself from the draft constitution.

The NAP's influence was greatly weakened, however, by a detailed exposure of its subversive aims and foreign connections made by Sardar Akbar Khan Bugti, chief of the powerful Bugti tribe in east Baluchistan. He had once been associated with the NAP, but during a visit to the U.K. he had become alarmed at the far-reaching plans of some party leaders to split off the NWFP and Baluchistan from the rest of Pakistan. The eventual goal was an armed rising on the lines of the one that had succeeded in Bangladesh. The Bugti chief had warned the plotters that he would make the plans public if they were not called off. This he did in a press conference in Lahore on January 31.

The veracity of these revelations was not questioned. Their serious character was underlined ten days later by the discovery, in the Iraqi embassy in Islamabad, of 70 cases of arms and ammunition of Soviet manufacture, imported under the cloak of diplomatic immunity from Baghdad, where a "Free Baluchistan" organization was located. Three other crates were found at the airport awaiting delivery to the embassy, and more were found in the house of the Iraqi military attaché. Pakistan broke off diplomatic relations with Iraq, but they were resumed in April after the latter country offered apologies.

In Baluchistan and the NWFP further friction occurred between the NAP and the central government, and on February 15 President Bhutto dismissed the NAP governors of both provinces and replaced them by Sardar Akbar Khan Bugti and Aslam Khattak. There were bitter complaints from NAP leaders against these appointments, which were echoed by the supporters of Pakhtunistan (an independent Pathan state) in Afghanistan. New governments were sworn in in both provinces. Meanwhile, on February 13, the governor of Sind resigned, following allegations that his brother had been distributing illegal arms, and Rana Liaquat Ali Khan, the widow of

Squatting Baluchistan tribesmen in the village of Mawand await gifts of radios, shoes, and lamps from the Pakistani government. Officials hoped to bring the people of this remote province into the mainstream of national life by introducing modern goods and services.

WIDE WORLD

UPI COMPIX

Water recedes in a section of Punjab Province, inundated in August 1973 by floods that left nearly 300 persons and 70,000 cattle dead.

Pakistan's first prime minister, became governor in his place. In Baluchistan and the NWFP the new governments acted with energy to restore order.

Opposition to the president and his Pakistan People's Party government was not confined to the NAP, as became clear when the Constitution Bill was introduced into the National Assembly on February 2. While there was general agreement on provincial autonomy and the division of powers, there were fears lest the new constitution might lead to a presidential rather than a parliamentary form of polity. These fears led to the formation of a "United Democratic Front" including all opposition.

After protracted maneuvers, the government accepted the more important of the opposition's proposals, and the new constitution was unanimously adopted in April. It provided for a bicameral legislature—a National Assembly of 200 members, in which political control was firmly vested, and a Senate of 10 members from each of the four provinces, 3 from the centrally administered tribal areas, and 2 from the federal capital area, to be elected by the provincial assemblies. The head of state was a constitutional president, bound to follow the advice of a prime minister responsible to Parliament. There were guarantees of fundamental rights, religious freedom, independence of the judiciary, and social justice, including an obligation on the state to provide the basic necessities of life. The new constitution took effect August 14. Chaudhri Fazal Elahi, who had been speaker of the National Assembly, became president, and Bhutto took over the post of prime minister.

In foreign affairs, the chief problem was the detention by India, contrary to the Geneva conventions, of more than 90,000 Pakistani prisoners of war. India's excuse was that Bangladesh was also a concerned party, and that until Pakistan recognized Bangladesh, nothing could be done. Bhutto refused to yield and, in the spring, India offered a tripartite plan under which Pakistan should repatriate all the Bengalis who wished to go to Bangladesh and receive the Biharis whom Sheikh Mujibur Rahman wanted to expel. In return it would get back all the prisoners except those whom Bangladesh wished to put on trial for war crimes. Pakistan still refused, although the National Assembly had given Bhutto authority to recognize Bangladesh in July. Finally, on August 29, after a second summit conference with India, agreement was reached on terms the National Assembly readily accepted. They involved a straightforward exchange of Pakistanis for Bengalis with no obligation to take all the Biharis in Bangladesh. (*See* INDIA.)

While the Kashmir question remained essentially stalemated, Bhutto, in November, suggested that the Pakistani-held portions could become a province of Pakistan until the question was settled. Later, his call for a one-day strike in support of self-determination led to student disturbances in Indian-held Kashmir; Bhutto's "interference" was subsequently denounced by the Kashmiri leader Sheikh Abdullah.

On the economic front, output in the basic industries was up 6%. Exports rose by 40% and exceeded the best performance of West and East Pakistan together before their separation. Increased expenditures had been made on all the social services and larger grants to all the provinces. There was an encouraging resumption of aid from abroad, leading to notable progress in the development sector, and agricultural production was improving. Unfortunately some of the high hopes based on these results were doomed by floods that devastated the Indus valley region.

The policy of bilateral friendly relations with all other countries continued. Relations with the U.S. and Britain warmed notably after Bhutto's visits to those countries. Relations with the U.S.S.R. also improved, while China, along with Iran and Turkey, remained a steady friend. However, difficulties with Afghanistan arose after a military coup d'etat in Kabul (*see* AFGHANISTAN) brought into power a regime pledged to promote secessionist movements in the NWFP and Baluchistan.

(L. F. RUSHBROOK WILLIAMS)

PAKISTAN

Education. (1969–70) Primary, pupils *c.* 5.1 million; secondary, pupils *c.* 530,000; vocational, pupils *c.* 28,000; primary, secondary, and vocational, teachers (1966–67) 131,925; teacher training, students *c.* 3,000; higher (including 7 universities with 14,425 students in 1966–67), students *c.* 97,090.

Finance. Monetary unit: Pakistan rupee, with (Sept. 17, 1973) a par value of PakRs. 9.90 to U.S. $1 (free rate of PakRs. 23.70 = £1 sterling). Gold, SDRs, and foreign exchange, state bank: (June 1973) U.S. $469 million; (June 1972) U.S. $284 million. Budget (1972–73 est.) balanced at PakRs. 8,509,000,000. National income: (1969–70) *c.* PakRs. 45 billion; (1968–69) *c.* PakRs. 41.6 billion. Cost of living (Karachi; 1963 = 100): (April 1973) 179; (April 1972) 151.

Foreign Trade. (1972) Imports PakRs. 6,353,000,000; exports PakRs. 6,442,000,000. Import sources: U.S. 22%; West Germany 9%; U.K. 9%; Japan 9%. Export destinations: Japan 16%; Hong Kong 14%; U.K. 8%; Italy 5%; U.S. 5%. Main exports (1971–72): cotton 28%; cotton yarn 18%; cotton fabrics 11%.

Transport and Communications. Roads (1972) 62,800 km. (including 11,600 km. main roads). Motor vehicles in use (1972): passenger 74,300; commercial 21,000. Railways: (1970–71) 8,572 km.; traffic (1971–72) 8,690,000,000 passenger-km., freight 7,010,000,000 net ton-km. Air traffic (1972): 1,142,300,000 passenger-km.; freight 58,504,000 net ton-km. Shipping (1972): merchant vessels 100 gross tons and over 131; gross tonnage 532,637. Telephones (including Bangladesh; Dec. 1971) 220,000. Radio licenses (June 1969) 1,339,000. Television receivers (including Bangladesh; Dec. 1970) 99,000.

Agriculture. Production (in 000; metric tons; 1972; 1971 in parentheses): wheat 6,891 (6,476); barley *c.* 95 (91); corn 760 (705); rice *c.* 3,600 (3,300); sugar, raw value 373 (552); dry beans *c.* 95 (*c.* 93); peanuts *c.* 40 (57); rapeseed and mustard seed *c.* 260 (269); tobacco *c.* 151 (150); cotton, lint 711 (708). Livestock (in 000; 1971–72): cattle *c.* 20,170; sheep *c.* 10,000; goats *c.* 15,000.

Industry. Production (in 000; metric tons; 1972): cement 2,847; crude oil (1971) 411; coal and lignite (1970) 1,249; natural gas (cu.m.; 1970) *c.* 3,500,000; electricity (excluding most industrial production; kw-hr.; 1965–66) 2,910,000; steel (1970) 175; sulfuric acid 32; soda ash (1970) 68; cotton yarn 296; woven cotton fabrics (m.) 686,000.

Palestine:
see Israel; Jordan

Panama

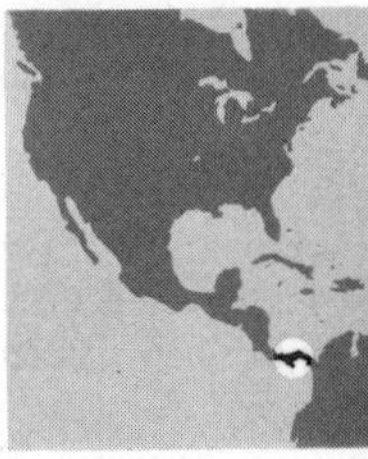

A republic of Central America, bisected by the Canal Zone, Panama is bounded by the Caribbean Sea, Colombia, the Pacific Ocean, and Costa Rica. Area: 29,208 sq.mi. (75,650 sq.km.). Pop. (1973 est.): 1,570,100. Cap. and largest city: Panama City (pop., 1973 est., 381,840). Language: Spanish. Religion (1971 est.): Roman Catholic 90%. President in 1973, Demetrio Lakas Bahas.

In maintaining his control of Panama during 1973, Brig. Gen. Omar Torrijos could boast that the National Guard had not fired a shot or hurled a tear gas bomb to disperse unruly and dissident crowds. But protests were not entirely absent, for in August Torrijos warned rebellious students in Chiriqui Province that deviation would not be tolerated. His tactics were, however, usually more in the nature of sympathy and agreement than of threat. Thus, he adopted the anti-imperialist, nationalist cry of the youth as public policy. Quietly, he replaced his own appointees when they displeased either the populace or himself as he did in Chiriqui and in removing the man heading the gambling board, the bingo commission, and a government publishing house.

During the year the government launched a program of rural aid to improve health and sanitation standards and increase food production. For these improvements several million dollars were available from the U.S. Agency for International Development (AID) and UNICEF. Such efforts were, however, of little immediate benefit to farmers who had been hit hard by inflation. Many, in a condition of near destitution, left their farms in search of more income in the towns. Torrijos countered these economic problems by continuing a program of public works. Panama could also fall back on the canal, which continued to be the largest employer and which, in 1971, paid out approximately $168 million in wages.

In regard to the canal, however, Panama wanted more than money. It wanted the Canal Zone fully integrated into its own territory. An adviser of the Panamanian Foreign Ministry called for an end of the "colonialism" imposed by the United States: its military presence, intelligence service, and psychological warfare. In a move that startled and angered the diplomatic arm of the U.S., he proceeded to disclose the negotiating position of the two nations. The concessions which the U.S. was willing to make included a substitution of a term of years instead of perpetuity for the life of the new agreement, a considerable extension of the jurisdiction of Panamanian courts and of the application of Panamanian law, a redefinition of the responsibility to keep order, a yielding of commercial services provided residents of the Canal Zone to the Panamanian business community, and an outright transfer to Panama of about one-third of the Canal Zone. These concessions were insufficient, and Panama rejected the terms.

The next move was promoted by Aquiline Boyd, Panama's ambassador to the UN and, by virtue of a rotating system, president of the Security Council. He succeeded in obtaining the approval of the members of that council to hold the meetings scheduled for March 15–21 in Panama, and at that time introduced a resolution calling for a new treaty consonant with Panama's aspirations for sovereignty over all of the isthmus. The U.S. found only Great Britain as an ally, and, therefore, in accordance with the rules of the Security Council, applied its rarely used veto to the resolution.

The sting of this bitter confrontation remained for only a few weeks. In July Panama invited a negotiating team from the U.S. to resume discussions. By October the U.S. had removed its air missiles and reduced its military manpower in Panama by 60% from the 1966 level. Appearing in U.S. newspapers was Panama's invitation to North American tourists to visit "the Hong Kong of the Western Hemisphere," "the Black Marlin Capital of the Seas," and "the friendliest people in the world." (ALMON R. WRIGHT)

WIDE WORLD

Brig. Gen. Omar Torrijos invited the UN Security Council to meet in Panama City in March 1973 to discuss the dispute between the U.S. and Panama over the 1903 Canal Zone Treaty.

PANAMA

Education. (1971–72) Primary, pupils 287,565, teachers 10,004; secondary and vocational, pupils 86,795, teachers 4,460; teacher training (1969–70), students 1,726, teachers 81; higher (at 2 universities), students 13,456, teaching staff 566.

Finance. Monetary unit: balboa, at par with the U.S. dollar, with a free rate (Sept. 17, 1973) of 2.41 balboas to £1 sterling. Gold, SDRs, and foreign exchange: (March 1973) U.S. $923.1 million; (March 1972) U.S. $580.9 million. Budget (1972 est.) balanced at 241 million balboas. Gross national product: (1971) 1,125,700,000 balboas; (1970) 1,019,400,000 balboas. Money supply (deposits only): (March 1973) 166.4 million balboas; (March 1972) 129 million balboas. Cost of living (Panama City; 1963 = 100): (2nd quarter 1973) 126; (2nd quarter 1972) 120.

Foreign Trade. Imports (1972) 438,390,000 balboas; exports 126,880,000 balboas. Net service receipts from Canal Zone (1971) 124.3 million balboas. Main import sources (1971): U.S. 35%; Venezuela 18%; Japan 8%. Main export destinations (1971): U.S. 49%; West Germany 18%; The Netherlands 6%; Mexico 5%. Main exports: bananas 55%; petroleum products 17%; shrimps 11%.

Transport and Communications. Roads (1970) 6,807 km. Motor vehicles in use (1971): passenger 55,600; commercial (including buses) 17,700. Railways (1971) 660 km. Shipping (1972): merchant vessels 100 gross tons and over 1,337 (mostly owned by U.S. and other foreign interests); gross tonnage 7,793,598. Telephones (Dec. 1970) 85,000. Radio receivers (Dec. 1970) 230,000. Television receivers (Dec. 1971) 158,000.

Agriculture. Production (in 000; metric tons; 1972; 1971 in parentheses): rice *c.* 102 (136); sugar, raw value *c.* 113 (85); bananas (1970) *c.* 900, (1969) 1,019; oranges (1971) *c.* 42, (1970) *c.* 42; coffee 5.6 (*c.* 5.6); cocoa (1971–72) 0.4, (1970–71) 0.5. Livestock (in 000; 1970–71): cattle 1,240; pigs 147; horses *c.* 157.

Industry. Production (in 000): cement (metric tons; 1969) 174; manufactured gas (cu.m.; 1971) 18,000; electricity (kw-hr.; 1970) 956,000.

Paraguay

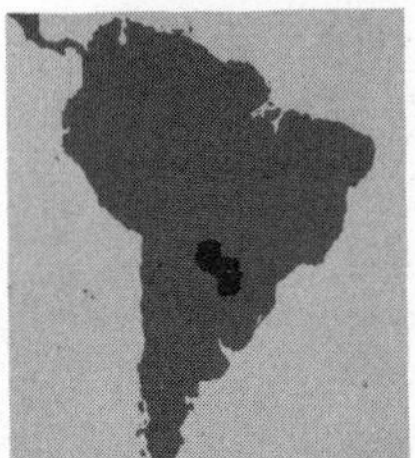

A landlocked republic of South America, Paraguay is bounded by Brazil, Argentina, and Bolivia. Area: 157,047 sq.mi. (406,752 sq.km.). Pop. (1972): 2,328,790. Cap. and largest city: Asunción (pop., 1972, 387,676). Language: Spanish (official), though Guaraní is the language of the majority of the people. Religion: Roman Catholic. President in 1973, Gen. Alfredo Stroessner.

In August 1973 General Stroessner was inaugurated to a fifth five-year term of office as president of the republic, which, if served, would result in an unbroken period of 24 years of rule by one man, something not seen elsewhere in Latin America in the 20th century. Stroessner was already in power when Gen. Juan Perón (*see* BIOGRAPHY) was expelled from Argentina in 1955; indeed, the two men had main-

Panama Canal Zone: *see* Dependent States; Panama

Paper Industry: *see* Forestry; Industrial Review

Papua New Guinea: *see* Dependent States

tained their friendship during Perón's exile, throughout which he traveled on a Paraguayan passport.

Nevertheless, despite Perón's triumphal return to Argentina, relations between the two countries steadily deteriorated during the year. No official Argentine representative of significant status attended Stroessner's inauguration ceremony in August. The reasons for the break lay firmly in a decision taken by the Paraguayan authorities midway through the year. This was the signing of the Itaipu treaty with Brazil to develop hydroelectric potential on the Paraná River, which borders both countries. In particular, a massive hydroelectric plant—designated Itaipu—was to be constructed, which would be the largest of its kind anywhere, with a capacity of 10.7 million kw. Cost of the project was expected to be about $2.4 billion, to be split equally between Brazil and Paraguay. The output from the plant would also be divided equally, which meant that Paraguay would have far more energy than it could possibly use and would sell back to Brazil all of its surplus. This sale was expected to realize the annual sum of about $100 million, marginally higher than Paraguay's annual export total. The benefits to Paraguay were enormous, and the development effort would receive a sustained boost for three or four decades. Against this had to be set the very high cost of the project.

Argentina was disturbed because of its own plans for hydroelectricity along a neighbouring stretch of the same waterway, which it had hoped to develop in conjunction with Paraguay. Not only was there a possibility of the water level of the river being altered by Itaipu to the detriment of Argentina's plans but also Paraguay was understandably reluctant to involve itself in additional foreign debt connected with the Paraná projects.

On the economic front, Paraguay enjoyed a highly prosperous year. This was entirely due to exceptionally high world prices for most Paraguayan exports, especially beef. In the first six months export revenue was higher than the annual total for all but one of the previous 20 years. Real growth in the economy was estimated at 5%, continuing the improvement of recent years. On the other hand, gross national product per head was only $250 annually, one of the lowest in Latin America. (M. J. SPENCE)

PARAGUAY

Education. (1970) Primary, pupils 431,743, teachers (including preprimary) 13,331; secondary and vocational, pupils 55,777, teachers 5,554; teacher training (1969), students 4,115, teachers (1968) 1,021; higher (including 2 universities), students *c.* 15,000, teaching staff *c.* 900.

Finance. Monetary unit: guaraní, with an official rate (Sept. 17, 1973) of 126 guaranies to U.S. $1 (free rate of 298 guaranies = £1 sterling). Gold, SDRs, and foreign exchange, central bank: (June 1973) U.S. $43,810,000; (June 1972) U.S. $19,830,000. Budget (1972 est.): revenue 12,186,000,000 guaranies; expenditure 13,019,000,000 guaranies. Gross national product: (1971) 82,110,000,000 guaranies; (1970) 73,110,000,000 guaranies. Money supply: (May 1973) 10,973,000,000 guaranies; (May 1972) 8,039,000,000 guaranies. Cost of living (Asunción; 1964 = 100): (June 1973) 143; (June 1972) 124.

Foreign Trade. (1972) Imports 10,394,400,000 guaranies; exports 10,657,200,000 guaranies. Import sources: U.S. 18%; Argentina 15%; West Germany 14%; U.K. 18%. Export destinations: Argentina 18%; West Germany 16%; U.S. 15%; U.K. 9%; The Netherlands 7%; Belgium-Luxembourg 5%. Main exports: meat 35%; timber 11%; tobacco 8%; oilseeds 7%.

Transport and Communications. Roads (1970) 11,225 km. Motor vehicles in use (1970): passenger 7,400; commercial (including buses) 10,100. Railways: (1970) 497 km.; traffic (1968) 28 million passenger-km., freight 22 million net ton-km. Navigable inland waterways (including Paraguay-Paraná river system; 1970) *c.* 3,000 km. Telephones (Dec. 1971) 20,000. Radio receivers (Dec. 1971) 175,000. Television receivers (Dec. 1970) 18,000.

Agriculture. Production (in 000; metric tons; 1972; 1971 in parentheses): corn *c.* 276 (255); cassava (1971) 1,690, (1970) 1,782; sweet potatoes (1971) 99, (1970) 99; soybeans *c.* 74 (52); peanuts *c.* 20 (20); dry beans *c.* 30 (32); sugar, raw value *c.* 65 (61); oranges (1971) 228, (1970) *c.* 225; bananas (1970) 249, (1969) *c.* 250; tobacco *c.* 18 (18); palm kernels *c.* 21 (*c.* 20); cotton, lint *c.* 13 (9); beef and veal *c.* 116 (*c.* 116). Livestock (in 000; 1971–72): cattle *c.* 5,950; sheep *c.* 320; pigs *c.* 550; horses *c.* 750; chickens (1970–71) *c.* 6,350.

Industry. Production (in 000; metric tons; 1971): cement 81; cotton yarn (1970) 12; electricity (kw-hr.) 236,000.

Payments and Reserves, International

The severe disturbances that periodically plagued international payments since 1967 erupted into a violent crisis in February 1973. The exchange rate structure that had been established by an agreement among the key governments at the Smithsonian Institution in Washington, D.C., in December 1971, was a fragile building, a fragile work of art. It attempted to restore, after the rather general regime of floating exchange rates from mid-August through mid-December 1971, a new, durable system of basically fixed exchange rates; but it failed. It failed in its immediate objective of restoring confidence so as to set in motion a reversal of the previous flight of funds out of U.S. dollars into European and Japanese currencies in search of protection or as outright speculation, as well as in its longer-run aim of bringing about an adjustment of the basic U.S. payments imbalances and the excessive current-account surpluses of West Germany, Japan, and a few other countries.

The failure of the Smithsonian venture was the result, in considerable part, of the fact that the 7.9% devaluation of the dollar against gold in December 1971—even taken together with the upvaluation of some other currencies—was almost universally regarded as inadequate, particularly since the U.S. authorities themselves were believed to have wanted a larger adjustment than they obtained. Furthermore, with regard to dollar inconvertibility, it made little difference that the price at which the Treasury did *not* sell gold was raised from $35 to $38 an ounce. In any event, the benefits of the devaluation to the U.S. balance of payments could have come only slowly.

The February Crisis. Against this background—and also against the background of Britain's decision in June 1972 to float the pound, which was regarded as further proof, if proof was needed, that the Smithsonian agreement had failed to restore confidence in international monetary stability—it came to be realized that there would be no progress toward a better basic balance in international payments so long as the foreign exchange markets remained critically unstable. In this atmosphere of unrest, the shock that in January 1973 ignited the crisis was the heavy flight out of the Italian lira into Swiss francs, with the dollar used as the vehicle currency, and Switzerland's unwillingness to accept these dollar inflows, which threatened its domestic anti-inflationary policies. To stem the outflows of capital and the loss of reserves, Italy established a floating exchange rate for financial transactions and Switzerland allowed its franc to float outright. These two moves were interpreted as further indications that governments had little choice but to float their currencies, and this experience brought about a new flight from the dollar, bigger than any previous one. The flight was by foreigners as well as by U.S. residents. By Friday, February 9, the situation had become untenable and most exchange markets were closed on Monday, February 12.

After a rapid round of consultations with the major U.S. trading partners, U.S. Treasury Secretary George Shultz announced on the evening of February 12 that the dollar would be devalued by 10% against special drawing rights (SDRs) and, hence, against gold, with the official monetary price of gold raised from $38 to $42.22 an ounce. (Congressional authorization for the devaluation was completed on September 7 and devaluation took place officially October 18, but had become effective in the foreign exchange markets on February 13.) Almost all industrial countries maintaining par or central values for their currencies left them unchanged, thus allowing the dollar devaluation to be fully reflected in the exchange rates of their currencies. Japan reluctantly allowed the yen to float temporarily to allow an additional appreciation against the dollar. Sterling and the Swiss franc remained on a floating basis and were joined by the Italian lira for commercial transactions.

The swift action by the U.S. contrasted with its refusal to devalue the dollar after Aug. 15, 1971, when the dollar was formally declared inconvertible. But in the circumstances of mid-February the underlying valuations of currencies, including the competitive position of the dollar, and their longer-run impact on trade were regarded as less critically important for the immediate future than the uncertainties stemming from the collapse of the Smithsonian exchange rate structure and the erosion of confidence in the stability of any fixed rates. The price of gold on the London market rose to $95 an ounce. There was widespread discussion of the possibility of a joint float of the European Economic Community (EEC) currencies in the event of renewed dollar inflows. In short, the markets remained unconvinced that the crisis was over, and on the night of March 1, in the wake of a sudden new flight from the dollar, the markets were closed until further notice.

It was believed that it would be futile to return to fixed exchange rates between the dollar and other key currencies. But rather than accept the complications, within the EEC framework, of complete floating, six of the Common Market countries—Belgium–Luxembourg, Denmark, France, West Germany, and The Netherlands—agreed to maintain fixed exchange rate relationships among themselves within a margin of 2¼% on either side of their nominal rates. At the same time, however, these EEC countries left the position of their currencies as a whole vis-à-vis the dollar to be determined by the market and abstained from any further support of the dollar through market intervention. Norway and Sweden subsequently joined this arrangement. In conjunction with the EEC decision to establish a fixed-rate currency grouping, West Germany upvalued the mark by 3%; and as a further protection against unwanted dollars, most countries participating in the joint float tightened and extended their existing exchange controls. Italy, Japan, Switzerland, and the United Kingdom, along with Ireland, whose currency remained at par with sterling, continued to float individually. Canada, a traditional floater, had resumed floating in June 1970. The U.S. dollar thus floated vis-à-vis the currencies of practically all the industrialized countries. A large majority of South American countries, and some in Asia and Africa, pegged their exchange rates to the dollar; others remained linked to sterling or the French franc. They consequently drifted downward or upward with the currencies to which their own currencies were pegged. The breakdown of the fixed exchange rate structure thus left the world with a regime of floating rates in which legal par values or central rates became nominal.

The EEC decision to engage in a joint float against the dollar left open the crucial question of whether such a float would be "clean" or subject to intervention by the U.S. Federal Reserve and the EEC central banks at their discretion. Within the EEC joint float, the stronger currencies were expected to assist their weaker brethren. On the other hand, as Secretary Shultz stated on March 17, the U.S. stood "prepared" to intervene "in a flexible manner, on an ad hoc basis, case by case"—a language that was interpreted by the markets to mean that any efforts to support the dollar would be minimal. In fact, for four months between March 19, when the markets reopened, and July 10, when—as pointed out later—the monetary authorities resumed intervention, the dollar was in the full sense, and for the first time, floating freely. (*See* Table I and Graph 1.)

Theoretically, a simple, effective, market-governed solution was achieved; in practical reality, despite a better trend in the U.S. balance of payments and the frequently voiced belief that the dollar had become undervalued, funds failed to flow back. On the contrary, the markets became increasingly concerned over the worsening of the U.S. inflation, and in May, shifts out of dollars into European currencies were resumed. By early July, the dollar was driven down to levels unjustified and undesirable on any reasonable assessment of the outlook for U.S. payments.

The sharpest fall of the dollar was against the West German mark and, with the mark, the EEC joint float came under increasing strain. After the publication of a report by a private economic institute recommending upvaluation of the mark as a wise course to reinforce existing anti-inflationary policies, pressure became so great that, on June 29, the mark was upvalued by 5½% but was kept within the EEC joint float.

Meanwhile, the dollar fell almost daily to new lows against the EEC currencies. This reflected the great volatility of exchange rates under a system of floating in unsettled and nervous foreign exchange markets where even modest pressures could cause large shifts

Table I. How the Currencies Fared: 1971–73

Currency	Parity on May 5, 1971 In dollars per unit	Appreciation or depreciation (−) against the U.S. dollar (%) May 5 to Dec. 18, 1971	Dec. 18, 1971, to March 19, 1973*	March 19* to July 6, 1973†	July 6† to Dec. 31, 1973†	Cumulative change May 5, 1971, to Dec. 31, 1973	Market rate on Dec. 31, 1973 In dollars per unit
Swiss franc	.228685	13.9	18.1	20.5	−14.1	39.1	.318200
German mark	.273224	13.6	14.4	24.5	−16.3	35.4	.370000
Austrian schilling	.038462	11.6	13.6	21.2	−14.0	32.1	.050800
Japanese yen	.002778	16.9	17.0	0.4	− 6.6	28.3	.003565
Dutch guilder	.276243	11.6	11.1	17.1	−11.6	28.3	.354400
Norwegian krone	.139999	7.5	11.1	16.6	−10.7	24.4	.174200
Belgian franc	.020000	11.6	11.1	16.8	−15.5	22.3	.024450
Danish krone	.133333	7.4	11.1	14.3	−12.9	18.9	.158500
French franc	.180044	8.6	11.1	19.7	−18.1	18.3	.213000
Swedish krona	.193304	7.5	5.5	14.9	−13.2	13.2	.218800
Italian lira	.001600	7.5	2.5	−1.6	− 5.1	2.9	.001646
British pound	2.400000	8.6	−5.6	4.0	− 9.3	−3.3	2.320000

*Based on nominal or middle rates except for the Swiss franc, Japanese yen, Italian lira, and British pound.
†Based on market rates.

Graph 1.

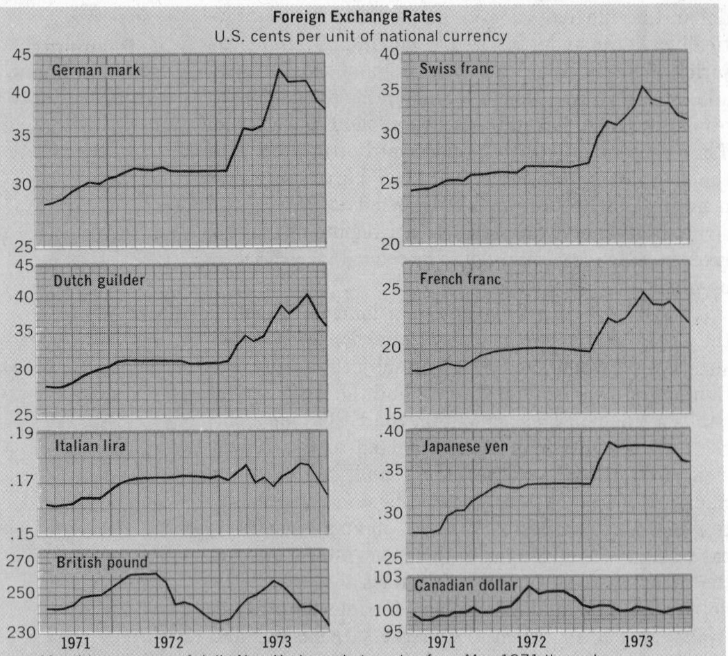

Monthly averages of daily New York market quotes from May 1971 through December 1973. Logarithmic scale shows proportionate change.
Source: U.S. Federal Reserve System, Board of Governors.

Graph 2.

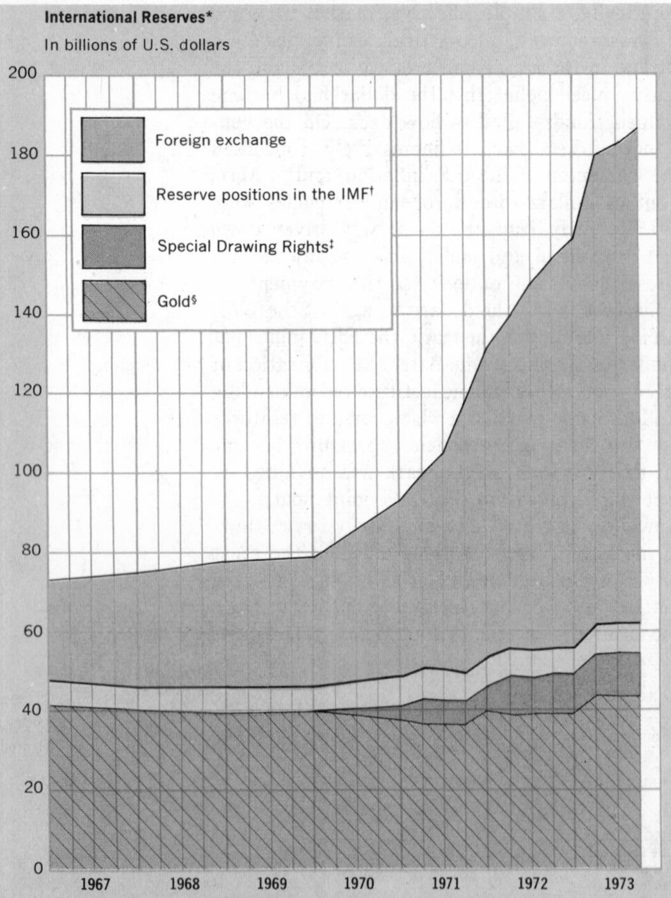

* Excluding the U.S.S.R., Eastern European countries, China, and other socialist economies.

† Amounts that can be drawn essentially automatically from the IMF, corresponding to members' gold subscriptions *plus* amounts of their currencies sold by the Fund to other members (net) *plus* outstanding lendings to the Fund.

‡ Special Drawing Rights are unconditional international reserve assets created by the IMF; they are allocated to participating members in proportion to their IMF quotas.

§ Valued at $35 an ounce from 1966 to September 1971; at $38 from December 1971 to December 1972; and at $42.22 thereafter.

Source: International Monetary Fund.

in rates. On the night of Sunday, July 8, the authorities of the key countries made it known, at a meeting held under the auspices of the Bank for International Settlements in Basel, Switz., that they would intervene "to maintain orderly markets" and that they had wound up earlier negotiations for major increases in mutual credits (the so-called swap lines) as well as for new arrangements covering exchange risks on floating rates. On July 10, the Federal Reserve itself, in agreement with the U.S. Treasury, initiated market intervention after it had announced that, if necessary, it would finance its exchange operations by drawings on intercentral bank credits, the total of which was increased from $11.7 billion to nearly $18 billion. The dollar's exposure to completely unsupported floating was, thus, of short duration.

The Rejuvenated Dollar. From all-time lows on July 6, the dollar immediately rocketed up against most European currencies; and its recovery continued for the remainder of the year, at first slowly, but in the last three months of 1973 strongly and, at times, dramatically (*see* Table I and Graph 1). At the year's end, the dollar had recovered the entire loss it had suffered between mid-May and early July in terms of ten major currencies (those of eight European countries, Canada, and Japan, on a trade-weighted basis).

The turnaround in the dollar's fortunes was attributable to a number of factors. The first was the markets' awareness that, as Secretary Shultz and Federal Reserve Chairman Arthur F. Burns stated jointly on July 18, "active intervention will take place in the future at whatever times and in whatever amounts are appropriate for maintaining orderly market conditions." Intervention, which had been sizable in July, tapered off with the passage of time. Basically, of course, the rejuvenated dollar reflected the growing market realization that, by early July, its depreciation had reached unrealistic proportions. The dollar had been depressed by the flight of funds. Imbalances due to short-term money flows could be expected to take care of themselves when the basic balance of payments—the balance on current account and long-term capital—showed clear signs of improvement. The critical factor was the imbalance in merchandise trade, which the devaluation of the dollar in December 1971 was intended to reverse by making U.S. goods cheaper in international markets and foreign goods more expensive in the U.S. It was acknowledged that this process would take time, but the only sign of a turnaround at the end of 1972 was a slight decline in the trade deficit. It was a good year for U.S. exports, but a disastrous one for the dollar value of U.S. imports, above all because of a very sharp rise in imports of manufactured goods.

This poor trade performance became, in early 1973, a crucial factor in the dollar crisis. The U.S. trade problem was too large to be corrected by the rather small devaluation of December 1971; even the second devaluation in February 1973 was regarded with skepticism. What then happened, however, was unpredicted and probably unpredictable. In March, the U.S. trade deficit narrowed, and in April a surplus was recorded. For the year as a whole, there was a modest surplus, which compared with a $7 billion deficit in 1972. Particularly striking was the rapid disappearance of the huge U.S. deficit with Japan. Exports rose at an extraordinary rate. Part of this was attributable to sales of agricultural products, and part to the world-wide industrial boom; but the improvement also reflected the lower rate of inflation in the U.S. than in other industrial countries and, far more important than this, the lagged effects of the depreciation of the dollar since 1971. In late 1973 the reversal in exchange rate trends, noted above, blunted somewhat the competitive edge enjoyed by U.S. exports earlier in the year. The change in U.S. international competitiveness resulting from the depreciation of the dollar also affected U.S. imports.

The balance of international flows of long-term private capital also moved in favour of the U.S. Most importantly, net flows of short-term funds were favourable, with the result that the balance of payments for the entire year was in much better shape (*see* Table II). Controls on private investments abroad were relaxed at the end of December.

Monetary Reserves. Against this background, and in an international monetary environment (it could not be called a system since there was nothing systematic in it) where exchange rates for many currencies were floating, changes in monetary reserves of governments and central banks had much less significance than in earlier years. For the most part, they merely reflected official intervention in the foreign exchange markets. In the first quarter of 1973, marked by the February–March crisis, total official holdings by governments and central banks of gold, foreign exchange, and SDRs, together with their IMF reserve positions, increased by a further $20 billion, to $179 billion; but from April through September they rose by $7 billion. During the last quarter, when Japan and West Germany lost dollar reserves in large amounts, the total declined. But even so, 1973 was the fourth year of massive expansion in global reserves (*see* Graph 2).

Of the increase in global reserves during the year, $4 billion was due to upvaluation of official gold stocks consequent upon the rise in the U.S. monetary price of gold in February. As to the remainder, it was mainly accounted for by the increase in official holdings of dollars. No further SDR allocation was made in 1973, following the $9.5 billion of 1970–72.

In September 1973, gold represented less than 25% of total reserves, as against more than 50% as recently as 1969. But calculations of this sort were based on the official price of gold and neglected, therefore, the judgment of the market, where the price in December 1973 was two-and-a-half times higher than the new U.S. Treasury price. If official gold stocks were valued near the market price, the proportion of gold in international liquidity in 1973 was about the same as in 1969, despite the $90 billion increase in foreign exchange reserves and the $9.5 billion in SDRs created during the period. Graph 2, which—as official statistics do—shows gold valued at $42.22 beginning with March 1973, fails, therefore, to give a realistic picture. Gold stocks were virtually frozen because no central bank would give up gold at the official price when the market price had soared above it. Gold remained "unused—but not unloved," as the Bank for International Settlements concluded in its 1973 report.

As in earlier years, the distribution of reserve gains among countries was very uneven (*see* Graph 3). The biggest gains during recent years were shown by Japan and West Germany; but Japan's dollar reserves declined sharply in the closing months of 1973, while those of West Germany also fell. U.S. monetary assets totaled $14.4 billion in November, including $11.7 billion of gold valued at $42.22 an ounce and $2.2 billion of SDRs; U.S. liabilities to foreign governments totaled $70 billion in November.

The year's experience—although still far too young for definite judgments—offered several lessons bearing directly and immediately on the discussions in 1974 about international monetary reforms. Among these lessons was, first of all, the renewed acceptance by governments of a large degree of responsibility for establishing exchange rates. In economic theorizing, a case was made, with verve and vehemence, for freely floating exchange rates so that balances of payments would always be in equilibrium and there would be no need for monetary reserves. If floating were to be between currency blocs, the need for reserves would be met on a regional scale.

Reality was not kind to theory. Governments, it is true, failed in the two starts they made to reestablish basically fixed exchange rates—at the Smithsonian in December 1971 and in Paris in February 1973; the currencies of most industrial countries floated. But the periods of free float were very short—from mid-March to early July 1973 and, previously, from mid-August to mid-December 1971. In 1972 and in January 1973, the dollar was supported, albeit along a downward sloping path, by several major central banks as they attempted to avoid any further appreciation of their own exchange rates. Beginning with mid-July 1973, the U.S. cooperated with other key countries to exert occasional influence on the speed and the size of market-induced changes in exchange rates for their currencies. Planned intervention did not define specific rate relationships; but—without opposing fundamental economic trends—it sought to

Graph 3.

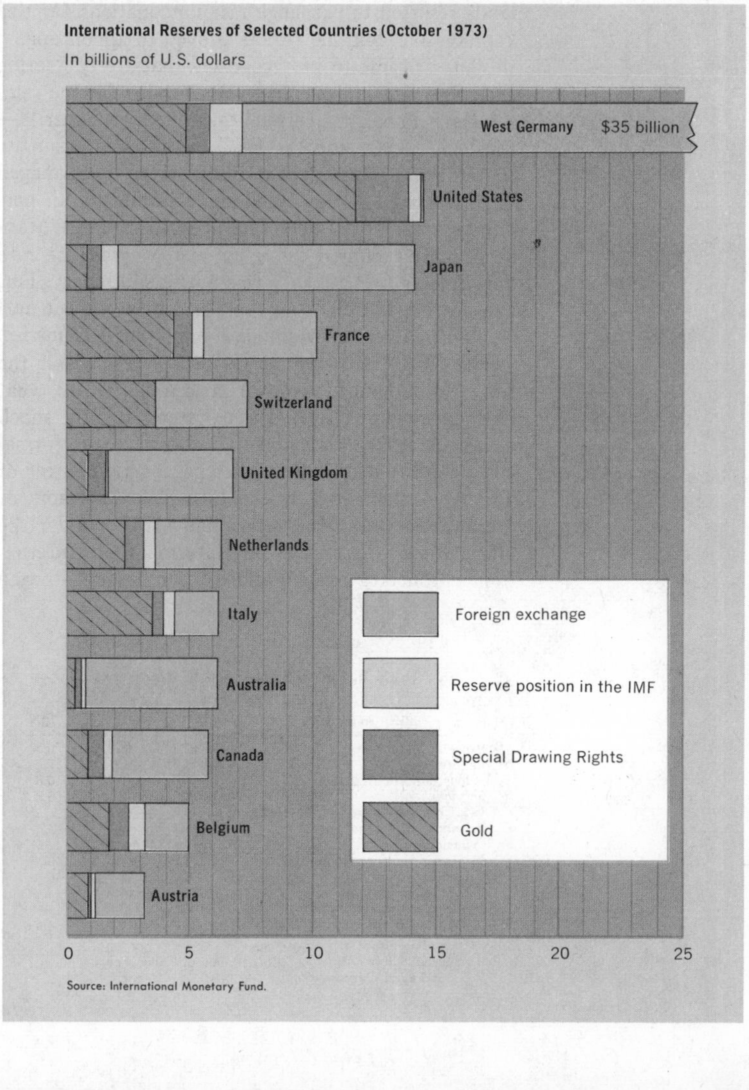

produce a steadying influence. This contrasted with the wide and erratic day-to-day fluctuations that were commonplace from mid-March through early July 1973 and, in the end, made the dollar clearly undervalued; its depreciation had been overdone, but proved reversible.

Second, the foreign exchange markets learned that economic realities—above all, comparative costs—are ultimately the decisive influence on rates at which currencies are exchanged. In the closing months of 1973, the dollar continued to strengthen against the European and Japanese currencies despite the question of the U.S. presidency and the unfinished business ahead of the U.S. to secure reasonable financial stability. The extent of the dollar's strength at the year's end should not be exaggerated; it was helped by the Middle East crisis and its consequences for oil supplies and prices, which were more serious for Europe and Japan than for the U.S. But, however imperfect, the dollar appeared marginally more promising than any of the other key currencies.

Third, by making imports more expensive, floating accentuated inflationary pressures in the U.S. The countries in South America, Asia, and Africa whose currencies depreciated with the dollar also found themselves exposed to increased inflationary pressures because of the rise in import prices and also because a rising price level made the inflation self-generating and the exchange rate depreciation continuous. On the other hand, exchange rate appreciation was often depicted as if it could, by decreasing import prices, help hold down inflation. West Germany and The Netherlands resorted to exchange rate upvaluations for this very reason; but the results proved disappointing.

Thus, it came to be recognized that freely floating exchange rates did not have much value for the relationships among the currencies of the key countries—the U.S., Japan, and the EEC. Not too surprisingly, therefore, the leading nations resorted to managed floating aimed at providing some stability and, perhaps, even some predictability in exchange rates. Managed floating offered a fair amount of exchange rate flexibility, but the change was not revolutionary. For, even before March 1973, there had been a great deal of managed flexibility among the industrial countries.

The "First Outline of Reform." Just about the time of the final breakdown in March 1973 of what had remained of the fixed-rate system after the shock of August 1971, when the U.S. abolished the formal convertibility of the dollar into gold, a Committee of Twenty—established by the Board of Governors of the International Monetary Fund (IMF) under the official title "Committee on Reform of the International Monetary System and Related Issues"—began to formulate and negotiate reforms. Its 20 members were appointed by six major countries (France, West Germany, the U.K., the U.S., Japan, and India) and by 14 groupings of other countries. The Committee was composed of finance ministers but the hard work was done by "deputies." It was anything but what its name suggested, for, with advisers and other officials, up to 200 people were reportedly present at its meetings, which made it an unwieldy organ for negotiation and decision. In September, at the IMF annual meeting in Nairobi, Kenya, the chairman of the deputies, Jeremy Morse, and four vice-chairmen presented to the ministers a report reflecting their views, and not those of the committee as a whole, under the title *First Outline of Reform*. It recorded agreement on some issues, and disagreement on others; where agreement was recorded, it was subject to further agreement on operational provisions as well as to eventual agreement on the reform as a whole. The ministers set a deadline of July 31, 1974, for the completion of basic agreement by the committee.

Judging from the *First Outline*, agreement was reached among the deputies in only three fields, and in these in a general manner. First, any new system would be based on a strengthened IMF. There would be no new brave world, at least not by design.

Second, in the reformed system, exchange rates would continue to be "a matter for international concern and consultation." "Competitive depreciation or undervaluation" would be avoided. The exchange rate mechanism would "remain based on stable but adjustable par values"; changes in par values, whenever appropriate, would be made "promptly." Countries might adopt floating rates "in particular situations, subject to Fund authorization, surveillance, and review." Taken as a whole, these words corresponded to the views the U.S. Treasury expressed in a document published on August 27: "We agree with other countries that stable but adjustable par values should be the 'center of gravity' of the new system. . . . But parities must not be allowed to become grossly inappropriate again. . . . Countries should be able to float their exchange rates, if that course is best suited to their needs—subject to international surveillance and in conformance with internationally agreed standards." With regard to controls, the *First Outline* expressed the wish that nations not use import or exchange controls; but they would cooperate in "actions" designed to limit "disequilibrating" capital flows and in arrangements to finance and offset them.

Third, SDRs would become "the principal reserve asset." They would also be "the *numéraire* in terms of which par values will be expressed." In ways not stated, allocations of SDRs would be "adequate" but not excessive. For the future, SDRs should be the principal means of reserve growth and an instrument—though not exclusive—of reserve management.

Disagreements remained on six critical issues. First, there was disagreement about how to establish the need for adjustments in exchange rates. In the U.S. view, as expressed in the August 27 document, whenever a country's monetary reserves rose or fell below a specified level over a specified period of time, such a country would be expected to adopt or reinforce policies to correct the imbalance (domestic policies, trade liberalization, capital liberalization, increased aid, or exchange rate changes, but not—except in extreme cases—import or exchange controls). If the country's reserves were to rise or fall beyond further specified points, the community of nations could apply

Table II. The U.S. Balance of Payments

In U.S. $000,000,000

Item	1971	1972	1973
Exports	42.8	48.8	70.3
Imports	45.5	55.7	69.2
Merchandise trade	−2.7	−6.9	0.8
Services	3.5	2.3	3.8
U.S. government grants and credits	−6.0	−5.1	...
Private long-term capital	−4.4	−0.1	...
Basic balance	−9.6	−9.8	2.5
Nonliquid short-term capital flows*	−13.1	−4.8	...
Allocations of SDRs	0.7	0.7	0
Balance on liquidity basis	−22.0	−13.9	...
Liquid short-term capital flows	−7.8	3.6	...
Balance on official settlements basis	−29.8	−10.3	−4.5

*Including errors and omissions.
Source: Adapted from U.S. Department of Commerce, *Survey of Current Business*.

graduated pressures on the recalcitrant country. The arrangement would provide an "objective indication" of payments imbalance and establish "a presumption" that adjustments were needed; but "the indicator system" would not be automatic, for the international body could override the indicator. The indicator system would, in the U.S. view, avoid undue delays. Consultations alone could not provide "the needed certainty in adjustment arrangements."

The U.S. views met with opposition. A reserve loss or gain would not necessarily be a sign of fundamental imbalance for it might originate from cyclical developments, from interest rate differentials, or from speculation. A better indicator might be the country's deficit or surplus in its basic balance of payments. However desirable it might be to make the concept of fundamental disequilibrium as concrete as possible, it was doubtful that really objective criteria could enable such situations to be identified by a rule of thumb. There was need for judgment.

The second disagreement revolved around the pressures that should be brought on countries with persistent payments surpluses that failed to take remedial action. The present IMF Charter is symmetrical in form by requiring surplus countries as well as deficit countries to take remedial action; but, in practice, the Fund did not match the pressures that compelled most deficit countries to take adjustment steps with comparable pressures on surplus countries. To make the new system truly symmetrical, therefore, an obligation would be imposed on surplus countries to control their surpluses either by internal policies or by upvaluing their currencies. These thoughts were opposed on the ground that one country's surplus is another country's deficit; that the rise in one country's reserves might be merely the consequence of some other country's misdeeds; and that the onus of taking remedial action would be put on the surplus country.

The third disagreement concerned convertibility—not the principle that all countries, including the U.S., should maintain convertibility of their currency into primary reserve assets of gold and SDRs, but whether the use of dollars (or sterling) as a reserve currency should be strictly limited. The U.S., with some support, took the position that if surplus countries were happy to receive dollars, such an option would introduce desired flexibility into the system. To limit increases in dollar reserves (once the "overhang" of unwanted dollars in the reserves of countries like Japan, West Germany, and Switzerland was disposed of) would require an overadjustment process in which exchange rate changes would be destabilizing for foreign trade as well as for domestic economies. There was need for some play in the system—for some unmanaged growth of reserves.

The fourth disagreement was about the nature of SDRs. Somehow, their effective yield would have to be made good enough for countries to want to hold them voluntarily, but not so attractive as to make them reluctant to part with them when in deficit. Somehow, too, the new SDRs would, hopefully, become an independent reserve asset, which would imply substituting some other guarantee for the present link with gold and changing the rules for their use.

The fifth disagreement was, not surprisingly, about gold. The U.S. maintained the view that the historic decline in the role of gold should continue, although it recognized that gold could not be demonetized overnight. All countries seemed to agree that the share of gold in global reserves would tend to decline as that of SDRs increased; but there was no agreement on how to phase out gold. Many countries believed that gold should be retained in the system and even that the SDR link with gold should be kept.

There was also disagreement about the monetary price of gold. Should it be kept unchanged after the two U.S. devaluations? Should it be raised? Should it be abolished or ignored, which would leave countries free, if they wished, to use gold in official settlements at prices related to the price in the international market? The EEC countries participating in the joint float agreed in 1973 to use gold, together with other reserve assets, for settlements within the EEC at market-related prices. At the year's end, this decision was still in suspense, but it came to be realized that such an EEC value for gold actually used would look much more like an "official" price than the $42.22 U.S. Treasury price, at which no settlements were made.

In November 1973, the U.S. and six other monetarily important countries, but not including France, which was not party to the arrangement, canceled the Washington emergency understanding they had reached among themselves in March 1968, in the midst of a severe gold crisis, to abstain from selling or buying gold at other than the $35 U.S. Treasury price then in force. The arrangement had been made at a time when the dollar was still convertible into gold and when the key governments wanted to preserve the fixed, although, of course, changeable, IMF exchange rates. In the drastically changed circumstances, the Washington understanding lost whatever usefulness it might have had. Its abrogation was interpreted by the U.S. as restoration of the right of monetary authorities to sell gold at higher prices than $42.22, as they are allowed to do under the IMF Charter, and by EEC countries as freedom to sell as well as buy at such prices. Whatever the outcome of these divergences of views might be, it appeared that gold would be unfrozen, but not that it would again become a dynamic component in the growth of reserves and the common denominator of currencies.

The sixth disagreement centred around the idea that less developed countries should be allocated more SDRs than would result from allocations proportionate to their quotas in the IMF, as at present. This idea, known as the "link" between SDRs and development aid, was opposed by the U.S., but favoured by South American, Asian, and African countries, and also by France. On strictly monetary grounds, the "link" would change the nature of SDRs, which are intended to finance the swings in payments, not persistent deficits. If the less developed countries should become the main debtors to the SDR system, confidence in SDRs would be hard to build up, especially if their share in the total allocations were large.

Thus, on the eve of 1974, the issues pending among the governments were difficult and explosive. They appeared even more intractable if the reforms were also framed with a view toward easing the accession of the Soviet Union and China to the IMF. As a matter of fact, the reforms had been on the official agenda for ten years. Lip service had long been paid to the need for the political will to agree and to manage the system. But a "new" monetary system cannot spring forth, full-blown, like Athena from the head of Zeus. It could only be an ongoing, evolutionary process.

(MIROSLAV A. KRIZ)

See also Commercial Policies; Commodities, Primary; Economy, World; Investment, International; Money and Banking; Prices; Trade, International.

Peace Movements

In the "Year of Watergate," the U.S. peace effort was confronted by dramatic changes in the domestic political climate. Peace leaders grappled with the opportunities afforded by the crises of legitimacy that racked the Nixon administration as the revelations of the Watergate hearings, the forced resignation of Vice-Pres. Spiro T. Agnew, and related developments exploded throughout the year. (*See* UNITED STATES.) The outbreak of yet another Arab-Israeli war dashed the hopes of peace leaders who had been encouraged by slight signs of flexibility both within and outside the Middle Eastern governments.

The striking fluidity of events and politics in 1973 was evident in the months following Pres. Richard Nixon's electoral triumph over dovish Sen. George McGovern in November 1972. Even in defeat, peace advocates had pointed to McGovern's capture of nearly 40% of the popular vote. Early in 1973 the protracted Paris negotiations—interrupted by the massive bombing of North Vietnam in late December 1972 and early 1973—finally culminated in an agreement formally ending the decade-long U.S. involvement in Vietnam. Peace leaders noted that hostilities among the Vietnamese continued and that U.S. forces were still actively supporting the Cambodian government, and they questioned the call for increased military spending despite the proclaimed end of the war and the alleged détente with China and the Soviet Union. Nevertheless, the country as a whole seemed to accept gratefully the U.S. withdrawal from Vietnam and the much-publicized return of the American prisoners of war. But this, the high-water mark of the administration's popularity during the year, was swiftly followed by the Watergate revelations and the steady attrition of the president's political base.

This postwar fragmentation of traditional political patterns demanded intensified and original responses from the peace movement. The trend from merely tactical protests to more basic involvement in longer-term political and educational efforts continued. A broadened coalition of public interest lobbies such as Common Cause (with over 250,000 members), the Council for a Livable World, and the Federation of American Scientists mounted full-scale attacks on vulnerable targets: corrupt methods of campaign financing, excessive military spending, and dominance of the executive in military and foreign policy. Many peace spokesmen urged the impeachment and trial of President Nixon himself, basing their demands—among other matters—on the president's military policies in Southeast Asia and the secret bombing of Cambodia in 1969 and early 1970, which, it was revealed during the year, had been systematically concealed through the falsification of military reports.

U.S. peace leaders also strongly supported full, broad, and unconditional amnesty for those who had resisted the draft, military service, or war during the Indochina conflict. Others examined the nature and political implications of the growing phenomenon of powerful multinational corporations. Peace tacticians also attempted to relate traditional peace concerns more effectively to environmental interests and the bread-and-butter concerns of the blue-collar worker. Finally, they examined communal methods of "living the nonviolent revolution" by establishing a national network of living centres where experiments in nonviolent social change could become a way of life rather than a part-time activity.

While the long-term goal of general and complete disarmament in a genuine world community still seemed distant, halting progress was made in challenging additional weapons systems, supporting the concept of arms limitation, and criticizing swollen military budgets. Most important, perhaps, was an emerging climate of opinion severely critical of traditional justifications for U.S. military and foreign policy. As the crises of the Nixon administration flowed over into the war-peace arena, both the dovish Senate and the more hawkish House showed an increasing readiness to challenge executive dominance in foreign policy. In early summer, as U.S. bombing in support of the Lon Nol regime in Cambodia reached massive proportions, Congress amended one major appropriations bill after another with a provision cutting off funds for the Cambodian effort. The president vetoed the bills and there were not enough votes in Congress to override, but as it became clear that the lack of appropriations would bring government to a halt, Nixon was forced to agree to end the bombing on August 15. Later both houses passed, over the president's veto, the War Powers Act placing strict limits on the president's ability to wage "undeclared" wars.

SANE, the Council for a Livable World, and the American Friends Service Committee were among those directing attention both to the escalating military budget and to the plethora of military assistance programs; of the 64 recipient nations, 25 were governed by the military or permitted no overt opposition to the prevailing regime. While opposition to such weapons systems as the Trident submarine and the proposed B-1 bomber was intense, some peace strategists urged a focus on less dramatic but more vulnerable sectors of military spending, such as waste in personnel, operations, and maintenance programs, the high ratio of support troops to combat troops, and

Swedish soldiers serving with the United Nations in Cyprus prepare to embark for the Middle East on Oct. 26, 1973, as the first troops of a peacekeeping force.

WIDE WORLD

flight pay for officers who did not fly. Finally, critics underlined U.S. arms supplies over many years to the Chilean military junta which overthrew the civilian Allende government. (*See* CHILE.)

A little publicized but highly important development involved the growth of peace research and curriculum efforts. The Consortium on Peace Research, Education and Development grew from 71 to 85 members, including over 70 academic institutions. Together with such organizations as the Canadian Peace Research Institute, the Peace Science Society (International), the Conference on Peace Research in History, the Institute for World Order (formerly the World Law Fund), and the Center for War/Peace Studies, peace researchers sponsored working meetings and curriculum and literature development. The publication of such works as Gene Sharp's *The Politics of Nonviolent Action* suggested the development of inclusive approaches to peacemaking.

One of the more surprising results of 1973 involved the virtual collapse of the U.S. government's efforts to prosecute "radical" members of the antiwar movement. The highly publicized trial of Daniel Ellsberg and Anthony J. Russo over release of the classified Pentagon papers ended with Judge William Byrne's dismissal of the charges. The judge cited "government misconduct" that included concealing the existence of government tapes of Ellsberg's phone conversations and a break-in of Ellsberg's psychiatrist's office by White House employees. While the case was still being tried, a covert offer to make Judge Byrne the head of the FBI had been made by presidential aide John D. Ehrlichman. Seventeen of the "Camden 28" were acquitted, and the prosecution itself recommended dismissal of charges against the remaining 10 defendants (one defendant had pleaded guilty to a misdemeanour). The jury found that although the defendants were guilty of breaking into a federal building and destroying draft records, their offense was stimulated and encouraged by the government's deliberate use of an agent provocateur. Finally, a Gainesville, Fla., jury dismissed government allegations against members of the Vietnam Veterans Against the War growing out of VVAW's antiwar protests at the Republican convention in Miami Beach in August 1972.

Over 150 delegates were present at the first National Conference on a Department of Peace, held at Skokie, Ill. Reviving an idea first proposed by Benjamin Rush in 1793, many delegates supported House Bill 4824, which anticipated the establishment of a National Department of Peace, a National Peace Academy, and a joint committee of the House and Senate on peace and international cooperation.

Appeals for universal amnesty for U.S. war resisters were matched by concern for the fate of over 100,000 political prisoners of the Saigon regime. Amnesty International, the American Friends Service Committee, and the Fellowship of Reconciliation were conspicuous leaders in a campaign calling for the end of torture and the swift release of such victims of the war. This effort was supplemented with legislative attempts to slash U.S. aid for police forces and the prison system of South Vietnam.

Anxious as they were for genuine détente, peace leaders, nevertheless, vigorously defended the rights of dissidents within the Soviet Union and other Communist countries. In June a statement demanding amnesty for dissenters in Communist nations was publicized during Soviet party leader Leonid I. Brezhnev's visit to the U.S. Among the more than 300 signatories

WIDE WORLD

Le Duc Tho, North Vietnam negotiator, signs a peace accord in Paris on June 13, 1973. Aimed at strengthening the January peace treaty signed with the United States, the accord was also signed by U.S. presidential adviser Henry Kissinger.

were such prominent peace advocates as the Rev. Philip Berrigan, Noam Chomsky, Dwight Macdonald, Lewis Mumford, William Sloane Coffin, Jr., and David McReynolds.

The Soviet government's attacks on liberal intellectuals, most notably physicist Andrey D. Sakharov (*see* BIOGRAPHY) and the distinguished writer Aleksandr I. Solzhenitsyn, caused significant repercussions in the U.S. scientific community. Some 150 scientists at the National Institute of Mental Health threatened not to cooperate with Soviet-U.S. scientific exchanges unless Soviet Jewish scientists were allowed to emigrate. Even the National Academy of Sciences' executive council threatened noncooperation in scientific exchanges over the Sakharov issue. What effect these gestures would have was problematic, but they suggested that criticism of the repression of intellectual freedoms would become more rather than less prominent as a result of warmer relations between the U.S. and the U.S.S.R.

The publication of Humanist Manifesto II stimulated a wide response among international leaders in religion, science, and philosophy. The manifesto criticized religious and political dogmatism, stressed that war and nationalism were obsolete, urged global ecological planning, and cautioned against a thoughtless retreat from technology. The manifesto was signed by more than 100 prominent figures, including Sakharov, B. F. Skinner and Sidney Hook (U.S.), Francis Crick (Great Britain), and others from India, Belgium, The Netherlands, Yugoslavia, and Canada. The 4,000-word document updated the 1933 Humanist Manifesto I, which had been signed, among others, by the philosopher John Dewey.

In related international developments, the sixth World Peace Through Law Conference attracted more than 2,500 judges and lawyers representing 123 countries to Abidjan, Ivory Coast. Their resolutions, while unofficial, urged that wars be outlawed, nuclear weapons controlled, terrorism ended, and UN development and human rights activities increased. Legal spokesmen from the Soviet Union and China had been invited but none attended.

The World Council of Churches voted to raise funds to assist Portuguese draft evaders and deserters who opposed their government's policies in Angola, Mozambique, and Guinea. The WCC also continued its support of stockholder divestment from firms doing business in South Africa and anticipated offering low-interest loans to individuals and groups in the poorest of the less developed countries.

The Moscow-oriented World Peace Council attracted a broad range of international, regional, and national organizations to its consultative meetings in March and its World Congress of Peace Forces in October. The March sessions drew nearly 200 representatives of 40 international groups and 81 national organizations from 60 countries. The October gathering in Moscow brought together more than 3,000 delegates from 141 countries, making the congress one of the largest of its type in recent history. Fourteen working bodies examined such topics as economic development, the environment, and scientific cooperation, as well as more explicitly political issues.

The council's successes contrasted sharply with the tight budget and restricted programs of the presumably nonaligned International Confederation for Disarmament and Peace (ICDP). Indeed, the ICDP staff was charged by some members with having tilted too far from a truly nonaligned position, especially in allegedly favouring North Vietnamese-National Liberation Front viewpoints over those of "third force" pacifists and neutralists in Vietnam.

An unusually varied collection of individuals, groups, and governments vigorously protested the decision of the French government to proceed with atmospheric nuclear testing over Mururoa Atoll in the South Pacific. The International Court of Justice, the World Health Organization, 56 nations voting at the 1972 UN Conference on the Human Environment in Stockholm, many governments bordering the Pacific including Japan, Peru, Australia, and New Zealand, trade unions, and peace protestors (who actually sailed into the testing area itself) were some of the critics. In France, Jean-Jacques Servan-Schreiber, publisher of *L'Express,* led the antitesting campaign.

A Japanese district court in Sapporo ruled that the nation's military "Self-Defense Forces" violated the "no war" clause of the Japanese constitution (art. 9). The September decision marked the first decisive court ruling on the subject since the controversial founding of the forces in 1950, and was cheered by pacifist spokesmen. They anticipated, however, that a definitive judgment by the Japanese Supreme Court would not occur for several years.

In the face of the Middle East war and the unstable cease-fire that followed, most peace leaders urged peace without victory for either side, recognition of the rights of both Israel and the displaced Palestinian refugees and of legitimate Arab interests, and support for the UN peacekeeping effort. Nonetheless, many adherents of the peace movement also maintained a deep emotional attachment to Israel, and others, especially in the churches, were inhibited from taking a neutralist stance by the spectre of resurgent anti-Semitism should Israeli recalcitrance be blamed for hardships growing out of the Arab oil boycott. The problem was typified by protests against the awarding of the Gandhi Peace Prize to the Rev. Daniel Berrigan because of a speech condemning Israeli militarism made earlier by Father Berrigan to a group of Arab students.

The pitfalls of awarding the Nobel Peace Prize to agents of governments were illustrated when the 1973 prize was given jointly to U.S. Secretary of State Henry Kissinger and Le Duc Tho, the North Vietnamese representative, for having negotiated the Vietnam "peace" agreement. While Kissinger said he would accept the prize, Tho declared he would be able to consider it only when "real peace is established in South Vietnam." In a most unusual gesture, two of the five-members of the Prize Committee resigned in protest against the award. (RICHARD O. HATHAWAY)

Penology:
see Prisons and Penology

Pentecostal Churches:
see Religion

Peru

A republic on the west coast of South America, Peru is bounded by Ecuador, Colombia, Brazil, Bolivia, Chile, and the Pacific Ocean. Area: 496,-222 sq.mi. (1,285,215 sq.km.). Pop. (1972 est.): 13.6 million, including approximately 52% whites and mestizos and 46% Indians. Cap. and largest city: Lima (pop., 1972 est., 3.3 million). Language: Spanish; Indians speak Quechuan or Aymara. Religion: Roman Catholic. President of the military government in 1973, Juan Velasco Alvarado.

During 1973 the government continued its attempts to blaze a trail between capitalism and Communism and in so doing made enemies of both the right and left. It did manage, however, to maintain economic growth and showed itself willing to be pragmatic about the application of doctrines.

The fourth anniversary of the agrarian reform scheme was celebrated in June with the handing over by government representatives of titles to more than 500,000 ha. of land, which would be farmed almost entirely by large-scale producers' cooperatives. At the

PERU

Education. (1970) Primary, pupils 2,750,000, teachers 64,004; secondary, pupils 674,000, teachers 21,863; vocational, pupils 223,300, teachers 6,333; teacher training, students 18,000, teachers 1,075; higher (at 27 universities), students 105,600, teaching staff (1968) 11,649.

Finance. Monetary unit: sol, with a principal official exchange rate (Sept. 17, 1973) of 38.70 soles to U.S. $1 and a free rate of 43.47 to U.S. $1 (104.76 soles = £1 pound sterling). Gold, SDRs, and foreign exchange, central bank: (June 1973) U.S. $479.1 million; (June 1972) U.S. $407.2 million. Budget (1971 actual): revenue 40,128,000,000 soles; expenditure 36,243,000,000 soles (capital expenditure 12,103,000,-000 soles). Gross domestic product: (1971) 262.1 billion soles; (1970) 236.2 billion soles. Money supply: (June 1971) 31,540,000,000 soles; (June 1970) 27,-250,000,000 soles. Cost of living (Lima and Callao; 1963 = 100): (April 1973) 250; (April 1972) 235.

Foreign Trade. (1972) Imports 30,628,000,000 soles; exports 36,497,000,000 soles. Import sources: U.S. 33%; West Germany 10%; Japan 8%; U.K. 5%; Canada 7%. Export destinations: U.S. 31%; Japan 15%; West Germany 11%. Main exports: fish meal 21%; copper 20%; sugar 8%; zinc 7%; iron ore 7%; silver 7%; coffee 5%; cotton 5%.

Transport and Communications. Roads (1972) 50,671 km. Motor vehicles in use (1972): passenger 256,400; commercial 136,100. Railways: (1969) 2,090 km.; traffic (1970) 248 million passenger-km., freight 410 million net ton-km. Air traffic (1971): 224 million passenger-km.; freight 17,790,000 net ton-km. Shipping (1972): merchant vessels 100 gross tons and over 655; gross tonnage 446,374. Telephones (Jan. 1972) 243,000. Radio receivers (Dec. 1970) 1,819,000. Television receivers (Dec. 1970) 395,000.

Agriculture. Production (in 000; metric tons; 1972; 1971 in parentheses): rice 477 (585); corn 643 (615); wheat 141 (122); barley *c.* 160 (159); potatoes 1,900 (1,968); sweet potatoes (1971) 168, (1970) 178; onions (1971) 158, (1970) 159; cassava (1970) 498, (1969) 450; dry beans *c.* 60 (58); sugar, raw value *c.* 920 (913); grapes *c.* 62 (63); oranges (1971) 254, (1970) 258; coffee 72 (71); cotton lint *c.* 70 (87); fish catch (1971) 10,611, (1970) 12,613. Livestock (in 000; 1971–72): cattle 4,310; sheep 16,918; pigs 2,071; goats *c.* 1,900; horses *c.* 600; poultry *c.* 22,000.

Industry. Production (in 000; metric tons; 1971): crude oil 3,053; coal (1970) 156; cement (1972) 1,427; iron ore (metal content; 1970) 6,119; pig iron 90; steel (1970) 94; lead (1970) 72; zinc 55; copper 33; tungsten concentrates (oxide content) 1; gold (troy oz; 1970) 95; silver (troy oz.) 38,400; fish meal 1,935; electricity (kw-hr.; 1970) 5,324,000.

same time, the government reassured small and medium-sized commercial farmers that there was no danger of their being "collectivized."

Worker enthusiasm for participation in industry was somewhat tempered by the government's decision that changes in industrial law were to be carried out under supervision of a committee of industrialists and government officials. After riots on May 24 in Chimbote, 3,000 striking workers were forced back to work under threat of dismissal. A number of union leaders were arrested.

The government's pragmatism did not help to increase confidence in itself or in the economy, since some of its actions contributed to a decline in private investment. In particular, the business community was worried both by the nationalization in May of the fish meal and fish oil industry (although this was in line with the government's policy of assigning to the state a major and direct role in developing and exploiting the country's natural resources) and by the publication in August of the plans for worker-owned-and-controlled companies. The U.S.-owned Cerro de Pasco Corp., the largest mining enterprise in Peru, was nationalized on December 31.

Public investment in 1973, however, was sustained at a high level (representing almost 50% of total investment); many of the contracts signed included a high degree of foreign participation. Reassuring words to foreign business interests followed announcement of a World Bank credit to Peru of $25 million for the agricultural development program. Progress was made in the petroleum sector, with many successful strikes and a commitment by Petroperú, the state petroleum company, to continue to invest in further exploration of jungle regions. In September the government banned the signing of further contracts with foreign oil companies, while allowing the 18 firms that already had contracts to continue prospecting.

Importance was also placed on new investment in mining, not only on the development of new deposits (such as those at Antamina and Cerro Verde) but also on the construction of refineries for zinc and of a copper manufacturing complex. The government hoped to double mining production by 1977. Peru also hoped to expand its embryonic motor vehicle industry.

The virtual disappearance of anchovies in 1972 and 1973, because of changes in ocean currents, caused severe disruption to the previously profitable fish meal industry. Plans to switch the emphasis toward fishing for human consumption included the construction of plants for processing fish, modernization of the fishing fleet, construction of new boats, and development of many small ports.

Economic growth was not seriously affected by the loss of fish meal production. Exports of fish meal stocks that had accumulated during 1971 and a recovery in exports of minerals in 1972 contributed to a trade surplus of $147 million in 1972. With large inflows of foreign capital, the balance of payments recorded a surplus of $42 million, compared with a deficit of $62 million in 1971. Unusual weather conditions caused a loss in agricultural production, but a growth rate of 5.9% in gross national product was nevertheless recorded.

Economic growth in 1973 was expected to be similar to that in 1972, as the fish meal industry was at a virtual standstill throughout the year. Industrialized nations responded fairly well to the $3 billion package of projects requiring external financing that Peru presented in June, and some offered substantial loans for development projects. Nevertheless, the high level of public foreign debt was disquieting, particularly as much of it was of a short-term nature.

In July Peru broke off diplomatic relations with France over French persistence in carrying out nuclear tests in the Pacific despite international protests. Commercial, consular, and cultural ties were maintained. (FRANCES KIRKHAM)

Philately and Numismatics

Philately. Serious philatelists who invested in rare stamps had no cause to worry about inflation during 1973. The prices of classic issues of all countries, especially those in fine condition and on the original covers, advanced well beyond the margin required to cover the depreciation of money. This was forcefully demonstrated by a sale held on October 4 by Stanley Gibbons Auctions in London, when 130 classic lots realized £228,505. The many new records set at the sale included £50,000 paid for an 1854 Bermuda provisional (the "Perot" stamp) on cover.

On the other hand, nonphilatelists investing in large quantities of common stamps received a shock when Harvey Michael Ross of Leeds, Eng., who traded as Harvey Michael Investments, was fined £37,500 and £4,000 costs on being found guilty of obtaining money by deception. He had sold vast quantities of obsolete British stamps with the promise that the purchasers could expect to receive 100% profit.

In February Robin West was appointed to take charge of the philatelic collections at the British Museum. He succeeded James Mackay, who in September 1972 had pleaded guilty to charges of theft of material on loan to the museum from the crown agents. West, a former police constable, had been a member of the Philatelic Squad at Scotland Yard which handled the Mackay case. The De La Rue reference collection, on permanent loan from Thomas De La Rue and Co. Ltd., was transferred from the British Museum to the National Postal Museum in June; the museum opened the first display from the collection in October.

Plans went forward for Canada's National Postal Museum, to be set up in Ottawa. A director of the museum and a board of governors were active under the direction of the Canada Post Office. One important donation was the collection of former prime minister Lester Pearson, whose widow made the presentation.

Two major international stamp exhibitions were held. At Munich, W.Ger., in May, the International Grand Prix was won by Count Alfredo Gerli of Italy for a collection of Sicilian stamps, and the National Grand Prix (for German stamps) went to Arthur Salm of the U.S. At Poznan, Pol., in August, the Grand Prix d'Honneur was awarded to Gunnar Roos of Sweden for a specialized Swedish collection and the Grand Prix International to Samad Khorshid of Iran for Persian stamps of 1863–80. The Grand Prix National (for Polish stamps) was won by Stanislow Dolinski of Poland. The Federation of Italian Philatelists instituted the Diena Medal, in memory of Maria Diena, to be awarded every third year to the philatelist who had gained the most points at international and national stamp exhibitions during the preceding three years.

The Philatelic Congress of Great Britain was held in London; Ilya Braunstein (Belgium), A. John Hubbard (U.K.), C. F. Rousseau (Luxembourg), and

Petroleum Industry: *see* Energy; Industrial Review

A U.S. memorial postage stamp honouring former president Lyndon B. Johnson was issued on Aug. 27, 1973, the 65th anniversary of his birth.
WIDE WORLD

Israel's 25th anniversary silver commemorative coin was released on May 7, 1973 (obverse: right; reverse: left). Two varieties of the coin were issued: brilliant uncirculated and proof.
AUTHENTICATED NEWS INTERNATIONAL

Australia issued a series of four cartoon stamps, including the above, to help ease that country's conversion to the metric system. Each stamp offers an example of how metric conversion will affect the people's daily lives.
AUSTRALIAN INFORMATION SERVICE

A new stamp issued by the United Kingdom on Oct. 2, 1973, honours the November 14 marriage of Princess Anne and Capt. Mark Phillips.
UPI COMPIX

A. M. A. van der Willigen (The Netherlands) signed the Roll of Distinguished Philatelists, and Thomas H. Wilcox of Liverpool, Eng., received the Philatelic Congress Medal. The Design Council's first award for print design went to the British Post Office for its 1972 commemorative and special stamps. The Isle of Man became postally independent on July 5 and issued its own definitive stamps and a single 15-pence commemorative. Isle of Man stamps were accorded international status although the island was still represented by Great Britain (as were the Channel Islands postal administrations of Guernsey and Jersey) at the Universal Postal Union.

The American Philatelic Society continued its "Black Blot" campaign against what it considered to be unnecessary stamps. For the first time it cited a U.S. issue, the Honoring Postal People series.

(KENNETH F. CHAPMAN)

Numismatics. A bill passed by the U.S. Congress and signed into law on Oct. 18, 1973, provided for the issuance of three coins (dollar, half-dollar, and quarter) with reverse designs appropriate to the 1976 bicentennial celebration of American independence. The Bureau of the Mint would select the three designs from those submitted in open competition. Consideration was still being given to creating a special piece of paper money, possibly a new $2 bill, for the same observance.

"Coin" collectors were becoming less concerned with completing date and mint sets of actual coins of the realm. Rather, they were more and more active in the fields of rare coins of the world, commemorative medals, silver ingots, and even such items as silver platters with artistic designs. The beautifully struck silver ingots, usually one ounce of fine silver, sold at $5 and up. The range of designs was almost unlimited, from Washington crossing the Delaware to Martha Mitchell. As people in many countries became more affluent, they were turning to collecting art objects, including rare coins. Europeans and Orientals, especially, were driving prices upward by buying coins of their countries from U.S. collectors.

As evidence of the hobby's healthy condition, the annual convention of the American Numismatic Association, held in Boston in August, had a record registered attendance of over 14,000. Perhaps in keeping with the times, the 27,000 members of ANA elected the first woman president in the organization's 82-year history.

While the U.S. did not issue any commemorative or other coins with new designs, numerous private mints and organizations issued medals during the year. As the American bicentennial approached, several medallic firms issued state and other medals referring to the occasion. After only two years (1971 and 1972) of issuing the U.S. Eisenhower dollar, during which nearly 285 million were struck, the Mint stopped producing it for circulation. However, it was included in the 1973 proof and special mint sets for collectors.

Many governments, but not the U.S., continued to issue special coins in connection with the UN Food and Agriculture Organization. Among nations issuing other special commemorative coins during the year were Austria (Max Reinhardt birth centennial), British Virgin Islands (300th anniversary of constitutional government), Canada (Royal Canadian Mounted Police founding centennial), Dominican Republic (25th anniversary of the Banco Central; this fine silver, dollar-size coin did not circulate because its silver value exceeded its face value), East Germany (125th anniversary of Otto Lilienthal's birth), Great Britain (entry into the EEC), and Hungary (125th anniversary of the 1848 revolution). The United Arab Emirates issued its first coinage in 1973, six denominations in all.

With the market price of silver and gold rising, noncollectors as well as numismatists were investing in coins of those metals. This was especially true in the U.S. where citizens were prohibited by law from buying and owning gold bullion. Twenty-dollar gold coins in nice condition sold for close to $200 each when gold reached its peak price in the spring of 1973. Meanwhile, as the price of copper rapidly approached the monetary value of the penny, the U.S. administration asked Congress for permission to mint pennies made from aluminum. (GLENN B. SMEDLEY)

See Postal Services.

Philippines

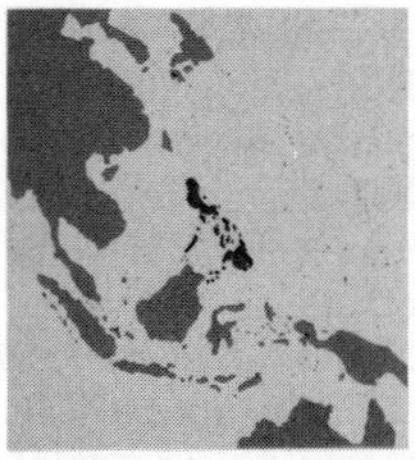

Situated in the western Pacific Ocean off the southeast coast of Asia, the Republic of the Philippines consists of an archipelago of about 7,100 islands. Area: 115,800 sq.mi. (300,000 sq.km.). Pop. (1973 est.): 40,218,819. Capital: Quezon City (pop., 1973 est., 896,173). Largest city: Manila (pop., 1973 est., 1,435,507). Language: Pilipino (based on Tagalog), English, Spanish, and many dialects. Religion (1960): Roman Catholic 84%; Aglipayan 5%; Muslim 5%; Protestant 3%. President in 1973, Ferdinand E. Marcos.

In January 1973 President Marcos (*see* BIOGRAPHY) assumed direct rule of the Philippines. Declaring that his action was based on a mandate from the people, he proclaimed the ratification of a new constitution on January 17, designed to replace the presidential form of government in the Philippines with a parliamentary one. He also signed two decrees indefinitely extending martial law, first imposed on Sept. 23, 1972, and suspending a constitutional provision for an "ad interim assembly" during the transition period before new national elections were held. Pending his call for the new elections, Marcos was to retain the powers of the president under the old constitution and of the prime minister under the new charter. On January 7 the president had postponed a constitutional referendum previously scheduled for January 15. He also renewed stringent restrictions on free speech.

In a nationwide broadcast assessing the previous 108 days of martial law, Marcos explained that he had reinstituted the strict curbs because enemies of the state were taking advantage of the debate on the proposed constitution to create anxiety, confusion, discord, and subversion. He described opponents of his "sweeping reforms" as left-wing Maoists, rightists, secessionists in the southern part of the country, and "clerical fascists," interpreted as a reference to some elements of the Roman Catholic Church. He asserted that rebels in Mindanao were being trained by foreigners and were "making the secessionist threat very real." He ordered that "rumour-mongering" be made punishable as subversive propaganda.

On January 17 the government announced that a survey of 35,000 citizens' assemblies indicated overwhelming support for the government position on continuation of martial law and ten other issues dealing with the new constitution. Petitioning lawyers argued later, however, that government agencies in charge of the referendum had "prefabricated and misrepresented the results." Under the new government, the citizens' assemblies would be the bodies through which the government would consult with the people. Marcos promised to convene the assemblies "when and if such meetings are deemed wise and necessary to resolve important national issues." The Supreme Court in April declared the new charter legal.

A nationwide plebiscite was held July 27 and 28, on a proposition permitting Marcos to remain in office beyond the December 1973 expiration of his current presidential term under the old constitution and to "continue the reforms he has initiated under martial law." The Commission on Elections reported on July 31 that 90% of the votes counted at the time were for

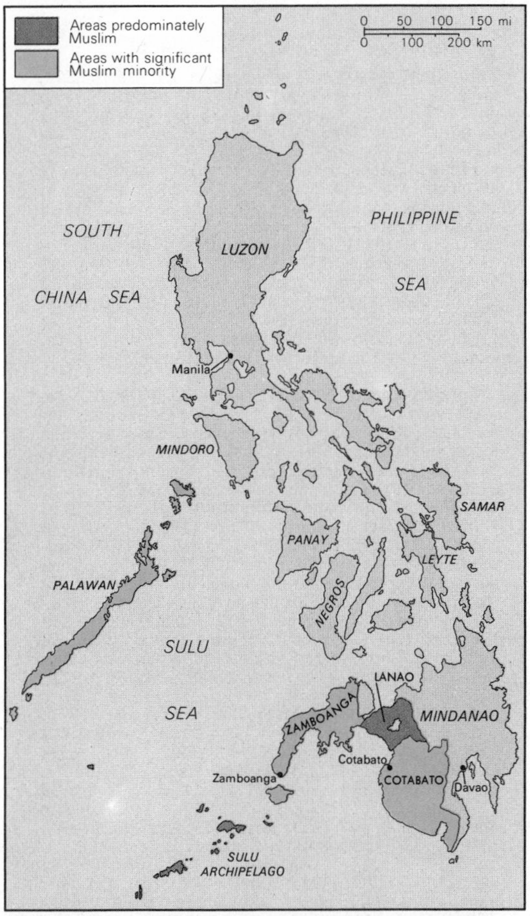

The map distinguishes regions inhabited by Muslim majorities or significant Muslim minorities in the heavily Roman Catholic Philippines. Muslim rebel guerrillas were active in these areas as well as neighbouring areas of Mindanao throughout 1973.

the proposition. Opposition Liberal Party leader Jovito Salonga, a former senator, called the results of the balloting invalid. He charged that martial law had prevented a free exchange of ideas and caused people to vote "yes" out of fear of reprisal.

Martial law was being eased to a degree in some areas. On May 11 President Marcos issued a decree lifting direct government supervision of all local and foreign information outlets. He abolished the government-controlled Mass Media Council and replaced it with the Media Advisory Council, the members of which were to be drawn from newspapers and radio and television. The body would review applications for permission to operate, but the president would have final authority. In December the government took control of the sale and distribution of crude oil and products in an effort to deal with the situation resulting from Arab oil cutbacks. The Philippines was exempted from the 5% cutback in Arab oil shipments in December after the government issued a statement calling for Israeli withdrawal from occupied Arab territories, and in late December it was listed among the "friendly nations" that would receive special treatment from the Arab oil-exporting countries.

In the south Marcos still faced the problem of the secessionist movement. Muslim insurgents had repeatedly clashed with government troops in Mindanao. Some non-Muslim Communists from Luzon Island were reported by the government to have joined the Mindanao rebels. On January 3 Marcos offered "selective amnesty" to the rebels and ordered a halt to military operations in Mindanao to permit the dis-

PHILIPPINES

Education. (1967–68) Primary, pupils 6,406,826, teachers 207,557; secondary and vocational (1968–69), pupils 1,502,346, teachers 49,652; higher (including 34 universities; 1968–69), students 627,104, teaching staff 27,733.

Finance. Monetary unit: peso, with (Sept. 17, 1973) an official rate of 6.78 pesos to U.S. $1 (free rate of 16.31 pesos = £1 sterling). Gold, SDRs, and foreign exchange, central bank: (June 1973) U.S. $845 million; (June 1972) U.S. $463 million. Budget (1972–73 est.): revenue 5,633,000,000 pesos; expenditure 5,639,000,000 pesos. Gross national product: (1971) 49,530,000,000 pesos; (1970) 41,180,000,000 pesos. Money supply: (June 1973) 7,091,000,000 pesos; (June 1972) 5,364,000,000 pesos. Cost of living (Manila; 1963 = 100): (May 1973) 199; (May 1972) 183.

Foreign Trade. (1972) Imports 9,159,000,000 pesos; exports 7,351,000,000 pesos. Import sources: Japan 32%; U.S. 27%; West Germany 5%; Australia 5%. Export destinations: U.S. 43%; Japan 32%; The Netherlands 6%. Main exports: coconut products 21%; sugar 19%; copper 17%; timber 16%.

Transport and Communications. Roads (1971) 73,532 km. Motor vehicles in use (1971): passenger 285,100; commercial (including buses) 182,300. Railways: (1970) 1,147 km.; traffic (1971) 699 million passenger-km., freight 83 million net ton-km. Air traffic (1971): 1,497,000,000 passenger-km.; freight 26,320,000 net ton-km. Shipping (1972): merchant vessels 100 gross tons and over 327; gross tonnage 924,564. Telephones (Jan. 1972) 351,000. Radio receivers (Dec. 1968) 1,633,000. Television receivers (Dec. 1971) 421,000.

Agriculture. Production (in 000; metric tons; 1972; 1971 in parentheses): rice 4,958 (5,100); corn 1,973 (2,013); sweet potatoes (1971) *c.* 700, (1970) 657; cassava (1970) 442, (1969) 506; copra *c.* 2,180 (*c.* 1,730); sugar, raw value *c.* 1,900 (1,815); coffee 52 (49); bananas (1970) *c.* 900, (1969) *c.* 896; tobacco 56 (56); rubber 22 (21); abaca (1971) *c.* 60, (1970) *c.* 70; pork *c.* 200 (*c.* 200); timber (cu.m.; 1971) 33,300, (1970) 33,700; fish catch (1971) 1,050, (1970) 990. Livestock (in 000; March 1972): cattle 1,933; buffaloes *c.* 4,600; pigs (1971) 7,050; goats (1971) 924; horses *c.* 300; chickens *c.* 60,000.

Industry. Production (in 000; metric tons; 1972): coal 39; iron ore (55–60% metal content) 2,203; chrome ore (oxide content; 1971) 150; manganese ore (metal content) 2.5; copper concentrates (metal content; 1971) 189; gold (troy oz.; 1971) 637; silver (troy oz.; 1971) 1,897; cement 2,902; electricity (kw-hr.; 1970) 8,666,000.

sidents to take advantage of his offer. He also announced a series of economic measures to improve the living conditions of the Mindanao Muslims. On April 17 the chief of the Armed Forces of the Philippines announced that the government had abandoned amnesty for the Muslim rebels. Fewer than 250 people had responded to Marcos' offer of pardon for surrendering their arms. The government then began planning a military offensive to crush the secessionist movement. On May 8 Marcos ordered the first military draft in the Philippines. (RAFAEL PARGAS)

Philosophy

The philosophical writings of 1973 continued to exhibit several trends of past years: a cautious resurgence of metaphysics that attempted to tie conceptions of reality to the presuppositions and findings of science; an increasing concern for the practical implications of value theories and concepts; and a continuing dissolution of the cultural and political boundaries separating philosophers.

A major interest was the nature and function of mind and its relation to the nonmental. In volume two of *Mind: An Essay on Human Feeling,* Susanne K. Langer treated the "great shift" from animal to human mentality as an evolutionary process in the central nervous system relating to specialized modes of symbolizing. *Belief, Language, and Experience* by Rodney Needham of Oxford was an attempt by empirical investigation to answer the question of whether belief is an experience. In *Thought,* Gilbert H. Harman held that some thoughts are in language, but others, as with those involved in perception, are not. In *Human Understanding,* vol. 1, Stephen Toulmin strongly opposed the current tendency to separate theoretical and practical knowledge. In *The Origin of Subjectivity,* Hiram Caton of the Australian National University defended the basic importance of Descarte's rationalistic method. Sir Karl Popper, in *Objective Knowledge,* opposed both positivism and traditional subjectivism with a realistic theory of knowledge.

Both personal and social morality were at issue as philosophers searched for ethical principles relating to such concrete problems as the nature of justice or sought philosophical support for such political action as revolution. *Democracy and Disobedience* by P. A. D. Singer assessed the ethical foundations of political philosophy. *Rules and Order,* the first volume of Friedrich A. Hayek's *Law, Legislation and Liberty,* was an analysis of the conditions necessary to the preservation of a free society.

A translation by David A. Ditworth and Valdo H. Vieglielmo of *Art and Morality* by Kitaro Nishida made available to Occidental readers a major work of the foremost representative of Japan's Kyoto school. Nishida held that the "true self" is an a priori immediacy that is the ground of all act, thought, and judgment. The vitality of value philosophy was also exhibited in two volumes published in English translation by Wladyslaw Tatarkiewicz of the University of Warsaw, *Nineteenth Century Philosophy* and *Twentieth Century Philosophy.*

Among historical and biographical works of special interest was John T. Blackmore's *Ernst Mach: His Work, Life, and Influence. Phenomenology and Natural Existence,* edited by Dale Riepe, was a volume of 29 essays in honour of the leader of American phenomenology, Marvin Farber. *Wittgenstein's Vienna* by Allan Janik and Stephen Toulmin graphically exhibited the socio-politico-intellectual context of Ludwig Wittgenstein's life before World War I. Finnish philosopher G. H. von Wright edited *Ludwig Wittgenstein: Letters to C. K. Ogden.*

There was evidence of an increasing interest in Muslim philosophy among non-Muslim thinkers. Charles Malik edited *God and Man in Contemporary Islamic Thought,* the proceedings of a Beirut philosophical symposium. A translation from the Persian *Danish Nameh* of part one of *Avicenna's Treatise on Logic* by F. Zabeeh was published at The Hague. *Muslim Studies* was a translation in two volumes by C. R. Barker and S. M. Stern of Goldziher's classical *Muhammedanische Studien* and the Muslim *Hadith.*

The XVth World Congress of Philosophy was held at Varna, Bulg., with the theme "Science, Technology, Man." A new quarterly, the *Journal of Chinese Philosophy,* edited by Chung-ying Chen and Antonio S. Cua, began publication at Dordrecht, Neth., and an international journal of philosophy, *Revolutionary World,* edited at the University of Bridgeport, Conn., was announced. A *Dictionary of the History of Ideas,* edited by Philip P. Wiener, comprised 311 articles by distinguished scholars. (STERLING M. MC MURRIN)

ENCYCLOPÆDIA BRITANNICA FILMS. *The Medieval Mind* (1969); *Spirit of the Renaissance* (1971); *The Reformation: Age of Revolt* (1973); *An Essay on War* (1973).

Phosphate:
see Mining

Photography

Annual developments in the photographic industry were to some extent linked with the occurrence of Photokina, the Cologne, W.Ger., exhibition generally held every two years. Thus during 1973 innovations shown at Photokina '72 gradually became available.

With the partial abdication of West Germany as the world's greatest producer of cameras, Japan grew rapidly in importance. Reaction against unfavourable trade balances, especially in the U.S., caused the Japanese government in late 1972 to restrain its exports. The Japanese Ministry of International Trade and Industry imposed one-year export controls on 19 categories of goods, including still cameras, interchangeable lenses, and 8-mm. motion-picture cameras.

In the still-camera sector, where exports had increased 30.6% in 1972, the figure for 1973 was held to 23.8%. Similarly, 8-mm. motion-picture cameras, which had shown a remarkable increase of 64.5% in 1972, were held to 47.5%, and interchangeable lenses, previously 53.5%, were tied to 32.5%. However, the reduction in trade caused by these controls was not high when compared with the total value of Japan's photographic exports. The most remarkable growth in turnover during 1973 was shown by Konishiroku, with a 28.1% increase in sales and a 90.6% rise in profits, though a smaller firm, Tokyo Kogaku, the makers of Topcon cameras, returned a profit increase of 166.7%.

The main growth was in 35-mm. single-lens reflex cameras. It was indicative of the inherent strength of the Japanese domestic market that sales rose despite an increase in prices. The revaluation of the yen produced a price differential of some 15% between domestic and export prices, leading to a certain amount of "gray market" trading. In an effort to stop this practice, manufacturers engraved their cameras according to the intended country of sale.

The manufacturing activities in Singapore of the West German manufacturer Rollei continued to be successful, largely because of the comparatively low labour costs. Trade turnover increased 50% in the U.S., 139% in Canada, 73% in the U.K., 57% in Switzerland, 49% in Austria, and 210% in France.

West Germany quoted turnover for 1972 as DM. 2,275,000,000, a rise of 2.3% over the previous year. Photographic equipment accounted for DM. 1,380,000,000 (+ 3%) and photochemicals for DM. 894.1 million (+ 1.4%). Photographic goods to the value of DM. 1,090,000,000 were imported; this represented an increase of 28.1% over the previous year, but it included products of West German firms that were manufactured abroad. Exports amounted to almost DM. 1.5 billion, of which over one-third went to the EEC, one-quarter to countries of the European Free Trade Area, and some 9% to the U.S. Exports to the EEC rose 28.8%. The continuing downward trend in U.S. trade was a consequence of the increased price of West German products, resulting from radical changes in the rate of exchange. One interesting trend was the establishment of trading relations with China, where electronic flash units were in particular demand. Leitz of Wetzlar, W.Ger., in addition to its connections with Minolta of Japan, set up a factory in Portugal, again because of lower labour costs.

Cameras. Most companies concentrated on producing the designs first announced in 1972, but some new designs were introduced during 1973. There was a general trend to convert 16-mm. cameras to take 110 film, Minolta being the first to achieve this. Agfa-Gevaert produced the Agfamatic 2000, a simple camera of small size (27 × 53 × 112 mm. [approximately 1 × 2 × $4\frac{3}{8}$ in.]) fitted with a three-element *f*/9.5 fixed-focus lens. Film transport and shutter cocking were accomplished by opening and shutting the camera in Minox fashion. X-type flashcubes were used for flash, and since these were fired mechanically, no battery was required. The Agfa Sensor release system was used, and the delicately balanced shutter release button assisted in minimizing camera shake.

The first joint product of the Minolta-Leitz partnership to be marketed was a compact 35-mm. camera with a vertically moving shutter made by Copal. The basic idea was to produce a camera of small size but with interchangeable lenses and through-the-lens metering, and to do this at a lower price than Leitz could achieve with the higher labour costs of West Germany. Olympus of Japan produced a single-lens reflex camera of unusually small dimensions (136 × 83 × 81 mm. [$5\frac{1}{2}$ × $3\frac{1}{4}$ × $3\frac{1}{4}$ in.]) and low weight (660 g. [$1\frac{1}{2}$ lb.]). Many of its components, such as lightweight curtain drums, had to be specially designed, contrary to the usual trend of ordering components from specialist firms.

The trend toward electronic shutters continued through 1973. Some of the latest models were of the type described as "aperture priority," meaning that the user selected the aperture and the camera set the shutter speed, which could be continuously variable between limits. In contrast, the older type was "shutter priority," with the photographer selecting the speed and the camera's metering system setting the lens aperture. Cameras following the new system included the Asahi Pentax ES, Cosina Hi-Lite EC, Minolta XM, Nikkormat EL, and the Yashica Electro AX.

A technical innovation was the use of light-emitting diodes in place of a moving needle in camera metering systems. The Fujica ST 801 used seven of these, in a vertical row visible at the side of the screen. Exposure was correct when the central one was il-

ANDRÉ KERTÉSZ

This striking 1959 photograph was among the works of André Kertész exhibited at the Hallmark Gallery in New York City early in 1973.

luminated, while the others indicated differing degrees of over- or underexposure. The Yashica Electro AX also utilized coloured lights to indicate exposure, though the system was not the same. One advantage of using lights was that the fragile meter pivot could be eliminated, but this had to be offset against any possible diminution in accuracy of setting and the distraction of coloured lights at the side of the viewfinder image.

Negative Colour Films. Kodacolor II film had been introduced in 1972 because no existing material was then capable of providing sufficiently fine grain or high enough definition for the production of acceptable colour prints from the very small 110 negatives. Early in 1973 the material was further improved. The changes included improved shelf life and latent image-keeping characteristics, increased resistance to formaldehyde fumes, and a modified magenta layer giving reduced granularity. Since this modification could demand a different setting on an automatic printer, the cartridge label now included the new Kodak corporate symbol, and the figure embossed on the cartridge side was changed from a roman II to an arabic 2. After processing, the new film could be distinguished from the old by a green edge stripe along both margins. The greater resistance to formaldehyde fumes might be thought to offer little advantage in practice. It had been reported, however, that vapours from the plywood used in some camera cases, and some permanent-press materials employed in clothing manufacture, could produce magenta fog on the original Kodacolor II. The new Kodacolor 2 126 size was introduced at the end of 1973, a few months behind schedule.

A new type of Eastman colour negative film, which was being developed for the motion-picture industry during 1973, could be considered the motion-picture analogue of Kodacolor 2, providing finer grain than previous materials and greater acutance. The film, coded 7247 for 16 mm. and 5247 for 35 mm., would be processed at higher temperatures than its predecessors and, like Kodacolor 2, used a new developing agent in the colour developer.

In the fall Agfa-Gevaert announced a new negative colour film for the 110 size. To distinguish it from the existing Agfacolor CNS, it was designated Agfacolor pocket special film, though it seemed probable that the same material would be available in larger sizes at a later date. It was a major improvement over the previous film in that the reduced number of coatings and thinner emulsion coatings caused less light diffusion during exposure, and the greater evenness of silver-halide structure reduced the subjective effect of grain in the resultant print. Of particular significance to the photofinisher was the fact that processing was unchanged from the original CNS procedure, so there would be no need to invest in new film-processing machines.

Transparency Colour Films. Major changes came from Eastman Kodak, which announced improved Kodachrome films for still and motion-picture use in May. Super 8 film would not be changed until a later date, but eventually the new materials would replace the older ones completely. The existing K-12 process could be regarded as obsolescent, being replaced by K-14 (perhaps K-13 never existed, having been omitted in deference to superstition). The new Kodachromes would not have better grain or sharpness, which were not really required, but the colour and tone reproduction were improved.

Reversal Colour Printing. The main advances in this sphere were made by Ciba-Geigy in Switzerland, and by Eastman Kodak. During 1973 a new Ektachrome reversal colour paper, on a resin-coated base, was used to an increasing extent, since it provided an alternative to the established method of producing colour prints from amateur colour transparencies through an intermediate colour negative. The new paper was somewhat faster than the Ektachrome colour paper that preceded it, and though the intrinsic contrast of the new material was lower, the higher colour saturation gave the impression of brilliance.

Early in 1973 Ciba-Geigy introduced an improved Cibachrome silver dye-bleach material for prints from transparencies. The reproduction of reds and greens was improved by the use of new azo dyes, and the sensitization was changed to allow easier printing of a wide variety of makes of transparency films. The new material was faster, and the print and transparency films had the same processing chemicals, though with different dye-bleach times. The dye-bleach bath no longer contained corrosive hydrochloric acid, which caused trouble with many processing machines. The other manufacturer of silver-dye bleach materials, Agfa-Gevaert, withdrew Agfachrome CU 410 early in 1973. It seemed probable that a development-type film on a resin-coated base would be introduced as a replacement.

Processing. The new materials introduced by Kodak required different processing solutions from their predecessors, and comparatively elevated temperatures (such as 100° F or 38° C) were employed. Processing times were shorter, and machines could be run faster, provided drying capacity remained adequate. The new chemistries were designed with the increasingly stringent requirements of antipollution legislation in mind. For example, the K-14 processing for the projected new Kodachromes used no prehardening bath, no magenta reversal bath, no phosphates except for sequestering agents, and no borax except for traces in the bleach bath.

Some processing firms installed 110 equipment during 1973, but others delayed a decision. A complete line of machines would be required. The small size of the negative, 13 × 17 mm., meant that films could be handled only in strips, and there were problems with dust. The printing room had to be air-conditioned, with a filtered air supply kept at a predetermined level of humidity, and the machinery required constant cleaning to prevent the buildup of dust-attracting static.

Electrolytic recovery of silver from used fixing solution was commonplace, but until 1973 it was not possible to use this process with the combined bleach-fix solutions used for colour films because the bleach tended to dissolve the silver as swiftly as electrolytic action deposited it. The difficulty was overcome by metering the flow of solution to the unit to balance the electrical current used, and to ensure that the silver deposit was hard and bright since, if it was soft and flocculent, the larger surface area would cause too much redissolving. The silver removed was about 98% pure, and the desilvered bleach could be treated for recirculation.

Exhibitions. No radical changes in style were noticeable at the larger exhibitions of amateur photography, exemplified by the London Salon. The 117th Royal Photographic Society's International Exhibition showed work from 23 countries. The general level of technique had continued to rise, and while this

POLAROID CORPORATION

Polaroid Land began marketing the SX-70 in 1973.
This single-lens reflex camera, which folds to compact size, uses a special film that self-develops outside the camera.

might not be discernible from one year to the next, it was immediately apparent when photographs shown in 1973 were compared with those of a decade earlier. The number of colour prints had not risen in the proportion that the sale of colour films would indicate. The expert amateur still tended to produce monochrome exhibition prints, while his vacation and family pictures were factory-processed colour. In general, there were more exhibition colour pictures from the U.S. than from Europe, and fewer from the otherwise prolific photographers of Singapore and Hong Kong.

The paramount importance of the generalized annual exhibition was severely challenged during 1973 by specialized exhibitions having a particular theme. Often such exhibitions offered attractive prizes, so it was not surprising that many of the best prints went there. An example was the Ilford £1,000 Print Competition, the main object of which was to show the excellent print quality obtainable with the monochrome material manufactured by that firm. The first prize was won by Peter Stone of the London *Daily Mirror* with a print entitled "The Victims of Vietnam." The Industrial Photography Awards Competition, organized by the *Financial Times* (London), continued to attract a large number of somewhat unimaginative pictures showing high technical competence.

Some exhibitions first introduced at Photokina in 1972 were still circulating during 1973. "The Creation" by Ernst Haas of New York, colour prints supposedly congruent with the text of Genesis, received far more complimentary notices when it was exhibited at the Kodak Galleries in London than on its original showing. The probable reason lay in the method of presentation. Kodak used the conventional light-hued walls in maze formation, with the widely separated pictures illuminated by hidden spotlights. This was obviously appreciated more than the avant-garde Photokina method of hanging prints on heavy wire mesh lit by fluorescent ceiling strips.

Among the many interesting specialized exhibitions of 1973 was one honouring the 75th birthday of the British sculptor Henry Moore. The photographer, Errol Jackson, built up an 8,000-negative archive of pictures taken during working sessions, and prints selected from these were shown. The National Geographic exhibition "Of Shoes–And Ships–And Sealing Wax" showed high-quality pictures with, as the title implied, a wide range of subjects. Included were cheetahs, baseball players, erupting volcanoes, Kennedy International Airport, camel trains, and retired coal miners. The New Mexico regional group of the Society for Photographic Education held some interesting exhibitions, ranging from albumen prints of fishermen in Whitby, Yorkshire, taken in the 1880s to contemporary surrealistic montages by Jerry Uelsmann. Among the most impressive shows was a 238-print retrospective of Eliot Porter.

(N. F. MAUDE)

See also Motion Pictures.

Physics

Energy. Satisfying the world's energy demands was a problem of immediate concern to physicists in 1973. Solutions ranged from an expansion of present methods to a major rethinking of energy technology. W. Bennett Lewis (*Proc. Roy. Soc. Edinburgh* A70: 219, 1972) defended the status quo by arguing that the earth's reserves of natural uranium were sufficient for many hundreds of years, even taking into account increases in population and power consumption. Therefore, the fission reactors in current use together with the breeder reactors under investigation should provide an adequate supply of energy for all needs. The disposal of radioactive waste is not a serious problem, it was claimed, though it would seem that a major portion of the earth's surface would have to be mined to a depth of at least one mile to collect sufficient uranium.

The most immediate alternative to nuclear fission as a source of power is nuclear fusion, which was being studied experimentally and theoretically in many laboratories throughout the world. In one of the more promising developments, laser light was used to implode pellets of heavy hydrogen (deuterium and tritium) to 10,000 times liquid density, thereby inducing efficient nuclear burning. More general interest in this approach was stimulated by the declassification of much of the work in the U.S. However, an editorial in *Physical Review Letters* indicated that there was still considerable pressure against the free publication of research.

The laser required must have high efficiency, high average power, short wavelength, and high energy. A study of the four most promising lasers available in 1973 (*Physics Today,* August 1973) indicated that none had the required characteristics. It was becoming obvious, therefore, as work on lasers continued, that a new laser would be required if laser fusion power production was to become a reality.

Laser power requirements may be lowered if a combined fission–fusion process proves feasible (*Nature,* 241:449, 1973). In this process milligram pellets of fissile material (*e.g.,* uranium-235) are coated with a mixture of deuterium and tritium. A laser pulse incident on these pellets triggers a chain reaction whereby fission in the uranium core is maintained and amplified because neutrons escaping from the core are reflected from the heavy hydrogen skin. The deuterium and tritium also provide extra neutrons when the high-temperature core causes fusion to occur.

Both Soviet (*ZhETF Pis. Red.* 5:286, 1972) and U.S. workers (*Physics Today,* March 1973) reported the apparent production, by compression techniques, of metallic hydrogen, which may eventually be important in fusion work. Theoretical considerations predicted that the metallic hydrogen is metastable (having only a slight margin of stability) with a stored energy density 30–40 times greater than TNT. Metastable metallic heavy hydrogen (deuterium) would have exciting applications in laser fusion.

Two totally different approaches to the power problem were described. The first (*J. Geophys. Res.* 77: 7,038, 1972) proposed utilizing the hot core of the earth to heat water. The basic idea was to drill a hole 5 km. (3 mi.) deep to rocks that are at a temperature of about 350° C; when cold water is poured down this borehole, it will cause the hot rocks to crack and thereby provide a large surface area for heat exchange processes. More cold water pumped down the bore will cause heated water to rise up a second borehole drilled into the cracked region. Calculations showed that, using a flow rate of 400 litres per second, 40 Mw. of power could be extracted initially and that this would only decline to 30 Mw. after more than 25 years.

The second method (*Physics Today,* January 1973) proposed extracting solar power from the sea by making use of ocean temperature gradients of, in some cases, 20° C over depths of 900 m. The warm water side of the heat engine would be maintained at 25° by radiation from the sun. The article concluded that the tropical oceans in the year 2000 could supply the world with energy at a per capita rate of consumption equal to that in the U.S. in 1970, and suffer only a 1° C drop in temperature at their surface. As a result, oceanic convection currents would increase and waters away from the tropics would be somewhat warmer.

Low-Temperature Physics. The application of quantum mechanics to the treatment of low-temperature phenomena in materials was now well established in view of our understanding of superfluidity in the normal isotope of liquid helium (^{4}He) and superconductivity in many metals. Atoms of ^{4}He obey Bose-Einstein statistics, which explain the superfluidity of the liquid ^{4}He by means of the "Bose-Einstein condensation." The Bose-Einstein condensation, which allows a certain percentage of the atoms to become superfluid (*i.e.,* exhibit zero viscosity), describes quantitatively the observed superfluid properties. On the other hand, the electrons in a metal obey Fermi-Dirac statistics (they have only a very small specific heat), and superconductivity can be understood in terms of this approach if one assumes that the electrons are paired together (Cooper pairs) when they transport current without electrical resistance through the metal. The light isotope of liquid helium (^{3}He) is also described by Fermi-Dirac statistics. It was argued theoretically that in a manner analogous to the superfluid behaviour of electrons in metals the atoms of ^{3}He should also pair up and show superfluid properties at a sufficiently low temperature. During 1973 the experimental evidence apparently in favour of superfluidity in ^{3}He was considerable.

The experimental work started as a search for antiferromagnetism in solid ^{3}He (*Phys. Rev. Lett.* 28: 885, 1972), and two phase changes (abrupt changes in energy level) were found, one at 2.7 mK (0.0027° K) and the other at 2 mK. Neither of these could be attributed to antiferromagnetism. It was then discovered that these transitions did not occur in the solid but in the liquid state (*Phys. Rev. Lett.* 29:920, 1972; 29:1227, 1972; 30:207, 1973), and the search was on for experimental justification of the superfluidity hypothesis. Recent measurements of specific heat revealed a phase change at 2–3 mK, which produced a discontinuity but no divergence in the specific heat. This type of phase change is characteristic of a transition from a normal to a superfluid state. Very recently all this was strongly supported by viscosity measurements indicating that the viscosity probably drops by three orders of magnitude below 2.6 mK (*Phys. Rev. Lett.* 30:962, 1973). (S. B. PALMER)

See also Astronautics; Astronomy; Chemistry.

ENCYCLOPÆDIA BRITANNICA FILMS. *Introduction to Lasers* (1973); *Introduction to Holography* (1973).

Pipelines:
see Energy; Transportation
Plastics Industry:
see Industrial Review
Platinum:
see Mining
Poetry:
see Literature

Poland

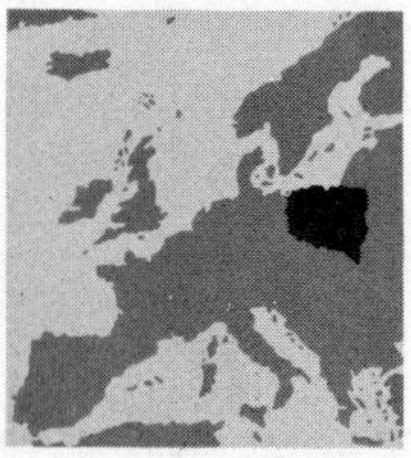

A people's republic of Eastern Europe, Poland is bordered by the Baltic Sea, the U.S.S.R., Czechoslovakia, and East Germany. Area: 120,725 sq.mi. (312,677 sq.km.). Pop. (1973 est.): 33,276,800. Cap. and largest city: Warsaw (pop., 1973 est., 1,369,000). Language: Polish. Religion: predominantly Roman Catholic. First secretary of the Polish United Workers' (Communist) Party in 1973, Edward Gierek; chairman of the Council of State, Henryk Jablonski; chairman of the Council of Ministers (premier), Piotr Jaroszewicz.

Economically, 1973 was a successful year for Poland. For the third consecutive year food prices remained frozen, while national income had risen annually, on average, by 9% since 1971 (instead of the 7% required in the original 1971–75 plan). Speaking on October 22, at the year's first national party conference, Gierek estimated total national income for 1973 at about 1,000,000,000,000 zlotys (30,000 zlotys per capita). Industrial production had risen during 1971–73 by 33% and agricultural output by 19%. According to the 1971–75 development plan, wages were expected to rise 18% over the five years; they had actually risen that amount in three years, and Gierek assured his audience that they would be rising by 5% annually during 1974 and 1975.

Housing remained the most painful social problem. The number of apartments completed during 1971–73 was 614,000 (20,000 more than had been planned). During 1974–75 about 515,000 more would be built, but at least 7 million would be required by 1990. The country had 22 plants producing prefabricated housing elements and 6 more were being built. In addition, six new cement plants were under construction. "At present," said Gierek, "30% of families have a monthly income of 2,000 zlotys or more per head, and only 10% earn less than 1,000 zlotys per head." Total investments in the national economy during 1971–75 would amount to 1,800,000,000,000 zlotys, 80% more than during 1966–70.

Turning to the problems of ideology, Gierek proclaimed that more than two million Polish Communists were faithful to the Leninist principle that "the socialist state must effectuate the dictatorship of the proletariat." Party membership meant "permanence of beliefs, hardness when in difficulty, and intransigence before adversaries of socialism." Gierek announced that all membership cards would be up for scrutiny before the seventh party congress, scheduled for 1976.

In order "to strengthen the socialist principles of

POLAND

Education. (1971–72) Primary, pupils 5,186,-500, teachers (1970–71) 217,800; secondary, pupils 578,300, teachers (1970–71) 19,200; vocational, pupils 1,753,100, teachers (1970–71) 63,600; teacher training (1969–70), pupils 39,-270, teachers 5,243; higher (including 18 universities), students 347,800, teaching staff 33,700.

Finance. Monetary unit: zloty, with (Sept. 17, 1973) an official exchange rate of 3.20 zlotys to U.S. $1 and a tourist rate of 33.20 zlotys to U.S. $1 (84 zlotys = £1 sterling). Budget (1972 est.): revenue 408.6 billion zlotys; expenditure 407.1 billion zlotys. National income (net material product): (1971) 854.5 billion zlotys; (1970) 749.2 billion zlotys.

Foreign Trade. (1972) Imports 19,612,000,-000 zlotys; exports 18,133,000,000 zlotys. Import sources: U.S.S.R. 30%; East Germany 11%; Czechoslovakia 9%; West Germany 8%; U.K. 5%. Export destinations: U.S.S.R. 37%; East Germany 8%; Czechoslovakia 7%; West Germany 5%. Main exports (1970): machinery 31%; coal 10%; iron and steel 7%; textiles and clothing 6%; meat and products 6%; ships and boats 5%.

Transport and Communications. Roads (1972) 302,421 km. (including 139 km. expressways). Motor vehicles in use (1972): passenger 656,872; commercial 293,021. Railways: (1971) 23,510 km. (including 4,010 km. electrified); traffic (1972) 38,781,000,000 passenger-km., freight 109,779,000,000 net ton-km. Air traffic (1972): 820.1 million passenger-km.; freight 9,-475,000 net ton-km. Shipping (1972): merchant vessels 100 gross tons and over 617; gross tonnage 2,012,659. Telephones (Dec. 1971) 1,971,-000. Radio licenses (Dec. 1971) 5,709,000. Television licenses (Dec. 1971) 4,709,000.

Agriculture. Production (in 000; metric tons; 1972; 1971 in parentheses): wheat 5,147 (5,-456); rye 8,149 (7,827); barley 2,750 (2,449); oats 3,260 (3,195); potatoes 48,735 (39,801); sugar, raw value *c.* 1,826 (1,713); rapeseed *c.* 450 (595); linseed *c.* 66 (75); dry peas *c.* 70 (66); onions 327 (337); tomatoes 394 (344); apples 548 (563); pears *c.* 110 (101); tobacco 85 (70); flax fibre *c.* 55 (60); butter *c.* 161 (128); cheese (1971) *c.* 250, (1970) 245; beef and veal (1971) 548, (1970) 563; pork (1971) 1,313, (1970) 1,279; timber (cu.m.; 1970) 18,300, (1969) 18,-100; fish catch (1971) 518, (1970) 469. Livestock (in 000; June 1972): cattle 11,452; horses 2,422; pigs 17,347; sheep 3,110; chickens *c.* 150,000.

Industry. Index of industrial production (1963 = 100): (1972) 212; (1971) 191. Fuel and power (in 000; metric tons; 1972): coal 150,-697; brown coal 38,221; coke (1971) 15,504; crude oil (1971) 395; natural gas (cu.m.) 5,821,-000; manufactured gas (cu.m.; 1971) 6,782,000; electricity (kw-hr.) 76,443,000. Production (in 000; metric tons; 1972): cement 13,984; iron ore (30% metal content) 1,660; pig iron 7,813; crude steel 13,477; aluminum (1971) 100; zinc (1971) 220; copper (1971) 93; lead (1971) 60; sulfuric acid 2,567; nitrogenous fertilizer (1971) 1,081; phosphate fertilizer (1971) 706; cotton fabrics (m.) 900,000; woolen fabrics (m.) 100,-000; rayon and synthetic fabrics (m.; 1971) 114,000; passenger cars (units) 90; commercial vehicles (units) 62. Merchant vessels launched (100 gross tons and over; 1972) 572,000 gross tons. New dwelling units completed (1971) 188,-000.

planning and management," a new administrative reform came into effect on Jan. 1, 1973, whereby the number of the smallest administrative units (*gromady* or villages) was reduced from 4,671 to 2,365. New larger units were set up (called *gminy* or communes), usually with first secretaries of the local Polish United Workers' Party as chairmen. New people's councils were elected on December 9.

The sixth congress of the United Peasants' Party (ZSL) reelected Stanislaw Gucwa as chairman of its Executive Committee and Edward Duda as first secretary in April. The party had 413,000 members, including 310,000 individual farmers. In April youth organizations merged into a single five-million-strong Federation of Socialist Unions of Polish Youth (FSZMP).

An important report on the Polish educational system, prepared by a committee of experts under Jan Szczepanski, a distinguished nonparty sociologist, appeared in Warsaw in April. The report proposed general comprehensive education for all, with a lengthening of the prespecialization period.

Gierek and Premier Jaroszewicz paid official visits to Czechoslovakia and East Germany in January and June, respectively. They were hosts to a Hungarian delegation in March and to a Bulgarian delegation in November, headed in both cases by Communist Party leaders (Janos Kadar and Todor Zhivkov). Gierek was cordially received by President Tito in Yugoslavia in May and by King Baudouin and the Belgian government in November. In July, Gierek met Soviet party leader Leonid I. Brezhnev in the Crimea. Jaroszewicz visited India in January, Turkey in May, and met Soviet Premier Aleksey N. Kosygin in Moscow in August. Henryk Jablonski, chairman of the Council of State, paid visits to Syria in February, to Cuba in April, and to Czechoslovakia in October. Stefan Olszowski, the foreign minister, was welcomed in Yugoslavia in April, in Denmark and Sweden in May, and in Italy in November. He was the first member of the Polish government to call at the Vatican since World War II. On November 12 he was received in private audience by Pope Paul VI.

A long-term agreement on the development of economic and industrial cooperation between Poland and Great Britain was signed in London on April 21 by Peter Walker, the British secretary of state for industry and trade, and Tadeusz Olechowski, the Polish minister of foreign trade. Julian Amery, minister of state at the British Foreign Office, visited Poland (September 26–October 1) to discuss problems of common interest with Polish leaders. In October, Valéry Giscard d'Estaing, the French minister of finance, was in Warsaw to examine with Polish ministers the state of Franco-Polish trade; on that occasion the three-year credit of Fr. 1.5 billion granted by France in 1972 was increased to Fr. 2,250,000,000. A three-day official visit to Warsaw by Walter Scheel, the West German foreign minister, in October was moderately successful in overcoming difficulties between the two countries. Frederick Dent, the U.S. secretary of commerce, attended a session of the joint Polish-American Trade Commission in Warsaw on September 26. David Rockefeller, chairman of the board of the Chase Manhattan Bank, visited Warsaw in January, and Henry Kearns, president of the U.S. Export-Import Bank, was there in April.

On September 13, at the city hall of Gdansk, the seven states bordering on the Baltic signed a convention to protect the fish of that sea and to fight the pollution of its waters. Quincentennial celebrations of the birth of Mikolaj Kopernik (Copernicus) took place during the year in Cracow, Torun, Olsztyn, and Frombork. A replica of the Warsaw monument of the Polish astronomer, the work of Bertel Thorvaldsen, was erected in Chicago near the Adler Planetarium.

Leopold Trepper, Jewish head of the "Red Orchestra," which had informed the incredulous Stalin of the date of Hitler's plan to attack the Soviet Union, was finally allowed to leave Poland in October, after he threatened to starve himself to death otherwise. He had already spent nine years in prison in the U.S.S.R. His passport allowed him to go anywhere but to Israel. (K. M. SMOGORZEWSKI)

Political Parties

The following table is a general world guide to political parties. All countries that were independent on Dec. 1, 1973, are included; there are a number for which no analysis of political activities can be given.

Parties are included in most instances only if represented in parliaments (in the lower house in bicameral legislatures), but the figures in the last column of the table do not necessarily add up to the

Police: *see* Crime

total number of seats in parliament because independents and certain small political groupings are sometimes omitted. The date of the most recent general election follows the name of the country.

The code letters in the affiliation column show the relative political position of the parties within each country; there is, therefore, no entry in this column for single-party states. There are obvious difficulties involved in labeling parties within the political spectrum of a given country. The key chosen is as follows: F—fascist; ER—extreme right; R—right; CR—centre right; C—centre; L—non-Marxist left; SD—social-democratic; S—socialist; EL—extreme left; and K—Communist.

The percentages in the column "Voting strength" indicate proportions of the valid votes cast for the respective parties, or the number of registered voters who went to the polls in single-party states.

COUNTRY AND NAME OF PARTY	Affiliation	Voting strength	Parliamentary representation
Afghanistan			
Monarchy abolished, July 17, 1973	—	—	—
Albania (1970)			
Albanian Labour (Communist)	—	100%	214
Algeria			
Military government since June 19, 1965	—	—	—
Andorra (1969)			
No parties	—	—	24
Argentina (1973)			
Frente Justicialista de Liberación (Frejuli)	R	49.6%	145
Alianza Popular Federalista	CR	14.6%	20
Unión Cívica Radical	C	21.3%	51
Alianza Popular Revolucionaria	L	7.1%	12
Others (including Fuerza Nueva and Marxist Frente de Izquierda Popular)	...	6.7%	15
Australia (1972)			
Country (Conservative)	R	...	20
Liberal	CR	...	38
Democratic Labor (DLP)	C	...	—
Australian Labor (ALP)	L	...	67
Austria (1971)			
Freiheitliche Partei Österreichs	R	5.4%	10
Österreichische Volkspartei	C	43.0%	80
Sozialistische Partei Österreichs	SD	50.0%	93
Kommunistische Partei Österreichs	K	1.4%	0
Bahamas			
Independence proclaimed July 10, 1973	—	—	—
Bahrain			
Emirate	—	—	—
Bangladesh (1973)			
Awami League	C	73%	293
Others	—	...	7
Barbados (1971)			
Democratic Labour Party	C	...	18
Barbados Labour Party	L	...	6
Belgium (1971)			
Volksunie (Flemish)	R	11.0%	21
Front Démocratique des Bruxellois Francophones / Rassemblement Wallon	R	11.4%	24
Parti pour la Liberté et le Progrès	CR	16.7%	34
Parti Social-Chrétien / Christelijk Volks-Partij	C	30.0%	67
Parti Socialiste Belge	SD	27.2%	61
Parti Communiste Belge	K	3.2%	5
Bhutan			
No parties	—	—	130
Bolivia			
Military government since Sept. 26, 1969	—	—	—
Botswana (1969)			
Botswana Democratic Party	C	...	24
Botswana People's Party	L	...	3
Botswana National Front	EL	...	3
Botswana Independent Party	L	...	1
Brazil (1970)			
Aliança Renovadora Nacional	CR	...	223
Movimento Democratico Brasileiro	L	...	87
Bulgaria (1971)			
Fatherland Front: Bulgarian Communist 266, Agrarian Union 100, Nonparty 34	—	99.9%	400
Burma			
Military government since March 2, 1962	—	—	—
Burundi			
Military government since Nov. 28, 1966	—	—	—
Cambodia (1972)			
Socio-Republican Party	—	...	26
Cameroon (1973)			
Cameroonian National Union	—	...	120
Canada (1972)			
Social Credit	R	7%	15
Progressive Conservative	CR	35%	107
Liberal	C	38.3%	109
New Democratic	L	17.8%	31
Central African Republic			
Military government since Jan. 1, 1966	—	—	—
Chad			
National Movement for Cultural and Social Revolution	—	...	...
Chile			
Military government since Sept. 11, 1973			
China, People's Republic of			
Communist (Kungchan-tang)	—	—	—
Colombia (1970)			
Alianza Nacional Popular	R	...	72
Partido Conservador / Partido Liberal	R / C	...	90
Congo			
Military government since September 1968	—	—	—
Costa Rica (1970)			
Partido de Liberación Nacional	R	...	32
Partido de Unificación Nacional	C	...	22
Acción Socialista	L	...	2
Cuba			
Partido Comunista de Cuba	—	—	—
Cyprus (1970)			
Greek-Cypriot			
Progressive Front	R	...	7
Unified Party	C	...	15
Democratic Centre Union	L	...	2
Independents	—	...	2
Progressive Party of Working People	K	...	9
Turkish-Cypriot			
National Solidarity	—	...	15
Czechoslovakia (1971)			
National Front	—	99.8%	350
Dahomey			
Military government since Oct. 26, 1972	—	—	—
Denmark (1973)			
Conservative	R	9.2%	16
Christian People's	CR	4.0%	7
Liberal Democratic (Venstre)	CR	12.3%	22
Radical-Liberal	C	11.2%	20
Justice	C	2.9%	5
Progress	C	15.9%	28
Centre Democratic	L	7.8%	14
Social Democratic	SD	25.7%	46
Socialist People's	EL	7.4%	11
Communist	K	3.6%	6
Dominican Republic (1966)			
Partido Reformista	R	...	48
Partido Revolucionario Dominicano	C	...	26
Ecuador (1968)			
Alianza Popular	R	...	...
Izquierda Democrática	L	...	...
Egypt (1971)			
Arab Socialist Union	—	...	338
El Salvador (1972)			
Partido de Conciliación Nacional	R	...	38
Union Nacional de Oposición	C	...	7
Partido Popular Salvadoreño	L	...	6
Equatorial Guinea (1968)			
Movimiento por Unión Nacional de Guiné Ecuadorial (MUNGE) / Idea Popular de Guiné Ecuadorial (IPGE) / Movimiento Nacional por Liberación de Guiné Ecuadorial (MONALIGE)	—	...	35
Ethiopia (1965)			
Imperial government with an elected Yeheg Memria (lower chamber)	—	—	250
Fiji (1972)			
Alliance Party (mainly Fijian)	—	...	33
National Federation Party (mainly Indian)	—	...	19
Finland (1972)			
Kansallinen Kokoomus Poulue (Cons.)	R	17.5%	34
Svenskapartiet (Swedish Party)	R	5.3%	10
Keskusliitto (Centre, ex-Agrarian)	C	16.4%	35
Christian League	C	2.5%	4
Kansan Poulue (Liberal)	C	5.1%	7
Rural Party	L	9.2%	18
Sosialidemokraatinen Poulue	SD	25.8%	55
People's Democratic League	K	17.1%	37
France (1973)			
Union des Démocrates pour la République (Gaullists)	CR	31.3%	185
Independent Republicans	CR	7.7%	54
Centre Démocratie et Progrès	C	3.9%	21
Other majority coalition	C	3.2%	15
Socialists	L	21.9%	89
Communists	K	20.6%	73
Left Radicals	EL	3.8%	12
Parti Socialiste Unifié and extreme left	EL	0.3%	3
Others	—	...	38
Gabon (1973)			
Parti Démocratique Gabonais	—	—	70
Gambia, The (1972)			
People's Progressive Party	C	...	28
United Party	L	...	3

COUNTRY AND NAME OF PARTY	Affiliation	Voting strength	Parliamentary representation
German Democratic Republic (1971)			
National Front	—	99.9%	434
Germany, Federal Republic of (1972)			
Nationaldemokratische Partei Deutschlands	F	0.6%	—
Christlich-Soziale Union	R	44.8%	48
Christlich-Demokratische Union	R		177
Freie Demokratische Partei	C	8.4%	41
Sozialdemokratische Partei Deutschlands	SD	45.9%	230
Deutsche Kommunistische Partei	K	0.3%	—
Ghana			
Military government since Jan. 13, 1972	—	—	—
Greece			
Military government since April 21, 1967	—	—	—
Guatemala (1970)			
Movimiento de Liberación Nacional	R	...	31
Partido Institucional Democrático	CR	42.9%	19
Democracia Cristiana Guatemalteca	C	21.5%	5
Partido Revolucionario	L	35.6%	...
Guinea (1968)			
Parti Démocratique de Guinée	—	—	75
Guyana (1973)			
People's National Congress	C	...	37
People's Progressive Party	EL	...	14
Others	—	...	2
Haiti			
Presidential dictatorship since 1957	—	—	—
Honduras (1971)			
Partido Nacional	R	...	33
Partido Liberal	C	...	32
Hungary (1971)			
Patriotic People's Front	—	98.9%	352
Iceland (1971)			
Independence (Conservative)	R	36.2%	22
Progressive	C	25.2%	17
Liberal Left	L	8.9%	5
Social Democratic	SD	10.4%	6
People's Union	EL	17.1%	10
India (1971)			
Jan Sangh (Hindu Nationalist)	ER	...	22
Swatantra (Freedom)	R	...	7
Dravida Munnetra Kazhagam	R	...	23
Ruling Congress	C	...	349
Opposition Congress	C	...	16
Praja Socialist	SD	...	2
Samyukta Socialist	S	...	3
Communist (pro-Soviet)	K	...	24
Communist (pro-Chinese)	K	...	25
Independents and others	—	...	43
Indonesia (1971)			
Sekber Golkar (Functional Groups)	—	...	261
Partai Nasional Indonesia	R	...	20
Nahdatul Ulama (Muslim Teachers)	R	...	58
Partai Sarikat Islam Indonesia (United Muslims)	C	...	10
Perti (Islamic Party)	C	...	2
Parmusi (Liberal Muslims)	C	...	24
Partai Keristen Indonesia (Protestants)	C	...	7
Partai Katholik	C	...	3
Partai Murba (Party of the Masses)	EL	...	0
West Irian	—	...	9
Iran (1971)			
Iran Novin (New Iran)	R	...	226
Mardom (People's) Party	C	...	36
Pan-Iranian Party	C	...	1
Religious groups	—	...	5
Iraq			
Military governments since 1958	—	—	—
Ireland (1973)			
Fianna Fail (Sons of Destiny)	C	46.2%	69
Fine Gael (United Ireland)	C	35.1%	54
Irish Labour	L	13.7%	19
Sinn Fein (We Ourselves)	—	1.1%	0
Others	—	3.9%	2
Israel (1973)			
Likud (Rally of Herut, Liberal Party, Free Centre, and State List)	R	...	39
Tora Front (Agudat Israel and Poalei Agudat Israel)	CR	...	5
National Religious	C	...	10
Independent Liberal	C	...	4
Civil Rights List (Mrs. Shulamit Aloni)	L	...	3
Maarakh (Alignment of Mapam, Mapai, Rafi, and Ahdut Avoda)	SD	...	51
Moked or Focus (pro-Israel Communist)	K	...	1
Rakah or New (pro-Soviet) Communist List	K	...	4
Pro-government Arabs	—	...	3
Italy (1972)			
Movimento Sociale Italiano	F	8.7%	56
Partito di Unita Monarchica	R		
Partito Liberale Italiano	CR	3.9%	20
Democrazia Cristiana	C	38.8%	267
Partito Repubblicano Italiano	C	2.9%	15
Partito Social-Democratico Italiano	L	5.1%	29
Partito Socialista Italiano	SD	9.6%	61
Partito Comunista Italiano	K	27.2%	179
Südtiroler Volkspartei	—	0.5%	3
Ivory Coast (1970)			
Parti Démocratique de la Côte d'Ivoire	—	...	100
Jamaica (1972)			
People's National Party	L	...	37
Jamaica Labour Party	L	...	15
Japan (1972)			
Komeito	CR	8.5%	29
Liberal-Democratic	CR	46.9%	271
Democratic Socialist	SD	7.0%	19
Socialist	S	21.9%	118
Communist	K	10.5%	38
Independents	—	—	16
Jordan			
Royal government, no parties	—	—	60
Kenya (1969)			
Kenya African National Union	—	—	171
Korea, North (1967)			
Korean Workers' (Communist) Party	...	100%	300
Korea, South (1973)			
Democratic Republican	—	38.7%	73
New Democratic	—	32.6%	52
Democratic Unification	—	10.1%	2
Independents	—	18.6%	19
Kuwait			
Princely government	—	—	30
Laos			
Royal government; pro-Communist Neo Lao Hak Sat party controls area bordering North Vietnam	—	—	—
Lebanon (1972)			
Maronites (Roman Catholics)	—	...	30
Greek Catholics (Melchites)	—	...	6
Armenian Catholics	—	...	1
Armenian Orthodox	—	...	4
Greek Orthodox	—	...	11
Other Christians	—	...	2
Sunni Muslims	—	...	20
Shia Muslims	—	...	19
Druzes (Muslim heretics)	—	...	6
Lesotho			
Constitution suspended Jan. 30, 1970	—	—	—
Liberia (1968)			
True Whig Party	—	...	41
Libya			
Military government since Sept. 1, 1969	—	—	—
Liechtenstein (1970)			
Vaterlandische Union	CR	...	8
Fortschrittliche Burgerpartei	C	...	7
Christlich-Soziale Partei	C	...	—
Luxembourg (1968)			
Parti Chrétien-Social	CR	35.3%	21
Parti Libéral	C	16.6%	11
Parti Ouvrier Socialiste	SD	32 3%	18
Parti Communiste	K	15.5%	6
Malagasy Republic			
Military government since Oct. 13, 1972	—	—	—
Malawi (1971)			
Malawi Congress Party	CR	...	58
Malaysia			
Malaya (1969)			
Federal Alliance Party	R	...	66
Panmalayan Islamic Party	R	...	12
Gerakan Rakyat Malaysia	C	...	8
Democratic Action (Chinese)	L	...	13
People's Progressive Party	K	...	4
Sarawak (1970)			
Federal Alliance Party	R	...	10
Opposition groups	L	...	14
Sabah (1970)			
Federal Alliance Party	R	...	6
Opposition groups	L	...	10
Maldives (1965)			
Government by the Didi family	—	...	54
Mali			
Military government since Nov. 19, 1968	—	—	—
Malta (1971)			
Nationalist Party	R	48.1%	27
Malta Labour Party	SD	50.8%	28
Mauritania (1965)			
Parti du Peuple Mauritanien	—	92%	40
Mauritius (1967)			
Independence Party (Indian-dominated)	C	...	39
Parti Mauricien Social-Démocrate	L	...	23
Mexico (1973)			
Partido Acción Nacional	CR	...	4
Partido Revolucionario Institucional	C	...	189
Partido Auténtico de la Revolución Mexicana	L	...	1
Monaco (1968)			
Union Nationale et Démocratique	—	...	18
Mongolia (1967)			
Mongolian People's Revolutionary Party	—	99%	295
Morocco (1970)			
Independents (pro-government)	CR	...	159
Popular Movement	C	...	60
Istiqlal	C	...	8
National Union of Popular Forces	L	...	1
Others	—	...	12
Nauru (1971)			
No political parties	—	...	18
Nepal			
Royal government since December 1960	—	—	—

COUNTRY AND NAME OF PARTY	Affiliation	Voting strength	Parliamentary representation
Netherlands, The (1972)			
Statkundig Gereformeerde Partij	R	2.2%	3
Boerenpartij (Farmers' Party)	R	1.9%	3
Anti-Revolutionaire Partij (Calvinist)	CR	8.8%	14
Christelijk Historische Unie (Protestant)	CR	4.8%	7
Katholieke Volkspartij	C	17.7%	27
Volkspartij voor Vrijheid en Democratie	C	14.4%	22
Democraten '66 (Nonconformist reformers)	C	4.2%	6
Democraten Socialisten-70	L	4.1%	6
Partij van de Arbeid	SD	27.4%	43
Pacifistisch Socialistische Partij	S	1.5%	2
Communistische Partij	K	4.5%	7
Five other parties	—	8.5%	10
New Zealand (1972)			
National (Conservative)	CR	41.0%	31
Labour Party	L	48.4%	56
Nicaragua (1967)			
Partido Liberal Nacionalista (Somoza)	R	...	36
Partido Conservador Tradicionalista	R	...	15
Partido Demócrata Cristiano	C	...	2
Partido Liberal Independenta	C	...	1
Niger (1970)			
Parti Progressiste Nigérien	—	...	50
Nigeria			
Military governments since Jan. 15, 1966	—	—	—
Norway (1973)			
Høyre (Conservative)	R	17.3%	29
Kristelig Folkeparti	CR	11.8%	20
Senterpartiet (Agrarian)	C	6.8%	21
Venstre (Liberal)	C	3.4%	1
Anti-EEC Venstre	C	2.3%	2
Arbeiderpartiet (Labour)	SD	35.5%	62
Socialist Electoral Alliance:		11.2%	16
Socialistisk Folkeparti	S		
Kommunistiske Parti	K		
Anders Lange Parti	—	5.0%	4
Oman			
Sultanate	—	—	—
Pakistan			
New constitution effective Aug. 14, 1973	...	...	...
Panama (1972)			
No political parties	—	—	505
Paraguay (1967)			
Partido Colorado (Stroessner)	R	69.4%	80
Partido Liberal Radical	C	21.5%	29
Partido Liberal	C	6.2%	8
Partido Revolucionario (Febrerista)	SD	2.8%	3
Peru			
Military government since Oct. 3, 1968	—	—	—
Philippines			
Martial law since Sept. 23, 1972	—	—	—
Poland (1972)			
Front of National Unity:	—	99.5%	
Polska Zjednoczona Partia Robotnicza			255
Zjednoczone Stronnictwo Ludowe			117
Stronnictwo Demokratyczne			39
Nonparty			49
Portugal (1973)			
Acção Nacional Popular	—	66.5%	150
Qatar			
Emirate	—	—	—
Rhodesia (1970)			
Rhodesian Front (European)	R	70%	50
Centre Party (mainly African)	C	10%	7
National People's Union (African)	L	...	1
Others (elected by councils of chiefs)	—	...	8
Romania (1969)			
People's Front:	—	99.75%	465
Partidul Comunist Romîn			
Nonparty			
Rwanda			
Military government since July 5, 1973	—	—	—
San Marino (1969)			
Partito Democratico-Cristiano	CR	...	27
Partito Social-Democratico	SD	...	11
Partito Socialista	S	...	7
Partito Communista (pro-Soviet)	K	...	14
Partito Communista (pro-Chinese)	K	...	1
Saudi Arabia			
Royal government	—	—	—
Senegal (1973)			
Union Progressiste Sénégalaise	—	...	100
Sierra Leone (1973)			
All People's Congress	—	...	84
Singapore (1972)			
People's Action Party	C	...	65
Four opposition parties	—	—	—
Somalia			
Military government since Oct. 21, 1969	—	—	—
South Africa (1970)			
Nationalist Party	R	...	117
United Party	C	...	47
Progressive Party	L	...	1
Spain (1971)			
Movimiento Nacional	—	...	558
Sri Lanka (Ceylon; 1970)			
United National	R	34.2%	17
Sri Lanka Freedom	CR	33.0%	91
Federal (Tamil)	C	4.4%	13
Lanka Sama Samaja (Trotskyist)	S	12.8%	15
Communist	K	3.0%	6
Sudan			
Military government since May 25, 1969	—	—	—
Swaziland			
Royal government	—	—	—
Sweden (1973)			
Moderata Samlingspartiet (ex-Höger)	R	14.3%	51
Centerpartiet (ex-Agrarian)	CR	25.1%	90
Folkpartiet (Liberal)	C	9.4%	34
Socialdemokratiska Arbetarepartiet	SD	43.5%	156
Vänsterpartiet Kommunisterna	K	5.3%	19
Switzerland (1971)			
National Action	R	...	4
Republican Movement	R	...	7
Conservative Christian Social People's	R	20.4%	44
Evangelical People's	R	1.9%	3
Swiss People's	CR	11.4%	23
Radical Democratic (Freisinnig)	C	21.3%	49
League of Independents	C	7.6%	13
Liberal Democratic	L	2.3%	6
Social Democratic	SD	23.1%	46
Communist (Partei der Arbeit)	K	2.7%	5
Syria			
Baath and military government	—	—	—
Taiwan (Republic of China)			
Nationalist (Kuomintang)	—	—	773
Tanzania (1970)			
Tanganyika African National Union (elected)	C	...	120
Zanzibar Afro-Shirazi Party (nominated)	L	—	52
Thailand			
Royal government	—	—	—
Togo			
Military government since Jan. 13, 1967	—	—	—
Tonga (1972)			
Legislative Assembly (partially elected)	—	—	21
Trinidad and Tobago (1971)			
People's National Movement	C	...	36
Action Committee for Dedicated Citizens	L	—	—
Tunisia (1969)			
Destourian Socialist Party	—	—	101
Turkey (1973)			
Nationalist Action	ER	3.4%	3
National Salvation	R	11.8%	49
Turkish Justice	CR	29.8%	149
Democratic	C	11.9%	44
Republican Reliance	C	5.3%	13
Republican People's	L	33.3%	185
Turkish Unity	EL	1.1%	1
Others	—	...	6
Uganda			
Uganda People's Congress	—	...	...
Union of Soviet Socialist Republics (1970)			
Communist Party of the Soviet Union	—	99.74%	767
United Arab Emirates			
Emirate	—	—	—
United Kingdom (1970)			
Conservative and Unionist	R	46.4%	330
Liberal	C	7.4%	6
Labour	L	43.0%	287
Others	—	...	7
United States (1972)			
Republican	CR	...	191
Democratic	C	...	244
Upper Volta (1970)			
Union Démocratique Voltaique	CR	...	37
Parti du Regroupement Africain	C	...	12
Mouvement de Libération Nationale	L	...	6
Uruguay			
Rule by Council of State as of June 1973	—	—	—
Venezuela (1973)			
Cruzada Civica Nacional	ER	4.3%	7
Unión Republicana Democrática	R	3.2%	5
COPEI (Social Christians)	C	30.2%	64
Acción Democrática	L	44.3%	102
Movimiento al Socialismo	SD	5.3%	9
Fuerza Democrática Popular	S	1.2%	2
Movimiento Electoral del Pueblo	EL	5.0%	8
Partido Comunista Venezuelano	K	1.2%	2
Others (four parties)	—	...	4
Vietnam, North (1971)			
Lao Dong (Communist Party)	—	...	420
Vietnam, South (1971)			
National coalition	—	...	152
Western Samoa (1973)			
No political parties	—	...	45
Yemen (Aden)			
National Liberation Front	—	—	—
Yemen (San'a')			
Republican regime since November 1967	—	—	—
Yugoslavia (1969)			
League of Communists of Yugoslavia; Socialist Alliance of the Working People	—	...	670
Zaire (1970)			
Mouvement Populaire de la Révolution	—	98.3%	420
Zambia (1973)			
United National Independence Party	—	80%	125

(K. M. SMOGORZEWSKI)

Political Science

Political scientists from 60 countries assembled in Montreal during Aug. 19–26, 1973, for the ninth triennial World Congress of Political Science, convened by the International Political Science Association (IPSA). It was the first to be held outside Western Europe. Attendance continued to increase: there were 1,044 participants at Montreal, as against 920 at the eighth congress (Munich, W.Ger., 1970) and 750 at the seventh congress (Brussels, 1967). The large delegations from the developing countries and Eastern Europe showed how much progress had been achieved in recent years in the internationalization of the discipline. There was one exception to the trend: for reasons unknown, only one of the 14 delegates expected from the U.S.S.R. attended.

A new formula was tried at the congress in an attempt to reduce the dispersion noticed at the previous one: the discussions were centred on two main themes, "Politics Between Economy and Culture," under the leadership of the retiring president of IPSA, Stein Rokkan of the University of Bergen, Nor., and "Key Issues in International Conflict and Peace Research," under the leadership of Karl W. Deutsch of Harvard University. The two themes had to be subdivided, however, into 12 and 8 panels, respectively, and there were also 8 research committees and 13 groups of specialists meeting officially at the congress, in addition to the many useful unofficial and unannounced meetings. The results of the new methods of organization were difficult to assess; though the congress generally seemed to be considered interesting, the dispersion did not appear to be less than at previous meetings: there were more than 100 working sessions.

For the first time at a political science congress, a demonstration of an automated system of bibliographic information retrieval was offered at Montreal (by a team working at the University of Pittsburgh under the auspices of the American Political Science Association [APSA]). The need to cope more efficiently with the rapidly expanding amount of information available to political scientists was increasingly felt by many teachers and researchers, but no satisfactory solution was in sight.

Meeting on the occasion of the congress, the council of IPSA, composed of delegates of the national political science associations, unanimously confirmed the election of Jean Laponce of the University of British Columbia as president and elected a new executive committee. It was decided to hold the tenth congress in Edinburgh, Scot., in 1976.

At Mannheim, W.Ger., in April, the European Consortium for Political Research (ECPR), established in 1970 and having a membership of more than 50 institutions, held eight simultaneous workshops on a variety of topics and its first council meeting. The meeting and various other workshops and summer schools intensified the efforts aimed at improving contacts among European political scientists. The ECPR also started publication of a quarterly journal, the *European Journal of Political Research.*

In the U.S. no member of the profession, however contemptuous of journalistic interest in current events, could avoid being concerned by the rapid changes in the international situation culminating in the end of the U.S. military involvement in Vietnam and the continued lowering of international tensions among the big powers, and by the Watergate scandal and related cases. The revelations of widespread corruption, political sabotage, and various illegal practices, directed or covered up by leading members of Pres. Richard Nixon's administration and White House staff, encouraged political scientists to think more realistically about possible remedies for defects in the political system. The many legal issues raised by litigation involving both President Nixon and former vice-president Spiro Agnew revived interest in constitutional law, which had been neglected somewhat in recent years. (*See* LAW; UNITED STATES.)

In the mail ballot conducted in November 1972, Avery Leiserson, of Vanderbilt University, Nashville, Tenn., was elected president of APSA for 1973–74.

(SERGE HURTIG)

ENCYCLOPÆDIA BRITANNICA FILMS. *The Presidency—Search for a Candidate* (1970); *The Progressive Era* (1971); *Where's Your Loyalty?* (1972); *Who Needs Rules?* (1972); *The United States Congress: Of, By and For the People* (2nd ed., 1973); *The United States Supreme Court: Guardian of the Constitution* (2nd ed., 1973); *President of the United States: Too Much Power?* (1973).

Populations and Areas

By mid-1973 UN estimates registered world population at 3,860,000,000 and the growth rate at roughly 2% each year. If this rate continued, the world would double its population in 35 years, with the most pronounced growth taking place in the poorer, less developed countries.

Because awareness of the effects of growing world population had increased dramatically since 1960, heroic efforts had been made, particularly in less developed countries, to curb growth as a way of heading off economic disaster. However, there was a considerable distance to go, and conditions and growth rates varied sharply from country to country. For example, a child born in 1973 in Nigeria could expect to live only long enough to reach his 37th birthday. A Swedish infant, however, could expect to live twice as long —72 years in the case of males and 77 years for females.

Life expectancy was to a large degree the product of affluence, and in the technologically developed countries of Europe and North America, as well as Australia, Japan, Israel, and New Zealand, the averages ran in the 60s and 70s. In the more temperate regions of Latin America and Asia, life expectancy averaged in the 50s, while in the tropical areas of Africa and Latin America the age range ran from the high 30s through the 50s. Among the factors contributing to shorter life expectancy in the less developed world

continued on page 559

Table I. The Ten Largest Nations by Area and Population*

Rank	Area in sq.mi.	Rank	Population
1 U.S.S.R.	8,600,340	1 China	800,721,000†
2 Canada	3,851,809	2 India	574,216,000
3 China	3,691,500	3 U.S.S.R.	250,000,000
4 United States	3,615,122‡	4 United States	210,157,000
5 Brazil	3,286,470	5 Indonesia	123,115,000
6 Australia	2,967,909	6 Japan	108,350,000
7 India	1,261,810	7 Brazil	101,607,600
8 Argentina	1,072,157	8 Bangladesh	75,000,000
9 Sudan	967,494	9 Nigeria	71,262,000§
10 Zaire	905,360	10 Pakistan	64,892,000†

*Areas are latest official data available; populations are for 1973.
†1972.
‡Excludes Great Lakes waters and territorial sea.
§Official estimate. UN estimate approximately 12 million lower.

Table II. World Census Data

POLITICAL UNIT	Year of census	ENUMERATED POPULATION Total	Male	Percent urban*	AGE DISTRIBUTION 0 to 14	15 to 44	45 and over	ECONOMICALLY ACTIVE Total	Agriculture	Mining and manufacturing
Afars and Issas	1960–61	81,200	...	57.4	...	...	...	...	...	...
Albania	1960	1,626,315	835,294	30.9	382,006†	1,244,249†	†	...	...	...
Algeria	1966	11,821,679	6,079,900	39.0	5,706,000	4,536,600	1,859,400	2,335,200	1,300,000	183,500
American Samoa	1970	27,159	13,682	28.3	12,879	10,872	3,408	5,094	110	1,166
Andorra	1971	20,550	...	...	...	...	...	...	...	...
Angola	1970	5,673,046	...	14.9	...	...	...	...	...	...
Antigua	1960	54,060‡	25,230	60.1	23,154§	20,964§	9,942§	16,873	12,564	4,084
Argentina	1970	23,364,431	11,601,155	...	...	...	...	...	...	...
Australia	1971	12,755,638	6,412,711	...	3,670,052	5,469,152	3,616,434	5,240,428	386,407	1,291,641
Austria	1971	7,456,403	...	51.9	...	...	...	...	...	...
Bahamas	1970	174,777	87,018	57.9	73,601	69,316	25,895	69,791	4,791	3,902
Bahrain	1971	216,078	116,314	78.1	95,640	90,994	29,444	60,301	3,990	8,464
Bangladesh	1961	50,840,235	26,348,843	5.2	23,440,000	20,137,000	7,263,000	17,443,000	14,872,000	...
Barbados	1970	238,141	110,470	...	87,190	88,672	59,367	83,669	17,815	11,532
Belgium	1970	9,650,944	4,721,866	...	...	...	...	...	...	...
Belize	1970	119,934	60,091	54.5	59,138	42,591	18,176	31,306	11,207	4,633
Bermuda	1970	52,330‡	26,293	7.0	15,520	24,206	12,604	33,948	983	5,837‖
Bhutan	1969	1,034,774	...	...	...	...	...	...	...	...
Bolivia	1950	2,704,165	1,326,099	...	1,070,900	1,185,600	447,700	...	...	...
Botswana	1971	574,094	262,121	8.4	264,530	198,019	100,042	51,408	11,564	6,129
Brazil	1970	93,204,379‡	46,330,629	55.9	38,865,773¶	44,048,881¶	10,289,725¶	29,545,293	13,071,385	5,263,805‖
British Solomon Islands	1970	160,998	85,179	7.0	71,761	66,326	22,911	13,690♀	3,182♀	960♀
British Virgin Islands	1970	10,298	5,481	21.9	3,788	4,237	1,647	3,842	298	195
Brunei	1971	136,256	72,772	63.6	59,136	59,555	17,256	40,012	4,776	4,666
Bulgaria	1965	8,227,866	4,114,167	46.4	2,083,368	3,816,669	2,327,829	4,267,793	1,891,398	1,124,885
Cambodia	1962	5,728,771	2,861,819	10.3	2,509,615	2,381,590	837,566	2,499,735	1,997,768	104,627
Canada	1971	21,568,310	10,795,370	76.1	6,380,898	9,419,692	5,767,720	...	...	...
Canal Zone	1970	44,198	24,254	5.8	14,061	22,588	7,549	9,776	123	281
Cape Verde Islands	1970	272,071	...	19.7	...	...	...	...	...	...
Cayman Islands	1970	10,652	4,840	...	3,960♂	5,526♂	763♂	...	...	...
Channel Islands										
Guernsey	1971	53,734	25,878	...	12,401	20,456	20,877	23,813	5,494	2,486
Jersey	1971	72,629	33,770	...	14,228	28,828	26,273	34,641	3,197	4,819
Chile	1970	8,853,140	4,321,500	76.0	3,456,700	3,729,320	1,547,300	2,607,360	552,340	490,740
Colombia	1964	17,484,508	8,614,652	52.8	8,155,529	7,022,627	2,306,352	5,134,125	2,427,059	737,240
Comoro Islands	1966	244,905‡	120,385	13.9	109,364	95,358	42,183	82,090	52,415	11,035
Cook Islands	1971	21,317	10,910	...	10,966	7,463	2,858	5,581	1,224	509
Costa Rica	1963	1,336,274‡	668,957	34.5	636,665	516,395	183,214	395,273	194,309	46,459
Cuba	1970	8,553,395‡	4,374,624	60.5	3,140,712♂	4,919,673♂	493,011♂	...	...	...
Cyprus	1960	573,566	281,983	35.9	221,656	226,612	125,298	241,823	93,287	37,718
Czechoslovakia	1970	14,361,557‡	6,989,486	55.6	3,289,533	6,192,976	4,879,048	6,989,411	1,040,605	3,359,259
Denmark	1970	4,937,784	...	79.9	1,146,400	2,049,700	1,757,400	...	...	...
Dominica	1970	69,549	32,968	46.2	34,118	22,543	12,888	19,617	7,720	1,551
Dominican Republic	1970	4,006,405	1,998,990	39.8	1,904,425	1,610,915	491,065	...	...	...
Ecuador	1962	4,476,007	2,236,476	36.0	2,014,505	1,839,160	622,342	1,442,591	800,390	215,617
Egypt	1966	30,075,858	15,175,554	41.2	...	...	...	...	...	...
El Salvador	1971	3,541,010	1,754,778	39.4	1,638,602	1,429,612	481,046	1,314,857	613,757	108,775
Equatorial Guinea	1960	245,989	132,293	...	...	...	...	...	...	...
Faeroe Islands	1970	38,612‡	...	...	...	...	...	...	...	...
Falkland Islands	1972	1,957	1,081	55.1	523¶	987¶	447¶	...	...	...
Fiji	1966	476,727	242,747	33.4	222,739	196,656	57,332	125,809	69,404	8,845
Finland	1970	4,622,299‡	2,233,658	50.9	1,120,287	2,068,345	1,433,527	2,128,537	428,991	722,796
France	1968	49,654,556‡	24,196,528	70.0	11,790,960	20,655,544	17,208,052	19,961,852	3,131,320	7,903,324
French Guiana	1967	44,392‡	24,078	66.5	16,613	18,732	9,047	...	...	...
French Polynesia	1971	119,168	...	...	...	...	...	...	...	...
Gabon	1970	950,009	455,339	26.9	336,493	393,875	219,641	...	...	...
Gambia	1973	494,279	251,704	...	204,968¶	232,744¶	55,485¶	...	...	...
Germany, East	1971	17,068,318	7,865,265	...	3,970,568	6,818,492	6,279,258	...	...	...
Germany, West	1970	60,650,599	28,866,724	...	14,058,277	24,821,968	20,770,360	26,493,512	1,990,514	12,956,672
Ghana	1970	8,559,313‡	4,247,809	28.9	4,015,965	3,439,456	1,103,892	3,133,047	1,790,806	...
Gibraltar	1970	26,833	12,914	100.0	5,662	10,819	8,191	9,160	...	146
Gilbert and Ellice Is.	1968	53,517	26,404	14.9	20,323	17,130	7,187	13,121	8,601	496
Greece	1971	8,768,640	4,280,060	53.2	2,180,220	3,710,960	2,877,460	3,283,880	1,330,320	560,860
Greenland	1970	46,531	24,425	...	20,198	20,305	6,028	...	...	...
Grenada	1970	96,542	44,556	...	...	...	...	...	...	...
Guadeloupe	1967	312,724‡	159,760	45.8	139,346	126,281	59,412	...	...	...
Guam	1970	84,996	47,362	25.5	33,701	41,162	10,133	22,112	157	1,386
Guatemala	1964	4,287,997	2,172,456	33.6	1,949,395	1,786,505	551,519	1,362,669	...	...
Guyana	1970	714,233	355,753	...	...	...	...	...	...	...
Honduras	1961	1,884,765	939,029	23.2	900,739	752,909	231,117	567,988	379,125	45,779
Hong Kong	1971	3,936,630	2,000,602	...	1,407,904	1,671,216	857,510	1,654,907	34,013	737,117
Hungary	1970	10,322,099	5,003,651	45.2	2,176,507	4,558,280	2,587,312	...	...	...
Iceland	1970	204,930‡	...	...	...	...	...	...	...	...
India	1971	547,949,809	283,936,614	19.9	...	...	...	183,605,325	126,011,684	...
Indonesia	1971	119,232,499‡	58,279,166	17.4	52,261,306	50,399,092	15,791,588	40,100,070	24,772,230	3,021,868
Iran	1966	25,078,923	12,981,665	38.1	11,887,006	10,146,859	3,754,857	7,584,085	3,168,515	1,293,912
Iraq	1965	8,261,527	4,205,201	44.1	3,857,901	2,922,015	1,267,499	...	...	...
Ireland	1971	2,978,248	1,495,760	52.2	...	...	...	1,119,531	273,079	224,053
Isle of Man	1971	56,289	24,461	55.7	11,187	18,696	26,406	...	...	...
Israel	1972	3,124,000	1,609,600	...	1,052,400	1,357,900	790,200	1,047,400	...	...
Italy	1971	54,025,211‡	26,381,955	...	...	...	...	18,749,799	3,240,856	...
Jamaica	1970	1,861,300	891,700	37.1	849,200	...	...	...	...	...
Japan	1970	104,665,171‡	51,238,700	72.1	25,081,700	52,929,100	26,305,900	52,409,200	10,149,000	13,695,700
Jordan	1961	1,706,226	867,597	47.4	774,516	680,126	251,584	389,978	137,757	41,932
Kenya	1969	10,942,705	5,482,381	9.9	5,291,312¶	4,567,536¶	1,083,857¶	...	...	...
Korea, South	1970	31,435,252	15,216,002	41.2	13,241,433	13,324,979	4,868,840	12,629,000	7,391,000	1,692,000
Kuwait	1970	738,663	419,886	...	319,299	353,210	66,154	233,534	4,060	39,263
Lesotho	1966	969,634	465,784	...	370,390	306,208	172,756	...	...	...
Liberia	1962	1,016,443	503,588	19.7	377,739	472,987	165,717	411,794	298,404	22,913
Libya	1964	1,564,369	813,386	24.6	683,431	630,379	249,160	405,258	146,709	43,636
Liechtenstein	1970	21,350	10,616	...	5,691	...	...	10,251	634	...
Luxembourg	1970	339,812	166,562	68.4	75,142	142,259	122,411	133,300	13,100	61,500
Macau	1970	248,118	127,365	100.0	93,398	109,024	46,214	...	...	...
Malawi	1966	4,039,583	1,913,262	5.0	1,774,766	1,645,740	619,077	...	...	...
Malaysia	1970	10,434,034	5,263,047	26.7	...	...	...	...	...	...

Table II. World Census Data *(Continued)*

POLITICAL UNIT	Year of census	ENUMERATED POPULATION Total	Male	Percent urban*	AGE DISTRIBUTION 0 to 14	15 to 44	45 and over	ECONOMICALLY ACTIVE Total	Agriculture	Mining and manufacturing
Maldives	1967	103,801‡	55,346	11.3	46,086	45,422	12,293	...	...	...
Malta	1967	314,216‡	150,598	94.3	93,759	136,884	83,573	94,367	7,109	22,893
Martinique	1967	320,030‡	155,212	45.8	139,262	120,406	60,211	89,464	22,746	8,091
Mauritius	1962	681,619	342,306	46.5	308,676	266,292	106,651	187,401	70,866	27,560
Mexico	1970	48,225,238‡	24,065,614	58.7	22,286,680	19,388,400	26,608,170	12,955,057	5,103,519	2,349,249
Monaco	1968	23,035‡	10,424	100.0	2,979	8,273	11,783	10,093	11	2,170
Mongolia	1969	1,197,600	597,400	44.0	...	...	...	...	...	...
Montserrat	1970	11,458	5,374	11.1	1,808	3,657	5,993	3,769	759	218
Morocco	1971	15,153,806	7,585,905	35.4	6,997,117	5,823,689	2,333,000	3,980,518	2,013,814	628,260
Mozambique	1970	8,233,834	...	...	...	...	...	...	...	...
Nauru	1966	6,048	3,696	0.0	2,420	2,943	694	2,504	2	1,727
Nepal	1971	11,555,983	5,738,780	...	4,674,578	5,113,071	1,768,334	...	...	...
Netherlands, The	1971	13,269,563	6,624,210	...	3,571,566	5,697,266	4,000,731	...	...	...
Netherlands Antilles	1960	192,538‡	94,811	...	79,683	77,069	35,786	59,806	1,029	16,059
New Caledonia	1969	100,579	52,591	41.6	34,964	46,028	19,587	39,185	13,357	7,152
New Hebrides	1967	76,582	40,626	12.0	34,917	31,707	9,958	35,133	28,681	875
New Zealand	1971	2,862,631	1,430,856	81.4	905,775	1,160,350	786,012	...	...	...
Nicaragua	1971	1,894,690	929,950	47.6	929,500	751,070	230,970	504,240	234,110	63,640
Nigeria	1963	55,670,046	28,112,118	16.1	23,925,586	26,959,145	4,785,324	18,267,669	10,209,122	2,205,476
Norway	1970	3,888,305	...	...	...	...	...	...	...	...
Pakistan	1972	64,892,000	34,417,000	...	...	...	...	...	...	...
Panama	1970	1,428,082	723,749	47.6	620,454	589,133	218,495	488,668	...	...
Papua New Guinea	1966	2,184,986	1,140,359	5.8	921,180	957,735	271,407	254,002	142,993	13,398
Paraguay	1972	2,328,790	1,152,744	37.6	...	...	...	...	...	...
Peru	1972	13,567,939	6,784,017	59.6	...	...	...	...	...	...
Philippines	1970	36,684,486	18,250,351	31.7	15,773,642	15,527,896	5,288,530	12,296,583	6,332,071	1,454,450
Poland	1970	32,589,209	15,834,525	52.3	8,606,338	14,964,555	9,018,316	15,927,000	4,890,000	...
Portugal	1970	8,545,120	4,053,040	...	2,426,360	3,496,260	2,622,500	3,143,940	987,400	742,300
Portuguese Guinea	1970	487,448	237,293	11.5	...	...	...	...	...	...
Portuguese Timor	1970	609,477	316,446	...	244,461	256,197	108,819	...	...	...
Puerto Rico	1970	2,712,033‡	1,329,949	58.1	990,920	1,138,462	582,551	...	...	...
Réunion	1967	416,525	203,497	42.8	189,997	163,253	62,166	94,334	27,845	6,910
Rhodesia	1969	5,099,340	2,567,081	16.8	2,385,907	2,082,996	591,194	...	...	...
Romania	1966	19,103,163	9,351,075	38.2	4,968,524	8,864,512	5,253,555	10,362,300	5,889,591	2,013,525
Rwanda	1970	3,735,585	1,784,862	3.2	1,637,307	1,471,821	626,457	...	...	...
St. Helena	1966	4,649	2,233	...	1,814	1,631	1,204	1,562	...	...
St. Kitts-Nevis-Anguilla	1970	45,457□	...	...	...	...	...	...	...	...
St. Lucia	1970	101,064	...	...	...	...	...	...	...	...
St. Pierre and Miquelon	1967	5,186	2,593	...	1,676	2,216	1,294	1,876	...	374
St. Vincent	1970	89,129	42,281	...	...	...	...	...	...	...
São Tomé and Príncipe	1970	73,631	37,017	11.6	32,359	28,900	12,192	...	...	...
Seychelles	1971	52,650	26,244	26.1	22,856	18,966	10,656	17,868	5,077	1,168◊
Sierra Leone	1963	2,180,355	1,081,123	...	800,404	1,016,240	363,711	...	682,588	88,846
Sikkim	1971	204,760	...	...	...	...	...	...	...	...
Singapore	1970	2,074,507	1,062,127	100.0	804,836	933,050	336,621	...	...	...
South Africa	1970	21,402,470	10,546,100	47.8	8,725,560	9,173,640	3,503,270	7,986,210	2,280,230	2,479,910
South West Africa	1970	746,328	379,136	24.9	...	...	...	...	...	...
Spain	1970	34,037,849	16,641,802	...	9,478,763	14,284,454	10,274,632	11,865,099	2,947,108	3,145,178
Spanish Sahara	1970	76,425	43,981	45.3	38,804	33,265	10,356	...	...	...
Sri Lanka	1971	12,711,143	6,525,948	22.4	5,808,863▲	6,902,280▲	▲	...	...	...
Surinam	1971	384,903	192,500	...	175,370▲	190,472▲	▲	...	...	...
Swaziland	1966	374,571	178,795	12.5	174,455	145,668	54,448	121,063	85,103	23,480
Sweden	1970	8,076,903‡	4,033,937	81.4	1,665,989	3,249,047	3,161,867	3,412,668	276,505	1,041,474◊
Switzerland	1970	6,269,783	3,089,326	52.0	1,466,533	2,750,816	2,052,434	3,005,139	229,293	1,451,975+
Syria	1970	6,304,685	3,233,110	43.5	3,106,120	2,318,448	880,117	1,570,776	751,519	436,491
Taiwan	1970	14,693,000	7,894,000	...	5,950,000	6,447,000	2,296,000	5,062,000	1,853,000	778,000
Tanzania	1967	12,313,469	6,005,894	5.5	5,398,445	4,932,236	1,960,130	5,577,567	5,078,038	96,502
Thailand	1970	34,220,000	16,970,000	...	15,527,000	13,997,000	4,597,000	16,312,000	13,399,000	575,000
Togo	1970	1,955,916	940,790	...	...	...	...	...	...	...
Tonga	1966	77,429	39,837	...	35,745	31,502	10,182	40,819	13,896	597
Trinidad and Tobago	1970	945,210	467,296	...	518,019⊕	415,087⊕	⊕	...	...	...
Trust Territory of the Pacific Islands	1970	90,940	46,482	...	41,700	34,784	14,456	13,377	935	426
Tunisia	1966	4,533,351	2,314,419	40.1	2,099,315	1,721,105	712,931	1,093,735	448,296	103,582
Turkey	1970	35,605,176	18,006,986	38.5	14,888,793	15,023,899	6,753,857	14,533,725	9,730,469	1,742,282
Turks and Caicos Islands	1970	5,558	2,635	...	2,618	1,797	1,143	...	...	...
Uganda	1969	9,548,847	4,818,449	7.7	4,404,291	3,791,156	1,350,865	...	...	...
Union of Soviet Socialist Republics	1970	241,720,134	111,399,377	56.3	69,973,962	109,616,467	62,129,705	...	...	...
United Kingdom	1971	55,360,000	26,890,000	...	13,498,900	21,549,000	20,518,500	...	...	...
United States	1970	203,211,926	98,912,192	73.5	57,900,052	83,436,603	61,875,271	...	...	...
Uruguay	1963	2,592,563	1,289,454	80.8	721,500	1,143,600	727,500	1,015,500	181,800	213,600
Venezuela	1971	10,721,522	5,364,365	75.5	4,485,431	4,464,357	1,411,734	3,068,784	645,027	619,285
Vietnam, North	1960	15,916,955	7,687,814	9.5	7,055,544**	7,556,129**	1,305,282**	8,119,286	6,377,024	537,761
Virgin Islands (U.S.)	1970	62,468‡	31,157	24.4	22,311	29,766	10,391	24,501	172	2,263
Western Samoa	1971	146,625	75,931	...	...	...	...	...	...	...
Yugoslavia	1971	20,522,972	10,077,282	...	5,500,255	9,660,846	5,361,871	8,889,846	3,902,963	1,574,512
Zambia	1969	4,056,995	1,987,011	29.6	1,878,861	1,646,486	527,648	1,159,698	...	...
DEMOGRAPHIC AND/OR SAMPLE SURVEYS										
Burundi	1962	2,319,540	1,104,266	...	...	...	...	...	...	...
Central African Republic	1959–60	1,177,000	577,000	6.8	429,000	661,000	81,000	610,000	461,000	52,000
Chad	1964	3,254,000	1,567,000	7.8	...	...	...	950,000	600,000	60,000
Congo††	1960–61	581,600	267,800	11.6	240,200	230,300	1,111,000	...	...	...
Dahomey††	1961	2,082,511	1,020,558	9.3	957,922	814,620	965,390	...	...	...
Malagasy Republic	1966	6,200,000	3,049,000	...	2,882,000	2,326,000	992,000	2,733,000	2,396,000	337,000
Mali	1960–61	3,680,000	1,829,000	11.2	1,551,100	1,553,100	573,800	...	...	...
Niger	1959–60	2,611,473	1,297,557	...	1,143,556	1,120,580	347,337	1,506,490	703,610	4,510
Senegal	1960–61	3,109,840‡	1,531,760	23.7	1,320,680	1,311,960	477,200	1,317,580	1,087,020	73,800
Upper Volta	1960–61	4,300,000	2,158,600	4.6	1,788,800	1,849,000	662,200	2,627,000	1,300,000	...

Note: Data reflect results of enumerations conducted 1960 to 1973, as available. Age groups may not add to country total.

*That population defined as urban by the political unit.

†0–9, 10 and over.
‡De jure population.
§0–15, 16–45, 46 and over.
‖Including public utilities and construction.

¶0–14, 15–49, 50 and over.
♀Estimated.
♂0–14, 15–64, 65 and over.
□Excluding Anguilla.
◊Including public utilities.

▲0–15, 16 and over.
+Including construction.
⊕0–21, 22 and over.
**0–15, 16–55, 56 and over.
††African population only.

Table III. Populations and Areas of the Countries of the World, Midyear 1972

Continent and state	Area in sq.mi.	Population in 000	Persons per sq.mi.
World total	57,945,604	3,791,594	72.3*
AFRICA	11,676,445	366,346	31.4
Algeria	896,588	15,270	17.0
Botswana	222,394	633	2.8
Bouvet Island (Norwegian)	23	—	—
British dependencies	311	61	—
Burundi	10,747	3,402	316.6
Cameroon	179,557	6,085	33.9
Central African Republic	240,377	1,676	7.0
Chad	495,752	3,791	7.6
Congo	132,000	1,150	8.7
Dahomey	43,475	2,869	66.0
Egypt	386,900	34,839	90.0
Equatorial Guinea	10,830	293	27.1
Ethiopia	471,800	25,933	55.0
French dependencies	10,733	840	—
Gabon	103,346	950	9.2
Gambia, The	4,467	485	108.6
Ghana	92,100	9,087	98.7
Guinea	94,925	4,092	43.1
Ivory Coast	123,483	4,526	36.7
Kenya	224,960	12,076	53.7
Lesotho	11,720	972	82.9
Liberia	43,000	1,617	37.6
Libya	675,000	2,084	3.1
Malagasy Republic	226,442	7,035	31.1
Malawi	45,747	4,666	102.0
Mali	478,822	5,257	11.0
Mauritania	398,000	1,150	2.9
Mauritius	720	857	1,190.3
Morocco	177,116	15,825	89.3
Niger	489,191	4,243	8.7
Nigeria	356,669	57,640	161.6
Portuguese dependencies	805,419	15,159	—
Rhodesia	150,803	5,690	37.7
Rwanda	10,169	3,896	383.1
Senegal	78,684	4,112	52.3
Sierra Leone	27,925	2,627	94.1
Somalia	246,154	2,941	11.9
South Africa	471,445	22,987	48.8
South West Africa (Namibia)	318,261	799	2.5
Spanish Sahara	102,703	91	0.9
Sudan	967,494	16,489	17.0
Swaziland	6,704	434	64.7
Tanzania	364,943	13,996	38.4
Togo	21,900	2,092	95.5
Tunisia	63,378	5,377	84.8
Uganda	91,452	10,462	114.4
Upper Volta	105,870	5,611	53.0
Zaire	905,360	23,222	25.6
Zambia	290,586	4,420	15.2
ANTARCTICA	5,500,000†	‡	—
Australian Antarctic Territory	2,472,000	—	—
British Antarctic Territory§	650,000	—	—
French Southern and Antarctic Lands	202,916	—	—
Norwegian dependencies	96‖	—	—
Ross Dependency (New Zealand)	160,000	—	—
ASIA (exclusive of U.S.S.R.)	10,726,066	2,124,741	198.1
Afghanistan	251,823	17,882	71.0
Australian dependencies	58	3	—
Bahrain	256	224	75.0
Bangladesh	55,126	75,000	1,360.5
Bhutan	18,000	1,093	60.7
Brunei (British protected state)	2,226	142	63.8
Burma	261,789	28,833	110.1
Cambodia	69,898	7,122	101.9
China	3,691,500	800,721	216.9
Cyprus	3,572	645	180.6
Hong Kong (British)	400	4,077	10,192.5
India (incl. Jammu and Kashmir)	1,261,810	563,494	446.6
Indonesia	782,658	121,630	155.4
Iran	635,932	30,550	48.0
Iraq¶	168,927	10,074	59.6
Israel	7,992	3,124	390.9
Japan	145,711	106,958	734.0
Jordan	36,832	2,467	67.0
Korea, North	46,800	14,680	313.7
Korea, South	38,022	32,369	851.3
Kuwait	6,880	914	132.8
Laos	91,400	3,106	34.0
Lebanon	3,950	2,410	610.1
Malaysia	127,316	10,910	85.7
Maldives	115	123	1,069.6
Mongolia	604,000	1,315	2.2
Nepal	54,362	11,467	210.9
Neutral Zone	7,000	...	—
Oman	82,000	699	8.5
Pakistan	307,374	64,892	211.1
Philippines	115,800	39,046	337.2
Portuguese dependencies	5,769	894	—
Qatar	4,400	170	38.6
Saudi Arabia¶	865,000	8,199	9.5
Sikkim (Indian protected state)	2,744	210	76.5
Singapore	226	2,147	9,500.0
Sri Lanka	25,332	13,033	514.5
Syria	71,498	6,678	93.4
Taiwan	13,893	15,130	1,089.0
Thailand	198,500	36,286	182.8
Turkey	300,948	37,010	123.0
United Arab Emirates	32,300	275	8.5
Vietnam, North	63,360	22,038	347.8
Vietnam, South	67,293	19,074	283.4
Yemen (Aden)	111,074	1,515	13.6
Yemen (San'a')	77,200	6,062	78.5

Continent and state	Area in sq.mi.	Population in 000	Persons per sq.mi.
EUROPE (exclusive of U.S.S.R.)	1,904,694	465,608	244.5
Albania	11,100	2,286	205.9
Andorra	179	21	114.8
Austria	32,375	7,488	231.3
Belgium	11,781	9,711	824.3
British dependencies	298	206	—
Bulgaria	42,823	8,578	200.3
Czechoslovakia	49,373	14,481	293.3
Denmark (incl. Faeroe Islands)	17,169	4,993	290.8
Finland	130,128	4,626	35.5
France	210,038	51,720	246.2
Germany, East	41,768	17,043	408.0
Germany, West (incl. W. Berlin)	95,980	61,674	642.6
Greece	50,944	8,940	175.5
Hungary	35,920	10,398	289.5
Iceland	39,769	209	5.3
Ireland	27,136	3,014	111.1
Italy	116,313	54,345	467.2
Liechtenstein	62	22	359.7
Luxembourg	999	348	348.3
Malta	122	319	2,614.8
Monaco	0.7	24	33,561.6
Netherlands, The	15,892	13,330	838.8
Norway (incl. Svalbard and Jan Mayen)	149,153	3,933	26.4
Poland	120,725	33,068	273.9
Portugal	35,383	8,590	242.8
Romania	91,700	20,663	224.8
San Marino	24	19	792.6
Spain	194,881	34,494	177.0
Sweden	173,732	8,122	46.8
Switzerland	15,943	6,422	402.8
United Kingdom	94,217	55,798	592.2
Vatican City	0.2	0.7	3,973.3
Yugoslavia	98,766	20,722	209.8
NORTH AND CENTRAL AMERICA	9,360,418	369,131	39.4
Barbados	166	240	1,469.9
Bahamas	5,382	185	34.4
British dependencies	10,368	738	—
Canada	3,851,809	21,848	5.7
Costa Rica	19,652	1,843	93.8
Cuba	42,827	8,749	204.3
Dominican Republic	18,658	4,305	230.7
El Salvador	8,098	3,760	464.3
French dependencies	1,211	687	—
Greenland (Danish)	840,000	47	—
Guatemala	42,042	5,409	128.7
Haiti	10,714	4,244	369.1
Honduras	43,277	2,687	62.1
Jamaica	4,244	1,923	453.1
Mexico	761,600	52,641	69.1
Netherlands Antilles (Dutch)	385	230	597.4
Nicaragua	49,759	1,988	40.0
Panama (excl. Canal Zone)	29,208	1,524	52.2
Trinidad and Tobago	1,980	1,043	526.8
United States	3,615,122	208,842	57.8
United States dependencies	3,916	2,921	—
OCEANIA	3,285,466	20,089	6.1
Australia	2,967,909	12,959	4.4
Australian dependencies	178,467	2,583	—
British dependencies	11,268	243	—
Canton and Enderbury Islands (U.K.-U.S.)	27	—	—
Fiji	7,055	545	77.3
French dependencies	8,725	254	—
Nauru	8	7	853.7
New Hebrides (Fr.-U.K.)	5,700	90	15.8
New Zealand	103,736	2,905	28.0
New Zealand dependencies	197	28	—
Tonga	225	91	404.4
United States dependencies	1,016	236	—
Western Samoa	1,133	148	130.6
SOUTH AMERICA	6,892,175	198,220	28.8
Argentina	1,072,157	23,923	22.3
Bolivia	424,165	5,195	12.2
Brazil	3,286,470	98,854	30.1
Chile	292,257	10,045	34.4
Colombia	439,735	22,461	51.1
Ecuador	109,483	6,508	59.1
Falkland Islands (British)	6,150	2	0.3
French Guiana	34,750	56	1.6
Guyana	83,000	754	9.1
Paraguay	157,047	2,329	14.8
Peru	496,222	13,568	27.3
Surinam (Dutch)	70,060	419	6.0
Uruguay	68,536	2,956	43.1
Venezuela	352,143	11,150	31.7
U.S.S.R.	8,600,340	247,459	28.8

Note: Populations given are latest official or UN estimates for midyear 1972. If no estimate for this date was available from either source, an estimate was made where information was sufficient or data for another date were inserted if information was insufficient to make an estimate. A dash (—) in the population column indicates none, or negligible; a dash in the density column indicates figure not meaningful; three dots (...) indicate data not available.

*Area of Antarctica omitted in calculating world density.

†Estimated area, including some unclaimed territory.

‡May reach a total of around 2,000 persons of all nationalities during the summer; authoritative figures are not available.

§Includes some territory claimed by Argentina and Chile.

‖Insular dependencies only. Norwegian claims in continental Antarctica are undefined.

¶Excluding Iraq-Saudi Arabia Neutral Zone of 7,000 sq.mi.

continued from page 555
were the high rates of infant mortality. As an index of health conditions within nations, prosperous and medically advanced Sweden had an infant mortality rate of 11.1 per 1,000 live births, while many of the nations of West Africa had rates exceeding 150 per 1,000. Surprisingly, the U.S., with an infant mortality rate of 18.5, lagged behind a dozen countries including Canada (17.6), East Germany (17.7), Finland (11.3), Japan (13), and The Netherlands (11.4).

Throughout most of the world there was a high correlation between wealth and low growth. Thus the U.S., the wealthiest nation per capita, had slowed its growth rate by mid-1973 to one of the lowest in the world and by far the lowest in the country's 200-year history. For the 12 months ended in June 1973, the birthrate was 15.3 births per 1,000 population; for the first half of 1973, it was 14.8. At the current 0.8% rate of growth, the U.S. could be expected to double its 210.3 million population in 87 years. Even if the birthrate continued to decline, the nation would continue to increase in population well into the 21st century. The large numbers of young people born during the "baby boom" of the 1940s and 1950s were entering their high reproductive years, and even if they opted for small families, as the trend seemed to indicate, some growth would be recorded.

Similar trends had been noted in a number of European countries where, as a result of years of declining fertility, population was nearing or had reached zero growth. Hungary was growing by 0.3% annually and could expect to double its 10.4 million people in 231 years. East Germany, where the death rate of 13.7 deaths per 1,000 population exceeded the birthrate of 11.7 and where 15% of the population was over 65, was actually losing population. In Austria the rate of growth was 0.1% annually, and West Germany reported zero population growth. Growth rates in Europe as a whole had slowed to 0.7%, meaning a doubling of the continent's 515 million population in 99 years. The European population was characterized by a high proportion of aged, 12% on the average, while a relatively low 25% were under age 15.

By contrast, the poor, less developed countries of Asia, Africa, and Latin America tended to have a high proportion of youth and a low proportion of aged. In Asia, where the rate of growth was 2.3%—meaning that the 2.2 billion population could double in only 30 years—40% of the people were under 15 and only 4% over 65. Oil-rich Kuwait continued to be the world's fastest growing nation, with a 9.8% annual rate of increase; the birthrate was 43 and the death rate was 7, but growth was also affected by immigration of Arabs from other nations attracted by Kuwait's high living standard. Iraq, Pakistan, Syria, the Philippines, and Thailand were growing fast enough to double their populations in 21 years. In each of these countries more than 42% of the population was under 15 and only a negligible percentage was over 65. In Iraq fully 48% was under 15.

In Africa the growth rate was still more rapid. If the current 2.5% growth rate continued, the continent's 374 million population could be doubled in 20 years. Throughout the continent birthrates ran in the high 40s per 1,000 (over 50 in Morocco, Liberia, Mali, Niger, Nigeria, and Angola), but death rates were also high, exceeding 21 in most of those countries. On the average, 44% of the population was under 15 and 3% over 65. Latin America had an average birthrate of 38 per 1,000, but the average death rate was only 10. At the current growth rate of 2.8%, this region could double its 308 million population in a generation—25 years. More than 42% of Latin America's population was under 15 and 4% was over 65. The most rapid growth was occurring in Mexico, the Dominican Republic, Venezuela, Ecuador, Paraguay, and Colombia. Brazil reported 101.3 million people and a growth rate of 2.8%. The slowest growth rates in Latin America occurred in the southernmost, temperate countries.

Against this background of high growth in the poorest nations and increasingly gloomy reports of economic instability and crisis around the world, there was a growing recognition that rising population added to tension and pressures. To deal with the issues raised, the UN announced its world population conference, scheduled to be held Aug. 19–30, 1974, in Bucharest, Rom. It was hoped that the conference—the first worldwide political gathering to address itself to the population question—would identify broad areas of agreement concerning population change, its relationship to economic and social development and to family well-being, and could formulate a World Population Plan of Action. UN Secretary-General Kurt Waldheim, in describing the conference, said: "It is my hope that the World Population Year and Conference will rank in the history of the United Nations among the great events of the seventies, and that they will bring us appreciably closer to the day when the world can say that the demographic problems facing us are understood and actions to solve them are under way." (WARREN W. EISENBERG)

See also Vital Statistics.

Portugal

A unitary corporative republic of southwestern Europe, Portugal shares the Iberian Peninsula with Spain. Area: 35,383 sq.mi. (91,641 sq.km.), including the Azores (905 sq.mi.) and Madeira (308 sq.mi.). Pop. (1972 est.): 8,523,600. Cap. and largest city: Lisbon (pop., 1972 est., 753,400). Language: Portuguese. Religion: Roman Catholic. President in 1973, Rear Adm. Américo de Deus Rodrigues Tomás; premier, Marcello José das Neves Alves Caetano.

Political stability was maintained during 1973, but the performance of the Portuguese economy was uneven. Premier Caetano was confirmed as undisputed

London policemen look stolidly ahead as demonstrators shout and wave placards protesting Portuguese Premier Marcello Caetano's visit to Britain in July 1973.

DAILY MAIL, LONDON/PICTORIAL PARADE

national leader by the convincing mandate the government obtained in the October 28 elections for 150 unopposed right-wing deputies in the National Assembly.

There were moves toward political liberalization during the year. A series of seven decrees published late in December 1972 granted a considerable measure of administrative and financial autonomy to the seven overseas provinces; Lisbon, however, retained the final say over their defense and foreign affairs. Angola and Mozambique were awarded the honorific title of state. There was more freedom of comment by the press; a law had been passed in November 1971 to ease press censorship, with the exception of matters relating to national security, but until 1973 little action had been taken to implement it. Despite this, the government continued to proscribe the role of political parties. It was also greatly concerned by the growth of urban guerrilla activities; for example, in October bombs destroyed part of the military headquarters in Oporto.

The policies of the government were subjected to international scrutiny and criticism during the year,

PORTUGAL

Education. (1969–70) Primary, pupils 989,676, teachers 27,753; secondary, pupils 265,462, teachers 17,053; vocational, pupils 135,979, teachers 8,385; teacher training, students 4,163, teachers 333; higher (including 5 universities), students 46,725, teaching staff 2,423.

Finance. Monetary unit: escudo, with (Sept. 17, 1973) a free rate of 23.30 escudos to U.S. $1 (56.20 escudos = £1 sterling). Gold, SDRs, and foreign exchange, official: (June 1973) U.S. $2,598,000,000; (June 1972) U.S. $1,966,000,000. Budget (1972 est.): revenue 36,877,000,000 escudos; expenditure 36,875,000,000 escudos. Gross national product: (1971) 194.9 billion escudos; (1970) 175.5 billion escudos. Money supply: (March 1973) 129,110,000,000 escudos; (March 1972) 99,750,000,000 escudos. Cost of living (Lisbon; 1963 = 100): (June 1973) 200; (June 1972) 179.

Foreign Trade. (1972) Imports 59,555,000,000 escudos; exports 35,063,000,000 escudos. Import sources: West Germany 15%; U.K. 13%; Angola 8%; U.S. 9%; France 6%; Italy 6%; Spain 5%. Export destinations: U.K. 23%; U.S. 11%; West Germany 7%; Angola 6%; Sweden 6%; Mozambique 5%; France 5%. Main exports: textile yarns and fabrics 18%; clothing 10%; machinery 10%; chemicals 7%; wine 6%; cork [illegible]%. Tourism (1971): visitors 3,867,000; gross receipts U.S. $299 million.

Transport and Communications. Roads (continent; 1971) 30,501 km. (including 77 km. expressways). Motor vehicles in use (1971): passenger 584,000; commercial 25,100. Railways: (1971) 3,563 km.; traffic (1972) 3,760,000,000 passenger-km., freight 829.2 million net ton-km. Air traffic (1971): 3,005,000,000 passenger-km.; freight 59,061,000 net ton-km. Shipping (1972): merchant vessels 100 gross tons and over 407; gross tonnage 1,027,070. Telephones (Dec. 1971) 809,000. Radio licenses (Dec. 1971) 1,411,000. Television licenses (Dec. 1971) 472,000.

Agriculture. Production (in 000; metric tons; 1972; 1971 in parentheses): wheat 585 (794); barley 55 (84); oats 71 (125); rye 167 (168); corn 517 (526); rice 163 (162); potatoes 1,093 (1,124); dry beans 47 (56); tomatoes (1971) *c.* 800, (1970) *c.* 800; figs (1970) *c.* 220, (1969) 221; oranges (1971) 85, (1970) 90; apples 105 (95); pears 67 (41); wine 726 (884); olives *c.* 380 (*c.* 290); olive oil 55 (42); meat (1971) 216, (1970) 210; timber (cu.m.; 1970) 6,400, (1969) 5,900; fish catch (1970) 498, (1969) 457. Livestock (in 000; 1970–71): sheep 5,690; cattle 1,100; pigs *c.* 1,400; goats *c.* 525; asses *c.* 153; poultry *c.* 13,740.

Industry. Fuel and power (in 000; 1972): coal (metric tons) 252; manufactured gas (Lisbon only; cu.m.) 129,000; electricity (kw-hr.) 8,676,000. Production (in 000; metric tons; 1972): iron ore (50% metal content) 44; steel 425; sulfuric acid 399; cement 2,743; tin 0.6; manganese ore (metal content; 1971) 1.8; tungsten concentrates (oxide content; 1971) 1.7; gold (troy oz.; 1971) 15; cotton yarn (1971) 83; woven cotton fabrics (1971) 47; preserved sardines (1971) 40; wood pulp (1971) 447; cork products (1971) 210.

Portuguese Overseas Provinces: *see* Dependent States

especially after June when Spanish priests accused the Portuguese armed forces of large-scale massacres of civilians in Mozambique. Demonstrations occurred during Caetano's visit to the United Kingdom (July 16–19) on the occasion of the 600th anniversary of the Anglo-Portuguese alliance.

Portugal was the only NATO country to facilitate the U.S. arms airlift to Israel during the October Middle East war, and when U.S. Secretary of State Henry A. Kissinger visited Lisbon in December, the Portuguese government was expected to solicit U.S. support for its campaign in Africa. Together with Rhodesia and South Africa, Portugal was cited by the Arab countries as a "colonialist and racist" regime that had given support to Israel and was subjected to a complete boycott of Arab oil shipments.

The Portuguese economy made reasonable progress during the year, but it was rather unevenly distributed. The rise in the gross domestic product was estimated at 7%, compared with 6.7% in 1972. The upswing in economic activity recorded in 1972 gathered momentum, with increases in consumption and in public and private investment and a continuing high level of imports of capital goods. The overall gains in industrial and agricultural output in 1973 were estimated at 10 and 2.5%, respectively, about the same as in 1972.

A rise in inflationary pressures gave cause for concern. It was unofficially calculated that the national average price level rose by 12–13% in 1973, compared with 10% per year in 1971 and 1972. In addition, the strong increase in the money supply that had occurred during 1971–72 continued. Most observers concluded that the measures adopted to counter inflation in the second half of 1972 were largely ineffective.

The external position remained strong. As in 1972, a large balance of payments surplus was recorded, with emigrants' remittances and proceeds from the tourist trade offsetting the traditional trade deficit. The adverse trade balance fell from U.S. $36 million in January–May 1972 to U.S. $25 million in the same period of 1973. Gross international reserves continued at a high level, reaching U.S. $2,625,000,000 at the end of May.

Prospects for long-term prosperity depended on the metropolitan economy being fully competitive with the advanced industrial countries of North America and Western Europe. The principal specific target of the fourth six-year development plan, to take effect from Jan. 1, 1974, was the achievement of an annual average growth rate of 7.5%.

The government continued to make great efforts to develop the economies of Angola and Mozambique, while maintaining their security in the face of guerrilla activities. Angola continued its rapid economic expansion, with spectacular increases in the output of mineral ores and industrial production. In Mozambique work proceeded on schedule on the giant Cabora Bassa dam and hydroelectric plant, despite sporadic guerrilla attacks. On completion the project would supply power to the whole state, thus helping to stimulate all-round expansion. (ROBIN CHAPMAN)

See also Dependent States.

Postal Services

With the admission of Bangladesh in February 1973, the United Arab Emirates in March, and East Germany in June, membership in the Universal Postal Union (UPU) rose to 149. The budget for the year was approximately $3,730,000. Topics discussed at the May session of the Executive Council included increasing technical aid to less developed countries, professional training, relations with the UN and other international bodies, the simplification of customs and tariffs, postal services to men at sea, and maximum use and security of airmail services. Also considered were forthcoming celebrations of the UPU's centenary and the 17th UPU Congress, scheduled for Lausanne, Switz., both in 1974.

In the United Kingdom 33,000 staff below senior management level, formerly employed in 20 different grades spread over five separate hierarchies, were incorporated into a single five-band structure to increase efficiency and open up wider career opportunities. The development of postal marketing continued. During the year the new sales force was extended to all commercial centres, and contracts were completed with many major customers. To help the sales drive, market research was stepped up to identify likely growth areas. Of the new services recently introduced for business users, Datapost was again particularly successful. A contract service guaranteeing prompt delivery of computer data and other urgent packages, Datapost had begun in 1970 as a purely internal U.K. service; by 1973 it was available to the U.S., The Netherlands, Brazil, Ireland, and Hong Kong, and was being extended to other countries.

The postal minibus service, which carried passengers as well as collecting and delivering mail, had been introduced in four rural U.K. areas in 1967; with the general decline in rural public transport, further requests for postal minibuses were received from local authorities during 1973. More than 20 such services were in operation.

In the field of automation, fully mechanized parcels offices were already functioning in Cardiff, Southampton, and Manchester, and new offices were being constructed in Belfast, Bristol, Newcastle, and East London. Standardized containers for conveying loose parcels between offices were developed, and plans for their introduction as replacements for the conventional mailbag where appropriate were far advanced. Fifteen letter offices were equipped with code-sorting machinery, although not all were yet fully operational. With the exception of a small area around Norwich, the introduction of postal codes in the U.K. was completed in July.

On July 5 the Manx postal administration took over the running of postal services on the Isle of Man. The Isle of Man Post Office Authority, although it issued its own stamps and made its own decisions, was represented in international affairs by the U.K. Ministry of Posts and Telecommunications.

In France the opening of the most modern automatic sorting centre at Orléans La Source on January 30 marked the culmination of years of research and the beginning of a large-scale modernization of the postal service. A vast covered hall comprised arrival, departure, indexing, and sorting sections, with administrative offices on the first floor. The "reader-indexer" machine could handle up to 43,200 letters an hour. There were also two new automatic sorting machines, the capacity of which could be increased by adding more modular units. The introduction of auxiliary equipment by 1975 was expected to increase the centre's handling capacity considerably beyond the 1973 level of 500,000 items per day.

MAC NELLY © 1973 CHICAGO TRIBUNE

"Well, not everybody thinks the mail service is lousy . . . we just got a letter of commendation from President Taft himself!"

Pressure on the services of the Deutsche Bundespost mounted in 1973: the overall traffic increase amounted to 4.6%, with intensity of growth varying in the different service branches. In the postal sector traffic decreased by 1.8%, while in telecommunications traffic increased by 8.6% over the previous year. The increased demand for telecommunications services and higher charges resulted in an increase in proceeds of 19.8%, to about DM. 19,650,000,000, corresponding to a 20.1% increase in revenues.

Although the revenue increase did not suffice to cover expenditures, the financial situation was favourably influenced by the fact that the increase in total revenues (19.6%) was greater than that in total expenditure (12.8%). As an example of the Bundespost's efficiency, traffic volume had increased by 85% during 1962–72, while the total number of personnel had increased by only 13.9%.

In the postal services efforts continued to reduce costs by a restriction of capital expenditure and a reduction of operating expenses. New fields of operation were opened for electronic data processing. The computer centres of the Deutsche Bundespost were equipped with 53 modern data-processing systems.

Among the more important developments in the Spanish postal service was the completion of a data-processing centre to take over accounting functions and extend mechanization of administrative processes in various departments. New communications centres were built in Salamanca and in six other cities; others in various districts were reorganized or extended. The new postal classification centre at Saragossa was completely automated, and transport installations were completed at the Barcelona centre. New mail trains were introduced: the Madrid–Levante, going to Valencia, Alicante, Murcia, and Cartagena; and the Madrid–Andalusia, serving the chief cities of southern Spain. Delivery routes totaling 8,489 km-days were permanently motorized, and a further 1,740 km-days were added on an experimental basis, bringing the cumulative total of motorized routes in operation up to 97,000 km-days.

Income of the postal and telegraphic services in Spain for 1972 amounted to 8,962,700,000 pesetas, 419 million pesetas (4.9%) over 1971. Expenses reached 11,125,000,000 pesetas, 13.2% above 1971. The number of letters and packets handled in 1972 totaled 4,235,000,000.

For the year ending March 31, 1973, record levels of business were attained by the New Zealand Post Office. Articles posted increased by 3.7% from 622 million to 645 million; telephone subscribers increased by 3.4% from 856,400 to 885,400; outward international telephone calls increased by 15% from 372,000 to 428,000; and international telex calls increased by 37.3% from 354,400 to 486,400. In keeping with worldwide trends, inland telegrams decreased by 1.4% from 5,080,000 to 5,012,000. Despite record business levels, however, the Post Office showed a trading loss of NZ$2 million. The Labour government, which took office in November 1972, announced a freeze on Post Office rates and charges for the following three years.

In the decade 1963–73 the domestic telephone traffic handled by the Australian Post Office increased fivefold and telex by 15-fold, while staff increased by less than one-quarter. The difference between traffic and staff growth was due largely to increased mechanization and improved operating techniques. By 1973 a national network comprising about three million exchange services was maintained; 92% of these were automatic, 83% having subscriber toll dialing service (STD) access.

During 1972–73 the Australian Post Office handled 2,787,000,000 articles of mail. Electronic equipment at the Sydney Mail Exchange, processing about 3.2 million letters a day, was being closely studied by overseas postal administrations. After six years of operation, the use of postal codes on mail in Australia rose to more than 89% by June 1973. Postal codes greatly assisted the processing of an increasing volume of mail. Bulk presorted mail, introduced in 1967, continued to increase in popularity.

Equipment for the mechanical and automatic sorting of mail matter was acquired for the two major mail handling centres of South Africa, Johannesburg and Cape Town, during the year. The two systems were to be in operation by 1975. Postal codes were introduced. Philatelic Services of the Department of Posts and Telegraphs in Pretoria served stamp collectors throughout the world. A mailing list was kept to inform interested parties of stamp news. (X.)

The U.S. Postal Service, in its second full year as a corporate-style, semi-independent government agency, substantially trimmed its traditionally large operating deficit and averted a probable nationwide

UPI COMPIX

A letter carrier with the Independent Postal System of America displays one of five postage stamp denominations included in a new series issued April 10, 1973.

mail strike by signing a new two-year labour agreement with major postal unions. But to pay for the costly wage settlement and to further reduce its annual operating loss, the Postal Service in September 1973 moved to raise postage rates an average 25%, to be effective in 1974. The higher rates, if approved by the Postal Rate Commission and the government's price controllers, would boost first-class postage to 10 cents an ounce from 8 cents and airmail rates to 13 cents from 11 cents.

The rate increase proposal, which would raise about $950 million for the Postal Service in the fiscal year ending June 30, 1974, was filed with the rate commission only two months after more than 600,000 postal union members ratified a new contract that called for pay increases averaging 7% in the first year and 4% in the second year of the contract. The agreement won postal workers a $700 pay boost on July 21, 1973, and a $400 raise in July 1974, plus fringe benefits worth about $250 over the two years.

Since labour costs represent about 85% of the Postal Service's annual expenditures, the request to increase rates was not surprising. But the size of the proposed increases startled many major businesses. The proposed rates would generate $1.2 billion annually in additional first-class revenues; $102 million in second-class, affecting newspapers and magazines; $276 million in third-class, for advertising circulars; and $34.5 million in fourth-class parcel post revenues. The increases for second-class mail users and senders of fourth-class books and records would take place in stages over several years.

Despite the higher rates, the Postal Service estimated in September that it would lose $352 million in fiscal 1974. However, in the fiscal year ended June 30, 1973, the Postal Service deficit was only $12,964,000, the smallest since 1945, when the old Post Office Department registered a surplus of $169,237,886. Revenues in fiscal 1973 rose to $9,805,442,000 from $9,346,943,000 in fiscal 1972, while spending totaled $9,818,306,000, compared with $9,522,378,000 in the previous year.

The improved financial showing was primarily due to higher postal rates that had gone into effect in July 1972 and again in September 1973, to an increase in mail volume, and to postal economies pushed in 1972 by Postmaster General Elmer T. Klassen. Mail volume in fiscal 1973 increased 2.9% to 89,700,000,000 pieces from 87,200,000,000 pieces the previous year, when volume had risen by only 200,000 pieces. The economies imposed, including a hiring freeze, created serious problems during the Christmas mailing season in 1972 and into early 1973. First-class and airmail delivery deteriorated seriously, while many third-class mail users complained that the Postal Service was deliberately delaying the delivery of their advertising circulars. During this period only about 60% of airmail pieces received overnight delivery, compared with the Postal Service's 70% service standard. Complaints from mail users and several U.S. congressmen prompted Klassen to tour all five postal regional headquarters during early 1973 to seek ideas to improve service. Postal managers were given more responsibility in hiring and in beginning new delivery services, and in February and March 6,000 additional employees were hired.

In a decision that aided its private mail delivery competitors, the Postal Service in July relaxed its private express statutes to allow some businesses to use other delivery firms to carry certain mail. The nine governors of the Postal Service suspended the private express statute for certain limited classes of business mail, including that delivered between a company's facilities and also data-processing materials. However, the Postal Service retained its delivery monopoly over all other first-class and addressed third-class mail.

As the year ended, the Postal Service faced new problems brought on by the energy crisis, although delivery of Christmas mail was accomplished more smoothly than had been anticipated. With airline schedules being cut back to conserve fuel, more long-distance mail was being shipped by train. However, some 80% of all mail was delivered by truck, and lower speed limits and other fuel-saving measures were expected to affect mail movement.

The Postal Rate Commission in January 1973 received the Postal Service's proposal for reclassifying its mail delivery system. The limited reclassification proposals provided various discounts for major mailers who sorted their own mail and also imposed surcharges for odd-sized and lightweight mail.

Among delivery changes begun in 1973, the Postal Service in July opened parcel post mail service between the U.S. and China by routing parcels via Hong Kong to Kwangchow. The Postal Service also raised to a maximum $300 the amount of a money order a customer could purchase at his local post office. (TIMOTHY D. SCHELLHARDT)

See also Philately and Numismatics; Telecommunications.

Prices

In most parts of the world, 1973 was a year of rapid economic growth and even more rapid inflation. This was certainly true of industrial countries, where a series of strong expansionary measures undertaken early in 1972 led to considerable "overheating" in 1973, especially in Western Europe. It was difficult to assess the extent to which excess demand influenced the acceleration in the rate of inflation, but the speed of recovery in many countries was such that it must have made a significant contribution to the process. At the same time, the worldwide boom produced a dramatic increase in demand for primary commodities, which, together with harvest failures, led to the biggest rise in commodity prices since the Korean War. At year's end, shortages of petroleum and petroleum-related products and of energy generally, apparent earlier but exacerbated by the Arab oil cutbacks, threatened to raise prices even higher.

As the persistently worsening inflation was becoming one of the most serious economic problems throughout the world, there seemed also to be a growing awareness that it was due to a complex combination of social and economic factors. Consequently, there was an increasing belief in many countries that a lasting solution was unlikely in the absence of a whole range of social as well as economic policies.

Consumer Prices. The worldwide acceleration in the rate of inflation can be seen from Table I, which shows that the cost of living increased at a lower rate in 1973 than a year earlier in only 11 of the 58 listed countries. The worst rates of inflation among developed countries were experienced in Italy (10.1%), Finland (9.9%), Japan (8.9%), Switzerland (8.5%), the U.K. (8.3%), and The Netherlands (8.1%). In Italy, apart from efforts to restrict the growth of bank credit, the authorities introduced an anti-inflationary package that included a temporary freeze on prices of a wide range of products, mainly foodstuffs and other essential consumer goods. Rents paid by lower income groups were frozen until Jan. 31, 1974. The price freeze was followed by the imposition of controls on the pricing policies of the large industrial enterprises.

In Japan higher import prices together with higher wages contributed to a sharp rise in the cost of living. The anti-inflationary policy introduced in Switzerland at the end of 1972 relied mainly on various measures designed to check the growth of the money supply. They were supplemented, however, by wage and price guidelines that determined price rises to be justified only so long as they did not exceed increases in costs.

In the U.K. the freeze on prices and incomes introduced in November 1972 ended early in 1973. It was followed by the so-called Stage Two of the program for controlling inflation, during which prices were allowed to rise only as the result of increases in "allowable" costs. There were also limitations on net profit

Table I. Cost of Living—Selected Countries

Country	Index (1963 = 100) 1971	1972	1973*	Annual % change 1963–70 (average)	Annual % changes over preceding year 1971	1972	1973†
Developed market economies							
Finland	155	166	178	5.6	6.1	7.1	9.9
Netherlands, The	152	164	174	5.0	7.8	7.9	8.1
Denmark	159	170	174	6.0	6.0	6.9	4.2
Japan	153	160	172	5.3	6.3	4.6	8.9
New Zealand	150	161	171	4.5	10.3	7.3	7.5
U.K.	148	159	169	4.4	9.6	7.4	8.3
Norway	149	160	169	4.9	6.4	7.4	7.6
Sweden	145	154	161	4.4	7.4	6.2	5.9
Italy	134	142	153	3.6	4.7	6.0	10.1
Switzerland	135	144	153	3.4	7.1	6.7	8.5
France	138	147	153	3.9	5.3	6.5	6.3
Austria	134	142	151	3.6	4.7	6.0	7.9
Belgium‡	134	142	149	3.7	3.9	6.0	7.2
Australia	132	139	147	3.1	6.4	5.3	6.5
Germany, West	127	134	142	2.8	4.9	5.5	7.6
Canada	130	136	142	3.4	3.2	4.6	6.0
U.S.	132	137	142	3.5	3.9	3.8	5.2
Less developed countries							
Indonesia	71,797	76,466	92,301	154.3	4.3	6.5	24.3
Uruguay	2,859	5,046	8,512	56.6	23.6	76.5	100.8
Chile	718	1,278	2,882	29.1	20.1	78.0	211.6
Brazil	1,300	1,514	1,658	40.5	20.1	16.5	13.1
Argentina	512	812	1,242	21.0	34.7	58.6	71.5
Vietnam, South	698	875	1,100	28.9	18.3	25.4	34.3
Cambodia	227	284	462	4.0	72.0	25.1	89.3
Laos	302	378	446	16.9	1.3	25.2	27.4
Yugoslavia	286	334	392	13.7	16.2	16.8	20.6
Korea, South	280	313	317	13.9	12.4	11.8	2.9
Colombia	214	245	290	10.2	8.6	14.5	23.9
Peru	220	236	250	10.9	6.8	7.3	6.4
Turkey‡	185	214	231	6.6	18.5	15.7	12.1
India	177	186	203	8.1	2.9	5.1	12.2
Bolivia	156	167	201	6.1	3.3	7.1	26.4
Israel	154	174	199	4.7	11.6	13.0	17.1
Portugal	163	180	196	5.6	11.6	10.4	10.1
Philippines	170	188	196	5.8	14.8	10.6	7.1
Spain	168	182	195	6.5	8.4	8.3	9.6
Ireland	158	172	186	5.5	9.0	8.9	10.7
Pakistan	144	156	175	4.6	5.1	8.3	15.9
Jamaica	145	154	170	4.5	6.6	6.2	14.1
Ecuador	146	158	169	4.4	8.1	8.2	9.7
South Africa§	133	142	152	3.2	6.4	6.8	9.4
Mexico‡	134	141	150	3.5	3.2	5.2	7.9
Syria	126	128	148	2.8	4.1	1.6	16.5
Tanzania‡	130	143	148	3.2	4.0	10.0	5.0
Sri Lanka	130	139	147	2.8	7.4	7.0	7.3
Tunisia	135	138	145	3.6	5.5	2.2	5.1
Ethiopia‡	144	135	144	5.2	0.0	−6.3	6.7
Puerto Rico	128	132	137	3.0	4.1	3.1	3.8
Greece	121	126	136	2.4	2.5	4.1	8.8
Iraq	121	127	135	2.3	3.4	5.0	6.3
Iran	119	126	135	1.9	4.4	5.9	5.5
Thailand	119	124	134	2.3	1.7	4.2	9.8
Dominican Republic	108	117	129	0.7	2.8	8.3	12.2
Singapore	110	112	127	1.1	1.9	1.8	14.4
Malta	116	120	128	1.9	1.8	3.4	9.4
Cyprus	114	120	126	1.4	3.6	5.3	5.9
Venezuela	115	120	122	1.6	2.7	3.4	3.4
Guatemala	106	107	118	1.0	−0.9	0.9	11.3

*January–June (average).
†First half 1973 over first half 1972.
‡Excluding rent.
§White population only.
Sources: International Monetary Fund, *International Financial Statistics;* United Nations, *Monthly Bulletin of Statistics;* International Labour Office, *Bulletin of Labour Statistics.*

Potash:
see Mining

Poultry:
see Agriculture and Fisheries

Power:
see Energy; Engineering Projects; Industrial Review

Presbyterians:
see Religion

margins on domestic sales. Prices of imported goods and fresh food subject to seasonal or external fluctuations were excluded from the controls. In Stage Three, introduced in the autumn, the various controls became somewhat more flexible.

The Netherlands was one of a small number of countries that revalued its currency in the hope of stabilizing prices. Earlier, at the end of 1972, the authorities had introduced price controls; they allowed price increases only if costs went up. However, in the production of goods no more than one-third of the increases in wage costs could be passed on in higher prices, and in the case of services only three-quarters of the increase could be passed on. The controls covered prices of goods and services sold on the home market.

A second group of developed countries experienced increases in the cost of living at what were until recently exceptionally high rates: Austria (7.9%), West Germany (7.6%), Norway (7.6%), New Zealand (7.5%), and Belgium (7.2%). In Austria the anti-inflationary program called for "extreme restraint" on wages and prices. A commitment was obtained from the labour unions not to negotiate for new wage agreements before the old ones expired. The authorities undertook not to support any price increases beyond the rate contemplated in transition to the new value-added tax system. Companies were asked to submit exact calculations along with their requests for price increases.

West Germany remained one of the very few countries in which the authorities refused to resort to direct control of prices and incomes. Instead, they continued to rely heavily on a tighter monetary policy. Thus, the stabilization programs introduced in 1973 consisted of fiscal and monetary measures and policies designed to increase competition. In contrast, Norway tried to combat inflation by means of exchange rate appreciation and incomes policies. Following government initiative a tripartite agreement was concluded early in 1973 between employers, labour unions, and the government. It relied mainly on higher subsidies and compensation of enterprises affected by the devaluations of other currencies. In New Zealand there was yet another freeze on prices and even a longer one on wages.

In only six industrial countries the cost of living increased by less than 7%. Most of them relied on what was becoming increasingly a rather familiar mixture of fiscal and monetary measures as well as direct controls of incomes and prices. In the U.S. many of the controls were discontinued early in 1973. However, in June a price freeze was imposed for 60 days. This was followed by Phase Four of the anti-inflationary policy. Mandatory and covering most sectors of the economy, it required an early notification of planned increases in wages and prices. Price increases were not to be higher than the rises in costs. The limitation on profit margins was also to continue. Exempt from the controls were: small businesses, public utility rates, interest rates, and rents. A special

Table II. Indices of Food Prices in Relation to Cost-of-Living Index

(1963 = 100)

Country	1970	1971	1972	1973*
Developed market economies				
Denmark	104	104	107	110†
U.K.	99	100	102	106†
Sweden	102	104	107	106†
Finland	104	101	103	105†
Japan	105	105	104	105
Canada	98	97	99	104
U.S.	99	98	99	104†
Norway	103	103	103	103†
France	98	99	101	102†
Australia	101	99	97	101
Belgium	101	99	100	101
Austria	100	99	98	99
New Zealand	101	99	97	98
Italy	96	96	96	97
Germany, West	95	94	94	95
Netherlands, The	98	94	93	93†
Less developed countries				
Chile	101	105	126	135‡
Vietnam, South	134	129	133	135
Cambodia	101	115	117	123
Indonesia	103	101	105	114
Thailand	111	109	112	114†
Pakistan	106	106	109	113
Philippines	118	116	118	111
India	109	107	106	110
Paraguay	96	99	101	109†
Yugoslavia	100	101	103	109
Puerto Rico	106	107	108	109
Colombia	97	96	100	108
Malta	103	101	102	108†
Greece	102	104	104	108
South Africa§	102	101	101	106
Ethiopia	109	108	101	105†
Sri Lanka	110	104	103	105
Argentina	99	104	107	105†
Singapore	98	99	99	104
Syria	104	103	102	104
Iran	100	102	104	104‡
Cyprus	102	103	105	104†
Ireland	96	95	98	103
Guatemala	101	100	100	103
Morocco	99	101	103	103‡
Peru	101	101	102	102
Kenya	103	104	104	102†
Iraq	99	99	99	101†
Mexico	102	101	101	101‡
Venezuela	96	96	99	100‡
Dominican Republic	98	101	98	98
Laos	83	82	89	95
Spain	94	94	94	95
Israel	93	95	91	92†
Portugal	98	95	94	91‡

*January–June (average) except where stated otherwise.
†January–July (average).
‡January–May (average).
§White population only.
Sources: United Nations, *Monthly Bulletin of Statistics;* International Labour Office, *Bulletin of Labour Statistics.*

Table III. Wholesale Prices for Selected Countries

Country	Index (1963 = 100) 1971	1972	1973*	Annual % change 1963–70 (average)	Annual % changes over preceding year 1971	1972	1973†
Developed market economies							
Finland	149	161	178	5.0	5.6	8.1	12.7
New Zealand	138	153	170	3.5	8.7	10.9	14.9
U.K.‡	138	147	153	3.6	7.8	6.5	6.3
Denmark	131	138	152	3.4	3.9	5.3	11.8
Sweden	130	137	146	3.4	3.2	5.4	7.4
France§	127	133	145	3.1	2.4	4.7	10.7
Canada	118	127	144	2.3	0.9	7.6	16.1
Netherlands, The	125	130	143	3.1	0.8	4.0	12.6
Italy	123	128	141	2.5	3.4	4.1	11.9
Norway	129	133	140	3.0	4.9	3.1	6.1
U.S.	121	126	138	2.3	4.1	4.1	11.3
Belgium	117	122	133	2.4	−0.8	4.3	10.8
Austria	128	134	132	2.9	4.9	4.7	0.8
Switzerland	114	118	127	1.6	1.8	3.5	8.5
Japan	112	112	123	1.6	0.0	0.0	10.8
Germany, West	112	116	121	1.0	4.7	3.6	6.1
Less de veloped countries							
Uruguay	2,821	5,357	9,796	56.9	18.9	89.9	122.8
Chile	785	1,335	3,281	31.1	17.9	70.1	223.6
Brazil	1,087	1,287	1,378	36.9	20.5	18.4	11.5
Argentina	436	770	1,130	17.7	39.3	76.6	66.4
Vietnam, South	372	495	626	17.7	19.2	33.1	34.3
Korea, South	235	267	277	11.6	8.8	13.6	4.9
Turkey	169	200	225	5.5	16.5	18.3	15.4
Yugoslavia§	179	199	214	6.5	15.4	11.2	10.9
Philippines	170	188	209	5.7	15.6	10.6	13.0
India	172	186	208	7.5	3.6	8.1	16.2
Tunisia	146	152	160	4.7	5.8	4.1	4.6
Syria	137	130	156	3.1	10.4	−5.1	17.3
Spain	132	141	151	3.2	5.6	6.8	7.9
South Africa	125	136	148	2.6	4.2	8.8	12.1
Thailand	117	126	146	2.3	0.0	7.7	19.7
Mexico	127	131	142	3.0	3.2	3.1	10.1
Greece	120	125	138	2.3	2.6	4.2	11.3
Iran	120	127	136	1.8	6.2	5.8	5.4
El Salvador	108	114	131	1.9	−5.3	5.6	19.1
Venezuela	120	124	128	2.1	3.4	3.3	4.1
Iraq	121	116	118	1.8	7.1	−4.1	2.6

*January–June (average).
†First half 1973 over first half 1972.
‡Prices of finished goods only.
§Prices of industrial products.
Sources: International Monetary Fund, *International Financial Statistics;* United Nations, *Monthly Bulletin of Statistics.*

UPI COMPIX

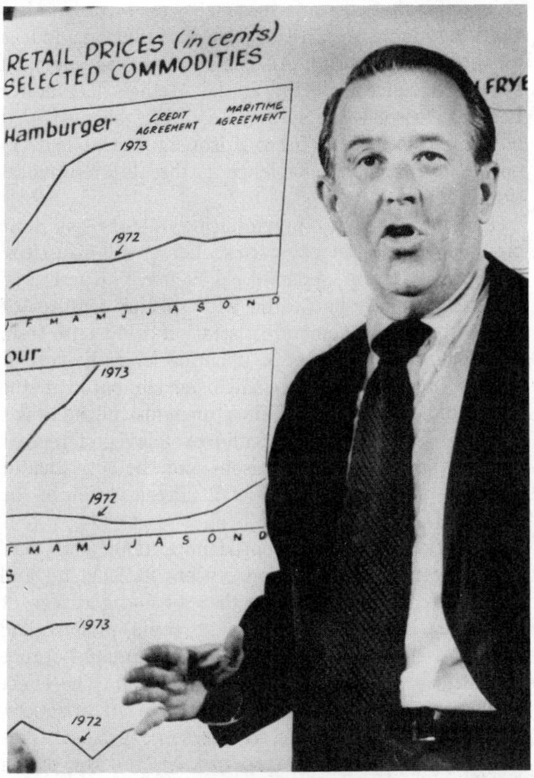

Sen. Henry M. Jackson demonstrates the relationship between the 1972 $1 billion Soviet grain deal and higher 1973 retail prices during a Washington, D.C., news conference held July 19, 1973.

two-stage program was instituted for food prices, but raw agricultural products were again excluded from the controls.

The problem of inflation was even more serious in the less developed countries; for instance, more than half of those included in Table I experienced rises in the cost of living of more than 10%. Most of the big increases took place in Latin America, notably Chile, Uruguay, and Argentina. In Chile the situation deteriorated even more after the military coup, when controls on prices were removed. Combined with a freeze on wages, this led to a sharp fall in real incomes of the majority of the population and, consequently, a sudden recession. On the other hand, there was a further reduction in the rate of inflation in Brazil, achieved mainly through tight control of wages and, to a lesser extent, prices.

Elsewhere, the highest rates of inflation were experienced in economies directly affected by the war in Southeast Asia: Cambodia, South Vietnam, and Laos. There was also a sharp deterioration in Indonesia after a few years of remarkable stabilization of prices.

On the whole, inflation gathered pace in the great majority of less developed countries as a result of increases in world prices, especially of foodstuffs. This was a particularly serious aspect of the problem, as high food prices hit hardest at the low-income groups, which spend a high proportion of their income on food.

The relatively higher increases in food prices are shown in Table II. (The figures were obtained in each case by dividing the index of food prices by the aggregate index of consumer prices. Hence, the figures over 100 indicate that prices of foodstuffs were rising faster than those of consumer goods and services as a whole, and vice versa.) Clearly, there were only a few countries in 1973 in which food prices did not increase at relatively higher rates. Sharp increases in food prices were even more widespread in less developed countries.

Wholesale Prices. The increases in wholesale prices, due in most countries to a combination of domestic and international factors, were both greater than those recorded for consumer prices and more ominous in the sense that it normally takes some time before they are reflected in a higher cost of living. In 1973 more than half of the industrial countries included in Table III had increases in wholesale prices of more than 10%, compared with only one country in 1972. In fact, in only one country did the index rise by less than 6%, a rate that was exceeded as recently as 1971 by only two countries. Moreover, the figures in Table III do not reflect the oil shortage and increases in oil prices that took place late in 1973. The situation deteriorated also in the less developed countries, where, with a few exceptions, the increases in wholesale prices were equally as dramatic as in the developed economies.

The main problem facing industrial countries toward the end of 1973—in addition to the oil crisis—was how to reduce the pressure on resources in their economies and stem a potentially dangerous tide of inflation without running once more into the problem of "stagflation"—the 1970–71 situation of severe wage-price inflation and stagnant consumer demand.

(MILIVOJE PANIC)

See also Commodities, Primary; Economy, World; Employment, Wages, and Hours; Income, National; Industrial Review; Investment, International; Merchandising; Money and Banking; Payments and Reserves, International; Stock Exchanges; Trade, International.

Prisons and Penology

The year opened more quietly than its predecessor; in the U.K. the most serious prison disturbance had occurred toward the end of 1972, when a major breakout at Gartree prison was barely foiled. The first prison unrest of 1973, a demonstration against the quality of food and general conditions, occurred at Saint Paul prison in Lyons, France, in April. It was followed by a much more serious mutiny in May involving about 200 prisoners who demanded, above all, speedier justice. Riot police were needed to bring this mutiny to an end, after 20 prisoners had been injured and much damage caused.

With the much reported riots at Toul prison in 1971 still in the public consciousness, there was real pressure on the French government to introduce reforms. On Aug. 1, 1973, Jean Taittinger, the minister of justice, obtained approval from the Council of Ministers for a bill to limit the period of detention of accused persons awaiting trial. This would end a major problem in the administration of French justice; previously about one-third of those held in detention were there on remand and awaiting trial, and the waiting period could last more than a year. For most accused, the maximum waiting period was reduced to six months and minor offenders were to be tried within 48 hours. But the French judiciary was already overburdened, and it was clear that financial provisions to increase the number of judges would have to be made in 1974.

A similar situation existed in Italy, where as many as half of those in detention were awaiting trial in 1973. During the year a series of riots spread through many Italian jails. The opening shots came, literally, at Fossany prison in northern Italy in July, when a

Printing:
see Industrial Review

prisoner shot three guards and barricaded himself in with two hostages. This was followed by a 26-hour rampage of violence and destruction at Rome's 19th-century Queen of Heaven prison after inmates had seized control. Trouble flared up in a dozen other jails, including those of Milan, Trieste, Civitavecchia, Avezzano, Veletri, Naples, and Catania.

Luxurious Rebibbia in Rome was no exception. In the separate women's section of Rebibbia, female prisoners organized a rooftop demonstration, chanting "Men, reforms, and Zagari." Whether they would eventually get conjugal visits remained to be seen, but they did obtain a promise from Mario Zagari, the Italian minister of justice, that he would follow up prison and penal code reform measures already before Parliament "with constant, inexorable pressure."

Late summer also saw new riots in U.S. prisons. At the Oklahoma state prison at McAlester, nearly 1,000 prisoners destroyed an entire industrial area in disturbances that lasted almost a week, involved the deaths of four inmates, and cost around $25 million. There was also trouble at the Ft. Leavenworth, Kan., federal penitentiary (one guard killed) and at the state prisons at Michigan City, Ind., and Stateville, Ill.

Prevention of Riots. A good deal was known about such disturbances in general. It had been summed up by the U.S. penologist Vernon Fox in his now famous remark: "The way to make a bomb is to build a strong perimeter and generate pressure inside" ("Why Prisoners Riot," *Federal Probation,* vol. 35, March 1971). His thinking was further refined by 1973 when it was found that, although pressure inside the strong perimeter was determined by two main factors—the kinds of inmates and the nature of the control system used—there also had to be a precipitating factor leading to the explosion itself (*see* P. H. Shapland, "Thoughts on Disturbances in Prison," *Prison Service Journal,* vol. 11, July 1973).

As for the kind of inmate, it was important to avoid having too high a concentration of long-term, psychologically abnormal, and aggressive prisoners in any one institution. Control was a question of regime and what might be called style of management, the important point being that easy and reasonably open communication could increase early awareness of tension and lead to appropriate action. Also important was sufficient space. Evidence collected at the Medical Center for Federal Prisons in Springfield, Mo., showed that physical closeness to other prisoners was at least as powerful a trigger to violence as threats or provocations.

The more general precipitating factors could be grouped into three categories: perceived injustices, general frustration, and external events. The perceived injustices usually had to do with specific features of prison treatment. General frustration could arise from boredom, the need to seek attention by some sort of action. Interestingly, this had been compared to the conditions behind certain kinds of industrial sabotage. External events included radio or television reports of disturbances in other prisons and the activities of outside organizations like PROP (Preservation of the Rights of Prisoners) in the U.K.

A special factor of potential importance was that, beginning in August, prison officers in England and Wales refused to work more than 14 hours a week of overtime. Previously, officers at some prisons had worked as much as 70 hours a week, largely because recruitment of new officers had fallen off. The effect of the partial overtime ban was to curtail prisoners' leisure activities, particularly in some prisons. This was a serious and risky step to take, and the prison officers' union no doubt realized that the action would lead to pressure on the government.

Parole Systems. A subject of considerable interest to comparative penology was parole. Pioneered in the U.S., parole existed mainly in English-speaking countries such as Australia, Canada, and the U.K. Countries with systems of criminal procedure and penal codes based on Roman law would have had some difficulty in introducing an exact parallel. France, West Germany, and Austria, for example, had systems of conditional release, but these were regulated by the penal codes, with little of the freedom of action that most parole boards enjoyed. Furthermore, conditional release was not normally accompanied by the kind of supervision and support in the community that were the hallmarks of true parole. The effect of conditional release on the prison population was relatively minor as compared with parole. It was really more akin to remission, which, in some countries, was an automatic shortening of the prison sentence that could only be lost by bad behaviour. Another and more sweeping measure to reduce the prison population was the declaration of periodic amnesties, used mainly in less developed countries.

Among the countries that did have parole, the basic principle might be the same but there were practical differences. Some of these were brought out at an Anglo-American Conference on the Treatment of Offenders, held in April and arranged by the Ditchley Foundation. In the U.K., for example, parole supervision was carried out by a probation officer, whereas the U.S. had separate parole officers whose sole function was to deal with parolees. Where indeterminate sentences existed, as in the state of California, the principal question posed by parole was "when?" Where sentences were determinate (that is, fixed) a second question was "whether?"

For prisoners serving determinate sentences, parole, if granted, constituted an earlier release and was therefore a source of hope. But it also introduced an element of uncertainty and anxiety that prisoners in

WIDE WORLD

Debris is scattered throughout a cell area after a riot by inmates of the Walpole (Mass.) State Prison on May 18, 1973. It took some 150 state policemen to quell the disturbance.

penal systems without parole did not experience. When the earliest date for parole consideration arrived—often after one-third of the sentence had been served—expectations were aroused, only to be dashed if parole was refused. If it was refused several times, considerable bitterness could ensue. There was still much argument as to whether and how much to tell individual prisoners of the reasons that had led to parole refusal. Most of those who favoured informing prisoners felt it was a matter of justice. Opponents feared it would lead to the growth of case law, greater formality, and inflexibility.

Many criminologists regarded parole decisions purely as exercises in risk prediction. Practical penologists tended to reject this view, partly because the known good parole predictors, such as school and work records, onset of delinquency, and number of types of offenses, usually lay in the past. The prisoner could do nothing about them, and this only served to increase his cynicism. In addition, it was important, in simple human terms, to take into account such factors as deterioration resulting from continued imprisonment and the possible saving of a marriage through early release (with consequent improvement in the chances of rehabilitation).

Looking at parole from a more general viewpoint, it could be seen as yet another gradation between complete loss of freedom in a penal institution and its total restoration. Other gradations already practiced in many penal systems in 1973 were work-release schemes (when the prisoner spent the last part of his sentence working in a factory or office but returned to the prison or hostel at night) and the frequent home leaves or furloughs provided in the Swedish penal system.

Special risks and special problems arose with certain types of sex offenders who were eligible for parole. The definition of what constituted a punishable sex offense differed from country to country. Thus, in many countries—including Denmark, The Netherlands, Sweden, and the U.K.—homosexual conduct between consenting adults in private was no longer punishable. All countries protected children, though the precise legal definition of what constituted a child or minor differed.

Those who offend against children—often because of fear of sexual contact with adults—constituted a special parole risk, especially if they already had a history of recidivism or if there was an element of compulsion in their offense. And while those who refused all treatment were unlikely to be paroled anywhere, by 1973 different countries had developed different solutions for those who were willing to undergo treatment.

A small percentage were treated successfully by intensive individual or group psychotherapy. Others, notably in Denmark, were treated by a modified form of castration in which the testicles were removed and replaced by plastic substitutes. Since this was an irreversible process, however, medical experts in other countries, such as the U.S. and the U.K., preferred antilibidinal drugs, usually certain types of female sex hormones that could be given orally or implanted under the skin. Oral treatment, either with sex hormones or with other medication, could be discontinued at any time and was suitable only for those already strongly motivated to control their sexual drive. Implants lasted over a period of months. Such treatment was sometimes preceded by aversion therapy while the potential parolee was still in prison. Results were reasonably encouraging, but much depended on the correct matching of patient with treatment.

RICHARD SEVERO—THE NEW YORK TIMES

A social worker leads inmates in a singing class at the State of Mexico Penitentiary outside Toluca. A model institution, it encouraged family visitations and condoned overnight conjugal visits.

Criticisms. Particularly in the U.S., increasing public concern over the state of the prison system was reflected in the appearance of several books aimed at the layman. The most widely publicized was *Kind and Usual Punishment,* in which Jessica Mitford made a devastating critique of existing penal institutions and concluded that prisons per se had outlived their usefulness and should be abolished.

While hardly ready to embrace such a radical solution, delegates to the fourth Conference of Heads of Prison Administrations, held in Oxford, Eng., in September under the auspices of the International Penal and Penitentiary Foundation, addressed many of the problems and deficiencies that had angered Mitford. The subject was "Communication and Democratization in the Penitentiary Field." This led to discussions on communications between staff members; between staff and inmates; and between the prison and the outside world, including access by the media to prisons and to the media by prisoners. Also touched on were such fairly contentious subjects as the possibility of negotiations by prisoners on such questions as earnings. Trade unions for prisoners were still some way off, and the difficulties of combining maximum security with real democracy were considerable. Nevertheless, a great deal of heartsearching about these questions had now begun. (HUGH J. KLARE)

See also Crime.

Profits

The data available on profits at the end of 1973 suggested that it was a banner year for the world's corporations, despite currency crises and monetary unrest. Only five countries publish current data on profits, the U.S., Canada, Great Britain, West Germany, and Japan, and new records were achieved in all but West Germany. But the data were misleading. They extended only to midyear for all of the countries cited except the U.S., where results for the third quarter were available. If the facts for the entire year had been recorded, they would probably have indicated that 1973 began well for profits but ended badly.

By the beginning of 1973, the cyclical expansion

of the free world's major economies had reached boom proportions. International trade continued its rapid expansion, notwithstanding the abandonment early in the year of fixed exchange rates and subsequent wide swings in currency values. As the year progressed, inflation, which had already reached disturbingly high rates in 1972, accelerated further. Capacity limits were reached in an increasing number of industries, both intensifying the inflationary effect of rising demand and creating bottlenecks that impeded further industrial expansion. In a number of countries, unit labour costs rose as wages outstripped productivity gains, adding cost-push to the prevailing demand-pull inflation. The governments of the countries concerned tried to stem the inflationary spiral, mainly through the use of restrictive monetary policies. In some cases they supplemented such measures with incomes policies bearing directly on wages, prices, and profits. By midyear the rapid surge of output in many countries was already beginning to moderate. This was largely a result of the retarding force of monetary restraint, but capacity limitations also played a role.

Even before the oil crisis began in October, profits were beginning to experience the eroding effects of these combined influences: slower growth of business volume, increased interest expense because of tight money conditions, rising unit labour costs, and, in some cases, direct government controls and sharply higher exchange rates. In the normal course of events, profits might have followed a typical cyclical pattern of decline. But this prospect was dramatically changed when, following renewed warfare by Egypt and Syria against Israel, the major Arab oil-producing countries decided to use their oil as a weapon for inducing the industrial world to pressure Israel into a settlement along the lines they desired. (*See* MIDDLE EASTERN AFFAIRS.)

The economic impact of these restrictions in oil supplies would depend on the duration of the curtailment. But by the end of 1973, it became apparent that the major non-Communist industrial nations could not escape some economic dislocation and, for a few, serious adverse effects were within the realm of possibility.

Table I. United States: Corporate Profits and Related Indicators

Period	Seasonally adjusted annual rates Profits (in $000,000,000): Before taxes (including inventory profits)	Inventory profits	After taxes	Seasonally adjusted: Profits per dollar of sales (cents)*	Ratio of profits (after taxes) to income originating in corporations (%)†	Ratio of price to unit labour cost index‡
1971: First quarter	75.8	5.0	38.8	4.0	8.5	96.6
Second quarter	79.2	5.0	40.8	4.2	8.8	97.4
Third quarter	82.0	6.1	43.9	4.2	9.3	97.5
Fourth quarter	80.2	3.6	43.8	4.1	9.1	97.7
1972: First quarter	87.3	6.6	46.7	4.2	9.4	97.5
Second quarter	89.1	6.7	47.7	4.2	9.3	98.3
Third quarter	92.2	6.9	49.3	4.3	9.5	99.8
Fourth quarter	98.6	7.3	52.7	4.4	9.8	101.3
1973: First quarter	111.9	15.4	59.2	4.7	10.5	103.4
Second quarter	121.3	21.4	63.9	4.8	11.1	105.4
Third quarter	121.9	17.0	64.0	—	10.8	107.3

*After taxes, all manufacturing.
†All industries.
‡Manufacturing; 1967=100.
Sources: *Survey of Current Business* (July and November 1973); *Business Conditions Digest* (November 1973).

Table II. Canada: Profits and Related Measures

Period	Seasonally adjusted annual rates (Can$000,000): Corporate profits before taxes (1)	Inventory profits (2)	Profits on operations before taxes (1)-(2)	Manufacturing industry indexes, seasonally adjusted, 1962=100: Labour income per unit of output	Profits per unit of output
1971: First quarter	7,816	492	7,324	119.6	89.3
Second quarter	8,616	840	7,776	120.3	99.5
Third quarter	9,576	752	8,824	120.0	111.1
Fourth quarter	9,924	568	9,356	120.1	104.1
1972: First quarter	10,232	1,248	8,984	121.0	119.0
Second quarter	10,696	576	10,120	122.4	116.7
Third quarter	10,728	1,004	9,724	125.1	114.0
Fourth quarter	11,688	1,256	10,432	125.2	118.9
1973: First quarter	13,232	1,736	11,496	124.5	148.7
Second quarter	13,864	1,968	11,896	127.3	138.9

Source: *Bank of Canada Review* (November 1973).

Table III. United Kingdom: Company Income and Related Indicators

Period	Seasonally adjusted quarterly rates company income (£000,000) Income arising in the United Kingdom: Total	Gross trading profits of companies	Rent and non-trading income	Income from abroad	Manufacturing industry indexes, seasonally adjusted, 1970=100: Output per person employed at 1970 prices	Wages and salaries per unit of output	Wholesale prices
1971: First quarter	2,608	1,406	582	620	101.1	105.4	106.3
Second quarter	2,693	1,445	600	648	103.2	105.9	108.7
Third quarter	2,708	1,435	634	639	104.5	108.3	110.3
Fourth quarter	2,757	1,470	644	643	104.4	109.9	110.8
1972: First quarter	2,830	1,499	673	658	104.8	111.8	112.1
Second quarter	2,970	1,614	704	652	108.3	115.2	113.5
Third quarter	3,161	1,692	771	698	108.7	118.8	115.6
Fourth quarter	3,376	1,779	798	799	112.7	119.6	118.0
1973: First quarter	3,759	1,950	904	905	117.2	117.3	119.5
Second quarter	3,810	1,988	944	878	117.3	121.1	120.1
Third quarter	—	—	—	—	—	—	124.0

Source: Central Statistical Office, *Economic Trends* (October 1973).

Table IV. West Germany: Profit and Income Developments

Period	Income from entrepreneurial activity and property in DM. 000,000; without adjustment for seasonal variation: Before income taxes	After income taxes	Share of national income (%)	1962=100; seasonally adjusted: Output per man-hour in industry	Unit labour costs	Industrial wholesale prices
1971: First half	84,730	66,650	30.7	164	136	112.0
Second half	97,430	78,390	31.8	166	141	113.1
1972: First half	91,110	73,480	30.3	172	142	115.0
Second half	103,600	81,420	31.1	178	146	117.2
1973: First half	102,030	79,320	30.1	186	148	121.7
July–August	—	—	—	186	156	124.7

Sources: *Wirtschaft & Statistik* No. 9 (1973); *Statistische Beihefte zu den Monatsberichten der Deutschen Bundesbank, Reihe 4* (November 1973).

United States. Corporate profits before taxes rose dramatically in the U.S. in the first half of 1973. The seasonally adjusted annual rate of increase was 54% from the final quarter of 1972 to the first quarter of 1973, and 34% from the first to second quarter (Table I). Profit margins also rose, from 4.4% at the end of 1972 to 4.8% by midyear 1973. Among the major influences contributing to these gains, one of the most important was inflation, which worked its effects on profits in two ways. The first and most readily identifiable in the data was through inventory profits. These arise from the difference between the inflated replacement cost of goods taken out of inventory and the lower cost at which those items are charged to production. Such profits reflect merely capital gains, as it were, and they are not properly regarded as earnings on operations. Yet they contributed no less than half of the gain in before-tax profits in the year between the third quarter of 1972 and the corresponding quarter of 1973. Never before in the history of the U.S. had inventory profits been so high.

The second major impact of inflation is not explicitly identifiable in the profits data. It is that, contrary to early business apprehensions, U.S. incomes policy was more effective in restraining wages than prices. The shift in January 1973 from mandatory controls to greater reliance on voluntary compliance resulted in so sharp a burst of price inflation that the authorities felt impelled to adopt a new freeze on most prices in June. The average size of wage settlements, on the other hand, declined in the first half of 1973. Thus, in spite of significant increases in unit labour costs, the increase in prices was greater and the ratio of profits after taxes to income originating in corporations was the highest since 1968.

The sweeping currency changes that occurred in 1973 also played a double role in increasing the profits of U.S. corporations. First, the relative decline in the value of the dollar increased U.S. international competitiveness, thereby stimulating sales of U.S. goods and services. In addition, the relative upward valuation of the Japanese yen and the European currencies increased the dollar value of local currencies earned by the foreign subsidiaries of U.S. corporations.

Canada. Corporate profits in Canada traced essentially the same pattern as in the U.S. (Table II). Before taxes, they rose at a seasonally adjusted annual rate of 53% between the fourth quarter of 1972 and the first quarter of 1973, and at a rate of 19% between the first and second quarters of 1973. Inventory profits, although large, played a relatively smaller role in the profits increase than they did in the U.S.; they accounted for 31% of the increase in the second quarter annual rate of profits above the level of 1972 as a whole.

As in the U.S., unit labour costs rose but prices climbed even faster. The result was a sharp increase in profits per unit of output.

United Kingdom. British data through mid-1973 gave little warning of the difficulties that were to plague the economy by the year's end. Output expanded at an exceptionally rapid rate at the beginning of the year and then continued to grow more moderately into the third quarter. The worldwide pretax income of British companies climbed 28% during the interval between the second quarters of 1972 and 1973 (Table III), and by mid-1973 it had reached the highest level in history. Gross trading profits arising in the U.K. (operating income before inventory valuation adjustment, depreciation, interest expense, and income taxes) were up 23% during the same period, while rent and nontrading income rose 34% and income from abroad, boosted by the marked depreciation of the pound sterling, surged 35%.

Although wage rates climbed rapidly (more than 15% between second quarter 1972 and second quarter 1973), much of the resulting impact on costs was moderated by productivity gains (8.3%). And, in Britain as in the U.S. and Canada, the increase in wages and salaries per unit of output (5.1%) was exceeded by the inflation of prices (7.3%). Thus, profit margins expanded.

West Germany. Profits in West Germany appeared to have fared reasonably well despite the upward valuation of the mark and governmental restraints on inflation. Exact results cannot be determined for the country because the published data combine corporate profits with professional income and with earnings from farming, rental, and lending activities. The resulting overall category is called income from entrepreneurial activity and property (IEP). While expansion in IEP had lagged behind the growth of national income in 1971 and 1972, the inflationary climate of 1973 permitted it to keep pace with other incomes, at least in the first half of the year. Before taxes IEP was up 12% over the first half of 1972 (Table IV). However, because advance payments of corporate income taxes rose particularly sharply, IEP after taxes advanced only 8%.

Corporate profits probably were not quite as high as the data on IEP would suggest. Wages and salaries per man-hour rose 12% between the first half of 1972 and that of 1973, while productivity increased only 8%. Accordingly, unit labour costs climbed 4.2%. And, while industrial prices gained 5.8% over the same period, the small spread between price and cost increases may not have sufficed, in the face of stagnant output and reduced profits on export sales, to increase corporate profits in the aggregate.

Japan. The year presented Japan with an initial period of rapid growth and the worst problem of inflation in more than two decades. By November wholesale prices were 22.3% above a year earlier. The adverse effects on profits of slower growth in the second quarter were evidently more than offset by the favourable impact of accelerating inflation, for corporate profits climbed rapidly in both the first and second quarters of 1973. By the second quarter, they were about 60% higher than in the comparable period of 1972. Profit margins, moreover, also expanded sharply.

The latest data, drawn from a survey of 539 corporations listed on the Tokyo Stock Exchange, suggested that both business volume and profits continued to expand into the third quarter of 1973. For the semiannual accounting period ended September 1973, these corporations reported a 16% gain in sales volume and a 24% increase in before-tax profits relative to the preceding period, compared with 15 and 39% gains, respectively, in the six-month period ended in March. (GERALD A. POLLACK)

See also Merchandising; Stock Exchanges.

Publishing

The pressure of economic conditions and commercial interests, the stringency or chaos of libel laws, changing public standards, failure to formulate clear definitions of obscenity, and the anxiety of governments to prevent news from being published that would endanger the national interest continued in 1973 to erode the right of publishers and their editors to decide what should be published. It was not, perhaps, surprising that the general admiration of the courage shown during 1972–73 by U.S. papers and magazines in bringing to light corruption in high places was sometimes tinged with envy of the conditions that had made it possible for them to do so while remaining free, or at least relatively so, of risk of prosecution or official censure.

As a result of the U.S. Supreme Court's "Caldwell decision" in June 1972, which held that reporters had no absolute right under the First Amendment to withhold confidential sources of information from grand juries, scores of newsmen and papers were faced with subpoenas. One of the most dramatic cases was that of William T. Farr, who, while covering the Charles Manson murder trial in 1970 for the *Los Angeles Herald-Examiner,* had published a story based on a witness's confidential testimony to prosecutors. Farr refused the judge's later order to reveal the source of his information and, after a lengthy legal struggle, was jailed in November 1972. After 46 days in jail, he was finally released in January, pending a new appeal. Other examples included the revelation in February that former U.S. Attorney General John Mitchell had authorized FBI wiretaps of several Washington correspondents' telephones and that these taps had continued for almost three years.

The unprecedented number of such actions prompted debate over the need for a federal "shield law." Faced with a welter of disagreement over what form the law should take, Congress postponed any decision. More than 20 states, however, had some

Psychiatry: *see* Medicine
Psychology: *see* Behavioural Sciences
Public Utilities: *see* Cooperatives; Energy; Industrial Review; Transportation

POPPERFOTO/PICTORIAL PARADE

Freed Rhodesian journalist Peter Niesewand arrived in London in May 1973 after experiencing a "living nightmare"—71 days in a tiny Rhodesian jail cell.

form of shield law protecting reporters. Worries that subpoena pressures could intimidate valuable sources of information into silence were alleviated somewhat by the number of spectacular "leaks" to U.S. journalists throughout 1973.

In France a political controversy with overtones of the U.S. Watergate affair erupted in December after a staff member of *Le Canard enchaîné* walked in upon "plumbers" installing eavesdropping equipment in the almost-completed new offices of the satirical weekly. The publication had taken the lead in revealing most of the scandals that had been cropping up within the French government since 1970 and had been dogged in its pursuit of the financial dealings of Gaullists especially. As charges that the bugs were the work of counterespionage forces under the interior minister, Raymond Marcellin, began to carry more weight than those claiming the whole thing was a circulation-building spoof, the affair was added to other issues threatening confidence in the Pierre Messmer government. Particularly disturbing were the implications behind Marcellin's statement in the National Assembly that the charges were a plot to discredit him and that those who get government secrets by bribery should not complain about being bugged.

Meanwhile, in many parts of the world, censorship and persecution of publishers, journalists, and authors were spreading, and Brazil, Cuba, Greece, Indonesia, and Singapore were added to the International Press Institute's list of countries in which the situation had deteriorated. In Chile, one of the few countries in Latin America with a tradition of press freedom, newspapers and books were publicly burned, and many papers and magazines were closed after a military coup overthrew Pres. Salvador Allende's government in September; those publications that remained were forced to submit to a military censor.

Newspapers. For all concerned with the position of newspapers, 1973 would be remembered as the year that saw the emergence of a problem that seemed unlikely to be soon resolved and that by midyear had assumed crisis proportions—a worldwide shortage of newsprint. The situation in India served both to indicate the scale of the problem and to illuminate its underlying causes. By October almost all the country's 521 daily papers, faced with closure, had drastically reduced size and stopped Sunday editions—in a country still incompletely covered by broadcasting and with a high growth potential for a multilingual press and a long tradition of liberal, outspoken journalism. Encouraged by a buyers' market during the 1960s the government had saved foreign currency by the bargain buying of newsprint. When the demand for newsprint began to rise with the 1972–73 advertising boom in the major industrialized countries, India was unable to buy newsprint anywhere at any price; producers were restricting supplies to regular, bulk-buying customers.

India's failure to foresee change in international economic conditions pinpointed the attitudes that had everywhere helped to cause the crisis. Recession during the 1950s and '60s had discouraged investment in newsprint plants, and although producers had urged the need to achieve stability of supply by raising prices gradually to a level high enough to permit long-term planning and expansion, newspaper owners, struggling to meet rising wage bills and printing costs, had refused to listen. The situation was neatly summed up by Harford Thomas in October in *The Guardian,* one of the U.K.'s leading national daily papers: "Demand can swing from stagnation to boom in six months, but it takes two or three years to build a paper-making machine, and up to 90 years to grow a tree."

Policies and problems in the world's main newsprint sources—Canada, the U.S., Japan, Sweden, Finland, the Soviet Union—intensified the crisis. U.S. newspapers became the first to feel the grim side-effects of the current prosperity. The bare facts of newspaper growth were encouraging: *Editor & Publisher International Year Book* reported that in the U.S. there were 1,441 evening newspapers in 1972, compared with 1,425 a year earlier; evening circulation jumped from 36,115,127, to 36,431,856. Morning dailies showed a slight decline in numbers (337, a loss of 2) and in circulation (26,078,386, a loss of 37,745), but 13 new Sunday and weekend papers appeared, for a total of 603, with a combined circulation of 50,000,669. The overall increase in papers and sales, coupled with an unexpected 10% jump in advertising during the first half of 1973, prompted sharp new demands for newsprint, which by midsummer were averaging 5.4% more than the 10.3 million tons consumed in 1972. Not only were Canadian paper mills, which supplied 65% of all U.S. newsprint, unprepared for the steep rise in U.S. requests, but summer strikes at many of their major installations cut daily production from 28,000 to 22,000 tons and a nationwide Canadian rail strike in August temporarily froze all newsprint supplies. By late August, many papers were cutting back on pages, newsstand copies, and advertising, and some were forced to drop at least one edition a week. Even the return to peak production by year's end could not solve matters, for Canadian mill capacities could not meet projected requirements, and producers seemed reluctant to commit the $50 million–$100 million that a new mill could cost, given the relatively low profits on newsprint sales. Elsewhere, fears of overproduction resulting from uncoordinated expansion, of a sudden slump in demand, and of the environmental consequences of modern tree-felling and replanting policies and methods were combining to slow down expansion. Both Sweden and Finland, for example, had halted development of their pulp and paper industries to reassess forest growth potentials and regeneration plans.

In the U.K., where during January–June news-

Behind major revelations of the "Washington Post" in the Watergate case were editor Barry Sussman (left) and reporters Bob Woodward (centre) and Carl Bernstein (right). They were largely credited with bringing the "Post" its 1973 Pulitzer Prize for public service in journalism.

WALTER BENNETT—TIME MAGAZINE © 1973 TIME INC.

print demand rose by 20%; the closing (in late May, because of low profits) of the country's third largest newsprint mill, which had provided 10% of its supply, alerted newspaper owners to the difficulties of planned investment that, by September, were recognized worldwide as among the industry's major long-term problems. As more mills shut down during the summer and wage disputes reduced production at others, local papers began to fear closure and by August were cutting or canceling editions. By September even the national papers, despite their protected positions as bulk buyers, were reducing the number of pages and editions, restricting advertising space, and lowering limits on returns from distributors.

As in the U.S., the shortage hit the U.K. during an unprecedented boom in advertising. Circulation figures showed a comparatively static sales situation. During January–June 1973 the eight national dailies had achieved a net increase of only 170,000 copies for a total of 14.5 million, while the seven national Sunday papers had lost 100,000 copies. Advertising revenues, however, were rising at a level of 20% for the national papers and in May most local evening papers reported a 279% rise for January and February. This proved a mixed blessing for, although local papers could use the boom to fill their coffers, national papers were committed to a policy of increasing revenue from sales rather than advertising. A round of cover-price rises planned for 1973 was prevented by the government's price freeze. But since the price freeze was widely regarded as being partly responsible for the advertising boom—firms prevented from declaring increased profits were spending them on advertising—it seemed likely that when restraints on profits were relaxed, the boom would end and the national dailies might well have to open 1974 with a round of price rises, without the bait of bigger papers.

In most countries soaring newsprint prices increased the need for papers to raise cover prices or seek government aid. In November the price of newsprint in the U.S. reached $200 a ton, a $25-a-ton increase; in Greece there were five increases during the year; while in the U.K., with two increases already permitted by the Price Commission and a further one set for January 1974 that was expected to carry the price per metric ton to well over £100 by October, prices of up to £160 per metric ton were being paid on a flourishing black market. In France, where the government increased its annual press subsidy of more than £30 million by £400,000, by November national political weeklies and dailies had been forced to raise cover prices, and further increases were planned for early 1974. Newsprint prices in Italy, where no daily paper had shown a profit since 1969, had long been above the international level because of a tariff designed to protect the Italian newsprint industry. In Belgium, where papers had for long been in financial straits despite their protected position in a country without commercial television, the government in January granted a subsidy for 1973 of BFr. 100 million, which would be doubled in 1974. This enabled West German newspaper publishers to claim, in a 70-page memorandum to the government, that theirs was one of the few European newspaper industries to receive no official help.

In a year in which the newspaper industry was relatively free from industrial disputes, two records were broken. In April a printers' wage dispute caused the first West German newspaper strike in 21 years; and in July in Athens a printers' wage claim led to the first union strike in Greece since the 1967 coup. In the U.K., although industrial unrest smoldered throughout the year, only a single protest day materialized nationally. The most notable strike was the nine-day one preceding the closure on June 30 of the *Nottingham Guardian Journal,* formed when the *Journal,* the U.K.'s second oldest paper, founded in 1710, had been bought in 1953 by its junior rival. A long and acrimonious jurisdictional dispute had been caused by introduction of a new photoprinting process.

A widely mourned death was that of the 141-year-old *Göteborgs Handels- och Sjöfartstidning,* one of Sweden's most influential dailies. With a 1972–73 circulation of only just over 48,000, it closed in September after its owners failed to persuade the Swedish publisher Bonnier to finance it.

In August the *Detroit News* became the most fully automated large newspaper in the U.S. with the opening of an automated printing plant north of Detroit that was electronically linked to its downtown headquarters. The International Typographical Union local complained in court that the *News*'s direct transmis-

Members of the Newspaper Guild of New York, representing 1,400 editorial, commercial, and miscellaneous employees, picket the "Daily News" 42nd Street entrance, Nov. 5, 1973, after the union rejected new contract terms.

WIDE WORLD

sion of copy from editors to print eliminated their jobs, but the issue was sent back to the paper and the union for arbitration. Labour snags continued to hold up similar automation at a number of other papers, including the *New York Times.* Contracts between the New York City dailies and 13 unions expired March 30, and after a two-day Newspaper Guild strike at the *Daily News* was settled in November, six unions remained without contracts. The two major St. Louis papers, the *Post-Dispatch* and the *Globe-Democrat,* were struck for more than five weeks in the fall; at issue was the new *Post-Dispatch* automated printing plant that threatened to eliminate the jobs of local teamsters' union members.

The most striking confrontation between commercial interests and the press came from Italy, where in May a right-wing Catholic magazine publisher, Edilio Rusconi, acquired 50% of the shares in the company publishing Rome's leading paper, *Il Messaggero,* sacked its editor, Alessandro Perrone, and replaced him by right-wing journalist and author Luigi Barzini. Perrone, who with his sisters owned the remaining shares, refused to regard his dismissal as valid and, backed by editorial and printers' union pickets, prevented Barzini from entering the building. While the ensuing legal battle was dragging on, Rusconi was accused of being backed financially by a right-wing oil magnate, Angelo Moratti, who, with the Fiat Motor Co., already owned 70% of Italy's major papers, and Ferdinando Perrone admitted that he had sold his shares to Rusconi because under his cousin Alessandro *Il Messaggero* had become "a mouthpiece for left-wing extremism." A "day of silence" in June was followed by a one-day strike by the staffs of *Il Messaggero* and the Genoese daily *Il Secolo XIX* (published by the same company) and by a long-term strike at *Il Messaggero* that was instituted on July 17.

What had begun as the farcical situation of a paper with two editors threatened to end as a full-scale confrontation between journalists and owners when, in September, a strike was called by reporters on *Il Corriere della Sera,* Milan's largest and most influential paper, and its sister paper, *Il Corriere d'Informazione.* They were demanding advance information on changes of financial control and consultative rights in editorial policy and appointments. Before May both papers had been owned by the Crespi family, who had then sold two-thirds of their shares to Fiat and Moratti. There was some reason for the (pre-oil embargo) headline in an Italian political weekly: "The press is drowning in a sea of petroleum."

During the year some notable cases focused attention on the function of the press. Its investigation of the Watergate affair (*see* UNITED STATES) earned the *Washington Post* the Pulitzer Prize for public service in journalism. Credit went to the *Post*'s investigative team of Bob Woodward and Carl Bernstein (*see* BIOGRAPHY), whose relentless pursuit drew new attention to investigative reporting. Although most papers lacked the money, manpower, or desire to risk large investments in long-range stories that might never pan out, some, like the *Boston Globe* and Long Island's *Newsday,* found their investigative teams coming up with consistently valuable scoops. Although White House Press Secretary Ronald L. Ziegler publicly apologized in May to the *Post* for his past denunciations of news stories that turned out to be accurate, the long war between reporters and the administration flared again as Watergate and related scandals continued to dominate the headlines. A "leak" to the *Wall Street Journal* first forced Vice-Pres. Spiro Agnew to reveal that he was under federal investigation, and a succession of subsequent stories led Agnew to charge that he was being pilloried in the press and that newsmen were trampling on both his rights and the secrecy of grand jury hearings. In an unprecedented move, a U.S. district court judge authorized the vice-president's attorneys to subpoena newsmen in an attempt to find out who was responsible for the leaks. Agnew's resignation the following week rendered that decision moot.

In the U.K. the example of the U.S. media probably served as a salutary contrast to the thalidomide case. In a campaign to force the drug manufacturers to make a more generous settlement to parents in whose children thalidomide had caused crippling mutations, the *Sunday Times* presented detailed investigations and revelations—including lists of shareholders who might bring pressure on the company—until injunctions prevented further publication. Paradoxically, a case of a different flavour pressed the point. In midsummer, two popular Sunday papers, the *News of the World* and *The People,* vied with each other over a revelation that a government minister had been associating with a call girl. It was alleged that photographs had been offered to the newspaper, which had handed them to the police, and that national security was involved. It later became known that the photographs had been taken by the paper. Although two ministers resigned, most of the outrage was directed at the press. (*See* UNITED KINGDOM.)

Elsewhere, interference with press freedom took a more acute form. One case to attract wide attention was that of Peter Niesewand, Rhodesian correspondent for *The Guardian,* the British Broadcasting Corporation, and several international news agencies. After Rhodesian police had searched his house in November 1972, Niesewand was arrested on Feb. 20, 1973, held under a detention order, charged under the Official Secrets Act for reports concerning guerrilla activity on the Rhodesia–Mozambique border, and given a two-year sentence. His defense was upheld on May 3 by the Rhodesian appeal court, but he was forced to leave the country within hours. The objectivity of Niesewand's reporting was widely acknowledged, and the case was seen as a warning ges-

AUTHENTICATED NEWS INTERNATIONAL

Jane Shuttleworth, manager of "Mother's," a highly profitable mail-order firm, thumbs through a recent catalog offering everything from windmills to butter churns. The company's publications carry no cover date and back issues are sold along with current ones.

ture to journalists made by the Rhodesian government. (PETER FIDDICK; PAUL GRAY)

Magazines. In most countries the magazine market had become so much a consumer industry that it often seemed that new magazines were produced to fill gaps in the market for as long as they lasted, rather than to allow writers to communicate with readers. In the U.K., for example, the sex war kept up, with gains all around and with *Mayfair* claiming particularly high figures by the autumn. But then came the uncertainty caused by the government's new bill to limit public display, a move aimed at motion picture houses and magazine shops alike. Paul Raymond, publisher of *Men Only,* said he would happily take nudes off the cover, since everyone would still know what was inside. Some publishers felt it necessary to reassure retailers that they would stand behind them if they were fined, although no significant prosecutions took place. The teen-age boom was to be seen in the circulation rises of such established magazines as *New Musical Express* (up by 30,000 to 204,512 copies weekly in January–June 1973), *Fabulous-208* (up by 58%), and *Mirabelle* (up by 46%), as well as in the launching of seven new ventures by the International Publishing Corp. (IPC) in the first five months of the year.

The changes in the women's magazine market—traditional centre of the consumer-oriented field—could be read in the same light. In October IPC launched *Candida,* a new weekly for younger women, and folded it inside two months, despite a £250,000 budget. The year was characterized by announcements of new launches, with three planned for early 1974. Morgan-Grampian's purchase of *Over Twentyone,* which Audrey Slaughter had launched in 1972 with the former staff of *Vanity Fair,* represented a departure for a company with many trade and technical titles. Other newcomers included Link House Publications, with a home-building monthly called *Inhabit.*

Other areas, however, were not so fortunate. The success of *Time Out,* originally an "underground" magazine but increasingly bought for its comprehensive guide to London's films, theatres, and other events, moved two journalists to raise the cash for a magazine aimed at those who might want the information without *Time Out*'s radical politics. *Inside London* lasted three issues.

Private Eye, the fortnightly satirical magazine whose reputation had been built on its challenge to the British libel laws, was justified in some of its earlier allegations of widespread corruption in the awarding of local government building contracts. In 1973 charges were brought against John Poulson, head of a bankrupt firm of architects, and others.

(PETER FIDDICK)

In the U.S. the fortunes, format, and headquarters of *Saturday Review* came almost full circle in 1973, two years after promoters Nicolas Charney and John Veronis had taken over the New York weekly, changed it into four monthlies over the objections of editor Norman Cousins (who had resigned in 1971), and moved it to California. In April the new publishers declared bankruptcy and Cousins moved immediately to acquire the magazine, uniting it in New York with his new venture, *World,* as a fortnightly. Another magazine with a new lease on life was the *Saturday Evening Post,* revised as a quarterly in 1971 and doing so well by mid-1973, with a circulation of over 800,000, that the Curtis Publishing Co. turned it into a bimonthly. Among the literary magazines the *Hudson Review,* still under the capable editorship of founder Frederick Morgan, celebrated its 25th anniversary, a rare event in a field that saw the recent deaths of such literary reviews as the *Kenyon Review, Midway,* and the *New Mexico Quarterly.*

The second phase of the U.S. Postal Service's ten-step 127% rate hike took effect in September but special congressional action gave consideration to smaller publishers who might be eliminated by the gigantic increase. Despite higher production costs, postal rates, and subscription rates, publishers reported an annual 8–10% revenue increase in 1973. The *Publishers Weekly* 1973 price index found that the average subscription price of the 2,861 titles in the U.S. was $16.20, an increase of $2.97, or 22%, over 1972. Despite some consumer resistance, the number of subscriptions actually increased.

It was also found that a well-designed, eye-catching cover could increase sales as much as 35%, especially at newsstands, although no formula could be seen among the 1973 attraction winners for the *Ladies' Home Journal, Time, Newsweek, Esquire,* or *New York Magazine.* The single common characteristic seemed to be involvement of the reader's personal life, his personal health, or his personal relationships, which meant covers about anything from sex to acupuncture. A more obvious trend in design, the smaller page size, which saved postage and paper costs, was followed by *Ladies' Home Journal* but resisted by *Better Homes and Gardens,* which insisted it would retain its traditional large format.

The midyear Supreme Court obscenity ruling that redefined obscenity laws in terms of community standards caused understandable concern, particularly on the part of men's magazine publishers. *Playboy* and its new companion, *Oui,* would attempt to adapt to the new ruling, but the English-based *Penthouse* and its new women's magazine companion, *Viva,* announced plans to fight the decision. The liberated woman's *Ms.* continued to enjoy a phenomenal success. Its expanding interests included preparation of a "magazine type" television program; recordings and books for children stressing the equality of boys and girls; and a subsidiary, Ms. Marketing, which would advise companies on "how to talk to women who are in the process of changing their lives." *Cosmopolitan* was being published in the U.K., Latin America, and Australia, in addition to the U.S., and doing quite well, in Britain at least. At the teen-age level *Ingenue* moved toward a more liberal stance in its editorial policy under a new owner, Twenty First Century Communications. Its competitor, Triangle's *Seventeen,* would continue to cover "contemporary social issues in a responsible way."

Several new magazines made news. *Good Food,* a Triangle publication, went on sale in 18,000 food store outlets, using the familiar pattern established by its sister, *TV Guide.* Downe Communications launched the monthly *Photo World,* which was unique in that it drew heavily for copy upon the French publication *Photo.* At a considerably less commercial level, two new poetry magazines showed every promise of success. The well-designed *Parnassus: Poetry in Review* was to appear twice a year and was more traditional in approach. But the *American Poetry Review* wore the newspaper format of *Rolling Stone,* was issued every two months, and made a serious effort to take the mystique out of poetry.

As elsewhere, most of the new titles issued recently in the U.S. reflected narrow but intense interest

World Daily Newspapers and Circulations, 1972–73*

Location	Daily newspapers	Circulation per 1,000 of population
AFRICA		
Algeria	4	20
Angola	4	15
Botswana	2	20
Cameroon	2	3
Central African Republic	1	0.3
Ceuta	1	58
Chad	1	0.2
Congo	3	...
Dahomey	2	0.7
Egypt	14	22
Ethiopia	9	2
Ghana	3	46
Guinea	1	1
Ivory Coast	2	10
Kenya	4	14
Liberia	1	4
Libya	7	...
Malagasy Republic	13	8
Mali	3	0.6
Mauritius	9	78
Melilla	1	60
Morocco	13	14
Mozambique	4	5
Namibia	3	...
Niger	1	0.5
Nigeria	15	6
Portuguese Guinea	1	...
Réunion	2	64
Rhodesia	4	15
Senegal	1	5
Seychelles	2	38
Sierra Leone	5	16
Somali Republic	2	2
South Africa	22	...
Sudan	13	8
Tanzania	4	5
Togo	3	6
Tunisia	4	16
Uganda	4	8
Zaire	7	9
Zambia	2	18
Total	199	
NORTH AMERICA		
Bahamas	3	162
Barbados	1	100
Belize (British Honduras	1	32
Bermuda	1	259
Canada	113	211
Costa Rica	8	101
Cuba	15	6
Dominican Republic	7	36
El Salvador	12	74
Guadeloupe	1	139
Guatemala	8	4
Haiti	7	16
Honduras	12	42
Jamaica	3	114
Leeward Islands	3	33
Martinique	2	126
Mexico	200	...
Netherlands Antilles	5	147
Nicaragua	7	51
Panama (incl. Canal Zone)	11	106
Puerto Rico	3	89
Trinidad and Tobago	3	131
United States	1,761	301
Virgin Islands	3	221
Total	2,190	
SOUTH AMERICA		
Argentina	176	179
Bolivia	21	42
Brazil	257	36
Chile	122	86
Colombia	36	109
Ecuador	25	41
French Guiana	1	37
Guyana	3	58
Paraguay	11	40
Peru	85	118
Surinam	6	59
Uruguay	31	140
Venezuela	42	93
Total	816	
ASIA		
Afghanistan	18	6
Bangladesh	10	...
Burma	44	15
Cambodia	26	22
China	392	19
Cyprus	12	133
Hong Kong	69	...
India	521	16
Indonesia	85	7
Iran	29	12
Iraq	4	...
Israel	75	146
Japan	170	510
Jordan	3	15
Korea, North	7	...
Korea, South	44	138
Kuwait	5	48
Laos	7	3
Lebanon	52	...
Macao	6	...
Malaysia	37	74
Mongolia	2	103
Nepal	30	3
Pakistan	124	...
Philippines	18	21
Ryukyu Islands	10	284
Saudi Arabia	5	7
Singapore	11	174
Sri Lanka	17	49
Syria	5	...
Taiwan	32	64
Thailand	35	24
Turkey	432	...
Vietnam, North	7	...
Vietnam, South	56	67
Yemen	5	18
Total	2,405	
EUROPE		
Albania	2	47
Austria	32	293
Belgium	55	...
Bulgaria	12	191
Czechoslovakia	28	252
Denmark	56	368
Finland	65	...
France	106	238
Germany, East	40	445
Germany, West	393	319
Gibraltar	2	222
Greece	107	76
Hungary	27	217
Iceland	5	449
Ireland	7	234
Italy	75	146
Luxembourg	8	560
Malta	6	...
Netherlands, The	93	311
Norway	81	396
Poland	44	217
Portugal	31	...
Romania	57	173
Spain	115	99
Sweden	114	534
Switzerland	99	374
U.S.S.R.	647	347
United Kingdom	106	463
Vatican City (Holy See)	1	...
Yugoslavia	24	85
Total	2,438	
OCEANIA		
American Samoa	1	90
Australia	58	321
Cook Islands	1	40
Fiji Islands	1	30
French Polynesia	4	91
Guam	2	244
New Caledonia	2	112
New Zealand	40	376
Niue	1	60
Tonga	2	16
Total	112	
Grand total	8,160	

*Only newspapers issued four or more times weekly are included. Areas not listed had no known daily newspapers.

Sources: *UN Statistical Yearbook 1972* (1973); *Newspaper Press Directory 1972; Editor & Publisher International Year Book 1973;* other secondary sources.

(WILLIAM A. HACHTEN)

areas: *Two Wheel Trip* (bicyclists); *Backpacker Magazine* (hikers); *Alaska Geographic; Country Women* (for women living on communes); *Folio* (a magazine trade journal); *Fly Fisherman; Happiness Holding Tank* (poetry); *Journal of Palestine Studies; Mysterious Barricade* (a little literary magazine); *Numus-West* (music); and *Sweet-Low Magazine* (health). Changing fashions and ways of life were reflected in new and modified titles: *Apartment Life,* born as an annual in 1969, proved popular enough to become a biweekly; *Singles* was intended for the unmarried one-third of the adult population; and *Couples* was directed to the 80% of the newly married who did not have and did not plan to have children for years. On the other hand, *American Baby* reported substantial ad revenue increases.

For writers and editors the most interesting new venture was *New Times,* the first news magazine to be launched in 30 years. Published by George Hirsch, who founded the successful *New York Magazine,* the biweekly had an impressive staff of contributing editors and writers to attempt to raise and answer questions for a better educated—and probably a younger—audience than was reached by either *Time* or *Newsweek. Money,* a Time, Inc., publication, proved to be one of the more successful new magazines. Giving advice on all aspects of personal finance, it was aimed at households with incomes of over $29,000—which went a long way toward explaining the lack of reluctance of 300,000 readers to pay a record $12–$15 a year for a subscription. Other new magazines included *The Chicagoan,* which promised to be a Midwestern version of *New York Magazine, Atlas,* revived and expanded after 17 months as a review of the world press, and *Homelife,* a weekly rival to *TV Guide,* sold in supermarkets at only five cents a copy. Polling 12 major agency media executives, Leon Garry of the *Media Industry Newsletter* found in August that, of 11 new titles in 1973, only three were given solid support: *New Times, Saturday Review/World,* and *Homelife.* Least likely to succeed were *Playgirl* (a somewhat sensational copy of *Playboy* for women), *Atlas, Gamblers World, Genesis* (a men's magazine), and *Singles,* while even odds were with *The Chicagoan, Players* (a black magazine), and *Viva.*

Following the success of *Kids,* established in 1970, the traditional reluctance of publishers to bring out new children's magazines gave way to enthusiasm. *Ebony Jr!* was the first national designed to appeal to black children. *Tube Talk,* a young person's guide to television, was meant to be included in newspapers as a monthly insert. Other entries that might win acceptance were *Dirtyfeet,* aimed at ages seven to ten, *Sesame Street* and *The Electric Company Guide,* complements of the two TV shows, and *Cricket,* for ages eight to ten and attracting 100,000 subscribers after four issues. Children's Communications Co., still in the planning stages, was to be tied to a TV news series by and for children.

One apparent casualty of the crackdown on dissidents in the Soviet Union was the suspension of the *Chronicle of Current Events,* the world-famous typewritten bulletin (a *samizdat* or "do-it-yourself" publication) that had reported political arrests and other news of dissidents since 1968. It had last appeared in October 1972. At the same time, the U.S.S.R. began publishing its first consumer magazine, a combination market analysis and critical buying guide, *Kommerchesky Vestnik.* The biweekly magazine was of more than passing interest outside the Soviet Union for the market guidance it gave to potential foreign suppliers. (WILLIAM A. KATZ)

Books. One of the most important events of the year was the Soviet Union's signing, with effect from May 27, of the Geneva Universal Copyright Convention, regarded as a contribution to Soviet–West détente and meaning that royalties would as a result be paid on such non-Soviet books as were published in the U.S.S.R. However, a decree passed on February 21, modifying Soviet law in connection with the convention, specified that copyright would apply not only to works first published in the Soviet Union but also to those "not published but found on the territory of the Soviet Union in any objective form." On September 20 the U.S.S.R. established a "copyright agency" as sole official channel between Soviet writers and Western publishers. A day later Nobel laureate Aleksandr Solzhenitsyn announced that he had begun circulating in *samizdat* form two chapters of his novel *The First Circle,* claiming that the terms of the convention should protect his words from pirate publication in the West. He followed this with a far more serious challenge to the agency's powers in December when he released for publication in Paris his first nonfiction work, *The Gulag Archipelago.* (*See* LITERATURE.) A further decree of September 27 had imposed whopping taxes (30–70%) on royalties earned by Soviet writers abroad.

In the U.K. a proliferation of small new publishing ventures pointed to the number of editors who had decided to gamble on their flair and go it alone. Distribution to book shops was often planned by arrangement with an established publisher. Of special interest was Quartet, founded in 1972, which launched "Midway" editions: new titles in bindings that were halfway between conventional paperbacks and hardcovers. Meanwhile, as paperback profits rose by comparison with the decline of hard-cover sales, no one was surprised when the British Printing Corp. announced plans to move into paperback publishing.

As had been expected, books were zero-rated when value-added tax (VAT) was introduced in Britain in 1973. It was hoped that other EEC countries would follow, but French publishers, for instance, were including VAT in their published prices. The small extra profit made from exported books reduced enthusiasm for zero-rating, a concept, in any case, unknown elsewhere in the EEC. A Green Paper on public lending rights (PLR) to provide compensation to authors for books borrowed from libraries was issued in 1972, and in 1973 a motion tabled in the House of Commons received 267 signatures. A private member's bill on PLR was to be introduced in the 1973–74 parliamentary session. In New Zealand authors were expected to benefit to the tune of £70,000 in 1973 as a result of PLR.

In January–June 1973, there were 16,644 titles published in the U.K., 1,177 more than in the corresponding period of 1972. Figures for 1972 showed that 33,140 titles were published, 602 more than in 1971. The number of fiction titles, although still forming much the largest category, continued to shrink, from 4,449 in 1970 to 3,759 in 1971 to 3,685 in 1972. Despite a successful campaign by the Educational Publishers' Council to reverse the decline in public expenditure per capita on books for schools, school textbooks dropped by 260 from the 1971 total of 2,040. Children's books, however, increased by 177 over the 1971 figure of 2,010. Publishers' turnover increased to an estimated £203,045,000, compared with £179,099,000 for 1971. While the value of book exports rose, the percentage of books exported was estimated to have dropped by about 3%.

West German book production in 1972 was estimated at something close to the 40,000 titles of 1971, with belles-lettres and children's books heading the lists. Paperbacks, despite higher retail prices, continued to be profitable, and showed a significant expansion in the fields of science, technology, and education. The international wave of interest in Hitler and the Third Reich also broke in West Germany. By autumn, the bulky "diary" of Joseph Goebbels, said to have reached the West from archives in Eastern Europe, had triggered a legal battle between publishers in Hamburg and New York. The value of all publishing in West Germany rose from DM. 618.9 million in 1971 to DM. 704.9 million in 1972. However, largely because of increased overhead costs, the economic outlook was less buoyant than the 11% increase that this turnover represented. Exports reached DM. 385.7 million, compared with DM. 327.9 million in 1971. Imports rose from DM. 164.6 million to DM. 184.3 million.

In Australia the number of new titles fell in 1972 and domestic sales dropped from A$16,888,000 to A$16,343,000—a decline partly offset by a rise in export sales from A$1,591,000 to A$2,040,000. But the figures did not reflect the general level of book demand, for imports continued to rise. The government helped relieve the somewhat gloomy outlook by setting up an Australian Literature Board with an annual budget of A$1.3 million, of which a substantial proportion was to be used in subsidizing genuinely Australian publishing firms.

Switzerland, with 6,849 titles published in 1972, topped its 1970 record by nearly 7%. Exports rose in value by 22% to SFr. 227.7 million and included increased exports to the U.K. and U.S. Imports also rose steadily, by 17.5% to SFr. 212.4 million, with books imported from East Germany almost doubling their 1971 value, reaching SFr. 1,830,000.

Danish book production again showed a remarkable rise in 1972 with 6,547 titles, 1,108 more than in 1971, but only 580 new paperback titles appeared as against 783 in 1971. Total turnover in 1971 was estimated at 353 million kroner, an increase of 33 million kroner, which, with prices rising by some 7–8%, represented an increase of only about 3%.

The South African government threatened to stiffen censorship laws by removing the right to appeal cen-

AUTHENTICATED NEWS INTERNATIONAL

"Big Little Books," highly popular in the 1930s and '40s, were being revived by Western Publishing Co. The new versions were soft-covered and slightly larger than the hardcover originals, one of which appears, lower left, in the photo.

sors' decisions to the courts. It denied "political sponsorship" in offering an inducement worth £1,500 to the U.K. publishers Hutchinson to go ahead with publication of Judge Gerald Sparrow's *Not What I Expected.* In India, Arthur Mee's *Book of Knowledge—Children's Encyclopaedia* sparked off riots in Srinagar, capital of Kashmir province, because of its alleged anti-Muslim content. In Turkey, left-wing book publishers Suleyman Ege and Muzaffer Erdost received prison sentences of up to 30 years "for propagating Communism."

The Frankfurt Book Fair duly and deservedly congratulated itself on reaching its quarter century. Publishers attending from over 50 countries numbered 3,817, and they exhibited some 248,000 books. In East Germany there were indications at the Leipzig Book Fair that an ideological thaw was under way, a notion reinforced by publication there of Stefan Heym's anti-Stalin novel, *The King David Report.* (x.)

The U.S. Supreme Court's 5–4 decision of June 21 setting forth new guidelines on obscenity upset the permissive earlier position that "redeeming social values" played a major factor in distinguishing what is and what is not pornographic. The court appeared to be substituting the nebulous criterion of whatever is "offensive to local standards," without being explicit as to whether such standards were for a neighbourhood, a borough or city, a town or state (although states were asked to be "detailed" in their legislative definitions). Within days after the ruling some booksellers were reportedly returning "thousands of unsold books" for fear of prosecution; on the other hand, the more daring retailers (notably in the big cities) revealed vastly increased sales of "books that might be banned." The effects of the decision, however, would not be seen until after state legislatures had enacted or rejected new legislation and tests of the new statutes could begin.

Relationships between the administration and book publishing were also strained. The budget for fiscal 1974 completely wiped out three major federal library programs that, with matching funds, had been expected to result in book expenditures of about $100 million for school and public libraries. Congress fought back by increasing appropriations, but the expected scenario of veto and efforts to override the veto was sufficient to make some publishers plan for sales declines of 10% in 1973 and of perhaps over 30% in 1974. Sales of school and college textbooks had already fallen slightly in 1972, a year of similar funding battles—by $1 million in the first category, by $4 million in the latter.

More significant, perhaps, was the announcement in July 1973 that the growth rate of publishing had sharply declined. Total sales rose from $3,083,000,000 in 1971 to $3,177,000,000 in 1972, for an increase of 3%; since World War II the growth rate had typically ranged between 5 and 9%. But the number of books published continued to mount. By mid-1973, 18,700 new books and new editions had been published, an increase over the same period in 1972 of 760 titles and, traditionally, more books are published in the second half of the year than in the first. (Total output in 1972 was 38,053, about 54% of which were published between July and December.) Thus, a trend continued that the publishers themselves saw as harmful—more books came to market than the public was willing or able to buy.

Puerto Rico:
see Dependent States

In a few areas, however, the public's willingness to buy seemed almost insatiable. Paperback "Gothic novels" and "family sagas" accounted for 21% of the paperbacks bought in 46 states in 1973. Paperback sales of adult titles had leaped from $48 million in 1971 to over $55 million in 1972, and appeared to be as much as 10% higher in 1973. Certainly the paperback houses were paying more than ever for reprint rights; paperback rights to the *Joy of Cooking* by Irma S. Rombauer and Marion Rombauer Becker were sold for a $1.5 million guarantee.

Another dollar record was broken with the publication of a four-volume reprint of Audubon's *The Birds of America,* priced at $6,960 per set and limited to 250 sets. In the category of reference books, two important works appeared. *Dictionary of the History of Ideas* was published by Scribner's. Described as a compendium of pivotal and recurrent ideas in the development of Western thought, it contained over 300 articles alphabetically arranged in four volumes. And the 15th edition of *Encyclopædia Britannica* was completed. It represented a revolution in encyclopaedia-making in both concept and presentation. Combining the reference and educational functions in a three-part work, the new encyclopaedia presented the range of human knowledge in 30 volumes.

Sex, diet, and psychiatry dominated the nonfiction best-seller lists in 1973, much as they did in 1972. (In the previous year, however, a newly written version of the Bible titled *The Living Bible* was released to booksellers late in the fall, and 750,000 copies were bought by year's end, with an additional 4,250,000 sold in other editions and outlets.) *Dr. Atkins' Diet Revolution,* although publicly criticized by the American Medical Association, was a best seller in both years, with over a million copies of the hard-cover edition in print. Another panacea for poundage, *Weight Watchers Program Cookbook* by Jean Nidetch, sold over 500,000 copies in six months of 1973. *The Joy of Sex* (available in two editions, the lesser-selling one without illustrations) was on the best-seller lists for nine months. *How to Be Your Own Best Friend,* a psychoanalytically oriented self-help book published by a new company, almost disappeared without a trace; when distribution was taken over by Random House, it led the fall best-seller list.

The fiction best seller, with about 250,000 copies sold during the year, was *Breakfast of Champions* by Kurt Vonnegut, Jr. (*see* BIOGRAPHY), whose audience had grown from a cult of college students and intellectuals to a vast national following. Close behind was Jacqueline Susann's *Once Is Not Enough,* followed by *The Hollow Hills* by Mary Stewart, queen of the Gothic novel. Other notable novels included Tom Wicker's *Facing the Lions* and Graham Greene's *The Honorary Consul.*

Two of the nonfiction best sellers precipitated litigation. Publication of Norman Mailer's text for the illustrated biography *Marilyn* was accompanied by complaints of alleged plagiarism and excessive quotation from two previous biographies of Marilyn Monroe. Louis Nizer's *The Implosion Conspiracy,* concerning the Rosenberg case (which led to the execution of a husband and wife as spies), was the subject of a $3 million suit by the Rosenberg sons alleging publication of correspondence without authorization.

The 1973 National Book Awards were won in the fiction category by John Barth for *Chimera* and by John Williams for *Augustus,* and in contemporary affairs by Frances FitzGerald's *Fire in the Lake,* a powerful recounting of the American role in Vietnam.

(LEONARD R. HARRIS)

Qatar

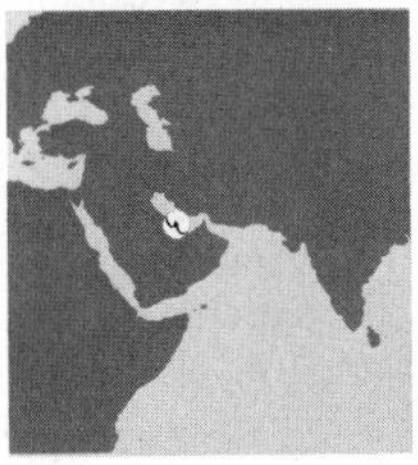

An independent emirate on the west coast of the Persian Gulf, Qatar occupies a desert peninsula east of Bahrain, with Saudi Arabia and the United Arab Emirates bordering on the south. Area: 4,400 sq.mi. (11,400 sq.km.). Pop. (1972 est.): 170,000. Capital: Doha (pop., 1971 est., 95,000). Language: Arabic. Religion: Muslim. Emir in 1973, Sheikh Khalifah ibn Hamad ath-Thani.

In 1973, Qatar's third year of independence, diplomatic relations were established with several more Arab and Western states. In January Qatar acquired 25% participation in the Shell Company of Qatar and the Qatar Petroleum Co. through agreements similar to those between Saudi Arabia and Kuwait and the oil companies. Oil output in 1972 was 11.4 million tons, compared with 10.4 million tons in 1971, and production increased to 6 million tons in the first half of 1973, as against 5.4 million tons in the first half of 1972. A 25% production cutback was imposed after the Arab-Israeli war in October.

Plans were announced for a major new airport near Doha capable of handling the Concorde supersonic airliner. On May 20 the new currency—the Qatar riyal divided into 100 dirhams—was introduced to replace the Qatar-Dubai riyal. (PETER MANSFIELD)

QATAR

Education. (1970–71) Primary, pupils 14,479, teachers 752; secondary, pupils 3,448, teachers 221; vocational, pupils 209, teachers 44; teacher training, students 237, teachers 38.

Finance and Trade. Monetary unit: Qatar riyal (which replaced the Qatar-Dubai riyal at par from May 20, 1973), with (Sept. 17, 1973) an official rate of 3.95 riyals to U.S. $1 (free rate of 9.55 riyals = £1 sterling). Budget (1972–73 est.) balanced at 700 million riyals. Foreign trade (1972): imports *c.* 600 million riyals; exports *c.* 1,590,000,000 riyals. Import sources: U.K. *c.* 41%; U.S. *c.* 18%; France *c.* 12%; Lebanon *c.* 12%; West Germany *c.* 10%; The Netherlands *c.* 5%. Export destinations: U.K. *c.* 27%; The Netherlands *c.* 25%; France *c.* 12%; Italy 11%; West Germany 7%. Main export crude oil.

Industry. Crude oil production (1972) 23,262,000 metric tons.

Race Relations

Existing racial and ethnic alliances at the national and international levels were generally maintained in 1973 by the presence of an external scapegoat—South Africa, Rhodesia, and Portugal for Africans and many other black or brown societies (although brown Asians provided useful internal alternative scapegoats in a number of African and other recently independent third world nations). Israel and Jewry had long been such a scapegoat for the Arab states, otherwise divided among themselves and internally by ideologies, types of regime, and socioeconomic inequalities. By the end of October, when an uneasy cease-fire had been negotiated in the latest Arab-Israeli war, Israel—as a result of stick-and-carrot policies instigated by oil-rich Libya and Saudi Arabia—had become a scapegoat for virtually all of black Africa and for many nonaligned nations.

MAHOOD—PUNCH / ROTHCO

"If I had known we were going to be the Token Whites I wouldn't have come!"

The anti-Israel campaign had never lacked a basic anti-Semitic component in the Soviet Union, where it continued to flourish. In 1973 anti-Semitic (*i.e.*, anti-Jewish) undertones became increasingly discernible in Arab and European anti-Zionism. Meanwhile, anti-Arab feelings and incidents increased in France, mainly in consequence of the large concentrations of Algerian migrant workers in major industrial cities. The Arabs were the chief target for French xenophobia; of the other two large recent migrant groups, black Africans tended to be regarded with paternalistic tolerance, while the Portuguese were seen as culturally compatible and assimilable.

Trouble and tension continued or flared up in other long-standing ethnic or religious minority situations: these included the Basque separatists in Spain; Kurds in Iraq; Tamils in Sri Lanka; Muslims in the Philippines; Roman Catholics in Northern Ireland; and Nagas in Indian-occupied Nagaland, where there was continued military repression combined with attempts to wipe out traditional culture and social organization. In the Western Hemisphere, particularly Brazil, the remote and primitive remnants of the Amerindian peoples were increasingly threatened with extinction as the roadbuilders and land barons moved into the interior. North American Indians were showing more ingenuity and adroitness in renegotiating their relations with the white majority, as were their models, the U.S. blacks, with their advances into the political arena. In Quebec Province, Canada, the separatists lost to the Liberals in the October elections, despite the widespread apprehensions of the English-speaking population.

In August Canada's Prime Minister Pierre Trudeau was host to the Commonwealth heads of government at a relaxed conference that foreshadowed a new lease on life for this worldwide grouping of large and small, democratic and authoritarian, less developed and developed, rural and urban states, representing most major racial, religious, and cultural groups. The traditional division between the "old white dominions" and the other nations was less conspicuous, Australia and New Zealand being represented by new Labour prime ministers who supported a number of third world causes, including the boycott on sports competition with white South African teams.

South Africa. Economic forces compelled the South African government to accept some economic liberalization in 1973, with the country changing from a mining and agricultural economy founded on cheap nonwhite labour to a modern high-technology econ-

Quakers:
see Religion

omy requiring more skilled and educated workers. The serious and long-standing shortage of white skilled workers meant that more and more black workers were being incorporated illegally or legally into the skilled urban working force, in addition to those thousands joining the unskilled labour force because of lack of work in the African "homelands."

In October Prime Minister B. J. Vorster appeared to be accepting the implications of this when he told Vic Feather, leader of a visiting British Trades Union Congress delegation investigating industrial apartheid, that he intended to allow black workers "collective bargaining rights"; later, he announced that the government would establish industrial training centres for Africans in the urban (white) areas. Such moves had for years been recommended by industrialists, but the prime minister in early November stressed their importance in an address to the right-wing Coordinating Council of South African Trade Unions (membership 200,000). He made it clear that, without any threat to white job security, the republic needed to make more productive use of its black workers if it were adequately to increase the growth rate and to limit black unemployment.

During the months preceding these developments South Africa had experienced an escalation of economic pressures. In January and February there were well-organized strikes for higher wages in Durban and Natal, involving approximately 65,000 workers: wage levels of R 8 a week for men and R 5 for women were revealed in some cases, far below the poverty datum line (PDL) for an African family of five in Natal of about R 83 a month. The police avoided direct confrontation with the strikers for several weeks, and there was an upsurge of support from white South Africans. Later the Department of Labour issued a list of minimum wages for workers in lower-paid jobs and about 30 trades (involving increases of up to 54%). The right to strike (in heavily limited circumstances) was restored to Africans in May under the Bantu Labour Relations Amendment Act; however, Chief Gatsha Buthelezi of KwaZulu called this a stopgap measure, and the Trade Union Council of South Africa, representing about 170,000 white and coloured workers, said that it entrenched the policy of treating Africans differently.

A policeman in Durban, S.Af., clubs a striking African worker to the ground after a protest march broke into disorder on Feb. 6, 1973. About 200 Africans were arrested and many injured as a series of strikes for higher wages threatened to shut down the port city.

UPI COMPIX

The wages campaign reopened the debate on investment in South Africa, with a call by the U.K. Anti-Apartheid Movement for a government investigation. In January the World Council of Churches had blacklisted 650 firms, 425 of them British, for being "directly involved" in investment in white-ruled Africa and thus strengthening "white oppression." At the same time, it announced that it had sold its own holdings in the listed companies at a total market value of about $1.5 million, and that African liberation movements would receive the lion's share of new grants, totaling nearly $200,000, for organizations combating racism. In April Chief Buthelezi criticized those advocating withdrawal of British capital and said it was a good way to precipitate revolution. Helen Suzman, sole Progressive Party member in the South African Parliament, also objected to the idea of withdrawal of foreign investment and said, "I am certain that the continued economic expansion of South Africa will prove to be the strongest weapon against apartheid."

Of some concern to South Africa was an International Labour Organization Workers' Section resolution taken in June in Geneva. It called for a stop to emigration and foreign investment and for a boycott of South African trade.

The increase in repressive measures that accompanied the economic liberalization included confiscation or denial of passports, deportations, and moves against black radicals, white liberals, students, the English-language press, and dissident churchmen. Government orders disabled the entire leadership of the black students' organization SASO, the Black People's Convention, and the Black Community Programme (BCP). The spearhead of the campaign against dissident white liberal and church organizations was the parliamentary Commission of Inquiry into Certain Organizations (CICO), which operated in secret. It had been asked to investigate the National Union of South African Students (NUSAS), whose membership was drawn from only the English-speaking universities; the South African Institute of Race Relations (a semiacademic body); the University Christian Movement (a largely black group, later defunct); and the Christian Institute of Southern Africa (an ecumenical church group). Each of these organizations received money from abroad, and each was critical of apartheid. None was accused of breaking the law, and none was opposed to a judicial inquiry. By October CICO's findings had led to the banning of eight NUSAS leaders; five passport withdrawals for the Christian Institute and the trial of its director, the Rev. Beyers Naudé, for refusing to give evidence to the commission; and passport withdrawals for Sonny Leon, leader of the Labour Party (in opposition to the government-created Coloured Persons' Representative Council), and H. Kleinschmidt of the South African Institute of Race Relations. The English-speaking press continued its scathing attacks on these and other less sophisticated instances of repression, including the public mass floggings of several hundred South West African People's Organization sympathizers, including women, by government-appointed tribal authorities in Namibia. (Floggings were later prohibited.) Vorster reacted by refusing to meet a deputation from the Newspaper Press Union, on the ground that some editors had refused to put their own houses in order.

Meanwhile, the leaders of South Africa's semi-autonomous black homelands or Bantustans were proceeding energetically with their own interpretations of separate development. Paramount Chief Kaiser Matanzima won a sweeping victory in the Transkei in late October, calling for independence within five years, more land, the africanization of government posts, and a federation of African homelands. Two weeks later a summit meeting of most of the black homeland leaders, including Chief Buthelezi of Kwa-Zulu and Chief Lucas Mangope of Bophuthatswana (bordering on Botswana), met in the Transkei capital of Umtata. They issued an eight-point program calling for the acceptance of federation as a long-term policy; meaningful consolidation of fragmented Bantustans; noncollaboration with Pretoria over the removal of Africans from urban areas to fit in with apartheid planning; unfettered rights to seek financial aid and personnel from UN agencies and church bodies; support in principle for a black bank; and opposition to any form of racial discrimination. Most significant was the federal concept, promoting black unity and cutting across the apartheid policy of establishing weak multiple tribal ethnic units in order to divide and rule blacks.

United Kingdom. Late in 1972 the arrival and emergency reception in Britain of approximately 28,500 Asian refugees from Uganda holding U.K. passports became confused with the long-standing debate on immigration policy and race relations in Britain. In November 1972, the debate focused on the Immigration Rules that were to come into force in January 1973, along with the Immigration Act of 1971, at the same time as Britain's formal entry into the EEC. This revived a "Little England" congeries of anti-European feelings and fears of massive coloured invasions. In the ensuing negative climate of opinion, the government was defeated in the House of Commons. Revised rules went into effect in February. The home secretary, Robert Carr, stated that while the government would "continue to accept its responsibility to U.K. passport-holders by admitting them in a controlled and orderly manner through the special voucher scheme," this was as much as could reasonably and realistically be done if good community relations were to be maintained; there would be no more mass inflows. Once again, therefore, tighter immigration curbs against coloured immigrants were being linked with better race or community relations, an association that the Community Relations Commission and other organizations concerned with aiding immigrants found damaging.

The new immigration legislation was intended to tidy up a complex welter of earlier immigration laws. In fact, it introduced further complications, including a system with four sets of immigration rules and eight major categories of prospective entrants with differing rights of entry. The retrospective aspect of the 1971 act (which had apparently gone unnoticed during parliamentary debates but which emerged as a result of the law lords' ruling, in June 1973, that illegal entrants who had entered Britain any time after March 9, 1968, could be removed at any time) was reported to be arousing insecurity and even possibilities of blackmail among Asian immigrants, an unknown but substantial minority of whom were thought to have entered Britain illegally. Feelings of insecurity were reinforced among the Pakistani community in particular by the Pakistan Bill 1973, regularizing the status of Pakistani citizens in Britain following the withdrawal of Pakistan from the Commonwealth in January 1972. Broadly speaking, those resident in Britain before Pakistan left the Commonwealth would be able to apply for registration as U.K. citizens up to six months (later extended to a year) from the date on which they completed five years' ordinary residence in the United Kingdom. An appeal by 31 Ugandan Asians, all U.K. passport-holders, against their exclusion from Britain under the Immigration Act, 1968, was pending before the European Commission on Human Rights in Strasbourg in late 1973.

The smuggling of illegal immigrants, mostly from India and Pakistan, into the U.K. via northern European ports was attracting counteraction by police and immigration authorities, with searches of boats and long-distance trucks, and of some houses and places of work. The home secretary said there would be no harassment and that individual cases would be treated humanely on their merits, but he rejected a general amnesty.

The total number of U.K. passport-holders from East Africa (and India after June 1972) admitted in 1972 was 34,825, as compared with 11,564 in 1971. In addition, another 25,025 persons were admitted from the New Commonwealth (nations that had achieved independence since World War II).

The virtual cessation of large-scale Commonwealth immigration meant that debate was increasingly focused on the numbers of those already in the U.K. and their likely increase in the future. Despite continued alarmist estimates, preliminary results of the 1971 census showed a total of 1,160,000 born in the New Commonwealth, or 2.1% of the population (about 26% of these were born in the West Indies and 40% in India and Pakistan). Including British-born children, the total coloured population was estimated at about 1.5 million. Distribution was uneven, with Greater London and the West Midlands showing the highest concentrations (6.4% and 5.1%, respectively).

By autumn 1973 almost all the Uganda Asians, who had been the major focus of public concern since August 1972, were "resettled" in the community. Full resettlement was, however, nowhere near achievement with so many having lost all their possessions and capital, with about one-quarter of those able to work unemployed, very many housed in expensive and overcrowded conditions, several hundred deprived of wage earners and household heads by immigration restrictions, and many too old or too handicapped to work effectively. As Commonwealth immigrants became settlers, expectations grew, and there were several instances of immigrant-led industrial action aimed at better jobs, more security, and higher status.

In May 1973 unemployment figures for coloured workers were 15,308, down by nearly 7,000 from May 1972, and representing 2.6% of all persons unemployed in Britain. Unemployment among black youths was connected with the general educational and other problems and needs of immigrant children in deprived urban areas, including inadequate language teaching, inappropriate teacher training, the absence of clearly formulated aims for multiracial schools, and the lack of suitable preschool facilities. This subject was reported on by the Parliamentary Select Committee on Race Relations and Immigration in September. Its inquiry of the previous year had been concerned with police-immigrant relations; there was some evidence of firm positive action by the police to improve these relations, but allegations of "muggings" by black adolescents and harassment of immigrants by a minority of police continued.

In its annual report the Race Relations Board stated that in 1972 the number of complaints of unlawful discrimination had increased from 813 to 845. In 648 cases in which an opinion was formed, 181 (28%) resulted in an opinion of discrimination. The board again called for wider powers, especially in the field of employment, but these were refused by the home secretary on the grounds that a limited law-enforcement role could not necessarily be combined with the much wider task of encouraging good managerial practices.

An upsurge of interest in black studies and black or third world arts and drama was noted in 1973, and Asian cultural, religious, and other associations continued active. The visiting West Indies cricket team gained a great victory, which boosted the morale of West Indians everywhere and attracted considerable coverage from the media, much of it sensational and biased. (SHEILA PATTERSON)

United States. Watergate scandals, war, and the energy crisis crowded race relations off the front pages of U.S. newspapers in 1973. Yet there were numerous significant racial events during the year, though the lack of progress that had characterized U.S. race relations in the 1970s continued.

Native American affairs marked the exception. In January, the federal government rejected the 20 demands of the protest group that had occupied the Bureau of Indian Affairs (BIA) offices two months earlier. The administration claimed that reservation reform was already under way and that any Indian rights to renegotiate treaties had been lost when Indians became U.S. citizens in 1924. Nevertheless, the government later asked for increased aid to Indians in its 1974 budget, shifted some Indian programs to the Department of Health, Education, and Welfare (HEW), and created an Office of Indian Rights within the Department of Justice.

At the close of February, the most serious and publicized Indian confrontation with the federal government in recent years began at Wounded Knee, S.D. Supporters of the American Indian Movement (AIM) seized the small town and barricaded themselves against surrounding federal agents. An agreement to end the siege on April 5 broke down three days later. Finally, on May 8, after 70 tense days, the occupation ended with the surrender of about 120 remaining protesters by the terms of an agreement signed on May 5. The lengthy confrontation witnessed about a dozen serious casualties, $240,000 in damage, and 300 arrests of persons trying to enter or leave the village. The government agreed to discuss Indian charges of broken treaties and compensation demands for lost lands once ceded to the Oglala Sioux. Significantly, a national survey conducted during the Wounded Knee occupation found most Americans in sympathy with the militant Indians.

UPI COMPIX

An elderly Oglala Sioux Indian near Wounded Knee, S.D., apparently supports at least one of the goals of the American Indian Movement, which seized the town on Feb. 27, 1973.

Native Americans also won concessions in the courts. In April, the U.S. Supreme Court let stand a previous ruling that exempted reservation land from local zoning laws. In June, a federal district court in Washington, D.C., forced the U.S. Department of the Interior to pay $106,000 in legal costs incurred by the Paiute Indians in their successful suit to block the department's attempt to divert water from their Nevada lake. And in July, the New Mexico Supreme Court ruled that the state could tax neither the reservation income of Indians on reservations nor reservation businesses owned by reservation Indians because only the federal government had jurisdiction.

But the full sweep of needed change for the Indians was yet to come. The Federal Trade Commission reported in June that trade and credit abuses were widespread on reservation trading posts in Arizona, New Mexico, and Utah. Largely white-owned and licensed by the BIA, these trading posts had prices 27% over the national average and 16.6% over the nearest off-reservation stores. The Census Bureau, in a June report based on 1970 data, found that almost half of the 793,000 recorded Indians in the U.S. lived in urban areas and that the number of Indians attending college had doubled since 1960. Nonetheless, the 1969 median family income for Indians was only $5,832, just slightly half that of whites. While only 11.6% of all U.S. families in 1969 were considered to be living in poverty, 33.3% of Indian families were. Conditions were especially acute on the reservations; median family income sank to $2,500 on Arizona's Papago Reservation and the median for school years completed on the Navajo Reservation was only 4.1.

Limited gains without fundamental social change also characterized 1973 for black Americans. A census report in February showed that blacks constituted 9% of college enrollment, compared with their total of 12% of college-age youth, and the college proportion of black males aged 18 and 19 had risen from 12% in 1964 to 23% in 1972. A survey of 25 social science textbooks reported in March by the Michigan Department of Education noted considerable improvement in the treatment of both blacks and Indians but inadequate presentations of women and Spanish heritage groups.

Black educational progress still had to rely largely upon the slow process of case-by-case victories in federal courtrooms. Much of this court action during 1973 was simply the continuation of legal battles that had extended over the past generation. Thus, 16 years after the much-publicized desegregation crisis involving a high school in Little Rock, Ark., the city's school board ratified an agreement with black plaintiffs for elementary school desegregation. Likewise, for Memphis, Tenn., the Supreme Court let stand in February a desegregation order that cut in half the black pupils attending all-black schools. In August, the Memphis plan was implemented peacefully, though private schools reportedly increased from 40 to 85. (However, a federal district judge in Alexandria, Va., cited an 1866 civil rights law and ruled that private schools cannot deny admission to blacks because of race.) In September, Alexandria began transporting 43% of its 7,700 elementary students to achieve about a two-to-one ratio of whites to blacks in each school. And one week after the 4th Circuit Court of Appeals upheld a lower court ruling for Prince Georges County, Md., extensive school desegregation began there.

The 6th Circuit Court of Appeals, sitting in Cincinnati, O., was particularly active. In April, it ordered implementation of a lower court plan for school desegregation in Chattanooga, Tenn., and in July upheld a desegregation plan for Knoxville, Tenn. But it was the 6th Circuit's 6–3 support in June of a desegregation plan involving Detroit and its suburbs that broke new legal ground. With increasing numbers of whites in suburbs and blacks in central cities, extensive urban desegregation of schools had become impossible unless plans combined suburban and central city children. The 6th Circuit's action came one month after the U.S. Supreme Court failed to overturn the 4th Circuit's denial of a similar metropolitan approach to school desegregation in Richmond, Va. Since the Supreme Court's refusal resulted from a 4–4 deadlock, no legal precedent was established.

Metropolitanism was also involved in two federal district court decisions in July. Judge S. H. Dillin found the state of Indiana guilty of maintaining segregated school systems and ordered the state legislature to devise a permanent desegregation plan for the entire Indianapolis metropolitan area. Judge A. J. Engel ordered the integration of teachers and administrators in Grand Rapids, Mich., but he rejected further student desegregation and a metropolitan plan. The Detroit, Indianapolis, and Grand Rapids decisions were all appealed.

Another significant legal trend involved Northern cities. The Supreme Court ruled 7–1 in June in a Denver, Colo., case that Northern cities with segregation practices would be treated like southern cities. In Boston in March, a federal administrative law judge found deliberate educational discrimination against blacks. His ruling could cost Boston schools $8 million in federal aid. Finally, in August, the Department of Justice filed a desegregation suit against the Omaha, Neb., school district.

Two other innovations emerged in this field in 1973. In Atlanta, a "compromise" was struck between the local chapter of the National Association for the Advancement of Colored People (NAACP) and the city's school board. In a 78% black system, busing demands were reduced so that 86 schools remained nearly all black in return for hiring of a black superintendent and other blacks in key administrative posts. The federal district court ordered the controversial plan into effect in April despite objections from NAACP lawyers. The national NAACP then suspended its Atlanta chapter.

A Washington, D.C., district court judge, in a sweeping order in February involving approximately three million students, required HEW to enforce the law and begin proceedings against states and school districts that HEW itself had previously found in noncompliance with college and school desegregation guidelines. One month later, HEW ordered 25 school districts and 2 states to submit new desegregation plans or face a cutoff of federal funds.

Federal courts were also involved in other minority problems. The Supreme Court decided in January that a defendant had a constitutional right to insist that potential jurors be questioned about possible racial prejudice, even in a state court. At the district court level, Hamtramck, Mich., in April was ordered to undertake a program of public housing construction and active fair-housing promotion to assure homes within the city for 4,000 black residents displaced by urban renewal. Bridgeport, Conn., was ordered to fill half of all vacancies among its police with blacks and Puerto Ricans until those groups constituted 15% of the force. This case represented a growing national effort to achieve proportional minority representation in urban police and fire departments. Under the Equal Employment Opportunity Act of 1972, the Justice Department filed suits charging discrimination in the hiring and promotion of blacks and Spanish-speakers by Boston's fire commissioner, Buffalo's police department, and Chicago's fire and police departments. In December the Chicago fire department reached an agreement with the Justice Department whereby half the firemen hired in the next five years would be either black or Spanish-surnamed and an allegedly biased hiring test would be scrapped.

The recently strengthened Equal Employment Opportunity Commission (EEOC) filed suits throughout 1973 charging employment discrimination against such firms as General Motors, Ford, General Electric, and Xerox as well as locals of such unions as the United Auto Workers and the International Longshoremen. And the commission joined the Department of Labor in a settlement with American Telephone and Telegraph under which the company paid women and minority employees compensation for past hiring and promotion restrictions. Also, a federal judge in Birmingham, Ala., ordered in May both United States Steel and the United Steelworkers to alter discriminatory hiring and seniority systems at the Fairfield Works, where 3,800 of 12,000 workers were black. The judge required back-pay compensation, a uniform seniority system, and specific hiring timetables.

Voluntary plans for minority employment in areas ranging from broadcasting to construction were not generally effective. The Federal Communications Commission reported that in 1972 only 6.6% of 130,-656 broadcasting employees were black, 3% Spanish-surnamed, 0.5% Oriental, and 0.4% native American. And New York City withdrew in protest from the federal government's "New York Plan" for minority inclusion in the building trades. The city claimed that only 537 minority trainees, instead of the intended minimum of 800, had actually found construction jobs over a one-year period. Meanwhile, minority groups unsuccessfully opposed the confirmation in January of Peter Brennan as secretary of labour.

Minority leaders perceived Brennan's appointment as yet another indication of Pres. Richard Nixon's opposition to their aspirations. They assailed the president's continued attacks against busing for school desegregation, his deferral of appropriated funds for aiding desegregating school districts, his use of the Department of Justice to oppose desegregation suits in court, and his elimination of the Office of Economic Opportunity and dozens of federal programs especially beneficial for racial minorities. The U.S. Commission on Civil Rights agreed with this negative assessment in its February report to Congress. The Commission charged that most federal agencies were failing to enforce adequately the nation's civil rights laws; it blamed this "steady erosion of the progress toward equal rights" on the lack of "Presidential leadership."

Not surprisingly, black trust in the government fell to its lowest point since the University of Michigan's national surveys began recording it in 1958. Unlike the 1960s, this estrangement did not typically express itself in public protests. The National Association for Community Development rally on the Capitol steps in Washington, D.C., on February 20 to protest program cuts was an exception, as was the Mexican-American march in Dallas, Tex., on July 28 to protest the police killing of a 12-year-old boy.

The more typical response was to enter politics. Even Black Panther leader Bobby Seale renounced violence and seriously campaigned for mayor of Oakland, Calif., finishing second to incumbent John Reading. Experienced blacks were more successful in mayoralty races throughout the country. In Los Angeles in May, Councilman Thomas Bradley (*see* BIOGRAPHY) defeated incumbent Sam Yorty with 56% of the votes in a reversal of their bitter race four years earlier. In Atlanta in October, Vice-Mayor Maynard Jackson defeated incumbent Sam Massell with 59% of the vote, while in November, State Sen. Coleman Young narrowly edged former police commissioner John Nichols to become mayor of Detroit, and Councilman Clarence Lightner won over businessman Wesley Williams to become mayor of Raleigh, N.C.

In addition, Mrs. Cardiss Collins, backed by Chicago Mayor Richard Daley, was elected to Congress from Illinois in June to replace her husband, who had died in an airplane crash. John Bass, a former city welfare director, was elected controller in St. Louis, the first black to hold the city's second highest office. The Democratic National Committee included 8 blacks and 2 Chicanos among its 25 new members.

These advances reflected the enormous grass roots growth in black political power since the enactment of the 1965 Voting Rights Act. By 1973, there were more than 2,600 black elected officials in the U.S., a 120% increase in four years. Almost half were in the 11 ex-Confederate states, a regional total over ten times that of 1964. At the Southern Governors' Conference meeting in September, Virgin Islands Gov. Melvin Evans was elected the first black chairman, succeeding Alabama Gov. George Wallace.

Black leaders kept a watchful eye on racially tense developments in the U.S. armed services. U.S. Rep. Ronald Dellums (Dem., Calif.) joined with the NAACP in attempting to reopen the case involving racial conflict in 1972 on the aircraft carrier "Kitty Hawk." The Navy had found only blacks guilty of rioting and assault. In February, the Navy confirmed that it had discharged 3,000 enlisted men, 14% of them black, as "a burden to the command," and also announced that it had embarked on a black recruitment drive. While blacks constituted fewer than 1% of the Navy's officers, black enrollment at Annapolis climbed from 11 in the class of 1974 to 150 in the class of 1977. Meanwhile, the Army promoted three blacks to brigadier general in May, raising the total number of black U.S. admirals and generals to 16.

Black and white militants received less attention during 1973. H. Rap Brown and three co-defendants were convicted in March of a 1971 robbery of a Manhattan bar; but in November Brown was released from long-standing charges of inciting a riot in Cambridge, Md. Nine Black Muslims were found guilty of inciting a riot in Baton Rouge by a Louisiana state court and given maximum 21-year sentences. Likewise, five former Ku Klux Klan members were found guilty in Detroit of conspiracy in connection with the bombing of school buses during a 1971 desegregation controversy in Pontiac, Mich.

Two black baseball stars received special notice: Monte Irvin, with the New York Giants in the early 1950s, was elected to baseball's Hall of Fame, and Henry Aaron of the Atlanta Braves achieved a lifetime total of 713 major league home runs, one shy of Babe Ruth's record. Two blacks rose to high religious posts. The Most Rev. Joseph Lawson Howze became auxiliary Roman Catholic bishop of Mississippi in January, and Margaret Haywood, a District of Columbia superior court judge, was elected to serve as moderator of the United Church of Christ.

(THOMAS F. PETTIGREW)

See also Cities and Urban Affairs; United States.

Refugees

In 1973, special operations entrusted to the Office of the United Nations High Commissioner for Refugees (UNHCR) by the secretary-general of the United Nations assumed even greater importance than in 1972. In the largest of these programs, UNHCR coordinated a vast UN emergency relief action in the southern Sudan designed to pave the way for the return of 180,000 Sudanese refugees from neighbouring countries and of 500,000 persons who were displaced within the country during 17 years of civil strife. After a preliminary phase in 1972, during which UNHCR airlifted urgently needed food and relief supplies to the southern Sudan and provided heavy equipment and hand tools for the repair of the shattered road system in the area, organized mass repatriation of refugees began early in 1973. UNHCR provided 80 vehicles, 50 to move the refugees from the settlements in which they had been living in the Central African Republic, Ethiopia, Uganda, and Zaire to reception centres along the frontier and 30 for use within the Sudan. After being registered and inoculated, and receiving food and identity cards, the returnees were taken back to their home villages.

The largest component in the UN plan was a massive gift of food from the United States. In addition, major allocations were made for medical care, including the procurement of medical supplies and equipment and the provision of building materials for the construction of hospitals and dispensaries and for the rebuilding and equipping of schools. A permanent bridge across the Nile at Juba, capital of the now autonomous Southern region, was also being built.

Another special operation, which began in 1972 and reached its final stages by the end of October 1973, concerned the Asians of undetermined nationality from Uganda. In November 1972, just before the deadline set by Ugandan authorities for the departure of all Asians not recognized as Uganda nationals, 4,500 Asians of undetermined nationality were removed to temporary reception centres in Europe. UNHCR's responsibility was threefold: to find permanent resettlement opportunities for all; to finance the transport of those accepted for resettlement to their countries of final destination; and, meanwhile, to cover the cost of cars and maintenance in transit. By the end of October, all but 164 had been accepted by 19 countries. Canada, the U.S., and the U.K. took the largest contingents, while Austria and Belgium allowed sub-

WIDE WORLD

Bihari women and children in a refugee camp at Muhammadpur, Bangladesh. Although they are Muslims, the socially isolated Biharis have been persecuted by the Bengali majority.

stantial numbers of those who had been admitted in transit to remain. Nearly $3.5 million was contributed to UNHCR by governments for this program.

A new special assignment of major proportions was given to UNHCR in September. It involved the repatriation of approximately 200,000 members of stranded minority groups in the South Asian subcontinent (Bengalis in Pakistan and non-Bengalis in Bangladesh). Even before the New Delhi agreement on repatriation of August 28, UNHCR had been engaged in a limited repatriation airlift, but on September 19 the main phase began, accompanied by an appeal for $14.3 million to complete the operation over the next four to six months. By October 22, seven governments had contributed $3.5 million in cash toward this target. In addition, the U.K. pledged the use of RAF aircraft for the airlift, while the U.S.S.R. made available an IV-18 airplane on a bilateral basis. The UNHCR airlift transported thousands of persons during the year.

Of the approximately 200,000 refugees who benefited from UNHCR's regular program, well over half were in Africa, thus following the pattern of recent years. The repatriation of the Sudanese solved one of the largest problems on that continent, but new difficulties were created as Hutus continued to flee from the ruling Tutsis in Burundi. By the end of October, they numbered 90,000 (Rwanda 10,000, Tanzania 45,000, and Zaire 35,000). In 1973, as it had done in 1972, UNHCR allocated approximately $2.2 million for emergency and settlement aid for this group of refugees. Refugees from colonial territories, such as Angolans in Zaire and Zambia, Mozambiquans in Tanzania and Zambia, and Portuguese Guineans in Senegal, also benefited from substantial UNHCR assistance. In addition, there was a relatively small movement of refugees from Rwanda into Burundi, Uganda, and Zaire. On the other hand, in Asia, Tibetan refugees in India and Nepal and Chinese in Macau reached a sufficient stage of resettlement to permit the cessation of UNHCR material assistance and the closing of the three branch offices concerned.

In Europe, though the number of refugees of European origin was relatively small, the sharp slowdown in migration opportunities that began in 1972 persisted in 1973, leading to extended delays for those wishing to resettle in other countries. Reception facilities in some countries of asylum in Europe were taxed by the arrival of relatively large numbers of Africans seeking asylum.

A new situation requiring urgent international aid arose in Chile in September following the violent change in regime. UNHCR's regional representative for Latin America flew into Santiago soon after the military coup and established working relationships with both the new government and the National Committee for Aid to Refugees, which set up emergency reception centres where refugees living in Chile could find shelter. The high commissioner followed up with an appeal to governments for resettlement opportunities for the approximately 2,000 refugees who had expressed a wish to leave Chile, and he allocated $340,000 from the UNHCR Emergency Fund, mostly for the transportation costs of refugees proceeding to other countries. (UNHCR)

See also Migration, International.

Religion

The year 1973 was marked by reassessment of the church's role, both as an organization and as a force in the life of the individual believer. In many respects, it was a time of retrenchment for churches throughout the world. There were indications of a return to theological conservatism and a questioning of the church's relation to social activism. The movement toward ecumenical unity faltered, and interdenominational organizations were faced with severe economic cutbacks.

The trend toward conservatism was dramatically demonstrated by the Lutheran Church-Missouri Synod. In a stormy convention, it reelected its fundamentalist president, adopted a statement of confession that included literal interpretation of the Bible, and backed the president in a fight with the president and faculty of its largest seminary. A liberal group organized in an effort to reverse the trend, but no split in the church body was contemplated. (See *Lutherans,* below.) On May 19 representatives of more than 260 Southern Presbyterian churches voted to form a new denomination in the first major Presbyterian schism since the Civil War. The dissidents claimed they could no longer remain loyal to a church that denied the infallibility of Holy Scriptures, supported the ordination of women, and engaged in social activism. (See *Presbyterian, Reformed, and Congregational,* below.)

In ecumenical matters, the United Presbyterian Church in the U.S.A. rejoined the Consultation on Church Union (COCU), a proposed merger of nine Protestant churches (the African Methodist Episcopal, African Methodist Episcopal Zion, and Christian Methodist Episcopal churches, the Christian Church [Disciples of Christ], the Episcopal Church, the Presbyterian Church in the U.S., the United Methodist Church, and the United Church of Christ). The United Presbyterians had withdrawn in 1972, al-

Radio:
see Television and Radio
Railroads:
see Transportation
Recordings:
see Music
Reformed Churches:
see Religion

though 12 years previously they had initiated the idea of a new 25-million member church.

Despite the United Presbyterian move, COCU was one of the indicators that the time had not come for real unity among the churches. According to observers, this was not because there was no theological consensus, but because no agreement could be reached on such practical matters as church property. Social, economic, and cultural factors seemed to be larger stumbling blocks to unity than theology.

In Britain the United Reformed Church invited other churches to engage in exploratory talks on union. (See *Presbyterian, Reformed, and Congregational,* below.) The synods of the two major Protestant churches in The Netherlands, the Netherlands Reformed Church and the Reformed Churches in The Netherlands, held a joint meeting for the first time since their break in 1886 and voted unanimously to establish a permanent common synod. In Canada the *Plan of Union* between the United Church of Canada, the Christian Church (Disciples of Christ), and the Anglicans encountered opposition from all sides. (See *United Church of Canada,* below.) Complex juridical problems prevented the United Methodists from joining the Church of North India, formed in 1970 by Anglicans, Presbyterians, Mennonites, some Baptists, and British Methodists. They might have another opportunity to join in 1974, but observers doubted whether this was legally possible.

The World Council of Churches observed its 25th anniversary on August 26. The Rev. Philip Potter, the general secretary, summarized the current state of the ecumenical movement by declaring that the picture of an "ecumenical ship"—the symbol of the WCC—riding smoothly on a slightly choppy sea should now be redesigned to show a vessel "rolling uneasily over the waves and in danger of being overwhelmed." He stressed communications as a prime problem. The National Council of the Churches of Christ in the U.S.A. elected Claire Randall as its general secretary; she succeeded R. H. Edwin Espy, who had served in the post for ten years.

The growth of the charismatic movement in the so-called main-line denominations became increasingly evident during the year. (See *Pentecostal Churches,* below.) The strongest opposition appeared to come from conservative and fundamentalist Christians, while moderates and liberals were more sympathetic.

Ted Patrick begins to "deprogram" Marc Manecke to rid him of beliefs acquired as a member of the Children of God, a fundamentalist sect. Patrick was hired by parents who felt their children had been brainwashed by a religious sect, to "rescue" and return them.

JOYCE DOPKEEN—THE NEW YORK TIMES

Archbishop Robert J. Dwyer, Portland, Ore., said the danger of Pentecostalism was that "it does not need the Church . . . . her authority . . . . her sacraments." On the other hand, church historian Jaroslav Pelikan of Yale declared that people who have deep religious experiences ought to be allowed to speak in tongues when other language fails.

The so-called Jesus Movement among young people was somewhat less in evidence. In some cases it had become institutionalized in small sects, while many of its youthful adherents had reentered more orthodox churches or drifted away to newer enthusiasms. Parents continued to attack such groups as the Children of God, which demanded that members leave their families to live a rigidly structured communal existence. Headlines were made by Ted Patrick (*see* BIOGRAPHY), who specialized in kidnapping young converts—at their parents' request—and "deprogramming" them through intensive psychological pressures. In at least one instance, his tactics were upheld in the courts. There was some resurgence of mystical, Eastern-inspired groups. The Divine Light Mission, led by the teen-age Maharaj Ji (*see* BIOGRAPHY), gained a large following; among its more notable adherents was Rennie Davis, a political activist of the '60s and one of the defendants in the Chicago Seven trial stemming from the disorder at the 1968 Democratic convention. A member of Hare Krishna ran for mayor of Atlanta, Ga.

Key 73, the broad-based evangelistic program "calling our continent to Christ" and backed, either officially or semiofficially, by practically all Christian denominations, did not achieve the dramatic success at first envisioned for it. At the beginning of the year, Jews objected to an implied anti-Semitism in some of the evangelistic methodology. Others were critical of the program because it ignored the religious pluralism of the U.S. or because it represented political and religious conservatism. All these criticisms were roundly denounced by many denominational leaders, although many admitted that Key 73 was too loosely structured and did not really reach the grass-roots level.

The Watergate scandal provided material for discussions of America's "civil religion." (*See* Special Report.) Churchmen on the whole condemned the amorality represented by the scandal and urged that church people subject the political order to a continuous judgment.

After four years of study, a major statement was issued by the Faith and Order Study Group on Christian-Jewish Relations, a group of Roman Catholic and Protestant scholars convened by the National Council of Churches with the Secretariat for Catholic-Jewish Relations of the National Conference of Catholic Bishops. It declared that "in Christ the Church shares in Israel's election without superseding it." The traditional view of many Christians that the validity of Judaism ended with the coming of Christianity conflicts, according to the scholars, with New Testament teachings. The study group also dealt extensively with issues relating to the state of Israel and declared that "the validity of the State of Israel rests on moral and juridical grounds." While the statement had not received official endorsement, it was transmitted to the churches for study and response.

Three U.S. Supreme Court decisions were of immediate concern to churches. By 5 to 4, the court ruled that material does not have to be "utterly without redeeming social value" to be declared obscene and/or pornographic. Roman Catholic spokesmen were divided on the issue. Methodist, Lutheran, and Southern Baptist groups agreed with the decision on the whole but warned that it could lead to repression. The decision striking down restrictive abortion laws created a divided house in Protestantism. While no Protestant church had said abortion should be approached casually, many denominations had taken liberal stands. The conservative National Association of Evangelicals called abortion "morally wrong" except in cases of rape or incest or when the mother's life was threatened. Clearly, no Protestant consensus existed, as contrasted with the Roman Catholic stand of open shock and disapproval. (See *Baptists,* below; LAW.) The decision striking down formulas providing aid to children in nonpublic schools proved a blow to the Roman Catholic parochial school system, which stood to lose large sums provided under mandated services legislation.

According to the 1973 *Yearbook of American and Canadian Churches,* released by the National Council of the Churches of Christ in the U.S.A., 62.4% of the U.S. population had a religious affiliation in 1972, an 0.8% decrease from the previous year. Of the total, 71,865,190 were listed as "Protestant" (including Latter-day Saints and others not "Protestant" in a strict sense). Roman Catholics were placed at 48,390,-990, Jews at 5,870,000, and Eastern Orthodox at 3,847,901. Taking all tabulation variables into account, church membership by and large remained at a standstill. The percentage remained the same as in 1970 and did not keep pace with the 1% population growth registered in 1971.

Although it would be difficult to deduce definitive trends, the statistical picture, according to *Yearbook* editor Constant H. Jacquet, Jr., challenged the widely held opinion that conservative churches were growing rapidly while liberal and main-line denominations were declining. The more liberal denominations did show losses but the more conservative showed smaller gains than in previous years and, in some cases, losses as well.

Among the 14 largest Christian churches in the U.S., only the Roman Catholic Church, the Southern Baptist Convention, and the Church of Jesus Christ of Latter-day Saints (Mormons) reported increased membership. Seven major Protestant denominations showed decreases: the United Methodist Church; the Lutheran Church-Missouri Synod; the Episcopal Church; the Lutheran Church in America; the United Presbyterian Church; the United Church of Christ; and the American Lutheran Church. Forty percent of Americans attended worship in a typical week, according to the Gallup Poll, but the percentage continued to decline.

Figures released in 1973 showed that religious book sales rose by $9 million in 1972 over 1971. Sales of Bibles increased in 1973, largely because of the appearance of the *Common Bible.* Hailed as the first genuine unity Bible, the *Common Bible* was the Revised Standard Version with a few textual changes in the New Testament. It had received unprecedented British Protestant, Roman Catholic, and Orthodox endorsement, as well as endorsements from U.S. churches. The New Testament of the *New International Bible,* a modern English translation sponsored by the New York Bible Society, appeared in the fall. *The Living Bible,* a "paraphrase" by Kenneth Taylor, led U.S. nonfiction best-seller lists in 1972 and early 1973. (ALFRED P. KLAUSLER)

PROTESTANTS

Anglican Communion. The chief official event of 1973 was the meeting of the Anglican Consultative Council, held in Dublin in July. It was attended by the archbishop of Canterbury, Michael Ramsey, and by two or three delegates from each of the Anglican churches throughout the world that together make up the Anglican Communion. This was the second meeting of the council since its establishment in 1968, the first having been held at Limuru, Kenya, in 1971. The council had been designed as "an instrument of common action" for the whole Anglican Communion, with the function of "developing agreed Anglican policies," but the first five years and two meetings of its existence were quite enough to prove the severe limitations under which it laboured.

Although meeting more frequently than the Lambeth Conference, the Consultative Council lacked the obvious authority of the larger episcopal gathering. Moreover, the very nature of the Anglican Communion as a fellowship of autonomous churches meant that the council could not fulfill the functions officially laid down for it. It had no power to commit constituent churches to any particular action or policy. Rather, it was as a think tank that the council appeared to justify its existence. Its resolutions chiefly emphasized the duty of Anglicans everywhere to concern themselves with social and economic issues, especially the plight of oppressed minorities. More specifically ecclesiastical topics were also touched on, but there were no clear-cut developments on such divisive issues as the ordination of women to the priesthood or the church's attitude toward the divorced.

On such matters, Anglicans continued to go their separate ways. Canada and Wales followed Hong Kong's earlier example by approving the ordination of women in principle, while England postponed any decision for a period likely to last at least two years. At the triennial General Convention of the Episcopal Church (U.S.), held in October in Louisville, Ky., an absolute majority of the House of Deputies approved the proposition, but it was defeated because of the bloc system of counting lay and clerical votes. England still maintained the traditional refusal of remarriage to the divorced, but other churches, such as Canada, decided to allow it. The Episcopalians adopted a new marriage canon that greatly liberalized the procedures regarding remarriage; the parish priest was given broader discretion in such cases, although final authority remained with the bishop. After agonizing debate, an international conference of the Mothers' Union decided, by a large majority, to admit divorced women to full membership whether they had remarried or not.

The rapidly changing character of the Anglican Communion was revealed by the publication in April of official statistics of membership. For the first time, just over half the 65 million members lived outside England. Of the 360 Anglican dioceses throughout the world, 225, with a nominal membership of 50 million, were in developed countries and 135, with a nominal membership of 15 million, belonged to the third world. This shifting balance, coupled with mistrust of the church-state connection in England, led to doubts about the future. Archbishop Ramsey admitted that there were Anglican churches overseas that "do not want to feel themselves in any way an English-led communion." He pinned his hopes on the close links between Anglican bishops throughout the world; on the primacy of Canterbury (a primacy of service, not privilege) as a symbolic focus of unity; and on the continuance of a distinctively Anglican ethos. As against these factors, two main countertrends were in evidence. One was the growing tendency of Anglican churches to go their own way on controversial issues, without regard to any consensus in the Anglican Communion as a whole. The other was the movement, especially strong in England itself, to discontinue use of the Prayer Book, which for centuries had served to unify Anglican faith and worship.

The Episcopalians were typical in this regard, as their General Convention voted overwhelmingly to continue liturgical experimentation. The convention elected the Rt. Rev. John Allin, bishop of Mississippi, as presiding bishop; a self-professed "middle-of-the-roader," he succeeded the liberal Bishop John Hines, who had announced his retirement in 1972. In other actions, membership in COCU was maintained while parishes were urged to explore relations with Roman Catholics at the local level. The $13,625,732 budget included continued appropriations for minority "empowerment" programs. (R. L. ROBERTS)

Baptists. The worldwide membership of Baptist churches had grown by over three million since 1968. At the beginning of 1973 it was calculated to be 32,804,398. The annual meeting of the Executive of the Baptist World Alliance (BWA), held in July at Einsiedeln, Switz., was attended by 282 Baptist leaders from 32 countries. The Alliance president, V. Carney Hargroves, noted that this was the largest attendance in history in both numbers and geographic representation. In addition to six business sessions, the delegates discussed papers presented by five study commissions: on doctrine, Christian teaching and training, missions and evangelism, religious liberty and human rights, and cooperative Christianity.

J. B. Underwood, chairman of the BWA's three-year World Mission of Reconciliation Through Jesus Christ, reported that 98 Baptist unions were joining in the worldwide program of evangelism. The Telegu churches of India reported that 13,095 persons had been baptized in one month. Nigerian Baptists reported similar professions of faith.

Though considerable persecution existed, the vitality of Baptists in Eastern Europe was significant. The Polish Baptist Union reported that evangelistic meetings were held in all churches in 1972 and 89 were baptized. A strain of the Jesus Movement had emerged among the young in Hungary, even though advance approval was required for Bible studies and other meetings and young people were warned they would be barred from the university if they persisted in their Christian faith. Both Romania and the U.S.S.R. indicated spectacular strides in evangelical faith, with Baptists providing strong leadership. The situation in Czechoslovakia was also encouraging.

Baptists in Ireland had had an unbroken record of growth since 1941, but in Wales membership was falling faster than in any other country. The Baptist Union of Great Britain and Ireland announced a small decrease in membership but an increase in the number of baptisms. Membership totaled 198,324, although attendance was about three times that size. Authorization was given for the production of a supplement to the *Baptist Hymn Book* (used in most English-speaking countries other than the U.S. and Canada). The supplement was to consist of hymns written or composed during the preceding decade, largely on modern themes.

Although Baptist churches in the U.S. experienced a decline in growth overall, Southern Baptists showed continuing numerical increases. This group grew by nearly 2% to 12,067,284, second only to the Roman Catholics among U.S. church bodies. The Southern Baptist foreign missionary force stood at more than 2,200, and its 34,500 churches reported a record of nearly 446,000 baptisms.

The fourth largest Baptist group in the U.S., the American Baptist Churches in the U.S.A., joined with the primarily black Progressive Baptists in the Fund of Renewal, a joint fund-raising effort for education and social justice with a goal of $7.5 million. American Baptists held their first biennial convention in Lincoln, Neb., a departure from annual meetings and a reflection of the church's recent reorganization. A peace prize was given to William Sloane Coffin, draft counselor and opponent of the war in Vietnam. In the tradition of concern about separation of church and state, the Baptist Joint Committee on Public Affairs and the American Baptists joined the National Council of Churches on the side of the fundamentalist, anti-Communist preacher Billy James Hargis in a suit aimed at getting his tax exemption reinstated.

Baptists took mixed positions on the issue of abortion. American Baptist Howard Moody, pastor of New York City's Judson Memorial Church, supported the Supreme Court decision allowing a woman to opt for abortion in consultation with her doctor within the first three months of pregnancy. He felt it had "saved the ecumenical movement, avoiding an all-out conflict between the Catholics and Protestants." Ironically, it might bring Catholics and many Protestants together in opposition, since much antiabortion activity was stemming from Protestant ranks. In Maryland a Baptist minister was leading the antiabortion fight although W. A. Criswell, former president of the Southern Baptist Convention, seemed satisfied with the ruling. Linda N. Coffee, lawyer for the plaintiff in the Supreme Court case and a Southern Baptist, said, "The Supreme Court decision does not absolve anyone of individual moral or religious responsibility."

(NORMAN R. DE PUY; RONALD WILLIAM THOMSON)

Christian Church (Disciples of Christ). Kenneth L. Teegarden was elected chief executive officer in 1973, succeeding A. Dale Fiers, who retired after nearly 25 years of leadership in the 1.3 million-member church. Teegarden became the second general minister and president, an office created in 1968 when the Disciples approved a major restructuring. He was a key figure in the restructure effort, having served as administrator for the commission that developed it. The election came at the church's biennial General Assembly in Cincinnati, O. The Assembly also elected Jean Woolfolk, a Little Rock, Ark., attorney and life insurance executive, as the first woman moderator.

As part of the continuing restructure, the United Christian Missionary Society was phased out during 1973. Its Division of Overseas Ministries and Division of Homeland Ministries were incorporated separately as divisions in the Disciples' general structure.

The Disciples followed up the 1972 visit of church leaders to Asia by reappointing a Quaker couple to a second two-year term in Hong Kong in a "people-to-people" Chinese-American friendship effort. The church also brought a Chinese journalist to the U.S., where he planned to study.

National City Christian Church in Washington, D.C., was the site of the funeral of former U.S. president Lyndon B. Johnson, who died January 22. Johnson was one of the most noted members of the church.

The World Convention of Churches of Christ (Disciples), a confessional body, moved its headquarters from New York City to Dallas, Tex.

(ROBERT L. FRIEDLY)

Christian Science. Recommitment to Christian healing was emphasized by the denomination during the year, which marked the opening of the Christian Science Church Center in Boston. The centre, which would serve as world headquarters for the Church of Christ, Scientist, was opened without ceremony after nearly five years of construction.

At the annual meeting in June, more than 12,000 church members were urged to build the spiritual resources of their movement throughout the world. During the year, individual members of the Christian Science Board of Directors toured Great Britain and Ireland and continental Europe. Christian Science Regional Youth Meetings were held in 12 countries, and 22 college organization meetings were held in the U.S. A new training program aimed at assisting the elderly in their own homes was taught in more than 20 cities in the U.S. and Canada.

Albert Bankart Crichlow of Trinidad and Tobago was named to the Christian Science Board of Lectureship in June, the first black member to become a lecturer. Other new members were Horacio Omar Rivas of Buenos Aires, Arg., and Harvey Wood of Chicago. The board had some 30 members who gave more than 4,000 public addresses each year.

David E. Sleeper was chairman of the board of directors for the year. Roy Garrett Watson of Boston was elected president of the Mother Church and Marc E. Engeler of Geneva, Switz., was named treasurer. Zadie Hatfield of Boston became the first woman to serve as executive manager of the Publishing Society.

(J. BUROUGHS STOKES)

Churches of Christ. The San Jose Church in Jacksonville, Fla., was a prime mover in coordinating the evangelistic effort known as Evangelism/73; it served as a clearinghouse for information from over 11,000 individual churches on the availability of evangelistic materials and resource persons. Reports of special evangelistic endeavours were received from 47 U.S. states and several other countries during the year. Three evangelistic films, entitled "One Way, One Truth, One Life," were produced for television.

Foreign evangelism continued to be a primary concern. The World Bible School, founded by *Action* editor Jimmie Lovell, aimed to expand the use of Bible correspondence courses, which were being studied by over 450,000 persons outside the U.S. Abilene (Tex.) Christian College opened its Missions Center.

There was a growing movement toward concentrating the efforts of individual churches in particular areas of the world. The San Fernando, Calif., church, for example, cut back on other programs to concentrate on the four families it was supporting in Zambia.

Many churches also increased benevolent activities in their local areas. Most of the 57 homes for orphans supported by the churches were placing greater emphasis on foster home care. Other local efforts included nine homes for the aged, elementary and high schools, nursery schools, and day-care centres. New buildings received less emphasis than in past years. An exception was the million-dollar plant constructed by the Hillsboro Church in Nashville, Tenn.

(M. NORVEL YOUNG)

Church of Jesus Christ of Latter-day Saints. Harold B. Lee, president of the church since July 1972, died in Salt Lake City, Utah, on Dec. 26, 1973. (*See* OBITUARIES.) The ruling body of the church became the Council of the 12 Apostles, headed by Elder Spencer W. Kimball who, following Mormon tradition, was named the church's 12th president on December 30.

WIDE WORLD

A new $70 million Christian Science headquarters opened in May 1973 in Boston. The modern 26-story building dwarfs the domed Mother Church and the tiny Romanesque stone church that was the original home of the First Church of Christ, Scientist in 1894.

During 1973 world membership rose to approximately 3.3 million, comprising more than 7,300 congregations (wards and branches) throughout the world. Approximately 700,000 members were located outside the U.S. The church's increasing internationalism was reflected in the organization of many stakes (dioceses) in such nations as Brazil and South Korea, and in the selection of Munich, W.Ger., as the site of the third area general conference, held in August.

The Young Men's and Young Women's Mutual Improvement Associations, which had functioned as auxiliaries of the church for approximately one hundred years, were reorganized into three organizations that grouped unmarried members by age under the direction of the local priesthood. The Church Welfare Program announced its intention to develop 20 autonomous welfare regions in the U.S., to meet emergency food and clothing needs of its members.

Construction was almost completed on a temple at Kensington, Md., that would serve the 300,000 members of the church living in the eastern U.S. and Canada. Five buildings in Nauvoo, Ill., significant to the Mormon sojourn there in the 1840s, were restored.

Following the Supreme Court decision on abortion, the First Presidency of the Church stated its opposition to abortion except under rare, extenuating circumstances. (LEONARD JAMES ARRINGTON)

Jehovah's Witnesses. The year 1973 was one of outstanding growth for the society of Christian ministers known as Jehovah's Witnesses. Within the year 193,990 new ministers (members) were baptized, bringing the total to 1,758,420 in 208 countries and territories. Altogether, they spent 300,468,678 hours preaching from door to door, made 131,657,832 return visits to interested persons, and conducted 1,209,549 free, weekly home Bible studies. In addition, 3,994,924 ministers in 31,850 congregations assembled on April 17 to commemorate the Lord's Evening Meal.

Beginning June 20, attention centred on the series of 69 "Divine Victory" international assemblies, scheduled to continue through Jan. 27, 1974. Tours and charters were arranged for delegates traveling to other countries. Attendance at the 41 assemblies concluded by August totaled 1,402,238, with 39,313 new ministers baptized. The principal talk was "Divine Victory —Its Meaning for Distressed Humanity."

Persecution in some African countries continued. Jehovah's Witnesses were banned in Kenya, and in Malawi, where many had returned after fleeing to Zambia in 1972, the government arrested a number who refused to join the ruling Malawi Congress Party.

During the year 12 new rotary presses were installed in Watch Tower Society offices throughout the world, bringing the total to 64. Circulation of *The Watchtower,* the official journal of Jehovah's Witnesses, reached 7.9 million in 74 languages. Its companion magazine, *Awake!,* attained a record circulation of 7.6 million in 29 languages. (N.H. KNORR)

Lutherans. The Lutheran Church-Missouri Synod, a citadel of theological conservatism for 126 years, remained true to that tradition in 1973. In the most tumultuous convention in its history, conservatives overwhelmed moderates and raised the threat of possible schism. Supporters of the rigid doctrinal stance of Jacob A. O. Preus (*see* BIOGRAPHY) returned him to the presidency on the first ballot and then backed him on every key issue.

Preus acknowledged that "the controversy in our midst" centred largely between the synodical president's office and the administration and faculty of Concordia Seminary in St. Louis, Mo., the largest school in the world for training Lutheran pastors. According to Preus, the authority of Scripture was being eroded by the seminary's use of the historical-critical method of Bible exposition.

Conservatives in the 2.8 million-member denomination scored a major victory when a series of scriptural and confessional principles formulated by Preus was elevated to the status of a doctrinal statement binding on all members of the Synod. Earlier, these principles, which insist on a literal interpretation of biblical events, had been repudiated by the Concordia faculty.

Then, in an action believed to be unprecedented in U.S. Protestantism, the Synod condemned John H. Tietjen, president of the seminary, and 45 of the 49 active faculty members, for "false doctrine running counter to the Holy Scriptures, the Lutheran Confessions, and synodical stance." Charges against Tietjen were referred to the seminary's board of control, which later dismissed him and then suspended the move pending study of its legality. Similar action seemed likely to oust many of the faculty. Meanwhile, some 800 moderates met and organized a "confessing movement" to challenge conservative dominance of the Synod. Terming the meeting "a rebellion . . . against God's . . . Word," Preus pleaded: "I pray that we will soon stop this protesting . . . and get back to the task of proclaiming the Gospel of Jesus Christ."

Kent S. Knutson, president of the 2.5 million-member American Lutheran Church, died on March 12 at the age of 48. David W. Preus, a cousin of J. A. O. Preus, was named to succeed him until 1974.

The Wisconsin Evangelical Lutheran Synod elected Oscar J. Naumann to his 11th two-year term as president. With 386,000 members, it was the fourth largest Lutheran body in the U.S. and was regarded as the most conservative.

U.S. Lutheran and Roman Catholic theologians, completing three years of concentrated study on the issue of papal primacy, agreed that "a basis has emerged upon which . . . fruitful discussions between our churches on this subject are possible." Formal findings would be published early in 1974. Next to be discussed, as the doctrinal dialogue entered its tenth year, would be the problem of papal infallibility.

Meeting for the first time in East Germany, the Executive Committee of the Lutheran World Federation (LWF) received into membership the Lutheran Church in the Philippines and the Evangelical Lutheran Church of Nigeria. It now had 88 member churches with a total constituency of 54.5 million. The Executive Committee also called on member churches in southern Africa "to clearly state, on the basis of their theological convictions, their opposition to the policy of separate development [for blacks and whites]."

LWF leaders also sent pastoral letters to four predominantly white churches in southern Africa suggesting that some churches might be expelled from the LWF if they failed to implement resolutions opposing apartheid. Four pastors of the white German Evangelical Lutheran Church in South West Africa asked to be sent back to Germany in an apparent clash over the denomination's failure to unite with two black churches, later merged in the United Evangelical Lutheran Church in South West Africa. Leaders of the latter body met for the second time with South African Prime Minister B. J. Vorster to protest "torturing and suffering" of people in Ovamboland.

The Evangelical Lutheran Church in New Guinea elected a national as bishop of the 350,000-member denomination. In Norway, Bishop Kaare Støylen was named to succeed Bishop Fridtjov Birkeli as spiritual leader of the diocese of Oslo and primate of the Lutheran Church of Norway. Members of the Lutheran Church in America and the American Lutheran Church gave $4,053,823 for Lutheran World Action, an annual financial appeal for a worldwide program of spiritual and material aid. For the fourth successive year, membership in Lutheran church bodies in North America declined, to 9,049,492 including 302,350 in Canada. The four-year loss of 189,782 members represented about 2% of the all-time high recorded in 1968. (ERIK W. MODEAN)

Methodists. In keeping with the recommendation of the 12th World Methodist Council, held at Denver, Colo., in 1971, Pentecost 1973 was observed as a worldwide day of commitment to mission. Major evangelism congresses were planned for 1974 in seven regions of the world. Each congress was to include a representative team of persons from other regions so that the global nature of the mission would be understood. Lent was to be devoted to a Bible study on the person and message of Jesus Christ, based on St. Luke's Gospel and especially written for the church by William Barclay.

The executive committee of the World Methodist Council met in Mexico City in July 1973, and for the first time arranged a consultation on missionary policy in addition to the usual plenary sessions. Many of the themes developed earlier in the year at the International Review of Mission at Bangkok, Thailand, arranged through the World Council of Churches, were considered. The main theme was "The Internationalization of Mission," which was seen as involving the replacement of traditional "sending" and "receiving" roles by new patterns of sharing between churches.

Another important theme was the growth of dialogue with other faiths. A report was given on the continuing conversations with the Roman Catholic Church, and members heard of growing ecumenical cooperation and experiment.

In the U.S. the United Methodist Church eliminated the last all-black annual conference, completed the new structural reorganization, and faced several trouble spots in overseas work. In the last of a series of mergers begun nine years earlier to end the Central (all Negro) Jurisdiction, two black conferences in Mississippi united in June with their white counterparts. At the next lower administrative level, only 8 of the 500-some districts remained segregated.

The denominational restructuring voted by the Quadrennial General Conference in 1972 came into being as 1973 opened. Among its more important features, nine national program agencies were combined into four boards, and board membership was made broadly representative. The annual conferences overwhelmingly ratified six amendments to the church's constitution; they included removal of male-oriented language from the constitution, elimination of a minimum age for General Conference delegates, and equalization of the numbers of ministerial and lay members at annual conferences.

Efforts were made to halt the declining number of missionaries overseas, a trend attributed partly to the growth of indigenous leadership and to nationalism in some countries. In 1973 the blame was placed primarily on lack of funds, caused by decreased giving as well as by inflation and devaluation of the U.S. dollar. The Board of Global Ministries established a minimum need for 922 missionaries, compared with the 950 on duty in mid-1973. Meanwhile, five persons from Japan, Indonesia, Mexico, and India began working in the U.S. as "missionaries in reverse."

About half of the 40,000 Methodist churches in the U.S. participated in the Key 73 evangelistic effort. Another interdenominational thrust was the challenge to investments in multinational corporations with policies antithetical to the churches' stands on colonialism and racism, particularly in southern Africa. Three large-scale Methodist gatherings occurred during the year: the assembly of the new United Methodist Women (8,000 in attendance); the quadrennial convocation of the laity (3,000); and the convocation of the unofficial United Methodists for Evangelical Christianity (2,000). Membership in the U.S. continued a slow decline, to 10,334,521, but giving for church-wide benevolences and administration rose 4% to a record $47,217,241.

The British Methodist Conference, meeting at Newcastle, approved legislation for far-reaching changes in church structures. The traditional departments of the Methodist Church were replaced by seven "divisions." Plans were being prepared to replace local church trustees by a central trust, with a local property committee as a subcommittee of the local church council. Also at the local level, the "leaders' meeting" was to be replaced by the church council, functioning through various committees. The Circuit Quarterly Meeting, now known as the Circuit Meeting, was to meet only twice a year with a reduced membership.

(PETER H. BOLT; WINSTON H. TAYLOR)

Pentecostal Churches. The unity and worldwide growth of the Pentecostal movement was demonstrated in September 1973 at the tenth World Pentecostal Conference in Seoul, South Korea. The conference met at the Central Full Gospel Church (Assemblies of God). Over 25,000 persons attended.

North American unity was demonstrated at the October meeting of the Pentecostal Fellowship of North America in Jacksonville and at the gathering of the Society for Pentecostal Studies in Cleveland, Tenn., in November. Twenty years of organized lay witness were celebrated at the July meeting of the Full Gospel Business Men's Fellowship International in New York City. Among individual church bodies, the International Church of the Foursquare Gospel marked its 50th anniversary in Los Angeles in February. The opening of a new graduate school of theology in Springfield, Mo., was announced at the biennial General Council of the Assemblies of God, held in Miami, Fla., in August. The Church of God (Cleveland, Tenn.) conducted an International Evangelism Congress in Mexico City. Far-reaching structural reforms were approved at the quadrennial General Conference of the Pentecostal Holiness Church.

The charismatic renewal gained further impetus. The Episcopal Charismatic Conference, including 300 priests, met at Dallas in February, and the Charismatic Communion of Presbyterian Ministers, with 400 members, at Ann Arbor, Mich., in March. Some 12,000 attended the International Lutheran Conference on the Holy Spirit in Minneapolis, Minn., in August. Leo Cardinal Suenens was the featured speaker at the 25,000-strong international conference of the Catholic Charismatic Renewal, held at Notre Dame, Ind., in June.

The Jubilee Conference in the U.K. was held May 12–19 at Minehead Somerset; 7,198 were registered and there were some 3,000 additional visitors. The general secretary reported that the number of churches remained at 549, with 418 accredited ministers. A Special Jubilee Rally was planned for Feb. 16, 1974, in Birmingham to mark the 50th anniversary of the first meeting of the Assemblies of God. Overseas missions opened a Bible College in Nairobi, Kenya, valued at between £80,000 and £100,000. Home missions were also active, with eight crusades held in 1972. Through Revivaltime Recordings Ltd., gospel tapes were being produced for cassette players.

The Pentecostal movement was also gaining momentum in France, in contrast to the declining popularity of the more orthodox churches. The number of Assemblies of God had increased from 264 in 1964 to more than 460 a decade later, and the number of ministers had risen from 167 to more than 240. The number of faithful was estimated at more than 40,000. The movement was also making headway among the gypsies, over 4,000 of whom held a convocation at Strasbourg in July. (AARON LINFORD; VINSON SYNAN)

Presbyterian, Reformed, and Congregational. The ongoing world monetary crisis seriously affected the work of the World Alliance of Reformed Churches (Congregational and Presbyterian) during 1973. An emergency budget, drawn up in April, included reductions of 28% for staff travel, 35% for bilateral dialogues, and 25% for executive committee meetings. The four executive staff members of the WARC decided to forgo the normal 7½% cost-of-living salary increase. Despite all this, it was estimated the WARC would end the year with a deficit of over $10,000 in a total budget of approximately $142,000.

In March a final text of the so-called Leuenberg Agreement was drafted by representatives of Lutheran, Reformed, and United churches in Europe. The agreement awaited approval by the churches, which were expected to sign the document before the end of 1974. The agreement was aimed at the creation of full altar and pulpit fellowship among the bodies involved.

The European Area Council of the Alliance met in Amsterdam, September 6–11. The theme of the assembly was "Who do you say that I am?," the question with which Christ challenged his followers. Main speakers were Hendrikus Berkof of Leiden University and Rabbi J. Soetendorp of Amsterdam. Daily Bible study was led by Hans-Ruedi Weber of the desk for biblical studies of the World Council of Churches.

The first working assembly of the United Reformed Church—formed in October 1972 by a merger of the Congregational Church in England and Wales and the Presbyterian Church of England—invited the Anglican, Baptist, Methodist, and Roman Catholic churches to share in discussions as to how unity in England could be furthered.

Another union involving an Alliance member church had gone almost unnoticed in September 1972. After years of negotiations, the United Congregational Church of Southern Africa united with the South African Association of the Disciples of Christ to form the United Congregational Church of Southern Africa.

Toward the end of 1972, the Rev. Zedequias Manganhela, president of the Presbyterian Church in Mozambique, and José Sidumo, an elder, were reported to have committed suicide while being held, without official charge, in a political prison. News of their deaths and of the months-long detention of some 30 other Presbyterian church leaders caused a worldwide stir. The WARC, through its general secretary, the Rev. Edmond Perret, registered a sharp protest and sent a demand for an independent inquiry to Portugal's prime minister, Marcello Caetano. The Alliance also appealed to Amnesty International, the UN Commission on Human Rights, and the International Commission of Jurists. On Dec. 31, 1972, news of the other churchmen's release from prison was received in Geneva. A subsequent report published by an Amnesty International investigator stated that Manganhela had obviously been subjected to torture.

Relationships between the WARC and the Roman Catholic Church were strengthened in February, when General Secretary Perret, together with executive secretaries Richmond Smith and Frederik Kaan, paid a working visit to the Vatican.

Delegates to the 185th General Assembly of the United Presbyterian Church in the U.S.A. (UPCUSA), held May 16–23, voted by 453 to 259 to reenter COCU; this reversed the action of the 1972 assembly, which had voted 411–310 to withdraw. The Rev. Clinton M. Marsh was elected moderator, the second black man to be so honoured. In June the 113th General Assembly of the Presbyterian Church in the United States (PCUS) chose the Rev. Charles E. S. Kraemer as moderator. The Rev. James E. Andrews was elected stated clerk, succeeding the Rev. James A. Millard, Jr., who had served in that capacity for 14 years. Efforts to unite PCUS and UPCUSA, the two largest Presbyterian denominations in the U.S., continued to move forward, although not as quickly as proponents had hoped.

On May 18–19 a "convention of sessions," claiming that the positions of PCUS were out of step with its constitutional and doctrinal requirements, voted overwhelmingly (349–16) to begin a new Presbyterian church in 1973. The first general assembly of the new conservative denomination, which adopted the name National Presbyterian Church, was held in Birmingham, Ala., in December. The group included about 75,000 members from 275 churches in Southern and Border states.

During the year, two Presbyterian denominations, the Orthodox Presbyterian Church and the Reformed Presbyterian Church, Evangelical Synod, which had been apart for more than 35 years, took steps toward possible union in 1975. In addition, the Reformed Church in America and the Christian Reformed Church, which had split in 1857, entered "an era of increased dialogue and explorations of possible co-operation." (FREDERIK H. KAAN; WILLIAM B. MILLER)

Religious Society of Friends. The American Friends Service Committee (AFSC) raised over $250,000 in a nationwide campaign for a North/South Vietnam Fund. Altogether the AFSC spent approximately $8.4 million on programs in the U.S. and 16 other countries. The Friends Committee on National Legislation celebrated 30 years of activity as the only registered religious lobby in Washington, D.C.

A Regional Asian Pacific Conference was held in Sydney, Austr., August 18–25, in conjunction with the 12th meeting of the Friends World Committee for Consultation. Quakers from 23 countries participated in the business sessions, and additional Friends from Asia and the Pacific area joined them for the conference. Edwin B. Bronner, Quaker historian at Haverford (Pa.) College, was named FWCC chairman for the next triennium.

In common with other churches, the Society of Friends in Britain gave thought during 1973 to its investment policy. Its central finance committee completed a report on "the right use of our financial resources," and Meeting for Sufferings (the central council of the society in Britain) expressed its continued concern to ensure right investment.

Adam Curle was appointed the first professor of peace studies at Bradford University, a chair established jointly by the university and the Society of Friends. The Northern Friends Peace Board celebrated its diamond jubilee with a series of regional consultations on its peace witness in a changing world. A conference in London in January, arranged by the Friends World Committee, brought together a wider representation of Quaker mission and service bodies than had ever before assembled for joint consultation.
(EDWIN BRONNER; CLIFFORD HAIGH)

Salvation Army. Salvation Army work began in Fiji and Venezuela in 1973, bringing to 81 the number of countries in which the Army was active. Gen. and Mrs. Erik Wickberg, in their last year of office as world leaders, conducted congresses in North America, Italy, and Finland and Ascension Day meetings in Switzerland.

Commissioner Arnold Brown, the chief of staff, conducted the 90th anniversary of Salvation Army work in Canada. During the commissioner's visit to Jamaica, Gov.-Gen. Sir Clifford Campbell opened the Army's new school for the blind.

Soldiers and officers from 31 territories met at the Netherlands Training College in Amstelveen for the fourth International Social Work Conference. In Bombay, Commissioner Brown opened the first Salvation Army All-India and Pakistan Medical Conference.

"Focus on the Family" was the theme of Salvation Army activities in the U.S., emphasizing the Army's concern for the family as the fundamental cement of society. Col. Ernest W. Holz was appointed national chief secretary for the U.S., succeeding Col. C. Emil Nelson, who retired. Colonel Holz, a fourth-generation Salvationist, had served as chief secretary for the Western Territory.

Disaster relief continued to be a vital part of Army service. Teams of workers, tons of relief supplies, and funds to buy needed items were sent to Nicaragua after the devastating earthquake of December 1972. Within minutes of the announcement of an air crash in Switzerland involving women from three small villages in Somerset, Eng., officers reported for duty at the villages concerned.

(ERNEST W. HOLZ; HARRY READ)

Seventh-day Adventists. Church membership reached a new high of 2,307,167 (including 477,790 in the U.S.). Tithes and offerings totaled $260 million. On March 14 the church began operation of the former U.S. Army 3rd Field Hospital in Saigon. A new $8 million medical facility in Sydney was opened in July. Devaluation of the U.S. dollar affected mission operations abroad and, to prevent retrenchment, the church called for a special offering. On one day—May 26—churches in the U.S. gave $1,176,904. The total received worldwide was $2,177,250.

The *Review and Herald,* the church's 123-year-old English-language official organ, began publication of a Spanish edition in July. For the first time, literature produced and sold by Adventist publishing houses topped $50 million for one year. In September two million copies of *Steps to Christ* by Ellen G. White were ordered from printers in Chicago. It was believed that this was the largest single order ever placed for a religious book. Approximately 17 million copies of *Steps to Christ* had been printed since it was first copyrighted in 1892.

Appropriations for missions and home-based programs, voted at the church's Annual Council of administrators in Washington, D.C., October 7–17, totaled $65,746,162, an increase of 10.3% over the previous year. The Seventh-day Adventist Welfare Service, the denomination's disaster relief arm, shipped 1,323,121 lb. of clothing and bedding, almost 3 million lb. of surplus food, and medical supplies valued at more than $500,000. (KENNETH H. WOOD)

Unitarians and Universalists. For Unitarians in the U.S., 1973 was a year of conferences. Grave social problems in the outside community added to the denomination's concerns, which included a 4.9% drop in adult membership and a 7% decline in church school enrollment. But if deepening involvement, serious goal-seeking, and new structures for discussion were any measure, foundations for enduring growth and change had been laid.

The 12th annual General Assembly of the Unitarian Universalist Association, held in Toronto, May 30–June 3, drew nearly a thousand delegates from 40 U.S. states and 8 Canadian provinces. Robert Nelson West and Joseph L. Fisher were reelected to four-year terms as president and moderator, respectively. A resolution was passed proposing establishment of a denominational office on homosexual affairs. The U.S. Congress was urged to enact a universal and unconditional amnesty for those who opposed the war in Vietnam. Support was voiced for the U.S. Supreme Court ruling on abortion and for the White House Senior Citizens' Charter designed to deal with the problems of the aging. Additional resolutions reflected concern with other contemporary political, social, and religious issues.

The biennial convention of the Unitarian Universalist Women's Federation, held in Toronto immediately preceding the General Assembly, attracted the largest delegations in years. "The Church as a Caring Community" was chosen as a new program priority, and resolutions were passed on amnesty and abortion. The board was reduced from 23 to 12 members.

Unitarian Universalists for Black and White Action reported advances in its programmatic approach to racism and racial justice. The other officially recognized denominational group seeking racial justice and empowerment, the Black Unitarian Universalist Caucus, challenged the sixth Annual Meeting's legal right to change its name to the Black Humanist Fellowship.

City-centre social and church problems brought 200 persons to Philadelphia from 43 churches in 29 Canadian and U.S. cities. Church survival, the church's relationship to its surroundings, and community rebuilding were analyzed in depth. On April 10–11, 50 prominent Americans of various faiths gathered in Washington, D.C., under UUA auspices to discuss ominous trends toward government interference with rights of speech, press, privacy, religion, and association.

"Sharing in Growth," a new program for cooperative assistance within the denomination, was begun. The Church of the Larger Fellowship launched the Eliot-Scott Endowment Fund to ensure continuance of its mail-order service to 3,447 isolated members in more than 90 countries.

The British General Assembly met in Bristol, April 16–19. The Rev. Jacob Davies was installed as president. Among the resolutions adopted was one calling for a commission to discuss ways and means of educating members in the problems raised by homosexuality.

Further discussions were held during the year with representatives of the Roman Catholic Church. A weekend meeting was held at Manchester College, Oxford, on "Natural Theology and the Liberal Religious Doctrine of Man."

Active steps were taken to help congregations implement an improved stipend scale for ministers and to make provisions for retirement housing. The Rev. F. M. Ryde was appointed editor of the denominational newspaper *The Inquirer* in succession to the Rev. J. Allerton.

(JOHN NICHOLLS BOOTH; B. L. GOLLAND)

United Church of Canada. The United Church had inherited a strong tradition of moral and social activism from its Congregational, Methodist, and Presbyterian background, and in 1973 it continued to urge the people and governments of Canada to further the cause of justice and human rights. Representations were made to the government of Canada to abolish capital punishment, provide an adequate guaranteed annual income, and liberalize sections of the Criminal Code and Public Hospitals Act dealing with birth control and abortion. The church was also deeply involved in the question of French-English relations.

As a rule the United Church preferred to make its witness in cooperation with other churches. During Lent it joined with four other denominations in signing a brief, presented to the public, which asked whether "relatively affluent Canadians are prepared to level off or even cut down on their living standards" in the interests of humanity. At the same time, the five churches pledged $275,000 to the World Council of Churches for reconstruction and reconciliation in Indochina.

The United Church faced a problem in connection with ordination. Some persons who were theologically educated and ordained were leaving the conventional ministry for a "ministry" of teaching or some other vocation, but without relinquishing ordained status. The result was a kind of identity crisis with respect to ordination, resulting in some uncertainty as to whether, in fact, new forms of ministry (such as counseling) should be considered as ministries. Much thought was being given to the matter, but there appeared to be no immediate solution.

The revised *Plan of Union* between the Anglican Church of Canada, the Christian Church (Disciples of Christ), and the United Church of Canada continued under study. However, the Anglicans appeared not only to have lost interest in union but to have developed significant opposition to it. Much of this centred around the Anglican General Synod's approval, in principle, of the ordination of women (which the United Church had had for 37 years). The Synod was accused of precipitate action, and there was considerable resistance to the principle itself. The United Church was also showing some indifference to union, partly because of Anglican backtracking. Nevertheless, cooperation between the denominations continued on the local level. (ARTHUR GUY REYNOLDS)

United Church of Christ. The membership of the United Church of Christ in 1973 stood at 6,635 congregations and 1,895,016 members. When the denomination came into being in 1957, it brought together four U.S. churches, the Congregational and Christian churches, which united in 1931, and the Evangelical Synod of North America and the Reformed Church in the United States, which merged in 1934.

Actions by two national bodies during 1972 had raised questions about the direction the denomination was taking. The Executive Council had questioned the future of COCU, and the Council for Christian Social Action had dismissed its entire staff and indicated that it would redirect its program. At the ninth General Synod, which met in St. Louis in June 1973, the delegates strongly reaffirmed the "ecumenical stance" of the United Church, supporting full participation in COCU and vigorous participation in the World and National Councils of Churches. The delegates also approved a proposal for creating a Center for Social Action, which would carry on the functions of the former Council for Christian Social Action and coordinate activities in this field.

While most other major Protestant denominations were engaged in significant efforts at restructure, the United Church opted to deal with this matter from the perspective of structural planning. There appeared to be no inclination toward major shifts in denominational structure, probably because power in the United Church was widely diffused and focused in the local congregations. The General Synod did approve a proposal to dissolve two national agencies, the Council for Lay Life and Work and the Council for Church and Ministry, and to create in their place an Office for Church Life and Leadership. This could be seen as an effort to address the problem of church leadership without separating professional and lay leadership. If approved by the regional bodies, the new arrangement would become effective July 1, 1974.

Other noteworthy actions of the General Synod included a decision, based on a proposal by the Task Force on Women in Church and Society, to revise the church's constitution in order to eliminate sexually biased language. The sum of $350,000 was provided in bail for the Wilmington Nine, a group of eight young blacks and one young white woman being held in prison in North Carolina pending appeal on charges arising out of a racial confrontation over school integration. Previously, the Commission for Racial Justice of the United Church had sent a staff member into Wilmington when a local UCC congregation became the focus of the conflict. Ninety-five delegates and visitors were sent by charter flight to the Coachella Valley of California to stand with the United Farm Workers in their struggle against grape growers and a rival union. (See *Presbyterian, Reformed, and Congregational,* above.) (ROBERT V. MOSS)

ROMAN CATHOLIC CHURCH

Pope Paul VI celebrated the tenth anniversary of his reign in June 1973. After ten turbulent years, he made a plea for renewal of spirit if the modern world was to be truly evangelized. But he looked forward rather than backward. The year had seen intense diplomatic activity on the part of the Vatican; in September the pope himself chaired an unprecedented gathering of nuncios and diplomatic staff aimed at coordinating and strengthening the Vatican's influence on international affairs.

The 1973 Conference on Security and Cooperation in Europe was the first international assembly since the 1815 Congress of Vienna to be attended by the Vatican as a full participant. The pope had already had some successes in Eastern Europe, where his right to appoint bishops to long-vacant sees had gradually been recognized. It had taken ten years of negotiation with Czechoslovakia before agreement was finally reached in February. Throughout the year the Vatican succeeded in developing and spreading its contacts in both the Middle and Far East. Israel's prime minister, Golda Meir, described her visit to the pope in mid-January as "an historic moment." But despite the cordiality and frankness of the exchanges, there was no sign that the Vatican, concerned also to extend its relations with Islam, would give official recognition to Israel. In December, prior to the opening meeting of the Middle East peace conference in Geneva, the pope asked that "the voice of the Vatican be heard" in any discussion of the disposition of the holy places in Jerusalem. On February 14 the pope had a successful meeting with Xuan Thuy, the North Vietnamese negotiator at the Paris peace talks; in April he received South Vietnam's Pres. Nguyen Van Thieu. Moves were made toward establishing a nunciature in China, but there was evident concern that this should not prejudice the position of Catholics in Taiwan.

It was also a year of preparation. On February 19 came the official announcement that the fourth Synod of Bishops would meet in October 1974. Its theme was to be the "evangelization of the peoples of the contemporary world." A 22-page document, later sent to the bishops, stressed human development and the importance of ecumenism as well as the main subject. Pentecost, June 10, saw the start of preparations for the Holy Year in 1975. The theme was to be one of reconciliation and the specific aim was to be the "interior renewal of man."

In Western Europe the role of the church in a secular society continued to arouse popular debate, and the relationship between the local churches and Rome produced the by now traditional tensions. Spanish bishops began the year by examining the 1953 Concordat with the state, which was now considered inadequate. Negotiations were eventually opened with the Vatican. May Day in Madrid saw an attack on members of the Catholic Working Youth organization by a group calling itself "Guerrillas for Christ the King." A week later Vicente Cardinal Enrique y Tarancon roundly condemned all forms of violent extremism, of both the right and the left. The cardinal also warned the government of the need to ease tensions, and on June 14 the new Spanish Cabinet recognized the need for "loyal cooperation" between church and state.

In The Netherlands the conflict continued between the local church and Rome over the appointment of bishops. A "solidarity group" from the diocese of Bishop J. M. Gijsen of Roermond distributed a tract strongly criticizing the bishop's opinions and activities during his first year. Replying to accusations that he "worked from an exclusively hierarchial model of the church" and did not accept a pluriform image of the church "in which all the members of the Body of Christ have their own specific function," the bishop insisted on his own role as leader and bridge builder and his responsibilities to those members of the church who did accept his function and authority.

The church in Africa came into the news with accounts of alleged massacres in Mozambique. The story broke in July, but as early as Nov. 25, 1972, priests had been on trial in Lourenço Marques for publicly condemning the murder of Africans by Portuguese troops. References by the pope to "atrocious massacres" in his midday address of Sunday, July 15, were soon taken by the press to refer to the atrocities. In Zaire, Pres. Mobutu Sese Seko continued to insist that the church must be "zaire-ized," but later in the year he announced his firm intention to "make his peace with the Catholic Church," provided the church was willing to go along with his policy of "African authenticity." The Rhodesian bishops continued their opposition to the government's policies.

Conflict between the Brazilian hierarchy and the government intensified during the year. In June the bishops of northeastern Brazil produced a sensational indictment of the regime, which was immediately banned. The bishops were concerned about the radical dechristianization of the country, but the root of the problem was seen as a regime described by Archbishop Fernando Gomes of Goîania as "omniscient, omnipresent, omnipotent, infallible, and unshakable." In August Bishop Félix Pedro Casaldáliga and his whole team of religious and secular priests found themselves on trial before a military court. In Chile the church had been taking a more conciliatory attitude toward the Marxist-inspired government of Salvador Allende when a military coup and his death cut short the experiment in September.

In the U.S. the Supreme Court's decision on abortion was fiercely criticized by the National Conference of Catholic Bishops in a pastoral in February. Less predictable was the statement of Joseph Howze, auxiliary bishop of Natchez-Jackson in Mississippi and one of the two black bishops in the U.S., that the Catholic Church there had been too white-oriented and the liturgy was too dependent on European culture. In California some 39 priests and 42 nuns, including several provincial superiors, were imprisoned as a result of their participation in the United Farm Workers and the teamsters' union dispute over the right to represent farm workers. Church leaders had been involved from the start in what was seen as a battle against blatant exploitation of poor farm workers, many of whom were of Mexican extraction. Father John Banks, spokesman for the United Farm Workers, was attacked, but a boycott of growers who refused to deal with the UFW gained widespread support. Bishop Sidney M. Metzger of El Paso, Tex., himself involved in a similar dispute over the rights of a predominantly Mexican-American work force, celebrated Mass in jail for the prisoners.

On the ecumenical front, there were further signs of encouraging if hesitant progress. Bishop Léon A. Elchinger of Strasbourg tentatively approached the possibility of intercommunion "in exceptional cases." In The Netherlands relations between the church and the Old Catholics, who had broken away in 1723, showed a distinct improvement, and the possibility of intercommunion was admitted. In January the archbishop of Canterbury visited France for the Week of Prayer for Christian Unity, and in May he marked British entry into the EEC at an ecumenical service in Brussels. In May Patriarch Shenouda III came to Rome as the pope's guest, the first visit of a Coptic patriarch of Alexandria since the Council of Chalcedon condemned Monophysitism in A.D. 451. (See *Eastern Churches,* below.) Having previously issued an agreed statement on the Eucharist, the joint Anglican-Roman Catholic commission reached "basic agreement" on the ministry. In February, for the first time, an official delegation from the World Alliance of

continued on page 595

WIDE WORLD

St. Patrick's Cathedral in New York City gleams after an $800,000 restoration that removed 90 years' accumulation of dust, grime, and lampblack.

THE ALTAR AND THE THRONE: CIVIL RELIGION IN AMERICA

By Martin E. Marty

Two U.S. Supreme Court decisions and the Senate Watergate hearings challenged millions of Americans in 1973 to rethink their views of the nation, its moral tendencies, and its informal support of religion. In the history of religions, these issues were usually referred to as having to do with "throne and altar." In 1776 Americans dismantled the throne and most of them thought they were building thick walls around altars. But in different terms the throne stands in the office of the presidency and in the religious use of governmental symbols. And the religious have never been content to restrict themselves to life before the altar. The new events made the year one of the most confusing in history as far as relations between civil and religious society were concerned.

Religion and the Supreme Court. Religious people of many stripes had had increasing difficulties with recent court decisions, since many of them tended to favour law-and-order approaches to civil life. They regarded the 1962 and 1963 decisions that banned formal prayer in the public schools as a sign of decay in the spiritual side of American life. Pres. Richard Nixon's "strict constructionist" court was to have reversed the trend.

Then, on Jan. 22, 1973, the high tribunal overthrew the antiabortion laws of Texas and Georgia and, in consequence, those of other states. A conservative Protestant journal spoke for millions when it said that the court "has clearly decided for paganism, and against Christianity." Many more liberal Protestant ethicists questioned the decision, and noted that religious people could depend less and less on the state to enforce their moral positions. The reaction of Roman Catholics was even more vehement. Antiliberal Archbishop Robert J. Dwyer in *Twin Circle* said that Jan. 22, 1973, would go down in history as a day of infamy. The somewhat more moderate John Cardinal Cody of Chicago confessed that January 22 was his "worst moment." If the Catholic press accurately represents the parishes, lay people began to question their own support of the government and their moral security under it.

The second decision, on June 25, was more restricted in its impact. The court majority declared state aid to nonpublic schools to be unconstitutional. "Separation of church and state" had always inhibited transmission of public funds to parochial schools, most of which were sponsored by Roman Catholics. As the financial crisis of such schools worsened, state after state had attempted to find legally acceptable means for such transmission. Now the court ruled out aid in any form.

Watergate. In the eyes of many religious people, the throne was already weakened when the Watergate revelations began. (*See* UNITED STATES: *Special Report*.) But why, it may be asked, should these political issues have religious implications?

Students of American history have long known that the legal separation of church and state did little to keep religious people from regarding the nation in more or less sacred terms, just as the government found ways to show favour to religion. During the Eisenhower era, a new religious tone was noticed in Washington. Its critics called it "Potomac Piety"; its admirers considered it to be moral leadership. In the Kennedy and Johnson years, at least until the Vietnamese war escalated, political and theological liberals welcomed another spiritual style. But in many ways the bonds were strongest in the Nixon administration.

In 1972 Gerald S. Strober and Lowell D. Streiker, in *Religion and the New Majority,* showed that traditional religion was among the most potent forces in American politics, and that it found its centre in the Nixon White House. The year 1973 began auspiciously. The inauguration was full of religious symbols, as inaugurations always are. There were follow-up religious services lauding the administration's spiritual achievements. Highly publicized prayer breakfasts extolled the virtues of the administration. Then came Watergate. It produced waves of shock in religious circles. The presidential mandate of 1972 had come from people who liked the administration's "law and order" motif, its support of religiously based "work ethics," its attacks on moral permissiveness, its encouragement of religion. Many of them now felt cheated.

Typical was the reaction of *Christianity Today,* which historically reflected the viewpoint of evangelist Billy Graham. The editors took at face value the president's claim that he was not personally involved, but he had a solemn responsibility as president and as a Christian to see that the matter was investigated. In general, conservatives were most wounded and angered, because they felt betrayed. Liberals merely felt their prejudices had been confirmed.

Some of the secular media even tried to tie the evangelicals to the Watergate morass. Thus author James Michener charged that the indicted Watergaters were not products of "permissive society" but devotees of the strict sermons preached in the White House. Some conservatives fought back by adopting the "new morality argument." They had learned to act as they did from antiwar and civil rights activists who appealed to a higher law for the sake of social justice.

The Threatened Tie. Meanwhile, the polls showed a decline of confidence in the moral tone of the government. The president convoked no East Room worship services during the half year after the scandal broke. His friend Billy Graham, who had long let word of his intimacy with the president be spread abroad, now claimed that he had little influence on high Washington figures.

Debate also raged in more liberal circles. In 1955 Jewish thinker Will Herberg had termed "idolatry" the temptation to worship the American Way of Life. In the climate of the Kennedy-Johnson era, sociologist Robert N. Bellah had wanted his confreres to regard what he called "civil religion" more positively. Many did, taking affirmative views of Jefferson and Lincoln as religious leaders and looking for spiritual moments in more recent American history.

During 1973 Bellah and his colleagues retreated in frustration and anger over what "civil religion" had turned out to be. The term itself was largely understood only in academic circles, but Republican Sen. Mark Hatfield gave it wider currency at a prayer breakfast in February. He scorned leaders who "appeal to the god of civil religion" for then "our faith is in a small and exclusive deity."

The issues were by no means settled; the throne was weak but not toppled. The faith of the religiously pious in America was shaken but not destroyed. Some continued to support the administration and others believed that, after unfair media and congressional attacks, it would regain its moral stature. Despite the crises of 1973, it was not likely that those who regarded themselves as citizens in two spheres, governmental and religious, would permanently lose faith in either one. But the task of relating the two had become significantly more complicated.

Martin E. Marty is a professor at the University of Chicago, an editor of The Christian Century, *author of numerous books on religion and American culture, and a contributor to* Encyclopædia Britannica *in the field of religious history.*

continued from page 593
Reformed Churches visited Rome to establish contact with the Secretariat for Christian Unity. In June a delegation from the Vatican met the Orthodox patriarch in Moscow to continue the dialogues begun in 1967.

The pope named 30 new cardinals in February. In January a document was issued from Rome announcing changes in the form for the Sacrament of the Sick, and the fasting laws for the sick were modified in March. Another document allowed bishops to establish lay ministries, readers, acolytes, and others according to the local need. Far more important was a 250-page directive issued by the Sacred Congregation for Bishops which set stiff new standards for a bishop's life-style. Bishops were to be "externally and internally poor"; they were expected to avoid authoritarianism and respect "liberty of opinion." Despite a vigorous reaffirmation of papal infallibility, directed at the liberal Swiss theologian Hans Küng (*see* BIOGRAPHY), Vatican documents continued to echo the spirit and language of Vatican II. (*See* VATICAN CITY STATE.) (PETER HEBBLETHWAITE)

EASTERN CHURCHES

The Orthodox Church. In contrast to the late Patriarch Athenagoras I, Dimitrios I, elected ecumenical patriarch of Constantinople in 1972, appeared to have adopted a rather cautious attitude in his relations with the other Orthodox churches and other Christians. At the same time, the resignation of Metropolitan Nikodim of Leningrad from the post of chairman of the Department of Foreign Affairs of the Russian Patriarchate, which occurred on May 30, 1972, had tended to limit the international initiatives of the Russian Church.

Whether influenced by these changes or not, Orthodox spokesmen throughout the world adopted a notably more critical attitude toward recent developments in the ecumenical movement. Thus, on the occasion of a visit by Patriarch Nicholas of Alexandria to Istanbul on March 10–20, 1973, the patriarchs of Constantinople and Alexandria urged "circumspection" toward certain tendencies in the World Council of Churches. In a much more explicit way, the bishops of the Orthodox Church in America, in an encyclical published on March 27, condemned "secularistic Christianity" and those "theories and understandings" of Christian ecumenism "which are radically different from those upon which it was founded." The Orthodox understanding of ecumenism as primarily a search for unity in faith was further stressed in special declarations by the patriarchates of Constantinople and Moscow during the August meetings of the Central Committee of the World Council of Churches.

A crisis involving political as well as canonical issues continued throughout the year in the Church of Greece. In November 1972, for the first time since the military junta came to power in 1967, a meeting of the entire hierarchy of Greece took place in Athens. It resulted in widespread criticism of Archbishop Ieronymos and his ecclesiastical regime, which many considered to have been imposed by the government. The archbishop attempted to submit formally to his synod those dioceses of northern Greece traditionally under the jurisdiction of Constantinople, provoking a sharp protest from the patriarch. On April 13, 1973, a supreme state authority, the Council of State, gave its support to the latter's claims and forced on the archbishop the election of a synod opposed to his views. In December the Holy Synod of the Greek Church accepted the archbishop's resignation and appointed Bishop Georgios of Kalavryta to replace him until an election could be held. Two weeks earlier, Ieronymos had interrupted a religious broadcast to say that he was being forced out of office but the broadcast was cut off before he could finish his statement.

Even more political was the crisis involving Archbishop Makarios, the president of Cyprus, and the bishops of Paphos, Kitium, and Kyrenia. The three bishops had tried to force Makarios' resignation from the presidency on the ground that Orthodox canons forbid clerics to assume political functions. When he refused to resign, the bishops attempted to strip him of his episcopal titles. In July 1973, however, the bishops themselves were deposed by a "major synod," composed of bishops from Greece as well as from the patriarchates of Alexandria, Antioch, and Jerusalem. It was widely assumed that Makarios' opponents, who had failed to invoke the canons when the archbishop was first elected president, were in fact representing the political interests of Greek ultranationalism.

The somewhat frustrating events in Greece and Cyprus did not prevent hopeful developments in Orthodox missionary expansion. In November 1972 the synod of the patriarch of Alexandria elected three indigenous bishops in East Africa. Previously, the Orthodox Church in East Africa had been governed by Greek bishops.

Eastern Non-Chalcedonian Churches. After his trips to Moscow and Istanbul (October 1972), Patriarch Shenouda III of the Coptic Church of Egypt visited Rome on May 5–10, 1973, and was received by Pope Paul VI. During his meetings with Orthodox leaders, the Coptic prelate had emphasized his readiness to continue the dialogue with the Orthodox Church and expressed the wish that agreements already reached unofficially between Orthodox and Non-Chalcedonian theologians might eventually be sanctioned by the hierarchy of both sides. In Rome the pope and the patriarch published a joint declaration of faith which professed a common understanding of the issue of Christ's identity, traditionally considered a dividing point between the churches. It appeared that the parallel visits of the Coptic patriarch to centres of the Orthodox and Roman Catholic worlds reflected his concern for defining evenhandedly the relations of the Coptic Church with the rest of Christendom.

The Ethiopian Patriarch Abuna Theophilos of Addis Ababa visited the U.S. in May 1973 as the guest of the National Council of Churches. He urged "a revitalized evangelical thrust in Africa," but without the system of "subjugation" that had characterized Western missions in the past. (JOHN MEYENDORFF)

JUDAISM

On Yom Kippur, the most solemn day in the Jewish calendar, Arab forces attacked Israeli-held territory. For the fourth time since Israel became a state, Jewish communities throughout the world mobilized to raise money and supplies in support of the Israeli war effort. The mood that followed the cease-fire, however, was a far cry from the elation that had succeeded the Six-Day War of 1967. Both in Israel and in the Diaspora there was a feeling that the Jewish state was increasingly isolated—a feeling that was intensified as the Arabs' use of the "oil weapon" led a number of countries to issue statements sympathetic to the Arab cause.

JOHN SOTO—THE NEW YORK TIMES

Chanting "Free Them Now," demonstrators march to New York City's Dag Hammarskjöld Plaza on the eve of Israel's 25th anniversary of nationhood. Their signs bear the names of Jews they said were being held in the Soviet Union.

Fears for the fate of Israel were compounded by the fear that, if hardships stemming from the oil shortage were perceived as the product of Israeli intransigence, the result might be a resurgence of anti-Semitism. This anxiety was voiced by several Jewish leaders in the U.S., although polls on the subject indicated that Americans on the whole did not blame the Israelis for the energy crisis and tended to believe the U.S. should stand firm in the face of "Arab blackmail." Jewish leaders expressed most disappointment in the reactions of some liberal Christian leaders who either remained silent or appeared to lean toward the Arab side. (*See* MIDDLE EASTERN AFFAIRS.)

Prior to the outbreak of hostilities in the Middle East, the position of Jews in the Soviet Union was the focal point of Jewish collective concern and action. Repeated appeals were made by Western Jewish communities and international Jewish organizations on behalf of those Soviet Jews who were forbidden to leave the U.S.S.R. and harassed for their Zionist convictions. It was pointed out, however, that concentration on the undeniable right to emigrate left unsolved the much greater problem of the majority of Soviet Jews, who wished to remain in the U.S.S.R. either as fully assimilated Soviet citizens or as Jews living in their country of birth. There were signs of growing anti-Semitism in the U.S.S.R., unalloyed by "anti-imperialist" and "anti-Zionist" phraseology. This was shown, for instance, by the behaviour of some sections of the Moscow public toward Israeli participants at the World Student Games in August, when Jewish supporters of the Israeli teams were beaten.

Gloomy views were expressed about the future of Latin-American Jewry. Yitzhak Goldberg, chairman of the Combined Jewish Communities in Latin America, was reported as saying that "Latin-American Jewry is headed for a catastrophe. . . . Israel is not prepared to acknowledge this predicament and does not help in accelerating the *aliya* [immigration] of Latin-American Jews." A contrasting opinion was given by Conservative rabbi Marshall Mayer of Buenos Aires, who saw the community's chief dangers in such problems as assimilation, mixed marriages, and the indifference of youth to Jewish values.

Similar dangers facing North American Jews were pointed out by Rabbi Joachim Prinz, chairman of the Governing Council of the World Jewish Congress, who saw "many discernible and definable phenomena which point to a possible disappearance of American Jewry within the next two generations. These include intermarriage of Jews with non-Jews, preoccupation of American Jews with Israel, and a diminishing of the liberal tradition within the American Jewish community."

Whether or not rabbis should officiate at mixed marriages became a burning issue during the year, precipitated by a spate of reports concerning their increasing frequency. A mixed marriage is defined as one in which one partner is an unconverted non-Jew. The New York Board of Rabbis voted on June 29 to limit its membership to rabbis "who neither officiate at mixed marriages nor make referrals to rabbis who officiate at mixed marriages." The Central Conference of American Rabbis (Reform), which included many rabbis who performed mixed marriages, passed a resolution at its June 1973 convention opposing participation by its members in such marriage ceremonies. In practice, rabbis who did solemnize mixed marriages would continue to do so, but with the knowledge that most of their colleagues disapproved of their policy.

Because of the centrality of Israel to the Jewish world, the election of Rabbi Shlomo Goren as the Ashkenazi chief rabbi and Rabbi Ovadia Joseph as the Sephardi chief rabbi of Israel had a wide significance. Rabbi Goren announced that his main priority would be to reestablish the Chief Rabbinate as the spiritual centre of the state of Israel and the entire Jewish world.

A minor tempest in a teapot was caused in the U.S. by Norman Jewison's film *Jesus Christ Superstar*. The American Jewish Committee objected to it on the ground that it reinforced the canard that "the Jews killed Jesus." On the other hand, many Jewish and non-Jewish leaders felt the film was so obviously stylized that no intelligent viewer would take it as anything more than fantasy.

The decisions of the U.S. Supreme Court against state support of parochial schools hurt the network of Jewish day schools, which were largely, but not exclusively, under Orthodox sponsorship. As a result, the Jewish Federations had been compelled to undertake an increasing share of the financial burden of the schools.

The Rabbinical Assembly of America (Conservative) announced that a majority of its Committee on Jewish Laws and Standards had approved the principle of counting women in the required quorum of ten (*minyan*). The quorum of ten for services went back to the use of the word *aida* (congregation) in the Pentateuch to describe the ten sons of Jacob (other than Joseph and Benjamin) and the ten spies (other than Joshua and Caleb). The Conservative movement had been proceeding steadily toward the equalization of women in Jewish law and ritual.

According to the latest statistical summary compiled by the American Jewish Committee, the world Jewish population was estimated at 14,236,000 at the end of 1971. About 7,169,000 (over 50%) were in North, Central, and South America; some 4 million were in Europe, 2,738,000 in Asia, 181,000 in Africa, and some 77,000 in Oceania. The countries with the largest Jewish populations were the U.S. (6,059,000), Israel (2,755,000), the U.S.S.R. (2,151,000), France

(550,000), Argentina (500,000), and the U.K. (410,-000). There was an increased flow of immigration to Israel: 55,880 in 1972, as compared with 41,930 in 1971 and 36,750 in 1970, though these figures included a category of "potential immigrants," some of whom decide, after a time, to return to their countries of origin. Of special significance was the emigration from the U.S.S.R.: 31,652 came in 1972, as against 12,839 in 1971 and 992 in 1970; in the first seven months of 1973 immigration from the Soviet Union totaled 16,-469—about 7% less than in the corresponding period of 1972. (JACOB B. AGUS; PAUL GLIKSON)

BUDDHISM

By far the most spectacular event in the world of Buddhism during 1972–73 was the tenth general conference of the World Fellowship of Buddhists (WFB), held in Colombo, Sri Lanka. About 250 delegates and observers from some 50 countries were in attendance. In her presidential address, Princess Poon Pismai Diskul of Thailand noted with satisfaction that the number of WFB regional centres has grown from 30 to 61 during the two decades of the organization's existence.

The first World Fellowship of Buddhist Youth was inaugurated at the closing session of the conference. Like its parent body, it would have its headquarters in Bangkok. It was expected that the WFB would soon form an international Buddhist Women's Conference and an Institute of Buddhist Education. One of the resolutions passed at the conference called on the WFB to keep in touch with UNESCO and other appropriate international organizations engaged in combating ignorance, hunger, poverty, disease, and social discrimination.

Sri Lanka observed the 66th anniversary of the death of Col. Henry Steel Olcott, the American theosophist who pioneered Buddhist education in the island, and the 75th anniversary of the Colombo YMBA. The Ven. Panditha Wimalakeerthi Sri Sumana Sirimalwatte Sri Ananda was elected as the new maha nayaka, the ranking prelate in Sri Lanka. The All Sri Lanka Buddhist Congress applauded the government's decision to close horse betting centres and casinos and was campaigning for the closing of all bars.

In India the Maha Mahinda Buddhist International Society added four new Buddhist mission centres, while the Maha Bodhi Society established a new medical centre in Bangalore. The Dalai Lama presided over the ceremony marking the conversion to Buddhism of 4,000 Harijans (former "untouchables") in New Delhi. Later he made a six-week tour of Europe—his first trip outside Asia—during which he met with Pope Paul VI in Rome.

Thailand now had two Buddhist universities and several Buddhist colleges. As the seat of the WFB headquarters, Bangkok was host to many international Buddhist conferences. The Standing Committee on Drug Abuse Control, under the chairmanship of Tan Eng Kong of the University of Malaysia, planned to carry on active programs in close coordination with the WFB headquarters and the regional centres in various countries. In Japan a Buddhist symposium on "Life Science and Buddhism" was held under the chairmanship of Shoson Miyamoto, professor emeritus of Tokyo University.

The formal signing of the Vietnam peace settlement in February in Paris failed to bring real peace to the Indochina peninsula. It was reported that some 500 Buddhist monks were among thousands of political prisoners held by the Saigon regime. In Cambodia the Communist forces still clung to the ancient city of Angkor Wat. The Swiss National Commission for UNESCO requested the director general of UNESCO and other authorities to intervene at once to ensure the protection of Angkor.

Soviet Buddhists, mostly Buryat Mongolians, were not faring well. While a new temple was built in Ivalgisky, the number of lamas had been drastically reduced over the years. According to a Swiss source, Bidya Dandaron, a prominent Buddhist and professor at the Buryat Social Science Institute, was sentenced in December 1972 to five years in a labour camp on a charge of heading an illegal, nonrecognized religious group. Meanwhile, members of the Asian Buddhist Committee for Promoting Peace met in Moscow and decided to set up an International Buddhist Commission to study the situation of Buddhism in Vietnam.

In the West, a new Buddhist centre was established in Oaken Holt, Farmoor, near Oxford, Eng., and a Buddhist meditation centre was being built in Rome. The Buddhist art exhibition in Cologne, W.Ger., was highly successful. In the U.S. a Buddhist spokesman in California opposed the teaching of divine creation in the state's schools.

(JOSEPH M. KITAGAWA)

ISLAM

The outbreak of war between Israel and its Arab neighbours in October overshadowed all specifically Islamic religious developments of the year. (*See* MIDDLE EASTERN AFFAIRS.)

Other Muslim nations were reportedly taking a greater interest in the situation of the Muslim minority in the Philippines. Serious open hostilities had been reported in December 1972. Attempted negotiations between Pres. Ferdinand Marcos and a number of Muslim leaders failed in January, and fighting continued in southern Mindanao through the spring. The direction of Muslim activist groups was passing out of the hands of the older village chiefs and into those of younger, more educated leaders. The government claimed that a former faculty member at the Philippines State University, N. Misuari, alleged to be a Maoist sympathizer, had assumed leadership of the insurgents and that Muslim fighting groups

KEYSTONE

Buddhist converts chant in prayer as they embrace their new religion at a mass conversion ceremony at New Delhi, India. The Dalai Lama administered the initiation ceremony on March 20, 1973.

were receiving Communist support. At least 5% of the Philippine population was Muslim. (*See* PHILIPPINES.)

More than half a million Muslim Biharis in Bangladesh remained in refugee camps or were living in conditions of serious poverty. The 1973 agreement between India and Pakistan included a promise to discuss the problem, together with that of the more than 200,000 Bengalis in Pakistan, but no concrete steps were undertaken. (*See* BANGLADESH; INDIA; PAKISTAN.) On May 22 two persons were killed and many injured in Srinagar, Kashmir, when more than a thousand Muslim students demonstrated to protest allegedly insulting references to Islam in the *Book of Knowledge*.

The Libyan government continued its efforts to enforce traditional Islamic laws and punishments. Sale and use of alcoholic beverages was prohibited, and in September it was announced that adultery would be punished by publicly inflicting the required 100 lashes on the guilty. A rising conservative religious mood seemed detectable in a number of Arab countries, said to be related in part to the activities of the officially banned Muslim Brotherhood. In late May, Libya announced the dismissal of two professors accused of membership in the Brotherhood.

Islam continued to spread and to increase its influence in Africa south of the Sahara. Some of the effect of this could be seen in the growing sympathy in that area for Arab attitudes toward Israel. More spectacular was the announcement by the Libyan News Agency in September that Pres. Albert Bernard Bongo of Gabon had converted from Roman Catholicism to Islam, taking the new name of Omar Bongo.

The Vatican's continued commitment to dialogue with non-Christian religions—including, specifically, Islam—was indicated by the appointment in March of Sergio Cardinal Pignedoli as prefect of the Secretariat for Non-Christians. This dialogue had been active for a number of years.

In November 1972 the Albanian Muslim community of New York and New Jersey had opened its own mosque; previously the Albanian Muslims, said to number some 8,000, had used mosques of other communities in the region. Relations between the Black Muslims and other Muslim groups became prominent in 1973. In January four gunmen, captured after holding nine persons hostage for two days in a Brooklyn sporting goods store, were identified as "Sunnis" disaffected with the Black Muslim movement; some 15 Sunni mosques were said to be active in New York City. At about the same time, seven "Hanafi" (*e.g.*, Sunni) Muslims were killed in Washington, D.C. Hanafi leaders blamed the Black Muslims while they, in turn, denied the charge and claimed they were not at war with other Muslim groups having a black membership. A number of blacks, including professional basketball star Kareem Abdul-Jabbar, spoke out in an effort to explain their differences with Black Muslim policies and teachings. In February the Arab Muslim community in Dearborn, Mich., said to be the largest in the U.S., filed suit against the city, alleging use of illegal tactics to force them to move so an industrial complex could be established in the area. (R. W. SMITH)

RELIGIONS OF ASIA

The hope and optimism so apparent in Asia immediately after World War II were no longer in evidence in 1973. In those days the attainment of independence by many Asian countries had seemed to promise a brighter future. The religions of Asia, traditionally characterized by a quietistic outlook and a goal of otherworldly spiritual liberation, had taken on an activist temper, stressing religious freedom as the prerequisite for man's freedom. By 1973, however, authoritarian regimes had replaced constitutional rule in a number of countries. The role of religion had been greatly circumscribed and in many instances political leaders expected religious leaders either to support national policies in toto or to take no part in public policy matters.

Early in 1973 over a thousand Buddhists and Hindus attended a conference for world peace, held at Kathmandu, Nepal. The motto of the conference was "Concord alone is commendable," taken from the Inscription of King Asoka. In 1972 India celebrated the 25th anniversary of its establishment as an independent "secular" state with a constitutional guarantee of religious freedom. According to an analysis of the 1971 census, there were six major religious groups in India, some of which, including the Muslims, had a higher growth rate than the Hindus. The census recorded 36,083 persons, or only 0.01% of the total population, as having no religious affiliation.

In south India the Society for the Prevention of Cruelty to Animals was campaigning against the practice of animal sacrifice in Hindu temples. Roman Catholic leaders expressed their concern to the prime minister over alleged "religious discrimination," aimed at the Christians in Orissa and Madhya Pradesh. Conversion from one religion to another had been punishable by law in both states, though the Orissa law was nullified by the courts in January. In April 1973 India took over the administration of its protectorate Sikkim, following a rebellion by the

BALDEV—THE NEW YORK TIMES

Hindu scholar holds a symbol of authority at a meeting in April of nearly 2,000 Hindu scholars at New Delhi, India. The nine-day convocation, the first such in centuries, was spent in recitation of the Vedas, the Hindu works that contain the essential tenets of the religion.

Estimated Membership of the Principal Religions of the World*

Religions	North America†	South America	Europe‡	Asia	Africa	Oceania§	World
Total Christian	224,933,250	163,567,000	372,425,700	87,396,500	98,862,000	20,609,000	967,793,450
Roman Catholic	128,995,500	157,831,000	179,684,000	46,456,500	34,587,000	4,395,000	551,949,000
Eastern Orthodox	4,117,000	54,000	67,380,700	2,135,000	17,410,000‖	484,000	91,580,700
Protestant¶	91,820,750	5,682,000	125,361,000	38,805,000	46,865,000♀	15,730,000	324,263,750
Jewish	6,344,475	680,700	3,983,750	3,064,050	297,950	73,000	14,443,925
Muslim♂	205,000	185,000	4,088,000	414,796,000	93,328,500	572,000	513,174,500
Zoroastrian□	—	—	—	180,600	450	—	181,050
Shinto◇	55,000	90,000	—	63,005,000	—	—	63,150,000
Taoist△	15,000	12,000	—	31,340,700	—	—	31,367,700
Confucian△	92,165	90,000	40,000	275,630,700	500	45,500	275,898,865
Buddhist✦	142,000	175,000	200,000	223,136,500	2,000	—	223,655,500
Hindu⊕	65,000	470,000	300,000	513,755,500	461,000	529,000	515,580,500
Totals	231,851,890	165,269,700	381,037,450	1,612,305,550	192,952,400	21,828,500	2,605,245,490
Population**	332,000,000	201,000,000	717,000,000	2,154,000,000	364,000,000	20,200,000	3,782,000,000

*Religious statistics are directly affected by war and persecution; for example, the expulsion of Asians from Uganda changes the estimate of the number of Hindus in Africa. There are about a million refugees in Africa, chiefly from the Sudan, Angola, Mozambique, Portuguese Guinea, Rwanda, Burundi, and Malawi, and about 18 million throughout the world.

†Includes Central America and the West Indies.

‡Includes the U.S.S.R., in which the effect of half a century of official Marxist ideology upon religious adherence is evident, although the extent of disaffiliation and disaffection is disputed. The same difficulty in estimating religious adherence obtains in other nations with officially Marxist governments, although the degree of persecution varies from country to country and from time to time.

§Includes Australia and New Zealand as well as islands of the South Pacific.

‖Including Coptic Christians.

¶Protestant statistics outside Europe usually include "full members" only, rather than all baptized persons, and are not comparable to those of ethnic religions or churches counting all adherents.

♀Including many sects and cults of recent appearance and rapid growth.

♂The chief base of Islam is still ethnic, although missionary work has lately been undertaken in Europe and America. In countries where Islam is the state religion, minority religions are frequently persecuted and reliable statistics are scarce.

□Zoroastrians are found chiefly in Iran and India.

◇A Japanese ethnic religion, Shinto has declined markedly since the Japanese emperor gave up the claim to divinity (1947); neither does it transplant readily with Japanese moving out from the homeland, as does Buddhism. Japanese religious statistics are problematical because adherents are frequently related to several different religions simultaneously.

△Figures on religions in China are highly speculative, since the effect of the Maoist-Marxist revolution has yet to be measured.

✦Buddhism has produced several modern renewal movements, with energetic missions outside traditional ethnic-Buddhist areas.

⊕Hinduism's strength in India has been enhanced by nationalism. Modern Hinduism has also developed several renewal movements with vigorous missions in Europe and America.

**Source: United Nations, Department of Economic and Social Affairs. Data refer to midyear 1972.

(FRANKLIN H. LITTELL)

National Congress and the State Congress against the Buddhist chogyal (king), Palden Thondup Namgyal (*see* BIOGRAPHY).

In Sri Lanka, where Sinhalese Buddhists and Hindu Tamils had had checkered relationships for years, the Tamil United Front (TUF) started a campaign to amend the 1972 constitution and demanded the participation of Tamil MPs in the National State Assembly. The fact that S. J. V. Chelvanayakam, leader of the TUF, resigned his seat in the National Assembly indicated the depth of the Hindu Tamils' feeling. The All-Ceylon Buddhist Congress protested the appointment of Christian principals to Buddhist schools and the admittance of Muslim girls to a Buddhist school called Vishaka Vidyalaya. The government, however, was determined not to allow discrimination in educational institutions.

The regime of U Ne Win in Burma was taking a cautious attitude toward religion in order not to alienate religious minority groups. Burma had been disturbed by a variety of insurgent movements, including the rebels of former prime minister U Nu's United National Liberation Front, which operated from northwestern Thailand. In Thailand, where the government was sensitive to the reactions of the Buddhist majority, a U.S. missionary of the Church of Jesus Christ of Latter-day Saints and his American friend served six months in jail and then were expelled from the country for taking a picture of one of them sitting on the head of a statue of Buddha.

Not much was known about the religious situation inside China, despite the increased contacts with that country. The U.S.S.R. banned Yoga on the ground that its philosophical ideas were idealistic and mystical and therefore socially and ideologically dangerous. A National Interreligious Consultation for Peace, held in Kyoto, Jap., in March 1973, discussed communication and cooperation among religions, international collaboration for peace, and restoration of man and establishment of humanity. (JOSEPH M. KITAGAWA)

WORLD CHURCH MEMBERSHIP

The study of religious statistics is still in its infancy. Some churches keep very exact information on their members but will not release the data to outsiders. Others, and this is particularly true of the ethnic religions and some branches of Christianity with centuries-old ethnic foundations, base their own reports on percentages of population figures. Pushing further, in some nations no census of any kind has as yet been taken.

Some religions have "adherents," others reckon "constituents," others count "communicants"; only on the mission fields of Christianity, Buddhism, Islam, and Hinduism are quite precise figures available. A typical instance is Sri Lanka. A reliable government report indicates there are about 6,200 Buddhist temples in the island with about 18,000 priests and 1,784 Hindu kovils (temples) with about 2,000 officiating kurukkals (priests). The number of adherents in both cases can only be estimated.

A second major problem for the statistician is the uncertainty of religious reports from areas of persecution. Many millions of the world's refugees are religious as well as cultural, political, or economic victims. Their exact religious composition can only be estimated, along with the numbers still left in their lands of origin. The effect of an enforced Marxist ideology in the U.S.S.R. and China, and in allied (Eastern Europe) or occupied (Tibet) areas, can only be hazarded. Some official Eastern Orthodox tables still show 100 million Russian Orthodox; a recent government study conceded 30 million "hard core" Christians. Presumably, some place in between is a figure that might be comparable to the statistics of active Christians in—for example—Spain or Sweden.

The data for countries with free churches, where membership is based upon a clear and uninhibited choice, are generally far more reliable than those for areas where government has intervened to sponsor or to persecute. That is to say, the statistics of membership of a Zen Buddhist Society in Boston or a Baptist congregation in Burma are "hard" figures; the Buddhist figures for Thailand and the Lutheran figures for Lower Saxony are considerably less dependable, if membership rather than very loose adherence is the issue. Accordingly, although the accompanying table is revised regularly to reflect the latest surveys and informed estimates, the reader is advised to use it with the awareness that mixed styles of reckoning are necessarily involved.

(FRANKLIN H. LITTELL)

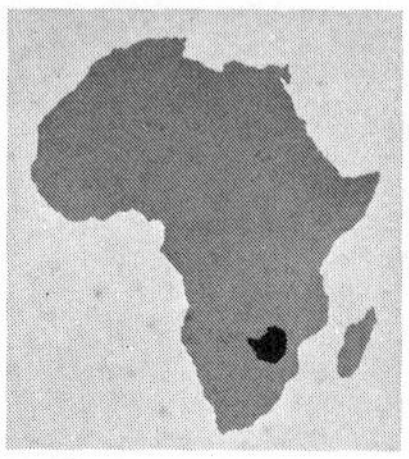

Rhodesia

Though Rhodesia declared itself a republic on March 2, 1970, it remained a British colony in the eyes of many other nations. It is bounded by Zambia, Mozambique, South Africa, and Botswana. Area: 150,803 sq.mi. (390,580 sq.km.). Pop. (1973 est.): 5,890,000, of whom 95% are African and 5% white. Cap. and largest city: Salisbury (urban area pop., 1973 est., 502,000). Language: English (official) and Bantu. Religion: predominantly traditional tribal beliefs; Christian minority. President in 1973, Clifford Dupont; prime minister, Ian D. Smith.

Rhodesian exports in 1972 were reported to have increased considerably, and the country's current account showed a small surplus in contrast to the marked deficit in 1971. The net balance of payments similarly showed a surplus after a deficit in the previous year. There was an increase, too, of 63,000 in the number of employed Africans. Industrial output in 1972 had continued to increase in spite of earlier predictions of a leveling-out process. Also, in spite of fears early in 1973 that the summer drought would have a seriously adverse effect on crop production, the harvest proved to be good. The mining industry, however, suffered as a result of devaluation of the U.S. dollar. In January 1973 came the news that the new Labor Party government in Australia had decided to ban wheat exports to Rhodesia, while in May action to tighten up sanctions was called for in the UN Security Council. A number of countries, notably Japan, West Germany, Switzerland, and The Netherlands, had been violating the UN embargo, while the U.S. had imported more than $12 million of strategic and critical commodities. Sir Alec Douglas-Home, the British foreign secretary, had stated that Britain was virtually the only country to bring prosecutions against sanction breakers, and supporters of sanctions received another setback in April when three Boeing jet airliners were delivered in Salisbury for use by Air Rhodesia. The Arab countries imposed a complete oil boycott on Rhodesia following the Arab-Israeli war, but at year's end its effect appeared to be minimal.

RHODESIA

Education. (1972) African: primary, pupils 715,835, teachers 17,230; secondary, pupils 29,170, teachers 1,418; vocational and teacher training, students 3,106, teachers 173. Non-African: primary, pupils 40,654, teachers 1,670; secondary, pupils 28,153, teachers 1,608; vocational and teacher training, pupils 3,963, teachers 214. African and non-African: higher (University of Rhodesia), students 978, teaching staff 195.

Finance. Monetary unit: Rhodesian dollar, with (Sept. 17, 1973) a free rate of *c.* R$0.56 to U.S. $1 (*c.* R$1.34 = £1 sterling). Budget (1971–72 est.): revenue R$229 million; expenditure R$236 million. Gross domestic product: (1971) R$1,208,000,000; (1970) R$1,067,900,000.

Foreign Trade. (1971) Imports R$282,380,000; exports R$277,240,000. Import sources (1965): U.K. 30%; South Africa 23%; U.S. 7%; Japan 6%. Export destinations (1965): Zambia 29%; U.K. 20%; South Africa 11%; West Germany 8%; Malawi 6%; Japan 5%. Main exports (1965): tobacco 51%; asbestos 12%; machinery 9%; clothing 6%; chemicals 5%.

Transport and Communications. Roads (1971) 77,962 km. Motor vehicles in use (1969): passenger 126,600; commercial (including buses) 52,000. Railways: (1971) 2,597 km.; freight traffic (including Botswana; 1970–71) 6,293,000,000 net ton-km. Telephones (Jan. 1972) 141,000. Radio receivers (Dec. 1970) 145,000. Television receivers (Dec. 1971) 51,000.

Agriculture. Production (in 000; metric tons; 1972; 1971 in parentheses): corn *c.* 1,400 (*c.* 1,179); millet *c.* 220 (*c.* 220); sugar, raw value *c.* 200 (*c.* 200); peanuts *c.* 130 (*c.* 122); tobacco *c.* 66 (*c.* 62); tea *c.* 2.3 (*c.* 2.3); cotton, lint *c.* 43 (*c.* 43); beef and veal (1970–71) *c.* 72, (1969–70) *c.* 70. Livestock (in 000; 1971–72): cattle *c.* 4,100; sheep *c.* 470; goats *c.* 700; pigs *c.* 150.

Industry. Production (in 000; metric tons; 1971): asbestos *c.* 80; coal *c.* 3,500; chrome ore (oxide content; 1970) *c.* 180; iron ore (metal content; 1970) *c.* 320; gold (troy oz.) *c.* 500; electricity (kw-hr.) 6,800,000.

Nevertheless, Rhodesian businessmen were becoming worried over the increasing government controls imposed both as a result of sanctions and because of increasing guerrilla activity. Admitting that the guerrillas were becoming more determined and were better trained than ever, the government closed the border with Zambia on January 9; there was also growing concern about a new threat of attacks from Mozambique. National military service was extended to a year, while reservists were called up more frequently for five weeks' operations, chiefly in the northeast. In January new regulations gave provincial commissioners power to impose collective fines on those considered guilty of assisting or harbouring guerrillas, or of murder, arson, and similar offenses. This move was criticized by Smith's white political opponents, who believed that it would win sympathy for the guerrillas. Nevertheless, the government seized cattle from tribesmen in the Chiweshe tribal trust lands for failing to report the presence of guerrillas. In a further attempt to reduce support for the guerrillas' activities the government decided in May to evacuate the African population of large areas along the northern border. In July, however, there was another setback when terrorists broke into a Jesuit mission school on the northern border and kidnapped 278 people, including 191 African children. In the course of the pursuit by security forces most of the captives were able to escape, but in September another guerrilla raid on villages located in the northeastern border area resulted in the capture of more than 90 children.

Attempts to promote discussions regarding a settlement of Rhodesia's future between the government and the African National Council, the recognized representative of black African opinion, encountered a number of obstacles. In February Bishop Abel Muzorewa, president of the ANC, claimed that six senior officials of his party had been arrested, and he immediately called off plans for settlement talks. Contact was renewed three weeks later, but progress was held up by the government's insistence that its settlement terms were nonnegotiable. Meanwhile, the ANC's status was challenged by an agreement signed in March between the two resistance movements, the Zimbabwe African National Union and the Zimbabwe African People's Union, which had been at loggerheads for ten years.

Throughout the year it became increasingly clear

Resources, Natural:
see Environment
Retail Sales:
see Merchandising

RHODESIAN MINISTRY OF INFORMATION

A photo supplied by the Rhodesian government is said to show "terrorists surrendering to security forces." Infiltrators had become increasingly troublesome to the white government.

that the British government had no intention of compromising its principles for the sake of a settlement. Prime Minister Smith, however, was under pressure from his own supporters and Rhodesian business interests to put an end to uncertainty and to produce convincing evidence that African opinion had changed since the Pearce Commission. (The commission had polled black Rhodesians in 1972 and found that the majority opposed a British-Rhodesian proposal of 1971 that would grant them slow and gradual political parity with whites.) In this dilemma he rejected completely the proposals for a settlement put forward by the ANC and instead pressed on with the policy of separate development, announcing in March the formation of two African regional authorities for Matabeleland and Mashonaland with responsibility for education, health, and general development and with powers of taxation. (KENNETH INGHAM)

Romania

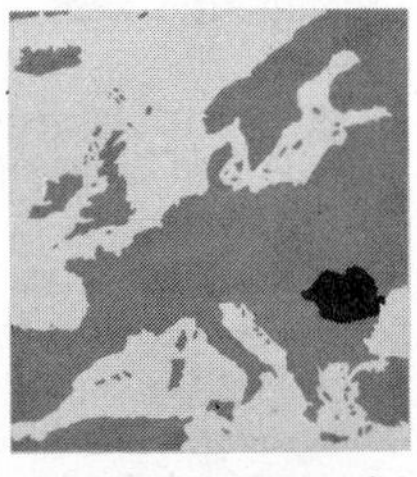

A socialist republic on the Balkan Peninsula in southeastern Europe, Romania is bordered by the U.S.S.R., the Black Sea, Bulgaria, Yugoslavia, and Hungary. Area: 91,700 sq.mi. (237,500 sq.km.). Pop. (1972 est.): 20,770,000, including (1968) Romanian 87.8%; Hungarian 8.4%. Cap. and largest city: Bucharest (pop., 1971 est., 1,591,784). Religion: Romanian Orthodox 70%; Greek Orthodox 10%. General secretary of the Romanian Communist Party and president of the State Council in 1973, Nicolae Ceausescu; chairman of the Council of Ministers (premier), Ion Gheorghe Maurer.

An eager traveler, President Ceausescu paid nine state visits to European and Latin-American countries during 1973, using every opportunity—as in previous years—to proclaim the sovereign independence of his country. In May he was in Rome to sign a ten-year accord with Italy on economic, industrial, and technical cooperation. On May 26 he was received in private audience by Pope Paul VI. On June 26–30 the Bonn government received him, and long-term agreements on economic, industrial, technical, scientific, and cultural cooperation were signed, as well as a solemn declaration in which the two governments affirmed the principles of their mutual relations and those of international collaboration. Ceausescu's meeting with Yugoslavia's President Tito at Brioni July 15–16 was almost a routine encounter of two friends and good neighbours. When the Middle East war broke out, Ceausescu offered Romania's mediatory services and in November invited Arab and Israeli officials to visit Bucharest. Only Israel responded, and Foreign Minister Abba Eban had talks with Ceausescu there on November 6. In December Ceausescu conferred with Pres. Houari Boumédienne in Algiers before flying on to Washington for talks with Pres. Richard Nixon.

A Romanian military delegation led by Gen. Ion Gheorghe, chief of the general staff, was warmly welcomed in Peking in June. On August 24 Premier Maurer had a meeting in Moscow with Aleksey N. Kosygin, the Soviet premier. The two statesmen discussed coordination between the Romanian and Soviet economic plans for 1976–80. The shah-in-shah of Iran visited Romania and on June 3 he and Ceausescu signed a 15-year economic agreement.

On July 4, during the general debate at the Conference on Security and Cooperation in Europe, in Helsinki, Fin., Romanian Foreign Minister Gheorghe Macovescu stated that the achievement of security on the European continent presupposed that relations among countries be based on the principles of equal

ROMANIA

Education. (1971–72) Primary and secondary, pupils 3,192,566, teachers 152,662; vocational, pupils 348,727, teachers 20,710; teacher training, students 22,634, teachers 1,421; higher (including 12 universities), students 148,428, teaching staff 14,470.

Finance. Monetary unit: leu, with (Sept. 17, 1973) an official exchange rate of 4.80 lei to U.S. $1 (12.20 lei = £1 sterling) and a tourist rate of 14.38 lei = U.S. $1 (35.30 lei = £1 sterling). Budget (1972 est.) balanced at 152,288,000,000 lei.

Foreign Trade. (1971) Imports 12,616,000,000 lei; exports 12,606,000,000 lei. Import sources: U.S.S.R. 23%; East Germany 7%; Czechoslovakia 7%; West Germany 7%; France 6%; U.K. 5%; Italy 5%. Export destinations: U.S.S.R. 27%; West Germany 10%; East Germany 6%; Czechoslovakia 6%; Italy 6%; China 5%. Main exports: machinery 24%; raw materials (minerals, metals, etc.) 13%; foodstuffs 13%; chemicals 8%; petroleum products 7%.

Transport and Communications. Roads (1971) 75,717 km. Motor vehicles in use: passenger (1969) *c.* 35,000; commercial (1970) 45,100. Railways (1971): 11,012 km.; traffic 18,811,000,000 passenger-km., freight 50,840,000,000 net ton-km. Air traffic (1971): 357.5 million passenger-km.; freight 6,266,000 net ton-km. Inland waterways in regular use (1971) 1,628 km. Shipping (1972): merchant vessels 100 gross tons and over 86; gross tonnage 445,622. Telephones (Dec. 1971) 727,000. Radio licenses (Dec. 1971) 3,106,000. Television licenses (Dec. 1971) 1,703,000.

Agriculture. Production (in 000; metric tons; 1972; 1971 in parentheses): wheat *c.* 6,100 (5,595); barley 839 (789); oats *c.* 150 (161); corn *c.* 8,800 (7,850); potatoes *c.* 2,760 (3,741); onions (1971) 292, (1970) 223; tomatoes (1971) 867, (1970) 720; sugar, raw value *c.* 597 (*c.* 499); sunflower seed *c.* 800 (791); dry beans *c.* 95 (94); soybeans *c.* 170 (165); dry peas *c.* 145 (123); plums (1971) 459, (1970) 697; apples *c.* 250 (253); wine *c.* 600 (*c.* 700); tobacco *c.* 30 (30); linseed *c.* 50 (58); hemp fibre *c.* 18 (*c.* 20); flax fibre *c.* 15 (17). Livestock (in 000; Jan. 1972): cattle 5,528; sheep 14,071; pigs 7,742; horses 654; poultry 61,262.

Industry. Fuel and power (in 000; metric tons; 1971): coal 7,123; lignite 13,782; coke (1970) 1,070; crude oil 13,794; natural gas (cu.m.) 26,719; manufactured gas (cu.m.) 536,000; electricity (kw-hr.) 39,454,000. Production (in 000; metric tons; 1971): cement 8,523; iron ore (30–35% metal content) 3,467; pig iron 4,382; crude steel 6,803; sulfuric acid 1,047; nitrogenous fertilizers (N content) 827; cotton yarn 121; cotton fabrics (sq.m.) 481,000; wool yarn 38; woolen fabrics (sq.m.) 70,000; newsprint 53; other paper (1970) 462; passenger cars (units) 9.1; commercial vehicles (units) 38. New dwelling units completed (1971) 150,000.

Rice:
see Agriculture and Fisheries

Roads:
see Engineering Projects; Transportation

Rockets:
see Astronautics; Defense

Roman Catholic Church:
see Religion

rights of all states; respect of every state's right to free existence, independence, and sovereignty; and noninterference in the internal affairs of states.

The 125th anniversary of popular revolutions in Transylvania, Walachia, and Moldavia was celebrated by large civic rallies in Blaj, Iasi, and Bucharest. Emphasizing the national and democratic character of the movements of 1848, Ceausescu said on all three occasions that—though they had been crushed by Russo-Turkish military interventions—these popular explosions marked the start of the victorious struggle for Romanian national unity.

On June 19 the plenary meeting of the Central Committee of the Romanian Communist Party decided to resume construction of the Danube–Black Sea canal across Dobruja. Work on the project, which had extensively employed forced labour, had been suspended in 1953, shortly after Stalin's death. At the same time a hydroelectric station would be built at Cernavoda and a new port constructed at Constanta Sud-Agigia. Another decision taken on the same day was the election of Elena Ceausescu, the president's wife, to the party's top policymaking body, the executive committee. Mrs. Ceausescu, a chemical engineer, was director-general of the Central Institute of Chemical Research.

In November Romania became the first Eastern European country to institute gas rationing and other energy-conserving measures, presumably as a result of the Arab oil cutback and possibly also because of an apparent failure to secure oil supplies from the Soviet Union. (K. M. SMOGORZEWSKI)

Rowing

East Germany and the Soviet Union dominated the world rowing scene in 1973, with West Germany the only other country to earn distinction. East Germany was the strongest nation in the men's and junior championships, but was eclipsed by the U.S.S.R. in the women's competition. Two significant features of 1973 were the decline in the number of countries contesting the European eights title, and the international baptism of two new rowing courses, one in Moscow and the other in Nottingham, Eng. Moscow was the site of the men's and women's European championships, which were held under the "European" label for the last time. Starting in 1974 they were to be replaced by the world championships, founded in 1972, which were to become an annual event except in Olympic years. There were 108 entries from 29 nations at Moscow but only 8 countries sent contestants in the eights. The overall entry was also lower than usual, probably because continually rising standards had led to more critical examination of selection criteria.

Cambridge pulls ahead of Oxford during their annual boat race on the River Thames, April 7, 1973. Cambridge won by 13 lengths.

KEYSTONE

Only 13 nations reached the finals in Moscow. East Germany walked away with the eights and also took the coxless fours and double sculls. The U.S.S.R. triumphed in coxed fours and coxed pairs, while Romania, in coxless pairs, collected its first gold medal in the championships since 1955. P. Kolbe of West Germany triumphed in single sculls. There were 53 boats from 18 nations contesting the five events in the women's European championships, in which East Germany recovered from its failure to win any event in 1972 by taking the coxless fours. However, it was the Soviet oarswomen who again dominated the racing by winning three titles for the third year in succession. They retained the eights and double sculls, but lost the coxed fours to The Netherlands. The third Soviet winner was G. Romashkin in single sculls.

The junior championships were used by the international rowing federation to try out the new British course at Nottingham, where 110 crews and scullers represented 26 nations. The East Germans won four events, taking their overall score to 19 titles out of the possible 28 since the championships became officially recognized in 1970. They successfully defended the double sculls and coxless pairs, lost the eights to West Germany, but completed their quadruple triumph with the coxed fours and coxed pairs. West Germany had a second win in coxless fours, and the seventh title went to N. Dovgan of the U.S.S.R. in single sculls.

At the Henley Royal Regatta the entry topped 250 for the first time since its foundation in 1839. U.S. crews competed in large numbers and won four trophies. For the first time the U.S. oarsmen were able to "loosen up" with two days of international racing preceding the regatta on the new Nottingham course. Their coaches claimed this sharpened their performance. Harvard University won the Ladies Plate for the first time; Princeton University captured the Thames Cup; a first Henley victory was recorded by Northeastern University in the Prince Philip Cup; and Potomac Boat Club triumphed in the Silver Goblets. Ridley College took the Princess Elizabeth Cup to Canada, Trud Kolomna scored a Soviet success in the Grand Challenge Cup, and Irishman S. Drea won the Diamond Sculls. In the 119th Oxford and Cambridge boat race, Cambridge won for the 67th time by a comfortable margin. (KEITH OSBORNE)

Rubber

The synthetic rubber industry experienced more changes in 1973 than in the entire preceding decade. Shortages of feedstocks (petroleum by-products used in synthetic rubber manufacture) curtailed production of almost all types. The styrene shortage threatened to prevent production of enough SBR (styrene-butadiene rubber) to meet 1974 consumption and

Table I. Natural Rubber Production

In 000 metric tons

Country	1968	1969	1970	1971	1972*
Malaysia	1,100	1,268	1,269	1,319	1,325
Indonesia	739	777	809	811	840†
Thailand	259	282	287	316	337
Sri Lanka	149	151	159	141	140
India	69	80	90	99	109
Liberia	64	67	83	74	64
Nigeria	56	61	65	56	54†
Zaire	32	35†	40†	40†	40†
Brazil	23	24	25	24	26
Others†‡	194	250	276	180	163
Total†‡	2,685	2,995	3,103	3,060	3,098

*Preliminary.
†Estimate.
‡May include statistical discrepancy.

Table II. Synthetic Rubber Production

In 000 metric tons

Country	1968	1969	1970	1971	1972*
United States	2,165	2,286	2,232	2,277	2,455
Japan	381	526	698	780	819
France	223	275	316	323	368
United Kingdom	237	273	306	277	307
Germany, West	238	292	302	306	300
Italy†	125	135	155	160	200
Canada	197	199	205	197	195
Netherlands, The	163	214	200	191	186
Germany, East	102	114	118	129	132†
Brazil	59	62	75	78	95
Poland	41	48	62	66	78
Romania	54	55	61	71	74†
Spain	27	35	39	45†	70†
Belgium†	25	35	50	60	60
Czechoslovakia	35†	40†	50†	52	52
Argentina	23	38†	39†	38†	44†
Australia	30	33	33	43	42
Mexico	34	36†	40†	45†	40†
South Africa	25	24	29	30	30
India	25	25	30	33	28
Bulgaria	—	—	—	5	15
Total†‡	4,908	5,495	5,855	6,083	6,515

*Preliminary.
†Estimate.
‡Includes estimated production for the Soviet Union and China (about 925,000 metric tons in 1972).
Source: International Rubber Study Group.

might affect 1973 production as well. Use of EPDM (ethylene propylene diene terpolymer), which had been subject to a serious overproduction problem, increased markedly, but this was threatened by the shortage of ethylene. U.S. production of synthetic polyisoprene, which, of the synthetics, most closely approximates natural rubber, was being severely limited by isoprene availability. Meanwhile, the oil-rich less developed nations and the Eastern European countries were expanding their capacity to manufacture synthetic rubber, particularly polyisoprene. This trend, if it continued, could result in the U.S. losing its position as the world's leading synthetic rubber producer.

The price situation was exemplified by the status of natural rubber. On Oct. 1, 1972, the New York spot price for no. 1 smoked sheet rubber was 18⅞ cents per pound. A year later, it was 34 cents. The high price had been influenced to some degree by large purchases by China and Japan during 1973 and by the dollar devaluation.

World production of natural rubber in 1972 was estimated at 3,098,000 metric tons, an increase of 38,000 tons over 1971. Production for 1973 was estimated at 3,366,000 metric tons. The management committee of the International Rubber Study Group (IRSG), meeting in London in June 1973, estimated world production and consumption of new rubber as follows: natural rubber supplies, including delivery from U.S. government stockpiles, 3,440,000 metric tons; synthetic rubber, 7,070,000 metric tons. It was estimated that some 3,360,000 metric tons of natural rubber and 6,970,000 metric tons of synthetic rubber would be consumed (*i.e.*, turned into manufactured products) in 1973. For the first time, estimates for synthetic rubber production included the U.S.S.R., nonmember countries in Eastern Europe, and China.

The U.S. remained the largest single buyer of natural rubber, using 650,679 metric tons in 1972. World consumption of natural rubber latex (dry basis) in 1972 was estimated at 282,500 metric tons. Statistics on world consumption of synthetic latices were incomplete, but the U.S. alone consumed 132,150 metric tons (dry basis) of the SBR type. World consumption of both natural and synthetic rubbers in 1972 was estimated at 9,620,000 metric tons. Production of reclaimed rubber fell to 280,000 metric tons, continuing a trend that began in the early 1960s.

A grading system for tread wear, traction, and high-speed performance of tires was being developed by the U.S. government, and it was proposed that tires sold after Sept. 1, 1974, have symbols denoting the type of service for which the tire was intended molded on the sidewall. This was encountering considerable opposition, however, since there was no agreement on definitive tests. The U.S. market was rapidly moving toward radial tires. Michelin of France, predominantly a manufacturer of radial tires, was invading the U.S. market with new plants in South Carolina. Two major developments in run-flat capabilities were announced. Pirelli's contribution was a cordless construction on a narrow rim so the rubber or rubberlike material was in compression. Dunlop, on the other hand, had a conventional-looking tire with special construction features; containers of material attached to the rim contained a combination ingredient that partially inflated the tire and lubricated the internal rubbing surfaces. Both were said to run about 100 mi. after a flat. (J. R. BEATTY)

Rwanda

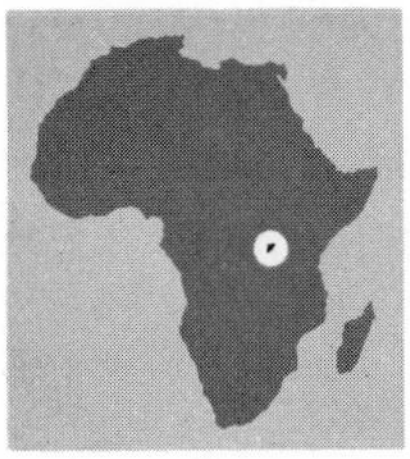

A republic in eastern Africa, Rwanda is bordered by Zaire, Uganda, Tanzania, and Burundi. Area: 10,169 sq.mi. (26,338 sq.km.). Pop. (1971 est.): 3,841,676, including (1970) Hutu 90%; Tutsi 9%; and Twa 1%. Cap. and largest city: Kigali (pop., 1971 est., 60,000). Language (official): French and Kinyarwanda. Religion (1970): animist 43%; Roman Catholic 46%; Protestant 7%; Muslim 1%. President in 1973, Grégoire Kayibanda until July 5; after that date the country was governed by the Commission for the Restoration of Peace under the leadership of Gen. Juvénal Habyalimana.

On July 5, 1973, the National Guard under Gen. Juvénal Habyalimana seized power in a bloodless coup and arrested President Kayibanda. The immediate provocation had been the president's intended constitutional changes, aimed at enabling him to seek re-election. A deeper cause was the resentment shown by northern tribes, to which Habyalimana belonged, against high administrative posts being held by the better-educated Tutsi minority.

Uganda and Burundi quickly indicated support for Rwanda's new governing body, the Commission for the Restoration of Peace, composed of senior army officers; it promised an end to tribalism and brotherhood for all Rwandans. Earlier in the year Burundi had accused Rwanda of organizing attacks on its territory, encouraging the massacre of Tutsi students at Butare University, dismissing Tutsi workers, and closing the border to Rwandan refugees.

In February Kayibanda and Pres. Julius Nyerere of Tanzania had formally opened the Rusumo Bridge on

Rugby Football:
see Football
Russia:
see Union of Soviet Socialist Republics
Russian Literature:
see Literature

RWANDA

Education. Primary (1970–71), pupils 415,566, teachers 7,047; secondary (1967–68), pupils 6,466; vocational (1967–68), pupils 912; teacher training (1967–68), students 1,464; secondary, vocational, and teacher training (1967–68), teachers 580; higher (1969–70), students 287, teaching staff 58.

Finance. Monetary unit: Rwanda franc, with (Sept. 17, 1973) a free rate of RwFr. 85.82 to U.S. $1 (RwFr. 206.83 = £1 sterling). Gold, SDRs, and foreign exchange, central bank: (June 1973) U.S. $15.6 million; (June 1972) U.S. $4,610,000. Budget (1969 est.): revenue RwFr. 1,636,618,000; expenditure RwFr. 1,664,000,000.

Foreign Trade. (1972) Imports RwFr. 3,223,600,000; exports RwFr. 1,755,900,000. Import sources (1971): Belgium-Luxembourg 22%; Japan 14%; West Germany 9%; U.S. 7%; U.K. 6%. Export destinations (1971): Kenya 61%; Belgium-Luxembourg 23%; Tanzania 5%. Main exports: coffee 45%; tin 28%.

Agriculture. Production (in 000; metric tons; 1971; 1970 in parentheses): sorghum *c.* 140 (156); dry beans *c.* 140 (144); dry peas *c.* 63 (65); potatoes *c.* 126 (126); sweet potatoes (1970) 417, (1969) 324; cassava (1970) 345, (1969) 283; coffee *c.* 15 (*c.* 14); tea (1972) *c.* 2, (1971) *c.* 1.7. Livestock (in 000; July 1971): cattle *c.* 740; sheep *c.* 230; pigs *c.* 60.

the Kagera River, giving landlocked Rwanda access to the sea via Tanzania. This was especially important because Uganda in 1972 had closed the common border, forcing Rwanda to airlift coffee exports to East African ports. (MOLLY MORTIMER)

Sailing

The year 1973 began with the recently introduced scheme of more lenient handicapping for older boats working to the advantage of the widely campaigned old 12-m. "American Eagle" sailed by Ted Turner, enabling it to win the Sydney-to-Hobart classic from the much-fancied Australian trio of "Apollo II," "Ginkgo," and "Ragamuffin." In February, while the ocean boats were engaging in the Southern Ocean Racing Conference (SORC) St. Petersburg circuit racing, based in Florida and the Caribbean, farther north on the American lakes the DN ice yachts were gathering for their world championship. In that competition the Soviet ace, Ain Vilde, streaked to victory, followed by Randy Johnson and Jan Gougeon of the U.S. The SORC circuit consisted of six races: St. Petersburg–Venice, St. Petersburg–Fort Lauderdale, Miami–Lucaya, Lipton Cup, Miami–Nassau, and Nassau Cup. "Muñequita" (SS37) won all its Class D races and took overall honours from Ted Turner in "Lightnin' " (SS38), with Ted Hood's "Robin" (Hood 38) third. Class A went to "Charisma" (SS56), Class B to "Alethea" (CC43), Class C to "Windquest" (CC39), Class D to "Muñequita" (SS37), and Class E to "Lightnin' " (SS38). "Cascade" might have won overall but for a course error.

Also in the West Indies, the Sunfish class, thought to be the largest in the world with numbers in the hundreds of thousands, mustered for its world championship. All 120 boats were supplied new from Akart for the event. Pierre Siegenthaler, sailing for the Bahamas but previously well known in the late 1950s for his Flying Dutchman sailing skills in Europe, won the title. In the well-tried 6-m. field Gary Mull appeared to have found a new formula with "St. Francis V," which outsmarted all its opposition quite easily. In the downwind Transpacific Yacht Club (Transpac) race from Los Angeles to Hawaii, victory went to the lightweights and small yachts, and for the first time in nearly 40 years a Hawaiian boat, Stuart Cowan's 35-ft. "Chutzpah," was the winner, from the 40-ft. "Ariana" and 42-ft. "Improbable."

It was interesting to see that many veteran sailors regularly appeared on the honours lists of the various classes. One such was Bruce Goldsmith, who won the Lightning class world title; the previous season he had been a reserve to Olympic gold medal winner Bud Melges for the United States in the Soling class.

The favoured U.S. entry "Ondine" leads the fleet at the beginning of the 3,500-mi. Cape Town–Rio race, later won by the Seychelles-registered yacht "Stormy."

A.F.P./PICTORIAL PARADE

WIDE WORLD

The U.S. six-metre sloop "St. Francis V" pulls ahead of Australia's "Pacemaker" to win the third race in the best-four-of-seven competition in the American-Australian Cup series.

Olympic gold medalist Serge Maury successfully defended his title in the Finn class. Two Danes dominated the Soling world championship sailed in France, Ib Ussing Andersen winning from Paul Jensen with Olympic silver medalist Stig Wennerström of Sweden finishing third. Another Dane, living in Canada, Hans Fogh, pulverized the Flying Dutchman class, in the absence of Rodney Pattisson, to take the world championship. The International Yacht Racing Union (IYRU) championships took place in Portugal with 470s and Lasers; probably to the surprise of most, Spain won the 470 title and placed third in the Laser class, indicating new sailing strength in that country.

The high spot for ocean racing yachtsmen was the Admiral's Cup series, finishing with the classic Fastnet race. Favourites Australia, Great Britain, and the United States were surprised by the West German team, led by sailmaker Hans Beilken sailing "Saudade." West Germany won the series and "Saudade" was the top-scoring yacht, with the beautiful "Recluta III" from Argentina second, and Britain's Carter-designed "Frigate," a particularly well-thought-out machine raced by Robin Aisher, third. The Australians were always near the front and finished second, but perhaps the sails of "Apollo II" and "Ginkgo," cut full to punch through the seas off Sydney Harbour, were not at their best in the choppy waters of the Solent and English Channel. The Fastnet began in good style but ended in total frustration for most of the 400 competitors as fickle winds and calms settled around the Scilly Isles and Plymouth. The big red Brazilian sloop "Saga" won the race from "Recluta III" and "Charisma" (U.S.).

The ton cup events all produced outstanding fast boats that did not win: "Ganbare" (U.S.) was the fastest one-tonner, "Bes" (Den.) the fastest half-tonner, and "Robber" (Swed.) the fastest quarter-tonner. However, the one-ton event was won by "Ydra" (Italy) from "Ganbare" and "Hann" (N.Z.); the half-ton by "Impensable" (France) from "Comfort II" (Swed.) and "Syrana III" (Nor.); and the quarter-ton by "Eygthene" (U.S.) from "Chien Jaune" (France) and "Timschal" (W.Ger.).

At the end of September the knifelike proa "Crossbow" raised its own world sailing speed record to 29.3 knots. The boat had been shortened by 5 ft. to 55 ft.; a foil had been added to the capsule, which now took the crew; and its sail area had been increased to just under 1,000 sq.ft. The Round-the-World-Race yachts left Portsmouth early in September on their first leg to Cape Town.

For the second time in four years John Jennings of St. Petersburg, Fla., won the Mallory Cup, emblematic of the North American men's sailing championship. Clark Thompson of Houston finished second. All eight competitors sailed 17-ft. Thistle class boats. "Baybea," a 12-m. yacht captained by Pat Haggerty of Sturgeon Bay, Wis., repeated its 1969 triumph in the Chicago-to-Mackinac Island race.

(ADRIAN JARDINE)

San Marino

A small republic, San Marino is an enclave in northeastern Italy, 14 mi. SW of Rimini. Area: 25 sq.mi. (61 sq.km.). Pop. (1972 est.): 18,706. Cap.: San Marino (metro. pop., 1971 est., 4,352). Language: Italian. Religion: Roman Catholic. San Marino is united with Italy by a customs union. The country is governed by two *capitani reggenti,* or coregents, appointed every six months by a Grand and General Council. Executive power rests with two secretaries of state: foreign and political affairs and internal affairs. From March 1973 the positions were filled, respectively, by Gian Luigi Berti and Giuseppe Lonfernini.

For the second successive year, the small republic faced a political crisis in 1973. Judged the gravest in 15 years, it began in late January, when the Cabinet resigned over a question of economic policy, and did not end until March. The new coalition Cabinet was formed by the Christian Democrats, the Socialists, and the Movement for the Defense of Constitutional Liberties (MDCL), a small splinter party. The Social Democrats, who with the Christian Democrats had ruled San Marino since 1957, were dropped from the Cabinet. The new coalition brought the Socialists to power for the first time since 1957 when they had joined with the Communists in a short-lived leftist government.

The 60-member Grand and General Council consisted of 27 Christian Democrats, 7 Socialists, 1 MDCL, 14 Communists, and 11 Social Democrats. With Communist support, Francesco Francini (Christian Democrat) and Primo Bugli (Socialist) were chosen as coregents on March 22. The government crisis ended five days later. In the Cabinet, secretaries Berti and Lonfernini were both Christian Democrats and Rémy Giacomini, the secretary of state for finance, budget, trade, and handicraft, was a Socialist.

On Sept. 10, 1973, the Grand and General Council, by a vote of 28–1, ended many legal restrictions on women. They could now be elected to the Council, could serve in any government post, and could engage in legal and financial transactions. They had received the right to vote in 1960.

(ROBERT D. HODGSON)

SAN MARINO

Education. (1969–70) Primary, pupils 1,580, teachers 89; secondary, pupils 843, teachers 62.

Finance. Monetary unit: Italian lira, with (Sept. 17, 1973) a free commercial (*valutaria*) rate of 564 lire to U.S. $1 (1,359 lire = £1 sterling); local coins are issued. Budget (1972 est.) balanced at 9,530,000,000 lire. Tourism (1970) *c.* 3 million visitors.

Sabah:
see Malaysia

St. Lucia:
see Dependent States

Salvador, El:
see El Salvador

Salvation Army:
see Religion

Samoa:
see Dependent States; Western Samoa

Sarawak:
see Malaysia

Satellites, Space:
see Astronautics

Saudi Arabia

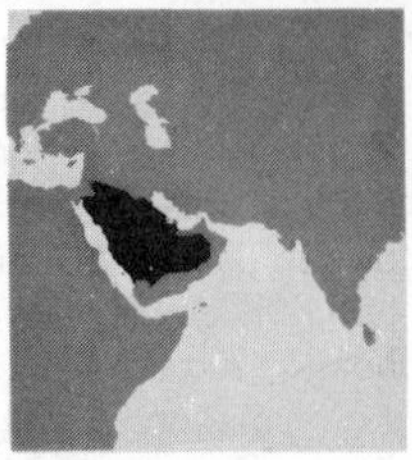

A monarchy occupying four-fifths of the Arabian Peninsula, Saudi Arabia has an area of 865,000 sq.mi. (2,240,000 sq.km.). Pop. (1973 est.): 8,115,000. Cap. and largest city: Riyadh (pop., 1965 est., 225,000). Language: Arabic. Religion: Muslim. King and prime minister, Faisal.

On Oct. 14, 1973, Saudi Arabia became the tenth Arab state to send forces against Israel in the fourth Arab-Israeli conflict since 1948. An immediate cutback in Saudi oil production of 10% was ordered on October 21 with further cutbacks of 5% each month until Israel withdrew from all occupied Arab territories, including East Jerusalem, and recognized the "legitimate rights of the Palestinian people." Under Saudi leadership, the Arab oil-producing countries cut off supplies to the U.S., The Netherlands, Portugal, Rhodesia, and South Africa, while manipulating cutbacks in supplies to other countries in a manner calculated to achieve support and prevent the formation of an anti-Arab front. Thus King Faisal (*see* BIOGRAPHY) warned against proposals to cut off oil from the West altogether as likely to weaken rather than strengthen the Arab cause, and the deputy oil minister, Prince Saud, pointed out that such a cutoff would affect the U.S. less than Europe and Japan, which were more favourable to Arab views. Late in the year the Saudi oil minister, Ahmad Zaki al-Yamani, and other Saudi representatives toured world capitals explaining the Arab position and warning against countermeasures. In mid-November it became clear that Saudi Arabia was not prepared to wait until 1982 for 51% control of its oil industry and was seeking immediate control.

King Faisal, monarch of oil-rich Saudi Arabia, became more significant in international affairs as the world faced an energy crisis and a new Middle East crisis in 1973.

G SIPAHIOGLU—LIAISON

By so dramatically forcing the issue, King Faisal turned from a conservative autocrat to an Arab hero overnight. It appeared that the "oil weapon," so long talked of, was a potent one—potent enough to cause a crisis within the Atlantic alliance, within the EEC, and between Israel and those it had come to regard as allies. Faisal's action showed that feudal autocracy and revolutionary radicalism could, apparently, work hand in hand to forge Egyptian manpower and Saudi oil money into a weapon of Islamic righteousness. The aim was simply to end U.S. support for "Zionism" (meaning Israel and Jews) and to reestablish a common front against Israel, including Egypt, Syria, and Jordan, with reduced dependence on the U.S.S.R.

Faisal secured the close collaboration of Egypt's Pres. Anwar as-Sadat (*see* BIOGRAPHY), who loosened his ties with Pres. Muammar al-Qaddafi (*see* BIOGRAPHY) of Libya, the Saudi monarch's strongest critic among Arab leaders. Faisal visited Cairo in May; the Egyptian president came to Saudi Arabia in August; and high-level contacts continued throughout the year. The Saudi subsidy to Jordan—whose aid from Libya and Kuwait had been cut off since 1970—was continued, and in May £10 million in aid for the Syrian Army was announced. The Palestinian guerrilla organization al-Fatah was allowed to open an office in Riyadh. Saudi oil income continued to increase rapidly. The 1973–74 budget of £2,300 million was £611 million above 1972–73, and 92.5% of the revenues came from oil. On August 1 the Saudi riyal was revalued by 5.078%. Saudi economic development continued apace and on January 31 King Faisal inaugurated the new £20 million Jiddah Port.

(PETER MANSFIELD)

SAUDI ARABIA

Education. (1970–71) Primary, pupils 422,744, teachers 17,435; secondary, pupils 81,141, teachers 3,973; vocational, pupils 848, teachers 224; teacher training, students 13,687, teachers 847; higher, students 8,492, teaching staff 697.

Finance. Monetary unit: riyal, with (Sept. 17, 1973) a par value of 3.55 riyals to U.S. $1 (free rate of 8.40 riyals = £1 sterling). Gold, SDRs, and foreign exchange, official: (June 1973) U.S. $3,110,000,000; (June 1972) U.S. $1,906,000,000. Budget (1972–73 est.) balanced at 13.2 billion riyals. Money supply: (March 1973) 4,591,000,000 riyals; (March 1972) 2,879,000,000 riyals.

Foreign Trade. (1971) Imports 3,626,000,000 riyals; exports 17.3 billion riyals. Import sources (1970): U.S. 14%; Lebanon 9%; Japan 8%; West Germany 8%; U.K. 6%. Export destinations (1970): Japan 21%; Italy 11%; The Netherlands 9%; U.K. 8%; France 6%; Bahrain 5%. Main exports (1970): crude oil 78%; petroleum products 16%.

Transport and Communications. Roads (1972) 14,150 km. (including 8,800 km. main roads). Motor vehicles in use (1972): passenger 51,100; commercial 37,200. Railways (1970): 610 km.; traffic 39 million passenger-km., freight 34 million net ton-km. Shipping (1972): merchant vessels 100 gross tons and over 35; gross tonnage 50,369. Telephones (Jan. 1972) 82,000. Radio receivers (Dec. 1971) 87,000. Television receivers (Dec. 1969) *c.* 50,000.

Agriculture. Production (in 000; metric tons; 1971; 1970 in parentheses): wheat *c.* 150 (*c.* 150); barley *c.* 35 (*c.* 34); millet *c.* 16 (*c.* 16); sorghum *c.* 52 (*c.* 52); dates *c.* 220 (*c.* 220). Livestock (in 000; 1970–71): cattle *c.* 320; sheep *c.* 3,300; goats *c.* 2,050; camels *c.* 560; asses *c.* 135.

Industry. Production (in 000; metric tons; 1971): cement 703; crude oil (1972) 285,915; electricity (excluding most industrial production; kw-hr.) 805,000.

Savings and Investment

Following a sharp rise in 1972, investment and savings in most of the industrial countries continued to increase in 1973, in both absolute and relative terms. This imparted additional stimulus to the economic upswing that had begun to gather momentum in the previous year. However, as the result of official policies designed to slow down the boom, contain inflationary pressures, and reduce imbalances in external accounts, there was some deceleration toward the end of the year.

The advance was associated with marked shifts in the type of investment spending on the one hand—most notably from housing toward productive facilities—and in the sources of savings on the other. To a large extent these changes were a reflection of cyclical positions and of the official policies, chiefly monetary policy, pursued by the authorities. Looked at in the wider perspective, this behaviour was in line with the cyclical pattern, except that the recovery in business investment spending came somewhat later than in the past and the acceleration in investment spending tended to be more modest.

In the U.S., where gross capital formation exercises a dominant influence on both the intensity of the upswing and the composition of output, total spending on fixed investment, after a large rise in 1972, moved up again, though at a somewhat slower rate. Within this total, there was a further acceleration in spending by industry on plant and machinery. However, expenditures on housing slowed down significantly, reaching a level only fractionally above that of 1972. Spending on additions to inventories remained (in relative terms) at approximately the same level as in the previous year. Foreign accounts showed a modest net investment abroad, as compared with net disinvestment in 1972.

The industrial upswing was accompanied by a decline in the financial deficit of federal, state, and local governments, a fall in disinvestment abroad, a slight rise in the financial surplus of the personal sector, and a modest rise in net financial requirements of the nonfinancial corporations. To a large extent these developments reflected tight monetary policy during the first nine months of the year, contributing to an improvement in household savings and accompanied by a slowing down of the willingness of the personal sector to incur additional debt.

The behaviour of investment in Canada was very similar to that in the U.S., with which Canada's economy is closely linked. The cyclical upswing, already strong in 1972, continued in 1973, to a large extent because of an even greater rise in total domestic fixed investment than in the previous year. As in the U.S., outlays on plant and machinery were the principal dynamic element, though public spending also advanced substantially. The expansion of these two types of spending was so great, in fact, that it comfortably exceeded an actual decline in expenditures on housing. Additional momentum to growth in total output was provided by a rise in the buildup of inventories and a fall in net foreign disinvestment.

As the year drew to a close, there was some evidence that private spending on productive capacity was beginning to lose momentum, with spending on inventories being increasingly hesitant. Total funds raised by domestic borrowers exceeded those obtained in 1972. This development was associated with pressures on interest rates, reflecting an increase in requirements for finance by the public sector and by nonfinancial corporations.

In the four main European countries, the U.K., West Germany, France, and Italy, the economic upswing and a rise in investment did not begin until around mid-1972. Thereafter, the pace accelerated, with business outlays in plant and equipment rising particularly rapidly but with spending on private housing slowing down significantly.

In the U.K., where economic recovery in the second half of 1972 had been led by a large rise in private consumption and, to a certain extent, by private housebuilding, 1973 saw an appreciable advance in investment outlays by the public sector on infrastructure facilities and by private industry and commerce on both plant and equipment and inventories. However, expenditures on private dwellings decelerated substantially, and external accounts showed an appreci-

Table I. Changes in Gross Domestic or National Product, Fixed Domestic Investment, Stock Building, and Foreign Balance in Main Industrial Countries

In percent

Country	Year	Increase in GDP or GNP	Change in total fixed domestic investment	Change in stock building*	Change in foreign balance*
U.S.†	1971	2.7	6.0	−0.2	−0.3
	1972	6.1	12.6	−0.1	−0.3
	1973‡	6.0	7.5	0	1.0
Canada†	1971	5.8	7.9	0.2	−0.6
	1972	5.8	3.6	0.3	−1.2
	1973‡	7.25	8.25	0	−0.75
U.K.§	1971	1.7	−0.5	−0.5	0.2
	1972	3.0	1.1	0	−1.6
	1973‡	6.75	4.25	1.75	0.5
West Germany†	1971	2.7	4.5	−1.8	−0.8
	1972	3.0	1.9	0	−0.1
	1973‡	6.25	2.75	0.75	2.0
France§	1971	5.5	5.6	−0.6	0.5
	1972	5.5	7.1	−0.1	−0.1
	1973‡	6.25	8.25	0.25	−0.25
Italy†	1971	1.6	−3.9	−1.2	1.1
	1972	3.5	−0.3	0.4	0.2
	1973‡	5.25	6.0	0.25	1.25
Japan*	1971	8.4	7.9	−2.4	1.7
	1972	9.6	11.1	−0.2	0.1
	1973‡	11.0	14.5	1.75	−1.0

*As a percentage of GDP or GNP in the previous year.
†Gross national product at market price.
‡All 1973 figures are estimates.
§Gross domestic product at market price.
Source: Organization for Economic Cooperation and Development, *Economic Outlook*, no. 14 (December 1973).

Table II. Changes in the Components of Gross Fixed Domestic Investments

In percent

Country	Year	Fixed public investment	Private residential	Private non-residential
U.S.	1971	—	30.5	−1.0
	1972	—	19.3	10.0
	1973	—	−0.75	10.75
Canada	1971	12.6*	18.9	3.3
	1972	0.7*	9.1	2.5
	1973	4.0*	7.0	10.0
U.K.	1971	2.2†	14.6	−5.0
	1972	−4.2†	21.2	2.2
	1973	2.0†	10.5	5.25
West Germany	1971	1.4*	9.2	5.1
	1972	−6.0*	13.6	0.4
	1973	−1.0*	3.0	3.5
France	1971	1.6*	4.0	8.9
	1972	5.5†	8.0	7.6
	1973	7.0†	6.5	9.75
Italy	1971	9.5*	−11.7	−6.6
	1972	3.0†	2.2	−4.7
	1973	0.5†	2.75	12.5
Japan	1971	24.5*	2.4	3.0
	1972	18.7†	13.6	6.75
	1973	8.25†	15.5	17.75

*Exclusive of nationalized industries and public corporations.
†Inclusive of nationalized industries and public corporations.
Source: Organization for Economic Cooperation and Development, *Economic Outlook*, no. 14 (December 1973).

able disinvestment. Large investment expenditures by the public sector increased its deficit substantially, raising, in turn, its requirements for savings. These were provided principally by domestic industry and commerce, and by way of a large deficit in external accounts. Net savings by households rose only moderately.

Total investment outlays rose appreciably in West Germany with public (including public corporations) and business expenditures on productive and allied facilities registering an exceptionally large advance. This was more than adequate to offset a significant deceleration in spending on private housing. With outlays on business investment accelerating and profitability under pressure, the business sector drew on savings generated by households.

In France, where fluctuations in total investment outlays and their various components tend to be somewhat smaller than in other industrial countries, the rise in total investment expenditures and the contribution this increase made to total output in 1973 were approximately the same as in 1972. While the private and public sectors both spent more on plant, machinery, and equipment, spending on housing slowed down moderately. Spending on inventories and net foreign investment rose, however, exerting a positive influence on domestic activity. To finance rising investment outlays, private business reduced its net savings while increasing indebtedness. Savings of households had fallen in 1972, together with borrowings, especially for housing, but these moved up again in 1973.

The recovery in Italy did not occur until the second half of 1972, and total investment outlay increased only moderately in 1973. In contrast with 1972, when investment spending by the public sector—and, above all, state enterprises—was one of the main dynamic elements, a moderate rise in expenditure on private housing and by private business on plant and equipment and inventories represented the bulk of the additional investment. As the result of increased capital outlays by public authorities and private industry, as well as a rise in the budget deficit, the net financial savings of these sectors declined and their indebtedness rose sharply.

The behaviour of investment in other European countries in 1973 was similar, in large measure because of the increasingly close degree of interdependence. There was a substantial rise in total outlays on investment in Belgium, The Netherlands, Scandinavia, Austria, and elsewhere, with most of the additional expenditures being undertaken by business and with spending on housing registering a marked slowdown.

In Japan the upturn in economic activity, which started early in 1972 under the stimulus of increased government investment and private expenditures on dwellings, continued in 1973. However, it was the rising outlay by business on additional productive facilities and inventories that provided the impetus. Public-sector spending on social infrastructure and private outlays on housing continued to exert approximately the same influence as in 1972, and there were some signs of deceleration toward the end of the year.

(T. M. RYBCZYNSKI)

See also Money and Banking; Profits; Stock Exchanges.

Table III. Savings and Investment in Main Industrial Countries in 1972

Country	Household	Nonfinancial enterprises	Public sector	Financial institutions	Foreign sector	Total
U.S. (in $000,000,000)	1972	1972	1972	1972	1972	1972
Gross savings	+191.2	+102.3	−13.2	+9.1	+8.4	+297.8
Gross physical investments	−157.8	−133.3		−4.6		−295.7*
Capital transfers and adjustments	+15.2	−15.0	−8.7	+2.3	+3.1	−3.1
Net financial savings	+48.6	−46.0	−21.9	+6.8	+11.5	−1.0
Financial assets	−117.5	−33.2	−11.9	−191.4	−19.4	−373.4
Indebtedness	+68.9	+79.1	+33.9	+184.6	+7.9	+374.4
U.K. (in £000,000)						
Gross savings	+3,717	+4,426	+3,102	+586		+11,831
Gross physical investments	−2,560	−4,207	−4,734	−592	−83	−12,093
Capital transfers and adjustments	−372	+378	+45	−51		−83*
Net financial savings	+785	+597	−1,587	−57	−83	−345
Financial assets†	−6,048	−3,203	+878	−18,389	−7,545	−34,307
Indebtedness†	+5,263	+2,606	+709	+18,446	+7,628	+34,652
West Germany (in DM. 000,000,000)						
Gross savings	+75.47	+93.04	+42.14	+9.72	−0.73	+219.64
Gross physical investments	—	−184.90	−30.51	−4.23	—	−219.64
Capital transfers and adjustments	−9.78	+24.51	−14.57	−0.86	+0.70	—
Net financial savings	+65.69	−67.35	−2.94	+4.63	−0.03	—
Financial assets	−73.95	−35.74	−14.58	−155.02	−16.35	−295.64
Indebtedness	+8.26	+103.09	+17.52	+150.39	+16.38	+295.64
Italy (in 000,000,000 lire)						
Gross savings‡	+11,315	+5,780	−2,995	+630	−830	+13,900
Gross physical investments	—	−8,185	−5,420	−300	—	−13,905
Capital transfers and adjustments	—	+870	−375	−170	−15	+310
Net financial savings	+11,315	−1,535	−8,790	+160	−845	+305
Financial assets	−11,815	−5,000	−1,640	−16,670	−5,090	−40,215
Indebtedness	+500	+6,535	+10,430	+16,510	+5,935	+39,910
Japan (in 000,000,000 yen)						
Gross savings	+14,603	+13,479	+7,077	—	—	+35,159
Gross physical investments	−8,649	−15,380	−9,090	—	—	−33,119
Capital transfers and adjustments	+4,632	−4,282	−350	—	−2,040	−2,040
Net financial savings	+10,586	−6,183	−2,363	—	−2,040	—
Financial assets	−18,062	−19,418	−4,331	−29,895	−1,300	−73,006
Indebtedness	+7,476	+25,601	+6,694	+29,895	+3,340	+73,006

Notes: For gross savings, gross physical investments, and capital transfers and adjustments: + means receipts and — means expenditure; for financial assets: — means spending on assets; for indebtedness: + means increase in indebtedness. Some of the totals may not add up due to rounding.

For the U.S., public sector includes federal, state, and local governments; financial authorities include monetary authorities, sponsored credit agencies, commercial banks, and private nonbank financial institutions; for the U.K., public sector includes central government, local authorities, and public corporations; for West Germany, enterprises includes housing and public sector includes social security funds; for Italy, public sector includes local authorities, social security funds, and autonomous government agencies; for Japan, government includes government financial institutions, administrative activities, local authorities, and nonfinancial public corporations.

*Equal to the total of foreign sector.

†Unidentified changes in financial assets and liabilities distributed equally between them.

‡Includes capital transfers.

Sources: U.S. Federal Reserve *Bulletin* (September 1973); U.K. Central Statistical Office, *National Income and Expenditure* (1973); West Germany and Japan: Organization for Economic Cooperation and Development, *Financial Statistics* No. 6D (1973); Italy: Bank for International Settlements, 43rd annual report.

Schools:
see Education

Scotland:
see United Kingdom

Sculpture:
see Art Exhibitions; Art Sales; Museums and Galleries

Securities:
see Savings and Investment; Stock Exchanges

Seismology

The possibilities of prediction and control of earthquakes assumed increased importance in 1973. The first phase of a field experiment to control earthquakes was completed at Rangely oil field in western Colorado. The experiment, conducted by the U.S. Geological Survey in cooperation with the Chevron Oil Co., was inspired by findings that associated a swarm of minor earthquakes in the Denver area in the mid-1960s with the pumping of waste material into deep wells at nearby Rocky Mountain Arsenal. The Rangely study demonstrated conclusively that minor earthquake activity could be turned on and off by the alternate pumping in and withdrawal of water from the substrata (in this instance at a depth of 6,000 ft.). The experiment gave hope that earthquake stresses could be relieved in areas of high seismic potential by causing minor activity and so preventing a buildup in stress of such proportions that it would result in a major catastrophe.

Another precursor phenomenon preceding an earthquake had been first described by three Soviet scientists in 1969 and subsequently had been noted by many researchers. This phenomenon, called dilatancy, occurs when a volume under stress expands, causing the pore pressure of internal fluids to drop and causing the crystalline strength to increase (phase I). This increase in strength eventually stops the expansion (phase II), after which the pores refill and the pore pressure increases again (phase III). The net result of this complex process leaves an expanded crystalline structure with a high pore pressure and a marked decrease in strength. This weakness results in an earthquake.

Yash P. Aggarwal of India, studying at the Lamont-Doherty Geological Observatory, New York City, investigated a swarm of microearthquakes in the Adirondack Mountains and found that a marked change in the ratio of the velocity of compressional waves to shear waves from foreshocks occurred. He showed that this was due to dilatancy and further reported that the change in velocity ratio was proportional to the size of the ensuing main shock of the series. C. H. Scholz and L. R. Sykes, also of Lamont-Doherty, found that dilatancy explains several precursor phenomena associated with earthquakes and that these can be used as measures of dilatancy. Tiltmeters could measure surface deformations, which would reach a maximum of several centimetres during the first phase when the material is expanding and the pore pressure is dropping.

The electrical resistivity of the rock is another measurable characteristic that decreases markedly during the expansion phase and continues to decrease through the next phases when the water is refilling the expanded pores. The trend would continue to the time of the earthquake, after which the resistivity would regain its equilibrium value. During the expansion-hardening (phase I) the minor seismic activity would cease, and during the entire expansion period on into the period of increasing pore pressure the flow of water into the expanded volume would be abnormally high. Thus, in a properly instrumented area, these factors could be used to establish a prediction sequence. It was also concluded that dilatancy is especially important because it is a process that actually triggers an earthquake rather than being just an indicator of conditions favourable to the occurrence of one.

Earthquakes were suggested as a source of energy for the geomagnetic dynamo within the earth that is thought to produce the earth's external magnetic field. J. T. Kuo and I. J. Won of Columbia University's School of Engineering and Applied Science calculated that about 0.05% of the energy of a large earthquake impacts the earth's solid inner core, causing oscillations in the earth's liquid outer core. They found that an earthquake of magnitude 8.5, such as the great Alaska shock of 1964, would set up oscillations as large as 60 cm. in amplitude that could continue for 10,000 years. Combined motions induced by thousands of earthquakes could cause the necessary fluid flow in the earth's outer core to produce the geomagnetic dynamo effect.

Earth scientists at the Massachusetts Institute of Technology developed a technique of high-resolution spectroscopy of the earth's free oscillations. The method involved the assumption of a source mechanism; *i.e.,* a simple model of the way the earth moved along a fault during a large earthquake. Given this assumption, the scientists found it possible to sum the traces of seismograms written at many stations, widely dispersed over the surface of the globe, in such a way to enhance the signal and subdue the noise (nonsignal vibrations). This increased manyfold the resolution for determining the long-term vibrational modes and served as a check on the validity of the assumed source model.

The seismic information gathered from the moon continued to be studied extensively. Scientists at the University of Texas counted several thousand shocks recorded on four lunar seismographs and identified hypocentres of 41 quakes. They found that the lunar tidal effect was the dominant factor in the lunar quake periodicity. The shocks to date occurred in two well-defined zones 100 to 300 km. wide and 2,000 km. in length, each lying on the near side of the moon along great circle arcs. Depths ranged from 800 to 1,000 km., as compared with the depth range of zero to 700 km. for earthquakes.

Correlation of lunar quakes with phenomena other than the lunar tide were found, including thermal moonquakes that begin to occur abruptly about two days after lunar sunrise and decrease rapidly after lunar sunset, and a phase lag in the seven-month tidal activity cycle that correlates with the effects of the

White vapour pours from the crater of a new volcano, born in the Pacific Ocean after a series of violent explosions. It lies in the Iwo Jima island chain.

© ASAHI SHIMBUN

six-year polar wobble of the moon. The evidence of these combined effects on lunar seismicity was quite marked and might lead to a better understanding of the effects of earth tides and the Chandler wobble on the seismicity of the earth. (RUTLAGE J. BRAZEE)

See also Disasters; Geology.

ENCYCLOPÆDIA BRITANNICA FILMS. *Earthquakes: Lesson of a Disaster* (1973).

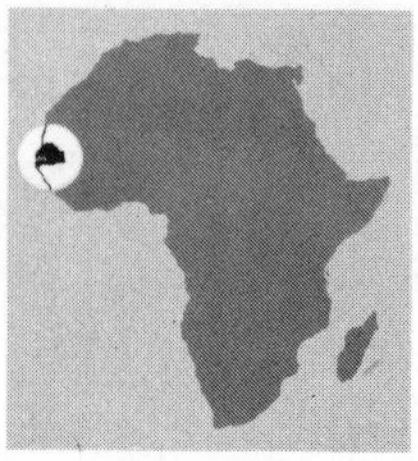

Senegal

A republic of northwestern Africa, Senegal is bounded by Mauritania, Mali, Guinea, and Portuguese Guinea, and by the Atlantic Ocean. The independent nation of The Gambia forms an enclave within the country. Area: 78,684 sq.mi. (203,793 sq.km.). Pop. (1972 est.): 4,112,000. Cap. and largest city: Dakar (pop., 1970 est., 580,000). Language: French (official); Wolof; Serer; other tribal dialects. Religion: Muslim 90%; Christian 6%. President in 1973, Léopold Sédar Senghor; premier, Abdou Diouf.

President Senghor was reelected in January 1973 for a further five-year term of office, with the approval of 99.97% of the electorate. He seemed the more assured of support in that all 100 deputies elected at the same time were members of the government party.

In February, however, serious unrest at the University of Dakar led to the expulsion of 55 students, and in March disturbances provoked by secondary school pupils broke out in the city centre. The authorities blamed the underground African Independence Party and the French Communist and trade-union movements. Further disturbances followed the death of a student in prison, and it was alleged that he had been murdered by the authorities. This led to a worsening of President Senghor's relations with the French left, who were also blamed for attacks on the Senegalese embassy in Paris in May and on its consulate in Rouen during Senghor's visit to France in September.

A test of strength between Senghor and Cheikh Fal, head of the multinational airline Air Afrique who made no secret of his designs on the Senegalese presidency, led to considerable tension between Senegal and Ivory Coast, where the airline had its headquarters.

A.F.P. / PICTORIAL PARADE

Dead cattle lie where there was once an oasis in Senegal, one of the sub-Saharan countries stricken by drought.

SENEGAL

Education. (1970–71) Primary, pupils 266,383, teachers (1968–69) 5,608; secondary, pupils 48,905, teachers (1968–69) 1,568; vocational (1967–68), pupils 10,608, teachers 354; teacher training, students 621, teachers (1965–66) 80; higher (University of Dakar), students 4,580, teaching staff 237.

Finance and Trade. Monetary unit: CFA franc, with (Sept. 17, 1973) a parity of CFA Fr. 50 to the French franc (free commercial rate of CFA Fr. 212.55 = U.S. $1; CFA Fr. 512.25 = £1 sterling). Budget (1972–73 est.) balanced at CFA Fr. 56.5 billion. Foreign trade (1972): imports CFA Fr. 70,550,000,000; exports CFA Fr. 54,412,000,000. Import sources: France 49%; U.S. 6%; West Germany 6%; Thailand 6%; Ivory Coast 5%. Export destinations: France 58%; Ivory Coast 5%; Mauritania 5%. Main exports (1971): peanut oil 21%; phosphates 11%; peanut oil cake 9%; fish and products 8%; peanuts 5%.

The Senegalese eventually secured Fal's removal. The affair also threatened the future of the Common Organization of Africa, Malagasy, and Mauritius (OCAM), of which Senghor was the current chairman.

Diplomatic relations with Guinea were broken off as a result of incessant verbal attacks by Guinean Pres. Sékou Touré. Senghor decided against a definitive break with Israel when Arab-Israeli hostilities broke out in October. However, Senegalese foreign policy continued to be pro-leftist.

Although Senegal seemed less badly hit by drought than its neighbours, Senghor was forced to deny allegations that his government had been taken unaware. (PHILIPPE DECRAENE)

Sierra Leone

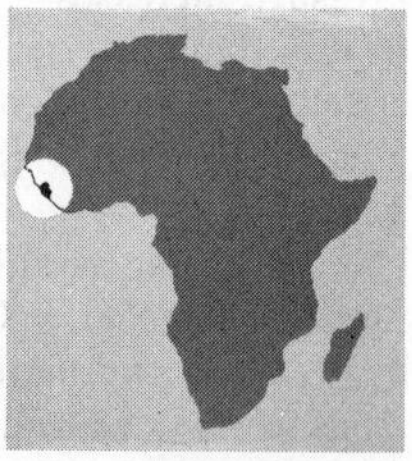

A republic within the Commonwealth of Nations, Sierra Leone is a West African nation located between Guinea and Liberia. Area: 27,925 sq. mi. (72,325 sq.km.). Pop. (1972 est.): 2,626,800, including (1963) Mende and Temne tribes 60.7%; other tribes 38.9%; non-African 0.4%. Cap. and largest city: Freetown (pop., 1972 est., 195,800). Language: English (official); tribal dialects. Religion: animist 66%; Muslim 28%; Christian 6%. President in 1973, Siaka Stevens; prime minister, Sorie Ibrahim Koroma.

The 1973 elections turned Sierra Leone into a virtual one-party state. After the 1972 ban on the United Democratic Party, the Sierra Leone People's Party remained the only opposition to the ruling All People's Congress Party (APC). By-elections early in 1973 provoked violence and the arrest of SLPP leader Salia Jusu-Sheriff. Opposition newspapers were closed because of their criticism of President Stevens' election policies. Parliament was dissolved on April 18, and the state of emergency, dating from October 1970, was prolonged. The prospect of elections in May produced further violence and death. SLPP candidates found it almost impossible to get nominations accepted. Many were held under arrest and on May 4 the remainder withdrew in protest, leaving the APC holding 81 out of the 97 seats, unopposed. For security during the election, Pres. Sékou Touré of Guinea lent four Soviet-built jets and two helicopters. On May 16 total victory was announced for the APC, which took 84 seats. Also seated were one independent, Desmond Fashole-Luke, and 12 unopposed

SIERRA LEONE

Education. (1969–70) Primary, pupils 154,848, teachers 5,011; secondary, pupils 29,058, teachers 1,364; vocational (1968–69), pupils 1,732, teachers 97; teacher training, students 879, teachers 129; higher, students 1,119, teaching staff 202.

Finance and Trade. Monetary unit: leone, with (Sept. 17, 1973) a free value of 0.83 leone to U.S. $1 (par value of 2 leones = £1 sterling). Budget (1971–72 est.): revenue 51.7 million leones; expenditure 50.6 million leones. Foreign trade (1972): imports 95,370,000 leones; exports 91,610,000 leones. Import sources: U.K. 23%; Japan 10%; West Germany 7%; Nigeria 7%; U.S. 7%; The Netherlands 6%. Export destinations: U.K. 64%; The Netherlands 7%; U.S. 6%; Japan 5%. Main exports: diamonds 62%; iron ore 11%.

Agriculture. Production (in 000; metric tons; 1972; 1971 in parentheses): rice 500 (460); cassava (1970) *c.* 65, (1969) *c.* 65; palm kernels *c.* 55 (*c.* 52); palm oil *c.* 62 (*c.* 60); coffee *c.* 6 (*c.* 7.5). Livestock (in 000; 1970–71): cattle *c.* 250; sheep *c.* 58; goats *c.* 158; chickens *c.* 3,000.

Industry. Production (in 000; metric tons; 1971): iron ore (metal content) 1,528; bauxite 590; diamonds (metric carats) 1,945; electricity (kw-hr.) 208,000.

chiefs, who by tradition joined the ruling party. In the new Cabinet, Vice-Pres. S. I. Koroma continued as prime minister and Luke became foreign minister.

The Ministry of Development, under guidance from the president, set a course to restructure the economy away from the wasting asset of minerals. Although 75% of the population was engaged in agriculture, food remained the third largest import. The development budget for 1972–75 had set aside 45% of its 30 million leone total for road development to open up the country for cash crops and to direct it onto an agricultural base. (MOLLY MORTIMER)

Singapore

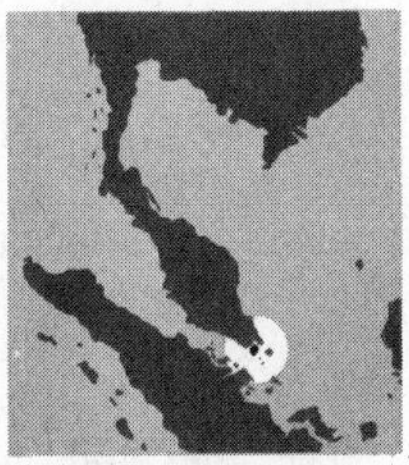

Singapore, a republic within the Commonwealth of Nations, occupies a group of islands, the largest of which is Singapore, at the southern extremity of the Malay Peninsula. Area: 226 sq.mi. (586 sq.km.). Pop. (1972 est.): 2,167,200, including 76% Chinese, 15% Malays, and 7% Indians. Language: official languages are English, Malay, Mandarin Chinese, and Tamil. Religion: Malays are Muslim; Chinese, mainly Buddhist; Indians, mainly Hindu. President in 1973, Benjamin Henry Sheares; prime minister, Lee Kuan Yew.

In his March 1973 budget speech Singapore's finance minister, Hon Sui Sen, described the island's future prosperity as dependent on multinational companies considering it an ideal offshore manufacturing base, especially in their hoped-for trade with China. It was hoped that the EEC too might take a more active interest in the region and so compensate in part for the phasing out of Commonwealth trade preferences between Britain and Singapore.

Vulnerability to outside economic forces was shown in the virtual halving of the growth in external trade, from 16.6% in 1971 to 8.6% in 1972. Japanese imports, following revaluation of the yen, had become more expensive; exports to Japan had not increased, and in some cases (such as rubber and petroleum products) had actually declined; trade with Britain had been further dampened by the floating of the pound; and trade with South Vietnam had declined after the winding down of the war there.

SINGAPORE

Education. (1971) Primary, pupils 357,936, teachers 11,949; secondary, pupils 139,251, teachers 5,938; vocational, pupils 20,334, teachers 1,421; higher (including 2 universities), students 14,269, teaching staff 1,292.

Finance and Trade. Monetary unit: Singapore dollar, with (Sept. 17, 1973) a free rate of Sing$2.35 to U.S. $1 (Sing$5.65 = £1 sterling). Budget (1972–73 est.): revenue Sing$1,449,100,000; expenditure Sing$1,448,700,000. Foreign trade (1972): imports Sing$9,539,200,000; exports Sing$6,150,300,000. Import sources: Japan 20%; Malaysia 16%; U.S. 14%; U.K. 7%. Export destinations: Malaysia 21%; U.S. 15%; Japan 6%; Hong Kong 6%; South Vietnam 5%; Australia 5%. Main exports: petroleum products 19%; machinery 16%; rubber 14%.

Transport and Communications. Roads (1972) 2,070 km. Motor vehicles in use (1971): passenger 163,200; commercial 40,800. Railways (1971) 39 km. (for traffic *see* MALAYSIA). Air traffic (apportionment of Malaysia-Singapore Airlines; 1971): 857 million passenger-km.; freight 16,653,000 net ton-km. Shipping (1972): merchant vessels 100 gross tons and over 28; gross tonnage 870,513. Shipping traffic (1972): goods loaded 21,757,000 metric tons, unloaded 36,214,000 metric tons. Telephones (Dec. 1971) 190,000. Radio licenses (Dec. 1971) 316,000. Television licenses (Dec. 1971) 159,000.

In order to stimulate foreign investment the government decided to invest equity up to 50% in foreign enterprises in Singapore, with an option for companies to buy back a substantial proportion of this later. A Sing$100 million fund was set aside under the control of the Development Bank of Singapore for this purpose and to give workers the training required to fit them for industries requiring a high level of technical skill. In August 1973 the government announced a joint venture with the Japanese Sumitomo Chemical Co. involving construction of a Sing$1 billion petrochemical complex.

After visiting Thailand in January Prime Minister Lee Kuan Yew gave support to a continued U.S. presence there against "relentless erosion through insurgency." In view of the U.S. withdrawal from the Vietnam conflict, and the uncertainty regarding the continued presence in the region of Australian, New Zealand, and British forces, he was determined to maintain good relations with Japan and the U.S.S.R. and in the fall of 1972 had granted two Soviet naval vessels repair facilities.

It was revealed during the year that Australia had for some time maintained a secret military intelligence unit in Singapore for the purpose of monitoring embassy radio messages throughout Southeast Asia. On September 17 a number of Australian troops began a withdrawal that was expected to bring home 1,200 men by February 1974, leaving 600 in Singapore.

Skiing

Aided by further improvements to equipment, additional installation of mechanical ascents, and more specialized group bookings by travel agents and airlines, the popularity of recreational skiing continued to increase in 1973 within most of the 46 member nations of the International Ski Federation (FIS). Ski clothing that was more colourful and varied in design added to the sport's initial attraction. Nordic skiing continued to infiltrate in North America and the European Alps. For the first time Nordic skis outsold Alpine skis in New England. Typical of fast-expanding ski resorts in the U.S. was Steamboat Springs, Colo.

Seventh-day Adventists: *see* Religion

Sheep: *see* Agriculture and Fisheries

Shinto: *see* Religion

Ships and Shipping: *see* Industrial Review; Transportation

Shipwrecks: *see* Disasters

Shoes: *see* Fashion and Dress

Sikkim: *see* Dependent States

Silk: *see* Industrial Review

Silver *see* Mining

Skating: *see* Hockey; Ice Skating; Sporting Record

WIDE WORLD

Gustavo Thoeni of Italy whips around poles of the Kandahar slalom at St. Anton, Aus., Feb. 4, 1973, on his way to an unprecedented third World Alpine Ski Cup championship.

Professional racing gained increased public interest in the U.S., though support for top amateur events did not match the keen following evident in Europe. In a season without the major biennial Alpine and Nordic world championships, the World Cup series and secondary competitions received closer attention. Ski bobbing, being easy to learn, gained a greater hold at snow sports centres, and special areas had to be allocated to keep enthusiasts away from conventional skiers' trails. On February 4 at Lausanne, Switz., the FIS agreed with the International Olympic Committee (IOC) and the four other concerned sports federations to designate Innsbruck, Aus., as host for the 1976 Olympic Winter Games. The original choice, Denver, Colo., had withdrawn.

Alpine Racing. The most consistently successful racers continued to be Gustavo Thoeni of Italy and Annemarie Proell (*see* BIOGRAPHY) of Austria, respectively the first man and woman to win the World Alpine Ski Cup for a third time, consecutively in each case. Whereas Miss Proell's impressive dominance put her triumph beyond serious doubt midway through the season, the men's outcome hinged on the final event, the giant slalom at Heavenly Valley, Calif., on March 24, when David Zwilling of Austria started only four points behind. Thoeni made the fastest first descent and played for safety in the second, to clinch the title by 15 points over Zwilling. Roland Collombin of Switzerland finished third overall.

Collombin scored the most World Cup downhill points during the season, with Thoeni winning the slalom and Hansi Hinterseer of Austria heading the giant slalom. Probably the best woman downhill skier yet seen, Miss Proell finished comfortably ahead of Monika Kaserer of Austria, with a rising French girl, Patricia Emonet, placing third overall. Miss Proell finished second to Miss Kaserer in the giant slalom, with Miss Emonet scoring highest in the slalom. Austria decisively gained the Nations' Cup, awarded for the highest aggregate points from the World Cup races. France, the previous winner, finished second and Switzerland, third.

In its seventh season, the World Cup was decided by 48 events, 24 each for men and women comprising 8 races apiece in the downhill, slalom, and giant slalom. The competition was spread over 23 selected sites in Austria, Canada, France, Italy, Japan, Switzerland, the U.S. (including Alaska for the first time), West Germany, and Yugoslavia. A new formula divided the series into three periods, a competitor's best 3 of 5 results counting in December 1972, 5 out of 9 in January 1973, and 6 out of 11 in February and March. Points were awarded to the first ten in each race, on a scale giving 25 points for first place down to one point for tenth.

The third Can-Am Ski Trophy competitions comprised 14 men's and 15 women's events, spanning seven weeks in January and February. The victors were Cary Adgate of the U.S. and Betsy Clifford of Canada. The second European Cup series winners were an Italian, Fausto Radici, and a French girl, Martine Couttet.

Jean-Claude Killy of France won the fourth annual Lange Cup and $68,625 in the professional series of 24 races at 12 meetings, again confined to North America. There remained little prospect of extending the circuit to Europe.

The fourth world ski-bob championships, on February 6–11 at Garmisch-Partenkirchen, W.Ger., produced overall men's and women's victories for Alois Fischbauer and Gertrude Geberth, both of Austria.

Nordic Events. The number of jumping hills approved by the FIS was increased to 151 in 17 countries; five of the hills were for ski flying, which differs from conventional jumping by emphasizing distance rather than style. The second annual world ski-flying championship, on March 9–11 at Oberstdorf, W.Ger., was won by Hans-Georg Aschenbach of East Germany, who finished only one-half point ahead of the title defender, Walter Steiner of Switzerland. The result was decided by only two jumps because fierce winds made it dangerous to hold third and fourth rounds, disappointing a crowd exceeding 50,000. Aschenbach, who jumped 157 and 152 m., admitted afterward that the hazardous conditions were frightening. During official training for the event, Heinz Wosipiwo, another East German, established a new world record with a leap of 169 m. Steiner cleared 179 m. but fell in landing.

The Four Hills tournament, from Dec. 30, 1972, to Jan. 6, 1973, was won for East Germany by Rainer Schmidt, followed by Aschenbach, with Sergey Boshkov of the Soviet Union third. Schmidt won the rounds on both West German hills, Oberstdorf and Garmisch-Partenkirchen, while in Austria Boshkov finished first at Innsbruck and Rudolf Hoehnl of Czechoslovakia triumphed at Bischofshofen.

The 81st Holmenkollen meeting near Oslo, Nor., on March 15–17 provided a show of Finnish cross-country strength. This was most notable in the women's 10 km., when Marjatta Kajosmaa, 35 and a mother of three, was followed by her compatriots Hilkka Kuntola and Helena Takalo, and in the men's 15 km., when Juha Mieto finished 24 sec. faster than runner-up Pål Tyldum of Norway.

Soviet skiers shone in the first contest for the world biathlon championships ever to be held in the U.S., which took place on March 1–3 at Lake Placid, N.Y. Aleksandr Tikhonov shot and skied his way to victory in the individual event, with his fellow Soviet competitor Gennadi Kovalev close behind for second place. Tor Svendsberget of Norway finished third. Tikhonov was also the power behind the U.S.S.R. team relay success. Norway finished only 5 sec. behind the Soviets, followed by East Germany.

(HOWARD BASS)

Soccer:
see Football

Social Services

One of the most obvious characteristics of social security systems in many countries was the relative frequency with which they were subject to change. The vast bulk of these modifications involved administrative and legislative changes in the existing programs, and while it was hardly feasible to explain why particular changes occurred without analyzing each national social security system, it was possible to detect certain trends and shifts in policies that were common to several countries. One of the most striking developments of recent years, and prominent also in 1973, was the special effort being made in a number of countries to extend and improve social security protection for certain categories of the population that might be considered to be particularly vulnerable or that had hitherto been comparatively neglected, such as the aged, women, and handicapped persons. The variety of provisions that were adopted to improve the social security coverage of these groups demonstrated how similar problems could be approached in strikingly different ways according to the country and its social security system.

Publication in the United Kingdom in late 1972 of the Green Paper *Proposals for a Tax-Credits System* aroused widespread interest in Britain and elsewhere in the possibility of radical changes in the structure of the social security system through the harmonizing of social security payments and tax allowances in a common system. A tax-credits system—in essence a variant of negative income tax systems that had been explored, particularly in the U.S., for some years—would, in the British proposals, replace major personal income tax allowances, which tended to favour families with higher incomes, with tax credits and the present system of family allowances and income supplements with credits for children. In cases where the credits to be granted exceeded the tax to be levied, the difference would be paid out as an addition to income.

Among the advantages claimed for the system were that there would be substantial administrative savings and that current inconsistencies and anomalies might

Social Security Programs, by Country, 1973*

Country	Old age, invalidity, survivors	Health, sickness, maternity	Work injury	Unemployment	Family allowances
	Type of program available				
Afghanistan			X		
Albania	X	X	X		X
Algeria	X	X	X		X
Argentina	X	X	X		X
Australia	X	X	X	X	X
Austria	X	X	X	X	X
Barbados	X	X	X		
Belgium	X	X	X	X	X
Bolivia	X	X	X		X
Botswana			X		
Brazil	X	X	X	X	X
Bulgaria	X	X	X	X	X
Burma		X	X		
Burundi	X		X		
Cambodia			X		X
Cameroon	X	X	X		X
Canada	X	X	X	X	X
Central African Rep.	X	X	X		X
Chad		X	X		X
Chile	X	X	X	X	X
China	X	X	X		
Colombia	X	X	X		X
Congo	X	X	X		X
Costa Rica	X	X	X		
Cuba	X	X	X		
Cyprus	X	X	X	X	
Czechoslovakia	X	X	X		X
Dahomey	X	X	X		X
Denmark	X	X	X	X	X
Dominican Rep.	X	X	X		
Ecuador	X	X	X	X	
Egypt	X	X	X	X	
El Salvador	X	X	X		
Ethiopia			X		
Fiji	X				
Finland	X	X	X	X	X
France	X	X	X	X	X
Gabon	X	X	X		X
Gambia, The			X		
Germany, East	X	X	X	X	X
Germany, West	X	X	X	X	X
Ghana	X	X	X	X	
Greece	X	X	X	X	X
Guatemala	X	X	X		
Guinea	X	X	X		X
Guyana	X	X	X		
Haiti	X	X	X		
Honduras	X	X	X		
Hungary	X	X	X	X	X
Iceland	X	X	X	X	X
India	X	X	X		
Indonesia		X	X		
Iran	X	X	X		X
Iraq	X	X	X		
Ireland	X	X	X	X	X
Israel	X	X	X	X	X
Italy	X	X	X	X	X
Ivory Coast	X	X	X		X
Jamaica	X		X		
Japan	X	X	X	X	X
Jordan			X		
Kenya	X	X	X		
Korea, South		X	X		
Laos			X		
Lebanon	X	X	X		X
Liberia			X		
Libya	X	X	X		
Luxembourg	X	X	X	X	X
Malagasy Rep.	X	X	X		X
Malawi			X		
Malaysia	X	X	X		
Mali	X	X	X		X
Malta	X	X	X	X	
Mauritania	X	X	X		X
Mauritius	X		X		X
Mexico	X	X	X		
Morocco	X	X	X		X
Nauru	X	X	X		X
Nepal	X				
Netherlands, The	X	X	X	X	X
New Zealand	X	X	X	X	X
Nicaragua	X	X	X		
Niger	X	X	X		X
Nigeria	X	X	X		
Norway	X	X	X	X	X
Pakistan		X	X		
Panama	X	X	X		
Paraguay	X	X	X		
Peru	X	X	X		
Philippines	X	X	X		
Poland	X	X	X		X
Portugal	X	X	X		X
Romania	X	X	X		X
Rwanda	X		X		
Saudi Arabia	X		X		
Senegal		X	X		X
Sierra Leone			X		
Singapore	X	X	X		
Somalia			X		
South Africa	X		X	X	X
Spain	X	X	X	X	X
Sri Lanka	X	X	X		
Sudan			X		
Swaziland			X		
Sweden	X	X	X	X	X
Switzerland	X	X	X	X	X
Syria	X		X		
Taiwan	X	X	X		
Tanzania	X	X	X		
Thailand			X		
Togo	X	X	X		X
Trinidad and Tobago	X		X		
Tunisia	X	X	X		X
Turkey	X	X	X		
Uganda	X		X		
U.S.S.R.	X	X	X		X
United Kingdom	X	X	X	X	X
United States	X	X	X	X	
Upper Volta	X	X	X		X
Uruguay	X	X	X	X	X
Venezuela	X	X	X		
Vietnam, North	X	X	X		
Vietnam, South		X	X		X
Western Samoa			X		
Yugoslavia	X	X	X	X	X
Zaire	X		X		X
Zambia	X		X		

*Data as of the beginning of 1973.
Source: U.S. Department of Health, Education, and Welfare, Social Security Administration, Office of Research and Statistics, *Social Security Programs Throughout the World: 1973.*

be obviated. Further, such a system would provide a more effective mechanism for redistributing income to those with the lowest incomes.

The less developed countries, given their low levels of national resources, faced very great difficulties in endeavouring to provide even minimum social security protection. One issue on which considerable discussion was taking place was whether preference should be given to the traditional social security programs (health insurance, accident insurance, pensions, family allowances, etc.) or to providing social services (such as maternity centres, child welfare facilities, and assistance with housing). Social insurance coverage in these countries tended to be confined to the relatively restricted sector of the population comprising wage or salary earners, and social services would, it was argued, reach a wider segment and meet more directly the primary needs of the community.

Social services were also the focus of attention in the U.S., where a series of disagreements and clashes between Congress and the Nixon administration over funding and operations of social action programs marked 1973 (*see* Special Report). In the end new regulations were promulgated for federal welfare and social services programs, the dismantling of the Office of Economic Opportunity was begun, and a large boost in Social Security payments and smaller compromise increases in several other programs were enacted.

An effort to raise minimum wages also produced a head-on collision between Congress and the White House. Congress passed a bill that would have raised the $1.60 an hour minimum in effect since 1968 for most workers to $2 an hour in 1973 and to $2.20 on July 1, 1974. It also would have extended coverage to local government employees. Pres. Richard Nixon vetoed the measure, contending that it was inflationary and would increase unemployment.

Another running battle between Congress and the administration concerned the Social Services Program for the poor, elderly, and disabled, set up under amendments to the Social Security Act. The federal government provided 75% matching grants to states, and for several years there was no limit on federal participation. But as states developed new programs, costs had zoomed, and in 1972 Congress put a $2.5 billion annual limit on federal outlays, with each state's share to be based on its percentage of the country's population. In February 1973, in line with a congressional directive, the Department of Health, Education, and Welfare announced new regulations for spending the federal Social Service funds. Angered state officials, lawmakers, welfare lobbyists, and others charged that the rules would penalize the working poor and would severely restrict the Social Service programs. HEW eased the regulations in May, then Congress suspended them until Dec. 31, 1974. Congressional opponents of the regulations said the suspension would give legislators a chance to work out a new system.

In August HEW issued a new set of regulations that reestablished secret state investigations of welfare applicants and recipients, gave states authority to cut or end welfare payments on short notice, and permitted them to develop their own methods for recovering overpayments within "reasonable limits." Welfare applications by mail and telephone were abolished. The Supreme Court did some welfare rule interpreting when it upheld a New York state law that required able-bodied welfare recipients to look for work or be put to work on public works projects. The court directed a lower court to determine whether the state law conflicted with sections of the Social Security Act.

The total number of welfare recipients dropped slightly in 1973. At the end of the fiscal year in June, there were 14,806,000 persons on welfare rolls, compared with 15,055,000 a year earlier. Of these, 10,912,000 received Aid to Families with Dependent Children; 1,845,000 got old-age assistance; 1,211,000 were on disability assistance, and 838,000 received other types of aid.

The federal food stamp program was extended through fiscal 1977, with certain alcoholics and drug addicts now eligible, and with allotments to be adjusted twice a year, instead of once, to keep up with the rising cost of living. The Department of Agriculture announced that the first boost, to affect 95% of the 12.3 million food stamp recipients, was planned for January 1974. An additional $220 million in federal subsidies was authorized to help hold down the costs of school lunch and nutrition programs for nearly 25 million children.

New Measures for the Aged. Increasing proportions of older people in populations, plus the effects of rapid inflation on the incomes of retired persons, gave added urgency to efforts to improve social security benefits for the aged. In the United Kingdom, in particular, public attention had been focused on the future development of state and occupational pensions since the publication in 1971 of the White Paper "Strategy for Pensions," the proposals of which were embodied in the Social Security Bill presented to Parliament in 1972 and ultimately adopted in 1973. The target date for the introduction of the new arrangement was April 1975. The new act replaced the current system of flat-rate and graduated contributions for wage and salary earners with earnings-related contributions (for employees 5.25% of earnings and for employers 7.5%, up to a ceiling). Although contributions would be earnings-related, retirement pensions from the basic scheme would continue to be a flat rate. In addition, employed persons would have to be covered by an approved occupational pension scheme or, if this was not available, by an independent reserve scheme to be set up by the government and maintained by contributions of 4% (2.5% for employers and 1.5% for employees) of the same range of earnings as the basic scheme.

As might be expected, regular old-age retirement benefits were increased in the majority of countries, but certain countries took additional steps to improve the benefits for persons who had had low incomes during their working years. For example, both Czechoslovakia and West Germany, in effect, recalculated the retirement benefits for persons whose low earnings had resulted in an inadequate pension. The measure adopted in West Germany was particularly interesting in that a hypothetical minimum earnings base was used to calculate retirement benefits for persons with over 25 years of coverage; this base amount could not be less than 75% of the average national earnings.

The U.S. joined the expanding number of countries that provide means-tested supplementary benefits for the aged and other categories under the social insurance system. This new program for needy persons who are 65 and over, or blind, or disabled was adopted in late 1972 and would begin paying benefits early in 1974. Norway also moved toward the establishment of a supplementary pension program that was to be financed through a special contribution of 1% of taxable income.

Also in the U.S. amendments to the Older Americans Act would expand federal spending and create new agencies to assist the elderly. Provisions included establishment of a national information clearinghouse on aging to collect, analyze, and distribute information on the needs of the elderly, creation of a Federal Council on Aging to promote the interests of older persons in all federal programs, authorizations of $50 million in fiscal 1974 and $60 million in 1975 for the National Older Americans Volunteer Program, Foster Grandparents, and other senior volunteer programs, and establishment of an employment program for persons 55 and older.

On June 30, 1973, Congress passed a 5.9% cost-of-living increase in the benefits to be paid to the nation's 30 million Social Security recipients after June 1974, in a bill that also increased to $2,400 a year the amount a recipient could earn without losing benefits. But another bill passed at the end of the year substituted a 7% boost in benefits in March 1974, to be followed by another of 4% in June. The wage base subject to the Social Security tax was also raised—to $13,200, for a maximum tax of $772.20 a year instead of the $12,600 that had been scheduled to take effect in January 1974. The December legislation also increased initial benefits to be paid by the new federal supplemental security income program.

There were also significant attempts to adapt social security systems more closely to the circumstances of persons nearing retirement age, including the introduction of preretirement benefits and flexible retirement provisions. Preretirement benefits, already in existence in West Germany, were also instituted in France and Finland to fill the need for income maintenance of persons approaching retirement age but unable to find reemployment. In France, this special benefit, amounting to 66% of average earnings during the last three months of employment, was paid, beginning at the age of 60, to wage and salary earners who had been unemployed for up to nine months, depending on age. The Finnish "unemployment pension" also began payment at the age of 60 and was granted to persons who had been receiving an unemployment benefit for at least 200 days during the last 52 weeks. The benefit was equal in amount to the invalidity pension that would be payable to the beneficiary at the relevant age.

There was also a move toward lower pensionable ages (*e.g.*, a pensionable age of 67 instead of 70 in Denmark and Norway), as well as toward more freedom for the insured to decide when he wished to retire. In West Germany the normal retirement age was 65, but a law adopted in 1972 permitted the beneficiary to receive his old-age pension with no reduction in amount as early as age 63 (62 in cases of invalidity) if he had been insured for 35 years.

Several countries also made important changes to adjust benefits to reflect increases in the cost of living. Belgium passed legislation to achieve quicker benefit increases following upward movement in the relevant indices. Japan introduced an automatic adjustment procedure, and the U.K. adopted an annual review of retirement pensions and related benefits in the state basic scheme.

Improved Protection for Women. One of the most striking trends in several national social security systems was the amelioration of the treatment of women. The growing number of working married women was undoubtedly prompting social security administrations to make improvements in maternity benefits and to participate to an increasing extent in the provision of day-care facilities for children.

Finland, for example, extended the period during which a maternity allowance was paid from 54 to 72 days. Italy changed its maternity provisions for working women to guarantee 80% of earnings, up to a maximum, during a five-month period, with a possibility of extending this period by six additional months with 30% of earnings. The Belgian health insurance program had, since late 1971, been paying a supplementary benefit of 15% of earnings during the 30-day period immediately following the birth—in addition to the regular 60% of earnings, up to a maximum.

In Czechoslovakia women who were insured in their own right had been eligible since 1971 for 26 weeks of leave with 90% of normal earnings. After expiration of paid maternity leave, unpaid leave could be extended up to two years to permit the mother to care for her child. A special allowance was also paid for two years to all women, regardless of whether they were employed before the birth, if in addition to the infant there were one or more school-age children in the family. This requirement was waived, however, for widows or divorced or unmarried mothers who had a dependent child.

In Sweden a proposal made during 1972 and eventually adopted in 1973 replaced the maternity insurance provisions with a "parents' insurance" that guaranteed a daily allowance equal to the regular sickness benefit (90% of earnings up to a maximum) for 180 days. This allowance could be paid to either the mother or the father, depending on which one stayed at home to care for the child. The allowance would also be granted to an employed mother or father who was absent from work to nurse a sick child under ten years of age, but for no more than ten days per year for each family.

The financing of day-care facilities received particular attention in Belgium, France, and Italy. In Belgium a special fund was created and would be financed by the family allowance branch. In Italy a 1% increase in the old-age pension contribution would be used to expand day-care facilities. In France the

continued on page 619

A group of Bronx teenagers "rap" with social worker Andi Stromberg (centre), director of "The Van," a mobile centre for troubled youth. "The Van" was funded by the Jewish Family Service and the Riverdale Y.M.-Y.W.H.A. in New York City.

MICHAEL EVANS—THE NEW YORK TIMES

SPECIAL REPORT

IS THERE A FUTURE FOR THE GREAT SOCIETY?

By William L. Taylor

In 1964 Lyndon B. Johnson inaugurated his Great Society by declaring war on poverty and promising to eradicate it within this century. Nearly a decade later, in 1973, Richard M. Nixon began his second term as president by declaring war on the Great Society, charging that its sponsors had promised much and delivered little and pledging a reduced but more effective federal presence in dealing with domestic problems.

In the early months, Nixon appeared assured of victory in his effort to dismantle the programs of the '60s and substitute his own. He seemed both willing and able to employ a wide array of powers to achieve his goals—refusing to spend money appropriated by Congress for Great Society programs, proposing severe budget cuts for the future backed by the threat of presidential veto if Congress did not submit, and offering a substitute package of revenue-sharing legislation under which the power and resources to shape domestic priorities would be ceded by the federal government to states and localities. As 1973 came to a close, the prospects of the Nixon administration were dimmer. The president's initiatives had been thwarted at key points by the courts and by Congress and, in the aftermath of the Watergate scandal, the leverage of the Office of the President seemed far less formidable. (*See* UNITED STATES: *Special Report.*)

Beneath the drama of confrontation between the executive and the coordinate branches of national government, other issues emerged. Debate mounted on the effectiveness of particular elements of Great Society programs and on whether President Nixon's "new federalism" constituted an abdication or simply a new definition of government responsibility. Some doubted the capacity of government to deal at all with long-entrenched problems of poverty, unemployment, disease, and racial injustice.

At stake were fundamental issues: what is the contemporary meaning of the constitutional commitment to "establish justice," "promote the general welfare," and assure the "equal protection of the laws"? How is the commitment to be implemented? In 1973 the answers were far from clear.

The Great Society. The landmarks of the Great Society were easy enough to identify. They included the Economic Opportunity Act of 1964, establishing the Office of Economic Opportunity (OEO) and new antipoverty programs; the Social Security Amendments of 1965, creating health insurance programs for the aged and needy through Medicare and Medicaid; the Elementary and Secondary Education Act of 1965, which constituted the first general school aid legislation and targeted money to schools with large concentrations of poor children; the Housing and Urban Development Act of 1968, which established for the first time a program to help low- and moderate-income families buy their own homes; and the Civil Rights Acts of 1964, 1965, and 1968, prohibiting racial discrimination in schools, employment, voting, housing, and public accommodations. Unquestionably, the mid-1960s were a period of legislative creativity matched only by the early years of the New Deal. But, in the minds of many, the strategies and ultimate goals of the Great Society were more difficult to discern.

In one sense, the Johnson programs could be viewed as an effort to complete the unfinished work of the New Deal. Franklin Roosevelt's New Deal sought to address the challenge of "one third of a Nation ill-clothed, ill-housed and ill-fed." The numbers had been substantially reduced in the intervening years, but by 1960 some 40 million people—one-fifth of the nation—remained in poverty. Through his Great Society programs, Johnson sought to reach people untouched by the legislation of the 1930s. Housing programs, for example, had become largely subsidies to the middle class, and had provided little assistance to the black or poor. In addition, Johnson sought to fill major gaps in the exercise of the "general welfare" powers of the national government by establishing a federal role in meeting the health care and education needs of citizens.

But there were important qualitative differences between the New Deal and Great Society approaches. Perhaps the most enduring legacy of the New Deal was Social Security for the elderly and disabled—a massive income transfer program that, along with other forms of pensions, retirement programs, and unemployment compensation, accounted for some $80 billion of the federal budget in 1973. The Johnson administration did not extend this principle of redistribution through direct income support as a means of raising the incomes of people in poverty.

Instead, Great Society measures fell largely into two other categories: (1) programs to help people obtain essential goods and services, such as housing, medical care, and food, through the private market; and (2) programs to make available or increase, largely through state and local governments, public services such as education, child care, and manpower training.

In enacting the first set of programs, the Johnson administration was able to muster the support of various producer lobbies—builders and developers, doctors and hospitals—that stood to gain from the increased ability of citizens to purchase their services. The genius of Johnson was that he was able to find the right formulas to overcome long-standing obstacles to the programs, such as fear of federal controls, and to balance neatly the motives of altruism and profit.

Programs to make better public services available to the poor also proceeded from premises that hardly seemed radical to most people. The principal assumption was that ingrained and inherited poverty and dependency had created in many poor families a pathology that made them different from others and prevented them from helping themselves. The remedy was to provide a range of critical services—manpower training, compensatory education, health care—that would give poor people the skills and the strength to extricate themselves from poverty. The direct creation of jobs for the poor, like direct income transfers, was at best a secondary objective of the Great Society. While a considerable number of new public service jobs were established as a by-product of the poverty program (and new positions in state and local agencies were opened by the Emergency Employment Act passed over President Nixon's objections), more far-reaching proposals, such as guaranteeing everyone a job by making government the "employer of last resort," were not seriously considered.

Other aspects of the Great Society were more controversial. If the poor were to help themselves, it was reasoned, they needed the confidence and skills to fight for their interests as aggressively as other groups do. Accordingly, the Community Action Program was established to provide skills in community and political organization. Energetic young lawyers were recruited into a legal services program to contest, in the courts, private and governmental practices that disadvantaged the poor. In addition, Great Society legislation made several departures from the usual method of furnishing public services. Many programs

---

William L. Taylor is director of the Center for National Policy Review of the Catholic University Law School, Washington, D.C. He is the author of Hanging Together: Equality in an Urban Nation (*1971*).

followed the pattern of providing federal money to state and local governments, which retained control over the administration of the public services (and sometimes the authority to decide whether they would be furnished at all). But some antipoverty programs created local structures that operated outside the control of state and local government. And overall responsibility for the programs was vested in a new federal entity, the OEO, less responsive to the interests of business, organized labour, and civil service bureaucracies than older Cabinet agencies. If the Johnson administration was not seriously embarking on an effort to nationalize public services, it was at least creating competitive structures that some perceived as a threat.

The Nixon Attack. President Nixon's assault on the Great Society stemmed from a variety of considerations—fiscal, political, and ideological.

The fiscal dilemma confronting the administration was not an inconsiderable one. As the programs enacted during the 1960s came to a full flower, their costs mounted rapidly. Programs to help people buy essential goods and services had accounted for only $1.1 billion in the federal budget in 1960. By 1973 the costs were estimated at $23 billion. Programs to provide public services had risen from $1.3 billion in 1960 to $14.9 billion in 1973. Taken together, the two sets of programs, which had accounted for less than 6% of all federal expenditures in 1960, constituted 23% of the budget by 1973.

Unwilling to permit large deficits in the federal budget for a sustained period, Nixon and his advisers were faced with three alternatives: to raise taxes and eliminate special advantages, to make significant reductions in the defense budget, or to put a brake on social programs. Having decided for political and policy reasons that tax reform was out and the defense budget was inviolable, the budget cutters had only one target left.

But all social programs did not suffer equally. No serious effort was made to stem the rapidly rising costs of the Social Security program, despite the fact that higher benefits meant repeated increases in the regressive payroll tax used to finance the program. Programs to assist people in buying essentials through the private market suffered to a limited extent. The administration sought to restrain the costs of the Medicare program by requiring patients to assume a larger share of the costs. More significantly, Nixon refused to spend any further funds to help low-income families purchase their own homes. This was one of the few areas in which administration action had an adverse impact on private business interests, but builders and developers were partially placated by administration promises that other steps would be taken to stimulate housing construction, although not for the poor. And the administration held out hope that it might eventually substitute a system of direct consumer allowances to enable low-income families to rent or buy their own homes—a prospect that was designed to appeal to another important segment of the housing industry, the landlords and real estate brokers.

The main burden of the budget cuts, however, fell on public service programs. The administration proposed to terminate emergency employment assistance and to cut back on manpower training and youth employment programs; to end federal assistance to community mental health centres; to make selective cuts in education programs, including a halt in aid to libraries; to eliminate the Model Cities program, and to dismantle the Community Action Program and abolish the OEO. While various justifications were offered for the cuts (the community mental health program was to be dropped on the ground that its workability had been demonstrated while others were attacked as unworkable), the focus on public service programs gibed neatly with the administration's political and ideological concerns.

Elimination of OEO and the Community Action Program was calculated to curb the abrasive confrontations that often accompanied federal efforts to help the poor assert their interests. In the words of Howard Phillips, appointed to preside over the dissolution of OEO, "the poor should not be treated as a class" because this was an approach "essentially in line with the Marxist ideal of setting class against class."

Public service programs that were administered through state and local governments were subject to other objections. While states and localities were theoretically free to accept or reject most grant-in-aid assistance, as a practical matter few could resist the lure of federal dollars, even when required to put up their own matching funds. This meant that priorities in meeting community needs were shaped in large measure by federal rather than local officials. Even more repugnant from the standpoint of Nixon strategists was the fact that the existing grant-in-aid system permitted officials in Washington to set conditions on the use of federal money. For example, officials of the Department of Housing and Urban Development might advise suburban counties that they would not be eligible for community development projects unless they agreed to permit low-cost housing to be built to help meet the needs of poor and black people. The danger was more potential than immediate; while red tape and time-consuming administrative procedures were a frequent adjunct of grant-in-aid programs, federal officials were rarely bold enough to use the programs as vehicles for accomplishing major social change. Nevertheless, the scope that existing laws afforded for "social planners" was a concern frequently voiced by the president in calling for a restructuring of federal programs.

To remedy these deficiencies, Nixon proposed to Congress that the great bulk of categorical domestic programs be eliminated and replaced by four major special revenue-sharing laws covering community development, education, manpower training, and law enforcement. Revenue sharing, a concept advanced by economist Walter Heller during the 1960s, was initially predicated on indications that state governments were going into serious debt because of inadequate tax sources, and that the "fiscal dividend" created by rapidly growing federal revenues could meet the need. When states began to run surpluses rather than deficits and the federal fiscal dividend failed to materialize, the rationale for revenue sharing shifted and Nixon strategists promoted it as a means of returning "power to the people."

Under general revenue sharing, a law enacted in 1972 as a forerunner to special revenue sharing, state and local governments were guaranteed more than $30 billion in federal funds over a five-year period. They were virtually unhampered in setting priorities for use of the funds, and other conditions attached to the law were minimal. For example, the federal government decided not to require that citizens be permitted a voice in determining how revenue-sharing allocations were to be used at the local level. Under the special revenue-sharing proposals, broad categories would be set out for expenditures in education, law enforcement, community development, and manpower training—but recipients, as a rule, would still have far more leeway in setting priorities than under existing categorical programs.

In addition, some of the special revenue-sharing proposals were designed to accomplish another kind of redistribution of resources. Under several Great Society laws, assistance was targeted directly to the poor or to areas where poor people were concentrated. Special revenue-sharing formulas tended to diffuse this aim. Under the "Better Communities" bill, for example, most central cities with deteriorating areas stood to lose money, while many suburban jurisdictions were slated to receive substantial sums for community development for the first time.

Reaction in the Courts and Congress. Of all the initiatives taken by the Nixon administration, none stirred more legal controversy than the decision to act immediately against Great Society programs by refusing to spend money appropriated by Congress to carry them out. While past presidents had occasionally impounded congressionally appropriated funds, Nixon sought to convert impoundment into a systematic instrument for accomplishing his broad policy objectives. Whole programs were terminated or expenditures deferred for lengthy periods of time on a variety of grounds—that spending would be inflationary, that the programs had proved ineffective or were philosophically objectionable, or that continued spending would be fruitless since the president had proposed that the programs be terminated or supplanted by revenue-sharing legislation. In the case of OEO, the Nixon administration sought to abolish an agency that Congress had authorized to function until 1974.

In a series of challenges to impoundments, the lower federal courts held uniformly that the executive branch had violated its legal responsibilities, principally the president's constitutional duty to "take care that the Laws are faithfully executed." If the Supreme Court ultimately sustained the position of the lower courts (or if Congress enacted a specific law circumscribing the use of impoundment), the administration would be deprived of one of the chief weapons it had used to reshape national priorities.

But even if presidential use of impoundment were curbed, almost the same ends could be accomplished through the presidential veto power over new congressional appropriations. Nixon had not hesitated to employ the veto in such areas as vocational rehabilitation, rural development, and emergency medical care, and in each case Congress failed to muster the two-thirds vote necessary to override (although sometimes by narrow margins). On issues such as curbing the ability of Legal Service lawyers to seek fundamental reforms through the courts, there was substantial sentiment in Congress in support of President Nixon's position.

If Congress was largely ineffective in defending its own programs, it had more success in thwarting the president's plans for substituting revenue-sharing schemes of his own. When the administration first put forth its plans, mayors and governors—plagued by the delays, restrictions, and red tape that accompanied categorical programs—eagerly supported the redistribution of authority promised in revenue sharing. But when it became clear that many jurisdictions would incur a substantial loss of aid, much of the support for the administration's proposals dissolved. Lacking strong public support, none of the special revenue-sharing bills was enacted into law by the end of 1973.

The result was stalemate. Many Great Society programs were curtailed and a few, like housing subsidies for low-income families, were terminated pending Supreme Court resolution of the impoundment issue. But neither the president nor congressional advocates of Great Society programs were able to establish supremacy, and the future direction of domestic policy remained undetermined.

The Uncertain Mood. Compounding the uncertainty over future directions was a growing debate among academic and policy experts who differed sharply in their assessments of the effectiveness of Great Society programs and in their beliefs about the appropriate objectives of government policy.

Defenders of the Great Society pointed to the fact that the number of people living in officially defined poverty has been reduced from about 40 million to 25 million in little more than a decade. Critics argued that the government definition of poverty was arbitrary and that, while it had been revised to take changes in living costs into account, the "reduction of poverty" really resulted from inflation and economic expansion.

Conservative critics of Great Society programs accepted the thesis that the poor are different but challenged the view that government could effectively assist them. Thus, administration adviser Irving Kristol disparaged manpower training programs, claiming that by the time people reach the age of 19 efforts to retrain them are futile. Others, relying on the findings of sociologist James Coleman that differences in school expenditures have very little effect on achievement, contended that federal expenditures on compensatory education are wasteful and ineffective.

Further, the conservative argument ran, the true objective of Great Society strategists was not equality of opportunity but equality of results—an idea antithetical to American principles. Equality of opportunity, these critics said, was established by the enactment of civil rights laws. When reformers seek to move further, to establish concrete goals for the employment of minorities in particular industries, for example, this is an unacceptable attempt to equalize results. The claim that such measures are needed to make up for past practices of discrimination in which government participated was rejected.

Critics on the left, on the other hand, faulted the Great Society for insufficient attention to equalizing results. For all the efforts of the '30s and the '60s, the distribution of wealth in the U.S. had not changed materially in 50 years. The top fifth of American families still had more than 40% of all income while the bottom fifth still had about 5%. Such basic inequities could be dealt with only through measures far bolder than those of the Great Society—direct redistribution of income, a major restructuring of work and its rewards, or other steps to establish political control over economic institutions.

Both sides often treated the incremental gains of the Great Society with disdain. School programs (including racial integration) that had improved children's reading scores, or job training programs that had produced marginal gains in employment and in income, for example, were dismissed as statistically insignificant, extremely expensive, or requiring too much time and effort. Increases in job satisfaction and in feelings of personal dignity that many poor and black people reported tended to go unnoticed because they were not statistically measurable. (On the other hand, some conservatives conceded that some black citizens had made substantial gains, but cited this as proof that "the problem has been solved.")

Defenders of Great Society programs conceded major deficiencies in liberal social policy of the '60s. High on their agenda was the conversion of the existing tangled welfare system into some form of guaranteed income. They agreed that federal benefits should be scaled to assist the near poor as well as the poor, removing some of the disincentives to work and allaying feelings of inequity that the Nixon administration had sought to exploit. Some also believed that until the poor and minorities were given access to jobs, homes, and services outside ghettos, federal policies could not be fully effective. Nevertheless, they argued, the Great Society provided a firm foundation on which to build.

In practical terms, the arguments of critics of the left and right tended to merge. In his widely discussed book *Inequality,* Christopher Jencks challenged the liberal assumption that public schools could be a powerful vehicle for promoting mobility of the poor. The achievement level of a child, Jencks said, is closely linked with his or her family background and not with any initiative the schools take to improve it. In any event, he concluded, school achievement is not closely related to economic success, which may depend on a variety of "noncognitive" factors—including individual character traits and luck. While there were major holes in Jencks's thesis, such as his confessed inability to trace the role of schools in influencing these "noncognitive" traits, his moral was clear: If reducing economic inequality was the goal, direct income redistribution—not school reform—was the way to achieve it. Conservatives drew a different moral, citing the book as evidence that such liberal initiatives as compensatory education, fiscal equalization, and school integration were unavailing. (*See* EDUCATION: *Special Report.*)

In short, while left and right proceeded from sharply different premises, they joined in the common refrain that "nothing we have tried, or are about to try, works." The mood of uncertainty and near paralysis thus produced was in striking contrast to that expressed by Roosevelt during the depression:

"The country needs, and unless I mistake its tenor, the country demands bold, persistent experimentation. It is common sense to take a method and try it. If it fails, admit it frankly and try another. But above all, try something."

Which of these two moods predominated in the '70s might well prove crucial for people still seeking to participate in a great—or even a good—society.

continued from page 615
funds devoted by the family allowance program to the operation of day-care centres were increased and, more importantly, a new allowance to defray the cost of day care for low-income families in which the mother was employed was instituted.

Significant changes affecting the status of women under social security systems were also made in the area of old-age and survivor's pensions. The French system reduced the age at which a survivor's benefit was payable to a widow from 65 to 55 and considerably relaxed the test of resources that applied to this pension. In the U.K. the basic widow's pension was granted at age 50, but a 1971 amendment provided for age-related pensions for widows who were between the ages of 40 and 50 at widowhood. The pensions tapered from 93% of the full-rate pension for the widow who was 49 at the time of her husband's death to 30% for the widow who was 40.

Legislation adopted in France and West Germany might be interpreted as those countries' first steps toward independent old-age pension protection for nonworking women. The French arrangement consisted of obligatory coverage under the general system for women who were receiving the single-wage allowance at the higher rate, that is, the family allowance benefit paid to families with a dependent child and only one wage or salary income. The contributions, calculated on the basis of a theoretical salary related to the current level of the minimum wage, would be paid to the old-age pension program on behalf of the women to be covered by the family allowance fund. To be eligible for a pension the woman had to be covered for at least 15 years.

The reform of the West German pension package for wage and salary workers in 1972 included among its provisions the extension of voluntary affiliation to all categories of the population not already compulsorily affiliated to an old-age program. One of the largest groups affected by this measure was nongainfully active persons, particularly housewives. Those who affiliated voluntarily would have considerable choice with respect to the amount and frequency of payment of their contributions. In order to qualify for an old-age pension, the insured had to, as in France, make contributions during at least 15 years. The law provided for the possibility, however, of making retroactive contributions back to 1956.

New Measures for the Handicapped. Judging from the amount of new legislation, many countries continued to be preoccupied with the need for improved protection for the handicapped and disabled. Belgium and the U.K., for example, introduced special constant attendance allowances for handicapped persons. The British regulations distinguished between handicapped persons who required attention or supervision both day and night and those who needed it only during the day or night.

In France an allowance for handicapped children was created, in addition to regular family allowances, to be paid for children up to the age of 20 who suffered from 80% disability. (Children in institutions receiving the special education allowance were not, however, eligible for this benefit.) A second new allowance was available for disabled adults between the ages of 20 and 65 who were unable to work, and, as was the case with the handicapped children's allowance, did not have resources that exceeded a specified maximum.

In the U.S. President Nixon signed a bill to provide federal aid to rehabilitate the handicapped, after having vetoed a more expensive measure. The legislation authorized $757.3 million for fiscal 1974 and $791.2 million for fiscal 1975, the bulk of the funds to go as grants to the states. The law required state rehabilitation agencies to serve the most severely handicapped first, a provision that was expected to open up vocational rehabilitation to many who could not get it in the past. Another bill expanded medical benefits to veterans by up to $407.9 million over five years.

GEORGE QUINN—CHICAGO TRIBUNE

A nun supervises children at the day-care centre in Chicago's Civic Center, said to be the first such service for children whose parents are involved in court proceedings.

Improvements for the Self-employed. The demand on the part of self-employed persons in many countries for "parity" in social security protection was hardly new, but some significant advances had been made in that direction. Both Belgium and France enacted legislation to bring the qualifying conditions and benefit levels of retirement plans for self-employed persons more closely into line with the provisions for wage and salary earners. In Finland a compulsory program was adopted to provide earnings-related pensions for farmers to supplement the flat-rate national pension, and in West Germany the extension of voluntary affiliation to the old-age pension program included the self-employed.

Some of the more noteworthy changes for the benefit of the self-employed occurred within health insurance plans. In both Denmark and Norway self-employed persons were now automatically insured for cash sickness benefits under the national health insurance schemes, whereas previously only employed persons were guaranteed such benefits. And in West Germany a health insurance plan, identical in most respects to those for wage and salary earners, was instituted in 1972 for the benefit of farmers.

In Belgium, the health insurance protection of the self-employed was considerably improved with the introduction of cash benefits to cover incapacity for work resulting from illness. (ISSA; DAVID M. MAZIE)

See also Education; Housing; Insurance; Medicine; Race Relations; Refugees; Taxation.

Sociology: *see* Behavioural Sciences

Soil Conservation: *see* Environment

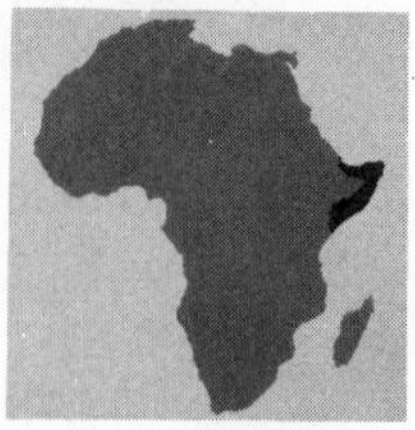

Somalia

A republic of northeast Africa, the Somali Democratic Republic, or Somalia, is bounded by the Gulf of Aden, the Indian Ocean, Kenya, Ethiopia, and Afars and Issas. Area: 246,154 sq.mi. (637,541 sq.km.). Pop. (1973 est.): 2,965,000, predominantly Hamitic, with Arabic and other admixtures. Cap. and largest city: Mugdisho (pop., 1969 est., 200,000). Language: Somali (official), Arabic, English, Italian. Religion: predominantly Muslim. President of the Supreme Revolutionary Council in 1973, Maj. Gen. Muhammad Siyad Barrah.

In 1973 the Somali tongue finally became the official language in Somalia, replacing English, Italian, and Arabic as the medium of written communication. This followed President Siyad's announcement in October 1972 that a modified Roman alphabet would become the official orthography.

The revolutionary government continued its efforts to achieve economic independence, especially self-sufficiency in basic foodstuffs. In this concluding year of its first three-year plan, major development projects were launched in agriculture, stock raising, and road building, and construction of a deepwater port for Mugdisho was begun.

In April, 18 members of the former government, in detention since 1969, were released. They included the former president, Aden Abdullah Osman, and the former opposition leader. Six others, including the former prime minister, Muhammad Haji Ibrahim Egal, were to be brought to trial.

The long-standing dispute between Somalia and Ethiopia over the Ogaden territory flared up again in May, at the Council of Ministers of the Organization of African Unity at Addis Ababa, Eth. Later, President Siyad agreed to the mediation of a good offices committee presided over by Gen. Yakubu Gowon of Nigeria. (VIRGINIA LULING)

SOMALIA

Education. (1969–70) Primary, pupils 31,589, teachers (including preprimary) 915; secondary, pupils 22,360, teachers 872; vocational, pupils 906, teachers 79; teacher training, students 168, teachers 10; higher, students 548, teaching staff 48.

Finance. Monetary unit: Somali shilling, with (Sept. 17, 1973) a free rate of 6.29 Somali shillings to U.S. $1 (15.16 Somali shillings = £1 sterling). Gold, SDRs, and foreign exchange, central bank: (June 1973) U.S. $34.1 million; (June 1972) U.S. $17.7 million. Budget (1973 est.): revenue 774 million Somali shillings; expenditure 773.2 million Somali shillings. Cost of living (Mugdisho; 1966 = 100): (April 1973) 112; (April 1972) 106.

Foreign Trade. (1972) Imports 523.1 million Somali shillings; exports 299.9 million Somali shillings. Import sources: Italy 23%; Japan 14%; Thailand 9%; Norway 8%; U.S. 5%; U.S.S.R. 5%; U.K. 5%. Export destinations: Saudi Arabia 40%; Italy 27%; U.S.S.R. 10%; Kuwait 5%. Main exports: livestock 50%; bananas 26%; meat and products 9%; hides and skins 7%.

Transport and Communications. Roads (1969) 13,396 km. Motor vehicles in use (1969): passenger 5,900; commercial (including buses) 8,000. There are no railways. Shipping (1972): merchant vessels 100 gross tons and over 148; gross tonnage 873,209. Telephones (Jan. 1971) *c.* 5,000. Radio receivers (Dec. 1970) 50,000.

Agriculture. Production (in 000; metric tons; 1971; 1970 in parentheses): millet and sorghum *c.* 50 (*c.* 50); cassava *c.* 25 (*c.* 25); sugar, raw value (1972) *c.* 50, (1971) *c.* 50; bananas *c.* 150 (*c.* 150). Livestock (in 000; 1971–72): cattle *c.* 2,850; sheep *c.* 4,000; goats *c.* 5,000; camels *c.* 3,000.

Sorghum Grains:
see Agriculture and Fisheries

South Africa

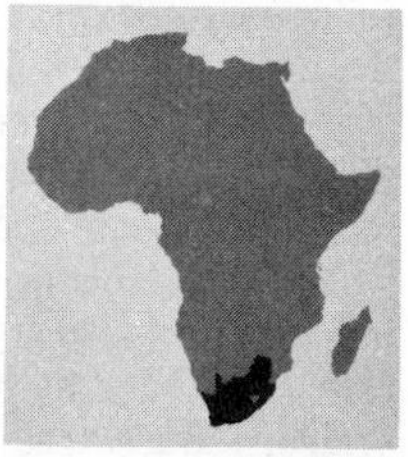

A republic occupying the southern tip of Africa, South Africa is bounded by South West Africa, Botswana, Rhodesia, Mozambique, and Swaziland. Lesotho forms an enclave within South African territory. Area: 471,445 sq.mi. (1,221,037 sq.km.), excluding Walvis Bay, 372 sq.mi. Pop. (1972 est.): 22,987,000, including (1970) Bantu 70.2%; white 17.5%; Coloured 9.4%; Asian 2.9%. Executive cap.: Pretoria (pop., 1971 est., 542,-200); judicial cap.: Bloemfontein (pop., 1971 est., 212,503); legislative cap.: Cape Town (pop., 1971 est., 721,350). Largest city: Johannesburg (pop., 1971 est., 1,315,741). Language: Afrikaans and English. Religion: mainly Christian, State president in 1973, Jacobus J. Fouché; prime minister, B. J. Vorster.

Domestic Affairs. A constitutional amendment adopted in the 1973 parliamentary session increased the membership of the House of Assembly from 160 to 165 apart from the six representatives of South West Africa. The Transvaal was allocated 76 seats, the Cape 55, Natal 20, and the Orange Free State 14. This was a gain of three seats for the Transvaal, two for Natal, and one in the Cape, and a loss of one seat for the Orange Free State, which was compensated by obtaining an increased number of provincial council members (28). In the other provinces the number of provincial councillors was the same as the number of MPs.

The former minister of the interior, T. J. A. Gerdener, who resigned from the Cabinet in June 1972 and later from the National Party, announced the formation of a new political party, the Democratic Party, with a policy aimed at solving the country's racial problems by gradually granting full political rights to the Coloureds and the Asians and independence to the Bantu, and ultimately establishing a commonwealth of states in southern Africa. In June a multiracial movement, Verligte (Enlightened) Action, was founded, mainly under liberal Afrikaans leadership, with a membership cutting across existing political party lines and with the object of enabling all population groups to share in planning the common future.

The publication of controversial interim reports by the parliamentary (Schlebusch) commission of inquiry into the activities of certain student and other organizations was followed by action against eight leaders of the National Union of South African Students, who were restricted for five years under the Suppression of Communism Act. A number of persons, including the director of the Christian Institute, C. F. Beyers Naudé, were subpoenaed to give evidence before the commission and were prosecuted when they refused to testify. In some cases passports were withdrawn. Bans were also imposed on a number of executive members of the (black) South African Students' Organization and of the Black Peoples' Convention. The commission investigated and condemned the activities of a church-sponsored sensitivity-training centre at Wilgespruit, Transvaal; its director, E. O'Keary, was served with a deportation order.

Under legislation passed in 1973 a commission was set up to review the whole body of South African laws and to streamline it by codification and the removal of anomalies. Another 1973 act required all foreigners who wished to work or study in South Africa to obtain permits before leaving for South Africa.

The budgetary provision for defense in 1973–74 was R 472 million, an increase of R 136.7 million over the actual expenditure for the previous year. This was accounted for largely by the cost of sophisticated armaments. Included in the total was R 136 million for land defense, R 43 million for air defense, R 28 million for maritime defense, R 62 million for guided missiles, and R 22.7 million for the purchase of ammunition. A guided missile research centre was opened at Somerset West in the Cape as part of the propulsion division of the National Institute for Defense Research, established for the development of a rocket motor for defense missiles.

As part of a program to acquire nearly 200 aircraft, the South African Air Force had on order 48 Mirage F1 fighters similar to those used by the French Air Force. A White Paper on defense tabled in April showed that South Africa was virtually self-sufficient for internal defense. Progress was made toward the manufacture of high performance gun propellants, army ammunition, aircraft gun ammunition, an advanced version of the Impala aircraft, and armoured cars. There were advances in missile and torpedo construction. A new scheme of national service permitting voluntary service over a continuous period of up to 24 months was instituted.

Work started on the project to link the Cape west coast with the iron ore field at Sishen in the north Cape. This involved the building of a harbour at Saldanha Bay and of a railway line from there to Sishen. Construction work was continued on the Richard's Bay harbour project, the completion of the first stage being set for February 1976. Provision was made for the preparatory work on the erection of a plant to manufacture enriched uranium at Pelindaba.

In the field of race relations the establishment of local legislatures in the partially self-governing Bantu homelands (Bantustans) was continued. General elections were held in the older areas, such as the Transkei, and for newly established homeland authorities. In each case Cabinets were formed with chief ministers and departmental ministers. In several homelands the party system was adopted.

Paramount Chief Kaiser Matanzima, Transkei chief minister, speculated that a plebiscite would be held at some future date to decide whether the territory should seek complete independence. Together with Chief Gatsha Buthelezi, his counterpart in KwaZulu (formerly Zululand), Matanzima advocated a federal union between the two states, with the possible future inclusion of other homelands, and leaders of six homelands met to discuss federation in November. Such proposals were rejected as premature by the central government. Plans for the territorial consolidation of the homelands into more cohesive units were finalized by the Department of Bantu Administration and Development and adopted by Parliament, despite vigorous opposition from Chief Buthelezi and some other homeland leaders, who claimed that the additional land offered them was inadequate. Criticism also came from white farmers whose land was earmarked for purchase under the consolidation scheme, which involved the eviction and transfer of 360,000 Bantu.

Efforts to encourage the decentralization of industries to areas bordering the homelands and the industrial development of the homelands themselves continued, with the help of economic concessions by the state. In the homelands the various development corporations and the local Bantu governments endeavoured to attract industries and capital investment and several factories were opened, mainly in the Transkei and KwaZulu. Statements by T. N. H. Janson, deputy minister of Bantu administration, emphasized the policy of improving the conditions of urban Bantu by a more considerate enforcement of the "pass" laws, better housing, and the provision of more facilities for recreation.

Widespread strikes by Zulu workers in and around Durban in January–February resulted in wage increases from which an estimated 50,000 workers benefited. Similar increases followed in other areas, in the general realization that average Bantu wages were well below the poverty line. The strikes—technically illegal—emphasized that Bantu workers, because of their inability under the law to join registered trade unions, had no legally recognized negotiating machinery or organized means of communication with employers. To remedy the position to some extent the Bantu Labour Relations Regulations Amendment Act, introduced by the minister of labour, Marais Viljoen, provided for negotiating channels and gave the government wide powers to improve wages and working conditions. The Bantu workers' right to strike was legalized within defined limits. In August the Trade Union Council of South Africa, representing over

SOUTH AFRICA

Education. (1968) European: primary, secondary, and vocational, pupils 820,626, teachers 38,472; teacher training, students 10,276, teachers 849; higher, students 48,726, teaching staff 5,019. African and other non-European: primary, secondary, and vocational, pupils 2,509,422, teachers 52,604; teacher training, students 7,380, teachers 651; higher, students 6,477, teaching staff 496.

Finance. Monetary unit: rand, with (Sept. 17, 1973) an official rate of R 0.67 to U.S. $1 (free rate of R 1.62 = £1 sterling). Gold, SDRs, and foreign exchange, official: (June 1973) U.S. $1,704,000,000; (June 1972) U.S. $982 million. Budget (1972–73 est.): revenue R 2,802,900,000; expenditure R 2,800,200,000. Gross national product: (1972) R 14,850,000,000; (1971) R 13,260,000,000. Money supply: (May 1973) R 2,948,000,000; (May 1972) R 2,406,000,000. Cost of living (1963 = 100): (June 1973) 154; (June 1972) 140.

Foreign Trade. (1972) Imports R 3,109,200,000; exports (excluding gold) R 2,069,700,000 (outflow of gold U.S. $1,505,000,000). Import sources: U.K. 21%; U.S. 17%; West Germany 15%; Japan 9%. Export destinations: U.K. 26%; Japan 13%; U.S. 7%; West Germany 6%. Main exports (excluding gold): fruit and vegetables 14%; diamonds 11%; wool 6%; textile yarns and fabrics 7%; iron and steel 7%; copper 5%.

Transport and Communications. Roads (1971) *c.* 320,000 km. (including *c.* 185,000 km. main roads). Motor vehicles in use (1970): passenger 1,535,000; commercial 394,000. Railways: (1971) 19,839 km.; freight traffic (including Namibia; 1972) 58,570,000,000 net ton-km. Air traffic (1971): 3,152,000,000 passenger-km.; freight 73,981,000 net ton-km. Shipping (1972): merchant vessels 100 gross tons and over 255; gross tonnage 511,190. Telephones (Dec. 1971) 1,624,000. Radio licenses (Dec. 1970) 2,014,000.

Agriculture. Production (in 000; metric tons; 1972; 1971 in parentheses): corn 9,630 (8,600); wheat 1,615 (1,670); oats 103 (97); sorghum (1971) 650, (1970) 445; potatoes *c.* 640 (*c.* 650); sugar, raw value *c.* 1,900 (1,865); peanuts 402 (404); sunflower seed 152 (131); oranges (1971) *c.* 481, (1970) *c.* 493; apples *c.* 250 (*c.* 250); wine *c.* 525 (577); tobacco *c.* 30 (*c.* 32); wool (1971) 53, (1970) *c.* 57; meat (1971) *c.* 617, (1970) *c.* 610; milk (1971) *c.* 2,840, (1970) 2,820; fish catch (1971) 1,084, (1970) 1,555. Livestock (in 000; June 1971): cattle *c.* 12,320; sheep 30,671; pigs *c.* 1,350; goats *c.* 5,600; horses *c.* 430; chickens (on farms and estates) *c.* 12,400.

Industry. Index of manufacturing production (1963 = 100): (1972) 167; (1971) 163. Fuel and power (in 000; 1972): coal (metric tons) 58,429; manufactured gas (cu.m.; 1971) 1,800,000; electricity (kw-hr.) 59,082,000. Production (in 000; metric tons; 1972): cement 6,112; iron ore (60–65% metal content) 11,172; pig iron 4,899; crude steel 5,343; copper ore (metal content) 152; asbestos (1971) 319; chrome (oxide content; 1971) 737; antimony concentrate (metal content; 1971) 14; manganese ore (metal content; 1971) 1,368; gold (troy oz.) 29,215; diamonds (metric carats; 1971) 7,031; fish meal (including Namibia; 1971) 273.

190,000 white, Coloured, and Asian workers in 50 trade unions, unanimously decided on the principle of establishing separate unions for Bantu employees in their industries. The government made it clear that Bantu trade unionism, registered by law, was contrary to its policy.

While retaining the policy of job reservation, the government agreed that, in view of the shortage of skilled workers, nonwhite workers could work in areas hitherto reserved for whites, provided the trade unions consented. Agreements to that effect were reached on the state railways, in the post office, and in the mining and some other industries.

In January a commission of inquiry was appointed, with both white and Coloured members, to investigate the political and socioeconomic conditions of the Coloured population. In the course of the year there were prolonged disturbances among the students of the Coloured University of the Western Cape. The university was closed for a time and some students were suspended or expelled; all students had to apply for readmission. A one-man judicial commission was appointed to investigate student grievances and student misconduct. The government nominated a Coloured man as rector for the first time to meet the demand that the Coloured people should have more say in the running of the university.

Student disturbances occurred at other universities after the banning of white and black student leaders. Demonstrations in Johannesburg and other centres led to arrests under the Riotous Assemblies Act.

Foreign Affairs. South Africa's credentials were rejected by a majority vote in the UN General Assembly in September. When the South African foreign minister, Hilgard Muller, was allowed to speak under a ruling by the president, most of the delegates staged a walkout during his speech. Resolutions condemning South Africa's policies were passed by various UN committees, with renewed calls for international sanctions. The International Labour Organization, meeting in Geneva, unanimously urged governments to sever all relations with and stop all investment in South Africa.

Relations between South Africa and neighbouring Lesotho deteriorated after the shooting in September by the South African police of five Lesotho nationals, along with six other Bantu mineworkers, in a riot at the Western Deep Levels mine at Carletonville, Transvaal.

The New Zealand government announced its intention to revoke all tariff preferences to South Africa from the end of 1973. Both New Zealand and Australia cut their traditional sports ties with South Africa in protest against its race policies.

The Economy. Presenting his budget for 1973–74 in March, the minister of finance, Nicholas J. Diederichs, defined its main purpose as the promotion of healthy economic growth. The forces pointing to an economic revival, he said, were strong and the country could look forward to a faster growth rate. While demand was playing no significant role in accelerating inflation, costs were likely to do so in the immediate future. There were grounds for hoping that when that factor had exerted its full pressure on prices the inflation rate would decline.

Measures to curb rising prices and living costs included a relaxation of import controls, cuts in sales tax, easing of bank credits, and an increase in labour productivity. The growth target rate for 1973 was set at 5.75%. The actual rate in 1972 was 4%.

The higher gold price on the free market was an important element in the economy. Largely because of the policy of mining lower grade ore, the volume of gold production fell while the value rose by about 33% in 1973. The life of older mines was lengthened and there were prospects of new mines being opened. Plans to open one new mine in the Free State were announced. The balance of payments deficit was reduced and gold and foreign exchange reserves rose.

When the U.S. dollar was devalued by 10% in February, the rand, though linked to the dollar, maintained its gold value. In June the rand was revalued against the dollar by 5% and by an average of 2–3% against foreign currencies generally. The effect was to make imports cheaper and to reduce the value of South African exports. Oil shipments to South Africa from Arab countries were cut off following the Arab-Israeli war. (LOUIS HOTZ)

Southeast Asian Affairs

If U.S. détente with China sent reverberations throughout Southeast Asia in 1972, the end of the Vietnam war created a nervous flutter in 1973. Fears spread through some Southeast Asian capitals that the winding down of the U.S. military commitment might create new security problems for local governments.

The nervousness progressively diminished as the major powers began indicating their intentions for the future. Although its troops were being withdrawn from Indochina and many of its bases were closing down, the U.S. made it clear that it would remain a watchful presence in the region. China continued to befriend established governments without showing any noticeable interest in assisting local Communist insurgents. Japan evinced interest in a bigger role in regional affairs, and the U.S. was openly suggesting that this role should include regional defense commitments. The Soviet Union, still committed to its theory of an Asian collective security arrangement, kept showing its flag everywhere and strengthening its diplomatic as well as military sinews in the region.

The overall lesson Southeast Asia learned from these postures was that the interplay of great powers would create its own stability in the region. It was clear that no one power would permit another to establish a hegemony in any one country. Southeast Asian states came to believe that they could maneuver and take advantage of the situation.

Given the above circumstances, the concept of Southeast Asia's neutralization, first officially projected by the Association of Southeast Asian Nations (ASEAN) in 1971, continued to be a debating point in 1973—but little else. Senior officials from the five ASEAN countries (Indonesia, Malaysia, Philippines, Thailand, and Singapore) met in Baguio in the Philippines in June. Some delegates reportedly advocated "some form of guarantee" of the neutralization plan from the big powers. But others did not welcome the proposal in the belief that guarantees might invite outside interference.

As if in direct response to the ASEAN officials, the U.S. ambassador to the Philippines, William Sullivan, said in Manila in October that neutralization was almost impossible for the countries of Asia. Sullivan, newly appointed to his post and known as a close collaborator of U.S. Secretary of State Henry A. Kissinger, bluntly made it clear that the U.S. intended to remain the dominant power in the Pacific at a time when a four-power equilibrium involving it, the Soviet Union, China, and Japan was emerging in the region.

Australia formally committed itself to the idea of neutralization when its federal Parliament opened in February. The governor-general, Sir Paul Hasluck, said in his speech that Australia would encourage other nations involved in the region to support the concept. He added that the establishment of the neutral zone in Southeast Asia would help phase out military arrangements such as the five-power defense pact, of which Australia was a member.

Australia's lukewarm attitude toward the five-power arrangement, and the consequent decline in its effectiveness, further accentuated the defense preoccupations of some governments. In May the prime minister of Singapore, Lee Kuan Yew, suggested the formation of a naval task force from the U.S., Western Europe, Australasia, and Japan to counter growing Soviet influence in the Indian and Pacific oceans. His argument was that the Soviet presence, though still very modest, would not become a threat "unless it becomes the predominant or exclusive task force in the area."

The proposal represented a considerable departure from Lee's stated positions in the past. Singapore was once outspoken in its apprehensions about the military potential of a resurgent Japan and was also the first Southeast Asian nation to extend facilities to Soviet fleets. If Lee's latest position on Japan and the Soviet Union was indicative of the search for new alignments in the post-détente Southeast Asia, his advocacy of U.S. policies in the region dramatized it even more. Having started out as a vehement critic of U.S. policies and even of American values, he became during 1973 an energetic salesman for the continued presence in the region of U.S. military forces. He traveled to Thailand to canvass support for his thesis that Thailand should be built up as a buffer against Indochinese Communism. The Lee stance, of course, went counter to the neutralization thesis that ASEAN as a whole had endorsed.

The year produced the usual quota of ideas for Asian togetherness. UN Secretary-General Kurt Waldheim asked for conditions conducive to the emergence of "a unified Asian political will." Waldheim's chief secretary, C. V. Narasimhan, suggested the creation of a pan-Asian political organization along the lines of those in Africa and Latin America. Australian Prime Minister Gough Whitlam, visiting Indonesia, called for a new grouping of Asian and Pacific nations in "an organization genuinely representative of the region, without ideological overtones, conceived as an initiative to help free the region from great power rivalries which have bedevilled its progress for so long." The proposal never left the ground, for Whitlam's host, President Suharto of Indonesia, was reported to have declined to back it.

The Asian Forum idea received a longer run, however. It had been aired the previous year by Pres. Ferdinand E. Marcos of the Philippines (*see* BIOGRAPHY). In their Kuala Lumpur meeting in February, ASEAN foreign ministers agreed to hold an Asian Forum "at an appropriate time in the future." It was reported that the proposal was to include all countries who would come under ASEAN's neutralization plan, which meant the five member countries plus Burma, Laos, Cambodia, and North and South Vietnam. Philippine Foreign Secretary Carlos Romulo made a fervent plea for the forum during a visit to Australia in September.

WIDE WORLD

U.S. Pres. Richard M. Nixon escorts Singapore's Prime Minister Lee Kuan Yew and his wife into the White House as they arrive for a state dinner on April 10, 1973.

ASEAN. One result of the peace settlement in Vietnam was that it gave new vitality to the Association of Southeast Asian Nations. Member countries realized that their best chance to face the uncertainties of the future was through coordinated policies. The differences among them were too deep to be papered over, but ASEAN's position as the premier regional organization was nevertheless reinforced.

A major preoccupation of ASEAN members was the question of relations with Communist countries. Clearly every member was pursuing its own interests; Malaysia established relations with both North Korea and North Vietnam. But there was a vague feeling that somehow they should coordinate their approach toward Communist countries in general and toward China in particular. Foreign ministers at their conference in Kuala Lumpur in February agreed to keep each other fully informed on the establishment of diplomatic relations with North Vietnam and on North Vietnamese activities in their respective countries after relations were established.

According to government sources, Singapore had pressed for the exchange of information on North Vietnamese activities in the various countries on the argument that North Vietnamese diplomatic missions could support local liberation fronts or other organizations. Malaysia on the other hand strongly pushed the idea of closer contacts with Hanoi on the plea that to ignore it any longer could be costly. North Vietnam's distinct lack of interest in any sort of contact with ASEAN was in striking contrast to continuous ASEAN debate over these matters.

China, however, engaged ASEAN's attention much more than Indochina. Again the different members of ASEAN seemed to be pulling in different directions. Malaysia was apparently most eager to establish full diplomatic relations with Peking. Singapore seemed to stand at the other extreme, although it already had economic contacts and was sending various groups of visitors to China. In between, the other members took their own particular lines. Indonesia, having once been very close to China, was wary of normalizing relations unless Peking first gave various assurances. Thailand went as far as exchanging sports teams but seemed unsure of how far to go beyond that. The Philippines expressed interest in contacts with China but was in no mood to relax its ties with Taiwan.

The most important ASEAN gathering of the year, the ministers' meeting at Pattaya near Bangkok in April, discussed security problems in the wake of the cease-fire agreement in Vietnam and also the question of enlarging ASEAN. A joint communiqué at the end of the three-day meeting made little or no reference to these topics, but instead was concerned with economic issues. It called on Japan to halt the expansion of its synthetic rubber industry.

Subsequently, ASEAN countries began studying a 147-page report by a UN team recommending a three-pronged program toward creating an ASEAN common market of 200 million people. The report urged trade liberalization; specialization by different countries in different manufactured items; and intra-regional agreements for large-scale industrial projects new to the region. As a first step, the report called for the establishment of an ASEAN Development Corporation that would channel approximately $3,750,000,000 over the following eight to ten years into agriculture, forestry, transportation and financial, monetary, and insurance services.

ECAFE. For the UN Economic Commission for Asia and the Far East, China's decision to participate was the big news of the year. A 14-man Chinese delegation went to Tokyo in April to attend the 29th general meeting of ECAFE. The Chinese used the occasion primarily for political purposes. They walked out on three occasions, when the Cambodian government representative and the leader of the South Vietnamese delegation rose to speak and when the South Korean foreign minister addressed the session. Surprisingly, however, they sat through the speech of the Soviet representative, who said that Chinese fear of Soviet power in Asia was the product of "a sick imagination."

As for China's official policy line at ECAFE, it was made clear by delegation leader An Chih-yuan who blamed imperialism and colonialism, "in particular by the superpowers," for the poverty in many less developed Asian countries. Although the Chinese dominated the headlines, they were not always able to have their own way. Over their objections, Bangladesh was admitted to ECAFE.

The Chinese role, however, led many observers to point out that ECAFE had reached a turning point in its history. Injection of a heavier dose of politics was not the only reason for this impression. After more than a decade, executive secretary U Nyun retired and was succeeded in June by Johann Bodwyn Maramis of Indonesia. U Nyun's term had seen an accumulation of grand plans on paper. The question in 1973 was whether the new executive secretary could usher in a period of action on these plans despite the politicization of the organization.

SEATO. Both the China-U.S. détente and the Vietnam cease-fire further eroded the position of the Southeast Asia Treaty Organization. The writing on the wall became clear when, in June, U.S. Sen. Frank Church (Dem., Ida.) moved to delete from the Department of State appropriation the U.S. contribution for the maintenance of SEATO's Bangkok headquarters. He withdrew the proposal only after colleagues had agreed to support committee hearings on the entire SEATO question.

When the SEATO Council met in New York in September for its annual session, the traditional personal welcome by the head of government of the host country was lacking. The newly appointed U.S. secretary of state, Henry Kissinger, did not participate. The communiqué issued at the end of the meeting showed that SEATO was to undergo a basic structural change. The emphasis in the future would be on support of the "internal security and development programs" of its two regional members, Thailand and the Philippines; its military and civilian staffs were to be completely integrated; the Military Planning Office was to be discontinued; and the organization's international staff was to be cut from 73 to about 50. Pakistan's previously announced withdrawal from the organization became final in November. France, which had not been active for some years, would end its formal membership in 1974.

(T. J. S. GEORGE)

Southern Rhodesia: *see* Rhodesia

Southern Yemen: *see* Yemen, People's Democratic Republic of

South West Africa: *see* Dependent States; South Africa

Soviet Bloc Economies

The Council for Mutual Economic Assistance (CMEA or Comecon), meeting in Prague, Czech., held its 27th plenary session June 5–8, 1973. The session was attended by delegations from Bulgaria, Cuba, Czechoslovakia, East Germany, Hungary, Mongolia, Poland, Romania, the U.S.S.R., and Yugoslavia. Observers from North Vietnam and North Korea were present. All the delegations were led by heads of government except Cuba and Yugoslavia.

Having examined the progress of the comprehensive program for economic integration of the member countries, which had been adopted in July 1971 by the plenary session in Bucharest, Rom., the CMEA decided to "do everything possible to develop still further the economic integration of socialist states, to consolidate and expand the brotherly contacts in all their aspects"—words identical to those used in the resolution of the April plenary meeting of the Central Committee of the Communist Party of the Soviet Union.

Opening the debate, Aleksey N. Kosygin, the Soviet premier, paid a great deal of attention to questions concerning specialization and cooperation in the field of industrial production and also to problems of socialist planning in the light of the tasks of expanding economic integration. He commented that with all the member countries embarking upon the coordination of their national economic plans for 1976–80, the most favourable conditions were being created for the successful solution of those questions.

Stanko Todorov, the premier of Bulgaria, warmly supported all the basic trends in the collective efforts for the implementation of the comprehensive program. Jeno Fock, the Hungarian premier, said that special attention in the coordination of national plans should be paid to questions whose solution would have a decisive influence on the development of a country's national economy and would simultaneously increase the effectiveness of the economy of the entire socialist community.

Horst Sindermann (*see* BIOGRAPHY), head of the East German delegation, underlined the importance of building machinery for the light and foodstuffs industries. In the opinion of Piotr Jaroszewicz, the Polish

Table I. Rates of Industrial Growth in Eastern Europe*

Country	1961–65	1966–70	1971	1972	1973†
U.S.S.R.	8.6	8.5	7.8	6.5	7.0
East Germany	5.9	6.4	5.5	6.0	7.6
Czechoslovakia	5.2	6.3	6.9	6.0	6.1
Poland	8.6	8.3	8.0	10.8	11.8
Hungary	8.1	6.1	5.0	5.5	6.6
Romania	13.0	11.8	11.5	12.0	14.6
Bulgaria	11.7	11.2	9.5	8.0	9.2

*Yearly average percentages.
†First six months.
Source: National statistics.

premier, plans for the economic development of the individual member countries had to form a common, coordinated, and broad framework for the entire community. Ion Gheorghe Maurer, the premier of Romania, emphasized his country's participation in the development of heavy industry within the CMEA, while Lubomir Strougal, the Czechoslovakian premier, stressed the point that the basic task of the present session was to determine ways and means for an even more intensive integration in the key branches of CMEA's national economies.

The communiqué issued at the end of the session expressed general satisfaction with the achievements of the comprehensive program during its first two years, pointing out that combined national income had increased by 11.6% and industrial production by more than 15% (Table I), while in the capitalist countries the corresponding increase was 8.8%. This brought the share of the CMEA countries in world industrial output up to 33%. Trade among the CMEA countries in 1972 was about 20% above that of 1970.

There was no denying that the CMEA countries achieved remarkable results in their industrial production. Between 1950 and 1972 their extraction of hard coal rose from 287.5 million to 640.3 million tons, and that of brown coal and lignite from 264.1 million to 640 million tons (Table II); generation of electric power jumped during the same period from 135,300,000,000 to 1,140,600,000,000 kw-hr.; extraction of crude petroleum rose from 43.6 million to 410.5 million tons; and production of crude steel increased from 34.9 million to 170.7 million tons.

The lion's share of the output in the area belonged, of course, to the Soviet Union, which in 1972 produced 70% of the hard coal, 32% of brown coal, 85.6% of natural gas, 96% of crude petroleum, 75.2% of electric power, and 74.1% of steel. Political considerations apart, these percentages demonstrated abundantly the commanding position of the U.S.S.R. within the CMEA bloc. It was the major supplier of its Eastern European partners in such raw materials as iron ore, cotton, natural gas, and crude petroleum. Though the Soviet Union was the second largest producer of crude petroleum in the world, it was becoming relatively short of that precious raw material for two reasons: first, its home consumption, as well as that of the whole CMEA area, was increasing faster than its extraction; and second, because crude petroleum and its products were the Soviet Union's most important single source of convertible currency, it exported in 1972 an estimated amount of 50 million tons of oil to the "capitalist" markets. Therefore, although the 1973 oil extraction in the U.S.S.R. was estimated at 424 million tons, Soviet imports of oil from the Arab countries, mainly from Iraq, continued to increase.

Considerable discrepancy persisted between the level of industrial production of the CMEA countries and the volume of their trade with the capitalist world. In 1972 the world's exports reached a total of $409.1 billion, including only $39.9 billion (9.7%) for the seven European CMEA countries; their part in the $425.4 billion world's imports was $40.3 billion, 9.5% (Table III). More than two-thirds of the total goods turnover of the CMEA countries was trade with each other.

The Prague session endorsed the agreement on cooperation between the CMEA and Finland that had been signed in Moscow on May 16. The premiers of the seven European member states signed an agreement on joint cooperation in the construction of the

Table II. Output of Basic Industrial Products in Eastern Europe in 1972

(In thousands of metric tons except for natural gas and electric power)

Country	Hard coal	Brown coal	Natural gas (million cu. m.)	Crude petroleum	Electric power (million kw-hr.)	Steel	Sulfuric acid	Cement
U.S.S.R.	450,000	205,000	220,800	393,600	858,000	126,000	13,692	104,400
Poland	150,696	38,220	5,820	396	76,428	13,476	2,568	14,400
East Germany	840	248,400	...	...	72,828	5,670	1,045	8,857
Czechoslovakia	27,540	85,572	...	192	51,348	12,732	1,189	8,040
Romania	7,200	13,800	27,000	14,100	43,400	7,400	1,162	9,200
Hungary	3,672	22,176	4,086	1,977	16,318	3,273	586	2,969
Bulgaria	384	26,868	...	248	22,271	2,121	514	3,910
Totals	640,332	640,036	257,706	410,513	1,140,593	170,672	20,756	151,776

Table III. Foreign Trade of Eastern Europe

(In $000,000)

Country	Exports			Imports		
	1960	1965	1972	1960	1965	1972
U.S.S.R.	5,564	8,176	15,383	5,628	8,058	16,069
East Germany	2,207	3,070	6,190	2,195	2,808	5,911
Poland	1,326	2,228	4,928	1,495	2,340	5,331
Czechoslovakia	1,929	2,689	4,921	1,816	2,673	4,668
Hungary	874	1,510	3,295	952	1,486	3,100
Bulgaria	572	1,176	2,612	633	1,178	2,557
Romania	717	1,102	2,603	648	1,077	2,620
Totals	13,189	19,951	39,932	13,367	19,620	40,256
Percentages of world trade	10.3%	10.6%	9.7%	9.9%	10%	9.5%

Source: National statistics.

Kiembayev asbestos enrichment plant in the Ural Mountains, which was expected to produce 500,000 tons of asbestos annually. On May 12–13 ministers responsible for electrical industries of the CMEA member countries decided to form an economic and scientific organization called Interelektro, which would coordinate research and production of all machinery and apparatus.

Following the Prague joint decision to "contact the EEC at a suitable time," Nikolay V. Faddeyev, the CMEA secretary-general, met in Copenhagen on August 27 with Ivar Nørgaard, at that time chairman of the EEC Council of Ministers. Faddeyev proposed that both organizations appoint delegations with a view to discussing possible cooperation. Nørgaard said that he would put the CMEA inquiry on the agenda of the Council of Ministers in Brussels; he also emphasized that the organizational differences between CMEA and the EEC needed careful scrutiny.

On April 6 the more than 5,000-km.-long pipeline bringing natural gas from the Tyumen basin in western Siberia to Czechoslovakia had crossed the Czechoslovakian-East German border and by the end of the year had reached Brandenburg. A branch of this pipeline was extended to Austria in the summer of 1973 and started operating; it would reach Italy in 1974. Another branch was being built from Bohemia to West Germany. The main pipeline had a diameter of 900 mm., and its maximum flow capacity was 7 million cu.m. of gas per day.

The building of the second Druzhba ("Friendship") oil pipeline from Almetyevsk in the U.S.S.R. to Poland, East Germany, Czechoslovakia, and Hungary was nearing completion. The first Druzhba, from its opening in August 1964 to March 1973, had supplied more than 100 million tons of oil from Almetyevsk to Plock in Poland. Beginning in May 1973 the Druzhba pipelines were being extended 1,800 km. eastward across the Urals to Samotlor, in the Tyumen area. According to a special correspondent of *Neues Deutschland*, the Samotlor basin would soon be producing 100 million tons of oil yearly and this would continue for many decades. (K. M. SMOGORZEWSKI)

See also Communist Parties.

Soviet Literature:
see Literature

Soviet Union:
see Union of Soviet Socialist Republics

Soybeans:
see Agriculture and Fisheries

Spacecraft:
see Astronautics

Space Exploration:
see Astronautics

Spain

A nominal monarchy of southwest Europe, Spain is bounded by Portugal, with which it shares the Iberian Peninsula, and by France. Area: 194,881 sq.mi. (504,741 sq.km.), including the Balearic and Canary islands. Pop. (1973 est.): 34,729,770, including the Balearics and Canaries. Cap. and largest city: Madrid (pop., 1973 est., 3,409,663). Language: Spanish. Religion: Roman Catholic. Prince of Spain and king-designate, Don Juan Carlos de Borbón y Borbón; chief of state in 1973, Gen. Francisco Franco Bahamonde; premiers, General Franco until June 9, Adm. Luis Carrero Blanco until December 20, and, from December 29, Carlos Arias Navarro.

Spain's slow advances toward shaping the post-Franco political system received a setback in December 1973 when Premier Carrero Blanco was assassinated, allegedly by Basque separatists, after only six months in office. On June 9, Carrero Blanco, who had been nominated vice-premier in 1972, was made premier (*presidente del gobierno*), a post held since the Civil War by General Franco himself. Franco retained his position as head of state. At the same time, numerous changes were made in the Cabinet; only seven of the members of the old Cabinet retained their posts.

The incoming government described its position as a continuation of the step-by-step development of the country that had been taking place since Franco came to power. It pledged itself to continue creating the legal framework for the country's future political development and to consider how the Spaniard-in-the-street might be brought into this process. Power nevertheless remained in the hands of Franco. It was evident that the caudillo intended no important changes in the political system during his lifetime.

Economic planning was de-emphasized in the government's statement, but the fact that a new ministry was created for this function gave weight to the government's tenet that social advance depended primarily on economic development. The importance of private enterprise in the development process was emphasized. Social justice would be advanced by improvements in basic education, and efforts would be made to promote equality of opportunity. The armed forces would be modernized in line with their objectives of maintaining Spanish independence and national integrity and defending the country's institutions. The keystone of the government's policy was the maintenance of law and order.

WIDE WORLD

Cleanup operations begin at the scene of an explosion in Madrid that killed Spanish Premier Luis Carrero Blanco Dec. 20, 1973. The first Western European head of government to be assassinated since 1934, Carrero Blanco had been installed in his post just months earlier by Gen. Francisco Franco.

In fact, the new government took over what appeared to be a very stable country. There were strikes and demonstrations, but no more than in previous years. Particularly noteworthy was the violence after May Day, when extreme right-wing demonstrators clashed with security forces following relatively peaceful labour marches. In November 113 persons, covering the whole spectrum of the opposition, were arrested in Barcelona as they met in the parish house of a Catholic church. Early in December, 14 Basque nationalists were arrested in connection with a series of bombings in the Basque provinces.

The assassination of Carrero Blanco, on December 20, had been carefully planned. Two young men, claiming to be artists, had rented a basement apartment near the church in Madrid where the premier habitually attended morning Mass; from there they tunneled under the street and planted the bomb that exploded under the premier's automobile, killing him, his chauffeur, and a police guard. The assassination coincided with the trial of ten leftist labour leaders charged with trying to organize an alternative to the

SPAIN

Education. (1969–70) Primary, pupils 3,789,135, teachers 129,244; secondary, pupils 1,371,078, teachers (1967–68) 34,119; vocational, pupils 354,227, teachers (1967–68) 22,688; teacher training, students 41,183, teachers 2,407; higher (including 27 universities), students 194,515, teaching staff (1967–68) 10,894.

Finance. Monetary unit: peseta, with (Sept. 17, 1973) a free rate of 56.82 pesetas to U.S. $1 (136.95 pesetas = £1 sterling). Gold, SDRs, and convertible currencies, central bank: (May 1973) U.S. $5,498,000,000; (May 1972) U.S. $3,714,000,000. Budget (1971 actual): revenue 364,033,000,000 pesetas; expenditure 363 billion pesetas. Gross national product: (1971) 2,542,000,000,000 pesetas; (1970) 2,253,000,000,000 pesetas. Money supply: (May 1973) 1,075,100,000,000 pesetas; (May 1972) 853.6 billion pesetas. Cost of living (1963 = 100): (June 1973) 201; (June 1972) 179.

Foreign Trade. (1972) Imports 434 billion pesetas; exports 244.4 billion pesetas. Import sources: EEC 33% (West Germany 12%, France 10%, Italy 6%); U.S. 16%; U.K. 8%; Saudi Arabia 5%. Export destinations: EEC 35% (France 12%, West Germany 12%, Italy 5%, The Netherlands 5%); U.S. 16%; U.K. 8%. Main exports: machinery 10%; fruit 8%; footwear 7%; textiles 7%; ships and boats 7%; iron and steel 5%. Tourism (1971): visitors 26,758,200; receipts U.S. $2,055,000,000.

Transport and Communications. Roads (1972) 141,951 km. (including 735 km. expressways). Motor vehicles in use (1972): passenger 3,254,801; commercial 818,144. Railways: (1971) 16,311 km. (including 3,782 km. electrified); traffic (1972) 14,393,000,000 passenger-km., freight 10,221,000,000 net ton-km. Air traffic (1972): 8,083,000,000 passenger-km.; freight 174,488,000 net ton-km. Shipping (1972): merchant vessels 100 gross tons and over 2,313; gross tonnage 4,300,055. Telephones (Dec. 1971) 5,129,000. Radio receivers (Dec. 1971) 7,174,000. Television receivers (Dec. 1971) 4,520,000.

Agriculture. Production (in 000; metric tons; 1972; 1971 in parentheses): wheat 4,563 (5,456); barley 4,358 (4,783); oats 440 (582); rye 263 (269); corn 1,921 (2,058); potatoes 5,516 (4,629); rice 346 (361); sorghum 157 (148); dry broad beans 102 (128); other dry beans *c.* 126 (106); tomatoes 1,617 (1,308); onions (1970) *c.* 970, (1969) 960; apples 695 (571); pears 403 (401); oranges 2,893 (2,100); lemons 177 (95); sugar, raw value *c.* 814 (1,046); sunflower seed 243 (256); bananas (1970) 330, (1969) 432; figs (1970) 148, (1969) 158; olive oil 485 (375); wine 2,645 (2,333); tobacco 30 (28); cotton, lint *c.* 50 (43); meat 901 (936); fish catch (1970) 1,499, (1969) 1,496. Livestock (in 000; 1971–72): cattle 4,249; pigs 7,423; sheep 16,668; goats 2,448; asses 361; chickens *c.* 47,000.

Industry. Index of industrial production (1963 = 100): (1972) 250; (1971) 213. Fuel and power (in 000; metric tons; 1972): coal 11,007; lignite 3,057; crude oil (1971) 120; manufactured gas (cu.m.) 2,453,000; electricity (kw-hr.) 68,140,000. Production (in 000; metric tons; 1972): cement 19,441; iron ore (50% metal content) 6,687; pig iron 6,078; crude steel 9,533; aluminum 148; copper 89; zinc 99; lead 92; sulfur (1971) 1,138; nitrogenous fertilizer (1971–72) 673; phosphate fertilizer (1971–72) 554; potash fertilizer (1971–72) 502; cotton yarn 80; cotton fabrics 87; wool yarn 38; rayon, etc., yarn and fibres 66; nylon, etc., yarn and fibres 107. Merchant vessels launched (100 gross tons and over; 1972) 1,134,000 gross tons.

official labour union, but the government claimed to have identified the assassins as Basque separatists. On December 29 Franco named Carlos Arias Navarro, a civilian who had been minister of the interior in Carrero Blanco's Cabinet, as the new premier.

In foreign affairs the government's stance was one of mutual respect and friendly noninterference. Particular mention was made of the value of relationships with Portugal and with the U.S. The claim of Spain to Gibraltar was repeated, and its traditional friendship with Arab countries was emphasized. Spain's relationship with the Roman Catholic Church was defined as filial and respectfully independent. Nevertheless, the dispute with Morocco over fishery limits continued without solution, while the question of the sovereignty of Gibraltar was again brought up at the UN and promised to drag on into the future. Diplomatic relations were established with East Germany in January and with the Peking government in March.

Negotiations for a new trade agreement with the enlarged EEC staggered on, largely centred on the need for Spain to sell its agricultural produce in the EEC market with fewer controls and duties. The previous agreement expired on Jan. 1, 1973, but was extended for one year in the absence of any scheme to replace it. Spain also continued to work toward a special relationship with Latin-American countries. A unique aid agreement was signed with the Andean Group, under which Spain would enjoy investment privileges in the member states.

The economy continued to do well, with a growth rate approaching 7%. Among important economic events of the year were the continuation of large-scale investment by electricity companies in nuclear-powered generating stations, and the official go-ahead given to the Ford Motor Co. to set up a major automobile plant in the Valencia region at a provisionally estimated cost of some U.S. $250 million. The government was pledged to the extension of expansive conditions, despite inflation and shortages of materials.

With prices showing no sign of slowing, the government acted to influence the market directly. A freeze on the prices of a wide range of goods and services was imposed for the last three months of the year, and a program of imports and duty suspensions was implemented to stabilize supplies of certain perishables. Thus it was hoped that domestic prices could be kept down at the expense of the country's extremely strong gold and foreign currency reserve position.

Catastrophic floods occurred in southeastern Spain in October, in which at least 500 were thought to have died. (*See* DISASTERS.) (RALPH DEANE)

Speleology

In 1973 new discoveries and more surveying in the Hölloch (the Swiss cave that is the second longest in the world) brought its length to 74½ mi. In the U.S.S.R. the Optimistitscheskaja Cave was explored to a total length of 57 mi., making it the third longest. A new plan of Organ Cave, in Greenbrier County, W.Va., showed it to be 34 mi. long. In England the length of the Easegill Cave system was extended to 17 mi. by the discovery of a new series of passages linking the bottom end of County Pot to the Lancaster Hole highway near Cornes Cavern.

A British karst research expedition spent six months in northwest Venezuela, investigating the area near

LONDON DAILY EXPRESS/PICTORIAL PARADE

Members of the West Australia Speleological Group examine the glittering beauty of a newly discovered chamber in the Augusta Jewel Cave system, Western Australia. They may have been the first explorers to enter the 100-ft.-high cave.

Curimagua. Many caves were explored for the first time, including the 1,000-ft.-deep Guarataro, the second deepest in South America. The abundant cave fauna was studied and also the hydrology of the underground water flows.

Bibima Cave in New Guinea was explored to a sump at a depth of 1,620 ft. by Kevan Wilde and others. It thus held the Southern Hemisphere depth record. A team from McMaster University in Canada descended into Yorkshire Pot, in the Rockies, the bottom of which they found sealed by a mud sump at 1,260 ft.; it became the deepest American cave north of Mexico.

Several important deep explorations took place toward the end of 1972. The Abîme Club Toulonnais found extensions in the Chourum des Aiguilles (Hautes-Alpes, France) that made it 3,215 ft. deep and thus the third deepest in the world. In the Gouffre du Cambou de Liard (Hautes-Pyrénées) a terminal sump was reached at 3,062 ft. A depth of 2,799 ft. was attained in the Sumidero de Callagua near Santander in northern Spain; the bottom of the cave was not reached, however, for the explorers were halted by a shaft for which they had no more tackle. Explorers from Trieste, Italy, were stopped by a lake at a depth of 2,411 ft. in the Abisso Enrico Davanzo. In the French Alps a three-man exploration team discovered the Scialet de Genieux, and by the end of the year they reached the bottom, at 2,215 ft.

A cave containing prehistoric wall paintings was discovered in the Alpes-Maritimes département of France. The discovery was by experts from the Museum of Prehistoric Anthropology at Monaco. A museum was opened at the cave of Chou-k'ou-tien, near Peking, the site of the discovery of Peking Man (*Sinanthropus pekinensis*).

The year marked the 300th anniversary of the Count de Nointel's descent on Dec. 22, 1673, into the Antiparos Cave in the Greek islands. This was an ambitious exploration involving the use of ladders and ropes. (T. R. SHAW)

Spanish Literature: *see* Literature

Spanish Sahara: *see* Dependent States

Spices: *see* Agriculture and Fisheries

Spirits: *see* Alcoholic Beverages

Sporting Record

ANGLING

Event	Winner	Country
WORLD CHAMPIONS		
Individual	P. Michels	Belgium
Team	Belgium	
U.K. CHAMPIONS		
Individual	A. Wright	
Team	Grimsby	

ARCHERY

Event	Winner	Country
WORLD CHAMPIONS		
Individual, men	V. Sidoruk	U.S.S.R.
Team, men	U.S.	
Individual, women	L. Myers	U.S.
Team, women	U.S.S.R.	

BADMINTON

Event	Winner	Country
THOMAS CUP (world team championship)		Indonesia
U.K. OPEN CHAMPIONS		
Men's singles	R. Hartono	Indonesia
Men's doubles	A. Chandra, L. Christian	Indonesia
Women's singles	M. Beck	U.K.
Women's doubles	M. Aizawa, E. Takenaka	Japan
Mixed doubles	D. Talbot, G. Gilks	U.K.
U.S. OPEN CHAMPIONS		
Men's singles	S. Johansson	Sweden
Men's doubles	D. Paup, J. Poole	U.S.
Women's singles	E. Twedberg	Sweden
Women's doubles	P. Bristol, D. Hales	U.S.
Mixed doubles	S. Johansson, E. Twedberg	Sweden

BIATHLON

Event	Winner	Country
WORLD CHAMPIONS		
Individual	A. Tikhonov	U.S.S.R.
Relay	U.S.S.R.	
Individual, junior	J. Szpunar	Poland
Relay, junior	Poland	

BILLIARDS

Event	Winner	Country
WORLD CHAMPIONS		
Professional	R. Williams	U.K.
Amateur	L. Driffield	U.K.

BOBSLEDDING

Event	Winner	Country
WORLD CHAMPIONS		
Two-man	W. Zimmerer, P. Utzschneider	West Germany
Four-man	R. Stadler (pilot)	Switzerland
EUROPEAN CHAMPIONS		
Two-man	W. Zimmerer, P. Utzschneider	West Germany
Four-man	W. Zimmerer (pilot)	West Germany

CANOEING

Event		Winner	Country
WORLD CHAMPIONS—MEN			
Kayak singles	500 m.	G. Csapo	Hungary
	1,000 m.	G. Csapo	Hungary
	10,000 m.	A. Shaparenko	U.S.S.R.
Kayak pairs	500 m.	V. Greshta, H. Hakol	U.S.S.R.
	1,000 m.	J. Deme, J. Ratkai	Hungary
	10,000 m.	J. Bako, H. Csapo	Hungary
Kayak fours	1,000 m.	Hungary	
Kayak relay		U.S.S.R.	
Canadian singles	500 m.	M. Darvas	Hungary
	1,000 m.	I. Patzaichin	Romania
	10,000 m.	V. Yurchenko	U.S.S.R.
Canadian pairs	500 m.	L. Khalidov, V. Slobodenyk	U.S.S.R.
	1,000 m.	T. Danielov, S. Covaliov	Romania
	10,000 m.	V. Chessyunas, Y. Lobanov	U.S.S.R.
WORLD CHAMPIONS—WOMEN			
Kayak singles	500 m.	N. Gopova	U.S.S.R.
Kayak pairs	500 m.	I. Kaschube, P. Borzym	East Germany
Kayak fours	500 m.	U.S.S.R.	

Event	Winner	Country
WORLD WILD-WATER CHAMPIONS—MEN		
Kayak singles	J. P. Burny	Belgium
Kayak singles team	West Germany	
Canadian singles	B. Heinemann	West Germany
Canadian singles team	West Germany	
Canadian pairs	G. Lefauconnier, F. P. Lefauconnier	France
Canadian pairs team	West Germany	
WORLD WILD-WATER CHAMPIONS—WOMEN		
Kayak singles	G. Grothaus	West Germany
Kayak singles team	West Germany	
Canadian pairs	K. Kremslehner, G. Ramelow	Austria
Canadian pairs team	West Germany	
WORLD SLALOM CHAMPIONS—MEN		
Kayak singles	N. Sattler	Austria
Kayak singles team	East Germany	
Canadian singles	R. Eiben	East Germany
Canadian singles team	Czechoslovakia	
Canadian pairs	J. Krejza, J. Polert	Czechoslovakia
Canadian pairs team	East Germany	
WORLD SLALOM CHAMPIONS—WOMEN		
Kayak singles	S. Spindler	East Germany
Kayak singles team	U.S.	
WORLD SLALOM CHAMPIONS—MIXED		
Canadian pairs team	U.S.	

CROSS-COUNTRY

Event		Winner	Country
INTERNATIONAL CHAMPIONS			
Men		P. Paivarinta	Finland
Women		P. Cacchi	Italy
Junior men		J. Brown	Scotland
Team, men		Belgium	
Team, women		England	
Team, juniors		Spain	
NATIONAL CHAMPIONS			
Belgium		W. Polleunis	
Canada	Men	G. McLaren	
	Women	G. Reiser	
East Germany		J. Haase	
Finland	Men	P. Paivarinta	
	Women	P. Virhonen	
France		N. Tijou	
Hungary	Men	L. Mecser	
	Women	Z. Volgyi	
Ireland		D. Walsh	
New Zealand	Men	N. Healey	
	Women	H. Thompson	
Norway	Men	R. Olsen	
	Women	G. Andersen	
Scotland		A. McKean	
U.K.	Men	*D. Bedford	
	Women	J. Smith	
U.S. (AAU)	Men	F. Shorter	
	Women	F. Larrieu	
Wales	Men	M. Thomas	
	Women	T. Bateman	
West Germany	Men	L. Philipp	
	Women	E. Tittel	

*R. Dixon (New Zealand) finished first in race but was ineligible to take U.K. title.

CURLING

Event	Winner
WORLD CHAMPIONS	Sweden

CYCLING

Event	Winner	Country
WORLD AMATEUR CHAMPIONS—TRACK		
Men		
Sprint	D. Morelon	France
Tandem sprint	J. Vackar, H. Vymazal	Czechoslovakia
Individual pursuit	K. Knudsen	Norway
1,000-m. time trial	J. Kierzkowski	Poland
Team pursuit	West Germany	
100-km. motor-paced	H. Gnas	West Germany
Women		
Sprint	S. Young	U.S.
Individual pursuit	T. Garkushina	U.S.S.R.
WORLD PROFESSIONAL CHAMPIONS—TRACK		
Sprint	R. van Lancker	Belgium
Individual pursuit	H. Porter	U.K.
100-km. motor-paced	C. Stam	The Netherlands
WORLD AMATEUR CHAMPIONS—ROAD		
Men		
100-km. team time trial	Poland	
Individual road race	R. Szurkowski	Poland
Women		
Individual road race	N. van den Broecke	Belgium

Event	Winner	Country
WORLD PROFESSIONAL CHAMPIONS—ROAD		
Individual road race	F. Gimondi	Italy
NATIONAL ROAD-RACE CHAMPIONS (professional unless otherwise stated)		
Belgium	F. Verbeek	
France	B. Thevenet	
Italy	E. Paolini	
Luxembourg	J. Schleck	
Netherlands, The	J. Zoetemelk	
Portugal	J. Agostinho	
Spain	D. Perurena	
Switzerland	J. Fuchs	
U.K., professional	B. Jolly	
amateur	G. Thomas	
women	B. Burton	
MAJOR PROFESSIONAL ROAD-RACE WINNERS		
Bordeaux-Paris	E. Mattioda	Italy
Criterium des As	G. Karstens	The Netherlands
Four Days of Dunkirk	F. Mertens	Belgium
Ghent-Wevelghem	E. Merckx	Belgium
Grand Prix des Nations	E. Merckx	Belgium
Liège-Bastogne-Liège	E. Merckx	Belgium
Midi-Libre	R. Poulidor	France
Milan-San Remo	R. de Vlaeminck	Belgium
Paris-Brussels	E. Merckx	Belgium
Paris-Nice	R. Poulidor	France
Paris-Roubaix	E. Merckx	Belgium
Paris-Tours	R. van Linden	Belgium
Tour of Belgium	L. Mortensen	Denmark
Tour of the Dauphiné	L. Ocana	Spain
Tour of Flanders	E. Leman	Belgium
Tour of France	L. Ocana	Spain
Tour of Italy	E. Merckx	Belgium
Tour of Lombardy	E. Merckx	Belgium
Tour of Luxembourg	S. Vasseur	France
Tour of Normandy	W. David	Belgium
Tour of Sardinia	E. Merckx	Belgium
Tour of Switzerland	J. Fuente	Spain
Super Prestige Pernod (Leading points-scorer in all classic races)	E. Merckx	Belgium
OTHER MAJOR ROAD-RACE WINNERS		
Tour of Britain	P. van Katwijk	The Netherlands
Tour de l'Avenir	G. Baronchelli	Italy
Berlin-Warsaw-Prague	R. Szurkowski	Poland
Grand Prix des Nations, Amateur	G. Bischoff	Switzerland

Event	Winner and country	Performance
WORLD AMATEUR RECORDS SET IN 1973		
Men		
200-m. flying start	N. Fredborg, Denmark	10.35 sec.
500-m. flying start	N. Fredborg, Denmark	27.50 sec.
1,000-m. time trial	N. Fredborg, Denmark	1 min. 4.49 sec.
4,000-m. time trial	K. Knudsen, Norway	4 min. 49.48 sec.
Women		
3,000-m. time trial	T. Garkushina, U.S.S.R.	3 min. 59.28 sec.
WORLD PROFESSIONAL RECORDS SET IN 1973		
Men		
1,000-m. time trial	P. Sercu, Belgium	1 min. 2.46 sec.

EQUESTRIAN SPORTS

Event	Winning rider and horse	Country
EUROPEAN CHAMPIONS		
Dressage, individual	R. Klimke, "Mehmed"	West Germany
Dressage, team	West Germany	
Show jumping, men	P. McMahon, "Penwood Forge Mill"	U.K.
Show jumping, women	A. Moore, "Psalm"	U.K.
Show jumping, junior	D. Johnsey, "Speculator"	U.K.
Driving, individual	A. Dubey	Switzerland
Driving, team	Switzerland	
3-day, individual	A. Evdokimov	U.S.S.R.
3-day, team	West Germany	

FENCING

Event	Winner	Country
WORLD CHAMPIONS—MEN		
Foil, individual	C. Noël	France
Foil, team	U.S.S.R.	
Épée, individual	R. Edling	Sweden
Épée, team	West Germany	
Sabre, individual	M. A. Montano	Italy
Sabre, team	Hungary	
WORLD CHAMPIONS—WOMEN		
Foil, individual	V. Nikonova	U.S.S.R.
Foil, team	Hungary	

FOOTBALL, ASSOCIATION

Event	Winner	Country
MAJOR TOURNAMENTS		
European Champions' Cup	Ajax Amsterdam	The Netherlands
European Cup-Winners' Cup	A.C. Milan	Italy
UEFA Cup	Liverpool	U.K.
South American Champions' Cup	Independiente	Argentina
UEFA Youth Cup	England	

Event		Winner	Country
NATIONAL CHAMPIONS (National Cup and League Winners)			
Belgium	Cup	Anderlecht	
	League	Brugge	
Bulgaria	Cup	CSKA Sofia	
	League	CSKA Sofia	
Czechoslovakia	Cup	Banik Ostrava	
	League	Spartak Trnava	
Denmark	Cup	Randers Freja	
East Germany	Cup	FC Magdeburg	
	League	Dynamo Dresden	
England	FA Cup	Sunderland	
	League Cup	Tottenham Hotspur	
	League	Liverpool	
Finland	Cup	Reipas Lahti	
	League	TPS Turku	
France	Cup	Lyons	
	League	Nantes	
Greece	Cup	Olympiakos Piraeus	
	League	Olympiakos Piraeus	
Hungary	Cup	Vasa Budapest	
	League	Ujpest Dozsa	
Ireland	Cup	Cork	
	League	Waterford	
Italy	Cup	Milan	
	League	Juventus	
Luxembourg	Cup	Jeunesse d'Esch	
	League	Jeunesse d'Esch	
Netherlands, The	Cup	NAC Breda	
	League	Ajax Amsterdam	
Northern Ireland	Cup	Glentoran	
Norway	Cup	Bran Bergen	
	League	Viking	
Poland	Cup	Legia Warsaw	
	League	Stal Mielec	
Portugal	Cup	Sporting Lisbon	
	League	Benfica	
Romania	League	Dinamo Bucharest	
Scotland	Cup	Glasgow Rangers	
	League Cup	Hibernian	
	League	Celtic	
Spain	League	Atletico Madrid	
Sweden	Cup	Malmö	
	League	Atvidaberg	
Switzerland	Cup	Zürich	
	League	Basel	
Wales	Cup	Cardiff City	
West Germany	Cup	Borussia Münchengladbach	
	League	Bayern Munich	
Yugoslavia	League	Red Star	

GYMNASTICS

Event	Winner	Country
WORLD UNIVERSITY GAMES—MEN		
Overall	N. Andrianov	U.S.S.R.
Floor exercises	N. Andrianov	U.S.S.R.
Parallel bars	S. Shukin	U.S.S.R.
Horizontal bar	S. Shukin	U.S.S.R.
Rings	F. Grecu	Romania
Pommeled horse	N. Andrianov	U.S.S.R.
Long horse vault	J. Cuervo	Cuba
Team	U.S.S.R.	
WORLD UNIVERSITY GAMES—WOMEN		
Overall	O. Korbut	U.S.S.R.
Floor exercises	O. Korbut	U.S.S.R.

WIDE WORLD

Event	Winner	Country
Asymmetrical bars	O. Korbut	U.S.S.R.
Beam	O. Korbut	U.S.S.R.
Horse vault	L. Bogdanova	U.S.S.R.
Team	U.S.S.R.	
EUROPEAN CHAMPIONS—WOMEN		
Overall	L. Tourischeva	U.S.S.R.
Floor exercises	L. Tourischeva	U.S.S.R.
Asymmetrical bars	L. Tourischeva	U.S.S.R.
Beam	L. Tourischeva	U.S.S.R.
Horse vault	A. Hellmann, East Germany, and L. Tourischeva, U.S.S.R. (tied)	
EUROPEAN CHAMPIONS—MEN		
Overall	V. Klimenko	U.S.S.R.

HANDBALL

Event	Winner
WORLD CHAMPIONS	
Men	Yugoslavia
Women	East Germany

JUDO

Event	Winner	Country
WORLD CHAMPIONS		
Lightweight	Y. Minami	Japan
Light-middleweight	T. Nomura	Japan
Middleweight	S. Fujii	Japan
Light-heavyweight	N. Sato	Japan
Heavyweight	C. Tagaki	Japan
Unlimited weight	H. Nimomiya	Japan
EUROPEAN CHAMPIONS		
Lightweight	S. Melnichenko	U.S.S.R.
Light-middleweight	D. Hoettger	East Germany
Middleweight	B. Jacks	U.K.
Light-heavyweight	J. L. Rouge	France
Heavyweight	S. Oieda	Spain
Unlimited weight	S. Novikov	U.S.S.R.
Team	U.S.S.R.	

MODERN PENTATHLON

Event	Winner	Country
WORLD CHAMPIONS		
Individual	P. Lednev	U.S.S.R.
Team	U.S.S.R.	

MOTORCYCLING

Event	Winner	Country
WORLD CHAMPIONS		
50 cc.	J. de Vries	The Netherlands
125 cc.	K. Andersson	Sweden
250 cc.	D. Braun	West Germany
350 cc.	G. Agostini	Italy
500 cc.	P. Read	U.K.
Sidecar	K. Enders	West Germany

RACKETS

Event	Winner	Country
WORLD CHAMPIONS	H. Angus	U.K.

ROLLER HOCKEY

Events	Winner
WORLD CHAMPIONS	Portugal
WORLD JUNIOR CHAMPIONS	Spain

ROLLER SKATING

Event	Winner	Country
WORLD FIGURE-SKATING CHAMPIONS		
Men	R. Dayney	U.S.
Women	S. Muellerbach	West Germany
Pairs	V. Handyside, L. Stoval	U.S.
Dance	K. Purachin, H. Stephens	U.S.

SAILING

Event	Winner	Country
WORLD CHAMPIONS		
Albatross	J. Herbert	U.K.
Contender	P. Hollis	Australia
Dragon	R. Eliasson	Sweden
Finn	S. Maury	France
Fireball	K. Brackwell, R. Butcher	U.K.
Flying Dutchman	H. Fogh	Denmark
Hornet	M. Goodwin, J. Lord	U.K.
O.K.	C. Roberts	New Zealand
Shark	J. Fitzpatrick	Canada
Snipe	F. Gancedo	Spain
Soling	U. Andersen	Denmark
Star	L. North	U.S.
Tempest	V. Mankin	U.S.S.R.
4-2-0	A. Wangel	Australia
5-0-5	P. White	U.K.
5.5 m.	E. Fay	U.S.
18 ft.	R. Holmes	Australia
16 ft.	D. Mackay	Australia
Vaurien	P. Bessec, Genevieve Routier	France
EUROPEAN CHAMPIONS		
Finn	C. Schroeder	East Germany
Finn Junior	V. Zaroslav	U.S.S.R.
Fireball	P. Durr	Switzerland
Flying Dutchman	H. Huettner	East Germany
Mirror Dinghy	P. Barnes	U.K.
Sharpie	A. van Veen	The Netherlands
Soling	D. Below	East Germany
Star	O. Meier	Switzerland
Tornado	R. White	U.K.
4-2-0	O. Hamerlijnck, R. Hamerlijnck	Belgium
4-7-0	H. Soderlund	Denmark
5-0-5	N. Loday	France

SPEEDWAY

Event	Winner	Country
WORLD CHAMPIONS		
Individual	J. Szczakiel	Poland
Team	U.K.	

WIDE WORLD

Event	Winner	Country
Individual, sand track	O. Olesen	Denmark
Individual, ice track	E. Kadyrov	U.S.S.R.

SQUASH RACKETS

Event	Winner	Country
MAJOR TOURNAMENT WINNERS		
World amateur, individual	C. Nancarrow	Australia
World amateur, team	Australia	
Australian amateur, men	Q. Zaman	Pakistan
Australian amateur, women	H. McKay	Australia
British open, men	J. Barrington	U.K.
British open, women	H. McKay	Australia
British amateur, men	C. Nancarrow	Australia
South African amateur, men	C. Nancarrow	Australia

TABLE TENNIS

Event	Winner	Country
WORLD CHAMPIONS		
Men's singles	Hsi En-ting	China
Men's doubles	S. Bengtsson, K. Johansson	Sweden
Women's singles	Hu Yu-lan	China
Women's doubles	M. Alexandru, M. Hamada	Romania, Japan
Mixed doubles	Liang Ko-liang, Li Li	China
Men's team	Sweden	
Women's team	South Korea	

TOBOGGANING

Event	Winner	Country
WORLD CHAMPIONS		
Men's individual	N. Rinn	East Germany
Men's pairs	B. Bredow, H. Hörnlein	East Germany
Women's individual	M. Schumann	East Germany
EUROPEAN CHAMPIONS		
Men's individual	N. Rinn	East Germany
Men's pairs	N. Hahn, N. Rinn	East Germany
Women's individual	M. Schumann	East Germany

TRAMPOLINE

Event	Winner	Country
EUROPEAN CHAMPIONS		
Men's individual	R. Tison	France
Men's pairs	S. Lobanov, N. Shmelyov	U.S.S.R.
Women's individual	O. Starykova	U.S.S.R.
Women's pairs	L. Levyna, O. Zarshchikova	U.S.S.R.

VOLLEYBALL

Event	Winner	Country
MAJOR CHAMPIONS		
World Championship, women	U.S.S.R.	
World University Games, men	U.S.S.R.	
World University Games, women	U.S.S.R.	
European Champions' Cup, men	CSKA Moscow	U.S.S.R.
European Champions' Cup, women	Nimse Budapest	Hungary
European Cup-Winners' Cup, men	Voroshilovgrad SV	U.S.S.R.
European Cup-Winners' Cup, women	CSKA Moscow	U.S.S.R.

WATER POLO

Event	Winner
WORLD CHAMPIONS	Hungary

WATER SKIING

Event	Winner	Country
WORLD CHAMPIONS—MEN		
Figures	W. Grimditch	U.S.
Jumps	R. McCormick	U.S.
Slalom	G. Athans	Canada
Overall	G. Athans	Canada
WORLD CHAMPIONS—WOMEN		
Figures	M. Carrasco	Venezuela
Jumps	L. A. Shetter	U.S.
Slalom	S. Maurial	France
Overall	L. St. John	U.S.
WORLD CHAMPIONS—MEN and WOMEN OVERALL	U.S.	
EUROPEAN CHAMPIONS—MEN		
Figures	V. Stehno	Czechoslovakia
Jumps	P. Seaton	U.K.
Slalom	L. Bjork	Sweden
Overall	L. Bjork	Sweden

WIDE WORLD

Event	Winner	Country
EUROPEAN CHAMPIONS—WOMEN		
Figures	W. Stahle	The Netherlands
Jumps	S. Maurial	France
Slalom	A. M. Fritsch	Austria
Overall	S. Maurial	France

WEIGHT LIFTING

Event	Winner and country	Performance
WORLD RECORD TOTALS (Established following the elimination of the press lift from competition)		
Flyweight	M. Nassiri, Iran	240 kg. (529 lb.)
Bantamweight	A. Kirov, Bulgaria	257.5 kg. (567½ lb.)
Featherweight	D. Shanidze, U.S.S.R.	277.5 kg. (611½ lb.)
Lightweight	M. Kirzhinov, U.S.S.R.	312.5 kg. (689 lb.)
Middleweight	N. Kolev, Bulgaria	337.5 kg. (743½ lb.)
Light-heavyweight	V. Rizhenkov, U.S.S.R.	355 kg. (781 lb.)
Middle-heavyweight	D. Rigert, U.S.S.R.	372.5 kg. (821 lb.)
Heavyweight	P. Pervushin, U.S.S.R.	400 kg. (882 lb.)
Super-heavyweight	V. Alekseyev, U.S.S.R.	417.5 kg. (921 lb.)

WRESTLING

Event	Winner	Country
WORLD GRECO-ROMAN CHAMPIONS		
Light-flyweight	V. Zhubkov	U.S.S.R.
Flyweight	G. Guergue	Romania
Bantamweight	J. Lipien	Poland
Featherweight	K. Lipien	Poland
Lightweight	S. Khizamutdinov	U.S.S.R.
Light-middleweight	I. Kolev	Bulgaria
Middleweight	L. Liberman	U.S.S.R.
Light-heavyweight	V. Rezantsev	U.S.S.R.
Heavyweight	N. Balbushin	U.S.S.R.
Super-heavyweight	A. Tomov	Bulgaria
WORLD FREESTYLE CHAMPIONS		
Light-flyweight	R. Dmitriev	U.S.S.R.
Flyweight	E. Javadpour	Iran
Bantamweight	M. Faravachi	Iran
Featherweight	Z. Abdulbekov	U.S.S.R.
Lightweight	L. Keaser	U.S.
Light-middleweight	M. Barzgar	Iran
Middleweight	V. Suilzhin	U.S.S.R.
Light-heavyweight	L. Tediashvili	U.S.S.R.
Heavyweight	I. Yarygin	U.S.S.R.
Super-heavyweight	S. Andyev	U.S.S.R.
Team	U.S.S.R.	
EUROPEAN GRECO-ROMAN CHAMPIONS		
Light-flyweight	G. Berceanu	Romania
Flyweight	J. Michalik	Poland
Bantamweight	C. Traykov	Bulgaria
Featherweight	N. Davidyan	U.S.S.R.
Lightweight	S. Khizamutdinov	U.S.S.R.
Light-middleweight	I. Kolev	Bulgaria
Middleweight	L. Andersson	Sweden
Light-heavyweight	V. Rezantsev	U.S.S.R.
Heavyweight	N. Balbushin	U.S.S.R.
Super-heavyweight	A. Tomov	Bulgaria
Team	Bulgaria	

(D. K. R. PHILLIPS)

See also Baseball; Basketball; Bowling and Lawn Bowls; Boxing; Chess; Contract Bridge; Cricket; Cycling; Football; Golf; Hockey; Horse Racing; Ice Skating; Motor Sports; Rowing; Sailing; Skiing; Swimming; Tennis; Track and Field Sports.

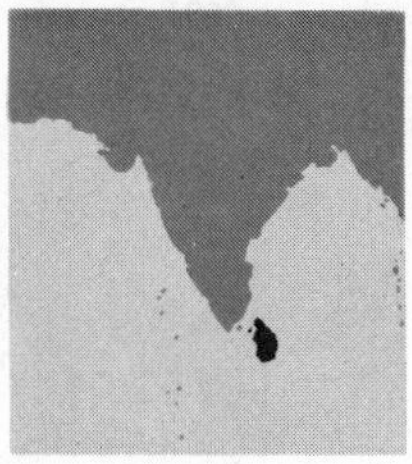

Sri Lanka

An Asian republic and member of the Commonwealth of Nations, Sri Lanka (Ceylon) occupies an island off the southeast coast of peninsular India. Area: 25,332 sq.mi. (65,610 sq.km.). Pop. (1972 est.): 13,022,000, including Sinhalese about 72%; Tamil 21%; Moors 7%. Cap. and largest city: Colombo (pop., 1972 est., 607,000). Language: Sinhalese (official), Tamil, English. Religion (1971): Buddhist 67%; Hindu 18%; Christian 7%; Muslim 7%. President in 1973, William Gopallawa; prime minister, Mrs. Sirimavo Bandaranaike.

In 1973 deterioration in the island's economy, which had been going on for some years, reached the crisis point. The causes were unfavourable terms of trade due in particular to world overproduction of tea, the island's main export; the rise in world prices of imports, causing strict control; the disproportionate percentage of the national revenue spent on welfare services, especially the free issue of rice; and some government mismanagement. Thus, there was a severe shortage of foreign exchange, despite drastic measures taken to conserve it, and a mounting foreign debt, the servicing of which amounted to SLRs. 2,730,000,000 a year.

The finance minister in his budget of November 1972 had introduced some measures for economic reform, which were not well received. The weekly free issue of rice was withdrawn from income-tax payers and their dependents; a "once-and-for-all" levy was imposed on private automobiles ranging from SLRs. 100 to SLRs. 600 according to age; and the rate for foreign exchange entitlement certificates on most moneys going out of the country was raised from 55 to 65%. The deficit of SLRs. 1,798,000,000 was to be met by borrowing, at home and from abroad. During the year sizable loans were received from several countries, including the United Kingdom, the United States, the Soviet Union, and China. Work on the Mahaweli River project under World Bank auspices was proceeding. Special concessions were offered to foreign investors in both the public and private sectors, the latter something of a reversal of government policy.

The economy, however, continued to worsen, and in September Prime Minister Bandaranaike broadcast a strong appeal to the people of Sri Lanka to step up the production of rice and other foods. She announced a rationing of food as severe as that during World War II. The free rice ration would be reduced to a half measure. Flour was to be rationed and the sugar ration reduced. As a small offset, low-paid employees were to get an extra 10% on their wages. Great efforts were being made to increase cultivation, and the armed forces were ordered to participate.

In the first half of 1973 public interest centred on two bills that concerned the press. Their object was to break the near monopoly of the family-owned Associated Newspapers, which had been consistently hostile to the government. One bill took steps to "broad base the ownership" of this company. The other, which caused acute controversy, set up a government-appointed Press Council. The appointment of two Constitutional Courts was necessary (the first having resigned over a clash with the National State Assembly) before the bill was declared constitutional. Subsequent stormy scenes in the Assembly culminated in a walkout by the opposition when the bill came up for debate. Government speakers maintained that the press remained free, except for a prohibition against publishing Cabinet proceedings, documents submitted to the Cabinet, official secrets, and government proposals relating to monetary, fiscal, exchange, and import controls and any other measures the publication of which before official release could adversely affect the country's economy. The opposition, both in the Assembly and in a number of public meetings, asserted that the bill would infringe the freedom of both the press and individuals.

In April Dudley Senanayake, twice prime minister, died (*see* OBITUARIES). His cremation was attended by two million mourners. He was succeeded in the leadership of the United National Party by J. R. Jayewardene. During the year this party won several by-elections.

In foreign affairs Mrs. Bandaranaike maintained her policy of nonalignment and pressed for the Indian Ocean to be declared a peace zone. She attended the Commonwealth heads-of-government conference in Ottawa in August, and in September the summit conference of nonaligned states in Algiers. Friendly relations were maintained with the Soviet Union and with China. With the latter the fifth five-year contract for a rubber-rice exchange was renewed, and the Chinese built a large conference hall in Colombo free of cost. Domestic policy continued to aim at making Sri Lanka a "socialist democracy," which led to government pressure on the upper and middle classes.

During the year a number of persons, including some Buddhist monks, were arrested on charges of having participated in the April 1971 attempt to overthrow the government. (SIDNEY A. PAKEMAN)

SRI LANKA

Education. (1969–70) Primary, pupils 2,298,200; secondary, pupils 342,300; vocational, pupils (state only) 7,565; primary, secondary, and vocational, teachers 94,113; teacher training, students 5,800, teachers (1967–68) 438; higher, students 14,400, teaching staff (1966–67) 1,064.

Finance. Monetary unit: Sri Lanka rupee, with (Sept. 17, 1973) an official rate of SLRs. 6.46 to U.S. $1 (SLRs. 15.57 = £1 sterling) and an effective tourist rate of SLRs. 10.65 to U.S. $1 (SLRs. 25.70 = £1 sterling). Gold, SDRs, and foreign exchange, official: (June 1973) U.S. $70 million; (June 1972) U.S. $64 million. Budget (1971–72 est.): revenue SLRs. 3,367,000,000; expenditure SLRs. 3,764,000,000. Gross national product: (1972) SLRs. 13,643,000,000; (1971) SLRs. 12,765,000,000. Money supply: (May 1973) SLRs. 2,434,000,000; (May 1972) SLRs. 2,124,000,000. Cost of living (Colombo; 1963 = 100): (June 1973) 151; (June 1972) 139.

Foreign Trade. (1972): Imports SLRs. 2,096,000,000; exports SLRs. 1,938,000,000. Import sources (1971): U.K. 12%; India 10%; Japan 9%; China 8%; West Germany 7%; Australia 6%; U.S. 5%; Burma 5%. Export destinations (1971): U.K. 17%; China 9%; U.S. 9%; Australia 5%. Main exports: tea 59%; coconut products 14%; rubber 13%.

Transport and Communications. Roads (1972) 21,990 km. Motor vehicles in use (1972): passenger 89,024; commercial 34,000. Railways: (1970) 1,536 km.; traffic (1970–71) 2,776,000,000 passenger-km., freight 339 million net ton-km. Air traffic (1972): 239,910,000 passenger-km.; freight 4,034,000 net ton-km. Telephones (Dec. 1971) 64,000. Radio receivers (Dec. 1969) 500,000.

Agriculture. Production (in 000; metric tons; 1972; 1971 in parentheses): rice 1,308 (1,397); cassava (1970) 354, (1969) 403; sweet potatoes (1971) 57, (1970) 72; onions (1971) 42, (1970) 37; tea *c.* 213 (*c.* 218); copra *c.* 240 (200); rubber *c.* 140 (*c.* 141). Livestock (in 000; June 1971): cattle 1,625; buffaloes 731; sheep 29; goats 546; pigs 90; chickens *c.* 6,900.

Industry. Production (in 000; metric tons; 1971): cement 386; salt 65; graphite 7.6; electricity (kw-hr.) 900,000.

Stamp Collecting: *see* Philately and Numismatics

Steel Industry: *see* Industrial Review

Stock Exchanges

The world's major stock markets generally experienced bearish patterns in 1973. Contributing to the poor environment for investment in stocks were rising rates of price inflation, record high short-term interest rates, uncertainty over the soundness of paper currencies, worldwide shortages of basic commodities, and social unrest. In fact, throughout 1973 stock market psychology seemed to be dominated by the unfavourable implications of the near-complete collapse of the post-World War II currency exchange system. Toward the end of 1973, the principal influence on stock price movements was the decision of the Organization of Arab Petroleum Exporting Countries to cut back oil exports to Europe and Japan, and to place a total embargo on oil shipments to the United States, The Netherlands, South Africa, Rhodesia, and Portugal.

Rising stock markets generally prevailed in countries that either were experiencing high levels of industrial production or were not directly affected by international monetary turmoil. Of the 17 major world stock price indexes, 11 posted lower figures at the end of 1973 than at the end of 1972. Within Europe, the United Kingdom, Switzerland, West Germany, The Netherlands, Denmark, and Sweden each showed bearish patterns. Higher stock markets prevailed in Norway, Italy, Spain, Austria, and Belgium, while France's index of stock prices showed no change. Outside of Europe, stock markets were bearish in the United States, Hong Kong, Australia, Japan, and South Africa. (*See* Table I.)

United States. The stock market in the United States was disappointing in 1973, as uncertainty and lack of monetary liquidity caused wide price fluctuations in a pronounced downtrend. Even though corporate profits achieved a record level, the leading stock price indexes declined about 17% for the year. Many individual stocks did much worse, with the median performer in the Media General composite of 3,450 common stocks off 39.6%. Trading volume was down on all the leading exchanges, and the price-earnings ratios at which blue-chip stocks were trading dropped from 16.4 times earnings at the beginning of the year to less than 10 by the year's end. The Dow Jones industrial average, which began the year with a record high of 1,051.70 on January 11, plunged to a three-year low of 788.31 on December 5. Volume on the New York Stock Exchange was off 2% and on the American Stock Exchange 31%, reflecting public disenchantment with stock market investments. The public movement out of the stock market was evidenced by a rapid decline in margin credit outstanding, diminished numbers of stockholders, and the expansion of deposits in banks and savings and loan institutions. Rising interest rates depressed the bond markets as well, and the volume of bond trading dropped sharply in comparison with 1972.

In the first half of 1973, the stock market dropped irregularly beginning in early January when the administration relaxed its Phase Two price control program and investors correctly anticipated a much higher rate of inflation. A rally in July arrested the downtrend, and another upsurge beginning in late August and lasting until October 12 prevented the decline from becoming a crash. During December a modest rally carried the market back above its low for the year and, with a margin requirement reduction anticipated, 1973 ended on a less bearish note.

The year's economic boom, in which gross national product rose by 11.5% and real economic growth at a rate of 6%, had a very uneven impact on the financial markets. Industrial production rose 8%, while after-tax profits of U.S. corporations reached $70 billion, more than 27% higher than the $55.4 billion of 1972. The unemployment rate dipped from 5% at the beginning of 1973 to a low of 4.5% in the autumn before climbing to 4.7% at the year's end. The wholesale price index experienced the worst annual rise in 25 years with a gain of 18.2% between 1972 and the end of 1973. The previous record was set in 1946 during the post-World War II inflation. Retail prices rose about 8% in 1973, led by refined petroleum products, which were up 125%. Prices of farm products rose 36.1%. The volume of housing starts was off drastically from an annual rate of 204,400 units in September 1972 to a level of 146,300 in September 1973, primarily because of the high cost of money. Mortgage rates were up to 9.5% in a tight money market for long-term credits.

The dollar was under pressure in international markets and was devalued for a second time on Feb. 12,

Illinois Gov. Daniel Walker, scissors aloft, prepares to cut a ticker tape ribbon to open the newest U.S. securities exchange, the Chicago Board Options Exchange, April 26, 1973.

UPI COMPIX

1973, by 10%. The money supply, the total of private checking accounts and deposits plus cash, rose by more than 5% during the year. The prime interest rate moved by steps from 6% in January to a high of 10% in September and October, dipped to 9.5% in November, and ended the year at 9.75%. External financing requirements of U.S. corporations were up from $55.5 billion in 1972 to $68.5 billion in 1973, but because of high interest rates and low stock prices most of this financing took the form of short-term loans and commercial paper. Net new stock issues accounted for $6.2 billion, down from the $10.9 billion level of 1972, while net new bond issues fell from $12.6 billion in 1972 to $8.3 billion in 1973.

Average prices on the New York Stock Exchange reflected a pronounced downtrend in 1973, with the highest levels on all the principal indexes achieved in January (Table II). The 500 stocks in Standard and Poor's composite index dropped from a January figure of 118.42, well above the corresponding January 1972 average of 103.20, to a low of 103.80 in August before the September and October recovery that preceded the December decline. The high for the year was 120.24 and the low was 92.16. On a year-to-year basis there was a net change of 20.50 points, or, in relative terms, a 17.37% drop from the final day of 1972 to the final day of 1973.

The 425 stocks in the industrial group, at 132.55 in January 1973, averaged 16% higher than the corresponding figure for January 1972. As a result of the slump, however, the industrial average fell below the corresponding 1972 levels by May and stayed there for the remainder of the year. The high for the year was 134.54 and the low 103.37. The percentage change from Dec. 31, 1972, to Dec. 31, 1973, was a decline of 17.24% in average prices.

Public utility stock prices eroded more or less steadily throughout 1973 with small breaks in the trend in May and September. From a high of 61.57, this group fell to a low of 43.91 and the year-to-year drop was 23.16%. The utilities had their worst year in more than five as the public remained disenchanted despite record earnings, low price-earnings ratios, and extraordinarily high dividend yields.

The railroad index was lower in every month of 1973 than it had been the previous year, continuing a long-term trend. From an average of 42.87 in January, the index fell to 33.76 in August before the small recovery of September. The emergence of the energy crisis in late 1973 resulted in a substantial boost to the railroad industry, and investors showed renewed interest in this group of stocks in December.

Common stock yields rose throughout most of 1973 with a small interruption in July. The average yield of 2.98% in January climbed slowly to a level of 3.43% in August. The spread in yields between high-grade stocks and bonds expanded during the year to a new record.

Government bond prices declined in 1973 in a continuous erosion of values (Table III). In January, the average price of a government bond was $65.89 per $100 bond, down from the level of $68.79 achieved in January 1972. By August 1973, the average had dropped to $58.71. Yields on government bonds were correspondingly higher month by month in 1973, rising from an average of 5.94% in January to 6.81% by August. On a year-to-year basis the yield in August 1973 was more than 22% higher than in August 1972.

Corporate bond prices fell more slowly than did government bonds in 1973, dropping from a high of $66 in January to $63.8 by July. They were below the levels of a year earlier in every month of 1973 (Table IV). Yields rose to the highest level in several years, creeping up from 7.15% in January to 7.68% by the end of the summer. Because of the tight money market, short-term rates pushed far above the long-term yields in a market reaction to inflation, price-control uncertainties, and realignments among world currencies. The diminished volume of new corporate and tax-exempt obligations also served to slow the rise in long-term bond yields.

Among the favourable factors affecting the stock market in 1973 were the economic boom, which resulted in a decline in the unemployment rate, the creation of 3.2 million additional jobs in the U.S., record profits, continued strong growth in personal income, a more than 10% gain in consumer spending, and the maintenance of sharply elevated business capital spending programs; other factors included a vastly strengthened dollar due to favourable shifts in the balance of payments, a limited budget deficit of about $5 billion, the end of U.S. military involvement in Vietnam, and relaxation of the tight money policy by the Federal Reserve Board.

Analysts blamed a host of factors for the unsettled state of the stock market in 1973. Investors were concerned about the government's economic policy, which abandoned Phase Two price controls in January, then

New York Stock Exchange prices and average daily volume, 1973.

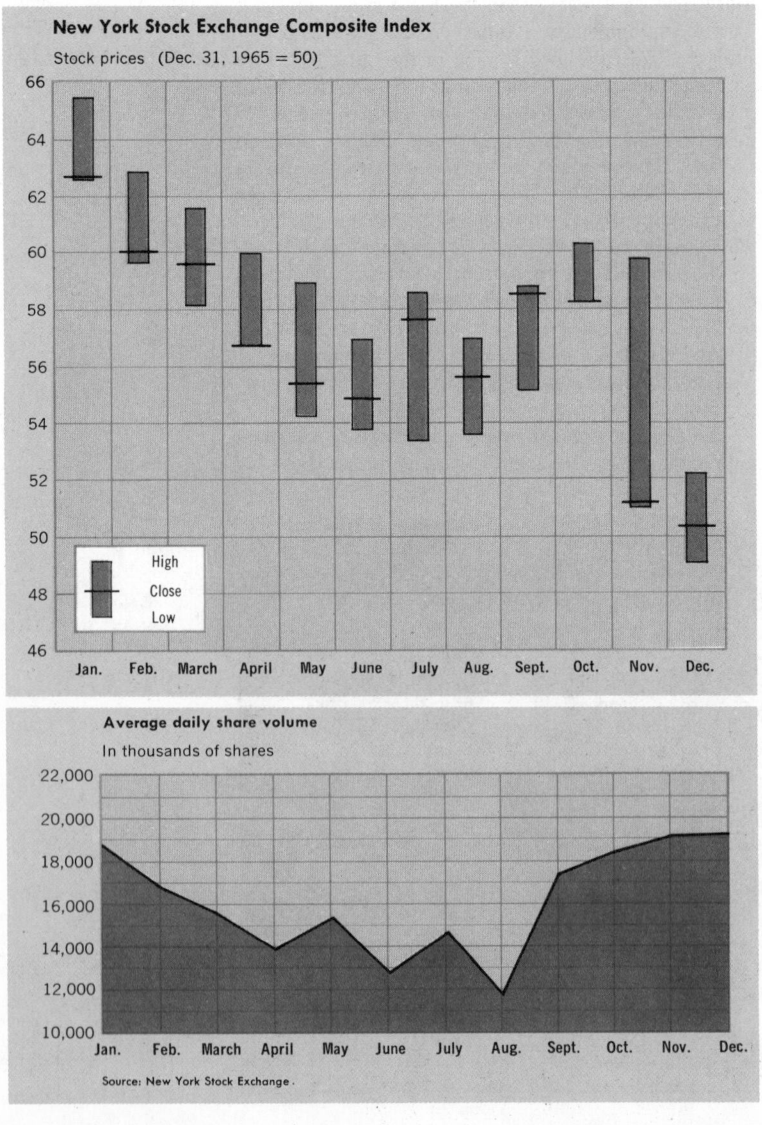

WIDE WORLD

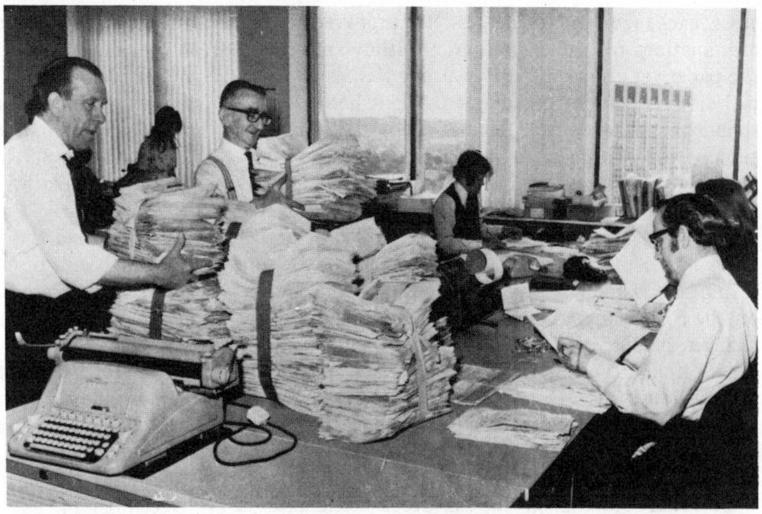

Thousands of applications for shares in Rolls-Royce Motor Holdings Ltd. are collected at the offices of N. M. Rothschild and Sons Ltd. in London, May 10, 1973, following the voluntary liquidation of the automakers.

applied a second price freeze, and finally instituted Phase Four price controls. The second devaluation of the dollar coupled with the threat of a credit crunch and a tight money policy raised concern about impending recession. The Watergate affair, the Equity Funding insurance scandal, the Arab-Israeli war, and the energy crisis all tended to cloud the investment outlook. High interest rates, the collapse of the housing boom, and accelerating worldwide inflation also served as market depressants.

Transactions on the New York Stock Exchange totaled 4,053,201,306 in 1973, a slight decline from the 4,138,187,706 in 1972. A record 2,081 issues were traded, with 241 recording advances for the year and 1,743 registering declines. On the American Stock Exchange trading volume declined 31% in 1973, with 759,840,245 shares traded as compared with 1,117,989,153 the previous year. The average daily turnover for the year fell to 3 million shares, down from the 1972 average of 4.4 million. On the Pacific Coast Stock Exchange, total transactions dropped to 214,730,113 from the 260,526,993 volume recorded in 1972. The market value of securities traded on the West Coast market fell from $8.1 billion in 1972 to $6,369,075,939 a year later. The number of new original listings, a measure of market interest, was only 48, the lowest in five years. The trading volume in the over-the-counter markets, as reported by the National Association of Securities Dealers, fell 37.7% in 1973 to a level of 1,615,816,300, down from 2,219,028,300 in 1972. Bond sales on the New York Stock Exchange declined to $4,424,671,800 in 1973, a more than 22% drop from the $5,444,117,100 record of 1972. The fall was sharper on the American Stock Exchange, from $728,524,000 in 1972 to $457,940,000 in 1973.

Stockbrokers had a disappointing year in 1973 despite moderately heavy volume. For the first 11 months of the year, the approximately 450 firms surveyed monthly by the New York Stock Exchange showed a composite $94.5 million loss. Much of the loss occurred because of falling stock prices, which resulted in both trading and inventory losses. More than 70 member firms of the exchange were forced to merge or go out of business, and membership prices on the New York Stock Exchange dropped to their lowest level in more than a decade. A number of competitive innovations increased the pressure on profit margins. These included discount brokerage houses providing lower commissions (and no advisory services) to small investors, a fight for the abolition of fixed commission rates, and the entry of commercial banks with automatic investment programs for checking account customers. The automated investment service idea, akin to the Monthly Investment Plan sponsored by member firms of the exchange, spread to include installment purchases of new securities, dividend reinvestment plans, and, in the case of some utilities, offers to sell corporate stock without fees or commissions. A potential source of new business was option trading, which began on the Chicago Board Options Exchange in April and enjoyed rising volume throughout the year. At 100 shares to an option contract, this provided a fresh speculative medium, and the major exchanges were considering trading in options directly.

The Securities and Exchange Commission (SEC) was active in 1973, emphasizing the need to provide fuller and more timely information to stockholders. Proposals were advanced for a uniform reporting system that would meet the requirements of the SEC, the National Association of Securities Dealers, and the

Index of industrial ordinary share prices on the London Stock Exchange, 1951–73.

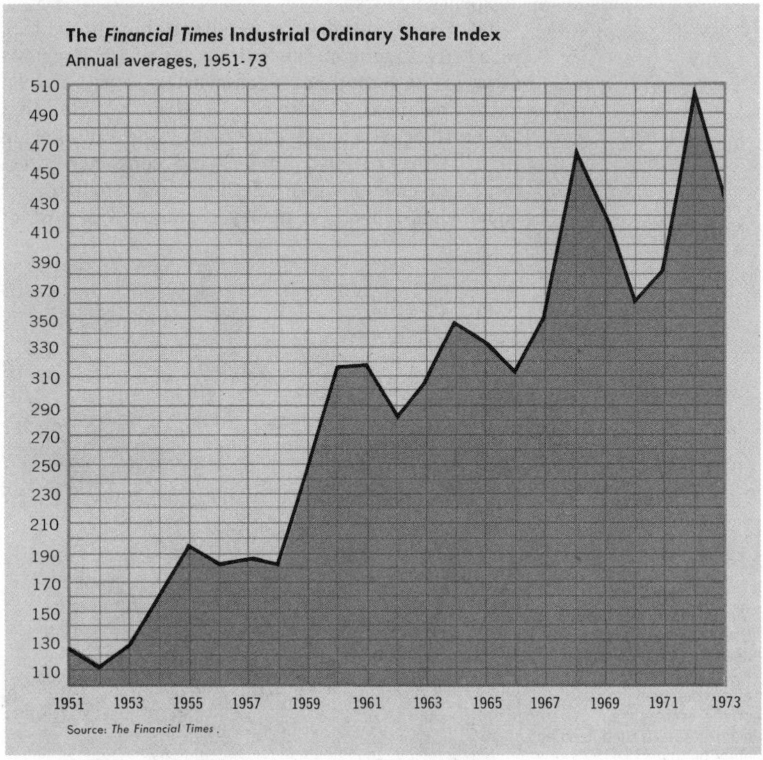

stock exchanges and would lead to improved annual examinations of brokerage houses without increasing the paperwork burden. Early warning signals of financial distress were regarded as crucial. A better correspondence between the Annual Report Form 10K submitted by corporations to the SEC and the information in the annual reports supplied to their stockholders was also recommended. The SEC advocated certified financial statements for the two most recent years rather than for only the most recent; sales and earnings breakdowns by line of business if reported on the SEC's annual 10K report; an explanation of changes in operating revenues and expenses; and a description of the corporation's stock performance for the previous two years and the dividend policy during that time. The SEC also urged companies to disclose in the financial reports some of the impact of inflation on their earnings.

Canada. Trading on the six stock exchanges in Canada rose to a record market value of $9.4 billion during 1973, up 3.5% from the previous record of $9.1 billion in 1972. Volume on the exchanges dropped 17.4% to 1.6 billion shares from 1.9 billion the previous year. On the Toronto Stock Exchange, which accounts for 71.7% of national trading value and 42.1% of national share volume, activity achieved record levels. Trading rose to $6.8 billion, up from $6.3 billion in 1972, while volume climbed to 655.7 million shares from 635.9 million a year earlier. The Montreal and Canadian stock exchanges suffered a decline in volume in 1973 from 330,130,000 shares in 1972 to 296,300,000 in 1973, a drop of 10.2%. However, values on these exchanges rose during the year from $2,060,000,000 in 1972 to $2,180,000,000 a year later. The Montreal and Canadian stock exchanges accounted for 23.1% of national trading value and 22.6% of national volume. The Vancouver Stock Exchange sustained a 34.5% decline in volume from 1972 to 1973 and a 38.3% reduction in values. This exchange accounted for only 5.1% of national trading value but 38.1% of national volume, reflecting its heavy involvement with inexpensive stocks.

The Canadian exchanges paralleled those in the U.S. with active trading in the first quarter of 1973, a slowdown in the second and third quarters, and a revival in the final months of the year. Analysts reported that "Everything was good except the stock market in 1973." Gross national product and consumer prices rose, and unemployment declined, but stock prices nonetheless fell. Tight money characterized most of the year, with bank prime rates moving upward from 6% at the beginning of the year to 9.5% by December. Bond yields rose across the board on a year-to-year basis: provincials increased to 8.7 from 7.9; municipals to 8.8 from 8.1; utilities to 8.9 from 8.2; and industrials to 8.8 from 8.1. Yields on 90-day treasury bills in Canada rose from a level of 3.7% in January to 4% by early March, 5% by May, and 6% in June. They finished the year at 6.3%. Yields on long-term Canada bonds began the year at 6.7%, reached 7% in March, fluctuated between 7.5 and 8% during the summer, and dipped to 7.25% in the last quarter of 1973. (IRVING PFEFFER)

Members of the London Stock Exchange crowd about several of 16 hexagonal pitches after the opening of the exchange's new marble-walled trading floor on June 11, 1973.

WIDE WORLD

Western Europe. In Great Britain, the *Financial Times* index of 30 industrial stocks traded on the London Stock Exchange declined 32% from the end of 1972 to the end of 1973. The index reached its 1973 high on January 10, and the low was established on December 14.

Weakness in stock prices began in mid-January following Prime Minister Edward Heath's announcement that the wage and price controls introduced on Nov. 6, 1972, not only would continue but would also be made more stringent. Particularly disturbing to investors was the government's decision that productivity gains had to be passed along to consumers in the form of lower prices. The decline from the January highs to mid-February amounted to 12%.

Although the British pound sterling had been floating without a fixed parity since June 1972, uncertainty over the outcome of the international currency crisis caused by the devaluation of the U.S. dollar on February 12 had a further adverse influence on equity investors. From February 9 to March 9, prices dropped 6%. The subsequent rebound, which lasted until early June, was largely a result of the country's booming economy. However, raw material and labour shortages placed a lid on business expansion policies. Moreover, the government was forced to permit relatively large price increases in basic commodities or face the likelihood of their diversion to eager foreign buyers. The ensuing slide in stock prices eventually reached a point in late August 15% below the lows recorded in March.

Following a relatively mild technical rally through October, stocks entered a new downward phase, which ultimately carried the stock price index to a level only slightly above that prevailing at the end of 1965. The decline was one of the steepest ever recorded on the London Stock Exchange. It was triggered by Britain's rising trade deficit (a record $715 million in October), followed by Prime Minister Heath's declaration of a national emergency stemming from the disruption of Britain's energy supplies, owing to shipping cutbacks from Arab oil exporters and work slowdowns by coal miners, railway engineers, and electrical-power engineers. To conserve the nation's dwindling fuel supplies, the government ordered a three-day workweek starting Jan. 1, 1974. During the week of December 10–14, the index of 30 industrial stocks experienced the biggest drop in both numerical and percentage terms ever recorded in a single week. At the end of December, stock prices were near the year's lowest level, 37% below the record high set on May 19, 1972.

The Swiss stock market also took a beating in 1973. After nosediving 15% from early February to mid-May, stock prices generated a technical rebound over the next two months which added 5% to equity values. Continued weakness of the U.S. dollar and British pound on European currency exchanges in mid-July touched off further selling. From July 14 to September

1, stock prices plunged 14%. This was followed by a strong rally, which saw prices advance 11% by November 3. The energy crisis caused by the cutbacks in Arab petroleum supplies, however, had a negative impact on Swiss investors. Consequently, stock prices fell below the September lows and ended the year 27% below the final figure for 1972.

The West German stock market in 1973 followed a bearish pattern similar to that in Great Britain and Switzerland, though the decline (21%) was not as severe. The chaos in European currency markets in early 1973 caused wide fluctuations on the stock market. Between mid-January and February 9, equity values tumbled nearly 6%. Prices remained relatively flat until March 12, when the government announcement of a 3% revaluation of the mark and an agreement with five other Common Market countries jointly to float their currencies against the U.S. dollar touched off a spirited rally. Stocks set their 1973 high on March 23.

The recovery, however, was short-lived. Steep increases in the general level of consumer prices, weakness in the U.S. dollar, and soaring gold prices necessitated drastic measures to curb inflation. On May 9, the government announced a 21-point program, including an 11% tax on investments, a rise in the Bundesbank's discount rate to 7%, and a tax surcharge on corporations and individuals in upper-income brackets. A $5\frac{1}{2}$% revaluation of the mark was ordered on June 29. Stocks declined an average of 18% from the beginning of May through July but regained 12% of their values over the next three months. However, investors feared that the reduction in Arabian oil shipments could trigger a severe world recession in 1974. The potential damaging consequences to West German exports was enough to drive equity values to their lowest levels of the year toward the end of 1973.

In The Netherlands, the price index of issues traded on the Amsterdam Stock Exchange was off 18% in 1973. After rising through the beginning of May, stock prices entered a downtrend that was still in progress as 1973 came to a close. Price inflation, which occurred at an annual rate of 9.2% in the second quarter, was one of the worst in Europe. Mirroring inflationary expectations, the yield on "treasury bill rates" rose to $10\frac{3}{4}$% in August, up from $4\frac{1}{4}$% at the end of 1972. The Dutch guilder was revalued about 5% in mid-September, without the permission of the International Monetary Fund or advance notice to the EEC. A brief recovery in equity values following the shock of revaluation was quickly aborted when the Arab countries announced a total embargo on oil shipments to The Netherlands. Moreover, The Netherlands remained in the "boycotted" category when Arab leaders ordered a relaxation of oil-export restrictions to Europe and Japan in late December.

Lower stock prices prevailed in Denmark and Sweden. From the end of 1972 to the end of 1973, equity values dropped 8% and 6%, respectively. The trend in equity prices in Denmark seemed to be heavily influenced by international monetary developments. In early February, stock prices showed a gain of 19% from the 1972 close. The chaos in European foreign exchange markets, however, created selling, which lowered equity values approximately 9% by mid-April. During the summer these losses were erased, but prices again fell in September. The failure of the International Monetary Fund's Committee of 20 to agree on a restructured world currency system at its annual meeting in Nairobi, Kenya, was a negative factor. Investor bearishness deepened further when it became apparent that the Arab oil cutbacks would extend into 1974. As 1973 came to a close, the Danish stock market was 24% below the year's high.

The Swedish economy was expected to grow 4% in 1973, compared with 2% the previous year and no growth in 1971. Nevertheless, there was a relatively high rate of price inflation. Voter discontent over the pace of economic recovery was reflected in the September elections, which raised the possibility that the Social Democrats, in power for the past 41 years, would not be able to rule effectively.

In Norway, stock prices staged a remarkable recovery following the electorate's rejection of EEC membership in late 1972. In fact, Norway experienced the largest increase (+84%) among the major world stock price indexes in 1973. From January through early July, stock prices surged ahead over 85% in a more or less straight line. On May 14 the Norwegian government signed an agreement with the EEC that

Stock trading on the New York Stock Exchange: yearly range of prices and number of shares sold, 1951–73.

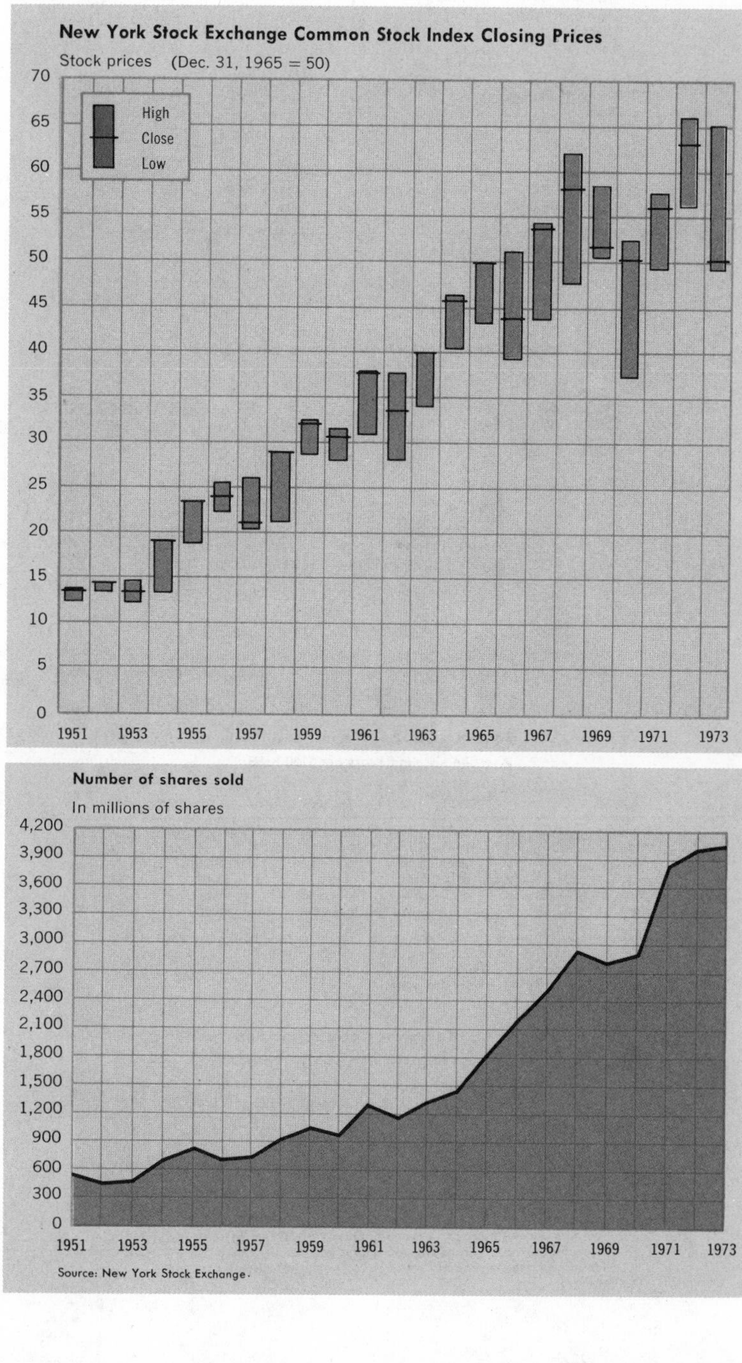

ultimately would eradicate all trade barriers. The first 20% reduction in tariffs on industrial products became effective on July 1. During the summer, profit-taking reduced prices 8%. Stocks already had resumed their uptrend when the October war between Israel and the Arabs erupted. Throughout 1973 the Norwegian part of the North Sea gave continuing evidence of containing huge quantities of oil and gas. Thus, the Arab oil cutbacks had favourable implications for Norwegian industry. The November 15 revaluation of the Norwegian krone by 5% caused investors to take profits, but stock prices still ended 1973 only 4% below the year's peak.

Table I. Selected Major World Stock Price Indexes*

Country	1973 range High	1973 range Low	Year-end indexes 1972	Year-end indexes 1973	Percent change
Australia	637	425	605	440	−27
Austria	2,788	2,401	2,397	2,484	+ 4
Belgium	142	113	121	125	+ 3
Denmark	194	141	161	148†	− 8
France	99	71	78	78	—
Germany, West	121	84	110	87	−21
Hong Kong	1,775	400	843	438	−48
Italy	147	98	100	114	+14
Japan	5,360	3,959	5,208	4,307	−17
Netherlands, The	172	113	156	128	−18
Norway	284	147	148	273†	+84
South Africa	292	215	270	223	−17
Spain	175	140	141	148†	+ 5
Sweden	390	297	356	333	− 6
Switzerland	460	298	444	326	−27
United Kingdom	510	306	505	344	−32

*Index numbers are rounded, and limited to countries for which at least 11 months' data were available.
†As of Dec. 26, 1973.
Sources: *Barron's*, *The Economist*, *Financial Times*, *Money Manager*, and *New York Times*.

Table II. U.S. Stock Market Prices and Yields

Month	Railroads (20 stocks) 1973	1972	Industrials (425 stocks) 1973	1972	Public utilities (55 stocks) 1973	1972	Composite (500 stocks) 1973	1972	Yield (200 stocks; %) 1973	1972
January	42.87	45.16	132.55	114.12	60.01	60.19	118.42	103.20	2.98	3.16
February	40.61	45.66	127.87	116.86	57.52	57.41	114.16	105.24	3.12	3.12
March	39.29	46.48	126.05	119.73	55.94	57.73	112.42	107.69	3.13	3.08
April	35.88	47.38	123.56	121.34	55.34	55.70	110.27	108.81	3.27	3.07
May	36.14	45.06	119.95	120.16	55.43	54.94	107.22	107.65	3.33	3.06
June	34.35	43.66	117.20	120.84	54.37	53.73	104.75	108.01	3.35	3.13
July	35.22	42.00	118.65	119.98	53.31	53.47	105.83	107.21	3.29	3.11
August	33.76	43.28	116.75	124.35	50.14	54.66	103.80	111.01	3.43	3.03
September	35.49	42.37	118.52	122.33	52.31	55.36	105.61	109.39		3.05
October		41.20		122.39		56.66	109.84	109.56		3.04
November		42.41		128.29		61.16		115.05		2.98
December		44.62		131.08		61.73		117.50		2.94

Source: U.S. Department of Commerce, *Survey of Current Business*. Prices are Standard and Poor's monthly averages of daily closing prices with 1941–43=10. Yield figures are Moody's index of 200 stocks.

Table III. U.S. Government Long-Term Bond Prices and Yields

Average price in dollars per $100 bond

Month	Average 1973	Average 1972	Yield (%) 1973	Yield (%) 1972	Month	Average 1973	Average 1972	Yield (%) 1973	Yield (%) 1972
January	65.89	68.79	5.94	5.62	July	60.87	69.23	6.53	5.57
February	64.09	68.32	6.14	5.97	August	58.71	69.55	6.81	5.54
March	63.59	68.43	6.20	5.66	September		68.06		5.70
April	64.39	67.66	6.11	5.74	October		68.09		5.69
May	63.43	68.59	6.22	5.64	November		69.87		5.50
June	62.61	69.05	6.32	5.59	December		68.68		5.63

Source: U.S. Department of Commerce, *Survey of Current Business*. Average prices are derived from average yields on the basis of an assumed 3% 20-year taxable U.S. Treasury bond. Yields are for U.S. Treasury bonds that are taxable and due or callable in ten years or more.

Table IV. U.S. Corporate Bond Prices and Yields

Average price in dollars per $100 bond

Month	Average 1973	Average 1972	Yield (%) 1973	Yield (%) 1972	Month	Average 1973	Average 1972	Yield (%) 1973	Yield (%) 1972
January	66.0	67.1	7.15	7.19	July	63.8	65.6	7.45	7.21
February	65.5	66.7	7.22	7.27	August		65.8	7.68	7.19
March	65.2	66.2	7.29	7.24	September		65.6		7.22
April	64.9	65.1	7.26	7.30	October		65.5		7.21
May	64.7	65.2	7.29	7.30	November		65.9		7.12
June	64.4	65.6	7.37	7.23	December		66.0		7.08

Source: U.S. Department of Commerce, *Survey of Current Business*. Average prices are based on Standard and Poor's composite index of A1+ issues. Yields are based on Moody's Aaa domestic corporate bond index.

The Italian stock market was a star performer in 1973. Its equity price index leaped 14%, despite substantial selling late in the year from fear of potential petroleum shortages. From January to mid-June, the upsurge in prices added 47% to equity values on the Milan Stock Exchange. Reflecting the economy's recovery from a three-year recession, industrial production rose at an annual rate of 38% in the second quarter, the highest in Europe. At the same time, inflationary pressures were not as strong as in other European countries. As a result, increases in "treasury bill rates," from 6% at the end of 1972 to a high of 7.7% in September, were relatively mild by European standards. The fall of Premier Giulio Andreotti's Cabinet brought the market's rise to an end. Investor confidence was somewhat restored after the new Cabinet, led by Premier Mariano Rumor, took office in mid-July. However, the new government's intention to fight inflation raised investors' fears that the economic recovery might be limited. The Arab oil squeeze reinforced such fears. The subsequent downswing in prices left equity values about 22% below the June 19 peak as 1973 came to a close.

Stock prices also were higher in Spain, rising by 5%. The bull market was triggered by a booming economy. The success of the Spanish government's efforts to attract foreign industry was reflected in record expenditures on new plant and equipment. Fixed capital investments were expected to increase nearly 15% in 1973 on top of the 7% gain reported in 1972. The Spanish peseta was revalued in relation to the U.S. dollar by 11% in February and by another 2% in July. Nevertheless, Spain's gold and foreign exchange reserves soared to record levels toward the end of 1973.

In Austria, the stock market recorded a bullish performance, up 4%. Equity values on the Vienna Stock Exchange rose 12% in the first six months of 1973. However, uncertainty over the outlook for the West German economy, which was Austria's major supplier and its principal market, caused the stock market to drop 7% from the end of September to the 1973 close.

The stock market in Belgium traced out a pattern similar to that of Italy. From the end of 1972 to the end of 1973 prices rose 3%. At the end of the second quarter industrial production was rising at an annual rate of nearly 10%, while the overall increase in price inflation was only 5%. The bull market would have been more vigorous had it not been for the threat of fuel shortages. The year's high, an all-time record, was reached on June 22.

Despite the seesaw movement of stock prices in France, leading stock averages ended 1973 unchanged from the 1972 close. The market was particularly robust during the first part of the year. In fact, stock prices through June rose nearly 20%. The anti-inflationary measures introduced by the government on Dec. 7, 1972, slowed the rapid growth of the money supply considerably without apparently reducing the pace of economic growth. The two-tier franc market also helped to insulate the nation against speculative international monetary movements. Moreover, French investors owned a significant proportion of the world's privately held gold. Thus, the rise in the price of gold from $65 per ounce at the start of 1973 to a record $127 in July added to the bullishness of investors.

Nevertheless, the unexpected devaluation of the Dutch guilder in mid-September aroused speculation of possible devaluation of the French franc and investor fears of runaway inflation. Before the month was over, the central bank's discount rate was increased to a record high (11%), minimum reserve requirements of French banks were lifted to 14% from 12%, and the rate on security loans jumped from 11 to $12\frac{1}{2}$%.

Further measures imposed by the government in early December included price, profit, and credit restrictions, as well as the advance payment of taxes. France's labour unions called a one-day general strike on December 7 to protest the government's failure to lower the inflation rate. Accordingly, equity prices ended 1973 21% below the year's high recorded on May 4.

Other Countries. After experiencing a bull market in 1972, stock prices in the British crown colony of Hong Kong plunged 48%, the biggest drop of world stock price indexes surveyed. The Hang Seng index, which measured 33 stocks traded on the Hong Kong exchange, was one of the most volatile in the world. The fluctuation from the record high on March 9 to the year's low on December 26 was over 77%.

The Australian stock market also showed a significant decline, of 27%. Downward pressure on stock prices was due mainly to currency readjustments, which resulted in a 20% revaluation of the Australian dollar against the U.S. dollar. Adding to investor woes was the indicated shift in economic policies brought about by the return to power of the Labor Party.

Prices on the Tokyo Stock Exchange also suffered in 1973. The market hit record highs two weeks prior to the international currency storm in February. The failure of world monetary leaders to agree on fixed currency rates raised the possibility of further repegging of the Japanese yen. Additionally, investors had to contend with predictions that the Arab oil cutbacks would plunge the country into the deepest economic recession since World War II. To combat fuel shortages and soaring inflation, the government imposed a state of emergency in December. The austerity measures included raising the central bank's discount rate to 9% from 7%, effective December 29. Both the rate and the amount of increase represented post-World War II records. Overall, equities lost 17% of their value in 1973.

The trend of stock prices in South Africa was likewise bearish. From year-end 1972 to the end of 1973, industrial share prices on the Johannesburg Stock Exchange dropped 17%. (ROBERT H. TRIGG)

See also Economy, World; Investment, International; Money and Banking; Savings and Investment.

Sudan

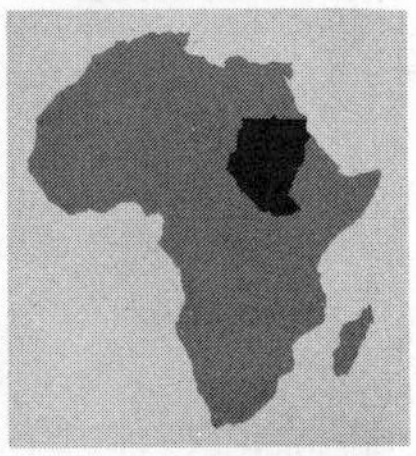

A republic of northeast Africa, the Sudan is bounded by Egypt, the Red Sea, Ethiopia, Kenya, Uganda, Zaire, the Central African Republic, Chad, and Libya. Area: 967,494 sq.mi. (2,505,813 sq.km.). Pop. (1973 est.): 16,901,000, including Arabs in the north and Negroes in the south. Cap. and largest city: Khartoum (pop., 1972 est., 300,000). Language: Arabic; various tribal languages in the south. Religion: Muslim in the north; predominantly animist in the south. President and prime minister in 1973, Maj. Gen. Gaafar Nimeiry.

The Sudanese capital, Khartoum, was brought sharply to world attention on March 1, 1973, when Palestinian guerrillas of the Black September group seized five diplomats at an evening reception at the Saudi Arabian embassy and later killed three of them —U.S. Ambassador Cleo A. Noel, Jr., outgoing U.S. chargé d'affaires George C. Moore, and the Belgian chargé d'affaires, Guy Eid. The guerrillas surrendered on March 4 and were held for the rest of the year in Sudanese prisons, awaiting their twice-postponed trial. President Nimeiry's handling of the incident did much to restore his waning popularity, but it also distracted world attention from the celebrations in March marking the first anniversary of the peace accord between north and south.

The resettlement of the southern region, after more than eight years of civil war, proceeded cautiously, and by November it was possible to hold general elections in the south. The new Regional People's Assembly was inaugurated in mid-December, and an executive council under Abel Alier was formed later in the month. Southern Sudanese refugees had been repatriated from Ethiopia and the Central African Republic by the end of June.

A permanent constitution, Sudan's first since independence in 1956, was introduced in May after extensive deliberation by the People's Assembly. The constitution incorporated the terms of the Addis Ababa accord for regional self-government in the south and codified the existing one-party system operated on the Egyptian model through the Sudanese Socialist Union (SSU). Introduction of the new constitution was accompanied by the formation of a new government, still headed by President Nimeiry as prime minister, and the release of political detainees, including former prime minister Sadiq al-Mahdi. The hope in liberal Sudanese circles that a new era of freedom of expression had been inaugurated was short-lived. Protests at the end of May over food and fuel shortages led President Nimeiry to offer his resignation, but the offer was quickly withdrawn and the president reminded the public that freedom was "not an open license to flout the law." In June a new State Security Law, outlawing opposition to the regime, was promulgated. It was followed by Communist and Muslim Brotherhood demonstrations against the regime in August, which led to several deaths; a railworkers' strike; and the

HENRI BUREAU—GAMMA

The bodies of U.S. diplomats Ambassador Cleo A. Noel, Jr., and former chargé d'affaires George C. Moore are lifted aboard a U.S. presidential jet at Khartoum for transfer to Washington, D.C., on March 5, 1973. The two were murdered by Black September commandos.

SUDAN

Education. (1969–70) Primary, pupils 610,798, teachers 12,370; secondary, pupils 172,486, teachers 9,030; vocational, pupils 1,181, teachers 151; teacher training, students 2,291, teachers 156; higher (including University of Khartoum), students 11,691, teaching staff 1,107.

Finance. Monetary unit: Sudanese pound, with (Sept. 17, 1973) a free rate of Sud£0.36 to U.S. $1 (Sud£0.87 = £1 sterling). Gold, SDRs, and foreign exchange, official: (June 1973) U.S. $40.8 million; (June 1972) U.S. $33.4 million. Budget (1971–72 est.): revenue Sud£189 million; expenditure Sud£178 million. Money supply: (June 1973) Sud£151,240,000; (June 1972) Sud£114,270,000. Cost of living (1963 = 100): (March 1973) 141; (March 1972) 127.

Foreign Trade. (1972) Imports Sud£111,560,000; exports Sud£124,350,000. Import sources: India 16%; U.K. 15%; China 7%; West Germany 6%; U.S.S.R. 5%. Export destinations: India 18%; China 12%; Italy 10%; West Germany 8%; Japan 8%; Egypt 6%. Main exports: cotton 61%; peanuts 8%; gum arabic 7%.

Transport and Communications. Roads (1970) *c.* 50,000 km. (mainly tracks, including 335 km. asphalted). Motor vehicles in use (1970): passenger 27,400; commercial (including buses) 16,500. Railways: (1970) 4,696 km.; freight traffic (1971) 2,636,000,000 net ton-km. Air traffic (1971): 167 million passenger-km.; freight 1,970,000 net ton-km. Navigable waterways (1970) 4,068 km. Telephones (Dec. 1971) 46,000. Radio licenses (Dec. 1970) *c.* 200,000. Television receivers (Dec. 1970) 45,000.

Agriculture. Production (in 000; metric tons; 1971; 1970 in parentheses): millet 325 (460); sorghum 2,152 (1,529); dry broad beans *c.* 13 (*c.* 12); peanuts (1972) *c.* 370, (1971) 381; sesame 271 (282); sugar, raw value *c.* 78 (*c.* 79); dates *c.* 72 (*c.* 72); bananas *c.* 10 (*c.* 10); cotton, lint *c.* 239 (*c.* 245); beef and veal *c.* 141 (*c.* 139); mutton and lamb *c.* 84 (*c.* 83). Livestock (in 000; 1970–71): cattle *c.* 13,650; sheep *c.* 13,200; goats *c.* 10,100; camels *c.* 3,100; asses *c.* 640.

Industry. Production (in 000; metric tons; 1971): salt 58; cement (1970) 156; electricity (kw-hr.) 259,000.

declaration of a state of emergency. The University of Khartoum was closed until November.

Sudan's role in Arab affairs remained uncertain until the outbreak in October of the war in the Middle East. Relations with Libya, accused of planning the Black September March murders in Khartoum, were clouded throughout 1973, but relations with Egypt brightened when presidents Anwar as-Sadat and Nimeiry met in Addis Ababa, Eth., in May. Sudanese troops, withdrawn from the Suez Canal in October 1972, returned to the battlefront on the third day of the war. (PETER KILNER)

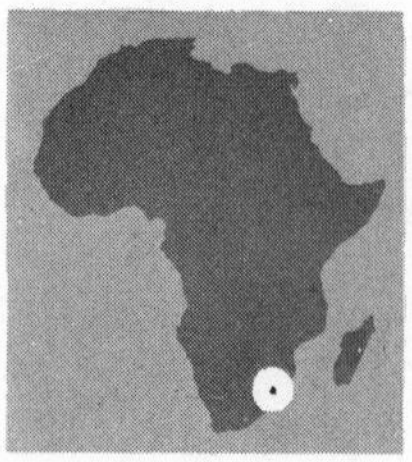

Swaziland

A landlocked constitutional monarchy of southern Africa, Swaziland is bounded by South Africa and Mozambique. Area: 6,704 sq.mi. (17,364 sq.km.). Pop. (1972 est.): 446,000. Cap. and largest city: Mbabane (pop., 1972 est., 17,850). Language: English and siSwati (official). Religion: Christian 60%; animist 40%. King, Sobhuza II; prime minister in 1973, Prince Makhosini Dlamini.

Swaziland, like Lesotho, reverted to traditional rule in 1973. During March, King Sobhuza II announced the creation of a national army in consultation with South African advisers. Previously each former High Commission territory (Swaziland, Lesotho, and Botswana) had maintained a paramilitary police force for internal security only. On April 12 the king, at a meeting of the nation at his royal kraal, repealed the 1968 constitution and announced his assumption of supreme power. He closed Parliament, placed his troops at strategic places, banned political activity, and introduced an act allowing 60 days' detention without trial. Traditional king-in-council rule (the Libandla was open to all male Swazis or their representatives and the king expressed their consensus) would last until the constitutional commission provided a constitution "suitable to Swaziland."

According to Prince Dlamini, the crisis leading to this change had arisen because the existing constitution had led to subversion and was "not part of Swazi traditional structure." The minister of finance added that severe industrial strife was being inflamed by political activities directed from Tanzania and the U.S.S.R. Opposition leader Ambrose Zwane was arrested in May with three fellow politicians for contravening the decree banning political parties and for appealing to the Organization of African Unity to overthrow the king.

Economic life continued to prosper in close relationship with South Africa. A new R 1 million tourist complex at Pigg's Peak brought total hotel investment to over R 15 million. A new road link to Mozambique to carry Swazi exports was begun, and in April a new asbestos agreement gave Swaziland a 40% equity interest in the Havelock Mine. In the second development plan, Britain agreed to contribute capital aid of £7 million over three years. (MOLLY MORTIMER)

SWAZILAND

Education. (1971) Primary, pupils 71,455, teachers 1,895; secondary, pupils 9,001, teachers 448; vocational, pupils 299, teachers (1969) 10; teacher training, students 332, teachers (1969) 31; higher (1969), students 66, teaching staff 15.

Finance and Trade. Monetary unit: South African rand, with (Sept. 17, 1973) an official rate of R 0.67 to U.S. $1 (free rate of R 1.62 = £1 sterling). Budget (1972–73 est.) balanced at R 20,355,000. Foreign trade (1971): imports R 47.8 million; exports R 56,034,000. Export destinations (1970): U.K. 25%; Japan 24%; South Africa 21%. Main exports: sugar 22%; iron ore 22%; wood pulp 17%; asbestos 11%; citrus fruit 8%; timber 6%.

Agriculture. Production (in 000; metric tons; 1972; 1970 in parentheses): corn 120 (105); rice *c.* 8 (7); sugar, raw value *c.* 180 (*c.* 183); cotton, lint *c.* 2 (2). Livestock (in 000; 1971–72): cattle 572; sheep 43; pigs 11; goats 262; poultry 399.

Industry. Production (in 000; metric tons; 1971): coal 150; iron ore (metal content) 1,480; asbestos 38; electricity (kw-hr.) 85,000.

King Sobhuza II assumed complete power in Swaziland in April 1973 with an army he had secretly raised and equipped. He is pictured here in traditional Swazi tribal attire.

WIDE WORLD

Strikes: *see* Labour Unions
Sugar: *see* Agriculture and Fisheries
Sulfur: *see* Mining
Surgery: *see* Medicine
Surinam: *see* Dependent States

Sweden

A constitutional monarchy of northern Europe lying on the eastern side of the Scandinavian Peninsula, Sweden has common borders with Finland and Norway. Area: 173,732 sq.mi. (449,964 sq.km.). Pop. (1973 est.): 8,137,400. Cap. and largest city: Stockholm (pop., 1972 est., 699,238). Language: Swedish, with some Finnish and Lapp in the north. Religion: predominantly Lutheran. King to Sept. 15, 1973, Gustaf VI Adolf and, from that date, Carl XVI Gustaf. Prime minister in 1973, Olof Palme.

The general election in September 1973 resulted in a deadlock between the Socialist and non-Socialist blocs. Both groups gained 175 seats in the Riksdag. The difference, in favour of the Communists and ruling Social Democrats, was only 3,798 (0.07%) of the 5,168,997 votes cast. Even before the election the Social Democrats had had fewer seats than the non-Socialist opposition, but they had managed to hold on to power with the help of the Communists. After the election even this support had evaporated. However, the government did not resign. Prime Minister Olof Palme said he intended to remain in office but did not exclude the possibility of a new election if the government suffered a defeat on a major issue in the Riksdag or if the parliamentary situation resulted in complete deadlock.

Anticipating a tough year, the government made an early start in improving its image. In October it presented a 2.5 billion kronor economic package to stimulate private consumption and create new jobs, and Palme reshuffled his Cabinet.

The main issues of the election campaign had been the economy, unemployment, and the government's increasingly Socialistic program. Throughout the campaign the government trailed the non-Socialist opposition in the opinion polls. The Social Democrats were in a difficult position: although the economy was improving, the results were not yet clear to the voters, and at the same time the non-Socialist parties had for the first time in years managed to agree on a common program. The election results (*see* POLITICAL PARTIES) were a clear encouragement to the Centre Party, the Conservatives, and the Communists and a minor catastrophe for the Liberals, who lost 24 seats. They were also a clear warning to the Social Democrats that their policies were appealing to a dwindling number of the electorate.

UPI COMPIX

The young King Carl XVI Gustaf, new monarch of Sweden, reads his first speech from the throne during official installation ceremonies at the Royal Palace in Stockholm, Sept. 19, 1973.

The budget for 1973–74, presented in January, was undramatic and for the second year in succession proposed no tax changes. The most important feature was a major extension and reorganization of health and unemployment insurance. According to the budget statement, although the economy was clearly recovering, there was little danger of it becoming overheated in 1973. The main aims of economic policy were full employment, rapid economic growth, a more uniform distribution of income, reasonable price stability, and balanced foreign payments. The budget statement declared that priority had been given to sickness and unemployment security, family policy, the working environment, and industrial development. Total expenditure was expected to rise by 8% to 66,245,000,000 kronor and revenue by 12% to 60,515,000,000 kronor. The largest appropriations went to the Ministries for Social Affairs and Education.

During 1973 the economy showed definite signs of emerging from the serious recession that had dogged it since 1970–71. During the first six months the industrial climate improved rapidly, and resource utilization by midyear was approximately at the same level as in the first quarter of 1969. Moreover, the balance of payments revealed continued signs of re-

SWEDEN

Education. (1971–72) Primary, pupils 658,000, teachers (1969–70) 30,620; secondary, pupils 504,000, teachers (1968–69) 36,701; vocational, pupils 74,000, teachers (1967–68) 16,019; teacher training, students 17,000; higher (including 9 universities), students 121,000, teaching staff (including teacher training) *c.* 7,000.

Finance. Monetary unit: krona, with (Sept. 17, 1973) a free rate of 4.19 kronor to U.S. $1 (free rate of 10.10 kronor = £1 sterling). Gold, SDRs, and foreign exchange, central bank: (June 1973) U.S. $2,274,000,000; (June 1972) U.S. $1,304,000,000. Budget (1973–74 est.): revenue 60,515,000,000 kronor; expenditure 66,245,000,000 kronor. Gross domestic product: (1972) 198,650,000,000 kronor; (1971) 183,410,000,000 kronor. Money supply: (June 1973) 20,010,000,000 kronor; (June 1972) 18,870,000,000 kronor. Cost of living (1963 = 100): (June 1972) 164; (June 1971) 153.

Foreign Trade. (1972) Imports 38,390,000,000 kronor; exports 41,652,000,000 kronor. Import sources: West Germany 19%; U.K. 13%; Denmark 8%; U.S. 7%; Norway 6%; Finland 6%. Export destinations: U.K. 15%; West Germany 10%; Norway 10%; Denmark 9%; U.S. 7%; Finland 6%; France 5%. Main exports: machinery 26%; motor vehicles 10%; paper 9%; iron and steel 8%; wood pulp 7%; timber 6%; ships and boats 5%.

Transport and Communications. Roads (1972) 113,000 km. (including 544 km. expressways; excluding 62,300 km. subsidized private roads open to the public). Motor vehicles in use (1972): passenger 2,456,940; commercial 145,400. Railways (1971): 12,181 km. (including 7,520 km. electrified); traffic 4,125,000,000 passenger-km., freight 15,658,000,000 net ton-km. Air traffic (including Swedish apportionment of international operations of Scandinavian Airlines System; 1972): 3,006,000,000 passenger-km.; freight 134,156,000 net ton-km. Shipping (1972): merchant vessels 100 gross tons and over 875; gross tonnage 5,632,336. Telephones (Dec. 1971) 4,506,000. Radio receivers (Dec. 1971) 2,924,000. Television licenses (Dec. 1971) 2,619,000.

Agriculture. Production (in 000; metric tons; 1972; 1971 in parentheses): wheat 1,150 (995); barley 1,883 (2,029); oats 1,629 (1,867); rye 363 (305); potatoes 1,137 (1,242); sugar, raw value *c.* 277 (271); rapeseed 325 (253); apples *c.* 150 (148); butter 44 (43); cheese 66 (66); beef and veal (1971) 146, (1970) 164; pork (1971) 248, (1970) 229; timber (cu.m.; 1971) 64,300, (1970) 60,000; fish catch (1971) 237, (1970) 295. Livestock (in 000; June 1972): cattle 1,861; sheep *c.* 330; pigs *c.* 2,300; horses *c.* 55; chickens (1971) 8,356.

Industry. Index of industrial production (1963 = 100): (1972) 153; (1971) 149. Production (in 000; metric tons; 1972): cement 3,731; electricity (83% hydroelectric in 1971; kw-hr.) 70,673,000; iron ore (60–65% metal content) 33,095; pig iron 2,342; crude steel 5,233; silver (troy oz.; 1971) 3,890; cotton yarn 7.9; rayon, etc., yarn and fibres 37; mechanical wood pulp (1971) 1,448; chemical wood pulp (1971) 6,386; newsprint 963; other paper (1971) 3,270. Merchant vessels launched (100 gross tons and over; 1972) 1,810,000 gross tons. New dwelling units completed (1972) 104,000.

covery, with foreign currency reserves the highest ever recorded. In spite of these developments, the nagging problem of unemployment (3%) displayed no signs of disappearing quickly. A 4.3 billion kronor surplus was estimated for the year, with consumer prices rising an average of 6%.

In response to international currency crises, the government took measures to defend the krona. In February it fixed the parity of the krona at an intermediate position between the devalued U.S. dollar and the European currencies that remained unchanged. This was tantamount to a 5% revaluation in relation to the dollar and those currencies that followed it and a 5% devaluation in relation to those that stayed unchanged. In March the Riksbank announced that the krona was floating against the dollar with the six EEC currencies.

In the Riksdag the government once again had a relatively easy year. Measures passed or considered included a new constitution, which removed remaining vestiges of power from the monarchy, reduced the voting age to 18, featured a charter of citizens' rights, and was to come into force on Jan. 1, 1975; the ratification of Sweden's trade agreement with the EEC; a law enabling the police to keep a closer watch on terrorist organizations such as Black September; a proposal to amalgamate Kreditbanken and Postbanken, two large state banking institutions; a bill allowing the use of state pension funds to purchase company shares; the inclusion of dental treatment in the national health insurance system; and a proposal to introduce more liberal marriage laws. To help meet fuel shortages caused by Arab oil cutbacks late in the year, it was announced that gasoline rationing would start early in 1974.

In September 90-year-old King Gustaf VI Adolf died and was succeeded by his grandson, Carl Gustaf (27), who took the title of King Carl XVI Gustaf. (*See* BIOGRAPHY; OBITUARIES.) Later in the same month one of Sweden's oldest newspapers, *Göteborgs Handels och Sjöfarts Tidning,* ceased publication.

The radical magazine *Folket i Bild/Kulturfront* published articles in May revealing the existence of a Swedish secret service organization called the Information Bureau (IB). The articles aroused widespread interest because they claimed that the IB authorized illegal break-ins, kept secret files on left-wing organizations, and cooperated with the secret services of foreign powers. The revelations, though not proven, led to intense public debate on the role of the secret service in a neutral country such as Sweden. Investigations of the articles and the two journalists who had written them were carried out by the chief prosecutor during the summer, and in the fall one of the journalists published a book with further information on the IB. In the meantime, a former IB agent came forward with additional details. In October the two journalists, the ex-agent, and two others were arrested.

A major scandal arose through investigations into the bankruptcy of Fulcrum, the holding company of the Wenner-Gren industrial and financial empire. In November these investigations led to the prosecution of, among others, 1955 Nobel medicine laureate Axel Hugo Theorell, charged with breach of trust in connection with the Wenner-Gren fund for medical research. "Loans" from the fund had allegedly been used to support ailing Wenner-Gren enterprises.

Sweden continued to be without a U.S. ambassador. After Prime Minister Palme's strong criticism of the Christmas bombing of Hanoi in 1972, the U.S. chief representative in Stockholm, John C. Guthrie, did not return from his Christmas leave. Later the U.S. refused to accept Yngve Möller as Sweden's new ambassador in Washington. In response to the bombing of North Vietnam by the U.S., there were large demonstrations in many places throughout Sweden, and all five political parties backed a national collection of names and money. The money was later donated to the rebuilding of a hospital in Hanoi. Sweden recognized East Germany in December 1972 and North Korea in April 1973. After the coup in Chile, the Swedish government cut off aid to that country.

(ALAN WILSON)

Swedish Literature: *see* Literature

Swimming

For the first time ever, the Fédération Internationale de Natation Amateur, the world governing organization for amateur aquatic sports, conducted a world championship tournament. Therefore, what should have been a relatively quiet post-Olympic year turned into one of the most exciting in swimming history, climaxed by the World Championships at Belgrade, Yugos., from August 31 through September 9. Swimmers produced 31 new world records (16 by East German women). The teen-age girls from East Germany replaced the United States women as the dominant power in world swimming, and the U.S. men had their supremacy narrowed by the retirement of such outstanding performers as Mark Spitz, Mike Burton, and Gary Hall.

With the retirement of Shane Gould, winner of three Olympic gold medals and at one time the holder of all women's world records in freestyle events, Australia also slipped from the highest rankings in world swimming. But the Australians did uncover a new teen-age star, Stephen Holland, 15, from Brisbane. Not fast enough to make the 1972 Olympic team, Holland completely shattered the world mark for the 1,500-m. freestyle of 15 min. 52.58 sec. set by Mike Burton in the 1972 Olympics. Holland burst from obscurity in the Australian world championship trials at Brisbane when he won his berth on the team by clocking 15 min. 37.8 sec. A little more than a month later at the finals, swimming against the U.S. distance ace, Rick DeMont, Holland further lowered his world mark to 15 min. 31.85 sec. and, along the way, reduced his 800-m. freestyle world standard from 8 min. 17.6 sec. to 8 min. 16.27 sec.

However, the big story in swimming was the rise of the East German women's team, which had begun to show promise at the 1972 Olympics when its young swimmers won four silver medals. At the World Championships, the East Germans completely shattered their opposition. Kornelia Ender, a 14-year-old schoolgirl, lowered Shane Gould's 58.5 sec. 100-m. freestyle world record by winning the event in 57.54 sec. In addition to her sensational freestyle marks, Miss Ender set world standards of 1 min. 2.31 sec. in the 100-m. butterfly and 2 min. 23.01 sec. in the 200-m. individual medley, though this mark was subsequently lowered by her teammate Andrea Huebner, 16, to 2 min. 20.51 sec. at Belgrade.

Among East Germany's other outstanding girls were Rosemarie Kother, 17, who erased the 200-m. butterfly world record by almost two seconds, clocking 2 min. 13.76 sec.; Ulrike Richter, 14, who lowered the 100-m. backstroke mark to 1 min. 4.99 sec.; Angela Franke, 15, who swam the 400-m. individual medley in a world record 5 min. 1.10 sec. at the Europe Cup meet; and Gudrun Wegner, 18, who broke Miss Franke's record with a time of 4 min. 57.51 sec. The East German 400-m. medley and 400-m. freestyle relay teams also set world records.

Novella Calligaris, 16, became the first Italian woman swimmer to break a world mark when she upset the U.S. 1,500-m. world record holder, Jo Harshbarger, to win the 800-m. freestyle at Belgrade. Miss Calligaris' time of 8 min. 52.97 sec. erased Keena Rothhammer's time of 8 min. 53.7 sec. set at the 1972 Olympics.

Earlier in the meet, Miss Rothhammer of the U.S. won the 200-m. freestyle and placed second to her teammate Heather Greenwood in the 400-m. freestyle. Melissa Belote won the 200-m. backstroke for the only other U.S. victory.

It was a different story in the men's competition as the U.S. won five individual events and swept the three relays, while the East Germans could gain but two victories. Rick DeMont, 17, from San Rafael, Calif., swam the 400-m. freestyle in 3 min. 58.18 sec., a feat as sensational as when Roger Bannister broke the four-minute mile in track. DeMont, who had won the same event at the Olympics in 1972 only to be disqualified for failure to pass the drug control test, trailed his Australian rival Brad Cooper for 350 m. Then, as in the Olympics, his final 50-m. sprint carried him to victory in world record time. Cooper also broke the four-minute barrier.

World records were set in both breaststroke events. John Hencken, 19, of Santa Clara, Calif., won the 100 m. in 1 min. 4.02 sec., and Great Britain's David Wilkie, 19, took the 200-m. event in 2 min. 19.28 sec. Roland Matthes, 22, of East Germany, who had not lost a backstroke race since 1967, won the 100 m. in 57.47 sec. and then lowered his previous world record in the 200 m. to 2 min. 1.87 sec.

Sweden's Gunnar Larsson, 22, Olympic gold medal winner in the 200-m. individual medley, again was the master in this event, winning in 2 min. 8.36 sec. Hungary's Andras Hargitay, 17, won the 400-m. individual medley with the second fastest clocking ever, 4 min. 31.11 sec. With the Olympic superstar Mark Spitz retired, the butterfly events were wide open. Canada's Bruce Robertson, 20, won the 100 m. in 55.69 sec., and Robin Backhaus, 18, of San Rafael won the 200 m. in 2 min. 3.32 sec.

A new U.S. freestyle star emerged from the meet. James Montgomery, 18, of Madison, Wis., in his first international competition won the 100 m. in 51.70 sec., only 0.5 sec. slower than Spitz's world mark, and the 200 m. in 1 min. 53.02 sec., just 0.3 sec. off Spitz's record. The U.S. quartet of Kurt Krumpholz, Robin Backhaus, Richard Klatt, and Montgomery were timed in 7 min. 33.22 sec. for a new world record in the 800-m. freestyle relay.

Diving. In early March, at Minsk, U.S.S.R., in an international competition of ten nations, the U.S. men failed to score in either the springboard or the platform as the Soviet Olympic champion Vladimir Vasin, 26, won the 3-m. springboard, and his teammate Nikolai Mikhailin won the 10-m. platform. The U.S. girls fared better as Cynthia Potter, 22, won the silver medal in the springboard behind East Germany's Krista Kohler, also 22. Sweden's Olympic champion, Ulrika Knape, 19, won the platform.

At the World Championships the U.S. men revived as Air Force Lieut. Phil Boggs, 23, won the 3-m. springboard, and his teammate Keith Russell, 25, placed second behind Italy's Klaus Dibiasi, 26, in the platform. Krista Kohler followed up her success at Minsk by winning the world championship 3-m. springboard title. In the platform, Miss Knape retained her world supremacy. (ALBERT SCHOENFIELD)

World Records Set in 1973

Event	Name	Country	Time
MEN			
400-m. freestyle	Rick DeMont	U.S.	3 min. 58.18 sec.
800-m. freestyle	Stephen Holland	Australia	8 min. 17.6* sec.
800-m. freestyle	Stephen Holland	Australia	8 min. 16.27 sec.
1,500-m. freestyle	Stephen Holland	Australia	15 min. 37.8* sec.
1,500-m. freestyle	Stephen Holland	Australia	15 min. 31.85 sec.
100-m. breaststroke	John Hencken	U.S.	1 min. 4.35 sec.
100-m. breaststroke	John Hencken	U.S.	1 min. 4.02 sec.
200-m. breaststroke	John Hencken	U.S.	2 min. 20.52 sec.
200-m. breaststroke	David Wilkie	U.K.	2 min. 19.28 sec.
200-m. backstroke	Roland Matthes	East Germany	2 min. 1.87 sec.
800-m. freestyle relay	U.S. national team (Kurt Krumpholz, Robin Backhaus, Richard Klatt, James Montgomery)	U.S.	7 min. 33.22 sec.

*Watch time, recorded in 1/10 increments.

Event	Name	Country	Time
WOMEN			
100-m. freestyle	Kornelia Ender	East Germany	58.25 sec.
100-m. freestyle	Kornelia Ender	East Germany	58.12 sec.
100-m. freestyle	Kornelia Ender (relay)	East Germany	57.61 sec.
100-m. freestyle	Kornelia Ender	East Germany	57.54 sec.
400-m. freestyle	Keena Rothhammer	U.S.	4 min. 18.07 sec.
800-m. freestyle	Novella Calligaris	Italy	8 min. 52.97 sec.
1,500-m. freestyle	Shane Gould	Australia	16 min. 56.9* sec.
1,500-m. freestyle	Jo Harshbarger	U.S.	16 min. 54.14 sec.
100-m. butterfly	Kornelia Ender	East Germany	1 min. 3.05 sec.
100-m. butterfly	Kornelia Ender	East Germany	1 min. 2.31 sec.
200-m. butterfly	Rosemarie Kother	East Germany	2 min. 15.05 sec.
200-m. butterfly	Rosemarie Kother	East Germany	2 min. 13.76 sec.
100-m. backstroke	Ulrike Richter	East Germany	1 min. 5.39 sec.
100-m. backstroke	Ulrike Richter (relay)	East Germany	1 min. 4.99 sec.
200-m. individual medley	Kornelia Ender	East Germany	2 min. 23.01 sec.
200-m. individual medley	Andrea Huebner	East Germany	2 min. 20.51 sec.
400-m. individual medley	Angela Franke	East Germany	5 min. 1.10 sec.
400-m. individual medley	Gudrun Wegner	East Germany	4 min. 57.51 sec.
400-m. freestyle relay	East Germany national team (Kornelia Ender, Andrea Eife, Andrea Huebner, Sylvia Eichner)	East Germany	3 min. 52.45 sec.
400-m. medley relay	East Germany national team (Ulrike Richter, Renate Vogel, Rosemarie Kother, Kornelia Ender)	East Germany	4 min. 16.84 sec.

*Watch time, recorded in 1/10 increments.

Switzerland

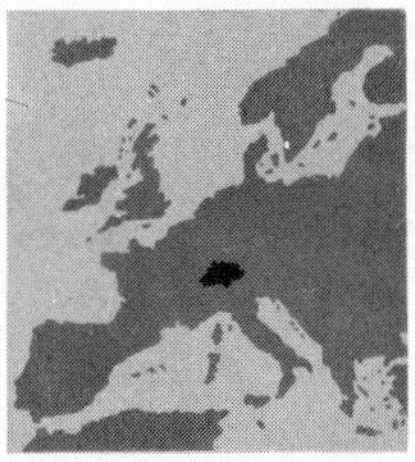

A federal republic in west central Europe consisting of a confederation of 25 cantons, Switzerland is bounded by West Germany, Austria, Liechtenstein, Italy, and France. Area: 15,943 sq.mi. (41,293 sq. km.). Pop. (1973 est.): 6,385,000. Cap.: Bern (pop., 1973 est., 159,100). Largest city: Zürich (pop., 1973 est., 416,100). Language (1970): German 65%; French 18%; Italian 12%; Romansh 1%. Religion (1970): Roman Catholic 49.4%; Protestant 47.7%. President in 1973, Roger Bonvin.

The "total revision" of the federal constitution, inaugurated in 1966, made some prudent progress with the publication of the report of the working group on Sept. 2, 1973. A second phase was begun with the setting up of an enlarged commission. The 1874 constitution, meanwhile, was the subject of various amendments and proposals for amendments. An important step, with regard to both domestic politics and the standing of Switzerland in the international community, was the abolition, by popular vote, of the historic articles forbidding public Jesuit activity and the foundation of new Roman Catholic convents.

The political scene was somewhat enlivened by a split in the right-wing National Campaign Against Foreign Domination. Its leader, James Schwarzenbach, was a fierce critic of the ascendancy of foreign elements (labour and capital) and of international organizations, the UN in particular.

The problem of how to deal with the increasing incidence of conscientious objection to compulsory military service was widely discussed. Rather surprisingly, the Federal Council approved the so-called Muenchenstein initiative, calling for a form of substitute civil service by conscientious objectors. Adoption of such substitution would require revision of art. 18 of the federal constitution. Both chambers of Parliament approved the proposal in principle, but protagonists of full-fledged recognition of the validity of conscientious objection were not wholly satisfied. The state of the Air Force was also a subject of heated debate. The Federal Council's much-delayed choice of 30 refurbished second-hand British Hunter planes, to be delivered in 1974 and 1975, was severely criticized by protagonists of a modern air defense system—the exact nature of which in a possible future war remained difficult to define.

The increase in benefits distributed in 1973 as a result of the eighth revision of the old-age pension scheme (financed by the contributions of employers and employees and from cigarette taxes) was expected to be followed by another increase, partly to compensate for the rising cost of living and partly as a further approach to a "genuine people's pension system."

The so-called peace agreement concluded in the 1930s between employers and employees of the important metal, machine, and watch industries, which had become the foundation of Switzerland's exceptionally peaceful industrial relations, was due to expire in 1974. Its revision was under discussion, with a view, in particular, to the inclusion of provisions for employee "participation."

At the opening of the Conference on Security and Cooperation in Europe, in Helsinki, Fin., Switzerland submitted a detailed plan for the peaceful settlement of conflicts through compulsory arbitration procedures. In the second phase of the conference, in Geneva, the project was rejected by the Soviet delegation as utopian. At the end of 1973 Switzerland was reported to be providing its good offices as protecting power to 27 countries at odds with one another over diverse issues. In Cuba alone Switzerland provided such services for ten countries.

The all-Swiss International Committee of the Red Cross was in a state of crisis, with some of its activities and failures being criticized at home and abroad. Marcel Naville resigned as president; Eric Martin was named to succeed him, and a reorganization of the committee's structures was undertaken.

The economic situation continued to be characterized by boom conditions, with a concomitant inflation of 8.2% for the year ended March 1973. The control measures instituted by the federal government in 1972, providing for a restriction of bank credits, export levies, amortizations, restrictions on building, and control of the movement of prices and wages, were extended for two years following a referendum held Dec. 2, 1973. As a result of the Arab oil embargo, speed limits, prohibition of Sunday driving, gasoline price increases, and rationing to retailers were among the measures introduced to save fuel. The fiscal burden on the Swiss population was still the lowest in Europe. Various socialist-inspired initiatives, at the cantonal and local level, were launched to increase taxation on higher incomes. Meanwhile, the state of the federal government's finances, as reported on Nov. 16, 1973, in the 1974 budget message, was described as "disastrous." It was hoped that the deficit would be reduced and a balance restored by the end of the 1970s through stringent economy measures and new taxes. (MELANIE STAERK)

SWITZERLAND

Education. (1969–70) Primary, pupils 487,583, teachers (excluding craft teachers; 1961–62) 23,761; secondary, pupils 306,786, teachers (full-time; 1961–62) 6,583; vocational, pupils 145,937; teacher training, students 11,300; higher (including 8 universities; 1971–72), students 44,624, teaching staff 4,318.

Finance. Monetary unit: Swiss franc, with (Sept. 17, 1973) a free rate of SFr. 3 to U.S. $1 (SFr. 7.24 = £1 sterling). Gold, SDRs, and foreign exchange, official: (June 1973) U.S. $8,222,000,000; (June 1972) U.S. $7,018,000,000. Budget (1973 est.): revenue SFr. 11,164,000,000; expenditure SFr. 11,360,000,000. Gross national product: (1972) SFr. 115.3 billion; (1971) SFr. 100.8 billion. Money supply: (May 1973) SFr. 54,310,000,000; (May 1972) SFr. 54,580,000,000. Cost of living (1963 = 100): (June 1973) 155; (June 1972) 143.

Foreign Trade. (1972) Imports SFr. 32,317,000,000; exports SFr. 26,014,000,000. Import sources: EEC 60% (West Germany 30%, France 14%, Italy 10%); U.K. 7%; U.S. 7%; Austria 5%. Export destinations: EEC 37% (West Germany 15%, France 9%, Italy 8%); U.S. 9%; U.K. 8%; Austria 6%. Main exports: machinery 31%; chemicals 22%; watches and clocks 11%; textile yarns and fabrics 7%. Tourism: visitors (1971) 6,920,100; gross receipts U.S. $875 million.

Transport and Communications. Roads (1972) 60,621 km. (including 465 km. expressways). Motor vehicles in use (1972): passenger 1,561,300; commercial 152,300. Railways: (1970) 5,000 km. (including 4,973 km. electrified); traffic (1972) 8,302,000,000 passenger-km., freight 6,703,000,000 net ton-km. Air traffic (1972): 5,783,000,000 passenger-km.; freight 218,477,000 net ton-km. Shipping (1972): merchant vessels 100 gross tons and over 33; gross tonnage 211,728. Telephones (Dec. 1971) 3,213,000. Radio licenses (Dec. 1971) 1.9 million. Television licenses (Dec. 1971) 1,403,000.

Agriculture. Production (in 000; metric tons; 1972; 1971 in parentheses): wheat 400 (441); barley 168 (170); oats 27 (41); rye 55 (51); corn *c.* 100 (*c.* 73); potatoes 1,000 (1,175); rapeseed 24 (24); apples *c.* 360 (*c.* 380); pears *c.* 190 (*c.* 190); sugar, raw value *c.* 66 (*c.* 74); wine 93 (82); milk *c.* 3,350 (3,160); butter 32 (29); cheese 94 (86); beef and veal 124 (134); pork 218 (204). Livestock (in 000; April 1972): cattle 1,841; sheep *c.* 293; pigs 1,878; horses 48; chickens *c.* 6,300.

Industry. Index of industrial production (1963 = 100): (1972) 149; (1971) 146. Production (in 000; metric tons; 1972): cement 5,712; aluminum (1971) 34; rayon, etc., yarn and fibre 9.8; nylon, etc., yarn and fibre (1971) 59; cigarettes (units; 1971) 30,935,000; watches (units; 1971) 51,811; manufactured gas (gasworks only; cu.m.; 1971) 386,000; electricity (kw-hr.) 31,443,000.

Syria

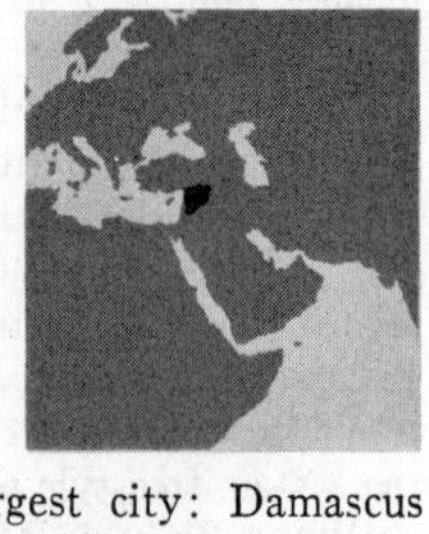

A republic in southwestern Asia on the Mediterranean Sea, Syria is bordered by Turkey, Iraq, Jordan, Israel, and Lebanon. Area: 71,498 sq.mi. (185,180 sq.km.). Pop. (1972 est.): 6,675,810. Cap. and largest city: Damascus (pop., 1970, 836,668). Language: Arabic (official); also Kurdish, Armenian, Turkish, and Circassian. Religion: predominantly Muslim. President in 1973, Gen. Hafez al-Assad; premier, Mahmoud Ayoubi.

On Oct. 6, 1973, the Jewish high holy day of Yom Kippur, Syria launched a massive offensive, in collaboration with Egypt, to try to recover territory in the Golan Heights occupied by Israel following the six-day Arab-Israeli war of 1967. After initial advances the Syrian forces were thrown back in fierce fighting until the front stabilized with Israeli troops less than 30 mi. from Damascus. Syria suffered severe losses in men and equipment and from Israeli air at-

SYNDICATION INTERNATIONAL LTD. / PHOTO TRENDS

Hunger forced this family to surrender in October 1973, after five days of hiding during Israeli occupation in the remote Syrian village of Jabta-al-Chatab. The young boy carries a white flag.

tacks on the Homs refinery, oil terminals at Baniyas and Tartus, power stations, and other installations. On October 20 the Syrian government said that Israeli bombing had virtually halted industrial and power production and caused several hundred civilian casualties. However, the military engagements with the Israelis were much more evenly matched than in 1967, and Syrian morale remained fairly high when the fighting ended. In particular, effective use of Soviet surface-to-air missiles meant that Israel did not have unchallenged command of the air. Syria delayed more than 24 hours before accepting UN Security Council Resolution 338 calling for a cease-fire on October 22, and a week later President Assad said that Syria was ready to resume fighting unless Israel withdrew from Arab territory. Syria refused to submit lists of Israeli prisoners, and instead stipulated a series of conditions and accusations. Israel, meanwhile, accused Syria of torturing and murdering Israeli prisoners. At least partly because of this dispute, Syria refused to participate in the Middle East peace conference that opened in Geneva December 21, despite last-minute trips to Damascus by U.S. Secretary of State Henry Kissinger and the Egyptian foreign minister. (*See* DEFENSE: *Special Report;* MIDDLE EASTERN AFFAIRS.)

Some indication of Syria's intentions had been given earlier in the year by renewed military action against Israel, which led to some severe clashes in December and January. In May President Assad paid an unexpected visit to Moscow to ask for Soviet military aid, which was subsequently increased and included the new SA-6 antiaircraft missiles. However, there was some Syrian disappointment with the Soviet failure to provide the most advanced weapons, and in September it was reported that the movement of the 1,800 Soviet military advisers in Syria had been restricted. Following the Arab Defense Council meeting in January, the Arab oil states provided substantial financial aid for the Syrian armed forces. Cooperation with Egypt became steadily closer during the year, but relations with Libya, Syria's third partner in the Arab federation, were cool as chief of state Muammar al-Qaddafi (*see* BIOGRAPHY) said he disagreed with Egypt's and Syria's battle plans and would limit his aid to Syria to £5 million. Relations with Jordan, on the other hand, improved. In December 1972 Syria had reopened the border, which had been closed for 18 months, and President Assad's summit meeting in Cairo in September 1973 with Pres. Anwar as-Sadat and King Hussein (*see* BIOGRAPHY) led to a resumption of diplomatic relations early in October and the dispatch of a Jordanian armoured brigade to the Syrian front during the fighting with Israel. On August 17 Syria reopened its borders with Lebanon, which it had closed on May 8 in protest against Lebanese actions against Palestinian guerrillas.

Following the resignation for health reasons of Abdul Rahman Khleyfawi on Dec. 21, 1972, the vice-president, Mahmoud Ayoubi, formed a new ten-member government with the key posts remaining in Baathist hands. On January 31 the National Assembly approved a new permanent constitution to replace the temporary constitution in force since 1969. This was approved by 97.6% of the votes in a referendum on March 12. The fact that this constitution referred to Syria as a "democratic, popular, socialist state" but for the first time in Syria's independent history did not refer to Islam as the state religion provoked serious rioting by orthodox Sunni Muslims in Homs and Hamah in February and March. Hostility was only partly allayed by the concession that the head of state would have to be Muslim, and there was further rioting in April in Damascus and Aleppo.

SYRIA

Education. (1969–70) Primary, pupils 845,130, teachers 23,431; secondary, pupils 281,254, teachers 10,651; vocational, pupils 10,445, teachers 892; teacher training, students 4,018, teachers 398; higher (including 2 universities), students 37,540, teaching staff 1,056.

Finance. Monetary unit: Syrian pound, with (Sept. 17, 1973) an official exchange rate of S£3.85 to U.S. $1 and a free rate of S£4.04 to U.S. $1 (nominal rate of S£9.74 = £1 sterling). Gold, SDRs, and foreign exchange: (Jan. 1973) U.S. $130 million; (June 1972) U.S. $100 million. Budget (1973 est.) balanced at S£3,413 million. Gross domestic product: (1971) S£7,562 million; (1970) S£6,433 million. Money supply: (Dec. 1972) S£3,133 million; (Dec. 1971) S£2,503 million. Cost of living (Damascus; 1963 = 100): (June 1973) 148; (June 1972) 123.

Foreign Trade. (1972) Imports S£2,060.6 million; exports S£1,097.6 million. Import sources: Italy 8%; West Germany 8%; U.S.S.R. 7%; Lebanon 7%; Japan 6%; France 6%; U.K. 5%. Export destinations: U.S.S.R. 20%; Lebanon 14%; Italy 11%; China 6%. Main exports: cotton 34%; crude oil 18%; wheat 8%.

Transport and Communications. Roads (1971) 16,710 km. (including 63 km. expressways). Motor vehicles in use (1971): passenger 31,700; commercial 17,500. Railways (1971): 1,259 km.; traffic 83,750,000 passenger-km., freight 125 million net ton-km. Air traffic (1971): 181 million passenger-km.; freight 1,723,000 net ton-km. Ships entered (1971) vessels totaling 15,553,000 net registered tons; goods loaded (1972) 31,688,000 metric tons, unloaded 2,292,000 metric tons. Telephones (Dec. 1971) 120,000. Radio receivers (Dec. 1970) 1,367,000. Television receivers (Dec. 1971) 118,000.

Agriculture. Production (in 000; metric tons; 1972; 1971 in parentheses): wheat 1,808 (662); barley 710 (123); lentils (1971) 87, (1970) 58; tomatoes (1971) *c.* 190, (1970) 192; apples *c.* 20 (*c.* 22); grapes *c.* 215 (*c.* 215); raisins *c.* 9 (*c.* 9); figs (1970) 44, (1969) 50; sugar, raw value *c.* 34 (*c.* 37); olives *c.* 125 (*c.* 110); tobacco (1971) 6.7, (1970) *c.* 8.9; cotton, lint *c.* 163 (157). Livestock (in 000; 1970–71): cattle *c.* 550; sheep *c.* 6,200; goats *c.* 770; horses *c.* 70; asses *c.* 230; chickens (Dec. 1970) 3,669.

Industry. Production (in 000; metric tons; 1971): petroleum products 1,997; crude oil (1972) 5,927; cement (1972) 1,056; cotton yarn 22; electricity (kw-hr.) 1,049,000.

Elections under the new constitution were held on May 25 for a new National Assembly. In the final results the Baathists won 122 seats, the Communists 8, independents 42, and various Nasserist groups 10. The opposition, which included Muslim Brothers and dissident Nasserists who had called for a boycott of the elections, won 4 seats. Although the Baathists could claim they had won 70% of the votes cast, the fact that only 40.6% of the electorate voted, probably reflecting Sunni Muslim opposition, was a blow to the regime. (PETER MANSFIELD)

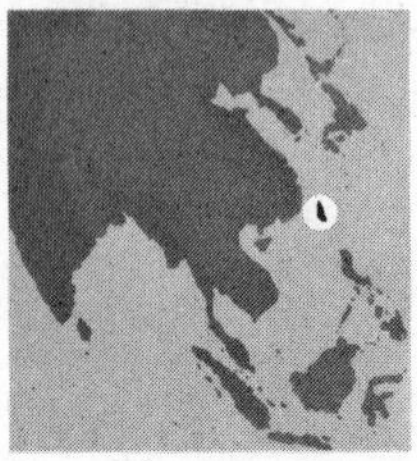

Taiwan

Taiwan, which consists of the islands of Formosa and Quemoy and other surrounding islands, is the seat of the Republic of China (Nationalist China). It is situated north of the Philippines, southwest of Japan and Okinawa, and east of Hong Kong. The island of Formosa has an area of 13,815 sq.mi.; including its 77 outlying islands (14 in the Taiwan group and 63 in the Pescadores group), the area of Taiwan totals 13,893 sq.mi. (35,981 sq.km.). Pop. (1973 est.): 15,-424,000. Cap. and largest city: Taipei (pop., 1973 est., 1,937,000). President in 1973, Chiang Kai-shek; premier (president of the Executive Yuan), Chiang Ching-kuo.

On Oct. 10, 1973, when the Nationalist government celebrated the 62nd anniversary of the revolution that founded the Republic of China, it had spent 24 years in exile on Taiwan. During the year the international position of the Republic of China further deteriorated, as Australia and New Zealand in December 1972 and Spain in March 1973 transferred their official recognition from the Nationalists to the Communist regime in Peking. Consequently, Portugal remained the only European country recognizing Taiwan, and the U.S. was the only major power that continued to maintain diplomatic relations with the Nationalists. However, more than 30 countries still maintained full diplomatic relations with Taiwan, and its existence was strengthened by continued economic growth and prosperity.

Administration. With the spectacular changes in international relations, the Nationalist government began to realize that Taiwan's survival as an independent entity depended increasingly on internal unity and strength rather than merely on international support. Under the leadership of Premier Chiang Ching-kuo, son of Pres. Chiang Kai-shek, comprehensive reform measures to promote efficiency and honesty in government as well as to broaden its domestic support were carried out.

Shortly after Chiang Ching-kuo's accession to the premiership in June 1972, Pres. Chiang Kai-shek, who reached 86 years of age on Oct. 31, 1973, was hospitalized. He did not take an active role in government affairs after his hospitalization. The younger Chiang's strong and more democratic leadership strengthened the administration by eliminating corruption and favouritism in government bureaucracy and appointing an unprecedented number of local-born Taiwanese to top-level offices, including the deputy premier, the governor of Taiwan, the mayor of Taipei, and heads of three key ministries: Defense, Interior, and Communications.

In addition to these appointments, the election of a few dozen local-born Taiwanese to the Legislative Yuan and the National Assembly helped to ease tensions between them and the minority exiles from the mainland. Premier Chiang's frequent visits to factories, rice fields, and fishing villages in connection with the rural reconstruction program helped raise public morale and create a sense of unity.

Economy. In spite of diplomatic setbacks the economy remained stable and prosperous; both industry and agriculture continued to grow, and the former replaced the latter as the mainstay of Taiwan's economy. More than 80% of exports came from industry, compared with 42% in 1961. However, the greater development of industry as compared with agriculture created difficult economic and social problems as people moved from the country to the city to find

TAIWAN

Education. (1971–72) Primary, pupils 2,439,505, teachers 61,386; secondary and vocational, pupils 1,232,438, teachers 59,481; teacher training (1969–70), students 528, teachers 14; higher (including 8 universities), students 222,505, teaching staff 18,029.

Finance. Monetary unit: New Taiwan dollar, with (Sept. 17, 1973) a par value of NT$38 to U.S. $1 (free rate of NT$92 = £1 sterling). Gold, SDRs, and foreign exchange, official: (June 1973) U.S. $1,241,-000,000; (June 1972) U.S. $606 million. Budget (1971–72 est.): revenue NT$56,482,000,000; expenditure NT$54,829,000,000. Gross national product: (1972) NT$387,270,000,000; (1971) NT$249,280,-000,000. Money supply: (May 1973) NT$69.9 billion; (May 1972) NT$47,120,000,000. Cost of living (1963 = 100): (May 1973) 139; (May 1972) 129.

Foreign Trade. (1972) Imports NT$100,791,000,-000; exports NT$116,650,000,000. Import sources: Japan 42%; U.S. 22%. Export destinations: U.S. 43%; Japan 13%; Hong Kong 8%; Canada 5%; West Germany 5%. Main exports: clothing 17%; telecommunications apparatus 13%; textile yarns and fabrics 12%; fruits and vegetables 8%; plywood 5%.

Transport and Communications. Roads (1971) 15,517 km. Motor vehicles in use (1971): passenger 55,100; commercial 47,600. Railways (1971): 3,839 km.; traffic 6,806,000,000 passenger-km., freight 2,614,000,000 net ton-km. Air traffic (1970): 954 million passenger-km.; freight 25,175,000 net ton-km. Shipping (1972): merchant vessels 100 gross tons and over 399; gross tonnage 1,494,903. Telephones (Jan. 1971) 403,000. Radio licenses (Dec. 1972) c. 1,460,-000. Television licenses (Dec. 1972) c. 1.1 million.

Agriculture. Production (in 000; metric tons; 1971; 1970 in parentheses): rice 2,314 (2,463); sweet potatoes 3,391 (3,441); cassava (1970) 308, (1969) 316; peanuts 98 (122); oranges (1970) c. 156, (1969) 123; tea 27 (28); sugar, raw value c. 750 (843); bananas 471 (462); tobacco 12 (21); pork c. 360 (354). Livestock (in 000; Dec. 1971): cattle 259; pigs 3,079; goats 174; chickens (1970) 14,269.

Industry. Production (in 000; metric tons; 1971): coal 4,097; crude oil 112; natural gas (cu.m.) 1,091,-000; electricity (kw-hr.) 15,171,000; cement 5,043; crude steel 643; salt 669; caustic soda 135; petroleum products (1970) 5,030; cotton yarn 105; paper 386.

A Taiwanese freighter lies grounded and burning on the bank of the Mekong River near the South Vietnamese-Cambodian border. Part of a convoy carrying oil, ammunition, and food to Phnom Penh, Cambodia, the ship was reportedly ambushed by Viet Cong, April 8, 1973.

WIDE WORLD

work. This became a serious problem in the countryside, where about 40% of the people lived. To accelerate the growth of the rural economy the government announced in January a two-year program to spend $102 million, designed to give farmers an increase in income and better working and living conditions.

The Economic Planning Commission predicted that, based on the gross national product of $4,439,000,000 in the first half of 1973, per capita income would rise from $372 in 1972 to $466 in 1973. This notable economic growth with its concomitant rise in living standards made a major contribution to defusing political and social dissatisfaction. The development of economic potential and the promotion of foreign trade figured prominently in the efforts for Taiwan's independent survival, and the government adopted a flexible and active policy in maintaining economic and trade relations with as many countries as possible. The U.S. remained Taiwan's largest trade partner, followed by Japan and Europe.

Status and Future of Taiwan. The two contending governments of China—Nationalist and Communist—shared the view that there is only one China, and that Taiwan is a province of China. The admission of Communist China to membership in the United Nations, replacing the Nationalists, dealt an irretrievable blow to the status of the Republic of China in the international community. Before and after its admission to the UN, Communist China made it a prerequisite for any country extending recognition to it to remove its official representation from Nationalist China and acknowledge that Taiwan is an integral part of China. All the countries that switched recognition or signaled a shift in policy except for the U.S. no longer maintained diplomatic relations with Nationalist China. Seven months after U.S. Pres. Richard Nixon's visit to Peking, Japan hastened to recognize Communist China in September 1972 and thus effectively severed diplomatic ties with the Nationalist regime. But despite the formal break, trade and travel between Japan and Taiwan continued to flourish.

The rapid improvement in relations between the U.S. and Communist China caused great concern to the Nationalists. Immediately after the two nations agreed to open governmental liaison offices, Taiwan issued a statement on February 22 reiterating its claim to being "the legitimate government elected by the people of China in accordance with the Constitution" and again declaring null and void any agreement reached between Washington and Peking. Taiwan feared that the establishment of the Chinese Communist liaison office in Washington would dilute the position and influence of its own diplomatic mission there.

In the wake of détente with Washington and facing an internal leadership struggle and the Soviet threat, Peking appeared to be unwilling or unable to seek a hasty solution to the Taiwan problem. Instead of immediate "liberation," it adopted a long-term policy of absorption. Just a week after the announcement of the exchange of liaison offices with the U.S., the Communist leaders issued a long message on February 28 inviting the Nationalists to start formal or private talks on the reunification of China. The message carried a warning that "the United States will neither maintain its relations with Taiwan for long at the expense of peaceful coexistence with China, nor allow Taiwan to cooperate with anybody [obliquely referring to the Soviet Union] to disrupt peace in the Asian and Pacific region." Nationalist officials scoffed at the suggestion, labeling it a Communist trick to damage relations between the U.S. and Taiwan.

(HUNG-TI CHU)

Tanzania

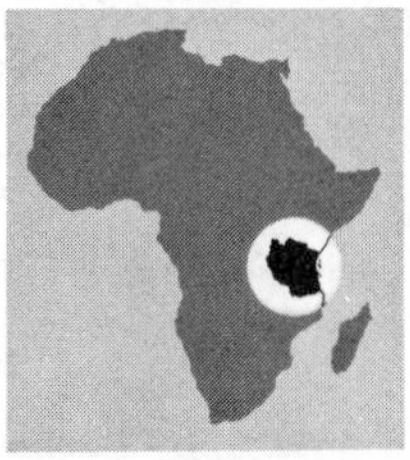

This republic, an East African member of the Commonwealth of Nations, consists of two parts: Tanganyika, on the Indian Ocean, bordered by Kenya, Uganda, Rwanda, Burundi, Zaire, Zambia, Malawi, and Mozambique; and Zanzibar, just off the coast, including Zanzibar Island, Pemba Island, and small islets. Total area of the united republic: 364,943 sq. mi. (945,203 sq.km.). Total pop. (1973 est.): 14,372,000, including (1966 est.) 98.9% Africans and 0.7% Indo-Pakistani. Cap. and largest city: Dar es Salaam (pop., 1972 est., 396,700) in Tanganyika. Language: English and Swahili. Religion (1967): traditional beliefs 34.6%; Christian 30.6%; Muslim 30.5%. President in 1973, Julius Nyerere.

In the early part of 1973 Tanzania underwent a series of crises in its relations with its northwestern neighbours. Difficulties between Uganda and Hutu-governed Rwanda induced the latter to try to strengthen its association with Tanzania, and Rwanda's minister of public works visited Dar es Salaam in February to sign an agreement on trade, tourism, immigration, air services, and security. In the same month a new bridge was opened over the Kagera River to link the two countries; this, together with the asylum given to Hutu refugees fleeing from Tutsi attacks in Burundi, led Burundi in May to accuse Tanzania of taking the side of the Hutu. The atmosphere of suspicion between Burundi and Tanzania had already been aggravated in March by an attack on a number of Tanzanian frontier villages by troops from Burundi who had killed nearly 100 Hutu refugees and several Tanzanians. Toward the end of May the Burundi government accused Tanzania of plotting an invasion, a charge that the latter firmly rejected, but in July Tanzanian dockworkers declared a boycott on the handling of Burundi cargoes in transit through Dar es Salaam.

The relationship between Tanzania and Uganda also deteriorated in March when 51 Ugandans were arrested in Dar es Salaam on charges of spying and 45 were expelled from the country. This was followed by mutual accusations between the two countries re-

Burundian refugees settle into a new life at Ulyankulu, a Tanzanian refugee camp established on what had been a game preserve. Civil upheavals in neighbouring countries had led an estimated 110,000 to flee to Tanzania, where humanitarian organizations cooperated in supporting resettlement camps.

AUTHENTICATED NEWS INTERNATIONAL

lating to alleged breaches of the Mugdisho agreement of 1972 by moving troops into their frontier zone. Although the tension was gradually reduced, the continuing presence in Dar es Salaam of former Ugandan president Milton Obote and of battalions of his troops in training camps kept relations cool. At the summit meeting of the Organization of African Unity (OAU) in Addis Ababa, Eth., in May, however, President Nyerere entered into a reconciliation pact with Pres. Idi Amin of Uganda as a result of initiatives taken by the latter and by Emperor Haile Selassie.

In spite of heavy criticism from many quarters of the late vice-president Sheikh Abeid Karume's regime in Zanzibar, his successor, Aboud Jumbe, was able to claim that the island's foreign reserves stood at more than £33 million at the end of 1972, compared with £1 million before the 1964 revolution. This optimistic picture was darkened by news of the trial, which began in May, of more than 80 persons accused of complicity in the assassination of Karume.

The economic situation in Tanzania appeared to offer mixed prospects. Progress on the Chinese-financed Tanzam railway continued. Accusations that Tanzania was becoming too dependent on Chinese aid received a counterblast when the World Bank estimated that aid of approximately $500 million would be made available from various quarters, excluding China, to assist in Tanzania's rural development program, which had been hit by an outbreak of coffee berry disease. It was feared not only that the revenue from the sale of coffee might be reduced but also that some of the better estates might have to be abandoned for lack of capital to maintain them.

(KENNETH INGHAM)

TANZANIA

Education. Tanganyika: (1970) primary, pupils 827,974, teachers 17,790; secondary, pupils 31,217, teachers 1,650; vocational, pupils 1,546, teachers 145; teacher training, students 4,092, teachers 306; higher (University of Dar es Salaam), students 2,060, teaching staff 308. Zanzibar: (1966) primary, pupils 35,000; secondary, pupils 1,700.

Finance. Monetary unit: Tanzanian shilling, with (Sept. 17, 1973) a par value of TShs. 6.90 to U.S. $1 (free rate of TShs. 16.67 = £1 sterling). Gold, SDRs, and foreign exchange: (June 1973) U.S. $133.7 million; (June 1972) U.S. $81.1 million. Budget (1971–72 est.): revenue TShs. 1,789,000,000; expenditure (including capital account) TShs. 2,778,000,000. Gross national product: (1971) TShs. 9,687,000,000; (1970) TShs. 9,125,000,000. Money supply: (May 1973) TShs. 2,255,000,000; (May 1972) TShs. 1,935,000,000. Cost of living (Dar es Salaam; 1963 = 100): (June 1973) 151; (June 1972) 142.

Foreign Trade. (Excluding trade with Kenya and Uganda; 1972) Imports TShs. 2,562,000,000; exports TShs. 2,152,000,000. Import sources: China 20%; U.K. 18%; Italy 8%; West Germany 8%; Iran 6%; Japan 6%; U.S. 5%. Export destinations: U.K. 16%; Indonesia 11%; Zambia 9%; India 8%; U.S. 7%; China 6%; Hong Kong 6%; West Germany 6%. Main exports: coffee 18%; sisal 7%.

Transport and Communications. Roads (1969) 16,743 km. Motor vehicles in use (1971): passenger 35,800; commercial (including buses) 38,000. Railways (1970) 1,998 km. (for traffic *see* KENYA). Construction of a *c.* 1,800-km. railway linking Dar es Salaam with Zambia began in 1970; completion was planned for 1974 (716 km. of track had been laid at the beginning of 1973). Air traffic: *see* KENYA. Shipping traffic (mainland only; 1972): goods loaded 1,256,000 metric tons, unloaded 2,801,000 metric tons. Telephones (Dec. 1971) 40,000. Radio receivers (Dec. 1971) 200,000. Television licenses (Dec. 1969) 4,000.

Agriculture. Production (in 000; metric tons; 1972; 1971 in parentheses): corn *c.* 600 (*c.* 541); sweet potatoes (1971) *c.* 320, (1970) 310; millet *c.* 140 (*c.* 138); sorghum *c.* 110 (*c.* 107); sugar, raw value *c.* 105 (*c.* 100); rice *c.* 190 (*c.* 185); cassava (1970) *c.* 1,500, (1969) *c.* 1,300; coffee 52 (*c.* 64); cotton, lint *c.* 65 (*c.* 65); sisal (1971) 181, (1970) 202; timber (cu.m.; 1970) 31,500, (1969) 30,500. Livestock (in 000; 1970–71): cattle *c.* 13,300; sheep *c.* 2,800; pigs *c.* 22; goats *c.* 4,450; asses *c.* 160; poultry *c.* 20,600.

Industry. Production (in 000; metric tons; 1971): cement 180; salt 37; magnesite (exports) 1; diamonds (metric carats) 837; electricity (excluding most industrial production; kw-hr.) 422,000.

Tariffs:
see Commercial Policies; Trade, International

Taxation

United States. There was little new legislation in U.S. taxation during 1973. The principal event of long-range interest in federal taxation was a three-week period of hearings by the Ways and Means Committee of the House of Representatives on various aspects of possible tax reform. Subsequently, Wilbur D. Mills (Dem., Ark.), chairman of the committee, said, "We are not going to windup with a tax system that meets the purist standards of the academician, but shuts off the wellsprings of economic progress—personal and business savings."

This statement indicated an appreciation of the breadth of the proposals but reassured those who feared that some of the drastic changes in the tax laws advocated under the name of reform would have serious adverse economic effects. The widely quoted sentence in Mills's remarks was regarded by many as the most significant single tax item of 1973.

Federal. The first session of the above mentioned hearings, from February 5 through February 28, involved statements by 56 witnesses invited by the Ways and Means Committee to represent all major points of view on 11 aspects of the tax law: (1) general objectives; (2) capital gains and losses; (3) capital recovery (investment credit, accelerated depreciation, etc.); (4) real estate; (5) farm operations; (6) minimum tax and tax shelters; (7) pensions, profit-sharing, and deferred compensation; (8) state and local bonds; (9) natural resources; (10) estate and gift taxes; and (11) taxation of foreign income. The principal topic omitted was the dual taxation of corporate and individual income, the problem of so-called double taxation of dividends, which had been relieved in one way or another in most industrial countries except the U.S.

The 11 volumes of testimony, including queries and comments by members of the committee and discussion among the panelists, constituted a superb compendium of material. It was generally agreed that it would serve for many years as the principal reference on issues of federal tax policy and alternative tax provisions regarding the subjects covered.

Witnesses before the committee included academic theorists, who often disagreed vigorously among themselves, leading tax practitioners, and representatives of industries and other groups especially concerned with different features of the tax law. A full range of opinion was represented.

One recurring difference in point of view developed in the panels. Some witnesses appeared to regard the tax system as something to be perfected for its own sake, according to their individual concepts of equity and other criteria of policy. In extreme forms, their proposals represented the "purist standards of the academician," to which Mills presumably referred. Other witnesses seemed to appraise the tax law as simply one element in a complex and inevitably imperfect social-political-economic structure. They typically believed that overemphasis on one feature, specifically on perfection of the tax law in terms of a theoretical ideal, would be at the expense of other equally or more important aspects of social institutions.

The hearings produced little in the way of new analysis or new proposals. Their value lay in the concise restatement of positions and in challenges and responses by protagonists of different points of view. The most general distinction to be drawn was between those who advocated a very broad base for income taxation and those who regarded differential taxation as essential as a matter of equity and to permit continued economic vitality.

In regard to equity, some public finance writers adopted a "net accretion" concept of income that included any appreciation in value of property as being equivalent, for purposes of income taxation, to wages, rents, interest, dividends, and other familiar forms of income. It also included such items of imputed income as the rental value of owner-occupied homes and the cash value of fringe benefits such as employer contributions to pension plans. On the basis of the net accretion concept, capital gains should be taxed in full as income. But this concept was regarded by others as an abstraction that did not conform either to popular understanding or to any principle of income determination in corporate or trust law. To them, taxation of long-term capital gains destined for reinvestment was a capital levy rather than a form of income taxation. This distinction was reflected in many of the panel discussions.

The broad-base position was reflected in virtually all the topics covered. The proposed changes not only included taxation of capital gains as ordinary income but also repeal of accelerated depreciation and investment credit provisions, removal of special allowances for real estate and farming, removal of tax exemptions from state and local bonds, and curtailment of depletion allowances to a recovery of cost.

Those who did not accept the net accretion broad-based concept of income based their objection on several grounds. In regard to capital gains, they contended that a mere appreciation in value is not spendable income and that if a gain is reinvested in other assets, a tax on the gain is a capital levy rather than a tax on income. They argued further that, with perpetual inflation, a minimum amount of increase in money value is necessary to maintain the real value of a capital sum; on this basis, they believed that taxation of the full amount of a gain was clearly a capital levy when it reduced the real value of capital.

The taxation of the income of foreign subsidiaries of U.S. corporations continued to be a major area of controversy in 1973, as it had been in 1972. The Burke-Hartke bill covering various aspects of foreign trade and legislation included several fundamental modifications of the tax law. The most drastic tax changes that would have been made by its adoption were abolition of the credit against the U.S. income tax for foreign income taxes, and taxation of the undistributed income of foreign subsidiaries of U.S. parent corporations. Both provisions were strongly advocated by labour organizations on the ground that U.S. corporations were responsible for decreased employment in the U.S. by "exporting jobs" to their foreign plants under the stimulus of lower taxes abroad.

There appeared to be little support for the Burke-Hartke bill in the House Ways and Means Committee, but discussion of the subject was active. Some changes in the tax treatment of foreign business income seemed possible as part of major tax revision. Though continuation of the foreign tax credit seemed probable, various compromises regarding the taxation of the retained earnings of foreign subsidiaries were proposed. One that created much interest was that a tax on the basis of retained earnings should be imposed only to the extent that distribution of income to the U.S. parent corporation did not meet some specified minimum standard.

A completely new situation developed at the end of 1973 when a large increase in the gasoline tax was suggested, along with or as an alternative to rationing, to reduce consumption of gasoline. One argument against the increase in tax was that the large revenue from it, perhaps in the tens of billions of dollars, would have a depressing effect on the economy unless the funds were immediately spent. Major programs for mass transit were mentioned as a reasonable use but they could not be started soon enough to absorb the revenues.

State and Local. The principal event in state and local taxation in 1973 was the proposal by Gov. Ronald Reagan of California for an amendment to the state constitution that would have limited the total tax revenue of the state to a specified and, over the years, a declining percentage of personal income within the state. The measure was complex, with many escape clauses to prevent actual reductions in expenditures and to provide for various contingencies. It was hailed by its supporters as a dramatic and effective device to impose a ceiling on spending and thereby force public and government attention on ways to achieve greater effectiveness in the use of public funds. Critics condemned it on the grounds that such a limitation should not be embodied in the constitution and that it would unduly curtail necessary government programs and shift burdens to counties, cities, and other taxing governmental units.

After a vigorous campaign on both sides, the amendment was substantially but not overwhelmingly defeated in a special election on November 6, in which it was the only state item on the ballot. The defeat was interpreted by some as an indication that voters were indifferent to tax burdens and had no objection to expensive government programs. Others argued that the defeat was due to the complexity and novelty of the proposal.

Barrel-clad James Nelson, of Wenonah, N.J., is asked to leave the New Jersey governor's office during a tax protest, April 26, 1973. Some 200 New Jersey residents who work in Pennsylvania were demonstrating against paying that state's income tax.

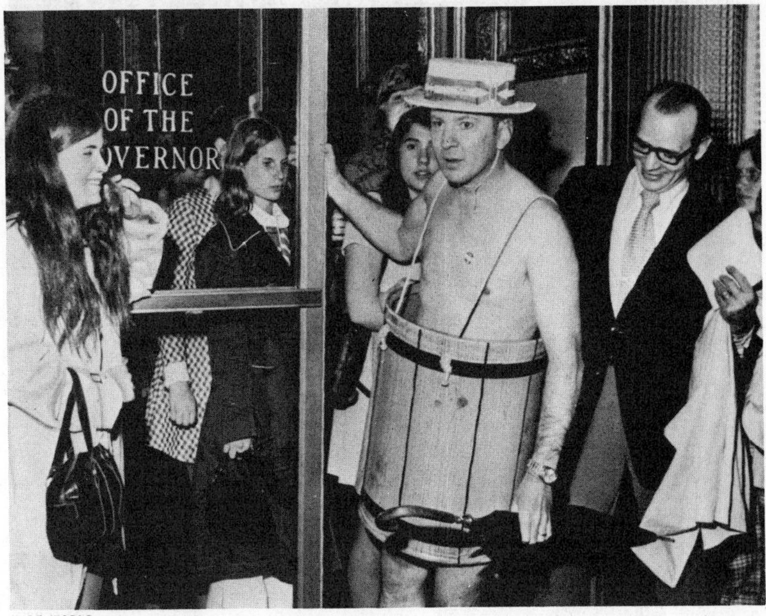

WIDE WORLD

There was increased interest in 1973 in legislation to modify property taxation to reduce the tax pressure for premature subdivision and development of agricultural land. It was recognized increasingly that when land was assessed on the basis of the value it could be sold for if converted to another use, an owner could be forced to sell because the tax absorbed more than the full income from a present and less profitable use. Tax relief by authorizing assessment for taxation on value in a present agricultural use was accepted as being in the public interest rather than a "tax subsidy" or "benefit" to farmers. Ohio in 1973 joined the states that had previously authorized "present use" instead of "best use" as a standard for land assessment. (DAN THROOP SMITH)

Europe. In Europe, fiscal harmonization had to be achieved within the EEC. Fiscal relations between the EEC and other countries also had to be considered. The EEC's interdependence with the Mediterranean countries existed in such matters as defense, trade, and labour supply; harmonization of tariffs and quotas was the long-term aim.

There was progress in a number of European Free Trade Association (EFTA) countries. In July 1972, a free trade agreement between Austria, Iceland, Portugal, Sweden, and Switzerland on the one hand and the enlarged EEC on the other was signed. The general effect of these agreements was to reduce customs duties, including those of a fiscal nature, over a number of years. Fiscal duties might be replaced by an internal tax that did not discriminate between imported and home-produced goods.

On Jan. 1, 1973, the United Kingdom, Ireland, and Denmark were admitted to the EEC, and a period of stress and strain in community relations was to be expected. Eventual monetary and fiscal harmonization was intended, but progress would be only gradual. By the end of the year all Common Market countries had the value-added tax (VAT), a first step toward fiscal integration. However, though VAT in each country was based on directives issued in 1967, the directives deliberately left some discretion in setting up the tax, in order to ease the transition. Thus, there were considerable differences in the application of VAT in each country. Ways to reduce these differences came under active consideration. The original six members of the EEC had agreed to pay up to 1% of VAT to the Brussels budget from 1975, but any differences with other countries would make the arrangement difficult to implement. France, the main instigator of VAT, announced that it would like to reduce heavy reliance on direct taxes to about 50% from the existing level of 58%. There were indications that Henri Simonet, the EEC commissioner for tax matters, might be willing to suggest some compromise.

Citizens picket the White House on Sept. 20, 1973, in response to news reports that U.S. Pres. Richard M. Nixon "apparently paid no income taxes for 1970–71." Nixon later made public his tax returns showing he had paid some income tax during those years.

UPI COMPIX

Directives had already been made relating to capital formation taxes and excise duties. Detailed studies on various aspects of company taxation could be subject to revision to take account of the views of the new members. The tax directorate of the EEC was reorganized at the same time as new members were admitted, and it remained to be seen how active the new directorate would be.

Most European countries suffered more or less the same rate of inflation, but only West Germany and Denmark made much use of increased taxes as a method of control, other countries preferring to try a mixture of monetary, credit, and wage measures. In a report published in June the European Commission examined the question of "tax havens" and called for joint EEC action to mitigate some abuses.

Austria. On Jan. 1, 1973, VAT was introduced at a standard rate of 16%, replacing a 5.5% turnover tax. A reduced rate of 8% applied to farm products, services, and certain other commodities. A new individual income tax was introduced, and important changes affecting corporate income taxes and business taxes were made. Interest was no longer deductible as a "special expense" under individual income tax. The presumed income from an owner-occupied house was abolished. Separate assessment of members of a household was introduced. Individual income tax started at 20% on the first 25,000 schillings of taxable income and proceeded in 12 steps to a top rate of 62%. Corporate profits, if undistributed, were taxed on a sliding scale that started at 30% on taxable income up to 200,000 schillings and, in seven steps, reached 55% on profits in excess of 1,142,800 schillings. Distributed profits were taxed at 50% of these rates.

Denmark. In March the government announced plans to stabilize the economy. Company income taxes were to be increased from 36 to 40%, and the allowance of 2.5% for paid-up share capital was abolished. Proposed increases in the depreciation allowances on machinery from 30 to 40%, to have taken place in 1973–74, were suspended. Refund of VAT on new houses was ended. Old-age pensions and child allowances were to be graduated according to income, and the latter abolished for high-income groups.

France. On January 1 France reduced the standard rate of VAT from 23 to 20%, while the lower rate of 7.5% was cut to 7%. VAT on beef, at 7.5%, was suspended for six months. These measures were intended to reduce prices of manufactured goods by 2%. The tax loss, estimated at Fr. 7.6 billion, would mostly be covered by the issuance of 15-year government securities.

Several tax scandals in France marked the intensification of the government's campaign against large-scale tax evasion. In 1972 it had emerged that former premier Jacques Chaban-Delmas had escaped paying income taxes altogether by making use of tax credits on dividends. Investigations into the Bordeaux wine business, started by tax inspectors in 1973, rocked the wine trade, and art dealer Daniel Wildenstein was charged with tax evasion running into many millions of francs.

Several tax reforms had been instituted in recent years. Late in 1972 the year's Finance Law was amended in respect to *societés civiles de moyens*—partnerships in a profession that shared the use of staff or assets—to relieve such partnerships of the possibility of being subject to corporation income tax. Other provisions changed the law governing the expenses of foreign establishments, and gave tax privileges, at the discretion of the minister of economic affairs and finance, to French enterprises investing in an industrial business in a designated less developed country. The law relating to the expenses of company executives was tightened up, and lump sum payments for expenses were to be treated as taxable income. In September 1973, following adoption by the Cabinet of his 1974 budget, Finance Minister Valéry Giscard d'Estaing announced several measures to achieve more justice in taxation, the most important being introduction by 1978 of the pay-as-you-earn system adopted by all other EEC members except Italy.

United Kingdom. The 1973 budget was one of consolidation. VAT was introduced at a flat rate of 10%. Children's clothing was zero-rated and—most controversially, in view of the high incidence of dental caries among British children—sweets (candy) and ice cream were given the same zero rating as other foods. Extensive use of zero rating in the U.K. did not conform to EEC practice.

A new unified system of personal taxation at the basic rate of 30% was introduced, and a substantial concession was given to those receiving investment income by charging the first £2,000 of such income at the 30% rate and not at the higher rate to which it had previously been subject.

The new imputation system of corporation tax was introduced as planned. Strong inducement was given to new investment: 100% of the cost of new plant and machinery could be written off against taxable profits in the first year of purchase, and any unused allowance could be carried forward against future profits without time limit. New industrial buildings received an initial first-year allowance of 40%, and additional help was given to companies in "development areas"—areas of high unemployment.

Ireland. The Republic of Ireland made headlines in September 1973 by announcing that it was to withdraw the 20-year tax holiday introduced in 1967 for the country's mining industry, a decision bitterly opposed by the companies concerned. One obvious advantage of fiscal cooperation in Europe was that such tax concessions would be regulated and, it was hoped, eliminated.

Italy. January 1 saw the start of the Italian tax reform program intended eventually to bring the tax structure more into line with other European countries. The new structure would derive the largest part of revenue from graduated direct taxes, and effectively tax companies and earnings from capital. The reform came at a time when Italy had a large balance of payments deficit and a large budget deficit; the latter was not helped by reported large-scale evasions of VAT, also introduced in January.

The standard VAT rate in Italy was 12%. A 6% rate applied to most food products, wine, beer, pharmaceutical goods, books, gas and electricity for domestic use, and to certain services. A higher rate of 18% applied to refined foods, gems, fur coats and certain valuable fabrics, perfume, private aircraft, and cars with engines exceeding 2,000 cc. No tax was applied to exports, or to various educational, welfare, and health organizations. As a transitional measure, over the first five years, reduced rates applied to a number of items. Certain essential foods would be taxed at 1% in 1973–74, 3% in 1975–76, and at 6% thereafter.

In January the new inheritance and gift tax was also introduced. The highest rate was 60%, as compared with 90% under the old system, but the new tax base was broader. The system provided for two taxes: estate tax levied on the value of the entire taxable estate or gift, and succession duty levied on the beneficiary unless there was close consanguinity. Only gifts of small value, transferred from hand to hand, were exempt. Other gifts had to be effected by a donation contract, and duty would be payable when the document was registered.

The Netherlands. The Netherlands revised its personal income tax from January, widening the income range applicable to each tax rate, making changes in personal and child deductions, giving special treatment to families of widowed or divorced parents or otherwise "incomplete" families, and exempting the child allowance from taxation. A person between 16 and 27 years old who, due to illness or infirmity, could not earn one-half of the income that a normal person that age could earn became considered as two persons for tax purposes if maintained by the taxpayer.

Sweden. A provisional tax on printed advertisements, introduced in Sweden in 1971, was replaced in November 1972 by a broader-based tax intended to avoid the discriminatory effects on the newspaper industry of the old tax. The tax was at the rate of 10% of the cost of the advertising except for non-technical newspapers, where the rate was 6%. Exemptions included cases where the yearly income from printing advertisements did not exceed 60,000 kronor per periodical. Mail-order houses were given special treatment, particularly those in competition with foreign mail-order firms.

Switzerland. Switzerland was preparing a program for a reform of taxation, and there was speculation that the changes could reduce the advantages of Switzerland as a tax haven. A proposal was made to introduce VAT to replace sales tax, and to attempt to harmonize the existing confused system of direct taxation imposed by the cantons.

West Germany. In an attempt to control inflation, a 21-point program was announced in May. Tax measures included a 10% income tax surcharge on all corporations and taxpayers with annual incomes of DM. 24,000 or more (double for married persons). The proceeds would be frozen in a special account and eventually applied to the employers' "assets accumulation scheme." It was also announced that government subsidies for new investments in depressed areas, and for research and development, would be reduced. The tax on gasoline was increased, and an 11% tax imposed, for no longer than two years, on investment goods, in an attempt to dampen down that expansive sector of the economy. (G. C. HOCKLEY)

See also Economics; Economy, World; Employment, Wages, and Hours; Government Finance; Social Services.

Tea:
see Agriculture and Fisheries

Telecommunications

In a year that was remarkable for developments in telecommunications technology rather than policy, the teetering progress of that mammoth infant, Britain's Post Office Corporation, received more than its usual share of attention. With plans for a £4,000 million modernization laid before the government, the Post Office gave its blessing to a type of telephone exchange that was neither the cheapest, the fastest, nor the most modern switching system available. Nevertheless, the government approved the plans in the spring of 1973. By the fall, inflation had bitten so deeply into the Post Office's finances that it had to declare that for the first time it had sustained an overall loss of over £64 million. Its telecommunications income jumped from £884.1 million in 1971–72 to a record £1,002.3 million, yet the previous £58 million profit had turned into a £9.7 million loss. Meanwhile, in the United States, the Federal Communications Commission (FCC) brought the nation's domestic telecommunications into the space age.

Telephones. Despite the vociferous objections of most of the manufacturing industries concerned, the British Post Office plans for modernization centred on the adoption of the TXE-4 electronic exchange. Western Electric in the U.S., Northern Electric in Canada, and Ericsson and Philips in Europe all had other electronic switching systems at a more advanced stage of development, and the British firms had hoped for a competitive system on which they could base a strong export effort. In theory the switching system with the greatest flexibility needed to cope with the rapid growth of telephone networks was one controlled by computer. The TXE-4 was not.

From the Post Office's point of view the TXE-4 had important advantages. It was simple to make, and, for industry tooled up to continue production of electromechanical switching systems like Strowger and crossbar, the reed-relay system of TXE-4 represented a comparatively small change. The Post Office telephone improvement plan between 1973 and 1980 envisaged £350 million for crossbar and an ever increasing volume of TXE-4s, costing up to £100 million.

Under strong political pressure, the Post Office commissioned the joint developers of TXE-4, Standard Telephone and Cables, to investigate the export possibilities of the switching system. Acting independently, General Electric Co. carried out an assessment which showed that, with modifications, TXE-4 could find markets abroad. The Post Office's final position was that TXE-4 could take some computer control. Meanwhile, it awarded a £100,000 development contract to GEC Telecommunications for work on the central processor for a new generation of computer-controlled telephone switching systems that it anticipated introducing for trunk switching in the late 1970s. The ultimate aim of the Post Office and manufacturers alike was the so-called System X, a range of fully electronic, computer-controlled exchanges capable of matching the Post Office's high-speed digital transmission system for the 1980s.

Switzerland's first satellite communications station was under construction during 1973, above the Rhône Valley in the canton of Valais. Nippon Electric Co. of Japan designed and supplied antenna and communications equipment.

VICTOR LUSINCHI—THE NEW YORK TIMES

The Bell Telephone System claimed a savings of $212 million on its manufacturing costs of $2.7 billion in 1972. Its subsidiary, Western Electric, had a program to cut the cost of new equipment being manufactured. As usual, a target cost was set, based on quantity production, but once this had been reached a study was made to see how costs could be further reduced by using changed design, new materials, or different manufacturing procedures. In 1972 the company made its cost-reducing teams available to its suppliers and saved two of them $1.1 million.

Misdialing was no longer merely a nuisance; it tied up many millions of dollars worth of exchange equipment annually. And even if his dialing was accurate, the busy executive who made his own calls could waste considerable time just in operating the dial. Therefore, automatic dialing was rapidly becoming essential. In the U.S. in 1973 automatic number callers became one of the fastest growing sectors of the telephone appliance business, mushrooming into a $100 million industry embracing about 200 firms. At the top of the market was an automatic dialer manufactured by Dasa Corp. It could hold 400 different telephone numbers on its magnetic tape memory but could only deal with 18-digit numbers. The British Post Office was evaluating an electronic dialer developed by Shipton Automation that could remember numbers of 31 digits. Bell Laboratories brought out a telephone that could dial any of 32 prerecorded numbers at the touch of a button. Slightly larger than a standard desk telephone, the instrument had a rotary dial for manual dialing and recording numbers and an array of buttons for those recorded. A "last number dialed" button allowed a caller who got a busy signal to redial automatically by touching the button.

The volume of telephone traffic across the Atlantic in 1973 was 30 million minutes per year. Calls from the U.S. accounted for nearly 13.5 million, compared with 2 million in 1960. The Post Office predicted that by 1976 some 130 million international telephone calls would be made to, from, or via the U.K. This was a massive growth from the 14 million calls made in 1965.

The U.S. Department of Commerce announced that the total gross capital investment by the nation's domestic telephone and telegraph industries should top $100 billion by the end of 1973; approximately $13 billion were invested in 1973. The department estimated that domestic telephone revenues would reach $27 billion in 1973 and climb to $53.9 billion per year by 1980. Telegraph and data transmissions revenues were estimated to be $1,450,000,000 in 1973 and were expected to rise to about $5 billion a year by the end of the decade. The department also predicted international telephone revenues of $597 million in 1973 and

$3.5 billion by 1980. International telegraph revenues were expected to be $840 million by 1980.

"Interconnects." In the U.S. the long-running battle on the right of interconnection continued. Microwave Communications, Inc. (MCI) and other specialized carriers brought action against AT & T to force the firm and its subsidiaries to provide them with entry into the nationwide telephone network. At issue in the dispute was the ever increasing private line business, in which large firms or organizations leased permanent intercity connections for voice or data transmissions at a cost cheaper than the normal fees paid for AT & T service. Several nationwide private line systems were under construction in 1973, and they were expected eventually to provide strong competition to AT & T's telephone line system. What MCI and the other specialized carriers wanted from AT & T was the same access to the national telephone system that AT & T subsidiaries had.

Joining the battle were companies that manufactured devices for attachment to telephones, such as call diverters, answering devices, and computer terminals. The objection of AT & T's Bell System was its claim that the devices could be harmful to the phone network if indiscriminately permitted to enter the system.

The FCC decided to explore the issue fully as the year drew to a close. It was expected that in early 1974 the legality of inserting customer-provided communications equipment into the telephone system would be resolved by either the FCC or a federal court. Meanwhile, MCI, most of whose customers were business firms with large communications needs for both voice and data transmissions, began offering service in a number of cities.

Late in September AT & T filed with the FCC a plan for the construction of a 24-city network to provide improved digital data transmission service. The plan was a second step in an overall program to improve digital service to 96 cities through AT & T's long lines department by 1976. The $3.8 million AT & T proposal would add 9,800 mi. of digital facilities to the AT & T system.

Satellites. Early in January the FCC approved a Western Union petition for a domestic communications satellite system. Western Union told the commission that it could probably have the system in operation in about one year. Western Union had already gained an advantage on its competitors in July 1972 when the FCC gave it permission to construct "at its own risk" three satellites for use in any system eventually approved. The $70 million Western Union system, to be called WESTAR, was expected to have its first satellite launch in about April 1974. The initial system would consist of two satellites, each containing 12 transponders, and five ground stations. Each transponder was to have a capacity of 600 two-way voice channels as well as data transmission and television capabilities.

In September the FCC approved the applications of five more company groups to build and orbit their own satellite communications systems. The American Satellite Corp. (jointly owned by Fairchild Industries, Inc., and Western Union International Inc.); RCA Global Communications Inc. and RCA Alaska Communications Inc.; GTE Satellite Corp. and National Satellite Services, Inc., a subsidiary of Hughes Aircraft; American Telephone and Telegraph Co.; and Communications Satellite Corp. (Comsat) were all given permission to proceed.

Comsat was authorized to spend about $180.6 million on four satellites to be used by AT & T. The latter firm was also authorized to spend $32.5 million on the construction of five satellite earth stations, while American Satellite received approval of a program calling for the expenditure of $18 million on an interim system of four earth stations and the leasing of channels from Telsat Canada for temporary use. Comsat planned to buy the four satellites from Hughes Aircraft, for a total of $65.9 million. Three of the satellites would be used in orbit and one would be an on-the-ground spare. Delivery of the first satellites was expected in late 1975. Under a long-term contract AT & T would lease the satellites from Comsat while building its own ground stations. AT & T's earth station facilities and the satellites would be integrated into the company's nationwide switched network to expand and diversify service to telephone users.

The satellites were to be placed in geostationary orbits about 22,300 mi. above the earth; each would have a design capacity for approximately 14,400 two-way, high-quality voice circuits. They were to be capable of providing service for the U.S. mainland, Alaska, Hawaii, Puerto Rico, and the Virgin Islands.

The world's first synchronous satellite solely for domestic communications came into operation over Canada early in the year, providing a capacity of 5,000 telephone channels or 12 high-quality TV channels, covering the whole of Canada. The television capacity was a dominant issue. Canada wanted to build up stable communities to exploit the mineral resources of the Arctic regions and, in the modern world, communities could not grow without the sustenance of television. There was also the problem of linking communities along the 200-mi.-wide strip bordering the U.S. where most Canadians lived. Without the satellite, the communication needs of the strip would have had to be met by extending U.S. communications networks into Canada.

Half the international calls between Britain and

Countries Having More Than 100,000 Telephones

Telephones in service, 1972

Country	Number of telephones	Percentage increase over 1962	Telephones per 100 population	Country	Number of telephones	Percentage increase over 1962	Telephones per 100 population
Algeria*	184,063	...	1.28	Luxembourg	118,664	89.1	34.40
Argentina	1,825,532	34.2	7.68	Malaysia‡	163,897	81.7	1.82
Australia*	4,151,622	74.3	32.62	Mexico	1,714,960	202.3	3.37
Austria	1,546,719	106.1	20.74	Morocco	171,544	29.1	1.12
Belgium	2,161,744	78.4	22.24	Netherlands, The	3,720,817	113.8	28.05
Brazil	2,064,950	85.0	2.12	New Zealand	1,281,105	59.8	44.04
Bulgaria	534,257	181.7	6.24	Norway	1,204,153	55.7	30.70
Canada	10,290,305	71.1	47.35	Pakistan§	211,088	124.2	0.18
Chile	389,609	76.6	4.26	Panama	107,129	226.1	6.93
Colombia	1,005,771	208.0	4.62	Peru	242,654	106.7	1.71
Cuba	274,949	26.2	3.16	Philippines	351,217	151.5	0.91
Czechoslovakia	2,111,996	89.6	14.63	Poland	1,970,856	105.9	6.00
Denmark	1,793,926	50.3	35.84	Portugal	809,380	89.6	9.34
Egypt†	365,000	49.3	1.14	Puerto Rico	355,763	153.4	12.79
Finland	1,289,592	97.1	27.83	Rhodesia	140,873	59.4	2.52
France	9,546,173	105.3	18.54	Romania	726,554	129.3	3.53
Germany, East	2,165,235	58.5	12.70	Singapore	189,847	181.3	8.92
Germany, West	15,245,686	134.2	24.88	South Africa	1,623,805	67.4	7.17
Greece	1,229,630	357.9	14.01	Soviet Union	11,980,000	134.0	4.86
Hong Kong	691,616	438.1	17.03	Spain	5,129,501	163.2	15.02
Hungary	873,194	85.4	8.42	Sweden	4,679,691	61.1	57.58
India	1,351,200	160.8	0.25	Switzerland	3,213,065	82.4	50.91
Indonesia	229,636	64.5	0.19	Syria	120,030	104.8	1.83
Iran*	307,500	190.4	1.06	Taiwan	492,307	309.2	3.28
Iraq*	119,650	120.6	1.24	Thailand	202,023	306.2	0.55
Ireland	323,826	75.9	10.90	Turkey	654,452	157.1	1.79
Israel	563,569	325.6	18.23	United Kingdom	16,143,102	87.5	28.88
Italy	10,321,581	167.3	19.09	United States	125,142,000	61.6	60.13
Japan	29,827,936	270.2	28.18	Uruguay	235,226	32.2	8.03
Korea, South	748,474	515.2	2.29	Venezuela	443,668	94.0	4.15
Lebanon*	192,000	189.2	6.78	Yugoslavia	820,860	196.9	3.99

*1971; increase (where given) over 1961. †1969. ‡West Malaysia only. §Includes Bangladesh.
Source: American Telephone and Telegraph Co., *The World's Telephones*, 1962 and 1972.

North America were being made by satellite in 1973, and safeguards against a satellite failure were therefore vital. In August a new £6 million communications satellite was launched to provide a spare in orbit, capable of handling 5,000 simultaneous calls.

With intense argument still raging across the Atlantic as to whether the airlines needed satellite navigation and, if so, who should provide and administer it, satellite navigation and communication for shipping took quiet but impressive steps forward. At the beginning of August, the European space ministers decided in Brussels to back a £30 million maritime satellite system. Meanwhile, the U.S. was putting its very long lead in satellite communications to good use. It was to have a maritime system operating in 1974 and a full-blown commercial system by 1976. Early in 1972 the U.S. Maritime Administration put forward a firm plan for a worldwide system to serve 4,460 of the largest vessels. By February 1973, however, the plan had to be dropped because of a budget cut. Fortunately, the U.S. Navy was looking for a communications satellite to fill a gap between the end of its Tacsat facility in September 1974 and the start of its FleetSatCom system two years later. In April, therefore, Comsat received a contract for a $70 million two-ocean system, to be shared by the U.S. Navy and civilian maritime interests.

However, most of the leading shipping nations were European, and the U.S.S.R. in particular had strong interests in keeping maritime communications out of U.S. control. This was quite different from the situation with Intelsat, where the U.S. had the lion's share of the traffic. The European Space Research Organization's OTS satellite would form the basis of a European maritime satellite project, with the U.K. supplying most of the electronics.

Cables. The largest single transatlantic cable began its journey to the bottom of the sea in June 1973. The £20 million cable, CANTAT 2, was to carry 1,800 simultaneous telephone conversations—more than all other transatlantic cables combined. Plans were also announced for a 4,000-conversation cable to be developed jointly by Britain, France, and the U.S. to come into service between the U.S. and France in 1976. Three new cable links from the U.K. to Europe, each capable of 1,260 simultaneous calls, came into service during the year. (DON BYRNE; LAURIE JOHN)

International Telecommunication Union. During 1973 membership in the International Telecommunication Union (ITU) increased to 146 with the accession to the International Telecommunication Convention of Qatar, East Germany, and Bangladesh. Papua New Guinea became the only associate member of ITU. The 28th session of the Administrative Council was held at ITU headquarters in Geneva, April 28–May 18. The council examined a report on technical cooperation during 1972. Under the ITU's various technical cooperation programs in less developed countries, 309 experts were on mission and 467 fellows were undergoing training abroad. The total cost of this assistance amounted to $8,971,377.

A Plenipotentiary Conference of the ITU met in Málaga-Torremolinos, Spain, from September 14 to October 25, for the purpose of revising the ITU's basic document. The new convention, which would come into force on Jan. 1, 1975, stressed the importance of the development of space radiocommunications.

(ITU)

ENCYCLOPÆDIA BRITANNICA FILMS. *The Information Machine* (1973); *An Introduction to Feedback* (1973).

Television and Radio

Radio and television sets in use throughout the world numbered more than 992 million in 1973. Virtually no country was without some form of radio service, and television was available in varying degrees in all industrial nations except South Africa, whose government was considering introducing it in 1975. Television sets throughout the world totaled 292 million, of which approximately 105 million, or 36%, were in the United States. Radio sets numbered about 700 million, with slightly more than half of those, or 355 million, in the U.S.

In television, the Soviet Union, with approximately 30 million sets, ranked second to the U.S., and Japan was third, with about 25 million, according to estimates compiled by *Broadcasting* for the 1974 *Broadcasting Yearbook*. Other *Broadcasting* estimates showed the United Kingdom with 20 million, West Germany 17 million, France 13 million, Italy 12 million, Canada 7.5 million, Spain 5.5 million, Poland 4.5 million, Argentina 3.8 million, Czechoslovakia 3,250,000, Australia and Sweden 3 million each, Yugoslavia 2.2 million, Austria 2.1 million, Hungary 2 million, Denmark 1.5 million, and Bulgaria 1,250,000.

There were approximately 6,390 television stations in operation throughout the world in 1973, and their distribution showed little change from recent years. About 2,100 were in the Far East, 2,000 in Western Europe, 910 in Eastern Europe, 906 in the U.S., 175 in South America, more than 80 in Canada, and 35 in Africa. Viewers' choices of programs varied widely, ranging from a single channel in some areas to ten or more in others. In the U.S. it was estimated that 98% of the television homes could receive three or more stations, 60% could receive seven or more, and 20% could receive ten or more.

More than 13,500 radio stations were operating or being built throughout the world in 1973. Most were of the amplitude modulation (AM) variety, but the number of frequency modulation (FM) stations continued to increase. The U.S. had 7,398, more than half of the world total, 3,026 of which were FM.

Organization. Achievements in technological organization for international distribution of television programs by satellite relays were much more successful in 1973 than the continuing attempts to achieve international harmony on future satellite uses. Distribution of special news coverage among countries by satellite, such as the signing of the Vietnam cease-fire agreements, the inauguration of U.S. Pres. Richard Nixon, funeral services for former president Lyndon Johnson, and developments in the Arab-Israeli war, had become routine. But efforts in the United Nations to reach agreement on more advanced international broadcasting via satellites in the future, from one country directly to home television sets in other countries, remained frustrated. The Soviet Union and Eastern Europe continued to insist that direct international broadcasts be subject to advance approval by each receiving nation. The U.S. adhered to its position that there should be an unhindered flow of information among countries, but it gained little support. Not only the Soviet bloc countries but also a growing number of small and emerging nations sided with the U.S.S.R. in demanding veto power over program importation. Aside from the prospect of having their peoples subjected to "foreign propaganda," the smaller countries feared that they would be swamped by the cultural programming of more advanced countries, weakening if not wiping out their native cultural identities.

Europe. The European Broadcasting Union (EBU) was honoured for its Eurovision activities in 1973 by receiving the first annual Directorate Award of the International Council of the National Academy of Television Arts and Sciences of the United States. The award, which followed a vote by the Academy's board of directors, was "for outstanding achievement in the arts and sciences or management of television so extraordinary as to give added lustre to the medium as an instrument of international communications and understanding." It was accepted by Charles Curran, president of the EBU and director general of the British Broadcasting Corporation (BBC).

The most significant event affecting Eurovision in 1973 was a unanimous decision by EBU's General Assembly that assured its future financial basis. This followed more than two years of detailed examination of the problem of the expense of Eurovision operations in the future, including the prospect of more high-cost, long-distance circuits being introduced to connect new small members situated on the periphery of the European broadcasting area.

The EBU General Assembly recognized that the establishment of such circuits was fair and reasonable and that they could be extended without discrimination to any new small members in accordance with the accepted philosophy of Eurovision as a mutually beneficial cooperative. One of the first countries to benefit from the assembly's decision was Turkey, which began to participate in Eurovision transmissions on a regular basis. Twenty-nine television services in 25 countries of the European broadcasting area were receiving the full Eurovision news exchange on a daily basis.

There was a marked increase generally in the number of Eurovision transmissions in the first half of 1973 (10.56%) compared with the same period in 1972. With the transmissions later in the year resulting from the Arab-Israeli war, the figures for 1973 were expected to set a record. Normally a decrease in traffic is expected in a year following one in which the Olympic Games are held.

In the area of interunion cooperation, several major events took place, including the second World Conference of Broadcasting Organizations in Rio de Janeiro, Braz., November 2–8, at the invitation of the Asociacion Interamericana de Radiodifusion and Associação Brasileira de Emissoras de Rádio e Televisão. The subjects discussed included not only communications satellites but also staff training, the problems of educational radio and television, and program exchange in the widest sense. Representatives of seven broadcasting unions as well as a North American delegation from the U.S. and Canada took part.

On the program level, the growing internationalization of television was evidenced by an increase in coproductions. As the cost of TV production mounted, many broadcasting organizations sought to share costs, particularly in the area of documentary and entertainment programming. An example was the BBC's coproduction agreement with Time-Life Broadcast Inc. In 1973 the world TV program market was recognized as becoming increasingly important, as a result of the awareness of export opportunities and the desire to recoup costs, especially by the strong producing countries (the U.S., U.K., and France). Many countries were unable to make their own programs to any large extent, and the international market, therefore, was becoming more important for them. Whereas some countries were able to provide a large part of their own programming—the U.S. made about 95% of its own output, and Japan 97.5%—many imported large quantities of material: Guatemala bought 84%, New Zealand 75%, Malaysia 71%.

Many countries expressed concern that the trade in television programs should not inhibit indigenous production, or project one nation's point of view on the world. There was also some anxiety about the imbalance in the flow of news material in the world TV news system. Many less developed countries urged more coverage of their affairs with less attention given to the developed world. This was discussed at a special meeting of broadcasting unions in Cologne, W.Ger., in May.

Apart from these moves on the international level, television remained embroiled with various governments as well as with all kinds of social and political pressure groups. There was, however, some amelioration in charges that had been heard in 1970–72 that TV was harmful and positively damaging to society and that it was in the hands of privileged minorities charged with reporting the news.

The Watergate revelations were certainly responsible in some ways for dampening criticism of the

WIDE WORLD

Members of scientist Jacques Yves Cousteau's expedition move cautiously among ice floes in preparation for a TV documentary on Antarctica. The four-part series, based on more than four months of exploration, was televised during the fall of 1973.

U.S. media, in particular television, which had been singled out by many U.S. politicians as biased against the Nixon administration. In Europe there continued to be some friction between broadcasters and national governments. In the U.K. the British government postponed its expected inquiry into television and radio services until the late 1970s, on the advice of the Television Advisory Committee. This group had reported at the end of 1972 that there would be no major changes in television distribution technology that would affect the whole population before the 1980s. The government decided, therefore, to allow the status quo to continue and renewed the legal instruments on which the BBC and the Independent Broadcasting Authority were based until 1981. The committee, under the chairmanship of Sir Robert Cockburn, also considered that other means of satellite and cable distribution would not be important for some time and that two new channels could become available in Britain before 1980 as a result of reengineering the existing systems.

Britain, however, did launch commercial radio in October 1973, when the first two stations began operations in London: London Broadcasting, specializing in news; and Capital Radio, which featured popular music and more general material. Another three stations were to open in 1974, preceding a 60-station network. The government also licensed five cable-television stations, the first of which had begun operation in July 1972.

In France, after revelations that there had been various abuses of the state broadcasting systems, mainly through the use of clandestine publicity, there was a major review of the Office de Radiodiffusion et Télévision Française (ORTF) in 1972. This resulted in a new statute and the appointment of a new president, Arthur Conte. Although himself a conservative Gaullist, Conte in 1973 defied the government by suggesting, with a letter as proof, that political interference and financial blackmail had been practiced by officials of the state in order to influence ORTF staff. Conte was dismissed and replaced in October by Marceau Long, former secretary-general responsible for administration at the Defense Ministry.

Proposals for establishing private broadcasting organizations in France were rejected, and the government monopoly was maintained. The minister of posts and telecommunications, however, would be able to grant licenses for cable and closed-circuit distribution outside the ORTF monopoly. The ORTF was to be supervised by the premier or one of his appointees.

In Canada a Green Paper on communications policy proposed by the minister of communications, Gérard Pelletier, called for the provision of fuller and more diverse Canadian sources of information, entertainment, and cultural and educational material of excellent quality; the development and preservation of high-quality telecommunications systems linking all parts of the country, so that as many Canadians as possible might have equitable access to the services provided; the efficient use of available skills and material resources; and the assurance of Canadian control, either through regulation or by restrictions on foreign ownership, of the entities offering telecommunications services of all kinds.

Throughout 1973 governments and industry in many countries extended their interest in cable television. In the U.K. four experimental stations—Greenwich, Bristol, Sheffield, and Swindon—were in operation by the end of 1973 with the small station of Wellingborough to follow. The stations were licensed until 1976 and could only broadcast local material. They were not allowed to advertise, and could not pass on their costs in higher subscriptions. No public money was involved.

Proposals for a number of cable-TV stations were made in France. They were likely to be based on rules and regulations differing from those in Britain; they would include an interest by the state organization, made up of the French post office and the ORTF. In addition, the local press, the municipalities, and private enterprise were to be involved. The proposals had to offer at least three ORTF channels, while another three were to be made available for the state corporations. Six others could be for public use.

In Italy the small cable-television company Telebiela broke the monopoly of Radiotelevisione Italiana (RAI) by redistributing foreign programs and making its own cable material, leading to a large increase in the number of cable-TV stations. An attempt by Premier Giulio Andreotti to stop the station's activities led to a major row in May within the Italian coalition government between the majority Christian Democrats and the small Republican Party, which favoured cable television. Andreotti was left without a majority, though he succeeded in stopping the development of cable television in Italy and maintaining the monopoly of RAI.

United States. U.S. homes equipped with colour television sets numbered 43.4 million as of Oct. 1, 1973, a gain of 12 million, or 38%, since July 1, 1972, according to estimates in *Broadcasting*. Virtually all network programs and most of those originated by individual stations were broadcast in colour; the chief exceptions were old movies filmed originally in black-and-white.

Cable television (CATV) failed to make as much progress in 1973 as many exponents had predicted it would after the FCC had adopted new rules in 1972 permitting it to expand from rural areas and small towns into larger cities. Its slow advance was attributed in part to the nation's unsettled economy; increases in interest rates were especially dampening in an industry like CATV, which depended heavily on outside financing for initial construction. Both internal and external pressures, particularly a campaign organized by the National Association of Broadcasters against pay-TV operations via CATV, and controversy over CATV efforts to relax FCC limits on the sports and entertainment programming carried by cable also played a part in the slowdown in CATV growth in 1973. In mid-1973 *Broadcasting* reported that 2,996 cable-TV systems were in operation in 5,663 U.S. communities, serving approximately 7,250,000 homes, about 10.1% of all U.S. TV homes, in comparison with about 5.4 million, or 9%, of all TV homes in 1972.

The prospect of U.S. domestic satellite operations beginning early in 1974 was foreseen after the FCC gave its go-ahead to six applicants: Western Union Telegraph Co. in January and five others, including American Telephone and Telegraph Co. (AT & T), Communications Satellite Corp. (Comsat), and RCA Corp., in September.

In a court case, NBC, ABC, and CBS failed in an effort to have a government antitrust suit against them dismissed or stayed on grounds that the basic charges—that the networks improperly control prime evening program time—are under the FCC's primary jurisdiction. In dismissing the networks' motions, however, U.S. District Judge Robert J. Kelleher also said in his October ruling that, in view of the "real and substantial problem" that might arise in trying to accommodate antitrust policies to those of the FCC, prosecution of the antitrust suits might be "unnecessary." The FCC, however, was reported by *Broadcasting* to be considering an even wider ranging inquiry that would investigate, among other things, network ownerships of stations, programs, and production facilities and perhaps reduce their interests in all three areas.

The administration of public broadcasting was torn by dissension during the first half of 1973, chiefly in a bitter jurisdictional dispute between the Corporation for Public Broadcasting (CPB), which allocated funds to the noncommercial stations and also demanded a key role in program selection, scheduling, and distribution, and the Public Broadcasting Service (PBS), which handled program scheduling and distribution and resisted CPB's attempts to become dominant in program matters. In late May, however, the two sides reached an accord and entered into a "partnership," in which, essentially, CPB would make program-funding decisions, PBS would retain jurisdiction over scheduling, the PBS network would be free to carry programs financed by foundations or other nongovernment sources as well as those funded through CPB, and a system of joint CPB-PBS review and appeals procedures would be established to reconcile future differences in these areas. In the meantime Congress passed and President Nixon signed a two-year, $120 million authorization bill for CPB funding in fiscal 1974 and 1975.

Broadcasters, meanwhile, remained under heavy pressures in 1973, although some of the forces changed in intensity. The Nixon administration's displeasure with television network news reporting, typified in earlier times by attacks by then Vice-Pres. Spiro Agnew and lesser officials, reached its most intense expression on October 26 when President Nixon, in a nationally televised news conference, branded network news the most "outrageous, vicious, distorted reporting" he had seen in "27 years of public life." It was by far the strongest attack the president had made and one of the first by any administration official since the Watergate scandal began to command national attention in the spring of 1973.

Pressures from minority groups and others dissatisfied with individual station operations continued to grow, reflected in most cases by petitions to the FCC to deny renewals of existing station licenses and in others by applications for the licenses themselves. A count by *Broadcasting* found 143 such cases pending in January 1973, up from approximately 100 six months earlier. Many stations under challenge undertook to negotiate settlements with their challengers, and some succeeded.

Broadcasters worked hard to get legislative relief from this problem. Clay Whitehead, director of the White House Office of Telecommunications Policy, had laid some groundwork in December 1972 when he said that broadcast license terms should be extended from the current three years to five, with the stations, in turn, taking responsibility for the programming they carry, whether locally originated or supplied by the networks. In the ensuing months, broadcasters were able to get scores of bills introduced in Congress to extend their license terms and provide varying degrees of relief from challengers. In mid-October the House Communications and Power Subcommittee voted out a bill that would provide for four-year licenses but also would direct the FCC to strip incumbent licensees of their stations if rival applicants promised a "clearly superior" program service.

Criticism of television programming for children remained another thorn for broadcasters in 1973, although the networks did curtail advertising in children's programming and introduced both new series and special programs presenting news and information as well as entertainment in child-oriented formats. The FCC, after lengthy hearings, was considering a ban on advertising in programs aimed at preschoolers, setting limits on advertising in all other children's programming, and requiring broadcasters to provide certain amounts of programming aimed at specific age groups, perhaps on weekday afternoons as well as on weekends.

Pay-cable, the CATV version of subscription television, was becoming a bigger and bigger threat in the opinion of many broadcasters in 1973. Over-the-air pay-TV, once a primary concern, had been virtually written off as a practical threat, but the number of cable systems offering special programs to subscribers willing to pay extra for them was beginning to grow. Research developed by the National Association of Theatre Owners and expanded by *Broadcasting* showed in October that pay-cable services were in operation on CATV systems serving more than 437,500 subscribers in 35 cities, and that 28 other cable systems, serving almost 260,000 subscribers, were preparing for pay-cable operations. What disturbed the broadcasters and theatre owners most were the types of programs that pay-cable subscribers found most appealing: feature movies and sports, two of television's mainstays.

Occasional bright spots appeared in the clouds over broadcasters in 1973. One of the brightest came in May when the U.S. Supreme Court reaffirmed the traditional view of broadcasters as public trustees having the journalistic responsibility for deciding what issues would be discussed on their stations and by whom, with the fairness doctrine—under which broadcasters must present all significant sides in dealing with important public issues—as the only constraint. The court's 7–2 decision, overturning a lower-court ruling, appeared to deal a serious blow to growing insistence by some groups that individuals and groups have a right of access to present their views directly through the broadcast media. The decision specifically struck down a lower-court interpretation of the fairness doctrine as requiring broadcasters to sell time for the presentation of editorial comment.

Programming. In its coverage of major news events, broadcasting repeatedly demonstrated its capacity to reach homes virtually throughout the world in 1973. Sending segments of news coverage from one country to another by satellite for inclusion in both network and local newscasts had become routine, as, in fact, had the sight of far-off events that once would have kept TV viewers at their sets for hours; public interest in the Skylab mission, for instance, was dwarfed by the attraction of the Senate Watergate hearings in progress at the same time. The public had come to expect coverage of such events and to take it for granted.

In entertainment programming, U.S.-produced Westerns, comedies, and mysteries remained among the top favourites in many countries. The most popular included "Bonanza," "Gunsmoke," "The Carol Burnett Show," "Bewitched," and "Perry Mason," all

WIDE WORLD

William Conrad was proving that leading men need not always be "tall, dark, and handsome." His TV series, "Cannon," barreled through a second year of high ratings in 1973 on the basis of the rotund actor's believability.

of which were being seen in scores of countries. U.S. TV film distributors, who had found foreign markets sluggish in the early 1970s, mounted a two-pronged campaign that appeared to increase sales and also produce higher prices. The Swedish broadcasting system, for example, agreed to double the going rate for a one-hour program from $1,000 to $2,000, and Spain agreed to pay $990 per hour rather than $660. Looking back, the distributors concluded that their estimate of $85 million in foreign sales in 1972 had been too low by about $10 million. For 1973 the figure was expected to approach $100 million.

United States. The FCC's prime-time access rule and its effect on television programming continued to generate controversy in 1973, and at the end of November the FCC moved to ease some of its restrictions. Since 1971 the rule had prohibited networks from providing more than three hours of prime-time programming to their affiliates in the 50 largest markets; in practice, however, all affiliates were affected. Thus, all had to provide their own programming for a total of four prime-time hours a week. FCC had hoped the rule would diversify the sources of programming as well as the programming itself, while also increasing the amount of community-oriented content offered by stations.

It appeared clear that the rule had fallen short of its objectives. Though supporters saw in it an opportunity for more "quality" programming and what some called an escape from "network dominance," it admittedly had accomplished relatively little in these areas. A study submitted to the FCC by four major independent producers early in the year reported that the number of program sources filling access time periods had declined in two years from 53 independent production companies to 34. The percentage of foreign-produced series in these periods had risen from 0.1 to 20%, and game shows in access periods had increased by 35%, to a point where they occupied almost half of all access time.

The same study also showed that virtually all syndicated programs scheduled in access time were revivals or continuations of programs formerly seen on the networks. The five most shown were "To Tell the Truth," "Truth or Consequences," "What's My Line?," "Hee Haw," and "The Lawrence Welk Show." In a report submitted later the FCC's economic consultant, Alan Pearce, also concluded that the rule had strengthened rather than weakened the networks' control over prime-time programming. The reduction in prime-time programming by the networks, Pearce said, created greater advertiser demand for commercial time in the network programming that remained.

After extensive hearings the FCC announced in late November that it was instructing its staff to draft changes that, among other things, would bar the networks only from the half-hour between 7:30 and 8:00 P.M. (Eastern Time) Monday through Saturday; affiliates in the 50 largest markets would be required to program 7:30–8:00 P.M. with nonnetwork material except for children's specials, documentaries, or public-affairs programs produced by the networks, which might be shown in one period per week. Those stations would also be required to devote "some portion" of their access periods to "minority-affairs programs, children's programs, and programs directed to the needs and problems of the station's community and coverage area." In addition, the half-hour from 7:00 to 7:30 P.M. would be removed from prime-time classification, making it available for network use.

The new television season that opened in September 1973 put heavier emphasis on drama, chiefly of the crime and courtroom variety, and on situation comedies. There were fewer 60-minute and 90-minute series and more half-hour entries. Both within regular programming and in documentaries and other special programs, television continued to try to come to grips with contemporary and often controversial problems and issues, such as abortion, drug abuse, homosexuality, and prison reform. Many of the new series, especially comedies, employed sexual references—though usually more suggestively than explicitly—far more than in the past. Critics' objections to what they called "permissiveness" in both theme and handling of many programs led the presidents of all three networks to speak out publicly in defense of television's need to deal with contemporary concerns in contemporary terms and to meet the changing tastes of the public, although all three also stressed that broadcasters must be careful to draw a line between what one called "liberty and license."

© CBS TELEVISION NETWORK

In "The Lie," Ingmar Bergman's first television drama, George Segal and Shirley Knight play an affluent suburban couple confronted with the barrenness of their married life. CBS aired the U.S. premiere, April 24, 1973.

Some programs earlier in 1973 had created intense controversy. When CBS scheduled "Sticks and Bones," a bitter allegorical drama about a blinded war veteran driven to suicide on his return home, for showing on March 9—when the first U.S. prisoners of war were beginning to return from Vietnam—more than one-third of the network's affiliates refused to carry it. CBS postponed the program, and when it was finally presented, on August 17, half of the normal network stations substituted movies or other local programming.

Another controversy developed over opposition, led by the U.S. Catholic Conference, to CBS's scheduling of reruns of a two-part episode dealing with abortion on the "Maude" comedy series, one of 1973's top-rated programs; when the reruns were presented, 39 stations out of a normal "Maude" lineup of 198 refused to show them. CBS, recognizing that abortion is a controversial question, granted free time for a Catholic Conference official and others to discuss the issue in one of its regular news reports.

In its 25th annual Emmy Awards balloting, the National Academy of Television Arts and Sciences voted "The Waltons," a wholesome, down-to-earth series about a Virginia mountain family during the Depression, as the best drama series of the 1972–73 season. "All in the Family" was again named the best comedy and "The Julie Andrews Hour," though dropped at the end of the season, was designated the most outstanding variety and musical series.

Sports continued to command large audiences and high prices in 1973. *Broadcasting* estimated that television and radio networks and stations paid $42,385,000 for broadcast rights to major league baseball games and $69,903,000 for professional and college football games. Both represented new records: the baseball total was up from *Broadcasting*'s 1972 estimate by $1.3 million, while football increased by almost $1 million. The football figure did not include a favourable law for TV voted by Congress in September; subsequently signed by President Nixon, it drastically changed the "blackout" policy under which professional football prohibited local live telecasts of home games. The law ended home-city blackouts for games that had been completely sold out 72 hours before game time. If the legislation was a boon for TV, however, it represented potential disaster for many radio stations, which collectively had paid an estimated $2,860,000 for football broadcast rights but stood to lose to television the bulk of the home-game audiences.

Complete, live coverage of the first round of the Senate Watergate hearings, stretching from May into August, totaled more than 319 network hours and, by *Broadcasting*'s estimates, cost ABC, CBS, and NBC at least $7 million and perhaps as much as $10 million. But it also attracted audiences substantially larger than the network entertainment programming it replaced. The hearings also produced the first rotation agreement among the networks, with ABC, CBS, and NBC each taking responsibility for full coverage on one hearing day out of three. They dropped the rotation pattern in the second phase of the hearings, and provided coverage primarily through the presentation of taped highlights on regular newscasts.

In radio a budding trend, so-called topless radio, involving explicit on-air discussion of sexual problems by telephone callers and program hosts, was cut short early in the year when the FCC fined one station $2,000 for allegedly "obscene" programming and the National Association of Broadcasters went on record condemning "tasteless and vulgar program content, whether explicit or by sexually oriented innuendo."

In public broadcasting, the Children's Television Workshop's "Sesame Street" for preschool children and its "The Electric Company" for second, third, and fourth graders remained the most conspicuously successful programs. Despite severe financial problems the Public Broadcasting Service introduced several new programs in the 1973 fall season, although some well received programs from earlier years had to be dropped at least temporarily. New entries included an interview series produced by the National Public Affairs Center for Television, a nine-part BBC adaptation of Leo Tolstoi's *War and Peace,* a five-part study of the five leading causes of death in the U.S., and a series of dramatic programs titled "Hollywood Television Theatre." Among PBS shows being dropped because they were unable to find adequate funding were two black-oriented series, "Soul!" and "Black Journal." Tony Brown, executive producer for the latter, subsequently announced plans for the formation of a Corporation for Blacks in Public Broadcasting to ensure that blacks get equal treatment with whites.

Europe. At the Geneva session of the Conference on Security and Cooperation in Europe (CSCE) the key role of television in any forthcoming improvement in East-West relations was well understood. Although the Soviet Union had always shown extreme suspicion of any plan for allowing Western expression on Soviet TV screens, Poland and Bulgaria had both produced plans for cooperative productions with the West in films, radio, and television.

Despite skepticism from some senior BBC and ORTF officials, the BBC itself suggested a series of Inter-European current affairs TV programs, to be screened 6 or 12 times annually. The programs would concern European problems and interests and be conducted by representatives of about 6 of the 35 CSCE participant states. The right to participate would rotate among the nations, and a balance of views would be the aim.

Among the most spectacular TV events of the year were the royal wedding in Britain and the war in the Middle East. The marriage of Princess Anne and Capt. Mark Phillips (*see* BIOGRAPHY) in Westminster Abbey, London, on November 14 was seen by up to 500 million viewers throughout the world, and gave ample proof of the British talent for colourful pageantry. As a result of administrative arrangements which had already been made between EBU and the Arab States Broadcasting Union, television viewers in Europe and North America were able to watch the Arab-Israeli war in October by means of daily satellite linkups.

Two major events involving EBU radio activities were a special stereophonic radio production of Darius Milhaud's immense opera *Christophe Colomb* (first performed in Berlin in 1930), which proved to be the most expensive joint radio undertaking of its kind in the history of broadcasting (undertaken in Brussels by Radiodiffusion Télévision Belge), and the first live stereophonic international relays in many parts of Western Europe. The first concert of the 1973–74 season from Vienna, Aus., on September 24, was broadcast live in stereo and relayed as such to eight countries.

The first intercontinental stereophonic transmission took place on May 15 when a concert given in

WIDE WORLD

Four years of court battles came to an end April 6, 1973, when comedians Tom (left) and Dick Smothers were awarded $766,300 in a breach-of-contract suit against CBS. The television network canceled their comedy series in April 1969.

Paris was relayed live to San Francisco in the U.S. The signals were conveyed across the Atlantic by an Intelsat 4 satellite and then, after demodulation and remodulation, transmitted over a television picture channel to San Francisco.

The issue of censorship and public taste remained firmly before British audiences in 1973, especially in view of a number of sensational events highlighted by the media. Of course, the U.S. Watergate hearings, watched by millions, led some to question as to how far TV could or should be used as an accusatorial medium; for some such reason the Independent Broadcasting Authority (IBA) in late January banned, two days before its scheduled screening, a program entitled "The Friends and Influences of Mr. John L. Poulson," part of the "World in Action" series. As a result many TV screens throughout Britain were blacked out several days later by a strike of protesting technicians and cameramen. Three months later a new version of the tale was unveiled with minimal revisions, skillfully tracing the rise and fall of Europe's once most successful architect, who now faced charges of corruption.

The screening of a controversial ITV program on Andy Warhol, pop artist and sex-film maker, was held up in January by decision of a Court of Appeal, but later was screened. Sports commentator Ross McWhirter had taken the case to court hoping for a total ban, but instead was forced to pay part of IBA's court expenses. Lord Denning, master of the rolls, said that it was for the IBA and not the courts to act as censor.

In the area of drama the BBC, on its second channel, offered an adaptation of Katherine Mansfield's brief life, interspersed with her own fictitious characters, all played, somewhat confusingly, by Vanessa Redgrave. A June documentary drama, "The Roses of Eyam," depicted the horrors of the 1665 plague-hit village of Eyam and the courage of its occupants who shut themselves off to stop the infection from spreading, sacrificing 260 of their original 350 inhabitants. Harlech TV produced John Hopkins' "Divorce His: Divorce Hers," built for and around Richard Burton and Elizabeth Taylor. Revealing with painfully repetitive tedium (in colour) the breakup of a wealthy marriage, it was most notable for its lavish sets, shot expensively on location in Rome. The BBC 2 serialization of Alberto Moravia's *Two Women* in June was a rather disappointing follow-up to the excellent BBC adaptations of previous novels—Heinrich Mann's *Der Untertan* (*Man of Straw*), Guy de Maupassant's *Bel-Ami,* Aldous Huxley's *Point Counter Point,* and the exceptional version of Jean-Paul Sartre's *Les Chemins de la liberté* ("The Roads to Freedom").

On the lighter side fatuous quizmasters continued to patronize, and mediocre nightclub entertainers to revel in their prejudices. ATV spent £150,000 on the "It's Tarbuck" comedy series, which squirted out its stock jokes on blacks, Jews, wives, mothers-in-law, Pakistanis, pop stars, dockers, homosexuals, and football players. Similar material was available in the "The Comedians" series. One successful comedy series was "Some Mothers Do 'Ave 'Em," polished slapstick with Michael Crawford portraying a walking disaster named Frank Spencer. After only two episodes it broke all records by attracting an audience of 12 million.

A BBC 2 highlight was Jacob Bronowski's series "The Ascent of Man," a more ambitious complement to Lord Clark's "Civilisation" in that it attempted to show man's entire cultural development. The program took three years to make and was filmed on location in 30 countries.

In 1972–73 the BBC broadcast 950 hours of sports (15% of output); this compared with 1,103 hours of talks, documentaries, and informational programs; 492 hours of drama; 451 hours of light entertainment; 143 hours of religion; and 122 hours of music. In the summer plans were disclosed for a four-year, 4,000-hour, £15 million sports schedule, designed to lead up to the Montreal Olympics in 1976. ITV in contrast had offered only 490 hours of sports, having at its disposal only one channel.

Helping to democratize TV away from being a mere spectator sport or soporific were a series of "do-it-yourself" TV shows ranging from the "Midweek" phone-in to "Open Door," an experiment in amateur production. "Open Door" began in April for 13 programs under the direction of Rowan Ayers; screened at 11:30 P.M., it was unobserved by 99% of viewers. Only extremists were banned from the programs, and requests from minority groups with views to express were so overwhelming that the series was given an additional run in the fall.

In The Netherlands the "Barend Servet Show," screened on Dec. 14, 1972, caused an uproar by including the first nude male on Dutch TV and a scene involving a woman resembling Queen Juliana peeling brussels sprouts and singing part of the national anthem. A dramatic highlight of Dutch TV was a play on euthanasia that used the record of a four-day-old court case as its basis.

In Sweden the interest of television in 1973 was largely concentrated on current affairs at home and abroad. TV reporter Erik Eriksson was one of the first Western journalists allowed into North Vietnam and the first permitted to provide regular news from there. His reporting attracted wide interest throughout the world. Because of favourable circumstances television was able to provide almost round-the-clock coverage of an airplane hijacking and of a six-day bank siege in Stockholm. (*See* CRIME.)

In other areas Swedish television had a successful year by winning first prize in the Montreux Festival competition for the best entertainment program with "The N.S.V.I.P.s" (Not So Very Important People). Starring Lee Hazlewood and Lill Lindfors, it won both the Golden Rose and the International Press jury prize. Swedish television also won the Prix Italia drama award for "Krocken" ("Crash"), by Bengt Bratt.

In November the French interview program "Radioscopie," produced by the France-Inter service, was gagged minutes before an intended hour-long interview with ORTF's ex-director general Arthur Conte, who had just published his account of his 16 months' service with ORTF, giving a series of unflattering portraits of members of the government including Pres. Georges Pompidou.

The Communist broadcasting services had no such problems as the French government. Communist broadcasting continued to stress the need for objective assessments of news but interpreted objectivity on a strictly dogmatic basis. Soviet television gave viewers a long look at a U.S. apparently on the verge of civil war in "Washington Correspondent," produced by the Belorusfilm cinema studio. Much use was made of real newsreels showing anti-Vietnam demonstrations, draft-card burning, and flag tearing, while the American dream as depicted in commercials and billboards was skillfully contrasted with popular unrest.

Japan. Japan celebrated its 20th anniversary of the beginning of TV broadcasting in 1973, and so journalists' comments and criticisms reexamining the condition of Japanese television were conspicuous in newspapers and magazines. Riding on the crest of the nation's high economic growth during the 1960s, Japanese television continued to expand. In Tokyo TV programs were available on seven different channels.

Both the government network NHK and all Japanese commercial broadcasters gave full TV coverage to Prime Minister Kakuei Tanaka's historic visit to China in September 1972. Japanese reporters were also allowed to visit North Korea. Their reports coincided with the excavation of an ancient tomb, together with some beautiful wall paintings, in the suburbs of Nara City, home of the ancient Japanese Imperial Court, revealing the ancient cultural relations between the two countries.

Australia. In Australia the return to power in late 1972 of the first Labor government in 23 years, and its establishment of a promised Department of the Media to control radio and television (previously handled by the postmaster general's department), meant that both media could expect more stringent programming impositions. They were not disappointed. Radio was required immediately to increase to 10% the amount of music broadcast by Australian performers, rising to 30% within three years; this was in addition to the existing 5% quota for works by Australian composers. To replace television's existing quota directives, a points system designed to raise standards of locally made programs was announced and began on Aug. 1, 1973, for a trial period of six months. It heavily favoured "culture" programs such as serious music and poetry.

(RUFUS W. CRATER; SOL TAISHOFF; MICHAEL TYPE; TERENCE HUGHES)

Amateur Radio. The launch of Oscar 6 (Orbiting Satellite Carrying Amateur Radio) late in 1972 marked the beginning of a new era of amateur radio in space, a second stage in the development of amateur satellite communications. During 1973 the amateur satellite program moved from a stunning but limited demonstration of scientific competence, imagination, and ingenuity to a capability of wider use by amateurs with ordinary equipment and operating skills. Oscar 6 contained a translator that received signals in the 145.9–146.0 MHz range (uplink) and retransmitted them at 29.45–29.55 MHz (downlink). In this manner more than 1,000 amateurs on all continents successfully conducted two-way communications via the satellite.

In June the FCC issued an announcement of proposed rulemaking, which, if implemented, would result in the reassignment of the upper megahertz of the 220–225 MHz amateur band to a new Class E citizens radio service. Believing that the proposed expansion of the citizens radio service through reallocation of present amateur frequencies was unjustified and unnecessary, the amateurs' representative organization, the American Radio Relay League, and thousands of individual amateurs registered strong opposition to the FCC's proposal. (MORGAN W. GODWIN)

See also Advertising; Astronautics; Motion Pictures; Music; Telecommunications.

ENCYCLOPÆDIA BRITANNICA FILMS. *Getting the News* (1967).

Tennis

Administrative problems again beset tennis during 1973, centring on the formation in September 1972 of the Association of Tennis Professionals (ATP) under the presidency of Cliff Drysdale of South Africa and the executive directorship of Jack Kramer of the United States. The new organization questioned the right of the International Lawn Tennis Federation (ILTF), the world's governing body since 1913, to suspend ATP members and demanded a share in the overall management of tournaments in which the association's members took part.

Matters came to a head when Nikki Pilic of Yugoslavia was suspended by his national association for not playing in the Davis Cup, a sentence later confirmed, though reduced in time, after appeal to the ILTF. The sentence barred Pilic from competing in the Italian championships and at Wimbledon. The Italian ruling body defied the ban and allowed Pilic to play. The Wimbledon authorities averred that the ILTF edict would be followed. ATP, on behalf of Pilic, appealed to the English High Court for an interim injunction to restrain both the Wimbledon authorities and the ILTF from enforcing the ban, doing so in the expectation that only a formal defense would be offered and that Pilic would be able to compete. However, a full defense of the action proved successful, whereupon ATP called on its members to boycott the Wimbledon championships. About 80 ATP members did so, leaving the men's entry at Wimbledon far short of its normal strength. Three ATP members, Roger Taylor of Great Britain, Ilie Nastase of Romania, and Ray Keldie of Australia, played despite the boycott. Taylor and Nastase were later fined $5,000 and Keldie $1,000 by ATP. Later in the year, accord was reached between ATP and the ILTF on the composition of a joint committee in control of tournaments.

There was also a dispute early in the year between the U.S. Lawn Tennis Association and some of the leading women players about an unsanctioned professional women's circuit of tournaments in the U.S. Agreement was later reached, though those players participating in the unsanctioned events were held not eligible to qualify for prize money in the Grand Prix series. In midsummer the leading women players organized themselves into an association of their own, the Women's International Tennis Association, with Billie Jean King (*see* BIOGRAPHY) as president.

The ILTF and World Championship Tennis (WCT) remained in accord. WCT, confining itself to the promotion of tournaments, successfully staged a two-group series of events throughout the world. The leaders in this competition qualified for a final tournament in Dallas in May that ranked as a major event of the year. WCT announced that for 1974 a threefold series of tournaments would engage 84 players. Difficulties for 1974 were indicated by the formation in the U.S. of World Team Tennis, with franchises granted to 16 cities competing on a league basis between May and August. Plans were for 48 men and 48 women to be put under contract with no possibility of their being able to take part in any of the traditional events staged in Europe at that time, except for Wimbledon.

Large prizes were earned by leading players. Top winner was Nastase, with $228,750. Stan Smith of the U.S. took $204,225, the second highest earnings. The U.S. Open championships at Forest Hills, N.Y., in September broke new ground in offering equal prize money for both the men's and women's singles, with $25,000 as the top prize in both cases.

A unique feature of the year was the staging of two highly publicized singles contests between a man and a woman. Bobby Riggs, born 1918, the Wimbledon champion of 1939, was involved in both. At Ramona, Calif., in May he beat Margaret Court, born 1942, 6–2, 6–1. At Houston in September Mrs. King, born 1943, defeated Riggs 6–4, 6–3, 6–3 before a crowd of 30,472, a record total for a tennis match.

Men's Competition. *Singles.* At the end of 1973 the ILTF Grand Prix competition was won by Nastase for the second successive year when he took the Masters' tournament staged in Boston. In the final he beat Tom Okker (Neth.) 6–3, 7–5, 4–6, 6–3.

The Australian championships for 1973 took place in Melbourne at the end of 1972. The defending titleholder, Ken Rosewall, was surprisingly beaten in his first match by Karl Meiler of West Germany, and the tournament was won by John Newcombe, who beat Onny Parun of New Zealand 6–3, 6–7, 7–5, 6–1 in the final.

The top four players in each of two groups, based on the outcome of 11 previous tournaments, qualified for the WCT final tournament at Dallas in May. They were Smith, the Australians John Alexander, Roy Emerson, Rod Laver, and Rosewall, Roger Taylor from the U.K., and Marty Riessen and Arthur Ashe of the U.S. In the semifinals Smith beat Laver 4–6, 6–4, 7–6, 7–5, and Ashe defeated Rosewall 6–4, 6–2, 5–7, 1–6, 6–2. Smith won the finals from Ashe 6–3, 6–3, 4–6, 6–4.

Nastase won the French championship for the first time, and without losing a set in any round. In the finals he defeated Pilic 6–3, 6–3, 6–0. The Romanian also won the Italian championship, being hard-pressed only in his semifinal match by the Italian Paolo Bertolucci 6–2, 3–6, 6–3, 3–6, 6–0. In the final he overwhelmed Manuel Orantes of Spain 6–1, 6–1, 6–1.

For Billie Jean King it was a very good year. Here representing the U.S., she overcomes Australian Kerry Harris during Wimbledon competition, June 29, 1973.

KEYSTONE

The men's entry for the Wimbledon championship was, because of the boycott by ATP, short of its normal standard. The top seed, Nastase, lost in the fourth round to Sandy Mayer of the U.S. Björn Borg of Sweden, only 17, distinguished himself and achieved wide popularity by his precocious skill. He reached the quarterfinals before losing to Roger Taylor. Jan Kodes of Czechoslovakia won the title, beating Alex Metreveli of the U.S.S.R. 6–1, 9–8, 6–3.

Newcombe won the most representative meeting of the year, the U.S. Open championship at Forest Hills. Kodes reached the final after defeating Smith in a notable semifinal contest 7–5, 6–7, 1–6, 6–1, 7–5. Newcombe then beat Kodes 6–4, 1–6, 4–6, 6–2, 6–3.

Doubles. Newcombe distinguished himself by taking four important titles with three different partners. He won the Australian with compatriot Mal Anderson, the French and Italian with Okker and the U.S. with Owen Davidson. The Wimbledon title was taken by Nastase and Jim Connors of the U.S. WCT staged a "World Doubles Championship" in Montreal in May. Smith and Bob Lutz won the final against Okker and Riessen 6–2, 7–6, 6–0.

Davis Cup. In zone competition for the Davis Cup Romania won section "A" of the European Zone, and Czechoslovakia triumphed in section "B." Australia defeated Japan and India to win the Eastern Zone, and the U.S. beat Mexico and Chile for the American Zone title. The contest with Chile was notable for the doubles match, which the U.S. won 7–9, 37–39, 8–6, 6–1, 6–3. In the interzone semifinals the U.S., led by Stan Smith and Marty Riessen, defeated Romania 4–1 at Alamo, Calif. John Newcombe and Rod Laver led Australia into the finals with a 4–1 triumph over Czechoslovakia at Melbourne.

In the finals, held at Cleveland, O., November 30–December 2, Australia decisively defeated the U.S. 5–0. Newcombe and Laver each won their singles matches from Smith and Tom Gorman and teamed together to take the doubles from Smith and Erik Van Dillen.

Women's Competition. *Singles.* The Grand Prix at the end of 1972 was won by Mrs. King. Her form during 1973 was marred by spells of injury, and the dominant player was Margaret Court of Australia. The latter won the Australian title for the 11th time in all. In the final she beat her compatriot Evonne Goolagong 6–4, 7–5 to win without the loss of a set. She was also conspicuously successful in the circuit organized by the women's professional group in the United States, winning 12 out of 16 tournaments. Mrs. Court won the French championship for the fifth time after a notable final of 6–7, 7–6, 6–4 against Chris Evert of the U.S. Mrs. Court did not challenge for the Italian title, and it was won by Miss Goolagong. She defeated Miss Evert 7–6, 6–0 in the finals.

Mrs. King came into her own at Wimbledon where she increased the number of titles won there to 17. Mrs. Court was beaten in the semifinals by Miss Evert 6–1, 1–6, 6–1. Mrs. King won her semifinal match against Miss Goolagong 6–3, 5–7, 6–3 and then beat Miss Evert in the finals 6–0, 7–5. Unlike the men's events, those for the women at Wimbledon represented the top world talent and contributed to the great spectator interest at the tournament. The attendance was 300,172, the second highest recorded figure.

In the U.S. Open championship at Forest Hills Mrs. King defaulted in the third round to her compatriot Julie Heldman because of illness. Mrs. Court won the title after three hard rounds. In the quarterfinals she beat Virginia Wade of Great Britain 7–6, 7–6 and in the semifinals Miss Evert 7–5, 2–6, 6–2. In the final she defeated Miss Goolagong 7–6, 5–7, 6–2.

Doubles. The most successful pair, in terms of major titles, was Mrs. Court and Miss Wade. They won the Australian, French, and U.S. titles. Miss Wade partnered Olga Morozova of the U.S.S.R. to take the Italian championship. Mrs. King and Rosemary Casals (U.S.) won at Wimbledon but were beaten in the Forest Hills finals by Mrs. Court and Miss Wade.

Federation Cup. Held in Bad Homburg, W.Ger., the international women's team championship was won by Australia for the sixth time. Miss Goolagong, Patti Coleman, and Janet Young made up the Australian team, and they did not lose a rubber in any of four matches, beating Japan 2–0, Indonesia 3–0, West Germany 3–0, and, in the final, South Africa 3–0.

Wightman Cup. The United States won 5–2 against Great Britain at the Longwood Cricket Club, Chestnut Hill, Mass. The U.S. team included Chris Evert, Patti Hogan, Linda Tuero, Marita Redondo and Jeanne Evert, while the British had Miss Wade, Veronica Burton, Glynis Coles, Lindsey Beaven, and Lesley Charles. (LANCE TINGAY)

Thailand

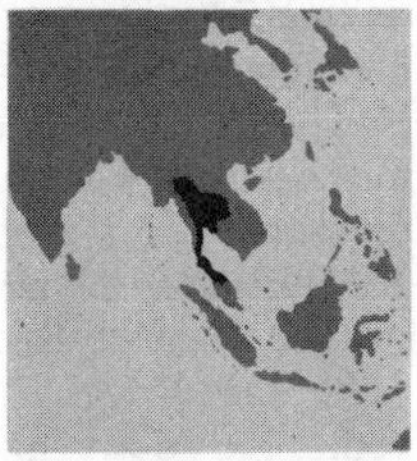

A constitutional monarchy of Southeast Asia, Thailand is bordered by Burma, Laos, Cambodia, and Malaysia. Area: 198,500 sq.mi. (514,000 sq.km.). Pop. (1973 est.): 36,320,000. Cap. and largest city: Bangkok-Thon Buri (pop., 1970, 2,495,286). Language: Thai. Religion (1964): Buddhist 93.7%; Muslim 3.9%. King, Bhumibol Adulyadej; prime ministers in 1973, Field Marshal Thanom Kittikachorn and, from October 14, Sanya Dharmasak.

When 1973 began, there was no suggestion of the national trauma it was going to bring. The powerful Col. Narong Kittikachorn, son of the prime minister, told an interviewer that the government was thinking of holding general elections in 1974, and there was the possibility that Gen. Prapas Charusathiara, the de facto strong man of the country, would become prime minister.

A Foreign Ministry spokesman said in February that Thailand had taken a firm decision to move toward neutrality based on the eventual evacuation of U.S. troops from the country. It was also announced that the U.S. was transferring the 7th Air Force headquarters from Danang in South Vietnam to Nakhom Phnom, northeast of Bangkok, and that Thailand was to receive more fighter-bombers from the U.S.

An embarrassment to the Thai government was the disclosure by a former U.S. ambassador to Laos that 15,000 to 20,000 U.S.-sponsored Thai troops were fighting in Laos. The official admission only confirmed the feeling that Thailand had decided, despite talk of neutrality, to fit itself into the U.S. post-cease-fire strategy for Indochina. In mid-May Prime Minister Thanom publicly stated that Thailand would continue to make military facilities available to the U.S. as long as there were violations of the Indochina peace agreement.

In June began the slow unsuspected buildup toward the shattering climax of October. Nine students of Bangkok's Ramkamhaeng University were expelled for publishing a magazine criticizing government leaders and university teachers. Students then staged a protest rally. Their demands included the completion of a constitution for Thailand within six months. This demand was pressed even after the expelled students were reinstated and the university rector resigned. Rallies, demonstrations, and vigils continued through July. Thereafter, students kept up private meetings and seminars aimed at putting pressure on the government on the one hand and winning popular support on the other.

On October 5 a student leader made a public speech calling for speedy completion of the constitution draft. Police rounded up 11 students, and Deputy Prime Minister Prapas announced that a plot to overthrow the government had been uncovered. Shock waves passed through Bangkok's many colleges, and the student protest began to swell rapidly. Some of the biggest rallies in Thai history took place in

THAILAND

Education. (1971–72) Primary, pupils 5,796,187, teachers (including preprimary; 1968–69) 127,737; secondary and vocational, pupils 582,466, teachers (state only) 16,138; teacher training (1968–69), students 22,634, teachers 2,293; higher (at 7 universities), students 45,237, teaching staff (1968–69) 5,470.

Finance. Monetary unit: baht, with (Sept. 17, 1973) a par value of 20 baht to U.S. $1 (free rate of 48.91 baht = £1 sterling). Gold, SDRs, and foreign exchange, official: (June 1973) U.S. $1,260,000,000; (June 1972) U.S. $1,033,000,000. Budget (1970–71 est.): revenue 21.8 billion baht; expenditure (including capital account) 28,645,000,000 baht. Gross national product: (1971) 144,590,000,000 baht; (1970) 136,330,000,000 baht. Money supply: (Dec. 1972) 24,680,000,000 baht; (Dec. 1971) 20,980,000,000 baht. Cost of living (Bangkok and Thon Buri; 1963 = 100): (June 1973) 138; (June 1972) 123.

Foreign Trade. (1972) Imports 30,869,000,000 baht; exports 22,111,000,000 baht. Import sources: Japan 40%; U.S. 13%; West Germany 7%; U.K. 5%. Export destinations: Japan 24%; U.S. 12%; The Netherlands 6%; Hong Kong 5%. Main exports: rice 20%; corn 9%; rubber 8%; tin 8%; tapioca 7%; kenaf 5%.

Transport and Communications. Roads (main; 1972) 17,686 km. Motor vehicles in use (1972): passenger 282,600; commercial 158,900. Railways (1970): 3,765 km.; traffic *c.* 3,860,000,000 passenger-km., freight *c.* 2,250,000,000 net ton-km. Air traffic (1972): 1,181,500,000 passenger-km.; freight 21,103,000 net ton-km. Shipping (1972): merchant vessels 100 gross tons and over 69; gross tonnage 108,271. Telephones (Dec. 1971) 202,000. Radio receivers (Dec. 1970) 2,775,000. Television receivers (Dec. 1969) 241,000.

Agriculture. Production (in 000; metric tons; 1972; 1971 in parentheses): rice 11,800 (13,570); corn 1,700 (2,300); peanuts *c.* 230 (*c.* 220); sweet potatoes (1971) *c.* 260, (1970) *c.* 250; sorghum *c.* 100 (*c.* 100); dry beans *c.* 230 (*c.* 230); soybeans *c.* 70 (*c.* 74); cassava (1970) 1,969, (1969) 1,932; sugar, raw value *c.* 960 (*c.* 825); bananas (1970) *c.* 1,200, (1969) *c.* 1,200; tobacco *c.* 99 (*c.* 95); rubber *c.* 336 (*c.* 316); cotton, lint *c.* 35 (*c.* 27); jute *c.* 10 (*c.* 12); kenaf *c.* 380 (*c.* 350); timber (cu.m.; 1970) 19,000, (1969) 18,700; fish catch (1971) 1,572, (1970) 1,448. Livestock (in 000; 1971–72): cattle *c.* 5,350; buffaloes *c.* 8,000; pigs *c.* 5,500; chickens *c.* 45,500.

Industry. Production (in 000; metric tons; 1972): cement 3,392; tin concentrates (metal content) 22; tungsten concentrates (oxide content; 1971) 2.3; lead concentrates (metal content; 1971) 2.2; electricity (kw-hr.; 1970) 4,543,000.

Textiles:
see Industrial Review

Bangkok, sometimes with as many as 400,000 participants. It also became evident that the students were receiving spontaneous support from the general public.

On October 13 the government unconditionally released the detained students and promised to promulgate a new constitution within a year. The concession was too little and too late, and the next day turned out to be Thailand's historic "bloody Sunday." Students rioted and riot police swung into action. Rumours of deaths spread, fanning the flames of students' fury. Pitched battles developed in many areas. Some army units, reportedly under Colonel Narong's orders, opened machine-gun and tank fire on student crowds. Two helicopter gunships fired on people in the university.

As became known later, the army chief, Gen. Kris Sivera, refused to bring in his men to suppress the students. In fact, he was thought to have implied that his troops would be used against Colonel Narong's.

By evening Thanom announced the resignation of his government. The king appointed Sanya Dharmasak, Thammasat University rector and former chief justice, as prime minister. Violence continued the next day, but ended when the announcement was made that Thanom, Prapas, and Narong had fled the country.

The new civilian government pledged to complete a constitution in six months. Exercising his little-used powers, the king in December convened a "national convention" of some 2,300 persons selected by himself and his advisers and charged them with electing a new National Assembly to replace the body appointed by the former military regime; this assembly, in turn, would ratify the new constitution. The convention, which met in a Bangkok racetrack, voted on December 19. The military and police who had made up 85% of the old assembly were eliminated; however, most of the 299 members elected to the new body were from the Bangkok area and many were public officials, the hoped-for representation for the rural areas and youth having failed to materialize. (T. J. S. GEORGE)

Theatre

Great Britain and Ireland. Growing criticism of the way in which the National Theatre was falling behind in its artistic and other obligations was met by the Board of Governors' decision to advance to Nov. 1, 1973, the date on which Lord Olivier was to hand over full management of the complex to Peter Hall. Hall, who had been appointed co-director in April, was entrusted with the task of successfully inaugurating the new theatre building in the fall of 1975. The building was to comprise two main auditoriums: the Olivier (seating 1,150), with its amphitheatre, and the Lyttelton (seating 900), with its proscenium stage, plus the flexible 200-seat Cottesloe studio theatre. A topping-out ceremony on May 2 was followed by the appointment of Michael Blakemore, Jonathan Miller, Harold Pinter, John Schlesinger, and Michael Kustow to the management and the departure of Olivier's literary manager, Kenneth Tynan. Although secret talks between the National Theatre and the Royal Shakespeare were admitted, speculation about the possibility of a merger between the capital's two leading subsidized theatres was dismissed by Hall as being premature.

Despite the unflattering nature of some of the essays and interviews published in Logan Gourlay's best-selling anthology *Olivier,* Lord Olivier's final year was not all criticism. John Dexter, who stayed on as a part-time director, was responsible for three of the season's hits: a modern verse version of Molière's *The Misanthrope* by the 36-year-old Yorkshire poet Tony Harrison; Peter Shaffer's latest excursion into the contortions of the human mind, entitled *Equus,* about a young lad obsessed by horses; and *The Party,* a modern drama about British Marxists specially commissioned from the Lancashire working-class playwright Trevor Griffiths, with its tailor-made role of a Scottish Trotskyite politician for Olivier. In the first two, Alec McCowen displayed his considerable versatility, first as Alceste and then as a troubled psychiatrist. Michael Blakemore's unusually inventive version of Chekhov's *The Cherry Orchard* was marred only by a lapse of taste in the final moments. Franco Zeffirelli paid a return visit (his third) to the National's stage at the Old Vic, directing Eduardo de Filippo's hilarious Neapolitan family comedy *Saturday, Sunday, Monday,* with Olivier once again shining inimitably in a minor role. Less successful, though bold in intent, was Roland Joffé's attempt to stage Euripides' *The Bacchae* in terms of African tribalism, using the Nigerian writer Wole Soyinka's new translation for the purpose.

Frank Dunlop, creator of the Young Vic, anticipated his theatre's separation from the parent body with a handsome new version of *Much Ado About Nothing,* premiered at the Biennial Europalia Arts Festival in Brussels even before opening in London, where revivals of *A Taste of Honey* and *Rosencrantz and Guildenstern Are Dead* were among the season's highlights. Also, at the temporary Bankside Globe Playhouse on the South Bank, Sam Wanamaker's annual festival boasted Charles Marowitz' savage interpretation of Eugène Ionesco's *Macbett* and Tony Richardson's modern-dress *Antony and Cleopatra* starring Vanessa Redgrave.

At the Royal Shakespeare Company's London home, the Aldwych, lovers of the international theatre bade a temporary farewell to Sir Peter Daubeny, knighted in the midyear honours list for his services to the theatre, and to his World Theatre Season, the tenth in the series, abandoned for one year because of its creator's ill health. The company's season included the first visit to Britain of the Vienna Burgtheater with Arthur Schnitzler's *Liebelei,* the Comédie Française in the British director Terry Hands's *Richard III* starring Robert Hirsch, and the British debut of the Brussels Théâtre du Rideau in Guillaume Apollinaire's *The Rotting Enchanter.* The main native attractions of the company were Eileen Atkins in Marguerite Duras' *Suzanna Andler,* transferred from the Yvonne Arnaud Theatre in Guildford; the massive Roman tetralogy staged by Trevor Nunn (from the previous year's Stratford Festival) and featuring Janet Suzman's Cleopatra, Nicol Williamson's Coriolanus, and John Wood's Brutus; a Pinter double bill with Peggy Ashcroft; and Nicol Williamson's popular one-man show. The company also staged a second experimental season at The Place, including a documentary about Sylvia Plath; the world premiere of Philip Magdalany's satire on U.S. mores, *Section Nine;* and works by David Rudkin, John Wiles, and Athol Fugard.

Fugard, with two black South African colleagues, was the author of the sensational antiapartheid *Sizwe Bansi Is Dead* at the Royal Court's small Theatre

Upstairs, which also fathered the mocking camp-show *The Rocky Horrow Show,* and *Sweet Talk* by the West Indian Michael Abbensetts, which won the author half the annual George Devine Prize and the job of the Royal Court's dramatist-in-residence. The principal new plays at the Royal Court were Samuel Beckett's *Not I* with Billie Whitelaw; Christopher Hampton's polemical drama of genocide in Brazil, *Savages,* with Paul Scofield; Edward Bond's *The Sea;* and David Storey's *Cromwell,* a Brecht-type drama of civil war, and *The Farm,* in which the Yorkshire author returned once more to the scene of his youth.

At the Hampstead Theatre Club, where Vivian Matalon handed over the directorship to Michael Rudman in the fall, the former was responsible for Tennessee Williams' *Small Craft Warnings* starring Elaine Stritch and the latter for Peter Handke's *A Ride Across Lake Constance.* Peter James, formerly of the Young Vic, staged *Macbeth* at the Shaw Theatre, where the National Theatre's Touring Company also stopped off with *Twelfth Night.* The other subsidized theatres kept the ball rolling with a varied repertoire that included *The Times* drama critic Irving Wardle's first play, *The Houseboy,* at the Open Space; *Hans Kohlhaas,* James Saunders' adaptation of a Heinrich Kleist novella, at the Greenwich, where Joan Plowright guested in *Rosmersholm* and the septuagenarian Elisabeth Bergner made her British stage comeback in Istvan Orkeny's *Cats Play;* Siobhan McKenna in *Juno and the Paycock* and J. B. Priestley's *An Inspector Calls* at the Mermaid; and, at the Stratford Theatre Royal, Joan Littlewood's 20th anniversary of her Theatre Workshop with among other delights a satire on socialized medicine and Maxwell Shaw's directing debut (C. G. Bond's *Sweeney Todd*).

The fringe theatre continued to flourish with a record number of new works, revivals, and lunchtime playlets at such sites as the Bush, the Soho Poly, the Howff, the Half Moon, the Almost Free, and the King's Head. At the last named the novelist William Trevor had some memorable one-act plays performed. Equally removed in spirit from the West End were the offerings at the Roundhouse, though several transferred from there to London's commercial theatres, among them *Joseph and the Amazing Technicolor Dreamcoat;* guest companies to be seen there were the regionally based Prospect Theatre with *Twelfth Night* and *The Royal Hunt of the Sun* and Steve Berkoff's London Theatre Group in *The Trial.*

The West End commercial theatre continued to thrive, thanks in part to increased seat prices, which helped both the established and the younger producers to keep their playbills filled for months on end with such popular hits as *The Constant Wife* starring Ingrid Bergman, *Design for Living* with Vanessa Redgrave, *Collaborators* with Glenda Jackson, *Habeas Corpus* with Sir Alec Guinness, *A Private Matter* with Alastair Sim, *Behind the Fridge* with Peter Cook and Dudley Moore, *A Doll's House* with Claire Bloom, *Absurd Person Singular* with Sheila Hancock, and Peter Ustinov's *The Unknown Soldier and His Wife,* with which the New London Theatre opened.

Other notable events in the calendar were the transfer of *Dandy Dick* to London from the Chichester Festival, where John Clements was replaced as manager at the end of the festival by Keith Michell; the reaching and overtaking by Agatha Christie's *The Mousetrap* of its 21st birthday, the occasion of a celebration given by its producer, Peter Saunders, for

CENTRAL PRESS/PICTORIAL PARADE

Members of the Chinese Acrobatic Theatre of Shanghai rehearse a bicycle spectacular in preparation for their debut at the London Coliseum, July 3, 1973. The show marked the first time they had performed outside China and the first visit of a Chinese theatrical company to Britain in more than 20 years.

the hundreds who had appeared in it since its opening; the renaming of the New Theatre as the Albery; and the publication by the Arts Council of Great Britain of an inquiry into the state of London's theatre and the growth of a public protest movement against the threat of random demolition of playhouses by property developers.

In Ireland the Dublin Theatre Festival was revived with a record number of world premieres to its credit, including, at the Abbey, Wilson John Haire's study of life in war-torn Belfast, *Bloom of the Diamond Stone;* at the Gate, Michael MacLiammoir's biographical *Prelude in Kazbek Street,* a semifictional play about the ballet world; and two premieres by non-Irish writers, U.S. playwright Harding Lemay's *The Joslyn Circle* and Scottish author Tom Gallacher's *The Only Street,* which later opened in London. A novelty at the Abbey's small Peacock substage was Hero Magee's *Red Biddy* starring Maire Keane. Brian Friel's drama about events in Belfast, *The Freedom of the City,* had dual premieres in Dublin and at London's Royal Court Theatre, while Patrick Galvin's *Nightfall to Belfast,* staged by the Lyric Players, showed that the theatre of that city was not to be silenced by political extremism.

France. The closing of the Théâtre National Populaire and the transfer of the title to Roger Planchon's regional theatre in Lyons left a gap in the Paris theatre not easily filled. Paris critics began to make the trip to Lyons that they formerly made to the Palais de Chaillot. Two outstanding productions there were Planchon's of his own play *Overboard,* a musical satire on the power of the mighty dollar, and Patrice Chereau's of Pierre de Marivaux's *La Dispute,* interpreting the 18th-century inquiry into the origins of human inconstancy in a highly original 20th-century manner. This play also came to Paris, where it became the *pièce de résistance* of the Autumn Festival. Under festival auspices Parisian theatregoers were able to savour the succulent outrage of Jorge Lavelli's handling of his fellow Argentine Copi's *The Four Twin Girls,* featuring cannibalism, nudity, and much else besides; the Groupe TSE's *Luxe,* a comic pastiche of the Paris music hall of the 1920s; Jerzy Grotowski's *Apocalipsis cum Figuris* restaged in the Sainte Chapelle; and in the same place Andrei Sherban's modern vision of *Elektra* in ancient Greek.

The third year of Pierre Dux's regime at the Comédie Française failed to fulfill the promise of earlier seasons despite Simon Eine's hopeful directing debut with Marivaux's *Island of Slaves* and a popular Alfred de Musset double bill. Its thunder was stolen by the Théâtre de la Ville with Lavelli's uproarious staging of a forgotten satire on Soviet foibles by Mikhail Bulgakov, *The Purple Island,* and Jean Mercure's production of Bertolt Brecht's *The Good Woman of Sezuan* starring Annie Doat. At the Théâtre de l'Est Parisien, Guy Rétoré staged an excitingly melodramatic *Macbeth* and played host to a company from Caen in Dieter Forte's German play about Martin Luther. Jean-Louis Barrault at the Récamier staged the world premiere of the stage version of Colin Higgins' *Harold and Maude* starring Madeleine Renaud; other U.S. imports included Israel Horovitz' *The First One, The Prisoner of Second Avenue, The Lion in Winter* (starring Edwige Feuillère), *Long Day's Journey into Night* with Georges Wilson and Suzanne Flon, and *The Karl Marx Play.*

New French plays of merit were conspicuous for their infrequency, exceptions being Victor Lanoux's thriller *The Tourniquet;* Jean Poiret's farcical *La Cage aux Folles;* Marcel Achard's *The Debauch;* Eduardo Manet's *The One-Eyed Man;* the new comedy by Barillet and Grédy, *A Rose for Breakfast;* Félicien Marceau's cynical *The Man in Question;* and last but far from least Ionesco's finest play since *Exit the King* called *Ce Formidable Bordel* (*This Hell of a Mess*), which called in question many contemporary assumptions.

Switzerland, Germany, Austria, Belgium, The Netherlands. In Zürich Harry Buckwitz continued his managerial regime with several outstanding productions, ranging from Maxim Gorki's *Yegor Bulichov and Others,* staged by the guest director from East Berlin, Manfred Wekwerth, to Friedrich Dürrenmatt's latest horror-comedy called *The Collaborator,* taken over by the author after Polish guest director Andrzej Wajda had walked out because of differences of opinion with him. A welcome newcomer at the tiny Neumarkt Theatre was Roland Merz, whose first play in Swiss dialect (*Strinckett*) smacked unmistakably of Samuel Beckett's influence.

In West Germany the recent change of several managers resulted in a variety of controversial productions. In Düsseldorf Ulrich Brecht's new regime was heavily attacked by orthodox press opinion but countered splendidly with two outstanding box-office hits: the world premier of Czechoslovakian playwright Pavel Kohout's philosophical drama about the motives behind the conduct of Shakespeare's Hamlet entitled *Poor Murderer,* and East German playwright Peter Rühmkorf's political parable *The Volsinii,* both banned in their countries of origin. In Cologne Hansgünther Heyme, nominated as manager for the ensuing season, staged a twofold Dionysiac frolic by giving *The Bacchae* and *The Frogs* in the same program. Thomas Bernhard's *The Idiot and the Madman* received its German premiere in Hamburg after its abortive world premiere at the previous season's Salzburg Festival. In Frankfurt Peter Palitzsch's new regime settled down nicely with several first-rate productions, Edward Bond's *Lear* among them. The same play was directed at the Munich Chamber Theatre by the English director William Gaskill, who also returned to Hamburg to put on *Galileo Galilei.* Two other guest directors in Munich were Arnold Wesker, directing his own *The Old Ones,* and the Romanian Liviu Ciulei, directing Ionesco's *Macbett* as a circus show. At the same city's second opera house in the Gärtnerplatz, Alexander Faris' musical version of Ustinov's *R loves J,* subsequently staged in English at the Chichester Festival, got a mixed reception. At Bochum Peter Zadek went from strength to strength with Tankred Dorst's study of a Quisling, based on the story of the Norwegian pro-Hitler writer Knut Hamsun and entitled *Ice Age,* and a modernistic *The Merchant of Venice,* deliberately presenting Shylock in an anti-Semitic manner as he would be seen by the Nazis; this became the major attraction of the Berlin Summer Theatre Festival. The year's Shakespeare Prize was awarded to Peter Brook.

In West Berlin the outgoing manager Hansjörg Utzerath's proudest success at the Free People's Theatre was Leopold Lindtberg's thrilling *Othello,* while Kurt Hübner's inaugural production there of *Macbeth* proved a deep disappointment. Dieter Dorn's scabrous production of *The Birds,* with Wilfried Minks's phallic costumes, was the best the Schiller had to offer on its main stage. The same director had an equally outrageous all-male version of *The Maids* at the Schlosspark, along with the German premiere of Beckett's *Not I,* with Brecht's daughter Hanne Hiob as the speaker, and the East German Heiner Müller's critique of Marxist society, *The Horatii,* not yet seen in the East, at the Studio Stage. The year's outstanding work at the Schaubühne am Halleschen Ufer was Peter Stein's drawn-out slapstick adaptation of Eugène Labiche's comedy about the evils of money-grubbing, *The Piggy-Bank,* performed as a satire on monopoly capitalism.

In East Berlin the Berliner Ensemble finally began to recover lost ground after Helene Weigel's death with Ruth Berghaus' amusing version of Brecht's *Turandot, or The Congress of Whitewashers* starring Curt Bois as the Chinese emperor, and her even more impressive productions of Peter Hacks's *Omphale* starring Ekkehard Schall as a lubricious Hercules and Müller's stage version of Fedor Gladkov's *Ce-*

Alastair Sim and Ralph Michael perform in the Chichester Festival production of "Dandy Dick." The play later transferred to London.

JOHN TIMBERS

ment. The oft-rewritten version of Volker Braun's socialist drama *The Sand Dumpers* at long last reached the stage of the Deutsches Theater, which also put on Hacks's *Amphitryon* (though his latest comedy, *Adam and Eva,* like so many other of his plays had to be world premiered in West Germany). At the Kammerspiele of this theatre, the talking point was Ulrich Plenzdorf's *The New Sorrows of Young W.*, taking its inspiration from Goethe's novel and telling the story of the tragic death (by suicide?) of an East German worker.

At Vienna's Burgtheater Gerhard Klingenberg continued his policy of foreign guest directors, notably Edward Bond, who made his directing debut with a surprisingly tame production of his own *Lear;* Jean-Louis Barrault with a carbon copy of his *The Would-Be Gentlemen* from Paris; and Erwin Axer from Warsaw with Thomas Bernhard's *A Feast for Boris.* At the Burg's small Akademie stage, Tom Stoppard's *Jumpers* won unexpected notoriety for Erika Pluhar's sexually frank portrayal of the role created in London by Diana Rigg.

In Brussels the season was dominated by the biennial Europalia festival, for which Jacques Huisman had Frank Dunlop over from London to direct an amusingly modern-dress production of *Pericles* at the National Theatre, while the Rideau competed with a series of English plays; Adrien Brine's original approach to Pinter's *Old Times* with Jean-Marie Fiévez' decor proved the most popular. After threats of being closed and having its ensemble disbanded, the Amsterdam Municipal Theatre was given a new lease on life when a new manager, Hans Croiset, took over, launching his season with an outstanding production of *King Lear* with Guus Hermus in the title role.

Italy. Giorgio Strehler's third version of Brecht's *Threepenny Opera* was dogged by illness and accidents but eventually opened in Prato before surfacing in Milan. Franco Enriquez' Rome City Theatre overcame a halting start with a sensational production of Pinter's *Old Times,* in which the director, Luchino Visconti, incurred the author's personal displeasure for having introduced unwarranted items of sexual deviation into the action. Previously Enriquez had invited Benno Besson from East Berlin to restage his celebrated *The Good Woman of Sezuan* at his theatre starring Valeria Moriconi. A new theatrical star was Manuela Kustermann, who shone in several productions, most strongly in John Webster's *The White Devil.* Rossella Falk formed her own acting troupe after the Giovani had disbanded. Notable regional events were Giancarlo Sbragia's stage adaptation of *The Iliad,* Luigi Squarzina's revival of Carlo Goldoni's *The New House* in Genoa, and Aldo Trionfo's of *King John* in Turin, where Trevor Griffiths' *Occupations* (about Antonio Gramsci and the Turin industrial disputes of the 1930s) received its Italian premiere.

Eastern Europe. The Moscow Arts Theatre occupied its new building with a repertoire of old-timers from previous decades, though the year's main draws included a first play by Gannadi Bokaryev, *The Steelworkers,* staged by Oleg Yefremov with all the theatre's accustomed realism. At the Sovremennik Galina, Volchok staged the Khirgizian writer Chingiz Aitmatov's *The Ascent to Fujiyama,* a study of a wartime collaborator's responsibility for the death of a friend. The Belorussian Andrey Makayonok's *A Pull Under the Tongue* was the year's most popular offering at the Satiric Theatre, while all Moscow rushed to the Maly to admire Mikhail Tsaryov as Clausen in Gerhart Hauptmann's *After Sunset.*

In Warsaw a new satire by Rozewicz brilliantly mounted by Jerzy Jarocki at the Dramatic and Jozef Szajna's latest multimedia antifascist collage at the Studio vied for popularity with Adam Hanuszkewicz' sombre production of *Macbeth* at the National and Maciej Prus's presentation of Stanislaw Witkiewicz' antifascist surrealist drama of the 1920s, *Gyubal Wahazar,* at the Ateneum. In Krakow Konrad Swinarski revived Adam Mickiewicz' *Forefathers' Eve* at the Stary Theatre, staging some of the action amid the spectators. A new work by the veteran Tibor Déry, *Fictitious Report About an American Pop Festival;* a stage adaptation by Karoly Kazimir and Tamas Ungvari of Graham Greene's *The Quiet American;* and Gyula Illyes' latest historical drama, *Brothers,* were the main offerings by Budapest theatres, which also mounted a skillful version of Natalia Ginsburg's *The Advertisement* starring Eva Ruttkai. A new work at Bucharest's National was Mihnea Gheorghiu's *Play Strindberg.* The most talked-of entries for the drama festival in Belgrade were those of the Hamburg Deutsches Schauspielhaus in Franz Xaver Kroetz's *Stallerhof* and the Glasgow Citizens' Theatre in Giles Havergal's androgynous *Twelfth Night.* The praise given to an avant-garde troupe from Ljubljana at the Novi Sad Festival was justly shared with a more orthodox presentation by Belgrade's Atelje 212, which also won favour in the capital with Dusan Kovasevic's sardonic *The Marathon Runners.*

Scandinavia. At Stockholm's Royal Dramatic Theatre Ingmar Bergman revived some of his earlier television techniques for Strindberg's *The Ghost Sonata* (which went on to win the highest praise at the Florence Festival in Italy). Frank Sundström's touring revival of Ibsen's *A Doll's House* featured the irresistible Bibi Andersson as Nora. Another unusual attraction was Peter Weiss's *Hölderlin,* which the dramatist rewrote for the Swedish premiere. Johan Bergenstråhle's imaginative staging of his own adaptation of Selma Lagerlöf's *The Saga of Gösta Berling* was the signal achievement at the City Theatre.

In Oslo the event of the year was Ibsen's *Brand* featuring the performance by Liv Ullmann (*see* BIOGRAPHY) as Agnes. In Copenhagen Bergman guest directed *The Misanthrope* at the Royal Theatre, where Ernst Bruun Olsen staged his own satire on Danish "isms," *The Flatterer.* Inkeri Kilpinen's dramatic onslaught on the pitiful failings of the welfare state, *The Other World,* was the unforeseen sensation of the Finnish National Theatre's repertoire in Helsinki. At the Turku City Theatre Kalle Holmberg's world premiere of the Australian-born writer Alan Seymour's stage version of Turkish novelist Yasar Kemal's *The Wind from the Plain* almost eclipsed Ralf Långbacka's production of *Galileo Galilei* in popularity.

(OSSIA TRILLING)

U.S. and Canada. The most striking trend in the U.S. theatre was the continuing decline of Broadway. According to *Variety,* the theatrical trade paper, the total number of "playing weeks" on Broadway during the 1972–73 season was the lowest for which figures exist, and the gross takings at the box office were the lowest in ten years. As the audience shrank, so did the number of productions, and talented people preferred —or were forced—to work elsewhere. Some attempts were made to reverse this trend, or at least slow it down. Two new commercial theatres, the Uris and the Minskoff, opened on Broadway during the 1972–73 season. A more significant opening was that of the Times Square Theatre Center, which sold theatre tickets at greatly reduced prices on the day of the performance and which had some success in attracting customers back to Broadway. But, in general, things were dim along the Great White Way.

Two of the more distinguished Broadway productions of the 1972–73 season were imported from noncommercial theatres. *The Changing Room* by the British writer David Storey, a naturalistic play about a group of rugby players, won the New York Drama Critics Circle Award as best play of the season; it was transferred to Broadway from the Long Wharf Theatre in New Haven, Conn. *The River Niger* by Joseph A. Walker, about a beleaguered father in Harlem, came from the Negro Ensemble Company.

Among the plays produced specifically for Broadway were new works by the two foremost living U.S. dramatists, Arthur Miller and Tennessee Williams. Miller's play (which opened in December 1972) was a comedy about Adam and Eve entitled *The Creation of the World and Other Business;* Williams' (March 1973) was a phantasmagoric drama entitled *Out Cry,* about a strange brother and sister. Both plays were failures. *The Sunshine Boys* (December 1972), Neil Simon's comedy about a pair of ancient vaudevillians, was a success but seldom a sellout in spite of enthusiastic reviews. *Finishing Touches,* a comedy by Jean Kerr, had a disappointing run. Musicals included *Irene,* the 1919 hit retooled into a vehicle for Debbie Reynolds, and *Seesaw,* a musical version of *Two for the Seesaw* by William Gibson. The most acclaimed musical of the season—the most impressive show to be created for Broadway during the year—was *A Little Night Music.* Produced and directed by Harold Prince, it was an adaptation of Ingmar Bergman's famous film *Smiles of a Summer Night,* with a waltzing musical score and brilliant lyrics by Stephen Sondheim (*see* BIOGRAPHY). But Prince and Sondheim were almost alone in their attempts to bring the Broadway musical comedy forward into the 1970s.

The off-Broadway commercial theatre was as deep into the doldrums as Broadway; economic realities weighed heavily on it, and artistic energies that might have given it some life had been channeled instead into the subsidized noncommercial theatres. A strange, surrealistic musical phenomenon entitled *Doctor Selavy's Magic Theatre,* with book by Richard Foreman, music by Stanley Silverman, and lyrics by Tom Hendry, opened at the end of 1972; it intrigued some spectators and angered others. There were two successful off-Broadway revues: *El Grande de Coca-Cola* from the U.K. and *National Lampoon's Lemmings,* a spin-off from a U.S. humour magazine, which featured an extended parody of the Woodstock rock festival.

In a Broadway revival of Clare Boothe Luce's 1936 success, "The Women," a coven of Park Avenue matrons compete to get—and keep—the most appropriate males. Here rivals resort to assault as Alexis Smith (right) attempts to make a lasting impression on Rhonda Fleming.

FRIEDMAN-ABELES

The Hot L Baltimore, a sentimentally naturalistic play by Lanford Wilson about the inhabitants of a rundown hotel, was produced by the Circle Theatre, an off-off-Broadway group, and successfully transferred to a regular off-Broadway house; it won the New York Drama Critics Circle Award as best American play of the season. *The Faggot* by Al Carmines, a musical revue about homosexuals, was another transfer from off-off-Broadway.

It became ever clearer during the year that artistic leadership in the U.S. theatre had passed to the noncommercial, institutional, resident theatres. Thus, perhaps the most important single event of the year was the take-over of the Vivian Beaumont Theatre in Lincoln Center, New York, by Joseph Papp's New York Shakespeare Festival. The Beaumont had been built as the headquarters of the Repertory Theatre of Lincoln Center; in October 1972 Jules Irving had resigned as director of the Repertory Theatre, effective at the end of the 1972–73 season. He was not replaced; instead, the Repertory Theatre went out of existence, and its premises were turned over to Papp's organization.

The Repertory had concentrated on classical revivals on the Beaumont's main stage and produced mostly new U.S. plays in the Forum downstairs; Papp announced his intention of producing mostly new U.S. plays on the main stage and Shakespeare in the Forum, which he renamed the Mitzi E. Newhouse Theatre. The Beaumont reopened under its new management in October 1973 with *Boom Boom Room,* a play by David Rabe about a Philadelphia go-go dancer; in November *Troilus and Cressida* opened in the Newhouse. Since the Shakespeare Festival retained control of its Public Theatre complex in downtown Manhattan, along with the Delacorte Theatre in Central Park and the portable Mobile Theatre, the move into Lincoln Center gave Papp control of no less than ten different stages and reinforced his claim to be considered the most powerful man in the U.S. theatre.

Ironically, the last season of the Repertory Theatre of Lincoln Center was one of its most successful. Its revival of *The Plough and the Stars* by Sean O'Casey featured distinguished performances by Roberta Maxwell and the late Jack MacGowran (*see* OBITUARIES). This was followed by *The Merchant of Venice,* directed by Ellis Rabb, and by Rabb's production of Tennessee Williams' *A Streetcar Named Desire,* with Rosemary Harris and James Farentino, *Streetcar* proved so successful that, recast and redirected, it was brought to Broadway. (1973 marked the 25th anniversary of the Williams play, and it was also produced in Cincinnati with Carrie Nye, in Chicago with Sandy Dennis, and in Los Angeles with Faye Dunaway and Jon Voight.)

Meanwhile, the New York Shakespeare Festival had a not particularly successful season in 1972–73. Late in 1972 *Wedding Band* by Alice Childress featured Ruby Dee and James Broderick as a pair of interracial lovers. A production of Chekhov's *The Cherry*

Orchard, with an all-black cast, featured James Earl Jones, Gloria Foster, Earle Hyman, and Ellen Holly. *The Orphan* by David Rabe, which tried to connect the Agamemnon-Clytemnestra legend to the Vietnam war, was the first failure for the author of *Sticks and Bones.* The festival's summer productions in Central Park were an unhappy *As You Like It* with Kathleen Widdoes and *King Lear* with James Earl Jones.

Other noncommercial theatres were also active in New York during the 1972–73 season. The Circle in the Square had a spectacular success with Chekhov's *Uncle Vanya,* directed by Mike Nichols and starring (among others) George C. Scott, Nicol Williamson, and Julie Christie. The American Place Theatre, which devoted itself to new U.S. plays, began its season with *Freeman* by Philip Hayes Dean, a drama set amid a black working-class family in a small industrial city in Michigan. Another of its offerings, a zany comedy called *Baba Goya* by Steve Tesich, was transferred to a regular off-Broadway house under the new title *Nourish the Beast.* Among the black theatres the Negro Ensemble Company sent *The River Niger* to Broadway, but the New Lafayette Theatre closed its doors.

Outside New York the regional repertory theatres continued, in many cases, to prosper. During the 1972–73 season, the American Conservatory Theatre in San Francisco played to 90% of capacity, the Hartford (Conn.) Stage Company played to 94.5% of capacity, and the Seattle Repertory Theatre played to 100% of capacity, according to figures released by those organizations. The Tyrone Guthrie Theatre of Minneapolis sent its production of *Of Mice and Men* by John Steinbeck on a ten-week tour of Minnesota, Nebraska, Iowa, Wisconsin, and the Dakotas.

In Washington, D.C., the Arena Stage presented the U.S. premiere of *A Public Prosecutor Is Sick of It All* by Max Frisch and offered a new musical, *Raisin* (adapted from *A Raisin in the Sun* by Lorraine Hansberry), which later went on to success on Broadway. Meanwhile, Arena productions of two U.S. plays, *Our Town* by Thornton Wilder and *Inherit the Wind* by Jerome Lawrence and Robert E. Lee, went on tour to Moscow and Leningrad. The Washington Theatre Club produced, in the spring of 1973, *The Enclave* by Arthur Laurents and the U.S. premiere of *The Ecstasy of Rita Joe* by the Canadian playwright George Ryga, an expressionistic play about modern Canadian Indians devastated by white civilization. The Folger Theatre Group began its 1973–74 season with the U.S. premiere of another Canadian play, *Creeps,* by David E. Freeman, about a workshop for victims of cerebral palsy. The American Theatre, a new venture, began operations with *Cervantes* by Norman Corwin, starring Richard Kiley.

The Long Wharf Theatre of New Haven, Conn., presented the U.S. premieres of two British plays: *Forget-Me-Not Lane* by Peter Nichols and *The Widowing of Mrs. Holroyd* by D. H. Lawrence. The Yale Repertory Theatre, also in New Haven, offered the world premiere of *The Mirror* by Isaac Bashevis Singer and the U.S. premieres of *Macbett* by Eugène Ionesco and *Lear* by Edward Bond, and scheduled the world premiere of *The Tubs* by Terrence McNally for December 1973.

For the 1973–74 season William Woodman took over as artistic director of the Goodman Theatre in Chicago and began his tenure with the U.S. premiere of *The Freedom of the City,* Brian Friel's drama about recent events in Northern Ireland.

It was not a great year for the avant-garde. Significantly, the year's most acclaimed plays, *The Hot L Baltimore, The River Niger,* and *The Changing Room,* were quite conventionally realistic or naturalistic in form. The Open Theatre presented a repertory of three productions—*Terminal, The Mutation Show,* and *Nightwalk*—on tour in the U.S. and Europe and then disbanded at the end of the year. Two companies noted for their collective collaborations had recourse to previously written scripts: André Gregory's Manhattan Project revived Samuel Beckett's *Endgame,* and Richard Schechner's Performance Group presented *The Tooth of Crime* by Sam Shepard and *The Beard* by Michael McClure. Two political theatres from the West Coast made an impression on tour: El Teatro Campesino, the theatrical arm of the Farm Workers Union, and the long-established radical theatre the San Francisco Mime Troupe. The Mime Troupe's production, *The Dragon Lady's Revenge,* presented the Vietnam war in terms of an old pseudo-Oriental B-movie and proved that effective political satire is still possible in the U.S.

While the U.S. theatre, particularly Broadway, was oppressed by a sense of malaise, theatre in Canada, stimulated by cultural nationalism and supported by extensive government grants, was growing and developing. Two main kinds of serious theatre had become established in Canada: the older festivals and regional theatres, devoted to an international repertory, and the newer, smaller theatres, devoted mainly to work by Canadian playwrights. Among the year's new Canadian plays were *You're Gonna Be All Right, Jamie Boy* by David Freeman (winner of the Toronto Drama Bench Award for his first play, *Creeps*); *Hosannah* by the French-Canadian playwright Michel Tremblay; *Of the Fields, Lately* by David French, which was produced in both Toronto and Montreal; and *The Donnellys* by James Rainey.

Among the more sedate, internationally minded companies, the Shaw Festival of Niagara-on-the-Lake, Ont., moved into an impressive new theatre with more

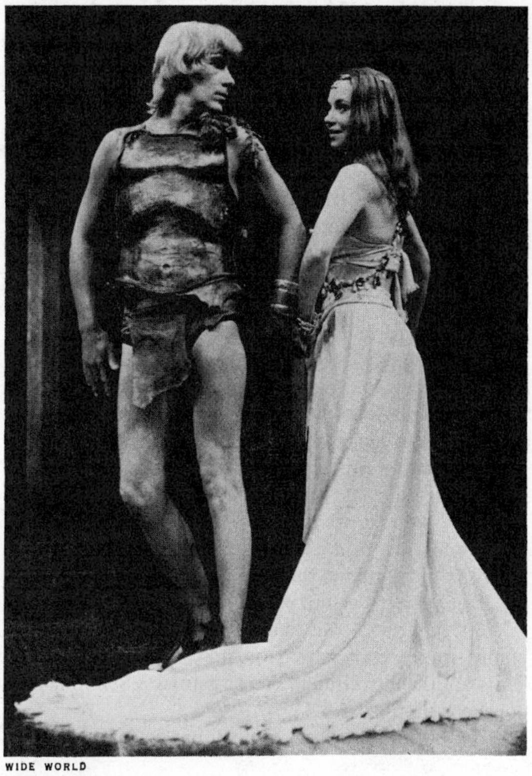

WIDE WORLD

Jean Gascon's staging of Shakespeare's "Pericles," with Nicholas Pennell as Pericles and Martha Henry as Thaisa, provided the high point of the 1973 Stratford (Ont.) Festival.

than twice the seating capacity of the festival's old premises and played to 97% of capacity with a repertory of *You Never Can Tell* and *Fanny's First Play* by George Bernard Shaw and *The Brass Butterfly* by William Golding. At two theatres it was announced that British artistic directors would replace Canadians: John Neville succeeded Sean Mulcahy at the Citadel Theatre, Edmonton, and Robin Phillips was to take over the leadership of the Stratford Festival from Jean Gascon after the 1974 season. Both appointments caused complaint in nationalistic circles.

Both wings of the Canadian theatre made their presence felt outside Canada. The Stratford Festival visited Denmark, The Netherlands, Poland, and the U.S.S.R. with its productions of *King Lear* and *The Taming of the Shrew;* the Factory Theatre Lab of Toronto appeared in London with several Canadian plays; and, as noted, plays by George Ryga and David Freeman were given U.S. productions in Washington, D.C. (JULIUS NOVICK)

See also Dance; Literature; Music.

ENCYCLOPÆDIA BRITANNICA FILMS. *Shaw vs. Shakespeare Part I: The Character of Caesar, Part II: The Tragedy of Julius Caesar, Part III: Caesar and Cleopatra* (1970).

Tobacco

The development of man-made tobacco substitutes took a step forward in mid-1973 with the announcement that Imperial Developments Ltd. was building a £10 million factory in Scotland to produce a new smoking material made of modified cellulose. This was the first serious manufacturing commitment to a synthetic tobacco. The company expected to make the material available to the world's tobacco product manufacturers in 1975. Also in Britain, Courtaulds, a manufacturer of man-made fibres, attracted considerable criticism by test-marketing a cigarette brand called Planet, consisting of 50% tobacco and 50% synthetic material, without first obtaining government health clearance. Courtaulds claimed the government had been kept fully informed.

Statistics for 1972 showed that world production of cigarettes continued to rise, but demand for cigars and smoking tobacco fell somewhat. Tobacco manufacturers generally had a better year than in 1971, particularly in the U.S. and the U.K., where cigarette output increased by 2 and 6%, respectively. Production rose only 1% in the original six EEC countries. The increase in Switzerland was also small, while little change was noted in Canada and Spain. In Sweden, however, a 12% increase was registered.

In the U.S. both production (599,100,000,000 units) and consumption (565,000,000,000 units) of cigarettes were at record levels, with filter-tipped cigarettes accounting for 84% of the total smoked. Consumption of large cigars and cigarillos fell 7% to an estimated 7,350,000,000 units, while production was down 10%. Production of small cigars rose to 4,000,000,000 units and consumption of smoking tobacco fell by 4%. It was expected that favourable economic conditions, an above-average increase in the 25–44 age group of the population, and a dampening of antismoking activity would combine to make 1973 a buoyant year.

U.K. cigarette manufacturers, with sales of 130,500,000,000 units in 1972, had one of their best years in some time. Cigar sales rose 3.7% to 1,410,000,000 units and hand-rolling tobaccos gained 3.8%, but pipe tobaccos dropped 5.6%.

Total world production of tobacco leaf in 1972, although marginally ahead of 1971, could not keep pace with the overall increase in consumption. With available supplies from the latest crop to be marketed falling short of manufacturers' demand, there was a rundown of inventories and a hardening of prices. Preliminary estimates put world production at about 10,500,000,000 lb., a gain of approximately 3%. The crops harvested fell short of early forecasts in several important tobacco-producing countries, largely because of unfavourable weather. Nevertheless, production was up in all areas except North America.

Production of flue-cured leaf—accounting for about two-fifths of the world total—remained at the 1971 level. India and Malawi both registered increases of one-third, and improved levels were noted in South Korea and Poland. In the U.S., however, the crop fell 4% to 1,000,000,000 lb., and in Canada flue-cured production declined 17% in spite of a 7% increase in the area sown. Lighter flue-cured crops were also harvested in the Philippines, Japan, and Brazil.

By contrast, world production of Burley rose by about one-fifth to a new record of approximately 1,100,000,000 lb. The U.S. contribution of 588 million lb. was an important factor, but substantial gains were reported from other countries including Mexico, Argentina, Brazil, and Yugoslavia. Marketing and weather problems cut production in Greece by about 25% to some 25 million lb. South Korea experienced a recovery from the poor 1971 crop, while in Japan good weather led to a high-yielding crop of good quality. Indications were that slightly less oriental and semioriental leaf was produced in 1972 than in 1971. The Greek crop, at 160 million lb., fell a little short of the previous year, while Turkish production rose some 6% to nearly 390 million lb.

The rundown of leaf stocks in 1972, combined with the expanding world demand for cigarettes, was expected to result in a significantly enlarged 1973 crop. Early estimates indicated that the harvested area in the U.S. was being increased by 5% and production by 2%, to 1,780,000,000 lb. Similarly, the area under flue-cured leaf in Ontario was expected to rise by nearly 20% to some 106,400 ac., yielding an expected crop of 250 million lb. In Argentina a heavier flue-cured crop was also expected. In the EEC, however, the area planted fell to 9,800 ac.

At the 47th session of the Committee on Commodity Problems of the UN Food and Agriculture Organization, held in Rome in late 1972, it was decided to set up a consultation group to examine various industry problems, including technical developments and the effect on international trade of national and regional policies. (VIVIAN RAVEN)

Togo

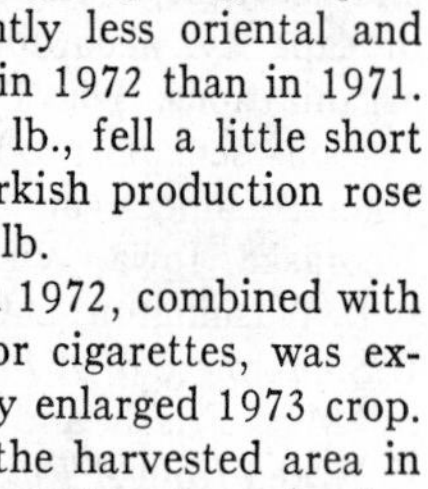

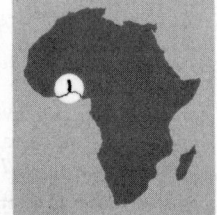

A West African republic, Togo is bordered by Ghana, Upper Volta, and Dahomey. Area: 21,900 sq.mi. (56,600 sq.km.). Pop. (1972 est.): 2,089,900. Cap. and largest city: Lomé (pop., 1972 est., 204,700). Language: French (official). Religion: animist; Muslim and Christian minorities. President in 1973, Gen. Étienne Eyadema.

In a major Cabinet reshuffle in August, Édouard Kodjo became responsible for finance and Michel Eklo for information. The latter was the driving force behind a marked radicalization of the regime and the

Theology: *see* Religion
Timber: *see* Forestry
Tin: *see* Mining
Titanium: *see* Mining

TOGO
Education. (1971–72) Primary, pupils 257,877, teachers 4,403; secondary, pupils 24,521, teachers 778; vocational, pupils 2,506, teachers 214; teacher training (1969–70), students 119, teachers 13; higher, students 1,369, teaching staff 93.
Finance. Monetary unit: CFA franc, with (Sept. 17, 1973) a parity of CFA Fr. 50 to the French franc (free commercial rate of CFA Fr. 212.55 = U.S. $1; free rate of CFA Fr. 512.25 = £1 sterling). Budget (1972 est.) balanced at CFA Fr. 12.3 billion.
Foreign Trade. (1972) Imports CFA Fr. 21,381,000,000; exports CFA Fr. 12,542,000,000. Import sources: France 38%; West Germany 10%; U.K. 8%; U.S. 5%; The Netherlands 5%. Export destinations: France 34%; The Netherlands 25%; West Germany 19%; Belgium-Luxembourg 6%. Main exports: phosphates 37%; cocoa 30%; coffee 21%.

development of a personality cult around the head of state. Both trends were known locally as "zairization" after the regime of Pres. Mobutu Sese Seko, of Zaire, whose experiment in "African authenticity" increasingly fascinated General Eyadema.

It was also significant that the president attended neither the summit of heads of state of the Common Organization of Africa, Malagasy, and Mauritius in May nor the summit of French-speaking African nations in Paris in November, being represented by a minister on both occasions. However, relations with France remained good, if somewhat more distant than previously, and the French secretary-general for African and Malagasy affairs, Jacques Foccart, visited Lomé in November. Relations with the Arab world and with Nigeria were considerably strengthened. On September 21 relations with Israel were broken off, and on October 30 General Eyadema paid an official visit to Libya, during which major cooperation agreements were concluded. Relations with Ghana, however, were gradually deteriorating, despite the exchange of visits and numerous messages of friendship. Ghana accused Togo of stirring up separatist feelings in the Volta region, while Togo accused Ghana of trying to strangle its economy. (PHILIPPE DECRAENE)

Tonga

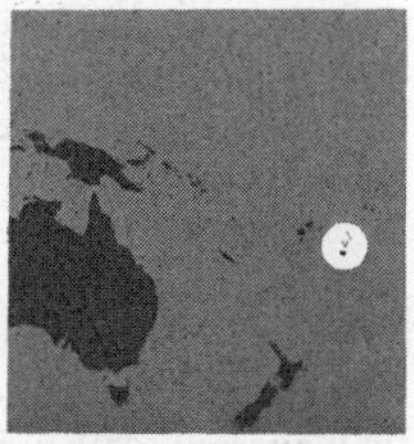

An independent monarchy and member of the Commonwealth of Nations, Tonga is an island group in the Pacific Ocean east of Fiji. Area: 225 sq.mi. (582 sq.km.). Pop. (1973 est.): 92,000. Cap.: Nukualofa (pop., 1972 est., 20,000). Language: English and Tongan. Religion: Christian. King, Taufa'ahau Tupou IV; prime minister in 1973, Prince Tu'ipelehake.

TONGA
Education. (1971) Primary, pupils 16,416, teachers (1970) 658; secondary, pupils 10,164, teachers (1967) 358; vocational, pupils 199; teacher training, students 92, teachers (1970) 6.
Finance and Trade. Monetary unit: pa'anga (dollar), with a free rate (Sept. 17, 1973) of 0.72 pa'anga to U.S. $1 (1.73 pa'anga = £1 sterling). Budget (1971–72 rev. est.): revenue 3,143,000 pa'angas; expenditure 3,162,000 pa'angas. Foreign trade (1971–72): imports 6,721,000 pa'angas; exports 2.2 million pa'angas. Import sources: New Zealand 34%; Australia 20%; U.K. 15%; Fiji 12%; Japan 5%. Export destinations: New Zealand 31%; U.K. 20%; The Netherlands 12%; West Germany 7%; Australia 7%. Main exports (1971): copra 50%; fruit and vegetables 29% (bananas 17%); desiccated coconut 14%.

WIDE WORLD

King Taufa'ahau Tupou IV, here with members of the royal family, follows a long line of rulers of Tonga. In 1973 he proposed formation of an alliance of China, Japan, Southeast Asia, and Tonga to ensure world unity and lasting peace.

With a rapidly increasing population and few industries, Tonga was hard hit in 1973 by low copra prices, a bad season for mangoes and breadfruit, and the increased cost of food. In April Hurricane Juliette struck the low-lying Ha'apai group, leaving 80% of the 15,000 people homeless and severely damaging crops. New Zealand gave hurricane relief totaling over NZ$100,000. Repair or replacement of schools was provided for in the first bilateral aid program between Tonga and New Zealand, about one-third of which was to be used to establish a livestock industry. Tourism expanded, and oil drilling resumed.

Another means of strengthening the economy was a regional shipping line. Tonga's Pacific Navigation Co. Ltd. and the Nauru Pacific Line agreed to cooperate in eliminating overlapping services pending the outcome of work on the financial and operational structure by the South Pacific Bureau for Economic Cooperation. Hopes for a passenger and cargo service on the New Zealand–Fiji–Tonga–Samoa run foundered when Nauru's "Enna G" became strike-bound in Wellington. The South Pacific Bureau provided supporting services for discussions in Brussels on the possible association of Tonga, Fiji, and Western Samoa with the EEC. It was regretted that copra and coconut products were not listed for special treatment.

(MARY BOYD)

Tourism

As 1973 drew to a close, the tourism industry faced an uncertain future. High rates of inflation and renewed pressures on currencies had combined to bring about a general slowing of international travel plans during the year, particularly in North America, and North Atlantic carriers reported only modest air traffic growth compared with 1972. However, these problems paled into insignificance beside the threat of an energy crisis that could seriously curtail transportation, the lifeblood of world tourism.

In Europe, where carless Sundays and other fuel-saving measures were adopted in the face of the Arab oil cutback in the fall, resorts dependent on the automobile reported reduced business and there were demands that governments take their special needs into account. Similar apprehensions were voiced in the U.S., where the administration urged reduced gas con-

Tornadoes: *see* Disasters; Meteorology

sumption and indicated the possibility of gas rationing in the spring. The full effect of the energy crisis on tourism, however, could not be gauged until more was known concerning its effect on long-distance travel, currently the fastest growing segment of the market. At year's end the extent of proposed reductions in airline schedules, the severity and duration of the Arab cutbacks, and the exact nature of the energy crisis over and above the Arab actions were imponderables, casting a shadow over earlier International Union of Official Travel Organization (IUOTO) predictions of 280 million international arrivals by 1980.

Since 1950 world tourism had grown at an average annual rate of 10% (12% for receipts), and by 1972 it accounted for 6% of the value of world export trade. For the first time, the number of international arrivals neared 200 million; recorded movements in 1972 reached 198 million, an increase of 9% over 1971. At $24.2 billion, receipts from international travel (excluding payments to carriers) were up 16%.

The decline of the U.S. dollar against the currencies of other major tourist nations brought changes in the shape of the tourist market. If U.S. tourists now found vacations abroad, particularly in Europe, more expensive, the reverse was a boom in travel to the Americas. Uncertainty in the international money markets was no cause for euphoria in any travel circles, however, and the net influence on travel was probably unfavourable. Tourism's support for an international currency free from fluctuations was reflected in plans, announced by the world's airlines, to abandon the U.S. dollar in favour of SDRs (Special Drawing Rights of the International Monetary Fund) as the basis for fare computations, and in the entry of tour operators into the exchange markets.

The currency situation also created problems for investors. In West Germany the large number of new luxury-class city hotels echoed hollowly to the boom that had failed to materialize. The crisis was aggravated by a shortage of qualified personnel, and rising construction costs put such pressure on occupancy rates that many new projects required 80% or higher occupancy to cover costs.

International Travel. A number of trends emerged as complete figures for 1972 became available. Hong Kong welcomed its millionth visitor and arrivals grew 19% overall. In Spain, where arrivals topped 30 million, a population of 34 million had played host to 32.5 million visitors in 1972, a growth of 24% over 1971. In Morocco arrivals of foreign tourists grew by 29%. With arrivals in neighbouring Tunisia numbering 780,000, a 28% increase, North Africa was rapidly becoming a major travel destination. Kenya continued to dominate the East African market with a winning combination of game-viewing and ocean-beach resort holidays; arrivals there rose 10% to 420,000. Despite internal unrest, neighbouring Uganda began a campaign to attract tourists. The wildlife parks of Africa were said to be "probably the best examples of the foresight and determination of governments of developing nations to preserve their natural resources in perpetuity."

International Tourist Arrivals

Region	1971	1972*	Percent change
Africa	3,120,000	3,520,000	13
Americas	34,910,000	36,000,000	†
Europe	134,240,000	148,100,000	10
Middle East	3,600,000	3,700,000	3
Pacific and East Asia	4,700,000	5,400,000	15
South Asia	930,000	940,000	1
Total	181,500,000	198,000,000	9

*Estimated.
†A change in the basis of recording statistics of international travel to Canada renders accurate comparison of 1972 with 1971 difficult.
Source: International Union of Official Travel Organisations, Geneva.

The year also saw further satisfactory progress in the traditional Mediterranean destinations. Arrivals in Egypt passed the half-million mark, a 26% increase over 1971. In Israel tourist arrivals were close to 750,000, but the percentage increase, at 11%, was smaller than in the preceding year. In Greece a 23% increase to 2.4 million was well ahead of 1971. A gain of almost 5% brought tourist accommodation arrivals in Italy to 13.6 million.

One noteworthy aspect of tourism in 1972 was the popularity of tropical island destinations. The opening of an international airport and the inauguration of regular air service to the Seychelles had brought an unprecedented 3,200 visitors in 1971. In another "pearl" of the Indian Ocean, Mauritius, already earning receipts of $7 million annually, the island's director of tourism took a firm stand to prevent tourism from despoiling the environment. Mauritian hotels were only two stories high—below the level of the palm trees.

A handful of nations remained responsible for the bulk of international tourist expenditures. Six countries, Canada, France, West Germany, Italy, the U.K., and the U.S., accounted for 60% of worldwide expenditures ($14.5 billion). Each of these "big spending" nations made cumulative outlays exceeding $1 billion; $4,856,000,000 came from the U.S., 14% more than in 1971, while $4,513,000,000 came from West Germany, an increase of 28%. With the mark increasing in value, travel expenditures of West Germans, expressed in U.S. dollars, accelerated at an unprecedented rate, surpassing the total spending of Canada, France, and the U.K. combined. West Germans traveling abroad spent nearly $2.7 billion more than foreign tourists spent in West Germany, surpassing even the notorious U.S. "travel gap," which itself was close to $2.2 billion.

Strong domestic economic growth, possibly combined with the fear that dollar prices for overseas travel would rise even higher in 1973, were major factors responsible for a record number—6.8 million—of U.S. residents traveling overseas in 1972. However, U.S. balance of payments experts observed that average dollar expenditures per tourist grew by only 2½% (compared with 14% for all tourists), indicating that higher prices had been offset by reductions in real expenditures. Thus the average U.S. tourist to Europe and the Mediterranean area visited 2.6 countries, compared with 3 countries before 1970.

Japanese spending on overseas travel surged forward by 52% during 1972, to $775 million, while the number of Japanese traveling abroad rose 35% to 1.4 million. More than half of these tourists went abroad for the first time. What the contemporary Japanese tourist wanted was "to see scenic beauty and how other people live." Package tours, which combined low air-fare costs with an easing of language difficulties, remained his preferred option. In 1972 more than 400,000 Japanese visitors arrived in the U.S.—34% more than in 1971—creating receipts of $205 million. For the first time, Japan led all overseas countries in travel to the U.S., and Amerioverseas countries in travel to the U.S., and Americans of Japanese origin found unexpected employment opportunities as part-time tour guides or assisting would-be souvenir shoppers from Tokyo and Osaka.

The second U.S. dollar devaluation in 14 months, which took place early in 1973, was viewed by many as a sign that—as far as U.S. originating travel was concerned—the party was about over. Departures to Europe in the first six months of 1973 grew by only 12%, or half the previous year's rate. In the same period, North Atlantic air travel also rose 12%, compared with 26% in 1972. North Atlantic traffic originating in North America remained sluggish throughout 1973 (although the number of North Atlantic charter passengers rose 38% in the first half of the year, possibly reflecting a new thrift among U.S. travelers). However, travel from Japan, West Germany, Austria, The Netherlands, South Africa, and Switzerland appeared to be poised for further expansion.

Not all destinations were profiting from the newly released spending power of the European countries and Japan. Arrivals in Spain in the first half of 1973 recorded only a 4% increase. The Bahamas (a destination highly dependent on U.S. traffic) showed an actual decrease in air arrivals; sea arrivals rose 11%, but the overall total was 1% below the first half of 1972. In Switzerland tourist nights in hotels showed no change in the first five months of the year, while in Japan traffic rose a moderate 5%.

Elsewhere, trade was somewhat brisker. Morocco reported foreign travel up by 22% in the first half of the year. In Sri Lanka there were 10,000 additional Western European arrivals, the largest number from France, and an overall increase of 50% was reported for the first half of 1973. In Greece, where the currency had stayed at par with the U.S. dollar, there was a 22% growth in arrivals in the first five months of the year. In the U.S. itself 1973 began well; arrivals rose 29% in the first four months of the year, and signs pointed to the beginning of a massive boom in the U.S. tourist trade. U.S. diplomatic missions were said to be swamped with visa applications as Europeans found that the dollar's successive devaluations had brought the long-awaited transatlantic vacation into their price bracket.

Selling Travel. In 1972 and 1973 there were signs of a growing awareness on the part of governments of the need to provide means appropriate for the realization of tourism's undoubted economic benefits. Even so, in some quarters the vital marketing function still seemed starved of funds. *The Times* (London), reviewing the development of tourism in the U.K., drew attention to a lack of harmonization of investment and other efforts and to the imbalance between sums available for hotel incentive schemes and funds for the promotion of Britain overseas. Stringent financial measures, said the journal, had obliged the British Tourist Authority to limit overseas advertising to black and white and to abandon more costly colour displays.

A need to face up to competition seemed to be behind the tripling of Italy's tourism promotion budget in 1973. Much of it was destined to fund the Italian National Tourism Authority (ENIT) offices in other European countries, the U.S., and South America.

The "Tourism Year of the Americas," launched in Panama City in December 1971, achieved considerable success in 1972. After four years of relative stagnation, spending by U.S. travelers in South America rose past $100 million to $113 million, an increase of 23%. One feature of the promotion was a life-size, talking statue of Christopher Columbus narrating the discovery of the Americas in four languages. Among the many other colourful and imaginative promotions of 1972 and 1973 were "Alpine High-life" in Switzerland, elephant roundups in Thailand, "Bonus Days" in Belgium, and, in Britain and Ireland, banquets and medieval-style repasts in historic settings.

In the changing world of travel, sales operators continued to work on tight profit margins, while the customer was still (nearly) always right. Whenever a particular currency encountered difficulties, tourists found themselves faced with modest but nonetheless irritating surcharges on their travel bills. Substantial liquidity was provided by the long lag that exists between the payment of deposits to the tour operator and the settlement of accounts of hotels, carriers, and other providers of services at the destination. The effect of the new uncertainty was that buyers of package tours now preferred to enter the market at the last possible moment. Operators were reportedly anxious about the tendency. The management dilemma thus created seemed certain to push up both costs and prices.

As to whether the client was always right, this too could no longer be left solely to the discretion of the operator or to the "small print" of the booking conditions. In Europe a number of governments, including those of the U.K. and West Germany, studied new measures of consumer protection aimed at shielding the traveler, as consumer, from certain abuses, the most common of which appeared to be double-booking and uncompleted hotel accommodation. Tour operators were disinclined to engage in special pleading, but observed that language, communications, and distance problems made it difficult to keep an eye on every resort.

Apart from ferry services, which depend on automobile traffic, shipping as a means of tourist transportation had sunk almost without a trace. But if sea

WIDE WORLD

A tugboat pushes the new Soviet luxury liner M.S. "Mikhail Lermontov" from her Hudson River berth in New York City as the liner begins a voyage to Leningrad via London. The 20,000-ton vessel's 11 decks can accommodate 700 passengers and 300 crew.

travel was dead—sea voyages accounted for less than 1% of U.S. overseas travel in 1973—cruises continued to grow in appeal. Some 657,000 U.S. residents, more than ever before, took cruises in 1972. With ships no longer simply the means of crossing from A to B, designers concentrated on sleek, smaller, heavily automated cruise ships with ample deck space. Enthusiasts believed that by the 1980s there would be cruise ships of catamaran design with glass-bottomed boats for undersea viewing of tropical marine life. In this new holiday horizon, airlines could cooperate (not compete) with shipping lines by speeding clients to tropical ports of embarkation. Back in 1973, a number of writers pointed to the shift to "open-class" cruising and the elimination of class privileges on board ship.

No one should be barred from tourist travel because of age or disability. Whenever and wherever the desire for travel exists, the means should be made available for satisfying that desire. In 1973 a number of ideas were put forward to help fulfill this ideal, among them a park for blind tourists with a braille nature trail—believed to be the first in the U.S.—in Michigan. While this was the most ambitious project of its type, gardens for blind tourists, with judicious arrangements of scented flower borders, had been developed earlier in England.

In Europe the enlarged EEC eliminated formalities and facilitated home exchanges among retired people. A retired person in Belgium who wished to live in another country long enough to learn the language and customs should be able to exchange homes with a retiree in, say, the U.K., for six months or a year. Both parties could then enjoy the stimulation of travel experience, considered so valuable for people in that age bracket.

Organization. In 1973 there was increasing government intervention in tourism, and wider responsibilities in many fields were given to tourism administrations. The appointment of the New Zealand minister of tourism to Cabinet rank was but one more sign of the political importance of tourism; the new appointee was the first Maori woman to become a minister of the crown and the first New Zealand woman to attain Cabinet rank. In the U.K. a move was made in Parliament to set up a tourism ministry to coordinate questions on the subject and to safeguard consumers by drawing up an industry code of conduct. In the U.S. government efforts were mobilized to reduce the "travel gap" to manageable proportions by the mid-1970s, while in Spain emphasis was placed on spreading the tourist season via development of winter-sports resorts.

The number of countries to have ratified the statutes of the intergovernmental World Tourism Organization (WTO), which would succeed the IUOTO, reached 50 in November; 51 ratifications would be necessary to set up the new body. At an Executive Committee meeting in Zambia in November 1972, delegates reached agreement on a contributions scale for the new body, a major negotiating breakthrough that paved the way for its prompt establishment. In the spring of 1973 a successful series of talks was held between the secretary-general of the IUOTO and the specialized agencies of the United Nations relating to the future responsibilities of the WTO. The prospect facing delegates at IUOTO's 23rd General Assembly in Venezuela, in October 1973, was that the new world body for tourism would come into operation before the close of 1974. (PETER SHACKLEFORD)

See also Transportation.

Toys and Games

For no apparent reason there was an unprecedented demand for toys and games during 1973. Profits of British toys and games firms practically doubled, and a similar growth pattern was seen throughout the world. But the boom brought problems of supply in its wake.

World shortages of raw materials, particularly plastics, board, and wood, held back production. Many of the larger companies closed their order books in midsummer. Retailers' shelves emptied in September and October, and most found it difficult to replenish stocks in time for the Christmas rush. By the end of the year suppliers of raw materials were operating on a quota system. Larger manufacturers obtained enough supplies to maintain some production, but many smaller companies were forced to close.

Exhibitors at the massive Nürnberg show in West Germany, and at the two major British trade fairs at Brighton and Harrogate, reported record orders for all lines, but lack of materials held back production of certain new products. This situation was further aggravated by difficulties in obtaining production equipment.

The supply situation in Britain tended to negate the potentially important innovation in terms of toy retailing during 1973, the opening of Argos cut-price stores. The Argos chain, a Green Shield Stamp subsidiary, burst onto the retailing scene in the middle of the year with more than 4,700 different items in stock, many of them toys. The shops carried a wide range of branded toys from the major manufacturers, many of them well below list price. Small toy retailers viewed the development with some concern, and there was talk of boycotting those manufacturers that supplied the cut-rate shops. However, because of the shortages, price became of less importance than avail-

Off on a tricycle built for 16 go a group of young Britons, testing the invention of engineer Carl Canty at Hull, Yorkshire, Eng. The machine weighs about 1¼ tons fully loaded.

SYNDICATION INTERNATIONAL LTD./PHOTO TRENDS

ability, and the Argos threat had not fully materialized at year's end.

The growth areas of 1973 were dolls, games, and preschool toys. The previous few years had seen a phenomenal increase in spending on dolls, so much so that in the U.S. 1973 was being called the "Year of the Doll." The introduction of fashion dolls had been one reason for the upsurge. These dolls had a constantly changing wardrobe for which outfits were specially manufactured and packaged. Mattel, which produced the Barbie doll, and Rovex, with its Sindie, both reported record orders in 1973, following massive sales during 1972. Dolls for boys, too, continued to sell, with Action Man, Cowboy Kid, and Mark Strong selling better than ever.

Increasing leisure time was obviously one of the factors contributing to increased sales of indoor games. Traditional board games such as Monopoly and Scrabble continued to top the charts, but many newcomers were introduced in 1973. The interest in chess sets reported in 1972 retained its impetus, and other traditional games, such as backgammon, had a high level of sales, especially in the U.S.

British toys exported well. Maintaining fixed prices was made possible by sterling devaluation and tariff reductions to the EEC markets, and many companies took advantage of the favourable price terms to push into new export areas.

The world's largest exporter of toys in 1973 was Hong Kong, toppling Japan from the top spot. Hong Kong's toy exports jumped by 11% in 1973 to £111 million, compared with Japan's £97 million. The U.S. remained Hong Kong's biggest market, with Britain in second place. Hong Kong also boosted its exports to the EEC by 30%, with sales worth £5.6 million during January–May.

The year saw the acquisition by Dunbee-Combex-Marx, a fast growing British toy conglomerate, of the U.K. trading activities of Mattel, the world's largest toy concern. The U.S. Mattel group had shaken the British toy trade when it entered the U.K. a few years earlier with Hot Wheels cars and hard-sell tactics. Lesney, makers of Matchbox Cars, was badly hit. However, the British manufacturers fought back, and the U.S. firm ran into trouble. As a result of negotiations, Dunbee-Combex-Marx was granted patent, trademark, and copyright rights on a royalty basis for five years to manufacture and market Mattel toys in both the U.K. and Ireland, thus allowing the group to add such names as Barbie, Hot Wheels, Mark Strong, and Rosebud to its line and making it Europe's second largest toy company.

Quaker Oats, the world's second largest toy manufacturer, also hit the headlines early in the year when it applied for a listing on the London Stock Exchange. The company, which owned Fisher-Price Toys and Marx Toys, was well pleased with the profits being turned out by its toy divisions and seemed likely to increase its market share even further.

With regard to safety, 1973 was a relatively quiet period. The controversy that had blown up in Britain in 1972 over the sale of realistic-looking toy guns, some of which were later used in holdups, died down. Toy pistol makers claimed that sales of their products remained unaffected.

Traditional toys had another good year. Chad Valley was typical of many manufacturers in claiming that by August 90% of its soft toys were sold out, and that future orders were being filled on an allocation basis. Plastics kits continued to sell well; a major manufacturer, Airfix, recorded a 31% increase in pretax profit to £1,936,000, and its highest turnover ever, £14.5 million, for the year 1972–73, 36% higher than the previous year. In Japan, however, three panda doll manufacturers went bankrupt as the great demand that had begun there in 1972 ended abruptly.

Possibly the biggest all-around increase of the year was in sales of television characters. The worldwide publicity generated by Walt Disney Productions to celebrate its 50th anniversary undoubtedly was a contributing factor. (A. A. WHITE)

Track and Field Sports

The year after an Olympic Games is generally a quiet one in track and field, but it was not so in 1973. Among men's world records that fell were the 800 m. and 880 yd., 10,000 m., 3,000-m. steeplechase, 110-m. hurdles, high jump, shot put, and javelin, and records were equaled over 100 yd. and 120-yd. hurdles. Women's world records that took place included the 100 m. and 200 m., 400 m. (equaled controversially), 800 m., 100-m. hurdles, shot put, discus, javelin, pentathlon, and 400-m. relay. The new recommended ruling that 800-m. runners should race the first 300 m. in lanes and the refusal of the International Amateur Athletic Federation (IAAF) council to accept electrical timing as mandatory for any world records were much discussed. The year-old rule regarding ties for first place in the high jump and pole vault, by means of which ties were broken by extra trials at the tying and then other heights, was abandoned from Oct. 1, 1973, after it had proved costly and unnecessary. After a well-publicized indoor season, the new professional circuit, the International Track Association based in the U.S., settled down to sit out the outdoor summer when several contracts to tour Europe fell through.

International Competition. Regarding the 800-m. recommendation, many spectators felt something vital was missing when they saw the runners only making contact with 500 m. left to run. Evidence suggested that the ruling helped to create a spate of fast times, for front runners were able to push ahead unimpeded. Most notable of these was Marcello Fiasconaro, who led all the way to a world record 1 min. 43.7 sec. in the Italy *v.* Czechoslovakia match in June. Earlier in the year Rick Wohlhuter (U.S.) had beaten the 880-yd. standard in 1 min. 44.6 sec. The major clash at 800 m., the Europa Cup final at Edinburgh in September, resulted in a win for Britain's Andy Carter over Yevgeniy Arzhanov (U.S.S.R.) and Dieter Fromm (East Germany). Arzhanov had beaten Wohlhuter and Carter earlier but never raced against Fiasconaro because of an unfortunate disqualification in the cup semifinal in Oslo in July. The Italian started too soon twice and was disqualified.

The standpoint of the IAAF over electrical timing seemed curious in view of the women's world sprint records made during the season. Renate Stecher's manually timed 10.8 sec. for 100 m. was more accurately 11.07 sec. on the electrical device in operation at the time. Similarly, Stecher's 22.1 sec. for the 200 m. was nearer to 22.6 sec. but the fast, certainly flattering, time was forwarded for ratification along with the 100-m. time. Also, in the women's 400 m., the former Mona-Lisa Strandvall (now Pursiainen) ran an officially accepted 51 sec., though the electrical timing indicated it should have been 51.3 (51.27) sec. Stranger still was the IAAF's decision that all timing in major games should be electrical coupled with its rejection of its technical committee's recommendation that for all world records in the sprint events, the timing should be electrical only and be accepted to 100ths of a second.

Men of the middle distance events were Belgian Emiel Puttemans, Briton Brendan Foster, Kenya's Ben Jipcho, and Filbert Bayi from Tanzania. The rugged Kenyan chopped the steeplechase world record down to 8 min. 19.8 sec. and then to a sensational 8 min. 14 sec. and was the only man to beat Bayi over 1,500 m. or over a mile. Bayi forged many fast times with his pace-setting tactics (first lap inside 54 sec.). In nine races in Europe he only lost to Jipcho, when they both narrowly missed the world mile record in Stockholm, Jipcho winning in 3 min. 52 sec. to Bayi's 3 min. 52.6 sec. In an earlier 1,500-m. race in Helsinki, Bayi won in 3 min. 34.6 sec. and dragged all 11 pursuers behind him home in under 3 min. 38.51 sec.—the greatest mass finish in track history. Puttemans was undefeated at his specialty events throughout the year, claiming the best 5,000 m. time of 13 min. 14.6 sec. in a solo run. He also bettered Jipcho in a hot 2-mi. race, and ran a 3 min. 56 sec. mile. Foster raced sparingly but brilliantly: he broke the world 2 mi. record with 8 min. 13.8 sec. (though Puttemans' time of 8 min. 13.2 sec. indoors in February was the fastest ever recorded for the distance), won the Amateur Athletic Association (AAA) 5,000 m. title (13 min. 23.8 sec.), and bettered veteran Harald Norpoth (West Germany) and Manfred Kuschmann (East Germany) in the Europa Cup 5,000 m. Dave Bedford (U.K.) emerged from injury and obscurity halfway through the year and devastated the AAA 10,000 m. championship, winning in a world record 27 min. 31 sec.

The sprint revelation of the season was Steve Williams of the U.S., who blitzed 100 yd. in 9.1 sec. to equal the world record and went undefeated over 100 m. and 200 m. throughout the year in Europe; previously, he had been known as a 400 m. runner. In the 400 m. Benny Brown (U.S.) and Maurice Peoples (U.S.) both ran 44.7 sec., though perhaps competitively the leader was West German Karl Honz who enjoyed a fine season, climaxed with his Europa Cup win. Peoples, however, did run a staggering 43.4 sec. for a 440-yd. relay leg in May, the fastest for the distance ever recorded anywhere at anytime. John Akii-Bua's 48.5 sec. in the African Games led the 400-m. hurdles rankings. Rod Milburn (U.S.) trimmed the world 110-m. hurdles record to 13.1 sec.

In the high jump Dwight Stones (U.S.), Olympic bronze medalist and not even 20 until December, surprised himself and the world by scaling 2.30 m. (7 ft. 6½ in.) in the U.S. *v.* West Germany match—the first 2.30-m. jump in history. Al Feuerbach (U.S.) blasted a shot put record of 21.82 m. (71 ft. 7 in.), and Hartmut Briesenick (East Germany) cracked his own European record with 21.67 m. Anatoliy Bondarchuk (U.S.S.R.) dominated the hammer as usual with several throws of more than 75 m. At the start of the season Klaus Wolfermann (West Germany) stunned the world with a superb javelin cast of 94.08 m. (308 ft. 8 in.) and in the Europa Cup threw 90.68 m. Ryszard Skowronek (Poland) piled up good decathlon scores, most notably 8,208 pt., while the injury-plagued Lennart Hedmark (Sweden) managed 8,188 pt. Perhaps the least-publicized event in track and field is walking, and the decision to cut back to just a 20-km. event for the 1976 Olympics and thereafter exclude the sport completely was a sad one for many.

Not surprisingly, East Germany's women utterly dominated the Europa Cup. They failed to win only the 1,500 m., high jump, shot put, and discus on their way to victory. There were two notable world records set during the contest: Faina Melnik (U.S.S.R.) threw the 1-kg. discus 69.48 m. (227 ft. 11 in.) and Ruth Fuchs (East Germany) cast 66.10 m. (216 ft. 10 in.) in the javelin. Just before the meet, an East German sprint relay team sped 42.6 sec. in Potsdam to recapture world domination in the 400-m. relay. Perhaps the most remarkable of women's world track records came from East Germany's Annelie Ehrhardt, who charged to a stunning 12.3 sec. for 100-m. hurdles (on hand timing), but better still was an 800 m. from Svetla Zlateva (Bulgaria) in 1 min. 57.5 sec. in Athens. In Edinburgh, however, it was East Germany's Gunnhild Hoffmeister who won the 800 m. in 1 min. 58.9 sec. from the Bulgarian. In the Europa Cup pentathlon contest Mary Peters (U.K.) lost her world record when Burglinde Pollak (East Germany) rolled up the remarkable total of 4,932 pt. In Varna, Bulg., Nadyezhda Chizhova (U.S.S.R.) became the first woman to surpass 70 ft. and 21 m. with 21.45 m. (70 ft. 4½ in.) in the shot put on September 29.

(JAMES COOTE)

United States Competition. The year was a surprisingly productive one for U.S. track and field athletes. Normally, following the heated competition of the Olympic Games there is a "down" year. Many Olympians retire from the sport, while others lack the incentive of striving to make the Olympic team. But whereas the heat of an Olympic year produced but one world record by U.S. performers, 1973 accounted for four individual and one relay world marks broken and two others equaled. In an unusually diversified effort, the records were scored in one throwing event, one jumping, one straightaway sprint, one oval run, one relay, and two hurdle races.

Rod Milburn, world track and field athlete of the year in 1971 and Olympic champion in 1972, put his name into the world record book three more times in one five-week period. First he matched his own 120-yd. high hurdle standard of 13 sec., at Eugene, Ore., on June 20. Then on July 6, in Zürich, Switz., the Southern University senior ran the 110-m. hurdles in 13.1 sec., cutting 0.1 sec. off the mark shared by

Rod Milburn (U.S.) bounds ahead of the field on his way to a new world record in the 110-m. hurdles at Zürich, Switz., July 6, 1973. His time was 13.1 sec.

KEYSTONE

himself and four others. He did it again at Siena, Italy, on July 22.

Rick Wohlhuter also earned multiple entry on the records list. He anchored the University of Chicago Track Club two-mile relay team when it ran the distance in 7 min. 10.4 sec. at Durham, N.C., May 12. Wohlhuter's leg was 1 min. 44.8 sec., equal to the fastest relay time ever, as he followed Tom Bach (1 min. 50.5 sec.), Ken Sparks (1 min. 47.1 sec.), and Lowell Paul (1 min. 48 sec.). At Los Angeles, on May 27, he made up for the frustration of falling in the Olympics by claiming the 880 yd. record with a time of 1 min. 44.6 sec.

Completing the record action on the track was Steve Williams of the San Diego Track Club. The 19-year-old dashed 100 yd. in 9.1 sec. at Fresno, Calif., on May 12, equaling the figure first set ten years earlier and tied by five others.

Two Pacific Coast Club teammates were responsible for the new world records in the field events. Al Feuerbach put the shot 71 ft. 7 in. at San Jose, Calif., on May 5. And Dwight Stones returned to the Munich Olympic Games stadium where he had earned third place in the high jump to leap 7 ft. $6\frac{1}{2}$ in.

All of the above were of course new U.S. records as well, and three more performances topped anything ever done before by U.S. citizens. All came in distance runs, with Steve Prefontaine of the University of Oregon accounting for two of them. He covered 6 mi. in 27 min. 9.4 sec. at Bakersfield, Calif., on March 24 and 5,000 m. in 13 min. 22.4 sec. at Helsinki, Fin., on June 26. Jeff Galloway of the Florida Track Club was timed in 47 min. 49 sec. in the seldom-run 10-mi. event on May 26 at Raleigh, N.C.

In team competition, UCLA won its third consecutive National Collegiate Athletic Association (NCAA) title with 52 pt. at Baton Rouge, La., June 5–9. The National Association of Intercollegiate Athletics championship went to Texas Southern University, scoring 81 pt. at Arkadelphia, Ark., May 23–25.

In three dual meets against European opponents, the U.S. national team won twice but lost the big one. It defeated West Germany 122–101 at Munich, July 11–12, and Italy, 143–78, at Turin, July 17–18. The loss came at the hands of the U.S.S.R., which won 121–112 at Minsk, July 23–24.

The indoor season was enlivened by the debut of professional track under the auspices of the new International Track Association (ITA). More than 60 athletes competed in 16 cities for prize money, which included $500 for a first-place finish and $500 for each world record broken. Although the group included many of the brighter stars of recent competition, attendance at the meets was not always large. World record holders Bob Seagren, Randy Matson, Jim Ryun, Kipchoge Keino, Lee Evans, and others were welcomed by large crowds in such diverse localities as New York City's Madison Square Garden and the Minidome of Pocatello, Ida. Crowds dipped to 5,000 in other cities though, and the average for the year was about 7,000 per meet. Evans, world record holder for 400 m., won the most money in the competition, $13,900, while Chris Fisher of Australia, Ryun, Brian Oldfield, and Warren Edmonson topped the $10,000 mark.

Oldfield was the brightest star in the record department, three times improving the world indoor shot put standard. He achieved 69 ft. $11\frac{1}{2}$ in. in Daly City, Calif., 70 ft. $9\frac{1}{2}$ in. in Albuquerque, N.M., and 70 ft. $10\frac{1}{4}$ in. in Salt Lake City, Utah. Another field event mark was surpassed by John Radetich, who high jumped 7 ft. $4\frac{3}{4}$ in. at Pocatello.

Indoor bests were set in five track events and equaled in two more. Evans ran 1 min. 2 sec. for 500 m. in San Diego, Calif., and 1 min. 16.7 sec. for 600 m. in Pocatello. The San Diego meet also saw Fisher cover 1,000 m. in 2 min. 19.7 sec., while the third record at Pocatello went to Edmonson, who sprinted the 100 m. in 10.2 sec. Larry James claimed the 500 yd. record with 53.9 sec. at Salt Lake City, where Mel Pender matched the 60 yd. standard of 5.8 sec. The 70 yd. record of 6.8 sec. was tied at Louisville, Ky., by Jean-Louis Ravelomarantsoa of the Malagasy Republic, Edmonson, and Harrington Jackson.

Steve Smith was the outstanding performer of the amateur segment of the indoor season. After raising the U.S. pole vault record to 17 ft. $8\frac{1}{2}$ in. at College Park, Md., on January 12, the Pacific Coast Club member twice topped the world standard. He vaulted 17 ft. 11 in. at Los Angeles on January 20 and 18 ft. $\frac{1}{4}$ in. at New York on January 26.

Feuerbach also set two world indoor marks, putting the shot 69 ft. $4\frac{1}{2}$ in. at Los Angeles on January 20 and 69 ft. $5\frac{3}{4}$ in. on January 27 at Portland, Ore. But the record soon fell to George Woods, who hit 69 ft. $9\frac{1}{2}$ in. at New York on February 23, while Oldfield

Table I. World 1973 Outdoor Records—Men

Event	Competitor, country, date	Performance
100 yd.	Steve Williams, U.S., May 12	9.1 sec.*†
800 m.	Marcello Fiasconaro, Italy, June 27	1 min. 43.7 sec.
880 yd.	Rick Wohlhuter, U.S., May 27	1 min. 44.6 sec.
1,000 m.	Danie Malan, South Africa, June 24	2 min. 16 sec.
2 mi.	Brendan Foster, U.K., August 27	8 min. 13.8 sec.
10,000 m.	David Bedford, U.K., July 13	27 min. 31 sec.
15 mi.	Seppo Nikkari, Finland, October 14	1 hr. 12 min. 22.6 sec.
25,000 m.	Seppo Nikkari, Finland, October 14	1 hr. 14 min. 55.6 sec.
2-mi. relay	Chicago Track Club, U.S., May 12	7 min. 10.4 sec.
6,000-m. relay	New Zealand, August 22	14 min. 40.4 sec.
3,000-m. steeplechase	Ben Jipcho, Kenya, June 19	8 min. 19.8 sec.
	Ben Jipcho, Kenya, June 27	8 min. 14 sec.
120-yd. hurdles	Rod Milburn, U.S., June 20	13 sec.*
110-m. hurdles	Rod Milburn, U.S., July 6	13.1 sec.
50,000 m. walk	Gerhard Weidner, West Germany, March 15	4 hr. 00 min. 27 sec.
High jump	Dwight Stones, U.S., July 11	7 ft. $6\frac{1}{2}$ in.
Shot put	Al Feuerbach, U.S., May 5	71 ft. 7 in.
Javelin	Klaus Wolfermann, West Germany, May 5	308 ft. 8 in.

*Ties record.
†Hand timing.

Table II. World 1973 Outdoor Records—Women

Event	Competitor, country, date	Performance
100 m.	Renate Stecher, East Germany, June 7	10.9 sec.*†
	Renate Stecher, East Germany, June 30	10.9 sec.*†
	Renate Stecher, East Germany, July 20	10.9 sec.*†
	Renate Stecher, East Germany, July 20	10.8 sec.†
200 m.	Renate Stecher, East Germany, July 1	22.4 sec.*‡
	Mona-Lisa Pursiainen, Finland, August 20	22.4 sec.*‡
	Renate Stecher, East Germany, July 21	22.1 sec.†
800 m.	Svetla Zlateva, Bulgaria, August 24	1 min. 57.3 sec.
1 mi.	Glenda Reiser, Canada, July 7	4 min. 34.9 sec.
	Paola Pigni-Cacchi, Italy, August 8	4 min. 29.5 sec.
400-m. relay	East Germany, September 1	42.6 sec.
3,200-m. relay	Bulgaria, August 12	8 min. 8.6 sec.
100-m. hurdles	Annelie Ehrhardt, East Germany, July 21	12.3 sec.†
Shot put	Nadyezhda Chizhova, U.S.S.R., August 28	69 ft. $6\frac{3}{4}$ in.
	Nadyezhda Chizhova, U.S.S.R., September 29	70 ft. $4\frac{1}{2}$ in.
Discus	Faina Melnik, U.S.S.R., May 25	221 ft. 3 in.
	Faina Melnik, U.S.S.R., July 11	221 ft. 9 in.
	Faina Melnik, U.S.S.R., September 7	227 ft. 11 in.
Javelin	Ruth Fuchs, East Germany, September 7	216 ft. 10 in.
Pentathlon	Burglinde Pollak, East Germany, August 14	4,831 pt.
	Burglinde Pollak, East Germany August 22	4,932 pt.

*Ties record.
†Hand timing.
‡Electrical timing.

WIDE WORLD

Steve Smith of the Pacific Coast Club, Long Beach, Calif., clears 18 ft. 1/4 in. to shatter his own world indoor pole vault record at the Wanamaker Millrose Games at Madison Square Garden, New York City, Jan. 26, 1973.

came along later with his three improvements on Woods's new mark.

Top indoor mark on the track was Tracy Smith's world 3 mi. best of 13 min. 7.2 sec., achieved at New York on February 23. Other track records were in less common events. Milburn hurdled 120 yd. in 13.3 sec., 50 yd. in 5.8 sec. (along with Tom Hill and Danny Smith), and 55 m. in 7 sec., the latter tying the record. Tommy White also matched a hurdle mark, 6.4 sec. for 50 m. Sprinter Herb Washington tied two figures, speeding 50 yd. twice in 5 sec. and 60 m. in 6.5 sec. U.S. indoor records fell to Prefontaine with 8 min. 24.8 sec. for the 2-mi. run and the University of Chicago Track Club with 7 min. 23.6 sec. for the 2-mi. relay.

The NCAA indoor title was captured by Manhattan with 18 pt. at Detroit, March 9–10. And in the second-ever U.S.-U.S.S.R. indoor dual meet the Europeans evened the score with a 84–76 victory in Richmond, Va., on March 16.

Among the women, several outdoor world records were achieved, but all were in seldom-contested events. Wendy Koenig covered the new 400-m. intermediate hurdles in 59.1 sec., Francie Larrieu ran 2 mi. in 10 min. 2.8 sec., and the Prairie View sprint medley relay team was timed in 1 min. 40.6 sec. but could not receive credit for a world record as the team included citizens of both the U.S. and Jamaica.

There was more success in breaking U.S. records, headed by Olympic medalist Kathy Schmidt, who achieved a new javelin mark three times. Her best was 208 ft. 1 in. In other standard events Larrieu ran the mile in 4 min. 38.7 sec., and Martha Watson long jumped 21 ft. 7¼ in. Larrieu gained still another mark by running 3,000 m. in 9 min. 16 sec., while Gale Fitzgerald raised the pentathlon record to 4,326 pt.

Larrieu also achieved a world indoor best, again in the mile, with a performance of 4 min. 35.6 sec. Other world indoor marks were claimed by Iris Davis, 5.5 sec. for 50 yd.; Mamie Rawlins and Lacey O'Neal, equaling the 50-yd. hurdle mark of 6.4 sec.; and Patty Johnson, 13.4 sec. for the 100-m. hurdles.

Four women sprinters joined the ITA professional tour. All were Olympians, headed by Wyomia Tyus Simburg, the only runner, male or female, to defend an Olympic 100 m. title, and including Barbara Farrell, Lacey O'Neal, and Vilma Charlton. Farrell equaled the world 60 yd. best with a 6.5 sec. clocking.

(BERT NELSON)

Trade, International

A marked acceleration in the rate of growth of the volume of world trade took place in 1972 and 1973, and by mid-1973 the total volume of world trade was almost 25% higher than it had been two years earlier. The main reason for the large increases in 1972 and 1973 was that the cyclical upswing in world economic activity generated a more than proportional increase in demand for imported goods. In both 1970 and 1971 the increase in world industrial production had been little more than 1% per annum; this accelerated to 7% in 1972, and in the first quarter of 1973 had reached a level almost 10% higher than in the corresponding period of 1972. As a result world demand, particularly from industrial countries, grew rapidly. The volume of imports into industrial countries, which had grown at the modest rate of 6% in 1971, increased by 10.6% in 1972 and by about 15% in 1973 (Table I). This rapid increase was achieved in 1973 despite the slowing down of the growth in U.S. imports. An encouraging feature of the world economic scene was that world trade continued to grow rapidly in 1972 and 1973 despite world monetary difficulties and major realignments of exchange rates.

A notable feature of world trade in 1972–73 was the marked recovery in exports from primary producing countries; these had been adversely affected by the slowdown in the industrial countries' demand in the previous years. Of particular importance was the very sharp increase in export prices of primary products. The average increase for all commodities (excluding oil) in 1972 was 13%, but these prices increased even more rapidly in 1973 and in the second quarter of that year had reached a level about 40% higher than one year earlier.

The value of world trade, measured in U.S. dollars, increased by 18% in 1972 and by 28% in the first half of 1973. However, the depreciation of the U.S. dollar in 1972 and 1973 meant that its use as a common unit of measurement for world trade gave rise to some distortion in the figures. The amount of trading activity was, in fact, better measured by volume figures, but from the point of view of the balance of payments positions of individual countries and regions value figures are essential. The effect of the devaluation of the U.S. dollar was to inflate the dollar value of trade of all other countries by the amount of the devaluation. Accordingly, in Table II the growth in value of world exports and imports is shown in terms of a fixed unit of measure, the International Monetary Fund (IMF) special drawing right (SDR). This shows that the growth in value of world trade was less in 1972 than in 1971 but confirms the rapid increase in 1973.

Primary Producing Countries. The exports of primary producing economies benefited from the upswing in economic activity in industrial economies, and the volume of their exports increased in 1972 and 1973 at a rate above the 6.8% average of the previous decade. In addition, these countries benefited greatly from the rapidly rising prices for primary products, which gathered momentum toward the end of 1972 and accelerated in 1973. The average export price of primary products (excluding petroleum) was 13% higher in 1972 than in 1971, and very large additional increases occurred in 1973. The average price index in the second quarter of 1973 was about 40% above its level of one year earlier. In addition to rising demand in the industrial economies, prices of some commodities were forced upward by temporary supply deficiencies in the markets for wheat, meat, cocoa, and sugar. An additional demand pressure forcing up prices stemmed from the international monetary crises, which encouraged the purchase of commodities as a means of either hedging against the risks of holding a particular currency or of engaging in outright speculation on exchange rate changes.

In 1972 the more developed primary producers benefited most from the increases in prices as these tended to be concentrated in commodities that they produced. Oil and sugar prices also rose rapidly, but this benefited only a limited number of other countries. The price increases in 1972 centred on nonfood agricultural products, which recorded a 23% increase as against 12% for food. Metal prices overall rose very little in 1972 but accelerated sharply in the early part of 1973 to reach a level by midyear that was 23% above one year earlier. Food prices in mid-1973 were one-third higher and agricultural nonfood prices were as much as 60% above the level of the previous year. The prices of copper and zinc were both over 50% higher in mid-1973 than one year earlier. Similar increases in this period were recorded in the world prices of rubber and cotton, while cocoa and wool prices doubled.

The overall balance of trade of the primary producing countries improved considerably in 1972 (Table III), and a further reduction in their overall deficit was recorded in 1973. As noted above, it was the more developed primary producers that benefited first from the increased demand and rising prices of primary products. Although their imports also rose considerably, both Australia and New Zealand recorded much larger trade surpluses in 1972 of $1.8 billion and $320 million, respectively, compared with $400 million and $13 million in 1971. The further increase in prices, particularly of wool, in 1973 increased their respective trade surpluses in the first half of 1973 to annual rates of $3.1 billion and $1 billion.

Among the less developed primary producing economies, fortunes varied in 1972 depending on price movements. In 1973, however, most areas benefited from the increase in prices. Exports in 1972 increased in value by 16% while the growth in imports was a more modest 13%. As a result the balance of trade of this group of countries swung from a deficit of $3.2 billion in 1971 to a small surplus of $100 million in 1972. The oil exporting countries again fared particularly well, increasing their combined trade surplus from $8.8 billion to $10.2 billion in 1972. In the first half of 1973 the less developed economies increased the volume of their imports by 10%, while their exports rose by 8.6%. Such was the favourable movement in the terms of trade, however, that their export earnings increased by more than the 20% rise in their spending on imports, and so a further improvement in their trade balance occurred.

The balance of trade of Latin-American countries as a group improved in 1972 as the overall deficit was reduced by $400 million. In individual countries the major changes were a reduction in the Venezuelan trade surplus by more than $1.5 billion and a reduction in the deficit in Argentina of almost $1 billion, almost removing that nation's deficit.

In Asia a number of large countries improved their trading positions in 1972, and the overall deficit was reduced by $1.3 billion. In both India and Pakistan exports increased, while imports were reduced. In India the improvement in the trade balance was $500 million, and in Pakistan it was $280 million; both countries recorded their first trade surpluses for many years. The fact that the less developed economies of Africa recorded an overall trade surplus was due entirely to the $1.9 billion surplus, based on oil exports, recorded by Libya. This surplus was, in fact, slightly lower than in 1971, and the other countries in Africa reduced their combined deficits by $600 million.

Table I. World Trade

Percent change from previous year
(Value in U.S. dollars)

Country		1969	1970	1971	1972	1973*
Imports						
World	value	13.9	14.6	11.5	17.1	27.7
	volume	11.4	9.2	5.7	9.2	8.0
Industrial countries	value	15.0	15.2	11.5	18.0	29.3
	volume	11.8	9.1	6.0	10.6	15.5
U.S.	value	8.5	10.8	14.1	21.5	22.5
	volume	5.3	3.5	8.5	13.7	7.9
Canada	value	14.5	1.8	15.7	21.9	21.7
	volume	12.0	−3.1	10.0	16.3	15.1
U.K.	value	5.3	8.9	10.5	16.5	27.0
	volume	20.3	16.3	−3.3	12.0	13.6
Germany, West	value	23.7	19.6	15.2	15.8	28.3
	volume	18.0	14.1	10.9	9.2	10.0
Japan	value	15.7	25.7	4.4	19.1	52.7
	volume	15.9	20.4	1.7	10.2	22.2
Primary producers	value	10.0	12.5	11.7	12.9	20.2
	volume	7.9	9.5	5.1	2.3	10.0
More developed areas	value	13.8	18.8	9.1	−3.4	25.8
	volume	10.5	12.7	2.7	0.7	...
Less developed areas	value	9.8	11.8	12.0	11.0	17.3
	volume	6.8	8.1	6.2	3.1	...
Oil exporters	value	9.9	10.2	18.0	14.0	...
	volume	7.5	7.5	11.5	8.2	...
Others	value	9.7	12.3	10.5	5.0	...
	volume	6.6	8.3	4.7	1.7	...
Exports						
World	value	14.6	14.8	11.9	18.1	27.6
	volume	10.6	9.0	6.1	8.5	9.4
Industrial countries	value	15.2	15.5	11.8	18.5	29.5
	volume	11.6	9.3	5.9	8.9	15.1
U.S.	value	9.7	13.7	2.1	12.6	37.2
	volume	6.3	8.0	−1.2	9.3	24.7
Canada	value	9.4	16.6	8.8	14.5	22.2
	volume	6.6	9.9	5.7	9.8	14.8
U.K.	value	14.1	9.9	15.4	8.8	16.1
	volume	10.8	2.7	6.1	1.5	13.9
Germany, West	value	16.9	17.7	14.2	18.4	33.8
	volume	12.1	8.5	6.7	8.6	18.1
Japan	value	23.3	20.8	24.3	19.0	27.2
	volume	18.0	14.5	17.5	5.5	6.8
Primary producers	value	12.2	12.3	11.1	17.5	22.8
	volume	9.5	8.3	6.5	7.3	8.6
More developed areas	value	15.5	12.3	9.7	24.4	46.3
	volume	11.8	7.8	6.5	10.8	...
Less developed areas	value	12.1	11.8	11.0	16.4	19.3
	volume	8.8	8.5	6.5	6.1	...
Oil exporters	value	8.5	11.9	30.0	23.7	...
	volume	12.9	9.0	8.5	7.2	...
Others	value	14.3	11.5	1.5	13.2	...
	volume	7.6	6.2	4.8	5.1	...

*First six months compared with first six months of 1972.
Sources: International Monetary Fund, *Annual Report;* United Nations, *Monthly Bulletin of Statistics.*

Table II. Growth in Value of World Trade in U.S. $ and SDRs

Percent increase from one year earlier

	1972	1973 first half
World imports—U.S. $	17.1	27.7
—SDRs	7.8	17.6
World exports—U.S. $	18.1	27.6
—SDRs	8.8	17.5

Source: International Monetary Fund, *Annual Report.*

Table III. Primary Producing Countries' Foreign Trade

In $000,000,000

Area	1971 Exports	1971 Imports*	1971 Balance of trade	1972 Exports	1972 Imports*	1972 Balance of trade
More developed countries†	20.8	30.0	−9.2	24.8	32.5	−7.7
Less developed countries‡	60.9	64.1	−3.2	71.4	71.3	+0.1
Latin America	14.1	15.8	−1.7	16.2	17.5	−1.3
West Indies	2.8	4.4	−1.6	3.2	4.9	−1.7
Middle East	15.0	9.7	+5.3	17.6	11.0	+6.6
Asia	16.2	21.3	−5.1	19.8	23.6	−3.8
Africa	12.2	11.8	+0.4	14.0	13.1	+0.9
Total‡	81.7	94.1	−12.4	96.2	103.8	−7.6

*Imports, in most cases, include freight and insurance charges.
†Australia, New Zealand, South Africa, and the less industrialized countries of Western Europe.
‡The total includes Pacific islands not shown separately.
Source: International Monetary Fund, *International Financial Statistics.*

TASS/SOVFOTO

The contract for construction of a transmission plant at the Soviet Union's Kama River truck complex was awarded to a West German company, which outbid U.S. companies for the job. Above, construction of an iron foundry at the complex.

Industrial Countries. Exports from industrial countries increased by almost 9% in terms of volume in 1972. This rate of increase was very much in line with the average for the previous decade but was distinctly larger than the increase recorded in 1971. The upswing in economic activity raised demand in all industrial economies for imports in 1972 and 1973, and, in addition, in 1973 imports of primary producing countries accelerated as their growing export earnings and comfortable level of reserves enabled them to increase foreign spending. The volume of exports of industrial economies was approximately 15% higher in the first half of 1973 than a year earlier; this growth, however, was not maintained and the increase for the year as a whole was somewhat less than this.

The largest growth in the value of exports in 1972 was recorded by the EEC countries, whose combined exports rose by 22%, compared with a growth of 14% in the previous year. EEC exports to Japan, which had declined by 5% in 1971, increased by 25% in 1972. Trade between EEC countries, which in a number of previous years had been the fastest growing segment of world trade, increased in 1972 by 22%. Japan and the U.K. were the only industrial countries whose exports grew less rapidly in 1972 than their average rate for recent years. U.S. exports, which had declined by 1% in volume terms in 1971, increased by 9% in 1972, a rate well above the average of 5.6% recorded over the previous decade.

Industrial countries' imports expanded sharply in 1972; in both volume and value terms the increase was much greater than in 1971. This increase accelerated even more in the first half of 1973 but remained just below the expansion of exports in terms of value.

The combined trade balance of industrial countries was reduced from a surplus of $3,550,000,000 in 1971 to a small surplus of $450 million in 1972, which increased slightly in the first half of 1973 (Table IV). This apparent movement toward overall balance on trade flows in 1972 concealed some widely divergent movements in individual countries that had serious implications not only for the surplus and deficit countries but for the entire international monetary system. The main feature of the industrial countries' trade was the sharp increase in the U.S. deficit, from

Trade of Selected Industrial Countries

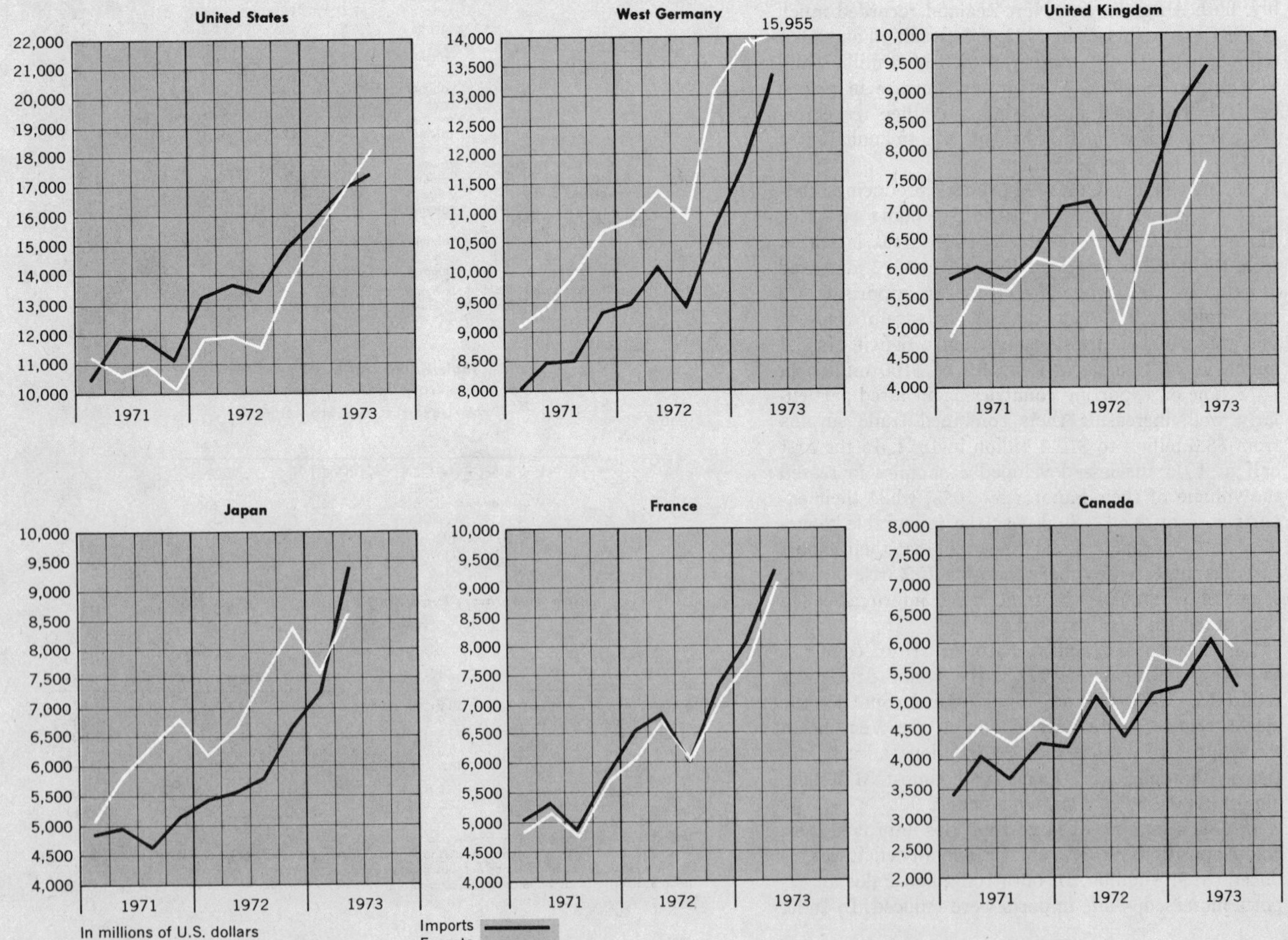

$1,460,000,000 to $5,880,000,000. There was an increase of more than $3 billion in the overall trade surplus of the original six EEC countries, but the U.K. deficit increased sharply. Further increases took place in the surpluses of the West German and Japanese economies, where the surpluses were already believed to be too large for future stability. Following the devaluation of the dollar and the upward revaluation of the yen, there were signs in 1973 of a reduction in both the U.S. deficit and the Japanese surplus. However, there was further growth in the West German surplus and in the British deficit.

The varying fortunes of these industrial countries can be clearly seen in Table V, which records their shares in total world exports of manufactured goods. The decline in the U.S. and U.K. share of total trade continued despite the depreciation of their currencies. On the other hand increases faster than those recorded for West Germany and Japan were prevented by upward revaluations of the mark and the yen.

Table IV. Trade of Industrial Countries

In $000,000,000

Country	1972 Exports	1972 Imports	1972 Balance of trade	1973* Exports	1973* Imports	1973* Balance of trade
U.S.	49.68	55.56	−5.88	58.39	62.53	−4.14
Canada	20.18	18.92	1.26	22.98	21.29	1.69
EEC†	153.16	153.22	−0.06	172.44	173.37	−0.93
Belgium	16.00	15.50	0.50	18.00	17.36	0.64
France	25.74	26.57	−0.83	29.40	30.35	−0.95
Germany, West	46.21	39.77	6.24	52.98	44.72	8.26
Italy	18.54	19.27	−0.73	18.89	21.35	−2.46
Netherlands, The	16.39	17.12	−0.73	19.68	19.99	−0.31
U.K.	24.35	27.85	−3.50	26.69	31.31	−4.62
Japan	28.60	23.47	5.13	32.32	28.02	4.30
Total	251.62	251.17	0.45	286.13	285.21	0.92

*First half of year, seasonally adjusted, at annual rate.
†This includes for all years the trade of Denmark, Ireland, and the U.K., who joined the EEC in January 1973.
Source: Organization for Economic Cooperation and Development, *Main Economic Indicators.*

Table V. World Exports of Manufactured Goods

Percent of total value

Year	Total value in $000,000,000*	United States	United Kingdom	West Germany	France	Italy	Japan	Others†
1960	52.4	21.6	16.5	19.3	9.6	5.1	6.9	21.0
1965	83.2	20.3	13.9	19.1	8.8	6.7	9.4	21.8
1968	114.8	20.1	11.6	19.4	8.2	7.3	10.6	22.8
1969	134.6	19.3	11.3	19.5	8.2	7.3	11.2	23.2
1970	155.0	18.5	10.8	19.8	8.7	7.2	11.7	23.3
1971	175.8	17.0	10.9	20.0	8.8	7.2	13.0	23.1
1972	205.7	16.2	10.1	20.3	9.3	7.6	13.3	23.3
1973‡	254.4	15.9	9.7	22.2	9.6	6.3	12.8	23.5

*Excluding special category exports (mostly arms).
†Belgium, Luxembourg, Canada, The Netherlands, Sweden, and Switzerland.
‡First half year (seasonally adjusted); value at annual rate.
Source: National Institute of Economic and Social Research, London.

Much international interest in world trade in 1972 and 1973 centred on the U.S. deficit and the Japanese surplus. It is to developments in these two countries, with their widely differing problems, that the remainder of this article is devoted.

The U.S. had recorded in 1971 its first trade deficit since 1935, and this deficit increased substantially in 1972 to reach a very serious level of almost $6 billion. Following the devaluation of the dollar in February 1973, there was a reduction in the deficit but it remained as a major problem. In 1972 the value of U.S. exports increased by 13%, as large an increase as had been recorded in any recent year. Imports, however, rose by about 14% in volume and, with rising prices, by 22% in value. The resulting increase in the U.S. trade deficit was not what had been expected at the time of the Smithsonian realignment of world currencies in December 1971. In particular, it had not been expected that the U.S. import bill would rise so dramatically in 1972. Various reasons, however, were given to explain this: (1) The devaluation of the dollar caused imports to be more expensive, and also world commodity prices were moving upward. (2) The cyclical upswing in the U.S. economy caused increased demand for all categories of imports. (3) Imports of manufactured goods, which had risen by 20% in 1971, rose by a further 27% in 1972. (4) Increased imports of oil to meet the soaring U.S. appetite for energy added an additional $1.1 billion to the import bill.

It soon became apparent that the magnitude of the problem could not be handled by the previous rather small devaluation of the dollar and that the unique international trading position of the U.S. had changed considerably over the past decade. Other industrial nations were beginning to catch up and overtake U.S. industry, which also was suffering from internal inflation. Accordingly, in February 1973 the dollar was devalued by 10%.

The U.S. trade deficit was sharply reduced in the second quarter of 1973, and for the first half year the deficit was well below the rate of 1972. The rate of growth of imports slowed down considerably in terms of volume, but due to devaluation the average price rose sharply and the value was 22% above the first half of 1972. There was a dramatic increase in both the volume and value of U.S. exports in the first part of 1973. Part of this gain, however, was temporary since it was due to exports of agricultural products reaching unprecedented levels as rising foreign demand coincided with worldwide crop shortages. Authorities hoped that the devaluation of the dollar would bring about the necessary improvement in the balance of trade, but it was far from clear to what extent the reduced deficit in the second quarter was due to devaluation or to temporary factors such as agricultural exports. Furthermore, about half the improvement in the trade balance in the second quarter was due to trade with Japan. U.S. exports were encouraged by official Japanese actions, while restrictions were imposed in Japan on "excessive" sales to the U.S. These restrictions, however, were lifted in September 1973.

The other major imbalance that the realignment of currencies at the end of 1971 was designed to cure was the Japanese surplus. The growth in the volume of Japanese exports fell to only 5% in 1972 due to a slower growth in demand in the major markets and a reduced share of some markets because of the 11% upward revaluation of the yen. However, the growth in the value of exports amounted to 19%, similar to the growth in the value of imports. It was noticeable that Japanese exporters were switching their attention from the U.S. market to Europe. Japanese sales to EEC countries in 1972 increased by 35%.

As the realignment of currencies appeared to be doing very little to reduce the Japanese surplus, a broadly based program of measures to promote imports and reduce exports was instituted in November 1972. These measures, combined with a rapid expansion of domestic demand and large-scale purchases of primary products, brought a reduction in the surplus in 1973 to an annual rate of $4.8 billion in the first quarter and $3.6 billion in the second quarter. The effect of these and other measures was readily apparent. In 1971 about 40% of the total Japanese trade surplus had come from trade with the U.S., but in the second quarter of 1973 Japan actually recorded a small deficit with the U.S. (A. G. ARMSTRONG)

See also Commercial Policies; Commodities, Primary; Payments and Reserves, International.

ENCYCLOPÆDIA BRITANNICA FILMS. *Rotterdam—Europort, Gateway to Europe* (1971).

Trade Unions: *see* Labour Unions

Traffic Accidents: *see* Disasters

Transportation

For many years transport policy, at least in developed countries, had been preoccupied primarily with two problems: how to accommodate the automobile in cities; and what to do about declining railways. By 1973 these problems were being overshadowed, not only in advanced countries, and not only on land but at sea and in the air, by two wider preoccupations: protection of an increasingly afflicted environment; and conservation of familiar energy resources that were suddenly beginning to look precious. The politically motivated petroleum cutbacks begun by the Arab oil-producing countries during the Arab-Israeli war in October, combined with astronomical increases in the price of oil on the world market, threatened at year's end to produce an energy crisis that could throw the world's transportation systems into disarray. But even before the Arab moves, the inexorable growth of worldwide demand for the movement of both people and goods had appeared to be on a collision course with the finite nature of the fuels that made such movement possible.

In the United States, 1973 would be remembered as the year in which the automobile, which had reigned supreme there for so long, was subjected to widespread curtailment in the interests of conserving fossil fuel. It was the year in which Europe's Concorde supersonic airliner continued to knock vainly at the door of the U.S. airlines. It was also the year in which providers of transport services found it increasingly difficult to do their job because nobody wanted roads, airports, or seaports on his doorstep.

Not surprisingly in these circumstances, politicians and transport planners began to display symptoms of schizophrenia, notably in Europe where the accession of three transport-conscious countries—Britain, Denmark, and Ireland—to the EEC brought fresh urgency to the European Commission's hitherto dilatory progress toward a Community transport policy. Because the EEC had been launched primarily for the furtherance of economic ends, such groping steps as had been taken toward a common transport policy before 1973 had been concerned mainly with ironing out market anomalies. Among six countries, this was difficult enough. With the accession of a seventh strong member (Britain), the conflict became even greater. So it was hardly surprising that policymaking was largely limited to such innocuous minutiae as standardizing the hours worked by truck drivers throughout the Community.

Bede Aircraft, Inc., of Cleveland, O., announced that it would manufacture the single-seat, 200+ mph BD-5 airplane for delivery in August 1974. It is, said the company, "the first new and modern design to come along in many years."

AUTHENTICATED NEWS INTERNATIONAL

As long as transport policy was seen primarily in economic terms, it remained a comparatively straightforward affair (on paper, at least) of getting costs and prices on a common basis, then letting market forces produce their own solutions. However, before the EEC seriously got down to formulating such a plan, its archproponent, Britain, was already proposing to drive a coach and horses through its own policy. Britain's 1968 Transport Act, which set a worldwide pattern by introducing specific subsidies for unprofitable but necessary services, was supposed to eliminate deficit financing on the railways and get them off the politicians' backs forever. By 1973, however, it was clear that British Rail's deficit, far from disappearing, was growing larger, and preparations for introducing new subsidies were under way.

This change of direction was made credible by the two considerations mentioned earlier: protection of the environment and conservation of energy, both of which were gratefully called in aid by the railways in their plea for a larger share of national investment. The same argument was likely to be used in Europe, where quality of life was being set alongside economic growth as an important EEC objective, and in the U.S., where the hard-pressed National Railroad Passenger Corporation (Amtrak) seemed to need ever more state aid and where the freight lines, already short of cars, were likely to inherit a greater share of freight from the oil-short truckers.

The railways were undoubtedly energy-conserving, compared with other transport modes. Therefore, they only stood to gain, as witness the investment in new mass-transit systems, refurbishing of old railways, and the projected Channel Tunnel rail link between Britain and France. How far the revival in high-capacity guided systems would go was impossible to say, since it depended so much on the extent and severity of the fuel shortage and on whether or not a clean, energy-conserving alternative to the internal combustion engine could be found.

While the experts continued to insist that the necessary breakthrough in battery technology was years away, the attraction of electricity as a clean, quiet, and fume-free means of propulsion for urban use was such that a whole range of experimental vehicles and systems were developed. One of the most remarkable to emerge in 1973 was the Dutch Witkar project, which aimed to provide a fleet of small, computer-controlled, battery-powered rental cars for movement around the old quarter of Amsterdam.

At sea the energy situation was conspicuous in the huge fleet of liquid-gas carriers under construction and in the scramble for oil stockpiles that kept tanker freight rates at record levels for much of the year. The effect of the Arab countries' cutback in oil shipments was still unclear at year's end. Concern for cleaner seas impelled the UN maritime arm, the Inter-Governmental Maritime Consultative Organization, to recommend a range of new measures to cut down pollution by oil and other harmful products.

In the air transport field, large new airports and fast new aircraft were resisted, while the new generation of quieter, wide-bodied jets was encouraged. Even the airship, so appropriate in many ways to the needs of the future, was taken out and given another dusting, though it bristled with operating problems. Walking, bicycling, and ballooning were on a rising market.

(MICHAEL BAILY)

World Transportation

Country	Railways: Route length in 000 km.	Railways Traffic: Passenger in 000,000 pass.-km.	Railways Traffic: Freight in 000,000 net ton-km.	Motor transport: Road length in 000 km.	Motor transport: Vehicles in use: Passenger in 000	Motor transport: Vehicles in use: Commercial in 000	Merchant shipping (Ships of 100 tons and over): Number of vessels	Merchant shipping: Gross reg. tons in 000	Air traffic: Total km. flown in 000	Air traffic: Passenger in 000,000 pass.-km.	Air traffic: Freight in 000,000 net ton-km.
EUROPE											
Austria	5.9*	6,668	9,817	95.4	1,325.0	128.0	11	31	10,755	476	6.1
Belgium	4.1	8,168	7,454	92.2	2,128.0	216.0	224	1,192	47,863	3,093	233.1
Bulgaria	4.2	6,701	15,813	35.7	c.17.0†	c.20.0†	149	742	7,830	313	5.8
Czechoslovakia	13.3	18,983	65,909	146.0	1,009.1	216.8	13	103	19,566	1,199	19.0
Denmark	2.0*	3,637*	1,926*	63.9	1,147.3	215.2	1,331	4,020	32,523‡	1,651‡	72.7‡
Finland	6.0	2,580	6,508	72.9	818.0	121.5	402	1,630	22,223	935	27.3
France	35.3	43,093	68,493	789.2	13,920.0	1,890.0	1,390	7,420	205,418	74,023	556.2
Germany, East (excluding Berlin)	14.5	19,931	44,710	c.160.0†	1,268.0	198.0	436	1,198	...	1,073	29.7
Germany, West (excluding Berlin)	32.8	39,065	64,865	418.6	16,324.0§	1,220.0§	2,546	8,516	146,240	10,452	700.7
Greece	2.6	1,635	748	35.5	301.9	130.2	2,241	15,329	31,380	2,965	46.5
Hungary	8.7	14,041	19,432	109.3	340.2	100.4	19	34	9,004	321	7.6
Ireland	2.2	818	500	87.2	418.1	44.5	97	182	22,281	1,623	80.0
Italy	20.1	35,370	17,097	287.4	12,475.0	986.0	1,684	8,187	153,461	9,502	323.7
Netherlands, The	3.1	8,114	3,071	81.4	3,117.4	346.5	1,452	4,972	95,699	7,857	479.6
Norway	4.2	1,620*	2,640*	74.2	854.2	161.6	2,826	23,507	43,116‡	2,526‡	90.4‡
Poland	23.5	38,781	109,779	302.4	656.9	293.0	617	2,013	16,506	820	9.5
Portugal	3.6	3,760	829	30.5	584.0	25.1	407	1,027	46,033	3,005	59.1
Romania	11.0	18,811	50,840	75.7	c.35.0†	45.1†	86	446	9,539	357	6.3
Spain	16.3	14,393	10,221	142.0	3,254.8	818.1	2,313	4,300	111,495	8,083	174.5
Sweden	12.2	4,125	15,658	c.175.3	2,456.9	145.4	875	5,632	53,889‡	3,006‡	134.2‡
Switzerland	5.0	8,302	6,703	60.6	1,561.3	152.3	33	212	78,345	5,783	218.5
U.S.S.R.	257.1	274,554	2,766,000	1,358.9†	c.1,500.0	c.4,500.0	6,851	16,734	...	88,331	1,876.7
United Kingdom	18.7‖	30,129‖	20,471‖	359.6	12,448.8	1,660.0	3,700	28,625	339,733	22,168	782.6
Yugoslavia	10.3	10,571	19,026	104.4	875.4	122.1	364	1,588	19,754	1,030	6.9
ASIA											
Burma	3.1	2,382	829	c.25.0	29.8†	31.0†	40	55	6,163	154	2.2
Cambodia (Khmer Republic)	0.6	90	10	c.11.0†	26.4	11.1	2	2	1,076	32	0.7
China	c.35.0†	45,670†	265,260†	c.800.0†	c.60.0†	c.400.0†	286	1,181	...	64†	2.0
India	60.0	118,309	127,407	1,021.8	646.5	346.0	412	2,650	59,510	4,556	151.3
Indonesia	7.9†	3,884†	655†	84.9	277.2	131.2	513	619	24,329	1,254	22.5
Iran	4.5	1,991	3,363	43.4	354.8	101.3	88	181	12,370	727	11.7
Iraq	2.5	467	1,310	12.8	53.5	42.3	41	121	5,304	253	2.7
Israel	0.8	388	421	c.9.3	201.1	82.5	99	698	33,063	3,356	103.3
Japan	27.9	301,491	60,265	1,037.6	12,531.0	9,820.0	9,433	34,929	228,456	13,695	593.4
Korea, South	5.4	8,750	7,086	40.6	67.6	70.8	446	1,057	c.15,630	749	39.1
Malaysia	1.8	672¶	1,108¶	c.28.5	308.9	73.3	99	149	15,185♀	857♀	16.7♀
Pakistan	8.6	8,690	7,010	62.8	74.3	21.1	131	533	28,798δ	1,142	58.5
Philippines	1.1	699	83	73.5	285.1	182.3	327	925	40,815	1,497	26.3
Syria	1.3	84	125	16.7	31.7	17.5	7	2	4,368	181	1.7
Taiwan	3.8	6,806	2,614	15.5	55.1	47.6	399	1,495	17,752†	954†	25.2†
Thailand	3.8†	c.3,860†	c.2,250†	17.7	282.6	158.9	69	108	20,429	1,181	21.1
Turkey	8.1	5,738	5,748	59.4	151.4	128.7	340	743	15,702	1,148	8.2
Vietnam, South	0.7	85	38	20.9†	58.4	29.2	39	32	9,421	434	4.0
AFRICA											
Algeria	4.0	1,014	1,531	78.4	165.0	90.8	40	133	12,439	643	4.4
Central African Republic	...	...	...	21.3	6.1	6.0†	...	...	1,774□	78□	7.6□
Chad	...	...	...	30.7	5.2	5.9	...	...	2,374□	89□	8.5
Dahomey	0.6†	84	94	6.9†	12.8	7.7	2	—	1,374□	74□	7.6□
Egypt	5.2†	6,772	3,340	c.50.0†	141.5	34.7	127	243	15,897	956	18.1
Gabon	0.4	...	...	6.1	7.1†	5.8†	6	2	2,904□	96□	7.8□
Ghana	1.0†	448	293	31.0	36.5†	27.0†	74	166	3,650	135	2.7
Ivory Coast	0.6	716	441	36.1	64.3	35.2	36	82	1,774□	80□	7.8□
Kenya	2.1†	4,529†◇	4,418◇	43.3	67.5	61.6	23	22	6,423▲	288▲	10.4▲
Malawi	0.6	74	218	10.7	12.7	10.1	...	...	1,645	54	0.7
Mali	0.6	77†	110†	14.5	13.9	2.8	...	...	1,874	58	2.5
Morocco	1.8	549	3,032	25.2	242.1	90.5	39	47	8,878	480	6.9
Nigeria	3.5	963	1,226	89.9	68.0	44.0	56	99	5,969	280	7.6
Rhodesia	2.6	...	6,293+	78.0	126.6†	52.0†	...	...	...	196	1.0
Senegal	1.0	322	188	15.4	40.4	22.8	39	16	1,914□	83□	7.7□
South Africa	19.8	...	58,570⊕	c.320.0	1,535.0†	394.0†	255	511	48,275	3,152	74.0
Tanzania	2.0	4,529†◇	4,418◇	16.7†	35.8	38.0	12	19	6,423▲	288▲	10.4▲
Uganda	1.2	4,529†◇	4,418◇	25.7	33.5	11.0	1	6	6,423▲	288▲	10.4▲
Zaire	5.3	751	2,482	140.0†	70.0†	27.5†	9	40	12,222	610	23.2
Zambia	1.4†	...	...	34.7†	61.6	34.1	1	6	5,978	320	6.5
NORTH AND CENTRAL AMERICA											
Canada	74.1	3,289	179,026	831.1	6,967.2	1,856.0	1,235	2,381	241,777	15,459	485.9
Costa Rica	0.8	c.57	c.13	18.7†	43.4	26.4	10	4	6,595	199	9.4
El Salvador	0.6†	...	...	10.7	35.9	20.9	10	2	...	...	...
Guatemala	0.9	...	106†	11.2	42.6†	24.4†	2	4	2,410	85	5.5
Honduras	1.0	...	...	5.2†	18.8†	16.9†	58	74	5,971	174	3.3
Mexico	19.8	4,362	22,374	109.2	1,520.1	592.8	216	417	65,367	3,571	45.3
Nicaragua	0.3	35†	13†	6.4	34.4†	8.7†	11	22	2,580	107	1.0
Panama	0.7	...	...	6.8†	55.6	17.7	1,337	7,794	...	...	...
United States	338.0	13,779	1,079,492	6,049.3	92,752.5	19,772.2	3,687	15,024	3,827,194	245,303	8,038.9
SOUTH AMERICA											
Argentina	39.5	12,183	12,284	283.8	1,680.0	788.0	343	1,401	51,240	2,700	66.5
Bolivia	3.5	271†	326†	25.6	c.19.2▲	c.28.8†	...	...	4,119	146	2.6
Brazil	31.8	11,232	17,358	1,138.4	2,324.3†	696.2†	444	1,885	108,120	5,959	265.6
Chile	9.8	2,481	2,718	63.7	193.0	135.7	134	382	23,965	1,142	55.2
Colombia	3.5	282	1,151	45.9	165.0	86.6	54	232	52,883	2,182	83.0
Ecuador	1.0†	85†	56†	18.3	27.0†	36.4†	21	57	10,178	209	5.0
Paraguay	0.5†	28†	22†	11.2†	7.4†	10.1†	26	22	...	...	...
Peru	2.1†	248†	410†	50.7	256.4	136.1	655	446	11,171	224	17.8
Uruguay	3.0†	...	...	c.42.0	c.121.0†	c.88.0†	39	143	2,420	27	0.1
Venezuela	0.5†	36†	13†	44.3	778.6	256.1	113	411	30,343	1,521	67.2
OCEANIA											
Australia	40.3*	...	25,260*	902.2	4,315.7	1,058.7	370	1,184	193,828	9,682	255.1
New Zealand	4.8	724	3,036	89.3	941.6	185.3	120	182	35,260	2,260	57.9

Note: Data are for 1971 or 1972 unless otherwise indicated.
(—) Indicates nil or negligible; (...) indicates not known; (c.) indicates provisional or estimated.
*State system only.
†Data given are the most recent available.
‡Including apportionment of traffic of Scandinavian Airlines System.
§Including West Berlin.
‖Excluding Northern Ireland.
¶Including Singapore.
♀Apportionment of traffic of Malaysia-Singapore Airlines Ltd.
δIncluding Bangladesh.
□Including apportionment of traffic of Air Afrique.
◇Total for Kenya, Tanzania, and Uganda (East African Railways Corp.).
▲Including apportionment of traffic of East African Airways Corp. and Caspair Ltd.
+Including traffic for Botswana.
⊕Including Namibia (South West Africa).

Sources: UN, *Statistical Yearbook 1972, Monthly Bulletin of Statistics, Annual Bulletin of Transport Statistics for Europe 1971*; Lloyd's Register of Shipping, *Statistical Tables 1972*; International Road Federation, *World Road Statistics 1973; Jahrbuch des Eisenbahnwesens 1973.*

(M. C. MacDONALD)

AVIATION

After several lean years the general health of the world air transport industry improved somewhat in 1973. Traffic and financial results did not come up to earlier expectations, however, especially in the U.S., where the airlines had hoped to shake off the effects of the recent financial depression.

Early estimates toward the end of the year indicated that passenger traffic in the U.S. in 1973 would not be more than 8 or 9% above 1972. In the first half of the year Pan American's revenue traffic was slightly below that of the same period in 1972, while United Air Lines and TWA each reported an 8% gain and American Airlines a 2% gain. Eastern Airlines had originally expected 10% growth, but revised its figure for the second half of the year from 8 to 6%. The smaller airlines took a brighter view, but it seemed unlikely that the industry as a whole would reach the 12% growth rate widely considered normal.

Freight traffic in the U.S. was stronger. During the first seven months of 1973, domestic freight was 17½% above the same period in 1972, and international freight was up 10%. On the North Atlantic the airlines reported weak scheduled traffic; in the first eight months the number of passengers rose less than 8% above the preceding year, and results in the peak months of July and August were particularly poor. This situation stemmed partly from the increase in charter traffic, which now accounted for about one-third of the total in this market.

The European flag airlines were in a better position during 1973. Traffic on intra-European routes grew by about 10%, and on intercontinental routes by as much as 20%. Their freight traffic was also strong, with growth at around 15%.

In May the International Civil Aviation Organization (ICAO) reported that 1972 traffic had been significantly better than that of the previous year. The final scheduled traffic results for all the ICAO member states, including the U.S.S.R. (but excluding China), were as follows (percentage change from 1971 in parentheses): passengers carried, 443 million (+8.8%); passenger-kilometres (number of passengers times distance flown), 555,000,000,000 (+12.1%); freight ton-kilometres (metric tons times distance flown), 14,900,000,000 (+13.7%); total ton-kilometres, 67,790,000,000 (+12%). ICAO's statistics showed that the U.S. accounted for about 45% of the world's scheduled airline traffic in ton-kilometres; the U.S.S.R. accounted for about 15½%, and the United Kingdom, Japan, France, and Canada for between 3 and 5% each. These six countries, in that order, had the largest air transport industries.

In 1973, for the first time, ICAO produced a detailed report on nonscheduled services, a subject on which information had been sparse in the past. In 1971, the latest year for which figures were available, nonscheduled traffic amounted to about 32% of the world total, or 83,000,000,000 passenger-kilometres out of a total of 256,000,000,000. More than one-quarter of the nonscheduled traffic was carried by the charter airlines based in Europe, reflecting the well established charter industry in that area. ICAO also estimated that total revenue from nonscheduled services worldwide was about $1.8 billion in 1971, split equally between charter carriers and the scheduled airlines' charter operations.

The financial situation of the major scheduled airlines in the U.S. in 1973 was gloomy. In the first eight months of the year—with the most profitable season behind them—Eastern, American, and Pan American all posted net losses. American's loss was $26.3 million, compared with a $12.4 million profit in the same period of 1972, and in the fall 74-year-old C. R. Smith was called out of retirement in an effort to regain the prosperity the company had enjoyed under his leadership. Two other major airlines, United and TWA, achieved profits, although TWA's outlook for the full year was dimmed by a strike of cabin attendants that grounded its planes for much of November and December. United emerged from a difficult period the previous year with an eight-month profit of $36.6 million, $25 million better than in the first eight months of 1972. Although Pan American's financial troubles were clearly not yet over, the premier U.S. international carrier appeared to have improved its position considerably in 1973, with its cost level running only about 7% above the previous year, against an industry average of more than 10%.

In Europe cost inflation was still a major problem in 1973, but the situation seemed less serious than in the U.S. In its fiscal year ended March 31, 1973, British Airways reported a £5.2 million net profit and a 6.7% return on net assets. This was British Airways' first fiscal year since the group was created by a merger of the two former state airlines, British European Airways (BEA) and British Overseas Airways Corporation (BOAC). During 1973 the merger was consolidated; the airline was now the largest outside the U.S. and the U.S.S.R.

One major problem still troubling the airline industry was the fall in revenue rates caused by the introduction of "promotional" fares—reduced-rate fares, such as excursions, subject to special conditions. The International Air Transport Association (IATA) noted that revenue per passenger-mile had sunk from 12 cents in 1950 to 2.5 cents in 1972. The situation was perhaps worst on the North Atlantic, where a high proportion of scheduled passengers traveled at reduced rates as a result of efforts to combat inroads by charter operators.

Efforts by the U.S., Canada, and Western European countries to clean up the illicit charters on the North Atlantic bore fruit in 1973. Illegal activities had developed because of the ease with which the rules attached to group charters—that all passengers should be bona fide members of a club or similar organization—could be circumvented. The chief countermeasure was the advance-booking charter (ABC), open to any member of the public prepared to commit himself to a booking a specified number of weeks in advance of the flight. It was felt that such a rule would deter businessmen and other full-fare passengers from taking advantage of the cheap rates. A memorandum of understanding on advance-booking charters was signed between the U.S. and Britain in March. The ABC fares introduced averaged about £80 ($190)—depending on the season, the number of passengers, and optional services—for a round trip between New York and northwestern Europe, a half to a quarter of the normal scheduled fares. The Europeans wanted to introduce the "part-charter" concept, whereby groups of charter passengers would be carried on scheduled services. This was resisted by the U.S. Civil Aeronautics Board (CAB), chiefly because of distinctions in U.S. law between scheduled and nonscheduled service.

On July 27 representatives of 42 airlines from both sectors of the industry met in Brighton, Eng., to discuss the relationship between scheduled services and charters and to try to reach a common position on charter prices. The meeting was the first of its kind; it failed to reach any generally acceptable conclusions, but observers noted that the mere holding of the event spelled out some hope for future cooperation. In order to attend such intraindustry consultations, U.S. airlines had to obtain CAB authorization. The CAB consented on the ground that Atlantic charters had become uneconomic. This view was supported when more than one airline withdrew from Atlantic charters during the year.

Developments on the political front included further moves to establish a common air transport policy within the EEC. In January the Transport Committee of the European Parliament called for greater technical and commercial cooperation among airlines and for the negotiation of multilateral rather than bilateral international agreements on landing rights. Other points were the need for common standards for the protection of the environment and for common action against hijacking.

Hijacking remained a major problem. It was the subject of a six-week conference organized by the ICAO which opened in Rome on August 28. Efforts were made to strengthen international law and to improve the existing Hague and Montreal conventions, but the meeting ended inconclusively. The U.S.S.R. demanded automatic extradition of hijackers to the state of registry of the aircraft, while Britain, France, and Switzerland insisted that countries failing to act against hijackers be suspended from the ICAO. One stumbling block was the continuing difference of opinion on what constituted permissible grounds for extradition and asylum.

Although an international convention aimed at limiting hijacking and other acts of terrorism failed to gain passage at the United Nations, the U.S. and Cuba concluded a five-year pact intended to curb hijacking between the two countries. Under the terms of the new pact both sides were required to prosecute severely or to extradite anyone hijacking a plane or boat. Political refugees facing death at home would still be allowed asylum, but only if they did not exact a ransom or cause physical injury in escaping. The agreement promised to provide a significant deterrent to hijackings to Cuba, which had long been a major haven for hijackers. Thus in 1969, when there had been 88 attempted hijackings worldwide, 70 of them successful, 58 had gone to Cuba; in 1970, of 84 attempts, 54 of which were successful, 31 had gone to Cuba; and in 1972, in 59 attempts, 24 of them successful, only 9 had gone to Cuba.

Vastly improved security procedures at the world's major airports were largely credited with the overall reduction in hijackings in 1973. At London's Heathrow Airport, for example, these procedures netted the following tally of weapons from passengers on British Airways in the first six months of 1973: 84 guns, 502 knives, and 255 swords; 1,722 rounds of ammunition; and 367 other weapons. In the U.S. the Federal Aviation Administration noted that the number of air travelers caught for possession of guns and drugs and for other crimes had declined sharply following the introduction of nationwide screening of all passengers. In the first six months of these searches 894 guns had been seized, 1,337 persons arrested for various offenses, and 1,505 persons refused permission to board aircraft, usually for declining to be searched. The cost to the airlines of this screening process was estimated to be at least $300 million a year, most of which was passed on to passengers in the form of increased fares and airport taxes.

By mid-October almost 11 months had passed without a successful hijacking in the U.S. Incidents continued in other countries, however, with the most spectacular being related to the situation in the Middle East. On July 20 a Japan Air Lines Boeing 747 en route to Tokyo was hijacked shortly after takeoff from Amsterdam by five terrorists. The aircraft eventually landed at Benghazi, Libya, where it was blown up by the hijackers after the passengers and crew had been allowed to leave. The demands made by the hijackers had been unclear; apparently their original aim had been the release of Kozo Okamoto, a Japanese Red Army terrorist sentenced to life imprisonment in Israel for his part in the 1972 massacre at Lod International Airport near Tel Aviv, but their plans had somehow misfired. On August 5 two Arab terrorists attacked airline passengers waiting at Athens airport to board a TWA flight to New York; 3 persons were killed and 55 wounded. Later the terrorists admitted to Greek police that they had intended to attack passengers boarding a TWA flight to Tel Aviv and had made a mistake. In a reversal of the usual situation, on August 16 an Arab gunman hijacked a Lebanese passenger plane en route from Benghazi to Beirut and forced it to land in Israel "to show Israelis that not all Arabs were enemies of Israel." On December 17 Arab terrorists opened fire with machine guns at the Rome airport and hurled incendiary bombs into a Pan American World Airways jetliner, killing 31. They then commandeered a Lufthansa airliner, killing one more, and flew to Athens, where they threatened to kill hostages in the plane unless two Palestinians were released. When Greece refused to negotiate, the five hijackers flew to Kuwait and surrendered to authorities.

One of the most serious crashes during 1973 occurred on February 21, when Israeli aircraft shot down a Libyan Arab Airlines Boeing 727 that had strayed into Israeli-controlled airspace over the Sinai Peninsula. The number of crew and passengers killed was 110. However, despite several other spectacular accidents involving heavy loss of life (*see* DISASTERS),

WIDE WORLD

In the drive to save fuel, U.S. Sen. Alan Cranston sets a fine example by pedaling himself to work in a Pedicar. The car is operated by two foot pedals and has five forward speeds, neutral, and reverse.

it seemed likely that when the final figures were known the accident record for 1973 might show some improvement over that for 1972. The ICAO reported in May that the 1972 figures had shown a deterioration from the preceding year. The number of fatal accidents per 100,000 aircraft landings was 0.41, the worst since 1963 (the U.S.S.R. was not included in the figures). The number of passengers killed was 1,205, compared with 857 in 1971, and the number of fatalities per 100 million passenger-kilometres was 0.26, compared with 0.21 in 1971 and 0.18 in 1970.

As airlines looked forward to 1974, one of their chief concerns was uncertainty over the oil supply. In the U.S. jet fuel allocations for the airlines beginning in early 1974, which had been set as low as 75% of 1972 levels, were pegged at 5% below 1972 usage in late December. Toward the end of the year most airlines announced curtailments in flight schedules and concomitant layoffs of personnel. In the short run, the reduction in flights and, hence, in the number of unfilled seats might improve the airlines' profitability position, but increases in fuel prices and the cost of mothballing planes made the long-run picture less optimistic. The CAB approved a 5% increase in domestic fares, effective December 1, to compensate for rising costs, and permission to raise international fares was announced later in the month. Some non-U.S. airlines were hit even harder. During the last week in December, for example, British Airways had to cancel most of its flights from U.S. cities because fuel supplies in London were almost exhausted.

(DAVID WOOLLEY)

COMMERCIAL MOTOR TRANSPORTATION

Freight. For road freight transport operators, 1973 began with confrontation with the environmentalists and ended with the spectre of a severe fuel shortage. Throughout the developed world economic growth had inevitably brought an increase in the movement of goods. This alone would have led to more and bigger vehicles but, in addition, road transport's share of freight traffic continued to outpace that of rail.

This growth in demand for road transport presented a dilemma for a society that needed the commodities moved but also sought to abate the consequent environmental disturbances. Environmental lobbies achieved token restrictions on trucks in many countries. France followed the West German example of banning trucks from the roads during the daytime on Sundays and public holidays. In Britain government proposals to restrict heavy trucks to certain roads, albeit on a voluntary basis, were reinforced in 1973 by the Heavy Commercial Vehicles (Control and Regulation) Act, which gave local authorities the power to direct trucks onto special routes.

The environmental problem affected attempts in the enlarged EEC to thrash out a common transport policy. Throughout 1973 the members wrestled with the basic matter of standard sizes and weights of freight vehicles. In this case the impasse could well be blamed on Britain's refusal to accept the Community's compromise of a maximum axle weight of 11 metric tons (10.8 long tons), as against the British limit of 10 tons—a small enough difference, considering the French had come down from their original demand for 13 tons.

Also stemming in large measure from environmental considerations was a new concern for the survival of railways as an alternative to road transport. State subsidies had become the order of the day, and massive financial subventions for the railways were made or planned in many countries. One result would be substantial increases in road taxes for heavy vehicles, both as a means of forcing traffic onto rail and as a source of revenue to offset railway subsidization. EEC member states were examining a Commission directive calling for a revision of taxes for freight vehicles of over 12 metric tons gross weight, in accordance with the wear and tear on the road caused by different categories of truck.

High taxation of heavy trucks and other restrictive measures were to be reinforced by control of the number of freight vehicles allowed to operate. Member states were to work out the statistical systems required to prevent overprovision of transport, and a strict system of Community authorizations for interstate journeys was to be introduced.

As the energy crisis worsened in the fall, truckers were confused and uncertain as to what the future had in store. In the U.S., Japan, and many European countries, gasoline rationing appeared to be a distinct possibility, perhaps by early 1974. Pres. Richard Nixon's call for a voluntary speed limit of 50 mph met with strong objections from truckers, who pointed out that their schedules would be delayed (and their incomes lowered accordingly) and that large trucks could not be run efficiently at such a low speed. Other complaints included fuel prices that were rising faster than freight rates and charges that illegally high prices for fuel were being charged by some roadside truck stops. To dramatize their grievances, some truckers attempted to block highways during the first week in December, and a week later a group of independent truckers called for a three-day work stoppage. Some relief was promised by the government, although the truckers were not entirely satisfied. Freight haulers were given a high priority under the government's fuel-allocation program, the Interstate Commerce Commission announced that it would streamline its procedures for reviewing freight rates in light of rising costs, and the Internal Revenue Service confirmed a number of cases of price-gouging by truck-stop operators. Late in the year Congress passed a bill setting a national speed limit of 55 mph and withholding highway funds from states that failed to comply. (ABE ALMAN)

Passenger. General worldwide interest in the preservation of the environment, the need to make towns and cities pleasant for those who lived, worked, or shopped in them, the need to cut down pollution, the folly of ever increasing urban roads schemes, and the obvious inefficiency of the private automobile in face of the growing fuel shortage, all began to convince politicians in 1973 that mass transit must be encouraged and improved. In the U.S. the fuel shortage in some areas even led fuel suppliers to publish advertisements exhorting car owners to make more use of buses. In other parts of the U.S., however, public and private bus companies had difficulty in obtaining sufficient supplies.

Another worldwide trend was toward greater public ownership of bus companies. Often this involved the merging of several transit systems to form one larger unit that provided and was responsible for all forms of public transportation—bus, streetcar, trolley bus, subway or underground, and ferries. Examples of this included the new Public Transport Commission in New South Wales, Austr., said to be the largest in the British Commonwealth after London.

In Britain the Local Government Act 1972, to take full effect in April 1974, created larger local authorities by merging numerous smaller ones. It also created two new metropolitan boroughs, with their own passenger transport authorities, in industrial urban areas comprising separate but almost indistinguishable conurbations made up of several adjoining towns and cities. A section of the act made all county councils responsible for public transport coordination and charged them, when conducting future transport planning, with giving attention to improvements in public transport facilities as well as to new road construction.

This act faded almost into insignificance, however, beside the U.S. Federal Highway Act of 1973, signed by President Nixon on August 13. This $23 billion, three-year bill opened the Highway Trust Fund, financed through gasoline, tire, and highway users' taxes and formerly devoted exclusively to road building, to mass transit. For the first time states and localities could set their own transport priorities and spend money on buses and exclusive traffic lanes for buses. The act also permitted substitution, on a dollar-for-dollar basis, of mass transit projects for "unbuilt interstate highway segments that are now no longer considered essential to the national system." It authorized the Urban Mass Transportation Administration (UMTA), which already administered a capital grant fund for new mass transit equipment, including vehicles, to spend an additional $3 billion. The Senate, backed by powerful road construction and automobile lobbies, had traditionally opposed the use of trust fund money for mass transit. Under the circumstances, the act was a sensible compromise, though scarcely a resounding victory for mass transit supporters.

But for public transport to succeed it had to be regular, reliable, and attractive. To help accomplish these ends, the U.S. Department of Transportation, through UMTA, sponsored a $25 million grant to three manufacturers, American General Corporation, GMC Truck and Coach Division, and the Flxible division of Rohr Industries, each of which was building a prototype of the advanced bus that would be the only one funded by UMTA under its capital grant program. The prototypes featured air suspension that lowered the vehicle to 12 in. above ground level at stops, a U-shaped lounge at the rear, larger seats with more legroom, a public address system, and lower noise levels. Individual groups of bus operators were also designing or evaluating advanced prototypes.

Concern about pollution and gasoline shortages renewed interest in streetcars or trams (the first new ones in 20 years were being built in the U.S. by Boeing), trolley buses, and battery-powered buses. The last were being developed in the U.S., Britain, West Germany, and Japan. Enthusiasm for trolley buses resulted in expansion plans in some Swiss towns, and orders for new vehicles were placed in Canada and the U.S. Other, more immediate plans to encourage bus travel included increased use of reserved lanes for buses in many city centres, introduction of new and more modern vehicles (often paid for by government funds), and experiments with reduced fares and multiride tickets. (JOHN M. ALDRIDGE)

PIPELINES

The oil companies' continuing success in the offshore search for oil and gas led to an upsurge in the construction of large-diameter pipelines to get finds ashore. Most of the activity was in the North Sea, where contractors were laying pipe in the deepest water yet encountered on a submarine route.

Work began in the spring of 1973 on two North Sea projects: a 115-mi., 32-in.-diameter pipeline linking British Petroleum's Forties oil field with a shore terminal at Cruden Bay, north of Aberdeen, Scot.; and a 235-mi. line to bring oil to Teeside from the Phillips group's Ekofisk discovery in the Norwegian sector of the North Sea. The BP project also involved construction of a 36-in.-diameter land line from Cruden Bay to the Grangemouth oil refinery on the Forth, 130 mi. away.

Both companies had hoped to complete construction work during the summer and early fall, before weather conditions became unsuitable for laying operations, but neither was able to do so. The BP operation was hit by a freak storm in July that delayed work for several weeks. The Phillips project was late in starting because of protracted negotiations with the Norwegian government, which eventually gained a 50% share in the company that would operate the pipeline.

Twin pipelines were also planned to bring gas 156 mi. from the North Sea Frigg field to a new reception terminal at St. Fergus in Aberdeenshire. A further 700 mi. of pipeline would be needed to feed the gas into the British distribution network. The Occidental group was planning a pipeline from its Piper oil field to the Orkney Islands. Controversy still surrounded a projected pipeline to bring oil from a cluster of major discoveries in the northern North Sea to Shetland, whose environment and traditional way of life would be profoundly changed thereby.

Positive steps were taken toward construction of the much discussed pipeline to link the Gulf of Suez to the Mediterranean. After several years of negotiations, the Egyptians rejected a European consortium's scheme and appointed U.S. contractors to build twin 42-in. pipelines from Ain Soukna on the Gulf of Suez to the Mediterranean coast just west of Alexandria. The line would be capable of handling 120 million tons of crude oil a year.

Contracts were signed in October for the first submarine pipeline across the Mediterranean. The 1,391-km. gas pipeline would run from the Hassi r'Mel gas field in Algeria through Tunisia, make a 156-km. submarine crossing to Sicily, cross the island, and make a second, 18-km. submarine crossing of the Messina Strait to Calabria in southern Italy. The total cost of the project was estimated at $700 million. When fully operational in 1980, it would deliver 11,000,000,000 cu.m. of gas a year for 25 years.

The 800-mi.-long, 48-in.-diameter trans-Alaska pipeline, which had been delayed for several years by conservationist and legal objections, received final approval from Congress in November, partly because of the serious shortage of crude oil that faced the U.S.; the relevant legislation was signed by President Nixon on November 16. The line would run from the North Slope oil fields to Valdez in southern Alaska. A feasibility study was begun on a $3 billion, 790-mi. gas pipeline from the North Slope to a liquefaction plant on the southern coast.

Agreement was reached on a route for the $5 billion, 48-in. gas pipeline to the U.S. from the MacKenzie Valley delta in northern Canada, close to the Alaskan North Slope. It would follow the MacKenzie River to Caroline in Alberta where it would divide into two 42-in. lines. Studies continued on a crude-oil pipeline from the MacKenzie delta to southern Canada and also on a 1,050-mi., 36-in. pipeline from Sable Island off Nova Scotia to Montreal.

In Europe, Druzhba II, parallel to the original 4,350-km. Druzhba pipeline linking the Siberian oil fields with Eastern Europe, was completed, and studies on a third line were started. The Czechoslovakian part of a gas pipeline capable of carrying 28,000,000,000 cu.m. of gas a year from the U.S.S.R. was finished on schedule. An extension of the line to West Germany opened October 1; other extensions would eventually take gas into France and Italy. A separate pipeline under construction to Finland might also be extended to move Soviet gas into Sweden.

A 285-mi. product pipeline, the longest in Britain, linking the Milford Haven refinery complex in South Wales with the Midlands and Manchester, was opened. (ROGER VIELVOYE)

RAILWAYS

With the general economic recovery, 1973 saw a significant upturn in freight carryings on the world's railways, although passenger traffic remained fairly static. Increased revenue, however, did little to prevent further deterioration in the financial position of most railways, and the vast majority of state-owned railways reported deficits. The West German Federal Railways had a deficit of some DM. 2.5 billion, while Japanese National Railways lost 340 billion yen in 1972. Less dramatic deficits were recorded in countries where government compensation was paid for unremunerative but socially necessary services—for example, commuter trains into big cities. British Rail reported a loss of £26 million in 1972 but, if various subsidies were taken into account, total support from the taxpayer was estimated at £140 million.

Privately owned railways in the U.S. had their best year in some time, but at 2.95% the rate of return on investment was still far from satisfactory. Operating revenues in 1972 were at an all-time high of $13.4 billion, but a $400 million increase in wages drained off most of the extra income. Nonetheless, capital expenditure for the year rose to $1,230,000,000. With 1973 traffic at record levels, grain shipments were particularly heavy, and piggyback traffic (road trailers moved by rail) climbed rapidly after two or three years in the doldrums. One major problem was a shortage of cars, especially for grain shipments.

Amtrak's new French-made turbo train, designed to run at speeds of up to 125 mph, prepares to leave Newark, N.J., for Chicago on its maiden long-distance test run, Aug. 10, 1973.

EDWARD HAUSNER—THE NEW YORK TIMES

In December, Congress passed legislation providing for reorganization of the Penn Central and six other bankrupt railroads in the northeastern U.S. Under the bill, an independent federal agency would be set up to design the new rail system, establish a corporation to run it, and issue up to $1.5 billion in guaranteed loans for purposes of acquisition and upgrading. In addition to the Penn Central, the railroads involved were the Ann Arbor, Boston & Maine, Central of New Jersey, Erie Lackawanna, Lehigh Valley, and the Reading.

Intercity passenger trains in the U.S. staged a modest comeback under the aegis of the quasi-governmental organization Amtrak. By May 1973 travel was 11% above the previous 12 months, and reduced losses were forecast for 1973–74. But with revenue still amounting to only half of operating expenses, Amtrak came under pressure to contribute more toward the costs of those railroads whose tracks it used, particularly Penn Central.

The Communist countries continued to make more use of railways than Western countries. Soviet Railways dominated the scene, with half the world's total tonnage (5 trillion ton-km.) hauled on one-tenth of the total route length. Soviet Railways was also the busiest passenger carrier, handling some 280,000,000,000 passenger-kilometres in 1972, compared with 330,000,000,000 for the whole of Europe and 17,000,000,000 for the U.S. The system most intensively used by passengers, Japanese National Railways, carried 190,000,000,000 passenger-kilometres in 1972 on only 21,000 route-kilometres.

Australian railways began a major reorganization in 1973, following the election of the first Labor government in many years. Ownership of Australia's railways was vested in the six states, and this had crippled efforts to create a national, uniform-gauge railway system that could benefit from long freight hauls between the main centres of population. Negotiations for a take-over of the state systems by the central government were begun, and work continued on a skeleton standard-gauge network linking the state capitals, starting with the link between Adelaide and the Sydney-Perth transcontinental main line at Crystal Brook. In Western Australia another mineral railway opened to serve the Robe River deposits, while the Hamersley Iron Railway was extended to Parraburdoo and modernized.

Expansion of railways had concentrated in particular sections of the transport market, although lines for general use continued to be built. The railhead of the 1,857-km. line from Dar es Salaam in Tanzania to Kapiri Mposhi in Zambia crossed the Zambian border in August 1973. Built with Chinese money and technical assistance, this important 1,067-mm.-gauge line was to be opened in 1975. Work began on the 843-km. iron-ore line from Sishen to Saldanha in South Africa. In Canada the British Columbia Railway continued to push toward the far north in search of mineral wealth. An agreement signed in July 1973 provided for two new links with Canadian National and an extension to Watson Lake near the British Columbia-Yukon border; continuation of this line to Dawson was contemplated.

The world's first electric railway to operate on North America's probable new standard voltage for electrification, 50 kv. at 60 Hz. single-phase, opened in 1973. The 81-mi. (130-km.) electrified Black Mesa and Lake Powell Railroad in Arizona, built to carry coal from a mine to a power station, featured automatic driving. Unlike the Muskingum Electric Railroad in Ohio, however, the trains would carry a driver as standby in case of failure.

Urban railways attracted heavy investment, as rapid transit and main-line commuter services were improved and expanded all over the world. The first Oakland section of San Francisco's Bay Area Rapid Transit (BART), which took a decade to build and cost $1.3 billion, had opened on Sept. 11, 1972, and the San Francisco line opened on Nov. 3, 1973. The connecting tunnel under San Francisco Bay was built but not yet in service. BART set new standards in speed, comfort, and automation. Unfortunately, it suffered such serious delays and teething troubles that other U.S. cities planning transit systems, including St. Louis, Mo., Seattle, Wash., Atlanta, Ga., Los Angeles, and Baltimore, Md., stopped short of ground breaking. The new Washington Metro, however, planned to open its first route in 1975. New York completed the two-level East River rail tunnel late in 1972, part of a construction program that would add 50 mi. (80 km.) to an already extensive rail network.

Frankfurt am Main and Hamburg, W.Ger., and Paris were among European cities building high-capacity rail links across their centres, but in the U.K. a similar project for Manchester was refused government aid in August 1973. In December 1972, Newcastle upon Tyne had received government authority and a 75% grant to build a £65 million rapid transit system. Contracts for an $80 million underground loop line in Melbourne, Austr., were placed in the summer.

The promise of higher speeds for intercity passengers brought further plans for new lines and for trains running at 250–300 kilometres per hour (kph). In 1972 work had begun on Japan's Shinkansen (new high-speed trunk line) network north of Tokyo, with lines to Morioka and Niigata. The former would continue through the newly constructed 52-km. Siekan Tunnel to link the islands of Honshu and Hokkaido by 1979. The International Union of Railways' master plan for linking major cities of Western Europe by 250-kph rail services would involve the construction of 6,000 km. of new line and improvement of a further 14,000 km. of existing trunk line. Work began in August 1973 on the first section of a new West German line—the Hannover–Kassel–Gemünden route—while in September the British and French governments announced their joint decision that a rail tunnel should be constructed under the English Channel and linked with a 130-km. line to London suitable for 250-kph trains.

Progress was made in developing trains to operate these faster services. French National Railways exceeded 300 kph with a gas-turbine-powered TGV.001 designed for the new Paris–Lyons route, while British Rail's diesel-powered Highspeed Train attained 230 kph during tests in June. Gas turbine failure, however, prevented BR's Advanced Passenger Train project from proceeding. A French-built high-speed train was placed in service on Amtrak's Chicago–St. Louis run, but was unable to attain maximum speed because of the condition of the roadbed.

More unconventional forms of high-speed guided transport materialized in Japan, West Germany, and the U.S., although the British Tracked Hovercraft project was scrapped in February. In West Germany Krauss-Maffei and MBB tested electromagnetic attraction systems, and a magnetic repulsion vehicle with cryogenic magnets began trials near Erlangen. A cryogenic vehicle was operated experimentally in Japan, and two tracked air-cushion vehicles of different design began trials at the U.S. government research centre at Pueblo, Colo.

(RICHARD ARTHUR HOPE)

WATER TRANSPORTATION

Shipping and Ports. Shipping has always thrived on famine and war. In 1973, with large parts of the human race suffering food shortages that in some cases approached famine, large quantities of grain had to be shipped from North America and Australia to the U.S.S.R. and China, and shipping unexpectedly prospered. War, however, failed to redound to the benefit of the shipping industry. Through most of the year tankers had prospered as a result of oil shortages in the U.S. and the gathering pace of the Japanese economy, but the cutbacks in oil production by the Arab oil-producing countries begun during the Arab-Israeli war in October, combined with complete boycotts of the U.S. and The Netherlands, threw the trade into confusion. In late October tanker freight rates in the Persian Gulf fell $20 per ton in one 24-hour period, and evidence that U.S.-controlled tonnage was not being loaded in some Persian Gulf areas led to a frantic rearrangement of schedules. Initially, at least, the dry-cargo side remained unaffected by the chaos in the tanker sector, although late in the year there were reports that some ships were stranded because of inability to obtain fuel.

For most of the year, however, there was a boom when most people had expected a slump. The slump of 1972 had been expected to continue because the amount of tonnage pouring from world shipyards seemed too great to be absorbed by world trade. Fulfilling orders placed in the heady days of the previous boom, yards were turning out ships as never before. By midyear the world fleet reached 290 million tons, compared with 268 million a year earlier and 247 million the year before that. Yet for much of the year rates were so high that tanker owners, and to a lesser extent owners of dry-cargo tramps, were making fortunes overnight.

As the fleet got bigger, so did individual ships. The effort to realize economies by getting bigger flows through larger, simpler systems was evident above all in the oil industry, where the tanker size rose for the first time to around the 500,000-ton mark. Globtik Tankers of London set the pace with a pair of 470,000-tonners built in Japan, soon to be topped by Shell with several 530,000-tonners under construction in France.

The snag in all this was that in the main oil-producing area—the Persian Gulf—and the main consumer areas—North Europe, Japan, and North America—nature had provided continental shelves permitting the approach of ships no larger than 100,000 tons in some cases and 250,000 tons in others. Several solutions to this problem were demonstrated. In both Japan and the Persian Gulf, artificial island ports for ships of 500,000 tons were being developed. At Dubai great tanks were set on the seabed offshore. Blasting, dredging, and construction to boost capacity went on at a number of other places, among them Rotterdam, Neth., and Le Havre, France, but the most widespread method was single-point mooring, which enabled a big ship to swing freely in deep water and discharge its cargo without ever coming into port at all. This was satisfactory from the oil industry's point of view, being flexible, efficient, and economical, but it was not so welcome to adjoining communities and to environmentalists, who saw the giant tankers as an ominous threat of further pollution.

Environmental considerations were much to the fore generally, reinforced by the close interest of the Inter-Governmental Maritime Consultative Organization, the UN's London-based maritime arm. IMCO announced more stringent construction rules in an effort to limit spillage from tankers caught in accidents. If internationally enforced, these rules would add materially to the cost of ships built in the traditional manner, so they had the effect of both inhibiting further rapid growth in the size of such vessels and inspiring some interesting new concepts. For example, the Onassis Group disclosed research on giant demountable tankers in which the cargo tanks could be detached from the propulsion unit.

Another branch of the UN, the UNCTAD (UN Conference on Trade and Development) organization at Geneva, was applying itself to a different branch of shipping. Less developed countries had long been dissatisfied with the extent to which world shipping, and therefore the carriage of their imports and exports, had been dominated by the developed countries. A series of conferences called by UNCTAD culminated at year's end in a meeting of plenipotentiaries in Geneva, held with the aim of drafting an international convention governing the liner trades of the world and, at the same time, providing a set of working rules that would help the less developed countries get more, and more out of, shipping. Not unnaturally, traditional shipowners, mainly from Europe and Japan, resisted, and the debate showed every sign of being a long, drawn-out affair.

Containerization took another big step forward as a fleet of nearly 20 second-generation cellular ships went into service on the important Europe–Far East trade route, and there were moves toward further intermodal transport of general cargo elsewhere. Facing up to mounting competition—particularly for higher valued freight—both from the airlines and from rail "land-bridges" across the U.S.S.R. and North America, container-ship operators were building faster as well as bigger vessels. The pioneering Sea-Land of New Jersey led the way with a fleet of 33-knotters—faster by far than any previous cargo ship.

The very high fuel consumption of these big, fast container ships inevitably generated renewed interest in nuclear power for merchant ships. While the first orders for genuinely commercial nuclear ships had yet to be placed, the concept began to seem more feasible.

(MICHAEL BAILY)

Inland Waterways. In terms of cost per ton-mile, the cheapest method of moving bulk cargoes from one place to another was by water. In view of this, and of the threatening fuel crisis, the developed nations might logically be expected to pay closer attention to the development of inland waterway transport in coming years. In fact, Europe, the U.S.S.R., and the U.S. all had long-term improvement and development plans in hand.

In Britain, where legislation passed in 1973 provided for radical reorganization of the nation's waterway system, prospects for the future were less promising. Under the new act, the former piecemeal structure of interdependent, although autonomous, bodies was to be replaced by ten Regional Water Authorities with overall responsibility for the entire system. Originally it was planned to abolish the British Waterways Board, the state industry that controlled 340 mi. of commercial waterways, and hand its functions over to the new regional authorities. There was, however, little provision for the expansion of water transport in the act, and, indeed, the industry anticipated a prolonged period of cutbacks and retrenchment. This was a cause for concern not only for the British inland water transport industry but also for its European counterparts. The British Waterways Board was becoming heavily involved with Denmark in the development of a new barge-carrying vessel, designed largely for the European system. Known as the BACAT (barge aboard catamaran), it was to carry 18 450-ton barges designed for the European waterway system or, alternatively, 10 European barges and 3 of the larger 850-ton barges built under U.S. patents.

These new transport systems were the inland water transport industry's answer to the "container revolution." Containers, it was believed, had been winning cargo from water to roads because of the ease of loading at ports and the shipping industry's increasing emphasis on container handling. First on the international scene with the barge-carrying ship was LASH (lighter aboard ship) Systems Inc. of New Orleans, La. By the end of 1973 there were nearly 30 ships built or under construction under LASH patents. Each carried up to 80 400-ton lighters. The advantage of the LASH method was that goods could be carried from Chicago to a Gulf Coast port and from there to Europe and as far inland as, say, Basel in Switzerland without having to be transferred or unloaded. LASH "mother ships" were rather large for European purposes, and it was thought there were good prospects for the smaller BACAT, which had a much shallower draft and could make greater use of shoaled estuary waters.

The British Waterways Board survived the government's reorganization scheme by accident rather than design—there were far too many minor acts of Parliament governing the board's affairs that needed amendment or revocation to make abolition practicable. However, the board's interest in BACAT lapsed for lack of funds, and the scheme was taken over by the Holland-America Line, which was to operate the vessels. The first BACAT ship was launched in the fall of 1973 and was scheduled to enter service in 1974.

The BACAT and LASH systems were expected to come into their own with the opening of the canal link between the Rhine and the Danube. If work remained on schedule, the link would come into operation in 1980, providing an access route to the Black Sea.

Another important factor affecting the inland water transport industry throughout the 1970s was expected to be the growing interest in protecting the environment. The U.S., Europe, and, increasingly, the Soviet Union all displayed concern at the problems caused by road transport. Oil pollution, noise, and the space needed for express highways were all cited by water transport operators as reasons for governments to support their schemes. The concept that was being presented was the "integrated transport system" where short-haul road transport would be used in conjunction with rail and water to provide door-to-door service. The idea had been pioneered in the U.S. and was generally accepted in Europe, but in Britain it had yet to catch on. However, the European Economic Community's well-developed water transport system could provide the impetus for Britain to accept the concept.

Britain's regional development problems met with scant sympathy in the EEC, and some economists believed that inland waterways could provide, in part, an answer to the development problems of the U.K.'s outlying regions. A number of inland ports capable of handling the new, large 750- to 850-ton barges, it was argued, could well provide the stimulus for industrial development that would otherwise require large subsidies or state aid. (GUY HAWTIN)

See also Cities and Urban Affairs; Engineering Projects; Industrial Review.

ENCYCLOPÆDIA BRITANNICA FILMS. *The Mississippi System: Waterway of Commerce* (1970); *The Great Lakes—North America's Inland Seas* (1971); *Rotterdam—Europort, Gateway to Europe* (1971); *Airplane Trip* (4th ed., 1973).

Trinidad and Tobago

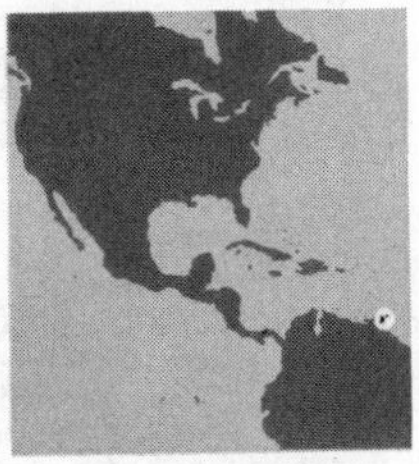

A parliamentary state and a member of the Commonwealth of Nations, Trinidad and Tobago consists of two islands off the coast of Venezuela, north of the Orinoco River delta. Area: 1,980 sq.mi. (5,128 sq.km.). Pop. (1972 est.): 1,043,000, including (1960) Negro 43.3%; East Indian 36.4%; mixed 16.3%. Cap. and largest city: Port-of-Spain (pop., 1971 est., 70,000). Language: English (official); Hindi, French, Spanish. Religion (1960): Christian 66%; Hindu 23%; Muslim 6%. Queen, Elizabeth II; governor-general in 1973, Ellis Clarke; prime minister, Eric Williams.

In September Prime Minister Williams announced that he would quit politics at the year's end, but in December he reversed this decision. The opposition, fragmented into nine splinter groups, had boycotted the previous elections, so that Williams' People's National Movement (PNM) dominated the House of Representatives with 34 out of 36 seats. It had also threatened to boycott any future elections unless certain conditions were met, including the abolition of voting machines, radio time for its candidates, the right to demonstrate, and impartial supervision of polls and registration. Despite relative economic well-being and educational progress, and the growing importance of recently discovered oil and gas fields, frustration over unemployment, inefficiency, corruption, and inequalities continued to fester.

Behind all the political uncertainties was an unstable economic situation, with a price inflation of 15.3% during the first six months of 1973, shattering Trinidad and Tobago's claim to be the most price-stable society in the West Indies. The five-year plan due to end in 1973 had already exceeded its original expenditure target by TT$33 million at the end of the fourth year, and there had been an adverse trade balance of almost TT$379 million in 1972. Hopes were pinned on negotiations to increase the royalty income on a barrel of crude oil from a very low U.S. $0.69. In July sugar crop operations terminated with an estimated production of nearly 184,000 tons, approximately 40,000 tons less than the previous year, attributed to a severe drought and the high incidence of malicious burning of cane. (SHEILA PATTERSON)

TRINIDAD AND TOBAGO

Education. (1969–70) Primary (state only), pupils 227,181, teachers 6,380; secondary (state only), pupils 28,457, teachers 1,343; vocational, pupils 4,679, teachers 273; teacher training, students 707, teachers 83; higher, students 2,218, teaching staff 348.

Finance and Trade. Monetary unit: Trinidad and Tobago dollar, with (Sept. 17, 1973) a free rate of TT$1.99 to U.S. $1 (par value of TT$4.80 = £1 sterling). Budget (1971 est.): revenue TT$342 million; expenditure TT$306 million (excludes TT$122 million capital expenditure). Foreign trade (1972): imports TT$1,448,100,000; exports TT$1,069,200,000. Import sources: U.S. 19%; U.K. 13%; Saudi Arabia 12%; Libya 12%; Venezuela 5%. Export destinations: U.S. 42%; U.K. 8%; Sweden 8%; ship and aircraft bunker stores 7%. Main exports: petroleum products 68%; crude oil 10%; sugar 6%.

Transport and Communications. Roads (classified; 1971) 4,230 km. Motor vehicles in use (1971): passenger 71,900; commercial (including buses) 19,100. Air traffic (1972): 545 million passenger-km.; freight 16,078,000 net ton-km. Ships entered (1971) vessels totaling 26,296,000 net registered tons; goods loaded (1971) 22,456,000 metric tons, unloaded 16,169,000 metric tons. Telephones (1971) 63,000; radio receivers 296,000; television licenses 45,000.

Agriculture. Production (in 000; metric tons; 1972; 1971 in parentheses): rice *c.* 10 (*c.* 10); sweet potatoes *c.* 20 (*c.* 19); oranges (1971) 11, (1970) 18; grapefruit (1971) *c.* 18, (1970) *c.* 15; sugar, raw value 236 (221); copra 13 (13). Livestock (in 000; 1970–71): cattle *c.* 65; pigs *c.* 53; goats *c.* 37; poultry *c.* 5,340.

Industry. Production (in 000; metric tons; 1971): crude oil 6,671; petroleum products 19,894; cement (1972) 286; nitrogenous fertilizers (1971–72) *c.* 95; electricity (kw-hr.) 1,226,000.

Tunisia

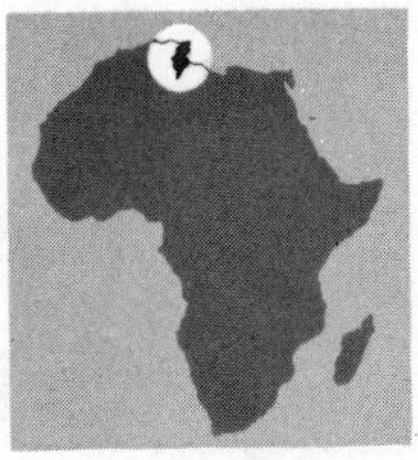

A republic of North Africa lying on the Mediterranean Sea, Tunisia is bounded by Algeria and Libya. Area: 63,378 sq.mi. (164,150 sq.km.). Pop. (1972 est.): 5,377,000. Cap. and largest city: Tunis (pop., 1966, 468,997). Language: Arabic (official). Religion: Muslim; Jewish and Christian minorities. President in 1973, Habib Bourguiba; prime minister, Hedi Nouira.

The question of succession continued to dominate Tunisian domestic affairs in 1973. In March, shortly after declaring that the prime minister would naturally succeed him, President Bourguiba announced that his successor was to be elected by universal suffrage.

Former prime minister Bahi Ladgham retired from politics in March, and two months later, in early June, the direction of the Destourian Socialist Party passed to Muhammad Sayah. This marked the beginning of a rise in Sayah's political fortunes, which by December had brought him the portfolio of assistant minister to the prime minister.

In February it was announced that former economics minister Ahmed Ben Salah, serving a ten-year prison sentence for treason and mismanagement of the economy, had succeeded in escaping. Later in the year his brother was charged with conspiring to bring about the escape and was sentenced to three years' imprisonment.

Relations with France were dominated by the problems of Tunisians already working in France and the flood of illegal immigrants continuing to arrive. Various specific incidents also affected relations between the two countries during the year. These included hunger strikes by Tunisian workers in Aix-en-Provence and Lyons in March, the expulsion of a number of Tunisian nationals from France in August, and alleged ill-treatment of a Tunisian teacher in Cannes in November. Three French ministers visited Tunis during the year: Social Affairs Minister Edgar Faure in January, Finance Minister Valéry Giscard d'Estaing in May, and Foreign Minister Michel Jobert in November.

Trucking Industry: *see* Transportation
Trust Territories: *see* Dependent States
Tungsten: *see* Mining

TUNISIA

Education. (1969–70) Primary, pupils 912,646, teachers 18,000; secondary, pupils 163,353; vocational (1968–69), pupils 50,587; secondary and vocational, teachers 6,931; teacher training (1968–69), students 8,207; higher (at University of Tunis), students 9,413, teaching staff (1968–69) 304.

Finance. Monetary unit: Tunisian dinar, with (Sept. 17, 1973) a par value of 0.44 dinar to U.S. $1 (free rate of 0.95 dinar = £1 sterling). Gold, SDRs, and foreign exchange, central bank: (June 1973) U.S. $267 million; (June 1972) U.S. $165.5 million. Budget (1972 est.) balanced at 175 million dinars. Gross national product: (1971) 741.6 million dinars; (1970) 648.7 million dinars. Money supply: (May 1973) 294,240,000 dinars; (May 1972) 262.8 million dinars. Cost of living (Tunis; 1963 = 100): (April 1973) 148; (April 1972) 138.

Foreign Trade. (1972) Imports 222,220,000 dinars; exports 150,330,000 dinars. Import sources: France 36%; U.S. 12%; Italy 10%; West Germany 9%. Export destinations: Italy 30%; France 21%; Spain 10%; West Germany 8%; Libya 5%. Main exports: olive oil 31%; crude oil 26%; phosphates 13%. Tourism (1971): visitors 608,700; gross receipts U.S. $107 million.

Transport and Communications. Roads (1972) 18,267 km. Motor vehicles in use (1972): passenger 78,300; commercial 41,700. Railways: (1971) 1,998 km.; traffic (1972) 510.8 million passenger-km., freight 1,441,900,000 net ton-km. Air traffic (1971): 316.9 million passenger-km.; freight 2,104,000 net ton-km. Telephones (Dec. 1971) 87,000. Radio licenses (Dec. 1970) 388,000. Television licenses (Dec. 1970) 51,000.

Agriculture. Production (in 000; metric tons; 1972; 1971 in parentheses): wheat 914 (600); barley 236 (140); oats 35 (22); potatoes 105 (*c.* 70); tomatoes 180 (*c.* 130); wine *c.* 90 (*c.* 90); dates *c.* 50 (*c.* 50); figs *c.* 15 (*c.* 15); olive oil 66 (167); oranges (1971) *c.* 64, (1970) *c.* 67; lemons (1971) *c.* 12, (1970) *c.* 12. Livestock (in 000; 1971–72): sheep *c.* 3,200; cattle *c.* 670; goats *c.* 450; camels *c.* 280; poultry *c.* 9,000.

Industry. Production (in 000; metric tons; 1972): crude oil 3,973; cement 629; iron ore (55% metal content) 890; phosphates (1971) 3,162; lead 25; sulfuric acid 433; electricity (excluding most industrial production; kw-hr.) 869,000.

The Tunisian leadership continued to adopt a highly individual attitude to the crisis in the Middle East. In June President Bourguiba declared that Israel's security as a nation must depend on the establishment of an equally secure Palestinian state and appealed to Tel Aviv to begin negotiations, apparently offering his personal mediation in the matter. During the summit meeting of nonaligned nations in Algiers in September Bourguiba postulated the creation of a union that would ultimately include the states of Algeria, Tunisia, Libya, and Mauritania. Visiting Paris in December on the eve of the Arab-Israeli peace talks in Geneva and the EEC summit meeting in Copenhagen, Bourguiba discussed with French Pres. Georges Pompidou the possibility of a conference of European oil consumers and Arab producers. (PHILIPPE DECRAENE)

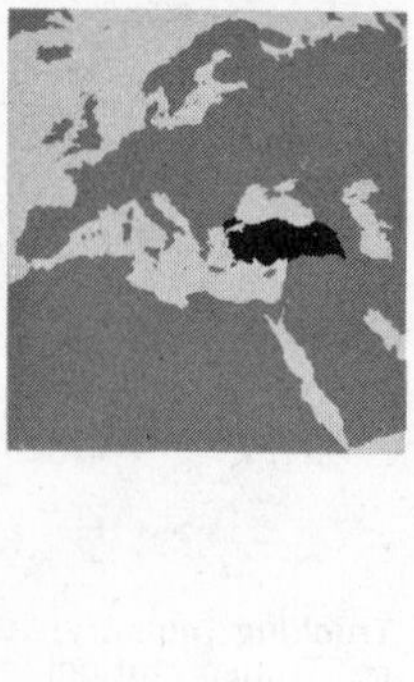

Turkey

A republic of southeastern Europe and Asia Minor, Turkey is bounded by the Aegean Sea, the Black Sea, the U.S.S.R., Iran, Iraq, Syria, the Mediterranean Sea, Greece, and Bulgaria. Area: 300,948 sq.mi. (779,452 sq.km.), including 9,150 sq.mi. in Europe. Pop. (1973 est.): 38,094,000. Cap.: Ankara (pop., 1970, 1,467,304). Largest city: Istanbul (pop., 1970, 2,041,658). Language: Turkish, Kurdish, Arabic. Religion: predominantly Muslim. Presidents in 1973, Gen. Cevdet Sunay until March 28 and, from April 6, Fahri Koruturk; prime ministers, Ferit Melen and, from April 15, Naim Talu.

TURKEY

Education. (1971–72) Primary, pupils 5,132,786, teachers 139,515; secondary, pupils 1,147,957, teachers 35,259; vocational, pupils 262,701, teachers 15,410; teacher training (1969–70), students 62,969, teachers 2,351; higher (including 9 universities), students 169,672, teaching staff 9,211.

Finance. Monetary unit: Turkish lira, with (Sept. 17, 1973) a par value of 14 liras to U.S. $1 (free rate of 35.28 liras = £1 sterling). Gold, SDRs, and foreign exchange, central bank: (June 1973) U.S. $1,793,000,000; (June 1972) U.S. $829 million. Budget (1971–72 est.) balanced at 38,472,000,000 liras. Gross domestic product: (1972) 229 billion liras; (1971) 187 billion liras. Money supply: (Dec. 1972) 28,330,000,000 liras; (Dec. 1971) 22,670,000,000 liras. Cost of living (Ankara; 1968 = 100): (May 1973) 172; (May 1972) 146.

Foreign Trade. (1972) Imports 21,520,000,000 liras; exports 11,880,000,000 liras. Import sources: West Germany 18%; U.S. 12%; U.K. 11%; Italy 11%; U.S.S.R. 8%; France 7%; Switzerland 5%. Export destinations: West Germany 21%; U.S. 12%; Switzerland 9%; Italy 6%; France 6%; U.K. 5%; U.S.S.R. 5%. Main exports: cotton 21%; hazelnuts 13%; tobacco 10%. Tourism (1971): visitors 494,000; gross receipts U.S. $63 million.

Transport and Communications. Roads (1972) 59,448 km. Motor vehicles in use (1971): passenger 151,400; commercial 128,700. Railways (1971): 8,135 km.; traffic 5,738,000,000 passenger-km., freight 5,748,000,000 net ton-km. Air traffic (1972): 1,148,000,000 passenger-km.; freight 8,207,000 net ton-km. Shipping (1972): merchant vessels 100 gross tons and over 340; gross tonnage 743,071. Telephones (Dec. 1971) 654,000. Radio licenses (Dec. 1971) 3,856,000. Television receivers (Dec. 1971) 102,000.

Agriculture. Production (in 000; metric tons; 1972; 1971 in parentheses): wheat 12,085 (13,594); corn 1,060 (1,135); rye 740 (895); barley 3,700 (4,170); oats 390 (455); rice 203 (292); tomatoes (1971) 1,900, (1970) 1,810; onions (1970) 748, (1969) 691; potatoes 2,000 (2,100); sunflower seed 570 (465); chick-peas (1971) 133, (1970) 109; dry beans 145 (153); lentils (1971) 101, (1970) 92; oranges (1971) 535, (1970) 523; lemons (1971) 152, (1970) 126; apples 850 (780); pears 200 (175); grapes 3,396 (3,853); raisins (1971) *c.* 315, (1970) *c.* 310; figs (1970) 214, (1969) 215; sugar, raw value *c.* 870 (910); olive oil 150 (52); tea *c.* 40 (34); tobacco 150 (154); cotton, lint *c.* 516 (522). Livestock (in 000; Dec. 1971): cattle 12,653; sheep 36,760; horses 1,027; asses 1,760; buffalo 1,026; goats 18,863; chickens 34,612.

Industry. Fuel and power (in 000; metric tons; 1972): crude oil 3,410; coal (1971) 5,116; lignite (1970) 4,500; electricity (kw-hr.) 11,141,000. Production (in 000; metric tons; 1972): cement 8,421; iron ore (metal content; 1971) 1,166; pig iron 1,130; crude steel 1,442; sulfur (1970) 70; sulfuric acid 28; nitrogenous fertilizer (1971) 74; phosphate fertilizer (1971) 76; manganese ore (metal content; 1971) 5; chrome ore (oxide content; 1971) 365; cotton yarn (factory only; 1970) 185; wool yarn (1970) 30.

At the beginning of 1973, politicians struggled with the military establishment, while the closing months of the year were dominated by a struggle among the politicians themselves. The seven-year term of office of the president, retired Gen. Cevdet Sunay, expired on March 28. On March 5 the chief of the general staff, Gen. Faruk Gurler, one of the signatories of the memorandum of March 12, 1971, which had secured the removal from office of the Justice Party (JP) administration headed by Suleyman Demirel, resigned from the armed forces. On March 6 he was appointed senator by the outgoing president and thus became available for election to the presidency.

However, when General Gurler's candidacy was put before the two houses of Parliament on March 13, he was opposed by candidates backed by the JP and by a breakaway from the latter, the Democratic Party, while the Republican People's Party (RPP) boycotted the election in protest against what it called improper pressures by the military. None of the candidates secured the necessary majority, and the deadlock continued through 14 ballots until April 6,

Tunnels: *see* Engineering Projects

when retired Adm. Fahri Koruturk (*see* BIOGRAPHY) was put up jointly by the JP, the RPP, and the Republic Reliance Party (RRP) and was elected by 365 votes against 87 for General Gurler and 51 for the leader of the Democratic Party. The last military signatory of the March 12 memorandum still on active service, Gen. Muhsin Batur, the commander of the Air Force, retired in August.

The RRP was formed on March 2 as a result of a merger between Turhan Feyzioglu's National Reliance Party and a number of defectors from Bulent Ecevit's RPP. The latter continued in opposition when, on April 15, independent Sen. Naim Talu formed a caretaker administration in which the JP held 13 portfolios, the RRP 5, and independents 7. The Talu government, which was endorsed by the Assembly on April 26 by 261 votes to 94, secured parliamentary approval of a number of measures favoured by the military. State security courts were set up to try subversion charges after the ending of martial law, which was gradually narrowed in scope and finally lifted on September 26 in the last two provinces (Istanbul and Ankara). Universities were subjected to a greater degree of public control. On June 13 the Assembly (and on June 22 the Senate) voted an agricultural reform law providing for the distribution of some 3.2 million ha. of land to about half a million farmers over 15 years.

In the meantime, there were several minor terrorist incidents, many arrests, and more trials of alleged subversives. Military courts continued to impose heavy sentences. Sentences of up to 15 years' imprisonment passed on the entire leadership of the dissolved Marxist Turkish Labour (or Workers') Party were confirmed by the Military Court of Appeal on April 26. Alleged violations of human rights in Turkey were discussed by the political committee of the Council of Europe, which on July 3 decided to set up a special group to keep the subject under review.

The demand for an amnesty to cover nonviolent political offenses was insistently put forward by the RPP in the campaign leading up to the elections of October 14. The elections, which took place without any major incidents, resulted in a stalemate; the left advanced, and there was a massive splitting of the centre and right-wing vote. (*See* POLITICAL PARTIES.) On October 28 President Koruturk entrusted the formation of the new government to Bulent Ecevit of the RPP. However, the latter's efforts to form a coalition with the National Salvation Party came to nothing, and he laid down his mandate on November 7. Subsequent efforts by Demirel and Talu also failed, and on December 29 the president asked Talu to form a coalition government to serve pending new elections in 1974.

A porter in Istanbul taxis passengers across a flooded street for one lira (about seven cents) during the spring rains, which often leave city streets under six or more inches of water.

WIDE WORLD

Turkey kept a low profile during the Middle East war. On October 9 the Foreign Ministry reiterated its support for UN Security Council resolution 242 and for the "legitimate rights" of Arab countries under it. On October 16 it stated that the joint defense base at Incirlik (near Adana) could only be used for NATO purposes.

The 50th anniversary of the founding of the Turkish republic was marked with great pomp on October 29. The inauguration of the Europe-to-Asia Bosporus bridge, built by an Anglo-West German consortium at a cost of £15 million, was the highlight of the celebrations. On December 25, Ismet Inonu, the first prime minister of the Turkish republic and a major figure in Turkish politics for more than 50 years, died (*see* OBITUARIES). (ANDREW MANGO)

See also Cyprus.

Uganda

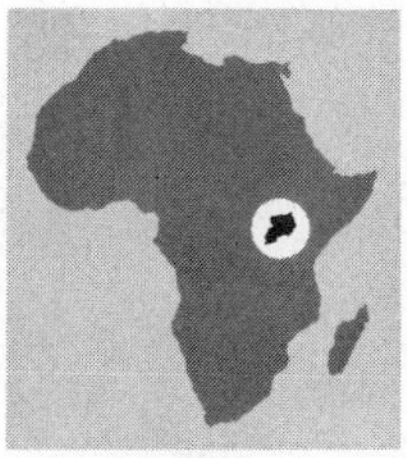

A republic and a member of the Commonwealth of Nations, Uganda is bounded by Sudan, Zaire, Rwanda, Tanzania, and Kenya. Area: 91,452 sq.mi. (236,860 sq.km.), including 15,236 sq.mi. of inland water. Pop. (1973 est.): 10,809,600, virtually all of whom are African. Cap. and largest city: Kampala (pop., 1969, 330,700). Language: English (official), Bantu, Nilotic, Nilo-Hamitic, and Sudanic. Religion: Christian, Muslim, traditional beliefs. President in 1973, Gen. Idi Amin.

Toward the end of 1972 President Amin sent a mission to North and South America in an attempt to extend Uganda's sources of foreign aid, and shortly afterward an embassy was established in Peking. It was, however, on the Muslim countries—Libya, Egypt, and Saudi Arabia—that Amin continued to rely most heavily for support. During the fourth Arab-Israeli war of October 1973 he visited Cairo and promised to send troops.

In February, 12 men found guilty of guerrilla activities were publicly executed by firing squad. Later in the month the president threatened to expel all members of the Luo tribe, whose homeland was just beyond the Kenya border. There were numerous cases of missing persons, and of unexplained murders, some of which Amin blamed on his enemies.

After two members of his Cabinet had resigned, the president sent the remaining members on 30 days' compulsory leave, extended later to 60 days. On their return to duty in May, Amin appointed them to administer the affairs of nationalized British companies and former Asian businesses.

Relations with Tanzania became strained in March after the arrest in Dar es Salaam of 53 Ugandans accused of spying. Amin placed the Army and Air Force on a war footing, and the Tanzanian foreign minister accused Uganda of moving troops to the border. Amin countered with the claim that a Tanzanian invading

UGANDA

Education. (1969) Primary, pupils 709,708, teachers 21,074; secondary, pupils 35,924, teachers 1,641; vocational, pupils 3,673, teachers 332; teacher training, students 4,328, teachers 318; higher (at Makerere University; 1970), students 1,949, teaching staff 350.

Finance and Trade. Monetary unit: Uganda shilling, with (Sept. 17, 1973) a par value of UShs. 6.90 to U.S. $1 (free rate of UShs. 16.68 = £1 sterling). Budget (1972–73 est.): revenue UShs. 1,525,000,000; expenditure UShs. 1,430,000,000. Foreign trade (excluding trade with Kenya and Tanzania; 1972): imports UShs. 806 million; exports UShs. 1,903,000,000. Import sources: U.K. 34%; Japan 10%; West Germany 9%; Italy 5%; U.S.S.R. 5%; India 5%; U.S. 5%. Export destinations: U.S. 22%; U.K. 19%; Japan 11%. Main exports: coffee 59%; cotton 19%; tea 7%; copper 6%.

Transport and Communications. Roads (1972) 25,714 km. Motor vehicles in use (1972): passenger 33,500; commercial 11,000. Railways (1970) 1,226 km. (for traffic *see* KENYA). Air traffic: *see* KENYA. Telephones (Dec. 1971) 34,000. Radio receivers (Dec. 1968) 531,000. Television receivers (Dec. 1971) 15,000.

Agriculture. Production (in 000; metric tons; 1972; 1971 in parentheses): millet *c.* 630 (*c.* 630); sorghum *c.* 330 (*c.* 330); sweet potatoes (1971) *c.* 713, (1970) *c.* 710; cassava (1970) *c.* 2,150, (1969) 2,321; peanuts *c.* 215 (*c.* 200); dry beans *c.* 270 (*c.* 270); coffee *c.* 200 (195); tea *c.* 24 (*c.* 18); sugar, raw value *c.* 145 (154); cotton, lint *c.* 87 (75); timber (cu.m.; 1971) 11,500, (1970) 11,400; fish catch (1971) 137, (1970) 129. Livestock (in 000; Dec. 1971): cattle *c.* 4,600; sheep *c.* 900; goats *c.* 1,950; pigs *c.* 85; chickens *c.* 10,500.

Industry. Production (in 000; metric tons; 1972): cement 166; copper, smelter 14; tungsten concentrates (oxide content; 1971) 0.14; salt (1971) 3; phosphates (1971) 24; electricity (excluding most industrial production; kw-hr.) 812,000.

force was moving toward the frontier, although an observer sent by the Somali government could find no such evidence. The situation was eased in May as a result of initiatives taken by Amin and Ethiopian Emperor Haile Selassie during the summit meeting of the Organization of African Unity in Addis Ababa, Eth. In the meantime, Amin had been strengthening his armed forces by the acquisition of eight fighter-bombers thought to have come from Libya, while both France and the U.S.S.R. appeared ready to supply him with arms. The United States, on the other hand, withdrew its ambassador from Kampala in April, closed its embassy in November, and cut off aid to Uganda.

The uncertain state of the country's economy led the president to question his earlier promise to pay compensation for properties taken over from noncitizen traders, although he justified his change of mind by accusing the noncitizens of having exploited Uganda for many years. A boycott by many foreign suppliers caused shortages of a number of consumer items.

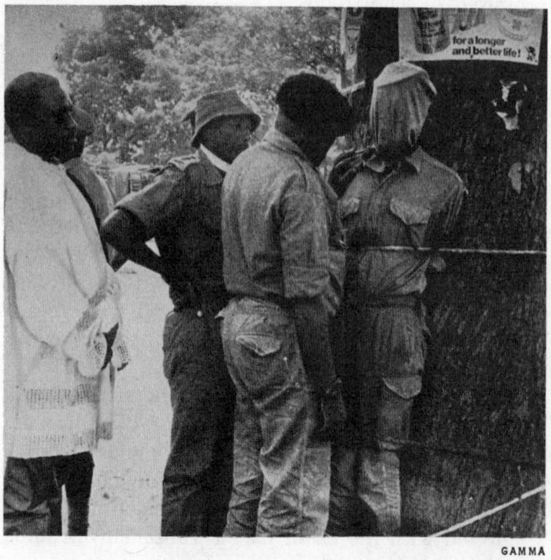

The last prayer for a prisoner convicted of treason and shot at Kampala on Feb. 10, 1973. Twelve prisoners were shot that day in Uganda as a warning to others.

GAMMA

Unemployment: *see* Employment, Wages, and Hours; Social Services

UNESCO: *see* United Nations

In August Amin announced the establishment of ten provinces in Uganda and promised a state supreme council consisting of himself as president, the prime minister or vice-president when appointed, the commanders of the Army, Air Force, and Navy, the chief of staff, and the ministers of defense and public administration. There was also to be a national forum comprising himself and his Cabinet, together with a representative of each county and municipal representatives from Kampala, Masaka, Jinja, and Mbale. Swahili would become the national language, gradually replacing English. Lake Edward was renamed Lake Idi Amin Dada. (KENNETH INGHAM)

See also Race Relations; Refugees.

Union of Soviet Socialist Republics

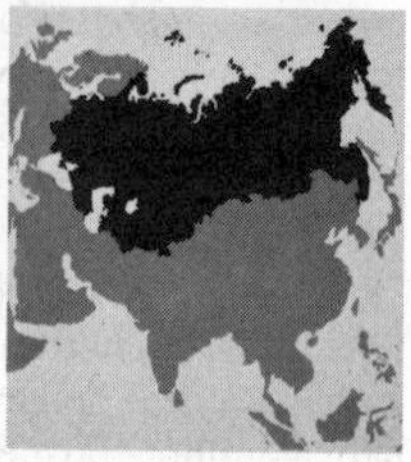

The Union of Soviet Socialist Republics is a federal state covering parts of eastern Europe and northern and central Asia. Area: 8,600,340 sq.mi. (22,274,900 sq.km.). Pop. (1972 est.): 247,459,000, including (1970) Russians 53%; Ukrainians 17%; Belorussians 4%; Uzbeks 4%; Tatars 2%. Cap. and largest city: Moscow (pop., 1972 est., 7.3 million). Language: officially Russian, but many others are spoken. Religion: about 40 religions are represented in the U.S.S.R., the major ones being Christian denominations. General secretary of the Communist Party of the Soviet Union in 1973, Leonid Ilich Brezhnev; chairman of the Presidium of the Supreme Soviet (president), Nikolay V. Podgorny; chairman of the Council of Ministers (premier), Aleksey N. Kosygin.

Domestic Affairs. The voices of dissidents within the Soviet Union continued to be heard, at least in other countries, during 1973. As in previous years, attention centred on Andrey D. Sakharov, a leading physicist (*see* BIOGRAPHY), and Aleksandr I. Solzhenitsyn, generally regarded as the greatest living Soviet novelist. The problem of allowing Jews to leave the Soviet Union for Israel also caused worldwide controversy. This aspect of internal affairs received an added, international dimension in 1973 with the beginning of the Conference on Security and Cooperation in Europe, in which the U.S.S.R. faced a confrontation with the West over negotiations dealing with the free movement of people and ideas across what used to be called the iron curtain.

Sakharov was perhaps the leading personality among Soviet dissenters. On July 3 the Swedish newspaper *Dagens Nyheter* published an attack by him on the one-party system in the Soviet Union, describing it as "antidemocratic in its essence." In the same article, he predicted that the authorities might react by putting pressure on himself and his family. The official Soviet news agency, Tass, replied nine days later with a statement that Sakharov's "activity in supplying the reactionary press with anti-Soviet slander" was intended "to smear his own country." A press campaign against Sakharov followed, including statements by leading Soviet intellectuals; Sakharov's achievements as a nuclear physicist seemed to have protected him from direct retaliation by the authorities. In September Sakharov's fellow dissident Solzhenitsyn reacted by proposing him for the Nobel Peace Prize.

Solzhenitsyn himself gave an interview to two Western correspondents at the end of August in which he spoke of threats against his life, and in September *Pravda* warned both men that "nobody is allowed to violate socialist legality." The establishment of a copyright agency in September gave the Soviet authorities control over one of the lines of communication between dissident writers and the outside world. This followed from Soviet membership in the Universal Copyright Convention, announced in May. The head of the new agency, Boris Pankin, stated that "the Soviet author cannot bypass our representation and approach a publisher directly and give him permission to publish. If he does so, he is violating Soviet law." Late in December Solzhenitsyn further outraged Soviet authorities by publishing in Russian in Paris *The Gulag Archipelago,* an account of police oppression and terror in the U.S.S.R. from 1918 to 1956. (*See* PUBLISHING.)

Dissent, and attempts to silence it, were by no means confined to Sakharov and Solzhenitsyn. In some cases leniency was shown. For example, in November the Ukrainian literary critic Ivan Dzyuba, sentenced to five years of imprisonment and five of exile for "anti-Soviet agitation," was pardoned, and the punishment of Andrey A. Amalrik, who completed one three-year sentence in May for "slandering the Soviet Union" and was sentenced to another three years in July, was reduced from imprisonment in a labour camp to exile. On the other hand, there were several reports during the year of particularly severe prison sentences inflicted on dissidents in the Ukraine. Some protesters, such as Zhores A. Medvedev and Valery N. Chalidze, were given permission to pursue their scientific work abroad, and, after they had left, were deprived of their citizenship and denied the right to return to the Soviet Union. There was a respite before and during the visit to the U.S. by General Secretary Brezhnev (*see* BIOGRAPHY), but shortly after his return the secret police stepped up its drive against the publishers of clandestinely circulated literature.

The regime deployed all its resources in the trial of Pyotr Yakir, a historian, and Viktor A. Krasin, an economist. These leading figures in the struggle for civil rights were arrested in 1972, and it was reported that they collaborated with the police during their interrogation. At their trial they pleaded guilty to charges of cooperating with anti-Soviet exiles and working as informers for foreign correspondents in Moscow. On September 1 they received relatively light sentences of three years in prison and three years' internal exile. The foreign press had been excluded from the trial, but on September 5 Yakir and Krasin were paraded at a press conference, where they repeated their admission of guilt. The Soviet authorities seemed satisfied that the trial had fulfilled its purpose of discrediting the dissidents, and it was reported unofficially in November that Yakir and Krasin had been released from prison.

The Soviet policy of seeking a workable modus vivendi with the United States was adversely affected by the pressure that the government put on Soviet Jews who expressed a desire to emigrate to Israel. Western opinion was particularly outraged by the so-called education tax levied on departing intellectuals to make them pay for the education they had received in the U.S.S.R. The first results of U.S. pressure came in March, just days after the visit to Moscow of George Shultz, the U.S. secretary of the treasury, who apparently told the Soviet leaders about moves in the U.S. Congress designed to prevent the granting of most-favoured-nation trading concessions to the Soviet Union; the U.S.S.R. waived emigration taxes for a small number of Jewish applicants for exit permits.

Toward the end of March it was reported that the law under which emigrants had to pay the education tax had been suspended. In July it was reported that committees of the Supreme Soviet, the legislature, had begun work on a new draft law on citizenship. It was expected to deal in precise terms with the right to emigrate and the effects of emigration on the right to citizenship. As Jews were the only Soviet citizens seeking to emigrate in any numbers, the discussion of new legislation obviously focused attention on their problem. In September the U.S.S.R. ratified the Interna-

A squadron of light tanks rumbles across Red Square during a military parade in Moscow on Nov. 7, 1973. It was believed to be the first public showing of these tanks, which have an antitank rocket over the gun.

WIDE WORLD

tional Covenant on Civil and Political Rights, first approved by the UN General Assembly in 1966; this guaranteed the right to emigration. The U.S.S.R., however, refused to accept an additional protocol giving the UN Commission on Human Rights the right to hear appeals from individuals, and the newspaper *Sovetskaya Rossiya* pointed out that the Communist countries had rejected a system of control over the implementation of the agreement, which "would have opened the way to infringement of the sovereignty of states and interference in their internal affairs."

Thus, the question of Jewish emigration was not resolved by any means, the fate of Valery Panov, formerly a leading dancer with the Kirov Ballet in Leningrad, being a case in point. Panov, a Jew, wanted to go to Israel with his wife, who was not a Jew; she also wanted to go, but the Soviet authorities said that she could not do so without the permission of her mother, who, it was claimed, refused to agree. Hunger strikes by the Panovs and appeals to the West proved useless. The outbreak of war in the Middle East in October created a new danger for Soviet Jewry, and a new wave of arrests of Jewish activists in Moscow, Leningrad, Kiev, and other Soviet cities was reported toward the end of the month.

Dissent in a totalitarian society always attracts excessive attention. On the whole, the great mass of people in the U.S.S.R. seemed relatively untouched by the controversies thrown up by the discontented intellectuals, and their preoccupations were perhaps more precisely mirrored by incidents such as a housing scandal reported from Tbilisi in the republic of Georgia in November, which led to the dismissal of the minister of trade of Georgia, his two deputies, the mayor of Tbilisi, and several other officials.

In terms of internal politics the most significant event of the year was the reconstitution in April of the Politburo, the supreme body of the Soviet Communist Party. Two of its members, Pyotr Y. Shelest and Gennady I. Voronov, were retired. Voronov, one of the party's leading agricultural experts, had disagreed with some of Brezhnev's investment policies in agriculture. His departure was linked to the appointments in February of Dmitry S. Polyansky as minister of agriculture and Fedor D. Kulakov as party secretary with special responsibility for farming. Both became members of the new Politburo, reflecting by their position the importance attached to the agricultural sector. Shelest's earlier dismissal from the post of first secretary of the Communist Party of the Ukraine in 1972, combined with ideological criticism of his book on the Soviet Ukraine, foreshadowed his total eclipse. He was reputed to have been a "hard-liner" on foreign policy, and his removal from the Politburo was seen as a strengthening of Brezhnev's policy of closer relations with the U.S. Andrey A. Gromyko, foreign minister for many years (*see* BIOGRAPHY), joined the Politburo, as did the minister of defense, Marshal Andrey A. Grechko (*see* BIOGRAPHY). The promotion of Gromyko and Grechko was interpreted as a signal of even greater emphasis on foreign policy and related defense matters. On the other hand, Yury V. Andropov, the head of the secret police, was moved from candidate to full membership, indicating perhaps that despite détente abroad there would be no relaxation of vigilance at home.

The Economy. In 1972 the major problem posed to the Soviet economy had been the failure of agriculture. This had serious repercussions on world food prices, as the U.S.S.R. had to purchase large quantities of grain on the world market. In 1973 the situation improved to an astonishing extent: the nation had a record grain harvest of about 215 million metric tons, exceeding the target by 17 million metric tons. This success owed much to weather, but it was also the result of greatly improved management techniques and greatly increased investments in fertilizers, irrigation, and land reclamation. By any standard, this was a tremendous achievement and must have added greatly to the self-confidence of the Soviet people and their leaders. It also demonstrated the wisdom of the decision taken by the late Nikita S. Khrushchev in 1953 to plow up the semiarid plains of Kazakhstan in central Asia. Khrushchev's "virgin lands" program ran into trouble in its early stages, threatening to make the area into a huge dust bowl, but tree planting, irrigation, and shallow plowing turned failure into success and Kazakhstan brought in its sixth successive record grain harvest.

The importance of the grain harvest must be seen in relation to the overall economic development of the Soviet Union. In 1972 the U.S.S.R. recorded its fifth

U.S.S.R.

Education. (1971–72) Primary and secondary, pupils 49,220,000, teachers (1969–70) 2,355,000; vocational and teacher training, pupils 4,420,000, teachers (1965–66) 251,000; higher (including 58 main universities), students 4,599,000, teaching staff (1965–66) 201,000.

Finance. Monetary unit: ruble, with (Sept. 17, 1973) an official exchange rate of 0.685 ruble to U.S. $1 (free rate of 1.65 rubles = £1 sterling). Budget (1972 est.): revenue 173.8 billion rubles; expenditure 173.6 billion rubles.

Foreign Trade. (1972) Imports 13,303,000,000 rubles; exports 12,734,000,000 rubles. Import sources: Sino-Soviet area 64% (East Germany 15%, Poland 11%, Czechoslovakia 10%, Bulgaria 9%, Hungary 7%). Export destinations: Sino-Soviet area 65% (East Germany 13%, Poland 10%, Czechoslovakia 10%, Bulgaria 9%, Hungary 7%, Cuba 5%). Main exports: machinery 24%; crude oil 9%; iron and steel 8%; timber 6%.

Transport and Communications. Roads (1969) 1,358,900 km. (including 540,000 km. surfaced roads in 1971). Motor vehicles in use: passenger (1969) *c.* 1.5 million; commercial (1965) *c.* 4.5 million. Railways (1971): 257,100 km. (including 135,400 km. public and 121,700 industrial); traffic 274,554,000,000 passenger-km., freight (1972) 2,766,000,000,000 net ton-km. Air traffic (1971): 88,331,000,000 passenger-km.; freight (1970) 1,876,700,000 net ton-km. Navigable inland waterways (1971) 144,600 km.; traffic 183,800,000,000 ton-km. Shipping (1972): merchant vessels 100 gross tons and over 6,851; gross tonnage 16,733,674. Telephones (Dec. 1971) 11,980,000. Radio licenses (Dec. 1971) 99.9 million. Television licenses (Dec. 1971) 39.3 million.

Agriculture. Production (in 000; metric tons; 1972; 1971 in parentheses): wheat 85,800 (98,760); barley 36,800 (34,571); oats 14,000 (14,650); rye 9,600 (12,787); corn 9,800 (8,597); rice 1,600 (1,429); millet (1971) 2,040, (1970) 2,100; potatoes 77,800 (92,655); sugar, raw value *c.* 9,000 (*c.* 8,220); sunflower seed 5,030 (5,663); linseed *c.* 500 (*c.* 540); dry peas *c.* 4,900 (*c.* 4,670); soybeans *c.* 540 (*c.* 535); wine 2,940 (2,820); cotton, lint *c.* 2,450 (*c.* 2,385); flax fibre 445 (485); tobacco *c.* 240 (*c.* 262); wool (1971) 254, (1970) 251; eggs (1971) *c.* 2,481, (1970) *c.* 2,222; meat (1971) *c.* 8,750, (1970) 8,765; milk (1971) 83,000, (1970) 82,900; butter (1971) *c.* 1,140, (1970) 1,067; cheese (1971) 466, (1970) 478; timber (cu.m.; 1970) *c.* 385,200, (1969) *c.* 374,200; fish catch (1971) 7,337, (1970) 7,252. Livestock (in 000; Jan. 1972): cattle 102,434; pigs 71,400; sheep 139,900; goats *c.* 5,400; horses (1971) 7,400; poultry (1971) 652,700.

Industry. Index of production (1963 = 100): (1972) 201; (1971) 189. Fuel and power (in 000; metric tons; 1972): coal and lignite 654,600; crude oil 395,900; natural gas (cu.m.) 220,900,000; manufactured gas (cu.m.; 1971) 33,929,000; electricity (kw-hr.) 846,600,000. Production (in 000; metric tons; 1972): cement 104,200; iron ore (60% metal content) 208,000; pig iron 84,600; steel 126,000; aluminum (1970) *c.* 1,100; copper (1971) *c.* 1,150; lead (1970) *c.* 440; zinc (1970) *c.* 610; manganese ore (metal content; 1971) 2,552; tungsten concentrates (oxide content; 1971) 8.8; magnesite (1971) *c.* 1,450; gold (troy oz.; 1969) 6,250; silver (troy oz.) 39,000; sulfuric acid 13,672; caustic soda 1,903; plastics and resins 2,030; fertilizers (plant nutrient content; 1971) nitrogenous 6,055, phosphate 2,772, potash 4,807; newsprint (1971) 1,152; other paper (1971) 5,934; cotton fabrics (sq.m.) 6,410,000; woolen fabrics (sq.m.) 681,000; rayon and synthetic fabrics (sq.m.) 1,170,000; passenger cars (units) 672; commercial vehicles (units) 595. New dwelling units completed (1971) 2,256,000.

foreign trade deficit since 1964, $700 million, caused largely by grain purchases abroad. The difficulties experienced in 1972 convinced the Soviet planners that they would have to reduce their growth targets for 1973, and at the beginning of the year it was announced that in 1973 gross industrial production would rise only 5.8% (as against 7.8% projected by the five-year plan), and that this would be weighted in favour of capital goods.

Despite the reduction in industrial investments, the Soviet government claimed that industrial targets were being met without difficulty, largely because of a substantial rise in labour productivity. The interim plan report, published halfway through 1973, showed that in fact industrial output rose 7%, compared with the 5.8% increase specified by the revised target for the year. Inflation seemed to have been held in check, with wages of industrial and office workers rising by 3% and those of collective farm workers by 5%. There was a marked expansion in the production of motor vehicles, machine tools, electrical equipment, chemicals, and farming implements.

The interim report also contained the usual catalog of industrial sectors that had failed to meet their plan targets. These included the production of certain chemicals (notably caustic soda and sulfuric acid), footwear, and some durable consumer goods. Among the most serious deficiencies was the output of bricks.

The global energy crisis lent special interest to the development of the West Siberian oil fields. The deposits at Agansk went into production, and West Siberia became the leading oil-producing area in the U.S.S.R. As there were no major oil-consuming industries in West Siberia, a 2,000-km. pipeline from the area to the Volga River was being built. On the whole, the U.S.S.R. faced the energy crisis with confidence. It reportedly had about half the world's resources of natural gas, vast oil and hydroelectric resources, and virtually inexhaustible coal reserves. The basic problem was to develop the technology to utilize and distribute these reserves.

In August the central statistical board of the U.S.S.R. announced that the nation's population had reached 250 million; of this total 121 million had been born since 1945. The balance of sexes, distorted by World War II, gradually was being restored. While in 1959 there were about 21 million more women than men, the margin in 1973 had been reduced to 18.6 million. Average life expectancy was 70.

Foreign Policy. The course of détente was pursued with single-minded determination during 1973. In June, Brezhnev went to Washington for talks with Pres. Richard Nixon and senior U.S. officials. According to Nixon's chief foreign-policy adviser, Henry Kissinger, the visit was intended to consolidate the recent improvements in Soviet-U.S. relations and to clear the way for the next, very complex stage of the talks on the limitation of strategic arms. The two leaders signed a series of functional agreements on oceanography, transport, agriculture, and the exchange of scientists. The two countries agreed to a total of $2 billion–$3 billion in trade over three years. It was also agreed that Nixon would go to Moscow in 1974 and Brezhnev would return to the U.S. in 1975. On his way back from Washington, the Soviet leader stopped in Paris for talks with French Pres. Georges Pompidou to reassure the French government that the Washington talks had not been concerned with deciding questions affecting the European allies of the U.S. and the Soviet Union.

WIDE WORLD

Soviet physicist Andrey Sakharov grasps his wife's hand during a news conference in their Moscow apartment. Mrs. Sakharov told Western newsmen that secret police told her she was "probably mentally ill" because she refused to help them persuade her husband to stop his dissident activities.

Brezhnev's visit to Bonn in May was equally important. It implied that the U.S.S.R. had abandoned its propaganda line about an allegedly militaristic threat from West Germany, which had been a means of holding the Warsaw Pact together for many years. The communiqué issued after talks between Brezhnev and Willy Brandt, the West German chancellor, reaffirmed their determination to adhere strictly to the four-power agreements on Berlin. A month earlier the U.S.S.R. agreed to supply West Germany with enriched uranium for a new nuclear power station. The Soviet offer was obviously designed to obtain West German cooperation in the expansion of the Soviet economy. Chemicals, electricity, and minerals were the main areas where the Soviets hoped to receive technological and financial aid from West Germany. In November the West German foreign minister, Walter Scheel, visited Moscow to continue discussions on economic collaboration.

Relations between Great Britain and the Soviet Union, which had been cool for some time, also improved. Sir Alec Douglas-Home, the British foreign and Commonwealth secretary, visited Moscow and Leningrad at the beginning of December. His talks with Soviet officials looked forward to the early signing of a ten-year agreement on economic, scientific, technological, and industrial cooperation, and it was also agreed that British Prime Minister Edward Heath would visit Moscow in the summer of 1974. Douglas-Home's visit had been preceded by exploratory talks conducted in Moscow in April by Peter Walker, the British secretary for trade and industry.

Apart from trade and economic cooperation, the West's relations with the Soviet Union were mainly determined by the issue of disarmament. In this area the crucial negotiations were those between the U.S. and the U.S.S.R. on strategic nuclear arms limitation (SALT). In September it was reported that the U.S.S.R. had achieved a major technological breakthrough in the development of nuclear multiple independently targeted reentry vehicles, indicating that by 1979 the Soviet Union would be able to match the U.S. in the number of deployable nuclear warheads. The fifth stage of SALT limited the number of Soviet missiles but not the weight or number of warheads. The U.S.S.R. also increased its capability in terms of submarine-launched missiles with the introduction into service of the Delta-class nuclear submarine.

In Eastern Europe, Soviet foreign policy appeared to concentrate on reassuring the U.S.S.R.'s allies about détente. During a visit to Bulgaria in September Brezhnev delivered a much publicized warning against

WIDE WORLD

U.S. presidential adviser Henry Kissinger is greeted at Moscow airport by First Deputy Foreign Minister Vasily V. Kuznetsov (left) and the Soviet ambassador to Washington, Anatoly F. Dobrynin, May 4, 1973.

a return to the cold war, speaking out against "reactionary forces trying to turn the tide" and arguing that all nations would profit from peace and security. President Tito of Yugoslavia visited Moscow in November for official talks with Brezhnev. There was little outward change in the Soviet Union's relations with China; despite periodic polemics in the Soviet press, there was no marked deterioration.

The major international crisis of 1973 was, of course, the outbreak of war between Israel and the Arabs in October. The Soviet Union appeared to be firmly committed to the Arab states, while the U.S. supported Israel. The fragile structure of détente appeared to be at risk, particularly when U.S. forces were put on alert allegedly to deter any possible Soviet move into the Middle East. The U.S.S.R. firmly denied ever having intended such a move, and subsequently used its influence with the Arabs to secure the implementation of the UN Security Council's call for a cease-fire. U.S. Secretary of State Kissinger went to the U.S.S.R. during the October crisis and his visit seemed to have served to reassure the Soviet government about U.S. intentions. Soviet policies during the crisis again demonstrated Moscow's awareness of its nuclear responsibilities in refusing a direct confrontation with the U.S., particularly as previous Soviet efforts had made it possible for the Arabs to face Israel on more equal terms.

At the height of the Middle East crisis, a Soviet-sponsored World Congress of Peace Forces met in Moscow and gave Brezhnev the opportunity to redefine the goals of Soviet foreign policy. He welcomed the conference as "a concentrated expression of positive changes" in the international system. "We are deeply convinced," he said, "that the current reversal from cold war to détente, from military confrontation to more solid security, to peaceful cooperation, is the main tendency in present-day international relations." On the Middle East he sounded intransigent: Israel's "aggression" was the cause of tension and conflict in the area, and the Soviet Union "firmly and consistently supports the Arab peoples' just demands." He promised that the U.S.S.R. would be prepared to participate in giving firm guarantees that would safeguard "the free and independent development of all states and peoples in the Middle East."

Throughout this major speech, Brezhnev returned to two main themes, the potential benefits of developing a global, well balanced system of international economic relations and the urgent need for measures aimed at achieving a military détente. Indeed, this concern seemed to reflect the current thrust of Soviet foreign policy—stability, economic development, and firm guarantees for the territorial status quo. But though he stated that "we oppose the export of revolution," Brezhnev made it clear that the cause of "changing the world" had not been abandoned. He declared that "no power on earth is capable of reversing the inexorable process of the renovation of social life" and that "the Soviet Union will always take sides with the forces of social progress." With doubtful logic, Brezhnev claimed that "this attitude does not conflict with the struggle for peace and for peaceful cooperation between states."

The resolution of this apparent contradiction would pose perhaps the major problem for Soviet foreign policy in future years. (OTTO PICK)

ENCYCLOPÆDIA BRITANNICA FILMS. *The Soviet Union: Epic Land* (1971); *The Soviet Union: A Student's Life* (1972); *The Soviet Union: Faces of Today* (1973).

United Arab Emirates

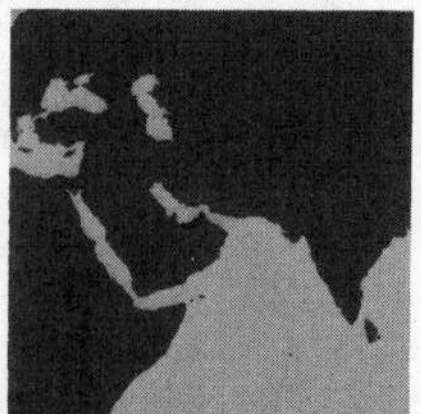

Consisting of seven emirates, the United Arab Emirates (the former Trucial States) is located on the eastern Arabian Peninsula. Area: 32,300 sq.mi. (83,657 sq.km.). Pop. (1973 est.): 320,000, of whom (1968) 68% were Arab, 15% Iranian, and 15% Indian and Pakistani. Cap.: Abu Dhabi town (pop., 1973 est., 60,000). Language: Arabic. Religion: Muslim. President in 1973, Sheikh Zaid ibn Sultan an-Nahayan; prime minister, Sheikh Maktum ibn Rashid al-Maktum.

In 1973 the United Arab Emirates' great and growing oil wealth enabled it to play a political role in the Middle East out of proportion to its size. Sheikh Zaid, of Abu Dhabi, consistently called for a unified stand by Arab oil producers and for the holding of an Arab

Unions:
see Labour Unions

Unitarians:
see Religion

United Arab Republic:
see Egypt; Libya

United Church of Canada:
see Religion

United Church of Christ:
see Religion

UNITED ARAB EMIRATES

Education. Primary and secondary (1968–69), pupils *c.* 12,000 (including 4,387 in Abu Dhabi), teachers (Abu Dhabi only) 223.

Finance. Monetary unit: dirham (introduced May 20, 1973, to replace the Qatar-Dubai riyal at par and the Bahrain dinar at the rate of 10 dirhams to one dinar), with (Sept. 17, 1973) a free rate of 3.95 dirhams to U.S. $1 (9.51 dirhams = £1 sterling). Budget (1973 est.) gross revenue *c.* 2 billion dirhams.

Foreign Trade. (1971) Imports *c.* U.S. $311.1 million; exports *c.* U.S. $727.5 million. Import sources: U.K. *c.* 36%; Japan *c.* 35%; Pakistan *c.* 6%; India *c.* 5%; Hong Kong 5%. Export destinations: Japan *c.* 57%; U.K. *c.* 29%; Sweden *c.* 5%. Main export crude oil.

Industry. Crude oil production (1971) 51,731,000 metric tons.

summit conference. In the October Arab-Israeli war the UAE was one of the leading advocates of cutting oil supplies to Israel's supporters.

The UAE Supreme Council, consisting of the rulers of the seven member states, met in July and decided on various measures to strengthen federal administration and improve common public services. In May a new uniform currency, the UAE dirham, was introduced, replacing the Bahrain dinar in Abu Dhabi and the Qatar-Dubai riyal in Dubai, with a fixed value in gold. With UAE reserves increasing rapidly, the dirham was expected to become one of the world's strongest currencies. Abu Dhabi oil production in 1973 was about 30% above 1972 levels before the October cutback, and Japan was taking an increasing share. A $37 million contract was signed with Kellogg International Corp. to build an oil refinery in Abu Dhabi, and in September Dubai signed a contract with British engineering firms to build what was described as the "world's biggest dry dock" in Dubai. It would be capable of handling million-ton tankers and would cost an estimated £91 million. A £40 million Eurodollar loan was raised for Abu Dhabi in October through one of London's leading merchant banks, Morgan Grenfell. The loan was made on the understanding that it would not be used for the purchase of arms. In December a new federal government was formed with Sheikh Maktum continuing as prime minister.

(PETER MANSFIELD)

United Kingdom

A constitutional monarchy in northwestern Europe and member of the Commonwealth of Nations, the United Kingdom comprises the island of Great Britain (England, Scotland, and Wales) and Northern Ireland, together with many small islands. Area: 94,217 sq.mi. (244,021 sq.km.), including 1,191 sq.mi. of inland water but excluding the crown dependencies of the Channel Islands and Isle of Man. Pop. (1972 est.) 55,789,000. Cap. and largest city: London (pop. [Greater London], 1972 est., 7,353,810). Language: English; some Welsh and Gaelic also are used. Religion: mainly Protestant. Queen, Elizabeth II; prime minister in 1973, Edward Heath.

On Jan. 1, 1973, the United Kingdom became a member of the European Economic Community. Although a historic date in British history, it was a change that brought few immediate consequences to the British people. Two of the new EEC commissioners were British, Sir Christopher Soames taking charge of external relations and George Thomson, regional policy. The British delegation to the first meeting of the enlarged European Parliament in January was led by Peter Kirk, who asked that the Parliament be made more powerful and influential. He submitted a memorandum prepared by the Conservative members of the British delegation suggesting changes to strengthen the Parliament's authority over the Commission and the Community budget—ideas stemming from British parliamentary practice.

Membership in the EEC continued to be a matter of disagreement in domestic politics, and the Labour Party chose to boycott the European Parliament, declining to nominate the 15 members it was entitled to send to Strasbourg. Labour continued to be critical of the EEC, complaining of "inward-looking Europeanism," and included in its prospective election program a pledge to renegotiate the terms of membership and to submit them to the approval of the electorate. Negotiation of the terms of membership was completed by agreement on the EEC's common agricultural policy, which came into effect on February 1, but during the year there were a number of occasions when British interests and views were in conflict with those of other member countries. Britain questioned the high farm prices fixed by the Community, and, though it was unable to win support for its proposal for a price freeze, it was able to secure much lower price increases than those advocated by the Commission.

Britain also stood aside from the Community's monetary exchange agreement, leaving the pound to float freely, while arguing that the member states should pool currency reserves. In this context Prime Minister Edward Heath (*see* BIOGRAPHY) claimed that Britain had consistently worked for Community rather than for United Kingdom interests, and he pressed for more rapid advances toward economic

LONDON DAILY EXPRESS/PICTORIAL PARADE

Princess Anne and Capt. Mark Phillips smile happily after their wedding in London's Westminster Abbey on Nov. 14, 1973. More than 500 million viewers observed the royal pageantry via television.

and monetary union. Earlier, in January, Heath had stressed the importance of developing a European foreign policy so that Europe could stand as "a valid partner" of the U.S. with a common policy toward the U.S.S.R. At the December meeting of the EEC foreign ministers in Brussels, Britain and West Germany clashed over the question of the financing of the regional development fund, which was of particular importance to Britain.

The Economy. Like most other countries of the developed world, Britain was caught up in the worldwide inflation of 1973. Economic developments were unforeseen, unprecedented, and often perverse. The Heath government had committed itself to a policy of sustained economic growth led by exports and accompanied by a counterinflationary program that had begun with a five-month prices and wages freeze announced in November 1972; this was to be followed by statutory limits on increases in wages, profits, and prices (called Stage Two) and renewed with some modifications in November (Stage Three). The Stage Two program was set out in a White Paper on January 17, and implemented, with some changes, by the Counter-Inflation Act and associated regulations. These laid down a code and established a Price Commission and a Pay Board (headed by, respectively, Sir Arthur Cockfield and Sir Frank Figgures; *see* BIOGRAPHY) to enforce it. Price control applied to all goods and services with exceptions for imports and fresh food. Prices were not to be increased above the level of increased costs per unit of output (with strict definition of allowable costs—only 50% of increased labour costs was allowable, the other 50% to be absorbed as an incentive to higher productivity). Prices were to be fixed at a level that would restrain profit margins to the average of the best two of the preceding five years. Profits on exports were exempt from control. Dividends were not to be increased by more than 5% over the previous year (with some exceptions). Companies with annual sales of more than £50 million (about 200) had to obtain advance approval for price increases, and smaller companies had either to report price increases or keep records. The objective in limiting pay increases was to keep spending power more in line with national output and to give priority for increases to the lower paid. The general principles laid down (with some particular exceptions) were that within a 12-month period increases should be limited to 4% of the average pay of the group of workers concerned plus £1 a week, the total increase not to exceed £250. Meanwhile, the trade unions had declared that they would not cooperate, and they refused to nominate members to the Price Commission and the Pay Board. There was an official but partial one-day protest strike on May 1.

Chinese Foreign Trade Minister Pai Hsiang-kuo takes leave of Prime Minister Edward Heath after a meeting at No. 10 Downing St., London, Jan. 15, 1973. Chinese Ambassador Sung Chih-kuang is at centre.

CENTRAL PRESS/PICTORIAL PARADE

Stage Three, taking effect in November, was to run for another 12 months. It continued the restraints of Stage Two within rather more generous limits, removed some anomalies, and tightened up control of some loopholes. Middle-ranking companies with annual sales of from £5 million to £50 million were required to notify the Price Commission of intended price increases, thus adding another 1,200 to the 200 biggest companies as those subject to most stringent control. The limit on pay increases was raised to 7% or £2.25 a week up to a £350 ceiling, with another 1% to remove anomalies affecting efficient use of manpower, premium payments for those working "unsocial hours," and "threshold" payments linked to increases in the retail price index above 7% during Stage Three.

These limits were based on assumptions that a 3.5% growth rate would be maintained and that the annual rate of inflation could be brought back to approximately 5% during 1974; also underlying them were the expectation that world commodity prices would level out and begin to decline and that the terms of trade (the ratio between export prices and import prices) would improve. In short, the Heath government was then still confident that it would be able to ride out whatever storms might lie ahead. Then, on November 13, with an oil crisis looming and an overtime ban in the coal mines, the government was obliged to declare a state of emergency and to lift the Bank of England's minimum lending rate to an unprecedented 13%. This followed the announcement that the October figures for visible trade showed a deficit of £298 million, later revised upward to £357 million. By the end of the year the U.K. was facing its worst economic crisis since World War II. With the price of Middle East oil increased fourfold in three months, the cost of oil imports was likely to raise the annual trade deficit by more than £1,000 million. Cuts in oil supplies led to a 10% reduction in deliveries to industrial and domestic consumers in November, but in some sectors cuts were more severe. Petrol (gasoline) became more difficult to obtain and preparations were made for rationing. When the coal miners banned overtime in pressing a wage claim beyond the limits of Stage Three, coal supplies to power stations and to industry were quickly affected. On December 13 the government ordered a three-day workweek to begin on Jan. 1, 1974, and a reduction of 35% in power consumption by continuous process (assembly-line) industries. In an emergency budget on December 17, £1,200 million was cut from projected public expenditure, a 10% surcharge on surtax of higher income ranges was imposed, a new tax on profits of property developers was introduced, and controls on hire purchase (installment buying) and bank advances were revived. The $3\frac{1}{2}$% growth target was abandoned and replaced by assumptions of nil growth. By the end of the year share prices on the London Stock Exchange had fallen by about 40% from the high point of May 1972—the biggest drop since the 1930s.

Yet the catastrophes of the year's last weeks concealed some notable achievements. Record trade deficits were accompanied by record exports (which topped £1,000 million a month for the first time in August, and again in September and October). Inflation was accompanied by a remarkably high rate of growth, 7.7% in the 12 months to November. The rate of inflation itself was relatively modest, with prices rising less than 10% during a period when costs of fuel and raw materials (largely imported) rose by more than 40%. Meanwhile, earnings, up 16% on the average with the average industrial wage reaching £40 a week for the first time, were running well ahead of prices. During the first half of the year there had been a boom in consumer spending, but it began to level off in the autumn. Unemployment had declined from the high levels recorded during the 1972–73 winter to 476,000 in December, the lowest figure since June 1969. However, another half million were laid off in anticipation of the three-day week.

Balance of payments difficulties had arisen from two main causes: the hectic increases in world commodity prices during the year; and the depreciation of the pound, by between 18 and 20% against other major trading currencies after it was left to float. The depreciation still further increased the cost of imports, while increasing the volume of exports needed to achieve a balance of visible trade. On top of this, the new policy for banking introduced in 1971, which created a freely competitive market for credit, had by October plainly run out of control and was aggravating demand pressures on the domestic economy—already showing symptoms of overheating. By the autumn the average prices of main imported commodities and food had doubled since 1971, oil and food each costing an extra £500 million or more a year. In August it seemed that commodity prices were leveling off and beginning to turn down, but after the Arab-Israeli war in October metal and oil prices began rising fast again. House and property prices had rocketed during the year and in June were reported to be 50% above mid-1972 levels. October saw the sharpest monthly increase in food prices—3.3%—since June 1955, an increase that lifted the cost of living as a whole by 2%.

Bank interest rates opened the year with a Bank of England minimum lending rate (MLR, equivalent to the former official bank rate) at 9% and eased to 7.5% by the end of June, but in July, owing to the uneasy state of the foreign exchanges and rising interest rates in other countries, the MLR was raised in successive weeks to 9% and then to 11.5% to protect the currency reserves. This in turn forced up housing mortgage rates to 10% in August and then 11% in September. These increases led the government to take special steps to protect first-time house buyers, for whom five-year loans were to be made available at 8.5%. The further rise of the mortgage rate to 13% on November 13 was quite without precedent. The high cost of loans and difficulty in raising mortgages checked the increase in house prices in the later months of the year. In December some of the so-called secondary banks operating retail "money shops" ran into difficulties and had to be rescued by the clearing banks and the Bank of England.

The 1973–74 budget was introduced on March 6, a month earlier than usual and before the acute difficulties of later months in the year had manifested themselves. Chancellor of the Exchequer Anthony Barber said that his intention was that the economy should grow at an annual rate of about 5% to the middle of 1974, and for this reason the budget was to be "broadly neutral" in effect. He said that in dealing with inflation and the balance of payments "we must not find ourselves compelled to bring growth to a halt."

Wage restraint policies inevitably led to industrial disputes when claims were rejected. There was a lengthy dispute in the gas industry, starting with a ban on overtime in January and leading to selective stoppages in February that disrupted industry and cut off supplies to some domestic consumers, notably in the West Midlands and London. Hospital ancillary workers were involved in scattered work stoppages for seven weeks in March and April. Civil servants took part in a one-day stoppage—a rare event in the civil service. Selective strikes took place in London schools by teachers seeking higher wages because of living in London. Railwaymen held one-day stoppages that dislocated rail transport, particularly in the London area. These claims were all ultimately settled within the terms of Stage Two. Postal workers accepted a settlement without resorting to industrial action.

Coal miners in April decided by ballot not to strike in support of a claim, but in November, after turning down an offer under Stage Three calculated to be

UNITED KINGDOM

Education. (1970–71) Primary, pupils 5,885,692, teachers (full-time) 207,283; secondary and vocational, pupils 3,608,062, teachers (full-time) 193,064; higher (44 universities only), students 259,604, teaching staff 34,103.

Finance. Monetary unit: pound sterling, with (Sept. 17, 1973) a free rate of £0.41 to U.S. $1 (U.S. $2.41 = £1 sterling). Gold, SDRs, and foreign exchange, official: (June 1973) U.S. $6,873,000,000; (June 1972) U.S. $6,964,000,000. Budget (1973–74 est.): revenue £17,451 million; expenditure £18,648 million. Gross national product: (1972) £61,190 million; (1971) £56,320 million. Money supply: (June 1973) £12,986 million; (June 1972) £11,753 million. Cost of living (1963 = 100): (June 1973) 173; (June 1972) 158.

Foreign Trade. (1972) Imports £11,155 million; exports £9,746 million. Import sources: EEC 24% (West Germany 7%, The Netherlands 6%, France 5%); U.S. 11%; Canada 5%; Sweden 5%. Export destinations: EEC 23% (West Germany 6%, France 5%, The Netherlands 5%); U.S. 12%; Ireland 5%. Main exports: machinery 28%; chemicals 10%; vehicles 9%; textile yarns and fabrics 5%. Tourism (1971): visitors 6,973,000; gross receipts U.S. $1,195,000,000.

Transport and Communications. Roads (1971) 359,622 km. (including 1,353 km. expressways). Motor vehicles in use (1971): passenger 12,448,782; commercial 1,660,000. Railways (excluding Northern Ireland; 1971): 18,738 km.; traffic 30,129,000,000 passenger-km., freight (1972) 20,471,000,000 net ton-km. Air traffic (1972): 22,168,000,000 passenger-km.; freight 782,602,000 net ton-km. Shipping (1972): merchant vessels 100 gross tons and over 3,700; gross tonnage 28,624,875. Ships entered (1970) vessels totaling 137,888,000 net registered tons; goods loaded (1971) 49,539,000 metric tons, unloaded 206,446,000 metric tons. Telephones (Dec. 1971) 16,143,000. Radio receivers (Dec. 1972) *c.* 18,980,000. Television licenses (Dec. 1972) 16,982,000.

Agriculture. Production (in 000; metric tons; 1972; 1971 in parentheses): wheat 4,760 (4,815); barley 9,238 (8,558); oats 1,255 (1,360); potatoes 6,441 (7,173); sugar, raw value *c.* 951 (1,179); apples *c.* 404 (529); pears *c.* 55 (72); dry peas *c.* 75 (73); dry broad beans (1971) 134, (1970) 160; tomatoes (1971) 110, (1970) 108; onions 195 (230); eggs *c.* 870 (877); milk 13,596 (12,732); butter 95 (65); cheese 182 (156); beef and veal 916 (954); mutton and lamb 220 (228); pork 977 (1,000); wool *c.* 28 (30); fish catch (1971) 1,107, (1970) 1,099. Livestock (in 000; June 1972): cattle 13,483; sheep 26,877; pigs 8,619; chickens 133,214.

Industry. Index of production (1963 = 100): (1972) 130; (1971) 126. Fuel and power (in 000; metric tons; 1972): coal 121,890; crude oil 83; natural gas (cu.m.) 25,098,000; manufactured gas (cu.m.; 1971) 11,650,000; electricity (kw-hr.) 266,000,000. Production (in 000; metric tons; 1972): cement 18,046; iron ore (28% metal content) 8,364; pig iron 15,319; crude steel 25,321; nitrogenous fertilizers (1971–72) 773; passenger cars (units) 1,921; commercial vehicles (units) 408; cotton fabrics (m.) 510,000; woolen fabrics (sq.m.) 183,000; rayon synthetic fabrics (m.) 469,000. Merchant vessels launched (100 gross tons and over; 1972) 1,242,000 gross tons. New dwelling units completed (1972) 331,000.

equivalent to a 16½% increase, the miners started a ban on overtime that threatened coal production at a time when oil supplies from Arab countries had been reduced. At about the same time, power station engineers banned out-of-hours work, which reduced electricity supplies, and rail services were disrupted when locomotive crews resorted to work-to-rule. Chronic unrest and disruptive stoppages in the automobile industry led the U.S. parent company of Chrysler to talk of withdrawing from the U.K. altogether.

Domestic Affairs. The Heath government completed three years out of its five-year term in June 1973, and the parties began to turn their minds to the likelihood of a general election in 1974. The Conservatives, blamed for rising prices and wage controls, suffered losses at by-elections and local government elections. Apart from the setbacks to their economic policies, they had been beset by growing criticism of what the prime minister himself had termed "the unacceptable face of capitalism." In May, while the Department of Trade and Industry investigated the affairs of the pan-African trading group Lonrho, Heath told the Conservative Women's annual conference "it is no part of our philosophy that by one device or another vast sums of money should pass hands at the heart of our financial system as personal rewards." His remarks were pertinent in the light of payments made to former Conservative Colonial Secretary Duncan Sandys as fees for a Lonrho consultancy and in compensation for its termination, these fees in part being paid into a Cayman Island tax haven.

Despite such revelations, the Labour Party failed to capitalize as much as might have been expected on Conservative unpopularity. For the Liberals, however, it was a year of by-election successes. They won the seats at Ripon, Isle of Ely, and Berwick-on-Tweed, and pushed into second place in other contests. Opinion polls at one time in September showed opinion split roughly equally between Conservatives, Labour, and Liberals, with the Liberals once momentarily in the lead. Labour suffered a wounding defeat at Lincoln when Dick Taverne retained the seat as a "Democratic Labour" independent after having resigned following a dispute with the official Labour Party over its opposition to joining the EEC.

A bomb blast in London's Great Scotland Yard, Whitehall, at the moment of explosion on March 8, 1973. Police suspected Irish terrorists in the incident, which was followed shortly afterward by another explosion near the Old Bailey.

CAMERA PRESS/PICTORIAL PARADE

In local government elections for the reformed local authorities that were due to come into operation in April 1974, Labour won control of all the seven main urban centres, including the Greater London Council. Of the 39 nonmetropolitan counties in England, Conservatives and associated independents won control of 20, and Labour 7. In Wales Labour won the four southern Wales counties, and Independents took control of three in central and northern Wales.

In expectation of a 1974 general election, the Labour Party adopted a lengthy "Programme for Britain" at its annual conference in October. This was described by Labour Party leader Harold Wilson as "socially relevant and radically progressive." Its main purposes were to shift the balance of power and wealth in the community to working people, to provide for more effective democratic control of industry, to eliminate poverty, and to improve the environment. Its preparation aroused controversy over a proposal to bring into public ownership the 25 largest private companies. This led Wilson to announce that a Labour government would not be bound by such a precise commitment. In general terms, however, the party was agreed on a substantial extension of public ownership. Roy Jenkins, formerly Labour chancellor of the Exchequer and deputy leader of the party, settled the differences over Europe that had led him to resign from the Labour shadow cabinet and returned to the opposition front bench with responsibility for Home Office affairs. Labour's poor performance in by-elections and in opinion polls had led to talk of a possible Liberal-Labour alliance. The idea was vehemently rejected by Labour leaders. The Liberal leader, Jeremy Thorpe (*see* BIOGRAPHY), also said there would be no pacts or deals.

Heath made one major change in his Cabinet when on December 2 he switched William Whitelaw, who had distinguished himself as secretary of state for Northern Ireland, to take charge of the Department of Employment. Francis Pym moved (like Whitelaw before him) from being government chief whip to take charge of Northern Ireland. Another change in the Cabinet came in May, when Lord Jellicoe, leader of the House of Lords, resigned after disclosing that he had had an association with a call girl. Lord Lambton, a junior minister at the Ministry of Defence, resigned for the same reason. Lord Windlesham, who had been minister of state at the Northern Ireland Office, replaced Lord Jellicoe as lord privy seal and leader of the House of Lords. The call-girl affair was investigated by the Security Commission, which found that there had been no leakage of classified information by the ministers concerned.

Transport. Three controversial and costly projects, the Concorde supersonic airliner, the third London airport at Maplin, and the Channel Tunnel (*see* ENGINEERING PROJECTS), were severely questioned by critics during the year. The Anglo-French Concorde had cost almost £1,000 million in its ten years of development, but only the British Overseas Airways Corp. (merged with British European Airways during the year to form British Airways) and Air France had placed firm orders, and many of the world's largest airlines had canceled provisional options on the ground that the plane would be uneconomic to operate. Production of five Concordes for British Airways and four for Air France continued. The cost (estimated at more than £1,000 million) and usefulness of the Maplin airport were challenged, and its target completion date was postponed to 1982.

Legislation. Among a number of important measures enacted during the 1972–73 session of Parliament was the Social Security Act, which provided for a new system of pensions based on occupational income-linked pension schemes run by employers and backed up by a basic state pension and an income-linked state reserve scheme. The Fair Trading Act established machinery to protect consumers against unfair trading practices. The Water Act set up ten regional water authorities for England and Wales; they were to manage water resources and to undertake an environmental cleanup of rivers and estuaries.

The Royal Family. Princess Anne, daughter of Queen Elizabeth II, was married on November 14 to Capt. Mark Phillips, an army officer in the Queen's Dragoon Guards (a tank regiment) and a member of the British Olympic Games equestrian team in 1968 (*see* BIOGRAPHY).

Foreign Policy. The 14-month-long "cod war" with Iceland over the latter's unilateral imposition of 50-mi. fishing limits ended in November after talks in London between Edward Heath and Iceland's Prime Minister Olafur Johannesson. The Icelandic government agreed to allow British trawlers to fish during the next two years within defined areas inside the 50-mi. limit but stipulated that the annual catch be reduced from 180,000 tons to 130,000 tons. (*See* ICELAND.)

When Egypt and Syria broke the Middle East cease-fire on October 6, their action was not met by any condemnation from the U.K. government but by an "evenhanded" ban on the sale of arms and spare parts for military equipment to both sides. However, while supplies already paid for by Israel were stopped, training of Egyptian helicopter pilots in the U.K. continued, and attack fighters were supplied to Saudi Arabia, a combatant state and the prime mover in the Arab oil embargo against Israel's allies. Britain's policy also involved denying facilities to the U.S. during its airlift of arms to Israel following a Soviet arms buildup, contributing to U.S. resentment at the lack of European support during the war and the confrontation with the U.S.S.R. When the oil embargo began to damage The Netherlands and it asked its EEC partners for an oil-sharing policy, Britain opposed such a scheme. In November Saudi Oil Minister Ahmed Yamani called Britain the Arabs' "number two friend" following France. Nonetheless, the U.K. was included in the cuts in oil supplies made by Arab producers.

Northern Ireland. Direct rule of Northern Ireland from London was extended for a second year to the end of March 1974, but a new chapter opened with the publication on March 20 of a White Paper called *Northern Ireland Constitutional Proposals.* This prepared the way for the Northern Ireland Assembly Act, which provided for the election of an assembly to replace the old Stormont Parliament. Next came the Northern Ireland Constitution Act, which laid down the guidelines for the restructuring of a Northern Ireland government. However, consensus proved hard to find, whether among intransigent politicians or against the background of the murderous vendetta that continued to be fought by both Roman Catholic and Protestant extremists. Terrorism spread to Britain in March, when car bombs exploded in London, in Whitehall and outside the Old Bailey (for which eight members of the Provisional IRA were later sentenced to life imprisonment), and again in August, when incendiary devices and carrier bag bombs were planted in London and letter bombs sent through the mails. There was a further outbreak of bomb incidents in London in December. On December 27 West German industrialist and honorary consul Thomas Niedermeyer was abducted from his Belfast home.

The new constitutional arrangements provided that Northern Ireland should remain part of the U.K. for as long as it was the wish of a majority of its people. The Assembly of 78 members was to be elected so as to give proportional representation to minority groups. Committees of the Assembly reflecting the balance of the parties were to be formed, and the chairmen of these committees were to form an executive. The White Paper also proposed institutional arrangements such as a "Council of Ireland" to provide for consultation and cooperation between Northern Ireland and the Republic of Ireland, an idea that was welcomed by the republic's prime minister, Liam Cosgrave (*see* BIOGRAPHY). As one by-product of these moves, a closer relationship developed between the U.K. and Ireland. A number of terrorists were arrested and imprisoned in the republic.

In the election for the Assembly on June 28, 72% of the electorate voted. About two-thirds of those voting could be taken to accept in principle the notion of power sharing between the Protestant and Catholic communities. Extremist candidates attracted remarkably few votes. Unionists accepting power sharing numbered 23 (led by Brian Faulkner, former Unionist prime minister); Unionists against power sharing 12; Democrat Unionist and Vanguard (militant Protestant parties) 15; the Catholic Social Democratic and Labour Party 19; and Alliance, the middle-of-the-road party of reconciliation, 8. Agreement on the composition of a Unionist and Republican coalition Northern Ireland Executive was announced on November 21; it consisted of six Unionists, four from the Social Democratic and Labour Party, and one from the Alliance Party. On December 9 agreement was reached on the formation of the Council of Ireland. (*See* Special Report.) (HARFORD THOMAS)

See also Ireland.

A wall sign in Belfast, N.Ire., reflects the mood of that city in 1973, which saw a continuation of conflict and violence between Protestant and Roman Catholic factions.

MICHAEL ST. MAUR—BLACK STAR

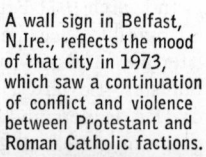

SPECIAL REPORT

THE IRISH DRAMA: A GLIMMER OF HOPE

By K. M. Smogorzewski

The confrontation of the two nationalisms in Northern Ireland, amplified by religious sectarianism and social unevenness, was by the end of 1973 as tense as it had been in the summer of 1968 when the curtain rose on the current violent episode. But a glimmer of hope had also appeared over the dark Ulster scene.

The Irish drama was the result of a 1920–21 English compromise that in actuality only postponed an unavoidable collision. Partition of a disputed territory is not an improbity provided that the division of nationalities is as equitable as possible. But the Anglo-Irish treaty of Dec. 6, 1921, had manifestly favoured the one-million-strong British-Protestant group by including in the historic, though territorially reduced, Ulster province a half million Irish Catholics—useful manpower in an industrialized region.

The Renewal of Violence. In the mid-1960s, when Terence O'Neill, a liberal-minded Ulster prime minister, tried to bring about a cordial relationship between Northern Ireland and the Republic to the south, suggesting also an end to the social and political discrimination against Ulster's Irish-Catholic minority, a plot within the ruling Unionist Party forced him to resign in April 1969. His successor, James Chichester-Clark, was too weak for the task assigned to him by the Orange Order, especially at a time when a division within the IRA, long an illegal military arm of the legal Sinn Fein party in the Republic, could only signal a more militant opposition. In December 1969 a schism within the Sinn Fein led to the formation of a "provisional Sinn Fein," with a "provisional IRA" as well. While the Provisionals were radical nationalists, the Officials presented themselves as supporters of a socialist united Ireland.

In March 1971 Brian Faulkner, a man of courage, firmness, and adaptability, became the Unionist Party's leader and prime minister. On August 9, with the approval of the new British prime minister, Edward Heath, Faulkner resorted to the internment of IRA leaders and militants. At the same time he published a program aimed at granting civil rights to the Irish Catholics. His attempt at isolating IRA fighters, hiding out in Irish-Catholic city areas, misfired for two reasons: the six members of the Social Democratic and Labour Party, representing electorally the bulk of the Irish Catholics, withdrew from the Parliament at Stormont and asked for its abolition; and, as this demand was identical with that of the IRA, the SDLP started a campaign against internment. The IRA, obviously not paralyzed, intensified its killings and bombings.

Against this background, on Sept. 27–28, 1971, Heath, John Lynch, prime minister of the Irish Republic, and Faulkner met at Chequers. The three remained "committed to their publicly stated positions on the constitutional status of Northern Ireland," but they agreed to condemn "any form of violence as an instrument of political pressure." But as terrorism in Ulster continued unabated, the British government concluded that the existing Stormont setting was not conducive to a political solution. Therefore, on March 30, 1972, the Northern Ireland (Temporary Provisions) Act, introducing Westminster's direct rule over the province, received royal assent. William Whitelaw, lord president of the council and leader of the House of Commons, was appointed secretary of state for Northern Ireland. He went to Belfast with the hope that the act would provide a fresh start and promote feelings of tolerance, fairness, and impartiality. Faulkner, however, expressed the fear that the British action, although it reaffirmed that Northern Ireland would not cease to be part of the United Kingdom "without the consent of the Parliament of Northern Ireland," would be interpreted as bowing to violence. William Craig (*see* BIOGRAPHY), a right-wing Unionist and leader of the newly created Vanguard Movement, went so far as to declare that he would rather proclaim Ulster's independence than be "submerged in an Irish Republic." But the SDLP, led by Gerard Fitt (*see* BIOGRAPHY), welcomed the act as "the first serious steps on the road to peace."

Whitelaw began his administration by releasing some of the internees and lifting a ban on marches, but his conciliatory moves had no effect. An additional 4,000 British troops were sent to Ulster in late July of 1972, bringing the total to 21,000. On July 31 troops moved into the IRA "no-go" areas of Londonderry and Belfast and began clearing Protestant barricades in East Belfast. By the end of 1973, 927 persons had been killed in Ulster since the first violence on Aug. 12, 1969, including 241 soldiers.

1973: A Crucial Year. Many important events took place during 1973. First, there was a change of government in Dublin. Following general elections on February 28, a coalition formed by Fine Gael and the Labour Party brought in Liam Cosgrave (*see* BIOGRAPHY) as prime minister—and Cosgrave was more diplomatic than Lynch had been in expressing the wish of every Irish statesman: the ultimate inclusion of Ulster in the Republic.

Later, on March 8 in Ulster, 58% of the electorate voted in the border referendum; 591,820 favoured union with the U.K., while 6,463 approved union with the Republic. The vast majority of abstentions were from those traditionally opposed to links with Great Britain. On March 20 the British government published a White Paper proposing a new framework for government in Northern Ireland. It called for a new assembly elected by a single transferable vote system of proportional representation applied to 12 multiseat constituencies. The assembly would elect its own presiding officer and an executive, but one no longer based upon any single party. Elections for the 78 seats in the new Assembly were held on June 28. Faulkner's Ulster Unionist Party won 23 seats; the nonsectarian Alliance Party, 8 seats; SDLP, 19; the Loyalist groups of Craig and Ian Paisley, 18; other Loyalists, 9; and the Labour Party, 1.

On September 17 Heath and Cosgrave met near Dublin—the first official visit to the Republic by a British prime minister since the state was established—to discuss the political and security situations in Ulster. On November 22 Whitelaw announced in the House of Commons that—after 6 months of negotiations at Stormont Castle, 20 months of direct rule, and more than 50 years of exclusively Orangist government—three political parties had agreed to form the first coalition administration in the history of Northern Ireland.

Finally, meeting at Sunningdale, Berkshire, Eng., on December 5–9, Heath, Cosgrave, and Faulkner agreed to form a Council of Ireland and a new system of combating terrorism in both North and South, while the Irish government "fully accepted and solemnly declared" that only the desire of a majority of the people of Northern Ireland would lead to a change in its status.

Cold blasts of "loyalist" opposition greeted Faulkner after the Sunningdale agreement. Craig and Paisley declared that they would destroy both the Executive and the Council of Ireland.

In Dublin the Provisional IRA expressed similar intentions. It would be relatively easy to silence the wild gunmen and bombers if Belfast, Dublin, and London acted in harmony, but how could wild "loyalists," who had their own gunners and were strong numerically, be neutralized? A great deal of water would continue to flow under the Liffey and Lagan bridges before the Irish dreams might come true.

K. M. Smogorzewski is a historian, journalist, and a regular contributor to the Britannica Book of the Year.

United Nations

Concerned with growing criticism of the organization he headed, UN Secretary-General Kurt Waldheim told a conference in May that, although the UN had been "oversold" in its early days, an equally unjustified trend existed now to "sell it short." Bilateral international action, by failing to take into account many countries' interests, was inadequate to meet contemporary problems, he asserted. The validity of his observations seemed borne out in the autumn when the UN faced yet another outbreak of war in the Middle East.

Middle East. Fighting between Israel, on the one hand, and Egypt and Syria, on the other, began on the Jewish high holy day of Yom Kippur (October 6). Early efforts to end hostilities were abortive. The Security Council held four inconclusive meetings in three days (October 8, 9, and 11), while the General Assembly interrupted its scheduled debates to hear from the principal belligerents. Observers with the UN Truce Supervision Organization (UNTSO) confirmed that Arab forces had crossed the 1967 cease-fire lines, but they were unable either to confirm or deny Arab reports of prior Israeli attacks. Neither the major powers nor the belligerents themselves seemed ready to accept a cease-fire order without a trial of arms.

The Security Council did not even meet to discuss the conflict for over a week. Meanwhile, U.S. Secretary of State Henry Kissinger went to Moscow on October 20 and hammered out a compromise resolution with Soviet party leader Leonid I. Brezhnev, which the two superpowers sponsored in the council on the night of October 21–22. The resolution, adopted in the early morning hours of October 22, called for a cease-fire in place, but the cease-fire did not take hold. The council then asked the secretary-general to arrange for the UN to supervise the Israeli-Egyptian front. Waldheim arranged for more patrols and passed on to the council a request from Finnish Maj. Gen. Ensio Siilasvuo, the head of UNTSO, for 43 additional officers.

Israel had crossed to the west bank of the Suez Canal before the October 22 truce call, but after the October 22 order it completely isolated the Egyptian 3rd Army. The council then decided on October 25 to adopt a third resolution, sponsored by eight "nonaligned" members, reiterating earlier cease-fire calls and also asking the secretary-general to send the vanguard of an emergency force to the Middle East and to prepare plans for a larger force that would include no nationals of permanent council members. The U.S. insisted on this provision in the face of a request by Egyptian Pres. Anwar as-Sadat for U.S. and Soviet military assistance in enforcing the October 22 cease-fire. The Soviet Union seemed to welcome this proposal, but the U.S. opposed it and actually ordered its armed forces on a "precautionary alert" on October 25 to counter Soviet moves that it interpreted as presaging unilateral Soviet intervention.

Besides dealing with the military situation, the council included two political provisos in its October 25 resolution. The first called on the parties concerned to start carrying out the council's November 1967 resolution, outlining a peace settlement that included Israeli withdrawal from territories occupied in 1967 and asking for security for all states in the area within recognized boundaries. The second provision of the resolution was that, concurrently with the cease-fire, immediate negotiations should start between the parties concerned with a view toward fashioning a just and durable peace.

PETER L. GOULD—KEYSTONE

Ambassador Leopoldo Benites of Ecuador, centre, is formally seated following election as president of the 28th UN General Assembly at its opening session, Sept. 18, 1973. On his right is UN Secretary-General Kurt Waldheim.

The council approved the secretary-general's plan for an emergency force on October 27 after amending its terms of reference. As finally agreed, they provided that the secretary-general could appoint the force commander with Security Council "consent" and that he could select the contingents for the force in consultation with the council, bearing in mind "equitable," not just "adequate," geographic representation. The terms gave the council active control over the secretary-general's actions, and the U.S.S.R. drove the point home by pressing to have 36 of its military men included in UNTSO.

On November 9 Waldheim directed General Siilasvuo to try to stabilize the cease-fire further by getting Egyptian and Israeli military officials to sign an accord, worked out by Kissinger in a visit to the Middle East, that allowed Egypt and Israel to settle the question of returning to the October 22 positions as part of a larger agreement to separate their forces under UN auspices. The accord also provided for the UN to supervise a corridor through which nonmilitary supplies could reach the encircled Egyptian troops, with an exchange of prisoners of war to follow as soon as UN troops replaced Israelis at crucial checkpoints. Representatives of the two sides signed the agreement on November 11, and the exchange of prisoners began November 15, at which time the UN took over supervision of supplies to the Egyptian troops.

Middle East tensions came to UN notice several times before the outbreak of the Yom Kippur war because of Israeli raids into Lebanon and Israeli actions against civilian aircraft. On April 21 the Security Council adopted a resolution condemning "the repeated military attacks conducted by Israel against Lebanon." On February 21 Waldheim expressed his shock and distress at an incident that day, when Israeli fighter planes shot down a Libyan civilian airliner over the Sinai desert with a loss of 106 lives. On August 15 the council unanimously condemned Israel for forcibly diverting and seizing a Lebanese airliner from Lebanese air space on August 10. Earlier, on July 26, the U.S. vetoed a council resolution favoured

Table I. Member States of the United Nations
Dec. 31, 1973

Afghanistan	Ecuador*	Laos	Saudi Arabia*
Albania	Egypt*	Lebanon*	Senegal
Algeria	El Salvador*	Lesotho	Sierra Leone
Argentina*	Equatorial Guinea	Liberia*	Singapore
Australia*	Ethiopia*	Libya	Somalia
Austria	Federal Republic	Luxembourg*	South Africa*
Bahamas	of Germany	Malagasy Rep.	Spain
Bahrain	Fiji	Malawi	Sri Lanka
Barbados	Finland	Malaysia	(formerly
Belgium*	France*	Maldives	Ceylon)
Belorussia*	Gabon	Mali	Sudan
Bhutan	Gambia, The	Malta	Swaziland
Bolivia*	German Democratic	Mauritania	Sweden
Botswana	Republic	Mauritius	Syria*
Brazil*	Ghana	Mexico*	Tanzania
Bulgaria	Greece*	Mongolia	Thailand
Burma	Guatemala*	Morocco	Togo
Burundi	Guinea	Nepal	Trinidad and
Cambodia	Guyana	Netherlands,	Tobago
(Khmer Rep.)	Haiti*	The*	Tunisia
Cameroon	Honduras*	New Zealand*	Turkey*
Canada*	Hungary	Nicaragua*	Uganda
Central African	Iceland	Niger	Ukraine*
Rep.	India*	Nigeria	U.S.S.R.*
Chad	Indonesia	Norway*	United Arab
Chile*	Iran*	Oman	Emirates
China*	Iraq*	Pakistan	United Kingdom*
Colombia*	Ireland	Panama*	United States*
Congo	Israel	Paraguay*	Upper Volta
Costa Rica*	Italy	Peru*	Uruguay*
Cuba*	Ivory Coast	Philippines*	Venezuela*
Cyprus	Jamaica	Poland*	Yemen (Aden)
Czechoslovakia*	Japan	Portugal	Yemen (San'a')
Dahomey	Jordan	Qatar	Yugoslavia*
Denmark*	Kenya	Romania	Zaire
Dominican Rep.*	Kuwait	Rwanda	Zambia

*Signatories to original Charter.

Table II. Council Membership
Years indicate date membership expires

Country	Security Council	Economic and Social Council*	Trusteeship Council
China	Permanent	1974	Permanent
France	Permanent	1975	Permanent
U.S.S.R.	Permanent	1974	Permanent
United Kingdom	Permanent	1974	Permanent
United States	Permanent	1973	†
Algeria		1975	
Australia	1974		†
Austria	1974		
Bolivia		1974	
Brazil		1975	
Burundi		1974	
Chile		1974	
Finland		1975	
Guinea	1973		
Haiti		1973	
Hungary		1973	
India	1973		
Indonesia	1974		
Japan		1974	
Kenya	1974		
Lebanon		1973	
Malagasy Rep.		1973	
Malaysia		1973	
Mali		1975	
Mongolia		1975	
Netherlands, The		1975	
New Zealand		1973	
Niger		1973	
Panama	1973		
Peru	1974		
Poland		1974	
Spain		1975	
Sudan	1973		
Trinidad and Tobago		1975	
Uganda		1975	
Yugoslavia	1973		
Zaire		1973	

*The General Assembly empowered an additional 27 member states of the sessional committees of the Economic and Social Council to serve on the council from Oct. 12, 1973, to Dec. 31, 1973.
†Administering authority.

by 13 members (China not voting) that would have expressed serious concern at Israel's failure to cooperate with UN Middle East peace efforts.

Other Activities. South Africa, Rhodesia, and Portugal continued to be the principal targets of the nonaligned countries and of several UN bodies. On September 14 the Committee of 24 called the South African situation "critical and explosive," and urged the international community to mobilize all its resources to end colonialism. The committee concentrated on giving concrete assistance to colonial peoples struggling for independence and on mobilizing international support for the "liberation struggle." On September 13 the Committee on Apartheid expressed its "utmost indignation" at the action of South African police in allegedly murdering a number of African mine workers in Carletonville. South Africa stated that its policemen had been forced to fire to protect themselves when surrounded in semidarkness by rioters. The Council for Namibia observed the first annual "Namibia Day" on August 24. On December 11 the Security Council voted to discontinue the private negotiations between the secretary-general and the South African government regarding Namibian independence.

The UN Disaster Relief Coordinator worked with UN specialized agencies and other groups to supply food and medicine to Pakistan, devastated by rain and floods, and to six West African states hit by prolonged drought. The Pakistani situation was the subject of a special session of the Economic and Social Council (Ecosoc) on September 17. A 20-member "Group of Eminent Persons to Study the Impact of Multinational Corporations on Development and International Relations" concluded the first of a series of hearings on September 14.

Membership in the UN rose to 135 on September 18 with the admission of the Bahamas and East and West Germany. Entry of the two Germanys was widely hailed as a historic step in liquidating the cold war and moving the organization toward universality. Leopoldo Benites (*see* BIOGRAPHY) of Ecuador was elected president of the 28th General Assembly.

(RICHARD N. SWIFT)

UNESCO. Two major conferences were organized during 1973. The 34th International Conference on Education, held in September at the Geneva headquarters of the International Bureau of Education, focused on the relationship between education, training, and employment. In Bucharest, Rom., in November, ministers of education from 32 European countries debated liberalizing the movement of scholars between nations.

UNESCO expanded its activities concerning the world drug problem. In September a seminar on the subject was organized in Paris. As a follow-up to International Book Year in 1972, UNESCO called a meeting of international experts to draw up plans for a world program for the promotion of books and reading. In the cultural field, UNESCO concentrated its efforts on the international campaign to preserve the Indonesian Buddhist sanctuary of Borobudur. A congress on "Sun in the Service of Mankind," held at Paris in July, attracted some 600 scientists. An extraordinary meeting of the UNESCO General Conference was held in October to consider how to meet a $12,652,100 deficit caused by the devaluation of the dollar. (RICHARD D. GREENOUGH)

See also Environment.

United States

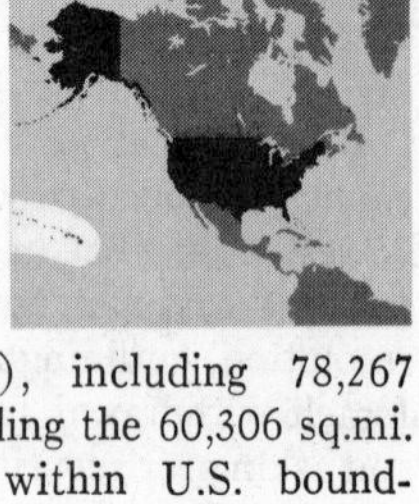

The United States of America is a federal republic composed of 50 states, 49 of which are in North America and one of which consists of the Hawaiian Islands. Area: 3,615,122 sq.mi. (9,363,123 sq.km.), including 78,267 sq.mi. of inland water but excluding the 60,306 sq.mi. of the Great Lakes that lie within U.S. boundaries. Pop. (1973 est.): 210,544,000, including (1970) white 87.3%; Negro 11.1%. Language: English. Religion (early 1970s est.): Protestant 72 million; Roman Catholic 48 million; Jewish 5.9 million; Orthodox 3,850,000. Cap.: Washington, D.C. (pop., 1972 est., 748,300). Largest city: New York (pop., 1972 est., 7,847,100). President in 1973, Richard Milhous Nixon.

Envisioned as a "Year of Europe" and the first year of a generation of peace, 1973 instead turned out to be a year of scandal and crisis for the United States. It was, above all, the year of Watergate—the name that became applied to the many and ever widening scandals and investigations that brought the administration of Pres. Richard Nixon (*see* BIOGRAPHY) to the brink of ruin.

The year began on a hopeful note, however. President Nixon had just been reelected by a near-record margin of popular and electoral votes. The end of the Vietnam war seemed, at last, to be imminent. And so Nixon appeared forceful and confident as he delivered his second inaugural address at the Capitol on January 20. "Above all else," he said, "the time has come for us to renew our faith in ourselves and in America. In recent years that faith has been challenged. . . . Let us pledge together to make these next four years the best four years in America's history, so that on its 200th birthday America will be as young and as vital as when it began, and as bright a beacon of hope for all the world."

Watergate. The faith that the president sought was soon to be shaken by the unfolding Watergate scandal. On June 17, 1972, five men carrying electronic surveillance equipment had been arrested inside the national headquarters of the Democratic Party, situated in Washington's Watergate office-apartment-hotel complex. Incredulity and a degree of amusement typified the initial public response to the bungled break-in. But it soon became known that the burglars had received money from the Finance Committee to Re-elect the President, Nixon's 1972 campaign organization. As one disclosure followed another, the amusement faded and the Watergate break-in became recognized for what it was: one segment of a much larger political spy puzzle involving espionage and sabotage, implicating White House officials and financed with hundreds of thousands of dollars in secret campaign funds.

In a little more than seven months, the five burglars and two of their accomplices had either pleaded guilty to or been convicted of felonies. A major break in the case occurred on March 23, 1973, the day the so-called "Watergate Seven" were sentenced. U.S. District Judge John J. Sirica (*see* BIOGRAPHY) read in court a letter from one of them, James W. McCord, Jr., in which McCord stated that other persons besides those convicted had been involved in the break-in. Perjury had been committed, he charged, and he also claimed that political pressure had been applied on the defendants to persuade them to plead guilty.

McCord's letter set in motion a dizzying succession of developments in the Watergate case. Reversing his earlier position of noncooperation, President Nixon said on April 17 that "All members of the White House staff will appear voluntarily when requested" by the Senate select committee established in February to investigate the Watergate case. The president added that he had begun "intensive new inquiries" into the Watergate affair on March 21 "as a result of serious charges which came to my attention." Without further elaboration, he said that there had been "major new developments in the case."

In a nationally televised address on April 30, Nixon said he took full responsibility for any improper activities connected with his 1972 presidential campaign and pledged that justice would be "pursued fairly, fully, and impartially." The president also announced the resignation of four men: H. R. Haldeman, White House chief of staff; John D. Ehrlichman, chief counselor for domestic affairs; John W. Dean III, presidential counsel (*see* BIOGRAPHY); and Attorney General Richard G. Kleindienst. Ehrlichman and Dean had been linked in press reports to efforts to cover up the Watergate case. At the same time, Nixon announced the nomination of Elliot L. Richardson (*see* BIOGRAPHY) to replace Kleindienst as attorney general. He said Richardson would have full charge of the administration's Watergate investigation and would have authority to appoint a special prosecutor in the case.

The president's speech did little to dispel mounting public concern about Watergate. A Gallup Poll published May 4 found that 40% of the 456 persons questioned did not think Nixon had told the whole truth in the speech. Of those polled 50% said they thought he had participated in a cover-up.

Meanwhile, a series of sensational developments directed attention to a seemingly unrelated case, the trial in Los Angeles of Daniel Ellsberg and Anthony J. Russo, charged with theft of the Pentagon papers. Judge William M. Byrne released a Department of Justice memorandum April 27 revealing that convicted Watergate conspirators G. Gordon Liddy and E. Howard Hunt, Jr., had burglarized the safe of Ellsberg's former psychiatrist in Beverly Hills, Calif. Three days later, Byrne announced from the bench that he had met with Ehrlichman early in April and had been "introduced" to the president. At the meeting with Ehrlichman, the possibility of Byrne's appointment as director of the FBI was discussed.

Finally, an FBI interview with Ehrlichman, made public May 1, disclosed that the former presidential aide had, at Nixon's request, ordered a secret White House investigation of the Pentagon papers case. It was this investigation that eventually led to the break-in at Ellsberg's psychiatrist's office. Attorneys

continued on page 710

Mrs. Nixon holds the family Bible as Chief Justice Warren Burger administers the oath of office to Pres. Richard M. Nixon at the outset of his second term, Jan. 20, 1973. Vice-Pres. Spiro T. Agnew, at right, was sworn in earlier.

PICTORIAL PARADE

Chronology of Watergate Events

1972

June 17. Five men, including James W. McCord, Jr., an official of the Committee for the Re-election of the President (CRP), were arrested inside the Democratic Party's headquarters at the Watergate building, Washington, D.C., with electronic eavesdropping equipment in their possession.

June 28. G. Gordon Liddy, a CRP lawyer, was discharged for refusing to answer FBI questions.

July 1. Former U.S. Atty. Gen. John Mitchell resigned as chairman of CRP.

August 29. Pres. Nixon declared that "no one in the White House staff, no one in this administration, presently employed, was involved."

September 15. U.S. grand jury returned an eight-count indictment against Liddy, former White House consultant E. Howard Hunt, Jr., and the five men arrested in the Watergate building.

October 10. Press reports stated that White House and CRP officials had conducted a massive campaign of political espionage and sabotage against the Democratic Party during the 1972 campaign.

October 22. Press reports stated that CRP official Jeb Stuart Magruder had authorized the expenditures for the bugging.

1973

January 30. Liddy and McCord were convicted on all charges against them; the five other defendants had pleaded guilty.

March 23. Watergate trial judge John Sirica disclosed a letter from McCord charging that persons other than those convicted had been involved in the case, that the defendants had been pressured to plead guilty, and that perjury had been committed at the trial.

March 24. McCord reportedly told Senate investigators that White House counsel John W. Dean III and Magruder knew about the Watergate bugging in advance.

April 17. Pres. Nixon said that there had been "major developments" in the Watergate affair as a result of a new White House investigation. Presidential Press Secy. Ronald L. Ziegler said that all previous statements denying White House involvement in Watergate were now "inoperative."

April 19. U.S. Atty. Gen. Richard Kleindienst dissociated himself from the investigation because of close personal relationships with figures involved.

April 27. Acting FBI Director L. Patrick Gray III resigned, following the disclosure that he had destroyed records he had received from Dean. Gray's nomination as permanent FBI director had been withdrawn on April 5.

April 30. White House Chief of Staff H. R. Haldeman, Special Presidential Assistant for Domestic Affairs John Ehrlichman, Dean, and Kleindienst resigned; Defense Secy. Elliot Richardson was nominated as attorney general. Pres. Nixon accepted responsibility for wrongdoing by his aides but denied any prior knowledge of the affair.

May 10. Mitchell, former Commerce Secy. Maurice H. Stans, chairman of the Nixon campaign's finance committee, former New Jersey Senate majority leader Harry L. Sears, and financier Robert L. Vesco were indicted on charges of conspiracy to defraud the U.S. and to obstruct justice. The indictments had grown out of the disclosure that Vesco, who had been charged with securities fraud, had made an illegal $200,000 contribution to CRP.

May 11. U.S. District Court judge William M. Byrne, Jr., declared a mistrial in the Pentagon papers case in Los Angeles and dismissed all charges against the defendants, Daniel Ellsberg and Anthony Russo; Byrne barred any further trial on the ground that the conduct of the government, which had included a break-in of Ellsberg's psychiatrist's office, had "incurably" affected future prosecution. Byrne himself had been approached in April by Ehrlichman on the possibility that he might be the next FBI director.

May 17. U.S. Senate Select Committee on Presidential Campaign Activities, under the chairmanship of Sen. Sam J. Ervin, Jr. (Dem., N.C.), opened its public hearings.

May 22. Pres. Nixon stated that it was now clear that "unethical, as well as illegal" acts occurred in the 1972 campaign, and that, therefore, "executive privilege will not be invoked as to any testimony concerning possible criminal conduct or discussions of possible criminal conduct."

May 25. Former U.S. Solicitor General Archibald Cox was sworn in as special prosecutor with full powers to investigate Watergate.

June 25. Dean testified before the Senate committee on his role in covering up the involvement of White House and CRP officials in the Watergate break-in and stated that Pres. Nixon had some knowledge of the cover-up.

July 16. Former White House aide Alexander P. Butterfield testified that all conversations in Nixon's offices in the White House and the Executive Office Building had been secretly recorded since early 1971.

July 23. Senate committee and Special Prosecutor Cox served subpoenas on the White House for Watergate-related tapes that Nixon had declined to supply.

July 26. Pres. Nixon refused to comply with the subpoenas. The Senate committee voted to seek a federal court order demanding compliance; Cox obtained a court order requiring Pres. Nixon to demonstrate why the tapes should not be produced.

July 30. Haldeman testified that he had listened, at Pres. Nixon's request, to two tapes and that they verified Nixon's contentions and contradicted Dean's.

August 7. White House lawyers filed a brief in federal court arguing that release of the tapes would violate the doctrine of separation of powers. The Senate committee recessed until September after having heard 33 witnesses and compiling more than 7,500 pages of testimony.

August 15. Pres. Nixon again accepted responsibility for Watergate but denied any personal involvement in the affair. He argued that release of the tapes would jeopardize the effectiveness of future presidents and urged that the nation turn its attention to "matters of far greater importance."

August 29. Judge Sirica ordered Pres. Nixon "to produce forthwith for the court's examination *in camera*" the subpoenaed tapes, granting a five-day stay to permit appeal.

September 4. Secret indictments on charges arising from the break-in of Ellsberg's psychiatrist's office were returned in Los Angeles against Ehrlichman, Liddy, Egil Krogh, Jr., and David Young.

September 20. Cox and Pres. Nixon's lawyer told the U.S. Court of Appeals for the District of Columbia that they had failed to reach an out-of-court settlement, as the court had urged on September 13.

September 24. Senate Watergate committee reopened its public hearings, the second phase of which was to cover "dirty tricks."

October 10. *Washington Post* reported that industrialist Howard Hughes had made a $100,000 cash contribution to Pres. Nixon, which had been kept for three years by Pres. Nixon's friend Charles ("Bebe") Rebozo and eventually returned. (Vice-Pres. Spiro T. Agnew resigned amid allegations of criminal activities unrelated to Watergate.)

October 12. Appeals court ordered Pres. Nixon to turn over the disputed tapes to Judge Sirica.

October 17. Judge Sirica dismissed the Senate Watergate committee's suit to obtain the White House tapes on the ground that the committee had failed to establish the court's jurisdiction in the dispute. Cox announced that criminal charges had been filed against three companies for having made illegal campaign contributions.

October 19. Pres. Nixon announced a compromise plan whereby summaries of the tapes would be made available to the court and the Senate committee; Cox was to stop trying to obtain presidential tapes and papers.

October 20. Cox, in a news conference, refused to stop his efforts to get presidential tapes and papers. Atty. Gen. Richardson resigned rather than obey Pres. Nixon's order to fire Cox and disband his task force; Deputy Atty. Gen. William Ruckelshaus also refused and was himself fired; Cox was finally fired by Solicitor Gen. Robert Bork, who was then named acting attorney general.

October 23. Pres. Nixon agreed to turn over to Judge Sirica the nine disputed tapes; eight impeachment resolutions were introduced in the House of Representatives. Cox was reported to have obtained a letter to Pres. Nixon from a dairy cooperative representative suggesting that higher import quotas on dairy products had been imposed in exchange for a large campaign contribution from the dairy industry.

October 31. White House counsel informed Judge Sirica that two of the nine subpoenaed tapes had never been made.

November 1. Pres. Nixon appointed attorney Leon Jaworski as special prosecutor and nominated Sen. William B. Saxbe (Rep., O.) attorney general.

November 4. *Time* magazine, in its first editorial in 50 years of publication, called for Nixon's resignation; a number of papers also echoed this call.

November 7. Senate Watergate committee began its third and final phase of investigation, focusing on campaign financing.

November 21. White House special counsel J. Fred Buzhardt told Judge Sirica that an 18-min. section of a tape of a June 20, 1972, conversation between Pres. Nixon and Haldeman consisted of "an audible tone and no conversation." Sirica ordered that the remaining subpoenaed tapes be turned over to him to ensure their safety.

November 26. White House complied with Judge Sirica's request.

November 27. Rose Mary Woods, Pres. Nixon's personal secretary, testified that she had accidentally erased five minutes of the June 20 tape, but could not account for the rest of the gap. The Senate Watergate committee suspended its hearings to give its staff more time to complete investigations.

December 17. Pres. Nixon allowed to become law without his signature a bill giving Judge Sirica's court jurisdiction over the Senate committee's subpoenas.

December 18. Senate Watergate committee voted to subpoena scores of White House documents relating to the Watergate break-in, its cover-up, and campaign financing.

December 21. Watergate-related portions of the subpoenaed tapes and documents were released to the special prosecutor by Judge Sirica.

December 31. Special Prosecutor Jaworski said in a year-end statement that a substantial number of criminal indictments could be expected in the next two months; to date 28 individuals and 9 corporations had faced criminal charges.

SPECIAL REPORT

THE SIGNIFICANCE OF WATERGATE

By Henry Steele Commager

Watergate, originally a bungled burglary, has become, like Tammany Hall or Teapot Dome, a valid symbol—for it represents fairly enough the philosophy that animates the Nixon administration as well as the bundle of practices and malpractices through which it has expressed that philosophy. For Watergate was no flash-in-the-pan operation. It was conceived and carried through by those close to the inner circle of the Nixon administration; its purpose was partisan advantage; it was financed by secret funds raised by the Committee for the Re-election of the President; it was justified by exalted claims of national security; and, although finally repudiated by the Nixon administration, the philosophy behind it was almost the official policy of the CRP, and, even after the exposure of Watergate, was invoked time and again to vindicate espionage, forged telegrams, the break-in at the office of Daniel Ellsberg's psychiatrist, and the exploitation of the Federal Bureau of Investigation, the Central Intelligence Agency, and the Internal Revenue Service for partisan advantage.

What then has Watergate come to symbolize?

First, it symbolizes the corruption of men in high office. In 1921 Lord Bryce, the distinguished British ambassador to Washington some years previously, could write that "not many American presidents have been brilliant and some have not risen to the full moral height of their position, but none has been base or unfaithful to his trust, none has tarnished the honour of the nation." We have indeed known corruption before, notably in the Grant and Harding administrations, but never before has corruption come so close to touching, if not engulfing, the president himself. Examples of corruption among both high and low in the Nixon administration are numerous and familiar. Second, Watergate symbolizes unconstitutionality in government—the question of breaking or at least of bending the highest law of the land. This second symbolical aspect of Watergate is of special significance here and therefore warrants closer examination.

Mr. Nixon has attempted to justify lawlessness in his policy actions on the grounds of either national security or executive privilege. The Watergate break-in itself was a lawless operation justified by the plea of national security. So was much of the president's conduct of his office, in both the domestic and the foreign arenas. National security dictated the wiretapping of the National Security Council itself; national security, coupled with the plea of executive privilege, justified the refusal to surrender the tapes of presidential discussions; national security was the purpose of the Huston plan to set up—temporarily of course—a police state; national security justified a secret war in Cambodia and justified lying to the Congress and the American people about it; national security authorized the dismissal of otherwise loyal civil servants who exposed the extravagance and inefficiency of great corporations; national security keeps secret from the Congress the activities of the CIA abroad, the policy documents of the information services, and the provisions of executive agreements. A phrase which justifies everything from Watergate to the operations of the CIA abroad must be strongly suspect.

Watergate, and all its attendant improprieties, was conceived and born in secrecy, and it was the discovery of Watergate, not its perpetration, that spread confusion and dismay in the Nixon ranks. Those who habitually resort to secrecy do so for two reasons: because they know that their deeds cannot stand the light of day, and because they do not trust the intelligence or judgment of the people. Mr. Nixon did not tell the American people the whole truth about the Vietnam war or hardly any of the truth about the Cambodian war; he did not tell them much of the truth about the use and abuse of congressional appropriations; he only very unwillingly has told them such truth about Watergate as he has so far divulged.

It is in connection with Watergate and the tapes, present and missing, that Mr. Nixon has asserted most vigorously his doctrine of executive privilege and immunity. This doctrine reflects his concept that not only his personal staff but also everyone in the administration owes loyalty primarily to the White House rather than to the Constitution and that the president is somehow entitled to a panoply of privileges and immunities that set him, in most matters, above the law. His claims to power that is almost imperialistic in both the foreign and the domestic arenas antedate Watergate and flourish independently of Watergate, but are rooted in that same arrogance from which Watergate itself emerged. Here Watergate is a symbol of a constitutional crisis.

One of the more serious contributions to that crisis is the Nixon administration's flagrant violation of the guarantees of the Bill of Rights: the resort to electronic surveillance without search warrants in the face of Supreme Court prohibition; the denial of the right of assembly and of petition in the mass arrest of thousands of Americans who gathered in Washington, D.C., in 1971 to exercise their constitutional right to protest the Indochina war; the widespread use of that most hateful weapon of the police state, the agent provocateur, to instigate and then to punish lawbreaking; the attempt—the first in U.S. history—to restrict the freedom of the press by applying prior censorship to newspapers; the connivance among high officials, including the attorney general, to deny due process, and equal protection of the laws, to the victims of the Kent State University and Jackson State College riots. It is undeniable that no other administration in our history has been so consistently antagonistic to civil liberties or so contemptuous of the Bill of Rights.

Is Watergate, then, to be a larger and more portentous symbol—a symbol of the breakdown of the principle of the supremacy of law and of constitutional government in the United States? Does it signify that the problems of government are now so importunate, and the laws and principles of the past so obsolete, that we must anticipate constitutional revolution?

Certainly there is no reason to suppose that the problems which confront the United States today cannot be resolved by traditional political and constitutional processes. It may be that the Nixon administration would have been unable to function as it has in the past five years if it had been required to observe the limits of these. The conclusion is not, however, that we should jettison the Constitution and ignore the laws, but that we should salvage it and abide by them. It is not, in recent years, the Constitution and the laws that have been found to be defective, but those who flout them.

The impact of Watergate on the institution of the presidency is another matter. The American presidency is an office that the Constitution prescribes, and one that presidents themselves realize and create as they live and work in it and face the problems of their time. George Washington gave the presidency its original character and shape; Andrew Jackson assured it a spe-

Henry Steele Commager has taught at Columbia University and at Amherst College in the U.S., as well as at the universities of Oxford and Cambridge. Although formally retired, he still teaches part-time at Amherst. A historian and writer of great authority and distinction, he has become known and appreciated for his critical interpretation of current events in the light of the American history he knows so well. The views here expressed, with typical forthrightness, are of course entirely his own.

cial relationship with the people; Abraham Lincoln exploited to the full the potentialities of its powers in wartime; Franklin Delano Roosevelt made it an instrument of social revolution; Dwight D. Eisenhower and John F. Kennedy, each in his own way, cultivated its symbolical and almost mythical character. Yet each succeeded in operating within the framework of the Constitution and the American political system and traditions. Alone of our presidents, Mr. Nixon seems to have found our Constitution and traditions too constricting and to have wrenched the presidency away from its constitutional and historical moorings. When one considers what a Washington, a Lincoln, or a Franklin Roosevelt faced, and compares what each was able to accomplish within the confines of law and Constitution with what Mr. Nixon has accomplished by transcending or evading both, one cannot be much impressed with the cogency of an argument for constitutional change.

But it is short-sighted to lodge responsibility for Watergate solely with the president and his associates. After all, the American people knew Mr. Nixon's record in the Congress, as vice-president, and as president when they reelected him by a thundering majority in 1972. And they had tolerated inadequacies and even illegalities in previous administrations. If Watergate is a natural product of what Mr. Nixon stands for, is it not equally an example of what the American people expect and tolerate in their leaders—and in their economy and society, too?

Pretty clearly there have occurred in the generation since World War II changes in the American mind and temper, not only in political but also in moral standards. There is a decline in political awareness. There is a readiness to accept official statements uncritically—statements such as those explaining our "commitment" in Vietnam, or submitting the claims of limitless executive privilege. There is a decline in that contempt for "the never-ending audacity of elected persons" which Walt Whitman expressed. There is a tolerance of official violence and lawlessness. There is a careless acceptance of the inevitability of corruption in politics as in business. There is a decline in the standards of integrity in public life. There is an assumption that government and business both manipulate the people, and an almost masochistic readiness to be manipulated. There is a widespread indifference to the guarantees of the Bill of Rights, and to the relation of civil liberties to the functioning of our constitutional and moral system. Most Americans have forgotten, if they ever knew, that somehow we got along for a century and a half without the FBI, the CIA, or security clearances and computerized records of our private lives, and were none the worse for it. And finally there is an ignorance of or indifference to such lessons as the past may have for us—our own past, and the past of mankind.

Have these attitudes been responsible for Watergate or changed our conception of the presidency?

If Mr. Nixon and his administration were to succeed in their high-handed policies, this might create precedents which it would be difficult to reverse. Fortunately this is more and more unlikely. If public opinion does not go so far as to support impeachment, neither will it support a continuation of those policies which have conjured up impeachment. In the face of public outcry and of the demands for restraint and cooperation by the Senate Watergate committee, by Judge John J. Sirica, and by two special prosecutors, Mr. Nixon has already abandoned his more extreme claims to be above the law and has gone on the defensive. And a president on the defensive can no longer endanger the integrity of our political or constitutional system.

Neither the presidency nor the Constitution will emerge unscathed from the crisis of Watergate. But the presidency and the Constitution have weathered other, albeit less serious, impairments and indignities, and will doubtless survive. They weathered the towering crises of the Civil War and Reconstruction, the tragic depressions of the 1890s and the 1930s, and the clamorous demands of the greatest of world wars. There is no reason to fear that they will not weather Watergate.

continued from page 707

for Ellsberg and Russo demanded that the charges of espionage, theft, and conspiracy against them be dismissed. Byrne did so on May 11. In granting the dismissal, the judge said that "bizarre events have incurably infected the prosecution of this case. The totality of the circumstances . . . offend 'a sense of justice.' "

The long reach of Watergate extended also to the so-called Vesco case. On May 10 former attorney general John N. Mitchell and former secretary of commerce Maurice H. Stans were indicted by a federal grand jury in New York City for their roles in the 1972 Nixon reelection campaign. Mitchell, who had directed the president's reelection campaign until July 1972, and Stans, who headed the Finance Committee to Re-elect the President, were each charged with three counts of conspiring to obstruct justice and six counts of perjury regarding the government's investigations of a secret $200,000 contribution made to the reelection committee in March 1972 by financier Robert L. Vesco (*see* BIOGRAPHY). Vesco, who was a defendant in a civil suit brought by the Securities and Exchange Commission and charged with looting four mutual funds of $224 million, was also indicted by the grand jury on one count of conspiracy and three counts of obstructing justice.

Senate Hearings. The steady flood of Watergate revelations served to heighten interest in the nationally televised hearings of the Senate select committee formed to investigate campaign irregularities in the 1972 election. Most of the early witnesses to appear before the committee, which began its public hearings May 17, were former officials of the Committee for the Re-election of the President. McCord, the former security director for the reelection committee and a convicted member of the Watergate burglary team, testified on May 18 that he had been offered executive clemency before the trial for his silence in the Watergate affair. The clemency offer, he said he was told, came from "the very highest levels of the White House."

The key witness in the Watergate hearings was Dean, the former presidential counsel, who testified for the entire week of June 25–29. While Dean's account was the first before the committee to directly accuse President Nixon of involvement in the Watergate cover-up, Dean asserted that Nixon did not "realize or appreciate at any time the implications of his involvement." Dean said, however, that Nixon had permitted the cover-up to continue even after Dean had told him about some of the cover-up plans. Dean added that Nixon had discussed with him the possibility of executive clemency for some of the Watergate conspirators and "hush money" payments to continue the cover-up.

Dean's statement detailed the "excessive concern" in the White House for data on antiwar activists and other political opponents of the administration. In support of this assertion, he produced from a White House file called "Opponents List and Political Enemies Project" the names of scores of prominent figures in the news media, organized labour, show business, and higher education. Dean suggested that concern about political opposition, along with the "do-it-yourself White House staff, regardless of the law," created the climate for the Watergate affair.

Dean described his superiors in the White House—former presidential aides Haldeman and Ehrlichman—as the principals in the efforts to conceal the ramifications of the Watergate break-in. But he also implicated, among others, former attorney general Mitchell, former special counsel to the president Charles W. Colson, former acting FBI director L. Patrick Gray III, presidential counsel Richard Moore, and former presidential aides Frederick C. LaRue and Gordon C. Strachan.

The questioning of Dean by committee members often centred on Dean's credibility as against that of the White House. Dean, however, refused to retreat from the allegations in his prepared statement, an extremely detailed document of 245 pages that took him six hours to read.

A number of the persons implicated by Dean subsequently were called as witnesses. Mitchell denied sworn testimony that he had approved the Watergate break-in and wiretapping of Democratic national headquarters, but acknowledged that he played a role in covering up the affair. Mitchell told the committee on July 10 that he did not tell President Nixon about Watergate cover-up actions for fear of crippling Nixon's 1972 reelection chances.

The former attorney general said that, to his knowledge, the president was unaware of the true story of the break-in and cover-up until long after his reelection. Mitchell's testimony directly contradicted that of Jeb Stuart Magruder, his former deputy director in the Nixon campaign organization, concerning two meetings where plans were discussed for the bugging of Democratic headquarters.

Of the remaining witnesses who testified during the televised portion of the Watergate hearings, former presidential aides Haldeman and Ehrlichman attracted the most attention. During four days in the witness chair, Ehrlichman testified and was questioned extensively on the 1971 break-in at the office of Ellsberg's psychiatrist. He said he had approved a "covert operation" that led to the break-in but insisted that he had not meant to approve a burglary. Nevertheless, Ehrlichman added, both he and President Nixon believed that the break-in was well within the president's constitutional powers to protect national security. Ehrlichman's testimony on this point provoked a series of sharp exchanges between him and Sen. Sam J. Ervin, Jr. (*see* BIOGRAPHY), the committee chairman, who argued that no law authorized the president to order an illegal act and that the Constitution specifically forbade "unreasonable" searches and seizures.

Much of Haldeman's testimony, which began July 30, was devoted to refuting statements made by Dean concerning when and how much Nixon knew of the Watergate cover-up. Dean had testified that on Sept. 15, 1972, the day the Watergate Seven were indicted for the break-in, he received congratulations from the president that the case had reached no higher than G. Gordon Liddy, the former legal counsel to Nixon's reelection and finance committees. Haldeman, who also attended the September 15 meeting, said that he disagreed with Dean's conclusion that Nixon was aware of the cover-up and was congratulating Dean on his efforts. Haldeman also disputed Dean's account of a March 13, 1973, meeting with Nixon during which, Dean alleged, the president said there would be no problem in raising $1 million for the seven Watergate defendants.

Tapes Controversy. Haldeman's testimony began with the startling announcement that he had listened at his home to a tape recording of the Sept. 15, 1972, meeting attended by himself, Nixon, and Dean. The existence of the White House tapes had been revealed only two weeks earlier by a surprise witness, Alexander P. Butterfield. Butterfield, a former White House aide, told the committee on July 16 that all of President Nixon's conversations in his White House and Executive Office Building offices were bugged and that his telephones in each office were tapped beginning in the spring of 1971. This meant that tape recordings of Nixon's conversations with Dean were a matter of record and could prove or disprove Dean's assertion that Nixon knew and approved of efforts to cover up the Watergate break-in.

The recording system, Butterfield said, would pick up any sound or conversation in the room, including the lowest tones. This was significant, for Dean had testified that, during a conversation with Nixon in his Executive Office Building office on April 15, 1973, the president mentioned "in a barely audible tone" that he had discussed executive clemency for one of the Watergate defendants. If Nixon did indeed say that, it was assumed, the recording system would have picked it up.

Butterfield's testimony touched off a long legal battle to force the White House to relinquish certain of its tapes to the Senate select committee, special Watergate prosecutor Archibald Cox (*see* BIOGRAPHY), and, ultimately, the federal grand jury in Washington that was investigating the Watergate case. In a letter sent to Nixon on July 17, Senate committee chairman Ervin asked that the president "provide the Committee with all relevant documents and tapes under control of the White House that relate to matters the Select Committee is authorized to investigate."

Replying to Ervin on July 23, Nixon said that the tapes, "which have been under my sole personal control, will remain so. None has been transcribed or made public and none will be." The committee immediately issued two subpoenas to Nixon, one for recordings of five of his meetings with Dean and the second for other documents related to Watergate. Nixon replied on July 26 that he would not hand over the tapes, thus setting the stage for a resolution of the issue in the courts.

Special Watergate prosecutor Cox, who had been appointed to the post by Attorney General Richardson, also was turned down by the White House when he requested access to tapes bearing on Watergate. Cox immediately issued a subpoena for the material he had asked for and, on July 26, he obtained a court order from Judge Sirica directing Nixon to show cause, by August 7, why he should not comply with the subpoena. At the same time, Sirica ruled that he had no authority to enforce the Senate committee's subpoena. In December Congress passed a bill granting him that authority.

Nixon suffered a severe setback when Judge Sirica handed down his decision in the tapes case on August 29. Sirica directed the president to turn over to him for private examination the tape recordings subpoenaed by Cox. The judge said that he was willing to recognize the validity of a claim of executive privilege "based on the need to protect presidential privacy" but that the courts must decide whether such a privilege had been properly claimed. He said that he was "simply unable to decide the question of privilege without inspecting the tapes" himself. The White House announced the following day that Nixon would appeal Sirica's order.

But the president fared no better in the U.S. Court of Appeals for the District of Columbia than he had in Sirica's U.S. District Court. The appeals court ruled on October 12 that Nixon must turn over his Watergate tape recordings to the U.S. District Court and declared that the president was "not above the law's commands." On the issue of executive privilege, the appeals court said, "The Constitution mentions no executive privileges, much less any absolute executive privileges."

When the appeals court's decision was announced, it was widely assumed that Nixon would take the final step of appealing to the U.S. Supreme Court. Instead, he set in motion the train of events known as the "Saturday night massacre." On October 19 the president announced a "compromise" plan to provide the U.S. District Court and Watergate investigators with a personally prepared summary of Watergate-related material on the tapes. The "authenticity" of the summary was to be assured by permitting Sen. John C. Stennis (Dem., Miss.) to listen to the tapes in question and "verify" that Nixon's summary was "full and accurate."

Cox had rejected the compromise plan, Nixon said, but he had decided to take "decisive actions" anyway in order to avert a "constitutional crisis." For that reason the president had decided not to seek Supreme Court review of the appeals court decision. And he announced that he had "felt it necessary" to direct Cox, "an employee of the Executive Branch, to make no further attempts by judicial process to obtain tapes, notes or memoranda of Presidential conversations."

Cox refused to comply with Nixon's order to desist from further court action to obtain White House material on Watergate, and he explained his position in a news conference on October 20. Then, at 8:24 P.M. that evening, the White House announced that Nixon had discharged Cox and Deputy Attorney General William D. Ruckelshaus. He also accepted the resignation of Attorney General Richardson. White House press secretary Ronald L. Ziegler said Richardson had resigned rather than fire Cox. Ruckelshaus was then asked to carry out the president's order to discharge the special prosecutor. When he refused, he was fired.

Cox's dismissal was finally carried out by Solicitor General Robert H. Bork, who was appointed acting attorney general. Nixon later appointed William B. Saxbe (Rep., O.) as attorney general.

The "Saturday night massacre" drew a massive and angry reaction from the public. Thousands of telegrams and letters of protest began arriving at the White House and the Capitol, and many of them advocated impeachment of the president. The outcry was so loud that Nixon was forced to back down from his refusal to release the tapes. Charles Alan Wright, chief of the president's Watergate legal defense team, announced in U.S. District Court on October 23 that "the President . . . would comply in all respects" with Sirica's order as modified by the appeals court.

The tapes controversy, however, was far from over. White House counsel J. Fred Buzhardt informed Sirica on October 31 that two of the subpoenaed White House tapes were nonexistent. The April 15, 1973, conversation between Nixon and Dean had not been recorded, Buzhardt said, because of an apparent malfunction of the recording system. Later, the White House said that the meeting went unrecorded because the machine ran out of tape. Buzhardt said the second conversation, a telephone exchange between Nixon and Mitchell, was not recorded because the president had used a phone not plugged into the White House recording system. He did not indicate why the nonexistence of the two tapes had not been disclosed by the White House earlier.

The two conversations in question were assumed crucial in determining how much the president knew about Watergate at two different times after the break-in. Mitchell had told the Senate select committee that Watergate had been the sole subject of discussion during the June 20 phone conversation. The April 15 conversation was the one in which Nixon, by Dean's account, mentioned having discussed executive clemency for a Watergate defendant with a White House aide.

Then, on November 21, Buzhardt disclosed in U.S. District Court that an 18-minute portion of still another taped Watergate conversation was missing. The conversation was between President Nixon and H. R. Haldeman on June 20, 1972, three days after the

UNITED STATES

Education. (1971–72) Primary, pupils 33,507,000, teachers 1,138,000; secondary and vocational, pupils 15,183,000, teachers 951,000; higher (including teacher training colleges), students 8,087,000, teaching staff (1966–67) 537,000.

Finance. Monetary unit: U.S. dollar, with (Sept. 17, 1973) a par value of U.S. $42.22 to one fine ounce of gold and a free rate of U.S. $2.41 to £1 sterling. Gold, SDRs, and foreign exchange, official: (June 1973) $13,830,000,000; (June 1972) $12,910,000,000. Federal budget (1973–74 est.): revenue $256 billion; expenditure $269 billion. Gross national product: (1972) $1,151,800,000,000; (1971) $1,050,400,000,000. Money supply: (June 1973) $259.5 billion; (June 1972) $239.7 billion. Cost of living (1963 = 100): (June 1973) 144; (June 1972) 136.

Foreign Trade. (1972) Imports $58,944,000,000; exports (excluding military aid of $560 million) $49,208,000,000. Import sources: Canada 27%; Japan 17%; West Germany 8%; U.K. 5%. Export destinations: Canada 25%; Japan 10%; West Germany 6%; U.K. 5%. Main exports: machinery 27%; motor vehicles 10%; chemicals 8%; cereals 7%; aircraft 6%.

Transport and Communications. Roads (1971) 3,758,839 mi. (including 34,589 mi. expressways). Motor vehicles in use (1971): passenger 92,752,500; commercial 19,772,200. Railways: (1971) 210,049 mi.; traffic (Class I only; 1972) 8,562,000,000 passenger-mi., freight (1971) 670,675,000,000 ton-mi. Air traffic (1972): 152,424,000,000 passenger-mi. (including internal services 123,905,000,000 passenger-mi.); freight 4,995,111,000 ton-mi. (including internal services 3,285,819,000 net ton-mi.). Inland waterways freight traffic (1970) 289,000,000,000 ton-mi. (including 104,000,000,000 ton-mi. on Great Lakes system and 126,000,000,000 ton-mi. on Mississippi River system). Shipping (1972): merchant vessels 100 gross tons and over 3,687; gross tonnage 15,024,148. Ships entered (including Great Lakes international traffic; 1971) vessels totaling 191,712,000 net registered tons; goods loaded (1972) 231,410,000 tons, unloaded 374,909,000 tons. Telephones (Jan. 1972) 125,142,000. Radio receivers (Dec. 1971) 336 million. Television receivers (Dec. 1971) 93 million.

Agriculture. Production (in 000; tons; 1972; 1971 in parentheses): corn 155,484 (157,950); wheat 46,342 (48,533); oats 11,120 (14,701); barley 10,164 (11,128); rye 827 (1,380); rice 4,258 (4,289); sorghum 23,145 (24,521); soybeans 38,487 (35,279); dry beans 901 (796); dry peas 105 (196); peanuts 1,645 (1,502); potatoes 14,707 (15,974); sweet potatoes (1971) 586, (1970) 670; tomatoes 6,780 (6,406); sugar, raw value 6,397 (5,879); apples 2,915 (3,040); pears 600 (702); oranges 8,696 (8,441); grapefruit (1971) 2,472, (1970) 2,187; lemons (1971) 782, (1970) 718; wine *c.* 1,262 (*c.* 1,853); raisins (1971) *c.* 249, (1970) 193; sunflower seed *c.* 386 (179); linseed 389 (509); tobacco 874 (853); cotton, lint 3,256 (2,514); butter 554 (571); cheese 1,305 (1,190); eggs 4,607 (4,665); beef and veal 11,321 (11,104); pork 6,727 (7,302); softwood timber (cu.ft.; 1971) 9,241,800, (1970) 8,687,400; hardwood timber (cu.ft.; 1971) 2,770,000, (1970) 2,900,000; fish catch (1971) 3,050, (1970) 3,031. Livestock (in 000; Jan. 1972): cattle 117,916; sheep (1971) 19,560; pigs 62,972; horses *c.* 8,000; chickens (1971) 442,783.

Industry. Index of production (1963 = 100): (1972) 150, (1971) 140; mining (1972) 122, (1971) 120; manufacturing (1972) 149, (1971) 139; electricity, gas, and water (1972) 191, (1971) 178; construction (1972) 122, (1971) 114. Unemployment: (1972) 5.6%; (1971) 6%. Fuel and power (in tons; 1972): coal 587,088; lignite (1971) 6,402; crude oil 515,282; natural gas (cu.ft.) 22,891,000,000; manufactured gas (cu.ft.) 910,200,000; electricity (kw-hr.) 1,853,389,000. Production (in 000; tons; 1972): iron ore (55–60% metal content) 84,814; pig iron 89,412; crude steel 133,102; cement (shipments) 78,240; newsprint 3,409; sulfuric acid 30,046; caustic soda 10,264; fertilizers (plant nutrient content; 1971–72) nitrogenous 9,169, phosphate 6,388, potash 2,432; plastics and resins (1971) 9,055; synthetic rubber 2,706; passenger cars (units) 8,824; commercial vehicles (units) 2,446. Merchant vessels launched (100 gross tons and over; 1972) 614,000 gross tons. New dwelling units started (1972) 2,374,000.

break-in. Nixon's personal secretary, Rose Mary Woods, later testified in court that she had inadvertently erased part of the conversation while listening to it on a tape recorder in her office. But she said she was responsible for only about 5 of the missing 18 minutes. Still later, Buzhardt acknowledged that the remaining subpoenaed tapes contained a number of spots without any "identifiable sound." At Judge Sirica's request, the subpoenaed tapes were placed in custody of the court. They were then to be analyzed by a panel of experts with a view to determining if they had been tampered with and if the apparently missing or erased portions could be restored. Sirica later listened to the tapes. He upheld Nixon's claim of executive privilege on parts of three of them and released the remaining tapes to the newly appointed special prosecutor, Leon Jaworski. (*See* Special Report.)

Other Controversies. While the tapes struggle raged on, trouble was piling up for President Nixon and his associates on other fronts. A number of questions were raised about the president's personal finances, especially as they related to the purchase of his homes at Key Biscayne, Fla., and San Clemente, Calif. Nixon, it was disclosed, had received substantial help in buying the properties from two wealthy friends, Charles G. ("Bebe") Rebozo and Robert H. Abplanalp (*see* BIOGRAPHY). But the full extent of their involvement remained unclear despite various explanations issued by the White House.

The use of government funds to improve the Key Biscayne and San Clemente estates also came in for criticism. A number of items paid for with public funds appeared to be ordinary household furnishings. But the White House insisted that the improvements at issue were dictated by security requirements. Also at issue was a federal income tax deduction of $576,000 claimed by President Nixon for turning over his pre-presidential papers to the National Archives.

Nixon and Rebozo were hard put to explain a $100,000 campaign contribution, made in two installments in 1969 and 1970, from the Howard Hughes organization. Rebozo said that he kept the money in a safe-deposit box in his bank and later returned it intact. Nevertheless, government investigators were looking into the possibility that Hughes's money had been donated in the expectation of receiving some favour from the government in return. Later in the year Hughes and four associates were indicted on charges of stock manipulation and conspiracy in connection with Hughes's 1969 acquisition of Air West Airlines.

A number of large corporations and business organizations found themselves under scrutiny for contributions to Nixon's 1972 reelection campaign. It was suggested that the International Telephone & Telegraph Corp. had pledged to contribute heavily to the Nixon campaign to ensure a favourable government ruling in a pending antitrust case. Similarly, many observers thought it more than coincidental that the administration raised milk-support prices shortly after the milk producers had pledged a large amount of money to the Nixon campaign.

One of the more sensitive Watergate-related investigations under way in 1973 concerned activities of "the plumbers," a clandestine White House security force whose primary mission was to plug leaks of government information. The break-in at Daniel Ellsberg's psychiatrist's office was one of the operations carried out by this group. President Nixon argued that any detailed investigation of the plumbers' activities might jeopardize national security. Archibald Cox's insistence on conducting such an investigation was said to be a major reason for his dismissal as special Watergate prosecutor. But Cox's successor, Jaworski, indicated that he intended to press forward with the probe. Egil Krogh, Jr., a former White House aide who headed the plumbers' unit, pleaded guilty November 30 to a civil rights charge growing out of the burglary of Ellsberg's psychiatrist's office. Also indicted for the burglary were Ehrlichman, Liddy, and David Young.

Agnew Resignation. The nation was momentarily diverted from the Watergate scandal when Vice-Pres. Spiro T. Agnew (*see* BIOGRAPHY) announced on August 6 that he had been informed he was under investigation for possible violations of criminal law. The investigation was being conducted by George Beall, U.S. attorney for Maryland, concerning allegations of kickbacks by contractors, architects, and engineers to officials of Baltimore County. Agnew had served as Baltimore County executive from 1962 to 1967 and as governor of Maryland from 1967 to 1968. The vice-president held a televised news conference on August 8 to deny any wrongdoing.

On October 10, however, Agnew resigned and pleaded no contest to a single federal charge of income tax evasion for the year 1967. In return, the Department of Justice agreed to drop all other pending charges against him and request leniency on the tax evasion charge. Agnew was fined $10,000 and placed on three years' unsupervised probation.

Only two days after Agnew's resignation, President Nixon announced that Rep. Gerald R. Ford (Rep., Mich.) was his choice to be the new vice-president. The Senate approved the nomination by a vote of 92–3 on November 27, and the House of Representatives by 387–35 on December 6.

There was speculation that Ford's succession to the vice-presidency would lead to renewed pressure on the House of Representatives to consider impeachment of President Nixon and renewed pressure on Nixon himself to resign from office. The House Judiciary Committee agreed to examine the possibility of im-

The Senate select committee investigating 1972 election campaign practices, including the Watergate scandal. Members, including counsel, are, from left: Sen. Lowell P. Weicker, Jr. (Rep., Conn.); Sen. Edward Gurney (Rep., Fla.); Chief Minority Counsel Fred Thompson; Sen. Howard Baker, Jr. (Rep., Tenn.); Sen. Sam J. Ervin, Jr. (Dem., N.C.), chairman; Chief Counsel Samuel Dash; Sen. Herman Talmadge (Dem., Ga.); Sen. Daniel K. Inouye (Dem., Hawaii); and Sen. Joseph M. Montoya (Dem., N.M.).

WIDE WORLD

peachment; its investigation was scheduled to begin in earnest early in 1974.

Foreign Affairs. For Americans, Watergate tended to overshadow several important developments in the nation's relations with other countries. But at least one major event received undivided attention. President Nixon announced on January 23 that his national security adviser, Henry A. Kissinger, had initialed a Vietnam war cease-fire agreement earlier that day in Paris. The accord, also initialed by North Vietnam's Le Duc Tho, contained the following principal provisions: a cease-fire throughout North and South Vietnam; complete withdrawal of all U.S. troops and military advisers and dismantling of U.S. bases in South Vietnam; and the return of all U.S. and other prisoners of war and civilians throughout Indochina along with the release of captured North Vietnamese and Viet Cong troops.

With the long Vietnam ordeal presumably over, Kissinger attempted to repair the frayed relations between the U.S. and Europe. In a major foreign policy address on April 23, he proposed a new relationship between the U.S., Western Europe, Canada, and Japan, described as a new "Atlantic Charter." Kissinger's address was regarded as the blueprint for the Nixon administration's "Year of Europe." To cap the year, President Nixon planned a tour of major Western European capitals in the autumn. But European leaders showed little enthusiasm for the Atlantic Charter, and Nixon's European trip was postponed indefinitely.

The visit to the United States in June of Soviet Communist Party leader Leonid I. Brezhnev appeared to demonstrate that the Soviet-U.S. détente was holding firm. On June 19 Brezhnev and Nixon signed a series of relatively minor executive agreements on oceanography, transportation, agricultural research, and cultural exchange. Two days later, they signed a declaration of principles to accelerate the strategic arms limitation talks (SALT) and complete a new arms limitation treaty by the end of 1974. Finally, on June 22, the two leaders signed an agreement designed to avert a nuclear war between the United States and the Soviet Union, or between one of them and any other country.

The half-forgotten war in Indochina returned to the news in midsummer when it was disclosed that U.S. Air Force bombers had been secretly bombing Cambodia in 1969 and 1970 while U.S. officials were publicly proclaiming respect for that country's neutrality. In a letter to Sen. Stuart Symington (Dem., Mo.) on July 16, Secretary of Defense James R. Schlesinger (*see* BIOGRAPHY) said the bombing raids had been "fully authorized" by senior military and civilian officials and that "special security precautions" had been taken to avoid public disclosure of the raids due to the sensitive diplomatic situation. Schlesinger later said that there were "legitimate questions" about the bombing of "what was nominally a neutral state" without consultation with Congress. On August 3, he announced that he had ordered U.S. military commanders to end "all combat activities" in Cambodia and Laos at midnight August 14.

Presidential envoy Henry Kissinger and North Vietnamese negotiator Le Duc Tho pause to greet newsmen after the first round of resumed peace talks in Paris, Jan. 23, 1973.

A.F.P./PICTORIAL PARADE

U.S. foreign policy was put to a severe test when war broke out between Israel and its Arab neighbours on October 6. Kissinger, who had been confirmed as secretary of state two weeks earlier, telephoned the Israeli and Egyptian foreign ministers with a plea to "avoid any escalation and continuation of the fighting." He also cabled King Hussein of Jordan and King Faisal of Saudi Arabia and asked them to "use their good office to urge restraint where they have the influence to do so." But these peace efforts were unavailing.

Kissinger flew to Moscow and conferred with Brezhnev on October 20–21 about the Middle East crisis. At first, it appeared that the secretary's mission had been a failure; the U.S. on October 25 placed its military forces on a "precautionary alert" in response to reports that the Soviet Union planned to send troops to the combat area. But the UN Security Council the same day adopted a resolution creating a truce observer force of smaller nations. The truce plan, it turned out, had been agreed upon by Kissinger and Brezhnev in Moscow.

A whirlwind tour of Middle Eastern capitals by Kissinger in early November led to the signing of a six-point cease-fire agreement by Egypt and Israel. Kissinger then flew on to Peking and Tokyo for talks with Chinese and Japanese leaders. His discussions with Chairman Mao Tse-tung and Premier Chou En-lai led to speculation that the U.S. and China might soon establish full diplomatic relations.

U.S. diplomatic maneuvering during the Middle East crisis had the unfortunate side effect of further straining relations with Western Europe. European members of NATO were irritated when the U.S. failed to consult them before placing its military forces on alert. Kissinger, in turn, expressed annoyance when a number of NATO governments balked at cooperating in the U.S. military reinforcement of Israel. In December the U.S. appropriated $2.2 billion for emergency security assistance for Israel.

Energy Crisis. The Middle East conflict was a major contributor to the U.S. "energy crisis." In retaliation for its support of Israel during the war, the Arab oil-producing nations placed an embargo on all petroleum shipments to the U.S.

To deal with the resulting fuel shortage, President Nixon said on November 25 that he would take a variety of actions to reduce consumption of energy, including a cutback in home heating-oil deliveries and a 15% reduction in gasoline production. The president called on the nation's service stations to close voluntarily each week from 9 P.M. Saturday to midnight Sunday. Homeowners were asked to lower their thermostats to 68° F to cope with the reduction in heating-oil deliveries. The president also urged a reduction of driving speed limits to 55 mph for intercity trucks and buses and to 50 mph for passenger cars, as well as reduction or elimination of ornamental lighting. Truck drivers staged extensive protests against the proposed speed limit.

Nixon requested from Congress legislation giving him broad emergency powers to deal with the energy crisis. After considerable argument and debate Congress adjourned late in December without acting on the request, the main stumbling block being a disagreement between the Senate and the House on "windfall profits" for the oil industry. Congress did pass two energy-conservation measures later signed into law by the president, a nationwide speed limit of 55 mph (subject to action by the states) and daylight saving time throughout the country for almost two years as of Jan. 6, 1974. In November the legislators had authorized the immediate construction of the trans-Alaska pipeline and gave President Nixon the power to allocate oil and oil products.

On December 27 federal energy director William E. Simon announced that a standby gasoline rationing system had been established. Stating that it could be put into effect by March 1, 1974, Simon also said that he remained optimistic that rationing could be avoided if the American public continued to cooperate in the conservation effort.

The Economy. The administration's reluctance to resort to rationing may have stemmed in part from its unhappy experiences in trying to manipulate the economy. The Phase Three economic program, which took effect in January 1973, terminated the mandatory wage and price controls of Phase Two except in the "problem areas" of food, health care, and construction. Business and labour were expected "to determine by themselves what conduct conforms reasonably to the guides" without requiring prior approval from the government, said Secretary of the Treasury George P. Shultz. Within three months, it was evident that the voluntary approach to wage-price control was not working.

Accordingly, President Nixon ordered on June 13 a freeze of up to 60 days on all "prices paid by consumers," except those on "unprocessed agricultural products at the farm levels, and rents." The president also announced that the Cost of Living Council would prepare new wage-price policies for Phase Four, which would impose "tighter standards and more mandatory compliance procedures" than under Phase Three.

The Phase Four program, unveiled on July 18, ended the price freeze and replaced it with a system of price controls similar to those in effect under Phase Two. However, price limits on beef, imposed March 29, were to remain in effect until September 12. Cattle raisers were incensed at being singled out for special treatment, and they withheld stock from meat-processing plants until the price freeze ended. A temporary beef shortage resulted.

But 1973 was a year of shortages in many areas of the economy. Food, fibre, and many important minerals all were in short supply. On July 5, the U.S. imposed export controls on 41 farm commodities in the categories of livestock feeds, edible oils, and animal fats in an attempt to prevent a shortage in domestic supplies. The surprise move followed the announcement June 27 of controls on feed-grain exports. Secretary of Commerce Frederick B. Dent said that the controls were necessary because foreign demand for feed supplements had increased after controls were imposed on soybean and cottonseed exports.

Continuing inflation and trade deficits led to a 10% devaluation of the dollar, effective February 12. According to exchange rates set by the International Monetary Fund, the par value of the dollar in relation to gold decreased from $38 to $42.22 an ounce. And yet speculative pressure on the dollar did not abate in European money markets.

Secretary of the Treasury Shultz at first resisted and then gave in to demands to intervene actively in support of the U.S. currency. When the dollar was plunging to new lows in early June, he described the situation as a "puzzling matter." He rejected pleas to intervene directly, but promised that President Nixon soon would take strong action to deal with inflation. A month later, however, Shultz announced in a joint statement with Federal Reserve Board Chairman Arthur F. Burns that the U.S. had intervened in New York foreign exchange markets to shore up the dollar's value and that "active intervention" would continue "at whatever time and in whatever amounts are appropriate for maintaining orderly market conditions." By the end of the year the dollar's position had improved, thanks largely to devaluation and the resulting improvement in the country's balance of trade, which showed its first quarterly surplus in four years in the third quarter.

Other Domestic Affairs. Congress dealt President Nixon a setback when it approved, over a Nixon veto, legislation to limit presidential war-making powers. For the first time in nine attempts in 1973, both houses of Congress on November 7 mustered the two-thirds majorities necessary to override a presidential veto. The measure, which immediately became law, required that the president report to Congress within 48 hours after committing forces to a foreign conflict or "substantially" enlarging the number of troops equipped for combat in a foreign country. The commitment would have to end within 60 days unless Congress authorized its continuation, but the deadline could be extended for 30 days if the president certified that the extension was necessary to complete the safe withdrawal of U.S. forces. Congress could order an immediate withdrawal within the 60- to 90-day

WIDE WORLD

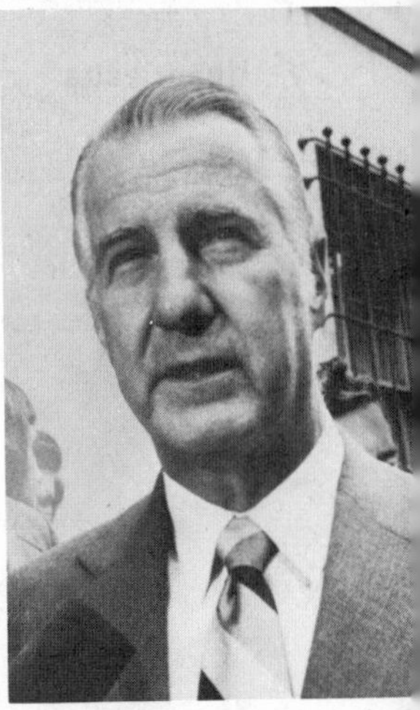

Spiro T. Agnew emerges from the federal courthouse in Baltimore, Md., Oct. 10, 1973, after pleading "no contest" to a charge of federal income tax evasion. Formal announcement of his resignation as the 39th vice-president of the United States was made the same day in Washington, D.C.

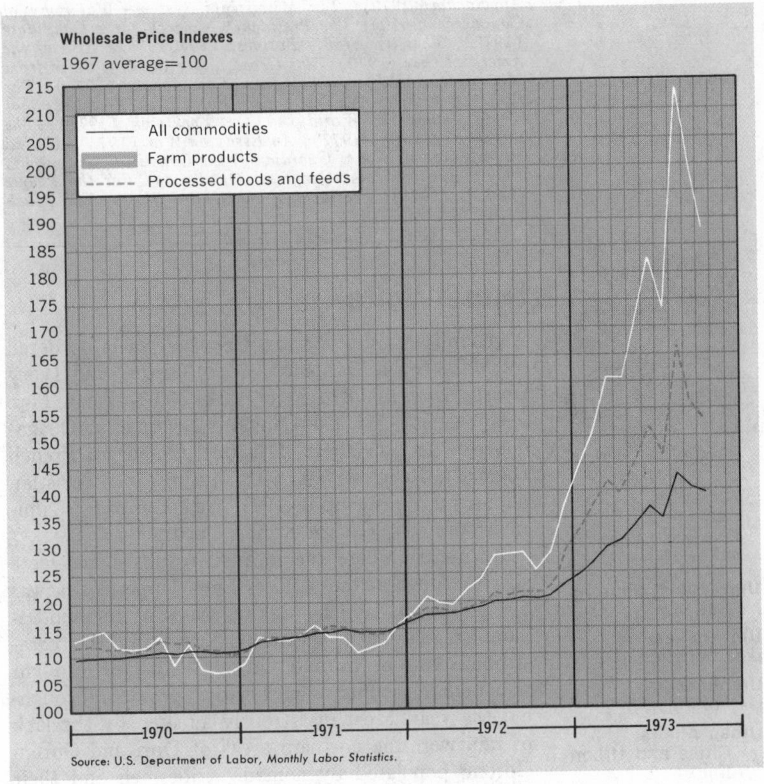

Source: U.S. Department of Labor, Monthly Labor Statistics.

period by passing a concurrent resolution that would not be subject to veto.

Among other major legislation approved in 1973, Congress enacted a bill providing for a four-year farm program with a new target price system for maintaining support programs for wheat, feed grains, and cotton. And in a major departure from past performance, Congress approved highway-construction legislation that permitted use of Highway Trust Fund money for urban mass transit systems.

The District of Columbia was granted partial home rule, subject to a referendum of District voters, and Social Security benefits were to be increased 11% in 1974. Congress also authorized $375 million over fiscal 1974–78 for the development of approximately 100 health maintenance organizations, comprehensive health services for a set annual or monthly fee.

With attention focused on Watergate, economic problems, and the energy crisis, three major U.S. ventures in space received less attention than they might have in calmer times. The Skylab program, the only ongoing U.S. man-in-space project, got off to a successful start when three astronauts spent a record 28 days living, working, and performing scientific experiments in an orbiting space station from May 25 to June 22. The mission produced many scientific dividends, including evidence that men could work effectively in space for extended periods with no apparent permanent health damage. As a result, the second Skylab team of astronauts was permitted to remain aboard the space station for 59½ days. A third Skylab crew was launched toward the orbiting space laboratory on November 10. (*See* ASTRONAUTICS.)

(RICHARD L. WORSNOP)

See also Race Relations.

ENCYCLOPÆDIA BRITANNICA FILMS. *The Industrial Revolution—Beginnings in the United States* (1968); *Midwest—Heartland of the Nation* (1968); *Produce—From Farm to Market* (1968); *Heritage in Black* (1969); *The Pacific West* (1969); *The Rise of Labor* (1969); *The South: Roots of the Urban Crisis* (1969); *Chicano from the Southwest* (1970); *The Industrial Worker* (1970); *Linda and Billy Ray from Appalachia* (1970); *The Mississippi System—Waterway of Commerce* (1970); *The Presidency—Search for a Candidate* (1970); *The Rise of Big Business* (1970); *The Rise of the American City* (1970); *The Great Lakes* (1971); *Jesse from Mississippi* (1971); *Johnny from Fort Apache* (1971); *The Progressive Era* (1971); *Valley Forge* (1971); *The Shot Heard Round the World* (1972); *Yorktown* (1972); *The Boston Tea Party* (1972); *An Essay on War* (1973); *United States Supreme Court: Guardian of the Constitution* (2nd ed., 1973); *United States Congress: Of, By and For the People* (2nd ed., 1973); *President of the United States: Too Much Power?* (1973).

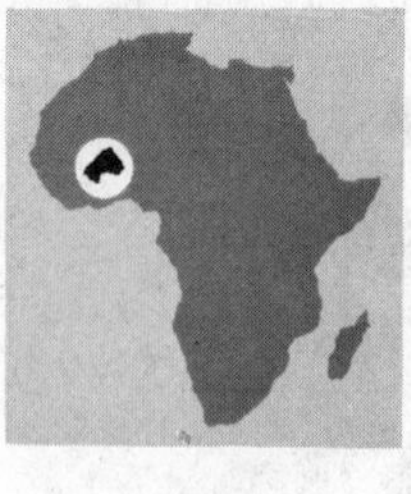

Upper Volta

A republic of West Africa, Upper Volta is bordered by Mali, Niger, Dahomey, Togo, Ghana, and Ivory Coast. Area: 105,870 sq.mi. (274,200 sq.km.). Pop. (1972 est.): 5,535,000. Cap. and largest city: Ouagadougou (pop., 1970 est., 110,000). Language: French (official). Religion: animist; Muslim and Christian minorities. President in 1973, Gen. Sangoulé Lamizana; premier, Gérard Kango Ouedraogo.

A country where the means of subsistence were sparse enough at the best of times, Upper Volta was one of the six French-speaking states of the sub-Saharan region most severely affected by the catastrophic lack of rainfall during 1973. The drought remained the country's most critical problem throughout the year. Most disastrously affected by the lack of rain were the northern areas of Dori and Gorom Gorom, populated by nomadic tribesmen and their herds. The advent of torrential rains during the month of August did nothing to improve the situation. Indeed, it merely served to aggravate the already appalling conditions and seriously hindered the efforts being made to bring relief to the stricken areas.

An intergovernmental committee was set up to coordinate efforts to bring relief and aid to the victims of the drought throughout the whole sub-Saharan region, and it established its headquarters in Ouagadougou. Upper Volta's minister of agriculture, Antoine Dakouré, was appointed head of the committee, and the capital became a clearinghouse for the reception and distribution of food and medical supplies coming in from all parts of the world for the relief of the surrounding territories.

In June and October General Lamizana paid visits first to France, to request from French Pres. Georges Pompidou an increase in French economic aid to the six drought-stricken countries, and then, with similar considerations in mind, to various other European capitals.

In September, at the conclusion of a conference of ministers held in Ouagadougou, the governments of the six affected countries (Mauritania, Senegal, Upper Volta, Mali, Chad, and Niger) formally requested a postponement of ten years in the settlement of their foreign debts. This conference was followed by a "summit" meeting of the chiefs of state of the six countries, at the conclusion of which Pres. Hamani Diori of Niger called for the setting up of a veritable "Marshall Plan" for the sub-Sahara.

In November it was announced publicly by General Lamizana that the armed forces would effect a complete restitution of power to a civilian government during the course of 1974. In the field of foreign affairs, the only event of any significance during the year was the breaking off of diplomatic relations with Israel in October.

(PHILIPPE. DECRAENE)

UPPER VOLTA

Education. (1970–71) Primary, pupils 132,420, teachers (including preprimary; 1968–69) 2,292; secondary, pupils 8,810, teachers (1968–69) 432; vocational, pupils 1,271, teachers (1967–68) 106; teacher training (1967–68), students 1,114, teachers 35; higher, (1968–69), students 122, teaching staff 19.

Finance. Monetary unit: CFA franc, with (Sept. 17, 1973) a parity of CFA Fr. 50 to the French franc (free commercial rate of CFA Fr. 212.55 = U.S. $1; CFA Fr. 512.25 = £1 sterling). Budget (1971 est.): revenue CFA Fr. 10,515,000,000; expenditure CFA Fr. 9,572,000,000.

Foreign Trade. (1972) Imports CFA Fr. 15,310,000,000; exports CFA Fr. 5,140,000,000. Import sources: France 48%; Ivory Coast 11%; West Germany 5%. Export destinations: Ivory Coast 46%; France 19%; Ghana 5%; Italy 7%; Mali 5%. Main exports: livestock 41%; cotton 20%; oilseeds 16%.

Uruguay

A republic of South America, Uruguay is on the Atlantic Ocean and is bounded by Brazil and Argentina. Area: 68,536 sq.mi. (177,508 sq.km.). Pop. (1972 est.): 2,956,300, including white 89%; mestizo 10%. Cap. and largest city: Montevideo (pop., 1972 est., 1,459,200). Language: Spanish. Religion: mainly Roman Catholic. President in 1973, Juan María Bordaberry.

Universalist Church: *see* Religion
Universities: *see* Education
Uranium: *see* Mining
Urban Affairs: *see* Cities and Urban Affairs

URUGUAY

Education. (1968–69) Primary, pupils 369,816, teachers 13,095; secondary (1969–70), pupils 123,426, teachers 9,668; vocational, pupils 35,648, teachers 3,048; teacher training (1969–70), students 7,049; higher, students 18,650, teaching staff (1963–64) 2,182.

Finance. Monetary unit: peso, with (Sept. 17, 1973) a free rate of 894 pesos to U.S. $1 (2,154 pesos = £1 sterling). Gold, SDRs, and foreign exchange, official: (Nov. 1972) U.S. $205 million; (Nov. 1971) U.S. $165 million. Budget (1971 est.): revenue 99.4 billion pesos; expenditure 116.7 billion pesos. Gross national product: (1971) 754,410,000,000 pesos; (1970) 596,920,000,000 pesos. Money supply: (June 1972) 154,674,000,000 pesos; (June 1971) 104,531,000,000 pesos. Cost of living (Montevideo; 1963 = 100): (March 1973) 8,416; (March 1972) 4,097.

Foreign Trade. (1972) Imports U.S. $186.6 million; exports U.S. $196.8 million. Import sources: Brazil 19%; Argentina 15%; U.S. 10%; West Germany 8%; Kuwait 7%; U.K. 6%. Export destinations: West Germany 13%; France 12%; Spain 11%; U.K. 7%; Italy 7%; The Netherlands 6%; Brazil 5%. Main exports: meat 47%; wool 35%; hides and skins 12%.

Transport and Communications. Roads (1970) *c.* 42,000 km. Motor vehicles in use (1970): passenger *c.* 121,000; commercial (including buses) *c.* 88,000. Railways (1970) 2,974 km. Air traffic (1972): 27,320,000 passenger-km; freight 147,000 net ton-km. Shipping (1972): merchant vessels 100 gross tons and over 39; gross tonnage 142,828. Telephones (Dec. 1971) 235,000. Radio receivers (Dec. 1971) 1.1 million. Television receivers (Dec. 1969) 250,000.

Agriculture. Production (in 000; metric tons; 1972; 1971 in parentheses): wheat 180 (302); barley 28 (32); oats 57 (60); potatoes 106 (150); sweet potatoes (1971) *c.* 81, (1970) 74; corn 141 (166); rice 128 (122); sorghum 57 (72); linseed 43 (49); sunflower seed 60 (49); sugar, raw value *c.* 70 (*c.* 67); oranges (1971) *c.* 60, (1970) 59; wine *c.* 90 (*c.* 85); wool (1971) 45, (1970) 47; beef and veal *c.* 380 (*c.* 370). Livestock (in 000; May 1972): cattle *c.* 8,600; sheep *c.* 18,000; pigs *c.* 400; horses *c.* 420; chickens *c.* 5,000.

Industry. Production (in 000; metric tons; 1971): cement 458; crude steel (1970) 16; petroleum products 1,627; electricity (excluding most industrial production; kw-hr.) 2,289,000.

Political unrest and uncertainty were rife in Uruguay during the first six months of 1973. Conflict arose between the armed forces and politicians over military investigations into allegations of corruption in public office. In February a demonstration of power by the armed forces in the streets of Montevideo led to the establishment of a National Security Council to advise the president directly. This was an important victory for the military, who had a majority vote on the council and who were also given the control of three important state-run organizations. Finally, in June, President Bordaberry (*see* BIOGRAPHY) dismissed Congress and determined to rule with a council of state. Still influenced by the military leaders, the president ordered the arrest of several political opponents. At the same time, restrictions were imposed on the national press.

The assumption of full powers of legislature by the president, with the close support of the armed forces, was a major turning point in Uruguayan political history. For most of the 20th century the country had been held up as a shining example of democracy in a continent not noted for its political stability. In reaction to the coup, a nationwide general strike was organized, factories were taken over, and students boycotted Montevideo University. Troops took over oil refineries and other key facilities. Striking bank clerks were arrested, drafted into the Army, and forced back to work at gunpoint. At the same time, the government increased wages of state employees by 25% and those of private sector workers by 31.48% in July. Workers demanded 60–80% increases and a return to constitutional rule. The Communist-controlled labour union federation was purged, and its secretary-general was arrested.

The long-term deterioration of the political structure was the direct result of a persistent decline in the country's economic position. Yet ironically 1973 witnessed a significant improvement at the very time the political structure was disintegrating. Uruguay was dependent on exports of beef and wool, and in a year when the prices of these as well as most primary products rose dramatically the country benefited enormously. In April a three-year nonpreferential trade agreement was signed with the EEC to allow steady access of Uruguayan beef to the European market. With beef exports at their highest level in five years, the balance of trade made a healthy recovery. This led to the relaxation of import restrictions, enabling capital goods, vital to long-term recovery, to be imported once again.

At the same time, payments of accumulated debts were speeded up in an effort to stimulate confidence abroad. Devaluations of the peso continued, but at a much slower rate than in 1972. Nevertheless, despite the overall improvement, the rate of inflation did not drop significantly.

WIDE WORLD

Troops patrol the streets of Montevideo June 28, 1973, one day after Pres. Juan María Bordaberry dismissed Congress and assumed the full powers of legislature.

In the early autumn the president and his military advisers presented to the nation a comprehensive five-year plan for recovery and development. It was significant that the plan was loosely based on the experience of the Brazilians; the Uruguayan military had already shown pro-Brazilian tendencies. The basis of the plan was to employ foreign capital as well as domestic savings to finance development projects, and to this end a first priority was the reform of the currency together with anti-inflation measures.

One basic aim of the plan was to disengage the public sector from ownership of the means of production. A large section of the Uruguayan economy was in the hands of the state; this was a throwback to the Socialist traditions of the interwar period. But the contemporary result was a flourishing bureaucracy and a glut of red tape. The plan also aimed to develop the industrial sector on the basis of Uruguay's most abundant raw materials, leather and wool. In the future the export of these two commodities in pure form was to be discouraged in favour of supplying the textile and leather-processing industries at home, whose products would eventually be exported—at a higher price. (M. J. SPENCE)

Vatican City State

This independent sovereignty is surrounded by but not part of Rome. As a state with territorial limits, it is properly distinguished from the Holy See, which constitutes the worldwide administrative and legislative body for the Roman Catholic Church. The area of Vatican City is 108.7 ac. (44 ha.). Pop. (1973): 722. As sovereign pontiff, Paul VI is the chief of state. Vatican City is administered by a pontifical commission of five cardinals, of which the secretary of state, Jean Cardinal Villot, is president.

The Vatican's external relations were marked by three important visits during 1973: by Israeli Prime Minister Golda Meir on January 15; Romanian Pres. Nicolae Ceausescu on May 26; and Polish Foreign Minister Stefan Olszowski on November 12. On each occasion Pope Paul explained his views on world peace, the situation of the church in the three countries, and, in the case of Israel, the question of the holy places. Ceausescu's visit was the first by a Romanian head of state, while relations with Poland had been strained for some time. Diplomatic relations were established with Cyprus, Australia, New Zealand, and Upper Volta. Other visitors included the presidents of West Germany and Paraguay. Planned visits by Pres. Habib Bourguiba of Tunisia and the foreign minister of Egypt were postponed because of the outbreak of war in the Middle East.

At the opening session of the Conference on Security and Cooperation in Europe, in Helsinki, Fin., the Holy See was represented by its "foreign minister," Msgr. Agostino Casaroli. In November Msgr. Casaroli visited Madrid for talks with the Spanish foreign minister and prominent churchmen to prepare the ground for revision of the 1953 Concordat with Spain. Following reports by Roman Catholic missionaries of atrocities committed by Portuguese troops in Mozambique (which were denied by Portugal), Pope Paul in July praised the missionaries for their honesty of purpose.

In March 30 new cardinals from six continents were created including, for the first time, a Pacific islander. In May the pope proclaimed that 1975 would be celebrated as a Holy Year, an event expected to bring millions of pilgrims to Rome. It was believed that the occasion might be marked by the beatification of Pope John XXIII. (MAX BERGERRE)

See also Religion.

U.S.S.R.:
see Union of Soviet Socialist Republics

Utilities, Public:
see Cooperatives; Energy; Industrial Review; Transportation

Venezuela

A republic of northern South America, Venezuela is bounded by Colombia, Brazil, Guayana, and the Caribbean Sea. Area: 352,143 sq.mi. (912,050 sq.km.). Pop. (1972 est.): 11,149,928, including mestizo 69%; white 20%; Negro 9%; Indian 2%. Cap. and largest city: Caracas (pop., 1972 est., 1,896,-947). Language: Spanish. Religion: predominantly Roman Catholic. President in 1973, Rafael Caldera.

The most significant event of 1973 took place in February with the Consensus of Lima, which heralded Venezuela's entry into the Andean Group economic association. The announcement came after prolonged negotiations between Venezuela and the other members of the group—Colombia, Chile, Bolivia, Ecuador, and Peru—over the terms of entry. When the

VENEZUELA

Education. (1971–72) Primary (including preprimary), pupils 1,918,655, teachers 54,387; secondary and vocational, pupils 564,167, teachers 15,665; teacher training (1969–70), students 13,841, teachers 1,184; higher (including 8 universities), students 99,-745, teaching staff 9,105.

Finance. Monetary unit: bolívar, with (Sept. 17, 1973) an official selling rate of 4.30 bolivares to U.S. $1 (free rate of 10.36 bolivares = £1 sterling). Gold, SDRs, and foreign exchange, central bank: (June 1973) U.S. $1,731,000,000; (June 1972) U.S. $1,384,-000,000. Budget (1972 est.): revenue 13,254,000,000 bolivares; expenditure 12,995,000,000 bolivares. Gross national product: (1970) 49,150,000,000 bolivares; (1970) 44,150,000,000 bolivares. Money supply: (March 1973) 9,593,000,000 bolivares; (March 1972) 8,293,000,000 bolivares. Cost of living (Caracas; 1963 = 100): (June 1973) 122; (June 1972) 119.

Foreign Trade. (1972) Imports 9,318,000,000 bolivares; exports 13,023,000,000 bolivares. Import sources (1971): U.S. 46%; West Germany 10%; Japan 8%; Italy 5%; Canada 5%; U.K. 5%. Export destinations (1971): U.S. 14%; Canada 12%; U.K. 6%. Main exports: crude oil and petroleum products 92%; iron ore 5%.

Transport and Communications. Roads (1972) 44,278 km. (including 586 km. expressways). Motor vehicles in use (1971): passenger 778,600; commercial 256,100. Railways (1970): 475 km.; traffic 36 million passenger-km., freight 13 million net ton-km. Air traffic (1972): 1,521,100,000 passenger-km.; freight 67,193,000 net ton-km. Shipping (1972): merchant vessels 100 gross tons and over 113; gross tonnage 411,242. Telephones (Jan. 1972) 444,000. Radio receivers (Dec. 1971) 1,750,000. Television receivers (Dec. 1971) 887,000.

Agriculture. Production (in 000; metric tons; 1972; 1971 in parentheses): corn 737 (713); rice 128 (153); sesame *c.* 132 (94); sweet potatoes (1971) 128, (1970) 123; potatoes 118 (120); cassava (1970) 317, (1969) 310; dry beans *c.* 50 (46); tomatoes (1971) 73, (1970) 87; cocoa (1972–73) 18, (1971–72) 19; bananas (1971) 989, (1970) 968; oranges (1971) 192, (1970) 184; sugar, raw value *c.* 530 (*c.* 511); coffee *c.* 66 (58); tobacco *c.* 14 (14); cotton, lint *c.* 16 (16); beef and veal *c.* 200 (*c.* 199). Livestock (in 000; 1970–71): cattle 8,499; pigs 1,671; sheep 104; horses 427; asses *c.* 500; poultry 20,430.

Industry. Production (in 000; metric tons; 1972): crude oil 169,006; natural gas (cu.m.; 1971) 9,365,-000; petroleum products (1970) 66,700; iron ore (64% metal content) 17,327; cement (1970) 2,318; gold (troy oz.; 1971) 19; diamonds (metric carats; 1971) 499; electricity (kw-hr.; 1971) 13,589,000.

group was formed in 1969, Venezuela backed out at the very last moment due to pressure from private industry, and its entry in 1973 reflected the change in public opinion in the intervening years.

As a result, Venezuela gained access to a market of 65 million people, as opposed to its domestic market of about 11 million. Integrated plans for industrialization would henceforth include Venezuela; petrochemical and metal-processing projects had already been announced, and more were to follow.

The change involved the close regulation of foreign capital within the country, together with restrictions on remittances of profits, dividends, and royalties. At the same time, foreign-owned firms would not be allowed to operate in certain sectors of the economy, and their activity was to be restricted in many others. This represented a vast change for Venezuela, which traditionally had enjoyed substantial foreign investment with minimal restrictions and regulations.

However, Venezuela would only become a full member of the Andean Group nations when all members, including Venezuela itself, had ratified the Consensus of Lima and deposited a copy of their ratification at the group's headquarters in Lima.

In the case of Venezuela, both Congress and President Caldera had signed the Consensus by mid-September, yet unaccountably the official notice had not been published. Since this was a requirement, the Consensus for all purposes remained unratified. Moreover, of the other five member nations, only three—Peru, Ecuador, and Colombia—appeared to have ratified the Consensus by the end of the year. Bolivian and Chilean plans were unknown.

Only after ratification could the integration schedule get under way. Initially, the schedule was to last 120 days, and within this time Venezuela was obliged to compile a list of products on which it wished to maintain existing tariff levels. At the end of that period tariffs on all other products would be lowered to the same level as those applied by the rest of the group (except Bolivia and Ecuador, which enjoyed special status), and all new foreign investment would be subject to government regulation.

Behind the move into the Andean Group was the fear of Venezuelan oil reserves eventually being exhausted. The economy was still very unevenly developed and depended heavily on the petroleum sector. Reserves were estimated at 13 billion bbl., about enough for only ten more years. Within that time the rest of the economy would have to be augmented to fill the gap.

Ironically, the oil situation changed almost beyond recognition during the year. Oil prices were raised again, and production increased slightly over the previous year's figures. But events outside Venezuela had a profound effect. The recognition of an "energy crisis" in the world led to a search for alternative sources of power as yet untouched. There existed in Venezuela a vast area in the Orinoco delta known as the Orinoco tar sands, estimated to contain approximately 700,000,000,000 bbl. of crude oil. The tar sands were an obvious energy source, but the one drawback was that the oil had a very heavy viscosity and would normally be too costly to recover. The threat of world shortages in the future, together with the threat to existing supplies following the Middle East war in October, combined to make the tar belt development a viable proposition. Even so, the project would require massive sums in investment, which would have to come from abroad. The stringent provisions of the Andean Group did allow foreign investment in industries that exported the vast majority of their output, and so no problem was envisaged in that respect. The problem was that the U.S., the most likely developer, would almost certainly require some form of guarantee of oil ownership, and the Venezuelans seemed unlikely to accept such a demand.

The economy continued in a very strong position, supported by the petroleum sector. Inflation rose to an annual rate of about 7%, though the government attempted to counter this by revaluing the bolívar by 3.5% against the dollar. This reflected the fact that, on the one hand, the inflation was "imported"—the result of world conditions—and, on the other hand, the bolívar was one of the strongest currencies in the world. National income per head was reported at $1,256 per year, comfortably above the "underdeveloped" level of $1,000.

In the presidential elections, held December 9, the winning candidate was Carlos Andrés Pérez of the opposition Acción Democrática. Pérez received about 48% of the vote, as against approximately 38% for his main opponent, Lorenzo Fernández of the ruling Comité de Organización Politica Electoral Independiente (COPEI). (M. J. SPENCE)

Veterinary Medicine

A new vesicular disease of swine, clinically indistinguishable from foot-and-mouth disease, appeared suddenly in Italy toward the end of 1972, and during 1973 outbreaks occurred in the U.K., Austria, Poland, France, and Hong Kong. Provisionally termed swine vesicular disease (SVD), it was caused by a porcine enterovirus first reported from Italy in 1966, when an outbreak in the Po Valley ran its course without spread or recurrence. Five primary outbreaks in England were attributed to illegally imported pork scraps in garbage fed to pigs, and by mid-April 84 secondary outbreaks had occurred in four English counties and in Scotland. Until SVD was positively diagnosed by laboratory analysis, these outbreaks had to be treated as foot-and-mouth disease, and ruminants in contact with affected swine were slaughtered. Altogether nearly 43,000 pigs were killed before the disease was believed to have been contained.

In the U.S. a few outbreaks of hog cholera (swine fever) during early 1973 prevented realization of the goal, set in 1962, of total eradication of the disease within a decade. State and federal officials, however, did anticipate a 12-month period of "no confirmed outbreaks" extending into 1974. Vaccination, which had paradoxically maintained reservoirs of the virus in improperly immunized swine, had been discontinued as scheduled midway through the program. Later emphasis was on rigorous sanitation and repopulation of previously infected premises. A continuing source of infection had been virus in garbage that was not adequately cooked before being fed to swine. A method for converting edible garbage into livestock feed, developed by two veterinarians in 1973, held the dual promise of eliminating this source of hog cholera and recycling a largely neglected resource into an economically useful product.

Throughout much of Europe and South America, foot-and-mouth disease continued to be the major animal disease problem, in terms of both incidence and measures required to hold it in check. The U.S.S.R., Turkey, Spain, and Greece accounted for

UPI COMPIX

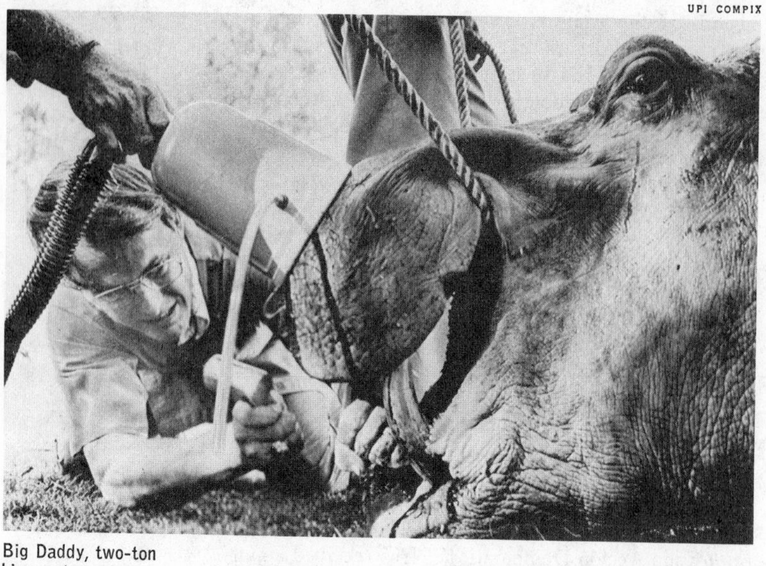

Big Daddy, two-ton hippopotamus and a favourite at Lion Country Safari in Texas, had trouble with a tooth, but the dentist wouldn't touch it. So veterinarian Joe Cannon did the job with hammer and chisel while Daddy, wide-eyed, slept. The hippo's mouth was held open with a rope.

most of the nearly 3,000 European outbreaks during 1972, and in early 1973 Spain experienced its worst outbreak in recent times. Of major significance was the reappearance of type A virus in southeastern Europe, where it had not been recorded for several years, and mass vaccination was reinstituted in many areas. In general, vaccination was prohibited in those countries where the disease had been minimal or absent for some time, including the U.K. and much of Scandinavia. Elsewhere sporadic outbreaks occurred, despite continuing compulsory or voluntary vaccination of several hundred million animals annually.

The problem of pet animal overpopulation was given increasing attention by animal-control officials and veterinary groups during 1973. With a projected increase of $4\frac{1}{2}\%$ per annum, it was estimated that the dog and cat population in the U.S. would more than double by late 1985, to about 200 million, unless stringent control measures were taken promptly. In 1971 Los Angeles had instituted the first municipal clinic for sterilization of dogs and cats, and in 1973 two additional clinics began operation there. Several other cities adopted similar programs. Federal legislation was proposed (but not acted upon) to aid in financing construction of such facilities. Animal-control and veterinary groups agreed, however, that surgical sterilization would be only a partial solution, and other means of contraception were studied. In late 1973 veterinarians in California began field trials of a vaginal plug requiring only a minute or so to insert, compared with about a half hour for the conventional spaying; early indications were that this technique should be effective. Other proposals included the addition of an antifertility agent to canned dog food, a contraceptive pill or injection, and an immunologic method (vaccination) applicable to males as well as females.

A new veterinary school at Louisiana State University, the 19th in the U.S., was scheduled to start its first class in January 1974. From 1944 to 1959 eight new schools had been established, and during the ensuing decade enrollments had more than doubled. By 1970 it had become evident that the two schools then in the active planning stage, at LSU and the University of Florida, would be insufficient to meet the increasing demand. Five or six additional schools were under consideration. Even so, it was estimated that there would be a shortage of some 4,000 veterinarians by 1980 unless facilities at existing schools were substantially increased. A major change in veterinary education had been a large increase in the number of women students admitted, from about 3% in 1963 to more than 20% a decade later. (J. F. SMITHCORS)

Vietnam

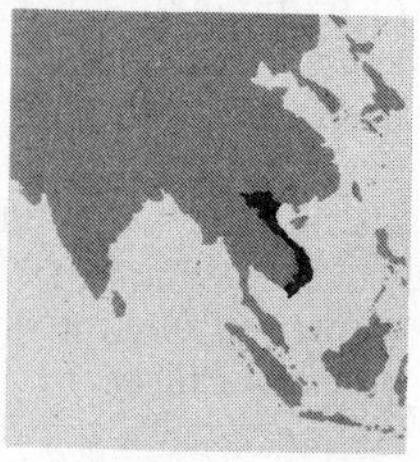

A country comprising the easternmost part of the Indochinese Peninsula, Vietnam was divided de facto into two republics in July 1954.

Republic of Vietnam (South Vietnam). This is bordered by North Vietnam (along the 17th parallel), the South China Sea, Cambodia, and Laos. Area: 67,293 sq.mi. (174,289 sq. km.). Pop. (1973 est.): 19,213,000. Cap. and largest city: Saigon (pop., 1972 est., 1,845,000). Language: Vietnamese. Religion: Buddhist; pagan; Confucian; Christian. President in 1973, Nguyen Van Thieu; premier, Tran Thien Khiem. The Provisional Revolutionary Government claimed legitimacy as one of two administrations pending resolution of the country's political future through elections.

Four years of frustrating negotiations appeared to bear fruit when, on Jan. 27, 1973, in Paris the Republic of Vietnam, the Provisional Revolutionary Government of South Vietnam (Viet Cong), the Democratic Republic of Vietnam, and the United States agreed to stop fighting while establishing means for the Vietnamese themselves to settle South Vietnam's political future. The "people's right to self-determination" and the whole of Vietnam's "independence, sovereignty, unity, and territorial integrity" were assured by the four principal signatories. Eight other governments acknowledged the agreement as part of an International Conference on Vietnam (China, Canada, the Soviet Union, Great Britain, Poland, Indonesia, Hungary, and France). As in the Geneva agreement of 1954, the demilitarized zone between North and South Vietnam was recognized as a provisional demarcation line.

Pending "free . . . general elections under international supervision" throughout South Vietnam, the Saigon administration remained in power and exercised control over the more heavily populated areas and most of the geographic territory. Communist authority extended over more remote regions inhabited by approximately 10% of the population.

The Paris agreement provided for establishment of a National Council of National Reconciliation and Concord, a tripartite body on which the Saigon government, the Communists, and undefined "neutralists" were to have equal representation. Decisions on forthcoming elections were to be based on unanimous agreement of the three factions.

U.S. and other foreign allied troops were to be withdrawn and bases dismantled within 60 days of the cease-fire, but the agreement made no provision for a pullback of North Vietnamese forces in the South. Hanoi's in-place force of 145,000 men, however, could not be strengthened. The U.S. and North Vietnam had reached agreement on the release of U.S. prisoners of war, but methods for exchanging Vietnamese military and political prisoners (the numbers of which could not be determined) were left to the Vietnamese parties. Responsibility for overseeing the cease-fire was given to an International Commission of Control and Supervision (ICCS), which initially consisted of a 1,160-member group drawn equally from Canada, Indonesia, Hungary, and Poland. Specific implementation of the cease-fire was left to two Joint Military Commissions, made up of representatives of the combatants, sitting as two and four parties.

Almost immediately after the cease-fire was to have gone into effect (2400 hours Greenwich Mean Time, January 27), violations were reported by both sides. The inauspicious beginnings prefigured the subsequent pattern of hostilities: lower levels of combat and casualties, but unimpeded warfare along the never-defined zones of control.

Of all the provisions of the Paris agreement, only the withdrawal of U.S. and other anti-Communist foreign combat units seemed to have been fully carried out. The final contingent of 68 U.S. Army, Navy, and Air Force personnel left Saigon's Tan Son Nhut Airport on March 29. North Vietnamese Lieut. Col. Bui Tin, a spokesman for Hanoi, observed at the farewell ceremony: "This is an historic day. It is the first time in 100 years there are no foreign troops on the soil of Vietnam." Only a few months later, in October, the Communists charged the U.S. with violating the agreement by keeping 20,000 U.S. military personnel behind in "civilian guises" as advisers to the South Vietnamese military. U.S. spokesmen denied the charge, saying the U.S. was "scrupulously observing" the Paris accord in every way. At the same time, U.S. officials reported the infiltration of 70,000 North Vietnamese troops, 400 tanks, and 200 artillery pieces into South Vietnam since the cease-fire. Mutual charges of noncompliance were symptomatic of the overall breakdown in the military and political agreements.

Canada's withdrawal from the ICCS at the end of July underscored the inability of that group to function effectively. (*See* Special Report.) Compelled to act only by unanimous agreement among its members and with no means to enforce compliance, the ICCS stagnated in impotence. Ideological intransigence in support of the warring factions, most blatantly by the Polish and Hungarian representatives, made it impossible to prevent renewed fighting or to pinpoint responsibility for increasing numbers of violations.

Iran replaced Canada on the ICCS, a move regarded more as a minimum diplomatic step to preserve the form of the cease-fire than as a means of effecting observance of the cease-fire itself.

According to the Saigon government, the Communists committed more than 26,000 violations in the first nine months of the cease-fire. The Provisional Revolutionary Government, at the same time, claimed 240,000 breaches by Saigon's forces. Both sides, in observed actions, were guilty of initiating varying levels of hostilities. Each claimed the necessity either for "actively" holding territory it already occupied or for taking "offensive" countermeasures to prevent encroachment by the opposition. While each side emphasized the alleged "defensive" character of its operations, the breakdown was ominous.

Figures released by the Saigon government in October revealed the grim failure of the Paris agreement to bring an end to the killing. Deaths among government troops were announced as 10,010, while an additional 1,690 civilians were reported to have died in combat. Saigon estimated Communist military deaths for the eight-month period at 36,451. Thus an average of nearly 180 Vietnamese had lost their lives each day since the fighting was supposed to have stopped.

On October 15 the Provisional Revolutionary Government issued orders to its troops "to redouble vigilance and to respond with arms and appropriate force anywhere as long as Saigon continues acts of war and sabotage."

President Thieu interpreted the order as part of an accelerating campaign to renew all-out hostilities on the part of the Viet Cong and the North Vietnamese. He said, "We must have timely actions to prevent the enemy from carrying out a new offensive like the offensive of March last year [1972]." The clear implication of preemptive operations came with maneuvering by Saigon and Communist troops in all four military regions of the South.

In Military Region I (comprising the five northernmost provinces), the two sides confronted each other with their greatest concentrations of force. About 80% of the region was under Communist control. Between 60,000 and 80,000 North Vietnamese regulars were believed to have been positioned there, bolstered by newly installed heavy artillery batteries, additional armour, surface-to-air missile sites, and the improved landing strips at the U.S.-abandoned airfields at Khe Sanh and Dong Ha, which could accommodate jet aircraft. Three of Saigon's best divisions secured a narrow coastal strip and guarded against anticipated Communist moves against the former imperial capital of Hue. While actual fighting in Military Region I was comparatively light during the year, the situation there remained potentially explosive.

To the south, in the predominantly mountainous area of Military Region II, action was heavier. Saigon forces employed extensive aerial and artillery pounding to dislodge the North Vietnamese from well-secured positions along the Laotian border and to discourage further incursions eastward. The provinces of Kontum and Pleiku saw the heaviest fighting, indistinguishable from the tempo of combat that had prevailed during most of the pre-cease-fire period. By improving previously neglected roads for all-weather use, the Communists established an efficient transportation network facilitating resupply and ready deployment of its troops and weapons. Saigon commanders in the region said the Communists still intended to sever South Vietnam by driving along the east-west routes to the South China Sea. Binh Dinh Province, on the coast, has been a Communist stronghold for decades and was seen as the eastern terminus

continued on page 723

"He wasn't killed in action. He laughed himself to death when he heard about the Nobel Peace Prize."

BACKES—NORDWEST ZEITUNG, OLDENBERG/ROTHCO

PEACEKEEPING IN VIETNAM: THE CANADIAN EXPERIENCE

By Charles Taylor

In late July 1973, Canada withdrew its 290 soldiers and diplomats from the International Commission of Control and Supervision in South Vietnam. The withdrawal marked the end of a 20-year effort by Ottawa to promote peace in the divided country. While the Canadians took professional pride in their performance under harrowing conditions, their Vietnam role had always been an exercise in futility. Despite their initial attempts to remain impartial, the Canadians were inevitably regarded as U.S. accomplices and were almost constantly at odds with their Communist counterparts. Many politicians and officials in Ottawa were left with a residue of bitterness against the United States, a feeling that Washington had once again bullied Canada into acting against its own best interests.

Since the French disengagement from Vietnam under terms of the 1954 Geneva agreement, Canada had served there with India and Poland on the International Control Commission. In its early months, the ICC had effectively supervised the repatriation of troops and the movement of civilian refugees between North and South. But the ICC became impotent as both sides began to violate the cease-fire provisions and the United States became entangled in a major ground and air war. With the Poles backing the Communist side and the Indians usually supporting the Poles, the Canadians became American surrogates on a commission that did little more than provide a tenuous air link between Saigon and Hanoi.

Nevertheless, Canada's service on the ICC made it a likely candidate for membership on the International Commission of Control and Supervision (ICCS), established by the Paris agreement signed by the United States, North Vietnam, South Vietnam, and the Provisional Revolutionary Government (PRG) on Jan. 27, 1973. As the outline of the new agreement began to emerge, Prime Minister Pierre Trudeau and External Affairs Minister Mitchell Sharp made clear that Canada's participation on a new truce commission could not be taken for granted, despite Canada's long history of peacekeeping—not only in Indochina but also in the Middle East, Cyprus, the former Belgian Congo, and the Indian subcontinent. This time Canada would cooperate only if the new body had teeth.

Somehow these brave words were forgotten in the flurry of a Canadian federal election and relentless pressure from Washington. Canada was named to the new ICCS without its formal consent and even before Ottawa had been officially informed. In the end, Canada joined Poland, Hungary, and Indonesia on a commission that lacked many of the practical guarantees Ottawa had deemed essential. When the first Canadian contingent arrived in Saigon on January 29, there was only one qualification: Canada reserved the right to withdraw after 60 days.

The First 60 Days. From the start, Ottawa was determined to show that it was not just Washington's spokesman on another powerless commission. Ambassador Michel Gauvin, a 53-year-old career diplomat known for his abrasive character, was chosen as Canada's senior commissioner and instructed to follow a tough, "open mouth" policy. At frequent press briefings, Gauvin pointed out that if the ICCS could not function properly, the whole world would be informed and the culprits identified. With their berets, green shorts, and knee-length socks, the Canadians looked like a team of scoutmasters, and that was how they often behaved.

But the Canadian strategy never really worked. As fighting flared up in South Vietnam—and continued in Laos and Cambodia—it became apparent that the United States, North Vietnam, South Vietnam, and the PRG were all breaking the Paris agreement. On the ICCS itself, Poland and Hungary faithfully followed the Communist line, while the Indonesians seemed anxious to avoid any serious confrontation. Inevitably, Gauvin found himself assailing his Communist colleagues and being assailed by them in turn.

Ottawa had hoped it could ensure that the ICCS would give fair treatment to the Saigon government without becoming its spokesman. Gauvin emphasized his willingness to investigate cease-fire complaints by the Communists and—if the evidence warranted—to find Saigon guilty. But as major battles raged beyond the range of the ICCS teams, the Communists—guilty of violations themselves—requested few such investigations.

In Ottawa there were conflicting pressures on—and within—the minority Liberal government. The opposition parties' increasing skepticism over Canada's role was shared by Sharp and most of his officials. On the other hand, Defense Minister James Richardson and the military seemed eager to continue, and other ministers were concerned about possible retaliation by Washington in crucial economic negotiations.

There was probably never much chance that Canada would withdraw after the first 60 days, if only for fear of being blamed for not trying hard enough. Few were surprised when Sharp announced in late March that Canada would continue on the ICCS until May 31 but would withdraw by June 30 unless all the parties showed a greater determination to make the cease-fire work.

Failure of a Mission. Still the fighting continued. ICCS helicopters and team sites came under frequent Communist fire, and one Canadian officer died when a helicopter was downed on April 7. Meanwhile, the commission was stalemated for six weeks by a dispute over the handling of a Canadian and Indonesian report concerning the infiltration of North Vietnamese troops.

Finally, on May 29, Sharp announced Canada's withdrawal, charging that the situation had not improved and that Canada's conception of how the commission should function had not been accepted. At the request of the United States, the original withdrawal date of June 30 was extended by one month. As the Canadians began to prepare for the pullout, there was one final humiliating experience: two of their officers were captured and detained for 18 days by the PRG.

The whole unhappy experience seemed certain to have important consequences. Even before Ottawa reluctantly agreed to join the commission, Canadians had entertained growing doubts about the general thrust of their foreign policy, with its emphasis on "quiet diplomacy," peacekeeping, and tacit support for most U.S. endeavours. Canada's experience also seemed likely to strengthen the growing feeling among many Canadians that Ottawa had often been too supine in the face of U.S. demands. As the Canadians were packing their bags in Vietnam, the publication of new portions of the Pentagon papers revealed how unwitting Canadian diplomats had been used by Washington in 1964–66 to further its policy in Vietnam. As both countries prepared for negotiations over vital economic questions, there was an increased awareness that Canadian interests often differ radically from those of the United States and that they must be stoutly defended.

Charles Taylor, foreign affairs writer for the Toronto Globe and Mail, *has served as his paper's bureau chief in Hong Kong, Peking, Nairobi, and London.*

YVES-GUY BERGES—GAMMA

Prisoners of war, held by the South Vietnamese at an air base near Saigon, gather to board trucks bound for Hue, Feb. 13, 1973, during a massive exchange of prisoners by North and South Vietnam.

continued from page 721

of such a corridor. While Route 1, which ran the breadth of South Vietnam, was open during 1973, traffic was generally restricted to the daytime.

Military Region III, principally to the northwest of Saigon, claimed a great share of attention, largely because of the threat posed by entrenched Communist forces (estimated at 75,000 men) less than 50 mi. from the capital. The area around Loc Ninh, in the province of Binh Long, served as the "liberation zone" command centre and ostensible capital of the Provisional Revolutionary Government (although Dong Ha in Military Region I was used for embryonic diplomatic activities because of its ready access to North Vietnam). Movement across the Cambodian border gave the Communists a ready flow of material and men for thrusts to Tay Ninh city, long coveted by the Viet Cong, and for securing territory acquired during the 1972 Easter offensive.

In the Mekong Delta, Military Region IV, each side engaged in comparatively minor "land-grabbing" after the cease-fire. The fighting was generally short-lived and apparently the result of tactical maneuvering—on Saigon's part to keep roads and waterways open for the transport of agricultural produce, on the Communists' part to maintain control over its pockets of authority. With its high population density and agricultural output, the Delta remained a prize, and there was little evidence to suggest any significant change in the status quo.

Nowhere in South Vietnam were geographic limits of control clearly delineated. Battlefield commanders never met to establish occupied zones or to work out arrangements for controlling breaches of the cease-fire. Direct contacts between the two sides were conducted by negotiators of the two-party Joint Military Commission in Saigon, but the meetings were held in an atmosphere of mutual hostility and became bogged down in procedural matters. Nothing of substance was agreed upon, and the talks were at a complete impasse. Late in December it was reported that Saigon and the Provisional Revolutionary Government had agreed in principle to resume prisoner exchanges, suspended in July. At the same time, the level of fighting was escalating. An estimated one-third of South Vietnam's gasoline supply for civilian use was destroyed in a rocket attack on a petroleum depot near Saigon early in December. Kissinger and Tho met once again in Paris on December 20, but the chief item of discussion was said to be an exchange of charges concerning the failure of the cease-fire.

Political solutions were equally elusive, and were made manifestly more difficult because of the continued fighting. Talks conducted near Paris were suspended indefinitely in October after 28 sessions in which nothing was achieved. The Provisional Revolutionary Government said Saigon was guilty of "continuous and flagrant violation" of the cease-fire agreement, while Saigon accused the Communists of "a discourteous and insolent attitude unacceptable among well-educated people and intolerable among negotiators seeking a peaceful solution."

At the core of the differences were sharply varying interpretations of the political provisions of the Paris agreement, which was admittedly ambiguous. To the

VIETNAM: Republic

Education. (1969–70) Primary, pupils 2,375,982, teachers 45,077; secondary, pupils 636,921, teachers 16,314; vocational, pupils 14,569, teachers 907; teacher training, students 3,923, teachers 92; higher, students 47,296, teaching staff 1,348.

Finance. Monetary unit: piastre, with (Sept. 17, 1973) an official exchange rate of 500 piastres to U.S. $1 (free rate of 1,206 piastres = £1 sterling). Gold, SDRs, and foreign exchange, central bank: (June 1973) U.S. $182 million; (June 1972) U.S. $204 million. Budget (1971 est.): revenue 239 billion piastres; expenditure 267 billion piastres. Gross national product: (1970) 804.4 billion piastres; (1969) 557.5 billion piastres. Money supply: (May 1973) 238,870,000,000 piastres; (May 1972) 233,920,000,000 piastres. Cost of living (Saigon; 1963 = 100): (June 1973) 1,162; (June 1972) 848.

Foreign Trade. (1971) Imports 222,757,000,000 piastres; exports 5,272,000,000 piastres. Import sources: U.S. 41%; Japan 20%; Taiwan 7%; France 7%. Export destinations: Japan 30%; France 19%; Hong Kong 24%; Singapore 6%. Main exports: fish 29%; rubber 28%.

Transport and Communications. Roads (1970) 20,917 km. Motor vehicles in use (1971): passenger 58,400; commercial (including buses) 29,200. Railways (1971): 684 km.; traffic 85.5 million passenger-km., freight 38 million net ton-km. Air traffic (1972): 434.3 million passenger-km.; freight 4,028,000 net ton-km. Telephones (Dec. 1971) 38,000. Radio receivers (Dec. 1970) 2.2 million. Television receivers (Dec. 1970) 450,000.

Agriculture. Production (in 000; metric tons; 1972; 1971 in parentheses): rice 6,215 (6,324); sweet potatoes (1971) 230, (1970) 220; cassava (1970) 216, (1969) 233; peanuts *c.* 32 (*c.* 32); dry beans *c.* 12 (*c.* 12); rubber *c.* 22 (*c.* 37); tea 5.8 (5.8); coffee *c.* 4.4 (4.4); fish catch (1971) 587, (1970) 517. Livestock (in 000; 1970–71): buffalo 565; cattle (1971–72) 898; pigs 3,848; goats 43; chickens *c.* 20,000.

Industry. Production (in 000; metric tons; 1971): cement 263; salt *c.* 120; cotton yarn 12; woven cotton fabrics (m.) 64,000; electricity (excluding most industrial production; kw-hr.; 1971) 1,343,000.

VIETNAM: Democratic Republic

Education. (1966–67) Primary and secondary, pupils 4,517,600, teachers 86,495; vocational, pupils 101,880, teachers 4,194; higher (including University of Hanoi), students (1970) *c.* 72,000, teaching staff (1966–67) 5,004.

Finance and Trade. Monetary unit: dong, with (Sept. 17, 1973) an official exchange rate of 2.35 dong to U.S. $1 (5.63 dong = £1 sterling) and a "tourist" rate of 13.24 dong to £1 sterling. Budget (foreign aid est.; 1971) *c.* 5 billion dong. Foreign trade (1965): imports *c.* 530 million dong; exports *c.* 290 million dong. Main import sources: U.S.S.R. *c.* 40%; China *c.* 25%; East Germany *c.* 9%; Czechoslovakia *c.* 8%; Poland *c.* 6%. Main export destinations: China *c.* 40%; U.S.S.R. *c.* 25%; Japan *c.* 9%; Czechoslovakia *c.* 6%; East Germany *c.* 5%.

Transport. Roads (1971) *c.* 13,500 km. Railways (1969) *c.* 780 km.

Agriculture. Production (in 000; metric tons; 1972; 1971 in parentheses): rice *c.* 5,500 (*c.* 5,000); corn *c.* 250 (*c.* 230); sweet potatoes *c.* 900 (*c.* 900); cassava (1970) *c.* 730, (1969) *c.* 700; peanuts (1970) *c.* 40, (1969) *c.* 46; tobacco *c.* 4 (*c.* 4); tea *c.* 2.8 (*c.* 2.8). Livestock (in 000; 1970–71): buffalo *c.* 1,700; cattle *c.* 880; pigs *c.* 6,800; horses 59.

Industry. Production (in 000; metric tons; 1971): coal *c.* 3,000; phosphate rock (oxide content) *c.* 1,050; salt *c.* 150; cement *c.* 500; cotton fabrics (m.; 1964) 105,200; paper (1964) 19; electricity (kw-hr.; 1964) 548,000.

ROGER PIC—GAMMA

A North Vietnamese survivor works to clear this residential quarter of Hanoi, devastated by the U.S. "Christmas bombings" of 1972.

Provisional Government, the agreement recognized the existence of a Communist administrative structure, a second government, parallel to Saigon's in every respect. To Saigon, the agreement maintained the republic's integrity and President Thieu's sole legal right to rule. Saigon refused to negotiate with the Communists as equals or co-representatives of the South Vietnamese people. National elections, to have been held by the end of the year, were never arranged. Saigon administered local and Senate balloting, as, it insisted, the constitution demanded. President Thieu held that he was abiding by the existing law, since the constitution had not been abrogated.

A key stumbling block to national reconciliation and concord was the inherent inability of the Paris-mandated council to be formed at all. Saigon and the Communists were to have equal representation with "neutralists" on the council, but it was never explained who would serve as "third force" representatives or how they would be appointed. The recognized parties made halting efforts to create "neutral" elements (favourable to each), but it was patently impossible to draw upon a middle-of-the-road that existed in spirit among many Vietnamese but had no embodiment as an identifiable political force.

President Thieu, meanwhile, strengthened his political authority and influence. Communists and Communist supporters were barred from any political activity (as spelled out in the constitution). A clampdown on opposition forces among the non-Communists virtually eliminated serious challenges at every level of government within Saigon's broad areas of control. Thieu's Democracy Party (Dan Chu) sought to extend its influence to the countryside, primarily through "revolutionary development cadres," and to bring government to the people. A program for decentralization of the national government was announced, but efforts to move civil servants out of Saigon into the less secure villages and hamlets were largely unsuccessful. To counter graft and corruption, Thieu felt compelled to dismiss six province chiefs at midyear.

The South Vietnamese legislative bodies lost what was left of their nominal opposition character during 1973. Elections were held on August 26 for 31 of the 60 seats in the Senate. Supporters of Thieu won them all; they were not even challenged, as opposition candidates refused to file in the belief that they could not hope to penetrate the election machinery created by the Saigon government.

Communists and their supporters were called upon to boycott the election, which the Provisional Revolutionary Government termed "illegal."

Former foreign minister Tran Van Lam was the unopposed victor in voting for presidency of the Senate, making him second in line to succeed Thieu. Friction developed between Thieu and Premier Khiem, whose own role in the government was largely reduced to ceremonial functions deemed unworthy of presidential participation. In the National Assembly, only 57 opposition deputies remained in office, a divided bloc reduced to ineffectual challenges of Thieu's growing dominance. Speakership of the lower house and all 18 committee chairmanships were held by members of the Democracy Party.

A deteriorating economic situation in South Vietnam created hardships and exerted great pressure on the government. Without direct U.S. assistance (which provided more than half of the country's operating funds), South Vietnam's entire political structure would be imperiled. To a large measure, it was the withdrawal of the massive U.S. presence that contributed to the crisis of converting to a peacetime economy. As many as 400,000 South Vietnamese were made jobless by the U.S. pullout. U.S. troops, at the height of the war, contributed an estimated $400 million annually to the local economy. There was no substitute for this ready inflow of hard currency.

Inflation was rampant, with the cost of living soaring 5% each month during the first three quarters of 1973. Foreign currency reserves were being depleted at a rate of $10 million a month. The gross national product fell more than 15% during the year, and there was little expectation that an early turnabout was in sight. Rising import prices, reflecting worldwide fluctuations in exchange rates, added to South Vietnam's economic problems. The country's imports were valued at about $750 million during the year (more than double the pre-1965 averages), while exports rose moderately to around $45 million. Exports in 1972 amounted to only 3% of imports; during 1960–64, the figure had been 26%.

South Vietnam's efforts to achieve even a modicum of self-sufficiency were made more difficult by the real uncertainty as to whether there would be a peaceful future. While essential items from abroad, including foodstuffs, fertilizers, and basic machinery, could be reduced—to the dissatisfaction of the people and the possible political benefit of the Communists—there were no acceptable alternatives. Economists saw an evident need for a reduction in overall government expenditures, particularly in military spending. Fifty-three percent of South Vietnam's $870 million budget went for defense purposes in 1973, and Saigon maintained a force of over a million men (including regulars, militiamen, and national police). Government officials contended, however, that any significant cutback would lead to Communist encroachments, and that, in turn, would only signal more costly fighting.

(ROBERT GORALSKI)

Democratic Republic of Vietnam (North Vietnam). This is bordered by China, the Gulf of Tonkin, the South China Sea, South Vietnam, and Laos. Area: 63,360 sq.mi. (164,103 sq.km.). Pop. (1972 est.): 22,040,000. Cap. and largest city: Hanoi (pop., 1970 est., 1,348,000). Language: Vietnamese. Religion:

COURTESY, U.S. NAVY

A U.S. Marine helicopter, with towrope attached, performs minesweeping duty among tall rocks in harbours northeast of Haiphong. Hydrofoil sleds, towed by helicopters, detonated the mines sown throughout the harbour system by the U.S. in 1972.

Buddhist; pagan; Confucian; Christian. Secretary of the Communist Party in 1973, Le Duan; president, Ton Duc Thang; premier, Pham Van Dong.

On January 28, the day after the cease-fire came into effect, Hanoi issued a statement informing its people of the terms of the settlement. The statement described the peace pact as a great victory for North Vietnam's struggle against U.S. aggression and as "the political and legal basis ensuring the fundamental national rights of our people and the sacred right of self-determination of our compatriots in the South." Cautioning that the struggle was not yet over, the statement emphasized the need to "strengthen solidarity, maintain high vigilance at all times and strive our best to consolidate the successes already won."

There were rallies and public speeches in North Vietnam to welcome the end of nearly three decades of warfare, but, on the whole, the North Vietnamese were cool and reserved in their rejoicing. On February 20 the National Assembly held a special session and heard Premier Pham Van Dong spell out the country's new tasks. Calling North Vietnam the inviolable outpost of the socialist system in Southeast Asia, he said: "The big victory just recorded has created even more favourable conditions for building socialism in the North . . . and bringing into play in a more positive way the effect of the Democratic Republic of Vietnam."

However, the peace so laboriously hammered out in Paris proved to be a tenuous arrangement in the field. A spate of public demonstrations—some of them violent—against official Communist negotiators took place in South Vietnam, apparently under government prodding. In one of the worst such incidents, four representatives of the Provisional Revolutionary Government were shot dead. Hanoi announced that it would suspend the release of U.S. prisoners, which was then in progress, and Washington promptly warned of retaliatory action.

Eventually, differences between Hanoi and Washington were settled to the satisfaction of both parties, but sporadic fighting in various parts of the South became an established pattern. Hanoi steadfastly backed the Paris agreement, shrewdly calculating that it had more to gain from peace than from renewed war. It said that the struggle in the South was now a political one and publicly stated its willingness to recognize the importance of a third force of neutralists in a future tripartite arrangement in Saigon.

But Hanoi made no secret of its determination to maintain military preparedness against the government in Saigon. Some saw the continued movement of men and equipment into the South as an effort to provide a base for the political struggle ahead in South Vietnam. Others, including Saigon, said the North was preparing for a major offensive in 1974.

In October North Vietnamese negotiator Le Duc Tho declined to accept the Nobel Peace Prize awarded to him along with U.S. Secretary of State Henry A. Kissinger. He explained that the time to consider accepting the prize would be after real peace had been established in Vietnam. (*See* NOBEL PRIZES.)

In April North Vietnam declined an invitation to send an observer to the conference of the Association of Southeast Asian Nations (ASEAN). The rejection was ostensibly on the ground that Thailand was host to the conference and "when the Vietnamese people were fighting against U.S. aggression, Thailand sent its troops to fight as mercenaries for the U.S. and let the latter use Thai territory as a base for its aggression." It was an open secret, however, that North Vietnam's main reason for not participating in the ASEAN meeting was its opposition to multilateral alliances in the region. It was willing to have bilateral relations with most of the ASEAN members.

In the same spirit of bilateralism, North Vietnam also entered into relations with various advanced nations. Japanese economic overtures were seriously considered, and prolonged negotiations were carried on concerning a variety of trade and aid projects including offshore oil exploration. Diplomatic relations with Japan were established in September. Other countries in which Hanoi showed special interest were Sweden, Australia, and India. Diplomatic circles believed that, in the era of peace, Hanoi was trying to reduce its dependence on the socialist bloc and strengthen ties with countries that were generally recognized as practicing independent foreign policies.

Nevertheless, Hanoi's need for reconstruction assistance was so pressing that it gave unexpected importance to negotiations in Paris aimed at getting war damage "compensation" from the U.S. The two countries agreed to create a joint economic commission to "develop the economic relations" between them. While the Nixon administration was apparently willing to sanction it, the aid project encountered serious trouble in Congress early in the year. A major bone of contention was whether reconstruction money should be funneled directly from the U.S. or through an international agency. Influential congressional opponents of the Vietnam war argued for a multinational program lest the U.S. try to control the flow of money and use it to put pressure on the recipients.

For all the newfound interest Hanoi showed in relations with non-Communist countries, its links with fraternal allies remained the bulwark of its foreign policy. In June delegations led by Le Duan and including Pham Van Dong began visiting them one by one. Part of their objective was to carry out the late Ho Chi Minh's instructions in his will that socialist allies who helped North Vietnam in its struggle must be personally thanked when the war was over, but the visits were also aimed at negotiating new aid agreements. The delegations visited North Korea, Mongolia, China, the Soviet Union, and Eastern European countries.

There were clear indications that new aid agreements were oriented toward economic reconstruction, although military requirements were still considered vital. Details of the agreements were not given, but they were believed to be generally one-year pacts pending the completion of a five-year plan that was under intensive preparation. A short-term plan launched immediately after the cease-fire aimed at completing "the restoration and development of the national economy" by 1975.

The extent to which the economy had been shattered by the war was never publicized. By midyear, however, official sources began claiming significant progress in rebuilding it. In line with previous practice, no absolute figures were given, but it was stated that the acreage under early spring crops had been increased by 6,000 ha. over that of the previous year and that the total output of spring rice was the highest in 15 years. In the first six months of the year, 138 public utility projects and 77 industrial projects were completed. Electricity output by mid-August had risen by 50% compared with the beginning of the year. The total productive capacity of industry in the second quarter of the year was 10% higher than in the first.

(T. J. S. GEORGE)

See also Defense.

Vital Statistics

In most countries having nearly complete registration, the trend to lower birthrates continued in 1972 and the early months of 1973. Death rates for these countries had fluctuated within a much narrower range in the preceding two decades; most of them showed small decreases from 1971 to 1972, although an appreciable number of countries reported slightly higher rates in 1972 and early 1973. The marriage rate had risen in most countries during the preceding decade, although several reported moderate declines. Between 1971 and 1972 and early 1973, slightly over half of the countries showed increases. The general pattern of recent years had not changed materially, but there was some indication that the birthrate might be beginning to level off again in the more technologically advanced countries.

Virgin Islands:
see Dependent States

Birth Statistics. In the U.S. the provisional crude birthrate declined from 17.3 births per 1,000 population in 1971 to 15.6 in 1972, or about 10%. The decrease continued in 1973; provisional data for the first eight months showed a fall of nearly 4% compared with the same period in 1972. The general fertility rate (births per 1,000 women 15–44 years of age) fell about 11%, from 82.3 in 1971 to 73.4 in 1972. The decline continued during the first eight months of 1973, to 69.4, compared with 73.1 for the corresponding 1972 period. The rate of natural increase (excess of births over deaths per 1,000 population) also continued to fall, from 8 in 1971 to 6.2 in 1972. (The U.S. population rose by about 1.3 million persons in 1972 as a result of natural increase.) The decline continued in the first part of 1973, as this rate fell from 6 in the first eight months of 1972 to 5.4.

The lower crude birthrates of recent years in the U.S. had occurred at the same time that the number of women in the childbearing ages (considered to be 15–44 years) had increased. Consequently, the general fertility rate, based on the number of women in the childbearing years, fell faster than the crude rate.

Provisional data indicated that the number of births and the crude birthrate declined in all U.S. states between 1971 and 1972. The lowest rate, 13.7 in 1972, occurred in the Middle Atlantic states, while the highest rates were reported for the mountain states, 18.7, and the west south central states, 18.2.

Data for 1969, the latest year for which final detailed statistics were available, showed that the crude birthrate for white persons, 16.9, was much lower than for all other race groups, 24.4. Five and one-half percent of all births to white mothers in 1969 were illegitimate; for all other races combined, the corresponding percentage was 32.5. The fall in the general fertility rate between 1960 and 1969 was about the same for white mothers, 27%, and for mothers of all other races, 25%.

The decline of the birthrate since roughly 1960 had occurred among mothers in all age groups, but was greater at the older ages. The rate for women 15–19 and 20–24 years fell about 26% and 36%, respectively, from 1960 to 1969, while for women 35–39 years and 40–44 years the rates fell 41% and 43%. The long-time trend was clearly toward fewer children per family. The rate for first births actually increased 5% between 1960 and 1969, while that for second births fell 20%; for third births, 41%; fourth births, 51%; fifth births, 52%; and sixth and higher order births, 54%.

Among countries where birth registration was at least 90% complete, UN reports indicated that the birthrate declined between 1971 and 1972 in 30 countries, increased in 3 countries, and did not change in 2. A similar pattern continued in the early months of 1973, when 19 of 29 countries reported decreases compared with 1972. The most recent official data for countries with incomplete registration and estimates made by the UN showed that birthrates around the world ranged from about 11 per 1,000 population to over 50. The highest rates, and consequently the highest rates of population increase, were in the less technologically advanced countries of Africa, Asia, and South America.

Death Statistics. The crude death rate (deaths per 1,000 population) in the U.S., which had fluctuated within narrow limits for 20 years, rose slightly in 1972 to 9.4, compared with 9.3 in 1971. In the first eight months of 1973 the number of deaths increased slightly over 1972, but the rate, 9.5, remained the same. Among age-specific rates, the largest change occurred for the oldest age group, 85 years and over, where the rate fell 7.6% between 1971 and 1972 and then rose 5.6% in the first seven months of 1973. In 1972 the lowest rates ever recorded in the U.S. were shown for: white males in the age groups 35–44, 55–64, and 85 and over; white females in the groups 35–44, 45–54, and 85 and over; and all other females in the groups 25–34, 35–44, 45–54, and 65–74.

The most recent available total age-adjusted death rates, for 1969, showed substantial differences between the sexes and between whites and all other races. The age-adjusted rate for males was 9.5 and for females, 5.5. For white persons the rate was 6.9 and for all others, 10.5. By major causes of death, the rates were much higher for males than for females, except for diabetes, and much lower for whites than for all other races, except for arteriosclerosis and bronchitis, emphysema, and asthma.

Table I. Life Expectancy at Birth, in Years, for Selected Countries

Country	Period	Male	Female
Africa			
Burundi	1965	35.0	38.5
Egypt	1960	51.6	53.8
Liberia	1970	50.8	57.4
Nigeria	1965–66	37.2	36.7
Upper Volta	1960–61	32.1	31.1
Asia			
Cambodia	1958–59	44.2	43.3
Hong Kong	1968	66.7	73.3
India	1951–60	41.9	40.6
Israel	1970	69.6	73.0
Japan	1968	69.1	74.3
Jordan	1959–63	52.6	52.0
Korea, South	1966	59.7	64.1
Pakistan	1962	53.7	48.8
Taiwan	1966	59.7	64.1
Thailand	1960	53.6	58.7
Europe			
Albania	1965–66	64.9	67.0
Austria	1970	66.3	73.5
Belgium	1963–66	67.6	73.7
Bulgaria	1965–67	68.8	72.7
Czechoslovakia	1966	67.3	73.6
Denmark	1968–69	70.7	75.6
Finland	1961–65	65.4	72.6
France	1969	67.6	75.3
Germany, East	1967–68	69.2	74.4
Germany, West*	1966–68	67.6	73.6
Greece	1960–62	67.5	70.7
Hungary	1968	66.6	71.9
Iceland	1961–65	70.8	76.2
Ireland	1960–62	68.1	71.9
Italy	1964–67	67.9	73.4
Netherlands, The	1970	70.7	76.5
Norway	1961–65	71.0	76.0
Poland	1965–66	66.9	72.8
Portugal	1970	65.3	71.0
Romania	1968	65.5	69.8
Spain	1960	67.3	71.9
Sweden	1967	71.9	76.5
Switzerland	1958–63	68.7	74.1
United Kingdom			
England and Wales	1968–70	68.6	74.9
Northern Ireland	1968–70	67.9	73.5
Scotland	1968–70	66.9	73.1
Yugoslavia	1967–68	64.3	68.9
North America			
Barbados	1959–61	62.7	67.4
Canada	1965–67	68.8	75.2
Costa Rica	1962–64	61.9	64.8
Guatemala	1963–65	48.3	49.7
Mexico	1965–70	61.0	63.7
Panama	1960–61	57.6	60.9
Puerto Rico	1959–61	67.1	71.9
United States	1970	67.1	74.8
Oceania			
Australia	1960–62	67.9	74.2
New Zealand	1960–62	68.4	73.8
South America			
Argentina	1965–70	64.1	70.2
Chile	1960–61	54.4	59.9
Peru	1960–65	52.6	55.5
Surinam	1963	62.5	66.7
Uruguay	1963–64	65.5	71.6
U.S.S.R.	1968–69	65.0	74.0

*Excluding West Berlin.
Source: United Nations, *Demographic Yearbook* (1971); official country sources.

The absence of any substantial decrease in the crude death rate during the preceding 20 years did not mean that no reductions of mortality had occurred. Significant decreases had occurred at all ages. The failure of the crude rate to fall was due primarily to the fact that the proportion of older people in the population had risen during this period.

The rankings of the ten leading causes of death in the U.S. in 1972 are shown below. Diabetes and certain causes of mortality in early infancy reversed their 1971 order, as did arteriosclerosis and cirrhosis of the liver. The rates for all causes, except the bronchitis and early infancy groups, rose slightly in 1972. The only significant change in the first seven months of 1973 was for bronchitis, emphysema, and asthma, which increased 7.4%.

Cause of death	Estimated rate per 100,000 population
All causes	942.2
Diseases of heart	361.3
Malignant neoplasms (cancer)	166.6
Cerebrovascular diseases	100.9
Accidents	54.6
Influenza and pneumonia	29.4
Diabetes mellitus	18.8
Certain causes of mortality in early infancy	16.4
Arteriosclerosis	15.8
Cirrhosis of the liver	15.7
Bronchitis, emphysema, and asthma	13.8

Comparison of crude death rates in the U.S. is limited by the effect of differing age composition. The lowest rates occur in the Western states, which have "younger" populations than the other sections of the country. The lowest rate in 1972 occurred in the mountain states, 8; and the highest in the east south central states, 10.2, and New England and the west north central states, 10.1.

The crude death rate in European countries had also shown only small year-to-year changes during the preceding decade or so. In the few countries of Africa, Asia, and South America that had reasonably complete

Table II. Birthrates and Death Rates per 1,000 Population and Infant Mortality per 1,000 Live Births in Selected Countries, 1972*

Country	Birth-rate	Death rate	Infant mortality	Country	Birth-rate	Death rate	Infant mortality
Africa				Romania†	19.6	9.5	42.4
Egypt	34.6†	13.1†	116.3‡	Spain	19.4	8.2	16.0
Kenya	17.2‡	3.8‡	55.0§	Sweden	13.8	10.4	11.1†
Mauritius	25.0	7.9	65.3	Switzerland	14.4	8.7	14.4†
Tunisia	37.1	7.5	77.7§	United Kingdom	14.9	12.1	17.6
Asia				England & Wales	14.8	12.1	17.2
Cyprus	22.0	6.5	25.0	Northern Ireland	19.4	11.0	21.0
Hong Kong	19.7	5.4	17.5	Scotland	15.1	12.5	19.0
Israel	27.2	7.2	23.7	Yugoslavia	18.2	9.1	43.2
Japan†	19.2	6.6	12.4	North America			
Kuwait†	42.8	4.6	37.4	Barbados	20.7	8.7	33.6
Lebanon	26.5†	4.5†	13.6‖	Canada	15.7	7.4	17.5†
Philippines†	25.4	6.6	62.0	Costa Rica	31.6	5.7	56.5†
Singapore	23.1	5.4	19.2	Cuba†	29.5	6.0	34.4
Thailand‡	33.3	6.5	25.5	El Salvador	40.7	8.6	52.4†
Europe				Guatemala†	41.7	14.1	83.1
Austria	13.8	12.6	25.1	Jamaica	34.3	7.2	30.9
Belgium	14.5	12.4	19.8	Mexico	42.6	8.7	61.3
Bulgaria	15.3	9.8	25.8	Panama	35.6	6.0	37.6†
Czechoslovakia	17.3	11.1	21.4	Puerto Rico†	25.6	6.5	27.5
Denmark	15.2	10.2	14.2‡	United States	15.6	9.4	18.5
Finland	12.7	9.6	11.3	Oceania			
France	16.9	10.6	16.0	American Samoa†	35.8	4.9	25.1
Germany, East†	11.7	13.7	18.0	Australia	20.5	8.5	17.3†
Germany, West	11.3	11.8	22.5	Fiji	27.8	4.9	21.4†
Greece†	16.0	8.3	26.9	Guam†	34.1	4.0	20.5
Hungary	14.7	11.4	32.9	New Caledonia†	35.1	8.9	31.7
Iceland	21.9	6.9	11.6	New Zealand	21.8	8.5	16.5†
Ireland	22.4	11.2	18.0†	Western Samoa	27.2	3.6	27.1
Italy	16.3	9.6	28.3†	South America			
Luxembourg	11.8	11.9	13.6	Ecuador‡	37.8	9.9	76.6
Netherlands, The	16.1	8.5	11.4	Paraguay‡	33.4	5.3	35.6
Norway	16.8	9.9	12.5†	Uruguay†	22.6	9.8	40.4
Poland	17.4	8.0	28.6	Venezuela	36.8	6.6	50.2†
Portugal	20.5	10.6	41.4	U.S.S.R.†	17.8	8.2	22.6

*Registered births and deaths only.
†1971.
‡1970.
§1969.
‖1960.
Sources: United Nations, *Population and Vital Statistics Report*; World Health Organization, *World Health Statistics Report*; various national demographic publications.

statistics, the trend of the death rate had been downward, reflecting improvement in health services and economic conditions. Among countries that had at least 90% complete registration, 13 reported higher rates in 1972, 18 reported lower rates, and in 3 the rate did not change. Among the countries for which data for the first part of 1973 were available, 14 showed higher rates, 7 lower, and 4 unchanged.

Infant and Maternal Mortality. The infant mortality rate (deaths under one year per 1,000 live births) continued its long downward trend in the U.S., falling to 18.5 in 1972 from 19.2 in 1971. The rates were the lowest ever recorded for infants of both sexes and nonwhites as well as whites. Improvement continued in the first eight months of 1973, when the rate declined to 17.7. Most of the decrease occurred among infants under 28 days old. While the rate for white infants 28 days to 11 months old increased slightly from 1971 to 1972, the rate for infants of all other races in this age group fell from 9.4 to 8.5. The total infant mortality rate for white infants, 16.3, was still much lower than for all others, 29.

Among countries with 90% or more complete registration, the infant mortality rate in 1971 or 1972 ranged from 11.1 for Sweden, 11.3 for Finland, and 11.4 for The Netherlands to 43.2 for Yugoslavia and 41.4 for Portugal. There was good evidence that many countries had rates well above 100, but precise figures were not available for most countries of Africa, Asia, and South America.

The provisional maternal mortality rate for the U.S. in 1972 was 24 per 100,000 live births. This was higher than the rate of 20.5 reported for 1971 but lower than for all other previous years. Comparison between countries of death rates for this cause, as well as other causes, was significantly limited by differences in the classification rules used.

Expectation of Life. The estimated expectation of life at birth in the U.S. in 1972 was 71.2 years, up slightly over 71.1 in 1971. The expectation of life at birth for the entire population in the U.S. had increased slightly more than one year during the preceding decade. In 1970, the latest year for which more detailed information was available, the average life expectancy of a male baby was 67.1 years and for a female baby, 74.8 years. Throughout the world in recent years, life expectancy for males had ranged from less than 40 years to over 70 years and for females, from less than 40 to over 75 years. (*See* Table I.)

Marriage and Divorce. The number of marriages rose to a record high in the U.S. in 1972, 2,269,000. The crude marriage rate (marriages per 1,000 population) increased to 10.9 in 1972, compared with 10.6 in 1971. However, higher rates had been recorded during several earlier periods, most recently in the years immediately after World War II. Both number and rate rose about 2% in the first eight months of 1973, continuing the upward trend that began in 1959. This was due primarily to the steady increase in the number of persons reaching marriageable age, caused in turn by the sharp rise in the number of births in the decade or so after World War II.

The more detailed U.S. statistics for 1969 revealed some interesting characteristics. The rates at which formerly married men (divorced plus widowed) remarried exceeded the rates at which previously unmarried men married, but the reverse was true for women. Also, for women the first-marriage rates at ages 18–19, and 20–24, by far the most frequent ages of marriage, fell 9% and 6%, respectively, between 1963 and 1969, while at ages 25–44 the rate rose 9%. The remarriage rates for women also declined at ages under 25 but increased at all other ages. Among men the picture was reversed. This sex difference might be due to the fact that there are usually more women than men in the population at the most frequent marrying ages and this disparity had been greater in recent years.

Among countries with at least 90% complete reporting, the marriage rate increased from 1971 to 1972 in 12 and decreased in 11, with no change in 3 countries. However, as in the U.S., most countries reported increases in the early months of 1973.

Differences between marriage rates in various countries are influenced by age composition of their populations, customary age at marriage, and the frequency of common law or consensual marriages that are not officially reported.

The estimated number of divorces and annulments granted in the U.S. increased in 1972 for the tenth consecutive year. The number, 839,000, and the crude rate per 1,000 population, 4, rose 9% and 8%, respectively, above the 1971 estimates. The upward trend of divorces coincided with the rise of the number of marriages. The crude divorce rate increased about 4% per year from 1962 to 1967 and about 11% per year from 1967 to 1972.

Latest detailed statistics on divorces in the U.S., for 1969, indicated that the median duration of marriages terminated by divorce or annulment in that year was 6.9 years. The average number of minor children affected was 1.3 per divorce. The number of children affected per divorce had increased slowly but steadily during the preceding 15 years.

Among the countries reporting divorces, the U.S. consistently had the highest rate. Next highest had been the U.S.S.R., Hungary, Czechoslovakia, Denmark, East Germany, and Sweden. The lowest rates occurred in countries of Africa, Asia, and South America where divorce was not recognized or was severely restricted by law and religious proscription. A National Center for Health Statistics study of reporting countries indicated that, as in the U.S., divorce rates had generally risen during the preceding decade.

(ROBERT D. GROVE)

See also Populations and Areas.

Western Samoa

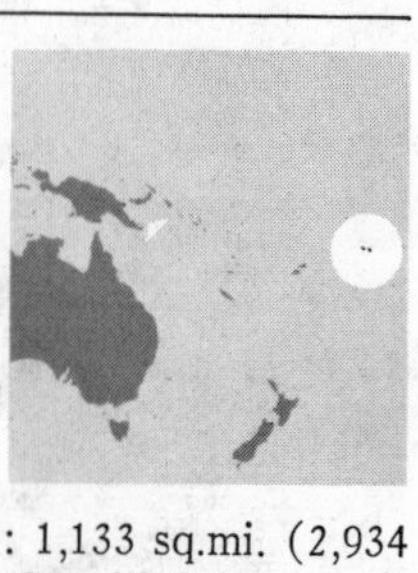

A constitutional monarchy and member of the Commonwealth of Nations, Western Samoa is an island group in the South Pacific Ocean, about 1,600 mi. E of New Zealand and 2,200 mi. S of Hawaii. Area: 1,133 sq.mi. (2,934 sq.km.), with two major islands, Savai'i (662 sq.mi.) and Upolu (435 sq.mi.), and seven smaller islands. Pop. (1973 est.): 151,000. Cap. and largest city: Apia (pop., 1971, 30,266). Language: Samoan and English. Religion: about 80% Protestant, 20% Roman Catholic. Head of state (*O le Ao o le Malo*) in 1973, Malietoa Tanumafili II; prime minister, Tupua Tamasese Lealofi IV.

A general election on Feb. 24, 1973, demonstrated strong continuity in post-independence politics. There were no political parties, but mounting challenges

continued on page 730

Wages and Hours: *see* Employment, Wages, and Hours
Wales: *see* United Kingdom
Warsaw Treaty Organization: *see* Defense
Water Resources: *see* Environment
Weather: *see* Meteorology
Welfare: *see* Social Services

WOMEN IN AMERICAN SOCIETY

By Lenore Hershey

There were more than 104 million women in the United States in 1973, outnumbering men (about 95 males to every 100 females). What kind of a year was it for American women who, 53 years after receiving the right to vote, were still conscious of inequalities, sexual discrimination, and all sorts of new pressures and problems augmenting the old ones?

On the positive side, it was a year of many definitive forward steps, political, legal, and economic. But, to match the continuing efforts of such activist women's groups as the National Organization for Women, there were also signs of status quo inertia and even a perceptible backlash to "women's lib," a term that had itself become out of date. ("The women's movement," "feminism," or "women's rights" were considered broader and less shrill labels.)

Women's power increased within both major political parties, and women's caucuses crossed party lines. Both parties had included commitments on issues of major concern to women in their 1972 platforms, and one woman, Rep. Shirley Chisholm of New York, had made a serious bid for the presidency.

The November 1972 election had resulted in an increase in the number of women in the U.S. Congress and in state legislatures. City councils, too, were becoming more and more open to women. In Congress, the only woman senator, Margaret Chase Smith, was defeated in 1972, but the election of 14 women to the House of Representatives (5 newly elected and 9 reelected) resulted in a net increase of one woman over the previous, 92nd Congress. In the state legislatures the number of women members rose 28.2%, from 344 to 441.

Perhaps the most striking item of legislation in the field was the Equal Rights Amendment to the U.S. Constitution, passed by the Senate in 1972 by a vote of 84 to 8. (The House had passed it in 1970.) Nine attempts by Sen. Sam Ervin, Jr., of North Carolina to amend this measure were defeated. At the end of 1973, the Equal Rights Amendment or, as it was familiarly known, ERA, had been ratified by 30 states of the 38 needed for final approval.

ERA, which provides that "Equality of rights under the law shall not be denied or abridged by the United States or by any state on account of sex," sharply divided women's groups. Opponents charged that the amendment would wipe out many rights and privileges women currently enjoyed, including alimony and freedom from the draft. Supporters, ranging from Pres. Richard Nixon to a broad spectrum of women's groups, felt that passage of the amendment would pave the way for relief of inequities and abolition of discriminatory practices without interfering with family responsibilities. ERA, they maintained, would not preclude adjustments based on real physical differences. Late in 1973, the AFL-CIO endorsed the amendment. Overshadowed by such issues as Watergate (in which, it should be noted, almost no women played major participatory roles), ERA moved slowly in 1973. Rep. Martha Griffiths (Dem., Mich.), one of the amendment's chief sponsors, expected such a lag in ratification, but felt that eventually it would be achieved.

A more dramatic change in the legal rights of women occurred in 1973. On January 22, with the landmark Supreme Court decision handed down in the cases of *Roe* v. *Wade* and *Doe* v. *Bolton,* the U.S. joined Great Britain, Sweden, Japan, and other countries where abortion is legal. The majority decision, written by Justice Harry Blackmun, indicated that a woman's right to decide for herself whether or not to bear a child is guaranteed under the Fourteenth Amendment. Many state laws would have to be revised to conform to the court's ruling. Meanwhile, anti-abortion forces continued to fight to protect "the right to life" of a potential human being, if necessary by nullifying the Supreme Court decision with a constitutional amendment. This clash of viewpoints would probably not be fully resolved for at least a generation.

In the areas of employment and education, women were changing the statistics. Women comprised 38% of the labour force and nearly 33 million women—more than 43% of those of working age—were employed outside the home. Most worked to support themselves and others. Some worked by choice, for fulfillment or to obtain a higher standard of living. But women still earned less than men. The average full-time annual income for women was $5,700, or 59% of the average for men working full time, and one-third of all employed women were clerical workers. Though job opportunities for women were expanding, there was still a long way to go.

Education, which plays an important role in occupational distribution, also showed a male bias. Although half of the nation's high school graduates were women, women constituted only 44% of those earning bachelor's degrees, 40% of those earning master's degrees, and a mere 14% of those awarded doctorates. Some change was seen in the professions. Women constituted 20% of the 1972 entering class of medical students, up from 13.5% in 1971. The percentage of women in law schools also rose, from 4.6% in 1967 to 12% in 1972. Nevertheless, here, too, much remained to be accomplished.

Many aspects of the changing role of women in the United States bore profound implications for the organization of the family and of society. In 1973 President Nixon appointed an advisory committee to study recommendations for furthering the cause of women. The year also saw the flowering of many feminist publications, including the successful *Ms.* magazine, created by and edited almost completely by women.

Another, supposedly "more traditional," women's magazine, *Ladies' Home Journal,* also took a forward step in recognizing the new status of women and their achievements. To counteract the Miss America Pageant and similar contests that emphasize only the physical and sexual attributes of women, the *Journal* in 1973 organized the first annual Women of the Year honours, for women doers, achievers, and shapers of American society. On the night of May 14, at the John F. Kennedy Center in Washington, D.C., in a CBS-TV network special sponsored by Clairol, eight women were presented to America, honoured both for their own accomplishments and as symbols of the total contribution women are making today. They were:

Public Affairs: *Shirley Chisholm,* black congresswoman, first woman to make a serious bid for the presidency; Economy and Business: *Katharine Graham,* president of the Washington Post Co.; Arts and Humanities: *Helen Hayes,* actress, author, humanitarian; Human Rights: *La Donna Harris,* long involved in Indian affairs; Voluntary Action: *Ellen Straus,* founder of "Call for Action," a nationwide radio citizen-assistance program; Quality of Life: *Mary Lasker,* benefactor, champion of medical research and beautification causes; Youth Leadership: *Nikki Giovanni,* young black poet; and Science and Medicine: *Virginia Apgar,* M.D., M.P.H., internationally recognized specialist in the problems of newborn infants.

These women and millions like them were proving that there were new horizons for women in America. Many women would find what they wanted by submerging themselves in their homes and families. Many would seek fulfillment by working, by doing volunteer work, or through political activities. All of these choices were to be respected and supported. But women's futures, like men's, would only improve as all Americans, male and female, found the courage to break through arbitrarily closed doors and to believe in the concept that every individual can go as high as her or his talents and determination can lead.

Lenore Hershey is the Editor of Ladies' Home Journal.

WESTERN SAMOA

Education. (1969) Primary, pupils 27,596, teachers 902; secondary, pupils 9,522, teachers 369; vocational, pupils 84, teachers 7; teacher training, students 271, teachers 17.

Finance and Trade. Monetary unit: Western Samoan dollar (tala), with (Sept. 17, 1973) a par value of WS$0.60 to U.S. $1 (nominal free rate of WS$1.44 = £1 sterling). Budget (1971 est.): revenue WS$6,478,000; expenditure WS$6,518,000. Foreign trade (1972): imports WS$13,640,000; exports WS$4 million. Import sources: New Zealand 31%; Australia 20%; Japan 15%; U.K. 8%; U.S. 6%; Fiji 5%. Export destinations: New Zealand 33%; West Germany 25%; The Netherlands 20%; U.S. 9%. Main exports: copra 45%; cocoa 28%; bananas 12%.

continued from page 728

from a younger, better-educated generation to older, more conservative, high-titled leaders. Moreover, a government that increased import duties and national indebtedness, while the cost of living skyrocketed and wages remained low, became increasingly unpopular.

The new Legislative Assembly of 45 Samoan members elected by *matai* (titled family heads) and 2 European members elected by universal adult suffrage contained 28 new members. Only 18 of the sitting members and 1 out of 5 Cabinet ministers seeking reelection were returned to their posts.

Increasing emphasis was placed on agricultural production and local industrialization. Parliamentary opposition succeeded in partly defeating government attempts to increase local revenues. The Bank of Western Samoa increased its share capital in order to expand its lending and other facilities after the government's decision to increase its shares to 50%. New Zealand undertook to increase its bilateral aid for 1973–74 by about 40% and admit at least 1,650 Samoan immigrants annually. For improved trade and shipping, the government looked to regional cooperation through the South Pacific Forum and the Pacific Islands Producers' Association.

In a resolution passed July 12, the Legislative Assembly condemned the French nuclear tests at Mururoa Atoll. (MARY BOYD)

Words and Meanings, New

With Project Apollo ended (in December 1972), **Skylab** became the word of the day, but the name of the most ethereal of Hellenic deities was perpetuated in the Apollo Telescope Mount (ATM) ultraviolet **spectroheliograph** used by the U.S. Skylab astronauts. Canada launched its own domestic satellite, **Anik** (Eskimo "little brother"), in geostationary orbit above the Equator. Europe decided to build **Spacelab,** a **sortie module** that would be taken into orbit by a reusable **space shuttle. Comet Kohoutek,** named for Lubos Kohoutek of the Hamburg (W.Ger.) Observatory, excited astronomers at the end of the year.

Both the U.S. Department of Labor and the U.K. Department of Employment computerized their help-wanted lists and called them **job banks,** whereas Launch Control at the John F. Kennedy Space Center computerized its countdown and called it **terminal sequencer.** On factory floors automation was extended to multipurpose robots called **unimates** in Europe and **versatrans** in the U.S. The electronic **sonobuoy** was devised as an effective sensor in antisubmarine warfare (ASW), and the **photic driver** was invented as an effective instrument for inducing transient faintness in urban guerrillas by combining strobe lighting with ultrasonic sound waves. The **tribometer** was invented to measure friction in machinery. To remove ambiguity from billion (one million millions in the U.K.; one thousand millions in the United States and France), it was proposed that the prefixes **tera** (from Greek *teras* "monster") and **giga** (from Greek *gigas* "giant") should be used instead.

Doomster, historically a Scottish judge, was revived as an appropriate label for those pessimists who, obsessed by a **doomwatch syndrome,** prophesied global **ecodoom** through **resource depletion** before the end of the century. The pessimists rejoined that their optimistic critics were themselves the victims of an **ostrich syndrome** when they buried their heads in the sand, refusing to face realities.

Conservationists and environmentalists alike declared that **global equilibrium,** nothing less, was their long-term aim. Following the recommendation of the UN General Assembly, not to mention the biblical example of Noah before the Flood, they applied the term **genetic banks** to those nature reserves in which rare and dying species of animals and birds would be preserved under permanent surveillance. In many cities **pedestrianization** implied the provision of car-free shopping precincts within easy walking distance of parking lots. The precincts would include shady walks or **pedestrian malls,** so named from the mall or mallet used in the once fashionable game of pall mall. Ideally, the precincts would lead off into areas of quietness or **islands of silence.**

Commuters were urged to keep their cars out of the city centres by using **park-and-ride railheads,** leaving their cars at suburban railway stations and finishing their journeys by public transport. **Transmodality** was coined as a blanket term to denote linked transportation by sea, road, rail, and inland waterway. Overweight continental trucks, plunging destructively through English towns and villages, were spontaneously christened **juggernauts** by local sufferers. This term found its way even into official documents, despite the fact that Sanskrit *Jagannatha* "world protector," avatar of Vishnu, signified the deity himself and not the enormous car in which his idol was conveyed.

Prefabricated **modular housing units** grew more and more elaborate. Oddly enough, structures of four stories or less were described as **low-rise** (as opposed to high-rise) buildings. More people than ever were buying or renting **katikias** on or near the coast of southern France for holidays or retirement.

After some time the noun phrase **postal code** became finalized in the U.K. as the simple compound **postcode.** The derivative **rebunk** was coined to denote "reestablishing a reputation previously damaged or destroyed by debunking." **Pathbreaking** was obviously a translation of German *Bahnbrechend*. More substantives in **-tron** appeared, modeled on electron (from *electric* + *on*). These included the botanists' **phytotron,** or electronic plant-breeder. The Anglo-Saxon suffix -dom was extended to **gurudom,** denoting the office of preceptor or spiritual guide in the realm of transcendental meditation. The Greek suffix -ology produced new derivatives like **acronymology, quasarology,** and **ufology** "the study of unidentified flying objects." With the widening of the EEC it was only natural that **Euro-** (**Eur-** before vowels) would become a prolific prefix, as in **Euro-**

West Indies: *see* Bahamas; Barbados; Cuba; Dependent States; Dominican Republic; Haiti; Jamaica; Latin-American Affairs; Trinidad and Tobago

Wheat: *see* Agriculture and Fisheries

Wines: *see* Alcoholic Beverages

Wool: *see* Agriculture and Fisheries; Industrial Review

World Bank: *see* Development, Economic

World Council of Churches: *see* Religion

Yachting: *see* Sailing

bank, Europatent, Europlane, Euroscience, and many more. The more euphonious **Euro-** was first used as a combining form instead of normal **Europo-** in the ad hoc compound **Euro-American** in 1928 (OED Supplement), but the style did not become firmly set until the advent of **Eurovision** (television of European range) in 1951.

Biofeedback was initiated by psychologists at the Rockefeller University in New York City. It involved the use of techniques for the precise measurement of bodily functions hitherto regarded as automatic and unconscious. It was not serious, but just a little unfortunate, that **quadraphonic** caught on as the technical term denoting four-channel sound recording in hi-fi instead of the properly formed Latin-Greek hybrid **quadriphonic,** or, better yet, all-Latin **quadrisonic** or all-Greek **tetraphonic.**

Numerous acronyms became current during the year, of which **Caad** and **Iris** merit special mention. The former stands for "computer aided architectural design" and the latter for "infrared intruder system," basically an electronic trip wire between transmitter and sensor. Two portmanteau words rose in status: the verb to **judder,** a blend of jump and shudder; and the noun **elint,** a telescoped form of **electronic intelligence.**

Among vogue words one noted **minuscule** with some misgiving because, strictly applicable to small lettering as opposed to majuscule, it was used merely as a pretentious substitute for "little, minute." **Catalyst** was another technical term that lost precision when nonchemists treated it as a kind of impressive synonym for "cause" or "agent." Another frequent favourite was **interface,** which likewise lost precision when, for instance, an instructor told his class that the emphasis in his course of lectures would lie "on the interfaces between research and development." To **erode,** etymologically "to gnaw off," and specifically a geologic term, enlarged its semantic field so widely that it came to be applied to the destruction or diminution of anything and everything from the value of the dollar to the native culture of the Eskimos. **Nub of truth** tended to supersede **moment of truth. Insightful** (German *Einsichtsvoll*) was heard early in the year and spread quickly. **Point in time,** as in "at that point in time" (rather than "at that time" or "then"), punctuated the testimony in the U.S. Senate Watergate hearings. **Consensus of opinion,** in the sense of collective judgment, "was sometimes clipped to **the consensus** (with obligatory definite article), and then, even in the quality press, it was misspelled **concensus.** (SIMEON POTTER)

Yemen, People's Democratic Republic of

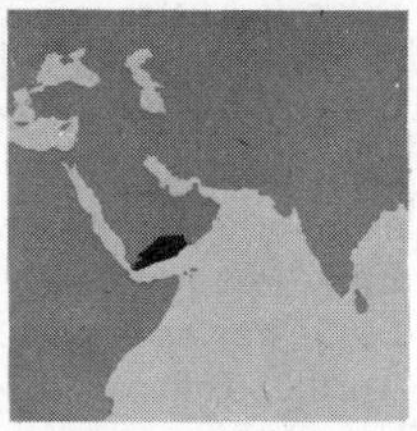

A people's republic in the southern coastal region of the Arabian Peninsula, Yemen (Aden) is bordered by Yemen (San'a'), Saudi Arabia, and Oman. Area: 111,074 sq.mi. (287,680 sq.km.). Pop. (1973 est.): 1,555,000. National cap. and largest city: Aden (pop., 1971 est., 184,000); administrative cap.: Madinat ash-Shab. Language: Arabic. Religion: Muslim. Chairman of the Presidential Council in 1973, Salem Ali Rubayyi; prime minister, Ali Nasir Muhammad Husani.

During 1973 discussions continued with the Yemen Arab Republic (YAR) government on the union between the two countries, which the two had agreed in October 1972 should take place by the end of 1973. Various difficulties arose because of mutual distrust and charges of armed aggression, and it was admitted that the union deadline would have to be postponed although spokesmen from Yemen (Aden) insisted that the objective remained. They accused elements in the YAR, supported by Saudi Arabia, of opposing the union and charged both Saudi Arabia and Oman of using mercenaries to attack the fifth and sixth governorates in the east to try to separate them from the rest of the country. They also alleged that Iranian troops were assisting Oman. Yemen (Aden) did show willingness to accept certain YAR terms, however: to grant an amnesty and permit exiles to return, and to allow the YAR to retain control over the Red Sea Karaman Islands.

In March Prime Minister Ali Nasir Muhammad toured Eastern European capitals and on his return said he had secured $32 million in loans and $5 million in aid for development. On April 30 the foreign minister, Muhammad Saleh Aulaqi, and 24 senior diplomats were killed in a DC-3 air crash while on a tour of the northeast. A new Cabinet formed on May 18 had few changes but contained two more ministers. When the Arab-Israeli war broke out in October, Aden expressed full support for the Arabs and, according to press reports, units of the country's Navy helped the Egyptians to blockade the Bab-el-Mandab straits at the southern end of the Red Sea.

(PETER MANSFIELD)

YEMEN, PEOPLE'S DEMOCRATIC REPUBLIC OF

Education. (1969–70) Primary, pupils 104,708, teachers 3,453; secondary, pupils 12,305, teachers 681; vocational, pupils 510, teachers 85; teacher training, students 235, teachers 29.

Finance and Trade. Monetary unit: Yemen dinar, with (Sept. 17, 1973) an official rate of 0.35 dinar to U.S. $1 (free rate of 0.83 dinar = £1 sterling). Budget (1970–71): revenue 13 million dinars; expenditure 18 million dinars. Foreign trade (1971): imports 64.9 million dinars; exports 43.1 million dinars. Import sources (1970): Iran 18%; Kuwait 13%; Japan 11%; United Arab Emirates 5%; U.K. 5%. Export destinations (1970): U.K. 25%; Japan 14%; Thailand 9%; Australia 6%; South Africa 6%; Spain 5%; Yemen (San'a') 5%. Main export petroleum products 74%.

Transport. Roads (1971) *c.* 4,500 km. (mainly tracks; including *c.* 220 km. with improved surface). Motor vehicles in use (1971): passenger 13,000; commercial (including buses) 3,900. There are no railways. Ships entered (1971) vessels totaling 6,598,000 net registered tons; goods loaded (1971) 3,322,000 metric tons, unloaded 4,286,000 metric tons.

Agriculture. Production (in 000; metric tons; 1971; 1970 in parentheses): millet and sorghum *c.* 75 (58); dates *c.* 8 (*c.* 8); cotton, lint 6 (5); fish catch (1970) 115, (1969) 53. Livestock (in 000; 1970–71): cattle *c.* 92; sheep *c.* 215; goats *c.* 870; camels *c.* 40.

Industry. Production (in 000; metric tons; 1971): salt 66; petroleum products 3,505; electricity (kw-hr.) 151,000.

Yemen Arab Republic

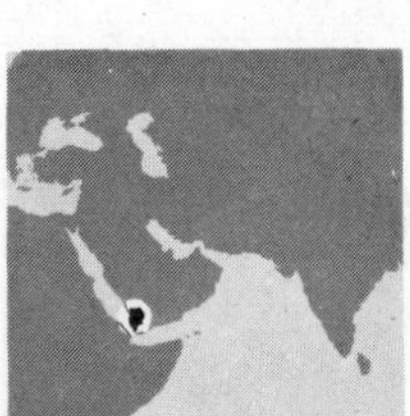

A republic situated in the southwestern coastal region of the Arabian Peninsula, Yemen (San'a') is bounded by Yemen (Aden), Saudi Arabia, and the Red Sea. Area: 77,200 sq.mi. (200,000 sq.km.). Pop. (1972 est.): 6,062,000. Cap. and largest city: San'a' (pop., 1970 est., 130,000). Language: Arabic. Religion: Muslim. President in 1973, Qadi Abdul Rahman al-Iryani; premier, Kadhi Abdullah al-Hagri.

YEMEN ARAB REPUBLIC

Education. (1969–70) Primary, pupils 72,107, teachers 1,533; secondary (1970–71), pupils 5,194, teachers (1967–68) 115; vocational (1970–71), pupils 4,057; teacher training, students 497, teaching staff (1965–66) 5.

Finance and Trade. Monetary unit: riyal, with (Sept. 17, 1973) an official rate of 4.50 riyals to U.S. $1 (free rate of 11.10 riyals = £1 sterling). Budget (1969–70 rev. est.): revenue *c.* 90 million riyals; expenditure *c.* 165 million riyals. Foreign trade (1972): imports 376.2 million riyals; exports 20.1 million riyals. Import sources: Australia 13%; Yemen (Aden) 11%; Japan 10%; France 8%; West Germany 7%; Saudi Arabia 6%; U.K. 5%; Egypt 5%. Export destinations: China 38%; Yemen (Aden) 22%; Saudi Arabia 11%; U.S.S.R. 9%; Italy 5%. Main exports: cotton 36%; coffee 27%; hides and skins 16%; kat 5%.

Agriculture. Production (in 000; metric tons; 1972; 1971 in parentheses): millet and sorghum *c.* 550 (*c.* 550); wheat *c.* 15 (*c.* 15); dates *c.* 60 (*c.* 60); coffee *c.* 3.6 (*c.* 3.6); cotton, lint *c.* 1 (*c.* 1). Livestock (in 000; March 1971): cattle *c.* 1,380; sheep *c.* 12,400; camels *c.* 59.

The replacement of Premier Mohsin al-Aini by Abdullah al-Hagri at the end of 1972 marked a move to the right and to closer relations with Saudi Arabia. It created new difficulties for plans to unite with the left-wing People's Democratic Republic of Yemen. However, talks on union continued throughout 1973 with the help of an Arab League mediator, and on May 1 a union draft charter was produced by a meeting of the political bureau of the Yemeni Union in Taez. While on a tour of Arab capitals in March, the premier agreed in Riyadh that the borders between Saudi Arabia and the republic should be those decided by the 1933 Saudi-Yemeni treaty of friendship. This provoked protests from Yemeni students.

On May 30 Sheikh Muhammad Ali Othman, the third member of the presidential council with President Iryani and the premier, was assassinated by men described by San'a' Radio as "elements from across the border," indicating the People's Democratic Republic. In August the government declared that 1,000 Yemenis had so far been killed in 360 sabotage operations, and a number of alleged saboteurs were publicly executed. A joint statement by the presidents of the two Yemens on September 13 pledged an end to aggression and the creation of an appropriate climate for an early agreement on union.

The economy grew at an annual rate of 6%, despite the burden of having to import high-priced grains. China provided £10 million to build the San'a'–Saada road; the United Arab Emirates contributed £7 million for projects that included a major educational program; Saudi Arabia was also giving educational and medical aid; and the U.S.S.R. had loaned more than £32 million. Early in the year a Mineral Resources Corp. was established, and the Royal Air Force made an aerial survey of the nation's natural resources. On September 26 the new San'a' International Airport, built with West German and British assistance, was opened. (PETER MANSFIELD)

Yugoslavia

A federal socialist republic, Yugoslavia is bordered by Italy, Austria, Hungary, Romania, Bulgaria, Greece, and Albania. Area: 98,766 sq.mi. (255,804 sq.km.). Pop. (1973 est.): 20,938,000. Cap. and largest city: Belgrade (pop., 1971, 774,744). Language: Serbo-Croatian, Slovenian, and Macedonian. Religion (1953): Orthodox 41.4%; Roman Catholic 31.8%; Muslim 12.3%. President of the republic and president of the League of Communists in 1973, Marshal Tito (Josip Broz); president of the Federal Executive Council (premier), Dzemal Bijedic.

Rapid growth of diplomatic, political, and economic links with the Soviet bloc was the main feature of Yugoslavia's foreign policy in 1973, while the domestic scene was characterized by continuation and intensification of the illiberal political course begun in December 1971.

During the Arab-Israeli war in October, Yugoslavia kept in close touch with the U.S.S.R. and gave overflying rights to Soviet transport planes carrying arms and supplies to Egypt and Syria. In November President Tito paid a four-day visit to the U.S.S.R. for talks with Soviet leaders about the Middle East and Soviet-Yugoslav relations. Economic cooperation with the U.S.S.R. was the main theme during a week-long visit paid to Yugoslavia in September by the Soviet premier, Aleksey N. Kosygin.

At the time of the visit by the Czechoslovak foreign minister, Bohuslav Chnoupek, in March, President Tito declared that problems arising out of the 1968 events in Czechoslovakia had been "overcome," and in October Czechoslovakia's Communist Party leader, Gustav Husak, paid a visit to Yugoslavia. Other top-level visitors from Soviet-bloc countries included the Polish party leader, Edward Gierek, in May, and the Hungarian party leader, Janos Kadar, in July. Also in July it was announced that a 500-km. pipeline would be built to carry crude oil from the Adriatic coast to northern Yugoslavia, Hungary, and Czechoslovakia. Stane Dolanc, secretary of the Yugoslav League of Communists' executive bureau, visited Bulgaria in February, but relations with that country remained cool until the November visit to Sofia by the Yugoslav foreign minister, Milos Minic. Dolanc also paid a visit to East Germany at the end of October.

President Tito convened a special assembly (Sabor) of the Yugoslav Federation on April 23 to unveil a new draft constitution and to confirm that Yugoslavia would remain faithful to its nonaligned foreign policy. Tito played a prominent role at the conference of nonaligned nations in Algiers in September. Yugoslavia's most prominent visitor from the West was the West German chancellor, Willy Brandt, in April. Yugoslavia's new vice-president, Mitja Ribicic, who replaced Rato Dugonjic on July 9, visited several Latin-American countries in October, including Argentina. Premier Bijedic visited Australia in March, but relations between the two countries cooled in April following the announcement that three Croat guerrillas of Australian citizenship had been executed. (*See* AUSTRALIA.)

In April President Tito's special security adviser, Gen. Ivan Miskovic, was dismissed, allegedly because of his advocacy of greater powers for the police. Vojin Lukic, who had been interior minister in Serbia before 1966, was sentenced to 18 months' imprisonment on April 28 for spreading "hostile propaganda"; on October 6 the sentence was increased by the Supreme Court to two and a half years of strict imprisonment. The purge of "liberal," "nationalist," and "technocratic" elements associated with the pre-1971 reform period continued, reaching a climax in October and November in Serbia with demands for expulsions from the party and other disciplinary measures against former liberal leaders. Numerous writers, filmmakers, and university professors were expelled from the

YUGOSLAVIA

Education. (1970–71) Primary, pupils 2,834,581, teachers 119,675; secondary, pupils 186,298, teachers 10,259; vocational, pupils 477,339, teachers 13,058; teacher training, students 16,873, teachers 1,117; higher (including 8 universities), students 282,546, teaching staff 16,783.

Finance. Monetary unit: dinar, with (Sept. 17, 1973) a free rate of 14.51 dinars to U.S. $1 (free rate of 34.98 dinars = £1 sterling). Gold, SDRs, and foreign exchange, central bank: (June 1973) U.S. $1,039,000,000; (June 1972) U.S. $467 million. Budget (1971 actual): revenue 29,682,000,000 dinars; expenditure 30,747,000,000 dinars. Gross material product: (1971) 204 billion dinars; (1970) 157 billion dinars. Money supply: (June 1972) 47,640,000,000 dinars; (June 1971) 37,620,000,000 dinars. Cost of living (1963 = 100): (June 1973) 418; (June 1972) 343.

Foreign Trade. (1972) Imports 54,957,000,000 dinars; exports 38,032,000,000 dinars. Import sources: West Germany 19%; Italy 13%; U.S.S.R. 9%; U.S. 6%; U.K. 5%; Czechoslovakia 5%; France 5%. Export destinations: U.S.S.R. 15%; Italy 14%; West Germany 12%; U.S. 7%; Czechoslovakia 6%; U.K. 5%. Main exports: machinery 13%; transport equipment 11%; nonferrous metals 10%; meat 7%; chemicals 6%; textile yarns and fabrics 5%. Tourism: (1971): visitors 5,238,700; gross receipts U.S. $360 million.

Transport and Communications. Roads (1971) 104,369 km. Motor vehicles in use (1971): passenger 875,365; commercial 122,105. Railways: (1971) 10,332 km.; traffic (1972) 10,571,000,000 passenger-km., freight 19,026,000,000 net ton-km. Air traffic (1972): 1,029,700,000 passenger-km.; freight 6,891,000 net ton-km. Shipping (1972): merchant vessels 100 gross tons and over 364; gross tonnage 1,587,585. Telephones (Dec. 1971) 821,000. Radio licenses (Dec. 1971) 3,476,000. Television licenses (Dec. 1971) 2,061,000.

Agriculture. Production (in 000; metric tons; 1972; 1971 in parentheses): wheat 4,862 (5,605); barley 487 (464); oats 267 (312); rye 120 (134); corn 7,906 (7,442); potatoes *c.* 2,985 (2,952); sunflower seed *c.* 277 (347); sugar, raw value *c.* 402 (429); dry beans *c.* 175 (173); onions (1971) 248, (1970) 266; tomatoes 372 (355); plums (1971) 817, (1970) 949; apples 316 (327); pears *c.* 115 (112); figs (1970) 22, (1969) 20; wine 626 (555); tobacco 58 (44); beef and veal (1971) *c.* 270, (1970) 245; pork (1971) *c.* 350, (1970) 339; timber (cu.m.; 1971) 16,900, (1970) 17,000; fish catch (1971) 49, (1970) 45. Livestock (in 000; Jan. 1972): cattle 5,148; sheep 8,326; pigs 6,216; horses 1,015; poultry 47,584.

Industry. Fuel and power (in 000; metric tons; 1972): coal 599; lignite 30,340; crude oil 3,198; natural gas (cu.m.) 1,242,000; manufactured gas (cu.m.) 190,000; electricity (kw-hr.) 33,178,000. Production (in 000; metric tons; 1972): cement 5,751; iron ore (35% metal content) 3,955; pig iron 2,050; crude steel 2,570; bauxite 2,196; antimony ore (metal content; 1971) 2; chrome ore (oxide content; 1971) 12; manganese ore (metal content; 1971) 5.7; aluminum 59; copper 130; lead 87; zinc 49; sulfuric acid 829; cotton yarn 101; wool yarn 42; wood pulp (1971) 518; newsprint 76; other paper (1971) 535.

party, and official pressure for Marxist indoctrination of youth increased toward the end of the year. The Roman Catholic Church and other religious groups came under attack in the press. On October 11 the Roman Catholic hierarchy issued a declaration condemning discrimination against religious believers in public life and demanding full guarantees for believers in the new constitution.

At a special conference of the Yugoslav League of Communists on May 10 and 11, Dolanc was reelected secretary of the party's executive bureau until the next party congress in the spring of 1974.

In June Yugoslavia signed a five-year nonpreferential trade agreement with the EEC, to replace the agreement signed in February 1970. In addition, Belgrade requested an improvement in the working and living conditions of the 600,000 Yugoslavs who were employed in EEC countries, but the European Commission replied that a solution was outside its jurisdiction. The strengthening of the EEC threatened to rob Yugoslavia of a good proportion of its Western European trade, especially its agricultural trade with Britain. The enlarged EEC accounted for half of Yugoslavia's trade, while Comecon accounted for less than one-third.

It was in this context that Belgrade moved to increase its economic links with the U.S. during the year, hoping thereby to present a plausible alternative to the EEC as a bargaining counter with it and with the U.S.S.R. In mid-January an agreement was signed whereby a U.S. government agency, the Overseas Private Investment Corporation (OPIC), would guarantee U.S. private investment in Yugoslavia. Plans were made to issue Yugoslav state bonds on Wall Street, and there was a possibility of U.S. participation in construction of a $250 million Yugoslav nuclear power plant.

Yugoslav exports during the first nine months of 1973 were 26% above the corresponding period in 1972, but imports rose 46%. In the same period industrial production increased by 7.2%, though labour productivity rose only 2.5% instead of 5% as planned, and the cost of living increased by about 20%. Yugoslavia's trade deficit was $1.1 billion, but invisible earnings (workers' remittances from the West and tourism) brought in $1.3 billion. In October a consortium of Western banks granted a group of Yugoslav banks a $64 million loan for the modernization of existing enterprises. (K. F. CVIIC)

Zaire

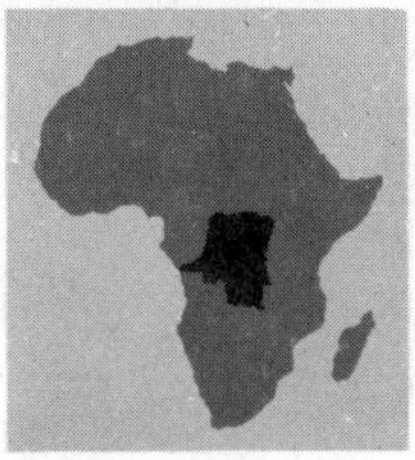

A republic of equatorial Africa, Zaire is bounded by the Central African Republic, Sudan, Uganda, Rwanda, Burundi, Tanzania, Zambia, Angola, Congo, and the Atlantic Ocean. Area: 905,360 sq.mi. (2,344,885 sq.km.). Pop. (1972 est.): 22,860,352. Cap. and largest city: Kinshasa (pop., 1973 est., 1,798,576). Language: French; Bantu dialects. Religion: animist approximately 50%; Christian 43%. President in 1973, Mobutu Sese Seko.

The formal recognition of Communist China by Zaire in November 1972 marked the beginning of a new relationship between the two countries. Early in the new year President Mobutu paid a ten-day visit to Peking as a result of which an agreement was concluded on economic and technical cooperation involving an interest-free loan from China of $100 million to assist in Zaire's agricultural development. Chou En-lai had suggested that Zaire break its diplomatic ties with Israel, and this it did on October 4.

This change in attitude toward China in no way affected Zaire's continuing friendship with major Western powers. After a tour of Europe the president announced in April that he had placed an order for 45 Mirage jet fighters and 30 Puma helicopters in France. A month later the West German cooperation minister, Erhard Eppler, visited Zaire and promised aid of $10.6 million, mainly for road construction. Mobutu hoped for further help from the same quarter to promote other projects. In June it was announced that Canada would supply Zaire with a long-term $36 million loan for help in constructing a pan-African telecommunications network. In December Mobutu paid a state visit to Great Britain.

The problem of finding employment for Zaire's own nationals led in late December 1972 to the banning of further foreign investment in small and medium-sized commercial enterprises, and on Nov. 30, 1973, sweeping nationalization measures were announced. The closing of the Rhodesia-Zambia frontier in January also threatened to create problems. Although the immediate effect seemed likely to be an increase in world copper prices, a matter of considerable importance to Zaire, there was some uncertainty as to the likely effects on the Benguela Railway, which extended through southern Zaire, of an increased demand for

Yiddish Literature: *see* Literature

ZAIRE

Education. (1970–71) Primary, pupils 3,088,011, teachers 70,000; secondary, pupils 253,234, teachers 11,755; vocational (1969–70), pupils 33,985, teachers 3,515; teacher training (1969–70), students 34,532, teachers 2,643; higher, students 12,363, teaching staff 1,386.

Finance. Monetary unit: zaire, with (Sept. 17, 1973) an official exchange rate of 0.50 zaire to U.S. $1 (free rate of 1.20 zaires = £1 sterling). Gold, SDRs, and foreign exchange, central bank: (June 1973) U.S. $114.7 million; (June 1972) U.S. $96,830,000. Budget (1971 est.): revenue 285,720,000 zaires; expenditure 249,560,000 zaires. Gross national product: (1970) 1,141,300,000 zaires; (1969) 938.1 million zaires. Money supply: (April 1973) 244,690,000 zaires; (April 1972) 202,470,000 zaires. Cost of living (Kinshasa; 1963 = 100): (May 1973) 493; (May 1972) 459.

Foreign Trade. (1970) Imports 266.5 million zaires; exports 367.7 million zaires. Import sources: Belgium-Luxembourg 24%; U.S. 11%; West Germany 10%; France 8%; U.K. 7%; Japan 7%; Italy 5%. Export destinations: Belgium-Luxembourg 43%; Italy 11%; U.K. 7%; France 7%. Main exports: copper 67%; diamonds 6%; coffee 5%.

Transport and Communications. Roads (1970) 140,000 km. Motor vehicles in use (1970): passenger 70,000; commercial 27,500. Railways (1971): 5,340 km.; traffic 751 million passenger-km., freight 2,482,000,000 net ton-km. Air traffic (1972): 610 million passenger-km.; freight 23,191,000 net ton-km. Shipping (1972): merchant vessels 100 gross tons and over 9; gross tonnage 40,221. Inland waterways (including Zaire [Congo] River; 1970) c. 13,700 km. Telephones (Dec. 1971) 41,000. Radio receivers (Dec. 1971) 75,000. Television receivers (Dec. 1971) 7,100.

Agriculture. Production (in 000; metric tons; 1972; 1971 in parentheses): rice *c.* 200 (195); corn *c.* 350 (306); sweet potatoes and yams (1971) *c.* 360, (1970) 350; cassava (1970) *c.* 10,000, (1969) 10,000; peanuts *c.* 180 (*c.* 180); dry peas *c.* 80 (*c.* 80); palm kernels *c.* 105 (*c.* 120); palm oil *c.* 180 (*c.* 197); coffee *c.* 81 (*c.* 78); sugar, raw value *c.* 45 (*c.* 42); rubber (exports) *c.* 40 (*c.* 40); cotton, lint *c.* 22 (*c.* 21); timber (cu.m.; 1970) 11,600, (1969) 11,600. Livestock (in 000; Dec. 1971): cattle *c.* 970; sheep *c.* 580; goats *c.* 1,700; pigs *c.* 450.

Industry. Production (in 000; metric tons; 1971): coal 112; copper 279; zinc 63; tin 1.4; manganese ore (metal content) 148; gold (troy oz.) 171; silver (troy oz.) 1,600; diamonds (metric carats) 12,677; electricity (kw-hr.) 3,718,000.

the transport of Zambia's copper. There were also fears that Rhodesian leader Ian Smith might attempt reprisals against Zambia that might also have repercussions in Zaire. In February, therefore, Mobutu joined Presidents Julius Nyerere and Kenneth Kaunda of Tanzania and Zambia at Arusha, Tanzania, in the first of four meetings during the year that attempted to deal with some of the immediate issues.

In spite of these uncertainties, Mobutu was anxious to press on with the expansion of Zaire's copper industry, aiming for a doubling of output by 1980. The immediate problem was to offset the balance of payments deficit created in part by overseas borrowings and the deterioration in the country's reserves that had resulted from the decline in the world price of copper. Future prosperity depended heavily on the copper market.

A problem of an entirely different character arose from the influx of thousands of refugee Hutus from Burundi, over the eastern border. With these foreign immigrants came also approximately 20,000 citizens of Zaire who had earlier moved to Burundi; the disturbed conditions in some of Zaire's smaller eastern neighbours suggested that the problem was likely to continue. In July the president had an amicable meeting with Pres. Idi Amin of Uganda, as a result of which Lakes Albert and Edward, which border the two countries, were renamed Lake Mobutu Sese Seko and Lake Idi Amin Dada. (KENNETH INGHAM)

Zanzibar:
see Tanzania

Zinc:
see Mining

Zoology:
see Life Sciences

Zambia

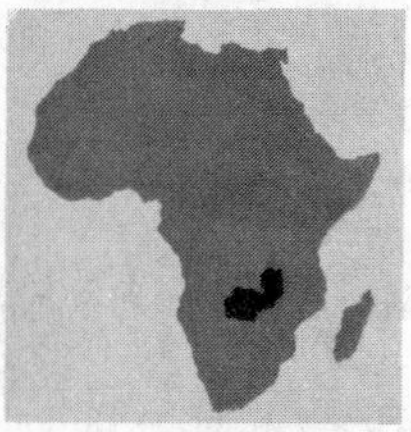

A republic and a member of the Commonwealth of Nations, Zambia is bounded by Tanzania, Malawi, Mozambique, Rhodesia, South West Africa, Angola, and Zaire. Area: 290,586 sq.mi. (752,614 sq.km.). Pop. (1973 est.): 4,635,000, of whom about 99% are Africans. Cap.: Lusaka (pop., 1973 est., 381,000). Language: English and Bantu. Religion: predominantly animist. President in 1973, Kenneth Kaunda; prime minister from December 10, Mainza Chona.

Zambia began 1973 as a one-party state on the basis of the constitution announced in December 1972. Simon Kapwepwe, leader of the former United Progressive Party (UPP), although released from jail in January after 11 months' imprisonment, said that he would not join the United National Independence Party (UNIP) as long as it remained a dictatorship. Nalumino Mundia, formerly deputy leader of the African National Congress (ANC), was detained in January, and in March 48 others were arrested in the Western Province, the stronghold of the ANC. On June 27, however, President Kaunda (*see* BIOGRAPHY) announced that the ANC leader, Harry Nkumbula, was to join the UNIP. Early in July, the new one-party constitution was republished with a number of amendments, including the ruling that there should be only one candidate for the presidency. In presidential and legislative elections held on December 5, Kaunda and the UNIP were duly reelected. A new 23-member Cabinet was formed on December 10, headed by Kaunda as president and minister of defense and with Mainza Chona as prime minister and minister of information and of national guidance and culture.

The country received a severe setback by the closing on January 9 of the Rhodesia-Zambia frontier as part of a campaign to check terrorist infiltration into Rhodesia. Coupled with the low prices offered for copper, this action threatened the country's economy, but when Rhodesia decided to reopen its frontier in February President Kaunda refused to respond. Meanwhile, Zambia continued to provide operational bases for terrorists threatening Angola, Mozambique, South West Africa, and South Africa, as well as Rhodesia. In February Presidents Kaunda, Julius Nyerere of Tanzania, and Mobutu Sese Seko of Zaire met in Arusha, Tanzania, to discuss the nationalist movements in the white-dominated states to the south and to try to evolve some means of reducing Zambia's dependence on trade routes through Rhodesia. This was followed by a visit to Zambia from a four-man UN commission, which submitted a report to the Security Council on the economic situation in Zambia. The commission suggested that Zambia would need aid of about 90 million kwachas if it was to sever its trade links with the south.

Meanwhile, reports on Zambia's internal resources were varied. Progress on the Tanzam Railway remained good. The opening on schedule of the Baluba copper mine also provided grounds for satisfaction. The new Indeni oil refinery in Ndola, however, presented difficulties as well as benefits. It was anticipated that the refinery would supply all the country's need for petroleum, but a use would have to be found for the quantities of heavy oil produced as a by-product of

ZAMBIA

Education. (1971) Primary, pupils 729,801, teachers (1970) 14,852; secondary and vocational, pupils 56,-000, teachers (1970) 2,465; teacher training, students 2,239, teachers (1970) 182; higher (1970), students 1,466, teaching staff 189.

Finance. Monetary unit: kwacha, with (Sept. 17, 1973) a par value of 0.64 kwacha to U.S. $1 (free rate of 1.55 kwachas = £1 sterling). Gold and foreign exchange, official: (June 1973) U.S. $221.4 million; (June 1972) U.S. $159.2 million. Budget (1972 est.): revenue 274 million kwachas; expenditure 297 million kwachas. Gross national product: (1970) 1,109,400,-000 kwachas; (1969) 1,192,600,000 kwachas. Cost of living (1963 = 100): (April 1973) 174; (April 1972) 166.

Foreign Trade. (1972) Imports 403,890,000 kwachas; exports 541,750,000 kwachas. Import sources (1971): U.K. 24%; South Africa 15%; U.S. 11%; Japan 7%; Rhodesia 5%; Italy 5%. Export destinations (1971): Japan 21%; U.K. 16%; Italy 11%; West Germany 9%; France 9%; China 7%. Main export copper 91%.

Transport and Communications. Roads (1969) 34,653 km. Motor vehicles in use: passenger (1971) 61,600; commercial (including buses) 34,100. Railways (1970) 1,430 km. Construction of a *c.* 1,800-km. railway linking Zambia with Dar es Salaam in Tanzania began in 1970; completion was planned for 1974. Air traffic (1972): 320.1 million passenger-km.; freight 6,484,000 net ton-km. Telephones (Dec. 1971) 57,000. Radio receivers (Dec. 1971) 80,000. Television receivers (Dec. 1971) 19,000.

Agriculture. Production (in 000; metric tons; 1972; 1971 in parentheses): corn *c.* 800 (*c.* 750); peanuts (1971) *c.* 103, (1970) *c.* 42; cassava (1970) *c.* 143, (1969) *c.* 145; millet and sorghum *c.* 250 (*c.* 250); sugar, raw value *c.* 51 (*c.* 42); tobacco *c.* 5.9 (6.5). Livestock (in 000; 1971–72): cattle *c.* 1,650; sheep *c.* 28; goats *c.* 190; pigs *c.* 110; chickens *c.* 7,000.

Industry. Production (in 000; metric tons; 1972): coal 959; copper (1971) 535; zinc 56; lead 26; electricity (kw-hr.; 1971) 1,168,000.

the refining process. This was expected to involve a changeover from coal to heavy oil as the main source of power in the copper mines, a blow to the recently developed coal mining industry. Agriculture presented other problems. Drought threatened the corn (maize) crop, and the government's program of assisting farming was not as successful as anticipated.

The fatal shooting by Zambian soldiers of two Canadian girl tourists on May 15 on the Rhodesian bank of the Zambezi River near the Victoria Falls did not prevent Canada's loaning 4,650,000 kwachas to assist Zambia in buying rolling stock in July. President Kaunda did not, however, attend the conference of Commonwealth heads of government in Ottawa in August. (KENNETH INGHAM)

Zoos and Botanical Gardens

Zoos. The days of huge collections of individual animals had passed. A new type of zoo was emerging, often comparatively small but concentrating on the breeding of rarer animals. For example, the recently opened Marwell Zoo at Winchester, Eng., aroused considerable interest by concentrating on the breeding of such rare species as scimitar-horned oryx—five of which had bred—Siberian tigers, Hartmann zebras, Przewalski's horses, and hunting dogs.

On a much larger scale, the San Diego Wild Animal Park at San Pasqual, Calif., proved not only that groups of animals bred far better in the park environment but also that they could be a very great public attraction. During its first year the park had one million visitors, double the number expected. Many animals produced young in this ideal habitat, including white rhinos and Arabian oryx.

There was a constant exchange of information among leading zoos about the breeding of rare animals, and this was one of the chief topics at the meeting of the International Union of Directors of Zoological Gardens, held at Tokyo in October 1973. The idea of studbooks to keep a check on rare animals was not a new idea; the Wisent or European Bison Studbook had been established 50 years earlier. However, three new studbooks were to be kept for maned wolf, bush dog, and spectacled bear. In keeping with the long-standing concern over the diminishing stock of several species of wild animals, zoo personnel welcomed the adoption of a Convention on International Trade in Endangered Species of Wild Fauna and Flora at a March 1973 conference in Washington, D.C. (*See* ENVIRONMENT.)

Many new zoo buildings were constructed during the year. Assiniboine Park Zoo in Winnipeg, Man., opened a $650,000 tropical house, containing reptiles, birds, and mammals; it attracted 300,000 visitors during the height of the winter, traditionally a poor time for zoo attendance. In England, London Zoo opened a completely new monkey and ape section at a cost of £250,000, while Chester Zoo continued to construct dry moat enclosures for its ever increasing ungulate collection. Taronga Zoo in Sydney, Austr., finished its Animals of the Night exhibit, and Oklahoma City Zoo completed an ambitious project called Condor Cliffs and Pampas Panorama.

The more successful zoos became at breeding animals, the more difficult it was to achieve a "first breeding" of a species. However, West Berlin bred the mountain anoa for the first time, as well as a Mayotte lemur, a subspecies of the brown lemur. Lincoln Park Zoo, Chicago, Ill., bred the Madagascan ground boa, which was thought to be a possible first. Whipsnade Park, Eng., recorded the birth of second-generation cheetah cubs, a species seldom bred until recent years.

A custody fight developed during the year over Patty Cake, a gorilla born in 1972 at the Central Park Zoo in New York City. Patty Cake had remained with her parents until March 1973, when she broke her arm and was taken to the Bronx Zoo for medical attention. At Bronx Zoo, where the baby gorilla was constantly attended by a human nurse, it was found that she was underweight and had intestinal parasites, and Bronx Zoo officials demanded that she remain with them so she could receive proper care. The matter was finally mediated by Ronald Nadler of the

A day-old female southern white rhinoceros, only the sixth member of this endangered species ever born in the U.S., stands beside its mammoth mother, Trina, at Lion Country Safari, near Dallas, Tex. The 150-lb. calf was born June 14, 1973.

UPI COMPIX

Yerkes Regional Primate Research Center, Atlanta, Ga., who determined that Patty Cake should be returned to Central Park because apes raised by their parents were more "socially competent and reproductively adequate."

The first giant pandas ever exhibited in Japan were received at the Ueno Zoological Gardens, Tokyo, presented to the people of Japan by China.

The rarest bird in the world was apparently the Mauritius kestrel, with only 10 or 12 specimens left in the wild. Many other birds of prey had declined at an alarming rate, and until recently had been rather neglected as breeding species in captivity. However, Woodland Park Zoological Gardens, Seattle, Wash., began a breeding program, Wisconsin bred a red-tailed hawk, and many other zoos were setting up breeding pairs of birds of prey. (G. S. MOTTERSHEAD)

Botanical Gardens. The California Arboretum Foundation, which sponsored the arboretum at Arcadia, celebrated its 25th anniversary in 1973. At the Botanischer Garten, Munich, W.Ger., popular interest in conservation was reflected in the establishment of a department for plants protected in West Germany; an alpine plant house was opened for the first time.

Experimental work continued in various botanical gardens on the cultivation of species requiring cooler conditions than those prevailing outside. Cool micro-environments in growth chambers with controlled illumination were successful in seed germination trials at the Royal Botanic Gardens, Kew, Eng. In previous years, arctic species had been successfully cultivated in small refrigerated greenhouses at Copenhagen and elsewhere. A much less elaborate process was used to cool large greenhouses at the Botanic Garden, Christchurch, N.Z. Two 24-in. diameter fans were installed at one end of each greenhouse, while at the opposite end a gauze jacket 5 ft. high and 16 ft. long with a 2-in. inner layer of wood-wool formed the entrance for incoming air. When the thermostatically controlled fans were activated, water trickled through the jacket, thus cooling the air entering the greenhouse. An air-conditioned greenhouse for the exhibition of plants requiring cooler temperatures was also being built at the Singapore Botanic Gardens.

Computerization and electronic data processing were assuming increasing importance in large botanical gardens. The Royal Botanic Garden, Edinburgh, Scot., for example, had resurveyed all its plant holdings and computerized the records. A catalog from the printout was in production.

In South Africa the 560-ha. National Botanic Gardens at Kirstenbosch continued to concentrate on indigenous flora. The upper regions on Table Mountain formed a reserve for plants native to the area, with management amounting to the removal of alien plants. Of the 50 ha. under cultivation, half were devoted to Proteaceae; by late 1973 most of the 13 South African genera, totaling over 400 species, were represented. A further five hectares were being developed for growing many of the 600 native species of Ericaceae. The first botanical garden in South West Africa (Namibia), at Windhoek, was being laid out for the display of succulent plants. Since the area was largely free of frost, it was expected that the delicate plants from the northern part of the country could be grown successfully. A new botanical garden in the Dominican Republic planned to collect palms and ferns.

Conservation formed an increasingly important aspect of many botanical gardens, in view of environmental pollution and the deterioration of botanical habitats. Seed banks of rare or endangered species were being assembled, and many gardens concentrated on the flora of their own regions for educational and scientific purposes. The refrigerated seed bank at the Royal Botanic Gardens, Kew, was being expanded into the foremost collection of its kind in the world.

Also at Kew, the site of the old herb garden was laid out with island beds displaying bulbous plants for all seasons. As part of the effort to enhance the educational function of the gardens, an orientation area was established in the Orangery and modernized, informative labeling was being used. The layout of special collections such as orchids, gesneriads, and succulents was modernized. The scientific role of the satellite garden at Wakehurst Place was established with the transference there of the plant physiology section. The garden itself was being developed rapidly; increased plantings of exotic species were made in areas cleared since the take-over by Kew.

(FRANK N. HEPPER)

ENCYCLOPÆDIA BRITANNICA FILMS. *Zoo's-Eye View: Dawn to Dark* (1973).

NEW YORK ZOOLOGICAL SOCIETY

One of the Bronx (N.Y.) Zoo's newest additions, an aerial tramway cable car, makes a trial run before opening to the public, May 5, 1973. The transit system, projected to have a maximum of 34 cars carrying 2,400 people an hour, allows riders a bird's-eye view not only of the zoo but also of much of the New York area.

CONTRIBUTORS

Names of contributors to the Britannica Book of the Year *with the articles written by them.*
The arrangement is alphabetical by last name.

AARSDAL, STENER. Economic Editor, *Børsen.* Press Officer, Chamber of Commerce, Copenhagen.
Denmark

ACCARDO, JOSEPH J. Washington Columnist.
Energy (*in part*)

AGRELLA, JOSEPH C. Turf Editor, *Chicago Sun-Times.* Author of *Ten Commandments for Professional Handicapping.*
Horse Racing (*in part*)

AGUS, JACOB B. Visiting Professor of Modern Jewish Philosophy, Dropsie University, Philadelphia, Pa. Author of *The Evolution of Jewish Thought; Dialogue and Tradition.*
Religion (*in part*)

ALDRIDGE, JOHN M. Assistant Editor and Passenger Transport Editor, *Motor Transport,* London.
Transportation (*in part*)

ALLABY, MICHAEL. Managing Editor of the *Ecologist,* Wadebridge, Eng. Author of *The Eco-Activists; Who Will Eat?; A Blueprint for Survival.*
Environment (*in part*)

ALLAN, J. A. Lecturer in Geography, School of Oriental and African Studies, University of London.
Libya

ALLEN, V. L. Professor of the Sociology of Industrial Society, University of Leeds, Eng. Author of *Power in Trade Unions; Trade Union Leadership; Trade Unions and the Government; Militant Trade Unionism; International Bibliography of Trade Unionism; Sociology of Industrial Relations.*
Labour Unions

ALMAN, ABE. Deputy Editor, *Motor Transport,* London.
Transportation (*in part*)

ALSTON, REX. Broadcaster and Journalist. Author of *Taking the Air; Over to Rex Alston; Test Commentary; Watching Cricket.*
Cricket

ANTONINI, GUSTAVO ARTHUR. Associate Professor, Center for Latin American Studies, University of Florida.
Dominican Republic

ARCHIBALD, JOHN J. Writer, *St. Louis Post-Dispatch.* Author of *Bowling for Boys and Girls.*
Bowling and Lawn Bowls (*in part*)

ARMSTRONG, A. G. Lecturer, Department of Economics, University of Bristol, Eng.
Investment, International; Trade, International

ARNOLD, BRUCE. Free-lance Journalist and Writer, Dublin.
Biography (*in part*); **Ireland**

ARRINGTON, LEONARD JAMES. Church Historian, Church of Jesus Christ of Latter-day Saints. Author of *Great Basin Kingdom: An Economic History of the Latter-day Saints.*
Religion (*in part*)

ASTROM, ERIC A. Executive Assistant to the President, The Ontario Jockey Club; Director, National Association of Canadian Race Tracks.
Horse Racing (*in part*)

AYTON, CYRIL J. Editor, *Motorcycle Sport,* London.
Motor Sports (*in part*)

BACHMAN, WILFRED A. Senior Editor, *The Oil and Gas Journal,* Tulsa, Okla.
Industrial Review (*in part*)

BAILY, MICHAEL. Shipping and Transport Correspondent, *The Times,* London.
Transportation (*in part*)

BARROS, SALVADOR. Literary Critic, *Vision.* Lecturer in Latin American Literature, University of Mexico.
Literature (*in part*)

BASS, HOWARD. Journalist and Broadcaster. Editor, *Winter Sports,* 1948–69; Winter Sports Correspondent, *Daily Telegraph,* London; *Christian Science Monitor,* Boston; *Canadian Skater,* Vancouver; *Skate,* London; *Skating,* Boston; *Ski Racing,* Denver; *Sportsworld,* London. Author of *The Sense in Sport; This Skating Age; The Magic of Skiing; Winter Sports; Success in Ice Skating; International Encyclopaedia of Winter Sports.*
Biography (*in part*); **Hockey** (*in part*); **Ice Skating; Skiing**

BEATTY, J. R. Senior Research Associate, B. F. Goodrich Research Center, Brecksville, O.
Rubber

BECKWITH, DAVID CAMERON. Correspondent, *Time* magazine, Washington, D.C.
United States Statistical Supplement: *Developments in the states in 1973*

BEDDOES, R. H. Sports Columnist, *Toronto Globe and Mail.*
Hockey (*in part*)

BEEMAN, WILLIAM J. Senior Economist, Board of Governors of the U.S. Federal Reserve System.
Government Finance (*in part*)

BELTRAN, WILLIAM. Senior Economic Research Officer, Lloyds and Bolsa International Bank Ltd., London.
Argentina; Colombia

BERÈS, PIERRE. Managing Director, Hermann Publishing Company, Paris. Expert in rare books.
Art Sales (*in part*)

BERGERRE, MAX. Correspondent ANSA for Vatican Affairs, Rome.
Vatican City State

BERGSTEIN, STANLEY F. Executive Secretary, Harness Tracks of America Inc.; Vice-President, United States Trotting Association.
Horse Racing (*in part*)

BICKELHAUPT, DAVID L. Professor of Insurance, College of Administrative Science, Ohio State University. Author of *Transition to Multiple-Line Insurance Companies.* Co-author of *General Insurance.*
Insurance

BILEFIELD, LIONEL. Technical Journalist.
Industrial Review (*in part*)

BLYTH, ALAN. Music Critic, London.
Music (*in part*)

BOBBITT, JOHN T. Executive Producer, Social Studies, Encyclopædia Britannica Educational Corporation. Films include *The Bill of Rights of the United States; The Congress; The Constitution of the United States; The Declaration of Independence by the Colonies; The Supreme Court; Productivity: Key to Plenty.*
Motion Pictures (*in part*)

BODDY, WILLIAM C. Editor, *Motor Sport.* Full Member, Guild of Motoring Writers. Author of *The Story of Brooklands; The 200 Mile Race; The World's Land Speed Record; Continental Sports Cars; The Sports Car Pocketbook; The Bugatti Story; History of Montlhéry; Vintage Years of the Morgan Three-wheeler.*
Motor Sports (*in part*)

BOLT, PETER H. Chaplain, Leys School, Cambridge, Eng. Secretary, British Committee, World Methodist Council. Author of *A Way of Loving.*
Religion (*in part*)

BOONSTRA, DICK. Assistant Professor, Department of Political Science, Free University, Amsterdam.
Biography (*in part*); **Netherlands, The**

BOOTH, JOHN NICHOLLS. Unitarian Universalist clergyman. Co-founder, Japan Free Religious Association. Author of *The Quest for Preaching Power; Introducing Unitarian Universalism.*
Religion (*in part*)

BOSWALL, JEFFERY. Producer of Sound and Television Programs, British Broadcasting Corporation Natural History Unit, Bristol, Eng.
Life Sciences (*in part*)

BOYD, MARY. Reader in History, Victoria University of Wellington, N.Z.
Fiji; Tonga; Western Samoa

BOYLE, C. L. Lieutenant Colonel, R.A. (retd.). Chairman, Survival Service Commission, International Union for Conservation of Nature and Natural Resources, 1958–63; Secretary, Fauna Preservation Society, London, 1950–63.
Environment (*in part*)

BRACKMAN, ARNOLD C. Author of *Indonesian Communism: A History; Southeast Asia's Second Front: The Power Struggle in the Malay Archipelago; The Communist Collapse in Indonesia.*
Indonesia

BRAIDWOOD, ROBERT J. Professor of Old World Prehistory, the Oriental Institute and the Department of Anthropology, the University of Chicago.
Archaeology (*in part*)

BRAZEE, RUTLAGE J. Senior Seismologist, Solid Earth Data Services Division, D62, NOAA, Boulder, Colo.
Seismology

BRICKHOUSE, JACK. Vice-President and Manager of Sports, WGN Continental Broadcasting Company.
Baseball (*in part*)

BRIERRE, ANNIE. Literary Critic, *La Croix Histoire Pour Tous; La Revue des Deux Mondes; France—U.S.A.* Author of *Ninon de Lenclos.*
Literature (*in part*)

BRONNER, EDWIN. Professor of History and Curator of the Quaker Collection, Haverford (Pa.) College. Author of *William Penn's Holy Experiment.* Editor, *American Quakers Today; An English View of American Quakerism.*
Religion (*in part*)

BURDIN, JOEL L. Associate Director, American Association of Colleges for Teacher Education; Director, ERIC Clearinghouse on Teacher Education. Author of *A Reader's Guide to the Comprehensive Models for Preparing Elementary Teachers.* Co-author of *Elementary School Curriculum and Instruction.*
Education (*in part*)

BURKE, DONALD P. Senior Editor, *Chemical Week.*
Industrial Review (*in part*)

BURKS, ARDATH W. Professor and Director, International Programs, Rutgers University, New Brunswick, N.J. Author of *The Government of Japan; East Asia: China, Korea, Japan.*
Japan

BUSHONG, ALLEN D. Associate Professor of Geography, University of South Carolina.
El Salvador; Honduras

BUTLER, FRANK. Sports Editor, *News of the World,* London. Author of *A History of Boxing in Britain.*
Boxing

BYRNE, DON. Associate Editor, *Traffic World Magazine,* Washington, D.C.
Telecommunications (*in part*)

CALASCIONE, JOHN. Press and Publications Officer, International Organization of Consumers Unions, The Hague, Neth.
Consumer Affairs (*in part*)

CAMPBELL, H. C. Chief Librarian, Toronto Public Library, Toronto.
Literature (*in part*)

CARSANIGA, GIOVANNI. Reader in Italian, University of Sussex, Eng.
Literature (*in part*)

CHALMEY, LUCIEN. Adviser, Union Internationale des Producteurs et Distributeurs d'Énergie Électrique, Paris.
Energy (*in part*)

CHAPMAN, KENNETH F. Editor, *Stamp Collecting;* Philatelic Correspondent, *The Times,* London. Author of *Good Stamp Collecting; Commonwealth Stamp Collecting.*
Philately and Numismatics (*in part*)

CHAPMAN, ROBIN. Senior Economic Research Officer, Lloyds and Bolsa International Bank Ltd., London.
Cuba; Haiti; Portugal; Latin-American Affairs

CHAPPELL, DUNCAN. Director, Law and Justice Study Center, Battelle Memorial Institute, Seattle, Washington. Co-author of *The Police and the Public in Australia and New Zealand; The Australian Criminal Justice System.*
Crime (*in part*)

CHAUSSIN, ROBERT. Government Civil Engineer, SETRA (Service d'études Techniques des Routes et Autoroutes), Bagneux, France.
Engineering Projects (*in part*)

CHU, HUNG-TI. Expert in Far Eastern Affairs. UN Area Specialist and Chief of Asia-Africa Section and Trusteeship Council Section, 1946–67; Professor of Government, Texas Tech. University, Lubbock, 1968–69.
China; Taiwan

CLEARY, BARBARA W. Production Coordinator, *Great Ideas Today.*
Biography (*in part*)

CLIFTON, DONALD F. Professor of Metallurgy, University of Idaho.
Metallurgy

COGLE, T. C. J. Technical Editor, *Electrical Review,* London.
Industrial Review (*in part*)

COOTE, JAMES. Athletics Correspondent, *The Daily Telegraph,* London. Author of *Olympic Report 1968; The Olympics 1972; A Picture History of the Olympics.*
Track and Field Sports (*in part*)

COPELAND, JAMES C. Associate Professor, Department of Microbiology, Ohio State University.
Life Sciences (*in part*)

COSTIN, STANLEY H. London Correspondent, *Nykytekstiili* (Finland); British Correspondent, *Herrenjournal International.* President, Men's Fashion Writers International.
Fashion and Dress (*in part*)

CRATER, RUFUS W. Chief Correspondent, *Broadcasting,* New York City.
Television and Radio (*in part*)

CROSSLAND, NORMAN. Bonn Correspondent, *The Guardian,* London, and British Broadcasting Corporation.
Biography (*in part*); Germany (*in part*)

CVIIC, K. F. Leader Writer and East European Specialist, *The Economist,* London.
Yugoslavia

DAIFUKU, HIROSHI. Director, Sites and Monuments Division, UNESCO, Paris.
Historic Buildings

DAVID, TUDOR. Managing Editor, *Education,* London.
Education (*in part*)

DAWBER, ALFRED. Textile consultant in all aspects of textile production. Specialized writer on textile, engineering, and electrical subjects.
Industrial Review (*in part*)

DEANE, RALPH. Economic Research Officer, Lloyds and Bolsa International Bank Ltd., London.
Spain

d'ECA, RAUL. Formerly Fulbright Visiting Lecturer on American History, University of Minas Gerais, Belo Horizonte, Braz. Co-author of *Latin American History.*
Brazil

DECRAENE, PHILIPPE. Member of editorial staff, *Le Monde,* Paris. Editor in Chief, *Revue française d'Études politiques africaines.* Author of *Le Panafricanisme; Tableau des Partis Politiques Africains.*
Cameroon; Central African Republic; Chad; Congo; Dahomey; Dependent States (*in part*); Gabon; Guinea; Ivory Coast; Malagasy Republic; Mali; Mauritania; Niger; Senegal; Togo; Tunisia; Upper Volta

DeGOES, LOUIS. Executive Secretary, Committee on Polar Research, National Academy of Sciences, Washington, D.C.
Antarctica

de la BARRE, KENNETH. Director, Montreal Office, Arctic Institute of North America.
Arctic Regions

DEMPSEY, GEOFFREY. Fellow of Institute of Practitioners in Advertising, J. Walter Thompson Co. Ltd., London.
Advertising (*in part*)

DENNERSTEIN, R. J. M. Associate Editor, *Encyclopædia Britannica,* London.
Biography (*in part*); Equatorial Guinea

DE PUY, NORMAN R. Executive Director, Division of Communication, American Baptist Churches, USA, Valley Forge, Pa. Author of *The Bible Alive.*
Religion (*in part*)

DILLARD, DUDLEY. Professor and Chairman, Department of Economics, University of Maryland. Author of *The Economics of John Maynard Keynes; Economic Development of the North Atlantic Community.*
Economics

DIRNBACHER, ELFRIEDE. Austrian Civil Servant.
Austria

EDLIN, HERBERT L. Publications Officer, Forestry Commission of Great Britain. Author of *Trees, Woods and Man; Wayside and Woodland Trees; Man and Plants; What Wood Is That?; Guide to Tree Planting and Cultivation.* Co-author of *Atlas of Plant Life.*
Environment (*in part*)

EDWARDS, JOHN. Research Fellow, Southampton (Eng.) University. Author of *Social Patterns in Birmingham.*
Housing

EISENBERG, WARREN W. Administrative Assistant to Rep. H. John Heinz III, Washington, D.C.
Populations and Areas

ENGELS, JAN R. Editor, *Vooruitgang* (Quarterly of the Belgian Party for Freedom and Progress).
Belgium; Biography (*in part*)

EWART, W. D. Editor and Director, *Fairplay International Shipping Journal.* Author of *Marine Engines; Atomic Submarines; Hydrofoils and Hovercraft; Building a Ship.* Editor of *World Atlas of Shipping.*
Industrial Review (*in part*)

FARR, D. M. L. Professor of History, Carleton University, Ottawa. Author of *The Colonial Office and Canada, 1867–1887; Two Democracies; The Canadian Experience.*
Canada

FENDELL, ROBERT J. New York Editor, *Automotive News.* Automobile Columnist for *Gentleman's Quarterly.* President Emeritus, International Motor Press Association. Co-author, *Encyclopedia of Motor Racing Greats.*
Motor Sports (*in part*)

FERRIER, R. W. Group Historian, British Petroleum.
Energy (*in part*)

FIDDICK, PETER. Feature Editor, *The Guardian*, London.
Publishing *(in part)*

FOWELL, R. J. Lecturer, Department of Mining Engineering, University of Newcastle upon Tyne, Eng.
Energy *(in part)*

FRANKLIN, HAROLD. Editor, *English Bridge Quarterly*. Bridge Correspondent, *Yorkshire Post; Yorkshire Evening Post*. Broadcaster. Author of *Best of Bridge on the Air*.
Contract Bridge

FREDRICKSON, DAVID A. Associate Professor of Anthropology, Sonoma State College, Rohnert Park, Calif.
Archaeology *(in part)*

FREEMAN, KENNETH C. Fellow, Department of Astronomy, Australian National University (Mt. Stromlo and Siding Spring Observatory), Australia.
Astronomy *(in part)*

FRIDOVICH, IRWIN. Professor of Biochemistry, Duke University Medical Center, Durham, N.C.
Life Sciences *(in part)*

FRIEDLY, ROBERT L. Director, Office of Communication, Christian Church (Disciples of Christ), Indianapolis, Ind.
Religion *(in part)*

FRIEDMAN, IRVING S. Professor in Residence and formerly Economic Adviser to the President of the International Bank for Reconstruction and Development, 1964–70. Author of *Exchange Controls and the International Monetary System; U.S. Foreign Economic Policy*.
Development, Economic

FROST, DAVID. Rugby Union Correspondent, *The Guardian*, London.
Football *(in part)*

FULLER, M. F. Lecturer in Economic and Social Statistics, Darwin College, University of Kent at Canterbury, Eng.
Income, National

GADDUM, PETER W. Chairman, H. T. Gaddum and Company Ltd., Silk Merchants, Macclesfield, Cheshire, Eng. President, International Silk Association, Lyons. Author of *Silk—How and Where It Is Produced*.
Industrial Review *(in part)*

GALVANO, FABIO. Special Correspondent, *Gazzetta del Popolo*, Turin, Italy.
Biography *(in part)*; **Italy**

GANADO, ALBERT. Lawyer, Malta.
Malta

GEORGE, T. J. S. Regional Editor, *Far Eastern Economic Review*, Hong Kong. Author of *Krishna Menon: A Biography; Lee Kuan Yew's Singapore*.
Biography *(in part)*; **Cambodia; Korea; Laos; Southeast Asian Affairs; Thailand; Vietnam** *(in part)*

GJESTER, FAY. Oslo Correspondent, *Financial Times*, London.
Norway

GLIKSON, PAUL. Secretary, Division of Jewish Demography and Statistics, Institute of Contemporary Jewry, the Hebrew University of Jerusalem, Israel.
Religion *(in part)*

GODWIN, MORGAN. W. Assistant Secretary, American Radio Relay League, Newington, Conn.
Television and Radio *(in part)*

GOLLAND, B. L. General Secretary, the General Assembly of Unitarian and Free Christian Churches, London.
Religion *(in part)*

GOLOMBEK, HARRY. British Chess Champion, 1947, 1949, and 1955. Chess Correspondent, *The Times* and *Observer*, London. Author of *Penguin Handbook on the Game of Chess; Modern Opening Chess Strategy*.
Chess

GOODWIN, R. M. Assistant Editor, *Encyclopædia Britannica*, London.
Horse Racing *(in part)*

GORALSKI, ROBERT. NBC News Washington Correspondent.
Vietnam *(in part)*

GOULD, DONALD W. Medical Correspondent, *The New Statesman*, London.
Drugs and Narcotics *(in part)*; **Medicine** *(in part)*

GRAHAM, JARLATH JOHN. Editor, *Advertising Age*.
Advertising *(in part)*

GRANGER, BILL. Reporter, *Chicago Sun-Times*. Teacher, Columbia College, Chicago. Free-lance Writer.
Biography *(in part)*

GRAY, PAUL. Contributing Editor, *Time* magazine.
Publishing *(in part)*

GREEN, BENNY. Jazz Critic, *Observer*, London; Record Reviewer, British Broadcasting Corporation. Author of *The Reluctant Art; Blame It on My Youth; 58 Minutes to London; Jazz Decade; Drums in My Ears*. Contributor to *Encyclopedia of Jazz*.
Music *(in part)*

GREENOUGH, RICHARD D. A. Former Chief English writer, Press Division, UNESCO, Paris. Author of *Africa Prospect; Children's Progress; Africa Calls*.
United Nations *(in part)*

GRIFFITHS, A. R. G. Lecturer in History, Flinders University of South Australia.
Australia; Biography *(in part)*; **Nauru**

GRINKER, ROY R., SR. Chairman, Department of Psychiatry, and Director, Psychiatric Institute, Michael Reese Hospital Medical Center, Chicago. Author of *Men Under Stress; Psychosomatic Research*. Co-author of *Borderline Syndrome*.
Medicine *(in part)*

GROVE, ROBERT D. Former Director, Division of Vital Statistics, U.S. Public Health Service. Co-author of *Vital Statistics Rates in the United States, 1900–1940; Vital Statistics Rates in the United States, 1940–1960*.
Vital Statistics

HACHTEN, WILLIAM A. Professor, School of Journalism and Mass Communication, University of Wisconsin, Madison.
Publishing *(in part)*

HAIGH, CLIFFORD. Editor, *The Friend*, London.
Religion *(in part)*

HAMILTON, DAVID. Professor of Economics, Department of Economics, University of New Mexico, Albuquerque. Author of *The Consumer in Our Economy; A Primer on the Economics of Poverty*.
Consumer Affairs *(in part)*

HARRIES, DAVID A. Chief Engineer, Mitchell Construction Ltd. and Kinnear Moodie Ltd., Peterborough, Eng.
Engineering Projects *(in part)*

HARRIS, LEONARD R. Executive Vice-President and Publisher, World Publishing Company.
Publishing *(in part)*

HASEGAWA, RYUSAKU. Editor, TBS-Britannica Ltd., Tokyo.
Biography *(in part)*

HATELY, DAVID. Associate Editor, *Encyclopædia Britannica*, London.
Biography *(in part)*; **Literature** *(in part)*

HATHAWAY, RICHARD O. Teaching Faculty, History and International Studies, Goddard College, Plainfield, Vt. Member, Board of Editors, *Current*.
Peace Movements

HAUSER, PHILIP M. Professor of Sociology and Director, Population Research Center, the University of Chicago. Editor of *Urbanization in Latin America*.
Cities and Urban Affairs *(in part)*

HAWKLAND, WILLIAM D. Professor of Law, University of Illinois. Author of *Sales Under Uniform Commercial Code; Cases on Bills and Notes; Commercial Paper; Transactional Guide of the Uniform Commercial Code; Cases on Sales and Security*.
Law *(in part)*

HAWLEY, H. B. Consultant, Human Nutrition and Food Science, Sherborne, Eng.
Food Processing *(in part)*

HAWTIN, GUY. Industrial Journalist, London.
Transportation *(in part)*

HEBBLETHWAITE, THE REV. PETER, S.J. Editor, *The Month*, London. Author of *Bernanos; The Council Fathers and Atheism; Understanding the Synod*. Editor of *Faith in Question; Talking with Unbelievers*.
Religion *(in part)*

HENDERSHOTT, MYRL C. Assistant Professor of Oceanography, Scripps Institution of Oceanography, La Jolla, Calif.
Oceanography

HEPPER, FRANK N. Principal Scientific Officer, Herbarium, Royal Botanic Gardens, Kew, Eng. Co-author of *Plant Collectors in West Africa*. Editor of *Flora of West Tropical Africa* (vol. ii and iii).
Zoos and Botanical Gardens *(in part)*

HOCKLEY, G. C. Senior Lecturer, Department of Economics, University College, Cardiff, Wales. Author of *Monetary Policy and Public Finance*. Co-author of *The Wealth of the Nation: The Balance Sheet of the United Kingdom, 1957–61*.
Taxation *(in part)*

HODGSON, ROBERT D. The Geographer, U.S. Department of State, Washington, D.C. Author of *The Changing Map of Africa*.
Andorra; Liechtenstein; Luxembourg; Monaco; San Marino

HOLLANDS, R. L. Hockey Correspondent, the *Daily Telegraph*, London. Co-author of *Hockey*.
Hockey *(in part)*

HOLZ, ERNEST W. National Chief Secretary and Colonel, Salvation Army, U.S.A.
Religion *(in part)*

HOPE, RICHARD ARTHUR. Editor, *Railway Gazette International*, London.
Transportation *(in part)*

HOPE, THOMAS W. President, *Hope Reports*, Rochester, N.Y.
Motion Pictures *(in part)*

HORN, PATRICE DAILY. Editor, *Behavior Today*; Senior Editor, *Psychology Today*, Del Mar, Calif.
Behavioural Sciences

HOTZ, LOUIS. Former editorial writer, the *Johannesburg* (S.Af.) *Star.* Co-author and contributor to *The Jews in South Africa: A History.*
South Africa

HUGHES, PHILIPPA. Economic Research Officer, Lloyds and Bolsa International Bank Ltd., London.
Mexico

HUGHES, TERENCE. Special Assistant, International Broadcast Institute, London.
Television and Radio (*in part*)

HUNNINGS, NEVILLE MARCH. General Editor, Common Law Reports Ltd., London. Editor of *Common Market Law Reports, European Law Digest,* and *Eurolaw Commercial Intelligence.* Author of *Film Censors and the Law.* Co-editor of *Legal Problems of an Enlarged European Community.*
Law (*in part*)

HURTIG, SERGE. Secretary General, Fondation Nationale des Sciences Politiques; Professor, Paris Institute of Political Studies. Former Secretary-General, International Political Science Association.
Political Science

IKER, SAMUEL R. Environment Correspondent, *Time* magazine, Washington, D.C.
Environment (*in part*)

INGHAM, KENNETH. Professor of History, University of Bristol, Eng. Author of *Reformers in India; A History of East Africa.*
Dependent States (*in part*); Kenya; Malawi; Rhodesia; Tanzania; Uganda; Zaire; Zambia

ISSA (INTERNATIONAL SOCIAL SECURITY ASSOCIATION), Geneva.
Social Services (*in part*)

ITU (INTERNATIONAL TELECOMMUNICATION UNION), Geneva.
Telecommunications (*in part*)

IULA. Research staff, International Union of Local Authorities, The Hague, Neth.
Cities and Urban Affairs (*in part*)

JACKSON, D. A. S. Research Officer, Department of Applied Economics, University of Cambridge; Fellow of St. Catharine's College, Cambridge.
Employment, Wages, and Hours

JACQUET, CONSTANT H. JR. Staff Associate for Information Services, Office of Research, Evaluation, and Planning, National Council of Churches. Editor, *Yearbook of American and Canadian Churches.*
United States Statistical Supplement: *Church Membership Table*

JARDINE, ADRIAN. Company Director and Public Relations Consultant. Secretary, Guild of Yachting Writers.
Sailing

JASPERT, W. PINCUS. Technical editorial consultant. European Editor, North American Publishing Company, Philadelphia, Pa. Member, Society of Photographic Scientists and Engineers. Editor of *Encyclopaedia of Type Faces.*
Industrial Review (*in part*)

JOHN, LAURIE. Producer, Science Unit, British Broadcasting Corporation (radio).
Telecommunications (*in part*)

JONES, C. M. Editor, *World Bowls; Lawn Tennis.* Author of *Winning Bowls; The Watney Book of Bowls; Bowls; How to Become a Champion.* Co-author of *Tackle Bowls My Way; Bryant on Bowls.*
Bowling and Lawn Bowls (*in part*)

JONES, W. GLYN. Professor of Scandinavian Studies, University of Newcastle upon Tyne, Eng. Author of *Johannes Jørgensens modne år; Johannes Jørgensen; Denmark.*
Literature (*in part*)

JOSEPH, LOU. Assistant Director, Bureau of Public Information, American Dental Association. Author of *Allergy—Facts and Fallacies.*
Medicine (*in part*)

JUNZ, HELLA B. Assistant Adviser, Board of Governors of the Federal Reserve System, U.S.
Government Finance (*in part*)

KAAN, FREDERIK H. Secretary of the Department of Cooperation and Witness, World Alliance of Reformed Churches (Presbyterian and Congregational), Geneva.
Religion (*in part*)

KAPLANSKY, IRVING. George Herbert Mead Distinguished Service Professor, Department of Mathematics, the University of Chicago.
Mathematics

KATZ, WILLIAM A. Professor, School of Library Science, State University of New York. Author of *Magazines for Libraries; Introduction to Reference Work.*
Publishing (*in part*)

KELLEHER, JOHN A. Editor, *The Dominion,* Wellington, N.Z.
Biography (*in part*); New Zealand

KENT, LOTTE. Editor, *Cooperative News Service,* International Cooperative Alliance, London.
Cooperatives

KERR, J. A. Lecturer, University of Birmingham, Eng.
Chemistry (*in part*)

KERRIGAN, ANTHONY. Editor and translator of *Selected Works* of Miguel de Unamuno (10 vol.). Author of *At the Front Door of the Atlantic.* Editor and Translator of works of Jorge Luis Borges.
Literature (*in part*)

KILLIN, ORLAND B. Professor of Industrial Education and Technology, Eastern Washington State College.
Industrial Review (*in part*)

KILNER, PETER. Editor, *Arab Report and Record.*
Algeria; Morocco; Sudan

KIMCHE, JON. Expert on Middle East Affairs, *Evening Standard,* London. Author of *There Could Have Been Peace: The Untold Story of Why We Failed with Palestine and Again with Israel.*
Israel

KIND, JOSHUA B. Associate Professor of Art History, Northern Illinois University. Author of *Rouault.*
Museums and Galleries (*in part*)

KIRKHAM, FRANCES. Economic Research Officer, Lloyds and Bolsa International Bank Ltd., London.
Peru

KITAGAWA, JOSEPH M. Professor of History of Religions and Dean of the Divinity School, the University of Chicago. Author of *Religions of the East; Religion in Japanese History.*
Religion (*in part*)

KLARE, HUGH J. Member of Parole Board for England and Wales; Member of the Council, International Penal and Penitentiary Foundations. Secretary, Howard League for Penal Reform 1950–71. Author of *People in Prison.*
Prisons and Penology

KLAUSLER, ALFRED P. Executive Secretary, Associated Church Press; Religion Editor, Westinghouse Broadcasting Company. Author of *Censorship, Obscenity and Sex; Growth in Worship.* Co-editor of *The Journalist's Prayer Book.*
Religion (*in part*)

KLIMOVICH, DONALD J. Social Policy Consultant.
Biography (*in part*)

KNECHT, JEAN. Former Assistant Foreign Editor, *Le Monde,* Paris; Permanent Correspondent in Washington and Vice-President of the Association de la Presse Diplomatique Française.
France

KNORR, N. H. President, Watch Tower Bible and Tract Society of Pennsylvania.
Religion (*in part*)

KOPPER, PHILIP. Free-lance Writer, Washington, D.C.
Biography (*in part*); Nobel Prizes

KOVAN, RICHARD W. Features Editor, *Nuclear Engineering International,* London.
Industrial Review (*in part*)

KRADER, BARBARA. President, Society for Ethnomusicology; Executive Secretary, International Folk Music Council, London, 1965–66.
Music (*in part*)

KRISTINSSON, VALDIMAR. Editor of *Fjarmalatidindi,* Reykjavik.
Iceland

KRIZ, MIROSLAV A. Vice-President, First National City Bank, New York City, 1958–73; Federal Reserve Bank of New York, 1945–58; Economic and Financial Department of the Secretariat of the League of Nations, 1936–45.
Economy, World; Payments and Reserves, International

KUBITSCHEK, H. E. Senior Biophysicist, Division of Biological and Medical Research, Argonne National Laboratory. Author of *Introduction to Research with Continuous Cultures.*
Life Sciences (*in part*)

LANGNESS, LEWIS LEROY. Associate Professor of Anthropology in Residence, Department of Psychiatry, Center for the Health Sciences, University of California, Los Angeles. Author of *Life History in Anthropological Science.* Co-author of *Melanesia: Readings on a Culture Area.*
Anthropology

LAST, G. C. Adviser, Imperial Ethiopian Ministry of Education and Fine Arts, Addis Ababa. Author of *A Regional Survey of Africa; A Geography of Ethiopia.* Co-author of *A History of Ethiopia in Pictures.*
Ethiopia

LEGUM, COLIN. Associate Editor and Commonwealth Correspondent, *Observer,* London. Author of *Must We Lose Africa?; Bandung, Cairo and Accra; Congo Disaster; Pan-Africanism—A Short Political Guide.* Co-author of *Attitude to Africa; South Africa; Crisis for the West; The Bitter Choice.* Editor of *Africa Contemporary Record; Travellers' Guide to Africa; Africa—A Handbook to the Continent.*
African Affairs; Biography (*in part*)

LENNOX-KERR, PETER. Editor and Publisher, *Textile Manufacturer,* Manchester. Author of *Index to Man-Made Fibres of the World; The World Fibres Book.* Editor of *Nonwovens 1971.*
Industrial Review (*in part*)

LINFORD, AARON. Editor of *Redemption Tidings,* weekly official organ of Assemblies of God in Great Britain and Ireland. Author of *Will the Church Go Through the Tribulation?; A Course of Study in Spiritual Gifts; The Baptism in the Holy Spirit; Living like Angels; Fabulously Rich; Divine Retribution.*
Religion (*in part*)

LITTELL, FRANKLIN H. Professor, Department of Religion, Temple University, Philadelphia, Pa. Co-editor of *Weltkirchenlexikon.*
Religion (*in part*)

LULING, VIRGINIA R. Social Anthropologist.
Somalia

McCLAM, WARREN D. Economist, Bank for International Settlements, Basel, Switz.
Money and Banking

MacDONALD, M. C. Director, Econtel Research Ltd., London. Editor, *World Series; Business Cycle Series.*
Agriculture (*in part*); Transportation (*in part*); *statistical sections of articles on the various countries*

MacDONALD, TREVOR. Manager, International Affairs, British Steel Corporation.
Industrial Review (*in part*)

McMANUS, IRENE. Associate Editor, *American Forests,* Washington, D.C.
Forestry

McMURRIN, STERLING M. Ericksen Distinguished Professor and Dean of the Graduate School, University of Utah. Co-author of *A History of Philosophy.*
Philosophy

MAILHOT, LAURENT. Associate Professor, Department of French Studies, University of Montreal. Author of *Le Théâtre Québécois; Albert Camus ou l'Imagination du Desert.*
Literature (*in part*)

MALLETT, H. M. F. Editor, *Weekly Wool Chart,* Bradford, Eng.
Industrial Review (*in part*)

MANGO, ANDREW. Orientalist and Broadcaster.
Biography (*in part*); Turkey

MANSFIELD, PETER. Formerly Middle East Correspondent, *Sunday Times,* London. Free-lance Writer on Middle East affairs.
Bahrain; Biography (*in part*); Egypt; Iraq; Jordan; Kuwait; Lebanon; Middle Eastern Affairs; Oman; Qatar; Saudi Arabia; Syria; United Arab Emirates; Yemen, People's Democratic Republic of; Yemen Arab Republic

MARCELLO, ALDO. Civil Engineer.
Engineering Projects (*in part*)

MARCUS, IRVING H. Publisher, *Wine Publications;* Columnist, *Wines and Vines.* Author of *Dictionary of Wine Terms; Lines About Wines; How to Test and Improve Your Wine Judging Ability.*
Alcoholic Beverages (*in part*)

MARSHALL, J. G. SCOTT. Horticultural Consultant.
Gardening (*in part*)

MARTENHOFF, JIM. Boating Editor, *Miami* (Fla.) *Herald.* Author of *How to Buy a Better Boat; Handbook of Skin and Scuba Diving.*
Motor Sports (*in part*)

MAUDE, N. F. Consultant Editor, *British Journal of Photography; Photo News Weekly.* Editor, *Photographic Processor.* Author of *Take Better Photos; Choosing a Camera.*
Photography

MAURON, PAUL. Director, International Vine and Wine Office, Paris.
Alcoholic Beverages (*in part*)

MAZIE, DAVID M. Associate of Carl T. Rowan, syndicated columnist. Free-lance Writer.
Social Services (*in part*)

MEADE, DAVID. Communication Director, Western Province, Congregation of the Passion.
Biography (*in part*)

MERMEL, T. W. Assistant to Commissioner for Scientific Affairs, Bureau of Reclamation, U.S. Department of the Interior, Washington, D.C. Chairman, Committee on World Register of Dams, International Commission on Large Dams. Author of *Register of Dams in the United States.*
Engineering Projects (*in part*)

MEYENDORFF, JOHN. Professor of Church History and Patristics, St. Vladimir's Seminary; Professor of History, Fordham University, New York City; Lecturer in Eastern Orthodoxy, Union Theological Seminary, New York.
Religion (*in part*)

MILES, PETER W. Professor of Zoology, University of Zambia, Lusaka.
Life Sciences (*in part*)

MILLARD, R. S. Deputy Director, Transport and Road Research Laboratory, Department of the Environment, Crowthorne, Berkshire, Eng.
Engineering Projects (*in part*)

MILLER, DANIEL. Student.
Biography (*in part*)

MILLER, WILLIAM B. Manager, Department of History, United Presbyterian Church, U.S.A.
Religion (*in part*)

MILLIKIN, SANDRA. Architectural Historian.
Architecture; Art Exhibitions

MINNES, GORDON. Secretary, Canadian Pulp and Paper Association.
Industrial Review (*in part*)

MITCHELL, K. K. Lecturer, Department of Physical Education, Leeds University. Hon. General Secretary, Amateur Basket Ball Association.
Basketball (*in part*)

MODEAN, ERIK W. Director, News Bureau, Lutheran Council in the U.S.A.
Religion (*in part*)

MODIANO, MARIO. Athens Correspondent, *The Times,* London.
Greece

MORGAN, HAZEL. Production Assistant (Sleevenotes and Covers), Creative Services Dept., E.M.I. Records Ltd., London.
Music (*in part*)

MORTIMER, MOLLY. Writer on Commonwealth and International Affairs. Author of *Trusteeship in Practice; Kenya.*
Botswana; Burundi; Commonwealth of Nations; Dependent States (*in part*); Gambia, The; Ghana; Lesotho; Maldives; Mauritius; Nigeria; Rwanda; Sierra Leone; Swaziland

MOSS, ROBERT V. President, United Church of Christ, New York City; President, American Association of Theological Schools, 1966–68. Author of *The Life of Paul; We Believe; As Paul Sees Christ.*
Religion (*in part*)

MOTTERSHEAD, G. S. Director-Secretary, Chester Zoo, Chester, Eng.
Zoos and Botanical Gardens (*in part*)

MULLINS, STEPHANIE. Historian.
Biography (*in part*)

NATOLI, SALVATORE J. Educational Affairs Director, Association of American Geographers. Co-author of *Dictionary of Basic Geography.*
Geography

NAYLOR, ERNEST. Professor of Marine Biology, University of Liverpool; Director, Marine Biological Laboratory, Port Erin, Isle of Man. Author of *British Marine Isopods.*
Life Sciences (*in part*)

NEILL, JOHN. Chief Chemical Engineer, Submerged Combustion Ltd. Author of Climbers' Club Guides; *Cwm Silyn and Tremadoc, Snowdon South;* Alpine Club Guide: *Selected Climbs in the Pennine Alps.*
Mountaineering

NELSON, BERT. Editor and Publisher, *Track and Field News.*
Track and Field Sports (*in part*)

NETSCHERT, BRUCE C. Vice-President, National Economic Research Associates, Inc., Washington, D.C. Author of *The Future Supply of Oil and Gas.* Co-author of *Energy in the American Economy: 1850–1975.*
Energy (*in part*)

NOEL, H. S. Editor in Chief, *World Fishing,* London.
Agriculture and Fisheries (*in part*)

NORMAN, GERALDINE. Saleroom Correspondent, *The Times,* London. Author of *The Sale of Works of Art.*
Art Sales (*in part*)

NOVALES, RONALD R. Professor of Biological Sciences, Northwestern University, Evanston, Ill. Member, Editorial Board, *American Zoologist.*
Life Sciences (*in part*)

NOVICK, JULIUS. Associate Professor of Literature, State University of New York at Purchase; Dramaturge, Juilliard Acting Company and Drama Division of the Juilliard School. Dramatic Critic for the *Village Voice* and *The Humanist.* Contributor to *The Nation;* the *New York Times.* Author of *Beyond Broadway: The Quest for Permanent Theatres.*
Theatre (*in part*)

O'LEARY, JEREMIAH A. Latin-American Correspondent, *Washington* (D.C.) *Evening Star-News.* Author of *Dominican Action—1965; Panama: Canal Issues and Treaty Talks—1967.*
Chile

OSBORNE, KEITH. Editor, *Rowing,* 1961–63. Hon. Editor, *British Rowing Almanack,* 1961–.
Rowing

OSTERBIND, CARTER C. Director, Bureau of Economic and Business Research, University of Florida. Editor, *Feasible Planning for Social Change in the Field of Aging.*
Engineering Projects (*in part*); Industrial Review (*in part*)

PAKEMAN, SIDNEY A. Historian. Author of *Ceylon.*
Sri Lanka.

PALMER, S. B. Lecturer, Department of Applied Physics, University of Hull, Eng.
Physics

PANIĆ, MILIVOJE. Head of Economic Division, National Economic Development Office, London.
Prices

PARGAS, RAFAEL. National Geographic Society, Washington, D.C.
Philippines

PARKER, SANDY. Fur Editor, *Women's Wear Daily.*
Furs

PARNELL, COLIN. Editor, *Wine and Spirit Trade International,* London.
Alcoholic Beverages *(in part)*

PARRY, V. J. Reader in the History of the Near and Middle East, School of Oriental and African Studies, University of London. Contributor to *New Cambridge Modern History; Cambridge History of Islam; Encyclopaedia of Islam.*
Cyprus

PARSONS, ANNE. Economic Research Officer, Lloyds and Bolsa International Bank Ltd., London.
Costa Rica, Guatemala

PATTEN, GEORGE P. Professor of Geography, Ohio State University.
Nicaragua

PATTERSON, SHEILA. Research Associate, Department of Anthropology, University College, London. Author of *Colour and Culture in South Africa; The Last Trek; Dark Strangers; Immigrants in Industry.*
Bahamas; Barbados; Dependent States *(in part)*; **Guyana; Jamaica; Migration, International; Race Relations** *(in part)*; **Trinidad and Tobago**

PENFOLD, ROBIN C. Public relations executive, Carl Byoir and Associates Ltd., London. Author of *A Journalist's Guide to Plastics.*
Industrial Review *(in part)*

PETERSON, VIRGIL W. Executive Director, Chicago Crime Commission, 1942–70. Author of *Gambling—Should It Be Legalized?; Barbarians in Our Midst.*
Crime *(in part)*

PETHERICK, KARIN. Crown Princess Louise Lecturer in Swedish, University College, London.
Literature *(in part)*

PETTIGREW, THOMAS F. Professor of Social Psychology, Harvard University. Author of *A Profile of the Negro American; Racially Separate or Together?*
Race Relations *(in part)*

PFEFFER, IRVING. Professor of Insurance and Finance, College of Business, Virginia Polytechnic Institute and State University. Author of *Insurance and Economic Theory; The Financing of Small Business.*
Stock Exchanges *(in part)*

PHILLIPS, D. K. R. Secretary-General, Association of Track and Field Statisticians. Contributor, *Sportsworld.* Editor, *World Sports Olympic Games Report.* Co-compiler of *Guinness Book of Olympic Records; Sportsworld International Athletics Annual.*
Sporting Record

PICK, OTTO. Professor of International Relations, University of Surrey, Guildford, Eng. Director, Atlantic Information Centre for Teachers, London.
Czechoslovakia; Union of Soviet Socialist Republics

PLATT, MAURICE. Consulting Engineer. Former Director of Engineering, Vauxhall Motors, Ltd. Author of *Elements of Automobile Engineering.*
Industrial Review *(in part)*

PLOTKIN, FREDERICK S. Associate Professor of English and Philosophy, University of Nevada, Las Vegas. Author of *Milton's Inward Jerusalem; Faith and Reason.*
Literature *(in part)*

POLLACK, GERALD A. Senior Economic Adviser, Exxon Corporation. Author of *Perspectives on the U.S. International Financial Position.*
Profits

POTTER, SIMEON. Emeritus Professor of English Language and Philology, University of Liverpool, Eng. Author of *Our Language; Language in the Modern World; Modern Linguistics; Changing English.*
Words and Meanings, New

PRAG, DEREK. Business Consultant and Free-lance Journalist. Director, London Information Office of the European Communities, 1965–73. Co-author of *Businessman's Guide to the Common Market.*
Biography *(in part)*; **European Unity**

PRASAD, H. Y. SHARADA. Director of Information, Prime Minister's Secretariat, New Delhi, India.
India

PREIL, GABRIEL. Writer. Hebrew and Yiddish poet. Author of *Israeli Poetry in Peace and War; Nof Shemesh Ukhfor* ("Landscape of Sun and Frost"); *Ner Mul Kokhavim* ("Candle Against the Stars"); *Mapat Erev* ("Map of Evening"); *Lieder* ("Poems"); *Haesh Vehadmama* ("The Fire and the Silence"); *Mitoch Leman Venof* ("Of Time and Place").
Literature *(in part)*

RANGER, ROBERT J. Assistant Professor, Department of Political Science, St. Francis Xavier University, Antigonish, Nova Scotia.
Defense

RAVEN, VIVIAN. Editor, *Tobacco,* London.
Tobacco

RAY, G. F. Senior Research Fellow, National Institute of Economic and Social Research, London.
Industrial Review *(in part)*

READ, HARRY. Director, Salvation Army International Information Services, London.
Religion *(in part)*

REICHELDERFER, FRANCIS W. Aeronautical and Marine Meteorology Consultant. Former Chief, Weather Bureau, U.S. Department of Commerce, Washington, D.C.
Meteorology

REID, J. H. Lecturer in German, University of Nottingham, Eng. Author of *Heinrich Böll: Withdrawal and Re-emergence.* Co-author of *Critical Strategies: German Fiction in the 20th Century.*
Literature *(in part)*

REYNOLDS, ARTHUR GUY. Registrar and Professor of Church History, Emmanuel College, Toronto.
Religion *(in part)*

RILEY, WALLACE B. Computers Editor, *Electronics* magazine.
Computers

ROBERTS, R. L. Editorial Consultant, *Church Times,* London.
Religion *(in part)*

ROBINSON, DAVID. Film Critic, *The Times,* London. Author of *Buster Keaton; Hollywood in the Twenties; The Great Funnies—A History of Screen Comedy; A History of World Cinema.*
Biography *(in part)*; **Motion Pictures** *(in part)*

ROSE, JOHN KERR. Senior Specialist in Natural Resources and Conservation, Congressional Research Service, Library of Congress, Washington, D.C.
Agriculture and Fisheries *(in part)*

RYBCZYNSKI, T. M. Economist, Lazard Brothers, London.
Savings and Investment

SAEKI, SHOICHI. Teacher, College of General Education, University of Tokyo.
Literature *(in part)*

SANDON, HAROLD. Former Professor of Zoology, University of Khartoum, Sudan. Author of *The Protozoan Fauna of the Soil; The Food of Protozoa; An Illustrated Guide to the Fresh-Water Fishes of the Sudan; Essays on Protozoology.*
Life Sciences *(in part)*

SARAHETE, YRJÖ. Secretary, Fédération Internationale des Quilleurs, Helsinki, Fin.
Bowling and Lawn Bowls *(in part)*

SCHATTMANN, S. E. Economist, London.
Germany *(in part)*

SCHELLHARDT, TIMOTHY D. Reporter, the *Wall Street Journal,* Washington, D.C.
Postal Services *(in part)*

SCHMITT, TILMAN. Brewery Engineer. Editor of *Brauwelt; Brauwissenschaft.*
Alcoholic Beverages *(in part)*

SCHOENFIELD, ALBERT. Editor, *Swimming World.*
Swimming

SCHULIAN, JOHN. Reporter, the *Baltimore Evening Sun.*
Basketball *(in part)*; **Football** *(in part)*

SERGEANT, HOWARD. Lecturer and Writer. Editor of *Outposts,* Walton-on Thames, Eng. Author of *The Cumberland Wordsworth; Tradition in the Making of Modern Poetry.*
Literature *(in part)*

SHACKLEFORD, PETER. Research Adviser, International Union of Official Travel Organisations (IUOTO), Geneva.
Tourism

SHARPE, MITCHELL R. Science Writer. Author of *Living in Space: The Environment of the Astronaut; Yuri Gagarin, First Man in Space; Satellites and Probes: The Development of Unmanned Space Flight.* Co-author of *Applied Astronautics; Basic Astronautics; Dividends from Space.*
Astronautics

SHAW, T. R. Commander, Royal Navy. Vice-President, British Speleological Association.
Speleology

SHERMAN, HARVEY R. Environmental Policy Division, Congressional Research Service, Library of Congress.
Agriculture and Fisheries *(in part)*; **Food** *(in part)*

SHIH, CONSTANT CHUNG-TSE. Senior Adviser on Trade Negotiations, United Nations Conference on Trade and Development (UNCTAD), Switzerland.
Commercial Policies

SHOREY, JOHN C. Lecturer in Economics, University College, Cardiff, Wales.
Merchandising

SIGNER, ROBERT A. Assistant National and Foreign Editor, *Chicago Daily News.*
Biography (*in part*)

SIMPSON, NOEL. Managing Director, Sydney Bloodstock Proprietary Ltd., Sydney, Austr.
Horse Racing (*in part*)

SKELDING, FRANK H. Director, Corporate Planning, Fluor Utah, Inc.
Energy (*in part*) ; **Mining** (*in part*) ; **United States Statistical Supplement:** *Principal Minerals table; Mineral Fuels and Electricity Production table.*

SMEDLEY, GLENN B. Governor, American Numismatic Association.
Philately and Numismatics (*in part*)

SMITH, DAN THROOP. Professor Emeritus, Harvard University ; Senior Research Fellow, Hoover Institution, Stanford (Calif.) University ; Director, Cambridge Research Institute ; Former Deputy to Secretary of the Treasury ; Former President, National Tax Association and Tax Institute of America. Author of *Federal Tax Reform ; Tax Factors in Business Decisions.*
Taxation (*in part*)

SMITH, R. W. Provost, Callison College, University of the Pacific, Stockton, Calif.
Religion (*in part*)

SMITHCORS, J. F. Editor, American Veterinary Publications, Inc., Santa Barbara, Calif. Author of *Evolution of the Veterinary Art; The American Veterinary Profession.*
Veterinary Medicine

SMOGORZEWSKI, K. M. Writer on contemporary history. Founder and Editor, *Free Europe*, London. Author of *The United States and Great Britain; Poland's Access to the Sea.*
Albania; Biography (*in part*) ; **Bulgaria; Hungary; Mongolia; Poland; Political Parties; Romania; Soviet Bloc Economies**

SPENCE, M. J. Economic Research Officer, Lloyds and Bolsa International Bank Ltd., London.
Paraguay; Uruguay; Venezuela

STAERK, MELANIE. Member, Swiss National Commission for UNESCO.
Switzerland

STARKMAN, MOSHE. Essayist in Yiddish and Hebrew ; Bibliographer. Former President, Yiddish P.E.N. Club ; New York Editor, *Hemshekh Anthology of American Yiddish Poetry.* Associate Editor, *Lexicon of Yiddish Literature.* Contributor, *Jewish Daily Forward*, New York.
Literature (*in part*)

STEVENSON, TOM. Garden Columnist, *Baltimore News American; Washington Post;* Washington Post-Los Angeles Times News Service. Author of *Pruning Guide for Trees, Shrubs and Vines; Lawn Guide; Gardening for the Beginner.*
Gardening (*in part*)

STOKES, J. BUROUGHS. Manager, Committees on Publication, The First Church of Christ, Scientist, Boston.
Religion (*in part*)

STOLER, PETER. Medical Editor, *Time* magazine, New York.
Medicine (*in part*)

STØVERUD, TORBJØRN. W. P. Ker Senior Lecturer in Norwegian, University College, London.
Literature (*in part*)

SUNDBLAD, ILMARI. Managing Editor, Finnish News Agency.
Finland

SWEETINBURGH, THELMA. Paris Fashion Correspondent for *International Textiles* (Amsterdam) and the British Wool Textile Industry.
Fashion and Dress (*in part*)

SWIFT, RICHARD N. Professor of Politics, New York University, New York City. Author of *International Law: Current and Classic.*
United Nations (*in part*)

SYNAN, VINSON. Division Chairman, Emmanuel College ; Pastor, Hartwell Pentecostal Holiness Church, Georgia. Author of *Emmanuel College—The First Fifty Years ; The Holiness-Pentecostal Movement.*
Religion (*in part*)

SZPAKOWSKI, ANDREW. Chief, Division of Standards, Research and Museums, UNESCO, Paris.
Museums and Galleries (*in part*)

TAISHOFF, SOL. Chairman and Editor, *Broadcasting*, Washington, D.C.
Television and Radio (*in part*)

TATTERSALL, ARTHUR. Textile Trade Expert and Statistician, Manchester, Eng.
Industrial Review (*in part*)

TAYLOR, WINSTON H. Director, Washington Office, Commission on Public Relations and United Methodist Information. Author of *Angels Don't Need Public Relations ; Ending Racial Segregation in the Methodist Church ; Toward an Inclusive Church.*
Religion (*in part*)

TERRY, WALTER. Dance Critic, *World* magazine. Author of *The Dance in America ; The Ballet Companion ; Miss Ruth: The "More Living Life" of Ruth St. Denis.*
Dance (*in part*)

THOMAS, HARFORD. City Editor, *The Guardian*, London.
Biography (*in part*) ; **United Kingdom**

THOMPSON, ANTHONY. Language Specialist, College of Librarianship, Aberystwyth, Wales. General Secretary, International Federation of Library Associations, 1962–70. Author of *Vocabularium Bibliothecarii ; Library Buildings of Britain and Europe.*
Libraries

THOMSON, RONALD WILLIAM. Former Assistant General Secretary, Baptist Union of Great Britain and Ireland. Author of *Heroes of the Baptist Church ; William Carey ; The Service of Our Lives ; A Pocket History of the Baptists.*
Religion (*in part*)

TINGAY, LANCE. Lawn Tennis Correspondent, the *Daily Telegraph*, London
Tennis

TRAIN, CHRISTOPHER JOHN. Assistant Secretary, Probation and After Care Department, Home Office, London.
Drugs and Narcotics (*in part*)

TRIGG, ROBERT H. Manager, Institutional Research, New York Stock Exchange.
Stock Exchanges (*in part*)

TRILLING, OSSIA. Vice-President, International Association of Theatre Critics. Co-editor and contributor, *International Theatre.* Contributor, BBC, *The Financial Times*, London.
Theatre (*in part*)

TYPE, MICHAEL. Assistant to the Secretary General, European Broadcasting Union, Geneva.
Television and Radio (*in part*)

UNHCR. The Office of the United Nations High Commissioner for Refugees, Geneva.
Refugees

UNNY, GOVINDAN. Agence France-Presse Special Correspondent for India, Nepal, and Ceylon.
Bangladesh; Bhutan; Biography (*in part*) ; **Burma; Dependent States** (*in part*) ; **Nepal**

UNO, HISASHI. Information Officer, Tokyo Office, United Nations.
Baseball (*in part*)

URQUHART, NORMAN R. Assistant Vice-President, in charge of Commodity Section, Economics Department, First National City Bank, New York City.
Commodities, Primary

VIANSSON-PONTÉ, PIERRE. Assistant Executive Editor and Senior Editorial Writer, *Le Monde*, Paris. Author of *Les Gaullistes ; The King and His Court ; Les Politiques ; Histoire de la République Gaullienne.*
Biography (*in part*)

VIELVOYE, ROGER. Industrial Journalist, London.
Transportation (*in part*)

VILLACA, ANTONIO CARLOS DA ROCHA. Editor, *Jornal Do Brasil*, Rio de Janeiro.
Literature (*in part*)

WADLEY, J. B. Writer and Broadcaster on cycling. Author of *Tour de France 1970 and 1971 ; Old Roads and New.*
Cycling

WARD-THOMAS, P. A. Golf Correspondent, *The Guardian*, London.
Golf

WEBB, W. L. Literary Editor, *The Guardian*, London and Manchester.
Literature (*in part*)

WEBSTER, PETER L. Assistant Professor, Department of Botany, University of Massachusetts, Amherst.
Life Sciences (*in part*)

WEEDEN, CYRIL. Assistant Director, Glass Manufacturers' Federation, London.
Industrial Review (*in part*)

WHITE, A. A. Editor, *Toys International*, London.
Toys and Games

WILE, JULIUS. Senior Vice-President, Julius Wile Sons & Co., Inc., New York City. Vice-President, New England Distillers, Inc., Teterboro, N.J. Chairman, Table Wine Committee, National Association of Alcoholic Beverage Importers, Inc. Lecturer on wines, School of Hotel Administration, Cornell University.
Alcoholic Beverages (*in part*)

WILLIAMS, DAVID L. Assistant Professor of Government, Ohio University.
Communist Parties

WILLIAMS, L. F. RUSHBROOK. Fellow of All Souls College, Oxford University, 1914–21 ; Professor of Modern Indian History, Allahabad, India, 1914–19. Author of *India Under the Company and the Crown ; The State of Pakistan ; What About India? ; Kutch in History and Legend.* Editor of *Handbook to India, Pakistan, Bangladesh, Nepal, and Sri Lanka.*
Afghanistan; Iran; Pakistan

WILLIAMS, PETER. Editor, *Dance and Dancers.*
Dance (*in part*)

WILLIAMSON, TREVOR. Chief Sports subeditor, the *Daily Telegraph*, London.
Football (*in part*)

WILSON, ALAN. Associate Editor, *Scanorama*, Bromma, Swed.
Biography (*in part*) ; **Sweden**

WILSON, J. TUZO. Professor of Geophysics and Principal, Erindale College, University of Toronto, Clarkson, Ontario. Author of *Continents Adrift*. Co-author of *Physics and Geology*.
Geology

WILSON, MICHAEL. Technical Editor, *Flight International*, London. Free-lance Writer.
Industrial Review (*in part*)

WOOD, KENNETH H. Editor, *The Advent Review and Sabbath Herald*. Author of *Meditations for Moderns; Relevant Religions*. Co-author of *His Initials Were F. D. N.*
Religion (*in part*)

WOOLLER, MICHAEL. Economic Research Officer, Lloyds and Bolsa International Bank Ltd., London.
Ecuador (*in part*)

WOOLLEY, DAVID. Editor, *Airports International*, London.
Transportation (*in part*)

WORSNOP, RICHARD L. Writer, Editorial Research Reports, Washington, D.C.
Biography (*in part*); **Liberia**; **United States**

WRIGHT, ALMON R. Retired Senior Historian, U.S. Department of State.
Panama

YOLLES, STANLEY F., M.D. Professor and Chairman, Department of Psychiatry, School of Medicine, Health Sciences Center, State University of New York at Stony Brook.
Drugs and Narcotics (*in part*)

YOPES, PAUL FREDERICK. Mining Engineer, Bureau of Mines, U.S. Department of the Interior, Washington, D.C.
Mining (*in part*)

YOUNG, J. C. Lecturer in Chemistry, University College of Wales.
Chemistry (*in part*)

YOUNG, M. NORVEL. Chancellor, Pepperdine University, Los Angeles. Editor of *Twentieth Century Christian; Power for Today*. Author of *Churches of Today*.
Religion (*in part*)

ZIMMERMAN, DONNA. Free-lance Writer.
Biography (*in part*)

Index

The black type entries are article headings in the *Book of the Year*. These black type article entries do not show page notations because they are to be found in their alphabetical position in the body of the book. They show the dates of the issues of the *Book of the Year* in which the articles appear. For example "Archaeology 74, 73, 72" indicates that the article "Archaeology" is to be found in the 1974, 1973, and 1972 *Book of the Year*.

The light type headings that are indented under black type article headings refer to material elsewhere in the text related to the subject under which they are listed. The light type headings that are not indented refer to information in the text not given a special article. Biographies and obituaries are listed as cross references to the articles "*Biography*" and "*Obituaries*" for the year in which they appear. References to illustrations are preceded by the abbreviation "il."

All headings, whether consisting of a single word or more, are treated for the purpose of alphabetization as single complete headings. Names beginning with "Mc" and "Mac" are alphabetized as "Mac"; "St." is treated as "Saint." All references below show the exact quarter of the page by means of the letters *a, b, c* and *d*, signifying, respectively, the upper and lower halves of the first column and the upper and lower halves of the second column. Exceptions to this rule are tables, illustrations, and references from biographies and the articles "*Energy*" and "*Industrial Review*."

A

C

D

E

F

G

H

I

J

K

L

M

N

O

P

Q

R

T

U

V

W

X

Y

Z

United States Statistical Supplement

Developments in the states in 1973

Although state governments avoided direct involvement in the Watergate domestic trauma of 1973, the year produced major events that altered long-established patterns, habits, and laws. Among the most notable developments were the invalidation of virtually every state abortion law, a marked upswing in concern with the ethical standards of public officials, and a halt to seemingly inexorable tax increases by state governments.

States were affected by an energy crisis that captured public awareness at year's end. A love-hate relationship developed in state relations with federal government funding policies. Although present methods of financing public schools were ruled constitutional, efforts to equalize spending between rich and poor school districts were accelerated. Legislative concern over drug abuse, consumer protection, and environmental problems was again at the fore.

Forty-nine states (all except Kentucky) held regular legislative sessions, and eight staged special sessions during the year.

Party Strengths. Thirty-one governors were Democrats in 1973; 19 were Republicans. For the third year in a row, November elections produced one statehouse gain for the Democrats, making the prospective 1974 majority 32 to 18. The gain came in New Jersey, where a scandal-plagued Republican administration was turned out. Democrats now had a numerical advantage in gubernatorial offices in every section of the country.

During 1973, Democrats controlled 25 legislatures while Republicans dominated 17. As a result of a New Jersey election in which Democrats gained a majority in both legislative houses, Republicans in 1974 would continue to hold two-house majorities in 17 states, while Democrats would have a majority in both legislative chambers of 26.

Federal-State Relations. Major problems developed almost immediately in the new compact between the federal and state governments. Shortly after the new State and Local Fiscal Assistance Act of 1972 began disbursing millions of new federal revenue-sharing dollars into state and local treasuries, the Nixon administration announced a series of program cuts and impoundments that seemed to take away many of the partnership gains achieved by the states.

The year started well enough. By mid-February, the federal treasury had doled out nearly $5.5 billion, one-third of it to state governments, as the first year's revenue-sharing payment. An equal amount was distributed to states and local governments by December during the second year payout. State officials hailed revenue-sharing as a welcome federal helping hand to hard-pressed state taxpayers; a survey by the General Accounting Office among state budget officials revealed that in 1973 revenue-sharing would help permit 18 states to grant some form of tax relief and 16 more to postpone future tax increases.

But President Nixon's belt-tightening budget message sent to Congress in early 1973 listed 113 federal programs to be terminated or markedly reduced, many of them directly affecting state services. The Office of Economic Opportunity was slated for abolition, low-interest loans for rural electrification and other projects were canceled, and programs were killed that provided aid for building hospitals, public service employment, regional medical centres, and mental health support. In addition, the budget message indicated Nixon was abandoning support for promised initiatives of the past, including property tax relief, welfare reform, and private school aid. Numerous states had counted upon federal help in those areas.

In many cases, the federal government did not publicly announce withdrawal of aid from state-supported programs, but simply withheld funds. Affected parties, including state governments, began filing lawsuits in federal courts to force payment of impounded funds. In the first impoundment case to reach the appellate level, *Missouri Highway Commission* v. *Volpe,* the 8th U.S. Circuit Court of Appeals ruled illegal the federal government's withholding of highway funds. The Justice Department elected not to appeal that ruling.

By year's end, according to a tabulation by Public Citizen, Inc., 38 suits had been filed in challenge to impoundment procedures, and decisions adverse to the federal government had been rendered in 34 of them. By and large, however, the funds continued to be withheld as lengthy appeals were perfected. In May, the state of Georgia asked the U.S. Supreme Court to speed matters by hearing its challenge to executive impoundment of $65.3 million in highway, education, and water pollution control funds. Although the U.S. solicitor general joined in the Georgia request, ten other states opposed it, preferring to see a pattern of lower court decisions develop before Supreme Court consideration. On October 9, the high court refused to set the case down on its original jurisdiction docket.

An initial analysis of usage of general revenue-sharing money revealed that only a small portion was being spent on nonessential services. In the first allocation, 23.5% was spent on public safety, 22% on education, 13.1% on transportation, 10.5% on general government, 7.6% on environment and conservation, 5.9% on health, and only 4.8% on recreation and culture.

Finance. For the first time in memory, state legislatures were generally able to level or even lower tax levies. Among states approving significant new tax legislation by late fall of 1973, nine states approved tax increases that were to raise $500 million in additional revenue, while 14 other states handed taxpayers reductions totaling just over $1 billion. Legislatures typically address tax matters during odd-numbered years; the $500 million net reduction in 1973 compares with a 1969 increase of $4 billion and a 1971 boost of $5 billion.

Massive increases in state tax yields in recent years prompted the leveling trend, according to the Tax Foundation: a combination of previous tax rate increases and economic growth increased state tax receipts by 43% in the past three years. Collections for the year ending March 31, 1973, jumped $10 billion (17%) over the prior year to a total of $66.2 billion. In addition, the advent of federal revenue-sharing brought $3.5 billion into state coffers in a 13-month period, helping authorities to postpone tax increases, proffer tax relief, or reform inequities in many jurisdictions.

Both tax increases and decreases were accomplished in the name of "tax reform" in 1973, a broad term encompassing property tax relief for the elderly and attempts to equalize assessment burdens. At least 21 states provided some form of property tax relief during the year. Corporation income tax increases provided the bulk of tax boosts, while other states were able to drop personal income and sales tax rates. No state imposed new sales, personal income, or corporate income taxes during the year.

State tax collections in the 1973 fiscal year totaled $59.9 billion, up 16.2% from the 1972 figure. Of the new total, $17.6 billion was from general sales and gross receipts taxes; $15.6 billion from selective sales taxes; $13 billion from individual income taxes; $4.4 billion from corporation income taxes; and $5.4 billion from motor vehicle and other licenses.

Figures accumulated in 1973 showed that state revenue from all sources totaled $112.3 billion in fiscal 1972, an increase of 15.5% from the preceding year. General revenue (excluding state liquor and state insurance trust revenue) was $98.5 billion, up 15.7%. Total state expenditures were $109.2 billion, an increase of 10.5%, creating a surplus for the year of $3.1 billion. General expenditures, not including outlays of the liquor stores and insurance trust systems, amounted to $98.8 billion, up 10.9% for the year. Of general revenue, 60.7% came from state taxes; 10.9% from charges and miscellaneous revenue, including education charges; and 28.4% ($28 billion) from the federal government.

The largest state outlay was $38.3 billion for education, of which $21.1 billion went to local public schools and $13.4 billion for state colleges and universities. Other major outlays were $19.2 billion for public welfare (a 17.9% increase over fiscal 1971), $9.6 billion for highways, and $5.1 billion for hospitals.

Administrative Structures, Powers. The trend toward consolidation and reorganization of state executive offices to meet changing needs and citizen demands continued. State legislatures in Arizona, California, Connecticut, Kentucky, Maine, Michigan, South Dakota, and Wyoming authorized reorganization of some executive departments. The new orders typically provided for more centralized control, either in the governor's office or in central administrative offices.

Presidential preference primaries were authorized for 1976 in Georgia and Nevada, bringing the number of states staging such elections to 26. Several political spokesmen called for establishment of national or regional primaries to replace the present system of state-by-state elections, but no concrete organizational moves developed.

A trend toward reforming court organization, noticeable in 1972, slowed somewhat, although South Dakota reorganized its judicial branch. The chief justices of Indiana, Mississippi, New Hampshire, Connecticut, and New Mexico were invited to deliver "state of the judiciary" messages before their legislatures, expanding a practice previously initiated by Colorado, Michigan, Alaska, Maryland, Oklahoma, and Kansas.

Voters in Rhode Island turned down a constitutional amendment that would have lengthened terms of state officers from two years to four.

Legislative Systems. Voters in Kentucky and Texas, in November balloting, turned down proposals that would have authorized annual legislative sessions. But a constitutional amendment requiring annual sessions was approved by Ohio voters May 8, bringing to 36 the number of states where legislatures meet every year.

Legislative reapportionment plans for Connecticut and Texas were approved by the U.S. Supreme Court June 18 and for Virginia February 21. In all three cases, relatively wide population deviation between the largest and smallest districts was allowed—as much as 16.4% in Virginia, 9.9% in Texas, and 7.8% in Connecticut. The high court stated in the Virginia case that the one-man, one-vote rule need not apply as strictly to apportionment of state legislatures as it does to congressional districting, and that preserving local political subdivision lines is a logical reason for drawing varying-sized districts.

Reregistration of Kentucky voters, required by a 1972 law, was completed in 1973, resulting in a reduction of state rolls by some 50,000 persons.

Pay raises authorized by the Washington legislature for state officials were slashed drastically by a voter initiative in November. Voters also turned down proposed legislative pay increases in Rhode Island and Texas.

A tabulation by the Council of State Governments revealed that the 50 states employ 7,563 legislators, including 1,978 senators and 5,585 members of the lower house.

Ethics. Increased public distrust of elected officials, augmented mightily by the Watergate scandal, put ethics at the forefront of 1973 political concerns in the states. To meet the challenge, an unprecedented number of states approved new codes of ethics for public officials, regulations on lobbyists, and laws ordering disclosure of campaign contributions and outside income. Resolutions calling for improved codes of ethics and reforms such as open meeting laws, conflict of interest regulation, and financial disclosure were approved overwhelmingly at annual meetings of the National Legislative Conference August 10 and the National Conference of Lieutenant Governors October 6. The measures were considered necessary "to restore public confidence in government."

New campaign finance disclosure laws were approved by several states, including Illinois, Nebraska, and New Jersey. New codes of ethics, including disclosure of outside income in some cases, were established by executive order or by legislation in Alabama, California, Illinois, Indiana, Maryland, Michigan, Missouri, Ohio, and Wisconsin.

Enforcement of ethics provisions produced unusual side effects. The Alabama law as written included news reporters covering state government in its financial disclosure provisions; several media representatives announced plans to fight the regulation as a First Amendment violation. In Ohio, the state supreme court upheld a law prohibiting candidates who fail to file timely reports of campaign income and expenses from seeking further office for five years. The ruling disqualified Donald Lukens, a state senator and a likely Republican nominee, from entering the 1974 gubernatorial race.

Nonetheless, the new spirit of morality failed to stop an unusually heavy number of bribery and extortion indictments during 1973 against current and former state officials.

New Jersey continued to be plagued with political corruption. John A. Kervick, state treasurer from 1958 to 1970, was indicted January 9 for conspiracy and extortion; he was accused of taking kickbacks from engineering firms seeking state business. Another former New Jersey treasurer, Joseph McCrane, was indicted May 24 with prominent GOP politician Nelson G. Gross for income tax fraud on campaign contributions in the 1969 race of incumbent Gov. William T. Cahill.

Oklahoma state treasurer Leo Winters was named in a nine-count mail fraud and extortion indictment by a federal grand jury May 31; he was accused of obtaining loans, gifts, and favours in return for depositing state funds in at least 13 selected banks.

Maryland State Rep. James A. Scott was accused April 3 by a federal grand jury of distributing 40 lb. of heroin; he was found murdered on July 13 in his Baltimore apartment building. Maryland State Sen. Clarence M. Mitchell III was indicted on April 10 on four counts of federal income tax evasion.

Former Illinois revenue director Theodore Isaacs and 7th U.S. Circuit Court of Appeals Judge Otto Kerner were sentenced April 19 to three years in prison and a $50,000 fine on multiple counts of fraud, perjury, bribery, and income tax evasion. The two were convicted February 19 on charges stemming from purchase and sale of racetrack stock while Kerner was Illinois governor.

Education. Two major U.S. Supreme Court decisions—one declaring constitutional the local property tax system of financing public schools, and the other extending court sanctions against school racial segregation into the North for the first time—dominated educational news in the states. Despite the high court ruling on financing, a trend toward equalizing public school spending between rich and poor areas continued, with numerous states taking steps to bring spending equity to less affluent areas.

In its 5–4 decision March 21 on school financing, *San Antonio School District* v. *Rodriguez,* the Supreme Court ruled that education was not a fundamental right protected by the Constitution despite its "undisputed importance" to individuals and society. Although the majority held that constitutional guarantees of equal protection under the laws thus were not violated by diverse spending, it added, "The need is apparent for reform in tax systems which may well have relied too long and too heavily on the local property tax."

Among states responding to the court advice were Arizona, Colorado, Florida, Kansas, Maine, Maryland, North Dakota, North Carolina, South Dakota, Utah, and Virginia, all of which significantly boosted state aid to local systems while apportioning additional funds to low-income areas. The Colorado legislature adopted a "power equalizing" formula advocated by some financing reformers; the formula rewards local districts that make strenuous taxing efforts by increasing state aid with each additional mill of local tax collected. It also places a limit on spending by wealthy districts in a further attempt to equalize spending.

Despite the Supreme Court ruling, the New Jersey Supreme Court declared April 3 that the state's school finance system was in violation of a state constitutional mandate for a "thorough and efficient" system of free public schools. Subsequently, the U.S. Supreme Court refused to review an appeal of the state court ruling filed by state legislators. However, Oregon voters May 1 defeated a tax proposal that would have provided state financing of public schools, severely limited local property taxes, increased personal and corporate income taxes, and introduced a new business profits tax. On September 25, the Illinois Supreme Court ruled that the state was not required to finance 50% of public school costs, despite the state constitution's declaration that primary responsibility for public school funding lay with the state. The court, based on records of the constitutional convention, ruled that the declaration constituted a goal rather than a duty.

On June 21, the Supreme Court served notice of its willingness to challenge racial segregation in Northern public schools. In *Keyes* v. *Denver School District,* the court ruled 8 to 1 that if an unofficial segregated racial pattern is found to be the result of deliberate actions by school authorities, then "all-out desegregation" must follow. The high court followed that ruling in November by agreeing to consider in 1974 whether a federal judge could lawfully order consolidation of Detroit and suburban Michigan school systems for purposes of redressing segregated conditions.

Efforts to provide public aid to the nation's hard-pressed parochial and private elementary-secondary schools suffered additional defeats in 1973. Courts in New Jersey, New Hampshire, and Washington struck down state attempts to partially finance such schools, and the U.S. Supreme Court further discouraged nonpublic school aid plans. In a series of decisions June 25, the high court invalidated New York and Pennsylvania laws providing grants and tax credits to parents of private school pupils, plus aid to private schools for testing, record keeping, maintenance, and repair. However, the court ruled that South Carolina could authorize building construction bonds for private colleges, some of which were religiously controlled.

In another Supreme Court ruling on higher education, a Connecticut law permanently prohibiting out-of-state university students from becoming eligible for lower in-state tuition rates was declared unconstitutional June 11.

Welfare. The Vermont legislature approved a pioneering system of subsidized dental care for children of low- and middle-income families in a law effective January 1974. The "denticaid" program covers children in low-income families through age 21; middle-income recipients are eligible through the sixth grade.

New York state's efforts to cut down on soaring relief expenditures continued. An expanded 11-page welfare application form was introduced in February, and starting in July, periodic face-to-face interviews were required to ensure that recipients continued to be eligible for benefits. The drive was spurred June 21 when the U.S. Supreme Court ruled constitutional New York's 1971 law requiring able-bodied welfare recipients to work; the ruling also reversed a lower court decision exempting from work persons receiving Aid to Families with Dependent Children program aid.

A trend toward updating of state disaster laws accelerated during 1973. New legislation was enacted in Arkansas, Georgia, Nebraska, North Dakota, Rhode Island, South Carolina, Texas, Virginia, and West Virginia, while significant amendments to existing disaster laws were approved in Colorado, New Hampshire, and New York. The revisions generally expanded civil defense contingencies, originated during concern over nuclear attack in the 1950s, to include provision for natural and man-caused disasters, especially weather abnormalities.

Health. State initiatives in health-related fields, like many other programs depending upon federal support, were severely limited during 1973 by impoundment of appropriated funds by the Nixon administration. Surveys revealed that more than $1 billion in authorized health program funds and $1.8 billion in social programs were impounded during fiscal 1973.

In a significant lower court ruling, a Michigan judge ruled July 10 that state funds could not be used to finance experimental psychosurgery on persons confined against their will in state institutions, even when the consent of the patient had been formally obtained.

Law and Justice. Attempts to revive the death penalty accelerated in 1973 as legislators and the general public refused to accept a June 1972 U.S. Supreme Court ruling on the question as final. During the year, 18 more states joined Florida and Ohio in passing new capital punishment laws that incorporate language designed to satisfy dicta in the high court's decision. But twice during the year the Supreme Court indicated it would not allow the end result of its ruling to be circumvented.

Confusion over the high court order existed because each of the nine justices submitted individual opinions in a 5–4 ruling. Only two of the majority declared that death per se constituted "cruel and unusual punishment," while three others ruled the penalty unconstitutional because of the "arbitrary" and "capricious" way it was meted out. Most of the new capital punishment laws made death mandatory for certain types of crimes, thus attempting to overcome the criticism of erratic imposition.

However, on April 2 the Supreme Court refused to allow a Pennsylvania prosecutor to argue that the death penalty was not capriciously or arbitrarily imposed in that state, and on November 12 it let stand a finding that New York's limited death penalty law was unconstitutional; the measure permitted capital punishment for only three types of crimes and provided for a separate jury trial for sentencing.

Massachusetts scored a victory for personal privacy when the U.S. Justice Department dropped a suit in October seeking access to the state's criminal data computer bank on behalf of the Small Business Administration and the Defense Investigative Services. Massachusetts allows access only to criminal justice agencies.

The Florida Supreme Court ruled July 18 that political candidates have a right to reply in newspapers to critical editorials. The defendant *Miami Herald* immediately launched an appeal in federal courts.

New judicial procedure rules were inaugurated in Arizona and Wisconsin, updating court practices and safeguarding litigants' rights.

In April, New Mexico became the 50th state to join the Interstate Compact on Juveniles. The compact was drafted in 1955 to provide for return to their home state of runaway youths and to create a system under which juvenile offenders can be supervised in other states.

Abortion. State laws regulating abortion procedures in 49 states were invalidated January 22 when the U.S. Supreme Court, in a landmark decision, ruled 7 to 2 that expectant mothers have a right to abortion in early stages of pregnancy. In a case from Texas, *Roe* v. *Wade,* the high court ruled that states may not restrict or prohibit voluntary abortions during the first three months, providing the operation is agreed to by an attending physician. In a companion case, the court ruled unconstitutional Georgia's more liberal antiabortion law, as it required residency prerequisites, approval by other doctors, and screening of applicants by a hospital committee. Only New York's abortion law appeared to meet the new guidelines as decreed by the court. Liberal abortion laws in Alaska, Hawaii, and Washington generally conformed to the ruling, but included residency requirements voided by the decision. The remaining 46 states' abortion laws were fully overturned.

The high court added that states may regulate abortion procedures during the second three months of pregnancy, but only in ways that relate to maternal health. During the last three months, states may regulate or prohibit abortion except where the operation is necessary to save the mother's life.

Although most states accepted the ruling, deep-seated opposition quickly became apparent. Attorneys general in Indiana and Montana claimed that the decision did not necessarily affect their state laws. Officials in Utah, Michigan, and Rhode Island attempted to pass new laws, superseding the high court ruling. But on April 16 the Supreme Court served notice it would not allow deviation from the new standards, turning down a petition for rehearing from Connecticut and 14 other states.

Legal Gambling. The trend toward easing of traditional strictures against betting and games of chance continued; the new attitude reflected changing public views toward the morality of gambling and an ever present need for painless sources of new state revenue.

Maine, Rhode Island, Ohio, and Illinois authorized state lotteries during 1973, bringing to eleven the number of states with legal statewide drawings. Other state gambling laws, typically approving bingo and raffles, were approved by legislatures in Michigan, Wisconsin, Washington, Oklahoma, and Virginia during the year.

A survey at year's end showed that 30 states then allowed pari-mutuel betting on horse racing, nine on dog racing. Off-track pari-mutuels were permitted only in Nevada and several New York cities, but plans were being formulated to extend the practice to other Northeast localities.

Drugs. Oregon became the first state to decriminalize marijuana use. A new law, hailed by reformers nationwide, made possession of an ounce or less punishable only by a maximum $100 fine, even for repeat violators.

New measures attempting to control abuse of dangerous drugs were approved in a dozen states. Typically, the new laws increased penalties for sale and use of "hard drugs" (illicit drugs other than marijuana), especially heroin, while easing strictures on marijuana possession in limited quantity.

Harsh new penalties for heroin sale were passed in a number of states, including Delaware, New York, and Vermont. The New York law was closely watched; it ordered life sentences for persons convicted of drug trafficking, with a minimum of 15 to 25 years prison time for sale of one ounce or more of hard drugs. The state also authorized appointment of 100 new judges and expenditures of $66.3 million for treatment and other expenses arising from the new legislation. By year's end, reports differed on early effectiveness of the new measure.

Texas, which previously boasted the nation's most severe penalties for marijuana use, approved a Controlled Substances law reducing possession of small amounts of marijuana from a felony to a misdemeanour.

Environment. Concern over deterioration of natural resources and a loss in the quality of life continued to be reflected in state legislatures. Laws tightening existing environmental regulations or establishing new protections were approved in Nevada, New Jersey, New Hampshire, North Dakota, South Dakota, and Wyoming. Hawaii initiated a population growth limitation study; courts okayed a scenic river protection law in Ohio and oil spill liability measures in Maine and Florida, and California sued four major auto makers, charging that new model cars exceeded state exhaust standards.

On June 11 the U.S. Supreme Court prohibited the federal Environmental Protection Agency from approving state air quality plans that permitted deterioration of existing air quality. The EPA had required only compliance with existing federal standards, even for states currently above standard. Eighteen states supported the environmentalist position while three filed briefs siding with EPA.

Environmental objections to the Alaska pipeline project, to bring oil from Prudhoe Bay to a port in southern Alaska, were brushed aside by Congress in authorizing the project in November. Federal courts had finally blocked the project in March, citing failure to meet environmental regulations, but the new law, approved during widespread concern over an energy crisis, specified removal of environmental roadblocks.

Energy Crisis. Early action by state governments failed to stave off a looming power shortage, largely due to shortages of oil, that preoccupied the nation at year's end.

At a September meeting, 36 state attorneys general called for a breakup of vertically integrated oil companies as a partial response to the problem. Connecticut and Florida filed antitrust suits against oil companies.

As the crisis grew more severe, several states inaugurated imaginative action in the face of federal indecision. Oregon Gov. Tom McCall banned unnecessary commercial and decorative lighting and unsuccessfully sought closing of public schools for a month to conserve energy. Sulfur-content fuel standards were relaxed in Massachusetts, New Hampshire, and New Jersey. Speed limits were reduced to 50 or 55 mph well before federal action in Massachusetts, Maryland, Montana, New Jersey, New York, North Carolina, Oregon, Pennsylvania, Rhode Island, Washington, and Vermont, and regional meetings of governors and other public officials were called to develop cooperative strategies for dealing with energy curtailment and to coordinate public policies.

On June 29, President Nixon named Colorado Gov. John A. Love as assistant to the president and director of the Energy Policy Office. Love resigned his post and assumed the new federal duties immediately, but on December 3 he left the Nixon administration, claiming that his job was to have little substance, thanks to the creation of a new Federal Energy Administration headed by former deputy treasury secretary William E. Simon.

At year's end, the first of several anticipated congressional energy measures had been signed into law: on December 15 President Nixon approved a bill that would put the nation on year-round daylight saving time beginning Jan. 6, 1974.

Obscenity. Efforts by states to control pornography and obscenity according to local standards of taste were approved by the U.S. Supreme Court in a historic series of opinions June 21 and 25. Prior to the rulings, materials were thought to be prosecutable only if they exceeded community standards as measured by a national norm. But the decision written by Chief Justice Warren Burger indicated that state or even local standards of obscenity could be applied to ban offensive materials. "It is neither realistic nor constitutionally sound to read the First Amendment as requiring that the people of Maine or Mississippi accept public depiction of conduct found tolerable in Las Vegas or New York City," Burger declared.

The court eliminated the requirement that a publication be "utterly without redeeming social value" in order to be banned. Instead, the ruling stated, states can enforce obscenity statutes against material that appeals to a prurient interest in sex, portrays specifically defined sexual conduct in an offensive way, and has no serious literary or artistic value.

Prosecutors nationwide generally hailed the new ruling as realistic and enforceable; civil libertarians decried it as a backward step toward censorship. On December 19, the Supreme Court agreed to review the case of a Georgia theatre manager who had been fined $750 under a state obscenity law for showing *Carnal Knowledge*, an R-rated film. His appeal was endorsed by the Association of American Publishers, the National Association of Theater Owners, and the Authors League of America, who hoped for clarification of the June opinions.

Prisons. A week-long riot at the Oklahoma state penitentiary, McAlester, in midsummer left four inmates dead and the prison physical plant in ruins. The trouble started July 27 when an estimated 800 rebellious inmates seized 21 hostages and set buildings ablaze. Gov. David Hall ordered in the National Guard July 29 and order was finally restored August 3. Damage was estimated at $20 million.

The warden and deputy warden of Holmesburg Prison, a holding facility in Philadelphia for inmates awaiting trial and sentencing, were stabbed to death by prisoners May 31. Two inmates accused in the slayings were being held in connection with killings of Philadelphia policemen.

Court decisions in Rhode Island, Kentucky, and Arizona ruled that a prisoner must be given a hearing and his Eighth Amendment rights secured before he can be transferred from state to state under the Interstate Corrections Compact. The compact, drafted in 1969 and ratified by 20 states, allows cooperative use of correctional facilities among signatory states.

Efforts to improve prison conditions continued on several fronts. A federal judge ended restrictions on the amount of mail sent or received by Kentucky prisoners, stopping censorship of outgoing mail and ordering that incoming letters to prisoners from attorneys, news media, or government officials could be inspected only in the inmate's presence. An agreement between state officials and prisoners' attorneys resulted in a bill of rights for Arizona prisoners, including guarantees of due process for inmates accused of breaking rules of conduct.

Efforts continued to lift restrictions on civil rights and employment opportunities of released prisoners. A national study revealed that nearly 2,000 restrictions on ex-convicts had been written on 350 occupations in various states. In the past two years, Arkansas, California, Florida, Illinois, and Washington enacted laws providing that an applicant can no longer be denied a driver's license solely because of a prior criminal offense.

Consumer Protection. Four more states—Hawaii, Kansas, New York, and Utah—adopted some form of no-fault insurance coverage during 1973. By mid-1974, limited or full-scale no-fault insurance systems were to be in effect in 13 states.

The trend toward legal protection from unscrupulous salesmen, especially door-to-door merchants, continued in several states. Laws regulating sales, typically providing for a cooling-off period on door-to-door transactions, were approved in Idaho, Minnesota, Nevada, Texas, and Virginia.

DAVID CAMERON BECKWITH

Area and Population

Area and population of the states

State	AREA in sq. mi. Total	Inland water*	POPULATION (000) July 1, 1970	July 1, 1972†	Percent change 1970–72
Alabama	51,609	549	3,451	3,510	1.7
Alaska	586,400	15,335	305	325	6.6
Arizona	113,909	334	1,792	1,945	8.5
Arkansas	53,104	605	1,926	1,978	2.7
California	158,693	2,120	19,994	20,468	2.4
Colorado	104,247	363	2,225	2,357	5.9
Connecticut	5,009	110	3,039	3,082	1.4
Delaware	2,057	79	550	565	2.7
Dist. of Columbia	69	8	753	748	−0.6
Florida	58,560	4,308	6,845	7,259	6.0
Georgia	58,876	602	4,602	4,720	2.6
Hawaii	6,424	9	774	809	4.5
Idaho	83,557	849	717	756	5.4
Illinois	56,400	470	11,137	11,251	1.0
Indiana	36,291	106	5,208	5,291	1.6
Iowa	56,290	258	2,830	2,883	1.9
Kansas	82,264	216	2,248	2,258	0.4
Kentucky	40,395	532	3,224	3,299	2.3
Louisiana	48,523	3,417	3,644	3,720	2.1
Maine	33,215	2,203	995	1,029	3.4
Maryland	10,577	703	3,937	4,056	3.0
Massachusetts	8,257	390	5,699	5,787	1.5
Michigan	58,216	1,197	8,901	9,082	2.0
Minnesota	84,068	4,059	3,822	3,896	1.9
Mississippi	47,716	493	2,216	2,263	1.2
Missouri	69,686	548	4,693	4,753	1.3
Montana	147,138	1,402	697	719	3.2
Nebraska	77,227	615	1,490	1,525	2.3
Nevada	110,540	752	493	527	6.9
New Hampshire	9,304	290	742	771	3.9
New Jersey	7,836	315	7,195	7,367	2.4
New Mexico	121,666	156	1,018	1,065	4.6
New York	49,576	1,637	18,260	18,366	0.6
North Carolina	52,712	3,645	5,091	5,214	2.4
North Dakota	70,665	1,208	618	632	2.2
Ohio	41,222	250	10,688	10,783	0.9
Oklahoma	69,919	1,032	2,572	2,634	2.4
Oregon	96,981	733	2,102	2,182	3.8
Pennsylvania	45,333	326	11,817	11,926	0.9
Rhode Island	1,214	156	951	968	1.8
South Carolina	31,055	783	2,596	2,665	2.7
South Dakota	77,047	669	666	679	2.0
Tennessee	42,244	482	3,932	4,031	2.5
Texas	267,338	4,499	11,254	11,649	1.9
Utah	84,916	2,577	1,069	1,126	5.3
Vermont	9,609	333	447	462	3.4
Virginia	40,815	977	4,653	4,764	2.4
Washington	68,192	1,483	3,414	3,443	0.8
West Virginia	24,181	102	1,746	1,781	2.0
Wisconsin	56,154	1,449	4,433	4,520	2.0
Wyoming	97,914	503	334	345	3.3
TOTAL U.S.	3,615,210	66,237	203,805	208,232‡	2.2

*Excludes the Great Lakes and coastal waters.
†Preliminary.
‡State figures do not add to total given because of rounding.
Source: U.S. Department of Commerce, Bureau of the Census, *Current Population Reports.*

Marriage and divorce rates

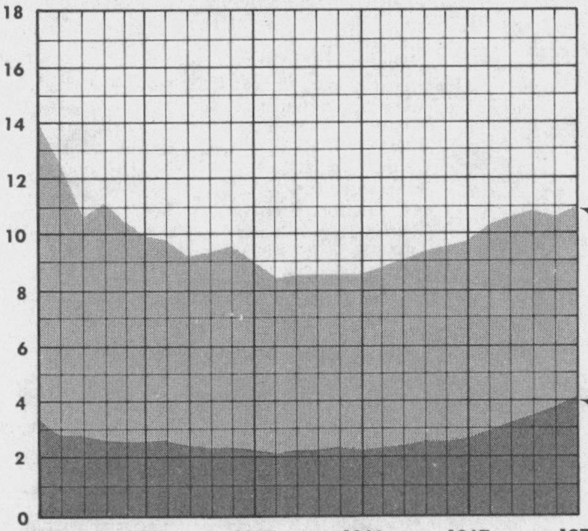

*Includes annulments.
Source: U.S. Department of Health, Education, and Welfare, Public Health Service, *Monthly Vital Statistics Report.*

Population change

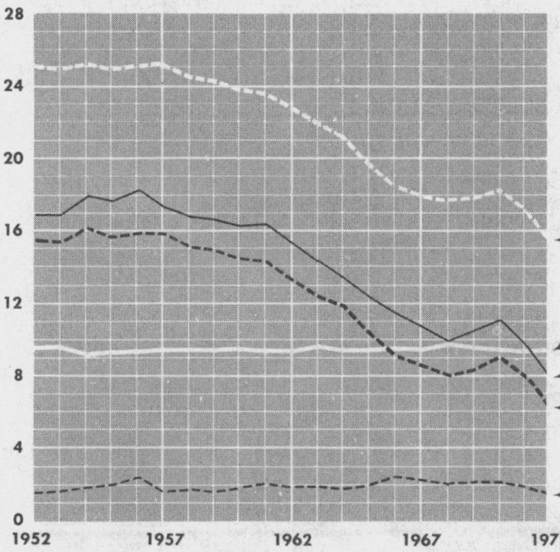

Source: U.S. Department of Commerce, Bureau of the Census, *Current Population Reports.*

Largest metropolitan areas

Name	POPULATION 1970 census	1972 estimate	% change 1970–72	land area (sq. mi.)	1972 density (per sq. mi.)
New York	9,973,716	9,943,800	—0.3	1,153	8,624
Chicago	6,977,611	7,084,700	1.5	3,719	1,905
Los Angeles-Long Beach	7,041,980	6,999,600	—0.6	4,069	1,720
Philadelphia	4,824,110	4,877,500	1.1	3,553	1,373
Detroit	4,435,051	4,488,900	1.2	3,916	1,146
Boston*	3,376,328	3,417,000	1.2	1,769	1,932
San Francisco-Oakland	3,108,782	3,131,800	0.7	2,480	1,263
Washington, D.C.	2,909,355	2,998,900	3.1	2,812	1,066
Nassau-Suffolk†	2,555,868	2,597,300	1.6	1,218	2,132
St. Louis	2,410,492	2,399,800	—0.4	5,208	461
Pittsburgh	2,401,362	2,395,900	—0.2	3,049	786
Dallas-Fort Worth‡	2,378,353	2,383,800§	0.2	6,109	390
Baltimore	2,071,016	2,125,000	2.6	2,259	941
Newark	2,057,468	2,082,000	1.2	1,008	2,065
Cleveland	2,063,729	2,045,500	—0.9	1,519	1,347
Houston	1,999,316	2,105,600§	5.3	6,794	310
Minneapolis-St. Paul	1,965,391	1,995,800	1.5	4,647	429
Atlanta	1,595,517	1,683,600	5.5	4,326	389
Anaheim-Santa Ana-Garden Grove	1,421,233	1,527,300	7.5	782	1,953
Seattle-Everett	1,424,605	1,399,600	—1.8	4,226	331
Milwaukee	1,403,883	1,423,200	1.4	1,456	977
Cincinnati	1,385,103	1,391,400	0.5	2,149	647
San Diego	1,357,854	1,443,100	6.3	4,261	339
Buffalo	1,349,211	1,353,100	0.3	1,590	851
Miami	1,267,792	1,331,100	5.0	2,042	652
Kansas City	1,273,926	1,303,600	2.3	3,341	390
Denver-Boulder	1,231,070	1,309,200	6.3	3,808	344
Tampa-St. Petersburg	1,088,549	1,189,000	9.2	2,045	581
Riverside-San Bernardino-Ontario	1,141,307	1,178,500	3.3	27,293	43
Indianapolis	1,111,352	1,128,000	1.5	3,072	367
San Jose	1,065,313	1,126,700	5.8	1,300	867
New Orleans	1,046,470	1,076,600	2.9	1,967	547
Columbus	1,017,847	1,057,700	3.9	2,460	430
Phoenix	969,425	1,053,000	8.6	9,155	115
Portland	1,007,130	1,036,300	2.9	3,650	284
Rochester	961,516	968,600	0.7	2,966	327
San Antonio	888,179	909,700§	2.4	2,527	360
Louisville	867,330	887,700	2.4	1,392	638
Dayton	852,531	857,300	0.6	1,708	502
Sacramento	803,793	851,300	5.9	3,434	248
Memphis	834,103	847,100	1.6	2,298	369
Hartford*	816,737	833,800	2.1	739	1,128
Bridgeport*	792,814	793,900	0.1	648	1,225
Albany-Schenectady-Troy	777,977	792,900	1.9	2,624	302
Providence-Warwick-Pawtucket*	769,789	782,600	1.7	680	1,151
Toledo	762,658	780,600	2.4	2,489	314
Birmingham	767,230	778,500	1.5	3,358	232
New Haven-West Haven*	744,948	760,800	2.1	604	1,260
Greensboro-Winston-Salem-High Point	724,129	745,100	2.9	3,214	232
Salt Lake City-Ogden‡	705,458	744,300	5.5	1,061	702
Oklahoma City	699,092	735,800	5.3	3,491	211
Nashville-Davidson	699,271	715,700	2.3	4,080	175
Norfolk-Virginia Beach-Portsmouth	687,576	683,000	—0.7	1,148	595
Akron	679,239	682,200	0.4	903	755
Worcester*	637,037	644,700	1.2	1,509	427

Standard Metropolitan Statistical Areas (SMSA's) defined by Census Bureau as of April 27, 1973.
*Metropolitan State Economic Area.
†New SMSA established since 1970 census.
‡Merger of two existing SMSA's since the 1970 census.
§Estimates not available for all counties in SMSA; total for 1972 is for available counties only.
Source: U.S. Department of Commerce, Social and Economic Statistics Administration, Bureau of the Census.

State population characteristics

mobility and housing

State	1970 Census pop. (000s)	% black	% same house last 5 years	Total house-holds (000s)	OWNER-OCCUPIED HOUSING: Median value ($000)	OWNER-OCCUPIED HOUSING: % total house-holds in	OWNER-OCCUPIED HOUSING: % black house-holds in	RENTED HOUSING: Median rent in $	RENTED HOUSING: % total house-holds in	RENTED HOUSING: % black house-holds in
Ala.	3,444	26.2	54.5	1,120	12.2	66.7	50.4	48	33.3	49.6
Alaska	300	3.0	26.9	79	22.7	50.3	25.2	171	49.7	74.8
Ariz.	1,771	3.0	41.3	539	16.3	65.3	49.3	90	34.7	50.7
Ark.	1,923	18.3	50.6	615	10.5	66.7	52.9	53	33.3	47.1
Calif.	19,953	7.0	43.5	6,574	23.1	54.9	39.1	113	45.1	60.9
Colo.	2,207	3.0	42.9	691	17.3	63.4	47.1	97	36.6	52.9
Conn.	3,032	6.0	57.5	933	25.5	62.5	22.9	105	37.5	77.1
Del.	548	14.3	54.0	165	17.1	68.0	49.9	89	32.0	50.1
D.C.	757	71.1	47.3	263	21.3	28.2	27.3	110	71.8	72.7
Fla.	6,789	15.3	44.1	2,285	15.0	68.6	48.7	92	31.4	51.3
Ga.	4,590	25.9	48.6	1,369	14.6	61.1	41.3	65	38.9	58.7
Hawaii	769	1.0	45.9	203	35.1	46.9	11.4	120	53.1	88.6
Ida.	713	0.3	48.7	219	14.1	70.1	29.1	70	29.9	70.9
Ill.	11,114	12.8	54.0	3,502	19.8	59.4	29.0	107	40.6	71.0
Ind.	5,194	6.9	53.8	1,609	13.8	71.7	51.0	82	28.3	49.0
Iowa	2,824	1.2	57.1	896	13.9	71.7	55.5	77	28.3	44.5
Kan.	2,247	4.8	51.1	727	12.1	69.1	54.1	75	30.9	45.9
Ky.	3,219	7.2	53.6	984	12.6	66.9	48.2	63	33.1	51.8
La.	3,641	29.8	55.8	1,052	14.6	63.1	47.1	62	36.9	52.9
Me.	992	0.3	58.3	303	12.8	70.1	30.8	69	29.9	69.2
Md.	3,922	17.8	51.5	1,175	18.7	58.8	37.7	110	41.2	62.3
Mass.	5,689	3.1	59.1	1,760	20.6	57.5	24.7	89	42.5	75.3
Mich.	8,875	11.2	55.3	2,659	17.5	74.4	53.4	93	25.6	46.6
Minn.	3,805	0.9	56.8	1,154	18.0	71.5	41.9	101	28.5	58.1
Miss.	2,217	36.8	55.4	637	11.2	66.3	49.1	46	33.7	50.9
Mo.	4,677	10.3	52.1	1,521	14.4	67.2	43.3	74	32.8	56.7
Mont.	694	0.3	50.4	217	14.0	65.7	24.3	71	34.3	75.7
Neb.	1,485	2.7	53.9	474	12.4	66.4	48.3	77	33.6	51.7
Nev.	489	5.7	36.2	160	22.4	58.5	38.7	123	41.5	61.3
N.H.	738	0.3	55.0	225	16.4	68.2	32.2	79	31.8	67.8
N.J.	7,168	10.7	57.6	2,218	23.4	60.9	33.6	111	39.1	66.4
N.M.	1,016	1.9	49.7	289	13.0	66.4	46.4	72	33.6	53.6
N.Y.	18,237	11.9	59.6	5,914	22.5	47.3	19.7	95	52.7	80.3
N.C.	5,082	22.2	53.8	1,510	12.8	65.4	45.5	59	34.6	54.5
N.D.	618	0.4	56.4	182	13.0	68.4	6.8	77	31.6	93.2
Ohio	10,652	9.1	54.8	3,289	17.6	67.7	44.6	83	32.3	55.4
Okla.	2,559	6.7	47.7	851	12.0	69.2	59.6	76	30.8	40.4
Ore.	2,091	1.3	44.7	692	15.4	66.1	45.5	86	33.9	54.5
Penn.	11,794	8.6	63.7	3,705	13.6	68.8	46.1	73	31.2	53.9
R.I.	947	2.7	57.4	292	18.2	57.9	24.7	65	42.1	75.3
S.C.	2,591	30.9	54.7	734	13.0	66.1	49.7	50	33.9	50.3
S.D.	666	0.2	57.1	201	11.4	69.6	23.1	69	30.4	76.9
Tenn.	3,924	15.8	52.6	1,213	12.5	66.7	43.7	62	33.3	56.3
Tex.	11,197	12.5	47.5	3,434	12.0	64.7	53.8	76	35.3	46.2
Utah	1,059	0.6	53.9	298	16.8	69.3	43.9	80	30.7	56.1
Vt.	444	0.2	54.9	132	16.4	69.1	38.4	76	30.9	61.6
Va.	4,648	18.5	50.3	1,391	17.1	62.0	51.5	92	38.0	48.5
Wash.	3,409	2.1	45.0	1,106	18.5	66.8	49.1	94	33.2	50.9
W.Va.	1,744	3.9	60.4	547	11.3	68.9	58.7	52	31.1	41.3
Wis.	4,418	2.9	57.8	1,329	17.3	69.1	34.2	91	30.9	65.8
Wyo.	332	0.8	48.1	105	15.3	66.4	37.8	72	33.6	62.2
TOTAL U.S.	203,212	11.1	53.0	63,450	17.0	62.9	41.6	89	37.1	58.4

Source: U.S. Dept. of Commerce, Bureau of the Census, *1970 Census of Housing; 1970 Census of Population.*

Church membership

Religious body	Total clergy	Inclusive membership
Adventist, Seventh-day	3,422	449,188
Baptist Bodies		
American Baptist Association	3,338	955,900
American Baptist Churches in the U.S.A.	7,599	1,484,393
Baptist General Conference	1,032	111,364
Baptist Missionary Association of America	2,500	199,640
Conservative Baptist Association of America	...	300,000
Free Will Baptists	3,600	203,000
General Baptists (General Association of)	1,200	70,000
National Baptist Convention of America	28,574	2,668,799
National Baptist Convention, U.S.A., Inc.	27,500	5,000,000
National Baptist Evangelical Life and Soul Saving Assembly of U.S.A.	137	57,674
National Primitive Baptist Convention, Inc.	601	1,645,000
Primitive Baptists	...	72,000
Progressive National Baptist Convention, Inc.	863	521,692
Regular Baptist Churches, General Assn. of	...	214,000
Southern Baptist Convention	54,150	12,065,333
United Free Will Baptist Church	784	100,000
Brethren (German Baptists): Church of the Brethren	2,026	179,686
Buddhist Churches of America	101	100,000
Christian and Missionary Alliance	1,259	136,154
Christian Church (Disciples of Christ)	6,749	1,352,211
Christian Churches and Churches of Christ	6,934	1,036,460
Christian Congregation	305	52,585
Church of God (Anderson, Ind.)	2,906	155,920
Church of the Nazarene	7,195	404,732
Churches of Christ	6,200	2,400,000
Congregational Christian Churches, Natl. Assn. of	459	85,000
Eastern Churches		
Albanian Orthodox Archdiocese in America	23	62,000
American Carpatho-Russian Orthodox Greek Catholic Church	68	108,400
Antiochian Orthodox Christian Archdiocese of New York and all North America	110	100,000
Armenian Apostolic Church of America	34	125,000
Armenian Church of America, Diocese of the (Including Diocese of California)	67	372,000
Bulgarian Eastern Orthodox Church	11	86,000
Greek Orthodox Archdiocese of North and South America	695	1,950,000
Orthodox Church in America	455	1,000,000
Romanian Orthodox Episcopate of America	49	50,000
Russian Orthodox Church in the U.S.A., Patriarchal Parishes of the	53	50,000
Russian Orthodox Church Outside Russia	168	55,000
Serbian Eastern Orth. Ch. U.S.A. and Canada	64	65,000
Syrian Orthodox Church of Antioch	14	50,000
Ukrainian Orthodox Church in the U.S.A.	131	87,745
Episcopal Church	11,566	3,062,734
Evangelical Covenant Church of America	671	68,771
Evangelical Free Church of America	...	70,490
Friends United Meeting	566	68,717
Independent Fundamental Churches of America	1,264	77,794
Jehovah's Witnesses	None	431,179
Jewish Congregations	6,400	6,115,000
Latter Day Saints		
Church of Jesus Christ of Latter-day Saints	17,133	2,185,810
Reorganized Church of Jesus Christ of L. D. S.	15,872	179,763
Lutherans		
American Lutheran Church	6,264	2,492,355
Lutheran Church in America	7,450	3,034,366
Lutheran Church—Missouri Synod	7,174	2,781,297
Wisconsin Evangelical Lutheran Synod	995	385,077
Mennonite Church	2,207	89,505
Methodists		
African Methodist Episcopal Church	7,089	1,166,301
African Methodist Episcopal Zion Church	5,500	940,000
Christian Methodist Episcopal Church	2,259	466,718
Free Methodist Church of North America	1,744	65,167
United Methodist Church	34,974	10,334,521
Moravian Church in America	213	56,825
North American Old Roman Catholic Church	111	60,098
Old Roman Catholic Church (English Rite)	201	65,128
Pentecostals		
Apostolic Overcoming Holy Church of God	350	75,000
Assemblies of God	12,087	1,099,606
Church of God	2,737	75,890
Church of God (Cleveland, Tenn.)	8,000	297,103
Church of God in Christ	6,000	425,000
Church of God in Christ, International	1,502	501,000
Church of God of Prophecy	5,195	59,535
International Ch. of the Foursquare Gospel	2,690	89,215
Pentecostal Church of God of America, Inc.	1,325	115,000
Pentecostal Holiness Church, Inc.	1,878	74,108
United Pentecostal Church, International	5,250	250,000
Polish National Catholic Church of America	144	282,411
Presbyterians		
Cumberland Presbyterian Church	710	88,738
Presbyterian Church in the U.S.	5,139	946,536
United Presbyterian Church in the U.S.A.	13,624	2,908,958
Reformed Bodies		
Christian Reformed Church	1,027	287,114
Reformed Church in America	1,470	372,681
Roman Catholic Church	57,332	48,460,427
Salvation Army	5,181	358,626
Spiritualists, International General Assembly	...	164,072
Triumph the Ch. and Kingdom of God in Christ	1,375	54,307
Unitarian Universalist Association	868	265,408
United Church of Christ	9,480	1,895,016
Wesleyan Church	2,925	84,499

Table includes churches reporting a membership of 50,000 or more and represents the latest information available. Source: National Council of Churches, *Yearbook of American and Canadian Churches*, 1974.

(CONSTANT H. JACQUET)

The Economy

Gross national product and national income

in billions of dollars

Item	1965	1970	1972	1973*
Gross national product	683.9	977.1	1,155.2	1,272.0
By type of expenditure				
Personal consumption expenditures	433.1	617.6	726.5	795.6
Durable goods	66.0	91.3	117.4	132.8
Nondurable goods	191.2	263.8	299.9	330.3
Services	175.9	262.6	309.2	332.6
Gross private domestic investment	107.4	136.3	178.3	198.2
Fixed investment	98.0	131.7	172.3	193.7
Changes in business inventories	9.4	4.5	6.0	4.5
Net exports of goods and services	6.9	3.6	−4.6	2.8
Exports	39.1	62.9	73.5	97.2
Imports	32.2	59.3	78.1	94.4
Government purchases of goods and services	136.4	219.5	255.0	275.3
Federal	66.8	96.2	104.4	107.3
State and local	69.6	123.3	150.5	168.0
By major type of product				
Goods output	346.6	466.7	535.4	599.6
Durable goods	139.5	182.5	214.1	242.4
Nondurable goods	207.1	284.1	321.2	357.3
Services	262.9	410.3	487.3	527.7
Structures	74.4	95.6	126.5	140.1

Item	1965	1970	1972	1973*
National income	562.4	800.5	941.8	1,038.2
By types of income				
Compensation of employees	393.9	603.9	707.1	774.9
Proprietors' income	56.7	66.9	74.2	81.5
Rental income of persons	19.0	23.9	24.1	24.6
Corporate profits and inventory valuation adjustment	74.9	69.2	91.1	107.9
Net interest	17.9	36.5	45.2	49.4
By industry division				
Agriculture, forestry, and fisheries	21.0	25.5	30.4	35.1
Mining and construction	35.3	50.5	59.9	65.5
Manufacturing	171.8	216.3	252.6	290.4
Nondurable goods	66.3	87.5	99.9	109.9
Durable goods	105.5	128.7	152.7	180.5
Transportation	23.1	29.7	36.0	38.5
Communications and public utilities	22.6	31.4	38.2	40.4
Wholesale and retail trade	84.2	121.2	139.7	149.7
Finance, insurance, and real estate	61.3	90.0	107.9	117.3
Services	63.7	102.7	120.1	131.4
Government and government enterprises	75.2	126.8	149.5	160.9
Other	4.2	4.6	7.5	8.9

*Second quarter, seasonally adjusted at annual rates.
Source: U.S. Department of Commerce, Office of Business Economics, *Survey of Current Business.*

Personal income per capita

State	1950	1960	1970	1972*
Alabama	$ 880	$1,489	$2,876	$3,333
Alaska	2,384	2,835	4,586	5,162
Arizona	1,330	2,032	3,620	4,300
Arkansas	825	1,374	2,864	3,357
California	1,852	2,708	4,444	5,002
Colorado	1,487	2,273	3,831	4,449
Connecticut	1,875	2,806	4,817	5,342
Delaware	2,132	2,758	4,353	4,983
District of Columbia	2,221	3,021	5,466	6,383
Florida	1,281	1,948	3,664	4,188
Georgia	1,034	1,640	3,354	3,846
Hawaii	1,386	2,369	4,557	4,995
Idaho	1,295	1,850	3,264	3,635
Illinois	1,825	2,649	4,486	5,126
Indiana	1,512	2,188	3,787	4,391
Iowa	1,485	1,987	3,750	4,318
Kansas	1,443	2,158	3,918	4,593
Kentucky	981	1,576	3,099	3,601
Louisiana	1,120	1,656	3,054	3,528
Maine	1,186	1,842	3,242	3,571
Maryland	1,602	2,342	4,287	4,897
Massachusetts	1,633	2,457	4,343	4,870
Michigan	1,701	2,324	4,133	4,817
Minnesota	1,410	2,114	3,855	4,332
Mississippi	755	1,206	2,597	3,063
Missouri	1,431	2,115	3,713	4,206
Montana	1,622	2,094	3,444	3,897
Nebraska	1,490	2,110	3,792	4,341
Nevada	2,018	2,856	4,552	5,215
New Hampshire	1,323	2,144	3,620	4,092
New Jersey	1,834	2,708	4,577	5,126
New Mexico	1,177	1,888	3,127	3,656
New York	1,873	2,749	4,731	5,319
North Carolina	1,037	1,562	3,218	3,721
North Dakota	1,263	1,714	3,069	3,718
Ohio	1,620	2,335	3,977	4,512
Oklahoma	1,143	1,862	3,332	3,802
Oregon	1,620	2,235	3,718	4,296
Pennsylvania	1,541	2,242	3,942	4,447
Rhode Island	1,605	2,219	3,918	4,399
South Carolina	893	1,379	2,933	3,448
South Dakota	1,242	1,782	3,164	3,716
Tennessee	994	1,544	3,075	3,640
Texas	1,349	1,926	3,573	4,045
Utah	1,309	1,968	3,221	3,745
Vermont	1,121	1,842	3,448	3,865
Virginia	1,228	1,841	3,650	4,258
Washington	1,674	2,349	3,984	4,476
West Virginia	1,065	1,596	3,034	3,574
Wisconsin	1,477	2,174	3,712	4,207
Wyoming	1,668	2,261	3,674	4,345
TOTAL U.S.	1,496	2,216	3,933	4,478

*Preliminary.
Source: U.S. Department of Commerce, Bureau of Economic Analysis, *Survey of Current Business.*

1972 Gross domestic product by industry and component*

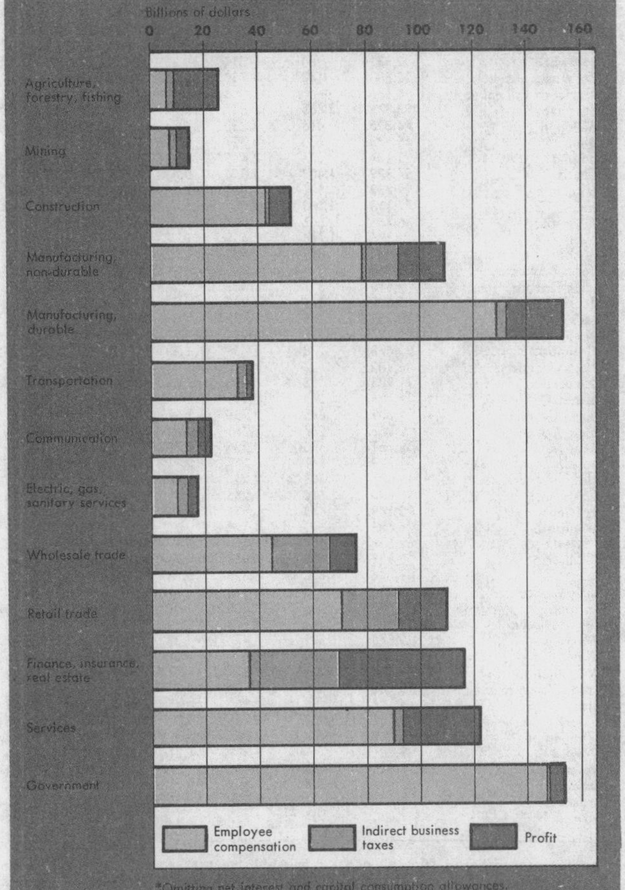

*Omitting net interest and capital consumption allowances.
Source: U.S. Department of Commerce, *Survey of Current Business.*

Farms and farm income

State	Number of farms 1973*	Land in farms 1973 in 000 acres	CASH INCOME, 1972, IN $000: Farm marketings: Crops	Farm marketings: Livestock and products	Government payments	Realized net income per farm 1972
Alabama	76,000	14,400	303,369	616,394	68,091	4,517
Alaska	310	1,710†	1,729	2,841	197	2,884
Arizona	6,000	39,200	342,253	479,986	49,013	28,185
Arkansas	69,000	17,400	730,139	673,596	81,624	8,133
California	63,000	36,200	3,268,272	2,205,784	122,433	20,506
Colorado	29,000	39,900	303,291	1,396,479	70,906	8,559
Connecticut	4,300	530	62,600	101,255	509	8,610
Delaware	3,600	700	51,447	103,186	1,975	14,165
Florida	34,000	14,500	1,198,524	464,033	18,183	20,691
Georgia	75,000	17,000	634,392	786,744	81,064	7,529
Hawaii	4,000	2,300	177,198	46,238	11,108	19,581
Idaho	27,600	15,500	410,289	397,734	51,067	10,367
Illinois	127,000	29,300	1,933,153	1,463,589	243,879	10,437
Indiana	107,000	17,500	860,394	967,171	133,101	6,076
Iowa	139,000	34,300	1,436,140	3,260,692	318,511	10,969
Kansas	84,000	49,900	921,044	1,899,276	246,409	10,756
Kentucky	125,000	16,100	492,067	593,327	36,837	3,891
Louisiana	48,000	11,800	506,944	323,639	50,953	8,381
Maine	7,400	1,670	89,425	155,248	1,295	8,702
Maryland	18,000	2,970	134,834	278,085	9,572	6,641
Massachusetts	5,700	700	70,067	83,768	478	5,314
Michigan	80,000	12,300	466,083	574,735	61,203	3,498
Minnesota	117,000	30,500	799,371	1,563,993	179,974	6,735
Mississippi	84,000	17,200	535,054	549,527	125,875	6,105
Missouri	138,000	32,800	701,799	1,237,845	150,203	5,065
Montana	25,100	62,700	266,536	495,517	103,169	13,105
Nebraska	70,000	48,100	765,031	1,915,112	233,324	9,730
Nevada	2,000	9,000	16,207	94,313	2,619	18,890
New Hampshire	2,500	540	15,203	42,829	461	5,545
New Jersey	8,100	1,035	135,840	90,194	3,676	2,956
New Mexico	11,800	47,200	105,704	471,737	42,503	9,303
New York	55,000	10,800	270,757	830,801	19,939	4,764
North Carolina	135,000	14,000	1,016,828	642,372	57,529	5,397
North Dakota	42,000	41,700	534,455	365,261	208,122	8,165
Ohio	117,000	17,400	781,205	875,527	89,578	4,598
Oklahoma	87,000	37,000	297,951	1,081,723	119,400	4,122
Oregon	33,000	19,700	355,433	288,767	24,558	5,953
Pennsylvania	71,000	9,900	249,047	840,966	22,892	3,169
Rhode Island	680	65	8,204	8,946	57	2,344
South Carolina	49,000	8,000	345,150	214,337	49,285	4,634
South Dakota	44,000	45,500	238,269	969,470	111,519	9,699
Tennessee	124,000	15,300	335,287	514,789	57,753	2,423
Texas	209,000	141,800	1,368,752	2,564,846	528,567	4,054
Utah	12,600	13,000	44,545	201,636	13,861	6,001
Vermont	6,400	1,810	18,349	160,981	828	9,654
Virginia	74,000	11,200	273,833	385,752	19,563	2,646
Washington	40,000	16,600	692,160	332,331	56,411	9,803
West Virginia	26,000	4,800	26,928	90,209	3,324	713
Wisconsin	106,000	19,700	251,644	1,598,147	57,106	5,771
Wyoming	8,200	35,500	51,535	293,786	20,595	13,121
Total U.S.	2,831,290	1,088,730	25,075,158	35,595,544	3,961,109	6,856

*Preliminary. †Exclusive of grazing land leased from the U.S. Government, Alaska farmland totals about 70,000 acres.
Source: U.S. Department of Agriculture, Economics Research Service.

Income by industrial source, 1972

State and region	SOURCES OF PERSONAL INCOME: Total personal income	Farm income	Govt. income disbursements*: Federal	Govt. income disbursements*: State, local	Private non-farm income†	SOURCES OF CIVILIAN INCOME % OF TOTAL: Total	Farms	Mining	Con-struc-tion	Mfg.	Whole-sale, retail trade	Finance, insur-ance, real estate	Transpor-tation, commun-ications, public util.‡	Service	Govt.§	Other
United States	$935,350	$24,073	$132,859	$96,011	$682,407	$720,373	%3.4	%1.0	%6.5	%27.6	%16.8	%5.5	%7.5	%15.6	%15.8	%0.3
New England	57,545	290	7,493	5,495	44,267	43,484	0.7	0.1	6.9	31.0	16.5	6.4	6.3	18.1	13.6	0.4
Maine	3,714	83	649	381	2,602	2,722	3.1	0.1	7.4	29.7	17.2	4.3	7.0	14.6	15.9	0.7
New Hampshire	3,270	20	487	261	2,503	2,503	0.8	0.2	7.8	33.3	16.8	5.3	6.2	15.7	13.6	0.3
Vermont	1,703	66	243	198	1,195	1,279	5.2	0.5	7.6	25.3	15.3	4.5	6.4	18.8	16.2	0.2
Massachusetts	28,096	53	3,651	2,871	21,522	21,106	0.3	0.1	6.8	28.1	17.0	6.4	6.6	20.1	14.2	0.4
Rhode Island	4,340	5	820	411	3,104	3,196	0.2	0.1	6.3	32.0	16.8	5.4	5.7	16.5	16.6	0.4
Connecticut	16,421	64	1,643	1,373	13,342	12,679	0.5	0.1	6.9	36.2	15.5	7.4	5.6	16.4	11.1	0.3
Mideast	215,493	834	29,092	24,297	161,270	165,917	0.5	0.4	6.0	27.2	16.4	6.8	8.0	17.7	16.7	0.3
New York	96,280	311	10,497	13,190	72,282	72,549	0.4	0.2	5.1	23.4	16.7	9.0	8.4	19.7	16.8	0.3
New Jersey	38,543	63	4,420	3,280	30,780	30,535	0.2	0.2	6.5	32.9	17.5	5.9	8.3	16.1	12.1	0.3
Pennsylvania	53,249	257	7,105	5,098	40,788	41,512	0.6	1.2	6.5	34.8	15.8	4.7	7.7	15.4	13.1	0.2
Delaware	2,931	60	314	269	2,289	2,253	2.8	0.1	7.2	39.8	14.2	4.4	5.5	12.8	13.0	0.2
Maryland	19,803	142	4,750	2,051	12,860	15,944	0.9	0.2	7.5	16.9	16.8	5.0	6.6	17.0	28.8	0.3
District of Columbia	4,686	—	2,006	409	2,272	3,123	—	0.1	3.5	4.9	8.5	3.7	5.4	26.2	46.5	1.2
Great Lakes	193,375	3,765	19,887	18,221	151,503	155,003	2.5	0.6	5.8	38.3	15.8	4.4	6.8	13.1	12.5	0.2
Michigan	44,325	416	4,138	4,740	35,032	35,996	1.2	0.4	5.4	44.3	14.7	3.5	5.3	12.3	12.7	0.2
Ohio	48,888	630	5,321	4,023	38,915	39,253	1.6	0.8	5.6	39.9	15.4	4.1	7.1	13.3	12.0	0.2
Indiana	23,101	687	2,449	1,946	18,019	18,841	3.7	0.5	6.0	41.6	14.6	4.0	6.5	11.1	11.8	0.2
Illinois	57,829	1,402	5,896	5,433	45,098	45,795	3.1	0.6	6.3	31.7	17.4	5.5	8.1	14.5	12.6	0.2
Wisconsin	19,232	631	2,084	2,079	14,439	15,117	4.3	0.2	6.0	35.9	15.9	4.3	6.1	13.0	14.0	0.3
Plains	71,118	6,206	9,561	6,816	48,535	54,518	11.6	0.7	6.0	22.6	17.5	4.9	8.0	13.8	14.6	0.3
Minnesota	16,746	867	1,884	1,892	12,102	13,161	6.7	1.2	6.4	24.4	18.0	5.2	8.3	14.5	15.1	0.2
Iowa	12,396	1,714	1,429	1,173	8,080	9,631	18.2	0.3	5.3	24.0	15.9	4.4	6.2	12.0	13.3	0.4
Missouri	20,403	865	2,932	1,737	14,868	15,637	5.6	0.6	5.9	26.7	18.0	5.1	9.2	14.6	14.0	0.3
North Dakota	2,363	399	445	250	1,269	1,707	23.8	0.9	8.2	5.5	18.4	3.7	7.5	13.3	18.5	0.2
South Dakota	2,512	511	433	268	1,300	1,879	27.7	1.3	5.0	8.3	16.3	3.6	6.0	12.9	18.5	0.4
Nebraska	6,642	868	915	599	4,260	4,982	17.8	0.2	6.4	15.7	17.5	5.5	8.4	13.5	14.7	0.3
Kansas	10,058	981	1,523	898	6,656	7,521	13.3	1.0	5.9	21.2	17.1	4.6	8.5	13.4	14.6	0.4
Southeast	171,827	6,072	30,292	15,991	199,473	130,971	4.7	1.7	7.4	25.6	17.0	5.0	7.6	14.1	16.6	0.3
Virginia	20,478	278	5,459	1,804	12,937	15,566	1.8	1.2	7.0	20.8	15.4	4.8	7.5	14.6	26.7	0.2
West Virginia	6,402	27	1,078	627	4,669	4,896	0.6	12.6	8.2	26.0	14.2	3.0	9.3	12.2	13.8	0.1
Kentucky	11,905	585	1,988	1,036	8,297	9,145	6.5	3.9	7.0	29.3	15.3	3.8	7.6	12.4	14.0	0.2
Tennessee	14,796	373	2,191	1,375	10,877	11,808	3.2	0.6	6.2	32.6	17.2	4.7	6.3	13.9	15.1	0.2
North Carolina	19,809	845	2,799	1,811	14,354	15,742	5.5	0.2	6.4	35.3	16.1	4.4	6.5	12.0	13.4	0.2
South Carolina	9,268	267	1,761	814	6,427	7,203	3.8	0.2	6.8	36.4	14.7	4.1	5.6	12.9	15.3	0.2
Georgia	18,451	590	2,880	1,724	13,256	14,689	4.1	0.4	6.7	26.1	19.2	5.8	8.4	13.1	15.8	0.4
Florida	31,779	941	5,677	2,912	22,250	22,272	4.4	0.4	10.2	13.9	20.1	7.1	8.5	18.7	16.1	0.6
Alabama	12,004	388	2,266	1,154	8,195	9,291	4.3	1.0	6.0	29.7	15.9	4.4	6.9	13.4	18.1	0.3
Mississippi	7,099	610	1,246	718	4,526	5,385	11.6	1.1	5.8	28.0	15.1	4.1	6.1	12.4	15.4	0.4
Louisiana	13,179	478	1,839	1,447	9,415	9,971	4.9	5.7	8.5	18.2	18.0	4.8	9.7	14.4	15.4	0.4
Arkansas	6,656	690	1,128	569	4,270	5,002	14.1	0.8	5.5	26.7	15.6	4.5	7.1	12.0	13.2	0.5
Southwest	68,568	2,499	11,494	6,348	48,227	51,535	5.0	3.8	7.5	19.0	18.7	5.7	7.9	15.3	16.8	0.3
Oklahoma	9,995	438	1,907	968	6,682	7,291	6.2	5.2	5.9	18.1	17.3	5.2	8.4	14.1	19.2	0.4
Texas	46,486	1,638	7,328	3,987	33,533	35,098	4.8	3.2	7.2	20.8	19.5	5.8	8.1	15.1	15.2	0.3
New Mexico	3,796	157	825	517	2,297	2,830	5.7	5.7	8.0	6.9	15.7	4.4	7.7	19.1	26.5	0.3
Arizona	8,292	266	1,435	877	5,715	6,316	4.3	4.7	11.0	15.8	16.9	6.0	6.3	16.2	18.4	0.4
Rocky Mountain	22,205	1,272	3,765	2,297	14,872	17,080	7.6	3.1	8.3	15.4	17.7	4.9	8.5	14.5	19.6	0.4
Montana	2,875	389	473	299	1,714	2,177	18.2	3.2	7.1	10.5	16.3	3.8	9.0	12.8	18.6	0.5
Idaho	2,858	332	433	278	1,814	2,225	15.3	1.5	7.4	17.3	17.2	3.9	7.0	13.9	15.9	0.6
Wyoming	1,494	129	231	174	960	1,122	11.8	11.1	9.8	7.0	14.1	3.3	10.7	11.4	20.5	0.3
Colorado	10,782	335	1,783	1,091	7,573	8,204	4.2	2.0	9.2	17.1	18.9	5.9	8.4	15.6	18.4	0.3
Utah	4,197	87	845	455	2,810	3,352	2.7	4.2	7.1	16.2	17.2	4.4	8.4	14.3	25.3	0.2
Far West	129,528	3,032	19,755	15,829	90,912	97,645	3.2	0.5	6.1	22.8	17.6	5.8	7.7	17.5	18.4	0.4
Washington	15,399	487	2,637	1,829	10,446	11,531	4.4	0.2	6.4	23.0	18.0	5.3	7.8	14.8	19.6	0.5
Oregon	9,354	249	1,301	1,011	6,793	7,246	3.5	0.2	6.5	25.8	19.0	4.8	8.2	14.5	17.0	0.5
Nevada	2,676	48	395	277	1,957	2,154	2.3	1.8	8.8	4.6	14.8	4.5	7.7	37.9	17.3	0.3
California	102,009	2,248	15,422	12,713	71,716	76,714	3.0	0.5	5.9	23.0	17.5	6.0	7.6	17.7	18.4	0.4
Alaska	1,671	1	538	263	868	1,289	0.1	3.1	11.3	5.7	13.7	3.6	11.5	12.0	36.9	2.1
Hawaii	4,020	103	982	455	2,480	2,932	3.6	—	11.1	7.6	17.3	6.3	9.7	18.4	25.6	0.4

Dollar figures in millions. *Consists of net income of farm proprietors', farm wages and other farm labor income less personal Social Security contributions. †Equals total personal income less farm income and government income disbursements. ‡Received by persons for participation in current production—consists of wage and salary disbursements, other labor income, and proprietors' income. §Does not include earnings of military personnel.
Source: U.S. Department of Commerce, Bureau of Economic Analysis, *Survey of Current Business*.

Principal minerals produced

in the United States and each state

Mineral (unit of production)	1970		1972	
	Quantity	Value in $000	Quantity	Value in $000
UNITED STATES		29,088,717		32,217,000‖
Mineral fuels		19,405,928		22,083,940
Petroleum, crude (000 42-gal. bbl.)	3,371,751	10,426,680	3,455,368	11,706,510
Coal (000 short tons)				
Bituminous and lignite*	602,932	3,772,622	595,386	4,561,983
Pennsylvania anthracite	9,729	105,341	7,106	85,251
Natural gas (000,000 cu.ft.)	21,920,642	3,745,680	22,531,698	4,203,236
Natural-gas liquids (000 gal.)				
Natural gasoline and cycle products	8,664,810	603,024	1,936,480	604,423
Liquefied petroleum gases	16,783,662	672,088	444,736	847,810
Nonmetallic minerals, except fuels		5,768,480		6,492,000‖
Stone† (000 short tons)	874,512	1,474,917	923,852	1,683,332
Cement§ (000 short tons)	73,704	1,365,769	78,350	1,688,559
Sand and gravel (000 short tons)	943,941	1,115,705	913,375	1,199,520
Salt (000 short tons)	45,804	303,523	45,022	296,772
Lime (000 short tons)	19,747	286,155	20,290	339,304
Clays (000 short tons)	54,853	267,912	59,456	303,022
Phosphate rock (000 short tons)	38,739	203,218	40,831	207,910
Sulfur, Frasch-process (000 long tons)	6,419	151,779	7,613	132,385
Potassium salts, K_2O equivalent (000 short tons)	2,729	98,123	2,659	106,680
Boron minerals (000 short tons)	1,041	86,827	1,121	95,882
Metals		3,914,309		3,641,000‖
Copper, recoverable (000 short tons)	1,720	1,984,484	1,665	1,704,796
Iron ore, usable (000 long tons)	87,176	941,739	77,884	950,365
Molybdenum, content of concentrate (000 lb.)	100,381	190,077	102,197	170,530
Lead, recoverable (000 short tons)	572	178,609	619	186,046
Zinc, recoverable (000 short tons)	534	163,650	478	169,803
Uranium (recoverable U_3O_8) (000 lb.)	24,682	149,464	25,758	162,272
Silver, recoverable (000 troy oz.)	45,005	79,696	37,233	62,737
Gold (troy oz.)	1,743,322	63,439	1,449,943	84,967
Alabama [21]		323,199		371,241
Coal, bituminous (000 short tons)	20,560	166,262	20,813	200,430
Cement† § (000 short tons)	3,689	58,715	2,767	59,798
Stone (000 short tons)	19,903	38,965	18,485	42,027
Petroleum, crude (000 42-gal. bbl.)	7,263	20,627	9,934	30,466
Lime (000 short tons)	749	10,286	739	11,751
Sand and gravel (000 short tons)	6,725	8,144	6,352	8,530
Clays† (000 short tons)	2,748	8,213	2,850	7,512
Alaska [24]		388,271		286,138
Petroleum, crude (000 42-gal. bbl.)	83,616	251,684	72,893	235,444
Natural gas (000,000 cu.ft.)	111,576	27,448	125,596	18,463
Arizona [8]		1,166,767		1,091,004
Copper, recoverable (000 short tons)	918	1,059,277	909	930,419
Molybdenum (000 lb.)	15,672	26,700	27,216	46,791
Sand and gravel (000 short tons)	17,822	19,804	24,842	32,420
Silver, recoverable (000 troy oz.)	7,330	12,981	6,653	11,210
Stone (000 short tons)	3,511	7,094	4,638	8,018
Gold (troy ounces)			102,996	6,036
Lime (000 short tons)			356	6,024
Arkansas [28]		225,622		241,179
Petroleum, crude (000 42-gal. bbl.)	18,035	51,760	18,519	58,335
Natural gas (000,000 cu.ft.)	181,351	29,560	166,522	28,808
Stone (000 short tons)	15,284	22,786	16,317	25,020
Bauxite (000 long tons)	1,869	26,293	1,634	21,010
California [3]		1,897,084		1,851,365
Petroleum, crude (000 42-gal. bbl.)	372,191	945,365	347,022	940,430
Cement (000 short tons)	9,305	173,126	9,086	182,308
Natural gas (000,000 cu.ft.)	649,117	208,367	487,278	179,318
Sand and gravel (000 short tons)	140,259	174,221	117,288	162,619
Boron minerals (000 short tons)	1,041	86,827	1,121	95,882
Stone (000 short tons)	46,399	66,950	37,213	65,811
Natural-gas liquids§ (000 gal.)	799,848	54,484	601,230	43,626
Salt, common (000 short tons)	1,656	14,407	1,621	14,860
Mercury (76-lb. flasks)	18,593	7,582	5,788	1,263
Colorado[19]		390,988		425,841
Molybdenum (000 lb.)	‡	‡	‡	‡
Petroleum, crude (000 42-gal. bbl.)	24,723	78,619	32,015	109,171
Coal, bituminous (000 short tons)	6,025	35,243	5,522	35,637
Sand and gravel (000 short tons)	22,261	24,190	28,318	34,631
Natural gas (000,000 cu.ft.)	105,804	15,553	116,949	19,297
Uranium (recoverable U_3O_8) (000 lb.)	2,727	15,832	1,877	11,825
Connecticut [45]		28,383		33,123
Stone (000 short tons)	8,338	16,915	8,719	19,695
Delaware [50]		1,615		2,871
Sand and gravel (000 short tons)	1,565	1,603	2,257	2,660
Florida [20]		300,042		424,287
Phosphate rock (000 long tons)	‡	‡	‡	‡
Stone† (000 short tons)	43,089	61,302	53,093	81,621
Georgia [27]		203,225		258,041
Clays (000 short tons)	5,684	110,149	6,227	132,322
Stone (000 short tons)	26,635	59,200	37,074	82,484
Hawaii [46]		28,965		28,074
Stone (000 short tons)	6,332	15,538	5,005	13,494
Idaho [35]		119,748		106,206
Silver, recoverable (000 troy oz.)	19,115	33,849	14,251	24,012
Lead, recoverable (000 short tons)	61	19,121	61,407	18,459
Zinc, recoverable (000 short tons)	41	12,578	39	13,720
Illinois [10]		688,697		769,737
Coal, bituminous (000 short tons)	65,119	320,705	65,523	402,481
Petroleum, crude (000 42-gal. bbl.)	43,747	141,994	34,874	121,013
Stone (000 short tons)	55,776	86,502	56,260	94,225
Sand and gravel (000 short tons)	43,926	60,155	39,929	61,696
Cement§ (000 short tons)	1,565	27,126	1,651	35,607
Fluorspar (000 short tons)	148	8,637	132	9,961
Indiana [22]		255,786		322,608
Coal, bituminous (000 short tons)	22,263	102,371	25,949	144,688
Stone (000 short tons)	25,818	45,215	27,511	50,919
Iowa [31]		120,822		134,496
Cement§ (000 short tons)	2,470	47,190	2,524	51,551
Stone (000 short tons)	25,305	41,119	27,457	48,642
Sand and gravel (000 short tons)	21,058	20,642	17,107	20,140
Gypsum (000 short tons)	1,136	4,223	1,380	5,714

Mineral (unit of production)	1970		1972	
	Quantity	Value in $000	Quantity	Value in $000
Kansas [15]		586,161		584,537
Petroleum, crude (000 42-gal. bbl.)	84,853	277,469	73,744	259,578
Natural gas (000,000 cu.ft.)	899,955	125,994	889,268	127,859
Helium§ (000,000 cu.ft.)	2,963	40,914	2,657	35,340
Stone (000 short tons)	15,161	22,406	14,547	23,849
Salt (000 short tons)	‡	‡	1,369	20,562
Kentucky [9]		847,465		976,910
Coal, bituminous (000 short tons)	125,305	711,163	121,188	824,691
Stone (000 short tons)	29,310	45,358	34,279	59,690
Petroleum, crude (000 42-gal. bbl.)	11,575	36,461	9,702	32,599
Louisiana [2]		5,182,617		5,411,543
Petroleum, crude (000 42-gal. bbl.)	906,907	3,061,558	891,827	3,201,659
Natural gas (000,000 cu.ft.)	7,788,276	1,583,137	7,972,678	1,626,426
Natural-gas liquids				
Petroleum gases, liquefied(000 gal.)	3,376,170	138,267	4,125,786	185,660
Natural gasoline (000 gal.)	2,374,092	174,637	1,219,364	167,768
Sulfur, Frasch-process (000 long tons)	3,618	89,489	3,765	‡
Salt (000 short tons)	13,584	64,854	13,514	67,464
Maine [47]		23,780		22,922
Sand and gravel (000 short tons)	12,971	6,888	11,818	7,535
Zinc (short tons)	9,114	2,792	5,820	2,066
Maryland [32]		88,216		115,501
Stone (000 short tons)	16,051	32,783	19,431	41,973
Sand and gravel (000 short tons)	12,951	20,434	12,594	26,557
Massachusetts [43]		50,360		52,428
Sand and gravel (000 short tons)	17,925	22,244	18,883	25,655
Michigan [13]		670,729		694,766
Iron ore, usable (000 long tons)	13,100	168,958	12,692	177,461
Cement § (000 short tons)	5,818	106,272	6,151	117,368
Copper, recoverable (000 short tons)	68	77,945	67	68,874
Sand and gravel (000 short tons)	53,092	54,646	59,467	65,445
Salt (000 short tons)	4,899	49,963	4,358	50,761
Stone (000 short tons)	41,687	49,501	39,754	50,317
Petroleum, crude (000 42-gal. bbl.)	11,693	36,246	12,990	41,556
Magnesium compounds, MgO equivalent (000 short tons)	412	38,055	378	31,484
Minnesota [14]		640,127		659,669
Iron ore, usable (000 long tons)	54,791	571,488	50,595	601,869
Sand and gravel (000 short tons)	46,851	38,802	36,792	33,454
Mississippi [29]		249,973		216,860
Petroleum, crude (000 42-gal. bbl.)	65,119	194,706	61,100	192,465
Natural gas (000,000 cu.ft.)	126,031	23,190	103,989	28,077
Missouri [18]		392,997		451,817
Lead, recoverable (000 short tons)	422	131,751	489	147,113
Cement§ (000 short tons)	‡	‡	4,357	82,757
Stone (000 short tons)	39,726	57,285	42,473	63,219
Iron ore, usable (000 long tons)	2,612	38,100	2,695	‡
Coal, bituminous (000 short tons)	4,447	19,526	4,551	23,667
Zinc, recoverable (000 short tons)	51	15,540	62	21,983
Montana [23]		313,015		307,676
Copper, recoverable (000 short tons)	120	138,955	123	126,064
Petroleum, crude (000 42-gal. bbl.)	37,879	105,403	33,904	103,924
Sand and gravel (000 short tons)	19,275	20,249	10,116	17,149
Silver, recoverable (000 troy oz.)	4,304	7,622	3,325	5,603
Nebraska [40]		72,657		73,675
Petroleum, crude (000 42-gal. bbl.)	11,451	35,384	8,705	29,423
Sand and gravel (000 short tons)	12,232	12,974	13,720	15,063
Nevada [30]		186,349		181,702
Copper, recoverable (000 short tons)	107	123,118	101	103,545
Gold (troy oz.)	408,144	17,472	419,748	24,597
Sand and gravel (000 short tons)	8,574	9,819	10,081	12,636
Stone (000 short tons)			3,329	5,926
Gypsum (000 short tons)	451	1,457	860	2,871
New Hampshire [48]		8,730		10,111
Sand and gravel (000 short tons)	6,529	4,753	6,020	6,256
New Jersey [33]		89,281		113,760
Stone (000 short tons)	15,164	40,677	18,654	53,083
Sand and gravel (000 short tons)	16,732	31,571	17,679	38,020
Zinc, recoverable (000 short tons)	29	8,788	38	13,524
New Mexico [7]		1,060,358		1,097,292
Petroleum, crude (000 42-gal. bbl.)	128,184	410,320	110,525	376,778
Natural gas (000,000 cu.ft.)	1,138,980	162,874	1,216,061	225,420
Copper, recoverable (000 short tons)	166	191,885	168	172,067
Potash, K_2O equivalent (000 short tons)	2,390	85,877	‡	‡
Natural-gas liquids§ (000 gal.)	1,531,015	62,727	1,604,274	75,659
Uranium (U_3O_8) (000 lb.)	11,574	69,970	10,808	68,091
New York [26]		299,564		266,585
Stone (000 short tons)	37,616	68,118	38,138	77,825
Salt (000 short tons)	5,990	47,254	5,604	43,866
North Carolina [42]		98,365		116,323
Stone (000 short tons)	30,363	54,121	32,297	62,741
Sand and gravel (000 short tons)	12,772	13,277	13,485	14,615
Feldspar (000 long tons)	345	5,173	440	6,030
Mica, scrap (000 short tons)	64	1,457	91	2,942
North Dakota [36]		96,047		98,086
Petroleum, crude (000 42-gal. bbl.)	21,998	67,107	20,624	67,647
Coal, lignite (000 short tons)	5,639	11,009	6,632	13,416
Ohio [12]		612,166		724,748
Coal, bituminous (000 short tons)	55,351	262,390	50,967	303,819
Stone (000 short tons)	47,244	81,506	48,498	90,821
Lime (000 short tons)	3,951	61,197	4,413	75,569
Sand and gravel (000 short tons)	42,069	57,506	53,506	59,932
Natural gas (000,000 cu.ft.)	52,113	14,123	89,995	35,271
Petroleum, crude (000 42-gal. bbl.)	9,864	32,914	9,358	35,179
Oklahoma [6]		1,137,267		1,210,728
Petroleum, crude (000 42-gal. bbl.)	223,574	712,419	207,633	709,033
Natural gas (000,000 cu.ft.)	1,594,943	248,811	1,806,887	294,523
Oregon [39]		68,101		76,516
Sand and gravel (000 short tons)	17,532	25,978	24,489	34,981
Stone (000 short tons)	13,439	20,948	10,915	18,380
Nickel, content of ore (000 short tons)	16	‡	17	‡

Principal minerals produced (continued)

Mineral (unit of production)		1970 Quantity	1970 Value in $000	1972 Quantity	1972 Value in $000
Pennsylvania [5]			1,096,053		1,231,485
Coal					
Bituminous	(000 short tons)	80,491	585,057	75,939	694,267
Anthracite	(000 short tons)	9,729	105,341	7,106	85,251
Cement§	(000 short tons)	8,084	129,424	8,665	168,409
Stone	(000 short tons)	66,241	120,187	67,307	124,340
Sand and gravel	(000 short tons)	18,504	33,915	18,757	36,804
Lime	(000 short tons)	1,887	29,279	1,891	33,802
Rhode Island [49]			4,386		4,291
Sand and gravel	(000 short tons)	‡	4,386	‡	4,291
South Carolina [38]			56,384		82,313
Stone	(000 short tons)	9,710	15,154	12,482	21,819
Sand and gravel	(000 short tons)	5,864	7,766	7,916	12,121
South Dakota [41]			61,576		65,200
Gold	(troy oz.)	578,716	21,059	407,430	23,875
Sand and gravel	(000 short tons)	16,556	16,656	12,748	14,793
Tennessee [25]			220,465		269,814
Stone	(000 short tons)	35,374	50,013	35,992	55,512
Coal, bituminous	(000 short tons)	8,737	40,372	11,260	81,386
Cement§	(000 short tons)	1,805	32,581	1,871	41,280
Zinc, recoverable	(000 short tons)	118	36,233	102	36,111
Sand and gravel	(C00 short tons)	6,715	10,639	10,839	15,328
Copper, recoverable	(000 short tons)	16	17,928	11	11,581
Texas [1]			6,402,462		7,211,551
Petroleum, crude	(000 42-gal. bbl.)	1,249,697	4,104,005	1,301,685	4,536,077
Natural gas	(000,000 cu.ft.)	8,357,716	1,203,511	8,657,840	1,419,886
Natural-gas liquids					
Natural gasoline	(000 gal.)	4,095,462	284,871	3,882,354	294,163
Petroleum gases, liquefied	(000 gal.)	8,575,434	334,850	226,624	428,319
Cement§	(000 short tons)	6,914	126,729	8,030	177,454
Stone	(000 short tons)	45,557	64,422	49,314	66,573
Utah [16]			606,093		542,809
Copper, recoverable	(000 short tons)	296	341,282	260	265,735
Petroleum, crude	(000 42-gal. bbl.)	23,370	65,603	26,570	80,773
Coal, bituminous	(000 short tons)	4,733	34,472	4,802	42.868
Gold	(troy oz.)	408,029	14,848	362,413	21,237
Sand and gravel	(000 short tons)	12,010	10,439	14,619	17,071
Silver, recoverable	(000 troy oz.)	6,030	10,678	4,300	7,245
Vermont [44]			27,843		34,868
Stone	(000 short tons)	1,514	19,088	3,300	26,170
Virginia [17]			374,321		489,791
Coal, bituminous	(000 short tons)	35,016	246,181	34,028	344,061
Stone	(000 short tons)	35,415	60,477	39,986	74,090
Sand and gravel	(000 short tons)	11,126	15,229	14,085	21,696
Washington [34]			90,922		109,806
Cement§	(000 short tons)	1,227	24,990	1,245	27,018
Sand and gravel	(000 short tons)	25,089	27,902	23,065	26,069
Stone	(000 short tons)	13,701	19,100	14,712	23,764
Zinc, recoverable	(000 short tons)	12	3,663	6	2,301
West Virginia [4]			1,285,364		1,430,632
Coal	(000 short tons)	144,072	1,142,245	123,743	1,275,813
Natural gas	(000,000 cu.ft.)	242,052	61,583	214,951	64,485
Stone	(000 short tons)†	9,740	16,722	11,649	21,293
Sand and gravel	(000 short tons)	4,396	11,473	5,765	15,031
Wisconsin [37]			87,670		89,353
Sand and gravel	(000 short tons)	41,103	35,107	36,430	31,324
Stone	(000 short tons)	17,577	25,167	19,394	29,681
Wyoming [11]			705,533		746,743
Petroleum, crude	(000 42-gal. bbl.)	160,345	469,811	140,011	432,071
Natural gas	(000,000 cu. ft.)	338,520	49,762	375,059	60,760
Uranium (U_3O_8)	(000 lb.)	6,346	38,768	8,544	53,827
Coal, bituminous	(000 short tons)	7,772	24,423	10,928	40,898

Figure in brackets is the rank of the states by value of 1972 mineral production. Boldface type indicates the state that leads in value of production for that mineral. Production is measured by mine shipments, sales, or marketable production (including consumption by producers). *Includes small quantity of anthracite mined in states other than Pennsylvania. †Excludes certain varieties. ‡Figure withheld to avoid disclosing confidential data. §For cement, portland and masonry figures combined; for helium, grade A and crude figures combined; for natural-gas liquids, natural gasoline, cycle products, and liquefied petroleum gases combined. ‖Rounded. Source: U.S. Department of the Interior, Bureau of Mines. (FRANK H. SKELDING)

Livestock and products, with fisheries, 1972

State	Cattle and calves (lbs.) Amount produced in 000	Cattle and calves Value in $000	Hogs and pigs (lbs.) Amount produced in 000	Hogs and pigs Value in $000	Sheep and lambs (lbs.) Amount produced in 000	Sheep and lambs Value in $000	Milk (lbs.) Amount produced in 000,000	Milk Farm value of milk produced in $000	Eggs Amount produced in 000,000	Eggs Gross income in $000	Chicken (lbs.) Amount sold plus farm con-sumption	Chicken Gross income in $000	Fisheries (lbs.) Commer-cial landings in 000	Fisheries Value in $000
Alabama	619,515	221,096	328,195	79,423	165	42	862	63,702	2,852	81,044	51,690	4,394	39,564†	18,326†
Alaska	1,238	373	176	84	*	*	18	2,045	7	526	117	22	390,137	80,733
Arizona	632,604	221,313	29,071	7,704	19,836	4,594	640	45,696	164	3,594	1,229	67	...	...
Arkansas	593,415	206,565	95,024	22,996	335	73	702	44,717	3,795	114,166	95,697	9,378	‡	‡
California	2,064,723	695,507	53,671	13,579	68,362	19,854	10,430	615,370	8,652	202,602	71,292	3,850	639,964	91,898
Colorado	1,855,575	664,954	130,244	32,431	82,959	24,085	919	64,514	297	8,291	6,049	393	...	...
Connecticut	24,940	6,385	2,579	645	255	74	651	49,411	924	38,731	16,553	1,573	4,911	1,498
Delaware	7,595	2,373	19,807	5,051	90	21	132	9,306	130	5,622	3,010	400	10,648	1,869
Florida	540,810	201,510	91,521	22,148	179	38	1,867	151,040	2,840	58,930	36,413	2,185	176,271	55,711
Georgia	555,065	181,614	536,973	129,410	154	34	1,235	88,796	5,465	159,851	96,484	9,069	17,544	6,802
Hawaii	56,880	15,762	10,938	4,441	...	...	136	14,669	204	7,990	1,429	143	14,686	5,097
Idaho	676,611	240,574	41,893	10,180	58,242	15,885	1,654	85,677	167	4,593	1,420	71	1,400	336
Illinois	1,183,565	390,873	2,748,356	692,586	17,616	4,219	2,799	164,301	1,778	37,486	26,342	6,664	5,701†	686†
Indiana	629,250	206,546	1,792,039	458,762	15,088	3,771	2,425	148,895	3,036	73,370	41,424	2,941	858†	181†
Iowa	2,942,354	1,005,564	4,944,163	1,250,873	41,978	12,425	4,506	240,620	2,256	44,180	34,667	2,254	3,518	352
Kansas	2,974,245	1,040,551	802,624	202,261	19,891	5,549	1,629	96,600	718	12,625	16,240	731	36	10
Kentucky	889,076	301,675	454,772	115,512	4,997	1,520	2,530	147,246	537	12,978	10,325	1,022	‡	‡
Louisiana	554,588	187,211	54,351	13,044	502	90	1,132	81,730	744	19,903	16,271	1,383	1,070,597†	71,916†
Maine	27,820	7,116	2,215	543	826	199	637	47,456	1,402	46,500	28,501	2,708	149,271	34,819
Maryland	103,649	34,135	58,561	14,757	1,111	281	1,548	107,741	334	12,609	7,258	813	67,636	18,261
Massachusetts	25,480	6,472	18,708	4,677	345	93	628	48,670	535	19,127	8,846	840	248,035	48,052
Michigan	494,178	152,947	269,573	68,741	11,783	3,227	4,916	302,826	1,523	33,380	22,807	1,939	14,213	2,985
Minnesota	1,500,552	462,416	1,269,241	318,579	29,009	8,225	9,580	495,286	2,584	44,143	32,361	1,456	11,583†	981†
Mississippi	660,000	227,617	166,210	42,550	354	69	983	66,844	2,299	77,017	55,728	5,907	260,216†	11,897†
Missouri	1,754,210	601,007	1,616,813	404,203	11,939	3,479	3,025	170,912	1,473	30,442	39,500	3,555	790	150
Montana	1,106,231	423,511	88,372	20,679	43,023	10,432	322	18,290	217	6,655	3,760	226	718	108
Nebraska	2,706,615	950,719	1,290,354	320,008	19,925	5,674	1,610	85,974	814	12,752	9,439	368	179	13
Nevada	205,965	73,556	2,750	682	10,702	2,860	143	8,837	3	75	41	2	...	...
New Hampshire	14,000	3,631	3,394	832	247	64	353	24,698	313	11,711	5,971	567	1,442	1,133
New Jersey	39,005	10,776	21,120	5,153	485	134	639	44,283	746	22,007	9,807	853	190,517	14,423
New Mexico	616,220	227,576	20,552	5,241	25,106	5,807	326	26,830	234	7,001	2,389	144	...	...
New York	346,727	100,466	27,628	6,879	4,298	1,175	10,190	652,160	2,271	59,046	38,436	2,998	37,377	22,123
North Carolina	242,878	75,955	639,394	156,652	590	151	1,535	113,897	3,433	98,413	96,344	10,887	175,410	11,827
North Dakota	866,683	306,230	121,116	29,310	22,562	5,480	982	44,583	153	2,767	3,821	172	395	40
Ohio	684,120	219,349	863,950	218,579	37,432	10,136	4,538	288,617	2,324	49,966	34,336	3,365	7,939†	1,026†
Oklahoma	2,054,205	720,675	158,867	39,081	6,335	1,769	1,235	76,940	502	13,219	9,704	786	‡	‡
Oregon	494,495	163,585	37,508	9,415	27,039	6,844	1,005	65,124	554	15,236	7,465	299	92,923	24,024
Pennsylvania	397,581	131,579	160,894	42,154	6,739	1,784	7,031	484,436	3,599	91,475	79,481	11,525	357	111
Rhode Island	1,329	385	2,632	658	78	21	69	4,996	57	2,337	805	77	86,376	12,443
South Carolina	191,955	66,638	218,239	53,032	35	8	518	39,109	1,381	34,755	25,345	2,027	22,365	7,961
South Dakota	1,713,529	598,403	710,858	174,871	74,503	19,578	1,569	80,019	814	12,210	14,002	561	3,159	253
Tennessee	743,820	247,024	329,002	81,592	1,394	365	2,161	130,740	1,113	34,318	18,497	1,850	‡	‡
Texas	4,718,505	1,684,053	455,190	109,246	167,965	47,735	3,381	244,446	2,685	75,404	48,310	5,024	117,000†	85,011†
Utah	242,581	84,302	15,598	3,571	52,916	14,140	874	53,052	295	6,834	2,771	152	...	...
Vermont	65,820	16,190	1,570	385	325	79	2,028	140,540	114	3,952	1,891	180	...	...
Virginia	454,840	136,890	192,480	47,735	13,198	3,649	1,760	118,096	825	28,187	20,250	2,187	663,845	25,992
Washington	413,746	141,676	28,739	7,328	6,753	2,025	2,307	148,571	1,035	22,856	14,216	668	120,458	38,496
West Virginia	124,525	42,250	22,387	5,485	10,984	2,825	345	23,322	261	7,743	5,248	598	...	...
Wisconsin	1,028,990	306,918	621,731	154,811	8,312	2,171	19,638	1,091,817	1,313	28,339	20,800	1,769	43,661†	2,521†
Wyoming	538,800	206,240	12,773	2,951	67,362	16,867	135	8,383	32	958	464	27	144	§
TOTAL U.S.	41,381,103	14,220,733	21,584,811	5,411,510	994,324	269,620	120,278	7,372,830	69,804	1,797,916	1,195,246	111,070	4,710,400	703,600

*Decrease in inventory and large death loss of sheep resulted in a deficit in number of pounds produced. †Catch in interior waters estimated. ‡Data not available. §Less than $500. Sources: U.S. Department of Agriculture, Statistical Reporting Service, Crop Reporting Board, *Chickens and Eggs, Meat Animals, Milk, Milk Production;* U.S. Department of Commerce, National Oceanic and Atmospheric Administration, National Marine Fisheries Service, *Fisheries of the United States.*

Value of construction contracts

in millions of dollars

State	1970	1971	1972 Total	1972 Non-residential	1972 Residential	1972 Non-building
Alabama	1,036	1,187	1,355	307	769	279
Alaska	238	259	374	112	108	154
Arizona	1,063	1,220	1,673	395	917	361
Arkansas	506	607	826	193	486	147
California	6,739	8,317	9,003	2,634	5,011	1,358
Colorado	834	1,151	1,705	473	939	293
Connecticut	1,154	969	1,222	499	495	228
Delaware	208	259	278	53	132	94
Dist. of Columbia	313	726	642	367	33	242
Florida	3,537	4,212	6,522	1,298	4,570	654
Georgia	1,555	2,124	2,533	643	1,421	468
Hawaii	601	502	666	201	353	111
Idaho	197	163	299	81	88	130
Illinois	3,596	3,956	4,853	1,878	2,041	935
Indiana	1,466	1,776	2,165	691	938	536
Iowa	701	752	822	245	332	244
Kansas	530	705	780	255	339	186
Kentucky	1,185	1,668	1,516	376	825	315
Louisiana	1,359	1,702	2,036	377	997	663
Maine	216	256	307	99	139	71
Maryland	1,270	1,655	1,746	544	897	305
Massachusetts	1,791	2,268	2,175	918	899	359
Michigan	2,950	3,034	3,450	1,011	1,597	843
Minnesota	1,094	1,332	1,327	414	605	307
Mississippi	570	929	885	202	495	188
Missouri	1,171	1,652	1,462	486	673	303
Montana	184	226	273	52	84	137
Nebraska	334	426	616	195	270	151
Nevada	364	432	631	95	443	93
New Hampshire	188	295	301	85	133	83
New Jersey	2,741	2,410	2,947	1,101	1,341	505
New Mexico	394	396	480	112	267	101
New York	5,589	5,786	6,063	2,187	2,818	1,558
North Carolina	1,722	2,041	2,638	668	1,439	593
North Dakota	296	189	331	60	89	182
Ohio	3,046	4,037	3,913	1,280	1,882	750
Oklahoma	754	941	1,330	326	635	369
Oregon	634	979	971	233	466	273
Pennsylvania	3,192	4,383	3,384	1,216	1,247	921
Rhode Island	194	231	207	47	127	33
South Carolina	883	989	1,322	337	798	187
South Dakota	160	255	211	54	80	78
Tennessee	1,562	1,528	1,876	512	1,088	277
Texas	4,119	4,969	5,836	1,887	2,962	987
Utah	334	417	509	133	272	105
Vermont	148	131	169	45	72	52
Virginia	1,891	2,547	2,749	609	1,667	473
Washington	1,478	1,155	1,545	529	589	426
West Virginia	846	609	590	100	227	263
Wisconsin	1,206	1,342	1,565	532	737	297
Wyoming	161	104	129	34	36	59
TOTAL U.S.	68,294	89,188	91,213	27,118	45,366	18,729

Source: U.S. Department of Commerce, Social and Economic Statistics Administration, Bureau of the Census, *Statistical Abstract of the United States 1973;* data compiled by F.W. Dodge Division, McGraw-Hill Information Systems Company.

Principal crops

of the United States, 1972

State	Corn, grain (bu.) Amount produced in 000	Corn Value in $000	Hay (tons) Amount produced in 000	Hay Value in $000	Soybeans for beans (bu.) Amount produced in 000	Soybeans Value in $000	Wheat (bu.) Amount produced in 000	Wheat Value in $000	Tobacco (lbs.) Amount produced in 000	Tobacco Value in $000	Cotton* lint (bales) Amount produced in 000	Cotton Value in $000	Sorghum grain (bu.) Amount produced in 000	Sorghum Value in $000	Potatoes (cwt.) Amount produced in 000	Potatoes Value in $000
Ala.	24,525	34,090	814	24,013	14,800	51,060	2,052	3,114	926	778	570	72,504	992	1,042	2,435	7,233
Alaska	...	...	...	...	...	...	...	...	...	...	...	...	...	...	...	...
Ariz.	525	840	1,372	46,648	...	...	11,390	19,268	...	...	610	86,376	10,608	17,397	2,400	6,840
Ark.	1,120	1,568	1,159	31,293	76,380	267,330	10,952	15,344	...	...	1,465	196,896	8,007	9,368	91	382
Calif.	21,500	37,625	8,159	277,406	...	...	23,340	45,076	...	...	1,750	247,800	17,424	29,098	21,991	66,821
Colo.	41,310	59,900	2,789	104,588	...	...	51,519	111,173	...	...	...	...	12,012	15,856	10,608	24,794
Conn.	...	...	150	7,200	...	...	...	...	5,720	16,280	...	...	...	...	609	2,436
Del.	13,962	19,268	52	1,976	4,025	13,283	825	1,405	...	...	...	...	...	...	1,287	4,440
Fla.	14,122	18,782	311	10,574	4,872	16,566	630	937	23,468	26,433	13	1,737	...	...	4,606	15,933
Ga.	77,480	106,922	912	30,096	10,050	35,678	2,800	5,058	114,386	99,582	360	44,064	990	1,218	...	...
Hawaii	...	...	...	...	...	...	...	...	...	...	...	...	...	...	...	...
Ida.	2,175	3,480	3,715	115,165	...	...	44,226	112,667	...	...	...	...	...	...	78,795	167,601
Ill.	988,740	1,315,024	3,373	92,758	262,150	930,633	54,000	100,709	...	...	1	94	5,460	6,279	400	1,080
Ind.	479,612	613,903	1,946	56,434	103,684	352,526	39,648	71,220	15,000	11,775	...	...	2,622	2,858	1,458	4,947
Iowa	1,191,300	1,465,299	6,827	146,781	217,800	773,190	1,238	3,029	...	...	...	...	4,080	4,651	682	1,978
Kan.	130,000	180,700	5,549	141,500	24,500	83,300	314,900	666,195	...	...	...	...	218,240	272,800	95	309
Ky.	83,248	116,547	2,772	84,546	25,060	87,710	7,020	12,139	437,581	340,934	4	518	1,360	1,482	150	593
La.	4,816	6,935	632	17,064	38,341	130,359	690	1,234	120	98	715	89,232	1,435	1,507	218	578
Me.	...	...	362	13,032	...	...	...	...	...	...	...	...	...	...	33,280	79,872
Md.	35,440	49,970	568	20,164	6,831	23,225	3,850	6,947	26,000	21,294	...	...	...	...	350	1,213
Mass.	...	...	205	9,635	...	...	...	...	1,898	6,020	...	...	...	...	592	2,368
Mich.	142,926	180,087	3,067	92,010	12,052	41,579	21,400	51,380	...	...	...	...	...	...	9,478	27,872
Minn.	455,607	523,948	8,163	175,505	93,100	321,195	49,292	103,221	...	...	...	...	...	...	13,050	32,318
Miss.	7,335	10,636	1,010	30,805	51,975	184,511	4,960	7,192	...	...	2,040	274,176	1,419	1,717	170	544
Mo.	220,000	286,000	5,533	149,391	112,000	386,400	36,075	71,867	5,980	4,664	425	59,160	26,980	32,376	66	297
Mont.	468	641	4,362	139,584	...	...	98,831	236,309	...	...	...	...	...	...	1,650	6,600
Neb.	537,680	688,230	7,203	169,271	24,618	83,701	94,572	202,811	...	...	...	...	128,376	160,470	1,393	3,086
Nev.	...	...	870	27,840	...	...	710	1,579	...	...	3	403	...	...	...	...
N.H.	...	...	163	7,335	...	...	...	...	...	...	...	...	...	...	141	606
N.J	3,848	5,657	266	12,768	986	3,402	1,330	2,484	...	...	...	...	...	...	2,106	7,582
N.M.	1,575	2,363	932	33,086	...	...	4,335	14,533	...	...	160	23,040	19,305	25,869	660	2,079
N.Y.	18,900	28,539	4,503	150,051	168	571	5,180	12,435	...	...	...	...	...	...	10,830	38,619
N.C.	108,000	140,400	509	19,342	27,750	98,513	6,975	14,001	679,230	579,816	130	16,848	3,740	4,189	1,930	6,610
N.D.	10,653	12,251	5,030	93,055	3,895	13,243	216,818	510,591	...	...	...	...	...	...	17,400	39,150
Ohio	279,000	371,070	3,134	89,319	81,810	278,154	46,305	89,686	22,505	16,278	...	...	...	...	2,485	8,250
Okla.	6,319	8,783	2,899	85,521	3,570	11,960	89,700	222,607	...	...	320	33,024	28,575	37,148	...	...
Ore.	891	1,337	2,279	75,207	...	...	36,848	89,442	...	...	...	...	...	...	14,436	37,253
Penn.	64,800	99,792	3,752	157,584	1,025	3,485	8,608	17,314	22,400	8,064	...	...	...	...	4,800	17,280
R.I.	...	...	17	816	...	...	...	...	...	...	...	...	...	...	907	2,177
S.C.	23,625	31,894	440	14,520	21,375	78,019	2,720	5,753	131,130	111,854	320	42,240	429	506	...	...
S.D.	152,832	168,115	7,082	131,017	7,337	24,946	53,619	126,220	...	...	...	...	12,432	13,054	738	1,624
Tenn.	32,340	45,923	1,781	50,759	28,566	95,696	7,680	12,164	122,040	91,867	535	69,336	1,624	1,916	371	1,632
Tex.	39,560	57,362	4,109	117,107	5,460	19,383	44,000	121,908	...	...	4,050	466,560	319,780	399,725	3,182	13,328
Utah	736	1,236	1,513	51,442	...	...	6,137	13,812	...	...	...	...	...	...	1,011	2,730
Vt.	...	...	851	37,444	...	...	...	...	...	...	...	...	...	...	209	899
Va.	41,666	56,666	1,817	65,412	8,050	28,578	8,066	14,338	114,260	92,090	2	177	714	800	4,145	14,784
Wash.	5,406	8,379	2,467	76,477	...	...	122,083	297,911	...	...	...	...	...	...	30,495	58,091
W.Va.	3,975	5,764	981	32,373	...	...	490	983	2,880	2,246	...	...	...	...	259	1,256
Wis.	203,585	248,374	10,203	290,786	4,060	13,601	901	1,948	23,235	12,728	...	...	...	...	11,075	34,233
Wyo.	2,125	3,081	1,786	54,473	...	...	8,060	15,750	...	...	...	...	...	...	1,456	2,912
TOTAL	5,473,727	7,017,381	128,389	3,661,973	1,276,290	4,451,797	1,544,775	3,433,754	1,748,759	1,442,801	13,473	1,724,185	826,604	1,041,326	294,490	751,230

*Excludes pima cotton (98,100 bales). Sources: U.S. Department of Agriculture, Statistical Reporting Service, Crop Reporting Board, *Crop Production* and *Crop Values.*

Principal manufactures, 1972

monetary figures in millions of dollars

Industry	Employees (000)	Cost of labor*	Cost of materials	Value of shipments	Value added by manufacture
Food and kindred products	1,543	$ 12,729	$ 78,375	$113,509	$ 35,399
Meat products	302	2,473	25,820	30,595	4,843
Dairy products	179	1,521	11,834	15,688	3,861
Canned, cured, frozen foods	269	1,719	8,139	13,211	5,031
Grain mill products	109	987	8,428	12,044	3,613
Beverages	221	2,113	7,524	14,313	6,986
Tobacco manufactures	69	514	3,430	6,138	2,704
Textile mill products	938	5,934	16,187	27,430	11,366
Apparel and other textile products	1,334	7,010	13,918	27,001	13,197
Lumber and wood products	539	3,853	10,235	18,112	7,861
Furniture and fixtures	460	3,187	5,333	11,231	6,012
Paper and allied products	635	6,042	16,411	29,565	13,181
Printing and publishing	1,022	9,460	9,519	28,709	19,250
Chemicals and allied products	857	8,899	25,204	58,115	33,081
Industrial chemicals	237	2,713	8,337	18,201	9,850
Plastics materials and resins	188	1,903	5,378	10,821	5,462
Drugs	136	1,481	2,117	8,279	6,270
Soap, cleaners, and toilet goods	104	993	3,419	9,362	5,980
Paints, allied products	68	651	2,028	3,856	1,828
Agricultural chemicals	38	353	1,707	2,993	1,234
Petroleum and coal products	137	1,630	22,226	28,299	5,841
Leather and leather products	273	1,590	2,867	5,781	2,971
Stone, clay, and glass products	592	5,295	8,669	20,708	12,092
Primary metal industries	1,172	12,513	36,106	59,013	23,405
Blast furnace, basic steel products	553	6,393	16,860	28,159	11,713
Iron, steel foundries	216	2,134	2,228	5,647	3,458
Primary nonferrous metals	58	615	4,244	5,950	1,693
Nonferrous drawing and rolling	188	1,835	9,012	12,713	3,754
Nonferrous foundries	75	669	969	2,100	1,137
Fabricated metal products	1,297	11,940	22,376	46,125	24,047
Machinery, except electrical	1,775	17,916	27,985	63,324	36,114
Engines, turbines	113	1,299	2,655	5,446	2,888
Farm machinery	124	$ 1,188	$ 2,949	$ 5,343	$ 2,502
Construction and related mach.	272	2,814	5,190	10,933	5,879
Metalworking machinery	275	2,912	2,519	7,499	5,049
Special industry machinery	181	1,758	2,422	5,916	3,592
General industrial machinery	255	2,516	3,435	8,264	4,889
Service industry machines	185	1,753	4,115	8,105	4,145
Office, computing machines	195	2,149	3,399	7,825	4,432
Electrical equipment and supplies	1,699	15,363	23,328	53,585	30,455
Electric test, distributing equip.	169	1,525	2,009	5,013	3,053
Electrical industrial apparatus	187	1,622	2,186	5,220	3,064
Household appliances	162	1,366	3,489	6,937	3,514
Electric lighting, wiring equip.	168	1,355	2,302	5,466	3,284
Radio, TV receiving equipment	108	794	2,871	4,924	2,124
Communication equipment	457	4,775	5,100	13,246	8,076
Electronic components, access.	324	2,788	3,434	8,491	4,954
Transportation equipment	1,666	18,853	58,378	96,327	39,131
Motor vehicles and equipment	824	9,772	44,110	67,150	23,348
Aircraft, parts	488	5,931	7,446	17,169	10,481
Ship, boat building, repair	173	1,616	1,825	4,050	2,256
Railroad equipment	52	543	1,371	2,500	1,132
Travel trailers, trailer coaches	96	720	2,829	4,155	1,372
Instruments and related products	391	3,628	4,351	13,839	9,510
Mechanical measuring, control devices	96	875	791	2,486	1,714
Medical instruments and supplies	87	733	1,013	2,770	1,780
Photographic equipment and supplies	90	1,057	1,357	5,503	4,086
Miscellaneous manufacturing industries	423	2,989	5,327	11,728	6,558
Ordnance and accessories	233	2,871	2,490	7,365	4,858
Ammunition, except small arms†	170	2,244	1,806	5,663	3,827
All establishments, including administrative and auxiliary	18,648	171,080	401,279	745,301	348,048

*Payroll only. †Includes guided missiles. Source: U.S. Department of Commerce, Bureau of the Census, *1972 Census of Manufactures, Advance Report, Industry Series.* (All data should be considered preliminary.)

Manufacturing activity by sector, 1971

selected industrial groups, percent of total value

State	Total value added by mfg. ($000,000)	Food	Textiles	Apparel	Lumber & wood	Paper prods.	Printing & publ.	Chemicals	Petroleum & coal	Rubber & plastics	Stone, clay, glass	Prim. metal ind.	Fabr. metal ind.	Machinery, etc., elec.	Electric equip.	Transport equip.	Instruments	Misc. mfg.
Ala.	4,531	7.5	8.9	7.6	4.6	8.7	2.6	11.8	*1.0*	6.2	3.4	16.1	5.5	1.2	4.0	6.1	0.2	*0.7*
Alaska	198	35.3	—	—	*13.3*	—	*7.2*	—	—	—	—	—	—	—	—	—	—	—
Ariz.	1,385	8.2	—	2.1	3.3	—	6.2	2.4	—	*0.7*	5.0	13.2	5.2	16.6	21.1	4.2	—	*1.3*
Ark.	2,420	13.9	2.5	4.9	8.3	9.2	4.3	5.3	1.4	4.9	*3.5*	3.9	5.2	4.6	11.1	*3.3*	—	2.2
Calif.	27,568	13.7	0.6	2.7	2.6	2.3	5.3	5.2	2.4	2.7	3.6	3.4	6.4	7.8	11.8	17.1	1.8	1.8
Colo.	2,089	24.0	—	0.7	*1.3*	1.2	6.9	3.3	*1.8*	4.2	*6.4*	6.0	7.2	9.1	6.2	2.9	2.2	*1.8*
Conn.	6,049	3.4	2.6	1.8	*0.3*	—	4.5	6.2	*0.3*	—	2.1	6.7	10.6	13.5	11.2	16.7	6.2	4.8
Del.	1,281	14.6	*0.9*	*1.0*	*0.1*	—	2.0	—	—	8.5	0.9	2.3	1.8	2.3	*0.8*	—	1.4	0.1
D.C.	380	12.4	—	—	—	—	75.4	—	—	—	*1.7*	—	*1.5*	*0.7*	—	—	—	—
Fla.	4,822	20.3	*0.7*	*5.1*	2.6	6.1	7.7	9.0	0.3	1.8	5.9	1.2	7.0	5.2	8.5	7.2	1.8	*0.6*
Ga.	6,533	11.9	18.5	8.3	3.3	*7.7*	3.3	6.8	—	3.0	3.2	1.9	3.2	2.5	3.4	18.2	—	1.2
Hawaii	435	58.4	—	*5.6*	*0.5*	—	*11.3*	—	—	—	6.2	—	*2.9*	*1.1*	—	—	—	*1.1*
Ida.	669	34.1	—	—	24.8	—	*3.5*	17.7	—	—	—	—	*2.5*	*2.3*	—	—	—	*0.7*
Ill.	22,790	13.6	0.3	1.6	0.6	2.7	8.5	8.6	1.6	2.7	3.0	7.6	10.0	15.4	12.3	4.2	3.1	2.0
Ind.	12,074	8.1	*0.1*	0.8	1.1	1.7	3.6	9.1	1.8	3.3	3.5	15.2	6.9	9.9	16.0	13.3	1.1	1.2
Iowa	3,941	27.5	*	—	1.4	2.1	5.7	8.7	†	4.8	*3.0*	2.8	5.7	20.0	8.6	3.1	*0.8*	2.3
Kan.	2,561	13.5	—	4.2	*0.2*	*1.9*	*7.1*	12.8	6.7	—	4.8	—	6.2	9.1	—	21.6	1.0	0.6
Ky.	5,168	13.0	0.7	4.5	1.4	1.8	4.4	7.9	—	2.9	2.3	6.7	5.0	14.0	16.3	5.5	1.4	1.0
La.	3,505	16.4	—	1.7	3.6	9.7	2.6	28.9	11.8	*0.2*	3.3	2.9	5.1	2.4	2.7	5.7	*0.2*	0.4
Maine	1,208	14.0	6.8	*2.1*	8.4	26.7	2.5	*1.4*	—	3.4	1.3	1.5	*2.0*	*2.5*	—	4.3	—	†
Md.	4,279	15.5	*0.7*	4.5	1.6	3.1	6.9	9.9	—	2.7	4.5	13.7	5.3	5.1	10.3	12.0	1.0	0.8
Mass.	9,567	6.7	3.5	4.6	0.6	5.4	7.3	5.5	—	4.9	2.3	2.8	6.7	14.4	15.0	3.4	7.3	3.8
Mich.	20,271	5.9	0.2	1.8	0.7	1.9	3.1	5.3	—	2.1	2.4	8.5	11.5	12.1	3.2	37.5	0.6	0.8
Minn.	4,827	18.5	*0.4*	1.0	2.2	9.3	8.2	4.7	1.3	—	2.4	*2.1*	5.8	21.0	5.6	3.9	3.9	*1.5*
Miss.	2,237	9.3	3.2	11.4	9.4	6.7	*1.7*	9.3	—	3.1	3.8	1.1	4.8	5.6	8.5	7.9	0.8	2.9
Mo.	7,525	13.2	0.2	3.9	1.2	2.7	7.4	8.7	1.1	1.7	3.0	3.3	5.5	6.8	7.2	24.4	*1.0*	1.3
Mont.	330	18.6	—	—	28.8	—	*8.1*	*3.8*	10.1	—	*5.0*	—	*1.2*	—	—	—	—	0.7
Neb.	1,594	35.5	—	*0.9*	*1.0*	—	4.9	5.2	—	—	*2.1*	3.8	6.2	*11.9*	8.8	5.0	4.4	*1.4*
Nev.	146	13.3	—	—	†	—	12.0	20.4	—	—	19.3	—	*4.3*	2.4	—	—	—	—
N.H.	1,089	7.2	6.8	2.0	4.6	10.5	4.6	*1.3*	—	5.9	*3.7*	2.8	3.1	13.0	18.2	2.0	1.0	1.5
N.J.	14,394	9.7	2.8	4.0	0.4	3.5	4.0	24.2	2.0	3.3	4.4	3.5	7.0	8.1	10.9	5.7	2.5	2.2
N.M.	273	*19.8*	—	—	—	—	*7.7*	3.6	2.9	*0.2*	*10.9*	—	*2.8*	*2.1*	6.2	—	—	*4.5*
N.Y.	28,862	7.9	2.1	10.9	0.5	2.8	14.2	6.9	0.3	1.6	2.5	3.4	4.7	8.6	9.1	7.2	10.8	3.7
N.C.	9,824	6.5	28.2	6.0	2.5	2.8	1.9	7.6	—	2.0	2.1	1.2	4.9	4.4	6.4	1.2	1.1	0.7
N.D.	189	35.8	—	—	—	—	*10.8*	—	—	—	—	—	*8.4*	10.5	—	—	—	1.0
Ohio	23,992	7.0	0.5	1.0	0.6	2.5	4.3	7.7	1.0	7.1	4.4	12.1	11.0	13.2	9.2	14.5	1.0	1.1
Okla.	1,834	13.3	—	3.8	*1.2*	1.4	6.5	*2.6*	5.1	6.2	*7.7*	3.1	10.2	16.7	*9.4*	8.2	†	1.7
Ore.	2,807	13.5	0.5	*1.1*	38.7	9.1	4.0	2.0	0.6	*0.4*	1.8	—	4.0	*5.6*	4.3	4.0	2.2	*1.2*
Penn.	21,964	8.9	3.2	5.8	0.9	3.6	4.3	7.5	1.9	2.5	4.2	16.9	7.8	9.9	9.2	6.0	2.2	1.9
R.I.	1,469	6.5	12.5	1.0	0.4	2.4	5.2	3.9	—	—	2.7	10.6	6.1	7.3	5.6	—	3.4	21.2
S.C.	4,235	3.9	34.0	7.5	*3.6*	6.5	*1.3*	17.5	—	2.0	2.8	1.1	2.6	7.6	4.0	1.1	1.2	1.5
S.D.	226	56.1	—	—	*4.2*	—	*9.1*	—	—	—	*6.9*	—	*5.7*	6.2	2.6	—	—	—
Tenn.	6,729	9.5	5.2	6.9	1.7	4.5	3.8	20.6	0.3	4.5	4.3	3.6	5.2	6.5	9.2	4.5	0.6	1.6
Tex.	13,794	12.3	0.4	3.6	1.4	2.2	3.8	20.9	11.4	2.1	3.7	5.2	6.8	7.4	5.1	9.1	—	0.7
Utah	864	11.9	—	3.9	*2.7*	1.0	6.0	2.2	*5.1*	*0.6*	4.7	—	7.4	7.8	6.0	13.4	—	*1.4*
Vt.	562	*7.5*	*0.8*	*0.8*	*6.7*	—	9.8	2.0	—	—	5.6	*1.3*	*2.1*	12.5	—	—	—	—
Va.	5,173	9.9	6.7	4.8	4.1	5.3	3.9	15.0	—	2.9	3.0	2.3	4.3	3.1	9.1	7.7	0.5	0.5
Wash.	4,117	13.4	—	1.4	15.3	9.2	4.5	4.0	—	*0.3*	2.3	7.7	2.7	3.3	1.1	21.5	—	1.4
W.Va.	2,388	3.8	*0.5*	1.3	*1.4*	0.9	2.7	35.2	0.4	—	13.3	20.6	4.3	3.3	4.9	—	1.8	0.8
Wis.	8,476	15.0	1.0	*0.9*	1.7	9.2	4.4	4.2	—	1.9	1.6	5.0	7.9	20.6	9.0	10.4	1.6	1.2
Wyo.	119	12.7	—	—	—	—	*9.5*	—	*36.3*	—	*8.0*	—	—	—	—	—	—	—
TOTAL U.S.	314,152	10.9	3.2	4.0	2.2	3.7	5.8	9.4	1.8	3.0	3.4	6.7	7.0	9.8	8.9	11.1	2.7	1.8

State and U.S. totals include estimates for all component industry groups, regardless of whether separate data are shown for each industry group. —Figure not shown because (1) no industry in this category; (2) industry too small (based on number of employees); or (3) to avoid disclosure of data for individual companies. Figures in italics indicate limited reliability. *Less than 0.05%. †Estimate of insufficient quality for publication. Source: U.S. Department of Commerce, Social and Economic Statistics Administration, Bureau of the Census, *Annual Survey of Manufactures · 1971.*

Retail sales

in millions of dollars

Kind of business	1960	1965	1970	1972
Durable goods stores	70,733	93,718	114,288	149,597
Automotive group	39,509	56,266	64,966	88,618
Passenger car, other automotive dealers	36,981	53,217	59,388	81,538
Tire, battery, accessory dealers	2,528	3,049	5,578	7,080
Furniture and appliance group	10,598	13,737	17,778	21,296
Furniture, home furnishings stores	6,770	8,538	10,483	12,552
Household appliance, TV, radio stores	3,828	4,223	6,073	6,998
Lumber, building, hardware, farm equipment group	14,819	16,274	20,494	26,692
Lumberyards, building materials dealers	8,618	9,302	11,995	15,970
Hardware stores	2,693	2,813	3,351	4,091
Nondurable goods stores	148,796	190,232	261,239	298,577
Apparel group	13,708	15,752	19,810	21,943
Men's, boys' wear stores	2,619	3,258	4,630	5,183
Women's apparel, accessory stores	5,329	6,243	7,582	8,382
Family clothing stores	2,728	2,981	3,360	3,856
Shoe stores	2,450	2,571	3,501	3,757
Drug and proprietary stores	7,530	9,335	13,352	14,508
Eating and drinking places	16,096	21,423	29,689	33,898
Food group	53,837	66,920	86,114	94,969
Grocery stores	48,339	61,068	79,756	88,296
Meat and fish markets	1,560	1,552	2,244	2,559
Bakeries	1,034	1,142	1,303	1,305
Gasoline service stations	17,594	21,765	27,994	31,056
General merchandise group	24,007	35,840	61,320	74,855
Department stores and dry goods general merchandise stores	16,994	27,939	55,812	68,890
Variety stores	3,899	5,320	6,959	7,747
Mail-order houses (department store merchandise)	1,857	2,581	3,853	4,994
Liquor stores	4,880	6,305	7,980	9,212
TOTAL	219,529	283,950	375,527	448,174

Source: U.S. Department of Commerce, Bureau of the Census, *Monthly Retail Trade.*

Services

Kind of service	NUMBER OF SERVICES		NUMBER OF EMPLOYEES†	
	1971*	1972	1971	1972
Hotels and other lodging places	51,444	51,302	800,918	828,532
Hotels, tourist courts, and motels	34,362	34,156	655,689	675,358
Rooming and boarding houses	7,009	6,905	102,902	106,984
Personal services	172,894	166,095	944,937	917,065
Laundries and drycleaning plants	44,446	42,224	449,271	416,706
Photographic studios	6,670	6,608	34,846	36,626
Beauty shops	70,716	70,309	272,994	278,061
Barber shops	21,669	18,203	45,588	38,283
Funeral service and crematories	13,077	12,922	67,492	67,876
Miscellaneous business services	94,806	97,255	1,589,941	1,670,653
Advertising	8,119	8,120	111,328	107,083
Credit reporting and collection	5,486	5,509	64,753	66,338
Duplicating, mailing, stenographic	5,189	5,284	60,768	60,206
Building services	16,122	16,735	292,680	317,650
Private employment agencies	5,499	5,300	47,938	51,380
Research and development laboratories	1,940	1,966	71,483	74,133
Business consulting services	19,733	21,179	288,603	301,982
Detective and protective services	3,570	3,822	163,700	182,665
Equipment rental and leasing	7,502	7,801	65,030	73,452
Photofinishing laboratories	1,621	1,609	39,124	40,878
Temporary help supply services	2,152	2,149	150,573	167,455
Auto repair, services, and garages	71,582	73,275	385,145	405,871
Automobile rentals, without drivers	5,301	5,405	63,044	66,538
Automobile parking	3,602	3,428	37,294	37,136
Automobile repair shops	55,437	56,852	224,375	235,901
Automobile laundries	4,798	5,038	45,468	50,693
Miscellaneous repair services	38,026	38,586	202,323	212,509
Radio and television repair	8,127	8,281	36,714	38,248
Motion pictures	10,977	11,076	189,630	186,501
Motion picture filming and distribution	2,853	2,973	58,201	53,726
Motion picture theaters	7,652	7,627	119,616	120,658
Other amusement and recreation services	37,312	37,143	440,169	467,716
Producers, orchestras, entertainers	5,795	5,695	58,211	57,041
Bowling and billiard establishments	8,853	8,424	93,666	95,461
Golf clubs and country clubs	4,721	4,763	89,793	93,586
Race tracks and stables	1,394	1,420	33,621	37,018
Medical and other health services	218,900	223,732	3,069,520	3,240,295
Physicians' and surgeons' offices	106,081	108,484	398,824	438,478
Dentists' and dental surgeons' offices	65,175	66,406	172,130	190,945
Hospitals	5,124	5,135	1,825,469	1,868,469
Medical and dental laboratories	7,172	7,389	56,516	60,330
Sanatoria, convalescent and rest homes	11,114	11,097	469,811	517,271
Legal services	69,360	70,456	249,853	269,904
Educational services	34,670	37,074	916,066	959,860
Elementary and secondary schools	24,963	26,496	331,370	364,964
Colleges and universities	1,869	1,930	461,742	462,286
Correspondence and vocational schools	3,372	3,474	54,668	53,006
Museums, botanical, zoological gardens	820	869	19,655	20,447
Nonprofit membership organizations	125,141	128,515	1,178,501	1,248,140
Business associations	11,881	11,999	74,258	75,129
Labor organizations	20,345	20,829	141,114	147,234
Civic and social associations	28,564	28,872	248,320	260,255
Religious organizations	45,252	46,096	307,328	326,427
Charitable organizations	6,609	6,768	149,119	160,074
Miscellaneous services	61,219	63,066	593,709	620,896
Engineering and architectural services	22,471	23,343	252,572	268,478
Nonprofit research agencies	3,551	3,640	104,208	110,818
Accounting, auditing, bookkeeping	30,172	30,958	210,136	213,826
TOTAL‡	989,523	1,000,729	10,634,134	11,102,077

*First quarter; each employer is counted once in each county for each industry in which it operates, regardless of the number of establishments operated. †Mid-March pay period. ‡Includes administrative and auxiliary businesses not shown separately. Source: U.S. Department of Commerce, Bureau of the Census, *County Business Patterns 1971* and *1972*.

Sales of merchant wholesalers

in millions of dollars

Kind of business	1960	1965	1970	1972
Durable goods	56,803	76,232	111,778	138,349
Motor vehicles, automotive equipment	7,883	10,945	20,203	26,951
Electrical goods	8,660	11,248	15,809	19,081
Furniture, home furnishings	2,910	3,392	5,343	6,322
Hardware, plumbing, heating equipment	6,422	7,947	10,643	13,483
Lumber, construction supplies	6,680	7,747	10,836	15,834
Machinery, equipment, supplies	14,287	20,279	28,515	35,057
Metals, metalwork (except scrap)	5,708	8,796	12,625	14,090
Scrap, waste materials	3,296	4,590	5,986	5,211
Nondurable goods	80,477	101,354	134,865	159,672
Groceries and related products	27,661	36,478	50,430	58,048
Beer, wine, distilled alcoholic beverages	7,424	9,496	12,862	15,000
Drugs, chemicals, allied products	5,370	6,859	9,619	11,681
Tobacco, tobacco products	4,164	4,856	6,118	6,873
Dry goods, apparel	6,675	8,614	10,391	13,010
Paper, paper products	4,153	5,234	7,317	8,187
Farm products	11,683	12,808	14,336	18,947
Other nondurable goods	13,346	17,008	23,792	28,015
TOTAL	137,281	177,587	246,643	298,111

Source: U.S. Department of Commerce, Bureau of the Census, *Monthly Wholesale Trade.*

Business activity

Category of activity	WHOLESALING			RETAILING			SERVICES		
	1960	1965	1970	1960	1965	1970	1960	1965	1970
Number of businesses (in 000)									
Sole proprietorships	306	265	274	1,548	1,554	1,689	1,966	2,208	2,507
Active partnerships	41	32	30	238	202	170	159	169	176
Active corporations	117	147	166	217	288	351	121	188	281
Business receipts (in $000,000)									
Sole proprietorships	17,061	17,934	21,556	65,439	77,760	89,315	23,256	29,789	40,869
Active partnerships	12,712	10,879	11,325	24,787	23,244	23,546	9,281	12,442	18,791
Active corporations	130,637	171,414	234,885	125,787	183,925	274,808	22,106	36,547	66,460
Net profit (less loss; in $000,000)									
Sole proprietorships	1,305	1,483	1,806	3,869	5,019	5,767	8,060	11,008	15,063
Active partnerships	587	548	557	1,612	1,654	1,603	3,056	4,402	6,189
Active corporations	2,130	3,288	4,441	2,225	4,052	5,217	849	1,505	1,199

Data refer to accounting periods ending between July 1 of year shown and June 30 of following year.
Source: U.S. Department of the Treasury, Internal Revenue Service, *Statistics of Income, U.S. Business Tax Returns,* and *Corporation Tax Returns.*

Commercial banks

Dec. 31, 1972

State	Number of banks	Total assets or liabilities $000,000	SELECTED ASSETS ($000,000) Loans*	Investments	Reserves, cash, and bank balances	SELECTED LIABILITIES ($000,000) Deposits Total	Demand	Time	Capital account
Ala.	277	7,804	4,128	2,395	1,031	6,792	3,319	3,473	578
Alaska	10	834	428	270	100	742	316	426	57
Ariz.	22	6,222	3,992	1,313	650	5,248	2,050	3,198	380
Ark.	253	4,830	2,578	1,360	761	4,231	2,141	2,090	358
Calif.	165	77,047	45,414	15,479	11,942	64,068	26,607	37,461	4,613
Colo.	291	7,074	4,260	1,521	1,042	6,030	3,095	2,934	487
Conn.	64	7,444	4,365	1,592	1,219	6,449	3,636	2,813	521
Del.	19	2,025	1,031	638	277	1,674	916	758	149
D.C.	16	3,720	2,124	914	593	3,205	1,970	1,235	304
Fla.	581	22,445	11,087	7,366	3,296	19,756	9,978	9,777	1,578
Ga.	437	12,178	7,429	2,332	1,872	9,929	5,476	4,453	953
Hawaii	11	2,442	1,463	582	285	2,131	943	1,188	189
Ida.	24	2,100	1,224	518	298	1,867	846	1,021	131
Ill.	1,155	55,122	30,756	15,431	6,635	45,644	19,351	26,294	3,988
Ind.	408	15,780	8,762	4,533	2,017	13,488	5,902	7,586	1,038
Iowa	670	9,588	4,699	2,990	1,197	8,387	4,751	4,751	716
Kan.	607	7,442	3,891	2,391	977	6,436	3,228	3,208	608
Ky.	341	8,066	4,307	2,346	1,215	7,052	3,733	3,319	587
La.	238	10,345	5,391	3,092	1,588	8,816	4,335	4,481	744
Me.	47	1,808	1,153	388	205	1,580	706	874	139
Md.	112	7,858	4,534	2,164	945	6,848	3,521	3,327	602
Mass.	155	16,239	9,350	3,330	2,672	12,920	8,125	4,795	1,225
Mich.	332	29,090	17,007	7,578	3,621	25,439	9,240	16,199	2,011
Minn.	737	13,570	7,509	3,889	1,619	11,457	4,933	6,524	953
Miss.	181	4,832	2,585	1,392	713	4,252	2,182	2,070	343
Mo.	677	16,662	8,895	4,895	2,406	13,976	7,582	6,394	1,292
Mont.	147	2,442	1,320	793	265	2,157	879	1,278	161
Neb.	446	5,374	3,139	1,374	725	4,658	2,376	2,282	401
Nev.	8	1,754	974	505	192	1,545	646	899	114
N.H.	78	1,511	988	315	165	1,308	581	727	128
N.J.	211	21,746	11,848	6,867	2,355	19,299	8,627	10,672	1,569
N.M.	72	2,509	1,418	642	378	2,201	980	1,220	172
N.Y.	305	141,422	77,356	23,147	31,303	109,040	63,924	45,116	10,223
N.C.	87	11,977	6,760	2,867	1,895	10,126	4,935	5,191	851
N.D.	170	2,210	1,081	882	202	1,967	806	1,161	170
Ohio	505	31,359	17,366	9,107	3,925	27,891	11,396	15,295	2,445
Okla.	441	8,622	4,450	2,603	1,288	7,409	3,637	3,772	656
Ore.	45	6,068	3,565	1,431	785	5,200	2,204	2,996	438
Penn.	437	43,626	25,489	10,976	5,386	35,807	15,342	20,465	3,400
R.I.	16	2,621	1,763	503	262	2,227	891	1,337	194
S.C.	94	3,734	2,134	932	535	3,208	1,985	1,223	286
S.D.	159	2,251	1,203	758	242	2,017	794	1,222	160
Tenn.	313	12,124	6,597	3,280	1,787	10,346	4,600	5,746	849
Tex.	1,238	41,208	22,599	10,010	6,958	34,697	18,694	16,004	2,813
Utah	53	2,856	1,700	645	412	2,460	1,143	1,317	202
Vt.	41	1,258	862	268	100	1,129	364	765	91
Va.	256	12,439	7,576	3,033	1,429	10,753	4,444	6,309	843
Wash.	90	8,438	5,110	1,743	1,135	7,051	3,151	3,900	540
W.Va.	203	4,502	2,360	1,558	463	3,869	1,598	2,270	367
Wis.	613	13,974	8,186	3,727	1,610	12,103	4,744	7,359	951
Wyo.	71	1,244	662	382	165	1,109	482	627	91
TOTAL	13,924	739,592	415,255	184,112	113,128	616,596	296,952	319,644	52,658

*Includes federal funds sold and securities purchased under agreements to resell.
Source: Federal Deposit Insurance Corporation, *Assets and Liabilities—Commercial and Mutual Savings Banks—Dec. 31, 1972, 1972 Report of Income.*

Life insurance, 1972

Number of policies in 000s; value in $000,000

State	Total: Number of policies	Total: Value	Ordinary: Number of policies	Ordinary: Value	Group: Number of certificates	Group: Value	Industrial: Number of policies	Industrial: Value	Credit*: Number of policies	Credit*: Value
Ala.	11,217	$25,567	1,431	$11,876	1,281	$9,211	6,692	$2,253	1,813	$2,227
Alaska	335	2,104	85	1,033	149	954	13	4	88	113
Ariz.	2,882	13,524	948	7,931	784	4,329	192	105	958	1,159
Ark.	2,402	10,148	717	5,281	491	3,446	567	289	627	1,132
Calif.	28,219	160,465	9,421	81,913	9,410	67,942	2,551	1,545	6,837	9,065
Colo.	3,714	19,135	1,442	11,165	994	6,391	350	251	928	1,328
Conn.	5,450	29,726	2,324	15,618	1,571	12,258	461	291	1,094	1,559
Del.	1,270	6,780	390	2,591	343	3,630	269	158	268	401
D.C.	3,058	10,061	411	2,893	994	5,987	551	296	1,102	885
Fla.	14,094	51,511	3,792	28,718	2,785	16,078	4,448	2,496	3,069	4,219
Ga.	11,852	38,030	2,443	18,968	1,735	13,083	4,931	2,673	2,743	3,306
Hawaii	1,345	9,034	476	4,992	535	3,594	8	4	326	444
Ida.	1,054	4,740	438	2,762	306	1,533	31	15	279	430
Ill.	21,392	101,432	8,619	54,004	5,407	40,407	3,729	2,097	3,637	4,924
Ind.	10,075	41,733	3,539	21,615	2,046	15,699	2,071	1,171	2,419	3,248
Iowa	4,536	21,509	2,312	13,381	980	6,409	314	149	930	1,570
Kan.	3,887	16,893	1,703	10,796	856	4,643	420	216	908	1,238
Ky.	5,823	19,574	1,695	10,080	914	6,784	1,884	933	1,330	1,777
La.	9,180	25,176	1,456	12,281	1,182	8,542	4,588	2,160	1,954	2,193
Me.	1,453	6,495	631	3,642	312	2,122	125	71	385	660
Md.	7,322	31,490	2,390	16,520	1,451	12,310	2,103	1,063	1,378	1,597
Mass.	9,266	46,066	3,976	24,367	2,255	18,894	1,246	697	1,789	2,108
Mich.	16,130	78,103	5,231	33,314	1,850	37,602	2,382	1,340	3,658	5,847
Minn.	5,530	28,971	2,229	15,209	1,850	11,713	346	169	1,105	1,880
Miss.	3,239	11,227	681	5,933	589	3,594	872	422	1,097	1,278
Mo.	8,583	37,693	3,325	19,442	1,996	14,802	1,615	869	1,647	2,580
Mont.	900	4,443	383	2,779	251	1,270	31	13	235	381
Neb.	2,471	11,974	1,193	7,610	522	3,424	162	80	594	860
Nev.	690	3,544	201	1,919	230	1,333	18	8	241	284
N.H.	1,283	5,811	589	3,461	238	1,750	149	83	307	517
N.J.	11,750	69,250	5,415	36,705	2,606	28,634	1,766	1,165	1,963	2,746
N.M.	1,509	6,878	464	3,507	425	2,690	131	76	489	605
N.Y.	27,497	157,043	11,778	79,422	6,949	68,331	2,834	1,663	5,936	7,627
N.C.	11,003	35,795	2,860	17,831	1,795	12,610	3,597	1,888	2,751	3,466
N.D.	845	3,886	366	2,411	217	1,072	6	3	256	400
Ohio	19,431	89,947	7,434	47,598	4,306	34,248	4,095	2,357	3,596	5,744
Okla.	3,943	18,595	1,449	10,064	827	6,505	502	286	1,165	1,740
Ore.	2,796	14,643	1,064	8,038	890	4,886	121	55	721	1,664
Penn.	23,980	94,812	9,276	51,204	4,690	34,756	5,580	2,992	4,434	5,860
R.I.	1,817	7,252	746	4,224	431	2,220	254	141	386	667
S.C.	6,887	18,235	1,806	8,934	911	6,017	2,819	1,528	1,351	1,756
S.D.	854	4,123	448	2,765	175	1,024	7	3	224	331
Tenn.	8,428	29,203	1,873	13,663	1,718	11,351	3,099	1,558	1,738	2,631
Tex.	19,212	87,069	6,404	47,844	4,085	30,411	3,355	1,962	5,368	6,852
Utah	1,732	7,895	592	4,142	584	3,091	122	50	434	612
Vt.	717	3,141	297	1,862	133	915	44	26	243	338
Va.	9,667	38,823	2,596	18,302	1,873	16,490	2,921	1,505	2,277	2,526
Wash.	4,143	23,285	1,644	12,830	1,484	9,186	221	98	794	1,171
W.Va.	2,934	10,342	825	4,674	585	4,315	681	383	843	970
Wis.	6,935	32,536	3,113	19,105	2,100	11,432	589	309	1,133	1,690
Wyo.	452	2,273	201	1,324	111	782	11	6	129	161
TOTAL U.S.	365,184	$1,627,985	125,122	$848,543	84,211	$630,700	75,874	$39,975	79,977	$108,767

*Insures borrower to cover loans in case of death.
Source: Institute of Life Insurance, *Life Insurance Book, 1973.*

Savings and loan associations

Dec. 31, 1972*

State	Number of assns.	Total assets ($000,000)	Per capita assets
Alabama	59	$1,912	$545
Alaska	3	148	456
Arizona	13	1,997	1,027
Arkansas	63	1,492	754
California	182	42,919	2,097
Colorado	48	3,462	1,469
Connecticut	35	2,128	690
Delaware	23	147	260
District of Columbia	17	3,229	4,317
Florida	131	16,082	2,215
Georgia	102	4,709	998
Guam	1	8	78
Hawaii	12	1,218	1,505
Idaho	11	422	558
Illinois	527	19,160	1,703
Indiana	182	4,904	927
Iowa	88	2,664	924
Kansas	94	2,993	1,326
Kentucky	127	2,575	780
Louisiana	106	3,107	813
Maine	24	309	300
Maryland	229	4,791	1,181
Massachusetts	178	5,172	894
Michigan	65	6,832	752
Minnesota	72	4,466	1,146
Mississippi	77	1,265	559
Missouri	131	6,311	1,328
Montana	16	390	543
Nebraska	46	2,008	1,317
Nevada	6	692	1,314
New Hampshire	22	491	637
New Jersey	296	9,562	1,298
New Mexico	37	755	709
New York	179	14,451	787
North Carolina	179	4,844	929
North Dakota	12	712	1,127
Ohio	461	17,798	1,651
Oklahoma	56	2,120	805
Oregon	28	2,333	1,069
Pennsylvania	552	11,002	923
Puerto Rico	9	628	224
Rhode Island	6	506	522
South Carolina	72	2,478	930
South Dakota	19	346	510
Tennessee	71	2,817	699
Texas	282	10,994	944
Utah	13	1,200	1,066
Vermont	7	123	267
Virginia	76	3,016	633
Washington	53	3,674	1,067
West Virginia	36	577	324
Wisconsin	127	5,465	1,209
Wyoming	13	255	738
TOTAL U.S.	5,448	$243,570	$1,175

*Preliminary. Components do not add to totals because of differences in reporting dates and accounting systems. Source: U.S. Savings and Loan League, *1973 Savings and Loan Fact Book.*

Retail food prices

in cents per pound, except as indicated

Commodity and unit	1960	1965	1970	1971	1972	1973*
Cereals and bakery prod.:						
Flour, wheat	11.1	11.6	11.8	12.0	11.9	13.5
Corn flakes (12 oz.)	25.8	28.9	32.2	33.4	31.2	31.2
Bread, white	20.3	20.9	24.3	25.0	24.7	25.8
Meats, poultry, and fish:						
Steak, round	105.5	108.4	130.2	136.1	147.7	174.8
Hamburger	52.4	50.8	66.2	68.1	74.4	94.2
Pork chops, center cut	85.8	97.3	116.2	108.1	124.6	145.0
Bacon, sliced	65.5	81.3	94.9	80.0	96.2	121.6
Frying chickens	42.7	39.0	40.8	41.0	41.4	58.7
Tuna fish, 6½ oz. can	32.5	32.0	39.8	44.0	45.5	47.6
Dairy products:						
Milk, fresh (grocery) (½ gal.)	24.7†	47.3	57.4	58.9	59.8	61.9
Butter	74.9	75.4	86.6	87.6	87.1	85.4
Cheese, American process (½ lb.)	34.3	37.7	50.4	52.8	54.3	57.6
Fruits and vegetables:						
Apples	16.2	17.8	21.9	23.5	24.6	27.9
Oranges, size 200 (doz.)	74.8	77.8	86.4	94.3	94.2	101.7
Potatoes	7.2	9.4	9.0	8.6	9.3	12.5
Lettuce (head)	17.3	25.5	29.9	34.1	34.1	43.9
Tomatoes	31.6	34.3	42.0	46.6	46.8	47.2
Other:						
Eggs, grade A, large (doz.)	57.3	52.7	61.4	52.9	52.4	67.7
Margarine	26.9	27.9	29.8	32.7	33.1	33.5
Sugar	11.6	11.8	13.0	13.6	13.9	14.4
Coffee	75.3	83.3	91.1	93.4	92.7	100.2

*April. †1 quart. Source: U.S. Department of Commerce, Bureau of the Census, *Statistical Abstract of the United States*. Data compiled by the U.S. Department of Labor, Bureau of Labor Statistics, *Retail Food Prices by Cities and Estimated Retail Food Prices by Cities*.

Unemployment trends

quarterly averages, seasonally adjusted

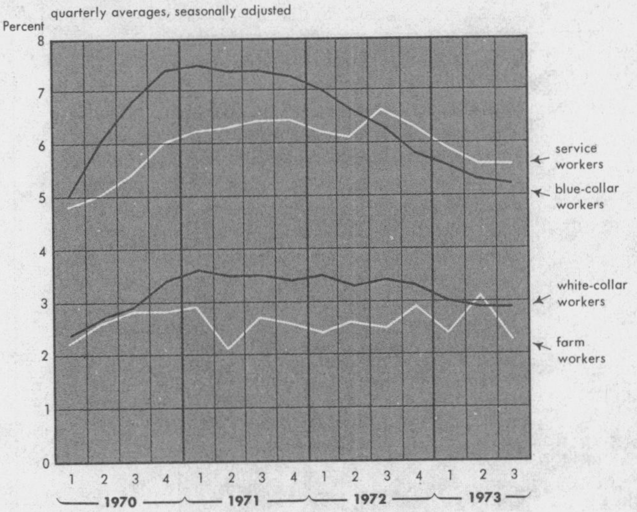

Source: U.S. Department of Labor, Bureau of Labor Statistics, *Monthly Labor Review*.

Average employee earnings

September figures

Industry	Average hourly earnings 1972	Average hourly earnings 1973*	Average weekly earnings 1972	Average weekly earnings 1973*
MANUFACTURING				
Durable goods	$4.11	$4.39	$171.39	$183.50
Ordnance and accessories	4.15	4.34	175.55	184.02
Lumber and wood products	3.38	3.67	140.27	150.47
Furniture and fixtures	3.11	3.32	127.51	132.80
Stone, clay, and glass products	3.99	4.24	169.18	179.35
Primary metal industries	4.75	5.16	199.50	220.33
Fabricated metal products	4.05	4.32	168.48	181.87
Nonelectrical machinery	4.33	4.60	183.59	197.34
Electrical equipment and supplies	3.72	3.92	151.78	159.54
Transportation equipment	4.80	5.13	203.52	218.54
Instruments and related products	3.74	3.91	152.97	159.92
Nondurable goods	3.51	3.75	140.40	150.00
Food and kindred products	3.61	3.88	148.01	160.63
Tobacco manufactures	3.35	3.66	126.97	143.47
Textile mill products	2.75	2.99	114.13	122.59
Apparel and related products	2.65	2.83	95.93	101.88
Paper and allied products	4.01	4.27	173.23	183.18
Printing and publishing	$4.56	$4.75	$175.56	$181.43
Chemicals and allied products	4.26	4.53	178.49	191.17
Petroleum and coal products	5.00	5.27	214.00	226.61
Rubber and plastics products	3.66	3.84	151.89	158.59
Leather and leather products	2.72	2.83	103.63	107.26
NONMANUFACTURING				
Metal mining	4.59	4.78†	192.32	200.28†
Coal mining	5.26	5.67†	215.13	227.37†
Oil and gas extraction	3.99	4.22†	170.37	181.04†
Contract construction	6.15	6.62	234.93	251.56
Local and suburban transportation	3.89	4.19†	161.82	176.82†
Electric, gas, and sanitary services	4.89	5.14†	202.45	213.82†
Wholesale trade	3.05	3.23	107.06	112.40
Retail trade	2.73	2.89	91.73	95.95
Hotels, tourist courts, and motels‡	2.27	2.33†	75.14	79.22†

*Preliminary. †August. ‡Excludes tips. Source: U.S. Department of Labor, Bureau of Labor Statistics, *Employment and Earnings*.

Consumer prices in selected cities, 1972

1967=100

Standard Metropolitan Statistical Area	Food	Housing	Rent	Home ownership	Apparel and upkeep	Medical care	Transportation	All items
U.S. average	123.5	129.2	119.2	140.1	122.3	132.5	119.9	125.3
Atlanta	124.4	131.8	117.0	142.8	118.7	139.6	113.0	125.5
Baltimore	124.7	130.9	112.6	149.3	123.8	142.5	116.7	126.3
Boston	123.7	133.3	129.2	147.6	124.3	134.7	119.5	127.1
Buffalo	123.5	133.1	120.1	137.3	126.1	126.1	117.9	126.6
Chicago	123.9	124.3	113.2	135.5	119.7	131.5	124.2	124.3
Cincinnati	124.5	124.5	109.6	138.1	122.9	136.5	123.8	124.7
Cleveland	123.3	126.3	113.0	131.8	123.8	144.0	126.0	126.5
Dallas	123.0	127.9	111.8	143.5	121.7	131.6	119.9	124.9
Detroit	122.9	133.3	120.2	147.7	118.3	141.4	116.5	126.2
Honolulu	123.2	124.3	127.7	130.9	120.5	127.5	123.0	122.8
Houston	125.0	128.7	110.9	142.8	125.7	135.3	114.8	125.2
Kansas City	123.6	126.1	110.7	140.0	127.5	129.1	118.4	124.0
Los Angeles	120.4	127.1	118.5	133.7	120.0	128.7	117.6	122.3
Milwaukee	120.6	126.4	117.9	133.2	126.8	128.1	119.3	123.7
Minneapolis-St. Paul	124.4	130.9	121.1	139.5	119.5	126.0	116.4	125.5
N.Y.-Northeastern N.J.	128.6	136.4	127.2	154.8	123.0	140.2	133.0	131.4
Philadelphia	124.4	130.6	124.4	143.7	120.0	142.1	125.1	127.0
Pittsburgh	122.8	129.7	117.0	143.4	123.6	128.7	121.2	125.3
St. Louis	122.5	122.4	108.6	129.2	120.3	125.8	120.1	122.3
San Diego	123.3	132.8	133.6	149.1	122.1	123.8	117.1	124.4
San Francisco-Oakland	121.4	130.5	129.2	138.5	121.7	127.1	120.4	124.3
Seattle	120.7	122.6	105.7	133.9	117.5	125.5	109.4	119.7
Washington, D.C.	125.8	128.8	118.6	140.9	125.0	139.9	123.6	126.9

Source: U.S. Department of Labor, Bureau of Labor Statistics.

Mortgage loan interest rates

conventional first mortgages

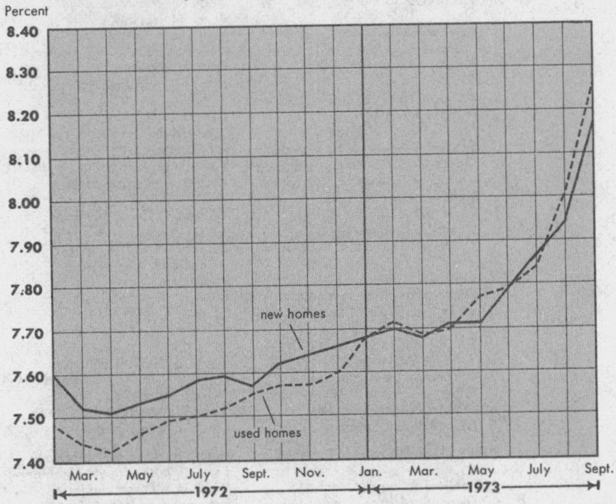

Source: Board of Governors of the Federal Reserve System, *Federal Reserve Bulletin*.

Stock market prices

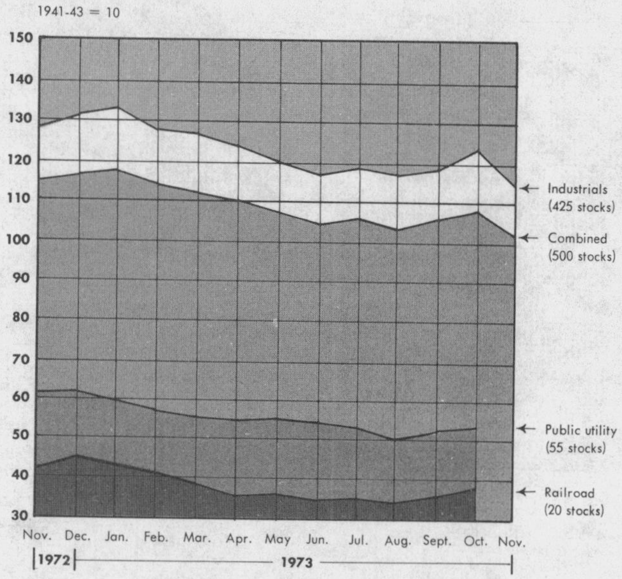

Source: U.S. Department of Commerce, Social and Economic Statistics Administration, Bureau of Economic Analysis, *Survey of Current Business*. Data compiled by Standard & Poor's Corporation.

Commodity prices (received by farmers)

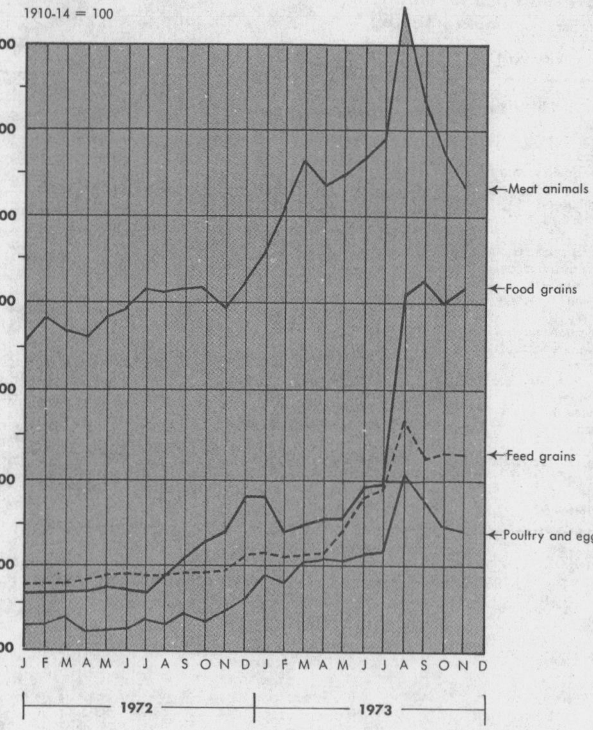

Source: U.S. Department of Commerce, Social and Economic Statistics Administration, Bureau of Economic Analysis, *Survey of Current Business*.

Government and Politics

The national executive

November 15, 1973

Department, bureau, or office	Executive official and official title
PRESIDENT OF THE UNITED STATES	Richard M. Nixon
Vice President	vacancy*
EXECUTIVE OFFICE OF THE PRESIDENT	
Counsellor to the President	Anne L. Armstrong Bryce N. Harlow
Counsellor to the President for Domestic Affairs	Melvin R. Laird
Assistant to the President	Peter M. Flanigan Gen. Alexander M. Haig (Ret.)
Assistant to the President and Press Secretary	Ronald L. Ziegler
Counsel to the President	Leonard Garment
Special Counsel to the President	J. Fred Buzhardt
Office of Management and Budget	Roy L. Ash, director
Council of Economic Advisors	Herbert Stein, chairman
National Security Council	†
Central Intelligence Agency	William E. Colby, director
Domestic Council	†
Office of the Special Representative for Trade Negotiations	William D. Eberle, special representative
Council on Environmental Quality	vacancy
Office of Telecommunications Policy	Clay T. Whitehead, director
Council on International Economic Policy	†
Special Action Office for Drug Abuse Prevention	Robert L. DuPont, director
Council on Economic Policy	George P. Shultz, chairman
Office of Economic Opportunity	Alvin J. Arnett, director
Federal Property Council	Anne L. Armstrong, chairman
Energy Policy Office	John A. Love, director
DEPARTMENT OF STATE	Henry A. Kissinger, secretary Kenneth Rush, deputy secretary
Political Affairs	William J. Porter, undersecretary
Economic Affairs	William J. Casey, undersecretary
Security Assistance	Curtis W. Tarr, undersecretary
Management	Curtis W. Tarr (acting), deputy undersecretary
Ambassador at Large	U. Alexis Johnson
DEPARTMENT OF STATE (continued)	
Counselor of the Department	vacancy
Agency for International Development	Daniel Parker, administrator
Permanent Mission to the Organization of American States	Joseph Jova, permanent representative
Mission to the United Nations	John A. Scali, permanent representative
African Affairs	David D. Newsom, asst. secretary
European Affairs	Walter J. Stoessel, asst. secretary
East Asian and Pacific Affairs	vacancy
Inter-American Affairs	Jack B. Kubisch, asst. secretary
Near Eastern and South Asian Affairs	Joseph J. Sisco, asst. secretary
DEPARTMENT OF THE TREASURY	George P. Shultz, secretary William E. Simon, deputy secretary
Monetary Affairs	Paul A. Volcker, undersecretary
Comptroller of the Currency	James E. Smith, comptroller
Bureau of Accounts	David Mosso, commissioner
Bureau of Customs	Vernon D. Acree, commissioner
Bureau of Engraving and Printing	James A. Conlon, director
Bureau of the Mint	Mary T. Brooks, director
Bureau of the Public Debt	H. J. Hintgen, commissioner
Internal Revenue Service	Donald C. Alexander, commissioner
Office of the Treasurer	Romona A. Banuelos, treasurer
Savings Bond Division	Jesse L. Adams, Jr., national director (acting)
U.S. Secret Service	H. Stuart Knight, director
Bureau of Alcohol, Tobacco and Firearms	Rex D. Davis, director
Consolidated Federal Law Enforcement Training Center	William B. Butler, director
DEPARTMENT OF DEFENSE‡	James R. Schlesinger, secretary William P. Clements, Jr., deputy secretary
Joint Chiefs of Staff	Adm. Thomas H. Moorer, chairman
Chief of Staff, Army	Gen. Creighton W. Abrams
Chief of Naval Operations	Adm. Elmo R. Zumwalt
Chief of Staff, Air Force	Gen. John D. Ryan

The national executive (continued)

Department, bureau, or office	Executive official and official title
DEPARTMENT OF DEFENSE (continued)	
Commandant of the Marine Corps	Gen. Robert E. Cushman
Department of the Army	Howard H. Callaway, secretary
Department of the Navy	John W. Warner, secretary
Department of the Air Force	John L. McLucas, secretary (acting)
	John L. McLucas, undersecretary
DEPARTMENT OF JUSTICE	
Attorney General	vacancy
Solicitor General	Robert H. Bork
Community Relations Service	Benjamin F. Holman, director
Law Enforcement Assistance Administration	Donald E. Santarelli, administrator
Antitrust Division	Thomas E. Kauper, asst. attorney general
Civil Division	Harlington Wood, Jr., asst. attorney general
Civil Rights Division	J. Stanley Pottinger, asst. attorney general
Criminal Division	Henry E. Peterson, asst. attorney general
Land and Natural Resources Division	Wallace H. Johnson, Jr., asst. attorney general
Tax Division	Scott P. Crampton, asst. attorney general
Administrative Division	Glen E. Pommerening, asst. attorney general
Federal Bureau of Investigation	Clarence M. Kelley, director
Bureau of Prisons	Norman A. Carlson, director
Immigration and Naturalization Service	James F. Greene, commissioner (acting)
Drug Enforcement Administration	John R. Bartels, administrator
U.S. Marshals Service	Wayne B. Colburn, director
Office of Watergate Special Prosecution Force	Leon Jaworski, special prosecutor
DEPARTMENT OF THE INTERIOR	Rogers C. B. Morton, secretary
	John C. Whitaker, undersecretary
Fish and Wildlife and Parks	Nathaniel P. Reed, asst. secretary
National Park Service	Ronald H. Walker, director
Sport Fisheries and Wildlife	Lynn Greenwalt, director
Energy and Minerals	Stephen A. Wakefield, asst. secretary
Office of Oil and Gas	Duke R. Ligon, director
Office of Coal Research	vacancy
Geological Survey	Vincent E. McKelvey, director
Bureau of Mines	vacancy
Land and Water Resources	Jack O. Horton, asst. secretary
Bureau of Land Management	Curtis J. Berklund, director
Bureau of Reclamation	Gilbert G. Stamm, commissioner
Commissioner of Indian Affairs	Morris Thompson
DEPARTMENT OF AGRICULTURE	Earl L. Butz, secretary
	J. Phil Campbell, undersecretary
Rural Development	William W. Erwin, asst. secretary
Rural Electrification Administration	David A. Hamil, administrator
Farmer's Home Administration	Frank B. Elliott, administrator
Marketing and Consumer Services	Clayton K. Yeutter, asst. secretary
Agricultural Marketing Service	Erwin L. Peterson, administrator
Commodity Exchange Authority	Alex C. Caldwell, administrator
International Affairs and Commodity Programs	Carroll G. Brunthaver, asst. secretary
Commodity Credit Corporation	Carroll G. Brunthaver, president
Conservation, Research, and Education	Robert W. Long, asst. secretary
Forest Service	John R. McGuire, chief
Soil Conservation Service	Kenneth E. Grant, administrator
Agricultural Economics	Don A. Paarlberg, director
Statistical Reporting Service	Harry C. Trelogan, administrator

Department, bureau or office	Executive official and official title
DEPARTMENT OF COMMERCE	Frederick B. Dent, secretary
	John K. Tabor, undersecretary
Domestic and International Business	Tilton H. Dobbin, asst. secretary
Economic Affairs	Sidney L. Jones, asst. secretary
Social and Economics Statistics Admin.	Edward D. Failor, administrator
Bureau of the Census	Vincent R. Barabba, director
Bureau of Economic Analysis	George Jaszi, director
Science and Technology	Betsy Ancker-Johnson, asst. secretary
Office of Environmental Quality	Sidney R. Galler, director
National Bureau of Standards	Richard W. Roberts, director
Patent Office	vacancy
Maritime Affairs	Robert J. Blackwell, asst. secretary
Tourism	C. Langhorne Washburn, asst. secretary
National Oceanic and Atmospheric Admin.	Robert M. White, administrator
DEPARTMENT OF LABOR‡	Peter J. Brennan, secretary
	Richard F. Schubert, undersecretary
Administration and Management	Fred G. Clark, asst. secretary
Manpower	William H. Kolberg, asst. secretary
Labor-Management Relations	Paul J. Fasser, Jr., asst. secretary
Employment Standards	Bernard E. DeLury, asst. secretary
Occupational Safety and Health	John H. Stender, asst. secretary
Labor Statistics	vacancy
DEPARTMENT OF HEALTH, EDUCATION, AND WELFARE‡	Caspar W. Weinberger, secretary
	Frank C. Carlucci, undersecretary
Education Division	Sidney P. Marland, Jr., asst. secretary
Office of Education	John Ottina, commissioner
National Institute of Education	Thomas K. Glennan, Jr., director
Health	Charles C. Edwards, M.D., asst. secretary
Public Health Service	
Food and Drug Administration	Sherwin Gardner, commissioner (acting)
National Institutes of Health	Robert S. Stone, director
Health Resources Administration	Harold O. Buzzell, administrator (acting)
Health Services Administration	Harold O. Buzzell, administrator
Center for Disease Control	David J. Sencer, director
Social and Rehabilitation Service	James S. Dwight, Jr., administrator
Social Security Administration	Arthur E. Hess, commissioner (acting)
DEPARTMENT OF HOUSING AND URBAN DEVELOPMENT‡	James T. Lynn, secretary
	Floyd H. Hyde, undersecretary
Community Planning and Development	vacancy
Housing Production and Mortgage Credit	Sheldon B. Lubar, asst. secretary
Housing Management	H. R. Crawford, asst. secretary
Equal Opportunity	Gloria E. A. Toote, asst. secretary
Policy Development and Research	Michael H. Moskow, asst. secretary
DEPARTMENT OF TRANSPORTATION‡	Claude S. Brinegar, secretary
	John W. Barnum, undersecretary
United States Coast Guard	Adm. Chester R. Bender, USCG, commandant
Federal Aviation Administration	Alexander P. Butterfield, administrator
Federal Highway Administration	Norbert T. Tiemann, administrator
National Highway Traffic Safety Admin.	vacancy
National Transportation Safety Board	John H. Reed, chairman
Federal Railroad Administration	John W. Ingram, administrator
St. Lawrence Seaway Development Corporation	David W. Oberlin, administrator
Urban Mass Transportation Administration	Frank C. Herringer, administrator

*Vacancy created by resignation of Spiro T. Agnew, Oct. 10, 1973.
†Council comprised of the President of the United States and certain other members.
‡August, 1973.

Senate

membership in 1973

State, name, and party	Term expires
Ala.—Allen, James B. (D)	1975
Sparkman, John (D)	1979
Alaska—Gravel, Mike (D)	1975
Stevens, Theodore F. (R)	1979
Ariz.—Goldwater, Barry (R)	1975
Fannin, Paul J. (R)	1977
Ark.—Fulbright, J. W. (D)	1975
McClellan, John (D)	1979
Calif.—Cranston, Alan (D)	1975
Tunney, John V. (D)	1977
Colo.—Dominick, Peter (R)	1975
Haskell, F. K. (D)	1979
Conn.—Ribicoff, Abraham (D)	1975
Weicker, Lowell P., Jr. (R)	1977
Del.—Biden, J. R. (D)	1979
Roth, William V., Jr. (R)	1977
Fla.—Gurney, Edward (R)	1975
Chiles, Lawton (D)	1977
Ga.—Talmadge, Herman (D)	1975
Nunn, Sam (D)	1979
Hawaii—Inouye, Daniel K. (D)	1975
Fong, Hiram L. (R)	1977
Ida.—Church, Frank (D)	1975
McClure, J. A. (R)	1979
Ill.—Stevenson, Adlai, III (D)	1975
Percy, Charles H. (R)	1979
Ind.—Bayh, Birch E., Jr. (D)	1975
Hartke, Vance (D)	1977
Ia.—Hughes, Harold (D)	1975
Clark, Richard (D)	1979
Kan.—Dole, Robert (R)	1975
Pearson, James B. (R)	1979
Ky.—Cook, Marlow W. (R)	1975
Huddleston, Walter (D)	1979
La.—Long, Russell (D)	1975
Johnston, J. B. (D)	1979
Me.—Muskie, Edmund S. (D)	1977
Hathaway, W. D. (D)	1979
Md.—Mathias, C. M., Jr. (R)	1975
Beall, J. Glenn, Jr. (R)	1977
Mass.—Kennedy, Edward M. (D)	1977
Brooke, Edward W. (R)	1979
Mich.—Hart, Philip A. (D)	1977
Griffin, Robert P. (R)	1979
Minn.—Humphrey, Hubert H. (D)	1977
Mondale, Walter F. (D)	1979
Miss.—Stennis, John (D)	1977
Eastland, James (D)	1979
Mo.—Eagleton, T. F. (D)	1975
Symington, Stuart (D)	1977
Mont.—Mansfield, Mike (D)	1977
Metcalf, Lee (D)	1979
Neb.—Hruska, Roman L. (R)	1977
Curtis, Carl T. (R)	1979
Nev.—Bible, Alan (D)	1975
Cannon, Howard W. (D)	1977
N.H.—Cotton, Norris (R)	1975
McIntyre, Thomas J. (D)	1979
N.J.—Williams, Harrison, Jr. (D)	1977
Case, Clifford P. (R)	1979
N.M.—Domenici, P. V. (R)	1979
Montoya, Joseph M. (D)	1977
N.Y.—Javits, Jacob K. (R)	1975
Buckley, James L. (C)	1977
N.C.—Ervin, Sam J., Jr. (D)	1975
Helms, Jesse (R)	1979
N.D.—Young, Milton R. (R)	1975
Burdick, Quentin N. (D)	1977
Ohio—Saxbe, William (R)	1975
Taft, Robert, Jr. (R)	1977
Okla.—Bellmon, Henry (R)	1975
Bartlett, D. F. (R)	1979
Ore.—Packwood, Robert (R)	1975
Hatfield, Mark O. (R)	1979
Penn.—Schweiker, R. S. (R)	1975
Scott, Hugh (R)	1977
R. I.—Pastore, John O. (D)	1977
Pell, Claiborne (D)	1979
S.C.—Hollings, Ernest F. (D)	1975
Thurmond, Strom (R)	1979
S.D.—McGovern, George (D)	1975
Abourezk, James (D)	1979
Tenn.—Brock, William E., III (R)	1977
Baker, Howard, Jr. (R)	1979
Tex.—Bentsen, Lloyd M., Jr. (D)	1977
Tower, John G. (R)	1979
Utah—Bennett, Wallace (R)	1975
Moss, Frank E. (D)	1977
Vt.—Aiken, George D. (R)	1975
Stafford, Robert T. (R)	1977
Va.—Byrd, Harry F., Jr. (I)	1977
Scott, W. L. (R)	1979
Wash.—Magnuson, Warren (D)	1975
Jackson, Henry M. (D)	1977
W.Va.—Byrd, Robert C. (D)	1977
Randolph, Jennings (D)	1979
Wis.—Nelson, Gaylord (D)	1975
Proxmire, William (D)	1977
Wyo.—McGee, Gale W. (D)	1977
Hansen, Clifford P. (R)	1979

House of Representatives

membership in 1973

State, district, name, and party

Ala.—1. Edwards, Jack (R)
2. Dickinson, W. L. (R)
3. Nichols, William (D)
4. Bevill, Tom (D)
5. Jones, Robert E., Jr. (D)
6. Buchanan, John H., Jr. (R)
7. Flowers, W. W. (D)
Alaska—Young, Don (R)*
Ariz.—1. Rhodes, John J. (R)
2. Udall, Morris K. (D)
3. Steiger, Sam (R)
4. Conlan, J. B. (R)
Ark.—1. Alexander, Bill (D)
2. Mills, Wilbur D. (D)
3. Hammerschmidt, J. P. (R)
4. Thornton, Ray (D)
Calif.—1. Clausen, Don H. (R)
2. Johnson, Harold T. (D)
3. Moss, John E. (D)
4. Leggett, Robert L. (D)
5. Burton, Phillip (D)
6. Mailliard, William S. (R)
7. Dellums, R. V. (D)
8. Stark, F. H. (D)
9. Edwards, W. Donlon (D)
10. Gubser, Charles S. (R)
11. Ryan, Leo J. (D)
12. Talcott, Burt L. (R)
13. Teague, Charles M. (R)
14. Waldie, Jerome R. (D)
15. McFall, John J. (D)
16. Sisk, B. F. (D)
17. McCloskey, Paul N., Jr. (R)
18. Mathias, Robert B. (R)
19. Holifield, Chet (D)
20. Moorhead, C. J. (R)
21. Hawkins, Augustus F. (D)
22. Corman, James C. (D)
23. Clawson, Del M. (R)
24. Rousselot, John H. (R)
25. Wiggins, Charles (R)
26. Rees, Thomas (D)
27. Goldwater, Barry, Jr. (R)
28. Bell, Alphonzo (R)
29. Danielson, George E. (D)
30. Roybal, Edward R. (D)
31. Wilson, Charles H. (D)
32. Hosmer, Craig (R)
33. Pettis, Jerry (R)
34. Hanna, Richard T. (D)
35. Anderson, Glenn M. (D)
36. Ketchum, W. M. (R)
37. Burke, Y. B. (D)
38. Brown, G. E., Jr. (D)
39. Hinshaw, A. J. (R)
40. Wilson, Bob (R)
41. Van Deerlin, Lionel (D)
42. Burgener, C. W. (R)
43. Veysey, Victor V. (R)
Colo.—1. Schroeder, P. (D)
2. Brotzman, D. G. (R)
3. Evans, Frank (D)
4. Johnson, J. P. (R)
5. Armstrong, W. L. (R)
Conn.—1. Cotter, William R. (D)
2. Steele, Robert H. (R)
3. Giaimo, Robert N. (D)
4. McKinney, Stewart B. (R)
5. Sarasin, Ronald A. (R)
6. Grasso, Ella T. (D)
Del.—duPont, Pierre S., IV (R)
Fla.—1. Sikes, Robert L. F. (D)
2. Fuqua, Don (D)
3. Bennett, Charles E. (D)
4. Chappell, William, Jr. (D)
5. Gunter, W. D., Jr. (D)
6. Young, C. William (R)
7. Gibbons, Sam (D)
8. Haley, James A. (D)
9. Frey, Louis, Jr. (R)
10. Bafalis, L. A. (R)
11. Rogers, Paul G. (D)
12. Burke, J. Herbert (R)
13. Lehman, William (D)
14. Pepper, Claude (D)
15. Fascell, Dante B. (D)
Ga.—1. Ginn, R. B. (D)
2. Mathis, Dawson (D)
3. Brinkley, Jack (D)
4. Blackburn, B. B. (R)
5. Young, Andrew (D)
6. Flynt, J. J., Jr. (D)
7. Davis, John W. (D)
8. Stuckey, W. S., Jr. (D)
9. Landrum, Phil M. (D)
10. Stephens, Robert G., Jr. (D)
Hawaii—1. Matsunaga, Spark M. (D)
2. Mink, Patsy (D)
Ida.—1. Symms, S. D. (R)
2. Hansen, Orval (R)
Ill.—1. Metcalfe, Ralph (D)
2. Murphy, Morgan (D)
3. Hanrahan, R. P. (R)
4. Derwinski, Edward J. (R)
5. Kluczynski, John C. (D)
6. Collier, H. R. (R)
7. Collins, Cardiss (D)†
8. Rostenkowski, Dan (D)
9. Yates, Sidney R. (D)
10. Young, S. H. (R)
11. Annunzio, Frank (D)
12. Crane, Philip M. (R)
13. McClory, Robert (R)
14. Erlenborn, J. N. (R)
15. Arends, Leslie C. (R)
16. Anderson, John B. (R)
17. O'Brien, G. M. (R)
18. Michel, Robert H. (R)
19. Railsback, Thomas F. (R)
20. Findley, Paul (R)
21. Madigan, E. R. (R)
22. Shipley, George E. (D)
23. Price, Melvin (D)
24. Gray, Kenneth J. (D)
Ind.—1. Madden, Ray J. (D)
2. Landgrebe, Earl F. (R)
3. Brademas, John (D)
4. Roush, J. Edward (D)
5. Hillis, Elwood H. (R)
6. Bray, William G. (R)
7. Myers, John (R)
8. Zion, Roger (R)
9. Hamilton, L. H. (D)
10. Dennis, David (R)
11. Hudnut, W. H., III (R)
Iowa—1. Mezvinsky, E. (D)
2. Culver, J. C. (D)
3. Gross, H. R. (R)
4. Smith, Neal (D)
5. Scherle, W. J. (R)
6. Mayne, Wiley (R)
Kan.—1. Sebelius, Keith G. (R)
2. Roy, William R. (D)
3. Winn, Larry, Jr. (R)
4. Shriver, Garner E. (R)
5. Skubitz, Joseph (R)
Ky.—1. Stubblefield, Frank A. (D)
2. Natcher, William H. (D)
3. Mazzoli, Romano L. (D)
4. Snyder, Gene (R)
5. Carter, Tim L. (R)
6. Breckinridge, J. B. (D)
7. Perkins, Carl D. (D)
La.—1. Hébert, F. Edward (D)
2. Boggs, Lindy (D)‡
3. Treen, David C. (R)
4. Waggonner, Joe D., Jr. (D)
5. Passman, Otto E. (D)
6. Rarick, John R. (D)
7. Breaux, John B. (D)
8. Long, Gillis W. (D)
Me.—1. Kyros, Peter (D)
2. Cohen, W. S. (R)
Md.—1. Bauman, Robert E. (R)§
2. Long, Clarence D. (D)
3. Sarbanes, Paul S. (D)
4. Holt, M. S. (R)
5. Hogan, Lawrence J. (R)
6. Byron, Goodloe E. (D)
7. Mitchell, Parren J. (D)
8. Gude, Gilbert (R)
Mass.—1. Conte, Silvio O. (R)
2. Boland, Edward P. (D)
3. Donohue, Harold D. (D)
4. Drinan, Robert F. (D)
5. Cronin, Paul W. (R)
6. Harrington, M. J. (D)
7. Macdonald, Torbert H. (D)
8. O'Neill, Thomas P., Jr. (D)
9. Moakley, J. J. (I)
10. Heckler, Margaret (R)
11. Burke, James A. (D)
12. Studds, Gerry E. (D)
Mich.—1. Conyers, John, Jr. (D)
2. Esch, Marvin (R)
3. Brown, Garry E. (R)
4. Hutchinson, Edward (R)
5. Vacancy‖
6. Chamberlain, Charles E. (R)
7. Riegle, D. W., Jr. (D)
8. Harvey, James (R)
9. Vander Jagt, Guy (R)
10. Cederberg, Elford A. (R)
11. Ruppe, Philip (R)
12. O'Hara, James G. (D)
13. Diggs, Charles C., Jr. (D)
14. Nedzi, Lucien N. (D)
15. Ford, W. D. (D)
16. Dingell, John D. (D)
17. Griffiths, Martha W. (D)
18. Huber, R. J. (R)
19. Broomfield, William S. (R)
Minn.—1. Quie, Albert H. (R)
2. Nelsen, Ancher (R)
3. Frenzel, William (R)
4. Karth, Joseph E. (D)
5. Fraser, Donald M. (D)
6. Zwach, John M. (R)
7. Bergland, Bob S. (D)
8. Blatnik, John A. (D)
Miss.—1. Whitten, Jamie L. (D)
2. Bowen, D. R. (D)
3. Montgomery, G. V. (D)
4. Cochran, Thad (R)
5. Lott, Trent (R)
Mo.—1. Clay, William (D)
2. Symington, James W. (D)
3. Sullivan, Leonor K. (D)
4. Randall, William J. (D)
5. Bolling, Richard (D)
6. Litton, Jerry (D)
7. Taylor, Gene (R)
8. Ichord, Richard H. (D)
9. Hungate, W. L. (D)
10. Burlison, Bill D. (D)
Mont.—1. Shoup, Richard G. (R)
2. Melcher, John (D)
Neb.—1. Thone, Charles (R)
2. McCollister, John Y. (R)
3. Martin, David (R)
Nev.—Towell, David (R)
N.H.—1. Wyman, Louis C. (R)
2. Cleveland, James C. (R)
N.J.—1. Hunt, John E. (R)
2. Sandman, Charles W., Jr. (R)
3. Howard, J. J. (D)
4. Thompson, Frank, Jr. (D)
5. Frelinghuysen, Peter, Jr. (R)
6. Forsythe, Edwin B. (R)
7. Widnall, William B. (R)
8. Roe, Robert A. (D)
9. Helstoski, Henry (D)
10. Rodino, Peter W., Jr. (D)
11. Minish, Joseph G. (D)
12. Rinaldo, M. J. (R)
13. Maraziti, J. J. (R)
14. Daniels, Dominick V. (D)
15. Patten, Edward J. (D)
N.M.—1. Lujan, Manuel, Jr. (R)
2. Runnels, Harold L. (D)
N.Y.—1. Pike, Otis G. (D)
2. Grover, James R., Jr. (R)
3. Roncallo, A. D. (R)
4. Lent, Norman F. (R)
5. Wydler, John W. (R)
6. Wolff, L. L. (D)
7. Addabbo, Joseph P. (D)
8. Rosenthal, Benjamin S. (D)
9. Delaney, James J. (D)
10. Biaggi, Mario (D)
11. Brasco, Frank J. (D)
12. Chisholm, Shirley (D)
13. Podell, B. L. (D)
14. Rooney, John J. (D)
15. Carey, Hugh L. (D)
16. Holtzman, E. (D)
17. Murphy, John M. (D)
18. Koch, Edward I. (D)
19. Rangel, Charles B. (D)
20. Abzug, Bella (D)
21. Badillo, Herman (D)
22. Bingham, J. B. (D)
23. Peyser, Peter A. (R)
24. Reid, Ogden R. (D)
25. Fish, Hamilton, Jr. (R)
26. Gilman, B. A. (R)
27. Robison, Howard W. (R)
28. Stratton, Samuel S. (D)
29. King, Carleton J. (R)
30. McEwen, Robert (R)
31. Mitchell, D. J. (R)
32. Hanley, James M. (D)
33. Walsh, W. F. (R)
34. Horton, Frank J. (R)
35. Conable, B., Jr. (R)
36. Smith, H. P., III (R)
37. Dulski, Thaddeus J. (D)
38. Kemp, Jack F. (R)
39. Hastings, James F. (R)
N.C.—1. Jones, Walter B. (D)
2. Fountain, L. H. (D)
3. Henderson, David N. (D)
4. Andrews, Ike F. (D)
5. Mizell, Wilmer (R)
6. Preyer, L. R. (D)
7. Rose, C. G., III (D)
8. Ruth, Earl B. (R)
9. Martin, J. G. (R)
10. Broyhill, James T. (R)
11. Taylor, Roy A. (D)
N.D.—Andrews, Mark (R)
Ohio—1. Keating, William J. (R)
2. Clancy, Donald D. (R)
3. Whalen, Charles W., Jr. (R)
4. Guyer, Tennyson (R)
5. Latta, Delbert L. (R)
6. Harsha, William H., Jr. (R)
7. Brown, Clarence J., Jr. (R)
8. Powell, Walter E. (R)
9. Ashley, Thomas L. (D)
10. Miller, Clarence E. (R)
11. Stanton, John W. (R)
12. Devine, Samuel L. (R)
13. Mosher, Charles A. (R)
14. Seiberling, John F., Jr. (D)
15. Wylie, Chalmers P. (R)
16. Regula, R. S. (R)
17. Ashbrook, John M. (R)
18. Hays, Wayne L. (D)
19. Carney, Charles J. (D)
20. Stanton, James V. (D)
21. Stokes, Louis (D)
22. Vanik, Charles A. (D)
23. Minshall, William E. (R)
Okla.—1. Jones, James R. (D)
2. McSpadden, C. R. (D)
3. Albert, Carl (D)
4. Steed, Tom (D)
5. Jarman, John (D)
6. Camp, J. N. H. (R)
Ore.—1. Wyatt, Wendell (R)
2. Ullman, Al (D)
3. Green, Edith (D)
4. Dellenback, John R. (R)
Penn.—1. Barrett, William A. (D)
2. Nix, Robert N. C. (D)
3. Green, William J., III (D)
4. Eilberg, Joshua (D)
5. Ware, John H., III (R)
6. Yatron, Gus (D)
7. Williams, L. G. (R)
8. Biester, E. G., Jr. (R)
9. Shuster, E. G. (R)
10. McDade, Joseph M. (R)
11. Flood, Daniel J. (D)
12. Vacancy ¶
13. Coughlin, R. L. (R)
14. Moorhead, William S. (D)
15. Rooney, Fred B. (D)
16. Eshleman, Edwin D. (R)
17. Schneebeli, Herman T. (R)
18. Heinz, H. John, III (R)
19. Goodling, George A. (R)
20. Gaydos, Joseph (D)
21. Dent, John H. (D)
22. Morgan, Thomas E. (D)
23. Johnson, Albert W. (R)
24. Vigorito, J. P. (D)
25. Clark, Frank M. (D)
R.I.—1. St. Germain, Fernand (D)
2. Tiernan, Robert O. (D)
S.C.—1. Davis, Mendel (D)
2. Spence, Floyd D. (R)
3. Dorn, W. J. Bryan (D)
4. Mann, James R. (D)
5. Gettys, Thomas S. (D)
6. Young, E. L. (R)
S.D.—1. Denholm, Frank E. (D)
2. Abdnor, James (R)
Tenn.—1. Quillen, James H. (R)
2. Duncan, John J. (R)
3. Baker, LaMar E. (R)
4. Evins, Joseph L. (D)
5. Fulton, Richard (D)
6. Beard, R. L., Jr. (R)
7. Jones, Edward (D)
8. Kuykendall, Dan (R)
Tex.—1. Patman, Wright (D)
2. Wilson, Charles (D)
3. Collins, James M. (R)
4. Roberts, Ray (D)
5. Steelman, Alan (R)
6. Teague, Olin E. (D)
7. Archer, William R. (R)
8. Eckhardt, Robert C. (D)
9. Brooks, Jack (D)
10. Pickle, J. J. (D)
11. Poage, W. R. (D)
12. Wright, James C., Jr. (D)
13. Price, Robert (R)
14. Young, John (D)
15. de la Garza, E. (D)
16. White, Richard C. (D)
17. Burleson, Omar (D)
18. Jordan, B. C. (D)
19. Mahon, George (D)
20. Gonzalez, Henry B. (D)
21. Fisher, O. C. (D)
22. Casey, Robert R. (D)
23. Kazen, Abraham, Jr. (D)
24. Milford, Dale (D)
Utah—1. McKay, Koln G. (D)
2. Owens, Wayne (D)
Vt.—Mallary, R. W. (R)
Va.—1. Downing, Thomas N. (D)
2. Whitehurst, G. W. (R)
3. Satterfield, D. E., III (D)
4. Daniel, R. W. (R)
5. Daniel, W. C. (D)
6. Butler, M. C. (R)
7. Robinson, James K. (R)
8. Parris, S. E. (R)
9. Wampler, William C. (R)
10. Broyhill, Joel T. (R)
Wash.—1. Pritchard, Joel (R)
2. Meeds, Lloyd (D)
3. Hansen, Julia Butler (D)
4. McCormack, Mike (D)
5. Foley, Thomas S. (D)
6. Hicks, Floyd V. (D)
7. Adams, B. (D)
W.Va.—1. Mollohan, R. H. (D)
2. Staggers, Harley O. (D)
3. Slack, John M., Jr. (D)
4. Hechler, Ken (D)
Wis.—1. Aspin, Leslie (D)
2. Kastenmeier, Robert W. (D)
3. Thomson, Vernon W. (R)
4. Zablocki, Clement J. (D)
5. Reuss, Henry S. (D)
6. Steiger, William A. (R)
7. Obey, David R. (D)
8. Froehlich, H. V. (R)
9. Davis, Glenn R. (R)
Wyo.—Roncalio, Teno (D)

*Sworn in March 14, 1973, to succeed Nick J. Begich (disappeared on a plane flight in Alaska; seat declared vacant). †Sworn in June 7, 1973, to succeed her husband, George W. Collins (deceased). ‡Sworn in March 27, 1973, to succeed her husband, Hale Boggs (disappeared on a plane flight in Alaska; seat declared vacant). §Sworn in Sept. 5, 1973, to succeed William O. Mills (deceased). ‖Seat vacated on Dec. 6, 1973, by Gerald R. Ford when he was sworn in as vice-president of the United States. ¶Vacancy caused by death of John P. Saylor on Oct. 28, 1973.

Supreme Court

Chief Justice of the United States:
Warren Earl Burger

Associate Justices:
William O. Douglas
William J. Brennan, Jr.
Potter Stewart
Byron R. White
Thurgood Marshall
Harry A. Blackmun
Lewis F. Powell, Jr.
William H. Rehnquist

The federal administrative budget

in millions of dollars; fiscal year ending June 30

Source and function	1972	1973 estimate	1974 estimate
Budget receipts	$208,649	$224,984	$255,982
Individual income taxes	94,737	99,400	111,600
Corporation income taxes	32,166	33,500	37,000
Excise taxes:			
Federal funds	9,506	9,683	10,198
Trust funds	5,971	6,287	6,600
Social insurance taxes and contributions (trust funds):			
Employment taxes and contributions	46,120	55,610	67,866
Unemployment insurance	4,357	5,262	6,267
Contributions for other insurance and retirement	3,437	3,667	4,029
Estate and gift taxes	5,436	4,600	5,000
Customs duties	3,287	3,000	3,300
Miscellaneous receipts:			
Deposit of earnings by the Federal Reserve System	3,252	3,350	3,700
Other miscellaneous receipts	381	625	422
Budget expenditures	231,876	249,796	268,665
National defense	78,336	76,435	81,074
Department of Defense military functions	75,151	74,200	78,200
Military assistance	806	600	800
Atomic energy	2,392	2,194	2,374
Defense-related activities	95	192	83
Deductions for offsetting receipts	−108	−751	−382
International affairs and finance	3,726	3,341	3,811
Conduct of foreign affairs	452	503	538
Economic and financial assistance	2,287	2,273	2,408
Foreign information and exchange activities	274	294	312
Food for Peace	993	847	766
Deductions for offsetting receipts	−280	−575	−213
Space research and technology	3,422	3,061	3,135
Agriculture and agricultural resources	7,063	6,064	5,572
Farm income stabilization	5,146	4,251	3,920
Rural housing and public facilities	877	657	717
Agricultural land and water resources	354	394	217
Research and other agricultural services	916	1,001	971
Deductions for offsetting receipts	−230	−239	−253
Natural resources and environment	3,761	876	3,663
Water resources and power	2,664	3,065	2,795
Land management	892	1,008	929
Mineral resources	112	151	131
Pollution control and abatement	763	1,148	2,128
Recreational resources	524	641	701
Other natural resources programs	153	174	191
Deductions for offsetting receipts	−1,347	−5,310	−3,214
Commerce and transportation	11,201	12,543	11,580
Air transportation	1,685	1,760	1,877
Water transportation	1,106	1,200	1,282
Ground transportation	5,210	5,564	5,536
Postal service	1,772	1,710	1,373
Advancement of business	645	1,476	548
Area and regional development	818	901	1,050
Regulation of business	168	175	168
Deductions for offsetting receipts	−203	−244	−254
Housing and community development	4,282	3,957	4,931
Community planning, management, and development	2,878	2,822	2,590
Low- and moderate-income housing aids	1,595	1,120	2,009
Maintenance of the housing mortgage market	−191	15	332
Deductions for offsetting receipts	*	*	*
Education and manpower	9,751	10,500	10,110
Elementary and secondary education	3,490	3,262	1,739
Higher education	1,434	1,496	1,635
Vocational education	521	557	308
Education revenue sharing	—	—	1,693
Other education aids	541	749	906
General science	567	573	586
Manpower training and employment services	2,894	3,486	2,847
Other manpower aids	318	393	411
Deductions for offsetting receipts	−13	−15	−15
Veterans benefits and services	10,731	11,795	11,732
Income security for veterans	6,833	7,025	6,814
Veterans education, training, and rehabilitation	1,960	2,597	2,521
Veterans housing	−317	−449	−269
Hospital and medical care for veterans	2,428	2,741	2,792
Other veterans benefits and services	318	363	360
Deductions for offsetting receipts	−491	−483	−486
Interest	20,582	22,808	24,672
Interest on the public debt	21,849	24,200	26,100
Interest on refunds of receipts	182	175	175
Interest on uninvested funds	6	5	5
Deductions for offsetting receipts	−1,455	−1,573	−1,608
General government	4,891	5,631	6,025
Legislative functions	311	329	383
Judicial functions	173	194	206
Executive direction and management	68	138	148
Central fiscal operations	1,647	1,774	1,852
General property and records management	725	902	917
Central personnel management	275	327	347
Law enforcement and justice	1,233	1,630	1,877
National capital region	450	506	634
Other general government	345	406	429
Deductions for offsetting receipts	−335	−576	−768
General revenue sharing	—	6,786	6,035
Allowances for contingencies, civilian agency pay raises	—	500	1,750
Undistributed intragovernmental transactions:			
Employer share, employee retirement	−2,768	−2,980	−3,157
Interest received by trust funds	−5,089	−5,401	−5,974

*Less than $500,000.
Source: Executive Office of the President, Office of Management and Budget.

Major legislation passed by the 93rd Congress in 1973

ECONOMY

Economic stabilization (PL 93-28; enacted April 30, 1973) Extended for one year the President's authority to establish wage and price controls.

Minimum wage (HR 7935; vetoed Sept. 6, 1973, sustained by House) Extended coverage of minimum wage legislation to 6.5–7.0 million additional workers; raised minimum wage to $2.20 by July 1, 1974.

ENERGY

Alaskan pipeline (PL 93-153; enacted Nov. 16, 1973) Authorized construction of the trans-Alaskan pipeline and prohibited further judicial review on environmental grounds.

Daylight savings time (93-182; enacted Dec. 15, 1973) Imposed year-round daylight savings time until the fourth Sunday of April, 1975, after which it would continue in effect an additional six months according to Uniform Time Act of 1966.

Fuel allocation (PL 93-159; enacted Nov. 27, 1973) Directed the President to initiate a program of petroleum and petroleum product allocation within 30 days of enactment.

FARMS—RURAL PROGRAMS

Farm program (PL 93-86; enacted Aug. 10, 1973) Established a four-year program for cash payments to farmers if farm prices fall below legally established target prices for wheat, feed grains, and cotton. Established a limit of $20,000 per individual farmer for subsidy payments; established a milk support rate of 80% of parity through March 31, 1975.

Rural electrification (PL 93-32; enacted May 11, 1973) Converted the loan program of the Rural Electrification Administration (REA) from a direct loan basis to one which would insure and guarantee loans for purposes defined by previous law.

FOREIGN AFFAIRS

Foreign aid (PL 93-189; enacted Dec. 17, 1973) Authorized $2,400,000,000 for general and military foreign aid during fiscal 1974.

Israel (PL 93-199; enacted Dec. 26, 1973) Authorized $2,200,000,000 in military and emergency aid for Israel during fiscal 1974.

GOVERNMENT

District of Columbia home rule (PL 93-198) Permitted election by residents of a mayor and 13-member city council; Congress, however, retained full budgetary control and veto power over city council legislation by concurrent resolution.

Franking (PL 93-191; enacted Dec. 18, 1973) Established for first time rules governing use of the franking privilege by members of Congress.

Office of Management and Budget, Director (S 518; vetoed May 18, 1973, sustained by House) Provided for Senate approval of the director and deputy director of the Office of Management and Budget.

War powers of the President (PL 93-148; enacted over Presidential veto Nov. 7, 1973) Set a 60-day limit to the period during which the President could commit U.S. troops to combat in foreign countries without Congressional approval.

MILITARY AFFAIRS

Indochina (PL 93-52; enacted July 1, 1974) Prohibited use of funds authorized by bill for support of U.S. combat operations in, over, or from off the shores of Cambodia, Laos, North Vietnam, and South Vietnam.

Military construction (PL 93-194; enacted Dec. 20, 1973) Appropriated $2,700,000,000 for military housing and installations in the U.S. and overseas during fiscal 1974.

Veteran's medical benefits (PL 93-82; enacted August 2, 1973) Increased programs and facilities available to veterans and dependents not covered by military insurance programs.

Weapons procurement (PL 93-155; enacted Nov. 16, 1973) Authorized $21,700,000,000 during fiscal 1974 for research, development, and procurement of weapons and weapon systems.

SOCIAL AFFAIRS

Emergency medical services

(S 504; vetoed Aug. 1, 1973) Authorized a three-year program of aid to state and local governments for emergency medical services.

(PL 93-154; enacted Nov. 16, 1973) Virtually identical with S 504 (above) but eliminated Public Service Hospital administrative changes which were unsatisfactory to the President in S 504.

Health Maintenance Organizations (HMO's) (PL 92-222; enacted Dec. 29, 1973) Authorized a five-year, $375,000,000 program to provide federal aid for the development of about 100 HMO's to provide health services for a set fee.

Health programs (PL 93-45; enacted June 18, 1973) Extended 12 major federal health programs through fiscal 1974, including several (Hill-Burton hospital construction, community mental health centers, etc.) which were to have been phased out by the President.

Social Security program

(PL 93-66; enacted July 9, 1973) Provided a 5.9% increase in social security benefits, effective July 1, 1974. Superseded by:

(PL 93-233; enacted Dec. 31, 1973) Provided a 7% increase in social security benefits, effective March, 1974 and a further 4%, effective June 1974.

TRANSPORTATION AND COMMUNICATIONS

Amtrak (PL 93-146; enacted Nov. 3, 1973) Authorized $154,000,000 during fiscal 1974 and expanded authority of National Railroad Passenger Corporation.

Highways—mass transit (PL 93-87; enacted Aug. 13, 1973) Authorized for first time (fiscal 1976) the use of Highway Trust Fund monies for financing of urban mass transit projects and programs.

Public broadcasting (PL 93-84; enacted Aug. 6, 1973) Authorized $130,000,000 for the Corporation for Public Broadcasting during fiscal 1974–75.

Sports broadcasting (PL 93-107; enacted Sept. 14, 1973) Prohibited local TV blackouts of sports events which were sold out three days in advance.

State executive officials

December 1973

State	Governor	Legislative seats: House	Legislative seats: Senate
Alabama	George C. Wallace(D)	106	35
Alaska	William A. Egan(D)	40	20
Arizona	Jack Williams(R)	60	30
Arkansas	Dale Bumpers(D)	100	35
California	Ronald Reagan(R)	80	40
Colorado	John D. Vanderhoof(R)*	65	35
Connecticut	Thomas J. Meskill(R)	151	36
Delaware	Sherman W. Tribbitt(D)	41	21
Florida	Reubin O'D. Askew(D)	120	40
Georgia	Jimmy Carter(D)	180	56
Hawaii	John A. Burns(D)	51	25
Idaho	Cecil D. Andrus(D)	70	35
Illinois	Daniel Walker(D)	177	59
Indiana	Otis R. Bowen(R)	100	50
Iowa	Robert D. Ray(R)	100	50
Kansas	Robert B. Docking(D)	125	40
Kentucky	Wendell H. Ford(D)	100	38
Louisiana	Edwin W. Edwards(D)	105	39
Maine	Kenneth M. Curtis(D)	151	33
Maryland	Marvin Mandel(D)	142	43
Massachusetts	Francis W. Sargent(R)	240	40
Michigan	William G. Milliken(R)	110	38
Minnesota	Wendell R. Anderson(D)	134	67
Mississippi	William L. Waller(D)	122	52
Missouri	Christopher S. Bond(R)	163	34
Montana	Thomas L. Judge(D)	100	50
Nebraska	J. James Exon(D)	49†	
Nevada	Mike O'Callaghan(D)	40	20
New Hampshire	Meldrim Thomson, Jr.(R)	400	24
New Jersey	William T. Cahill(R)	80	40
New Mexico	Bruce King(D)	70	42
New York	Malcolm Wilson(R)‡	150	60
North Carolina	James E. Holshouser, Jr.(R)	120	50
North Dakota	Arthur A. Link(D)	102	51
Ohio	John J. Gilligan(D)	99	33
Oklahoma	David Hall(D)	101	48
Oregon	Tom McCall(R)	60	30
Pennsylvania	Milton J. Shapp(D)	203	50
Rhode Island	Philip W. Noel(D)	100	50
South Carolina	John C. West(D)	124	46
South Dakota	Richard F. Kneip(D)	70	35
Tennessee	Winfield Dunn(R)	99	33
Texas	Dolph Briscoe(D)	150	31
Utah	Calvin L. Rampton(D)	75	29
Vermont	Thomas P. Salmon(D)	150	30
Virginia	Linwood Holton(R)	100	30
Washington	Daniel J. Evans(R)	98	49
West Virginia	Arch A. Moore, Jr.(R)	100	34
Wisconsin	Patrick J. Lucey(D)	99	33
Wyoming	Stanley K. Hathaway(R)	62	30

*Succeeded John A. Love (resigned) in July 1973. †Unicameral. ‡Succeeded Nelson A. Rockefeller (resigned) in December 1973.
Source: Council of State Governments, *The Book of the States*, Supplements I and II.

State government revenue, expenditure, and debt

1972 in thousands of dollars

State	General revenue: Total	State taxes	General sales	Individual income	Intergov-ernmental	Charges & misc.	General expenditure: Total	Education	Highways	Public welfare	Hospi-tals	Debt: Total	Issued 1972	Retired 1972
Alabama	1,521,514	817,671	257,780	118,994	536,534	167,309	1,502,465	680,586	267,806	255,180	79,391	838,477	105,061	36,252
Alaska	416,556	102,084	...	39,112	168,131	146,341	575,197	208,225	114,250	33,705	9,127	373,854	66,655	12,395
Arizona	942,616	595,413	224,078	94,577	227,313	119,890	946,173	455,888	167,221	70,520	31,877	89,248	3,075	2,796
Arkansas	812,020	459,780	144,673	70,150	286,486	65,754	747,258	300,195	157,681	141,548	31,651	111,152	9,314	9,807
California	11,603,633	6,740,222	2,006,100	1,838,503	3,928,279	935,132	11,061,661	3,326,906	1,289,012	3,342,582	289,919	6,132,166	637,247	233,079
Colorado	1,146,167	602,183	187,813	174,269	358,132	185,852	1,133,554	490,357	202,946	226,543	57,520	121,131	6,110	5,130
Connecticut	1,482,426	988,539	358,630	60,968	321,129	172,758	1,559,231	518,536	220,325	268,413	120,048	2,351,967	348,350	121,662
Delaware	396,379	256,733	...	90,688	80,183	59,463	410,886	200,165	55,982	46,853	17,044	488,645	70,000	29,827
Florida	2,860,535	1,989,970	875,775	...	639,372	231,193	2,725,018	1,273,649	535,609	306,742	102,851	1,121,757	243,025	42,400
Georgia	2,021,976	1,198,035	425,442	239,900	645,063	178,878	1,950,722	847,434	285,443	393,921	115,719	984,360	95,880	42,646
Hawaii	666,373	388,861	186,368	120,063	174,812	102,700	765,145	306,878	60,607	90,613	45,254	789.647	130,000	22,960
Idaho	355,698	200,062	51,704	50,191	118,333	37,303	349,679	136,041	78,777	39,746	6,143	37,929	1,400	1,208
Illinois	5,403,618	3,397,848	1,104,671	843,251	1,626,742	379,028	5,101,635	1,935,791	906,762	1,237,859	269,254	1,769,876	207,780	69,451
Indiana	1,933.504	1,187,234	437,168	283,669	434,787	311,483	1,883,405	916,443	377,587	214,325	113,278	605,691	62,670	21,091
Iowa	1,220,925	759,410	218,725	202,158	316,016	145,499	1,275,560	524,653	322,388	149,726	50,003	117,756	12,680	2,757
Kansas	894,145	527,813	179,557	95,345	241,868	124,464	891,279	358,157	184,850	144,266	62,828	214,641	6,200	10,402
Kentucky	1,494,733	860,927	318,068	156,369	450,290	183,516	1,576,389	617,848	402,763	222,273	54,659	1,810,228	358,684	38,321
Louisiana	1,978,428	1,105,116	277,765	105,354	536,632	336,680	1,959,465	771,623	333,516	305,965	128,621	1,128,275	206,093	41,636
Maine	502,167	276,461	102,678	28,179	165,469	60,237	489,043	158,531	101,189	92,151	18,968	273,369	39,000	17,323
Maryland	1,943,688	1,272,413	291,968	456,854	415,538	255,737	2,106,295	790,578	310,317	328,710	120,607	1,425,117	232,440	73,042
Massachusetts	2,917,332	1,805,694	200,337	743,628	875,719	235,919	2,949,113	878,072	235,625	929,206	193,440	2,323,606	423,880	106,207
Michigan	4,688,009	3,062,365	987,737	728,885	1,115,861	509,783	4,531,982	1,831,774	597,557	1,025,237	231,622	1,351,183	240,782	75,508
Minnesota	2,154,193	1,324,439	270,128	483,215	547,775	281,979	2,172,599	971,942	307,038	288,212	98,838	633,786	70,105	25,465
Mississippi	1,069,741	588,236	281,845	54,655	379,521	101,984	1,056,044	415,213	207,825	185,272	39,111	534,364	57,840	20,068
Missouri	1,722,050	1,050,346	367,375	256,801	530,053	141,651	1,681,423	718,164	322,014	325,716	90,016	139,210	2,676	7,447
Montana	387,579	182,817	...	68,082	159,810	44,952	370,663	133,087	117,168	40,007	12,201	94,955	89	4,042
Nebraska	579,292	319,480	99,985	54,170	170,381	89,431	558,359	204,593	124,784	86,083	37,373	83,176	14,690	2,499
Nevada	292,259	180,871	59,992	...	83,996	27,392	290,026	118,772	65,298	25,435	5,261	55,085	14,372	1,848
New Hampshire	271,086	139,175	...	6,618	84,312	47,599	311,121	84,426	74,263	41,712	21,936	182,705	300	14,235
New Jersey	2,894,448	1,626,285	579,557	23,258	851,244	416,919	2,998,721	919,600	457,226	682,433	173,048	2,567,558	515,720	73,840
New Mexico	690,101	356,373	136,319	44,088	219,855	113,873	635,665	309,045	115,327	78,789	13,823	140,110	20,308	15,686
New York	11,165,198	7,018,509	1,532,795	2,514,557	3,164,766	981,923	12,353,127	4,361,254	924,346	2,843,425	866,949	10,259,823	1,602,487	262,814
North Carolina	2,268,888	1,460,869	325,417	361,816	567,047	240,972	2,189,450	1,104,684	370,310	244,783	119,768	538,267	57,923	37,496
North Dakota	338,834	157,807	60,970	19,506	108,110	72,917	329,564	117,126	76,928	35,755	11,783	55,998	17,590	1,015
Ohio	3,542,843	2,189,413	743,617	111,269	879,848	473,582	3,521,000	1,343,148	706,276	612,257	198,801	1,965,302	757,507	129,229
Oklahoma	1,269,387	649,377	113,196	97,759	413,840	206,170	1,253,852	478,909	205,666	303,865	56,522	753,944	95,287	100,094
Oregon	995,940	507,914	...	251,226	339,542	148,484	1,082,165	370,943	238,983	144,479	37,388	923,503	128,500	37,238
Pennsylvania	5,613,379	3,862,969	979,280	730,641	1,276,413	473,997	5,720,710	2,385,165	886,860	1,057,664	349,897	4,264,717	591,755	136,079
Rhode Island	492,170	300,907	91,082	66,416	132,668	58,595	485,615	172,052	36,442	126,654	37,609	390,234	35,177	19,706
South Carolina	1,106,295	682,916	245,497	127,708	293,898	129,481	1,073,605	495,419	166,633	92,442	57,375	531,791	191,453	49,581
South Dakota	302,433	133,347	60,732	...	102,672	66,414	302,444	118,799	74,631	39,077	9,723	39,629	4,657	643
Tennessee	1,509,975	887,450	354,508	13,598	475,037	147,488	1,447,079	582,733	302,920	225,720	75,602	592,383	103,555	23,941
Texas	4,377,493	2,571,960	827,401	...	1,272,253	533,280	4,139,849	1,969,772	782,865	725,198	208,017	1,341,263	238,197	97,547
Utah	608,111	307,915	117,720	74,096	212,113	88,083	615,904	326,115	116,376	69,201	19,623	97,016	2,870	6,616
Vermont	306,159	158,253	21,566	46,102	101,345	46,561	323,977	116,744	65,623	53,394	11,788	331,479	47,980	14,218
Virginia	1,971,096	1,188,766	259,452	365,379	503,546	278,784	1,921,325	836,437	384,097	240,920	129,525	350,094	36,450	32,347
Washington	1,929,649	1,174,568	608,164	...	498,283	256,798	1,908,341	839,035	340,611	318,032	60,123	981,560	160,323	45,415
West Virginia	939,425	529,385	224,410	89,152	334,912	75,128	974,685	331,006	373,962	104,692	32,024	685,771	80,000	22,251
Wisconsin	2,398,223	1,628,043	383,346	594,697	518,824	251,356	2,366,906	913,572	252,077	319,768	118,342	800,691	136,520	15,206
Wyoming	233,306	97,145	37,560	...	86,506	39,655	234,476	81,927	75,366	13,927	7,414	38,180	4,300	12,624
TOTAL	98,631,995	59,870,369	17,618,951	12,995,916	27,981,259	10,780,367	98,809,850	38,348,012	15,380,128	19,190,996	5,049,704	53,832,669	8,494,957	2,225,091

Fiscal year ending June 30, 1972, except Alabama, Sept. 30; New York, Mar. 31; and Texas, Aug. 31.
Source: U.S. Department of Commerce, Bureau of the Census, *State Government Finances in 1972.*

Education

Federal funds supporting education

in thousand dollars

Funds	1968	1970	1972	1974*
Supporting education in educational institutions	7,804,454	9,222,139	11,901,721	12,868,823
Grants, total	7,201,173	8,615,843	11,325,086	12,462,906
Elementary-secondary education	2,967,004	3,212,418	3,856,527	4,062,779
Higher education	3,262,988	3,814,332	4,963,464	5,937,467
Vocational-technical and continuing education (not classifiable by level)	971,181	1,589,093	2,505,095	2,462,660
Loans, total	603,281	606,296	576,635	405,917
Student loan program, National Defense Education Act	226,303	295,173	515,072	380,341
College facilities loans	376,978	311,123	61,563	25,576
Other funds for education and related activities	3,605,629	3,428,724	4,553,964	5,037,412
Applied research and development	1,142,350	1,236,749	1,497,999	1,649,000
School lunch and milk programs	543,845	676,196	1,213,075	1,273,263
Training of federal personnel	1,138,333	691,694	961,215	1,115,027
Library services	136,099	170,135	165,096	150,744
International education	272,008	193,464	122,740	139,098
Other	372,994	460,486	593,839	710,280

*Estimated data.
Source: U.S. Department of Health, Education, and Welfare, Office of Education, *Digest of Educational Statistics.*

Cost of attending college

in current dollars

Expenditure	1964–65		1969–70		1974–75*	
	Public	Private	Public	Private	Public	Private
Tuition and required fees						
Universities	298	1,297	427	1,809	648	2,606
Other 4-year institutions	224	1,023	306	1,470	432	2,142
2-year institutions	99	702	179	1,034	248	1,472
Board rates						
Universities	462	515	540	608	661	747
Other 4-year institutions	402	479	483	543	571	639
2-year institutions	361	464	465	546	590	643
Charges for dormitory rooms						
Universities	291	390	395	503	559	679
Other 4-year institutions	241	308	347	408	587	545
2-year institutions	178	289	309	413	472	567

Data are for the entire academic year and are average charges per full-time resident degree-credit student. *Estimated.
Source: U.S. Department of Health, Education, and Welfare, Office of Education, *Digest of Educational Statistics.*

Level of school completed

25 years old and over, by race

Level of school completed	April 1940	April 1950	April 1960	March 1970	March 1972
Less than 5 years elementary school, percent:					
White	10.9	8.7	6.7	4.2	3.7
Nonwhite	41.8	31.4	23.5	14.7	12.8
4 years of high school or more, percent:					
White	26.1	35.5	43.2	57.4	60.4
Nonwhite	7.7	13.4	21.7	36.1	39.1
4 years of college, or more, percent:					
White	4.9	6.4	8.1	11.6	12.6
Nonwhite	1.3	2.2	3.5	6.1	6.9
Median school years completed, percent:					
White	8.7	9.7	10.8	12.2	12.3
Nonwhite	5.7	6.9	8.2	10.1	10.5

Source: U.S. Department of Health, Education, and Welfare, Office of Education, *Digest of Educational Statistics.* Data compiled by U.S. Department of Commerce, Bureau of the Census.

Years of school completed

by ethnic origin and age: March 1972*

Origin	Total (000)	Percent distribution by years of school completed						
		Elementary			High school		College	
		0 to 4 years	5 to 7 years	8 years	1 to 3 years	4 years	1 to 3 years	4 years or more
Total, 25 years old and over	111,133	4.6	8.3	11.9	17.0	35.2	10.9	12.0
Male	52,351	5.0	8.6	12.1	16.1	31.4	11.4	15.4
Female	58,782	4.2	8.0	11.8	17.8	38.7	10.5	9.0
25 to 34 years old	26,517	1.1	3.0	3.8	15.0	43.9	15.4	17.9
German	3,353	0.5	0.6	2.3	10.6	51.1	15.6	19.2
Italian	104.6	0.9	2.4	3.3	13.0	51.1	12.8	16.5
Irish	2,009	0.3	2.7	3.4	15.0	46.2	16.1	16.3
French	755	0.4	4.5	4.0	18.1	41.2	18.4	13.2
Polish	661	0.0	0.6	1.2	9.5	47.5	17.1	24.1
Russian	245	0.0	0.0	0.0	1.6	28.6	18.0	51.8
English, Scottish, Welsh	3,632	0.3	0.9	2.0	11.0	40.6	18.8	26.3
Spanish	1,300	6.8	14.9	11.4	21.5	31.5	9.6	4.2
Other	10,930	1.0	2.9	3.6	16.6	43.2	15.6	17.1
Not reported	2,587	1.5	4.0	6.5	19.0	44.7	11.7	12.6
35 years old and over	84,616	5.7	10.9	14.5	17.6	32.5	9.5	10.2
German	10,868	2.0	7.4	18.9	16.1	36.1	9.3	10.2
Italian	4,117	8.7	10.5	17.0	19.7	31.9	6.1	6.0
Irish	7,415	3.4	9.6	14.9	18.5	35.2	8.8	9.5
French	2,244	4.5	12.2	15.1	18.5	32.3	9.4	8.0
Polish	2,442	6.7	9.8	19.5	19.0	30.8	7.1	7.0
Russian	1,199	4.6	5.0	10.9	10.9	33.7	14.2	20.6
English, Scottish, Welsh	14,142	1.8	5.8	11.3	15.7	35.7	14.3	15.4
Spanish	2,592	25.5	21.9	11.4	14.4	16.7	5.1	5.1
Other	31,617	6.9	10.9	13.5	18.5	31.4	8.9	9.8
Not reported	7,982	7.6	13.7	16.1	18.4	29.9	7.3	7.0

*25 years of age and over.
Source: U.S. Department of Commerce, Social and Economic Statistics Administration, Bureau of the Census, *Current Population Reports.*

Universities and colleges

state statistics

State	NUMBER OF INSTITUTIONS fall, 1972		Enrollment* fall, 1972	EARNED DEGREES CONFERRED† 1971–1972		
	Total	Public		Bachelor's and first professional	Master's, except first professional	Doctor's
Alabama	51	30	110,514	14,110	2,700	290
Alaska	3	1	11,698	400	200	10
Arizona	20	14	110,468	8,850	3,300	430
Arkansas	19	8	52,198	7,850	1,200	130
California	217	115	1,063,043	81,550	21,800	3,620
Colorado	32	21	115,657	13,500	3,700	710
Connecticut	46	20	129,911	12,530	4,500	560
Delaware	7	3	24,263	1,700	500	80
District of Columbia	20	3	80,067	8,140	4,800	620
Florida	64	36	225,232	22,590	5,300	760
Georgia	61	28	135,710	16,720	4,700	490
Hawaii	13	8	35,155	3,200	1,100	80
Idaho	9	6	31,534	2,940	500	60
Illinois	138	50	414,208	46,630	14,300	2,250
Indiana	44	6	194,132	25,730	8,900	1,460
Iowa	54	18	98,036	16,110	2,800	760
Kansas	52	28	104,365	13,360	3,000	420
Kentucky	36	8	102,765	14,010	2,900	200
Louisiana	23	12	131,999	15,680	3,500	420
Maine	17	4	32,885	4,770	800	30
Maryland	48	25	150,483	13,920	3,400	590
Massachusetts	118	30	298,152	34,510	11,600	1,930
Michigan	87	42	344,149	40,160	13,700	1,930
Minnesota	59	28	154,938	20,380	2,900	660
Mississippi	41	24	74,823	9,430	1,700	240
Missouri	70	22	182,738	22,070	6,200	700
Montana	12	9	27,197	4,240	700	80
Nebraska	27	13	63,161	10,780	1,400	240
Nevada	6	5	14,353	1,300	300	20
New Hampshire	19	4	27,620	4,500	600	60
New Jersey	58	25	228,313	21,310	5,900	590
New Mexico	11	8	46,721	4,600	1,300	200
New York	225	79	838,278	80,400	31,000	3,640
North Carolina	113	68	155,109	21,580	3,600	780
North Dakota	12	9	27,356	4,240	700	130
Ohio	101	32	351,398	48,260	10,100	1,530
Oklahoma	40	26	118,746	13,420	3,000	500
Oregon	40	20	93,450	11,080	3,400	530
Pennsylvania	146	31	401,636	54,940	12,900	1,760
Rhode Island	13	3	46,891	5,300	1,400	220
South Carolina	46	22	78,248	8,730	1,100	130
South Dakota	16	6	28,217	5,070	900	60
Tennessee	62	19	143,241	18,330	3,400	520
Texas	134	79	446,153	47,620	10,000	1,460
Utah	13	9	73,228	10,000	2,100	420
Vermont	18	5	24,715	3,250	700	30
Virginia	70	36	157,158	16,360	3,300	400
Washington	43	31	151,649	17,760	3,600	620
West Virginia	24	14	60,833	8,420	1,300	110
Wisconsin	58	28	175,066	24,430	5,000	1,030
Wyoming	8	8	15,011	1,440	300	90
United States	2,664	1,179	8,202,921	918,200	238,000	34,580

Excludes service academies. *Excludes non-degree-credit students. †Estimated.
Source: U.S. Department of Health, Education, and Welfare, Office of Education, *Digest of Educational Statistics, Education Directory, 1972–73, Higher Education.*

Public elementary and secondary schools

Fall 1972 estimates

State	Enrollment: Elementary	Enrollment: Secondary	Instructional staff: Total*	Instructional staff: Principals and supervisors	Instructional staff: Teachers, elementary	Instructional staff: Teachers, secondary	Teachers' average annual salaries: Elementary	Teachers' average annual salaries: Secondary	Student-teacher ratio: Elementary	Student-teacher ratio: Secondary	Expenditure per pupil†
Alabama	407,737	375,646	35,432	1,702	16,523	17,207	$ 8,024	$ 8,184	24.7	21.8	$ 739
Alaska	58,155	27,200	4,611	720	2,338	1,804	14,549	14,404	24.9	15.1	1,398
Arizona	385,278	156,506	25,241	921	16,248	7,005	10,155	11,160	23.7	22.3	1,022
Arkansas	245,457	213,600	21,955	734	10,008	10,603	7,209	7,508	24.5	20.1	619
California	2,750,000	1,820,000	208,500	11,000	112,000	77,500	11,360	12,350	24.6	23.5	937
Colorado	312,960	265,040	28,714	1,330	12,264	12,280	9,589	9,963	25.5	21.6	895
Connecticut	478,528	195,001	39,263	1,990	19,343	14,825	10,300	11,000	24.7	13.2	1,141
Delaware	71,950	62,367	7,140	370	3,070	3,295	10,430	10,770	23.4	18.9	1,083
District of Columbia	83,869	56,049	7,773	425	3,798	2,750	...	...	22.1	20.4	1,211
Florida	769,700	667,500	77,300	3,865	34,012	33,239	9,100	9,400	22.6	20.1	841
Georgia	686,601	397,801	52,468	2,531	29,914	20,023	7,916	8,613	23.0	19.9	722
Hawaii	98,700	81,400	9,920	720	4,945	3,455	10,660	10,750	20.0	23.6	970
Idaho	91,847	92,816	10,580	542	3,793	5,677	7,491	7,803	24.2	16.3	...
Illinois	1,480,475	907,524	119,605	6,808	60,824	45,676	10,700	11,865	24.3	19.9	1,058
Indiana	656,578	563,370	59,350	3,450	26,600	25,900	9,600	10,120	24.7	21.8	833
Iowa	449,615	199,259	38,854	2,175	16,565	15,776	9,101	10,213	27.1	12.6	1,007
Kansas	277,675	213,901	28,386	1,404	12,970	12,557	8,329	8,669	21.4	17.0	870
Kentucky	450,213	264,394	34,945	1,565	19,400	11,980	7,660	8,075	23.2	22.1	649
Louisiana	511,298	335,221	42,598	2,105	22,306	18,187	8,933	9,297	22.9	18.4	855
Maine	177,393	70,055	12,307	650	6,721	4,456	8,699	9,424	26.4	15.7	789
Maryland	508,312	412,923	48,066	3,191	21,562	20,765	10,910	11,417	23.6	19.9	1,082
Massachusetts	670,000	520,000	68,381	4,620	29,036	28,475	10,440	10,600	23.1	14.6	1,060
Michigan	1,160,128	1,032,610	101,090	5,890	37,769	51,731	11,600	12,200	30.7	20.0	...
Minnesota	475,839	435,240	49,070	2,615	21,455	22,700	9,789	11,231	22.2	19.2	1,089
Mississippi	302,200	224,118	26,295	1,692	13,158	10,226	6,787	7,100	23.0	21.9	651
Missouri	737,884	292,124	52,000	3,025	24,600	22,075	8,917	9,271	30.0	13.2	837
Montana	116,980	55,076	9,651	400	4,982	3,518	8,461	9,696	23.5	15.7	895
Nebraska	183,000	145,000	18,940	880	9,300	8,760	8,200	9,300	19.7	16.6	700
Nevada	72,756	58,917	6,238	386	2,906	2,505	10,721	11,030	25.4	23.5	904
New Hampshire	96,788	71,265	8,457	435	4,137	3,385	8,890	9,238	23.4	21.1	841
New Jersey	991,000	523,000	91,750	5,150	41,400	35,600	11,050	11,460	23.9	14.7	1,216
New Mexico	155,102	133,725	13,772	897	6,460	5,810	8,368	8,537	24.0	23.0	799
New York	1,879,000	1,632,000	206,197	13,824	88,300	93,300	12,040	12,700	21.3	17.5	1,424
North Carolina	799,709	358,840	54,672	2,645	32,674	16,707	8,877	9,454	24.5	21.5	753
North Dakota	94,319	47,216	7,750	320	4,450	2,685	7,762	8,664	21.2	17.6	825
Ohio	1,465,500	950,950	115,800	6,400	55,150	50,250	9,100	9,650	26.6	18.9	883
Oklahoma	324,000	290,000	30,326	1,600	14,820	13,006	7,750	8,000	22.7	22.3	663
Oregon	278,863	198,724	25,590	1,560	11,740	9,740	9,412	9,720	23.8	20.4	939
Pennsylvania	1,229,100	1,139,300	121,800	5,000	52,600	57,200	10,400	10,800	23.4	19.9	1,100
Rhode Island	116,937	72,756	10,819	558	5,481	4,003	10,200	10,498	21.3	18.2	1,075
South Carolina	400,000	240,000	31,200	1,600	16,080	10,920	7,890	8,175	24.9	22.0	702
South Dakota	110,222	52,016	9,079	450	5,212	2,949	7,638	8,253	21.1	17.6	803
Tennessee	541,221	350,554	40,200	1,950	21,300	14,900	8,040	8,700	25.4	23.5	692
Texas	1,475,622	1,218,780	142,900	7,444	68,549	60,788	8,735	8,735	21.5	20.0	974
Utah	162,775	142,164	13,624	764	5,950	5,775	8,500	8,610	27.4	24.6	698
Vermont	68,514	44,801	7,274	452	3,165	3,185	8,380	8,890	21.6	14.1	1,151
Virginia	665,310	404,035	57,300	3,800	30,500	23,000	9,268	10,033	21.8	17.6	866
Washington	412,792	377,710	39,038	2,918	17,462	15,858	10,215	10,988	23.6	23.8	...
West Virginia	265,225	177,882	18,947	1,625	8,795	7,917	7,968	8,430	26.9	22.5	702
Wisconsin	574,918	420,305	53,543	2,401	27,208	23,934	10,130	10,737	21.1	17.6	1,071
Wyoming	45,025	40,992	5,162	315	2,260	2,337	9,300	9,700	19.9	17.5	909
TOTAL U.S.	26,794,070	19,027,673	2,350,233	129,276	1,122,103	978,199	9,823	10,460	23.9	19.5	966

Kindergartens are included in the elementary schools; junior high schools, in the secondary schools. *Includes librarians, guidance and psychological personnel and related educational workers. †Based on average daily membership. Source: National Education Association, Research Division, *Estimates of School Statistics, 1972–73* (Copyright 1973. All rights reserved. Used by permission).

Government expenditure on education, 1970-71

in millions of dollars

State	Total expenditure: State	Total expenditure: Local*	Local schools: State	Local schools: Local*	Institutions of higher education: State	Institutions of higher education: Local*	Other education: State	Other education: Local*
Alabama	302	455	7	455	229	—	67	—
Alaska	111	91	51	91	44	—	15	—
Arizona	175	432	—	395	155	37	20	—
Arkansas	123	239	—	239	97	—	27	—
California	1,263	4,621	19	4,442	1,105	547	140	—
Colorado	273	495	—	477	251	18	22	—
Connecticut	215	689	—	689	142	—	73	—
Delaware	82	164	6	164	62	—	15	—
District of Columbia†	226	—	180	—	46	—	—	—
Florida	335	1,438	8	1,293	250	146	77	—
Georgia	379	765	29	759	296	6	53	—
Hawaii	290	‡	188	‡	159	—	13	—
Idaho	64	120	—	115	51	5	13	—
Illinois	815	2,512	16	2,335	661	177	137	—
Indiana	479	1,078	—	1,078	411	2	69	—
Iowa	242	703	—	670	205	33	37	—
Kansas	174	470	—	433	157	37	17	—
Kentucky	273	494	3	494	221	—	50	—
Louisiana	265	611	8	610	223	1	35	—
Maine	95	157	2	157	74	—	19	—
Maryland	271	1,636	—	960	209	65	62	—
Massachusetts	346	1,126	—	1,123	282	3	64	—
Michigan	830	2,203	—	2,088	686	115	143	—
Minnesota	437	1,034	—	1,034	405	—	32	—
Mississippi	148	336	3	301	116	34	29	—
Missouri	252	891	—	851	227	41	31	—
Montana	78	144	—	143	67	2	11	—
Nebraska	121	299	—	261	107	3	14	—
Nevada	28	109	—	109	24	—	4	—
New Hampshire	69	121	—	121	59	—	10	—
New Jersey	395	1,657	—	1,564	283	93	113	—
New Mexico	123	225	2	225	108	—	13	—
New York	1,238	5,305	—	4,870	764	435	474	—
North Carolina	367	848	10	787	308	61	49	—
North Dakota	80	115	—	113	67	2	12	—
Ohio	630	1,993	—	1,875	560	118	70	—
Oklahoma	231	400	3	399	190	1	38	—
Oregon	202	497	—	470	177	27	25	—
Pennsylvania	857	2,357	62	2,320	469	37	326	—
Rhode Island	99	163	—	163	77	—	22	—
South Carolina	191	410	18	410	114	—	59	—
South Dakota	75	152	—	152	68	—	7	—
Tennessee	262	596	—	596	215	—	47	—
Texas	726	2,101	18	2,010	638	92	70	—
Utah	159	218	—	218	145	—	14	—
Vermont	65	79	—	79	51	—	14	—
Virginia	361	873	—	873	285	‡	76	—
Washington	499	793	39	793	427	—	33	‡
West Virginia	140	278	—	278	119	—	21	—
Wisconsin	521	1,042	—	890	446	152	75	—
Wyoming	42	94	—	88	35	5	8	—
United States	15,800	43,613	491	41,275	12,448	2,337	2,861	‡

*Estimates subject to sampling variation. †Federal expenditure. ‡Less than $500,000. Source: U.S. Department of Commerce, Social and Economic Statistics Administration, Bureau of the Census, *Governmental Finances in 1970–71.*

Universities and colleges, 1972-73

Selected list of four-year schools

Institution	Location	Year founded	Total students	Faculty	Bound library volumes
ALABAMA					
Alabama A. & M.	Normal	1875	3,100	156	122,354
Alabama State U.	Montgomery	1874	2,704	115	125,352
Auburn U.	Auburn	1856	12,895	850	760,000
Birmingham-Southern	Birmingham	1856	1,031	86	100,000
Florence State U.	Florence	1873	3,104	165	113,300
Jacksonville State U.	Jacksonville	1883	5,066	253	177,202
Livingston U.	Livingston	1835	1,450	81	42,525
Miles	Birmingham	1905	1,242	78	—
Samford U.	Birmingham	1842	2,703	168	183,407
Troy State U.	Troy	1887	6,075	190	115,000
Tuskegee Inst.	Tuskegee Institute	1881	2,965	246	195,000
U. of Alabama	University	1831	12,586	617	1,092,000
U. of Montevallo	Montevallo	1896	3,100	160	115,000
U. of South Alabama	Mobile	1963	4,686	329	180,000
ALASKA					
Alaska Methodist U.	Anchorage	1957	1,005	67	49,075
U. of Alaska	Fairbanks	1917	2,739	305	305,000
ARIZONA					
Arizona State U.	Tempe	1885	30,445	1,072	1,316,300
Northern Arizona U.	Flagstaff	1899	8,888	460	254,233
U. of Arizona	Tucson	1885	26,558	1,634	693,450
ARKANSAS					
Arkansas Polytech.	Russellville	1909	2,272	107	66,000
Arkansas State U.	State University	1909	6,477	224	198,000
Harding	Searcy	1924	1,908	110	102,425
Henderson State	Arkadelphia	1929	3,000	150	104,000
Ouachita Baptist U.	Arkadelphia	1886	1,360	88	85,000
Southern State	Magnolia	1909	2,325	113	70,000
State Col. of Arkansas	Conway	1907	4,500	237	140,000
U. of Arkansas	Fayetteville	1871	12,131	800	685,000
U. of A. at Little Rock	Little Rock	1927	4,171	148	102,642
U. of A. at Monticello	Monticello	1909	1,958	102	56,650
CALIFORNIA					
Art Center Col. of Design	Los Angeles	1930	1,002	110	8,500
Biola	La Mirada	1908	1,781	135	95,000
California Arts & Crafts	Oakland	1907	1,378	132	20,000
California Inst. of Tech.	Pasadena	1891	1,428	591	239,000
California Lutheran	Thousand Oaks	1959	1,226	67	64,182
Cal. State, Bakersfield	Bakersfield	1965	1,700	130	80,000
Cal. State, Dominguez Hills	Dominguez Hills	1962	3,700	250	98,000
Cal. State, Hayward	Hayward	1959	11,753	687	367,000
Cal. State, Long Beach	Long Beach	1949	29,399	1,357	502,000
Cal. State, San Bernardino	San Bernardino	1967	2,335	155	143,294
Cal. State Polytech. U.	Pomona	1956	9,000	545	177,715
Cal. Polytech. State U.	San Luis Obispo	1901	10,738	716	324,949
Cal. State U., Chico	Chico	1887	10,763	700	325,000
Cal. State U., Fresno	Fresno	1911	14,800	960	343,000
Cal. State U., Fullerton	Fullerton	1959	16,258	640	389,000
Cal. State U., Los Angeles	Los Angeles	1947	23,500	1,301	531,000
Cal. State U., Northridge	Northridge	1958	23,709	1,450	87,000
Cal. State U., Sacramento	Sacramento	1947	17,500	895	367,000
Cal. State U., San Diego	San Diego	1897	25,806	1,620	12,644
Cal. State U., San Francisco	San Francisco	1899	18,928	1,296	432,000
Chapman	Orange	1861	3,600	257	98,763
Col. of Notre Dame	Belmont	1851	1,506	105	69,716
Golden Gate	San Francisco	1901	4,700	200	77,651
Humboldt State	Arcata	1913	6,406	380	149,754
La Verne	La Verne	1891	1,210	74	65,500
Loma Linda U.	Riverside	1905	3,150	500	255,000
Loyola U.	Los Angeles	1911	3,822	231	447,454
‡Mt. St. Mary's	Los Angeles	1925	1,180	113	106,377
Naval Postgraduate Sch.	Monterey	1909	1,700	300	282,000
Occidental	Los Angeles	1887	1,737	138	247,908
Pacific Union	Angwin	1882	1,583	150	80,097
Pasadena	Pasadena	1902	1,236	72	119,102
Pepperdine U.	Los Angeles	1937	3,117	195	114,215
Saint Mary's	Moraga	1863	1,188	115	98,000
San Diego City	San Diego	1914	2,750	145	52,000
San Jose State	San Jose	1857	26,000	1,240	547,000
Sonoma State	Rohnert Park	1960	4,411	250	132,974
Stanford U.	Stanford	1885	11,197	1,289	3,584,123
Stanislaus State	Turlock	1960	2,568	181	100,401
U. of California	Berkeley	1868	103,440	8,529	11,500,000
U. of C., Berkeley	Berkeley	1868	28,000	2,495	4,009,595
U. of C., Davis	Davis	1905	13,497	906	909,422
U. of C., Irvine	Irvine	1964	5,845	480	450,688
U. of C., Los Angeles	Los Angeles	1919	27,000	1,800	3,038,828
U. of C., Riverside	Riverside	1868	5,717	592	643,941
U. of C., San Diego	La Jolla	1912	6,000	466	813,447
U. of C., Santa Barbara	Santa Barbara	1944	12,100	690	844,765
U. of C., Santa Cruz	Santa Cruz	1965	3,097	324	346,241
U. of Pacific	Stockton	1851	4,100	265	278,000
U. of Redlands	Redlands	1907	1,923	110	172,272
U. of San Francisco	San Francisco	1855	6,243	411	335,981
U. of Santa Clara	Santa Clara	1851	6,085	306	245,465
U. of Southern California	Los Angeles	1880	19,100	883	1,452,590
West Coast U.	Los Angeles	1909	1,135	125	4,670
Whittier	Whittier	1901	2,184	105	95,025
Woodbury	Los Angeles	1884	1,900	75	18,000
COLORADO					
Adams State	Alamosa	1921	2,700	167	123,848
Colorado	Colorado Springs	1874	1,821	140	244,032
Colorado Sch. of Mines	Golden	1874	1,520	141	137,754
Colorado State U.	Fort Collins	1870	14,600	1,108	808,000
Fort Lewis	Durango	1911	2,275	118	81,251
Metropolitan State	Denver	1965	6,750	350	92,049
Regis	Denver	1877	1,324	108	65,000
Southern Colorado State	Pueblo	1933	4,950	356	125,000
†U.S. Air Force Academy	USAF Academy	1954	4,201	638	320,000
U. of Colorado	Boulder	1876	31,802	2,729	1,503,187
U. of Denver	Denver	1864	8,517	635	714,000
U. of Northern Colorado	Greeley	1890	9,619	581	323,305
Western State	Gunnison	1901	2,800	137	97,882
CONNECTICUT					
Central Connecticut State	New Britain	1849	9,155	663	192,864
Eastern Connecticut State	Willimantic	1889	2,775	198	60,799
Fairfield U.	Fairfield	1942	2,284	164	112,414
Quinnipiac	Hamden	1929	2,719	215	69,369
Sacred Heart U.	Bridgeport	1963	1,945	108	70,125
Southern Connecticut St.	New Haven	1893	12,107	636	202,033
Trinity	Hartford	1823	1,939	144	478,260
†U.S. Coast Guard Acad.	New London	1876	1,100	121	90,000
U. of Bridgeport	Bridgeport	1927	7,861	549	219,413
U. of Connecticut	Storrs	1881	19,972	1,213	808,492
U. of Hartford	West Hartford	1877	8,290	498	111,473
U. of New Haven	West Haven	1920	4,601	291	66,105
Wesleyan U.	Middletown	1831	1,574	248	657,217
Western Connecticut St.	Danbury	1903	4,208	228	104,452
Yale U.	New Haven	1701	8,857	1,411	5,829,035
DELAWARE					
Delaware State	Dover	1891	1,835	105	55,974
U. of Delaware	Newark	1833	10,600	700	766,987
DISTRICT OF COLUMBIA					
American U.	Washington	1893	14,508	706	431,274
Catholic U.	Washington	1887	6,667	572	854,823
D.C. Teachers	Washington	1851	2,500	155	116,084
George Washington U.	Washington	1821	14,295	1,948	541,876
Georgetown U.	Washington	1789	8,470	636	669,619
Howard U.	Washington	1867	10,315	1,400	657,173
FLORIDA					
‡Barry	Miami	1940	1,245	115	82,195
Bethune-Cookman	Daytona Beach	1872	1,127	61	60,000
Eckerd	St. Petersburg	1958	1,025	75	94,005
Florida A. & M. U.	Tallahassee	1887	4,011	295	211,476
Florida Atlantic U.	Boca Raton	1961	5,122	360	313,665
Florida Inst. of Tech.	Melbourne	1958	1,800	158	57,425
Florida Southern	Lakeland	1885	1,620	110	120,297
Florida State U.	Tallahassee	1857	16,606	1,300	916,805
Florida Tech. U.	Orlando	1968	5,569	324	107,226
Jacksonville U.	Jacksonville	1934	2,727	167	148,627
Rollins	Winter Park	1885	3,540	200	155,986
Stetson U.	DeLand	1883	2,640	145	141,524
U. of Florida	Gainesville	1853	20,240	2,260	1,487,303
U. of Miami	Coral Gables	1925	14,441	1,267	953,457
U. of South Florida	Tampa	1960	16,104	799	305,852
U. of Tampa	Tampa	1931	2,181	142	124,000
U. of West Florida	Pensacola	1963	3,811	201	169,663
GEORGIA					
Albany State	Albany	1903	1,798	133	58,571
Armstrong State	Savannah	1935	2,300	119	72,020
Atlanta U.	Atlanta	1865	1,048	113	241,000
Augusta	Augusta	1925	2,604	125	101,198
Clark	Atlanta	1869	1,118	107	45,327
Columbus	Columbus	1958	3,562	146	56,450
Emory U.	Atlanta	1836	5,368	2,007	966,459
Fort Valley State	Fort Valley	1895	2,286	114	100,430
Georgia	Milledgeville	1889	2,325	121	95,839
Georgia Inst. of Tech.	Atlanta	1885	7,199	556	703,516
Georgia Southern	Statesboro	1906	5,300	329	172,212
Georgia Southwestern	Americus	1926	2,100	139	57,598
Georgia State U.	Atlanta	1913	15,693	720	336,681
Mercer U.	Macon	1833	1,850	110	159,534
†Morehouse	Atlanta	1867	1,130	84	297,296
North Georgia	Dahlonega	1873	1,383	96	89,828
Oglethorpe U.	Atlanta	1835	1,020	42	44,394
Savannah State	Savannah	1890	2,120	105	70,956
‡Spelman	Atlanta	1881	1,067	90	30,819
U. of Georgia	Athens	1785	25,560	2,095	1,158,047
Valdosta State	Valdosta	1906	3,913	182	108,667
West Georgia	Carrollton	1933	5,696	285	123,949
HAWAII					
Church Col. of Hawaii	Laie	1955	1,205	75	70,000
U. of Hawaii	Honolulu	1907	23,044	1,469	1,130,632
IDAHO					
Boise State	Boise	1932	7,626	301	110,660
Idaho State U.	Pocatello	1901	8,095	300	137,972
Lewis-Clark State	Lewiston	1955	2,352	120	55,583
Northwest Nazarene	Nampa	1913	1,018	66	64,810
U. of Idaho	Moscow	1889	6,437	520	727,112
ILLINOIS					
Augustana	Rock Island	1860	2,174	138	152,172
Aurora	Aurora	1893	1,039	94	69,258
Bradley U.	Peoria	1897	5,206	404	208,969
Chicago State U.	Chicago	1869	5,723	326	186,119
Concordia Teachers	River Forest	1864	1,500	93	100,110
De Paul U.	Chicago	1898	9,194	504	309,189
Eastern Illinois U.	Charleston	1895	8,264	663	246,542
Elmhurst	Elmhurst	1871	2,731	178	83,846
Illinois Inst. of Tech.	Chicago	1892	6,518	762	165,879

†Men's schools, ‡Women's schools; the others are coeducational.

Universities and colleges (continued)

Institution	Location	Year founded	Total students	Faculty	Bound library volumes
Illinois State U.	Normal	1857	17,169	908	486,279
Illinois Wesleyan U.	Bloomington	1850	1,641	130	123,856
Knox	Galesburg	1837	1,349	104	145,840
Lake Forest	Lake Forest	1857	1,096	104	119,945
Lewis	Lockport	1930	2,440	104	57,303
Loyola U.	Chicago	1870	13,787	630	600,621
Millikin U.	Decatur	1901	1,716	141	116,000
Monmouth	Monmouth	1853	1,275	104	128,702
‡Mundelein	Chicago	1930	1,362	95	90,027
National Col. of Ed.	Evanston	1886	2,605	149	74,337
Northeastern Illinois State	Chicago	1869	5,380	300	185,361
Northern Illinois U.	DeKalb	1895	21,313	1,289	604,709
North Park	Chicago	1891	1,223	110	123,851
Northwestern U.	Evanston	1851	15,571	2,375	2,364,720
Olivet Nazarene	Kankakee	1907	1,670	88	95,487
Quincy	Quincy	1860	2,004	117	151,829
Rockford	Rockford	1847	1,324	109	78,000
Roosevelt U.	Chicago	1945	6,536	250	260,330
Rosary	River Forest	1901	1,234	106	127,364
Schools of the Art Inst.	Chicago	1866	1,500	84	95,256
Southern Illinois U.	Carbondale	1869	20,347	2,500	1,403,535
at Edwardsville	Edwardsville	1869	12,856	558	474,041
U. of Chicago	Chicago	1892	8,962	1,133	3,090,127
U. of Illinois	Urbana	1868	30,877	3,681	4,609,238
Chicago Circle Campus	Chicago	1965	18,290	1,170	439,375
Western Illinois U.	Macomb	1899	12,527	664	319,418
Wheaton	Wheaton	1860	1,959	153	157,687
INDIANA					
Anderson	Anderson	1917	1,618	117	116,294
Ball State U.	Muncie	1918	17,923	891	556,362
Butler U.	Indianapolis	1855	4,355	250	217,750
De Pauw U.	Greencastle	1837	2,173	150	300,354
Earlham	Richmond	1847	1,070	108	177,069
Goshen	Goshen	1894	1,250	125	109,000
Hanover	Hanover	1827	1,033	92	105,704
Indiana Central	Indianapolis	1902	2,118	119	64,033
Indiana State U.	Terre Haute	1865	12,870	1,500	469,399
Indiana U.	Bloomington	1820	65,389	3,459	2,341,672
Manchester	North Manchester	1889	1,323	108	97,352
Purdue U.	Lafayette	1869	35,864	3,905	964,616
†Rose-Hulman Inst. of Tech.	Terre Haute	1874	1,050	67	37,704
St. Francis	Fort Wayne	1890	1,990	101	71,410
St. Joseph	Rensselaer	1889	1,150	83	120,631
‡St. Mary's	Notre Dame	1844	1,753	96	116,336
Taylor U.	Upland	1846	1,370	80	88,785
Tri-State	Angola	1884	1,380	91	48,536
U. of Evansville	Evansville	1854	4,600	260	122,555
U. of Notre Dame	Notre Dame	1842	8,054	645	1,093,191
Valparaiso U.	Valparaiso	1859	4,469	296	241,713
IOWA					
Briar Cliff	Sioux City	1930	1,096	60	61,658
Central U. of Iowa	Pella	1853	1,162	96	83,820
Coe	Cedar Rapids	1851	1,138	87	124,812
Drake U.	Des Moines	1881	7,130	385	327,418
Graceland	Lamoni	1895	1,240	89	67,500
Grinnell	Grinnell	1846	1,234	110	196,113
Iowa State U.	Ames	1858	17,909	1,400	831,023
Loras	Dubuque	1839	1,452	96	197,288
Luther	Decorah	1861	1,974	143	162,047
Marycrest	Davenport	1939	1,017	84	81,000
Morningside	Sioux City	1894	1,548	75	103,849
Parsons	Fairfield	1875	1,204	86	130,115
St. Ambrose	Davenport	1882	1,293	96	84,547
U. of Dubuque	Dubuque	1852	1,004	66	110,758
U. of Iowa	Iowa City	1847	19,239	3,293	1,584,865
U. of Northern Iowa	Cedar Falls	1876	9,011	502	345,329
Wartburg	Waverly	1852	1,309	89	90,440
KANSAS					
Fort Hays Kansas State	Hays	1902	4,840	275	235,000
Kansas State	Pittsburg	1903	5,037	285	331,880
Kansas State Teachers	Emporia	1863	6,302	415	435,734
Kansas State U.	Manhattan	1863	13,771	748	600,081
U. of Kansas	Lawrence	1866	19,116	1,099	1,568,807
Washburn U.	Topeka	1865	4,974	177	116,000
Wichita State U.	Wichita	1895	12,098	492	306,991
KENTUCKY					
Asbury	Wilmore	1890	1,022	86	81,129
Bellarmine	Louisville	1950	1,577	92	71,887
Berea	Berea	1855	1,324	125	175,784
Cumberland	Williamsburg	1889	1,688	100	59,204
Eastern Kentucky U.	Richmond	1906	9,235	453	353,996
Georgetown	Georgetown	1829	1,310	91	100,000
Kentucky State	Frankfort	1886	1,754	145	99,793
Morehead State U.	Morehead	1922	5,895	379	211,916
Murray State U.	Murray	1922	6,633	377	232,415
Spalding	Louisville	1814	1,081	100	107,998
Thomas More	Ft. Mitchell	1921	1,605	142	73,000
U. of Kentucky	Lexington	1865	18,911	1,238	1,153,774
U. of Louisville	Louisville	1798	10,182	1,402	634,968
Western Kentucky U.	Bowling Green	1906	9,879	610	431,247
LOUISIANA					
Grambling	Grambling	1901	3,663	203	93,285
Louisiana State U.	Baton Rouge	1860	34,265	3,520	1,830,409
L.S.U. in Baton Rouge	Baton Rouge	1860	18,827	1,487	1,348,290
L.S.U. in New Orleans	New Orleans	1958	11,546	487	212,920
Louisiana Tech U.	Ruston	1894	7,133	465	171,711
Loyola U.	New Orleans	1912	4,727	192	171,711
McNeese State	Lake Charles	1939	5,602	337	112,217
Nicholls State U.	Thibodaux	1948	5,155	172	110,383
Northeast Louisiana U.	Monroe	1931	8,237	327	160,469
Northwestern State U.	Natchitoches	1884	6,188	330	178,102
Southeastern Louisiana U.	Hammond	1925	5,605	279	128,146
Southern U.	Baton Rouge	1880	9,457	534	276,318
Tulane U.	New Orleans	1834	9,447	950	1,071,638
U. of Southwestern La.	Lafayette	1898	10,300	615	278,736
Xavier U.	New Orleans	1925	1,439	131	91,384
MAINE					
Bates	Lewiston	1864	1,204	86	154,716
Bowdoin	Brunswick	1794	1,090	100	443,978
Colby	Waterville	1813	1,514	120	270,985
U. of Maine, Farmington	Farmington	1864	1,344	95	47,188
U. of Maine, Orono	Orono	1865	9,486	658	437,155
U. of Maine, Portland-Gorham	Portland	1957	6,107	215	249,231
MARYLAND					
Bowie State	Bowie	1867	2,658	137	63,000
Columbia Union	Takoma Park	1904	1,134	80	80,000
Coppin State	Baltimore	1900	1,205	83	55,000
Frostburg State	Frostburg	1898	1,815	130	109,645
‡Goucher	Baltimore	1885	1,096	120	151,177
Johns Hopkins U.	Baltimore	1876	8,871	994	2,085,435
Loyola	Baltimore	1852	3,471	138	89,000
Maryland Inst. Col. of Art	Baltimore	—	1,050	90	27,000
Morgan State	Baltimore	1867	5,313	279	152,420
Mt. St. Mary's	Emmitsburg	1808	1,131	78	92,461
Salisbury State	Salisbury	1925	1,547	76	96,937
Towson State	Baltimore	1866	10,950	422	150,000
†U.S. Naval Academy	Annapolis	1845	4,200	550	325,000
U. of Maryland	College Park	1807	37,000	4,283	1,049,600
Western Maryland	Westminster	1867	2,463	161	87,410
MASSACHUSETTS					
American International	Springfield	1885	2,474	157	95,000
Amherst	Amherst	1821	1,223	141	449,321
Assumption	Worcester	1904	1,384	100	119,711
Babson	Babson Park	1919	1,767	92	51,299
Bentley	Waltham	1917	3,600	123	59,274
Boston	Chestnut Hill	1863	11,111	1,165	828,749
Boston State	Boston	1852	5,200	450	88,000
Boston U.	Boston	1869	17,000	3,300	831,519
Brandeis U.	Waltham	1947	2,921	368	455,301
Bridgewater State	Bridgewater	1840	6,970	404	88,914
Clark U.	Worcester	1887	3,080	264	282,575
Emerson	Boston	1880	1,712	143	47,000
‡Emmanuel	Boston	1919	1,187	118	90,077
Fitchburg State	Fitchburg	1894	3,000	185	73,000
Framingham State	Framingham	1839	4,360	253	80,851
Harvard U.	Cambridge	1636	20,000	5,700	8,451,187
‡Radcliffe	Cambridge	1879	1,300		167,320
Holy Cross	Worcester	1843	2,451	181	286,000
Lowell State	Lowell	1894	2,359	169	85,684
Lowell Tech. Inst.	Lowell	1895	8,670	258	149,035
Mass. Inst. of Tech.	Cambridge	1861	7,717	950	1,314,070
Merrimack	North Andover	1947	2,574	178	71,521
‡Mt. Holyoke	South Hadley	1837	1,837	208	331,457
North Adams State	North Adams	1894	2,024	65	62,558
Northeastern U.	Boston	1898	36,874	2,055	366,495
Salem State	Salem	1854	6,535	268	86,435
‡Simmons	Boston	1899	2,513	329	172,567
Smith	Northampton	1871	2,595	240	793,067
Southeastern Mass. U.	North Dartmouth	1895	4,403	300	112,219
Springfield	Springfield	1885	2,657	145	100,049
Stonehill	North Easton	1948	1,840	123	59,152
Suffolk U.	Boston	1906	5,754	227	119,825
Tufts U.	Medford	1852	5,288	1,824	448,111
U. of Massachusetts	Amherst	1863	24,493	1,411	925,373
‡Wellesley	Wellesley	1870	1,796	217	452,482
Western New England	Springfield	1919	3,343	223	56,569
Westfield State	Westfield	1839	2,609	144	63,436
‡Wheaton	Norton	1834	1,261	115	144,168
Williams	Williamstown	1793	1,575	140	377,557
Worcester Polytech. Inst.	Worcester	1865	2,381	160	98,000
Worcester State	Worcester	1874	3,958	189	79,740
MICHIGAN					
Adrian	Adrian	1859	1,318	111	76,256
Albion	Albion	1835	1,735	147	165,024
Alma	Alma	1886	1,203	86	89,295
Andrews U.	Berrien Springs	1874	2,191	204	238,041
Aquinas	Grand Rapids	1923	1,400	110	87,460
Calvin	Grand Rapids	1876	3,047	182	274,942
Central Michigan U.	Mt. Pleasant	1892	13,885	797	251,195
Detroit Inst. of Tech.	Detroit	1891	1,048	85	40,730
Eastern Michigan U.	Ypsilanti	1849	18,420	965	287,287
Ferris State	Big Rapids	1884	7,705	416	188,497
General Motors Inst.	Flint	1919	3,075	218	50,000
Grand Valley State	Allendale	1960	4,174	171	128,796
Hillsdale	Hillsdale	1844	1,085	65	49,002
Hope	Holland	1866	2,029	165	137,101
Kalamazoo	Kalamazoo	1833	1,297	80	150,000
Lake Superior State	Sault Ste. Marie	1946	1,415	95	50,225
Lawrence Inst. of Tech.	Southfield	1932	4,000	180	35,808
Marygrove	Detroit	1910	1,038	75	150,094
Mercy	Detroit	1941	1,620	113	76,500
Michigan State U.	East Lansing	1855	41,649	2,493	1,759,942
Michigan Tech. U.	Houghton	1885	4,394	300	265,845
Northern Michigan U.	Marquette	1899	7,976	395	187,342
Oakland U.	Rochester	1957	7,069	311	173,249
Saginaw Valley	University Center	1964	1,957	75	61,950
U. of Detroit	Detroit	1877	9,561	593	407,223
U. of Michigan	Ann Arbor	1817	39,986	4,733	4,396,525
Wayne State U.	Detroit	1868	36,765	1,850	1,367,553
Western Michigan U.	Kalamazoo	1903	20,456	1,084	713,644

Institution	Location	Year founded	Total students	Faculty	Bound library volumes
MINNESOTA					
Augsburg	Minneapolis	1869	1,521	125	123,339
Bemidji State	Bemidji	1913	4,779	280	184,175
Bethel	St. Paul	1871	1,044	89	72,655
Carleton	Northfield	1866	1,542	158	212,946
Concordia	Moorhead	1891	2,278	168	144,791
Gustavus Adolphus	St. Peter	1862	1,918	135	117,318
Hamline U.	St. Paul	1854	1,232	89	120,535
Macalester	St. Paul	1885	1,946	174	197,558
Mankato State	Mankato	1867	14,000	725	272,010
Moorhead State	Moorhead	1887	4,783	282	160,262
‡St. Catherine	St. Paul	1905	1,303	114	176,540
St. Cloud State	St. Cloud	1869	9,308	410	325,808
†St. John's U.	Collegeville	1857	1,566	127	217,803
St. Mary's	Winona	1912	1,023	85	101,000
St. Olaf	Northfield	1874	2,650	185	246,800
†St. Thomas	St. Paul	1885	1,813	138	146,254
U. of Minnesota	Minneapolis	1851	65,249	8,262	3,112,526
Winona State	Winona	1858	3,573	208	116,230
MISSISSIPPI					
Alcorn A. & M.	Lorman	1871	2,677	116	71,734
Delta State	Cleveland	1924	2,774	164	89,943
Jackson State	Jackson	1877	5,058	300	96,417
Mississippi	Clinton	1826	2,370	130	125,894
‡Mississippi State	Columbus	1884	2,238	139	150,892
Mississippi State U.	State College	1878	10,334	767	372,233
Mississippi Valley State	Itta Bena	1946	2,138	132	72,281
U. of Mississippi	University	1848	8,300	350	464,373
U. of Southern Mississippi	Hattiesburg	1910	7,800	550	345,801
MISSOURI					
Central Missouri State	Warrensburg	1871	12,572	562	315,330
Drury	Springfield	1873	2,544	170	79,171
Evangel	Springfield	1955	1,165	73	54,300
Harris Teachers	St. Louis	1857	1,169	87	48,300
Lincoln U.	Jefferson City	1866	2,345	147	99,976
Missouri Southern	Joplin	1949	2,924	110	68,434
Missouri Western	St. Joseph	1915	3,147	158	43,835
Northeast Missouri State	Kirksville	1867	5,894	278	155,303
Northwest Missouri State U.	Maryville	1905	5,135	293	123,702
Rockhurst	Kansas City	1910	2,075	140	83,000
St. Louis U.	St. Louis	1818	10,490	1,749	710,241
School of the Ozarks	Point Lookout	1906	1,048	68	70,000
Southeast Missouri State	Cape Girardeau	1873	6,757	382	192,821
Southwest Baptist	Bolivar	1878	1,059	67	70,000
Southwest Missouri State	Springfield	1906	9,000	550	189,432
‡Stephens	Columbia	1833	1,980	179	98,132
U. of Missouri-Columbia	Columbia	1839	20,811	1,604	1,589,115
U. of M.-Kansas City	Kansas City	1929	9,018	441	435,949
U. of M.-Rolla	Rolla	1870	4,289	407	192,876
U. of M.-St. Louis	St. Louis	1963	9,750	336	182,103
Washington U.	St. Louis	1853	10,599	3,268	1,421,349
Webster	St. Louis	1915	1,600	100	30,000
‡William Woods	Fulton	1870	1,172	73	106,000
MONTANA					
Carroll	Helena	1909	1,034	70	49,087
Eastern Montana	Billings	1927	3,680	154	95,250
Great Falls	Great Falls	1932	1,032	60	48,000
Montana State U.	Bozeman	1893	8,113	548	561,331
Northern Montana	Havre	1929	1,125	86	58,314
U. of Montana	Missoula	1893	7,586	400	479,537
Western Montana	Dillon	1883	1,072	50	52,733
NEBRASKA					
Chadron State	Chadron	1911	2,107	132	95,953
Concordia Teachers	Seward	1894	1,500	93	95,423
Creighton U.	Omaha	1878	3,916	659	297,887
Kearney State	Kearney	1905	5,514	250	134,777
Nebraska Wesleyan U.	Lincoln	1887	1,056	104	103,251
Peru State	Peru	1867	1,012	54	68,568
U. of Nebraska	Lincoln	1869	20,130	1,117	976,310
U. of N. at Omaha	Omaha	1908	12,711	604	291,744
Wayne State	Wayne	1891	2,322	125	102,752
NEVADA					
U. of Nevada-Las Vegas	Las Vegas	1964	3,570	154	266,824
U. of Nevada-Reno	Reno	1874	7,228	400	413,075
NEW HAMPSHIRE					
Dartmouth	Hanover	1769	3,149	364	1,030,749
Franklin Pierce	Rindge	1962	1,077	83	29,461
Keene State	Keene	1909	2,706	125	80,000
New England	Henniker	1946	1,150	99	47,978
Plymouth State	Plymouth	1870	2,637	128	96,989
†St. Anselm's	Manchester	1889	1,674	126	71,675
U. of New Hampshire	Durham	1866	10,529	734	560,126
NEW JERSEY					
Bloomfield	Bloomfield	1868	1,600	103	65,895
Drew U.	Madison	1866	2,854	276	327,024
Fairleigh Dickinson U.	Rutherford	1941	18,693	550	371,602
Glassboro State	Glassboro	1923	11,266	450	120,059
Jersey City State	Jersey City	1927	7,000	330	126,274
Monmouth	West Long Branch	1933	5,240	283	131,954
Montclair State	Upper Montclair	1908	12,864	574	154,569
Newark Engineering	Newark	1881	4,434	280	79,213
Newark State	Union	1855	12,376	683	133,120
Princeton U.	Princeton	1746	5,398	919	2,314,323
Rider	Trenton	1865	5,700	315	206,176
Rutgers U.	New Brunswick	1766	35,229	2,387	1,611,649
St. Peter's	Jersey City	1872	4,500	350	132,989

Institution	Location	Year founded	Total students	Faculty	Bound library volumes
Seton Hall U.	South Orange	1856	9,155	475	283,584
Stevens Inst. of Tech.	Hoboken	1870	2,192	167	59,767
Trenton State	Trenton	1855	10,630	585	205,059
Upsala	East Orange	1893	1,853	129	119,429
William Patterson	Wayne	1855	9,306	378	161,993
NEW MEXICO					
Eastern New Mexico U.	Portales	1934	5,685	195	146,093
New Mexico Highlands U.	Las Vegas	1893	2,400	120	117,569
New Mexico State U.	Las Cruces	1889	10,600	405	319,902
Santa Fe	Santa Fe	1947	1,228	75	60,300
U. of Albuquerque	Albuquerque	1940	2,470	124	55,300
U. of New Mexico	Albuquerque	1889	17,717	835	720,124
Western New Mexico U.	Silver City	1893	1,387	76	78,719
NEW YORK					
Adelphi U.	Garden City	1896	8,000	599	226,028
Alfred U.	Alfred	1857	2,241	181	157,829
Canisius	Buffalo	1870	3,972	280	157,146
City U. of New York	New York	1847	142,441	8,815	2,900,000
Bernard M. Baruch	New York	1968	12,407	827	112,932
Brooklyn	Brooklyn	1930	31,415	1,412	541,000
City	New York	1847	19,955	1,654	866,135
Herbert H. Lehman	Bronx	1931	13,230	852	187,548
Hunter	New York	1870	24,406	1,463	332,515
Queens	Flushing	1937	27,975	1,839	383,898
Richmond	Staten Island	1965	3,388	207	140,000
York	Jamaica	1966	2,608	225	54,264
Clarkson Tech.	Potsdam	1895	2,499	210	101,261
Colgate U.	Hamilton	1819	2,283	163	272,170
Columbia U.	New York	1754	14,475	4,500	4,241,130
‡Barnard	New York	1889	1,904	197	125,402
Teachers	New York	1887	5,199	403	380,000
Cooper Union	New York	1859	1,011	177	88,272
Cornell U.	Ithaca	1865	15,525	1,616	3,779,990
D'Youville	Buffalo	1908	1,196	107	91,919
Elmira	Elmira	1855	3,266	145	107,808
Fordham U.	Bronx	1841	13,800	780	927,159
Hartwick	Oneonta	1928	1,600	117	101,988
Hobart & William Smith	Geneva	1822	1,600	107	140,985
Hofstra U.	Hempstead	1935	12,015	760	520,000
Houghton	Houghton	1883	1,168	85	87,596
Iona	New Rochelle	1940	3,106	200	119,081
Ithaca	Ithaca	1892	4,025	383	180,000
Juilliard	New York	1905	1,121	200	37,683
Le Moyne	Syracuse	1946	1,614	133	100,895
Long Island U.	Greenvale	1926	7,252	321	437,000
†Manhattan	Bronx	1853	4,336	310	192,357
Manhattanville	Purchase	1841	1,264	137	188,082
Marist	Poughkeepsie	1929	1,700	105	69,212
†Marymount	Tarrytown	1918	1,007	101	80,000
Mercy	Dobbs Ferry	1950	1,605	99	61,589
‡Molloy	Rockville Centre	1955	1,127	106	52,500
‡Nazareth	Rochester	1924	1,742	110	117,744
‡New Rochelle	New Rochelle	1904	1,480	105	105,000
New School	New York	1919	17,000	2,000	86,576
New York Inst. of Tech.	Old Westbury	1955	4,520	200	110,000
New York U.	New York	1831	40,126	4,662	2,111,570
Niagara U.	Niagara University	1856	3,210	176	133,723
Pace	New York	1906	9,708	539	218,792
Polytechnic Inst.	Brooklyn	1854	3,597	255	203,943
Pratt Inst.	Brooklyn	1887	4,412	447	242,744
Rensselaer Polytech.	Troy	1824	5,018	441	208,947
Rochester Inst. of Tech.	Rochester	1829	10,587	803	96,987
Rosary Hill	Buffalo	1948	1,222	120	72,925
Russell Sage	Troy	1916	3,404	235	112,017
St. Bonaventure U.	St. Bonaventure	1859	2,525	173	163,588
St. Francis	Brooklyn	1884	2,499	120	80,206
St. John Fisher	Rochester	1948	1,300	90	74,843
St. John's U.	Jamaica	1870	13,025	677	597,551
St. Lawrence U.	Canton	1856	2,200	146	211,335
St. Rose	Albany	1920	1,516	105	85,946
Siena	Loudonville	1937	1,791	129	132,652
Skidmore	Saratoga Springs	1911	1,820	159	146,893
State U. of New York	Albany	1948	166,363	8,461	6,675,000
SUNY at Albany	Albany	1844	13,905	795	611,478
SUNY at Binghamton	Binghamton	1946	7,604	416	371,701
SUNY at Buffalo	Buffalo	1846	22,321	929	1,575,872
SUNY at Stony Brook	Stony Brook	1957	11,413	609	632,292
State U. Colleges					
Brockport	Brockport	1867	10,023	509	228,504
Buffalo	Buffalo	1867	10,895	522	263,103
Cortland	Cortland	1868	5,565	295	179,035
Fredonia	Fredonia	1867	5,129	279	206,454
Geneseo	Geneseo	1871	5,905	314	196,293
New Paltz	New Paltz	1885	7,880	365	231,795
Oneonta	Oneonta	1887	5,890	338	247,546
Oswego	Oswego	1861	8,528	421	274,892
Plattsburgh	Plattsburgh	1889	5,754	293	195,358
Potsdam	Potsdam	1867	4,844	296	199,434
Syracuse U.	Syracuse	1870	22,000	881	1,548,733
Union Col. & U.	Schenectady	1795	2,652	211	283,800
†U.S. Merchant Marine Acad.	Kings Point	1938	1,016	91	68,000
†U.S. Military Acad.	West Point	1802	3,894	525	345,000
U. of Rochester	Rochester	1850	7,877	2,174	1,179,204
Vassar	Poughkeepsie	1861	2,041	200	416,338
Wagner	Staten Island	1883	3,124	145	143,751
Yeshiva U.	New York	1886	7,057	2,500	568,000
NORTH CAROLINA					
Appalachian State U.	Boone	1903	6,793	357	225,940
Atlantic Christian	Wilson	1902	1,749	103	84,409
Campbell	Buie's Creek	1887	2,220	118	93,919
Catawba	Salisbury	1851	1,094	84	84,852
†Davidson	Davidson	1837	1,000	90	172,893
Duke U.	Durham	1838	8,682	1,392	2,231,519

Universities and colleges (continued)

Institution	Location	Year founded	Total students	Faculty	Bound library volumes
East Carolina U.	Greenville	1907	9,192	604	432,296
Elizabeth City State U.	Elizabeth City	1891	1,024	82	71,500
Elon	Elon College	1889	1,696	99	81,268
Fayetteville State U.	Fayetteville	1877	1,798	96	76,232
Guilford	Greensboro	1837	1,611	124	137,468
High Point	High Point	1924	1,070	70	81,759
Johnson C. Smith U.	Charlotte	1867	1,015	73	67,019
Lenoir Rhyne	Hickory	1891	1,318	103	74,513
Mars Hill	Mars Hill	1856	1,337	102	82,327
‡Meredith	Raleigh	1891	1,229	91	59,520
N. Carolina A. & T. St. U.	Greensboro	1891	4,197	274	305,724
N. Carolina Central U.	Durham	1910	3,470	269	246,785
Pembroke State U.	Pembroke	1887	1,902	108	63,446
St. Augustine's	Raleigh	1867	1,234	73	55,044
Shaw U.	Raleigh	1865	1,047	84	42,634
U. of North Carolina	Chapel Hill	1795	46,342	3,870	3,010,647
N. Carolina St. U., Raleigh	Raleigh	1887	13,000	1,100	550,329
U. of N.C. at Chapel Hill	Chapel Hill	1789	19,160	1,800	1,819,669
U. of N.C. at Charlotte	Charlotte	1965	4,480	292	137,059
U. of N.C. at Greensboro	Greensboro	1891	6,720	473	345,218
U. of N.C. at Wilmington	Wilmington	1947	1,849	135	82,012
Wake Forest U.	Winston-Salem	1834	3,615	558	450,190
Western Carolina U.	Cullowhee	1889	5,780	326	140,671
Winston-Salem State U.	Winston-Salem	1892	1,536	109	85,892
NORTH DAKOTA					
Dickinson State	Dickinson	1916	1,460	90	56,859
Minot State	Minot	1913	2,462	140	68,837
North Dakota State U.	Fargo	1890	6,696	328	230,240
U. of North Dakota	Grand Forks	1883	8,067	435	367,190
Valley City State	Valley City	1889	1,025	65	75,979
OHIO					
Antioch	Yellow Springs	1852	2,275	142	190,254
Ashland	Ashland	1878	2,388	256	159,011
Baldwin-Wallace	Berea	1845	2,691	215	153,088
Bowling Green State U.	Bowling Green	1910	15,963	730	431,223
Capital U.	Columbus	1850	2,276	150	149,267
Case Western Reserve U.	Cleveland	1826	8,647	1,500	1,175,262
Central State U.	Wilberforce	1887	2,525	158	100,099
Cleveland State U.	Cleveland	1964	13,642	643	289,705
Defiance	Defiance	1850	1,049	75	65,383
Denison U.	Granville	1831	2,044	157	188,411
Findlay	Findlay	1882	1,151	68	64,113
Heidelberg	Tiffin	1850	1,222	114	108,976
Hiram	Hiram	1850	1,185	95	116,446
John Carroll U.	Cleveland	1886	4,000	250	199,012
Kent State U.	Kent	1910	19,793	1,020	648,012
Kenyon	Gambier	1824	1,241	103	141,995
Marietta	Marietta	1835	2,088	150	177,355
Miami U.	Oxford	1809	15,371	670	597,192
Mt. Union	Alliance	1846	1,205	112	145,000
Muskingum	New Concord	1837	1,220	101	128,000
Oberlin	Oberlin	1833	2,572	240	695,442
Ohio Northern U.	Ada	1871	2,254	160	143,075
Ohio State U.	Columbus	1870	50,804	3,015	2,539,716
Ohio U.	Athens	1804	22,000	935	606,279
Ohio Wesleyan U.	Delaware	1842	2,423	179	341,895
Otterbein	Westerville	1847	1,330	91	91,589
Steubenville	Steubenville	1946	1,217	72	72,900
U. of Akron	Akron	1870	17,700	1,277	363,848
U. of Cincinnati	Cincinnati	1819	29,506	2,805	1,156,971
U. of Dayton	Dayton	1850	8,265	459	317,359
U. of Toledo	Toledo	1872	14,903	670	842,607
Wilberforce U.	Wilberforce	1856	1,217	46	43,000
Wittenberg U.	Springfield	1845	2,771	279	227,929
Wooster	Wooster	1866	1,750	160	199,000
Wright State U.	Dayton	1967	9,950	440	188,569
Xavier U.	Cincinnati	1831	5,964	292	179,494
Youngstown State U.	Youngstown	1908	12,868	760	262,344
OKLAHOMA					
Bethany Nazarene	Bethany	1899	1,528	86	83,308
Cameron	Lawton	1909	4,262	150	66,152
Central State U.	Edmond	1890	10,050	386	162,752
East Central State	Ada	1909	2,831	125	148,906
Langston U.	Langston	1897	1,111	79	110,000
Northeastern State	Tahlequah	1846	5,088	229	156,200
Northwestern State	Alva	1897	2,109	92	84,994
Oklahoma Baptist U.	Shawnee	1911	1,460	104	90,681
Oklahoma Christian	Oklahoma City	1950	1,149	44	66,155
Oklahoma City U.	Oklahoma City	1904	2,245	160	144,513
Oklahoma Liberal Arts	Chickasha	1908	1,015	62	70,746
Oklahoma Panhandle St.	Goodwell	1909	1,268	65	53,011
Oklahoma State U.	Stillwater	1890	18,655	777	1,073,583
Oral Roberts U.	Tulsa	1963	1,375	100	118,500
Phillips U.	Enid	1906	1,307	101	177,104
Southeastern State	Durant	1909	3,425	161	106,825
Southwestern State	Weatherford	1901	5,018	210	131,241
U. of Oklahoma	Norman	1890	16,988	706	1,158,596
U. of Tulsa	Tulsa	1894	5,541	320	411,524
OREGON					
Eastern Oregon	La Grande	1929	1,700	114	78,467
Lewis and Clark	Portland	1867	2,352	120	133,228
Linfield	McMinnville	1849	1,000	89	74,983
Oregon Col. of Education	Monmouth	1856	3,500	250	113,383
Oregon State U.	Corvallis	1868	14,100	1,320	643,189
Oregon Technical Inst.	Klamath Falls	1947	1,400	110	31,957
Pacific U.	Forest Grove	1849	1,168	101	87,703
Portland State U.	Portland	1955	12,467	764	360,000
Reed	Portland	1908	1,208	113	220,000
Southern Oregon	Ashland	1926	4,206	285	119,790
U. of Oregon	Eugene	1872	13,848	1,285	1,104,320
U. of Portland	Portland	1901	1,816	112	146,091
Willamette U.	Salem	1842	1,617	142	140,542

Institution	Location	Year founded	Total students	Faculty	Bound library volumes
PENNSYLVANIA					
Albright	Reading	1856	1,407	110	127,341
Allegheny	Meadville	1815	1,690	122	196,971
Bloomsburg State	Bloomsburg	1839	4,941	280	149,069
‡Bryn Mawr	Bryn Mawr	1885	1,421	234	348,647
Bucknell U.	Lewisburg	1846	2,878	228	374,803
California State	California	1852	5,615	378	146,769
‡Carlow	Pittsburgh	1929	1,053	95	68,168
Carnegie-Mellon U.	Pittsburgh	1967	4,500	575	377,508
‡Chestnut Hill	Philadelphia	1924	1,128	70	84,221
Cheyney State	Cheyney	1837	2,400	210	115,808
Clarion State	Clarion	1867	4,000	280	203,796
Delaware Valley	Doylestown	1896	1,184	78	54,163
Dickinson	Carlisle	1773	1,551	107	173,023
Drexel U.	Philadelphia	1891	10,100	550	310,367
Duquesne U.	Pittsburgh	1878	8,261	450	315,600
East Stroudsburg State	East Stroudsburg	1893	3,419	217	187,863
Edinboro State	Edinboro	1857	7,155	479	247,754
Elizabethtown	Elizabethtown	1899	1,608	126	89,665
Franklin and Marshall	Lancaster	1787	1,950	156	212,568
Gannon	Erie	1944	2,832	177	96,503
Geneva	Beaver Falls	1848	1,293	126	91,692
Gettysburg	Gettysburg	1832	1,847	145	193,321
Grove City	Grove City	1876	2,090	123	97,741
Gwynedd-Mercy	Gwynedd Valley	1948	1,088	124	37,500
‡Immaculata	Immaculata	1920	1,473	90	89,146
Indiana U.	Indiana	1875	10,500	600	407,012
Juniata	Huntingdon	1876	1,200	102	140,000
King's	Wilkes-Barre	1946	2,555	135	113,411
Kutztown State	Kutztown	1866	4,850	270	146,672
Lafayette	Easton	1826	1,948	167	273,618
La Salle	Philadelphia	1863	7,000	450	155,513
Lebanon Valley	Annville	1866	1,233	102	93,042
Lehigh U.	Bethlehem	1865	5,303	526	549,381
Lincoln U.	Lincoln University	1854	1,079	98	108,108
Lock Haven State	Lock Haven	1870	2,237	186	207,741
Lycoming	Williamsport	1812	1,553	97	92,000
Mansfield State	Mansfield	1857	3,078	240	112,480
‡Marywood	Scranton	1915	2,214	162	104,382
Millersville State	Millersville	1855	5,849	330	228,279
Moravian	Bethlehem	1807	1,440	92	114,168
Muhlenberg	Allentown	1848	1,781	121	146,962
Pennsylvania State U.	University Park	1855	62,368	3,467	1,165,822
Philadelphia Col. of Art	Philadelphia	1876	1,532	152	31,780
Phila. Col. of Tex. & Sci.	Philadelphia	1884	2,051	144	45,213
Point Park	Pittsburgh	1960	2,523	202	88,247
Robert Morris	Pittsburgh	1921	3,999	98	46,283
St. Francis	Loretto	1847	1,570	83	108,385
St. Joseph's	Philadelphia	1851	6,625	264	123,068
†St. Vincent	Latrobe	1846	1,027	75	174,393
Shippensburg State	Shippensburg	1871	5,246	303	204,712
Slippery Rock State	Slippery Rock	1889	5,100	356	263,547
Susquehanna U.	Selinsgrove	1858	1,537	100	90,828
Swarthmore	Swarthmore	1864	1,145	155	347,803
Temple U.	Philadelphia	1884	29,754	2,882	1,029,544
Thiel	Greenville	1866	1,400	97	85,967
U. of Pennsylvania	Philadelphia	1740	17,939	1,726	2,329,401
U. of Pittsburgh	Pittsburgh	1787	27,709	1,915	1,456,573
U. of Scranton	Scranton	1888	2,400	150	131,538
Ursinus	Collegeville	1869	1,862	145	97,893
Villanova U.	Villanova	1842	9,400	480	444,147
Washington & Jefferson	Washington	1781	1,045	84	142,707
Waynesburg	Waynesburg	1849	1,009	77	85,208
West Chester State	West Chester	1812	8,106	512	238,067
Westminster	New Wilmington	1852	1,919	117	117,190
Widener College	Chester	1821	2,522	185	91,443
Wilkes	Wilkes-Barre	1933	3,436	192	119,020
York	York	1941	2,400	98	66,975
PUERTO RICO					
Catholic U.	Ponce	1948	6,763	294	140,000
Inter American U.	San German	1912	9,145	178	182,745
U. of Puerto Rico	Rio Piedras	1903	25,448	1,397	1,088,831
RHODE ISLAND					
Brown U.	Providence	1764	5,658	586	1,390,186
Bryant	Smithfield	1863	3,600	94	56,567
Providence	Providence	1917	3,175	268	143,304
Rhode Island	Providence	1854	7,058	341	135,475
Rhode Island Sch. of Design	Providence	1877	1,119	108	44,344
U. of Rhode Island	Kingston	1892	9,656	862	437,616
SOUTH CAROLINA					
Baptist	Charleston	—	1,918	95	50,425
Benedict	Columbia	1870	1,477	88	59,047
†The Citadel	Charleston	1842	2,606	158	113,799
Clemson U.	Clemson	1889	8,647	651	453,046
Furman U.	Greenville	1826	2,135	160	187,090
South Carolina State	Orangeburg	1896	2,543	145	110,729
U. of South Carolina	Columbia	1801	19,288	784	934,739
Winthrop	Rock Hill	1886	3,694	204	192,054
Wofford	Spartanburg	1854	1,010	73	110,763
SOUTH DAKOTA					
Augustana	Sioux Falls	1860	1,978	145	98,282
Black Hills State	Spearfish	1883	1,979	115	59,990
Dakota State	Madison	1881	1,118	69	57,762
Northern State	Aberdeen	1901	3,025	163	121,772
S. Dakota Mines & Tech.	Rapid City	1885	1,506	113	109,677
South Dakota State U.	Brookings	1883	6,520	399	230,281
U. of South Dakota	Vermillion	1882	5,300	386	308,456

Institution	Location	Year founded	Total students	Faculty	Bound library volumes
TENNESSEE					
Austin Peay State U.	Clarksville	1929	3,445	165	121,200
Carson-Newman	Jefferson City	1851	1,611	111	103,188
David Lipscomb	Nashville	1891	1,963	105	93,793
East Tennessee State U.	Johnson City	1911	9,798	662	288,056
Fisk U.	Nashville	1867	1,341	120	163,835
George Peabody	Nashville	1875	1,980	235	1,300,000
Knoxville	Knoxville	1875	1,100	100	53,094
Lee	Cleveland	1918	1,000	62	48,621
Memphis State U.	Memphis	1909	19,323	776	391,176
Middle Tennessee State U.	Murfreesboro	1911	7,964	477	217,902
Southern Missionary	Collegedale	1892	1,313	110	61,344
Southwestern	Memphis	1848	1,022	103	134,373
Tennessee State U.	Nashville	1909	4,225	276	183,710
Tennessee Tech. U.	Cookeville	1915	6,000	297	205,716
U. of Tennessee	Knoxville	1794	22,161	1,342	1,122,691
Vanderbilt U.	Nashville	1872	6,432	1,358	1,301,391
TEXAS					
Abilene Christian	Abilene	1906	3,046	175	161,550
Angelo State U.	San Angelo	1928	3,528	145	91,342
Austin	Sherman	1849	1,077	91	94,305
Baylor U.	Waco	1845	6,750	398	511,570
Bishop	Dallas	1881	1,755	142	88,936
Dallas Baptist	Dallas	1898	1,375	89	69,471
East Texas State U.	Commerce	1889	8,003	488	321,617
Hardin-Simmons U.	Abilene	1891	1,647	110	277,995
Houston Baptist	Houston	1960	1,086	65	59,790
Howard Payne	Brownwood	1889	1,255	73	85,156
Incarnate Word	San Antonio	1881	1,608	106	87,138
Lamar U.	Beaumont	1923	10,600	425	228,904
McMurry	Abilene	1922	1,500	86	97,176
Midwestern U.	Wichita Falls	1922	3,847	200	142,395
North Texas State U.	Denton	1890	14,321	990	716,525
Our Lady of the Lake	San Antonio	1911	2,180	135	100,693
Pan American U.	Edinburg	1927	6,233	221	105,612
Prairie View A. & M.	Prairie View	1876	3,995	240	130,000
Rice U.	Houston	1891	3,200	400	660,574
St. Edward's U.	Austin	1871	1,215	90	61,494
St. Mary's U.	San Antonio	1852	3,692	160	130,000
Sam Houston State U.	Huntsville	1879	9,631	360	372,053
Southern Methodist U.	Dallas	1911	9,609	720	1,164,600
Southwest Texas State U.	San Marcos	1899	10,684	462	216,323
Stephen F. Austin State U.	Nacogdoches	1923	9,227	413	203,993
Sul Ross State U.	Alpine	1920	2,274	130	132,592
Tarleton State	Stephenville	1899	2,885	147	111,667
Texas A & I U.	Kingsville	1925	8,081	414	262,140
Texas A. & M. U.	College Station	1876	13,816	1,300	716,260
Texas Christian U.	Forth Worth	1873	6,252	450	660,354
Texas Southern U.	Houston	1947	5,530	260	202,615
Texas Tech U.	Lubbock	1923	19,554	1,355	1,062,483
Texas Wesleyan	Fort Worth	1891	1,784	100	89,934
‡Texas Woman's U.	Denton	1901	5,602	300	422,219
Trinity U.	San Antonio	1869	3,108	231	184,280
U. of Dallas	Irving	1956	1,327	113	80,124
U. of Houston	Houston	1927	24,805	1,455	664,469
U. of St. Thomas	Houston	1947	1,510	124	43,374
U. of Texas System	Austin	1883	67,535	6,073	3,650,800
U. of Texas at Arlington	Arlington	1895	13,569	710	288,929
U. of Texas at Austin	Austin	1881	39,503	3,328	2,427,000
U. of Texas at El Paso	El Paso	1913	11,348	442	290,613
West Texas State U.	Canyon	1910	6,371	285	168,761
UTAH					
Brigham Young U.	Provo	1875	25,467	1,137	1,039,000
Southern Utah State	Cedar City	1897	1,726	106	59,908
U. of Utah	Salt Lake City	1850	23,633	1,900	1,178,985
Utah State U.	Logan	1888	7,950	650	408,533
Weber State	Ogden	1889	9,772	355	147,038
VERMONT					
Castleton State	Castleton	1867	1,332	88	38,630
Goddard	Plainfield	1938	1,600	68	50,000
Middlebury	Middlebury	1800	1,848	130	233,568
†Norwich U.	Northfield	1819	1,054	107	101,734
St. Michael's	Winooski	1903	1,279	105	54,466
U. of Vermont	Burlington	1791	8,425	1,019	579,858
VIRGINIA					
Eastern Mennonite	Harrisonburg	1917	1,005	100	59,106
George Mason	Fairfax	1957	3,110	160	62,034
Hampton Inst.	Hampton	1868	2,485	208	132,000
‡Hollins	Hollins College	1842	1,084	93	122,225
Longwood	Farmville	1839	2,286	145	122,128
Lynchburg	Lynchburg	1903	1,600	107	72,016
Madison	Harrisonburg	1908	4,574	327	159,556
Mary Washington	Fredericksburg	1908	1,999	160	211,087
Old Dominion U.	Norfolk	1930	9,201	426	228,508
‡Radford	Radford	1910	3,584	261	128,906
Roanoke	Salem	1842	1,251	79	88,634
U. of Richmond	Richmond	1830	4,286	332	200,279
U. of Virginia	Charlottesville	1819	12,300	1,200	1,699,151
Virginia Commonwealth U.	Richmond	1838	14,132	1,061	257,715
†Virginia Military Inst.	Lexington	1839	1,128	106	191,099
Virginia Polytech. Inst.	Blacksburg	1872	9,568	970	626,955
Virginia State	Petersburg	1882	3,222	216	143,735
Virginia Union U.	Petersburg	1865	1,137	81	94,390
†Washington & Lee U.	Lexington	1749	1,567	150	285,554
William & Mary	Williamsburg	1693	5,259	431	561,814
WASHINGTON					
Central Washington St.	Ellensburg	1891	7,424	424	182,024
Eastern Washington St.	Cheney	1890	5,981	369	193,886
Gonzaga U.	Spokane	1887	2,800	210	237,049
Pacific Lutheran U.	Tacoma	1890	2,985	206	136,139
Seattle Pacific	Seattle	1891	1,812	165	81,040
Seattle U.	Seattle	1891	2,929	190	145,160
U. of Puget Sound	Tacoma	1888	2,974	245	157,148
U. of Washington	Seattle	1861	30,765	2,200	1,876,900
Walla Walla	College Place	1892	1,667	127	127,935
Washington State U.	Pullman	1890	13,732	851	853,458
Western Washington St.	Bellingham	1899	9,600	590	236,352
Whitman	Walla Walla	1859	1,042	94	157,198
Whitworth	Spokane	1890	1,577	96	63,527
WEST VIRGINIA					
Alderson-Broaddus	Philippi	1871	1,024	75	55,043
Bethany	Bethany	1840	1,078	75	102,993
Bluefield State	Bluefield	1895	1,010	83	51,016
Concord	Athens	1872	1,747	107	81,672
Fairmont State	Fairmont	1867	3,320	180	87,953
Glenville State	Glenville	1872	1,360	82	64,701
Marshall U.	Huntington	1837	7,794	399	200,331
Morris Harvey	Charleston	1888	2,837	178	62,849
Salem	Salem	1888	1,375	69	69,000
Shepherd	Shepherdstown	1871	1,843	93	68,686
West Liberty State	West Liberty	1837	3,950	223	95,303
W. Virginia Inst. of Tech.	Montgomery	1895	2,452	148	69,578
West Virginia State	Institute	1891	3,434	154	108,856
West Virginia U.	Morgantown	1867	15,203	834	684,503
West Virginia Wesleyan	Buckhannon	1890	1,525	128	94,504
WISCONSIN					
Beloit	Beloit	1846	1,663	125	219,566
Carroll	Waukesha	1846	1,200	93	108,898
Carthage	Kenosha	1847	1,616	106	67,143
Lawrence U.	Appleton	1847	1,350	130	171,600
Marquette U.	Milwaukee	1864	10,834	720	550,184
St. Norbert	West De Pere	1898	1,549	104	85,594
U. of W.—Eau Claire	Eau Claire	1916	8,900	545	200,233
U. of W.—Green Bay	Green Bay	1969	4,579	271	187,218
U. of W.—La Crosse	La Crosse	1909	6,497	431	184,272
U. of W.—Madison	Madison	1848	33,943	2,102	2,417,024
U. of W.—Milwaukee	Milwaukee	1956	20,959	2,304	663,974
U. of W.—Oshkosh	Oshkosh	1871	11,300	750	198,927
U. of W.—Parkside	Parkside	1965	4,102	237	159,113
U. of W.—Platteville	Platteville	1866	4,542	340	153,866
U. of W.—River Falls	River Falls	1874	3,756	285	195,410
U. of W.—Stevens Point	Stevens Point	1894	9,193	418	200,567
U. of W.—Stout	Menomonie	1893	4,903	375	121,435
U. of W.—Superior	Superior	1896	2,886	224	154,012
U. of W.—Whitewater	Whitewater	1868	8,189	561	287,697
WYOMING					
U. of Wyoming	Laramie	1886	8,500	628	465,344

Living Conditions

Participation in outdoor recreation, 1972

Activity	Participants (millions)	Participants as percentage of total population*	Total person-days of participation (millions)†	Average number of person-days per participant
Camping in remote or wilderness areas	7.7	5	57	7.5
Camping in developed camp grounds	17.5	11	153	8.8
Hunting	22.2	14	299	13.5
Fishing	38.0	24	278	7.3
Riding motorcycles off the road	7.4	5	58	7.8
Hiking with a pack, mountain/rock climbing	8.6	5	45	5.2
Nature walks	26.7	17	149	5.6
Walking for pleasure	54.2	34	496	9.2
Bicycling	16.7	10	214	12.8
Horseback riding	8.7	5	51	5.9
Water skiing	8.5	5	54	6.4
Sailing	4.1	3	32	7.9
Other boating	23.3	15	126	5.4
Outdoor pool swimming	28.5	18	257	9.0
Other swimming outdoors	53.8	34	487	9.0
Golf	7.7	5	63	8.2
Tennis	8.6	5	81	9.5
Playing other outdoor games or sports	35.0	22	339	9.7
Going to outdoor sports events	18.9	12	97	5.1
Visiting zoos, fairs, amusement parks	38.7	24	123	3.2
Sightseeing	59.8	37	363	6.1
Picnicking	74.4	47	405	5.4
Driving for pleasure	54.5	34	405	7.4
Snow skiing	7.2	5	58	8.1
Snowmobiling	7.2	5	104	14.3
Other winter sports	24.8	16	259	10.4

*Population 12 years old and over.
†Participation by a person during any part of a day counted as one person-day.
Source: U.S. Department of Commerce, Bureau of the Census, *Statistical Abstract of the United States 1973;* data compiled by U.S. Bureau of Outdoor Recreation.

Social insurance beneficiaries and benefits

State	Old-age and survivors insurance		Disability insurance		Medicare enrollment,* July 1, 1971	Unemployment insurance state programs	
	Beneficiaries, end of December 1972	Benefits, calendar year 1972	Beneficiaries, end of December 1972	Benefits, calendar year 1972		Beneficiaries, year ending June 30, 1973	Benefits, year ending June 30, 1973 (in 000)
Alabama	431,818	$532,703	80,780	$98,727	339,288	65,600	$34,421
Alaska	12,587	17,703	1,908	2,417	6,963	18,042	16,463
Arizona	229,664	338,527	32,328	45,538	170,136	30,483	18,919
Arkansas	299,863	354,535	57,760	67,035	245,447	39,687	20,240
California	2,193,322	3,349,507	317,071	480,347	1,840,832	753,049	602,970
Colorado	228,943	330,097	25,810	35,920	194,424	26,911	15,141
Connecticut	344,479	584,834	32,290	50,264	294,011	149,895	128,576
Delaware	58,862	90,660	7,363	10,661	46,184	20,715	9,533
Dist. of Columbia	72,722	100,037	9,738	13,156	68,888	20,107	25,102
Florida	1,239,007	1,830,738	132,908	188,821	999,318	69,371	38,085
Georgia	482,974	606,528	98,209	118,495	380,431	48,392	30,042
Hawaii	68,463	96,243	7,950	10,882	47,563	26,411	25,943
Idaho	90,744	128,392	11,737	15,953	71,325	21,516	11,350
Illinois	1,276,046	2,038,532	122,882	188,163	1,110,699	238,983	194,663
Indiana	614,356	948,152	69,134	100,130	502,068	110,618	46,349
Iowa	404,980	588,947	34,439	48,162	357,751	37,116	26,675
Kansas	306,243	444,715	24,749	34,763	272,470	37,499	20,199
Kentucky	424,883	536,093	79,217	93,139	349,029	78,572	42,299
Louisiana	388,486	488,200	85,319	97,432	314,385	82,338	59,859
Maine	144,154	204,067	17,761	22,458	122,282	42,289	22,795
Maryland	371,563	560,637	40,743	60,049	303,367	85,381	64,874
Massachusetts	706,499	1,137,392	66,558	97,370	640,109	223,295	236,584
Michigan	995,612	1,575,088	132,811	199,807	778,574	303,369	214,791
Minnesota	488,234	692,664	37,889	53,069	420,417	92,086	64,309
Mississippi	294,522	321,811	59,208	64,292	231,942	23,970	10,311
Missouri	652,122	934,394	79,484	106,925	570,328	117,889	71,982
Montana	87,688	126,258	11,081	14,993	70,965	18,468	11,410
Nebraska	208,769	298,419	15,538	21,075	186,596	24,728	14,999
Nevada	45,226	71,326	6,753	10,288	33,905	27,191	22,387
New Hampshire	99,415	154,928	9,239	13,099	83,829	20,354	7,809
New Jersey	838,067	1,899,049	88,940	138,693	707,234	‡	307,015
New Mexico	105,749	136,007	21,387	23,691	76,953	19,226	13,388
New York	2,262,747	3,786,705	239,714	366,729	1,979,948	657,483	593,293
North Carolina	582,399	733,766	95,808	118,321	432,015	80,100	29,415
North Dakota	85,130	112,621	7,334	8,808	69,350	9,074§	7,922
Ohio	1,202,330	1,852,794	147,193	215,960	1,013,997	176,746	119,224
Oklahoma	348,329	472,424	51,035	65,791	305,578	41,913	26,768
Oregon	288,059	434,921	36,496	53,667	233,054	66,880	41,902
Pennsylvania	1,526,171	2,402,715	168,087	259,481	1,294,611	400,502	364,946
Rhode Island	122,820	193,939	14,359	20,668	106,160	45,068	33,710
South Carolina	278,664	344,604	58,258	70,728	201,450	34,154	18,674
South Dakota	98,045	130,275	8,638	10,679	82,635	7,221	3,445
Tennessee	493,957	619,701	85,958	104,666	399,407	76,990	38,101
Texas	1,251,485	1,669,825	164,013	206,227	1,024,331	108,793	69,111
Utah	101,173	150,798	11,040	15,569	80,127	26,440	17,878
Vermont	58,718	85,599	7,014	9,115	50,388	15,206	13,013
Virginia	477,746	639,888	77,409	99,365	377,916	33,300	16,341
Washington	406,676	622,184	45,962	68,806	331,798	146,977	124,348
West Virginia	254,799	346,852	63,847	84,232	202,687	50,991	25,239
Wisconsin	584,055	883,042	57,621	82,809	485,188	93,580	80,599
Wyoming	37,932	55,713	3,734	5,201	31,660	5,403	2,813
U.S. TOTAL†	25,204,445	$37,121,884	3,271,486	$4,473,180	20,914,896	4,950,372	$4,056,224

*Includes hospital and/or medical insurance. †Includes data for American Samoa, Guam, Puerto Rico, Virgin Islands and for beneficiaries or enrollees living abroad for all categories except unemployment insurance state programs, for dollar figures only. ‡Data not available. §Preliminary. Source: U.S. Department of Health, Education, and Welfare, Social Security Administration, Office of Research and Statistics.

Health personnel and facilities

	Physicians Dec. 31, 1972	Dentists Dec. 31, 1972	Registered Nurses 1972*	Hospital facilities Sept. 30, 1972		Nursing homes 1971	
				Hospitals	Beds	Facilities	Beds
Alabama	3,301	1,173	10,235	148	27,910	200	13,745
Alaska	251	125	2,030	26	1,695	8	653
Arizona	3,176	951	12,383	82	10,520	85	5,359
Arkansas	1,899	679	5,033	95	11,075	223	15,501
California	41,043	14,077	103,385	635	121,674	4,395	149,672
Colorado	4,168	1,405	15,515	96	14,816	218	17,212
Connecticut	6,292	2,060	23,612	67	21,449	384	22,150
Delaware	806	255	4,389	14	4,998	35	1,944
District of Columbia	3,210	646	5,545	21	12,367	74	2,786
Florida	12,358	4,189	38,398	205	50,257	381	36,712
Georgia	5,405	1,690	17,423	172	32,816	287	23,168
Hawaii	1,302	534	4,117	31	5,806	135	2,303
Idaho	744	387	3,755	52	3,567	67	4,262
Illinois	16,326	6,259	60,806	301	87,479	1,060	67,809
Indiana	5,648	2,341	21,481	135	37,268	537	33,622
Iowa	3,029	1,477	17,812	147	21,593	759	34,278
Kansas	2,744	1,093	12,655	161	18,652	484	22,128
Kentucky	3,585	1,279	11,734	130	19,754	349	18,894
Louisiana	4,598	1,451	11,524	152	26,174	217	15,049
Maine	1,210	469	7,440	52	8,448	298	7,772
Maryland	8,118	2,039	22,462	84	32,080	203	15,507
Massachusetts	12,844	4,005	56,567	207	57,582	980	50,915
Michigan	11,942	4,741	46,681	245	59,975	570	44,147
Minnesota	6,083	2,686	23,638	196	32,846	609	42,041
Mississippi	1,919	647	6,288	108	16,664	137	7,245
Missouri	6,531	2,389	18,823	153	36,598	501	32,486
Montana	774	393	4,429	67	4,746	104	4,473
Nebraska	1,851	967	9,798	106	11,700	255	15,172
Nevada	616	271	2,564	23	2,838	44	1,459
New Hampshire	1,122	384	7,044	35	6,414	143	5,670
New Jersey	11,227	4,488	51,061	137	49,648	567	31,798
New Mexico	1,275	383	4,077	59	6,326	61	3,339
New York	45,040	14,735	125,794	416	178,962	1,133	85,312
North Carolina	5,995	1,791	21,366	162	35,360	862	19,479
North Dakota	593	281	3,653	63	5,580	110	6,215
Ohio	14,848	5,210	57,052	242	75,714	1,223	61,425
Oklahoma	2,730	1,063	8,698	142	17,763	424	27,771
Oregon	3,345	1,524	11,382	85	12,026	322	18,038
Pennsylvania	18,682	6,656	96,414	317	110,041	767	58,680
Rhode Island	1,628	484	6,638	22	7,951	194	6,736
South Carolina	2,610	808	10,187	87	19,019	120	7,669
South Dakota	543	293	3,852	64	6,358	155	7,153
Tennessee	5,008	1,813	12,051	156	32,149	241	14,763
Texas	14,192	4,864	40,372	550	76,484	976	73,360
Utah	1,649	701	4,531	37	4,793	143	4,782
Vermont	886	231	4,521	21	4,257	102	3,045
Virginia	6,270	2,057	23,935	127	36,938	342	16,105
Washington	5,338	2,361	21,953	129	18,243	405	30,270
West Virginia	1,972	675	7,314	84	15,861	125	3,902
Wisconsin	5,764	2,602	23,318	184	33,417	510	39,732
Wyoming	346	169	1,922	31	2,814	34	1,697
United States	325,789†	123,349‡	1,127,657	7,061	1,549,665	22,558	1,235,405

*Preliminary. †Including 65 in the Canal Zone, 48 in U.S. Pacific Islands, and 32,466 retired or not classified, who are not distributed by state. ‡Including 9,098 federally employed who are not distributed by state. Sources: American Medical Association, *Profile of Medical Practice, 1973;* American Dental Association; American Nurse's Association; American Hospital Association; U.S. Department of Health, Education, and Welfare, Public Health Service.

Crime rates per 100,000 population

for states and cities

Unit	MURDER* 1968	MURDER* 1972	FORCIBLE RAPE 1968	FORCIBLE RAPE 1972	ROBBERY 1968	ROBBERY 1972	AGGRAVATED ASSAULT 1968	AGGRAVATED ASSAULT 1972	BURGLARY 1968	BURGLARY 1972	LARCENY† 1968	LARCENY† 1972	AUTO THEFT 1968	AUTO THEFT 1972
STATE														
Alabama	11.8	14.1	11.1	18.8	41.0	68.6	168.5	211.7	617.5	776.1	420.4	557.8	170.7	195.0
Alaska	10.5	9.5	21.7	**41.8**	52.7	66.5	90.6	252.6	747.3	970.8	778.7	1,287.1	482.3	498.2
Arizona	6.3	7.3	18.7	33.4	86.7	120.8	151.9	287.4	1,167.4	1,615.9	936.3	1,251.3	421.2	429.8
Arkansas	8.1	10.4	17.3	17.3	39.6	54.8	151.7	162.2	514.0	663.1	413.4	594.8	94.2	104.2
California	6.0	8.8	**29.9**	39.7	192.5	238.6	194.6	253.7	**1,644.5**	**1,949.2**	1,075.0	1,435.1	621.4	681.3
Colorado	5.4	8.3	26.1	38.4	96.5	141.4	135.0	217.3	917.0	1,580.1	800.7	1,479.7	420.6	589.3
Connecticut	2.5	3.2	8.0	8.9	45.0	79.1	73.7	107.9	964.4	956.8	606.9	845.4	376.1	469.1
Delaware	7.7	6.9	12.7	14.2	101.7	130.1	75.7	234.9	820.4	1,249.4	516.1	1,035.9	409.2	491.2
Florida	11.9	12.7	18.1	26.4	159.9	189.4	263.3	**326.0**	1,327.0	1,605.1	801.5	1,394.4	319.9	366.1
Georgia	**13.9**	**18.5**	13.5	20.8	47.5	134.3	141.0	204.0	660.8	1,081.7	447.5	702.9	236.4	306.7
Hawaii	2.8	6.8	7.2	21.3	22.6	55.4	52.4	72.1	1,363.8	1,335.6	796.1	1,122.4	505.8	398.4
Idaho	2.3	3.8	8.4	15.6	11.8	20.6	51.1	103.4	470.6	754.6	485.5	1,052.4	118.2	183.9
Illinois	8.1	8.8	16.4	23.3	211.5	260.1	172.0	215.9	683.6	846.1	492.0	686.7	441.0	443.0
Indiana	4.7	6.0	13.2	20.3	98.5	106.6	78.0	100.9	691.0	880.9	526.9	810.8	392.3	348.1
Iowa	1.7	1.7	6.8	8.6	25.0	26.7	35.0	50.3	474.1	521.6	431.2	683.3	164.6	169.1
Kansas	3.7	4.0	13.2	17.8	47.5	68.9	85.8	119.1	615.6	906.6	508.7	791.0	205.5	232.0
Kentucky	8.9	9.8	10.2	15.7	60.1	83.2	85.4	117.1	522.5	650.2	455.1	609.0	332.2	281.8
Louisiana	9.5	13.2	16.4	23.0	90.3	133.4	198.4	252.8	678.0	903.1	510.5	788.5	282.6	356.4
Maine	3.0	5.3	6.7	7.8	8.8	21.1	41.8	69.6	452.4	698.0	250.7	560.8	128.1	155.5
Maryland	9.3	12.5	26.0	26.0	**275.6**	324.1	**312.0**	288.6	1,310.2	1,111.7	764.5	1,082.2	605.0	534.2
Massachusetts	3.5	3.7	9.5	13.5	74.3	152.8	76.7	125.2	868.3	1,242.3	545.7	881.4	**806.6**	**972.4**
Michigan	7.3	11.0	26.5	29.3	210.7	289.3	168.9	225.6	1,106.0	1,582.3	753.0	1,208.0	425.5	473.9
Minnesota	2.2	2.4	10.9	14.7	81.2	84.4	45.9	72.9	801.8	927.2	576.1	817.0	351.1	337.3
Mississippi	9.9	15.4	7.6	17.5	13.2	39.9	114.3	240.0	313.7	540.0	180.7	346.8	72.0	120.5
Missouri	8.8	8.3	23.3	25.5	153.6	175.6	143.2	174.0	976.6	1,100.6	513.3	699.7	446.4	470.5
Montana	3.3	2.5	7.2	10.8	18.2	33.2	59.3	103.5	567.8	708.2	549.1	821.4	198.4	247.0
Nebraska	2.3	2.9	7.2	13.9	49.6	52.7	87.3	103.5	507.4	556.7	391.6	729.0	302.4	261.6
Nevada	5.5	13.5	17.4	34.0	142.8	190.1	112.6	192.0	1,282.1	1,757.5	1,010.6	**1,486.1**	449.7	563.4
New Hampshire	1.4	1.7	2.7	7.0	10.3	13.4	25.4	41.6	371.1	596.6	255.3	592.6	141.3	124.8
New Jersey	5.1	6.5	11.3	16.9	123.6	210.1	96.1	140.8	1,011.9	1,194.3	671.1	878.3	518.5	586.2
New Mexico	6.2	11.1	20.5	32.7	49.5	119.0	164.7	253.1	925.7	1,402.1	853.8	1,230.0	321.9	369.5
New York	6.5	11.0	13.7	22.4	328.4	**467.4**	187.6	243.2	1,332.4	1,256.3	**1,104.2**	923.2	571.7	565.0
North Carolina	9.7	12.8	11.0	14.2	35.3	62.3	288.4	325.3	499.4	752.0	364.3	618.3	137.6	148.2
North Dakota	1.1	1.3	4.6	4.9	5.8	8.9	16.2	30.9	239.0	357.1	286.7	530.2	80.6	90.7
Ohio	5.3	7.5	12.4	19.9	102.0	160.6	80.7	111.4	659.4	901.3	479.4	717.8	380.2	442.6
Oklahoma	6.4	7.0	15.2	19.0	48.5	63.6	103.1	143.1	689.8	942.9	533.5	661.3	212.2	264.6
Oregon	3.2	5.5	17.2	26.3	76.5	109.5	100.0	156.3	945.1	1,468.8	818.5	1,290.2	270.6	386.6
Pennsylvania	4.0	6.0	9.7	15.2	83.2	145.6	73.5	100.6	551.2	742.3	299.2	437.1	275.8	333.5
Rhode Island	2.4	1.3	3.7	8.3	49.3	81.7	81.9	159.1	1,089.6	1,124.0	646.9	996.9	765.5	896.2
South Carolina	13.6	16.8	14.3	21.4	42.8	66.0	146.0	281.6	629.6	992.3	371.2	695.9	176.2	213.2
South Dakota	3.8	1.2	10.2	11.3	19.3	15.6	52.4	83.2	430.1	472.8	359.8	587.3	103.5	107.4
Tennessee	8.7	11.3	11.6	19.9	71.2	101.1	129.0	186.7	719.1	894.3	390.3	587.4	267.4	300.9
Texas	10.6	12.3	14.6	23.8	81.4	118.2	160.9	196.6	932.7	1,206.7	561.1	768.6	302.9	329.3
Utah	2.9	2.9	11.1	18.3	33.7	62.3	68.5	99.7	741.3	913.2	703.5	1,167.3	255.2	277.7
Vermont	2.6	1.7	7.3	10.8	6.2	10.6	21.1	73.2	496.0	738.3	168.0	497.6	85.8	114.1
Virginia	8.3	9.6	14.0	19.5	63.5	109.4	149.7	159.1	692.7	790.0	449.3	678.0	248.5	266.6
Washington	3.6	4.2	17.1	21.8	98.4	87.6	93.7	137.0	1,019.5	1,381.4	843.7	1,197.6	297.1	331.3
West Virginia	5.5	6.1	4.4	8.2	25.5	31.6	73.2	83.2	349.8	413.0	236.3	405.1	92.0	109.7
Wisconsin	2.2	2.8	6.2	8.3	33.1	36.7	39.2	48.6	503.8	638.5	456.9	815.4	204.1	232.7
Wyoming	6.3	4.1	8.9	13.9	12.4	33.9	60.6	96.2	545.1	596.2	575.9	958.0	136.8	203.8
METROPOLITAN AREA														
Baltimore	13.6	17.6	37.9	31.4	454.5	507.7	**506.1**	399.9	1,675.9	1,356.2	974.4	1,115.9	786.8	622.9
Boston	4.4	4.6	10.2	15.1	96.5	201.3	83.4	129.4	831.8	1,112.6	572.2	836.1	935.7	**1,104.8**
Chicago	10.7	11.5	21.4	28.5	304.5	373.8	228.2	257.9	759.6	919.8	537.8	712.9	595.3	609.1
Cleveland	9.6	16.1	11.2	27.0	185.7	302.7	89.5	137.2	610.7	849.3	506.0	509.4	838.3	1,101.2
Detroit	11.3	17.3	34.5	33.1	377.5	507.1	192.7	263.6	1,403.0	1,855.9	918.5	1,357.3	674.3	783.9
Houston	**14.7**	17.3	21.4	30.1	232.3	255.9	202.3	156.6	1,321.7	1,711.4	687.0	818.4	542.2	580.0
Los Angeles-Long Beach	8.6	12.8	**45.0**	**56.0**	272.7	377.7	319.5	406.6	1,932.5	2,237.3	1,280.4	1,365.6	846.7	975.8
Minneapolis-St. Paul	3.8	3.8	19.6	26.2	167.0	165.8	81.7	129.5	1,254.3	1,408.8	867.7	1,166.6	639.9	597.0
Newark	8.2	10.7	19.7	28.5	266.2	382.1	176.5	217.6	1,455.3	1,426.5	868.5	873.0	725.6	764.7
New York	8.5	**19.1**	17.0	37.0	**485.1**	**877.4**	258.3	**423.6**	1,707.6	1,747.4	**1,485.3**	1,100.2	772.2	889.5
Philadelphia	6.7	10.7	13.5	19.9	115.4	254.7	114.2	155.8	653.2	1,021.3	337.3	545.2	328.6	580.4
Pittsburgh	2.9	3.9	12.7	19.1	149.9	151.4	88.0	110.4	730.3	717.6	532.8	484.6	589.4	401.5
St. Louis	11.8	12.7	26.8	34.5	220.3	277.6	177.0	234.8	1,238.3	1,500.1	535.7	776.3	689.8	751.3
San Francisco-Oakland	7.7	8.6	27.5	45.2	377.0	341.9	196.5	247.3	**2,118.6**	**2,045.4**	972.7	**1,488.8**	**966.2**	828.7
Washington, D.C.	9.5	12.4	21.0	42.0	378.9	375.0	187.8	239.9	1,357.6	1,123.7	735.8	1,079.1	725.8	608.1

Boldface type indicates highest rate for that crime among the states or the listed metropolitan areas. *Includes nonnegligent manslaughter. †$50 and over. Source: U.S. Department of Justice, Federal Bureau of Investigation, *Uniform Crime Reports.*

Public assistance

June 1973

State	NUMBER OF RECIPIENTS: Old-age assistance	Aid to dependent children*	Aid to the permanently and totally disabled	Aid to the blind	General assistance	AVERAGE MONEY PAYMENTS: Old-age assistance	Aid to dependent children, per recipient	Aid to the permanently and totally disabled	Aid to the blind	General assistance
Alabama	107,394	164,903	20,068	1,994	93	$ 73.04	$21.42	$ 79.90	$103.77	$ 12.48
Alaska	2,025	11,836	1,537	96	478	118.42	71.37	169.99	172.07	46.47
Arizona	12,727	71,768	10,239	439	2,879	79.48	34.79	88.96	86.63	70.81
Arkansas	56,525	85,782	13,150	1,653	1,187	68.64	32.12	82.72	91.40	5.94
California	288,203	1,363,178	210,122	13,984	47,958	112.21	63.51	151.70	166.33	79.96
Colorado	26,283	98,431	12,780	338	3,967	74.81	54.53	82.62	78.77	83.62
Connecticut	7,009	116,727	10,282	236	18,897†	81.42	71.65	126.02	107.60	58.19
Delaware	2,990	30,747	2,028	332	3,888	90.44	33.53	116.00	121.95	30.77
Dist. of Columbia	4,180	102,445	10,421	218	4,058	94.62	61.63	117.28	124.97	121.25
Florida	67,752	311,989	24,459	2,226	20,700†	82.03	27.07	92.07	91.59	—
Georgia	83,189	336,968	40,447	3,134	3,369	57.65	30.04	68.03	73.56	25.75
Hawaii	3,096	45,147	2,539	90	14,063	106.97	80.81	149.74	131.47	65.48
Idaho	3,044	19,572	3,351	94	—	69.92	54.17	94.87	99.53	—
Illinois	31,980	772,039	87,354	1,712	61,885	67.05	63.08	107.77	111.38	94.86
Indiana	13,748	172,453	10,713	1,189	—	57.00	40.54	63.97	82.87	—
Iowa	11,369	81,021	3,136	1,019	8,300†	69.36	54.99	92.31	103.58	—
Kansas	8,669	70,950	6,588	398	8,180	62.08	59.59	79.40	79.25	73.55
Kentucky	52,495	153,438	19,195	2,012	—	68.25	36.40	95.48	93.33	—
Louisiana	104,152	259,487	23,281	2,103	9,476	73.71	24.31	60.36	81.93	51.86
Maine	11,532	68,918	6,551	261	11,405	74.28	39.56	112.27	111.24	20.90
Maryland	9,789	220,505	19,544	414	15,697	67.17	45.28	92.65	103.05	92.97
Massachusetts	56,303	296,680	27,558	2,941	38,889	102.64	96.60	148.92	147.99	80.90
Michigan	38,338	593,102	50,596	1,658	51,238	70.39	67.18	113.42	111.10	105.16
Minnesota	12,664	124,760	14,260	807	10,393†	61.76	73.23	95.87	102.45	55.85
Mississippi	80,973	179,823	27,866	2,090	1,157	54.16	14.37	65.38	66.83	12.10
Missouri	89,498	238,919	23,852	4,050	15,060	82.98	31.03	86.92	104.96	63.63
Montana	2,468	20,707	2,927	173	1,289	56.59	42.50	87.59	84.63	23.44
Nebraska	6,506	39,377	6,145	270	—	65.40	43.75	105.75	129.74	—

Public assistance

(continued)

State	NUMBER OF RECIPIENTS: Old-age assistance	Aid to dependent children*	Aid to the permanently and totally disabled	Aid to the blind	General assistance	AVERAGE MONEY PAYMENTS: Old-age assistance	Aid to dependent children, per recipient	Aid to the permanently and totally disabled	Aid to the blind	General assistance
Nevada	2,554	13,565	—	119	—	76.03	36.98	—	86.22	—
New Hampshire	4,420	23,558	1,398	250	2,662	170.79	69.57	148.19	162.92	30.73
New Jersey	19,385	416,098	20,710	958	13,255	80.29	71.18	112.46	98.66	145.63
New Mexico	7,580	59,309	9,852	378	195	55.57	32.88	75.48	70.25	62.39
New York	109,064	1,232,310	163,569	4,313	180,814	102.90	79.37	129.11	122.01	72.08
North Carolina	30,367	150,960	32,905	4,414	4,047	78.45	34.69	84.39	92.98	12.08
North Dakota	3,814	14,313	1,968	54	336	95.14	62.56	111.43	110.39	19.47
Ohio	43,790	486,129	48,319	2,410	51,939	64.31	45.52	87.75	85.42	51.82
Oklahoma	52,258	96,732	21,808	1,078	3,296	67.46	39.17	101.22	107.53	8.85
Oregon	7,026	75,561	9,326	702	2,045	73.65	53.43	97.03	108.36	59.11
Pennsylvania	37,320	619,475	42,141	5,933	87,094	68.22	63.35	98.64	110.59	101.14
Rhode Island	3,832	48,782	5,192	137	12,300	73.13	63.89	112.54	117.47	48.77
South Carolina	17,195	114,533	13,581	1,877	505	52.52	22.03	62.13	72.38	36.29
South Dakota‡	3,200	21,400	1,833	104	845‡	64.86	54.67	80.37	96.27	13.83
Tennessee	45,782	191,390	30,567	1,635	4,126	54.99	31.39	74.35	76.66	11.24
Texas	172,504	432,106	28,813	3,723	—	54.63	30.85	74.99	82.23	—
Utah‡	2,310	43,155	5,200	161	1,173	79.41	55.72	89.81	106.61	69.23
Vermont	3,965	19,839	2,674	83	—	74.65	67.09	117.73	110.08	—
Virginia	13,727	163,467	12,806	1,304	9,243	76.42	48.94	97.28	102.65	73.98
Washington	16,711	142,210	27,138	430	4,264	76.65	66.06	107.41	118.61	90.83
West Virginia	12,534	71,653	11,883	548	2,440	104.71	40.21	91.04	112.24	14.45
Wisconsin‡	19,190	145,655	9,701	744	13,072	158.01	79.24	142.62	94.34	58.21
Wyoming	1,155	7,034	921	33	253	66.01	48.17	82.41	...	27.44
Total U.S.	1,824,584	10,640,906	1,193,294	77,319	759,572	$ 78.78‖	$54.19‖	$107.85‖	$110.51‖	$ 73.21‖

*Includes children and parents or caretaker relatives in families in which these adults were included in determining amount of assistance. †Estimated.
‡Data for May; June data not available. §Excludes Idaho, Indiana, Kentucky, Nebraska, Nevada, and Vermont. ‖Includes Guam, Puerto Rico, and the Virgin Islands.
Source: U.S. Department of Health, Education, and Welfare, Social Security Administration, *Social Security Bulletin*.

Transport, Energy, and Communication

Transportation

State	ROAD AND STREET MILEAGE Jan. 1, 1973: Total*	Municipal mileage	Rural mileage: State controlled	Rural mileage: Locally controlled	AUTOMOBILES, TRUCKS, AND BUSES registrations, in 000, 1972: Total	Private, commercial: Auto-mobiles	Private, commercial: Trucks and buses	Publicly owned†	RAILROAD MILEAGE OWNED Jan. 1, 1972: Total	Class 1	AIRPORTS‡ Jan. 1, 1973: Total	Private	CIVIL AIRCRAFT Jan. 1, 1972: Total	Active
Alabama	85,347	17,924	19,738§	47,410	2,227	1,740	456	31	4,567	4,097	128	37	2,182	1,697
Alaska	8,631	1,391	4,343	1,561	149	99	43	6	20	—	766	219	3,341	2,697
Arizona	49,301	6,308	5,484	19,571	1,302	964	315	23	2,052	1,879	198	96	3,186	2,405
Arkansas	77,885	9,487	12,918	53,760	1,070	728	326	16	3,582	3,316	155	83	2,095	1,686
California	166,472	45,676	14,278	71,467	12,852	10,488	2,170	194	7,385	6,593	754	468	21,909	17,442
Colorado	82,024	7,580	8,394	65,955	1,680	1,264	388	28	3,572	3,460	214	140	2,812	2,307
Connecticut	18,624	13,229	1,518	3,877	1,860	1,687	150	23	664	609	79	64	1,366	1,080
Delaware	5,136	797	4,339§	—	323	267	51	5	291	—	30	27	460	382
District of Columbia	1,099	1,099	—	—	259	232	16	12	30	12	7	2	27	12
Florida	96,774	25,698	17,134	52,552	4,836	4,111	656	68	4,157	3,732	329	215	7,345	5,794
Georgia	100,240	15,067	15,779	68,391	2,959	2,366	557	37	5,420	4,029	231	122	3,744	3,042
Hawaii	3,709	1,012	893	1,727	447	389	51	7	—	—	48	33	362	266
Idaho	55,991	3,157	4,734	25,950	550	378	156	16	2,668	2,478	169	46	1,459	1,163
Illinois	130,428	27,989	13,357	88,840	5,644	4,881	702	61	10,822	8,949	749	664	7,035	5,666
Indiana	90,973	15,629	10,267	65,021	2,909	2,300	584	24	6,405	3,425	208	143	4,021	3,346
Iowa	112,930	13,768	9,086	90,007	1,917	1,442	440	35	7,903	7,642	244	133	3,056	2,550
Kansas	134,683	11,322	10,118	113,149	1,692	1,214	452	26	7,776	7,752	307	185	3,494	2,795
Kentucky	69,639	5,751	23,904§	39,375	1,968	1,510	432	26	3,504	3,093	76	26	1,246	1,054
Louisiana	53,645	11,180	14,189‖	27,953	1,942	1,508	410	24	3,753	3,445	260	190	2,652	2,144
Maine	21,444	2,521	10,936¶	7,829	565	449	109	7	1,666	1,509	153	109	846	684
Maryland	26,737	4,181	4,985	17,427	2,130	1,825	283	23	1,110	564	99	78	2,294	1,852
Massachusetts	29,692	23,554	1,194	4,895	2,822	2,532	255	34	1,430	1,286	117	90	2,394	2,018
Michigan	118,060	20,232	7,968	87,200	5,011	4,241	698	71	6,159	4,093	383	253	6,625	5,511
Minnesota	128,064	17,444	11,383	97,335	2,368	1,863	472	33	7,700	7,579	276	135	4,211	3,400
Mississippi	66,824	6,977	9,723	49,885	1,249	918	312	20	3,653	3,170	134	64	1,820	1,440
Missouri	115,590	15,536	30,069	69,270	2,618	2,021	572	25	6,337	5,708	319	215	3,715	2,977
Montana	77,906	2,386	12,126	53,876	584	373	201	10	4,981	4,916	176	59	1,578	1,286
Nebraska	98,547	6,880	9,594	81,666	1,081	774	291	16	5,420	5,420	289	196	2,041	1,657
Nevada	49,659	1,921	6,151§	41,587	399	294	93	12	1,574	1,413	112	55	1,174	906
New Hampshire	14,974	4,839	3,049	6,966	436	366	63	7	817	680	46	32	675	531
New Jersey	32,336	18,731	1,562	12,030	3,859	3,440	346	72	1,742	913	192	167	3,644	2,983
New Mexico	68,075	4,885	11,704	45,326	711	494	201	16	2,120	2,046	131	66	1,509	1,225
New York	107,295	40,779	12,930	53,551	7,119	6,325	689	104	5,595	4,652	442	373	6,419	5,172
North Carolina	86,611	14,179	71,004§	—	3,220	2,510	626	84	4,144	2,944	228	167	3,193	2,597
North Dakota	106,316	3,168	6,662	95,188	464	287	167	9	5,108	5,108	193	105	1,253	979
Ohio	109,547	23,724	16,947	68,847	6,224	5,470	694	60	7,804	4,524	522	417	7,155	5,783
Oklahoma	107,881	14,338	11,501	82,008	1,887	1,321	537	29	5,332	5,240	273	154	4,177	3,292
Oregon	99,531	6,567	9,285	35,258	1,496	1,218	250	28	3,068	2,521	258	159	3,088	2,442
Pennsylvania	114,144	24,229	42,372	46,689	6,311	5,435	822	54	8,273	5,485	514	446	5,640	4,526
Rhode Island	5,472	4,450	499	523	536	473	58	6	146	113	15	8	247	206
South Carolina	59,938	7,019	31,822	20,629	1,497	1,197	275	25	3,059	2,116	120	61	1,412	1,109
South Dakota	82,790	2,978	8,736	69,454	463	310	141	11	3,505	3,505	114	43	1,085	887
Tennessee	80,577	11,954	8,299	59,115	2,294	1,811	449	33	3,214	2,826	120	50	2,212	1,827
Texas	250,546	51,834	61,604	136,082	7,316	5,520	1,673	122	13,563	12,873	1,167	889	12,694	9,889
Utah	47,331	4,468	4,828	22,090	741	533	192	15	1,750	1,686	87	34	966	792
Vermont	14,567	1,011	2,575	10,802	261	214	43	4	766	325	47	34	324	259
Virginia	61,826	9,278	49,539§	—	2,603	2,148	409	47	3,895	3,270	209	155	2,299	1,883
Washington	80,279	9,993	14,071	39,530	2,242	1,689	507	46	4,887	4,394	258	150	4,443	3,488
West Virginia	36,170	3,643	31,833§	—	874	664	195	14	3,569	3,159	50	27	824	684
Wisconsin	103,822	14,375	10,788	78,591	2,379	1,963	381	35	5,926	5,885	281	181	3,257	2,615
Wyoming	40,631	1,289	5,881	20,948	274	172	95	7	1,812	1,805	85	44	739	627
TOTAL U.S.	3,786,713	613,426	712,093	2,252,023	118,620	96,418	20,454	1,741	204,696	176,239	12,362	7,909	165,745	133,055

*Includes federally controlled rural roads. †Excludes vehicles owned by the military services. ‡Includes seaplane bases, heliports, and military fields having joint civil-military use.
§Includes mileage of state-controlled county roads. ‖Includes mileage designated as farm-to-market. ¶Includes the state-aid system.
Sources: Interstate Commerce Commission; U.S. Department of Transportation, Federal Aviation Administration; Federal Highway Administration.

Mineral fuels and electricity production

in trillion British thermal units

Year	MINERAL FUELS: Total production	Bituminous coal and lignite	Anthracite	Crude petroleum	Natural gas: Liquids	Natural gas: Dry	ELECTRICITY*: Hydropower	ELECTRICITY*: Nuclear power
1966	51,741	13,507	329	16,925	18,894†		2,029	57
1967	58,265	11,982	274	25,335	18,250†		2,344	80
1968	61,763	12,481	258	24,607‡	2,445	19,580	2,342	130
1969	64,979	12,509	224	26,029‡	2,392	21,020	2,659	146
1970	67,143‡	12,488	210	27,049‡	2,488	22,029	2,650	229
1971‡	68,790	11,857‡	186	28,045‡	2,525	22,819	2,862‡	404
1972§	72,242	12,454	150	30,381	2,584	23,125	2,972	576

Represents outputs of hydropower and nuclear power converted to theoretical energy inputs calculated from national average heat rates for fossil-fueled steam-electric plants provided by the Federal Power Commission using 10,432 Btu per net kilowatt-hour in 1967; 10,398 Btu in 1968; 10,447 Btu in 1969; 10,494 Btu in 1970; and 10,498 Btu in 1971 & 1972 for hydropower. Energy input for nuclear power in 1971 & 1972 is converted at an average heat rate of 10,660 Btu per net kilowatt-hour based on information from the Atomic Energy Commission.

*Includes installations owned by manufacturing plants and mines, as well as government owned and public utilities.

§Preliminary. ‡Revised. †Wet, unprocessed.

Source: U.S. Department of the Interior, Bureau of Mines. (FRANK H. SKELDING)

Intercity transportation

by type of transport

FREIGHT, in billions of ton-miles

Year	Total traffic	Railroads	Motor vehicles	Inland waterways	Oil pipelines	Airways
1960	1,330	595	285	220	229	0.8
1961	1,326	586	296	210	233	0.9
1962	1,387	616	309	223	238	1.3
1963	1,469	644	336	234	253	1.3
1964	1,556	679	356	250	269	1.5
1965	1,651	721	359	262	306	1.9
1966	1,759	762	381	281	333	2.3
1967	1,776	742	389	281	361	2.6
1968	1,839	757	396	291	391	2.9
1969	1,895	774	404	303	411	3.2
1970	1,936	771	412	319	431	3.3
1971*	1,930	746	430	307	444	3.4

PASSENGERS, in billions of passenger-miles

Year	Total traffic	Private automobiles	Airways	Bus (excludes schoolbus)	Railroads	Inland waterways
1960	784	706	34	19	22	2.7
1961	791	714	35	20	21	2.3
1962	818	736	37	22	20	2.7
1963	853	766	43	23	19	2.8
1964	896	802	49	23	18	2.8
1965	920	818	58	24	18	3.1
1966	971	856	69	25	17	3.4
1967	1,021	890	87	25	15	3.4
1968	1,079	936	101	25	13	3.4
1969	1,138	977	120	25	12	3.8
1970	1,185	1,026	119	25	11	4.0
1971*	1,230	1,071	120	26	9	4.1

*Preliminary. Source: U. S. Department of Commerce, Bureau of the Census, *Statistical Abstract of the United States 1973.*

Communications facilities

State	Post Offices July 1, 1973	COMMERCIAL BROADCAST STATIONS, 1972: Radio AM	Radio FM	TV	Public TV stations 1971	TELEPHONES* January 1, 1973: Total	Residential	NEWSPAPERS: Daily Number Feb. 1, 1973	Daily Circulation Sept. 30, 1972	Weekly April 1, 1973† Number	Weekly Circulation	Sunday Number Feb. 1, 1973	Sunday Circulation Sept. 30, 1972
Alabama	662	136	56	16	8	1,762,900	1,333,200	24	742,885	109	419,960	16	654,459
Alaska	196	16	3	7	—	...	...	7	76,253	9	13,708	1	18,397
Arizona	214	59	18	11	2	1,166,400	823,100	12	480,893	58	191,939	4	401,571
Arkansas	685	84	41	8	1	993,500	743,900	35	438,471	126	315,937	12	342,568
California	1,153	232	157	49	9	14,381,400	10,197,000	127	5,835,642	439	5,320,450	39	4,915,438
Colorado	419	65	30	11	1	1,592,500	1,111,500	26	756,331	138	382,806	9	650,003
Connecticut	249	38	21	5	3	2,185,000	1,608,700	28	966,722	50	339,518	7	639,066
Delaware	57	10	5	—	—	410,300	300,700	5	179,838	13	87,416	1	23,204
District of Columbia	1	6	7	6	1	959,100	479,800	2	953,679	...	...	2	1,008,446
Florida	468	194	97	25	9	5,103,100	3,698,300	52	2,166,084	135	549,363	32	2,053,244
Georgia	660	171	67	16	10	2,820,800	2,072,800	34	1,037,291	165	492,898	11	975,854
Hawaii	77	24	4	10	2	414,600	301,300	5	238,101	2	19,132	2	195,794
Idaho	271	43	7	7	1	...	...	15	193,602	55	106,844	5	152,934
Illinois	1,288	121	107	24	5	7,640,900	5,540,000	93	4,034,892	561	2,883,231	19	2,456,996
Indiana	764	86	77	18	4	3,201,700	2,441,500	79	1,691,311	195	534,382	19	1,172,499
Iowa	964	72	43	13	1	1,751,100	1,341,600	42	949,307	350	713,082	9	814,221
Kansas	708	58	29	12	2	1,411,900	1,064,000	52	663,731	241	452,713	14	457,240
Kentucky	1,334	106	64	12	13	1,610,100	1,206,000	26	773,472	138	490,878	12	583,805
Louisiana	541	91	45	16	1	1,980,600	1,488,400	26	822,651	90	283,273	13	729,491
Maine	505	36	15	7	4	553,600	418,300	10	273,986	36	145,249	1	109,319
Maryland	426	53	34	7	1	2,739,500	2,002,400	12	744,448	66	576,729	4	705,905
Massachusetts	439	63	40	11	2	3,745,600	2,616,500	46	2,159,857	143	915,863	8	1,522,632
Michigan	871	125	84	22	4	5,586,000	4,193,000	55	2,509,960	283	1,430,157	14	2,245,491
Minnesota	876	87	45	12	4	2,454,100	1,828,600	32	1,127,557	316	707,891	11	1,074,125
Mississippi	477	100	42	9	1	1,032,400	789,600	21	355,193	96	242,878	8	246,475
Missouri	998	106	50	24	2	2,979,500	2,195,500	54	1,804,911	273	719,473	13	1,472,082
Montana	388	41	8	12	—	398,800	289,200	13	193,828	72	148,432	8	189,290
Nebraska	558	48	17	14	9	974,800	731,800	19	494,872	204	435,977	4	361,098
Nevada	99	21	10	7	1	397,400	255,400	7	152,796	18	42,010	4	142,352
New Hampshire	249	27	13	3	5	486,200	365,400	9	174,176	32	185,014	1	58,474
New Jersey	520	35	27	4	—	5,208,600	3,857,500	31	1,711,899	204	1,361,805	7	1,090,486
New Mexico	341	57	19	7	1	568,500	388,000	19	230,928	31	151,321	14	213,189
New York	1,639	159	98	28	9	12,555,500	8,600,500	78	7,313,484	400	1,986,394	22	6,398,892
North Carolina	790	202	75	19	6	2,713,600	2,035,700	50	1,327,643	136	505,863	20	974,195
North Dakota	469	27	10	12	1	354,900	264,300	11	156,967	89	163,380	3	62,009
Ohio	1,087	118	112	27	8	6,667,900	4,992,000	96	3,549,237	263	1,579,012	20	2,378,354
Oklahoma	650	66	36	10	3	1,645,100	1,197,100	52	869,224	203	332,841	42	828,640
Oregon	366	78	20	13	2	1,337,600	969,300	22	673,248	93	487,616	5	549,923
Pennsylvania	1,816	171	118	23	9	7,966,600	6,028,400	106	3,990,312	227	1,377,931	11	2,814,370
Rhode Island	56	15	7	2	1	573,600	421,300	7	315,357	13	81,013	2	211,353
South Carolina	399	102	42	11	5	1,371,800	1,021,900	17	579,231	76	259,380	7	455,478
South Dakota	429	30	10	10	4	366,800	283,800	13	177,877	145	192,908	4	125,094
Tennessee	595	148	68	16	5	2,225,700	1,665,600	34	1,161,425	124	430,323	14	960,803
Texas	1,546	286	129	56	5	7,122,400	5,108,000	111	3,297,879	476	1,204,448	82	3,294,968
Utah	230	32	10	3	3	683,500	497,500	5	264,861	51	126,184	4	258,895
Vermont	293	18	6	2	4	265,200	189,200	9	119,667	15	37,993	1	3,127
Virginia	933	125	60	12	5	2,812,400	2,021,700	32	1,032,167	112	564,199	13	743,420
Washington	494	97	42	15	6	2,143,800	1,556,700	24	1,028,570	132	994,267	13	979,452
West Virginia	1,052	60	26	9	2	827,700	628,700	29	490,631	82	246,464	9	388,916
Wisconsin	794	99	77	18	3	2,606,500	1,909,900	37	1,221,665	239	701,589	6	843,390
Wyoming	174	29	1	3	—	216,600	152,300	10	80,223	29	65,207	3	53,242
United States	31,270	4,273	2,229	694	189	130,968,100	95,226,100	1,761‡	62,510,242‡	7,553	31,997,341	605‡	50,000,669‡

*Excluding Alaska and Hawaii. †Excluding District of Columbia. ‡Adjusted to account for double listing of newspapers published near state borders whose circulation is divided between two states.

Sources: U.S. Postal Service; Federal Communications Commission; U.S. Department of Health, Education, and Welfare, National Center for Educational Statistics, *Broadcast and Production Statistics of Public Television Licensees: Fiscal Year 1971;* American Telephone and Telegraph Co.; The Editor & Publisher Co., Inc., *International Year Book*-1973 (Copyright 1973. All rights reserved. Used by permission); American Newspaper Representatives, Inc.

Foreign Trade and Affairs

Major trading partners, by value

in millions of dollars

Country	EXPORTS 1970	EXPORTS 1972	IMPORTS 1970	IMPORTS 1972
North America	12,430	16,096	13,018	17,364
Canada	9,079	12,415	11,092	14,909
Mexico	1,704	1,982	1,218	1,632
South America	2,796	3,146	2,561	2,979
Argentina	441	400	172	201
Brazil	840	1,243	670	942
Chile	300	187	157	83
Colombia	395	317	269	284
Venezuela	759	924	1,082	1,298
Europe	14,817	16,160	11,395	15,740
Belgium and Luxembourg	1,195	1,138	696	968
France	1,483	1,610	942	1,369
Germany, West	2,741	2,811	3,127	4,249
Italy	1,353	1,430	1,316	1,756
Netherlands	2,536	2,658	528	639
Spain	712	930	353	600
Sweden	543	472	399	601
Switzerland	700	672	459	619
Turkey	315	317	70	106
United Kingdom	2,536	2,658	2,194	2,986
Asia	10,105	11,376	9,644	15,128
Hong Kong	406	489	944	1,249
India*	572	350	298	427
Indonesia	266	308	182	278
Iran	326	559	67	199
Israel	592	558	150	222
Japan	4,652	4,965	5,875	9,064
Korea, South	643	735	370	708
Pakistan*	325	183	80	40
Philippines	373	366	472	484
Taiwan	527	631	549	1,294
Vietnam, South*	352	318	†	†
Australia and Oceania	1,189	1,035	871	1,145
Australia	986	843	611	807
Africa	1,502	1,501	1,090	1,578
Libya	108	85	39	116
South Africa	563	602	290	325
Total	43,224	49,768	39,952	55,555

*Excludes "special category" shipments. †Less than $5,000,000.
Source: U.S. Department of Commerce, Domestic and Industrial Business Administration, *Overseas Business Reports*.

Major commodities traded, 1972

in millions of dollars

Item	Total*	Canada	American Republics	Western Europe	Far East†
Total Exports	49,768	12,415	6,471	15,342	9,340
Agricultural commodities					
Grains and preparations	3,505	138	357	872	1,295
Fruits, nuts and vegetables	734	297	45	239	114
Tobacco, unmanufactured	639	2	5	389	199
Soybeans	1,508	77	17	843	464
Cotton, including linters, wastes	518	43	3	98	348
Nonagricultural commodities					
Ores and scrap metals	508	77	51	180	198
Coal, coke and briquettes	1,019	277	71	317	351
Petroleum products	442	64	81	153	85
Chemicals	4,134	693	908	1,446	661
Machinery	13,509	3,535	2,181	3,314	1,904
Agricultural machines, tractors, parts	1,076	419	249	190	72
Electrical apparatus	3,699	872	633	1,170	662
Transport equipment‡	7,461	3,577	793	1,466	803
Aircraft, civilian, and parts for all aircraft	2,608	194	193	1,141	642
Paper manufactures	726	152	151	261	57
Metal manufactures	828	334	127	175	70
Iron and steel mill products§	800	291	152	154	97
Textile yarn, fabrics and clothing	753	152	145	212	115
Other exports	12,684	2,706	1,384	5,223	2,579
Total imports	55,555	14,909	5,772	15,420	14,322
Agricultural commodities					
Meat and preparations	1,223	76	271	235	3
Fish, including shellfish	1,205	247	235	229	294
Fruits, nuts and vegetables	846	31	445	154	157
Coffee	1,182	—	800	2	44
Sugar	824	—	494	3	234
Nonagricultural commodities					
Alcoholic beverages	824	198	8	607	5
Pulp and waste paper	500	484	‖	8	‖
Ores and scrap metal	1,022	441	243	24	40
Petroleum, crude and partly refined	2,607	978	527	8	124
Petroleum products	1,693	132	656	148	24
Chemicals	2,015	439	82	940	276
Machinery	7,916	1,657	335	2,959	2,914
Transport equipment	9,484	4,571	37	2,601	2,263
Automobiles, new	5,705	2,593	‖	1,973	1,138
Iron and steel-mill products§	2,743	197	97	1,239	1,153
Nonferrous base metals	1,754	798	199	389	243
Textiles other than clothing	1,528	38	71	591	765
Other Imports	18,189	4,622	1,272	5,283	5,783

*Includes areas not shown separately. †Includes Japan, East and South Asia.
‡Excludes parts for tractors. §Excludes pig iron. ‖Less than $500,000.
Source: U.S. Department of Commerce, Domestic and International Business Administration, *Overseas Business Reports*.

Major recipients of foreign assistance

in millions of dollars; fiscal years ending June 30

Program and country	1966	1969	1972	Total loans and grants 1946–72*
Total	7,634	7,570	11,114	173,542
By program				
Economic assistance programs	5,144	4,304	6,412	113,914
Agency for International Development	2,677	1,690	2,072	53,533
Loans	1,306	723	625	15,591
Grants	1,370	966	1,446	37,946
Food for Peace	1,558	1,179	1,223	20,847
Export-Import Bank loans	347	703	2,086	15,405
Other economic programs	549	655	646	23,165
Military assistance programs	2,490	3,266	4,702	59,628
By country				
Africa				
Algeria	19	2	22	217
Ethiopia	66	33	44	485
Ghana	9	30	15	300
Guinea	7	22	1	110
Ivory Coast	6	8	22	111
Kenya†	20	4	5	97
Liberia	12	14	20	308
Morocco	64	56	74	960
Nigeria	31	87	40	423
Tunisia	22	50	53	798
Zaire	39	11	8	495
Asia				
Cambodia	‡	‡	245	863
India	909	478	129	9,382
Indonesia	24	243	269	1,808
Iran	176	136	158	2,770
Israel	127	160	425	2,610
Jordan	66	26	109	871
Korea, South	500	732	860	11,379
Laos	112	130	272	1,756
Pakistan	157	118	171	4,878

Program and country	1966	1969	1972	Total loans and grants 1946–72*
Philippines	44	65	130	2,481
Sri Lanka (Ceylon)	14	26	17	200
Taiwan§	137	89	276	5,911
Thailand	93	208	91	1,747
Turkey	287	223	254	6,403
Vietnam, South	1,599	2,022	2,837	17,984
Canada	—	5	19	144
Europe				
France	11	—	19	9,712
Germany, West	3	—	3	5,088
Greece	103	93	96	4,229
Italy	22	51	22	6,466
Netherlands	—	—	44	2,606
Norway	34	—	37	1,357
Spain	104	52	522	2,913
United Kingdom	86	31	51	9,758
Yugoslavia	136	33	87	3,093
Latin America				
Argentina	63	71	65	1,028
Bolivia	40	32	65	624
Brazil	377	58	343	4,533
Chile	122	92	21	1,654
Colombia	117	134	143	1,607
Dominican Republic	112	31	32	528
Ecuador	32	14	13	386
Guatemala	10	82	18	403
Mexico	33	16	54	1,268
Panama	15	18	64	342
Peru	52	24	76	862
Venezuela	21	5	54	577
Oceania				
Australia	106	132	109	1,104
New Zealand	7	—	—	144
Trust Territory of the Pacific Islands	18	40	57	395

Obligations and loan authorizations for economic assistance are on a gross basis, military assistance on a program basis, and cumulative total on a net basis (reflecting total deobligations).
*Includes post-war relief period (1946–48), Marshall Plan period (1948–52), and Mutual Security Act period (1953–61). †Excludes share of east Africa regional aid. ‡Less than $50,000.
§Total includes $218.5 million to mainland China (1946–50). Source: U.S. Department of State, Agency for International Development.